D1272488

Encyclopedia of Opera on Screen

Encyclopedia
of
Opera on Screen

A Guide to More Than 100 Years
of Opera Films, Videos, and DVDs

Ken Wlaschin

Yale University Press   New Haven and London

The author and publisher are grateful to the American Film Institute and the British Film Institute for providing film stills. All other illustrations in the book are from the author's collection.

Designed by Scott Wlaschin

Set in Times New Roman type

Printed in the United States of America by Vail Ballou Press

Library of Congress Cataloging-in-Publication Data

Wlaschin, Ken.

    Encyclopedia of opera on screen : a guide to more than 100 years of opera films, videos, and DVDs / Ken Wlaschin.

      p.   cm.

    Includes bibliographical references and index.

    ISBN 0-300-10263-1 (hardcover: alk. paper)

    1. Opera in motion pictures—Encyclopedias. 2. Operas—Films and video adaptations—History and criticism.

ML 102.O6W55 2004

791.43′657—dc22

2004041519

A catalogue record for this book is available from the British Library.

The paper in this book meets the guidelines for permanence and durability of the Committee on Production Guidelines for Book Longevity of the Council on Library Resources.

10 9 8 7 6 5 4 3 2 1

CONTENTS

Introduction

This is a guide to the thousands of films, videos, and DVDs featuring operas and opera singers made since 1896. There is no other guide like it so it should be a useful reference tool for those interested in opera and operetta on screen.

Opera on the screen goes back to the beginnings of cinema, and Thomas Edison predicted its future at once. In 1893 he told *The New York Times* that "my intention is to have such a happy combination of photography and electricity that a man can sit in his own parlor, see depicted upon a curtain the forms of the players in opera upon a distant stage and hear the voices of the singers." In 1894 he told *Century Magazine,* "I believe that in coming years grand opera can be given at the Metropolitan Opera House in New York with artists and musicians long since dead."

We are the heirs of Edison's dream, the first generation to have access in our homes to a century of screen opera. A large majority of the films and television programs of operatic interest are now available in DVD, VHS, and LD formats, and it is quite easy to survey the riches of the opera legacy at home. Though audio has dominated the home experience of opera for the past 100 years, video is likely to dominate the next 100 by way of the DVD. With the emergence of DVDs as the major video format of the 21st century, the home opera experience has been enormously enhanced with excellent sound and picture quality and many extras. As opera is as much theater as music, this change should help make the art more popular.

This guide is intended to show what has been filmed or taped and what it is possible to view. It has been organized alphabetically as an encyclopedia with entries on operas, operettas, zarzuelas, singers, composers, writers, conductors, directors, and subjects of interest. The net is wide and inclusive and includes operas composed for film and television, operas that exist only electronically, operas with cinema content, films with opera content, and singers whose opera career was only on the movie screen.

Major opera singers have their own entries with descriptions of their concert videos and cross-references to their screen operas. As most opera singers have also sung in operettas, traditional operettas that have been filmed or videotaped are discussed, including some composed only for the screen. The entries on composers include screen biographies and cross-references to their operas that have been filmed or taped. There are also entries on conductors, stage directors. TV directors, opera houses, cities, and production groups.

The video market has noticeable gaps, but this should improve with the growing popularity of DVD. Many once-rare operas now can be easily viewed, and many more will become available. Any opera that has been televised is probably on tape somewhere and could be published at a future date as many older television productions have been made available in recent years.

In addition to the chronological entries of the screen versions of operas, there are entries on films of related interest that either use music from the opera or are based on the same story. Early and silent versions of operas are listed after the more recent ones as being of more specialized interest. Operas that were more fashionable in the early years of the 20th century often have many silent versions and few in the sound era.

The Carmen story is by far the major literary source and has the largest number of screen versions. Also popular are *La Traviata* and *The Barber of Seville,* followed by *Tosca, Pagliacci, Don Giovanni, Aida, The Magic Flute,* and *La bohème.* The most popular composer, measured by the number of screen biographies, is Mozart, though Verdi has the largest number of different operas on screen.

The most popular opera personalities are the three tenors Plácido Domingo, Luciano Pavarotti, and José Carreras, and the three sopranos Joan Sutherland, Kiri Te Kanawa, and Teresa Stratas, with Domingo the leader in the number of videos. The major screen opera directors are Kirk Browning and Brian Large, each with more than 200 operas taped for television and video. The most prolific director of opera on film is Carmine Gallone, followed by Jean-Pierre Ponnelle.

Operas and operettas are listed in their original language, except for Slavic operas which are described under their English titles. Accent marks used in European languages are retained. Opera and film titles are capitalized in the style used in the language; this is the practice of *The New Grove Dictionary of Opera* and Schwann catalogs, though it is not usually followed on opera video covers.

The New Grove Dictionary of Opera has been used as the definitive source of information about operas, though its Slavic spellings are not always followed. Kurt Gänzl's *Encyclopedia of Musical Theatre* is the most complete single source of data about operettas and musical comedies. Information about films and television programs comes from *The American Film Institute Feature Film Catalogs*, *Variety*, *The New York Times,* catalogs, journals, and videos.

When it is known, the video company that distributes, or once distributed, an opera is named. Distribution is always in flux, and the companies handling videos often change. Almost all companies can now be accessed on the Internet, library or second-hand copies are available if there is no current distributor. When a film or video is available for viewing at one of the television or film museums, this is noted.

If a video company is English, French, Italian, or German, it's video are usually available in the PAL or SECAM video systems, not the American NTSC system. These must be played on a multi-standard or European video player. DVDs have regional codes: Region 0 DVDs can be played on any machine, Region 1 only on American and Canadian machines, and Region 2 only on European and Japanese machines. Many machines on the market will play all regions.

A name printed in SMALL CAPS indicates it has its own entry with further information. Starred films and videos (***) are recommended for their quality, and there may be more than one for the same opera.

I would like to thank the large number of people who have helped with this book. Harry Haskell of Yale University Press was the most patient and understanding of editors. He recruited a group of film and opera experts from around the world who provided invaluable suggestions, corrections, and additions, including notably Richard Fawkes, Tom Glasow, Mary K. Hunter, Joe Pearce, John Pennino, John Snelson, Paul Spehr, and John Walker. I was greatly aided by many other people at Yale University Press, but especially Lauren R. Shapiro, Jeffrey Schier, Mary C. Traester, and Jessie Dolch. Finally I would like to express my gratitude to advisors David Meeker, Kirk Browning, and Andrzej Rzepczynski, to my designer son Scott Wlaschin, and to my artist wife Maureen Kennedy Martin.

Ken Wlaschin
Los Angeles

ABBREVIATIONS

ABC (Australia): Australian Broadcasting Corporation
ABC (USA): American Broadcasting Company
AFI: American Film Institute
BBC: British Broadcasting Corporation
BFI: British Film Institute
BHE: British Home Entertainment
BIP: British International Pictures
CBC: Canadian Broadcasting Company
CBS: Columbia Broadcasting System
CCC: CCC Television, Berlin
CNN: Cable News Network
DEFA: Deutsche Filmakademie (film studio)
DG: Deutsche Grammophon (recording company)
DVD: Digital Video Disc
EMI: Electrical and Music Industries (recording company)
GB: Great Britain
HBO: Home Box Office
HDTV: High-Definition Television
LD: Laserdisc
LWT: London Weekend Television
MPI: MPI Home Entertainment (video company)
MPRC: Music Performance Research Center
MTR: Museum of Television and Radio
NBC: National Broadcasting Company
NDR: Norddeutscher Rundfunk, Hamburg (TV company)
NFTA: National Film and Television Archive
NHK: Nippon Hoso Kyokai (Japan Broadcasting Corporation)
NLD: NLD Home Video
NRK: Norsk Rikskringkasting, Oslo (TV company)
NTSC: National Television Standards Committee (US video system)
NVC: National Video Corporation
NYPL: New York Public Library
PAL: Phase Alternation Line (European video system)
PBS: Public Broadcasting System
PRC: Producers Releasing Company (film company)
RAI: Radiotelevisione Italiana (TV company)
RKO: RKO-Radio Pictures (film company)
RTE: Radio Telefis Eireann (TV company)
RTVE: Radio Television Española (TV company)
SECAM: (French television system)
SFB: Sender Freies, Berlin (TV station)
TDK: Tokyo Denkikagaku Kogyo (recording company)
UCLA: University of California–Los Angeles
UFA: Universum Film Aktien Gesselschaft (film company)
V&E: V & E Home Video
VAI: Video Artists International (video company)
VHS: Video Home System (videocassette format)

SUBJECT ENTRIES

Encyclopedia of Opera on Screen

A

ABARBANELL, LINA
German-born American soprano (1879–1963)

Lina Abarbanell sang Hansel in the first performance of Humperdinck's *Hänsel und Gretel* at the Metropolitan Opera in 1905. Her voice was too light for the Met, but she became popular in Broadway operettas such as *Madame Sherry* (1910), having already had success in such roles in Europe. She became involved in movies late in her career. The Abarbanell family, including Judith and Lorraine, sang in Yiddish opera films such as THE CANTOR'S SON (1937) while Sam Abarbanell produced movies and Lina became a talent scout/producer. She is credited with discovering movie stars June Allyson and Vera Ellen, and several of her stage productions went to Hollywood, including *The Big Knife* and *The Country Girl*.

ABBADO, CLAUDIO
Italian conductor (1933–)

Milan-born conductor Claudio Abbado is featured on a number of opera videos, and a book he wrote about TEATRO ALLA SCALA was made into a film in 1990. He has been conducting professionally since 1958, was music director of VIENNA State Opera from 1986 to 1991, and is part of a musical dynasty with father, brother, and nephew. His opera videos include UN BALLO IN MASCHERA (1975), IL BARBIERE DI SIVIGLIA (1972), CARMEN (1984), LA CENERENTOLA (1981), ELEKTRA (1989), FEDORA (1997), FIERRABRAS (1988), FROM THE HOUSE OF THE DEAD (1992), KHOVANSHCHINA (1989), LOHENGRIN (1990), LE NOZZE DI FIGARO (1992), LUCIANO PAVAROTTI (1996), SERGEI PROKOFIEV (1993), DER ROSENKAVALIER (1992 film), GIOACHINO ROSSINI (1985), SIMON BOCCANEGRA (1978), VERDI REQUIEM (1982/2001), IL VIAGGIO A REIMS (1984/1988), and WOZZECK (1987).

1985 Claudio Abbado: Lux Aeterna
Norbert Behharz's film shows Abbado rehearsing the *Verdi Requiem* at La Scala, St. Mark's Church, and a Milan rehearsal room. Those being rehearsed are Montserrat Caballé, Cecilia Gasdia, Peter Dvorsky, Chris Merritt, Samuel Ramey, Lucia Valentini-Terrani, and the La Scala Orchestra and Chorus. Color. In German with English subtitles. 119 minutes. Naxos/Arthaus DVD.

1996 Claudio Abbado: A Portrait
Paul Smaczny's film about the conductor shows him at work in Salzburg, Paris, and Venice with the Berlin and Vienna Philharmonic Orchestras, the Gustav Mahler Youth Orchestra, and the Chamber Orchestra of Europe. He talks about his musical ideas, and there are comments from other conductors. Color. 60 minutes. Arthaus DVD.

ABC TELEVISION (AUSTRALIA)

ABC, the Australian Broadcasting Corporation in Sydney, is the primary source of televised operas and videos from the SYDNEY Opera House, most notably many operas starring JOAN SUTHERLAND. It has also telecast many contemporary operas, from Menotti's AMAHL AND THE NIGHT VISITORS and AMELIA AL BALLO to Australian works such as THE SUMMER OF THE SEVENTEENTH DOLL and VOSS.

ABC TELEVISION (USA)

ABC television, the American Broadcasting Company, telecast the first live operas from the METROPOLITAN OPERA and also commissioned two American TV operas. In November 1948, ABC telecast the Met season opening night of OTELLO; in November 1949, the Met opening night of DER ROSENKAVALIER; and in November 1950, the Met opening night of DON CARLO to an estimated 4 million viewers. ABC then ended its prestigious but expensive collaboration with the Met (there do not appear to be telecine versions of these telecasts). ABC's original American operas were THE THIRTEEN CLOCKS (1953), based on the James Thurber story, and THE FINAL INGREDIENT (1965), set in a World War II prison camp. It also featured opera on its OMNIBUS program, including the 1957 THE BALLAD OF BABY DOE.

ABDUCTION FROM THE SERAGLIO, THE
See ENTFÜHRUNG AUS DEM SERAIL, DIE

ABDUCTION OF FIGARO, THE
1984 parody opera by Schickele

In a seacoast town "in Spain or Italy or somewhere," Figaro lies on his deathbed in the palace of Count Alma Mater with wife Susanna Susannadonna, Doctor Al Donfonso, and servant Pecadillo. Donna Donna comes looking for Donald Giovanni as things begin to go absurdly wrong for three hours of parody gently mocking

Mozart's *Le nozze di Figaro, Don Giovanni,* and *The Abduction from the Seraglio.* There is even a "Dance of the Seven Pails." PETER SCHICKELE's satirical three-act opera *The Abduction of Figaro* (composed and written as if by his alter ego P.D.Q. Bach and subtitled *A Simply Grand Opera*) is an inventive pastiche premiered by the Minnesota Opera at the Orpheum Theater in Minneapolis April 24, 1984, with Schickele conducting. It is scored for a standard orchestra plus ukulele and electric and steel guitars.

***1984 Minnesota Opera
American stage production: Michael Montel (director), Peter Schickele (conductor, Minnesota Opera Orchestra, Chorus, and Ballet), John Lee Beaty (set designer).
Cast: Arthur Kraemmer (Figaro), Dana Krueger (Susanna Susannadonna/Mama Geno), Marilyn Brustadt (Donna Donna), Lisbeth Lloyd (Blondie), Bruce Ford (Pecadillo,) Michael Burt (Donald Giovanni), Jack Walsh (Schlepporello), LeRoy Lehr (Al Donfonso/Pasha Shaboom/Papa Geno), Will Roy (Captain Kadd), John Ferrante (Opec).
Video: VAI VHS. Telecast by KRMA-TV, Denver, in December 1985. Kaye S. Lavine (director). Color. In English. 144 minutes.
Comment: This is the only Schickele opera on video. Bruce Ford, who created the role of Pecadillo, later became famous as a Rossini tenor in Europe.

ABERFAN
1977 television opera by Pannell

Aberfan, a mining village in Wales, was the site of a major disaster in 1966 when a rain-soaked slag heap avalanched upon the town, killing 144 people, 116 of them children. Canadian composer Raymond Pannell's television opera *Aberfan,* libretto by Beverly Pannell and composer, was commissioned for CBC Television and won the Salzburg Television Opera Prize in 1977.

CBC Television
Canadian TV production: John Thomson (director), Raymond Pannell (conductor, CBC Orchestra).
Cast: Gary Relyea (Collie), Mary Morrison (Mother), Glyn Evans (Charlie).
Telecast in Canada in 1977 by CBC. Color. In English. 50 minutes.

ABRAHAM, PAUL
Hungarian composer (1892–1960)

Paul Abraham (in Hungary it's Pál Ábrahám) has never been an American favorite, but his operettas were per-

formed in Canada and England and continue to be popular in continental Europe. VIKTORIA UND IHR HUSSAR has been staged in Montreal, London, and Paris and filmed twice. BALL IM SAVOY, which starred opera singer Gitta Alpar on stage and screen, was presented in London by Oscar Hammerstein II, who wrote a new book for it. DIE BLUME VON HAWAII is still prominent in the central European repertory. Abraham also wrote memorable film musicals such as *Die Privatsekretärin* (1931), which was filmed in four languages and became Victor Saville's *Sunshine Susie* when it was transposed to England. Abraham was Jewish so he had to flee from Berlin when the Nazis took over and then had to leave Vienna, Budapest, and Paris. He ended up in New York where he wrote no more operettas.

ACCUSED, THE
1961 TV monodrama by John Strauss

A woman accused of being a witch is about to be condemned at a trial in Puritan Salem. She charges her accusers of wanting to destroy everything that is good and then shocks them by revealing she is pregnant. John Strauss's 30-minute one-character opera *The Accused,* libretto by Sheppard Kerman, premiered on CBS Television on May 7, 1961.

1961 Camera Three, CBS
American TV production: John McGiffert (director), Julius Rudel (conductor, CBS Orchestra), Neil De Luca (set designer).
Cast: Patricia Neway (the woman).
Telecast live June 4, 1961. John Desmond (director). Black and white. In English. 30 minutes.
Comment: This was the composer's only opera.

ACQUA CHETA, L'
1920 operetta by Pietri

Giuseppe Pietri's 1920 operetta *L'acqua cheta* (Still Waters), his most popular musical stage work, is the story of Ida and her sister Anita and their relationships with their men friends. Based on a stage play by Augusto Novelli, its most popular number was the ensemble "Oh com'è bello guidare i cavalli."

1992 Italian TV: Operette, che Passione!
Italian TV studio production: Sandro Massimini (director/producer), Roberto Negri (pianist), Sandro Corelli (choreographer).
Cast: Sandro Massimini, Daniela Mazzucato, Max René Cosotti.
Video: Ricordi (Italy) VHS. Pierluigi Pagano (director). Color. In Italian. About 19 minutes.

Comment: Highlights of operetta on Italian TV series *Operette, che Passione!* Includes songs "Canzone della Rificolona," "Su, le stelle sorridone chete," and "Serenata."

ADAM, ADOLPHE
French composer (1803–1856)

Adolphe Adam, the opéra-comique composer "of catchy little tunes that one can whistle," according to waspish HECTOR BERLIOZ, is best known today for his ballet *Giselle*. However, he also wrote many operas, and five of them are on CD. On video, there is only LE POSTILLON DE LONJUMEAU; it is especially liked in German-speaking countries where tenors enjoy showing off their high notes in a tuneful fashion. It has been televised at least twice in Germany, and there is a film version.

ADAM, THEODOR
German bass-baritone (1926–)

Theodor Adam has a big voice and a commanding presence even on the small screen and has been a major figure in German opera since his 1949 debut in Dresden. He was a star performer at that opera house, especially noted for his performances in works by Wagner, Handel, and Beethoven. Two of his best roles are as Caesar in Handel's GIULIO CESARE (1977) and as Pizarro in Beethoven's FIDELIO (1968 and 1977). He can also be seen in concert with the BERLIN Deutschen Staatsoper in 1976 and performing WAGNER excerpts in Leipzig in 1988. His other opera videos include ARIADNE AUF NAXOS (1999), LUDWIG BEETHOVEN (1971), BERLIN (1976), CAPRICCIO (1990), THE ETERNAL ROAD (1999), DER FREISCHÜTZ (1985), and DIE ZAUBERFLÖTE (1991).

ADAMO, MARK
American composer (1968–)

Mark Adamo has had remarkable success with his first opera, LITTLE WOMEN, a lyrical work based on the novel by Louisa May Alcott composed to his own libretto. It premiered at Houston Grand Opera's Opera Studio in March 1998 and was so popular it was revived, broadcast, telecast, and issued on CD. Adamo, best known as a composer of choral work and a music critic, is a graduate of New York University and the Catholic University of America in Washington, D.C.

ADAMS, DONALD
English bass (1929–1996)

Bristol-born Donald Adams was principal bass with the D'Oyly Company from 1953 to 1969 and a mainstay of its GILBERT AND SULLIVAN productions. He is featured in 12 videos of Gilbert and Sullivan operas, including a 1967 D'Oyly Carte THE MIKADO, an operetta in which he appeared more than 2,000 times. He toured the world with the Gilbert and Sullivan For All company (a group he organized with Thomas Round), and this company filmed eight abridged versions of the operettas. In 1983, he began a new career singing bass roles in grand operas at Covent Garden and the English National. He was appearing in *Don Pasquale* at the Royal Opera when he died. His other Gilbert and Sullivan videos are THE GONDOLIERS (1972), H.M.S. PINAFORE (1972), IOLANTHE (1972), THE MIKADO (1972), PATIENCE (1982), THE PIRATES OF PENZANCE (1972), RUDDIGORE (1967/1972/1982), THE SORCERER (1982), and THE YEOMEN OF THE GUARD (1972).

ADAMS, JOHN
American composer (1947–)

John Adams has won critical and audience favor for his operas on contemporary subjects that feature an attractive minimalist vocal style and memorable melodies. His collaboration with stage director PETER SELLARS has helped gain wide attention for his work. NIXON IN CHINA (1987) is one of the most publicized modern operas, a trendsetting media event that originated what became known as the "CNN opera." *The Death of Klinghoffer* (1991), based on the hijacking of the cruise ship *Achille Lauro*, is both admired and controversial. *I Was Looking at the Ceiling and Then I Saw the Sky* (1995) is based around a Los Angeles earthquake. The multimedia EL NIÑO (2000), a nativity opera/oratorio, premiered at the Théâtre du Châtelet in Paris, and the DVD of the performance won the *Gramophone* magazine award as the best of 2001. Adams is said to be currently the most performed American composer. Born in Massachusetts, he began his musical studies at Dartmouth and Harvard universities and made his reputation on the West Coast.

1998 John Adams: Minimalism and Beyond
Portrait of the composer centered around his choral work *Harmonium*. Adams analyses the piece, while Simon Rattle conducts a rehearsal with the City of Birmingham Symphony Orchestra. Color. In English. 52 minutes. Films for the Humanities & Sciences VHS.

2002 Portrait of John Adams
This 60-minute portrait of the composer is an introduction to a concert of music by Adams and his American contemporaries. Adams talks about himself and his operas in a genuinely interesting and modest manner. Color. 120 minutes Arthaus DVD.

ADÈS, THOMAS

English composer (1971–)

Thomas Adès had a rapid rise to celebrity as pianist, conductor, and composer, but it was his 1995 chamber opera POWDER HER FACE that brought him wide media attention. The story and staging of this story about a scandalous real-life duchess attracted international discussion, and music critics hailed Adès as England's most exciting young composer. The opera, staged around the world and filmed for BBC, led to commissions from Covent Garden and Glyndebourne. Adès, born in London, began to compose in 1990; *Powder Her Face* was his first opera.

1999 Thomas Adès

British television documentary about Adès that examines his career and allows him to explain his musical ideas. It includes scenes of rehearsals for his chamber opera *Powder Her Face* and his large-orchestral work *Asyla*. Gerald Fox directed. Color. In English. 50 minutes.

ADLER, PETER HERMAN

Czech-born American conductor (1899–1990)

Peter Herman Adler was one of the triumvirate who created NBC OPERA THEATRE and made American television opera into a major cultural force. He was musical and artistic director of the series with SAMUEL CHOTZINOFF as producer and KIRK BROWNING as director from 1949 to 1959. Their productions included everything from the first TV opera, AMAHL AND THE NIGHT VISITORS, to the first American production of WAR AND PEACE. He also staged the excellent opera sequences in THE GREAT CARUSO, the most popular opera film ever. In 1969, he created the NET OPERA Company for National Educational Television in collaboration with Browning, and they produced some of the most innovative TV operas seen up to that time. Original NET Opera production ended in 1973 when Henze's opera RACHEL THE CUBANA exploded its small budget.

ADLER, RICHARD

American composer (1921–)

Met soprano Risë Stevens starred in Richard Adler's 1958 TV musical *Little Women,* while Gordon MacRae was the featured performer in his 1958 TV musical *The Gift of the Magi.* Adler is best known, however, for his Broadway musicals. With fellow New Yorker Jerry Ross (1926–1955), he created *The Pajama Game* (1954) about a labor dispute in a factory; it was later filmed with Doris Day. They had another success in 1955 with *Damn Yankees,* the story of a Washington Senators fan who wants so much to help his team beat the Yankees that he signs a Faustian pact with the Devil; it was filmed with its stage star Gwen Verdon.

ADRIANA LECOUVREUR

1902 opera by Cilea

FRANCESCO CILEA's theatrical melodrama focuses on an actress of the Comédie-Française in the 18th century. Her ill-fated love for Maurizio ends with her death, poisoned by a jealous princess. The libretto by Arturo Colautti is based on a play by Scribe and Legouve about a real actress. The opera has been a favorite of sopranos of a certain age since Angelica Pandolfini and Enrico Caruso launched it in 1902, and it is much liked by set designers who enjoy being theatrically monumental. The composer was especially fond of MAGDA OLIVERO in the title role and brought her out of retirement in 1951 to sing it once again; she continued to do so for another 40 years.

1976 NHK Lirica Italiana

Japanese stage production: Gianfranco Masini (conductor, NHK Symphony Orchestra and Chorus).

Cast: Montserrat Caballé (Adriana Lecouvreur), José Carreras (Maurizio), Fiorenza Cossotto (Princess de Bouillon), Attilio D'Orazi (Michonnet), Ivo Vinco (Prince de Bouillon).

Video: Legato Classics VHS. Taped live in Tokyo on September 20, 1976. Color. In Italian. 145 minutes.

1978 Teatro San Carlo

Italian stage production: Giuseppe De Tomasi (director), Eduardo Müller (conductor, Teatro San Carlo Orchestra and Chorus).

Cast: Montserrat Caballé (Adriana Lecouvreur), José Carreras (Maurizio), Maria Luisa Nave (Princess de Bouillon), Enrico Serra.

Video: Bel Canto Society VHS. Taped in April 1978 for French television. Color. In Italian. 143 minutes.

1984 Australian Opera

Australian stage production: John Copley (director), Richard Bonynge (conductor, Elizabethan Sydney Orchestra and Chorus).

Cast: Joan Sutherland (Adriana Lecouvreur), Anson Austin (Maurizio), Heather Begg (Princess de Bouillon), John Wegner (Prince de Bouillon), John Shaw (Michonnet).

Video: Sony VHS. Hugh Davison (director). Color. In Italian with English subtitles. 135 minutes.

Comment: Sutherland sings well, but this is not a role suited for her acting talents.

1989 Teatro alla Scala

    Italian stage production: Lamberto Puggelli (director), Gianandrea Gavazzeni (conductor, Teatro La Scala Orchestra and Chorus), Paolo Bregni (set designer).

    Cast: Mirella Freni (Adriana Lecouvreur), Peter Dvorsky (Maurizio), Fiorenza Cossotto (Princess de Bouillon), Ivo Vinco (Prince de Bouillon), Alessandro Cassis (Michonnet).

    Video: Image Entertainment DVD/Home Vision VHS. Taped June 2, 1989. Brian Large (director). Color. In Italian with English subtitles. 157 minutes.

    Comment: Freni is a dramatic Adriana and Dvorsky an imposing Maurizio in this monumental production, finely conducted by Gavazzeni and nicely staged by Puggelli.

***2000 Teatro alla Scala

    Italian stage production: Lamberto Puggelli (director), Roberto Rizzi Brignoli (conductor, Teatro La Scala Orchestra and Chorus), Paolo Bregni (set designer).

    Cast: Daniella Dessì (Adriana Lecouvreur), Sergei Lerin (Maurizio), Olga Borodina (Princess de Bouillon), Giorgio Giuseppini (Prince de Bouillon), Caro Guelfi (Michonnet).

    Video: TDK DVD. Taped in January 2000. Lamberto Puggelli (director). Color. In Italian with English subtitles. 138 minutes.

    Comment: The 1989 production was first class but this one is even better with superb performances by Dessì and Lerin.

Related films

1910 Adrienne Lecouvreur

Sarah Bernhardt plays Adrienne in the French film *Adrienne Lecouvreur*, based on the play. It was directed by Albert Capellani and Louis Mercanton for Pathé. Black and white. Silent. About 10 minutes.

1918 Adriana Lecouvreur

Biana Stagno-Bellincioni stars in the Italian feature film *Adriana Lecouvreur*, based on the play. It was directed by Ugo Falena for Tespi Film. Black and white. Silent. About 80 minutes

1938 Adrienne Lecouvreur

Soprano Yvonne Printemps is Adrienne, with Pierre Fresnay as her Maurice in the French film *Adrienne Lecouvreur*, based on Scribe and Legouve's play and directed by Marcel l'Herbier. June Astor is the Duchess of Bouillon, André Lefaur is the Duke of Bouillon, and Pierre Larquey is Michonnet. F. A. Wagner was cinematographer. In France the film used music by Maurice Thiriet, but in Italy it was shown with a score based on the opera music. Black and white. In French. 110 minutes.

1942 Vertigine

Beniamino Gigli performs the aria "No, più nobile" from *Adriana Lecouvreur* in this film. He plays a disgruntled opera singer who breaks up with his girl and gambles away his money. See VERTIGINE.

1993 Philadelphia

Maria Callas is heard singing "Io son l'umile ancella" from *Adriana Lecouvreur* in this film starring Tom Hanks as an opera lover dying of AIDS. Jonathan Demme directed. Color. 119 minutes.

1995 Magda Olivero: The Last Verismo Soprano

Magda Olivero, the composer's favorite Adriana, is featured in the role in two excerpts on the video *Magda Olivero: The Last Verismo Soprano*. She is heard singing the role at the age of 26 in a 1938 film, then is pictured singing the role in 1993 at the age of 83. Black and white and color. 59 minutes. Bel Canto Society VHS.

AFRICAINE, L'

1865 opera by Meyerbeer

L'Africaine (The African Woman) is the best of the spectacular "grand operas" in the French manner by GIACOMO MEYERBEER, invoking the age of Portuguese exploration with great passion and glorious music. Eugène Scribe's libretto revolves around the adventures of explorer Vasco da Gama who returns to Portugal after a long voyage bringing as captives Nelusko and Sélika, the "African woman" of the title. She loves Vasco, Vasco loves Ines, and Nelusko loves Sélika. On the next voyage, they are shipwrecked in Africa near where Sélika is a queen, and the power structure is reversed. The tenor aria "O paradis sorte de l'onde," sung by Vasco da Gama, is well-known in its Italian version as "O paradiso" through being popularized by Enrico Caruso. The opera is usually presented in Italy in Italian as *L'Africana*.

***1988 San Francisco Opera

    American stage production: Lotfi Mansouri (director), Maurizio Arena (conductor, San Francisco Opera Orchestra and Chorus), Wolfram Skalaicki (set designer).

    Cast: Shirley Verrett (Sélika), Plácido Domingo (Vasco da Gama), Ruth Ann Swenson (Ines), Justino Diaz (Nelusko), Michael Devlin (Don Pedro), Philip Skinner (Don Diego).

    Video: Image Entertainment and Arthaus (GB) DVD/Kultur and Home Vision VHS/Pioneer LD. Brian Large (director). Color. In French with English subtitles. 192 minutes.

    Comment: Old-fashioned but grandiose and finely sung by Verrett and Domingo and boldly conducted by Arena.

Early/related films

1927 Vitaphone film with Hackett
Chicago Opera tenor Charles Hackett sings the aria "O paradiso" in Italian in this early sound film made by the Vitaphone company. Black and white. 8 minutes.

1929 MGM film with Ruffo
Italian baritone Titta Ruffo made three early opera sound films for MGM. On the first, he performs, in costume and in Italian, Nelusko's invocation "Adamastor, re dell'onde profonde." Black and white. About 8 minutes.

1934 La Buenaventura
Enrico Caruso Jr., playing an opera singer in this American Spanish-language film, sings "O paradiso" in Italian. *La Buenaventura* is an adaptation of Victor Herbert's operetta THE FORTUNE TELLER.

1935 Forget-Me-Not
Beniamino Gigli sings "O paradiso" in Italian in this film about an opera singer married to a woman who may leave him. See FORGET-ME-NOT.

1935 El Cantante de Napoles
Enrico Caruso Jr. sings "O paradiso" in Italian in this American Spanish-language film loosely based on the life of his father. Howard Bretherton directed. Black and white. 77 minutes.

1946 Voglio Bene Soltanto a Te
Beniamino Gigli plays a tenor making a movie who fancies a female costar and sings "O paradiso" from *L'Africana*. See VOGLIO BENE SOLTANTO A TE.

1949 Song of Surrender
Wanda Hendrix plays a recording of Enrico Caruso singing "O paradiso" on a gramophone in 1906 in the film *Song of Surrender* and the music becomes central to the plot. See SONG OF SURRENDER.

1950 The Toast of New Orleans
Maria Lanza sings "O paradiso" in this film about a Louisiana fisherman who becomes an opera star in turn-of-the-century New Orleans with help from Kathryn Grayson. See THE TOAST OF NEW ORLEANS.

1956 Serenade
Mario Lanza sings "O paradiso" with Ray Heindorf and orchestra in this film about an opera singer with emotional problems. See SERENADE.

1979 Prince Charles Backstage at Covent Garden
Prince Charles promotes a fundraising campaign at the ROYAL OPERA HOUSE in Covent Garden backstage during a production of *L'Africaine*.

AFRICAN-AMERICAN OPERA

There have been African-American composers since the 19th century, but you won't find many operas by them on film or video. The most widely available is SCOTT JOPLIN'S TREEMONISHA, taped by HOUSTON GRAND OPERA in 1982. William Grant Still was the first African-American composer to have an opera televised, A BAYOU LEGEND by Opera/South in 1974, but it is not available as a commercial video. Anthony Davis is one of the best-known contemporary black opera composers, but his operas are only on CD. African-American singers have been more fortunate in recent years, but it took a long time; black singers were not allowed to sing with major American white opera companies until the 1930s. Caterina Jarboro was the first, singing with Chicago Civic Opera in 1933 after achieving stardom in Europe. TODD DUNCAN, the creator of Porgy in PORGY AND BESS, was the first at New York City Opera, singing Tonio in *Cavalleria rusticana* in 1945. MARIAN ANDERSON was the first at the Met, singing Ulrica in *Un ballo in maschera* on January 7, 1955. ROBERT MCFERRIN was the first black man to sing at the Met, playing Amonasro in *Aida* on January 27, 1955. There is no film of these breakthrough performances, but black singers began to be seen on screen in opera in the 1940s. ANNE BROWN, who created the role, played Bess in the PORGY AND BESS sequence of the 1945 film *Rhapsody in Blue*, and LEONTYNE PRICE starred in *Tosca* on NBC Television in 1955 (some southern stations refused to air it). African-Americans are an important part of the opera world today, so it is no surprise that hundreds of videos are available featuring them in every kind of operatic role.

2000 Aida's Brothers and Sisters
Aida's Brothers and Sisters: Black Voices in Opera is a revealing examination of the situation of African-American opera singers in America. Among those interviewed or featured in archival film are MARIAN ANDERSON, ROBERT MCFERRIN, GRACE BUMBRY, KATHLEEN BATTLE, LEONTYNE PRICE, JESSYE NORMAN, SHIRLEY VERRETT, SIMON ESTES, BARBARA HENDRICKS, PAUL ROBESON, and members of the Opera Ebony company. George Shirley, Martina Arroyo, Edward Said, and Bobby McFerrin (son of Robert) are among those who discuss black singers, Negro spirituals, and the fight to overcome racism in the opera house. Rosalyn Story, author of *And So I Sing, African-American Divas of Opera and Concert*, provides an historical perspective. Jan Schmidt-Garre and Marieke Schroeder made the film,

telecast on PBS in February 2000. Color. In English. 85 minutes.

AGNESE DI HOHENSTAUFEN
1829 opera by Spontini

GASPARE SPONTINI's grand historical opera *Agnese von Hohenstaufen* was composed to a German libretto by Ernest Rapuach, but it is usually performed now in an Italian version as *Agnese di Hohenstaufen*. It's a complex and rather emotional love story set among aristocratic intrigues during the 12th century. Agnes, a cousin of Emperor Henry VI, is in love with Heinrich, the son of the emperor's Guelph enemy Henry the Lion.

1986 Teatro dell'Opera di Roma
Italian stage production: Tonino del Colle (director), Maximiano Valdes (conductor, Teatro dell'Opera di Roma Orchestra).

Cast: Montserrat Caballé (Agnes), Veriano Luchetti (Heinrich), Silvano Pagliuca, Glenys Linos.

Video: Bel Canto Society/Premiere Opera/Opera Dubs VHS. Telecast November 8, 1986. Color. In Italian. 158 minutes.

Comment: Caballé first sang the role in an RAI Italian radio broadcast in 1970.

AGRIPPINA
1709 opera by Handel

GEORGE FRIDERIC HANDEL composed this opera while he was living in Italy, where he had the extremely powerful Cardinal Vincenzo Grimani as his libretto writer. The cardinal's contribution ensured its success, and it made Handel famous. The fictional story concerns Roman Emperor Claudius's conniving second wife Agrippina and her schemes to obtain the crown for her son Nero. She is willing to murder for it.

1985 Schwetzingen Festival
German stage production: Michael Hampe (director), Arnold Östman (conductor, London Baroque Players), Maurice Pagano (set designer).

Cast: Barbara Daniels (Agrippina) David Kuebler (Nero), Claudio Nicolai (Ottone), Carlos Feller (Lesbo), Günter von Kannen (Claudius), Janice Hall (Poppea).

Video: Kultur/Home Vision VHS. Thomas Olofsson (director). Color. In Italian with English subtitles. 160 minutes.

Comment: Daniels sings this difficult music brilliantly, tenor Kuebler does well in a role written for a castrato, Östman conducts with feeling, and Pagano's sets are striking.

Early film

1911 Cines film
Enrico Guazzoni wrote and directed the Italian film *Agrippina* for Cines with Adele Bianchi Azzarilli as the scheming Agrippina. Cesare Moltini as Aniceto, Signora Sturla as Locusta, and Signor Dolfini as a slave. Black and white. Silent About 18 minutes. Print survives in Dutch Film Archive.

AGUA, AZUCARILLOS Y AGUARDIENTE
1897 zarzuela by Chueca

Summer in Madrid at the end of the 19th century. Street vendors cry their wares ("agua, zucarillos, aguardiente," that is, water, candy, brandy), and the sellers in the Recoletos Gardens are doing good business. Lovestruck poet Asia, feisty water seller Pepa, her rebellious rival Manuela, and their men friends spend a complicated day in the park sorting out their intertwined love lives, but all ends well. Federico Chueca's "sainete" *Agua, azucarillos y aguardiente*, libretto by Miguel Ramos Carrión, is one of the composer's most popular zarzuelas.

1995 Teatro Calderón, Madrid
Spanish stage production: José Luis Moreno (director), José A. Irasforza (conductor, Teatro Calderón Orchestra and Chorus), Julian Perez Muñoz (set designer), Alhambra Ballet.

Cast: Rosa Martin, Pepa Rosado, Pepe Ruiz, Antonia Pantoja, David Muro, Pedro Pablo Juárez, Guadalupe Sánchez.

Video: Metrovideo VHS. José Ignado Ortega (director). Telecast live by RTVE. Color. In Spanish. 65 minutes.

Comment: Lively dances and pleasant choral numbers, but the acting styles seem to have been left over from the 19th century.

***2000 Jarvis Conservatory, Napa
American stage production: Daniel Helfgot (director), Philip J. Bauman (conductor, Jarvis Conservatory Orchestra), Peter Crompton (sets), William Jarvis (producer/translator).

Cast: Lizette Amado (Asia), Gisella Monclova (Pepa), Joanna Foutz (Manuela), Celeste Mann (Dona Simona), Andrew Moore (Serafin), Harry Baechtel (Lorenzo), Christopher Fernandez (Vincente), Joe Lewis (Don Aquilino).

Video: Jarvis Conservatory VHS. Dave Drum (director). Color. Dialogue in English, singing in Spanish with English subtitles. 60 minutes.

Comment: Delightfully sung, acted, and staged with a large cast and good production values, from dancing nannies to singing wafer sellers. The video director captures the spirit of the production, and the orchestra helps one appreciate the enduring appeal of Chueca's music.

AIDA
1871 opera by Verdi

GIUSEPPE VERDI's *Aida* is the most popular of the 19th-century "grand operas," and its grandiose spectacle and stirring music have made it a favorite at outdoor arenas like Verona where elephants can join the triumphal march. Its spectacle has also made it a favorite of filmmakers. Librettist Antonio Ghislanzoni focuses the story on the daughter of an Ethiopian king who is a captive slave in Egypt. Aida has fallen in love with Radames, the man chosen to lead the Egyptian army, and he loves her in return, but the Pharaoh's jealous daughter Amneris also fancies Radames. Aida's love and their split loyalties eventually lead to betrayal and death for both lovers. The opera premiered in Cairo soon after the opening of the Suez Canal.

1949 NBC Television
American TV production: Doug Rodgers (film director), Arturo Toscanini (conductor, NBC Symphony Orchestra and Robert Shaw Chorale).

Cast: Herva Nelli (Aida), Richard Tucker (Radames), Eva Gustavson (Amneris), Giuseppe Valdengo (Amonasro), Dennis Harbour (Pharaoh), Norman Scott (Ramfis), Teresa Stich-Randall (Priestess).

Video: BMG/RCA VHS and LD. Telecast March 26 and April 2, 1949. Black and white. In Italian with English narration before each act. 149 minutes.

Comment: Historic concert version of the opera with 82-year-old Toscanini conducting. It's rather formal but wonderful all the same.

1953 Fracassi film
Italian feature film: Clemente Fracassi (director), Renzo Rossellini (conductor, RAI Italian State Radio Orchestra), Pietro Portalupi (cinematographer), Flavio Mogherini (set designer), Oscar Film (production).

Cast: Sophia Loren (Aida, sung by Renata Tebaldi), Lois Maxwell (Amneris, sung by Ebe Stignani), Luciano della Marra (Radames, sung by Giuseppe Cam-

Aida (1953): Clemente Fracassi's film of the opera was promoted by Sol Hurok as a spectacular epic with music.

8

pora), Amonasro (Afro Poli, sung by Gino Bechi), Giulio Neri (Ramfis, sung by Antonio Cassinelli).

Video: Image Entertainment DVD/Bel Canto Society VHS. Color. In Italian with English narration. 95 minutes.

Comment: This famous film was launched like a live spectacle by impresario Sol Hurok and was promoted as the first opera film in color. It was a truly major production for its time, with grandiose sets and top La Scala and Rome Opera singers, but the opera is considerably abridged from the standard stage version of around 160 minutes.

1956 NHK Lirica Italiana

Japanese stage production: Carlo Piccinato (director), Vittorio Gui (conductor, NHK Symphony Orchestra and Lyric Opera of Nikikai and Fujiwara Chorus), Enzo Deho (set designer).

Cast: Antonietta Stella (Aida), Umberto Borsa (Radames), Giulietta Simionato (Amneris), Gian Giacomo Guelfi (Amonasro), Carlo Cava (Ramfis), Antonio Cassinelli (Pharaoh).

Telecast in Japan in NHK series *Lirica Italian.* Filmed live in Tokyo September 29, 1956. Black and white. In Italian. 163 minutes.

Comment: First production telecast in the invaluable NHK series; not currently on video.

1961 NHK Lirica Italiana

Japanese stage production: Carlo Piccinato (director), Franco Capuana (conductor, NHK Radio Symphony Orchestra and Nikikai and Fujiwara Opera Chorus). Enzo Deho (set designer).

Cast: Gabriella Tucci (Aida), Mario del Monaco (Radames), Giulietta Simionato (Amneris), Aldo Protti (Amonasro), Paolo Washington (Ramfis), Silvano Pagliuca (Pharaoh).

Video: VAI VHS/Dreamlife (Japan) LD. Filmed live in Tokyo October 13, 1961, for NHK series *Lirica Italiana.* Black and white. In Italian with English subtitles. 163 minutes.

Comment: Creaky production but valuable for performances by Tucci, del Monaco, and Simionato.

***1966 Arena di Verona

Italian stage production: Herbert Graf (director), Franco Capuana (conductor, Arena di Verona Chorus and Orchestra), Pino Casarini (set designer).

Cast: Leyla Gencer (Aida), Carlo Bergonzi (Radames), Fiorenza Cossotto (Amneris), Anselmo Colzani (Amonasro), Bonaldo Giaiotti (Ramfis), Franco Pugliese (Pharaoh).

Video: Hardy Classic DVD/Bel Canto Society VHS. Cesare Barlacchi (director). Black and white. In Italian. 160 minutes.

Comment: Acting styles and production values have changed a lot at Verona in the past 40 years, but these splendid voices have never been superseded.

1976 Orange Festival

French stage production: Pierre Jourdan (director), Thomas Schippers (conductor, Torino Regio Teatro Orchestra).

Cast: Grace Bumbry (Amneris), Gilda Cruz-Romo (Aida), Peter Gougaloff (Radames), Ingvar Wixell (Amonasro).

Video: Lyric VHS/Dreamlife (Japan) DVD/LD. Pierre Jourdan (film director). Color. In Italian. 149 minutes.

Comment: This fine open-air production at the Roman amphitheater in Orange is truly international with a Mexican Aida, Bulgarian Radames, American Amneris, Swedish Amonasro, and French director.

***1981 Arena di Verona

Stage production: Giancarlo Sbragia (director), Anton Guadagno (conductor, Arena di Verona Orchestra and Chorus), Vittorio Rossi (set designer).

Cast: Maria Chiara (Aida), Nicola Martinucci (Radames), Fiorenza Cossotto (Amneris), Carlo Zardo (Ramfis), Giuseppe Scandola (Amonasro), Alfredo Zanazzo (Pharaoh).

Video: HBO Cannon/NVC Arts (GB) VHS. Brian Large (director). Color. In Italian with English subtitles. 150 minutes.

Comment: The Arena di Verona, an open-air Roman amphitheater seating 25,000, is the perfect spectacular setting for *Aida.* This production has real grandeur, with sets of a size most designers can only dream about. Large provides a better view of the opera than the real audience has, and the singing is as notable as the sets.

1981/1989 Opera Stories

Laserdisc highlights version of the above Arena di Verona production. Charlton Heston narrates the story from Egypt, where Keith Cheetham filmed him in 1989. Color. In English and Italian with English subtitles. 52 minutes. Pioneer Artists LD.

1981 San Francisco Opera

American stage production: Sam Wanamaker (director), García Navarro (conductor, San Francisco Opera Orchestra and Chorus), Douglas Schmidt (set designer).

Cast: Margaret Price (Aida), Luciano Pavarotti (Radames), Stefanie Toczyska (Amneris), Simon Estes

(Amonasro), Kurt Rydl (Ramfis), Kevin Langam (Pharaoh).

Video: Warner Music NVC Arts (GB) DVD/VHS. Telecast November 15, 1981, live by satellite to Europe. Brian Large (director). Color. In Italian with English subtitles. 163 minutes.

Comment: Pavarotti's first Radames and Price's first Aida, shown live to European television audiences, is a good old-fashioned production with grand sets and fancy costumes. The audience loves it.

1985 Metropolitan Opera

American stage production: John Dexter (director), James Levine (conductor, Metropolitan Opera Orchestra and Chorus), David Reppa (set designer).

Cast: Leontyne Price (Aida), James McCracken (Radames), Fiorenza Cossotto (Amneris), Simon Estes (Amonasro), John Macurdy (Ramfis), Dimitri Kavrakos (Pharaoh).

Video at the MTR. Brian Large (director). Telecast live January 3, 1985, on PBS. Color. In Italian with English subtitles. 150 minutes.

Comment: One of Price's greatest performances, but it has not been issued on commercial video.

1985 Teatro alla Scala

Italian stage production: Luca Ronconi (director), Lorin Maazel (conductor, Teatro alla Scala Orchestra and Chorus), Mauro Pagano (set designer).

Cast: Maria Chiara (Aida), Luciano Pavarotti (Radames), Ghena Dimitrova (Amneris), Juan Pons (Amonasro), Nicolai Ghiaurov (Ramfis). Paata Burchuladze (Pharaoh).

Video: Image Entertainment and Arthaus (GB) DVD/Kultur and Home Vision VHS/Pioneer LD. Derek Bailey (director). Telecast July 12, 1985, in Italy. Color. In Italian with English subtitles. 160 minutes.

Comment: Very impressive production. Ronconi wanted spectacular sets, and designer Pagano certainly provided them. He also added extra piquancy to the Act II scene in Amneris's rooms by filling them with seminude serving women.

1988 Fellbom film

Swedish feature film: Claes Fellbom (director), Kerstin Nerbe (conductor, Swedish Folk Opera Orchestra and Chorus), Jorgen Persson (cinematographer).

Cast: Margareta Ridderstedt (Aida), Niklas Ek (Radames, sung by Robert Grundin), Ingrid Tomasson (Amneris), Jan Van Der Schaaf (Amonasro).

Color. In Swedish with English subtitles. 116 minutes.

Comment: Fellbom's film, a fascinating attempt to create a primitive setting for the opera with Egyptian society envisioned as a barbaric kingdom, was shot entirely on location on the island of Lanzarote. When it premiered at AFI's Cinetex Film Festival in Las Vegas, it was reviewed by *Variety* as the "topless" *Aida* because of the women's costumes.

1988 Teatro Regio, Parma

Italian stage production: Mauro Bolognini (director), Donato Renzetti (conductor, Orchestra Sinfonica dell'Emilia-Romagna and Teatro Regio Chorus), Mario Ceroli (set designer).

Cast: Maria Chiara (Aida), Nicola Martinucci (Radames), Elena Obraztsova (Amneris), Bruno Pola (Amonasro), Cesare Siepi (Ramfis).

Video: Bel Canto Society VHS. Color. In Italian. 162 minutes.

1989 Metropolitan Opera

American stage production: Sonja Frisell (director), James Levine (conductor, Metropolitan Opera Orchestra and Chorus), Gianni Quaranta (set designer).

Cast: Aprile Millo (Aida), Plácido Domingo (Radames), Dolora Zajick (Amneris), Paata Burchuladze (Ramfis), Dimitri Kavrakos (Pharaoh), Sherrill Milnes (Amonasro).

Video: DG DVD/VHS/LD. Brian Large (director). Taped October 7, 1989; telecast December 27, 1989. Color. In Italian with English subtitles. 158 minutes.

Comment: Millo is an intense Aida and Domingo a powerful Radames with strong support from Levine. Rodney Griffin created impressive dance sequences, and the telecast won an Emmy Award as the Outstanding Classical Program in the Performing Arts.

1994 Royal Opera

English stage production: Elijah Moshinsky (director), Edward Downes (conductor, Royal Opera House Orchestra and Chorus), Michael Yeargan (set designer).

Cast: Cheryl Studer (Aida), Dennis O'Neill (Radames), Luciana D'Intino (Amneris), Robert Lloyd (Ramfis), Alexandru Agache (Amonasro).

Video: Kultur DVD and VHS/Home Vision VHS/Pioneer LD. Brian Large (director). Color. In Italian with English subtitles. 152 minutes.

Comment: Excellent production values, including superb dance sequences choreographed by Kate Flatt. The singing, however, is just okay.

1997 St. Margarethen Opera Festival

Austrian stage production: Martin Dubowitz (director), Giorgio Croci (conductor, Stagione d'Opera Italiana Orchestra and Chorus), Manfred Wabo (set designer).

Cast: Pauletta de Vaughn (Aida), Bruno Sebastian (Radames), Adriana Nicolai (Amneris), Walter Donati (Amonasro).

Video: Beckmann/Cascade (GB) DVD. Color. In Italian with English subtitles. 80 minutes.

Comment: Spectacle dominates this production filmed at the ancient Roman quarry of St. Margarethen in Austria in what is claimed to be "the biggest open-air stage in Europe," with seating for 3,800. Hundreds of extras, including three elephants and a dozen horses, are impressive. The singing is not.

***2001 Teatro Verdi, Busseto

Italian stage production: Franco Zeffirelli (director/set designer). Massimiliano Stefanelli (conductor, Arturo Toscanini Foundation Orchestra and Chorus).

Cast: Adina Aaron (Aida), Scott Piper (Radames), Kate Aldrich (Amneris), Giuseppe Garra (Amonasro), Enrico Giuseppe Iori (Ramfis), Paolo Pecchioli (Pharaoh).

Video: TDK DVD/Live Opera Heaven VHS. Franco Zeffirelli (director). Taped live January 27, 2001. Color. In Italian with English subtitles. 188 minutes

Comment: This production in Verdi's birth city was staged to mark the centenary of the composer's death. Teatro Verdi is a small 19th-century theater, so this is an intimate rather than a grandiose production, and all the better for it. The young singers were selected by the Toscanini Foundation and trained by tenor Carlo Bergonzi, who lives in Busseto.

Early/related films

1911 Edison film
Mary Fuller plays Aida in the Edison studio film *Aida* based on the Verdi opera with Marc MacDermott as Radames, Miriam Nesbitt as Amneris, and Charles Ogle as the Pharaoh. The film premiered May 6, 1911, with live *Aida* music, and contemporary critics thought it a magnificent "reproduction" of the opera. Oscar Apfel and J. Searle Dawley wrote and directed. Black and white. Silent. About 15 minutes.

1911 Film d'Arte Italiana film
Bianca Lorenzoni plays Aida in this Italian *Aida* from the Film d'Arte Italiana company, with Virgilio Frigerio as Radames and Rina Agozzino Alessio as Amneris. Black and white. Silent. About 12 minutes. Print in Dutch film archive.

1914 The Nightingale
Ethel Barrymore plays a street singer who becomes an opera star at the Met by singing the title role in *Aida*. The plot of this American film foreshadows what would occur at the Met four years later, when Rosa Ponselle became an opera star with no prior experience. Black and white. Silent. About 30 minutes.

1927–1930 Vitaphone films with Martinelli
Met tenor Giovanni Martinelli made three Vitaphone sound films in 1927 and 1930 featuring excerpts from *Aida*. In two, he sings "Celeste Aida"; in the third, he joins mezzo-soprano Ina Bourskaya in a Radames-Amneris duet. Black and white. Each film about 8 minutes.

1935 Stars Over Broadway
James Melton auditions at the Met with "Celeste Aida" and seems set on an opera career until his manager (Pat O'Brien) diverts him into better paying jobs in radio and clubs. At the end of the film, he returns to opera and makes his debut in *Aida* at the Met. William Keighley directed for Warner Brothers. Black and white. In English. 89 minutes.

1936 Sinfonie di cuori
Beniamino Gigli plays an opera singer loved by a married woman who collapses while he is on stage singing "Celeste Aida" with the Bavarian State Opera Orchestra and Chorus. See SINFONIE DI CUORI.

1951 The Great Caruso
Enrico Caruso (Mario Lanza) makes his first appearance on an opera stage in this film biography, playing a spear-bearer in an Italian regional production of *Aida*. When he is famous, he is cast as Radames for his first appearance at the Met. After Dorothy Kirsten as Aida sings "Numi, Pieta" at a rehearsal, he performs "Celeste Aida." They appear together on the Met stage in the "La fatale pietra" tomb scene with Blanche Thebom as Amneris. Peter Herman Adler staged and conducted the opera sequences. See THE GREAT CARUSO.

1959 For the First Time
In Mario Lanza's last film, he is typecast as a temperamental opera singer who is always missing performances and behaving badly; his screen career closes ironically with the Triumphal March from *Aida*. George Stoll was music director and Rudolph Maté, director. Color. 97 minutes. MGM-UA VHS.

1958 Price concert
Leontyne Price sings the role of Aida in the third act of the opera at a Radio-Canada TV concert telecast October 23, 1958. William McGrath is Radames, Napoleon Bisson is Amonasro, and the Radio-Canada Orchestra plays the music. François Bernier directed. Black and white. 30 minutes.

1960 The Girl With a Suitcase

Valerio Zurlini's film *La ragazza con la valigia* has as its heroine a young woman named Aida (Claudia Cardinale). As she walks down her boyfriend's staircase, "Celeste Aida" is played on a phonograph (Beniamino Gigli is the singer). Black and white. In Italian. 113 minutes.

1962 Voice of Firestone

Leontyne Price, one of the great interpreters of Aida, sings "O patria mia" on the *Voice of Firestone* television show. Howard Barlow conducts. Telecast December 30, 1962. Black and white. In Italian with English introduction. About 7 minutes. On anthology *A Firestone Verdi Festival.* VAI VHS.

1987 The Aida File

Informative and entertaining documentary about the opera, examining its origins and featuring footage of past performances by great Aidas, plus interviews with Eva Turner, Renata Tebaldi, Grace Bumbry, Carlo Bergonzi, and Luciano Pavarotti. The docu-drama scenes were shot in Parma and at the La Scala Museum with George Barker playing Verdi and Colin Jeavons as libretto writer Antonio Ghislanzoni. Producer Hilary Chadwick and director Derek Bailey created the film for the British TV South Bank Show. Color. 78 minutes. Kultur/Home Vision VHS.

1989 Getting It Right

Randal Kleiser's English film about a man looking for Ms. Right features a scene at the opera *Aida* with the music performed by the Sofia National Opera Orchestra and Chorus. The on-stage singers are Anne-Marie Owens, Vivian Tierney, and John Cashmore. During the opera Jesse Birdall meets Lynn Redgrave, who seduces him. Color. 102 minutes.

1994 Domingo at Verona

Plácido Domingo celebrated 25 years of appearances at the Arena di Verona with a program of staged opera scenes, including Act III of *Aida* with Domingo as Radames. Nello Santi conducts the Arena Orchestra. Color. 90 minutes. On VHS.

1999 The Prompter

Norwegian film about a prompter (Hege Schøyen) rehearsing a production of *Aida* while getting ready to marry. Aida is played by Liv Gunhild Tandberg, Radames by Richard Edgar-Wilson, and Amneris by Anne-Lise Bernsten; Carlo Barsotti is the stage director. The film has rehearsal and performances scenes of the opera. See THE PROMPTER.

AKHNATEN
1984 opera by Glass

Egyptian Pharaoh Akhnaten, a visionary leader ahead of his time, creates a religion in 1875 B.C. based around an all-powerful god. His subjects eventually rebel against monotheism and restore the old gods. PHILIP GLASS's minimalist three-act opera *Akhnaten,* libretto by the composer created in collaboration with Shalom Goldman, Robert Israel, Richard Riddell, and Jerome Robbins, was premiered by Stuttgart State Opera March 24, 1984, and staged by Houston Grand Opera October 12, 1984. *Akhnaten* is the third of Glass's trilogy of "portrait" operas, after *Einstein on the Beach* and *Satyagraha* and includes passages in Akkadian, Egyptian, and biblical Hebrew. It was voted the third most popular opera of the 20th century by readers of *BBC Music Magazine* in a 1999 poll.

1984 Philip Glass: A Composer's Notes

Documentary about Glass, subtitled *Philip Glass and the Making of an Opera,* featuring simultaneous productions of *Akhnaten* in Germany and America. Achim Freyer directed the production at the Wurttemberg State Theater in Stuttgart with PAUL ESSWOOD as Akhnaten, Milagro Vargas as Nefertiti, and Dennis Russell Davies conducting. David Freeman directed the Houston Grand Opera production with Christopher Robson as Akhnaten, Marta Senn as Nefertiti, and John DeMain conducting. Michael Blackwood directed the film, photographed by Mead Hunt. Color. 87 minutes. VAI VHS.

ALAGNA, ROBERTO
French tenor (1963–)

Roberto Alagna gained international acclaim in 1994 for his performance at Covent Garden in *Roméo et Juliette,* and this led to a film version with his wife, soprano ANGELA GHEORGHIU. Born in Paris of Sicilian parents, Alagna studied privately and is bilingual in French and Italian. He made his operatic debut at Glyndebourne in 1988 as Alfredo in *La traviata* and has also sung Hoffmann in *Les contes d'Hoffmann,* Rodolfo in *La bohème,* and the Duke in *Rigoletto.* His opera videos include DON CARLOS (1996), L'ELISIR D'AMORE (1996), JAMES LEVINE (1996), A MIDSUMMER NIGHT'S DREAM (1999 film), ROMÉO ET JULIETTE (1984/2002), ROYAL OPERA HOUSE (1996), TOSCA (2001), LA TRAVIATA (1992), and VERDI REQUIEM (2001).

1999 Classics on a Summer Evening

Alagna and wife Angela Gheorghiu perform a program of operatic favorites by Bizet, Puccini, and Verdi in a concert staged July 11, 1999, in the square in front of the Semper Opera House in Dresden. Giuseppe Sinopoli conducts the Dresden Semper Opera Orchestra and Chorus, and Hans Hulscher directed the video. Color. 101 minutes. EMI DVD.

ALBANESE, LICIA
Italian-born American soprano (1913–)

Licia Albanese, noted for her Puccini and Verdi heroines, was Toscanini's choice to sing Violetta in *La traviata* and Mimì in *La bohème* in his NBC radio broadcasts. She made her debut in Milan in 1934 and her first appearance at the Metropolitan Opera in 1940; she also sang with the Met that year in the first American opera telecast. She was so well received she decided to move to the United States and become an American citizen. Albanese won great praise for the intensity of her singing, and her performances are widely available on record. She played Desdemona in *Otello* in the first complete opera telecast from the Metropolitan, performed with Mario Lanza in his 1956 film *Serenade,* sings on the soundtrack of the 1979 film THRILLER, and is featured in the *Tosca* documentary *I Live for Art.* She retired from the Met in 1966. See also METROPOLITAN OPERA (1940/1953), OTELLO (1948), TOSCA (1983 film), and ARTURO TOSCANINI (1985).

1951 Licia Albanese in Opera and Song
Albanese finished her career before extensive televising of operas, but she left some TV records, including an appearance on the *Voice of Firestone* television series. Her performance, taped February 19, 1951, includes an aria from *Pagliacci.* Black and white. 26 minutes. VAI VHS.

1956 Serenade
Licia Albanese plays herself in this Hollywood feature film. She appears on a New York opera theater stage resembling the Met singing Desdemona opposite Mario Lanza as Otello. It is his Met debut, but he abandons Albanese on stage when Joan Fontaine doesn't turn up for the performance. See SERENADE.

ALBERGHETTI, ANNA MARIA
Italian-born American soprano (1936–)

Italian-born Anna Maria Alberghetti began her career splendidly singing Monica in the 1951 film of Menotti's THE MEDIUM. Paramount thought she might be another Deanna Durbin and had her sing an aria in the Bing Crosby musical *Here Comes the Groom.* She was fine as a girl with a good opera voice in the 1953 film *The Stars are Singing* with the Met's LAURITZ MELCHIOR. After that, her films were less musical and less interesting. High points of her later career include a Tony Award for the Broadway music *Carnival* and a TV production of

KISMET (1967) with José Ferrer. She also worked with the Long Beach Civic Light Opera Company. In addition to the films listed below, she appeared in the nonmusical westerns *The Last Command* (1955) and *Duel at Apache Wells* (1957).

1951 Here Comes the Groom
Alberghetti, playing a blind war orphan, gives a touching performance of Gilda's aria "Caro nome" at the beginning of this enjoyable musical. She is auditioning in Paris for an American conductor who decides to adopt her and arrange for her to sing at the Met. Most of the singing in the film, however, is by Bing Crosby who has to get married so he can adopt orphans. Frank Capra directed. Black and white. 113 minutes. Paramount VHS.

1953 The Stars Are Singing
Alberghetti plays a 15-year-old Polish girl who jumps ship in New York and hides out from the police with family friend Lauritz Melchior, a former Metropolitan Opera star. She has a good voice and demonstrates it singing "Una voce poco fa" from *Il barbiere di Siviglia,* "Sempre libera" from *La traviata,* and a duet with Melchior. Norman Taurog directed this pleasant film for Paramount. Color. 99 minutes. Paramount VHS.

1957 Ten Thousand Bedrooms
Alberghetti is a gold digger in Rome throwing herself at millionaire Dean Martin in this old-fashioned musical directed by Richard Thorpe. Color. 114 minutes. Paramount VHS.

1960 Cinderfella
Alberghetti plays a princess opposite comedian Jerry Lewis in her last film. Frank Tashlin directed. Color. 90 minutes.

ALBERNI, LUIS
Spanish-born American character actor (1887–1962)

Luis Alberni is not from the world of opera, but for moviegoers during the 1930s and 1940s he was the personification of opera stereotypes. Whether he was portraying an opera singer, maestro, singing teacher, prompter, or impresario, he usually climbed to impressive heights of frenzy and temperament. He acted opposite opera singers such as Grace Moore, Marion Talley, and Michael Bartlett and even sang the baritone part of the *Lucia* sextet to a haddock in FOLLOW YOUR HEART. *The New York Times* hailed him as its favorite screen musician saying, "Mr. Alberni may not know one note from another, but he has done so much of this sort of thing for the screen that he achieves a fervor comparable to that of an inspired conductor in the throes of *L'Africaine*." Alberni's other operatic films include THE FORTUNE TELLER (1934), ONE NIGHT OF LOVE (1934), METROPOLITAN (1935), LOVE ME FOREVER (1935), WHEN YOU'RE IN LOVE (1937), and WONDER MAN (1945), where he prompts an opera starring Danny Kaye. He is Svengali's roommate in the 1931 version of the TRILBY story. Alberni made more than 135 films and is a small delight in all of them.

ALBERT, EUGEN D'
German composer (1864–1932)

Eugen d'Albert was truly international, a Euro composer ahead of his time. His family came from Italy, his name was French, his parents were Germans living in England, he was born in Scotland, he became a Swiss citizen, and he died in Latvia. Although he wrote many operas, only one has remained in the repertoire, and it is naturally the most international. TIEFLAND (1903) is a German opera based on a Catalan play composed in the Italian verismo style. Maria Callas helped build her early reputation singing in it.

ALBERT HERRING
1947 opera by Britten

Benjamin Britten's popular comic opera *Albert Herring*, libretto by Eric Crozier, is based on a de Maupassant story transposed to England. Albert Herring is picked to be the virgin May Day King in a small Suffolk village when no virgin May Queen can be found. After he is crowned, he has a little too much to drink and ends ups disqualifying himself for the crown.

1978 St. Louis Opera
American stage production: Lou Galterio (director), John Moriarty (conductor, St. Louis Symphony Orchestra), John Kasarda (set designer).

Cast: James Hoback (Albert Herring), Pauline Tinsley (Lady Billows), Joyce Gerber (Florence Pike), Mallory Walker (Mrs. Upfold), David Ward (Budd), Stephen Dickson (Sid), Evelyn Petro (Nancy), Judith Christin (Mrs. Herring).

Video: House of Opera DVD/VHS. Telecast by WNET and BBC. Brian Large (director). Color. In English. 150 minutes.

***1985 Glyndebourne Festival
English stage production: Peter Hall (director), Bernard Haitink (conductor, London Philharmonic Orchestra and Glyndebourne Festival Chorus), John Gunter (set designer).

Cast: John Graham-Hall (Albert Herring), Patricia Johnson (Lady Billows), Felicity Palmer (Flor-

ence), Elizabeth Gale (Miss Wordsworth), Richard van Allan (Budd), Alan Opie (Sid), Jean Rigby (Nancy).

Video: Kultur/Home Vision VHS. Telecast by BBC. Robin Lough (director). Color. In English. 145 minutes.

Comment: Superb production, finely conducted, excellent cast.

ALCESTE
1767 opera by Gluck

Alceste, Queen of Thessaly, is a rather noble wife who promises to sacrifice herself to the gods if her husband King Admète will recover from an illness. He does, and she keeps her promise, but all ends well with a little supernatural help from Apollo. CHRISTOPH WILLIBALD GLUCK's opera *Alceste* was ahead of its time when it premiered in 1767, the second of his reform operas with librettist Ranieri de' Calzabigi, based on the play by Euripides. The French version has a libretto by the wonderfully named Marie François Louis Gand Leblanc du Roullet.

1998 Drottningholm Court Theatre
Swedish stage production: Marianne Mörck (director), Arnold Östman (conductor, Drottningholm Court Theatre Orchestra and Chorus).

Cast: Teresa Ringholz (Alceste), Justin Lavender (King Admète), Margreth Weivers, Lars Martinsson.

Telecast August 9, 1998, by STV Swedish Television. Thomas Olofsson (director). Color. In Italian. 137 minutes.

***1999 Théâtre du Châtelet
French stage production. Robert Wilson (director/set designer/lighting), John Eliot Gardiner (conductor, English Baroque Soloists and Monteverdi Choir).

Cast: Anne Sofie von Otter (Alceste), Paul Groves (King Admète), Dietrich Henschel, Yann Beuron, Ludovic Tezier, Frédéric Caton.

Video: Image Entertainment/Arthaus (GB) DVD. Brian Large (director). Color. In French with English subtitles. 134 minutes.

Comment: Wilson makes the opera as interesting visually as it is musically.

Related films

1982 Full Circle
Dame Janet Baker rehearses and performs in *Alceste* at Covent Garden in the documentary film *Full Circle*. She is pictured on stage singing the aria "Divinités du Styx" with Charles Mackerras conducting the Royal Opera House Orchestra. Bob Bentley's excellent film follows

Baker's final opera season. Color. In English. 75 minutes. Kultur VHS.

1997 The Golden Age
Documentary about the music created during the reign of Queen Elizabeth and featuring music by Byrd, Purcell, Monteverdi, and Lully. It includes scenes from *Alceste* performed by Anthony Rooley and the Consort of Musicke. Part of the series *Music in Time*. Color. In English. 60 minutes. Films for the Humanities & Sciences VHS.

ALCINA
1735 opera by Handel

Sorceress Alcina lures men to her enchanted island and turns them into beasts when she tires of them. When she captures the crusader Ruggiero, his lover Bradamante comes looking for him disguised as her brother Ricciardo. Alcina's general loves Alcina's sister Morgana, who fancies Ricciardo. It gets more complicated, but the hero and his lover win out in the end. HANDEL's *Alcina*, libretto based on a tale in Ariosto's *Orlando Furioso*, premiered at Covent Garden and has become quite popular in recent years. The pastiche opera THE SORCERESS is based around the plot of *Alcina*.

1990 Grand Théâtre de Genève
Swiss stage production: Philippe Berling (director), William Christie (conductor, Suisse Romande Orchestra and Grand Théâtre de Genève Chorus), Carlo Tommasi (set designer).

Cast: Arlene Augér (Alcina), Della Jones (Ruggiero), Kathleen Kuhlmann (Bradamante), Donna Brown (Morgana), Jorge Lopez-Yanez (Oronte), Gregory Reinhart (Melisso), Martina Musacchio (Oberto).

Video: House of Opera DVD/VHS. Telecast by TSI Swiss Television May 25, 1990. Michel Dami (director). Color. In Italian. 186 minutes.

1999 Stuttgart State Opera
German stage production: Jossi Wieler and Sergio Marabito (directors), Alan Hacker (conductor, Stuttgart State Orchestra and Chorus).

Cast: Catherine Naglestad (Alcina), Alice Coote (Ruggiero), Helene Schneiderman (Bradamante), Catriona Smith (Morgana), Rolf Romei (Oronte), Claudia Mahnke (Oberto).

Video: Arthaus DVD. János Darvas (director). Color. In Italian with English subtitles. 159 minutes.

Comment: Deconstructionist modernist production savaged by critics, with 40 minutes of Handel's music cut and most cast members having to take off their clothes at various times.

ALDA, FRANCES
New Zealand–born American soprano (1879–1952)

Frances Alda is noted for many things besides her splendid voice and her long, notable career at the Metropolitan Opera. She is the focal point of a great many opera anecdotes as she had a quick temper, was often involved in quarrels and lawsuits, and was a "close friend" of conductor ARTURO TOSCANINI and Met director GIULIO GATTI-CASAZZA, whom she later married. She was once hired to train GANNA WALSKA, the opera singer who became the prototype for the singer in *Citizen Kane*. Her entertaining 1937 autobiography is titled *Men, Women and Tenors*.

1927/1930 Vitaphone films
"Madame Frances Alda," as she was described, starred in three sound short films made by the Vitaphone Corporation in 1927, 1929, and 1930. She sings "The Star Spangled Banner" on the 1927 film, "The Last Rose of Summer" from *Martha* and the "Birth of Morn" on the 1929 film, and "Ave Maria" from *Otello* on the 1930 film. Black and white. Each film about 8 minutes. Bel Canto Society VHS.

2001 Bride of the Wind
American soprano Renée Fleming plays Alda in this film about the early life of Alma Mahler (played by Sarah Wynter). In the last scene, Fleming/Alda sings Alma's "Laue Sommernacht," accompanied by Jean-Yves Thibaudet on piano, one of the most memorable moments in the film. Bruce Beresford directed. Color. In English. 99 minutes.

ALEGRÍA DE LA HUERTA, LA
1900 zarzuela by Chueca

Spain in the Huerta region of Murcia at the end of the 19th century during the Fuensanta Festival. Carola, known as "la alegría de la huerta," is attracted to Alegrias, but he is too shy to speak of his love. After many misunderstandings, they finally get together. Federico Chueca's zarzuela *La alegría de la huerta* (The Joy of La Huerta), libretto by Antonio Paso and Enrique García Álvarez, premiered at the Teatro Eslava in Madrid on January 20, 1900. It is a very folksy zarzuela with most of the characters speaking Murcian dialect.

1940 Levante film
Spanish feature film: Ramón Quadreny (director), Ramon de Banos and Francisco Gibert (cinematographers), Levante Films, Barcelona (production company).

Cast: Flora Santacruz, Maruja Catalá, Matilde Artero, Dora Sánchez, Salvador Castillo, Federico Hergueta, Daniel Benítez.

Black and white. In Spanish. 82 minutes.

1995 Teatro Calderón, Madrid

Spanish stage production: José Luis Moreno (director), José A. Irasforza (conductor, Teatro Calderón Orchestra and Chorus), Julian Perez Muñoz (set designer), Alhambra Ballet.

Cast: Jesús Ladiz (Alegrias), Guadalupe Sánchez (Carola), Mario Valdivieso (Juan Francisco), David Muro (Troncho), Tia García (Tío Piparro)

Video: Metrovideo VHS. Telecast live by RTVE. José Ignado Ortega (director). Color. In Spanish. 66 minutes.

***2001 Jarvis Conservatory, Napa

American stage production: Daniel Helfgot (director), Philip J. Bauman (conductor, Jarvis Conservatory Orchestra), Peter Crompton (sets), William Jarvis (producer and translator).

Video: Jarvis Conservatory DVD/VHS. Dave Drum (director). Color. Dialogue in English, singing in Spanish with English subtitles. 57 minutes.

Comment: Delightfully sung, acted, danced, and staged, with good cast and production values.

ALEGRÍA DEL BATALLÓN, LA
1909 zarzuela by Serrano

JOSÉ SERRANO's zarzuela *La alegría del batallón*, libretto by Carlos Arniches and F. Quintana, has an antimilitaristic theme. It takes place in the 1870s during the second phase of the Carlista civil war and points out the harsh realities of military life while ridiculing the comic self-importance of soldiers.

1936 Centinela, Alerta!

Spanish feature film: Jean Grémillon (director), Luis Buñuel (producer/screenplay), José María Beltrán (cinematographer). Filmófono, Madrid (production company).

Cast: Angelillo, Ana María Custodio, Mari Tere, Luis Heredia, Mary Cortés, Luis Buñuel (voice of a peasant).

Black and white. In Spanish. 90 minutes.

Comment: This Buñuel/Grémillon collaboration was one of the most popular films in the zarzuela genre, admired by critics as well as audiences. Neither filmmaker took a screen credit.

Early film

1924 CCHP/PACE film

Spanish feature film: Maximiliano Thous (director and screenwriter), Jose Gaspar (cinematographer), CCHP (Madrid) and PACE, Valencia (production companies).

Cast: Anita Giner Soler, Francisco Gómez Rosell, Leopoldo Pitarch, Julio M. Simón, Pepita Bastida.

Black and white. Silent. 76 minutes.

Comment: Screened with the zarzuela music played live.

ALEKO
1893 opera by Rachmaninoff

Aleko, composed as a graduation exercise by the 19-year-old SERGEI RACHMANINOFF, was immediately staged at the Bolshoi Opera and launched the composer's career. It was an even bigger success four years later, when Chaliapin sang the title role in a Kirov production, and the opera entered the Russian repertory. The libretto, by Vladimir Nemirovich-Danchenko, is based on Pushkin's story *The Gypsies* and is a kind of one-act variation on *Carmen*. Young Aleko joins a group of gypsies because he is attracted by gypsy Zemfira. When she decides to leave him for another man, he kills her.

1954 Kirov Opera

Soviet feature film: Grigory Roshal and Serge Sidelev (directors), Lenfilm (production company).

Cast: Alexander Ognivtsev (Aleko), Mark Reizen, I. Soubkovaskaja, S. Kouznetsov, and B. Elatogorova.

Black and white. In Russian. 61 minutes.

Comment: Film of a stage production of the opera in Leningrad, with location scenes added to open it up, including river and sea views.

1986 USSR Television

Soviet TV film: Victor Okunzov (director), Dimitri Kitaenko (conductor, Moscow Philharmonic and USSR TV and Radio Chorus), Pavel Sasjadko (cinematographer), Vladimir Lebedov (set designer).

Cast: Yevgeny Nesterenko (Aleko), Nelli Volshaninova (Zemfira, sung by Svetlana Volkova), Vladimir Golovin (Zemfira's father, sung by Vladimir Matorin), Maria Papasjan (old Gypsy woman, sung by Raisa Kotova).

Video: Lyric VHS/Dreamlife (Japan) LD. Color. In Russian. 62 minutes.

Comment: All roles except Aleko are played by actors with their singing dubbed by opera singers. The soundtrack is on CD.

ALLEN, THOMAS
English baritone (1944–)

Thomas Allen, who has sung at the Royal Opera for more than 30 years, began his career with Welsh National Opera in 1969 in *La traviata* and came to Covent Garden in 1971 to sing Donald in *Billy Budd*. By the age of 25, he was considered one of the best British baritones in half a century, but he did not make his debut at the Metropolitan Opera until 1981. Allen, who has won wide praise as Don Giovanni, became the first Englishman to sing the part at La Scala in 1987, a portrayal that is on video. He can be seen on video in BILLY BUDD (1988), LA BOHÈME (1982), CARMINA BURANA (1981/1989), COSÌ FAN TUTTE (1975/1996), THE CUNNING LITTLE VIXEN (1995), DON GIOVANNI (1989/1991), THE HOUSE (1995), MANON LESCAUT (1983), LE NOZZE DI FIGARO (1985), IL RITORNO D'ULISSE IN PATRIA (1985), and ROYAL OPERA HOUSE (1986).

1992 Songs of Northumbria
Allen returns home for a gala concert in Durham Cathedral to mark its 900th anniversary in company with Sheila Armstrong and the Northumbrian Chamber Orchestra and Chorus. The regional songs range from nursery rhymes to mining disaster ballads. Color. 70 minutes. Mawson and Wareham Music (England) VHS.

ALPAR, GITTA
Hungarian soprano (1900–1991)

Gitta Alpar (in Hungary it's Alpár) began her career in Budapest in 1923 and became popular in coloratura roles in Munich and Vienna. She had great success in Berlin as Violetta, the Queen of the Night, and the leading roles in operettas by Millöcker and Lehár. Her biggest hit was DIE DUBARRY, the operetta that starred Grace Moore when it came to New York. Alpar had to leave Germany in 1933 when the Nazis came to power, going first to Austria and then to the United States. Married to actor/director Gustav Fröhlich, she appeared in many films in Germany, Austria, England, and America, including a version of Paul Abraham's operetta BALL IM SAVOY.

1932 Die—Oder Keine
Die—Oder Keine (She or Nobody) features Alpar as a prima donna appearing in a production of *La traviata*, an opera in which she had been popular on the Berlin stage. She also wins the love of a young prince and helps him defeat his rivals for the throne. Gustav Fröhlich directed, with music by Otto Stransky. *The New York Times* gave high praise to Alpar when the film opened in the United States. Black and white. In German. 92 minutes.

1932 Gitta Endeckt ihr Herz
Gitta Discovers Her Heart is an autobiographical operetta film. Alpar plays a Hungarian singer named Gitta who becomes famous singing in Berlin. Husband Gustav Fröhlich directed and plays the young composer she loves and helps make a success. The music is by Nikolaus Brodszky and Hansom Milde-Meissner. Black and white. In German. 92 minutes.

1936 Guilty Melody
Alpar plays an opera singer in this odd British film that mixes espionage with music. She sings arias by Gounod and Verdi, while her impresario husband Nils Asther, secretly a spy, sends coded messages on her records. British intelligence officer John Loder suspects Alpar of being the spy. Based on Hans Rehfisch's novel *The Guilty Voice*. Richard Potter directed. Black and white. In English. 75 minutes.

1936 Le Disque 413
The French version of *Guilty Melody* also stars Alpar but has a different supporting cast, cinematographer, and scriptwriter. The actors include Jules Barry, Jean Galland, and Cecile Meunier. Richard Potter again directed. Black and white. In French. 82 minutes.

1941 The Flame of New Orleans
Gitta Alpar is seen on stage as Lucia in *Lucia di Lammermoor* opposite Anthony Marlowe as Edgardo in the opening scene of this René Clair film. While the Donizetti opera is being presented at the New Orleans Opera House, Marlene Dietrich is baiting a honeyed trap for a rich man. Black and white. In English. 78 minutes.

ALTMAN, ROBERT
American film director (1925–)

Robert Altman, best known for films such as *M*A*S*H*, *Nashville*, and *Gosford Park*, has also directed operas and written a libretto. His first stage production was *The Rake's Progress*, produced in Lyons and Ann Arbor. William Bolcom and Ardis Krainik of Lyric Opera of Chicago saw the Michigan production and invited Altman to collaborate on Bolcom's opera MCTEAGUE. Altman cowrote the libretto, directed the stage production in October 1992, and made a documentary about it. Altman's only opera film, one of the episodes in ARIA, is based on Rameau's LES BORÉADES (1987). His 2001 film *Gosford Park* has helped bring IVOR NOVELLO's music back into fashion.

17

ALWYN, WILLIAM
English composer (1905–1985)

William Alwyn, who is known for his fine film scores, wrote no operas, but he created opera arias for two English films. In the 1947 suspense film *Take My Life*, Greta Gynt plays an opera singer who has to prove her husband did not murder an old girlfriend. Gynt is seen on stage performing an opera aria created for the film by Alwyn, with the actual singing done by Victoria Sladen. For the 1954 *Svengali*, he composed the aria "Libera me," performed on stage by Trilby (Hildegarde Neff) at the end of the film, with the actual singing done by Elisabeth Schwarzkopf. A recent CD of film music by Alwyn features these arias sung by Susan Bullock. Alwyn's many film scores include *The Rake's Progress* (1945), *Odd Man Out* (1946), and *The Crimson Pirate* (1953).

***AMADEUS
1984 American film about Mozart

This multiple Academy Award winner is the best of the many films about Wolfgang Amadeus Mozart, with a superb screenplay by Peter Shaffer based on his play. Czech-born American director Milos Forman knows his Mozart and does a fine job of re-creating the period and the attitudes of the protagonists. He has outstanding collaborators: Twyla Tharp staged the opera scenes in the Tyl Theater in Prague (where *Don Giovanni* had its premiere), Neville Marriner conducted the Academy of St. Martin-in-the-Fields Orchestra, Miroslav Ondricek was the cinematographer, and Saul Zaentz produced.

The film begins in 1823 with composer Antonio Salieri (F. Murray Abraham) dying and claiming to have killed Mozart (Tom Hulce). He narrates the story of Mozart's rise to fame and shows his great appreciation of Mozart's genius. He is deeply jealous, however, as he cannot compete on the same level, so he sets out to destroy him. Mozart marries Constanze (Elizabeth Berridge) against the wishes of his father Leopold (Roy Dotrice) after impressing Austrian Emperor Joseph II (Jeffrey Jones) with his ability (the one important historical figure who does not appear in the movie is Mozart's librettist Lorenzo da Ponte).

Four Mozart operas are staged in the film. First is a brief scene from *Die Entführung aus dem Serail*, the first important opera in the German language.

Next is an extended scene from *Le nozze di Figaro*, after Mozart brags to the emperor about its long and complicated sextet. Miro Grisa is Figaro (sung by Samuel Ramey), Zuzana Kadlecova is Susanna (sung by Isobel Buchanan), Helena Cihelnikova is the countess (sung by Felicity Lott), Karel Gult is the count (sung by Richard Stilwell), Magda Celakovska is Cherubino (sung by Anne Howells), Slavena Drasilova is Barbarina (sung by Deborah Rees), Eva Senkova is Marcellina (sung by

Patricia Payne), Ladislav Kretschmer is Antonio (sung by Willard White), Leos Kratochvil is Basilio (sung by Alexander Oliver), Bino Zeman is Curzio (sung by Robin Leggate), and Jaroslav Mikulin is Bartolo (sung by John Tomlinson).

After a scene showing Salieri's triumph with his opera *Axur* (Christine Ebersole is Cavalieri, sung by Suzanne Murphy), there is a production of *Don Giovanni* with a memorable last act scene; the commendatore's statue bursts onto the stage as if he were Mozart's father coming back from the grave to chastise his son. Jan Blazek is the commendatore (sung by John Tomlinson), Karel Fiala is Don Giovanni (sung by Richard Stilwell), and Zdenek Jelen is Leporello (sung by Willard White).

The scenes around the composition of *Die Zauberflöte* show Mozart's relationship with showman/librettist Emanuel Schikaneder (Simon Callow). Callow (who was Mozart in the original stage production of the play) is shown on stage creating the role of Papageno (sung by Brian Kay) with Lisabeth Bartless as Papagena (sung by Gillian Fisher). A visually striking scene shows the arrival of the Queen of the Night (Milada Cechalova, sung by June Anderson).

Finally, Mozart composes his *Requiem* after a commission from a mysterious masked visitor (actually Salieri) and works on it as a final memorial, even when he is deathly ill. He dictates its final parts to Salieri, dies, and is buried like a pauper.

After Salieri finishes his portrait of Mozart's life and achievements, he tries to kill himself but fails.

Amadeus won eight Oscar Awards: best picture, director, actor (Abraham), screenplay, art direction (Patrizia Van Brandenstein/Karel Cerny), costume design (Theodor Pistek), makeup (Paul Leblanc/Dick Smith), and sound (Mark Berger, Tom Scott, Chris Newman, and Todd Boekelheide). It was nominated for best cinematography, editing (Michael Chandler/Nena Danevic), and actor (Hulce). The 160-minute Technicolor Panavision film was distributed theatrically by Columbia Pictures. Warner DVD/HBO Cannon VHS/Pioneer LD (Director's cut Double Disc DVD has commentary by director and writer and documentary film *The Last Laugh*).

Amadeus (1984): Mozart (Tom Hulce) conducts the Vienna court orchestra in Milos Forman's Oscar-winning film.

AMAHL AND THE NIGHT VISITORS
1951 TV opera by Menotti

This was the first opera created for television and marked the coming of age of TV. Written, composed, and staged by GIAN CARLO MENOTTI for NBC Opera Theatre as a Christmas Eve special for Hallmark, it was commissioned by SAMUEL CHOTZINOFF and proved so popular it was repeated annually for years in the Hallmark Hall of Fame series. The story, inspired by Bosch's painting *The Adoration of the Magi*, tells of a crippled boy whose family is visited on Christmas Eve by the Three Kings (Balthazar, Kaspar, and Melchior) on their way to Bethlehem with gifts. Food for them is provided by neighbors. When Amahl offers his crutch as a gift, he is miraculously healed and joins the kings on their visit to the Holy Child, carrying his crutch. *Amahl* is one of the most popular and widely staged American operas and has been telecast in most Western European countries, starting in Holland in 1953. Listed below are the American, English, and Australian films and telecasts.

1951 NBC Opera Theatre
American TV production: Gian Carlo Menotti (director), Samuel Chotzinoff (producer), Thomas Schippers (conductor, NBC Orchestra), Eugene Berman (set/costume designer), John Butler (choreographer).

Cast: Rosemary Kuhlmann (Mother), Chet Allen (Amahl), David Aiken (Melchior), Leon Lishner (Balthazar), Andrew McKinley (Kaspar), Francis Monachino (Page).

Video: UCLA and the MTR. Telecast live December 24, 1951, on NBC. Kirk Browning (director). Black and white. In English. 60 minutes.

Comment: *Amahl and the Night Visitors* was the first production in the Hallmark Hall of Fame series and was presented seven more times. Bill McIver and Kirk Jordan played Amahl in later versions. The telecast on December 20, 1953, was the first version in color. Videos at UCLA Film and Television Archive.

1953–1955 BBC Television
English TV productions: Christian Simpson (director), Stanford Robinson (conductor, Wigmore Ensemble in 1953 and 1954, Sinfonia of London in 1955), Michael Yates (set designer), Michael de Lutry (choreographer).

Cast: Gladys Whitred (Mother), Charles Vignoles (Amahl, 1953 and 1954), Graham Saunders (1955), John Cameron (Melchior), Scott Joyn (Balthazar), John Lewis (Kaspar).

Telecast live December 20, 1954; December 24, 1954; and December 20, 1955. Black and white. In English. 50 minutes.

Comment: Success of the telecast led to repeats in 1954 and 1955 with essentially the same cast and crew.

1957 ABC Television, Australia
Australian TV production: Christopher Muir (director), Joseph Post (conductor, Melbourne Symphony Orchestra), John Peters (set designer), Laurel Martyn (choreographer).

Cast: Joyce Simmons (Mother), Anthony Monopoli (Amahl), Neil Easton (Melchior), Neil Warren-Smith (Balthazar), Victor Franklin (Kaspar).

Telecast live by ABC Television December 18, 1957. Black and white. In English. 50 minutes.

1959 BBC Television
English TV production: Christian Simpson (director), Bryan Balkwill (conductor, Royal Philharmonic Orchestra and Glyndebourne Festival Chorus), Roy Oxley (set designer), Maria Fay (choreographer).

Cast: Elsie Morison (Mother), Christopher Nicholls (Amahl), Hervey Alan (Melchior), Forbes Robinson (Balthazar), John Kentish (Kaspar).

Telecast live December 24, 1959. Black and white. In English. 50 minutes.

Amahl and the Night Visitors (1951): Amahl (Chet Allen) and his mother (Rosemary Kuhlmann) in the first television opera.

1963–1965 NBC Opera Theater
American TV productions: Samuel Chotzinoff (director), Herbert Grossman (conductor, NBC Orchestra and Chorus), Frank Skinner (set designer).

Cast: Martha King (Mother), Kurt Yaghjian (Amahl), John McCollum (Kaspar), Richard Cross (Melchior), Willis Patterson (Balthazar).

Video at the MTR. Kirk Browning (director). Black and white. In English. 48 minutes. Video.

Comment: The production was videotaped at Webster Hall in 1963, and this video was shown in 1964 and 1965. Menotti was not involved in the production, and this led to cancellation of the series. Soundtrack was issued on LP.

1968 BBC Television
English TV production: Michael Hayes (director), James Lockhart (conductor, Ambrosian Opera Chorus and Philharmonia Orchestra), Philippe Perrottet (choreographer).

Cast: April Cantelo (Mother), Paul Boucher (Amahl), Joseph Ward (Kaspar), Forbes Robinson (Melchior), Don Garrard (Balthazar).

Telecast December 25, 1968. Michael Hayes (director). Black and white. In English. 50 minutes.

***1978 Worldvision film
English feature film: Arvin Brown (director), Jesus Lopez-Cobos (conductor, Ambrosian Opera Chorus and Philharmonia Orchestra), John Coquillon (cinematographer), Robert Jones (sets), Ivy Baker Jones (costumes), Worldvision (production company).

Cast: Teresa Stratas (Mother), Robert Sapolsky (Amahl), Giorgio Tozzi (Melchior), Willard White (Balthazar), Nico Castel (Kaspar).

Video: Artisan/VAI VHS. Telecast in the United States December 24, 1978, on NBC. Color. In English. 52 minutes.

Comment: Shot on location in Israel and in London. Visually splendid, with a formidable cast.

2001 Zambello film
This apparently excellent film of the opera is in limbo. Francesca Zambello shot it in Spain for producer Fiona Morris and BBC Wales. Pablo Strong plays Amahl with his daydreams turned into magical visions. The film was to have been televised December 25, 2001, but the rights were not cleared, and it cannot presently be shown.

AMAMI, ALFREDO!
1940 film with opera content

Opera diva Maria Cebotari, who had sung the role of Violetta on stage, stars in *Amami, Alfredo!* (Love Me, Alfredo!) as Maria Dalgeri, a famous singer whose life parallels her role in *La traviata*. It was made following the success of a similar film based on *Madama Butterfly*. After she persuades La Scala to present an opera by her fiancé, novice composer Giacomo Varni (Claudio Gora), Maria is threatened by the illness that struck down the heroine of *La traviata*. When she is unable to continue to sing, the opera impresario loses interest in the new opera,

despite praise from Arrigo Boito. Luckily, it's a poor diagnosis, and she really isn't sick so there's a happy ending, and the new opera is performed as well as a lot of Verdi music. The other opera singers are tenor Giovanni Malipiero and baritone Mariano Stabile. Guido Cantini wrote the screenplay, Anchise Brizzi was cinematographer, Riccardo Zandonai composed the new music, Luigi Ricci conducted the orchestra, and Carmine Gallone directed for Grandi Film Storici. Black and white. In Italian. 86 minutes. On VHS.

AMARA, LUCINE
Armenian-American soprano (1925–)

Lucine Amara made her debut at the Metropolitan Opera in 1950 in DON CARLO and sang the Celestial Voice in the pioneering Met telecast of the opera. She began her career in the chorus at San Francisco Opera but became a regular at Glyndebourne, where she was known for her performances in Italian operas. She was not, however, Italian; her Armenian birth name was Armaganian and she was born in Hartford. She can be seen in the opera montage scenes in the 1951 Caruso film biography THE GREAT CARUSO, in a 1953 METROPOLITAN OPERA gala telecast at the Museum of Television and Radio, and in a BELL TELEPHONE HOUR video singing with RICHARD TUCKER (1961) in a duet from Pagliacci.

AMATO, PASQUALE
Italian-born American baritone (1878–1942)

Neapolitan Pasquale Amato was a colleague of Enrico Caruso at the Metropolitan Opera and played Jack Rance opposite Caruso's Dick Johnson in the world premiere of *La Fanciulla del West* at the Met in 1910. Amato made his debut in his native Naples in 1900, was soon at La Scala and Covent Garden, and first sang at the Metropolitan in 1908. He was at the Met until 1921 and then taught opera in New York and Louisiana. He appeared in only two films, but he left many recordings.

1928 A Neapolitan Romance
Amato is featured in the Vitaphone sound short *Pasquale Amato in A Neapolitan Romance* singing the Toreador aria from *Carmen* and the Neapolitan song "Torna a Surriento." Black and white. About 8 minutes.

1928 Glorious Betsy
Amato plays Napoleon in this patriotic part-talkie American film but does not sing. Dolores Costello, Conrad Nagel, and Betty Blythe star in a tale about Napoleon's younger brother falling in love with an American woman. Alan Crosland directed. Black and white. 80 minutes.

AMELIA AL BALLO
1937 opera by Menotti

Amelia is determined to go to the ball no matter what happens. When her husband finds out about her lover upstairs, he ends up in the hospital, the lover goes to prison, and Amelia goes to the ball with a police inspector. Gian Carlo Menotti's *opera buffa Amelia al Ballo* (Amelia Goes to the Ball), a boudoir romp with a sparkling score, was his first stage success and a breakthrough for the 24-year-old composer. He wrote the mock-serious libretto in Italian, but the opera premiered in English (translation by George Mead) at the Philadelphia Academy of Music on April 1, 1937, and was staged by the Metropolitan Opera the following year.

1957 Teatro dell'Opera, Rome
Italian stage production: Margarita Wallmann (director), Oliviero de Fabritiis (conductor, Teatro dell'Opera Orchestra).
Cast: Margherita Carosio (Amelia), Rolando Panerai (Husband), Giacinto Prandelli (Lover).
Telecast live January 9, 1957, on RAI Italian television. Lino Procacci (director). Black and white. In English. 50 minutes.

1965 Cuvilliés Theater, Munich
German stage production: Trude Kolman (director), Menhard von Zallinger (conductor), Elisabeth Urbancic (set designer), George C. Winkler (German translation).
Cast: Ingeborg Hallstein (Amelia), Keith Engen (Husband), David Thaw (Lover), Brigitte Fassbaender (Friend), Carl Christian Kohn (Chief of Police).
Telecast by Bavarian TV September 12, 1965. Hans-Joachim Scholz (director). Black and white. In German. 48 minutes.

1966 ABC Television, Australia
Australian TV production: Peter Page (director), Walter Stiasny (conductor, Sydney Symphony Orchestra), Desmond Downing (set designer).
Cast: Rae Cocking (Amelia), Ronald Jackson (Husband), Peter Baillie (Lover), Florence Taylor (Friend), John Brosnan (Chief of Police).
Telecast on ABC on May 11, 1966. Peter Page (director). Black and white. In English. 50 minutes.

AMERICAN FILM INSTITUTE

The American Film Institute (AFI), the major cultural film organization in the United States, was founded by President Lyndon Johnson in 1967. It has offices and a conservatory in Los Angeles and film theaters in Washington, D.C., and Silver Spring, Maryland. The *AFI Catalogs of American Feature Films* by decade are an invaluable source of information about opera and opera singers in American cinema since 1893. AFI has also presented an opera-on-film series at its National Film Theater in the Kennedy Center in Washington in collaboration with the Washington Opera, and in its Los Angeles International Film Festival (AFI Fest). AFI is a leader in the film preservation movement and has restored several early opera films.

AMFITHEATROF, DANIELE
Russian-born American composer (1901–1983)

Daniele Amfitheatrof, who began his professional career as assistant conductor at La Scala, wrote an IMAGINARY OPERA that is central to the plot of Max Ophuls's great 1934 film *La signora di tutti*. He began to work in Hollywood in 1938, where he wrote scores for Ophuls's *Letter From an Unknown Woman* (1948), SALOME (1953), *Major Dundee* (1965), and many other films.

AMICA
1905 opera by Mascagni

Pietro Mascagni's little-known *verismo* opera *Amica*, libretto in French by Paul Bérel (Paul de Choudens), premiered at Monte Carlo. It has never had great success although it has been revived and recorded. It is set in Piedmont. Amica is the niece of Camoine, who wants to marry her off to Giorgio so he can marry Maddalena. However, she actually loves his brother Rinaldo and runs off with him. The composer conducted performances in Italy, and its success led to a 1916 Italian film by Enrico Guazzoni made with Mascagni's cooperation and screened with the opèra music. Katia Ricciarelli sings the role of Amica in a 1995 recording conducted by Marco Pace.

1916 Guazzoni film
Italian feature film: Enrico Guazzoni (director), Cines (production company).
Cast: Leda Gys (Amica), Amleto Novelli, Augusto Mastipietri, Augusto Poggioli.
Black and white. Silent. About 60 minutes.

AMORE DEI TRE RE, L'
1913 opera by Montemezzi

ITALO MONTEMEZZI's *The Love of Three Kings* used to be a popular opera and was considered a near masterpiece, but it has almost vanished from the repertory. Sem Benelli's libretto from his play is set in Italy in the 10th century and revolves around the loves of the Princess

Fiora. She has been forced to marry blind King Archibaldo's son Prince Manfredo, but she really loves Prince Avito. When the king catches her with her lover, he strangles her and spreads poison on her lips. Lover and husband both kiss her lips and die. The king is left alone.

1962 NBC Opera Theatre
American TV production: Samuel Chotzinoff (director), Alfred Wallenstein (conductor, NBC Orchestra), Ed Wittstein (set designer), Joseph Machlis (English translation).

Cast: Phyllis Curtin (Princess Fiora), Giorgio Tozzi (King Archibaldo), Richard Torigi (Prince Manfredo), Frank Poretta (Prince Avito).

Telecast live February 25, 1962, on NBC. Kirk Browning (director). Color. In English. 93 minutes.

Comment: Browning used eight cameras to show off an elaborate four-level castle set.

1983 Providence Opera
American stage production: William Radka (director), Alvaro Cassuto (conductor, Providence Opera Orchestra), Preston McClanahan (set designer).

Cast: Louise Cash (Princess Fiora), John Seabury (King Archibaldo), Lawrence Cooper (Prince Manfredo), Michael Harrison (Prince Avito).

Video: House of Opera DVD/VHS. Ray Fass (director). Color. In Italian with English narration before each act. 100 minutes.

AMRAM, DAVID
American composer (1930–)

Philadelphia-born David Amram, who composed for theater, film, and opera house, began writing music for Ford's Theater in Washington in 1951 and later became music director of Joseph Papp's Shakespeare Festival in New York. His first opera, THE FINAL INGREDIENT (1965), written for television, revolves around a Passover supper in a World War II concentration camp. His second, *Twelfth Night* (1968), was based on the Shakespeare play revised by Papp. His notable film scores include *Splendor in the Grass* and *The Arrangement* for Elia Kazan and *The Manchurian Candidate* for John Frankenheimer.

AND DAVID WEPT
1971 TV opera by Laderman

King David falls in love with the beautiful Bathsheba and arranges to get rid of her husband Uriah the Hittite. The biblical love affair is told in flashbacks by dancers, as the lovers and Uriah describe how it began in lust and ended in tears. Ezra Laderman's opera *And David Wept*, libretto by Joseph Darion, premiered on CBS Television on April 8, 1971, on commission by CBS News. It had its stage premiere at the 92nd Street YMHA in New York on May 31, 1980.

1971 CBS Television
American TV production: Alfredo Antonini (conductor, CBS Orchestra).

Cast: Rosalind Elias (Bathsheba), Ara Berberian (Uriah).

Telecast live April 8, 1971. Color. In English. 60 minutes.

AND THE SHIP SAILS ON
See E LA NAVE VA.

ANDERSON, JUNE
American soprano (1952–)

Boston-born June Anderson made her debut at the New York City Opera in 1978 as Queen of the Night in *Die Zauberflöte*. Since then, her coloratura mastery has been heard everywhere, from Covent Garden to the Met. She is known for *bel canto* roles and has developed a strong stage presence to go with her powerful voice, which has been compared with Joan Sutherland's. She is well represented on video, impressive as Cunegonde in the 1989 CANDIDE, memorable in a 1989 PARIS celebration of the opening of the new Bastille Opera, excellent in a 1991 LUCIANO PAVAROTTI concert, and superb as ADELINA PATTI in a 1993 film about the 19th-century diva. See also LA DONNA DEL LAGO (1992), LA FILLE DU REGIMENT (1984), JAMES LEVINE (1996), LUCIA DI LAMMERMOOR (1983), LUISA MILLER (1988), METROPOLITAN OPERA (1991), NORMA (2001), OPERA NORTH (1992), OTELLO (Rossini 1988), PARIS (1989), RICCIARDO E ZORAIDE (1990), and SEMIRAMIDE (1990).

1984 Amadeus
Anderson is heard as the Queen of the Night singing "Die Hölle Rache" in a visually striking scene staged by Twyla Tharp in this Academy Award–winning Mozart film biography. Milada Cechalova plays the queen on screen. See AMADEUS.

1989 June Anderson: The Passion of Bel Canto
French documentary showing the soprano rehearsing, singing, and talking about her *bel canto* roles in cities around Europe. Anderson says she enjoys her roles as "crazy ladies." She is seen as Lucia in *Lucia di Lammermoor* at Covent Garden, Amina in *La sonnambula* at La Scala, Marie in *The Daughter of the Regiment* at the Opéra-Comique in Paris, Desdemona in Rossini's *Otello* in a production by Jean-Pierre Ponnelle, and Elvira in *I*

puritani in a production by André Serban. Color. 57 minutes. VIEW VHS.

ANDERSON, MARIAN
American contralto (1897–1993)

Marian Anderson, one of the real-life heroines of opera, paved the way for the great African-American divas of today. She never had the chance to become an opera star herself, as her Metropolitan Opera debut did not take place until 1955, when she was long past her prime, but she was still the first African-American to sing a solo role at the Met, Ulrica in *Un ballo in maschera*. As much as for her voice ("A voice like yours is heard only once in a hundred years" said Toscanini), she was memorable for her integrity. A central moment in her career was an outdoor concert at the Lincoln Memorial in Washington, D.C., in 1939, after the Daughters of the American Revolution refused her permission to sing in Constitution Hall. Anderson was then hired by 20th Century–Fox to sing at the premiere of the film *Young Mr. Lincoln* in Springfield, Illinois, where, ironically, she was refused as a guest at the Lincoln Hotel. She can be seen with other opera singers in the 1956 all-star telecast PRODUCERS' SHOWCASE.

1953 Meet the Masters: Marian Anderson
Jules Dassin directed this film for the *Meet the Masters* series; it features Anderson in a program of spirituals and Schubert lieder and includes a reconstruction of her 1935 introductory concert. There are also scenes of her home life and her Connecticut farm. World Artists. Black and white. 27 minutes. Kultur VHS.

1957 The Lady From Philadelphia
Edward R. Murrow's film about Anderson's goodwill tour of Southeast Asia for the State Department premiered on Murrow's CBS Television program *See It Now* December 30, 1957. She sings 15 songs and arias, ranging from "Ave Maria" to "Mon coeur s'ouvre à ta voix," as she visits seven countries from Korea to India. The film won warm praise, and the State Department arranged to show it in 70 countries. The soundtrack is on record. Black and white. 60 minutes. Video at the MTR.

1969 The Lady in the Lincoln Memorial
Short film tracing the career of Anderson from her childhood through her early church and concert hall successes to her triumphs in Europe and America. Highlight is Anderson's performance at the Lincoln Memorial in 1939. Color. 18 minutes.

1977 Peerce, Anderson, & Segovia
One segment of this video is a 20-minute compilation history of the life and career of Anderson, probably based on Jules Dassin's 1953 film. It begins with a re-creation of her Town Hall concert of 1935; shows her in recital singing "Deep River," "Ave Maria," and other favorites; and includes interviews and historic film of her 1939 concert at the Lincoln Memorial. Black and white. 20 minutes. Kultur VHS.

1991 Marian Anderson
Film portrait produced by Dante J. James for WETA, with interviews and concert scenes from the 1930s to the 1960s and a section about her Metropolitan Opera role. Includes interviews with Isaac Stern, Martin Feinstein, Jessye Norman, and Mattiwilda Dobbs. Anderson, 94 when the film was made, reflects on her life and music. Juan Williams wrote the script and Avery Brooks narrates the film. Color. 60 minutes. PBS VHS.

ANDREA CHÉNIER
1896 opera by Giordano

This romantic *verismo* opera by Italian composer UMBERTO GIORDANO, set at the time of the French Revolution, was written by the ubiquitous Luigi Illica. Based on the life of poet André Chénier, it centers on his love for aristocrat Maddalena. She is also loved by a former servant who becomes the revolutionary leader Gérard. Despite sacrifices all round, the lovers end up on the guillotine. *Andrea Chénier* offers a wonderful opportunity for a divo tenor to show off. Maddalena's aria "La mamma morta" has become widely known because it was featured in the film *Philadelphia*.

***1955 RAI Television
Italian TV film: Angelo Mario Landi (director), Angelo Questa (conductor, RAI Milan Orchestra and Chorus).

Cast: Mario Del Monaco (Andrea Chénier), Antonietta Stella (Maddalena), Giuseppe Taddei (Gérard), Luisa Mandelli (Bersi), Maria Amadini (Contessa).

Video: Bel Canto Society/Legato Classics VHS. Black and white. In Italian. 116 minutes.

Comment: Del Monaco, one of the great interpreters of *Andrea Chénier*, was at the peak of his powers when he sang in this production. Stella and Taddei are also in fine form.

1961 NHK Lirica Italiana
Japanese stage production: Franco Capuana (conductor, NHK Symphony Orchestra).

Cast: Mario Del Monaco (Andrea Chénier), Renata Tebaldi (Maddalena), Aldo Protti (Gérard), Anna Di Stasio (Bersi).

Video: VAI VHS. Filmed in Tokyo October 1, 1961. Black and white. In Italian with English and Japanese subtitles. 118 minutes.

Comment: The combination of Del Monaco and Tebaldi would be hard to improve upon, although the quality of the production is not the highest.

1973 RAI Television

Italian TV film: Václav Kaslik (director), Bruno Bartoletti (conductor, RAI Symphony Orchestra), Susanna Egri (choreographer).

Cast: Franco Corelli (Andrea Chénier), Celestina Casapietra (Maddalena), Piero Cappuccilli (Gérard), Giovanni di Rocco (Bersi), Gabriella Carturan (Contessa).

Video: Hardy Classic DVD/Bel Canto Society VHS. Color. In Italian. 117 minutes.

Comment: Corelli is in fine form singing and acting in one of the roles most associated with him

1981 Vienna State Opera

Austrian stage production: Otto Schenk (director), Nello Santi (conductor, Vienna Philharmonic), Rolf Glittenberg (set designer).

Cast: Plácido Domingo (Andrea Chénier), Gabriela Beňačková (Maddalena), Piero Cappuccilli (Gérard), Fedora Barbieri (Madelon), Rohangiz Yachmi (Bersi), Czeslawa Slania (Contessa).

Video: Bel Canto Society VHS. Otto Schenk (director). Color. In Italian. 161 minutes.

1985 Teatro alla Scala

Italian stage production: Lamberto Puggelli and Antonello Madau Diaz (directors), Riccardo Chailly (conductor, Teatro alla Scala Orchestra and Chorus), Paolo Bregni (set designer), Luisa Spinatelli (costume designer).

Cast: José Carreras (Andrea Chénier), Eva Marton (Maddalena), Piero Cappuccilli (Gérard), Nella Veri (Countess).

Video: Bel Canto Society and Home Vision (US) VHS/NVC Arts (GB) VHS/Pioneer Artists LD. Brian Large (director). Color. In Italian with English subtitles. 130 minutes.

Comment: Massive production, impressive sets, colorful costumes based around the French tricolor.

1985 Royal Opera

English stage production: Michael Hampe (director), Julius Rudel (conductor, Royal Opera House Orchestra), William Orlandi (set designer).

Cast: Plácido Domingo (Andrea Chénier), Anna Tomowa-Sintow (Maddalena), Giorgio Zancanaro (Gérard), Cynthia Buchan (Bersi), Patricia Johnson (Contessa).

Video: Kultur VHS. Humphrey Burton (director). Color. In Italian with English subtitles. 119 minutes.

Comment: Well produced but not very exciting.

1985/1989 Opera Stories

Laserdisc highlights version of above production for *Opera Stories* LD series. Charlton Heston provides introduction and narration from Paris where he was filmed by Keith Cheetham in 1989. Color. In English and Italian with English subtitles. 52 minutes. Pioneer Artists LD.

1996 Metropolitan Opera

American stage production: Nicolas Joël (director), James Levine (conductor, Metropolitan Opera Orchestra and Chorus), Hubert Monloup (set/costume design).

Cast: Luciano Pavarotti (Andrea Chénier), Maria Guleghina (Maddalena), Juan Pons (Gérard), Wendy White (Bersi), Judith Christin (Contessa).

Telecast April 23, 1997; taped live October 15, 1996. Brian Large (director). Color. In Italian with English subtitles. 130 minutes.

Early/related films

1909 André Chénier

Léonce Perret directed this French film of the opera titled *André Chénier*. It was shown in cinemas with Giordano's music. Black and white. Silent. About 10 minutes.

1909 Andrea Chénier

This Italian film of the opera titled *Andrea Chénier* was made by Roma Film of Torino and shown in cinemas in England in Agusut 1909 with Giordano's music. Black and white. Silent. About 9 minutes.

1937 Solo Per Te

Beniamino Gigli appears on stage in a scene from *Andrea Chénier* in this film in which he plays a famous opera singer married to a soprano (Maria Cebotari) with a past. See SOLO PER TE.

1955 Andrea Chénier

Giordano's music is used as the score of this *Andrea Chénier*, a narrative adaptation of the opera directed by Clemente Fracassi. Michel Auclair is Andrea Chénier, Antonella Lualdi is Maddalena, and Raf Vallone is

Gérard. Italian/French coproduction. Black and white. In Italian or French. 97 minutes.

1993 Philadelphia

Tom Hanks, a lawyer dying of AIDS, listens to Maria Callas sing Maddalena's aria "La mamma morta," in which she tells how her mother died when a French Revolution mob burned down her house. It's his favorite aria, and his playing it for his lawyer (Denzel Washington) is a crucial moment in their relationship. The Callas recording was made in 1955 for EMI with Tullio Serafin conducting the Philharmonia Orchestra. Jonathan Demme directed the film for TriStar. Color. 119 minutes. On VHS.

ANDRIESSEN, LOUIS
Dutch composer (1939–)

Louis Andriessen has worked with English filmmaker PETER GREENAWAY on two operas, one for television, the other for the stage, both using cinema techniques. Their 1993 British TV opera M IS FOR MAN, MUSIC AND MOZART is a combination of song, dance, and ritual created for the Not Mozart series. Their 1994 Dutch stage opera ROSA: DEATH OF A COMPOSER, about a composer who lives in an abattoir and writes music for Western films, attracted international attention and was filmed by Greenaway. Andriessen's best-known earlier operas include the collaborative *Reconstructie* (1969) and *De materie* (1989).

ANIMATED OPERA

Some of the most enjoyable opera films have been animated cartoons featuring music by Rossini, Wagner, Mozart, and other composers in unusually inventive ways. Rossini's overtures to *Il barbiere di Siviglia* and *William Tell* have been especially popular with animators. The great animated opera films include CHUCK JONES's WHAT'S OPERA, DOC? and THE RABBIT OF SEVILLE, WALT DISNEY's THE WHALE WHO WANTED TO SING AT THE MET, and WALTER LANTZ's *The Barber of Seville*. Other notable creators include Tex Avery and Friz Freleng at WARNER BROTHERS, GIANINI AND LUZZATI, GEORGE PAL, LOTTE REINIGER, and PAUL TERRY. See also BABES IN TOYLAND, IL BARBIERE DI SIVIGLIA, LA BELLE HÉLÈNE, CARMEN, LA DAMNATION DE FAUST, DICK DEADEYE, ELVERHØJ, LA FORZA DEL DESTINO, LA GAZZA LADRA, GUILLAUME TELL, HÄNSEL UND GRETEL, L'HISTOIRE DU SOLDAT, JOHN THE HERO, THE LEGEND OF THE INVISIBLE CITY OF KITEZH, THE MIKADO, OPERA IMAGINAIRE, OPERAVOX, THE PIRATES OF PENZANCE, RHEINGOLD, RIGOLETTO, RUDDIGORE, THE SNOW MAIDEN, TURANDOT, WARNER BROS. CARTOONS, and DIE ZAUBERFLÖTE. Generic animation films not listed under individual operas are described below.

1935 Opera Night

Paul Terry and Frank Moser created this American film about a night at the opera. Black and white. 6 minutes.

1952 Off to the Opera

American Connie Rasinski drew this animated opera film. Color. 7 minutes.

1955 Stage Door Magoo

Mr. Magoo (voiced by Jim Backus) causes chaos at the opera. Dick Shaw was the writer, Pete Burness was director, and Stephen Bosustow was producer. Color. 7 minutes.

1967 The Opera Caper

Paramount cartoon from the series *Go-Go Toons* started by Shamus Culhane and finished by Ralph Bakshi. Color. 7 minutes.

1969 The World in Opera

Polish animator Jerzy Kotowski created this lively animated opera film. Color. 8 minutes.

1972 Opera

Italian cartoon about opera by animation genius Bruno Bozzetto. Animated comic lampoons of opera scenes form the background to commentary about modern madnesses. Color. 11 minutes.

1996 All the Great Operas...in 10 Minutes

Kim Thompson spoofs the plots of famous operas in a deadpan manner in this humorous animated film, which notes the body count. Color. In English. 10 minutes. Videos.com VHS.

ANNA BOLENA
1830 opera by Donizetti

Anna Bolena is the earliest of GAETANO DONIZETTI's regularly performed operas. Felice Romani's libretto tells the story of Anne Boleyn (Anna Bolena in Italian), the second wife of English King Henry VIII (Enrico VIII), and her tribulations as the king attempts to get rid of her so he can marry lady-in-waiting Jane Seymour (Giovanna Seymour). It has one of Donizetti's great mad scenes, when Anne reveals her love for Lord Percy and her hatred of Henry and Jane as she awaits execution in the Tower of London. Joan Sutherland's recording of the opera is much admired.

Canadian stage production: Lotfi Mansouri (director), Richard Bonynge (conductor, Canadian Opera Company Orchestra and Chorus).

Cast: Joan Sutherland (Anna Bolena), James Morris (Enrico VIII), Judith Forst (Giovanna Seymour), Janet Stubbs (Smenton), Michael Myers (Lord Percy), Gideon Saks (Rochefort), Ben Heppner (Hervey).

Video: VAI DVD/VHS. Telecast September 30, 1984, on CBC. Color. In Italian with English subtitles. 157 minutes.

Comment: Sutherland is splendid in this lavish production at Toronto's O'Keefe Center.

1985 Avery Fisher Hall, New York

American concert production: Richard Bonynge (conductor, New York City Opera Orchestra and New York Choral Artists).

Cast: Joan Sutherland (Anna Bolena), Gregory Yurisch (Enrico VIII), Judith Forst (Giovanna Seymour), Cynthia Clarey (Smeaton), Jerry Hadley (Lord Percy), Jan Opalach (Lord Rochefort), Gran Wilson (Hervey).

Telecast November 25, 1985, in *Live From Lincoln Center* series. Kirk Browning (director). Color. In Italian. 178 minutes.

ANOUSH

1912 opera by Tigranyan

Anoush, a young woman living in an Armenian mountain village with her brother Mossi, is in love with his best friend, the shepherd Saro. At a wedding party, Saro defeats Mossi in a wrestling match meant to be a draw, is ostracized by the villagers, and eventually killed by the humiliated Mossi. Anoush throws herself off a cliff. Armen Tigran Tigranyan's colorful opera *Anoush,* based on an epic poem by Hovannes Toumanian, is the Armenian national opera, and much of its music is based on Armenian folk forms and melodies. It was staged privately in Erevan in 1912, but the first public performance did not take place until 1935 when it was produced by the Spendiarian Opera and Ballet Company. It was staged in the United States in Armenian for the first time in 2001 by Michigan Opera Theater, with Anoush sung by Aline Kuta and Hasnik Papian.

1996 Yerevan Opera

Armenian stage production: Produced by Alexander Spendiarov's Academic Opera and Ballet Company at the Yerevan Opera House.

Cast: Cast not listed on VHS.

Video: PE-KO VHS (available online from Narek.com). Color. In Armenian, no subtitles. 120 minutes.

Comment: Best of the VHS versions of the opera; more professionally staged, taped, and sung.

1999 Shrine Auditorium, Los Angeles

American stage production: Tigran Levonian (director), Yuri Davtyan and Michael Avetissian (conductors).

Cast: Anahit Mikhitarian (Anoush), Drastamat Petrosian (Saro), Konstantin Simonian (Mossi).

Video: Parseghian Records VHS (sold by Narek.com). M. Parseghian (director). Taped on January 23, 1999. Color. In Armenian. 130 minutes.

Comment: Produced at the Shrine Auditorium in Los Angeles by the National Academic Theater of Opera and Ballet of Armenia while it was on tour. Taped mostly in longshot, it is very uninvolving.

Related film

1971 Gohar Gasparian

Gohar Gasparian, a Soviet-Armenian film produced by Grigory Melik-Avakyan as a showcase for the Armenian soprano, includes a scene in which she sings Anoush's final aria. Armenfilm Studio. Color. In Armenian and Russian. 70 minutes. Not on VHS.

ANTHOLOGIES

Many opera anthologies, guides, and compilations have been released on film and video with multiple opera scenes and excerpts. They are mostly excerpts from operas that already exist in more complete form on film or video, but some are unique. Those with music by a single composer are listed under the composer's entry; those taken from the TV programs BELL TELEPHONE HOUR, ED SULLIVAN SHOW, and VOICE OF FIRESTONE are listed under those entries.

The Art of Singing

Superb British collection of opera singers on screen from Caruso, Martinelli, and de Luca to Callas, Price, and Sutherland. See THE ART OF SINGING.

Classic Opera

Television appearances by top opera singers, mostly in color with splendid sound. Featured in arias and duets are Leontyne Price, Roberta Peters, Robert Merrill, Beverly Sills, Anna Moffo, Richard Tucker, Maria Callas, Lily Pons, Joan Sutherland, Marilyn Horne, Renata Tebaldi, Franco Corelli, Eileen Farrell, Birgit Nilsson, Jan Peerce, and Dorothy Kirsten. Sources and dates are not identified but most seem to have originated on *The Ed Sullivan Show.* Released in 1996. Color and black and white. 90 minutes. MIA (England) VHS.

Classics in Vision

Sampler of 12 scenes from the Decca video catalogue, most with opera content, including excerpts from *Rigoletto, Tosca, Lucrezia Borgia,* and *Le nozze di Figaro.* The singers include José Carreras, Cecilia Bartoli, Kiri Te Kanawa, Luciano Pavarotti, Plácido Domingo, Joan Sutherland, and Sherrill Milnes. Released in 1994. Color. In original languages with English subtitles. 60 minutes. Decca VHS.

Essential Opera 1 and 2

Two introduction-to-opera compilation videos, each featuring stars in 12 scenes from famous operas such as *The Barber of Seville, La bohème, Carmen,* and *Tosca.* The singers include Cecilia Bartoli, José Carreras, Plácido Domingo, Maria Ewing, Mirella Freni, Raina Kabaivanska, Leo Nucci, Joan Sutherland, Luciano Pavarotti, and Kiri Te Kanawa. The opera scenes are excerpts from existing videos. Compilation released in 1990. Color. In original languages with English subtitles. Each 82 minutes. Decca/London VHS/LD.

First Opera Film Festival

Film consisting of highlight versions of five operas staged at the Rome Opera House in 1948: CARMEN, DON PASQUALE, FRA DIAVOLO, GUILLAUME TELL, and LE NOZZE DI FIGARO. Most roles are played by actors and dubbed by singers such as Tito Gobbi, Cloe Elmo, and Piero Biasini. Olin Downes introduces the operas, and Angelo Questa conducts the Rome Opera House Orchestra. George Richfield produced the film, released in the United States by Classic Pictures. Black and white. In Italian. 90 minutes. See individual operas for details.

Great Moments in Opera

This is a superb compilation video of performances on *The Ed Sullivan Show.* See THE ED SULLIVAN SHOW.

Great Puccini Love Scenes

Not just Puccini but rather a 1998 compilation of scenes from videos of operas by Puccini, Verdi, Strauss, and Offenbach filmed at various opera houses. Kiri Te Kanawa, Plácido Domingo, Raina Kabaivanska, and Mirella Freni are featured in excerpts from favorites such as *Madama Butterfly, Tosca,* and *Otello.* Color. 111 minutes. Kultur VHS.

Great Singers of Russia

Two videos featuring Russia's greatest singers in historic performances. *Volume One: From Chaliapin to Reizen* includes Chaliapin, Pirogov, Lemeshev, Mikhailov, Shpiller, Lisitsian, Nelepp, and Reizen. *Volume Two: From Petrov to Kazarnovskaya* includes Petrov, Andzhaparidze, Arkhipova, Piavko, Rudenko, Nesterenko,

Obraztsova, Atlantov, Kasrashvili, Borodina, Hvorostovsky, and Kazarnovskaya. Ljuba Kazarnovskaya acts as host, and Ivan Petrov, Irina Arkhipova, and Joan Dornemann are interviewed. Black and white and color. VAI VHS.

Great Voices From CBC

Compilation of telecasts by singers appearing on CBC Toronto from 1957 to 1965. They include Marian Anderson singing spirituals, Maureen Forrester with songs, Marilyn Horne singing arias from *Semele* and *Semiramide,* George London performing an aria from *Faust,* Peter Pears with Elizabethan songs, Imgard Seefriend with a Schubert song, and Richard Tucker and Lisa Della Casa with a duet from *Madama Butterfly.* 52 minutes. VAI VHS.

History of Italian Music

Italian series by Elio Rumma tracing chronologically the history of opera and other forms of music in Italy. Each video is about an hour long and is devoted to a subject such as *Opera Buffa in Naples.* Released in 1988. Color. In Italian. About 60 minutes. Mastervideo (Italy) VHS.

Legends of Opera

American collection of opera singers on film and video including Bergonzi, Callas, Caruso, Christoff, Del Monaco, Gigli, Milanov, Ponselle, Siepi, Supervia, Taddei, Tebaldi, Tetrazzini, Tucker, and Wunderlich. Released in 1996. Mostly black and white. 77 minutes. Legato Classics VHS.

Music in the 20th Century

John Huszar and FilmAmerica's 10-part series on modern music contains several entries of operatic interest. *Fire and Ice,* the first program, has excerpts and discussions of operas by Wagner and Debussy. *Musical Stages,* the eighth program, focuses on opera and musical theater. Televised in 1997. Color. In English. FilmAmerica VHS.

Musikalisches Rendezvous

Compilation of highlights from DEFA opera films made in East Berlin in 1962, including DER BETTEL STUDENT, DIE LUSTIGEN WEIBER VON WINDSOR, ZAR UND ZIMMERMANN, and LE NOZZE DI FIGARO. Color. In German. 83 minutes. See individual operas for details.

The Music of Man

Canadian series about the history of music, eight 60-minute programs on four videos with Yehudi Menuhin as narrator and guide. Opera composers discussed include Monteverdi, Lully, Mozart, Beethoven, and Verdi. Richard Bocking and John Thomason directed. Released in 1987. Color. In English. Home Vision VHS.

My World of Opera

Kiri Te Kanawa gives a tour of the Royal Opera House and introduces scenes from operas. They include Te Kanawa singing the *Der Rosenkavalier* trio with Barbara Bonney and Anne Howells, Robert Lloyd in *Don Carlo*, José Carreras in *Andrea Chénier*, Plácido Domingo in *Les contes d'Hoffmann*, Janet Baker in *Orfeo ed Euridice*, Domingo and Mirella Freni in *Ernani*, Vladimir Atlantov in *Otello*, plus *Die Fledermaus*, *La bohème*, and *Nabucco*. Keith Cheetham directed and Robin Scott produced the video released in 1992. Color. 59 minutes. Teldec VHS.

Opera Favorites

Plácido Domingo and Kiri Te Kanawa in scenes from six operas. Te Kanawa is Rosalinde, Hildegarde Heichele is Adele, and Hermann Prey is Eisenstein in *Die Fledermaus* at the Royal Opera House. Domingo is Hoffmann in *Les contes d'Hoffmann* at Covent Garden with Agnes Baltsa as Giulietta and Dick Johnson in *La Fanciulla del West* at Covent Garden. At the Arena di Verona, Te Kanawa is Desdemona, and Vladimir Atlantov is Otello in *Otello*. At La Scala, Domingo is Ernani and Mirella Freni is Elvira in *Ernani*. The compilation ends at Covent Garden with Domingo as Des Grieux and Te Kanawa as Manon in *Manon Lescaut*. Released in 1988. Color. In original languages with English subtitles. 59 minutes. HBO VHS.

Opera Titans

Excellent compilation documentary of vintage film material featuring great opera singers at their best, including Björling, Caniglia, Carosio, Del Monaco, De Taranto, Gigli, Schipa, Tagliavini, and Tetrazzini. Black and white and color. 65 minutes. Bel Canto Society VHS.

See How Great They Sound

DVD compilation issued in 2001 to demonstrate the quality of opera and classical music performance in the new format. It includes 21 numbers and features singers Cecilia Bartoli, Andrea Bocelli, José Carreras, Plácido Domingo, Jessye Norman, Luciano Pavarotti, and Bryn Terfel. Color. Universal Classics DVD.

Stars of Bel Canto

Belgian TV compilation of studio appearances by nine singers during the 1960s. Renata Tebaldi, Regina Resnik, Leonie Rysanek, Giulietta Simionato, Roberta Peters, Hilde Gueden, George London, Lawrence Winters, and Fernando Corena sing arias by Rossini, Offenbach, Verdi, Puccini, Mozart, and Bizet. RTBF Radiotélévision Belge Française. Black and white. 60 minutes.

ANTHONY ADVERSE
1936 American film with opera content

Olivia de Havilland becomes a great opera star (and the mistress of Napoleon) in this big-budget blockbuster with an Academy Award–winning score by Erich Wolfgang Korngold and operatic sequences created by Aldo Franchetti. Based on a best-selling historical swashbuckler by Hervey Allen, *Anthony Adverse* stars Fredric March as Adverse, de Havilland as his wife Angela (who becomes opera diva Mlle. George), and Gale Sondergaard as a nasty villainess (she won an Oscar for her leer). The sprawling story concerns Adverse's adventures in America and Africa as well as France and Italy. Natale Carossio staged the opera sequences, de Havilland's singing was dubbed by Diana Gaylen, and Leo F. Forbstein conducted the Vitaphone Orchestra. Sheridan Gibney wrote the screenplay, Tony Gaudio won an Oscar for his cinematography, and Mervyn LeRoy directed for producer Hal B. Wallis and Warner Bros. Black and white. In English. 139 minutes.

ANTONY AND CLEOPATRA
1966 opera by Barber

Samuel Barber's operatic version of Shakespeare's play was commissioned to open the new Metropolitan Opera House at Lincoln Center on September 16, 1966. The premiere was dominated by the extravagant staging of Franco Zeffirelli and badly received by critics. The libretto is mostly Shakespeare's words arranged by Zeffirelli, who condensed the play to 17 scenes. It was later revised and shortened by Barber with help from Gian Carlo Menotti, and this version has been more popular.

1991 Lyric Opera of Chicago

American stage production: Elijah Mojinský (director), Richard Buckley (conductor, Lyric Opera of Chicago Orchestra and Chorus), Michael Yeargan (set/costume designer).

Cast: Catherine Malfitano (Cleopatra), Richard Cowan (Antony), Jacques Trussel (Octavius), Eric Halfvarson (Enobarbus), Wendy White (Charmian), Nancy Maultsby (Iras), Michael Wadsworth (Agrippa), Paul Kreider (Dolabella), Philip Zawisza (Eros), William Walker (Alexas).

Taped in October 1991; telecast December 16, 1991, on PBS in *Great Performances* series. Kirk Browning (director). Color. In English. 118 minutes.

Comment: Revised Menotti version. It was well received but is not available on commercial video.

Related films

1966 The New Met: Countdown to Curtain

Preparations for the opening of *Antony and Cleopatra* at the new Metropolitan Opera House at Lincoln Center in 1966. Leontyne Price is seen rehearsing the role of Cleopatra with conductor Thomas Schippers; director Franco Zeffirelli has problems with a giant turntable that won't work; and general manager Rudolf Bing is threatened with a walkout by the orchestra. Robert Drew directed this documentary film telecast on the *Bell Telephone Hour* on NBC November 20, 1966. Black and white. 60 minutes. Kultur VHS.

1972 Heston/Neil film

The most interesting film of the Shakespeare play, for comparison purposes, is the 1972 version directed by Charlton Heston with Heston as Antony and Hildegard Neil as Cleopatra. Color. In English. 160 minutes.

1983 Spoleto Festival USA

Menotti's production of *Antony and Cleopatra* at the 1983 Spoleto Festival in Charleston is featured in the video *Festival! Spoleto, USA*. Brief scenes from the opera are shown. Kirk Browning directed the telecast June 27, 1983. Color. 60 minutes.

ARABELLA

1933 opera by Richard Strauss

RICHARD STRAUSS's delightful opera, set in Vienna in 1860 at Carnival time, concerns Arabella and her sister Zdenka and their suitors and how their love affairs get sorted out. The role of Arabella is a demanding one, calling for a silvery soprano voice untroubled by high notes. It also helps if she is quite beautiful. This was the last of the operas written by Hugo von Hofmannsthal for Strauss.

***1960 Bavarian State Opera

German stage production: Rudolf Hartmann (director), Joseph Keilberth (conductor, Bavarian State Opera Orchestra and Chorus), Helmut Jürgens (set designer).

Cast: Lisa Della Casa (Arabella), Dietrich Fischer-Dieskau (Mandryka), Anneliese Rothenberger (Zdenka), Ira Malaniuk (Adelaide), Karl Christian Kohn (Waldner), Georg Paskua (Matteo), Eva Maria Rogner (Fiakermilli).

Video: House of Opera DVD and VHS/Legato Classics VHS. Black and white. In German. 175 minutes.

Comment: Video is not of the best quality, but the production, conducting, and cast are outstanding.

1977 Vienna State Opera

Austrian TV film: Otto Schenk (director, based on his Vienna State Opera production), Sir Georg Solti (conductor, Vienna Philharmonic and Vienna State Opera Chorus), Jan Schulbach (set designer) Wolfgang Treu (cinematographer).

Cast: Gundula Janowitz (Arabella), Bernd Weikl (Mandryka), Sona Ghazarian (Zdenka), René Kollo (Matteo), Edita Gruberova (Fiakermilli), Martha Mödl (Fortune teller).

Video: London/Polygram VHS/LD. Telecast December 19, 1977. Otto Schenk (director). Color. In German with English subtitles. 149 minutes.

1984 Glyndebourne Festival

English stage production: John Cox (director), Bernard Haitink (conductor, London Philharmonic Orchestra and Glyndebourne Festival Chorus), Julia Trevelyan Oman (set/costume design).

Cast: Ashley Putnam (Arabella), John Brocheler (Mandryka), Gianna Rolandi (Zdenka), Keith Lewis (Matteo), Gwendolyn Bradley (Fiakermilli).

Video: Warner NVC Arts DVD/EMI & HBO VHS. John Vernon (director), Color. In German with English subtitles. 160 minutes.

Comment: Putnam is the glory of this production, for both her singing and her acting.

***1994 Metropolitan Opera

American stage production: Otto Schenk (director), Christian Thielemann (conductor, Metropolitan Orchestra and Chorus), Günther Schneider-Siemssen (set designer).

Cast: Kiri Te Kanawa (Arabella), Wolfgang Brendel (Mandryka), Marie McLaughlin (Zdenka), David Kuebler (Matteo), Natalie Dessay (Fiakermilli).

Video: DG DVD/VHS. Taped November 3, 1994; telecast November 1, 1995, on PBS. Brian Large (director). Color. In German with English subtitles. 160 minutes.

Comment: Top notch on all fronts and most sensitively staged, with Te Kanawa in wonderful form.

ARAGALL, GIACOMO

Spanish tenor (1939–)

Giacomo Aragall, one of the world's top tenors and a major force in Spanish singing, was born in Barcelona, studied in Milan, and made his debut at La Fenice in Venice in 1963. He sang at La Scala for three years and arrived in Covent Garden in 1966 as the Duke in *Rigoletto*. He was again the Duke in the Verdi opera at the Metropolitan in 1968 and in San Francisco in 1972. See SEVILLE (1991), TOSCA (1984), LA TRAVIATA (1984 film), and VERONA (1988).

ARAIZA, FRANCISCO
Mexican tenor (1950–)

Francisco Araiza is one of the top Mozartian tenors but is also popular in Rossini and Verdi operas. He studied with Mexican soprano Irma Gonzalez, made his debut in Mexico City in 1970, and went to Europe in 1975. He sang in 1983 at Covent Garden *(Don Pasquale)*, in 1984 in San Francisco *(La Cenerentola),* and at the Met *(Die Entführung aus dem Serail).* He is featured on many videos, including four Mozart operas. See LA CENERENTOLA (1981/1988/1996 film), COSÌ FAN TUTTE (1983), DON GIOVANNI (1989 Parma and La Scala), DIE ENTFÜHRUNG AUS DEM SERAIL (1980), FALSTAFF (1982), MANON (1983), MOZART (1991), THE PHANTOM OF THE OPERA (1989), IL RITORNO D'ULISSE IN PATRIA (1980), DER ROSENKAVALIER (1979), ROSSINI (1985), DIE SCHÖPFUNG (1990), SEMIRAMIDE (1980), IL VIAGGIO A REIMS (1984), and DIE ZAUBERFLÖTE (1983/1991).

ARGENTINA, IMPERIO
Spanish singer (1906–2003)

Imperio Argentina (born Magdalena Nilo del Rio in Buenos Aires) was the leading Spanish female film star of the 1930s, famous for singing, dancing, and acting in musicals directed by Benito Perojo or her husband Florian Rey. Her most popular Spanish movie was *Morena Clara* (1936), and she made a version of CARMEN in 1938. Her most notable films are the Italian TOSCA (1940), on which Renoir and Visconti worked, and the Spanish film of Granados's opera GOYESCAS (1942). She also made films in Germany and Argentina. She made a comeback in 1986 at the age of 80, when director José Luis Borau featured her singing again in the Spanish film *Tata Mia.*

ARGENTO, DARIO
Italian film director (1943–)

Italian director Dario Argento specializes in stylish horror films, often featuring opera music. His horrific 1987 film TERROR AT THE OPERA centers around a production of Verdi's bad-luck opera MACBETH in Parma. The supernatural 1979 *Inferno* features an appropriate chorus from NABUCCO on its soundtrack. His 1973 *The Five Days,* about the Milan Revolution of 1848, features the La Scala Orchestra playing excerpts from LA GAZZA LADRA. His 1998 version of THE PHANTOM OF THE OPERA includes music from CARMEN, LAKMÉ, and FAUST.

ARGENTO, DOMINICK
American composer (1927–)

Dominick Argento, one of the most successful modern American opera composers, created the screen opera THE DREAM OF VALENTINO, which premiered at the Washington Opera in 1994. Based on the life of silent film star Rudolph Valentino, it uses movie techniques to enhance its Hollywood background. Argento's operatic adaptation of THE ASPERN PAPERS (1988) was telecast from the Dallas Opera. Argento has composed 13 operas, including *Postcard From Morocco* (1972), *The Voyage of Edgar Allen Poe* (1976), and *Miss Havisham's Fire* (1979). He won the Pulitzer Prize for Music in 1975 for his song cycle *From the Diary of Virginia Woolf.*

ARIA
1987 English opera film

English producer Don Boyd asked 10 well-known directors to make a film around an opera aria of their choice. The result was the controversial *Aria,* which closed the Cannes Film Festival in 1987 and opened AFI Fest in Los Angeles in 1988. Some episodes are better than others, but all are innovative interpretations of opera music; some of the filmmakers had directed opera on stage. Critics have tended to dismiss this film because it falls in that uncertain area between cinema and opera, but most of the episodes stand up well to repeated viewing. They are described under their operas: ARMIDE (Jean-Luc Godard), UN BALLO IN MASCHERA (Nicolas Roeg), LES BORÉADES (Robert Altman), LA FORZA DEL DESTINO (Charles Sturridge), LOUISE (Derek Jarman), PAGLIACCI (Bill Bryden), RIGOLETTO (Julien Temple), TRISTAN UND ISOLDE (Franc Roddam), DIE TOTE STADT (Bruce Beresford), and TURANDOT (Ken Russell). Color. 90 minutes. Image Entertainment DVD/Lightyear VHS/LD.

ARIADNE AUF NAXOS
1912 opera by Richard Strauss

RICHARD STRAUSS and librettist Hugo von Hofmannsthal had problems working out the final form of this sophisticated opera-within-an-opera. The first version combined Molière's musical play of 1670, *Le Bourgeois Gentilhomme,* with the opera *Ariadne auf Naxos,* which was presented as an entertainment after the dinner that ends the play. It was way too long (six hours), so Hofmannsthal revised it and dropped the play. The second version, the one performed today, is a witty story about an *opera seria* company putting on a production for an 18th-century patron and learning that a light comedy troupe will perform with it simultaneously. The leading roles are all sopranos, and there is great rivalry between the very serious Prima Donna, the effervescent comedy troupe leader Zerbinetta, and the deeply concerned Composer. See also LE BOURGEOIS GENTILHOMME.

1955 NBC Opera Theatre

American television production: John Schwartz (director), Peter Herman Adler (conductor, Symphony of the Air Orchestra), Samuel Chotzinoff (producer), Reuben Ter-Arutunian (set/costume designer), John Wood (English version of *Le bourgeois gentilhomme*), George and Phyllis Mead (English version of *Ariadne auf Naxos*).

Ariadne cast: Wilma Spence (Ariadne), Virginia MacWatters (Zerbinetta), Robert Marshall (Bacchus), Joan Marie Moynagh (Echo), Robert Goss (Harlequin), Joan Carroll (Naiad).

Bourgeois cast: Wally Cox (M. Jourdain), Anita Darian (Nicole), Charlotte Rade (Mme. Jourdain), Ross Martin (Dorante), Roy Dean.

Video at the MTR. Telecast live February 27, 1955. Kirk Browning (director). Black and white. In English. 90 minutes.

Comment: Ambitious NBC production attempting to re-create the premiere staging using abridged versions of opera and play. Comic arias are sung in English, *seria* music is sung in German.

1978 Vienna State Opera

Austrian stage production: Filippo Sanjust (director and set/costume design), Karl Böhm (conductor, Vienna Philharmonic Orchestra), Unitel (production company).

Cast: Gundula Janowitz (Prima Donna/ Ariadne), Edita Gruberova (Zerbinetta), Trudeliese Schmidt (Composer), René Kollo (Tenor/Bacchus), Walter Berry (Music Master), Heinz Zednik (Dancing Master/Brighella), Kurt Equiluz (Scaramuccio).

Telecast January 11, 1979, on ORF Austrian Television. John Vernon (film director). Color. In German. 128 minutes.

Comment: The prologue is staged in a realistic 18th-century setting and the opera-within-the-opera in stylized sets.

***1988 Metropolitan Opera

American stage production: Bodo Igesz (director), James Levine (conductor, Metropolitan Opera Orchestra and Chorus), Oliver Messel (set designer), Jane Greenwood (costume design).

Cast: Jessye Norman (Prima Donna/Ariadne), Kathleen Battle (Zerbinetta), Tatiana Troyanos (Composer), James King (Tenor/Bacchus), Franz Ferdinand Nentwig (Music Master), Dawn Upshaw (Echo), Barbara Bonney (Naiad), Gweneth Bean (Dryad), Stephen Dickson (Harlequin).

Video: DG DVD/VHS/LD. Taped March 12, 1988; telecast April 27, 1988. Brian Large (director). Color. In German with English subtitles. 154 minutes.

Comment: Traditional production with a terrific trio of American sopranos heading the cast and a notable trio of nymphs adding to the enjoyment.

1988 Gran Teatre del Liceu, Barcelona

Spanish stage production: Jean-Pierre Ponnelle (director/set designer), Janos Kulka (conductor, Gran Teatre del Liceu Symphony Orchestra).

Cast: Mechtild Gessendorf (Prima Donna/Ariadne), Edita Gruberova (Zerbinetta), Trudeliese Schmidt (Composer), Paul Frey (Tenor/Bacchus), Barry Mora (Music Master), Brigitte Hahn (Echo), Julie Kaufman (Naiad), Andrea Bönig (Dryad), Wolfgang Rausch (Harlequin).

Video: House of Opera DVD/Legato Classics VHS. Antonio Chic (director). Color. In German with Spanish subtitles. 131 minutes.

1991 Florentine Opera

American stage production: Jay Lesenger (director), Joseph Rescigno (conductor, Milwaukee Symphony Orchestra), J. M. Deegan and Sarah G. Conly (set/costume design).

Cast: Linda Roark-Strummer (Prima Donna/Ariadne), Erie Mills (Zerbinetta), Sharon Graham (Composer), Gary Bachlund (Tenor/Bacchus), Peter Strummer (Music Master), David Ronis (Dance Master).

Telecast May 29, 1991, on WMVS, Milwaukee. Bill Werner (director). Color. In English. 133 minutes.

1999 Dresden Semper Opera

German stage production: Marco Arturo Marelli (director), Sir Colin Davis (conductor, Dresden Staatskapelle and Semperoper Chorus).

Cast: Susan Anthony (Ariadne), Iride Martinez (Zerbinetta), Sophie Koch (Composer), Jon Villars (Bacchus), Theo Adam (Music Master), Friedrich-Wilhelm Junge (Major-Domo).

Video: Arthaus Musik (GB) DVD. Felix Breisach (director). Color. In German with English subtitles. 130 minutes.

Comment: Marelli updates the opera to the present day and sets it at an art gallery vernissage with guests wandering around drinking champagne and barely acknowledging the performers. Critics were not impressed.

ARIANE
1958 opera by Martinů

Czech composer BOHUSLAV MARTINŮ wrote his last opera *Ariane* (Ariadne) to his own French libretto based on Georges Neveux's play *Le voyage de Thésée*. It's a variation on the Greek myth about Ariadne and her relationship with Theseus during his time in Crete fighting the Minotaur. It was created for a bravura soprano (the composer was an admirer of Maria Callas) and features a coloratura aria as its final number. The music is almost romantic and quite powerful.

***1994 Czech Television
Czech TV production: Tomás Simerda (director), Václav Neumann (conductor, Czech Philharmonic Orchestra), Vladimir Soukénka (set designer).
Cast: Celina Lindsley (Ariadne), Norman Phillips (Theseus), Richard Novák (Minotaur), Vladimir Dolezal (Burun), Miroslav Kopp (Guard), Ludek Vele (Old Man).
Video: Opera d'Oro VHS. Tomás Simerada (director). Color. In French. 44 minutes.
Comment: Lindsley, an American who recorded the opera with this cast for a Supraphon CD, is made up to look like Callas. She sings well, and the stylized sets help create an unreal mythical world.

ARIODANTE
1735 opera by Handel

GEORGE FRIDERIC HANDEL's opera *Ariodante* tells the story of the tribulations of Princess Ginevra (Guinevere), daughter of the King of Scotland. She is in love with Prince Ariodante (mezzo-soprano role originally sung by a castrato) but is falsely accused of infidelity by the villain Polinesso. When he is proved wrong and killed, the lovers are reunited. The vocally difficult opera, which has never really entered the Handel repertory, is set in Edinburgh, though it is based on a work by Antonio Salvi derived from Ariosto's *Orlando Furioso*.

***1996 English National Opera
English stage production: David Alden (director), Ivor Bolton (conductor, English National Opera Orchestra and Chorus).
Cast: Ann Murray (Ariodante), Joan Rodgers, (Princess Ginevra), Christopher Robson (Polinesso), Lesley Garrett (Dalinda), Paul Nilon (Lurcanio), Mark Le Brocq (Odoardo), Gwynne Howell (King of Scotland).
Video: Image Entertainment/Arthaus (GB) DVD. Color. In Italian with English subtitles. 177 minutes.
Comment: Alden originally staged the opera in 1993 as a coproduction of English and Welsh National

Operas. It was revived and videotaped in 1996 and revived again in 2002.

ARKHIPOVA, IRINA
Russian mezzo-soprano (1925–)

Irina Arkhipova began singing professionally in 1954 and made her debut at the Bolshoi in 1956 as Carmen. She quickly became one of the top stars of Bolshoi, originating roles in new operas and traveling with the company abroad. She was particularly admired for her Azucena in IL TROVATORE at the Orange Festival in 1972, a performance that is on video. In 1988, she sang the role of Ulrica at Covent Garden. She can be seen with the Bolshoi Opera as Irina in BORIS GODUNOV (1978), as Marfa in KHOVANSHCHINA (1979), and as Carmen opposite Mario Del Monaco in CARMEN (1959). See also ANTHOLOGIES (Great Singers of Russia), BOLSHOI OPERA (1989/1999), BORIS GODUNOV (1963 film), MARIO DEL MONACO (1979), and TCHAIKOVSKY (1970).

1959 Irina Arkhipova Recital
Arkhipova was filmed in recital for Moscow TV singing arias from some of her favorite operas, including *Carmen, Aida, Boris Godunov,* and other Russian works. Black and white. In Russian. 70 minutes.

ARLESIANA, L'
1897 opera by Cilea

Bizet wrote the incidental music for the premiere of Alphonse Daudet's French play *L'arlésienne,* which later became the basis of Francesco Cilea's Italian opera *L'Arlesiana* (The Woman From Arles), libretto by Leopoldo Marenco. Like *Carmen,* it is the story of a man (Federico) who loses his heart to a cruel woman, the woman from Arles (she never appears on stage). After he learns the truth about her, he agrees to marry Vivetta at the urging of his mother, Rosa Mamai. Just before the marriage, he is reminded of the woman from Arles and kills himself. Caruso first became known through the premiere of this opera.

1979 Flemish Opera
Flemish Belgian stage production: Eddy Verburggen (director), André Vandernoon (conductor, Antwerp Philharmonic Orchestra and Royal Opera of Ghent Chorus), Jean Marlier (sets).
Cast: Bruno Sebastian (Federico), Lia Rottrei (Vivetta), Maryse Patric (Rosa Mamai), Jean Lafont (Baldassare), Bert Olsson (Metifio).
Video: House of Opera/Lyric VHS. Color. In Italian. 61 minutes.

1939 Casa Lontana
Beniamino Gigli sings the sad tenor aria "È la solita storia del pastore" on stage in the opera after his wife tells him she is leaving him for another man. The aria affects him so much that he then disappears. See CASA LONTANA.

1956 Serenade
Mario Lanza sings Federico's lament "È la solita storia del pastore" with Ray Heindorf and orchestra in this film about an opera singer with emotional problems. See SERENADE.

ARMENIAN OPERA

Armenian opera and operetta began while the Armenian people were living in Turkey in the 19th century, but it is now centered in the Armenian capital of Erevan (formerly Yerevan). The first operetta composer was Chouhajian, best known for *The Chick-pea Seller;* soprano GOHAR GASPARIAN starred in a film based on it. The first opera composer was Tigran Tchukhatjian. His 1868 *Arshak II* is considered the first Armenian grand opera; it was staged in the United States by San Francisco Opera in 2001. ARMEN TIGRANIAN's 1912 ANOUSH, however, holds pride of place as the Armenian national opera; there are two productions on video. There have been several Armenian opera singers of note, with Gasparian and LUCINE AMARA the best known.

ARMIDE
1686 opera by Lully

JEAN-BAPTISTE LULLY's opera, libretto by Philippe Quinault based on Tasso's epic poem *La Gerusalemme liberata,* is the story of the enchantress Armida (Armide in the opera). She bewitches the Crusader knight Rinaldo (Renaud), who had earlier resisted her charms, and they live happily together for a time. He is eventually rescued by his knight friends Artemidorus and Ubalde, who arrive with magic weapons.

1987 University of Western Australia
Australian stage production: Colin O'Brien (director), Ivor Keys (conductor, University Collegium Musicum), Philippa O'Brien (set/costume design). Cast: Jane Manning (Armide), John Foster (Renaud), Lorentz Lossius (Ubalde), Christopher Waddell (Hidraoth, King of Damascus), Margo Robertson (Phénice), Lisa Brown (Sidonie).

Telecast in Australia in 1987. Gerald Wright and Eric Hawkins (directors). Color. In French. 133 minutes.

1911 La Gerusalemme liberata
Fernando Negri-Pouget plays Armida in this four-reel Italian epic based on the Tasso poem that was the basis of the opera libretto. Amleto Novelli is Tancredi, Emilio Ghione is Rinaldo, and Gianna Terribili-Gonzales is Clorinda. Director Enrico Guazzoni spent five months making the film for Cines with a cast of 800. Released in the United States as *The Crusaders or Jerusalem Delivered.* Black and white. About 60 minutes.

1987 Aria
Jean-Luc Godard creates an updated version of the opera's story of a heroic knight held in a spell by a sorceress. His episode of the film ARIA is set in the Weider bodybuilding gym in Paris. Two frustrated young women wander around the gym trying to get a response from musclemen frozen in enchantment. The music is sung by Rachel Yakar, Zeger Vandersteene, and Daniele Boorst, with Philippe Herreweghe conducting the Ensemble Vocal et Instrumental de la Chapelle Royale. Color. In French. About 10 minutes.

2000 Le roi danse
The King Dances is a lavish French film biography of composer Lully (played by Boris Terral), which features music and scenes from *Armide* and other Lully operas. See LE ROI DANSE.

ARRIETA, EMILIO
Spanish composer (1823–1894)

Pascual Emilio Arrieta y Corera wrote many operas but is primarily remembered as a composer of zarzuelas. The most popular is the 1855 Italian-influenced MARINA, which is close to being a full-scale opera and has been compared with Donizetti. It has remained in the repertory of most Spanish-speaking countries, with recent productions in Spain, Mexico, and Venezuela.

ART OF SINGING, THE
1996 anthology of opera singers

The Art of Singing: Golden Voices of the Century is an outstanding British collection of opera singers performing on film and video. It begins with Enrico Caruso, has Vitaphone films of Giovanni Martinelli and Giuseppe de Luca, and features Rosa Ponselle's *Carmen* screen test, Kirsten Flagstad's film version of "Hojotoho," Maria

Callas's Lisbon *La traviata* appearance, and Jussi Björling singing Rodolfo to Renata Tebaldi's Mimì on television. The other singers include Feodor Chaliapin, Ezio Pinza (playing Chaliapin singing a scene from *Boris Godunov*), Beniamino Gigli, Tito Gobbi, Richard Tauber, Lawrence Tibbett, Lauritz Melchior, Leontyne Price, and Joan Sutherland. Commentary is provided by Thomas Hampson, Kirk Browning, Magda Olivero, and others; excerpts are of excellent quality; and written notes are by John Steane. Based on a BBC TV production by Donald Sturrock. Color and black and white. 116 minutes. NVC Arts DVD/Warner Music (GB) VHS/LD.

ASHLEY, ROBERT
American composer (1930–)

Robert Ashley's television and video operas have helped redefine the meaning of "opera" in a mixed-media world and have many admirers in the avant-garde world. He feels that TV/video artists should create re-viewable works of art that, like musical compositions, can be experienced a number of times. Born in Michigan, and a disciple of John Cage, Ashley has composed a dozen television operas that mix music with spoken and written texts and unusual visual imagery. The best known is PERFECT LIVES (1980), which has been telecast in England and the United States and is available on commercial VHS. The 14-hour MUSIC WITH ROOTS IN THE AETHER (1976) involves six other composers. Most of Ashley's operas belong to three groups: ATALANTA (ACTS OF GOD), *Perfect Lives,* and *Now Eleanor's Idea.* His 1999 DUST features homeless street people, including one who is able to converse with God when under the influence of morphine.

1983 Robert Ashley (4 American Composers)
Peter Greenaway's film about Robert Ashley focuses on the origin, composition, and design of his opera *Perfect Lives.* Segments of it are shown based around performances in a London theater with Ashley as storyteller, "Blue" Gene Tyranny on keyboards, and Jill Kroesen and David Van Tieghem as singers. Ashley uses a multitude of video monitors and multiple images. Channel Four. Color. 60 minutes. Mystic Fire VHS.

ASPERN PAPERS, THE
1988 opera by Argento

Opera diva Juliana Borereau lives with her spinster niece Tina in a villa by Lake Como in Italy in 1895. A scholar who arrives seeking lodging is actually seeking a lost opera composed by Aspern for Juliana in 1835. The action switches between 1835 and 1895. DOMINICK ARGENTO'S *The Aspern Papers,* libretto by the composer based on the Henry James novella, shifts the location from Venice to Lake Como and makes Aspern a Bellini-like composer instead of a poet. It was premiered by Dallas Opera on November 19, 1988, with Elisabeth Söderstrom as the diva Juliana.

1988 Dallas Opera
American stage production: Mark Lamos (director), Nicola Rescigno (conductor, Dallas Symphony Orchestra), John Conklin (set/costume designer).

Cast: Elisabeth Söderström (Juliana), Frederica von Stade (Tina), Richard Stilwell (Lodger), Neil Rosenshein (Aspern), Katherine Ciesinski (Sonia), Eric Halfvarson (Barelli).

Video at the MTR. Taped in November 1988 and telecast on PBS on June 9, 1989. Kirk Browning (director). Color. In English. 120 minutes.

ASQUITH, ANTHONY
English film director (1901–1968)

Anthony Asquith's 36-year career in cinema included two films with notable opera content. *The Importance of Being Earnest* (1952) features ironic use of an aria from RIGOLETTO. *On Such a Night* (1955) is a charming film about a young American attending a performance of LE NOZZE DI FIGARO at the Glyndebourne Festival where Sesto Bruscantini and Sena Jurinac are singing. Asquith also directed the opera *Carmen* on stage at Covent Garden and made Covent Garden ballet films.

ATALANTA (ACTS OF GOD)
1982 video opera by Ashley

Robert Ashley's 1982 video opera *Atalanta (Acts of God),* libretto by the composer loosely based on the Greek myth of Atalanta, premiered in 1985 at the Museum of Contemporary Art in Chicago. It consists of three 90-minute episodes, with each episode concerning a different person. Atalanta was a swift huntress who successfully avoided marriage by winning races, until she was tricked by three golden apples.

1984 Atalanta Strategy
Atalanta Strategy is a highlights version of the opera. Based on "Willard," the second episode, it consists of seven scenes: "The Immigration Office" (with Ronald Vance, Willem Dafoe, Norman Frisch, Jim Johnson, Anna Kohler, Annie Roth, and Kate Valk); "The Interview" (Ashley talks to Jeffrey M. Jones about the opera); "The Flying Saucer" (Kate Valk and Ron Vawter portray aliens in a space ship discussing humans); "Willard Anecdote & Chorales" (voice-over by Ashley with keyboard solos by "Blue" Gene Tyranny and chorus by Rebecca Armstrong and David Van Tiegham); "Character Reference" (with Ashley); "The Mule in the Tree" (with Jac-

queline Humbert); and "The Mystery of the River" (with Margaret Ahrens and Marjorie Merrick). Lawrence Brickman designed and directed. Color. In English. 28 minutes. Lovely Music VHS.

ATLANTOV, VLADIMIR
Russian tenor (1939–)

Vladimir Atlantov has become widely known through singing in Western opera houses from La Scala to Covent Garden. He is the son of an opera singer, made his debut at the Kirov Opera in 1963, became a member of the Bolshoi Opera in 1967, and has toured widely with the company. He made his Covent Garden debut in 1987 in OTELLO and can be seen in this role in a 1982 Arena di Verona video. He can also be seen in three Russian operas: KHOVANSHCHINA (1989), THE QUEEN OF SPADES (1983/1992), and THE STONE GUEST (1967). See also ANTHOLOGIES (Great Singers of Russia), TCHAIKOVSKY (1970), and VERONA (1990).

ATTILA
1846 opera by Verdi

Italians who first experienced GIUSEPPE VERDI's opera in 1846 felt it was a portrait of their time, with Italy once again overrun by barbarians. They loved its patriotism, and it still stirs the blood today with its magnificent early Verdian rhythms. Temistocle Solera's libretto is the story of Attila the Hun who, after conquering most of Italy, has stopped to celebrate in the town of Acquileia. Woman warrior Odabella swears revenge on him for killing her father and stabs him on the day she promised to marry him.

1985 Arena di Verona
Italian stage production: Giuliano Montaldo (director), Nello Santi (conductor, Orchestra and Chorus of the Arena di Verona), Luciano Ricceri (set designer).
Cast: Yevgeny Nesterenko (Attila), Maria Chiara (Odabella), Silvano Carroli (Ezio), Veriano Luchetti (Foresto).
Video: Home Vision VHS. Brian Large (director). Color. In Italian with English subtitles. 120 minutes.
Comment: Russian bass Nesterenko has a voice built to conquer the giant Arena di Verona as well as the Romans and he dominates this magnificent production with its grandiose sets. Montaldo, an Italian filmmaker, gives the opera narrative drive.

1987 Teatro La Fenice
Italian stage production: Gian Franco De Bosio (director), Gabriele Ferro (conductor, Teatro La Fenice Orchestra and Chorus), Emanuele Luzzati (set designer).
Cast: Samuel Ramey (Attila), Linda Roark-Strummer (Odabella), William Stone (Ezio), Veriano Luchetti (Foresto), Aldo Bottion (Uldino), Giovanni Antonini (Leone).
Video: Image Entertainment DVD/Bel Canto Society and Home Vision VHS. Taped live January 23, 1987. Ilio Catani (director). Color. In Italian with English subtitles. 118 minutes.
Comment: American basso Ramey is a very impressive Attila.

**1991 Teatro alla Scala
Italian stage production: Jérôme Savary (director), Riccardo Muti (conductor, Teatro alla Scala Orchestra and Chorus), Michel Lebois (set designer).
Cast: Samuel Ramey (Attila), Cheryl Studer (Odabella), Giorgio Zancanaro (Ezio), Kaludi Kaludov (Foresto), Ernesto Gavazzi (Uldino), Mario Luperi (Leone).
Video: Image Entertainment DVD/Kultur and Home Vision VHS. Christopher Swann (director). Color. In Italian with English subtitles. 115 minutes.
Comment: Ramey and Studer are both impressive, Savary keeps the production lively, and Muti conducts with great skill. For all-around value, this is probably the best available video.

Related film

1970 La strategia del ragno
Bernardo Bertolucci's superb film *The Spider's Stratagem,* based on a Borges story, revolves around a plot to kill Mussolini during a performance of *Rigoletto* in a provincial city. Music from *Attila* is also featured in the film, which stars Giulio Brogi and Alida Valli. Color. In Italian. 98 minutes. On VHS.

AUBER, DANIEL
French composer (1782–1871)

Daniel Auber wrote light operas that were immensely popular in their time and are usually thought of as the forerunners of operetta. He is as important historically as Rossini, though none of his operas is currently available in modern commercial videos. His most popular works were FRA DIAVOLO, a kind of French Robin Hood story; LA MUETTE DE PORTICI, a revolutionary opera that once had a very wide appeal; and MANON LESCAUT, a version of the Prévost novel made before Massenet and Puccini created their more popular versions.

AUDEN, W. H.

British poet/librettist (1907–1973)

W. H. Auden was the most prominent 20th-century poet involved in writing opera and called himself an "opera addict." He began by collaborating with Benjamin Britten on *Paul Bunyan* in 1941 and then wrote THE RAKE'S PROGRESS for Stravinsky in 1948 in tandem with his longtime companion, opera expert Chester Kallman. They also wrote librettos for Nicolas Nabokov and Hans Werner Henze and created English-language versions of Kurt Weill's *The Seven Deadly Sins* and *The Rise and Fall of the City of Mahagonny* and Mozart's *Die Zauberflöte* and *Don Giovanni*.

AUDRAN, EDMOND

French composer (1840–1901)

Edmond Audran, a hugely popular composer in his time and an international rival of Lecocq, is not widely known today outside France. He had a fine gift for melody, and many of his airs are still popular. His comic operas continue to be produced on the French stage. The best known and most enduring is his opéra-comique LA MASCOTTE, which was made into a French film in 1935. His *Le Grand Mogol* and *La Poupée* are on French CDs.

AUFSTIEG UND FALL DER STADT MAHAGONNY

1930 opera by Weill

KURT WEILL's German opera *Aufstieg und Fall der Stadt Mahagonny* (Rise and Fall of the City of Mahagonny), libretto by Bertolt Brecht, is based on a *songspiel* (Weill's phrase) that they enlarged after the success of *The Threepenny Opera*. It's set in Mahagonny, an imaginary city of pleasures and criminals located in Alabama. Jenny Hill and Jim Mahoney have a love affair based on money, but he is eventually executed for not paying his whiskey bill. The tone is cynical and satirical but more than merely anticapitalistic. The "Alabama Song," sung in English by Jenny and the other whores, is one of Weill's best-known songs.

1965 BBC Television

English TV production: Philip Saville (director), Lawrence Leonard (conductor, English Chamber Orchestra), Roger Andrew (set designer), Sydney Newman (producer).

Cast: Anne Pashley (Jenny Hill), Emile Belcourt (Jim Mahoney), Monica Sinclair (Begbick), Inia Te Wiata (Trinity Moses), Trevor Anthony.

Telecast on BBC in March 1965. Philip Saville (director). Black and white. In English. 90 minutes.

1976 Hessischer Rundfunk, Frankfurt

German TV production: Rudolf Küfner (director), Christian Stalling (conductor, Hessischer Radio-Television Orchestra).

Cast: Julia Migenes (Jenny Hill), Karl Walter Böhm (Jim Mahoney), Charlotte Berthold (Begbick), Kurt Marschner (Fatty), Toni Blankenheim (Trinity Moses), Eberhard Katz (Jack), Karl Heinz Lippe (Bill), Norbert Berger (Joe), Peter Schmitz (Toby).

Video: House of Opera DVD/VHS. Bert Rhotert (director). Color. In German. 102 minutes.

1979 Metropolitan Opera

American stage production: John Dexter (director), James Levine (conductor, Metropolitan Opera Orchestra and Chorus), Jocelyn Herbert (set/costume designer), David Drew and Michael Geliot (English translation).

Cast: Teresa Stratas (Jenny), Richard Cassilly (Jim), Astrid Varnay (Begbick), Cornell MacNeil (Moses), Ragnar Ulfung (Fatty), Arturo Sergi (Jacob), Vern Shinall (Billy), Paul Plishka (Joe), Michael Best (Toby).

Video at the MTR. Telecast live November 27, 1979. Brian Large (director). Color. In English. 110 minutes.

***1998 Salzburg Festival

Austrian stage production: Peter Zadek (director), Dennis Russell Davies (conductor, Vienna Radio Symphony Orchestra and Vienna State Opera Chorus), Richard Peduzzi (set designer), Verena Weiss (choreographer).

Cast: Catherine Malfitano (Jenny), Jerry Hadley (Jim), Gwyneth Jones (Begbick), Roy Cornelius Smith (Fatty), Wilbur Pauley (Trinity Moses), Udo Holdort (Jake Smith), Dale Duesing (Pennybank Bill), Norbert Berger (Joe), Toby Spence (Toby).

Video: Kultur and Arthaus DVD/Premiere Opera VHS. Telecast August 29, 1998. Brian Large (director). Color. In German with English subtitles. 159 minutes.

Related films

1973 Harry Smith four-screen film

Avant-garde filmmaker Harry Smith created a bizarre version of the opera using four screens and the 1956 Lotte Lenya recording as soundtrack. The imagery is of New York and its underground celebrities in the 1970s (including Allen Ginsberg) plus homemade animation. First presented in New York with four 16-mm projectors more or less synchronized, the film was restored and shown in a Weill celebration at the Getty Center in Los Angeles in June 2002.

1979 Mahagonny songspiel

Peter Schweiger wrote and directed this Swiss Television adaptation of the *Mahagonny* songspiel that provided the basis for the opera. Clementine Patrick is Jessie, Brigitte Suschni is Bessie, Arley Reece is Charlie, Paul Späni is Billy, Allen Evans is Bobby, and Hans Franzen is Jimmy. The music is played by a 10-piece band led by Armin Brunner. Color. In German. 32 minutes. House of Opera/Opera Dubs VHS.

AVE MARIA

1936 film with opera content

Italian tenor Beniamino Gigli plays an opera singer mourning his lost love, Maria. He becomes involved with a Paris nightclub singer (Käthe Von Nagy) sent to trap him by her manager (Harald Paulsen). She ends up falling in love with him (he's such a nice guy) and then tries to kill herself out of shame. There is a clever use of a staging of *La traviata* (Erna Berger playing Violetta to Gigli's Alfredo) to comment on the action. Nagy identifies with the courtesan Violetta during the Act I duet "Un dì felice" but is devastated in Act II when Alfred throws his gambling winnings at her. Gigli is seen early in the film singing "Ave Maria" in church and sings it again at the end to express his forgiveness for Nagy. At the beginning of the film, he sings "Che gelida manina" from *La bohème* on stage and "Di quella pira" from *Il trovatore* in a Paris concert. The music is performed by the Berlin State Opera Orchestra and Cathedral Boys Choir led by Alois Melichar. Bruno Mondi was cinematographer, George C Klaren wrote the screenplay, and Johannes Riemann directed the film in Italian and German versions for Itala Film. It premiered at the Venice Film Festival where it won the prize for best musical. Black and white. In Italian with English subtitles. 89 minutes. Bel Canto Society/House of Opera/Live Opera/Lyric/Opera Dubs VHS.

B

BAA BAA BLACK SHEEP
1993 opera by Berkeley

British composer Michael Berkeley and librettist David Alouf based their opera on Rudyard Kipling's autobiographical story *Baa Baa Black Sheep*, which they superimposed on the *Jungle Book* tales. The boy Punch is in a bleak British seaside boarding house with his sister Judy and begins to create imaginary jungle characters based on the people he knows. He identifies himself with Mogli, the hero of the stories. The opera was premiered July 3, 1993, at the Cheltenham Festival by Opera North, recorded live and then telecast.

1993 Opera North
English stage production: Jonathan Moore (director), Paul Daniel (conductor, English Northern Philharmonic Orchestra and Opera North Chorus), David Blight (set/costume designer), Roger Monk (choreographer).

Cast: Malcolm Lorimer (Punch/Mogli the boy), William Dazely (Mogli the man), Ann Taylor-Morley (Judy/Grey Wolf), George Mosley (Father), Eileen Hulse (Mother), Fiona Kimm (Auntirosi/Baldeo), Henry Newman (Captain/Akela), Philip Sheffield (Harry/Sheer Khan), Mark Holland (Bhini/Baloo), Clive Bayley (Meeta/Bagheera).

Telecast by the BBC in 1993. Barrie Gavin (director). Color. In English. 100 minutes.

BABEL OPÉRA
1985 Belgian film with opera content

Babel Opéra, ou La Répétition de Don Juan is a Belgian film by master director André Delvaux built around preparations for a production of *Don Giovanni* at the Théâtre Royale de la Monnaie in Brussels. It is a "parallel opera"–style story with "real" characters in the film becoming involved in situations similar to those in the opera. François (François Beukelaers), who is planning this ambitious production of the opera, is married to Sandra (Alexandra Vandernoot) but is trying to seduce Stéphane (Stéphane Escoffier), who is loved by his assistant Ben (Ben van Ostade). The singers in the opera are José van Dam as Don Giovanni, Ashley Putnam as Donna Anna, Stuart Burrows as Don Ottavio, Christiane Eda-Pierre as Donna Elvira, and Pierre Thau as the Commendatore. Denise Debbaut, Jacques Sojcher, and Delvaux wrote the screenplay, and Michel Baudour was cinematographer. Color. In French. 94 minutes.

BABES IN TOYLAND
1903 operetta by Herbert

VICTOR HERBERT's operetta is as much fun for adults as for children with an inventive libretto by Glen MacDonough, memorable tunes by the composer, and a wonderful fairy tale setting. It tells the story of two children who escape from their wicked uncle to Mother Goose Land and become involved with nursery rhyme characters. The tuneful "March of the Toys" and "Toyland" remain popular, and there have been many screen adaptations of the operetta.

1934 MGM film
American feature film: Charles Rogers and Gus Meins (directors), Hal Roach (producer), Nick Grinde and Frank Butler (screenplay), Harry Jackson (music director), Art Lloyd and Francis Corby (cinematographers).

Cast: Stan Laurel (Stannie Dum), Oliver Hardy (Ollie Dee), Felix Knight (Tom-Tom), Charlotte Henry (Little Bo Peep), Johnny Downs (Little Boy Blue), Jean Darling (Curly Locks), Marie Wilson (Mary Quite Contrary), William Burress (Toy Maker), Ferdinand Munier (Santa Claus), Virginia Karns (Mother Goose).

Video: Goodtimes VHS (as *March of the Wooden Soldiers*). Black and white. In English. 78 minutes.

Comment: Most of the Herbert score is retained, and the film is quite fun. Most of the singing is by Knight, who later became a Metropolitan Opera tenor.

1950 NBC TV: Musical Comedy Time
American TV production: Alexander Kirkland (director/adaptation), Harry Sosnick (conductor, Harry Sosnick Orchestra), Robert Gundlach (set designer).

Cast: Dennis King (Dr. Electronic), Robert Weede (Santa Claus), Edith Fellows (Bo Peep), Dorothy Jarnac, Gil Lamb, Robert Dixon.

Telecast live December 25, 1950. William Corrigan (director). Black and white. In English. 60 minutes.

1954 NBC TV: Max Liebman Presents
American TV production: Max Liebman and Bill Hobin (directors); Charles Sanford (conductor); Neil Simon, Will Glickman, William Freidberg, Fred Saidy (adaptation).

Cast: Barbara Cook (Jane Piper), Wally Cox (Toymaker), Dennis King (Tom-Tom), Dave Garroway (Santa Claus), Jack E. Leonard (Silas Barnaby), Ellen

Barrie (Joan), Mary Mace (Widow Piper), Jack Powell (Clown), Jo Sullivan (Bo Peep).

Telecast December 18, 1954, and December 24, 1955. Bill Hobin (director). Color. In English. 90 minutes.

1960 NBC TV: Shirley Temple's Storybook

American TV studio production: Sheldon Keller (director/adaptation), William Scharf (conductor).

Cast: Shirley Temple (Floretta), Jonathan Winters (Uncle Barbary), Angela Cartwright (Jane), Michel Petit (Allen), Jerry Colonna, Joe Besser.

Telecast December 25, 1960. Color. In English. 60 minutes.

1961 Disney film

American feature film: Jack Donohue (director); Ward Kimball, Joe Rinaldi, and Lowell S. Hawley (screenwriters); George Bruns (conductor); Edward Colman (cinematographer).

Cast: Ray Bolger (Barnaby), Ed Wynn (Toymaker), Annette Funicello (Mary Contrary), Tommy Sands (Tom Piper), Tommy Kirk (Grumio), Kevin Corcoran (Boy Blue), Mary McCarty (Mother Goose), Ann Jillian (Bo Peep), Henry Calvin (Gonzorgo), Gene Sheldon (Roderigo).

Video: Walt Disney Home Video VHS. Color. In English. 126 minutes.

Comment: Critics disliked the film, but it got Academy Award nominations for music and costumes.

1986 Donner film

American TV film: Clive Donner (director), Paul Zindel (screenplay), Leslie Bricusse (conductor and additional music).

Cast: Drew Barrymore, Richard Mulligan, Eileen Brennan, Keanu Reeves, Jill Schoelen, Pat Morita.

Telecast December 19, 1986, on NBC. Color. In English. 150 minutes.

Comments: Critics didn't much like this film, as little of Herbert's score survived. "Toyland" and "March of the Wooden Soldiers" are heard, but most of the music is by Bricusse.

1997 MGM film

American animated feature film: Charles Grosvenor, Toby Bluth, and Paul Sabella (directors); John Loy (screenplay); Toby Bluth (production design); Mark Waters (score and new songs).

Voices: James Belushi, Christopher Plummer, Catherine Cavadini, Lacey Chabert, Bronson Pincot, Charles Nelson Reilly, Raphael Sbarge.

Video: MGM-UA Home Video VHS. Color. In English. 74 minutes.

Comment: Surprisingly effective version of the tale. Three Herbert numbers are retained, including an impressive "March of the Toys" sequence with giant toy soldiers. The colorful animation for the film seems to have been done in Asia.

BACCALONI, SALVATORE
Italian bass (1900–1969)

Salvatore Baccaloni, in addition to being a good-humored star at La Scala and the Met, acted in a number of films, usually as the comic father. He began his American opera career in 1930 in Chicago and was a regular at the Met until 1962. He kept his opera and movie careers separate and made no opera films. His film career began in 1956 opposite Judy Holliday and Richard Conte in Richard Quine's *Full of Life*, the story of a New York Italian couple expecting a baby. In 1958, he was in Frank Tashlin's *Rock-a-Bye Baby* with Jerry Lewis and Marilyn Maxwell, and then in Michael Kidd's *Merry Andrew* with Danny Kaye and Pier Angeli. In 1960, he appeared in Joshua Logan's *Fanny*, a Marcel Pagnol adaptation with Charles Boyer and Leslie Caron. In 1962, he was in Mel Shavelson's *The Pigeon That Took Rome*, playing the father of Elsa Martinelli.

BACCHAE, THE
1991 Swedish opera by Börtz

Swedish composer Daniel Börtz's opera *Backanterna* (The Bacchae), libretto by filmmaker INGMAR BERGMAN, is based on a rather nasty Euripides play meant to show the foolishness of fundamentalism as seen in the tragedy of the last great matriarchy. Bergman changed Euripides' chorus of Bacchantes into individual characters, so their murdering fury in the second act could appear more realistic, and Börtz's music is full of insistent rhythms and percussive climaxes. The opera, written at the instigation of Bergman, premiered at the Royal Opera Stockholm November 2, 1991, under Bergman's direction.

1992 Royal Opera, Stockholm

Swedish stage production: Ingmar Bergman (director), Kjell Ingerbretsen (conductor, Royal Opera House Orchestra and Chorus), Lennart Mörk (set and costume designer).

Cast: Sylvia Lindenstrand (Dionysus), Peter Mattei (Pentheus), Laila Andersson-Palme, (Tiresias), Sten Wahlund (Cadmus), Anita Soldh (Agave), Mariane Orland, Berit Lindholm.

Video at the MTR. Telecast on Swedish SVT Television. Ingmar Bergman (director). Color. In Swedish. 129 minutes.

Comment: Soundtrack was released as a CD.

Related film

Börtz, Bergman and the Bacchae

Swedish documentary about the production of *The Bacchae* that shows composer Börtz and director/librettist Bergman in rehearsal plus interviews with others in the production. Mans Reuterswürd directed the documentary. Color. In Swedish. 57 minutes. Video at the MTR.

BACH, JOHANN SEBASTIAN
German composer (1685–1750)

Johann Sebastian Bach did not compose operas, more the pity, though his cantatas are nearly the equivalent. However, some of his works have been produced on stage as operas, and others have been filmed with opera singers. There have been three telecasts of *Coffee Cantata,* four of *St. John's Passion,* and five of *St. Matthew Passion,* including the famous film described below.

1950 Matthau-Passion

Austrian feature film: Ernst Marischka (director and screenplay), Herbert von Karajan (conductor, Vienna Philharmonic and Viennese choirs), Václav Vich (cinematographer).

Singers: Elisabeth Schwarzkopf, Elisabeth Höngen, Walter Ludwig, Karl Schmitt-Walter, Hans Braun, Raoul Aslan.

Black and white. In German. 90 minutes.

Comment: The film was commissioned for the 200th anniversary of the composer's death and features paintings of the life of Christ by Michelangelo, Raphael, Leonardo da Vinci, Rubens, and other masters.

BACH, P.D.Q.
Mythical German composer (1807–1742)

American musical jester and broadcaster Peter Schickele invented this member of the Bach family and attributed parodistic pieces of baroque and classical music to him. P.D.Q. Bach supposedly composed eight operas, starting with *The Stoned Guest,* presented in Carnegie Hall in 1967. See PETER SCHICKELE for his operas.

BACQUIER, GABRIEL
French baritone (1924–)

Gabriel Bacquier, born in Béziers, began his career in 1950 and quickly became one of the most popular opera singers on the circuit. He has sung in most of the major opera houses, and his admirers feel that his voice and his acting have grown in power and quality with the years. Falstaff is one of his great roles. See LES CONTES D'HOFFMANN (1993), DON GIOVANNI (1978), DON

PASQUALE (1979/1991), FALSTAFF (1979), GIANNI SCHICCHI (1981), THE LOVE FOR THREE ORANGES (1989), LE NOZZE DI FIGARO (1980), and LA PÉRICHOLE (1982).

BAILEY, DEREK
English television director

Derek Bailey is one of the leading television opera directors, and his excellent work can been seen on a wide array of opera videos shot around the world from Glyndebourne, English National Opera, and Covent Garden to La Scala, La Fenice, and the Bolshoi. He has also made first-class documentaries about the opera AIDA (1987 film) and JOAN SUTHERLAND (1991). His operas include AIDA (1985), BORIS GODUNOV (1987), DON GIOVANNI (1995), EUGENE ONEGIN (1998), FIDELIO (1991), GLORIANA (1984), JENŮFA (1989), KATYA KABANOVA (1988), THE KNOT GARDEN (1986), A LIFE FOR THE TSAR (1992), MADAMA BUTTERFLY (1986), MITRIDATE, RE DI PONTO (1991), LE NOZZE DI FIGARO (1994), ORPHÉE AUX ENFERS (1983), PUNCH AND JUDY (1984), RUSALKA (1986), SALOME (1992), SEMELE (1999), LA TRAVIATA (1987/1992), and TRIAL BY JURY (1982).

BAJADERE, DIE
1921 operetta by Kálmán

EMMERICH KÁLMÁN's popular 1921 operetta *Die Bajadere,* libretto by Julius Brammer and Alfred Grünwald, features an operetta within an operetta. The heroine is the prima donna of an operetta called *La Bayadère,* who is being pursued by an Eastern prince. It was a major hit in Vienna and was staged in New York in 1922 as *The Yankee Princess* with Vivienne Segal as the star.

1992 Bajadera

Italian TV studio production: Sandro Massimini (director/producer), Roberto Negri (pianist), Sandro Corelli (choreographer).

Cast: Sandro Massimini (host), Daniela Mazzucato, Max René Cosotti.

Video: Ricordi (Italy) VHS. Pierluigi Pagano (director). Color. In Italian. About 17 minutes.

Comment: Highlights of the operetta known in Italy as *Bajadera* on Italian TV series *Operette, che Passione!* Songs include "Un piccolo bar," "Oh Bajadera," "Quando in cielo ridino le stelle," and "Ci si dié la man."

BAKER, JANET
English mezzo-soprano (1933–)

Dame Janet Baker, who began her career in 1956, was especially admired for her performances in operas by Handel and Gluck. She created the role of Kate in the

1971 TV version of Benjamin Britten's *Owen Wingrave* and sang the role at Covent Garden. She retired from opera in 1982 after performing in MARIA STUARDA at the English National Opera and ORFEO ED EURIDICE at Glyndebourne. Some of her best performances are preserved on video, and there is also an excellent biography on video. See also DIDO AND AENEAS (1966), GIULIO CESARE (1984), GLYNDEBOURNE (1992), OWEN WINGRAVE (1971), IL RITORNO D'ULISSE IN PATRIA (1973), and SYDNEY (1984).

1982 Full Circle: Her Last Year in Opera
Baker describes her final opera season and talks about her career in Bob Bentley's documentary film. Her stage career had begun 26 years earlier at Glyndebourne, so she makes her farewell from that stage. She is seen preparing for Gluck's *Alceste* at Covent Garden, rehearsing *Maria Stuarda* in English for television, and performing at Carnegie Hall and Haddon Hall in Scotland. The film ends with Baker's performance in *Orfeo ed Euridice* at Glyndebourne. John Copley, Charles Mackerras, Janine Reiss, Martin Isepp, Peter Hall, and Raymond Leppard also appear. Color. 75 minutes. Kultur VHS.

1987 Christmas at Ripon Cathedral
Baker is in fine voice in this video of a Christmas concert with Robert Hardy at Ripon Cathedral in Yorkshire. It includes a Baker's dozen of carols from "Mary Had a Baby" to "Come All Ye Faithful." Also performing are the Huddersfield Choral Society, the Black Dyke Mills Band, and organists Simon Lindley and Robert Marsh. Terry Henebery directed for Yorkshire Television. Color. 55 minutes. Home Vision VHS.

BALADA, LEONARDO
Spanish-born U.S. composer (1933–)

Leonardo Balada, a Catalan from Barcelona, came to the United States in 1956 as a student and remained as a teacher and composer. His first opera, the 1982 *Hangman, Hangman!* based on a cowboy ballad, is a satire about the American West with a thief as hero. His major opera, CRISTÓBAL COLÓN (1982), which tells the story of Columbus's voyage, premiered in his native Barcelona with José Carreras and Montserrat Caballé in the main roles.

BALALAIKA
1936 British operetta by Posford

GEORGE POSFORD's romantic operetta *Balalaika*, libretto by Eric Maschwitz, is the bittersweet story of a Russian aristocrat Cossack officer who falls in love with a revolutionary ballerina at the time of the Russian Revolution.

When the revolution succeeds, he has to flee to Paris and work as a waiter. Eventually the couple are reunited and love wins outs. The operetta premiered at the Adelphi Theatre in London and was later produced in the United States. Joan Sutherland includes two numbers from it on her album *The Golden Age of Operetta*, "At the Balalaika" and "Cossacks' Song."

1939 MGM film
American feature film: Reinhold Schunzel (director); Leon Gordon, Charles Bennett, and Jacques Deval (screenplay); Joseph Ruttenberg and Karl Freund (cinematographers); Herbert Stothart (music director); William Axt (conductor).

Cast: Nelson Eddy (Count Peter Karagin), Ilona Massey (Lydia), Charlie Ruggles (Nicki), Frank Morgan (Danchenoff), William Woolf King (Sibirsky), Joyce Compton (Masha), Lionel Atwill (Marakov), C. Aubrey Smith (General Karagin).

Video: MGM/UA Home Video. Black and white. In English. 91 minutes.

Comment: The plot is somewhat altered, and music is added to this film. It includes an imaginary Rimsky-Korsakov opera based on *Scheherazade,* supposedly staged at the Imperial Opera House, devised by Stothart with help from Bob Wright and Chet Forest, the team that transmuted Borodin's music into *Kismet.* There is also an excerpt from *Carmen.*

BALFE, MICHAEL
Irish composer (1808–1870)

Dublin-born Michael Balfe was one of the most popular light opera composers of the 19th century, but fashions have changed and his operas are no longer performed. His best-known opera, THE BOHEMIAN GIRL (1843), which contains the famous aria "I dreamt I dwelt in marble halls," has been filmed several times and is available on CD. Balfe was one of the three "Irish" opera composers (Vincent Wallace and Julius Benedict are the others) who dominated British opera in the 19th century before Gilbert and Sullivan.

BALL IM SAVOY
1932 operetta by Abraham

PAUL ABRAHAM's *Ball im Savoy* (Ball at the Savoy) was highly successful when it premiered in Germany with Hungarian opera diva Gitta Alpar playing its heroine, opera singer Anita Helling. It was translated into English by Oscar Hammerstein II for a London production, where it had 148 performances, but it never went to New York. The story revolves around jealous behavior during a honeymoon that threatens to break up a marriage. Alfred Grünwald and Bela Löhner-Beda wrote the libretto.

1935 Bál a Savoyban

Hungarian feature film: Stefan Szekeley (director), Hunnia Film (production company).

Cast: Gitta Alpar (Anita Helling), Hans Jaráy (Baron André von Wollheim), Rosi Barsony (Mary von Wollheim), Felix Bressart (Birowitsch).

Black and white. In Hungarian. 82 minutes.

Comment: This was the first musical film made in Hungary.

1955 Ball im Savoy

German feature film: Paul Martin (director), Cental and Europa Film (production company).

Cast: Nadja Tiller, Eva-Engeborg Scholz, Rudolf Prack.

Color. In German. 90 minutes.

1992 Ballo al Savoy

Italian TV studio production: Sandro Massimini (director/producer), Roberto Negri (pianist), Sandro Corelli (choreographer).

Cast: Sandro Massimini, Sara Dilena, Max René Cosotti.

Video: Ricordi (Italy) VHS. Pierluigi Pagano (director). Color. In Italian. About 19 minutes.

Comment: Highlights and history of the operetta, known in Italy as *Ballo al Savoy,* on TV series *Operette, che Passione!* Includes songs "O Mister Brown," "È tanto bello in giro la sera andar," and "Tangolita."

BALLAD OF BABY DOE, THE
1956 opera by Moore

DOUGLAS MOORE's frontier opera about the Colorado mining era and the romance of Baby Doe Tabor has a memorable libretto by John Latouche. It premiered at the Central City Opera House and arrived at the New York City Opera in 1958, with Beverly Sills as Baby Doe. The opera is based on events concerning the love triangle of silver mining magnate Horace Tabor, his wife Augusta, and his lady love Baby Doe McCourt. At one time it was ranked as the Great American Opera; during the 1976 bicentenary celebrations, it was given five professional productions.

1957 ABC Television: Omnibus

American TV production: Michael Myerberg (director), Sylvan Levin (conductor, Symphony of the Air), Donald Oenslager (set designer).

Cast: Virginia Copeland (Baby Doe), William Johnson (Horace Tabor), Martha Lipton (Augusta), Evelyn Lear (Augusta's friend), Margery Mayer (Mama McCourt).

Telecast February 10, 1957, on ABC Television. Charles S. Dubin (director). Black and white. In English. 57 minutes.

Comment: Lipton created the role of Augusta in the Central City premiere.

1962 American Music Theater

American TV production: Martin O'Carr (director), Alfredo Antonini (conductor, CBS Television Orchestra).

Cast: Beverly Sills (Baby Doe), Douglas Moore (composer).

Video at the MTR. Telecast March 4, 1962, on WCBS-TV. Martin O'Carr (director). Black and white. In English. 30 minutes.

Comment: Sills re-creates her New York City Opera triumph as Baby Doe. She sings highlights from the opera and talks with composer Moore.

1976 New York City Opera

American stage production: Harold Prince (director), Judith Somogi (conductor, New York City Opera Orchestra and Chorus), Donald Oenslager (set designer).

Cast: Ruth Welting (Baby Doe), Richard Fredricks (Horace Tabor), Frances Bible (Augusta).

Telecast April 21, 1976, in *Live From Lincoln Center* series. Kirk Browning (director). Color. In English. 120 minutes.

1992 Lancaster Opera

American stage production: Lancaster Opera Company at Fulton Theater in Lancaster, Pennsylvania.

Cast: Andrea Rose Folan (Baby Doe), John Darrenkamp (Horace Tabor).

Video: Opera Dubs VHS. Color. In English. 131 minutes.

Comment: Poor quality, nonprofessional VHS videotaped from a balcony. Darrenkamp is a Lancaster native.

**1995 Des Moines Metro Opera

American stage production: Robert Larsen (director/conductor, Des Moines Metro Opera Orchestra and Chorus).

Cast: Evelyn del la Rosa (Baby Doe), Richard L. Richards (Horace Tabor), Gwendolyn Jones (Augusta), Anne Larson (Mama McCourt), Paul Geiger (William Jennings Bryan).

Video: Premiere Opera/Opera Dubs VHS. Telecast by Iowa Public Television. Jerry Grady (director). Color. In English. 170 minutes.

Comment: Best available VHS. Good regional production, good orchestra, well sung.

BALLO IN MASCHERA, UN

1859 opera by Verdi

GIUSEPPE VERDI's *Un ballo in maschera* (A Masked Ball) was a controversial opera in its time because it showed the assassination of a king, Sweden's Gustavus III, slain in 1792 at a masked ball. The censors objected, so Verdi moved the venue to 17th-century Boston and changed the king into colony governor Riccardo. The story concerns his love for Amelia, the wife of his best friend; her love for him; their honorable behavior; and an assassination plot. Producers often change the setting back to Sweden or to another time or place, and this is reflected in the videos. Luciano Pavarotti stars in two of the operas available on video.

1967 NHK Lirica Italiana

Japanese film of stage production: Bruno Nofri (director), Oliviero de Fabritiis (conductor, NHK Symphony Orchestra and Nikikai and Fujiwara Opera Chorus).

Cast: Carlo Bergonzi (Riccardo), Antonietta Stella (Amelia), Mario Zanasi (Renato), Lucia Danieli (Ulrica), Margherita Guglielmi (Oscar).

Video: Lyric VHS. Filmed live at Metropolitan Hall, Tokyo. Color. In Italian. 140 minutes.

Comment: Modest staging, terrific cast, American setting of the opera.

1975 Royal Opera House

English stage production: Otto Schenk (director), Claudio Abbado (conductor, Royal Opera Orchestra and Chorus), Jürgen Rose (set/costume designer).

Cast: Plácido Domingo (Riccardo), Katia Ricciarelli (Amelia), Pierro Cappuccilli (Renato), Elizabeth Bainbridge (Ulrica), Reri Grist (Oscar).

Video: Kultur DVD/VHS. John Vernon (director). Color. In Italian with English subtitles. 148 minutes.

***1980 Metropolitan Opera

American stage production: Elijah Moshinsky (director), Giuseppe Patanè (conductor, Metropolitan Opera Orchestra and Chorus), Peter Wexler (set designer), Peter J. Hall (costume designer).

Cast: Luciano Pavarotti (Riccardo), Katia Ricciarelli (Amelia), Louis Quilico (Renato), Bianca Berini (Ulrica), Judith Blegen (Oscar).

Video: Pioneer DVD/LD and Bel Canto Paramount VHS. Telecast live February 16, 1980. Brian Large (director). Color. In Italian with English subtitles. 150 minutes.

Comment: Superb cast, modernistic sets, time of the opera moved to the eve of the American Revolution.

1987 Opera Company of Philadelphia

American stage production: Sonja Frisell (director), Emerson Buckley (conductor, Opera Company of Philadelphia Orchestra and Chorus), John Conklin (set designer).

Cast: Luciano Pavarotti (Gustavo III), Susan Marie Pierson (Amelia), Mark Rucker (Renato), Anita Berry (Ulrica), Nuccio Focile (Oscar).

Telecast December 20, 1987, on PBS. Kirk Browning (director). Color. In Italian with English subtitles. 150 minutes.

Comment: Nine young singers, who won the Opera Company of Philadelphia/Luciano Pavarotti International Voice Competition, perform with Pavarotti, who donated his services. Setting of the opera moved back to Sweden.

***1991 Metropolitan Opera

American stage production: Piero Faggioni (director/set and costume designer/lighting), James Levine (conductor, Metropolitan Orchestra and Chorus).

Cast: Luciano Pavarotti (Gustavo III), Aprile Millo (Amelia), Leo Nucci (Renato), Florence Quivar (Ulrica), Harolyn Blackwell (Oscar).

Video: DG DVD/VHS. Taped January 26, 1991; telecast May 22, 1991. Brian Large (director). Color. In Italian with English subtitles. 137 minutes.

Comment: Set in Sweden as originally envisioned by Verdi, this is the best of the available videos.

Early/related films

1911 Film d'Arte Italiana film

Writer/director Ugo Falena made the Italian color film *Un ballo in maschera* in 1911 for Film d'Arte Italiana in Rome. The story is the same as the opera. Alfredo Robert is King Gustavo, Bianca Lorenzoni is his beloved Amelia, and Ignazio Mascalchi is Amelia's husband Renato, his assassin. Color. Silent. About 10 minutes.

1937 Solo Per Te

A backstage murder in this film during a performance of *Un ballo in maschera* reflects what is happening in the opera. Beniamino Gigli plays an opera singer married to a soprano (Maria Cebotari) with a secret. See SOLO PER TE.

1938 Fram för Framgang

Jussi Björling plays a young tenor in the Swedish film comedy *Fram för Framgang* and sings the aria "Di tu se fedele" from *Un ballo in maschera*. Gunnar Skaggund directed. Black and white. In Swedish. 89 minutes. Bel Canto Society VHS.

1975 The Adventure of Sherlock Holmes's Smarter Brother
An 1891 production of *Un ballo in maschera* in London is the setting of the climax of this Sherlock Holmes comedy. Opera singer Gambetti (Dom DeLuise) is to pass secret documents to Moriarty (Leo McKern) during a performance of the opera, conducted by Tony Sympson. The wine at the ball is drugged, the chorus collapses, and Moriarty is bested by Sherlock's brother Sigi (Gene Wilder). Wilder directed. Color. 91 minutes.

1987 Aria
Nicolas Roeg creates an ironic variation on the story of *Un ballo in maschera* for his episode of the opera film ARIA. In 1931 Vienna, King Zog of Albania (Teresa Russell cast against gender) sneaks out of the opera house for an assignation with a baroness (Stephanie Lane). The opera being performed is *Un ballo in maschera*, and Zog has to fight off an assassination attempt outside the theater. The singers (from a 1966 recording) are Carlo Bergonzi, Leontyne Price, Robert Merrill, Shirley Verrett, and Reri Grist. Erich Leinsdorf conducts the RCA Italiana Opera Orchestra. Color. In Italian. About 10 minutes.

BALTSA, AGNES
Greek mezzo-soprano (1944–)

Agnes Baltsa, who was born in Lefkas, Greece, and studied singing in Athens and Munich, made her stage debut in Frankfurt in 1968 as Cherubino and her American debut in Houston as Carmen. Her performance as Carmen has been particularly admired for its dramatic quality and earthiness, but her repertoire is wide ranging. See CARMEN (1987), LES CONTES D'HOFFMANN (1981), COSÌ FAN TUTTE (2000), DON CARLO (1986), DER ROSENKAVALIER (1984), and VERDI REQUIEM (1982).

1991 José Carreras and Friends
Baltsa joins José Carreras and other singers for a friendly recital, accompanied by the London Arts Orchestra led by Jacques Delacôte. Color. 60 minutes. Kultur VHS.

BÁNK BÁN
1861 opera by Erkel

Ferenc Erkel's 1861 Hungarian opera *Bánk bán* is the story of a famous 13th-century rebellion against a hated queen led by the heroic Bánk bán. Based on a play by Jószef Katona, it is considered Hungary's most important opera of the 19th century. Bánk ("bán" signifies his noble rank) is viceroy of the country in 1213 while King Endre is off fighting a war. Queen Gertrude, however, is not Hungarian but Meranian, and she has appointed her countrymen to positions of power. They have exploited the country, and famine is widespread. While Bánk travels around the country learning about this, his wife Melinda is pursued at court by the queen's brother Otto. When Bánk discovers how bad the situation is, he leads an uprising in which the queen and her courtiers are killed. The stirring patriotic music has been compared to middle-period Verdi.

2002 Káel film
Hungarian feature film: Csaba Káel (director) Gábor Mészöly (screenplay), Vilmos Zsigmond (cinematographer), András Werner (producer).
Cast: Atilla Kiss B. (Bánk Bán), Andrea Rost (Melinda, his wife), Eva Marton (Queen Gertrude), Dénes Gulyás (Prince Otto of Meran, Gertrude's brother), Kolos Kováts (Endre II, King of Hungary).
Color. In Hungarian with English subtitles. 117 minutes.
Comment: Oscar-winning cinematographer Zsigmond *(Close Encounters of the Third Kind)* returned to Hungary to shoot this superb film of the opera with first-time director Káel. It is a big-budget film for Hungary, at more than $2.5 million, and every penny is on the screen.

Related film

1914 Curtiz film
A feature film of the play *Bánk bán* was made in 1914 by Hungarian director Mihály Kertéz, later famous in Hollywood as Michael Curtiz, director of *Casablanca*. Actors from Jenö Jankovic's theater in Kolozsvar play the main roles. Bánk bán is played by László Bakó, his wife Melinda by Erzsi Paulay, Queen Gertrude by Mari Jászai, and the peasant Tiborc by István Szentgyörgyi. The film was usually screened with the opera music performed live. Black and white. Silent. About 60 minutes.

BARBE-BLEUE
1866 opéra-bouffe by Offenbach

JACQUES OFFENBACH's *Barbe-bleue* is a satirical version of the Bluebeard legend, composed to a libretto by Henri Meilhac and Ludovic Halévy. Bluebeard's wives are not killed but are given sleeping potions and come back for vengeance at the end. The best-known modern production was the creation of Germany's Walter Felsenstein.

1973 Komische Oper Berlin
German film of stage production: Walter Felsenstein (director), Karl-Fritz Voigtmann (conductor, Komische Oper Berlin Orchestra and Chorus), Paul Lehmann (set designer).

Cast: Hans Nöcker (Bluebeard), Rudolf Asmus (Popolani), Anny Schlemm (Boulotte), Werner Enders (Bobeche).

Video: Classic VHS/Dreamlife (Japan) DVD. Georg Mielke (film director). Color. In German. 138 minutes.

Comment: Felsenstein's *Ritter Blaubart* was his most popular production for the Komische Oper and was repeated many times over the years.

Early film

1902 Electro Talking Bioscope
An aria from the operetta was presented with sound and picture in Holland in September 1902. Alber's Electro Talking Bioscope was brought from France and used equipment acquired from Clement Maurice at the 1900 Paris Exhibition. Black and white. In French. About 3 minutes.

BARBER, SAMUEL
American composer (1910–1981)

Samuel Barber is best known to the general public through the film *Platoon*, which used his "Adagio for Strings" so effectively. "Adagio" is said to be the most popular American classical composition of the 20th century and has been used in several films, including *Lorenzo's Oil* and *The Best Intentions*. Barber's fine operas, on the other hand, have had mixed receptions, although VANESSA now seems likely to become a repertory staple and ANTONY AND CLEOPATRA was popular in its revival. Both have been telecast and are on CD but not on commercial video.

1977 Happy Birthday, Samuel Barber
CBS Camera Three television program celebrating the composer's birthday, with Barber talking about his career to James Tocco. Esther Hinds performs an aria from *Antony and Cleopatra*. Roger Englander produced and directed the March 6, 1977, telecast. Color. 30 minutes. Video at the MTR.

BARBER OF SEVILLE, THE
See IL BARBIERE DI SIVIGLIA

BARBERILLO DE LAVAPIÉS, EL
1874 zarzuela by Barbieri

El barberillo de Lavapiés (The Little Barber of Lavapiés) is the most popular zarzuela by Spanish composer FRANCISCO BARBIERI, and its songs have become a part of Spanish culture. Its hero, Lamparilla, is a Figaro-type

barber in working-class Madrid in 1766 who has a sweetheart named Paloma. They are caught up in a conspiracy to replace a hated prime minister and end up hiding the aristocrat Estrella and her fiancé. Luis Mariano de Larra wrote the libretto.

1968 Teatro Lirico Español
Spanish TV film: Juan de Orduña (director), Federico Moreno Torroba (conductor, Orquesta Lírica Española), Jose Perera Cruz (leader, Coro Cantores de Madrid), Federico G. Larraya (cinematographer).

Cast: Luis Sagi-Vela (Lamparilla), Maria Carmen Ramirez (Paloma), Dolores Perez, Francisco Saura, Ramon Alonso, Luis Frutos.

Video: Metrovideo (Spain) VHS. Shot in 35mm for RTVE Spanish Television. Juan de Orduña (director). Color. In Spanish. 96 minutes.

Related film

1991 Zarzuela Royal Gala Concert
Paloma Perez Inigo sings the "Canción de Paloma" from *El barberillo de Lavapiés* in Plácido Domingo's zarzuela concert at the National Music Auditorium in Madrid. She is accompanied by the Madrid Symphonic Orchestra. Enriques Garcia Asensio directed. Color. 69 minutes. Kultur VHS.

BARBIERE DI SIVIGLIA, IL (Paisiello)
1782 opera by Paisiello

GIOVANNI PAISIELLO's opera *Il barbiere di Siviglia* (The Barber of Seville), which preceded Rossini's more famous version by 34 years, has fallen into undeserved neglect but continues to be staged and televised. The story is more or less the same as that of the Rossini opera, except librettist Giuseppe Petroselli follows the Beaumarchais source play more closely. Barber Figaro helps Count Almaviva, disguised as a student, win Rosina despite the opposition of her guardian Bartolo.

1991 Teatro Accademico, Mantua
Italian stage production: Flavio Trevisan (director), Gregorio Goffredo (conductor, Orchestra di Camera di Mantova), Mario de Carlo (set designer).

Cast: Luca Caselin (Figaro), Maria Grazia Bonelli (Rosina), Alessandro Safina (Almaviva), Gerardo Spinelli (Bartolo), Lorenzo Regazzo (Basilio).

Video: House of Opera/Lyric VHS. G. Franco Campigotto (director). Telecast in Italy by RAI. Color. In Italian. 119 minutes.

Related film

1975 Barry Lyndon

Stanley Kubrick's film of the Thackeray novel features the Cavatina from Paisiello's *Il barbiere di Siviglia* in keeping with the 18th-century setting of the story. Ryan O'Neal stars. Color. 183 minutes.

BARBIERE DI SIVIGLIA, IL (Rossini)

1816 opera by Rossini

GIOACHINO ROSSINI's opera *Il barbiere di Siviglia* (The Barber of Seville) has been an audience favorite for nearly 200 years. Cesare Sterbini based his libretto on the famous Beaumarchais play, whose story is continued in *Le nozze di Figaro.* Set in Seville, it tells how the matchmaking barber Figaro helps Count Almaviva marry the beautiful Rosina despite opposition from her guardian Bartolo. *Barber* is one of the most filmed operas, beginning with a French version in 1903. One of the famous recordings features Maria Callas and Tito Gobbi, but there is no film of them together in the opera. Gobbi was filmed with other Rosinas, and Callas was filmed singing "Una voce poco fa" in concert. Videos of the opera with Cecilia Bartoli, Teresa Berganza, and Maria Ewing are critical favorites.

1933 Le barbier de Séville

French feature film: Hubert Bourlon and Jean Kemm (directors), Pierre Maudru (screenplay), Marcel Lucine (cinematographer), L. Masson (conductor), Robert Gys (set designer).

Cast: André Baugé (Figaro), Hélène Robert (Rosine), Jean Galland (Almaviva), Pierre Juvenet (Bartholo), Fernand Charpin (Basile), Josette Day (Suzanne), Monique Rolland (Chérubin), Yvonne Yma (Marceline).

Video: Video Yesteryear VHS. Black and white. In French. 93 minutes.

Comment: This film combines Rossini's opera with Mozart's *Le nozze di Figaro* and tells the story of both using music from both. There are also plot changes; for example, Rosina and Almaviva get married during the music lesson.

1946 Rome Opera

Italian film of stage production: Mario Costa (stage and film director), Giuseppe Morelli (conductor, Rome Opera House Orchestra and Chorus), Massimo Terzano (cinematographer).

Cast: Tito Gobbi (Figaro), Nelly Corradi (Rosina), Ferruccio Tagliavini (Almaviva), Vito de Taranto (Bartolo), Italo Tajo (Basilio).

Video: Bel Canto Society/Lyric/Pickwick (GB) VHS. Black and white. In Italian with English narration by Deems Taylor. 93 minutes.

Comment: Essentially a record of a Rome Opera production. Tagliavini was popular in the United States at the time of the film's release, so his name was put on American cinema marquees.

1947 Paris Opéra-Comique

French film of stage production: Jean Loubignac (stage director), André Cluytens (conductor, Opéra-Comique Orchestra and Chorus), Claude Dolbert (film director), René Colas (cinematographer).

Cast: Roger Bussonet (Figaro), Raymond Amadé (Almaviva), Lucienne Jourfier (Rosine), Roger Bourdin (Basile), Louis Musy (Bartholo), Renée Gilly (Marceline).

Video: René Chateau (France) VHS. Black and white. In French. 90 minutes.

Comment: Sung in French with spoken dialogue. Well made and well acted, an excellent record of a French production of the period.

1948 First Opera Film Festival

Italian film of stage production: Enrico Fulchigoni (stage director), Angelo Questa (conductor, Rome Opera House Orchestra and Chorus), Edmondo Cancellieri (film director), George Richfield (producer).

Cast: Tito Gobbi (Figaro), Pina Malgharini (Rosina, sung by Angelica Tuccari), Mino Russo (Almaviva, sung by Cesare Valletti), Gino Conti (Bartolo, sung by Giulio Tomei).

Video: Bel Canto Society/Lyric VHS. Black and white. In Italian with English voice-over by Olin Downes. About 24 minutes.

Comment: Highlights version of the opera sung in Italian, filmed on stage at Rome Opera House with singers from La Scala and Rome; part of an anthology film.

1952 NBC Opera Theatre

American TV production: Charles Polacheck (director), Peter Herman Adler (conductor, Symphony of the Air Orchestra), Samuel Chotzinoff (producer), Carl Kent (set designer), Townsend Brewster (English translation).

Cast: Ralph Herbert (Figaro), Virginia Haskins (Rosina), Davis Cunningham (Almaviva), Emile Renan (Bartolo), Carlton Gauld (Basilio).

Telecast live March 6, 1952. Kirk Browning (director). Black and white. In English. 60 minutes. Video at MTR.

1955 Figaro il barbiere di Siviglia

Italian feature film: Camillo Mastrocinque (director), Jacques Rachmilovic (orchestra conductor for opera sequences), Leo Benvenuti and Piero De Bernardi (screenplay), Alvaro Mancori (cinematographer).

Cast: Tito Gobbi (Figaro), Irene Gemma (Rosina, sung by Giulietta Simionato), Armando Francioli (Almaviva, sung by Nicola Monti), Cesco Baseggio (Bartolo, sung by Vito De Taranto), Giulio Neri (Basilio).

Video: Bel Canto Society/Lyric VHS. Color. In Italian. 93 minutes.

Comment: Many of the opera's musical numbers are cut, and the film has spoken dialogue replacing the recitatives.

1959 Bavarian State Opera

German stage production: Herbert List (director), Joseph Keilberth (conductor, Bavarian State Opera Orchestra), Max Bignens (set/costume designer).

Cast: Hermann Prey (Figaro), Erika Köth (Rosina), Fritz Wunderlich (Almaviva), Hans Hotter (Bartolo), Max Proebstl (Basilio).

Video: Bel Canto Society/Lyric VHS. Herbert List (director). Telecast December 25, 1959. Black and white. In German. 140 minutes.

Comment: Primarily of interest as a record of famous singers of the era.

***1972 Ponnelle film

German-French feature film: Jean-Pierre Ponnelle (director/set designer), Claudio Abbado (conductor, Teatro alla Scala Orchestra and Chorus), Ernst Wild (cinematographer).

Cast: Hermann Prey (Figaro), Teresa Berganza (Rosina), Luigi Alva (Almaviva), Enzo Dara (Bartolo), Paolo Montarsolo (Basilio).

Video: DG DVD/VHS/LD. Color. In Italian with English subtitles. 142 minutes.

Comment: One of the best films of the opera, with terrific performances all around. Ponnelle is highly inventive with a mobile camera that helps bring out the best of Rossini. This is a companion to his film of *Le nozze di Figaro,* which was shot on the same sound stage.

1972 Who's Afraid of Opera? series

English TV film: Ted Kotcheff (director), Richard Bonynge (conductor, London Symphony Orchestra), George Djurkovic (set designer), Claire Merrill (screenplay), Nathan Kroll (producer).

Cast: Tom McDonnell (Figaro), Joan Sutherland (Rosina), Ramon Remedios (Almaviva), Spiro Malas (Bartolo), Clifford Grant (Basilio), Larry Berthelson puppets.

Video: Kultur VHS. Color. In English and Italian. 30 minutes.

Comment: Highlights version of an opera made for young audiences, with Sutherland telling the story to puppets. Dialogue in English, arias in Italian.

1975 Knebworth House

English TV film: Peter Seabourne (director), John J. Davies (conductor, Classical Orchestra), Peter Murray (English translation).

Cast: Michael Wakeham (Figaro), Margaret Eels (Rosina), Edmund Bohan (Almaviva), Malcolm Rivers (Bartolo), Philip Summerscales (Basilio).

Telecast on BBC. Color. In English. 54 minutes.

Comment: Seabourne filmed this highlights version in Knebworth House in Hertfordshire.

1976 New York City Opera

American stage production: Sarah Caldwell (director/conductor, New York City Opera Orchestra and Chorus), Helen Pond (set designer), Herbert Senn (costume design), John Goberman (producer).

Cast: Alan Titus (Figaro), Beverly Sills (Rosina), Henry Price (Almaviva), Donald Gramm (Bartolo), Samuel Ramey (Basilio).

Video: Paramount VHS/Pioneer LD. Telecast live November 3, 1976. Kirk Browning (director). Color. In Italian with English subtitles. 156 minutes.

Comment: Sills is a sparkling Rosina in this quirky production with the cast costumed like their roles; Figaro is striped like a barber pole, Rosina wears feathers like a bird in a cage, Lindoro/Almaviva wears student books, and Bartolo carries a key cane. The effect is odd and sometimes silly but certainly original and quite fun. This was the first live TV opera telecast with subtitles.

***1982 Glyndebourne Festival

English stage production: John Cox (director), Sylvain Cambreling (conductor, London Philharmonic Orchestra and Glyndebourne Festival Chorus), William Dudley (set/costume designer).

Cast: John Rawnsley (Figaro), Maria Ewing (Rosina), Max-René Cosotti (Almaviva), Claudio Desderi (Bartolo), Ferruccio Furlanetto (Basilio).

Video: Home Vision VHS/Pioneer Artists LD. Dave Heather (director). Color. In Italian with English subtitles. 156 minutes.

Comment: Ewing is alluring, Rawnsley zesty, and Cosotti dashing in this inventive production. The bright sets enliven the comedy, and the singing is a treat.

1984 Maestro's Company Puppets

Australian puppet film: William Fitzwater (director), Silvio Varviso (conductor, Naples Rossini Orchestra), Jim George (producer), Marcia Hatfield (series creator).

Voices of puppets: Manuel Auseni (Figaro), Teresa Berganza (Rosina), Ugo Benelli (Almaviva), Fernando Corena (Bartolo), Nicolai Ghiaurov (Basilio).

Video: VAI VHS. Color. Dialogue in English, arias in Italian. 30 minutes.

Comment: Highlights version for children with Maestro's Company puppets rehearsing the opera under an abandoned theater.

1988 Schwetzingen Festival

German stage production: Michael Hampe (director), Gabriele Ferro (conductor, Stuttgart Radio Symphony Orchestra and Cologne City Opera Chorus), Mauro Pagano (set/costume designer).

Cast: Gino Quilico (Figaro), Cecilia Bartoli (Rosina), David Kuebler (Almaviva), Robert Lloyd (Basilio), Carlos Feller (Bartolo).

Video: Arthaus DVD and RCA VHS/LD. Claus Viller (director). Color. In Italian with English subtitles. 157 minutes.

Comment: Bartoli established her reputation in this entertaining production and justly so. She is quite magnificent, radiant in personality and a delight to see and hear.

1988 Metropolitan Opera

American stage production: John Cox (director), Ralf Weikert (conductor, Metropolitan Opera Orchestra and Chorus), Robin Wagner (set designer).

Cast: Leo Nucci (Figaro), Kathleen Battle (Rosina), Rockwell Blake (Almaviva), Enzo Dara (Bartolo), Ferruccio Furlanetto (Basilio).

Video: DG VHS. Taped December 3, 1988; telecast February 17, 1989. Brian Large (director). Color. In Italian with English subtitles. 161 minutes.

Comment: Battle steals the show with a sparkling performance in this big but rather unexciting production.

1992 Netherlands Opera

Dutch stage production: Dario Fo (director), Alberto Zedda (conductor, Netherlands Chamber Orchestra and Netherlands Opera Chorus).

Cast: David Malis (Figaro), Jennifer Larmore (Rosina), Richard Croft (Almaviva), Renato Carecchi (Bartolo), Simone Alaimo (Berta).

Video: Image Entertainment DVD. Hans Hulscher (director). Color. In Italian with English subtitles. 153 minutes.

Comment: Italian Nobel Prize–winning writer-director Dario Fo turned to opera for the first time in 1987 with this production, staging it as a kind of carnival with entertainers in *commedia dell'arte* style; it was so popular it was revived and videotaped.

2001 Zurich Opera

Swiss stage production: Grischa Asagaroff (director), Nello Santi (conductor, Zurich Opera House Orchestra and Chorus), Luigi Perego (set designer).

Cast: Manuel Lanza (Figaro), Vesselina Kasarova (Rosina), Reinaldo Macias (Almaviva), Carlos Chausson (Bartolo), Nicolai Ghiaurov (Basilio).

Video: TDK EuroArts DVD. Taped in April 2001. Felix Breisach (director). Color. In Italian with English subtitles. 161 minutes.

Comment: Updated to the 1930s in art deco style, with revolving sets in the shape of Spanish fans. Almaviva arrives on a motorbike and Figaro on a bicycle.

Early/related films

1903 Le barbier de Séville

The first film of the opera was *Le barbier de Séville*, created in 1903 by French pioneer Georges Méliès. It was a long film for its time, 402 meters and seven scenes, and was publicized as a genuine "reproduction" of the opera with sound. Rossini's music was played on discs with the film in screenings. In Rome, the system was called the Cinematofonio and in Florence the Cinetofonio. Distributed in United States in 1904 by Kleine. Black and white. In Italian. About 15 minutes.

1908 La calunnia

La calunnia is an Italian sound film of Basilio's famous aria "La calunnia è un venticello." It was produced by a film studio in Pisa specializing in sound films, but the singer is unknown. Black and white. In Italian. About 4 minutes.

1908 Barbarenen i Sevilla

Barbarenen i Sevilla is a Swedish sound film of the aria "Una voce poco fa," sung by Swedish soprano Sigrid Arnoldsen. N. H. Nylander directed the film, which was made with the Biophon sound system and produced by Svenska Biografteatern. There is also a Danish version made for Kosmorama. Black and white. In Swedish. About 4 minutes.

1910 Le barbier de Séville

Georges Berre is Figaro, Jean Périer is Almaviva, and Jeane Bertiny is Rosine in the French film *Le barbier de Séville*, which features scenes from the opera. Made for Pathé. Black and white. Silent. About 10 minutes.

1910 Il barbiere di Siviglia arias
Three arias from *Il barbiere di Siviglia* were filmed with sound by Itala Film of Turin in 1910. Local singers were filmed and recorded, and the recordings were synchronized with the projected films. They were all titled *Il barbiere di Siviglia,* followed by the name of the aria, "La calunnia...," "Largo al factotum," and "Manco un foglio..." (part of Bartolo's "A un dottore della mia sorte"). Black and white. In Italian. Each about 4 minutes.

1913 Il barbiere di Siviglia
Eleuterio Rodolfi is Figaro, Ubaldi Stefani is Almaviva, and Gigetta Morano is Rosina in the Italian film *Il barbiere di Siviglia,* directed by Luigi Maggi for the Ambrosio studio of Turin. Ernesto Vaser plays Bartolo, and Umberto Scalpellini is Basilio. The film, based on both opera and play, was released in America in 1914. The same team earlier made a version of *Le nozze di Figaro.* Black and white. Silent. About 30 minutes.

1915 The Barber of Seville
The sound film *The Barber of Seville* was copyrighted in the United States in 1915 by German sound film pioneer Oskar Messter. Black and white. In Italian. About 4 minutes.

1923 Il barbiere di Siviglia
The Italian brothers Azeglio and Lamberto Pineschi invented a camera that recorded sound on film and used it to make a highlights version of *Il barbiere di Siviglia.* Gabriella Di Veroli sings the role of Rosina and Giovanni Manurita sings Almaviva. The contemporary critics were impressed. Black and white. In Italian. About 20 minutes.

1927 Vitaphone film with De Luca
This Vitaphone sound film is titled *Giuseppe De Luca of the Metropolitan Opera Company as Figaro singing "Largo al Factotum" from The Barber of Seville.* He is accompanied by the Vitaphone Symphony Orchestra. Black and white. In Italian. About 7 minutes.

1928 RCA film with Granforte
Italian baritone Apollo Granforte bounces on stage in Figaro costume with guitar and sings the aria "Largo al factotum" in an energetic style with full orchestra in this early Australian sound film. It was made by RCA with its Photophone system while he was on tour in Australia with Melba. Black and white. In Italian. About 6 minutes. Lyric VHS.

1928 Movietone film with Bonelli
American baritone Richard Bonelli performs "Largo al factotum" from *The Barber of Seville* for the Fox studio for a film series titled *Movietone Numbers.* Black and white. About 8 minutes.

1929 Figaro
Gaston Ravel's French film *Figaro* is based on the entire Beaumarchais trilogy. It follows the story from *The Barber of Seville* through *The Marriage of Figaro* to *The Guilty Mother.* Edmund Van Duren is Figaro, Tony D'Algy is the Count, Arlette Marchal is Rosine, Marie Bell is Suzanne, and Jean Weber is Cherubin. Black and white. In French. 76 minutes.

1930 MGM film with Ruffo
Italian baritone Titta Ruffo made three opera films for MGM in 1929 and 1930, singing in costume. On the second he performs Figaro's "Largo al factotum." The soundtrack of the aria has also been issued on record. Black and white. About 8 minutes.

1931 Figaro e la sua gran giornata
Figaro's Great Day is an excellent Italian film about a touring opera company staging the Rossini opera in a provincial city. Directed by the very able Mario Camerini, it was a major hit in its time. Gianfranco Giachetti stars as an opera teacher who agrees to sing the role of Figaro with the company when the baritone quits. Rossini's music is played by an orchestra conducted by Felice Lattuada. Black and white. In Italian. 80 minutes.

1934 Apples to You
Billy Gilbert stars in *Apples to You*, a Hal Roach comedy based on *The Barber of Seville.* He plays a burlesque theater impresario hired to revive the fortunes of a bankrupt opera company. He does this with an amazing version of *Barber*, lacing the opera with burlesque routines and "20 Beautiful Barberettes." The opera audiences in the film love it; Peter Sellars, take note. Black and white. In English. 20 minutes.

1935 El Cantante de Napoles
Enrico Caruso Jr. sings an aria from *The Barber of Seville* in this American Spanish-language film, loosely based on the life of his father. Howard Bretherton directed. Black and white. 77 minutes.

1937 Broadway Melody of 1938
An opera-loving racehorse wins its big race when baritone Igor Gorin (who plays a barber) sings Figaro's "Largo al factotum" over the racetrack loudspeakers. This is a central plot point of this delightful musical. See BROADWAY MELODY OF 1938.

1937 Our Gang Follies of 1938
Alfalfa decides to give up crooning like Bing Crosby and turn to opera. He dreams of his operatic future, making his debut as Figaro in *The Barber of Seville*. He sings "I am the barber of Seville" on the stage of the Cosmopolitan Opera while sharpening a razor, is roundly booed, and ends up singing in the street. When he wakes up, he happily goes back to crooning in this enjoyable *Our Gang* musical. Marvin Hatley was musical director, but Alfalfa's aria is a very long way from Bizet. Gordon Douglas directed. Black and white. 20 minutes. Platinum Disc DVD and on VHS.

1938 El barbero de Sevilla
This Spanish film, made in Germany by Benito Perojo during the Spanish Civil War, is a zarzuela version of the story. Estrillita Castro, Roberto Rey, Raquel Rodrigo, and Miguel Ligero star. Black and white. In Spanish. 88 minutes.

1940 Bitter Sweet
The Jeanette MacDonald/Nelson Eddy screen version of Noël Coward's operetta features MacDonald singing Rosina's cavatina "Una voce poco fa." See BITTER SWEET.

1941 Citizen Kane
Dorothy Comingore makes a miserable attempt at singing "Una voce poco fa," and vocal coach Fortunio Bonanova tells her husband Charles Kane (Orson Welles) that she has no future as an opera singer. Kane pays no attention. See CITIZEN KANE.

1941 Notes to You
An alley cat sets up a sheet music stand on a backyard fence and begins to sing Figaro's "Largo al factotum" to the intense annoyance of Porky Pig, who is trying to sleep. Friz Freleng directed this Warner Bros. cartoon. Color. About 7 minutes.

1944 The Barber of Seville
The Woody Woodpecker cartoon *The Barber of Seville* is one of the great screwball comedies. Woody substitutes for barber Figaro and sings the aria "Largo al factotum" while he gives shaves and haircuts. Walter Lantz produced, James Culhane directed, and Darrell Calker conducted the music. Color. 7 minutes.

1946 The Whale Who Wanted to Sing at the Met
Willie, the opera-singing whale with the voice of Nelson Eddy, imagines he is about to be discovered and auditions all over the ocean with Figaro's "Largo al factotum." See THE WHALE WHO WANTED TO SING AT THE MET.

1948 NBC Television
NBC telecast excerpts from *Il barbiere di Siviglia* on December 25, 1948, in preparation for the formation of NBC Television Opera. Samuel Chotzinoff was producer, Kirk Browning was director, and Peter Herman Adler was conductor. Singers not known.

1948 For the Love of Mary
Deanna Durbin sings a comic rendition of "Largo al factotum" in this film in which she plays a telephone operator. Frederick De Cordova directed for Universal. Black and white. 90 minutes.

1948 Back Alley Oproar
Sylvester the Cat tries out his vocal style with Figaro's "Largo al factotum" as Elmer Fudd tries to sleep in this remake of the Warner Bros. cartoon *Notes to You*. Friz Freleng directed. Color. 7 minutes.

1949 House of Strangers
Lawrence Tibbett is heard on the soundtrack of this film singing "Largo al factotum"; he let the studio use his recording if they gave him a screen credit. The film revolves around Italian-American banker Edward G. Robinson, who loves opera, and his dysfunctional family. Joseph Mankiewicz directed for Fox. Black and white. 101 minutes.

1950 Figaro qua, Figaro la
Italian comic Toto stars in this Italian film based around the opera. It uses Rossini's music and the plot and characters of the opera, but it is mostly farce. Toto plays Figaro, Isa Barzizza is Rosina, Gianni Agus is Almaviva, and Guglielmo Barnabò is Bartolo. Carlo Ludovico Bragaglia directed. Black and white. In Italian. 85 minutes.

1950 The Rabbit of Seville
Bugs Bunny has a grand time to music from *The Barber of Seville* in this brilliant cartoon. Elmer Fudd chases Bugs onto the stage of the Hollywood Bowl. When the curtain goes up, the rabbit is the barber and Elmer is his customer. See THE RABBIT OF SEVILLE.

1952 The Magical Maestro
Tex Avery's classic cartoon revolves around the music of *The Barber of Seville*. A magician transforms a baritone in various strange ways as he tries to sing. Warner Bros. 7 minutes.

1953 Melba
Patrice Munsel portrays opera diva Nellie Melba in this British film biography and sings "Una voce poco fa" from *The Barber of Seville*. See NELLIE MELBA.

1955 Girolamo marionettes

Condensed version of the opera performed by marionettes of the Teatro Girolamo in Milan. The singing voices belong to Graziella Sciutti (Rosina), Antonio Pirino (Almaviva), Walter Monachesi, and Bruno Scalchiero, accompanied by the Rome Opera Orchestra. Filmeco. Color. Sung in Italian with English narration. 26 minutes.

1961 Une Aussi Longue Absence

Director Henri Colpi uses the romantic tenor aria "Ecco ridente in cielo" in a magical moment as the lovers reunite in this Cannes Grand Prize winner. The film is the story of a woman who finds her lost husband. Color. In French. 90 minutes.

1963 8½

The *Barber* overture is used in a key moment in Federico Fellini's portrayal of a movie director in a creative crisis. Marcello Mastroianni escapes into fantasies and memories in a hotel washroom as the overture swells up on the soundtrack. Black and white. In Italian. 138 minutes.

1964 Bell Telephone Hour

Judith Raskin and William Walker of the Met are featured in a duet from *The Barber of Seville* on the *Bell Telephone Hour* TV program telecast January 14, 1964. Sid Smith directed. Color. 60 minutes. Video at MTR.

1972 Lollipop Opera

Author-artist Don Freeman uses the music from *The Barber of Seville* to tell an animated tale about a boy's visit to a barber. He draws the shop and customer and then mixes animation with live action. Color. 9 minutes.

1979 Breaking Away

The overture to *The Barber of Seville* is heard on the soundtrack during the big bicycle race in this film about an Indiana boy who wants to be like his Italian cycling heroes. Peter Yates directed; Steve Tesich won an Oscar for his screenplay. Color. 100 minutes.

1980 Hopscotch

Tito Gobbi's recording of "Largo al factotum" is used ironically in this amiable spy comedy, as Walter Matthau works out his escape from murderous CIA pursuers. Matthau even sings it to a Austrian border guard, who thinks it's by Mozart. Ronald Neame directed from Brian Garfield's novel. Color. 104 minutes.

1985 Prizzi's Honor

The *Barber* overture is featured in this John Huston film about the Prizzi crime family and a love affair between killers-for-hire Jack Nicholson and Kathleen Turner. Color. 130 minutes.

1987 Dark Eyes

Nikita Mikhalkov's film about turn-of-the-century Italian roué Marcello Mastroianni has an elegant use of "Una voce poco fa." At an aristocratic health resort, Evelina Megnagi (voice of Magali Damonte) sings the aria at the start of his long affair with a married Russian woman. He spends most of the movie remembering her. Color. 118 minutes.

1993 Mrs. Doubtfire

Robin Williams sings a parody of Figaro's "Largo al factotum" as he records the voices of cat and canary animated cartoon characters during the opening scenes of this movie. Chris Columbus directed. Color. 125 minutes.

1995 Operavox film

Moscow animation studio Christmas Films created a model animation version of *The Barber of Seville* for the British Operavox series. The Welsh National Opera Orchestra plays a specially recorded score. Gareth Jones was music editor. Color. 27 minutes.

1999 The Lost Lover

The last act ensemble "Di si felice innesto" is performed by the Hungarian Radio Chorus and Falloni Chamber Orchestra in this British-Italian film. The story concerns Jews and Palestinians in modern Israel and love across religious barriers. Robert Faenza directed. Color. 79 minutes.

2000 Our Lady of the Assassins

The protagonist of the Colombian film *La virgen de los sicarios*, which takes place amidst the violence of Medallín, buys a stereo and listens to Maria Callas sing "Una voce poco fa." Barbet Schroeder directed. Color. In Spanish. 98 minutes. Paramount VHS.

BARBIERI, FRANCISCO
Spanish composer (1823–1894)

Francisco Asenjo Barbieri, one of the most popular Spanish composers of zarzuelas, is best known for EL BARBERILLO DE LAVAPIÉS and *Pan y Toros*. He wrote his first zarzuela in 1850 and completed more than 70, all premiered in Madrid. He also made major contributions to Spanish music as a writer, historian, and teacher.

BARBIER VON BAGDAD, DER
1858 opera by Cornelius

PETER CORNELIUS's comic opera *Der Barbier von Bagdad* (The Barber of Baghdad) is based on tales from *The Arabian Nights*. Cornelius himself wrote the libretto, which tells the story of Nureddin's love for Margiana and the unhelpful assistance he gets from an eager barber with the grand name of Abdul Hassan Ali Ebn Bekar. Nureddin gets the girl, but the barber gets the best music, including a fine buffo patter song. The opera, comparable to the work of Nicolai and Lortzing, is rarely performed outside German-speaking countries.

1974 Bavarian Television
German TV production: Herbert Junkers (director), Heinrich Hollreiser (conductor, Bavarian Radio-Television Orchestra and Chorus), Gerd Krauss (set designer).
Cast: Adalbert Kraus (Nureddin), Sylvia Geszty (Margiana), Karl Ridderbusch (Barber), Gerhard Under (Kadi), Trudeliese Schmidt (Bostana).
Telecast October 13, 1974, in Germany. Herbert Junkers (director). Color. In German. 90 minutes.
Comment: Available with this cast and conductor on CD but not on video.

BARCLAY, JOHN
British baritone (1892–1978)

John Barclay was born in England but moved to the United States in 1921 to establish a recital and recording career. He sang on two of the early Vitaphone sound films. His best-known movie is the 1939 British color film of THE MIKADO, for which he returned to England to sing the title role.

1927 Barclay Sings Pagliacci
The full title of this Vitaphone sound film is *John Barclay Offering Impersonations of Famous Characters Singing the Prologue from Pagliacci*. It features the Prologue plus Mephisto's Serenade from *Faust*, an aria from *Boris Godunov,* and the "Toreador Song" from *Carmen*. Black and white. About 10 minutes.

1927 Barclay Sings Faust
The full title of this Vitaphone sound film is *John Barclay Offering His Famous Character Interpretations of Mephisto's Calf of Gold*. He performs "The Calf of Gold" from Gounod's *Faust* plus songs by Damrosch and Logan. Black and white. About 10 minutes.

BARITONES AND BASSES

Baritones, bass-baritones, and basses seem to be gaining ground on tenors in popularity, as the acclaim given Bryn Terfel has demonstrated. In an earlier era, basso Feodor Chaliapin was a major celebrity. While the deep-voice singers often play villains, they also have many of the great buffo roles and comedy arias. In Mozart operas, the baritones are far ahead of the mere tenors, from Figaro to Don Giovanni.

1995 Six Great Basses
Compilation of performances by six noted basses (Boris Christoff, Giulio Neri, Tancredi Pasero, Ezio Pinza, Cesare Siepi, and Norman Treigle) and a notable baritone (Tito Gobbi). Christoff is shown in the death scene of *Boris Godunov* in 1978; Pasero sings "La calunnia" from *The Barber of Seville* in 1943; Neri sings with Gobbi in scenes from *Rigoletto* in 1947 and *La forza del destino* in 1949; Pinza sings the *Don Giovanni* duet "Là ci darem la mano" with Blanche Thebom in the 1947 film *Rehearsal;* and Treigle is shown in the revival scene in *Susannah* in 1958 with wife Loraine. Black and white and color. 68 minutes. Bel Canto Society VHS.

BARRY, GERALD
Irish composer (1952–)

Gerald Barry created the 1995 television opera THE TRIUMPH OF BEAUTY AND DECEIT for Channel 4 in England, basing it on Handel's oratorio *The Triumph of Time and Truth* and using the same characters. Born in Clarecastle and educated in Holland, Germany, and Austria, he began composing vocal works in 1977. After the short 1981 theater pieces *Cinderella* and *Snow White*, he composed the three-act opera *The Intelligence Park* on commission from the Institute of Contemporary Arts in London, which premiered in 1990. Set in Dublin in 1753, it is an opera about writing an opera and centers on a composer in love with a castrato; the music is based on Bach chorales.

BARSTOW, JOSEPHINE
English soprano (1940–)

Josephine Barstow joined Sadler's Wells in 1967, made her debut at Covent Garden in 1969, and first sang at the Metropolitan in 1977 as Musetta. Her repertoire ranges from classic Mozart and Verdi to modern Tippett and Britten. She can be seen on video at Glyndebourne in IDOMENEO (1974) singing the role of Elettra, in MACBETH (1972) as Lady Macbeth, and in the title role of SALOME (1994) in a Netherlands production. She played Queen Elizabeth in a 1999 Opera North telecast of Benjamin Britten's GLORIANA and Miss Wingrave in a 2001 TV production of Britten's OWEN WINGRAVE. See also GIUSEPPE VERDI (1994).

BARTERED BRIDE, THE
1866 opera by Smetana

BEDŘICH SMETANA's *Prodaná nevěsta* (The Bartered Bride) is the quintessential Czech opera and the standard against which all other Czech operas are measured. It has charm galore, with its roots in Bohemian folk music, and has remained popular in central Europe. The libretto by Karel Sabina tells the story of the lovers Mařenka and Jeník. Each contrives an elaborate stratagem so they can marry after she has been betrothed to another. The opera's popularity is reflected in the many films based on it.

***1932 Ophuls film
German feature film: Max Ophuls (director); Curt Alexander (screenplay); Reimar Kuntze, Franz Koch, and Herbert Illig (cinematographers); Reichsliga Film (production).

Cast: Jarmila Novotná (Mařenka), Willy Dom-graf-Fassbaender (Jeník), Max Nadler (Mayor), Karl Valentin (Brummer), Paul Kemp (Wenzel), Annemarie Sörensen (Esmeralda), Otto Wernicke (Kezal), Herman Kner (Mícha).

Video: Bel Canto Society/Lyric/Opera Dubs VHS. Black and white. In German as *Die Verkaufte Braut*. 76 minutes.

Comment: Ophuls's film is a delight, one of the most enjoyable opera films and a cinema classic.

1933 Espofilm film
Czech feature film: Jaroslav Kvapil and Emil Pollert (directors); Karel Degl, Václav Vich, and Otto Heller (cinematographers), Espofilm (production).

Cast: Ota Horáková (Mařenka), Vladimir Toms (Jeník), Jaroslav Gleich (Vašek), Emil Pollert (Kezal), Jan Konstantin (Krušina), Dobroslava Sudíkova (Ludmila).

Film: Black and white. In Czech as *Prodaná nevěsta*. 80 minutes.

Comment: Straightforward film of the opera, shot in Prague as a kind of authentic Czech answer to the German version. It was the third Czech film of the opera and the first with sound.

1957 ABC Television, Australia
Australian TV production: Christopher Muir (director), Clive Douglas (conductor, Victoria Symphony Orchestra and Melbourne Singers), John Peters (set designer), Rex Reid (choreographer).

Cast: Elsie Morison (Mařenka), Victor Franklin (Jeník), Muriel Luyk (Ludmila), Keith Nelson (Kezal), Raymond MacDonald (Wenzel), June Barton (Esmeralda), Alan Eddy (Mícha).

Video: House of Opera DVD/VHS. Black and white. In English as *The Bartered Bride*. 117 minutes.

Comment: Lively and enjoyable English-language version shot at ABC Studios, Melbourne.

1975 Bavarian Television
German TV film: Václav Kaslík (director), Jaroslav Krombholc (conductor, Munich RadioTelevision Orchestra and Chorus), Karel Vacek (set designer), Bavaria Film (production).

Cast: Teresa Stratas (Marie), René Kollo (Hans), Walter Berry (Kecal), Janet Perry (Esmeralda), Margarethe Bence (Ludmila), Alexander Malta (Mícha), Jörn W. Wilsing (Krušina).

Telecast April 18, 1976, on ARD. Color. In German as *Die Verkaufte Braut*. 120 minutes.

1976 Barrandov film
Czech feature film: Václav Kaslík (director), Jaroslav Krombholc (conductor, National Theater Orchestra, Prague), Barrandov Studios.

Cast: Vanda Svarcova (Mařenka, sung by Gabriela Beňačková), Petr Skarke (Jeník, sung by Ivo Zedek), Cesmir Randa (Kecal), Vaclav Sioup (Vasek).

Color. In Czech as *Prodaná nevěsta*. 119 minutes.

1978 Metropolitan Opera
American stage production: John Dexter (director), James Levine (conductor, Metropolitan Opera Orchestra and Chorus), Josef Svoboda (set designer), Tony Harrison (English translation).

Cast: Teresa Stratas (Mařenka), Nicolai Gedda (Jeník), Jon Vickers (Vasek), Martti Talvela (Kecal), Colette Boky (Esmeralda), Elizabeth Coss (Ludmila), Derek Hammond-Stroud (Krušina).

Video at the NYPL/MTR. Telecast live November 21, 1978, on PBS. Kirk Browning (director). Color. In English as *The Bartered Bride*. Color. 130 minutes.

1981 Filip film
Czech TV film: Frantisek Filip (director), Zdenek Kosler (conductor, Czech Philharmonic Orchestra and Chorus).

Cast: Gabriela Beňačková (Mařenka), Peter Dvorský (Jeník), Miroslav Kopp (Vasek), Richard Novák (Kecal), Indrich Jindrák (Krušina), Marie Vesela (Ludmila), Jaroslav Horácek (Mícha).

Video: Topaz (Germany) VHS. Telecast on DFF, Berlin, April 16, 1982. Color. In Czech as *Prodaná nevěsta*. 132 minutes.

Comment: Colorful production, with the director stressing the folkloristic elements. Supraphon CD has the same cast.

1982 Vienna State Opera

Austrian stage production: Otto Schenk (director), Adam Fischer (conductor, Vienna Staatsoper Orchestra), Max Kalbeck (German translation).

Cast: Lucia Popp (Marie), Siegfried Jerusalem (Hans), Karl Ridderbusch (Kezal), Heinz Zednik (Wenzel), Gertrude Jahn (Ludmila), Gabriele Sima (Esmeralda).

Telecast on ORF Austrian Television April 25, 1982. Otto Schenk (director). Color. In German as *Die Verkaufte Braut*. 142 minutes.

***1998 Royal Opera at Sadler's Wells

English stage production: Francesca Zambello (director), Bernard Haitink (conductor, Royal Opera House Orchestra and Chorus), Alison Chitty (set designer), Kit Hesketh Harvey (English translation).

Cast: Soile Isokoski (Mařenka), Jorma Silvasti (Jeník), Franz Kawlata (Kecal), Gwynne Howell (Krušina), Heather Begg (Ludmila), Anne Howells (Hata), Ian Bostridge (Vašek), Colette Delahunt (Esmeralda), Robert Tear (Ringmaster), Jeremy White (Mícha).

Video: House of Opera DVD/VHS. Telecast December 19, 1998, by BBC. Caroline Speed (director). Color. In English as *The Bartered Bride*. 179 minutes.

Comment: Highly enjoyable production with fine cast, superb conductor, and great director.

Early/related films

1908 Pathé film

German Pathé sound film of a scene and aria from the opera, made in 1908 and screened with the music on a phonograph. Black and white. In German. About 4 minutes.

1913 National Theater, Prague

A condensed version of the opera, performed by the Czech National Theater on an open-air stage in Prague on May 16, 1913, was filmed live by director Max Urban and cinematographer Václav Münzberger. Marie Slechtova played Mařenka, Tadeusz Dura was Jeník, Adolf Krössing was Vašek, Emil Pollert was Kecal, and Emil Burian was Krušina. The film was screened in cinemas with live music from the opera. Black and white. Silent. About 45 minutes. Apparently no prints survive.

1922 Kmínek film

The second Czech film of the opera was made in 1922 by Oldrich Kmínek with Tommy Falley-Novtony as cinematographer. Laura Zelenská is Mařenka, Frantisek Smolík is Jeník, Frantisek Beransky is Vašek, Karel Noll is Kecal, and Frantisek Kudlacet is Krušina. It was screened with live music. Black and white. In Czech. Silent. About 70 minutes. Print survives in the Czech Film Archive.

1948 NBC Television

The NBC telecast excerpts from *The Bartered Bride* in English on December 25, 1948, in preparation for the formation of NBC Television Opera. Samuel Chotzinoff was producer, Kirk Browning was director, and Peter Herman Adler was conductor. Singers not known.

1999 Man on the Moon

The overture to *The Bartered Bride*, performed by the New York Philharmonic led by Leonard Bernstein, is heard on the soundtrack of this Jim Carrey biopic about comedian Andy Kaufman. Milos Forman directed. Color. 118 minutes. On video.

BARTLETT, MICHAEL
American tenor (1903– ?)

Michael Bartlett was born in Massachusetts, studied in Milan, and made his debut in Trieste in 1928 in *Lucia di Lammermoor*. In the United States, he joined the Franco-Italo Opera Company, sang on the Jack Benny radio show in 1934, and made his film debut as himself in the 1935 film *Love Me Forever*. He starred in a film of Charles Cuvillier's operetta THE LILAC DOMINO in England in 1937 and then returned to the stage. In 1939, he starred in Clarence Loomis's folk opera *Susanna, Don't You Cry* and joined the San Francisco Opera where he sang opposite Jarmila Novotná in *Madama Butterfly*. In 1944, he was Romeo to Jeanette MacDonald's Juliette in a Chicago Opera production of Gounod's *Roméo et Juliette*. He continued to sing into his 60s.

1935 Love Me Forever

Bartlett made his film debut as himself in this Grace Moore film, singing Rodolfo opposite her Mimì in the climactic stage production of *La bohème*. She plays a soprano who gets to sing the opera at the Met with the help of a gangster. The film features a mockup of the Met and a caricature of Met manager Giulio Gatti-Casazza. See LOVE ME FOREVER.

1935 She Married Her Boss

Bartlett plays a rich playboy who fancies Claudette Colbert in this romantic comedy. Her boss is Melvyn Douglas. Gregory La Cava directed. Columbia. Black and white. 90 minutes.

1936 The Music Goes Round

Bartlett plays himself and sings the title song as if it were an operatic aria in this Columbia movie about a showboat troupe. Harry Richman and Rochelle Hudson star. Victor Schertzinger directed. Columbia. Black and white. 85 minutes.

1936 Follow Your Heart

Bartlett plays a gifted tenor opposite former Met soprano Marion Talley in this quirky Republic film. This is a down-home opera film, written tongue-in-cheek; for example, the sextet from *Lucia di Lammermoor* is a comic number, with Bartlett singing the tenor part to a ham. See FOLLOW YOUR HEART.

BARTÓK, BÉLA
Hungarian composer (1881–1945)

Béla Bartók has the ability to strike universal chords with his music, possibly because of his remarkable use of folk music and legend. His only opera, BLUEBEARD'S CASTLE, invites interpretations on multiple musical, psychological, and historical levels. His main connection with film was through his collaborator Béla Belazs, a noted screenwriter and film theorist. Bartók's ballet *The Miraculous Mandarin* has been turned into a quasi-operatic Hungarian film by Miklos Szinetar.

1964 Bartók

Ken Russell's television biography of the composer, one of his most successful, intercuts shots of Bartók with his music and scenes from *Bluebeard's Castle* and *The Miraculous Mandarin*. Russell's extravagant style includes an acetylene torch, a steel mill furnace, and a rocket launch in the *Bluebeard* section. Black and white. 60 minutes.

1989 After the Storm

This program, subtitled *The American Exile of Bela Bartók*, focuses on the last five years of the composer's life, which he spent as a research fellow at Columbia University. Donald Sturrock directed for the BBC and Hungarian television. Color. 75 minutes. Home Vision/Films for the Humanities & Sciences VHS.

BARTOLI, CECILIA
Italian mezzo-soprano (1966–)

Cecilia Bartoli made her stage debut in 1987 and attracted wide attention in 1988 singing Rosina in IL BARBIERE DI SIVIGLIA in Cologne, Schwetzingen, and Zurich. In a very short time, she became one of the most talked-about singers in the world, noted especially for her interpretations of Rossini, Mozart, and Vivaldi. She made

her debut at the Met as Despina in a fine 1996 production of *Così fan tutte* in 1996, and sang there again in *La Cenerentola* and *Le nozze di Figaro*. The hype does not seem to have harmed her, and her delightful stage personality and superb voice promise an enduring career. She can be seen at the beginning of her career meeting HERBERT VON KARAJAN in a 1987 documentary and singing in a MOZART REQUIEM in Vienna in 1991. In recent years, she has been promoting Vivaldi operas, and two videos are available of her singing music from them. See LA CENERENTOLA (1995/1997), COSÌ FAN TUTTE (1996/2000), DON GIOVANNI (1999), A MIDSUMMER NIGHT'S DREAM (1999 film), LE NOZZE DI FIGARO (1998), and ANTONIO VIVALDI (1999/2000).

1992 Cecilia Bartoli: A Portrait

Excellent two-part documentary by David Thomas. Part One is biographical, with Bartoli recording Rossini at La Fenice in Venice, practicing with her mother, talking about her life, and discussing Rossini and Mozart. Part Two is a concert at the Savoy Hotel in London with Gyorgy Fischer at the piano. She sings arias by Rossini, Mozart, Vivaldi, and Pergolesi and gives two encores. Color. 107 minutes. London VHS/LD.

1998 Cecilia Bartoli: Live in Italy

Bartoli, filmed live at a recital in the magnificent Teatro Olimpico in Vicenza in June 1998, performs songs and arias by Bellini, Berlioz, Bizet, Caccini, Donizetti, Giordani, Handel, Montsalvatge, Mozart, Rossini, Schubert, Viardot, and Vivaldi. She is accompanied by pianist Jean-Yves Thibaudet and the Sonatori de la Gioiosa Marca. Brian Large directed the video. Color. 114 minutes. Decca DVD/Polygram VHS.

1999 Cecilia and Bryn at Glyndebourne

Bartoli and Bryn Terfel perform scenes from *The Barber of Seville, Don Giovanni, L'elisir d'amore,* and *Le nozze di Figaro* at the Glyndebourne Festival in 1999, with Myung-Whung Chung conducting the London Philharmonic Orchestra. Brian Large directed. Color. 90 minutes. Telecast by BBC. Opus Art (GB) DVD.

2001 Cecilia Bartoli Sings Mozart

Bartoli sings "Bella mia flamme," "Resta, oh cara," "Giunse alfin al moment," and other pieces by Mozart, with Nikolaus Harnoncourt conducting. Color. 60 minutes. Naxos DVD.

BARYTON
1985 Polish film with opera content

Baryton (The Baritone) centers around a famous opera baritone who returns to Poland in 1933 as Hitler is coming to power. The filmmaker uses a soap opera–like story of operatic intrigues to spotlight the rise of fascism. Baritone Antonio Taviatini (Zbigniew Zapasiewicz), who has been singing abroad for 25 years, returns to his hometown with plans to build an opera house with his own money. He brings with him an entourage of wife, secretary, business manager, and other hangers-on who are plotting their own schemes. Artur Netz (Piotr Froncewski) is the ambitious secretary who wants to become the new opera house director and is having an affair with the singer's wife Sophie (Malgorzata Pieczynska) to further his scheme. Meanwhile, the baritone is losing his voice before a fundraising recital, his hotel room is being bugged by the local fascist party, and his business manager is plotting to steal the opera house funds. In the end, not surprisingly, it is a German who controls what is going to happen. The film premiered at the Montreal Film festival. Feliks Falk wrote the screenplay, Jerzy Satanowsky was music director, Witold Adamek was cinematographer, and Janusz Zaorski directed. Color. In Polish. 95 minutes.

BASTIANINI, ETTORE
Italian baritone (1922–1967)

Ettore Bastianini, whose remarkable voice was stilled at the early age of 45, began as a bass in Rome in 1945 and switched to baritone in 1951. He made his debut at the Met in 1953 as Germont and sang many other roles there and at La Scala. He was especially noted for his passionate singing of Verdi roles. See LA FORZA DEL DESTINO (1958) and IL TROVATORE (1957).

BATTLE, KATHLEEN
American soprano (1948–)

Kathleen Battle was brought up in a small town in Ohio, learned about opera by watching television broadcasts, and made her debut with the New York City Opera in 1976. She has sung in most of the major opera houses, including the Met and Covent Garden, and her attractive stage presence is evident in her recital videos. She is also noted for her temperament, which led to professional clashes and a much-publicized parting of the ways with the Met. See AFRICAN-AMERICAN OPERA (2000), ARIADNE AUF NAXOS (1988), IL BARBIERE DI SIVIGLIA (1988), CARMINA BURANA (1989), CARNEGIE HALL (1991), DON GIOVANNI (1987), L'ELISIR D'AMORE (1991), HERBERT VON KARAJAN (1987), LE NOZZE DI FIGARO (1985), METROPOLITAN OPERA (1983/1991), DER ROSENKAVALIER (1992 film), SOPRANOS AND MEZZOS (1995), and DIE ZAUBERFLÖTE (1991).

1990 Spirituals in Concert
Battle teams with Jessye Norman at Carnegie Hall for a program of spirituals. The divas, dressed in contrasting shades of blue, interact beautifully as they sing in a variety of styles. Battle is particularly fine singing "Swing Low, Sweet Chariot" and in duet with flautist Hubert Laws. James Levine leads the orchestra and a 70-member chorus. Brian Large directed. Color. 91 minutes. DG/Cami VHS.

1991 Battle at the Metropolitan Museum
A formal recital with pianist Warren Jones in front of the Egyptian Temple of Dendur at the Metropolitan Museum in New York. Battle, wearing a striking formal red dress, performs 17 arias and songs from Mozart and Puccini to Strauss and Gershwin. Her voice is stunning. Humphrey Burton directed. Color. 55 minutes. Cami/Polygram VHS.

1992 Baroque Duet
Battle and jazz trumpeter Wynton Marsalis make a recording and are filmed by Susan Froemke, Peter Gelb, Albert Maysles, and Pat Jaffe. The film shows rehearsals, a recording session and studio performance, plus Battle visiting her hometown in Ohio and Marsalis performing with friends. John Nelson conducts the Orchestra of St. Luke's. The recording was filmed by Michael Chapman. Color. 85 minutes. Cami VHS.

1995 Kathleen Battle and Thomas Hampson
Battle and Hampson join forces for this *Live From Lincoln Center* concert telecast March 1, 1995. They perform arias and duets by Mozart, Rossini, Massenet, Verdi, Lehár, and Korngold in the first half and American musical theater tunes in the second. During the interval, Sherrill Milnes hosts a backstage segment with Battle and Hampson talking about their work. Color. 90 minutes.

BAYOU LEGEND, A
1941 opera by Still

WILLIAM GRANT STILL's opera *A Bayou Legend* was composed in 1941 to a libretto by his wife Verna Arvey and was first staged in 1974 by Opera/South in Jackson, Mississippi. They based the story on a Mississippi legend they found in a book in the Los Angeles Public Library. Clothilde rejects Leonce because she wants to marry Bazile, whom she says is the father of her unborn child. The spirit maiden Aurore, who loves Bazile, tells him this is not true, so Clothilde accuses him of witchcraft to gain revenge. The villagers hang him, and his spirit joins Aurore's.

1979 Opera/South

American TV film: John Thompson (director), Leonard de Paur (conductor, Opera/South Orchestra and Jackson State University Chorus), Bobby Mason (choreographer), Curtis W. Davis (producer).

Cast: Raeschelle Potter (Clothilde), Gary Burgess (Bazile), Peter Lightfoot (Leonce), Carmen Balthrop (Aurore), Cullen Maiden (Father Lestant), François Clemmons (Minstrel).

Telecast June 15, 1981, on PBS. Color. In English. 120 minutes.

Comment: Filmed on location on a Mississippi bayou in 1979 with the Opera/South cast.

BAYREUTH

Not many composers have the ego to build an opera house to present only their own operas, but Richard Wagner did. His Bayreuth Festspielhaus, completed in 1876, remains a place of Wagnerian pilgrimage and controversy for the composer's heirs. Its epic construction is often featured in biographical films about Wagner, most notably in Tony Palmer's grandiose biopic. Many videos are available of operas filmed on stage at Bayreuth. See DER FLIEGENDE HOLLÄNDER (1985), GÖTTERDÄMMERUNG (1980/1992), LOHENGRIN (1982/1990), DIE MEISTERSINGER VON NÜRNBERG (1984), PARSIFAL (1981), DAS RHEINGOLD (1980/1991), DER RING DES NIBELUNGEN (1980/1991), SIEGFRIED (1980/1992), TANNHÄUSER (1978/1990), TRISTAN UND ISOLDE (1983), RICHARD WAGNER, and DIE WALKÜRE (1980/1991).

1960 Wagner in Modern Dress

Phänomen Bayreuth (distributed in English as *Wagner in Modern Dress*) is a German film about rehearsals at Bayreuth for the 1959 and 1960 festivals. It features Wieland and Wolfgang Wagner, Rudolf Kempe, Wolfgang Sawallisch, Anja Silja, Hans Knappertsbusch, Lorin Maazel, and Jerome Hines. Werner Lütje directed for Nord-Sud Television. Black and white. In German or English. 33 minutes.

1976 100 Years of Bayreuth

Film portrait of the Bayreuth Festival on its 100th anniversary, made to celebrate Wagner's achievements. It includes scenes from the 1976 production of the *Ring* cycle under the direction of Pierre Boulez. Color. In German. 40 minutes.

1980 Wagner and Bayreuth

Hans Jürgen Rojek wrote and directed this German film about Wagner's association with the city of Bayreuth and the building of his opera house. Color. In English or German. 27 minutes. Goethe Institute Inter Nationes VHS.

1985 Wagner in Bayreuth

Wolfgang Wagner presents an introduction to Wagner followed by excerpts from 10 operas staged at Bayreuth from 1978 to 1985. Colin Davis, Woldemar Nelsson, Pierre Boulez, Horst Stein, and Daniel Barenboim conduct the Bayreuther Festspiele Orchestra and Chorus in performances by an array of singers. Brian Large directed the video. Color. In German. 60 minutes. Philips LD.

1994 Die Verwandlung der Welt in Musik

The Transformation of the World in Music is a documentary about Bayreuth today by German filmmaker Werner Herzog, who has staged Wagner operas. It features interviews with Wolfgang Wagner, Daniel Barenboim, and Plácido Domingo, plus scenes from stagings of *Parsifal, The Flying Dutchman,* and *Tristan und Isolde.* Unitel/ZDF. Color. In German. 90 minutes.

BBC TELEVISION
British Broadcasting Corporation Television

BBC Television was the first in the world to present opera on TV, 25 minutes of highlights from Albert Coates's opera PICKWICK, telecast on November 13, 1936. The following year a complete LA SERVA PADRONA was telecast. From 1936 to September 1939, when BBC Television closed down for the war, 30 operas were presented. Lionel Salter gives a wonderful description of this amazing early venture into TV opera in two articles in *Opera* magazine, but it does not appear that any of this pioneering material was preserved on film. The BBC began to telecast opera again after the war on November 26, 1946, with *The Beggar's Opera,* and it began outside broadcasts of opera from the New London Opera Company in 1947 with DON GIOVANNI. The first opera commissioned by the BBC was Arthur Benjamin's *Mañana,* telecast in 1956. The first BBC live broadcast from Covent Garden was delayed until 1968 because of union disagreements. BBC Television opera is now a regular part of viewing in the United Kingdom; there are entries for BBC under most of the operas listed in this book.

BEAR, THE
1967 opera by Walton

Young widow Madame Popova mourns her husband and is looked after by old servant Luka. When boorish neighbor Smirnov demands payment for a debt made by her husband, she gets so angry she challenges him to a duel. While he shows her how to use a pistol, they fall in love and decide to get married. William Walton's genial opera *The Bear,* libretto by Paul Dehn based on a play by Chekhov, includes affectionate allusions to several other operas.

1970 BBC Television

English TV production: Rudolf Cartier (director), William Walton (conductor, BBC Orchestra), Richard Wilmot (set/costume designer).

Cast: Regina Resnik (Mme. Popova), Thomas Hemsley (Smirnov), Derek Hammond Stroud (Luka).

Telecast in 1970 on BBC TV. Color. In English. 48 minutes.

1990 Teatro Nacional de São Carlos, Lisbon

Portuguese stage production: Luis Miguel Cintra (director), João Paulo Santos (conductor, Teatro Nacional de São Carlos Orchestra), Cristina Reis (set/costume designer).

Cast: Marina Ferreira (Mme. Popova), Jorge Vaz de Carvalho (Smirnov), José Manuel Coelho (Luka).

Telecast April 29, 1992, on RTP Portuguese Television. Color. In Portuguese as *O Urso*. 47 minutes.

BEATRICE

1959 TV opera by Hoiby

Beatrice is a novice in a 13th-century Belgian convent. Although highly religious, she feels she has to leave the convent when she falls in love with Prince Bellidor. Her place is taken by the Virgin Mary, and the convent's statue of Mary vanishes. Fourteen years later, Beatrice returns broken in spirit, and the statue reappears. Lee Hoiby's three-act opera *Beatrice*, libretto by Marcia Nardi based on Maurice Maeterlinck's *Soeur Béatrice*, was commissioned by WAVE-TV in Louisville, Kentucky, to celebrate the opening of its new television center. It was premiered on television and then staged at the Columbia Auditorium in Louisville.

1959 Kentucky Opera

American TV production: Moritz Bomhard (stage director), Robert Whitney (conductor, Louisville Orchestra), George Tuell (set designer).

Cast: Audrey Nossaman (Beatrice), Richard Lohr (Bellidor), Elizabeth Johnson (Abbess), Robert Fischer (Father Justinian), David Clenny (Timothy), Bonnie Bounnell (Sister Eglantine), Mary Treiz (Sister Anna).

Telecast October 23, 1959, on WAVE-TV. Burt Blackwell (director). Black and white. In English. 90 minutes.

BEATRICE DI TENDA

1833 opera by Bellini

Milan in 1418. Filippo Visconti gets a dukedom through his marriage to Beatrice but now wants to abandon her for Agnese. Orombello, who loves Beatrice but was re-jected by her, testifies against her, and she is condemned to death. Vincenzo Bellini's opera *Beatrice di Tenda*, libretto by Felice Romani based on a ballet by Antonio Monticini, is a vehicle for a prima donna. It was composed for Giuditta Pasta and is best known today through a 1966 recording made by Joan Sutherland.

2000 Bellini Conservatory, Palermo

Italian stage production: Carlo Rizzi (conductor, Bellini Conservatory Orchestra).

Cast: Donia Palade (Beatrice), Renata Daltin, Salvatore Fisichella.

Video: House of Opera/Opera Classics VHS (nonprofessional video shot from the audience). Color. In Italian. 165 minutes.

Related films

1999 Ladies Room

John Malkovich takes his mistress to the opera to see *Beatrice di Tenda* while his pregnant wife is absent (he thinks). Most of the action takes places in the women's restroom, where we hear bits of the opera but never actually see it. The credits do not indicate which recording was used. Gabriella Cristiani directed. Color. In English. 90 minutes. On VHS.

1999 Les Enfants du Siècle

Edith Gruberova, the Vienna Youth Choir, and the ORF Symphony Orchestra perform music from *Beatrice di Tenda* in this French film about the love affair of George Sand (Juliette Binoche) and Alfred de Musset (Benoît Magimel). Diane Kurys directed. Color. In French. 108 minutes.

BEÁTRICE ET BÉNÉDICT

1862 opera by Berlioz

Sicily around 1700 as soldiers begin to return from fighting the Moors. Hero is glad to see Claudio, but their relationship is pretty standard romantic. Beátrice welcomes Bénédict with mocking banter, and they have to be tricked into admitting their love for each other. Hector Berlioz's opera *Beátrice et Bénédict*, libretto by the composer, is a version of Shakespeare's play *Much Ado About Nothing*, with the emphasis on Beátrice and Bénédict and the addition of a pedantic orchestral conductor named Somarone. For some reason the French changed Shakespeare's "Benedick" into "Bénédict."

1979 Boston Symphony

American concert production: Seiji Ozawa (conductor, Boston Symphony Orchestra and Tanglewood Festival Chorus).

Cast: Karan Armstrong (Beátrice), Stuart Burrows (Bénédict), Gwendolyn Killebrew.

Video: House of Opera DVD/VHS. Color. In French. 120 minutes.

BEAUMARCHAIS, PIERRE-AUGUSTIN
French playwright (1732–1799)

Pierre-Augustin Caron de Beaumarchais wrote three plays, the Figaro trilogy, which became the basis for more than 40 operas. The great ones were by Mozart (LE NOZZE DI FIGARO) and Rossini (IL BARBIERE DI SIVIGLIA), but there are also notable operas by Paisiello (IL BARBIERE DI SIVIGLIA) and Massenet (*Chérubin*). He also wrote an excellent original libretto for Antonio Salieri, TARARE, in which a king is deposed—this daringly just two years before the French Revolution. Beaumarchais is the main character in John Corigliano's 1991 opera THE GHOSTS OF VERSAILLES (which also draws from the lesser-known third play in his Figaro trilogy, *La mère coupable*) and in Cools's 1931 operetta *Beaumarchais*. His life was as fascinating as his operas; he rose from watchmaker to literary great and friend of kings and queens (he bought his title) to spy to friend of the American Revolution. He appears as a character in many films about his era, including James Whale's *The Great Garrick* (1937, played by Lionel Atwill), Sacha Guitry's *Si Versailles m'étais conté* (1954, played by Bernard Dhéran), and *Si Paris nous étais conté* (1955, played by Aimé Clariond) and the French TV film *Voltaire* (1977, played by Gérard Caillaud).

1972 Figaro-ci, Figaro-là
French television film about Beaumarchais and his life, in which he is seen as the prototype for Figaro. Jean-François Poron plays Beaumarchais with a strong supporting cast that includes Isabelle Huppert and Marie-Christine Barrault. Hervé Bromberg directed. Color. In French. 120 minutes.

1996 Beaumarchais, l'insolent
Opulent French feature film about Beaumarchais, played by Fabrice Luchini, based on a play by Sacha Guitry. The film describes his social climbing and his womanizing life during which he finds time to write his famous plays while acting as a spy for the king and helping supply arms for the American Revolution (and getting swindled by Ben Franklin). Outstanding period re-creation by director Eduard Molinaro, who wrote the screenplay with Jean-Claude Brisville. Color. In French. 100 minutes.

BECCE, GIUSEPPE
Italian composer (1877–1973)

Giuseppe Becce occupies an important place in the history of early opera film. In 1913, he portrayed Wagner in Oskar Messter's biofilm RICHARD WAGNER and also composed the score, the first specially composed for a German silent film. He quickly became the most important composer of scores for German silent films and edited the definitive collection of film themes. He continued to work for a very long time; one of his later scores was for a 1954 film of the opera HÄNSEL UND GRETEL.

BECHI, GINO
Italian baritone (1913–1993)

Gino Bechi, the leading Italian dramatic baritone of his time, was born in Florence, made his debut in *Empoli* in 1936, and sang regularly at Rome and La Scala from 1938 to 1953. He also made guest appearances at Covent Garden and other opera houses until 1961. Bechi was featured in a dozen Italian films, usually in singing roles, sometimes just as a voice. Two of his films were cinema versions of operas, AIDA (1953) and LA TRAVIATA (1967), and he is one of the operatic stars of FOLLIE PER L'OPERA.

1943 Fuga a due voci
A film company can't find the right plot for Bechi, its baritone star. He tells them a tale about missing a train, spending the night with a girl who also missed it, and ending up in jail with her. It becomes the story of the film *Fugue for Two Voices*. Bixio wrote charming songs for the film. Carlo Ludovico Bragaglia directed. Black and white. In Italian. 66 minutes.

1945 Pronto, chi parla?
In *Pronto, chi parla?* (Hello, Who's Speaking?), Bechi plays a famous singer who poses as his butler to woo and win countess Annette Bach. He sings the prologue to *Pagliacci* and other arias. Carlo Ludovico Bragaglia directed. Released in the United States as *The Voice of Love*. Black and white. In Italian. 80 minutes.

1946 Torna a Sorrento
Bechi stars opposite Adriana Benetti in the romantic musical *Return to Sorrento*. She has lost her fiancée, and he helps her look for him. After a few songs, they fall in love. Carlo Ludovico Bragaglia directed. Black and white. In Italian. 88 minutes.

1948 Arrivederci, Papá!
Bechi plays an opera singer undergoing a midlife career crisis. A philosopher tells him he is about to meet the woman of his life and have two children. And so he does.

Camillo Mastrocinque directed. Black and white. In Italian. 86 minutes.

1947 Il segreto di Don Giovanni

Bechi plays an opera singer with an irresistible charm for women, including Silvana Pampanini. When he loses his voice, he despairs and decides to end his life by hiring killers. When he changes his mind, he has problems. This cinematic *opera buffa* was released in the United States as *When Love Calls*. Mario Costa directed. Black and white. In Italian. 85 minutes.

1947 Amanti in fuga

Bechi play 17th-century composer Alessandro Stradella in the rather grim historical musical *Lovers in Flight*. After he has a love affair in Venice with Ortensia Foscarini (Annette Bach), daughter of the Inquisitor, her father orders Stradella killed. Giacomo Gentilomo directed. Black and white. In Italian. 83 minutes.

1949 Signorinella

The song "Signorinella mio" was the inspiration for this Bechi musical with Antonella Lualdi. The plot revolves around a confidence swindle. Mario Mattoli directed. Black and white. In Italian. 87 minutes. Opera Dubs/Lyric VHS.

1950 Una voce nel tuo cuore

Bechi and Beniamino Gigli appear in opera sequences in *A Voice in Your Heart*. Vittorio Gassman plays a war correspondent who loves a nightclub singer who wants to sing opera. Alberto D'Aversa directed. Black and white. In Italian. 98 minutes.

1954 Canzoni a due voci

Songs for Two Voices is an excuse to allow Bechi and Tito Gobbi to sing. Gobbi is a famous baritone and Bechi is his voice in this fantasy directed by Gianni Vernuccio. Black and white. In Italian. 84 minutes.

1955 Schubert

Bechi plays baritone Johann Vogl, composer Franz Schubert's friend and ideal interpreter, in this Italian film biography. See SCHUBERT.

1957 La chiamavan Capinera

Bechi plays a famous baritone in his last film, *The Woman Called Capinera*. Fairground singer Irene Galter (Capinera) comes to live with Bechi and falls in love with his son. Piero Regnoli directed. Black and white. In Italian. 95 minutes.

BED AND SOFA
1996 screen opera by Pen

This stage work, promoted as a "silent movie opera," is based on the 1926 Soviet film *Bed and Sofa,* a satirical comedy by Abram Room about a trio of working folk living in a one-room apartment. The married couple (Ludmilla and Nikolai) sleep on the bed and the friend (Volodya) sleeps on the sofa. When the husband goes away for a time, the friend moves into the bed. Polly Pen's 90-minute chamber opera, libretto by Laurence Klavan, premiered in February 1996.

1996 Vineyard Theater

American stage production: André Ernotte (director), Alan Johnson (conductor, Vineyard Theater Orchestra), G. W. Mercier (sets/costume designer).

Cast: Terri Klausner (Ludmilla), Michael X. Martin (Nikolai), Jason Workman (Volodya).

BEDFORD, STEUART
English conductor (1939–)

Steuart Bedford, who began conducting with *Albert Herring* while still at Oxford, has been associated with the operas of Benjamin Britten during most of his career. He conducted the first stage performance of *Owen Wingrave* at Covent Garden in 1973 and the premiere of *Death in Venice* at Aldeburgh the same year. He made his debut at the Met in 1974 with *Death in Venice* and conducted *Billy Budd* there in 1997. He also conducted the first British production of Britten's opera/operetta *Paul Bunyan*. All of his videos are of Britten operas. See BILLY BUDD (1997), DEATH IN VENICE (1981), and THE TURN OF THE SCREW (1990).

BEECHAM, SIR THOMAS
English conductor (1879–1971)

Sir Thomas Beecham is not well represented on film, though he left a strong legacy on disc. The founder of the London and Royal Philharmonic orchestras was one of the major figures in opera in England, and his recording of *La bohème* is considered by many to be the best ever. Beecham conducted the orchestra for a 1936 British film biography of Mozart called WHOM THE GODS LOVE, is seen conducting the orchestra in the 1951 Powell/Pressburger film THE TALES OF HOFFMANN, is featured in a 1995 documentary about great CONDUCTORS, and is portrayed on screen by Henri Szeps in a 1980 TV play about NELLIE MELBA.

1990 Beecham

British docu-drama about the conductor (played by Timothy West) from his early years through the first English productions of Strauss's *Elektra*, *Salome*, and *Der Rosenkavalier*. The music is performed by the Halle Orchestra. Color. In English. 90 minutes. Films for the Humanities & Sciences VHS.

BEESON, JACK
American composer (1921–)

Indiana-born Jack Beeson, who began composing tuneful and accessible operas in 1950, tends to favor American subjects. He is particularly fond of William Saroyan, with two of his operas, *Hello Out There* and MY HEART'S IN THE HIGHLANDS, based on plays by the Armenian-American writer. LIZZIE BORDEN tells the story of the legendary Massachusetts murder trial protagonist while *Captain Jinks of the Horse Marines* was inspired by an early American play. Beeson's operas mix folk idioms with operatic lyricism; most are on record although not on commercial video.

Captain Jinks of the Horse Marines

Beeson and librettist Sheldon Harnick based their 1975 light opera *Captain Jinks of the Horse Marines* on a 1916 play by Clyde Fitch. Jinks bets a friend he can seduce visiting opera singer Aurelia Trentoni, but the two fall in love and the bet becomes a problem. There is no video of the opera, but the play was made into a feature film in 1916 by Essanay, with Ann Murdock as Aurelia and Richard Travers as Captain Jinks. Fred E. Wright directed. Black and white. 70 minutes.

BEETHOVEN, LUDWIG VAN
German composer (1770–1827)

We owe a debt to Mozart's *Magic Flute* collaborator Emanuel Schikaneder for getting Ludwig van Beethoven started in the opera field. Schikaneder commissioned him to compose an opera to his libretto *Vestas Feuer*, but Beethoven abandoned it to work on an opera called *Leonore*, which eventually became FIDELIO. Beethoven's life seems to have appealed to filmmakers, perhaps because his scowl, deafness, and temperament are seen as cinematic, but most of the films tend to romanticize him. He also appears in biographies about other composers, including SCHUBERT (1941), MOZART (1942), and ROSSINI (1943).

1936 The Life and Loves of Beethoven

Abel Gance's French film *Un grand amour de Beethoven* (The Life and Loves of Beethoven) stars Harry Baur as Beethoven. It's a big romantic movie, if not quite as grandiose as the director's *Napoleon,* and has many powerful scenes, including one demonstrating the composer's deafness. Gance's bravura direction is as impressive as the music, arranged by Louis Masson. Supporting actors include Annie Ducaux as Thérèse Brunswick, Jean-Louis Barrault as Karl Beethoven, Jany Holt as Giulietta Guicciardi, and Marcel Dalio as Steiner. Gance wrote the screenplay, and Robert LeFebvre and Marc Fossard were cinematographers. Black and white. In French with English subtitles. 135 minutes. Connoisseur VHS.

1941 The Melody Master

Albert Basserman plays Beethoven in this Hollywood version of Schubert's life. Schubert's friend Anna (Ilona Massey) shows the deaf Beethoven the *Unfinished Symphony* and he hears it in his head. He says Schubert is a genius and vows to help him, but dies before he can. Reinhold Schunzel directed the film (aka *New Wine*), released in England as *The Great Awakening*. Black and white. In English. 89 minutes. Video Yesteryear VHS.

1949 Eroica

Austrian film biography based around the creation of the "Eroica" Symphony. Ewald Balser gives a sensitive portrayal of Beethoven under the direction of H. W. Kolm-Veltée and Karl Hartl. The cast includes Marianne Schonauer and Judith Maria Holzmester. Color. In German. 100 minutes.

1962 The Magnificent Rebel

Walt Disney film about the young Beethoven (Karl Böhm) was shot in Vienna with careful attention to period detail. Also in the cast are Ernst Nadhering, Ivan Desny, and Gabriele Parks. George Tressler directed, Joanne Court wrote the screenplay, and Goran Strindberg was the cinematographer. Technicolor. 94 minutes.

1969 Beethoven 1814

Herbert Vesely's German documentary looks at Beethoven's life in Vienna in 1814 and examines his compositions of that year. Orchestra rehearsals of the third *Leonore* overture are also featured, with Vjaceslaw Neumann conducting. Color. In English. 14 minutes. Goethe Institute Inter Nationes film.

1970 Ludwig van Beethoven

Hans Conrad Fischer made this fine documentary film for the Beethoven bicentennial; it describes Beethoven's life through narration; visual and audio collages of houses, concert halls, manuscripts, letters, photographs, and other memorabilia; and his music, including an excerpt from *Fidelio*. Screenplay by Erich Koch; cinematography by Ivan Putora. Color. In German. 100 minutes.

1970 Beethoven—Tage aus einem Leben

Russian actor Donatas Banionis, who bears a close resemblance to the composer, is the star of the East German film *Beethoven—Days From a Life*. It presents reflective episodes from the life of Beethoven in Vienna from 1813 to 1819. Stefan Lisewiski is Johann Beethoven, Hans Tuscher is Karl Beethoven, Renate Richter is Josephine, and Fred Delmare is Maelzel. Horst Seeman directed and wrote the screenplay with Gunter Kundert for DEFA. Color. In German. 110 minutes.

1971 Beethoven's Birthday

Leonard Bernstein narrates this documentary, subtitled *A Celebration in Vienna*, which was made to show how Vienna marked the composer's 200th birthday. It includes excerpts from a production of *Fidelio* with Gwyneth Jones, James King, and Theo Adam. Humphrey Burton produced and directed. Color. In English. 60 minutes. Video at the MTR.

1981 Bernstein/Beethoven

Eleven-part series devoted to the music of Beethoven as analyzed and performed by Leonard Bernstein with the Vienna Philharmonic. Program Four discusses *Fidelio*. The series was directed by Humphrey Burton and screened on CBS in 1981. Color. Videos at the MTR.

1985 Beethoven's Nephew

Paul Morrissey's film revolves around the composer's supposed obsession with his nephew; one critic described it as "a high-minded subject with some genuine low-down fun." Wolfgang Reichmann plays Beethoven, Dietmar Prince is his nephew, and Natalie Baye is Leonore. Morrissey and Mathieu Carriere wrote the screenplay. Color. In English. 103 minutes.

1989 Beethoven

Anthony Quayle and Balint Vaszonyi visit Beethoven's home in Bonn and talk about his life and music while actors re-create scenes from his turbulent life in Vienna. Made for Klassix 13 series. Color. 60 minutes. MPI Home Entertainment VHS.

1992 Beethoven Lives Upstairs

Beethoven rents the upstairs room in a house and impresses a young boy. This Canadian film, shot in Vienna with a good deal of music, is pleasant and innocuous and meant for young viewers. It stars Neil Munro, Ilya Woloshyn, and Fiona Reid and won an Emmy Award. Heather Conkie wrote the screenplay, and David Devine directed. Shown on HBO in its Composers Series. Color. In English. 52 minutes. Sony Classical VHS.

1994 Immortal Beloved

Gary Oldman plays Beethoven in this big-budget romantic biography, written and directed by Bernard Rose and shot on location in Europe and Prague. It focuses on the relationship between the composer and the supposed woman of his life, the "immortal beloved" of the title. The glory of the film is the music performed by Sir Georg Solti and the London Symphony Orchestra and singers such as Renée Fleming. Columbia Pictures. Color. In English. 123 minutes.

1996 Famous Composers: Ludwig van Beethoven

Video documentary about the life and music of the composer, featuring excerpts from his works. Color. 30 minutes. Kultur VHS.

2001 Great Composers: Beethoven

BBC Television documentary about the life and career of Beethoven, narrated by Kenneth Branagh, with commentary from experts and excerpts from performances. Color. In English. 60 minutes. Warner Music Vision/NVC Arts DVD.

Early/related films

1909 Beethoven

The first Beethoven film biography seems to have been the 1909 French film *Beethoven* produced by the Eclair Company. Black and white. Silent. About 14 minutes.

1909 The Origin of Beethoven's Moonlight Sonata

The Edison Studio made a romantic Beethoven film in 1909 titled *The Origin of Beethoven's Moonlight Sonata*. It was restored by the American Film Institute in 1999 and shown at the AFI's Los Angeles Film Festival. Tinted. Silent. About 13 minutes.

1918 Beethovens Lebensroman

Fritz Kortner plays Beethoven in *Beethoven's Life Story*, an Austrian feature film about the composer. Emil Justitz directed for Sascha Film, and Oskar Nedbal arranged Beethoven's music for its screenings. Aka *Der Martyrer seines Herzens*. Black and white. Silent. About 75 minutes.

1927 The Life of Beethoven

Fritz Kortner plays Beethoven again in this major Austrian film biography made for the Beethoven centenary and directed by Hans Otto Löwenstein. Ernst Baumeister is Haydn, Lillian Gray is Countess Guiccardi, Heinz Altringen is Ries, and Will Schmieder is Prince Liechnowsky. Produced by Allianz. Black and white. Silent. About 70 minutes.

1954 Napoleon

Erich von Stroheim plays Beethoven in this French film about Napoleon. It contains a famous scene in which an angry Beethoven crosses out his dedication of his "Eroica" Symphony to Napoleon. Sacha Guitry directed. Color. In French. 182 minutes.

BEGGAR'S OPERA, THE
1718 opera by Gay and Pepusch

The Beggar's Opera is the most famous ballad opera and the ancestor of operas by Gilbert and Sullivan and Brecht and Weill. It is also the only opera usually considered to have been created by its writer, JOHN GAY, rather than by its composer/arranger, Johann Pepusch. *The Beggar's Opera* is the cynical story of the highwayman Macheath and his involvement with several women, including Polly Peachum, Lucy Lockit, and Jenny Diver. He is betrayed and imprisoned and given a purely arbitrary reprieve. Jonathan Swift suggested the story to Gay when the idea of a corrupt gang of crooks, whores, and informers as protagonists was a novelty. The opera still has bite; apparently the corruption and hypocrisy that Gay satirized have not gone away.

1937 BBC Television

British TV production: Stephen Thomas (director), Hyam Greenbaum (BBC Orchestra), Marian Wilson (choreographer).

Cast: Frederic Ranalow (Macheath), Joan Collier (Polly Peachum), Sybil Evers (Lucy Lockit), Valerie Hay (Jenny Diver), Scott Russell (Peachum), Elizabeth French (Mrs. Peachum).

Telecast live May 18, 1937, on BBC. Black and white. In English. 43 minutes. No copy known.

1952 CBS Television Workshop

American TV production: Dick Linroum (director), Lehman Engel (conductor, CBS Orchestra), Henry May (set designer), Norris Houghton (producer).

Cast: Steven Douglas (Macheath), Doretta Morrow (Polly), Joseph Silver (Peachum), Odette Myrtil (Mrs. Peachum), Karen Lindgren (Lucy).

Video at the MTR. Telecast live March 2, 1952, on CBS. Dick Linroum (director). Black and white. In English. 30 minutes.

1953 Brook film

British feature film: Peter Brook (director), Dennis Cannan and Christopher Fry (screenplay), Guy Green (cinematographer), Arthur Bliss (music director), Georges Wakhévitch and William C. Andrews (art directors).

Cast: Laurence Olivier (Macheath) Stanley Holloway (Lockit), Dorothy Tutin (Polly Peachum), Yvonne Furneaux (Jenny Diver), Daphne Anderson (Lucy Lockit), George Devine (Peachum), Mary Clare (Mrs. Peachum), Hugh Griffith (Beggar), Athene Seyler (Mrs. Trapes), Margot Grahame (Actress).

Video: Warner VHS. Color. In English 90 minutes.

Comment: Olivier and Holloway do their own singing; the other actors are dubbed.

1973 Chelsea Theater Center

American TV production: George Cappannelli (director).

Cast: Timothy Jerome (Macheath), Leila Martin (Polly), June Gable (Lucy), Gordon Connell, Howard Ross, John Long, Joe Palmieri, Jill Eikenberry.

Telecast on cable television. Edward F. Simon (director). Color. In English. 120 minutes.

Comment: TV adaptation of Obie-winning stage production by Cappannelli.

1983 BBC Television

British TV production: Jonathan Miller (director), John Eliot Gardiner (conductor, English Baroque Soloists), Sally Gilpin (choreographer).

Cast: Roger Daltrey (Macheath), Carol King (Polly), Stratford Johns (Peachum), Patricia Routledge (Mrs. Peachum), Rosemary Ashe (Lucy Lockit).

Video: Image Entertainment DVD/Home Vision and Polygram VHS/Philips LD. Color. In English. 135 minutes.

Comment: Singing is fine and filming is lively, so this should be an exciting video, but somehow it isn't; it just never catches fire.

1987 Opera Do Malandro

Brazilian feature film: Ruy Guerra (director); Chico Buarque, Orlando Senna, and Ruy Guerra (screenplay); Chico Buarque (music).

Cast: Edson Celulari, Claudia Ohana, Elba Ramalho, Nev Latorraca.

Video: Virgin Vision VHS. Color. In Portuguese with English subtitles. 108 minutes.

Comment: Loose adaptation of *Beggar's Opera* set in Brazil in the 1940s. Smalltime crook seduces daughter of prostitution ring boss and gets in hot water. Distributed in the United States by Samuel Goldwyn.

1991 Zebrácká Opera

Czech feature film: Jerí Menzel (director), Jan Klusak (original music and conductor), Barrandov Film (production).

Cast: Josef Abraham (Macheath), Libuše Sifrankova (Jenny), Barbara Leichnerova (Polly), Veronika Freimanova (Lucy), Marian Labuda (Peachum).

Color. In Czech. 102 minutes.

Comment: Based on a 1972 play by Václav Havel, derived from Gay opera. Characters and story are basically the same, although Havel updates the story and creates contemporary relevance.

BEHRENS, HILDEGARD
German soprano (1937–)

Hildegard Behrens sings Brünnhilde in two DER RING DES NIBELUNGEN cycles on video, the 1989 Bavarian State Opera production conducted by Wolfgang Sawallisch and the 1990 Met production conducted by James Levine. She is also formidable playing Electra in two different operas, Mozart's IDOMENEO (1982) and Strauss's ELEKTRA (1994). She is a fine Marie in WOZZECK (1987), a powerful TOSCA (1985), and an excellent Senta in DER FLIEGENDE HOLLÄNDER (1989). She made her debut in Freiburg in 1971, first came to Covent Garden as Leonore, and arrived at the Met as Giorgetta in *Il Tabarro*. See DIE FRAU OHNE SCHATTEN (1980), GÖTTERDÄMMERUNG (1989/1990), SALOME (1998 film), SIEGFRIED (1989/1990), GEORG SOLTI (1978), and DIE WALKÜRE (1989/1990).

1987 Hildegard Behrens, A Portrait
Peter Adam filmed this documentary about Behrens for the BBC in England, with interviews and excerpts from her performances. Color. 60 minutes.

BELISARIO
1836 opera by Donizetti

Belisarius (Belisario), the brilliant Byzantine general who reconquered the West for Roman Emperor Justinian, also aroused his intense jealousy. In GAETANO DONIZETTI's opera *Belisario,* libretto by Salvatore Cammarano, he is arrested after being accused by his wife Antonina of killing their son Alamiro and plotting to seize the throne. He is led from captivity by his daughter Irene, finds his son still alive, and leads a final defense of the empire before dying. Now a rarity, the opera was very popular in its era.

1997 Graz Festival
Austrian stage production: Sabine Loew (director), Dan Ratiu (conductor, Graz Philharmonic Orchestra and Chorus), Jörg Kossdorff (set designer).

Cast: Jacek Strauch (Belisario), Inez Salazar (Antonina), Natalia Biorro (Irene), Sergei Homov (Alamiro), Konstantin Sfiris (Giustiniano), Walter Pauritsch (Eutropio).

Video: Premiere Opera/House of Opera VHS. Telecast November 29, 1997, in Austria. Color. In Italian. 105 minutes.

BELLA DORMENTE NEL BOSCO, LA
1922 opera by Respighi

La bella dormente nel bosco (The Sleeping Beauty in the Woods) is OTTORINO RESPIGHI's best opera and an attractive musical fairy tale. It has never entered the repertory, although it had great success around the world, because Respighi composed it for Vittorio Podrecca's puppet theater, the Teatro dei Piccoli. The singers sit with the orchestra and lend their voices to the puppets. The opera has unusual singing roles, including a spindle that pricks the princess asleep and spiders who weave a protective web around her. Gian Bistolfi's libretto follows the Perrault fairy tale closely, but Beauty's sleep here lasts into the 20th century.

1954 CBS Television: Omnibus
American TV production: Robert Banner (director), George Bassman (conductor, CBS Orchestra) Julius Rudel (chorus director), Henry May and Gene Callahan (set designers), Leslie Renfield (costume designer), Arnold Schulman (English translation), William Engvick (lyrics).

Cast: Jo Sullivan (Princess), Jim Hawthorne (Prince Charming), Nadia Witkowska (Good Fairy), Rosemary Kuhlmann (Queen), Frank Rogier (King), Helen Scott (Nurse), Gloria Lane (Witch), and Leon Lishner (Ambassador).

Video at the MTR. Telecast by CBS on January 26, 1954. Robert Banner (director). Black and white. In English. 55 minutes.

BELL TELEPHONE HOUR
American television series (1959–1968)

The *Bell Telephone Hour* premiered on television in 1959, after 10 years on radio, and was an important addition to TV opera. JOAN SUTHERLAND made her U.S. debut on the program in 1961, and major singers were regular guests. They included FRANCO CORELLI, GIUSEPPE DI STEFANO, ROBERT MERRILL, ANNA MOFFO, BIRGIT NILSSON, LEONTYNE PRICE, RENATA TEBALDI, JON VICKERS, and RICHARD TUCKER. One program was devoted to the opening of the new Met with ANTONY AND CLEOPATRA, another to the Aldeburgh Festival and composer BENJAMIN BRITTEN. Other programs featured staged scenes from classic operas such as IL BARBIERE DI SIVIGLIA and FAUST, directed by TV opera specialists like ROGER ENGLANDER and KIRK BROWNING.

1947 Rehearsal
Ezio Pinza and Blanche Thebom star in this documentary about the *Bell Telephone Hour* radio show, predecessor

of the TV program. It shows the singers at a Monday afternoon rehearsal for the NBC program. Pinza sings Tosti's "L'Ultima Canzone," Thebom sings "Amour! viens aider ma faiblesse" from *Samson et Dalila*, and they join on the duet "Là ci darem la mano" from *Don Giovanni*. The film, a Peabody Award winner, ends with Pinza singing as the rehearsal fades into the formal evening performance. Donald Voorhees conducts the Bell Telephone Orchestra. Black and white. 24 minutes. Bel Canto/Video Yesteryear VHS.

1959–1966 Great Stars of Opera

Twenty opera stars who sang on the *Bell Telephone Hour* telecasts between 1959 and 1966 are shown in performance in color on DVD and VHS. The performers and opera excerpts are Franco Corelli and Régine Crespin *(Un ballo in maschera, Tosca)*, Giuseppe Di Stefano *(Manon)*, Eileen Farrell *(Tristan und Isolde)*, George London *(Boris Godunov)*, Victoria de los Angeles *(La bohème)*, Robert Merrill and Robert Peters *(The Barber of Seville)*, Anna Moffo and Nicolai Gedda *(La traviata)*, Birgit Nilsson *(Turandot, Götterdämmerung)*, Leontyne Price *(Aida, Il trovatore)*, Giulietta Simionato and Jon Vickers *(Aida)*, Risë Stevens *(Natoma)*, Joan Sutherland *(Lucia di Lammermoor)*, Renata Tebaldi *(Madama Butterfly)*, and Richard Tucker and Lucine Amara *(Pagliacci)*. Donald Voorhees conducts the Bell Telephone Hour Orchestra and Chorus. Color. The VAI and Kultur DVD (120 minutes) features the singers above, while the longer VAI VHS version (two tapes of 83 and 89 minutes) also has performances by Teresa Berganza, Phyllis Curtin, Lisa Della Casa, Regina Resnik, Teresa Stratas, and Theodor Uppman.

1961–1968 Joan Sutherland

Sutherland's 13 appearances on *The Bell Telephone Hour* from 1961 to 1968, mostly in color, are available on DVD and VHS. VHS Volume One has arias and scenes from *Crispino e la Comare, Ernani, Hamlet* (the Mad Scene in black and white), *Lakmé, Norma, I puritani,* and *Rigoletto* (the quartet with Gedda, Gobbi, and Miller). Volume Two has arias and scenes from *Lucia di Lammermoor* (the sextet with Gedda, Gobbi, Hines, Miller, and Anthony), *Otello* ("Willow Song" in black and white), *La sonnambula, Tosca,* and *La traviata*. Donald Voorhees conducts the Bell Telephone Hour Orchestra. Color. 102 minutes VAI DVD/VHS.

1967 First Ladies of the Opera

Birgit Nilsson, Leontyne Price, Joan Sutherland, and Renata Tebaldi appeared on this *Bell Telephone Hour* special January 1, 1967, singing arias and talking with Donald Voorhees, conductor of the Bell Telephone Hour Orchestra. Nilsson sings "Dich teure Halle" from *Tannhäuser* and "In questa reggia" from *Turandot*. Price sings

"Io son l'umile ancella" from *Adriana Lecouvreur* and "Pace, pace, mio Dio" from *La forza del destino*. Sutherland sings the "Bell Song" from *Lakmé* and "Io non sono più l'Annetta" from the Ricci brothers's comic opera *Crispino e la comare*. Tebaldi finishes the program with "Voi lo sapete" from *Cavalleria rusticana* and "Suicidio" from *La Gioconda*. Henry Jaffe produced; Charles R. Meeker directed. Color. 53 minutes. VAI VHS.

1968 Opera: Two to Six

Superb *Bell Telephone Hour* program of great operatic ensembles. Joan Sutherland and Tito Gobbi sing the duet from Act II of *Tosca*. Phyllis Curtin, Nicolai Gedda, and Jerome Hines join for the trio from *Faust*. Sutherland and Gobbi team with Gedda and Mildred Miller for the quartet from *Rigoletto*. Curtin, Miller, Gedda, and Hines are joined by Charles Anthony for the quintet from *Die Meistersinger*. And finally the sextet from *Lucia di Lammermoor* is sung by Sutherland, Gobbi, Miller, Gedda, Anthony, and Hines. Donald Voorhees conducts the Bell Telephone Hour Orchestra and talks to the singers. Henry Jaffe produced; Charles R. Meeker directed. Color. 52 minutes. Kultur VHS.

BELLE ET LA BÊTE, LA
1946 Cocteau film

Jean Cocteau's classic 1946 French film *La Belle et la Bête* retells the romantic fairy tale of Beauty and the Beast most beautifully and poetically. It has had a powerful effect on opera composers, make-up artists, and set designers, with at least three quasi-operas based on it. Beauty is portrayed in the film by Josette Day, with Jean Marais superbly effective as the Beast. Cocteau wrote the screenplay, cinematographer Henri Alekan created the stunning black-and-white images, and Georges Auric composed a wonderful score for the film (which has not really been bettered by the opera composers).

1982 Stage work by Bill Nelson

Bill Nelson's score for a stage adaptation of the film by the Yorkshire Actor's Company is not strictly a screen opera, although his music, plus gesture and dialogue, helps re-create the effect of the film. It was staged in 1982 after the success of a collaboration between the composer and the company on a stage version of the silent film *The Cabinet of Dr. Caligari*.

1994 Screen opera by Philip Glass

PHILIP GLASS's 1994 screen opera *Beauty and the Beast* is an attempt to literally make the movie into an opera. It was composed to be presented with four soloists singing the same words the actors recite on screen while the film is projected without sound. Whether the Glass music improves the words or the images dominate his atmospheric score is debatable, but it is certainly unusual. The 100-minute opera premiered in New York on December 8, 1994, at the Brooklyn Academy of Music with Glass leading the Philip Glass Ensemble. Alexandra Montano sang Belle and Gregory Purnhagen was the Beast.

1994 Screen opera by Mathias Ruegg
Swiss composer Mathias Ruegg created a version of the Cocteau film for his Vienna Art Orchestra. Ruegg's version does not include scenes from the movie. Instead, it features slide projections of text and shapes from several of Cocteau's films, including *La Belle et la Bête*, *Orphée*, and *The Blood of a Poet*, plus a Cocteau-like statue that comes to life. When the 80-minute opera was staged at the Huddersfield Festival on Contemporary Music in November 1994, Corin Curshellas sang Beauty and tuba player Jon Sass was the voice of the Beast.

BELLE HÉLÈNE, LA
1864 opéra-bouffe by Offenbach

La belle Hélène (Beautiful Helen) is a humorous operetta by JACQUES OFFENBACH, libretto by Henri Meilhac and Ludovic Halévy, based on the legend of Helen of Troy, the most beautiful woman in the world. It features the usual cast of Homeric Greek heroes from husband Menelaus to heroic Achilles but delights in telling how Helen rationalizes her seduction by Paris. Hortense Schneider starred in the Paris production, Lillian Russell in the New York version, Anna Moffo in a 1974 German film, and Karan Armstrong in a 1975 New York City Opera production.

1974 Unitel film
Austrian TV film: Axel von Ambesser (director), Franz Allers (conductor, Stuttgart Radio-Television Orchestra), Gerd Krauss (set designer), Unitel (production company).

Cast: Anna Moffo (Helen) René Kollo (Paris), Josef Meinrad (Menelaus), Hans Kraemmer (Agamemnon), Ivan Rebroff (Calchas), Harald Serafin (Achilles), Karin Meier (Pandora), Urda Meier (Medusa).

Telecast January 19, 1975, on ZDF German television. Shot in 35mm. Color. In German as *Die Schöne Helena*. 110 minutes.

***1999 Théâtre du Châtelet, Paris
French stage production: Laurent Pelly (director and set/costume designer), Marc Minkowski (conductor, Les Musiciens du Louvre and Grenoble Choir), Théâtre Musical de Paris (production).

Cast: Felicity Lott (Helen), Yann Beuron (Paris), Michel Sénéchal (Menelaus), Laurent Naouri (Agamemnon), François Le Roux (Calchas), Marie-Ange Dorodovitch (Orestes), Eric Huchet (Achilles).

Video: TDK DVD. Color. In French with English subtitles. 127 minutes.

Comment: Great fun! Presented as the fantasy of a bored, sex-starved Parisian housewife who dreams she is the most beautiful woman in the world. And she has a wonderful imagination.

2000 Zurich Opera
Swiss stage production: Helmut Lohner (director), Nikolaus Harnoncourt (conductor, Zurich Opera House Chorus and Orchestra), Jean-Charles de Castellbajac (set/costume designer).

Cast: Vesselina Kasarova (Helen), Deon van der Welt (Paris), Liliana Nichteanu (Orestes), Carlos Chausson, Volker Bogel, Oliver Widmer.

Video: Image Entertainment/Arthaus (GB) DVD. Harmut Schroder (director). Color. In French with English subtitles. 151 minutes.

Related film

1957 Reiniger film
Animation pioneer Lotte Reiniger made an abbreviated, animated silhouette version of the operetta in 1957. Color. In French. 12 minutes.

BELLINI, VINCENZO
Italian composer (1801–1835)

VINCENZO BELLINI is one of the big three of early 19th-century Italian opera, although he had only 10 years during which to compose his masterpieces. He was born in Catania, began his career in Naples in 1825, and became famous in 1826 when IL PIRATA premiered in Milan. His mastery of the art of *bel canto* was amply demonstrated in I CAPULETI ED I MONTECCHI, LA SONNAMBULA, BEATRICE DI TENDA, and NORMA. He died soon after I PURITANI was produced in Paris in 1835. Relatively few commercial videos of Bellini's operas are available but many are on alternative DVD and VHS, as well as several biographical films with opera scenes. He is a character in the 1943 film MARIA MALIBRAN and two films about the Ricordi publishing firm. Domenick Argento's opera THE ASPERN PAPERS features an opera composer modeled on Bellini.

1935 The Divine Spark
Romantic film about Bellini and his love for singer Maddalena Fumaroli, made in English and Italian versions by opera film specialist Carmine Gallone. A lavish production for its period, the English version stars Phillips Holmes as Bellini, Marta Eggerth as Maddalena, Benita Hume as Giuditta Pasta, and Edmond Breon as Rossini. The film tells us that Bellini was a dreamy romantic in-

spired to write the aria "Casta diva" because of his feelings for Maddalena. Black and white. In English or Italian. 81 minutes. On VHS.

1935 Casta diva
The Italian version of the above film stars Sandro Palmieri as Bellini with Marta Eggerth again in the role of Maddalena, Bruna Dragoni as Giuditta Pasta, Achille Majeroni as Rossini, and Gualtiero Tumiata as Paganini. Walter Reisch wrote the screenplay. It was named Best Italian Film at the 1935 Venice Film Festival. Black and white. In Italian. 95 minutes.

1942 La sonnambula
Bellini's love affair with a sleepwalker inspired his opera *La sonnambula.* Anyway that's what this film claims, and the music is certainly by Bellini. It's loosely based on the relationship between Bellini and Giuditta Turina, the most famous of his many lovers, and is set at Lake Como where the composer recovered from an illness in 1830, the year before the premiere of the opera. Roberto Villa plays Bellini, Germana Paolieri is Giuditta Turina, and Anita Farra is Giuditta Pasta, the singer who created Amina on stage. Piero Ballerini directed. Black and white. In Italian. 88 minutes.

1954 Casta diva
Carmine Gallone's Technicolor remake of his 1935 Bellini biography. This version stars Maurice Ronet as Bellini, with Antonella Lualdi as Maddalena Fumaroli, Nadia Gray as Giuditta Pasta, and Fausto Tozzi as Donizetti. The plot is more or less the same, with Maddalena again inspiring Bellini to write "Casta diva" so *Norma* can be a success. There are extracts from *Norma, Il pirata,* and *La sonnambula* as well as Donizetti's *Lucia di Lammermoor.* The singers are Cesare Formichi, Caterina Mancini, Giulio Neri, and Gianni Poggi; the music is performed by the Rome Opera Chorus and Orchestra led by Oliviero De Fabritiis. France/Italy. Color. In Italian, French, or English. 98 minutes. Bel Canto Society VHS (in English).

1954 Casa Ricordi
Bellini (Maurice Ronet) dies as *I puritani* is being premiered in this grand Hollywood-on-the-Tiber Italian opera film, the romanticized story of the publishing house with an all-star cast of Italian singers. See RICORDI.

1955 Un palco all'opera
Enrico De Melis plays Bellini in this Italian film that has a section devoted to his relationship with Maria Malibran (Liliana Gerace). Siro Marcellini directed. Color. In Italian. 98 minutes.

1995 La famiglia Ricordi
Kim Rossi Stuart plays Bellini in Mauro Bolognini's four-part TV film *The Ricordi Family,* which traces the history of the publishing firm and Italian opera from 1808. See RICORDI.

BELSHAZZAR
1745 oratorio by Handel

GEORGE FRIDERIC HANDEL's oratorio *Belshazzar,* composed to an English libretto by Charles Jennes, is sometimes staged by opera companies. It tells the story of King Belshazzar of biblical and Babylonian fame. Handel was very taken with the story of the great king and composed a fine aria for Belshazzar's mother, Nitocris, describing the tragic fate of empires. The famous writing on the wall is interpreted by Daniel just before the Persians triumph.

1985 Hamburg State Opera
German stage production: Harry Kupfer (director), Gerd Albrecht (conductor, Hamburg Philharmonic State Orchestra and State Opera Chorus), Wolfgang Gussmann (set designer).

Cast: Walter Raffeiner (Belshazzar), Helen Donath (Nitocris), Jeanne Piland (Cyrus), Jochen Kowalski (Daniel), Harald Stamm (Gobrias).

Video: Goethe Institute Inter Nationes VHS. Telecast on NDR German television. Günther Bock (director). Color. In English. 139 minutes.

BENATZKY, RALPH
Moravian composer (1884–1957)

Ralph Benatzky is remembered today for his spectacular operetta IM WEISSEN RÖSSL (White Horse Inn) and his Strauss pastiche operetta *Casanova* with its famous "Nun's Chorus." He was a popular songwriter in Vienna in the 1910s, but his greatest success came later in Berlin with the lavish *White Horse Inn.* He also composed a famous Vienna stage musical about Hollywood called *Axel an der Himmelstür* with Zarah Leander as star. Benatzky was very prolific; he is said to have created 5,000 songs, 250 film scores, and 92 stage shows.

BENEDICT, JULIUS
German/English composer (1804–1885)

Sir Julius Benedict, a student of Weber and friend of Maria Malibran, was an opera composer and conductor in Austria and Italy before going to England, where he found his greatest fame. He was involved with all the big three "Irish" operas popular in 19th-century Britain. He produced Michael Balfe's THE BOHEMIAN GIRL and Vincent Wallace's MARITANA at Drury Lane and won wide popularity with his own opera THE LILY OF KILLARNEY. He was also associated with Jenny Lind, acting as her conductor and accompanist.

BENJAMIN, ARTHUR
Australian composer (1893–1960)

Australian Arthur Benjamin has an important place in screen opera history as the first composer to create an opera for BBC Television. He was apparently chosen to write the 1956 Latin American–oriented MAÑANA because he had had success with a prize-winning opera on BBC radio and with the piano composition *Jamaican Rumba*. His first opera, the one-act comedy *The Devil Take Her*, was staged in London in 1931 with Sir Thomas Beecham conducting; it was revived and telecast in Australia in 1962. His second opera, the Italian-style comedy *Prima Donna*, was composed in 1933 but not staged until 1949; it has now been televised in England, Canada, and Australia. His major opera is A TALE OF TWO CITIES, a full-length adaptation of the Dickens novel. It was one of the four winners in the 1951 Festival of Britain Opera Competition, premiered on BBC radio's Third Program in 1953, was staged at Sadler's Wells in 1957, and adapted for television and telecast by the BBC in 1958.

BENVENUTO CELLINI
1838 opera by Berlioz

It's Shrove Tuesday in Rome in 1532. Benvenuto Cellini has been commissioned to create a statue of Perseus but plans instead to elope with Teresa, daughter of the Papal treasurer. His plans are thwarted by rival sculptor Fieramosca and the Pope, who comes to his studio to demand the statue by midnight—or else. Hector Berlioz's opera *Benvenuto Cellini*, libretto by Léon de Wailly and August Barbier, is based on the imaginative autobiography of the Florentine artist.

1987 Teatro Communale, Florence
Italian stage production: Elijah Moshinsky (director), Vladimir Fedoseyev (conductor, Orchestra and Chorus of the Maggio Musicale Fiorentino).
Cast: Chris Merritt (Cellini), Cecilia Gasdia (Teresa), Victor Braun (Fieramosca), Jules Bastin (Balducci), Elena Zilio (Ascanio), Agostino Ferrin (Cardinal).
Video: House of Opera DVD and VHS/Lyric VHS. Telecast by RAI. Color. In French. 165 minutes.

BERESFORD, BRUCE
Australian film director (1940–)

Australian director Bruce Beresford, known for such memorable movies as *The Getting of Wisdom* and *Tender Mercies,* has also become a stage director of opera. Two of his films have operatic content. His episode of the 1987 opera film ARIA is a romantic homage to Korngold's DIE TOTE STADT. His Oscar-winning 1989 film *Driving Miss Daisy* features an aria from Dvořák's RUSALKA.

BERG, ALBAN
Austrian composer (1885–1935)

Alban Berg is known for only two operas, WOZZECK and LULU, both derived from works by major writers. Berg's operas have become staples of the international repertory, and his reputation continues to grow. They are strangely popular despite their pessimism and their musical difficulty, perhaps because of the strong emotions he explores and his unique style. He apparently composed slowly and painfully, but he infused his operas with enormous feeling.

1992 The Secret Life of Alban Berg
Soprano Kristine Ciesinski sings selections from *Lulu* and *Wozzeck* while traveling around Europe and America exploring Berg's secret inner life. Norman Bailey plays Dr. Schön and the Animal Tamer in the *Lulu* excerpt, and Edgar Howard conducts the BBC Symphony Orchestra. Color. In English. 50 minutes. Films for the Humanities & Sciences VHS.

BERGANZA, TERESA
Spanish mezzo-soprano (1934–)

Teresa Berganza was born in Madrid and made her debut in France in 1957 in *Così fan tutte*. Her rich, warm voice helped her became one of the most admired singers of her generation, particularly admired in Rossini operas and in *Carmen*. In the 1980s, she appeared mostly in recitals. Berganza's great voice and personality are featured in two major opera films: in Losey's 1978 DON GIOVANNI, she plays Zerlina; in Ponnelle's 1972 IL BARBIERE DI SIVIGLIA, she sings Rosina. See IL BARBIERE DI SIVIGLIA (1984), BELL TELEPHONE HOUR (1959–1966), CARMEN (1980), L'ITALIANA IN ALGERI (1957), PARIS (1989), and SEVILLE (1991).

BERGER, ERNA
German soprano (1900–1990)

Erna Berger made her debut at the Dresden Staatsoper in 1925 in *Die Zauberflöte* as First Boy and later became one of the world's most famous interpreters of the Queen of the Night. She can be seen in the role in a 1942 film about MOZART and singing a duet from *La traviata* with Beniamino Gigli in the 1936 film AVE MARIA. Berger sang at Salzburg from the 1930s to the 1950s and sings Zerlina in the classic 1954 film of DON GIOVANNI. She made her first appearance at the Met in 1949 as Sophie in DER ROSENKAVALIER. See CONDUCTORS (1993), DIE LUSTIGEN WEIBER VON WINDSOR (1940 film), and LE NOZZE DI FIGARO (1949/1959 film).

BERGMAN, INGMAR
Swedish film director (1918–)

Swedish filmmaker Ingmar Bergman has filmed two operas, featured opera in his fiction films, directed opera on stage, and written an opera libretto. His 1973 film *Tröll-flojten* (Swedish for DIE ZAUBERFLÖTE) is one of the great opera films and a fine introduction to the Drottningholm Opera House. His love of Mozart is shown in three other movies. In the 1952 *Face to Face*, the score is based on Mozart themes. In the 1960 *The Devil's Eye*, he gives his version of the Don Giovanni legend. In the 1967 *Hour of the Wolf*, a tiny Tamino performs an aria from *Die Zauberflöte* on a miniature stage. Bergman wrote the libretto for Daniel Börtz's opera THE BACCHAE, which he staged and then directed for television.

Börtz, Bergman and the Bacchae
Swedish documentary about the production of the Daniel Börtz opera *The Bacchae*, written at the instigation of Bergman. It shows Börtz and Bergman in rehearsal and has interviews with others involved in the production at the Stockholm Royal Opera. Mans Reuterswärd directed the documentary. Color. In Swedish. 57 minutes. Video at the MTR.

BERGONZI, CARLO
Italian tenor (1924–)

The golden-voiced Italian tenor Carlo Bergonzi made his debut in 1948, sang at La Scala from 1953 to 1970, and was a regular at the Met from 1956 to 1988. He recorded more than 40 roles, mostly Verdi, and some consider him the heir of Gigli in singing style and voice quality. Bergonzi's voice is featured on the soundtrack of the film MOONSTRUCK and in the *Un ballo in maschera* episode of ARIA. He now lives in Verdi's hometown of Busetto, where he helped select the singers for a fine commemorative production of *Aida* in 2001; he can be seen in that

opera himself in a 1966 Arena di Verona video. See AIDA (1966/1987 film), UN BALLO IN MASCHERA (1967), BOLSHOI OPERA (1989), L'ELISIR D'AMORE (1989), GIACOMO LAURI-VOLPI (1983), JAMES LEVINE (1996), LUCIA DI LAMMERMOOR (1967/1986 film), LUISA MILLER (1986), OPERA IMAGINAIRE (1993), TENORS (1990/1997), and ARTURO TOSCANINI (1988).

1985 Bergonzi Celebrates Gigli
In October 1985, Bergonzi gave a recital at Carnegie Hall celebrating the art of Beniamino Gigli by performing 19 songs and arias that Gigli made popular. The recital was later videotaped in a studio before an invited audience. Bergonzi is accompanied on piano by Vincenzo Scalera, with George Jellinek as host. The recital won warm praise from *The New York Times*, which noted the continuing quality of Bergonzi's singing. The video includes a pictorial essay by Jellinek comparing the careers of Bergonzi and Gigli. Color. 87 minutes. V&E VHS.

1989 Legends of Opera
Bergonzi as Nemorino sings two arias on stage in a dress rehearsal of *L'elisir d'amore* in a small New Jersey theater. He was 65 at the time and still sounds pretty good. The arias, "Quanto è bella" and "Un furtiva lagrima," are on the video *Legends of Opera*. Color. In Italian. 8 minutes. Legato Classics VHS.

BERKELEY, MICHAEL
English composer (1948–)

Michael Berkeley has composed two operas to librettos by Australian novelist David Malouf. BAA BAA BLACK SHEEP, based on Kipling stories, was warmly received when it was premiered by Opera North at the Cheltenham Festival in 1993, recorded, and telecast. The other collaboration was the chamber opera *Jane Eyre*, based on the Charlotte Brontë novel. Berkeley, who was born in London and studied at the Royal Academy, has also composed an oratorio with a radical message, *Or Shall We Die?*

BERLIN

Berlin is home to three notable opera houses. Most famous is the Staatsoper Unter den Linden, formerly in East Berlin, which began life as the Lindenoper in 1742. The present building dates from 1955. Near it is the Komische Oper, which opened in 1966 and usually presents comic operas. Biggest is the Deutsche Oper, which dates from 1961. All three are fine places to see quality opera in person or on video. See BARBE-BLEUE (1973), THE CUNNING LITTLE VIXEN (1965), FIDELIO (1970), GIULIO CESARE (1977), LES HUGUENOTS (1990), DER JUNGE

LORD (1968), MACBETH (1987), OTELLO (1969), PARSIFAL (1993), SALOME (1990), DIE TOTE STADT (1986), and TRISTAN UND ISOLDE (1993).

1976 Gala Unter den Linden
East German film celebrating the Staatsoper Unter den Linden opera house records a gala evening featuring major stars performing arias identified with them. The singers are Theo Adam, Eberhard Büchner, Celestina Casapietra, Renate Hoff, Fritz Hubner, Isabella Nawe, Harald Neukirch, Ruggiero Orofino, Martin Ritzmann, Peter Schreier, Gisela Schröter, Ingeborg Springer, Reiner Suss, Anna Tomowa-Sintow, Uta Trekel-Burkhardt, and Siegfried Vogel. DEFA. Color. In German. 90 minutes.

1989 Berlin: capitale de l'opéra
Claire Newman directed *Berlin: Opera Capital*, a French TV documentary focusing on Berlin's reputation for innovative opera production. It includes footage of Harry Kupfer rehearsing a production of *Les contes d'Hoffmann* in Berlin. Made by France 3. Paris. Color. In French. 60 minutes.

1990 The German Center: Kroll
Story of a famous but now-vanished opera house, the Kroll Opera in Berlin, which opened in 1844 on the Platz der Republik, the "German Center." Caruso was among those who sang there, Johann Strauss was house conductor for two years, and Otto Klemperer began his conducting career there in 1927. It was closed in 1931 and torn down in 1951. Jörg Moser-Metius wrote and directed the film. Color. In English or German. 58 minutes. Goethe Institute Inter Nationes VHS.

BERLIOZ, HECTOR
French composer (1803–1869)

Berlioz wrote five operas, but he did not have much luck with them during his lifetime. His first surviving opera, the 1838 BENVENUTO CELLINI, was a failure when it premiered, and he had problems getting later operas on stage in any form. In recent years, LES TROYENS and LA DAMNATION DE FAUST have been successfully staged and are now on commercial videos. BEÁTRICE ET BÉNÉDICT and *Benvenuto Cellini* have both been telecast and are on alternative videos. Berlioz's desperate life has also inspired screen biographies. The popular conception of Berlioz is reflected in Claude Chabrol's thriller *Un Double Tour*, in which a murderer likes to conduct work by Berlioz.

1941 La symphonie fantastique
Jean-Louis Barrault plays Berlioz in this romantic French film about his life and love affairs. Renée Saint-Cyr is singer Marie Martin, who dies while singing one of his arias, and Lise Delamare is his actress-wife Harriet Smithson. The music is played by the Conservatory Orchestra of Paris conducted by Marius-Paul Guillot. Christian-Jaque directed. Black and white. In French. 95 minutes.

1992 I, Berlioz
Tony Palmer's powerful film biography, starring Corin Redgrave as the composer, concentrates on the opera *Les Troyens* and the difficulties Berlioz had in creating and staging it. The film includes three sizable extracts from the opera, performed by Zurich Opera, with Ludmilla Schemtschuk as Dido, Giorgio Lamberti as Aeneas, Agnes Habereder as Cassandra, and Vesselina Kasarova as Anna. Ralf Weikert conducts the Zurich Opera Orchestra and Chorus. Filmed for *The South Bank Show*. Color. In English. 90 minutes.

BERNSTEIN, LEONARD
American composer (1918–1990)

Leonard Bernstein, like George Gershwin, wrote music that appealed to both popular and classical music lovers. TROUBLE IN TAHITI and its sequel, A QUIET PLACE, are close to being traditional operas, but opera companies have also staged the operatic operetta CANDIDE, the operatic musical WEST SIDE STORY, and the operatic MASS. Bernstein considered them so close to opera he recorded them with opera singers along with his musical ON THE TOWN. Other important stage works are also beginning to enter the opera repertory, including the joyful 1953 musical *Wonderful Town* and the political musical *1600 Pennsylvania Avenue*. Bernstein was also, of course, one of the major conductors of his time, principal conductor of the New York Philharmonic Orchestra for 10 years and a conductor of operas at the Met and La Scala. He conducted the first performance of Marc Blitzstein's adaptation of *The Threepenny Opera* in 1952, the premiere of *Candide* in 1956, and the premiere of Lukas Foss's *Introductions and Goodbyes* in 1960. He was a remarkable educator, able to explain musical ideas with great clarity, and he had a major television career, beginning with *Omnibus* in 1954; there are more than 250 Bernstein TV programs at the Museum of Television and Radio. Selected programs only are listed below. See BEETHOVEN (1971/1981), CONDUCTORS (1995), PAUL HINDEMITH, (1964), and DIE SCHÖPFUNG (1986).

1949–1969 Hollywood films
Bernstein's earliest connection with Hollywood movies was through the screen adaptation of *On the Town* in

1949. He was nominated for an Oscar for his score for *On the Waterfront* (1954) and appears in *Satchmo the Great* (1957) and *A Journey to Jerusalem* (1969).

1954–1958 Omnibus TV
Bernstein won his first Emmy Award in 1957 for his *Omnibus* TV programs, which were telecast from 1954 to 1958. In the March 23, 1958, program "What Makes Opera Grand?" Bernstein examined facets of opera, with excerpts from *Carmen, Faust, Tristan und Isolde*, and *La bohème*. Videos at the MTR.

1958 Wonderful Town
Bernstein's 1953 musical *Wonderful Town,* created with lyric writers Betty Comden and Adolph Green, was based on the 1940 play *My Sister Eileen.* It tells the romantic story of two sisters and their adventures in Greenwich Village and has entered the repertory of some opera houses. It was never filmed, but a TV adaptation was made in 1958 with Rosalind Russell, Sidney Chaplin, Jacquelyn McKeever, and Joseph Buloff. Mel Ferber directed. Black and white. 120 minutes. Video at the MTR.

1958–1973 Young People's Concerts
Bernstein telecast these programs on CBS from 1958 to 1973 with the New York Philharmonic. He was an enthusiastic teacher, and he explains many forms of music, including opera, on these award-winning programs. He also talks about composers from Beethoven to Charles Ives. Roger Englander produced and directed the telecasts. Bernstein Society/Sony VHS.

1973 The Unanswered Question
Six-part musical lecture series in which Bernstein examines music using Noam Chomsky's ideas as a springboard as he conducts the Boston Symphony and Vienna Philharmonic. The series originated as the Charles Eliot Norton Lectures at Harvard in 1973 and was telecast in 1976. Humphrey Burton was producer. Color. 15 hours. Kultur DVD/VHS.

1974–1989 Great Performances
Bernstein conducted many concerts and recitals for the *Great Performances* TV series on PBS. They range from Tanglewood to Vienna and from Mahler to Brahms. Humphrey Burton directed most of them. Videos at the MTR.

1988 Leonard Bernstein at 70
Emmy Award–winning record of Bernstein's birthday gala, directed by Kirk Browning. The performers include Barbara Hendricks, Christa Ludwig, Kurt Ollmann, Beverly Sills, Michael Tilson Thomas, Dawn Upshaw, Frederica von Stade, John Williams, and the Boston Symphony Orchestra. Color. 126 minutes.

1993 The Gift of Music
Ambitious documentary attempting to tell the story of Bernstein's musical life. There are scenes of Bernstein at the 1947 Prague Festival and on *Person to Person* in 1955, performance extracts, extracts from operas and musicals, archival film footage, and comments from friends. Lauren Bacall narrates; Horant Hohlfeld directed for LWT. Color. 90 minutes. DG VHS.

1993 Leonard Bernstein's Place
A 75th birthday salute to Bernstein at Alice Tully Hall in Lincoln Center. Family members and friends remember him, including Lauren Bacall, Isaac Stern, Wynton Marsalis, and Phyllis Newman. Color. 87 minutes.

1994 Bernstein on Broadway
Highlights video with excerpts from three of Bernstein's Broadway productions recorded by opera singers. Featured are *On the Town* with Tyne Daly, Frederica von Stade, Thomas Hampson, and Samuel Ramey; *Candide* with Jerry Hadley, June Anderson, Christa Ludwig, Kurt Ollmann, and Adolph Green; and *West Side Story* with Kiri Te Kanawa, José Carreras, and Tatiana Troyanos. Color. 90 minutes. On DVD and VHS.

1997 Leonard Bernstein's New York
Exploration of New York elements in Bernstein's work, focusing on the three musicals set in the city, *On the Town, Wonderful Town,* and *West Side Story.* Performers include Dawn Upshaw, Audra McDonald, Mandy Patinkin, Judy Blazer, Richard Muenz, and Donna Murphy. Eric Stern conducts the Orchestra of St. Luke's; Hart Perry directed. Color. In English. 55 minutes. Warner Vision/NVC Arts (GB) VHS.

1998 Leonard Bernstein: Reaching for the Note
Susan Lacy's documentary for the American Masters series explores Bernstein's life and music from 1943 to the end of his career. It includes interviews with collaborators and family and scenes from *Candide, Trouble in Tahiti, A Quiet Place,* and *Mass.* The DVD also includes a discography. Telecast by PBS October 10, 1998. Color. 90 minutes. Winstar DVD/DG VHS.

BERTOLUCCI, BERNARDO
Italian film director (1940–)

Bernardo Bertolucci, the Oscar-winning director of *The Last Emperor* and *Last Tango in Paris,* has been described as having an "operatic sensibility." The Parma-born director admits to strong influences from Verdi, and certainly three of his films have overt opera content. LA LUNA (1978) focuses on an American opera singer in Italy and her operatic tour. *The Spider's Stratagem* (1970) revolves around a plot to kill Mussolini during a performance of RIGOLETTO. *Novecento* is an epic film about Italy and the influence of Verdi.

1976 Novecento (1900)

Novecento (1900) is an epic film about Italy but also an homage to Giuseppe Verdi. The two boys who are the protagonists of the film are born on January 27, 1901, the day on which Verdi died. Twentieth-century Italian history is surveyed across their families, who live in Verdi's Emilia-Romagna region. There is Verdi music on the soundtrack and even a hunchback clown called Rigoletto. Robert De Niro and Gérard Depardieu star. Color. In Italian. 320 minutes. On VHS.

BEST FILMS ABOUT OPERA

There are a surprising number of excellent feature films about opera and operas singers going back to the silent era. Here are some subjective assessments.

The **most popular** is THE GREAT CARUSO, which stars Mario Lanza as the legendary tenor; several singers say they turned to opera because of this film. The opera establishment never loved it, but the public adored it.

The **best biography** is Milos Forman's AMADEUS, which brings Mozart and his time truly alive. Also of real worth is INTERRUPTED MELODY, the sleek story of the courageous soprano Marjorie Lawrence.

The **funniest** opera film is undoubtedly A NIGHT AT THE OPERA in which the Marx Brothers send up operatic extravagance with mad enjoyment and turn *Il trovatore* into a near farce. Nearly as funny is René Clair's French film LE MILLION, which preceded and influenced it.

The **most powerful** opera film is FITZCARRALDO, Werner Herzog's extraordinary tale about a fanatic Caruso fan who tries to build an opera house in the middle of the Amazon jungle.

The **most exotic** is FARINELLI with its amazing portrayals of the era of the castratos in opera. The sound of the created voice is incredible.

The **most surrealistic** is E LA NAVE VA, Federico Fellini's amazing tale about a boat full of opera singers on their way to an operatic funeral, which turns out to be their own.

The **best portrayal of the difficulties (and joys) of staging an opera** is MEETING VENUS, in which everything that can go wrong does and yet opening night still takes places.

The **most romantic film with opera content** is MOONSTRUCK in which *La bohème* helps mismatched lovers find unexpected happiness.

The **most famous opera horror film** is THE PHANTOM OF THE OPERA, which has been filmed a number of times but is at its operatic best in the 1943 version with Nelson Eddy.

The **best silent film with opera content** is the original 1925 version of THE PHANTOM OF THE OPERA, with Lon Chaney creating one of cinema's most memorable monsters.

The **most horrific** is TERROR AT THE OPERA by Dario Argento, based around a truly unlucky production of Verdi's *Macbeth*.

The **most bizarre** is certainly FOLLOW YOUR HEART, a down-home opera film for the horse opera folks with the *Lucia* sextet as a comedy number sung to hams and haddocks.

The **best mystery** opera film is the clever B-picture CHARLIE CHAN AT THE OPERA, with Boris Karloff as the baritone of your worst nightmares. The French film DIVA is also full of clever thrills and good singing.

The **best animated films** are WHAT'S OPERA, DOC? (Bugs Bunny meets Wagner) and THE WHALE WHO WANTED TO SING AT THE MET (Nelson Eddy gets to sing at the Met in three voices).

The **best non-opera film with operatic content** is Orson Welles's CITIZEN KANE, which features one of the most famous opera scenes in the movies: Mrs. Kane trying and failing to sing a difficult aria created by Bernard Herrmann.

BEST OPERA ON FILM

The best operas on film are usually operas made by major filmmakers. The consensus best film and probably the most popular is Francesco Rosi's 1984 CARMEN, though Ingmar Bergman's 1974 *The Magic Flute* (DIE ZAUBERFLÖTE) has a lot of admirers. Patrick J. Smith voted for these two as the best opera films when he was editor of *Opera News*.

There are others who like Franco Zeffirelli's 1982 LA TRAVIATA, Joseph Losey's 1978 DON GIOVANNI, Max Ophuls's 1932 THE BARTERED BRIDE, Gianfranco De Bosio's 1976 TOSCA, and Michael Powell and Emeric Pressburger's 1951 *The Tales of Hoffmann* (LES CONTES D'HOFFMANN).

Julie Taymor's stunning 1992 film of her production of Stravinsky's OEDIPUS REX is also a strong contender, as are Jean-Pierre Ponnelle's films, including his 1974 MADAMA BUTTERFLY, 1978 L'ORFEO, and 1981 LA CENERENTOLA.

The best silent opera film is the 1915 CARMEN, in which Geraldine Farrar shows why she was a great star in both opera and cinema.

Finally, there is "best film" support for a less well-known movie, described by the British film journal *Sight & Sound* as "an almost forgotten picture with some claim to being the most successful filmed opera." This is Gian Carlo Menotti's 1951 THE MEDIUM, the only modern stage opera filmed by its composer. It is as effective today as it was when it was made. It may not be the best opera per se, but *Opera News* called it "the most cinematic opera on film."

BEST OPERA ON VIDEO

The best operas shot on videotape rather than film are records of live performances at major opera houses. The quality of the work by the masters of video techniques such as Brian Large and Kirk Browning is such that it often enhances the stage performances. Since the advent of DVD and the huge improvement in sound and picture, video directors are starting to be recognized for their artistry.

"Best" in this context, however, usually depends on the stage production itself and the quality of the singers involved. Nearly every production shot live at, for instance, the Metropolitan, San Francisco, Covent Garden, Glyndebourne, La Scala, or Salzburg, is finely made and worth watching.

Videos that have been strongly admired by critics include the Met's FRANCESCA DA RIMINI and THE GHOSTS OF VERSAILLES, Glyndebourne's ALBERT HERRING and DEATH IN VENICE, English National Opera's MARY STUART and PETER GRIMES, La Scala's LA FANCIULLA DEL WEST, Kirov's THE FIERY ANGEL, Bolshoi's THE QUEEN OF SPADES, Bayreuth's DIE WALKÜRE (1980), Bavarian Opera's DIE ZAUBERFLÖTE, and San Francisco's TURANDOT.

One of the best recent opera videos is the 1993 Australian Opera production of LA BOHÈME staged by Baz Luhrmann. It was so impressive that he ended up staging it on Broadway.

The best series of opera videos may be the eight Mozart operas taped at the DROTTNINGHOLM COURT THEATRE by Thomas Olofsson for Swedish TV with Arnold Östman conducting relatively unknown singers. They are presented with 18th-century sets, and the orchestra dresses in period costume and plays period instruments. All eight are a pleasure to watch and listen to and are probably close to what Mozart experienced.

BEST OPERETTA ON FILM

Operettas have not been well treated by the cinema, possibly because they have been out of fashion for 70 years. Most of the operetta films were made during the 1930s, and often much of the original music was abandoned in the filming.

The most popular operettas on film in America have been the Jeanette MacDonald/Nelson Eddy pictures for MGM, which are enjoyable but treat their source material with little respect. MAYTIME, which is the best, is probably furthest from its stage original.

The best French film is Straus's TROIS VALSES filmed by Ludwig Berger in 1938 with its stage star Yvonne Printemps. The best English film is the 1939 THE MIKADO directed by Victor Schertzinger, which features stars of the D'Oyly Carte Opera Company.

The best German film operetta is probably Werner Heymann's CONGRESS DANCES directed by Erik Charell, but it did not originate on stage. The most impressive German film of a stage operetta is a 1975 version of Strauss's DIE ZIGEUNERBARON with a starry cast headed by Wagnerian tenor Siegfried Jerusalem.

The best operetta film of all, however, may be the 1934 U.S. movie *The Merry Widow* (DIE LUSTIGE WITWE). It was directed by the masterful Ernst Lubitsch and stars Maurice Chevalier and Jeanette MacDonald, with English lyrics by Lorenz Hart. It's a film liked even by those who dislike operettas.

BEST OPERETTA ON VIDEO

There is not a wide choice in this area on commercial video, as few operettas have been videotaped live in America in recent years. On the other hand, many excellent productions have appeared on European television, and quite a few are available on alternative videos and from European companies.

One of the best U.S. videos is the 1955 TV production of Herbert's NAUGHTY MARIETTA with Patrice Munsel and Alfred Drake; it was directed by Max Liebman, who did a good job of making the operetta into a fine screen experience.

The most televised operetta is Strauss's DIE FLEDERMAUS, and several good video versions are available featuring top singers. Most impressive is the 1983 Covent Garden production with Kiri Te Kanawa as Rosalinde and Hermann Prey as Eisenstein in a video by Humphrey Burton.

BETROTHAL IN A MONASTERY
1946 opera by Prokofiev

Richard Brinsley Sheridan's farcical English play *The Duenna* (1775) was the basis of Sergei Prokofiev's romantic *opera buffa*–style *Betrothal in a Monastery*. The libretto, by Mira Mendelson and Prokofiev, features a complicated scheme that finally results in the right people getting married to each other in an 18th-century Seville monastery. Don Jerome wants to marry daughter Luisa to rich Mendoza, but she wants to marry Antonio. Her duenna decides to nab the rich man for herself. The romanticism is probably heart-felt; Prokofiev left his wife for the young librettist.

1997 Kirov Opera

Russian stage production: Vladislav Pasi (director), Valery Gergiev (conductor, Kirov Opera Orchestra and Chorus), Alla Koyenkova (set designer).

Cast: Nikolai Gassiev (Don Jerome), Anna Netrebko (Luisa), Larissa Diadkova (Duenna), Marianna Tarasova (Clara), Sergei Aleksashkin (Mendoza), Yevgeny Akimov.

Video: Philips VHS. Taped by NHK Tokyo and EuroArts Entertainment. Aarno Cronvall (director). Color. In Russian. 156 minutes.

Comment: The same cast is on CD.

BETTELSTUDENT, DER
1882 operetta by Millöcker

KARL MILLÖCKER, once as popular for his operettas as Johann Strauss, had his greatest success with *Der Bettelstudent* (The Beggar Student), a combination of romance and revolutionary politics. Librettists F. Zell and Richard Genée set the story in Cracow in Poland in 1704, when Poland was occupied by Saxony. Saxon governor Colonel Ollendorf, who had been slapped by Countess Nowalska's daughter Laura for being fresh, takes his revenge by tricking her into marrying Symon, a poor student he has freed from prison and disguised as a rich count. The two fall in love, as do Laura's sister Bronislawa and Symon's friend Jan. All ends happily when Polish rule is reestablished and Symon is made a real count for his patriotic heroism. The operetta has been popular all over the world, including a 1945 Athens production starring Maria Callas as Laura. There are many film versions, and it has been telecast in Germany several times.

1931 Aafa film

German feature film: Viktor Janson (director), Hans Zerlett (screenplay), Guido Seebar (cinematographer), Felix Günther (music director), Aafa Film (production company).

Cast: Jarmila Novotná (Tania), Hans Heinz Bollmann (Carl), Paul Westermeier (Ollendorf), Hansl Arnstaedt (Countess), Fritz Schulz, Hans Juray, Truus van Aalten.

Black and white. In German. 64 minutes.

Comment: The first European sound film of an operetta, shot in German and English with different casts. The plot is modernized, with the Countess urging her daughter to marry Ollendorf and, after a masked ball, deciding to marry him herself.

1931 Amalgamated film

English feature film: John Harvel and Victor Hansbury (directors), John Stafford and Hans Zerlett (screenplay), Amalgamated Film (production).

Cast: Shirley Dale (Tania), Lance Fairfax (Carl), Margaret Halstan (Countess), Frederick Lloyd (Ollendorf), Jerry Verno (Jan).

Black and white. In English. 64 minutes.

Comment: This English film, titled *The Beggar Student,* was shot at the same time and has the same plot as its German counterpart above. It opened theatrically in New York in 1933.

1936 UFA film

German feature film: Georg Jacoby (director), Walter Wasserman and C. H. Diller (screenplay), Karl Vass and Georg Bruckbauer (cinematographers), Alois Melchior (music director), UFA (production).

Cast: Carola Höhn (Laura), Johannes Heesters (Simon), Marika Rökk (Bronislawa), Bernhold Ebbecke (Jan), Ida Wüst (Countess), Fritz Kampers (Ollendorf).

Video: BMG (Germany) VHS in the series *Die großen UFA Klassiker.* Black and white. In German. 89 minutes.

Comment: Best of the early German versions, it was shown theatrically in the United States and helped make Rökk a movie star.

1956 Carlton film

West German feature film: Werner Jacobs (director), Fritz Boetiger (screenplay), Carlton Film (production company).

Cast: Waltraud Haas (Laura), Gerhard Riedmann (Simon), Gustav Knuth (Ollendorf), Elma Karlowa (Countess).

Color. In German. 95 minutes.

1957 DEFA film

East German feature film: Hans Müller (director), A. Arthur Kuhnert (screenplay), DEFA (production company).

Cast: Bert Fortell, Albert Garbe, Eberhard Krug.

Color. In German. 87 minutes.

Comment: Shot in East Berlin and released with the odd title of *Mazurka der Liebe.*

1977 Seregi film

Hungarian TV film: Laszlo Seregi (director), Herbert Magg (conductor, Hungarian Television Orchestra and Chorus).

Cast: Harvath Tivadar (Ollendorf), Marika Németh (Countess), Zsuzsa Domonkos (Laura), József Kovács (Simon), Maria Sempléni (Bronislawa), József Virágh (Jan).

Video: European Video Distributors VHS. Color. In Hungarian with English subtitles. 90 minutes.

Comment: The singing is reasonable, the costumes colorful, the acting adequate, and the style only a little kitschy. The Hungarian title is *Koldusdiák*.

1986 Gärtnerplatz Theater, Munich

German stage production: Roland Velte (director), Tristant Schick (conductor, Gärtnerplatz Theater Orchestra), Jörg Zimmermann (set designer).

Cast: Jo Ella Todd (Laura), Kurt Schreibmayer (Simon), Marita Dummers (Countess), Lambert Hamel (Ollendorf), Eva-Christine Reimer (Bronislawa).

Video. House of Opera VHS. Telecast in Germany May 8, 1986. Karlheinz Hundorf (director). Color. In German. 125 minutes.

Early/related films

1908 Messter film

Henny Porten, Germany's first film star, and her father Franz star in a Messter sound film directed by Franz featuring an aria sung by Ollendorf. Black and white. In German. About 4 minutes. Print survives in German archive.

1922 Steinhoff film

Feature version of the operetta made in Germany in 1922 and directed by Hans Steinhoff. Black and white. Silent About 70 minutes.

1927 Fleck film

Harry Liedtke and Hans Junkermann, popular German actors of the silent era, star in this feature film of the operetta. Jacob and Luise Fleck produced and directed. Black and white. Silent. About 70 minutes.

1962 Musikalisches Rendezvous

This anthology of DEFA opera films made in East Berlin includes highlights from Hans Müller's 1957 film of the operetta. Color. In German. 83 minutes.

BETTONI, VINCENZO
Italian bass (1881–1954)

Vincenzo Bettoni made his opera debut in 1902 and began his long career at Teatro alla Scala in 1905. He was a popular partner for Conchita Supervia in Rossini operas in the 1920s and sang Don Alfonso in *Così fan tutte* in the first Glyndebourne season. He continued to sing until 1950 and can be seen in comic form in two films in the 1930s featuring Pergolesi's LA SERVA PADRONA.

BEZANSON, PHILIP
American composer (1916–1975)

Philip Bezanson, who taught music at Iowa University and Amherst, is known primarily as a composer of choral and chamber music, but he also wrote two operas, *Western Child* and *Stranger in Eden*. *Western Child* was first performed at the State University of Iowa in 1959 and then revised and presented on NBC Television as the television opera GOLDEN CHILD.

BIBALO, ANTONIO
Italian-born Norwegian composer (1922–)

Antonio Bibalo has composed a number of notable operas based on literary works, including adaptations of Tennessee Williams's THE GLASS MENAGERIE, Ibsen's *Ghosts*, Shakespeare's *Macbeth*, and Strindberg's *Miss Julie*. After studies in Trieste, where he was born, and then London, he moved to Norway in 1957. His international breakthrough came in 1965 with the Hamburg State Opera production of *The Smile at the Foot of the Ladder*, based on a story by Henry Miller. He has also had success with ballet and instrumental works.

BIG BANGS
2000 TV series about classical music

Composer Howard Goodall's five-part survey of key moments in the development of Western classical music devotes one program to opera. It begins with Monteverdi and his *Orfeo* and looks at Mozart *(Le nozze di Figaro)*, Offenbach, Verdi, and John Adams, among others. Color. 60 minutes. Films for the Humanities & Sciences. VHS.

BILLY BUDD
1951 opera by Britten

BENJAMIN BRITTEN's all-male opera tells what happens when pure evil meets pure goodness. The libretto by E. M. Forster, based on a novella by Herman Melville, is set on a British warship. The good Billy Budd is press-ganged into service on the ship and persecuted by the evil master-of-arms John Claggart. When Budd accidentally kills Claggart, Captain Vere is forced to hang him, though it seems he could have spoken in his defense. The opera is told as a memory by the haunted Vere.

1952 NBC Opera Theatre

American TV studio production: Samuel Chotzinoff (producer), Peter Herman Adler (conductor, Symphony of the Air Orchestra), William Molyneux (set designer).

Cast: Theodor Uppman (Billy Budd), Andrew McKinley (Captain Vere), Leon Lishner (Claggart), David Williams, Paul Ukena, Robert Holland, Kenneth Smith, Robert Gross.

Video at the MTR. Telecast live on October 19, 1952. Kirk Browning (director). Black and white. In English. 90 minutes.

Comment: This was the American premiere of the opera. Uppman created the role of Billy Budd on stage in England.

1966 BBC Television

English TV production: Basil Coleman (director), Charles Mackerras (conductor, London Symphony Orchestra and Ambrosian Opera Chorus), Tony Abbott (set designer).

Cast: Peter Glossop (Billy Budd), Peter Pears (Captain Vere), Michael Langdon (Claggart), John Shirley-Quirk (Mr. Redburn), Robert Tear (Novice), David Bowman, Bryan Drake, David Kelly, Kenneth MacDonald.

Telecast on BBC on December 11, 1966. Black and white. In English. 158 minutes.

***1988 English National Opera

English stage production: Tim Albery (director), David Atherton (conductor, English National Opera Orchestra), Tom Cairns and Antony McDonald (set designers).

Cast: Thomas Allen (Billy Budd), Philip Langridge (Captain Vere), Richard van Allan (Claggart), Neil Howlett, Philip Guy-Bromley, Clive Bayley, Edward Byles.

Video: Image Entertainment DVD/Kultur and Home Vision VHS. Barrie Gavin (director). Color. In English. 157 minutes.

1997 Metropolitan Opera

American stage production: John Dexter (director), Steuart Bedford (conductor, Metropolitan Opera Orchestra and Chorus), William Dudley (set/costume designer).

Cast: Dwayne Croft (Billy Budd), Philip Langridge (Captain Vere), James Morris (Claggart), Victor Braun (Mr. Redburn), James Courtney (Mr. Flint), Julien Robbins (Lt. Ratcliffe), Bradley Garvin (First Mate), Kevin Short (Second Mate), Kim Josephson (Donald), John Osborn (Maintop), Tony Stevenson (Novice), Bernard Fitch (Squeak).

Taped March 11, 1997; telecast June 3, 1998. Brian Large (director). Color. In English. 160 minutes.

BIOGRAPHIES
Fictional films about opera people

There are a quite a number of enjoyable film biographies of opera composers, singers, and other personalities. Most are highly romanticized and usually more fiction than history, but all have interesting re-creations of historical opera productions.

The most successful at the box-office was THE GREAT CARUSO (1951) with Mario Lanza as the great tenor, but Milos Forman's Oscar-winning Mozart biography AMADEUS (1984) has won the most critical acclaim.

In addition to many other films about MOZART, there are movies devoted to composers BELLINI, BIZET, DONIZETTI, GERSHWIN, GILBERT AND SULLIVAN, HANDEL, HERBERT, KERN, NICOLAI, MASCAGNI, OFFENBACH, RIMSKY-KORSAKOV, RODGERS, ROMBERG, ROSSINI, SCHUBERT, JOHANN STRAUSS, VERDI, VIVALDI, and WAGNER.

In addition to many other films about CARUSO, there are movies devoted to singers MARIA CALLAS, LINA CAVALIERI, FARINELLI, JULIÁN GAYARRE, SALOMEA KRUSCENISKI, MARJORIE LAWRENCE, JENNY LIND, MARIA MALIBRAN, NELLIE MELBA, JOSÉ MOJICA, GRACE MOORE, and ADELINA PATTI.

Two fascinating films are available about an opera publishing company, Italy's influential RICORDI firm, and one about an impresario (SOL HUROK). Most of the great librettists are ignored, but there are films about some writers who were also librettists, including BEAUMARCHAIS and MOLIÈRE.

BIOPHON FILMS
Early German sound films (1903–1911)

Biophon films were one-reel movies with sound supplied by gramophone records, and many were of opera and operetta arias. They were developed by Oskar Messter, beginning in 1903 in Germany and were widespread in Sweden and Denmark within a year. Production of them seems to have finished about 1911. The films usually featured a famous aria in a scene from an opera. It appears that about 300 to 400 were made, though not many survive. The difficulty in presenting them was not the film or the record but the poor loudspeaker systems in the theaters. Biophon films are listed under operas when known.

BIRTWISTLE, HARRISON
English composer (1934–)

Harrison Birtwistle, considered by many to be the leading opera composer in England today, is best known for his first opera, PUNCH AND JUDY (1968), created for the Aldeburgh Festival, and GAWAIN (1991), televised from

Covent Garden. He was musical director of the National Theatre for many years, where he learned a good deal about stage techniques. His opera *The Mask of Orpheus* (1986) includes electronic inserts and requires action at an accelerated pace, like silent movie comedies of the Keystone Cops genre. *Yan Tan Tethera,* also premiered in 1986, was commissioned for television. His very cinematic THE SECOND MRS. KONG (1995), inspired by the RKO film *King Kong,* premiered at the Glyndebourne Festival and was filmed by the BBC.

BITTER SWEET
1929 operetta by Coward

Bitter Sweet, NOËL COWARD's deliberately old-fashioned Viennese-style operetta, was inspired by Strauss's *Die Fledermaus.* It tells the story of Sari, an upper-class English lady, who elopes with her music teacher Carl. They have a good life in Vienna until he dies in a duel with a count protecting her good name. Afterwards she becomes a famous singer. Like its Viennese model, the operetta has a big waltz, "I'll See You Again," and a rousing gypsy song "Zigeuner." Coward wrote both music and libretto.

1933 British and Dominion film
English feature film: Herbert Wilcox (director), Lydia Hayward and Monckton Hoff (screenplay), F. A. Young (cinematographer), British and Dominion (production).

Cast: Anna Neagle (Sarah) Fernand Gravey (Carl), Miles Mander (Captain Auguste von Lutte), Esme Percy (Hugh).

Black and white. In English. 93 minutes.

1940 MGM film
American feature film: W. S. Van Dyke (director), Victor Saville (producer), Lesser Samuels (screenplay), Herbert Stothart (musical director), Allen Davey (cinematographer), MGM (studio).

Cast: Jeanette MacDonald (Sarah), Nelson Eddy (Carl), George Sanders (Baron von Tranisch), Ian Hunter (Lord Shayne).

Video: MGM-UA VHS. Color. In English 92 minutes.

Comment: Includes most of Coward's songs plus bits of *La bohème* and *The Barber of Seville.* MacDonald is dressed in Adrian's plushest creations.

BIZET, GEORGES
French composer (1838–1875)

Parisian Georges Bizet began his professional career with the comic operetta *Le Docteur Miracle,* which won a competition organized by Offenbach and was staged in 1857. His career ended in 1875 with the seeming failure of the tragic opera CARMEN. He was never to know that he had composed what was to become the most popular opera of all time and added the Carmen story to the realm of myth. Bizet wrote other fine and popular operas, such as *The Pearl Fishers* (LES PÊCHEURS DE PERLES) and *The Fair Maid of Perth,* but he is acclaimed and will continue to be remembered for *Carmen.*

1930 Georges Bizet
"Musical novelty" about the composer made by James Fitzpatrick, the creator of the famous *Travelogues.* Black and white. In English. 10 minutes.

1938 Georges Bizet, Composer of Carmen
Expanded 37-minute English version of above film with Bizet played by Dino Gavani and Mme. Bizet by Madeleine Gibson. The romantic story revolves around the first production of *Carmen,* with Julie Suedo as Carmen and Webster Booth as Don José. After its failure, Bizet dies of a broken heart. W. K. Williamson wrote the screenplay and James Fitzpatrick directed the film, which was screened with their companion movies about Chopin and Liszt.

1942 Hommage à Georges Bizet
French film about the life of the composer, including excerpts from *Carmen.* The main singer is Yvonne Gouverné with Julien Bertheau as the poet. Louis Cuny wrote and directed. Black and white. In French. 36 minutes.

1952 Immortal Bizet
Short film telling the story of the composer's life and using his homes in Paris and Italy as setting. The film features selections from several operas. Black and white. 26 minutes.

1988 Bizet Concert in Soissons Cathedral
Montserrat Caballé stars in this Bizet concert filmed at the Soissons Cathedral in France. Highlight is a performance of the cantata *Clovis and Clotilda* with Caballé, tenor Gerard Garino, bass Boris Martinovich, and the Lille National Orchestra conducted by Jean-Claude Casadesus. Color. 95 minutes. Kultur VHS.

1995 Bizet's Dream
Maurice Godin plays Bizet in this film in the "Composers Series" aimed at young audiences and first shown on HBO. A girl learns that Bizet is composing an opera about a soldier and gypsy and, as her soldier father is away in Spain, she begins to imagine he has been seduced by someone like Carmen. Brittany Madgett plays the girl and Micaëla, Yseult Lendvai is Genevieve and

Carmen, Vlastimil Harapes is her father and Don José, and R. H. Thomson is Delaborde and Escamillo. Ondrej Lenard conducts the Slovak Philharmonic Orchestra of Bratislava, with singing by tenor Gurgen Ousepian. A bit of *Carmen* is shown on stage at the end. David Devine directed the film shot in the Czech Republic. Color. In English. 60 minutes. Sony Classical VHS.

BJÖRLING, JUSSI
Swedish tenor (1911–1960)

Jussi Björling is one of the great tenors of the century, and some prefer his radiant voice to all others. He joined the Royal Swedish Opera in Stockholm in 1930, began to sing in England and America in the late 1930s, and was soon a favorite at the Met. His voice recorded exceptionally well, and his records remain popular. His recording of *La bohème,* with Victoria de los Angeles as Mimì and Thomas Beecham conducting, is considered by many critics to be the best. Björling sang in the Met's pioneer 1950 telecast of DON CARLO, in three Swedish feature films, and in television shows, but there is no video of him in a complete opera.

1938 Fram för Framgang
Björling plays a young tenor in *Fram för Framgang* (Heading for Success), a Swedish comedy about his path to success and his relationship with a playwright and an actress. He sings the aria "Di tu se fedele" from *Un ballo in maschera* and four songs. Gunnar Skaggund directed. The film opened in the United States when Björling was at the Met in 1938. Black and white. In Swedish. 89 minutes. Bel Canto Society VHS (also includes scene of Björling in *Aida*)/Live Opera VHS.

1948 En Svensk Tiger
Björling plays an opera singer like himself in *En Svensk Tiger* (A Swedish Tiger), a Swedish film by Gustaf Edgren. It includes music from *Don Giovanni, Les contes d'Hoffmann,* and *L'Africaine.* The "tiger" of the title is Edvin Adolphson, and the supporting cast includes Margareta Fahlen, Sven Lindberg, and Marianne Löfgren. Black and white. In Swedish. 87 minutes.

1950 Jussi Björling in Opera and Song 1 and 2
Björling appeared on the *Voice of Firestone* television series three times. *Volume One* (40 minutes) has scenes from telecasts on March 6, 1950, and November 19, 1951, with arias and duets from *Faust, La bohème, Princess Pat,* and *Pagliacci,* with his wife Anna-Lisa as partner. *Volume Two* (26 minutes) features the tenor on a November 20, 1950, telecast singing the "Flower Song" from *Carmen* and the "Neapolitan Love Song" from *Princess Pat.* Black and white. VAI VHS.

1953 Resan till Dej
Björling is a featured performer in his third Swedish film *Journey to You,* directed by Stig Olin. Appearing with him are Alice Babs, Sven Lindberg, and Karl-Arne Holmsten. Color. In Swedish. 88 minutes.

1977 Jussi Björling's Saga
Swedish documentary with musical scenes from two of Björling's movies and interviews with colleagues and family. His brother Karl narrates, and there are comments from Fred Schang, Robert Merrill, and Fedora Barbieri. Black and white and color. In Swedish. 99 minutes. Bel Canto Society VHS.

BLACK RIVER
1989 opera by Schultz

Black River is an Australian opera about race relations with music by Andrew Schultz and libretto by Julianne Schultz. A group of people take shelter from a storm in a jail, where an aboriginal has been found hanged. Discussion on how this could have happened leads to an examination of the realities of the relationship between aboriginals and whites in Australia.

1993 Lucas film
Australian feature film: Kevin Lucas (director), Roland Peelman (conductor, Seymour Group). Linus Onus and Tim Ferrier (set designers).

Cast: Maroochy Barambah, John Pringle, Akiko Nakajima, Clive Birch, James Bonnefin.

Color. In English. 56 minutes.

Comment: Winner of the Grand Prix at Opera Screen Festival in Paris. Toured in Australian film festival.

BLAKE, ROCKWELL
American tenor (1951–)

Rockwell Blake made his debut as Lindoro in Washington in *L'italiana in Algeri* and at the Met in 1981 in the same role. He has become especially popular in France, where critics consider him to be the finest Rossini tenor of our time. He sings regularly at the Rossini Festival in Pesaro and at the Aix-en-Provence Festival. See IL BARBIERE DI SIVIGLIA (1988), LA CENERENTOLA (1980), DON GIOVANNI (1992), LA DONNA DEL LAGO (1990/1992), ELISABETTA, REGINA D'INGHILTERRA (1985/1991), MITRIDATE (1983), OTELLO (Rossini/1988), GIOACHINO ROSSINI (1992), and ZELMIRA (1989).

BLEDSOE, JULES
American baritone (1898–1943)

Jules Bledsoe created the role of Joe in Jerome Kern's SHOW BOAT and thus introduced the world to the glorious aria "Ol' Man River." He can be seen in the part in the 1929 film. He also created the role of Tizanne in William Harling's Broadway opera *Deep River* in 1926 and Voodoo Man in Shirley Graham Dubois's *Tom-Tom* in Cleveland in 1932. Bledsoe, born in Texas, sang with Chicago and Cleveland opera companies and the Aeolian Opera Association. In Holland, he sang with the Italian Opera Company as Rigoletto, Amonasro, and Boris Godunov. His only other film was *Drums of the Congo* (1942), in which he plays Kalu and performs musical numbers with Prince Modupe's Congo Choir.

BLEGEN, JUDITH
American soprano (1941–)

Montana-born Judith Blegen, who began her career at the Santa Fe Festival, learned her craft in Italy and Germany, starting in Spoleto in 1963. She sang a wide variety of roles in Nuremberg, Vienna, and Salzburg; made her debut at the Met in 1970 as Papagena; and went to Covent Garden in 1975 as Despina. Blegen is particularly admired for the purity and sweetness of her voice. See UN BALLO IN MASCHERA (1980), L'ELISIR D'AMORE (1979/1981), DIE FLEDERMAUS (1986), HÄNSEL UND GRETEL (1982), GIAN CARLO MENOTTI (1976), METROPOLITAN OPERA (1975/1983/1986), DER ROSENKAVALIER (1982), DIE SCHÖPFUNG (1986), and SPOLETO (1966).

BLISS, ARTHUR
British composer (1891–1975)

Sir Arthur Bliss is a major figure in film music as well as classic musical; his score for the 1936 film *Things to Come* has been particularly popular and influential. He prepared the music for the 1953 film of THE BEGGAR'S OPERA, and he composed the scores of *Conquest of the Air, Christopher Columbus,* and *Seven Waves Away.* He composed only two operas. After the success of *The Olympians* on stage in 1949, BBC Television commissioned the opera TOBIAS AND THE ANGEL, which was telecast in 1960.

BLITZSTEIN, MARC
American composer (1906–1964)

Marc Blitzstein was the most overtly political American opera/music theater composer, a true believer in agitprop. His stage works occupy territory halfway between opera and musical theater, and critics do not always consider them operas. He wrote his best-known work, THE CRADLE WILL ROCK (1937), with encouragement from Bertolt Brecht, and its staging was a political event in itself with the cast locked out of the theater, so director Orson Welles had to lead the audience to an alternate location. It was so popular it became the first Broadway musical work to have an original cast album. Blitzstein's most important stage work could turn out to be REGINA (1949), an impressive large-scale Broadway opera based on Lillian Hellman's play *The Little Foxes.*

BLOND ECKBERT
1994 opera by Weir

JUDITH WEIR's opera *Blond Eckbert,* libretto by the composer based on a mystifying but fascinating 1796 German story by Ludwig Tiech, was premiered by English National Opera in 1994. Eckbert has his wife Berthe tell her life story to Walther. She was raised by an old woman with a dog and a bird that laid jewels, and she later ran away with the jewels. Walther says he knows the name of the dog, so Eckbert kills him and Berthe dies. Eckbert goes to the old woman's house where explanations of the psychodrama are revealed.

1994 English National Opera
English stage production: Tim Hopkins (director), Sian Edwards (conductor, English National Opera Orchestra), Nigel Lowry (set designer).
Cast: Nicholas Folwell (Eckbert), Anne-Marie Owens (Berthe), Nerys Jones (Bird), Christopher Ventris (Walther/Hugo/Old Woman).
Telecast July 3, 1994, on Channel 4. Margaret Williams (director). Color. In English. 70 minutes.

BLOSSOM TIME
See DAS DREIMÄDERLHAUS

BLUE MONDAY
1922 mini-opera by Gershwin

"Like the white man's opera the theme will be Love! Hate! Passion! Jealousy!" sings gambler Joe as this mini-opera opens. Before it's over, his sweetheart Vi will shoot him dead because she thinks he's been unfaithful. George Gershwin's first opera, *Blue Monday,* libretto by B. G. De Sylva, focuses for 25 minutes on love, jealousy, and murder in a Harlem bar. It premiered in New York in 1922 as part of the *George White Scandals of 1922* but was withdrawn for being too downbeat. Ferde Grofé reorchestrated it in 1925 for presentation at Carnegie Hall as *135th Street.*

1953 Omnibus, CBS Television

American TV production: Valerie Bettis (director), George Bassman (conductor, CBS Orchestra).

Cast: Etta Warren (Vi), Rawn Spearman (Joe), Jimmy Rushing, Lorenzo Fuller, Warren Coleman, Bill Dillard.

Telecast March 29, 1953. Seymour Robbie (director). Black and white. In English. 25 minutes.

Comment: This is Ferde Grofé's orchestrated version, titled *135th Street*.

1981 RTSI Swiss Television

Swiss TV production: Sergio Genni (director), Marc Andrae (conductor, Orchestra della Svizzera Italiana), Jimmy Ortelli (set/costume designer).

Cast: La Verne Williams (Vi), Howard Haskin (Joe), Raymond Bazemore (Mike), Daniel Washington (Tom), Ivan Thomas (Sam). Oswald Russell (Sweetpea).

Telecast by RTSI Italian Swiss Television on October 26, 1981. Color. In English. 25 minutes.

Comment: Soundtrack has been issued on CD.

Related film

1945 Rhapsody in Blue

The Gershwin film biography *Rhapsody in Blue* features an abridged version of *Blue Monday,* including the numbers "Blue Monday Blues," "Has Anyone Seen My Joe?" and "135th Street Blues." Irving Rapper directed for Warner Bros. Black and white. 139 minutes. Warner VHS.

BLUEBEARD'S CASTLE
1918 opera by Bartók

BÉLA BARTÓK composed only one opera, but it was a highly original one with a brilliant libretto by Béla Balazs based on the Bluebeard legend. *A Kekszakallu Herceg Vara,* also translated as *Duke Bluebeard's Castle,* is the symbolic story of an inquisitive woman who marries a reticent man. She insists in looking behind seven closed doors in his castle despite grim rumors she has heard.

1963 Powell film

German TV film: Michael Powell (director), Milan Horvath (conductor, Zagreb Philharmonic), Hannes Staudinger (cinematographer), Hein Heckroth (production designer)

Cast: Norman Foster (Bluebeard), Ana Raquel Sartre (Judith).

Telecast December 15, 1963, by SDR German television. Color. In German. 60 minutes.

Comment: Powell creates reflections of Bluebeard's torment through decor and lighting.

***1980 Szinetar film

Hungarian TV film: Miklos Szinetar (director), Sir Georg Solti (conductor, London Philharmonic Orchestra), Gabor Bachmann (set designer), Judith Schaffer (costume designer), Hungarofilm (production company).

Cast: Kolos Kováts (Bluebeard), Sylvia Sass (Judith).

Video: London VHS. Color. In Hungarian with English subtitles. 58 minutes.

Comment: Visual and aural feast in 35mm. It begins at night with the wife's arrival at Bluebeard's castle, and each door she opens becomes a treat for the eyes and the imagination.

1988 Megahey film

English TV film: Leslie Megahey (director), Adam Fischer (conductor, London Philharmonic Orchestra), Bruce Macadie (set designer), Anna Buruma (costume designer).

Cast: Robert Lloyd (Bluebeard), Elizabeth Laurence (Judith).

Video: Teldec VHS. Color. In Hungarian with English subtitles. 64 minutes.

Comment: The story is told as if it is taking place in Bluebeard's mind. When Bluebeard's new wife visits a room and brings back a souvenir, he weeps like the walls of his castle. The film won the 1989 Prix Italia Music Prize.

1989 Metropolitan Opera

American stage production: Göran Järvefelt (director), James Levine (conductor, Metropolitan Opera Orchestra), Hans Schavernoch (set designer), Chester Kallman (English translation).

Cast: Samuel Ramey (Bluebeard), Jessye Norman (Judith).

Telecast March 31, 1989; taped February 1, 1989. Brian Large (director). Color. In English. 70 minutes.

BLUME VON HAWAII, DIE
1931 operetta by Abraham

Die Blume von Hawaii (The Flower of Hawaii) is an operetta by Hungarian composer PAUL ABRAHAM with an exotic international plot. An Hawaiian princess working as a French waitress in Paris falls in love with an American officer. She is taken back to Hawaii to marry the king, but true romance finally wins out in the end. The operetta, with a libretto by Alfred Grünwald and Bela Löhner-Beda, was quite popular in Montreal for a time and is still in the Berlin repertory.

1933 Rio film

German feature film: Richard Oswald (director), Heinz Goldberg (screenplay), Reimar Kuntz (cinematographer), Rio Film (production company).

Cast: Marta Eggerth (Princess), Hans Fidesser, Ivan Petrovitch, Hans Junkermann, Ferdinand Hart, Eugen Rex, Baby Gray.

Black and white. In German. 85 minutes.

Comment: Stagy production but strong cast.

1953 Arion film

German feature film: Geza von Cziffra (director), Arion Film (production company).

Cast: Ursula Justin, Mario Litto, William Stelling, Rudolf Platte.

Film: Color. In German. 95 minutes.

Comment: Plot is changed; story is now about actresses who want to get acting roles and the men to go with them.

1992 Fiore d'Haway

Italian TV production: Sandro Massimini (director/producer), Roberto Negri (pianist), Sandro Corelli (choreographer).

Cast: Sandro Massimini, Sonia Dorigo, Tadamici Oriè.

Video: Ricordi (Italy) VHS. Pierluigi Pagano (director). Color. In Italian. About 19 minutes.

Comment: Highlights of the operetta, known as *Fiore d'Haway* in Italy, on TV series *Operette, che Passione!* Includes songs "Un paradiso in riva al mare," "Un bambolino piccolino," "My golden baby," and "Bimbe floride."

BOCCACCIO
1879 operetta by Suppé

The most popular operetta by FRANZ VON SUPPÉ, with music worthy of a comic opera and a fine libretto by F. Zell and Richard Genée. It tells the story of Italian writer Boccaccio and his life in 14th-century Florence, where his tales scandalized his fellow citizens. Using various intrigues, he wins the love of beautiful Fiametta, the daughter of the duke. Maria Callas made her stage debut in this operetta in 1940 in Athens at the Royal Opera.

1940 Venus-Scalera film

Italian feature film: Marcello Albani (director); Luigi Bonelli, Marcello Albani, and Maria Basaglia (screenplay); Massimo Terzano (cinematographer); Venus-Scalera Film (production company).

Cast: Clara Calamai (Giannina/Boccaccio), Silvana Jachino (Fiametta), Osvaldo Valenti (Berto), Luigi Amirante (Scalza).

Black and white. In Italian. 80 minutes.

Comment: Plot is heavily revised. Calamai, star of Visconti's film *Ossessione,* plays the writer's niece Giannina, who disguises herself as Boccaccio. This causes problems for her cousin Berto, who is also pretending to be Boccaccio.

1972 ZDF German Television

German TV film: Georg Marischka (director), Hermann Hildebrandt (conductor, Bavarian Radio-Television Orchestra), Elena Ricci and Heinz Brendel (set designers), ZDF (production company).

Cast: Erland Hagegaard (Boccaccio), Patricia McCrew (Fiametta), Toni Blankenheim (Scalza), Charlotte Berthold (Beatrice), Dorothy Chryst (Isabella), Harald Serafin (Lotteringhi).

Telecast November 3, 1972. Color. In German. 90 minutes.

Early film

1920 Curtiz film

Hungarian Michael Curtiz, later the director of *Casablanca,* shot a feature film based on the operetta in Austria, after he had moved from Budapest to Vienna. It was screened with the operetta music played lived. Black and white. Silent. About 65 minutes.

BOCELLI, ANDREA
Italian tenor (1959–)

Blind Italian tenor Andrea Bocelli is not greatly admired by opera aficionados, but he has become one of the most famous "opera" singers in the world all the same through recitals and TV appearances. He has appeared on stage in two operas, *Werther* in Detroit and *La bohème* in Caligari, and has made complete recordings of *La bohème* and *Il trovatore.* His CDs and DVDs are best-sellers, and a number of new opera lovers say they discovered the art through Bocelli. His CD of arias from Verdi operas was conducted by Zubin Mehta.

1997 A Night in Tuscany

Bocelli returns home to Tuscany and performs arias and songs from his CDs *Romanza* and *Viaggio Italian.* Color. 50 minutes. Polygram DVD/VHS.

2000 Christmas Glory

Bocelli joins Charlotte Church and Bryn Terfel in a Christmas concert at Westminster Abbey with the Westminster Abbey Choir and City of London Sinfonia. Color. 60 minutes. Polygram DVD/VHS.

2001 Tuscan Skies

Portrait of Bocelli featuring performances and scenes of his life in Tuscany. Black and white and color. 60 minutes. Universal DVD/VHS.

BOHÈME, LA
1896 opera by Puccini

GIACOMO PUCCINI's *La bohème*, one of the most melodious of all operas, with unforgettable arias and great romantic ensembles, has done more to create romantic ideas about Bohemian life than any other work. Early films of the opera are based more on Henri Murger's source novel *Scènes de la vie de bohème* than on the poetic libretto by Giuseppe Giacosa and Luigi Illica. At least that's what the film producers claimed when the opera was still in copyright. *La bohème* is the story of four Bohemians who share an apartment in Paris in the 1830s. Poet Rodolfo has a wistful love affair with seamstress neighbor Mimì, and painter Marcello has a tempestuous relationship with flirtatious Musetta, while philosopher Colline and musician Schaunard complete the quartet. Mimì dies of consumption after four acts of the most romantic music ever written.

1948 Cambridge Theatre

English stage production: Campbell Logan (stage director), Alberto Erede (conductor, Cambridge Theater Orchestra).

Cast: Daria Bayan (Mimì), James Johnston (Rodolfo), Tony Sympson (Musetta), Stanley Pope (Marcello), Ian Wallace (Colline), Sidney Snape (Schaunard).

Telecast April 19, 1948, on BBC. Philip Bates (film director). Black and white. 108 minutes.

1949 NBC Opera Theatre

American TV production (Act IV only): Samuel Chotzinoff (producer), Peter Herman Adler (conductor, Symphony of the Air Orchestra).

Cast: Evelyn Case (Mimì), Glen Burris (Rodolfo), Virginia Cards (Musetta), Norman Young (Marcello), Edwin Steffe (Colline).

Video at the MTR. Telecast live February 2, 1949. Kirk Browning (director). Black and white. In English. 30 minutes.

Comment: First opera telecast by NBC Opera Theater although only Act IV was presented.

1953 Omnibus, CBS Television

American TV production: Bob Banner (director), Alberto Erede (conductor, Metropolitan Orchestra and Chorus), Rolf Gerard (set/costume designer), Howard Dietz (English translation).

Cast: Nadine Conner (Mimì), Brian Sullivan (Rodolfo), Brenda Lewis (Musetta), Frank Guarrera (Marcello), Norman Scott (Colline), Clifford Harvuot (Schaunard).

Video: Video Yesteryear VHS. Telecast live February 22, 1953, on CBS. Bob Banner (director). Black and white. In English. 71 minutes.

1956 NBC Opera Theatre

American TV production: Samuel Chotzinoff (producer), Peter Herman Adler (Symphony of the Air Orchestra, NBC Opera Chorus, Columbus Boy Choir), Ed Wittstein (set designer), Joseph Machlis (English translation)

Cast: Dorothy Coulter (Mimì), John Alexander (Rodolfo), Jan McArt (Musetta), Richard Torigi (Marcello), Thomas Tipton (Colline), Chester Watson (Schaunard).

Video at the MTR. Telecast live November 18, 1956. Kirk Browning (director). Color. In English. 150 minutes.

***1965 Semmelroth film

Italian studio film: Wilhelm Semmelroth (director), Franco Zeffirelli (stage director/set designer), Herbert von Karajan (conductor, Teatro alla Scala Theater Orchestra and Chorus), Werner Krien (cinematographer).

Cast: Mirella Freni (Mimì), Gianni Raimondi (Rodolfo), Adriana Martino (Musetta), Rolando Panerai (Marcello), Ivo Vinco (Colline), Gianni Maffeo (Schaunard).

Video: DG DVD/VHS. Color. In Italian with English subtitles. 105 minutes.

Comment: This superb film, shot in 35mm in a Milan studio and based on Zeffirelli's stage production at La Scala, uses music prerecorded by Karajan in Munich. Highlights version in *Great Moments* VHS series.

1977 Metropolitan Opera

American studio production: Fabrizio Melano (director), James Levine (conductor, Metropolitan Opera Orchestra), Pier Luigi Pizzi (set designer).

Cast: Renata Scotto (Mimì). Luciano Pavarotti (Rodolfo), Maralin Niska (Musetta), Ingvar Wixell (Marcello), Paul Plishka (Colline), Allan Monk (Schaunard), Italo Tajo (Benoit).

Video at the MTR. Telecast live March 15, 1977. Kirk Browning (director). Color. In Italian with English subtitles. 120 minutes.

Comment: First opera televised from the new Met home at Lincoln Center.

***1982 Metropolitan Opera

American stage production: Franco Zeffirelli (director/set designer), James Levine (conductor, Metropolitan Opera Orchestra and Chorus).

Cast: Teresa Stratas (Mimì), José Carreras (Rodolfo), Renata Scotto (Musetta), Richard Stilwell (Marcello), James Morris (Colline), Allan Monk (Schaunard), Italo Tajo (Alcindoro).

Video: Pioneer DVD/Bel Canto Paramount VHS. Kirk Browning (director). Taped January 16 and telecast January 20, 1982. Color. In Italian with English subtitles. 141 minutes.

Comment: This Met production is a visual and an audio treat; even the sets get applause. The DVD includes s 20-minute documentary *Zeffirelli on Bohème*.

1982 Royal Opera House

English stage production: John Copley (director), Lamberto Gardelli (conductor, Royal Opera House Orchestra), Julia Trevelyan Oman (set designer).

Cast: Ileana Cotrubas (Mimì), Neil Shicoff (Rodolfo), Marilyn Zschau (Musetta), Thomas Allen (Marcello), Gwynne Howell (Colline), John Rawnsley (Schaunard).

Video: Arthaus DVD/HBO and NVC Arts (GB) VHS/Pioneer LD. Brian Large (director). Color. In Italian with English subtitles. 115 minutes.

Comment: First-class all-around production and cast, with Cotrubas at her most memorable.

1982/1989 Opera Stories

Charlton Heston narrates a highlights version of the above Royal Opera production, with introductions filmed in the Latin Quarter in Paris by Keith Cheetham in 1989. Color. In Italian with English subtitles. 50 minutes. Pioneer Artists LD.

1983 Philadelphia Opera

American stage production: Gian Carlo Menotti (director), Oliviero de Fabritiis (conductor, Philadelphia Opera Orchestra), Franco Colavecchia (set designer).

Cast: Luciano Pavarotti (Rodolfo), Leila Guimaraes (Mimì), Mary Jane Johnson (Musetta), Franco Sioli (Marcello), Laszlo Polgar (Colline), Ivan Konsulov (Schaunard).

Telecast on PBS in 1983. Kirk Browning (director). Color. In Italian. 120 minutes.

Comment: Pavarotti performs with the winners of an international competition for young singers. Nine million people, the largest audience for an opera in public TV history, watched the telecast.

1986 Tianquiao Theater, Beijing

Chinese stage production: Gian Carlo Menotti (director), Leone Magiera (conductor, Genoa Opera Orchestra and Chorus), Franco Colavecchia (set designer).

Cast: Luciano Pavarotti (Rodolfo), Fiamma Izzo d'Amico (Mimì), Madelyn Renee (Musetta), Roberto Servile (Marcello), Francesco Ellero D'Artegna (Colline), Jeffrey Mattsey (Schaunard).

Video: Kultur VHS. Color. In Italian with English subtitles. 120 minutes.

Comment: Filmed in Beijing's Tianquiao Theater during Genoa Opera's China tour; the location is more interesting that the production.

1988 Comencini film

Italian feature film: Luigi Comencini (director), James Conlon (conductor, National Orchestra of France and Radio France Choir), Armando Nannuzzi (cinematographer), Daniel Toscan du Plantier and Gaumont (production).

Cast: Barbara Hendricks (Mimì), Luca Canonici (Rodolfo, sung by José Carreras), Angela Maria Blasi (Musetta), Gino Quilico (Marcello), Richard Cowan (Schaunard), Francesco Ellero D'Artegna (Colline).

Video: Erato VHS. Color. In Italian with English subtitles. 107 minutes.

Comment: Comencini filmed the opera straight, but he added ideas such as having Mimì initiate her meeting with Rodolfo by pretending her candle has gone out.

**1989 San Francisco Opera

American stage production: Francesca Zambello (director), Tiziano Severini (conductor, San Francisco Opera Orchestra and Chorus), David Mitchell (set designer).

Cast: Mirella Freni (Mimì), Luciano Pavarotti (Rodolfo), Sandra Pacetti (Musetta), Gino Quilico (Marcello), Nicolai Ghiaurov (Colline), Stephen Dickson (Schaunard), Italo Tajo (Benoit/Alcindoro).

Video: Kultur DVD/VHS and Arthaus (GB) DVD. Brian Large (director). Color. In Italian with English subtitles. 111 minutes.

Comment: Zambello, one of the best opera directors now working, pushes a cast of stars to memorable performances.

***1993 Australian Opera, Sydney

Australian stage production: Baz Luhrmann (director), Julian Smith (conductor, Australian Opera and Ballet Orchestra), Catherine Martin (set designer).

Cast: Cheryl Barker (Mimì), David Hobson (Rodolfo), Christine Douglas (Musetta), Roger Lemke (Marcello), Gary Rowley (Colline), David Lemke (Schaunard).

Video: Image Entertainment DVD/VHS/LD. Geoff Nottage (director). Telecast in Australia December 1, 1993. Color. In Italian with English subtitles. 112 minutes.

Comment: Luhrmann, known for the movies *Moulin Rouge* and *Strictly Ballroom*, directs the opera as a 1950s Paris love story with a young cast to give it a fresh feeling. These Bohemians live behind a rooftop neon sign that proclaims "L'Amour" and the subtitles reference to Sartre and Mary Poppins. The production was such a success it went to Broadway in 2002.

1997 New York City Opera

American stage production: Graziella Sciutti (director), George Manahan (conductor, New York City Opera Orchestra and Chorus), Michael Anania (set designer).

Cast: Cassandra Riddle (Mimì), Raymond Very (Rodolfo), Jane Thorngren (Musetta), Robert Perry (Marcello), Brian Matthews (Colline), James Bobick (Schaunard), William Ledbetter (Alcindoro).

Telecast March 26, 1997, in *Live From Lincoln Center* series on PBS. Kirk Browning (director). Color. In Italian with English subtitles. 140 minutes.

Early/related films

1910 Edison film

Enrico Berriel directed this American *La bohème*, featuring scenes from the opera, for the Edison studio. Maria Mokryszka is Mimì and Vittorio Lois is Rodolfo. The film was shown in theaters with live music from the opera. Black and white. Silent. About 12 minutes. Film survives in American archives.

1910 Pathé film

Albert Capellani directed this *La bohème*, said to be based on the Murger play, for Pathé in France. Paul Capellani, Suzanne Révonne, and Juliette Clarens are the stars. Black and white. Silent. About 15 minutes.

1911 Cines film

Orlando Ricci stars as Rodolfo in this Italian *La bohème* made for Cines in Rome. Black and white. Silent. About 15 minutes

1916 La Vie de Bohème

Alice Brady, who plays Mimì in the film, sang Mimì's introductory aria from the theater stage when this American film premiered. *La Vie de Bohème* was based on the Murger novel, but it used Puccini's music as live orchestral accompaniment. Paul Capellani is Rodolfo, Zena Keefe is Musetta, Chester Barnett is Marcello, and D. J. Flanagan is Schaunard. Albert Capellani directed for Paragon-World. Black and white. Silent. About 70 minutes.

1917 Cosmopoli film

Leda Gys is Mimì in this Italian *La bohème*, directed by Amleto Palermi for Cosmopoli Film in Rome. Luigi Serventi is Rodolfo, Camillo De Rossi is Marcello, Bianca Lorenzoni is Musetta, Vittorio Pierri is Colline, and Alberto Casanova is Schaunard. The film was based on both opera and novel and was to be accompanied by Puccini's music, but the composer refused his permission (in regional theaters, the pianists usually ignored the ban). Black and white. Silent. About 70 minutes.

La bohème (1917): Mimi (Lyda Gys) and Rodolfo (Luigi Serventi) in Amleto Palermi's film based on the opera.

1923 Righelli film

Wilhelm Dieterle plays Rodolfo with Maria Jacobini as Mimì in this German *La bohème* directed by Gennaro Righelli. Hans Krähly and Righelli adapted the Murger-Puccini story. Black and white. Silent. About 80 minutes.

1926 MGM film

Lillian Gish is Mimì with John Gilbert as Rudolphe in this American *La bohème*, the most famous silent film of the story. Renée Adorée is Musette, George Hassell is Schaunard, Edward Everett Horton is Colline, and Gino Carrado is Marcel. The film follows the plot of the opera, but the publisher refused to allow the studio to use Puccini's music, so MGM commissioned a new score by William Axt to be played with the film. King Vidor directed. Black and white. Silent. About 96 minutes.

1926 Mi chiamano Mimì

This Italian children's film, which takes its title from Mimì's introductory aria, tells the story of *La bohème* with child actors younger than age 10. This Italian answer to the American *Our Gang* films was written and directed by Washington Borg. Black and white. Silent. About 60 minutes.

1934 Evensong

Evelyn Laye sings Mimì's "Mi chiamano Mimì" on stage at an audition, and her performance launches her career in this British film inspired by Nellie Melba's career. At the end of the film, Conchita Supervia sings Musetta's show-off waltz "Quando me'n vo" on stage as the aging diva watches jealously. See EVENSONG.

1935 Mimì

Gertrude Lawrence is Mimì with Douglas Fairbanks Jr. as Rudolphe in this British film. It's an adaptation of the Murger novel, but it still uses music from the opera. Carol Goodner is Musette, Harold Warrender is Marcel, Richard Bird is Colline, and Martin Walker is Schaunard. Paul Stein directed. Black and white. In English. 94 minutes. Video Yesteryear VHS.

1936 Ave Maria

Italian tenor Beniamino Gigli sings "Che gelida manina" from La bohème in a formal concert at the beginning of this Italian-German film. He plays a singer mourning for a lost love. See AVE MARIA.

1937 Zauber de Bohème

Zauber de Bohème (The Charm of La Bohème) is a "parallel" story of La bohème in which what happens to the opera characters is reflected in the lives of the screen characters. Marta Eggerth and Jan Kiepura play opera singers who want to sing together. When Eggerth learns she is dying of tuberculosis, she goes away so he can have a career without worrying about her. They become famous separately and finally appear on stage together in La bohème. At the end of the opera, she dies on cue, like Mimì. See ZAUBER DE BOHÈME.

1939 La Vida Bohemia

American Spanish-language film based on the story of the opera but without the music. The film has titles informing the audience that the poet and flowermaker got married secretly and so were not really immoral lovers. Rosita Diaz is sweet as Mimì, while Gilbert Roland is fine as Rodolfo. Joseph Berne directed. Columbia Pictures. Black and white. In Spanish. 88 minutes.

1940 It's a Date

Deanna Durbin sings "Musetta's Waltz" in this Universal film. She plays the daughter of a Broadway star who wins a role her mother wanted. William Seiter directed. Black and white. 100 minutes.

1940 Bitter Sweet

The MacDonald-Eddy screen version of Noël Coward's operetta also includes selections from La bohème. See BITTER SWEET.

1940 Ritorno

Beniamino Gigli plays himself in this musical starring Marte Harell that has a scene from La bohème; Mafalda Favero provides the voice for Harell. See RITORNO.

1942 La Vie de Bohème

Maria Dennis plays Mimì and Louis Jourdan is Rodolfo in this film by Marcel L'Herbier based on the Murger novel; it uses the opera music as score. Gisele Pascal is Musette, André Roussin is Marcel, Louis Salou is Colline, and Alfred Adam is Schaunard. France-Italy. Black and white. In French or Italian. 92 minutes.

1942 Vertigine

Beniamino Gigli sings Rodolfo opposite Tito Gobbi as Marcello in the La bohème sequence of this film with Liva Caloni as Mimì, Tatiana Menotti as Musetta, and Gino Conti as Colline. Gigli plays an opera singer who breaks up with his girl and gambles away his money. See VERTIGINE.

1942 La donna è mobile

In La donna è mobile, tenor Ferruccio Tagliavini plays a school teacher with a great voice. On a visit to Rome, he is discovered as a singer and performs arias from La bohème, La sonnambula, Lohengrin, and L'elisir d'amore. Mario Mattoli directed.. Black and white. In Italian. 78 minutes.

1947 Her Wonderful Lie

The 1937 German film Zauber de Bohème was such a success it was remade as an American film with the same stars, Jan Kiepura and Marta Eggerth. Shot in English in Italy, it again parallels the "real" life of two Parisian opera singers with the story of Mimì and Rodolfo. The "wonderful lie" is the heroine's denial of her love for the hero so he can be a success. After they become successful and sing La bohème together, she dies like Mimì. Angelo Questa leads the Rome Opera House Orchestra in the music. See HER WONDERFUL LIE.

1950 Grounds for Marriage

Kathryn Grayson plays a New York opera star who appears on stage as Mimì in La bohème despite a doctor's disapproval. Richard Atkinson plays her Rodolfo. The plot revolves around her relationship with ex-husband Van Johnson. See GROUNDS FOR MARRIAGE.

1951 The Great Caruso

Enrico Caruso (Mario Lanza), seen on stage at the Met as Rodolfo in this romantic film biography, sings "Che gelida manina" to Dorothy Kirsten as Mimì. Former Met tenor Jean de Reszke (Alan Napier) applauds and the audience joins in. Peter Herman Adler staged and conducted the sequence. See THE GREAT CARUSO.

1953 So This Is Love
Kathryn Grayson plays soprano Grace Moore in this biopic, which finishes with her on stage at the Met singing "Mi chiamano Mimì." See SO THIS IS LOVE.

1953 Melba
Patrice Munsel plays opera diva Nellie Melba in this British film biography and sings an aria from *La bohème*. See NELLIE MELBA.

1955 Interrupted Melody
Marjorie Lawrence, played by Eleanor Parker in this film biography with singing by Eileen Farrell, is seen on stage in Monte Carlo as Musetta singing "Quando me'n vo." See INTERRUPTED MELODY.

1956 Serenade
Mario Lanza and Jean Fenn join voices on "O soave fanciulla" with piano accompaniment by Jacob Gimpel in this film about an opera singer with emotional problems. See SERENADE.

1979 Thriller
Sally Potter's feminist film examines the victim role Mimì has in the opera and reconstructs her death as possible murder. Colette Laffont plays Mimì and Rose English is Musetta, with much of the film told through performance photos and music. The singing voices are Licia Albanese as Mimì, Tatiana Menotti as Musetta, and Beniamino Gigli as Rodolfo. See THRILLER.

1987 Moonstruck
This film, virtually an homage to *La bohème,* begins in front of the Metropolitan Opera as *La bohème* billboards are put up. Nicolas Cage takes his brother's fiancée Cher to see the opera; we are shown Act II with Renata Tebaldi and Carlo Bergonzi singing and Martha Collins and John Fanning acting (the stage scenes were actually shot in Toronto and directed by Lotfi Mansouri). Musetta's Waltz and Mimì's Farewell are also on the soundtrack. See MOONSTRUCK.

1990 Maggio Musicale
Ugo Gregoretti's Italian film *Maggio Musicale* revolves around a production of *La bohème* in Florence with Shirley Verrett and Chris Merritt as Mimì and Rodolfo. This is a gentle satire on Italian opera people, with Malcolm McDowell as the troubled producer. See MAGGIO MUSICALE.

1990 Awakenings
Nicolai Gedda and Mirella Freni are heard singing "O soave fanciulla" in this fascinating film based on the experiences of neurologist Dr. Oliver Sacks. The music is performed by the Rome Opera House Orchestra led by Thomas Schippers. Robin Williams and Robert De Niro star as doctor and patient under the direction of Penny Marshall. Color. 121 minutes.

1992 La Vie de Bohème
Finnish director Aki Kaurismäki's bittersweet narrative adaptation of the Murger novel is set in a timeless though modern Paris. The plot revolves around painter Rodolfo, poet Marcello, and composer Schaunard and their love affairs with Mimì and Musette. Color. In French. 100 minutes.

1994 Heavenly Creatures
Kate Winslet is heard singing Mimì's "Sono andati" in this New Zealand film set in the early 1950s. The story is about two strange teenage girls. Peter Jackson directed. Color. 95 minutes. On video.

2000 Italian for Beginners
Soundtrack snippets from *La bohème* are an important mood component of this romantic Danish film about a group of Copenhagen folk taking evening classes in Italian. Lone Scherfig directed. Color. In Danish. 112 minutes.

BOHEMIAN GIRL, THE
1838 opera by Balfe

Fame is fleeting for some famous operas and their composers. Despite his 19th-century fame, Irish composer MICHAEL BALFE is known today mostly because of one aria from the opera *The Bohemian Girl*. "I dreamt I dwelt in marble halls" is sung by the heroine of the opera, Arline, as she dreams of her original home. It's a dream with a basis in fact, as she is actually the daughter of Count Arnheim, kidnapped as a child from her father's castle by gypsies. The libretto is by Alfred Bunn. There are early films and a complete version on CD, but no modern videos except a Laurel and Hardy comedy.

1936 Hal Roach film
American feature film: Hal Roach (producer), James Horne (director), Nathaniel Shilkret (music director).

Cast: Stan Laurel (Stan Laurel), Oliver Hardy (Oliver Hardy), Jacqueline Wells (Arline), Darla Hood (Arline as child), Felix Knight (Gypsy singer), Mae Busch (Mrs. Hardy), Antonio Moreno (Devilshoof),

Thelma Todd (Gypsy queen's daughter), William P. Carlton (Count Arnheim).

Video: MGM VHS. Black and white. In English. 74 minutes.

Comment: This famous comic version of *The Bohemian Girl* is the only sound film/video of the opera. It's not bad at all, if hardly the opera, and Felix Knight (later a Met tenor) sings well. The plot is basically unchanged, with Laurel and Hardy playing gypsy pickpockets who find and raise the stolen child Arline. "I dreamt I dwelt in marble halls" is nicely sung by Arline over breakfast in their gypsy caravan.

Early/related films

1909 Pathé film
The earliest film of the opera was made by Pathé Frères in France and released in the United States in a tinted version. Color. Silent. About 7 minutes.

1922 Knoles film
This is the opera libretto filmed without the music, featuring England's leading movie star of the period, Ivor Novello. Harley Knoles directed this British film for Alliance Film with Novello as Thaddeus, Gladys Cooper as Arline, C. Aubrey Smith as Devilshoof, Constance Collier as Queen of the Gypsies, and Ellen Terry as the nurse Buda. High point of the film is an elaborate visualization of the aria "I dreamt I dwelt in marble halls," which was accompanied by live music when the film was screened. Black and white. Silent. About 85 minutes.

1927 Cameo Opera
Pauline Johnson stars as Arline opposite Herbert Langley as Thaddeus in this British *Song Films* highlights version. Live singers and orchestra performed the arias in synchronization with the screen. H. B Parkinson directed for the *Cameo Opera* series. Black and white. Silent. About 15 minutes.

1945 Salome, Where She Danced
Selections from *The Bohemian Girl* are featured in the Universal film *Salome, Where She Danced,* one of the all-time delightfully bad movies. Yvonne De Carlo, who became a star on the strength of her torrid dancing in this movie, plays a 19th-century dancer-spy who comes to the American West and gets a town named after her. Laurence Stallings wrote the screenplay and Charles Lamont directed. Color. In English. 90 minutes.

1986 Fanfare for Elizabeth
Jessye Norman sings "I dreamt I dwelt in marble halls" at the Royal Opera House in London on April 21, 1986. Her performance was part of *Fanfare for Elizabeth,* an all-star gala in honor of the queen. Color. 90 minutes. House of Opera VHS and video at the MPRC.

1993 The Age of Innocence
Martin Scorsese's adaptation of Edith Wharton's novel features the aria "I dream I dwelt in marble halls." Michelle Pfeiffer and Daniel Day-Lewis star in the film. Columbia. Color. 132 minutes.

BOHEMIOS
1904 zarzuela by Vives

Spanish composer AMADEO VIVES's famous zarzuela *Bohemios* (The Bohemians), like the Puccini and Leoncavallo *La bohème* operas that preceded it, was inspired by the Henri Murger novel and takes place in the Paris Latin Quarter around 1840. The Bohemians in focus here are penniless composer Roberto, who is writing an opera called *Luzbel,* and his poet/librettist friend Victor. Aspiring opera singer Cossette, who lives next door, falls in love with Roberto through listening to his music. She ends up singing a love duet from his opera with him at an audition for Papá Girard. *Bohemios* was written by Guillermo Perrín and Miguel de Palacios and has been popular with audiences. It has been filmed three times.

1937 Elías film
Spanish feature film: Francisco Elías (director, screenplay, set designer), Camillo Lemoine (producer), José Gaspar (cinematographer).

Cast: Amparo Bosch (Roberto), Emilia Aliaga (Cossette), Roma Taeni, Antonio Gaton, Fernando Vallejo, Antonio Palacios, Luis Villasiul.

Film: Black and white. In Spanish. 90 minutes.

Comment: Roles are played by zarzuela singers. Shot in Barcelona.

1968 Teatro Lirico Español
Spanish TV film: Juan de Orduña (director), Federico Moreno Torroba (conductor, Orquesta Lírica Española), Jose Perera Cruz (conductor, Coro Cantores de Madrid), Manuel Tamayo (screenplay), Federico G. Larraya (cinematographer).

Cast: Julián Mateos (Roberto, sung by Carlo del Monte), Dianik Zurakowska (Cossette, sung by Josefina Cubeiro), Antonio Durán (Victor, sung by Enrique del Portal), José Franco (Papá Girard, sung by Ramón Sola), Antonio Martelo (Marcelo, sung by Octavio Alvarez).

Video: Metrovideo (Spain) VHS. Shot in 35mm for RTVE Spanish television. Juan de Orduña (director). Color. In Spanish. 85 minutes.

Early film

1905 de Banos film

Ricardo de Banos directed this *Bohemios* in Spain in 1905 with a cast headed by El Mochuelo and Antonio del Pozo. It was one of four zarzuela films he made that year, all screened with their music live. Black and white. Silent. About 10 minutes.

BÖHM, KARL

Austrian conductor (1894–1981)

Karl Böhm, one of the most popular opera conductors, was particularly admired for conducting Mozart operas, two of which are on film. He was also a good friend of Richard Strauss, who dedicated an opera to him, and videos are available of Strauss operas he conducted. He is featured in the documentary *Great Conductors of the Third Reich,* which portrays him as a strong supporter of the Nazis. See ARIADNE AUF NAXOS (1978), CONDUCTORS (1955), ELEKTRA (1981/1981 film), DIE ENTFÜHRUNG AUS DEM SERAIL (1980), FIDELIO (1970), DIE FLEDERMAUS (1971), LE NOZZE DI FIGARO (1976), and SALOME (1974).

1994 I Remember...Dr. Karl Böhm

Subtitled *His Life—His Music,* this documentary portrait of the conductor was created to celebrate the 100th anniversary of the conductor's birth on August 28, 1894. The video was made by Horant H. Hohlfeld. Color. In German. 60 minutes.

BOHNEN, MICHAEL

German bass-baritone (1887–1965)

Michael Bohnen sang at the Metropolitan Opera regularly from 1923 to 1932 and at the Deutsche Opernhaus in Berlin from 1933 to 1945. He was intendant of the Berlin Städtische Oper from 1945 to 1947 and continued to sing on stage until 1951. He was married for a number of years to American soprano Mary Lewis. Bohnen is featured in several German opera and operetta films made during the 1920s and 1930s, including a 1926 DER ROSENKAVALIER with Richard Strauss and one that claimed to be a "film opera," the 1930 *Zwei Kravaten* (see OPERAS AS MOVIES). In the Beniamino film SOLO PER TE (1937), he is the villainous person from Maria Cebotari's secret past. In the film WIENER BLUT (1932), he portrays Johann Strauss and writes some memorable waltzes. He was also a featured actor in a number of nonmusical movies. See TIEFLAND (1922), VIKTORIA UND IHR HUSSAR (1931), and DER ZIGEUNERBARON (1927).

1929 Sajenko, the Soviet

Bohnen was billed as the bass-baritone from the Metropolitan Opera in this German film, a story about Russian refugees in Berlin. Bohnen plays the Soviet spy Sajenko opposite Suzy Vernen as a princess. Erich Waschneck directed. Black and white. About 80 minutes.

1934 Gold

In the German film *Gold,* Bohnen plays a mining scientist with a method of creating gold, Brigitte Helm plays his daughter, and Hans Albers is the German engineer who opposes him. Karl Hartl directed. Black and white. In German. 120 minutes.

1935 Der Gefangene des Königs

Bohnen plays brawny King Augustus the Strong in this German historical film. Augustus was a Saxon Elector who was King of Poland from 1697 to 1733. Franz Koch directed. Black and white. In German. 105 minutes.

1935 Liselotte von der Pfalz

Bohnen plays King Louis XIV of France in this historical drama, shown in the United States as *The Private Life of Louis XIV.* Renate Müller is Princess Liselotte. Carl Froelich directed. Black and white. In German. 91 minutes.

1936 August Der Starke

Bohnen is powerful king Augustus the Strong for a second time on screen. The king has a weakness for wine and women, especially Lil Dagover. Paul Wegener directed. Black and white. In German. 105 minutes.

1939 Das Unsterbliche Herz

Bohnen has a minor role in *The Immortal Heart,* a film about Peter Henlein, the man who invented the pocket watch in 1510. Veit Harlan directed. Black and white. In German. 104 minutes.

1940 Achtung! Feind Hört Mit!

Bohnen has a small role in this spy movie starring Kirsten Heiberg. Arthur Maria Rabenalt directed. Black and white. In German. 100 minutes.

1940 Der Liebe Augustin

Bohnen gets to sing again in this Austrian musical about a famous 18th-century Viennese beer cellar singer. E. W. Emo directed. Black and white. In German. 94 minutes.

1940 Die Rothschilds

Bohnen has a small role in this film about the Rothschild banking family. It was banned after the war. Erich

Waschneck directed. Black and white. In German. 94 minutes.

1943 Münchhausen
This famous color fantasy extravaganza features Bohnen as Count Karl von Braunschweig. Hans Albers plays Baron Münchhausen. Josef von Backy directed. Color. In German. 130 minutes.

1945 Meine Herren Söhne
Bohnen has a small role in this family-style movie starring Monika Burg. Robert A. Stemmle directed. Black and white. In German. 85 minutes.

BOITO, ARRIGO
Italian composer/librettist (1842–1918)

Arrigo Boito was a fine composer and an equally great librettist. His texts for Verdi's FALSTAFF and OTELLO are among the finest ever written, and he deserves a lot of credit for helping to persuade the composer to write his last two operas. Boito studied at the Milan Conservatory and wrote the text for Verdi's *Inno delle Nazione* a year after graduation. His other notable librettos include LA GIOCONDA for Ponchielli, and a revision of Verdi's SIMON BOCCANEGRA. He composed two operas to his own librettos. MEFISTOFELE, a version of the Faust legend based on the Goethe novel, is far different from Gounod's and remains in the repertory. The other, NERONE, is not widely performed although the publication of its libretto was a major literary event in its time. Arrigo's brother Camillo was also a fine writer; one of his stories provided the basis for Visconti's operatic film *Senso*.

BOLCOM, WILLIAM
American composer (1938–)

William Bolcom, who moves among jazz, cabaret, and classical music in company with his wife, Joan Morris, avoids European styles in his operas. He began with the "cabaret opera" *Dynamite Tonight*, composed to a libretto by constant collaborator Arnold Weinstein. He followed it with the cabaret opera *Casino Paradise* and then wrote the score for the independent film *Hester Street* (1975). He was awarded the Pulitzer Prize for Music in 1988 for his *Twelve New Etudes* for piano. His first major opera was MCTEAGUE, based on the film *Greed* and the novel that inspired it. It was premiered by Lyric Opera of Chicago in 1992 in a production by ROBERT ALTMAN. *A View from the Bridge*, based on the Arthur Miller play, was premiered by Lyric Opera in 1999. Its success led Lyric Opera to commission further operas, starting with *A Wedding* based on Altman's 1978 film.

BOLES, JOHN
American baritone (1895–1969)

Texas baritone John Boles was a mainstay of the Hollywood operetta in its heyday during the 1930s after he had won fame on Broadway. He was the Red Shadow in the first film of THE DESERT SONG in 1929 and the singing hero of the even more successful RIO RITA the same year. In 1934, he costarred with Gloria Swanson in a film of Jerome Kern's operetta MUSIC IN THE AIR. He sang with Met soprano GLADYS SWARTHOUT in two movies, the 1935 *Rose of the Rancho* and the 1938 *Romance in the Dark*. In the latter, he had the chance to try his voice out on a real opera duet, joining her in "Là ci darem la mano" from *Don Giovanni*. Boles is probably best known today, however, for his nonsinging roles, especially as Dr. Frankenstein's friend in the 1931 *Frankenstein* and as the romantic lead in the 1937 *Stella Dallas*.

BOLSHOI OPERA
Moscow opera house (1856–)

The Bolshoi (the word means *Grand*) Opera is the principal opera house in Russia and one of the most famous in the world. The original theater was built in 1825, and the present building dates from 1856. It can be seen in all its glory in a number of videos. See BORIS GODUNOV (1978/1987), CARMEN (1959), EUGENE ONEGIN (1993), IOLANTA (1963), KHOVANSHCHINA (1979), A LIFE FOR THE TSAR (1992), THE MAID OF ORLEANS (1881), MLADA (1992), PRINCE IGOR (1951), QUEEN OF SPADES (1983), and THE SNOW MAIDEN.

1951 Bolshoi Koncert
Bolshoi Koncert, released in the United States as *The Grand Concert,* is an opera/dance recital film directed by Vera Stroyeva, who also shot notable films of operas. The first 45 minutes of *Koncert* features excerpts from *Prince Igor* with Alexander Pirogov as Igor, Yevgeniya Smolenskaya as his wife, and Maxim Mikhailov as Khan Konchak; Olga Lepeshinskaya is principal dancer in the Polovetsian Dances sequence. Other highlights include Mark Reizen singing an aria from *A Life for the Tsar* and Ivan Kozlovsky singing Lensky's aria from *Eugene Onegin*. Black and white. In Russian. 105 minutes.

1989 Great Gala for Armenia
An all-star gala concert was held at the Bolshoi Opera in 1989 to raise money for victims of an earthquake in Armenia. The singers included Yevgeny Nesterenko, Alfredo Kraus, Hermann Prey, Carlo Bergonzi, and Irina Arkhipova. Color. 120 minutes. Kultur VHS.

1999 Russian Opera at the Bolshoi
Documentary portrait of the Bolshoi Opera including the theater, its operatic productions, and its major singers. Photographs, recordings, and archival footage bring its history alive, with early scenes of Feodor Chaliapin and Ivan Kozlovsky, but most of the video consists of scenes from Bolshoi stage productions. Galina Vishnevskaya, Elena Obratsova, and Irina Arkhipova are among the singers. Black and white and color. Singing in Russian with English subtitles. 112 minutes. Kultur/Bel Canto Society VHS.

BOLVARY, GEZA VON
Hungarian film director (1897–1961)

Geza von Bolvary began directing in Hungary in 1920, but he worked mainly in Austria and Germany. He specialized in music films, including many based on operas or operettas, often in collaboration with screenwriter Ernst Marischka. One of their most interesting and influential films was the 1937 ZAUBER DER BOHÈME, a "parallel" story of *La bohème* in that what happens to the opera characters is reflected in the lives of the "real" screen characters. His operetta films include Zeller's DER VOGELHÄNDLER (1935), Heuberger's DER OPERNBALL (1939), Strauss's DIE FLEDERMAUS (1946), and Lehár's SCHÖN IST DIE WELT (1954), plus three with music by Robert Stolz: ZWEI HERZEN IN DREIVIERTELTAKT (1930), DIE LUSTIGEN WEIBER VON WIEN (1931), and FRÜH-JAHRSPARADE (1934). He directed JARMILA NOVOTNÁ in *Die Nacht der Grossen Liebe* in 1933 and BENIAMINO GIGLI in the 1940 RITORNO, and made a narrative version of Donizetti's LA FILLE DU RÉGIMENT in 1953.

BONANOVA, FORTUNIO
Spanish baritone (1896–1969)

Fortunio Bonanova is better known as a film actor than as an opera singer, but he sang widely in Europe during the 1920s. He began his opera career in Madrid, appeared as Escamillo in *Carmen* in Paris, and toured Europe and Latin America. He reached Broadway in 1930 and then moved on to Hollywood. His first film, however, was made in 1922 in Spain, a version of the classic *Don Juan Tenorio*, and he was featured in Spanish-language shorts at the beginning of the sound era. His Hollywood career began in 1932 with *A Successful Calamity*, in which he played a musician sponsored by Mary Astor. In the Grace Moore film biography SO THIS IS LOVE, he plays Dr. P. Mario Mariofiti who helps to restore her lost voice. His greatest role came in the Orson Welles film CITIZEN KANE; he plays the despairing vocal coach of would-be opera singer Susan Alexander Kane. When she attempts to sing "Una voce poco fa," he lets us know that she can't make the grade. His many other films include *Tropic*

Holiday, The Black Swan, Five Graves to Cairo, Blood and Sand, An Affair to Remember, Double Indemnity, For Whom the Bell Tolls, The Moon Is Blue, and *September Affair.* He also appeared in Mexican films and TV series.

BONELLI, RICHARD
American baritone (1887–1980)

Richard Bonelli studied under Jean de Reszke in Paris and made his debut at the Brooklyn Academy in 1915 as Valentin in *Faust.* He established his reputation in Europe with the San Carlo Opera and then returned to the United States for performances in Chicago and San Francisco. He made his debut at the Metropolitan in 1932 as Germont opposite Rosa Ponselle's Violetta. He was usually cast in Verdi operas but also sang Valentin and Tonio.

1928 Movietone films
Bonelli starred in two sound films for Fox in 1928 in a series titled *Movietone Numbers,* which were intended to compete with the Vitaphone opera shorts. He performs the prologue from *Pagliacci* on one and "Largo al factotum" from *The Barber of Seville* on the other. Black and white. Each about 8 minutes.

1933 Enter Madame
Bonelli and Nina Koshetz are the featured singers in this romantic comedy partially set in the world of opera. There are selections from *Cavalleria rusticana, Tosca,* and *Il trovatore.* The film is mainly about millionaire Cary Grant and his marriage to opera singer Elissa Landi. Elliott Nugent directed. Paramount. Black and white. 81 minutes.

1941 There's Magic in Music
Bonelli joins Met colleague Irra Petina in this film about a burlesque singer (Susanna Foster) who is transformed into an opera diva at a music camp. It includes selections from *Carmen, Faust,* and Meyerbeer's *Dinorah.* Andrew L. Stone directed. Also known as *The Hard-boiled Canary.* Paramount. Black and white. 80 minutes.

BONYNGE, RICHARD
Australian conductor (1930–)

Richard Bonynge rose to fame as a conductor with his wife Joan Sutherland and conducts all her operas on video. He was also an opera scholar and, as Sutherland's career advisor, helped her to build an unusual repertory of operas by Bellini and other lesser known composers. He began conducting operas with his wife in 1963, first with *Faust* in Vancouver and then with *La sonnambula* in San Francisco. His operas and TV programs on video, most but not all with Sutherland, include ADRIANA LECOUVREUR (1984), ANNA BOLENA (1984/1985), IL BARBIERE DI SIVIGLIA (1972), DIE CSÁRDÁSFÜRSTIN (1990), DIALOGUES DES CARMÉLITES (1985), DON GIOVANNI (1978), FAUST (1973), LA FILLE DU RÉGIMENT (1972/1986), DIE FLEDERMAUS (1982/1990), HAMLET, VICTOR HERBERT (1973), LES HUGUENOTS (1990), LAKMÉ (1976/1976/1987 film), LUCIA DI LAMMERMOOR (1973/1982/1986), LUCREZIA BORGIA (1977/1980), DIE LUSTIGE WITWE (1988), MARIA STUARDA (2000), METROPOLITAN OPERA (1972/1983/1986), MIGNON (1973), NORMA (1978/1981), IVOR NOVELLO (1975), LE NOZZE DI FIGARO (1972), LA PÉRICHOLE, (1973), I PURITANI (1985), RIGOLETTO (1973), SEMIRAMIDE (1986), LA TRAVIATA (1973), IL TROVATORE (1983), and DIE ZAUBERFLÖTE (1986). For the many concerts and programs he conducted with his wife, see JOAN SUTHERLAND.

1972/1973 Who's Afraid of Opera?
Bonynge conducts the London Symphony Orchestra while Sutherland stars in highlight versions of operas for young audiences, telling the story to puppets and performing the leading roles. The operas are IL BARBIERE DI SIVIGLIA, LA FILLE DU REGIMENT, FAUST, LUCIA DI LAMMERMOOR, MIGNON, LA PÉRICHOLE, RIGOLETTO, and LA TRAVIATA. George Djurkovic designed the sets and Richard. Color. Each 30 minutes. Kultur VHS.

BOORMAN, JOHN
English film director (1933–)

John Boorman, known for such powerful dramatic films as *Point Blank* and *Deliverance,* has featured Wagnerian opera music in several of his movies. *Excalibur* (1981) includes extracts from PARSIFAL, GÖTTERDÄMMERUNG, and TRISTAN UND ISOLDE. *Hope and Glory* (1987) features music from DIE MEISTERSINGER that seems to help a World War II blimp to soar.

BORÉADES, LES
1763 opera by Rameau

The Boreads of the title are descendants of the wind god Boreas. Their queen wants to marry a non-Boread and decides to abdicate for love, but the gods work out a better solution. JEAN-PHILIPPE RAMEAU's opera *Les Boréades,* composed to a libretto by Louis De Cahusac, has been recorded by John Eliot Gardiner but is rarely staged. It was considered subversive in its time because the abdication of monarchs was thought to be a bad idea. Folklore holds that the Paris Opera house burned down during its rehearsals.

1987 Aria
ROBERT ALTMAN's episode of the opera film ARIA derives from a legend that inmates of French insane asylums during the 18th century were invited to the opera once a year. In the film, they attend a performance of *Les Boréades* at the Ranelagh Theater in Paris. Altman made the film after staging *The Rake's Progress* in Lyons, the final scene of which is set in a Hogarthian lunatic asylum. The stage performance of the opera is never shown in the film; we see only the audience. The actors include Genevieve Page as the brothel keeper, Julie Hagerty, Bertrand Bonvoisin, Cris Campion, and Delphine Rich. The singers are Jennifer Smith, Anne-Marie Rodde, and Philip Langridge, with John Eliot Gardiner conducting the Monteverdi Choir and English Baroque Soloists. Charles Dill ends his book *Monstrous Opera, Rameau and the Tragic Tradition* (Princeton University Press/1998) with a four-page examination of this fascinating film.

BORIS GODUNOV
1869 opera by Mussorgsky

MODEST MUSSORGSKY's *Boris Godunov* was completed in 1869, first performed in 1874, and promoted to success by Rimsky-Korsakov with a revised orchestration (which purists disapprove of today). It became popular in the West when Chaliapin began singing the role of Boris in the great opera houses. Mussorgsky based his libretto on a Pushkin tragedy. Boris Godunov murders Dimitri, the young heir, so he can become Tsar. When another young man, Grigory, pretends to be Dimitri, many people believe him, and Boris is full of doubts. The opera has been quite popular with filmmakers, and music from it is often featured in telecast tributes like one honoring NICOLAI GHIAUROV in 1986 and one celebrating KIROV OPERA at Covent Garden in 1992.

1954 Stroyeva film
Soviet feature film: Vera Stroyeva (director/screenplay), Vasily Nebolsin (conductor, Bolshoi Theater Orchestra and Chorus), V. Nikolayev (cinematographer), Mosfilm (production).

Cast: Alexander Pirogov (Boris), Gyorgy Nellep (Dimitri), Larissa Avdeyeva (Marina), Maksim Mikhailov (Pimen), Aleksei Krivchenya (Varlaam), Ivan Kozlovsky (Fool).

Video: Corinth/House of Opera VHS/Image Entertainment LD. Color. In Russian with English subtitles. 105 minutes.

Comment: Impressive film with massive sets, huge crowds, elaborate costumes, and location scenes shot in monasteries and Moscow streets and at the Kremlin.

Boris Godunov (1954): Alexander Pirogov as Boris in Vera Stroyeva's Soviet film of the opera.

1961 NBC Opera Theatre

American TV production: Samuel Chotzinoff (producer), Peter Herman Adler (conductor, Symphony of the Air Orchestra), Ed Wittstein (set designer), John Gutman (English translation).

Cast: Giorgio Tozzi (Boris), Frank Poretta (Dimitri), Gloria Lane (Marina), Jeanette Scovotti (Xenia), Richard Cross (Pimen), Andrew McKinley (Shuisky), Spiro Malas (Varlaam), Lee Cass (Rangoni), Joan Caplan (Nurse).

Video: Lyric VHS. Telecast on March 26, 1961. Kirk Browning (director). Black and white. In English. 120 minutes.

1962 Voice of Firestone

American TV production: Howard Mitchell (conductor, Firestone Orchestra).

Cast: Jerome Hines (Boris).

Video: VAI VHS *Jerome Hines in Opera and Song.* Telecast November 18, 1962. Black and white. In Russian with English introduction. 12 minutes.

Comment: Extended scenes from opera, staged with sets and extras, beginning with the Coronation and including the Farewell and Death of Boris.

**1978 Bolshoi Opera

Russia stage production: Leonid Baratov (director), Boris Khaikin (conductor, Bolshoi Theater Orchestra and Chorus).

Cast: Yevgeny Nesterenko (Boris), Vladislav Piavko (Dimitri), Artur Eisen (Varlaam), Irina Arkhipova (Marina), Valery Yaroslavtsev (Pimen), Andrei Solokov (Shuisky), Galina Kalinina (Xenia), Aleksei Maslennikov (Fool).

Video: Kultur/Bel Canto Society VHS. Boris Pokrovsky (director). Color. In Russian with English subtitles. 174 minutes.

Comment: Nesterenko is a magnificent Boris, both singing and acting in this traditional realistic Bolshoi production.

1980 Paris Opéra

French stage production: Joseph Losey (director), Rousslan Raichev (conductor, Paris Opéra Orchestra and Chorus), Emile Aillaud (set/costume designer)

Cast: Ruggero Raimondi (Boris), Wieslaw Ochman (Dimitri), Kenneth Riegel (Shuisky), Victoria Cortez (Marina), Peter Memen (Pimen), Aage Haugland (Varlaam), Roger Soyer (Rangoni), Jules Bastin (Nikitine), Christine Barbaux (Xenia).

Video: House of Opera/Lyric VHS. Telecast in France August 24, 1980. Dirk Sanders (director). Color. In Russian. 179 minutes.

1987 Bolshoi Opera

Russian stage production: Irina Morozova (director, based on production by Leonid Baratov), Alexander Lazarev (conductor, Bolshoi Opera Orchestra and Chorus).

Cast: Yevgeny Nesterenko (Boris), Vladislav Piavko (Dimitri), Tamara Sinyavskaya (Marina), Alexander Vedernikov (Pimen), Artur Eisen (Varlaam), Nelya Lebedeva (Xenia), Tatiana Yerastova (Fyodor), Vladimir Kudryashov (Shuisky).

Video: Home Vision VHS. Derek Bailey (director). Color. In Russian with English subtitles. 171 minutes.

Comment: More or less the same production as the 1978 Bolshoi video, but Nesterenko is 20 years older here and less exciting.

1989 Zulawski film

Polish feature film: Andrzej Zulawski (director), Mstislav Rostropovich (conductor, National Symphony Orchestra, Oratorio Society and Choral Arts Society of Washington), Andrzej Jaroszewic and Pierre-Laurent Chenieux (cinematographers), Nicolas Dvigoubsky (set designer).

Cast: Ruggero Raimondi (Boris), Kenneth Riegel (Shuisky), Delphine Forest (Marina, sung by Galina Vishnevskaya), Romuald Tesarowicz (Varlaam), Bernard Lefort (Pimen, sung by Paul Plishka), Pavel Slaby (Dimitri, sung by Vyacheslav Polosov), Pavel Slaby (Simpleton, sung by Nicolai Gedda).

Color. In Russian. 115 minutes.

***1990 Kirov Opera

Russian stage production: Stephen Lawless (director, based on London production by Andrei Tarkovsky), Valery Gergiev (conductor, Kirov Theater Orchestra and Chorus), Nicholas Dvigoubsky (set/costume designer).

Cast: Robert Lloyd (Boris), Alexei Steblianko (Dimitri), Olga Borodina (Marina), Alexandr Morozov (Pimen), Vladimir Ognovenko (Varlaam), Sergei Leiferkus (Rangoni), Larissa Dyatkova (Fyodor), Yevgeny Boitsov (Shuisky).

Video: Philips DVD/VHS/LD. Humphrey Burton (director). Color. In Russian with English subtitles. 221 minutes.

Comment: Soviet filmmaker Andrei Tarkovsky, who created this stage production at the Royal Opera, Covent Garden, in 1983, died in 1986, but the Kirov restaged it as closely as possible. Like his great films, it is striking visually and dramatically.

1993 Grand Théâtre de Genève

Swiss stage production: Stein Winge (director), Edo De Waart (conductor, Orchestre de la Suisse Romande and Chorus of the Grand Théâtre de Genève), Göran Wassberg (set designer).

Cast: Samuel Ramey (Boris), Vesselina Zorova (Marina), John Tomlinson (Pimen), Eirian James (Fyodor), Lesley Garrett (Xenia), Antony Rolfe Johnson (Shuisky), Kim Begley (Dimitri), Henk Smit (Varlaam).

Video: House of Opera DVD/VHS. Michel Dami (director). Color. In Russian with French subtitles. 140 minutes.

Early/related films

1907 Boris Godunov

This *Boris Godunov* was the first fiction film made in Russia. It features scenes from the Pushkin play, on which the opera is based, filmed at the Eden summer theater in St. Petersburg. Ivan Shuvalov directed. Black and white. Silent. About 11 minutes.

1927 Vitaphone film with Barclay

English baritone John Barclay sings an aria from *Boris Godunov* in the style of Chaliapin in this Vitaphone sound film. Black and white. In Russian. About 10 minutes.

1953 Ukrainian Concert Hall

Ukrainian basso Boris Gmirya (aka Borys Hmyrya) is the star of the 1953 Soviet concert film *Ukrainian Concert Hall,* and his number from *Boris Godunov* is the highlight of the concert. Boris Barnett directed. Color. In Russian with English subtitles. 52 minutes.

1953 Tonight We Sing

Ezio Pinza plays Chaliapin and sings the Coronation and Death scenes from *Boris Godunov* in this film about impresario Sol Hurok. See TONIGHT WE SING.

1963 Panorama of Russia

The Soviet documentary *Pesni Rossii* (Panorama of Russia), basically a musical tour of the USSR with opera singers Irina Arkhipova and Boris Shtokolov, includes an excerpt from *Boris Godunov*. Yefil Uchitel directed. Black and white. In Russian. 65 minutes.

1966 The Opera Makers

Documentary about preparations for a production of *Boris Godunov* at the Chicago Lyric Opera with Nicolai Ghiaurov as Boris and Bruno Bartoletti conducting the Chicago Lyric Opera Orchestra and Chorus. The filmmakers, who follow the production from casting through the first night, are writer Hal Wallace, cinematographer Morry Bleckman, and director Al Schwartz. Produced for WBKB-TV in Chicago. Color. In English. 60 minutes.

1986 Boris Godunov

This *Boris Godunov* is an epic, non-operatic Soviet film based on the Pushkin poem and directed by Sergei Bondarchuk, who made the seven-hour Soviet film of *War and Peace*. Bondarchuk plays Boris himself with a supporting cast that includes Alexander Soloviev, Adriana Bierdjinskay, and Antatoli Romanchine. Color. In Russian. 164 minutes.

BORKH, INGE
Swiss soprano (1921–)

Lyric/dramatic soprano Inge Borkh was most famous for her performances as Salome and Elektra. They are widely available on record, but there appears to be only one video of her in performance. She sings the role of Jocasta in Stravinsky's OEDIPUS REX (1961 film) on a Leonard Bernstein television program.

BORODIN, ALEXANDER
Russian composer (1833–1887)

Alexander Borodin tried to be both chemist and composer so, not surprisingly, he did not have time to finish most of his operas. He labored over PRINCE IGOR for 18 years, for example, and never completed it. What we see on stage is a completion made by colleagues Rimsky-Korsakov and Glazunov, although the magnificent melodies are all Borodin's. To the non-opera public, Borodin is best known as the man who wrote the original music for the pastiche operetta KISMET, a success on stage and screen and one of the classics of music theater.

1948 Song of My Heart

Robert Barron plays Borodin in this much-disliked American film about Tchaikovsky. See PYOTR TCHAIKOVSKY.

BOSE, HANS-JÜRGEN VON
German composer (1953–)

Munich-born Hans-Jürgen von Bose is not well known in the United States, but he has written and composed two operas based on American novels. The most ambitious is *Schlachthof,* with libretto by the composer, based on Kurt Vonnegut's novel *Slaughterhouse 5* about the fire-bombing of Dresden during World War II. It premiered at the Munich Festival in 1996. (An American film of the novel was made in 1972 by George Roy Hill.) Bose's other American opera is 63: DREAM PALACE, with libretto in English and based on a novel by James Purdy, which premiered in Munich in 1990. Bose's best-known opera is DIE LEIDEN DES JUNGEN WERTHERS, an adaptation of Goethe's *The Sorrows of Young Werther,* first staged at Schwetzingen in 1986. Three of Bose's operas have been telecast in Germany.

1987 Hans-Jürgen von Bose
German documentary about Bose made for the *Young German Composers* TV series. It includes scenes from his ballet *Das Nacht au Belie* and opera *Die Leiden des jungen Werthers* plus extracts from his *Three Songs.* Detlef-Michael Behrens directed. Color. In English or German. 17 minutes. Goethe Institute Inter Nationes VHS.

BOSTON

Boston has always been one of the opera centers of the United States, and for a time at the turn of the century the Boston Opera Company was a major rival for the Met. The city has premiered many famous operas, including George Gershwin's PORGY AND BESS in 1935 and Leonard Bernstein's CANDIDE in 1956. SARAH CALDWELL established her innovative Opera Company of Boston in 1958 and staged many notable productions, and many NET OPERA productions were produced from Boston with Boston orchestras. Boston Lyric Opera, founded in 1976, has been very popular. See also BÉATRICE ET BÉNÉDICT (1979) and OEDIPUS REX (1973).

BOULEZ, PIERRE
French conductor/composer (1925–)

Pierre Boulez was not attracted to opera when he was a composer; in fact, he suggested that opera houses should be blown up. He changed his mind when he became an opera conductor. His DER RING DES NIBELUNGEN cycle at Bayreuth in 1980 was the first to be televised and made available on video, and DAS RHEINGOLD, DIE WALKÜRE, SIEGFRIED, and GÖTTERDÄMMERUNG have all been issued separately. He conducted the music for Peter Patzak's

1987 film *Richard and Cosima,* and he can be seen in person in Richard Leacock's film about IGOR STRAVINSKY (1968) and two films about ARNOLD SCHOENBERG (1989/1998). See BAYREUTH (1976/1985), LULU (1979), PELLÉAS ET MÉLISANDE (1992), RICHARD WAGNER (1987/1998), and TRISTAN UND ISOLDE (1967).

1989 Pierre Boulez—The Birth of Gesture
Oliver Mille's documentary centers around classes given by Boulez at Villeneuve-les-Avignon in July 1988. He is shown advising young conductors as they direct the InterContemporain Ensemble. There is also footage of Boulez in rehearsal in 1988 with the BBC Symphony Orchestra and Jessye Norman as well as extracts from compositions by Boulez sung by Phyllis Bryn-Julson. Color. In French. 55 minutes.

BOURGEOIS GENTILHOMME, LE
1670 comédie-ballet by Lully and Molière

Jean-Baptiste Lully wrote the music for *Le Bourgeois Gentilhomme* (The Would-Be Gentleman) to a libretto by Molière in 1670. Although it's really a play with songs and dances, it's a close relative of opera and has been quite influential in various way. Monsieur Jourdain is a wealthy bourgeois who wants to emulate the nobility. He won't allow his daughter to marry anyone except an aristocrat but gets tricked into believing that the man she wants to wed is a Grand Turk. Hugo von Hofmannsthal and Richard Strauss devised a way to combine the play with their opera *Ariadne auf Naxos;* it would be performed as an entertainment after the dinner that concludes the play in the presence of Jourdain. When the combination was staged in 1912, it was way too long (more than six hours), so Hofmannsthal had to revise it and the Molière play was cut. The second shorter version is the one commonly staged.

1955 NBC Opera Theatre
American television production: John Schwartz (director), Peter Herman Adler (conductor, Symphony of the Air Orchestra), Samuel Chotzinoff (producer), Reuben Ter-Arutunian (set/costume designer), John Wood (English version of *Le bourgeois gentilhomme*), George and Phyllis Mead (English version of *Ariadne auf Naxos*).

Bourgeois cast: Wally Cox (M. Jourdain), Charlotte Rade (Mme. Jourdain), Anita Darian (Nicole), Ross Martin (Dorante).

Ariadne cast: Wilma Spence (Ariadne), Virginia MacWatters (Zerbinetta), Robert Marshall (Bacchus), Joan Marie Moynagh (Echo), Robert Goss (Harlequin), Joan Carroll (Naiad).

Video at the MTR. Telecast live February 27, 1955. Kirk Browning (director). Black and white. In English. 90 minutes.

Comment: This ambitious NBC production attempts to re-create the original staging with abridged versions of opera and play. Comic arias are sung in English; *seria* music is sung in German.

1958 Comédie Française film
French feature film: Jean Meyer (director), André Jolivet (conductor), Jean-Baptiste Lully (composer), Henri Alekan (cinematographer).

Cast: Louis Seigner (M. Jourdain), Andrée de Chauveron (Mme. Jourdain), Micheline Boudet (Nicole), Jean Piat (Cléonte), Jean Meyer (Covielle), and Michèle Grellier (Lucile).

Video: Video Yesteryear VHS. Color. In French with English subtitles. 96 minutes.

BOWMAN, JAMES
English countertenor (1941–)

James Bowman is one of the singers who has helped popularize the countertenor voice. He made his debut as Oberon at Aldeburgh in Benjamin Britten's A MIDSUMMER NIGHT'S DREAM in 1967 and became well known singing the role around the world; he can be seen in it at Glyndebourne on a 1981 video. Bowman is well suited to both modern and baroque operas, but he has been particularly associated with Handel. He is the villainous Ptolemy in English National Opera's 1984 English-language production of Handel's GIULIO CESARE, and he plays the castrato Nicolini who originated the role of RINALDO in the film *Honour, Profit and Pleasure*. In Tony Palmer's 1981 film of Britten's DEATH IN VENICE, he is the voice of Apollo. See also BENJAMIN BRITTEN (2001), COUNTERTENORS (2000), DIDO AND AENEAS (1995), and ORLANDO FURIOSO (1978).

BRAVO, IL
1839 opera by Mercadante

The original source of Italian composer Saverio Mercadante's 1839 opera *Il Bravo* is American writer James Fenimore Cooper's 1831 novel *The Bravo, A Venetian Story;* it was turned into a libretto by Gaetano Rossi and Marco Marcello. The setting is 16th-century Venice, and the "bravo" of the title is an assassin under the control of the governing Council of Ten. He is hired by Teodora to kidnap her daughter but then reveals that he is the girl's father. It gets even more complicated.

1990 Festival della Valle d'Itria
Italian stage production: Bruno Aprea (conductor, Orchestra Internazionale d'Italia and Bratislava Philharmonic Chorus).

Cast: Dino di Dominico (the Bravo), Adelisa Tabiado (Teodora), Stefano Antonucci (Foscari), Janet Perry (Violetta), Sergio Bertocchi (Pisani).

Video: House of Opera DVD and VHS/Opera Dubs VHS. Color. In Italian. 165 minutes.

Comment: Staged in Palazzo Ducale in Martina Franca for the Festival della Valle d'Itria

BRECHT, BERTOLT
German librettist/dramatist (1898–1956)

Poet-playwright Bertolt Brecht is important in the operatic world for his collaborations in Germany with composer KURT WEILL from 1927 to 1933. Together they revolutionized ideas about the musical stage, notably with the hugely successful DIE DREIGROSCHENOPER but also with HAPPY END, DER LINDBERGHFLUG, AUFSTIEG UND FALL DER STADT MAHAGONNY, and DIE SIEBEN TODSÜNDEN. Both men fled the Nazi regime and ended up in the United States, but they never worked together there. Brecht had a strong influence on American opera composer MARC BLITZSTEIN, whom he encouraged to write THE CRADLE WILL ROCK, and Blitzstein returned the favor by helping make *The Threepenny Opera* successful in the United States after its initial failure.

BREEN, BOBBY
Canadian-born American boy soprano (1927–)

Bobby Breen, who began his vocal career on the Eddie Cantor radio show and was the singing equivalent of Shirley Temple for RKO, featured opera arias in his films. He became an instant star, with his opera-oriented first film, the 1936 *Let's Sing Again,* and made seven more in a similar style. Also successful were *Rainbow on the River, Make a Wish,* and *Hawaii Calls.* After his movie career ended in 1942, Breen became a nightclub singer.

1936 Let's Sing Again
Breen plays the son of an opera singer who runs away from an orphanage and joins a once-famous Italian tenor in a traveling theater. The tenor has lost his voice, but he has kept the opera records he made in his early years; with them he teaches Breen to sing opera arias, beginning with "La donna è mobile." The boy is a hit in the show and eventually is reunited with his father. See LET'S SING AGAIN.

BRETÓN, TOMÁS
Spanish composer (1850–1923)

Tomás Bretón y Hernandez, one of the best known composers of zarzuelas, devoted much of his life to trying to create truly Spanish operas. The most successful was LA DOLORES, which has been staged around the world and filmed. He is also remembered for the hugely popular zarzuela LA VERBENA DE LA PALOMA (1894), which features a realistic portrayal of working-class Madrid street life; it is ranked among the great works of the genre and has been filmed three times.

BRIGANDS, LES
1869 opéra-bouffe by Offenbach

JACQUES OFFENBACH's satirical operetta *Les brigands* is the story of an Italian bandit gang as satirically imagined by creative librettists Ludovic Halévy and Henri Meilhac. Business is bad for the bandits as there are far bigger thieves in banks and government. Bandit chief Falsacappa's daughter Fiorella and chocolate shop owner Fragoletto have a flirtation, but it is the Duke of Mantua who wins her heart. Meanwhile the Carabinieri police threaten, but they always arrive too late. *Les brigands* is the French counterpart of a Gilbert and Sullivan satire, a pleasant diversion with infectious melodies and double-dyed deception. It was very popular in the 19th century and has had many recent revivals.

***1989 Opéra de Lyon
French stage production: Louis Erlo and Alain Maratrat (directors), Claire Gibault (conductor, Opéra de Lyon Orchestra and Chorus), Gian Maurizio Fercioni (set designer), Jean-Marie Bergis (cinematographer).
Cast: Michel Trempont (Falsacappa), Valérie Chevalier (Fiorella), Colette Alliot-Lugaz (Fragoletto), Jean-Luc Maurette (Duke of Mantua), Ricardo Cassinelli (Pietro), Georges Gautier (de Campo-Tasso), Jan-Luci Viala (Gloria-Cassis).
Video: Image Entertainment DVD/Home Vision/Pioneer VHS. Yves-André Hubert (director). Color. In French with English subtitles. 122 minutes.
Comment: The high jinks of the Italian bandits are here transposed to gangland Chicago and a gigantic but well-utilized three-level set.

BRIGNONE, GUIDO
Italian film director (1887–1959)

Guido Brignone, who began working in the cinema in 1913, directed films from 1930 to 1958 and was a specialist in music movie, often featuring opera tenors. He helped create tenor TITO SCHIPA's cinema career with the hit movie VIVERE (1937); directed tenor Beniamino Gigli in MAMMA (1941), VERTIGINE (1942), and VOGLIO BENE SOLTANTO A TE (1946); and produced three of tenor GIUSEPPE LUGO's films. He made a film version of the opera LA WALLY (1931) and directed biographies of GIOVANNI PERGOLESI (1932) and MARIA MALIBRAN (1943), with Maria Cebotari as the diva.

BRITTEN, BENJAMIN
English composer (1913–1976)

Benjamin Britten almost single-handedly revived the reputation of British opera. His 1945 PETER GRIMES created a sensation, and nearly every work afterwards was accepted as an instant classic. His sympathy for innocence badly treated is seen in many of his operas, including PETER GRIMES, THE RAPE OF LUCRETIA, and BILLY BUDD. Some critics see in this a reflection of his problems in being gay in a less-tolerant era; the potency of his last opera, DEATH IN VENICE, based on the Thomas Mann novel, is seen as a particular example of this. Britten's lifetime companion PETER PEARS had roles in almost all of his operas. The first operas by Britten to be televised were LET'S MAKE AN OPERA (incorporating *The Little Sweep*) on BBC in 1950, and BILLY BUDD on NBC TV in 1952, while OWEN WINGRAVE (1971) was actually composed for television. Britten also composed music for several films, including memorable scores for documentaries, and founded the famous Aldeburgh Festival in Suffolk. He was given a peerage in 1976 shortly before his death. Most of his other operas are also available on video, including ALBERT HERRING, CURLEW RIVER, GLORIANA, A MIDSUMMER NIGHT'S DREAM, NOYE'S FLUDDE, and THE TURN OF THE SCREW, plus the oratorio WAR REQUIEM.

1936–1938 British documentary films
Britten wrote music for British documentary films from 1936 to 1938. The most famous is *Night Mail*, a film poem about a mail train, on which he collaborated with poet W. H. Auden, who later wrote the libretto for Britten's opera *Paul Bunyan*. His other documentary films include *Coal Face*, *The Savings of Bill Blewit*, *Line to Tschierva*, *The Calendar of the Year*, *The Tocher*, *Advance Democracy*, and *The Way to the Sea*. They were all made for the GPO (General Post Office) and other government film units.

1937 Love From a Stranger
Britten wrote the score for only one fiction feature film, a suspense thriller about a woman who thinks she may have married a maniac. It stars Ann Harding and Basil Rathbone and is based on an Agatha Christie story. Rowland V. Lee directed. Black and white. In English. 90 minutes.

1959 Benjamin Britten

John Schlesinger was at the beginning of his career when he directed this fine documentary about Britten for the BBC Television *Monitor* series. Black and white. In English. 60 minutes.

1963 Britten at 50

Humphrey Burton produced this BBC Television tribute to Britten for the composer's 50th birthday. Britten and Peter Pears make appearances, W. H. Auden talks about their collaboration, Michael Tippett talks about music, and there are clips from films such as *Night Mail* and excerpts from operas such as *Peter Grimes*. Gennadi Rozhdestvensky conducts the London Symphony Orchestra; Huw Wheldon is moderator. Black and white. In English. 65 minutes.

1966 Rehearsal and Performance with Peter Pears

Britten rehearses and performs his "Nocturne for Tenor, Seven Obbligato Instruments and Strings" with Peter Pears and the CBC Vancouver Chamber Orchestra. Produced by CBC Vancouver. Black and white. In English. VAI DVD/VHS.

1967 Britten and His Aldeburgh Festival

The *Bell Telephone Hour* and *BBC* celebrate the 20th anniversary of the founding of the Aldeburgh Festival. Extracts from *A Midsummer Night's Dream* and *The Burning Fiery Furnace* are included, plus interviews with Peter Pears and other Britten associates. Humphrey Burton produced; Tony Palmer directed. Black and white. In English. 55 minutes. Video at the MTR.

1980 A Time There Was...

Peter Pears supplies the narrative framework for Tony Palmer's documentary *A Time There Was...A Profile of Benjamin Britten*, which focuses on Brittten's operas. Participants include E. M. Forster, Leonard Bernstein, Julian Bream, Frank Bridge, Paul Rotha, Rudolf Bing, and Mstislav Rostropovich. There is also archival and home movie footage. The film won the 1980 Italia Prize for the production company London Weekend Televison. Color. In English. 102 minutes. Kultur VHS.

1992 The British Documentary Movement

The British Documentary Movement is a six-part series examining the growth and development of the British documentary film movement; *Volume Three* is devoted to Britten, and his contribution is considered especially important because of *Night Mail* and *Coal Face*. Color and black and white. In English. 60 minutes. Kino Video VHS.

2001 Benjamin Britten: The Hidden Heart

British TV documentary about Britten concentrating on three major works, with excerpts from *Peter Grimes, Death in Venice,* and the *War Requiem*. The interviewees include James Bowman, John Britten, John Evans, Donald Mitchell, Heather Harper, and Sue Phipps. Teresa Griffiths directed for Channel 4. Color. In English. 60 minutes.

BROADWAY MELODY OF 1938
1937 American film with opera content

Opera baritone Igor Gorin portrays an operatic barber named Nicki Papaloopas in this entertaining musical about an opera-loving racehorse. The first shot of the movie shows crowds in front of the old Metropolitan Opera building and highlights posters of *Carmen*. An orchestra plays Escamillo's music, and a voice is heard singing the "Toreador Song." The camera pans right to a barber shop, where barber Gorin is singing the aria while shaving customer Buddy Ebsen. Racehorse owner Eleanor Powell finds that when Gorin sings Figaro's "Largo al factotum" from *The Barber of Seville*, her horse can win steeplechase races. The horse has to win so Robert Taylor can finance a Broadway show that is to star Powell. With Gorin and Rossini's help, it does, and the show goes on. The film also features Judy Garland singing "Dear Mr. Gable" and Sophie Tucker singing "Some of These Days." Jack McGowan and Sid Silvers wrote the screenplay, William Daniels was cinematographer, and Roy Del Ruth directed for MGM. Black and white. 113 minutes. MGM-UA VHS.

BRODERNA MOZART
1986 Swedish film with opera content

Broderna Mozart (The Mozart Brothers) is a Swedish film by Suzanne Osten about staging *Don Giovanni*, with more than a hint of homage to the Marx Brothers and *A Night at the Opera*. A stage director wants to stand the "old war-horse opera" on its head and create a vital new production. The singers lose hair and clothes, the musicians get angry, and the union becomes outraged. Only the ghost of Mozart seems happy with what is happening. Many of the actors in the film are from the Stockholm Opera. Etienne Glaser plays the stage director; Loa Falkman is Eskil, who plays Don Giovanni on stage; Agneta Ekmannder is Marian, who plays Donna Elvira; Lena T. Hansson is Ia and Donna Anna; Helge Skoog is Olof and Don Ottavio; Grith Fjelmose is Therese and Zerlina; Rune Zetterstrom is Lennart and Leporello; Krister Sit Hill is Philip and Masetto; and Niklas Ek is the Commendatore. Etienne Glaser, Niklas Radström, and Osten wrote the screenplay; Hans Weilin was cinematographer; Björn Jason Lindh was music director; and

Bengt Forslund produced for the Swedish Film Institute. Color. In Swedish with English subtitles. 98 minutes. Facets VHS.

BROKEN MELODY, THE
British and Australian films with opera content

The Broken Melody has been a popular movie title since the early silent era; three films with the title focus on the writing of an imaginary opera.

The first was a 1929 British silent film based on a play by Herbert Keith and James Leader. An exiled prince in Paris (Georges Galli) falls in love with a singer and writes an opera for her, but he then returns to his wife. Fred Paul directed for Welsh-Pearson.

More far-fetched is a 1934 British film in which a French composer (John Garrick) marries an opera diva (Margot Graham) and writes her an opera. When it flops, he becomes enraged, kills her lover, and is sent to Devil's Island. He escapes a few years later, returns to his first love (Merle Oberon), and writes a successful opera based on his experience. The governor of Devil's Island attends the premiere and recognizes his former prisoner but is so impressed he reveal nothing. Vera Allinson and Michael Hankinson wrote the screenplay, Sydney Blythe was cinematographer, and Bernard Vorhaus directed the 84-minute film for Twickenham Films.

Finally there is a 1937 Australian film based on a novel by Fred J. Thwaites and titled simply *Broken Melody* (without "The"). Lloyd Hughes stars as a man suffering from depression who discovers he has so much musical talent that he can sit down without training and write an opera. He does, too; it is hugely successful, and he wins back his girl. George Heath was cinematographer, Thwaites and Frank Harvey wrote the screenplay, and Ken G. Hall directed.

BROOK, PETER
English director (1925–)

Peter Brook was director of productions at the Royal Opera House from 1947 to 1950, but he then left to concentrate on theater and film. He made his first opera film in 1953, THE BEGGAR'S OPERA with Laurence Olivier, but won more praise 30 years later with the three 1983 films of his minimalist Paris production of Bizet's CARMEN. Brook's film career began in 1943, but stage rather than screen has always been his main love. See CARMEN (1978 film).

BROSCHI, RICCARDO
Italian composer (1698–1756)

Riccardo Broschi, the brother of the famous castrato male soprano Farinelli, wrote several operas for him.

Farinelli's most famous aria, "Son qual nave ch'agitata," was composed by Broschi for the pasticcio opera *Artaserse*, which premiered in London in 1734. It is featured in the 1994 film FARINELLI and is pretty impressive.

BROWN, ANNE
American soprano (1912–)

Anne Brown created one of the great roles in American opera in 1935—Bess in George Gershwin's PORGY AND BESS. She can be seen singing "Summertime" in the *Porgy and Bess* sequence of the 1945 Gershwin biography *Rhapsody in Blue* and is featured in the 1998 documentary *Porgy and Bess: An American Voice*. Brown was discouraged by American intolerance of African-Americans and emigrated to Norway, where she married a lawyer. Her 1979 autobiography was a best-seller in Scandinavia but was never published in the United States.

BROWNING, KIRK
Television opera director (1921–)

Kirk Browning is the D. W. Griffith of television opera, one of the major pioneers of the operatic screen, and he continues to work creatively still today. Browning essentially invented the vocabulary of filming opera for TV in America, and he directed most of the early TV opera productions. He began at NBC-TV in 1948 and became director of NBC OPERA THEATRE in 1949 under NBC music director Samuel Chotzinoff. He collaborated with conductor Peter Herman Adler on NBC and NET OPERA and also worked on the BELL TELEPHONE HOUR. He directed the first *Live From Lincoln Center* and *Live From the Met* telecasts; worked with opera companies in Washington, Chicago, Philadelphia, and Dallas on their telecasts; and won numerous awards, including an Emmy for his 1979 LA GIOCONDA. His style varies by the opera, but he is noted for his restless camera and emphasis on close-ups. Browning also helped create many TV operas, including Menotti's AMAHL AND THE NIGHT VISITORS, Stravinsky's THE FLOOD, Pasinetti's THE TRIAL OF MARY LINCOLN, and Foss's GRIFFELKIN. He directed more than 100 of the operas for television listed in this book, and there are more than 170 videos directed by Browning at the Museum of Television and Radio. He continues to work steadily. His recent productions include new America operas such as A STREETCAR NAMED DESIRE (1998) and CENTRAL PARK (1999), a new New York City Opera production of the classic PORGY AND BESS (2002), and repertory favorites such as LA BOHEME (1997), HÄNSEL UND GRETEL (1997), LE NOZZE DI FIGARO (1991), PAGLIACCI (1992), and DER SCHAUSPIELDIREKTOR (1990).

1986 Metropolitan Opera Seminar

Panel discussion with Browning at the Museum of Broadcasting (now the Museum of Television and Radio) on October 1, 1986. He talks about Metropolitan Opera telecasts with Robert M. Batscha. Color. 58 minutes. Video at the MTR.

1990 Bell Telephone Hour Seminar

Same as the panel discussion above, but on October 1, 1990. He talks about the *Bell Telephone Hour* telecasts with Robert Sherman. Color. 22 minutes. Video at the MTR.

BRUNDIBÁR
1938 Czechoslovakian opera by Krása

HANS KRÁSA created the children's opera *Brundibár* (The Bumble Bee) for a Prague orphanage using a libretto by Adolf Hoffmeister. Based on a Czech fairy tale, it tells how two children get the better of evil organ grinder Brundibár with the help of friendly animals. Krása's opera became known when the Nazis allowed a showcase production in the TEREZIN (Theresienstadt) prison camp for the International Red Cross. Krása later died in Auschwitz. The opera has been revived in recent years because of growing interest in music suppressed by the Nazis; it is now on CD and has been filmed and telecast.

1990 CST Czech Television

Czech TV film: Klaas Rusticus (director), Mario Klemens (conductor, FISYO Film Symphony Orchestra), Michael Dana (set designer), CST, Prague (production company).

Cast: Lucie Maradova, Daniel Jarzavek, Barbara Humhansova, Thomas Durs, Jan Müller, Thomas Prochazka.

Telecast October 9, 1990, on CST. Klaas Rusticus (director). Color. In Czech. 34 minutes.

1994 Mecklenburg Opera

English stage production: John Abulafia (director), Anne Manson (conductor, Mecklenburg Opera Ensemble and New London Children's Choir), Christ Baugh (set/costume designer), Maria Pattinson (choreographer), BBC Television (production).

Cast: John Addison, Catherine Hooper, Susie Plett, David Nowell-Smith, Emily Attree, Daniel Parnes, Sam Ritchie, Rebecca Bainbridge.

Telecast by BBC in 1995. Simon Broughton (director). Color. In English 28 minutes.

Comment: The production is based on designs by Frantizek Zelenka, which survived from Terezin; it was filmed at the Harrow School Theatre.

Related film

1994 The Music of Terezin

Simon Broughton's documentary film about the music and musicians of Terezin features scenes of the original Terezin production of *Brundibár*, filmed by camp officials for a Nazi propaganda film. Color. In English. 30 minutes.

BRUSCANTINI, SESTO
Italian bass-baritone (1919–2003)

Sesto Bruscantini, who began his career in Rome in 1946, was popular at the Glyndebourne Festival in the 1950s in Mozart and Rossini operas. He made his first appearance there as Don Alfonso in a telecast production of COSÌ FAN TUTTE in 1951 and then sang Guglielmo, Figaro, and Dandini. He was the archetypal Glyndebourne Mozart Figaro, made a famous recording of LE NOZZE DI FIGARO in 1955 with Sena Jurinac as the Countess, and can be seen with her on stage in the opera in the 1955 film *On Such a Night*. See DON PASQUALE (1955), L'ELISIR D'AMORE (1981), FALSTAFF (1960), LA FAVORITA (1971), LA FORZA DEL DESTINO (1978), GLYNDEBOURNE (1955), L'ITALIANA IN ALGERI (1957), METROPOLITAN OPERA (1983), and LA TRAVIATA (1973).

BRUSON, RENATO
Italian baritone (1936–)

Renato Bruson, a fine *bel canto* baritone, has sung 17 Donizetti operas and is also popular in Verdi. He made his debut in Spoleto in 1961 as Count di Luna, came to the Metropolitan as Enrico in *Lucia di Lammermoor* in 1969, and made his debut at La Scala as Antonio in Donizetti's *Linda di Chamounix*. He now sings around the world in a wide variety of roles, ranging from Falstaff to Don Giovanni, and has been featured in many opera videos, including three of *Nabucco*. See CAVALLERIA RUSTICANA (1982), DON GIOVANNI (1989), I DUE FOSCARI (1988), ERNANI (1982), FALSTAFF (1982), GIOVANNA D'ARCO (1989), LUCIA DI LAMMERMOOR (1992), LUISA MILLER (1979), MACBETH (1987), METROPOLITAN OPERA (1983), NABUCCO (1981/1986/1998), and GIUSEPPE VERDI (1989).

1992 Renato Bruson

This video about the baritone was created for the Italian opera television series *I grandi della lirica*. Color. In Italian. 60 minutes. Center (Italy) VHS.

BRYDEN, BILL
English director (1942–)

Bill Bryden, who directed the PAGLIACCI segment of the 1987 film ARIA, is primarily a theater director but he has a continuing association with opera on stage. He wrote the libretto for the 1975 opera *Hermiston*, and he staged a famous production of *Parsifal* in 1988 set in a bomb-damaged cathedral like Coventry. His films include the excellent *Ill Fares the Land* (1982).

BUCCI, MARK
American composer (1924–)

New Yorker Mark Bucci writes operas and musicals for stage and television in a singable contemporary lyric style; most have been staged. His 1953 musical adaptation of James Thurber's THE THIRTEEN CLOCKS, starring Met soprano Roberta Peters, premiered on ABC in 1953. His best-known opera is probably the one-act *Tale for a Deaf Ear*, presented by the New York City Opera in 1958 but not televised. THE HERO, a 1965 TV opera commissioned by Lincoln Center and shown on National Educational Television, won the Prix Italia in 1966.

BUENAVENTURA, LA
See THE FORTUNE TELLER.

BUMBRY, GRACE
American mezzo-soprano (1937–)

Grace Bumbry won a Metropolitan Opera audition in 1958, but she didn't make her Met debut until 1965. Her career really began in Paris in 1960 and then took off in 1961 when, as Venus, she became the first African-American to sing at Bayreuth. She sings a wide range of roles but is especially noted for her Carmen, Tosca, and Amneris. See AFRICAN-AMERICAN OPERA (2000), AIDA (1976/1987 film), CARMEN (1967/1994 film), DON CARLO (1983), HERBERT VON KARAJAN (1995), JAMES LEVINE (1996), METROPOLITAN OPERA (1983), NABUCCO (1979), PORGY AND BESS (1998 film), ROYAL OPERA HOUSE (1979), and TOSCA (1983 film).

1972 The Art of Grace Bumbry
Bumbry performs arias from Massenet's *Le Cid*, Tchaikovsky's *The Maid of Orléans*, and Verdi's *Un ballo in maschera*, plus songs by Brahms, Liszt, Schumann, and Wolf. Jacques Beaudry conducts the Orchestra of Radio-Canada, Montréal, with John Newmark on piano. Telecast January 7, 1973. Black and white. 39 minutes. VAI VHS.

BUÑUEL, LUIS
Spanish film director (1900–1983)

Luis Buñuel, one of the masters of cinema, seems to have been obsessed by Richard Wagner's operas, especially *Tristan und Isolde,* as he often featured Wagner music in his films. His first, *Un chien andalou* (1928), has music from TRISTAN UND ISOLDE. *L'Âge d'or* (1930) uses music from *Tristan und Isolde* and SIEGFRIED. *Wuthering Heights* (1954) uses themes from *Tristan und Isolde* as its entire music track. *That Obscure Object of Desire* (1977) features a duet from DIE WALKÜRE. Buñuel was also involved in Spanish opera and zarzuela films. His first job in Paris was as set designer for a production of Manuel de Falla's *El retablo de maese Pedro*. In 1935, he began to produce, write, and direct zarzuela films although he did not want his name on the credits. His 1935 adaptation of Guerrero's DON QUINTIN EL AMARGAO was so successful that he remade it in Mexico 16 years later as *La hija del engaño*. His 1936 film of Serrano's LA ALEGRÍA DEL BATALLÓN was also a big success. Finally, LUCIA DI LAMMERMOOR has an intriguing but famously unexplained connection to his 1960 film *The Exterminating Angel:* the guests mysteriously trapped in the film have all come from a production of this opera, including the soprano who sang Lucia.

BURCHULADZE, PAATA
Georgian bass (1951–)

Georgian basso Paata Burchuladze made his debut in his native Tbilisi in 1976, went to Covent Garden in 1984 as Ramfis, and sang Don Basilio at the Metropolitan Opera in 1989. He has become internationally popular in a wide variety of roles but especially in Russian operas. He was one of the stars celebrating TCHAIKOVSKY at a 1993 Covent Garden gala. See AIDA (1985/1989), DON GIOVANNI (1987), GEORGIAN OPERA, KHOVANSHCHINA (1989), MEFISTOFELE (1989), NABUCCO (1986), and PRINCE IGOR (1990).

BURTON, HUMPHREY
English producer/director (1931–)

Humphrey Burton, one of the most creative producer/directors of opera for television and video, has worked for BBC, London Weekend Television, and Channel 4. He has produced or directed the videos of many of the stage productions at Glyndebourne and Covent Garden, and he has also made several fine films about performers and composers including KATHLEEN BATTLE (1991), LUDWIG VAN BEETHOVEN (1971/1981), LEONARD BERNSTEIN (1973/1974), BENJAMIN BRITTEN (1963/1967), THOMAS HAMPSON (1991), GEORG SOLTI (1990), IGOR STRAVINSKY (1982), JOAN SUTHERLAND (1991), and

LOTTE LENYA (1964). In 1965, he made a famous film, *The Golden Ring,* about the first complete recording of DER RING DES NIBELUNGEN. His opera videos include ANDREA CHÉNIER (1985), BORIS GODUNOV (1990), CANDIDE (1989), DIE ENTFÜHRUNG AUS DEM SERAIL (1986), ERMIONE (1995), EUGENE ONEGIN (1994), DIE FLEDERMAUS (1983/1990), LULU (1996), MACBETH (1972), MANON LESCAUT (1983/1998), MOZART REQUIEM (1988/1991), LE NOZZE DI FIGARO (1973), PÉLLEAS ET MÉLISANDE (1999), PRINCE IGOR (1990), RODELINDA (1998), DIE SCHÖPFUNG (1986), LA TRAVIATA (1994), WAR AND PEACE (1991), and WEST SIDE STORY (1984 film).

BUSCH, FRITZ

German conductor (1890–1951)

The peripatetic Fritz Busch began conducting in 1909 in Riga and became music director of Stuttgart Opera in 1918. He was in charge of Dresden Staatsoper from 1922 to 1933, when he was fired for his anti-Nazi attitude. He moved to England to become music director of the new Glyndebourne Festival where he especially emphasized Mozart operas. From there he went to Argentina, Denmark, and Sweden, pausing to work with the Metropolitan Opera for a few years in the late 1940s. In 1948 he conducted OTELLO for the Met opening night and made history; it was the first complete opera ever to be televised live. In 1951 he return to Glyndebourne where he conducted four Mozart operas, including COSÌ FAN TUTTI, which was telecast by the BBC. His recordings of Mozart operas at Glyndebourne continue to be treasured. See CONDUCTORS (1993/1994).

C

CABALLÉ, MONTSERRAT
Spanish soprano (1933–)

One of the great voices of the 20th century, Montserrat Caballé made her debut in Basle in 1956 singing Mimì and won acclaim in New York in 1965 as Lucrezia Borgia. Caballé, a proud and supportive Catalan, helped launch countryman José Carreras on his career. They have starred together in films and stage productions, some on video. She has devoted more time in recent years to recitals and concerts than operas, but she remains one of the great interpreters of Italian opera. See ADRIANA LECOUVREUR (1976/1978), AGNESE DI HOHENSTAUFEN (1986), GEORGES BIZET, (1988), JOSÉ CARRERAS (1992), CRISTÓBAL COLÓN (1989), LA FORZA DEL DESTINO (1978), JULIÁN GAYARRE (1986), GLYNDEBOURNE (1992), IL GUARANY (1986 film), HENRY VIII (2002), LUCIA DI LAMMERMOOR (1999 film), METROPOLITAN OPERA (1972/1983), NORMA (1974/1974), ROBERTO DEVEREUX (1977), GIOACHINO ROSSINI (1985), SALOME (1979), SEMIRAMIDE (1980), SEVILLE (1991), TOSCA (1979/1979/1983 film), IL TROVATORE (1972), VERDI REQUIEM (1980/1985 film), VERONA (1988), and VIAGGIO A REIMS (1988/1988 film).

1975 Caballé at Her Most Ravishing
Caballé, in concert in Spain, sings six arias from five Puccini operas (*La bohème, Gianni Schicchi, Manon Lescaut, Tosca,* and *Turandot*) with Gianfranco Masini conducting. She is at the peak of her powers, and the audience loves her. Black and white. Arias sung in Italian. 26 minutes. Bel Canto Society VHS.

1983 Montserrat Caballé: The Woman, the Diva
Antonio Chic's documentary examines the person as well as the singer. Caballé talks about her husband and family and sings with consummate brilliance. There are arias from her favorite operas, including *Giulio Cesare, Adriana Lecouvreur, La bohème, La forza de destino,* and *Mefistofele,* plus songs and zarzuela arias. She comes across as a warm human being as well as a splendid singer. Color. 65 minutes. Kultur VHS.

1983 Caballé Subjugates La Scala
Caballé's recital at La Scala on March 26, 1983, followed her withdrawal from *Anna Bolena* the year before. This time she triumphed with a program including arias by Spontini, Cherubini, Bellini, Vives, and Rossini. Color. In Italian. 118 minutes. Bel Canto Society VHS.

1989 Caballé and Carreras in Moscow
The two Catalan stars appear in concert together at the Bolshoi Opera. The program includes 19 solos and four duets, with compositions by Bellini, Verdi, Vivaldi, Tosti, Granados, Scarlatti, and others. They are accompanied on piano by Miguel Zanetti. Color. 60 minutes. Kultur VHS.

1990 Evviva Bel Canto/Le Grande Primadonne
These two videos are from one concert with Caballé appearing with Marilyn Horne at the Philharmonie Hall in Munich. They work well together and seem to give each other inspiration, notably on a magnificent duet from *Semiramide.* They also sing arias and duets by Vivaldi, Meyerbeer, Rossini, Handel, Puccini, Offenbach, and Mercadante. Nicola Rescigno leads the Munich Rundfunk Orchestra; Evelyn Paulman and Helmut Rost directed the videos. Color. 47/41 minutes. MCA video.

1993 Montserrat Caballé
Chris Hunt's fine documentary film about the diva's life and career traces her life from the early years. She is shown in performance and rehearsal and tells fascinating anecdotes. There are comments from Joan Sutherland, Plácido Domingo, José Carreras, and Cheryl Studer. Made for the South Bank Show. Color. 60 minutes.

1993 Christmas Concert from the Vatican
Caballé is the operatic star of this Vatican Christmas concert telecast by RAI TV. Renato Serio conducts the St. Cecilia National Academy Symphony Orchestra. Color. 97 minutes.

1999 Concerto de Pasqua
Caballé and her daughter Monserrat Marti join forces for an Easter Sunday Concert at Santa Maria degli Angeli Basilica in Rome. They sing "Ave Maria" by Verdi *(Otello),* Mascagni *(Cavalleria rusticana),* and Donizetti; four pieces from Handel's *Messiah;* and other religious works by Bellini, Bernstein, and Massenet with the Cappella Giulia St. Peter's Chorus and Orchestra del Festival di Pasqua. Color. In Italian. 70 minutes. Trinidad Entertainment DVD.

CABALLERO, MANUEL FERNÁNDEZ
Spanish composer (1835–1906)

Manuel Fernández Caballero is one of the major zarzuela composers, best known for GIGANTES Y CABEZUDOS and LOS SOBRINOS DEL CAPITÁN GRANT. He began as a violinist and conductor, started to compose zarzuelas in 1854, and became successful after spending time in Cuba absorbing new musical ideas. Caballero wrote more than 100 zarzuelas; his works are especially popular in South America.

CABINET OF DR. CALIGARI, THE
1981 musical stage work by Nelson

Robert Wiene's expressionist 1919 German film *The Cabinet of Dr. Caligari,* one of the first great horror movies, was widely influential for its stylist acting and powerful set design. Conrad Veidt, Werner Krauss, and Lil Dagover star in a paranoiac story about a hypnotist who uses a somnambulist to commit murders. Carl Mayer and Hans Janowitz wrote the screenplay. It was turned into a quasi-opera in 1981 by composer Bill Nelson, who created an electronic music score based on the film for an English stage production. The Yorkshire Actors' Company used the music in their theatrical adaptation of the film to complement storytelling through gesture, mime, and dance.

CACOYANNIS, MICHAEL
Greek film director (1922–)

Michael Cacoyannis, who began his moviemaking career in 1953, is known for classic films such as *Zorba the Greek* (1964) and *Electra* (1961). He has not made any opera films, but he has directed opera on stage. One of his most notable productions was an American opera derived from *Electra* staged at the Metropolitan in 1967, Marvin David Levy's *Mourning Becomes Electra,* based on the Eugene O'Neill play, which starred Evelyn Lear and Sherrill Milnes.

CAGE, JOHN
American composer (1912–1992)

It might seem unlikely for John Cage to write opera, given his predilection for indeterminacy, but in fact much of his work is theatrical in a nonnarrative way, like the radio play *Roaratorio: An Irish Circus on Finnegans Wake.* His operas grew out of his idea that he was the "maker of a camera who allows someone else to take the picture." In a sense, his nonnarrative operas are created by the performers, who sing arias from old European op-

eras at random. They're called simply *Europeras* 1 and 2, 3 and 4, and 5, and they combine elements of traditional European opera production in bewildering, infuriating, and fascinating ways.

1983 4 American Composers: John Cage
Peter Greenaway's film about Cage in his British *4 American Composers* series centers around a performance celebrating Cage's 70th birthday and links other works, including *Roaratorio: An Irish Circus on Finneganss Wake, Double Music, Music for Marcel Duchamp, Indeterminacy, Song Books, Branches,* and *Inlets.* Color. In English. 60 minutes. Mystic Fire VHS.

1995 From Zero: John Cage
Cage talks about music, harmony, chance, and the influence of Zen Buddhism, *Finnegans Wake,* and Marcel Duchamp on his work. Counterpointing the discussion is a performance of Cage's *Fourteen* by the Ives Ensemble with light and camera score designed by Andrew Culver. Color. In English. 51 minutes. Films for the Humanities & Sciences VHS.

CALDWELL, SARAH
American conductor/director (1924–)

Sarah Caldwell, who founded the Boston Opera Company in 1958, was also the first woman to conduct opera at the Metropolitan (*La traviata* in 1976). She won much praise for her innovative productions, including little-known and modern operas; she held the American premieres of Rameau's classic HIPPOLYTE ET ARICIE, Session's *Montezuma,* and Zimmermann's DIE SOLDATEN. Among her telecast productions, often working with NET OPERA, were a pioneering 1957 LA FINTA GIARDINIERA, a daring 1965 version of Nono's INTOLLERANZA 1960, and a bizarrely costumed 1976 IL BARBIERE DI SIVIGLIA starring Beverly Sills.

1973 What Time Is the Next Swan?
A short film of a behind-the-scenes visit to the Boston Opera Company as Caldwell rehearses with performers and works with staff. The film shows the preparation and planning for a Boston Opera production. Color. 8 minutes.

CALL OF THE FLESH
1930 fiction film with opera content

Ramon Novarro stars as Juan, a cantina singer in Seville, whose teacher Esteban (Ernest Torrence), a once-famous opera performer, wants him to become an opera singer as well. Juan does badly in an audition in Madrid, as he is judged to lack heart in his singing, but Esteban uses his influence to get him a debut performance anyway. Juan is in love with Maria (Dorothy Jordan), a novice at a convent, but her brother Enríque (Russell Hopton) persuades Juan to give her up to the church. He rejects her by pretending to be in love with his singing partner Lola (Renée Adorée), but it breaks his heart. At his debut opera performance, he sings a passionate rendition of Des Grieux's aria "Ah! Fuyez, douce image" from Massenet's *Manon* (his supposed final farewell to Manon) and collapses on stage. Lola regrets the deception that caused the collapse and tells Maria the truth. The lovers are reunited. Novarro also sings the cavatina "Quanto è bella" from *L'Elisir d'amore*, the aria "Questa o quella" from *Rigoletto*, and songs by Herbert Stothart and Clifford Grey. Dorothy Farnum and John Colton wrote the screenplay, Merritt B Gerstad was cinematographer and Charles Brabin directed the 100-minute film for MGM in English and Spanish-language versions.

CALLAS, MARIA
American/Greek soprano (1923–1977)

Maria Callas is the reason many people have become attracted to opera and she is certainly one of the greatest female opera singers of the 20th century. Born Cecilia Sophia Anna Maria Kalogeropoulos in New York City in 1923, she made her debut in Athens in 1940 and became famous in Italy in the late 1940s with the help of conductor Tullio Serafin. Film directors Luchino Visconti and Franco Zeffirelli influenced her and directed her in operas on stage, although unfortunately not in films. She ended her public career in 1965, returned for a concert tour during 1973–1974, and died in 1977 at the age of 53. Callas's career ended before televising operas became common, and there is no video of her in a complete opera, although there are two versions of Act II of TOSCA. What does survives gives a powerful indication of how she could immerse herself in a role and effectively become the character she portrayed.

1956 Ed Sullivan Show
Callas made her American TV debut on the *Ed Sullivan Show* on CBS on November 25, 1956. Rudolf Bing introduces her in a scene from *Tosca* staged by John Gutman. George London sings Scarpia with Dimitri Mitropoulos conducting the Metropolitan Opera Orchestra. Black and white. 18 minutes. Video at the MTR.

1958 Edward R. Murrow Person to Person
Callas made her second American television appearance on the Edward R. Murrow *Person to Person* show on CBS on January 24, 1958. Murrow talks to her about her life and career. Black and white. 60 minutes. Video at the MTR.

1958 LisbonTraviata
A fabled pirate recording of Callas singing *La traviata* in Lisbon was the subject of a 1989 play by Terrence McNally. Real film of Callas in Lisbon is included in the video *Legends of Opera;* she is shown being interviewed at the Lisbon airport and briefly on stage in *La traviata* in Act II with Alfredo Kraus. Black and white. In Italian and French. 7 minutes. Legato Classics VHS.

1958 La Callas Toujours...
This is the most notable Callas video, a gala concert televised live from the Palais Garnier in Paris on December 19, 1958. The first half features arias from *Norma, Il barbiere di Siviglia,* and *Il trovatore.* The second half is a staging of Act II of *Tosca* with Callas joined by Tito Gobbi as Scarpia and Albert Lance as Cavaradossi. Georges Sebastian conducts the Paris Opéra Orchestra and Chorus; Roger Benamou. directed the telecast. Black and white. French narration. 107 minutes. EMI Classics DVD and VHS/Pioneer Artists LD.

1959/1962 In Concert: Hamburg 1959, 1962
These two live concerts of Callas taped performing in Hamburg, originally issued separately on VHS, are now available in better quality on DVD. She sings wonderfully in both concerts, truly living her roles. In 1959, the music is from *Macbeth, Il barbiere di Siviglia, Don Carlo, Il pirata,* and *La vestale,* all operas she sang at La Scala. In 1962, she sings arias from *Carmen, Ernani, Le Cid,* and *La Cenerentola,* operas she had not performed on stage, plus *Don Carlo.* Nicola Rescigno, who conducted her American debut in Chicago in 1954, leads the Hamburg NDR Symphony Orchestra in the 68-minute concert May 15, 1959. Georges Prêtre, who conducted her *Norma* and *Tosca* in Paris, leads the NDR Orchestra in the 67-minute concert March 16, 1962. Black and white. EMI DVD/Kultur VHS.

1962 Covent Garden Gala Concert
Callas was the featured singer in this November 4, 1962, concert at the Royal Opera House with Giuseppe Di Stefano. She sings "Tu, che le vanità" from *Don Carlo* and the Habanera and Séguidille from *Carmen.* Georges Prêtre conducts the Royal Opera House Orchestra. Sir David Webster makes introductions, and Bill Ward directs for ATV television. Black and white. In French and Italian. 60 minutes. EMI Classics VHS.

1964 Callas in Tosca at the Royal Opera
This is the only visual record of Callas on stage in an actual performance of opera, Act II of *Tosca* at the Royal Opera House in London. Renato Cioni is Cavaradossi and Tito Gobbi is Scarpia, with Carlo Felice Cillaro conducting and Franco Zeffirelli directing. Telecast live February 9, 1964, by ATV television with Bill Ward as the

TV director. Black and white. In Italian. 41 minutes. EMI Classics VHS.

1962/1964 Maria Callas at Covent Garden
This is the DVD version of the two Callas performances at the Royal Opera House described above, but with higher quality sound. Black and white. In French and Italian. 70 minutes. EMI DVD.

1968 The Callas Conversations
Callas looks relaxed and elegant in her Paris apartment talking with Lord Harewood about her career, early life, preparations for performing, and ideas about interpretation, especially for *Norma, Tosca,* and *La traviata. The Callas Conversations* was produced by John Culshaw and directed by Barrie Gavin. It was first shown in 50-minute segments on BBC Television in December 1968. Color. 100 minutes. Bel Canto Society VHS (includes as an extra *Callas in Paris* in 1965).

1968 Werner Schroeter 8mm films
German filmmaker Werner Schroeter, who was obsessed with Callas in his early years, made three 8mm films about her in 1968: *Callas Walking Lucia* (3 minutes), *Maria Callas Portrait* (17 minutes) and *Maria Callas singt 1957 Rezitativ und Arie der Elvira aus Ernani 1844 von Giuseppe Verdi* (15 minutes).

1970 Medea
Callas is superb in the only movie she ever made, though it is not the Cherubini opera and she does not sing. She portrays the Medea of the Euripides tragedy, under the direction of Italian filmmaker Pier Paolo Pasolini. These two great artists create a memorable film, with Callas at her most emotional and charismatic and Pasolini at his most powerful and lucid. The film tells the story of Medea's horrific revenge on Jason after he betrays her. Color. In Italian with English subtitles. 118 minutes. VAI VHS.

1974 Callas Reveals Herself
Callas talks about herself in a revealing manner in these once suppressed interviews dating from 1974. She is interviewed in English and Italian by conductor Antonino Votto. Black and white and color. In English and in Italian with English subtitles. 49 minutes. Bel Canto Society VHS.

1978 Callas in Japan
Video of a concert Callas gave in Japan while she was on her last tour. Color. 56 minutes. Video at the NFTA.

1978 Vissi d'Arte
Alain Ferrari created this French TV documentary about Callas to examine what was unique about her work, both vocally and artistically. Through interviews with collaborators, directors, and conductors, he shows the demands Callas made on those she worked with and how it influenced her artistry. Color. In French. 75 minutes. On video.

1978 Callas: A Documentary
Revealing portrait of the singer, written and directed by critic John Ardoin. It begins with her funeral in Paris and has excellent interviews with friends and colleagues, from Franco Zeffirelli to Gian Carlo Menotti. Footage of Callas in performance is also included. Color. 90 minutes. Bel Canto Society VHS.

1983 Callas
International television tribute to Callas introduced by Leonard Bernstein with live performances by singers from La Scala in Milan, Covent Garden in London, the Opéra in Paris, and the Lyric in Chicago, all linked by satellite. Also includes interviews and film clips. Color. 150 minutes.

1987 La Divina: A Portrait
Tony Palmer's documentary traces Callas's life and career from birth to death, intercutting archival footage with interviews. Franco Zeffirelli is especially interesting as he tries to explain her magic as a singer and her relationship with Aristotle Onassis. The film opens and closes with scenes from her 1958 Paris debut, but it also includes rare newsreel and interview material. There are excerpts of her performing arias from *Il barbiere di Siviglia, Carmen, Don Carlo, La Gioconda, Norma, Il pirata, Tosca, Il trovatore,* and *La sonnambula.* Color and black and white. 90 minutes. Arthaus DVD/Pioneer Artists LD.

1988 Maria Callas: Life and Art
This informative documentary about Callas by Alan Lewens and Alastair Mitchell follows her career intelligently in chronological format. There are excerpts from most of her films and videos, interviews with those who knew her well, and many insights into her life and singing. She is seen performing arias from *Tosca, Il barbiere di Siviglia, Carmen, Cavalleria rusticana,* and *L'elisir d'amore.* Black and white. 80 minutes. EMI DVD/Kultur VHS/Pioneer LD.

2002 Callas Forever
Franco Zeffirelli's impressionistic movie stars Fanny Ardant as a believable Callas (she played the singer on stage for a year in the play *Master Class*). Zeffirelli imagines

105

that Callas agreed to make a film of *Carmen* in the last year of her life and that this brings her out of depression and seclusion. Jeremy Irons plays her (fictional) gay manager, with Joan Plowright as her journalist friend. Ennio Guarnieri, who shot the Callas *Medea*, was cinematographer. Zeffirelli wrote the screenplay with Martin Sherman. Color. In English. 108 minutes.

Related films

1988 Onassis: The Richest Man in the World
Jane Seymour gives a fiery performance as Callas in this highly fictional American TV movie based on a book by Peter Evans. Raul Julia plays Aristotle Onassis, Anthony Quinn is his father, and Francesca Annis is Jackie Kennedy. Waris Hussein directed. Color. 200 minutes. On VHS.

1992 Casta diva: Tribute to Maria Callas
Callas is honored at a concert in the open-air Herodion Theater on the Athens Acropolis. "Casta diva" and other arias associated with Callas are sung by Mariella Devia, Raina Kabaivanska, Daniela Dessì, and Francesca Pedaci. Lending support are Giuseppe Sabbatini, Giacomo Prestia, and Paolo Coni. Irene Pappas makes introductions, and Gianluigi Gelmetti conducts the Stuttgart Radio Symphony Orchestra. Color. 111 minutes. Lyric VHS.

1993 Philadelphia
Tom Hanks, a lawyer dying of AIDS, listens to Callas sing Maddalena's aria "La mamma morta" from *Andrea Chénier,* in which she tells how her mother died when a mob burned down her house during the French Revolution. It's his favorite aria, and playing it for his lawyer (Denzel Washington) is a crucial moment in their relationship. The Callas recording was made in 1955 for EMI with Tullio Serafin conducting the Philharmonia Orchestra. She is also heard singing "Ebben...ne andrò lontano" from *La Wally* and "Io son l'umile ancella" from *Adriana Lecouvreur.* Jonathan Demme directed for TriStar. Color. 119 minutes. On VHS.

CAMBIALE DI MATRIMONIO, LA
1810 opera by Rossini

La cambiale di matrimonio (The Bill of Marriage) is GIOACHINO ROSSINI's first professional opera, a one-act comedy written when he was only 18. It revolves around a marriage bill that becomes the cause of romantic confusion. Sir Tobias Mill tries to marry off his daughter Fanny to rich Canadian Slook, who has the bill, so her lover Edoardo Milfort has to find a quick solution. Gaetano Rossi wrote the libretto.

1989 Schwetzingen Festival
German stage production: Michael Hampe (director), Gianluigi Gelmetti (conductor, Stuttgart Radio Symphony Orchestra), Carlo Tommasi (set designer), Carlo Diappi (costume designer).
Cast: Janice Hall (Fannì), David Kuebler (Edoardo), John Del Carlo (Tobia), Alberto Rinaldi (Slook), Amelia Felle (Clarina).
Video: Teldec VHS/Pioneer LD. Claus Viller (director). Color. In Italian with English subtitles. 85 minutes.
Comment: This charming Cologne Opera production was staged, with other early Rossini operas, in a celebratory cycle in the Rococo Schlosstheater for the Schwetzingen Festspiele.

CAMBRELING, SYLVAIN
French conductor (1948–)

Sylvain Cambreling made his conducting debut at Lyons in 1975 with *La Cenerentola,* worked in Paris and at Glyndebourne, and became music director of La Monnaie in Brussels in 1981. He has been guest conductor at Geneva, La Scala, Salzburg, and the Met, and some of his productions at Glyndebourne, Geneva, Monnaie, and Salzburg are on video. See IL BARBIERE DI SIVIGLIA (1982), FAUST (1999), LA FINTA GIARDINIERA (1990), KATYA KABANOVA (1998), MIREILLE (1981), THE RAKE'S PROGRESS (1996), and LES TROYENS (2000).

CAMEO OPERAS
1927 British film series

Cameo Operas, a 1927 British film series, condensed well-known operas to about 20 minutes of silent film and presented them with live vocalists and cinema orchestras. They were produced by John E. Blakeley and directed by H. B. Parkinson for *Song Films.* Parkinson also produced the earlier series *Tense Moments in Opera.* The operas selected for the series are a reflection of what interested the British movie-going public at the time. See (all 1927): The BOHEMIAN GIRL, CARMEN, LA FILLE DU RÉGIMENT, FAUST, THE LILY OF KILLARNEY, MARITANA, MARTHA, RIGOLETTO, DER RING DES NIBELUNGEN, SAMSON ET DALILA, LA TRAVIATA, and IL TROVATORE.

CAMERA
1994 TV opera by Moore

In Anthony Moore's television opera *Camera,* libretto by Peter Blegvad based on a story by Dagmar Krause, tax collector Forecast is sent to a derelict house to collect arrears from a woman named Melusina. She says her house is a country called Camera and only the laws of imagination are in effect. He returns to his office without the taxes and is fired. A more ruthless tax collector is sent to complete the job.

1994 Channel 4
English TV production: Jane Thorburn (director), Anthony Moore (conductor, Balanescu Quartet).

Cast: Dagmar Krause (Melusina), John Harris (Forecast), Quentin Hayes (Taft), Nicole Tibbels (Hardwick), Ewart James Waters (The Clock).

Telecast by Channel 4 on February 6, 1994. Jane Thorburn (director). Color. In English. 53 minutes.

CAMERA THREE
CBS Television series (1953–1978)

The adventurous CBS art and culture series *Camera Three* presented opera in a bare-bones recital format. Its extreme low budget and early Sunday morning time slot meant it could present almost anything that didn't cost much money. There were programs devoted to composers and performers such as SAMUEL BARBER, DOROTHY KIRSTEN, THOMAS PASATIERI, and MICHAEL TIPPETT; historic operas such as Baldassare Galuppi's IL FILOSOFO DI COMPAGNA and Mozart's DER SCHAUSPIELDIREKTOR; and modern operas such as THE ACCUSED, THE CRADLE WILL ROCK, and THE FOUR NOTE OPERA. CBS dropped the series in 1978 but PBS revived it in 1979 with new and repeat programs. ROGER ENGLANDER was producer and director for three years.

CAMPANARI, GIUSEPPE
Italian baritone (1855–1927)

Giuseppe Campanari made his debut at the Metropolitan in 1894 and had a major success as Ford in the U.S. premiere of *Falstaff* the following year. He was much liked as Figaro in both the Mozart and Rossini operas and sang more than 500 performances with the Met before retiring in 1912. He made a number of recordings and was featured in one early sound film, a 1917 CARMEN.

CAMPORA, GIUSEPPE
Italian tenor (1923–)

Giuseppe Campora made his debut in 1949 as Rodolfo in Bari and soon was performing around the world, from New York to Buenos Aires. He made many recordings, mostly of Verdi and Puccini operas. Opera film enthusiasts know him as the voice declaring love for Sophia Loren in the 1953 Italian movie of AIDA (he dubbed Radames). He did the same thing in Carmine Gallone's 1955 movie of MADAMA BUTTERFLY, dubbing the voice of Pinkerton. He can be seen performing on a *Voice of Firestone* TV program.

1958 Lisa Della Casa in Opera and Song
Campora is featured with soprano Lisa Della Casa on a *Voice of Firestone* telecast on September 22, 1958. He sings "Recondita armonia" from *Tosca* and joins the soprano on the opening and closing songs by Idabelle Firestone. Black and white. 30 minutes. VAI VHS.

CANCIÓN DEL OLVIDÓ, LA
1916 zarzuela by Serrano

In a small town in the Kingdom of Naples in 1799, Roman princess Rosina hatches an elaborate plan to capture the womanizing Captain Leonello with the help of the musician Toribio impersonating a prince. The romantic plot revolves around the song the "Cancion del Olvidó" (Song of Forgetting). Jose Serrano's delightful zarzuela *La cancion del olvidó*, libretto by Federico Romero and Guillermo Fernández Shaw, premiered in Valencia in 1916.

1969 Teatro Lirico Español
Spanish TV film: Juan de Orduña (director), Federico Moreno Torroba (conductor, Orquesta Lírica Española), Jose Perera Cruz (conductor, Coro Cantores de Madrid), Federico G. Larrya (cinematographer).

Singers: Josefina Cubeiro, Dolores Perez, Vicente Sardinero, Francisco Saura.

Actors: María Cuadra, Juan Luis Gallardo, José Perera, José Sacristán, Luchy Soto.

Video: Metrovideo (Spain) VHS. Shot in 35mm for RTVE Spanish television. Juan de Orduña (director). Color. In Spanish. 85 minutes.

CANDIDE
1956 operetta by Bernstein

LEONARD BERNSTEIN's *Candide* veers from opera to high-octane operetta, but it seems likely to enter the opera house repertory. Based on Voltaire's sharply funny and still relevant satire, it tells the story of the naive couple Candide and Cunegonde. They start off believing the optimistic teachings of the philosopher Pangloss, who says that this is the best of all possible worlds. After a series of disasters, they find that such a philosophy is of little relevance in the real world. The libretto for the original Broadway production was by Lillian Hellman, with lyrics by so many writers it became a joke. The original production was not a success, and the libretto has been revised a number of times. The marvelous overture has become a concert standard, and Cunegonde's aria "Glitter and Be Gay" has become a favorite of coloratura sopranos.

1986 New York City Opera

American stage production: Harold Prince (director), Scott Bergeson (conductor, New York City Opera Orchestra and Chorus), Clark Dunham (set designer).

Cast: David Eisler (Candide), Erie Mills (Cunegonde), John Lankston (Voltaire/Pangloss), Deborah Darr (Paquette), Muriel Costa-Greenspon (Old Lady), Scott Reeve (Maximilian).

Telecast November 12, 1986, in the PBS series *Live From Lincoln Center.* Kirk Browning (director). Color. In English. 148 minutes.

1989 Barbican Center, London

English concert production: Humphrey Burton (director), Leonard Bernstein (conductor, London Symphony Orchestra and Chorus).

Cast: Jerry Hadley (Candide), June Anderson (Cunegonde), Adolph Green (Pangloss), Christa Ludwig (Old Lady), Kurt Ollmann (Maximilian).

Video: Polygram DVD/VHS/LD. Humphrey Burton (director). Color. In English. 147 minutes.

Comment: It looks like an oratorio, but it sounds like an opera in this revised concert version. Anderson is particularly fine singing the "Glitter" aria, Adolph Green is a delight, and Christa Ludwig is a joy.

CANIGLIA, MARIA
Italian soprano (1905–1979)

Maria Caniglia was born in Rome, studied in Naples, and made her debut in Turin. She became a regular at La Scala and sang at Covent Garden and the Met in the late 1930s. She brought a warm humanity to her specialty Verdi roles, but she was also a much admired Tosca. She made a few Italian films, usually dubbing the opera arias, and is one of the featured singers in the 1948 film FOLLIE PER L'OPERA. She sings the Puccini arias in Carmine Gallone's 1940 film of MANON LESCAUT, and she is the voice of Tosca in his 1956 film TOSCA. See also ANTHOLOGIES (Opera Titans), TEATRO ALLA SCALA (1943), and TOSCA (1993 film).

1947 Il vento mi ha cantato una canzone
Caniglia plays a singer in *The Wind Sang Me a Song,* an Italian musical starring Laura Solari and Alberto Sordi. It's the story of a musician who succeeds in his ambitions with the help of an amateur. Camillo Mastrocinque directed. Black and white. In Italian. 95 minutes.

CANTANTE DE NAPOLES, EL
1935 American film with opera content

Enrico Caruso Jr. plays opera star Enrico Daspurro in *El cantante de Napoles* (The Singer From Naples), an American Spanish-language film based on Enrico Caruso Sr.'s life. As a young man in Naples, he dreams of singing at La Scala and eventually succeeds with help from Mona Maris. Caruso Jr. sings arias from *Il trovatore, Il barbiere di Seviglia* and *L'Africaine,* plus Neapolitan songs. Emilia Leovalli plays his mother, and Carmen Rio is his sweetheart. Betty Reinhardt wrote the script, based on a novel by Arman Chelieu, and Howard Bretherton directed. Black and white. In Spanish. 77 minutes.

CANTOR'S SON, THE
1937 "Yiddish film opera"

The Cantor's Son (*Dem Khazns Zund* in Yiddish) was planned as the first of six "Yiddish film operas" to be produced by Sidney M. Goldin for Eron Pictures, but he died so the film had to be finished by Ilya Motyleff. The "opera" is the story of Shloimele, a cantor's son from Belz in Eastern Europe, who runs off with a theater troupe and ends up in New York. Fifteen years later, he achieves success as a singer on stage and radio and becomes a popular cantor. He returns home to Belz and is reunited with his family and his old love Rivkele. Moishe Oysher is Shloimele, Florence Weiss is his singing partner Helen, Judith Abarbanell is Rivkele, and Lorraine Abarbanell is Rivkele as a child. Alexander Olshanetsky composed the music and conducted the orchestra, Louis Freiman wrote the screenplay, and Frank Zucker was cinematographer. Black and white. In Yiddish with English subtitles. 90 minutes.

CANZONE DEL CUORE, LA
1937 Italian-German film with opera content

Beniamino Gigli stars opposite Geraldine Katt in *La canzone del cuore* (Song of the Heart), a musical about an opera singer and a princess. She plays piano for him as a favor after he fires his pianist at a hotel rehearsal, and he asks her to play for his encore that evening at a concert. When an American woman visits Gigli's hotel room later that night, the princess's fiancé suspects a romance and breaks off their engagement. After a series of complications, it gets sorted out. Gigli has the opportunity to sing arias from *Martha* and *Lohengrin,* plus songs by Giuseppe Becce and Ernesto de Curtis. Karl Heinz Martin directed for Bavaria Film, Franz Koch was cinematographer, and Giuseppe Becce conducted the music. The German title is *Die Stimme des Herzens,* but it is also know as *Der Sänger Ihrer Hoheit.* Released March 1937. Black and white. In German. 91 minutes. House of Opera/Lyric VHS.

CANZONE DEL SOLE, LA
1933 Italian film with opera content

Italian tenor GIACOMO LAURI-VOLPI plays himself in *La canzone del sole* (The Song of the Sun), a musical film with an original score by Pietro Mascagni, arranged by Giuseppe Becce. The film begins with the tenor on stage at a formal concert singing Arturo's cavatina "A te, o cara, amor talora" from *I puritani* and the title song by Mascagni. It ends with a full-scale production of Meyerbeer's *Gli ugonotti (Les Huguenots)* at the Arena di Verona with Lauri-Volpi singing the lead role of Raoul. Vittorio De Sica plays his lawyer, who gets mistaken for the tenor by a beautiful German woman (Lilian Dietz), who idolizes Lauri-Volpi. They begin a love affair, and we see picture-postcard views of Italy from Venice to Capri. Giovacchino Forzano wrote the screenplay, Augusto Tiezzi was cinematographer, and Max Neufeld directed for Italfono. The film was shot in Berlin, and a German version was also made titled *Das Lied Der Sonne.* Shown in the United States as *Song of the Sun.* Black and white. In Italian. 80 minutes. (Lengthy extracts are included in the RAI Italian TV documentary *Ricordi di Giacomo Lauri-Volpi,* which is on American VHS.)

CAPELLO DI PAGLIA DI FIRENZE, IL
1945/1955 opera by Rota

A horse eats a lady's straw hat, and this causes a multitude of problems for a man about to get married. The situation is finally resolved by the wedding gift of an identical hat. NINO ROTA's light-hearted musical farce *Il capello di paglia di Firenze,* known in English as *The Italian Straw Hat,* is one of the most popular modern Italian operas. The libretto, by Nino and Ernesta Rota, is based on the same French play by Eugène Labiche that inspired a classic 1927 film by René Clair. The opera is completely tonal, even quoting music from Rota's films, and looks back to the glories of Rossini and *opera buffa.* Rota wrote the opera in 1945 but it was not finalized and performed until 1955.

1977 RAI Italian Television

Italian TV production: Ugo Gregoretti (director), Nino Rota (conductor, RAI Radio-Television Orchestra and Chorus).

Cast: Ugo Benelli (Fadinard), Daniela Mazzucato (Elena), Alfredo Mariotti (Nonancourt), Mario Basioli (Beaupertuis), Viorica Cortez (Baroness).

Video: House of Opera DVD/VHS. Ugo Gregoretti (director). Color. In Italian. 108 minutes.

Comment: The soundtrack is also on CD.

1999 Opéra National de Lyon

French stage production: Claudia Stavisky (director), Claire Gibault (conductor, Opéra National de Lyon Orchestra and Chorus), Lila Kendaka (set/costume designer).

Cast: Alain Gabriel, Alketa Cela, Christophe Fel, Marie-Thérèse Keller.

Telecast December 31, 1999, in France. Pierre Cavassilas (director). Color. In French. 110 minutes.

CAPPUCCILLI, PIERO
Italian baritone (1926–)

Piero Cappuccilli, who was born in Trieste, made his debut in Milan in 1957 in *Pagliacci.* His international career began in 1960 when he sang *La traviata* at the Metropolitan and recorded *Lucia di Lammermoor* with Maria Callas. By 1964, he was one of the leading baritones in the world, singing regularly at La Scala and other major opera houses and was considered one of the great interpreters of Verdi. He had to give up his opera career after a serious car accident in 1992, but his greatness can still be enjoyed in a number of opera videos and tributes. See ANDREA CHÉNIER (1973/1985), UN BALLO IN MASCHERA (1975), DON CARLO (1986), LA FORZA DEL DESTINO (1978), NICOLAI GHIAUROV (1986), LUCIA DI LAMMERMOOR (1986 film), OTELLO (1976/1982), LUCIANO PAVAROTTI (1991), SIMON BOCCANEGRA (1976/1978), IL TABARRO (1983), IL TROVATORE (1978), and VERONA (1990).

CAPRICCIO
1942 opera by Richard Strauss

The relative importance of words and music in opera is the self-referential focus of this philosophical opera by RICHARD STRAUSS. The libretto, by the composer and conductor Clemens Krauss, set in a castle in Paris in 1775, revolves around Countess Madeleine and her two suitors. Olivier is a poet, and Flamand is a composer and they have a heated debate on the value of words and music in opera. The suitors are asked to write an opera using the people present as the characters. They do but the countess is still unable to choose. The opera premiered in Munich during World War II.

1975 Glyndebourne Festival

English stage production: John Cox (director), Andrew Davis (conductor, London Philharmonic Orchestra and Glyndebourne Festival Chorus), Dennis Lennon (set designer).

Cast: Elisabeth Söderström (Countess), Håkan Hagegård (Count), Ryland Davies (Flamand), Dale Duesing (Olivier), Marius Rintzler (La Roche), Kerstin Meyer (Clairon), Hugues Cuénod (Taupe).

Video: House of Opera DVD and VHS/Legato Classics VHS. Color. In German with English subtitles. 143 minutes.

Comment: Cox updated this fine stage production to the 1920s although apparently the Strauss estate does not approve of modern dress productions.

1990 Salzburg Festival

Austrian stage production: Johannes Schaaf (director), Horst Stein (conductor, Vienna Philharmonic Orchestra), Andreas Reinhardt (set/costume designer).

Cast: Anna Tomowa-Sintow (Countess), Wolfgang Schöne (Count), Eberhard Büchner (Flamand), Andreas Schmidt (Olivier), Iris Vermillion (Clairon), Theo Adam (La Roche), Heinz Zednik (Taupe).

Video: House of Opera DVD and VHS/Legato Classics VHS. Johannes Schaaf (director). Color. In German with English subtitles. 146 minutes.

Comment: Schaaf has the opera begin in the 1920s and then regress to the 18th century.

1993 San Francisco Opera

American stage production: Stephen Lawless (director), Donald Runnicles (conductor, San Francisco Opera Orchestra), Mauro Pagano (set designer).

Cast: Kiri Te Kanawa (Countess), Håkan Hagegård (Count), Simon Keenlyside (Olivier), David Kuebler (Flamand), Tatiana Troyanos (Clairon), Victor Braun (La Roche), Michel Sénéchal (Taupe).

Video: Kultur & Arthaus DVD/London VHS & LD. Peter Maniura (director). Color. In German with English subtitles. 155 minutes.

Comment: Clairon was Troyanos's last stage role before her death.

CAPULETI ED I MONTECCHI, I
1830 opera by Bellini

I Capuleti ed i Montecchi (The Capulets and the Montagues) is VINCENZO BELLINI's version of the Romeo and Juliet story. Felice Romani's libretto is based on the original Italian stories rather than Shakespeare's play, but the plot is essentially the same. The leading roles are for women singers: Juliet is as a soprano and Romeo is a mezzo. Romeo was composed for the diva Giuditta Grisi, who created the role when the opera premiered at La Fenice in 1830. The final duet between the two lovers is much admired, especially by lesbian opera lovers.

1991 Teatro La Fenice

Italian stage production: Ugo Tesitore (director), Bruno Campanella (conductor, Teatro La Fenice Orchestra and Chorus). Pier Luigi Pizzi (set/costume designer).

Cast: Katia Ricciarelli (Juliet), Diana Montague (Romeo), Dano Raffanti (Tebaldo), Marcello Lippi (Capellio), Antonio Salvador (Lorenzo).

Video: Kultur VHS. Allan Miller (director). Color. 60 minutes.

Comment: Highlights version of the opera filmed for the series *My Favorite Opera* with the focus on Ricciarelli. Rehearsals and staged scenes are shown in the order they appear in the opera.

CARDILLAC
1926/1952 opera by Hindemith

PAUL HINDEMITH's first full-length opera, created in 1926 and heavily revised in 1952, is based on a novella by E. T. A. Hoffmann with libretto by Ferdinand Lion. It tells the bizarre story of psychotic goldsmith René Cardillac and his strange behavior at the Paris court of King Louis XIV. Unable to give up his creations, he murders his clients to recover them. His story is counterpointed by his daughter's love affair.

1986 Bavarian State Opera

German stage production: Jean-Pierre Ponnelle (director/set designer), Wolfgang Sawallisch (conductor, Bavarian State Opera Orchestra).

Cast: Donald McIntyre (Cardillac), Maria de Francesca-Cavazza (Daughter), Robert Schunk (Police Officer), Hans Günter Nöcker (Gold Merchant), Josef Hopferwieser (Gentleman), Doris Soffel (Lady).

Telecast in Germany November 17, 1985. Brian Large (director). Color. In German. 89 minutes.

CARMEN
1875 opéra-comique by Bizet

The story of Carmen has transmuted into a genuine modern myth and has become one of the most popular literary sources for movies. The idea of a strong, sensual woman killed by an ordinary man she has seduced and abandoned seems to have universal resonance. It is the largest single entry in this book, with more than 70 films and videos from around the world. Early films often claim to be based on the source story by Prosper Mérimée rather than the libretto by Henri Meilhac and Ludovic Halévy for GEORGES BIZET's opera, but this was usually for copyright reasons. The role is written for a mezzo-soprano but many sopranos have sung it, including JULIA MIGENES, who starred in the superb FRANCESCO ROSI film version. One famous Carmen, RISË STEVENS, became associated with the role before she had sung it on stage because of her appearance in it in the film *Going My Way*. MARIA EWING can be seen in three different versions on video opposite three different Don Josés. There are many non-operatic movies feature arias or other references to the opera; a selection of these is included below.

1931 Gipsy Blood

British film: Cecil Lewis (director), Walter C. Mycroft and Cecil Lewis (screenplay), Malcolm Sargent (conductor, New Symphony Orchestra), British International Pictures (production).

Cast: Marguerite Namara (Carmen), Thomas Burke (Don José), Lance Fairfax (Escamillo), Lester Matthew (Zuniga), Mary Clare (Factory Girl), Dennis Wyndham (Le Doncaïre), Lewin Mannering (Innkeeper), Hay Petrie (Remendado).

Video: Operavideo VHS. Black and white. In English. 79 minutes.

Comment: The opera is heavily abridged and the arias are sung in English. Namara, an American famous at the time for the role, had just finished touring in a stage production when this film was made. Distributed theatrically in the United States as *Carmen*.

1948 First Opera Film Festival

Italian stage production: Enrico Fulchigoni (director), Angelo Questa (conductor, Rome Opera House Orchestra and Chorus), George Richfield (producer).

Cast: Fernanda Cadoni (Carmen, sung by Cloe Elmo), Giacinto Prandelli (Don José), Tito Gobbi (Escamillo), Pina Malgharini (Micaëla).

Video: Bel Canto Society/Lyric VHS. Edmondo Cancellieri (director). Black and white. In Italian with English narration. 25 minutes.

Comment: Highlights version of the opera filmed on stage at the Rome Opera House with singers from La Scala and Rome Opera. Made for the anthology film *First Opera Film Festival*. Elmo, a famous La Scala mezzo, made her debut at the Met in 1947. Cadoni, who plays Carmen on screen but does not sing, was also a noted mezzo-soprano.

1950 CBS Opera Television Theater

American TV production: Henry Souvaine (producer), Boris Goldovsky (conductor, CBS Television Orchestra).

Cast: Gladys Swarthout (Carmen), Robert Rounseville (Don José), Robert Merrill (Escamillo).

Telecast live January 1, 1950. Byron Paul (director). Black and white. In French. 75 minutes.

Comment: The first opera telecast in a CBS opera series narrated by Lawrence Tibbett.

1950 NBC Opera Theatre

American TV studio production: Charles Polacheck (director), Peter Herman Adler (conductor, Symphony of the Air), George Jenkins (set designer), Samuel Chotzinoff (producer), Lillian Foerster and Townsend Brewster (English translation).

Cast: Vera Bryner (Carmen), David Poleri (Don José), Andrew Gainey (Escamillo), Guy Tano (narrator), Elizabeth Carron, Beatrice Bush-Kane, Morley Meredith, Robert Goss.

Telecast live December 17, 1950. Kirk Browning (director). Black and white. In English. 60 minutes.

Comment: Story of the opera is told in flashback by Don José from his prison cell. Vera Bryner is Yul Brynner's sister; he added an "n" to his name.

1952 Metropolitan Opera

American stage production: Tyrone Guthrie (director), Fritz Reiner (conductor, Metropolitan Opera Orchestra and Chorus), Rolf Gérard (set designer).

Cast: Risë Stevens (Carmen), Richard Tucker (Don José), Robert Merrill (Escamillo), Nadine Conner (Micaëla).

Video at the MTR (but only 40 minutes of Act IV). Clark Jones (director). Telecast on December 11, 1952. Black and white. In French. 150 minutes

Comment: Famous production partially captured for posterity when it was telecast on closed-circuit television to 31 theaters in 27 cities to an audience 70,000. The *Variety* reviewer said he was shocked by the cleavage Stevens displayed.

1953 NBC Opera Theatre

American TV production: Charles Polacheck (director), Peter Herman Adler (conductor, NBC Symphony Orchestra and Chorus), William Molyneux (set designer), Samuel Chotzinoff (producer).

Cast: Vera Bryner (Carmen), Robert Rounseville (Don José) Warren Galjour (Escamillo), John Boles (Commentator).

Telecast live October 31, 1953. Kirk Browning (director). Color. In English. 60 minutes.

Comment: First color telecast of an opera. It was shot in the Colonial Theater in New York and could be seen in color only by an invited audience, but they judged it a colorful success.

1959 Voice of Firestone

American TV production: Alfred Wallenstein (conductor, Voice of Firestone Orchestra).

Cast: Rosalind Elias (Carmen), Nicolai Gedda (Don José), Robert Merrill (Escamillo).

Video: VAI VHS in *Firestone French Opera Gala*. Telecast April 27, 1959. Black and white. In French with English introductions. 20 minutes.

Comment: Highlight scenes from the opera with sets and extras as featured on the *Voice of Firestone* television show.

1959 Bolshoi Opera

Soviet stage production: Alexander Melik-Pahavev (conductor, Bolshoi Theatre Orchestra).

Cast: Irina Arkhipova (Carmen), Mario Del Monaco (Don José), Pavel Lisitsyan (Escamillo).

Video: VAI VHS. Black and white. Sung in Italian and Russian. 68 minutes.

Comment: Selected scenes from a June 1959 Bolshoi production with Del Monaco singing in Italian and the others in Russian.

1962 BBC Television

English TV production: Rudolph Cartier (director), Charles Mackerras (conductor, London Philharmonic Orchestra and Glyndebourne Festival Chorus and Ealing Boys' Grammar School Choir), Clifford Hatts (set designer), Christopher Hassall (English translation).

Cast: Rosalind Elias (Carmen), Raymond Nilsson (Don José), John Shirley-Quirk (Escamillo).

Telecast December 20, 1962. Black and white. In English. 101 minutes.

Comment: Cartier eliminated spoken dialogue and the role of Micaëla for this version and added film of Seville as background.

1967 Herbert von Karajan film

Swiss studio stage film: Herbert von Karajan (film/stage director and conductor, Vienna Philharmonic Orchestra and Vienna State Opera Chorus), Ernst Wild and François Reichenbach (cinematographers), Georges Wakhévitch (set/costume designer).

Cast: Grace Bumbry (Carmen), Jon Vickers (Don José), Justino Diaz (Escamillo), Mirella Freni (Micaëla), Olivera Miljakovic (Frasquita), Julia Hamari (Mercédès), Robert Kerns (Moralès), Anton Diakov (Zuniga).

Video: Philips VHS/LD. Color. In French with English subtitles. 167 minutes.

Comment: Karajan filmed his Salzburg Festival production in 35mm on his studio stage with help from Wild and Reichenbach. The cast is terrific, and Bumbry is a magnificent Carmen, but Karajan does not succeed in making the opera come alive. The film opened theatrically in New York July 26, 1970.

1979 Vienna State Opera

Austrian stage production: Franco Zeffirelli (director/set designer), Carlos Kleiber (conductor, Vienna State Opera Orchestra and Chorus),

Cast: Elena Obraztsova (Carmen), Plácido Domingo (Don José), Juri Mazurok (Escamillo), Isobel Buchanan (Micaëla).

Telecast by ORF Austrian television. Franco Zeffirelli (director). Color. In French. 177 minutes.

Comment: Zeffirelli's opulent and influential Vienna production won him wide acclaim.

1980 Paris Opéra

French stage production: Piero Faggioni (director), Pierre Dervaux (conductor, Paris Opéra Orchestra and Chorus), Ezio Frigerio (set/costume designer).

Cast: Teresa Berganza (Carmen), Plácido Domingo (Don José), Ruggero Raimondi (Escamillo), Katia Ricciarelli (Micaëla),

Video: House of Opera DVD/VHS and Lyric VHS. Telecast May 14, 1980. Pierre Badel (director). Color. In French. 158 minutes.

***1983 La Tragédie de Carmen

French feature films: Peter Brook (director/screenplay), Jean Claude Carrière (screenplay), Sven Nykvist (cinematographer), Marius Constant (conductor), Micheline Rozan (producer).

Casts: Hélène Delavault/Eva Saurova/ Zehava Gal (Carmen), Howard Hensel/Laurence Dale (Don José), Agnes Host/Véronique Dietschy (Micaëla), Jake Gardner/John Rath (Escamillo).

Video: Home Vision VHS (with Delavault as Carmen). Telecast in Europe in all three version. Color. In French with English subtitles. 82 minutes.

Comment: Brook's minimalist Paris stage production was a slimmed-down neorealistic version of the opera with Micaëla, for example, shown as a tough-minded country girl who has a knife fight with Carmen over Don José. Brook filmed it three times on stage with different Carmens, each version with four singers, two actors, and 15 musicians.

***1984 Francesco Rosi film

French/Italian film: Francesco Rosi (director), Tonino Guerra and Francesco Rosi (screenplay), Pasqualino De Santis (cinematographer), Lorin Maazel (conductor, National Orchestra of France, Radio France Chorus and Children's Choir), Enrico Job (set/costume designer), Antonio Gades (choreographer), Patrice Ledoux (producer), Daniel Toscan du Plantier and Gaumont (production).

Cast: Julia Migenes (Carmen), Plácido Domingo (José), Ruggero Raimondi (Escamillo), Faith Esham (Micaëla), Susan Daniel (Mercédès), Lillian Watson (Frasquita), François Le Roux (Morales), Jean-Paul Bogart (Zuniga), Julie Guiomar (Lillas Pastia).

Video: Columbia TriStar DVD/VHS. Color. In French with English subtitles. 151 minutes.

Comment: Rosi's film is a model for what a great opera movie can be, and it works nearly as well on the small screen as in the cinema. He uses the spoken dialogue of the original stage production to create effective cinema as well as fine opera. Migenes as Carmen acts as well as she sings, and her sensual personality is at the center of the drama. Domingo is at his best as a country boy in the army with a potential for violence brought to the surface by Carmen; Raimondi is a grand full-of-himself Escamillo; and Esham is touching as the girl-from-back-home. Maazel conducts with sizzle, and De Santis's cinematography is as glorious as the music. This is reportedly the biggest-selling opera on DVD. The film was distributed theatrically by Columbia/TriStar.

Carmen (1984): Julia Migenes-Johnson stars as a fiery Carmen in Francesco Rosi's film of the opera.

1984 New York City Opera

American stage production: Frank Corsaro (director), Christopher Keene (conductor, New York City Opera Orchestra and Chorus), Franco Colavecchia (set designer).

Cast: Victoria Vergara (Carmen), Jacques Trussel (Don José), Marianna Christos (Micaëla), Robert Hale (Escamillo).

Telecast September 26, 1984, on PBS for *Live From Lincoln Center* series. Kirk Browning (director). Color. In French. 210 minutes.

Comment: Corsaro's controversial production updated the opera to the 1930s during the Spanish Civil War. Carmen is portrayed as an anti-Franco loyalist, with Don José as a fascist soldier.

1984 Teatro alla Scala

Italian stage production: Piero Faggioni (director), Claudio Abbado (conductor, Teatro alla Scala Orchestra and Chorus).

Cast: Shirley Verrett (Carmen), Plácido Domingo (Don José), Alida Ferrarini (Micaëla), Ruggero Raimondi (Escamillo).

Video: House of Opera DVD/VHS. Telecast December 7, 1984, on RAI television. Color. In French. 210 minutes.

***1985 Glyndebourne Festival

British stage production: Peter Hall (director), Bernard Haitink (conductor, London Philharmonic Orchestra and Glyndebourne Festival Chorus), John Bury (set/costume designer).

Cast: Maria Ewing (Carmen), Barry McCauley (Don José), David Holloway (Escamillo), Marie McLaughlin (Micaëla).

Video: Home Vision VHS. Robin Lough (director). Color. In French with English subtitles. 175 minutes.

Comment: Ewing gives an electrifying performance as Carmen in Hall's starkly realistic production. This is the first of three versions of *Carmen* on video featuring Ewing; she was married to Hall when this production was taped.

1986 Vancouver Opera

Canadian stage production: Lucian Pintile (director).

Cast: Jean Stillwell (Carmen), Jacques Trussel (Don José), Tom Fox (Escamillo), Martha Collins (Micaëla).

Video: Lyric VHS. Telecast June 17, 1986. Tony Gilbert (director). Color. In English. 180 minutes.

Comment: Updated version of the opera presented as a fantasy play-within-a-play at a carnival in a Latin American country. Escamillo is a rock singer, and Micaëla is blind.

1987 Metropolitan Opera

American stage production: Paul Mills (director), James Levine (conductor, Metropolitan Opera Orchestra and Chorus), John Bury (set/costume designer).

Cast: Agnes Baltsa (Carmen), José Carreras (Don José), Samuel Ramey (Escamillo), Leona Mitchell (Micaëla), Myra Merritt (Frasquita), Diane Kesling (Mercédès), Anthony Laciura (Le Remendado), Bruce Hubbard (Le Dancaïre), Ara Berberian (Zuniga), Vernon Hartman (Moralès), Nico Castel (Lillas Pastia).

Video: DG DVD/VHS. Brian Large (director). Taped February 28, 1987; telecast April 1, 1987. Color. In French with English subtitles. 172 minutes.

Comment: Production is effective, cast is strong, and Baltsa is a believably earthy Carmen, but there are more memorable versions of the opera on video.

***1989 Earl's Court, London

English stage production: Steven Pimlott (director), Jacques Delacote (conductor, National Philharmonic, Ambrosian Opera Chorus), Stefanos Lazaridis (set designer).

Cast: Maria Ewing (Carmen), Jacques Trussel (Don José), Alain Fondary (Escamillo), Miriam Gauci (Micaëla), Paco Peña flamenco troupe (dancers).

Video: Image Entertainment/Stax DVD/Arena (GB) VHS. Gavin Taylor (director). Color. In French with English subtitles. 165 minutes.

Comment: Mammoth production using a giant set in the round. It reportedly cost $10 million to stage, with a cast of 500, including singers, dancers, horse riders, fire eaters, and musicians. It's well sung and surprisingly enjoyable. Ewing is once again a marvel.

1991 Royal Opera

British stage production: Nuria Espert (director), Zubin Mehta (conductor, Royal Opera House Orchestra and Chorus), Gerardo Vera (set designer).

Cast: Maria Ewing (Carmen), Luis Lima (Don José), Gino Quilico (Escamillo), Leontina Vaduva (Micaëla), Judith Howarth (Frasquita), Jean Rigby (Mercédès).

Video: Image Entertainment DVD/Kultur and Home Vision VHS/Pioneer Artists LD. Barrie Gavin (director). Color. In French with English subtitles. 164 minutes.

Comment: Ewing, who had already won wide recognition in the role at Glyndebourne and Earl's Court, acts quite differently here, more open and flirtatious under the direction of Spanish actress–turned–director Espert.

1997 Metropolitan Opera

American stage production: Franco Zeffirelli (director/set designer), James Levine (conductor, Metropolitan Opera Orchestra and Chorus).

Cast: Waltraud Meier (Carmen), Plácido Domingo (Don José), Angela Gheorghiu (Micaëla), Sergei Leiferkus (Escamillo), Mary Dunleavy (Frasquita), Kristine Jepson (Mercédès).

Telecast December 29, 1997; taped March 25, 1997. Gary Halvorson (director). Color. In French with English subtitles. 175 minutes.

1998 St. Margarethen Opera Festival

Austrian stage production: Wolfgang Werner (producer), Gianfranco de Bosio (director), Giorgio Croci (conductor, Stagione d'Opera Italiana Orchestra and Chorus and Budapest Hanved Ensemble), Bernhard Kratza (set designer).

Cast: Malgorzata Walewska (Carmen), Mario Malagnini (Don José), Boaz Senator (Escamillo), Ulrike Sonntag (Micaëla), Barcelona Flamenco Dance Theater (dancers).

Video: Festspiele St. Margarethen (Germany) VHS. Color. In French, with introduction in German. 60 minutes.

Comment: Spectacle dominates this abridged production of the opera filmed at the ancient Roman quarry of St. Margarethen in Austria, "the biggest open-air stage in Europe," with seating for 3,800. The set is an entire village with lots of children, but Micaëla looks rather like a Heidi.

2002 Glyndebourne Festival

British stage production: David McVicar (director), Philippe Jordan (conductor, London Philharmonic Orchestra and Glyndebourne Festival Chorus), John Bury (set/costume designer).

Cast: Anne Sofie von Otter (Carmen), Marcus Haddock (Don José), Laurent Naouri (Escamillo), Lisa Milne (Micaëla).

Video: BBC Opus Arte DVD. Taped live on August 17, 2002. Sue Judd (director). Color. In French with English subtitles. 220 minutes.

Comment: Von Otter's first Carmen attracted a good deal of attention in England, with McVicar describing his sumptuous production of the opera as "the first ever musical." The double DVD set includes documentary material about the opera, costumes, choreography, cast, and Glyndebourne.

Early/related films

1894 Carmencita

Thomas Edison's film *Carmencita*, made in his Black Maria studio in March 1894, features a Spanish dancer named Carmencita. In Bizet's *Carmen*, the heroine says her name is "Carmencita." It is not recorded whether this Carmencita danced to Bizet's music, but it seems probable. Black and white. Silent. About 30 seconds.

1896 Eidoloscope bullfight

A film of an actual bullfight was featured in a stage production of *Carmen* in 1896. It was shot in Mexico City with the widescreen Eidoloscope camera/projector and shown in a production of *Carmen* by the Rosabel Morrison company at the Lyceum Theater in Elizabeth, New Jersey. Black and white. Silent. About 1 minute.

1902 Bioscope aria

An aria from *Carmen* was featured in a sound film shown in September 1902 by Alber's Electro Talking Bioscope in the Netherlands. Singer unknown. Black and white. In French. About 3 minutes.

1906 Bitzer film

D. W. Griffith's cameraman G. W. Bitzer shot an early American *Carmen* in a New York studio for the American Mutoscope and Biograph company. Black and white. Silent. About 7 minutes.

1907 Chronophone

The 1907 British sound film *Carmen,* which features several arias and scenes from the opera, was made by Arthur Gilbert for Gaumont using the Chronophone sound-on-disc system. Black and white. In French. About 12 minutes.

1908 Pineschi sound films

The Pineschi company of Rome made two sound films in the 1908 featuring arias from *Carmen,* "Mia tu sei" and "Toreador." Black and white. Each about 3 minutes.

1908 Toreador Song

Antonio Cataldi is featured singing the "Toreador Song" from *Carmen* in a sound film made in Brazil with a synchronized record. Black and white. In French. About 4 minutes.

1909 Film d'Arte Italiana

Vittoria Lepanto, one of the top Italian stars of the period, has the lead in this *Carmen* directed by Gerolamo Lo Savio for the Film d'Arte Italiana studio of Rome and based on the opera. Alberto Nepoti is Don José and Annibale Nichi is Escamillo. Black and white. Silent. About 10 minutes.

1909 Torero Song "Carmen"

The American Lubin company made a sound film for its Bizet series titled *Torero Song "Carmen."* Escamillo's aria was synchronized with the film using the Lubin sound system with a disc. Black and white. In French. About 4 minutes. NFTA in London has the sound disc.

1910 Films d'Art film

André Calmettes directed this French *Carmen* in 1910 with the ballerina Régine Badet as Carmen; she had made her debut as a solo dancer in *Carmen* at the Opéra-Comique in 1904. Dancer/actor Max Dearly plays Don José. The film was presented with live singers at the Battersea Arts Centre in London in 1999. Films d'Art Pathé production. Black and white. Silent. About 12 minutes.

1913 Monopol film

Marion Leonard stars as Carmen in this American *Carmen* produced by the Monopol company. This was one of two rival feature films of *Carmen* made in 1913

and was the first released. Black and white. Silent. About 45 minutes.

1913 Thanhouser film

Thanhouser studio star Marguerite Snow plays Carmen in this rival American *Carmen* released one month after the Monopol film. Her costars are William Garwood and William Russell. Theodore Marston directed. Black and white. Silent. About 45 minutes.

1915 Toreador Song

German sound film pioneer Oskar Messter made the film *Toreador Song* with his synchronized sound-on-disc system for his Berlin Biophon Theater. It was copyrighted in the United States in 1915 but probably was made earlier. Black and white. In French. About 4 minutes.

1915 Farrar/De Mille film

Geraldine Farrar, who had sung *Carmen* at the Metropolitan Opera, made her cinema debut in the role in Cecil B. De Mille's famous film *Carmen.* It was very popular and launched Farrar on a successful film career. Wallace Reid is Don José, Pedro De Cordoba is Escamillo, William Elmer is Morales, Jeanie Macpherson is Frasquita, and Anita King is Mercédès; there is no Micaëla. William C. De Mille wrote the screenplay, Alvin Wyckoff was the cinematographer, and S. L. Rothapfel prepared the musical accompaniment. De Mille claimed that the opera owners wanted too much money for rights so he used only the Mérimée story, but nobody believed him. A 50-piece symphony orchestra played the opera music on opening night with Hugo Riesenfeld conducting. Produced for Lasky-Paramount. Color tinted. Silent. About 76 minutes. Kino DVD/VHS (with original score performed by the Olympia Chamber Orchestra), and VAI DVD/VHS (with reconstruction of the Riesenfeld score by Gillian Anderson, who conducts the London Philharmonic).

1915 Bara/Walsh film

Theda Bara stars as Carmen in this rival *Carmen* film produced by the Fox studio and directed by Raoul Walsh. It was released on the same day as the Geraldine Farrar film, and it won reasonable acceptance, although critics felt that vamp Bara was not well cast as a tempestuous gypsy. Don José is Einar Linden, and Escamillo is Carl Harbaugh. Black and white. Silent. About 75 minutes.

1916 Charlie Chaplin's Burlesque on Carmen

Charlie Chaplin's Burlesque on Carmen was written and directed by Chaplin who plays a soldier called Darn Hosiery; Edna Purvience is his enticing Carmen. This is a very funny movie with many Chaplinesque delights, including satirical jabs at opera acting and the rival movies of Geraldine Farrar and Theda Bara. There is even a happy ending; the knife Chaplin uses to kill Carmen is a palpable fake. Produced for Essanay. Black and white. Silent. About 60 minutes.

1916 Cines film
Belgian-born American opera diva Marguerite Sylva, who sang the role of Carmen on stage 600 times around the world, stars in the Italian film *Carmen* and won praise from critics for her intense performance opposite André Habay as Don José. Giovanni Doria and August Turchi directed for Cines. Black and white. Silent. About 75 minutes.

1917 Webb Singing Pictures
Met baritone Giuseppe Campanari plays Escamillo in this *Carmen*, a sound film of highlights of the opera; he performs the Toreador Song with soprano Marie Conesa, tenor Salvatore Giordano, and bass Léon Rothier. The film, made by Webb Singing Pictures, premiered at the Cohan and Harris Theatre in New York in the presence of Enrico Caruso and Met colleagues. George Webb was an early sound film entrepreneur. Black and white. In French. About 10 minutes.

1918 Lubitsch film
Ernst Lubitsch's famous *Carmen* stars Pola Negri as Carmen with Harry Liedtke as Don José. It was made in Germany and based more on the novel than the opera, but the video includes Bizet's music as score. Lubitsch and Negri won high praise from U.S. critics and had notable Hollywood careers later. The film was titled *Carmen* in Germany, but it was released in the United States in 1921 as *Gypsy Blood*. Black and white. Silent. About 75 minutes. On VHS.

1919 Bos film
Dutch actress Annie Bos plays Carmen in the Dutch feature film *Carmen* shot in the Netherlands in 1919. Black and white. Silent. About 70 minutes.

1920 Vollrath film
A feature film of *Carmen* was produced in Mexico in 1920 by Germán Camus with Ernest Vollrath directing. Black and white. Silent. About 65 minutes.

1922 Tense Moments From Operas
Patricia Fitzgerald is Carmen, Ward MacAllister is Don José, and Maresco Maresini is Escamillo in this British highlights film made for the series *Tense Moments From Operas*. George Wynn directed and H. B. Parkinson produced for Master/Gaumont. Black and white. Silent. About 10 minutes.

1922 Carmen Jr.
Three-year-old child star Baby Peggy plays an infant Carmen in *Carmen Jr.*, a two-reel comedy. Black and white. Silent. About 20 minutes.

1926 Feyder/Meller film
Raquel Meller is Carmen in the famous French *Carmen* directed by Jacques Feyder. Meller is superb as the gypsy temptress and has a fine partner in Louis Lerch as Don José. *The New York Times* called it "vastly superior" to earlier screen versions of the story. Feyder based his realistic film on the Mérimée source novel, but there are overtones of the opera. Produced by Albatros Film. Black and white. Silent. About 75 minutes.

1927 Vitaphone film with Martinelli
Met tenor Giovanni Martinelli plays Don José and sings selections from Act II of *Carmen* in a Vitaphone sound film. He is joined by contralto Jeanne Gordon as Carmen on three of the excerpts and is accompanied by the Vitaphone Symphony Orchestra. Black and white. In French. About 10 minutes.

1927 Vitaphone film with Barclay
English baritone John Barclay performs the "Toreador Song" in "imitation of a famous character" in the Vitaphone sound film *John Barclay Sings the Toreador Song*. Black and white. In French. About 10 minutes.

1927 The Loves of Carmen
Dolores Del Rio is a memorable Carmen in this version of the Carmen story, the second directed by Raoul Walsh. Don Alvarado plays Don José, but it is Victor McLaglen as Escamillo that Carmen really pursues. Bizet's influence was fully acknowledged; a prologue of music from the opera was performed at the New York premiere and selections played during the film. Critics praised Del Rio's fiery performance. Black and white. Silent. About 93 minutes.

1927 Cameo Opera
Zeda Pascha plays Carmen opposite Herbert Langley as Don José in this highlights version of *Carmen*. Live singers and orchestra performed in synchronization with the scenes on screen. H. B. Parkinson directed for the series *Song Films*. Black and white. Silent. About 20 minutes.

1928 Vitaphone film with Amato
Baritone Pasquale Amato sings the Toreador aria from *Carmen* in this 1928 Vitaphone sound short titled *Pasquale Amato in A Neapolitan Romance*. Black and white. 8 minutes.

1928 Pinschewer film
Julius Pinschewer's German animated film of *Carmen* was screened with music from the Bizet opera. Black and white. Silent. About 7 minutes.

1928 Campus Carmen
Carole Lombard stars in the Mack Sennett comedy short *Campus Carmen*. Black and white. Silent. About 10 minutes.

1929 Vitaphone film with Painter
"Eleanor Painter, The Lyric Soprano" sings, in costume, the Habanera from *Carmen* in this sound short made for Vitaphone. Black and white. About 9 minutes.

1929 The Cocoanuts
The first Marx Brothers film *The Cocoanuts* features a famous burlesque of the Habanera titled "Tale of the Shirt." The lyrics revolve around repetition of the phrase "I want my shirt" and grow in strength as a formidable chorus joins the Marx Brothers in ribbing the man who wants his shirt. Paramount. Black and white. In English. 96 minutes.

1929 Vitaphone film with Gentle
Met mezzo-soprano Alice Gentle sings the Habanera from *Carmen* in this Vitaphone sound short recorded at the old Manhattan Opera House. Black and white. About 8 minutes.

1932 Operalogue
An English-language highlights film of *Carmen* was produced for the American Operalogue series in 1932. Lew Seller directed for Educational Films. Black and white. In English. 28 minutes.

1933 Reiniger film
German silhouette artist Lotte Reiniger's animated film *Carmen* is still widely admired. It is one of the most famous early "artistic" cartoons. Black and white. 10 minutes.

1935 The Melody Lingers On
George Houston is featured as Don José in scenes from *Carmen* in this romantic film. He plays an opera singer, a captain in the Italian army during World War I, who returns home in 1917 for a Red Cross benefit performance of the Bizet opera. David Burton directed. Black and white. In English. 85 minutes.

1936 Dyer film
England animator Anson Dyer made a charming burlesque version of *Carmen* based on the Stanley Holloway character Sam as matador. Color. 9 minutes.

1937 Broadway Melody of 1938
The first shot of this movie shows crowds in front of the old Metropolitan Opera and posters of *Carmen*. An orchestra plays Escamillo's music and a voice is heard beginning the "Toreador Song." The camera pans right to a barber shop, where a barber (played by baritone Igor Gorin) is singing the aria while shaving Buddy Ebsen. Roy Del Ruth directed. MGM. Black and white. 110 minutes.

1938 Carmen la de Triana
Imperio Argentina plays Carmen in this Spanish version of the story, directed by Florian Rey and shot in Berlin during the Spanish Civil War. The basic music is Bizet, but there are many new songs. Also in the cast are Rafael Rivelles, Manuel Luna, and Alberto Romea. Black and white. In Spanish. 102 minutes.

1938 Andalusische Nachte
The German version of the above *Carmen la de Triana* features Imperio Argentina singing in German under the direction of Herbert Maisch. The cast includes Friedrich Benfer, Erwin Biegel, and Karl Kousner. Black and white. In German. 102 minutes.

1939 Balalaika
The "Toreador Song" and the "Gypsy Song" from *Carmen* are featured in this Nelson Eddy/Ilona Massey musical about the Russian Revolution. He plays a prince; she's a cabaret singer. Reinhold Schunzel directed. Black and white. 102 minutes.

1941 There's Magic in Music
Susanna Foster sings an aria from *Carmen* in this film about a burlesque singer taken to a summer music camp. After she meets Met stars Richard Bonelli and Irra Petina, she is transmuted into an opera singer. Andrew L. Stone directed. Also known as *The Hard-Boiled Canary*. Paramount. Black and white. 80 minutes.

1941 Ridin' the Cherokee Trail
This low-budget Tex Ritter Western contains what is surely the most bizarre version of the "Toreador Song" in the movies. It has to be seen to be believed. See RIDIN' THE CHEROKEE TRAIL.

1942 I Married an Angel
The last of the Jeanette MacDonald–Nelson Eddy films is an adaptation of a Rodgers and Hart musical about a man

who dreams he marries an angel. It also includes the Chanson bohème from *Carmen* "Les tringles des sistres tintaient." W. S. Van Dyke directed. Black and white. 84 minutes.

1943 Christian-Jaque film
Viviane Romance plays Carmen opposite Jean Marais as Don José in the French film *Carmen* based on the opera libretto and using Bizet's music as score. This is an elaborate and colorful film, splendidly made and well directed by period film specialist Christian-Jaque. Black and white. In French. 105 minutes.

1943 Amadori film
Nini Marshall stars in the Argentine comedy *Carmen* based on the opera. She plays a dressmaker who gets hit on the head at the opera house while watching *Carmen* and dreams she is part of the action on stage. It turns into an updated burlesque, with the smugglers dealing in black market tires. Luis Cesar Amadori directed. Sono Film. Black and white. In Spanish. 96 minutes.

1944 Going My Way
Met diva Risë Stevens sang Carmen at the Met in this film before she had actually performed the role on stage, but it helped identify her with the part. Bing Crosby, playing a priest who needs to raise money for his church, goes backstage at the Met and watches with admiration as his friend Stevens sings the Habanera. Leo McCarey directed for Paramount. Black and white. 126 minutes. Paramount VHS.

1948 The Loves of Carmen
Rita Hayworth is Carmen in this Hollywood version of the story set in 1820 Seville with Glenn Ford as the soldier captivated by her. Hayworth is beautiful and the film is quite pleasant, but the music is by Mario Castelnuovo-Tedesco, not Bizet. Charles Vidor directed for Columbia. Color. 99 minutes.

1949 Everybody Does It
Paul Douglas sings the Toreador aria in this film about a businessman who discovers he has an operatic voice (the voice belongs to New York City Opera baritone Stephen Kemalyan). The film was based on James Cain's story *Career in C Major*. Edmund Goulding directed. Black and white. 98 minutes.

1950 Grounds for Marriage
Kathryn Grayson and Van Johnson appear in a *Carmen* dream sequence, narrated by Milton Cross, and Johnson sings arias by both Don José and Escamillo through the magic of dubbing. Vladimir Risin staged the opera ex-

cerpts, and Robert Z. Leonard directed for MGM. Black and white. 90 minutes.

1950 The Toast of New Orleans
Maria Lanza sings the "Flower Song" from *Carmen* in this musical about a Louisiana fisherman in turn-of-the-century New Orleans. He becomes an opera star with help from Kathryn Grayson. Norman Taurog directed. MGM. Color. 97 minutes.

1953 Carmen Proibita
Aña Esmeralda plays a Spanish dancer called Carmen in *Carmen Proibita* (Forbidden Carmen), an Italian film based on a modern version of the story. Fausto Tozzi is the José she seduces and corrupts. Giuseppe Maria Scotese directed. A Spanish version was made at the same time titled *Siempre Carmen* and directed by Alejandro Perla. Black and white. In Italian or Spanish. 93 minutes.

1955 Interrupted Melody
Opera diva Marjorie Lawrence, played by Eleanor Parker in this film biography, is seen on stage in *Carmen* singing the seguidilla "Pres des remparts de Séville." It is very well done, with the singing by Eileen Farrell. See INTERRUPTED MELODY.

1956 Serenade
The Carmen myth is central to James Cain's novel *Serenade* and the Mario Lanza film based on it. The hero is an opera singer, his favorite opera is *Carmen,* and his real-life Carmen is a rich American woman. The Escamillo counterpart is a Mexican woman who fights figurative bulls; she nearly kills Carmen to save him. The book is more resonant than the film, but director Anthony Mann keeps it interesting. Warner Bros. Color. 121 minutes.

1959 Carmen, la de Ronda
Carmen, la de Ronda is a revised Spanish version of the story set in Spain during the Napoleonic wars. Sara Montiel is Carmen, a Spanish cabaret singer who falls in love with a French soldier named José and tries to save his life. Tulio Demicheli directed and Benito Perojo produced. Distributed in America as *The Devil Made a Woman*. Color. In Spanish. 98 minutes.

1962 The Drama of Carmen
Leonard Bernstein examines the opera using Metropolitan Opera singers and Broadway actors in the television show *Ford Presents Leonard Bernstein: The Drama of Carmen*. Jane Rhodes and William Ovis sing the roles of Carmen and Don José while Zohra Lampert and James Congdon play them in the spoken version. Bernstein

contrasts the original opera with its spoken dialogue and the later sung version and conducts the New York Philharmonic. William A. Graham directed the telecast. Black and white. 60 minutes.

1962 Black Tights

Zizi Jeanmaire is Carmen, Roland Petit is Don José, and Henning Kronstam is the toreador in a 30-minute ballet version of *Carmen* featured in this French film. Petit created the choreography, and Terence Young directed the film. The French title is *Les Collants Noirs*. Color. 120 minutes.

1962 Carmen di Trastevere

Giovanna Ralli is Carmen in *Carmen di Trastevere*, an Italian attempt to transfer the story to the working-class district of Trastevere in Rome. Don José is a policeman, and his rival is now a motorcyclist. Opera film specialist Carmine Gallone directed. Black and white. In Italian. 90 minutes.

1970 The Clowns

Federico Fellini features the Toreador music in this brilliant Italian film about the world of clowns. Color. In Italian. 93 minutes.

1972 Carmen: The Dream and the Destiny

Huguette Tourangeau is Carmen, Plácido Domingo is Don José, and Tom Krause is Escamillo in this documentary about a Hamburg production of the opera directed by Regina Resnik. The film shows rehearsal and performance and explores the history of the opera. Alain Lombard conducts the Hamburg Opera Orchestra. Swansway Productions. 90 minutes. Print at the NFTA.

1976 The Bad News Bears

Themes from *Carmen* are featured rather ironically as the score of this excellent satirical comedy. Michael Ritchie's fable about a Little League baseball team stars Walter Matthau and Tatum O'Neal. Color. 103 minutes.

1978 Peter Brook and the Tragedy of Carmen

Documentary film about Peter Brook and his bare-bones production of *Carmen* at the Théâtre des Bouffes du Nord in Paris. After the libretto is revised with screenwriter Jean Claude Carrière and music director Marius Constant, the result is a highly theatrical production with four singers, two actors, and 15 musicians. Brook used three casts on the production for 150 performances. Tony Cash directed for London Weekend Television. Color. 52 minutes.

1978 Carmen, la que Contaba 16 Años

Mayra Alejandra stars as Carmen in *Carmen, la que Contaba 16 Años* (Carmen, Who Was Only 16), a Venezuelan version of the story set in the harbor of La Guaira. Director Roman Chalbaud follows the story fairly closely in its new setting and ends the film with Don José killing Carmen at a bullring. Color. In Spanish. 102 minutes.

1978 To Forget Venice

Franco Brusati's *Dimenticare Venezia*, which features the Habanera from *Carmen*, takes place at the home of a dying opera star who has some complicated relationships. The film received an Oscar nomination for Best Foreign Language film. Color. In Italian. 107 minutes. On VHS.

1983 Saura film

Laura Del Sol dances the role of Carmen in Carlos Saura's superb flamenco film *Carmen* with a screenplay based on the opera and the novella. Choreographer Antonio Gades discovers Carmen as an untrained dancer and hires her for a production of *Carmen*. He falls in loves with her, finds her fickle, and kills her when she betrays him. Arias from *Carmen* are sung by Regina Resnik as Carmen, Mario Del Monaco as Don José, and Tom Krause as Escamillo. Color. In Spanish with English subtitles. 101 minutes. On VHS.

1983 First Name Carmen

Jean-Luc Godard's updated version of the story, *Prénom Carmen*, is more Godard than Bizet, but it includes snatches of music from the opera. Maruschka Detmers is Carmen, a terrorist rather than a smuggler, but still a femme-fatale. She seduces a policeman called Joseph and leads him to a life of crime. She's also an aspiring filmmaker, with a film director uncle played by Godard. Color. In French. 85 minutes. On VHS.

1988 Jessye Norman Sings Carmen

Behind-the-scenes film of Jessye Norman making a recording of *Carmen* in Paris. She is observed recording, giving a press conference, and talking about her interpretation. Neil Shicoff is Don José and Simon Estes is Escamillo for the Philips recording, with Seiji Ozawa conducting the National Orchestra of France and Radio France Chorus. The film was made by Susan Froemke, Peter Gelb, Albert Maysles, and Charlotte Zwerin. Color. In English and French with subtitles. 59 minutes. Cami VHS.

1994 The Hudsucker Proxy

Grace Bumbry sings the Habanera on the soundtrack as Tim Robbins dances with a Carmen figure in a dream. The music is played by the Paris Opera Orchestra and Chorus led by Rafael Frübeck de Burgos. The film is an odd Capra-esque fantasy about an innocent running a big business. Joel Coen directed. Color. 111 minutes. On VHS.

1995 Operavox
The British Pizzazz animation studio created this computer-enhanced live-action animated version of *Carmen* for the British Operavox series. The Welsh National Opera Orchestra plays the music. Julian Smith was music editor. Color. 27 minutes.

1995 Babe
A trio of mice briefly sing the "Toreador Song" in this Australian children's fantasy about a pig that wants to herd sheep. Chris Noonan directed. Color. 91 minutes. On VHS.

1996 Pevec film
Natasa Barbara Gracner stars as a hooker Carmen in the Slovenian film *Carmen*, a retelling of the mythic tale set in the urban underworld of Slovenia. Sebastian Cavazza plays the Don José role. Metod Pevec directed. Color. 94 minutes.

1998 The Phantom of the Opera
Dario Argento's horrific version of *The Phantom of the Opera*, with Julian Sands as the Phantom, features the Habanera from *Carmen*. Ennio Morricone conducted. Color. 99 minutes.

1999 Magnolia
Magnolia is a street in the Los Angeles Valley area where people live very complicated lives. A quiz kid correctly identifies the Habanera in an English translation and then tries to sing it in French. His version shifts into the aria as sung (rather better) by Leontyne Price on a record being played in a down-scale apartment. Price is accompanied by the Vienna Philharmonic led by Herbert von Karajan. Paul Thomas Anderson wrote and directed the fim. Color. 188 minutes.

2000 When Brendan Met Trudy
The Habanera from *Carmen* is featured on the soundtrack of this Irish film about a schoolteacher (Peter McDonald) who becomes involved with a female burglar (Flora Montgomery). Kieron J. Walsh directed. Color. 94 minutes.

2001 The Car Man
Superb modern ballet set to the music of *Carmen*, with choreography and direction by Matthew Bourne. Set in a small midwestern American town in the 1960s, it tells the story of a drifter who comes to town, seduces the wife of a garage owner, and then murders him with her help. Les Brotherston designed the sets; Ross MacGibbon directed the film. Color. 100 minutes. Warner Vision (GB) DVD.

2002 Carmen—A Hip Hopera
Beyoncé Knowles plays Carmen in this hip hop version of the story with Mekhi Phifer as the man she dazzles. Robert Townsend directed. Color. In English. 88 minutes. NLD DVD.

2003 Aranda film
Vincent Aranda's Spanish film *Carmen* is based on the Mérimée novella rather than the opera and imagines that Don José tells the writer his tragic love story while in prison. Paz Vega plays the Carmen who destroys him. In Spanish. 110 minutes.

CARMEN JONES
1943 "American opera" by Hammerstein/Bizet

OSCAR HAMMERSTEIN II's adaptation of Bizet's *Carmen* is so different from the original that it deserves its own entry here. While it respects its source, *Carmen Jones* is an ocean away from Henri Meilhac and Ludovic Halévy's libretto and the original Prosper Mérimée story. Gypsy Carmen is transformed into Carmen Jones, a worker in a World War II parachute factory. Don José is an American army corporal named Joe, hometown girlfriend Micaëla is now called Cindy Lou, and bullfighter Escamillo is neatly transmuted into boxing champion Husky Miller. The "Toreador Song" is changed into a splendid "Stand Up and Fight," the Habanera is turned into "Dat's Love," the seguidilla is "Dere's a Café on the Corner," and the Chanson bohème is the splendid "Beat Out Dat Rhythm on a Drum." Joe tells Cindy Lou that "You Talk Just Like My Maw," and the Smugglers' Quintet becomes "Whizzin' Away Along de Track." The central story is essentially the same: Carmen seduces Joe and gets him to desert the army. When she leaves him, he kills her. *Carmen Jones* opened at the Broadway Theatre in New York in 1943 with alternating Carmens, Muriel Smith and Muriel Rahn. Marilyn Horne made her operatic debut in the 1954 film version, dubbing Dorothy Dandridge. The opera was revived at the Old Vic in London in 1992 to great success, named best stage musical of the year and recorded. It was presented in New York in January 2001 in the series *Musicals in Mufti*.

1954 Preminger film
American feature film: Otto Preminger (director), Harry Kleiner (screenplay), Sam Leavitt (cinematographer, in CinemaScope), Samuel Goldwyn (producer), Herbert Ross (choreography), Twentieth Century-Fox (studio).

Cast: Dorothy Dandridge (Carmen Jones, sung by Marilyn Horne), Harry Belafonte (Joe, sung by La-Vern Hutcherson), Husky Miller (Joe Adams, sung by Marvin Hayes), Olga James (Cindy Lou), Pearl Bailey (Frankie), Diahann Carroll (Myrt, sung by Bernice Peterson), Nick Stewart (Dink, sung by Joe Crawford), Brock Peters (Sergeant Brown), Sandy Lewis (T-Bone), Mauri Lynn (Sally).

Video: Fox DVD/VHS/LD. Color. In English. 105 minutes.

Comment: A much undervalued film. It won a Golden Globe Award as Best Musical in 1954, Dandridge was nominated for a Best Actress Oscar, Horne made her operatic debut, and Bailey gave a truly memorable performance of "Beat Out Dat Rhythm on a Drum."

Carmen Jones (1954): Dorothy Dandridge and Harry Belafonte, the doomed lovers in Otto Preminger's film.

CARMINA BURANA
1937 scenic cantata by Orff

CARL ORFF's *Carmina Burana* (Songs of Beuren), which he called a "scenic cantata," is neither opera nor oratorio in the traditional sense, but it was meant to be staged and danced with orchestra and choir in the pit. It has been produced by opera directors such as Jean-Pierre Ponnelle and has influenced contemporary opera. Orff used as his "libretto" a collection of poems dating to the 12th and 13th-century discovered in the Benedictine Cloister in Bavaria. The thread of narrative that runs through the cantata concerns the workings of fate/ fortune, and there are sections devoted to spring, the tavern, and seduction, with solos for soprano, tenor, and baritone.

1975 Ponnelle film
German TV film: Jean-Pierre Ponnelle (director/set designer), Kurt Eichhorn (conductor, Munich Radio-Television Orchestra, Bavarian Radio-Television Chorus and Tölz Boys Choir), Pet Halmen (costumes).

Singers: Lucia Popp, John Van Kesteren, Hermann Prey.

Video: RCA DVD/BMG VHS. Color. In Latin and German. 78 minutes.

Comment: The set is a representation of an ideal medieval Europe, including a ruined church; the female singers are dressed in white (Popp wears a wimple) while the men are in Bohemian gear with beards. DVD includes the composer talking about the work. Soundtrack of the film is on CD.

1981 Cardiff Festival of Choirs
Welsh stage production: Terry de Lacey (producer), Walter Weller (conductor, Royal Philharmonic Orchestra, Cardiff Polyphonic Choir, Dyfed Choir, and Llandaff Cathedral Choristers).

Cast: Norma Burrowes, Kenneth Bowen, Thomas Allen.

Video: Kultur VHS. Terry de Lacey (director). Color. In Latin and German with English subtitles. 60 minutes.

1989 Berlin Philharmonic Hall
German stage production: Christian Greube (producer), Seiji Ozawa (conductor, Berlin Philharmonic Orchestra, Shin-Yu Kai Chorus, Boys' Choir of the Staats-und-Domchor, Berlin).

Cast: Kathleen Battle, Frank Lopardo, Thomas Allen.

Video: Philips VHS. Barrie Gavin (director). Telecast on PBS on December 31, 1989. Color. In Latin and German. 62 minutes.

Comment: Title cards used were made from original manuscripts. A highlights version is available in the *Great Moments* video series.

Related film

1999 The Bachelor
"O Fortuna" from *Carmina Burana* is heard on the soundtrack of this film, performed by the Slovak Philharmonic Chorus and CSR Symphony Orchestra led by Carl Orff. The film is a remake of Buster Keaton's *Seven Chances* about a bachelor (Chris O'Donnell) who has to marry to inherit a fortune. Gary Sinyor directed. Color. 102 minutes.

CARNEGIE HALL
American concert hall

Carnegie Hall, the most famous concert hall in America, has crowned the reputation of opera singers from Caruso to Callas. Despite an attempt to replace this 1891 repository of musical memory with an orange skyscraper,

Carnegie Hall looks set to celebrate another century of music. It has been the subject of two films and appears as a character in movies such as *On the Town, Unfaithfully Yours,* and *Home Alone 2.* It is also the subject of America's most famous classical music joke. Question: "How do you get to Carnegie Hall?" Answer: "Practice!"

1947 Carnegie Hall

This pleasant film is a fiction framework for a series of numbers by classical stars of the period. Karl Lamb's script centers around a lady who works at the Hall and dreams that her pianist son will one day play there. Ezio Pinza performs arias from *Don Giovanni* and *Simon Boccanegra,* Risë Stevens sings arias from *Carmen* and *Samson et Dalila,* Lily Pons sings the "Bell Song" from *Lakmé,* and Jan Peerce sings "O Sole Mio." The other performers are Bruno Walter, Leopold Stokowski, Artur Rubinstein, and Jascha Heifetz. William Miller was cinematographer; Edgar G. Ulmer directed. Produced by Federal Films. Black and white. 134 minutes. Kino DVD/Allegro and Bel Canto Society VHS.

Carnegie Hall (1947): Risë Stevens and Lily Pons are among the many stars of this classic music film.

1991 Carnegie Hall at 100

This splendid documentary, subtitled *A Place of Dreams,* celebrates the centennial of the hall and includes archival footage of opera personalities who sang there. Marilyn Horne is interviewed, Leonard Bernstein talks about his first appearance, and Lily Pons performs her party piece, the "Bell Song." The hero of the film is Isaac Stern; he organized the group that saved the building from being torn down in 1961. Sara Lukinson wrote the film and

Peter Rosen directed it. Color. 57 minutes. RCA Victor VHS/LD.

1991 Carnegie Hall Live at 100

A gala at Carnegie Hall to celebrate its 100th birthday. The performers include Plácido Domingo, Marilyn Horne, Leontyne Price, and Samuel Ramey, with Zubin Mehta conducting. The gala was telecast on PBS in May 1991. Color. 57 minutes.

1991 A Carnegie Hall Christmas

Kathleen Battle and Frederica von Stade perform seasonal favorites in this Carnegie Hall concert on December 8, 1991. Their program includes the "Evening Prayer" from Humperdinck's *Hansel and Gretel,* "Mariä Wiegenlied," and "Gesu Bambino." Also appearing are Wynton Marsalis, Nancy Allen, the American Boys Choir, and the Christmas Concert Chorus and Orchestra of St. Luke's led by André Previn. Brian Large directed the video. Color. 88 minutes. Sony VHS.

1998 Carnegie Hall Opening Night 1998

George Gershwin's 100th birthday is celebrated at Carnegie Hall with excerpts from *Porgy and Bess* and other Gershwin works. The singers are Audra McDonald, Brian Stokes Mitchell, and Frederica von Stade, with Michael Tilson Thomas conducting the San Francisco Symphony Orchestra. Brian Large directed the video on September 23, 1998. Color. In English. 87 minutes. Telecast by PBS September 30, 1998.

CAROUSEL

1945 "operatic musical" by Rodgers and Hammerstein

Carousel is one of the most powerful of the great musicals produced by RICHARD RODGERS and OSCAR HAMMERSTEIN II; they said they imagined it in operatic terms. The story is derived from Ferenc Molnar's 1921 play *Liliom,* with the setting transferred to a 19th-century New England fishing village. Carnival barker Billy Bigelow marries factory worker Julie Jordan but, as they have no money, they move into Cousin Nettie's home. He is killed during a robbery attempt but is allowed to return to Earth for a good deed and to sing "You'll Never Walk Alone" to his daughter. Counterpointing their story is the plain but satisfying marriage of Carrie to Mr. Snow. The role of Nettie is usually performed by an opera contralto, the beginning of an Rodgers and Hammerstein tradition of having a big aria for a mezzo in their musicals, here the famous "You'll Never Walk Alone." In the 1956 film, it was Claramae Turner; in the 1967 TV production, it was Patricia Neway. *Carousel* has been sung and recorded by many opera singers and seems likely to enter the opera house repertory. Neil Rishoi wrote a long article about it in *Opera Quarterly* in 2002, describing it as an "operatic musical."

1956 Twentieth Century-Fox film

American feature film: Henry King (director), Charles G. Clarke (CinemaScope cinematography), Phoebe and Henry Ephron (screenplay), Alfred Newman (music director), Ken Darby (vocal arrangements), Agnes de Mille and Rod Alexander (choreographers).

Cast: Gordon MacRae (Billy Bigelow), Shirley Jones (Julie Jordan), Claramae Turner (Nettie), Barbara Ruick (Carrie), Robert Rounseville (Mr. Snow).

Video: Fox DVD/VHS. Color. In English. 128 minutes.

Comment: A good deal of music has been cut from the stage version but MacRae, Jones, and Turner sing what is left quite wonderfully and King is a fine director of Americana.

1967 ABC Television

American TV production: Paul Bogart (director), Jack Elliott (music director), Jan Scott (set designer), Edward Villella (choreographer), Sidney Michaels (screenplay), Norman Rosemont (producer).

Cast: Robert Goulet (Billy Bigelow), Mary Grover (Julie Jordan), Patricia Neway (Nettie), Marlyn Mason (Carrie), Jack De Lon (Mr. Snow).

Telecast May 7, 1967, in *Armstrong Circle Theater* series. Paul Bogart (director). Color. In English. 120 minutes.

CARRERAS, JOSÉ

Spanish tenor (1946–)

José Carreras has become one of the most popular tenors of our time, amply demonstrated by his participation in the THREE TENORS concerts and his many recordings, films, and videos. He made his debut in his hometown of Barcelona in 1970, was aided in his early career by fellow Catalan MONTSERRAT CABALLÉ, and quickly won acclaim in the major opera houses. He has starred in a feature film, playing Catalan tenor JULIÁN GAYARRE, and his warm personality comes across well in his many opera videos. His weakest moments (he would probably agree) came when he was miscast singing in the American musicals WEST SIDE STORY (1984 film) and SOUTH PACIFIC (1986). Carreras had a long fight against leukemia, but he made a courageous comeback and conquered it. He has said that his role models were ENRICO CARUSO and MARIO LANZA, and he has sung concerts in honor of both. See ADRIANA LECOUVREUR (1976/1978), ANDREA CHÉNIER (1985), LA BOHÈME (1982/1988), CARMEN (1987), CRISTÓBAL COLÓN (1989), DON CARLO (1986), LA FORZA DEL DESTINO (1978), FRANZ LEHÁR (1998), NICOLAI GHIAUROV (1986), I LOMBARDI ALLA PRIMA CROCIATA (1984), LUCIA DI LAMMERMOOR (1981/1999 film), METROPOLITAN OPERA (1983/1986), MOZART REQUIEM (1994), OPERA NORTH (1992), ROBERTO DEVEREUX (1977), SEVILLE (1991), SLY (2000), STIFFELIO (1993), TOSCA (1979/1979), LA TRAVIATA (1973), TURANDOT (1983), GIUSEPPE VERDI (2001), VERDI REQUIEM (1982), VERONA (1988), VIENNA (1991/1992), WERTHER (1986 film), and ZURICH (1984).

1984 Carreras and Ricciarelli in Concert

Carreras and Katia Ricciarelli join in a concert, including a duet from *Aida*. The other operas featured are *Adriana Lecouvreur, L'Arlesiana, Le Cid, Il corsaro, Poliuto, La traviata,* and *La Wally*. Bruno Amaducci conducts. Color. 66 minutes. Bel Canto Society VHS.

1985 Silent Night with José Carreras

Christmas journey in Austria with Carreras filmed in and around Salzburg. The tenor talks about Christmas, visits the place where "Silent Night" was composed, and sings it with style. He also performs other favorites, including "White Christmas" and "Come All Ye Faithful." Color. 40 minutes. On VHS.

1987 José Carreras in Concert

Carreras gives a concert at the Komische Oper in East Berlin on January 9, 1987, and receives enormous applause. He sings music by Puccini, Tosti, Bellini, Leoncavallo, Cilea, Respighi, Ginastera, and Sorozabal. Vincenzo Scalera accompanies on piano. Color. 90 minutes. Kultur VHS.

1988 José Carreras Comeback Recital

Carreras's comeback recital at Peralada Castle in Spain in 1988 carries an emotional charge as it was his first appearance after being hospitalized with leukemia. He sings music by Tosti, Hahn, Duparc, Massenet, Mompou, Turina, Puccini, Grieg, and Lara. The closing number is a very strong "Granada." He is accompanied by pianist Vincenzo Scalera. Color. 82 minutes. Kultur VHS.

1990 Music Festival in Granada

Carreras performs music by Scarlatti, Bononcini, Tosti, Puccini, de Falla, Turina, Ginastera, and Nacho in a summer music festival concert in Granada. Color. 93 minutes. Kultur VHS.

1990 Carreras: Four Days on the Road

Documentary about the four days Carreras spent working on the film *Misa Criolla*. He follows in the footsteps of his ancestors from Barcelona to Mallorca, and he prepares for his journey to the Mission Dolores in California where he will perform in Ariel Ramirez's *Misa Criolla*.

Andrea Thomas directed. Color. 31 minutes. Kultur VHS.

1990 Misa Criolla
Carreras sings Ariel Ramirez's *Misa Criolla* (La Palabra y la Voz) in a performance shot in the Mission Dolores in San Francisco. Carlos Caballé conducts. Color. 60 minutes. Kultur VHS.

1991 Carreras Sings Andrew Lloyd Webber
Carreras sings the songs of Andrew Lloyd Webber with Marti Webb, Jane Harrison, Stephanie Lawrence, and the St. Paul's Cathedral Choir. Richard Harroway directed the video. Color. 55 minutes. Teldec VHS.

1991 José Carreras and Friends
An evening of arias, duets, and songs with Carreras, Katia Ricciarelli, Agnes Baltsa, and Ruggero Raimondi. They are accompanied by the London Arts Orchestra, led by Jacques Delacôte. Color. 60 minutes. Kultur VHS.

1992 José Carreras: A Life Story
Chris Hunt's excellent biography of the singer includes a version of "La donna è mobile," recorded by the tenor when he was seven years old. Hunt shows Carreras's rise to success, his fight against leukemia, his triumphant return, and his first Three Tenors concert. There are comments from Caballé, Domingo, and Pavarotti, plus interviews with the singer and his father. Color. 60 minutes. London VHS.

CARSEN, ROBERT
Canadian opera director

Robert Carsen, who was born in Toronto, has become one of the most successful new opera directors with his popular productions being staged around the world. The best known, which is on a San Francisco Opera video, is his fine production of Boito's *Mefistofele*. It was his first major production (Geneva, 1988) and it made his international reputation as it traveled on to San Francisco, Chicago, Houston, Turin, and the Met. Carsen, who began his opera directing career with long years as an assistant in Spoleto and Glyndebourne, has since had major successes with *Le nozze di Figaro, Cendrillon,* and *A Midsummer Night's Dream*, all of which have traveled around the world. See MANON LESCAUT (1991), MEFISTOFELE (1989), and SEMELE (1999).

CARUSO, ENRICO
Italian tenor (1873–1921)

Caruso was the first opera singer to become famous on record. He had a phonogenic voice, the acoustical equivalent of the cinema's photogenic face, and the primitive recording apparatus loved him. Caruso was born in Italy and became a star there, but his main career was at the Metropolitan Opera from 1903 to 1920 as the center of the Met's Golden Age. Caruso was signed up by the movie moguls, of course, and there was talk of a silent version of *Pagliacci*. But the camera didn't love him in the way the recording machine did. His films were not successful, and his movie career was brief. His voice, however, is still being used in films, and there are several entertaining film biographies. THE GREAT CARUSO is by far the most popular opera film ever made, and Werner Herzog's film FITZCARRALDO, which centers around Caruso, is one of the best.

1905 Pagliacci film
On November 13, 1905, at the Gran Salon Excelsior in Rome, Caruso was the featured singer in a sound film of *Pagliacci*. As information about this film is from contemporary advertisements, it could be that another actor appeared on screen, miming to Caruso's recording. The film apparently does not survive, and the company that made it is not known.

1908 Synchronoscope
Jules Greenbaum's Synchronoscope was an early attempt at synchronizing a recording with a film image. Universal Pictures founder Carl Laemmle exhibited one at the Majestic Theater in Evansville, Indiana, in the summer of 1908, and the program reportedly included a "sound film" with Caruso singing an aria. No copies are known.

1912 Cinephonograph
Caruso is reported to have sung the Sextet from *Lucia di Lammermoor* with basso Pol Plançon in a legendary Edison Studio attempt to synchronize sound and image. Caruso did make records of the Sextet during this period, but not with Plançon, and no such film has been found.

1917 Webb's Singing Pictures
Caruso turned up in person at the Cohan and Harris Theatre in New York on January 14, 1917, for the premiere of an early attempt at sound cinema by George Webb's Singing Pictures. An actor was seen on screen in costume in a scene from *Pagliacci* while Caruso's voice (on a recording) was heard singing the aria "Vesti la giubba" over loudspeakers. A second film featured actors on screen in *Rigoletto*, with Caruso singing "La donna è

mobile." No copies of the film are known, but the screening was reviewed by *Variety*.

1918 My Cousin
Caruso is pretty good in his first feature film, playing the double role of a great opera singer and his poor American cousin. It includes scenes at the Met, shows Caruso's dressing room, and shows him silently singing in *Pagliacci*. Caruso's film career never took off, but it is not true that he was a bad actor; he is quite watchable, and his personality shines through. See MY COUSIN.

1919 The Splendid Romance
In Caruso's second film, he played Prince Cosimo, an aristocrat sought out in Rome by American Ormi Hawley, who wants to be an opera singer. They have a romance. The film was made by Artcraft in its New York studio for Famous Players–Lasky, directed by Edward José, and written by Margaret Turnbull. It was reportedly released in June 1919, but apparently not in the United States. There are no contemporary reviews, and no prints are known. Black and white. Silent. About 74 minutes.

Enrico Caruso acted in only two films, in 1918 and 1919, but his cinematic legacy is amazingly large.

1935 El cantante de Napoles
Enrico Caruso Jr. plays opera star Enrico Daspurro in *El cantante de Napoles* (The Singer from Naples), an American Spanish-language film based on Caruso Sr.'s life. As a young man in Naples, he dreams of singing at La Scala and eventually succeeds. Caruso Jr. sings arias from *Il trovatore*, *The Barber of Seville*, and *L'Africaine*. See EL CANTANTE DI NAPOLES.

1949 Song of Surrender
Caruso on record is the focus of this film set in a small New England town in 1906. Wanda Hendrix, wife of pu-

ritanical Claude Raines, buys a gramophone at an auction when other townspeople scorn it as the instrument of the devil. It comes with some Caruso records, and she falls in love with his voice and opera music. See SONG OF SURRENDER.

1951 The Great Caruso
Mario Lanza plays Caruso in this romantic biography, one of the most popular opera films ever made. See THE GREAT CARUSO.

1951 Enrico Caruso, leggenda di una voce
Ermanno Randi plays Caruso (singing by Mario Del Monaco) in this romantic Italian film biography. See ENRICO CARUSO, LEGGENDA DI UNA VOCE.

1956 The Day I Met Caruso
Frank Borzage's charming film about Caruso's meeting with a Quaker girl was made for the Screen Directors Playhouse. Lotfi Mansouri, who later became an opera director, plays Caruso, with his singing provided by Caruso recordings, and Sandy Descher is the little girl who meets Caruso on a Boston train to New York and is won over by his voice. Zoë Atkins's screenplay is based on a story by Elizabeth Bacon Rodewald. Black and white. 30 minutes.

1960 Pay or Die
Caruso received blackmail threats from the Mafia-like Black Hand while he was singing at the Met in 1909. This real event is incorporated into this period American crime thriller set in New York City's Italian neighborhood. Howard Caine plays Caruso and is seen on stage at the Met performing an aria from *Lucia di Lammermoor* (sung by David Poleri.) The plot to kill Caruso is thwarted by heroic Italian police detective Ernest Borgnine. Richard Wilson directed. Black and white. 109 minutes. Allied Artists VHS.

1980 A Toast to Melba
Augustus Harris plays Caruso in this Australian TV play about soprano Nellie Melba (played by Robyn Nevin). Jack Hibbert wrote the play, Alan Burke directed. Color. 70 minutes. See NELLIE MELBA.

1985 The Grey Fox
Richard Farnsworth, an aging train robber in the early years of the 20th century, overhears an outdoor phonograph playing Caruso's recording of "M'apparì" from *Martha*. He talks to the woman with the phonograph and their joint love of Caruso leads to a relationship. Philip Borsos directed this fine Canadian film. Color. 92 minutes. Media VHS.

1987 Melba

Australian opera tenor Anson Austin plays Caruso in this Australian TV miniseries about Nellie Melba. See NELLIE MELBA.

1987 Aria

The final episode of the opera film *Aria* features John Hurt, who enters an opera house and makes up as a clown. On stage he has a vision of a girl he once loved, mimes to Caruso's recording of "Vesti la giubba" from *Pagliacci,* and dies. Bill Bryden directed. See ARIA.

1994 Omaggio a Caruso

Tribute to Caruso is a gala evening in honor of Caruso at the San Carlo Opera House in his native Naples. The singers are José Carreras, Shirley Verrett, and Lucio Dalla, and there are memories and anecdotes as well as music. Walter Licastro directed. Color. 147 minutes.

1995 Tenors of the 78 Era, Volume One

One section of this video is devoted to Caruso, with extracts from *Aida, L'Africana, L'elisir d'amore, La Juive, Pagliacci,* and *Il trovatore.* Four critics talk about his singing. Black and white and color. 86 minutes. Bel Canto Society VHS.

1998 The Original Three Tenors

Mary Ellis, aged 98 when this documentary was made, was apparently the last person then alive who sang with Caruso, and she talks about the experience. Richard Fawkes's film for BBC Television looks at the careers of tenors Caruso, Gigli, and Björling, with commentary by Nigel Douglas. Color and black and white. 50 minutes.

1998 Enrico Caruso: Voice of the Century

Peter Rosen's documentary, made for A&E Television, tells the Caruso story using archival footage and interviews with son Enrico Jr. and admirers Plácido Domingo, Luciano Pavarotti, and Beverly Sills. There is information about his romances and marriages as well as his singing. Black and white/color. In English. 44 minutes. Bel Canto Society VHS as *Caruso: A Documentary.*

CASA LONTANA
1939 film with opera content

Italian tenor Beniamino Gigli plays an Italian opera tenor in *Casa Lontana* (Far From Home) who is on trial for killing a man; his story is told in flashbacks from the courtroom. He is first seen on stage in two scenes from Riccardo Zandonai's *Giulietta e Romeo* at the Teatro Massimo in Palermo, with Livia Caloni as Juliet. A chorus dancer (Kirstein Heilberg) flirts with him on stage, and he later marries her. They break up after a mix-up

when she tries to get money to bail out her old dance troupe, but he thinks she has left him for another man. On stage that night in Cilea's *L'Arlesiana* (not surprisingly the story of a man who loses his heart to a cruel woman), he sings the sad tenor aria "È la solita storia del pastore" and then disappears. We see him next in lower-class bars in America where he becomes a Pagliacci-like clown singing in a nightclub (he doesn't sing Leoncavallo, he sings Zandonai's "Canzone del Clown"). The couple are reunited when she comes to sing in the same club, and he sings the *Fedora* aria "Amor ti vieta" at a reception. She is being blackmailed so he confronts her blackmailer (Hans Olden) in a park; the blackmailer draws a gun and is accidentally shot by Gigli during their struggle. There is a witness, and the killing is judged self-defense. Gigli returns to the opera stage in *Lucia di Lammermoor* and sings the Act I love duet "Verranno a te sull'aure" with Livia Caloni as the movie ends. Johannes Meyer shot the film in Rome for Itala Film, in Italian as *Casa Lontana* and in German as *Der Singende Tor.* Alberto Spaini and L. A. C. Muller were the screenwriters, Werner Brandes was the cinematographer, and Luigi Ricci conducted the music. The film was shown in the United States as *Legittima Difesa/Self Defense.* Black and white. In Italian. 84 minutes. House of Opera/Lyric/Opera Dubs VHS.

CASA RICORDI
See RICORDI.

CASA VERDI
Milan retirement home

The Casa Verdi in Milan is a retirement home for opera singers founded in 1902 by composer Giuseppe Verdi. Many of its residents were major stars of the opera world in their youth. Casa Verdi, always a place of fascination to opera enthusiasts, has been the subject of two documentaries.

1943 Casa Verdi

Italian director Giovanni Paolucci made several documentaries in the 1940s about aspects of Italian life and music. *Casa Verdi,* about the Milan retirement home and its opera singers, was made at the height of World War II. Black and white. In Italian. 30 minutes.

1985 Tosca's Kiss

Il Bacio di Tosca, released in America as *Tosca's Kiss,* is a feature-length Swiss film about the Casa Verdi. Director DANIEL SCHMID, who has directed opera on stage, focuses on singers Sara Scuderi, Giovanni Puligheddu, Leonida Bellon, Salvatore Locapo, and Giuseppe Manacchini. They consider themselves as resting between jobs, and they still keep suitcases packed in case they might be suddenly called to sing at the Met. They are more than willing to demonstrate a scene from *Tosca* in a phone booth. Schmid's film is filled with opera music as well as warmth, humor, conflict, and delight. Color. In Italian with English subtitles. 87 minutes. VAI VHS.

CASE, ANNA
American soprano (1889–1984)

Anna Case, who made her debut at the Metropolitan Opera in 1909, sang Sophie in the first Met performance of *Der Rosenkavalier* in 1913. She stopped performing in opera in 1920, but she continued to give concerts until 1931. Her voice was highly phonogenic and recorded well in the early systems so she is featured on nearly 100 Edison recordings. Her screen career was slight; she played a singer in a silent feature film in 1918, and she was featured in one of the first Vitaphone sound films, with her Met connection highly publicized. Case became Irving Berlin's mother-in-law in 1931 when she married millionaire Clarence H. Mackay; his daughter Ellin had married Berlin in 1926.

Met soprano Anna Case made history singing in a short shown before the first American sound feature, *Don Juan* (1926).

1918 The Hidden Truth
Case plays a singer in a mining town in her only feature film, a romantic Western directed by Julius Steger. The plot revolves around her taking on another woman's identity because of love. Select Pictures. Black and white. About 70 minutes.

1926–1927 Vitaphone films
Case's cinematic moment of glory arrived with the premiere of the John Barrymore film *Don Juan* on August 6, 1926. She was a featured performer in this famous prelude to the sound era, starring in the Vitaphone short *La Fiesta* with the Metropolitan Opera House Chorus. The sheet music for *Don Juan* carries a banner announcement: "Sung by Anna Case of the Metropolitan Opera." *La Fiesta* is available with the other Vitaphone shorts featured that historic evening on an LD with *Don Juan*. Case's second Vitaphone short, made in 1927, features her singing Stephen Foster's "Old Folks at Home." Black and white. Each about 7 minutes. On VHS and LD.

CASERÍO, EL
1926 zarzuela by Guridi

Basque composer JESÚS GURIDI's zarzuela *El caserío* (The Homestead) is set in the Basque countryside and uses Basque rhythms and musical instruments. The libretto by Guillermo Fernández Shaw and Federico Romero is a country love story. Middle-aged Santi has a nice farm and intends to leave it to his young relatives Ana Mari and José Miguel, if they will marry. When José doesn't want to settle down, Santi says he will marry the girl himself. *El Caserío*, considered one of the masterpieces of the zarzuela genre, was a huge success in its time and includes a famous sword dance.

1969 Teatro Lirico Español
Spanish TV film: Juan De Orduña (director), Federico Moreno Torroba (conductor, Spanish Lyric Orchestra and Madrid Chorus), Jesús María Arozamena (screenplay), Federico Larraya (cinematographer).

Singers: Dolores Pérez, Rosa Sarmiento, Luis-Sagi-Vela, Carlo del Monte, Enrique del Portal.

Actors: Mary Francis, Jose Mareno, Armando Calvo, Antonio Duran, Teresa Hurtado, Venando Muro, Valentín Tornos.

Video: Metrovideo (Spain) VHS. Shot in 35mm for RTVE Spanish television. Color. In Spanish. 105 minutes.

CASTELNUOVO-TEDESCO, MARIO
Italian-born American composer (1895–1968)

Mario Castelnuovo-Tedesco wrote operas for both screen and stage. His first opera, *La Mandragola,* premiered at La Fenice in Venice in 1925. Because of growing anti-Semitism, he left Italy in 1939 and settled in Los Angeles, where he composed movie music and became a U.S. citizen. His movie operas are *The Loves of Fatima,* created for *Everybody Does It* (1949); and *Il Ritorno de Cesare,* composed for *Strictly Dishonorable* (1951). For details, see IMAGINARY OPERAS IN FILMS. His other film scores include a CARMEN movie with Rita Hayworth, *The Loves of Carmen* (1948). Two of his stage operas were based on Shakespeare, *The Merchant of Venice* (1956) and *All's Well That Ends Well* (1958).

CASTRATOS

Castratos were male sopranos or contraltos, castrated when young to preserve high voices with masculine power. Many early operas were written for them, and for a period castrato were the highest paid singers. Handel wrote many of his operas for their voices, and the castrato Farinelli was enormously popular. No one today knows what they really sounded like, but Farinelli reportedly had a range of three and a half octaves and could sing 250 notes in a row or hold a single note for a minute. It must have been impressive. The last opera written for a castrato was Meyerbeer's 1824 *Il crociato in Egitto*. Most roles composed for castratos are now sung by contraltos and countertenors. The era of the castrato in opera has been explored in several fiction films, including a rather good one about Farinelli.

1964 Le voce bianche
Le voce bianche (White Voices) is an Italian film about castratos set in 18th-century Italy. Paolo Ferrari tries to sell his brother as a castrato but ends up having to take his place. He bribes the surgeon not to perform the operation and enjoys a special position with women until fate catches up with him. There are several elegant operatic scenes. Pasquale Festa Campanile and Massimo Franciosa wrote and directed the film. Color. In Italian. 103 minutes.

1989 Les voix du serail
The Voices of the Seraglio is a televised concert of music written for castratos presented at the 1989 Marrakesh Festival in Morocco. The singers include Charles Brett, Elisabeth Vidal, Aris Christofellis, and Paulo Abel Donascimento. Color. In French. 60 minutes. Lyric VHS.

1992 The Reluctant Angels
Michael Bartlett's documentary, subtitled "The World of the Castrati," explores the why and how of the era of the castratos. The practice seems to have grown up at first because women were not allowed in the Vatican choir and on the Italian stage. Most castratos came from poor families who found out that successful singers could become very wealthy. The film journeys from Venice to Dresden, with arias sung by countertenor Jochen Kowalski. Color. English narration. 56 minutes. Opera Dubs VHS.

1994 Farinelli
Gérard Corbiau's film is a visually opulent biography of the most famous castrato, focusing on his relationships with his composer brother Riccardo, teacher Nicola Porpora, and Handel. There are elaborate re-creations of opera productions of the period. See FARINELLI.

CAT AND THE FIDDLE, THE
1931 operetta by Kern

JEROME KERN's 1931 *The Cat and the Fiddle* is called a "musical romance" but is usually considered a successful attempt to put the traditional operetta into a contemporary form. OTTO HARBACH wrote the lyrics and book about a love affair between two composers. Romanian Victor Florescu is working in Brussels on his serious opera, *The Passionate Pilgrim*, when American composer Shirley Sheridan helps him out with her jazzier style. Their music harmonizes in the operetta they create together.

1934 MGM film
American feature film: William K. Howard (director), Sam and Bella Spewack (screenplay), Herbert Stothart (music director), Harold Rosson and Charles Clarke (black and white cinematography), Ray Rennahan (Technicolor cinematography).

Cast: Jeanette MacDonald (Shirley), Ramon Novarro (Victor), Frank Morgan (Jules), Charles Butterworth (Charles), Jean Hersholt (Professor Beriter), Vivienne Segal (Odette).

Video: MGM Home Video VHS. Color. In English. 90 minutes.

Comment: The stage plot is changed, but all the songs are retained. The couple are still composers, but Victor's lack of success leads to their breakup. When he needs help on an operetta, she returns and true love takes over as the film changes from black and white into glorious three-strip Technicolor.

CATALANI, ALFREDO
Italian composer (1854–1893)

Alfredo Catalani, a romantic composer who died young and is sometimes compared to Puccini, is remembered primarily for his opera LA WALLY. It has a heated plot about a mountain woman and her ill-fated love affair. The libretto is by Luigi Illica, who wrote *La bohème* and other Puccini operas. Catalani suffered from a persecution complex in the latter part of his life, intensified by a continuing illness, and died a year after the premiere of *La Wally*. The cinematic public became aware of one of the glories of Catalani's opera in 1981 when the film DIVA used its best-known aria as a plot point.

CAVALIERE DEL SOGNO, IL
1946 Italian film about Donizetti

Il cavaliere del sogno is an Italian fiction film about Gaetano Donizetti with Amadeo Nazzari portraying the composer. His life is told in flashback from his deathbed, with many scenes shot on location in his native Bergamo. The plot is mostly concerned with his complicated love affair with aristocrat Luisa di Cerchiara (Mariella Lotti). When she marries an Austrian prince, the jealous prince has Donizetti put in an insane asylum, so she has to win his freedom by promising never to see him again. The film includes ample excerpts from Donizetti operas. Tito Schipa plays French tenor Gilbert Duprez, who created the role of Edgardo in *Lucia di Lammermoor;* he also sings excerpts from *L'elisir d'amore* and *Don Pasquale.* Mario Ferrerari is the jealous prince, Dina Sassoli is Donizetti's wife Virginia, and Rubi D'Alba is Baroness Scotti. Vittorio Nino Novarese wrote the screenplay, Arturo Gallea was cinematographer, Alessandro Cicognini was the music director, and Camillo Mastrocinque directed the film released in the United States in 1952 as *The Life of Donizetti.* Black and white. In Italian. 85 minutes. VIEW VHS (with dialogue in dubbed English).

CAVALIERI, LINA
Italian soprano (1874–1944)

Lina Cavalieri, publicized as the "most beautiful woman in the world," was as famous for her extravagant lifestyle and beauty as for her voice, but she was a notable singer. Born in poverty in Viterbo, she had a career as a café singer before making her opera debut in *La bohème* in Naples in 1900 and going on to sing in Paris and at Covent Garden and other major opera houses. She made her American debut at the Metropolitan in 1906 opposite Caruso in Giordano's *Fedora* and then sang at the Manhattan and Chicago Opera Houses. After marrying tenor Lucien Muratore, her fourth husband, she starred in a series of silent films with reasonable success. Cavalieri had a preference for opera roles that allowed display of costume and jewels, so it is not surprising she began her film career in *Manon Lescaut.* She died in a freak accident during an air raid on Florence in 1944. Gina Lollobrigida portrayed her in a film biography.

1914 Manon Lescaut
Cavalieri made her film debut as Manon, the beautiful convent girl who becomes a courtesan. Her husband Lucien Muratore plays her lover, the Chevalier des Grieux. The film was supposedly based on the Abbé Prévost source novel rather than the Puccini opera, which was in copyright. Herbert Hall directed for the Playgoers Film Company. Black and white. Silent. About 80 minutes.

1915 La sposa della morte
Cavalieri's second film, *The Bride of Death,* was made in Italy for Tiber Film under the direction of Emilio Ghione. Her tenor husband Lucien Muratore was again featured along with Alberto Collo, Ida Carloni Talli, and Luigi Scotto. Black and white. Silent. About 75 minutes.

1916 La rosa di granata
Cavalieri's third film, *La rosa di granata,* was also made in Italy with Emilio Ghione directing. Appearing with her are husband Lucien Muratore, Diomira Jacobini, and Kally Sambucini. Black and white. Silent. About 75 minutes.

1917 The Eternal Temptress
Cavalieri plays a princess of extraordinary beauty living in Venice and loved madly by every man she meets. The melodramatic plot centers around secret papers and her sacrifice for the man she loves. Emile Chautard directed for Famous Players. Black and white. Silent. About 72 minutes.

Lina Cavalieri, publicized as the "most beautiful woman in the world," strikes a dramatic post on a postcard from the 1910s.

1918 Love's Conquest
Cavalieri is Gismonda, the beautiful Duchess of Athens, in this film based on Sardou's play *Gismonda.* She has many suitors but loves only her son. In the end, she falls for the huntsman who rescues him from kidnappers. Edward José directed for Famous Players. Black and white. Silent. About 70 minutes.

1918 A Woman of Impulse
In this film Cavalieri is the Parisian prima donna Leonora "La Vecci." The film has faint autobiographical elements, as the singer, like Cavalieri, comes from a poor Italian family and cannot afford voice lessons until a rich admirer pays for them. Lucien Muratore has a small role. Edward José directed for Famous Players. Black and white. Silent. About 60 minutes.

1919 The Two Brides
Cavalieri is Diana di Marchesi, the beautiful daughter of a sculptor. The plot revolves around a lifelike statue of her created by her father and her love for two different men. Edward José directed for Famous Players. Black and white. Silent. About 72 minutes.

1921 Amore che ritorna
Cavalieri's last film, an Italian melodrama called *Love that Returns,* is listed in her credits but does not appear to have been reviewed and may not have been completed.

1955 La donna più bella del mondo
Gina Lollobrigida plays Cavalieri in *La donna più bella del mondo* (The Most Beautiful Woman in the World), an Italian film biography of the diva released in America as *Beautiful But Dangerous.* It pictures Cavalieri's rise from singing in the cheapest of cafés to the best of opera houses. Mario Del Monaco is the singing voice of tenor Gino Sinimberghi. See LA DONNA PIÙ BELLA DEL MONDO.

CAVALLERIA RUSTICANA
1890 opera by Mascagni

PIETRO MASCAGNI's instantly famous opera *Cavalleria rusticana,* based on a story by Giovanni Verga, is his only opera in the repertory and has been a favorite for Italian-American filmmakers as both story and mood setter. Francis Ford Coppola's *The Godfather Part III* has its final sequence set at a production of the opera, and Martin Scorsese's *Raging Bull* also uses music from the opera to good effect. Giovanni Targioni-Tozzetti and Guido Menasci's libretto tells a story of infidelity and revenge in a Sicilian village. Turiddu has seduced Santuzza and is having an affair with Alfio's wife Lola. Jealous Santuzza tells Alfio of the affair, and he challenges Turiddu to a duel. Turiddu asks his mother Lucia to look after Santuzza, who is pregnant, as he knows he will be killed in the duel.

1952 Vinti/Rhodes film
Italian-American film of abridged production: Carlo Vinti and Marion Rhodes (directors/producers), Anthony Stivanello (stage director), Giuseppe Bambos-chek (conductor, Opera Cameos Orchestra and Chorus), Jon Ericson (narrator), R. M. Savini (presenter).

Cast: Rina Telli (Santuzza), Mario Del Monaco (Turiddu), Richard Torigi (Alfio).

Video: Lyric/Bel Canto Society VHS. Color. In Italian. 45 minutes.

Comment: Shown theatrically December 1953 in double bill with *La traviata,* telecast in 1954 on the *Opera Cameos* series.

1960 NBC Opera Theatre
American TV production: Samuel Chotzinoff (producer), Peter Herman Adler (conductor, Symphony of the Air Orchestra), Joseph Machlis (English translation).

Cast: Virginia Copeland (Santuzza), David Poleri (Turiddu), Jan McArt (Lola), Chester Ludgin (Alfio), Anna Carnevale (Mamma Lucia).

Telecast live January 31, 1960. Kirk Browning (director). Color. In English. 75 minutes.

1961 NHK Lirica Italiana
Japanese stage production: Giuseppe Morelli (conductor, NHK Symphony Orchestra and Chorus).

Cast: Giulietta Simionato (Santuzza), Angelo Lo Forese (Turiddu), Attilio d'Orazi (Alfio), Anna di Stasio (Lola), Amalia Pini (Mamma Lucia).

Video: VAI VHS. Taped live in Tokyo October 21, 1961, for the NHK *Lirica Italiana* series. Black and white. In Italian with English and Japanese subtitles. 72 minutes.

1968 Falck film
Italian studio film: Åke Falck (film director), Giorgio Strehler (stage director), Herbert von Karajan (conductor, Teatro alla Scala Chorus and Orchestra), Ernst Wild (cinematographer), Unitel (production).

Cast: Fiorenza Cossotto (Santuzza), Gianfranco Cecchele (Turiddu), Giangiacomo Guelfi (Alfio), Adriana Martino (Lola), Anna di Stasio (Mamma Lucia).

Video: London VHS. Color. In Italian. 73 minutes.

Comment: Based on Strehler's La Scala production, mostly shot in a studio but opened up with location shots of Sicilian landscapes. Released theatrically in the United States with film of *Pagliacci.*

1978 Metropolitan Opera
American stage production: Franco Zeffirelli (director/set designer), Fabrizio Melano (staging), James Levine (conductor, Metropolitan Opera Orchestra and Chorus).

Cast: Tatiana Troyanos (Santuzza), Plácido Domingo (Turiddu), Vern Shinall (Alfio), Isola Jones (Lola), Jean Kraft (Mamma Lucia).

Video at the MTR. Telecast live on PBS April 5, 1978, in double bill with *Pagliacci*. Kirk Browning (director). Color. In Italian. 70 minutes.

***1982 Zeffirelli film

Italian feature film: Franco Zeffirelli (director), Georges Prêtre (conductor, Teatro alla Scala Orchestra and Chorus), Armando Nannuzzi (cinematographer), Gianni Quaranta (art director), Anna Anni (costumes).

Cast: Elena Obraztsova (Santuzza), Plácido Domingo (Turiddu), Renato Bruson (Alfio), Fedora Barbieri (Mamma Lucia), Axelle Gall (Lola).

Video: Decca and Philips DVD/VHS/LD. Color. In Italian. 69 minutes.

Comment: Zeffirelli shot this realistic film on location in the Sicilian village of Vizzini and on stage in Milan, basing it on his La Scala stage production. Outstanding singing, acting, and directing.

1990 Teatro Comunale, Siena

Italian stage production: Mario Monicelli (director), Baldo Podic (conductor, Philharmonia Orchestra of Russe).

Cast: Shirley Verrett (Santuzza), Kristjan Johannsson (Turiddu), Ettore Nova (Alfio), Rosy Orani (Lola), Ambra Vespasiani (Mamma Lucia).

Video: VAI VHS. Peter Goldfarb (director). Color. In Italian. 80 minutes.

Comment: Verrett introduces the opera and describes its history and plot.

1992 New York City Opera

American stage production: Jonathan Eaton (director), Steven Sloan (conductor, New York City Opera Orchestra and Chorus), Paul Short (set designer).

Cast: Sharon Graham (Santuzza), Craig Sirianni (Turiddu), Max Wittges (Alfio), Melanie Sonnenberg (Lola), Dulce Reyes (Mamma Lucia).

Telecast September 20, 1992, on PBS in the series *Live From Lincoln Center*. Kirk Browning (director). Color. In Italian with English subtitles. 75 minutes.

Comment: The opera setting is moved to an Italian neighborhood in New York City in the late 19th century.

Early/related films

1906 Cinemafono Pagliej

Cinemafono Pagliej, an Italian sound-on-disc company specializing in opera films, screened a film featuring an aria from *Cavalleria rusticana* at the Sala Umberto I in Rome from May 19 to July 30, 1906. Black and white. In Italian. About 4 minutes.

1908 Gallo film

An Italian film of the Verga and Mascagni story titled *Cavalleria rusticana* and directed by Mario Gallo was screened in Italy in 1908. Black and white. Silent. About 10 minutes.

1909 Jasset film

French film of the opera and Verga play directed by Victorin Jasset for the Éclair company. It stars Charles Krauss, Dupont Morgan, Eugénie Nau, and Mme. Barry. Black and white. Silent. About 10 minutes.

1910 Grasso film

Sicilian actor Giovanni Grasso, who often portrayed Alfio on the stage, is featured in the role in this *Cavalleria rusticana*, an Italian film of the Verga/Mascagni story. Black and white. Silent. About 15 minutes.

1916 Sanzogno/Flegrea film

Two Italian films of *Cavalleria rusticana* were made in 1916. This version was authorized by the Sanzogno publishing house and produced by the Flegrea film company. Mascagni objected to both films, sued to stop them, and lost both times. Ubaldo Maria Del Colle directed and played Turiddu with Tilde Pini as Santuzza, Bianca Lorenzoni as Lola, and Ugo Gracci as Alfio. Black and white. Silent. About 50 minutes.

1916 Verga/Tespi film

The second of the two 1916 films of *Cavalleria rusticana* was authorized by writer Giovanni Verga and produced by the Tespi film company. Mascagni again objected and sued to stop it, but lost. Gemma Bellincioni, who had created the role on stage in 1890, plays Santuzza with Luigi Serventi as Turiddu, Gioacchino Grassi as Alfio, and Bianca Virginia Camagni as Lola. Ugo Falena and Mario Gargiulo directed. Black and white. Silent. About 50 minutes.

1924 Gargiulo film

Mario Gargiulo directed a second version of *Cavalleria rusticana* in 1924 with Sicilian actor Giovanni Grasso, famous for playing Alfio. Tina Xeo is Santuzza, Livio Pavanelli is Turiddu, Lia Di Marzio is Lola, and Mary-Cleo Tarlarini is Nunzia. The film was supposedly based on the Verga story. Black and white. Silent. About 70 minutes.

1927 Vitaphone film with Gigli

Beniamino Gigli sings three selections from *Cavalleria rusticana* on this Vitaphone sound film with support from baritone Millo Picco and contralto Minnie Egener. Black and white. In Italian. About 10 minutes.

1932 Vendetta

Vendetta is an American highlights version of *Cavalleria rusticana* created for the Operalogue series and directed by Lew Seller for Educational Films. Black and white. In English. 28 minutes.

1934 Enter Madame

Elissa Landi (dubbed by Nina Koshetz) sings an aria from *Cavalleria rusticana* in this film about a glamorous opera singer who marries millionaire Cary Grant. Elliott Nugent directed for Paramount. Black and white. In English. 83 minutes.

1939 Palermi film

Isa Pola plays Santuzza in this *Cavalleria rusticana,* with Leonardo Cortese as Turiddu, Carlo Ninchi as Alfio, Doris Duranti as Lola, and Bella Starace Sainati as Nunzia. It was meant to be an adaptation of the Mascagni opera, but the composer refused to cooperate so the Verga novel became the basis for the story and Alessandro Cicognini wrote new music. Amleto Palermi directed for Scalera film. Released in the United States in 1947. Black and white. In Italian. 75 minutes.

1951 The Great Caruso

Enrico Caruso (Mario Lanza) is shown on stage in two productions of *Cavalleria rusticana* in this romantic biography. In the first, in an Italian regional opera house, he is just rising to fame. In the second, he is a star in a major production in Rio di Janeiro. See THE GREAT CARUSO.

1952 Because You're Mine

Mario Lanza sings the final aria from *Cavalleria rusticana* in this film about an opera star drafted into the army. Alexander Hall directed. Color. 103 minutes. MGM-UA VHS.

1953 Fatal Desire

Opera film specialist Carmine Gallone directed this Italian narrative version of *Cavalleria rusticana,* basing it on both the opera and the Verga novel. It has Tito Gobbi as an off-screen singing voice; the on-screen actors are Anthony Quinn as Alfio, May Britt as Santuzza, Kerima as Lola, Ettore Manni as Turiddu, and Virginia Balistieri as Mamma Lucia. Oliviero De Fabritiis conducted the music; Carlo Ponti produced the film. Shown in the United States as *Fatal Desire.* Color. In Italian. 106 minutes.

1963 Simionato/Corelli duet

Franco Corelli as Turiddu and Giulietta Simionato as Santuzza join in duet at a piano rehearsal of the opera at La Scala in 1963. A film of the scene is included in the video *Legends of Opera.* Black and white. In Italian. 4 minutes. Legato Classics VHS.

1990 The Godfather Part III

A production of *Cavalleria rusticana* at the Teatro Massimo opera house in Palermo, Sicily, is the focus of the final scene of this Francis Ford Coppola film. Michael Corleone (Al Pacino) is there to see his son Anthony make his operatic debut as Turiddu. Plot and revenge threads converge in counterpoint to the unfolding opera, culminating in an assassination attempt on the steps of the opera house. The opera performers are Franc D'Ambrosio as Anthony and Turiddu (sung by Gianni Lazzari), Elena Lo Forte as Santuzza (sung by Madelyn Renée Monti), Corinna Vozza as Lucia, Angelo Romero as Alfio (sung by Paolo Gavanelli), and Madelyn Renée Monti as Lola. Anton Coppola conducts the Orchestra and Chorus of the Academia Musicale Italiana. Color. In English with opera scenes in Italian. 162 minutes. Paramount VHS.

2002 Minor Mishaps

This Danish film about a dysfunctional family features music from *Cavalleria rusticana* on the soundtrack. Annette K. Olesen directed. Color. In Danish. 109 minutes.

CAVANI, LILIANA
Italian film director (1936–)

Liliana Cavani, probably best known in the United States for her controversial 1974 film *The Night Porter,* began directing in 1966 and won her critical reputation with historical films on St. Francis, Galileo, and Nietzsche. She has also become a stage opera director, with highly praised La Scala productions of LA TRAVIATA in 1992 and *La vestale* in 1994. She also filmed the 50th anniversary concert of the rebuilt TEATRO ALLA SCALA.

CAVE, THE
1993 screen opera by Reich

American composer STEVE REICH describes his visually complex opera *The Cave* as "documentary music video theater." It's a collaboration with his wife, video artist Beryl Korot, and uses five video screens to show the underpinnings of the Middle East conflict. The focus is the Cave of the Patriarchs in Hebron where Abraham is supposed to be buried, long a center of conflict. The music is based around film interviews with Jews, Muslims, and Americans talking about Abraham, Sarah, Isaac, and Hagar. The screens provide text, imagery, and documentary information. The opera, not yet on video, is performed by the Steve Reich Ensemble and singers Cheryl Bensman

Rowe, Marion Beckenstein, James Bassi, and Hugo Munday on CD.

1993 Austrian Television
Peter Payer's documentary *The Cave* features extracts from the opera and an interview with Reich. It was made for Austrian television (ORF) in Vienna and telecast in 1993. Color. In German. 30 minutes.

CBC TELEVISION OPERA

The Canadian Broadcasting Company (CBC) regularly produces operas and operettas, and many are shown on U.S. television. The most widely seen are Gilbert and Sullivan comic operas, including THE GONDOLIERS, H.M.S. PINAFORE, IOLANTHE, THE MIKADO, and THE PIRATES OF PENZANCE. Canadian opera singers who now have world reputations, such as JON VICKERS and TERESA STRATAS, often made their screen opera debut on CBC. Other opera productions on video include EUGENE ONEGIN (1986 film), HÄNSEL UND GRETEL (1970), DER LUSTIGE WITWE (1988 film), PAGLIACCI (1955), PETER GRIMES (1970), LA RONDINE (1970), and DIE ZAUBERFLÖTE (1987).

CBS TELEVISION OPERA

The Columbia Broadcasting System (CBS) began televising opera in 1950 with its series *Opera Television Theater*. These were staged studio productions created under the direction of baritone Lawrence Tibbett and producer Henry Souvaine. The first was a New Year's Day 1950 telecast of CARMEN in French, with Gladys Swarthout, followed the same year with LA TRAVIATA in English, with Elaine Malbin. The series ended because CBS could not find sponsors, but the network continued to present opera and operetta in other formats. The 1962 world premiere of Igor Stravinsky's THE FLOOD was a major media event; Ed Sullivan featured opera on the ED SULLIVAN SHOW, including METROPOLITAN OPERA performers; CAMERA THREE was adventurous in its choice of subject; and OMNIBUS presented unusual operas and operettas. Other CBS presentations included THE BEGGAR'S OPERA (1952), GALLANTRY, MADAMA BUTTERFLY (1957), MARTIN'S LIE, THE MEDIUM (1948), OEDIPUS REX (1951), THE PIRATES OF PENZANCE (1955), THE RED MILL (1958), THE SECOND HURRICANE, TOSCA (1956), LA TRAVIATA (1950), TRIAL BY JURY (1950/1953), and THE TRIALS OF GALILEO.

CEBOTARI, MARIA
Moldovan soprano (1910–1949)

Maria Cebotari (born Cebutaru), one of the leading sopranos in Germany during the Nazi era, made her debut as Mimì in Dresden in 1931, created Aminta in Strauss's *Die Schweigsame Frau* in 1935, and sang in Vienna, Salzburg, and Covent Garden. Her attractive voice and personality translate well to records and film. She plays MARIA MALIBRAN in a film about the diva, appears as Teresina Stolz in a 1938 VERDI biography, and sings opposite Beniamino Gigli in the 1937 film SOLO PER TE. Her operatic "parallel" films were much liked, including IL SOGNO DI BUTTERFLY (1939), based around *Madama Butterfly*, and AMAMI, ALFREDO! (1940), based around *La traviata*. Cebotari's early death at age 39 and career in Nazi Germany meant that she never had the chance to become as well known internationally as she might have. Cebotari's birth town, Chisinau, is now the capital of the independent country of Moldova, and a street in the city center bears her name.

1936 Mädchen in Weiss
Cebotari's voice is the chief attraction of her debut film, *The Girl in White*, a Cinderella-type musical set in prerevolutionary St. Petersburg. Her aristocratic fiancé (Ivan Petrovich) doesn't want her to sing, but she goes ahead anyway, like her mother before her. Her tenor partner is Norberto Ardelli. Viktor Janson directed. Shown in the United States in 1939 as *Alles die Treue*. Black and white. In German. 83 minutes.

1937 Stark Herzen
Lost UFA-studio film about a production of *Tosca* during a Communist uprising in Hungary in 1918. Cebotari plays the actress who sings the role of Tosca, heading a cast that includes Gustav Diessl and René Deltgen. Herbert Maisch directed the film, which was banned and apparently no longer exists. Black and white. In German. 79 minutes.

1942 Odessa in fiamme
Cebotari is a Romanian opera singer seeking her young son in war-torn Europe in *Odessa in Flames*, an Italian-Romanian film directed by Carmine Gallone. When the boy is taken to Odessa, she follows; her husband eventually rescues them. The film was shown at the Venice Film Festival in 1942. Black and white. In Italian or Romanian. 83 minutes.

CENDRILLON

1899 opera by Massenet

JULES MASSENET's version of the Cinderella story, *Cendrillon,* is no longer a fashionable opera, but it is quite charming all the same. His librettist, Henry Cain, follows the Perrault fairy tale more closely than Rossini's librettist. Cinderella has a weak father (Pandolfe), wicked stepmother (Madame de la Haltière), and vile stepsisters (Noémie and Dorothée). She goes magically and glamorously to the ball, meets Prince Charming, and leaves her glass slipper behind. The role of Prince Charming was written for a soprano.

1979 National Arts Center, Ottawa

Canadian stage production: Brian Macdonald (director), Mario Bernardi (conductor, National Arts Center Orchestra).

Cast: Frederica von Stade (Cinderella), Delia Wallis (Prince Charming), Ruth Welting (Fairy Godmother), Maureen Forrester (Madame de la Haltière), Michele Boucher (Noémie), Louis Quilico (Pandolfe).

Video: House of Opera DVD and VHS/Lyric VHS. Jean-Yves Landry (director). Color. In French. 146 minutes.

1982 Théâtre Royal de la Monnaie

Belgian stage production: Gilbert Deflo (director), Jacques Delacôte (conductor, National Opéra Orchestra).

Cast: Frederica von Stade (Cinderella), Ann Murray (Prince Charming), Britt-Marie Aruhn (Fairy Godmother), Jocelyne Taillon (Madame de la Haltière), Katarina Moesen (Noémie), Gisèle Ory (Dorothée), Jules Bastin (Pandolfe).

Telecast June 4, 1982, in Belgium. Eddy Verburggen (director). Color. In French. 184 minutes.

Early/related films

1899 Méliès film

Georges Méliès's *Cendrillon* was inspired by the 1899 premiere of Massenet's opera in Paris. It was an epic production for its time with 20 scenes, a cast of 35, and delightful special effects. With such a popular theme and the opera to publicize it, Méliès had a surefire hit. The film is like the opera, but the screen version has many more attractive young women. Tinted. Silent. About 7 minutes.

1902 Alber's film

An early sound film featuring an aria from *Cendrillon* was shown at the September 1902 screenings of Alber's Electro Talking Bioscope in the Netherlands. Black and white. In French. About 3 minutes.

CENERENTOLA, LA

1817 opera by Rossini

GIOACHINO ROSSINI's charming *La Cenerentola* (Cinderella) is not quite the story of the fairy tale as we know it; there is no magic, no fairy godmother, no stepmother, and no glass slipper. The prince's elderly tutor Alidoro takes over the godfather role, the stepmother is transmuted into a stepfather, and a silver bracelet replaces the glass slipper, but the stepsisters, Clorinda and Tisbe, are as mean as always. Cinderella's stepfather, Don Magnifico, is a comic character, counterpointed by the prince's valet Dandini, who impersonates the prince for plot reasons. The libretto, by Jacopo Ferretti, is closely based on a French libretto by Charles Étienne, not the Perrault fairy tale. This is an *opera buffa* delight, with grand comedy, memorable music, amazing ensembles, touching arias, and a very happy ending. Cinderella's real name, it seems, is Angelina.

1948 Cerchio film

Italian feature film: Fernando Cerchio (director), Oliviero de Fabritiis (conductor, Rome Opera Orchestra and Chorus), Mario Albertelli (cinematographer), Carlo Egidi and Mauro Fabri (art directors).

Cast: Lori Randi (Cinderella, sung by Fedora Barbieri), Gino del Signore (Prince), Vito de Taranto (Don Magnifico), Fiorella Carmen Forti (Clorinda), Franca Tamantini (Tisbe, sung by Fernanda Cadoni Azzolini), Afro Poli (Dandini), Enrico Formichi (Alidoro).

Video: VIEW (USA)/Multimedia (Italy) VHS. Black and white. In Italian (VIEW video has English narration). 94 minutes.

Comment: This was a famous film in its day, the first screen version of a then-little-known Rossini opera. It was shot in palaces near Milan and Turin on a sizable budget, but it is rather badly dated.

1980 New York City Opera

American stage production: Lou Galterio (director), Brian Salesky (conductor, New York City Opera Orchestra and Chorus), Rouben Ter-Arutunian (set designer), Gimi Beni (English translation).

Cast: Susanne Marsee (Cinderella), Rockwell Blake (Prince), James Billings (Don Magnifico), Gianna Rolandi (Clorinda), Rosemary Fredi (Tisbe), Alan Titus (Dandini), Ralph Bassett (Alidoro).

Telecast on PBS on November 6, 1980. Kirk Browning (director). Color. In English. 179 minutes.

***1981 Ponnelle film

Italian feature film: Jean-Pierre Ponnelle (director and set/costume designer), Claudio Abbado (conductor, Teatro alla Scala Orchestra and Chorus).

Cast: Frederica von Stade (Cinderella), Francisco Araiza (Prince), Paolo Montarsolo (Don Magnifico), Margherita Guglielmi (Clorinda), Laura Zannini (Tisbe), Claudio Desderi (Dandini), Paul Plishka (Alidoro).

Video: DG DVD/VHS/LD. Jean-Pierre Ponnelle (director). Color. In Italian with English subtitles. 152 minutes.

Comment: Based on Ponnelle's famous Teatro all Scala production and shot there on 35mm without an audience, this is one of the most enjoyable opera films.

1983 Glyndebourne Festival

English stage production: John Cox (director), Donato Renzetti (conductor, London Philharmonic Orchestra and Glyndebourne Festival Chorus), Allen Charles Klein (set designer).

Cast: Kathleen Kuhlmann (Cinderella), Laurence Dale (Prince), Claudio Desderi (Don Magnifico), Marta Taddei (Clorinda), Laura Zannini (Tisbe), Alberto Rinaldi (Dandini), Roderick Kennedy (Alidoro).

Video: HBO VHS. John Vernon (director). Color. In Italian with English subtitles. 152 minutes.

Comment: Genial but not a memorable production, staged in a fairy tale manner.

1988 Salzburg Festival

Austrian stage production: Michael Hampe (director), Riccardo Chailly (conductor, Vienna Philharmonic), Mauro Pagano (set/costume designer).

Cast: Ann Murray (Cinderella), Francisco Araiza (Prince), Walter Berry (Don Magnifico), Angela Denning (Clorinda), Daphne Evangelatos (Tisbe), Gino Quilico (Dandini), Wolfgang Schöne (Alidoro).

Video: Image Entertainment/Arthaus (GB) DVD/Home Vision and HBO VHS/Pioneer LD. Claus Viller (director). Color. In Italian with English subtitles. 160 minutes.

1995 Houston Grand Opera

American stage production: Robert De Simone (director), Fabio Sparvoli (staging), Bruno Campanella (conductor, Houston Grand Opera Orchestra and Chorus).

Cast: Cecilia Bartoli (Cinderella), Raúl Giménez (Prince), Enzo Dara (Don Magnifico), Laura Knoop (Clorinda), Jill Grove (Tisbe), Alessandro Corbelli (Dandini), Michele Pertusi (Alidoro).

Video: Decca DVD/London VHS. Brian Large (director). Taped at a November 1995 performance. Telecast on PBS April 3, 1996. Color. In Italian with English subtitles. 150 minutes.

Comment: Bartoli is great fun to watch and splendid to hear—a spirited Cinderella.

1997 Metropolitan Opera

American stage production: Cesare Lievi (director), James Levine (conductor, Metropolitan Opera Orchestra and Chorus), Maurizio Balo (set/costume designer).

Cast: Cecilia Bartoli (Cinderella), Ramón Vargas (Prince), Simone Alaimo (Don Magnifico), Alessandro Corbelli (Dandini), Joyce Guyer (Clorinda), Wendy White (Tisbe), Michele Pertusi (Alidoro).

Telecast December 28, 1998; taped November 3, 1997. Brian Large (director). Color. In Italian with English subtitles. 150 minutes.

2000 Royal Opera

English stage production: Patrice Caurier and Moshe Leiser (directors), Mark Elder (conductor, Royal Opera House Orchestra and Chorus), Christian Fenouillat (set designer).

Cast: Sonia Ganassi (Cinderella), Juan Diego Flórez (Prince), Simone Alaimo (Don Magnifico), Marcin Bronikowski (Dandini), Lea-Marian Jones (Clorinda), Nicole Tibbels (Tisbe).

Video: House of Opera DVD/VHS. Color. In Italian with English subtitles. 152 minutes.

Related film

1996 Celestial Clockwork

This romantic fantasy film is based on *La Cenerentola*. A young Venezuelan woman abandons her bridegroom at the altar and heads for Paris to become an opera singer like her role model Maria Callas, whose poster winks at her when she arrives. She ends up starring in a production of *La Cenerentola*. Spanish actress Ariadna Gil plays the young woman; Venezuelan director Fina Torres wrote and directed. The excerpts from the opera in the film are from a 1980 recording with Lucia Valentini Terrani as Cinderella, Francisco Araiza, Elsa Maurus, Domenico Trimarchi, and the West German Radio-Television Chorus and Capella Coloniensis led by Gabriele Ferro. Color. In French. 85 minutes.

CENTRAL PARK
1999 opera trilogy by Drattell/Torke/Beaser

Three one-act operas—*The Festival of Regrets, Strawberry Fields,* and *The Food of Love*—under the collective title *Central Park* were premiered at Glimmerglass Opera on August 8, 1999, and reprised at New York City Opera in November. They have been called "writer operas" because playwrights were commissioned to create librettos set in New York City's Central Park and the composers were brought in afterward. The principal singers, each appearing in two operas, were Lauren Flanigan and Joyce Castle.

1999 Glimmerglass Opera

American stage production: Mark Lamos (director), Stewart Robertson (conductor, Glimmerglass Opera Orchestra and Chorus), Michael Yeargan (set designer).

Telecast on PBS on January 19, 2000, but taped in August 1999. Kirk Browning and Mark Lamos (directors). Color. In English. 117 minutes.

The Festival of Regrets

Deborah Drattell's *The Festival of Regrets*, libretto by Wendy Wasserstein, is about Greta and her domineering mother, who meet Greta's ex-husband and his non-Jewish girlfriend at the annual New Year's ceremony at Central Park's Bethesda Fountain.

Cast: Joyce Castle (Mother), Lauren Flanigan (Greta), Matthew Dibattista (Wesley), John Hancock (Frank), Margaret Lloyd (Jessica), Joshua Winograde (Rabbi).

Strawberry Fields

Michael Torke's *Strawberry Fields*, libretto by A. R. Gurney, follows a confused old lady who thinks that Central Park is the Metropolitan Opera. She enjoys herself until her children try to take her to a retirement home.

Cast: Joyce Castle (Old Lady), Jeffrey Lentz (Student), Daniel Ihasz (Workman), John Hancock (Son), Enrique Abdala (Boy), Kelly E. Kaduce (Girl), Troy Cook (Panhandler), Barbara Lemay (Nurse), Margaret Lloyd (Daughter).

The Food of Love

Robert Beaser's *Food of Love*, libretto by Terrence McNally, is about a homeless woman in Central Park who tries to give away her baby, whom she can no longer care for, but no one will take it.

Cast: Lauren Flanigan (Woman), Troy Cook (Policeman), Jennifer Anne Cooper (Au Pair), Maggie G. Kuch (Little Girl), Matthew Dibattista (Hot Dog Vendor), Kelly E. Kaduce (Rich Lady), Derrick L. Parker and Torrance Blaisdell (Frisbee Players), Joshua Winograde (Painter), Enrique Abdala (Man With Sun Reflector), Margaret Lloyd (Woman With Sun Reflector), Jeffrey Lentz (Man with Cell Phone), Stephen Gaertner (Zoo-

keeper), John Hancock (Elderly Man), Cynthia Jansen (Elderly Woman).

C'EST LA GUERRE
1961 opera by Petrovics

Emil Petrovics's opera *C'est la guerre,* libretto by Miklós Hubay, is a love triangle set in a Budapest apartment in 1944 during the German occupation. Husband and Wife, who are hiding a Deserter friend, are spied on by the Janitress and an invalid Neighbor. The Janitor discovers that the Wife is having an affair with the Deserter, and she betrays them to the Germans. Husband and Deserter are shot, and Wife jumps off the balcony. The opera premiered on radio in 1961, was staged in 1962, and telecast in 1964.

1964 Hungarian State Opera

Hungarian stage production: Miklos Szinetar (director), Tamas Blum (conductor, Hungarian State Opera Orchestra).

Cast: Mária Mátyás (Wife), György Melis (Husband), Robert Ilosfalvy (Deserter), Margit Szilvassy (Janitor), Tibor Udvardy (Neighbor).

Telecast September 27, 1964. Black and white. In Hungarian. 90 minutes.

CHABRIER, EMMANUEL
French composer (1841–1894)

The eclectic French composer Emmanuel Chabrier was influenced by both Offenbach and Wagner, but he managed to create his own delightful style out of the amalgam. His best-known works are the comic operas L'ÉTOILE (1877) and *Le roi malgré lui* (1887), and the somewhat Wagnerian *Gwendoline* (1886).

CHALIAPIN, FEODOR
Russian bass (1873–1938)

Feodor Chaliapin (or Fyodor Shalyapin as *Grove Opera* now calls him) is the most famous bass of the early 20th century with an unforgettable voice still impressive on more than 200 records. He was influential both in restoring acting to the opera stage and in popularizing Russian opera. His career began in Tbilisi in 1892, he reached La Scala in 1901, and he sang at the Metropolitan in 1907. He was noted for his Russian roles, but he was also liked as Mefistofele, Don Basilio, and Don Quichotte. His acting style can be seen in G. W. Pabst's 1935 film of DON QUIXOTE and in a 1915 Russian film about IVAN THE TERRIBLE. Ezio Pinza plays him in the Sol Hurok biopic TONIGHT WE SING. Hollywood actor Feodor Chaliapin Jr. is his son.

1940 Yakov Sverdlov

In Sergei Yutkevich's official Soviet film biography of the first president of the Soviet Republic, one of the people portrayed (by Nicolai Okhlopkov) is Chaliapin. Black and white. In Russian. 100 minutes.

1972 Chaliapin

This Soviet film by Mark Donskoi appears in many filmographies and was certainly a long-planned project of the director. However, it does not appear to have been made.

1999 Fyodor Chaliapin

Documentary film about Chaliapin portraying his rise to international fame. It begins with his becoming a member of the Mamontoff Opera Company in 1896 where he learns the roles that later made him famous. The story is told with photographs, archival footage, and interviews. Black and white and color. 30 minutes. Kultur VHS.

2000 Chaliapin the Enchanter

Documentary film by Elisabeth Kapnist about the singer. There are interviews with his daughter and with Boris Pokrovsky and Sergei Leiferkus, plus evidence of Chaliapin's own opinions of his contemporaries. Color and black and white. 50 minutes. Warner NVC Arts (GB) VHS.

CHANCE, MICHAEL
English countertenor (1955–)

Michael Chance made his opera debut in 1983 at the Buxton Festival in Cavalli's *Giasone* and quickly became popular in both baroque and modern operas. He has recorded operas by Monteverdi, Purcell, and Gluck and is also liked in oratorio. He is featured in videos of Handel's ACIS AND GALATHEA (1985) and MESSIAH (1992), Britten's DEATH IN VENICE (1990), Purcell's THE FAIRY QUEEN (1995), and Monteverdi's L'INCORONAZIONE DI POPPEA (1998) and *Vespers of the Blessed Virgin*. He is one of the performers in David Thomas's 2000 documentary COUNTERTENORS.

CHAPÍ, RUPERTO
Spanish composer (1851–1909)

Ruperto Chapí (y Lorente) created many kinds of music drama, including operas, but he is best known for his zarzuelas. He first became famous in the genre in 1882 with LA TEMPESTAD, followed by *La bruja* and EL REY QUE RABIÓ. Most popular with the movie industry has been LA REVOLTOSA, which has been filmed four times. *La chavala* was filmed in 1914 and 1925, and *La bruja* was made into a silent film in 1923. Juan de Orduña, who

made a series of zarzuela films for Spanish television in 1968, starred in silent versions of *La revoltosa, El rey que rabió,* and *La chavala.*

CHARLIE CHAN AT THE OPERA
1936 operatic murder mystery movie

Boris Karloff plays an opera baritone (sung by Tudor Williams) suffering from amnesia with a desire for revenge. He is suspected of murdering a woman on stage, but detective Charlie Chan (Warner Oland) has his doubts. This was one of the best of the low-budget Chan films based on the Honolulu detective created by Earl Derr Biggers. OSCAR LEVANT composed an imaginary opera called *Carnival* for this film, with overture, prelude, marches, and arias. The libretto by William Kernell was created around a Méphistophélès costume used by Lawrence Tibbett in *Metropolitan*. It was given to the Chan picture to be worn on stage by Karloff in the stabbing scene, with Nedda Harrington as the soprano (sung by Zaruni Elmassian). Levant discusses this opera in his autobiography *A Smattering of Ignorance,* and Irene Hahn Atkins analyzes it in *Source Music in Motion Pictures*. H. Bruce Humberstone directed for Twentieth Century-Fox. Black and white. 66 minutes. Fox/Key Video VHS.

Charlie Chan at the Opera (1936): Chan (Werner Oland) studies baritone murder suspect Boris Karloff in costume.

CHARPENTIER, GUSTAVE
French composer (1860–1956)

Gustave Charpentier, the very model of a Parisian Montmartre Bohemian, affected its lifestyle and eventually created a great opera out of that atmosphere. LOUISE is the story of a girl who chooses Bohemian life in sin with an artist over obedience to her parents. It was considered quite scandalous when it premiered, but today it is viewed as a romantic tribute to Paris, and its aria "Depuis le jour" has become a soprano standard. Charpentier was strongly involved in the making of a film of the opera with Grace Moore as Louise. He also wrote a sequel, *Julien*, but it was not a hit.

CHEAT, THE
1915 American film made into opera

The Cheat, a 1915 Paramount movie directed by Cecil B. De Mille, was the first film to become the basis of an opera. French composer Camille Erlanger used *The Cheat* screenplay as the basis of the libretto for his 1921 opera *Forfaiture*. The film, about the relationship between a rich Japanese man (Sessue Hayakawa) and a woman in desperate need of money (Fannie Ward), was famous for a scene in which he brands her on the shoulder with his seal. Erlanger saw the film in Paris in 1916 and was so impressed he obtained permission to make it into an opera; it was staged at the Opéra-Comique in Paris in 1921, two years after his death, with a libretto by P. Milliet and A. De Lorde based on the screenplay. Hector Turnbull and Jeanie Macpherson wrote the screenplay and Alvin Wyckoff was the cinematographer. The film has been remade three times: in the United States in 1923 with Pola Negri and in 1931 with Tallulah Bankhead, and in France in 1937 as *La Forfaiture* with Sessue Hayakawa reprising his original role under the direction of Marcel L'Herbier. French critics consider the 1915 movie to be as important in the development of film as *Citizen Kane*. Black and white. Silent. About 75 minutes.

CHÉREAU, PATRICE
French director (1944–)

Patrice Chéreau, a successful theater and film director, first began to work in opera in 1969. He is best known for staging the complete *Ring* cycle at Bayreuth in 1976, setting it in Wagner's 19th century with the Rhinemaidens as whores cavorting around a hydroelectric dam and the gods wearing aristocratic Victorian dress. It was quite controversial in its time but also hugely influential. It was also the first complete version of the tetralogy to be televised and issued on video. He can be seen at work on it in the 1980 documentary film *The Making of the Ring*, which is included with the video of his DIE WALKÜRE (1980). Chéreau's notable movies include *Danton* and *Queen Margot*. See GÖTTERDÄMMERUNG (1979), DER RING DES NIBELUNGEN (1980), KATERINA ISMAILOVA (2000 film), LULU (1979), DAS RHEINGOLD (1980), SIEGFRIED (1980), and WOZZECK (1994).

CHICAGO

Chicago has been a major site for opera since the middle of the 19th century. It was especially famous when Mary Garden was its prima donna from 1910 to 1933 and vast sums were spent on premieres such as THE LOVE FOR THREE ORANGES. The major company today, the Lyric Opera of Chicago, dates from 1954 and became known for importing top stars like Maria Callas, Tito Gobbi, and Renata Tebaldi. It has mounted many important and adventurous productions and is now one of the five or six top opera companies in the United States. The smaller Chicago Opera Theater, founded in 1974, has been even more adventurous, with an emphasis on modern American operas such as Floyd's *Susannah* and Hoiby's *Summer and Smoke*. See ANTONY AND CLEOPATRA (1991), BORIS GODUNOV (1966 film), MARIA CALLAS (1983), EUGENE ONEGIN (1985), FAUST (1988), DER LUSTIGE WITWE (1983 film), McTEAGUE (1991), SUMMER AND SMOKE (1980), and SUSANNAH (1986).

CHILD IS BORN, A
1955 TV opera by Herrmann

A Bethlehem innkeeper and his wife turn away Joseph and his expectant wife Mary because soldiers have taken all the rooms, but the wife offers them use of the stable. After the soldiers leave, the innkeeper and his wife join shepherds and wise men in taking gifts to the newborn child. Bernard Herrmann's 30-minute television opera *A Child Is Born*, libretto by Stephen Vincent Benét with lyrics by Maxwell Anderson, is the story of the Nativity as seen by the innkeeper's wife. It premiered on General Electric Theater on CBS Television December 25, 1955. Two Metropolitan Opera singers had the main roles; Theodor Uppman was the innkeeper and Nadine Conner was his wife. The opera soundtrack was released as an LP, with Ronald Reagan as narrator. Benét's libretto originated as a 1942 verse play for the radio show *Cavalcade of America*.

1955 CBS Television
American TV production: Don Medford (director), Mort Abrams (producer), Bernard Herrmann (conductor, CBS Orchestra), Roger Wagner (choral director).

Cast: Theodor Uppman (Innkeeper), Nadine Conner (Innkeeper's Wife), Robert Middleton, Harve Presnell, Roger Wagner Chorale.

Telecast December 25, 1955, on CBS. Black and white. In English. 30 minutes.

CHOCOLATE SOLDIER, THE
1908 operetta by Straus

OSCAR STRAUS's *Der Tapfere Soldat* (The Chocolate Soldier) is based on George Bernard Shaw's 1894 play *Arms and the Man*. Its central character is a Serbian soldier named Bumerli, nicknamed the "chocolate soldier" because he keeps chocolates in his cartridge box rather than bullets. He wins the heart of Nadine, daughter of a colonel in the enemy Bulgarian Army, through his nonheroic behavior. Shaw let Straus use the play for an operetta on the condition that he receive no royalties, a condition he regretted when the operetta became a world success. The German title translates as *The Valiant Soldier* and the German libretto is by Rudolf Bernauer and Leopold Jacobson; however, the operetta was more successful and more true to Shaw in its English translation by Stanislaus Stange. It opened in New York in 1909 and in London in 1910 as *The Chocolate Soldier* and has been popular ever since. The hit tune is Nadine's memorable "My Hero," probably the most popular song Straus ever wrote. All screen versions are in English as the original German version seems to have dropped out of the repertory. The famous American film of the operetta has a different plot, but the TV adaptations stick close to Shaw's story.

1941 MGM film

American feature film: Roy Del Ruth (director), Leonard Lee and Keith Winter (screenplay), Karl Freund (cinematographer), Herbert Stothart (music director).

Cast: Risë Stevens (Maria Lanyi), Nelson Eddy (Karl Lang), Nigel Bruce (Bernard Fischer), Florence Bates (Madame Helene).

Video: MGM Home VHS. Black and white. 102 minutes.

Comment: Shaw wanted more money for the rights than MGM wanted to pay, so his story was dropped. Molnar's *The Guardsman* was adapted for use with the Straus music, plus excerpts from *Tannhäuser* and *Samson et Dalila*. Stevens and Eddy play a husband and wife team starring in a musical comedy called *The Chocolate Soldier*. When he becomes suspicious of her fidelity, he disguises himself as a Cossack and tries to seduce her. She strings him along.

1950 NBC Television

American TV production: William Corrigan (director), Harry Sosnick (conductor, Harry Sosnick Orchestra), Robert Gundlach (set designer), Lester O'Keefe (TV adaptation), Bernard L. Schubert (producer).

Cast: Mimi Benzell (Nadine Popoff), Wilbur Evans (Bumerli), Bill Gilbert (Popoff), Betty Oaks (Mascha), Muriel O'Malley (Aurelia).

Telecast live on NBC on October 30, 1950. William Corrigan (director). Black and white. In English. 59 minutes.

1955 NBC Television

American TV production: Max Liebman (producer), Frederick Fox (set designer), Neil Simon, William Friedberg, and Will Glickman (TV adaptation).

Cast: Risë Stevens (Nadine Popoff), Eddie Albert (Bumerli), Akim Tamiroff (General Masakroff), Will Scholz (General Kirovitch).

Telecast live on NBC on June 4, 1955. Bill Hobin (director). Black and white. In English. 90 minutes.

Comment: Stevens stars in the operetta for the second time but this time within the Shaw plot.

Early film

1914 Stange film

The first film of the operetta was made in 1914 by the people who had introduced it to the New York stage in 1909. Stanislaus Stange, who wrote the English libretto and lyrics and directed the operetta on Broadway, directed the film with Walter Morton. The Broadway cast is featured in the film. Alice Yorke is Nadina Popoff, Tom Richards is Lieutenant Bumerli, Lucille Saunder is Aurelia Popoff, and Francis J. Boyle is Massakroff. Fred C. Whitney, who brought the operetta to the United States, produced the film under the auspices of the Daisy Feature Film Company. It was screened with live music from the operetta score. Black and white. Silent. About 75 minutes.

CHOTZINOFF, SAMUEL
Russian-born U.S. producer (1889–1964)

Samuel Chotzinoff, one of the great pioneers of screen opera, was instrumental in the creation of TV opera. As NBC music director, he was the first to commission an opera especially for television, Gian Carlo Menotti's AMAHL AND THE NIGHT VISITORS (1951). He founded and ran NBC OPERA THEATRE from 1949 to 1964 in association with conductor PETER HERMAN ADLER and director KIRK BROWNING, and he commissioned an impressive number of operas; the series ended with his death. Chotzinoff, who began his musical career as a pianist and music critic, was the person who persuaded Toscanini to return to the United States in 1937 to lead the NBC Symphony Orchestra. In 1939 he commissioned Menotti's 1939 radio opera *The Old Maid and the Thief*. He felt it was his responsibility to bring opera to the wider American public; he once told *Time* magazine that "television is the only hope of opera in America."

CHRISTIE, WILLIAM
American conductor (1944–)

William Christie was music director at Dartmouth College before moving to Paris in 1971. He founded his orchestra Les Arts Florissants in 1979 and has since become known for superb productions of French baroque operas, including Lully's *Atys* (1987) and *Thésée* (1998) and Charpentier's *Médée*. His production of Antonio Sacchini's DARDANUS (1995) is featured in James Ivory's film *Jefferson in Paris*. He is also associated with the operas of Handel and Gluck, and there are videos of his productions of ALCINA (1990), RODELINDA (1998), and THEODORA (1996).

1994 William Christie et les Arts Florissants
French TV documentary about Christie and his orchestra and their performances of baroque operas. The focus is on *Médée*, but there are also excerpts of Christie productions of Lully's *Atys*, Marais' *Alcione*, Purcell's *The Fairy Queen*, and Rameau's *Les Indes galantes* and *Castor et Pollux*. The film was made over a three-year period by Andrea Kirsch. Color. In French. 70 minutes.

CHRISTINÉ, HENRI
French composer (1867–1941)

Henri Christiné was born in Switzerland, but his career as an operetta composer took place in Paris. He first achieved fame as a song writer, and then he had a big success with his 1918 operetta PHI-PHI, about the Greek sculptor Phidias. Equally successful was the 1921 DÉDÉ, which starred Maurice Chevalier. Both were made into French films. The song "Valentine," which became Chevalier's theme song, was composed by Christiné for a 1925 revue.

CHRISTMAS CAROL, A (Herrmann)
1954 TV opera

Victorian miser Ebenezer Scrooge discovers the meaning of Christmas after seeing Christmases past, present, and future. He befriends nephew Bob Cratchit's family and finds joy in giving. Bernard Herrmann's 60-minute television opera *A Christmas Carol*, libretto by Maxwell Anderson based on Charles Dickens's 1843 novel of the same name premiered on CBS Television December 23, 1954.

1954 CBS Television
American TV production: Ralph Levy (director), Bernard Herrmann (conductor, CBS Orchestra and Roger Wagner Chorale), Edward Boyle (set designer), Donald Saddler (choreographer).
Cast: Marilyn Horne (singer), William Olvis (singer), David Venesty (singer), Fredric March (old Scrooge), Craig Hill (young Scrooge), Basil Rathbone (Marley), Bob Sweeney (Bob Cratchit), Christopher Cook (Tiny Tim), Sally Fraser (Spirit of Christmas Past), Ray Middleton (Spirit of Christmas Present), Queenie Leonard (Mrs. Cratchit).

Video: Classic TV VHS. Telecast December 23, 1954. Black and white. In English. 60 minutes.

CHRISTMAS CAROL, A (Musgrave)
1979 opera

Thea Musgrave's two-act opera *A Christmas Carol*, libretto by the composer based on Charles Dickens's 1843 novel, was commissioned by Virginia Opera, which premiered it in Norfolk on December 7, 1979. Musgrave added two scenes to the story: young Scrooge's rejection of his first love Belle, and a mourning scene for Tiny Tim's death.

1982 Royal Opera at Sadler's Wells
English stage production: David Farrar (director), Peter Mark (conductor, London Sinfonietta and Chorus), Miguel Romere (set designer), Alex Reid (costumes).
Cast: Frederick Burchinal (Ebenezer Scrooge), Murray Melvin (Spirit of Christmas), Robin Leggate (Bob Cratchit), Sandra Dugdale, Elizabeth Bainbridge, Eiddwen Harrhy, Forbes Robinson.
Telecast in December 1982 by Granada Television in England. Color. In English. 110 minutes.

CHRISTOFF, BORIS
Bulgarian bass (1914–1993)

Boris Christoff, one of the world's great basses, was the most famous Bulgarian opera singer of his time. He won recognition after his debut at Covent Garden in 1949 as Boris Godunov and was equally admired for his Philip II in *Don Carlo*. Christoff, who was born in Plovdiv, studied in Rome and Salzburg. His career was slowed by the war but he finally made his opera debut in 1946 at the Teatro Argentina singing Colline in *La bohème*. After his successes in the roles of Boris Godunov and Philip II, they became virtually his property for many years, and his recordings of them are famous. He can be seen in one complete opera on video, a 1958 LA FORZA DEL DESTINO, and in excerpts of others.

1956 NBC Festival of Music
Christoff is featured in the death scene from *Boris Godunov* in this NBC program in the *Producer Showcase* series. He is supported by Nicola Moscona, Michael Pollock, and Kirk Jordan with Alfred Wallenstein conducting the NBC Symphony of the Air Orchestra. It was telecast December 10, 1956. Black and white. In English. 30 minutes.

1962 Profile in Music: Boris Christoff

Christoff is seen in staged performances of scenes from two operas in this British television program. He sings "Ella giammai m'amo" from *Don Carlo* and the death scene from *Boris Godunov*. He is accompanied by the Philharmonia Orchestra led by Marcus Dods. Patricia Foy produced the program; John Freeman narrates. Black and white. In English. 30 minutes. Video at the MPRC.

1972 Christoff as Philip II

Christoff, on stage as King Philip II in *Don Carlo,* sings his aria "Ella giammai m'amo" in an excerpt from a 1972 production on the video *Legends of Opera*. Color. In Russian. 7 minutes. Legato Classics VHS.

1976 Profilo di una voce

The 62-year-old basso performs arias and is interviewed by Italian critic Giorgio Gualerzi on this Swiss TV program. Included are Osmin's aria from *Die Entführung aus dem Serail*, the Calumny aria from *The Barber of Seville*, and the death scene from *Boris Godunov*. B. Amaducci conducts the RTSI (Radiotelevisione della Svizzera Italiana) Orchestra. Color. In Italian. 65 minutes.

CHRISTUS

1893 sacred opera by Rubinstein

Russian pianist/composer Anton Rubinstein (1829–1894) is best known as a piano virtuoso but he also composed a number of operas, 11 of them with biblical subjects. The last was the "sacred opera" *Christus,* German libretto by H. A. Bulthaupt, relating the life and death of Christ in seven episodes. While it is hardly known today, it was obviously popular in the early years of the 20th century as it inspired one of the longest early sound opera films.

1912 Messter Tonbild film

German film producer Oskar Messter produced his longest sound film (Tonbild) of Rubinstein's "spiritual opera" *Christus* with extensive scenes. The 35-minute movie was shown with the opera music and singing played on linked synchronized records. It was one of the last opera films that Messter made. Black and white. In German. About 35 minutes.

CHU CHIN CHOW

1916 operetta by Norton

Frederic Norton's *Chu Chin Chow*, libretto by Oscar Asche, is a romantic tale about a slave girl and a robber based on the story of Ali Baba and the Forty Thieves. It was one of the greatest operetta successes of the London stage, running for 2,238 performances during World War I. Critics said it was silly escapism, but it has pleasant tunes, including the popular "Robbers Chorus," and has been filmed twice. The Chu Chin Chow of the title is a disguise adopted by robber chief Hassan, who owns the treasure cave that opens with the famous phrase "Open Sesame."

1934 Gainsborough film

British feature film: Walter Forde (director), Edward Knoblock, L. DuGarde Peach and Sidney Gilliat (screenplay), Mutz Greenbaum (cinematographer), Michael Balcon (producer), Gainsborough (production company).

Cast: Anna May Wong (Zahrat), George Robey (Ali Baba), Fritz Kortner (Hassan), Pearl Argyle (Marjanah), Dennis Hoey (Rakham).

Black and white. In English. 103 minutes.

Early film

1923 Wilcox film

The first film of the operetta was made in Berlin by Herbert Wilcox with Betty Blythe as Zohrat, Herbert Langley as Hassan, and Judd Green as Ali Baba. Norton's music was played live when the film was screened. Black and white. Silent. About 130 minutes.

CHUECA, FEDERICO

Spanish composer (1846–1908)

Federico Chueca, a noted conductor as well as the composer of more than 40 zarzuelas, had a gift for melody and the ability to capture the essence of various types of Spanish music. Many of his colorful musicals have remained popular, especially LA GRAN VÍA (celebrating a Madrid street), LA ALEGRÍA DE LA HUERTA (celebrating a festival in the Murcia area), and AGUA, AZUCARILLOS Y AGUARDIENTE (celebrating the street vendors in Madrid parks).

CHURCH, CHARLOTTE

British soprano (1986–)

Welsh schoolgirl soprano Charlotte Church has sung opera arias in concert, on CD, and on video but has not appeared on the opera stage. She became famous after her first solo concert at the age of 13 when the resulting CD, *Voice of an Angel*, became a bestseller (it's also on DVD and VHS). Despite her popularity, she has few admirers in the world of opera.

1999 Charlotte Church: Voice of an Angel
Church was filmed in her first concert at the age of 13 singing an array of classical and popular music. Color. 67 minutes. Sony DVD/VHS.

2000 Christmas Glory From Westminster Abbey
Church sings in a Christmas program at Westminster Abbey with tenor Andrea Bocelli and baritone Bryn Terfel, backed by the Westminster Abbey Choir and City of London Sinfonia. Color. 60 minutes. Sony DVD/VHS.

2000 Charlotte Church in Jerusalem
Church performs in a concert at the Tower of David in Jerusalem, broadcast on PBS. Included are arias from *Carmen*, *Gianni Schicchi*, and *Martha* and music from *Cavalleria rusticana* and *La forza del destino*. Color. 49 minutes. Sony DVD/VHS.

2000 Charlotte Church in the Holy Land
Church sings Christmas classics at holy sites in Jerusalem, including the Dormition Abbey and Church of the Nativity. Color. 49 minutes. Sony DVD/VHS.

2001 Entertainment from Cardiff, Wales
Church returned to her hometown of Cardiff for a concert in September 2001 with a program including an aria from *Carmen*. Color. 90 minutes. Sony DVD/VHS.

CIBOULETTE
1923 operetta by Hahn

French composer REYNALDO HAHN's best-known operetta *Ciboulette*, libretto by Robert de Flers and Francis de Croisset, is set in Les Halles in 1867; it is virtually an homage to the light operas of that era. Ciboulette is a Parisian market girl who is having a bad time with her fickle suitor Antonin. After she becomes an operetta singer, he returns to her. *Ciboulette* is of special interest to admirers of *La bohème* as one of its main characters is the poet Rodolfo from that opera, now 30 years older and calling himself Duparquet. In one scene, he sings of his sad love affair with Mimì.

1935 Claude Autant-Lara film
French feature film: Claude Autant-Lara (director), Jacques Prévert (screenplay), Curt Courant (cinematographer).
Cast: Simone Berriau (Ciboulette), André Urban (Duparquet), Robert Burnier (Antonin), Guy Ferrant (Roger), Thérèse Dorny (Zénobie), Madeleine Guitty (Mère Pingret), Armand Dranem (Père Grenu).
Black and white. In French. 100 or 75 minutes.
Comment: This was quite a controversial film in its time. Librettist de Croisset attacked it for diverging from the stage text, and director Autant-Lara disavowed it when the producers cut it to 75 minutes from the original 100.

1985 Monte Carlo Opera
French TV production: Pierre Jourdan (director), Cyril Diederich (conductor, Monte Carlo Opera Philharmonic Orchestra and Chorus), André Brasilier (set/costume designer).
Cast: Agnes Host (Ciboulette), Jacques Jansen (Duparquet), Antonine Norman (Antonin), Mariel Berger (Zenobie), Nicolas Rivenq (Roger), Madeleine Robinson, François Perrot.
Video: Opera Dubs VHS. Color. In French. 123 minutes.
Comment: Postmodern production that begins with Hahn telling to his maid Françoise the story of the operetta he is composing. It then fades into Act I on stage at the Monte Carlo Opera House and cuts back and forth between narrator and operetta.

CID, LE
1885 opera by Massenet

The chivalric saga of the Cid ("lord" or "chief") is the national epic of Spain. The heroic 11th-century Spanish knight Don Rodrigo (called Rodrigue in the opera) drives the Moors from Spain, but he suffers in his private life because of a duel he was forced to have with the father of Chimène, the woman he loves. Jules Massenet's grand opera *Le Cid*, based on the play by Corneille, was hugely popular in its time but has dropped from the repertory despite its memorable music. It was revived with great success by Washington Opera in 1999 in a coproduction with Teatro de la Maestranza in Seville, Spain. The libretto is by Édouard Blau, Adolphe d'Ennery, and Louis Gallet. The role of Rodrigue was created by Jean de Reszke, who also performed it at the Met.

1999 Washington Opera
American stage production: Hugo de Ana (director and set/costume designer), Emmanuel Villaume (conductor, Kennedy Center Opera House Orchestra and Washington Opera Chorus).
Cast: Plácido Domingo (Don Rodrigue, Le Cid), Elisabète Matos (Chimène), Angela Turner Wilson (the Infanta), Kimm Julian (King of Spain), Hao Jiang Tian (Don Diègue), William Parcher (Count of Gormas).
Telecast August 19, 2001, on PBS; taped in November 1999. Brian Large (director). Color. In French with English subtitles. 130 minutes.

Related film

1961 El Cid

Charlton Heston stars as El Cid with Sophia Loren as Chimène in Samuel Bronston's spectacular 70mm movie version of the story, shot in Spain and directed by Anthony Mann. Philip Yordan and Ben Barzman wrote the screenplay, and Miklos Rosza composed the stirring music. Color. 184 minutes.

CILEA, FRANCESCO
Italian composer (1866–1950)

The early careers of Francesco Cilea and promising new singer Enrico Caruso were richly intertwined at the turn of the century. Caruso starred in the premieres of Cilea's two major operas at the Teatro Lirico in Milan, and they helped make him famous. L'ARLESIANA in 1897 was Caruso's first major world premiere and a big success. An even greater triumph, however, came with ADRIANA LECOUVREUR, which premiered November 6, 1902. Six days later, Caruso recorded an aria from the opera, "No, più nobile," one of his earliest and best records. *Adriana Lecouvreur* is still the most popular of Cilea's operas.

CIMAROSA, DOMENICO
Italian composer (1749–1801)

Domenico Cimarosa composed wonderful tunes, witty ensembles, and enjoyable comic operas, so he was deservedly popular in the 18th and 19th centuries. He was born in Naples, rose to fame in 1772 with his opera *Le stravaganze del conte*, and was soon popular all over Europe. He was court composer in St. Petersburg, Naples, and Vienna (where he replaced Salieri), and he wrote more than 60 operas. Today he is mostly remembered for only one, the delightful IL MATRIMONIO SEGRETO, although IL MAESTRO DI CAPPELLA remains popular in Italy.

CINEMAFONO PAGLIEJ
Italian sound opera series in silent film era

The Cinemafono Pagliej system of synchronizing movies with sound-on-disc, also known as the Melocinephonos Pagliej and described as a "cinematografo cantabile," was used primarily to present opera films. It was invented by Pasquale Pagliej of Rome and exhibited at the Sala Umberto I in Rome from May 19 to July 30, 1906. The opera films shown were LA TRAVIATA ("De' miei bollenti spiriti" and "Addio! del passato"), IL TROVATORE (solo, duet, trio), CAVALLERIA RUSTICANA, ERNANI, and RIGOLETTO. On March 28, 1908, a screening at the Politeama Pisano in Pisa featured Titta Ruffo in *Rigoletto*. On March 1,

1908, a screening at the Teatro Goldoni in Livorno featured soprano Teresina Burzio and baritone Magini-Coletti in the duet "Mira d'acerbe lacrime" from *Il trovatore;* the couple appeared in person after the show to thank the public. On April 19, 1908, a screening in Pisa featured "Stride la vampa" and "Di quella pira" from *Il trovatore,* "Suona la tromba" from I PURITANI, and a scene from *La traviata*. On May 19, 1908, a screening in a Lumière program in Rome featured the duet "Sì, vendetta!" from *Rigoletto*. Aldo Bernardini describes this fascinating early effort to combine opera and sound in the cinema in his books *Cinema muto italiano: Industria e organizzazione dello spettacolo 1905–1909* (1981) and *Cinema italiano delle origini: Gli ambulati* (2001).

CINESI, LE
1754 opera by Gluck

CHRISTOPH WILLIBALD GLUCK's *Le cinesi* (The Chinese Women) originated as a palace entertainment for future Empress Maria Theresa. Metastasio's libretto is a kind of light-hearted *opera seria* about three young ladies suffering from boredom. The fashion of the time was *chinoiserie,* so the ladies are supposedly Chinese. Lisinga and her friends are showing off their dramatic abilities to each other when her brother Silango interrupts. They play scenes and sing arias. He plays Sivene's lover with a little too much feeling for jealous Tangia, who imitates and mocks him. Lisinga sings a tragic aria. They end up dancing.

1987 Schwetzingen Festival

German stage production: Herbert Wernicke (director and set/costume designer), René Jacobs (conductor, Concerto Cologne Orchestra).

Cast: Kurt Streit (Silango), Sophie Boulin (Sivene), Christina Högman (Lisinga), Eva Maria Tersson (Tangia).

Video: Home Vision VHS. Claus Viller (director). Color. In Italian with English subtitles. 69 minutes.

Comment: Elegant entertainment.

CINOPÉRA
1985 French opera documentary

Cinopéra, a French television documentary, examines the art of opera on film through interviews, analysis, and excerpts. It ranges over many opera movies, with discussions by Eric Lipman, Levon Sayan (who created the first opera film festival in 1976), and Daniel Toscan du Plantier (who has produced many major opera films). Subjects discussed include Gina Lollobrigida's acting in the 1948 PAGLIACCI, Franco Zeffirelli's direction of LA TRAVIATA and OTELLO, Julia Migenes-Johnson's contribution to Rosi's CARMEN, Ruggero Raimondi's work in Losey's DON GIOVANNI, Plácido Domingo's style as film actor, and Sophia Loren's acting in the 1952 LA FAVORITA. Yvon Gerault directed. Color. In French. 90 minutes. Premiere/Lyric VHS.

CITIZEN KANE
1941 American film with opera content

KIRI TE KANAWA recorded an opera aria composed for this movie by BERNARD HERRMANN, one of the reasons why *Citizen Kane* is among the more interesting films with opera content. Herrmann wrote the IMAGINARY OPERA *Salammbô* for the film because director ORSON WELLES wanted an opera in which the soprano heroine is on stage as the curtain goes up and has to sing over a powerful orchestra. This is a disaster for Kane's singer wife Susan Alexander, whom he has forced into an opera career. The actress is Dorothy Comingore, but the singing is by soprano Jean Forward, a professional who forced herself to sound amateurish and could barely be heard over the booming orchestra. It's a great scene with many ramifications, including the sacking of Kane's critic friend Joseph Cotten. The *Salammbô* aria sounds quite splendid in Te Kanawa's recording. In another memorable scene, Comingore attempts to sing Rosina's "Una voce poco fa" to the despair of her opera coach Fortunio Bonanova, the former Met baritone. Bonanova knows she can't make the grade, but Kane won't allow her to quit. William Randolph Hearst, one of the prototypes for Kane, did have an opera singer girlfriend named Sibyl Sanderson, but she was a success. She went to Paris and seduced composer Jules Massenet, who wrote operas for her. A better prototype is Chicago newspaper magnate Harold McCormick, who promoted a somewhat untalented Polish soprano named GANNA WALSKA. He hired Met diva Frances Alda to develop her voice, and he arranged for her to star in Leoncavallo's opera *Zazà* at the Chicago Opera Company, of which he was chief funder. Like Susan Alexander, Walska had a disastrous experience and fled the city before the premiere. Welles kept notes on the Walska affair. Produced by RKO. Black and white. 119 minutes. Warner DVD/VHS.

CIVIL WARS, THE
1984 opera/media event by Glass/Wilson

Designer/director/librettist ROBERT WILSON and composer PHILIP GLASS conceived *the CIVIL warS: a tree is best measured when it is down* as a multimedia event for the 1984 Los Angeles Olympics art festival. Based on Mathew Brady's photographs of the American Civil War, each act was to be by a different composer. The finished opera would have been the longest ever produced, but it became too expensive and the production was canceled;

only the sections with music by Glass have been staged. *Act V: The Rome Section,* commissioned by Rome Opera, premiered in Rome on March 26, 1984, and has been recorded.

1984 Civil Wars: Cologne Section
German TV production: Robert Wilson (director/set designer), Philip Glass (conductor, Philip Glass Ensemble), Yoshito Yabar (costumes).

Cast: Ingrid Andrée, Anna Henke, Fred Hospowsky, Hannelore Lübeck, Georg Peter-Pilz, Rainer Philippi, Ilse Ritter.

Telecast on WDR TV on June 24, 1984. Jürgen Flimm (director). Color. In English. 150 minutes.

Comment: The libretto by Wilson is based on a play by Heiner Müller.

Related film

2000 Le Secret
An excerpt from *The Civil Wars, Act V—The Rome Section* is used on the soundtrack of this French film about a married woman (Anne Coësens) involved in a secret love affair. Virginie Wagon directed. Color. 108 minutes.

Citizen Kane (1941): Failed Kane (Orson Welles) and his failed opera singer wife (Dorothy Comingore) fill in the long hours.

CLAIR, RENÉ
French film director (1898–1981)

René Clair became famous in France during the silent era for comedies such as *The Italian Straw Hat* and even more famous during the sound era for musicals such as *Sous les toits de Paris*. He also made fine movies in England and America. Opera is used with great skill in two of his films: The delightful 1931 French *opéra-bouffe* film LE MILLION was very probably the model for the Marx Brothers' A NIGHT AT THE OPERA and features one of the great opera house comedy scenes. The 1941 American film *The Flame of New Orleans* opens with LUCIA DI LAMMERMOOR on stage, with Hungarian diva Gitta Alpar as Lucia, and sets the mood for the film.

CLAVELES, LOS
1929 zarzuela by Serrano

Tangled romances in Madrid from the perfume factory Los Claveles to a bar and a church, but all ends well, especially for Rosa and Fernando. José Serrano's one-act *Los claveles* (The Carnations), libretto by Luis Fernandez and Ansel C. Carreno, has been filmed three times with well-known singers in the starring roles. It helped modernize the zarzuela genre with its up-to-date working-class people and attitudes.

1935 Ardavin/Ontanon film
Spanish feature film: Eusebio Fernandez Ardavin and Santiago Ontanon (directors), José Maria Beltrán (cinematographer), Campa Film, Valencia (production company).
Cast: Maria Arias, Maria Amparo Bosch, Mario Gabarro, Anselmo Fernández, Ramón Cebrián, Maria Zaldivar.
Black and white. In Spanish. 85 minutes.

1960 Lluch film
Spanish feature film: Miguel Lluch (director), A. Campa (screenplay), Ricardo Albiñana (cinematographer), IFI Film, Barcelona (production company).
Cast: Lilián de Celis, Maruja Tamayo, Conchita Bautista, José Campos y Zori.
Color. In Spanish. 86 minutes.

1995 Teatro Calderón, Madrid
Spanish stage production: José Luis Moreno (director), José A. Irasforza (conductor, Teatro Calderón Orchestra and Chorus), Julian Pérez Muñoz (set designer).
Cast: María Rodríguez (Rosa), Rafael Lledó (Fernando), Enrique del Portal (Evaristo), Pepe Ruiz (Bienvenido), Antonia Pantoja (Paca), David Muro (Goro), Alhambra Ballet (dancers).
Video: Metrovideo (Spain) VHS. Telecast by RTVE. José Ignado Ortega (director). Color. In Spanish. 65 minutes.

CLEMENZA DI TITO, LA
1791 opera by Mozart

La clemenza di Tito (The Clemency of Titus), MOZART's last *opera seria*, is set in Rome in A.D. 80 and is the story of an unsuccessful assassination plot against the Emperor Titus. In the end, he pardons the plotters. The opera was not an original text (it was adapted by Caterina Mazzolá from a Metastasio libretto), but it fits well with the composer's usual themes of betrayal and forgiveness. There are excellent videos, one filmed by Jean-Pierre Ponnelle on location in Rome, and two taped at notable stage performances in Sweden and England.

***1980 Ponnelle film
French feature film: Jean-Pierre Ponnelle (director), James Levine (conductor, Vienna Philharmonic Orchestra and Vienna State Opera Chorus), Giovanni Agostiniucci (set designer), Pet Lalmen (costumes).
Cast: Eric Tappy (Tito), Tatiana Troyanos (Sesto), Carol Neblett (Vitellia), Anne Howells (Annio), Catherine Malfitano (Servilia), Kurt Rydl (Publio).
Video: DG VHS/LD. Color. In Italian with English subtitles. 135 minutes.
Comment: Ponnelle shot the film on location in Rome, including the Arch of Titus in the Roman Forum, the Baths of Caracalla, and the Villa Adriana in the Tivoli Gardens. He opens the opera with fascinating images and expert camera work and creates surrealistic effects with dummy figures. The soundtrack was prerecorded with the same cast as for his Salzburg Festival stage production.

1987 Drottningholm Court Theatre
Swedish stage production: Göran Järvefelt (director), Arnold Östman (conductor, Drottningholm Court Theatre Orchestra and Chorus).
Cast: Stefan Dahlberg (Tito), Anita Soldh (Vitellia), Lani Poulson (Sesto), Maria Hoeglind (Annio), Pia-Marie Nilsson (Servilia), Jerker Arvidson (Publio).
Video: Philips VHS/LD. Thomas Olofsson (director). Color. In Italian with English subtitles. 145 minutes.
Comment: One of a series of intimate Mozart operas filmed at the Drottningholm Court Theatre. Östman wears a period costume, like his orchestra members, who perform on period instruments. The set designs are from the 18th century.

***1991 Glyndebourne Festival
English stage production: Nicholas Hytner (director), Andrew Davis (conductor, London Philharmonic Orchestra and Glyndebourne Festival Chorus), David Fielding (set designer).

Cast: Philip Langridge (Tito), Ashley Putnam (Vitellia), Diana Montague (Sesto), Martine Mahé (Annio), Elzbieta Symytka (Servilia), Peter Rose (Publio).

Video: Image Entertainment and Arthaus (GB) DVD/Home Vision VHS/Pioneer LD. Robin Lough (director). Color. In Italian with English subtitles. 150 minutes.

Comment: Hytner's modernist production, with tilted, eye-catching sets that go well with the Roman costumes, provides strong characterizations.

CLIMAX, THE
1944 American film with opera content

An imaginary opera is the central focus of the 1944 Universal movie *The Climax*. Vienna opera house physician Boris Karloff killed the woman who sang it 10 years before at the Royal Opera, and he thinks of it as sacred to her memory. When young soprano Susanna Foster is engaged to revive it, he tries to stop her by using a spray to make her lose her voice. She recovers and sings the opera, with the help of boyfriend Turhan Bey. The opera is seen and heard on stage a number of times during the film. Edward Ward composed the music to a libretto by producer/director George Waggner, based around themes by Chopin and Schubert, and Lester Horton staged the opera sequences. The film was meant to be a sequel to the 1943 *The Phantom of the Opera* with Foster, Nelson Eddy, and Claude Raines, but the men were not available this time. Hal Mohr and W. Howard Greene were the cinematographers; Lynn Starling and director Curt Siodmak wrote the screenplay, based on a 1910 play by Edward Locke. Color. 85 minutes. Universal MCA VHS.

This was the second film of the play. Universal produced a version in 1930 with a slightly different plot but still revolving around a young opera soprano (Kathryn Crawford) and an evil doctor (LeRoy Mason) who uses a spray to make her lose her voice. This 1930 *Climax* was written by Julian Josephson and Lillian Ducey and directed by Renaud Hoffman. Black and white. 65 minutes.

CLOCLO
1924 operetta by Lehár

The light-hearted FRANZ LEHÁR operetta *Cloclo* centers around a musical comedy star whose manager, Anton, causes her constant trouble by planting imaginative stories in the gossip press. Eventually, one of the stories affects her love life and causes her real problems. Béla Jenbach wrote the libretto.

1935 Die Ganze Welt Dreht sich um Liebe
Austrian feature film: Viktor Tourjansky (director), Werner Brandes (cinematographer), Hans Sass-

mann with Ernst and Hurbert Marischka (screenplay based on *Cloclo*).

Cast: Marta Eggerth (Ilona Ratkay), Leo Slezak (Adalbert von Waldenau), Rolf Wanka (Peter), Ida Wüst (Helene), Hans Moser (Anton).

Black and white. In German. 87 minutes.

Comment: Eggerth is in fine form and lights up the film. Released in the United States with the title *The World in Love*.

The Climax (1943):The new soprano at the Vienna Opera House (Susanna Foster) is shown pearls by mad doctor Boris Karloff.

CLOUZOT, HENRI-GEORGES
French director (1907–1977)

Henri-Georges Clouzot, the Hitchcock of France, directed two of the great French thrillers, *The Wages of Fear* and *Les Diaboliques*. He also filmed a modernized non-operatic version of MANON LESCAUT (1949) and two other films of musical interest. In his 1966 film *Karajan: Early Images,* he puts his cameras in unusual places and conveys the intensity of the music and KARAJAN's conducting through camera movements, odd angles, and jump cuts. In his 1967 film of the VERDI REQUIEM, shot at La Scala, his powers as a filmmaker are also wonderfully evident.

CLOWN AT MIDNIGHT, THE
1998 Canadian horror film with opera content

The Clown at Midnight is set in an opera house and begins as the audience leaves a performance of *Pagliacci*. A man in clown costume enters the dressing room of the woman who played Nedda and stabs her to death. The singer who played Canio disappears and is presumed to have been the murderer, but he is never caught. Fifteen years later, the murdered woman's daughter (Sarah Lassez) comes to the now closed theater with a group of teenagers. They have been drafted to clean it up by a schoolteacher (Margot Kidder), as it is to be opened for school performances. Theater owner Christopher Plummer turns up to wish them well. During an all-night work session, a man in clown costume kills Kidder and many of the students before he is caught. The film, shot in the Walker Theater in Winnipeg, features music from *Pagliacci* performed by the Slovak Philharmonic Choir and Czechoslovak Radio Symphony Orchestra of Bratislava. Kenneth J. Hall wrote the screenplay, and Jean Pellerin directed. Color. In English. 91 minutes. Artisan VHS.

CNN OPERAS

The relatively new genre of operas about contemporary events and people, initiated by John Adams, Alice Goodman, and Peter Sellars with NIXON IN CHINA, has been dubbed the CNN opera, borrowing the name from the Cable News Network. Some have been telecast and are available on video, and most are on CD. *Nixon in China,* which is on its way to becoming a modern classic, describes President's Nixon's historic visit to China in 1972. It was followed in 1991 by Adams, Goodman, and Sellars's *The Death of Klinghoffer,* about the hijacking of the cruise liner *Achille Lauro.* In 1986, Adams teamed with Sellars and librettist June Jordan to create an opera based on the 1994 Los Angeles earthquake, *I Was Looking at the Ceiling and Then I Saw the Sky.* Other American composers have focused on contemporary personalities. Anthony Davis's *X, The Life and Times of Malcolm X* (1986), libretto by Thulani Davis, is the story of the black Muslim leader. John Moran's *The Manson Family* (1990), libretto by the composer, is a portrait of the murderous cult leader Charles Manson and his deadly "family." Ezra Laderman's *Marilyn* (1993), libretto by Norman Rosten, examines the life and death of Marilyn Monroe. Stewart Wallace's *Harvey Milk* (1995), libretto by Michael Korie, concerns the murder of the gay San Francisco politician. Wallace and Korie also created *Hopper's Wife* (1997), in which artist Edward Hopper marries gossip columnist Hedda Hopper and actress Ava Gardner becomes his model. In Michael Daugherty's opera *Jackie O* (1997), libretto by Wayne Koestenbaum, Jackie Kennedy meets Aristotle Onassis, Elizabeth Taylor, and Grace Kelly at a party at Andy Warhol's Factory; sings a duet with Maria Callas; and remembers her life with John F. Kennedy. Jake Heggie's *Dead Man Walking* (2000), libretto by Terrence McNally, is about Sister Jean Prejean and a man on death row. Cary John Franklin's *Loss of Eden* (2002), libretto by Michael Patrick Albano, centers around the kidnapping and murder of Charles Lindbergh's infant son in 1932. Contemporary-themed operas are also in vogue in England. Thomas Adès's opera POWDER HER FACE (1995), libretto by Philip Hensher, is based on the scandalous life of the Duchess of Argyll. Richard

Thomas's JERRY SPRINGER: THE OPERA (2002), libretto by Steward Lee, raises the talk-show host to operatic status. Jonathan Dove's 2002 WHEN SHE DIED: DEATH OF A PRINCESS (2002), libretto by David Harshent, is based on the death of Princess Diana. The concept has also spread to the birthplace of opera. Filippo del Corno's *Non Guardate al Domani* (2002), libretto by Angelo Miotta, deals with the kidnapping and murder of Italian prime minister Aldo Moro by the Red Brigade in 1978.

COATES, ALBERT
English composer (1882–1953)

Eric Coates wrote nine operas, including the very British *Samuel Pepys* (1929) and PICKWICK (1936) even though he completed his musical education in Germany and began his career in Russia *Pickwick* has a secure niche in the history of music as it was the first televised opera, presented on BBC Television on November 13, 1936, 10 days before it premiered at Covent Garden. Twenty-five minutes of scenes from the opera were shown in a "special adaptation for television." Two orchestral interludes from Pickwick later achieved popularity as the *Pickwich* Scherzo and the *Cricket* Fugue.

COME MORÌ BUTTERFLY
1917 film with opera content

Italian soprano Rosina Storchio created the role of Madama Butterfly at its disastrous La Scala premiere in 1904; but she was hissed for her performance and said she would never sing the role again. However, she did finally agree to star in a 1917 Italian film based on the opera. She plays a famous opera singer named Rosa D'Alba who is about to marry poet Dario D'Antri, but her glamorous sister Silvana (Alma Lyser) arrives and steals him away. She tries to forget him by devoting herself to her singing career, but cannot. Finally, during a performance of *Madama Butterfly,* she kills herself on stage in the last act like Cio-Cio-San. Giuseppe Adami wrote the screenplay; Emilio Graziani-Walter directed for Savoia Film of Torino. Black and white. Silent. About 70 minutes. This is apparently a lost film.

COMENCINI, LUIGI
Italian film director (1916–)

Luigi Comencini, who began his movie career just after World War II, is best known in the United States for his popular 1953 film *Bread, Love and Dreams* starring Gina Lollobrigida. His 1988 film of the opera LA BOHÈME stars American soprano Barbara Hendricks as Mimì. He films the opera straight but adds his own ideas about the story, such as having Mimì initiate her meeting with Rodolfo by only pretending her candle has gone out so she can see him alone.

COMTE ORY, LE

1828 opera by Rossini

Gioachino Rossini's rather far-fetched but fun *Le Comte Ory* (Count Ory), libretto by Eugène Scribe and Charles-Gaspard Delestre-Poirson, was his last comedy. It's set around the year 1200. Womanizing Count Ory learns of the loneliness of Countess Adèle and her companion Ragonde, who have taken vows of chastity while their men are away at the Crusades. He and two lustful friends enter their castle disguised as nuns with the aim of seducing them. The Rabelaisian story is based on a medieval legend.

1997 Glyndebourne Festival

English stage production: Jérôme Savary (director), Andrew Davis (conductor, London Philharmonic Orchestra and Glyndebourne Festival Chorus), Ezio Toffolutti (set/costume designer).

Cast: Annick Massis (La Comtesse Adèle), Marc Laho (Le Comte Ory), Diana Montague (Isolier), Ludovic Tézier (Raimbaud), Jane Shaulis (Dame Ragonde), Julien Robbins (Le Gouverneur).

Video: House of Opera DVD/VHS and NVC Arts (GB) VHS. Brian Large (director). Color. In French with English subtitles. 103 minutes.

CONDUCTORS

The great opera conductors have been recorded for posterity on film like the great singers. Material on them goes back to the silent era, especially in Germany, where "director films" were a virtual genre. Most modern videos of stage opera performances automatically include scenes of the conductors at work. A major series of videos about conductors was held at the Museum of Television and Radio in New York in 1994 with 50 hours of taped performances. Videos about individual conductors are described under their names; multiple conductor videos are listed below.

1913–1917 Dirigentenfilme

German interest in high culture led filmmakers such as Oskar Messter to create a new genre of musical film, the *Dirigentenfilme* (director film). Famous conductors such as Ernest von Schuh, Arthur Nikisch, Felix Weingartner, and Oskar Fried were shown in action in a unique manner. Historian Ennio Simeon, in his study *Music in German Cinema Before 1918,* says: "The screen was divided into an upper and lower half. The upper half showed the conductor from behind, as he would be seen by the public, while the lower half, which the audience could not see, displayed him to the instrumentalists in such a way they could really be conducted by him." No other film records are known of most of these conductors. Excerpts

from some are featured in the Bel Canto Society *Great Conductors* videos.

1993 Great Conductors, Volume I

Bel Canto Society video compilation showing nine conductors at work: Bruno Walter, Leo Blech, Fritz Busch, Joseph Keilberth, Ferenc Fricsay, Karl Elmendorff (an excerpt from *Gotterdämmerüng* at Bayreuth), Hans Knappertsbusch (with Erna Berger and Torsten Ralf), Carl Schuricht, and Erich Kleiber. 60 minutes. Bel Canto Society VHS.

1994 Great Conductors, Volume 2

Second Bel Canto Society video compilation of conductors at work: Arthur Nikisch (in a "Dirigentenfilme"), Pietro Mascagni, Fritz Busch, Richard Strauss, Arturo Toscanini, Sergiu Celibidache, Bruno Walter, Igor Stravinsky, Wilhelm Furtwängler, Hans Knappertsbusch, Charles Munch, Hermann Scherchen, Karl Böhm, Josef Krips, Herbert von Karajan, Georg Solti, Rafael Kubelik, and Lorin Maazel. 80 minutes. Bel Canto Society VHS.

1995 The Art of Conducting: Great Conductors of the Past

This superb video, based on a BBC TV series, features sixteen giants of the conducting world and includes the 1913 film of Arthur Nikisch demonstrating his technique. The other conductors are John Barbirolli, Thomas Beecham, Leonard Bernstein, Wilhelm Furtwängler, Herbert von Karajan, Otto Klemperer, Serge Koussevitsky, Fritz Reiner, Leopold Stokowski, Richard Strauss, George Szell, Bruno Walter, Fritz Busch (with a 1932 Dresden *Tannhäuser*), Arturo Toscanini (with a 1944 *La forza del destino*), and Felix Weingartner (with a 1932 *Der Freischütz*). Sue Knussen directed the video, which won *Gramophone*'s Best Video of the Year award. Color and black and white. In English. Teldec DVD, 164 minutes/Teldec VHS, 117 minutes.

1995 Great Conductors of the Third Reich

Subtitled "Art in the Service of Evil," this is a survey of conductors working in Germany during the Nazi era. They are Wilhelm Furtwängler, Herbert von Karajan, Karl Böhm, Leo Blech, Hans Knappertsbusch, Clemens Krauss, and Max von Schillings. Performance footage includes *William Tell* and *Die Meistersinger*. Newsreel material shows Hitler and Goebbels. Black and white. 70 minutes. Bel Canto Society VHS.

1998 The Art of Conducting: Legendary Conductors of a Golden Era

Follow-up to the award-winning 1995 *The Art of Conducting* video and equally interesting. The conductors here are Sergiu Celibidache, André Cluytens, Wilhelm

Furtwängler, Herbert von Karajan, Erich Kleiber, Willem Mengelberg, Evgeny Mravinsky, Charles Munch, Hermann Scherchen, and Vaclav Talich. Marcos Klorman produced the video, which includes performance material and interviews. Color and black and white. 115 minutes. Teldec (GB) DVD/VHS.

CONGRESS DANCES
1931 German operetta film

Congress Dances, the English version of the best-known and most popular German operetta film, stars England's Lillian Harvey in a frothy tale about aristocratic dalliance at the 1815 Congress of Vienna. The Russian Tsar has a fling to splendid music by Werner Heymann. The film was made in three languages. Henri Garat is Harvey's love in the English and French *(Le Congrès s'amuse)* versions. The German version, *Der Kongress Tanzt,* pairs her with Willy Fritsch. Karl Hoffmann was the cinematographer, Norbert Falk and Robert Liefmann wrote the script, Erich Pommer produced for the UFA studio, and Erik Charell directed. Black and white. 92 minutes. On VHS.

CONLON, JAMES
American conductor (1950–)

James Conlon, who recorded LA BOHÈME for Luigi Comencini for his 1998 film and MADAMA BUTTERFLY for Frederic Mitterand for his 1995 film, made his debut at Menotti's Spoleto Festival in 1971. He conducted the first performance of the revised version of Barber's ANTONY AND CLEOPATRA in 1975 at Juilliard, where he had studied, and he made his Met debut in 1976. He became chief conductor at the Cologne Opera in 1989. See DON GIOVANNI (1991), DON QUICHOTTE (2000), SEMIRAMIDE (1990), and TOSCA (1978).

CONNER, NADINE
American soprano (1907–2003)

Nadine Conner was born in Los Angeles and began her career in the film capital in 1940 singing Marguerite in *Faust.* She made her debut at the Metropolitan Opera in 1941 as Pamina in *Die Zauberflöte,* sang in Europe in the 1950s, and remained a regular at the Met until 1960. She can be seen in telecasts as Micaëla in a 1952 CARMEN and as Mimì in a 1953 LA BOHÈME. She starred in the classical music film OF MEN AND MUSIC, and she appeared in a 1953 *Voice of Firestone* show with GEORGE LONDON.

CONSUL, THE
1950 opera by Menotti

GIAN CARLO MENOTTI's political opera *The Consul,* which won a Pulitzer Prize, has been presented in more than 20 countries. It can be interpreted as a sinister modern variation on *Tosca,* for it also revolves around getting a visa to leave a police state. Menotti's plot is set somewhere in Europe in the late 1940s and tells the story of freedom fighter John Sorel and his wife Magda. He has to flee the country because the secret police want to arrest him, but he wants his wife to get a visa from a foreign consulate and follow him. She tries but is blocked by a kafkaesque bureaucracy. After her baby dies, she kills herself in a vain attempt to stop Sorel from returning for her. The lead roles were created on stage by Cornell MacNeil as Sorel, Patricia Neway as Magda, and Marie Powers as the Mother.

1951 BBC Television
English TV production: Julia Smith (director), Eric Robinson (conductor, BBC Orchestra), James Bould (set designer).

Cast: Patricia Neway (Magda), Marie Powers (Mother), Russell George (Sorel), Leon Lishner (Police Agent), Gloria Lane (Secretary), David Aiken (Mr. Kofner).

Telecast on BBC Television on May 28, 1951. Julia Smith (director). Black and white. In English. 120 minutes.

1952 Cleveland Play House
American TV production: Earl Keyes (director), Harold Fink (conductor), Frederick McConnell and George Dembo (set designers).

Cast: Mary Simmons (Magda), Salvatore Colluras (Sorel), Zelma George (Mother), Shirley Abrams (Secretary), Jack Lee (Magician), Michael Sandry (Mr. Kofner), Edgar Power (Police Agent).

Telecast in February 1952 on WEWS, Cleveland. Earl Keyes (director). Black and white. In English. 60 minutes.

1954 Canadian Television
Canadian TV production: Herman Geiger-Torel (director), Sydney Newman (producer).

Cast: Theresa Gray (Magda), Glenn Gardiner (Sorel), Nellie Smith (Mother), Andrew Macmillan (Police Agent), Joanne Ivey (Secretary), Jan Rubes (Mr. Kofner).

Telecast January 17, 1954, on CBC. Black and white. In English. 116 minutes.

1962 Australian Television

Australian TV production: Christopher Muir (director), George Tintner (conductor).

Cast: Loris Synan (Magda), Morris Williams (Sorel), Justine Rettick (Mother), Dorothy Deegan (Secretary), Charles Skase (Police Agent), Leslie Coe (Mr. Kofner), Lorenzo Nolan (Magician).

Video: Premiere Opera VHS. Telecast on ABC Australian TV December 12, 1962. Black and white. In English. 115 minutes.

1963 Vienna Volksoper

German stage production: Rudolph Cartier (director), Franz Bauer-Theussl (conductor, Vienna Volksoper Orchestra), Rosalia Chladek (choreographer), Robert Posik (set designer), Werner Gallusser (German translation).

Cast: Melita Muszely (Magda), Eberhard Wächter (Sorel), Res Fischer (Mother), Willi Ferenz (Police Agent), Gloria Lane (Secretary), Friedrich Nidetzky (Mr. Kofner), Laszlo Szereme (Magician).

Video: Premiere Opera VHS. Telecast on Austrian TV on April 19, 1963. Black and white. In German. 114 minutes.

1978 Spoleto Festival, USA

American stage production: Gian Carlo Menotti (director), Christopher Keene (conductor, Spoleto Festival Orchestra), Corey Gordon Wong (set designer).

Cast: Marvalee Cariaga (Magda), David Clatworthy, Fredda Rakusin, Vern Shinall, Jerold Siena.

Video at the New York Public Library. Telecast March 29, 1978, by PBS. Kirk Browning (director). Color. In English. 115 minutes.

1998 Spoleto Festival, Italy

Italian stage production: Gian Carlo Menotti (director), Richard Hickox (conductor, Spoleto Festival Orchestra), Fausto Fiorito (set designer).

Cast: Susan Bullock (Magda), Louis Otey (Sorel), Jacalyn Bower-Kreitzer (Mother), Charles Austin (Police Agent), Victoria Livengood (Secretary), Herbert Eckhoff (Mr. Kofner), Giovanna Manci (Foreign Woman), Robin Blitch (Anna Gomez), Malin Fritz (Vera Boronel), John Horton Murray (Magician).

Video: Premiere Opera/Opera Dubs/Live Opera VHS. Telecast on RAI in October 1998. Paolo Longobardo (director). Color. In English. 138 minutes.

CONTES D'HOFFMANN, LES

1881 opera by Offenbach

JACQUES OFFENBACH's only opera, *Les contes d'Hoffmann* (The Tales of Hoffmann), is now more popular than his operettas. It provided the basis for a memorable Powell and Pressburger film, and its Barcarolle is as famous as the Cancan from *Orpheus in the Underworld*. The story revolves around fantasy writer E. T. A. Hoffmann, who describes three failed love affairs as he sits in a pub waiting for his new love, Stella. Olympia turns out to be a mechanical doll and is destroyed by Coppélius. Antonia, weakened by illness, dies when the evil Dr. Miracle gets her to sing. Giulietta, a courtesan in Venice, is hired by Dapertutto to steal Hoffmann's soul. All three women are apparently aspects of Hoffmann's present love, and all four women are often sung by the same soprano. Hoffmann's rival/enemy in each episode is also usually sung by the same baritone. Jules Barbier's libretto is based on stories by the real Hoffmann, who lived from 1776 to 1822 and also wrote operas. (Note: The *Metropolitan Opera Annals* and other Met reference books spell the character name "Dapertutto" as "Dappertutto," but French sources, *New Grove*, and author E. T. A. Hoffmann use only one *p*.)

1950 NBC Opera Theatre

American TV production: Charles Polacheck (director), Peter Herman Adler (conductor, Symphony of the Air Orchestra), Otis Riggs (set designer), Samuel Chotzinoff (producer).

Cast: Davis Cunningham (Hoffmann), Dorothy Etherige (Olympia, sung by Barbara Gibson), Dorothy Warenskjold (Antonia, Stella), George Britten (Lindorf, Coppélius, Dr. Miracle).

Telecast live on May 1, 1950. Kirk Browning (director). Black and white. In English. 60 minutes.

Comment: The Giulietta episode is cut.

***1951 Powell/Pressburger film

English feature film: Michael Powell and Emeric Pressburger (directors/screenwriters), Thomas Beecham (conductor, Royal Philharmonic Orchestra and Sadler's Wells Chorus), Christopher Challis (cinematographer), Hein Heckroth (set designer), Frederick Ashton (choreographer), Dennis Arundell (English translation).

Cast: Robert Rounseville (Hoffmann), Moira Shearer (Stella and Olympia, sung by Dorothy Bond), Ann Ayars (Antonia), Ludmilla Tcherina (Giulietta, sung by Margherita Grandi), Robert Helpmann (Lindorf, Coppélius, Dapertutto, and Dr. Miracle, sung by Bruce Dargavel), Pamela Brown (Nicklausse, sung by Monica Sinclair).

Video: Somm DVD/Home Vision VHS/Criterion LD. Technicolor. In English. 127 minutes.

Comment: One of the classics of opera film, this is a visual feast, as important for the way it looks as for the way it sounds. Powell and Pressburger made it after *The Red Shoes* in the same colorful style using many of the same actors. The film is correctly titled *The Tales of Hoffmann* with two *n*'s, although the title is misspelled "Hoffman" in film reference books.

1970 Felsenstein film

German feature film: Walter Felsenstein (director/screenwriter), Georg Mielke (co-director/co-screenwriter), Karl-Fritz Voigtmann (conductor, Komischer Oper Orchestra), Otto Merz and Hans-Jurgen Reinecke (cinematographer), DEFA (studio).

Cast: Hans Nocker (Hoffmann), Melitta Muszely (Olympia, Antonia, Giulietta, Stella), Rudolf Asmus (Lindorf, Coppélius, Dr. Miracle, Dapertutto).

Video: House of Opera DVD/VHS and Lyric VHS. Color. In German. 125 minutes.

Comment: Felsenstein's film is based on his famous 1958 Komischer Oper production in East Berlin and seems to have been stylistically influenced by Soviet filmmakers such as Eisenstein. The German title is *Hoffmanns Erzählungen*.

1970 Kaslík film

German TV film: Václav Kaslík (director, based on stage production by Rolf Liebermann), Christoph von Dohnanyi (conductor, Bavarian State Opera Orchestra and Chorus), Josef Svoboda (set designer).

Cast: Jon Piso (Hoffmann), Sylvia Geszty (Olympia, Antonia, Giulietta, Stella), Thomas Tipton (Lindorf, Coppélius, Dr. Miracle, Dapertutto).

Telecast on ZDF German television on December 25, 1970. Color. In German. 140 minutes.

1974 Seabourne film

English TV film: Peter Seabourne (director), John J. Davies (conductor, Classical Orchestra).

Cast: Kenneth Woollam (Hoffmann), Susan Miasey (Olympia), Valerie Masterson (Antonia), Janette Kearns (Giulietta), Malcolm Rivers (Coppélius, Dr. Miracle, Dapertutto).

Telecast on BBC Television. Color. In English. 52 minutes.

Comment: English highlights film shot for *Focus on Opera* series at Knebworth House, Hertfordshire.

1981 Royal Opera

English stage production: John Schlesinger (director), Georges Prêtre (conductor, Royal Opera House Orchestra and Chorus), William Dudley (set designer), Maria Bjornson (costume designer).

Cast: Plácido Domingo (Hoffmann), Luciana Serra (Olympia), Ileana Cotrubas (Antonia), Agnes Baltsa (Giulietta), Deanne Bergsman (Stella), Robert Lloyd (Lindorf), Geraint Evans (Coppélius), Robert Tear (Spalanzani), Nicola Ghiuselev (Dr. Miracle), Siegmund Nimsgern (Dapertutto), Philip Gelling (Schlemil), Claire Howell (Nicklausse).

Video: Warner NVC Arts DVD/VHS & Pioneer LD. Brian Large (director). Color. In French with English subtitles. 150 minutes.

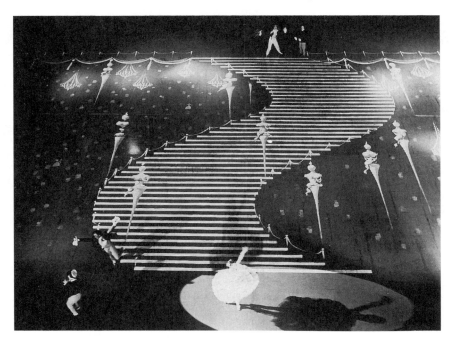

Les Contes d'Hoffmann (1951): A spectacular dance sequence in Michael Powell and Emeric Pressburger's film.

1988 Teatro Regio, Parma

Italian stage production: Beppe De Tomasi (director), Alain Guingal (conductor, Orchestra Sinfonica dell'Emilia-Romagna and Teatro Regio Chorus), Ferruccio Villagrossi (set designer).

Cast: Alfredo Kraus (Hoffmann), Ruth Welting (Olympia), Barbara Hendricks (Antonia), Jolanda Omilian (Giulietta), Nicolo Ghiuselev (Lindorf, Coppélius, Dr. Miracle, Dapertutto), Elena Zilio (Nicklausse).

Video: Bel Canto Society/House of Opera DVD and VHS. Color. In French. 174 minutes.

1988 Metropolitan Opera

American stage production: Otto Schenk (director), Charles Dutoit (conductor, Metropolitan Opera Orchestra and Chorus), Günther Schneider-Siemssen (set designer).

Cast: Neil Shicoff (Hoffmann), Gwendolyn Bradley (Olympia), Tatiana Troyanos (Giulietta), Roberta Alexander (Antonia), Pauline Andrey (Stella), James Morris (Lindorf, Coppélius, Dr. Miracle, Dapertutto), Susan Quittmeyer (Nicklausse).

Video: DG VHS/LD. Taped January 8, 1988; telecast March 2, 1988, on PBS. Brian Large (director). Color. In French with English subtitles. 180 minutes.

1993 Opéra de Lyon

French stage production: Louis Erlo (conductor), Kent Nagano (conductor, Lyons Opera Orchestra and Chorus).

Cast: Daniel Galvez-Vallejo (Hoffmann), Natalie Dessay (Olympia), Barbara Hendricks (Antonia), Isabelle Vernet (Giulietta), José van Dam (Lindorf, Coppelius, Dr. Miracle, Dapertutto), Gabriel Bacquier (Spalazan, Crespel, Schlemil), Brigitte Balleys (Nicklausse).

Video: Image Entertainment DVD/Home Vision VHS/Pioneer LD. Pierre Cavassilas (director). Color. In French with English subtitles. 158 minutes.

Comment: Erlo's eccentric production is retitled *...des Contes d'Hoffmann*. The setting is a madhouse with drab, gray walls; Olympia is a catatonic inmate on a trolley; Giulietta is the matron; and Stella wears evening dress but is bald.

Early/related films

1911 Hoffmanns Erzählungen

The first film of the opera was a silent Austrian version made in Vienna in 1911; Offenbach's music was arranged by Erich Hiller to accompany the film in cinemas. Luise Kolm, Anton Kolm, Jakob Fleck, and Claudis Veltée wrote and directed the film, which features actors from the Vienna stage. Black and white. Silent. About 15 minutes.

1912 Barcarolle

This early sound film of the Barcarolle was made by German sound film pioneer Oskar Messter for his Biophon Theater in Berlin with synchronized picture and record. It was copyrighted in the United States in 1915 but was made earlier, probably in 1912. Black and white. In German. About 3 minutes.

1914 Hoffmanns Erzählungen

Richard Oswald directed this German film of the opera, which follows the opera closely, with prologue and three episodes with the three women. Kurt Wolowsky is young Hoffmann, Erich Kaiser-Titz is old Hoffmann, Kathe Oswald is Stella, Ruth Oswald is Antonia, Alice Scheel-Hechy is Olympia, Thea Sandten is Giulietta, and Werner Krauss is Dapertutto. Manfred Noa was the set designer and Ernst Krohn, the cinematographer. Black and white. Silent. About 50 minutes.

1923 Hoffmanns Erzählungen

Max Neufeld directed this Austrian film of the opera, adapted for the screen by Josef Malina. It stars Dagny Servaes, Friedrich Feher, Eugen Neufeld, Max Neufeld, Karl Ehmann, and Viktor Franz. Black and white. Silent. 78 minutes.

1934 Barcarolle

The film *Barcarolle,* based on the melodies of *Les contes d'Hoffmann,* is set at Carnival time in Venice and centers around a young man willing to risk his life for a bet on a woman. It was made in German and French versions. The German film stars Gustav Fröhlich and Lida Baarova, and the French film has Edwige Feuillère and Pierre Richard-Willm. Gerhardt Lamprecht directed both. Black and white. In German or French. 83 minutes.

1998 Life is Beautiful

Régine Crespin and Shirley Verrett sing the Barcarolle as Roberto Benigni watches a pair of performers on a stage in Arezzo, Italy, in the 1930s. Benigni also directed this extraordinary comedy about a concentration camp survivor and won Oscars for his performance and for the film Italian title is *La vita è bella.* Color. 116 minutes

1999 Topsy-Turvy

Composer Arthur Sullivan (Allan Corduner) enjoys himself in a Paris brothel while a pianist warbles the Doll Song from *Les contes d'Hoffmann.* Mike Leigh's fine film explores the difficult relationship between Sullivan and librettist William S. Gilbert (Jim Broadbent). Color. 160 minutes.

COPELAND, STEWART
American composer (1952 -)

Stewart Copeland is a rock musician who has also composed operas. *Holy Blood and Crescent Moon*, about the Crusades, was commissioned by Cleveland Opera which premiered it in 1989. HORSE OPERA, about Old West fantasies, premiered on Channel Four television in England in 1994.

COPLAND, AARON
American composer (1900–1990)

Aaron Copland, one of the most popular modern classical American composers, is also noted for his film scores; he won an Academy Award for one. He wrote two operas, but neither was a real success. THE SECOND HURRICANE, which deals with students helping out during a natural disaster, was given its premiere in 1937 by Orson Welles before he went to Hollywood. Leonard Bernstein revived it for television. *The Tender Land,* the story of a young woman's coming of age in the Midwest, was created for television. After NBC rejected it, Copland revised it for the stage. It premiered at the New York City Opera in 1954. A CD version was released in 1989, but there is no video.

1939–1988 Hollywood films
Copland began writing scores for Hollywood films in 1939 with *The City*. He was nominated for Oscars for his scores for *Of Mice and Men, Our Town,* and *North Star* and won an Academy Award for *The Heiress* in 1949. He also gained acclaim for *The Red Pony* and *Love and Money*. Copland adapted some of his film scores into orchestral suites, the most popular being *The Red Pony*.

1961 Aaron Copland's Birthday Party
Leonard Bernstein and the New York Philharmonic celebrate Copland's birthday on CBS Television. The program features William Warfield singing Copland songs, Bernstein conducting Copland works, and Copland conducting *El Salon Mexico*. Roger Englander directed the telecast on February 12, 1961, for the *Young People's Concerts* series. Black and white. 60 minutes.

1972 Copland on Copland
Copland discusses his work and career with Karl Haas, who made the program, and there is an excerpt from the film *The City*. Copland is shown in his garden, at his piano composing, and at his desk orchestrating. Black and white. 30 minutes. Video at the MTR.

1976 The Copland Portrait
A film made by the U.S. Information Service as a portrait of the composer's life, work, and music. He is shown with friends discussing his career and significant moments in his life. Color. 29 minutes.

1980 An American Birthday: Copland at 80
Copland conducts the American Symphony in *Fanfare for the Common Man* and *Short Symphony* for this birthday concert at Carnegie Hall. He also narrates *A Lincoln Portrait* as Leonard Bernstein conducts. Telecast by Bravo. Color. 40 minutes.

1985 Aaron Copland: A Self-Portrait
Allan Miller's film, formatted as an autobiography, traces the career of the composer and the creation of his music, with the composer explaining how his style developed.. There are performance excerpts and interviews with Leonard Bernstein, Ned Rorem, Michael Tilson Thomas, and Agnes de Mille. Vivian Perlis was the writer and Ruth Leon the producer of the film telecast on PBS in October 1985. Color. In English. 60 minutes. Films for the Humanities & Sciences VHS.

2001 Fanfare for America: The Composer Aaron Copland
A documentary looking at how Copland created an American sound in his music with biographer Howard Pollock talking about events in Copland's life. Hugh Wolff conducts the Frankfurt Radio Symphony Orchestra in excerpts from Copland works. Color. In English. 59 minutes. Films for the Humanities & Sciences VHS.

COPLEY, JOHN
English director (1933–)

John Copley became a leading London stage director in the 1970s with notable productions at Covent Garden and the English National Opera. He began to work internationally during the 1980s, moving from Europe to Sydney to New York and producing operas with major stars. He is particularly noted for his ability to work with singers. See ADRIANA LECOUVREUR (1984), JANET BAKER (1982), LA BOHÈME (1982), L'ELISIR D'AMORE (1991), LA FORZA DEL DESTINO (1988 film), GIULIO CESARE (1984), LUCIA DI LAMMERMOOR (1986), MARIA STUARDA (1982), LE NOZZE DI FIGARO (1991), SEMIRAMIDE (1986/1990), and TOSCA (1986).

COPPOLA, FRANCIS FORD
American film director (1939–)

Francis Ford Coppola, after filming *The Godfather* in 1972, directed the stage production of Gottfried von

Einem's opera *The Visit of the Old Lady* for San Francisco Opera. Its success resulted in invitations from Vienna and the Met to direct productions for them, and he had plans to stage *La bohème* for Joseph Papp. None of these happened, but he has featured opera in his movies. Coppola says that the smoke at the beginning of *Apocalypse Now* (1979) signals that the film is an opera and says *Turandot* was his model for the bodies in the compound. The unforgettable use of the "Ride of the Valkyries" music from DIE WALKÜRE during the helicopter attack has helped make this scene one of the most memorable in all cinema. In *The Godfather III* (1990), the climax of the film revolves around a production of CAVALLERIA RUSTICANA at the Teatro Massimo opera house in Palermo. The Coppola name, appropriately, actually has an operatic history in Italy; Giuseppe and Pietro Coppola composed operas in Naples in the 18th and 19th centuries.

COQ D'OR, LE

See THE GOLDEN COCKEREL.

CORBIAU, GÉRARD
Belgian film director (1945–)

Gérard Corbiau wrote and directed three of the most interesting opera-oriented films of recent years after he spent time making TV music programs. LE MAÎTRE DE MUSIQUE (The Music Teacher) (1987) stars Belgian bass-baritone JOSÉ VAN DAM as a retired opera singer who becomes an extraordinary teacher for two young students. FARINELLI (1994) is the story of the famous 18th-century castrato and features vivid period reconstructions. LE ROI DANSE (The King Dances) (2000) is a portrayal of the life and achievement of the founder of French opera, Jean-Baptiste Lully. All three films have large amounts of opera music.

CORELLI, FRANCO
Italian tenor (1921–2003)

A cult has emerged around this Italian tenor in recent years, so there was real excitement when his 1958 San Carlo performance in LA FORZA DEL DESTINO with Renata Tebaldi and an all-star cast was released from Italian TV archives. The Modena-born tenor made his debut in 1951 in Spoleto in *Carmen* and sang widely around the world during the 1950s and 1960s. He had a special relationship with Maria Callas and often sang with her. He was a favorite at the Metropolitan Opera and sang 368 performances at the Met from 1961 through 1975. There are also videos of Corelli in concert, compiled by the Bel Canto Society, mostly off-air television tapings. See ANDREA CHÉNIER (1973), CAVALLERIA RUSTICANA (1963 film), TENORS (1997), and TOSCA (1956).

1959 Voice of Firestone
Corelli appeared on the *Voice of Firestone* television program on June 2, 1963, and sang three arias and two songs. The arias are the "Brindisi" and "Addio alla madre" from *Cavalleria rusticana* and "Non piangere, Liù" from *Turandot*. Wilfrid Pelletier conducts the Voice of Firestone Orchestra. Black and white. 35 minutes. VAI VHS titled *Renata Tebaldi and Franco Corelli*.

1962–1964 Bell Telephone Hour
The video collection *Corelli—Di Stefano—Vickers* showcases the three tenors as they appeared on the Bell Telephone Hour television show. Corelli sings an aria from *Tosca*, a duet with Lisa Della Casa from *Tosca*, and a duet from *Un ballo in maschera* with Régine Crespin. Donald Voorhees conducts the Bell Telephone Hour Orchestra. Color. 36 minutes. VAI VHS.

1971 Corelli in Concert
In this recital by Corelli taped in 1971 he performs arias from *L'Africana, Andrea Chénier, La bohème, Le Cid, La fanciulla del West,* and *Rigoletto*. Alberti Venturi conducts the orchestra. Color. 51 minutes. Bel Canto Society VHS.

1996 Corelli's Favorite Corelli
Compilation video by Stefan Zucker of performances Corelli himself liked includes numbers from *Aida, Carmen, Cavalleria rusticana, Il trovatore, Turandot,* and Verdi's *Requiem*. Color. 38 minutes. Bel Canto Society VHS.

CORIGLIANO, JOHN
American composer (1938–)

John Corigliano had real success with his first major opera, THE GHOSTS OF VERSAILLES. It premiered at the Metropolitan Opera in 1991 to critical praise, was a hit when telecast, is a consistent seller on video and LD, and has been revived by the Met. Corigliano had some success with earlier dramatic works. His 1970 *Naked Carmen* is based on the Bizet opera although it uses unusual instruments and singers and is available on record only. He also wrote the Oscar-nominated score for Ken Russell's film *Altered States* (1980) and the score for Hugh Hudson's film *Revolution* (1985).

CORNELIUS, PETER
German composer (1824–1874)

Peter Cornelius is not well known in the United States but holds an important position in the development of modern German opera. Liszt urged him to write his opera DER BARBIER VON BAGDAD and then conducted the premiere in 1858. It does not always help to have famous admirers, however; the premiere was a fiasco, Cornelius had to leave town, and the opera was not performed again until after his death when it became his most popular opera. Cornelius was also a close friend of Wagner, who encouraged him to write opera as well, and the result, *Der Cid,* had a successful premiere in 1865. His last opera, *Gunlöd,* was not completed when he died in 1874.

CORONATION OF POPPEA, THE

See L'INCORONAZIONE DI POPPEA.

CORSARO, FRANK

American director (1924–)

Frank Corsaro made his operatic debut at the New York City Opera in 1958 directing Floyd's *Susannah* and later staged the premieres of American operas by Floyd, Hoiby, and Pasatieri. Although he began naturalistically with the NYCO, he has become known for his brilliant staging of fantasy operas by Sendak, Prokofiev, Ravel, Humperdinck, and Janáček. See CARMEN (1984), THE CUNNING LITTLE VIXEN (1983), L'ENFANT ET LES SORTILÈGES (1987), HÄNSEL UND GRETEL (1997/1998), L'HEURE ESPAGNOLE (1987), HIGGLETY PIGGLETY POP! (1985), THE LOVE FOR THREE ORANGES (1982), MADAMA BUTTERFLY (1982), TREEMONISHA (1982), and WHERE THE WILD THINGS ARE (1985).

CORTE DE FARAÓN, LA

1910 zarzuela by Lleó

VICENTE LLEÓ's only famous zarzuela is *La corte de faraón* (The Court of the Pharaoh), set in ancient Egypt in the time of the Pharaohs and based on the biblical story of Joseph and Potiphar's wife. Its tone has some of the qualities of a Cecil B. De Mille film—sex and history mixed with vaudevillian grandeur—but the tone is much more satirical. *La corte de faraón* had censorship problems because of its risqué dialogue and scanty feminine costumes, and it has been banned at various times.

1985 Sánchez film
      Spanish feature film: José Luis García Sánchez (director/screenplay), Rafael Azcona (screenplay), José Luis Alcaine (cinematographer), Andrea d'Odorico (art director), Lince Films (production).
      Cast: Ana Belén, Fernando Fernán Gómez, Antonio Banderas, Josema Yuste, Agustín González, Mary Carmen Ramírez.
      Color. In Spanish. 96 minutes.
      Comment: This is a postmodern version of the zarzuela. An amateur company is performing it in Madrid in the late 1940s when a priest objects. Police stop the show and take the cast members to jail in their Egyptian costumes. While the police investigate, there are flashbacks of scenes from the zarzuela, and relationships within the company are explored. The actors are judged to be political agitators and are kept in prison.

CORTI, AXEL

Austrian film director (1933–)

Axel Corti, who was born in Paris but made his reputation directing film and theater in Austria, is known for movies such as *Welcome in Vienna* and *The Refusal.* He has included opera music in his films about Vienna and directed opera on film and stage. His 1976 production of Lortzing's ZAR UND ZIMMERMANN with Hermann Prey is on video.

COSÌ

1995 Australian film with opera content

This delightful Australian comedy about a therapeutic production of Mozart's *Così fan tutte* in a mental hospital is warmly humorous fun, almost an homage to the healing power of opera. A young first-time director (Ben Mendelsohn) is persuaded by a Mozart-mad inmate (Barry Otto) to stage *Così fan tutte* with a cast that includes a pyromaniac, a junkie, a nympho, a stutterer, and a knife-wielder. The accompaniment is played by a lithium-addicted pianist who hates Mozart. None of inmates can understand Italian, but they produce the opera anyway and actually succeed in a bizarre way. The fine cast includes Toni Collette, Rachel Griffiths, Colin Friels, Aden Young, Jacki Weaver, Pamela Rabe, Paul Chubb, and David Wenham with Greta Scacchi in a cameo appearance. Louis Nowra, who had written libretti for two operas, wrote the screenplay for the film, basing it on his stage play. Ellery Ryan was the cinematographer and Mark Joffe directed for Smiley Films. Distributed in the United States by Miramax. Color. In English. 100 minutes. Miramax VHS.

COSÌ FAN TUTTE

1790 opera by Mozart

Così fan tutte (literally, Thus Do All Women) looks slight at first sight, but it may well be MOZART's and librettist LORENZO DA PONTE's most complex opera. Unlike their other collaborations, it is an original story with only six characters. Everything is balanced and orderly (or so it seems), as it tells the tale of two men testing the love of their fiancées with the connivance of an old cynic and a chameleon-like servant. The opera went out of fashion during the 19th century because it was considered immoral, and it was not popular with filmmakers during the silent era, reflecting its unfashionable status at the time. Its revived reputation has resulted in many modern films and videos.

1951 Glyndebourne Festival

English stage production: Carl Ebert (director), Fritz Busch (conductor, London Philharmonic Orchestra and Glyndebourne Festival Chorus), Rolf Gérard (set designer).

Cast: Sena Jurinac (Fiordiligi), Alice Howland (Dorabella), Marko Rothemüller (Guglielmo), Richard Lewis (Ferrando), Sesto Bruscantini (Don Alfonso), Isa Quensel (Despina).

Telecast live by BBC Television. Black and white. In Italian. 140 minutes.

1958 NBC Opera Theatre

American TV production: Samuel Chotzinoff (producer), Peter Herman Adler (conductor, NBC Symphony of the Air Orchestra and Chorus), Ed Wittstein (set/costume designer), Ruth and Thomas Martin (English translation).

Cast: Phyllis Curtin (Fiordiligi), Frances Bible (Dorabella), Mac Morgan (Guglielmo), John Alexander (Ferrando), James Pease (Don Alfonso), Helen George (Despina).

Telecast live by NBC on April 6, 1958. Kirk Browning (director). Black and white. In English. 59 minutes.

1970 Kaslik film

Austrian feature film: Vaclav Kaslik (director), Karl Böhm (conductor, Vienna Philharmonic Orchestra and Chorus), Jan Stallich (cinematographer), Milos Ditrich (set designer), Beta Film (production).

Cast: Gundula Janowitz (Fiordiligi), Christa Ludwig (Dorabella), Olivera Miljakovic (Despina), Luigi Alva (Ferrando), Hermann Prey (Guglielmo), Walter Berry (Don Alfonso).

Color. In Italian. 159 minutes.

Comment: This is the earliest version of the opera on film, shot in baroque settings in eight scenes that are introduced by *commedia dell'arte* figures bearing captions and icons. It opened theatrically in New York on July 23, 1970.

1975 Glyndebourne Festival

English stage production: Adrian Slack (director), John Pritchard (conductor, London Philharmonic Orchestra and Glyndebourne Festival Chorus), Emanuele Luzzati (set designer).

Cast: Helena Döse (Fiordiligi), Sylvia Lindenstrand (Dorabella), Danièle Perriers (Despina), Thomas Allen (Guglielmo), Anson Austin (Ferrando), Franz Petri (Don Alfonso).

Video: VAI/Opera d'Oro VHS. Dave Heather (director). Color. In Italian with English subtitles. 150 minutes.

Comment: Traditional but quite enjoyable.

***1984 Drottningholm Court Theatre

Swedish stage production: Willy Decker (director), Arnold Östman (conductor, Drottningholm Court Theatre Orchestra and Chorus), Tobias Hoheisel (set/costume designer).

Cast: Anne Christine Biel (Fiordiligi), Maria Hoeglind (Dorabella), Magnus Linden (Guglielmo), Lars Tibell (Ferrando), Ulla Severin (Despina), Enzo Florimo (Don Alfonso).

Video: Thorn EMI VHS/Philips LD. Thomas Olofsson (director). Color. In Italian with English subtitles. 141 minutes.

Comment: Sheer delight, an effervescent but complex version of this multifaceted opera videotaped in an intimate 18th-century theater with the orchestra in period costumes playing authentic instruments. During the overture, the cast members are shown arriving by bus, bike, and foot, and this segues into the opening stage scene. There is nothing apparently dark about this production and its young cast, but appearances are deceptive; hidden under the charm is a good deal of Bergmanesque concern about the frailty of human beings.

1988 Ponnelle film

Austrian feature film: Jean-Pierre Ponnelle (director), Nikolaus Harnoncourt (conductor, Vienna Philharmonic Orchestra and Chorus), Wolfgang Treu (cinematographer).

Cast: Edita Gruberova (Fiordiligi), Delores Ziegler (Dorabella), Luis Lima (Ferrando), Ferruccio Furlanetto (Guglielmo), Teresa Stratas (Despina), Paolo Montarsolo (Don Alfonso).

Video: London VHS/LD. Color. In Italian with English subtitles. 178 minutes.

1989 Teatro alla Scala

Italian stage production: Michael Hampe (director), Riccardo Muti (conductor, Teatro alla Scala Orchestra and Chorus), Mauro Pagano (set/costume designer).

Cast: Daniela Dessi (Fiordiligi), Delores Ziegler (Dorabella), Josef Kundiak (Ferrando), Alessandro Corbelli (Guglielmo), Adelina Scarabelli (Despina), Claudio Desderi (Don Alfonso).

Video: Image Entertainment DVD/Home Vision VHS. Taped April 15, 1989. Ilio Catani (director). In Italian with English subtitles. 186 minutes.

Comment: Lavish, large-scale production, but this intimate opera seems lost on such a huge stage.

***1989 Sellars film

Austrian studio film: Peter Sellars (director), Craig Smith (conductor, Viennā Symphonic Orchestra and Arnold Schoenberg Choir), Adrianne Lobel (set designer), Dunya Ramicova (costume designer).

Cast: Susan Larson (Fiordiligi), Janice Felty (Dorabella), Frank Kelley (Ferrando), James Maddalena (Guglielmo), Sue Ellen Kuzma (Despina), Sanford Sylvan (Don Alfonso).

Color. London VHS/LD. In Italian with English subtitles. 184 minutes.

Comment: Sellars tries to give the opera contemporary relevance by setting it in a small-town diner called Despina's and the characters are modern in dress and attitude. The interpretation is bleak and the subtitles slangish, but the production is intelligent and well thought out, and it justifies its modernity. It was filmed in a Vienna television studio, but Sellars originated the concept at the Pepsico Summerfare Festival in Purchase, New York.

1990 Australian Opera

Australian stage production: Göran Järvefelt (director), Ross A. Perry (staging), Peter Robinson (conductor, Victoria State Orchestra and Australian Opera Chorus), Carl Friedrich Oberle (set/costume designer).

Cast: Yvonne Kenny (Fiordiligi), Fiona Janes (Dorabella), David Hobson (Ferrando), Jeffrey Black (Guglielmo), Rosamund Illing (Despina), John Pringle (Don Alfonso).

Video: Pioneer Artists LD. Peter Butler (director). Color. In Italian with English subtitles. 170 minutes.

***1992 Théâtre du Châtelet, Paris

French stage production: John Eliot Gardiner (director/conductor, English Baroque Soloists and Monteverdi Choir), Carlo Tommasi (set/costume designer).

Cast: Amanda Roocroft (Fiordiligi), Rosa Mannion (Dorabella), Rodney Gilfry (Guglielmo), Rainer Trost (Ferrando), Eirian James (Despina), Claudio Nicolai (Don Alfonso).

Video: DG Archiv DVD/VHS/LD. Peter Mumford (director). Color. In Italian with English subtitles. 193 minutes.

Comment: Outstanding direction and conducting by Gardiner, with an excellent cast.

1996 Metropolitan Opera

American stage production: Lesley Koenig (director), James Levine (conductor, Metropolitan Opera Orchestra and Chorus), Michael Yeargan (set/costume designer).

Cast: Carol Vaness (Fiordiligi), Susanne Mentzer (Dorabella), Jerry Hadley (Ferrando), Dwayne Croft (Guglielmo), Cecilia Bartoli (Despina), Thomas Allen (Don Alfonso).

Telecast December 30, 1996; taped February 27, 1996. Brian Large (director). Color. In Italian with English subtitles. 180 minutes.

Comment: Bartoli steals the limelight as a lively Despina in her Met debut.

2000 Zurich Opera

Swiss stage production: Jürgen Flimm (director), Nikolaus Harnoncourt (conductor, Zurich Opera House Orchestra and Chorus).

Cast: Cecilia Bartoli (Fiordiligi), Liliana Nikiteanu (Dorabella), Roberto Sacca (Ferrando), Oliver Widmer (Guglielmo), Agnes Baltsa (Despina), Carlos Chausson (Don Alfonso).

Video: Arthaus DVD (with behind-the-scenes documentary). Brian Large (director). Color. In Italian with English subtitles. 175 minutes

Comment: Flimm makes Don Alfonso a college philosophy professor and Ferrando and Guglielmo his students. The bet is a cold-blooded experiment.

Related films

1971 Sunday Bloody Sunday

There is a nice use of the trio "Soave sia il vento" in the British film *Sunday Bloody Sunday*. A love triangle ends when Murray Head decides to leave both Peter Finch and Glenda Jackson and go to America. Finch reacts by putting on a record of the trio sung by Pilar Lorengar, Yvonne Minton, and Barry McDaniel. This is, effectively, a Mozartian resolution, for it allows him to express his emotional best wishes for the trip without speaking. Joseph Losey directed. Color. In English. 110 minutes. On video.

1978 Portrait of Solti

The trio "Soave sia il vento" is used as ironic commentary in the TV documentary *Portrait of Solti*. It is played over grim newsreel scenes of German tanks rolling into Hungary at the beginning of World War II. Color and black and white. 60 minutes. On video.

1989 My Left Foot

Irish artist/cerebral palsy victim Christy Brown (Daniel Day-Lewis) plays the optimistic tenor aria "Un' aura amorosa" on his phonograph in this fine film directed by Jim Sheridan. Day-Lewis won an Oscar for his performance. Color. 103 minutes.

1992 Così fan tutte

Despite its title, this Italian film directed by Tinto Brass has very little to do with the opera; one Italian critic called it an insult to the memory of Mozart. Color. In Italian. 99 minutes

1995 Così

Fascinating Australian comedy about a production of *Così fan tutte* in a mental hospital. The inmates can't speak Italian but produce the opera anyway and actually succeed in an odd way. See Così.

2000 The House of Mirth

Music from *Così fan tutte* is featured several times in writer/director Terence Davies's fine adaptation of Edith Wharton's novel. Society folk enter a New York opera house on opening night in 1906 to the Overture (played by La Petite Bande). Ferrando's aria "La mia Dorabella" is heard as the heroine of the film, Lily (Gillian Anderson), leaves indiscreetly with a man and is observed by her lover. The trio "Soave sia il vento" is performed over an image of a New York country estate turning wintry as rain lashes a pond; the image dissolves into the warm, glowing water of the Mediterranean and a yacht carrying Lily. The music is performed by the Slovak Philharmonic Chorus. Color. 140 minutes.

2000 The Captive

Sisters Dorabella and Fiordiligi are heard performing a duet on the soundtrack of this Belgian movie, which is about an obsessive lover whose girlfriend may be involved in a lesbian relationship. Chantal Akerman directed. Color. 118 minutes.

COSSIRA, EMILE
French tenor (1854–1923)

Emile Cossira was one of the first opera singers to be both seen and heard on the movie screen. One of his most famous roles was as Romeo in the Gounod opera ROMÉO ET JULIETTE, and he was featured singing an aria from it in a pioneering sound film shown at the Paris Exhibition of 1900. Cossira was at the Paris Opéra from 1888 to 1891, sang the role of Romeo at Covent Garden in 1891, and was the first French Tristan in 1896. He was noted for the stylishness of his singing.

COSSOTTO, FIORENZA
Italian mezzo-soprano (1935–)

Fiorenza Cossotto, born among the rice paddies of Vercelli, made her debut at La Scala in 1957. She sang there regularly and was welcomed at the other major opera houses, from Covent Garden to Berlin. She made her debut at the Met in 1968 as Amneris, and American audiences also admired her fine singing. See ADRIANA LECOUVREUR (1976/1989), AIDA (1966/1981/1985),

CAVALLERIA RUSTICANA (1968), LA FAVORITA (1971), MOZART (1967), IL TROVATORE (1985), and VERDI REQUIEM (1967).

COSTA, MARIO (composer)
Italian composer (1858–1933)

Taranto-born composer Mario Costa, who began as a Neapolitan songwriter, first found success on stage with the 1909 light opera *Il Capitan Fracassa*. His greatest success, and one of the classics of the light opera genre in Italy, is SCUGNIZZA, first performed in 1922. It is still popular.

COSTA, MARIO (director)
Italian film director (1908–)

Director Mario Costa, who is credited with discovering Gina Lollobrigida, began his movie career in 1938 with a documentary based on the music of Respighi's *The Fountains of Rome*. After the war, he made a number of opera films, including a 1946 IL BARBIERE DI SIVIGLIA that spearheaded the postwar Italian opera film boom. His films usually featured the top Italian opera singers of the period, including a 1947 movie with GINO BECHI and the all-star FOLLIE PER L'OPERA (1948). His other opera films include L'ELISIR D'AMORE (1947), MANON LESCAUT (1955), and PAGLIACCI (1948).

COSTA, MARY
American soprano (1932–)

Mary Costa began her film career with *Marry Me Again* in 1953 and then married its director, Frank Tashlin. She made her opera debut in *The Bartered Bride* in Los Angeles in 1958, joined the San Francisco Opera company, and was invited to London in 1962 to sing Violetta at Covent Garden. She made her debut at the Metropolitan Opera in 1964 in the same role. Costa made four feature films and appeared on a 1963 *Voice of Firestone* TV program as Marguerite in FAUST. She played opera singer Jetty Treffz in the 1972 film *The Great Waltz*, based on a JOHANN STRAUSS pastiche operetta, and performed in a 1973 Canadian TV tribute to VICTOR HERBERT.

1953 Marry Me Again

Costa's first Hollywood film was a comedy directed by Frank Tashlin. It stars Robert Cummings as an aviator romancing beauty contest winner Marie Wilson. Costa plays Wilson's best friend. Black and white. 73 minutes.

1957 The Big Caper

Costa's second film was a crime drama directed by Robert Stevens. Costa and Rory Calhoun pose as a married couple in a town in order to set up a robbery. Life in the town reforms them, and they undo the planned crime. Black and white. 84 minutes.

1959 Sleeping Beauty

Costa won praise for giving voice to the princess in this Disney animated feature: "Mary Costa's rich and expressive voice for the title character gives substance and strength to it," noted *Variety;* "It is a stronger voice than Disney ordinarily uses and its choice was wise." The music was adapted by George Bruns from Tchaikovsky's *Sleeping Beauty* ballet, and Costa was particularly admired singing "Once Upon a Dream." The film is based on the Perrault version of the fairy tale. Clyde Geronimi directed. Color. 75 minutes. Disney VHS.

COTRUBAS, ILEANA
Romanian soprano (1939–)

Ileana Cotrubas made her debut in Bucharest in 1964 and quickly won recognition in the major opera houses. She sang Mimì at La Scala in 1975 and at the Met in 1977. Her voice has a truly touching quality in roles like Mimì and Violetta, and this is especially evident in the video of LA BOHÈME made at Covent Garden in 1982. Cotrubas retired from the opera stage in 1989, but she came back for special occasions, such as a Three Sopranos recital to challenge the tenors. See LES CONTES D'HOFFMANN (1981), DON CARLO (1985), LA GAZZA LADRA (1984), IDOMENEO (1982), METROPOLITAN OPERA (1983), A MIDSUMMER NIGHT'S DREAM (1981), LE NOZZE DI FIGARO (1973), GIACOMO PUCCINI (1989), RIGOLETTO (1977), SOPRANOS AND MEZZOS (1991), LA TRAVIATA (1981), VERONA (1988), WERTHER (1991), and DIE ZAUBERFLÖTE (1982).

COUNTERTENORS

The revival in popularity of countertenors (male altos), which began with England's Alfred Deller, continues apace with a widening number of roles and singers to fill them. Not only are countertenors prominent on video in the operas of Handel and other baroque composers, they can also been heard in modern operas written for them, including works by Britten and Glass. Countertenors with entries in this book include JAMES BOWMAN, MICHAEL CHANCE, PAUL ESSWOOD, JOCHEN KOWALSKI, and CHRISTOPHER ROBSON.

2000 Countertenors

David Thomas's documentary film *Countertenors,* made for the English television program *The South Bank Show,* takes a close look at the countertenor phenomenon. The featured performers are James Bowman, Michael Chance,

and Andreas Scholl. Color. In English. 60 minutes. Warner (GB) DVD (includes 70 minutes of singing not used in the TV film) and VHS.

COUPS DE ROULIS
1928 operetta by Messager

André Messager's operetta *Coups de Roulis* is a musical love story set on a warship, with echoes of *H.M.S. Pinafore.* Albert Willemetz's libretto, based on a novel by Maurice Larrouy, centers around Béatrice, who is loved by the ship's captain and a humble ensign, and Béatrice's government minister father Puy Pradal, who gets involved with an Egyptian actress named Sola Myrrhis.

1931 de la Cour film

French feature film: Jean de la Cour (director/screenplay), Paul Cotteret and Robert Le Febvre (cinematographers), Jean d'Eaubonne (set designer).

Cast: Max Dearly (Puy Pradel), Edith Manet (Béatrice), Lucienne Herval (Sola Myrrhis), Pierre Magnier (Commandant Gervil), Roger Bourdin (Ensign Kermao).

Black and white. In French. 115 minutes.

COWARD, NOËL
English composer (1899–1973)

Noël Coward is best known as a wit, playwright, song writer, entertainer, and musical comedy composer, but he also wrote a deliberately old-fashioned Viennese operetta. BITTER SWEET was inspired by Strauss's *Die Fledermaus,* and like its Viennese predecessor it has a gypsy song, "Zigeuner," and a big waltz, "I'll See You Again." Coward wrote both libretto and music.

COX AND BOX
1866 operetta by Sullivan

Sir Arthur Sullivan's operetta *Cox and Box, or the Long Lost Brothers,* was composed as a private entertainment before his collaboration with William S. Gilbert The libretto, by Francis C. Burnard, tells the farcical story of two men who share a rented room without knowing it. Cox works by day and Box works by night, and landlord Bouncer gets double rent for their room. They also share the same unwanted widow and turn out to be long lost brothers.

1939 NBC Television

NBC experimented with the new medium of television by presenting excerpts from *Cox and Box* in July 1939. There weren't many viewers as a TV set cost a small fortune at the time (around $800) and programming was limited to only a few hours a week.

1948 New York University Players

American TV production: Albert M. Greenfield (director/conductor, New York University Orchestra).

Cast: William Whalen (Cox), Stanley Weiler (Box), Earle Woodberry (Bouncer).

Telecast December 1, 1948, from WPIX, New York. Black and white. In English. 60 minutes.

Comment: Produced by students at New York University, with the music played by the university orchestra led by their professor, who also directed.

1982 Gilbert and Sullivan Collection series

English studio production: David Alden (director), Judith De Paul (producer), Alexander Faris (conductor, London Symphony Orchestra and Ambrosian Opera Chorus), Allan Cameron (set designer), George Walker (executive producer).

Cast: John Fryatt (Box), Russell Smythe (Cox), Tom Lawler (Bouncer).

Video: Braveworld (GB) VHS. Dave Heather (director). Color. In English. 55 minutes.

CRADLE WILL ROCK, THE
1937 "play in music" by Blitzstein

While workers struggle to organize in Steeltown, various groups end up at a night court. Prostitute Moll sings of her joy in finding a nickel when she had no money for food and condemns the society that condemns her, saying it's easy to be moralistic when you have plenty to eat. Labor organizer Larry Foreman explains how and why the cradle will rock. *The Cradle Will Rock,* MARC BLITZSTEIN's first major "play in music," was influenced by the Weill/Brecht political opera *The Threepenny Opera.* It was created after encouragement from Brecht, who was enthusiastic about "Nickel Under the Foot," which became the most popular left-wing aria in American opera. The premiere was almost blocked by the funders who, under political pressure, had the theater closed. Director ORSON WELLES simply moved cast and audience to the nearby Venice Theater, where the opera premiered June 16, 1937, with Blitzstein on stage playing piano. He was the only one there, as the union had warned the actors not to go on stage. Welles asked them to sing from seats in the auditorium instead, and Olive Stanton, who played Moll, was first. She sang the opening "Nickel" aria so movingly she inspired the others. The opera became famous and had a long and successful run. It has been revived many times.

1986 The Acting Company

American TV production: John Houseman (stage director), Bruce Minnix (TV director), Michael Barrett (pianist).

Cast: Patti LuPone (Moll), Randle Mell (Larry Foreman), Casey Biggs (Gus Polock), Mary Lou Rosato (Mrs. Mister), David Schramm (Mr. Mister), Michele-Denise Woods (Ella Hamer), Tim Robbins, James Harper, Charles Shaw-Robinson.

Telecast January 26, 1986, on WGBH for PBS. Bruce Minnix (director). Color. In English. 90 minutes.

Comment: TV version of a production staged in 1983 by Houseman and The Acting Company at the American Place Theatre in New York City. Tim Robbins had a small role.

1999 Cradle Will Rock

American feature film: Tim Robbins (director/screenplay), Jean-Yves Escoffier (cinematographer), Richard Hoover (set designer), Touchstone Pictures (production company).

Cast: Hank Azaria (Marc Blitzstein), Angus Macfadyen (Orson Welles), Emily Watson (Olive Stanton), Cary Elwes (John Houseman), Cherry Jones (Hallie Flanagan), Ruben Blades (Diego Rivera), John Cusack (Nelson Rockefeller), Joan Cusack (Hazel Huffman), Vanessa Redgrave (Countess LaGrange), Susan Sarandon (Margherita Sarfatti), John Turturro (Aldo Silvano), Olly Jean Harvey, Audra McDonald, Bill Murray, Eddie Vedder.

Video: Disney DVD/VHS. Color. In English. 134 minutes.

Comment: *Cradle Will Rock* is based on the premiere of the opera, but it also includes other 1930s political events, such as Mexican mural artist Diego Rivera's clash with Nelson Rockefeller. Watson sings "Moll's Song," Olly Jean Harvey sings "Nickel Under the Foot," Audra McDonald sings "Joe Worker," and Susan Sarandon and Eddie Vedder duet on "Croon-Spoon."

Related film

1967 Blitzstein's Cradle

Blitzstein's Cradle is a Camera Three TV program featuring scenes from the opera in recital form. Color. In English. 30 minutes. New York State Education Department VHS.

CREATION, THE

See DIE SCHÖPFUNG.

CRESPIN, RÉGINE

French soprano (1927–)

Régine Crespin, who was born in Marseilles and made her debut in 1950, began to sing at the Paris Opéra in 1951. She rose to international fame singing French and German operas and was particularly noted as the Marschallin and Sieglinde. She made her first appearance at the Metropolitan in 1962 and sang in a 1987 Met telecast of DIALOGUES DES CARMÉLITES. She had an affection for Offenbach, recorded many of his operettas, and sings in a 1981 Paris Opéra production of LA GRANDE-DUCHESSE DE GÉROLSTEIN. She was also a notable TOSCA and is seen in the role in the 1983 documentary *I Live for Art*. Crespin retired from the stage in 1991 and became a popular singing teacher. See also BELL TELEPHONE HOUR (1959–1966), FRANCO CORELLI (1962–1964), and THE MEDIUM.

1974 Régine Crespin Recital
Crespin gives a recital on French television with the Orchestre National de France conducted by Jean Doussard. The program includes works by Massenet, Wagner, and Berlioz. Yvonne Courson directed for INA (Institut National de l'Audiovisuel). Color. In French. 25 minutes.

1985 Tribute to Régine Crespin
This French TV documentary includes an interview with the singer and performance excerpts from *Ariadne auf Naxos, Tosca,* and *La Grand-Duchesse de Gérolstein.* She is also seen in rehearsals of *Die Walküre* with Herbert von Karajan. Color. In French. 88 minutes. Opera Dubs VHS.

2003 Régine Crespin
A collection of performances by Crespin taken from French TV archives and dating from 1964 to 1972. It includes excerpts from *Les Troyens, La damnation de Faust,* and *Les nuits d'eté,* plus songs by Schumann, Schubert, Poulenc, and others. 68 minutes. EMI Classics DVD.

CRISPINO E LA COMARE

1850 opera by Luigi and Federico Ricci

LUIGI AND FEDERICO RICCI's *Crispino e la comare* (Crispino and the Fairy) was one of the most successful comic operas in Italy in the 19th century. It's a fantasy about a poor cobbler who is saved from suicide by a fairy godmother. The fairy helps him realize his desire to be-

come a fashionable doctor, but then success goes to his head. In the end, she decides to change him back into a cobbler. The libretto by Francesco Maria Piave (who wrote nine librettos for Verdi, including *Rigoletto* and *La traviata*) sews medical satire and buffo fun onto infectious melodies. Crispino's wife Annetta has a memorable aria, "Io non sono più l'Anneta," a favorite of Galli-Curci and Tetrazzini and sung on video by Joan Sutherland. Its famous buffo trio, sung by arguing doctors, was made into a sound film in Italy in 1910.

1989 Savona Festival
Italian stage production: Paolo Carignani (conductor, San Remo Symphony Orchestra and Francesco Cilea Chorus).

Cast: Roberto Coviello (Crispino), Daniele Lojarro (Annetta), Simone Alaimo (Fabrizio), Antonio Marani (Mirabolano), Serena Lazzarini (Fairy).

Video: House of Opera/Lyric VHS. Color. In Italian. 100 minutes.

Comment: This is the only modern video of this rare opera, but it's a nonprofessional version shot from the audience. A CD is available of the same Savona production.

Early/related films

1910 Itala Film sound films
Three numbers from the opera were filmed and recorded by Itala Film of Turin in 1910 and were screened in cinemas as synchronized sound films. The three were "Una volta un ciabattino...," "Vuoi tornare...," and "Terzetto dei Dottori." Black and white. In Italian. Each about 3 minutes. No prints are known.

1918 De Riso film
Camillo De Riso directs and plays Crispino in *Crispino e la comare,* an Italian feature film made for the Ambrosio Studio. Also in the cast are Emma Saredo as Annetta, Carlo Benetti, Olga Benetti, and Lea Giunchi. Black and white. Silent. About 50 minutes.

1938 Sorelli film
Ugo Céresi plays Crispino in this Italian film based on the opera and using its music as soundtrack. Silvana Jachino is the Marchesina, Mario Pisu is the young painter, and Guglielmo Sinaz is the doctor. Piero Pupilli was cinematographer and Vincenzo Sorelli directed for Caesar Film. Black and white. In Italian. 72 minutes.

1967 Joan Sutherland aria
Joan Sutherland sings the aria "Io non sono più l'Annetta" from the opera on *The Bell Telephone Hour* with Orchestra and Chorus led by Donald Voorhees. The

performance is on the VAI DVD *Joan Sutherland—Complete Bell Telephone Hour Performances* and on the VAI VHS *First Ladies of the Opera*.

CRISTÓBAL COLÓN
1989 opera by Balada

LEONARDO BALADA's opera *Cristóbal Colón* (Christopher Columbus), libretto by A. Gala, tells the story of Columbus's voyage to America in flashbacks. The opera, composed to mark the 500th anniversary of the journey, features a range of music styles, from Catalan and Andalusian tunes to Native American elements. It was well received by critics at its Barcelona premiere when José Carreras and Montserrat Caballé sang the principal roles of Columbus and Queen Isabella.

1989 Gran Teatre del Liceu
Spanish stage production: M. Alcantara (conductor, Gran Teatre de Liceu Orchestra).

Cast: José Carreras (Columbus), Montserrat Caballé (Queen Isabella), Victoria Vergara, Carlos Chausson.

Video: House of Opera DVD and VHS /Lyric and Opera Dubs VHS. Taped live at the September 24, 1989, premiere. Color. In Spanish. 118 minutes.

CRITICS, THE
1998 British documentary with opera content

The four-part British TV documentary *The Critics* includes one section devoted to London opera critics Martin Hoyle, David Fingleton, Tom Sutcliffe, Rodney Milnes, and Hugh Canning. According to the film, opera critics are very passionate and opinionated, even about what other opera critics write and might not speak to each other for years if they disagree. It seems, however, that opera critics are less feared than other critics because their reviews are often not read until the production has finished its run. Jon Ronson made the documentary for Channel 4. Color. In English. 60 minutes.

CSÁRDÁSFÜRSTIN, DIE
1915 operetta by Kálmán

Die Csárdásfürstin (The Gypsy Princess) is EMMERICH KÁLMÁN's most successful and enduring operetta. A Budapest cabaret singer named Sylva is in love with a German prince named Edwin. They face a lot of problems, but after much confusion, love wins out. In the course of the story Sylva becomes known as the Gypsy Princess. The operetta arrived in America in 1917 as *The Riviera Girl* in an adaptation by P. G. Wodehouse and Guy Bolton, with new songs by Jerome Kern. It was staged in London in 1921 as *The Gipsy Princess*. It has been filmed many times in German, Hungarian, and Russian. The Hungarian title is *Csárdáskirályno*.

1934 Jacoby film
German feature film: Georg Jacoby (director), Hans H. Zerlett and B. E. Lüthge (screenplay), Hans-Otto Borgmann (music director), Carl Hoffmann (cinematographer), UFA Film (production).

Cast: Marta Eggerth (Sylva), Hans Söhnker (Prince Edwin), Paul Kemp, Inge List.

Video: House of Opera/Lyric Opera Dubs/BMG (Germany) VHS. Black and white. In German. 95 minutes.

Comment: There is a memorable performance of the "Swallow Song" in an elevator.

1934 Princesse Czardas
French feature film: André Beucler and George Jacoby (directors), Hans H. Zerlett and B. E. Lüthge (screenplay), Hans-Otto Borgmann (music director), Carl Hoffmann (cinematographer), UFA Film (production).

Cast: Meg Lemonnier (Sylva), Jacques Pills (Prince Edwin), Lyne Clevers (Countess Stasi), Marcel Vibert, Lucien Dayle, Marfa Dhervilly.

Black and white. In French. 85 minutes.

Comment: This is the French version of the Jacoby German film listed above and was shot at the same time.

1951 Jacoby film
German feature film: George Jacoby (director), Willy Mattes (music director), B. E. Lüthge (screenplay), Bruno Mondi (cinematographer), Styra Film (production company).

Cast: Marika Rökk (Sylva), Johannes Heesters (Prince Edwin), Franz Schafheitlin (Leopold), Hubert Marsischka (Feri).

Color. In German. 94 minutes.

Comment: Jacoby returned to the operetta to film it in color.

1971 Szinetár film
Hungarian feature film: Miklós Szinetár (director), Bert Grund (conductor, Graunke Symphony and Zigeuner Orchestras and Choruses), Thomas Vayer (set designer), Mafilm (production company).

Cast: Anna Moffo (Sylva), René Kollo (Prince Edwin), Dagmar Koller (Countess Stasi), Zoltan Latinovits (Miska), Sándor Németh, Irén Psota.

Color. In Hungarian. 97 minutes.

Comment: Released in America as *The Czardas Queen*.

1990 Australian Opera

Australian stage production: Brian Douglas (director), Richard Bonynge (conductor, Australian Opera Orchestra and Chorus), Kenneth Powell (set designer).

Cast: Deborah Riedel (Sylva), Anson Austin (Prince Edwin), Roxane Hislop (Countess Stasi), Roger Lemke (Count Boni).

Video: House of Opera VHS. Virginia Lumsden (director). Taped July 25, 1990. Color. In English. 120 minutes.

1991 Mörbisch Seefestspiele

Austrian stage production: Sandor Nemeth (director), Kataline Varadi (conductor, Seefestspiele Mörbisch Chorus and Orchestra), Pantelis Dessyllas (set designer), Lazlo Pethö (choreographer).

Cast: Sona Ghazarian (Sylva), Michael Roider (Prince Edwin), Gaby Bischof (Countess Stasi), Karl Dönch (Leopold), Budapest State Opera ballet.

Video: ORF (Austria) VHS. Sylvia Dönch (director). Color. In German. 67 minutes.

Comment: Opulent, large-scale outdoor production with a formidable cast of dancers.

1992 La Principessa della Czarda

Italian stage production: Sandro Massimini (director), Roberto Negri (conductor, theater orchestra), Umberto Di Nino (set designer), Don Lurio (choreographer).

Cast: Sonia Dorigo (Sylva), Edoardo Guarnera (Prince Edvino), Sandro Massimini (Count Boni), Gabriele Villa (Miska), Vincenzo De Angelis (Feri).

Video: Ricordi (Italy) VHS. G. F. Principe and Pier Luigi Pagano (directors). Color. In Italian. 121 minutes.

Early films

1919 Leyde film

Ida Russka stars as the Gypsy Princess in this Austrian feature film of the operetta written and directed by Emil Leyde. The cast includes Max Brod, Karl Bachmann, and Susanne Bachrich. Black and white. Silent. About 70 minutes.

1927 Schwarz film

Liane Haid is the Csardas Princess in this elaborate German/Hungarian feature film of the operetta. The music was played live with the film in theaters. Ladislaus Vajda and Wilhelm Thiele wrote the screenplay; Hans Schwarz directed. Black and white. Silent. 85 minutes.

CUNNING LITTLE VIXEN, THE
1924 opera by Janáček

LEOŠ JANÁČEK's Czechoslovakian opera *The Cunning Little Vixen* (*Příhody Lišky Bystroušky* in Czech) takes place in a netherworld between reality and fantasy, with its principal characters both animals and people. Janáček based the libretto on a tale by Rudolf Těsnohlídek that tells the story of Vixen Sharp-Ears and the Forester who captures her. After she escapes, mates with the Fox, and has cubs, she is killed by a poacher.

1965 Komische Oper, Berlin

German studio production: Walter Felsenstein (TV and stage director), Vaclav Neumann (conductor, Komische Oper Orchestra and Chorus), Rudolf Heinrich (set designer).

Cast: Imgart Arnold (Vixen Sharp-Ears), Rudolf Asmus (Forester), Manfred Hopp (Fox), Ruth Schob-Lipka (Forester's Wife), Werner Enders (Schoolmaster).

Video: Dreamlife (Japan) VHS/LD. Telecast April 18, 1965, on DFF, Berlin. Black and white. In German. 104 minutes.

Comment: Felsenstein re-created his Komische Oper production in a Berlin TV studio. Asmus was noted for his performances as the Forester.

1983 New York City Opera

American stage production: Frank Corsaro (director), Scott Bergeson (conductor, New York City Opera Orchestra and Chorus), Maurice Sendak (set/costume designer), Jessica Redel (choreographer).

Cast: Gianna Rolandi (Vixen Sharp-Ears), Richard Cross (Forester), Nadia Pelle (Fox), Beverly Evans (Forester's Wife), John Lankston (Schoolmaster).

Video at the NYPL. Telecast November 9, 1983, in the *Live From Lincoln Center* series. Kirk Browning (director). Color. In English. 100 minutes.

Comment: The fairy tale sets and costumes created by Sendak enchanted audiences and critics.

***1995 Théâtre du Châtelet, Paris

French stage production: Nicholas Hytner (director), Sir Charles Mackerras (conductor, Orchestre de Paris and Chorus), Bob Crowley (set/costume designer) Jean-Claude Gallotta (choreographer).

Cast: Eva Jenis (Vixen Sharp-Ears) Thomas Allen (Forester), Jan Minutillo, Libuše Márova, Ivan Kusnjer, Josef Hajna, Richard Novak, Jean-Philippe Marlière, Sarah Connolly, Florence Bonnafous.

Video: Image Entertainment/Arthaus (GB) DVD. Brian Large (director). Color. In Czech with English subtitles. 98 minutes.

Comment: Excellent dance scenes, convincing performances, fine singing, and a memorable production by Hytner.

2003 Dunbar animated film
English animated film: Geoff Dunbar (director), Kent Nagano (conductor, New London Children's Choir, BBC Singers and Deutsches Symphony Orchestra).

Cast: Christine Buffle (Vixen Sharp-Ears) Grant Doyle (Forester), Richard Coxon (Fox), Keel Watson (Harašta), Matt Baker (Dog), Richard Robert (Cock), Andrew Foster-Williams (Badger).

Video: BBC Opus Arte DVD. Color. In Czech with English subtitles. 75 minutes.

Comment: Excellent condensed animated version of the opera based on the newspaper strip drawings by Czech painter Stranislaw Lolek that inspired Janáček to compose the opera. It looks wonderful but its seriously cut.

CURA, JOSÉ
Argentine tenor (1962–)

José Cura, one of the most popular new tenors on the international opera scene (he was once dubbed the "fourth tenor"), acquired new admirers when he sang the role of Alfredo in the live LA TRAVIATA telecast from Paris in 2000. He made his stage debut in 1992 in Verona in Henze's *Pollicino*, his American debut in 1995 in Chicago in *Fedora*, and his London debut the same year in *Stiffelio*. His first CD consisted of tenor arias from Puccini operas, and he has participated in television programs about GIACOMO PUCCINI (2000) and GIUSEPPE VERDI (2001). His other operas on video include IRIS (1985), TOSCA (2000), and IL TROVATORE (2002).

CURLEW RIVER
1964 church opera by Britten

A madwoman asks a ferryman to take her across the Curlew River to a child's grave that has become a shrine; she think it is the grave of her son who was stolen from her. When his ghost appears, she is restored to sanity. Benjamin Britten's *Curlew River*, a "parable for church performance" with libretto by William Plomer, was inspired by a Japanese Noh play. It has an all-male cast and is performed as if it were being presented by medieval monks. It premiered in Orford Church in Suffolk with Peter Pears as the madwoman and has been televised.

1998 Birmingham Touring Opera
British TV studio production: Karen Whiteside (TV director), Toby Wilsher (stage director), Simon Hal-sey (conductor, Birmingham Contemporary Music Group), Teresa McCann (set/costume designer, based on Wilsher's stage designs).

Cast: Neill Archer, Jeremy Huw Williams, Quentin Hayes, Matthew Best.

Telecast: Karen Whiteside (director). Color. In English. 80 minutes.

Comment: BBC Wales Television production, based on a stage production created by Wilsher for the City of Birmingham Touring Opera. It was shot mostly in a London studio, with some location filming in Hampshire.

1998 Aix-en-Provence Festival
French TV production: Mathias Ledoux (TV director), Yoshi Oida (stage director), David Stern (conductor, The European Academy of Music).

Cast: Michael Bennett, Jussi Järvenpää, Andrew Rupp, Jachi Yang, Ulas Inan Inac, Kim Tal, Fernando Cobo, Nicolas Bauchau.

Telecast in 1998. Mathias Ledoux (director). Color. In English. 70 minutes.

Comment: Based on a stage production created by Japanese director Yoshi Oida for the Aix-en-Provence Opera Festival. It emphasizes the Noh play origins of the opera.

CURTIZ, MICHAEL
Hungarian-born American film director (1888–1962)

Michael Curtiz, whose *Casablanca* is one of the icons of the American cinema, began his career in his native Hungary in 1912. In his early years he made several opera-related movies in Hungary and Austria. They included films of Flotow's MARTHA in 1913, Wedekind's LULU in 1918, Lehár's DIE LUSTIGE WITWE in 1918, and Suppé's BOCCACCIO in 1920. In Hollywood he filmed Friml's THE VAGABOND KING (1956). His 1938 film *The Adventures of Robin Hood* was partially based on the REGINALD DE KOVEN light opera *Robin Hood*.

CYRANO DE BERGERAC
1913 opera by Damrosch

American composer WALTER DAMROSCH was one of the most influential figures in American music in the first half of the century as conductor and composer. His opera *Cyrano de Bergerac*, which uses Edmund Rostand's play as libretto, was premiered at the Metropolitan Opera on February 27, 1913. It was well received but was considered overly long and is no longer in the repertory.

1922 Genina film

Italian director Augusto Genina based his 1922 film *Cirano di Bergerac* on the Rostand play and followed the original exactly like Damrosch. When the silent film came to America in 1925, the Damrosch score was considered the perfect accompaniment. The film opened at the Colony Theater, accompanied by music from the Damrosch opera, and won praise from critics. Pierre Magnier plays Cyrano de Bergerac, with Linda Moglia as Roxanne and Angelo Ferrari as Christian. Black and white. In Italian. About 95 minutes.

CZINNER, PAUL

Hungarian opera film director (1890–1972)

Paul Czinner, one of the most notable opera film pioneers, began making movies in Austria in 1919 and moved his cinema career to England and America after the Nazis came to power. He was married to actress Elisabeth Berger, who starred in many of his films, including *Catherine the Great* and *As You Like It*. He turned to ballet and opera films in the 1950s. His 1954 Salzburg Festival DON GIOVANNI is one of the earliest complete operas filmed in performance on stage and was a harbinger of the multi-camera live TV operas of the future. In 1960, he filmed DER ROSENKAVALIER at Salzburg, preserving a classic performance by Elisabeth Schwarzkopf. He also made a short film about SALZBURG.

D

DAISI
1923 opera by Paliashvili

Daisi (Twilight), the second opera of Georgian composer ZAKHARY PALIASHVILI, became the first Georgian opera staged in Georgia when it premiered at the Georgia National Opera House in Tbilisi in 1923. V. Guniya's libretto, based on Georgian poems, is a romantic and highly patriotic folk legend set in 18th-century Georgia. Two men are rivals for a woman during a period when the country is being attacked by a foreign power. Love and patriotism are intertwined.

1966 Sanishvili film
Georgian feature film: Nikolai Sanishvili (director), Dudar Margiev (cinematographer), Djansug Charkviani and Valeriano Tunia (assistants), Gruzia Film (production company).

Singers: Medea Amiramashvili, Tamara Gurgenidze, Zurab Andjaparidze.

Actors: Nana Kipiani, Dahli Tushishvili, Otar Koberidze, Kartolso Miradishvili

Color. In Georgian. 73 minutes.

Comment: The film stresses the necessity of struggling against foreign invaders, even in the midst of a love affair. The Georgian actors seen on the screen are dubbed by Georgian opera singers.

DALIBOR
1868 opera by Smetana

BEDŘICH SMETANA's opera *Dalibor*, which occupies a place in Czechoslovakia comparable to that of *Fidelio* in Germany, expresses similar patriotic ideas about national freedom. Josef Wenzig's libretto also has a story reminiscent of the Beethoven opera but without the happy ending. Dalibor is in prison for attacking a castle and killing a high official. Milada, the sister of that official, has fallen in love with Dalibor. She disguises herself as a boy musician to get into the prison and dies in an attempt to rescue him. So does he.

1956 Krska film
Czech feature film: Vaclav Krska (director).

Cast: Karel Fiala (Dalibor, sung by Beno Blachut), Vera Heroldava (Milada, sung by Milada Šubrtová), Jana Ryabarova (Jitka, sung by Libuše Domaninska), Karel Bednar (King).

Black and white. In Czech. 92 minutes.

Comment: Czech actors portray the characters on screen, with singing dubbed by Czech opera singers.

DAL MONTE, TOTI
Italian soprano (1893–1975)

Toti Dal Monte, once proclaimed by Melba as her successor, remains a major cult figure for opera enthusiasts in Italy, and her records are still popular. Dal Monte made her debut in 1916 at La Scala and in 1924 sang Lucia and Gilda at the Metropolitan Opera. She starred in four Italian films, one of which is available on an American video.

1940 Il carnevale di Venezia
Critics thought the best thing about *The Venice Carnival* was Dal Monte's singing of arias from *Lucia di Lammermoor* and *La sonnambula*. She plays a retired opera singer whose daughter is supposed to sing for the Carnival. When the daughter panics, the mother sings instead. Giacomo Gentilomo and Giuseppe Adami directed. Black and white. In Italian. 68 minutes.

1944 Fiori d'arancio
Orange Blossoms, Dal Monte's second movie, was made in Venice at the end of 1944 during wartime chaos, and few people saw it. It was based on a play by André Birabeau and directed by the journalist Dino Hobbes Checchini. Black and white. In Italian. 70 minutes.

1949 Il vedovo allegro
The Merry Widower, written and directed by Mario Mattoli, features Dal Monte in a supporting role, but she does get to sing. The film has a slight story about a revue performer. Black and white. In Italian. 90 minutes.

1954 Cuore di mamma
Dal Monte plays a retired opera singer in her last film, *Heart of a Mother,* and gets her final chance to sing on screen. The simple plot revolves around love complications after false accusations about a jewel theft. Luigi Capuano directed. Black and white. In Italian. 87 minutes. Bel Canto Society VHS.

DAMNATION DE FAUST, LA
1846 légende dramatique by Berlioz

Aging scholar Faust sells his soul to Méphistophélès for youth, love, and glory and ends up betraying Marguerite, the woman he loves. He goes to Hell and she goes to Heaven. HECTOR BERLIOZ based the libretto of his dramatic cantata *La damnation de Faust* (The Damnation of Faust) on Goethe's *Faust*. He did not originally intend it for the stage, but he later had plans to adapt it for an English opera company. That didn't happen, but there still have been many attempts to stage it.

1985 Opera Company of Philadelphia
American stage production: Bernard Uzan (director), Serge Baudo (conductor, Opera Company of Philadelphia Orchestra and Germantown Friends School Choir), Mark Morton (set designer).

Cast: Nadine Denize (Marguerite), Curtis Ryan (Faust), James Morris (Méphistophélès), Jules Bastin (Brander).

Telecast by PBS March 30, 1986. Alan Skog (director). Color. 150 minutes.

1989 Royal Albert Hall, London
English concert production: Sir Georg Solti (conductor, Chicago Symphony Orchestra and Chorus).

Cast: Anne Sofie von Otter (Marguerite), Keith Lewis (Faust), José van Dam (Méphistophélès), Peter Rose (Brander).

Video: London VHS. Taped August 28, 1989. Rodney Greenberg (director). Color. In French. 133 minutes.

1998 Royal Albert Hall, London
English concert production: Caroline Speed (BBC producer), Andrew Davies (conductor, BBC Symphony Orchestra, Chorus, and Singers).

Cast: David Rendall, Bryn Terfel, Ann Murray, Donald Maxwell.

Telecast on BBC July 17, 1998. Robert Coles (director). Color. In French. 140 minutes.

***1999 Salzburg Festival
Austrian stage production: Alex Olle and Carlos Padrissa (directors), Silvain Cambreling (conductor, Berlin Staatskapelle, San Sebastian Orfeón Donostiarra, and Tölzer Knabenchor), Jaume Plenso (set/costume designer).

Cast: Vesselina Kasarova (Marguerite), Paul Groves (Faust), Willard White (Méphistophélès), Andreas Macco (Brander), La Fura dels Baus theater company.

Video: Naxos/Arthaus DVD. Alexandra Tarta (director). Taped August 25, 1999. Color. In French with English subtitles. 146 minutes.

Comment: The avant-garde Catalan theater company La Fura dels Baus reimagine the story as a science fiction tale. This innovative production, staged with visual pyrotechnics, won a Gramophone Award. It is not just theatrically surprising, it is also finely sung and acted.

Early/related films

1898 Damnation de Faust
Damnation de Faust is an early George Méliès film of the opera, the predecessor of the much longer and more ambitious film he made in 1903. Black and white. Silent. About 1 minute.

1903 Faust aux Enfers, ou La damnation de Faust
French film pioneer George Méliès created his epic adaptation of the Berlioz opera *Faust aux Enfers, ou La damnation de Faust* in 1903. It was considered epic because of its extreme length (9 minutes) and 15 spectacular tinted scenes, with much of the film devoted to Faust being taken to Hell after the death of Marguerite. Méliès himself plays Méphistophélès. Shown in the United States as *The Damnation of Faust*. Tinted color. Silent. About 9 minutes.

1992 The Ride to the Abyss
Swiss animator Georges Schwitzgebel's expressionistic animated version of scenes from the opera featuring the Berlioz music. Color. 10 minutes.

1992 L'Affaire Faust
French animator Jacques Houdin created this updated version of the Faust story using the Berlioz music for its soundtrack. Color. 5 minutes.

DAMROSCH, WALTER
American composer/conductor (1862–1950)

Walter Damrosch, who was born in Germany but spent most of his life in the United States, was an influential figure in American music as both composer and conductor. He wrote four operas, two of which were produced at the Metropolitan Opera, CYRANO DE BERGERAC (1913) and *The Man Without a Country* (1937). They were well received but have not remained in the repertory. He directed the Damrosch Opera Company in New York from 1894 to 1899, presenting German operas in competition with the Italian and French operas at the Met.

DANCING YEARS, THE
1939 operetta by Novello

IVOR NOVELLO's charming 1939 operetta *The Dancing Years,* lyrics by Christopher Hassall, is set in Vienna in 1910. Composer Rudi Kleber meets and falls in love with operetta star Maria Ziegler, who persuades her lover Prince Charles to help Kleber get his operetta *Lorelei* staged. They live together for a while, but his involvement with another woman causes a break, and she marries the prince. Many years later Maria reveals that Kleber is the father of her son. Novello played Rudi in the stage production with former Met star Mary Ellis as Maria.

1950 French film
British feature film: Harold French (director), Warwick Ward and Jack Whittingham (screenplay), Louis Levy (music director), Frank Staff (choreographer), Associated British Pictures (production company).

Cast: Dennis Price (Rudi), Gisèle Préville (Maria, sung by Vanessa Lee), Anthony Nicholls (Prince), Patricia Dainton (Grete), Olive Gilbert (Frau Kurt).

Color. In English 97 minutes.

DANGEROUS LIAISONS, THE
1994 opera by Susa

Decadent sexuality and seductive power games in the 18th century revolve around the aristocratic rake Valmont and the manipulative Marquise de Merteuil. Valmont's dangerous seductions of Cecile de Volanges and Madame de Tourvel lead to love and tragedy. CONRAD SUSA's three-hour opera *The Dangerous Liaisons,* libretto by Philip Littell based on the 1782 epistolary novel *Les liaisons dangereuses* by Pierre Choderlos de Laclos, premiered at San Francisco Opera on September 10, 1994, and was televised but not issued on video. The opera maintains the wit and style of the novel, although the libretto was probably influenced by three early films based on the book.

1994 San Francisco Opera
American stage production: Colin Graham (director), Donald Runnicles (conductor, San Francisco Opera Orchestra and Chorus), Gerard Howland (set/costume designer).

Cast: Thomas Hampson (Valmont), Frederica von Stade (Merteuil), Renée Fleming (Mme. de Tourvel), Judith Forst (Madame de Volanges), Mary Mills (Cecile de Volanges), David Hobson (Chevalier de Danceny), Johanna Meier (Madame de Rosemond).

Telecast October 17, 1994. Gary Halvorson (director). Color. In English. 150 minutes.

Related films

1959 Vadim film
Roger Vadim's *Les liaisons dangereuses* is an updated French version of the story. Gérard Philippe plays Valmont, with Jeanne Moreau as his intrigue-spinning partner, Annette Stroyberg as Tourvel, Jeanne Valérie as Cecile, and Jean-Louis Trintignant as Danceny. Black and white. In French. 105 minutes.

1988 Frears film
Stephen Frears's film *Dangerous Liaisons* is based on Christopher Hampton's stage play, an adaptation of the novel. John Malkovich is Valmont with Glenn Close as Merteuil, Michelle Pfeiffer as Tourvel, Uma Thurman as Cecile, and Keanu Reeves as Danceny. Color. In English. 120 minutes.

1989 Forman film
In Milos Forman's *Valmont,* scripted by Jean-Claude Carriere, Colin Firth plays Valmont with Annette Bening as Merteuil, Meg Tilly as Tourvel, Fairuza Balk as Cecile, and Jeffrey Jones in the Danceny role. Color. In English. 137 minutes.

DANZA DELLE LIBELLULE, LA
1916/1922 operetta by Lehár/Lombardo

FRANZ LEHÁR's operetta was first staged in German in 1916 in Vienna, where it was called *Der Sterngucker* and told the story of an astronomer involved with three women. It was a failure. It was an even bigger failure in English in New York in 1917, where it was staged as *The Star Gazer*. It was saved from extinction when it was translated into Italian and revised by Italian entrepreneur CARLO LOMBARDO. He worked with Lehár to transform it into the Italian operetta *La danza delle libellule* (The Dance of the Dragonflies), which premiered in Milan in 1922. In the new libretto, the protagonist is a duke in search of a wife (he finally decides on a widow), and there are elaborate dances. This version was a hit, especially for the song "Gigolettes," and it returned to Vienna in its new form as *Libellentanz*. It was then staged in England in 1924 as *The Three Graces* and revived in Milan in 1926 as *Gigolette*.

1990 Milano Theater
Italian stage production: Sandro Massimini (director), Roberto Negri (conductor, theater orchestra), Umberto Di Nino (set designer), Don Lurio (choreographer).

Cast: Edoardo Guarnera (Duke of Nancy), Simona Bertini (Elena, widow Cliquot), Sandro Massimini (Bouquet Blum), Annalena Lombardi (Tutù Gratin), Donatella Zapelloni (Carlotta Pommery), Gabriele Villa (Piper), Giorgio Valente (Gratin).

Video: Ricordi (Italy) VHS. Color. In Italian. 112 minutes.

1992 Italian TV: Operette, che Passione!

Italian TV production: Sandro Massimini (director, producer, host), Roberto Negri (pianist), Sandro Corelli (choreographer).

Cast: Sandro Massimini, Daniela Mazzucato, Max René Cosotti.

Video: Pierluigi Pagano (director). Color. In Italian. About 19 minutes. Ricordi (Italy) VHS.

Comment: Highlights and history of the operetta on the Italian TV series *Operette, che Passione!* Includes songs "Gigolettes," "Neve e gel," and "Entrata di Carlo."

DA PONTE, LORENZO
Italian librettist (1749–1838)

Lorenzo Da Ponte, who wrote some of the most beautiful words in opera for MOZART, is deservedly one of the best known of opera librettists as the Da Ponte–Mozart operas stand on an operatic peak all their own. Surprisingly, Da Ponte has been mostly ignored in the many Mozart film biographies, including *Amadeus*. His highly enjoyable *Memoirs* make his life seem fictional, even if it actually happened. Born Emmanuele Conegliano (his father was Jewish but converted to Christianity), he borrowed his name from the Bishop of Ceneda, was ordained a priest, and then was exiled from Venice for womanizing and politics. He had a gift for poetry and soon became chief librettist at the Austrian court, writing popular operas for SALIERI, Martín y Soler, and Mozart, often simultaneously. His mistress Adriana Ferrarese was the first Fiordiligi. After he left Vienna, he moved on to Paris and London and finally to New York; he taught at Columbia University and became an opera impresario. He is buried in New York. His enduring memorials are the Mozart operas COSÌ FAN TUTTE, DON GIOVANNI, and LE NOZZE DI FIGARO.

DARDANUS
1784 opera

Antonio Sacchini's *Dardanus* revolves around the adventures of Dardanus, founder of the royal house of Troy, and describes how he won his wife Iphise from his rival Antenor. The libretto by Nicolas-François Guillard is based on a libretto used by Jean-Philippe Rameau for his 1739 version of the story.

1995 Jefferson in Paris

Sacchini's *Dardanus* was a big success when Thomas Jefferson was living in Paris, so it is justifiably featured in the 1995 film *Jefferson in Paris*. Director James Ivory includes an elaborate re-creation of the Paris staging with dancing and singing. Jean-Paul Fouchécourt is Dardanus, Sophie Daneman is Iphise, and William Christie conducts Les Arts Florissants orchestra. The opera house is the setting for the return of Jefferson (Nick Nolte) to Maria Cosway (Greta Scacchi). Color. 139 minutes.

DARGOMIZHSKY, ALEXANDER
Russian opera composer (1813–1869)

Alexander Dargomizhsky, the first important Russian opera composer after Glinka, is known for three operas. The first was *Esmeralda*, based on a novel by Victor Hugo. Second was *Rusalka*, based on a poem by Pushkin, and it became a favorite of Russian singers such as Chaliapin. Dargomizhsky's last opera, THE STONE GUEST, a variation on the Don Giovanni story based on a Pushkin poem, is his masterpiece and is still in the Russian repertory. A Soviet film of *The Stone Guest* was distributed internationally.

DAUGHTER OF THE REGIMENT, THE
See LA FILLE DU RÉGIMENT.

DAVIS, ANDREW
English conductor (1944–)

Sir Andrew Davis became music director of Glyndebourne Festival Opera in 1989, where he gained international fame for his triumphs with the Janáček operas KATYA KABANOVA (1988) and JENŮFA (1989). Although he has worked at the Met, Covent Garden, and Chicago, all his video operas are from Glyndebourne. See CAPRICCIO (1975), LA CLEMENZA DE TITO (1991), LE COMTE ORY (1997), EUGENE ONEGIN (1994), GLYNDEBOURNE (1992), THE MAKROPOULOS CASE (1995), NEW YEAR (1991), PELLÉAS AND MÉLISANDE (1999), THE QUEEN OF SPADES (1992), and BRYAN TERFEL (1995).

DAVIS, COLIN
English conductor (1927–)

Sir Colin Davis began his opera conducting career in 1958 conducting *Die Entführung aus dem Serail* at Sadler's Wells Opera in 1958 and won renown when he replaced Otto Klemperer for a Festival Hall production of *Don Giovanni* in 1959. He made his Royal Opera debut in 1965 with *Le nozze di Figaro*, became its music director in 1971, and conducted more than 30 operas there. He conducted the premieres of Michael Tippett's THE KNOT GARDEN in 1970 and *The Ice Break* in 1977. Many of his productions are on video. See ARIADNE AUF NAXOS (1999), BAYREUTH (1985), MOZART REQUIEM (1984), PETER GRIMES (1981), THE PHANTOM OF THE OPERA (1989), ROYAL OPERA HOUSE (1979), SAMSON ET DALILA (1981), DER SCHAUSPIELDIREKTOR (1991), TANNHÄUSER (1978), TOSCA (1979), THE TURN OF THE SCREW (1982), WERTHER (1986 film), and DIE ZAUBERFLÖTE (1991).

DEAD, THE
1987 opera film by Huston

JOHN HUSTON's wonderful last film *The Dead* is not ostensibly about opera, but opera is central to its story. Based on a story by one-time opera singer James Joyce, it revolves around a 1904 New Year's Eve party in Dublin where one of the guests is a professional opera tenor. The conversation is often about opera, including *La bohème*, which has just premiered in Dublin. The discussion ranges from Verdi to *bel canto* and ends with talk about Caruso and memories of another great tenor. There is a touching scene in which one of the elderly women giving the party performs Elvira's aria "Son vergin vezzosa" from *I puritani*. It is sung in English as "Arrayed for the Bridal" by Cathleen Delany, who sings badly but charmingly over a montage of mementos. The final scene of the film, the memory of a long-dead love, is triggered by the tenor singing "The Lass of Aughrim." Color. 82 minutes. Vestron VHS.

DEATH IN VENICE
1973 opera by Britten

BENJAMIN BRITTEN's *Death in Venice* is based on a novella by Thomas Mann, which has also made into a notable film by Luchino Visconti. Myfanwy Piper's libretto tells the story of Gustav von Aschenbach, a world-famous German writer who goes to Venice on holiday and falls in love with a young boy named Tadzio. Cholera strikes the city, but he is unable to leave and dies. The roles of the characters who lead the writer to his destiny are sung by the same baritone, while the boy does not sing but dances. The opera is structured with the vocal scenes connected by dance interludes. This was Britten's last opera.

1981 Palmer film
English feature film: Tony Palmer (director), Steuart Bedford (conductor, English Chamber Orchestra), Nick Knowland (cinematographer), Ian Spink (choreographer), Charles Knode (costume designer).
Cast: Robert Gard (Aschenbach), John Shirley-Quirk (Traveler, Fop, Gondolier, Hotel Manager, Barber,

Players Leader, Voice of Dionysus), James Bowman (Voice of Apollo), Deanne Bergsma (Tadzio's Mother).
Video: London (GB) VHS. Color. In English. 132 minutes.
Comment: The film was shot on location in Venice. Bedford had conducted the premiere, and Shirley-Quirk and Bergsma had created their roles on stage.

1990 Glyndebourne Touring Opera
English stage production: Stephen Lawless (director), Graeme Jenkins (conductor, London Sinfonietta and Glyndebourne Opera Chorus), Martha Clarke (choreographer), Tobias Hoheisel (set/costume designer).
Cast: Robert Tear (Aschenbach), Alan Opie (Traveler, Gondolier, Hotel Manager), Michael Chance (Voice of Apollo), Christopher Ventris (Hotel Porter), Gerald Finley (English Clerk), Paul Zeplichal (Tadzio), Cathryn Pope (Tadzio's Mother).
Video: Kultur and Arthaus DVD/Home Vision and Virgin (GB) VHS/Pioneer LD. Robin Lough (director). Color. In English. 137 minutes.

Related film

1971 Visconti film
This superb adaptation of the Thomas Mann source novel makes a useful companion to the Britten opera and possibly influenced it. Director Luchino Visconti and co-scripter Nicola Badalucco, like Britten, emphasize that this is a story of homosexual love. Dirk Bogarde as Aschenbach is made up to look like German composer Gustav Mahler, and Mahler's music is used as score. Bjorn Andresen is Tadzio, Silvana Mangano is his mother, and Romolo Valli is the hotel manager. Color. In English or Italian. 130 minutes. Warner Home Video VHS.

DEBURAU
1926 operetta by Messager

André Messager's operetta *Deburau* tells the story of a celebrated Paris mime Jean-Gaspard Deburau and how he falls in love with courtesan Marie Duplessis. As she is the model for Violetta of *La traviata*, she naturally prefers Armand Duval. It breaks his heart, but a later encounter with her encourages him to pass on his theatrical secrets to his son. The operetta was composed for Sacha Guitry, who also wrote the libretto and filmed it.

1950 Guitry film
French feature film: Sacha Guitry (director/screenplay), Noël Ramettre (cinematographer).

Cast: Sacha Guitry (Jean-Gaspard Deburau), Lana Marconi (Marie Duplessis), Jean Danet (Armand Duval), Michel François (Charles Deburau).

Black and white. In French. 93 minutes.

DEBUSSY, CLAUDE
French composer (1862–1918)

Claude Debussy, one of the revolutionaries of modern music, had plans for many operas, but he completed only one. PELLÉAS ET MÉLISANDE, based on a play by Maurice Maeterlinck, is one of the most influential modern operas. Debussy's version of the story of El Cid, RODRIGUE ET CHIMÈNE, was nearly finished when he died, and it has been completed and staged. Debussy also had projects to make operas out of Edgar Allan Poe stories; one of them, *La Chute de la Maison Usher,* has been completed by others and staged.

1965 The Debussy Film
Oliver Reed plays Debussy in Ken Russell's BBC Television film, which centers around a group of people making a film about Debussy. The lives of the actors and the characters they portray begin to interact. Vladek Sheybal, for example, plays both the film director and the character who takes photographs of Debussy in the film-within-the-film. The film is an ingenious study in reflexive self-referential biography and was very adventurous for its time. Melvyn Bragg co-scripted. Black and white. In English. 60 minutes.

1998 Claude Debussy
An examination of the impressionistic techniques Debussy used in his music, with selections conducted by Leonard Bernstein and Herbert von Karajan. From the video series *Harmonics: The Innovators of Classical Music.* Color. In English. 28 minutes. Films for the Humanities & Sciences VHS.

DE CORDOBA, PEDRO
American bass (1881–1950)

Pedro De Cordoba, a New Yorker of Cuban and French parents, began his career as an opera bass but is better known for his movies. He was tall, good looking, and gaunt and became a popular Hollywood character actor playing aristocratic Latinos. He made a large number of films, but few of them have operatic connections, and he was never a screen singer. His first film, however, was the 1915 Cecil B. De Mille version of CARMEN; he portrays the bullfighter Escamillo opposite opera diva GERALDINE FARRAR, and he also appeared with her in De Mille's 1915 *Temptation.* His memorable movies include *Captain Blood, The Mark of Zorro, Blood and Sand, Saboteur,* and *The Song of Bernadette.*

DÉDÉ
1921 operetta by Christiné

Maurice Chevalier helped make HENRI CHRISTINÉ's tuneful French operetta *Dédé* into a major success on the Paris stage. He played Robert, the friend of Dédé (André Urban) who has bought a fashionable shoe shop so he can meet married Odette without compromising her. The shop employees are all beautiful young women, hired from the Casino de Paris chorus line, but their efficient and even more beautiful supervisor Denise came to the shop from a law firm. Albert Willemetz wrote the libretto.

1934 Guissart film
French feature film: René Guissart (director), Jacques Bousquet and Jean Boyer (screenplay), Jacques Constant (set designer).

Cast: Albert Prejean (Robert), Danielle Darrieux (Denise), Mireille Perrey (Odette), Claude Dauphin (Dédé), René Bergon (Chausson), Louis Baron (Leroy-det).

Video: René Chateau (France) VHS. Black and white. In French. 75 minutes.

DEEP IN MY HEART
1954 American film biography of Romberg

José Ferrer plays composer Sigmund Romberg in this lively film biography that traces his operetta career from its earliest days and shows off many of his best songs. Met soprano Helen Traubel plays the jolly woman who runs the restaurant where his career begins. Ferrer is superb previewing a spoof stage show called *Jazz A Doo* by singing all the parts, duetting with Traubel on "Leg of Mutton," duetting with Rosemary Clooney (his real-life wife) on "Mr. and Mrs.," and performing a moving rendition of "When I Grow Too Old to Dream." Traubel is in grand form singing "You Will Remember Vienna," "Auf Wiedersehn," "Softly as in a Morning Sunrise," and "Stouthearted Men." Doe Avedon plays Romberg's wife, Merle Oberon is lyricist Dorothy Donnelly, Walter Pidgeon is J. J. Shubert, and Paul Henried is Florenz Ziegfeld. The guest stars and their songs are Howard Keel ("Your Land and Mine"), Jane Powell and Vic Damone ("Will You Remember"), Tony Martin and Joan Weldon ("Lover Come Back to Me"), Cyd Charisse and James Mitchell ("One Alone"), Gene and Fred Kelly ("I Love to Go Swimmin' With Women"), Ann Miller (dancing to "It"), William Olvis ("Serenade"), and Vic Damone ("The Road to Paradise"). Roger Edens produced, Leonard Spielgass wrote the screenplay, Adolf Deutsch was music director, Eugene Loring was the choreographer, George J. Folsey was the cinematographer, Cedric Gibbons was the art director, and Stanley Donen directed for MGM. Color. 132 minutes. MGM-UA VHS/LD.

DEHN, PAUL
English librettist (1912–1976)

Paul Dehn was a professional screenwriter who took time out to write opera librettos, including *The Bear* for William Walton and *A Dinner Engagement* and *Castaway* for Lennox Berkeley. He had greater success writing for the movies, winning an Oscar for his story for *Seven Days to Noon* in 1950 and a British Academy Award for his screenplay for *Orders to Kill* in 1958.

DE KOVEN, REGINALD
American composer (1859–1920)

Reginald De Koven was one of the most popular American composers of light operas and operettas at the end of the 19th century. His 1891 *Robin Hood* was a major success in its time and the source of the still popular wedding song "O, promise me." There was even a sequel called *Maid Marian*.

1938 The Adventures of Robin Hood
De Koven's music was not used in this famous film because a rival studio had acquired rights for the comic opera, but the screenplay is partially based on the Harry B. Smith libretto. We know this because the De Koven/Smith version of the story is the only one in which Robin and Sir Guy duel over Maid Marian, and the movie would not be the same without that marvelous sword fight. Errol Flynn is Robin, Basil Rathbone is Guy, and Olivia de Havilland is Marian. Erich Wolfgang Korngold wrote the new score, and Michael Curtiz and William Keighley directed. Color. 102 minutes. Warner Home Video VHS.

1981 S.O.B.
Blake Edwards features the hit song from De Koven's opera at the end of his Hollywood satire. Julie Andrews sings "O Promise Me" rather well. Color. 121 minutes.

DELIBES, LÉO
French composer (1836–1891)

Léo Delibes used to be better known as the composer of the ballet *Coppelia* than for his operas. This changed when British Airways began to use the Flower Duet from LAKMÉ in their commercials and made him an operatic favorite with the general public. Tchaikovsky was a great admirer of Delibes's operas, which include *Le Roi l'a dit, Jean de Nivelle,* and *Kassya.*

DELIUS, FREDERICK
English composer (1862–1934)

Frederick Delius is not usually thought of as an opera composer, but he wrote several in the early part of his career. The most successful and the only one presently on video is the bucolic love story A VILLAGE ROMEO AND JULIET.

1968 Song of Summer
Ken Russell's elegiac film about Delius stars Max Adrian as the composer at the end of his life; he struggles to finish his last compositions with help from Eric Fenby (Christopher Gable). Color. In English. 50 minutes. BFI DVD.

DELLA CASA, LISA
Swiss soprano (1919–)

Lisa Della Casa won praise for her performances in Mozart and Wagner operas but is probably best known for Strauss's Arabella. She made her debut in Solothurn in 1941, soon became a regular at the Zurich Stadttheaterm, and then sang at the Met from 1953 to 1967. She retired from the stage in 1974. She can be seen on video in ARABELLA in a 1963 German production, as Donna Elvira in a 1954 Salzburg DON GIOVANNI, as Marguerite in a 1963 Bell Telephone Hour FAUST, and in videos of *Voice of Firestone* TV shows.

1958/1962 Voice of Firestone
Lisa Della Casa in Opera & Song is a selection of highlights from her appearances on *Voice of Firestone* television shows in 1958 and 1962. On one program she performs arias and scenes from *La bohème* in collaboration with tenor Nicolai Gedda, including "O soave fanciulla." On the other program she sings *Tosca* with Giuseppe Campora and Richard Tucker and *La bohème* with Tucker. She also performs songs by Idabelle Firestone. Black and white. 30 minutes.

1970 Portrait of Lisa Della Casa
Heinz Liesendahl made this documentary portrait of Della Casa for WDR German television. She talks about her career and sings arias by Mozart, Strauss, and Puccini. Color. In German. 32 minutes.

DELLO JOIO, NORMAN
American composer (1913–)

Pulitzer Prize–winning composer Norman Dello Joio, who has written operas for both stage and television, considers *Blood Moon* the most important. The story of a 19th-century actress who crossed color lines, it was premiered by San Francisco Opera in 1961 but has not been revived. He has written three operas about St. Joan, including THE TRIAL AT ROUEN (1956), which he created for the NBC Opera Theatre. His other TV operas are *All is Still* (1971), a monologue based on a letter from Mozart to his father, and *The Louvre* (1965), which won an Emmy Award. Dello Joio has also written scores for films and television shows, most famously for the 1956 *Air Power* TV series.

1958 The Seven Lively Arts
Dello Joio talks about the sources of his ideas and techniques in this program created for *The Seven Lively Arts* series. He discusses the influence of his organist father, uses a piano to explain patterns in his music, and discusses his score for the *Air Power* TV series. Lending support are conductor Alfredo Antonini, a symphony orchestra, a ballet company, and a Japanese pianist. The program was telecast February 16, 1958. Black and white. 60 minutes.

DEL MONACO, MARIO
Italian tenor (1915–1982)

Mario Del Monaco is in the tradition of those Italian tenors who feel that powerful voices were meant to thrill audiences, and so he did, from his debut in Milan in 1941 until his retirement in 1975. He began his international career at Covent Garden in 1946 with the San Carlo Company and made his first appearance at the Met in 1950. He was admired for his Otello, which he recorded and sang around the world, but his range of roles included even Wagner. He began appearing in movies in 1949 and had a modest but successful cinema career. He plays Francesco Tamagno, the tenor who created the role of Otello, in two films, a 1953 biography of GIUSEPPE VERDI and a 1954 biography of the RICORDI opera publishers. He plays the tenor Roberto Stagno, who created the role of Turiddu in *Cavalleria rusticana*, in a 1952 film about PIETRO MASCAGNI. He was the voice of ENRICO CARUSO in a 1951 Italian film about the tenor, and he was the voice of Gino Sinimberghi in a 1955 film about LINA CAVALIERI. He can be seen on stage in OTELLO in 1954 and 1961 videos. Other operas televised in Italy and Japan and on video include AIDA (1961), ANDREA CHÉNIER (1958/1961), MADAMA BUTTERFLY (1957), PAGLIACCI (1961), RIGOLETTO (1954), and IL TROVATORE (1957).

1948 L'Uomo dal Guanto Grigio
Del Monaco plays a tenor fresh from the country in Camillo Mastrocinque's Italian thriller. He's a bit naive, but he sings some arias, wins Annette Bach, and solves the crime. The film was released in America (as *The Man with the Grey Glove*) on the strength of Del Monaco's popularity. Black and white. In Italian. 85 minutes.

1955 Guai ai Vinti!
Del Monaco has a small role in *Getting in Trouble!*, a didactic Italian film about abortion. Two women are raped during World War I and become pregnant; only one has an abortion. Lea Padovani and Anna Maria Ferrero are the women; Raffaello Matarazzo directed. Black and white. In Italian. 100 minutes.

1959 Legends of Opera
Del Monaco sings the "Flower Song" from *Carmen* on stage in Tokyo on the video *Legends of Opera*. Black and white. In Italian. 4 minutes. Legato Classics VHS.

1960 Schlussakkord
Ljuba Welitsch and Del Monaco are the opera singers featured in this German/Italian film revolving around the premiere of an opera in Salzburg. There are the usual problems of love, suspicion, jealousy, and hate. Wolfgang Liebeneiner directed. Black and white. In German. 102 minutes. Lyric/Opera Dubs videos.

1966 Ein Sängerporträt
Portrait of a Singer is a German documentary about Del Monaco with excerpts from *Tosca, Turandot, Rigoletto, La bohème, Il trovatore,* and *Otello*. It was shot on 35mm for WDR Television in Germany. Color. 29 minutes.

1969 Del Monaco at His Most Thrilling
German television concert with Del Monaco singing arias from *The Barber of Seville, Macbeth, Norma, Otello, Il trovatore, Turandot,* and *Die Walküre*. Black and white. 37 minutes. Bel Canto Society VHS.

1978 Primo Amore
Del Monaco is director of a retirement home for show business personalities in the Italian film *First Love*. Ugo Tognazzi plays a retired star who begins a love affair with Ornella Muti. Dino Risi directed. Color. In Italian. 112 minutes. Opera Dubs VHS.

1979 Mario Del Monaco in Moscow
De Monaco sings in recital with Russian mezzo-soprano Irina Arkhipova in a Soviet television program, with music by Verdi, Bizet, and Leoncavallo. Color. 61 minutes.

1992 Mario Del Monaco
Television program about the tenor made for the Italian opera series *I Grandi della Lirica*. Color. In Italian. 60 minutes. Center (Italy) video.

1995 Del Monaco: The Singing Volcano
On this compilation video Del Monaco sings selections from *Cavalleria rusticana, Giulietta et Romeo, Madama Butterfly, Pagliacci,* and *Werther.* The excerpts are taken from tapes and films made between 1952 and 1960, plus a 1978 interview. Black and white and color. English subtitles. 37 minutes. Bel Canto Society VHS.

DE LOS ANGELES, VICTORIA
See LOS ANGELES, VICTORIA DE.

DE LUCA, GIUSEPPE
Italian baritone (1876–1950)

Giuseppe De Luca's impressive career, which began in 1897, includes the world premieres of Cilea's *Adriana Lecouvreur* and Puccini's *Madama Butterfly* (as Sharpless). He sang at La Scala for eight years and at the Met for 22 seasons between 1915 and 1946. In New York, he created another famous role, Puccini's Gianni Schicchi in *Il Trittico.* De Luca made many recordings and can be seen in three Vitaphone films.

1927–1928 Vitaphone films
De Luca, billed as "of the Metropolitan Opera Company," appeared in three sound films for the Vitaphone company. In the first, he sings one of his specialties, Figaro's "Largo al factotum" from *The Barber of Seville.* In the second, he sings the Quartet from *Rigoletto,* with Beniamino Gigli as the Duke, Marion Talley as Gilda, and Jeanne Gordon as Maddalena. In the third, he joins Gigli in the Friendship Duet from Act I of Bizet's *The Pearl Fishers,* sung in Italian. Black and white. Each film about 7 minutes. Bel Canto Society VHS.

DELVAUX, ANDRÉ
Belgian film director (1926–2002)

André Delvaux, one of Belgium's and the world's great modern filmmakers, had wide recognition for films such as *The Man Who Had His Hair Cut Short* (1968) and *Rendezvous in Bray* (1971). His fascinating BABEL OPERA (1985) revolves around a production of *Don Giovanni* at the Théâtre Royal de la Monnaie in Brussels.

DeMAIN, JOHN
American conductor (1944–)

John DeMain has conducted a large number of premieres, especially for Houston Grand Opera. He first became widely known when he conducted the 1976 Houston production of PORGY AND BESS, which went on to Broadway; in 2002 he conducted a production by New York City Opera that was televised. His telecast operas in Houston include Floyd's WILLIE STARK in 1981, Joplin's TREEMONISHA in 1982, Glass's AKHNATEN in 1985, and Adams's NIXON IN CHINA in 1987. DeMain began his opera career on television in 1969 as assistant conductor to Peter Herman Adler at NET Opera. In 1972 he joined the New York City Opera and in 1978 became principal conductor for Houston.

DEMME, JONATHAN
American film director (1944–)

Jonathan Demme, who won an Oscar for *The Silence of the Lambs,* began his Hollywood career in the 1970s with B-pictures for Roger Corman. He has created some of the more thought-provoking Hollywood films; his 1993 AIDS-oriented film *Philadelphia* has a notable use of opera, especially the MARIA CALLAS version of "La Mamma Morta" from ANDREA CHENIER.

DE PALMA, BRIAN
American film director (1940–)

Brian De Palma, whose films have stylistic similarities to those of Alfred Hitchcock, is known for such shocking thrillers as *Carrie, Body Double,* and *Wise Guys.* Like other Italian-American directors, he occasionally has opera in his films. In *The Untouchables* (1987), he uses PAGLIACCI for ironic counterpoint. Al Capone (Robert De Niro) is shown at the opera shedding a tear for the clown on stage (voice of Mario Del Monaco singing "Vesti la giubba") while incorruptible policeman Jim Malone (Sean Connery) is killed by Capone's men.

DE PAOLIS, ALESSIO
Italian tenor (1893–1964)

Alessio De Paolis made his debut at Bologna in 1919 and sang Fenton in *Falstaff* at La Scala in 1923. He was a top tenor in Italy for 15 years before going to the Metropolitan Opera in 1938 where, incredibly, he sang for 26 more years. He seems to have appeared in only one film.

1932 La cantante dell'opera
De Paolis and soprano Laura Pasini, both singing at La Scala at this time, are featured in the opera scenes in this

colorful Italian film. The plot revolves around a young opera singer in Venice and her involvement with an American man who is not what he seems. Nunzio Malasomma directed. Black and white. In Italian. 90 minutes.

DE SEGUROLA, ANDRÉS

See SEGUROLA, ANDRÉS DE.

DESERET

1961 TV opera by Kastle

American composer LEONARD KASTLE was working for the NBC Opera Theatre when it produced this opera about Mormon leader Brigham Young and his last romance. "Deseret" was the Mormon's name for their country before it was forced to become the American state of Utah. Librettist Anne Howard Bailey sets the opera in Young's mansion at the time of the Civil War. It tells how the 68-year-old Young decides to give up Anne, his proposed 25th wife, to Union Army Captain James Lee. The opera was premiered by NBC Opera Theatre on January 8, 1961, and Kastle later revised it for stage production as a three-act opera.

1961 NBC Opera Theatre

American TV production: Samuel Chotzinoff (producer), Peter Herman Adler (conductor, NBC Opera Theatre Orchestra), Jan Scott (set designer).

Cast: Kenneth Smith (Brigham Young), Judith Raskin (Anne), John Alexander (Capt. James Lee), Rosemary Kuhlmann (Sarah), Marjorie McClung, Mae Morgan.

Video at the MTR. Kirk Browning (director). Telecast January 8, 1961. Color. In English. 120 minutes.

DESERT SONG, THE

1926 operetta by Romberg

SIGMUND ROMBERG's *The Desert Song* may not be grand opera but it is certainly grand operetta, as the many films and stagings of this classic piece of melodic hokum demonstrate. It has been staged at New York City Opera, and it was the first operetta filmed during the sound era. The libretto by OTTO HARBACH, OSCAR HAMMERSTEIN II, and Frank Mandel tells the story of a mysterious cloaked figure called the Red Shadow who leads the Moroccan Riffs against the French. He is actually Pierre Birbeau, the supposedly wimpy son of the French governor. He secretly loves, and eventually wins, Margot, the fiancée of his bitter rival, French Army commander Fontaine. The operetta's famous songs include "The Riff Song" and "One Alone." Only one version is on video.

1929 Del Ruth film

American feature film: Roy del Ruth (director), Bernard McGill (cinematographer), Harvey Gates (screenplay), Vitaphone/Warner Bros. (production).

Cast: John Boles (Pierre/Red Shadow), Carlotta King (Margot), Edward Martinedel (General Birabeau), John Miljan (Capt. Fontaine), Louise Fazenda (Susan), Johnny Arthur (Benjamin), Myrna Loy (Azuri).

Black and white and color. In English. 106 minutes.

Comment: The first operetta filmed with sound, made soon after it premiered on stage. It was advertised as the "first all-singing and all-talking operetta," with a chorus of 132 voices and 109 musicians. Some sequences were shot in the two-color Technicolor process.

1932 The Red Shadow

American film: Warner Bros. (production studio).

Cast: Alexander Gray (Paul/Red Shadow), Bernice Claire (Margot).

Black and white. In English. 20 minutes.

Comment: Warner Bros. made many short films based on their own musicals, as the costs were minimal. Gray and Claire had sung their roles in stage productions.

1943 Florey Film

American feature film: Robert Florey (director), Robert Buckner (screenplay), Bert Glennon (cinematography), Charles Rovi (art director), Warner Bros. (production studio).

Cast: Dennis Morgan (Paul/Red Shadow), Irene Manning (Margot), Bruce Cabot (Capt. Fontaine), Lynne Overman (Johnny Walsh), Gene Lockhart (Père Fan Fan).

Color. In English. 96 minutes.

Comment: As this version of the story was made during World War II, it was updated to 1939 and the Germans were made the real villains. To make it more realistic, the songs are featured as nightclub numbers.

1953 Humberstone film

American feature film: H. Bruce Humberstone (director), Max Steiner (music director), Robert Burks (cinematographer), Stanley Fleischer (art direction), Warner Bros. (studio).

Cast: Gordon MacRae (Paul/Red Shadow), Kathryn Grayson (Margot), Steve Cochran (Capt. Fontaine), Raymond Massey (Youssef), Dick Wesson (Benjamin), Ray Collins (Gen. Birabeau).

Video: Warner Home Video VHS. Color. In English. 110 minutes.

Comment: This is the best of the film versions, much helped by Steiner's musical arrangements.

1955 NBC Television
American TV production: Max Liebman (producer), Charles Sanford (conductor, NBC Orchestra), Frederick Fox (set designer), Rod Alexander (choreographer).

Cast: Nelson Eddy (Red Shadow), Gale Sherwood (Margot), Otto Krueger (Gen. Birabeau), John Conte (Capt. Fontaine), Salvatore Baccaloni (Ali Ben Ali).

Video at the MTR of kinescope in black and white. Telecast live May 7, 1955. Bill Hobin (director). Color. In English. 90 minutes.

Comment: Eddy and Sherwood were appearing together in nightclub music theater at this time.

DESTINN, EMMY
Czech soprano (1878–1930)

Emmy Destinn (Ema Destinnová), the Czech soprano who became a patriotic heroine to her country, made her debut in 1898 in Berlin as Santuzza and sang there for 10 years. She made her first appearance at the Metropolitan Opera in 1908 as Aida, and in 1910 she created the role of Minnie in the premiere of *La fanciulla del West*. She was an important part of the Met's Golden Age and a recording artist of great merit, but she was also an important Czech patriot. Her birth name was Ema Kittlovà, but she changed it to Destinnová after her singing teacher.

1913 The Power of Singing
Destinn's only film (apparently lost) was a German short called *Die Macht des Gesangs oder Die Loewenbraut* (*The Power of Singing* or *The Lion's Bride*), produced in Berlin by Hans Ewers. The title comes from of a poem by Friedrich Schiller. In the film, she sings an aria from inside a lion's cage, probably to demonstrate the power of singing. Black and white. Silent. About 10 minutes.

1979 Divine Emma
Bozidara Turzonovova stars as Destinn in *Bozská Ema,* a Czech film biography released in the United States as *Divine Emma.* It is as much about her love for her country as it is about her opera career; it begins with her triumphal tour of America while World War I rages in Europe and the United States remains neutral. When she returns home, she is put in prison as a spy by the Austro-Hungarian authorities, but eventually she is allowed to tour the country singing patriotic songs. The film was directed by Jiri Krejcik, written by Krejcik and Zdenek Mahler, and photographed by Miroslav Ondricek. Color. In Czech with English subtitles. 110 minutes.

DEVIL AND KATE, THE
1899 opera by Dvořák

ANTONÍN DVOŘÁK'S Czech opera *The Devil and Kate* (Čert a Káča) is a comic tale centering around a strong-minded woman named Kate. She dances with a devil called Marbuel at a village fair and then goes off to his home at his invitation. Home turns out to be Hell, but Kate proves to be too much for this devil. With the help of the shepherd Jirka, she saves and reforms the local princess and makes everything turn out right. The libretto by Adolph Wenig is based on a Czech folk tale.

1988 Theatre Royal, Wexford Festival
Irish stage production: Francesca Zambello (director), Albert Rosen (conductor, RTE [RadioTelefisEireann] Symphony Orchestra and Wexford Festival Chorus), Neil Peter Jampolis (set designer).

Cast: Anne Marie Owens (Kate), Peter Lightfoot (Marbuel), Kristine Ciesinski (Princess), Joan Davies (Kate's Mother), Marko Putkonen (Lucifer), Joseph Evans (Jirka), Alan Fairs (Marshall), Kathleen Tynan (Chambermaid), Philip Guy Bromley (Hell's Gatekeeper).

Video: House of Opera DVD and VHS/Lyric VHS. Color. In English. 115 minutes.

Comment: Very enjoyable production with the overture played over scenes of Wexford.

DEVILS OF LOUDUN, THE
1969 opera by Penderecki

The opera begins by saying that the devil cannot be trusted even when he tells the truth. Father Grandier is accused of corrupting the nuns in a convent, especially its prioress Mother Jeanne. The truth is much more complicated. KRZYSZTOF PENDERECKI's remarkable *The Devils of Loudun,* an operatic version of what happened to a priest and a group of nuns in 17th-century Loudun, has been widely produced. Erotic fantasies in a religious setting with blasphemy for spice apparently can count on popularity, even if the music is difficult. The opera premiered in Hamburg in German as *Die Teufel von Loudun,* but it is based on an English play by John Whiting derived from a book by Aldous Huxley.

1969 Hamburg State Opera
German stage production: Konrad Swinarski (director), Marek Janowski (conductor, Hamburg State Opera Orchestra and Chorus), Lydia and Jerzy Skarynski (set/costume designers), Rolf Liebermann (producer).

Cast: Andrzej Hiolski (Father Grandier), Tatiana Troyanos (Mother Jeanne), Cvetka Ahlin (Sister Claire), Ursula Boese (Sister Louise), Helga Thieme (Sister Gabrielle), Bernard Ladysz (Father Barré), Horst

Wilhelm (Father Mignon), Heinz Blankenburg (Mannoury), Kurt Marschner (Adam), Ingeborg Krüger (Philippe).

Telecast July 5, 1970, on NDR German television. Joachim Hess (film director). Color. In German. 110 minutes.

Related film

1970 The Devils

Ken Russell's film, like Penderecki's opera, is based on the play by Whiting and the book by Huxley. This may be Russell's most bizarre film, but it's hysterically fascinating. Oliver Reed plays Father Grandier with Vanessa Redgrave as Mother Jeanne. The film score is by Peter Maxwell Davies. Color. In English. 111 minutes.

DEW, JOHN
English director (1944–)

English director John Dew, who studied with Walter Felsenstein and Wieland Wagner, began to direct opera in Germany in 1971. He has worked at the Deutsche Oper, Berlin, and is particularly well known for updating classic operas, such as his 1993 production of LES HUGUENOTS.

1993 Portrait of John Dew, Opera Producer
Hubert Orthkemper made this documentary about the English producer for German television. It shows Dew at work on an opera and explores his career up to 1993. Color. In German. 44 minutes.

DEXTER, JOHN
English director (1925–1990)

John Dexter began his directing career producing plays for the English Stage Company and the National Theatre. His first opera was *Benvenuto Cellini,* staged at Covent Garden in 1966. He became director of productions for the Metropolitan Opera in 1974, and many of his productions there have been telecast and are on video. See AIDA (1985), THE BARTERED BRIDE (1978), DON CARLO (1980/1983), DON PASQUALE (1979), LA FORZA DEL DESTINO (1984), LULU (1980), RIGOLETTO (1981), and AUFSTIEG UND FALL DER STADT MAHAGONNY (1979).

DIALOGUES DES CARMÉLITES
1957 opera by Poulenc

Dialogues of the Carmelites is an opera based on a movie screenplay. The story originated in the memoirs of a nun who survived the French Revolution; her story was turned into a novel by German writer Gertrude von Le Fort. Austrian priest Raymond-Leopold Bruckberger wrote a film script based on the novel and asked French novelist Georges Bernanos to write the dialogue. The screenplay was judged uncinematic by producers, even though Bruckberger later made a film from it, so Bernanos turned it into a stage play in 1948. Composer FRANCIS POULENC saw the play and wrote a libretto based on it, but the opera, completed in 1953, was not staged until 1957. It tells the story of a group of nuns during the French Revolution who are forced to become martyrs. Blanche de la Force is the fragile new nun who decides to join her sister nuns when they are led to the guillotine by Prioress Madame Lidoine.

1957 NBC Opera Theatre
American TV production: Samuel Chotzinoff (producer), Peter Herman Adler (conductor, Symphony of the Air Orchestra and NBC Opera Chorus), Trew Hocker (set designer).

Cast: Elaine Malbin (Blanche de la Force), Leontyne Price (Madame Lidoine), Rosemary Kuhlmann (Mother Marie), Patricia Neway (Madame de Croissy), Judith Raskin (Sister Constance), David Lloyd (Priest), Robert Rounseville (Chevalier de la Force).

Telecast live December 8, 1957, on NBC. Kirk Browning (director). Color. In English. 120 minutes.

1985 Australian Opera
Australian stage production: Elijah Moshinsky (director), Richard Bonynge (conductor, Elizabethan Sydney Orchestra and Australian Opera Chorus) John Bury (set/costume designer).

Cast: Isobel Buchanan (Blanche de la Force), Joan Sutherland (Madame Lidoine), Heather Begg (Mother Marie), Ann-Marie MacDonald (Sister Constance), Patricia Price (Mother Jeanne), Geoffrey Chard (Marquis de la Force), Paul Ferris (Chevalier de la Force), Lone Kopple (Madame de Croissy).

Video: Sony VHS. Henry Prokop (director). Color. In English. 155 minutes.

1987 Canadian Opera
Canadian stage production: Lotfi Mansouri (director), Jean Fournet (conductor, Canadian Opera Orchestra).

Cast: Irena Welhasch (Blanche), Carol Vaness (Madame Lidoine), Maureen Forrester (Madame de Croissy), Janet Stubbs (Mother Marie), Harolyn Blackwell (Sister Constance), Mark DuBois (Chevalier de la Force).

Telecast on CBC on January 25, 1987. Norman Campbell (director). Color. In English. 180 minutes.

1987 Metropolitan Opera

American stage production: John Dexter (director), Manuel Rosenthal (conductor, Metropolitan Opera Orchestra and Chorus), David Reppa (set designer).

Cast: Maria Ewing (Blanche), Jessye Norman (Madame Lidoine), Régine Crespin (Madame de Croissy), Florence Quivar (Mother Marie), Betsy Norden (Sister Constance), David Kuebler (Chevalier de la Force).

Telecast May 6, 1987; taped April 4, 1987. Brian Large (director), Color. In French with English subtitles. 180 minutes.

***1999 Opéra National du Rhin, Strasbourg

German stage production: Marthe Keller (director), Jan Latham-Koenig (conductor, Strasbourg Philharmonic Orchestra and Opéra National du Rhine Chorus), Jean-Pierre Capeyron (set designer).

Cast: Ann-Sophie Schmidt (Blanche), Valérie Millot (Madame Lidoine), Hedwig Fassbender (Mother Marie), Nadine Denize (Madame de Croissy).

Video: Arthaus DVD. Don Kent (director). Color. In French with English subtitles. 149 minutes.

Comment: Keller allows her cast to tell this moving and disturbing story without trying to add frills, and it works wonderfully.

Related film

1959 Bruckberger film

The French feature film *Dialogues des Carmélites* is based on the novel and original screenplay, and it makes a fascinating comparison with the opera. It was directed by Raymond-Leopold Bruckberger, the priest who wrote the screenplay that inspired the opera, and Philippe Agostini. The script of the film is credited to Bruckberger and Agostini. The story is basically the same: a young nun learns the spirit of sacrifice during the Terror of the French Revolution. Jeanne Moreau is Mère Marie, Pascale Audret is Blanche, Alida Valli is Mère Thérèse, Madeleine Renaud is the nun who dies, and Pierre Brasseur is the people's commissar. Moreau won a Best Actress award for her performance. Black and white. In French. 112 minutes.

DICK DEADEYE
1975 pastiche Gilbert and Sullivan operetta

This pastiche operetta, in the form of a British animated film, is based on the characters of William S. Gilbert, the music of Arthur Sullivan, and the drawings of Ronald Searle. It was created by animator Bill Melendez, and the graphics are its chief delight. The main character is Dick Deadeye, the villain of *H.M.S. Pinafore*, transformed here into a hero commissioned by the queen to undertake a dangerous mission. He is joined in his adventure by Little Buttercup, Yum-Yum, the twins Nanki and Poo, a Modern Major General, and other GILBERT AND SULLIVAN characters. Some of the songs have recognizable lyrics; others have new words by Robin Miller. The voices belong to John Baldry, Barry Cryer, George A. Cooper, Miriam Karlin, Victor Spinetti, Linda Lewis, and Peter Reeves. Leo Rost and Robin Miller wrote the libretto; Jimmy Horowitz arranged and conducted the music. Color. In English. 80 minutes. Proscenium Entertainment VHS.

DICK TRACY
1990 American film with opera content

American opera composer Thomas Pasatieri *(Washington Square, Three Sisters)* created an opera for Warren Beatty's film *Dick Tracy*. In the movie *Die Schlumpf* is performed on stage by Marvalee Cariaga and Michael Gallup. It looks and sounds like a Wagnerian pastiche, but it is shown only in long shot from where Tracy (Warren Beatty) and Tess Trueheart (Glenne Headley) are seated in the opera house. His wrist radio goes off and he leaves saying, "I'll be back; I want to see how it ends." When he returns many hours later, the scene is still in progress. The excerpt is brief (apparently more was filmed), but for satirical purposes it is made to seem very long indeed. Beatty directed the film, Jim Cash and Jack Epps Jr. wrote the screenplay based on the Chester Gould comic strip, and Vittorio Storaro was the cinematographer. Stephen Sondheim, who wrote new songs for the film, won an Oscar for "Sooner or Later," and Harold Michelson won another for his colorful set designs. Color. 103 minutes.

DIDO AND AENEAS
1689 opera by Purcell

Queen Dido of Carthage has fallen in love with Prince Aeneas, who fled from Troy at the end of the Trojan War and is a guest at her court. An envious sorceress sends a false messenger from the gods to tell Aeneas he must leave the island and abandon Dido. Dido is heartbroken and dies, watched over by her confidante Belinda. HENRY PURCELL's *Dido and Aeneas* is usually considered the first great English opera and often ranked as the best before the 20th century although, oddly, it was probably written for and premiered at a girls' school. Nahum Tate's libretto is based on the story as told in Virgil's *Aeneid*. The aria known as "Dido's Lament" ("When I am laid in earth") has become popular in its own right.

1951 Elizabethan Theatre Opera

English stage production (highlights): Bernard Miles (director), Geraint Jones (conductor, Mermaid Theater Orchestra).

Cast: Kirsten Flagstad (Dido), Maggie Teyte (Belinda).

Video at the MPRC in London. Black and white. In English. 10 minutes.

Comment: Scenes from a famous production of the opera at the Mermaid Theatre in London. BBC Television shot the film at a stage rehearsal on September 14, 1951, with both singers in costume.

1962 NET Opera

American TV production: Boris Goldovsky (director/conductor, New England Conservatory of Music Student Orchestra), Henry May (set/costume designer).

Cast: Joy McIntyre (Dido), Justino Diaz (Aeneas), Junetta Jones (Belinda), Mary M. Hagopian (Sorceress), Eric Davies (Sailor).

Telecast on April 25, 1961, on WGBH. Black and white. In English. 60 minutes.

1966 Glyndebourne Festival

English stage production: Franco Enriquez (director), John Pritchard (conductor, London Philharmonic Orchestra and Glyndebourne Festival Chorus), Lorenzo Ghighlia (set designer).

Cast: Janet Baker (Dido), Thomas Hemsley (Aeneas), Elizabeth Robson (Belinda), Yvonne Minton (Sorceress), Ryland Davies (Sailor), Lorna Elias (Second Woman), Clare Walmesley (First Witch/Voice of Mercury), Elizabeth Robson (Second Witch).

Telecast on BBC in England. John Vernon (director). Color. In English. 60 minutes.

1986 Reggio Emilia Opera

Italian stage production: Pier Luigi Pizzi (director), M. Francombe (conductor, Reggio Emilia Opera Orchestra and Chorus).

Cast: Margarita Zimmermann (Dido), Nicolas Rivenq, Fiorella Pediconi, Nathalie Stutzmann, Susanna Anselmi, Alessandra Ruffini.

Video: House of Opera DVD/VHS and Lyric VHS. Color. In English. 60 minutes.

Comment: Taped for telecast by RAI Italian television at Teatro Romolo Valli in Reggio Emilia.

1995 BBC Television

BBC Television film: Peter Maniura (film and stage director), Richard Hickox (conductor, Orchestra and Chorus of the Collegium Musicum 90), Niek Kortekaas (set/costume designer).

Cast: Maria Ewing (Dido), Karl Daymond (Aeneas), Rebecca Evans (Belinda), Sally Burgess (Sorceress), Patricia Rozario (Second Woman), Mary Plazas (First Enchantress), Pamela Helen Stephen (Second Enchantress), Jamie McDougall (Aeneas's Lieutenant), François Testory (Mercury), James Bowman (Voice of Mercury).

Video: NVC Arts (GB) VHS. Peter Maniura (film director). Telecast November 18, 1996, on PBS. Color. In English. 55 minutes.

Comment: Maniura filmed this opulent version of the opera at Hampton Court House in England with the camera constantly on the move.

***1995 Mark Morris film

Canadian film: Barbara Willis Sweete (director), Mark Morris (choreographer), Milan Podsedley (cinematographer), music performed by Tafelmusic Orchestra and Chamber Choir.

Cast: Mark Morris (Dido/Sorceress, sung by Jennifer Lane), Guillermo Resto (Aeneas, sung by Russell Braun), Ruth Davidson (Belinda, sung by Ann Monoyios), Tina Fehlandt (First Witch, sung by Shari Saunders), Rachel Murray (Second Woman, sung by Shari Saunders), William Wagner (Second Witch, sung by Meredith Hall), Meredith Hall (voice of Spirit), Kraig Patterson (Sailor).

Video: Image Entertainment DVD. Color. In English. 56 minutes.

Comment: Highly effective dance/opera version conceived and choreographed by Morris with the roles doubled by dancers and singers dressed in black.

Related films

1989 Stradivari

Giacomo Battiato's Italian film about the life of a violin maker, played by Anthony Quinn, features a scene from *Dido and Aeneas*. Angelo Maggi is the opera singer. Color. In Italian. 115 minutes.

1994 Opera: Words and Music

Three extracts from *Dido and Aeneas* are featured in this program that examines the use of recitative and arias in opera. Part of the series *Understanding Music*. Color. In English. 25 minutes. Films for the Humanities & Sciences VHS.

2000 The Man Who Cried

Sally Potter's Anglo-French film about Jews and opera in Paris during World War II features "Dido's Lament" in two scenes, both sung by Czech soprano Iva Bittová. See THE MAN WHO CRIED.

DIDUR, ADAMO
Polish bass (1874–1946)

Adamo Didur was born in Poland in 1874, made his debut in Rio de Janeiro in 1894, and sang with Warsaw Opera, La Scala, and Covent Garden. The most important segment of his career was at the Met, where he made his debut in 1908; he remained with the company for 25 years and was a notable Figaro, a fine Almaviva, and an outstanding Boris. He left a film record of his singing style before returning to Poland.

1927 Vitaphone film
Didur joins tenor Giovanni Martinelli and an unseen soprano in excerpts from *Aida* in this 1927 Vitaphone opera film. It was shot at the Manhattan Opera House and seems to have been Didur's only film. Black and white. In Italian. About 9 minutes.

DIETZ, HOWARD
American librettist (1896–1983)

Howard Dietz wrote English adaptations of LA BOHÈME and DIE FLEDERMAUS for 1953 Metropolitan Opera productions that aroused so much interest they were sold as books. Small wonder. Dietz was one of the great Hollywood publicists and more or less created the public image of MGM. He is credited with the company's trademark Leo the Lion, Latin motto *Ars Gratia Artis,* and Greta Garbo campaigns. At the same time, he was a successful opera and musical comedy lyricist and librettist. His shows included *The Little Show* (1929) and *The Band Wagon* (1931). His autobiography *Dancing in the Dark* (1975) tells all. He appeared in person in a 1953 METROPOLITAN OPERA TV program.

DIMITROVA, GHENA
Bulgarian soprano (1940–)

Ghena Dimitrova made her debut in Sofia in 1966 in one of her most famous roles, Abigaille in *Nabucco*. She began to sing in Western Europe in 1975, and her powerful voice was first heard in America in Dallas in 1982 in *Ernani*. She made her Metropolitan debut in 1988 as *Turandot*, another of her great roles, and she sang often at La Scala and the Arena di Verona. She can be seen on video as Abigaille in NABUCCO at Verona in 1982 and La Scala in 1986, as TURANDOT at Verona in 1983, as Giselda in I LOMBARDI ALLA PRIMA CROCIATA at La Scala in 1984, and as Amneris in AIDA at La Scala in 1985. She participated in a 75th anniversary VERONA gala in 1988.

DINORAH
1859 opera by Meyerbeer

Giacomo Meyerbeer's comic opera *Dinorah,* libretto by Michel Carré and Jules Barbier, is the story of a woman who goes crazy when her husband abandons her on their wedding day. After many adventures, they are reunited and her reason is restored. The opera has dropped out of the repertory, so there are no videos and only one CD, but its famous "Shadow Song" ("Ombre légére") remains popular and has been featured in Hollywood movies.

1941 Rio Rita
Kathryn Grayson sings the coloratura waltz aria "Shadow Song" from *Dinorah* in this 1941 film of Harry Tierney's operetta *Rio Rita*. Grayson plays the Rio Rita role. Black and white. 91 minutes.

1941 There's Magic in Music
Susanna Foster sings the "Shadow Song" in this film about a burlesque singer at a summer music camp. She meets Met stars Richard Bonelli and Irra Petina and is soon transmuted into on opera singer. Andrew L. Stone directed. Also known as *The Hard-Boiled Canary*. Paramount. Black and white. 80 minutes.

DIRECTORS: OPERA ON FILM

More than a thousand film directors have made opera films, but only a limited number can be highlighted here. They are of four types. First, and best known, are the filmmakers with major cinematic reputations whose opera films are among the glories of the genre; they include INGMAR BERGMAN, LUIS BUÑUEL, LUIGI COMENCINI, ABEL GANCE, JOSEPH LOSEY, MAX OPHULS, MICHAEL POWELL, FRANCESCO ROSI, and FRANCO ZEFFIRELLI. Second are the filmmakers who, although they have made a number of excellent opera films, are not as widely recognized as they deserve to be, including Italians CARMINE GALLONE and MARIO COSTA and Russians VLADIMIR GORIKKER, VERA STROYEVA, and ROMAN TIKHOMIROV. Third are the directors whose work is not well known in cinematic circles because their films were made primarily for TV presentation. They include JEAN-PIERRE PONNELLE, who made 16 important opera films; film and stage director WALTER FELSENSTEIN, whose innovations had a wide influence; PIERRE JOURDAN, whose films of operas at the Orange Festival are models of their kind; JOACHIM HESS, who directed Hamburg operas for Rolf Liebermann; VÁCLAV KASLÍK, who was an opera composer as well as a fine director; and Spain's JUAN DE ORDUÑA, who directed a fine series of zarzuelas. Finally there are the composers who have directed films of their own operas, a small group led by GIAN CARLO MENOTTI.

DIRECTORS: OPERA ON TV

The pioneer television and video opera directors have not received the recognition they deserve, and they are often not listed in reference books. KIRK BROWNING and BRIAN LARGE, for example, who directed most of the Metropolitan Opera telecasts and videos, do not have entries in the *Metropolitan Opera Encyclopedia*. Opera on the small screen could not have developed so well without their craft and genius in creating effective images of live opera. Most of the pioneers who helped create the genre are still working. Browning, the first great director in the field, developed television opera on American television along with ROGER ENGLANDER, who collaborated with Menotti and Bernstein. The dominant director in the field today is England's ubiquitous BRIAN LARGE, who has written about the subject in *Grove*. Other British TV opera directors of note are DEREK BAILEY, HUMPHREY BURTON, BARRIE GAVIN, DAVE HEATHER, PETER MANIURA, and JOHN VERNON. Also important are THOMAS OLOFSSON, who directed the Drottningholm Mozart videos; and CLAUS VILLER, who made many of the Schwetzingen Festival videos. Filmmakers who have directed the videos of their own stage productions include INGMAR BERGMAN, PETER BROOK, PETER HALL, PETER SELLARS, and FRANCO ZEFFIRELLI.

DIRINDINA, LA

1715 intermezzo buffo by D. Scarlatti

Music teacher Don Carissimo fancies his pupil Dirindina and is jealous of her friend Liscione. When she is offered a role at the Milan opera, and he sees her rehearsing the part of Dido, he foolishly tries to save her from her fake suicide. Domenico Scarlatti's *La Dirindina*, libretto by Girolamo Gigi, is a stinging satire on *opera seria* and was to have premiered with Scarlatti's *Ambleto* in 1715; however, its cast felt the satire was too pointed so they had it banned. It got staged 10 years later and is now ranked among the best of the intermezzi that helped create comic opera.

1996 Villa Medicea, Poggio a Caiano

Italian stage production: Goffredo Gori (director), Riccardo Cirri (conductor, Ars Cantus Chamber Orchestra).

Cast: Patrizia Cigna (Dirindina), Ernesto Palacio (Liscione), Giorgio Gatti (Don Carissimo), Siliana Fedi (Didone), Gabriele Ara (Ambleto).

Video: Hardy Classic VHS. Filmed live September 15, 1996, by Prato Filmstudio Ventidue. Silvia Scali (director). Color. In Italian. 40 minutes.

Comment: The music is played on period instruments in a simple but charming production in Poggio a Caiano, a small town near Florence.

DISNEY, WALT

American film producer (1901–1966)

Walt Disney was the genius behind the greatest animation studio in the history of movies and the creator of such cinematic icons as Mickey Mouse and Donald Duck. He also created many impressive films featuring opera and operetta music, including the remarkable THE WHALE WHO WANTED TO SING AT THE MET. Most Disney animated films are musicals, and most Disney feature films from *Snow White and the Seven Dwarfs* to *Beauty and the Beast* are really film operettas. Listed below are some of his films with opera music

1935 The Band Concert

Mickey Mouse conducts a band playing opera tunes in the park in his first color film. After the audience cheers selections from the opera *Zampa,* the band plays the *William Tell* Overture. Donald Duck interrupts in his own inimitable fashion. Wilfred Jackson directed. Color. 7 minutes.

1936 Mickey's Grand Opera

Mickey Mouse, the first great star of the Disney studio, is featured in his earlier and funnier years in this opera cartoon. Wilfred Jackson directed. Color. 7 minutes.

1940 Fantasia

This Disney classical musical extravaganza features a famous melody from Ponchielli's opera *La Gioconda* in one of its more memorable scenes. The "Dance of the Hours" is performed in the film by a pink hippopotamus with an alligator as her partner and a ballet corps of ostriches and elephants. Color. 120 minutes.

DI STEFANO, GIUSEPPE

Italian tenor (1921–)

Giuseppe Di Stefano accompanied MARIA CALLAS on her last tour in 1973 and was still in reasonable voice. He had made his debut in 1946 in Reggio Emilio as Des Grieux in Manon, began to sing at La Scala in 1947, and arrived at the Met in 1948; he sang there regularly until 1952 and made his last appearance in 1965. His great period of recording with Callas and Tito Gobbi in the 1950s resulted in a legacy of disc masterpieces. He can be seen in several performances on film and video, including playing the tenor Luciano Buffarotti in an enjoyable 1980 TV production of DER SCHAUSPIELDIREKTOR, and in videos about Callas. He is a featured singer on the soundtrack of Martin Scorsese's films *Mean Streets* and *Goodfellas.* In recent years he has been explaining his technique in master classes.

1953 Canto per te
Di Stefano stars in the film *I Sing for You* as a tenor who has trouble with a detective who covets his girl (Hélène Remy). He is given ample opportunity to sing but not enough to save the film from being ordinary. Marino Girolami directed. Black and white. In Italian with English subtitles. 96 minutes. Bel Canto Society/Live Opera VHS.

1962–1964 Bell Telephone Hour
The VAI VHS collection *Corelli—Di Stefano—Vickers* showcases the three tenors as they appeared on the *Bell Telephone Hour* television show. Di Stefano sings "Ah, fuyez!" from *Manon*. Donald Voorhees conducts the Bell Telephone Hour Orchestra. Color. 36 minutes. VAI VHS.

1987 Maria Callas: Life and Art
Di Stefano is seen in performance with Maria Callas on the final night in Japan of their 1973–1974 recital tour, and they're both splendid. He is interviewed about their relationship and talks of her with warmth and admiration. Alan Lewens and Alistair Mitchell produced. Black and white. 80 minutes. Kultur VHS.

Diva (1981): Wilhelmenia Wiggins Fernandez is the diva in Jean-Jacques Beineix's French thriller *Diva*.

DIVA
1981 French film with operatic content

Wilhelmenia Wiggins Fernandez plays African-American opera singer Cynthia Hawkins in this stylish French thriller by Jean-Jacques Beineix. She is wonderfully mysterious, because she refuses to allow her voice to be recorded. An admirer secretly tapes her singing "Ebben…ne andrò lontana," an aria from Catalani's opera *La Wally*, at the Théâtre des Bouffes du Nord in Paris. The tape, which gets confused with a tape about a drug king, is central to the plot. The film, which made Fernandez famous and renewed interest in Catalani's opera, is based

on a French crime novel by Delacorta. The aria is heard twice in the film with Fernandez accompanied by the London Symphony Orchestra led by Vladimir Cosma. Color. In French with English subtitles. 117 minutes. MGM/UA Home Video.

DOLLARPRINZESSIN, DIE
1907 operetta by Fall

The "princess" of Leo Fall's charming Viennese operetta *Die Dollarprinzessin* (The Dollar Princess) is Alice, the daughter of New York millionaire and coal king John Couder. The loves and problems of the wealthy father and sought-after daughter are the focus of the plot, headed by cabaret singer Olga, who passes herself off as a countess to try to snare Couder. The operetta is set in New York and Canada rather than Vienna but the music doesn't sound much different. The principal waltz of the operetta was so popular it helped the New York stage production run for 200 performances. A. M. Willner and Fritz Grünbaum wrote the libretto.

1971 Überall TV film
German TV film: Klaus Überall (director), Bert Grund (conductor, Kurt Graunke Symphonic Orchestra), Peter Scharff (set designer).
Cast: Horst Niendorf (John Couder), Gabriele Jacoby (Alice), Tatiana Ivanov (Olga), Gerhardt Lippert (Fredy), Regina Lemnitz (Daisy), Stefan Behrens (Hans).
Telecast on ORF Austrian Television on September 25, 1971. 35mm film. Color. In German. 87 minutes.

Early films

1908 "Wir tanzen Ringelreih'n"
Alfred Duskes's German sound film of the duet "Wir tanzen Ringelreih'n" from *Die Dollarprinzessin* was screened with synchronized music from a record. The singers are Arnold Riech (Hans) and Hélène Winter (Daisy). Black and white. In German. About 3 minutes.

1910 "Entresangen"
Charles Magnusson directed this Swedish sound film made with the Biophon system. It features the aria "Entresangen" from *Die Dollarprinzessin,* sung by Carl Barcklind. Black and white. In German. About 3 minutes.

1927 Die Dollarprinzessin un ihre sechs Freier
Liane Haid, Hans Albers, and George Alexander star in this feature-length version of the operetta made in Germany by Felix Basch. The film was retitled *Die Dollarprinzessin un ihre sechs Freier.* Black and white. Silent. About 80 minutes.

DOLORES, LA
1895 opera by Bretón

Dolores, a maid in a 19th-century Spanish inn, has a great many suitors, including soldier Rojas, barber Melchior, student Lázaro, and wealthy Patricio. Lázaro kills Melchior while protecting Dolores, but she insists on taking the blame. Tomás Bretón's opera *La Dolores*, libretto by the composer based on a play by José Feliú y Codina, premiered in Madrid on March 16, 1896. It has been produced in many countries and is especially valued for its use of Spanish musical idioms.

1940 Rey film
Spanish feature film: Florian Rey (director, screenplay), Enrique Guerner (cinematographer), CINFESA (production company).

Cast: Conchita Piquer (Dolores), Manuel Luna (Melchior), Riccardo Merino (Lázaro), Guadalupe Muñoz Sampedro, Pablo Hildago.

Video: Divisa Ediciónes (Spain) VHS. Black and white. In Spanish. 107 minutes.

Early/related films

1908 Jiménez film
Enrique Jiménez made this Spanish version of *La Dolores* in Barcelona in 1908. The cast includes Jiménez, Marsal, Bozo, Carrasco, Gallar, and Valar y Vives. Black and white. Silent. About 10 minutes.

1923 Thous film
Ana Giner plays Dolores in the Spanish feature *La Dolores* shot in Valencia and featuring a genuine bullfight. José Latorre is Lázaro and Leopoldo Pitarch is Melchior. Maximiliano Thous wrote and directed. Black and white. Silent. About 90 minutes.

1991 Zarzuela Royal Gala Concert
Plácido Domingo sings an aria from *La Dolores* in this concert in the National Music Auditorium in Madrid accompanied by the Madrid Symphonic Orchestra. Enriques Garcia Asensio directed. Color. In Spanish. 69 minutes. Kultur VHS.

DOLOROSA, LA
1930 zarzuela by Serrano

Brother Rafael, a painter who has become a monk, is working on a portrait of the Virgin Dolorosa; it reflects his unhappiness about Dolores, a woman he loved and lost. When she turns up with an illegitimate baby and abandoned by her lover, there is a scandal. In the end, she and Brother Rafael are reconciled, and he leaves the monastery to go off with her. José Serrano's *La Dolorosa*, libretto by Juan José Lorente, was said to have been inspired by the death of the composer's son.

1934 Grémillon film
Spanish feature film: Jean Grémillon (director), Jacques Monterault (cinematographer).

Cast: Agustin Godoy, Rosita Diaz Gimeno, Mary Amparo Bosch, Pilar Carcia.

Black and white. In Spanish. 100 minutes.

Comment: Critics consider this one of the best films in the zarzuela genre, comparable to Grémillon's classic French films.

1996 Teatro Calderón, Madrid
Spanish stage production: José Luis Moreno (director), José A. Irasforza (conductor, Teatro Calderón Orchestra and Chorus), Julian Perez Muñoz (set designer).

Cast: María Rodríguez (Dolores), Rafael Lledó (Rafael), Vicente Lacárcel (Prior), Pepa Rosado (Juana), Enrique del Portal (José), Amelia Font (Nicasia), P. P. Juárez (Perico), Alhambra Ballet (dancers)

Video: Metrovideo VHS. José Ignado Ortega (director). Telecast live by RTVE. Color. In Spanish. 72 minutes.

***1996 Jarvis Conservatory
American stage production: Daniel Helfgot (director), Monroe Kanouse (conductor, Jarvis Conservatory Orchestra), Peter Crompton (set designer), Carlos Carvajal (choreographer), William Jarvis (producer/translator).

Cast: Karen Carle (Dolores), Jorge Gomez (Rafael), Ross Halper (Perico), Juan Sánchez-Lozano (Prior), Roderick Gomez (Friar Lucas), Suzanne Lustgarten (Nicasia), Ramón Perez (Bienvenido).

Video: Jarvis Conservatory DVD/VHS. Milt Wallace (director). Color. Dialogue in English; singing in Spanish with English subtitles. 54 minutes.

Comment: Finely produced, sung, and acted, with good production values and excellent music.

DOMGRAF-FASSBÄNDER, WILLI
German baritone (1897–1978)

Willi Domgraf-Fassbänder, the father of mezzo-soprano Brigitte Fassbaender, was the principal lyric baritone at the Berlin Staatsoper from 1930 to 1946. He sang Figaro at Glyndebourne on the opening night in 1934 and later returned as Guglielmo and Papageno. He also appeared in several opera films, including Max Ophuls's famous 1932 version of THE BARTERED BRIDE, a notable 1949 LE NOZZE DI FIGARO, and a 1934 biographical film about CARL MARIA VON WEBER.

DOMINGO, PLÁCIDO
Spanish tenor (1941–)

Plácido (or Placido) Domingo may be the best tenor of our time, with a remarkable voice that has allowed him a wide repertory. He can be seen in an enormous number of operas on film and video, more than Pavarotti and over a much wider range of roles. Born in Madrid but raised in Mexico, he began his career in 1957 singing zarzuelas with his parents before making his American debut in Dallas in 1961, as Arturo in *Lucia di Lammermoor*. He began to build his international reputation in Israel from 1962 and was soon established as one of the best tenors in the world; the THREE TENORS concerts confirmed his prominence. Since becoming artistic director of the Washington and Los Angeles opera companies, he has encouraged adventurous programming in both cities.

Domingo is featured in two of the best classic opera films, Rosi's CARMEN (1984) and Zeffirelli's LA TRAVIATA (1982), but he has never been afraid to take risks with new operas, such as Menotti's GOYA (1986) and Moreno Torroba's IL POETA (1980), or neglected ones such as Gomes's IL GUARANY (1994). He has remained attached to his zarzuela roots, including singing in EL BARBERILLO DE LAVAPIÉS (1991 film), EL GATO MONTÉS (1994), LUISA FERNANDA (1963), and MARINA (1963) and participating in ZARZUELA (1991) concerts. He has also sung in operettas such as LA DUCHESSA DEL BAL TABARIN (1963), DIE FLEDERMAUS (1983), DER GRAF VON LUXEMBURG (1963), and DIE LUSTIGE WITWE (1963).

His telecasts and videos of operas include L'AFRICAINE (1988), AIDA (1989), ANDREA CHÉNIER (1979, 1985), UN BALLO IN MASCHERA (1975), CARMEN (1979, 1980, 1984, 1997, 1972 film), CAVALLERIA RUSTICANA (1978, 1982), LE CID (1999), LES CONTES D'HOFFMANN (1981), LA DOLORES (1991 film), DON CARLO (1983), ERNANI (1982), LA FANCIULLA DEL WEST (1983, 1991, 1992), FEDORA (1993), FRANCESCA DA RIMINI (1984), LA GIOCONDA (1986), LOHENGRIN (1990), LUISA MILLER (1979, 1980), MADAMA BUTTERFLY (1974), MANON LESCAUT (1980, 1983), OTELLO (1979, 1986, 1993), PAGLIACCI (1975, 1978, 1982), RIGOLETTO (1977), SAMSON ET DALILA (1980), SIMON BOCCANEGRA (1995), STIFFELIO (1993), IL TABARRO (1994), TOSCA (1976, 1985, 1992), LES TROYENS (1983), and TURANDOT (1988).

He has participated in televised concerts and TV programs with friends, including MONTSERRAT CABALLÉ (1993), JOSÉ CARRERAS (1992), ANGELA GHEORGHIU (1994), SHERRILL MILNES (1985), JESSYE NORMAN (1991), BEVERLY SILLS (1981), KIRI TE KANAWA (1988) and SHIRLEY VERRETT (1985).

He has participated in celebrations at BAYREUTH (1994), CARNEGIE HALL (1991), METROPOLITAN OPERA (1972, 1983, 1986, 1991), PARIS (1989), SEVILLE (1991), VERONA (1988, 1994), and VIENNA (1992, 1993, 1994), and has appeared in tribute programs about ENRICO CARUSO (1998), MARIO LANZA (1983), FRANZ LEHAR (1998), and PYOTR TCHAIKOVSKY (1993).

1984 A Year in the Life of Plácido Domingo
Revel Guest follows a busy Domingo around the world with a camera for a year. He rehearses with Kiri Te Kanawa for *Manon Lescaut*, Katia Ricciarelli for *Otello*, and Marilyn Zschau for *La Fanciulla del West*. He makes his debut as a conductor at Covent Garden with *Die Fledermaus* and performs in *Tosca, The Tales of Hoffmann, Ernani, Otello, La Fanciulla del West, Manon Lescaut,* and Zeffirelli's film of *La traviata*. Color. 105 minutes. Kultur VHS.

1987 An Evening with Plácido Domingo
Domingo in concert at Wembley Arena in London on June 21, 1987. He sings arias and duets by Giordano, Puccini, Verdi, Lehár, and Spanish composers with mezzo Marta Seen and baritone Eduard Tumagian. Eugen Kohn conducts the English Chamber Orchestra; Madeleine French directed. 55 minutes. Image Entertainment DVD/Kultur VHS.

1989 Great Arias With Domingo and Friends
Domingo in concert with four singers in Paris. He sings "Quando le sere al Plácido" from *Luisa Miller*, Shirley Verrett sings "Vissi d'arte," and they duet on "Non sono tuo figlio" from *Il trovatore*. Barbara Hendricks sings "Senza mamma, o bimbo" from *Suor Angelica*, Simon Estes performs Iago's "Credo," and Wang Yan Yan sings an aria from *Don Carlos*. Lorin Maazel conducts the National Orchestra of France, André Frederick directed the video. Color. 46 minutes. VIEW VHS.

1990 Plácido Grandisimo
Domingo and friends in a Seville Stadium concert. Julia Migenes joins him for scenes from *Carmen* and then sings arias from *La Rondine* and *Porgy and Bess*. Domingo sings "E lucevan le stelle," joins Guadalupe Sanchez on a duet from Penella's *El gato montés*, and teams with guitarist Ernesto Bitetti on songs by Manuel Alejandro. Eugene Kohn and Alejandro conduct the National Symphonic Orchestra of Spain. Juan Villaescusa filmed the concert. Color. 60 minutes. Kultur VHS.

1990 Songs of Mexico Volumes 1 and 2
Two travelogue-like videos of Domingo performing songs on location in Mexico with Mexican folksingers, mariachi bands, and folk dancers. Color. Each 60 minutes. On VHS.

1991 Concert for Planet Earth
Domingo filmed in concert in Rio de Janeiro. He sings arias from *L'Africaine, Tosca,* and *Candide* and duets

with mezzo Denyce Graves in a scene from *Carmen*. He is joined by the Wynton Marsalis septet, Antonio Carlos Jobim, and violinist Sarah Chang. John De Main of the Houston Opera leads the Rio de Janeiro Municipal Theater Orchestra. Color. 60 minutes. Sony VHS.

1991 Domingo and Rostropovich Concert
Domingo in an open-air concert at the ancient Roman Theater in Merida, Spain. He sings Lensky's aria from *Eugene Onegin* and is joined by Olga Borodina for a duet from *Carmen*. Rostropovich performs the Haydn Cello Concerto in C and joins Domingo on Massenet's "Elegie," with the tenor singing and playing the piano. Eugene Kohn and the two star performers conduct the St. Petersburg Kirov Theater Orchestra. Juan Villaescusa directed the video. Color. 60 minutes. Kultur VHS.

1991 Domingo Live From Miami
Domingo filmed in concert in the Miami Arena. He sings arias from *L'Africaine*, *Lucia di Lammermoor*, *Tosca*, *La del Manoja de Rosas*, and *Luisa Fernanda* and joins soprano Ann Panagulias in duets from Donizetti's *L'elisir d'amore* and Penella's *El gato montés*. She sings arias from *Don Pasquale* and *Gianni Schicchi*. Eugene Kohn leads the Symphonic Orchestra of Miami; Francisco Suarez filmed the concert. Color. 60 minutes. Kultur VHS.

1994 Plácido Domingo—Live in Prague
Domingo in concert at the Royal Hall in Prague with Angela Gheorghiu on April 24, 1994. Eugen Kohn conducts the Czech Symphony Orchestra in a recital that includes arias and duets by Mozart, Donizetti, Meyerbeer, Puccini, Verdim and Penella. The video was later released in England under Gheorghiu's name because of her sudden rise to fame. Tomás Simerada directed the video. Color. 60 minutes. Kultur VHS/Beckman (GB) DVD.

1994 European Concert 1992
Plácido Domingo joins Daniel Barenboim and the Berlin Philharmonic Orchestra in a celebration at the Basilica of the Royal Monastery of San Lorenzo of the Escorial in Spain on May 1, 1992. Domingo is in fine form in a concert that includes music from *Don Carlo*, *La forza del destino*, *La damnation de Faust*, *Die Meistersinger von Nürnberg*, *Die Walküre*, and *Götterdämmerung*. Color. 125 minutes. TDK DVD.

1994 Tales at the Opera
Four films about Domingo made as a series by BBC Television. The first, shot in Vienna, features his debut in *Die Walküre*. The second, made in Los Angeles, shows Domingo conducting *La bohème*. The third features him at the Met in *Otello*, and the fourth is built around a production of Gomes's *Il Guarany* in Bonn. Daniel Snow-

man and Martin Rosenbaum produced. Color. Each 55 minutes.

1994 Domingo at Arena di Verona
Gala on August 9, 1994, celebrating Domingo's 25th anniversary as a performer at the Arena di Verona. It features scenes from operas, with sets and costumes, including Domingo as Rodolfo in *La bohème* and Radames in *Aida*. Drazen Siriscevic directed. Color. In Italian. 60 minutes. Telecast in America on the A&E cable network.

1995 Plácido Domingo: A Musical Life
Documentary about the tenor from his early days in Mexico and Israel to his later triumphs around the world. He is seen in scenes from *Otello*, *The Tales of Hoffmann*, *Rigoletto*, and *L'Africaine*, as well as recording a zarzuela and relaxing with his family. His wife Marta also appears. Mike Csaky directed. Color. 90 minutes. Kultur VHS.

2001 Moulin Rouge
Domingo provides the singing voice for the Man on the Moon in this innovative musical by opera producer Baz Luhrmann. Color. In English. 128 minutes.

DOMINO NOIR, LE
1837 opéra-comique by Auber

Le Domino Noir (The Black Domino) was one of the most popular of DANIEL AUBER's operas, performed a thousand times at the Opéra-Comique in Paris. It's the story of a man who falls in love with a woman wearing a "black domino" mask at a masked ball in Spain. The woman, Lady Angela, continues to reemerge in various garbs and fascinates him every time. Finally the mystery is unraveled and they get married. The only screen version is a silent movie.

1929 Janson film
This silent feature film directed by Victor Janson was based on the libretto of the opera and was shown in cinemas with the opera music played live. Harry Liedtke plays Orazio de Massarena, Vera Schmiterlow is his beloved Angela, and Hans Junkermann is the Conte de St. Lucar. Aafa Film. Black and white. About 80 minutes.

DOÑA FRANCISQUITA
1923 zarzuela by Vives

AMADEO VIVES's *Doña Francisquita*, one of the major Spanish zarzuelas, based on Lope de Vega's play *La discreta enamorada* updated to the mid-19th century, is set during Carnival time in Madrid. Francisquita loves the student Fernando, but he fancies the actress Aurora. Fernando's widowed father Don Matías courts Francisquita, and she encourages him to make Fernando jealous. Fernando woos Francisquita to make Aurora jealous, and then it really gets complicated, but it all works out somehow in the end. The libretto is by Federico Romero and Guillermo Fernández Shaw.

1934 Behrendt film

Spanish feature film: Hans Behrendt (director), Enrique Guerner (cinematographer), Jean Gilbert (music director).

Cast: Raquel Rodrigo (Francisquita), Fernando Cortes (Fernando), Matilde Vazquez (Aurora), Antonio Palacios (Cardona).

Black and white. In Spanish. 88 minutes.

Comment: Contemporary critics thought the singing was very good.

1952 Vajda film

Spanish feature film: Ladislaus Vajda (director), Antonio Ballesteros (cinematographer), Benito Perojo (producer).

Cast: Mirtha Legrand (Francisquita, sung by Marimi del Pozo), Emma Penella (Aurora, sung by Luly Bergman), Armando Calvo, Antonio Casal, Manola Moran.

Black and white. In Spanish. 90 minutes.

Comment: A much more lavish production than the 1938 film, with spectacular Carnival scenes.

1988 Gran Teatre del Liceu, Barcelona

Spanish stage production José Luis Alonso (director for Teatro Lirico Nacional de la Zarzuela), M. Valdes (conductor, Gran Teatre del Liceu Orchestra and Chorus).

Cast: Enedina Lloris (Francisquita), Alfredo Kraus (Fernando), Rosalina Mestre (Aurora), Josep Ruiz (Cardona), Maria Rus (Doña Francisca), Tomas Alvarez (Don Matias).

Video: House of Opera/Opera Dubs VHS. Francisco Montolo (director). Color. In Spanish. 135 minutes.

***2001 Jarvis Conservatory, Napa

American stage production: Daniel Helfgot (director), Philip J. Bauman (conductor, Jarvis Conservatory Orchestra), Peter Crompton (set designer), Mario la Vega and Maria del Sol (choreographers), William Jarvis (producer/translator).

Cast: Kristin Peterson (Francisquita), Jimmy Kansas (Fernando), Heather Antonissen (Aurora), Rián Villaverde (Cardona), Ilse Apéstegui (Doña Francisca), Mark Urbina (Don Matias).

Video: Jarvis Conservatory VHS. Milt Wallace (director). Color. Dialogue in English; singing in Spanish with English subtitles. 133 minutes.

Comment: Very enjoyable production, nicely staged with good singers.

Related film

1991 Zarzuela Royal Gala Concert

Plácido Domingo and zarzuela singers perform the "Coro de Románticos" from *Doña Francisquita* in a concert in the National Music Auditorium in Madrid accompanied by the Madrid Symphonic Orchestra. Enriques Garcia Asensio directed. Color. In Spanish. 69 minutes. Kultur VHS.

DON CARLOS/DON CARLO
1867 opera by Verdi

A young man (Don Carlo) and a young woman (Elisabetta) fall in love, but she is forced to marry his father. As the father is Philip II of Spain, they have a major problem. Throw in a Grand Inquisitor of doubtful morality, a noble friend (Rodrigo), a scheming rival (Eboli), and a heap of political intrigue, and you have grand soap opera. It's an overheated story, but GIUSEPPE VERDI's music turns it into a great opera, and it only requires half a dozen magnificent singers to make it sound right. The original French libretto by Joseph Mery and Camille du Locle is based on Schiller's verse play *Don Carlos*. In French, as *Don Carlos*, the opera was not a success, but when it was translated into Italian and sung as *Don Carlo*, it became a major hit. Most videos of the opera are in Italian and are titled *Don Carlo*.

1950 Metropolitan Opera

American stage production: Margaret Webster (director), Fritz Stiedry (conductor, Metropolitan Opera Orchestra), Rolf Gérard (set designer).

Cast: Jussi Björling (Don Carlo), Delia Rigal (Elisabetta), Fedora Barbieri (Eboli), Cesare Siepi (Philip II), Robert Merrill (Rodrigo), Jerome Hines (Grand Inquisitor), Lucine Amara (Celestial Voice).

Telecast live November 6, 1950. Black and white. In Italian with introductions to each scene by Milton Cross. 225 minutes.

Comment: Pioneering ABC telecast to an estimated 4 million viewers on opening night of the 1950–1951 Met season. Webster was the first woman to stage a Met production.

1980 Metropolitan Opera

American stage production: John Dexter (director), James Levine (conductor, Metropolitan Opera Orchestra and Chorus), David Reppa (set designer).

Cast: Vasile Moldoveanu (Don Carlo), Renata Scotto (Elisabetta), Tatiana Troyanos (Eboli), Paul Plishka (Philip II), Sherrill Milnes (Rodrigo), Jerome Hines (Grand Inquisitor).

Video at the MTR. Taped February 21, 1980; telecast April 12, 1980. Kirk Browning (director). Color. In Italian with English subtitles. 205 minutes.

1983 Metropolitan Opera

American stage production: John Dexter (director), James Levine (conductor, Metropolitan Opera Orchestra and Chorus), David Reppa (set designer).

Cast: Plácido Domingo (Don Carlo), Mirella Freni (Elisabetta), Nicolai Ghiaurov (Philip II), Grace Bumbry (Eboli), Ferruccio Furlanetto (Grand Inquisitor), Louis Quilico (Don Rodrigo).

Video: Pioneer Classics DVD/VHS/LD and Paramount VHS. Brian Large (director). Taped March 26, 1983; telecast February 1, 1984. Color. In Italian with English subtitles. 214 minutes.

Comment: These singers are perfectly fitted for their roles in this fine production.

1985 Royal Opera

English stage production: Luchino Visconti (director/set designer), Christopher Renshaw (restaging), Bernard Haitink (conductor, Royal Opera House Orchestra and Chorus).

Cast: Luis Lima (Don Carlo), Ileana Cotrubas (Elisabetta), Robert Lloyd (Philip II), Joseph Rouleau (Grand Inquisitor), Giorgio Zancanaro (Rodrigo), Bruna Baglioni (Eboli).

Video: Home Vision VHS. Brian Large (director). Color. In Italian with English subtitles. 204 minutes.

Comment: Visconti created this sumptuous production way back in 1958, and its success helped restore the opera to the repertory. This reprise was seen as a close reproduction of the original version.

1986 Salzburg Festival

Austrian stage production: Herbert von Karajan (director/conductor, Berlin Philharmonic Orchestra, Bulgarian National Opera Chorus, Vienna State Opera Chorus and Salzburg Chamber Choir).

Cast: José Carreras (Don Carlo), Fiamma Izzo d'Amico (Elisabetta), Agnes Baltsa (Eboli), Piero Cappuccilli (Rodrigo), Ferruccio Furlanetto (Philip II), Matti Salminen (Grand Inquisitor).

Video: Sony VHS/LD. Ernst Wild (film director). Color. In Italian. 179 minutes.

Comment: One of the operas filmed by Herbert von Karajan for his "Legacy for Home Video" series.

1992 Teatro alla Scala

Italian stage production: Franco Zeffirelli (director/set designer), Riccardo Muti (conductor, Teatro alla Scala Orchestra and Chorus), Anna Anni (costume designer).

Cast: Luciano Pavarotti (Don Carlo), Samuel Ramey (Philip II), Daniela Dessi (Elisabetta), Luciana d'Intino (Eboli), Paolo Coni (Rodrigo), Alexander Anisimov (Grand Inquisitor).

Video: EMI Classics VHS/Pioneer LD. Franco Zeffirelli (director). Color. In Italian with Italian subtitles. 182 minutes.

1996 Théâtre du Châtelet

French stage production: Luc Bondy (director), Antonio Pappano (conductor, Orchestre de Paris and Théâtre du Châtelet Chorus), Gilles Aillaud (set designer).

Cast: Robert Alagna (Don Carlos) Karita Mattila (Elizabeth), Waltraud Meier (Eboli), Thomas Hampson (Rodrigue), José van Dam (Philip II), Eric Halfvarson (Grand Inquisitor).

Video: Bel Canto Society/NVC Arts (GB) DVD and VHS. Yves André Hubert (director). Color. In French with English subtitles. 211 minutes.

Early/related films

1909 Cines film

Italian film of scenes from the opera produced by the Cines studio. It was released in America in September 1909 as *Don Carlos* and screened with music from the opera. Black and white. Silent. About 10 minutes.

1909 Film d'Art film

French film of scenes from the opera directed by André Calmettes for the Société du Film d'Art with cast headed by Paul Mounet, Dehelly, and Bartet. Released in America in May 1910 as *Don Carlos* and screened with Verdi music. Black and white. Silent. About 14 minutes.

1921 Antamoro film

Italian feature film based on the opera and the Schiller play. It was directed by Giulio Antamoro, a moviemaker known primarily for religious films. Alfredo Bertone, Elena Lunda, and Enrico Roma have the main roles. Black and white. Silent. About 70 minutes.

1955 Interrupted Melody

Interrupted Melody begins in the Australian outback where aspiring opera soprano Marjorie Lawrence (Eleanor Parker) wins a competition to study in Paris with her performance of Eboli's aria "O don fatal" from *Don Carlos*. The singing voice belongs to Eileen Farrell. See INTERRUPTED MELODY.

1999 Angela's Ashes

The aria "È lui! desso! L'Infante" is featured in this film about the desperately poor Irish childhood of Frank McCourt and the difficult life of his mother Angela, played by Emily Watson. Alan Parker directed. Color. In English. 146 minutes.

2002 The Sum of All Fears

The aria "Io la vidi," sung by Thomas Harper with the Czechoslovak Radio Symphony Orchestra and Slovak Philharmonic Chorus, is featured on the soundtrack of this Tom Clancy thriller. Ben Affleck stars as Jack Ryan; Phil Alden Robinson directed. Color. In English. 123 minutes.

DON CÉSAR DE BAZAN
1872 opera by Massenet

JULES MASSENET's fading reputation has meant that this opera has dropped almost out of sight, but it was very popular with filmmakers in the early part of the century. It's based on the play by Adolphe d'Ennery and Philippe Dumanoir, which also inspired Vincent Wallace's English opera MARITANA. Don César is a nobleman who becomes the surrogate husband for the gypsy Maritana when she attracts the interest of the Spanish king.

Early films

1909 Eclair film

Victorin Jasset directed this French film of the opera for the Eclair company. It stars Charles Krauss, Harry Bauer, Marie de l'Isle, and Suzanne Goldstein. Black and white. Silent. About 10 minutes.

1912 Reliance film

Irving Cummings directed an American film based on the opera for the Reliance company. Black and white. Silent. About 15 minutes.

1915 Kalem film

This American feature film is called *Don Caesar de Bazan* although the screenplay was apparently based on Wallace's opera *Maritana*. The plots, however, are virtually the same. Robert G. Vignola directed it for the Kalem studio. Black and white. Silent. About 70 minutes.

DON GIL DE ALCALÁ
1932 opera by Penella

Spanish composer MANUEL PENELLA's *Don Gil de Alcalá* is one of his most popular operas. Set in 18th-century Mexico, it focuses on the adventures of Captain Don Gil de Alcalá and his rescue of convent girl Estrella from having to marry the elderly Spanish nobleman Don Diego. Penella, who also wrote the libretto, went to Mexico in 1938 to supervise the making of a film based on the opera and died while he was there.

1938 El Capitan Aventurero

Mexican feature film: Arcady Botelier (director), screenplay based on libretto of *Don Gil de Alcalá*.

Cast: José Mojica (Don Gil de Alcalá), Manolita Saval (Estella), Alberto Marti (Don Diego), Carlos Orellana (Sergeant), Margarita Mora (Marquesa), Sara Garcia, Eduardo Arozamena.

Video: Bel Canto Society/Lyric VHS. Black and white. In Spanish. 91 minutes.

Comment: The film, which allows Mexican tenor Mojica ample time to sing Penella's melodies, was also distributed in America.

DON GIOVANNI
1787 opera by Mozart

MOZART's *Don Giovanni* reached the cinema as early as 1900 when a sound film of a scene from the opera was shown at the Paris Exposition. A silent version was made in 1922, and arias have been featured regularly in films since the coming of sound. It was one of the three operas written in Italian for Mozart by LORENZO DA PONTE, who tells the great libertine's story brilliantly (he was rumored to have had help from his friend Casanova). Many consider this the greatest opera ever written. George Bernard Shaw wrote an ironic sequel called *Don Juan in Hell*, which describes what happens to the main characters in the opera when they meet up in Hell. There are also many films from Spanish-speaking countries titled *Don Juan Tenorio*, but they are based on a famous Spanish play and not the opera.

1947 New London Opera Company

English stage production: Clifford Evans (director), Alberto Erede (conductor), Joseph Carl (set designer).

Cast: Bruce Boyce (Don Giovanni), Italo Tajo (Leporello), Rachel Ravina (Donna Anna), Elizabeth Theilmann (Donna Elvira), Murray Dickie (Ottavio),

Daria Bayan (Zerlina), Ian Wallace (Masetto), Marco Stefanoni (Commendatore).

Filmed live for telecast by BBC Television. Black and white. In English. 120 minutes.

1954 RAI Italian Television

Italian television production: Max Rudolf (conductor, RAI Chorus and Orchestra of Torino).

Cast: Giuseppe Taddei (Don Giovanni), Italo Tajo (Leporello), Maria Crutis Verna (Donna Anna), Carla Gavazzi (Donna Elvira), Cesare Valletti (Ottavio), Elda Ribetti (Zerlina), Vito Susca (Masetto), Antonio Zerbini (Commendatore).

Video: Warner Fonit DVD. Black and white. In Italian. 163 minutes.

1954 Salzburg Festival

English film of stage production: Paul Czinner and Alfred Travers (film directors), Herbert Graf (stage director), Wilhelm Furtwängler (conductor, Vienna Philharmonic Orchestra and Vienna State Opera Chorus), S. D. Onions (cinematographer).

Cast: Cesare Siepi (Don Giovanni), Otto Edelmann (Leporello), Elisabeth Grümmer (Donna Anna), Lisa della Casa (Donna Elvira), Erna Berger (Zerlina), Anton Dermota (Don Ottavio), Walter Berry (Masetto), Deszö Ernster (Commendatore).

Video: DG/Universal DVD/VAI VHS. Color. In Italian. 129 minutes.

Comment: One of the earliest complete operas filmed in performance, shot on an open-air stage without an audience. It was widely promoted and released theatrically in both the United States and England. While it is certainly dated, it is a fascinating trip back in time to see a top-notch cast perform in the style of its era.

1954 Kolm-Veltée film

Austrian feature film: H. W. Kolm-Veltée (director and screenplay, with Alfred Uh and Ernest Henthaler), Prof. Birkmeyer (conductor, Vienna Symphony Orchestra), Willy Sohm-Hannes Fuchs (cinematographer).

Cast: Cesare Danova (Don Giovanni, sung by Alfred Poell), Josef Meinrad (Leporello, sung by Harald Progelhof), Marianne Schonauer (Donna Anna, sung by Anny Felbermayer), Lotte Tobisch (Donna Elvira, sung by Hanna Loeser), Evelyn Cormand (Zerlina, sung by Anny Felbermayer), Jean Vinci (Don Ottavio, sung by Hugo Meyer-Welfing), Hans von Vorsody (Masetto, sung by Walter Berry), Fred Hennings (Commendatore, sung by Gottlob Frick), Vienna State Opera Ballet.

Color. In German with English subtitles. 89 minutes.

Comment: Kolm-Veltée's shortened film version eliminates many arias and turns the opera into a kind

of swashbuckler with duels in the Errol Flynn style. It was released theatrically in America by Times Films as *Don Juan*.

1954 Vienna State Opera Mozart Ensemble

Austrian stage production: Alfred Stöger (director), Rudolf Moralt (conductor, Vienna Philharmonic).

Cast: Paul Schöffler (Don Giovanni), Erich Kunz (Leporello), Carla Martiris (Donna Anna), Hilde Zadek (Donna Elvira), Hilde Gueden (Zerlina), Ludwig Weber (Commendatore).

Video: Taurus (Germany) VHS. Color. In German. 30 minutes.

Comment: Highlights version of the opera included in the anthology film *Unsterblicher Mozart* (Immortal Mozart) with two other Mozart operas.

1960 NBC Opera Theatre

American stage production: Samuel Chotzinoff (producer), Peter Herman Adler (conductor, Symphony of the Air), Don Shirley (set designer), W. H. Auden and Chester Kallman (English translation).

Cast: Cesare Siepi (Don Giovanni), James Pease (Leporello), Leontyne Price (Donna Anna), Helen George (Donna Elvira), Judith Raskin (Zerlina), Charles K. L. Davis (Don Ottavio), John Reardon (Masetto), John Macurdy (Commendatore).

Telecast live April 10, 1960. Kirk Browning (director). Black and white. In English. 160 minutes.

1961 Deutsche Oper Berlin

German film of stage production: Carl Ebert (director), Ferenc Fricsay (conductor, Deutsche Oper Berlin Orchestra and Chorus), George Wakhevitch (set/costume designer).

Cast: Dietrich Fischer-Dieskau (Don Giovanni), Walter Berry (Leporello), Elisabeth Grümmer (Donna Anna), Pilar Lorengar (Donna Elvira), Erika Köth (Zerlina), Donald Grobe (Don Ottavio), Ivan Sardi (Masetto), Josef Greindl (Commendatore).

Video: Lyric VHS. Telecast September 24, 1961. Black and white. In German. 166 minutes.

Comment: This historic production, which reopened the Deutsche Oper Berlin after World War II, was filmed live in 16mm at its dress rehearsal.

1977 Glyndebourne Festival

English stage production: Peter Hall (director), Bernard Haitink (conductor, London Philharmonic Orchestra and Glyndebourne Festival Chorus), John Bury (set designer).

Cast: Benjamin Luxon (Don Giovanni), Stafford Dean (Leporello), Rachel Yakar (Donna Elvira), Horiana Branisteanu (Donna Anna), Leo Goeke (Don Ottavio), Elizabeth Gale (Zerlina), John Rawnsley (Masetto), Pierre Thau (Commendatore).

Video: Opera d'Oro/VAI VHS. Dave Heather (director). Color. In Italian with English subtitles. 173 minutes.

Comment: Controversial production set in the Victorian period, but Hall certainly obtains memorable performances from the singers.

***1978 Losey film

French/Italian/German feature film: Joseph Losey (director/screenplay, with Franz Salieri and Patricia Losey), Lorin Maazel (conductor, Paris Opéra Orchestra and Chorus), Gerry Fisher and Carlo Poletti (cinematographers), Daniel Toscan du Plantier (producer).

Cast: Ruggero Raimondi (Don Giovanni), José van Dam (Leporello), Edda Moser (Donna Anna), Kiri Te Kanawa (Donna Elvira), Teresa Berganza (Zerlina), Kenneth Riegel (Don Ottavio), Malcolm King (Masetto), John Macurdy (Commendatore), Eric Adjani (Valet).

Video: Columbia TriStar DVD/Kultur VHS/Pioneer LD. Technicolor. In Italian with English subtitles. 177 minutes.

Comment: One of the great opera films. Losey shot it on location in Vicenza near Venice with unusual visual concepts. It opens at a glass factory where Don Giovanni is on a visit, accompanied by Donna Anna. Leporello's Catalogue aria is a visual joke as the "catalogue" is a scroll that unrolls down the stairs.

Don Giovanni (1978): Don Giovanni (Ruggero Raimondi) seduces Zerlina (Teresa Berganza) in Joseph Losey's film.

1978 Metropolitan Opera

American stage production: Herbert Graf (director of original production), Patrick Tavernia (stager), Richard Bonynge (conductor, Metropolitan Opera Orchestra and Chorus), Eugene Berman (set designer).

Cast: James Morris (Don Giovanni), Gabriel Bacquier (Leporello), Joan Sutherland (Donna Anna), Julia Varady (Donna Elvira), Huguette Tourangeau (Zerlina), John Brecknock (Don Ottavio), Allan Monk (Masetto), John Macurdy (Commendatore).

Video at the MTR. Kirk Browning (director). Telecast live March 16, 1978. Color. In Italian with English subtitles. 190 minutes.

***1987 Drottningholm Court Theatre

Swedish stage production: Göran Järvefelt (director), Arnold Östman (conductor, Drottningholm Court Theatre Orchestra), set design based on an early production in the theater.

Cast: Håkan Hagegård (Don Giovanni), Erik Saedén (Leporello), Helena Döse (Donna Anna), Birgit Nordin (Donna Elvira), Anita Soldh (Zerlina), Gösta Winbergh (Don Ottavio), Tord Wallström (Masetto), Bengt Rundgren (Commendatore).

Video: Philips VHS/LD. Thomas Olofsson (director). Color. In Italian with English subtitles. 155 minutes.

Comment: Charming intimate production in a baroque theater that dates from Mozart's era, with the orchestra in period costumes playing period instruments finely led by Östman.

1987 Salzburg Festival

Austrian stage production: Michael Hampe (director), Herbert von Karajan (conductor, Vienna Philharmonic Orchestra and Vienna State Opera Chorus), Mauro Pagano (set/costume designer), Ernst Wild (cinematographer).

Cast: Samuel Ramey (Don Giovanni), Ferruccio Furlanetto (Leporello), Anna Tomowa-Sintow (Donna Anna), Julia Varady (Donna Elvira), Kathleen Battle (Zerlina), Gösta Winbergh (Don Ottavio), Alexander Malta (Masetto), Paata Burchuladze (Commendatore).

Video: Sony DVD/VHS/LD. Claus Viller (director). Color. In Italian. 193 minutes.

Comment: Stolid production like most of Karajan's "Legacy for Home Video" series.

1989 Teatro alla Scala

Italian stage production: Giorgio Strehler (director), Riccardo Muti (conductor, La Scala Opera Orchestra and Chorus), Ezio Frigerio (set designer).

Cast: Thomas Allen (Don Giovanni), Claudio Desderi (Leporello), Edita Gruberova (Donna Anna),

Ann Murray (Donna Elvira), Suzanne Mentzer (Zerlina), Francisco Araiza (Don Ottavio), Natale de Carolis (Masetto), Sergei Koptchak (Commendatore).

Video: Image Entertainment DVD/Home Vision VHS. Carlo Battistoni (director). Color. In Italian with English subtitles. 176 minutes.

Comment: Sumptuous production by Strehler using many of the innovative theatrical techniques he originated at Milan's Piccolo Teatro.

1989 Teatro Regio, Parma

Italian stage production: Mario Corradi (director), Hans Graf (conductor, Orchestra Sinfonica dell'Emilia-Romagna "Arturo Toscanini" and Teatro Regio Chorus).

Cast: Renato Bruson (Don Giovanni), Domenico Trimarchi (Leporello), Winifred Faix Brown (Donna Anna), Daniela Dessi (Donna Elvira), Adelina Scarabelli (Zerlina), Francisco Araiza (Don Ottavio), Marcello Grisman (Masetto), Matthias Holle (Commendatore).

Video: Bel Canto Society VHS. Color. In Italian. 190 minutes.

1990 Sellars film

American/Austrian feature film: Peter Sellars (director), Craig Smith (conductor, Vienna Symphony and Arnold Schoenberg Choir), George Tsypin (set designer).

Cast: Eugene Perry (Don Giovanni), Herbert Perry (Leporello), Dominique Labelle (Donna Anna), Lorraine Hunt (Donna Elvira), Ai Lan Zhu (Zerlina), Carroll Freeman (Don Ottavio), Elmore James (Masetto), James Patterson (Commendatore).

Video: London VHS/LD. Color. In Italian with English subtitles. 190 minutes.

Comment: Sellars sets his bleak modern *Don Giovanni* in the back streets of Harlem; the Don is a vicious drug addict, and Leporello is his doppelganger, with the roles played by twin brothers. Sellars's vision is striking, but it's so dark we lose sympathy for the Don and the other characters. Filmed in a Vienna TV studio.

1990 Metropolitan Opera

American stage production: Franco Zeffirelli (director/set designer), James Levine (conductor, Metropolitan Opera Orchestra and Chorus).

Cast: Samuel Ramey (Don Giovanni), Ferruccio Furlanetto (Leporello), Carol Vaness (Donna Anna), Karita Mattila (Donna Elvira), Dawn Upshaw (Zerlina), Jerry Hadley (Don Ottavio), Philip Cokorinos (Masetto), Kurt Moll (Commendatore).

Telecast October 31, 1990; taped April 2 and 5, 1990. Brian Large (director). Color. In Italian with English subtitles. 190 minutes.

1991 Cologne Opera

German stage production: Michael Hampe (director), James Conlon (conductor, Cologne Gurzenich Orchestra and Cologne Opera Chorus), Hartmut Warneck (set designer).

Cast: Thomas Allen (Don Giovanni), Ferruccio Furlanetto (Leporello), Carolyn James (Donna Anna), Carol Vaness (Donna Elvira), Andrea Rost (Zerlina), Kjell-Magnus Sandvé (Don Ottavio), Reinhard Dorn (Masetto), Matthias Holle (Commendatore).

Video: Arthaus Musik DVD. José Montes-Baquer (director). In Italian with English subtitles. 173 minutes.

1991 Grand Théâtre de Genève

Swiss stage production: Mathia Langhoff (director), Armin Jordan (conductor, Orchestra de la Suisse Romande and Chorus of the Grand Théâtre de Genève), Jean-Marc Stehle (set/costume designer).

Cast: Thomas Hampson (Don Giovanni), Willard White (Leporello), Marilyn Mims (Donna Anna), Nancy Gustafson (Donna Elvira), Della Jones (Zerlina), John Aler (Don Ottavio), François Harismendy (Masetto), Carsten Harboe Stabell (Commendatore).

Video: House of Opera DVD/VHS and Lyric VHS. Color. In Italian. 189 minutes.

1991 Stavovské Theatre, Prague

Czech stage production: David Radok (director), Charles Mackerras (conductor, Prague National Theater Chorus and Orchestra), Simon Caban (set designer).

Cast: Andrei Bestchastney (Don Giovanni), Ludek Vele (Leporello), Nadezhda Petrenko (Donna Anna), Jírina Marková (Donna Elvira), Alice Randova (Zerlina), Vladimír Dolezal (Don Ottavio), Zdenek Harvánek (Masetto), Dalibor Jedlicka (Commendatore).

Video: am@do (GB) DVD. Michal Caban (director). Color. In Italian with English subtitles. 152 minutes.

Comment: The Stavovské Theatre in Prague, where *Don Giovanni* premiered in 1787, reopened in December 1991 with this production of the opera featuring a mostly Czech cast.

1992 Ruggero Raimondi: My Favorite Opera

Documentary film: Paul Smaczny/Clara Fabry (film directors), Luca Ronconi (stage director), Riccardo Chailly (conductor, Teatro Communale Orchestra and Chorus), Margherita Palli (set designer).

Cast: Ruggero Raimondi (Don Giovanni), Alessandro Corbelli (Leporello), Jane Eaglen (Donna Anna), Daniele Dessi (Donna Elvira), Adelina Scarabelli (Zerlina), Rockwell Blake (Don Ottavio), Giovanni Fulanetto (Masetto), Andrea Silvestrelli (Commendatore).

Video: Kultur VHS. Color. In Italian with English narration and English subtitles. 60 minutes.

Comment: This documentary in the *My Favorite Opera* series shows Raimondi rehearsing and performing scenes from *Don Giovanni* at the Teatro Communale in Bologna. The complete opera was telecast on RAI Italian television on July 29, 1991, but it is not on a commercial video.

1995 Glyndebourne Festival

English stage production: Deborah Warner (director), Yakov Kreizberg (conductor, Orchestra of the Age of Enlightenment and Glyndebourne Festival Chorus), Hildegarde Bechtler and Nicky Gillibrand (set/costume designers).

Cast: Gilles Cachemaille (Don Giovanni), Steven Page (Leporello), Hillevi Martinpelto (Donna Anna), Adrianne Pieczonka (Donna Elvira), Juliane Banse (Zerlina), John Mark Ainsley (Don Ottavio), Roberto Scaltriti (Masetto), Gudjon Oskarsson (Commendatore).

Video: Arthaus DVD/Warner Vision (GB) VHS. Derek Bailey (director). Color. In Italian with English subtitles. 176 minutes.

Comment: Exciting though somewhat controversial modern dress production with the ball scene set in a disco. This is an unglamorous portrait of the Don, who is portrayed like a street hood woman chaser.

1999 Zurich Opera

Swiss stage production: Jürgen Flimm (director), Nikolaus Harnoncourt (conductor, Zurich Opera Orchestra and Chorus), Erich Wonder (set designer).

Cast: Rodney Gilfry (Don Giovanni), Laszlo Polgar (Leporello), Cecilia Bartoli (Donna Elvira), Isabel Rey (Donna Anna), Liliana Nikiteanu (Zerlina), Roberto Sacca (Don Ottavio), Oliver Widmer (Masetto), Matti Salminen (Commendatore).

Video: Naxos/Arthaus DVD. Brian Large (director). Color. In Italian with English subtitles. 187 minutes (with 24-minute behind-the-scenes documentary).

2000 Metropolitan Opera

American stage production: Franco Zeffirelli (director/set designer), James Levine (conductor, Metropolitan Opera Orchestra and Chorus).

Cast: Bryn Terfel (Don Giovanni), Ferruccio Furlanetto (Leporello), Renée Fleming (Donna Anna), Solveig Kringelborn (Donna Elvira), Hei-Kyung Hong (Zerlina), Paul Groves (Don Ottavio), John Relyea (Masetto), Sergei Koptchak (Commendatore).

Telecast December 27, 2000, on PBS; taped October 14, 2000. Gary Halvorson (director). Color. In Italian with English subtitles. 191 minutes.

Comment: This is a reprise of Zeffirelli's popular 1990 production.

Early/related films

1900 First sound opera film

Victor Maurel, the French baritone who created the roles of Iago, Falstaff, and Tonio, is seen and heard singing an aria from *Don Giovanni* in the first sound opera film. It was shown in Paris on June 8, 1900, at Clément Maurice's Phono-Cinéma-Théâtre at the Paris Exhibition with a synchronized phonographic cylinder providing the sound. Also on the program were films of Maurel in *Falstaff* and Emile Cossira in *Romeo et Juliette*. Black and white. In Italian. About 3 minutes.

1905/1908 Don Juan

Albert Capellani made the French Pathé film *Don Juan* in 1905 with a cast headed by Paul Capellani and Henry Desfontaines. It was rereleased in Germany in 1908 as a sound film with an aria from the opera played on a phonograph. Black and white. In Italian. About 7 minutes.

1911 La fin de Don Juan

Victorin Jasset directed this early French film of scenes from the opera for the Éclair company. A contemporary critic noted how pleasant it was to see films based on operas because one could imagine the music that accompanied the scenes. Black and white. Silent. About 10 minutes.

1922 Tense Moments From Operas

J. R. Tozer plays Don Giovanni in this British highlights version of the opera made for the series *Tense Moments From Opera*. Pauline Peters is Zerlina, Lillian Douglas is Donna Anna, and Kathleen Vaughan is Donna Elvira. Real singers behind the stage performed with the film. Edwin J. Collins directed. Black and white. Silent. About 10 minutes.

1922 Don Juan et Faust

Marcel L'Herbier directed this French feature based on a novel that combined the two legends into one story. Jaque Catelain is a sympathetic Don Juan, Vanni Marcoux is an evil Faust, and Marcelle Pradot is the Donna Anna they both desire. Gaumont. Black and white. Silent. About 80 minutes.

1929 Vitaphone film with Hackett

Chicago Opera tenor Charles Hackett sings Don Ottavio's aria "Il mio tesoro" from *Don Giovanni* in this sound film made by the Vitaphone company. Black and white. In Italian. 8 minutes.

1932 The Great Lover
Adolphe Menjou plays a Don Juan–esque opera star philanderer who seduces women with the help of the duet "Là ci darem la mano." He is seen on stage at the Met in *Don Giovanni* with Irene Dunne. Harry Beaumont directed. MGM. Black and white. 79 minutes.

1937 Solo per te
Beniamino Gigli sings a duet with himself as both Don Giovanni and Zerlina as he has fun with his version of "Là ci darem la mano." He plays an opera singer married to a soprano (Maria Cebotari) with a secret in her past. See SOLO PER TE.

1940 Her First Romance
Shy Edith Fellows sings the duet "Là ci darem la mano" with Chicago opera star Wilbur Evans at a dance soon after they meet in this Monogram film. Naturally he immediately asks her to marry him. Black and white. In English. 77 minutes.

1942 Don Giovanni
Dino Falconi directed the Italian narrative film *Don Giovanni* that tells more or less the same story as the opera and uses Mozart's music as its score. Adriano Rimoldi is Giovanni, Dina Sassoli is Donna Anna, and Elena Zasreschi is Donna Elvira. Black and white. In Italian. 85 minutes.

1945 The Picture of Dorian Gray
Lord Harry Wotton (George Sanders) invites Dorian Gray (Hurd Hatfield) to the opera to hear de Reszke sing soon after Gray has seduced and caused the suicide of pub entertainer Angela Lansbury. He leaves singing "Là ci darem la mano." Albert Lewin directed. Black and white. In English. 110 minutes.

1947 It Happened in Brooklyn
Kathryn Grayson teams with Frank Sinatra on the duet "Là ci darem la mano" in this story about a group of Brooklynites trying to break into musical show business. Richard Whorf directed. Black and white. In English. 105 minutes.

1949 Kind Heart and Coronets
Dennis Price, sitting in an English prison death cell writing his memoirs, remembers how his opera singer father sang Don Ottavio's aria "Il mio tesoro" to his mother and then eloped with her. She was cut off by her aristocratic family, so Price has bumped them all off in revenge. Robert Hamer directed this enjoyable black comedy. Black and white. 104 minutes.

1950 The Toast of New Orleans
Maria Lanza and Kathryn Grayson perform the duet "Là ci darem la mano" in this pleasant film about a Louisiana fisherman who becomes an opera star in turn-of-the-century New Orleans. See THE TOAST OF NEW ORLEANS.

1967 Felsenstein Inszeniert
American filmmaker Michael Blackwood shot the German TV documentary *Felsenstein Director* for NDR while Walter Felsenstein was rehearsing the second act of *Don Giovanni* at the Berlin Komische Oper in 1966. Color. In German. 67 minutes.

1967 Mozart in Prague: Don Giovanni 67
Dietrich Fischer-Dieskau (Don Giovanni), Birgit Nilsson (Donna Anna), and Peter Schreier (Don Ottavio) are filmed during rehearsals and recording of *Don Giovanni* in Prague. Karl Böhm conducts the Prague National Theater Chorus and Orchestra. Wolfgang Esterer directed this TV film. Color. 60 minutes.

1970 Don Giovanni
Carmelo Bene's purposely outrageous experimental Italian film *Don Giovanni* is loosely based on the opera; the music he created for it might be called mock-Mozart. Bene plays Don Giovanni, Lydia Mancinelli is the woman, Gea Marotta is her daughter, and Salvatore Vendittelli is the Commendatore. Color. In Italian. 80 minutes.

1980 Don Juan, Karl-Liebknecht-Strasse 78
Siegfried Kuhn's film revolves around the problems a Berlin opera producer confronts in a provincial theater in East Germany as he tries to stage *Don Giovanni*. His personal problems parallel the opera, especially his relations with the women portraying Donna Anna and Donna Elvira. The main actors are Hilmar Thate, Beata Tyszkiewicz, Ewa Szykulska, and Helmut Strassburger. DEFA. Color. In German. 99 minutes.

1984 Amadeus
Milos Forman's Mozart biopic has a memorable scene of the Commendatore's statue bursting onto the stage in the Tyl Theater in Prague when *Don Giovanni* has its premiere. The statue is presented as if it were Mozart's father coming back from the grave to chastise his errant son. The scene was staged by Twyla Tharp with Neville Marriner conducting the orchestra. Karel Fiala plays Don Giovanni (sung by Richard Stilwell), Zdenek Jelen is Leporello (sung by Willard White), and Jan Blazek is the Commendatore (sung by John Tomlinson). See AMADEUS.

1985 Babel Opera

Babel Opéra, ou La Répétition de Don Juan is a Belgian film by André Delvaux built around preparations for a production of *Don Giovanni*. The "real" characters in the film are involved in situations similar to those in the opera. José van Dam is Don Giovanni, Ashley Putnam is Donna Anna, Stuart Burrows is Don Ottavio, Christiane Eda-Pierre is Donna Elvira, and Pierre Thau is the Commendatore. See BABEL OPERA.

1986 Broderna Mozart

The Mozart Brothers is a Swedish film by Suzanne Osten about a production of *Don Giovanni*. The stage director wants to stand the "old war-horse opera" on its head and create a vital new production so the singers lose hair and clothes, the musicians get angry, and the union is outraged. Only the ghost of Mozart seems happy. Many of the actors are from the Stockholm Opera. Loa Falkman is Don Giovanni, Agneta Ekmannder is Donna Elvira, Lena T. Hansson is Donna Anna, Helge Skoog is Don Ottavio, Grith Fjelmose is Zerlina, Rune Zetterstrom is Leporello, and Krister Sit Hill is Masetto. See BRODERNA MOZART.

1987 Harry Kupfer Rehearses Don Giovanni

Rainer Milzkott directed this TV documentary for Berlin's SFB Television showing German director Harry Kupfer at work while staging a production of *Don Giovanni*. Color. In German. 44 minutes.

1987 Babette's Feast

This Academy Award–winning Danish film has two scenes featuring *Don Giovanni*. A French opera singer (Jean-Philippe Lafont) is first seen on stage in *Don Giovanni*. When he goes on holiday to a Jutland village, he is attracted to the pious daughter (Hanne Stensgaard, singing by Tina Kiberg) of the local Lutheran pastor and offers to give her lessons. After a seductive session singing "Là ci darem la mano," she decides to gives up singing. Years later, the singer sends the French chef Babette (Stéphane Audran) to the woman with a request for sanctuary (she is a Communard fleeing from 1871 Paris) and sets in motion the banquet that climaxes the film. Gabriel Axel directed. Color. In Danish with English subtitles. 102 minutes. On DVD & VHS.

1987 Karajan in Salzburg

This documentary about Herbert von Karajan at the 1987 Salzburg Festival has extensive scenes of rehearsals and the opening of *Don Giovanni* with Samuel Ramey as the Don. Susan Froemke, Peter Gelb, and Deborah Dickson directed the film. Color. In English and German. 84 minutes. On VHS.

1992 Don Gio

Czech filmmakers who worked with Milos Forman on *Amadeus* created this experimental version of the Don Giovanni story. Don Giovanni is sung by Andrej Bescasny and Zdenek Klumpar, Leporello by Ludek Vele, Zerlina by Bara Basikova, and Donna Elvira by Jirina Markova. Mozart's music is played by the National Theatre Orchestra conducted by Jose Kuchinka. Directors Simon Caban and Michal Caban intercut opera and rehearsals with modern music and contemporary events. Color. In Czech with English subtitles. 88 minutes.

1995 Guarding Tess

This Hollywood comedy drama about a bodyguard and a wayward first lady features Leporello's aria "Madamina, il catalogo é questo" sung by Giuseppe Taddei with the Philharmonia Orchestra conducted by Carlo-Maria Giulini. Shirley MacLaine and Nicolas Cage are the stars; Hugh Wilson wrote and directed the film. Color. 98 minutes.

1999 The Lost Lover

Zerlina's aria "Vedrai, carino" from *Don Giovanni* is featured in this British-Italian film about Jews and Palestinians in modern Israel and love across religious barriers. Robert Faenza directed. Color. 79 minutes.

2000 The Contender

The Minuet from *Don Giovanni* is performed by harpist John Carrington in this film about a woman senator (Joan Allen) nominated for vice president. Rod Lurie directed. Color. 126 minutes.

2000 The Tao of Steve

Donna Anna's aria "Non mir dir" and the seductive duet "Là ci darem la mano" are featured in this film about a womanizer (Donal Logue) who finally finds true love. Jenniphr Goodman directed. Color. 86 minutes.

2002 xXx

Rob Cohen's action film *xXx* stars Vin Diesel as a sports daredevil government agent who has to save the world. Meanwhile the soundtrack features two numbers from *Don Giovanni*, the aria "Fin ch'han dal vino" and the duet "Batti, batti, o bel Masetto" Color. 124 minutes.

DON GIOVANNI: LEPORELLO'S REVENGE

2000 Canadian opera film by Sweete

Barbara Willis Sweete's film *Don Giovanni: Leporello's Revenge* (shown on U.S. television in 2001 as *Don Giovanni Unmasked*) is a dualist revisionist version of the

Mozart–da Ponte opera with Leporello as the central character; Russian baritone Dmitri Hvorostovsky plays both Leporello and the Don. It begins in a screening room (filmed in color) with producer Leporello in evening dress showing his cast the black-and-white film of the opera that he has made which is supposed to be his revenge. He sings Leporello's lines from the screening room while on screen he plays and sings Don Giovanni. No lines of the opera libretto are changed, but only scenes in which Leporello is present are used. Donna Elvira is more central in Leporello's version, Donna Anna and Zerlina less so. Barbara Dunn Prosser plays Donna Elvira (sung by Liesel Fedkenheur), Dominque Labelle is Donna Anna, Krisztina Szabó is Zerlina, Michael Colvin is Don Ottavio, Gary Relyea is the Commander, and Alain Coulombe is Masetto. Florence Ilia has the silent dancing role of Donna Elvira's maid, Donna Fedore is the choreographer, René Ohashi is the cinematographer, and Richard Bradshaw conducts the Canadian Opera Company Orchestra (the sound track is on a CD). Sweete made the film for Rhombus Media of Canada. Color and black and white. 60 minutes.

DONIZETTI, GAETANO
Italian composer (1797–1848)

Gaetano Donizetti, who was born in Bergamo in 1797 and composed his first opera in 1818, wrote 67 operas, many still in the repertory. His first great opera was ANNA BOLENA, which premiered in 1830. It was followed by L'ELISIR D'AMORE in 1832 and LUCIA DI LAMMERMOOR in 1835. Also still popular are DON PASQUALE, LA FAVORITA, LA FILLE DU RÉGIMENT, LUCREZIA BORGIA, MARIA STUARDA, and ROBERTO DEVEREUX. His last opera was the 1844 *Caterina Cornaro*. Donizetti is well served on film and video; nine operas are on commercial video and several others have been telecast and are available from alternative distributors, including BELISARIO, IL DUCA D'ALBA, LINDA DI CHAMOUNIX, MARIA DI ROHAN, and SANCIA DE CASTIGLIA. *La fille du régiment* and *Maria Stuarda* are available on video in English versions as *The Daughter of the Regiment* and *Mary Stuart*.

1946 Il cavaliere del sogno
Il cavaliere del sogno (The Dream Knight) is an Italian fiction film about the composer with Amedeo Nazzari playing Donizetti. His life is told in flashback from his deathbed, with many scenes shot on location in his native Bergamo. Shown in the United States as *The Life of Donizetti*. See IL CAVALIERE DEL SOGNO.

1954 Casa Ricordi
Donizetti (Marcello Mastroianni) tames a temperamental diva during rehearsals for the premiere of *L'elisir d'amore*. At least that is what happens in this film about the Ricordi opera publishing firm. See RICORDI.

1954 Casta diva
Fausto Tozzi has the role of Donizetti in Carmine Gallone's biographical film about rival composer Vincenzo Bellini. See VINCENZO BELLINI.

1955 Un palco all'opera
Eduardo De Santis plays Donizetti in this Italian film that features a section about his relationship with Luisa (Elena Kleus). Siro Marcellini directed. Color. In Italian. 98 minutes.

1987 La famiglia Ricordi
Alessandro plays Donizetti in this four-part TV miniseries about the Italian opera publishing family. See RICORDI.

DONNA DEL LAGO, LA
1819 opera by Rossini

GIOACHINO ROSSINI's opera *La donna del lago* is based on Sir Walter Scott's poem *The Lady of the Lake* as adapted by libretto writer Andrea Leone Tottola. Set in 16th-century Scotland during the time of James V, it revolves around the king's unrequited love for Elena, the lady of the lake. He is traveling in disguise and staying in an enemy household; the lady is the daughter of his chief enemy, and she doesn't like him at all. The score is one of Rossini's best.

1990 Teatro Regio, Parma
Italian stage production: Gae Aulenti (director), Arnold Östman (conductor, Teatro Regio Orchestra and Chorus), Lorenza Codignola (set designer).

Cast: Cecilia Gasdia (Elena), Rockwell Blake (King James), Kathleen Kuhlmann (Malcolm), Luca Canonici (Rodrigo), Boris Martinovich (Douglas).

Video: Lyric VHS. Color. In Italian. 153 minutes.

Comment: Östman, whose Drottningholm Mozart opera videos are highly regarded, does an equally impressive job leading the Parma orchestra.

1992 Teatro alla Scala
Italian stage production: Werner Herzog (director), Riccardo Muti (conductor, Teatro alla Scala Orchestra and Choir), Maurizio Balo (set designer).

Cast: June Anderson (Elena), Rockwell Blake (King James), Chris Merritt (Rodrigo), Martine Dupuy (Malcolm), Giorgio Surjan (Douglas), Marilena Laurenza (Albina).

Video: Image Entertainment DVD/Home Vision VHS. Ilio Catani (director). Color. In Italian. 167 minutes.

DONNA PIÙ BELLA DEL MONDO, LA
1955 Italian film with opera content

Italian soprano Lina Cavalieri, who made her American debut at the Metropolitan in 1906 opposite Caruso in Giordano's *Fedora*, was as famous for her extravagant lifestyle and beauty as for her voice and was publicized as the "most beautiful woman in the world." The Italian film biography of the diva titled *La donna più bella del mondo* (The Most Beautiful Woman in the World) stars Gina Lollobrigida as Cavalieri. It shows her rise from the slums of Viterbo to the cheapest of cafés to the best of opera houses after making her debut in *La bohème* in Naples in 1900. Lollobrigida, who once trained to be an opera singer, sings Tosca's aria "Vissi d'arte." Mario Del Monaco is the singing voice of Gino Sinimberghi, the tenor who loves Cavalieri. Vittorio Gassman plays ardent Russian Prince Sergio, and Robert Alda is nasty conductor Doria. Robert Z. Leonard directed. The film was released in America as *Beautiful But Dangerous* and is available on video with that title. Color. In Italian. 104 minutes. Live Opera VHS.

DON PASQUALE
1843 opera by Donizetti

GAETANO DONIZETTI's popular comic opera *Don Pasquale* has a highly entertaining libretto by Giovanni Ruffini and the composer. Foolish old miser Don Pasquale opposes his nephew Ernesto's marriage to Norina. When he seeks a wife for himself through Dr. Malatesta, an elaborate trick is set in motion with Norina posing as his wife and making his life a misery. Afterwards Pasquale is happy for her to marry his nephew. There are excellent patter songs, delightful comic scenes, and wonderful arias and duets.

1948 First Opera Film Festival
Italian stage production: Enrico Fulchigoni (director), Angelo Questa (conductor, Rome Opera House Orchestra and Chorus), George Richfield (producer).

Cast: Tito Gobbi (Malatesta), Giulio Tomei (Don Pasquale, sung by Luciano Neroni), Pina Malgharini (Norina, sung by Angelica Tuccari), Mino Rosso (Ernesto, sung by Cesare Valletti).

Video: Bel Canto Society/Lyric VHS. Edmondo Cancellieri (film director). Black and white. In Italian with English voice-over by Olin Downes. 23 minutes.

Comment: Highlights version of opera sung in Italian and filmed on stage at the Rome Opera House with singers from La Scala and Rome. Made for an anthology film titled *First Opera Film Festival*.

1955 RAI Italian Television
Italian TV film: Alessandro Brissoni (director), Alberto Erede (conductor, RAI Orchestra and Chorus).

Cast: Italo Tajo (Don Pasquale), Sesto Bruscantini (Malatesta), Alda Noni (Norina), Cesare Valletti (Ernesto).

Video: Bel Canto Society/Hardy Classics (France) VHS. Black and white. In Italian. 110 minutes.

1979 Welsh National Opera
Welsh film of stage production: Basil Coleman (film director), Richard Armstrong (conductor, Welsh National Opera Chorale and Welsh Philharmonia), Roger Andrews (set designer).

Cast: Geraint Evans (Don Pasquale), Lillian Watson (Norina), Russell Smythe (Malatesta), Ryland Davies (Ernesto).

Video: Pickwick Video (England) VHS. Color. In Italian with English subtitles. 112 minutes.

1979 Metropolitan Opera
American stage production: John Dexter (director), Nicola Rescigno (conductor, Metropolitan Opera Orchestra and Chorus), Desmond Heeley (set designer).

Cast: Gabriel Bacquier (Don Pasquale), Beverly Sills (Norina), Alfredo Kraus (Ernesto), Håkan Hagegård (Malatesta), Nico Castel (Notary).

Telecast May 17, 1980; taped January 11, 1979. Kirk Browning (director). Color. In Italian with English subtitles. 115 minutes.

1990 RAI Italian Television
Italian TV film: Frank de Quell (director), Evelino Pidò (conductor, Sinfonia Varsovia), Salvatore Russo (set/costume designer).

Cast: Alfredo Mariotti (Don Pasquale), Susanna Rigacci (Norina), Bruno Pola (Malatesta), William Matteuzzi (Ernesto).

Video: Lyric VHS. Color. In Italian. 110 minutes.

1991 Barbara Hendricks: My Favorite Opera
Documentary film: Márta Mészaros (film director), Patricia Gracis (stage director), Gabriele Ferro (conductor, Warsaw Sinfonietta and Festival Chorus), Lauro Crisman (set designer).

Cast: Barbara Hendricks (Norina), Gabriel Bacquier (Don Pasquale), Gino Quilico (Malatesta), Luca Canonici (Ernesto).

Video: Kultur VHS. Color. In English. 60 minutes.

Comment: This documentary in the *My Favorite Opera* series shows Hendricks preparing and performing scenes of *Don Pasquale* at the Aix-en-Provence Festival.

Early/related films

1927 Meine Tante, Deine Tante
Henny Porten plays Norina in this loose German film adaptation of the Donizetti opera by Walter Supper. W. R. Heymann wrote new music for the film directed by Carl Froelich. The cast also includes Ralph Arthur Roberts, Angelo Ferrari, and Harry Grunwald. Black and white. In German. About 75 minutes.

1934 La Buenaventura
Enrico Caruso Jr., playing an opera singer in this American film, sings Ernesto's aria "Com'è gentil." *La Buenaventura* is an adaptation of Victor Herbert's THE FORTUNE TELLER. William McGann directed for Warner Bros. Black and white. In Spanish. 77 minutes.

1940 Don Pasquale
This Italian film is a narrative version of the story using the libretto of the opera as its script and Donizetti's music as its score. Armando Falconi plays Don Pasquale, Laura Solari is Norina, Franco Coop is Malatesta, and Maurizio D'Ancora is Ernesto. Camillo Mastrocinque directed. Black and white. In Italian. 98 minutes.

DON QUICHOTTE
1910 opera by Massenet

JULES MASSENET's opera *Don Quichotte* is based on Cervantes's novel about the aged, idealistic, and somewhat mad Spanish knight Don Quixote, known in France as Don Quichotte. Henri Cain's libretto concentrates on the Don's relationship with his ideal woman Dulcinea (Dulcinée in French) and on his death. Ironically it also reflects Massenet's own life in its mocking story about an elderly man infatuated with a young girl. The girl in his case was singer Lucy Arbell, for whom he wrote the role of Dulcinée. The role of Quichotte was written for Feodor Chaliapin, who recorded the finale. When G. W. Pabst decided to make a film of the novel many years later, he persuaded Chaliapin to reprise the role of Quixote. The opera has been telecast several times in Europe.

2000 Opéra de Paris-Bastille
French stage production: Gilbert Deflo (director), James Conlon (conductor, Orchestra and Chorus of the Opéra National de Paris).

Cast: Samuel Ramey (Don Quichotte), Carmen Oprisanu (Dulcinée), Jean-Philippe Lafont (Sancho), Jaël Azzaretti (Pedro), Allison Cook (Garcias), Jean-Pierre Trévisani (Rodriguez), Gérard Théruel (Juan).
Video: Opera Direct/House of Opera DVD/Premiere Opera VHS. François Roussillon (director). Color. In French. 125 minutes.

Related films

1933 Don Quixote/Don Quichotte
Feodor Chaliapin plays the knight of La Mancha in G. W. Pabst's film of episodes from the Cervantes novel. There is music and singing in the film, but the music is by Jacques Ibert, not Massenet. The film was made in two versions. In the English version, George Robey is Sancho Panza, Sidney Fox is Dulcinea, and Miles Mander is the Police Captain. In the French version, Dorville is Sancho Panza, Renée Valliers is Dulcinée, and Charles Martinelli is the Police Chief. At the end of the film, the sane but sad knight returns home, and his books about chivalrous adventures are burned. One book burns in reverse and is revealed to be the history of the knight Don Quixote. Ibert's music is played by an orchestra conducted by Alexander Drajomisjky. Black and white. In English or French. 82 minutes. Lyric/Opera Dubs VHS.

1986 Nicolai Ghiaurov: Tribute to a Great Basso
Bulgarian bass Nicolai Ghiaurov appears in an extended scene from *Don Quichotte* in the video *Nicolai Ghiaurov: Tribute to a Great Basso*. The sequence begins with filmed scenes of the sheep episode and concludes with Ghiaurov on stage in Quichotte's death scene. Color. 79 minutes. VIEW VHS.

DON QUINTIN EL AMARGAO
1924 zarzuela by Guerrero

JACINTO GUERRERO's tuneful zarzuela *Don Quintin el Amargao* has been filmed twice by master filmmaker Luis Buñuel. The libretto by Carlos Arniches and José Estremera is pure melodrama. Don Quintin had abandoned his little girl when his unfaithful wife claimed he was not the father. Many years later the dying wife admits she lied out of spite, so the father sets out to find his long lost daughter. The young woman has run away from her adopted parents and married, but he eventually finds her.

1935 Don Quintin el Amargao
Spanish feature film: Luis Buñuel (director, producer, editor, screenplay), Luis Marquina (credited on screen as director), José Maria Beltrán (cinematogra-

pher), José Maria Torres (set designer), Filmófono (production).

Cast: Alfonso Muñoz (Don Quintin), Ana Maria Custodio (Teresa), Luisita Esteso (Felisa), Fernando Granada (Paco), Isabel Noguera (Margot).

Black and white. In Spanish. 85 minutes.

Comment: Buñuel's film was a huge commercial success even though he kept his name off the official credits.

1951 La Hija del Engaño

Mexican feature film: Luis Buñuel (director), José Ortiz Ramos (cinematographer), Raquel Rojas and Luis Alcoriza (screenplay), Edward Fitzgerald (set designer), Ultramar Films (production).

Cast: Fernando Soler (Don Quintin), Alicia Caro (Marta), Rubén Rojo (Paco), Nacho Contla (Jonrón).

Black and white. In Spanish. 80 minutes.

Comment: Buñuel's Spanish version of the zarzuela was so successful that his Mexican producer persuaded him to remake it using the title *La Hija del Engaño*. It follows the original closely although some character names are changed. It was shown in the United States as *Daughter of Deceit*.

Early film

1925 Noriega film

The first version of the zarzuela was a Spanish film directed by Manuel Noriega and scripted by Carlo Primelles. It stars Juan Nada as Don Quintin, Lina Moreno, and Consuelo Reyes. It was produced by Cartago Films of Madrid. Black and white. Silent. 75 minutes.

DOWNES, EDWARD
English conductor (1924–)

Sir Edward Downes began his long association with the Royal Opera in 1952 and conducted his first opera there in 1953. During his half century of working at Covent Garden, he has conducted most of the standard repertory and become known for his knowledge of Russian opera. He was director of Australian Opera from 1972 to 1976 and conducted the first opera presented at the new Sydney Opera House; it was an epic production of WAR AND PEACE (1973) and is available on DVD. In 1981 he conducted Prokofiev's unfinished opera MADDALENA at Graz, after completing it himself. See AIDA (1994), RIGOLETTO (2000), ROYAL OPERA HOUSE (1986), SALOME (1992), and STIFFELIO (1993).

DOWN IN THE VALLEY
1948 opera by Weill

KURT WEILL's American folk opera has become one of his most popular works, partially because of its strong libretto by Arnold Sundgaard but also for its wonderful use of folk song. It begins with the Leader's song "Down in the Valley," which tells the story of the opera. Brack Weaver is in jail for killing Thomas Bouché in a fight over Jennie Parsons and has been sentenced to die. On the eve of his execution, he escapes to spend the night with Jennie but returns to his death cell at dawn. Weill originally wrote the opera for radio.

1950 NBC Opera Theatre

American TV production: Charles Polacheck (director), Peter Herman Adler (conductor, Symphony of the Air Orchestra and NBC Opera Chorus), William Smith (set designer), Samuel Chotzinoff (producer).

Cast: Marion Bell (Jennie), William McGraw (Brack), Kenneth Smith (Leader/Preacher), Ray Jacquemont (Thomas), Richard Barrows (Jennie's father), Roy Johnston (Prison Guard).

Telecast live January 14, 1950. Kirk Browning (director). Black and white. In English. 50 minutes.

Comment: This was NBC Opera Theatre's official premiere after four experimental telecasts. It starred Marion Bell, who had created the role of Jennie, and the cast made a recording of the opera under Weill's supervision. It was a studio production, but there were film inserts of a valley and a train at the beginning and fields and clouds at the end.

1961 BBC Television

English TV production: Douglas Craig (director), Charles Mackerras (conductor, Pro Arte Orchestra), Desmond Chinn (set designer).

Cast: Stephanie Voss (Jennie), Joseph Ward (Brack), Bernard Turgeon (Leader), John Hauxvell (Preacher), Richard Golding (Thomas), Mark Baker (Jennie's father), Edmund Donleavy (Prison Guard).

Telecast August 29, 1961. Charles R. Rogers (director). Black and white. In English. 30 minutes.

1984 Channel 4 Television

English TV film: Peter Weigl (film director), Frank Cvitanovich (stage director), Carl Davis (conductor, orchestra and Ambrosian Singers).

Cast: Linda Lou Allen (Jennie), Hutton Cobb (Brack), Van Hinman (narrator), Phil Brown (Jennie's father), Bob Sessions (Thomas), Kenny Andrews (Peters).

Telecast on Channel 4 in England. Color. In English. 51 minutes.

DREAM OF VALENTINO, THE

1994 screen opera by Argento

DOMINICK ARGENTO's Hollywood-style opera *The Dream of Valentino*, libretto by Charles Nolte, tells the story of film star Rudolph Valentino from his quick rise to mythical fame to his sudden death and includes large screen projections of films and Hollywood images. It was premiered at Washington Opera on January 15, 1994, with Robert Brubaker as Valentino; Suzanne Murphy as screenwriter June Mathis, who promoted him; Julia Ann Wolf as Natacha Rambova, who shaped his career; Joyce Castle as movie star Alla Nazimova; Edrie Means as Valentino's first wife Jean Acker; Julian Patrick as the Mogul; and Dan Dressen as Marvin Heeno, the Mogul's nephew. Ann-Margret Pettersson was stage director, Valentino designed the costumes, John Conklin designed the sets, and Christopher Keene conducted the Washington Opera Orchestra and Chorus.

DREIGROSCHENOPER, DIE

1928 opera by Weill

Die Dreigroschenoper (The Threepenny Opera) is an adaptation of John Gay's *The Beggar's Opera* as rewritten by BERTOLT BRECHT with new music by KURT WEILL. Brecht kept the outline of the original but poured his ideas about society, corruption, love, crime, and justice into the libretto, while Weill composed a most tuneful popular opera. It tells the story of petty crook Macheath (Mack the Knife) and his love affair with Polly Peachum, daughter of the chief of beggars. When he commits the sin of marrying her, he sets in motion a series of events that leads him to the gallows. The opera was an enormous hit in Germany and was made into a famous film but was not popular in the United States until it was revived in New York in 1954 in a new translation by MARC BLITZSTEIN. The song "Mack the Knife" became a popular hit. Weill's wife Lotte Lenya has played Jenny on both stage and screen.

1931 Pabst German film

German feature film: G. W. Pabst (director); Leo Lania, Bela Balazs, and Ladislaus Vajda (screenplay); Fritz Arno Wagner (cinematographer); Andrei Andreiev (set designer); Nero Films (production company).

Cast: Rudolf Forster (Macheath), Lotte Lenya (Jenny), Caroline Neher (Polly Peachum), Fritz Rasp (Peachum), Ernst Busch (Street Singer), Valeska Gert (Mrs. Peachum), Reinhold Schunzel (Tiger Brown).

Video: Bel Canto Society/Nelson VHS/Voyager LD. Black and white. In German with English subtitles. 112 minutes.

Comment: Theo Mackeben, who conducted the stage performances, worked with Weill to adapt the op-

era. Brecht and Weill sued Pabst because he altered the libretto and music, but critics still rank the film as one of the great achievements of German cinema. The film was distributed in the United States by Janus.

1931 Pabst French film

French feature film: G. W. Pabst (director); André Mauprey, Solange Bussi, and Ninon Steinhoff (adaptation of German screenplay); Fritz Arno Wagner (cinematographer); Andrei Andreiev (set designer); Nero Films (production company).

Cast: Albert Prejean (Macheath), Odette Florelle (Polly Peachum), Margo Lion (Jenny), Bill Bocketts (Street Singer), Gaston Modot (Peachum), Lucy de Matha (Mrs. Peachum), Jacques Henley (Tiger Brown).

Video: René Chateau (France) VHS. Black and white. In French. 90 minutes.

Comment: Pabst's French film of the opera, made at the same time and titled *L'Opéra de Quat'Sous*, uses the same sets and lighting but has a different all-French cast. While it looks much like the German film, it has quite a different tone sung in French.

1963 Staudte film

American/German feature film: Wolfgang Staudte (director/screenplay with Günther Weisenborn), Peter Sandloff (music director), Roger Fellous (cinematographer), Embassy Pictures (production).

Cast: Sammy Davis Jr. (Street Singer), Curt Jurgens (Macheath), Hildegarde Knef (Jenny), June Ritchie (Polly Peachum, partially sung by Maria Korber), Marlene Warrlich (Lucy Brown), Gert Frobe (Peachum), Hilde Hildebrand (Mrs. Peachum), Lino Ventura (Tiger Brown).

Video: Video Yesteryear VHS. Color. In English or German. 124 minutes.

Comment: Davis is fun but this is a poor film shot in English and German versions.

1989 Mack the Knife

Israeli/American film: Menahem Golan (director/screenplay), Dov Seltzer (music director), Cannon Film (production).

Cast: Raul Julia (Macheath), Julia Migenes (Jenny), Roger Daltrey (Street Singer), Rachel Roberts (Polly Peachum), Richard Harris (Peachum), Julie Walters (Mrs. Peachum), Bill Nighy (Tiger Brown).

Video: Columbia TriStar VHS/LD. Color. In English. 122 minutes.

Comment: Despite an all-star cast, this lavish but dull English-language version doesn't work; the fault probably lies with the director.

Related films

1979 La città delle donne
Federico Fellini's fantasy film *City of Women,* which concerns the power of women, features "Mack the Knife" on the soundtrack. Color. In Italian. 139 minutes.

1994 Quiz Show
Robert Redford's film concerns a 1950s television scandal. Music from *The Threepenny Opera* is used to show the similarities between the sleazy behavior of the characters in the film and the crooks in the opera. Bobby Darin sings "Mack the Knife" over the opening credits, and Lyle Lovett performs it over the closing credits. Color. 130 minutes.

DREIMÄDERLHAUS, DAS
1916 operetta by Schubert/Berté

It is ironic that FRANZ SCHUBERT, one of the great composers for the voice, wrote 14 operas without success but became popular as an operetta composer a century after his death. *Das Dreimäderlhaus* (The House of the Three Girls) is a pastiche operetta cobbled together by Heinrich Berté from Schubert melodies. It tells the (fictional) story of Schubert's love for Hannerl, who has sisters called Hederl and Haiderl. He is too shy to woo her and loses her to his poet friend Schober. The libretto by A. M. Willner and Heinz Reichert is based on a novel. The operetta was a hit in 20 languages, with Richard Tauber playing the lead role in Germany and England. In England the operetta was first called *Lilac Time* and then *Blossom Time;* in France it was *Chanson d'Amour* and in America *Blossom Time.* The American version was arranged by Sigmund Romberg, who recomposed the score to a new libretto, but his version is not on video.

1934 Blossom Time
English feature film: Paul L. Stein (director); Otto Kanturek (cinematographer); John Drinkwater, Roger Burford, Paul Perez, and G. H Clutsam (screenplay); BIP (production company).

Cast: Richard Tauber (Schubert), Jane Baxter (Vicki), Carl Esmond (Rudi).

Video: Bel Canto Society/Premiere Opera VHS. Black and white. In English. 91 minutes.

Comment: Tauber played the role on stage in London in 1933. In this version, set in Vienna in 1836, Schubert loves Vicki but helps her win the count she loves. Originally released in America as *April Romance.*

1936 Drei Mäderl um Schubert
German feature film: E. W. Emo (director); Alois Melichar (music director); Arthur Pohl, Hanns Sassmann, and E. W. Emo (screenplay); Eduard Hoesch (cinematographer).

Cast: Paul Hörbiger (Schubert), Else Elster (Hannerl), Maria Andergast (Haiderl), Gretl Theimer (Hederl), Gustav Waldau (Tschoell), Julia Serda (his wife).

Black and white. In German. 88 minutes.

Comment: Shown in England and the United States as *Three Girls and Schubert.*

1958 Marischka film
Austrian feature film: Ernst Marischka (director/screenplay), Bruno Mondi (cinematographer), Aspa Film (production company).

Cast: Karl-Heinz Böhm (Schubert), Johanna Matz (Hannerl), Rudolf Schock (Schober), Gustav Knuth (Tschöll), Magda Schneider (Frau Tschöll), Gerda Siegl (Hederl), Ewald Balser (Beethoven).

Color. In German. 90 minutes.

Comment: Shown in England and the United States as *The House of the Three Girls.*

Early film

1917 Oswald film
Richard Oswald directed an early silent German film version of the operetta screened in theaters with the Schubert music. Black and white. About 70 minutes.

DREI WÄLZER
See TROIS VALSES.

DRESDEN

Dresden, founded in the 12th century, has been a center for German opera since the 18th century when the Grosses Operhaus opened. In the 19th century, Wagner began his rise to fame there, premiering *Rienzi, Die fliegende Holländer,* and *Tannhäuser* at the Royal Opera House. During the 20th century, the city hosted the premieres of nine operas by Richard Strauss. The Royal (aka Semper) Opera House has been destroyed a number of times, including being bombed in 1945, but it reopened in 1985 with its signature opera *Die Freischütz.* Harry Kupfer became chief director of Dresden State Opera in 1972 and helped it earn an international reputation for quality productions. See ARIADNE AUF NAXOS (1999), DIE ENTFÜHRUNG AUS DEM SERAIL (1980), DER FREISCHÜTZ (1985), and THE TALE OF TSAR SALTAN (1978).

2000 Concert from Semper Opera, Dresden
Giuseppe Sinopoli conducts the Dresden Semper Oper Orchestra and Chorus in celebration of the 450th anni-

versary of the Sachsische Staatskapelle Dresden. The music includes the overture to *Rienzi*, plus music by Weber, Vivaldi, and Richard Strauss. Color. In German with English subtitles. Naxos DVD.

DROTTNINGHOLM COURT THEATRE
Swedish opera house (1766–)

The baroque Drottningholm Court Theatre (Drottningholm Slottsteater) near Stockholm, built for the Swedish royal family, is one of the most beautiful old opera houses in the world. Operas are presented with their original machinery and 18th-century sets, while the orchestra dresses in period costume and plays period instruments. The theater was seen on film in a reconstruction in Ingmar Bergman's *The Magic Flute* but has become better known through a series of superb videos of Mozart operas filmed by Thomas Olofsson for Swedish TV with conductor Arnold Östman. As a group, these are among the finest screen operas and are also on LD and DVD. See LA CLEMENZA DI TITO (1987), COSÌ FAN TUTTE (1984), DON GIOVANNI (1987), DIE ENTFÜHRUNG AUS DEM SERAIL (1991), LA FINTA GIARDINIERA (1988), IDOMENEO (1991), LE NOZZE DI FIGARO (1981), and DIE ZAUBERFLÖTE (1974/1989).

1967 Drottningholm Court Theatre
Swedish film demonstrating the glories of the Drottningholm Court Theatre and showing how its decor is unchanged after two centuries. The ancient groove-and-shutter machinery is pictured in action during a performance of Gluck's *Iphigenia in Aulis*. Color. In English or Swedish. 28 minutes.

DUBARRY, DIE
1931 operetta by Millöcker/Mackeben

KARL MILLÖCKER and THEO MACKEBEN's operetta *Die Dubarry* (The Dubarry) was very popular in the 1930s and was staged in English in London and New York in 1932. Metropolitan opera diva Grace Moore starred in the New York production, and her success led to her being invited back to Hollywood to become a movie star. Originally an 1879 Millöcker operetta called *Gräfin Dubarry*, it was revised by Theo Mackeben in 1931 using a new libretto by Paul Knepler and J. M. Welleminsky. The revised version, which premiered in Berlin with Hungarian opera diva Gitta Alpar as Dubarry, tells the story of a milliner's assistant in Paris who marries a count and becomes the mistress of Louis XV. It does not follow history very closely. There are many nonmusical versions of the story starring everyone from Theda Bara to Martine Carol.

1935 I Give My Heart
English feature film: Marcel Varnay (director); Claude Friese-Greene (cinematographer); Frank Launder, Roger Burford, and Kurt Siodmak (screenplay); BIP (production company).

Cast: Gitta Alpar (Madame Dubarry), Owen Nares (Louis XV), Arthur Margetson (Count Dubarry), Patrick Waddington (René).

Black and white. In English. 91 minutes.

Comment: "I Give My Heart" is the English version of the operetta's hit song. Gitta Alpar created the role of Madame Dubarry on stage. The film was shown in New York in 1938 with the title *The Loves of Madame Dubarry*.

1975 ZDF German Television
German TV film: Werner Jacobs (director), Wolfgang Ebert (conductor, Bavarian Television Symphony Orchestra), Sergiu Singer (set designer).

Cast: Gail Robinson (Madame Dubarry), Peter Pasetti (Louis XV), Julia Migenes (Margot), Wolfgang Preiss (Count Dubarry), Barry McDaniel (René).

Telecast in Germany May 17, 1975. Black and white. In German. 90 minutes.

DUCA D'ALBA, IL
1839/1882 opera by Donizetti

Amelia and her lover Marcello lead a revolt against Spanish control of Flanders. When Marcello finds out that he is the illegitimate son of the hated Spanish leader, the Duke of Alba, he prevents Amelia from assassinating him by sacrificing his own life. Gaetano Donizetti's opera *Il duca d'Alba* was begun by Donizetti in 1830 using a French libretto by Eugène Scribe and Charles Duveyrier but was never finished. It was completed in an Italian translation by Donizetti's pupil Matteo Salvi and others after his death and premiered in Rome in 1882. Scribe also used the plot as the basis of Verdi's 1855 *Les vêpres siciliennes*. The aria "Spirto gentil," featured in Donizetti's *La favorite,* was actually created for this opera.

1992 Spoleto Festival, Italy
Italian stage production: Filippo Sanjust (director), Alberto Maria Giuri (conductor, Spoleto Festival Orchestra and Chorus).

Cast: Michaela Sburlati (Amelia), Cesar Hernandez (Marcello), Alan Titus (Duke of Alba).

Video: Premiere Opera/Opera Direct/House of Opera VHS. Color. In Italian. 150 minutes.

DUCHESSA DEL BAL TABARIN, LA
1917 operetta by Lombardo

Italian composer CARLO LOMBARDO's 1917 operetta *La Duchessa del Bal Tabarin* is an adaptation of Bruno Granichstädten's 1911 Austrian operetta *Majestät Mimì* with a new libretto by A. Franci and C. Vizzotto. It was a big success in its reincarnation and became popular in Spain as well as Italy. The story focuses on the love affair of a Ruritanian prince and a Paris cabaret performer called Frou-Frou of the Bal Tabarin. The operetta has entered the zarzuela repertory as *Frou-Frou del Tabarin* and has also been called that in Italy.

1963 Mexican television film
Mexican TV film: Plácido Domingo (director), Max Factor (production company).

Cast: Plácido Domingo (Prince), Marta Ornelas (Frou-Frou), Ernestina Garfias, Franco Inglesias.

Telecast in Mexico as *Frou-Frou del Tabarin*. Black and white. In Spanish. 90 minutes.

Comment: Domingo, who began his career in Mexico, filmed a series of zarzuelas for sponsor Max Factor in 1963. No known copies.

1975 Italian television films
Italian TV film: Gianni Grimaldi (director, screenplay).

Cast: Martine Brochard, Fabrizio Moroni, Carmen Scarpitta, Jacques Berthier.

Telecast in Italy as *Frou-Frou del Tabarin*. Color. In Italian. 88 minutes.

1992 Italian TV: Operette, che Passione!
Italian TV production: Sandro Massimini (director/producer), Roberto Negri (pianist), Sandro Corelli (choreographer).

Cast: Sandro Massimini, Sonia Dorigo, Max René Cosotti.

Video: Pierluigi Pagano (director). Color. In Italian. About 19 minutes. Ricordi (Italy) VHS.

Comment: Highlights of the operetta on the Italian TV series *Operette, che Passione!* Includes songs "Frou-Frou del Tabarin" and "Ombre siamo nella notte."

Early film

1917 Cyrius film
La duchessa del Bal Tabarin, an Italian silent feature film version of the operetta, was shown in cinemas with recordings of the main songs played live at the appropriate times. Olga Paradisi is Frou-Frou, Americo de Giorgio is Ottavio, Edy Darclea is Edi, and Alessandro des Varennes is the minister. Nino Martinengo directed for Cyrius Film. Black and white. About 60 minutes.

DUE FOSCARI, I
1844 opera by Verdi

GIUSEPPE VERDI's tragic opera *I due Foscari* (The Two Foscari) is one of the few operas in which evil wins out. Francesco Maria Piave wrote the libretto based on Lord Byron's play *The Two Foscari*, set in Venice in 1457 when the city was at the height of its power. The elderly Doge Francisco Foscari is unable to stop his son Jacopo from being exiled after a false accusation of murder. The son dies and the Doge is forced to resign and dies. His archenemy Jacopo Loredano is jubilant.

1988 Teatro alla Scala
Italian stage production: Pier Luigi Pizzi (director/designer), Gianandrea Gavazzeni (conductor, Teatro alla Scala Orchestra and Chorus).

Cast: Renato Bruson (Francesco Foscari), Alberto Cupido (Jacopo Foscari), Linda Roark-Strummer (Lucrezia), Luigi Roni (Loredano), Renato Cazzaniga (Barbarigo), Monica Tagliasacchi (Pisani), Aldo Bottion (Sante).

Video: Castle/Fonit Cetra (Italy) VHS. Tonino Del Colle (director). Color. In Italian. 100 minutes.

2000 Teatro di San Carlo, Naples
Italian stage production: Werner Düggelin (director), Nello Santi (conductor, Teatro San Carlo Orchestra and Chorus).

Cast: Leo Nucci (Francesco Foscari), Vincenzo La Scola (Jacopo Foscari), Alexandrina Pendatchanska (Lucrezia), Danilo Rigosa (Loredano), Leopoldo Lo Sciuto (Barbarigo), Birgit Eger (Pisana).

Video: TDK DVD. George Blume (director). Color. In Italian with English subtitles. 114 minutes.

Related films

1923 I Foscari
Amleto Novelli, the most famous Italian actor of the silent era, stars as Jacopo Foscari in an Italian adaptation of the Byron play titled *I Foscari*. The cast includes Alberto Collo, Nini Dinelli, Vittorio Pieri, and Lia Miari; Mario Almirante directed. Verdi's music was played live with the film at screening. Black and white. Silent. About 72 minutes.

1942 I Due Foscari
Rossano Brazzi plays Jacopo Foscari in this adaptation of the Byron play that uses Verdi's music from the opera, arranged by Fernando Previtali, as its soundtrack. Carlo

Ninchi is the Doge Foscari and Regina Bianchi is Lucrezia. Enrico Fulchigoni directed for Scalera Film. Black and white. In Italian. 85 minutes.

DUKE BLUEBEARD'S CASTLE
See Bluebeard's Castle.

DUNCAN, TODD
American baritone (1903–1998)

Todd Duncan created the most famous male role in American opera, Porgy in George Gershwin's Porgy and Bess, but continued to teach voice at Howard University. Duncan, who made his debut in 1934 in *Cavalleria rusticana* with the Aeolian Opera company, also created the role of Lord's General in Vernon Duke's musical *Cabin in the Sky* in 1940 and Stephen Kumalo in Kurt Weill's "musical tragedy" *Lost in the Stars* in 1949. Duncan was the first African-American member of New York City Opera, making his debut as Tonio in *Cavalleria rusticana* on September 28, 1945. He acted in two movies, the 1942 jazz film *Syncopation* and the 1955 prison film *Unchained,* and is featured in documentaries about *Porgy and Bess* and Marian Anderson.

DURBIN, DEANNA
Canadian soprano (1921–)

Deanna Durbin may not have been an opera singer on stage but she introduced a lot of moviegoers to opera music. She was originally signed by MGM to portray Ernestine Schumann-Heink in a film biography, but the contralto became ill and the film was canceled. Durbin then moved to Universal where her singing coach was Spanish bass Andrés de Segurola, formerly of the Met. Her first feature, the 1936 *Three Smart Girls,* was a huge success and Durbin quickly became a top star. Her producers usually found room for opera arias in her films, including one in 1947 in which she duets with Met tenor Jan Peerce. There was even a souvenir songbook of opera arias from her movies. Two of her films were based on operettas, the 1940 *Spring Parade,* based on Frühjahrsparade, and the 1948 Up in Central Park. Durbin's active film career ended in 1948, but she still has many fans. Her films with operatic content are listed below.

1937 100 Men and a Girl
Durbin sings the "Libiamo" aria from *La traviata* in this picture about the spunky talented daughter of a musician. Her costar is conductor Leopold Stokowski. Henry Koster directed. Universal. Black and white. 83 minutes.

1938 That Certain Age
Durbin gets a crush on Melvyn Douglas and sings "Daydreams" ("Ah! Je veux vivre") from Gounod's *Roméo et Juliette.* Edward Ludwig directed. Universal. Black and white. 95 minutes.

1939 Three Smart Girls Grow Up
Durbin sings "The Last Rose of Summer" from *Martha* and Weber's "Invitation to the Dance" in this film about three sisters and their romantic attachments. Henry Koster directed. Universal. Black and white. 87 minutes.

1939 First Love
Durbin sings an English version of "Un bel dì" from *Madama Butterfly.* The aria ends with her Prince Charming rescuing her. She also performs a song based on a Strauss waltz. Henry Koster directed. Universal. Black and white. 84 minutes.

1940 It's a Date
Durbin sings "Musetta's Waltz" from *La bohème* and Schubert's "Ave Maria." She plays the daughter of a Broadway star who wins the role her mother wanted. William Seiter directed for Universal. Black and white. 100 minutes.

1943 The Amazing Mrs. Holliday
Durbin sings "Vissi d'Arte" from *Tosca* in this story about a missionary and Chinese orphans. Jean Renoir directed most of the film, but Bruce Manning completed it for Universal. Black and white. 96 minutes.

1943 His Butler's Sister
Durbin sings the tenor aria "Nessun dorma" from *Turandot* at a butler's ball in this charming film about a girl and a composer. She also sings songs by Victor Herbert. Frank Borzage directed with flair. Universal. Black and white. 94 minutes.

1948 For the Love of Mary
Durbin is a White House telephone operator in her last film and performs a comic version of Figaro's "Largo al factotum" from *The Barber of Seville.* Frederick De Cordova directed. Universal. Black and white. 90 minutes.

DUST
1999 television opera by Ashley

A group of homeless street people sing the stories of their lives. One man, who lost his legs in a war, converses with God while under the influence of morphine. Unfortunately God talks too fast to be understood. Robert Ashley's electronic "television opera" *Dust,* libretto by the composer, was premiered in Japan in collaboration with Japanese video artist Yukihiro Yoshihara. It had its American premiere at The Kitchen in New York City on April 14, 1999, with the singers standing by television monitors featuring images related to their stories.

1999 The Kitchen
American TV production: Yukihiro Yoshihara (director of TV visuals), "Blue" Gene Tyranny (synthesizer), Tom Hamilton (mixing board).

Cast: Robert Ashley, Sam Ashley, Thomas Buckner, Jacqueline Humbert, Joan LaBarbara.

Color. In English. 90 minutes.

DVOŘÁK, ANTONÍN
Czech composer (1841–1904)

Antonín Dvořák is known to most Americans as the composer of the *New World Symphony* as his operas have never really entered the international repertory. He wrote 10 of them, however, and they are quite popular in the Czech Republic. By far the most performed and admired is RUSALKA, a version of the Undine legend that contains a much-performed soprano aria called "Song of the Moon." The other fairly popular Dvořák opera is the fun and folksy THE DEVIL AND KATE.

1993 Dvořák in Prague: A Celebration
American tribute to Dvořák shot at Smetana Hall in Prague with the Boston Symphony Orchestra conducted by Seiji Ozawa. Frederica von Stade sings the "Song of the Moon." Brian Large directed the video. Color. 90 minutes. Sony VHS.

1997 Dvořák
Documentary about Dvořák and his music in *The Great Composers* series with the music played by the Moscow Symphony Orchestra led by David Palmer. Color. 24 minutes. Films for the Humanities & Sciences VHS.

DVORSKY, PETER
Czech tenor (1951–)

Peter Dvorsky, who made his debut in Bratislava in 1972, has sung around the world from La Scala and Covent Garden to the Metropolitan. Although he sings Slavic operas, he is equally well known for his performances in Puccini and Verdi. Dvorsky is featured in three of PETR WEIGL's opera films, RUSALKA (1978), THE LOVE OF DESTINY (1983), and WERTHER (1985). He has also starred in Czech and Slovakian TV opera productions, including an excellent THE BARTERED BRIDE (1981) and repertory standards such as *La bohème* and *Tosca*. Two appearances at La Scala are on video, MADAMA

BUTTERFLY (1986) and ADRIANA LECOUVREUR (1989), as well as two concerts at the VERONA Arena (1988/1990). He can be seen as Edgardo in LUCIA DI LAMMERMOOR in Geneva in 1983, Nemorino in L'ELISIR D'AMORE in a 1984 Czech film, Lensky in EUGENE ONEGIN in Chicago in 1985, and Des Grieux in MANON LESCAUT in Barcelona in 1990. He is also featured in a 1985 film of the VERDI REQUIEM.

E

EATON, JOHN
American composer (1935–)

John Eaton, whose operas focus on icons of literature and history, began composing operas while a student at Princeton. The 1957 *Ma Barker* is based on the life of a 1930s gang leader. *Heracles,* based on plays by Sophocles and Seneca, was the opening event at Indiana University's Music Center in 1972. MYSHKIN, based on Dostoevsky's *The Idiot,* was telecast on PBS by Indiana University Opera Theatre in 1973, and his children's opera THE LION AND ANDROCLES was telecast in 1974. *Danton and Robespierre,* about the French Revolution, premiered in 1978, and *The Cry of Clytaemnestra,* based on Aeschylus's *Agamemnon,* was staged in 1980. *The Tempest,* libretto by Andrew Porter based on the Shakespeare play, was premiered by Santa Fe Opera in 1985. In 1993 the composer created the Eaton Opera Company of Chicago in collaboration with the New York New Music Ensemble.

ECHO ET NARCISSE
1779 opera by Gluck

GLUCK wrote this little opera at the end of his career to a libretto by Ludwig Von Tschoudi based on a tale in Ovid's *Metamorphoses.* Echo loves Narcissus but he loves only his own image. In despair she dwindles into a voice and causes Narcissus to suffer. The god Amor won't allow him to die of despair as well, so he restores Echo to life. The opera was successfully revived at the Schwetzingen Festival in 1987.

1987 Schwetzingen Festival
German stage production: Herbert Wernicke (director, set/costume designer), René Jacobs (conductor, Concerto Cologne Orchestra).
Cast: Kurt Streit (Narcisse), Sophie Boulin (Echo), Deborah Massell (Amor), Peter Galliard (Cynire), Gertrude Hoffstedt (Egle), Hanne Krogen (Thanais), Eva Marie Tersson (Sylphie).
Video: Home Vision VHS. Claus Viller (director). Color. In French with English subtitles. 99 minutes.

Comment: A charming production, the first in the 20th century.

EDDY, NELSON
American baritone (1901–1967)

Nelson Eddy began his career on stage singing Gilbert and Sullivan roles with the Savoy Opera Company in Philadelphia. He made his opera debut as Amonasro in *Aida* with the Philadelphia Civic Opera in 1924 and sang with them for six years. He even sang at the Metropolitan Opera House in *Pagliacci* and *Wozzeck,* although not with the Met company. Eddy began his MGM film career in 1933 and was teamed with JEANETTE MACDONALD in 1935 for NAUGHTY MARIETTA. They stayed a popular team for eight years with the operetta films ROSE-MARIE (1936), MAYTIME (1937), SWEETHEARTS (1938), THE GIRL OF THE GOLDEN WEST (1938), BITTER SWEET (1940), THE NEW MOON (1940), and I MARRIED AN ANGEL (1942). Eddy had a strong career apart from MacDonald teamed with Ilona Massey in BALALAIKA (1939), Risë Stevens in THE CHOCOLATE SOLDIER (1941), Susanna Foster in THE PHANTOM OF THE OPERA (1943), Charles Coburn in a 1944 film of KURT WEILL's *Knickerbocker Holiday,* and Gale Sherwood in a 1955 TV version of THE DESERT SONG. He even gave voice to a singing whale in one of the best animated opera films, THE WHALE WHO WANTED TO SING AT THE MET. His other musical films are listed below. Eddy continued to make films until 1947 and then switched to television. He toured with Sherwood as partner in the 1950s and sang in nightclub acts until the end of his life.

1937 Rosalie
Eddy sings Cole Porter in this MGM musical about a romance between West Point cadet Eddy and princess-in-disguise Eleanor Powell. His songs include "In the Still of the Night" and "Rosalie." W. S. Van Dyke directed. Black and white. 122 minutes.

1939 Let Freedom Ring!
Eddy plays the masked hero The Hornet who fights for the ranchers against railroad villain Edward Arnold and wins the heart of Virginia Bruce. He also sings songs like "America" and "Dusty Road." Ben Hecht wrote the screenplay and Jack Conway directed. 100 minutes.

1947 Northwest Outpost
Eddy's last film was a musical Western made for Republic with a score by operetta composer Rudolf Friml. Ilona Massey costars in a story set in a Russian trading post in 19th-century California. Allan Dwan directed. Black and white. 91 minutes.

1992 Nelson and Jeanette: America's Singing Sweethearts

Michael Lorentz's documentary about MacDonald and Eddy, written by Elayne Goldstein and hosted by Jane Powell, includes clips from most of their films. Produced by WTTW Chicago and Turner Entertainment and shown on PBS in 1993. Color. 57 minutes. On VHS and at the MTR.

EDISON, THOMAS ALVA
Opera film visionary (1847–1931)

The inventor of the phonograph and the cinema was an opera film visionary who dreamt of "Kinetoscope operas with phono." He began describing it as early as 1888 and, in 1993, told *The New York Times* that his intention was "to have such a happy combination of photography and electricity that a man can sit in his own parlor, see depicted upon a curtain the forms of the players in opera upon a distant stage and hear the voices of the singers." In 1894, he told *Century Magazine:* "I believe that in coming years grand opera can be given at the Metropolitan Opera House in New York with artists and musicians long since dead." Edison's company made a number of silent opera films, including a famous *Parsifal*. See AIDA (1911), LA BOHÈME (1910), CARMEN (1894), ENRICO CARUSO (1912), FAUST (1909), MARTHA (1899), DER LUSTIGE WITWE (1908 film), and PARSIFAL (1904).

1940 Young Tom Edison

Hollywood biography with Mickey Rooney as Edison trying out his first experiments under the direction of Norman Taurog. MGM. Black and white. 82 minutes.

1940 Edison, the Man

Edison grows up to becomes Spencer Tracy and invent almost everything you can think of in this film directed by Clarence Brown. MGM. Black and white. 107 minutes.

ED SULLIVAN SHOW, THE
CBS television series (1948–1971)

The Ed Sullivan Show, the most important television variety show in the 1950s (known as *The Toast of the Town* from 1948 to September 1955) often featured opera singers and scenes. One of the first was Roberta Peters, who appeared in 1950 after her walk-on debut at the Met as Zerlina in *Don Giovanni.* Anna Moffo and Joan Sutherland each appeared six times. In November 1953, the TV show was broadcast live from the Met stage with an excerpt from *Carmen* with Risë Stevens and Richard Tucker. In 1956, Sullivan and the Met agreed to do five programs together. The first, on November 26, 1956, featured Maria Callas in a scene from *Tosca*. The second featured Dorothy Kirsten and Mario Del Monaco in *Madama Butterfly*. Audience response was so poor that the agreement was ended. The Met's final appearance on the show was on March 10, 1957, when Renata Tebaldi and Richard Tucker sang a duet from *La bohème*.

1996 Great Moments in Opera

Compilation video with 95 minutes of operatic highlights from *The Ed Sullivan Show* with opera stars of the '50s, '60s, and '70s. The singers performing arias and duets include Maria Callas, Nedda Casei, Franco Corelli, Eileen Farrell, Marilyn Horne, Dorothy Kirsten, Robert Merrill, Anna Moffo, Birgit Nilsson, Jan Peerce, Roberta Peters, Lily Pons, Leontyne Price, Beverly Sills, Lillian Sukis, Joan Sutherland, Renata Tebaldi, and Richard Tucker. Color and black and white. 116 minutes. Kultur DVD/Consumer Video VHS.

EGGERTH, MARTA
Hungarian soprano (1912–)

Hungarian soprano Marta Eggerth and her Polish tenor husband JAN KIEPURA were the MacDonald and Eddy of German cinema. She began her career in opera and usually sang opera in her films, two of them based on LA BOHÈME. However, most of her movies were operettas, including adaptations of Abraham's DIE BLUME VON HAWAII, Kálmán's DIE CSÁRDÁSFÜRSTIN (1934), and Lehár's CLOCLO, DAS LAND DES LÄCHELNS, WO DIE LERCHE SINGT, and DER ZAREWITSCH. She played VINCENZO BELLINI's love Maddalena Fumaroli and sang his music in the biopics *Casta diva* and *The Divine Spark* directed by Carmine Gallone in 1935. Eggerth came to the United States with Kiepura in 1938 when he was engaged to sing at the Met, and they appeared on stage in *La bohème* in Chicago. She was featured in two Hollywood films with Judy Garland, neither very flattering to her style of singing. In 1944, she and Kiepura starred in *The Merry Widow* on Broadway and toured it around the world. Kiepura died in 1966, but Eggerth was still singing in her 80s, including Sondheim's *Follies;* she appeared in a TV program about operetta composer ROBERT STOLZ in 1990. Most of her important theatrical films are listed below, but she also appeared in many TV shows.

1932 Where Is This Lady?

Eggerth starred in English and German versions of this film operetta by Franz Lehár written by Billy Wilder. Eggerth is Steffi, a Viennese charmer who helps a bankrupt banker turn his bank into a nightclub. Her English costars are Owen Nares, George Arthur, and Wendy Barrie. Lazlo Vajda and Victor Hanbury directed. Black and white. In English. 77 minutes.

1932 Es War Einmal ein Walzer

Once There Was a Waltz is the German version of the Billy Wilder/Franz Lehár movie described above. Eggerth's costars are Paul Hörbiger, Rolf von Goth, and Lizzie Natzler. Viktor Janson directed. Black and white. In German. 77 minutes.

1932 Kaiserwalzer

Eggerth is the main singer in this musical by composer Nico Dostal based on themes composed by his operetta colleagues Strauss, Millöcker, and Suppé. The cast includes Willi Eicheberger, Paul Hörbiger, and Hansi Niese. Black and white. In German. 89 minutes.

1932 Der Frauendiplomat

Former Vienna State Opera tenor Leo Slezak appears opposite Eggerth in this musical comedy set in the world of diplomats. Max Hansen, Theo Lingen, and Anton Poinner lend support, Hans May wrote the music, and E. W. Emo directed. Black and white. In German. 70 minutes.

1934 The Unfinished Symphony

Romantic British-Austrian film about composer Franz Schubert and his impossible love for Count Esterhazy's daughter Caroline, played by Eggerth. Eggerth sings Schubert's "Ave Maria." Willi Forst directed versions in English and German. The German title is *Schuberts Unvollendete Symphonie*. Black and white. 90 minutes.

1935 Die Blonde Carmen

The Blonde Carmen is a German film operetta with Eggerth singing up a storm opposite Wolfgang Liebeneiner. He's a librettist who thinks theater women are no good, so Eggerth sets out to prove him wrong. Leo Slezak and Ida Wüst lend support, Franz Grothe wrote the music, and Viktor Janson directed. Black and white. In German. 98 minutes.

1942 For Me and My Gal

Eggerth plays a glamorous singing star who almost teams up with Gene Kelly at the urging of Judy Garland in this MGM musical about a vaudeville team aiming for the big time. Eggerth sings "Do I Love You?" very nicely. Busby Berkeley directed. Color. 104 minutes. MGM/UA VHS.

1943 Presenting Lily Mars

Eggerth has a large role as the star rival of Judy Garland in this MGM musical about a girl with theatrical dreams. Eggerth demonstrates her high notes singing three songs, including "Is It Really Love" and "When I Look at You." Garland parodies her accent and singing style in a funny but rather unkind scene. Norman Taurog directed. Color. 104 minutes. MGM/UA VHS.

1949 La Valse Brillante

Eggerth plays a singer receiving threatening letters in this French musical, and Kiepura plays a tenor hired to be her bodyguard. He solves her problems nicely and ends up as her singing partner and husband. The music is mostly by Mozart and Verdi. Jean Boyer directed. Produced by Vox Film. Black and white. In French. 95 minutes.

EIKA KATAPPA
1969 German film with opera content

Experimental German director Werner Schroeter is obsessed with opera. *Eika Katappa,* his first feature, is a celebration of opera in an extravagant, funny, and sometimes hysterical manner mixing scenes from dozens of operas in a frenzied manner. The film begins with a preview of coming attractions, including a skinny Siegfried and a tough Brünnhilde, and it ends with a survey of opera highlights. Among the operas featured are *Un ballo in maschera, Carmen, Ernani, Fidelio, La forza del destino, Hamlet, I puritani, Rigoletto, Il trovatore, Tosca,* and *La vestale.* There are also extracts from films such as Buñuel's *Un Chien Andalou;* music by Beethoven, Penderecki, and Johann Strauss; and songs by Conchita Supervia, Milva, and Caterina Valente. The actors include Magdalena Montezuma, Gisela Trowe, Carla Aulaulu, Alix von Buchen, Rosy-Rosy, Rita Bauer, Camille Calabrese, and Rosa von Praunheim. Schroeter wrote the screenplay, arranged the musical montage, and photographed the film with Robert van Ackeren. Color. In German and Italian. 144 minutes.

EINSTEIN ON THE BEACH
1976 opera by Glass

Einstein on the Beach, the influential opera created by composer PHILIP GLASS and playwright ROBERT WILSON, is one of the most famous minimalist productions and was staged with great success in opera houses in Europe and at the Met after its premiere in Avignon. The opera takes an offbeat aural and visual look at Einstein as scientist, musician, humanist, and theorist of the atomic bomb. The music is scored for four soloists and chorus of 12 with chamber orchestra.

1976 Avignon Festival

There is no commercial video of the opera but Wilson's original production at the Avignon Theatre Festival in France was videotaped. It runs for four hours and 40 minutes without intervals, with four acts connected by "knee plays." The character Einstein appears as a violinist positioned between the stage and the orchestra pit. Color. 280 minutes. Video source unknown.

1986 Einstein on the Beach: The Changing Image of Opera

Mark Obenhaus's film is a behind-the-scenes documentary about the revival of the opera at the Brooklyn Academy of Music in 1984. Glass and Wilson are shown working on the production, and there are scenes of the opera in rehearsal and performance. Telecast January 31, 1986. Color. 60 minutes. Direct Cinema film/VHS.

1985 A Composer's Notes

The "Spaceship" episode from *Einstein on the Beach* is performed in this documentary by the Philip Glass Ensemble, although most of the film is devoted to *Akhnaten*. Michael Blackwood directed the film. Color. 87 minutes. VAI VHS.

EISENSTEIN, SERGEI
Soviet film director (1898–1948)

Film director Sergei Eisenstein was also an opera director and enthusiast, and opera affected much of his life. As a young man he queued all night to see Chaliapin in *Boris Godunov* although later, when Chaliapin wanted him to direct a film of *Don Quichotte,* he refused. Chaliapin played Ivan the Terrible in Rimsky-Korsakov's opera *The Maid of Pskov* and reprised the role in a 1915 Russian film that Eisenstein studied when preparing his own film about Ivan. In 1940, Eisenstein staged Wagner's *Die Walküre* at the Bolshoi Opera during the era of the nonaggression pact with Germany. Eisenstein's production was controversial, so his hopes for a complete *Ring* cycle ended. He also wanted to stage Prokofiev's opera *War and Peace* so it is hardly surprising that he conceived IVAN THE TERRIBLE as virtually a film-opera with Prokofiev music. It has been described as the most operatic film ever made. Eisenstein's earlier *Alexander Nevsky* also has operatic overtones and music by Prokofiev.

1925/1937 Battleship Potemkin

Eisenstein's 1925 Soviet film *Battleship Potemkin* (Bronenosets Potemkin) inspired a Soviet opera with the same name in 1937. Film and opera tell the story of a mutiny in Odessa in 1905 by sailors on the battleship *Potemkin.* Ukrainian composer Oles Semenovich Chishko wrote his Potemkin opera to a libretto by S. D. Spassky. It was produced at the Kirov and Bolshoi Operas and became one of the popular revolutionary operas of its time. German composer Edmund Meisel wrote an influential score to accompany the silent Eisenstein film, but the sound version issued by the USSR in 1950 used a score by Soviet composer E. Kriouskov.

EISINGER, IRENE
German-born English soprano (1903–1994)

Irene Eisinger, German-born but a favorite at Glyndebourne after she left Germany in 1933 (she was Jewish), sang the role of Despina in the first complete recording of *Così fan tutte* made at Glyndebourne in 1935. She made her debut in Basle in 1926 and sang in Berlin, Vienna, Prague, and Salzburg before moving to England. She was noted for her performances in Mozart operas but also sang in operettas. Eisinger starred in a number of German films in the 1930s, including a 1931 version of Jarno's operetta DIE FÖRSTER-CHRISTL, which used mostly Mozart music. She made two movies with music by operetta composer ROBERT STOLZ, the international hit ZWEI HERZEN IN DREIVIERTELTAKT (Two Hearts in 3/4 Time) and DIE LUSTIGEN WEIBER VON WIEN. She had a small role in the 1939 British film *Young Man's Fancy* directed by Robert Stevenson.

***E LA NAVE VA
1983 Italian film with opera content

E la nave va (And the Ship Sails On) is an operatic fantasy by FEDERICO FELLINI featuring a ship full of opera personalities on a luxury liner sailing from Naples in 1914. They are headed for the island birthplace of diva Edmea Tetua (Janet Suzman), whose ashes are to be scattered there and whose life is remembered in flashback as they travel. The passengers include singers, musicians, journalists, aristocrats, and an Austrian grand duke. At one point, the singers descend to the boiler room and serenade the stokers in an operatic competition. After a boatload of Serbian refugees is picked up, the liner is sunk by an Austrian battleship to music by Rossini and Verdi, including the overture from *Forza del Destino.* Earlier there is an ironic use of the "Soldiers' Dance" from *William Tell;* in the opera Austrian soldiers force the local women to dance with them to this tune. The opera singer characters are soprano Ildebranda Cuffari (Barbara Jefford, sung by Mara Zampieri), tenor Aureliano Fuciletto (Victor Poletti, sung by Giovanni Bavaglio), soprano Inez Ruffo Saltini (sung by Elizabeth Norberg-Schulz), mezzo Teresa Valegnani (sung by Nucci Condo), tenor Sabatino Lepari (sung by Carlo Di Giacomo), basso Ziloev (sung by Boris Carmeli), mezzo Maria Augusta Miceli, and tenor Bruno Beccaria. Gianfranco Plenezio conducted the RAI Symphony Orchestra and Chorus and arranged the music with texts for the opera passages written by Andrea Zanzotto. Fellini and Tonino Guerra wrote the screenplay, and Giuseppe Rotunno was the brilliant cinematographer. Color. In Italian with English subtitles. 138 minutes. Criterion DVD.

ELDER, MARK
English conductor (1947–)

Mark Elder began as a chorister and bassoon player and turned to conducting at Cambridge. He worked at Glyndebourne and Sydney, but his major recognition came after he joined English National Opera in 1974. He conducted more than 30 operas for them, including Jonathan Miller's famous RIGOLETTO (1982), and helped established the company's world reputation through tours. He has also conducted at Covent Garden. Elder selected and conducted the GIUSEPPE VERDI (1994) opera extracts used in the TV documentary *The Life of Verdi*. His other operas on video include LA CENERENTOLA (2000), GLORIANA (1984), and RUSALKA (1986).

ELEKTRA
1909 opera by Richard Strauss

RICHARD STRAUSS asked HUGO VON HOFMANNSTHAL if he could use the playwright's German version of Sophocles's tragedy as the libretto for an opera. Hofmannsthal agreed, thus beginning a long and fruitful collaboration. The opera describes how Elektra (Electra in English) seeks revenge for the death of her father King Agamemnon. While he was away at the Trojan War for 10 years, Queen Klytemnästra (Clytemnestra) took Aegisth (Aegisthus) as her lover, and they killed Agamemnon when he returned. Elektra's brother Orest (Orestes) has been sent into exile, and her younger sister Chrysothemis is ineffectual. Electra dreams of what will happen when Orestes finally returns.

1969 Hamburg State Opera
German feature film: Joachim Hess (film and stage director), Leopold Ludwig (conductor, Hamburg Philharmonic Orchestra and State Opera Chorus), Herbert Kirchhoff (set designer), Rolf Liebermann (producer).

Cast: Gladys Kuchta (Elektra), Regina Resnik (Klytemnästra), Ingrid Björner (Chrysothemis), Hans Sotin (Orest), Helmut Melchert (Aegisth).

Color. In German. 107 minutes.

Comment: Filmed in 35mm in a Hamburg TV studio but based on a stage production by Hamburg State Opera. Released theatrically in America.

1980 Metropolitan Opera
American stage production: Paul Mills (director), James Levine (conductor, Metropolitan Opera Orchestra and Chorus), Rudolf Heinrich (set designer).

Cast: Birgit Nilsson (Elektra), Mignon Dunn (Klytemnästra), Leonie Rysanek (Chrysothemis), Donald McIntyre (Orest), Robert Nagy (Aegisth).

Video: Pioneer Classics DVD and LD/Paramount VHS. Brian Large (director). Taped February 16, 1980; telecast January 28, 1981. Color. In German with English subtitles. 110 minutes.

Comment: Birgit Nilsson is 61 but still in good voice, and the audience loves her.

1981 Friedrich film
Austrian feature film: Götz Friedrich (film and stage director), Karl Böhm (conductor, Vienna Philharmonic Orchestra and Vienna State Chorus Concert Ensemble), Rudolf Blahacek (cinematographer), Josef Svoboda (set designer).

Cast: Leonie Rysanek (Elektra), Astrid Varnay (Klytemnästra), Dietrich Fischer-Dieskau (Orest), Catarina Ligendza (Chrysothemis), Hans Beirer (Aegisth).

Video: London VHS/LD. Color. In German with English subtitles. 117 minutes.

Comment: Filmed on location in Vienna in a ruined landscape with a bleak, expressionist style and a good deal of rain.

1989 Vienna State Opera
Austrian stage production: Harry Kupfer (director), Claudio Abbado (conductor, Vienna State Opera Orchestra and Chorus), Hans Schavernoch (set designer).

Cast: Eva Marton (Elektra), Brigitte Fassbaender (Klytemnästra), Cheryl Studer (Chrysothemis), Franz Grundheber (Orest), James King (Aegisth).

Video: Image Entertainment (USA) and Arthaus (GB) DVD/Home Vision VHS/Pioneer Classics LD. Brian Large (director). Color. In German with English subtitles. 108 minutes.

1991 Orange Festival
French stage production: Jean-Claude Auvray (director), Marek Janowski (conductor, Radio France Philharmonic Orchestra and Chorus), Bernard Arnould (set designer).

Cast: Gwyneth Jones (Elektra), Leonie Rysanek (Klytemnästra), Elizabeth Connell (Chrysothemis), Simon Estes (Orest), James King (Aegisth).

Video: Opera Direct/House of Opera DVD and VHS/Lyric VHS. Maté Rabinovsky (director). Color. In German with French subtitles. 104 minutes.

1993 South Australian State Opera
Australian stage production: Bruce Beresford (director), Richard Armstrong (conductor, Adelaide Symphony Orchestra and South Australian State Opera Chorus), John Stoddart (set designer).

Cast: Marilyn Zschau (Elektra), Yvonne Minton (Klytemnästra) Claire Primrose (Chrysothemis), Florian Cemy (Orest), Robert Grand (Aegisth).

Video: House of Opera/Legato Classics VHS. Peter Butler (director). Color. In German with English subtitles. 108 minutes.

1994 Metropolitan Opera

American stage production: Otto Schenk (director), James Levine (conductor, Metropolitan Opera Orchestra and Chorus), Jurgen Rose (set/costume designer).

Cast: Hildegard Behrens (Elektra), Brigitte Fassbaender (Klytemnästra), Deborah Voigt (Chrysothemis), Donald McIntyre (Orest), James King (Aegisth).

Telecast September 12, 1994; taped January 22, 1994. Brian Large (director). Color. In German with English subtitles. 110 minutes.

Early/related films

1909 Electra

Italian film of the story distributed in America by G. W. Bradenburgh. Black and white. Silent. About 15 minutes.

1910 Elektra

Mary Fuller plays Elektra in this Vitagraph film inspired by the success of the Strauss opera. Maurice Costello is Orest. The film, released in April 1910, was screened with live music although not always by Strauss. Black and white. Silent. About 15 minutes.

1961 Electra (Sophocles)

Anna Synodinou is Electra in this film of the play by Sophocles that provided the basis for the opera libretto. Ted Zarpas filmed it on stage at the ancient outdoor Epidaurus Theater, with G. Eptamenitis as cinematographer. Black and white. In Greek. 115 minutes.

1961 Electra (Euripides)

Irene Papas is Electra with Aleka Katselli as Clytemnestra in this famous film by Michael Cacoyannis based on the Euripides tragedy. It was filmed on location in Mycenae and Argos with Walter Lassally as cinematographer. Mikis Theodorakis wrote the music. Black and white. In Greek. 110 minutes.

1981 The Filming of Elektra

Norbert Beilharz shot this German documentary about the making of the Götz Friedrich film of *Elektra* with Leonie Rysanek and Dietrich Fischer-Dieskau. Conductor Karl Böhm is shown in rehearsal with the singers and the Vienna Philharmonic Orchestra. Color. In German. 90 minutes.

ELIAS, ROSALIND
American mezzo-soprano (1929–)

Rosalind Elias began her opera career with the New England Opera in 1948 and joined the Metropolitan in 1954. She sang in more than 600 performances with the Met and was a featured singer in the Met premieres of VANESSA and ANTONY AND CLEOPATRA. She can be seen at the Met in a 1982 video of HÄNSEL UND GRETEL as the Witch and in a 1975 Danny Kaye TV program about the METROPOLITAN OPERA. She sang the title role in CARMEN on a *Voice of Firestone* TV show in 1959 and in a BBC TV production in 1963. She is Baba the Turk in a 1977 Glyndebourne Festival production of THE RAKE'S PROGRESS.

ELISABETTA, REGINA D'INGHILTERRA
1815 opera by Rossini

Queen Elisabetta (Elizabeth) of England wants to honor the Earl of Leicester for his victory over the Scots, but he is unhappy to find Matilda (whom he secretly married) and his brother Enrico (Henry) among the hostages. After he is betrayed by Norfolk and declines to marry the queen, she puts him in prison. When Norfolk's villainy is eventually discovered, the queen pardons Leicester and gives him up to his wife. Giovanni Schmidt based his romantic libretto for Gioachino Rossini's opera *Elisabetta, regina d'Inghilterra* on a play derived from the novel *The Recess* by Sophie Lee. Although this Rossini opera is not well known, its overture is famous; it was recycled for *The Barber of Seville*.

1985 Teatro Regio, Turin

Italian stage production: Gianfranco De Bosio (director), Gabriele Ferro (conductor, Teatro Regio di Torino Orchestra and Chorus), Aldo di Lorenzo (set designer).

Cast: Lella Cuberli (Elisabetta), Antonio Savastano (Leicester), Daniela Dessì (Matilda), Rockwell Blake (Norfolk).

Video: Hardy Classics DVD/VHS. Color. In Italian with English subtitles. 150 minutes.

1991 Teatro San Carlo, Naples

Italian stage production: Alberto Zedda (conductor, San Carlo di Napoli Chorus and Orchestra).

Cast: Anna Caterina Antonacci (Elisabetta), Chris Merritt (Leicester), Sumi Jo (Matilda), Rockwell Blake (Norfolk).

Video: Premiere Opera VHS. Color. In Italian. 135 minutes.

ELISIR D'AMORE, L'

1832 opera by Donizetti

L'elisir d'amore (The Elixir of Love/The Love Potion) has always been one of GAETANO DONIZETTI'S most popular comic operas, helped by an entertaining libretto by Felice Romani based on a Scribe original. Shy peasant Nemorino loves beautiful Adina but she lives in a fantasy world and ignores him. He buys an alcoholic love potion from quack medicine man Dr. Dulcamara that makes him drunk and drives annoyed Adina into the arms of his rival, Sergeant Belcore. A second bottle of elixir and Nemorino is in the army, but Adina realizes she loves him and buys his enlistment paper back. The famous tenor aria "Una furtiva lagrima" is sung by Nemorino.

1947 Costa film

Italian feature film: Mario Costa (director), Mario Bava (cinematographer), Giuseppe Morelli (conductor, Rome Opera Orchestra and Chorus), Aldo Calvo and Liberto Petrassi (set designers).

Cast: Gino Sinimberghi (Nemorino), Nelly Corradi (Adina), Tito Gobbi (Belcore), Italo Tajo (Dulcamara), Loretta di Lelio (Giannetta), Gina Lollobrigida (friend of Adina).

Video: Bel Canto Society/Applause VHS. Black and white. In Italian with English subtitles. 75 minutes (originally 85 minutes).

Comment: This classic film, shown theatrically in the United States as *The Wine of Love,* was Lollobrigida's second film. It was originally released with introduction and commentary by Milton Cross.

1954 Brissoni TV film

Italian TV film: Alessandro Brissoni (director), Mario Rossi (conductor, RAI Milan Orchestra and Chorus).

Cast: Cesare Valletti (Nemorino), Alda Noni (Adina), Renato Capecchi (Belcore), Giuseppe Taddei (Dulcamara), Raimonda Stamer (Giannetta).

Video: Bel Canto Society VHS. Black and white. In Italian. 112 minutes.

1959 NHK Lirica Italiana

Japanese film of stage production: Alberto Erede (conductor, NHK Symphony Orchestra and Chorus).

Cast: Ferruccio Tagliavini (Nemorino), Alda Noni (Adina), Paolo Montarsolo (Dulcamara), Arturo La Porta (Belcore), Santa Chissari (Giannetta).

Video: Legato Classics VHS. Filmed live in Osaka on March 6, 1959. Black and white. In Italian with Japanese subtitles. 96 minutes.

Comment: Tagliavini was famous for his performances as Nemorino and is in grand form here, but the video shows its age.

1979 Cincinnati Opera

American stage production: James de Blasis (director), Byron Dean Ryan (conductor, Cincinnati Opera Orchestra and Chorus), Henry Heymann (set designer).

Cast: Jon Garrison (Nemorino), Judith Blegen (Adina), Andrew Foldi (Dulcamara), Julian Patrick (Belcore), Deborah Longwith (Giannetta).

Telecast January 5, 1980, on PBS. Kirk Browning (director). Color. In English. 120 minutes.

Comment: English-language version set in the Texas Panhandle in the 1840s. The action takes place at a ranch corral and outside the local saloon.

1981 Metropolitan Opera

American stage production: Nathaniel Merrill (director), Nicola Rescigno (conductor, Metropolitan Opera Orchestra and Chorus), Robert O'Hearn (set designer).

Cast: Luciano Pavarotti (Nemorino), Judith Blegen (Adina), Brent Ellis (Belcore), Sesto Bruscantini (Dulcamara), Louise Wohlafka (Giannetta).

Video: Pioneer DVD/Paramount VHS/Pioneer LD. Telecast live March 2, 1981. Kirk Browning (director). Color. In Italian with English subtitles. 132 minutes.

Comment: The opera is set in the Basque area in the 19th century. Pavarotti is superb in what became one of his signature roles.

1984 DeQuell film

Czechoslovakian feature film: Frank DeQuell (director), Piero Bellugi (conductor, Bratislava Radio Symphony).

Cast: Melanie Holliday (Adina), Miroslav Dvorsky (Nemorino), Alfredo Mariotti (Belcore), Armando Ariostini (Dulcamara), Bozena Plonyova (Giannetta).

Video: European Video VHS/Dreamlife (Japan) DVD. Color. In Italian. 80 minutes.

Comment: Picturesque but abridged film version shot on location in the Slovakian countryside with Adina as a vivacious school teacher and Nemorino as a lovesick house painter.

1991 Metropolitan Opera

American stage production: John Copley (director), James Levine (conductor, Metropolitan Opera Orchestra and Chorus), Beni Montresor (set designer).

Cast: Luciano Pavarotti (Nemorino), Kathleen Battle (Adina), Juan Pons (Belcore), Enzo Dara (Dulcamara), Korliss Uecker (Giannetta).

Video: DG VHS/LD. Brian Large (director). Taped November 16, 1991; telecast December 23, 1992. Color. In Italian with English subtitles. 129 minutes.

***1996 Opéra de Lyon

French stage production: Frank Dunlop (director), Evelino Pidò (conductor, Opéra de Lyon Orchestra and Chorus), Roberto Platé (set designer).

Cast: Roberto Alagna (Nemorino), Angela Gheorghiu (Adina), Roberto Scaltriti (Belcore), Simone Alaimo (Dulcamara), Elena Dan (Giannetta).

Video: Decca DVD/London VHS. Brian Large (director). Telecast August 12, 1998, in the United States on PBS. Color. In Italian with English subtitles. 130 minutes.

Comment: Superb production updated to rural Italy in the 1930s with two of the best singer/actors of our time having a grand time. So does the audience.

2002 Macerata Opera Festival

Italian stage production: Saverio Marconi (director), Niel Muus (conductor, Marchigiani Choir and Orchestra), Roberto Platé (set designer).

Cast: Aquiles Machado (Nemorino), Valeria Esposito (Adina), Enrico Marrucci (Belcore), Erwin Schrott (Dulcamara).

Video: TDK DVD. Color. In Italian with English subtitles. 173 minutes.

Comment: Performed in the Sferisterio Arena without opera pit. Nothing special but adequate.

Early/related films

1909 Alessandro Bonci film

Itala Film of Torino, which specialized in sound-on-disc films, released a film titled *L'elisir d'amore: "Una furtiva lagrima,* in 1908. The tenor heard on the record was the famous Alessandro Bonci. Black and white. In Italian. About 3 minutes.

1914 The Elixir of Love

The American film *The Elixir of Love,* made by the Imp company, was based on the libretto of the opera. Black and white. Silent. About 20 minutes.

1930 Call of the Flesh

Ramon Novarro sings the cavatina "Quanto è bella" from *L'elisir d'amore* in this MGM film about a café singer who turns to opera. See CALL OF THE FLESH.

1935 Forget Me Not

Beniamino Gigli sings "Una furtiva lagrima" in this film about an older opera singer married to a young woman who almost leaves him. See FORGET ME NOT.

1941 L'elisir d'amore

The Italian narrative film *L'elisir d'amore* tells the opera story in flashback. Love potion salesman Dr. Dulcamara makes a return visit to the village where his elixir solved Nemorino's love problem 20 years before and finds that Nemorino and Adina's son has the same problem. Armando Falconi is Dulcamara, Margherita Carosio is Adina, Roberto Villa is Nemorino, Giuseppe Rinaldi is their son, Carlo Romano is Belcore, and Jone Salinas is Giannetta. Ferruccio Tagliavini and Vincenzo Bettoni do the singing. Amleto Palermi directed the film, released in the United States as *Elixir of Love.* Black and white. 85 minutes. In Italian. Bel Canto Society VHS.

1942 La donna è mobile

In *La donna è mobile,* tenor Ferruccio Tagliavini plays a school teacher with a great voice. On a visit to Rome, he is discovered as a singer and performs arias from *La bohème, La sonnambula, Lohengrin,* and *L'elisir d'amore.* Mario Mattoli directed.. Black and white. In Italian. 78 minutes.

1946 Voglio bene soltanto a te

Beniamino Gigli plays a tenor making a movie. He falls for a female costar, but she prefers a younger man so he sings "Una furtiva lagrima." Giuseppe Fatigati directed. Black and white. In Italian. 80 minutes. Lyric/Opera Dubs VHS.

1947 On the Old Spanish Trail

Operatic gypsy Tito Guizar sings "Una furtiva lagrima" as he plays his guitar in his jail cell. This Roy Rogers Western was directed by William Witney for Republic. Color. In English. 72 minutes.

1949 Song of Surrender

Wanda Hendrix plays a recording of Enrico Caruso singing "Una furtiva lagrima" on a gramophone in 1906 in this U.S. film and the music becomes central to the plot. See SONG OF SURRENDER.

1950 I cadetti di Guascogna

Ferruccio Tagliavini sings "Una furtiva lagrima" in this Italian film about army draftees arranging a fundraising show for stranded actors. See FERRUCCIO TAGLIAVINI.

1951 Bellissima

Luchino Visconti's film, which opens with *L'elisir d'amore* being performed in a Rome broadcast studio, makes unusual use of themes from the opera; one gradually realizes that the magic elixirs of today are the movies. A film company announces that it is looking for a child actress, and Anna Magnani sets out to get her little girl the role. The film director is played by veteran Alessandro Blasetti, whose every appearance is accompanied by music associated with Dulcamara. Visconti uses Nemorino's aria "Quanto è bella" ("How Beautiful She Is") as ironic theme music for Magnani's quite unbeautiful child. Franco Mannino arranged and conducted the music. Black and white. In Italian. 112 minutes.

1985 Prizzi's Honor

A tenor is singing "Una furtiva lagrima" on stage during a Prizzi mob family celebration toward the climax of the film when the event is fire bombed by rival gangsters. John Huston directed. Color. 130 minutes. Vestron VHS.

1989 Bergonzi/Peters rehearsal

Carlo Bergonzi (aged 65) plays Nemorino opposite Roberta Peters (aged 59) as Adina in scenes from a dress rehearsal of *L'elisir d'amore* in a small New Jersey theater. He still sounds pretty good singing "Quanto è bella" and "Una furtiva lagrima." Alfredo Silipigni conducts. The scenes are on the video *Legends of Opera*. Color. In Italian. Lyric VHS.

1992 Lorenzo's Oil

George Miller features "Una furtiva lagrima" as sung by Tito Schipa in this harrowing film about a boy dying of a seemingly incurable disease. Parents Susan Sarandon and Nick Nolte refuse to accept his fate and set out to find a cure. Color. 135 minutes.

ELLIS, MARY

American soprano (1897–2003)

New York–born Mary Ellis made her debut at the Metropolitan Opera in 1918 creating the role of the novice Suor Genovieffa in the premiere of *Suor Angelica*. She sang opposite both Caruso and Chaliapin in major operas but after four years decided to switch from opera to operetta and acting. In 1924 she created the title role in Rudolf Friml's *Rose Marie* on Broadway, and in 1932 she moved to England and became an English star in the West End production of Jerome Kern's *Music in the Air* in 1933. Her London stage shows included IVOR NOVELLO's *Glamorous Night* in 1935, *The Dancing Years* in 1939, and *Arc de Triomphe* in 1943, in a role based on diva Mary Garden. Her film career began with *Bella Donna* in 1934 and ended with *The Three Worlds of Gulliver* in 1960. She continued to work in television

and appeared in a documentary about Caruso when she was 98. She was considered the world's oldest actress when she died at the age of 105.

1934 Bella Donna

Ellis made her film debut in this British film about a woman who tries to poison her husband because of her love for an Egyptian. It was based on a Robert Hichens play and directed by Robert Milton. Black and white. 91 minutes.

1935 All the King's Horses

Ellis made her American screen debut in this Ruritanian operetta based on a stage musical by Edward Horan. It's a kind of musical *Prisoner of Zenda* with Carl Brisson playing both a king and an actor who looks like him. Ellis is his rather confused queen. Frank Tuttle directed. Paramount. Black and white. 85 minutes.

1936 Fatal Lady

The New York Times called this "a prima donna's vehicle, duly affording Miss Ellis opportunities of singing choice bravura passages in nearly every world capital." She plays an opera diva who runs away after accusations of murder and joins another opera company under a false name. Backstage intrigue and murder follow her. See FATAL LADY.

1936 Paris in Spring

Ellis plays a Paris nightclub singer opposite Tullio Carminati, a count who loves her. She ignores him until he makes her jealous by wooing young Ida Lupino. The songs are by Harry Revel and Mack Gordon. Lewis Milestone directed. Paramount. Black and white. 82 minutes.

1960 The Three Worlds of Gulliver

Ellis's last theatrical film was a British fantasy based on *Gulliver's Travels* with Kerwin Matthews as Gulliver. Ellis plays Queen Brobdingnag, the 40-foot-tall ruler of the giants. Jack Sher directed. Color. 98 minutes.

1998 The Original Three Tenors

Mary Ellis, 98 when this documentary was made and apparently the last person alive who had sung with Caruso, talks about the experience. Richard Fawkes's documentary for BBC Television looks at tenors Caruso, Gigli, and Björling, with commentary by Nigel Douglas. Color and black and white. 50 minutes.

ELMO, CLOE
Italian mezzo-soprano (1909–1962)

Cloe Elmo, a leading mezzo-soprano at La Scala from 1936 to 1945, began her career in Cagliari in 1934. She came to the Metropolitan Opera in 1947, sang Mistress Quickly in a Toscanini telecast of FALSTAFF in 1950, made a number of American recordings, and returned to La Scala in 1951. She plays Cherubino in a 1948 Italian film of LE NOZZE DI FIGARO and provided the voice for CARMEN in another film the same year.

ELVERHØJ
1828 stage work by Kuhlau

Elverhøj (The Elf Hill) is not strictly an opera, but it became the patriotic equivalent in Danish stage music history. Friedrich Kuhlau (1786–1832), a major Danish composer, wrote five singspiels but his most important stage work is *Elverhøj*, a play by Johan Ludwig Heiberg for which he wrote songs and music. Created for a royal wedding, it tells the story of a girl raised by elves. Kuhlau based the music on Danish folk tunes arranged to fit the incidents in the play. One of the songs, "Kong Christian stod ved højen mast" (King Christian stood by the high mast), became the Danish national anthem.

1939 Methling film
Svend Methling's feature film, produced by Palladium and based on an adaptation by Gunnar Robert Hansen, gives prominence to Kuhlau's music. The stars are Nicolai Neilendam, Carlo Wieth, Eva Heramb, and Peter Poulson. Black and white. In Danish. 80 minutes.

1965 Barfod film
Bent Barfod, one of the leading animation artists of Denmark, made an animated cartoon version of the story in 1965. Color. In Danish. About 10 minutes.

Early films

1902 Children's Dance
The "Children's Dance" from *Elverhøj* is performed by the Royal Danish Ballet in this film. The soloists are Gudrun Christen and Helga Smith. Black and white. Silent. About 3 minutes. Print in the Danish Film Archive.

1909 Der vanker en Ridder
The first sound film of *Elverhøj* was a short showing singer Solborg Fjeldsøe performing the aria "Der vanker en Ridder." It was produced by the Talende company. Black and white. In Danish. About 4 minutes.

1910 Biorama film
Jørgen Lund directed this film of *Elverhøj* and played the role of King Christian IV himself. Carl Petersen is Erik Walkendorff, Agnes Lorentzen is Elisabeth Munk, Franz Skondrup is Albert Ebbesen, and Victoria Petersen is Elisabeth. Biorama Film produced. Black and white. Silent. About 18 minutes.

1910 Fotorama film
Gunnar Helsengreen directed this film version of *Elverhøj* with Philip Bech as King Christian IV. Johannes Rich is Erik Walkendorf, Marie Nidermann is Elisabeth Munk, Pater Malberg is Albert Ebbesen, Martha Helsengreen is Martha, and Jenny Roelsgaard is Agente. Fotorama Film produced. Black and white. Silent. About 16 minutes.

EMMELINE
1996 opera by Picker

Emmeline is a reworking of the Oedipus myth transposed to 19th-century New England. Emmeline, a 13-year-old mill worker, is seduced by her boss and sent away to have a baby that she is forced to give up for adoption. Twenty years later she marries a young man whom she discovers, to her horror, is her own son. Tobias Picker's first opera, *Emmeline*, libretto by J. D. McClatchy based on a novel by Judith Rossner, was commissioned by Santa Fe Opera, which premiered it July 27, 1996, with Patricia Racette as Emmeline and Curt Peterson as her son-husband Matthew. The opera was warmly received by most critics, televised and issued on video and CD, and then reprised by New York City Opera with Racette again in the title role. Picker's opera is composed in the tonal conservative style now associated with many modern American operas and includes jazz syncopation and the hymn "Rock of Ages."

1996 Santa Fe Opera
American stage production: Francesca Zambello (director), George Manahan (conductor, Santa Fe Opera Orchestra), Robert Israel (set designer).

Cast: Patricia Racette (Emmeline), Curt Peterson (Matthew), Victor Ledbetter (Mr. Maguire), Anne-Marie Owens (Aunt Hannah), Kevin Langan (Henry Mosher), Melanie Sarakatsannis (Sophie), Josepha Gayer (Mrs. Bass), Herbert Perry (Pastor Avery).

Telecast April 2, 1997, for the PBS *Great Performances* series. Color. In English. 115 minutes.

EMPRESS, THE
1993 TV opera by Gough

Composer Orlando Gough, librettist David Gale, director Jane Thorburn, and producer Mark Lucas were asked to create a TV opera by Avril MacRory for England's Channel 4. They adapted a wordless play by Frank Wedekind called *The Empress of Newfoundland*. A doctor prescribes marriage as a cure for the Empress of Newfoundland, who is ill. She rejects suitors who represent mind, money, and power and chooses the strongest man in the world. When he leaves her, she kills herself.

1993 Channel 4 Television
English TV film: Jane Thorburn (director), Mark Lucas (producer).

Cast: Amanda Dean (Empress of Newfoundland), Valerie Morgan (Prime Minister), Richard Stuart (Doctor), Mike Ahearne (Strong Man, sung by Jeremy Birchal).

Telecast September 26, 1993, on Channel 4. Color. In English. 30 minutes.

ENESCU, GEORGE
Romanian composer (1881–1955)

George Enescu, Romania's greatest composer, wrote only one opera, the 1936 *Oedipe*. Romanians consider it a masterpiece, but it has never been popular outside Romania and is rarely staged elsewhere. The libretto by Edmund Flegg, partially based on the Sophocles Theban trilogy, tells the tragic story of Oedipus from birth to death in an expressionist manner.

1981 Bucharest Opera
Romanian stage production: Mihail Brediceanu (conductor, Bucharest Opera Orchestra and Chorus).

Cast: David Ohanesian (Oedipe), Dan Zancu, J. Grigorescu, M. Vanerg.

Video: Color. In Romanian. 155 minutes. Opera Dubs VHS.

Comment: Ohanesian is famous in Romania in the role of Oedipus and recorded it in 1966 with the Bucharest Opera.

Related films

1995 Mihailescu TV film
Florin Mihailescu filmed Romanian stage director Andrei Serban at work on his 1995 Romanian National Opera production of Enescu's *Oedipe*. The film is a coproduction of, Romsat Tele 7 abc, Panoceanic Romania, and Fundatia Culturala Romana. Color. In Romanian with English subtitles. 58 minutes. Editura Video VHS.

1996 Someone Has Killed the Sphinx
Adrian Mihai's video documentary examines Romanian cultural life as seen through the staging of Enescu's *Oedipe* by Andrei Serban at the Romanian National Opera House in August 1995. Bass-baritone Sever Barnea is Oedipe, mezzo Mihaela Agachi is Meropa, and contralto Lucia Cicoare is the Sphinx. There are interviews with Serban, singers, and opera officials. Screened at the Romanian Cultural Center in New York on February 29, 1996. Color. In Romanian. 64 minutes. Mihai DVD/VHS.

ENFANT ET LES SORTILÈGES, L'
1925 opera by Ravel

French novelist Colette wrote the libretto *L'enfant et les sortilèges*, the delightful MAURICE RAVEL opera about a naughty child sent to his room for misbehavior. In a tantrum he destroys toys, furniture, and books and assaults the family cat. The maltreated objects comes to life and the scene moves outdoors where the child finally redeems himself with an act of kindness.

1986 Netherlands Dance Theatre
Dutch stage production: Hans Hulscher (director), Lorin Maazel (conductor, Paris Orchestre National/RTF Chorus), Jiří Kylián (choreographer), John Macfarlane (set/costume designer).

Cast: Marly Knoben (Child, sung by Françoise Ogéas), Roslyn Anderson (Mother, sung by Janine Collars), Nacho Duato (Cat, sung by Camille Maurane).

Video: Home Vision VHS. Color. In French. 50 minutes.

Comment: This is a dance video with an opera soundtrack. The Netherlands Dance Theatre dancers perform on the stage, but the soundtrack comes from a 1961 recording.

***1987 Glyndebourne Festival
English stage production: Frank Corsaro (director), Simon Rattle (conductor, London Philharmonic Orchestra, Glyndebourne Festival Chorus and Trinity Boys Choir), Maurice Sendak (set/costume designer), Ronald Chase (slides/animation), Jenny Weston (choreographer).

Cast: Cynthia Buchan (Child), Fiona Kimm (Mother/Cat), Malcolm Walker (Tomcat/Clock), François Loup (Armchair/Tree), Hyacinth Nicholls (Louis XV Chair/Bat), Thierry Dran (Teapot/Frog), Louise Winter (Cup), Nan Christie (Fire), Carolyn Blackwell (Princess).

Video: Home Vision VHS. Tom Gutteridge (director). Color. In French with English subtitles. 46 minutes.

Comment: The star of this highly enjoyable production is American Maurice Sendak, who designed the eye-catching sets and costumes.

1993 Opéra de Lyon

French stage production: Moshe Leiser and Patrice Caurier (directors), Didier Punto (conductor, Atelier Lyrique de l'Opéra de Lyon), Christian Rätz (set designer).

Cast: Isabelle Eschenbrenner (Child), Marie Boyer (Mother/Chinese Cup/Dragonfly), Nathalie Dessay (Fire), Sylvaine Davene (Nightingale), Catherine Dubosc (Princess), Jean-Louis Meunier, Christophe Lacassagne, Christopher Goldsack, Doris Lamprecht.

Telecast in France in 1993. Moshe Leiser and Patrice Caurier (directors), Color. In French with English subtitles. 45 minutes.

ENFANTS TERRIBLES, LES

1996 screen opera by Glass

A brother and sister have a quasi-incestuous relationship, and the games they play with each other lead to tragedy. Philip Glass's third operatic version of a classic film by Jean Cocteau, *Les Enfants Terribles,* mixes singing, dancing, and speaking. Cocteau's hothouse tale of brother and sister first appeared as a 1929 novel and was made into a film in 1952 by Jean-Pierre Melville with screenplay by Cocteau and Melville. Glass's adaptation was staged by his choreographer collaborator Susan Marshall and premiered at the Brooklyn Academy of Music in 1996. Sister Lise was sung by Christine Arand and danced by Kristen Hollinsworth, Krista Langberg, and Eileen Thomas. Brother Paul was sung by Philip Cutlip and danced by Hans Beenhakker, Mark DeChiazza, and John Heginbotham. Dargelos and Agathe were sung by Valerie Komar and danced by Susan Blankensop. Hal Cazalet was the Narrator.

ENGLANDER, ROGER

American TV director/producer (1935–)

Roger Englander, one of the pioneers of television opera, was involved with early productions of operas by Gian Carlo Menotti for NBC Television, including THE MEDIUM and THE TELEPHONE in 1948 and THE OLD MAID AND THE THIEF in 1949. He directed a 1960 production of Aaron Copland's opera THE SECOND HURRICANE and produced a tribute to the composer in 1961. He was a producer/director with the BELL TELEPHONE HOUR and CAMERA THREE series and also worked on many of LEONARD BERNSTEIN's TV programs. Much of his later TV work was in non-operatic classical music and he also produced stage productions. He wrote an excellent beginner's guide to opera, *Opera, What's All the Screaming About?*, which includes photographs of some of his early TV productions.

ENGLISH NATIONAL OPERA

The English National Opera, which presents operas in English in the Coliseum in London, began at the Old Vic, then became the Sadler's Wells Opera, and was renamed English National Opera in 1973. The ENO is innovative and adventurous in its productions with new English operas, lesser known French works, and radical stagings of classics. Its presentations of modern American operas, such as a recent staging of *Nixon in China,* have been highly influential. Its famous productions on video include Jonathan Miller's Mafia-style RIGOLETTO (1982) and the award-winning SERSE (1988), but there are also notable productions of ARIODANTE (1996), BILLY BUDD (1988), BLONDE ECKBERT (1994), THE FAIRY QUEEN (1995), GIULIO CESARE (1984), GLORIANA (1984), MARIA STUARDA (1982), THE MIKADO (1987), PETER GRIMES (1994), RUSALKA (1986), SEMELE (1999), and STREET SCENE (1992).

ENRICO CARUSO, LEGGENDA DI UNA VOCE

1951 Italian film about Caruso

Italian tenor Mario Del Monaco is the singing voice of Enrico Caruso in *Enrico Caruso, leggenda di una voce,* a romantic Italian film about the singer's early years. Ermanno Randi plays Caruso, with Gina Lollobrigida as Stella, the woman he loves. Like its American rival, *The Great Caruso,* it is highly fictional but still enjoyable although it has much smaller production values. Based on Frank Thies's novel *Leggenda Napoletana,* it concentrates on Caruso's childhood and rise to fame. It begins in Naples with the boy Caruso (Maurizio Di Narda) singing for an outdoor café crowd and arousing the interest of opera lover Proboscide (Ciro Scafa) who introduces him to his niece Stella. Caruso sneaks into a performance of *La Damnation di Faust* in the Teatro San Carlo and decides he wants to be an opera singer. His father (Gaetano Verna) opposes the idea, and when his mother (Maria von Tasnady) dies, he quits singing for eight years. Proboscide finally finds him and persuades him to sing again with help from Stella. Music maestro Vergine (Lamberto Picasso) takes him as a pupil and has him demonstrate what a real voice is to his other pupils. He sings a series of arias later associated with Caruso, including "Amor ti vieta" from *Fedora,* "O paradiso" from *L'Africana,* "Una furtiva lagrima" from *L'elisir d'amore,* and "M'apparì" from *Martha.* He auditions on stage at Teatro San Carlo singing the arioso "Vesti la giubba" from *Pagliacci* and breaking into a sob in the last line. Watching him is composer Leoncavallo who says Caruso will become the greatest interpreter of his opera and insists that the sob should be used in future performances. Stella is also watching, but she decides she should go away and allow Caruso to become a great singer. When he finds she has gone to Sicily with her father, who wants her to marry a rich man, he quits his studies and joins an opera company that is going to Sicily. There is another tenor in the company, so he is not allowed to sing leading roles and is full of despair. When they reach Sicily and he sees Stella arriving at the opera house for a performance of *Andrea Chenier,* he decides to jump off a cliff, but she finds him and tells him she loves him. The company tenor becomes ill, so Caruso replaces him and goes on stage as Andrea and sings "Un dì, all'azzurro spazio." The audience erupts in a standing ovation and demands an encore. Caruso has become The Great Caruso. Carlo Franci was music director for the film, directed by Giacomo Gentilomo; written by Fulvio Palmieri, Giovanna Soria, and Maleno Malenotti; and photographed by Tinto Santoni. The 91-minute film was released in the United States in a dubbed version as *The Young Caruso.* Triton DVD (includes film of Caruso's funeral, a scrapbook biography, and 48 minutes of recordings) and Bel Canto Society VHS (includes excerpt from Caruso's film *My Cousin* plus documentary film of Caruso).

ENTER MADAME
1922 and 1934 films with opera content

Two Hollywood films have been based on the 1920 operatic play *Enter Madame* by Gilda Varesi and Dolly Byrne, the story of a prima donna whose nonstop opera career almost wrecks her marriage. In the silent 1922 version, Clara Kimball Young plays Italian prima donna Lisa Della Robia, who cancels an Italian opera tour to return to New York to confront her husband (Elliott Dexter) when he files for divorce. She wins him back with a little guile. Harry Garson directed for Metro. In the 1934 sound version, Elissa Landi plays Lisa and is married to millionaire Cary Grant. When he gets tired of never seeing her during a European opera tour while he follows in her wake, he returns to America and files for divorce, claiming his marriage has been a "charming nightmare." She returns to fight the divorce and a rival women and wins him back operatically. Soprano Nina Koshetz provides the singing voice for Landi, partnered with Met baritone Richard Bonelli. The film features scenes from *Tosca, Cavalleria rusticana,* and *Il trovatore* staged by the Los Angeles Opera Company. Gladys Lehman and Charles Brackett wrote the screenplay, Theodor Sparkuhl and William C. Mellor were the cinematographers, and Elliott Nugent directed for Paramount. Black and white. In English. 83 minutes.

ENTFÜHRUNG AUS DEM SERAIL, DIE
1782 opera by Mozart

Die Entführung aus dem Serail (The Abduction from the Seraglio), a singspiel with spoken dialogue that premiered at the Burgtheater in Vienna on July 16, 1782, is considered the first major opera in German. Gottlieb Stephanie's libretto tells the story of nobleman Belmonte's attempt to rescue his captive lover Konstanze from the palace of the Pasha Selim in 16th-century Turkey. Belmonte's servant Pedrillo loves her servant Blonde and the unfriendly guard Osmin lusts after her. In the end, as in most MOZART operas, there is forgiveness and understanding. *Abduction* has been popular with filmmakers in recent years but was not filmed during the silent era.

1954 NBC Opera Theatre
American TV production: Samuel Chotzinoff producer), Peter Herman Adler (conductor, Symphony of the Air Orchestra), Rouben Ter-Arutunian (set designer).
Cast: Nadja Witkowska (Konstanze), David Cunningham (Belmonte), Virginia Haskins (Blonde), David Lloyd (Pedrillo), Leon Lishner (Osmin), Norman Rose (Pasha Selim).
Video at the MTR. Kirk Browning (director). Telecast October 31, 1954. Color. In English. 90 minutes.

1954 Mozart Ensemble, Vienna State Opera
Austrian stage production: Alfred Stöger (director), Rudolf Moralt (conductor, Vienna Philharmonic).
Cast: Wilma Lipp (Konstanze), Rudolf Christ (Belmonte), Emmy Loose (Blonde), Peter Klein (Pedrillo), Ludwig Weber (Osmin).
Video: Taurus (Germany) VHS. Color. In German. 30 minutes.
Comment: Highlights version of opera included on the anthology film *Unsterblicher Mozart* (Immortal Mozart) with two other Mozart operas.

1970 NET Opera Theater
American TV production: Kirk Browning (director), Peter Herman Adler (conductor, Boston Symphony Orchestra), Robert Israel (set designer).
Cast: Elaine Cormany (Konstanze), Grayson Hirst (Belmonte), Carolyn Smith-Meyer (Blonde), John Lankston (Pedrillo), Spiro Malas (Osmin), Michael Kermoyan (Pasha Selim).
Video at the MTR. Telecast October 18, 1970, on PBS. Kirk Browning (director) Color. In English. 90 minutes.

Comment: Experimental chroma-keyed production with abstract sets. Patterned backdrops and solid color flat props give the opera a two-dimensional feeling.

1980 Glyndebourne Festival

English stage production: Peter Wood (director), Gustav Kuhn (conductor, London Philharmonic Orchestra and Glyndebourne Festival Chorus), William Dudley (set designer).

Cast: Valerie Masterson (Konstanze), Ryland Davies (Belmonte), Lillian Watson (Blonde), James Hoback (Pedrillo), Willard White (Osmin), Joachim Bissmeier (Pasha).

Opera d'Oro/VAI VHS. Dave Heather (director). Color. In German with English subtitles. 145 minutes.

1980 Dresden State Opera

German stage production: Harry Kupfer (stage and film director), Peter Gulke (conductor, Dresden State Opera Orchestra and Chorus).

Cast: Carolyn Smith-Meyer (Konstanze), Armin Ude (Belmonte) Rolf Tomaszewaki (Osmin), Barbara Sternberger (Blonde), Uwe Peper (Pedrillo), Werner Haseleu (Pasha Selim).

VIEW VHS/Dreamlife (Japan) LD. Color. In German. 129 minutes.

1980 Bavarian State Opera

German state production: August Everding (director), Karl Böhm (conductor, Bavarian State Opera Chorus and Orchestra), Max Bignens (set/costume designer), Unitel (production).

Cast: Edita Gruberova (Konstanze), Francisco Araiza (Belmonte), Reri Grist (Blonde), Norbert Orth (Pedrillo), Martti Talvela (Osmin), Thomas Holtzman (Pasha).

DG VHS. Karl-Heinz Hundorf (director). Color. In German with English subtitles. 146 minutes.

Comment: Superbly conducted by one of the great Mozart conductors in the year before his death. The singers are terrific and the production is adequate.

1982 Salzburg Marionette Theater

Austrian puppet production: Karl-Heinz Hundorf (director), Ferenc Fricsay (conductor, Berlin RIAS Orchestra and Chorus), Günther Schneider-Siemssen (set designer).

Voices: Maria Stader (Konstanze), Ernst Haefliger (Belmonte), Rita Streich (Blonde), Martin Vantin (Pedrillo), J Greindl (Osmin).

Cascade DVD. Telecast on ORF Austrian Television. Color. In German. 60 minutes.

Comment: The Salzburg Marionette Theater specializes in shortened versions of operas and operettas

using recordings of operas. The Fricsay recording, made in 1954, includes dialogue. Peter Ustinov introduces the opera, and the DVD includes a behind-the-scenes documentary.

1987 Royal Opera

English stage production: Elijah Moshinsky (director), Georg Solti (conductor, Royal Opera House Orchestra and Chorus), Timothy O'Brien and Sidney Nolan (set designers).

Cast: Inga Nielsen (Konstanze), Deon van der Walt (Belmonte), Lillian Watson (Blonde), Kurt Moll (Osmin), Lars Magnusson (Pedrillo), Oliver Tobias (Pasha Selim).

Video: Home Vision VHS/NVC Arts (GB) VHS/Pioneer LD. Humphrey Burton (director). Color. In German with English subtitles. 140 minutes.

1989 Salzburg Festival

Austrian stage production: Johannes Schaaf (director), Horst Stein (conductor, Vienna Philharmonic and State Opera Chorus), Andreas Reinhardt (set designer).

Cast: Inga Nielsen (Konstanze), Deon van Der Walt (Belmonte), Lillian Watson (Blonde), Heinz Zednik (Pedrillo), Kurt Rydl (Osmin), Ulrich Wildgruber (Pasha).

Telecast January 5, 1990, for the PBS *Great Performances* series. Johannes Schaaf (director). Color. In German with English subtitles. 150 minutes.

***1990 Drottningholm Court Theatre

Swedish stage production: Harald Clemen (director), Arnold Östman (conductor, Drottningholm Court Theatre Orchestra).

Cast: Aga Winska (Konstanze), Richard Croft (Belmonte), Elisabet Hellstrom (Blonde), Beng-Ola Morgny (Pedrillo), Tamäs Szüle (Osmin), Emmerich Shaeffer (Pasha Selim).

EMI VHS/Philips LD. Thomas Olofsson (director). Color. In German with English subtitles. 130 minutes.

Comment: Delightful production shot in the intimate Drottningholm Court Theatre with the orchestra performing in costume on period instruments.

1998 Stuttgart State Opera

Austrian stage production: Hans Neuenfels (director), Lothar Zagrosek (conductor, Stuttgart State Opera Orchestra and Chorus).

Singers: Catherine Naglestad (Konstanze), Matthias Klink (Belmonte), Roland Bracht (Osmin), Kate Ladner (Blonde), Heinz Göhrig (Pedrillo).

Video: Arthaus DVD. János Darvas (director), Color. In German with English subtitles. 178 minutes.

Comment: The roles are doubled (each singer paired with an actor), except nonsinging Selim, who complains about this. Layers of symbolism are combined with anachronistic gags and horrific visuals in a fascinating though complicated mix. Neuenfels's postmodern production won the 1999 Bavarian Theatre Prize.

2002 Teatro della Pergola, Florence

Italian stage production: Eike Gramss (director), Zubin Mehta (conductor, Maggio Musicale Fiorentino Orchestra and Chorus), Christoph Wagenknecht (set designer).

Cast: Eva Mei (Konstanze), Rainer Trost (Belmonte), Patrizia Ciofi (Blonde), Mehrzad Montazeri (Pedrillo), Kurt Rydl (Osmin), Markus John (Pasha Selim).

TDK DVD. George Blume (director). Color. In German with English subtitles. 136 minutes.

Comment: Traditional but excellent in all ways.

Related films

1958 A Night at the Harem
Animation pioneer Lotte Reiniger made a silhouette version of the opera in 1958 called *A Night at the Harem*. Color. 14 minutes.

1971 Giorgio Strehler Rehearses
Giorgio Strehler is shown working on his famous staging of the opera, originally created for the 1965 Salzburg Festival, which features *commedia dell'arte* ideas and shadow silhouettes of singers. Norbert Beilharz directed. Color. In German. 60 minutes.

1994 Guarding Tess
Shirley MacLaine, a former First Lady, falls asleep during a scene from *Die Entführung aus dem Serail* and is woken by bodyguard Nicolas Cage. The opera singers seen on stage are Julie Kursawa and Michael Consoli, but the duet "Ich gehe, doch rate ich dir" is actually sung by Günther Missenhardt and Elzbieta Szmytka with the Vienna Symphony conducted by Bruno Weil. Hugh Wilson wrote and directed the film. Color. 98 minutes.

1999 Mozart in Turkey
Elijah Moshinsky and his cast and crew are filmed during a production of *Die Entführung aus dem Serail* at the Topkapi Palace in Istanbul. Director Mick Csáky combines documentary material about the production with scenes from the opera. The performers are Paul Groves, Yelda Kodalli, Désirée Rancatore, Lynton Atkinson, Peter Rose, and Oliver Tobias; Sir Charles Mackerras conducts the Scottish Chamber Orchestra and Chorus. Moshinsky talks about his approach to Mozart, and Alev Lytle Croutier, author of a book on harems, discusses the historical background of the story. Color. In English. 89 minutes. Films for the Humanities & Sciences VHS.

ERKEL, FERENC
Hungarian composer (1810–1893)

Ferenc Erkel, the most important 19th-century Hungarian opera composer, wrote many operas, but they are mostly unknown outside Hungary. The most famous and important is the 1861 BÁNK BÁN, which has been made into a feature film shown in American cinemas in 2002. Also popular is *Hunyadi László,* which has been telecast. Recordings of both operas are on the Hungaroton label.

ERNANI
1844 opera by Verdi

GIUSEPPE VERDI's fifth opera, a full-blooded melodrama, made him internationally famous. Francesco Maria Piave's libretto, based on Victor Hugo's play *Hernani,* tells the story of three men who desire the same woman in 16th-century Spain. Elvira is the fiancée of Silva but loves the nobleman-turned-bandit Ernani. When Don Carlo, the king of Spain, takes her hostage, the other two plot against him. In the end Ernani wins Elvira but then has to kill himself because of a pledge of honor he made to Silva. Don't ask. The music redeems all.

***1982 Teatro alla Scala

Italian stage production: Luca Ronconi (director), Riccardo Muti (conductor, Teatro alla Scala Orchestra and Chorus), Ezio Frigerio (set designer).

Cast: Plácido Domingo (Ernani), Mirella Freni (Elvira), Renato Bruson (Don Carlo), Nicolai Ghiaurov (Silva).

Video: Bel Canto Society and HBO (USA) VHS/NVC Arts (GB) VHS. Preben Montell (director). Color. In Italian with English subtitles. 135 minutes.

1982/1989 Opera Stories
Laserdisc highlights version of above 1982 La Scala production with Charlton Heston narrating the story from a Spanish castle and the plains of Aragon. Keith Cheetham filmed the Heston material in 1989. Color. In English and Italian with English subtitles. 52 minutes. Pioneer Artists LD.

1983 Metropolitan Opera

American stage production: Pier Luigi Samaritani (director/set designer), James Levine (conductor, Metropolitan Opera Orchestra and Chorus).

Cast: Luciano Pavarotti (Ernani), Leona Mitchell (Elvira), Sherrill Milnes (Don Carlo), Ruggero Raimondi (Silva).

Video: Pioneer Classics DVD/Bel Canto Paramount VHS. Kirk Browning (director). Taped December 17, 1983; telecast December 21, 1983. Color. In Italian with English subtitles. 142 minutes.

Comment: Pavarotti dominates this beautifully sung Met production.

Early/related films

1906 Cinemafono Pagliej sound film
CINEMAFONO PAGLIEJ, an Italian sound-on-disc company specializing in opera aria films, screened a film featuring an aria from *Ernani* at the Sala Umberto I in Rome from May 19 to July 30 in 1906. Black and white. In Italian. About 4 minutes.

1908 Pineschi sound film
The Italian Pineschi company, which specialized in sound-on-disc films featuring arias from operas, released one called *"Ernani"* in 1908. Black and white. In Italian. About 3 minutes.

1909 Itala sound film
Itala Film of Torino released a sound-on-disc film in 1909 titled *Ernani: "Oh sommo Carlo..."*. Black and white. In Italian. About 3 minutes.

1909 Capellani film
Albert Capellani directed this *Ernani*, a French film of the story for Pathé. It stars Henry Krauss, Jeanne Delvair, and Paul Capellani. Black and white. Silent. About 10 minutes.

1910 Gasnier film
Italy's first and greatest film diva Francesca Bertini stars as Elvira in scenes from the Verdi opera under the direction of Louis Gasnier. Black and white. Silent. About 10 minutes.

1911 Barcelona film
A Spanish film of the opera was produced in 1911 by the Barcelona Film company featuring highlight scenes from the opera. Black and white. Silent. About 10 minutes.

1972 Il caso Pisciotta
Eriprando Visconti's Italian film *The Pisciotta Case* features excerpts of music from *Ernani*. A magistrate investigates the killing of bandit Salvatore Giuliano's chief lieutenant by the Mafia. Color. In Italian. 98 minutes.

1982 Fitzcarraldo
This film contains a most unusual historical staging of the opera in Brazil. Fitzcarraldo (Klaus Kinski) travels thousands of miles to see a Teatro Amazonas production of *Ernani* starring Enrico Caruso and Sarah Bernhardt (a singer in the pit provides vocals for the non-operatic Bernhardt). He arrives just as it is ending. The scene, staged by Werner Schroeter, is sung by Mietta Sighele, Veriano Luchetti, and Dimiter Petkov for the actors seen on stage. The music is played by the Venice Philharmonic. Color. In German with English subtitles. 157 minutes. Warner VHS.

ERWARTUNG
1909 monodrama by Schoenberg

Erwartung (Expectation) is a one-act one-person opera about a woman looking for her lover in a forest in the moonlight and worrying out loud about his infidelity with another woman. She eventually comes upon his bloody corpse, but by then we suspect that she may have been the one who killed him. ARNOLD SCHOENBERG's powerful opera, libretto by Marie Pappenheim, was composed in 1909 but not premiered until 1924. It is now considered one of the modern opera classics.

1989 Metropolitan Opera
American stage production: Göran Järvefelt (director), James Levine (conductor, Metropolitan Opera Orchestra), Hans Schavernoch (set designer).

Cast: Jessye Norman (the Woman).

Telecast March 31 1989, on PBS in the *Metropolitan Opera Presents* series. Brian Large (director). Color. In German with English subtitles. 30 minutes.

Comment: This performance is on CD but not on a commercial VHS although noncommercial copies are available at various university libraries.

ESSWOOD, PAUL
English countertenor (1942–)

Paul Esswood made his debut in 1968 and quickly became one of the best-known countertenors in the world, singing around the world in both modern and baroque operas. He was featured in the famous Ponnelle-Harnoncourt Monteverdi opera cycle at Zurich in the late 1970s and created the title role of Akhnaten in the Philip Glass opera. See AKHNATEN (1985), L'INCORONAZIONE DI POPPEA (1979), and IL RITORNO D'ULISSE IN PATRIA (1980).

ESTES, SIMON
American bass-baritone (1938–)

Simon Estes began his career with the Deutsche Oper singing Ramfis in *Aida* and then won praise in Wagnerian roles; in 1978, he became the first African-American man to sing at Bayreuth, starring as the Dutchman in DER FLIEGENDE HOLLÄNDER (his 1985 performance there is on video). In 1982, he made a triumphal entry to the Metropolitan as the Landgrave in *Tannhäuser*. He also sings Italian and Russian operas and was the first Porgy at the Metropolitan in 1985. See also AIDA (1981/1985), CARMEN (1988 film), ELEKTRA (1991), HENRY VIII (2002), IL RITORNO D'ULISSE IN PATRIA (1980), and SALOME (1990).

1989 Great Arias with Domingo and Friends
Estes performs Iago's "Credo" in this Paris concert with Plácido Domingo. Lorin Maazel conducts the National Orchestra of France; André Frederick directed. Color. 46 minutes. VIEW VHS.

1990 Concert for Peace
Estes sings with Frederica von Stade in a concert in Oslo, Norway, with arias by Mozart and Handel, spirituals, and the fourth movement of Mahler's Symphony No. 4. Audrey Hepburn and Gregory Peck hosted the program telecast on PBS in 1991. Color. 55 minutes.

ETERNAL ROAD, THE
1937 pageant opera by Weill

The epic story of the Jewish people as it is told in the Bible. KURT WEILL's spectacular three-hour pageant opera *The Eternal Road*, libretto by Ludwig Lewisohn based on the Franz Werfel play *Der Weg der Verheissung*, premiered at the Manhattan Opera House on January 4, 1937, with a cast that included Lotte Lenya, Sam Jaffe, and Sidney Lumet under the direction of Max Reinhardt. It was well received by critics and popular with audiences but was a financial disaster and not staged again for another 62 years. Chemnitz Opera in Germany produced a scaled-down version in 1999 that was reprised at the Brooklyn Academy of Music in February 2000.

1999 Chemnitz Opera
German stage production: Michael Heinicke (director), John Mauceri (conductor, Robert Schumann Philharmonie and chorus from Chemnitz Opera, Cracow Opera, and Leipzig Synagogue), David Sharis (set designer).

Cast: Theo Adam, Siegfried Vogel, Peter Schmidt.

Telecast March 22, 2000. Color. In English. 180 minutes.

Related film

2001 The Eternal Road: Encounter With the Past
Ron Frank's documentary tells how the production of *The Eternal Road* at Chemnitz came about. It uses modern and archival footage to describe the place and the event, placing it in the context of the rise of Hitler. Shown on PBS. Color. 57 minutes.

ÉTOILE, L'
1877 opéra-bouffe by Chabrier

EMMANUEL CHABRIER's charming comic opera *L'étoile* (The Star) is about a mythical king caught in a Catch 22 quandary. King Ouf I likes to hold a public execution once a year, and his choice for victim this year is a peddler named Lazuli. However, his astrologer says their stars are tied together and advises the king that he will die 24 hours after Lazuli. The peddler is quickly made into a person of importance by the king and even wins the hand of Princess Laoula. Lazuli is a mezzo-soprano trouser role.

1986 Opéra de Lyon.
French stage production: Louis Erlo (director), John Eliot Gardiner (conductor, Lyons Opera Orchestra and Chorus).

Cast: Colette Alliot-Lugaz (Lazuli), George Gautier (King), Ghyslaine Raphanel (Princess), François Le Roux (Hérisson de Porc Epic), Antoine David (Tapioca).

Video: Image Entertainment DVD/House of Opera and Polygram (France) VHS. Bernard Maigrot (director). Color. In French. 105 minutes.

EUGENE ONEGIN
1879 opera by Tchaikovsky

A deceptively simple but resonant bittersweet love story provides the basis for *Eugene Onegin* (*Yevgeny Onegin* in Russian), TCHAIKOVSKY's best-loved opera. The libretto by Konstantin Shikovsky and the composer, based on a famous Pushkin novel written in verse, tells of the love of innocent Tatyana for world-weary aristocrat Eugene Onegin. She writes him a passionate love letter, but he rejects her and flirts with her sister, the fiancée of his friend Lensky. They duel over this, and Lensky is killed. Years later Onegin discovers that he loves Tatyana but it is too late; she is now married to Prince Gremin and will not leave him. Tatyana's "Letter Aria" is one of the most famous in Russian opera.

1958 Tikhomirov film

Soviet feature film: Roman Tikhomirov (director), Alexander Ivanovsky (screenplay), Boris Haikin (conductor, Kirov Opera Orchestra and Chorus), Yevgeny Shapiro (cinematographer), Lenfilm (production).

Cast: Ariadna Shengelaya (Tatyana, sung by Galina Vishnevskaya), Vadim Medvedev (Eugene Onegin, sung by Yevgeny Kibkalo), Igor Ozerov (Lensky, sung by Anton Gregoriev), Svetlana Nemolyneva (Olga, sung by Larissa Avdeyeva), Ivan Petrov (Gremin).

Video: Corinth/Kultur VHS and Image Entertainment LD. Color. In Russian with English subtitles. 106 minutes.

Comment: Tikhomirov, who specialized in movies of Russian operas, shot the film on location with actors dubbed by notable singers from the Kirov. It includes effective cross-cutting and flashbacks but is cut from the stage opera.

1962 Bavarian State Opera

German stage production: Rudolf Hartman (director), Joseph Keilberth (conductor, Bavarian State Opera Orchestra and Chorus), Helmut Jurgens (set designer).

Cast: Ingeborg Bremert (Tatyana), Hermann Prey (Eugene Onegin), Fritz Wunderlich (Lensky), Brigitte Fassbaender (Olga), Mino Yahia (Gremin).

Video: Opera Direct/Lyric VHS. Black and white. In German. 135 minutes.

Comment: An outstanding cast, especially Wunderlich, but the quality of the video image is low.

1968 Bavarian Television

German TV film: Václav Kaslik (director), Vaclav Neumann (conductor, Bavarian State Opera Orchestra and Chorus), Gerd Krauss (set designer).

Cast: Teresa Stratas (Tatyana), Hermann Prey (Eugene Onegin), Wieslaw Ochman (Lensky), Julia Hamari (Olga), Peter Lagger (Gremin).

Video: Opera Direct/Lyric VHS. Color. In German. 150 minutes.

1984 Kirov Opera

Russian stage production: Elena Gorbunova (director), Yuri Temirkanov (conductor, Kirov Opera Orchestra and Chorus).

Cast: Tatyana Novikova (Tatyana), Sergei Leiferkus (Eugene Onegin), Yuri Marusin (Lensky), Larissa Dyatkova (Olga), Nikolai Okhotnikov (Gremin), Evgenya Gorskovskaya (Madame Larina).

Video: Kultur VHS. Vasily Tarasiok (director). Color. In Russian with English subtitles. 155 minutes.

Comment: Poor sound and poor images but a great cast.

1985 Chicago Lyric Opera

American stage production: Pier Luigi Samaritani (director and set/costume designer), Bruno Bartoletti (conductor, Lyric Opera Orchestra and Chorus).

Cast: Mirella Freni (Tatyana), Wolfgang Brendel (Eugene), Peter Dvorsky (Lensky), Sandra Walker (Olga), Nicolai Ghiaurov (Gremin), Chicago City Ballet.

Video: Home Vision VHS. Kirk Browning (director). Color. In Russian with English subtitles. 157 minutes.

1988 Weigl film

Czech feature film: Petr Weigl (director/screenplay), Georg Solti (conductor, Royal Opera House Orchestra and John Aldis Choir), Dodo Simoncic (cinematographer).

Cast: Magdaléna Vásáryová (Tatyana, sung by Teresa Kubiak), Michal Docolomansky (Eugene Onegin, sung by Bernd Weikl), Emil Horváth (Lensky, sung by Stuart Burrows), Kamila Magálová (Olga, sung by Julia Hamari), Premysl Koci (Gremin, sung by Nicolai Ghiaurov), Antonie Hegerlikova (Madame Larina, sung by Anna Reynolds).

Video: Decca-London DVD/VHS/LD. Color. In Russian with English subtitles. 116 minutes.

Comment: Weigl's beautiful film, shot on location with Czech actors dubbed by opera singers, unfortunately loses about 40 minutes of the stage score.

1994 Glyndebourne Festival

English stage production: Graham Vick (director), Andrew Davis (conductor, London Philharmonic Orchestra and Glyndebourne Festival Chorus), Richard Hudson (set designer).

Cast: Yelena Prokina (Tatyana), Wojciech Drabowicz (Eugene Onegin), Martin Thompson (Lensky), Louise Winter (Olga), Frode Osen (Gremin), Yvonne Minton (Larina).

Video: Warner Vision (GB) VHS. Humphrey Burton (director). Color. In Russian with English subtitles. 156 minutes.

1998 Baden-Baden Festival

German stage production: Nikolaus Lehnhoff (director), Gennadi Rozhdestvensky (conductor, European Union Opera Orchestra and Chorus), Markus Meyer (set designer).

Cast: Orla Boylan (Tatyana), Vladimir Glushchak (Onegin), Michael König (Lensky), Anna Burford (Olga).

Video: Kultur and Arthaus (GB) DVD. Derek Bailey (director). In Russian with English subtitles. Color. 150 minutes.

Comment: New young European singers were chosen for this production by the European Union Opera at the Festspielhaus.

Early/related films

1911 Goncharov film

This Russian film by Vasilij Goncharov was the first based on the Tchaikovsky opera. A. Goncharova is Tatyana, Andrei Gromov is Lensky, and P. Biryukov is Onegin. Black and white. Silent. About 14 minutes. Print in the Russian Film Archive.

1935 Anna Karenina

Anna Karenina (Greta Garbo) and her lover Count Vronsky (Fredric March) attend a production of *Eugene Onegin* at the Moscow Opera after she has left her husband. Their presence is considered a scandal. The opera was chosen by music director Herbert Stothart for its ironic effect as it is about a woman who refuses to leave her husband for a lover. Seen on stage is the Act I "Dance of the Peasants." Clarence Brown directed. Black and white. 95 minutes.

1970 Tchaikovsky

Innokenti Smoktunovsky plays Tchaikovsky in this stolid Soviet biography that includes a scene from *Eugene Onegin*. See PYOTR TCHAIKOVSKY.

1971 The Music Lovers

Ken Russell's bizarre biography of Tchaikovsky includes the "Letter Song" from *Eugene Onegin* sung by April Cantelo. See PYOTR TCHAIKOVSKY.

1986 Onegin

Onegin is a film of John Cranko's ballet adaptation of the Tchaikovsky opera and Pushkin poem. Sahina Sallemann is Tatyana, Frank Augustyn is Eugene Onegin, Jeremy Ranson is Lensky, and Cynthia Lucas is Olga. Norman Campbell directed, and Kurt-Heinz Stolze arranged the music. Telecast November 9, 1986, on CBC-TV. Color. 120 minutes.

1999 The Talented Mr. Ripley

The Act II duel scene featuring Lensky's aria is an ironic highlight of this film of the Patricia Highsmith thriller; the protagonist Ripley (Mark Damon) also kills his closest friend. The actors on stage are Francesco Bovino as Lensky, Roberto Valentini as Onegin, Stefano Canettieri as Zaretsky and Marco Foti as Onegin's valet. The singers are Nicolai Gedda (Lensky), Yuri Mazurok (Onegin), and Dimter Stanchev (Zaretsky), with Emil Tchakarov conducting the Sofia Festival Orchestra. Anthony Mingella wrote and directed the film. Color. 139 minutes.

1999 Onegin

This English film of the Pushkin novel, directed by Martha Fiennes, is a visual feast as shot by English cinematographer Remi Adefarasin (exteriors filmed in St. Petersburg). Ralph Fiennes as Onegin and Liv Tyler as Tatyana are outstanding and well supported by Toby Stephens as Lensky and Lena Headey as Olga. No music from the Tchaikovsky opera is used but there is an excerpt from *Fidelio*. Color. In English. 106 minutes.

2000 Cast Away

Prince Gremin's aria describing his love for his wife is featured in this film about a marooned FedEx executive (Tom Hanks) surviving alone for several desperate years on a desert island. It's sung, appropriately, by a FedEx delivery man in Moscow. Robert Zemeckis directed. Color. 143 minutes.

EVA
1911 operetta by Lehár

Eva, The Factory Girl has never been one of FRANZ LEHÁR's most popular operettas, but it still has fans in Spain and Italy. The story revolves around the love life of factory worker Eva and her efforts to stave off unwanted attention from factory owner Octave Flaubert. By the end of the operetta, however, she has agreed to marry him. *Eva* was staged in both London and New York in the 1910s, and its big waltz was quite popular. The libretto is by A. M. Willner and Robert Bodanzky.

1935 Riemann film

Austrian feature film: Johannes Riemann (director), Ernst Marischka (screenplay), Eduard Hoesch (cinematographer).

Cast: Magda Schneider (Eva), Hans Rühmann (Octave), Hans Söhnker, Adele Sandrock, Hans Moser.

Black and white. In German. 94 minutes.

1992 Italian TV: Operette, che Passione!

Italian TV production: Sandro Massimini (director/host), Roberto Negri (pianist), Sandro Corelli (choreographer).

Singers: Sandro Massimini, Sonia Dorigo, Max René Cosotti.

Video: Ricordi (Italy) VHS. Pierluigi Pagano (director). Color. In Italian. About 19 minutes.

Comment: Highlights of operetta on the Italian TV series *Operette, che Passione!* Includes songs "Sia pur chimera, felicità," "Oh Parigina bella ed elegante," and "Perchè tremate così."

1918 Deesy film

1918 Deesy film
This feature film of the Lehár operetta was made in Hungary during the period of the Councils' Republic. Alfred Deesy directed. Black and white. Silent. About 60 minutes.

EVANGELIMANN, DER
1895 opera by Kienzl

Wilhelm Kienzl's religious opera *Der Evangelimann* (The Evangelist) was a popular opera in the early years of the century, but it is now almost unknown outside Germany. Based on a story by Leopold Meissner with libretto by the composer, it tells the story of a bitter rivalry between brothers. Johannes is jealous of Matthias, who is having a secret love affair with Martha. In his anger, Matthias sets fire to a barn, but it is Johannes who is blamed and sent to prison. Many years later after a time in prison, Johannes returns as an evangelical preacher and forgives his dying brother.

1964 Theater am Gärtnerplatz
German stage production: Herbert List (director), Kurt Eichhorn (conductor), Ekkehard Grübler (set designer).
Cast: Julius Patzak (Matthias), Heinz Friedrich (Johannes), Hedi Klug (Martha), Heinz Herrmann (Friedrich Engel), Eva Maria Gorgens (Magdalena).
Telecast by ZDF German Television in 1964. Karlheinz Hundorf (director). Black and white. In German. 86 minutes.

Early film

1924 Union film
Elisabeth Bergner plays Martha in the 1924 German film *Der Evangelimann* based on the opera. The other actors are Paul Hartmann, Hanni Weisse, Heinrich Peer, and Jacob Feldhammer. Forrest Holger-Madsen directed for Union Film. Black and white. Silent. About 75 minutes.

EVANS, GERAINT
Welsh baritone (1922–1992)

Sir Geraint Evans, one of the best-liked Welsh opera singers, was particularly admired in comic roles such as Don Pasquale and Falstaff. He joined Covent Garden in 1948 and created roles in two operas by Benjamin Britten. He became a regular at Glyndebourne in Mozart roles and sang Falstaff at the Metropolitan in 1964. There is a film of him as FALSTAFF (1960) at Glyndebourne, a video of his DON PASQUALE (1979) with the Welsh National Opera, and a video of his performance as Coppélius in LES CONTES D'HOFFMANN (1981) at Covent Garden.

EVENSONG
1934 British film with opera content

Evensong is a thinly disguised fictional biography of Australian diva NELLIE MELBA based on a roman á clef novel by Beverly Nichols, her private secretary and the ghost writer of her autobiography. Evelyn Laye plays Maggie O'Neill, an Irish singer who elopes with a young musician (Emlyn Williams) and is molded into the opera diva Irela (a name derived from Ireland, as Melba's was derived from Melbourne) by an ambitious impresario (Fritz Kortner). After an audition with the aria "Mi chiamano Mimì" from *La bohème*, she quickly becomes famous and sings in the great opera houses of Europe. In Vienna, she begins an affair with an Austrian archduke (Carl Esmond), who throws her a bouquet of flowers laced with jewels after watching her sing Violetta in *La traviata;* the "Brindisi" party scene is shown on stage with Australian tenor Browning Mummery as Alfredo (Mummery sang Rodolfo to Melba's Mimì in her last Covent Garden *La bohème*). The love affair is interrupted by the start of World War I, so she does not see him again until 1934, by which time she is worrying about new young singers replacing her in the public fancy. CONCHITA SUPERVIA plays Baba, the Spanish singer who challenges her supremacy. After she hears Supervia sing Musetta's waltz "Quando me'n vo" quite wonderfully at a rehearsal, she realizes her time is almost over. At the performance, the audience cheers Baba and ignores Irela. Her friends try to persuade her to retire, but she refuses and dies alone in her dressing room listening to her old records.
Ironically, it was Supervia who was to die tragically young not long after making the film. Also in the cast is Alice Delysia, a once-famous singing star. Dorothy Farnum wrote the screenplay based on Nichols's and Edward Knoblock's play derived from the novel. Mutz Greenbaum was cinematographer, Louis Levy was music supervisor, Michael Balcon produced, and Victor Saville directed for Gaumont-British. Black and white. 83 minutes. Bel Canto Society/Live Opera/Lyric VHS.

EVERYBODY DOES IT
1949 American film with opera content

Paul Douglas plays a businessman whose wife (Celeste Holm) wants to be an opera singer, but it turns out he's the one with a voice. He is taken up by a successful opera diva (Linda Darnell) who tries to launch his career by starring him opposite her in a new opera called *The Loves of Fatima*. The premiere is an epic and very funny failure as Douglas takes so many pills and potions to gain courage that he ends up falling down and knocking over the sets. The film was based on James Cain's story *Career in C Major,* already filmed in 1939 as WIFE, HUSBAND AND FRIEND. MARIO CASTELNUOVO-TEDESCO wrote the exotic Fatima opera for the movie, including arias for soprano, baritone, and chorus. Douglas is dubbed by New York City Opera baritone Stephen Kemalyan, who sings the "Toreador Song" from *Carmen* for him. Darnell is dubbed by San Francisco Opera soprano Helen Spann. Edmund Goulding directed; Nunnally Johnson wrote the screenplay. Black and white. In English. 98 minutes.

EWING, MARIA
American mezzo-soprano (1950–)

Maria Ewing can be watched on video changing from a delightful Cherubino in LE NOZZE DI FIGARO (1976) to an alluring CARMEN (1985/1989/1991) to a depraved SALOME (1992), and she is wonderful as all three. Ewing, who began her career in 1973 under the guidance of James Levine, broke into the big time in 1976 singing Cherubino at Salzburg and the Met. Her other Met roles include Rosina, Carmen, Zerlina, Dorabella, and Blanche in DIALOGUES DES CARMÉLITES (1987). She was also popular at Glyndebourne under the direction of then husband Peter Hall and can be seen there in IL BARBIERE DI SIVIGLIA (1982) and L'INCORONAZIONE DI POPPEA (1984). See DIDO AND AENEAS (1995), JAMES LEVINE (1996) MOZART REQUIEM (1988), and LA PÉRICHOLE (1982).

Everybody Does It (1949): Linda Darnell stars in the spoof opera *Fatima e Solimano,* created for the film by Mario Castelnuovo-Tedesco.

F

FAIRY QUEEN, THE
1692 semi-opera by Purcell

Henry Purcell's five-act semi-opera *The Fairy Queen,* libretto by an unknown writer based on Shakespeare's play *A Midsummer Night's Dream,* premiered at the Dorset Garden Theatre in London in 1692 but was not staged in the United States until 1932. It mostly follows the plot of the play, with various human and supernatural beings involved in complicated love stories.

1995 English National Opera
English stage production: David Pountney (director), Nicholas Kok (conductor, English National Opera Orchestra and Chorus), Quinny Sacks (choreographer).
Cast: Yvonne Kenny (Titania), Thomas Randle (Oberon), Simon Rice (Puck), Richard van Allan (Theseus), Michael Chance, Jonathan Best, Mary Hegarty, Yvonne Barclay, Janis Kelly, George Mosley.
Image Entertainment (USA)/Arthaus (GB) DVD. Video: Barry Gavin (director). Color. 134 minutes. In English.
Comment: Controversial production with much cross-dressing and other zany goings-on and gags. It mostly ignores the dialogue of the original and tells the story primarily through dance.

Related films

Films of Shakespeare's play
Shakespeare's play *A Midsummer Night's Dream,* the source of the opera, has been filmed a number of times. The most famous version is a 1935 U.S. film directed by Max Reinhardt and William Dieterle with a starry cast headed by James Cagney and Olivia de Havilland. More authentic is a 1968 British film directed by Peter Hall with Diana Rigg, David Warner, and members of the Royal Shakespeare Company. Less popular is a 1996 RSC version directed by Adrian Noble. There is also a 1966 film of the ballet version with music by Mendelssohn.

2002 Talk to Her
Jennifer Vyvyan sings *The Fairy Queen* aria "O let me weep, forever weep" with the English Chamber Orchestra on the soundtrack of the Spanish film *Hable con ella* (Talk to Her) directed by Pedro Almodovar. The sad story revolves around male friendship, desire, and women in comas in hospitals. Color. In Spanish. 112 minutes.

FALENA, UGO
Italian film director (1875–1931)

Italian pioneer filmmaker Ugo Falena directed many early cinema versions of operas and opera subjects, often starring diva Francesca Bertini. He usually worked for the Film d'Arte Italiana and Bernini Film companies. See ADRIANA LECOUVREUR (1918), UN BALLO IN MASCHERA (1911) CAVALLERIA RUSTICANA (1916), FRANCESCA DA RIMINI (1910), GUGLIELMO TELL (1911), LUISA MILLER (1911), RIGOLETTO (1910), SALOME (1910), LA TRAVIATA (1909), TRISTANO E ISOTTA (1911) and IL TROVATORE (1909).

FALL, LEO
Austrian composer (1873–1925)

Leo Fall was not very successful as an opera composer, but he became a rival for Franz Lehár and Oscar Straus when he turned to operetta. He had a genuine gift for melody and is sometimes considered the Viennese equivalent of Offenbach. He first won fame with DER FIDELE BAUER and DIE DOLLARPRINZESSIN in 1907 and DIE GESCHIEDENE FRAU in 1908. The most popular of his later operettas are DIE ROSE VON STAMBUL (1916) and MADAME POMPADOUR (1922), often considered his masterpiece. Many of his operettas were staged in New York and London, and some are still popular on stage in Germany. Joan Sutherland included six of his arias on her influential record album *The Golden Age of Operetta.*

FALLA, MANUEL DE
Spanish composer (1876–1946)

Manuel De Falla is the most important Spanish composer of the 20th century, but his effect on opera has been relatively small. He created two popular one-act operas, *La vida breve* (1904) and EL RETABLO DE MAESE PEDRO (1923). The cantata *Atlántida,* which was unfinished at his death, has also found admirers. De Falla composed six zarzuelas, but they have not found popularity.

1990 When the Fire Burns...
Documentary film about the composer that includes an extract from his opera *La vida breve* with Gabriel Moreno as the singer and Carmen Casarrubios as the dancer.

There are extracts from other major musical works plus interviews and views of places associated with his music. Edward Atienza narrates; Larry Weinstein directed. Color. In English and Spanish with English subtitles. 84 minutes. London VHS (with *El retablo de maese Pedro*).

FALSTAFF (Salieri)
1799 opera by Salieri

ANTONIO SALIERI's sparkling *opera buffa Falstaff, ossi Le Tre Burle* (Falstaff or The Three Pranks), libretto by Carlo Prosperpo Defranceschi, is based on *The Merry Wives of Windsor;* it concentrates on Falstaff's relationship with the Fords and Pages and leaves out the young lovers. A non-Shakespearean addition shows Mrs. Ford pretending to be German and speaking a mixture of German and Italian. It premiered in Vienna in 1799 as one of the first operas based on a Shakespeare play. Although it has been overshadowed by Verdi's version, it remains an enjoyable work and has been successfully revived.

1995 Schwetzingen Festival
German stage production: Michael Hampe (director), Arnold Östman (conductor, Stuttgart Radio Symphony Orchestra), Carlo Tommasi (set/costume designer).

Cast: John Del Carlo (Falstaff), Teresa Ringholz (Alice Ford), Delores Ziegler (Mistress Slender), Dwayne Croft (Ford), Carlos Feller (Bardolfo), Jake Gardner (Slender), Darla Brooks (servant).

Video: Arthaus DVD. Agnes Meth and Claus Viller (directors). Color. In Italian with English subtitles. 120 minutes.

FALSTAFF (Verdi)
1893 opera by Verdi

Falstaff was VERDI's last opera, and many critics consider it his masterpiece. Librettist Arrigo Boito made a brilliant adaptation of Shakespeare's *The Merry Wives of Windsor* with additions from the Henry IV plays. It premiered at La Scala with VICTOR MAUREL as Falstaff, and seven years later Maurel was filmed in the role in the first sound opera film. The vain, fat knight Sir John Falstaff is caught sending the same love letter to both Alice and Meg. Alice's husband Ford is suspicious, and Falstaff ends up in the Thames in a laundry basket. He is humiliated a second time when he agrees to meet Alice in the forest.

1950 NBC Television
American TV concert: Arturo Toscanini (conductor, NBC Symphony Orchestra and Robert Shaw Chorale), Don Gillis (producer).

Cast: Giuseppe Valdengo (Falstaff), Herva Nelli (Alice Ford), Frank Guarrera (Ford), Nan Merriman (Meg Page), Cloe Elmo (Mistress Quickly), Teresa Stich-Randall (Nannetta).

Telecast live on NBC. Doug Rodgers (director). Black and white. In Italian. 141 minutes.

1960 Glyndebourne Festival
English stage production: Carl and Peter Ebert (directors), Vittorio Gui (conductor, Royal Philharmonic Orchestra and Glyndebourne Festival Chorus), Osbert Lancaster (set/costume designer).

Cast: Geraint Evans (Falstaff), Ilva Ligabue (Alice Ford), Sesto Bruscantini (Ford), Oralia Dominguez (Mistress Quickly), Alice Maria Rota (Meg Page), Mariella Adani (Nannetta), Juan Oncina (Fenton), Hugues Cuénod (Dr. Cajus).

Video: Copy of telecast in the National Film and Television Archive, London. Telecast September 15, 1960, by the BBC. Peter Ebert and Noble Wilson (directors). Black and white. In Italian. 145 minutes.

1976 Glyndebourne Festival
English stage production: Jean-Pierre Ponnelle (director), John Pritchard (conductor, London Philharmonic Orchestra and Glyndebourne Festival Chorus).

Cast: Donald Gramm (Falstaff), Kay Griffel (Alice Ford), Benjamin Luxon (Ford), Nucci Condo (Mistress Quickly), Reni Penkova (Meg Page), Elizabeth Gale (Nannetta), Max-René Cosotti (Fenton).

Video: Opera d'Oro/VAI VHS. Dave Heather (director). Color. In Italian with English subtitles. 123 minutes.

Comment: Ponnelle was in peak form when he staged this exuberant production emphasizing the comedy aspects of the opera.

***1979 Friedrich film
Austrian TV film: Götz Friedrich (director), Sir Georg Solti (conductor, Vienna Philharmonic Orchestra, Vienna State Opera Chorus, Berlin Deutsch Opera Chorus and Schönberg Boys Choir), Jörg Neumann (set designer).

Cast: Gabriel Bacquier (Falstaff), Karan Armstrong (Alice Ford), Richard Stilwell (Ford), Márta Szirmay (Mistress Quickly), Sylvia Lindenstrand (Meg Page), Jutta-Renate Iholoff (Nannetta), Max-René Cosotti (Fenton).

Video: London VHS/LD. Color. In Italian with English subtitles. 126 minutes.

Comment: Friedrich shot the film on 35mm on a sound stage with postsynchronized singing so performers have the chance for lively acting. One of the most impressive videos of the opera.

1982 Salzburg Festival

Austrian stage production: Herbert von Karajan (director/conductor, Vienna Philharmonic Orchestra and Vienna State Opera Chorus), Günther Schneider-Siemssen (set designer).

Cast: Giuseppe Taddei (Falstaff), Raina Kabaivanska (Alice Ford), Rolando Panerai (Ford), Christa Ludwig (Mistress Quickly), Trudeliese Schmidt (Meg Page), Janet Perry (Nannetta), Francisco Araiza (Fenton).

Video: Sony VHS/LD. Ernst Wild (director). Color. In Italian. 135 minutes.

Comment: Solid, conventional, and a bit dull, like most of the Karajan films of operas.

1982 Royal Opera

English stage production: Ronald Eyre (director), Carlo Maria Giulini (conductor, Royal Opera House Orchestra and Chorus), Hayden Griffin (set designer).

Cast: Renato Bruson (Falstaff), Katia Ricciarelli (Alice Ford), Leo Nucci (Ford), Brenda Boozer (Meg Page), Lucia Valentini-Terrani (Mistress Quickly), Barbara Hendricks (Nannetta), Dalmacio Gonzalez (Fenton).

Video: Bel Canto Society (USA)/NVC Arts (GB) VHS and Pioneer LD. Brian Large (director). Color. In Italian with English subtitles. 141 minutes.

1982/1989 Opera Stories

Laserdisc highlights version of above 1982 Royal Opera production with Charlton Heston introducing scenes from London. Keith Cheetham filmed the framework material in 1989. Color. In English and Italian with subtitles. 52 minutes. Pioneer Artists LD.

1992 Metropolitan Opera

American stage production: Franco Zeffirelli (director and set/costume designer), Paul Mills (staging), James Levine (conductor, Metropolitan Orchestra and Chorus).

Cast: Paul Plishka (Falstaff), Mirella Freni (Alice Ford), Bruno Pola (Ford), Marilyn Horne (Mistress Quickly), Susan Graham (Meg Page), Barbara Bonney (Nannetta), Frank Lopardo (Fenton).

Video: DG VHS/LD. Brian Large (director). Taped October 10, 1992; telecast September 13, 1993. Color. In Italian with English subtitles. 126 minutes.

Comment: Zeffirelli designed and staged the original 1964 production restaged by Mills with emphasis on the humor.

1999 Royal Opera

English stage production: Graham Vick (director), Bernard Haitink (conductor, Royal Opera House Orchestra and Chorus).

Cast: Bryan Terfel (Falstaff), Barbara Frittoli (Alice Ford), Bernadette Manca di Nissa (Mistress Quickly), Désirée Rancatore, Robert Frontali, Gwynne Howell.

Video: Naxos/BBC DVD/Premiere Opera VHS. Color. 130 minutes.

Comment: Controversial farce-style production that reopened the Royal Opera House, Covent Garden, in December 1999.

***2001 Teatro Verdi, Busseto

Italian stage production: Ruggero Cappuccio (director), Riccardo Muti (conductor, Teatro alla Scala Orchestra and Chorus).

Cast: Ambrogio Maestri (Falstaff), Barbara Frittoli (Alice Ford), Roberto Frontali (Ford), Bernadette Manca di Nissa (Mistress Quickly), Anna Caterina Antonacci (Meg Page), Inva Mula (Nannetta), Juan Diego Flórez (Fenton).

Video: TDK DVD. Pierre Cavassillas (director). Color. In Italian with English subtitles. 118 minutes.

Comment: This is a replica of a 1913 production that Toscanini conducted in this small theater in Verdi's birthplace featuring facsimiles of the original sets. It was staged for the Verdi centenary, and critics have been fulsome in their praise of the singers, production, conductor, and orchestra.

2001 Aix-en-Provence Festival

French stage production: Herbert Wernicke (director), Enrique Mazzola (conductor, Orchestre de Paris and Chorus of the European Academy of Music of Aix-en-Provence).

Cast: Willard White (Falstaff), Geraldine McGreevy (Alice Ford), Marcus Jupither (Ford), Nora Gubisch (Mistress Quickly), Charlotte Hellekant (Meg Page), Miah Persson (Nannetta), Yann Beuron (Fenton).

Video: Arthaus DVD. Chloé Perlemuter (director). Color. In Italian with English subtitles. 125 minutes.

Comment: The setting is updated to the United States around 1910 with resultant racial overtones. It has had few admirers.

Early/related films

1900 First sound opera film

Victor Maurel, the French baritone who created the role of Falstaff at La Scala, was seen and heard as Falstaff in the first sound opera film, made by Clément Maurice. It was shown in Paris on June 8, 1900, at the Phono-Cinéma-Théâtre at the Paris Exhibition using a synchronized phonographic cylinder. Also on the program were films of Maurel in *Don Giovanni* and Emile Cossira in *Roméo et Juliette*. Black and white. About 3 minutes.

Silent Films

There are many early *Falstaff* films based on the Shakespeare play, but they do not appear to have a connection to the opera. French film critic Jean Mitry says that a 1911 French film by Henri Desfontaines was based on the opera libretto, but Shakespeare expert Robert Hamilton Ball disagrees in his book *Shakespeare on Silent Film.*

Shakespeare Films

The most interesting modern film based on Shakespeare is Orson Welles's 1966 *Falstaff,* also known as *Chimes at Midnight.* Like the Verdi opera, it is a combination of all the plays in which Falstaff appears, and Welles is superb in the role. Black and white. In English. 115 minutes.

FANCIULLA DEL WEST, LA
1910 opera by Puccini

The Girl of the Golden West was the name of the American play by David Belasco on which PUCCINI based his opera *La fanciulla del West.* The libretto by Carlo Zangarini and Guelfo Civinini follows the play fairly closely. Minnie, the "girl" of the title, runs a saloon in a gold mining town and falls in love with stranger Dick Johnson. He turns out to be a bandit wanted by the miners, but she saves his life anyway by playing a desperate poker game with Sheriff Jack Rance. The opera premiered at the Metropolitan Opera with Toscanini conducting Enrico Caruso as Johnson, Emmy Destinn as Minnie, and Pasquale Amato as Rance. The popularity of the play is shown by the many non-operatic films based on it during the silent era. Plácido Domingo currently owns the role of Johnson on video with three versions at different opera houses. The "realism" of this opera makes Americans understand how the Japanese must feel about *Madama Butterfly.*

1963 NHK Lirica Italiana

Japanese stage production: Oliviero de Fabritiis (conductor, NHK Symphony Orchestra and Chorus).

Cast: Antonietta Stella (Minnie), Gastone Limarilli (Dick Johnson), Anselmo Colzani (Jack Rance), Mario Guggia (Nick), Arturo La Porta (Sonora).

Video: Opera Direct/Lyric VHS. Filmed live November 2, 1963, in Tokyo for NHK's *Lirica Italiana* series. Color. In Italian. 140 minutes.

1983 Royal Opera House

English stage production: Piero Faggioni (director, costume designer, lighting), Nello Santi (conductor, Royal Opera House Orchestra and Chorus), Ken Adams (set designer).

Cast: Carol Neblett (Minnie), Plácido Domingo (Dick Johnson), Silvano Carroli (Jack Rance), Gwynne Howell (Jake), Robert Lloyd (Ashby), Francis Egerton (Nick).

Video: NVC Arts DVD/HBO VHS. John Vernon (director). Color. In Italian with English subtitles. 139 minutes.

Comment: Set designer Ken Adams is probably better known as the designer of the James Bond films.

1991 Teatro alla Scala

Italian stage production: Jonathan Miller (director), Lorin Maazel (conductor, Teatro alla Scala Orchestra and Chorus), Stephanos Lazaridis (set designer).

Cast: Mara Zampieri (Minnie), Plácido Domingo (Dick Johnson), Juan Pons (Rance), Marco Chingari (Jake), Luigi Roni (Ashby), Sergio Bertocchi (Nick).

Video: Image Entertainment DVD/Home Vision VHS. Telecast in Italy July 22, 1991, on RAI. John Michael Phillips (director). Color. In Italian with subtitles. 142 minutes.

1992 Metropolitan Opera

American stage production: Giancarlo Del Monaco (director), Leonard Slatkin (conductor, Metropolitan Opera Orchestra and Chorus), Michael Scott (set/costume designer)

Cast: Barbara Daniels (Minnie), Plácido Domingo (Dick Johnson), Sherrill Milnes (Rance), Yanni Yannissis (Jake), Julien Robbins (Ashby), Anthony Laciura (Nick).

Video: DG VHS. Brian Large (director). Taped April 8, 1992; telecast June 10, 1992. Color. In Italian with English subtitles. 140 minutes.

Early/related Films

1915 Lasky film

Cecil B. De Mille directed the first film of the David Belasco play with Mabel Van Buren as the Girl, House Peters as Johnson, and Theodore Roberts as Rance. Jesse Lasky acquired the movie rights to Belasco's theatrical productions, and Belasco said the film achieved a realism he could not match on stage. Black and white. Silent. About 70 minutes.

1923 First National film

Sylvia Breamer stars as the Girl with J. Warren Kerrigan as Johnson and Russell Simpson as Rance in this film of the play directed by Edwin Carewe for First National. Black and white. Silent. About 65 minutes.

1930 First National film

Ann Harding is Minnie, James Rennie is Dick Johnson, and Harry Bannister is Rance in this film based very closely on the Belasco play. John Francis Dillon directed for First National. Black and white. 78 minutes.

1938 MGM film

MGM did not want to pay to use Puccini's music for their film of the Belasco play so it commissioned a new score from Sigmund Romberg. Jeanette MacDonald plays saloon owner Mary smitten by bandit Nelson Eddy and plays poker for his life. Robert Z. Leonard directed. See THE GIRL OF THE GOLDEN WEST.

1993 The Man Without a Face

Mel Gibson plays a 78 rpm record of Jussi Björling singing Johnson's aria "Ch'ella mi creda libero" as he sits alone in his house reciting the opening lines of the *Aeneid.* Gibson also directed this film about a teacher with a scarred face who mentors a 12-year-old with problems. Color. 114 minutes.

FARINELLI
Italian soprano castrato (1705–1782)

Farinelli was a famous castrato soprano and a major cultural figure in 18th-century Europe. He was born Carlo Broschi, trained by composer Nicola Porpora, and made his debut in Naples in 1720. It was said he had a three-and-one-half-octave range, could sing 250 notes in a row, and was able to sustain a single note for a minute. Farinelli lived in London for three years singing with Handel's competitors and then quit the stage. He spent the next two decades in Spain singing for and advising King Philip V and King Ferdinand VI about opera, music, and horses. After retiring to Bologna, he was visited by the great musicians of the time, including Mozart and Gluck.

1994 Farinelli

Gérard Corbiau's film is a visually opulent biography that focuses on Farinelli's relationships with his composer brother Riccardo, his teacher Nicola Porpora, and Handel. There are elaborate re-creations of opera productions of the period. Among the featured castrato arias are Porpora's "Alto Giove" from *Polifemo,* Broschi's "Son qual nave" from *Artaserse,* and "Ombra fedele anch'io" from *Idaspe.* They are staged with the supposed sound of a male soprano, created artificially by fusing the voices of soprano Ewa Mallas-Godlewska and countertenor Derek Lee Ragin. The sound is extraordinary but it is impossible to know if it is historical. Also featured are arias from Handel's *Rinaldo* and Hasse's *Cleofide.* Farinelli is played by Stéfano Dionisi with Jeroen Krabbe as Handel and Enrico Lo Verso as Riccardo. The superb

production design is by Gianni Quaranta, and the music is played by Christophe Rousset with Les Talens Lyriques. Color. In Italian, French, and English with English subtitles. 100 minutes. Columbia TriStar VHS.

FARNACE
1727 opera by Vivaldi

Farnace, the king of Pontus, is married to Tamiri, the daughter of Berenice, the queen of Cappodocia, but Berenice wants to destroy him. She almost does, with the help of Roman legions, but she repents at the last moment. Antonio Vivaldi's opera *Farnace,* libretto by Antonio Maria Lucchini, was one of his most popular and was widely performed in its time.

1991 Festival della Valle d'Itria

Italian stage production: Egisto Marcucci (director), Massimiliano Carraro (conductor, Solisti dell'Orchestra Sinfonia de Graz), Maurizio Balo (set/costume designer).

Cast: Susan Long Solustri (Farnace), Raquel Pierotti (Berenice), Serena Lazzarini (Tamari), Marina Bolgan (Selinda), Susanna Anselmi (Pompeo), Gabriella Morigi (Gilade), Tiziana Carraro (Aquilio).

Video: House of Opera DVD/VHS. Taped July 1991. Color. In Italian.

Comment: Staged in Palazzo Ducale in Martina Franca for Festival della Valle d'Itria.

FARRAR, GERALDINE
American soprano (1882–1967)

Geraldine Farrar, a Massachusetts-born soprano who made her early career in Germany, joined the Metropolitan Opera in New York in 1906. She made her debut as Juliet in Gounod's *Roméo et Juliette* and was one of the glories of the Met's Golden Age. She sang at the Met until 1922 in a variety of roles but was most popular as Butterfly and Carmen. Her success on stage in CARMEN led producer Jesse Lasky to invite her to make films, and she starred in a film version in 1915. Even without her voice, she had great appeal and a winning personality and became a real movie star. She was helped by having a major filmmaker, CECIL B. DE MILLE, as the director of her first six films. She was so popular that her numerous female fans became known as Gerryflappers. She made 14 films before giving up the movies in 1920. Lou Tellegen, who acts in some of her films, was her husband at the time.

1915 Carmen

Farrar made her film debut as Carmen in Cecil B. De Mille's famous *Carmen.* It was very popular and

launched Farrar on her film career. Wallace Reid is Don
José, Pedro De Cordoba is Escamillo, William Elmer is
Morales, Jeanie Macpherson is Frasquita, and Anita King
is Mercedes; there is no Micaëla. William C. De Mille
wrote the screenplay, Alvin Wyckoff was the cinematographer, and S. L. Rothapfel prepared the musical accompaniment. A 50-piece symphony orchestra played the opera music on opening night with Hugo Reisenfeld
conducting. Jesse Lasky–Paramount film. Color tinted.
Silent. About 76 minutes. Kino VHS/DVD (new score)
and VAI VHS (reconstruction of Riesenfeld score).

1915 Maria Rosa

Farrar made this Cecil B. De Mille film before *Carmen,*
supposedly as a cinematic warm-up, but it was not released until afterwards. She plays a Catalan woman who
is the center of a bitter rivalry between two men, Wallace
Reid and Pedro de Cordoba. Paramount. Black and
white. Silent. About 70 minutes.

1915 Temptation

Farrar plays an opera singer, the villain is an opera impresario (dressed like the Met's Giulio Gatti-Casazza),
and the hero is an opera composer. Farrar almost has to
make the ultimate sacrifice to help the composer but is
saved in the nick of time. Cecil B. De Mille directed with
an eye on the Metropolitan Opera. Paramount. Black and
white. Silent. About 70 minutes.

1916 Joan the Woman

Farrar is outstanding as Joan of Arc in this superb Cecil
B. De Mille epic about the French heroine. It was written
by Jeanie Macpherson, who had played Frasquita in
Carmen. The story is framed within a soldier's dream
during World War I in France. Wallace Reid plays the
English lover who betrays her. Partially in color. Silent.
About 120 minutes. Image Entertainment DVD.

1917 The Woman God Forgot

Farrar portrays a daughter of Montezuma who falls in
love with a Spanish captain during the Cortez invasion of
Mexico. She betrays her people but finds consolation in
Christianity under the direction of one of that religion's
great promoters, director Cecil B. De Mille. An Artcraft
production. Black and white. Silent. About 70 minutes.

1917 The Devil Stone

The last Farrar film directed by De Mille and produced
by Jesse Lasky. She plays a Breton fisherwoman in a
story about a priceless emerald with a curse on it. She
later gets rich, so she has a chance to wear the fine
clothes her fans expected. An Artcraft production. Black
and white. Silent. About 70 minutes.

Met soprano Geraldine Farrar, shown in her dressing room on a
film set, was also a glamorous movie star during the 1910s.

1918 The Hell Cat

Farrar's first film for Goldwyn Pictures. She plays Pancho O'Brien, the high-spirited, beautiful daughter of an
Irish ranch owner. She is loved by the sheriff but prefers
the outlaw in this melodramatic love story. Reginald
Barker directed. Black and white. Silent. About 80 minutes.

1918 The Turn of the Wheel

Farrar is a beautiful American woman on vacation in
Monte Carlo who falls in love with a gambler and helps
him win a fortune. When he's arrested for murdering his
wife, she sets out to find who really did it. Reginald
Barker directed for Goldwyn. Black and white. Silent.
About 70 minutes.

1919 Flame of the Desert

Farrar plays Isabelle Channing, a lady who falls in love
with a charming sheik (Lou Tellegen) in Egypt. A few
reels later, he rescues her and turns out to be a noble
Englishman in disguise. Reginald Barker directed for
Goldwyn. Black and white. Silent. About 70 minutes.

1919 Shadows

Farrar is now a devoted wife and mother, but she was
once a dance hall girl in Alaska. A friend of her husband
finds out and tries to blackmail her. Milton Sills is her

costar. Reginald Barker directed for Goldwyn. Black and white. Silent. About 70 minutes.

1919 The Stronger Vow

This is a kind of Spanish grand opera variation on *Romeo and Juliet* with Farrar in love with the man (Milton Sills) she believes killed her brother in a family feud. Reginald Barker directed for Goldwyn. Black and white. Silent. About 80 minutes.

1919 The World and Its Women

Farrar plays a famous opera singer and is seen on stage in a scene from Massenet's *Thais*. Off stage she is in love with a Russian prince (Lou Tellegen) who rescues her from the Bolshevists during the revolution. They escape to America together. Frank Lloyd directed for Goldwyn. Black and white. Silent. About 80 minutes.

1920 The Woman and the Puppet

Pierre Louys wrote the novel and play on which the film is based but the influence of *Carmen* is evident. Farrar is a Spanish cigarette maker who dances wonderfully and is loved by a nobleman. She scorns him because she believes he has tried to buy her. Reginald Barker directed for Goldwyn. Black and white. Silent. About 80 minutes.

1920 The Riddle: Woman

Farrar's last film was directed by Edward José, the man who directed Caruso's and Cavalieri's unsuccessful movies. He was obviously bad luck for opera singers; Farrar hated him and the film so much that she gave up moviemaking. The story derives from a Danish play about a woman blackmailed by a former lover. Pathé. Black and white. Silent. About 80 minutes.

FARRELL, EILEEN

American soprano (1920–2002)

Eileen Farrell began her career in concerts and didn't make her stage debut until after singing opera on screen. She was the voice of opera singer Marjorie Lawrence in the 1955 film biography INTERRUPTED MELODY and made her theatrical debut in 1956 as Santuzza in Tampa. Her first appearance at the Metropolitan came in 1960 as Gluck's Alceste, and in 1962 she opened the Met season as Maddalena in *Andrea Chenier;* she sang at the Met for five seasons. She became popular for crossover pop performances after 1959 when she substituted for Louis Armstrong at the Spoleto Festival in Italy but was equally noted for her Wagnerian and Verdi heroines on the concert stage. Farrell made no more films, but she did sing on television and left a splendid legacy of records. See BELL TELEPHONE HOUR (1959–1966), THE ED SULLIVAN SHOW (1996), and SPOLETO (1959).

1955 Interrupted Melody

Farrell is outstanding as the voice of Marjorie Lawrence in this well-crafted film biography that includes scenes from *La bohème, Il trovatore, Madama Butterfly, Carmen, Samson et Dalila, Die Götterdämmerung,* and *Tristan und Isolde.* See INTERRUPTED MELODY.

1960 The Creative Performer

Farrell sings the "Suicidio" aria from *La Gioconda* with the New York Philharmonic on Leonard Bernstein's CBS television program *The Creative Performer.* William A. Graham directed. Black and white. 60 minutes. Video at the MTR.

1969 Eileen Farrell: A Portrait

Farrell sings arias and songs and appears in scenes from operas in this CBC documentary. The arias are from *Aida* and *Madama Butterfly;* the songs are by Fauré, Gershwin, and Poulenc; and the scenes are from *La forza del destino* and *La Gioconda.* Black and white. 60 minutes. VAI VHS.

FATAL LADY

1936 American film with opera content

Opera diva Mary Ellis plays an opera diva falsely accused of a murder in *Fatal Lady.* She runs away and is singing under an alias in a South American opera house when a second murder occurs. She is acquitted but her reputation is destroyed. The murderer is eventually found out by her longtime admirer Walter Pidgeon. *The New York Times* called this "a prima donna's vehicle, duly affording Miss Ellis opportunities of singing choice bravura passages in nearly every world capital." The movie features two IMAGINARY OPERAS sung by Ellis. The first is *Isabelle,* with music by Gerard Carbonara and libretto by David Ormont; the second is *Bal Masque,* with music by Gerard Carbonara and Victor Young with a libretto by Sam Coslow. There are also excerpts from Rossini's *William Tell.* Boris Petroff staged the operatic numbers. Marshall Sohl plays a tenor who performs with Ellis, Russell Hicks is an opera house manager, and Tudor Williams is a major domo. Sam Ornitz wrote the screenplay, Leon Shamroy was cinematographer, and Edward Ludwig directed for Paramount. Black and white. In English. 72 minutes.

FAUST

1859 opera by Gounod

CHARLES GOUNOD's opera was by far the most popular opera in the world at the beginning of the century and its arias among the best known. The Faust legend itself is one of the favorite subjects of filmmakers, with at least 50 movies, most of them based to a certain extent on the opera, and Gounod's music was played with silent film versions even when they weren't connected to the opera. The opera itself is based on Goethe's play, but the focus of Jules Barbier and Michel Carré's libretto is on Faust's love affair with Marguerite. Faust promises his soul to Méphistophélès if he can become young again and have Marguerite. After she has been seduced, her brother Valentin challenges Faust to a duel and is killed. Marguerite goes mad, kills her baby, is sentenced to death, and is forgiven by heaven. The opera is a central plot concept in THE PHANTOM OF THE OPERA movies.

1936 Hopkins film

British feature film: Albert Hopkins (director), Oktavijan Milet (cinematographer), Fred Swann (producer), Publicity Pictures (production).

Cast: Webster Booth (Faust), Anne Ziegler (Marguerite), Dennis Hoey (Méphistophélès).

Color. In English. 63 minutes.

Comment: Highlights version sung in English and filmed in early color system. Critics did not like it much then and do not now. Ziegler and Booth were the British equivalents of MacDonald and Eddy, while Hoey went on to Hollywood to play Inspector Lestrade to Basil Rathbone's Sherlock Holmes.

1949 Faust and the Devil

Italian-American feature film: Carmine Gallone (director), Leopold Marchand (screenplay), Vaclav Vich (cinematographer), Gregor Rabinovitch (producer), Cineopera/Columbia (production).

Cast: Gino Mattera (Faust), Nelly Corradi (Marguerite, sung by Onelia Fineschi), Italo Tajo (Méphistophélès), Gilles Quéant (Valentin), Cesare Barbetti (Siébel, sung by Onofrio Scarfoglio), Thérèse Dorny (Martha).

Black and white. In Italian. 90 minutes.

Comment: This film is a bit of an operatic melange as it is based on Gounod's *Faust* and Boito's *Mefistofele* and uses music from both plus a bit from Berlioz's *La Damnation di Faust*. The Italian title is *La leggenda di Faust*.

1963 Voice of Firestone

American TV production: Harry John Brown (conductor, Voice of Firestone Orchestra).

Cast: Richard Tucker (Faust), Mary Costa (Marguerite), Jerome Hines (Méphistophélès).

Video: VAI VHS titled *French Opera Gala*. Telecast June 16, 1963. Black and white. In French with English introductions. 16 minutes.

Comment: Highlights version of the opera featured on the last *Voice of Firestone* TV show, with the singers performing in formal wear before abstract sets.

1973 NHK Lirica Italiana

Japanese stage production: Paul Ethuin (conductor, NHK Symphony Orchestra and Chorus).

Cast: Alfredo Kraus (Faust), Renata Scotto (Marguerite), Nicolai Ghiaurov (Méphistophélès), Lorenzo Saccomani (Valentin), Milena Dal Piva (Siébel), Anna Di Stasio (Marthe), Guido Mazzini (Wagner).

Video: Opera Direct/House of Opera/Legato Classics VHS. Taped live September 9, 1973, in Tokyo for the NHK *Lirica Italiana* series. Color. In Italian. 159 minutes.

Comment: A notable cast with three fine singers although the production is ordinary.

1973 Who's Afraid of Opera?

English TV film: Ted Kotcheff (director), Richard Bonynge (conductor, London Symphony Orchestra), George Djurkovic (set designer), Claire Merrill (screenplay), Nathan Kroll (producer).

Cast: Joan Sutherland (Marguerite), Ian Caley (Faust), Joseph Rouleau (Méphistophélès), Peter Van Der Stolk (Valentin), Margreta Elkins (Siébel), Larry Berthelson (puppets).

Video: Kultur VHS. Color. In English and French. 30 minutes.

Comment: Highlights version made for young audiences with Sutherland telling the story to puppets. Dialogue is in English, arias are in French.

1975 Paris Opéra

French stage production: Jorge Lavelli (director), Charles Mackerras (conductor, Paris Opéra Orchestra and Chorus), Max Bignes (set/costume designer).

Cast: Nicolai Gedda (Faust), Mirella Freni (Marguerite), Roger Soyer (Méphistophélès), Tom Krause (Valentin), Jean-Louis Soumagnas (Wagner), Renée Suphan (Siébel), Jocelyne Taillon (Marthe).

Video: Opera Direct/House of Opera/Lyric VHS. Telecast March 30, 1976. Yves-André Hubert (director). Color. In French. 159 minutes.

1979 Lyric Opera of Chicago

American stage production: Alberto Fassini (director), Georges Prêtre (conductor, Chicago Lyric Opera Orchestra), Pier Luigi Samaritani (set/costume designer).

Cast: Alfredo Kraus (Faust), Mirella Freni (Marguerite), Nicolai Ghiaurov (Méphistophélès), Richard Stilwell (Valentin), Robert Wilber (Wagner), Katherine Ciesinski (Siébel), Geraldine Decker (Marthe).

Telecast January 2, 1980 on PBS; taped in September 1979. Brian Large (director). Color. In French. 139 minutes.

1985 Philadelphia Opera

American stage production: Grethe Holly (director), Serge Baudo (conductor, Philadelphia Opera Orchestra), Franco Colavecchia (set designer).

Cast: Alain Vanzo (Faust), Valerie Masterson (Marguerite), James Morris (Méphistophélès), Gino Quilico (Valentin), Marta Senn (Siébel).

Telecast April 7, 1985, on PBS. Brian Large (director). Color. In French. 141 minutes.

1987 Teatro Regio, Parma

Italian stage production: Beppe De Tomasi (director), Alain Guingal (conductor, Emilia-Romagna Symphony Orchestra and Teatro Regio Chorus).

Cast: Alfredo Kraus (Faust), Anna Maria Gonzalez (Marguerite), Nicolo Ghiuselev (Méphistophélès), Roberto Coviello (Valentin), Ambra Vespasiani (Siébel), Wilma Colla (Marta), Tito Tortura (Wagner).

Video: Hardy Classics DVD/Bel Canto Society VHS. Color. In French. 190 minutes.

Comment: Mainly of interest for Kraus to contrast with his 1973 video.

Early/related films

1897 Faust

Two of the first opera films were of Gounod's *Faust*, produced by the Lumière Brothers in Paris in 1897 and directed by Georges Hatot. In the first, Marguerite appears in a vision to Faust after which he calls for Méphistophélès, who magically materializes. In the second, Faust accepts Méphistophélès's conditions, is transformed from poor old scholar to rich young man, and worships Marguerite when she appears. Black and white. Silent. Each film about 1 minute.

1898 Faust et Marguerite

French filmmaker George Méliès's first Faust film shows Méphistophélès drawing a sword across Marguerite's throat, causing her to disappear and Faust to appear in her place. It was distributed in the United States in 1900 by Edison. Black and white. Silent. About 1 minute.

1898 Faust and Méphistophélès

British film pioneer G. A. Smith, who invented Kinemacolor, made a Faust film the same year as Méliès. Méphistophélès conjures up a vision of Marguerite to persuade Faust to sign a pact for his soul. Faust is transformed into a young man. Black and white. Silent. About 1 minute.

1900 Faust and Marguerite

Edwin S. Porter, later famous for making *The Great Train Robbery,* directed a version of the Faust story for the Edison company. Black and white. Silent. About 3 minutes.

1902 Faust et Méphisto

Alice Guy-Blaché, the first woman director, filmed this brief adaptation of the opera for Gaumont. Black and white. Silent. About 3 minutes.

1902 Faust Opera (Colored Views)

Faust Opera (Colored Views) was the announcement made for the September 1902 screenings of Alber's Electro Talking Bioscope in the Netherlands. The film used sound and film equipment purchased at the Paris Exhibition of 1900. Black and white. In French. About 3 minutes.

1904 La Damnation du Docteur Faust

The Damnation of Dr. Faust, George Méliès's second version of the Faust legend, is a colorful epic adaptation of the Gounod opera in 20 scenes. Méliès himself plays Méphistophélès. Also known as *Faust et Marguerite.* Tinted. Silent. About 14 minutes.

1907 First complete opera film

Arthur Gilbert's 1907 English film of *Faust* is the first complete opera to be filmed, at least according to the *Guinness Book of Records.* It was made in the Gaumont Chronophone sound-on-disc system and advertised as the "complete opera with 22 arias" on disc. Black and white. In French. About 66 minutes.

1908 Messter films

Two early German sound films were made of *Faust* for Oskar Messter's Berlin Biophon-Theater. Henny Porten, who plays Marguerite, is directed by her father Franz. The "Jewel Song" is sung by Sigrid Arnoldson and the duet by Arnoldson and Johannes Sembach. Black and white. In German. Each about 3 minutes.

1909 Deutsche Bioscop film

The "Soldiers' Chorus" from *Faust* is featured on this early German sound film made by Deutsche Bioscop. Black and white. In German. About 3 minutes.

1909 Edison film

This adaptation of the opera, written and directed by J. Searle Dawley under the supervision of Edwin S. Porter, was intended to be the first of an Edison series of films of operas. William J. Sorelle plays Méphistophélès. Contemporary critics called it a classic. Black and white. Silent. About 12 minutes.

1910 Pathé film
Ferdinand Zecca stars in this hand-colored French film directed by Henri Andreani and Georges Fagot for Pathé. It was distributed with a score based on the Gounod opera. Color. Silent. About 18 minutes.

1910 Animatophone film
A British sound film of scenes from the opera was made in the Animatophone system by David Barnet. The arias sung on screen were synchronized with phonograph records. Black and white. In French. About 10 minutes.

1910 Cines film
Enrico Guazzoni directed this Italian version of the story for Cines with Fernanda Negri-Pouget as Margherita, Alfredo Bracci as Faust, and Ugo Bazzini as Mefistofele. Black and white. Silent. About 18 minutes. Print in British and Dutch film archives.

1910 Éclair film
The French Éclair company made this sound film of an aria from the opera with a Paris Opera basso. His recording of the aria was played on a synchronized phonograph. Black and white. In French. About 4 minutes.

1911 Hepworth film
This British Hepworth sound film of scenes from *Faust* uses the Vivaphone system with the movie images synchronized to records. Hay Plumb is Faust, Claire Pridelle is Marguerite, Jack Hulcup is Méphistophélès, and Frank Wilson is Valentin. Cecil Hepworth directed. Black and white. In French. About 15 minutes.

1913 Hlavsa film
Czech director/singer Stanislav Hlavsa was influenced by Méliès when he made this Czech film based on the opera. He played Méphistophélès and toured the country with the film singing the role from behind the screen. Antonin Pech produced the film, which has an important place in early Czech cinema. Black and white. Silent. About 30 minutes.

1915 Sloman film
Edward Sloman directed and played Méphistophélès in this two-reel British film of the story. Black and white. Silent. About 30 minutes.

1915 Biophone film
This British sound film of arias from the opera was made by the Commercial Biophone company. Black and white. In French. About 10 minutes.

1916 The Woman Who Dared
Beatriz Michelena, who plays an opera singer in this American feature film, is seen on stage in her most famous role as Marguerite in *Faust*. The scenes were staged by her father Fernando Michelena, who had been an opera tenor. California Motion Picture Corporation. Black and white. Silent. About 80 minutes.

1918 Find the Woman
Alice Joyce plays a soprano with the French Opera Company in New Orleans in this film and is seen as Marguerite in the Gounod opera. Tom Terriss directed for Vitagraph. Black and white. Silent. About 70 minutes.

1918 Mefistofele e la leggenda di Faust
Mario Gargiulo directed this Italian film version of the Faust story for Flegrea Film in 1918. Black and white. Silent. About 65 minutes.

1919 The Price Woman Pays
This unusual film incorporates scenes from an uncompleted 1916 film of *Faust* starring Beatriz Michelena as Marguerite and William Pike as Faust, directed by George Middleton. The California Motion Picture Corporation, which produced it, used the completed footage in *The Price Woman Pays* by having its heroine (Lois Wilson) dream the Faust story after reading the book. She learns a lesson from what happens to Marguerite, wakes up, and is very careful of men from then on. Frank Hatch wrote the screenplay, and George Terwilliger directed. Black and white. Silent. About 90 minutes.

1922 Tense Moments From Operas
Sylvia Caine plays Marguerite with Dick Webb as Faust and Lawford Davidson as Méphistophélès in this *Faust*, a British highlights version made for the series *Tense Moments From Operas*. Gordon Hopkin is Valentin and Minnie Rayner is Martha. The music was played live with the film. Challis Sanderson directed for Gaumont. Black and white. Silent. About 15 minutes.

1922 Bourgeois film
Jeanne Leduc plays Marguerite with Georges Wague as Méphistophélès and Maurice Varny as Faust in this French *Faust* based on the opera. Gérard Bourgeois directed. Critics praised it warmly. Black and white. Silent. About 72 minutes.

1922 Don Juan et Faust
Marcel L'Herbier directed this French feature based on a novel that merged the Don Juan and Faust legends into one story. Jaque Catelain is a sympathetic Don Juan, Vanni Marcoux is an evil Faust, and Marcelle Pradot is

the Donna Anna they both desire. Gaumont. Black and white. Silent. About 80 minutes.

1926 Murnau film
F. W. Murnau made this German *Faust* with Emil Jannings as Méphistophélès, Gosta Ekmann as Faust, and Camilla Horn as Marguerite. It was based on Goethe, Marlowe, and German folktales but supposedly not on the opera. Black and white. Silent. About 80 minutes.

1927 Cameo Operas
Margo Lees is Marguerite, Herbert Langley is Faust, and A. B. Imeson is Méphistophélès in this British highlights version made for the *Cameo Operas* series. Live singers and a small orchestra performed in synchronization with the screen. H. B. Parkinson directed. Black and white. Silent. About 18 minutes.

1927 Barclay on Vitaphone
English baritone John Barclay sings arias from *Faust* on two Vitaphone sound films made in 1927. On one he performs "The Calf of Gold," on the other "Mephisto's Serenade." Black and white. In English. Each about 8 minutes.

1929 Kurenko on Movietone
Russian-born America soprano Maria Kurenko sings the aria "Anges purs" from *Faust* on this sound short made for the Metro Movietone series in 1928. Black and white. In French. About 8 minutes.

1929 Hackett on Vitaphone
Tenor Charles Hackett of the Chicago Opera plays Faust in this two-reel Vitaphone sound film of Act I of the opera. Bass Chase Baromeo is his Méphistophélès, and the music is played by the Vitaphone Symphony Orchestra. Black and white. In French. About 20 minutes.

1930 Martinelli on Vitaphone
Giovanni Martinelli plays Faust in this Vitaphone sound film of the Prison Scene. Yvonne Bourdon is Marguerite and Louis d'Angelo is Méphistophélès in the famous trio with the music played by the Vitaphone Symphony Orchestra. Black and white. In French. About 10 minutes.

1933 Facing the Music
The "Jewel Song" from *Faust* is sung by José Collins as an opera star persuaded to take her genuine jewels on stage as a stunt. Of course, they are stolen in this British musical comedy directed by Harry Hughes. Black and white. In English. 69 minutes.

1936 San Francisco
Jeanette MacDonald impresses Clark Gable by singing Marguerite's prayer aria "Anges purs." MacDonald is appearing in *Faust* at the Tivoli Opera House, and Gable goes on opening night to stop the show. He changes his mind when he hears her. See SAN FRANCISCO.

1937 La Grand Illusion
Jean Renoir's magnificent World War I prison film uses the "Anges purs" aria in a rather different way. It's sung by the French prisoners with extra words to warn new arrivals to hide their gold and watches from their German captors. Black and white. In French. 117 minutes.

1941 There's Magic in Music
Susanna Foster sings "Anges purs" from *Faust* in this film about a burlesque singer taken to a summer music camp. She meets Met stars Richard Bonelli and Irra Petina and is soon transmuted into on opera singer. Andrew L. Stone directed. Also known as *The Hard-Boiled Canary*. Paramount. Black and white. 80 minutes.

1942 I Married an Angel
The last of the MacDonald-Eddy films was this adaptation of a Rodgers and Hart musical about a man who dreams he marries an angel. MacDonald naturally has to sing Marguerite's prayer "Anges purs." W. S. Van Dyke directed. Black and white. 84 minutes.

1949? Pirogov as Méphistophélès
This excerpt from a Soviet feature film of the 1940s features the Russian bass Alexander Pirogov as Méphistophélès singing the "Serenade." Black and white. In Russian. 10 minutes.

1953 Tonight We Sing
Bass Feodor Chaliapin (Ezio Pinza), soprano Elsa Valdine (Roberta Peters), and tenor Gregory Lawrence (voice of Jan Peerce) perform the Act V trio from *Faust* in this film about impresario Sol Hurok. Peters also sings the "Jewel Song" and joins Peerce in the love duet. See TONIGHT WE SING.

1960 Faust
This is a filmed record of Goethe's play as staged at the Hamburg Deutsches Schauspielhaus by Gustaf Gründgens. Will Quadflieg is Faust, Gründgens is Mefisto, and Ella Büchi is Gretchen. Peter Gorski directed the film shown in America in 1963. Color. In German. 128 minutes.

1963 Bell Telephone Hour
The NBC TV program *The Bell Telephone Hour* presented the prison scene from *Faust* on November 22, 1963. Lisa della Casa is Marguerite, Nicolai Gedda is Faust, and Cesare Siepi is Méphistophélès. Sid Smith directed. Black and white. In French. 60 minutes. Video at the MTR.

1965 Chroniques des France No. 14
This French Pathé-Cinéma news film shows Jean-Louis Barrault preparing a production of *Faust* at the Met in September 1965. Seen in rehearsal and performance are Nicolai Gedda as Faust, Gabriella Tucci as Marguerite, and Cesare Siepi as Méphistophélès along with designer Jacques duPont, choreographer Flemming Flindt, and conductor George Prêtre. Part of the October 2 opening night is shown. Black and white. In French. 7 minutes. Print in the NFTA in London.

1983 Faust in Film
German documentary with silent film versions of the Faust story shown in counterpoint to Gustaf Gründgens's stage production of the Goethe play. Gerd Albrecht, Hauke Lange-Fuchs, and Steffen Wolf wrote and directed. Color and black and white. In English. 36 minutes. Goethe Institute Inter Nationes VHS.

1993 The Age of Innocence
Martin Scorsese's adaptation of Edith Wharton's novel begins, like the book, with the principal characters attending a production of *Faust* in the 1870s. The plot begins to unfold as we observe Faust and Marguerite on stage in Act III (they sing in Italian). A similar ill-fated love affair becomes the central concern of the film, and the opera is featured later in ironic counterpoint when the affair is forced to end. Linda Faye Farkas plays Marguerite on stage with Michael Rees Davis as Faust. Columbia. Color. 132 minutes.

1994 Svankmajer film
Czech animator Jan Svankmajer's kafkaesque *Faust* takes an ordinary man in Prague and turns him into Faust in a puppet production of the Gounod opera. A strange but powerful movie. Color. In Czech. 60 minutes.

1995 The American President
Michael Douglas plays a widowed president who becomes romantically involved with a lobbyist (Annette Bening). Director Rob Reiner features an aria from *Faust* on the soundtrack. Color. 115 minutes.

1998 The Phantom of the Opera
Dario Argento's horrific version of *The Phantom of the Opera*, with Julian Sands as the Phantom, features the overture to *Faust* on the soundtrack. Ennio Morricone conducted. Color. 99 minutes. On DVD and VHS.

FAVORITA, LA / LA FAVORITE
1840 opera by Donizetti

Italian GAETANO DONIZETTI created this popular work as a French opera called *La favorite*, but outside France most productions are now in Italian as *La favorita*. Fourteenth-century Spanish monk Fernando falls in love with Leonora, not realizing that she is the mistress of King Alfonso XI. With her as inspiration, he becomes a soldier hero, returns in glory, and marries her. When he discovers her past, he renounces the marriage and returns to monastic life. She pleads for forgiveness and dies. The libretto is by Alphonse Royer and Gustav Vaëz. The popular tenor aria "anges si pure" is usually sung in Italian as "Spirto gentil."

1952 Barlacchi film
Italian feature film: Cesare Barlacchi (director/screenplay/set designer), Massimo Dallamano (cinematographer), Nicola Rucci (conductor, Rome Opera Orchestra).

Cast: Sophia Loren (Leonora, sung by Palmira Vitali Marini), Gino Sinimberghi (Fernando, sung by Piero Sardelli), Franca Tamantini (Ines, sung by Miriam Di Giove), Paolo Silveri (King Alfonso XI), Alfredo Colella (Baldassare).

Video: VIEW/Video Yesteryear VHS. Black and white. In Italian with English narration. 80 minutes.

Comment: Loren was called Sofia Lazzaro when this much abridged film version of the opera was made.

1971 NHK Lirica Italiana
Japanese stage production: Oliviero De Fabritiis (conductor, NHK Symphony Orchestra).

Cast: Fiorenza Cossotto (Leonora), Alfredo Kraus (Fernando), Sesto Bruscantini (King Alfonso), Marisa Zotti (Ines), Ruggero Raimondi (Baldassare), Augusto Pedroni (Don Gasparo).

Video: Bel Canto Society VHS. Taped live September 13, 1971, in Tokyo. Color. In Italian. 152 minutes.

Early/related films

1902 Alber's Electro Talking Bioscope
Dutch sound film picturing an aria from *La favorite*, one of the opera films featured at Alber's Electro Talking Bioscope screening in Holland in September 1902. Black and white. In French. About 3 minutes.

1909 Itala sound films
Itala Film of Torino released two sound-on-disc films of arias from *La Favorita* in 1909, "Spirto gentil..." and "Una vergine." Black and white. About 3 minutes each.

1911 Film d'Arte Italiana film
Amelia Cattaneo stars as Leonora in this Italian film shot mostly in color. Lamberto Picasso is Fernando, Dillo Lombardi is King Alfonso XI, and Georges Denola directed. The film was coproduced with Pathé, which distributed it in America. Color and black and white. Silent. About 12 minutes

1946 Voglio bene soltanto a te
Beniamino Gigli plays a tenor making a movie who falls for a young costar and has a chance to sing an aria from *La favorita*. See VOGLIO BENE SOLTANTO A TE.

FEDORA
1898 opera by Giordano

UMBERTO GIORDANO's opera *Fedora* has some similarities to *Tosca*, perhaps because both are based on plays written by Sardou for Sarah Bernhardt. It is no longer fashionable on the stage although its great tenor aria "Amor ti vieta" remains popular. Arturo Colautti created the melodramatic libretto. Russian princess Fedora goes to Paris to avenge the murder of her fiancé and falls in love with Loris, whom she believes is his murderer. Her plans for revenge cause multiple deaths; she kills herself when she discovers too late that the killing of her fiancé was justified.

1993 Teatro alla Scala
Italian stage production: Gianandrea Gavazzeni (conductor, Teatro alla Scala Orchestra and Chorus).

Cast: Mirella Freni (Fedora), Plácido Domingo (Loris).

Video: Opera Direct/Lyric VHS. Color. In Italian. 120 minutes.

1997 Metropolitan Opera
American stage production: Beppe de Tomasi (director), Roberto Abbado (conductor, Metropolitan Opera Orchestra and Chorus), Ferruccio Villagrossi (set designer).

Cast: Mirella Freni (Fedora), Plácido Domingo (Loris), Aïnhoa Arteta (Olga), Dwayne Croft (De Siriex).

Telecast October 29, 1997, on PBS; taped April 26, 1997. Brian Large (director). Color. In Italian. 117 minutes.

Comment: The production originated at Barcelona's Gran Teatre del Liceu.

1998 Teatro Massimo, Palermo
Italian stage production: Beppe de Tomasi (director), Stefano Ranzani (conductor, Teatro Massimo Orchestra), Ferruccio Villagrossi (set designer).

Cast: Mirella Freni (Fedora), Sergei Larin (Loris), Adelina Scarabelli, Stefano Antonucci, Monica Di Siena, Giorgio Merighi.

Video: Bel Canto Society VHS. Color. In Italian. 117 minutes.

Comment: The production originated at Barcelona's Gran Teatre del Liceu.

Early/related films

1916 Caesar film
Francesca Bertini stars as Fedora in this Italian feature film based on the Sardou play. Carlo Benetti is Loris with Olga Benetti as Olga. Giuseppe De Loguoro and Gustavo Serena directed for Caesar Film of Rome. Black and white. Silent. About 90 minutes.

1939 Casa Lontana
Beniamino Gigli sings the aria "Amor ti vieta" at a gala reception in this Italian film. He plays an opera singer whose wife has returned after a bitter misunderstanding. See CASA LONTANA.

1942 Fedora
Camillo Mastrocinque's narrative film is based on the opera libretto and uses Giordano's music as its score. Luisa Ferida is Fedora with Amedeo Nazzari as Loris and a supporting cast that includes Osvaldo Valenti, Rina Morelli, and Sandro Ruffini. Ferida and Valenti were fanatical fascists and were both shot by partisans at the end of the war. Black and white. In Italian. 90 minutes.

1999 One More Kiss
The aria "Amor ti vieta" is performed by South American tenor Tito Beltrán on the soundtrack of this British film about a woman (Valerie Edmond) dying of cancer who returns to Scotland to seek out an old flame. The opera singer on stage is Julian Jensen, the opera lovers on stage are Kim Hicks and Tim Francis, and the opera buff is Nigel Pegram. Vadim Jean directed. Color. 102 minutes.

FELDMAN, MORTON
American composer (1926–1987)

Morton Feldman was an avant-garde composer in the John Cage mode although he created his style of atonal organized sound before meeting with Cage in 1950. His one opera is, not surprisingly, highly unusual, with a nonnarrative 87-word, 16-line libretto by Samuel Beckett. NEITHER, an eventless composition for soprano in which not much happens, premiered at the Teatro dell'Opera in Rome on May 13, 1977. The opera it mostly closely resembles is Schoenberg's ERWARTUNG, likewise an interior monologue for soprano. Feldman also wrote music for another Beckett drama, the radio play *Words and Music* (1987).

FELLINI, FEDERICO
Italian film director (1920–1994)

Federico Fellini became famous in 1954 with his Oscar-winning film LA STRADA, transmuted into an opera in 1982 by Czech composer Václav Kaslík. He attracted even more attention in 1960 with *La Dolce Vita,* and he was recently voted the greatest film director of all time in a *Sight and Sound* poll of filmmakers. Fellini said he did not understand opera so he did not direct operas on stage, but opera music features in many of his films. It is the central focus of E LA NAVE VA (1983), about the funeral of an opera diva with operatic music by Verdi and Rossini. In his 1963 film *8½,* the overture to IL BARBIERE DI SIVIGLIA is played at a key moment. In his 1970 film *The Clowns,* there are excerpts from "The Ride of the Valkyries" from DIE WALKÜRE and the Toreador music from CARMEN. "Mack the Knife" from DIE DREIGROSCHENOPER is featured on the soundtrack of his 1979 fantasy *City of Women.*

FELSENSTEIN, WALTER
Austrian director (1901–1975)

Walter Felsenstein was one of the most influential modern opera producers. Although much of his work was done behind the Iron Curtain in East Berlin at the Komische Oper, his ideas permeated opera production around the world. Essentially, he believed opera was as much theater as it was music, so that the acting was as important as the singing—a radical concept at the time. His ideas have been so assimilated that what was once revolutionary now seems less than surprising; nevertheless, his fine qualities as a director can still be experienced in his films. His 1955 FIDELIO was especially influential as for a long time it was the only film of the opera and was shown widely. See also BARBE-BLEUE, (1973), THE CUNNING LITTLE VIXEN (1965), DON GIOVANNI (1966), LE NOZZE DI FIGARO (1976), OTELLO (1969), and LES CONTES D'HOFFMANN (1970).

1967 Felsenstein Inszeniert
Felsenstein Director was made by American documentarian Michael Blackwood while Felsenstein was rehearsing the second act of *Don Giovanni* in Berlin in 1966. It shows him at work and commenting on his ideas. Made for NDR German Television. Color. In German. 67 minutes.

1972 Walter Felsenstein, a Portrait
German television documentary film about the career of the director, showing aspects of his productions and discussing his ideas about opera on stage. Made for Hessischer Rundfunk. Color. In German. 62 minutes.

FERNANDEZ, WILHELMENIA
American soprano (1949–)

Wilhelmenia Wiggins Fernandez was the African-American soprano who became famous singing an aria from *La Wally* in the 1981 French thriller DIVA. She played a mysterious opera singer who refused to allow her voice to be recorded so an admirer secretly taped her singing "Ebben...ne andrò lontana"; the tape becomes a hot property. Fernandez made her debut in 1982 singing Musetta in *La bohème* with the New York City Opera. She played Carmen Jones in the first London production of the opera and was even an operatic guest on *Sesame Street.*

1991 La Grouchiata
Wilhelmenia Fernandez is a delight in this episode of *Sesame Street,* which tries to show young viewers the joys of opera. Puppet opera star Grundgetta prefers screaming to singing so she quits the show. Wilhelmenia has to step in and save the day singing in *La traviata.* Color. 30 minutes.

FERRER, JOSÉ
American actor-singer (1909–1992)

Puerto Rico–born José Ferrer was an actor, director, and singer whose primary career was in the movies, but he also sang in operas, operettas, and musicals. In 1960, he was featured at Santa Fe Opera in the title role of Puccini's *Gianni Schicchi.* In 1964, he won acclaim on Broadway singing the prince in Noël Coward's musical *The Girl Who Came to Supper.* In 1967, he played the title role in a television production of the pastiche operetta KISMET. He won a Tony and an Oscar playing Cyrano de Bergerac on stage and on film and is a delight as SIGMUND ROMBERG in the 1954 film *Deep in My Heart* singing opposite Helen Traubel. Even when he isn't singing, his voice is a sonorous marvel.

FIDELE BAUER, DER
1907 operetta by Fall

Austrian composer LEO FALL's 1907 operetta *Der fidele Bauer* (The Merry Peasant) was his first success and one of the most popular state musicals of its time. Victor Léon's libretto tells the story of an old-fashioned German peasant Mathaeus who idolizes his son and makes sacrifices in order to give him an education. When the son goes to Vienna and eventually finds a wife, he is too embarrassed by his peasant family to invite them to his wedding. They visit him anyway and it all works out for the best. The operetta was staged in London as *The Merry Peasant*.

1951 Marischka film

Austrian feature film: Hubert Marischka (director and screenplay), Hans Schneeberg (cinematographer).

Cast: Paul Hörbiger (Mathaeus), Erich Auer (Heini), Marianne Wischmann (Vivian).

Black and white. In German. 90 minutes.

Comment: The story is somewhat altered and the woman the son loves is now an American.

1971 Theater an der Wien

Austrian stage production: Axel von Ambesser (director), Rudolf Bibl (conductor, Theater an der Wien Orchestra), Willy Schatz (set designer).

Cast: Josef Meinrad (Mathaeus), Alois Aichhorn (Stefan), Marianne Schönauer (Amélie), Ulli Fessl (Alice), Fritz Muliar (Lindoberer), Dolores Schmidinger (Red Lisi).

Telecast November 14, 1971, on ORF Austrian television. Color. In German. 85 minutes.

Early film

1927 Seitz film

Hungarian actor S. Z. Sakall, who later became popular in Hollywood movies, is one of the stars of this German production with English actress Ivy Close and German actors Werner Krauss, Mathias Wieman, and Leo Peukert. It was screened with Fall's music played live. Franz Seitz directed. Black and white. Silent. About 75 minutes.

FIDELIO

1814 opera by Beethoven

BEETHOVEN's opera had its premiere in the form we know it in Vienna in 1814. Leonore disguises herself as the young man Fidelio so she can work in the Seville jail and try to rescue her husband Florestan. The jailer's daughter Marzelline takes a fancy to her, and the evil Pizarro has plans to kill her husband as soon as he can. The opera is filled with Beethoven's ideas about liberty, heroism, and the triumph of hope. The libretto in its final form is by George Friedrich Treitschke and Josef Sonnleithner. It is Beethoven's only opera.

1955 Felsenstein film

Austrian feature film: Walter Felsenstein (director and screenplay with Hans Eisler), Fritz Lehmann (conductor, Vienna Philharmonic Orchestra and Vienna Opera Chorus), Niklaus Hayer (cinematographer), Erich Bertin (music director).

Cast: Claude Nollier (Leonore, sung by Magda Laszlo), Richard Holm (Florestan), Hannes Schiel (Don Pizarro, sung by Heinz Rehfuss), Sonja Schöner (Marzelline), George Reiter (Rocco, spoken by George Weiter), Erwin Gross (Don Fernando, sung by Alfred Poli), Fritz Berg (Jaquino).

Black and white. In German with English subtitles. 90 minutes.

Comment: Felsenstein sets the film in a massive fortress and internalizes the music with visual symbolism, including waterfalls, falling rocks, and flowery meadows. The acting is somewhat stagy, rather like the silent cinema stereotype.

1959 NBC Opera Theatre

American TV production: David Sarser (director), Samuel Chotzinoff (producer), Peter Herman Adler (conductor, NBC Opera Theatre Orchestra), Trew Hocker (set designer), Joseph Machlis (English translation).

Cast: Irene Jordan (Leonore), John Alexander (Florestan), Lee Cass (Don Pizarro), Judith Raskin (Marzelline), Chester Watson (Rocco), Fred Cushman (Jaquino), Kenneth Smith (Don Fernando).

Video at the MTR. Telecast live November 8, 1959. Kirk Browning (director). Color. In English. 120 minutes.

1968 Hamburg State Opera

German TV film: Guenther Rennert (stage director), Leopold Ludwig (conductor, Hamburg Philharmonic State Orchestra and State Opera Chorus), Wilhelm Reinking (set designer), Hannes Schlinder (cinematographer), Rolf Liebermann (producer).

Cast: Anja Silja (Leonore), Richard Cassilly (Florestan), Theo Adam (Don Pizarro), Lucia Popp (Marzelline), Ernest Wiemann (Rocco), Hans Sotin (Don Fernando), Erwin Wohlfahrt (Jaquino).

Film: Joachim Hess (director). Color. In German. 128 minutes.

Comment: This film was shown theatrically in America.

1970 Deutsche Oper Berlin

German TV film: Gustav Rudolf Sellner (film and stage director), Karl Böhm (conductor, Deutsch Oper Berlin Orchestra), Ernst Wild (cinematographer), Wilhelm Reinking (set/costume designer).

Cast: Gwyneth Jones (Leonore), James King (Florestan), Gustav Neidinger (Don Pizarro), Olivia Miljakovic (Marzelline), Josef Greindl (Rocco), Martti Talvela (Don Fernando), Donald Grobe (Jaquino).

Video: Decca VHS. Color. In German. 115 minutes.

Comment: This film is based on a Deutsche Oper Berlin stage production but it was shot in a Berlin studio.

1977 Orange Festival

French stage production: Alfred Wopmann (stage director), Pierre Jourdan (film director), Zubin Mehta (director, Israel Philharmonic Orchestra and London New Philharmonia Chorus), Marco Arturo Marelli (set designer).

Cast: Gundula Janowitz (Leonore), Jon Vickers (Florestan), Theo Adam (Don Pizarro), Stella Richmond (Marzelline), William Wilderman (Rocco), Misha Raitzin (Jaquino).

Video: Dreamlife (Japan) VHS/LD. Color. In German. 120 minutes.

Comment: Filmed live on stage without an audience.

1978 Vienna State Opera

Austrian stage production: Otto Schenk (director), Leonard Bernstein (conductor, Vienna Philharmonic Orchestra).

Cast: Gundula Janowitz (Leonore), René Kollo (Florestan), Hans Sotin (Don Pizarro), Lucia Popp (Marzelline), Manfred Jungwirth (Rocco), Adolf Dallapozza (Jaquino).

Video: House of Opera VHS. Telecast on ORF Austrian TV. Otto Schenk (director). Color. In German. 145 minutes.

1979 Glyndebourne Festival

English stage production: Peter Hall (director), Bernard Haitink (conductor, London Philharmonic Orchestra and Glyndebourne Festival Chorus), John Bury (set designer).

Cast: Elisabeth Söderström (Leonore), Anton de Ridder (Florestan), Robert Allman (Don Pizarro), Elizabeth Gale (Marzelline), Curt Appelgren (Rocco), Michael Langdon (Don Fernando), Ian Caley (Jaquino).

Video: Opera d'Oro/VAI VHS. Dave Heather (director). Color. In German with English subtitles. 130 minutes.

***1991 Royal Opera House

English stage production: Adolf Dresen (director), Christoph von Dohnányi (conductor, Royal Opera House Orchestra and Chorus), Margit Bardy (set/costume designer).

Cast: Gabriela Beňačková (Leonore), Josef Protschka (Florestan), Monte Pederson (Don Pizarro), Marie McLaughlin (Marzelline), Robert Lloyd (Rocco), Hans Tschammer (Don Fernando), Neill Archer (Jaquino).

Video: Image Entertainment and Arthaus (GB) DVD/Home Vision VHS/Pioneer LD. Derek Bailey (director). Color. In German with English subtitles. 129 minutes.

Comment: Thoughtful, effective production.

2000 Metropolitan Opera

American stage production: Jürgen Flimm (director), James Levine (conductor, Metropolitan Opera Orchestra and Chorus), Robert Israel (set designer).

Cast: Karita Mattila (Leonore), Ben Heppner (Florestan), Falk Struckmann (Don Pizarro), Jennifer Welch-Babidge (Marzelline), René Pape (Rocco), Robert Lloyd (Don Fernandez), Matthew Polenzani (Jaquino).

Taped October 28, 2000; telecast December 26, 2002, on PBS. Color. In German with English subtitles. 130 minutes.

Related films

1937 Yoshiwara

Max Ophuls's 1937 film about a Japanese woman (Michiko Tanaka) who sells herself to a brothel to provide for her little brother features an homage to *Fidelio*. Her Russian protector (Pierre Richard Willm) takes her on an imaginary train ride to the opera and teaches her how to applaud. The opera, appropriately, is about another self-sacrificing woman. Black and white. In French. 88 minutes.

1970 Fidelio: A Celebration of Life

Leonard Bernstein takes a look at Beethoven's "flawed masterpiece" and discusses its story and problems. Four selections from Act II are presented, preceded by analysis and plot summary. This film was a part of Bernstein's *Young People's Concert* series on television. Black and white. 54 minutes. Video at the MTR.

FIERRABRAS

1823 opera by Schubert

FRANZ SCHUBERT's opera *Fierrabras* was composed in 1823 but didn't get staged until 1897. It was then ignored until 1988 when it was revived at the Vienna State Opera. Josef Kupelwieser's libretto evokes the legend of Charlemagne and his heroic knight Roland. Moorish prince Fierrabras loves Charlemagne's daughter Emma while Roland loves Fierrabras's sister, Florinda. All ends more or less well after many complications.

1988 Vienna State Opera

Austrian stage production: Ruth Berghaus (director), Claudio Abbado (conductor, Chamber Orchestra of Europe and Arnold Schoenberg Chorus), Hans-Dieter Schaal (set designer).

Cast: Thomas Hampson (Roland), Josef Protschka (Fierrabras), Karita Mattila (Emma), Ellen Shade (Florinda), Peter Hofmann (Ogier), Robert Holl (Charlemagne), Robert Gambill (Eginhard).

Video: House of Opera/Opera Direct DVD/Lyric VHS. P. W. R. Lauscher (director). Color. In German. 120 minutes.

Comment: Berghaus sets the action in a timeless era with abstract modernist sets.

FIERY ANGEL, THE
1927 opera by Prokofiev

SERGEI PROKOFIEV's opera *Ognennyi Angel* (The Fiery Angel) premiered in Paris in 1954 after the composer's death and is now considered one of his finest works. Based on a symbolist novel by Valery Bryussov with libretto by the composer, it is the sexually charged story of 16th-century mystic Renata who has visions of a fiery angel lover named Madiel. Her friend Ruprecht tries to help her and fights a duel on her behalf, but she ends up being tried as a witch.

1993 Kirov Opera

Russian stage production: David Freeman (director), Valery Gergiev (conductor, Kirov Opera Orchestra and Maryinsky Theater Chorus), David Roger (set designer).

Cast: Galina Gorchakova (Renata), Sergei Leiferkus (Ruprecht), Yevgeny Boitsov (Jacob Glock), Vladimir Galuzin (Agrippa), Larissa Diadkova (Fortuneteller), Konstantin Pluzhnikov (Mephistopheles), Sergei Alexashkin (Faust), Vladimir Ognovenko (Inquisitor), St. Petersburg Maryinsky Acrobatic Troupe (Renata's demons).

Video: Arthaus DVD/Philips VHS & LD. Brian Large (director). Color. In Russian. 124 minutes.

Comment: Superb production, fine singers, overheated story, the breakthrough role for Gorchakova.

FILLE DE MADAME ANGOT, LA
1872 operetta by Lecocq

CHARLES LECOCQ's tuneful operetta *La fille de Madame Angot* (Madame Angot's Daughter) is not well known today, but it was hugely popular internationally in its time. It takes place in Paris during the French Revolution. Clairette, the orphan daughter of fishwife Madame Angot, is in love with radical poet Ange Pitou, but her marriage has been arranged to wigmaker Pomponnet. Pitou,

however, prefers actress Mlle. Lange, an old school friend of Clairette's, so sparks fly. The libretto is by Clairbille, Siraudin, and Koning.

1935 SFPC film

French feature film: Jean Bernard-Derosne (director), Jean Jacques Bernard (screenplay), Montéran and Lucien Jaulin (cinematography), SFPC (production company).

Cast: Moniquella (Clairette), André Baugé (Ange Pitou), Danièle Brégis (Mlle. Lange), Robert Arnoux (Pomponnet), Arletty (Ducoudray).

Black and white. In French. 85 minutes.

FILLE DU RÉGIMENT, LA
1840 opera by Donizetti

GAETANO DONIZETTI's *La fille du régiment* was composed to a French libretto but is usually staged in Anglophone countries in English as *The Daughter of the Regiment*. In any language it's a romp, the colorful story of Marie, who was found on a battlefield as a child and raised by a French regiment as its mascot. She wants to marry Tonio, but a marquise intervenes saying Marie is her long-lost niece and must marry a nobleman. After some rollicking fun and lots of bugle and drum playing, everything works out for the best. The French libretto is by J. H. Vernoy de Saint-Georges and Jean-François Bayard. Donizetti also wrote an Italian version.

1933 Billon film

French feature film. Pierre Billon (director); Hans Zerlett and Hans Hannes (screenplay); Otto Heller, Kurt Neubert, and Ernst Mühlrad (cinematographers); Vandor Film (production).

Cast: Anny Ondra (Mary), Pierre Richard Willm (Lord Robert), Marfa Dhervilly (Lady Diana), Claude Dauphin (Lt. Williams), Paul Asselin (Sergeant Bully).

Black and white. In French. 90 minutes.

Comment: Billon's film modernizes the opera, moves the setting to Scotland, turns the French regiment into Scottish Highlanders, and Anglicizes the names. It was shot in Austria.

1933 Lamac film

Austrian feature film: Karel Lamac (director); Hans Zerlett and Hans Hannes (screenplay); Otto Heller, Kurt Neubert, and Ernst Mühlrad (cinematographers); Vandor Film (production).

Cast: Anny Ondra (Mary), Werner Fuetterer (Lord Robert), Adele Sandrock (Lady Diana), Willi Stettner (Lt. Williams), Otto Wallburg (Sergeant Bully).

Black and white. In German. 90 minutes.

Comment: This German-language version of the opera *Die Tochter des Regiment* was shot in Austria at the same time as the French film above with the same changes in plot and names and a mostly different cast.

1972 Who's Afraid of Opera?

English TV film: Ted Kotcheff (director), Richard Bonynge (conductor, London Symphony Orchestra), George Djurkovic (set designer), Claire Merrill (screenplay), Nathan Kroll (producer).

Cast: Joan Sutherland (Marie), Ramon Remedios (Tonio), Spiro Malas (Sergeant Sulpice), Monica Sinclair (Marchioness), Larry Berthelson puppets.

Video: Kultur VHS. Color. In English and French. 30 minutes.

Comment: Highlights version of the opera made for young audiences, with Sutherland telling the story to puppets. Dialogue in English, arias in French.

***1974 Wolf Trap Park

American stage production: Lotfi Mansouri (director), Charles Wendelken-Wilson (conductor, Filene Center Orchestra and Wolf Trap Company Chorus), Beni Montresor (set designer), Ruth and Thomas Martin (English translation).

Cast: Beverly Sills (Marie), William McDonald (Tonio), Spiro Malas (Sergeant Sulpice), Muriel Costa-Greenspon (Marquise).

Video: VAI DVD/VHS. Kirk Browning (director). Color. In English. 118 minutes.

Comment: Sills is delightfully exuberant and really seems to enjoys herself in this lively English-language production, her first complete TV opera and the first from Wolf Trap. It helped make her a media star.

1984 Teatro Regio, Parma

Italian stage production: Beppe De Tomasi (director), Angelo Campori (conductor, Orchestra Sinfonica dell'Emilia-Romagna and Teatro Regio Chorus), Antonio Mastromattei (set designer).

Cast: June Anderson (Marie), Alfredo Kraus (Tonio), Roberto Coviello (Sulpice), Rosa Laghezza (Marquise).

Video: Bel Canto VHS. Color. In French. 124 minutes.

1986 Australian Opera

Australian stage production: Sandro Sequi (director), Richard Bonynge (conductor, Elizabethan Sydney Orchestra and Australian Opera Chorus), Henry Bardon (set designer).

Cast: Joan Sutherland (Marie), Anson Austin (Tonio), Gregory Yurisch (Sulpice), Heather Begg (Marquise).

Video: Kultur DVD/VHS. Peter Butler (director). Color. In French with English subtitles. 122 minutes.

Comment: Sutherland is in terrific voice in this enjoyable French-language production.

1996 Teatro alla Scala

Italian stage production: Filippo Crivelli (director), Donato Renzetti (conductor, Teatro alla Scala Opera Orchestra and Chorus), Franco Zeffirelli (set designer).

Cast: Mariella Devi (Marie), Paul Austin Kelly (Tonio), Bruno Praticó (Sulpice), Ewa Podleś (Marquise).

Video: TDK DVD. Tina Protasoni (director). Color. In French with English subtitles. 134 minutes.

Early/related films

1898 American Mutoscope

A very early film of a scene from this opera was made in July 1898 in the New York City studio of the American Mutoscope Company. It was distributed with the title *The Daughter of the Regiment*. Black and white. Silent. About 2 minutes.

1900 Phono-Cinéma-Théâtre

La Scala opera singer Polin performs an aria from *La fille du régiment* in one of the first sound films. It premiered at the Phono-Cinéma-Théâtre at the Paris Exhibition of 1900. Black and white. In French. About 3 minutes.

1909 Deutsches Mutoscop

German sound film featuring the aria "Weiss nich die Welt" from the German version of *Die Regimentstochter*. It was made by the Deutsches Mutoscop und Biograph company. Black and white. In German. About 4 minutes.

1913 Cines film

The Italian film company Cines made a version of the Donizetti opera in 1913 with the Italian title *La figlia del reggimento*. It was shown in the United States and England and reviewed as a "well-staged adaptation." Black and white. Silent. About 20 minutes.

1915 Pittaluga film

Another long Italian film of the opera was made two years later, also titled *La figlia del reggimento*. It was distributed by Pittaluga. Black and white. Silent. About 40 minutes.

1920 Vidali film
The popularity of the opera was so strong in Italy at this time that a third version of the opera was produced, again titled *La figlia del reggimento.* Liliane de Rosny is Mary (not Marie) opposite Umberto Mozzato as Toni. Enrico Vidali directed for Subalpina Films of Turin. Black and white. Silent. About 50 minutes.

1927 Cameo Operas
Kitty Barling is Marie in this British *Song Films* highlights version with Oscar Sosander as Tonio and Algernon Hicks as Baron Bertrand. It was screened with singers and orchestra. H. B. Parkinson directed for the series *Cameo Operas.* Black and white. Silent. About 20 minutes.

1929 Behrendt film
English film star Betty Balfour was brought to Berlin to star as Marie in a feature version of the opera as adapted by Hans Zerlett. Alexander D'Arcy is the man she loves and Kurt Gerron is the Sergeant. Hans Behrendt directed this German-British coproduction. Black and white. Silent. About 80 minutes.

1930 A Lady's Morals
Grace Moore plays prima donna Jenny Lind in this American film biography and performs the soldierly "Rataplan" number. Sidney Franklin directed. The British title is *Jenny Lind.* Black and white. In English. 75 minutes.

1944 La hija del regimiento
Mapy Cortes plays Maria in this Spanish-language film based on the Donizetti opera made in Mexico under the direction of Jamie Salvador. It was released by Aguila Films as *La hija del regimiento.* Black and white. In Spanish. 86 minutes.

1953 Bolvary film
Antonella Lualdi is the daughter in this narrative film of the opera made in three languages with Isa Barzizza, Hannelore Schroth, Michel Auclair, and Theo Lingen. The Italian version is called *La figlia del reggimento,* the German is *Die Tochter der Kompanie,* and the French is *La fille du régiment.* Geza von Bolvary directed all three with help from Tullio Covazi in Italy. Black and white. In Italian, German, or French. 90 minutes.

1953 Melba
Patrice Munsel plays opera diva Nellie Melba in this British film biography and sings "Chacun le sait" from *La fille du régiment.* See NELLIE MELBA.

1954 Athena
Jane Powell sings the aria "Chacun le sait" from the opera in the film *Athena,* a musical about health fads. Richard Thorpe directed. Color. 96 minutes.

1999 Any Given Sunday
The opera's Finale is heard on the soundtrack of this Oliver Stone film about the tribulations of professional football players. It's performed by the Munich Radio Orchestra led by Marcello Panni. Color. 150 minutes.

FILMMAKERS ON THE STAGE

A number of major filmmakers, in addition to making opera films, have turned to directing operas on stage. This has become more common in recent years and appears to be a growing trend. The first and most influential were Luchino Visconti and Franco Zeffirelli, whose stage work is as important as their filmmaking. Some of the other notable film directors who have directed opera on stage include ROBERT ALTMAN, ANTHONY ASQUITH, BRUCE BERESFORD, INGMAR BERGMAN, PETER BROOK, LILIANA CAVANI, FRANCIS FORD COPPOLA, AXEL CORTI, SERGEI EISENSTEIN, ISTVÁN GAÁL, CLAUDE GORETTA, PETER GREENAWAY, PETER HALL, WERNER HERZOG, JOHN HUSTON, JAROMIL JIREŠ, HERBERT ROSS, KEN RUSSELL, JOHN SCHLESINGER, DANIEL SCHMID, WERNER SCHROETER, ISTVÁN SZABÓ, and ANDREI TARKOVSKY.

FILMZAUBER
1912 operetta about the movies by Kollo

Filmzauber (Film Magic) was the first opera or operetta with cinema as its subject. It was a big hit in Berlin in 1912 and was staged with equal success in London and New York in 1913 as *The Girl on the Film.* The story concerns a film company making a movie about Napoleon in a small village. The "girl" of the title is a society lady on the run who pretends to be a boy to get a part in the film. *Filmzauber* was composed by Germany's WALTER KOLLO with help from Willy Bredschneider to a libretto by Rudolf Bernauer and Rudolph Schanzer. For England and the United States, James T. Tanner wrote the libretto, Adrian Ross wrote the lyrics, and ALBERT SIRMAY (SZIRMAI) composed new songs. The stars in the London and New York productions were George Grossmith, Emmy Wehlen, and Madeleine Seymour. There is no film version.

FILOSOFO DE CAMPAGNA, IL
1754 opera by Galuppi

Baldassare Galuppi's comic opera *Il filosofo de campagna* (The Country Philosopher), libretto by playwright

Carlo Goldoni, was the most popular opera of their collaboration and was staged all over the Europe. It centers around the philosophical country farmer Nardo and the connivances of the maid Lesbina. She sets out to help Eugenia, who does not want to marry Nardo, and then decides to marry him herself.

1960 CBS Television

American TV production: John Desmond (director), Alfredo Antonini (conductor, CBS Television Orchestra), Camera Three (production).

Cast: Salvatore Baccaloni (Nardo), Barbara Meister, Arlene Saunders, William Lewis, Ezio Flagello.

Telecast on February 7, 1960. John Desmond (director). Black and white. In Italian. 30 minutes.

Comment: Structured as a highlights recital with excerpts and scenes from the opera presented in a semi-staged manner.

FINAL INGREDIENT, THE
1965 TV opera by Amram

Jewish prisoners in a World War II concentration camp are short one ingredient for their forbidden Passover supper and stage a breakout to get the needed egg. David Amram's TV opera *The Final Ingredient*, libretto by Arnold Weinstein based on a TV play by Reginald Rose, was commissioned for Passover by the ABC Television series *Directions '65* and telecast in 1965.

1965 ABC Television

American TV production: Robert Delaney (director), David Amram (conductor, ABC Symphony Orchestra), John Dappers (set designer).

Cast: William Covington (Aaron), Joseph Sopher (Aaron's Father), Ezio Flagello (Walter), Malcolm Smith (Eli), Richard Frisch (Felix), Alan Baker (Max), Thomas Motto (Rabbi), Brown Bradley (Sigmund), John Fiorito (Herr Fedwebel), Robert Lancaster (Corporal), James Olesen (Private), Sara Mae Endich, Elaine Bonazzi, Marija Kova (Three Women).

Telecast April 11, 1965, on ABC. Robert Delaney (director). Color. In English. 60 minutes.

Comment: The opera was so popular it was repeated annually for years; the soundtrack was released on a CD in 1996.

FIND THE WITNESS
1927 American film with operatic murder mystery

American opera star Rita Calmette (Rita LaRoy) is the murder victim in the low-budget mystery *Find the Witness,* originally released as *A Slug for Cleopatra.* The opera singer's magician husband the Great Mordini (Henry Mollison) is the chief suspect as he had left her and she followed him to Los Angeles to create a scandal. Newspaperman Larry McGill (Charles Quigley), with help from Calmette's secretary Linda (Rosalind Keith), finally solves the mystery. There's not much opera in this operatic mystery written by Grace Neville and Fred Niblo Jr. and based on a story by Richard Sale. Virgil Miller and Allen Siegler were the cinematographers, and David Selman directed for Columbia Pictures. Black and White. In English. 58 minutes.

FINTA GIARDINIERA, LA
1775 opera by Mozart

MOZART was 18 when he composed this entertaining opera to a libretto attributed to Giuseppe Petrosellini. *La finta giardiniera* (The False Woman Gardener) is the story of a marchioness who pretends to be the gardener Sandrina so she can look for her fiancé Count Belfiore. He believes her dead because he stabbed her in a quarrel. She is hired by old and foolish Don Achise who falls in love with her. Meanwhile, the maid Serpetta wants to marry the old man and rejects the advances of the countess's servant, also in disguise. Sandrina reveals her identity to save her fiancé from the charge of murdering her after numerous amorous and identity complications.

1957 NET Opera

American TV production: Sarah Caldwell (director/conductor, Boston University Symphony Orchestra), Jack Brown (set designer), WGBH (production).

Cast: Polyna Zagaretou (Sandrina), Merle Puffer (Belfiore), James Billings (Don Achise), Rolda Ringo (Serpetta), Lesli Loosli (Arminda), Rosalin Hupp (Ramiro), Richard Christopher (Nardo).

Telecast November 2, 1957, on WGBH. Black and white. In English. 131 minutes.

***1988 Drottningholm Court Theatre

Swedish stage production: Göran Järvefelt (director), Arnold Östman (conductor, Drottningholm Court Theatre Orchestra and Chorus).

Cast: Britt-Marie Aruhn (Sandrina), Richard Croft (Belfiore), Stuart Kale (Don Achise), Ann Christine Biel (Serpetta), Eva Pilat (Arminda), Annika Skoglund (Ramiro), Petteri Salomaa (Nardo).

Video: Philips VHS/LD. Thomas Olofsson (director). Color. In Italian with English subtitles. 149 minutes.

Comment: Charming production, nicely sung, and wonderfully performed in the intimate Swedish Royal theater.

1990 Théâtre Royal de la Monnaie

Belgian stage production: Karl-Ernst Hermann (director, set/costume designer), Ursula Herrmann (codirector), Silvain Cambreling (conductor, Théâtre Royal de la Monnaie Orchestra).

Cast: Joanna Kozlowska (Sandrina), Marek Torzewski (Belfiore), Ugo Benelli (Don Achise), Elzbieta Szmytka (Serpetta), Malvina Major (Arminda), Lani Poulson (Ramiro), Russell Smythe (Nardo).

Telecast April 7, 1991. O. Herrmann and W. Ooms (directors). Color. In French. 148 minutes.

FIREFLY, THE

1912 operetta by Friml

An Italian street singer travels to Bermuda as a cabin boy and ends up as an opera star. RUDOLF FRIML replaced Victor Herbert as composer of this operetta after Herbert quarreled with prima donna Emma Trentini and refused to work with her again. Friml wrote a fine score to Otto Harbach's libretto, including three hit songs, "Giannina Mia," "Love Is Like a Firefly," and "Sympathy." The operetta's most famous number, "The Donkey Serenade," was not in the original stage show but was created for the film version.

1937 MGM film

American feature film: Robert Z. Leonard (director); Frances Goodrich, Albert Hackett, Ogden Nash (screenplay); Herbert Stothart (music director); Oliver T. Marsh (cinematographer); Cedric Gibbons (art director).

Cast: Jeanette MacDonald (Nina Maria), Allan Jones (Don Diego), Henry Daniell (General Savary), Warren William (Major de Rouchemont), George Zucco (Secret Service Chief), Billy Gilbert (Innkeeper).

Video: MGM-UA DVD/VHS. Black and white. In English. 131 minutes.

Comment: MGM abandoned the stage libretto in favor of a new story but kept most of the songs. The new setting is Spain during the Napoleonic War with France. MacDonald plays a singer called "The Firefly," secretly a Spanish spy. Jones introduced "The Donkey Serenade" and became famous for it.

FIRST OPERA FILMS

1894: First film with possible opera content is Thomas Edison's *Carmencita* made in March 1894 with Spanish dancer Carmencita. In Bizet's *Carmen*, the heroine is hailed as "Carmencita" when she first appears to sing and dance the Habanera. It is not known if this Carmencita danced to Bizet's music but it is probable. About 30 seconds.

- **1896:** First film seen in an opera was a bullfight shown in an 1896 production of *Carmen* by the Rosabel Morrison company at the Lyceum Theater in Elizabeth, New Jersey. It was shot in Mexico City using the Eidoloscope camera/ projector. About 30 seconds.

- **1897:** First film based on an opera uses Gounod's *Faust* as source and was directed by Georges Hatot for the Lumière Brothers in Paris in 1897. It's in two parts: Marguerite appears in a vision to Faust; he calls for Méphistophélès and agrees to his contract; he is transformed from poor old scholar to rich young man; Marguerite reappears. About 2 minutes.

- **1898:** First film of an opera was a condensed version of Donizetti's *The Daughter of the Regiment* shot in July 1898 at a New York City studio by American Mutoscope. About 2 minutes.

- **1898:** First film of an actual opera was William Paley's *The Opera of Martha*, shot in 1898 and screened at the Eden Musée in New York in January 1899. Four singers from the Castle Square Opera Company perform five scenes from the Flotow opera on stage in costume in front of sets. The opera arias were sung live by singers behind the screen. The film was sold to Thomas Edison in July 1899 and released as an Edison film in 1900. About 15 minutes.

- **1898:** First Georges Méliès opera film was the one-minute *Faust et Marguerite*, shot in 1898 and based on the Gounod opera.

- **1898:** First films about opera composers were made in 1898 by Italy's first filmmaker, Leopoldo Fregoli. They satirized Verdi, Rossini, Mascagni, and Wagner.

- **1899:** First film based on a contemporary opera was *Cendrillon*, shot by Georges Méliès in 1899 and inspired by the Massenet opera, which premiered the same year.

- **1900:** First opera films with sound were shown at the Phono-Cinéma-Théâtre at the Paris Exhibition on June 8, 1900. Victor Maurel sang arias from *Don Giovanni* and *Falstaff*, and Emile Cossira sang an aria from *Roméo et Juliette*. In a later film the same year Polin sang an aria from *La fille du régiment*.

- **1900:** Edwin S. Porter, later director of *The Great Train Robbery*, made *Faust and Marguerite* for the Edison company. About 3 minutes.

- **1902:** An aria from *Carmen* was featured in a sound film shown in September 1902 by Alber's Electro Talking Bioscope in the Netherlands. About 3 minutes.

- **1902:** The first woman director, Alice Guy-Blaché, filmed *Faust et Méphisto* for Gaumont in 1902. About 3 minutes.

- **1904:** The first epic opera films were made in 1904. Edwin S. Porter's 20-minute *Parsifal,* based on the Wagner opera, was filmed in eight scenes for Edison. George Méliès's 14-minute *The Damnation of Dr. Faust,* based on the Gounod opera, was filmed in 20 scenes.

- **1907:** First complete opera to be filmed was a sound version of Gounod's *Faust,* according to the *Guinness Book of Records.* Arthur Gilbert's 1907 English film was advertised as the "complete opera with 22 arias." The music was played on records synchronized using the Chronophone sound-on-disc system. About 60 minutes.

- **1913:** First complete opera to be filmed in America was *Pagliacci,* according to the *Guinness Book of Records.* It was a three-reel film made in 1913 by the Vi-T-Ascope Co. using the Vi-T-Phone sound system. About 45 minutes.

- **1930:** First full-length opera adapted for the screen with sound and photographed as a movie rather than a stage production was Auber's *Fra Diavolo.* Mario Bonnard shot this 90-minute film in 1930 in French, Italian, and German versions with Croatian tenor Tino Pattiera as the star.

- **1931:** First sound era film of a full opera was *Pagliacci,* shot on stage on Long Island in 1931 by Italian-Americans of the San Carlo Grand Opera Company. Joe W. Coffman directed the 80-minute movie, and the San Carlo Symphony Orchestra played the music.

FIRST OPERAS ON TELEVISION

- **1936:** First opera shown on TV was Albert Coates's English opera *Pickwick.* About 25 minutes of scenes from the opera were telecast by BBC Television on November 13, 1936, before its Covent Garden premiere.

- **1937:** First opera televised in its entirety was Pergolesi's *La Serva Padrona,* shown in September 1937 on BBC Television.

- **1938:** First opera on German television was Mozart's *Der Schauspieldirektor,* telecast by the Paul Nipkow Sender station in Berlin in 1938.

- **1939:** First opera on U.S. television was an amateur version of *Carmen* shown on NBC's experimental W2XBS in November 1939. The Miniature Opera Company staged scenes from the opera with child singers. NBC also presented three programs of excerpts from Gilbert and Sullivan comic operas, *The Pirates of Penzance* in June, *Cox and Box* in July, and *H.M.S. Pinafore* in September.

- **1940:** First opera shown on U.S. television with professional singers was *Pagliacci.* The Metropolitan Opera staged the first act at NBC's Radio City TV studio in March 1940.

- **1943:** First telecasts of complete operas in the United States were performed in 1943 in English by the Hartford Opera Workshop on the Schenectady station WRGB-TV. Menotti's *The Old Maid and the Thief* and Offenbach's *Le mariage aux lanternes* were telecast as a double bill in May, and Humperdinck's *Hänsel und Gretel* was performed in December.

- **1944:** Herbert Graf presented excerpts and shortened versions of four operas on NBC Television: *La bohème, The Barber of Seville, Carmen,* and *Pagliacci.*

- **1946:** First opera broadcast on BBC Television, after having closed down for the war in September 1939, was *The Beggar's Opera* on November 26, 1946.

- **1948:** First full-length opera telecast from an opera house stage was Verdi's *Otello* from the Metropolitan Opera on November 29, 1948.

- **1953:** First color telecast of an opera was NBC Opera Theatre's *Carmen* on October 31, 1953, with Vera Bryner as Carmen.

- **1950s:** First French opera telecasts began in the early 1950s with a series directed by Henri Spade including *Mireille, Don Quichotte,* and *Manon Lescaut.*

- **1958:** First live telecast from the Paris Opéra was the Maria Callas gala evening on December 19, 1958.

- **1961:** First international opera telecast was June 3, 1961, when a Stuttgart State Opera production of *Tosca* with Renata Tebaldi inaugurated a consortium of European stations.

FIRST OPERETTAS ON FILM

- **1896:** First operetta film may have been made by Germany's Max Skladanowsky at the end of 1896. Operetta stars Fritzi Massary and Josef Gianpietro reportedly appeared in a scene from *Der Vogelhändler* or *Der Bettelstudent.*

- **1902:** First U.S. operetta film was a 1902 Lubin movie featuring a scene from *The Mikado.*

- **1902:** First French operetta film was a 1902 scene of Offenbach's *Barbe-Bleue.* An aria was presented with sound and picture in Holland in September 1902.

- **1929:** First operetta filmed complete with sound was Sigmund Romberg's *The Desert Song,* advertised in June

1929 as the "first all-singing and talking operetta." John Boles starred as the Red Shadow in this Warner Bros. movie.

• **1929:** First European operetta filmed during the sound era was Oscar Straus's *Hochzeit in Hollywood*. It premiered on stage in Vienna in December 1928 and by September 1929 was showing in American movie houses as *Married in Hollywood*. It was advertised by Fox as "the first Viennese operetta."

FISCHER-DIESKAU, DIETRICH
German baritone (1925–)

Dietrich Fischer-Dieskau, as famous for lieder as for opera, retired in 1993, but his recordings maintain his reputation as one of the major singers of our time. He made his debut in 1948 in *Don Carlo* in Berlin and became known for a studied, intellectual style. He said he did not want to be a screen opera singer, so he did not make films and rarely appeared on TV. Luckily, a small legacy of his work is available on video, including a 1961 Berlin DON GIOVANNI (as the Don), a 1971 Hamburg DIE ZAUBERFLÖTE (as the Speaker), a 1976 Hamburg LE NOZZE DI FIGARO (as the Count), and a 1981 Vienna ELEKTRA (as Orest). Derek Jarman's 1988 film of Britten's WAR REQUIEM uses his 1963 recording as its soundtrack.

1990 Winterreise
The great baritone was 65 when he was filmed in Berlin in a performance of Schubert's *Winter Voyage* song cycle. He first performed them in 1948, and nearly half a century later his voice is still impressive. He is accompanied on piano by Murray Perahia. Rodney Greenberg directed the video. Color. In German. 70 minutes. Sony VHS/LD.

1992 Master Class
Fischer-Dieskau at 67 gives a master class to young singers in Berlin. He talks about opera and lieder, emphasizing Mozart, Schubert, and Schumann. Bruno Monsaingeon directed the video for Idéale Audience. Color. In German. 90 minutes.

1997 An Autumn Journey
Documentary about Fischer-Dieskau with interviews, archival footage, scenes showing him preparing to conduct, and a concert of Schubert songs he gave at the Nürnberg Opera House in 1991. Color. In German with English subtitles. 188 minutes. NVC Arts (GB) VHS.

***FITZCARRALDO
1982 German film with opera content

WERNER HERZOG's *Fitzcarraldo* is one of the great films about opera, the story of a man so obsessed with Enrico Caruso that he decides to build an opera house for him in the Amazon jungle. Klaus Kinski stars as opera-mad Fitzcarraldo, whose ideas about opera dominate the film. It begins with Kinski and his mistress Molly (Claudia Cardinale) rowing 1,200 miles to Manaus to hear the last few moments of Caruso on stage with Sarah Bernhardt in *Ernani* in the Teatro Amazonas. He decides to open a shipping route on the Amazon and raise the money to bring opera to the jungle even if he has to haul a ship over a mountain to do it. The ship is called the *Molly Aida,* and the film is filled with opera talk and music by Verdi, Bellini, Leoncavallo, Meyerbeer, and Massenet. Caruso's voice is heard on a phonograph at various times singing arias from *Pagliacci* ("Vesti la giubba), *L'Africana* ("O paradiso"), and *La bohème* ("O Mimì, tu più no torni"). When a missionary says he can't cure Indians of their "notion that normal life is an illusion behind which lies the reality of dreams," Fitzcarraldo comments that he is also "a man of the opera." "Il Sogno" from *Manon* and the Quartet from *Rigoletto* are also heard in the film. At the end of the movie there are scenes from *I puritani* on the boat with Isabel Jimenz de Cisneros as Elvira and Liborio Simonella as Arturo accompanied by the Lima Repertory Symphony Orchestra. The opening *Ernani* scene, staged by Werner Schroeter, is sung by Mietta Sighele, Veriano Luchetti, and Dimiter Petkov with actors on stage and music by the Venice Philharmonic. Color. In German. 157 minutes. Warner Bros. DVD/VHS.

FLAGSTAD, KIRSTEN
Norwegian soprano (1895–1962)

Kirsten Flagstad had an extraordinary career. She was about to retire in 1933 after a modestly successful career in Scandinavia when she was engaged to sing at Bayreuth in small roles. By the following year, she was being promoted as one of the best Wagnerian singers of the century. She made her debut at the Metropolitan Opera in 1935 at the age of 40 as Sieglinde in *Die Walküre* and was such a powerful singer that she did not, in fact, retire for another 20 years. She made only one film, *The Big Broadcast of 1938*, in which she sings Brünnhilde's "Hojo-to-ho!" from DIE WALKÜRE. She can also be seen in a 1951 BBC Television program as Dido in scenes from Purcell's DIDO AND AENEAS.

FLEDERMAUS, DIE

1874 operetta by Johann Strauss

Die Fledermaus (The Bat) is JOHANN STRAUSS's most popular operetta and has honorary opera status in most opera houses. The libretto by Carl Haffner and Richard Genée is based on *Le réveillon* by Henri Meilhac and Ludovic Halévy. The philandering Eisenstein has been sentenced to jail for a minor infraction, but he goes first to a masked ball given by Prince Orlofsky at the urging of his friend Falke. His wife Rosalinde disguises herself and goes to the ball to catch her husband flirting. Their maid Adele goes to the ball with her sister Ida pretending to be an actress. Rosalinde's old flame Alfred goes to jail pretending to be Eisenstein. Falke set all this up in revenge for a trick played on him once when he was wearing a bat costume. The ball scene usually includes guest stars. *Die Fledermaus* is one of the most filmed and televised operettas.

1931 La chauve-souris

French feature film: Karel Lamac and Pierre Billon (directors), Hans Zerlett and Karl Forest (screenplay), Otto Heller (cinematographer), Lucien Aguettand and Heinz Fenchal (set designers).

Cast: Anny Ondra (Arlette), Marcelle Denya (Caroline Gaillardin), Mauricet (Isodore Gaillardin), George Bury (Alfred), Ivan Petrovich (Orlofsky).

Black and white. In French. 80 minutes.

Comment: The first sound film of the operetta was made in Paris at the Pathé Studios in Joinville in French and German versions.

1931 Die Fledermaus

German feature film: Karel Lamac (director), Hans Zerlett and Karl Forest (screenplay), Otto Heller (cinematographer), Heinz Fenchal (set designer).

Cast: Anny Ondra (Adele), Georg Alexander (Eisenstein), Betty Werner (Rosalinde), Ivan Petrovich (Orlofsky), Oskar Sima (Frank), Hans Junkermann.

Black and white. In German. 80 minutes.

Comment: German version of the first sound film of the operetta made in Paris at the Pathé Studios in Joinville.

1933 Waltz Time

English feature film: William Thiele (director), A. P. Herbert (screenplay), Gaumont-British (production).

Cast: Evelyn Laye (Rosalinde), Fritz Schultz (Eisenstein), Gina Malo (Adele), Parry Jones (Alfred), Ivor Barnard (Falke), George Baker (Orlofsky).

Black and white. In English. 82 minutes.

Comment: In this adaptation, Eisenstein is a writer researching a book at a masked ball in Vienna, but he is still conned by his wife in disguise. It was distributed in the United States.

1937 Verhoeven film

German feature film: Paul Verhoeven (director), W. Wasserman and C. H. Diller (screenplay), Alois Melichar (conductor, Berlin Philharmonic), Bruno Mondi (cinematographer).

Cast: Lida Baarova (Lida Baarova), Hans Sohnker (Hans Weigel), Frieda Czepa (Hanni, the maid), Georg Alexander (Wentine), Robert Dorsay (Franz), Hans Moser (Ruber).

Black and white. In German. 105 minutes.

Comment: Sohnker plays a tenor celebrating his 300th performance as star of *Die Fledermaus*. He has become so bat-obsessed that when he falls asleep, he dreams the operetta, with his wife and friends in the various roles.

1946 Bolvary film

German feature film: Geza von Bolvary (director), Alois Melichar (conductor).

Cast: Marte Harell (Rosalinde), Johannes Heesters (Eisenstein), Dorit Kreysler (Adele), Siegfried Breuer (Orlofsky), Willi Dohm (Falke), Willy Fritsch (Frank).

Color. In German. 100 minutes.

Comment: Agfa color film made at the end of World War II in Barrandov Studios in Prague. The negative was seized by the Soviets, who premiered the film in East Berlin in 1946. It was released in the United States in 1958.

1950 NBC Opera Theatre

American TV production: Charles Polacheck (director), Peter Herman Adler (conductor, NBC Opera Orchestra and Chorus), Paul Barnes (set designer), Samuel Chotzinoff (producer), Ruth and Thomas Martin (English translation as *The Bat*).

Cast: Ethel Barrymore Colt (Rosalinde), Edward Kane (Eisenstein), Adelaide Bishop (Adele), Gene Barry (Orlofsky), Ray Jaquemot (Falke), Joseph Mordino (Alfredo).

Telecast live March 6, 1950, on NBC. Kirk Browning (director). Black and white. In English. 60 minutes.

1953 Metropolitan Opera on Omnibus

American TV production: Herbert Graf (director), William Spier (producer), Eugene Ormandy (conductor, Metropolitan Opera Orchestra), Rolf Gerard (set designer), Garson Kanin (English libretto), Howard Dietz (lyrics).

Cast: Brenda Lewis (Rosalinde), Charles Kullman (Eisenstein), Lois Hunt (Adele), Jarmila Novotná

(Orlofsky), Thomas Hayward (Alfred), John Brownlee (Falke).

Video at the MTR. Telecast live January 2, 1953, on CBS Television. Bob Banner (director). Black and white. In English. 65 minutes.

Comment: TV version of a famous Metropolitan Opera, the centerpiece of Rudolph Bing's first season as general manager.

1955 Oh Rosalinda!!

English feature film: Michael Powell and Emeric Pressburger (directors/screenplay), Christopher Chalis (cinematographer), Heinz Heckroth (production designer).

Cast: Rosalinda (Ludmilla Tcherina, sung by Sari Barabas), Michael Redgrave (French Colonel Eisenstein), Adele (Anneliese Rothenberger), Anton Walbrook (Dr. Falke, sung by Walter Berry), Mel Ferrer (American Captain Alfred, sung by Alexander Young), Anthony Quayle (Russian General Orlofsky), Dennis Price (British Major Frank, sung by Dennis Dowling).

Video: Live Opera VHS. Color. In English. 101 minutes.

Comment: Deliberately artificial version of the operetta set in post–World War II occupied Vienna. The songs have new lyrics, and the sets look like sets. The film opens with Falke explaining his practical joke.

1962 von Cziffra film

Austrian feature film: Geza von Cziffra (director/screenplay), Kurt Edelhagen (conductor, Vienna State Opera Orchestra), Willy Winterstein (cinematographer), Fritz-Jüptner Jonstorff and Alexander Sawcznski (set designer).

Cast: Marianne Koch (Rosalinde), Peter Alexander (Eisenstein), Marika Rökk (Adele), Boy Gobert (Orlofsky), Rolf Kutschera (Alfred), Gunther Philipp (Pista von Bundassy), Willy Millowitsch (Frank).

Video: Taurus/German Language Video Center VHS. Color. In German. 107 minutes.

Comment: The libretto has been somewhat changed and the era moved to the turn of the century.

1966 Flagermusen

Danish feature film: Annelise Meineche (director), John Hilbard and Vilmer Sørensen (screenplay), Ole Lytken (cinematographer), Ole Høyer (music director).

Cast: Lily Broberg (Rosalinde), Poul Reichhardt (Eisenstein), Ghita Nørby (Adele), Grethe Morgensen (Orlofsky), Holger Juul-Hansen (Falke), Karl Steggera (Frank), Dario Campeotto (Alfred).

Color. In Danish with English subtitles when released in England by Gala. 99 minutes.

Comment: Dance scenes by the Royal Danish Ballet and Pantomime Theatre of Copenhagen.

1972 Vienna State Opera

Austrian film: Otto Schenk (stage and film director), Karl Böhm (conductor, Vienna Philharmonic Orchestra and State Opera Chorus).

Cast: Gundula Janowitz (Rosalinde), Eberhard Wächter (Eisenstein), Renate Holm (Adele), Wolfgang Windgassen (Orlofsky), Erich Kunz (Frank).

Video: Taurus (Germany) VHS. Color. In German. 137 minutes.

1982 Australian Opera

Australian stage production: Anthony Besch (director), Richard Bonynge (conductor, Elizabethan Sydney Orchestra and Australian Opera Chorus), John Stoddart (set/costume designer), David Pountnoy and Leonard Hancock (English translation).

Cast: Joan Sutherland (Rosalinde), Robert Gard (Eisenstein), Monique Brynnel (Adele), Heather Begg (Orlofsky), Anson Austin (Alfred), Michael Lewis (Falke).

Video: Sony VHS. Hugh Davison (director). Taped July 10, 1982. Color. In English. 142 minutes.

1983 Royal Opera

English stage production: Leopold Lindberg and Richard Gregson (directors), Plácido Domingo (conductor, Royal Opera House Orchestra and Chorus), Julia Trevelyan Oman (set/costume designer).

Cast: Kiri Te Kanawa (Rosalinde), Hermann Prey (Eisenstein), Hildegarde Heichele (Adele), Doris Soffel (Orlofsky), Benjamin Luxon (Falke), Dennis O'Neill (Alfred).

Video: Warner NVC Arts DVD & VHS/HBO VHS. Taped December 31, 1983. Humphrey Burton (director). Color. Dialogue in English, singing in German with English subtitles. 175 minutes.

Comment: The ball scene guests include Charles Aznavour, Dame Hilda Bracket, Wayne Eagling, Evadne Hinge, and Merle Park.

1983/1989 Opera Stories

Laserdisc highlights version of above Royal Opera House production. Charlton Heston tells the story of the operetta from Vienna in framing material shot in 1989. Color. 52 minutes. In English and German with English subtitles. Pioneer Artists LD.

1986 Metropolitan Opera

American stage production: Otto Schenk (director), Jeffrey Tate (conductor, Metropolitan Opera Orchestra and Chorus), Günther Schneider-Siemssen (set designer).

Cast: Kiri Te Kanawa (Rosalinde), Håkan Hagegård (Eisenstein), Judith Blegen (Adele), Tatiana Troyanos (Orlofsky), David Rendall (Alfred), Michael Devlin (Falke).

Video at the MTR. Telecast live December 31, 1986. Kirk Browning (director). Color. 210 minutes.

Comment: Strong cast assembled for a live New Year's Eve telecast. Joanne Woodward hosted the evening.

***1987 Bavarian State Opera

German stage production: Otto Schenk (director), Carlos Kleiber (conductor, Bavarian State Opera Orchestra and Chorus), Günther Schneider-Siemssen (set designer).

Cast: Pamela Coburn (Rosalinde), Eberhard Wächter (Eisenstein), Janet Perry (Adele), Brigitte Fassbaender (Orlofsky), Wolfgang Brendel (Falke), Josef Hopferwieser (Alfred).

Video: DG DVD/VHS. Brian Large (director). Color. In German with English subtitles. 146 minutes.

Comment: Much praised production, the most enjoyable on video although it doesn't have the star power of other versions.

1990 Royal Opera

English stage production: John Cox (director), Richard Bonynge (conductor, Royal Opera Orchestra and Chorus), Julia Trevelyan Oman (set/costume designer), John Mortimer (English translation).

Cast: Nancy Gustafson (Rosalinde), Louis Otey (Eisenstein), Judith Howarth (Adele), Jochen Kowalski (Orlofsky), Anthony Michaels-Moore (Falke), Bonaventura Bottone (Alfred).

Video: Image Entertainment (USA) and Arthaus (GB) DVD/Home Vision VHS/LD. Humphrey Burton (director). Color. In English. 121 minutes.

Comment: Joan Sutherland bids farewell to Covent Garden as a party guest in this spirited production. She sings duets with guests Luciano Pavarotti and Marilyn Horne and a nostalgic "Home Sweet Home" emulating her Australian predecessor Nellie Melba.

1992 Italian TV: Operette, che Passione!

Italian TV production: Sandro Massimini (director/producer), Roberto Negri (pianist), Sandro Corelli (choreographer).

Singers: Sandro Massimini, Daniela Mazzucato, Max René Cosotti.

Video: Pierluigi Pagano (director). Color. In Italian. About 19 minutes. Ricordi (Italy) VHS.

Comment: Highlights of the operetta as *Il Pipistrello* on the Italian TV series. Songs include "Deli-

oziose che maniere," "Aria di Adele," and "Inno allo champagne."

2001 Salzburg Opera

Austrian stage production: Hans Neuenfels (director), Marc Minkowsi (conductor, Salzburg Mozarteum Orchestra and Arnold Schoenberg Choir).

Cast: Mireille Delunsch (Rosalinde), Christoph Homberger (Eisenstein), Malin Hartgelius (Adele), David Moss (Orlofsky).

Video: Arthaus DVD. Color. In English. 170 minutes.

Comment: Critics and audiences savaged this radically chic and somewhat silly updating of the operetta with contempory dialogue and over much sexuality.

Early films

1908 Duskes film

A trio from *Die Fledermaus* is pictured and sung by Edmund Binder and Hermine Hoffman in this early German sound film directed by Alfred Duskes. Black and white. In German. About 3 minutes. Film survives in a German archive.

1912 Messter Tonbild

German film producer Oskar Messter produced one of his longest sound films (Tonbilder) of *Die Fledermaus* featuring extensive scenes from the operetta. It was shown with the music played on several synchronized records. Black and white. In German. About 20 minutes.

1923 Mack film

This German feature version of the operetta, directed by Max Mack, stars Lya de Putti as Rosalinde with support from Harry Liedtke, Paul Heidemann, Eva May, Ernst Hoffman, and Wilhelm Bendow. It was screened with live music. Black and white. Silent. About 85 minutes.

FLEMING, RENÉE
American soprano (1960–)

Renée Fleming, who made her professional debut in Salzburg in 1986, has become one of the leading American sopranos in recent years, creating roles in three operas. She was Rosina in John Corigliano's THE GHOSTS OF VERSAILLES at the Metropolitan Opera in 1991 (telecast in 1992 and on video), Mme. de Tourvel in Conrad Susa's THE DANGEROUS LIAISONS at San Francisco Opera in 1994 (telecast in 1994), and Blanche Dubois in André Previn's A STREETCAR NAMED DESIRE at San Francisco Opera in 1998 (telecast in 1998 and on video). She also sang the title role in the first Met production of Carlisle Floyd's classic opera SUSANNAH. Her international repertoire is equally strong, including telecast performances at the Met singing Desdemona in OTELLO in 1995, the Countess in LE NOZZE DI FIGARO in 1998, and Donna Anna in DON GIOVANNI in 2000. She sang the Marschallin in DER ROSENKAVALIER in a televised 1992 Berlin concert. She has also begun to be seen and heard in fiction feature films.

1994 Immortal Beloved

Fleming's voice is featured on the soundtrack of this big-budget romantic biography of Beethoven. See LUDWIG VAN BEETHOVEN.

1999 A Midsummer Night's Dream

Fleming's voice is featured on the soundtrack of this version of the Shakespeare play directed by Michael Hoffman. Color. 115 minutes.

2001 Bride of the Wind

Fleming plays New Zealand–born Met soprano Frances Alda in this film about the life of Alma Mahler (Sarah Wynter) and performs Alma's songs. In the last scene, she sings "Laue Sommernacht," accompanied by Jean-Yves Thibaudet on piano, one of the most memorable moments in the film. Bruce Beresford directed. Color. In English. 99 minutes.

FLIEGENDE HOLLÄNDER, DER
1843 opera by Wagner

Der Fliegende Holländer (The Flying Dutchman), the earliest WAGNER opera in the repertory, is based on a tale by Heinrich Heine, but it was already a folk legend when he wrote it. It tells of a Dutch ship captain condemned to sail around the world until he is redeemed by the love of a faithful woman; he is allowed to land every seven years to search for her. When he docks in Norway, he meets Senta, who is obsessed with his legend and falls in love with him. When he sails away because he thinks she has been unfaithful, she throws herself off a cliff and provides his redemption.

1964 Herz film

East German feature film: Joachim Herz (director), Rolf Leuter (conductor, Leipzig Gewandhaus Orchestra and Leipzig Opera Chorus), DEFA (production).

Cast: Anna Prucnal (Senta, sung by Gerda Hannemann), Fred Dueren (Dutchman, sung by Rainer Lüdeke), Gerd Ehlers (Daland, sung by Hans Krämer), Mathilde Danegger (Mary, sung by Katrin Wölzl), Herbert Graedke (Erik, sung by Rolf Apreck), Hans-Peter Reineck (Steersman, sung by Friedrich Hölze).

Video: On DVD and VHS. Black and white. In German. 98 minutes.

1975 BBC Television

English TV production: Brian Large (director), David Lloyd-Jones (conductor, Royal Philharmonic Festival Orchestra and Ambrosian Opera Chorus).

Cast: Gwyneth Jones (Senta), Norman Bailey (Dutchman), Stafford Dean, Robert Ferguson, Keith Erwen, Joan Davies.

Telecast December 27, 1975, on BBC and then on PBS in America. Color. In English. 145 minutes.

1975 Bavarian State Opera

German film of stage production: Václav Kaslik (director), Wolfgang Sawallisch (conductor, Bavarian State Opera Orchestra and Chorus), Unitel (production).

Cast: Catarina Ligendza (Senta), Donald McIntyre (Dutchman), Bengt Rundgren (Daland), Ruth Hesse (Mary), Hermann Winkler (Erik).

Telecast April 27, 1975, on ZDF German Television. Shot in 35mm. Color. In German. 118 minutes.

***1984 Bayreuth Festival

German stage production: Harry Kupfer (director), Woldemar Nelsson (conductor, Bayreuth Festival Orchestra and Chorus), Peter Sykora (set designer).

Cast: Lisbeth Balslev (Senta), Simon Estes (Dutchman), Matti Salminen (Daland), Anny Schlemm (Mary), Robert Schunk (Erik), Graham Clark (Steersman).

Video: House of Opera DVD/Philips VHS/LD. Brian Large (director). Color. In German with English subtitles. 136 minutes.

Comment: The story is told from the point of view of Senta in this excellent, thought-provoking, and finely sung production.

1989 Savonlinna Opera Festival

Finnish stage production: Juhani Pirskanen (director), Ilkka Bäckman (producer), Leif Segerstam (conductor, Savonlinna Opera Festival Orchestra and Chorus), Juhani Pirskanen (set/costume designer).

Cast: Hildegard Behrens (Senta), Franz Grundheber (Dutchman), Matti Salminen (Daland), Anita Välkki (Mary), Raimo Sirkiä (Erik), Jorma Silvasti (Steersman).

Video: Teldec VHS/LD. Telecast November 4, 1989. Aarno Cronvall (director). Color. In German with English subtitles. 139 minutes.

Comment: Shot in the open-air courtyard of the 15th-century Olavinlinna Castle in Finland.

1991 Bavarian State Opera

German stage production: Henning von Gierke (director/set designer), Wolfgang Sawallisch (conductor, Bavarian State Opera Orchestra and Chorus).

Cast: Julia Varady (Senta), Robert Hale (Dutchman), Jaako Ryhänen (Daland), Anny Schlemm (Mary), Peter Seiffert (Erik), Ulrich Ress (Steersman).

Video: EMI VHS/LD. Eckhart Schmidt (director). Color. 135 minutes. In German.

Early/related films

1918 Harmonie film

Leo Schützendorf stars as the Dutchman with Olga Desmond as Senta in the German feature film *Der Fliegende Holländer*. Hans Neumann directed for Harmonie Film. Black and white. Silent. About 70 minutes.

1919 Delog film

The German Delog company, which made this silent version of *Der Fliegende Holländer,* had an original answer to the silence of screen opera. They sent the film on tour with the company's own soloists, chorus, and orchestra. Black and white. About 70 minutes.

1923 The Flying Dutchman

This American feature film is based on the Wagner opera, but writer-director Lloyd B. Carleton departs considerably from the libretto. Philip falls asleep reading *The Flying Dutchman* and imagines he is the accursed sailor. He becomes involved with Melissa, who is unable to be faithful, but her sister Zoe redeems him. Lawson Butt is Philip, Nola Luxford is Melissa, and Ella Hall is Zoe. R. C. Pictures/FBO. Black and white. Silent. About 70 minutes.

1950 Pandora and the Flying Dutchman

This Hollywood version of the story is set in Spain with James Mason as the Dutchman and Ava Gardner as the woman who dies to save him from all that traveling. Albert Lewin directed. Color. 123 minutes. Kino DVD and VHS.

2000 Shadow of the Vampire

The Overture to *The Flying Dutchman* is featured in this film about F. W. Murnau (John Malkovich) during the production of *Nosferatu,* the first Dracula movie. Max Schreck (Willem Dafoe) turns out to be a real vampire. E. Elias Merhige directed. Color. 91 minutes.

FLOOD, THE
1962 "musical drama" by Stravinsky

Igor Stravinsky's TV opera *The Flood,* his only work created for television, tells the story of humankind from Adam and Eve to Noah and the Flood with song, dance, mime, narration, and orchestra. CBS asked Stravinsky to compose a work for television, and he decided on a dance/drama about Noah after visiting Venice and seeing its flooded streets (or so he said). Robert Craft based the libretto on the story as told in the Bible and English miracle plays and wrote it for actors and dancers as well as singers. Noah and his wife wear masks, and the animals on the ark are toys. It was premiered on CBS Television on June 14, 1962, and given its stage premiere by Santa Fe Opera on August 21, 1962.

1962 CBS Television

American TV production: Kirk Browning (director), Robert Craft (conductor, Columbia Symphony Orchestra and Chorus), George Balanchine (choreographer), Rouben Ter-Arutunian (set designer).

Actors: Laurence Harvey (Narrator), Sebastian Cabot (Noah), Elsa Lancaster (Noah's wife), Paul Tripp (The Caller).

Singers: Richard Robinson (Lucifer), John Reardon and Robert Oliver (God).

Dancers: Jacques d'Amboise (Adam/Lucifer), Suzanne Farrell (Eve), Edward Villella (Satan), Ramon Segarra (Noah), Joysann Sidimu (Noah's wife), New York City Ballet.

Video at the MTR. Telecast June 14, 1962, on CBS. Kirk Browning (director). Black and white. In English. 23 minutes.

Comment: One of the major events of operatic television, but it has never been released on commercial video.

***1985 Drupsteen video

Dutch TV production: Jaap Drupsteen (director/designer), Robert Craft (conductor, Columbia Symphony Orchestra and Chorus).

Soundtrack voices: Laurence Harvey (Narrator), Sebastian Cabot (Noah), Elsa Lancaster (Noah's wife), Paul Tripp (The Caller), Richard Robinson (Lucifer), John Reardon and Robert Oliver (God).

Actors: Julian Beusker (Adam), Silvia Millecam (Eve), Pauline Daniels (Lucifer), Rudi Van Vlaanderen (Noah), Kitty Courbois (Noah's wife), Rudolf Grasman, Emile Linssen and Carel Willink (God), Fried Keesttulst (Noah's Son), Liesbeth Coops and Annet Malherbe (Wives).

Video: Kultur/Home Vision VHS. Color. In English. 23 minutes.

Comment: This inventive production uses the original CBS soundtrack as the basis of a new video production featuring amazing electronic wizardry. The imagery is stunning and completely different from the original; the nudity of Adam and Eve is an indication of the changing times.

FLÓREZ, JUAN DIEGO
Peruvian tenor (1973–)

Juan Diego Flórez, one of the most highly acclaimed new tenors, made his breakthrough when he took over the tenor role in Rossini's *Matilde de Shabran* at Pesaro in 1996. It was his professional debut after studies at the Curtiz Institute in Philadelphia. He sang at La Scala the same year, then at Covent Garden, Paris, and Vienna, reaching the Met in 2002 as Almaviva in *Il barbiere di Siviglia*. He has become one of the leading interpreters of *bel canto* roles and can be seen on DVD as Ramiro in Rossini's LA CENERENTOLA at Covent Garden in 2000 and as Fenton in FALSTAFF at Busseto in 2001.

FLOTOW, FRIEDRICH VON
German composer (1812–1883)

Friedrich von Flotow composed a large number of operas in the 19th century but is known today for only one, the 1847 MARTHA. At the turn of the century *Martha* was an opera house regular and a great favorite of Caruso. Its tenor aria "Ach so fromm" remains popular, especially when sung in Italian as "M'apparì," but the opera itself is currently out of fashion in the English-speaking world. All the videos are in German. There is also still interest in Flotow's 1844 "serious" opera *Alessandro Stradella* and his 1859 operetta *La veuve Grapin.*

FLOYD, CARLISLE
American composer (1926–)

Carlisle Floyd has been one of the most popular American opera composers for half a century, and his works are continually staged. Like Gian Carlo Menotti, he writes his own librettos and is loved by producers and audiences who aren't concerned about his critical neglect. SU-SANNAH (1956), his most popular opera, is a modern version of the biblical story of Susannah and the Elders. Its seamless combination of folk idiom and classical opera style has helped it become one of the most performed American operas. Floyd wrote his first opera, *Slow Dusk,* in 1949, followed by *The Fugitives* in 1951. The third was *Susannah,* which made his reputation. *Wuthering Heights,* based on the Emily Brontë novel, was produced in 1958, followed by *The Passion of Jonathan Wade* in 1962. The comic opera THE SOJOURNER AND MOLLIE SINCLAIR, about Scottish settlers and patriotism, was created for South Carolina television in 1963. It was followed by *Markheim* in 1966, the popular *Of Mice and Men* in 1970, and *Bilby's Doll* in 1976. WILLIE STARK, based on Robert Penn Warren's novel *All the King's Men,* was premiered in Houston in 1981 to great acclaim and was televised nationally. *Cold Sassy Tree,* based on Olive Ann Burns's novel, premiered in 2000.

FLYING DUTCHMAN, THE
See FLIEGENDE HOLLÄNDER, DER.

FOCILE, NUCCIA
Italian soprano (1961–)

Sicilian Nuccia Focile is one of the rising stars of the international opera world, with an agile voice and fine acting ability. She first won attention for her comic roles, with particular success as Nannetta in *Falstaff* in Cardiff in 1988. She has also been acclaimed for her portrayals of Violetta and Tatyana and for her Ascanio in the Neapolitan rarity LO FRATE 'NNAMORATO. She sang in concert with Luciano Pavarotti in 1993 and made her Met debut as Mimi in *La bohème* in 1995. See UN BALLO IN MASCHERA (1987), L'ITALIANA IN ALGERI (1987), and PLATÉE (1986).

FOLLIE PER L'OPERA
1948 Italian film with opera content

Follie per l'opera (Mad About Opera) is a romantic opera film about the Italian community in London that organizes a concert with Italian opera stars to raise funds to rebuild a Soho church. Gina Lollobrigida and Carlo Campanini are the concert organizers, and the singers who appear in concert are Tito Gobbi, Beniamino Gigli, Gino Bechi, Tito Schipa, and Maria Caniglia. Mario Costa directed, Mario Monicelli and Steno wrote the screenplay, and Mario Bava was cinematographer. Black and white. In Italian. 95 minutes. Bel Canto Society/House of Opera/Premiere Opera VHS.

1950 Soho Conspiracy
The English film *Soho Conspiracy* is a cut-price remake of *Follie per l'opera* with a different cast but the same plot and the same opera singers as guest stars; their scenes are simply lifted from the earlier film. Jacques Lebreque and Zena Marshall are the concert organizers here, with Cecil H. Williamson as director. Black and white. In English. 85 minutes.

FOLLOW YOUR HEART
1936 American film with operatic content

Republic Pictures, the studio best known for Gene Autry cowboy films and thrill-a-minute serials, was a new studio in 1936 and needed a prestige picture to establish itself as something more than just a B-picture film factory. This was the time of the Grace Moore opera film boom in Hollywood so opera seemed the hot ticket, but there weren't many unsigned big-name singers around. Studio chief Herbert J. Yates and producer Nat Levine recalled the publicity around Marion Talley's Met debut and thought they could garner prestige with a relatively high-budget opera film. And so the bizarre *Follow Your Heart* was born. Talley plays a soprano with an eccentric Kentucky farm family. When Uncle Tony (Luis Alberni at his most frenzied) brings his down-on-its luck opera company to the old homestead, she ends up as the star of an operetta composed by tenor Michael Bartlett. This is truly a down-home opera film for the folks, written tongue-in-cheek by top writers Nathaniel West, Lester Cole, and Samuel Ornitz. Talley is introduced singing her first aria lying on a cellar floor poking a furnace. She sings the Page aria from *Les Huguenots* in a haymow accompanied by a phonograph and teams with Bartlett on the Raoul/Valentine duet "Tu l'as dit" from the same opera. The *Lucia di Lammermoor* sextet is turned into a comedy number with Bartlett singing to a baked ham while baritone Luis Alberni addresses a haddock. Talley sings rather splendidly despite all this, especially the selection from Thomas's *Mignon*, the opera that had made her famous years before. Hugo Riesenfeld devised the music settings, Clarence Music led the Hall Johnson Choir, and Harry Grey was music supervisor. John Mescall and Allyn C. Jones were cinematographers and Aubrey Scotto directed. Black and white. 82 minutes. Opera Dubs VHS.

FORFAITURE
1921 screen opera by Erlanger

Camille Erlanger's opera *Forfaiture,* the first to be based on a motion picture scenario, used as source material the 1915 Paramount movie *The Cheat.* The film, directed by Cecil B. De Mille, tells of the relationship between a rich Japanese man (Sessue Hayakawa) and a woman in desperate need of money (Fannie Ward). Erlanger (1863–1919) is best known for a 1906 opera called *Aphrodite,* which was introduced by Mary Garden. He saw the De Mille picture in Paris in 1916 and was so impressed he obtained permission to make it into an opera. Hector Turnbull and Jeanie Macpherson wrote the screenplay, which was refashioned into a libretto by P. Milliet and A. De Lorde. The opera was staged at the Opéra-Comique in Paris in 1921, two years after Erlanger's death, but was performed only three times. There do not appear to be any recordings.

FORGET-ME-NOT
1935 film with opera content

BENIAMINO GIGLI plays a famous opera singer who marries a much younger woman (Joan Gardner) rebounding from a failed love affair. She is tempted to leave Gigli when she meets her former love a few years later, but she stays true. Gigli is shown on an operatic world tour that allows him to sing arias from *Rigoletto* ("La donna è mo-

bile"), *Martha* ("M'appari"), *L'Africana* ("O paradiso"), and *L'elisir d'amore* ("Una furtiva lagrima"), and there is also music from *Carmen, Faust, La favorita, Lohengrin, Mignon,* and *Il trovatore.* This was Gigli's first feature film, and it was made in English, Italian, and German versions to reach the widest possible audience. It takes its title from its theme song "Non ti scordar di me" (Forget-Met-Not) written by Ernesto De Curtis. Gigli sings it a number of times in the film, and it has remained popular in Italy; Pavarotti featured it in the Los Angeles *Three Tenors* concert. The other cast members include Hugh Wakefield as Gigli's manager, Ivan Brandt as the former lover, and Jeanne Stuart as a troublemaking friend. Zoltan Korda directed the English version; screenplay by Hugh Gray and Arthur Wimperis, with cinematography by Hans Schneeberg. It premiered in England in March 1936 and came to America in 1937, retitled *Forever Yours.* Augusto Genina directed the Italian and German versions titled *Non ti scordar di me* and *Vergiss mein nicht,* respectively, with slightly different casts. Black and white. In English. 72 minutes. Bel Canto Society VHS/HBO LD.

Forget-Me-Not (1935): Beniamino Gigli on stage as Pagliacci in a film about an opera singer with love problems.

FORMAN, MILOS
Czech-born U.S. film director (1932–)

The first movie that Milos Forman saw was a silent version of Smetana's opera *The Bartered Bride.* That was in 1937 in Czechoslovakia and it made a lasting impression. Forman won acclaim in the late 1960s for the Czech new wave films *Loves of a Blonde* and *The Fireman's Ball,* but he moved to the United States in 1969 after the USSR invaded Czechoslovakia. His American movies include the Oscar-winning *One Flew Over the Cuckoo's Nest.* In 1984 he returned to Czechoslovakia to make AMADEUS, a brilliant biographical tribute to Mozart who premiered two of his operas in Prague. See also THE DANGEROUS LIAISONS (1989 film).

FORRESTER, MAUREEN
Canadian contralto (1930–)

Maureen Forrester, noted for her witty characterizations as well as for her splendid voice, sang mainly in concert in the early part of her career but turned to opera in 1962. Her success was rapid and she was soon invited to sing on the stages of most of the major opera houses of the world, including the Met and La Scala. She can be seen in a number of videos of televised screen operas, including a 1975 Canadian version of Menotti's THE MEDIUM with Forrester as Madame Flora. See CENDRILLON (1979), DIALOGUES DES CARMÉLITES (1987), HANSEL AND GRETEL (1970), and IOLANTHE (1984).

1982 Portrait of Maureen Forrester
Auréle Lecoste directed this portrait of Forrester for a Canadian TV program. She talks about her life and career and sings arias by Offenbach, Dvořák, Ponchielli, and Gershwin. John Newmark accompanies her on piano. Color. In English. 60 minutes.

FÖRSTER-CHRISTL, DIE
1907 operetta by Jarno

Hungarian composer GEORG JARNO's *Die Förster-Christl* (The Forester's Daughter) is his most popular operetta and has been filmed a number of times. Gerhard Buchbinder's libretto tells the tuneful and bittersweet story of an tentative romance between Christl, the beautiful daughter of a forester, and Austrian Emperor Josef II. She has gone to see him in Vienna to plead for the life of her soldier lover. Romantic sparks fly, but he dutifully sends her home. The operetta was staged in New York as *The Girl and the Kaiser*.

1931 Zelnick film
German feature film: Friedrich Zelnick (director), Alfred Frank and Bruno Granischstaedten (screenplay), Mutz Greenbaum and Akos Farkas (cinematographers), Walter Sieber (music director), Transocean Film (production).

Cast: Irene Eisinger (Christl), Paul Richter (Kaiser Josef), Oskar Karlweiss (Mozart), Fritz Daghofer (Christl's father), André Pilot (Corporal Franzl).

Black and white. In German. 90 minutes.

Comment: This was Zelnick's second film of the operetta (he made a silent version in 1925), and it includes many added songs based on music by Mozart. Eisinger, an opera star in Berlin when the film was made, was Jewish and had to leave Germany in 1933, but she became an even bigger star at Glyndebourne, especially in Mozart operas. The film was shown in the United States in 1931.

1952 Rabenalt film
German feature film: Arthur Maria Rabenalt (director); Fritz Boettger, Joachim Wedekind, and Friedl Behn-Grund (cinematographers); Bruno Uher (music director); Carlton Film (production).

Cast: Johanna Matz (Christl), Karl Schönbock (Kaiser Josef), Angelika Hauff (Ilona), Will Quadflieg (Joseph), Ivan Petrovich (Count), Jochen Hauer (Forester), Oskar Sima (Leisinger).

Black and white. In German. 95 minutes.

1962 Gottlieb film
German feature film: Franz-Josef Gottlieb (director), Franz Grothe (music director), Dieter Wedekind (cinematographer), Janne Furch and Fritz Böttger (screenplay), Carlton Film (production).

Cast: Sabine Sinjen (Christl), Peter Weck, Sieghardt Rupp.

Black and white. In German. 96 minutes.

Early film

1925 Zelnick film
Friedrich Zelnick's first film of the operetta was silent but it was shown in cinemas with live music. He tried again in 1931 with sound. William Dieterle, who later became an American film director, is one of the stars along with Harry Liedtke and Eduard von Winterstein. Black and white. About 75 minutes.

FOR THE FIRST TIME
1959 American film with opera content

In Mario Lanza's last film, he is typecast as a temperamental opera singer who is always missing performances and behaving badly until he meets a deaf girl in Capri (Johanna von Koszian) who reforms him. There is plenty of opera music (including *Così fan tutte*) and a grand tour of European opera houses. He is seen in the rain outside the Rome Opera House singing arias from *Rigoletto* and on stage in costume in *Pagliacci* ("Vesti la giubba"), *Otello* (final scene), and *Aida;* his screen career closes ironically with the Triumphal March from *Aida*. George Stoll was music director and Rudolph Maté directed for Corona film. Color. 97 minutes. MGM-UA VHS.

FORTUNE TELLER, THE
1898 operetta by Herbert

VICTOR HERBERT's operetta *The Fortune Teller,* which revolves around a gypsy fortune teller, is naturally filled with tuneful Hungarian gypsy music. Harry B. Smith's libretto tells the story of rich heiress Irma and gypsy fortune teller Elvira, who looks just like her. Both roles were created on stage by Alice Nielsen in a production that also featured opera singer Marguerita Sylva. The operetta is still being staged; there was a recent off-Broadway production by Light Opera of Manhattan.

1934 La Buenaventura

American feature film: William McGann (director), Warner Bros. (production).

Cast: Enrico Caruso Jr. (Enrico Baroni), Anita Campillo (Irma/Elvira), Luis Alberni (Fresco), Alfonso Pedroza (Sandor).

Black and white. In Spanish. 77 minutes.

Comment: Spanish-language adaptation of the operetta made by Warner Bros. in Los Angeles. It includes most of Herbert's songs, with new lyrics, plus arias from the operas *Don Pasquale*, *L'elisir d'amore*, and *L'Africana*.

FORZA DEL DESTINO, LA

1862 opera by Verdi

One of the more overheated plots in all opera. Don Alvaro accidentally shoots Donna Leonora's father, who has caught them trying to elope. Her brother Don Carlo swears revenge, so the lovers have to separate. Leonora becomes a hermit with the help of Father Guardiano, while Alvaro becomes a monk in a nearby monastery. Don Carlo finds him and is killed in a resultant duel, but manages to stab his sister before dying. Alvaro retreats into prayer. GIUSEPPE VERDI's melodramatic opera *La forza del destino* (The Force of Destiny), libretto by Francesco Maria Piave based on a Spanish play and set in 18th-century Spain, was commissioned by the Imperial Theatre of St. Petersburg where it was premiered in 1862. There is a video of a production at the same theater using the same sets and score.

1949 Gallone film

Italian feature film: Carmine Gallone (director), Gabriele Santini (conductor, Rome Opera House Orchestra and Chorus), Mario Corsi, Ottavio Poggi and Lionello De Felice (screenplay), Aldo Giordani (cinematographer).

Cast: Nelly Corradi (Leonora, sung by Caterina Mancini), Gino Sinimberghi (Don Alvaro, sung by Galliano Masini), Tito Gobbi (Don Carlo), Mira Vargas (Preziosilla, sung by Cloe Elmo), Giulio Neri (Padre Guardiano), Vito de Taranto (Fra Melitone).

Video: Bel Canto Society (USA)/Pickwick (GB)/Multimedia (Italy) VHS. Black and white. In Italian. 110 minutes.

Comment: Gobbi was 36 when he starred in this abridged film version of the opera shot in natural settings near Rome; most of the other actors are dubbed by notable opera singers.

1952 Opera Cameos

American TV production of abridged Act II: Carlo Vinti (director), Giuseppe Bamboschek (conductor), Joseph Vinti (screenplay), Hugh LaRue (narrator).

Cast: Rina Telli (Leonora), Lloyd Harris (Don Carlo), Nicola Moscona (Padre Guardiano).

Telecast live November 16, 1952, on WPIX, New York. Black and white. In Italian. 30 minutes.

***1958 Teatro di San Carlo

Italian stage production: Francesco Molinari-Pradelli (conductor, Teatro di San Carlo Orchestra and Chorus).

Cast: Renata Tebaldi (Leonora), Franco Corelli (Don Alvaro), Ettore Bastianini (Don Carlo), Boris Christoff (Padre Guardiano), Oralia Dominguez (Preziosilla), Renato Capecchi (Fra Melitone).

Video: Hardy Classics DVD/Bel Canto Society VHS. Telecast March 15, 1958, by RAI. Black and white. In Italian. 156 minutes.

Comment: Historic performance in Naples with an all-star cast. Picture quality of the RAI archival copy is poor, but the sound is wonderful and the singers are magnificent. On the DVD, Tebaldi is interviewed about her role in the opera.

1978 Teatro alla Scala

Italian stage production: Giovanni Foiani (director), Giuseppe Patanè (conductor, Teatro alla Scala Opera Orchestra and Chorus).

Cast: Montserrat Caballé (Leonora), José Carreras (Don Alvaro), Piero Cappuccilli (Don Carlo), Nicolai Ghiaurov (Padre Guardiano), Maria Luisa Nave (Preziosilla), Sesto Bruscantini (Melitone).

Video: House of Opera/Lyric VHS. Telecast in the United States in 1980: Color. In Italian with English subtitles. 155 minutes.

1984 Metropolitan Opera

American stage production: John Dexter (director), James Levine (conductor, Metropolitan Opera Orchestra and Chorus), Eugene Berman (set designer).

Cast: Leontyne Price (Leonora), Giuseppe Giacomini (Don Alvaro), Leo Nucci (Don Carlo), Isola Jones (Preziosilla), Bonaldo Giaiotti (Padre Guardiano), Enrico Fissore (Fra Melitone).

Video: Pioneer Classics DVD/LD and Bel Canto Paramount VHS. Taped March 24, 1984; telecast October 31, 1984. Kirk Browning (director). Color. In Italian with English subtitles. 179 minutes.

1996 Metropolitan Opera

American stage production: Giancarlo Del Monaco (director), James Levine (conductor, Metropolitan Opera Orchestra and Chorus), Michael Scott (set/costume designer).

Cast: Sharon Sweet (Leonora), Plácido Domingo (Don Alvaro), Vladimir Chernov (Don Carlo), Gloria Scalchi (Preziosilla), Robert Scandiuzzi (Padre Guardiano), Bruno Pola (Fra Melitone).

Telecast September 11, 1996; taped March 12, 1996. Brian Large (director). Color. In Italian with English subtitles. 180 minutes.

1998 Kirov Opera

Russian stage production: Elijah Moshinsky (director), Valery Gergiev (conductor, Kirov Opera Orchestra and Chorus), Andrei Voitenko (set reconstruction).

Cast: Galina Gorchakova (Leonora), Gegam Grigorian (Don Alvaro), Nikolai Putilin (Don Carlo), Sergei Alexashkin (Padre Guardiano), Marianna Tarasova (Preziosilla), Georgy Zastavny (Fra Melitone).

Video: Kultur and Arthaus DVD/Kultur and Bel Canto Society VHS. Taped at Maryinsky Theatre, St. Petersburg, in July 1998; telecast in the United States June 28, 2000. Brian Large (director). Color. In Italian with English subtitles. 160 minutes.

Comment: Produced at the theater where the opera premiered. The original St. Petersburg score was used, and the sets are based on the original designs.

Early/related films

1911 Film d'Arte Italiana film

This Italian adaptation of *La forza del destino* stars Aurelia Cattaneo as Leonora, Achille Vitti as Don Alvaro, Ignazio Mascalchi as Don Carlo, and Paolo Cantininelli as the Marquis. It was produced by the Societa Italiana per Film d'Arte in Rome and exceptionally well reviewed. Black and white. Silent. About 20 minutes.

1911 Pathé film

French Pathé film version of the opera titled *La force du destin*. Critics praised it for being a good screen adaptation. Black and white. Silent. About 14 minutes.

1948 Up in Central Park

Deanna Durbin sings "Pace, pace, mio dio" from *La forza del destino* in this film of Sigmund Romberg's New York operetta. She plays the daughter of a Tweed crony in love with reporter Dick Haymes. William Seiter directed. Black and white. 88 minutes.

1976 Glanzmann film

The animated film *La forza del destino* was created by Hans Glanzmann at the London International Film School. It tells the tragic destiny of a man seduced by a woman. Color. 3 minutes.

1983 E la nave va

A luxury liner full of opera people sailing from Naples in 1914 is sunk by a battleship while the overture from *La forza del destino* is played. Federico Fellini directed. See E LA NAVE VA.

1986 Jean de Florette/Manon of the Spring

The overture of *La forza del destino* is used effectively in these French films that tell a harsh story about the force of destiny. They were directed by Claude Berri and based on a novel by Marcel Pagnol. Color. In French. 122 and 113 minutes.

1987 Aria

Charles Sturridge directed a lyrical black-and-white *La forza del destino* episode of the anthology film ARIA. It shows children Nicola Swain, Jack Kyle, and Marianne McLoughlin in church, stealing a car, and learning about violence. They seem to need the protection asked for in "La vergine degli Angeli," sung by Leontyne Price as Leonora. Thomas Schippers conducts the RCA Italiana Orchestra. Color. In Italian. 10 minutes.

1988 Making Opera

This Canadian documentary, subtitled "The Creation of Verdi's *La forza del destino*," revolves around a production of the opera by the Canadian Opera Company. It follows the preparations of the 500 people involved with the opera and shows how it looked when it was staged and telecast in Canada in August 1988. John Copley is stage director; the cast includes Stefka Evstatieva (Leonora), Ernesto Veronelli (Don Alvaro), Allan Monk (Don Carlo), and Judith Forst (Preziosilla) Maurizio Arena conducts, Anthony Azzopardi directed the film, and Ron Stannett was the cinematographer. Color. In English. 88 minutes. VIEW VHS.

1994 Desperate Remedies

The music of *La forza del destino* is central to this rather bizarre New Zealand film about a 19th-century woman (Jennifer Ward-Lealand) and her odd relationships. The film opens with her cracking her whip to the overture and includes a moment of understanding set to the aria "Pace, pace, mio dio," sung by Carvel Carroll. Peter Scholes arranged and conducted the music, and Peter Wells and Stewart Main directed the film. Color. 101 minutes.

1999 Being John Malkovich

The aria "Pace, pace, mio dio," sung by Eva Urbanova with Prague Symphony Orchestra, is played by puppeteer John Cusack to accompany street performance of Abelard and Heloise story in this surrealistic film. The plot revolves around idea that people can live inside actor John Malkovich's head for 15-minute periods. Spike Jonze directed. Color. 112 minutes

FOSS, LUKAS
German-born U.S. composer (1922–)

Pianist-conductor-composer Lukas Foss has composed three very enjoyable and still popular operas. *The Jumping Frog of Calaveras County* (1949) is based on the famous Mark Twain story and has entered the small theater repertory. The whimsical *Introductions and Good-byes* (1960), created for the Spoleto Festival, is also still staged. Foss's best-known opera is the devilish folktale GRIFFELKIN, which he composed for NBC Opera Theatre. It premiered on television in 1955 but has been staged three times since, the last an excellent 1993 New York City Opera production.

FOSTER, SUSANNA
American soprano (1924–)

Susanna Foster was gifted with an extraordinary voice; although she never appeared on the opera stage except in movies, she did become a star on the operetta stage. Foster was signed for a film by MGM at the age of 11 as a child prodigy who could sing F above high C. She and her family moved to Hollywood in 1935, but the film that was to have been called *B Above High C* was never made and she returned to voice lessons. She was then signed by Paramount, which featured her in four films, starting with *The Great Victor Herbert* in 1939. After that she went to Universal for eight more pictures, including her best movie, the 1943 THE PHANTOM OF THE OPERA and the Boris Karloff thriller THE CLIMAX. In 1948 she quit filmmaking and appeared in a West Coast production of the operetta *Naughty Marietta*. She later joined the Cleveland Light Opera Company and toured in *The Merry Widow*. In 1955 she sang in *Brigadoon* and *Show Boat*. See also VICTOR HERBERT (1939).

1941 There's Magic in Music
Foster plays burlesque singer Toodles LaVerne who is taken by Allan Jones to a summer music camp where she meets Met stars Richard Bonelli and Irra Petina and is transmuted into on opera singer. She performs arias from *Carmen, Faust,* and Meyerbeer's *Dinorah* ("Shadow Song") plus a *Carmen-Faust* medley with new lyrics by Edwin Lester. Andrew L. Stone directed. Also known as *The Hard-Boiled Canary*. Paramount. Black and white. 80 minutes.

1941 Glamour Boy
Foster is the girl whom Jackie Cooper loves in this story about a grown-up child star hired to coach a kid in a remake of his old success *Skippy*. She sings "Sempre libera" from *La traviata* and two songs. Ralph Murphy directed. Paramount. Black and white. 79 minutes.

1942 Star Spangled Rhythm
Foster is one of many guests in this all-star Paramount extravaganza featuring every star on the lot in a show for the navy. It was her last film for the studio. George Marshall directed. Black and white. 99 minutes.

1943 Top Man
Foster appears opposite Donald O'Connor in this putting-on-a-show musical with silent movie diva Lillian Gish as her mother. Foster's hit song in the film is "Wrap Your Troubles in Dreams." Charles Lamont directed for Universal. Black and white. 74 minutes.

1944 The Climax
Foster upsets Boris Karloff when she sings arias from the imaginary opera *The Magic Voice* in this thriller. Karloff plays a doctor who years before killed a singer who sang the same opera. See THE CLIMAX.

1944 Bowery to Broadway
Jack Oakie and Donald Cook have rival beer gardens in old New York. Foster is one of the Universal stars who sings for them when they join forces to produce musicals. Charles Lamont directed. Black and white. 94 minutes.

1944 Follow the Boys
Foster has a cameo role as herself in this all-star Universal musical with Orson Welles, Jeanette MacDonald, et al. Edward Sutherland directed. Black and white. 122 minutes.

1944 This Is the Life
Foster is a singer, the fickle girlfriend of Donald O'Connor, but she really fancies an older man, Patrick Knowles. She sings some popular songs, including "With a Song in My Heart." Felix Feist directed. Universal. Black and white. 87 minutes.

1945 Frisco Sal
A Western mystery film but Foster still gets to sing. She plays a woman who goes West to find the man who killed her brother. George Waggner directed for Universal. Black and white. 94 minutes.

1945 That Night With You

Foster's last film was a kind of musical screwball comedy that featured her singing a feminine version of *The Barber of Seville* and not liking either the idea or the make-up. She plays a singer who becomes a Broadway success. William A. Seiter directed for Universal. Black and white. 84 minutes.

FOUR NOTE OPERA, THE
1972 opera by Johnson

Tom Johnson says his minimalist postmodern *The Four Note Opera,* which uses only the notes A, B, D, and E, was influenced by Pirandello's *Six Characters in Search of an Author.* The libretto, by Johnson and Robert Kushner, has the singers describe the music they sing. Like Pirandello's characters, the singers are aware they are performers and their destiny is to be obedient to the score. After it was telecast by CBS, Netherlands Opera mounted its European premiere.

1972 CBS Television Camera Three

American TV production: Ivan Cury (director), Erick Steinman (conductor/pianist).

Cast: Julie Kennedy (soprano), Martha Novick (contralto), Roger Owens Childs (tenor), William Barone (baritone), Giuseppe Garofalo (bass).

Telecast on *Camera Three* on CBS Television. Color. In English. 30 minutes.

FOUR SAINTS IN THREE ACTS
1934 opera by Thomson

Virgil Thomson's opera *Four Saints in Three Acts* shocked America when it premiered in Hartford in 1934. It had no discernible plot, was too playful to be serious, and had black Americans portraying white saints in 16th-century Spain. Gertrude Stein's libretto became infamous and the aria "Pigeons on the grass alas" a catchphrase for humorists. In other words, *Saints* broke the boundaries of what American opera dared to be, and its influence is still noticeable. It is often considered the true beginning of modern American opera. It is also quite a lot of fun, with excellent music and grand words.

1934 Hartford premiere

Thomson's friend Julien Levy filmed scenes of the 1934 premiere in Hartford with a 16mm camera. They show key moments in the opera, including St. Ignatius's "Pigeons on the grass alas" aria and finale, and give a good impression of the style of the "cellophane" production. John Huszar includes three minutes of Levy's film in his fine documentary *Virgil Thomson at 90.* Thomson discusses the opera and sings an aria, which is then performed (rather better) by Betty Allen. Telecast November 30, 1986, on PBS. Color. 60 minutes. FilmAmerica VHS.

1970 Thomson rehearsing Saints

Thomson plays piano and rehearses Edward J. Pierson in the "Pigeons on the grass alas" aria, then Pierson joins Claudia Lindsey and Betty Allen in singing excerpts from the opera. The scenes are in Perry Miller Adato's 1970 documentary *Gertrude Stein: When This You See, Remember Me.* Thomson was filmed at Stein's country house in France talking about the opera. "When this you see, remember me" is sung by the chorus in the final scene of *Four Saints.* Color. 89 minutes. Meridian VHS.

FOURTH TENOR, THE
2002 American film with opera content

The Fourth Tenor is an operatic comedy starring Rodney Dangerfield as Lupo, a New York restaurant owner who wants to become an opera singer. He has fallen in love with Gina (Annabelle Gurwitch), one of the singing waitresses in his restaurant, but she says she can love only a man who sings opera. He goes to Rome to study with crooked voice coach Vincenzo (Richard Libertini) and is nearly chased out of Italy after his horrible stage debut. He is saved by opera star Rosa (Anita De Simone), whose wine-making family has a secret wine that can turn anyone into a rival for Pavarotti. Lupo returns to New York to impress Gina with his new voice but then discovers he really loves Rosa. Unfortunately, she is about to marry another man (Vincent Schiavelli). *The Fourth Tenor* is pleasant, unassuming hokum that opera lovers will enjoy as it never takes itself seriously. Dangerfield wrote the script with director Harry Basil, basing it partly on his own early experiences as a singing waiter. Ken Blakey was the cinematographer and Dawn Soler was the music supervisor. Universal Studios. Color. 97 minutes.

FRA DIAVOLO
1830 opera by Auber

DANIEL AUBER's most famous comic opera, *Fra Diavolo* (Brother Devil), is based on legends about a Robin Hood–type bandit in southern Italy who was hanged by Napoleon. In Eugène Scribe's libretto he is not very altruistic and seems mostly just interested in robbing. He disguises himself as a marquis and goes to a tavern where he plans to rob an English lord and lady. Lorenzo dreams of capturing the bandit and claiming a reward so he can marry Zerlina, the innkeeper's daughter. *Fra Diavolo* was one of the most popular operas of the 19th century and has been filmed and telecast several times.

1930 Bonnard film

Feature film: Mario Bonnard (director, screenplay with Nunzio Malasomma and Hedy Knorr), Giuseppe Becce (music director), Nicolas Farkas (cinematographer).

Cast, French and Italian versions: Tino Pattiera (Fra Diavolo), Madeleine Breville (Anita), Armand Bernard (Scaramanzia), Alex Bernard (Marquis).

Cast, German version: Tino Pattiera (Fra Diavolo), Brigitte Horney (Anita), Kurt Lilien, Heinrich Heilinger.

Black and white. In French, German, or Italian. 90 minutes.

Comment: This was the first full-length opera adapted for the screen with sound and photographed as a movie rather than a stage production. The dialogue is spoken and the action is of the swashbuckling type. Bonnard made French, Italian, and German versions with Pattiera as Diavolo in all three. He was a Croatian tenor who sang in Chicago in the early 1920s, and he is the only opera singer in the film except for the chorus. The Italian version was released in the United States in 1931.

1933 The Devil's Brother

American feature film: Hal Roach (director), Jeanie MacPherson (screenplay), Art Lloyd and Hap Depew (cinematographers), MGM (production).

Cast: Dennis King (Fra Diavolo), Stan Laurel (Stanlio), Oliver Hardy (Ollio), Lucille Brown (Zerlina), Thelma Todd (Lady Pamela), Arthur Pierson (Lorenzo).

Video: MGM/UA VHS/LD. Black and white. In English. 88 minutes.

Comment: Bonnard's film was the model for this Laurel and Hardy film also known as *Fra Diavolo*. King is the only singer in the film, and there is not a lot of opera left in it, although this is one of the more amusing Laurel and Hardy sound films.

1948 First Opera Film Festival

Italian stage production: Enrico Fulchigoni (director), Angelo Questa (conductor, Rome Opera House Orchestra and Chorus), George Richfield (producer).

Cast: Nino Adami (Fra Diavolo), Palmira Vitali-Marina (Lady Pamela), Luciano Neroni (Giacomo), Gino Conti (Matteo), Giacinto Prandelli, Magda Laszlo (Zerlina).

Video: Bel Canto Society/Lyric VHS. Edmondo Cancellieri (film director). Black and white. In Italian with English voice-over by Olin Downes. 25 minutes.

Comment: Highlights version of the opera sung in Italian and filmed on stage at the Rome Opera House with singers from La Scala and Rome. Made for the anthology film *First Opera Film Festival*.

Early/related films

1906 Messter film

This German *Fra Diavolo* was shot in 1906 with opera singers Hedwig Francillo-Kaufmann and Albert Kutzner seen on screen singing. It was filmed and recorded by Oskar Messter for his Biophon-Theater in Berlin. The music was played on a phonograph synchronized with the movie. Black and white. In German. About 3 minutes.

1909 Capellani film

This *Fra Diavolo* is a French film of the story directed by Albert Capellani for Pathé and starring Jean Angelo and Germaine Rouer. Black and white. Silent. About 10 minutes.

1912 Solax film

This *Fra Diavolo* is an American feature-length adaptation of the opera made by the first woman film director, Alice Guy-Blaché, for her Solax company. Billy Quirk is Fra Diavolo, Blanche Cornwall is Zerlina, George Paxton is Lord Allcash, Fanny Simpson is Lady Allcash, and Darwin Karr is Lorenzo. It was warmly received by contemporary critics, who felt it augured well for the future of opera on the screen. Black and white. Silent. About 45 minutes.

1913 Ambrosio film

Italian narrative film based on the story of Fra Diavolo and produced by the Ambrosio company. Black and white. Silent. About 20 minutes.

1915 Éclair film

French narrative film based on the story of Fra Diavolo and made for the Éclair company. Black and white. Silent. About 30 minutes.

1922 Tense Moments From Opera

Gordon Hopkirk is Fra Diavolo in this British highlights version made for the series *Tense Moments From Opera*. Vivian Gibson is Zerlina, Lionel Howard is Lorenzo, and Amy Willard is Lady Allcash. Challis Sanderson directed for Master film. Black and white. Silent. About 12 minutes.

1924 Zeppieri film

Emilio Zeppieri directed a feature-length sound version of *Fra Diavolo* with opera singers. Their voices were recorded and the film was screened with synchronized music using the Zeppieri Fotocinema system. Apparently it didn't work very well as it was pulled from circulation after the first few screenings. Bosia film. Black and white. In Italian. About 70 minutes.

1925 Roberti/Gargiulo film

This *Fra Diavolo* tells the story of the bandit Michel Pezza on whom the Fra Diavolo legend is based but it is not the opera. Gustavo Serena stars as Diavolo; Roberto Roberti and Mario Gargiulo wrote and directed. About 75 minutes.

1938 Marionette

Beniamino Gigli sings an aria from *Fra Diavolo* in this Italian film about a famous tenor who performs with a marionette show. See MARIONETTE.

1942 Zampa film

Enzo Fiermonte plays Diavolo in this *Fra Diavolo* based on a play rather than the opera. The story is about the same. Luigi Zampa directed. Black and white. In Italian. 90 minutes.

1952 Donne e Briganti

Amedeo Nazzari plays Diavolo in *Women and Bandits*, an Italian film of the story directed by Mario Soldati. Black and white. In Italian. 88 minutes.

1962 I Tromboni di Fra Diavolo

Francisco Rabal stars as Fra Diavolo in *The Trombones of Fra Diavolo*, an Italian film directed by Giorgio C. Simonelli. It uses music from the opera as its soundtrack. Color. In Italian. 90 minutes.

1962 La Leggenda di Fra Diavolo

Tony Russell plays Fra Diavolo in *The Legend of Fra Diavolo*, an Italian film about the legendary bandit directed by Leopold Savona. Color. In Italian. 90 minutes.

FRANCESCA DA RIMINI

1914 opera by Zandonai

The tragic story of the 13th-century Italian lovers Paolo and Francesca, which has similarities to the Tristan and Isolde legend, originated in Dante's *Inferno* and has inspired more than 30 operas. The best known is RICCARDO ZANDONAI's 1914 version *Francesca da Rimini*, composed to a libretto by Tito Ricordi and based on a play written by Gabriele D'Annunzio for Eleanora Duse. Paolo is sent by his brother Giociotti to bring back bride-to-be Francesca. They fall in love, are eventually found out by the brother, and are killed. The opera was produced at the Metropolitan Opera in 1916 soon after its premiere in Milan and was revived in 1984. The popular story inspired many early films that have no direct connection with the opera, but two of them were based on the D'Annunzio source play.

***1984 Metropolitan Opera

American stage production: Piero Faggioni (director), James Levine (conductor, Metropolitan Opera Orchestra and Chorus), Ezio Frigerio (set designer).

Cast: Renata Scotto (Francesca), Plácido Domingo (Paolo), Cornell MacNeil (Gianciotto), William Lewis (Malatestino), Isola Jones (Smadragdi), Richard Fredericks (Francesca's brother).

Video: Pioneer Classics DVD and LD/Paramount VHS. Taped April 7, 1984; telecast January 30, 1985. Brian Large (director). Color. In Italian with English subtitles. 148 minutes.

Comment: Outstanding production that has stood the test of time.

Early/related films

1908 Vitagraph film

The American film *Francesca da Rimini*, based on the D'Annunzio play, was produced by the Vitagraph studio with Florence Turner (Francesca), Paul Panzer, and Edith Storey. J. Stuart Blackton directed. Black and white. Silent. About 10 minutes.

1908 Comerio film

The Italian film *Francesca da Rimini*, based on the D'Annunzio play, was produced by the Comerio studio of Milan in February 1908. Mario Morais directed. Black and white. Silent. About 10 minutes.

1910 Film d'Arte Italiana

Francesca Bertini stars in this Italian *Francesca da Rimini* directed by Ugo Falena for the Film d'Arte Italiana studio and based on the D'Annunzio play. Francesco Di Gennaro, Stanislao Ciarli and Gustavo Conforti lend support. Black and white. Silent. About 10 minutes.

1910 Pathé film

The French film *Francesca da Rimini*, based on the D'Annunzio play, was produced by the Pathé studio with Jeanne Delvair (Francesca), Jacques Gretillat, and Paul Capellani. Albert Capellani directed. Black and white. Silent. About 10 minutes.

1912 Vitagraph film

Florence Turner reprises her role as Francesca in this second Vitagraph *Francesca da Rimini*, based on the D'Annunzio play. William Raymond and Hector Dean have the other main roles. J. Stuart Blackton directed. Black and white. Silent. About 15 minutes.

FRASER-SIMSON, HAROLD
British composer (1872–1944)

Harold Fraser-Simson is best known for the hugely popular comic opera THE MAID OF THE MOUNTAINS; it had 1,352 consecutive performances in London during the 1910s and was the must-see operetta for World War I soldiers. Joan Sutherland featured its best-known aria, "Love Will Find a Way," on her *Golden Age of Operetta* album. Before *Maid,* Fraser-Simpson wrote the 1911 comic opera *Bonita,* but it was considered old-fashioned even in its time. After the long run of *Maid,* he wrote two more operettas for its star José Collins. His biggest later success was a musical version of Kenneth Grahame's children's classic *Toad of Toad Hall* as dramatized by A. A. Milne.

FRASQUITA
1922 operetta by Lehár

FRANZ LEHÁR's *Frasquita* is the story of a gypsy woman and her protracted love-hate relationship with a man called Armand. He starts off planning to marry Dolly, but he gives her up to his friend Hippolyt when he finds that he actually prefers Frasquita. Richard Tauber played Armand when the operetta premiered in Vienna in 1922. It came to London in 1925 but didn't make it to New York until 1953. Several notable opera sopranos have found the role of Frasquita to their liking, including Conchita Supervia, Jarmila Novotná, and Ilona Massey.

1934 Lamac film
Austrian feature film: Carl Lamac (director), Franz Lehár (conductor, Vienna Philharmonic), George C. Klaren (screenplay), Eduard Hoesch (cinematographer), Atlantis Film (production).

Cast: Jarmila Novotná, (Frasquita), Hans Heinz Bollmann (Armand), Heinz Ruhmann (Hippolyt), Charlotte Dauder (Dolly), Hans Moser (Jaromir).

Black and white. In German. 82 minutes.

FRATE 'NNAMORATO, LO
1731 comic opera by Pergolesi

GIOVANNI PERGOLESI is best known for his delightful intermezzo LA SERVA PADRONA, but his full-scale comic opera *Lo frate 'nnamorato* (The Beloved Brother) was his first success. The dialogue is in Neapolitan dialect, and this apparently prevented the opera from being widely known in other Italian cities. The complicated libretto by Gennaro Antonio Federico (who wrote *La serva padrona*) tells the story of the Neapolitan twin sisters Nina and Nena. They think they love Ascanio, but he turns out to be their long-lost brother. He is the ward of rich Marcaniello, who has designs on the sisters, while his daughter Lucrezia fancies Ascanio. The La Scala revival production of the opera is on CD and video.

1990 Teatro alla Scala
Italian stage production: Robert De Simone (director), Riccardo Muti (conductor, Teatro alla Scala Orchestra and Chorus), Mauro Carosi (set designer).

Cast: Amelia Felle (Nena), Bernadette Manca Di Nissa (Nina), Nuccia Focile (Ascanio), Alessandro Corbelli (Marcaniello), Luciana D'Intino (Lucrezia), Ezio Di Cesare (Carlo), Elizabeth Norberg-Schulz (Vanella), Nicoletta Curiel (Cardella), Bruno De Simone (Don Pietro).

Video: Image Entertainment DVD/Home Vision VHS. John Phillip (director). Color. In Italian with English subtitles. 132 minutes.

Comment: This major rediscovery was arranged by Muti and De Simone at La Scala and most expertly and authentically produced.

FRAU, DIE WEISS, WAS SIE WILL, EINE
1932 operetta by Straus

Oscar Straus's operetta *Eine Frau, die weiss, was sie will* (A Woman Who Knows What She Wants) was written for aging operetta diva Fritzi Massary, who starred in the Berlin premiere. She played Manon, an aging singing musical actress somewhat like herself. Her illegitimate daughter Vera, who does not know about their relationship, has fallen in love with a man who prefers her mother. Mother agrees to give him up. Alfred Grünwald wrote the bittersweet libretto. The operetta went to London in 1933 as *Mother of Pearl* by A. P. Herbert with Alice Delysia as star. It has been filmed twice.

1934 Binovec film
Czechoslovak feature film: Václav Binovec (director), Vilem Werner and Jaroslav Mottle (screenplay), Jan Stallich and Otto Heller (cinematographers), Slavia Film (production)

Cast: Markéta Krausová (Manon), Jiri Steimar (Rón), Truda Grosslichtová (Vera), Frantisek Paul (Veverka).

Black and white. In Czech. 82 minutes.

Comment: Shot and set in Prague with a somewhat altered plot, but the mother-daughter relationship is similar.

1934 Janson film
German feature film: Viktor Janson (director), Peter Francke and Ernst Hasselbach (screenplay), Eduard Hoesch and Jan Stallich (cinematographers), Werne Schmidt-Boelcke (music director).

Cast: Lil Dagover (Manon), Anton Edthofer, Maria Beling, Hans Junkermann, Kurt Bespermann.

Hunnia Film. Black and white. In German. 82 minutes.

Comment: Shot in Prague at the same time as the Czech version.

1957 Rabenalt film

German feature film: Arthur Maria Rabenalt (director).

Cast: Lilli Palmer (Angela/Julia), Maria Sebaldt, Peter Schütte.

Bavaria Film. Color. In German. 101 minutes.

Comment: In this rewritten and somewhat surrealistic version, Palmer plays both the singing star and her virtuous granddaughter.

FRAU IM HERMELIN, DIE
1919 operetta by Gilbert

German composer JEAN GILBERT's tuneful operetta *De Frau im Hermelin* (The Woman in Ermine) is set in a castle near Verona in 1810 during the Russian invasion. The castle has been taken over by a colonel and his regiment, and the countess has to fend off his advances and save her husband from being shot. The "woman in ermine" of the title is a ghost who defends the castle during times of peril. Rudolf Schanzer and Ernest Welisch wrote the libretto. This was Gilbert's most Lehár-like operetta and was staged in London in 1921 as *The Lady of the Rose* with Phyllis Dare as its star. It reached New York in 1922 as *The Lady in Ermine* with lyrics by Lorenz Hart.

1930 Bride of the Regiment

American feature film: John Francis Dillon (director); Humphrey Pearson (screenplay); Al Dubin, Al Bryan, Eddie Ward (songs); First National (production).

Cast: Vivienne Segal (Countess Anna-Marie), Walter Pidgeon (Colonel Vultow), Alan Prior (Count Adrian Beltrami), Myrna Loy (Sophie).

Black and white. In English. 80 minutes.

Comment: Most of Gilbert's music is replaced with new songs. In Australia the film was called *The Lady of the Rose*.

1949 That Lady in Ermine

American feature film: Ernst Lubitsch and Otto Preminger (directors), Samson Raphaelson (screenplay), Leon Shamroy (cinematographer), Leo Robin and Frederick Hollander (songs), Twentieth Century–Fox (production).

Cast: Betty Grable (Francesca/Angelina), Douglas Fairbanks Jr. (Colonel/Duke), Cesar Romero (Mario), Walter Abel (Major Horvath).

Color. In English. 89 minutes.

Comment: Lubitsch died during filming so Preminger completed the movie. The actors play double roles with parallel stories in the 19th and 16th centuries. Most of Gilbert's music was again replaced with songs.

Early film

1927 First National film

Silent screen diva Corinne Griffith stars as the resourceful woman with an ermine weapon in *The Lady in Ermine,* a feature version of the operetta directed by James Flood for First National Pictures. Francis X. Bushman is the invading general and Eoinar Hasen is her husband. The film was shown in cinemas with Gilbert's music played live. Black and white. Silent. About 70 minutes.

FRAU LUNA
1899 operetta by Lincke

Frau Luna (Lady Moon) is PAUL LINCKE's most popular operetta and has become symbolic of Berlin, especially since his Berlin theme tune "Berliner Luft" was incorporated into it. The operetta originated as an 1899 fantasy about a group of Berliners visiting the moon via balloon, where they meet Frau Luna, the lady-in-the-moon. It's an Offenbach-type burlesque, and many of Lincke's other songs have been added to it over the years. The songs remain popular, and the operetta is still being staged and telecast in Germany today. It was produced in London in 1911 as *Castles in the Air.*

1941 Lingen film

German feature film: Theo Lingen (director), Ernst Marischka (screenplay), Ekkehard Kyrath (cinematographer) Majestic Film (production).

Cast: Lizzi Waldmuller, Fita Benkhoff, Irene von Meyendorff, Georg Alexander, Theo Lingen.

Black and white. In German. 96 minutes.

Comment: The story is changed considerably but the songs are retained; it is now a backstage romance set in 1899 during the opening run of *Frau Luna* on stage in Berlin.

1976 ZDF German Television

German television film: Eugen York (director), Werner Schmidt-Boelcke (conductor, Bavarian Radio-Television Orchestra).

Cast: Ingeborg Hallstein (Frau Luna), Willi Brokmeier (Prince Sternschnuppe), Beate Granzow (Stella), Harald Juhnke (Theophil), Edith Hancke (Frau Pusebach), Stefan Behrens (Steppke).

Telecast January 1, 1976, on ZDF German Television. Color. In German. 90 minutes.

FRAU OHNE SCHATTEN, DIE
1919 opera by Richard Strauss

RICHARD STRAUSS's *Die Frau ohne Schatten* (The Woman Without a Shadow) is a "magic fairy tale," a highly symbolic opera with an original libretto by HUGO VON HOFMANNSTHAL. The empress, daughter of the King of the Spirits, is without a shadow, a sign of her childlessness. She must find one to keep the emperor from being turned to stone, so she makes a bargain to buy the shadow of the wife of the dyer Barak. In the end she decides not to take the other woman's shadow when she finds the harm this action will cause. Her humanity results in happiness all around.

***1980 Opéra de Paris
French stage production: Nikolaus Lehnhoff (director), Christoph von Dohnányi (conductor, Orchestre du Theatre National de l'Opéra de Paris).

Cast: Gwyneth Jones (Empress), Hildegarde Behrens (Dyer's Wife), René Kollo (Emperor), Walter Berry (Dyer), Mignon Dunn, Hélène Garetti, Eliane Lublin, Annick Dutertre.

Video: House of Opera DVD/VHS. Telecast November 21, 1980, on TF1 French Television. Yves-André Hubert (director). Color. In German. 183 minutes.

Comment: This is considered one of the finest ever productions of the opera.

1992 Salzburg Festival
Austrian stage production: Götz Friedrich (director), Sir Georg Solti (conductor, Vienna Philharmonic and Vienna State Opera Chorus), Rolfe Glittenberg (set designer).

Cast: Cheryl Studer (Empress), Eva Marton (Dyer's Wife), Thomas Moser (Emperor), Robert Hale (Dyer), Marjana Lipovsek (Nurse), Bryn Terfel (Spirit-Messenger).

Video: Decca/London DVD/VHS/LD. Brian Large (director). Color. In German with English subtitles. 203 minutes.

Comment: Studer is in terrific form, but the production is somewhat minimalist.

FREGOLI, LEOPOLDO
Italian filmmaker (1867–1936)

Italian stage performer Leopoldo Fregoli, promoted as the "Protean Artiste" in England, is considered the first Italian film director. He was a quick-change illusionist who transformed himself into famous people, including composers Rossini and Verdi conducting their operas. Fregoli saw the first Lumière films in 1896, constructed what he called a "Fregoligraphe" shortly afterwards, and made 25 short films in 1897. These were screened at stage performances when he would stand behind the screen and sing or talk in synchronization with the moving pictures.

1898 Maestri di musica
Fregoli's famous film of great opera composers, *Maestros of Music*, is one of the first opera films and survives in an Italian film archive. Illusionist Fregoli is seen on screen as Rossini, Verdi, Mascagni, and Wagner conducting their own operas as the music of each composer is played live. In England the film was titled *Fregoli the Protean Artiste* and distributed by film pioneer R. W. Paul. Black and white. Silent. About 6 minutes.

1981 Fregoli
Luigi Proietti plays Fregoli in this Italian television film about the illusionist director. It shows his rise in the world of theater and his discovery of his ability to transform himself. He travels to Paris where he makes his entry into the world of cinema through collaboration with the film pioneer Lumière brothers. Lucia Drudi Demby, Robert Lerici, and director Paolo Cavara wrote the screenplay. The film was telecast in Italy on RAI Television in four parts in April and May 1981. Color. In Italian. 240 minutes.

FREISCHÜTZ, DER
1821 opera by Weber

Die Freischütz (The Freeshooter) is CARL MARIA VON WEBER's best-known opera. Max has to win a shooting contest if he is to marry Agathe. At midnight in the Wolf's Glen he obtains seven magic bullets from the evil spirit Samiel. In the competition, the seventh bullet will be controlled by Samiel and aimed at Agathe. A holy hermit intervenes, however, and the bullet kills the villainous huntsman Kaspar instead. Friedrich Kind's libretto is based on a tale from the *Gespensterbuch* by Johann Apel and Friedrich Laun. The Wolf's Glen scene became one of the central images of 19th-century German romanticism.

1968 Hamburg State Opera
German television film: Joachim Hess (director), Rolf Liebermann (producer), Leopold Ludwig (conductor, Hamburg State Opera Orchestra and Chorus), Hannes Schindler (cinematographer), Polyphon Film (production).

Cast: Ernst Kozub (Max), Arlene Saunders (Agathe), Tom Krause (Ottokar), Edith Mathis (Aennchen), Bernard Minetti (Samiel), Gottlob Frick (Kaspar), Hans Sotin (Hermit).

Color. In German. 127 minutes.

Comment: This TV film based on a Hamburg State Opera stage production was released theatrically in both the United States and Germany.

1981 Wurttemberg State Opera

German stage production: Achim Freyer (director/set designer), Dennis Russell Davies (conductor, Wurttemberg State Opera Orchestra and Chorus), Hans Joachim-Haas (lighting).

Cast: Toni Krämer (Max), Catarina Ligendza (Agathe), Raili Viljakainen (Aennchen), Wolfram Raub (Samiel), Wolfgang Schöne (Ottokar), Wolfgang Probst (Caspar).

Video: Home Vision VHS. Hartmut Schottler (director). Color. In German with English subtitles. 150 minutes.

Comment: Mysterious and intriguing production with impressive sets, nightmarish lighting, and excellent singing.

1985 Dresden Semper Opera

German stage production: Joachim Herz (director), Wolf-Dieter Hauschild (conductor, Dresden State Opera Chorus and Orchestra).

Cast: Reiner Goldberg (Max), Jana Smitkova (Agathe), Andrea Ihle (Aennchen), Hans-Joachim Ketelsen (Ottokar), Ekkehard Wlaschiha (Caspar), Theo Adam (Hermit).

Video: Dreamlife (Japan) LD. Color. In German. 148 minutes.

Comment: *Der Freischütz* was the signature opera of Dresden's Semper Opera House and was chosen to re-open the rebuilt theater on February 13, 1985.

1999 Hamburg State Opera

German stage production: Peter Konwitschny (director), Ingo Metsmacher (conductor, Hamburg Philharmonic Orchestra), Gabriele Koerbl (set/costume designer).

Cast: Poul Elming (Max), Charlotte Margiono (Agathe), Wolfgang Rauch (Ottokar), Jörg-Michael Koerb (Samiel), Albert Dohmen (Caspar), Sabine Ritterbusch (Aennchen), Dieter Weller (Cuno), Simon Yang (Hermit).

Video: House of Opera (USA)/Arthaus (GB) DVD. Felix Breisach (director). Color. In German with English subtitles. 160 minutes.

Early/related films

1908 Messter film

Henny Porten, Germany's first important film star, plays Agathe in this Messter Biophone sound film based on a recording of an aria from the opera. Porten's father Franz, a former opera singer, directed the film in a Berlin studio. Black and white. In German. About 3 minutes.

1917 Deutsche Lichtspielopern film

A feature-length film of *Die Freischütz* was made in Germany in 1917 by Deutsche Lichtspielopern Gesellschaft GmbH, a company founded in 1915 to produce German film operas. Screenings were accompanied by music and singing. Black and white. Silent. About 70 minutes.

1954 Konsul Strotthoff

Der Freischütz excerpts are featured in the German film *Konsul Strotthoff* set in Salzburg. They counterpoint a love triangle story revolving around a singer studying at the Salzburg Mozarteum. Erich Engel directed. The film was released in America as *Melody Beyond Love*. Black and white. In German. 103 minutes.

1967 Five Girls to Deal With

Evald Schorm's Czech film *Pet Holek na Krku* (Five Girls to Deal With) revolves around performances of *Der Freischütz* staged by a repertory company in the city of Liberec. The girls attend every night because they are infatuated with the tenor; the romanticism of the opera is counterpointed with the girls' romantic behavior. Black and white. In Czech. 100 minutes.

1994 Enyedi film

Hungarian filmmaker Ildiko Enyedi, who won an Oscar nomination for *My 20th Century,* based her narrative film *Der Freischütz* on the Weber opera but updated it to Budapest in the 1990s. Max is a policeman married to Eva. He makes a pact with the Devil who gives him six bullets that never miss. Gary Kemp is Max, Sadie Frost is Eva, and Alexander Kajdanovski is the Devil. Released in the United States as *Magic Hunter*. Color and black and white. In Hungarian and German. 110 minutes.

1999 24 Hours in London

Agathe's cavatina "Und ob die Wolke" is heard on the soundtrack of this British gangster film about a turf war started by an American woman. Alexander Finbow directed. Color. 95 minutes.

2000 Little Otik

The Overture to *Der Freischütz* is featured on the soundtrack of this Czech fantasy about a baby who is carved out of a tree stump and comes alive. Jan Svankmejer directed. Color. In Czech. 131 minutes.

FRENI, MIRELLA
Italian soprano (1935–)

Mirella Freni, who sang at the Metropolitan Opera for seven seasons between 1966 and 1985, began her career in Italy but has sung in most major opera houses. She is often identified by moviegoers with *Madama Butterfly* as she starred in Jean Pierre Ponnelle's 1974 film version and her recordings of the opera were featured in the films *Fatal Attraction* and *M. Butterfly*. She can be seen in many videos of operas, including ADRIANA LECOUVREUR at La Scala in 1989, LA BOHÈME in a 1965 Franco Zeffirelli production and at San Francisco Opera in 1989, CARMEN in Salzburg in 1967, DON CARLO at the Met in 1983, ERNANI at La Scala in 1982, EUGENE ONEGIN at Chicago in 1985, FALSTAFF at the Met in 1992, FAUST in Paris (1975) and Chicago (1988), and especially in FEDORA at La Scala (1993), a role she reprised at the Met in 1998. Her other screen operas include MANON LESCAUT (1990), LE NOZZE DI FIGARO (1976), OTELLO (1974), SIMON BOCCANEGRA (1978), and LA TRAVIATA (1975). She appeared in METROPOLITAN OPERA telecasts in 1983, 1986, and 1991 and with her Bulgarian basso husband NICOLAI GHIAUROV in his 1986 video biography.

1985 Freni and Siepi Concert
Freni joins basso Cesare Siepi in an Italian concert of favorite arias. The program includes selections from *Don Carlo, Gianni Schicchi, Mefistofele, Philemon et Baucis, Simon Boccanegra,* and *Tosca.* Bruno Amaducci conducts. Color. 48 minutes. Bel Canto Society VHS.

FRICK, GOTTLOB
German bass (1906–1994)

Gottlob Frick, one of the great basses of the century, recorded a wide range of operas but is usually thought of as one of the masters of Wagner. He began to sing professionally in Germany in 1927 and was a regular at Covent Garden from 1957 to 1967. He left only a small legacy of film performances. He can be seen as Hagen in a film about the recording of DER RING DES NIBELUNGEN in 1965 and as Kaspar in a 1968 film of DER FREISCHÜTZ. In his other two films, DON GIOVANNI (1954) and the biopic *The Life and Loves of Mozart* (1955), he's simply a memorable voice on the soundtrack.

FRIEDERIKE
1928 operetta by Lehár

Richard Tauber played the great German writer Goethe in the Berlin premiere of the bittersweet FRANZ LEHÁR operetta *Friederike*. Friederike is his first love, a young woman who loves him as much as he loves her. She realizes, however, that unless she gives him up, he will never leave the village and become what he is destined to be. She makes him believe that she no longer cares, so he leaves for Weimar. When he returns years later, he discovers the truth but it is too late. Its most famous aria is Friederike's question, "Warum hast du mich wachgeküsst?"(Why did you kiss my heart awake?) The operetta was staged in New York in 1937 as *Frederika*.

1932 Friedmann-Frederich film
German feature film: Fritz Friedmann-Frederich (director/screenplay), Werner Brandes and Werner Bohne (cinematographers), Indra Film (production).

Cast: Mady Christians (Friederike), Hans Heinz Bollmann (Goethe), Veit Harlan (Duke of Weinmar), Ida Wüst (Magdalena).

Black and white. In German. 90 minutes.

FRIML, RUDOLF
Czech-born U.S. composer (1879–1972)

Rudolf Friml created a style of music so uniquely recognizable as his own that musical satirist Tom Lehrer could write a lyric describing a tune as "quite Rudolph Frimly." One of the last major American composers of European-style operettas, he began his career in his native Prague but moved to New York in 1904. In 1912 Victor Herbert quarreled with Emma Trentini, so Friml was asked to create a new operetta for her. He composed THE FIREFLY, and it launched him on a long career in music theater. Friml had major success with European-style operettas such as ROSE-MARIE (1924) and THE VAGABOND KING (1925), but he was less successful with American-style musicals such as *Cinders*. His 1927 operetta *The White Eagle* is based on the same play as Cecil B. De Mille's 1913 debut film *The Squaw Man*. As European operettas became outmoded, Friml switched to Hollywood work and composed music for films ranging from Jeanette MacDonald's 1930 operetta THE LOTTERY BRIDE to NELSON EDDY's 1947 Western *Northwest Outpost*.

FROM THE HOUSE OF THE DEAD
1930 opera by Janáček

LEOŠ JANÁČEK's powerful opera *From the House of the Dead* (Z Mrtvého Domu) is an adaptation of Dostoevsky's autobiographical 1862 novel *Memoirs From the House of the Dead*. Set in a prison camp in Siberia, it begins with a prisoner being flogged. Despite the grimness of the story, the opera is considered exhilarating and uplifting. For many in Czechoslovakia, it was a prophetic opera about the Communist future.

1969 NET Opera

American TV production: Kirk Browning (director), Peter Herman Adler (producer/conductor, Boston Symphony Orchestra), Francis Mahard (set designer).

Cast: Robert Rounseville (Gorjanchikov), John Reardon (Siskov), David Lloyd (Skuratov), Harry Danner (Alyosha), Frederick Jagel (Luka).

Telecast December 2, 1969, on PBS. Kirk Browning (director). Black and white. In English. 90 minutes.

Comment: Adler added flashbacks to this expressionistic English-language TV version of the opera. This was its American premiere.

1992 Salzburg Festival

Austrian stage production: Klaus Michael Gruber (director), Claudio Abbado (conductor, Vienna Philharmonic Orchestra and Vienna State Opera Chorus), Eduardo Arroyo (set/costume designer).

Cast: Nicolai Ghiaurov (Gorjanchikov), Philip Langridge (Skuratov), Monte Pederson (Siskov), Barry McCauley (Luka), Heinz Zednik (Shapkin), Elzbieta Szymtka (Alyeya).

Video: DG VHS. Brian Large (director). Color. In Czech with English subtitles. 93 minutes.

FRÜHJAHRSPARADE

1934/1954 operetta by Stolz

A young Hungarian woman travels from a country village to Emperor Franz Josef's Vienna where, of course, she finds true love. ROBERT STOLZ's operetta *Frühjahrsparade* (Spring Parade) was originally a 1934 Hungarian film operetta with a screenplay by Ernst Marischka. The film was remade twice (once in Hollywood) before it was turned into a stage opera and presented at the Vienna Volksoper on March 25, 1954.

1934 Bolvary film

Hungarian feature film: Geza von Bolvary (director), Ernst Marischka (screenplay), Joseph Pasternak (producer).

Cast: Franziska Gaal, Paul Hörbiger, Theo Lingen, Annie Rosar.

Black and white. In Hungarian or German. 97 minutes.

Comment: The film, shot in Vienna, won the Best Musical award at the 1934 Venice Film Festival.

1940 Spring Parade

American feature film: Henry Koster (director), Bruce Manning and Felix Jackson (screenplay, based on Ernst Marischka's screenplay), Joe Valentine (cinematographer), Charles Previn (music director), Joe Pasternak (producer), Universal Studios (production).

Cast: Deanna Durbin (Ilonka Tolnay), Robert Cummings (Harry Marten), Mischa Auer (Gustav), Henry Stephenson (Emperor).

Video: Universal VHS. Black and white. In English. 89 minutes.

Comment: Pasternak had produced the original film version in Vienna. Stolz, who was living in Hollywood at this time, provided new songs, including the Oscar nominee "Waltzing in the Clouds."

1955 Ein Deutschmeister

Austrian feature film: Ernst Marischka (director and screenplay).

Cast: Romy Schneider, Paul Hörbiger, Hans Moser, Magda Schneider.

Color. In German. 92 minutes.

Comment: Marischka had written the screenplay for the original movie.

FULL CIRCLE

1968 opera by Orr

Scottish composer Robin Orr (1909–) wrote the one-act opera *Full Circle* for Scottish Opera as a companion to Stravinsky's *L'Histoire du Soldat* and scored it for the same instruments. The libretto, by Sydney Goodsir Smith, is in Clydeside dialect and tells the story of an unemployed man during the Depression. He is driven to steal and is arrested for killing a policeman.

1968 Scottish Opera

Scottish stage production: Bryan Izzard (director), Alexander Gibson (conductor, Scottish Opera Chamber Orchestra).

Cast: William Elvin (David McGee), Sheila McGrow (Jean McGee), John Robertson.

Video: Copy at the NFTA in London. Telecast October 8, 1968. Ian Watt-Smith (director). Color. In English. 47 minutes.

FURTWÄNGLER, WILHELM

German conductor (1886–1954)

Wilhelm Furtwängler was admired for his ability as a conductor, but he remains controversial for his political attitudes because he stayed in Germany during the Nazi era. He is featured in two videos about CONDUCTORS, *Great Conductors of the Third Reich* and *The Art of Conducting: Great Conductors of the Past.* The only film with him conducting a complete opera is the 1954 DON GIOVANNI shot in Salzburg.

G

GAÁL, ISTVÁN
Hungarian film director (1933–)

István Gaál began directing short films in 1957 and acquired an international reputation in 1970 with his feature *The Falcons.* His film of Gluck's opera ORFEO ED EURIDICE, which premiered at the Venice Film Festival in 1985, was shot in natural settings but retained its quality of a mythological dream.

GALLANTRY
1958 opera by Moore

This parody of a TV soap opera is a tangled tale of romantic involvements and satiric commercials. Dr. Gregg flirts with Nurse Lola who is engaged to Donald who arrives on a stretcher and asks about the doctor's wife. Douglas Moore's 35-minute opera *Gallantry,* libretto by Arnold Sundgaard, premiered at Columbia University in 1958. Critics thought it was jazzy and tuneful, and it has become popular with small opera companies.

1962 CBS Television

American TV production: Martin Carr (director), Alfredo Antonini (conductor, CBS Symphony Orchestra).

Cast: Ronald Holgate (Dr. Gregg), Laurel Hurley (Nurse Lola), Charles Anthony (Donald), Martha Wright (narrator/commercials performer).

Video: Live Opera VHS. Telecast August 8, 1962. Black and white. In English. 35 minutes.

Comment: Jan Peerce introduced the opera in a TV program titled *Arias and Arabesques.*

GALLONE, CARMINE
Italian film director (1886–1973)

Carmine Gallone, who specialized in opera films, probably made more films in the genre than any other theatrical filmmaker. He started making movies in 1913 and was an active filmmaker until the 1960s. The public and often the Italian critics usually liked his films, but he has not gained an international reputation or following. He was one of the inventors of the "parallel" opera film, in which a modern story parallels the plot of the opera, notably IL SOGNO DI BUTTERFLY (1939), AMAMI, ALFREDO! (1940), and HER WONDERFUL LIE (1947). His films may not be to everyone's taste, but they are made with an understanding of both cinema and opera. Most are superior to their Hollywood operatic equivalents, and as a group they provide a wide-ranging portrait of Italian opera and its singers. They include LA BOHÈME (1947 film), CARMEN (1962 film), CAVALLERIA RUSTICANA (1953), FAUST (1949), LA FORZA DEL DESTINO (1949), MADAMA BUTTERFLY (1955), MANON LESCAUT (1940 film), RIGOLETTO (1947), TOSCA (1946 film/1956), LA TRAVIATA (1947), and IL TROVATORE (1949). *Casa Ricordi,* a history of Italian opera through the story of the RICORDI publishing firm, is his epic achievement. His other operatic biographical films were about BELLINI (1935/1954), MOZART (1940), PUCCINI (1952), and VERDI (1938), and he directed films starring MARIA CEBOTARI (1942), BENIAMINO GIGLI (1937/1938/1950), and JAN KIEPURA (1930/1934/1936).

GALUPPI, BALDASSARE
Italian composer (1706–1785)

Baldassare Galuppi was an important figure in 18th-century Italian opera, no surprise, as he composed more than 100 operas. He was a notable *opera seria* composer, but he was also one of the creators of the comic opera. His collaboration with Venetian playwright Carlo Goldoni marked a major advancement in the development of *opera buffa.* The most successful of their operas was IL FILOSOFO DI CAMPAGNA (The Country Philosopher), first staged in 1756 and telecast in America in 1960.

GANCE, ABEL
French film director (1889–1981)

French film genius Abel Gance, known to the wider public for his epic 1927 film *Napoleon,* was involved with a number of films of operatic interest during his long career. The most important is LOUISE, a 1938 film based on the opera by Gustave Charpentier and starring Grace Moore. Also of note are his 1934 *La dame aux camélias* starring YVONNE PRINTEMPS, with music by Reynaldo Hahn; and his 1936 biography *Un grand amour de Beethoven,* starring Harry Baur as BEETHOVEN.

GANNE, LOUIS
French composer (1862–1923)

Louis Ganne began writing operettas in 1893 and had his first real success with the 1899 opéra-comique LES SALTIMBANQUES, helped by its colorful circus setting. It is still his best-known stage work, and it has remained a favorite in France. Ganne was also a noted conductor and was especially popular for his concerts at the Monte Carlo Opera. His operettas *Hans, le joueur de flûte* (1906) and *Rhodope* (1910) were both produced at Monte Carlo before being staged in Paris.

GARDEN, MARY
Scottish-born U.S. soprano (1874–1967)

Mary Garden, who came to live in the United States as a child, made her opera debut in Europe singing the title role of *Louise* in Paris in 1900. Her success in French operas led to Massenet writing *Chérubin* for her in 1905. She made her U.S. debut in 1907 in *Thaïs* at the Manhattan Opera House and was acclaimed as the greatest singing actress in the world. In 1910, she began a 20-year association with the Chicago Grand Opera. Her great rival was Geraldine Farrar, so it was not surprising that she followed Farrar into movies. Garden was hired by the Goldwyn Studio at $10,000 a week for two pictures, beginning with her great New York operatic success. Her personality and acting style did not translate to the screen as had Farrar's, and she did not have an expert director such as Cecil B. De Mille to help her. Her film career ended as quickly as it began.

1917 Thaïs
Garden's first film was intended to be a "picturization" of her opera success so it was obviously not conceived cinematically. Most of the film showed Garden posing in a statuesque opera manner. Audiences, not surprisingly, didn't care for it. The plot is more or less the same as the opera and revolves around the loves of the courtesan Thaïs and the monk who saves her soul (Hamilton Revelle). It was shot at the Goldwyn Studios in Fort Lee, New Jersey, with location scenes in Florida. Frank H. Crane and Hugo Ballin directed. It was publicized as the first film ever shown at the Vatican. Black and white. Silent. About 60 minutes.

1918 The Splendid Singer
Garden's second and last film was a modern story set during World War I. She plays a woman who had once loved a wealthy German but is now married to an American doctor. She ends up on the war front and is shot as a spy by her German lover. Audiences didn't like this film either. Edwin Carewe directed. Black and white. Silent. About 80 minutes.

1953 So This Is Love
Mabel Albertson plays Garden in this glossy film biography of Grace Moore (Kathryn Grayson). Garden is Moore's role model idol who persuades her to go to Europe and train to be opera singer. See SO THIS IS LOVE.

GARDINER, JOHN ELIOT
English conductor (1943–)

John Eliot Gardiner is known for his promotion of early music and period-style performance of operas, especially those of Mozart. He began his career conducting Monteverdi while still at university, and he talks about his interest in conducting on a Monteverdi video (see below). He filmed an excellent series of Mozart operas at the Théâtre du Châtelet in Paris, including DIE ENTFÜHRUNG AUS DEM SERAIL (1991), COSÌ FAN TUTTE (1992), and LE NOZZE DI FIGARO (1993), in addition to DIE ZAUBERFLÖTE (1995) in Amsterdam and the MOZART REQUIEM (1991) in Barcelona. He conducted the music for Jonathan Miller's 1983 film of THE BEGGAR'S OPERA, Barrie Gavin's 1992 film of Britten's WAR REQUIEM, and Tony Palmer's 1995 film about HENRY PURCELL. Robert Altman used his recording of LES BORÉADES for his episode of the 1987 film ARIA. There are videos of his productions of HIPPOLYTE ET ARICIE (1983) at Aix-en-Provence, L'ÉTOILE (1986) and PELLÉAS ET MÉLISANDE (1987) in Lyons, MANON LESCAUT (1998) at Glyndebourne, and ORFEO ED EURIDICE (1999) and ALCESTE (1999) at the Théâtre du Châtelet.

1989 Vespro della Beata Vergine
Gardiner travels around Venice talking about MONTEVERDI's life as a composer and how his own interest in conducting was inspired by his love of Monteverdi. Afterwards he leads a performance of the *Vespers of the Blessed Virgin* in St. Mark's Basilica. Color. In English and Latin. 111 minutes. Archiv VHS.

GARGIULO, MARIO
Italian film director (1895–?)

Mario Gargiulo was a workhorse director of the early Italian cinema and filmed a number of opera story adaptations from 1916 to 1926, mostly for Flegrea Film. They included two versions of CAVALLERIA RUSTICANA (1916, 1926), FAUST (1918), FRA DIAVOLO (1925), MANON LESCAUT (1918), and MIGNON (1921). Sicilian silent film diva Tina Xeo starred in four of them.

GARLAND, JUDY
American musical entertainer (1922–1969)

Judy Garland is one of the great American singers but she didn't do much to further the cause of opera in her films. As she tells us in *Babes in Arms,* "If I sang a duet from an opera, Mr. Verdi would turn over in his grave." In fact, she represented the jazzy opposite end of the musical spectrum in three films. She sang "hot" against classical opponents and seemed to enjoy poking fun at the operatic manner.

1936 Every Sunday
Garland is matched again the operatic Deanna Durbin in this MGM short, her first film. She and Durbin both sing

to help save their town's park concerts. Judy is hot and jazzy while Deanna sings the classical "Il Bacio." Black and white. 20 minutes.

1939 Babes in Arms
Garland partners with Betty Jaynes in the "Opera vs. Jazz" section of this memorable musical. Roger Edens created the words and most of the music for a five-part number about twin sisters with different musical tastes. Judy swings a jazzy *Barber of Seville* number while Betty has to sing the sextet from *Lucia di Lammermoor* all by herself. It's very clever, but opera comes out a poor second. Black and white. 96 minutes.

1943 Presenting Lily Mars
Hungarian opera soprano Marta Eggerth is Garland's rival in this MGM musical about a girl with theatrical ambitions. Eggerth sings well in her European manner, but Garland parodies her accent and singing style in a funny if rather unkind scene. Norman Taurog directed. Color. 104 minutes.

1946 Till the Clouds Roll By
MGM biography of Jerome Kern with highlights of his career and a potted version of *Show Boat*. Garland sings some of his songs. Richard Whorf directed. Color. 137 minutes

1948 Words and Music
MGM biography of Richard Rodgers and Lorenz Hart with Garland singing two of their songs. Norman Taurog directed. Color. 119 minutes.

GARRETT, LESLEY
English soprano (1955–)

Lesley Garrett is one of England's most popular sopranos and her albums, such as *A Soprano in Red,* have become best-sellers. She made her debut in 1980 at the English National Opera and has sung in modern and classic operas at Wales, Wexford, Glyndebourne, and other venues. She can be seen in a number of opera videos, including ARIODANTE (1996), BORIS GODUNOV (1993), THE MIKADO (1987), SERSE (1988), and STREET SCENE (1992).

1998 Lesley Garrett Tonight
Six BBC TV programs featuring Garrett with singing and dancing colleagues. In the first program, Bryan Terfel and Garrett perform numbers from *Porgy and Bess,* and Michael Ball teams up with her on the Papagana-Papagena duet from *The Magic Flute*. In the second, blind tenor Andrea Bocelli joins her in excerpts from *La bohème* and *Carmen*. Peter Robinson conducts the BBC

Concert Orchestra; Mike Leggott directed. Color. In English. Each 60 minutes.

GASDIA, CECILIA
Italian soprano (1960–)

Verona-born Cecilia Gasdia, who began her career as Giulietta in *I Capuleti e i Montecchi* in Florence in 1981, has become known for her *bel canto* roles and coloratura technique. She sang in most major European opera houses before coming to the Metropolitan in 1986 as Juliet in Gounod's *Roméo et Juliette*. She has recorded a wide range of Italian operas by Rossini, Verdi, Donizetti, and Puccini and can be seen on a number of opera videos, including BENVENUTO CELLINI (1987), LA DONNA DEL LAGO (1990), GIANNI SCHICCHI (1983), MAOMETTO II (1986), MOÏSE ET PHARAON (1984), THE RAKE'S PROGRESS (1982), TURANDOT (1983), IL VIAGGIO A REIMS (1988), and ZELMIRA (1989). She can be seen in concert with other SOPRANOS at 1991 concerts in Venice and Caracalla and in a 1985 film about the VERDI REQUIEM.

2000 Cenacolo Concert
Gasdia and Pietro Ballo are the star performers at a Cenacolo (The Last Supper) Concert held at the Santa Maria delle Grazia Basilica in Milan, the location of the famous Leonardo da Vinci painting. The concert, arranged for the 2000 Jubilee celebrations, features Gasdia singing music by Handel, Verdi, Mozart, and Vivaldi with Donato Renzetti conducting the Orchestra I Pomeriggio Musicali. Carlo Di Palmo was the cinematographer, and Enrico Castiglione directed. Color. In Italian. 70 minutes. Trinidad Entertainment DVD.

GASPARIAN, GOHAR
Armenian soprano (1922–)

Coloratura soprano Gohar Gasparian, one of Armenia's most famous opera singers, was born in the Armenian colony in Cairo where she made her debut. She moved to Soviet Armenia in 1948 where she became the principal soprano of the Spendiarian Opera and Ballet Company in 1949. She has sung around the world, including England and America, and portrayed the heroines of most of the Armenian operas, but she also sings Russian, Italian, and French opera. She has been an instructor at the Komitas Conservatory in Yerevan.

1971 Gohar Gasparian
Gohar Gasparian, a Soviet-Armenian film produced by Grigory Melik-Avakyan as a showcase for the soprano, consists of 11 scenes, each with a different aria. Two are from famous Armenian operas: Anoush's final aria from Armen Tigranian's 1912 *Anoush* and an aria from Tigran

Tchukhatjian's 1868 *Arshak II.* The others are the Mad Scene from *Lucia di Lammermoor,* Oxana's aria from Mussorgsky's *Christmas Eve,* the Queen of the Night's first aria from *Die Zauberflöte,* Auber's "A Burst of Laughter," Ter-Tatevosyan's "Song of Armenia," Grieg's "Solvejg's Song," and the Bach-Gounod's "Ave Maria." Armenfilm Studio. Color. In Armenian and Russian. 70 minutes.

1979 Gariné

Gasparian stars as Gariné, the heroine of this 1979 film of an operetta by Armenian composer Chouhajian, known in English as *The Chick-pea Seller.* It's a love story set in 19th-century Istanbul. Chouhajian, who lived in Istanbul, was the creator of the first operettas in Turkey. Color. In Armenian. 93 minutes.

GASPARONE
1884 operetta by Millöcker

KARL MILLÖCKER's last major operetta, a romance set in Sicily in the 1820s and written by F. Zell and Richard Genée, is still performed. Gasparone is the name of a bandit evoked by almost every character in the operetta and blamed for almost everything that happens, but he is never actually seen. Widowed Countess Carlotta falls in love with Erminio after he rescues her from a danger he himself devised. However, she has promised to marry the mayor's son if he will help her on an important matter. True love, as always, wins out. With the help of the bandit, of course.

1937 Jacoby film

German feature film: Georg Jacoby (director), Hans Leip, Werner Eplinius, Rod Ritter (screenplay), Peter Kreuder (music director), Konstantine Irmen-Techet (cinematographer), UFA (production).

Cast: Marika Rökk (Ita), Johann Heesters (Erminio), Edith Schollwer (Carlotta), Leo Slezak (Nasoni), Heinz Schorlemmer (Sindulfo), Oskar Sima (Massaccio)

Video: PTM (Germany) DVD/VHS. Black and white. In German. 92 minutes.

Comment: The film was distributed in America in the 1930s.

1983 Vienna Volksoper

Austrian stage production: Robert Herzl (director), Rudolf Bibl (conductor, Vienna Volksoper Orchestra and Chorus)

Cast: Marjon Lambriks (Carlotta), Karl Dönch (Nasoni), Ossy Kolmann (Sindulfo), Adolf Dallapozza (Malfatti), Peter Baillie (Massaccio), Helga Papouschek (Sora).

Telecast June 11, 1984, on ORF Austrian Television. Sylvia Dönch (director). Color. In German. 155 minutes.

GATO MONTÉS, EL
1916 opera by Penella

MANUEL PENELLA's *El gato montés* (The Mountain Cat), libretto by the composer, has the best-known melody in Spanish music, a pasodoble that has become the theme music of the Spanish bullfight. *El gato montés* is roughly the Spanish equivalent of the French *Carmen* with a love triangle involving the bandit the Wildcat, the bullfighter Rafael, and the Gypsy Soleá. There is a major scene at the Seville bullring, and all three end up dead. The opera was first staged in the United States in New York in 1922 in English as *The Wildcat.* Plácido Domingo has been promoting it in recent years, producing it in Los Angeles, recording it in Spain, and featuring it in a film about Seville.

1935 Pi film

Spanish feature film: Rosario Pi (director), Manuel Penella (screenplay), Agustin Macasoli (cinematographer), Cifesa (production).

Cast: Pablo Hertogs (The Wildcat), Maria del Pilar Lebron (Soleá), Mary Cortes, Joaquín Valle, Consuela Company, Juan Baroja, José Rueda.

Video: Diva Ediciónes (Spain) VHS. Black and white. In Spanish. 89 minutes.

Comment: This was the first Spanish feature film directed by a woman. Pi also made a film version of Pablo Luna's zarzuela *Molinos de Viento.*

1994 Los Angeles Music Center

American stage production: Emilio Sagi (director), Miguel Roa (conductor, Music Center Opera Orchestra), Julian Gahan (set designer).

Cast: Plácido Domingo (Rafael), Verónica Villarroel (Soleá), Justino Diaz (The Wildcat).

Telecast October 5, 1994; taped January 1994. Gary Halvorsen (director). Color. In Spanish with English subtitles. 115 minutes.

Comment: Based on a production created at the Teatro Lirico National de la Zarzuela in Madrid.

Early film

1924 Tiger Love

The first film of the opera was made in the United States after the New York stage success of *The Wildcat* in an adaptation written by Howard Hawks before he became a director. He changed the plot considerably and gave it a new name, but it was screened with Penella's music played live. Antonio Moreno is the Wildcat, Estelle Taylor is Marcheta, G. Raymond Nye is El Pezuño, and Manuel Camero is Don Ramón. George Melford directed for Paramount. Black and white. Silent. About 70 minutes.

GAVAZZENI, GIANANDREA
Italian conductor (1909–)

Gianandrea Gavazzeni began as an opera composer, but he turned to conducting in 1940 and withdrew his operas in 1949. He has been especially associated with Teatro alla Scala, most of his videos are of La Scala productions, and was he was even artistic director of the theater for a period during the 1960s. He has also conducted orchestras around the world, from Moscow to Chicago, and including the Met. See ADRIANA LECOUVREUR (1989), I DUE FOSCARI (1988), FEDORA (1993), GIANNI SCHICCHI (1983), I LOMBARDI ALLA PRIMA CROCIATA (1984), SUOR ANGELICA (1983), IL TABARRO (1983), and ZAZÀ (1995).

GAVIN, BARRIE
English TV opera director

Barrie Gavin has directed a number of excellent operas and documentaries for television, many available on video and several of them unique. The operas include BAA BAA BLACK SHEEP (1993), BILLY BUDD (1988), CARMEN (1991), CARMINA BURANA (1989), INÉS DE CASTRO (2000), MLADA (1992), NEITHER (1990), PETER GRIMES (1994), RUDDIGORE (1982), STREET SCENE (1992), WAR REQUIEM (1992), and KURT WEILL (1994). The documentaries include programs about MARIA CALLAS (1968), GIUSEPPE VERDI (1994), and KURT WEILL (1994 and 1995)

GAWAIN
1991 opera by Birtwistle

Sir Gawain, a knight at King Arthur's court, accepts a challenge from the visiting Green Knight. He is required to visit the Green Chapel where he is entertained by Sir Bertilak and Lady de Hautdesert. After three days, he fights the Green Knight. Harrison Birtwistle's *Gawain,* libretto by David Harsent, is a massive work based on the 14th-century poem *Sir Gawain and the Green Knight.* It was premiered at the Royal Opera in Covent Garden and broadcast and telecast.

1991 Royal Opera
English stage production: Di Trevis (director), Elgar Howarth (conductor, Royal Opera House Orchestra), Alison Chitty (set designer).

Cast: François Le Roux (Gawain), Elizabeth Laurence (Lady de Hautdesert), John Tomlinson (Sir Bertilak), Richard Greager (Arthur), Penelope Walmsley-Clark (Guinevere), Marie Angel (Morgan Le Fay), Kevin Smith (Bishop Baldwin), Omar Ebrahim (Fool).
Video: House of Opera DVD/VHS. Telecast April 17, 1992, on BBC. Peter Maniura (director). Color. In English with English subtitles. 191 minutes.

GAY, JOHN
English librettist (1685–1732)

The only opera usually credited to its libretto writer rather than its composer is John Gay's THE BEGGAR'S OPERA, a ballad opera that premiered in London in 1728. His composer partner on it was Johann Pepusch who compiled the popular songs for the opera and wrote its overture. Gay's work changed the face of English theater, although his other ballad operas, such as *Polly* (which was banned) and *Achilles,* have not remained in the repertory. However, Gay became wealthy through his first beggarly production. His influence has continued into the 20th century, inspiring the Weill-Brecht *The Threepenny Opera* and even a Brazilian variation.

GAYARRE, JULIÁN
Spanish tenor (1844–1890)

Julián Gayarre, the most famous Spanish tenor of the 19th century, was born near Pamplona, studied in Madrid and Milan, and made his debut in Varese in 1867. He was quickly recognized as one of the great tenors and was invited to sing in the major opera houses; he created the role of Enzo in *La Gioconda* in 1876. Gayarre collapsed on stage in Madrid in 1889 while singing in *Les pêcheurs de perles* and died at age 45. He has become a symbol of Spanish opera and is the subject of two biographical films.

1959 Gayarre
Spanish tenor Alfredo Kraus plays Gayarre in this Spanish film and sings many of the arias associated with Gayarre. Among the operas featured are *Don Pasquale, La favorita, Rigoletto, I puritani, Lucia di Lammermoor,* and *Les pêcheurs de perles.* Luz Marquez plays his love Luisa and Lina Huarte appears as the diva Adelina Patti. Domingo Viladomat directed. Color. In Spanish. 100 minutes. Bel Canto Society/Premiere Opera/Lyric VHS.

1986 Final Romance
José Carreras plays Gayarre in *Romanca Final,* a Catalan biopic that tells of the tenor's rise to fame and his love for his childhood sweetheart. The film has fascinating recreations of the 19th-century opera milieu as well as first-

class singing, with excerpts from *Il Guarany, Les pêcheurs de perles, La favorita, L'elisir d'amore, Martha, Un ballo in maschera,* and *Lohengrin.* Montserrat Caballé makes an appearance to sing with Carreras in a production of *Il Guarany.* Romano Gandolfi leads the Orchestra and Chorus of the Theatre del Liceu. José M. Forque directed. Color. In Spanish with English subtitles. 120 minutes. Kultur VHS.

GAZZA LADRA, LA
1817 opera by Rossini

La gazza ladra (The Thieving Magpie) is a mixture of drama and comedy, what was once called an *opera semiseria,* and has one of ROSSINI's most famous overtures. Giovanni Gherardini based the libretto on a French comedy. The magpie thief of the opera causes real trouble when it steals a silver spoon. The maid Ninetta is accused of the theft and, because of circumstantial evidence, is sentenced to be hanged by the mayor who is angry because she has rejected him as a suitor. Her father Fernando ends up in jail trying to save her, and her lover Giannetto seems unable to help. She is saved only at the end by the discovery of the real thief.

***1984 Cologne Opera
German stage production: Michael Hampe (director), Bruno Bartoletti (conductor, Cologne Gurzenich Orchestra and Cologne Opera Chorus), Maurice Pagano (set/costume designer).
Cast: Ileana Cotrubas (Ninetta), David Kuebler (Giantess), Brent Ellis (Fernando), Alberto Rinaldi (Mayor), Carlo Feller (Fabrizio), Elena Zilio (Pippo).
Video: Home Vision VHS/Pioneer LD. José Montes-Baquer (director). Color. In Italian with English subtitles. 176 minutes.
Comment: Convincing, powerful production with fine singing.

Related films

1954 The Thieving Magpie
Johnny Green conducts the MGM Symphony Orchestra in the overture to *La gazza ladra* in the CinemaScope short *The Thieving Magpie.* Color. 9 minutes.

1964 La gazza ladra
Emanuele Luzzati and Giulio Giannini's animated *La gazza ladra,* based on the overture to the opera, is one of the masterpieces of animation and one of the world's best-known cartoons. The film story, however, has no relation to the opera. A king and his noblemen ride out to hunt birds, but instead a magpie steals the king's crown, and the birds attack the hunters. The patterns and colors of the film create the effect of a medieval painting. Color. 10 minutes.

1971 A Clockwork Orange
Music from *The Thieving Magpie* is featured on the soundtrack of Stanley Kubrick's dystopian vision of England in the not-too-distant future. Color. 136 minutes.

1973 Le Cinque Giornate
Dario Argento's *Le Cinque Giornate* tells of the five days of the Milan revolution against the Austrians in 1848. It features music from *La gazza ladra* performed by the Teatro alla Scala Orchestra. Color. In Italian 126 minutes.

GEDDA, NICOLAI
Swedish tenor (1925–)

Nicolai Gedda made his debut in Stockholm in 1951, sang at La Scala in 1953 as Don Ottavio, and arrived at Covent Garden in 1955. The focus of his career, however, was the Metropolitan Opera. He sang there for 22 seasons, beginning in 1957, in a variety of roles, including Anatol in the premiere of Samuel Barber's VANESSA. His other screen operas include THE BARTERED BRIDE (1978), BORIS GODUNOV (1989), CARMEN (1959), FAUST (1963/1965/1975), ROMÉO ET JULIETTE (1963), and DIE ZAUBERFLÖTE (1971). For other performances, see BELL TELEPHONE HOUR (1968), LISA DELLA CASA (1958), METROPOLITAN OPERA (1983), OPERA IMAGINAIRE, VOICE OF FIRESTONE (1950–1963), and ROBERT STOLZ (1990).

1985 Nicolai Gedda in Concert
The Bel Canto Society has compiled two videos of excerpts from Gedda concerts. Volume One (49 minutes) features arias from *Fedora* and *L'Arlesiana* plus Russian songs. Volume Two (33 minutes) includes arias from *L'elisir d'amore, Paganini, The Merry Widow, The Land of Smiles, Giuditta,* and *Eugene Onegin.* Color. Bel Canto Society VHS.

GENCER, LEYLA
Turkish soprano (1924–)

Leyla Gencer studied in Istanbul, made her debut in Ankara in 1950, and began to sing in Italy in 1953. She was Madame Lidone in the premiere of *Dialogues des Carmélites* at La Scala in 1957 and soon after began to sing around the world in a variety of roles. Her voice is unique and her style absorbing. It can be experienced on video in two of her great Verdi roles, in the title role of ÀIDA in 1963 and 1966 and as Leonora in IL TROVATORE in 1957.

GENÉE, RICHARD
German librettist/composer (1823–1895)

Richard Genée was one of the great operetta librettists, mainly in partnership with Camillo Walzel, who wrote under the pen name F. Zell. His major achievement is the 1874 DIE FLEDERMAUS for Johann Strauss on which he worked out melodic as well as plot ideas. He wrote other librettos for Strauss (EINE NACHT IN VENEDIG), Suppé (BOCCACCIO), and Millöcker (DER BETTELSTUDENT, GASPARONE). His biggest success as a composer was the operetta NANON (1877), which was filmed in Germany with diva Erna Sack as star.

GENEVIÈVE DE BRABANT
1899 marionette opera by Satie

Erik Satie's marionette opera *Geneviève de Brabant*, libretto by J. P. Contamine de Latour based on a legend, was created for puppets and piano and later scored for orchestra. Geneviève is the wife of Sifroy who has gone to war and left his chamberlain Golo in charge. Golo tries and fails to seduce her, so he has her sent to prison for adultery as revenge. She escapes into the forest when her husband returns and the truth finally comes out.

1989 Little Angel Marionette Theatre
English TV production: John Wright (director), Robert Ziegler (conductor, The Matrix Ensemble), Lyndie Wright (set designer).
Voices: Yvonne Barclay (Geneviève), Omar Ebrahim (Golo), Tilda Swinton (Narrator).
Telecast January 14, 1990, on Channel 4. Color. In English. 38 minutes.

GENTLE, ALICE
American mezzo-soprano (1885–1958)

Alice Gentle, who began her opera career at Manhattan Opera in 1909, made her debut at the Met in 1918. She was brought to Hollywood in 1930 during the first musical boom, where she starred in two Technicolor operettas, Gershwin's SONG OF THE FLAME and Kálmán's GOLDEN DAWN. She made her final movie appearance in a small role in *Flying Down to Rio.*

1929 Vitaphone film
Gentle sings the Habanera from *Carmen* in this Vitaphone sound short recorded at the old Manhattan Opera House. Black and white. About 8 minutes.

1934 Flying Down to Rio
Gentle has a tiny role as a featured singer in this RKO musical that launched the screen collaboration of Fred Astaire and Ginger Rogers and made the Carioca into a national dance craze. The music is by Vincent Youmans with lyrics by Edward Eliscu and Gus Kahn. Black and white. 80 minutes.

GEORGIAN OPERA

Georgian opera history began in the capital Tbilisi in 1851 when the first opera house opened in what was then a part of Russia. All of the operas performed in the 19th century were Italian or Russian, but Georgian operas began to be staged in 1919. ZAKHARY PALIASHVILI is considered the father of Georgian opera and the opera theater in Tbilisi is named after him. His opera DAISI has been filmed. The famous bass PAATA BURCHULADZE is probably the best known of the many Georgian opera singers.

GERGIEV, VALERY
Russian conductor (1953–)

Valery Gergiev began to work at the Kirov in 1977, was named chief conductor of the Armenian State Opera in 1981, and became artistic director and chief conductor of the Kirov Opera House in 1988. He has made it one of the most admired in the world, with many notable productions of Russian operas and a fine re-creation of the original production of Verdi's LA FORZA DEL DESTINO (1998), which premiered there. Many of his productions at the Kirov are on video. See BETROTHAL IN A MONASTERY (1997), BORIS GODUNOV (1997), THE FIERY ANGEL (1993), LA FORZA DEL DESTINO, HÉRODIADE (1994), KHOVANSHCHINA (1992), KIROV OPERA HOUSE (1992), PARSIFAL (1991 film), THE QUEEN OF SPADES (1992/1999), RUSLAN AND LYUDMILA (1995), SADKO (1994), SOPRANOS AND MEZZOS (1990), PYOTR TCHAIKOVSKY (1993/2000), and WAR AND PEACE (1991).

GERSHWIN, GEORGE
American composer (1898–1937)

George Gershwin is one of America's greatest opera and music theater composers as well as one of its finest songwriters. He was involved with four "operas." The first was BLUE MONDAY (1922), an all-black cast mini-opera work created for a revue and almost a sketch of what was to come. Second was the "romantic opera" SONG OF THE FLAME (1925), which is really a Broadway operetta. Third was the "Jewish opera" *The Dybbuk,* commissioned by the Metropolitan Opera in 1929; it was never completed. Last was the magnificent PORGY AND BESS (1935), probably the greatest opera yet produced in America, although it took 50 years for it to reach the Met stage. Gershwin's success in importing jazz and blues idioms into other forms of music has been widely copied, and his stage and film scores are among the best of their kind. Born in Brooklyn as Jacob Gershvin, he studied classical piano and harmony but then turned to popular music and was writing hits as early as 1919. His concerto *Rhapsody in Blue* made him famous, and his tone poem *An American in Paris* consolidated his reputation in the classical world. He composed 22 musical comedies; his musical satire *Of Thee I Sing* won the Pulitzer Prize in 1931. He died tragically young while working in Hollywood on the movie *The Goldwyn Follies.*

1945 Rhapsody in Blue

This is a romantic Hollywood film version of Gershwin's life and musical career with Robert Alda as the composer and Ray Turner dubbing his piano playing. His lyricist brother Ira Gershwin is played by Herbert Rudley. The film contains an extract from Gershwin's mini-opera *Blue Monday,* arias from *Porgy and Bess,* and a performance of *Rhapsody in Blue.* Irving Rapper directed. Black and white. 139 minutes. Warner VHS.

1998 Carnegie Hall Gershwin Tribute

Gershwin's 100th birthday is celebrated at Carnegie Hall with excerpts from *Porgy and Bess* and other Gershwin music. The singers are Audra McDonald, Brian Stokes Mitchell, and Frederica von Stade with Michael Tilson Thomas conducting the San Francisco Symphony Orchestra. Brian Large directed the taping on September 23, 1998; telecast by PBS September 30, 1998. Color. In English. 87 minutes.

GESCHIEDENE FRAU, DIE
1908 operetta by Fall

LEO FALL's 1908 operetta *Die geschiedene frau* (The Divorcée) traveled from Vienna to London and New York in 1910 as *The Girl in the Train.* Viktor Leon's libretto was considered slightly scandalous at the time; most of the first act is set in a Dutch divorce court where a woman accuses her husband of infidelity in a railway sleeper. It's a misunderstanding and they remarry at the end. Joan Sutherland recorded a medley of tunes from the operetta in her influential album *The Golden Age of Operetta.*

1953 Jacoby film

Marika Rökk stars as the scandalous divorcée opposite Johannes Heesters in this modern German film version of the operetta. The cast includes Trude Hesterberg and Hans Nielsen with Konstantin Tschet as cinematographer. Georg Jacoby directed. Black and white. In German. 100 minutes.

Early film

1926 Janson film

Mady Christians stars as the divorced woman in this 1926 German film of the operetta directed by Victor Janson. Carl Drews was the cinematographer. The film was shown in cinemas with Fall's music played live. Black and white. Silent. About 75 minutes.

GHEORGHIU, ANGELA
Romanian soprano (1965–)

Angela Gheorghiu, born in Ajud and trained in Bucharest, began to sing internationally from 1990 in Vienna, London, Zurich, and New York. She became one of the most talked-about sopranos in the world after winning acclaim in 1994 as Violetta in LA TRAVIATA at Covent Garden with Sir Georg Solti conducting. Since her marriage, she and her tenor husband Roberto Alagna have been hailed as the first couple of opera. She can be seen in her breakthrough performance as Violetta in London with Solti. Her screen operas with Alagna include a superb 1996 L'ELISIR D'AMORE and a 2001 film of Gounod's ROMÉO ET JULIETTE. She played Micaëla in a 1997 Met telecast of CARMEN, but it has not been released on video.

1994 Domingo and Gheorghiu in Prague

The soprano is featured in concert in Prague on April 24, 1994, with tenor Plácido Domingo. Domingo was a much bigger star at the time and the original telecast was under his name; after the success of her London Violetta, the video was rereleased in England under her name. She sings duets with Domingo from *La traviata, Otello,* and *L'elisir d'amore* plus the arias "Porgi amor" from *Le nozze di Figaro,* "Ebben...ne andrò lontana" from *La Wally,* and the Romanian aria "Muzika" by Grigoriu. The music is performed by the Czech Symphony Orchestra under the direction of Eugen Kohn. Thomas Simerda directed the video. Color. 80 minutes. Bechmann (GB) DVD and VHS/Kultur (USA) VHS.

1999 Classics on a Summer Evening

Gheorghiu and husband Roberto Alagna perform a program of operatic favorites by Bizet, Puccini, and Verdi in a live concert staged on July 11, 1999, in the square in front of the Semper Opera House in Dresden. Giuseppe Sinopoli conducts the Dresden Opera Orchestra and Chorus. Hans Hulscher directed the video. Color. 101 minutes. EMI DVD.

2001 Live From Covent Garden

Gheorghiu gives a recital at the Royal Opera House in London with Ion Marin conducting the Royal Opera

House Orchestra. She sings arias from *Norma, Louise, Adriana Lecouvreur, Rinaldo, My Fair Lady, Le nozze de Figaro, Gianni Schicchi, Madama Butterfly,* and *Turandot.* Dominic Best directed the video, taped June 8, 2001. Color. 72 minutes. EMI DVD (includes interview, discography, and photos).

GHIAUROV, NICOLAI
Bulgarian bass (1929–)

Nicolai Ghiaurov, the most famous Bulgarian opera singer of our time and one of the most impressive bassos of any country, made his debut in Sofia in 1955 as Don Basilio in *The Barber of Seville* and began his international career in Bologna in 1958 as Méphistophélès in FAUST. He first sang at Covent Garden in 1962 and at the Metropolitan in 1965. His popular roles include the title role in BORIS GODUNOV, Philip II in DON CARLO, and Don Quichotte. His other screen operas include AIDA (1986), LA BOHÈME (1989), ERNANI (1982), LA FORZA DEL DESTINO (1978), FROM THE HOUSE OF THE DEAD (1992), EUGENE ONEGIN (1985/1988), SIMON BOCCANEGRA (1978), and KHOVANSHCHINA (1989). He also can be seen in Clouzot's 1967 film of the VERDI REQUIEM at La Scala and in a 1983 METROPOLITAN OPERA gala.

1986 Nicolai Ghiaurov: Tribute to a Great Bass
Bulgarian TV documentary about the basso featuring Ghiaurov, wife Mirella Freni, and friends. He is shown in solo performance, singing with José Carreras and Piero Cappuccilli, and in rehearsal with Herbert von Karajan. The program begins with a staged performance of the Golden Calf aria from *Faust* and includes excerpts from *Don Quichotte, La bohème, Simon Boccanegra, The Barber of Seville,* and *Boris Godunov.* Freni sings with him in the sequences from *Faust* and *La bohème.* Color. 82 minutes. VIEW VHS.

GHOSTS OF VERSAILLES, THE
1991 opera by Corigliano

The Ghosts of Versailles is set beyond time where history and theater mingle with ghosts. French playwright Beaumarchais is in love with Marie Antoinette, who feels that her trial and execution were unfair. Beaumarchais tries to change history by rewriting his plays, but his characters will no longer take his orders. Marie Antoinette finally decides she has to accept her fate. American composer JOHN CORIGLIANO's grand opera *The Ghosts of Versailles,* commissioned by the Metropolitan Opera, premiered with great success in 1991. William M. Hoffman's libretto borrows characters from the Beaumarchais Figaro trilogy, including the third play *La mère coupable. Ghosts* is a delightful mixture of Mozart, Rossini, Strauss, Turkish dance, 12 tone, and sheer spectacle,

but the musical influence is primarily Mozart and Rossini, who created operas from the first two Figaro plays.

***1992 Metropolitan Opera
American stage production: Colin Graham (director), James Levine (conductor, Metropolitan Opera Orchestra and Chorus), John Conklin (set/costume designer).

Cast: Teresa Stratas (Marie Antoinette), Håkan Hagegård (Beaumarchais), Gino Quilico (Figaro), Marilyn Horne (Samira), Graham Clark (Bégears), Judith Christin (Susanna), Renée Fleming (Rosina), Peter Kazaras (Almaviva), Stella Zambalis (Cherubino).

Video: DG VHS/LD. Taped January 10, 1992; telecast September 14, 1992. Brian Large (director). Color. In English. 180 minutes.

Comment: Terrific production, brilliantly staged, and superbly sung by an all-star cast. The video not only captures the spectacle but almost enhances it.

Related film

1938 Marie Antoinette
Norma Shearer stars as Marie Antoinette in this lavish big-budget film that had the same problem as the opera: how to make a frivolous queen into a sympathetic character. Scripters Donald Ogden Stewart, Claudine West, and Earnest Vajda do a good job, and art director Cedric Gibbons creates a bigger-than-life Versailles for this opulent MGM epic. W. S. Van Dyke directed. Black and white. 149 minutes.

GIANINI AND LUZZATI
Italian film animators/designers

Italian animation masters Giulio Gianini (1927-) and Emanuele Luzzati (1921-)became famous in 1964 for one of the most popular opera-inspired animated films. *The Thieving Magpie* (LA GAZZA LADRA) is based on the Overture to the Rossini comic opera; it tells of three kings who make war on birds but get outwitted by a magpie. In 1968 they created L'ITALIANA IN ALGERI (The Italian Girl in Algiers), also inspired by a Rossini comic opera. In 1974 they made an animated version of Puccini's TURANDOT and in 1977 a version of Mozart's DIE ZAUBERFLÖTE with a live Papageno. Luzzati has also designed sets for stage productions of operas, including COSÌ FAN TUTTE (1975) and MACBETH (1972).

GIANNINI, VITTORIO
American composer (1903–1966)

Vittorio Giannini came from a family of opera singers. His sister Dusolina helped him get his first opera, the three-hour *Lucedia,* staged in Munich in 1934, and she created the role of Hester Prynne when his opera *The Scarlet Letter* was produced in Hamburg in 1938. He also wrote radio operas for CBS during the 1930s, including a version of the legend of Beauty and the Beast. His most popular opera, however, is THE TAMING OF THE SHREW, based on the Shakespeare play. It captured national attention as an NBC Opera Theatre production in 1954. Giannini's *The Servant of Two Masters* (1967), based on the Goldoni play, has also been well received.

GIANNI SCHICCHI
1918 opera by Puccini

Giacomo Puccini's one-act opera *Gianni Schicchi* is best known for its soprano aria "O mio babbino caro," sung by Gianni Schicchi's daughter Lauretta. The libretto by Gioachino Forzano tells the story of a crafty medieval Florentine who devises a way to get a man's will changed after he has died. This is modern *opera buffa* and very clever in plot and music. It is the third opera in PUCCINI's triptych *Il Trittico,* with *Il Tabarro* and *Suor Angelica,* and had its world premiere with these other two at the Metropolitan Opera in 1918.

1951 NBC Opera Theatre
American TV production: Charles Polacheck (director), Samuel Chotzinoff (producer), Peter Herman Adler (NBC Opera Orchestra). H. M. Crayon (set designer), Townsend Brewster (English translation).

Cast: Ralph Herbert (Gianni Schicchi), Virginia Haskins (Lauretta), Robert Marshall (Rinuccio).

Telecast live February 11, 1951, on NBC, and repeated live on May 1, 1952. Kirk Browning (director). Black and white. In English. 60 minutes.

1975 CBS Television
American TV production: Patricia Foy (director).

Cast: Zero Mostel (Gianni Schicchi), Norma Burrowes (Lauretta), Robert Bowman, David Hillman, Richard van Allan.

Telecast November 28 1975, on CBS. Black and white. In English. 60 minutes.

1981 Metropolitan Opera
American stage production: Fabrizio Melano (director), James Levine (conductor, Metropolitan Opera Orchestra and Chorus), David Reppa (set designer).

Cast: Gabriel Bacquier (Gianni Schicchi), Renata Scotto (Lauretta), Philip Creech (Rinuccio).

Telecast live November 14, 1981, as part of *Il Trittico.* Kirk Browning (director). Color. In Italian with English subtitles. 50 minutes.

1983 Teatro alla Scala
American stage production: Sylvano Bussotti (director), Gianandrea Gavazzeni (conductor, Teatro alla Scala Orchestra and Chorus).

Cast: Juan Pons (Gianni Schicchi), Cecilia Gasdia (Lauretta) Yuri Marusin (Rinuccio).

Video: Home Vision VHS (issued with *Il Trittico*). Brian Large (director). Color. In Italian with English subtitles. 50 minutes.

Comment: Gasdia's "O mio babbino caro" is particularly fine.

Related films

1970 Gianni Schicchi
This *Gianni Schicchi* is an American documentary film about preparations for a production of the opera by the music department at Pennsylvania State University. It was made by students of the University's Theatre Arts Department. Black and white. In English. 23 minutes.

1985 A Room With a View
James Ivory features two excerpts from *Gianni Schicchi* in this superb film based on an E. M. Forster novel and set, like the opera, in Florence. An aria comparing the city to a tree in flower ("Firenze è come un albero fiorito") is heard on the soundtrack as Judi Dench and Maggi Smith go exploring while Lauretta's aria "O mio babbino caro" (sung by Kiri Te Kanawa) is heard at a key moment while confused Helena Bonham Carter is discovering herself. Color. 115 minutes.

1997 G.I. Jane
Lauretta's aria "O mio babbino caro" is heard on the strenuous soundtrack of this film about a woman (Demi Moore) training very hard to be a Navy SEAL. Ridley Scott directed. Color. 124 minutes.

1998 A Soldier's Daughter Never Cries
Francis Fortesque (Anthony Roth Costanzo) sings "O mio babbino caro" in this film about an American writer (Kris Kristofferson) and his family living in Paris during the 1960s. James Ivory directed. Color. In English. 127 minutes.

1999 Mystery Men
Miriam Gauci sings "O mio babbino caro" with the Belgian Television (BRT) Philharmonic Orchestra on the soundtrack of this odd film about comic strip superheroes with problems. Kinka Usher directed. Color. 120 minutes.

2000 Italian for Beginners

Italian opera music, including a snippet from *Gianni Schicchi,* is an important component of this Danish film about a group of Copenhagen folk taking evening classes in Italian. Lone Scherfig directed. Color. In Danish. 112.

2001 Very Annie-Mary

Annie-Mary (Rachel Griffiths) sings the aria "O mio babbino caro" to her best friend from the top of a bakery truck in this delightful offbeat Welsh film. See VERY ANNIE-MARY.

2001 Captain Corelli's Mandolin

Italian Army officer Nicolas Cage sings a tiny bit of "O mio babbino caro" as he describes his opera club to a newcomer on the Greek island of Cephalonia during World War II. He tells the newcomer not to prefer Donizetti to Verdi, mocks Hitler with a "Heil Puccini" greeting, and shows a strong dislike for Wagner. John Madden directed the film based on a popular novel. Color. 131 minutes.

GIFT OF THE MAGI, THE
1997 TV opera by Rautavaara

A young married couple, deeply in love but without money to buy Christmas presents, sell their dearest possessions to buy gifts for each other. Minna sells her glorious long hair to buy Joel a chain for his watch; he sells his watch to buy her combs for her hair. Finnish composer Einojuhani Rautavaara's opera *The Gift of the Magi,* libretto by the composer based on a famous story by O. Henry, was created for Finnish television as a Christmas opera. He expands the story slightly and brings in a few other characters, but keeps the essence of the fable.

***1997 YLE Finnish Television

Finnish TV film: Hannu Heikinheima (director), Petri Sakari (conductor, Tapioli Sinfonietta), Raimo Hartzell (cinematographer), Gabrielle Faust (producer).

Cast: Pia Freund (Minna), Jaakko Kortekangas (Joel).

Video: Kultur VHS. Telecast by YLE TV. Color. In Finnish with English subtitles. 45 minutes.

Comment: Wonderfully produced, acted, and sung. O. Henry would have liked it.

GIGANTES Y CABEZUDOS
1898 zarzuela by Caballero

MANUEL FERNÁNDEZ CABALLERO's folksy zarzuela *Gigantes y cabezudos* gets its odd title from Carnival figures called "giants and bigheads." The story is set during Carnival time in Zaragoza in Spain and centers around the love affair of orphan Pilar and soldier Jesús. The other main characters are the town policeman Timoteo, his wife Antonia, Pilar's uncle Isidoro, and the sergeant who fancies Pilar and tells lies about Jesús. Miguel Echegaray wrote the libretto.

1968 Teatro de Fomento de la Artes, Madrid

Spanish stage production: Juan de Orduña (director), Federico Moreno Torroba (conductor, Orquesta Lírica Española) Jose Perera Cruz (conductor, Coro Cantores de Madrid), Federico G. Larrya (cinematographer).

Singers: Isabel Rivas (Pilar), Carlo del Monte, Rosa Sarmiento, Jesus Aguirre, Ramon Alonso.

Telecast in 1968 on TVE Spanish Television. Color. In Spanish. 100 minutes.

1996 Teatro Calderón, Madrid

Spanish stage production: José Luis Moreno (director), José A. Irasforza (conductor, Teatro Calderón Orchestra and Chorus), Julian Pérez Muñoz (set designer), Alhambra Ballet.

Cast: Maria Rodríguez (Pilar), Rafael Lledó (Jesús), Pepa Rosado (Antonia), Enrique del Portal (Uncle Isidoro), Pepin Salvador (Timoteo), Santiago Muriente (Vicente), Pedro D. Juárez (Sergeant).

Video: Metrovideo (Spain) VHS. Telecast live by RTVE. José Ignado Ortega (director). Color. In Spanish. 49 minutes.

2002 Jarvis Conservatory, Napa

American stage production: Daniel Helfgot (director), Philip J. Bauman (conductor, Jarvis Conservatory Orchestra), Peter Crompton (set designer), Maria del Sol and Mario La Vega (choreographers), William Jarvis (producer/translator).

Cast: Marcos Solá, Todd Peterson, Aurora Frias, Carolina Ibañez, Cristian Almodovar, Javier Beatto.

Video: Jarvis Conservatory DVD/VHS. Dave Drum (director). Color. Dialogue in English, singing in Spanish with English subtitles. 56 minutes.

Early film

1925 Atlántida film

Carmen Viance stars as Pilar in this popular silent film of the zarzuela written and directed by Florián Rey for the Atlántida film company of Madrid. The cast includes José Nieto, Marina Torres, Guillermo Muñoz, Francisco Marti, and comic José Gimeno, the Ben Turpin of the Spanish cinema. Alberto Arroyo was cinematographer. The film was screened with live music from the zarzuela. Black and white. Silent. 80 minutes.

GIGLI, BENIAMINO
Italian tenor (1890–1957)

Beniamino Gigli possessed one of the great voices of the 20th century, and his recordings seem likely to keep him popular for a long time to come. He made his debut in Italy in 1914 and was one of the stalwarts of the Metropolitan Opera during the 1920s, virtually the successor to Caruso. He returned to Italy in 1932 after declining to accept a cut in salary asked for because of the Depression. He was, sadly, a favorite of Mussolini and a supporter of fascism, but the Italian public loved him all the same. He began making fiction movies in English, Italian, and German in 1935 and can be seen in 18 features and six Vitaphone shorts. He is by no means one of the great film actors, but his screen personality is attractive and his incredible voice carries all else before. Most of his films are available on video, although it is sometimes difficult to separate them as they are in three languages with different titles and casts. His only film based on an opera is RIDI, PAGLIACCIO, a 1943 film about the genesis of PAGLIACCI. His other films are listed below with brief descriptions only as most have their own entries with full details. CARLO BERGONZI presented a concert in Gigli's honor at Carnegie Hall in 1985 and organized a memorial event in VERONA in 1990.

Feature films

1935 Forget-Me-Not/Non ti scordar di me
Gigli plays an older opera singer who marries a young woman rebounding from a failed love affair. There are three versions: Zoltan Korda directed *Forget-Me-Not* in English while Augusto Genina directed *Non ti scordar di ne* in Italian and *Vergiss mein nicht* in German. See FORGET-ME-NOT.

1936 Ave Maria
Gigli is an opera singer with a lost love who falls for Paris torch singer Käthe Von Nagy; she tries to trap him but ends up falling in love. Gigli sings arias from *La bohème* and *Il trovatore* and appears on staged in *La traviata*. Johannes Riemann directed Italian and German versions. See AVE MARIA.

1936 Sinfonie di cuori/Du bist mein Glück
Isa Miranda plays opposite Gigli in this melodramatic musical about a mother who loses her daughter because of her love for opera star Gigli. Karl Heinz Martin directed Italian and German versions. See SINFONIE DI CUORI.

1937 La canzone del cuore/Die Stimme des Herzens
Gigli is an opera singer and Geraldine Katt is a princess who plays piano for him, the cause of a mistaken identity mix-up. Gigli sing arias from *Martha* and *Lohengrin*. Karl Heinz Martin directed Italian and German versions. See LA CANZONE DEL CUORE.

1937 Solo per te/Mutterlied
Gigli plays an opera singer married to a singer (Maria Cebotari) who has a secret past. Bass-baritone Michael Bohnen is the man from that past who joins their opera company. Carmine Gallone directed Italian and German versions. See SOLO PER TE.

1938 Giuseppe Verdi
In this Italian film about the composer, Gigli plays tenor Raffaele Mirate, the tenor who created the role of the Duke in *Rigoletto*. He is seen practicing "La donna è mobile" with Verdi (Fosco Giachetti) in a gondola in Venice before the premiere. Carmine Gallone directed. See GIUSEPPE VERDI.

1938 Marionette/Dir gehört mein Herz
Journalist Carla Rust hears aristocrat Gigli singing in a vineyard on his estate and thinks she has discovered a great peasant tenor. He allows her to promote him but she finds out she's been deceived. Carmine Gallone shot the film on location in Rome and Naples in Italian and German. See MARIONETTE.

1939 Casa lontana/Der singende Tor
Gigli plays an opera singer whose ballerina wife leaves him for another man. He meets her again in South America and kills her blackmailer in self-defense. Johannes Meyer directed Italian and German versions. See CASA LONTANA.

1940 Ritorno/Traummusik
Gigli plays himself in this film starring Marte Harell. She has been cast in the opera *Penelope* and wants Gigli to be her Ulysses. Scenes from the imaginary opera were created by Riccardo Zandonai. Geza Von Bolvary directed Italian and German versions. See RITORNO.

1941 Mamma/Mutter
A three-handkerchief opera movie. Gigli's aging mother (Emma Gramatica) prevents his wife from running off with another man by running through the rain while Gigli is on stage tearfully singing *Otello*. Mamma dies from the strain, but she dies happy. Guido Brignone directed the film in Rome in Italian and German versions. See MAMMA.

1942 Vertigine/Tragödie einer Liebe

Gigli plays the "most famous tenor in the world" who breaks up with his girl and gambles away his money because of another woman. His true love eventually rescues him. A high point is when Gigli sings opposite Tito Gobbi in *La bohème*. Guido Brignone directed Italian and German versions. See VERTIGINE.

1944 Silenzio, si gira!/Achtung Aufnahme

Gigli is a famous opera singer who gets a girl he fancies a role in his latest film. He becomes jealous when she prefers a younger actor and stops filming out of spite. He also sings arias from *Rigoletto* and *Lohengrin*. Carlo Campogalliani directed the film in Rome in Italian and German versions See SILENZIO, SI GIRA!

1946 Voglio bene soltanto a te

Gigli plays a tenor making a movie in Rome who fancies a female costar who prefers a younger man. The film includes arias from *L'Africana*, *L'elisir d'amore*, *Lohengrin*, *La favorita*, *Martha*, *Tannhäuser*, and *Die Walküre*. Giuseppe Fatigati directed. See VOGLIO BENE SOLTANTO A TE.

1948 Follie per l'opera

Follie per l'opera (Mad About Opera) is a romantic film about Gina Lollobrigida and other Italians in London organizing a concert to raise funds to rebuild a church. Gigli is one of the opera singers who participate. Mario Costa directed. See FOLLIE PER L'OPERA.

1950 Taxi di notte

Gigli plays a taxi driver who sings opera for his customers for extra tips. The story happens within a 48-hour period in Rome, and Gigli has the chance to sing Donizetti and Leoncavallo as well as some Italian folk songs. Carmine Gallone directed. See TAXI DI NOTTE.

1950 Una voce nel tuo cuore

Gigli and baritone Gino Bechi play themselves as opera singers, and their operatic sequences are the best moments in the film. Vittorio Gassman stars as a war correspondent who loves a nightclub performer who wants to be an opera singer. Alberto D'Aversa directed. Shown in America as *A Voice in Your Heart*. Black and white. In Italian. 98 minutes.

1953 Carosello Napoletano

Carosello Napoletano features Gigli's voice but he does not appear in person as the film tells the story of Naples in music and dance from the 16th century to the present. Also on the soundtrack are Carlo Tagliabue, Mario Cioffi, and Marinelli Meli. Sophia Loren stars. Ettore Giannini directed the film released in the United States as *Neapolitan Carousel*. Color. In Italian. 116 minutes. Bel Canto Society VHS.

Documentaries/related films

1927–1928 Vitaphone films

Gigli began his movie career in America singing in six Vitaphone sound films shot at the old Manhattan Opera Theater in 1927 and 1928. They include selections from *La Gioconda* ("Cielo e mar"), *The Pearl Fishers* (a classic duet in Italian with baritone Giuseppe De Luca), *Lucia di Lammermoor* (duet with soprano Marion Talley), *Rigoletto* (Quartet with De Luca, Talley, and contralto Jeanne Gordon), and *Cavalleria rusticana* (with baritone Millo Picco and contralto Minnie Egener). There is also "A program of concert favorites." Black and white. In Italian. Each film about 8 minutes.

1937 When You're in Love

Gigli is heard singing "M'apparì" on a phonograph record in this Hollywood film about an opera singer, played by Grace Moore. Robert Riskin directed for Columbia. Black and white. 104 minutes.

1960 Beniamino Gigli, una voce nel mondo

Beniamino Gigli, A Voice in the World, an Italian TV film about the singer written by Enrico Roda and directed by Giorgio Ferroni, traces the life and career of the singer from his early years. There are versions in English, Italian, and German. Black and white. 40 minutes.

1994 Ritratto di Beniamino Gigli

Italian television documentary about the singer broadcast in 1994. It featured interview materials and scenes with Gigli singing. Color. In Italian. 60 minutes.

GILBERT AND SULLIVAN
English librettist and composer of comic operas

The poet and the composer, different as they were, are almost never separated on film and video so they are considered here together. William S. Gilbert (1836–1911) wrote the words, Arthur Sullivan (1842–1900) wrote the music, and Richard D'Oyly Carte forged their collaboration. Together they created the Savoy Operas, a species of comic opera or operetta unique to the English-speaking world. Sullivan was first in the field and wrote the music for COX AND BOX before teaming with Gilbert. Their first effort together went over the heads of audiences, so it wasn't until the 1875 TRIAL BY JURY that the collaboration took off. The team wrote 14 operettas, most of which remain popular; THE MIKADO, THE PIRATES OF PENZANCE, and H.M.S. PINAFORE are the most often filmed and telecast, but there are also excellent videos of

THE GONDOLIERS, IOLANTHE, PATIENCE, PRINCESS IDA, RUDDIGORE, THE SORCERER, THESPIS, TRIAL BY JURY, and THE YEOMEN OF THE GUARD. The D'Oyly Carte Opera Company, which controlled copyrights until 1961, has also been captured on film at different periods. There do not appear to be videos of the team's last operettas, *Utopia Limited* and *The Grand Duke*, but there is one of a pastiche called DICK DEADEYE. Two comprehensive series of the operettas have been made and are described below.

Gilbert and Sullivan For All series
Eight of the operettas were filmed in 1972 by the *Gilbert and Sullivan for All* touring group formed by bass Donald Adams and tenor Thomas Round. These are heavily abridged versions, each about 50 minutes, made for television and schools. They were shown on PBS, with introductions, and are now available on VHS from Musical Collectables, the marketing arm of the Gilbert and Sullivan Festival. Peter Seabourne directed, John Seabourne produced, Trevor Evans wrote the adaptations, David Maverovitch was cinematographer, and Peter Murray conducted the Gilbert and Sullivan Festival Orchestra and Chorus. The series was also called the *World of Gilbert and Sullivan.*

Gilbert and Sullivan Collection series
Eleven of the operettas were produced by George Walker in 1982 as *The Gilbert and Sullivan Collection* with top performers and technical crews. Former Met soprano Judith de Paul was line producer with Allan Cameron designing the sets and Alexander Faris conducting the London Symphony Orchestra and Ambrosian Opera Chorus. They were shot at Twickenham Studios in England with one week for rehearsal and one week of shooting; the actors performed live to playback of the music. The majority of these productions are excellent.

1937 The Girl Said No
This little-known American film contains portions of *The Mikado* and other Gilbert and Sullivan operettas performed in a traditional manner by members of the old New York Gilbert and Sullivan Opera Company. William Danforth, who plays the Mikado, was said to have performed it for 25 years on stage. The other Savoyards are Frank Moulan, Vivian Hart, and Vera Ross. See THE GIRL SAID NO.

1940 Lillian Russell
Nigel Bruce plays Gilbert with Claude Allister as Sullivan in this American film biography of singer Lillian Russell. She starred in many of their operettas, but they are only minor characters in the film. Irving Cummings directed. Black and white. 127 minutes.

1953 The Story of Gilbert and Sullivan
Maurice Evans is Sullivan with Robert Morley as Gilbert in this lavish British film biography by Frank Launder and Sidney Gilliat. It tells the story of their career intertwined with that of theater manager D'Oyly Carte (Peter Finch). The singers include Martyn Green, Owen Brannigan, Webster Booth, Elsie Morison, and Marjorie Thomas; the screenplay is based on a book by Leslie Bailey. The film was shown in America as *The Great Gilbert and Sullivan.* Color. In English. 109 minutes. Musical Collectables VHS.

The Story of Gilbert and Sullivan (1953): Sheet music from the British film starring Robert Morley and Maurice Evans.

1974 Gilbert and Sullivan
This is a documentary about the Savoy Opera masters made for the Music Shop television series. It is hosted by Jerry H. Bilik and focuses on the growth of the partnership and the nature of their genius. Color. In English. 27 minutes. Michigan Media VHS.

1982 Gilbert & Sullivan: Their Greatest Hits
Royal Albert Hall concert presented as if Gilbert and Sullivan were present in Victorian costume to celebrate the centenary of the first presentation of *Iolanthe.* They discuss their operettas as they listen to their most famous compositions, performed by the D'Oyly Carte Singers in costume backed by a 1,000-voice choir. Michael Heyland directed the concert, Alan Birkinshaw directed the video. Color. 54 minutes. View DVD/VHS and Vestron VHS.

1999 Topsy-Turvy

The creation of *The Mikado* is central to this superb Mike Leigh film about the difficult relationship between Gilbert (Jim Broadbent) and Sullivan (Allan Corduner). It begins with the premiere of *Princess Ida* in 1884 and ends with the triumph of *The Mikado* in 1885 and includes music from *The Sorcerer* and *The Yeomen of the Guard*. See TOPSY-TURVY.

GILBERT, JEAN

German composer (1879–1942)

Jean Gilbert, whose operetta career was primarily in Berlin, is little remembered in the English-speaking world today, but his operettas were once quite popular in London and New York. The most successful was the 1910 DIE KEUSCHE SUSANNE (Modest Susanne); it was staged in most major cities, filmed in five countries, and remains popular in Latin America. DIE KINOKÖNIGEN (The Cinema Queen), first produced in Berlin in 1913, was one of the first operettas about the movies; it was staged in London in 1914 as *The Cinema Star* with Jack Hulpert, Cicely Courtneidge, and Fay Compton and then in New York as *The Queen of the Movies*. His operetta DIE FRAU IM HERMELIN (The Lady in Ermine), staged in New York in 1922, has been filmed three times. He also worked as music director on German films the 1930s, including the movie version of DOÑA FRANCISQUITA (1934).

GIOCONDA, LA

1876 opera by Ponchielli

La Gioconda is AMILCARE PONCHIELLI's most famous opera and the only one still in the repertory. Even those who have never seen it on stage recognize music from it. The famous "Dance of the Hours" ballet is memorably performed by pink hippopotami in Disney's *Fantasia*, and the aria "Cielo e mar" is a favorite recital piece for tenors. The strong, if somewhat melodramatic, libretto by Arrigo Boito is based on Victor Hugo's play *Angélo, tyran de Padou*. Set in Venice, it tells the story of street singer La Gioconda, Prince Enzo whom she loves, her blind mother La Cieca, Laura whom Enzo loves, and the villain Barnaba, who loves Gioconda and causes quite a lot of trouble. It's even more complicated when you watch it.

1980 San Francisco Opera

American stage production: Lotfi Mansouri (director), Kurt Herbert Adler (conductor, San Francisco Opera Orchestra and Chorus), Gerlinde Dill (choreographer of "Dance of the Hours" ballet).

Cast: Renata Scotto (La Gioconda), Luciano Pavarotti (Enzo), Matteo Manuguerra (Barnaba), Margarita Lilova (La Cieca), Ludmilla Semtschuk (Laura), Kurt Rydl (Alvise).

Telecast in April 1980, like a miniseries, one act each night following a documentary about its production. Color. In Italian with English subtitles. 170 minutes.

Comment: Memorable both for its fine singing and for a famous feud between Scotto and Pavarotti; after he took a disputed solo bow, she refused to take her final bow and remained in her dressing room.

1986 Vienna State Opera

Austrian stage production: Filippo Sanjust (director/designer), Adam Fischer (conductor, Vienna State Opera Orchestra and Chorus), Pantellis Dessyllas (set designer).

Cast: Eva Marton (La Gioconda), Plácido Domingo (Enzo), Matteo Manuguerra (Barnaba), Margarita Lilova (La Cieca), Ludmilla Semtschuk (Laura), Kurt Rydl (Alvise).

Video: Arthaus DVD/Kultur and Home Vision VHS. Hugo Käch (director). Color. In Italian with English subtitles. 169 minutes.

Comment: Almost the same cast as the San Francisco production, but this version is available on commercial video. Stolid traditional production but fine singing from Marton and Domingo.

Early/related films

1927 Gigli on Vitaphone

Beniamino Gigli sings extracts from the second act of *La Gioconda* in this sound film made by Vitaphone at the old Manhattan Opera House in New York. It begins with "Sia gloria ai canti dei naviganti" and ends with the aria "Cielo e mar!" He is accompanied by the Vitaphone Symphony Orchestra. Black and white. In Italian. About 9 minutes.

1946 Il tiranno di Padova

The Tyrant of Padua is an Italian film based on the Victor Hugo play *Angélo, tyran de Padou*, which provided the basis for the libretto of the opera. Clara Calamai stars as the street singer Tisbe with Carlo Lombardi as Angelo and Elsa De Giorgi as Catarina. Max Neufel directed. Black and white. In Italian. 91 minutes.

1951 The Great Caruso

Enrico Caruso (Mario Lanza) is shown on stage in his first major success, *La Gioconda*, singing "Cielo e mar!" Peter Herman Adler staged and conducted the opera sequences; Richard Thorpe directed the film. Color. 109 minutes. MGM-UA VHS/DVD.

1953 La Gioconda

Boito's libretto is the screenplay of this Italian narrative film and Ponchielli's music is used as the score, but there is no singing. Alba Arnova is La Gioconda, Paolo Carlini is Enzo, Elena Kleus is Laura, and Peter Trent is Alvise. Giacinto Solito directed. Black and white. In Italian. 88 minutes.

1970 Tucker sings "Cielo e mar"

Tenor Richard Tucker sings the aria "Cielo e mar" from *La Gioconda* on stage in a 1970 concert. The aria is included on the video *Legends of Opera*. Black and white. In Italian. 5 minutes. Legato Classics VHS.

1980 Opening Night: The Making of an Opera

Documentary about the production of *La Gioconda* at the San Francisco Opera in 1980. The film is informative about what goes on backstage, from troubles at rehearsals to instructions to ushers. Kurt Herbert Adler, 75, is the conductor and Lotfi Mansouri the director. Memorable is Renata Scotto's feud with Luciano Pavarotti. Telecast April 13, 1980, preceding the telecast of the opera. Color. In English. 60 minutes.

GIORDANO, UMBERTO

Italian composer (1867–1948)

Umberto Giordano's FEDORA has more or less remained in the repertory, and he had other popular successes during his life, but it is really the love of tenors for ANDREA CHÉNIER which has kept his reputation alive. The opera has become a regular part of the international repertory because it offers wonderful opportunities for a divo tenor to show his quality. In modern times it has been a specialty of Franco Corelli, Plácido Domingo, Mario Del Monaco, and José Carreras, all of whom can be seen in the opera on video.

GIOVANNA D'ARCO

1845 opera by Verdi

Giovanna d'Arco (Joan of Arc) is GIUSEPPE VERDI's romantic and quite unhistorical version of the story of the Maid of Orleans, composed to a libretto by Temistocle Solera based on a Schiller play. Giovanna (Joan) urges French King Carlo VII (Charles) and his troops on to victory after hearing celestial voices. Giovanna and Carlo fall in love, but she knows it is impossible. Her father Giacomo denounces her as a witch, saying she is in league with the Devil. When the French begin to lose the next battle, however, she rushes to help them and inspires victory. During the fighting she is killed. *Giovanna d'Arco* was perceived as a patriotic opera about the Austrian occupiers when it was first staged.

1989 Teatro Comunale, Bologna

Italian stage production: Werner Herzog and Henning von Gierke (directors), Richard Chailly (conductor, Bologna Teatro Comunale Orchestra and Chorus and Parma Chorus), Henning von Gierke (set/costume designer).

Cast: Susan Dunn (Giovanna), Vincenzo La Scola (Carlo VII), Renato Bruson (Giacomo), Pietro Spagnoli (Talbot).

Video: Teldec VHS/LD. Werner Herzog and Keith Cheetham (directors). Color. In Italian with English subtitles. 128 minutes.

Comment: A straightforward production that highlights the strengths of the opera.

GIRL OF THE GOLDEN WEST, THE

1938 operetta film by Romberg

MGM's operetta film *The Girl of the Golden West* is based on the same David Belasco play as Puccini's opera *La fanciulla del West*. As the studio did not want to pay for music rights it would not afterwards own, it commissioned a new score from Sigmund Romberg. It is not his best score, and it hardly bears comparison to the opera, but it is adequate. In this version of the story, Minnie is called Mary (Jeanette MacDonald), but she still runs a saloon called the Polka in 19th-century California. Nelson Eddy is bandit Ramerez who falls in love with her and takes her to a ball disguised as Lt. Richard Johnson. Sheriff Jack Rance (Walter Pidgeon) sets a trap by spreading news that a shipment of gold will be stored in the Polka. Rance is suspicious when Ramerez shows up, but Mary defends him and invites him to her cabin. Nina Martinez (Priscilla Lawson), an old girlfriend of Ramerez, betrays him and he is shot. Mary hides the wounded bandit in her loft and plays poker with Rance for his life. When he finds out she cheated to win, she agrees to marry Rance if he will let Ramerez go. On the day of their marriage, Ramerez returns. Rance realizes Mary truly loves him and lets her have the bandit as husband. Romberg's songs for the operetta, lyrics by Gus Kahn, did not become popular, and the musical high point of the film is MacDonald singing the Gounod/Bach "Ave Maria." Herbert Stothart was music director, Isabel Dawn and Boyce DeGaw wrote the imaginative screenplay, Oliver T. Marsh was cinematographer, and Robert Z. Leonard directed. Black and white. 120 minutes. MGM-UA VHS.

GIRL SAID NO, THE

1937 American film with opera content

This little-known movie is a kind of Gilbert and Sullivan time capsule, as it contains scenes of their comic operas as they were performed in a traditional manner by members of the old Gilbert and Sullivan Opera Company of New York. William Danforth, who sings the role of the Mikado, is said to have performed it for 25 years on stage. In the film, Danforth (playing old Savoyard William Hathaway) and his screen wife Beatrice (fellow Savoyard Vera Ross) own a restaurant where they can sing Gilbert and Sullivan with former colleagues Frank Moulan and Vivian Hart. When bookie Jimmie Allen (Robert Armstrong, the hero of *King Kong*) arranges a staging of *The Mikado* with the Savoyards at a theater to which he has access through a friend, Hathaway and his wife sell their restaurant to back the show. Unfortunately, it is actually a swindle arranged by Jimmie to get revenge on Pearl (Irene Hervey), whom he promised star billing in a show—for a fee. Although he had planned to run off with the money, he falls in love with Pearl and confesses all to the Savoyards. They decide to put on the show anyway, with Frank Moulan as Ko-Ko and Carita Crawford as Yum-Yum, and it's a big hit. In *The Mikado* scenes, Danforth plays the Mikado. The Gilbert and Sullivan songs featured in the film include "A Wandering Minstrel I," "The Mikado's Song," "The Flowers That Bloom in the Spring," "Three Little Maids From School," and "The Lord High Executioner" from *The Mikado;* "I'm Called Little Buttercup" and "I Am the Monarch of the Sea" from *H.M.S. Pinafore;* "A Policeman's Lot Is Not a Happy One" from *The Pirates of Penzance;* and "The Magnet and the Churn" from *Patience.* Betty Laidlaw and Robert Lively wrote the screenplay, Ira Morgan was the cinematographer, and Andrew Stone directed for Grand National Films. The film is also known as *With Words and Music.* Black and white. In English. 63 minutes. Video Yesteryear VHS.

GIUDITTA
1934 operetta by Lehár

Working-class housewife Giuditta runs off with Italian Army officer Octavio and becomes a night club dancer when he becomes a cabaret pianist. Jarmila Novotná starred as Giuditta, with Richard Tauber as Octavio when FRANZ LEHÁR's operetta *Giuditta* premiered at the Vienna State Opera in 1934. Its biggest hit was Novotná's waltz aria "Meine Lippen sie küssen so heiss." *Giuditta* has never been among Lehár's most popular works, but it has fine roles for opera singers. The libretto is by Paul Knepler and Fritz Löhner.

1970 ORF Austrian Television
Austrian TV film: Günther Hassert (director), Wolfgang Ebert (conductor, Berlin Symphony Orchestra and RIAS Chorus).
Cast: Teresa Stratas (Giuditta), Rudolf Schock (Octavio), Maria Tiboldi (Anita), David Thaw (Pierrino), Joachim Hansen (Antonio).

Telecast October 29, 1970, on ORF Austrian Television. Filmed in 35mm. Günther Hassert (director). Color. In German. 97 minutes.
Comment: Lavish production with young Stratas in good form.

Related film

1993 Schindler's List
The operetta's famous aria, "Meine Lippen sie küssen so heiss" is played on piano at a Nazi party celebrating the opening of a new factory which will utilize Jewish workers under the direction of Oskar Schindler (Liam Neeson). Director Steven Spielberg is being ironic; Lehar was Jewish and yet somehow a favorite composer of Hitler. Black and white. 195 minutes.

GIULIETTA E ROMEO
1922 opera by Zandonai

Riccardo Zandonai's opera *Giulietta and Romeo*, libretto by Arturo Rossato, is the familiar Romeo and Juliet story but is based on the original Italian stories rather than the Shakespeare play. Tybalt is here Tebaldo, and a much more important character, but most of the other people in the rival families are not seen nor is Friar Lawrence. In this opera, the lovers die dramatically at the same time. This was Zandonai's most popular opera after FRANCESCO DA RIMINI, but it has faded from the repertory. It was telecast in Italy in 1961, and there is an LP version with Antonietta Mazza-Medici as Giulietta and Angelo lo Forese as Romeo.

Related film

1939 Casa Lontana
Beniamino Gigli and Livia Calona are seen on stage in two scenes from the opera at the Teatro Massimo in Palermo, including the balcony scene in which Gigli sings the aria "Giulietta! son io!" Gigli plays an opera singer who meets his dancer wife on stage during the opera. See CASA LONTANA.

GIULIO CESARE IN EGITTO
1724 opera by Handel

GEORGE FRIDERIC HANDEL's opera *Giulio Cesare in Egitto* (Julius Caesar in Egypt) is not based on the Shakespeare play but is set in Egypt; it focuses on the relationships between Cesare and Cleopatra and her brother Tolomeo (Ptolemy). Tolomeo kills Pompey and is killed by Sesto (Sextus) when he tries to rape Pompey's widow Cornelia. The libretto by Nicola Haym, based on a libretto by Bussani, is in Italian although the opera was written for English audiences in London. This is currently the most popular of Handel's operas, with three very different videos in German, English, and Italian with the role of Caesar (written for an alto castrato) sung on by a bass-baritone, a mezzo-soprano, and a counter-tenor.

1977 Berlin State Opera

German stage production: George F. Mielke (director), Ehard Fischer (staging), Peter Schreier (conductor, Berlin State Opera Orchestra and Chorus), Gustaf Hoffman (set designer).

Cast: Theo Adam (Cesare), Celestina Casapietra (Cleopatra), Siegfried Vogel (Tolomeo), Annelies Burmeister (Cornelia), Eberhard Büchner (Sesto), Günther Leib (Achilla).

Video: VIEW VHS. Color. In German. 124 minutes.

1984 English National Opera

English stage production: John Copley (director), Sir Charles Mackerras (conductor, English National Opera Orchestra and Chorus), John Pascoe (set designer), Michael Stennett (costume designer), Brian Trowell (English translation).

Cast: Janet Baker (Cesare), Valerie Masterson (Cleopatra), James Bowman (Tolomeo), Sarah Walker (Cornelia), Della Jones (Sesto), John Tomlinson (Achilla).

Video: Image Entertainment and Arthaus (GB) DVD/HBO VHS/Pioneer LD. John Michael Phillips (director). Color. In English. 180 minutes.

Comment: The production originated in 1979, but it was filmed in 1984 at the Limehouse Studios in London. Several arias have been cut, the recitatives trimmed, and Sextus's role reduced, but this is still a superb production. Cleopatra has an impressive collection of dresses.

1990 Sellars film

American-German film: Peter Sellars (director), Craig Smith (conductor, Dresden Sachsische Staatskapelle).

Cast: Jeffrey Gall (Cesare), Susan Larson (Cleopatra), Drew Minter (Tolomeo), Mary Westbrook-Geha (Cornelia), Lorraine Hunt (Sesto), James Maddalena (Achilla).

Video: London VHS/LD. Color. In Italian with English subtitles. 151 minutes.

Comment: Sellars updates the opera to the near future with Caesar an American president staying at the Nile Hilton and Cleopatra something like an Egyptian Valley girl. The film, based on his production at the Monnaie Théâtre in Brussels, was shot at the DEFA studios in Babelsberg.

Related film

2001 Invincible

Werner Herzog's film *Invincible,* the story of a Samson-like Jewish strongman in 1930s Poland and Germany, features an aria from *Giulio Cesare* performed in German, "Ohne Trost, ohne alles Hoffen." Color. In German. 132 minutes.

GIUSTINO
1737 opera by Handel

Giustino (Justin) was a peasant who rose through the army ranks in the Roman Empire of the East and became Emperor Justin I in A.D. 518. In GEORGE FRIDERIC HANDEL's not-very-historical opera, based on a libretto by Pietro Pariati, he rescues Leoncasta, the emperor's sister, from a bear, and Arianna, the widow of the former emperor, from a sea monster. He is discovered to be the missing brother of the noble tyrant Vitaliano, so Emperor Anastasio rewards him with a share of the throne and a royal bride. The role was originally sung by an alto castrato.

1985 Komische Oper Berlin

German stage production: Harry Kupfer (director), Hartmut Haenchen (conductor, Komische Oper Orchestra and Chorus), Valery Levental (set designer).

Cast: Jochen Kowalski (Giustino), Michael Rabsilber (Anastasio), Dagmar Schellenberger (Arianna), Violetta Madjarowa (Leocasta), Bernd Grabowsky (Amanzio), Günter Neuman (Vitaliano), Hans-Martin Nau (Polidarte), Barbara Steenberg (Fortuna).

Video: House of Opera DVD/VHS and Dreamlife (Japan) DVD/VHS. Annelis Thomas (director). Telecast February 21, 1986, in East Germany. Color. In German. 120 minutes.

GIVE US THIS NIGHT
1936 American film with opera content

A Sorrento fisherman (JAN KIEPURA) with a fine voice throws rotten eggs at a poor tenor (Alan Mowbray) during a performance of *Il trovatore* in Naples and is chased by the police. The company soprano (GLADYS SWARTHOUT) hears Kiepura sing in church and falls in love with his voice. She persuades him to sing with her in a new opera based on *Romeo and Juliet* that has been created for her by Maestro Marcello Bonetti (Philip Merivale). His mother, however, doesn't want him to sing opera because his father deserted her after he became a famous tenor. After many problems, his mother changes her mind, and the couple end up on stage together in the opera, in love just like Romeo and Juliet.

When they kiss, they get a standing ovation. ERIC WOLFGANG KORNGOLD composed the IMAGINARY OPERA *Romeo and Juliet* for the film after his success as a stage opera composer in Europe. He was music director of the film and an old friend of Kiepura's. Edwin Justus Mayer and Lynn Starling wrote the screenplay, Victor Milner was the cinematographer, and Alexander Hall directed for Paramount. Black and white. 73 minutes. House of Opera VHS.

GLAMOROUS NIGHT
1935 operetta by Novello

An opera diva in a tiny country leads an army of gypsies to save a weak king from being overthrown by an evil prime minister. Met soprano Mary Ellis starred as gypsy prima donna Militza Hajos in IVOR NOVELLO's operatic operetta when it premiered at the Theatre Royal in 1935. Militza has been King Stefan's mistress for years, opposing wicked Baron Lydyeff's plans to take over the country. She falls in love with visiting British inventor Anthony Allen, who saves her life, but has to give him up for the good of her country. In the operetta, Militza is seen rehearsing and starring in a production of an operetta called *Glamorous Night*. Christopher Hassall wrote the lyrics for the songs.

1937 Associated British Pictures film
  English feature film: Brian Desmond Hurst (director), Dudley Lesie and Hugh Brooke (screenplay), Fritz Arno Wagner (cinematographer).
  Cast: Mary Ellis (Militza), Barry McKay (Anthony Allen), Otto Kruger (King Stefan), Victor Jory (Baron Lydyeff).
  Black and white. In English. 81 minutes.
  Comment: Olive Gilbert of the Carl Rosa Opera Company appears in the film's opera sequence.

GLASS, PHILIP
American composer (1937–)

Philip Glass is the best-known American opera composer in the world. The Baltimore-born minimalist has had popular acceptance of the operas EINSTEIN ON THE BEACH, staged in 1976 at the Avignon Festival and the Met; SATYAGRAHA, which focuses on Gandhi in South Africa and was premiered by Netherlands Opera in 1980; and AKHNATEN, the story of the pharaoh who tried to introduce monotheism to ancient Egypt, which was staged in Stuttgart and Houston in 1984. His growing popularity led the Metropolitan Opera to commission the elaborate Columbus/spaceship opera *The Voyage* staged at the Met in 1992. He has also had success transmuting classic films by Jean Cocteau into operas with ORPHÉE (1993), LA BELLE ET LA BÊTE (1994), and LES ENFANTS TER-

RIBLES (1996). MONSTERS OF GRACE, a digital film opera created with Robert Wilson, was unveiled in 1998 at UCLA. His film scores are an integral part of Godfrey Reggio's visual new age films *Koyaanisqatsi* (1983) and *Powaqqatsi* (1988) and add greatly to the power of films such as *Mishima* (1985), *The Thin Blue Line* (1988), and *A Brief History of Time* (1992). He has also composed for Hollywood movies, including *Breathless* (1983), *Hamburger Hill* (1987), *Candyman* (1992), *Kundun* (1997), and *The Truman Show* (1998).

1976 Music With Roots in the Aether
Glass talks about his work and performs a scene from *Einstein on the Beach* and parts of *Music in 12 Parts: Part 2* with the Philip Glass Ensemble on this video made by composer Robert Ashley. See MUSIC WITH ROOTS IN THE AETHER.

1979 Skyline: Philip Glass
Television program about the composer with excerpts from various compositions and portions of the opera *Einstein on the Beach*. The program was produced by Peggy Daniel and directed by John Merl. Color. 60 minutes.

1983 Philip Glass: 4 American Composers
Peter Greenaway based this film portrait of Glass around performances at London's Sadler's Wells Theatre. Glass talks about his work, and the Philip Glass Ensemble performs passages from *Einstein on the Beach* and *Glassworks*. Transatlantic Films. Color. In English. 60 minutes. Mystic Fire VHS.

1985 Philip Glass: A Composer's Notes
Most of the film is devoted to productions of *Akhnaten* in Stuttgart and Houston, but the spaceship episode from *Einstein on the Beach* is also performed by the Philip Glass Ensemble. Michael Blackwood directed. Color. 87 minutes. VAI VHS.

GLASS MENAGERIE, THE
1998 chamber opera by Bibalo

The glass menagerie is a collection of fragile glass animals owned by Laura, the shy daughter of former Southern belle Amanda. When her poet brother Tom brings a friend home to meet Laura, the delicate structure of the family collapses. Norwegian composer ANTONIO BIBALO's *The Glass Menagerie*, libretto by the composer, is an adaptation of Tennessee Williams's 1944 play. It was staged in New York in 2002 by Operaworks.

1998 Opera Vest, Bergen
  Norwegian stage production: Hilde Andersen (director), Ingar Bergby (conductor, BIT 20 Orchestra), Kristin Trop (set/costume designer).
  Cast: Toril Carlsen, Ann-Helen Moen, Jerker Dahlin, Marcus Jupiter.
  Telecast by NRK Norwegian Television in 1999. Frode Krogh (director). Color. In English. 80 minutes.

GLASS MOUNTAIN, THE
1948 English film with opera content

An English composer (Michael Denison) is shot down in the Italian Alps during World War II and falls in love with an Italian woman (Valentina Cortese) who helps him to survive. She tells him the legend of the glass mountain, and he writes an opera based on it when he returns to England and his wife (Dulcie Gray). TITO GOBBI and Elena Rizzieri star in the finished opera, *The Glass Mountain,* with the music played by La Fenice Opera Orchestra conducted by Franco Ferrara. NINO ROTA created the IMAGINARY OPERA for the film, and its theme music became popular in England during the 1950s. Henry Cass directed the film and wrote the screenplay with four other writers while William McLeod was cinematographer. The Italian version is called *La montana di cristallo.* Black and white. In English or Italian. 91 minutes. Bel Canto Society/House of Opera/Live Opera VHS.

The Glass Mountain (1948): Tito Gobbi sings this aria in an opera titled *The Glass Mountain* in this British film.

GLINKA, MIKHAIL
Russian composer (1804–1857)

Mikhail Glinka, the father of Russian opera, was the first Russian composer to become known abroad. He wrote two operas, the Italianate A LIFE FOR THE TSAR (1836) and the more genuinely Russian RUSLAN AND LYUDMILA (1842), both still popular in Russia. Glinka, who pioneered many types of Russian national music, has been the subject of two major Soviet screen biographies.

1946 The Great Glinka
Boris Chirkov plays Glinka in this Soviet film biography by Lev Arnshtam. Valentina Serova is Glinka's wife, Peter Aleynikov is Pushkin, Vasili Merkuriev is Ulynanich, and Boris Livanov is Tsar Nicholas I. The film traces Glinka's search for a Russian musical idiom and includes highlights from *A Life for the Tsar* sung by members of the Bolshoi Opera. The cinematography is by Alexander Shelenkov and Chen Yu-lan, the set designs by Vladimir Kaplunovsky, and the music direction by Vissarion Shebalin. The film was shown in the United States in 1947. Mosfilm. Black and white. In Russian. 98 minutes.

1952 Man of Music
Boris Smirnov plays Glinka in this Soviet film biography directed by Grigori Alexandrov. It focuses on Glinka's music more than his life and features stagings of scenes from *A Life for the Tsar* and *Ruslan and Lyudmila.* Critics were impressed with the musical sequences. Sviatoslav Richter is Liszt, Lyubov Orlova is Ludmilla Glinka, I. Durasov is Pushkin, and B. Vinogradova is soprano Giuditta Pasta. The film was released in the United States in 1953 as *Man of Music.* Color. In Russian. 100 minutes.

GLORIANA
1953 opera by Britten

BENJAMIN BRITTEN wrote *Gloriana* on commission from the Royal Opera House to celebrate the coronation of Queen Elizabeth II. It was not well received at its premiere, but it has since been reevaluated and restored to a position of importance. The opera concentrates on the later years of the reign of Elizabeth I and focuses on the tragic relationship between the queen and the Earl of Essex. This was also the subject of Donizetti's opera ROBERTO DEVEREUX, but librettist William Plomer says Lytton Strachey's *Elizabeth and Essex* was his starting point. Joan Cross played the queen in the premiere with Peter Pears as Essex.

1984 English National Opera

English stage production: Colin Graham (director), Mark Elder (conductor, English National Opera Orchestra and Chorus), Alix Stone (set designer).

Cast: Sarah Walker (Queen Elizabeth), Anthony Rolfe Johnson (Essex), Richard van Allan (Sir Walter Raleigh), Elizabeth Vaughan (Lady Rich), Alan Opie (Cecil).

Video: HBO VHS. Derek Bailey (director). Color. In English. 146 minutes.

Comment: This intense production by the English National Opera was an important step in the reevaluation of the opera.

1999 Opera North

English TV film: Phyllida Lloyd (director), Paul Daniel (conductor, English Northern Philharmonic and Opera North Chorus), Anthony Ward (set/costume designer).

Cast: Josephine Barstow (Queen Elizabeth), Tom Randle (Essex), Advid Ellis (Mountjoy).

Telecast December 25, 1999, on BBC TV. Phyllida Lloyd (director). Color. In English. 109 minutes.

Comment: The film is half onstage opera with the other half showing backstage events mirroring the opera; Barstow is central to both halves.

Related film

1939 The Private Lives of Elizabeth and Essex

This colorful film version of the story stars Bette Davis as Elizabeth, and one English critic felt that Sarah Walker had modeled herself on Davis for the English National Opera production of the opera. The film is based on Maxwell Anderson's play *Elizabeth the Queen*. Errol Flynn plays Essex; Michael Curtiz directed for Warner Bros. Color. 106 minutes. Warner's VHS.

GLUCK, CHRISTOPH WILLIBALD
Austrian composer (1714–1787)

Christoph Gluck was influential in reforming ideas about what operas should be, working with librettist Ranieri de' Calzabigi to make operas musical dramas rather than showcases for singers to demonstrate their skill. Gluck composed his early operas in Italy and Vienna, but he spent the later part of his career in Paris writing operas in French. His most famous opera is ORFEO ED EURIDICE (1762), a retelling of the Greek myth, and there are several versions on video. Many critics consider *Iphigénie en Tauride* his masterpiece, but there is also a good deal of interest in *Iphigénie en Aulide;* both are based on plays by Euripides. His small-scale operas such as LE CINESI (1754) and ECHO ET NARCISSE (1779) are most enjoyable.

1979 Dimenticare Venezia

One of Gluck's most famous arias is "Oh del mio dolce ardor" from the 1770 opera *Paride ed Elena,* the story of Paris and Helen. It is featured in Franco Brusati's 1979 Italian film *Dimenticare Venezia* (Forget Venice) sung by Adriana Martino. Much of the film takes place at the home of an opera soprano. Color. In Italian. 107 minutes.

1988 Christoph Willibald Gluck, Portrait

Christine Eichel's film about the composer was made for the 200th anniversary of his death. It centers around scenes from two of his most important operas, *Orfeo ed Euridice* and *Iphigénie en Tauride,* and an exhibition of Gluck opera sets and costume designs. The production of *Orfeo* in Kassel was directed by Herbert Wernicke. Color. In English. 44 minutes. Inter Nationes VHS.

GLYNDEBOURNE
English opera festival

Glyndebourne Festival, which opened in 1934 with *Le nozze di Figaro,* is noted for its Mozart productions and innovative stagings, including productions directed by Peter Hall and Peter Sellars. In recent years it has staged many rarely seen operas by Handel and Rossini. Glyndebourne was one of the first opera houses to telecast operas, starting with BBC in the 1950s and continuing to the present day with Southern, TVS, and Channel 4. A large number of Glyndebourne productions are available on video, many with Dave Heather as director and Humphrey Burton as producer, including an excellent 1973 *Le nozze di Figaro.* There are also videos showing the history of the old and the new theaters. See ALBERT HERRING (1985), ARABELLA (1984), IL BARBIERE DI SIVIGLIA, (1982), CAPRICCIO (1975), CARMEN (1985), LA CENERENTOLA (1983), LA CLEMENZA DI TITO (1991), LE COMTE ORY (1997), COSÌ FAN TUTTE (1951/1975), DEATH IN VENICE (1990), DIDO AND AENEAS (1966), DON GIOVANNI (1977/1995), L'ENFANT ET LES SORTILÈGES (1987), DIE ENTFÜHRUNG AUS DEM SERAIL (1980), ERMIONE (1995), EUGENE ONEGIN (1994), FALSTAFF (1960/1976), FIDELIO (1979), L'HEURE ESPAGNOLE (1987), HIGGLETY PIGGLETY POP! (1985), IDOMENEO (1974/1983), L'INCORONAZIONE DI POPPEA (1984), INTERMEZZO (1983), JENŮFA (1989), KATYA KABANOVA (1988), THE LOVE FOR THREE ORANGES (1982), LULU (1996), MACBETH (1972), THE MAKROPOULOS CASE (1995), MANON LESCAUT (1998), A MIDSUMMER NIGHT'S DREAM (1981), NEW YEAR (1991), LE NOZZE DI FIGARO (1973/1994/1996), ORFEO ED EURIDICE (1982), PELLÉAS AND MÉLISANDE (1999), LA PIETRA DEL PARAGONE (1965), PORGY AND BESS (1992), THE QUEEN OF SPADES (1992), THE RAKE'S PROGRESS (1977), THE RAPE OF LUCRETIA (1987), RODELINA (1998), IL RITORNO D'ULISSE IN PATRIA (1973), THE SECOND MRS. KONG (1995), THEODORA

(1996), LA TRAVIATA (1987), WHERE THE WILD THINGS ARE (1985), and DER ZAUBERFLÖTE (1978).

1955 On Such a Night
Anthony Asquith's famous short film promotes the experience of seeing opera at the Glyndebourne Festival. David Knight plays an American who goes to see *Le nozze di Figaro* at the Glyndebourne Festival, and Sesto Bruscantini as Figaro and Sena Jurinac as the Countess are seen performing on stage. Oliver Messel designed the sets. Frank North was cinematographer, and Paul Dehn wrote the script. Color. 37 minutes.

1992 The Glyndebourne Gala
The final gala evening at the old Glyndebourne was an all-star recital. Frederica von Stade is a joy singing "Voi che sapete" while Montserrat Caballé is extraordinary singing Desdemona's "Willow Song." Also appearing are Janet Baker, Kim Begley, Geraint Evans, Cynthia Haymon, Felicity Lott, Benjamin Luxon, Ruggero Raimondi, and Elisabeth Söderström. Andrew Davis and Bernard Haitink conduct the London Philharmonic Orchestra, and Christopher Swann directed the tape that was telecast in the United States by Bravo. Color. 112 minutes. Image Entertainment DVD/Kultur VHS.

1994 Glyndebourne: The House that George Built
This documentary film about the history of Glyndebourne and its new opera house was filmed by Christopher Swann over three years. It begins with a meeting at which Sir George Christie's group decides to knock down and rebuild the opera house, and it continues through design, demolition, and reopening. The film was first shown on British television when Glyndebourne reopened on May 28, 1994, with *Le nozze di Figaro*. Color. 90 minutes. Praxis (GB) VHS.

1999 Cecilia and Bryn at Glyndebourne
Cecilia Bartoli and Bryn Terfel perform scenes from *Il barbiere di Siviglia, Don Giovanni, L'elisir d'amore,* and *Le nozze di Figaro* at the Glyndebourne Festival in 1999. Myung-Whung Chung conducts the London Philharmonic Orchestra; Brian Large directed the video. Opus Arte (GB) DVD.

GOBBI, TITO
Italian baritone (1913–1984)

Tito Gobbi, one of the great baritones of the 20th century, starred in many opera and operatic films. He made his stage debut in 1936 and his film debut one year later when he played a singer in the medieval epic *I Condottieri*. He appears in films as both singer and actor; while his acting is good, his singing is better. He was featured in a number of postwar Italian films of complete operas, all available on video. He sings in a re-creation of the premiere of IL BARBIERE DI SIVIGLIA in a 1954 film about the RICORDI opera publishing company and stars in films of the opera made in 1946, 1948, and 1955. He appears in films about GIUSEPPE VERDI made in 1938 and 1953, and he plays baritone Giorgio Ronconi, who created the title role of *Nabucco,* in the 1953 film. He is one of the Italian singers who appear in a London concert in the 1948 film FOLLIE PER L'OPERA. Gobbi was a notable partner for MARIA CALLAS in her golden years and can be seen as Scarpia with her in Act II of TOSCA on stage at Covent Garden in 1964. See also L'ELISIR D'AMORE (1947), LA FORZA DEL DESTINO (1950), GUILLAUME TELL (1947), LUCIA DI LAMMERMOOR (1948), PAGLIACCI (1949), RIGOLETTO (1947), IL SOGNO DI BUTTERFLY (1939), TOSCA (1946 film), and LA TRAVIATA (1948).

1937 I Condottieri
Gobbi made his debut as Nino the Singer in this epic, one of a number of supposedly historical films made during the Mussolini era with history twisted to justify the fascists. It's the story of a Medici and his "black shirts" in the 16th century. There's lots of spectacle, but not much truth. It was directed by Luis Trenker, who starred himself as Giovanni, and was released in the United States as *Giovanni De Medici, the Leader.* Black and white. In Italian. 88 minutes.

1942 Vertigine
Gobbi is Marcello opposite Beniamino Gigli as Rodolfo, Liva Caloni as Mimì, Tatiana Menotti as Musetta, and Gino Conti as Colline in the *La bohème* sequence of this film. Gigli plays an opera singer who gambles away his money because of a woman. See VERTIGINE.

1943 Musica proibita
Gobbi has an operatic double role in this film playing both a famous baritone and his son. The son wants to marry the niece of a woman the father had been involved with years before. She opposes the marriage after she hears Gobbi sing the "Forbidden Music" of the title and learns his name. The film, spiced with opera tunes, was directed by Carlo Campogalliani. Black and white. In Italian with English subtitles. 93 minutes. Bel Canto Society VHS (as *A Tito Gobbi Feast* with added Gobbi arias) and House of Opera/Video Yesteryear VHS.

1945 07...Tassi
In *07...Taxi,* Gobbi plays a widowed taxi driver who becomes involved with a young actress (Vera Carmi). They fall in love, break up, and finally marry. The film, started in 1943 by Marcello Pagliero, was interrupted by the war and finally completed in 1945 by Alberto D'Aversa. Black and white. In Italian. 76 minutes.

1946 O sole mio

Gobbi is an Italian-American army officer/singer parachuted into Naples during the famous "four days of Naples." Gobbi broadcasts coded messages to the Allies through radio songs until a woman betrays him. The music is based on themes from Leoncavallo. Giacomo Gentilomo directed. Black and white. In Italian. 90 minutes. House of Opera/Live Opera VHS.

1946 Les beaux jours du roi Murat

Gobbi plays a singing revolutionary in the Kingdom of Naples in *The Beautiful Days of King Murat;* he charms his way into the palace and nearly gets himself executed. This French-Italian film, which costars Claude Génia and Junie Astor, has the Italian title of *L'eco della gloria.* Théophile Pathé directed. Black and white. In French or Italian. 85 minutes.

1950 The Glass Mountain

Gobbi plays an Italian partisan opera singer named Tito who stars in an opera called *The Glass Mountain* in this World War II story. The IMAGINARY OPERA was composed for the film by NINO ROTA. Elena Rizzieri sings with Gobbi in the opera scenes, while Franco Ferrara conducts La Fenice Opera Orchestra. See THE GLASS MOUNTAIN.

1952 The Firebird

Gobbi plays an opera singer who falls in love with ballet dancer Ellen Rasch in this odd Swedish-Italian film made in English. Gobbi's singing is the highlight of the film, which includes excerpts from *Don Giovanni,* and Rasch is seen in excerpts from ballets. The film originated as two Gevacolor ballet shorts, and the Gobbi material was added to create a feature. Hasse Ekman directed. The Swedish title is *Edlfageln,* in Italian it's *L'uccello di fuoco.* Color. In English. 100 minutes.

1954 Songs for Two Voices

Canzoni a due voci is more or less an excuse to allow Gobbi and Gino Bechi a chance to sing on screen. Gobbi is a famous baritone who hides out when he discovers that someone wants to kill him; Bechi plays his voice, which seems to have a mind of its own. This operatic fantasy was directed by Gianni Vernuccio. Black and white. In Italian. 84 minutes.

GODARD, JEAN-LUC
French film director (1930–)

Jean-Luc Godard, arguably the most influential European director of the modern era, became instantly famous with his 1959 *A bout de souffle* (Breathless). His versions of classic stories, which are as individualistic as his con-temporary films, sometimes have operatic connections. His episode of the opera film ARIA is based around Lully's ARMIDE. His 1983 updating of the CARMEN story, *First Name Carmen,* turns her into a modern-day terrorist and a filmmaker. His 1996 MOZART film *For Ever Mozart* is a self-referential work about reality and art.

GOLDEN CHILD
1960 "Christmas folk opera" by Bezanson

Christmas Eve at Sutter's Fort in 1849 at the peak of the century California Gold Rush. Prospectors are celebrating by drinking and fighting when a family arrives in a covered wagon. They are greeted with hostility, but the true spirit of Christmas returns when Martha gives birth to a child. PHILIP BEZANSON's "Christmas folk opera" *Golden Child,* libretto by Paul Engle, was titled *Western Child* when it was first performed on July 28, 1959, at the University of Iowa in Iowa City. An adaptation of the Nativity story, it was heavily revised for presentation on the *Hallmark Hall of Fame* television show.

1960 NBC Television: Hallmark Hall of Fame

American TV production: Robert Hartung (director), Herman Grossman (conductor, NBC Orchestra), Warren Clymer (set designer), Peter Herman Adler (music director).

Cast: Jerome Hines (Captain Sutter), Patricia Neway (Martha), Brenda Lewis (Sara), Stephen Douglass (Martin), Patricia Brooks (Annabelle), Chester Ludgin, Judy Sanford, Enrico Di Giuseppe, David Lloyd, John Wheeler.

Video at the MTR. Telecast December 16, 1960, on NBC Television. Black and white. In English. 60 minutes.

GOLDEN COCKEREL, THE
1909 opera by Rimsky-Korsakov

NIKOLAI RIMSKY-KORSAKOV's last and greatest opera, *Zolotoi Petushok,* was first produced in the West as the Diaghilev ballet *Le Coq d'Or* with the singers performing from theater boxes. It was later restored to its authentic operatic form and is now known in English as *The Golden Cockerel.* It's an antiwar satire based on a Pushkin poem with a libretto by Vladimir Bielsky. An astrologer gives a cockerel with a gift of prophecy to King Dodon to warn him of danger. When the King falls in love with the queen of Shemakha, the astrologer wants her as his payment. The queen's aria, "Hymn to the Sun," has become popular outside the opera.

1971 New York City Opera

American stage production: Giga Denda (director/choreographer), Jules Rudel (conductor, New York City Opera Orchestra and Chorus), Ming Cho Lee (set designer), Antal Dorati and James Gibson (English translation).

Cast: Beverly Sills (Queen of Shemakha), Norman Treigle (King Dodon), Syble Young (Golden Cockerel), Enrico Di Giuseppe (Astrologer), Muriel Greenspon (Amelfa), Edward Pierson (General Polkan), Gary Glaze (Prince Guidon), David Smith (Prince Afron).

Telecast live September 11, 1971, on Tele-PrompTer cable TV. Kirk Browning (director). Color. In English. 120 minutes.

Related films

1947 Song of Scheherazade

Met tenor Charles Kullman sings the soprano aria "Hymn to the Sun" in this biopic about composer Rimsky-Korsakov. Walter Reisch directed. See RIMSKY-KORSAKOV.

1950 Grounds for Marriage

Opera singer Kathryn Grayson sings the "Hymn to the Sun" at a rehearsal as she begins to becomes reinvolved with ex-husband Van Johnson. Robert Z Leonard directed. Black and white. 90 minutes.

1953 Mood Contrasts

Mary Ellen Bute created this abstract film as a visual interpretation of music from Rimsky-Korsakov operas. The "Hymn to the Sun" is contrasted to "The Dance of the Tumblers" from *The Snow Maiden*. Color. 7 minutes.

GOLDEN DAWN

1927 operetta by Kálmán

Hungarian composer EMMERICH KÁLMÁN created this American operetta during a visit to New York when his *Gypsy Princess* was a Broadway hit. *Golden Dawn,* composed with Herbert Stothart to a libretto by Oscar Hammerstein and Otto Harbach, is an odd and somewhat dubious achievement. The setting is Germany-controlled East Africa during World War I, but the music is Viennese and the songs better suited for Mayfair. White actors in blackface play the Africans, and the plot is ludicrous. Dawn, a blonde African princess who doesn't know she is white, falls in love with British officer Tom Allen, who is being held prisoner by the Germans. The black overseer Shep is the baddie, and his hit song is about his whip. The score was liked, so the operetta ran for half a year although some considered it ridiculous even at the time. It was filmed and was, not surprisingly, a critical and box-office flop.

1930 Warner Bros. film

American feature film: Ray Enright (director), Walter Anthony (screenplay), Devin Jennings and Frank Good (cinematographers), Louis Silvers (music director).

Cast: Vivienne Segal (Dawn), Alice Gentle (Mooda), Noah Beery (Shep Keyes), Walter Woolf (Tom Allen), Lupino Lane (Pigeon).

Video: Warner Bros. LD. Black and white. In English. 75 minutes.

Comment: Some critics rate this as the worst operetta ever filmed. It was made in early two-color Technicolor, and *The New York Times* reviewer felt that even the color was weird. Gentle, the Metropolitan Opera mezzo who plays the African woman who reared Dawn, has two songs and performs them rather well in a dark, powerful voice. Beery, in blackface as the villainous overseer, sings his whip song splendidly.

GOLONDRINAS, LAS

1914 lyric drama by Usandizaga

JOSÉ MARIA USANDIZAGA is one of the most famous Basque composers, and his opera *Las golondrinas* (The Wanderers) is a permanent fixture in the Spanish repertory. It's a tragic love story about a group of traveling players, led by Puck who loves Cecilia and is loved by Lina. Cecilia pretends to love Puck to spite Lina but, when she scorns him, Puck kills her. *Las golondrinas* was written as a zarzuela but converted into an opera by the composer's brother. Gregorio Martinez Sierra wrote the libretto.

1969 Teatro Lirico Español

Spanish TV film: Juan De Orduña (director), Federico Moreno Torroba (conductor, Spanish Lyric Orchestra and Madrid Chorus), Manuel Tamayo (screenplay), Federico Larraya (cinematographer).

Cast: Diana Zurakowska (Lina, sung by Josefina Cuberio), José Moreno (Puck, sung by Vincente Sardinero), Maria Silva (Cecilia, sung by Isabel Rivas), Antonio Durán (Juanito), Carlos Casaravilla (Roberto, sung by Ramone Alonso).

Video: Metrovideo (Spain) VHS. Shot in 35mm for RTVE Spanish Television. Juan De Orduña (director). Color. In Spanish. 95 minutes.

GOMES, CARLOS

Brazilian composer (1836–1896)

Carlos Gomes is the best known Brazilian opera composer, mostly because of the success of IL GUARANY in

Europe. He was born in Campinas, studied in Rio de Janeiro at the Imperial Conservatory with an Italian teacher, and had his first opera, *A noite do castelo,* produced in 1861. He spent most of the later part of his life in Italy, where *Il Guarany* won him renown after its premiere at La Scala in 1870. It was produced in Rio the same year. Gomes's later successes include *Salvator Rosa* (1874) and *Lo schiavo* (1889). *Il Guarany* was in the international opera repertory for many years, and it remains popular in Brazil.

1948 Guarany

This Italian film biography, starring Antonio Vilar as Gomes, is the story of Gomes's life from his childhood in Brazil, where some of the film was shot, to his opera success in Italy. Mariella Lott is Lindita, Anita Vargas is the composer's mother, and Luigi Pavese is his father. Gomes's music is used as the score for the film, which was written and directed by Riccardo Freda, better known for his horror films. Black and white. In Italian. 85 minutes.

GONDOLIERS, THE

1889 comic opera by Gilbert and Sullivan

The Gondoliers or The King of Barataria is the last of the GILBERT AND SULLIVAN operettas still regularly performed. Set in Venice, it has a complicated story about gondolier twin brothers Marco and Giuseppe. One of them is really a prince, and he was married as a child to Casilda, the daughter of the duke and duchess of Plaza-Toro. This is a problem because no one knows which one is the prince, and they are already married to Gianetta and Tessa. The Grand Inquisitor orders them to rule the kingdom of Barataria jointly until things get sorted out. The music is among the best in the Savoy operas.

1972 Gilbert & Sullivan for All series

English highlights film: Peter Seabourne (director), Peter Murray (conductor, Gilbert and Sullivan Festival Orchestra and Chorus), David Maverovitch (cinematographer), Trevor Evans (adaptations), John Seabourne (producer).

Cast: Helen Landis (Duchess of Plaza-Toro), John Cartier (Duke), Thomas Round (Marco Palmieri), Michael Wakeham (Giuseppe Palmieri), Donald Adams (Grand Inquisitor), Gillian Humphreys (Gianetta), Ann Hood (Tessa), Joy Roberts (Casilda).

Video: Musical Collectables VHS. Color. In English. 50 minutes.

1982 Gilbert and Sullivan Collection series

English studio production: Peter Wood (director), Judith De Paul (producer), Alexander Faris (conductor, London Symphony Orchestra and Ambrosian Opera Chorus), Allan Cameron (set designer), George Walker (executive producer).

Cast: Anne Collins (Duchess of Plaza-Toro), Eric Shilling (Duke of Plaza-Toro), Francis Egerton (Marco), Tom McDonnell (Giuseppe), Keith Michell (Grand Inquisitor), Nan Christie (Gianetta), Fiona Kimm (Tessa), Sandra Dugdale (Casilda).

Video: CBS/Fox and Opera World/Braveworld (GB) VHS. Dave Heather (director). Color. In English. 111 minutes.

1983 Stratford Festival

Canadian TV production: Brian Macdonald (director/choreographer), Berthold Carrière (conductor, Stratford Festival Orchestra and Chorus), Douglas McLean and Susan Benson (set/costume designers), John Banks (adaptation), Melvyn Morrow (additional lyrics).

Cast: Douglas Chamberlain (Duchess of Plaza-Toro), Eric Donkin (Duke of Plaza-Toro), John Keane (Marco), Paul Massel (Giuseppe), Richard MacMillan (Grand Inquisitor), Marie Baron (Gianetta), Karen Skidmore (Tessa), Deborah Milsom (Casilda).

Video: Connaisseur/Home Vision VHS. Norman Campbell (director). Color. In English. 154 minutes.

Comment: This is a TV production based closely on an updated Stratford Festival. It features a male singer as the duchess and has many rewritten lyrics.

1989 Australian Opera

Australian stage production: Brian Macdonald (director), Frank Dobbs (conductor, Elizabethan Philharmonic Orchestra and Australian Opera Chorus), Susan Benson (set/costume designer), John Banks (adaptation), Melvyn Morrow (additional lyrics).

Cast: Graeme Ewer (Duchess of Plaza-Toro), Robert Gard (Duke of Plaza-Toro), David Hobson (Marco), Roger Lemke (Giuseppe), Christine Douglas (Gianetta), Susanne Johnston (Tessa).

Video: Image Entertainment DVD/Polygram (GB) VHS. Martin Coombes (director). Color. In English. 150 minutes.

Comment: Based closely on the updated Stratford Festival production described above with a male singer as the duchess.

Related film

1999 The Talented Mr. Ripley

"We're Called Gondoliers" is sung playfully by Ripley (Mark Damon) and Peter Smith Kingsley (Jack Davenport) in this film version of a Patricia Highsmith thriller. Anthony Mingella wrote and directed the film. Color. 139 minutes.

GOOD FRIDAY 1663

1995 English TV opera by the Westbrooks

Good Friday 1663 is an English television opera composed by Mike and Kate Westbrook to a libretto by Helen Simpson. A pregnant 17-year-old (Belinda), trapped in a loveless marriage, sits in church in 1663 listening to a gloomy Good Friday sermon by Parson Snakepeace. She remembers and visualizes her love affair in London with Celadon and her forced marriage in Suffolk to Squire Clodpoll. The opera was commissioned by Channel 4.

1995 Channel 4 film
English TV film: Frank Cvitanovich (director), Peter Jaques (producer), Tom Hannan (art director).
Cast: Kate Westbrook (sings all roles except the Parson), Simon Grant (Parson Snakepeace), Trilby James (Belinda), Jay Simon (Celadon), Geoffrey Hughes (Squire Clodpoll), John Savident (Sir Porly Spatchcock), Julie Legrand (Aunt Champflower).
Telecast March 12, 1995, on Channel 4. Color. In English. 51 minutes.
Comment: The opera was filmed on location in Suffolk.

GORCHAKOVA, GALINA

Russian soprano (1962–)

Galina Gorchakova emerged from Siberia to become the prima donna of the Kirov Opera in St. Petersburg. She first attracted international attention singing Tatyana in *Eugene Onegin* in Sverdlovsk in 1988 and was much admired as Renata in Prokofiev's THE FIERY ANGEL (1993). She can be seen on video as Tatyana with the Bolshoi Opera in EUGENE ONEGIN (1993), as Gorislava with the Kirov Opera in RUSLAN AND LYUDMILA (1996), and as Leonora with the Kirov Opera in LA FORZA DEL DESTINO (1998). She played Lisa to Plácido Domingo's Hermann in a televised production of THE QUEEN OF SPADES at the Met in 1999.

GORETTA, CLAUDE

Swiss film director (1929–)

Claude Goretta is known for such internationally successful films as *The Lacemaker* (1977) and *The Girl From Lorraine* (1980), both made with notable sensitivity. His controversial film version of the Monteverdi opera ORFEO premiered at the Venice Film Festival in 1985.

GORIKKER, VLADIMIR

Russian opera film director(1925-)

Soviet filmmaker Vladimir Gorikker specialized in creating films of classic Russian operas. They were made as real movies and shot on outdoor locations with actors portraying the opera personages and the singing dubbed by top opera stars. His 1965 version of Rimsky-Korsakov's THE TSAR'S BRIDE has been particularly admired for its visual and vocal qualities, but all of his films have quality. See IOLANTA (1963), MOZART AND SALIERI (1962), and THE STONE GUEST (1967).

GORIN, IGOR

Ukrainian/American baritone (1904–1982)

Igor Gorin was born in the Ukraine but his family moved to Vienna after the Soviet Revolution. He made his debut at the Vienna Volksoper in 1930, emigrated to the United States in 1933, and began to sing on American radio programs. He first appeared on screen in the 1937 MGM movie *Broadway Melody of 1938,* singing arias from *Carmen* and *The Barber of Seville,* and he was a regular guest on the *Voice of Firestone* opera TV series during the 1950s. After starring in NBC Opera Theatre productions of LA TRAVIATA (1957) and RIGOLETTO (1958), he made his debut at the Met on February 10, 1964, singing the role of Germont in *La traviata.* It was his only appearance. Two years later, he sang Ford opposite Norman Foster's Falstaff in a film of Otto Nicolai's DIE LUSTIGEN WEIBER VON WINDSOR. In retirement, he taught at the University of Arizona.

1937 Broadway Melody of 1938
Gorin plays barber Nicki Papaloopas in this musical about an opera-loving racehorse. The first shot shows crowds in front of the old Metropolitan Opera building and posters of *Carmen.* An orchestra plays Escamillo's music and a voice is heard singing the "Toreador Song." The camera pans right to a barber shop where Gorin is singing the aria while shaving customer Buddy Ebsen. Eleanor Powell finds that when Gorin sings Figaro's "Largo al Factotum," her horse can win steeplechase races. See BROADWAY MELODY OF 1938.

1951–1952 Igor Gorin in Opera and Song
Gorin is seen in performances on *Voice of Firestone* television programs in 1951 and 1952 in this video of highlights from the series. He sings arias from *La traviata, Pagliacci, The Barber of Seville,* and *Hérodiade,* plus a selection of popular songs including "The Way You Look Tonight" and "For You Alone." Howard Barlow conducts the orchestra. Black and white. 55 minutes. VAI VHS.

GÖTTERDÄMMERUNG
1876 opera by Wagner

Götterdämmerung (The Twilight of the Gods) is the fourth and final opera in RICHARD WAGNER's epic RING DES NIBELUNGEN tetralogy. Hagen, son of Alberich, plots to get back the Ring. The hero Siegfried is given a drug at the castle of Gunther and Gutrune that obliterates his love for Brünnhilde. He agrees to marry Gutrune, abducts Brünnhilde as a bride for Gunther (having magically assumed his form), and takes the Ring from her. When Siegfried's memory starts to return, Hagen kills him. The distraught Brünnhilde, when she discovers how Siegfried was tricked, rides her horse into his funeral pyre, setting fire to the world and destroying Valhalla. The Rhine floods, and the Ring is restored to the Rhine Maidens. The era of the Gods is over.

1979 Bayreuth Festival

German film of stage production: Patrice Chéreau (director), Pierre Boulez (conductor, Bayreuth Festival Orchestra and Chorus), Richard Peduzzi (set designer), Jacques Schmidt (costume designer).

Cast: Gwyneth Jones (Brünnhilde), Manfred Jung (Siegfried), Jeannine Altmeyer (Gutrune), Franz Mazura (Gunther), Gwendolyn Killebrew (Waltraute), Fritz Hubner (Hagen), Hermann Becht (Alberich), Norma Sharp (Woglinde), Ilse Gramatzki (Wellgunde), Marga Schiml (Flosshilde), Ortrun Wenkel, Gabriele Schnaut, Katie Clarke (Norns).

Video: Philips DVD/VHS/LD. Brian Large (director). Shot in 35mm. In German with English subtitles. 249 minutes.

Comment. Chéreau's famous Bayreuth Festival Centenary production, updated to the 19th century, was first staged in 1976 but not taped until 1979.

1989 Bavarian State Opera

German stage production: Nikolaus Lehnhoff (director), Wolfgang Sawallisch (conductor, Bavarian State Opera Orchestra and Chorus), Erich Wonder (set designer).

Cast: Hildegard Behrens (Brünnhilde), René Kollo (Siegfried), Lisbeth Balslev (Gutrune), Hans Gunter Nocker (Gunther), Waltraud Meier (Waltraute), Matti Salminen (Hagen), Ekkehard Wlaschiha (Alberich).

Video: EMI VHS. Shokichi Amano (director). Color. In German with English subtitles. 230 minutes.

Comment: This a very modernist production with symbolic high-tech sets.

***1990 Metropolitan Opera

American stage production: Otto Schenk (director), James Levine (conductor, Metropolitan Opera Orchestra and Chorus), Gunther Schneider-Siemssen (set designer), Rolf Langenfass (costume designer).

Cast: Hildegard Behrens (Brünnhilde), Siegfried Jerusalem (Siegfried), Hanna Lisowska (Gutrune), Anthony Raffell (Gunther), Christa Ludwig (Waltraute), Matti Salminen (Hagen), Ekkehard Wlaschiha (Alberich), Kaaren Erickson (Woglinde), Diane Kesling (Wellgunde), Meredith Parsons (Flosshilde), Gweneth Bean, Joyce Castle, Andra Grubers (Norns).

Video: DG DVD/VHS/LD. Brian Large (director). Taped April 18 and May 5, 1990; telecast June 21, 1990, on PBS. Color. In German with English subtitles. 252 minutes.

Comment: Solidly traditional production with naturalistic sets, the only version on video staged the way Wagner might have done it. German opera lovers have been known to travel to New York to see Met productions for this very reason.

1992 Bayreuth Festival

German stage production: Harry Kupfer (director), Daniel Barenboim (conductor, Bayreuth Festival Orchestra and Chorus), Hans Schavernoch (set designer).

Cast: Anne Evans (Brünnhilde), Siegfried Jerusalem (Siegfried), Eva-Maria Bundschuh (Gutrune), Bodo Brinkman (Gunther), Waltraud Meier (Waltraute), Gunter von Kannen (Alberich), Philip Kang (Hagen).

Video: Teldec VHS/LD. Horant H. Hohlfeld (director). Color. In German with English subtitles. 230 minutes.

Comment: Modernist production set in a mythological future with minimalist science fiction–style sets.

1996 Jutland Opera

Danish stage production: Klaus Hoffmeyer (director), Francesco Cristofoli (conductor, Aarhus Symphony Orchestra), Lars Juhl (set/costume designer).

Cast: Stig Anderson (Siegfried), Lisbeth Balslev (Brünnhilde), Aage Haugland (Hagen), Jørgen Klint (Alberich).

Video: Musikhuset Aarhus (Denmark) VHS. Telecast on Danmarks Radio, Copenhagen. Thomas Grimm (director). Color. In German. 232 minutes.

Related films

1932 Rehearsal at Bayreuth

Frida Lieder (Brünnhilde) and Max Lorenz (Siegfried) are seen on stage at Bayreuth rehearsing the Dawn Duet with Winifred Wagner watching Karl Elmendorff conduct. On the video *Legends of Opera*. Black and white. In German. 2 minutes. Legato Classics VHS.

1955 Interrupted Melody

Marjorie Lawrence (Eleanor Parker) insists on galloping her horse into the flames on stage at the Met during the Immolation Scene arguing that no sensible horse would walk into a fire. The voice heard on screen belongs to Eileen Farrell. See INTERRUPTED MELODY.

1965 The Golden Ring

The Golden Ring: The Making of Solti's "Ring" is about the recording of *Götterdämmerung* in Vienna in 1964 with Georg Solti and the Vienna Philharmonic. Birgit Nilsson is Brünnhilde, Wolfgang Windgassen is Siegfried, Claire Watson is Gutrune, Dietrich Fischer-Dieskau is Gunther, and Gottlob Frick is Hagen. The film, made for the BBC by Humphrey Burton, is a fascinating story about how this classic Decca recording was conceived and created by producer John Culshaw. Black and white. In English. 87 minutes. London VHS/LD.

1990 Highlander II—The Quickening

Christopher Lambert, Highlander hero of this fantasy set in a dismal future where the world is about to end, goes to the opera for a little relaxation. The opera, appropriately, is *Götterdämmerung*. Birgit Nilsson as Brünnhilde is heard on the soundtrack singing with the Vienna Philharmonic Orchestra conducted by Georg Solti, from the classic 1964 recording. Color. 100 minutes.

2001 The Officers' Ward

Siegfried's Funeral March, played by the Chicago Symphony Orchestra, is featured on the soundtrack of the French film *La chambre des officiers*, a story about disfigured World War I soldiers. Francis Dupeyron directed. Color. 132 minutes.

GOUNOD, CHARLES
French composer (1818–1893)

Charles Gounod was considered one of the major opera composers at the end of the 19th century when FAUST was the favorite opera of Queen Victoria and most opera houses, but his reputation has been in decline for the past 100 years. Only *Faust* has remained in the standard repertory, and even it is accused of sentimentality. The decline in Gounod's reputation can be measured by the films made of his operas; there were a great many at the beginning of the century and very few during recent years. Gounod's other major operas are MIREILLE (1864) and ROMÉO ET JULIETTE (1867). Gounod's "Ave Maria," based on Bach, is very popular with opera singers on record and in recitals.

1904 Cinéma-Gramo-Théatre

Mme. Lise Landouzy of the Paris Opéra-Comique sings Gounod's "Ave Maria," accompanied by her husband on cello, in this early French sound film using a system called Cinéma-Gramo-Théatre. It was produced by Henri Joly and George Mendel. Black and white. In French. 3 minutes.

1960 I Survive My Death

A Czech opera singer in a World War II Nazi concentration camp sings Gounod's "Ave Maria" instead of the usual "Internationale" in a key scene in this Czech film. Vojtech Jasny directed. The Czech title is *Prezil Jsem Sviu Smrt*. Black and white. In Czech. 92 minutes.

Goya (1986): Goya (Plácido Domingo) and the Duchess of Alba (Victoria Vergara) in the Washington Opera premiere.

GOYA
1986 opera by Menotti

GIAN CARLO MENOTTI's three-act opera *Goya* was created for Plácido Domingo for presentation at the Kennedy Center by the Washington Opera. The libretto by Menotti tells the story of the Spanish painter Goya and his difficult relationships with the Duchess of Alba and the Queen of Spain, who are vicious rivals. This was the first opera telecast from the Kennedy Center, and the premiere audience received it politely, but it was a critical failure so no further productions were planned. Menotti revised the opera and relaunched it at the Spoleto Festival in 1991 where it was recorded.

1986 Washington Opera

American stage production: Gian Carlo Menotti (director), Rafael Frühbeck de Burgos (conductor, Washington Opera Orchestra) Pasquale Grossi (set/costume designer).

Cast: Plácido Domingo (Goya), Victoria Vergara (Duchess of Alba), Karen Huffstodt (Queen Maria Luisa), Louis Otey (Martin Zapater), Howard Bender (King Charles IV), Stephen Dupont (Godoy).

Video: House of Opera VHS. Telecast November 28, 1986, on PBS. Kirk Browning (director). Color. In English. 150 minutes.

GOYESCAS
1916 opera by Granados

Spanish composer ENRIQUE GRANADOS premiered *Goyescas,* his most famous opera, at the Metropolitan Opera on January 28, 1916, the first opera in the Spanish language presented in a major American opera house. Set in Madrid around 1800 and based on a piano suite by the composer, it features a libretto by Fernando Periquet inspired by Goya paintings. The bullfighter Paquiro is engaged to the singer Pepa, but he flirts with the aristocratic Rosario and arouses the animosity of her lover, Captain Fernando. The two men end up dueling, and Fernando is killed. The opera has a famous intermezzo and a noted aria, "La maja y el ruiseñor." It is on CD.

1942 Ibero Americana film

Spanish feature film: Benito Perojo (director/screenplay) José Munoz Molleda (conductor, Madrid Symphonic Orchestra), Michel Kelber and Cecilio Paniagua (cinematographers), Sigfrido Burman (set designer), Ibero Americana (production).

Cast: Imperio Argentina (Petrilla/Countess de Gualda), Rafael Rivelles (Capt. Fernando), Armando Calvo (Don Louis Alfonso), Ramón Martori (Mayor).

Black and white. In Spanish. 97 minutes.

Comment: The plot is considerably altered. Argentina plays both of the women who love Fernando, who supposedly resemble each other closely. The film was distributed in the United States in 1944 by Universal.

GRAF, HERBERT
American opera director (1904–1973)

Herbert Graf, best known for his work as a stage director with the Philadelphia, Metropolitan, and Zurich Opera companies, was also an innovative pioneer in television opera. NBC hired him in 1944 as director of opera production and telecast excerpts and shortened versions of *La bohème, The Barber of Seville, Carmen,* and *Pagliacci.* He directed the 1948 Metropolitan Opera opening night OTELLO (the first complete opera televised live from an opera house), the 1949 Met opening night DER ROSENKAVALIER (also televised), the 1950 CBS Opera Television Theater LA TRAVIATA, and the 1956 Sol Hurok TV gala PRODUCERS' SHOWCASE. He discusses his TV work in his 1951 book *Opera for the People.* Many of his later opera productions are on video, including his Salzburg DON GIOVANNI (1954), Zurich OTELLO (1961), Verona AIDA (1966), and Met DON GIOVANNI (1978).

GRÄFIN MARIZA
1924 operetta by Kálmán

Beautiful Hungarian Countess Mariza hires disguised Count Tassilo to work on her estate and then falls in love with him, although she is pursued by the boorish Baron Zsupán. *Gräfin Mariza* (Countess Mariza), EMMERICH KÁLMÁN's most popular operetta after *Die Csárdásfürstin,* includes one of his best-known melodies; it was sung in English as "Play Gypsies, Dance Gypsies" when it was produced on Broadway in 1926. The libretto is by Julius Brammer and Alfred Gruenwald. (The Countess is called Maritza in the U.S. and English productions.)

1932 Roto film

German feature film: Richard Oswald (director), Fritz Friedmann-Frederich (screenplay), Heinrich Gärtner (cinematographer), Roto Film (production).

Cast: Dorothea Wieck (Countess Mariza), Hubert Marischka (Count Tassilo), Charlotte Ander, Ferdinand von Alten, Anton Pointner, S, Z. Sakall.

Black and white. In German. 110 minutes.

Comment: Marischka had created the role of Count Tassilo in the Vienna premiere of the operetta.

1958 Constantin film

German feature film: Rudolf Schündler (director), Janne Furch (screenplay), Constantin Film (production).

Cast: Christine Görner (Countess Mariza), Rudolf Schock (Count Tassilo), Renate Ewert (Lisa), Gunther Philipp (Baron Zsupán), Hans Moser (Ferdinand), Lucie Englisch (Franzi), Alice and Ellen Kessler.

Video: Taurus/German Language Video Center VHS. Color. In German. 110 minutes.

1973 Unitel film

German TV film: Eugen York (director), Wolfgang Ebert (conductor, Vienna Symphony Orchestra and Vienna Operetta Choir), Rolf and Alexandra Becker (screenplay), Otto Pischinger (set designer), Unitel (production).

Cast: Erzsebet Hazy (Countess Mariza), René Kollo (Count Tassilo), Dagmar Koller (Lisa), Ljuba Welitsch (Princess Bozeno), Kurt Huemer (Baron Zsupán), Olivera Miljakovic (Manja).

Video: Taurus (Germany) VHS. Color. In German. 102 minutes.

Comment: Shot in 35mm on location in the countryside with plenty of colorful dancing and inventive Busby Berkeley–like camera movements.

1992 Italian TV: Operette, che Passione!

Italian TV production: Sandro Massimini (director/producer), Roberto Negri (pianist), Sandro Corelli (choreographer).

Singers: Sandro Massimini, Sara Dilena, Tadamici Oriè.

Video: Pierluigi Pagano (director). Color. In Italian. About 19 minutes. Ricordi (Italy) VHS.

Comment: Highlights of the operetta in Italian on the Italian TV series *Operette, che Passione!* Songs include "Se vieni a Varasdin," "Vien Tzigon," and "Il trillare delle viole."

Early film

1925 Steinhoff film

Vivian Gibson plays the countess with Harry Liedtke as Count Tassilo in this early German feature film of the operetta. It was directed by Hans Steinhoff, who also filmed *Die Fledermaus* and *Der Bettelstudent*. Black and white. Silent. About 70 minutes.

GRAF VON LUXEMBURG, DER
1909 operetta by Lehár

FRANZ LEHÁR's *Der Graf von Luxemburg* (The Count of Luxembourg), libretto by Alfred Maria Willner and Robert Bodansky, is the story of René, the penniless Count of Luxembourg. As he is in need of money, he agrees to marry opera singer Angèle Didier for a substantial payment. The marriage is arranged so she will have a title and be able to marry Prince Basil; it takes place without either seeing the other. Naturally, they later fall in love but don't know they are already married to each other. After various problems are solved, they become a happy couple. The operetta was staged in English in London in 1911 and in New York in 1912.

1957 CCC film

German feature film: Werner Jacobs (director), CCC (production).

Cast: Renate Holm (Angèle), Gerhard Riedmann (René), Germaine Damar.

Color. In German. 90 minutes.

1963 Mexican Television

Mexican TV film: Director and conductor unknown, Max Factor company (production).

Cast: Plácido Domingo (Count of Luxembourg) Marta Ornela (Angèle), Pepita Embil, Plácido Domingo Sr.

Black and white. In Spanish. 80 minutes.

Comment: A family film, with Domingo's wife as Angèle and his father and mother in the other main roles. The film, sponsored by Max Factor, has not been located and could be lost.

1972 Unitel film

German TV film: Wolfgang Glück (director), Walter Goldschmidt (conductor, Kurt Graunke Symphony Orchestra), Gerd Staub (set designer), Unitel/ORF/ZDF (production).

Cast: Eberhard Wächter (Count), Lilian Sukis (Angèle), Erich Kunz (Prince Basil), Peter Frölich (Armand Brissard), Helga Papouschek (Juliette Vermont), Jane Tilden (Countess Stasa).

Video: Taurus (Germany) VHS. Color. In German. 96 minutes.

Comment: Filmed in 35mm.

1992 Il Conte de Lussemburgo

Italian TV production: Sandro Massimini (director/producer), Roberto Negri (pianist), Sandro Corelli (choreographer).

Cast: Sandro Massimini, Sara Dilena, Max René Cosotti.

Video: Ricordi (Italy) VHS. Pierluigi Pagano (director). Color. In Italian. About 19 minutes.

Comment: Highlights of the operetta, sung in its Italian version as *Il Conte de Lussemburgo,* on the Italian TV series *Operette, che Passione!* Songs include "Lei di qui lui di là" and "Cuoricin, tesorin."

Early films

1909 Messter Tonbild

German film producer Oskar Messter produced one of his longest sound films (Tonbilder) of *Der Graf von Luxemburg*. The 143-meter film included several scenes from the operetta and was shown with the music played on synchronized records. Black and white. In German. About 10 minutes.

1926 Chadwick film

George Walsh stars as René, the penniless count, in this American silent film version of the operetta directed by Arthur Gregor for Chadwick Films. Helen Lee Worthing plays the actress Angèle with Michael Dark as the Duke. It was screened with live music from the operetta. Black and white. In English. About 70 minutes.

GRANADOS, ENRIQUE
Catalan composer (1867–1916)

Enrique Granados is one of the best-known Catalan composers, especially for his opera GOYESCAS and his piano compositions. His Catalan operas, known only in Barcelona during his lifetime, include *Petrarca, Follet,* and *Picarel,* all written to librettos by Catalan poet Apeles Mestres. His most famous opera, *Goyescas,* premiered at the Metropolitan Opera in 1916. The composer was returning home from the Met premiere when he was killed when his ship was torpedoed in the English Channel.

GRANDE BRETÈCHE, LA
1957 TV opera by Hollingsworth

STANLEY HOLLINGSWORTH's opera *La grande Bretèche* was commissioned by the adventurous NBC Opera Theatre. Harry Duncan's libretto is based on a famous Balzac story that has been made into an opera by five composers. It's a grim tale about a countess whose lover is walled up in a closet by a jealous husband after she denies that he is there.

1957 NBC Opera Theatre
American TV production: John Schwartz (director), Peter Herman Adler (conductor, Symphony of the Air Orchestra), Gerald Ritholz (set designer), Samuel Chotzinoff (producer).

Cast: Gloria Lane (Countess Marie), Hugh Thompson (Count Robert, the husband), Davis Cunningham (Bagos, the lover), Adelaide Bishop (Rosalie, the maid), Gimi Beni (Gorenflot, the handyman).

Telecast February 10, 1957, on NBC Television. Kirk Browning (director). Color. In English. 45 minutes.

GRANDE-DUCHESSE DE GÉROLSTEIN, LA
1867 opéra-bouffe by Offenbach

JACQUES OFFENBACH's *La Grande-Duchesse de Gérolstein* (The Grand Duchess of Gérolstein), a satire about war and petty German principalities, was one of his greatest successes. Its popularity continued to the time of Lillian Russell, who sang its famous "Saber Song" to President Cleveland in one of the first long-distance phone calls. It was written for Offenbach's very good friend Hortense Schneider to a libretto by Henri Meilhac and Ludovic Halévy. The duchess fancies Private Fritz so she promotes him to commander-in-chief of her army to the dismay of bombastic General Boum. As Fritz prefers Wanda, he soon loses his promotion.

1979 Théâtre du Capitole de Toulouse
French stage production: Robert Dhéry (director), Michel Plasson (conductor, Théâtre du Capitole de Toulouse Orchestra and Chorus).

Cast: Régine Crespin (Grand Duchess), Charles Burles (Fritz), Michel Trempont (Boum), Danièle Castaing (Wanda).

Video: House of Opera DVD and VHS/Lyric and Opera Dubs VHS. Claude Dagues (director). Color. In French. 120 minutes.

Comment: Crespin, who seems fond of Offenbach, has recorded many of his operettas. She reprised the role of the Grand Duchess in San Francisco in 1983.

1992 Italian TV: Operette, che Passione!
Italian TV production: Sandro Massimini (director/producer), Roberto Negri (pianist), Sandro Corelli (choreographer).

Cast: Sandro Massimini, Sonia Dorigo, Max René Cosotti.

Video: Pierluigi Pagano (director). Color. In Italian. About 16 minutes. Ricordi (Italy) VHS.

Comment: Highlights and history of the operetta on the Italian TV series *Operette, che Passione!* Includes songs "Ah, que j'aime les militaires" and "Il generale Bum-Bum."

GRANFORTE, APOLLO
Italian baritone (1886–1975)

Apollo Granforte began his career in Argentina, where he made his debut in 1913. He sang with Melba on Williamson tours in Australia in 1924 and 1928 and became a regular at La Scala during the 1930s. He sang in a wide variety of operas, from Mascagni's *Nerone* to Wagner's *Parsifal,* but was especially admired in Rossini and Verdi. He can be seen as Rossini's Figaro in a short film made in Australia in 1928 and in a 1938 feature film biography of GIUSEPPE VERDI.

1928 Granforte Sings *The Barber of Seville*
Granforte bounces on stage in Figaro costume with his guitar and sings the "Largo al factotum" aria in an energetic manner with the backing of a full orchestra. He made this sound film in Australia while he was on tour with Melba. The title on the screen is "Efftee Presents Signor Apollo Granforte of La Scala, Milan, and the

Williamson-Imperial Grand Opera Company. Selections from 'The Barber of Seville' (Rossini)." The film was made by RCA with its Photophone Recording system. Black and white. In Italian. About 6 minutes. Lyric VHS.

GRAND HOTEL
1987 TV opera by Kortekangas

Finnish composer Olli Kortegangas's television opera *Grand Hotel,* libretto by Arti Melleri, was commissioned by the Finnish Broadcasting Company and won the Salzburg TV Opera Prize. It was composed for two singers playing seven roles, three choirs, an actor, and a chamber orchestra.

1987 YLE Finnish Television
Finnish TV production: Arto Haellstroem (director), Esa-Pekka Salonen (conductor, Avanti! Ensemble).

Cast: Sauli Tiilikainen (baritone roles), Eeva-Liisa Saarinen (mezzo-soprano roles), Kauko Laurikainen (actor).

Telecast September 12, 1987, on YLE. Color. In Finnish. 39 minutes.

GRAN SCENA OPERA, LA
1981 satirical opera group

La Gran Scena Opera Company of New York is a satirical male theatrical opera troupe that has been successful in poking gentle fun at opera around the world. It was founded in 1981 by Ira Siff who, in addition to being artistic director, stars as Madame Vera Galupe-Borszkh, a "traumatic" soprano known as La Dementia. His singing, like that of his colleagues, is unusual and quite funny.

1985 La Gran Scena in Munich
This La Gran Scena show was staged for the Munich Theater Festival and taped by Bavarian Television; it features the company in scenes from *Die Walküre, Semele, La bohème, Lucia di Lammermoor, Carmen,* and *La traviata.* The performers are Ira Siff, Keith Jurosko, Philip Koch, Bruce Hopkins, Luis Russinyol, Charles Walker, Dennis Raley, and Dan Brack. Ross Barentyne is music director, Kenneth M. Young designed the costumes, and Christopher Banner designed the wigs and make-up. Siff, Peter Schloser, and Jane Whitehill were the stage directors, and Christina Haberlik directed the video. Color. In English with arias in the original languages. 112 minutes. VAI VHS.

GRAN VÍA, LA
1886 zarzuela by Chueca and Valverde

Federico Chueca and Joaquín Valverde's *género chico* zarzuela *La Gran Vía,* with a revue-style libretto by Felipe Pérez y González, is a celebration of the creation of a new central street in Madrid. It was so popular it ran for four years and was staged in the United States, England, and Italy. The characters are mostly personifications of streets, buildings such as the Elíseo dance hall, and allegorical figures such as the Gentleman and the Stroller. There is almost no plot, but the cheerful music creates its own narrative.

1995 Teatro Calderón, Madrid
Spanish stage production: José Luis Moreno (director), José A. Irasforza (conductor, Teatro Calderón Orchestra and Chorus), Julian Pérez Muñoz (set designer).

Cast: Amelia Font (Elíseo), Mar Abscal (Menegilda), Santiago Muriente (Comadrón), Pedro Pablo Juárez, Enrique del Portal (Thief), David Muro (Thief), Alhambra Ballet (dancers).

Video: Metrovideo (Spain) VHS. Telecast live by RTVE. José Ignado Ortega (director). Color. In Spanish. 49 minutes.

***1996 Jarvis Conservatory, Napa
American stage production: Daniel Helfgot (director), Monroe Kanouse (conductor, Jarvis Conservatory Orchestra), Peter Crompton (set designer), Carlos Carvajal (choreographer), William Jarvis (producer/translator).

Cast: Andrew Moore (Stroller), Martin Philip (Gentleman), Abraham Aviles (Midwife), Virginia Voulgaris (Main Street), Sarah Rosemond (Injury Street), Ellen Cowan (Menegilda).

Video: Jarvis Conservatory DVD/VHS. Milt Wallace (director). Color. Dialogue in English, singing in Spanish with English subtitles. 60 minutes.

Comment: Delightfully sung and danced evocation of turn-of-the-century Madrid with a large cast of personified streets, maids, ladies, police officers, sailors, thieves, and allegorical figures.

Related films

1910 "Ladroni" (terzetto)
Italian sound film of the trio "Ladroni" (Thieves) from *La Gran Vía* made by the Itala Film company of Turin. The number was performed by three men on screen with the singing from a synchronized disc recording. The zarzuela was quite popular in Italy at the time. Black and white. In Italian. 4 minutes.

2000 "Chotis del Elíseo Madrileño"

"Chotis del Elíseo Madrileño," an aria sung by the personified dance hall Elíseo in *La Gran Vía*, is performed in concert style by soprano Camille Zamora with help from tenor Andrew Moore and baritone Keir Murray. Philip J. Bauman conducts the Jarvis Conservatory Orchestra. The delightful performance is included as extra on the Jarvis Conservatory VHS of *Agua, Azucarillos y Aguardiente*. Color. Sung in Spanish with English subtitles. About 10 minutes.

GRAYSON, KATHRYN

American soprano (1922–)

Kathryn Grayson was the successor to Jeanette MacDonald at MGM during the 1940s and 1950s, singing the difficult soprano roles in films based on operettas or featuring opera arias. Grayson, born Zelma Kathryn Hedrick in North Carolina, grew up wanting to be an opera diva. She had a florid coloratura soprano voice, photographed well, and was a fine star for MGM in its musical heyday. She made an adequate operatic partner for Mario Lanza and Lauritz Melchior and was able to sing enough opera to star as Grace Moore in a biopic. She was featured in the 1941 film version of the operetta RIO RITA, in which she sings an aria from Meyerbeer's opera DINORAH, but her greatest successes were her partnerships with Howard Keel in SHOW BOAT (1951) and *Kiss Me Kate* (1943) and with Gordon MacRae in THE DESERT SONG (1953). THE VAGABOND KING with Oreste in 1956 was her last film. In 1960, she went on stage in productions of the operas *Madama Butterfly*, *La bohème*, and *La traviata*. In 1961, she turned to operettas and was on stage in *The Merry Widow*, *Naughty Marietta*, and *Der Fledermaus*. Her films with operatic content are listed below.

1941 Andy Hardy's Private Secretary

Grayson, in her first film, plays a high school student hired by fellow student Mickey Rooney to sort out his mixed-up affairs. She sings the "Mad Scene" from *Lucia di Lammermoor* at the school graduation ceremony. George Seitz directed for MGM. Black and white. 101 minutes.

1943 Thousands Cheer

Grayson sings the aria "Sempre libera" from *La traviata* in this all-star film in which she is the love interest of army private Gene Kelly. George Sidney directed. Black and white. 126 minutes.

1946 Two Sisters From Boston

Kathryn Grayson plays opposite Met tenor Lauritz Melchior in the 1890s musical. She sings in a saloon to earn money but really wants to get into opera. Her family think she's already an opera star so she has to pretend to be one and sneak on stage with Melchior. They team on IMAGINARY OPERAS called *My Country*, based on music by Liszt, and *Marie Antoinette*, based on music by Mendelssohn. See TWO SISTERS FROM BOSTON.

1947 It Happened in Brooklyn

Grayson stars opposite Frank Sinatra in a story about Brooklynites trying to break into musical show business. She sings the "Bell Song" from *Lakmé* and teams up with Sinatra for the duet "Là ci darem la mano" from *Don Giovanni*. Richard Whorf directed. Black and white. 105 minutes.

1949 That Midnight Kiss

Grayson stars opposite Mario Lanza in his first film. She's an heiress who wants to be an opera singer; he's a truck driver with a great voice. There is music from *Aida*, *Cavalleria rusticana*, and *L'elisir d'amore*. See THAT MIDNIGHT KISS.

1950 The Toast of New Orleans

Grayson plays the prima donna of the French opera house in turn-of-the-century New Orleans, and Mario Lanza is a Louisiana fisherman who becomes an opera star through her tutoring. She is seen on stage in scenes from *Mignon* and *Madama Butterfly*. Cio-Cio-San was said to be her favorite opera role. See THE TOAST OF NEW ORLEANS.

1950 Grounds for Marriage

Grayson plays an opera star who returns to New York after success in Europe. She sings arias from *Mignon* and *Le nozze di Figaro*, sings "Hymn to the Sun" from *The Golden Cockerel*, appears on stage as Mimì in *La bohème*, and appears in a dream sequence *Carmen*. The plot revolves around her relationship with ex-husband Van Johnson. See GROUNDS FOR MARRIAGE.

1953 So This Is Love

Grayson plays diva Grace Moore in this film about her struggle to become an opera star. She finishes the film on stage at the Metropolitan Opera as Mimì in *La bohème* singing "Mi chiamano Mimì." See SO THIS IS LOVE.

GREAT CARUSO, THE

1951 American film with opera content

Mario Lanza plays Enrico Caruso in *The Great Caruso*, one of the most popular and influential films ever made about opera. It's a highly romantic biography, partially based on a book by Caruso's American wife, with all the legends as facts, but it is still good entertainment. It did a great deal to make the wider public interested in opera, and singers such as José Carreras and Plácido Domingo have acknowledged its influence on them. Ann Blyth plays Caruso's American wife Dorothy Benjamin, Dorothy Kirsten is Met soprano Louise Heggar (his regular stage partner in the film, presumably modeled on Louise Homer), Jarmila Novotná is temperamental prima donna Maria Selko, Alan Napier is Met tenor Jean Reszke, Eduard Franz is Met manager Giulio Gatti-Casazza, and Paul Javor is baritone Antonio Scotti. The film opens with Caruso's birth in Naples, glances at his early preoperatic life, and then shows his rise to fame as a spear bearer in AIDA, singing in *Tosca,* making a breakthrough in CAVALLERIA RUSTICANA, and achieving fame in LA GIOCONDA. After success at Covent Garden in 1902 in RIGOLETTO, he goes to New York to sing in AIDA and triumphs in LA BOHÈME. After a whirlwind world tour (IL TROVATORE in Paris, *Rigoletto* in Berlin, TOSCA in Madrid, and *Cavalleria rusticana* in Rio de Janeiro), he returns to New York to marry Dorothy, although first he cries his heart out with the PAGLIACCI lament "Vesti la giubba" at a concert when she does not appear. They elope, and a baby girl is born while he performs in the LUCIA DI LAMMERMOOR sextet on stage. A year later he is seen using ether to quell a cough, and he dies on stage singing "The Last Rose of Summer" in MARTHA. In real life, Caruso's last Met appearance was in Halevy's *La Juive* on December 24, 1920; he died the following August of a lung ailment. Singers seen in the staged opera sequences include Blanche Thebom, Teresa Celli, Nicola Moscone, Giuseppe Valdengo, Lucine Amara, and Marina Koshetz. The opera sequences were staged and conducted by Peter Herman Adler, and Richard Thorpe directed the film for MGM. (Arias recorded for the film's soundtrack album, but not included in the final film, are "Questa o quella" and "Parmi veder le lagrime" from *Rigoletto,* "Recondita armonia" from *Tosca,* and "Una furtiva lagrima" from *L'elisir d'amore.*) Color. 109 minutes. MGM-UA DVD/VHS.

GREAT LOVER, THE
American film series with opera content

The Great Lover originated as a 1915 Broadway play by Leo Ditrichstein and Frederick and Fanny Hatton about a love affair between a famous opera baritone and a rising young soprano. It was filmed in 1920 and again in 1932. A third film, to star Ezio Pinza, Jan Peerce, Roberta Peters, and Robert Merrill, was announced in 1952 but never made.

1920 Goldwyn film
John Sainpolis stars as famous baritone Jean Paurel, who becomes engaged to American soprano Claire Adams. She has just returned from study in Europe and joined his opera company. Prima donna Rose Dion becomes jealous, as does young singer John Davidson. Paurel loses his voice and eventually gives up the girl to the young man, who turns out to be his son. Several scenes take place on the opera house stage. Frank Lloyd directed for Goldwyn Pictures. Black and white. Silent. About 70 minutes.

1932 MGM film
Adolphe Menjou stars as the famous opera baritone and philanderer Jean Paurel who seduces women by singing Don Giovanni's "Là ci darem la mano." He is attracted to American singer Irene Dunne and arranges for her to come to the Metropolitan. There is much backstage strife as he wins her, loses his voice, and finally gives her up to her true love. The film features *Don Giovanni* on stage at the Met plus arias from *Die Walküre, The Barber of Seville,* and *Roméo et Juliette.* In real life Dunne had wanted to be an opera singer, but the Met turned her down. Harry Beaumont directed for MGM. Black and white. 79 minutes.

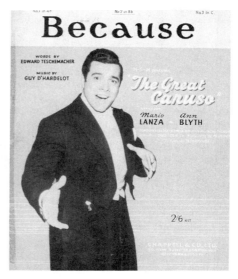

The Great Caruso (1951): Sheet music for popular song performed by Enrico Caruso (Mario Lanza) in this romantic film.

GREAT PERFORMANCES
PBS opera series (1975–)

This PBS television series is a kind of cultural umbrella brand name rather than a particular program but includes many operas. It has presented many European as well as American productions.

GREEK
1988 opera by Turnage

MARK-ANTHONY TURNAGE's opera *Greek* is a modern variation of the Oedipus legend set in London's East End with the plague seen as unstoppable unemployment and racism. The protagonist Eddy discovers he has killed his father and married his mother. The opera was commissioned for the Munich Biennale by Hans Werner Henze and then staged at the Edinburgh Festival and the English National Opera. The libretto, by the composer and Jonathan Moore, is based on a play by Stephen Berkoff with the same title. *Greek* was well received by critics, who interpreted it as an anti-Thatcher political statement.

1990 BBC Television
English TV production: Jonathan Moore (director), Richard Bernas (conductor, The Almeida Ensemble), David Blight (set/costume designer), Keith Alexander (producer).

Cast: Quentin Hayes (Eddy), Fiona Kimm (sister, wife, Sphinx), Richard Stuart (father, café manager, police chief), Helen Charnock (mother, waitress, Sphinx).

Video: RM Arts (GB) VHS. Peter Maniura (director). Color. In English. 81 minutes.

GREEK PASSION, THE
1961 opera by Martinů

BOHUSLAV MARTINŮ's opera *The Greek Passion,* libretto in English by the composer, is based on Nikos Kazantzakis's novel *Christ Recrucified.* It is set in a Greek village where young Manolios becomes identified with Christ after the priest Grigoris selects him for the role in a Passion play. A young widow named Katerina is chosen to play Mary Magdalene and her lover Panait to be Judas. After refugees arrive in the village and are aided by Manolios against the priest's wishes, Katerina falls in love with him. He is killed by Panait.

1981 Indiana University Opera Theater
American stage production: Ross Allen (director), Bryan Balkwith (conductor, Indiana University Opera Theater Orchestra and Chorus), Max Rothlisberger (set designer), Brian Large (English translation).

Cast: Larry Paxton (Manolios), Rebecca Field (Katerina), Tim Nobel (Grigoris), David Rampy (Panait), Rudolf Neufeld (Kostandis), Joannes Kosters (Fotis).

Video at the New York Public Library. Taped April 11, 1981; telecast April 4, 1982, on Bravo. Phillip Byrd (director). Color. In English. 145 minutes.

Comment: This university production was the American premiere of the opera.

1999 Simerda film
Czech feature film: Tomas Simerda (director), Sir Charles Mackerras (conductor, Brno State Philharmonic Orchestra, Prague Philharmonic Chorus and Kuhn Children's Chorus), Mijo Adzic (set designer).

Singers: John Mitchinson (Manolios), Helen Field (Katerina), John Tomlinson (Grigoris), Jeffrey Lawton (Panait), Philip Joll (Kostandis), Geoffrey Moses (Fotis), Arthur Davies (Yannakos), Rita Cullis (Lenio).

Color. In English. 90 minutes.

Comment: Filmed on location on an island in the Adriatic with the actors dubbed by English singers from a Supraphon recording. It was produced for screening on Czech television.

GREENAWAY, PETER
English film director (1942–)

Peter Greenaway writes and directs operas as well as films and also makes documentaries about opera composers. He began as painter, turned to films in 1965, and became internationally known in 1982 for his first feature, *The Draughtsman's Contract,* which featured a Purcell-esque score by Michael Nyman. There were also operatic qualities in his subsequent films, including *The Cook, the Thief, His Wife and Her Lover* and *Prospero's Books.* In 1993 he began to collaborate with Dutch composer LOUIS ANDRIESSEN, and they created the television opera M IS FOR MAN, MUSIC AND MOZART. In 1994 he wrote the libretto and staged Andriessen's opera ROSA, DEATH OF A COMPOSER, using cinematic techniques; when it was revived in 1998, he filmed it. Greenaway made fascinating documentaries about composers ROBERT ASHLEY, JOHN CAGE, PHILIP GLASS, and MEREDITH MONK for the series *4 American Composers.*

GRÉMILLON, JEAN
French film director (1902–1959)

French filmmaker Jean Grémillon, known for films such as *Remorques* and *Le ciel est à vous,* wanted to become a professional musician after seeing Debussy's *Pelléas et Mélisande* 15 times but turned to cinema in 1923. In 1934 he made a film based on a famous Spanish opera, Jose Serrano's LA DOLOROSA. In 1935 he shot the musical *La valse royale,* the French version of the German operetta *Königswalzer.* In 1936 he collaborated with fellow filmmaker Luis Buñuel and directed a much-liked zarzuela film based on Serrano's LA ALEGRÍA DEL BATALLÓN.

GRIFFELKIN
1955 TV opera by Foss

LUKAS FOSS's opera *Griffelkin,* commissioned by NBC Opera Theatre with a libretto by Alastair Reid, is based on a fairy tale called *The Little Devil's Birthday* told to Foss when he was a boy; it is intended to be an opera with appeal for both children and adults. Griffelkin is a little devil whose birthday present is a day in our human world to create mischief. The experience changes him, as he finds he likes things in this world—and especially one little girl. He is so corrupted that he commits a good deed, is expelled from Hell, and is forced to become a human. The opera was first staged at Tanglewood in 1956 and was revived by New York City Opera in 1993.

1955 NBC Opera Theater
American TV production: Robert Joffrey (director), Peter Herman Adler (conductor, Symphony of the Air Orchestra), Rouben Ter-Arutunian (set designer), Robert Joffrey (choreographer), Samuel Chotzinoff (producer).
Cast: Adelaide Bishop (Griffelkin), Mary Kreste (Devil's Grandmother), Mignon Dunn (Voice of Statue), Andrew McKinley (Voice of Mailbox), Alice Richmond (Mother), Oliver Andes (Boy), Rose Geringer (Girl), Lee Cass (Policeman), Robert Holland (Shopkeeper).
Video at the MTR. Kirk Browning (director). Telecast November 6, 1955, on NBC. Black and white. In English. 60 minutes.

GROSS TENOR, DER
1930 German film with operatic content

Emil Jannings plays a world-famous opera tenor named Alberto Winkelmann in *Der Gross Tenor* (The Great Tenor), a German film made at the height of Jannings's stardom. There are opera house scenes in Germany, Brazil, and Austria and scenes of Jennings on stage in *Otello* and *Lohengrin* with his singing dubbed. The film shows his pampered, philandering life, his jealousy about a rising singer, the loss of his voice, and his eventual redemption. Renate Müller plays his faithful wife, with Evaristo Signorini as his rival. Hans Müller and Robert Liebmann wrote the screenplay, Günther Rittau and Konstantin Tschet were the cinematographers, and Hans Schwartz directed for UFA. The film is also known as *Liebling der Götter*. Black and white. In German. 103 minutes.

GROUNDS FOR MARRIAGE
1950 American film with operatic content

Kathryn Grayson plays an opera star who returns to New York after enjoying success in Europe. She sings the "Hymn to the Sun" from *The Golden Cockerel* at a rehearsal and then starts to becomes reinvolved with former husband Van Johnson. They divorced because she spent so much time on her opera career. She appears on stage as Mimì in *La bohème,* despite a doctor's disapproval, with Richard Atchkinson as her Rodolfo. She participates in a *Carmen* dream sequence with Johnson while Milton Cross narrates the opera story; Johnson sings arias by

both Don José and Escamillo through the magic of dubbing. She also sings arias from *Mignon* and *Le nozze di Figaro*. Vladimir Resing staged the excerpts from the operas, Allen Rivkin and Laura Kerr wrote the screenplay based on a story by producer Samuel Marx, John Alton was the cinematographer, and Robert Z. Leonard directed for MGM. Black and white. 90 minutes.

GUADAGNO, ANTON
Italian-born American conductor (1925–2002)

Anton Guadagno, principal conductor of Palm Beach Opera in Florida for 19 years, studied in Italy and began his career in South America. He made his American debut in 1952, worked for many years with opera companies in Philadelphia and Cincinnati, and conducted at the Vienna Staatsoper for 30 seasons. His operas on video include spectacular open-air productions of AIDA at the Arena di Verona in 1981 and OTELLO at the St. Margarethen Opera Festival in 2002. He conducted for Roberto Alagna and Angela Gheorghiu's 2002 film of ROMÉO ET JULIETTE and for Carlo Bergonzi's TENORS concert at the Arena di Verona in 1990.

GUARANY, IL
1870 opera by Gomes

This opera, which made Brazilian composer CARLOS GOMES famous when it premiered at La Scala in 1870, is the only opera by a 19th-century Latin American composer to enter the repertory, and it is still the best-known Brazilian opera. Antonio Scalvini and Carlo D'Ormeville wrote the libretto, which tells the story of the Guarani Indian Peri and his love for the Portuguese noblewoman Cecilia (it is set around 1560 near Rio de Janeiro). A Spanish adventurer named Gonzales is the chief villain. *Il Guarany* is modeled on Italian opera, but it sounds different as it incorporates Brazilian Indian melodies and rhythms into the score. It was admired by Verdi and presented in most major opera houses during the 19th century, and its arias were recorded by Caruso, Gigli, and Destinn. It was rarely staged outside Brazil in modern times until Plácido Domingo, who admires it, starred in productions in Bonn in 1994 and Washington, D.C., in 1996.

1986 Teatro Campinas, Sao Paulo
Brazilian stage production: Benito Juarez (conductor, Campinas Municipal Symphony Orchestra).
Cast: Ivo Lessa (Peri), Niza de Castro Tank (Cecilia), Eduardo Janho-Abumrad (Don Antonio), Nelson N. Di Marzio (Gonzales).
Video: Opera Dubs VHS. Telecast by RTC. Color. In Italian with Portuguese titles. 148 minutes.

1994 Bonn Opera

German stage production: Werner Herzog (director), John Neschling (conductor, Bonn Opera Orchestra and Chorus), Maurizio Baló (set designer).

Cast: Plácido Domingo (Peri), Veronica Villarroel (Cecilia), Carlos Alvarez (Gonzales) Hao Jiang Tian (Don Antonio).

House of Opera DVD/VHS. Donald Sturrock (director). Color. In Italian with English subtitles. 55 minutes.

Comment: Rehearsal highlights from the BBC TV film series *Plácido Domingo's Tales at the Opera*, produced by Daniel Snowman and Martin Rosenbaum. Domingo introduces the opera and explains how it had long been his ambition to sing in it. The cast is about the same as that for the 1996 Washington Opera production.

1996 Sofia National Opera

Bulgarian stage production: Plamen Kartaloff (director), Júlio Medaglia, (conductor, Sofia National Opera Orchestra and Chorus), Cyro Del Nero (set designer).

Cast: Roumen Doykov (Peri), Krassamira Stoyanova (Cecilia).

Video: Premiere Opera/House of Opera VHS. Telecast October 25, 1996, by Bulgarian National Television. Color. In Italian. 145 minutes.

Early/related films

1916 O Guarani

O Guarani was made in Brazil during the silent era as what was known as a "singing" film. Singers stood behind the screen and sang arias from the opera (in Portuguese) as the characters appeared to sing on screen. Georgina Marchiani played Cecilia. Black and white. Silent. About 40 minutes.

1923 Aversano film

Feature version of the opera made in Italy by Salvatore Aversano, a big production for its time and praised for its advanced special effects. Gino Soldarelli plays Peri with Elisenda Annovazzi as Cecilia and Camillo de Rossi as Gonzales. Black and white. Silent. About 70 minutes.

1948 Freda film

Riccardo Freda's biographical film about the composer, *Guarany*, features extracts from the opera and tells how it came to be written. Antonio Vilar plays Gomes, and the composer's music is used as the film score. Black and white. In Italian. 85 minutes.

1970 Terre em transe

An excerpt from *Il Guarany* is featured in the Brazilian film *Terre em transe* directed by Glauber Rocha. The film revolves around a political murder. Color. In Portuguese with English subtitles. 110 minutes.

1986 Romanca Final

José Carreras and Montserrat Caballé sing the roles of Peri and Cecilia in the re-creation of the premiere of *Il Guarany* in the Catalan film *Romanca Final*. The music is performed by the Orchestra and Choir of the Liceu Theatre led by Romano Gandolfi. Jose M. Forque directed the movie, a biography of 19th-century Navarese tenor Julián Gayarre. Color. In Spanish with English subtitles. 120 minutes. Kultur VHS.

GUEDEN, HILDE
Austrian soprano (1917–1988)

Hilde Gueden made her debut at the Volksoper in Vienna in an operetta by Robert Stolz. After singing in Zurich, Munich, and Salzburg, she became a member of the Vienna State Opera. She appeared at the Metropolitan for nine seasons where she was much admired for her vocal technique. She can be seen as Zerlina in DON GIOVANNI and Cherubino in LE NOZZE DI FIGARO in 1954 Vienna State Opera productions, and in a 1953 *Ed Sullivan Show* TV program about the METROPOLITAN OPERA. She is heard on the soundtrack of a 1955 Austrian film about MOZART.

GUERRERO, JACINTO
Spanish composer (1895–1951)

Jacinto Guerrero y Torres, one of the most popular Spanish composers of zarzuelas, first became known through the song "Hymn to Toledo." He created more than 200 musical stage works, in addition to composing for films and revues, and was a major promoter of the zarzuela genre. His best-known zarzuelas are *Los gavilanes* (1923); DON QUINTIN EL AMARGAO (1924), which was filmed by Luis Buñuel; and the Don Quixote story EL HUÉSPED DEL SEVILLANO (1926).

GUILLAUME TELL
1829 opera by Rossini

Guillaume Tell (Guglielmo Tell/William Tell) has the most famous overture in opera, so much so that an intellectual was once defined as a person who could listen to it and not think of *The Lone Ranger*. GIOACHINO ROSSINI's last opera was composed in Paris in French to a libretto by Étienne de Jouy and Hippolyte-Louis-Florent and is based on a play by Schiller. However, most of the versions on video are in Italian, and only the French speak of a *Guillaume Tell* overture. The opera tells the legendary story of the Swiss rebel patriot archer who was forced to shoot an apple off his son's head. The main characters are Guillaume Tell; his conspiratorial friends Walter Furst and Arnold Melcthal; Austrian princess Mathilde, who loves Arnold; Tell's son Jemmy; Tell's wife Hedwige; and the tyrant Gesler. The story has been filmed many times since 1901, although most of the early films are based on the legend or the Schiller play. The overture has been as popular with animated filmmakers as with *Lone Ranger* fans.

1948 First Opera Film Festival

Italian stage production: Enrico Fulchigoni (director), Angelo Questa (conductor, Rome Opera House Orchestra and Chorus), George Richfield (producer).

Cast: Tito Gobbi (Guglielmo Tell), Pina Malgarini (Mathilde, sung by Gabriella Gatti), José Soler (Arnoldo).

Video: Bel Canto Society/Lyric VHS. Edmondo Cancellieri (film director). Black and white. In Italian with English voice-over by Olin Downes. 25 minutes.

Comment: Highlights version of the opera filmed on stage at the Rome Opera House with singers from La Scala and Rome. It was produced for the anthology film *First Opera Film Festival*.

1987 Zurich Opera

Swiss stage production: Daniel Schmid (director), Nello Santi (conductor, Zurich Opera Orchestra and Chorus).

Cast: Antonio Salvadori (Guglielmo Tell), Maria Chiara (Matilde), Salvatore Fisichella (Arnoldo), Alfred Muff (Gesler), Margaret Chalker (Jemmy), Nadine Asher (Hedwige).

Video: House of Opera/Lyric VHS. Daniel Schmid (director). Color. In Italian. 172 minutes.

1991 Teatro alla Scala

Italian stage production: Luca Ronconi (director), Riccardo Muti (conductor, Teatro alla Scala Orchestra and Chorus), Gianni Quaranta (set designer).

Cast: Giorgio Zancanaro (Guglielmo Tell), Cheryl Studer (Matilde), Chris Merritt (Arnoldo), Luigi Roni (Gesler), Amelia Felle (Gemma), Giorgio Surjan (Gualitiero).

Image Entertainment DVD/Home Vision VHS. Luca Ronconi (director). Color. In Italian with English subtitles. 242 minutes.

Early/related films

1911 Film d'Arte Italiana film

Ugo Falena directed *Guglielmo Tell*, an Italian adaptation of the Schiller play for the Film d'Arte Italiana studio with Joseph Kaschmann and Bianca Lorenzoi as the stars. Black and white. Silent. About 10 minutes.

1925 Harder film

Emil Harder directed this Swiss feature film based on the opera libretto and shown in America with live music from the opera. Felix Orell is Tell, George Roberts is Albrecht, and Robert Kleiner is Gesler with support from Heinrich Gretler, Elizabeth Jaun, and Helene Kassewitcz. Black and white. Silent. About 75 minutes.

1927 Henry Hadley Conducts

Henry Hadley, who wrote operas as well as conducting, was featured in one of the early Vitaphone sound films conducting the New York Philharmonic Orchestra in a performance of the *William Tell* Overture. Black and white. About 8 minutes.

1933/1956 The Lone Ranger

The *William Tell* Overture was used as the theme music for *The Lone Ranger* radio show when it started in 1933. When the series moved to television in 1949 with Clayton Moore as star, the Rossini theme music became even better known. There have been many movies about the character, but the most "authentic" is the 1956 *The Lone Ranger* derived from the TV series. Moore plays the Lone Ranger, Stuart Heisler directed. Color. 86 minutes.

1934 Wilhelm Tell

German version of the story starring Conrad Veidt as Tell with music by Herbert Windt, shown in United States as *The Legend of William Tell*. Heinz Paul directed for Terra Film. Black and white. In German. 85 minutes.

1934 William Tell

William Lantz cartoon using the Overture as its score, directed by William Nolan. Black and white. In English. 7 minutes.

1935 The Band Concert

Disney's Mickey Mouse conducts an animated band in a park in his first color film. The cartoon audience cheers selections from *Zampa*, and then the band plays the *William Tell* Overture until Donald Duck interrupts. Wilfred Jackson directed. Color. 7 minutes.

1940 Popeye the Sailor Meets William Tell

The king of spinach meets the king of the bow and arrow to Rossini's music in this lively animated cartoon. Dave Fleischer directed and Max Fleischer produced for Paramount. Color. 7 minutes.

1947 Overture to William Tell

Walter Lantz made this animated cartoon for his *Musical Miniatures* series, basing it on the overture to the Rossini opera and featuring his cartoon character Wally Walrus. Dick Lundy directed. Color. 7 minutes.

1948 Guglielmo Tell

Italian narrative version of the story based on the Schiller play and using Rossini's music as score. Gino Cervi plays Guglielmo Tell with Allegra Sander as Mathilde, Monique Orban as Berta, and Paul Muller as Gessler. Fernando Previtali directed. Black and white. In Italian. 91 minutes.

1948 A Song Is Born

The *William Tell* Overture is featured in this Danny Kaye movie about an encyclopedist who needs to learn about jazz. Howard Hawks directed this remake of his *Ball of Fire*. Color. 111 minutes.

1983 E la nave va

A luxury liner full of opera people sailing from Naples in 1914 for the funeral of a famous opera singer is sunk by an Austrian battleship. Earlier there is ironic use of the "Soldiers' Dance" from *William Tell;* in the opera Austrian soldiers force Swiss women to dance with them to this tune. Federico Fellini directed. See E LA NAVE VA.

1971 A Clockwork Orange

The *William Tell* Overture is featured on the soundtrack of Stanley Kubrick's dystopian vision of England in the not-too-distant future, as imagined by Anthony Burgess. Color. 136 minutes.

1991 Nello Santi's My Favorite Opera

Nello Santi is the focal point of this documentary in the *My Favorite Opera* series. Director Tomas Simerda mixes scenes from the opera with interviews with the conductor and views of the Swiss countryside where the opera takes place. Lee Roisum sings Tell, Maria Chiara is Matilde, Salvatore Fisichella is Arnold, and Santi conducts the Svizzera Italiana Orchestra. Color. 60 minutes. Kultur VHS.

1993 Ludwig 1881

Helmut Berger stars in this German film about an attempt by King Ludwig II of Bavaria to present Schiller's *Wil-liam Tell* in 1881 in its original setting at Lake Lucerne. Donatello Dubini directed. Color. In German. 90 minutes.

GURIDI, JESÚS

Basque composer (1886–1961)

Jesús Guridi, one of the most popular Basque musicians, composed a number of zarzuelas and operas in the Basque language. The libretto of his opera *Mirentxu* (1910) is in Basque and includes quotes from Basque folk music, while his opera *Amaya* (1920) is based on a famous Navarese novel. His most famous work, however, is the Basque zarzuela EL CASERÍO (1926), considered one of the masterpieces of the genre.

H

HACKETT, CHARLES
American tenor (1889–1942)

Massachusetts tenor Charles Hackett began his opera career in Italy and France, made his debut at the Metropolitan Opera in 1919, and sang with the Chicago Opera from 1922 to 1935. He was able to sing at Covent Garden with Melba. His recordings include duets with Rosa Ponselle, and he continued singing professionally until 1939. He can be heard in fine form on a 1935 Met broadcast of Gounod's *Roméo et Juliette.*

1927–1929 Vitaphone films
Hackett made seven Vitaphone sound opera films during the period from 1927 to 1929 and was described on them as the "leading tenor of the Chicago Civic Opera Co." The films include a duet from *Roméo et Juliette* with Rosa Low and arias from *Rigoletto, Don Giovanni, L'Africana, Faust,* and *Sadko* plus various art songs. Black and white. Each about 8 minutes.

HADLEY, JERRY
American tenor (1952–)

Jerry Hadley made his debut as Lyonel in *Martha* in Sarasota in 1978 and then sang with New York City Opera for several seasons in a wide range of roles. His European career began in Vienna in 1982 as Nemorino in *L'elisir d'amore;* afterwards, he sang in most of the major European opera houses. He made his debut at the Metropolitan Opera in 1987 as Des Grieux in *Manon.* Hadley is featured in a large number of videos and was chosen by Leonard Bernstein to be his final Candide. He can also be seen in concert with FREDERICA VON STADE in 1990 and at a Mozart gala at the VERONA Arena in 1991. His screen operas include ANNA BOLENA (1985), AUFSTIEG UND FALL DER STADT MAHAGONNY (1998), CANDIDE (1989), COSÌ FAN TUTTE (1996), DON GIOVANNI (1990), IDOMENEO (1983), MADAMA BUTTERFLY (1982), MESSIAH (1992), MOZART REQUIEM (1988), THE RAKE'S PROGRESS (1992/1996), and IL RE PASTORE (1989).

HAGEGÅRD, HÅKAN
Swedish baritone (1945–)

Håkan Hagegård delighted audiences in 1973 as the superb Papageno in Ingmar Bergman's film of DIE ZAUBERFLÖTE although he was then an unknown baritone singing in Swedish. The part was his debut role at Sweden's Royal Opera in 1968; he has since become one of the most popular baritones in the world. He made his first appearance at the Metropolitan as Malatesta in DON PASQUALE (1979) and later created the role of Beaumarchais in Corigliano's THE GHOSTS OF VERSAILLES in 1991. His other screen operas include DON GIOVANNI at Drottningholm (1987), CAPRICCIO at Glyndebourne (1975) and San Francisco (1992), DIE FLEDERMAUS at the Met (1986), and a film of THE RAKE'S PROGRESS (1995).

HAHN, REYNALDO
Venezuelan-born French composer (1875–1947)

Reynaldo Hahn, one of the leading modern composers of French operettas, was also a specialist in conducting Mozart, a notable singer, and an intimate friend of Proust. His biggest success was CIBOULETTE (1923), which is set in Les Halles in 1867 and is virtually an homage to the operettas of Messager and Lecocq. He also wrote a popular operetta with Mozartian themes called *Mozart,* which premiered with YVONNE PRINTEMPS as the composer. His last operetta was *Malvina* (1935). Hahn also composed an opera, *Le merchant de Venise,* and movie music, including *La dame aux camélias* with Printemps.

HAITINK, BERNARD
Dutch conductor (1929–)

Bernard Haitink, one of the major opera conductors of the world, is well represented on video. He can be seen leading the London Philharmonic Orchestra at the Glyndebourne Festival, often for Peter Hall productions, and at Covent Garden where he was music director and conducted a tribute to TCHAIKOVSKY (1993). See ALBERT HERRING (1985), ARABELLA (1984), THE BARTERED BRIDE (1998), CARMEN (1985), DON CARLO (1985), DON GIOVANNI (1977), FALSTAFF (1999), FIDELIO (1979), GLYNDEBOURNE (1992), THE HOUSE (1995), IDOMENEO (1983), THE LOVE FOR THREE ORANGES (1982), GUSTAV MAHLER (1974 film), A MIDSUMMER NIGHT'S DREAM (1981), LE NOZZE DI FIGARO (1994), OEDIPUS REX (1984), PRINCE IGOR (1990), THE RAKE'S PROGRESS (1977), ROYAL OPERA HOUSE (1999), PYOTR TCHAIKOVSKY (1993), LA TRAVIATA (1987), and DIE ZAUBERFLÖTE (1978).

HALÉVY, FROMENTAL
French composer (1799–1862)

Fromental Halévy wrote about 40 operas, many of them grand in the manner of Meyerbeer, but only LA JUIVE (The Jewess) is currently available on CD. Halévy was also much appreciated for the comic opera *L'éclair* and the grand opera *La reine de Chypre*. His operas are not currently fashionable, but there are Vitaphone films of Giovanni Martinelli in scenes from *La juive,* and there is a documentary about a Vienna production in 1999.

HALKA
1848 opera by Moniuszko

STANISLAW MONIUSZKO's *Halka* was the first Polish "grand opera," and it is still the most famous as it has become a national icon and its arias a part of Polish popular culture. Although it has not entered the international repertory, it has been filmed and is available on DVD and CD. The story has similarities to that of *Madama Butterfly*. Halka is the heroine, a village girl seduced and abandoned by aristocrat Janusz who is marrying another woman. Jontek, who loves Halka, tries to help but she goes mad and kills herself on Janusz's wedding day. Wlodzimierz Wolski's libretto is based on a story by Kazimierz Wojcicki.

1937 Rex film
Polish feature film: Juliusz Gardan (film director), Leon Schiller (stage director), Jakub Jonilowicz and Albert Wywerka (cinematographers), Stefan Norris and Jacques Rotmil (production designers), Rex Film (production company).

Cast: Liliana Zielinska (Halka, sung by Ewa Bandrowska-Turska), Wladislaw Ladis-Kiepura (Jontek), Witold Zacharewicz (Janusz).

Black and white. In Polish. 90 minutes.

Comment: Ladis-Kiepura was the brother of Jan Kiepura and the leading tenor of the Hamburg Opera at this time. The film, a huge success in Poland, was distributed in America by Star Film.

1997 Narodowy Theater
Polish stage production: Maria Foltyn (director), Antoni Wicherek (conductor, Teatr Narodowy Orchestra and Chorus), Jadwiga Jarowsiewicz (set designer).

Cast: Tatiana Zacharczuk (Halka), Vladimir Kuzmienko (Jontek), Suska Wichenek.

Video: House of Opera DVD. Mariana Pyszniak (director). Color. In Polish. 120 minutes.

Early/related films

1913 Pulchalski film
The first screen adaptation of Moniuszko's opera was a 1913 film, one of the earliest Polish movies. Edward Pulchalski adapted the libretto for the screen and directed the film, which was presented in cinemas with the opera music. Black and white. Silent. About 15 minutes.

1940 Overture to Glory
Moishe Oysher plays a cantor attracted to opera in this American Yiddish film. He is befriended by composer Stanislaw Moniuszko, who persuades him to sing the role of Jontek in *Halka* at the Warsaw Opera, and he is seen on stage performing Jontek's most famous aria. Although he is a success, he eventually returns to his religious calling. See OVERTURE TO GLORY.

HALL, PETER
English director (1930–)

Sir Peter Hall is known primarily for theater and opera direction, but he has also had a lively cinema career. His films include *The Homecoming, Perfect Friday,* and *Three in Two Won't Go.* He directed a film of Shakespeare's *A Midsummer's Night's Dream,* and his stage production of Britten's opera based on the play is on video. Hall began directing opera in 1957 at Sadler's Wells and has been a regular at Covent Garden and Glyndebourne. Many of his opera stage productions are on video. See ALBERT HERRING (1985), CARMEN (1985), DON GIOVANNI (1977), FIDELIO (1979), L'INCORONAZIONE DI POPPEA (1984), A MIDSUMMER NIGHT'S DREAM (1981), NEW YEAR (1991), LE NOZZE DI FIGARO (1973), ORFEO ED EURIDICE (1982), IL RITORNO D'ULISSE IN PATRIA (1973), SALOME (1991), and LA TRAVIATA (1987).

HALLMARK HALL OF FAME
American television series (1951–)

The *Hallmark Hall of Fame* television series began on NBC on December 24, 1951, with the premiere of Menotti's TV opera AMAHL AND THE NIGHT VISITORS. It was a major success and was repeated in the following years. The Hallmark series, which continues to the present day, has featured other operas and operettas, including Bezanson's Nativity opera GOLDEN CHILD and Gilbert and Sullivan's THE YEOMEN OF THE GUARD. The Hallmark programs are preserved at the UCLA Film and Television Archive, which mounted a major tribute in 1991.

HAMLET
1868 opera by Thomas

Ambroise Thomas had resounding success with *Hamlet* and MIGNON in the 19th century, but both had faded from the repertory until recently. The libretto for *Hamlet,* by Michel Carré and Jules Barbier, drastically simplifies and alters the Shakespeare play. Ophelia, not surprisingly, has a notable mad scene, but Hamlet does not die at the end; he is told by the ghost of his father to kill Claudius and become king, which he does. Various attempts have been made in modern times to create an ending more in keeping with the play because English speakers know it. Modern operatic Hamlets include Thomas Hampson, Sherrill Milnes, Bo Skovhus, and Thomas Allen, all of whom have starred in telecasts of the opera. Richard Bonynge staged it in Sydney in 1982 with Milnes, but the available video is not very satisfactory as it was shot from the audience. In Bonynge's version Hamlet dies after he kills Claudius, from wounds inflicted by Laertes.

2001 Toulouse at Théâtre du Châtelet, Paris

Paris stage production: Nicolas Joël (director), Michel Plasson (conductor, Toulouse Orchestra and Chorus), Ezio Frigerio (set designer).

Cast: Thomas Hampson (Hamlet), Nathalie Dessay (Ophelia), José Van Dam (Claudius), Michelle DeYoung (Gertrude), Marc Laho (Laertes).

House of Opera VHS. Brian Large (director). Color. In French. 134 minutes.

Comment: Hampson has also sung the role on stage in Monte Carlo (1994), San Francisco (1996), and Paris (2000) and has recorded it.

HAMMERSTEIN II, OSCAR
American lyricist/librettist (1895–1960)

Oscar Hammerstein II is the major bridge between the worlds of European-style operetta and American musical comedy. His collaborations with composers SIGMUND ROMBERG and RUDOLF FRIML on one side and JEROME KERN and RICHARD RODGERS on the other are especially notable. His European-style operettas, such as THE DESERT SONG and THE NEW MOON, are deservedly popular, but it was his ground-breaking American-style "operettas" such as SHOW BOAT (with Jerome Kern) and OKLAHOMA! (with Richard Rodgers) that created the modern musical as we know it. Hammerstein also transformed Bizet's *Carmen* into the American opera CARMEN JONES. Oscar Hammerstein II's impresario grandfather Oscar I created the old Manhattan Opera House. See also BALL IM SAVOY, CAROUSEL, MUSIC IN THE AIR, ROSE-MARIE, and SOUTH PACIFIC.

1946 Till the Clouds Roll By

Paul Langton portrays Oscar Hammerstein II in this film biography of composer Jerome Kern and (to a limited degree) Hammerstein. It ends with their triumph with *Show Boat.* Richard Whorf directed. MGM. Color. 137 minutes. Silver Screen VHS.

HAMPE, MICHAEL
German director (1935–)

Michael Hampe, who became intendant of Cologne Opera in 1975, has staged a large number of operas that are on video, many of them from the Schwetzingen and Salzburg festivals. His entertaining 1988 production of IL BARBIERE DI SIVIGLIA at Schwetzingen launched Cecilia Bartoli on her international career. His productions of comic operas are especially enjoyable. See AGRIPPINA (1985), ANDREA CHÉNIER (1985), LA CAMBIALE DI MATRIMONIO (1989), LA CENERENTOLA (1988), COSÌ FAN TUTTE (1989), DON GIOVANNI (1987/1991), FALSTAFF (SALIERI, 1995), LA GAZZA LADRA (1984), IDOMENEO (1991), L'INCORONAZIONE DI POPPEA (1993), L'ITALIANA IN ALGERI (1987), IL MATRIMONIO SEGRETO (1986), DIE MEISTERSINGER VON NÜRNBERG (1988), L'OCCASIONE FA IL LADRO (1992), IL RITORNO D'ULISSE IN PATRIA (1985), LA SCALA DI SETA (1989), IL SIGNOR BRUSCHINO (1989), and THE TURN OF THE SCREW (1990).

HAMPSON, THOMAS
American baritone (1955–)

Indiana-born Thomas Hampson studied singing in Los Angeles, but he made his debut in Düsseldorf in 1981. He sang a variety of roles in small European and American opera houses and then had great success in Switzerland singing in DON GIOVANNI (1991) and *The Barber of Seville.* He made his debut at the Metropolitan as Almaviva in *Le nozze di Figaro* in 1986 and is now popular around the world. He is particularly noted for his stage presence in Mozart operas and Thomas's HAMLET (2000). He helped revive Schubert's virtually unknown opera FIERRABRAS (1988), and he created the role of Valmont in Conrad Susa's THE DANGEROUS LIAISONS (1994). He plays the Dark Fiddler in Petr Weigl's 1989 film of Delius's A VILLAGE ROMEO AND JULIET, Rodrigue in DON CARLOS in Paris in 1996, Macbeth in MACBETH in Zurich in 2001, and is one of the sailor trio in the 1992 Barbican concert of ON THE TOWN. He can be seen in telecast galas at ZURICH Opera in 1984 and the METROPOLITAN OPERA in 1991 and celebrating ROSSINI at Lincoln Center in 1992.

1991 Mahler Concerts in Vienna

Hampson sings Mahler songs at concerts in 1989 and 1991 in Vienna. "Five Rückert Songs" and "Songs of a

Wayfarer" were taped in 1991 with Leonard Bernstein conducting the Vienna Philharmonic, and Mahler's "Kindertotenlieder" were taped in 1989. Humphrey Burton directed. Color. In German. 70 minutes. DG VHS.

1995 Kathleen Battle and Thomas Hampson
Battle and Hampson join forces for a *Live From Lincoln Center* concert March 1, 1995. They perform arias and duets by Mozart, Rossini, Massenet, Verdi, Lehár, and Korngold in the first half and American music theater tunes in the second. In the interval they talk about their work. Color. 90 minutes.

1999 Carte Blanche: Thomas Hampson
The Royal Concertgebouw of Amsterdam offered Hampson carte blanche for seven concerts, a symposium, and a master class. These resulted in several videos, including a 49-minute documentary by B. Schoewert shot in Amsterdam and Vienna during 1997–1998 and a 52-minute documentary by Pieter Vorekamp of Hampson leading a master class in February 1998.

HAMPTON, HOPE
American soprano (1897–1982)

Hope Hampton was a movie star who decided to become an opera star. The Texas-born singer-actress, née Kennedy, arrived in Hollywood as a beauty contest winner and immediately found a sugar daddy. Wealthy Jules E. Brulatour set up a film company for her, and she starred in 13 films, from *The Bait* and *A Modern Salome* in 1920 to *The Unfair Sex* in 1926. She plays an opera singer in *Star Dust* (1921), and she starred in the first *Gold Diggers* film in 1923. In 1927 she began to study singing, and in 1928 she made her opera debut in Philadelphia as Manon in the Massenet opera. In 1929 Warner Bros. made a Vitaphone film of her in the role. She made her debut with San Francisco Opera in 1930 as Marguerite in *Faust* opposite Ezio Pinza. In the 1930s she sang leading roles in *Thaïs* and *La bohème* with regional opera companies. In 1938 she was featured in a Hollywood film singing "Musetta's Waltz" from *La bohème*. She made her last film in 1961. Her films with some opera relevance are listed below.

1920 A Modern Salome
This film was inspired by the Oscar Wilde play that provided the basis for the Strauss opera. Hampton plays a woman who causes a lot of problems for people before she dreams she is the biblical Salome and reforms. Black and white. Silent. About 80 minutes.

1921 Star Dust
Hampton plays a singer who goes to New York, has problems, is discovered by a voice teacher, and becomes an opera star. She makes her debut in Massenet's *Thaïs*. The story came from a Fannie Hurst novel. Hobart Henley directed. First National. Black and white. Silent. About 75 minutes.

1929 Hope Hampton in the Fourth Act of Manon
Hampton's stage debut in Philadelphia in Massenet's *Manon* in 1928 led to her being asked to appear in a sound film of excerpts from the opera. This one-reel Vitaphone film features scenes from Act IV of the opera with accompaniment by the Vitaphone Symphony Orchestra and Chorus. Black and white. In French. About 10 minutes.

1938 The Road to Reno
Hampton is on stage singing "Musetta's Waltz" from *La bohème* in the opening scenes of this film. She plays a New York opera singer who wants to divorce her ranch owner husband Randolph Scott. S. Sylvan Simon directed for Universal. Black and white. In English. 68 minutes.

HANDEL, GEORGE FRIDERIC
German/English composer (1685–1759)

George Frideric Handel was long remembered as the creator of the oratorio MESSIAH rather than as an opera composer. This has changed dramatically in recent years, and he is now equally famous as the German composer who wrote Italian operas for the English. Most of his operas have been revived in modern productions and are on CD and video, and many of his oratorios have been given theatrical productions. Handel's life has been the subject of several films, and he is a central character in a film about the divo castrato FARINELLI. See AGRIPPINA, ALCINA, ARIODANTE, BELSHAZZAR, GIULIO CESARE IN EGITTO, GIUSTINO, ISRAEL IN EGYPT, OTTONE, RINALDO, RODELINA, SERSE, THE SORCERESS, TAMERLANO, and THEODORA.

1942 The Great Mr. Handel
Wilfred Lawson plays the composer in this British film about Handel's fall from royal favor and his rise again after composing *Messiah*. The plot mainly concerns Handel's feud with the Prince of Wales (Max Kirby). The film includes arias from *Serse,* the overture to *Alcides,* and a little *Water Music*. Elizabeth Allen plays prima donna Mrs. Cibber (sung by Gladys Ripley), Malcolm Keen is Lord Chesterfield, and Hay Petrie is the valet Phineas. Norman Walker directed from a screenplay by Gerald Elliott and Victor MacClure. Black and white. 103 minutes.

1953 Christmas Chorale

J. B. Sloan's short film is based on *The Great Mr. Handel*. After a contemporary Christmas scene, Handel's interest in the Hatton Garden Foundling Hospital is shown, and the film ends with the *Messiah* chorus "For unto us a child is born." G.H.W. Production. Black and white. 25 minutes.

1985 Honor, Profit and Pleasure

Simon Callow plays Handel in this fine British film biography written and directed by Anna Ambrose. It begins with a performance of *Rinaldo,* Handel's first opera in London, beautifully reconstructed with a feeling for period and performance style. There is a delightful scene when Handel, in Italy in search of sopranos, is serenaded in a coach by two of them. Alan Devlin plays Handel's friend James Quin, who narrates the film; Jean Rigby is Susannah Cibber; Christopher Benjamin is Heidegger; T. P. McKenna is Jonathan Swift; John Moffatt is Richard Steele; and James Villiers is Richard Addison. Anne Skinner was the producer, Peter MacDonald was the cinematographer, Peter Luke was the coscripter, and Nicholas Kraemer was music director and conductor of the Raglan Baroque Players. Color. 70 minutes. Films for the Humanities & Sciences VHS.

1985 God Rot Tunbridge Wells!

Trevor Howard plays the dying Handel in John Osborne's biographical teleplay *God Rot Tunbridge Wells!* It was commissioned to mark the 300th anniversary of Handel's birth and is set on the day in 1759 on which he witnessed a performance of *Messiah* by the Tunbridge Wells Ladies Music Circle. Tony Palmer directed for Ladbroke Productions. Color. 130 minutes.

1990 Handel's Resurrection

German film by Klaus Lindemann based on Stefan Zweig's novel *Händels Augerstehung*. The soloists are soprano Gundula Janowitz, mezzo Marga Hoeffgen, and trumpeter Maurice André, with Karl Richter conducting the Munich Bach Orchestra and Choir. The actors are Heinrich Schweiger, Enrico Dondi, and Mike Gwilym. Color. In German. 100 minutes.

1995 The Madness of King George

Handel's music is used as the score for this superb English film, performed by a baroque orchestra led by Nicholas Kraemer. Nicholas Hytner directed from a screenplay by Alan Bennett based on his play. Color. 105 minutes.

1996 A Night With Handel

Arias and duets by Handel are performed in modern London settings during a 24-hour period. Sarah Connolly sings "Scherza infida" while watching a couple in a London square, Alastair Miles sings Zoroaster's aria from *Orlando* in a psychiatrist's chair, Rosa Mannion and John Mark Ainsley join in a duet from *Il Moderato* as commuters hurry to work, and Claron McFadden and Christopher Robson are lovers singing a duet from *Sosarme* in an Italian café. Harry Bicket leads the Orchestra of the Age of Enlightenment, Jonathan Keates imagined the settings, and Nicholas McGegan and David Field set the context. Alex Maregno directed the film for Channel 4. Color. 60 minutes. Warner/NVC Arts DVD.

1996 Famous Composers: George Frideric Handel

Documentary video about the life and music of the composer with excerpts from his works. Color. 30 minutes. Kultur VHS.

1998 George Frederic Handel

An examination of Handel's career in London with the focus on his operas and oratorios, including *Orlando, Rinaldo, Giulio Cesare, Solomon,* and *Messiah.* Part of video series *Harmonics: The Innovators of Classical Music.* Color. In English. 28 minutes. Films for the Humanities & Sciences VHS.

HANNIBAL
2001 American film with opera content

Patrick Cassidy created a mini-opera called *Vide Cor Meum* (See Your Heart) for the film *Hannibal;* the libretto is based on Dante's *La Vita Nuova,* in which he describes his first attempts at poetry and his famous meeting with Beatrice. This IMAGINARY OPERA is staged in costume in a palace in Florence, Italy, by Cassidy and Hans Zimmer as if it were one of the early operas created by the Camerata around 1600. Bruno Lazzaretti sings the role of Dante and Danielle de Niese is Beatrice with the music played by the Lyndhurst Orchestra led by Gavin Greenaway. Only about a minute of the opera is seen, but there is more on the film soundtrack album. Attending the performance are serial killer Hannibal Lecter (Anthony Hopkins) and the policeman who is trying to catch him (Giancarlo Giannini). The film is a sequel to *The Silence of the Lambs* and carries on the gruesome adventures of Lecter. Ridley Scott directed. Color. 131 minutes.

HÄNSEL UND GRETEL
1893 opera by Humperdinck

Hänsel und Gretel (Hansel and Gretel) is the only opera by Germany's ENGELBERT HUMPERDINCK that has remained popular. As it is a major musical achievement as well as a children's favorite, it is likely to survive a few more centuries. The libretto, by Adelheid Wette based on a Grimm Brothers story, tells of the adventures of two children who wander off one day and end up at the gingerbread cottage of a witch. She tries to bake them in an oven, but she ends up in it herself while the children she had previously captured magically reappear. The opera, one of the first to be telecast complete in the United States, is usually performed in English in America and England.

1937/1939 BBC Television

English TV productions: Stephen Thomas (director), Hyam Greenbaum (conductor, BBC Orchestra), Andrée Howard (choreographer), Ernest Irving (English translation).

Cast: Charlotte Leigh/Robert Berek (Hansel), Jane Bowles/Muriel Pavlov (Gretel), Vivienne Chatterton/H. D. C. Pepler (Witch).

Telecast live December 23, 1937, and January 15, 1939. Black and white. In English. 55 minutes.

1943 Hartt Opera Workshop

American TV production: Elemer Nagy (director), Moshe Paranov (conductor, Julius Hartt School of Music Orchestra and Chorus), Elemer Nagy (set designer), Truba Kaschmann (choreographer).

Cast: Students from the Julius Hartt School of Music Opera Workshop.

Telecast live December 23, 1942, on WRGB-TV. Robert Stone (director). Black and white. In English. 90 minutes.

Comment: One of the first operas telecast complete in America. WRGB-TV was General Electric's pioneer station in Schenectady, New York.

1948 NBC Kraft Television Theatre

American TV production: Stanley J. Quinn (director), Sam Morgenstern (conductor, Co-Opera Company Chorus), Joan Slessinger and Margaret Diehl (pianists).

Cast: William McLocklin (Hansel), Florence Forsberg (Gretel), Marion Selee (Witch), Dean Mundy (Mother), Harry Wayne (Father).

Telecast live December 22, 1948, on NBC. Stanley J. Quinn (director). Black and white. In English. 60 minutes.

1950 NBC Opera Theatre

American TV production: Charles Polacheck (director), Peter Herman Adler (conductor, NBC Symphony of the Air), Henry Crayon (set designer), Samuel Chotzinoff (producer), Townsend Brewster (English translation).

Cast: David Lloyd (Hansel), Virginia Haskins (Gretel), Claramae Turner (Witch), Frances Lehnerts (Mother), Paul Ukena (Father).

Video at the MTR. Telecast live December 25, 1950, on NBC. Kirk Browning (director). Black and white. In English. 60 minutes.

1954 Kimemins Puppets film

German puppet film: John Paul (director), Franz Allers (conductor, Allers Orchestra and Apollo Boys Choir), Padraic Colum (screenplay), Evalds Dajevskis (set designer), James Summers (puppet creator), Giuseppe Becce (music arranger), Michael Myerberg (producer).

Puppet voices: Constance Brigham (Hansel and Gretel), Anna Russell (Witch), Mildred Dunnock (Mother), Frank Rogier (Father), Delbert Anderson (Sandman), Helen Boatwright (Dew Fairy), Apollo Boys Choir (Angels and Children).

Video: VIEW DVD/VHS (with "making of" documentary). Color. In English. 75 minutes.

Comment: The electronic puppets called Kimemins are the stars of this charming film of the opera that won warm praise from critics.

**1981 Everding film

Austrian feature film: August Everding (director), Sir Georg Solti (conductor, Vienna Philharmonic Orchestra and Boys Choir), Gerhard Janda and Friedrich Hechelmann (set/costume designers), Wolfgang Tren (cinematographer), Unitel (production).

Cast: Brigitte Fassbaender (Hänsel), Edita Gruberova (Gretel), Sena Jurinac (Witch), Helga Dernesch (Mother), Hermann Prey (Father), Norma Burrowes (Sandman), Elfriede Höbarth (Dew Fairy).

Video: London VHS. Color. In German with English subtitles. 109 minutes.

Comment: Charming production filmed as if the opera were being performed for children in a small theater.

***1982 Metropolitan Opera

American stage production: Nathaniel Merrill (director), Bruce Donnell (staging), Thomas Fulton (conductor, Metropolitan Opera Orchestra and Chorus), Robert O'Hearn (set/costume designer), Norman Kelley (English translation).

Cast: Frederica von Stade (Hansel), Judith Blegen (Gretel), Rosalind Elias (Witch), Jean Kraft (Mother), Michael Devlin (Father), Diane Kesling (Sandman), Betsy Norden (Dew Fairy).

Pioneer Classics DVD/LD and Bel Canto Paramount VHS. Telecast live December 25, 1982. Kirk Browning (director). Color. In English. 104 minutes.

Comment: A delight, as good as one could hope for, with superb singing, acting, and directing.

1997 Juilliard Opera

American stage production: Frank Corsaro (director), Randall Behr (conductor, Juilliard Opera Orchestra and Chorus), Maurice Sendak (set/costume designer).

Cast: Jennifer Marquette (Hansel), Sari Gruber (Gretel), Mariana I. Karpatova (Witch and Mother), Samuel Hepler (Father).

Telecast December 17, 1997, on PBS. Kirk Browning (director) for *Live From Lincoln Center* series. Color. In German with English subtitles. 105 minutes.

Comment: Sendak's fairy-tale sets and costumes are the colorful stars of this fine production.

1998 Zurich Opera

Swiss stage production: Frank Corsaro (director), Franz Welser-Möst (conductor, Zurich Opera Orchestra and Children's Choir), Maurice Sendak (set/costume designer).

Cast: Liliana Nikiteanu (Hansel), Malin Hartelius (Gretel), Volker Vogel (Witch), Gabriele Lechner (Mother), Alfred Muff (Father), Maartin Jankova (Sandman), Milena Jotowa (Dew Fairy).

Video: TDK (GB) DVD. Ruth Käch (director). Color. In German with English subtitles. 90 minutes.

Comment: Swiss reprise of Corsaro's Juilliard production with Sendak's sets and costumes. Welser-Möst makes it all seem real.

Related films

1954 Reiniger film

Animation pioneer Lotte Reiniger made an abbreviated animated silhouette version of the opera in 1954. Color. 10 minutes.

1954 Schronger film

German narrative version of the Grimm fairy tale with songs but not by Humperdinck. The cast includes Jurgen Miksch, Mara Inken Bielenberg, and Ellen Frank. Walter Janssen directed for Schronger Films. Color. Released in the United States by Hemdale in a dubbed English-language version. Color. 52 minutes.

1958 NBC Television

Risë Stevens plays the Mother in this NBC-TV production and won praise for her performance of Humperdinck's "Lullaby." The rest of the composer's music was not used but was replaced by songs by Alec Wilder. Red Buttons is Hansel, Barbara Cook is Gretel, Hans Conreid is the Witch, Rudy Vallee is the Father, and Stubby Kaye

is the Town Crier. Paul Bogart directed. Black and white. In English. 60 minutes.

1984 Maestro's Company puppets

A group of children discover puppets rehearsing *Hänsel und Gretel* under an old theater. The Australian Maestro's Company staged the scenes with the puppets dubbed by opera singers. The singing voices belong to Brigitte Fassbaender (Hansel), Lucia Popp (Gretel), Anny Schlemm (Witch), Walter Berry (Father), and Julia Hamari (Mother) with the music played by the Vienna Philharmonic Orchestra led by Georg Solti. William Fitzwater directed. Color. Dialogue in English, arias in German. 30 minutes. VAI VHS.

1987 Cannon film

Cloris Leachman plays the Witch in this Cannon film that uses Humperdinck's music mostly as background score although there is some singing by the children and the Father. Hugh Pollard is Hansel, Nicola Stapleton is Gretel, David Warner is the Father, and Emily Richards is the Mother. Len Talen directed for Cannon Film. Color. In English. 84 minutes. Cannon VHS.

HANSON, HOWARD
American composer (1896–1981)

Howard Hanson, who was born in the same tiny Nebraska town as Hollywood movie mogul Daryl Zanuck, wrote a good deal of music but only one opera. *Merry Mount* was staged at the Metropolitan Opera in 1934 with Lawrence Tibbett in the leading role of Wrestling Bradford and Tullio Serafin as conductor. It was a huge success, with 50 curtain calls, but it is no longer in the repertory. Richard L. Stokes based the libretto on Nathaniel Hawthorne's story *The Maypole of Merry Mount*, a tale of witchcraft and sexual obsession among the Puritans.

1957 Merry Mount

Howard Hanson, director of the Eastman School of Music when this film was made, explains how a composer conveys the ideas and emotions of the characters in an opera. Hanson uses his opera *Merry Mount* to demonstrate. The film, shot in 16mm, was made for the series *Music as a Language*. Black and white. In English. 29 minutes.

HAPPY END
1929 musical by Weill and Brecht

Happy End is KURT WEILL and BERTOLT BRECHT's successor to their hit *The Threepenny Opera*, although it has never had the same popularity. Some of its songs, however, are among their best known, including "Surabaya Johnny" and "Bilbao Song." It tells the story of Salvation Army officer Lilian Holliday who reforms a gang of criminals in Chicago after falling for the charms of dance hall boss Bill Cracker. The libretto is by Elisabeth Hauptmann, writing as Dorothy Lane.

1986 Arena Stage, Washington, D.C.
American stage production: Garland Wright (director), Martha Schlamme (host). Cast: Judith Anna Roberts, Marilyn Caskey, Casey Biggs, Kevin McClaron, Richard Bauer, Joe Palmiere, Lisabeth Pritchett, Henry Strozier.
Telecast January 19, 1986, on PBS. Greg Harney (director). Color. In English. 120 minutes.

HARBACH, OTTO
American librettist (1873–1963)

Otto Harbach, although not as influential as Oscar Hammerstein II, was one of the principal creators of the words for major American operettas during their classic period. Both librettist and lyricist, he worked most famously on operettas with Rudolf Friml (THE FIREFLY and ROSE-MARIE), Sigmund Romberg (THE DESERT SONG), George Gershwin (SONG OF THE FLAME), Emmerich Kálmán (GOLDEN DAWN), and Jerome Kern (THE CAT AND THE FIDDLE). His many notable musicals include *No No Nanette,* with Vincent Youmans, and *Roberta,* with Kern.

HARNONCOURT, NIKOLAUS
Austrian conductor (1929–)

Nikolaus Harnoncourt, one of the leading exponents of the period instrument opera, formed the Vienna Concentus Musicus in 1953 to perform early music. He conducted his first Monteverdi opera in 1971 and subsequently made a number of films of Monteverdi and Mozart operas, usually in collaboration with director Jean-Pierre Ponnelle. See LA BELLE HÉLÈNE (1996), COSÌ FAN TUTTE (1988), IDOMENEO (1988), L'INCORONAZIONE DI POPPEA (1979), MITRIDATE (1986), LE NOZZE DI FIGARO (1996), ORFEO (1978), and IL RITORNO D'ULISSE IN PATRIA (1980).

HARRY AND WALTER GO TO NEW YORK
1976 American film with operatic content

New York City in the 1890s. Vaudevillians–turned–bank robbers James Caan and Elliott Gould don exotic Eastern costumes and join star Lesley Ann Warren on stage in a comic opera called *The Kingdom of Love.* A secret tunnel to a bank is under the theater, and they are trying to delay the show so their gang can finish the robbery before Michael Caine's rival gang arrives. The duo improvise songs and dances and improve the show so much (there is nowhere for it to go but up) that they get standing ovations at the end. The IMAGINARY OPERA created by David Shire with Alan and Marilyn Bergman, really an operetta, is truly bad, but it was meant to be that way. Carmine Coppola plays its conductor in the film, John Byrum and Robert Kaufman wrote the screenplay, Laszlo Kovacs was the cinematographer, and Mark Rydell directed for Columbia. Color. 123 minutes.

HART, LORENZ
American lyricist (1895–1943)

The greatest song lyricist of the 20th century never collaborated on an opera, but he did write English words for two operettas, Jean Gilbert's *The Lady in Ermine* and Franz Lehár's *The Merry Widow. Lady* was presented on the New York stage, and the *Widow* lyrics were used in Ernst Lubitsch's film of the operetta with Jeanette MacDonald and Maurice Chevalier. Hart also wrote the lyrics of a wartime patriotic song for Metropolitan Opera tenor Jan Peerce. His lengthy collaboration with composer RICHARD RODGERS culminated in one of the greatest of all American musicals, *Pal Joey.* In the 1948 Rodgers and Hart film biography *Words and Music,* he is portrayed (bizarrely) by Mickey Rooney. See DIE FRAU IM HERMELIN, DER LUSTIGE WITWE (1934), and JEANETTE MACDONALD (1932/1934).

HÁRY JÁNOS
1926 opera by Kodály

ZOLTÁN KODÁLY's Hungarian opera *Háry János* celebrates the imagination and virtues of a bragging old veteran whose fantastic adventures reflect the qualities and folk music of his country. He tells how he rescued a French princess, won a battle against Napoleon, and gained the love of the emperor's wife. However, he turns her down, saying he prefers to return to his native village and his first love, Orzse. The libretto, by Bela Paulini and Zsolt Harsany, is based on an epic comic poem by János Garay. It seems that Háry János was a real person and the poet simply passed on the story he was told. The opera music is widely known because of the orchestral suite based on it.

1965 Szinetar film
Hungarian feature film: Miklos Szinetar (director), János Ferencsik (conductor, Budapest Philharmonic Orchestra and Budapest Opera Chorus), Lorant Kezdi (set designer), Mafilm (production).
Cast: Adam Szirtes (Háry János, sung by Gyorgy Melis), Maria Medgyesi (Orzse, sung by Maria

Matyas), Teri Torday (Princess Marie-Louise, sung by Judith Sandor), Laszlo Markus (Ebelastin, sung by Jozsef Reti), Gyula Bodrogi (Napoleon), Manyi Kiss (Empress, sung by Eva Gombos).

Color. In Hungarian. 109 minutes.

HAUNTED MANOR, THE
1865 opera by Moniuszko

Polish composer STANISLAW MONIUSZKO's opera *Straszny Dwór* (The Haunted Manor) is not as well known as *Halka,* possibly because it was banned after its premiere (one aria was considered a little too patriotic). It's a comic opera about two soldier brothers and the women they decide to wed immediately after a night in the haunted house of the title. The libretto, by Jan Checinski, is based on a story by Kazimierz Wojcicki. It's available on CD in a 1978 Cracow production.

1986 Grzesinski film
Polish feature film: Marek Grzesinski (director), Robert Satanowski (conductor, Warsaw Grand Theater Orchestra and Chorus), Irena Bieganska (set/costume designer).

Cast: Andrzej Hiolski (Miecznik), Izabella Klosinska (Hanna), Elzbieta Panko (Jadwiga), Stanislaw Kowalski (Stefan), Leonard Mroz (Zbigniew), Krzysztof Szmyt (Pan Damazy), Krystyna Szostek-Radkowa (Czesnikowa).

Video: Polart/Contal/House of Opera VHS. Color. In Polish. 134 minutes.

HAYDN, FRANZ JOSEF
Austrian composer (1732–1809)

Franz Josef Haydn wrote many operas and considered them among his most important works; some of his contemporaries ranked them over Mozart's. They have been neglected until recently but are now beginning to be re-evaluated. There are a dozen on CD, and an equal number have been telecast in Europe. On the other hand, his great dramatic oratorio DIE SCHÖPFUNG (The Creation), based on Milton's *Paradise Lost,* is so popular that it is available in multiple versions. Haydn appears as a character in several feature films; he is played by Ernst Baumeister in a 1927 film about BEETHOVEN and by William Vedder in a 1948 film about MOZART. His statue is one of the narrators in Michael Nyman's TV opera LETTERS, RIDDLES AND WRITS.

1984 Haydn and Mozart
Haydn's life, times, and career are explored and illustrated by André Previn on Volume One of the series *The Story of the Symphony* by Herbert Chappell. It finishes with a performance of Haydn's Symphony No. 87 by Previn and the Royal Philharmonic Orchestra. Color. In English. 90 minutes. Home Vision VHS.

1990 Haydn at Esterháza
Chris Hunt's film focuses on the composer's life and work at Prince Esterházy's palace, where he conducted hundreds of operas, with explanatory comments from H. C. Robbins Landon, Christopher Hogwood, and Melvyn Bragg. At the end of the biography section, Hogwood leads the Academy of Ancient Music in performances of three Haydn symphonies. Color. In English. 100 minutes.

1996 Haydn and the Esterházys
Documentary about Haydn and the music he composed during his years with the Esterházys, with an excerpt from his opera *Il mondo della luna.* Part of the *Man and Music* series. Color. 53 minutes. Films for the Humanities & Sciences VHS.

1997 Haydn
Portrait of the composer and his music with excerpts from his works, including *The Creation,* played by the Moscow Symphony Orchestra led by David Palmer. Part of the video series *The Great Composers.* Color. In English. 25 minutes. Films for the Humanities & Sciences VHS.

HEATHER, DAVE
English TV opera director(1943-)

Dave Heather is one of the pioneers of television opera directing, and there are videos of his work from as early as 1972. He directed most of the Glyndebourne Festival telecasts for Southern Television, and the majority on are commercial video. In 1982 he directed the Gilbert and Sullivan opera series for George Walker. See IL BARBIERE DI SIVIGLIA (1982), COSÌ FAN TUTTE (1975), COX AND BOX (1982), DON GIOVANNI (1977), DIE ENTFÜHRUNG AUS DEM SERAIL (1980), FALSTAFF (1976), FIDELIO (1979), THE GONDOLIERS (1982), L'HEURE ESPAGNOLE (1987), IDOMENEO (1974), IOLANTHE (1982), MACBETH (1972), A MIDSUMMER NIGHT'S DREAM (1981), LE NOZZE DI FIGARO (1973), PATIENCE (1982), PRINCESS IDA (1982), THE RAKE'S PROGRESS (1977), IL RITORNO D'ULISSE IN PATRIA (1973), THE SORCERER (1982), KIRI TE KANAWA (1978), THE YEOMEN OF THE GUARD (1982), and DIE ZAUBERFLÖTE (1978).

HENDRICKS, BARBARA
American soprano (1948–)

Barbara Hendricks was born in Arkansas, studied science at the University of Nebraska, and didn't consider music as a career until she was 20. In 1969 she went to Juilliard to study with Jennie Tourel, and her musical life began. She made her debut in San Francisco in 1974 in Cavalli's *Ormindo* and then began to sing in opera houses around the world. In 1982 she made her debut in Paris as Juliette in Gounod's ROMÉO ET JULIETTE and sang Nanetta in FALSTAFF at Covent Garden the same year. She came to the Metropolitan Opera in 1986 as Sophie in *Der Rosenkavalier*. Luigi Comencini chose her to play Mimì in his 1988 film of LA BOHÈME, and Márta Mészaros made a 1991 film about her performing on stage in DON PASQUALE. She sings in two televised concerts in PARIS in 1989, one at the Bastille Opera and one with PLÁCIDO DOMINGO. Her most unusual video is a strange production of LES CONTES D'HOFFMANN in Lyons in 1993, in which she plays Antonia as a catatonic inmate in a madhouse.

1988 Fauré/Poulenc Concert
Hendricks in a live concert at the Saint Denis Basilica in France with Fauré's *Requiem* and Poulenc's *Gloria*. Hendricks is partnered with baritone Carl-John Falkam while Jean-Claude Casadesus conducts the Lille National Orchestra. Mate Rabinovsky directed for French television. Color. 70 minutes. Kultur VHS.

1990 Barbara Hendricks
Jean-Luc Leon directed this French documentary about the soprano. She is seen on the set of Comencini's film of *La bohème*, at the Met with Brigitte Fassbaender for a production of *Der Rosenkavalier*, at La Scala for *Le nozze di Figaro* with conductor Riccardo Muti, and in Berlin for *Rigoletto* with conductor Silvio Varsivo. She is also shown at home studying a role. Made for France's La Sept. Color. In French. 47 minutes. Kultur DVD.

HENRY VIII
1883 opera by Saint-Saëns

CAMILLE SAINT-SAËNS's French opera *Henry VIII*, about the much-married English king, was popular in the late 19th century, but it has never entered the international repertory like his *Samson et Dalila*. The libretto, by Léonce Détroyat and Armand Silvestre, tells of Henry's split with the Catholic Church when he divorces Catherine of Aragon to marry Anne Boleyn, the former lover of Spanish ambassador Don Gomez.

1991 Théâtre Impérial, Compiègne
French stage production: Alain Guingal (conductor, French Lyric Orchestra and Rouen Theatre Chorus).

Cast: Philippe Rouillon (Henry VIII), Michèle Command (Catherine of Aragon), Lucile Vignon (Anne Boleyn), Alain Gabriel (Don Gómez de Feria).

Video: House of Opera/Lyric VHS. Color. In French. 180 minutes.

Comment: This restored 19th-century theater reopened in September 1991 with this production; it's on CD with the same cast.

2002 Gran Teatre del Liceu, Barcelona
Spanish stage production: Pierre Jourdan (director), José Collado (conductor, Gran Teatre del Liceu Orchestra and Chorus), Guillermo Auger (set designer).

Cast: Simon Estes (Henry VIII), Montserrat Caballé (Catherine of Aragon), Nomeda Kazlaus (Anne Boleyn), Charles Workman (Don Gómez de Feria).

Video: Premiere Opera VHS. Taped January 17, 2002. Color. In French. 180 minutes

HENZE, HANS WERNER
German composer (1926–)

Hans Werner Henze, one of the most influential modern German composers, has created a number of unusual stage works and composed scores for several important films. His first full-length opera was the 1952 *Boulevard Solitude*, a modernized version of the *Manon Lescaut* story. His best-known opera is probably the bizarre satire DER JUNGE LORD, whose leading character turns out to be an ape. His operas *Elegy for Young Lovers* and *The Bassarids* have English librettos by poet W. H. Auden and his partner Chester Kallman. His American TV opera RACHEL LA CUBANA, about a Cuban singer, was well received but its cost overruns led to the demise of original opera on National Educational Television. His films include Alain Resnais's *Muriel* and Volker Schlondorff's *Young Torless, The Lost Honor of Katarina Blum*, and *Swann in Love*.

HERBERT, VICTOR
Irish-born U.S. composer (1859–1924)

Victor Herbert, the most important of the American Viennese-style operetta composers, composed more than 30 stage works starting in 1894, and he dominated the Broadway scene at the beginning of the 20th century. His major operettas can be as vocally demanding as operas and were often written for opera sopranos such as Alice Nielsen, FRITZI SCHEFF, and Emma Trentini. Herbert, who was born in Dublin and brought up in Germany, came to the United States as a cellist when his wife was engaged to sing at the Metropolitan Opera. He is probably best known for the operettas NAUGHTY MARIETTA, BABES IN TOYLAND, and THE RED MILL. Seven of his operettas have been filmed, and there is even a Hollywood film about his career. *Rosalie*, which he co-composed with George Gershwin, was also filmed but without the Herbert-Gershwin music. Herbert also wrote two operas,

Natoma and *Madeleine,* which are more or less forgotten today despite their real quality. His other operettas with entries in this book are THE FORTUNE TELLER, MLLE. MODISTE, OLD DUTCH, and SWEETHEARTS.

1939 The Great Victor Herbert
Walter Connolly plays Herbert in this romantic film that masquerades as a biography, although it is really the story of a couple who sing his music. Mary Martin and Allan Jones star in Herbert's operettas until Jones's career starts to decline and Martin's to rise. In the end their daughter Susanna Foster becomes a star in a revival of *The Fortune Teller* singing "Kiss Me Again" with a remarkable B above high C. The film features performances of many Herbert songs, from "Ah, Sweet Mystery of Life" to the "March of the Toys." Andrew L. Stone directed for Paramount. Black and white. 84 minutes. On VHS.

1946 Till the Clouds Roll By
Paul Maxey plays Victor Herbert in this all-star film biography of Jerome Kern. Richard Whorf directed. MGM. Color. 137 minutes. Silver Screen VHS.

1973 The Music of Victor Herbert
Canadian television tribute to Victor Herbert featuring performances of his songs by Mary Costa, Anna Shuttleworth, Judith Forst, and Robert Jeffrey. Richard Bonynge accompanies on piano. Color. In English. 60 minutes. Opera Dubs VHS.

HERE'S TO ROMANCE
1935 American film with opera content

Italian tenor Nino Martini plays opera singer Nino Donelli, a promising student of diva Ernestine Schumann-Heink. She thinks he can become the greatest singer in the world, and through her help, he is sent to study opera in Paris with financial assistance from Genevieve Tobin. Love problems make his Paris debut a disaster, but he finally triumphs in *Tosca* at the Metropolitan. He also sings arias from *Manon, Cavalleria rusticana,* and *Pagliacci.* Ernest Pascal and Arthur Richman wrote the screenplay, L. W. O'Connell was the cinematographer, and Alfred E. Green directed for Twentieth Century-Fox. Also known as *Melody of Life.* Black and white. In English. 83 minutes.

HERO, THE
1965 TV opera by Bucci

A man is acclaimed a hero for shooting a murderer on Far Rockaway Beach, but he doesn't remember how it happened. When his memory returns, he realizes that he killed the man unnecessarily and decides to drown himself. Marc Bucci's 12-minute television opera *The Hero,* libretto by David Rogers based on Frank Gilroy's story "Far Rockaway," was commissioned by Jac Venza to celebrate the third anniversary of Lincoln Center for the Performing Arts. It was televised with a ballet and a play based on the same story. The opera won the Prix Italia in 1966.

1965 Lincoln Center for the Performing Arts
American stage production: Jac Venza (director and producer).

Cast: Arthur Rubin (Home Sagrin), Anita Darian (Evelyn Sagrin), Elaine Bonazzi (Psychiatrist), John Thomas (Announcer), Kirsten Falke (Girl), Keith Kaldenberg (Policeman), Chester Watson (Minister), Gordon B. Clarke (Mayor), Jack Dabdoud (Boss), William Glassman (Murderer).

Telecast September 24, 1965, on PBS. Kirk Browning (director). Color. In English. 12 minutes.

HÉRODIADE
1890 opera by Massenet

JULES MASSENET's French opera *Hérodiade* is a somewhat different version of the biblical Salome story as filtered through a romantic libretto by Paul Milliet, based on a story by Flaubert. Salome, a much nicer person than in the Strauss opera, fancies John the Baptist (Jean), while Herod desires Salome. She refuses Herod's attentions but wins Jean's love. Both end up in jail waiting to be beheaded. Neither Herod nor his wife Herodias (Hérodiade) know that Salome is Herodias's long-lost daughter. When Salome finds out, she is so distressed she kills herself.

1994 San Francisco Opera
American stage production: Lotfi Mansouri (director), Valery Gergiev (conductor, San Francisco Opera Orchestra), Gerard Howland (set designer).

Cast: Renée Fleming (Salome), Plácido Domingo (Jean), Dolora Zajick (Hérodiade), Juan Pons (Hérode), Kenneth Cox (Phanuël).

Video: Sony Classics VHS. Color. In French with English subtitles. 175 minutes.

HÉROLD, FERDINAND
French composer (1791–1833)

Ferdinand Hérold was one of the most popular composers of the 19th century, and his 1831 opera ZAMPA was almost constantly on stage. He was a mainstay of the Paris Opéra-Comique during the early 19th century, and his other major opera, *Le Pré aux clercs* (1832), was almost as much of a hit as *Zampa*. But fashions fade, and his operas are no longer fashionable, although the *Zampa* overture remains popular at open-air band concerts. *Le Pré aux clercs* and *Le muletier* are on French CDs, and his ballet *La fille mal gardée* is on video.

HERRMANN, BERNARD
American composer (1911–1975)

Bernard Herrmann is best known as one of the great movie composers, but he also wrote operas. His soprano aria for the imaginary opera *Salammbó*, created for the 1941 film CITIZEN KANE, has been recorded by Kiri Te Kanawa. His short Christmas operas, A CHILD IS BORN (1955) and A CHRISTMAS CAROL (1954), were premiered on CBS Television. His grand opera *Wuthering Heights*, libretto by Lucille Fletcher, based on Emily Brontë's novel, was recorded in 1966 and staged by Portland Opera in 1982. Herrmann was brought to Hollywood by Orson Welles and wrote scores for more than 40 films, including Alfred Hitchcock's *Psycho* and Martin Scorsese's *Taxi Driver*. They often contain allusions to opera, especially Wagner. The music in the love scene on the train in *North by Northwest* is a variation on the love theme in *Tristan und Isolde,* while *Vertigo* contains a variation of the "Magic Fire" music from *Die Walküre.*

HERVÉ
French composer (1825–1892)

Hervé (Louis August Joseph Florimond Ronger) is the father of French operetta, the precursor of Offenbach. His most important light opera, and the only one on film, is the 1883 MAM'ZELLE NITOUCHE. It's an almost autobiographical story of a convent organist, who writes operettas, and a convent girl, who wants to go on stage. Like the protagonist, Hervé led a double life in his early years working simultaneously as church organist and operetta composer. His other popular operettas include *Chilpéric* (1868) and *Le petit Faust* (1869).

HER WONDERFUL LIE
1947 American-Italian film with opera content

Her Wonderful Lie is a "parallel" story of *La bohème* in that what happens to the people in the opera parallels the lives of the "real" people we see in the film. It originated as the 1937 Austrian film ZAUBER DE BOHÈME, which was such an international success that Columbia Pictures decided to remake it in English in Italy with the same stars. JAN KIEPURA and MARTA EGGERTH play the Parisian opera singers whose story parallels that of Mimì and Rodolfo. The "wonderful lie" is the heroine's denial of her love for the hero so he can become a success without having to worry about her. Like Mimì, she is dying of consumption, but she doesn't want him to know. Both become successful, however, and finally get to sing *La bohème* together. She dies at the end of the opera, just like Mimì. They also get to sing a bit of *Martha*. Janis Carter plays her Musetta-like friend; Douglass Dumbrille is her rich protector; Sterling Holloway, Marc Platt, and Gil Lamb are his Bohemian friends; Franklin Pangborn is a cat lover; and John Abbott plays an orchestra conductor. The real conductor is Angelo Questa with the Rome Opera House Orchestra. Ernst Marischka, Hamilton Benz, and Rowland Leigh wrote the screenplay; Arturo Gallea was the cinematographer and Carmine Gallone directed for Cineopera and Columbia Pictures. The Italian title of the film is *Addio, Mimì!* Black and white. In English. 89 minutes. House of Opera VHS.

HERZOG, WERNER
German film director (1942–)

Werner Herzog, one of the great filmmakers of our time, is also a director of opera on stage. His magnificent opera film FITZCARRALDO, the story of a Caruso-obsessed opera fanatic in Brazil, explores the meaning of opera in a highly unusual way. His vampire film *Nosferatu* features music from DAS RHEINGOLD; his aboriginal film *Where the Green Ants Dream* uses music by Wagner; his strongman film *Invincible* features the aria "Ombra mai fu" from SERSE; and his film *Woyzeck* has the same story as the Berg opera WOZZECK. His stage productions have been as well received as his films. GIOVANNA D'ARCO, produced at Bologna in 1989 is on video along with his LOHENGRIN at Bayreuth in 1989, LA DONNA DEL LAGO at La Scala in 1992, and TANNHÄUSER in Naples in 1998. He worked with Plácido Domingo to revive Gomes's IL GUARANY in Berlin in 1994, and he made a documentary about BAYREUTH the same year.

HESS, JOACHIM
German opera film director(1943 -)

Joachim Hess directed a number of opera films in collaboration with producer Rolf Liebermann while Liebermann was in charge of the Hamburg State Opera. An impressive group of them were screened in New York in 1970 at an opera film festival. See THE DEVILS OF LOUDUN (1969), FIDELIO (1969), DER FREISCHÜTZ (1968), LE NOZZE DI FIGARO (1967), ORPHÉE AUX ENFERS (1968), WOZZECK (1967), ZAR UND ZIMMERMANN (1968), and DIE ZAUBERFLÖTE (1971).

HESTON, CHARLTON
American actor (1923–)

Charlton Heston, one of the monuments of the American cinema, is best known for epic roles such as Moses and

Ben Hur, but he is also quite good talking about opera. He is featured on an LD series called *Opera Stories* in which he introduces highlights from operas and describes the stories behind them from supposed actual locations. The LDs include about 50 minutes of scenes from productions at Covent Garden, La Scala, and Verona. The framing material with Heston was written by Gerald Sinstadt and filmed by Keith Cheetham in 1989. See AIDA (1981), LA BOHÈME (1982), ERNANI (1982), FALSTAFF (1983), DIE FLEDERMAUS (1983), MANON LESCAUT (1983), OTELLO (1982), TOSCA (1984), and IL TROVATORE (1985).

HEUBERGER, RICHARD
Austrian composer (1850–1914)

Richard Heuberger, an Austrian music critic and teacher, also composed operas and operettas. He is mostly remembered today for his 1898 operetta DER OPERNBALL (The Opera Ball), which has similarities to *Die Fledermaus*. It has been filmed three times and continues to be staged in Vienna. Heuberger was the first person to compose music for *The Merry Widow* libretto, but his attempt was rejected by the producers so Lehár took over.

HEURE ESPAGNOLE, L'
1911 opera by Ravel

MAURICE RAVEL composed this clock-watcher's delight to a risqué vaudeville by Franc-Nohain set in Toledo. *L'heure espagnole* (The Spanish Hour) is the time every Thursday when clock maker Torquemada leaves his wife Concepción alone and goes off to wind the town clocks. The wife plans to meet her lover during this hour, but it gets complicated when there is more than one suitor. The first two end up stuck in grandfather clocks while she dallies with the mule driver Ramiro.

1961 NET Opera
American TV production: Boris Goldovsky (director and conductor, New England Conservatory of Music Student Orchestra), Robert Simon (English translation).

Cast: Gertrude Pepin (Concepción), Richard Beauregard (Torquemada), Adib Fazah (Ramiro), William Conlon (Gonzalve), Lucien Oliverie (Don Inigo Gomez).

Telecast September 3, 1961 on WGBH. Black and white. In English. 50 minutes

***1987 Glyndebourne Festival
English stage production: Frank Corsaro (director), Sian Edwards (conductor, London Philharmonic Orchestra and Glyndebourne Festival Chorus), Maurice

Sendak (set/costume designer), Ronald Chase (slides and animated films).

Cast: Anna Steiger (Concepción), Rémy Corazza (Torquemada), François Le Roux (Ramiro), Thierry Dran (Gonzalve), François Loup (Don Ingo Gomez).

Video: Home Vision VHS/LD. Dave Heather (director). Color. In French with English subtitles. 50 minutes.

Comment: Sendak's colorful designs and Corsaro's inventive direction make this great fun.

HIGGLETY PIGGLETY POP!
1985 opera by Knussen and Sendak

American artist and author MAURICE SENDAK, whose colorful children's books are both controversial and delightful, was inspired to create the fairy tale *Higglety Pigglety Pop!* by his Sealyham terrier Jennie. The pampered dog sets out to explore the world in search of "something more than everything" and meets lions, pigs, cats, and babies. She eventually becomes the star of a Mother Goose theater. English composer OLIVER KNUSSEN set the witty story to impressionistic music. The opera premiered at Glyndebourne in 1985, and a definitive version was staged in Los Angeles in 1990.

***1985 Glyndebourne Festival
English stage production: Frank Corsaro (director/choreographer), Oliver Knussen (conductor, London Sinfonietta), Maurice Sendak (set/costume designer).

Cast: Cynthia Buchan (Jennie), Deborah Rees (Plant, Baby, Mother Goose), Andrew Gallacher (Pig, Tree low voice), Neil Jenkins (Cat, Milkman, Tree high voice), Rosemary Hardy (Maid, Baby's Mother voice), Stephen Richardson (Lion).

Video: Home Vision VHS/LD. Christopher Swann (director). Color. In English. 60 minutes.

Comment: Bright, cheerful, tuneful fun with wondrous costumes and set designs by Sendak and fine direction by Corsaro.

HINDEMITH, PAUL
German composer (1895–1963)

Paul Hindemith, one of the most influential composers of the century, emigrated to the United States in 1940 after the Nazis banned his work for being degenerate. He composed a number of operas, including CARDILLAC, a bizarre story about a psychotic goldsmith; *Mathis der Maler*, about a radical painter in 16th-century Germany; and THE LONG CHRISTMAS DINNER, libretto by Thornton Wilder, about a dinner that lasted for 90 years.

1964 The Genius of Paul Hindemith

Leonard Bernstein pays tribute to Hindemith on a 1964 CBS Television *Young People's Concert* soon after the composer's death. He talks about the importance of his music and leads the orchestra in excerpts, including a section of *Mathis der Maler.* Roger Englander directed the telecast on February 23, 1964. Black and white. 60 minutes. Video at the MTR.

HINDENBURG
1998 screen opera by Reich and Korot

A musical/video portrait of the German zeppelin that caught fire and crashed in New Jersey on May 6, 1937. Tenors and sopranos sing about what is happening while film of its construction, flight, and crash are shown and the famous broadcast by Herb Morrison describing the disaster is heard. Steve Reich's 25-minute multimedia opera *Hindenburg,* libretto by the composer created with video artist Beryl Korot, premiered at the Spoleto Festival USA in Charleston, South Carolina, on May 23, 1998. *Hindenburg,* described by Reich as "documentary music video theater," was sung by tenors Gerard O'Beirne, Steve Trowell, and Robert Kearnley and sopranos Micaela Haslam and Olive Simpson. It was reprised at the Brooklyn Academy of Music in October 1998.

2002 Three Tales

The *Hindenberg* is one of three Reich/Korot multi-media operas performed by the Steve Reich Ensemble with Synergy Vocals on this DVD (packaged with an audio-only CD). The other operas on the DVD are *Bikini* and *Dolly.* Color. 59 minutes. Nonesuch DVD.

HINES, JEROME
American bass and composer (1921–2003)

Jerome Hines, a six-foot, six-inch basso who sang for 40 consecutive years with the Metropolitan Opera, was noted for his portrayals of Boris Godunov and Philip II. He also composed a religious opera called *I Am the Way,* in which he portrayed Christus; an excerpt can be seen on a *Voice of Firestone* video. Hines made his debut in San Francisco in 1941 as Nerone and joined the Met in 1946, where he sang most of the great bass roles. He sang also in Europe, including at La Scala and Bayreuth and with the Bolshoi. In 1989 he returned to sing in New Orleans 45 years after his first appearance there. In 2001 he appeared as the Grand Inquisitor in a production of *Don Carlo* at the New England Conservatory of Music in Boston. He was married to soprano Lucia Evangelista. See BAYREUTH (1960), BELL TELEPHONE HOUR (1968), BORIS GODUNOV (1962), DON CARLO (1950/1980), FAUST (1963), GOLDEN CHILD (1960), ELEANOR STEBER (1950–1954), and JOAN SUTHERLAND (1961–1968).

1951–1963 Jerome Hines in Opera and Song

Highlights video featuring Hines in performance on six *Voice of Firestone* TV programs broadcast over 12 years. He sings arias from *Faust, The Magic Flute, Porgy and Bess,* and Thomas's *Le Caïd* plus songs by Tosti, Speaks, and Rodgers. His portrayal of Boris Godunov is featured in an 11-minute excerpt from November 18, 1962. His sacred opera *I Am the Way* is shown in a 10-minute excerpt telecast on March 31, 1963; Hines sings Christus, Mildred Miller is Mother Mary, William Walker is St. Peter, and David Starkey is St. John. Black and white. 58 minutes. VAI VHS.

HISTOIRE DU SOLDAT, L'
1918 opera/ballet by Stravinsky

A soldier on his way home from war meets the Devil and exchanges his violin for a magic book. He wins a princess but eventually loses his soul. IGOR STRAVINSKY's *L'Histoire du soldat* (The Soldier's Tale) is sometimes classified as a ballet, although it is also included in opera books such as George Martin's *The Companion to Twentieth Century Opera.* The ambiguity is understandable as *The Soldier's Tale* is situated somewhere between opera and ballet with a narrated story told through and heightened by music and dance but without singing. Nowadays it is seen as a predecessor of postmodern opera. Swiss poet Charles F. Ramuz wrote the French libretto, which is based on a Russian folktale.

1963 Birkett film

English film: Michael Birkett (director/screenplay), Derek Hudson (conductor, Melos Ensemble), Dennis Miller (cinematographer).

Cast: Robert Helpmann (Devil), Brian Phelan (Soldier), Svetlana Beriosova (Princess).

Color. In English. 52 minutes.

Comment: Filmed on location in English villages, woodlands, and mansions.

1983 Netherlands Dance Theater

Dutch stage production: Jirí Kylián (director/choreographer), David Porcelijn (conductor, Netherlands Dans Theater Orchestra).

Cast: Aryeh Weiner (Devil, narration by Philip Clay), Nacho Dutao (Soldier, narration by Pierre-Marie Escourrou), Karin Heyninck (Princess), Gabriele Cattano (Storyteller).

Video: Philips VHS/LD. Torbjörn Ehrnvall (director). Color. In French. 40 minutes.

1984 Blechman film

American animated film: R. O. Blechman (director/designer), Gerard Schwarz (conductor, Los Angeles Chamber Orchestra).

Voices: Max Von Sydow (Devil), Dusan Makavejev (Soldier), Galina Panova (Princess), André Gregory (Narrator).

Video: MGM/UA VHS. Christian Blackwood (director). Color. In English. 56 minutes.

Comment: Blechman is best known as a cartoonist for the *New Yorker*.

Related film

1996 Devil's Dance from *A Soldier's Tale*

An examination of how Stravinsky creates effects in this work by the use of unpredictable rhythms. The music is performed by the Scottish Chamber Orchestra led by William Conway. Part of the video series *The Score: Classical Music Appreciation Through Listening*. Color. In English. 15 minutes. Films for the Humanities & Sciences VHS.

HITCHCOCK, ALFRED

English film director (1899–1980)

Music is an essential element in Alfred Hitchcock's films, and eight of his protagonists are musicians. *Waltzes From Vienna*, one of his lesser known films, revolves around the supposed JOHANN STRAUSS father/son rivalry. In *Shadow of a Doubt*, the villainous uncle (Joseph Cotten) is associated with Lehár's MERRY WIDOW waltz and becomes known as the Merry Widow murderer. Hitchcock's musical collaborator Bernard Herrmann would sometimes pay homage to Wagner in his scores for him. The music for the love scene on the train in *North by Northwest* is a tongue-in-cheek variation of the love theme from *Tristan und Isolde*, while the score for *Vertigo* contains a variation on the Magic Fire music from *Die Walküre*.

H.M.S. PINAFORE

1878 comic opera by Gilbert and Sullivan

H.M.S. Pinafore or The Lass That Loved a Sailor is one of the most often filmed GILBERT AND SULLIVAN Savoy operas and was a hit from its first appearance. The target of Gilbert's satire is the British Navy and class distinctions. First Lord of the Admiralty Sir Joseph Porter, who tells us he started as an office boy, asks for the hand of Captain Corcoran's daughter Josephine, who loves the common sailor Ralph Rackstraw. Their relationship seems impossible until Little Buttercup reveals that she mixed up two babies many years ago, and so sailor Ralph is really the captain and vice versa.

1939 NBC Television

NBC experimented with the new medium of television by presenting excerpts from *H.M.S. Pinafore* in September 1939, featuring Ray Heatherton as Ralph Rackstraw. There weren't many viewers; a TV set cost a small fortune at the time (up to $800), and programming was limited to a few hours a week.

1944 Provincetown Players Light Opera

American TV production: Irwin Shayne and Tony Ferreira (producers, for WAGB Television Workshop), John Grahame and Norman Rosen (TV adaptation), music by Provincetown Players Light Opera Theatre Orchestra and Chorus.

Cast: Joseph De Stefano, Ione Di Caron, James Gales, Robert Feytl, Josephine Lombardo, Charles Kingsley, Cecile Carol, Andrew Duvries.

Telecast live August 14, 1944, on WAGB, DuMont, New York. Black and white. In English. 50 minutes.

Comment: Historic live telecast. Critics weren't overwhelmed but thought it was better than other TV musicals and showed promise of what television might become.

1956 Ashley puppets

American TV production: Barry Shear (producer/director), Paul Ashley (puppet creator), Tom Elwell (set designer), Harriet Neill and Gloria Pauley (costume designers).

Singing voices: Martyn Green (Sir Joseph Porter), Leslie Rands (Captain Corcoran), Muriel Harding (Josephine), Leonard Osborne (Ralph Rackstraw), Ella Halman (Little Buttercup), Darrell Fancourt (Dick Deadeye).

Speaking voices: Paul Ashley, Claude McCann, Michael King, George Nelle.

Telecast April 9, 1956, on WABD, New York. Black and white. In English. 90 minutes.

Comment: Puppet replicas of the operetta characters speak with the voices of off-camera actors and sing with the voices of a 1949 D'Oyly Carte Opera Company Decca recording. The set was a 12-foot duplicate of the *Pinafore*. Critics called it an imaginative success.

1959 NBC Television: Omnibus

American TV production: Norman Campbell (director), Samuel Krachmalnick (conductor, NBC Television Orchestra), Henry May (set designer), Saul Bolasni (costume designer), Dania Krupska (choreographer).

Cast: Cyril Richard (Sir Joseph Porter), William Chapman (Captain Corcoran), Jacqueline McKeever (Josephine), Loren Driscoll (Ralph Rackstraw), Irene Byatt (Little Buttercup), Nathaniel Frey (Dick Deadeye).

Telecast live May 10, 1959, on NBC. Black and white. In English. 51 minutes.

1960 Stratford Festival
Canadian TV film: Norman Campbell (film director), Tyrone Guthrie (stage director), Louis Applebaum (conductor, CBC Orchestra).

Cast: Eric House (Sir Joseph Porter), Harry Mossfield (Captain Corcoran), Marion Studholme (Josephine), Andrew Downie (Ralph Rackstraw), Irene Byatt (Little Buttercup), Howard Mosson (Dick Deadeye).

Black and white. In English. 90 minutes.

Comment: Campbell's film was based on a Stratford Festival production by Guthrie. It was released in the United States on 16mm film by Contemporary Films.

1973 D'Oyly Carte Opera Company
English TV production: Michael Heyland (stage director), John Sichel (film director), Royston Nash (music director/conductor).

Cast: John Reed (Sir Joseph Porter), Michael Rayner (Captain Corcoran), Pamela Field (Josephine), Malcolm Williams (Ralph Rackstraw), Lyndsie Holland (Little Buttercup), John Ayldon (Dick Deadeye).

Video: Magnetic Video/ITC (GB) VHS. John Sichel (director). Color. In English. 78 minutes.

1972 Gilbert and Sullivan for All series
English highlights film: Peter Seabourne (director), Peter Murray (conductor, Gilbert and Sullivan Festival Orchestra and Chorus), David Maverovitch (cinematographer), Trevor Evans (adaptation), John Seabourne (producer).

Cast: John Cartier (Sir Joseph Porter), Michael Wakeham (Captain Corcoran), Valerie Masterson (Josephine), Thomas Round (Ralph Rackstraw), Helen Landis (Little Buttercup), Donald Adams (Dick Deadeye).

Video: Musical Collectables VHS. Color. In English. 50 minutes.

***1982 Gilbert and Sullivan Collection series
English studio production: Michael Geliot (director), Judith De Paul (producer), Alexander Faris (conductor, London Symphony Orchestra and Ambrosian Opera Chorus), Allan Cameron (set designer), George Walker (executive producer).

Cast: Frankie Howerd (Sir Joseph Porter), Peter Marshall (Captain Corcoran), Meryl Drower (Josephine), Michael Bulman (Ralph Rackstraw), Della Jones (Little Buttercup), Alan Watts (Dick Deadeye).

Video: CBS Fox/Braveworld (GB) VHS. Rodney Greenberg (director). Color. In English. 90 minutes.

Comment: One of the best versions of Gilbert and Sullivan on video. Howerd gives a delightful performance, and Faris shows the high quality of the music.

Early/related films

1906 Chronophone film
Early British sound film with Iago Lewis singing "I Am the Captain of the *Pinafore*." Arthur Gilbert directed it for Gaumont using the Chronophone sound system. Black and white. In English. About 3 minutes.

1937 The Girl Said No
This little-known American film contains scenes from Gilbert and Sullivan operettas performed in a traditional manner by members of the old Gilbert and Sullivan Opera Company of New York. It includes "I'm Called Little Buttercup" and "I Am the Monarch of the Sea" from *H.M.S. Pinafore*. See THE GIRL SAID NO.

1988 Permanent Record
A scene from *H.M.S. Pinafore* featuring "I'm Called Little Buttercup" is performed in this American high school movie about a teenage suicide. Marisa Silver directed. Color. 91 minutes.

HOCHZEIT IN HOLLYWOOD
1928 operetta by Straus

OSCAR STRAUS's operetta *Hochzeit in Hollywood* (Married in Hollywood) premiered in Vienna on December 21, 1928, and then crossed the Atlantic with surprising speed. It became the first European operetta to be made into a sound film in Hollywood, premiering in New York on September 23, 1929. The libretto, by Leopold Jacobson and Bruno Hardt-Warden, tells the story of a Ruritanian prince who falls in love with an American operetta singer. After his family forces them to break up, she goes home and becomes a Hollywood movie star. When he is forced to flee to America after a revolution, he gets a job playing a prince in one of her films, and they are reunited.

1929 Married in Hollywood
American feature film: Marcel Silver (director), Harlan Thompson (screenplay), Edward Royce (music director), Fox Film (production).

Cast: J. Harold Murray (Prince Nicholai), Norma Terris (Mary Lou Hopkins), Walter Catlett (Joe Glitner), Lennox Pawle (King Alexander), Evelyn Hall (Queen Louise).

Black and white and color. In English. 106 minutes.

Comment: *The New York Times* loved the movie and its songs, but only 12 minutes of it survive at the UCLA Film and Television Archive.

HOCKNEY, DAVID
English painter (1937–)

David Hockney, one of the most important living artists, has made notable contributions to opera set design; his seemingly simple but extraordinarily effective use of bright color and design have enlivened many productions. He began in 1975 with a remarkable design for THE RAKE'S PROGRESS at Glyndebourne and an equally impressive DIE ZAUBERFLÖTE. and stopped in 1992 with *Die Frau ohne Schatten* in 1992. His eleven opera sets include a *Tristan und Isolde* for the Los Angeles Opera and a TURANDOT for San Francisco. His work looks nearly as impressive on video as it does on stage.

2003 The Colors of Music
Documentary film about Hockney and his work as a designer of sets for operas. Maryte Kavaliauskas and Seth Schneidman's shot the film with Hockney's full cooperation as he worked out his ideas with the sets and models of the stages. Color. 85 minutes. Film distributed by Arte/AVRO.

HODDINOTT, ALUN
Welsh composer (1929–)

Alun Hoddinott, who founded the Cardiff Music Festival in 1967, began writing operas in 1974 after a long career composing only instrumental music. He has shown a fondness for the fiction of Robert Louis Stevenson and has based two operas on Stevenson stories. First was *The Beach of Falesa*, libretto by Flyn Jones, which Welsh National Opera premiered in 1974. Second was THE RAJAH'S DIAMOND, libretto by Myfanwy Piper, which premiered on BBC Wales in 1979; it starred Welsh baritone Geraint Evans, one of Hoddinott's favorite singers. Piper, who created the libretto for Benjamin Britten's TV opera OWEN WINGRAVE, also collaborated with Hoddinott on *The Trumpet Major* and *What the Old Man Does Is Always Right*. His other TV opera, *Murder the Magician*, libretto by J. Morgan, was premiered on Harlech Television in 1976.

HOFMANNSTHAL, HUGO VON
Austrian poet and librettist (1874–1929)

Librettist Hugo von Hofmannsthal's 23-year collaboration with composer RICHARD STRAUSS is said to have helped restore the word to equality with the music in opera; Strauss even composed an opera on the relative importance of word and music, *Capriccio,* after his death. Hofmannsthal's collaboration with Strauss began when the composer asked to use his adaptation of Sophocles's tragedy *Electra* as the basis for an opera. Their ELEKTRA was an international success, as were most of their other operas, although DER ROSENKAVALIER is usually considered their crowning achievement. See ARABELLA, ARIADNE AUF NAXOS, and DIE FRAU OHNE SCHATTEN.

HOIBY, LEE
American composer (1926–)

Lee Hoiby, one of the most successful modern American opera composers, has based most of his operas on literary works. He first won acclaim with *The Scarf,* based on a Chekhov story, which premiered at the Spoleto Festival in 1958; and BEATRICE, based on a Maeterlinck story, which premiered on a Kentucky television station in 1959. His other successes include *Natalia Petrovna* (revised as *A Month in the Country*), based on a Turgenev novel; SUMMER AND SMOKE, based on a Tennessee Williams play; *The Tempest,* based on the Shakespeare play; and *A Christmas Carol,* based on the Dickens story. He also had success with the witty monodramas *The Italian Lesson,* based on a Ruth Draper monologue; and *Bon Appetite!,* based on a Julia Childs recipe.

HOLLINGSWORTH, STANLEY
American composer (1924–)

Stanley Hollingsworth became the youngest American composer to write an opera for television when NBC Opera Theatre telecast his LA GRANDE BRETÈCHE in 1957. It's based on a grim Balzac story about a husband who seals his wife's lover behind a wall. He has also had success with fairy-tale operas such as *The Mother, The Selfish Giant,* and *Harrison Loved His Umbrella.* Hollingsworth, who studied with Gian Carlo Menotti, was musical director of the Spoleto Festival in Italy in 1960.

HOLLYWOOD BOWL

The Hollywood Bowl, one of the largest and most atmospheric outdoor opera venues in the world, with 17,619 seats, has a small place in screen opera history. Two Hollywood operatic films are set in the Bowl: the cinematic opera VOICES OF LIGHT had its Los Angeles premiere there, and ZUBIN MEHTA was filmed conducting there. The first opera presented at the Bowl was William Parker's *Fairyland* in 1915, and regular seasons began in 1922. Lawrence Tibbett made his opera debut at the Bowl in *Aida* in 1923, Felix Knight in *La traviata* in *1935,* and George London in *La traviata* in 1941.

1936 Moonlight Murder

A tenor is killed at the Bowl during a performance of *Il trovatore,* and detective Chester Morris has to find the person whodunit. The Bowl itself got the best reviews when this low-budget murder mystery opened ("the best part of the film is the setting," said *Variety*). See MOONLIGHT MURDER.

1937 Music for Madame

Italian tenor Nino Martini wins fame singing at the Hollywood Bowl at the climax of this enjoyable musical. Conductor Alan Mowbray (a caricature of Leopold Stokowski) is the one who gives him the chance. See MUSIC FOR MADAME.

HONEGGER, ARTHUR
French composer (1892–1955)

Arthur Honegger wrote seven dramatic works that can be loosely called operas and about 40 film scores, including famous ones for Abel Gance; he was very interested in the new medium of film. Honegger's best-known operatic works are *Antigone* (1927), JEANNE D'ARC AU BÛCHER (1938), and *L'aiglon* (1937). He wrote three operettas, including the scandalous *Les aventures du roi Pausole* (1930), a risqué tale about a king with 1,000 wives based on a novel by Pierre Louÿs. Honegger's scores for films include Gance's *Napoleon,* Bernard's *Les Misérables,* Pabst's *Mademoiselle Docteur,* and Asquith's *Pygmalion.* His score for the Gance film *La Roue,* about a locomotive, was adapted into the concert piece *Pacific 231.* In 1949 Jean Mitry made a film about the music, also titled *Pacific 231.*

HOPKINS, ANTONY
English composer (1921–)

Antony Hopkins is best known for his film scores, such as *The Pickwick Papers* (1953) and *Billy Budd* (1962), and the opera *Lady Rohesia* (1948), which critics have likened in eccentricity to the zany Hollywood comedy *Hellzapoppin.* He was also a radio broadcaster and wrote a radio opera called *Scena.* His comic opera *Hands Across the Sky* was premiered by the Intimate Opera Company at Cheltenham Town Hall in 1959.

1960 Hands Across the Sky

Hopkins's comic opera, libretto by G. Snell, was presented on BBC Television soon after its stage premiere. Eric Shilling, Julia Shelley, and Stephen Manton sang the main roles, and Charles Lefeaux directed. Telecast July 2, 1960. Black and white. In English 45 minutes. Film at the NFTA, London.

HORNE, MARILYN
American mezzo-soprano (1934–)

Marilyn Horne, who studied singing in Los Angeles with Lotte Lehmann, made her screen debut at the very beginning of her career by dubbing Dorothy Dandridge's voice in the 1954 film CARMEN JONES. She made her stage debut the same year, singing Hata in *The Bartered Bride* in Los Angeles and then went to Europe where her career blossomed working with Joan Sutherland. Her performances in Rossini operas have been particularly admired, and she is one of the main singers in the 1992 ROSSINI Birthday Bicentennial concert at Lincoln Center. She is also featured in the METROPOLITAN OPERA Centennial Gala in 1983, CARNEGIE HALL Centennial Gala in 1991, and ROSSINI Bicentennial Gala in 1992 as well as the SOPRANOS TV programs *Donne e divas* (1990) and *Queens From Caracalla* (1991). Her TV appearances include appearances on THE ED SULLIVAN SHOW and an episode of *The Odd Couple* sitcom (she played a Carmen who wouldn't sing unless Jack Klugman was Don José). Her screen operas include CARMEN (1954), A CHRISTMAS CAROL (1954), DIE FLEDERMAUS (1990), FALSTAFF (1993), THE GHOSTS OF VERSAILLES (1992), L'ITALIANA IN ALGERI (1986), ORLANDO FURIOSO (1978/1990), SEMIRAMIDE (1980/1986/1990), and TANCREDI (1981).

1981 Sutherland, Horne, Pavarotti Concert

Horne, Luciano Pavarotti, and Joan Sutherland compete for honors in a *Live From Lincoln Center* concert telecast on March 23, 1981. Horne sings "Mura felici" from *La donna del lago* and teams with Pavarotti in a duet from *La Gioconda;* all three join in trios from *Norma, Beatrice di Tenda,* and *Il trovatore.* Richard Bonynge conducts the New York City Opera Orchestra. Color. 150 minutes.

1983 American Songbook

Horne celebrates her 50th birthday, and the 30th anniversary of her opera debut, in a recital at Avery Fisher Hall. The program includes songs by Foster, Kern, and Copland plus spirituals and folk songs. Leonard Slatkin leads the American Symphony Orchestra. Telecast December 28, 1983. Color. 60 minutes.

1985 A Gala Concert

Horne and Joan Sutherland sing some of their finest collaborations in a concert at the Sydney Opera House. They include arias and duets from *Norma, Lakmé, Les contes d'Hoffmann, Don Pasquale, Samson et Dalila, Fra Diavolo, Semele, Alcina, La donna del lago, La cambiale di matrimonio, Semiramide,* and *Les Huguenots.* Richard Bonynge conducts. Color. 142 minutes. Arthaus DVD/ Kultur VHS.

1990 Evviva Bel Canto/Le Grande Primadonne

These two videos are from one concert with Horne and Montserrat Caballé performing in concert at the Philharmonie Hall in Munich. They sing arias and duets by Vivaldi, Meyerbeer, Rossini, Handel, Puccini, Offenbach, and Mercadante, with the highlight a duet from *Semiramide*. Nicola Rescigno leads the Munich Rundfunk Orchestra. Evelyn Paulman and Helmut Rost directed. Released as two videos. Color. 47 and 41 minutes. MCA VHS.

1994 Marilyn Horne: A Portrait

Horne celebrates her 60th birthday on a British TV program. She talks about her career, explains her ideas about singing, and performs in operas by Rossini and Vivaldi. Nigel Wattis directed for London Weekend Television and Bravo. Color. 52 minutes. Arthaus DVD.

HORSE OPERA

1994 TV opera by Copeland

An office clerk, who likes to pretend to be a cowboy, gets hit on the head and believes he wakes up in the Old West in company with Wyatt Earp, Jesse James, and Billy the Kid. Stewart Copeland's TV opera *Horse Opera*, libretto by Jonathan Moore based on Anne Caulfield's play *Cowboys*, premiered on English television in 1994.

1994 Channel 4

    English TV film: Bob Baldwin (director), Ryan Walmsley (set designer), Diana Mosely (costume designer), Initial Film (production).

    Cast: Philip Guy-Bromley, Rik Mayall, Michael Attwell, Edward Tudor Pole, Gina Bellman.

    Telecast February 13, 1994, on Channel 4. Shot in 16mm. Color. In English. 52 minutes.

HOTTER, HANS

German bass-baritone (1909–)

Hans Hotter, an authentic Wagnerian in all aspects of style, power, and grandeur, began singing Wagner in the 1930s and quickly became the world's leading Wagnerian bass-baritone; he remained so until his retirement from major roles in 1972. He also directed the *Ring* Cycle at Covent Garden. Hotter made a number of films in Germany and Austria between 1939 and 1950, mostly sentimental stories or musicals but also a 1943 version of PAGLIACCI in which he sang the Prologue. His operas on video are few, but he can be seen as King Mark in a 1967 Osaka production of TRISTAN UND ISOLDE and as Bartolo in a 1959 Munich production of IL BARBIERE DI SIVIGLIA.

1939 Mutterliebe

Hotter plays a country boy in *Mother Love*, a family-style Austrian film directed by Gustav Ucicky. Käthe Dorsch and Paul Hörbiger are his costars. Black and white. In German. 102 minutes.

1942 Brüderlein fein

Hotter's second film was this Austrian biography of the Viennese poet Ferdinand Raimund. Marte Harell, Hans Holt, and Winnie Markus are also featured. Hans Thimig directed. Black and white. In German. 100 minutes.

1943 Seine beste Rolle

Hotter is the star of *His Best Role*, a Czech-German musical shot in Prague during the worst days of World War II. The cast includes Marina von Ditmar, Paul Dahlke, and Camilla Horn. Otto Pittermann directed. Black and white. In German. 90 minutes.

1950 Grosstadtnacht

Night in the Big City is an Austrian musical featuring opera arias sung by Hotter. Hans Wolff directed. Black and white. In German. 82 minutes.

1950 Sehnsucht des Herzens

Yearnings of the Heart is a German film about a singer who falls in love with a married woman. Hotter stars opposite Linda Caroll and Rainer Penkert. Paul Martin directed. Black and white. In German. 78 minutes.

HOUSE, THE

1995 documentary about the Royal Opera House

This is the ultimate opera house documentary, a six-part BBC Television film showing the inner workings of the Royal Opera House in all its glories, complications, and problems. Director Michael Waldman's cameras filmed the meetings and work of the staff of "The House" from October 1993 to June 1994, and the edited six hours are probably the most candid film portrait ever made of a major opera institution. When the series was first televised, it aroused mixed interpretations as there are a good few heroes and villains. Among the insiders seen at their best or worst in the film are general director Jeremy Isaacs, stage director Trevor Nunn, and a marketing director with a mission. The series begins with American soprano Denyce Graves losing her voice just before the press performance of *Carmen* and literally collapsing; Magali Damonte has to be flown in from Paris to sing the role. The box office manager is fired by the public affairs director. Designer Maria Bjornson gets way behind trying to design sets simultaneously for *Kát'a Kabanová* and *The Sleeping Beauty*. Thomas Allen flies in as a last-minute savior substitute for Jeffrey Black to sing Almaviva. Bernard Haitink is not pleased with the naked Rhine Maidens. The documentary was telecast on PBS and is on VHS. Color. In English. 360 minutes.

HOUSTON, GEORGE
American tenor (1900–1944)

George Houston, who studied at Juilliard, joined the American Opera Company to sing in operettas such as *New Moon* and *Casanova* and made his first film, *The Melody Lingers On,* in 1935. He often played opera singers in his early films, most famously in the 1938 MGM JOHANN STRAUSS biography *The Great Waltz,* in which he portrayed Imperial Opera star Fritz Schiller. Most of his films, however, were not musical. He was George Washington opposite Cary Grant in *The Howards of Virginia,* Marshall Duroc with Greta Garbo in *Conquest,* and the cowboy hero the Lone Rider for the PRC studio in a series of low-budget Westerns. His films of some operatic interest are listed below.

1935 The Melody Lingers On
Houston plays Carlo Salvini, an opera tenor army captain, who returns home in 1917 for a benefit performance of *Carmen;* he is shown on stage as Don José in several scenes from the opera. He meets and marries pianist Josephine Hutchinson, and years later their son also becomes an opera singer. United Artists. Black and white. 85 minutes.

1935 Let's Sing Again
Houston plays Leon Alba, the opera singer father of Bobby Breen. Breen inherits his father's voice and becomes a singer even though they are separated until the end of the movie. See LET'S SING AGAIN.

HOUSTON GRAND OPERA

The adventurous and innovative Houston Grand Opera, housed in the Wortham Center since 1978, is noted for championing modern American opera. Between 1974 and 2000 it premiered 25 new operas, including works by Mark Adamo, John Adams, Leonard Bernstein, Carlisle Floyd, Philip Glass, Tod Machover, Henry Mollicone, Meredith Monk, Thomas Pasatieri, Michael Tippett, and Stewart Wallace. It has also arranged major revivals of operas by Scott Joplin, George Gershwin, and Kurt Weill as well as outstanding productions of European operas. A number of its productions have been telecast, and some are on video. See AKHNATEN, LA CENERENTOLA (1995), LITTLE WOMEN (2000), NIXON IN CHINA (1987), STREET SCENE (1994), TREEMONISHA (1982), and WILLIE STARK (1981).

HOWARD, KATHLEEN
Canadian mezzo-soprano (1873–1956)

Kathleen Howard had three careers in her long life as opera singer, fashion editor, and movie actress. Her opera career began in Metz in 1907; she sang with the Metropolitan Opera from 1916 to 1928, creating the role of Zita in *Gianni Schicchi* in 1918. She was welcomed by other opera companies and made records for Edison and Pathé. During this period she became a costume expert, so after she left the Met in 1928, she was appointed fashion editor of *Harper's Bazaar.* She worked there until she began her Hollywood career in 1934. She made movies until 1950; none of them have opera content, but many are classics. Her first movie was the stylish 1934 *Death Takes a Holiday* and her last the classy 1950 *The Petty Girl,* but she is best known for her memorable performances as W. C. Fields's nagging wife in *It's a Gift* (1934), *You're Telling Me* (1934), and *The Man on the Flying Trapeze* (1935). Her later films include *Ball of Fire* (1941), *Laura* (1944), and the Jerome Kern musical *Centennial Summer* (1946).

HUÉSPED DEL SEVILLANO, EL
1926 zarzuela by Guerrero

Spanish composer JACINTO GUERRERO's zarzuela *El huésped del sevillano* focuses on an imaginary incident in the life of *Don Quixote* creator Miguel Cervantes; it supposes that this event inspired him to write a story titled *La ilustre fregona* (The Noble Kitchen Maid). An aristocrat (Don Diego) kidnaps the beautiful daughter of a swordsmith (Raquel), but she is rescued by a painter (Juan Luis) and his page (Rodrigo) with the help of a kitchen maid (Constancia). Cervantes is not mentioned by name in the zarzuela but is simply "the huésped" (guest) at the Sevillano Inn. He is, however, quite recognizable. The libretto, by Enrique Reoyo and Juan Ignacio Luca de Tena, is also a hymn of praise to the city of Toledo in its golden age.

1939 Arte film
Spanish feature film: Enrique del Campo (director), Arte Films (production).
Cast: Luis Sagi-Vela, Charito Leonís, Marta Ruel, Julio Castro, Manuel Kayser (Cervantes).
Black and white. In Spanish. 88 minutes.

1969 Teatro Lirico Español
Spanish TV film: Juan de Orduña (director), Federico Moreno Torroba (conductor, Orquesta Lírica Española), Jose Perera Cruz (conductor, Coro Cantores de Madrid), Manuel Tamayo (screenplay), Federico G. Larrya (cinematographer).

Cast: María Silva (Raquel, sung by Dolores Pérez), Manuel Gil (Juan Luis, sung by Carlo del Monte), Maria José Alfonso (Constancia, sung by Rosa Sarmiento), Antonio Durán (Rodrigo, sung by Enrique del Portal), Angel Picazo (Cervantes), Rubén Rojo (Don Diego, sung by Luis Frutos).

Video: Metrovideo (Spain) VHS. Shot in 35mm for RTVE Spanish Television. Juan de Orduña (director). Color. In Spanish. 85 minutes.

HUGUENOTS, LES
1836 opera by Meyerbeer

GIACOMO MEYERBEER's *The Huguenots,* the second of the composer's spectacular collaborations with librettist Eugène Scribe, was one of the most popular operas of the 19th century and is grand opera in all senses. It requires seven major singers, gigantic sets, and elaborate production values to tells its story of events leading up to the horrific St. Bartholomew's Day massacre of Protestant Huguenots by French Catholics. The plot revolves around Queen Marguerite de Valois and a love affair between Protestant aristocrat Raoul de Nangis and Catholic noblewoman Valentine; both die in the massacre. The other main roles in the opera are Count de Nevers, Count de St. Bris, Urbain, and Marcel. The opera is usually performed in Italy as *Gli ugonotti* and in Germany as *Die Hugenotten.*

1990 Australian Opera
Australian stage production: Lotfi Mansouri (director), Richard Bonynge (conductor, Elizabethan Sydney Orchestra and Australian Opera Chorus), John Stoddart (set designer), Michael Stennet (costume designer), Lois Strike (choreographer).

Cast: Joan Sutherland (Marguerite de Valois) Amanda Thane (Valentine), Anson Austin (Raoul), John Pringle (Count de Nevers), John Wegner (Count de St. Gris), Clifford Grant (Marcel), Suzanne Johnston (Urbain).

Video: Kultur DVD/Bel Canto Society and Home Vision VHS. Virginia Lumsden (director). Color. In French with English subtitles. 200 minutes.

Comment: This was Sutherland's last performance in Sydney. She sings "Home Sweet Home" (emulating Melba) for the audience after the opera ends.

1990 Deutsche Oper Berlin
German stage production: John Dew (director), Stefan Soltesz (conductor, Deutsche Oper Berlin Orchestra and Chorus).

Cast: Angela Denning (Marguerite de Valois), Lucy Peacock (Valentine), Richard Leech (Raoul), Lenus Carlos (Count de Nevers), Harmut Welker (Count de St.

Bris), Martin Blasius (Marcel), Camille Capasso (Urbain).

Video: Arthaus DVD. Brian Large (director). Color. In German (as *Die Hugenotten*) with English subtitles. 156 minutes.

Comment: Set in a modern divided Berlin, this abridged and updated adaptation attempts to connect past and present forms of bigotry.

Early/related films

1902 Electro Talking Bioscope
An aria from the opera was seen and heard in Holland in September 1902 in a sound film featured in screenings by Alber's Electro Talking Bioscope. Black and white. In French. About 3 minutes.

1909 Gaumont film
French director Louis Feuillade, later famous for his serials, shot an early version of the story for Gaumont in 1909. Black and white. Silent. About 12 minutes.

1933 La canzone del sole
Italian film that ends with a live production of *Gli ugonotti* in the open-air Arena di Verona with Giacomo Lauri-Volpi starring as Raoul. Three scenes from the opera are shown. Also in the cast is mezzo-soprano Gianna Pederzini. See LA CANZONE DEL SOLE.

1936 Follow Your Heart
Marion Talley sings the Page aria from *Les Huguenots* in a hayloft, accompanied by a phonograph, and then teams with Michael Bartlett on the Raoul/Valentine duet "Tu l'as dit." See FOLLOW YOUR HEART.

1937 Maytime
Jeanette MacDonald plays an opera singer in 19th-century Paris who is shown on stage as the queen's page Urbain in a production of *Les Huguenots* at the Paris Opéra. She is introduced by Tudor Williams as Raoul's servant Marcel and then sings the Page Aria ("Une dame noble et sage") while admirer Nelson Eddy watches from the front row. See MAYTIME.

1951 Madame de…
Max Ophuls's stylish study of relationships features ironic theme music from *Les Huguenots.* The plot revolves around earrings that countess Danielle Darrieux pawns, husband Charles Boyer retrieves, and baron lover Vittorio De Sica returns with unfortunate consequences. Shown in America as *The Earrings of Madame de....* Black and white. In French. 100 minutes.

HUMPERDINCK, ENGELBERT
German composer (1854–1921)

Engelbert Humperdinck used to be known only as the composer of the hugely successful opera HÄNSEL UND GRETEL, a favorite of children and adults around the world since its premiere in 1893. He is now also known as the composer whose name was appropriated by a British pop singer. Fortunately, Humperdinck's musical brilliance in *Hansel and Gretel* is likely to keep him in the limelight long after the pop star is forgotten. Humperdinck's other major opera, still occasionally performed, is the 1897 *Königskinder*. He also composed one of the earliest important film scores, at producer Max Reinhardt's request, for the 1912 spectacular *Das Mirakel*.

HUROK, SOL
American impresario (1889–1974)

Russian-born American impresario Sol Hurok helped popularize opera in America by touring famous singers such as Russian basso Feodor Chaliapin. Among the many singers whose reputations were enhanced by Hurok were Marian Anderson, Jan Peerce, and Roberta Peters. Hurok even made an Italian film of an opera famous, the 1953 Italian AIDA starring Sophia Loren, by launching it as if it were a live spectacle.

1953 Tonight We Sing
Hurok is romanticized in the 1953 film biography TONIGHT WE SING, where he is portrayed by David Wayne. His famous stars are played by modern equivalents. See TONIGHT WE SING.

1956 Producers' Showcase
Hurok produced this operatic all-star TV program featuring Leonard Warren, Zinka Milanov, Roberta Peters, Jan Peerce, Marian Anderson, Blanche Thebom, Mildred Miller, and Risë Stevens. See PRODUCERS' SHOWCASE.

HUSTON, JOHN
American film director (1906–1987)

John Huston, whose splendid directing career began with *The Maltese Falcon* in 1941, featured opera in his films THE DEAD and *Prizzi's Honor* and also directed opera on stage. The Metropolitan Opera was the first to approach him, an offer to direct *La fanciulla del West*, but he turned the Met down saying that its approach was shabby. La Scala then gave him the chance to direct Richard Rodney Bennett's *The Mines of Sulphur*, which he accepted; it premiered in Milan on March 1, 1966. Critics called it a success, but Huston never directed op-

era on stage again. His love of opera, however, is very evident in *The Dead*, his last film.

1966 The Life and Times of John Huston
This documentary about Huston was made at the time he was directing Richard Rodney Bennett's *The Mines of Sulphur* at La Scala. The film includes interviews and scenes of him working as he talks about his past, his philosophy of life, his successes, and his failures. Black and white. 60 minutes.

1985 Prizzi's Honor
A tenor is singing "Una furtiva lagrima" on stage at a Prizzi family celebration when the event is fire bombed by rival gangsters. The film centers around the love affair between killers-for-hire Jack Nicholson and Kathleen Turner and their relationship with the Prizzi crime family. The parodistic use of Rossini, Verdi, Puccini, and Donizetti contributes to the texture of many scenes. Tomasina Baratta is the opera singer and Alexandra Ivanoff is the soprano in the wedding scene. *The Barber of Seville* overture is also featured. Color. 130 minutes. Vestron VHS.

HYTNER, NICHOLAS
English director (1956–)

Nicholas Hytner, one of the most original of the newer theater/opera directors, became equally well known as a film director after the success of *The Madness of King George* (which uses music by HANDEL as its soundtrack) and *The Crucible*. His first opera production was *The Turn of the Screw* for Kent Opera, and he also directed KING PRIAM (1985) and *Le nozze di Figaro* for Kent. His controversial 1991 LA CLEMENZA DI TITO at Glyndebourne is on video, as is his splendid 1988 SERSE by the English National Opera and his imaginative 1995 THE CUNNING LITTLE VIXEN at the Châtelet in Paris. Hytner has staged a number of plays for the Royal Shakespeare Company and the National Theatre, and he also produced the musical *Miss Saigon*.

I

IDOMENEO, RE DI CRETA
1781 opera by Mozart

Idomeneo, re di Creta (Idomeneus, King of Crete) is the official name of MOZART's first major opera but the videos are titled simply *Idomeneo* as was its original poster. It's an impressive *opera seria*, considered by some critics to be the best ever. Idomeneo, on his way home after leading the Cretans in the Trojan War, has been shipwrecked; he promises the god Neptune that he will sacrifice the first person he sees if allowed to return home. That person turns out to be his son Idamante, who is in love with the Trojan princess Ilia. Elettra (Electra), who has also taken refuge on the island, is also in love with Idamante and madly jealous. Neptune wants his pledge honored. The libretto, by Giambattista Varesco, is based on Antoine Danchet's French libretto *Idoménée,* derived from a Greek myth. Mozart had casting problems so the role of Idamante was written for both tenor and soprano; most productions use the tenor version, but there is an excellent Metropolitan Opera video of the soprano version.

1966 BBC Television
English TV production: Benjamin Britten (conductor, BBC Orchestra).

Cast: Peter Pears (Idomeneo), Heather Harper (Ilia), Anne Pashley (Idamante), Rae Woodland (Elettra), Robert Tear (Arbace).

Black and white. In Italian. 66 minutes.

Comment: The complete opera does not survive, but the NFTA has a 66-minute video of Act II.

1974 Glyndebourne Festival
English stage production: John Cox (director), John Pritchard (conductor, London Philharmonic Orchestra and Glyndebourne Festival Chorus), Roger Butlin (set designer).

Cast: Richard Lewis (Idomeneo), Bozena Betley (Ilia), Leo Goeke (Idamante), Josephine Barstow (Elettra), Alexander Oliver (Arbace), John Fryatt (High Priest), Dennis Wicks (Voice of Neptune).

Video: Opera d'Oro/VAI VHS. Dave Heather (director). Color. In Italian with English subtitles. 127 minutes.

***1982 Metropolitan Opera
American stage production: Jean-Pierre Ponnelle (director, set/costume designer), James Levine (conductor, Metropolitan Opera Orchestra and Chorus).

Cast: Luciano Pavarotti (Idomeneo), Ileana Cotrubas (Ilia), Frederica von Stade (Idamante), Hildegard Behrens (Elettra), John Alexander (Arbace), Timothy Jenkins (High Priest), Richard J. Clark (Voice of Neptune).

Video: Pioneer Classic DVD/LD and Bel Canto Paramount VHS. Taped November 6, 1982, telecast January 26, 1983. Brian Large (director). Color. In Italian with English subtitles. 185 minutes.

Comment: A starry cast with Pavarotti in great form and von Stade as good a soprano Idamante as you could wish for.

1983 Glyndebourne Festival
English stage production: Trevor Nunn (director), Bernard Haitink (conductor, London Philharmonic Orchestra and Glyndebourne Festival Chorus), John Napier (set designer).

Cast: Philip Langridge (Idomeneo), Yvonne Kenny (Ilia), Jerry Hadley (Idamante), Carol Vaness (Elettra), Thomas Hemsley (Arbace), Anthony Roden (High Priest), Roderick Kennedy (Voice of Neptune).

Video: HBO VHS. Christopher Swann (director). Color. In Italian with English subtitles. 180 minutes.

1988 Kreihsl film
Austrian feature film: Michael Kreihsl (director/screenplay), Nikolaus Harnoncourt (conductor, Mozart Orchestra and Zurich Opera Chorus).

Cast: Pepi Griesser (Idomeneo), Elke Heinbücher (Ilia), Joachim Bauer (Idamante), Marisa Fernandino (Elettra), Hjalmar Este (Arbace), Uli Hoffmann (High Priest).

Color. In German. 102 minutes.

Comment: The film was produced by the Vienna Music School and was presented at the Ghent and Gothenburg film festivals.

***1991 Drottningholm Court Theatre
Swedish stage production: Michael Hampe (director), Arnold Östman (conductor, Drottningholm Court Theatre Orchestra), Martin Rupprecht (set/costume designer).

Cast: Stuart Kale stars (Idomeneo), Ann-Christin Biel (Ilia), David Kuebler (Idamante), Anita Soldh (Elettra), John-Eric Jacobsson (Arbace), Lars Tibel (High Priest), Olle Skold (Voice of Neptune).

Video: Philips VHS/LD. Thomas Olofsson (director). RM Arts. Color. In Italian with English subtitles. 142 minutes.

Comment: Delightful authentic production from the baroque Drottningholm Court Theatre with the orchestra playing period instruments.

Related film

1975 Barry Lyndon
The march from *Idomeneo* is featured on the soundtrack of this Stanley Kubrick film based on Thackeray's novel about the adventures of an Irishman in wartorn 18th century Europe. Ryan O'Neal stars. Color. 183 minutes.

1993 Philadelphia
This Hollywood film, about a gay lawyer with AIDS (Tom Hanks), features Lucia Popp on the soundtrack singing Idamante's aria "Non temer, amato bene" accompanied by the Vienna State Opera Orchestra led by John Pritchard. Color. 119 minutes.

I DREAM TOO MUCH
1935 American film with opera content

Metropolitan Opera soprano Lily Pons made her film debut opposite Henry Fonda in this enjoyable RKO picture. Her delightful personality comes through well in her portrayal of a rising opera singer married to aspiring composer Fonda. His opera *Echo and Narcissus* is not a success, but it becomes one when it is turned into a musical comedy. Pons sings her signature aria "Bell Song" from *Lakmé*, "Caro nome" from *Rigoletto*, and songs by Jerome Kern and Dorothy Fields. She insisted that her husband-to-be André Kostelanetz conduct the orchestra accompanying her arias. Lucille Ball plays Pons's best friend in one of her earliest screen roles. Edmund North and James Gow wrote the screenplay, David Abel was the cinematographer. and John Cromwell directed. Black and white. 85 minutes. Nova/Turner VHS.

I'LL TAKE ROMANCE
1937 American film with opera content

Metropolitan Opera soprano Grace Moore plays an opera diva romanced by Melvyn Douglas in a rather simplistic story; it revolves around whether she should sing in Buenos Aires or Paris. Melvyn Douglas plays the man who wants her to go to Argentina, and their relationship evolves into love after a couple of kidnappings. Helen Westley plays Madame Della, Moore's dominating aunt, while Stuart Irwin is Douglas's best friend Pancho. Moore is seen on stage in New York as Violetta in the "Libiamo" sequence from Act I of *La traviata* and in the Quintet and Finale of *Martha*. She also sings the Gavotte from *Manon* ("Obéissons quand leur voix appelle") and the Act I duet with Pinkerton from *Madama Butterfly*

before she capitulates to love. Wilhelm von Wymetal Jr. staged the opera sequences, Isaac Van Grove conducted the orchestra, George Oppenheimer and Jane Murfin wrote the screenplay, Lucien Andriot was the cinematographer, Oscar Hammerstein II wrote the title tune, and Edward H. Griffith directed for Columbia Pictures. This was Moore's last U.S. film before she left for Europe to make LOUISE with Abel Gance. Black and white. 85 minutes. Live Opera VHS.

IMAGINARY OPERAS IN FILMS

A large number of imaginary operas have been created for the movies as a part of the plot, usually to allow the stars to behave or sing in ways that a traditional opera might not encompass. They have never been transferred to the stage as they are only segments of operas, but an aria created by Bernard Herrmann for an imaginary opera in *Citizen Kane* has been recorded by Kiri Te Kanawa and appears to have a life of its own. The composers of these fascinating imaginary operas include such stage opera composers as Erich Wolfgang Korngold, Riccardo Zandonai, Kurt Weill, Herbert Stothart, Nino Rota, Oscar Levant, and Mario Castelnuovo-Tedesco. Irene Kahn Atkins discusses some of them in her fine study *Source Music in Motion Pictures*.

1931 Les bohémiens
The imaginary opera *Les bohémiens*, seen in the climactic scenes of the René Clair film LE MILLION, is only vaguely related to Murger. There are two scenes on stage at the Opéra-Lyrique Théâtre in Paris. A duet titled "Alone in the forest" is sung by tenor Sopranelli (Constantin Stroesco) and soprano Mme. Ravellina (Odette Talazac) with the romantic leads (Annabella and René Lefèvre) hidden behind the scenery. Later in a gypsy camp, the Bohemians sing about their happiness, the tenor wins a duel for his soprano's honor, and his dying rival sings to his mother. The film centers around the hunt for a lottery ticket hidden in a coat the tenor is wearing. Rival groups charge on stage to try to seize it, so the opera ends in chaos. *Les bohémiens* was composed by Georges van Parys with Philippe Parès and Armand Bernard.

1934 La signora di tutti
An unnamed imaginary opera is at the center of Max Ophuls's film LA SIGNORA DI TUTTI, and its plot is described in detail. It is about a young officer who is magically healed by a woman after he is shot. She becomes his lover and goes on a military campaign with him, but the emperor takes the woman away from him. The officer ends up in prison totally mad. In the film Isa Miranda is taken to the opera by a married man and his wife, and they fall in love as he is describing the opera plot. The

opera music is by Daniel Amfitheatrof, who began his career at La Scala.

1934 Devil's Island
A French composer escapes from Devil's Island and writes an opera based on his experiences there. He had been sent there for killing his opera singer wife's lover. The governor of Devil's Island attends the premiere of the opera and recognizes his former prisoner, but he says nothing. The imaginary opera is featured in the British film THE BROKEN MELODY.

1935 Venetian Moon
Imaginary opera created by Edward Lockton and Rudolph Sieczynski for the English film *Heart's Desire*. Richard Tauber plays a Venetian gondolier in the London premiere of the opera, supposedly composed by Carl Harbord. See RICHARD TAUBER.

1936 Romeo and Juliet
German opera composer Erich Wolfgang Korngold created an imaginary *Romeo and Juliet* opera for the 1936 Hollywood film GIVE US THIS NIGHT, with a plot much like that of the Shakespeare play. Jan Kiepura, who was a friend of Korngold's, and Gladys Swarthout fall in love and star in the stage production of *Romeo and Juliet* in the movie.

1936 Carnival
Oscar Levant composed an opera called *Carnival* for the 1936 film CHARLIE CHAN AT THE OPERA with overture, prelude, marches, and arias. The libretto by William Kernell was created around a Mephistopheles costume worn by Lawrence Tibbett in the film METROPOLITAN, which was given to the low-budget Chan picture to be worn onstage by a baritone in a stabbing scene. Boris Karloff plays the baritone (singing dubbed by Tudor Williams), who is suffering from amnesia and a desire for revenge. Levant discusses his opera in his autobiography *A Smattering of Ignorance*.

1936 Isabelle and Bal Masqué
The 1936 Mary Ellis movie FATAL LADY features two imaginary operas. The first to be seen is *Isabelle*, with music by Gerard Carbonara and libretto by David Ormont. The second is *Bal Masqué*, with music by Carbonara and Victor Young with a libretto by Sam Coslow. Ellis plays an opera diva who runs away after being accused of a murder; she sings in both operas under a false name.

1937 Regina della Scala
Regina della Scala (Queen of La Scala) is an imaginary opera about Teatro alla Scala opera house by a young composer that is to be premiered by his prima donna lover at La Scala. It is featured in the 1937 Italian film REGINA DELLA SCALA, a movie designed to glorify the Milan theater. Antonio Veretti wrote the music.

1937 Czaritza
Herbert Stothart created *Czaritza*, a 19th-century French opera set in Russia, for the 1937 film MAYTIME. It is supposedly written by a Rossini-like Paris composer for American prima donna Jeanette MacDonald and is to premiere in New York. Stothart based the opera on themes from Tchaikovsky's Fifth Symphony; about 10 minutes of it are staged at the climax of the film with MacDonald and Nelson Eddy in the leading roles. Also seen on stage in the opera are Alex Kandiba as the Black Prince and M. Morova as the contralto. It was staged by Wilhelm von Wymetal Jr. who also wrote the lyrics.

1937 Broken Melody
An Australian (Lloyd Hughes) is suffering from depression but discovers he has so much musical talent that he can sit down and write a hugely successful opera. The imaginary opera is featured in the 1937 Australian film BROKEN MELODY.

1939 Balalaika
An imaginary Rimsky-Korsakov opera based on *Scheherazade* is staged at the Imperial Opera House in the MGM operetta film BALALAIKA. It was devised by Herbert Stothart with help from pastiche masters Bob Wright and Chet Forest, the team that transmuted Borodin's music into the operetta *Kismet*. Nelson Eddy and Ilona Massey are the stars of the opera and the film, which is set at the time of the Russian Revolution.

1939 Arlesiana
Arlesiana was composed by Sam Pokrass to a libretto by Armando Hauser for the film WIFE, HUSBAND AND FRIEND. Opera soprano Nina Koshetz supplies the singing voice for Binnie Barnes, who plays an opera diva, while Emery Darcy sings for Warner Baxter and T. Chavrova for his wife in the movie, Loretta Young. The film, based on James Cain's story *Career in C Major*, was remade in 1949 as *Everybody Does It*, with another imaginary opera.

1940 Penelope
Italian opera composer Riccardo Zandonai created the imaginary opera *Penelope* for the 1940 Beniamino Gigli film RITORNO (*Traummusik* in German). It's a retelling of the *Odyssey* story about Ulysses's wife Penelope, who waited faithfully for 20 years for his return. In the film, composer Rossano Brazzi has created the opera for his soprano friend Marte Harell, and she asks Gigli to be her

Ulysses. A scene from the opera is shown, with Mafalda Favero supplying the singing voice for Harell.

1941 Salammbô

Kiri Te Kanawa recorded an aria from this imaginary opera created by Bernard Herrmann for CITIZEN KANE. Herrmann wrote *Salammbô* because director Orson Welles wanted a peculiar kind of opera, one in which the soprano is on stage as the curtain goes up having to sing over a powerful orchestra. In the film, this is a disaster for Kane's singer wife Susan Alexander, whom he has forced into an opera career. The actress on stage is Dorothy Comingore, but the singing is by soprano Jean Forward, a professional who forced herself to sound amateurish. The *Salammbô* aria sung professionally by Te Kanawa actually sounds rather good.

1943 Amour et Gloire

The 1943 Universal film of THE PHANTOM OF THE OPERA includes scenes and arias from two imaginary operas created by composer Edward Ward. The first, a charming, melodious French opera called *Amour et Gloire,* is based on music by Chopin with lyrics by Wilhelm von Wymetal Jr., who staged it. Nelson Eddy stars opposite soprano Susanna Foster in the opera, and Foster hits some fine high notes as the Phantom (Claude Rains) listens.

1943 Le Prince de Caucasie

The second opera created by Edward Ward for the 1943 Universal film THE PHANTOM OF THE OPERA is a fiery Russian drama, *Le Prince de Caucasie,* based on themes from Tchaikovsky's Fourth Symphony. George Waggner wrote the English libretto, Wilhelm von Wymetal Jr., staged it, and Max Rabinowitz did the Russian translation. Nelson Eddy, Tudor Williams, and Nicki André perform in the opera, which stops when a giant chandelier comes crashing down; the Phantom (Claude Rains) has cut the chain holding it up.

1944 The Magic Voice

An imaginary opera is the central focus of the 1944 Universal movie *The Climax.* Boris Karloff killed the woman who sang it 10 years before at the Royal Opera, and he thinks it is sacred to her memory. Susanna Foster plays a singer chosen to revive the opera, and Karloff, the opera house doctor, sets out to stop her. Edward Ward composed the music to libretto and lyrics by George Waggner, basing it around themes by Chopin and Schubert.

1945 Columbus

Kurt Weill created a 12-minute comic opera with librettist Ira Gershwin for the time travel film WHERE DO WE GO FROM HERE? It is heard on Columbus's mutinous ship just before land is sighted. Benito (Carlos Ramirez) sings about the mutiny, saying the world is flat; Columbus (Fortunio Bonanova) defends his voyage for the queen saying the world is round; and time traveler Bill Morgan (Fred MacMurray) tells the crew what they are about to discover.

1945 Testimony Opera

An aria for an imaginary comic opera was created for Danny Kaye for the 1945 Goldwyn movie *Wonder Man.* Kaye is about to testify against a gangster who killed his brother. When the gangster's mob chases him, he escapes onto an opera stage and sings his testimony as an aria to the district attorney in the audience. Sylvia Fine created the words and music for this bizarre aria. The opera singers on stage with Kaye are Noël Cravat, Nick Thompson, Nino Pipitone, and Baldo Minuti. Luis Alberni is the disturbed prompter, and Aldo Franchetti is the orchestra conductor.

1946 My Country

My Country is an imaginary opera based on music by Franz Liszt featured in the 1946 film TWO SISTERS FROM BOSTON. Lauritz Melchior plays a Metropolitan Opera tenor who sings some of it on stage with Kathryn Grayson. Charles Previn arranged the music.

1946 Marie Antoinette

Marie Antoinette is an imaginary opera by Charles Previn, based on music by Felix Mendelssohn, that is staged at the Met at the end of the 1946 MGM film TWO SISTERS FROM BOSTON. Lauritz Melchior plays the Met tenor who sings the role of French King Louis XVI and Kathryn Grayson is his Marie Antoinette; they are dressed in period costumes with dozens of extras, a massive set, and a 500-foot-wide reproduction of the Old Met interior.

1947 Take My Life

William Alwyn created an imaginary opera and aria for the 1947 British suspense film TAKE MY LIFE. Greta Gynt, who plays an opera star married to a man accused of murder, is seen performing the aria in an opera house, although it is actually sung by Victoria Sladen. On a recent CD of music by Alwyn, it is performed by Susan Bullock.

1949 The Loves of Fatima

Mario Castelnuovo-Tedesco created an opera called *The Loves of Fatima* for the 1949 film EVERYBODY DOES IT with arias for soprano and baritone. Paul Douglas sings the baritone role with Linda Darnell as the soprano in its premiere by the American Scala Opera Company. His singing is performed by New York City Opera baritone Stephen Kemalyan, while Darnell's is by San Francisco

Opera soprano Helen Spann. The premiere is a comic disaster as Douglas takes so many stimulants to get courage that finally he falls down on stage and knocks over the sets.

1949 The Princess
Mario Lanza and Kathryn Grayson make their opera debut in an imaginary opera called *The Princess* in the 1949 film THAT MIDNIGHT KISS. Charles Previn based it on themes from Tchaikovsky's Fifth Symphony. Lanza is a truck driver with a great voice while Grayson is an heiress who wants to be an opera singer.

1949 The Glass Mountain
Tito Gobbi stars in the imaginary opera *The Glass Mountain,* created by Nino Rota for the 1949 film THE GLASS MOUNTAIN. Elena Rizzieri sings with Gobbi in the opera scenes and Franco Ferrara conducts the La Fenice Opera Orchestra. Michael Denison, who plays the opera's composer, falls in love with Valentina Cortese after his plane crashes in the Italian Alps. A theme from the opera became popular in England during the 1950s.

1951 Il Ritorno de Cesare
Mario Castelnuovo-Tedesco created this opera for the 1951 MGM film STRICTLY DISHONORABLE. The opera singer is Ezio Pinza who belts out the bass aria "Il Ritorno de Cesare" with Janet Leigh as his sword bearer. He plays an operatic Don Juan, while she is an innocent who falls in love with him. He has to marry her to save her reputation—or so he says.

1962 Saint Joan
The opera *Saint Joan,* composed by the Phantom, is the centerpiece of the 1962 British film THE PHANTOM OF THE OPERA. Herbert Lom plays the Phantom with Heather Sears as the young soprano Christine. The Phantom teaches her how to sing his opera and saves her life when a chandelier falls. Edwin Astley was the actual composer.

1976 The Kingdom of Love
Bank robbers James Caan and Elliott Gould don costumes and join star Lesley Ann Warren in the imaginary operetta *The Kingdom of Love* in the film HARRY AND WALTER GO TO NEW YORK. A secret tunnel to the bank is under the theater, and they are trying to delay the show until their fellow crooks can finish the robbery. David Shire created the operetta with Alan and Marilyn Bergman.

1989 Don Juan Triumphant
Misha Segal wrote an aria of the Phantom's lost opera *Don Juan Triumphant* for a 1989 version of THE PHANTOM OF THE OPERA. The imaginary opera, which is described in Leroux's source novel, is sung in the film by Christine (Jill Schoelen). Robert Englund plays the Phantom in this film in which the setting is transposed to 19th-century Covent Garden.

1990 Die Schlumpf
Thomas Pasatieri's imaginary opera *Die Schlumpf,* created for the 1990 film *Dick Tracy,* is performed on stage by Marvalee Cariaga and Michael Gallup. It looks and sounds like a Wagnerian pastiche, but it is only shown in long shot from where Dick Tracy (Warren Beatty) and Tess Trueheart (Glenne Headley) are seated in the opera house. The excerpt is brief, although apparently more was filmed. In the film, it is apparently meant to be very, very long as Tracy leaves the theater, stays away for hours, and comes back to see the same scene still in progress.

2001 Vide Cor Meum
Patrick Cassidy created the mini-opera *Vide Cor Meum* (See Your Heart) for the film HANNIBAL; it uses words from Dante's *La Vita Nuova* as libretto, describing his first attempts at poetry and his meeting with Beatrice. The opera is staged in costume in a palace in Florence, Italy, by Cassidy and Hans Zimmer as if were one of the early operas presented by the Camerata in the 1600s. Bruno Lazzaretti sings Dante, Danielle de Niese is Beatrice, and the music is played by the Lyndhurst Orchestra led by Gavin Greenaway. Only about a minute of the opera is seen in the film, but there is more on the film soundtrack album. Attending the performance are serial killer Hannibal Lecter (Anthony Hopkins) and the policeman who is trying to catch him (Giancarlo Giannini).

I MARRIED AN ANGEL
1942 American film with opera content

The last of the Jeanette MacDonald/Nelson Eddy operetta films is a version of the 1938 Rodgers and Hart musical *I Married an Angel,* with added opera numbers for the stars. Ironically, Rodgers and Hart originally wrote the musical for the screen, but the screenplay was rejected by the Hays Office; it considered the story of a man who marries an angel to be "blasphemous and sacrilegious." Eddy plays a Hungarian banker whose playboy lifestyle is about to cause his ruin. After a young typist (MacDonald) comes to a costume party in angel costume, Eddy has a dream in which he marries a real angel (MacDonald again). When he wakes up, he decides to reform and proposes to the woman in the angel costume. MacDonald sings "Anges purs" from *Faust* and joins Eddy on "Les tringles des sistres tintaient" from *Carmen.* The songs are good and the singing is fine, but the film itself is a disappointment. Herbert Stothart arranged the music, Anita Loos wrote the screenplay, Ray June was the cinematographer, and W. S. Van Dyke directed for MGM. Black and white. 84 minutes. MGM/UA VHS.

IMPRESARIO, THE

See SCHAUSPIELDIREKTOR, DER.

IM WEISSEN RÖSSL

1930 operetta by Benatzky

RALPH BENATZKY's *Im weissen Rössl* (At the White Horse Inn), a spectacular and rather nostalgic operetta-revue, was a major hit during the 1930s in Berlin, Vienna, Paris, London, and New York. Its slight plot (libretto by Erik Charell and Hans Mueller) revolves around Josefa, the owner of the famous White Horse Inn in St. Wolfgang, Austria, and her relationship with her headwaiter Leopold and a lawyer named Siedler. She thinks she loves the lawyer (he is actually interested in young Ottilie, daughter of business mogul Giesecke), but the waiter is really the man for her; this is pointed out to her by good-hearted Emperor Franz Josef during a visit to the inn. Siedler is happy to settle for Ottilie. The basic score is by Benatzky, but there are songs by other composers, including Robert Stolz and Robert Gilbert. The White Horse Inn actually exists and has become very popular with tourists because of the operetta.

1935 Lamac film

Austrian/German feature film: Carl Lamac (director), Ralph Benatzky and Fritz Wallner (screenplay), Eduard Hoesch and Ludwig Zahn (cinematographers), Ralph Benatzy (music director).

Cast: Christl Mardayn (Josefa), Herman Thimig, Theo Lingen, Willi Schaeffers, Annie Markart.

Black and white. In German. 84 minutes.

1948 La Hosteria del Caballito Blanco

Argentine feature film: Benito Perojo (director), Gerardo Rinaldi (screenplay), Pablo Tabernero (cinematographer), J. Muller and Leo Benatzky (music directors), Elmelco (production).

Cast: Elisa Galve (Josefa), Juan Carlos Thorry, Tilde Thamar, Susanita Canales, Hector Calcagno.

Black and white. In Spanish. 90 minutes.

Comment: This lavish Argentine film of the operetta was a big hit in Buenos Aires. Thorry plays a singer who visits the inn incognito to help boost its reputation.

1952 Carlton film

Austrian feature film: Willi Forst (director), Eric Charell (producer), Carlton Film (production).

Cast: Johanna Matz (Josefa), Walter Müller (Leopold), Johannes Heesters (Siedler), Marianne Wischmann (Ottilie), Paul Westermeier (Giesecke), Rudolf Forster (Emperor Franz Josef).

Video: Kinowelt (Germany), VHS. Color. In German. 94 minutes.

Comment: Charell, the librettist and producer of the stage show, created this spectacular Agfacolor film with Austrian scenery almost as attractive as the songs. *The New York Times* called it an "ageless delight."

1960 L'Auberge du Cheval Blanc

Austrian-French feature film: Werner Jacobs (director).

Cast: Karin Dor (Josefa), Peter Alexander, Adrian Hoven, Günther Philipp, Estella Blain, Serner Finch, Erick Jelde.

Video: Editions Montparnasse (France) VHS for French version as *L'Auberge du Cheval Blanc*. Color. In French or German. 95 minutes.

Comment: Colorful and folksy version shot on location in French and German versions at the real White Horse Inn. This film is apparently screened daily for those visiting the inn.

1979 Hauff film

German TV film: Eberhard Hauff (director).

Cast: Margot Werner (Josefa), Helmuth Lohner (Leopold), Claus Ebert (Siedler), Petra Maria Grühn (Ottilie), Henning Schlüter (Giesecke), Erik Frey (Emperor Franz Josef).

Telecast December 29, 1979, on ARD in Germany. Color. In German. 102 minutes.

1985 Seefestspiele Mörbisch

Austrian stage production: Robert Herzl (director) Franz Bauer-Theussl (conductor, Seefestspiele Mörbisch Chorus and Orchestra).

Cast: Dagmar Koller (Josefa), Rudolf Buczolich (Leopold), Harald Serafin (Siedler), Elizabeth Kales (Ottilie), Karl Dönch (Giesecke), Franz Stoss (Emperor Franz Josef).

Video: ORF (Austria) VHS. Sylvia Dönch (director). Color. In German. 140 minutes.

Comment: Opulent large-scale outdoor production with a big cast of singers and dancers.

1992 Al Cavallino Bianco

Italian TV studio production: Sandro Massimini (director/producer), Roberto Negri (pianist), Sandro Corelli (choreographer).

Cast: Sandro Massimini, Tadamici Oriè.

Video: Pierluigi Pagano (director). Color. In Italian. About 19 minutes. Ricordi (Italy) VHS.

Comment: Highlights of operetta sung in Italian as *Al Cavallino Bianco* on the TV series *Operette, che Passione!* Includes songs "Al Cavallino è l'hotel più bel," "Meglio val sorridere," and "Occhione blu."

INCORONAZIONE DI POPPEA, L'
1642 opera by Monteverdi

CLAUDIO MONTEVERDI's last surviving opera, *L'incoronazione di Poppea* (The Coronation of Poppea), has become quite popular in recent years, perhaps because the villains triumph for a change. The story, loosely based on Roman history, tells of the love of the Emperor Nero for the beautiful Poppea and her desire to become empress in place of Octavia. The philosopher Seneca's opposition to a change of wife results in an order for his execution. An attempt to murder Poppea by Drusilla backfires. Octavia is divorced and exiled, and the adulterous couple reign in full triumph. Of morality there is very little.

***1979 Ponnelle film
Swiss film: Jean-Pierre Ponnelle (director/designer), Nikolaus Harnoncourt (conductor, Monteverdi Ensemble and Choir of the Zurich Opera House), Unitel Film (production).
Cast: Rachel Yakar (Poppea), Eric Tappy (Nerone), Trudeliese Schmidt (Octavia), Matti Salminen (Seneca), Janet Perry (Drusilla), Paul Esswood (Ottone).
Video: London VHS/LD. Color. In Italian with English subtitles. 161 minutes.
Comment: Visually stimulating and musically exciting film based on Ponnelle and Harnoncourt's acclaimed Monteverdi cycle at the Zurich Opera House. It has basically the same cast as the stage production with countertenors in the castrato roles and Amore sung by a boy soprano.

1984 Glyndebourne Festival
English stage production: Peter Hall (director), Raymond Leppard (conductor, London Philharmonic Orchestra and Glyndebourne Chorus), John Bury (set designer).
Cast: Maria Ewing (Poppea), Dennis Bailey (Nerone), Cynthia Clarey (Octavia), Robert Lloyd (Seneca), Elizabeth Gale (Drusilla), Dale Duesing (Ottone).
Video: HBO VHS. Robin Lough (director). Color. In Italian. 148 minutes.
Comment: The characters are dressed in Renaissance clothes in accordance with Hall's idea that the opera reflects the ideas of the time of its composition (1642) rather than those of ancient Rome.

1993 Schwetzingen Festival
German stage production: Michael Hampe (director), René Jacobs (conductor, Cologne Concerto Orchestra).

Cast: Patricia Schuman (Poppea), Richard Croft (Nerone), Kathleen Kuhlmann (Octavia), Harry Peters (Seneca), Darla Brooks (Drusilla), Jeffrey Gall (Ottone).
Video: Arthaus DVD. José Montes-Baquer (director). Color. In Italian with English subtitles. 150 minutes.
Comment: Hampe staged this austere production at the Schwetzingen Festival with few props but excellent atmosphere.

1998 BBC Wales
Welsh TV production: David Alden (director), Rinaldo Allesandrini (conductor, BBC Wales Orchestra), Paul Steinberg (set designer).
Cast: Catrin Wyn Davies (Poppea), Paul Nilon (Nerone), Sally Burgess (Octavia), Gwynne Gowell (Seneca), Dominique Visse (Amore), Michael Chance, Linda Kitchen.
Video: House of Opera VHS. Margaret Williams (director). Color. In Italian with English subtitles. 175 minutes.
Comment: Titled simply *Poppea,* this is a TV adaptation of Alden's Welsh National Opera production filmed for BBC Wales at the Lyceum Theatre in London. It was shown in five 35-minute segments with the story recapped each time, like a soap opera.

Early/related films

1911 Poppea ed Ottavia
Italian film version of the story in eight scenes starring Maria Gasparini as Poppea. It was produced by Latium Film of Rome. Black and white. Silent. About 15 minutes.

1969 Laughter in the Dark
Tony Richardson's film of the Nabokov novel *Laughter in the Dark* uses seduction music from Monteverdi's opera to accompany a similar situation. Nicol Williamson plays a married man whose obsession with young Anna Karina ruins his life. Color. 101 minutes.

INDIAN QUEEN, THE
1695 semi-opera by Purcell

Henry Purcell's last important opera *The Indian Queen,* libretto adapted from a play by John Dryden and Sir Robert Howard, tells the story of Mexican Queen Zempoalla and her struggle again Peruvian invaders led by Montezuma. There are no commercial videos of the complete opera but it is on CD.

2000 Le goût des autres
This popular French film about an industrialist in love with an actress features the duet "Let us wander, not unseen" from *The Indian Queen*. It is from a recording made in 1945 by Kathleen Ferrier and Isobel Baillie with Gerald Moore on piano. Agnès Jaoui directed the film. Color. 112 minutes.

INÉS DE CASTRO
1996 opera by Macmillan

In 14th-century Portugal, Crown Prince Pedro is in love with Spanish Princess Inés de Castro. She is considered an enemy of the state when their countries go to war. When Pedro defies the wishes of his father King Alfonso and secretly marries her, the king is outraged, sends him off to battle, and has her murdered. After Alfonso's death, King Pedro has her corpse crowned queen. JAMES MACMILLAN's Scottish opera *Inés de Castro,* libretto by John Clifford based on his play, created a scandal when it premiered in Edinburgh in 1996. It was considered over-the-top lurid with a coronation scene with a corpse, a bag with severed heads of children, and a graphic description of torture. Objectors didn't seem to care that the bizarre but supposedly true story of Inés de Castro had already been the subject of more than 20 operas during the past 200 years, including a 1976 American version by Thomas Pasatieri.

2000 Scottish Opera
Scottish stage production: Jonathan Moore (director), Richard Armstrong (conductor, Scottish Opera Orchestra and Chorus), Chris Dyer (set designer).
Cast: Helen Field (Ines), Jon Garrison (Pedro), Simon Thorpe (Pacheco), Stafford Dean (King Alfonso).
Telecast February 12, 2002, on BBC Television. Barrie Gavin (director). Color. In English. 120 minutes.

INNOCENZA ED IL PIACER, L'
Operas by Gluck

The video set *L'Innocenza ed il Piacer* is composed of two short operas by Christoph Willibald Gluck staged together at Schwetzingen in 1988. See LE CINESI and ECHO ET NARCISSE.

INTERMEZZO
1924 opera by Richard Strauss

RICHARD STRAUSS wrote his own libretto for *Intermezzo,* an autobiographical opera derived from an incident in his marriage. The main characters are based on his wife Pauline, a temperamental former opera singer, and himself. In the opera, Christine, the annoying wife of conductor Robert Storch, has a flirtation with young Baron Lummer but soon drops him. She then becomes incensed when she discovers a love letter apparently meant for her husband, and she threatens to divorce him. It is simply a misunderstanding, and all ends well.

1963 Bavarian State Opera
German stage production: Rudolf Hartmann (director), Joseph Keilberth (conductor, Bavarian State Opera Orchestra and Chorus), Jean-Pierre Ponnelle (set designer).
Cast: Hanny Steffek (Christine), Hermann Prey (Robert Storch), Ferry Gruber (Baron Lummer), Gertrude Freedman (Anna).
Video: Premiere Opera/Legato Classics VHS. Lothar Tanhauser (director). Color. In German. 143 minutes.

***1983 Glyndebourne Festival
English stage production: John Cox (director), Gustav Kuhn (conductor, London Philharmonic Orchestra and Glyndebourne Festival Chorus), Martin Battersby (set designer), Andrew Porter (English translation).
Cast: Felicity Lott (Christine), John Pringle (Robert Storch), Ian Caley (Baron Lummer), Elizabeth Gale (Anna).
Video: Kultur/Home Vision VHS. David Buckton (director). Color. In English. 155 minutes.

***INTERRUPTED MELODY
1955 American film with opera content

Curtis Bernhardt's excellent film biography of Australian-born American opera diva Marjorie Lawrence, based on her 1949 autobiography *Interrupted Melody,* is one of the best American films about opera. It includes well-staged and finely sung scenes of classic operas integrated into a quite moving story for which William Ludwig and Sonya Levien deservedly won Academy Awards. While it is not accurate in all its details, it certainly captures the spirit of her story. Lawrence recorded arias for the film, but they were not used; the voice heard belongs to Eileen Farrell. *Interrupted Melody* begins in the Australian outback where Lawrence (Eleanor Parker) wins a competition to study in Paris by singing Eboli's aria "O don fatal" from *Don Carlos.* After studies in Paris, she makes her debut in Monte Carlo in 1932 singing Musetta in *La bohème* (in real life, it was as Elisabeth in *Tannhäuser*). There she meets Dr. King (Glenn Ford), the man she will later marry. She begins a tour of regional opera houses in Ravenna, and there are stage scenes of her as Leonora in *Il trovatore,* Cio-Cio-San in *Madama Butterfly,* and

Carmen in *Carmen*. She is invited to Paris in 1933 to sing Delilah in *Samson et Dalila* (in real life, it was Ortrud in *Lohengrin;* she never sang the mezzo role of Delilah on stage), and she is shown on stage singing "Mon coeur s'ouvre à ta voix." Her brother (Roger Moore) comes from Australia to be her manager, and in 1935 she goes to the Met to sing Brünnhilde in *Götterdämmerung* (in real life it was Brünnhilde in *Die Walküre)*. During the rehearsal of the Immolation Scene, she insists on galloping her horse into the flames after arguing with the director that no sensible horse would walk into a fire. She marries King and goes on a South American tour after an argument. She collapses during a rehearsal of *Tristan und Isolde* while singing the Liebestod, with Tudor Williams as King Mark, and is diagnosed with polio. Her husband gives up his practice to care for her, but she is so despondent that she refuses to try to move by herself. He finally has to use a ruse to make her make an effort. As she can no longer bear to listen to her old opera records, he puts her "Mon coeur s'ouvre à ta voix" on a phonograph and leaves the room. She is so angry that she crawls across the floor and knocks it over. Her recovery begins. (In real life, Lawrence never recorded this aria). She begins to sing again in a wheelchair, first for soldiers in hospital (a touching "Somewhere Over the Rainbow") and then on an overseas tour. She returns to the Met in 1943 to sing *Tristan und Isolde,* seated. At the end of the Liebestod, she stands up before dying and collapsing onto Tristan. The Met audience gives her a standing ovation. Parker was nominated for an Academy Award for her terrific performance, Helen Rose was nominated for her costume design, and Saul Chaplin deserved one as music director. Joe Ruttenberg and Paul Vogel photographed the stylish 106-minute film in color and CinemaScope for MGM. MGM-UA VHS.

INTOLLERANZA 1960
1961 opera by Nono

Luigi Nono's experimental and politically radical opera *Intolleranza 1960* has only a slight narrative. The libretto by the composer, based on an essay by Angelo Maria Ripellino titled *Materiali per un'opera,* incorporates poems by Brecht, Mayakovsky, and others with prose narrative by Sartre, Fucík (Nazi interrogations), et al. The central "story" is about an immigrant refugee who gets arrested and thrown into a camp. He escapes with an Algerian, becomes friends with a sympathetic woman, and eventually meets intolerance head-on in the form of a flood. The only screen production of the opera, rather surprisingly, was an American television adaptation with Beverly Sills in a leading role and the innovative Sarah Caldwell directing.

1965 NET Opera
   American TV production: Sarah Caldwell (director), Bruno Maderna (conductor, Opera Company of Boston Orchestra), Joseph Svoboda (set designer), Jan Skalicky (costume designer).
   Cast: Lawrence White (Refugee), Beverly Sills (Friend of Refugee), Ercole Bertolino (Algerian), Margaret Roggero (Woman), Gus Hoekman (Tortured Man).
   Telecast on NET in 1966. Greg Harney and Fred Barzyk (directors). Color. In English. 115 minutes.

IOLANTA
1892 opera by Tchaikovsky

Iolanta, the virginal blind daughter of King René, has been kept away from the very idea of sight, but it turns out she can be cured if she wants to see light. After she falls in love with Count Vaudémont, she is made to believe she has to be cured to save his life. TCHAIKOVSKY's opera *Iolanta,* libretto by Modest Tchaikovsky based on a Danish play by Henrik Hertz, was presented in its Soviet film version in the United States as *Yolanta,* although the Sovexport publicity brochure calls it *Yolande* in both English and French.

1963 Gorikker film
   Soviet (Latvian) feature film: Vladimir Gorikker (director/screenplay), Boris Khaikin (conductor, Bolshoi Opera Orchestra and Chorus), Vadim Mass (cinematographer) Riga, Latvia (production studio).
   Cast: Natalya Rudnaya (Iolanta, sung by Galina Oleynichenko), Fyodor Nikitin (King René, sung by Ivan Petrov), Yuri Petrov (Count Vaudémont, sung by Surab Andzhaparidze), Alexander Belyavsky (Duke Robert, sung by Pavel Lisitsian), Pyotr Glebov (Ibn-Hakia, sung by Vladimir Valaitis), Valentina Ushakova (Martha, sung by Eugenio Verbitskaya), Valdis Sandberg (Bertrand, sung by Valeri Yaroslavtev).
   Color. In Russian. 82 minutes.
   Comment: Opera film specialist Gorikker created this charming film with the actors on screen dubbed by Bolshoi Opera singers.

IOLANTHE
1882 comic opera by Gilbert and Sullivan

Iolanthe or The Peer and the Peri is an enjoyable combination of fantasy and satire with the House of Lords involved in a fairyland frolic. Iolanthe is a fairy who was banished years before for marrying a mortal; she now has a grown-up son named Strephon. The other fairies entreat their queen to forgive Iolanthe; Strephon's fiancée Phyllis becomes jealous of his beautiful mother; the Lord Chancellor and Peers of the Realm get involved; Strephon becomes a Peer to try to solve his problems;

and everything gets turned topsy-turvy. Arthur Sullivan's music is outstanding, and William S. Gilbert's lyrics are among his best.

1972 Gilbert & Sullivan for All series

English highlights film: Peter Seabourne (director), Peter Murray (conductor, Gilbert and Sullivan Festival Orchestra and Chorus), David Maverovitch (cinematographer), Trevor Evans (adaptation), John Seabourne (producer).

Cast: Helen Landis (Fairy Queen), John Cartier (Lord Chancellor), Gillian Humphrey (Phyllis), Anne Hood (Iolanthe), Thomas Round (Earl Tolloller), Michael Wakeham (Strephon), Donald Adams (Earl of Mountararat).

Video: Musical Collectables VHS. Color. In English. 50 minutes.

1982 Gilbert and Sullivan Collection series

English studio production: Christopher Renshaw (director), Judith De Paul (producer), Alexander Faris (conductor, London Symphony Orchestra and Ambrosian Opera Chorus), Allan Cameron (set designer), George Walker (executive producer).

Cast: Anne Collins (Fairy Queen), Derek Hammond-Stroud (Lord Chancellor), Kate Flowers (Phyllis), Alexander Oliver (Strephon), Beverly Mills (Iolanthe), Richard van Allan (Private Willis), David Hillman (Earl Tolloller), Thomas Hemsley (Earl of Mountararat).

Video: CBS Fox/Braveworld (GB) VHS. Barrie Gavin (director). Color. In English. 116 minutes.

1984 Stratford Festival

Canadian stage production: Brian Macdonald (director and choreographer), Berthold Carrière (conductor, Stratford Festival Orchestra and Chorus), Susan Benson (set/costume designer), Jim Betts and John Banks (libretto adaptation).

Cast: Maureen Forrester (Fairy Queen), Eric Donkin (Lord Chancellor), Marie Baron (Phyllis), Paul Massel (Strephon), Katharina Megli (Iolanthe), Stephen Beamish (Earl Tolloller), Douglas Chamberlain (Earl of Mountararat).

Image Entertainment DVD/Home Vision VHS/LD. James Guthro (director). Color. In English. 138 minutes.

Comment: The operetta is presented as if it were being staged by a second-rate touring company in a provincial city. Forrester is a delight as the grande dame of the company who plays the Fairy Queen.

IPHIGÉNIE EN TAURIDE
1781 opera by Gluck

Iphigenia, daughter of Agamemnon, was the subject of two plays by Euripides, both turned into operas by Christoph Willibald Gluck. This was the most popular as in it Iphigenia does not die as a Trojan War sacrifice at Aulis. Instead goddess Artemis substitutes a hind in her place and transports her to Tauris to be her priestess where she is forced by the cruel King Thoas to sacrifice strangers who come to the island. Gluck's opera *Iphigénie en Tauride*, libretto in French by Nicolas-François Guillard, tells of the arrival of her brother Orestes and his friend Pylades, the death of Thoas, and the end of the custom of human sacrifice. In modern times the role of Iphigénie is often associated with Maria Callas.

2001 Zurich Opera

Swiss stage production: Claus Guth (director), William Christie (conductor, La Scintilla Orchestra & Zurich Opera House Chorus).

Cast: Juliette Galstian (Iphigénie), Rodney Gilfry (Oreste), Deon van der Walt (Pylade), Anton Scharinger (Thoas).

Video: Arthaus DVD. Thomas Grimm (director). In French with English subtitles. 166 minutes.

Comment: DVD includes documentary *Gluck: The Reformer* by Reiner Moritz.

IRIS
1898 opera by Mascagni

PIETRO MASCAGNI's influential opera *Iris* reflected his interest in the Japanese subjects fashionable at the time it was created. It has a libretto by Luigi Illica, one of the authors of Puccini's similarly themed *Madama Butterfly*, but *Iris* was written earlier so it probably influenced the Puccini opera. Iris is the name of the heroine, an innocent Japanese girl who is kidnapped by her rich admirer Osaka and placed in a brothel run by Kyoto. She kills herself when she is discovered by her blind father and cursed. *Iris* helped spark a vogue for Oriental and Eastern settings for operas.

1985 Tokyo Television

Japanese stage production: Michiyoshi Inoue (conductor, New Japan Philharmonic Orchestra).

Cast: Masimo Miwako (Iris), Yamadi Yoshishisa (Osaka), Kimara Tosimitu (Kyoto).

Live Opera/Lyric VHS. Telecast August 2, 1985, in Japan. Color. In Japanese and Italian. 100 minutes.

Comment: Telecast of a stylish Tokyo stage production with Japanese cast. The opera is introduced in Japanese but sung in Italian.

1985 Rome Opera

Italian stage production: Gianluigi Gelmetti (conductor, Rome Opera House Orchestra and Chorus).

Cast: Daniela Dessì (Iris), José Cura (Osaka), Robert Servile (Kyoto), Nicolai Ghiaurov (Father).

House of Opera VHS. Color. In Italian. 110 minutes.

Comment: The same cast can be heard on a CD.

I SING FOR YOU ALONE
1932 multilingual Italian film with opera content

Italian tenor Tito Schipa plays a tenor who has a great voice but suffers from crippling stage fright. He allows his voice to be used by a friend, who becomes an opera star, but he eventually wins recognition for himself. Mario Bonnard shot the film in three languages at the Caesar Studio in Rome with different casts supporting Schipa, and it seems to have been popular in all three versions. The English version, also known as *Three Lucky Fools,* features a supporting cast headed by Roy Gilbert, Al Andrews, Claire Vaudry, and Lester Charles. The Italian version, *Tre uomini in frac,* features Eduardo and Peppino De Filippo and Assia Norris. The French version, *Trois hommes in habit,* features Alfred Pasqual, Jean Gobet, and Simone Vaudry. Michele Galdieri wrote the screenplay with Bonnard; Giovanni Vitrotti and Ferdinando Martini were the cinematographers; and Dan Caslar, Umberto Mancini, and Giulio Bonnard were in charge of the music. Black and white. Originally 70 minutes; English version is 57 minutes. Bel Canto Society VHS (English and French versions)/Live Opera VHS (English version).

ISRAEL IN EGYPT
1738 oratorio by Handel

GEORGE FRIDERIC HANDEL's dramatic *Israel in Egypt,* with its strong emphasis on choruses, has become one of his most popular oratorios. It opens with the Israelites lamenting the death of Joseph and telling about the plagues in Egypt that led to their being allowed to depart and escape across the Red Sea. The miracle of their liberation is celebrated with exciting choruses and exhilarating solos. The libretto, based on Exodus and Psalms, is probably by Handel himself.

1991 Greenberg film

Scottish feature film: Rodney Greenberg (director), John Currie (conductor, John Currie Singers, Edinburgh Festival Chorus, Scottish National Orchestra Chorus, and Jerusalem Symphony Orchestra).

Singers: Irene Drummond and Lyndall Trotman (sopranos), John Hearne and Stephen Roberts (basses), Christine Cairns (contralto), Stuart Patterson (tenor).

Video: SISU Home Entertainment VHS. Color. In English with English subtitles. 90 minutes.

Comment: Greenberg filmed the oratorio live on the shores of the Red Sea in Israel, using the actual location of the drama magnificently. The text of the oratorio appears as subtitles.

ITALIANA IN ALGERI, L'
1813 opera by Rossini

L'italiana in Algeri (The Italian Woman in Algiers) was GIOACHINO ROSSINI's first full-length comic opera, and it remains one of his most enjoyable. The libretto by Angelo Anelli is high-spirited fun, a comic counterpoint to Mozart's *Die Entführung aus dem Serail.* Set in Algiers in the early 1800s, it tells the story of Isabella, an Italian woman captive who bewitches and outwits her blustering captor, the Bey Mustafà. After causing him to behave in a most foolish manner, Elvira restores the Bey to his wife and escapes with her lover Lindoro.

1957 RAI Television, Milan

Italian TV production: Mario Lanfranchi (director), Nino Sanzogno (conductor, Milan RAI Orchestra and Chorus), Luca Crippa (designer).

Cast: Teresa Berganza (Isabella), Alvinio Misciano (Lindoro), Mario Petri (Mustafà), Rena Gary Falachi (Elvira), Sesto Bruscantini (Taddeo), Valerio Meucci (Haly).

Video: Bel Canto Society/Lyric VHS. Black and white. In Italian. 118 minutes.

Comment: Lanfranchi sets the opera in a kind of Arabian Nights fairy-tale land.

1986 Metropolitan Opera

American stage production: Jean-Pierre Ponnelle (director/designer), James Levine (conductor, Metropolitan Opera Orchestra and Chorus).

Cast: Marilyn Horne (Isabella), Douglas Ahlstedt (Lindoro), Paolo Montarsolo (Mustafà), Myra Merritt (Elvira), Allan Monk (Taddeo), Spiro Malas (Haly).

Video at the MTR. Telecast live January 11, 1986. Brian Large (director). Color. In Italian with English subtitles. 150 minutes.

***1987 Schwetzingen Festival

German stage production: Michael Hampe (director), Ralf Weikert (conductor, Stuttgart Radio Symphony Orchestra and Bulgarian Men's Chorus of Sofia), Mauro Pagano (set/costume designer).

Cast: Doris Soffel (Isabella), Robert Gambill (Lindoro), Gunther von Kannen (Mustafà), Nuccia Focile (Elvira), Enrico Serra (Taddeo), Rudolf A. Hartmann (Haly), Susan McLean (Zulma).

Video: ArtHaus Musik DVD/RCA VHS and LD. Claus Viller (director). Color. In Italian with English subtitles. 149 minutes.

Comment: Outstanding production in a beautiful 18th-century palace.

1998 Teatro Regio, Parma

Italian stage production: Pier Luigi Pizzi (director/designer), Daniele Callegari (conductor, Orchestra Sinfonica dell'Emilia-Romagna and Teatro Regio Chorus).

Cast: Anna Maria Di Micco (Isabella), William Matteuzzi (Lindoro), Michele Pertusi (Mustafà), Annamaria Dell'Oste (Elvira), Bruno Praticò (Taddeo), Riccardo Novaro (Haly).

Video: Bel Canto Society VHS. Color. In Italian. 145 minutes.

1998 Paris Opéra

French stage production: Andrei Serban (director), Bruno Campanella (conductor, Opéra National de Paris Orchestra and Chorus), Marina Draghici (set/costume designer).

Cast: Jennifer Larmore (Isabella), Bruce Ford (Lindoro), Simone Alaimo (Mustafà), Alessandro Corbelli (Taddeo), Jeanette Fischer.

Telecast in France in 1998; taped at Palais Garnier in May 1998. André Flederick (director). Color. In Italian. 145 minutes.

Related film

1968 Gianini and Luzzati film

Italian animation masters Giulio Gianini and Emanuele Luzzati, who became famous in 1964 for the Rossini-inspired cartoon of the overture to *The Thieving Magpie,* followed it with another Rossini opera. Their cartoon version of *L'italiana in Algeri* was also popular. Color. 8 minutes.

IVAN THE TERRIBLE
Russian Tsar (1530–1584)

Tsar Ivan IV Vasilyevich, the 16th-century Grand Duke who became the first Russian Tsar and a symbol of absolutist rule, has been the central character of several operas, films, and ballets. The first two films were based on operas, Rimsky-Korsakov's notable *The Maid of Pskov* and Raoul Gunsbourg's now forgotten *Ivan le Terrible.* Paul Leni's 1924 German film *Das Wachsfigurenkabinett* has Ivan as a principal character, and Yuri Tarich's 1926 Soviet film *Wings of the Serf* (released in the West as *Ivan the Terrible*) revolves around him, but they have no apparent operatic connections. Eisenstein's magnificent two-part *Ivan the Terrible,* however, is highly operatic with a memorable score by Prokofiev. A Soviet ballet was later created around its music, and the ballet has been filmed.

1915 Rimsky-Korsakov's Ivan the Terrible
One of Feodor Chaliapin's most popular opera roles in Russia was Ivan the Terrible in Nikolai Rimsky-Korsakov's 1873 opera *Pskovityanka* (The Maid of Pskov, or Ivan the Terrible). The opera tells how Ivan spared the city of Pskov after the intercession of his daughter Olga. Chaliapin reprised the role in a 1915 Russian film of the opera called *Tsar Ivan Vasilyevich Grozny,* produced and directed by A. Ivanov-Gai. Chaliapin was paid a generous 25,000 rubles and the film was meant to celebrate his 25th year on the stage, but it did not become popular. Chaliapin apparently hated it, although Eisenstein studied it when he made his own Ivan film. Sharez Film. Black and white. In Russian. About 80 minutes.

1915 Gunsbourg's Ivan le Terrible
Raoul Gunsbourg aka Ginsberg (1859–1955), a Bucharest-born French impresario who managed opera houses in Moscow and St. Petersburg during the 1880s, became director of the Monte Carlo Opera in 1893. He wrote six operas, the second of which was the 1910 *Ivan le Terrible.* Chaliapin sang the title role in its premiere production, although he said harsh things about it in his memoirs. In 1915 Enrico Guazzoni made an Italian film version of the opera. His *Ivan il Terrible* stars Amleto Novelli as Ivan, Matilde Di Marzio as the Romanov, Leda Gys as Elena, and André Habay as Vladimir. Cines Film. Black and white. In Italian. About 60 minutes.

1946 Eisenstein's Ivan the Terrible
Sergei Eisenstein's epic film *Ivan Groznyi* (Ivan the Terrible) is not based on either of the above operas, but they inspired the Soviet filmmaker to create an operatic film around the Tsar. James Agee once described Eisenstein's film as "a visual opera, with all of opera's proper disregard of prose-level reality." Eisenstein was working at the Bolshoi Opera staging Wagner's *Die Walküre* just before making the film, so opera was very much on his mind. He was also hoping to stage composer Sergei Prokofiev's opera *War and Peace,* but that was not going to be possible so instead Prokofiev wrote the music for Eisenstein's film. Nikolai Cherkassov plays Ivan in one of the great Soviet film performances. The film was made in two parts: the first, finished in 1944, tells of Ivan's early life and struggles; the second, completed in 1946 with color sequences, focuses on the boyars' plot. Black and white and color. In Russian with English subtitles. 188 minutes.

1977 Prokofiev's Ivan the Terrible

Prokofiev's music for Eisenstein's film was transmuted into a ballet choreographed and staged by Yuri Grigorovich in 1975. It was so popular that the ballet was filmed by Grigorovich and Vadim Derbenev with the original stage cast. Yuri Vladimirov stars as the dancing Ivan with Natalya Bessmertnaya as his wife Anastasia and Boris Akimov as Prince Kurbsky. Color. 92 minutes.

IVORY, JAMES
American film director (1928–)

James Ivory began to work with Indian producer Ismail Merchant in 1963, and the team has made an astonishing number of beautiful movies, many based on literary classics. A Merchant-Ivory film is almost considered a genre. Although Ivory has not filmed actual operas, his movies often use opera to great effect. These include *Jefferson in Paris* (1995), with an elaborate staging of ANTONIO SACCHINI'S opera *Dardanus;* and *A Room With a View* (1985), with its fine use of Puccini arias from GIANNI SCHICCHI and LA RONDINE.

J

JACKSON
2002 American film with opera content

Jackson is an unusual film about the homeless men and bag ladies of Los Angeles as they also like to sing opera. As the sun rises in the opening scene, a young black crack addict (Shawnette Sulker), seated in a burned-out car, sings "Una furtive lagrima" from *L'elisir d'amore* with tears streaming down her face. Nearby, an old homeless drunk (Richard Brown) nurses a bottle of Colt 45 and also sings the aria as the music swells. A dangerously insane young man in filthy clothes and with wild hair argues violently with invisible people and begins to sing the Champagne Aria from *Don Giovanni*. An aggressive panhandler at the entrance to a Hollywood Boulevard subway station sings Ibn-Hakia's Monologue from Tchaikovsky's *Iolanta*. A young woman sings an aria from *Madama Butterfly* while an older one sings an aria from *Carmen*. J. F. Lawton, who directed and wrote the screenplay, uses opera music to enhance the universal humanity of the people who live on skid row. The singers who perform the arias, many who have sung professionally, were made up to look like street people. The story of the film is basic—a day in the life of two homeless men, Barry Primus and Charles Robinson. When a rich man (Steve Guttenberg) gives Primus a $20 bill (a "Jackson" in street language because it has the portrait of Andrew Jackson on it), he and Robinson have a day on the town. The movie was shot digitally on location in Los Angeles streets by Jack Conroy, who photographed *My Left Foot* and *The Field*. Director/producer Lawton is best known for writing the screenplays of films such as *Pretty Woman* and *Under Siege*. Color. In English. 90 minutes.

JACOBS, RENÉ
Belgian conductor and countertenor (1946–)

René Jacobs began his musical career as a countertenor, making his debut in 1974 in Cavalli's Erismena, and then founded his own group, Concerto Vocale. He has specialized in baroque opera and can be heard on many recordings, but he does not sing on the available videos of operas he has conducted. See LE CINESI (1987), ECHO ET NARCISSE (1987), and L'INCORONAZIONE DI POPPEA (1993).

JACOBS, WERNER
German film director (1909–)

Werner Jacobs, who began working in the cinema as an editor during the 1930s, started directing features in 1952. He has never been a critical favorite, although his films have usually been popular with audiences. Jacobs adapted a number of German and Austrian operettas for the screen in French and German versions, including DER BETTELSTUDENT (1956), DER GRAF VON LUXEMBURG (1957), DIE LUSTIGE WITWE (1962), and IM WEISSEN RÖSSL (1960).

JANÁČEK, LEOŠ
Czech composer (1854–1928)

Leoš Janáček's operas have shown an amazing growth in popularity and critical esteem during the past 70 years. He didn't have an opera staged in a major opera house until 1916, when he was 62 years old, but a burst of creativity during the last years of his life resulted in one of the major operatic legacies. He created a unique sound, partially through his decision to set words to their sound as spoken in Czech rather than as sung. His popularity today is shown by the large number of videos of his operas including THE CUNNING LITTLE VIXEN, FROM THE HOUSE OF THE DEAD, JENŮFA, KATYA KABANOVA, and THE MAKROPOULOS CASE. His music has also begun to be used on the soundtrack of feature films as different as *Don's Party* and *The Unbearable Lightness of Being*.

1983 Leoš Janáček: Intimate Excursions
An extraordinary British puppet film about Janáček's operas created by the brothers Quay and Keith Griffiths. The puppet Janáček reminisces about his life and introduces excerpts from his operas, in which he also acts, including *Diary of One Who Vanished, The Cunning Little Vixen, The Makropoulos Case, From the House of the Dead, The Excursion of Mr. Broucek,* and *The Glagolitic Mass.* The singers include Pacel Kuhn, Bohumir Vichm, and Libuše Pylova; the music is played by the Czech Philharmonic Orchestra and Prague National Theatre Orchestra. Color. In English and Czech. 27 minutes.

JANOWITZ, GUNDULA
German soprano (1937–)

Gundula Janowitz was born in Berlin, but she began her professional opera career at the Vienna Staatsoper and sang there for 30 years. She came to the Met in 1967 as Sieglinde and also sang regularly at Salzburg and Bayreuth. She can be seen on video in a range of roles, from Ariadne to Fiordiligi to Leonore. See ARIADNE AUF NAXOS (1978), COSÌ FAN TUTTE (1970), FIDELIO (1977), DIE FLEDERMAUS (1972), and LE NOZZE DI FIGARO (1980).

JARMAN, DEREK
English film director (1942–1994)

Derek Jarman is best known as a filmmaker, but he had first trained as an artist and worked as a designer in both theater and cinema. He created the sets for John Gielgud's controversial *Don Giovanni* at the Coliseum in 1968, and he designed the sets and costumes for Ken Russell's innovative THE RAKE'S PROGRESS in Florence in 1982. His 1988 film of Benjamin Britten's WAR REQUIEM is of operatic interest (he virtually turns it into an opera), and he directed one of the most effective episodes of the 1987 opera film ARIA around Charpentier's LOUISE.

JARNO, GEORG
Hungarian composer (1868–1920)

Hungarian composer Georg Jarno wrote tuneful Viennese-style operettas, but his work has never been well known in the United States. One of his operettas, the 1907 DIE FÖRSTER-CHRISTL, has remained in the German stage repertory and has been filmed at least four times. His last operetta, *Die Csikós-Baroness,* was also turned into a film.

1930 Die Csikós-Baroness
The Czardas Baroness is a Hungarian-style operetta based on a story by Sándor Petöfi with a libretto by Fritz Grünbaum. It was finished in 1920, the year Jarno died, and was an immediate success. It was made into a German film 10 years later with Gretl Theimer, Ernst Verebes, Julius Falkenstein, and Ida Wüst. Jakob Fleck and Luise Fleck directed for Hegewald Film. Black and white. In German. 93 minutes.

JARVIS CONSERVATORY
American center for the zarzuela

The Jarvis Conservatory in Napa, California, has been a center of zarzuela activity in the United States since 1995, and 10 of its superb stage productions have been professionally videotaped. They feature talented young casts and are the best possible introduction to the genre. Jarvis makes them available free to public TV stations, educational institutions, and libraries so they've been seen by hundreds of thousands of viewers, but they are also for sale to individuals. Their classic zarzuelas currently available on DVD and VHS with entries in this book include AGUA, AZUCARILLOS Y AGUARDIENTE, LA ALEGRÍA DE LA HUERTA, LA DOLOROSA, DOÑA FRANCISQUITA, GIGANTES Y CABEZUDOS, LA GRAN VÍA, LUISA FERNANDA, LA REVOLTOSA, and LA VERBENA DE LA PALOMA. They are all first-rate. The Jarvis Conservatory is at 1711 Main Street, Napa, California 94559 (e-mail: info@jarvisconservatory.com).

JEANNE D'ARC AU BÛCHER
1938 dramatic oratorio by Honegger

ARTHUR HONEGGER described *Jeanne d'Arc au bûcher* (Joan of Arc at the Stake) as a "dramatic oratorio" and it is certainly full of drama. Paul Claudel's libretto tells the story of Joan's triumph and martyrdom with spectacular pageantry. It may not be a full-fledged opera, but, as staged by Roberto Rossellini in the major opera houses of Europe in 1953, it is assuredly a first cousin. The role of St. Joan, a spoken one, was performed on stage and film by Ingrid Bergman in Rossellini's revival.

1954 Giovanna d'Arco al rogo
Italian feature film: Roberto Rossellini (director/screenplay), Angelo Spagnolo (conductor, Teatro di San Carlo Opera House Orchestra and Chorus), Gabor Pogany (cinematographer), Bianca Gallizia (choreographer).
Actors: Ingrid Bergman (Giovanna d'Arc), Tullio Carminati (Fra Domenico), Giacinto Prandelli (Procus), Augusto Romani (Heurtebise), Agnese Dubbini (Mrs. Botti).
Singers: Miriam Pirazzini (St. Catherine), Marcella Pobbe (Virgin Mary), Florence Quartararo (St. Margaret), Pina Esca, Gianni Avolant.
Color. In Italian. 80 minutes.
Comment: Rossellini made this film version after directing the oratorio on stage in 1953 at San Carlo, La Scala, Paris Opéra, and the Stoll Theatre in London.

1993 Saito Kinen Festival
Japanese stage production: Seiji Ozawa (conductor, Saito Kinen Festival Orchestra).
Cast: Marthe Keller (Jeanne d'Arc), Georges Wilson (Frère Dominque), Christine Barbaux, John Aler.
Video: Japanese LD. Color. In French. 90 minutes.
Comment: Based on an earlier production by Ozawa with Keller that was recorded in France in 1989.

1996 NHK Tokyo Television
Japanese TV production: Isao Takashima (director), Charles Dutoit (conductor, NHK Symphony Orchestra, Nikai Chorus and Little Singers of Tokyo), Henning von Gierke (set designer).
Cast: Julie Vincent (Jeanne d'Arc), Guy Provost (Frère Dominque), Raymond Bouchard, Rie Hamada.
Telecast February 16, 1997, in Japan; taped December 6, 1996, at NHK Hall in Tokyo. Yo Asari (director). Color. In French. 75 minutes.

Related film

1986 August Everding Directs

This is a German film by Werner Lütje about a production of the oratorio by August Everding for Bavarian State Opera in Munich. Joan is played by Andrea Jonasson and Dominic by Christian Quadflieg. The film follows the rehearsals and shows the production as it develops form. Color. In English. 26 minutes. Inter Nationes VHS.

JENSEITS DES STROMES
1922 screen opera by Hummel

Jenseits des Stromes (The Other Side of the River) is said to be the first opera written expressly as a movie. It was the creation of Berlin opera composer Ferdinand Hummel (1855–1928), who wrote seven operas for the stage, the most famous being the 1893 *Mara*. They are all forgotten today, and his film opera shares their fate. It was composed for singers and orchestra during the silent cinema era, and its score was literally on the screen. A strip of musical notation ran from left to right at the bottom of the image on screen as the picture progressed to provide guidance to the singers and orchestra in the theaters showing the film. Not many did, and no copy is known.

JENŮFA
1904 opera by Janáček

LEOŠ JANÁČEK's opera *Jenůfa* (Její Pastorkyňa/Her Stepdaughter) is based on a 1904 dialect play by Gabriela Preissová. It is a highly realistic portrayal of peasant life, and it made Janáček famous when it was staged in Prague in 1916. The grim story revolves around a young peasant woman named Jenůfa, who becomes pregnant by the miller Števa. The baby is murdered by her stepmother, the Kostelnička, when it becomes an obstacle to Jenůfa's marriage to Laca. The play itself has been filmed twice in Czechoslovakia, once with the singer who created the role of the Kostelnička.

***1989 Glyndebourne Festival

English stage production: Nikolaus Lehnhoff (director), Andrew Davis (conductor, London Philharmonic Orchestra and Glyndebourne Festival Orchestra), Tobias Hoheisel (set designer).

Cast: Roberta Alexander (Jenůfa), Anja Silja (Kostelnička), Philip Langridge (Laca), Mark Baker (Števa), Alison Hagley (Karolka), Sarah Pring (Barena).

Video: Kultur and Arthaus DVD/Home Vision VHS. Derek Bailey (director). Color. In Czech with English subtitles. 118 minutes.

Comment: Excellent production, finely conducted, with a believable cast.

1997 National Theatre, Prague

Czech stage production: Josef Prudek (director), Jiri Belohlavek (conductor, National Theatre Opera Orchestra and Chorus), Petr Perina (set designer).

Cast: Helena Kaupova (Jenůfa), Eva Urbanova (Kostelnička), Jan Vacik (Laca), Ludovic Ludha (Števa).

Video: House of Opera DVD/VHS. Tomas Simerda (director). Color. In Czech. 120 minutes.

Related films

1929 Mesták film

Gabriela Horvátová, the singer who created the role of the Kostelnička in the premiere of Janáček's opera, reprises the role in Rudolf Mesták's film of the play by Gabriela Preissová. The Czech film features portraits of Janáček and Preissová at its beginning. Thilda Ondra plays Jenůfa, Stanislav Sedlácek is Laca, and Václav Norman is Števa. Black and white. Silent. 73 minutes.

1938 Cikán film

Miroslav Cikán's Czech film of the original dialect play by Gabriela Preissová is close in story to the opera. Marie Glázrová plays Jenůfa with Leopolda Dostalová as the Kostelnička, Ladislav Bohác as Laca, and Jiri Dohnal as Števa. Jaroslav Blazek was cinematographer. Black and white. In Czech. 75 minutes.

JEPSON, HELEN
American soprano (1904–1997)

Helen Jepson made her opera debut in Philadelphia in 1928 in *Le nozze di Figaro* and her Metropolitan Opera debut seven years later in the premiere of John Seymour's *In the Pasha's Garden*. She sang in San Francisco as Flotow's *Martha* and in Chicago as Massenet's *Thaïs*, with coaching from Mary Garden. Paramount put Jepson under contract in 1935 during the opera film boom, but the studio never used her. She was supposed to star in Grand National's *Something to Sing About* with James Cagney, but that didn't happen either. She finally appeared in a Samuel Goldwyn movie, *The Goldwyn Follies,* when he needed a photogenic prima donna. It was her only film, but she continued to sing opera on stage until 1944.

1938 The Goldwyn Follies

Jepson plays an opera singer named Leona Jerome in this Goldwyn film. She is first seen on stage in *La traviata* as Violetta with Met tenor Charles Kullman as Alfredo as they perform "Libiamo" and "Sempre libera." Producer

Adolphe Menjou, who is seeking an opera singer for a film, hires her, and she has a small role in the rest of the movie. *The Goldwyn Follies* is a musical kaleidoscope with songs by George Gershwin (who died while it was being made), including "Love Walked In" and "Love Is Here to Stay." Ben Hecht's tongue-in-cheek screenplay revolves around an ordinary girl (Andrea Leeds) hired by producer Menjou as an expert on ordinary people. George Marshall directed. Color. 115 minutes.

JERITZA, MARIA
Czech soprano (1887–1982)

Maria Jeritza, who combined glamour with a remarkable voice and real acting ability, still has many admirers. She also had four husbands, one of whom was U.S. film producer Winfield Sheehan. He was head of production at Fox during the 1930s, and he built her a showcase house in Beverly Hills where guests reportedly dined on gold plates. Dietrich Arndt's 1931 novel *Bagage, Reigen um eine Sängerin* is based on her rather glamorous life. Jeritza was a favorite in Vienna for two decades in the Puccini roles of Tosca, Minnie, and Turandot, and she was equally popular at the Met. She created the role of Ariadne in Strauss's *Ariadne auf Naxos* and the empress in his *Die Frau ohne Schatten* and was the first to star in Korngold's *Die tote Stadt* and Janáček's *Jenůfa* in Vienna and New York. She was also much admired in operettas by Strauss and Suppé. Unfortunately, she made only one film.

1933 Grossfürstin Alexandra
Grossfürstin Alexandra (Grand Duchess Alexandra) is an Austrian film starring Jeritza as a Russian grand duchess who flees to Vienna after the revolution and becomes an opera singer. Franz Lehár wrote the original music for this musical set in Czarist Russia and postwar Vienna. Jeritza looks beautiful and sounds splendid in scenes from *Aida* and *La forza del destino*. Paul Hartmann plays Grand Duke Michael, and Leo Slezak is Duke Nikolai. Wilhelm Thiele directed. Black and white. In German. 85 minutes.

1983 I Live for Art—Tosca
Jeritza is talked about quite a lot in this Tosca documentary, especially by Ljuba Welitsch, who considers her the best Tosca ever. Jeritza is pictured singing on stage in *Aida* in her Austrian film where she tells her teacher that she wants to sing the role of Tosca; he tells her she will have to wait until she is ready. Muriel Balash made the documentary. Color. In English. 91 minutes. Kultur VHS.

JÉRUSALEM
1847 opera by Verdi

Toulouse viscount Gaston marries Hélène, but his jealous brother Roger causes his exile after a bungled assassination attempt. Roger becomes a hermit in the Holy Land, and Gaston and Hélène are captured by the Saracens. Roger helps rescue them and then dies heroically fighting alongside Gaston during the battle for Jerusalem. VERDI's French opera *Jérusalem* is a grand opera adaptation of his 1843 Italian opera I LOMBARDI. It is still set during the First Crusade, but the French librettists Alphonse Royer and Gustave Vaëz changed the plot and character names while Verdi composed new music and altered the old. *Jérusalem* was well received at its Paris Opéra premiere, but it has never really entered the repertory.

1986 Teatro Regio, Parma
Italian stage production: Renzo Giacchieri (director), Donato Renzetti (conductor, Orchestra Sinfonica dell'Emilia-Romagna and Teatro Regio Chorus), Fiorenzo Giorgi (set designer).
Cast: Katia Ricciarelli (Hélène), Veriano Luchetti (Gaston), Cesare Siepi (Roger), Wilma Colla (Isaure), Gianfranco Manganotti (Raymond), Alfonso Marchica (Adhemar), Eftimio Micalopoulos (Emir).
Video: House of Opera DVD & VHS/Premiere Opera & Bel Canto Society VHS. Color. In French. 174 minutes.

2000 Teatro Carlo Felice, Genoa
Italian stage production: Ermanno Olmi and Piergiorgio Gay (directors), Michel Plasson (conductor, Orchestra and Chorus of Teatro Carlo Felice, Genoa).
Cast: Verónica Villaroel (Hélène), Ivan Momirov (Gaston), Carlo Colombara (Roger), Federica Bragaglia (Isaure), Giorgio Casciarri (Raymond), Carlo di Cristoforo (Adhemar), Reda El Wakil (Emir).
Video: TDK DVD. Paola Longobardo (director) Color. In French with English subtitles. 166 minutes

JÉRUSALEM, SIEGFRIED
German tenor (1940–)

Siegfried Jerusalem is noted primarily for his performances in Wagner, but he can be seen in a lighter vein on video in Strauss's operetta DER ZIGEUNERBARON (1975). It was his first professional singing appearance; he enjoyed it so much that he decided to stop being a bassoon player and become a singer. It was the right decision. He made his opera debut with the Stuttgart Opera in 1975 in *Fidelio* and quickly rose to fame at Bayreuth as Lohengrin, Siegmund, and Siegfried. He became a member of Deutsche Oper in 1978 and made his first appearance at the Metropolitan in 1980 as Lohengrin. A number of his

Met performances have been telecast and are on video. See THE BARTERED BRIDE (1982), GÖTTERDÄMMERUNG (1990), DER MEISTERSINGER VON NÜRNBERG (1984), PARSIFAL (1981/1993), DAS RHEINGOLD (1980/1990), and SIEGFRIED (1990/1992).

JESSEL, LÉON

German composer (1871–1942)

Léon Jessel, a talented German-Jewish composer killed by the Nazis in 1942, wrote 16 operettas and some clever piano pieces such as "The Parade of the Tin Soldier." He is best remembered today for the charming operetta DAS SCHWARZWALDMÄDEL (The Black Forest Girl). It premiered at the Komische Oper in Berlin in 1917 with a rustic libretto by August Niedhart, and it has been a favorite of film and TV directors ever since.

JOHNSON, TOM

American composer (1939–)

Tom Johnson first became known as a music critic for *The Village Voice* helping promote new opera composers such as Robert Ashley and Philip Glass. He turned to composing himself in 1967 and won popularity in 1972 with THE FOUR NOTE OPERA, which used only A, B, D, and E. It was telecast and then staged by Vienna, Paris, and Dutch opera companies. His next opera was *Masque of Clouds*, a collaboration with librettist Robert Kushner, staged at The Kitchen in 1976. Johnson moved to Paris in 1982 where he began to write operas with French and German librettos. The most famous is *Riemannoper* (1986), which is based on definitions from the German music dictionary *Riemann Musik Lexikon*.

JOHN THE HERO

1904 folk opera by Kacsóh

PONGRAC KACSÓH's folk opera *János Vitéz* (John the Hero) is hardly known in America and England, but it is the most popular "Hungarian" light opera in Hungary in contrast to the "Viennese" operettas of Emmerich Kálmán. Based on a patriotic epic poem by Sándor Petőfi with a libretto by Jenő Keltai and Károly Bakonyi, it tells of the fantastic adventures of a peasant soldier named John. After being driven out of his country home by his stepmother and finding military glory, he travels to the underworld to find his lost love. The opera, which incorporates Hungarian folk music in its score, has been filmed and televised.

1938 Gaál film

Hungarian feature film: Béla Gaál (director/screenplay).

Black and white. In Hungarian. 91 minutes.

Comment: Gaál was one of the major Hungarian directors of the 1930s. His film of the opera had great success in Hungary and was distributed in the United States.

Early/related films

1917 Illés film

Alfred Deesy, one of the most popular Hungarian actors of the 1910s, plays John the Hero in this feature version of the opera filmed by Jenő Illés. It was shown in cinemas with Kacsóh's music played live. Black and white. Silent. About 65 minutes.

1973 Johnny Corncob

The first full-length animated feature film made in Hungary was Marcell Jankovic's *János Vitéz*, known in English as *Johnny Corncob*. It is based on Sándor Petőfi's epic poem, the source of the opera, but it includes music by Kacsóh from the opera. Color. In Hungarian. 70 minutes.

JONES, CHUCK

American animation director (1912–2002)

Chuck Jones, one of the great masters of film animation, worked at Warner Bros. from 1938 to 1963 and created many of the studio's most inventive cartoons. His Bugs Bunny, Daffy Duck, and Road Runner cartoons are amazing in their vitality and humor. His greatest achievements, however, are the opera cartoons *What's Opera, Doc?* and *The Rabbit of Seville*. Jones was greatly assisted by his writing partner Michael Maltese.

1949 Long-Haired Hare

This was Jones's first attempt to wed Bugs Bunny to the music of Rossini's *The Barber of Seville*. It features the tough-talking rabbit and the aria "Largo al factotum." Color. 7 minutes.

1950 The Rabbit of Seville

Bugs Bunny has a grand time to music from *The Barber of Seville*. Hunter Elmer Fudd chases Bugs onto the stage of the Hollywood Bowl, and the curtain goes up showing Bugs as barber and Elmer as customer. See THE RABBIT OF SEVILLE.

1952 Operation: Rabbit

Bugs Bunny meets Wiley E. Coyote in this superb cartoon filled with music from Wagner's *Ring* operas, including Siegfried's theme and the *Rheingold* music heard in Alberich's cave. Carl Stalling arranged the music and Michael Maltese wrote the script. Color. 7 minutes.

1957 What's Opera, Doc?
One of the great animated opera films, admired even by Picasso for its awe-inspiring art, a brilliant pastiche of Wagner written by Michael Maltese. Elmer Fudd hunts Bugs Bunny singing "Kill da wabbit, kill da wabbit" to the "Ride of the Valkyries" music so Bugs disguises himself as Brünnhilde. See WHAT'S OPERA, DOC?

JONES, GWYNETH
Welsh soprano (1936–)

Dame Gwyneth Jones began her remarkable career as a mezzo-soprano in Zurich in 1962, but she made her reputation as Lady Macbeth with the Welsh National Opera and the Royal Opera. She was soon a regular at Covent Garden, Bayreuth, Vienna, and other opera houses, making her debut at the Metropolitan in 1972 as Sieglinde. Her powerful voice and strong stage presence can be experienced on a number of videos, including the 1980 Bayreuth DER RING DES NIBELUNGEN series, in which she sings Brünnhilde. See also AUFSTIEG UND FALL DER STADT MAHAGONNY (1998), ELEKTRA (1991), FIDELIO (1970), DER FLIEGENDE HOLLÄNDER (1975), DIE FRAU OHNE SCHATTEN (1980), GÖTTERDÄMMERUNG (1980), DER ROSENKAVALIER (1979), SIEGFRIED (1980), TANNHÄUSER (1978), TRISTAN UND ISOLDE (1993), IL TROVATORE (1964 film), LA VOIX HUMAINE (1990), and DIE WALKÜRE (1980).

1988 Gwyneth Jones in Concert
Live concert in 1988 with Simon Streatfield leading the Quebec Symphony Orchestra. Jones is featured in arias from her favorite operas, including *Tosca, Tannhäuser,* and *The Merry Widow.* Color. 53 minutes. VAI VHS.

JOPLIN, SCOTT
American composer (1868–1917)

Scott Joplin is the Chopin of ragtime, the composer who perfected this style of music and created masterpieces in it such as "The Maple Leaf Rag." He was much admired in the early years of the century, but he was almost forgotten when Joshua Rifkin and the film *The Sting* made him famous all over again. His recognition as an opera composer was late arriving. His great opera TREEMONISHA was performed only once in his lifetime; because no one else was interested, he produced it himself in Harlem in 1915 with only a piano. It was such a failure that it helped push him toward insanity and early death. The opera was virtually forgotten for 50 years, but it won warm admiration in 1972 when it was finally staged pro-

fessionally. It is now considered the earliest of the great American operas, and it won a posthumous Pulitzer Prize for Joplin in 1974.

1977 Scott Joplin
Billy Dee Williams plays Joplin in this enjoyable film biography in which his rise to success and his ambition to write the opera *Treemonisha* are central. The cast includes Art Carney as publisher John Stark, Margaret Avery as his wife, Eubie Blake, Godfrey Cambridge, and Sam Fuller. Christopher Knopf wrote the screenplay; Jeremy Paul Kagan directed. Color. 96 minutes.

JŌRURI
1985 opera by Miki

Blind Japanese puppeteer Shōjo discovers that his wife Otane has fallen in love with his assistant Yosuke. He writes a play telling them how they can have a romantic suicide. "Jōruri" is the name of the kabuki singing style used in the puppet show. Japanese composer Minoru Miki's opera *Jōruri*, libretto by Colin Graham based on a puppet play by Monzaemon Chikamatsu, was commissioned by Opera Theater of St. Louis. The opera's score includes three Japanese instruments in a Western-style orchestra. After its premiere in St. Louis, staged by Graham in 1985, it was reprised in Tokyo in 1988 and taped live at the Nissei Theater.

1988 Opera Theater of St. Louis
American stage production in Japan: Colin Graham (director), Joseph Rescigno (conductor, Opera Theater of St. Louis Orchestra and Chorus).

Cast: Andrew Wentzel (Shōjo), Faith Esham (Otane), John Brandstetter (Yosuke), Carol Freeman (Visitor).

Video: Japanese VHS/LD. Taped November 15, 1988. Nirasawa (director). Color. In English with Japanese subtitles. 160 minutes.

JOURDAN, PIERRE
French film director (1940-)

Pierre Jourdan has directed several films of operas on stage at the Orange Festival in France, most of them intended for television. The best known are his 1977 FIDELIO with Gundula Janowitz, shot on stage without an audience, and a live 1974 NORMA with Montserrat Caballé. His postmodern 1985 CIBOULETTE is highly entertaining, and he had international distribution for his 1970 film with Rudolph Nureyev, *I Am a Dancer.* Some of his Orange Festival films are on video and others are on Japanese DVD and LD. See AIDA (1976), HENRY VIII (2002), Auber's MANON LESCAUT (1990), MIGNON

(1992), Tristan und Isolde (1973), and Il trovatore (1972).

JUANA, LA LOCA
1979 opera by Menotti

Spanish queen Juana la Loca is betrayed by father, husband, and son, who all want to take the kingdom of Castile from her. Her father is Ferdinand V, the king who created the Spanish Inquisition; her husband is Philip I, the king who created the Habsburg dynasty in Spain; her son Carlos is Holy Roman Emperor Charles V, the most powerful monarch in Europe in his time. She doesn't have a chance. Gian Carlo Menotti's three-act opera *Juana, La Loca* (aka *La Loca*), libretto by the composer, takes place over 60 years from Juana's marriage in 1496 to her death in prison in 1555. The opera, which premiered at San Diego Opera on June 3, 1979, was commissioned for Beverly Sills, who sang Juana. Her three betrayers are all sung by the same baritone.

1979 San Diego Opera
American stage production: Tito Capobianco (director), Calvin Simmons (conductor, San Diego Opera Orchestra), Mario Vanarelli (set/costume designer).
Cast: Beverly Sills (Juana), John Brocheler (Felipe, Fernando, Carlos), Robert Hale (Bishop Ximenes), Susanne Marsee (Doña Manuela), Jane Westbrook (Nurse), Joseph Evans (Miguel de Ferrara), Carlos Chausson (Marques de Denia),
Video: Live Opera VHS. Color. In English. 120 minutes.

1982 Spoleto Festival
Italian stage production: Gian Carlo Menotti (director), Herbert Gietzen (conductor, Spoleto Festival Orchestra and Westminster Choir), Pasquale Grossi (set/costume designer).
Cast: Pamela Myers (Juana), Brian Schexnayder (Felipe, Fernando, Carlos), Boris Martinovich (Bishop Ximenes), Petra Malakova (Doña Manuela), Corinna Vozza (Nurse), Robert Lyon (Miguel de Ferrara), Angelo Nosotti (Marques De Denia).
Telecast in 1982. Color. In English. 120 minutes.

Related film

2001 Juana la Loca
This Spanish narrative film, written and directed by Vicente Aranda, stars Pilar López de Ayala as Spanish Queen Juana. In this version of the story, Juana is madly in love with Felipe. The film was released in America with the title *Mad Love*. Color. In Spanish with English subtitles. 123 minutes

JUIVE, LA
1835 opera by Halévy

Fromental Halévy's grand opera *La juive* (The Jewess) is not in fashion today, so it is not available complete on video, but it was hugely popular during the 19th century. The jewess of the title is Rachel, seemingly the daughter of the goldsmith Eléazar. She has fallen in love with Prince Léopold, who had disguised himself as a Jew. When she refuses to convert to Christianity, Cardinal de Brogni has her thrown into a boiling cauldron. Eléazar then reveals that she was actually de Brogni's long-lost daughter. Eugène Scribe wrote the overheated libretto. The opera is on CD with José Carreras as Eléazar and Julia Varady as Rachel.

1927 Vitaphone films
Giovanni Martinelli made two one-reel sound films of numbers from the opera for the Vitaphone company in 1927. In one, he sings Eléazar's aria "Va prononcer la mort." In the other, he plays Eléazar opposite bass Louis d'Angelo as Cardinal de Brogni, and they sing the Act IV duet in costume in a staged scene. Black and white. About 6 minutes each. Bel Canto Society VHS.

1999 The Making of La Juive
A documentary about the Vienna State Opera's production of *La juive* that premiered in October 1999 with Neil Shicoff as Eléazar. Scenes from the opera are shown in rehearsal and on stage. Gunter Kramer was the stage director, and Simone Young conducted the Vienna State Opera Orchestra and Chorus. Color. 60 minutes. Premiere Opera VHS.

JULIETTA
1938 opera by Martinů

Bohuslav Martinů's Czech opera *Julietta: Snář* (Julietta: or the Key of Dreams) is based on Georges Neveux's enigmatic play *Juliette ou la clé des songes*. It's a rather mysterious surrealistic opera set somewhere out of time and concerns a man seeking an illusion of the past. Michel is the man who is looking for the dream that is Julietta. In the town where she lives, nobody has any memory of the past; the end of the opera seems to be more or less the same as its beginning.

1969 Kaslík film
Czech TV film: Václav Kaslík (director), Jaroslav Krombholc (conductor, Prague National Theater Orchestra and Chorus), Josef Svoboda (set designer).
Cast: Erzsebet Hazy (Julietta), René Kollo (Michel), Martha Mödl, Nigel Douglas.
Color. In Czech. 105 minutes.

Related film

1951 Juliette ou la clé des songes
French director Marcel Carné made a famous film version of the Georges Neveux play that provided the libretto for the opera. Gérard Philipe stars as the dreamer Michel with Suzanne Cloutier as the mysterious Juliette. Joseph Cosma composed the music. Black and white. In French. 90 minutes.

JUNGE LORD, DER
1965 opera by Henze

HANS WERNER HENZE's opera *Der junge Lord* (The Young Lord) was commissioned by Berlin's Deutsche Opera, which premiered it in 1965. Based on a story by Wilhelm Hauff, libretto by Ingeborg Bachmann, it has been called a tribute to Italian *opera buffa*. A young English lord arrives in a small German town in 1830 and upsets the local gentry with his odd behavior. The main characters are Luise and Wilhelm, who fall in love. The lord himself is finally discovered to be a performing ape.

1968 Deutsche Oper, Berlin
German film of stage production: Gustav Rudolf Sellner (film/stage director), Christoph von Dohnanyi (conductor, Berlin Deutsche Oper Chorus and Orchestra), Unitel (production).

Cast: Edith Mathis (Luise), Donald Grobe (Wilhelm), Barry McDaniel (Secretary), Loren Driscoll (Barrat), Charles Williams, Lisa Otto, Margarete Anst, Vera Little.

Color. In German. 136 minutes.

Comment: The film was shown theatrically in the United States.

JURINAC, SENA
Yugoslav soprano (1921–)

Sena Jurinac, who made her debut in 1942 in Zagreb, was particularly admired during her early career for her performances in Mozart and became a favorite at the Glyndebourne Festival. She sang Dorabella in *Così fan tutte* with the Glyndebourne company at Edinburgh in 1948 and later appeared as the Countess and both Donnas in *Don Giovanni*. She made a famous recording of LE NOZZE DI FIGARO in 1955 at Glyndebourne with Sesto Bruscantini as Figaro, and they can be seen on stage in it in Anthony Asquith's film *On Such a Night*. Her repertory also included Strauss, Verdi, Berg, and Humperdinck operas. She can be seen as Octavian in Paul Czinner's Salzburg film of DER ROSENKAVALIER (1960), as Marie in a German WOZZECK (1967), and as the Witch in HÄNSEL UND GRETEL (1981).

K

KABAIVANSKA, RAINA
Bulgarian soprano (1934–)

Raina Kabaivanska is particularly liked as Madama Butterfly and Tosca, but she has a wide range of roles. She made her debut in Sofia in 1957, sang regularly at La Scala and the Metropolitan from the beginning of the 1960s, and soon became popular all over the world for her warm voice and agreeable stage personality. She is one of the singers in a notable SOPRANOS concert in Venice in 1991, joins LUCIANO PAVAROTTI in a celebration in Reggio Emilia the same year, and participates in a tribute to MARIA CALLAS in Athens in 1992. Her screen operas include FALSTAFF (1982), MADAMA BUTTERFLY (1983), PAGLIACCI (1968), TOSCA (1976/1983 film/1993), and IL TROVATORE (1978).

KACSÓH, PONGRAC
Hungarian composer (1873–1923)

Pongrac Kacsóh is little known in the United States but he is a national hero in Hungary. His 1904 folk opera *János Vitéz* (JOHN THE HERO), adapted from a patriotic epic poem by Sándor Petőfi, is the most popular "Hungarian" operetta, in contrast to the "Viennese" operettas of Emmerich Kálmán. Kacsóh also wrote *Mary Ann* (1908), an operetta based on Israel Zangwill's English play *Merely Mary Ann,* and a few other stage works, but nothing could measure up to *John the Hero.*

KAISER VON ATLANTIS, DER
1943 opera by Ullmann

Der Kaiser von Atlantis (The Emperor of Atlantis) centers around an emperor who forces people to make all-out war. Death is so dismayed by the senseless killing that he abdicates and refuses to allow people to die. The emperor has to capitulate by offering himself as Death's first new subject. The other main characters are the Drummer, Pierrot the Soldier, the Girl, and the Loudspeaker, which introduces characters and describes what is happening. Jewish composer VIKTOR ULLMANN and librettist Peter Kien created the opera in the Terezin (Theresienstadt) concentration camp on the back of SS deportation forms

but were sent to Auschwitz before they could stage it. The opera, with its echoes of Weill and Hindemith, has been revived in recent years because of interest in music suppressed by the Nazis. See also TEREZIN OPERAS.

1978 BBC/WDR/ORF Television
International TV production: John Goldschmidt (director), Kerry Woodward (conductor, London Sinfonietta), Gerd Krauss (set/costume designer), BBC/WDR/ORF (producers).

Cast: Sigmund Nimsgern (Emperor), Alexander Malta (Death), Teresa Stratas (Drummer), Richard Lewis (Pierrot), Rüdiger Wohlers (Soldier), Janet Perry (Girl).

Color. In German. 64 minutes.

Comment: Goldschmidt staged the opera in a set designed like a concentration camp with barbed wire and prison spotlights. It won the Prix Italia.

Related film

1994 The Music of Terezin
Simon Broughton's documentary film about the music and musicians of Terezin features staged scenes of *Der Kaiser von Atlantis.* Color. In English. 30 minutes.

KAIVOS
1963 TV opera by Rautavaara

Finnish composer EINOJUHANI RAUTAVAARA's *Kaivos* (The Mine), a 12-tone examination of liberty and state control, was inspired by the Hungarian uprising against the Soviets in 1956; it tells the story of a miners' strike that is crushed by the Party. Because of its strong political content during a period when Finland was nervous about its relationship with the USSR, the Finnish National Opera rejected it, so Rautavaara adapted it for TV.

1963 YLE Finnish Television
Finnish TV production: Seppo Wallin (director), Jorna Panula (conductor, YLE Radio Symphony Orchestra), Jorma Lindfors (set designer).

Cast: Mariaheidi Rautavaara (Ira), Matti Lethinen (Simon), Pekky Nuotio (Marko), Aarne Vainio (Pastor), Harri Nikkonen (Prefect), Pentti Tuominen (Old Man), Timo Mustakallio (Miner).

Telecast April 10, 1963, on YLE Finnish Television. Color. In Finnish. 84 minutes.

KALICH, BERTHA
Romanian soprano (1874–1939)

Bertha Kalich began her opera career in Bucharest singing *Carmen* and *Il trovatore.* She emigrated to the United States in 1895, sang in New York productions of Offenbach's *La Belle Hélène* and Strauss's *The Gypsy Baron,* and then moved into nonmusical theater. She toured in the play *Marta of the Lowlands,* the basis of the opera *Tiefland,* and starred in a film version of it in 1914. She made three other films in 1916 for Fox, but her film career did not take off.

1914 Marta of the Lowlands
Kalich repeats her stage success as a woman of the mountains who is kept by a rich man but married off by him to another. The play has the same literary source as Eugen d'Albert's opera *Tiefland.* J. Searle Dawley directed for Famous Players. Black and white. Silent. About 70 minutes.

1916 Slander
A clever seducer sets out to destroy Kalich's happy marriage so she will be free to wed him. She discovers his duplicity and returns to her husband. Will S. Davis directed for Fox. Black and white. Silent. About 70 minutes.

1916 Ambition
Kalich, the wife of an ambitious attorney, leaves him when she finds out that he wants to give her to another to advance his career. James Vincent directed for Fox. Black and white. Silent. About 70 minutes.

1916 Love and Hate
An evil man tells lies about Kalich so her husband will divorce her, but the truth comes out in the end. James Vincent directed for Fox. Black and white. Silent. About 80 minutes.

KÁLMÁN, EMMERICH
Hungarian composer (1882–1953)

Emmerich Kálmán is out of fashion in the United States today, as are most other traditional operetta composers, but he retains a strong following in central Europe. As he wrote lovely melodies, it is likely that his star will rise again. In the meantime, his major operettas can be enjoyed on German videos. Although Kálmán was Hungarian, he modeled his operettas on the Viennese style created by Strauss and Lehár, and he premiered most of them in Vienna. His greatest success came with DIE CSÁRDÁSFÜRSTIN in 1915, but GRÄFIN MARIZA, DIE ZIRKUSPRINZESSIN, and DIE BAJADERE were also popular. In 1927 he went to New York to collaborate with Oscar Hammerstein on the bizarre Broadway operetta GOLDEN DAWN. He also wrote music for films. Like many other composers, Kálmán had to flee when the Nazis took over Austria. He eventually settled in the United States and continued to compose until his death in 1953.

1931 Ronny
Kálmán wrote this German film operetta for Käthe von Nagy with Willy Fritsch as her romantic partner. It has the surefire operetta plot of the prince and the poor girl who wins his heart. In this variation, the prince writes an operetta that stars the girl. Reinhold Schunzel directed for the UFA studio. Black and white. In German. 87 minutes.

1958 Die Csárdaskönig
The Czardas King, subtitled *The Emmerich Kálmán Story,* is a German film biography of the composer. Gerhard Riedmann stars as Kálmán in what is essentially a potpourri of scenes and songs from his best-known operettas. Camilla Spira plays Mrs. Kálmán, Rudolf Schock is the tenor János, and Marina Orschel is Vera. Harald Philip directed for the CCC production group. Color. In German. 96 minutes.

KANAWA, KIRI TE
See TE KANAWA, KIRI.

KARAJAN, HERBERT VON
Austrian conductor (1908–1989)

Herbert von Karajan was deeply involved with opera and film during much of his career, and he made sure that he left a screen legacy of his work. After he became director of the Salzburg Festival, he filmed virtually every opera he produced. His early telecasts were produced by the German company Unitel and have been released on Deutsche Grammophon VHS. He later formed the Telemondial company and filmed his operas himself aided by cinematographer Ernst Wild and audio producer Michel Glotz. Karajan also oversaw the editing of the videos. Most of his operas are available commercially, and there are many others showing him conducting non-operatic music. He was also involved in a few feature films; he conducted the *St. Matthew Passion* for a 1950 Austrian film in honor of JOHANN SEBASTIAN BACH and the Wagnerian score for the 1955 film LUDWIG II. Unfortunately, he tarnished his reputation by joining the Nazi party in both Germany and Austria; he is featured prominently in the documentary *Great Conductors of the Third Reich.* See LA BOHÈME (1965), CARMEN (1966), CAVALLERIA RUSTICANA (1968), CONDUCTORS (1955), DON CARLO (1986), DON GIOVANNI (1987), FALSTAFF (1982), MADAMA BUTTERFLY (1974), OTELLO (1974), PAGLIACCI (1968), DAS RHEINGOLD (1978), DER ROSENKAVALIER (1960/1984), and VERDI REQUIEM (1967).

1966 Karajan: Early Images

French filmmaker Henri-Georges Clouzot filmed these extraordinary images of Karajan at work. He conveys the intensity of the music and Karajan's conducting through camera movements, unusual angles, and jump cuts. Black and white. 95 minutes. DG VHS/LD.

1978 Impressions of Herbert von Karajan

Czech director Vojtech Jasny created this informative bilingual documentary for British and German television to mark the 70th birthday of the conductor. Color. In English (50 minutes) or German (60 minutes).

1975/1978 Karajan Conducts

Karajan leads the Berlin Philharmonic at New Year's Eve programs in 1975 and 1978. The programs include opera overtures and intermezzi from *L'Amico Fritz, La forza del destino,* and *Tannhäuser.* Karajan himself directed the videos. Color. DG VHS/LD.

1987 Karajan in Salzburg

The 79-year-old Karajan, shown at work during the 1987 Salzburg Festival, talks about the 43 films he has made as his legacy and shows his video editing room. *Don Giovanni, Tannhäuser,* and *Tristan und Isolde* are seen in rehearsal and performance with Jessye Norman (*Tristan und Isolde*), Kathleen Battle and Samuel Ramey (*Don Giovanni*), Julia Varady, and others. He talks with two then-rapidly-rising young singers, Sumi Jo and Cecilia Bartoli. Susan Froemke, Peter Gelb, and Deborah Dickson made this excellent documentary. Color. In English and German. 84 minutes. Sony VHS.

1995 Herbert von Karajan

Documentary about the composer with extensive archival footage and commentary by Dr. Oliver Rathkolb. It includes a scene from Karajan's 1987 Salzburg production of *Carmen,* with Grace Bumbry as Carmen and Jon Vickers as Don José. Black and white and color. 80 minutes. Bel Canto Society VHS.

KASLÍK, VÁCLAV
Czech composer/conductor (1917–1989)

Václav Kaslík, who directed a number of operas and operettas for film and television, also composed screen operas. His 1961 TV opera *Krakatit* (see below) is based on a story by Karel Čapek, and his 1980 stage opera LA STRADA is based on Federico Fellini's film *La Strada.* Kaslík was also a highly respected conductor and the founder of a grand opera house in Prague. The films he directed that are on video include LES CONTES D'HOFFMANN (1970), JULIETTA (1969), RUSALKA (1962), and ZIGEUNERLIEBE (1974).

1961 Krakatit

Kaslík's TV opera *Krakatit* is based on a 1925 novel by Karel Čapek, the Czech writer who gave the world the word "robot." The novel, published in English as *An Atomic Fantasy,* is the prophetic story of an inventor who discovers atomic power and finds that people want to make bombs out of it. In the opera, the tenor inventor struggles to keep his explosive away from deep-voiced militants. It was telecast March 5, 1961, on CST Czech Television. Black and white. In Czech. 90 minutes.

KASTLE, LEONARD
American composer (1929–)

Leonard Kastle, who helped stage Menotti's operas on Broadway, was a music director on the ambitious NBC Opera Theatre, and his first two operas, THE SWING (1956) and DESERET (1961), were commissions for the company. Many of his operas are set in 19th-century America. *Deseret* deals with Mormon leader Brigham Young, *The Pariahs* is about American whalers, and *The Calling of Mother Ann* and *The Journey of Mother Ann* are concerned with the Shakers.

KATERINA ISMAILOVA
See LADY MACBETH OF THE MTSENSK DISTRICT.

KATYA KABANOVA
1921 opera by Janáček

LEOŠ JANÁČEK's powerful *Katya Kabanova* (Kát'a Kabanová), a harrowing portrait of adultery, guilt, and suicide, is based on Russian writer Alexander Ostrovsky's 1859 play *The Thunderstorm.* Katya, the frustrated wife of timid Tichon, is dominated by her shrewish mother-in-law Kabanicha, but she is able to share spiritual ideas with her friend Varvara. She becomes infatuated with Boris and has a secret affair with him while her husband is away. When he returns during a thunderstorm, Katya makes a guilt-stricken public confession of her adultery. After a reunion with Boris, she drowns herself in the Volga.

1977 Hudecek film

Czech feature film: Václav Hudecek (director), Jaroslav Krombholc (conductor, National Theater of Prague Orchestra and Chorus).

Cast: Katerina Machackova (Katya Kabanova, sung by Drahomíra Tikalova), Slavka Budinova (Kabanicha, sung by Ludmilla Komancová), P. Starke (Boris, sung by Beno Blachut), Eva Hudeckova (Varwara, sung by Ivana Mixova), J. Faltynek (Tichon, sung by Boris Vich).

Color. In Czech. 88 minutes.

Comment: The film was shot on location in 35mm with the actors miming to a 1959 recording of the opera with Czech singers.

***1988 Glyndebourne Festival

English stage production: Nikolaus Lehnhoff (director), Andrew Davis (conductor, London Philharmonic Orchestra and Glyndebourne Festival Chorus), Tobias Hoheisel (set/costume designer).

Cast: Nancy Gustafson (Katya Kabanova), Barry McCauley (Boris), Felicity Palmer (Kabanicha), Louise Winter (Varvara), Ryland Davies (Tichon), John Graham-Hall (Váňja), Donald Adam (Dikoj).

Video: Kultur and Arthaus DVD/Kultur, Home Vision, and Virgin (GB) VHS. Derek Bailey (director). Color. In Czech with English subtitles. 100 minutes.

Comment: An outstanding production all around, with a superb performance by Gustafson and memorable sets based on Russian art.

1998 Salzburg Festival

Austrian stage production: Christoph Marthaler (director), Silvain Cambreling (conductor, Czech Philharmonic Orchestra and Slovak Philharmonic Chorus), Anna Viebrock (set/costume designer).

Cast: Angela Denoke (Katya Kabanova), David Kuebler (Boris), Jane Henschel (Kabanicha), Henk Smits, Hubert Delamboye, Rainer Trost.

Video: TDK (GB) DVD/House of Opera DVD and VHS. Christoph Marthaler (director). Color. In Czech. 120 minutes.

Comment: This is an updated version of the opera set in a shabby Hungarian apartment house block during the Communist era where everyone can see what is going on. Critic Matthew Rye felt it gave the opera a voyeuristic feeling similar to Hitchcock's *Rear Window*.

KEENLYSIDE, SIMON
English baritone (1959–)

Simon Keenlyside is one of the new generation of baritones and a fine actor as well as singer. He had great success in *Billy Budd* in Glasgow in 1992, and his career has widened from Glasgow and Hamburg to Geneva, Paris, and Milan. He can be seen on video as the poet Olivier opposite Kiri Te Kanawa in a 1992 San Francisco production of CAPRICCIO.

KENNY, YVONNE
Australian soprano (1950–)

Yvonne Kenny, who was born in Sydney, made her professional debut in London in 1975 and then became a regular at Covent Garden. She has since returned to Australia for performances with the Australian Opera, but her fine coloratura technique has made her in demand all over the world. She participates in a ROYAL OPERA HOUSE tribute to Queen Elizabeth in 1986, performs in WILLIAM WALTON's opera *Troilus and Cressida* in a 1987 film about the composer, is the voice of MELBA in a 1987 Australian TV film about the diva, and is heard singing an aria from RINALDO on the soundtrack of the 2000 Australian film *The Monkey's Mask*. Her operas on video include COSÌ FAN TUTTE (1990), THE FAIRY QUEEN (1995), IDOMENEO (1983), DIE LUSTIGE WITWE (2001), MITRIDATE (1983/1986), DER SCHAUSPIELDIREKTOR (1991), and DIE ZAUBERFLÖTE (1986).

KERN, JEROME
American composer (1885–1945)

Most of the many musicals of Jerome Kern, one of the finest composers of the century, are outside the boundaries of this reference book, but three can be considered American operettas and have been staged in opera houses. SHOW BOAT, which greatly enlarged the operetta format and is very close to being an opera, was the first to enter the opera house repertory, and it has been recorded by opera singers. Kern participated in the American adaptation of Emmerich Kálmán's operetta *Die Csárdásfürstin,* staged in New York in 1917 as *The Riviera Girl*. His 1931 THE CAT AND THE FIDDLE, a kind of modernized operetta, was filmed in 1934 with Jeanette MacDonald. His 1932 MUSIC IN THE AIR, also filmed, is set in a Central European operetta milieu and features an operetta singer as one of its stars. Kern wrote as brilliantly for the cinema as for the stage, including such classic movies as *Swing Time* and *Cover Girl,* and was the subject of a film biography.

1946 Till the Clouds Roll By

This all-star MGM film biography of Jerome Kern contains highlights from his musical career and a potted version of *Show Boat*. Robert Walker plays Kern, and the singers include Judy Garland, Frank Sinatra, Kathryn Grayson, Dinah Shore, Tony Martin, Angela Lansbury, Caleb Peterson, and Lena Horne. Richard Whorf directed. Color. 137 minutes. Silver Screen VHS.

KEUSCHE SUSANNE, DIE
1910 operetta by Gilbert

Die keusche Susanne (Modest Susanne), an ironic operetta about people pretending to be more virtuous than they really are, centers around a baron caught at the Moulin Rouge in Paris. German composer JEAN GILBERT is not much remembered in the English-speaking world today, but this operetta was once popular internationally. It was staged in London as *The Girl in the Taxi*, with

Yvonne Arnaud in the leading role, and has been filmed in six countries. It remains popular on stage in Latin America, where it has become part of the zarzuela repertory, and it was presented as a Spanish zarzuela in Miami in 1978.

1926 Eichberg film

German feature film: Richard Eichberg (director), Hans Stürm (screenplay), Heinrich Gertner (cinematographer), Jacques Rotmil (set designer).

Cast: Lillian Harvey (Susanne), Willy Fritsch (René), Hans Junkermann, Willy Fritsch.

Black and white. Silent. About 78 minutes.

Comment: The first film of the operetta made British singer-dancer Lillian Harvey famous even though it was shot before the coming of sound.

1937 The Girl in the Taxi

English feature film: André Berthomieu (director), Austin Melford and Val Valentine (screenplay), Roy Clark (cinematographer), British Unity Pictures (production).

Cast: Frances Day (Suzanne), Henri Garat (René), Lawrence Grossmith (Baron), Jean Gillie (Jacqueline), Mackenzie Ward (Robert).

Black and white. In English. 72 minutes.

Comment: Filmed in London in English as *The Girl in the Taxi* and in French as *La Chaste Suzanne* (see below) with a different cast.

1937 La Chaste Suzanne

French feature film: André Berthomieu (director), Jean Boyer (screenplay), Roy Clark (cinematographer).

Cast: Meg Lemonnier (Suzanne), Henri Garat (René Boisiurette), Raimu (Baron), Blanchette Brunoy (Jacqueline), Serge Flateau (Hubert).

Black and white. In French. 90 minutes.

1945 La Casta Susanna

Argentine feature film: Benito Perojo (director/screenplay), Paul Misraki (music director).

Cast: Martha Legrand, Tilda Thamar, Jack Petersen, Raimundo Pastore.

Black and white. In Spanish. 89 minutes.

Comment: Zarzuela film specialist Perojo made this film during his period of exile from Spain.

1952 El Casto Susano

Mexican feature film: Joaquin Pardavé (director), Filmex (production company).

Cast: Not known.

Black and white. In Spanish. 87 minutes.

Comment: This Mexican version of the operetta turns the protagonist into a man.

1964 La Casta Susanna

Argentine feature film: Luis César Amadori (director/screenplay with Jesus Arozamena), Antonio Ballesteros (cinematographer), Gregorio Segura (music director).

Cast: Gracita Morales, Isabel Garcés, Chonette Laurent, Armand Mestral.

Color. In Spanish. 90 minutes.

KHOVANSHCHINA
1886 opera by Mussorgsky

Khovanshchina (The Khovansky Affair), an epic historic opera, was left unfinished by MODEST MUSSORGSKY when he died in 1881; it was completed by Rimsky-Korsakov in 1886 and later revised by Stravinsky and then by Shostakovich. The opera, inspired by the bicentenary of Tsar Peter the Great, describes a plot at the beginning of Peter's reign. The complicated libretto by Mussorgsky and Vladimir Stassov concerns the struggle of a group of radicals, led by Prince Ivan Khovansky, and their collaboration with the Old Believers, led by dissenter Dosifei. Khovansky's son Andrei and Old Believer prophetess Marfa have a hopeless love affair, and all ends badly. There are, rather surprisingly, four screen versions of the opera using different orchestrations.

***1959 Stroyeva film

Soviet feature film: Vera Stroyeva (director), Dimitri Shostakovich, Anna Abramova and Stroyeva (screenplay), Yevgeny Svetlanov (Bolshoi Opera Ballet and Orchestra), A. Borisov (set designer), Dimitri Shostakovich (orchestration).

Cast: Alexei Krivchenya (Ivan Khovansky), Mark Reizen (Dosifei), Kira Leonova (Marfa), Anton Grigoriev (Andrei Khovansky), Vladimir Petrov (Prince Golitsyn), Yevgeny Kibkalo (Shaklovity), Vera Gromova (Emma), Maya Plistetskaya (Persian dancer).

Video: Corinth VHS/LD. Color. Wide screen. In Russian with English subtitles. 131 minutes.

Comment: This is an abridged version of the opera (about 50 minutes) but an excellent film.

1979 Bolshoi Opera

Russian stage production: Yuri Simonov (conductor), Bolshoi Theater Orchestra and Chorus), Nikolai Rimsky-Korsakov (orchestration).

Cast: Alexander Vedernikov (Ivan Khovansky), Yevgeny Nesterenko (Dosifei), Irina Arkhipova (Marfa), Georgi Andruschenko (André Khovansky), Evgeny Raikov (Golitsyn), Vladislav Romanovsky (Shaklovity), Vitaly Vlasov (Scribe).

Video: Kultur and Bel Canto Society VHS. Color. In Russian with English subtitles. 181 minutes.

***1989 Vienna State Opera
Austrian stage production: Alfred Kirchner (director), Claudio Abbado (conductor, Vienna State Opera Orchestra and Chorus, Slovak Chorus of Bratislava, and Vienna Boys' Choir), Erich Wonder (set designer), Joachim Herzog (costume designer), Dimitri Shostakovich (orchestration, with final scene by Igor Stravinsky).

Cast: Nicolai Ghiaurov (Ivan Khovansky), Paata Burchuladze (Dosifei), Ludmila Semtschuk (Marfa), Vladimir Atlantov (Andrei Khovansky), Yuri Marusin (Golitsyn), Anatoly Kocherga (Shaklovity), Joanna Borowska (Emma).

Video: Image Entertainment DVD/Home Vision VHS. Brian Large (director). Color. In Russian with English subtitles. 182 minutes.

Comment: The most powerful and effective of the stage versions. Finely directed and conducted and well sung.

1992 Kirov Opera
Russian stage production: Fyodor Lopukhov (director, staged by L. Baratov), Valery Gergiev (conductor, Kirov Orchestra, Chorus, and Ballet), F. Fedorovsky (set designer), Dimitri Shostakovich (orchestration).

Cast: Bulat Minzhilkiev (Ivan Khovansky), Nikolai Okhotnikov (Dosifei), Olga Borodina (Marfa), Yuri Marusin (Andrei Khovansky), Konstantin Pluzhnikov (Golitsyn), Tatiana Kratsova (Emma).

Video: Philips Classics VHS/LD. Brian Large (director). Color. In Russian with English subtitles. 210 minutes.

KIENZL, WILHELM
Austrian composer (1857–1941)

Wilhelm Kienzl was strongly influenced by Richard Wagner (he had attended the premiere of the *Ring* at Bayreuth in 1876), but he eventually found his own style and success with the 1895 religious opera DER EVANGELIMANN (The Evangelist). It was a popular opera in the early years of the 20th century, especially in German-speaking countries, although it is now almost unknown outside Germany. Kienzl's other operas include *Don Quixote* (1898) and *Der Kuhreigen* (1911), but only *Der Evangelimann* continues to be staged.

KIEPURA, JAN
Polish tenor (1902–1966)

Jan Kiepura was a major star of the Vienna State Opera from 1926 to 1937, and he was also popular at La Scala and the Paris Opéra. He starred in 19 films in Germany, England, France, and the United States, and most of them feature opera. His Hungarian soprano wife MARTA EGGERTH often appeared with him, and they became a popular team on film and stage, including two "parallel" films based on *La bohème*. He made his U.S. debut in Chicago in 1937 in *Tosca*, an opera with which he was often identified. He sang *La bohème* at the Met in 1938, continued to sing in opera in America until 1942, and then began a long run on Broadway in *The Merry Widow* with his wife. In 1952 the couple starred in a film version of Lehár's operetta DAS LAND DES LÄCHELNS.

Polish tenor Jan Kiepura was as popular in the movies in the 1930s as he was in the leading operas houses.

1930 City of Song
Kiepura plays a Neapolitan singer brought to London by an English socialite (Betty Stockfield), who wants him to have professional training. He is unable fit in to English society and returns to his first love (Heather Angel) in Naples. The film was also shot in German, as *Die singende Stadt* with Brigitte Helm, and in Italian as *La città canora*. In America it was shown as *Farewell to Love*. Carmine Gallone directed this popular musical for UFA with a screenplay by Miles Malleson, Hans Szekley, and C. H. Dand. Black and white. 101 minutes. Bel Canto Society/House of Opera VHS.

1932 Tell Me Tonight
Kiepura is an Italian tenor in Switzerland who changes places with a fugitive and falls in love with the mayor's daughter. He sings arias from *La bohème, Rigoletto, La*

traviata, and *Martha,* plus songs by Mischa Spoliansky. See TELL ME TONIGHT.

1934 My Song for You
Kiepura plays a famous tenor brought to Vienna to star in *Aida;* a young woman he fancies uses his influence to get her boyfriend a job in the opera. Kiepura sings a splendid "Celeste Aida" and "Di quella pira" with ringing high Cs. See MY SONG FOR YOU.

1934 My Heart Is Calling
Kiepura is the tenor of an opera company stranded in Monte Carlo with Marta Eggerth as a stowaway. Their efforts to get an engagement at the Monte Carlo Opera fail, so they end up performing *Tosca* on the opera house steps. See MY HEART IS CALLING.

1935 Ich liebe alle Frauen
I Love All Women is a German musical with music by operetta king Robert Stolz. Kiepura plays a singer, as usual, and has support from Lien Deyers and Theo Lingen. Carl Lamac directed. Black and white. In German. 94 minutes. House of Opera/Opera Dubs VHS.

1936 Opernring
Kiepura plays a singing taxi driver who becomes a successful opera tenor and gets to sing in *Turandot* at the Vienna State Opera. Kiepura's costars are Friedl Czepa and Theo Lingen. Carmine Gallone directed this Austrian film, which won a prize at the Venice Film Festival in 1936. The English release title was *Thank You, Madame.* Black and white. In German. 91 minutes.

1936 Give Us This Night
Kiepura and Gladys Swarthout are the stars of this American film about opera singers. When a tenor singing badly in *Il trovatore* is nearly booed off stage, Kiepura demonstrates his own fine voice and causes a riot. Swarthout refuses to sing with the old tenor, so Kiepura replaces him. See GIVE US THIS NIGHT.

1937 Zauber de Bohème
Kiepura and Eggerth play opera singers who want to sing together in *La bohème.* When Eggerth learns she is dying of tuberculosis, she goes away so he can have a successful career without worrying about her. They become famous separately and finally appear on stage together in *La bohème.* At the end of the opera she dies, just like Mimì. See ZAUBER DE BOHÈME.

1947 Her Wonderful Lie
Zauber de Bohème was such a success it was remade with Kiepura and Eggerth again matching their "real" life with the story of Mimì and Rodolfo. The "wonderful lie" is the heroine's denial of her love for the hero so he can be a success. After they become successful and sing *La bohème* together, she is able to die just like Mimì. See HER WONDERFUL LIE.

1949 La valse brillante
Kiepura plays a tenor hired to be soprano Eggerth's bodyguard after she receives threatening letters. He solves her problems and ends up as her singing partner and husband. The music is mostly by Mozart and Verdi. Jean Boyer directed for Vox film. Black and white. In French. 95 minutes.

1994 125 Years of the Vienna State Opera
Austrian documentary about the Vienna State Opera celebrating its 125th birthday. It includes vintage excerpts of past stars, including Kiepura. Color. In German. 60 minutes. House of Opera VHS.

KING, JAMES
American tenor (1925–)

James King, born in the historic cowtown Dodge City made famous in Western movies, began his opera career singing in Florence. He moved on to San Francisco in 1961 and reached the Metropolitan in 1966 as Florestan in *Fidelio.* King was particularly popular in Wagner and Strauss operas in Germany. See ARIADNE AUF NAXOS (1988), ELEKTRA (1989/1991/1994), FIDELIO (1970), GEORGE LONDON (1964), IL RITORNO D'ULISSE IN PATRIA (1985), DIE TOTE STADT (1983), and DIE WALKÜRE (1977 film).

KING AND I, THE
1951 operetta by Rodgers and Hammerstein

English governess Anna Leonowens travels to Siam to teach King Mongkut's children and finds dealing with the autocratic monarch her major challenge. Richard Rodgers's Broadway operetta *The King and I,* libretto by Oscar Hammerstein based on Anna's diaries and Margaret Landon's novel *Anna and the King of Siam,* opened in New York in 1951. Yul Brynner played the King, Gertrude Lawrence was Anna, John Stewart was the Crown Prince, Doretta Morrow was Tuptim, Jerome Robbins arranged the choreography, and John van Druten directed.

1956 Twentieth Century-Fox film
American feature film: Walter Lang (director), Ernest Lehman (screenplay), Alfred Newman and Ken Darby (music directors), Leon Shamroy (cinematographer, CinemaScope).

Cast: Yul Brynner (King), Deborah Kerr (Anna, sung by Marni Nixon), Rita Moreno (Tuptim), Carlos Riva (Lun Tah, sung by Reuben Fuentes), Terry Saunders (Lady Thiang).

Video: Fox DVD/VHS. Color. In English. 133 minutes.

Comment: Brynner won an Academy Award for his performance, and Newman and Darby won the Oscar for their music score.

KING OF HEARTS
1995 television opera by Torke

King of Hearts is an English TV opera composed by American Michael Torke to a libretto by English writer/director Christopher Rawlence. The story is a love triangle set in contemporary London involving two teachers and a therapist. There are evocations of *Madame Bovary* and the opera that she attends in the novel, *Lucia di Lammermoor*. The opera was staged at Aspen in the summer of 1996.

1995 Channel 4
English TV production: Christopher Rawlence (director).

Cast: Hilton McRae (Antoine), Lynne Davies (Helen), Omar Ebrahim (Charles).

Telecast February 26, 1995, on Channel 4 in England. Color. In English. 51 minutes.

KING PRIAM
1962 opera by Tippett

MICHAEL TIPPETT's *King Priam*, libretto by the composer based on Homer's *Iliad*, focuses on King Priam of Troy and, through him, on the meaning of love, violence, war, and death. The opera begins with the birth of Paris, examines the horrors of the Trojan War caused by his love for Helen, and ends compassionately with Priam's death. The deaths of Patroclus, Hector, Achilles, and Paris precede his and are seen to be linked. Tippett described the opera as about "the mysterious nature of human choice."

***1985 Kent Opera
English stage production: Nicholas Hytner (director), Roger Norrington (conductor, Kent Opera Orchestra and Chorus), David Fielding (set designer).

Cast: Rodney Macann (King Priam), Janet Price (Hecuba), Sarah Walker (Andromache), Howard Haskin (Paris), Anne Mason (Helen of Troy), Omar Ebrahim (Hector), Neil Jenkins (Achilles), John Hancorn (Patroclus), Christopher Gillet (Hermes).

Video: Kultur/Home Vision VHS. Robin Lough (director). Color. In English. 135 minutes.

Comment: An outstanding production made timelessly modern by using sandbags and barbed wire as its basic set.

KING'S RHAPSODY
1949 operetta by Novello

Prince Nikki, who has lived in exile in Paris with his mistress Marta for many years, has to return to his country after his father dies to become king. He marries Princess Cristiane but later is forced to abdicate so he returns to Paris. Cristiane rules the country until their son grows up and becomes king. Ivor Novello's operetta *King's Rhapsody* premiered in London at the Theatre Royal, Drury Lane, with Novello as the Prince, Vanessa Lee as Cristiane, and Phyllis Dare as Marta. The most popular number was Lee's "Someday My Heart Will Awake," and she reprised her role as Cristiane in a British TV production in 1957 opposite Griffith Jones. Novello died while *King's Rhapsody* was in its successful second year.

1955 Everest film
British feature film: Herbert Wilcox (director); Pamela Bower, A. P. Herbert, and Christopher Hassall (screenplay); Max Green (cinematographer); Everest (production); British Lion (distributor).

Cast: Anna Neagle (Marta), Errol Flynn (Prince), Patrice Wymore (Princess), Martita Hunt (Queen Mother), Finlay Currie (King Paul).

Color. In English 93 minutes.

Comment: The film did not have the success of the stage production as it was made on a low budget with the wrong cast.

KINOKÖNIGEN, DIE
1913 operetta about the movies by Gilbert

German composer Jean Gilbert's *Die Kinokönigen* (The Cinema Queen) was the second operetta about the movies. It opened in Berlin in March 1913, and it reached London in 1914 as *The Cinema Star* and New York as *The Queen of the Movies*. The "queen" is a movie actress who pretends to be a princess to trick a stuffy businessman into acting in a film. Gilbert's operetta, composed to a libretto by Georg Okonkowski and Julius Freund, had first been staged in Hamburg as *Die Elfte Muse* (The Eleventh Muse). The English adaptation was by Glen MacDonough with lyrics by Edward Paulton. Jack Hulpert, Cicely Courtneidge, and Dorothy Ward had the main roles in London, and Alice Dovey, Frank Moulan, and Valli Valli were the stars in New York. Irving Berlin wrote new songs for the U.S. production.

KIRKOP, ORESTE
Maltese tenor (1923–1998)

Oreste Kirkop, who starred in the 1956 Hollywood movie of THE VAGABOND KING opposite Kathryn Grayson, was publicized by Paramount simply as "Oreste" with the hope that he might turn out to be another Mario Lanza. However, he had none of the screen personality of Lanza, the film was a failure, and he was never given another chance. He sang in *La bohème* in Las Vegas in 1957, toured with NBC Opera Theatre, played the Duke in a 1958 NBC color telecast of RIGOLETTO, and returned to England. Kirkop, who was born in the tiny British colonial island country of Malta, made his debut in its capital city Valletta in *Cavalleria rusticana,* and then began to sing in Italy. His career took off in England where he sang with the Carl Rosa Opera Company in 1951, joined Sadler's Wells Opera in 1952, and sang at Covent Garden. He played Canio in a BBC TV production of *Pagliacci* that was seen by Paramount scouts and resulted in his Hollywood venture.

1956 Bing Presents Oreste
Paramount promoted its new singer Oreste with help from Bing Crosby in this VistaVision film special. Oreste sings "Vesti la giubba" from *Pagliacci* and joins Crosby on pop songs. Color. 10 minutes.

KIROV OPERA HOUSE
St. Petersburg opera theater

The Kirov Opera House in St. Petersburg (formerly Leningrad), once the Russian Imperial Court Theater, has gone back to its original name of Maryinsky Theater. The Kirov was the site of the premiere of Verdi's LA FORZA DEL DESTINO (where it was reprised and telecast in 1998) and many Russian operas, including Tchaikovsky's *The Queen of Spades.* It is featured in a number of Soviet opera videos, most of them conducted by artistic director Valery Gergiev, and it staged the operas for the 1952 Soviet film RIMSKY-KORSAKOV. Its major singers in recent years have included SERGEI LEIFERKUS and GALINA GORCHAKOVA, and its operas on video include ALEKO (1954), BETROTHAL IN A MONASTERY, (1997), BORIS GODUNOV (1990), EUGENE ONEGIN (1984), THE FIERY ANGEL (1993), KHOVANSHCHINA (1992), PRINCE IGOR (1962), THE QUEEN OF SPADES (1992), RUSLAN AND LYUDMILA (1996), SADKO (1994), and WAR AND PEACE (1991).

1992 Welcome Back, St. Petersburg
A gala evening at the Royal Opera House, Covent Garden, with the Kirov Opera and Ballet and the Kirov Opera Orchestra. There are selections from works by Borodin, Drigo, Minkus, Mussorgsky, Prokofiev, Rimsky-Korsakov, and Tchaikovsky. Highlights include arias from Tchaikovsky's *The Enchantress* and Mussorgsky's *Salammbô,* and the Kromy Forest scene from *Boris Godunov.* Valery Gergiev conducts the opera scenes and Viktor Fedotov the ballet numbers. Color. In Russian with English subtitles. 90 minutes. Philips VHS.

KIRSTEN, DOROTHY
American soprano (1910–1992)

Dorothy Kirsten was a protégé of Grace Moore so it was natural for her to appear in the movies. When she sang *Louise* at the Metropolitan Opera in 1947, she dedicated the performance to Moore. Kirsten made her debut in 1940 with the Chicago Grand Opera Company in *Manon,* performed with New York City Opera and San Francisco Opera, and came to the Met in 1945 as Mimì in *La bohème.* She continued to sing at the Met until 1979, but she also performed on radio and screen. She can be enjoyed in two films and several television appearances.

1950 Mr. Music
Kirsten plays herself as Bing Crosby's guest star in this enjoyable Paramount musical. She sings a wonderful stage duet with Crosby, "Accidents Will Happen," written by James Van Heusen and Johnny Burke; she's on the opera side of the stage, he's on the Vaudeville side, but their voices intertwine. Crosby's problems as a Broadway composer provide the plot. Richard Haydn directed. Black and white. 113 minutes. Paramount VHS.

1951 The Great Caruso
Kirsten has a major role in this popular film. She plays Metropolitan Opera soprano Louise Heggar, Caruso's regular stage partner in the film (seemingly modeled on Louise Homer), and she performs with Caruso (Mario Lanza) in several opera scenes. She sings "Numi, Pieta" at a rehearsal of *Aida,* and they appear together on stage in the "La fatale pietra" tomb scene; she plays Mimì to his Rodolfo in a Met production of *La bohème;* and she participates in a kitschy but amusing *Lucia di Lammermoor* sextet as he awaits the birth of his child. See THE GREAT CARUSO.

1955 Colgate Comedy Hour
Kirsten sang an opera aria on this NBC television program. Mannin Ostroff directed. Black and white. 60 minutes. Video at the MTR.

1957 Ed Sullivan Show
Kirsten performs in two scenes from *Madama Butterfly* opposite Mario Del Monaco as Pinkerton. The scenes were excerpts from a Met production restaged for a 1957

Ed Sullivan Show on CBS. Black and white. About 15 minutes. Video at the MTR.

1959/1962 Voice of Firestone

The video *Dorothy Kirsten in Opera & Song* features Kirsten in opera scenes from 1959 and 1962 *Voice of Firestone* telecasts. She is seen as Minnie in an extended scene of the poker game in *La Fanciulla del West,* with Mario Sereni as Jack Rance; she sings "Vissi d'arte" from *Tosca;* she duets with Thomas L. Thomas on "And This Is My Beloved" from *Kismet;* and she partners with Sereni on the song "Romance." Black and white. 23 minutes. VAI VHS.

1978 An Occasion With Dorothy Kirsten

The *Camera Three* CBS Television program devoted a program to the singer and called it *An Occasion With Dorothy Kirsten.* She sings a bit and then talks about her life and career. The program was telecast April 18, 1978. Color. 30 minutes. Video at the MTR.

KISMET
1953 Borodin pastiche operetta

The pastiche operetta *Kismet,* created by Robert Wright and George Forrest, is based on themes by Russian composer ALEXANDER BORODIN, mostly from the opera *Prince Igor.* It tells the story of the witty Arabian poet-beggar Hajj and his success as a sorcerer deceiving a wicked Wazir in Baghdad. In a subplot, the young Caliph woos and wins Hajj's daughter Marsinah. The book, by Charles Lederer and Luther Davis, was based on a 1911 play by Edward Knoblock that had been filmed with Ronald Colman as Hajj. The memorable songs include "A Stranger in Paradise" and "Baubles, Bangles, and Beads." *Kismet* seems to have found a permanent place in the operetta repertory and continues to be revived.

1955 MGM film

American feature film: Vincent Minnelli (director), Charles Lederer and Luther Davis (screenplay), Joseph Ruttenberg (cinematographer), André Previn and Jeff Alexander (music supervisors), Cedric Gibbons and Preston Ames (production designers), Jack Cole (choreographer).

Cast: Howard Keel (Hajj), Ann Blyth (Marsinah), Vic Damone (Caliph), Sebastian Cabot (Wazir), Dolores Gray (Lalume).

Video: MGM-UA VHS. Color. In English. 113 minutes.

1967 ABC Television

American television production: Bob Henry (director), Norman Rosemont (producer), Jack Regas (choreographer).

Cast: José Ferrer (Hajj), Anna Maria Alberghetti (Marsinah), George Chakiris (Caliph), Hans Conreid (Wazir), Barbara Eden (Lalume).

Telecast October 24, 1967, on ABC. Color. In English. 90 minutes.

KLEIBER, CARLOS
German conductor (1930–)

Carlos Kleiber, whose father Erich was also a famous conductor, is one of the best-known orchestra leaders in the field today. He has conducted orchestras at Covent Garden, Edinburgh, and most of the other major European opera houses. His opera productions on video include CARMEN (1979), DIE FLEDERMAUS (1987), OTELLO (1976), and DER ROSENKAVALIER (1979/1994).

1991 Vienna New Year's Day Celebration

Kleiber conducts the Vienna Philharmonic's 150th anniversary celebration with the focus on Viennese operetta. The singers include José Carreras, Plácido Domingo, and Richard Tauber (on film). Color. In German. 60 minutes.

KLEMPERER, OTTO
German conductor (1885–1973)

Otto Klemperer, one of the great visionary conductors of the century, began his career in 1906 in Berlin with the Offenbach operetta *Orphée aux Enfers.* He was soon in demand all over Germany and was the director of the Kroll Theater during the 1920s, where he premiered classics such as Stravinsky's *Oedipus Rex.* His German career ended when the Nazis took over, and he decided to leave for America. He returned to Europe in 1947 to conduct in Budapest, and he helped to raise the opera company there to a high level. He made his debut at Covent Garden in 1961 with *Fidelio.*

1985 Otto Klemperers lang Reise durch sein Zeit

Phil Bregstein's documentary *Otto Klemperer's Long Journey Through His Time* puts the conductor's life in the context of history as he talks about opera and his career. His promotion of modern composers caused him problems in both Nazi Germany and Communist Hungary, but he also had problems in the United States where his passport was withdrawn during the anti-Communist witch hunt era. Made for the German and Austrian TV companies WDR and ORF. Black and white. In German. 90 minutes.

1995 The Art of Conducting: Great Conductors of the Past

An informative video, based on a BBC series, featuring 16 giants of the conducting world, including Klemperer; Sue Knussen directed. Color and black and white. 117 minutes. Teldec VHS.

KNIGHT, FELIX
American tenor (1908–1998)

Felix Knight's stage opera career began after he had finished his film operatic career. He worked first for Hal Roach in Laurel and Hardy versions of light operas. He is Tom-Tom in the 1934 BABES IN TOYLAND, and does most of the singing, and a gypsy singer in the 1936 THE BOHEMIAN GIRL, where he is again the main singer. He made his opera debut in *La traviata* at the Hollywood Bowl in 1935 and won a Metropolitan Opera competition in 1938, but he did not make his Met debut until 1946. He stayed with the company until the arrival of Rudolph Bing. He spent his career after that singing in recitals and nightclubs.

KNOT GARDEN, THE
1970 opera by Tippett

Michael Tippett's *The Knot Garden,* libretto by the composer, focuses on a married couple, Thea and Faber, and their daughter Flora. Mangus, a psychoanalyst, decides to have them act our their problems by portraying characters from Shakespeare's *The Tempest* with himself as Prospero and two gay friends as Ariel and Caliban. It was premiered at Covent Garden in 1970 with Colin Davis conducting.

1986 Opera Factory, London
English stage production: David Freeman (director), Howard Williams (conductor, London Sinfonietta).

Cast: Christine Botes (Thea), Tom McDonnell (Faber), Janis Kelly (Flora), André Cardino (Mangus), Marie Angel (Denise), Nigel Robson (Dov), Omar Ebrahim (Mel).

Telecast in 1986 on Channel 4. Derek Bailey (director). Color. In English. 60 minutes.

KNUSSEN, OLIVER
English composer/conductor (1952–)

Glasgow-born Oliver Knussen, who spent his early musical years experimenting with concert work, became known as an opera composer through his collaborations with American author/illustrator Maurice Sendak. Together they created two of the most popular modern children's operas, HIGGLETY PIGGLETY POP! and WHERE THE WILD THINGS ARE. Knussen has become one of the leading conductors of modern music and a respected advisor to musical festivals.

KODÁLY, ZOLTÁN
Hungarian composer (1882–1967)

Zoltán Kodály, who ranks with Bartók as one of the major modern Hungarian composers, has greatly influenced other Hungarian composers. He is known to most of the rest of the world primarily for his folksy 1926 opera HÁRY JÁNOS; it celebrates the imagination of a bragging veteran whose fantastic adventures reflect the qualities and folk music of his country.

KOLLO, RENÉ
German tenor (1937–)

René Kollo is the grandson of Walter Kollo, the composer who wrote the first operetta about the movies. He was born in Berlin, began his career in operetta, and made his opera debut in Düsseldorf in 1965. He began in light lyric roles and was featured in television films of classic operettas, but he then shifted to heavier roles, including Wagnerian tenor parts. He became a regular at Bayreuth and made his first appearance at the Met in 1976 as Lohengrin. He is also much admired as *Otello* and for his Russian opera roles. His many opera and operetta videos include ARABELLA (1977), ARIADNE AUF NAXOS (1978), THE BARTERED BRIDE (1976), LA BELLE HÉLÈNE (1974), DIE CSÁRDÁSFÜRSTIN (1971), FIDELIO (1978), DIE FRAU OHNE SCHATTEN (1980), GÖTTERDÄMMERUNG (1989), GRÄFIN MARIZA (1973), JULIETTA (1969), DAS LAND DES LÄCHELNS (1973), OBERON (1968), OEDIPUS REX (1973), SIEGFRIED (1989), TANNHÄUSER (1994), TRISTAN UND ISOLDE (1983/1993), WIENER BLUT (1974), and DIE ZAUBERFLÖTE (1975 film). He can also be seen honoring RUDOLF SCHOCK in a 1983 TV gala and singing in a concert at the ARENA DI VERONA in 1988.

KOLLO, WALTER
German composer (1878–1940)

Walter Kollo, who was one of Germany's top music theater composers during the early years of the century, wrote the first operetta about the movies. It was titled FILMZAUBER when it was first staged in Berlin in 1912, and it became *The Girl on the Film* when it went to London and New York in 1913. The story revolves around a film company's efforts to make a movie about Napoleon. Kollo's romantic 1913 operetta WIE EINST IM MAI, which provided the basis for Sigmund Romberg's operetta *Maytime,* is still popular in Germany where it continues to be staged and filmed in its original form. Tenor René Kollo is Walter's grandson and appeared in a Berlin stage production of *Wie einst im Mai* in 1966.

KORJUS, MILIZA
Polish soprano (1902–1980)

Coloratura soprano Miliza Korjus, who starred in two films and was nominated for an Academy Award for her only Hollywood movie, was born in Warsaw of Swedish and Estonian parents. She sang for many years in Berlin, Vienna, Brussels, and Stockholm opera houses but is mainly remembered today for her starring role in *The Great Waltz*. MGM publicists promoted her with the slogan "Miliza Korjus rhymes with gorgeous." It worked; she received considerable acclaim and was nominated for Best Supporting Actress. Not long afterwards, she had an automobile accident and moved to Mexico where she made one more film. She returned to the United States for a concert in Carnegie Hall in 1944 and then moved to Los Angeles. Her fine coloratura voice can also be enjoyed on recordings.

1938 The Great Waltz
Korjus plays Carla Donner, a singer with the Imperial Opera who falls in love with JOHANN STRAUSS (Fernand Gravet). He loves her as well, but he marries sweetheart Poldi (Luise Rainer). Korjus sings his waltzes, gets him a publisher, and inspires him to write the operetta *Die Fledermaus*. Most of the singing in the film is by Korjus, and critics felt it was done well. The film was a big success. Julien Duvivier directed for MGM. Black and white. In English. 100 minutes.

1942 Caballería del Imperio
Caballería del Imperio (Chivalry of the Empire) is a Mexican film musical that begins with Korjus on stage in Vienna in 1864 singing with Johann Strauss conducting. She is hired to sing Mexico and arrives during the era of Emperor Maximilian and Empress Carlotta. When bandits invade a restaurant where she is dining, she tells them she is the ambassador from Strauss to Mexico. They believe her after she sings, even though it's Bellini's "Casta diva" rather than Strauss. The film also features Mexican tenor Pedro Vargas. Miguel Contreras Torres directed. Black and white. In Spanish. 139 minutes. Opera Dubs VHS.

KORNGOLD, ERICH WOLFGANG
Moravian-born American composer (1897–1957)

Erich Wolfgang Korngold was a major opera composer in Europe before he went to Hollywood to create what he called "operas without singing," his poetic description of film scores. There are certainly few opera scores more memorable than those he composed for *The Adventures of Robin Hood* or *The Sea Hawk*. He wrote an IMAGINARY OPERA called *Romeo and Juliet* for the 1936 Hollywood film GIVE US THIS NIGHT, and he worked on the 1956 RICHARD WAGNER biopic *Magic Fire*. His most successful opera on stage was the symbolist DIE TOTE STADT (1920), which has come back into fashion and is on video.

2003 Erich Wolfgang Korngold: The Adventures of a Wunderkind
Barrie Gavin's 90-minute documentary about the composer, narrated by Samuel West, is the central section of this DVD with interesting interviews with friends and colleagues. There is also 45 minutes of performances of Korngold compositions. Black and white & color. 144 minutes. Arthaus DVD.

KOSHETZ, MARINA
Russian-born American soprano (1912–2001)

Marina Koshetz, who followed her mother Nina onto the opera stage and into movies, studied music in France. She first appeared in movies during the 1930s using the name Marina Schubert (her father's name) including *All the King's Horses* (with Mary Ellis), *Millions in the Air*, and *Little Women*. She began to sing with the San Francisco Opera in 1941 (Tatiana in *Eugene Onegin*), made her debut at the Met in *The Fair at Sorochinsk*, and sang opera at the Hollywood Bowl in 1945. She appeared opposite Lauritz Melchior in two films, and she played an opera singer opposite Mario Lanza in THE GREAT CARUSO. She had small singing roles in a number of films during the 1950s and 1960s, including *On the Riviera*, *The Singing Nun*, and *The Busy Body*.

1946 Two Sisters From Boston
Koshetz plays an innkeeper's daughter in this turn-of-the-century New York musical starring Met tenor Lauritz Melchior and Kathryn Grayson. See TWO SISTERS FROM BOSTON.

1948 Luxury Liner
Koshetz partners with Lauritz Melchior in a duet from *Aida* in this delightful MGM shipboard musical. Jane Powell stars as the stowaway daughter of the captain; Richard Whorf directed. Color. 98 minutes. MGM-UA VHS.

KOSHETZ, NINA
Ukrainian-born American soprano (1891–1965)

Nina Koshetz, the Kiev-born daughter of a Bolshoi tenor, made her debut in 1913 with the Zimin Opera Company. She performed in Russia until 1920 and then went to Chicago to sing in the premiere of Prokofiev's *The Love for Three Oranges*. She continued to sing around the world until 1940 when she retired to Hollywood and opened a restaurant. She also worked in movies, starting in 1926 in France with the film *Casanova*. Her daughter Marina, born in Moscow, was also an opera singer and appeared in films.

1926 Casanova
Nina Kochitz (her name on the film credits) plays Countess Vorontzvo in this epic French film version of the story of the great lover. Casanova is played by Ivan Mojoukine, and the cast includes many other Russian expatriates. Alexandre Volkoff directed. Black and white. In French. 110 minutes.

1934 Enter Madame
Koshetz sings arias from *Tosca* and *Cavalleria rusticana* for Elissa Landi in this charming film about a glamorous opera singer who marries millionaire Cary Grant. See ENTER MADAME.

1938 Algiers
Koshetz plays Tania in this American remake of the French film *Pépé le Moko*. Charles Boyer and Hedy Lamar are the stars; John Cromwell directed. Black and white. 95 minutes.

1939 Wife, Husband and Friend
Koshetz provides the voice for Binnie Barnes, who plays an opera diva, in this film of James Cain's story *Career in C Major*. Warner Baxter and Loretta Young star as would-be opera singers. See WIFE, HUSBAND AND FRIEND.

1944 Our Hearts Were Young and Gay
Koshetz plays an old-style grand opera diva in this fine comedy directed by Lewis Allen. The film is based on a book by two women who had enjoyed themselves in 1920s Paris and wrote about the life that late they led. Paramount. Black and white. 81 minutes.

1944 Summer Storm
Koshetz is a singer in 1912 provincial Russia in this Chekhov story about a judge who falls for a loose-living lady. George Sanders and Linda Darnell star; Douglas Sirk directed. Black and white. 106 minutes.

1947 The Chase
Koshetz has a supporting role to Michèle Morgan and Robert Cummings in this film noir set in Cuba and based on a Cornell Woolrich novel. Arthur Ripley directed. Black and white. 86 minutes.

1950 It's a Small World
Koshetz has a small role in this odd Hollywood film about smallness. Midget Paul Dale, who stars, has a difficult time until he gets adjusted to his small size. William Castle directed. Black and white. 68 minutes.

1952 Captain Pirate
Koshetz has a supporting role in this pirate movie starring Louis Hayward and Patricia Medina. Ralph Murphy directed for Columbia. Black and white. 85 minutes.

1956 Hot Blood
Koshetz's last film, directed by Nicholas Ray, stars Jane Russell and Cornel Wilde in a story about gypsies. Columbia. Black and white. 85 minutes.

KOWALSKI, JOCHEN
German countertenor (1954–)

Jochen Kowalski, who made his debut with the Komische Opera while still a student, has become one of the most popular countertenors in the world. He sings both modern and baroque opera, but he is especially noted for his roles in Gluck and Handel operas, most famously as Orfeo in the Berlin and London ORFEO ED EURIDICE (1991). His other operas on video include BELSHAZZAR (1985), DIE FLEDERMAUS (1990), GIUSTINO (1985), THE HAUNTED MANOR (1986), and MITRIDATE, RE DI PONTO (1991).

1992 The Reluctant Angels
Kowalski sings famous arias composed for castratos in Michael Bartlett's documentary. The film journeys from Venice to Dresden as it explores the castrato era. Color. English narration. 56 minutes. Opera Dubs VHS.

KRÁSA, HANS
German composer (1899–1944)

Hans Krása was born in Prague, worked all over Europe, and died in Auschwitz. His first opera, based on a story by Dostoyevsky, was composed in 1933. He is remembered today primarily for his simple but highly effective children's opera BRUNDIBÁR. It was created in 1938 for the children at a Prague orphanage, and he and the Jewish children took it with them when they were deported to the concentration camp at Terezin. It was staged there in

1943 for the International Red Cross as a show piece for a Nazi propaganda film. It continues to be revived.

KRAUS, ALFREDO
Spanish tenor (1927–1999)

Lyric tenor Alfredo Kraus, known in Spain for performances in zarzuelas was well as operas, was a singer's singer, a *tenore di grazia*. He made his debut in Cairo in 1956 and then rose to prominence in Italy and Spain, singing with MARIA CALLAS in 1958 (the fabled Lisbon *La traviata*) and with Joan Sutherland in 1959 in *Lucia di Lammermoor*. He can be seen in many operatic films and videos, including a splendid performance in a Spanish film as the 19th-century Navarese tenor JULIÁN GAYARRE. He has taken part in filmed concerts in New York (1983 for the METROPOLITAN OPERA/1996 for James Levine), ZURICH (1986 for the Operhaus), PARIS (1989 for the Bastille Opera), Moscow (1989/BOLSHOI OPERA), Madrid (1991/OPERA STARS IN CONCERT), and Seville (1991/GALA LIRICA). He often sang the title role in FAUST (1973/1979/1987) and was a notable Edgardo for June Sutherland in a Metropolitan Opera production of LUCIA DI LAMMERMOOR (1982) and for JUNE ANDERSON (1989) in a Covent Garden production. There are also videos of him in the operas LES CONTES D'HOFFMANN (1988), DON PASQUALE (1979), LA FAVORITA (1971), LA FILLE DU RÉGIMENT (1984), RIGOLETTO (1987), ROMÉO ET JULIETTE (1985), and WERTHER (1987/1991) and the zarzuelas DOÑA FRANCISQUITA (1988) and MARINA (1980/1987).

1958 El vagabundo y la estrella
Kraus plays an opera singer opposite dancer Aña Esmeralda in the Spanish musical film *El vagabundo y la estrella* (The Vagabond and the Star). He sings arias from *Lucia di Lammermoor, I puritani, La bohème, Il trovatore,* and *Serse.* Mateo Cano and Jose Luis Merino directed. Color. In Spanish. 80 minutes. Bel Canto/Opera Dubs/Lyric VHS.

KRAUSE, TOM
Finnish baritone (1934–)

Finland's Tom Krause began his opera career in Berlin as Escamillo in *Carmen* and has been popular in the role ever since. He made his first appearance at the Metropolitan Opera in 1967 as Almaviva in *Le nozze di Figaro.* Krause now sings in a wide range of modern and traditional operas in German and Italian in opera houses around the world. See CARMEN (1972/1983 films), FAUST (1975), DER FREISCHÜTZ (1968), LE NOZZE DI FIGARO (1968), OEDIPUS REX (1973), and THE PALACE (1995).

KRUSCENISKI, SALOMEA
Ukrainian soprano (1872–1952)

Salomea Krusceniski (or Kruszelnicka) was one of the great singing actresses of the operatic stage and an important interpreter of the roles of Butterfly, Salome, and Aida. She made her debut in Lvov in 1892 and her first appearance in the West in Trieste in 1896 in *La forza del destino.* As an outspoken Ukrainian patriot, she became unpopular in Russia, so after 1903 she sang mostly in Italy. One of her most famous performances was as Madama Butterfly in the successful revised production of Puccini's opera in Brescia in May 1904 after its failure at La Scala in February. She was the first to sing Salome and Elektra at La Scala, sang splendidly with Caruso, and remained a major star until her retirement from opera in 1925. In 1927 she made a patriotic tour of the United States singing to Ukrainian audiences.

1982 The Return of Butterfly
Elena Safonova stars as Salomea Krusceniski in V*ozrast-chenié Batterflai,* a Soviet Ukrainian film about the soprano. The film shows her life and studies and has many opera scenes, including her triumph in *Madama Butterfly.* See THE RETURN OF BUTTERFLY.

KUBRICK, STANLEY
American film director (1928–2000)

Stanley Kubrick, who began making movies in 1951, won international acclaim in 1957 for the antiwar film *The Paths of Glory.* Three of his films have notable operatic and musical interest: *Barry Lyndon* (1975) uses instrumental operatic music in keeping with the period of the film, including the Cavatina from Paisiello's *The Barber of Seville* and the March from Mozart's *Idomeneo.* There is also music by Bach, Handel, Schubert, and Vivaldi. His film *2001: A Space Odyssey* (1968) is closely identified with music by Richard Strauss through its evocative use of "Thus Spake Zarathustra," but it also has music by Johann Strauss and György Ligeti. *A Clockwork Orange* (1971) succeeds in making Beethoven's music an integral part of the story.

KULLMAN, CHARLES
American tenor (1903–1983)

Charles Kullman, who sang with the Metropolitan Opera for 25 seasons in a wide variety of roles, was noted for his pleasing stage personality. After studies at Yale and Juilliard, he made his debut as Pinkerton in 1929 with the American Opera Company. Afterwards he went to Europe and built his career in Berlin, Vienna, Salzburg, and Covent Garden. He returned to the United States and began his long Metropolitan career in 1935 by singing in

Faust. He can be seen on video in two Hollywood feature films and as Eisenstein in a famous 1953 Metropolitan Opera production of DIE FLEDERMAUS.

1938 The Goldwyn Follies
Kullman is seen on stage as Alfredo in *La traviata* performing "Libiamo" and "Sempre libera" with Helen Jepson as Violetta. Film producer Adolphe Menjou, who is seeking an opera singer for a film, sees the performance and hires Jepson, but not Kullman. *The Goldwyn Follies* is a musical with songs by George Gershwin. George Marshall directed. Color. 115 minutes.

1947 Song of Scheherazade
Kullman plays Dr. Klin, the physician of a Russian navy ship on which Lt. Nikolai Rimsky-Korsakov is traveling in 1865. It is one of the main roles in the film, and he performs quite a lot of Rimsky-Korsakov music, including even the soprano aria "Hymn to the Sun" from *The Golden Cockerel.* Jean-Pierre Aumont plays the composer in this Universal film that is poor biography but enjoyable kitsch. Walter Reisch directed, with musical direction from Miklos Rozsa. Color. 107 minutes.

KÜNNEKE, EDWARD
German composer (1885–1953)

Edward Künneke was one of the German operetta composers whose work was so popular in London and New York during the 1920s. His most successful operetta was the 1921 DER VETTER AUS DINGSDA (The Cousin From Nowhere), which was staged in both London and New York and filmed twice. Also popular were *Marriage in Crisis* (1921) and *Casino Girls* (1923). He wrote the Offenbach-esque *The Love Song* (1926) for the Schuberts in New York, and he had a hit in London with *The Song of the Sea* (1928). Künneke composed 25 operettas, and the best bear comparison with Lehár.

1960 Eduard Künneke Tribute
Hans Homeberg produced this German television tribute to the composer on what would have been his 75th birthday. It features highlights from his career, and there are interviews with Hans Carste, Willy Stech, Heinz Hentsche, and his singer-daughter Evelyn Künneke. Black and white. In German. 40 minutes.

KUPFER, HARRY
German opera director (1935–)

The innovative German stage director Harry Kupfer made his debut with the opera *Rusalka* in 1958, became chief director of Dresden State Opera in 1972, and headed the Komische Oper in Berlin for 21 years until 2002. His highly original interpretation of *Der Fliegende Holländer* at Bayreuth in 1978 made him world famous, and his high-tech production of the *Ring* cycle in 1991 aroused even more interest. His *Elektra* for the Welsh National Opera in 1978 was a revelation to British critics, as was his ORFEO ED EURIDICE at Covent Garden in 1991. Kupfer was the spiritual heir of Walter Felsenstein for radical productions, many of which are on video. See BELSHAZZAR (1985), ELEKTRA (1989), DIE ENTFÜHRUNG AUS DEM SERAIL (1976), DER FLIEGENDE HOLLÄNDER (1985), GIUSTINO (1985), GÖTTERDÄMMERUNG (1992), THE LEGEND OF THE INVISIBLE CITY OF KITEZH (1995), PARSIFAL (1992), DAS RHEINGOLD (1991), SALOME (1994), SIEGFRIED (1992), DIE SOLDATEN (1988), THE TALE OF TSAR SALTAN (1978), and DIE WALKÜRE (1991).

1987 Harry Kupfer Rehearses *Don Giovanni*
Documentary showing Harry Kupfer staging a production of *Don Giovanni*. Rainer Milzkott directed it for SFB TV. Color. In German. 44 minutes.

1989 Der musik Theater macher Harry Kupfer
Music Theater Creator Harry Kupfer is a German TV documentary about the achievements of Kupfer. It was filmed by Lothar Spree for ZDF and ORF. Color. In German. 80 minutes.

1989 Berlin: Capitale de l'Opéra
Berlin: Opera Capital, a French TV documentary about opera in Berlin, includes scenes of Kupfer rehearsing *Les contes d'Hoffmann*. Claire Newman directed for FR 3. Color. In French. 60 minutes.

KURENKO, MARIA
Russian-born American soprano/contralto (1890–1980)

Maria Kurenko, who was born in Siberia, studied in Moscow and sang at the Bolshoi before coming to the United States in 1925. She sang opera in Chicago, Los Angeles, and New York, including *A Life for the Tsar,* but she mostly gave recitals and concerts. She continued to record into the 1950s and is probably best known for her many records of Rachmaninoff songs. She made an early sound film for Metro Movietone in 1929.

1929 Metro Movietone
Kurenko sings two arias on a short sound film she made for the Metro Movietone series in 1928, "Anges purs" from *Faust* and "The Last Rose of Summer" from *Martha*. Black and white. About 8 minutes.

L

LABYRINTH
1963 TV opera by Menotti

A young couple on their honeymoon get lost trying to find the key to their room in a grand hotel. A hurrying bellboy, a mysterious spy, an old chess player, and other strange people are no help. When the couple open doors, they see strange things. A traditional opera is staged behind one door, an astronaut floats through space behind another, a train full of water is behind a third. GIAN CARLO MENOTTI's enigmatic television opera *Labyrinth: An Operatic Riddle,* libretto by the composer, premiered on NBC Opera Theatre. It was not well received and was not repeated, despite its interesting special effects.

1963 NBC Opera Theatre
American TV production: Gian Carlo Menotti (director), Samuel Chotzinoff (producer), Herbert Grossman (conductor, Symphony of the Air Orchestra), Warren Clymer (set designer).
Cast: Judith Raskin (Bride), John Reardon (Groom), Elaine Bonazzi (Spy), Robert White (Old Chess Player), Beverly Wolff (Executive Director), Leon Lishner (Desk Clerk/Death).
Video at the MTR. Telecast March 3, 1963, on NBC. Kirk Browning (director). Black and white. In English. 45 minutes.

LADERMAN, EZRA
American composer (1924–)

Ezra Laderman has written four screen operas, three for television and one about a movie star. The most famous is THE TRIALS OF GALILEO, an examination of the life and ideas of the Italian astronomer, televised in 1967 and later staged as *Galileo Galilei.* The 1971 TV opera AND DAVID WEPT is the story of the biblical David and Bathsheba. The 1973 TV opera THE QUESTIONS OF ABRAHAM concerns the Jewish patriarch and his search for answers. Laderman's opera *Marilyn,* about the life and death of MARILYN MONROE, was staged in 1984 at the New York City Opera.

LADY MACBETH OF THE MTSENSK DISTRICT
1934 opera by Shostakovich

DIMITRI SHOSTAKOVICH's opera *Lady Macbeth of the Mtsensk District,* libretto by the composer and Alexander Preis, is based on a famous Russian story by Nikolai Leskov. Katerina Ismailova is a bored housewife who has an affair with her servant Sergei. When her father-in-law Boris discovers this, she poisons him. Finally she and Sergei murder her husband Zinovy. They are exiled to Siberia where Sergei seduces another woman; Katerina drowns her rival and herself. The opera premiered in Leningrad in 1934 and was considered a success until Stalin went to see it in December 1935 and disapproved. *Pravda* published a vicious attack on the opera in January 1936, and the opera was immediately withdrawn. It did not surface again until after Stalin's death in 1962, when Shostakovich presented a revised version as *Katerina Ismailova.* This was filmed with Russian soprano Galina Vishnevskaya as Katerina. In the post-Soviet era, the original opera has been revived, filmed, and recorded. Vishnevskaya, who discusses the two versions in her autobiography, sings and acts in the film of the revised version, while her recorded voice is used in the film of the original version. Both films are well made but both abridge the 150-minute stage opera score by nearly a third.

1966 Katerina Ismailova
Soviet feature film: Mikhail Shapiro (director), Konstantin Simeonov (conductor, Shevchenko Opera and Ballet Theater Orchestra of Kiev), Rostislav Davydov (cinematographer).
Cast: Galina Vishnevskaya (Katerina Ismailova), V. Trepyak (Sergei, sung by Artem Inozemtsev), Alexandrovich Sokolov (Boris, sung by A. Verdernikov), V. Reka (Zinovy, sung by T. Gavirolova).
Pioneer LD. Color. In Russian. 116 minutes.
Comment: Abridged by about 35 minutes but superbly photographed in natural settings.

***1999 Lady Macbeth of Mtsensk
Czech feature film: Peter Weigl (director), Mstislav Rostropovich (conductor, London Philharmonic Orchestra and Ambrosian Opera Chorus).
Cast: Markéta Hrubeÿová (Katerina Ismailova, sung by Galina Vishnevskaya), Michal Dlouhý (Sergei, sung by Nicolai Gedda), Petr Hanicinec (Boris, sung by Dimiter Petkov), Václav Necká (Zinovy, sung by Werner Krenn), Robert Tear (Peasant).
Image Entertainment DVD. Color. In Russian with English subtitles. 100 minutes.

Comment: Weigl uses the 1978 EMI recording of the opera as soundtrack with Czech actors playing the characters on screen. Abridged by about 50 minutes.

Related films

1962 Siberian Lady Macbeth
Polish director Andrzej Wajda's film is based on the source Leskov story and uses the Shostakovich music as its score. Olivera Markovic plays Katerina and Lujba Tadic is Sergei. Wajda shot the film on locations in Yugoslavia. Black and white. In Polish. 94 minutes.

1994 Katia Ismailova
Valeri Todorovski's Russian film, based on a modernized version of the Leskov story, stars Ingeborga Dapkounaite as Katerina. Shostakovich's music is not used. Color. In Russian. 88 minutes.

2000 Intimacy
Music from *Katerina Ismailova* is featured in the Anglo-French film *Intimacy,* about a hyper-intense love affair. Mark Rylance and Kerry Fox are the lovers; Patrice Cheréau directed. The music is performed by the Prague Symphony Orchestra Color. In English and French. 120 minutes.

LAKMÉ
1883 opera by Delibes

British Airways promoted the "Flower Duet" ("Dôme épais") from LÉO DELIBES's opera in commercials seen worldwide, and this probably helped make *Lakmé* a popular favorite once again, although its showy "Bell Song" ("Ou va la jeune Hindoue") has never fallen from favor. This has always been Delibes's best-known opera, rivaling the ballets *Coppélia* and *Sylvia* in popularity. Far

Katerina Ismailova (1966): Galina Vishnevskaya in the Soviet film of a revised and retitled *Lady Macbeth of the Mtsensk District.*

East–themed operas were popular in France at the end of the 19th century, so librettist Edmond Gondinet and Philippe Gille couldn't go wrong in adapting Pierre Loti's novel *Rarahu*. It is set in 19th-century India. Lakmé, daughter of Brahmin priest Nilakantha, falls in love with British army officer Gérald and it leads to her doom. Coloratura sopranos such as Lily Pons have been particularly fond of the "Bell Song."

1976 Australian Opera

Australian stage production: Norman Ayrton (director), Richard Bonynge (conductor, Elizabethan Sydney Orchestra), Desmond Digby (set designer).

Cast: Joan Sutherland (Lakmé), Huguette Tourangeau (Mallika), Clifford Grant (Nilakantha), Henri Wilden (Gérald), John Pringle (Frédéric).

Video: Home Vision VHS. John Charles (director). Taped August 18, 1976. Color. In French. 153 minutes.

Comment: Sutherland is not very convincing as a demure Indian temple priestess, but she sings so well it really doesn't matter.

Early/related films

1906 Lakmé: Les Stances

Early British sound film of a scene from the opera. The music was synchronized on a phonograph when the film was shown. Black and white. About 3 minutes.

1906 Chronophone film

An excerpt from *Lakmé* was featured on this French sound film made by Leon Gaumont with the Chronophone system. It may be identical with the English film above. Black and white. About 3 minutes.

1933 A Brahmin's Daughter

American highlights version of the opera directed by Howard Highness for Kindle–De Valley. Black and white. In English. 22 minutes.

1935 I Dream Too Much

Lily Pons made her film debut in this RKO picture playing a rising opera singer and takes the opportunity to sing her signature "Bell Song." John Cromwell directed. Black and white. 85 minutes. Turner VHS.

1937 Love and Hisses

French actress Simone Simon, playing a French singer in this American film, performs the "Bell Song" under the direction of Sidney Lanfield. Black and white. 84 minutes.

1947 It Happened in Brooklyn

Kathryn Grayson sings the "Bell Song" in this story about Frank Sinatra and a group of Brooklynites trying to break into show business. Richard Whorf directed. Black and white. 105 minutes.

1947 Carnegie Hall

Lily Pons sings the "Bell Song" on stage at Carnegie Hall in this feature film, a fictional framework for a series of concert numbers by classical music stars. See CARNEGIE HALL.

1976 Joan Sutherland Making *Lakmé*

This documentary about the Australian Opera production of *Lakmé* with Joan Sutherland follows it from initial concept through design, casting, costuming, and rehearsal to opening night. Sutherland is shown rehearsing the "Bell Song" and the "Flower Duet" with Huguette Tourangeau, while conductor Richard Bonynge supervises. Color. In English. 60 minutes. Mastervision VHS.

1987 Someone to Watch Over Me

Ridley Scott's film about a cop (Tom Berenger) who becomes involved with the woman he is guarding (Lorraine Bracco) features the "Flower Duet" from *Lakmé* on the soundtrack. Mady Mesplé and Danielle Millet are the singers with Alain Lombard conducting the Paris Opéra-Comique Orchestra. Color. 106 minutes.

1987 I've Heard the Mermaid Singing

The "Flower Duet" is featured on the soundtrack of this sexually ambiguous Canadian film about a young innocent and lesbian activity in a trendy art gallery. Patricia Rozema directed. Color. 83 minutes.

1987 Five Corners

Joan Sutherland sings the "Bell Song" on the soundtrack of this film about Jodie Foster and her problem boyfriend. Richard Bonynge conducts the Monte Carlo Opera Orchestra. Tony Bill directed the film. Color. 94 minutes.

1993 The Hunger

The highlight of Tony Scott's modern vampire movie features beautiful vampire Catherine Deneuve in bed with Susan Sarandon. The music on the soundtrack is, of course, the "Flower Duet." Color. 97 minutes.

1993 True Romance

The "Flower Duet" is featured on the soundtrack of this Tony Scott film, which has a screenplay by Quentin Tarantino. The odd couple at the center of the film somehow live happily ever after. Color. 119 minutes.

1993 Carlito's Way
Brian DePalma's film about a criminal trying to go straight features Joan Sutherland on the soundtrack in an excerpt from *Lakmé*. Al Pacino and Sean Penn are the film's stars. Color. 144 minutes.

1995 The American President
The "Flower Duet," sung by Mady Mesplé and Danielle Millet, is featured on the soundtrack of this film about a love affair between a widowed president (Michael Douglas) and a journalist (Annette Bening). Alain Lombard conducts the Orchestre du Théâtre National de l'Opéra-Comique in the recording. Color. 98 minutes.

1998 The Phantom of the Opera
Dario Argento's horrific version of *The Phantom of the Opera*, with Julian Sands as the Phantom, features the "Bell Song" from *Lakmé*. Ennio Morricone conducts. Color. 99 minutes.

LAMAC, KAREL
Czech film director (1897–1952)

Prague-born Karel (aka Karl) Lamac wrote, directed, and sometimes acted in about 265 films in five languages in six countries (Czechoslovakia, Austria, Hungary, Germany, France, and England), and many of them have opera and operetta content. He was married to Hitchcock's *Blackmail* star Anny Ondra (she became famous through his films), and they were major contributors to the growth of Czech cinema. Although never highly ranked by cineastes, and mostly ignored in film histories, Lamac's movies are well-made, entertaining, and important in the history of opera and operetta on film. See LA FILLE DU RÉGIMENT (1933), DIE FLEDERMAUS (1931), FRASQUITA (1934), JAN KIEPURA (1935), DIE LANDSTREICHER (1937), MAM'ZELLE NITOUCHE (1931), POLENBLUT (1934), LE POSTILLON DE LONJUMEAU (1936), IM WEISSEN RÖSSL (1935), WO DIE LERCHE SINGT (1936).

LAND DES LÄCHELNS, DAS
1929 operetta by Lehár

FRANZ LEHÁR's *Das Land des Lächelns* (The Land of Smiles) is about a Viennese woman who marries a Chinese prince and goes to live with him in Peking. She finds life there not as she had imagined and wants to return home, but she is prevented until the intervention of an old suitor. The operetta was made famous by Richard Tauber, who starred as Prince Sou-Chong in productions in Vienna, London, and New York. In London the operetta was titled *The Land of Smiles;* in New York it was called *Yours Is My Heart*, after its hit song "Dein ist mein ganzes Herz." The libretto, by Ludwig Herzer and Fritz Lohner, is based on an earlier Lehár operetta.

1930 Tauber film
German feature film: Max Reichmann (director); Leo Lasko, Anton Kuh, and Curt J. Braun (screenplay); Reimar Kuntze (cinematographer); Richard Tauber Tonfilm (production).
Cast: Richard Tauber (Prince Sou-Chong), Mary Losseff (Lisa), Hans Mierendorff, Bruno Kastner, Karl Platen, Margit Suchy, Max Schreck.
Video: Premiere Opera/Opera Dubs VHS. Black and white. In German. 89 minutes.
Comment: Tauber's company produced this film only a year after its stage premiere in Berlin in 1929.

1952 Berolina film
German feature film: Hans Deppe (director), Axel Eggebrecht and Hubert Marischka (screenplay), Kurt Schulz (cinematographer), Alois Melichar (music director), Berolina Film (production).
Cast: Jan Kiepura (Prince Sou), Marta Eggerth (Lisa Licht), Paul Hörbiger (Prof. Licht),Walter Muller (Gustl), Karin Dassel (Mi).
Video: Opera Dubs/Lyric VHS. Black and white. In German. 114 minutes.
Comment: The plot is somewhat altered. Sou is now a Siamese prince who meets a Viennese operetta soprano and marries her. They return to Bangkok, where some of the film was shot, for their Easterner-married-to-Westerner problems.

1973 Rabenalt film
German TV film: Arthur Maria Rabenalt (director), Wolfgang Ebert (conductor, Stuttgart Radio-Television Orchestra), Herta Pischinger-Hareiter (set designer), Unitel (production).
Cast: René Kollo (Sou-Chong), Birgit Pitsch-Sarata (Lisa), Dagmar Koller (Mi), Heinz Zednik (Count Gustav), Fred Liewehr (Count Lichtenfels), South Korean State Ballet (dancers).
Telecast on ZDF German Television on September 28, 1973. Shot in 35mm. Color. In German. 98 minutes.

1989 Seefestspiele Mörbisch
Austrian stage production: Robert Herzl (director), Uwe Theimer (conductor, Seefestspiele Mörbisch Chorus and Orchestra).
Cast: Otoniel Gonzaga (Sou-Chong), Ulrike Steinsky (Lisa), Elisabeth Kales (Mi), Franz Waechter (Count Gustav).
Video: ORF VHS. Sylvia Dönch (director). Color. In German. 120 minutes.

Comment: Opulent large-scale outdoor Seefestspiele Mörbisch production with a formidable cast of Chinese dancers.

1992 Il paese del sorriso

Italian TV studio production: Sandro Massimini (director/producer), Roberto Negri (pianist), Sandro Corelli (choreographer).

Cast: Sandro Massimini, Daniel Mazzucato, Max René Cosotti.

Video: Pierluigi Pagano (director). Color. In Italian. About 19 minutes. Ricordi (Italy) VHS.

Comment: Highlights of the operetta sung in Italian on the TV series *Operette, che Passione!* Includes songs "Chi nella nostra vita accese amor," "Duetto del tè," and "Tu che m'hai preso il cuor."

LAND OF SMILES, THE

See *Land des Lächelns, Das.*

LANDSTREICHER, DIE

1899 operetta by Ziehrer

Die Landstreicher (The Vagabonds) is Austrian composer KARL MICHAEL ZIEHRER's most popular operetta. It tells the story of a resourceful vagabond team, husband (August) and wife (Bertha), who find a diamond necklace and a large bank note. Being clever scam artists, they find many ways to take advantage of their unexpected fortune. The operetta, libretto by Leopold Krenn and Carl Lindau, went to Broadway in 1901 with the title *The Strollers.*

1937 Lamac film

German feature film: Karel Lamac (director), Geza von Cziffra (screenplay), Edgar Ziesemer (cinematographer), Paul Hühn (music director), Aco Film (production).

Cast: Paul Hörbiger (August), Lucie Englisch (Bertha), Erika Drusovich, Rudolf Carl, Rudolf Platte, Gretl Theimer.

Black and white. In German. 89 minutes.

LAND WITHOUT MUSIC

1936 film with light opera content

In a bankrupt Ruritanian country, the ruling Princess Regent (Diane Napier) bans music with the hope that its obsessively musical people will concentrate on making money. Opera tenor Mario Carlini (Richard Tauber), American newspaper reporter Jonah J. Whistler (Jimmy Durante), and Whistler's daughter (June Clyde) lead a revolution so the people can get their music back. Tauber gets to sing some pleasant light opera tunes by Oscar

Straus and wins the hand of the princess (not surprising, she's played by his wife). Rudolph Bernauer, Marian Dix, and L. DuGarde Peach wrote the screenplay; John W. Boyle was cinematographer; and Walter Ford directed for Capitol Films. Shown in America as *Forbidden Music.* Black and white. 80 minutes. Bel Canto Society VHS.

LANG, FRITZ

German film director (1890–1976)

Fritz Lang, who made notable films in Germany, France, and the United States, created an epic movie version of *Die Nibelungen* with a wonderful sequence of Siegfried vs. the Dragon, but he did not use Wagner's music. He did, however, feature Wagner in his 1953 U.S. film *The Blue Gardenia,* where Isolde's death music signals a crime of passion. See DER RING DES NIBELUNGEN (1924 film) and TRISTAN UND ISOLDE (1953 film).

LANGRIDGE, PHILIP

English tenor (1939–)

Philip Langridge made his debut at Glyndebourne in 1964 in a minor role but afterwards sang there as Florestan, Don Ottavio, Tito, and Idomeneo. He has also been a regular at the English National Opera and Covent Garden while singing at other European opera houses. He has won particular acclaim for his performances in modern operas by Berg, Birtwistle, Britten, Janáček, Stravinsky, and Tippett, many of which are on video. See BILLY BUDD (1988/1997), LES BORÉADES (1987), LA CLEMENZA DI TITO (1991), FROM THE HOUSE OF THE DEAD (1992), IDOMENEO (1983), JENŮFA (1989), THE MIDSUMMER MARRIAGE (1984), OBERON (1986), OEDIPUS REX (1992), PETER GRIMES (1994), THE SECOND MRS. KONG (1995), THE TURN OF THE SCREW (1982), and WOZZECK (1987).

LANTZ, WALTER

Animated film producer (1900–1994)

Walter Lantz, who created such popular cartoon characters as Woody Woodpecker and Andy Panda, received an Academy Award in 1979 in recognition of his contributions. Several of his films use classical music from Rossini to Chopin to Suppé.

1944 The Barber of Seville

This Woody Woodpecker cartoon, one of the great screwball cartoons, is built around the overture to *The Barber of Seville.* Woody substitutes for barber Figaro and sings the "Largo al factotum" while he gives bizarre shaves and haircuts. Lantz produced and James Culhane directed. Color. 7 minutes.

1947 Overture to William Tell
This Walter Lantz *Musical Miniature,* based on the overture to the Rossini opera *William Tell,* features the character Wally Walrus. Dick Lundy directed. Color. 7 minutes.

LANZA, MARIO
American tenor (1921–1959)

Mario Lanza does not get an entry in standard opera reference books such as *The New Grove Dictionary of Opera* but he should. His influence was important, and many of today's top tenors, including José Carreras and Plácido Domingo, have commented on the effect he had on their careers. As much as any singer, Lanza helped popularize opera with the wider public. *The Great Caruso* may not be historically accurate or remarkable cinematically, but it is still the most popular opera film ever made. Lanza, born Alfred Arnold Coccozza in Philadelphia, auditioned for Serge Koussevitzky in 1942, and this led to a scholarship and an appearance at Tanglewood in Nicolai's *Die lustigen Weiber von Windsor.* His film career began in 1949 at MGM with *That Midnight Kiss,* where he played a truck driver who becomes an opera singer. His best film is the 1951 *The Great Caruso,* in which he performs opposite opera singers in a romantic biography of his role model. He sang in only one film actually based on an opera or operetta, but he does not appear on screen in the 1954 THE STUDENT PRINCE, although his voice alone made it a success. Personality, alcohol, barbiturate problems, obesity, and perhaps the Mafia helped end his brief career. For the record, Lanza did perform opera on stage; he sang Pinkerton in *Madama Butterfly* with the New Orleans Opera. His popularity on disc and video remains strong; 50 million copies of his records have been sold, and Philadelphia has named a park in his honor.

1949 That Midnight Kiss
Lanza stars opposite Kathryn Grayson in his film debut and sings arias from *Aida, L'elisir d'amore,* and *Cavalleria rusticana.* He's a truck driver, she's an heiress who wants to be an opera singer, they fall in love. The film launched his career into high gear. See THAT MIDNIGHT KISS.

1950 The Toast of New Orleans
Lanza is a Louisiana fisherman who becomes an opera star with help from Kathryn Grayson in this film set in turn-of-the-century New Orleans. There is music from *L'Africaine, Don Giovanni, Linda di Chamounix, Madama Butterfly, Martha, Mignon,* and *La traviata.* See THE TOAST OF NEW ORLEANS.

1951 The Great Caruso
Lanza plays Enrico Caruso in the most popular opera film ever made and sings on stage in operas with Dorothy Kirstein and other opera performers. The film is a romantic biography, with the legends seen as facts, but it is good entertainment. See THE GREAT CARUSO.

1952 Because You're Mine
Lanza is an opera star drafted into the army who falls in love with the sister (Doretta Morrow) of his sergeant (James Whitmore). When he works in the kitchen, his buddies serenade him to the tune of the *Lucia di Lammermoor* sextet, "Renato is a potato expert." The film includes the final aria from *Cavalleria rusticana* and the "Addio" duet from *Rigoletto.* This was Lanza's last film for MGM as an actor. Alexander Hall directed. Color. 103 minutes. MGM-UA VHS.

1954/1957 Lanza Live!
Lanza sings arias from *Tosca* and *The Vagabond King* in this 1954 TV program and three songs in the 1957 program. The are also interviews with Mario and Betty Lanza. Black and white. 35 minutes. Bel Canto Society VHS.

1956 Serenade
Lanza is a singer with emotional problems in this adaptation of James M. Cain's novel. He's the protégé of Joan Fontaine, and he even quits the Met stage during his debut as Otello when Fontaine doesn't turn up. See SERENADE.

1958 The Seven Hills of Rome
Lanza, a TV singer who goes to Rome to look for a lost woman friend, ends up finding true love with an Italian. The plot is about his rise to success after he wows them belting "Questa o quella" from *Rigoletto.* There is a good deal of Rome tourist scenery and a bizarre scene in which he imitates American pop singers. Roy Rowland directed. Color. 104 minutes. MGM-UA video.

1959 For the First Time
In Lanza's last film, he is typecast as a temperamental opera singer who is always missing performances and behaving badly. He is seen in the rain outside the Rome Opera House singing arias from *Rigoletto* and on stage in costume in *Pagliacci* ("Vesti la giubba"), *Otello* (the final scene), and *Aida;* his screen career closes ironically with the Triumphal March from *Aida.* See FOR THE FIRST TIME.

1983 Mario Lanza, the American Caruso
Plácido Domingo hosts this documentary about Lanza's career, which includes praise for his singing ability from

several opera singers who worked with him. Domingo says that seeing Lanza in the film *The Great Caruso* inspired him to become an opera singer while Anna Moffo, Kathryn Grayson, and Joe Pasternak also have some good things to say. Jo Ann G. Young wrote the script, and John Musilli directed the film. Color. 68 minutes. Kultur DVD/VHS.

1987 A Time to Remember
An Italian boy (Ruben Gomez) makes Lanza his role model and is encouraged to become an opera singer by his parish priest (Donald O'Connor). He finally succeeds with the help of a small Christmas miracle. In the film he goes to see Lanza's movie *The Great Caruso* several times. Thomas Travers directed. Off Hollywood VHS.

1991 Tribute to Mario Lanza
José Carreras salutes his idol in a recital at the Royal Albert Hall in London and sings Lanza favorites such as "Be My Love," "Serenade," "Because You're Mine," and "Una furtiva lagrima." Enrique Ricci conducts the BBC Concert Orchestra and English Concert Chorus. Declan Lowney directed. Color. 83 minutes. Teldec VHS.

1994 Heavenly Creatures
Lanza is worshipped (literally) by two teenage girls (Kate Winslet and Melanie Linsky) in this bizarre New Zealand film set in the early 1950s. They have an altar for their operatic god, and they attend his films as often as they can; Lanza's records and songs are recurrent symbols. To prevent being separated, the girls kill the mother of one of them. Frances Walsh wrote the screenplay based on real events, and Peter Jackson directed before he became famous with the *Lord of the Rings* trilogy. Color. 95 minutes.

LARGE, BRIAN
English TV opera director (1939–)

Brian Large, one of the two major television opera directors, is England's counterpart to U.S. pioneer KIRK BROWNING. Large uses fewer close-ups and has a less restless camera than Browning, tending to favor medium shots and more painterly compositions. He directed Benjamin Britten's TV opera OWEN WINGRAVE in 1971, became the chief director of opera for BBC Television in 1974, and now directs the Metropolitan Opera telecasts. One of his major achievements was directing the telecast of DER RING DES NIBELUNGEN at Bayreuth in 1980. His expertise can be seen in his informative entry on "Filming, videotaping" in *The New Grove Dictionary of Opera* and in his books on Smetana and Martinů. A very large number of the videos made from opera house telecasts around the world are the work of Large and are listed in

this book; there are too many to list, but they include nearly every major opera, sometimes more than once.

1980 The Making of the Ring
Large makes a rare personal appearance talking about his work in this documentary by Peter Weinberg, which shows the filming of the 1980 Bayreuth *Ring*. The documentary is included with the box set of the performance. Color. In English and German with English subtitles. About 40 minutes. Philips DVD/VHS/LD.

LARMES DU COUTEAU, LES
1928 chamber opera by Martinů

Satan appears as tempter in various disguises, even as a hanged man, in BOHUSLAV MARTINŮ's little-known one-act chamber opera *Les larmes du couteau* (The Tears of the Knife). The imaginative and highly surrealistic libretto by French poet Georges Ribemont-Dessaignes is set to a jazzy score that features banjo and saxophone.

1998 Czech Television
Czech TV production: Jirí Nekvasil (director), Jiri Belohlávek (conductor, Prague Chamber Philharmonic), Ondrej Nekvasil (set designer).
Cast: Lenka Smídová, Hana Jonásová, Roman Janál,
Telecast and taped in Prague in August 1998. Jirí Nekvasil (director). Color. In Czech. 27 minutes.

LARMORE, JENNIFER
American mezzo-soprano (1960–)

Atlanta-born Jennifer Larmore, who attracted a good deal of international critical attention with her 1995 debut album of Handel and Mozart arias, has also made a name for herself in the international opera world. She made her stage debut in France in 1986 and her Met debut in 1995 as Rosina; she can be seen as Rosina in a video of a Netherlands Opera production of IL BARBIERE DI SIVIGLIA (1992). In 1998 she sang Isabella in a telecast of a Paris Opéra production of L'ITALIANA IN ALGERI. Larmore, who is married to bass-baritone William Powers, has made recordings of operas by Berlioz, Bizet, Donizetti, Gluck, Handel, Humperdinck, Mozart, Rossini, and Verdi.

2001 Jennifer Larmore in Recital
Larmore performs arias from Handel's *Hercules* and *Semele*, Rossini's *Semiramide*, and Bizet's *Carmen* at a recital at Purchase College Performing Arts Center in New York on January 5, 2001. The program also has songs by Barber, Barroso, Debussy, Heggie Herbert, Obradors,

Purcell, Quilter, Rossini, and Weill. Antoine Palloc accompanies on piano. Color. 82 minutes. VAI DVD/VHS.

LA SCALA
See Teatro alla Scala.

LAURI-VOLPI, GIACOMO
Italian tenor (1892–1979)

Giacomo Lauri-Volpi, who could sing with ease a high D above high C, made his last public appearance at the age of 85 hitting a high B while singing "La donna è mobile." Lauri-Volpi was born in Rome, made his debut in 1919, and was a star attraction at La Scala and Verona from 1922 through the 1940s. He sang at the Metropolitan from 1923 to 1933, and he continued to perform in public until 1959 when he retired to Spain. He also wrote studies of singers and singing. His continued reputation is mainly based on his recordings, but he also left a few films in which he can be seen singing during his best years.

1933 La canzone del sole
Lauri-Volpi plays himself in *Song of the Sun,* an Italian feature film that ends at the Arena di Verona where he sings Raoul in Meyerbeer's *Gli ugonotti (Les Huguenots).* His role in the film is primarily as singer, including arias from *I puritani* and the title song by Pietro Mascagni. See LA CANZONE DEL SOLE.

1950 Il Caimano del Piave
Lauri-Volpi has a reportedly autobiographical scene in this film about an incident during World War I in Piave. It is Christmas, so the Italian troops ask their captain to sing a carol. Lauri-Volpi does so, and his voice floats so beautifully over the trenches that the troops on both sides stop fighting and listen. Black and white. In Italian. 100 minutes.

1983 Ricordi di Giacomo Lauri-Volpi
Memories of Giacomo Lauri-Volpi begins with a concert in Spain where the 85-year-old tenor sings "La donna è mobile" to warm applause. Next are lengthy extracts from the film *La canzone del sole,* probably the best audiovisual record of the singer in his early years, especially his performance in *Les Huguenots* at the Arena di Verona. Italian mezzo-soprano Gianna Pederzina, who sang there with him, remembers the experience, and tenors Franco Corelli and Carlo Bergonzi express their admiration for him. Rodolfo Celetti and Tonino del Colle made the documentary for Italian TV. Color and black and white. In Italian. 90 minutes. Opera Dubs VHS.

LAWRENCE, MARJORIE
Australian soprano (1909–1979)

Marjorie Lawrence was mainly known in U.S. opera circles for her portrayals of Wagner heroines at the Metropolitan, although she sang a wide range of roles around the world. After studies in Paris, she made her stage debut in Monte Carlo in 1932 as Elisabeth in *Tannhäuser,* her Paris Opéra debut in 1933 as Ortrud in *Lohengrin,* and her Metropolitan Opera debut as Brünnhilde in *Die Walküre.* She continued to sing at the Met until 1941 when she was stricken with polio. She courageously refused to quit, resuming her stage career in 1943 in roles in which she could be seated. In 1946 she returned to the Paris Opéra to sing Amneris. Lawrence published her autobiography *Interrupted Melody* in 1949, and it became the basis of a film.

1955 Interrupted Melody
This fine film biography contains opera sequences from Lawrence's debut in Monte Carlo through her success in Paris and her triumphs at the Met to her return to the stage after being stricken by polio. Lawrence recorded arias for Eleanor Parker, who portrays her, but they were not used; the voice on screen belongs to Eileen Farrell. See INTERRUPTED MELODY.

LECOCQ, CHARLES
French composer (1832–1918)

Charles Lecocq replaced Offenbach as the king of French operetta with his brilliant and tuneful 1872 masterpiece LA FILLE DE MADAME ANGOT. He was seriously crippled and perhaps this inspired him to favor romance over reality; his operettas are the triumph of escapism over satire and mockery. Lecocq, who once shared first prize with Bizet in an Offenbach operetta competition, had continuing success with *Giroflé-Girofla, La petite mariée,* and *Le petit duc.* These operettas are available on French CDs, but only *La fille de Madame Angot* has been filmed.

LEGEND OF THE INVISIBLE CITY OF KITEZH, THE
1907 opera by Rimsky-Korsakov

NIKOLAI RIMSKY-KORSAKOV's epic *Skazaniye o nevidomom grade Kitezhe I deve Fevronii (The Legend of the Invisible City of Kitezh and the Maiden Fevroniya)* is a heroic, patriotic, religious opera set in medieval times telling of a miracle that made a city invisible and saved it from invading Tartars. The libretto, by Vladimir Belsky, is based on Russian legend, and the Maiden Fevroniya, who prays for the miracle that saves the city, is considered a saint. The opera, with its religious mystical theme, has been called the Russian *Parsifal*. The music depicting the battle of Kerzhenets is particularly powerful.

***1995 Bregenz Festival

Austrian stage production: Harry Kupfer (director), Vladimir Fedoseyev (conductor, Vienna Symphony, Sofia Chamber Choir, and Chorus of the Russian Academy, Moscow), Hans Schavernoch (set designer), Reinhard Heinich (costume designer)

Cast: Yelena Prokina (Fevroniya), Pavel Danilyuk (Prince Yury), Sergei Naida (Prince Vsevolod), Vladimir Galuzin (Grishka Kuterma), Vladimir Vanev (Burunday).

Video: Telecast July 20, 1995. Color. In Russian. 178 minutes. House of Opera VHS.

Related film

1971 The Battle of Kerzhenets

This hugely effective animated portrayal of the battle at the center of the opera, with magnificent images based on medieval frescoes and Russian icons, uses the powerful Rimsky-Korsakov music to great effect. It shows the people before the battle, the Maid appearing to make the city vanish, the Russian Army drawn up to meet the waves of Tartars, the Tartars' total defeat, and the reappearance and rebuilding of the city. *The Battle of Kerzhenets* was produced by two of the best Soviet animation directors, Ivan Ivanov-Vano and Yuri Norstein, and is considered one of the masterpieces of the genre. It won the Grand Prize at the Zagreb Animation Festival in 1972. Color. No dialogue. 20 minutes. Jove VHS.

LEGEND OF TSAR SALTAN, THE
See THE TALE OF TSAR SALTAN.

LEHÁR, FRANZ
Austro-Hungarian composer (1870–1948)

Franz Lehár, the leading operetta composer of the 20th century, is likely to remain popular for a few more centuries, especially because of *The Merry Widow,* which has entered the opera repertory. Lehár, who was born in Hungary but spent most of his life in Austria and Germany, wrote so many infectious melodies that he is sometimes called the Puccini of the operetta. He was an avid cinema-goer, enjoyed the films of his operettas, and even acted in some of the films made about him. His music was featured with early silent films, such as *Mit Herz und Hand fürs Vaterland* (1915), and in the 1930s he composed music for films starring RICHARD TAUBER (*Die grosse Attraktion,* 1931), MARTA EGGERTH (*Where Is This Lady?,* 1932), MARIA JERITZA (*Grossfürstin Alexandra,* 1933), and JARMILA NOVOTNÁ (*Der Kosak und die Nachtigall,* 1935). Many of his operettas remain popular and have been filmed and telecast. See CLOCLO, LA DANZA DELLE LIBELLULE, EVA, FRASQUITA, FRIEDERIKE, GIUDITTA, DER GRAF VON LUXEMBURG, DAS LAND DES LÄCHELNS, DIE LUSTIGE WITWE, PAGANINI, SCHÖN IST DIE WELT, WO DIE LERCHE SINGT, DER ZAREWITSCH, and ZIGEUNERLIEBE.

1914 Die ideale Gattin

Lehár's Spanish-themed 1913 operetta *Die ideale Gattin* (The Ideal Wife) was made into a silent film in Austria in 1914. The actors include director-to-be Ernst Lubitsch and Lyda Salmonova. Hans Heins Ewers directed. Black and white. Silent. About 50 minutes.

1923 Franz Lehár

This Austrian feature film about the composer was made with Lehár's cooperation in Vienna by Thalia Film. He also wrote a score, based on his operetta melodies, that was played live with the film. Wilhelm Thiele and Hans Torre directed. Black and white. Silent. About 70 minutes.

1925 Franz Lehár, der Operettenkönig

Franz Lehár, the Operetta King is another tribute to the composer made in Vienna, this one by Allianz Film. Lehár himself appears in the film playing piano and conducting a rehearsal. Music from his operettas was played with the film in theaters. Alfred Deutsch-German directed. Black and white. Silent. About 80 minutes.

1927 Das Fürstenkind

Lehár's operetta *Das Fürstenkind* (The Prince's Child), first staged in 1909, was made into a feature film in Austria in 1927. It's the story of a brigand, his beautiful daughter, and the American naval officer she loves. The operetta music was played live with the film. Jacob and Luise Fleck directed. Black and white. Silent. About 90 minutes.

1927 Der Rastelbinder

Lehár's operetta *Der Rastelbinder* (The Tinker), first staged in 1910 was made into an Austrian feature film in 1927. Viktor Léon's libretto, set in Slovakia, Vienna, and an army barracks, tells the story of an ill-matched engaged couple. The cast includes Ellen Davis as Mitzi, Franz Glawatsch as her father, Louis Treumann (creator of Danilo in *The Merry Widow*), Hanna Andrée, and Mary Hadar. The operetta music was played live with the film. Maurice Armand Mondet, Heinz Hanus, and Arthur Göttlein directed. Black and white. Silent. About 86 minutes.

1929 Franz Lehár

This feature film about Lehár includes his friends Liesl Goldarbeiter (Miss Austria that year), Viktor Léon, Ida Ruska, Victor Fleming, Ossi Fuhrer, Hans Otto Löwenstein, Karl Juiles, and Fritz Heller. Lehár wrote a score for it, and Hans Otto Löwenstein directed for Norbert Film. Black and white. Silent. 90 minutes.

1930 Wiener Liebschafter

Wiener Liebschafter (Viennese Loves) is a French-German film operetta with original music by Lehár. The French version *(Amours Viennoise)* stars Janie Marèse, Lyne Clèvers, Roland Toutain, and Michel Duran under the direction of Jean Choux. The German version stars George Alexander, Betty Bird, Max Schipper, and Lotte Lorring. Black and white. 72 minutes.

1998 Magic Music: A Tribute to Franz Lehár

Plácido Domingo, José Carreras, Thomas Hampson, Andrea Rost, and other admirers pay homage to the composer in Bad Ischl on the 50th anniversary of his death. The program is mainly their singing the best-known songs from *The Merry Widow* and others operettas. Marcello Viotti conducts the Budapest Philharmonic Orchestra; Bernd Hellthaler directed the video. Telecast on ORF Austrian Television on August 2, 1998. Color. 90 minutes.

LEHMANN, LOTTE
German-born U.S. soprano (1888–1976)

Lotte Lehmann, who originated roles in two of Richard Strauss's operas before being driven out of Austria by the politics of 1938, began her career in Berlin and Hamburg. She moved to Vienna in 1916, where she established her international reputation, and she made her debut at the Met in 1934. Lehmann continued to give recitals until 1951, and she can be seen singing in a film made when she was 60. Her voice is well served on her many recordings

1948 Big City

Lehmann sings four songs in her sole film appearance: Brahms's Lullaby, "The Kerry Dance," "Traümerei," and "God Bless America." She plays the mother of Danny Thomas in this story about racial tolerance involving Jews, Catholics, and Protestants. Margaret O'Brien plays an orphan adopted by a minister, a cantor, and an Irish cop. Norman Taurog directed for MGM. Black and white. 103 minutes.

1961 Lotte Lehmann, Master Classes Vol. 1

Lehmann talks about arias identified with her career and shows how to sing the Marschallin's monologue from *Der Rosenkavalier* and "Dove sono" from *Le nozze di Figaro* in classes at the Music Academy of the West in Santa Barbara. Filmed by KQED/Thirteen. Color. In English. 56 minutes. VAI VHS.

1966 NBC Television: Open Mind

Lehmann and other Met stars talk about the Golden Age of the Metropolitan Opera shortly after the razing of the old theater on the program *Open Mind*. Telecast April 17, 1966, on NBC. Black and white. 30 minutes. Video at the MTR.

LEHNHOFF, NIKOLAUS
German director (1939–)

Videos and DVDs have given the world the chance to see the brilliance of stage director Nikolaus Lehnhoff from his powerful RING cycle at Bavarian State Opera in Munich to his brilliant stagings of Janáček operas at Glyndebourne. Especially memorable is his production of TRISTAN UND ISOLDE with Birgit Nilsson at Orange in 1973, which is on video. See EUGENE ONEGIN (1998), DIE FRAU OHNE SCHATTEN (1980), GÖTTERDÄMMERUNG (1989), JENŮFA (1989), KATYA KABANOVA (1988), THE MAKROPOULOS CASE (1995), DAS RHEINGOLD (1989), SIEGFRIED (1989), and DIE WALKÜRE (1989).

LEIDEN DES JUNGEN WERTHERS, DIE
1986 German opera by Bose

German composer HANS-JÜRGEN VON BOSE's opera *Die Leiden des jungen Werthers* (The Sorrows of Young Werther) is based on the same Goethe novel as Massenet's WERTHER. Bose and Filippo Sanjust's libretto, however, is surrealistic rather than romantic, as it combines scenes from the novel with visions, dreams, and poems by Goethe, Lenz, and Hölderlin. The basic story, however, is the same. Werther falls in love with Lotte, but when he goes away a while, she marries Albert. When Werther returns and finds she cannot return his love, he shoots himself. The opera premiered at the Schwetzingen Festival.

1986 Hamburg State Opera

German stage production: Marco Arthur Marelli (director, set/costume designer), Hans Zender (conductor, Stuttgart Suddeutscher Rundfunk Orchestra and Stuttgart Schola Cantorum Madrigal Quintet).

Cast: François Le Roux (Werther), Hildegarde Hartwig (Lotte), Albert Dohmen (Albert), David Knutson (Heinrich), Linda Plech (Lisa).

Video: Inter Nationes VHS. Jose Monte-Baczuer (director). Color. In German. 117 minutes.

LEIFERKUS, SERGEI
Russian baritone (1946–)

Sergei Leiferkus was born in Leningrad and spent his early years at the Kirov Opera where he made his debut as Prince André in *War and Peace*. In 1978 he toured Britain with the Kirov; he was so well received that he decided to make London his home. He sings regularly at Covent Garden and the Metropolitan and is popular in Italian as well as Russian operas. His Russian roles remain his strongest suit, however, and he is particularly liked as Tomsky in *The Queen of Spades* (he has the role in three videos). See BORIS GODUNOV (1990), CARMEN (1997), EUGENE ONEGIN (1984), THE FIERY ANGEL (1993), OTELLO (1992), PRINCE IGOR (1990), THE QUEEN OF SPADES (1992 Vienna, Kirov, and Glyndebourne), ROTHSCHILD'S VIOLIN, SAMSON ET DALILA (1998), TCHAIKOVSKY (1993), and TOSCA (1994).

LEMESHEV, SERGEI
Russian tenor (1902–1977)

Sergei Lemeshev made his debut in 1926 at Sverdlovsk and joined the Bolshoi Opera in 1931. A combination of personal charm, acting ability, and a fine voice made him an instant star; it also helped that he studied with Stanislavsky at the Bolshoi Opera Studio. He remained a leading tenor with the Bolshoi into the 1950s, singing the Russian repertoire as well as Italian opera. He began to direct in 1951 and published his memoirs in 1968.

1940 A Musical Story
Lemeshev made his film debut as the star of *Muzikalnaya Istoriya,* the first Soviet sound film to have an operatic theme. He plays a driver sent by his fellow workers to the State Music Conservatory, where he falls in love with dispatcher Zoya Fyodorova and wins her over rival Erast Garin. Lemeshev won particular praise for his performances of arias from *Eugene Onegin*. The film, which also features music by Bizet, Flotow, Borodin, and Rimsky-Korsakov, was distributed in America in 1941. Black and white. In Russian. 80 minutes.

1941 Kino-Concert 1941
Lemeshev sings arias from *Rigoletto* and *Martha* in *Kino-Concert 1941,* a Soviet concert musical released in the West with the odd title *Russian Salad*. The six directors were Adolf Minkin, Herbert Rappaport, Sergei Timoshenko, I. Menaker, M. Tsekhanovsky, and M. Shapiro. Black and white. In Russian. 86 minutes.

1947 Sergei Lemeshev Recital
A documentary film showing Lemeshev singing at a recital filmed by Ostankino. Black and white. In Russian. 60 minutes.

LEMNITZ, TIANA
German soprano (1897–1994)

Tiana Lemnitz, a fine lyric soprano who made her debut at Heilbronn in 1920, joined the Berlin Staatsoper in 1934 and remained with that company until she retired in 1957. She also sang at Covent Garden in a number of roles during the mid-1930s. She sings the role of the Countess in a 1949 film of LE NOZZE DI FIGARO and appears in an opera recital scene in a German narrative film. Her relationship with the Nazi party during the war has been controversial.

1939 Altes Herz wird wieder Jung
Lemnitz is featured in the opera scene in this German feature film with Berlin Staatsoper tenor Max Lorenz. Emil Jannings and Maria Landrock star in this family-type comedy directed by Erich Engel. English title: *An Old Heart Becomes Young*. Black and white. In German. 81 minutes.

LEONCAVALLO, RUGGERO
Italian composer (1857–1919)

Struggling composer Ruggero (or Ruggiero) Leoncavallo became world famous in 1892 with PAGLIACCI after 15 long years of trying to get his operas produced. The Naples-born composer was already 35 when his one-act opera about a group of traveling players won him international recognition, but he was never again to find such success. His earlier operas did not become popular, and his excellent *La bohème* (revived in London in 2000) was overshadowed by Puccini's more popular version. The only other Leoncavallo opera currently on video and CD is ZAZÀ; the rest are more or less forgotten outside Italy. Leoncavallo also wrote operettas in an attempt to make money, the best known being LA REGINETTA DELLE ROSE. *Pagliacci,* however, is his masterpiece, and it remains one of the most popular operas on stage, film, television, and video. There are at least 15 films and videos of it, and many movies that feature its music.

LET'S MAKE AN OPERA
1949 play/opera by Britten

Let's Make an Opera, libretto by Eric Crozier, is a framing play in which children and adults prepare and present the chamber opera *The Little Sweep*. In the *Sweep* opera, set in Suffolk in 1810, the eight-year-old apprentice chimney sweep Sam meets up with a group of children when he goes to sweep the nursery chimney at Iken Hall. Juliet, Rowan, and the other children help him escape from his master Black Bob.

1950 BBC Television

English film of stage production: Basil Coleman (stage director), Norman Del Mar (conductor, BBC Television Orchestra).

Cast: Alan Woolston (Sam), Norman Lumsden (Black Bob), Anne Sharpe (Juliet), Pamela Woolmore (Rowan), Gladys Parr (Miss Baggott), Max Worthley (Alfred), Michael Nicholls (Gay), Jean Galton (Sophie), Paul Nedland (Johnnie), Clive Wyatt (Hughie), Shirley Eaton (Tina).

Telecast February 5, 1950, by BBC. Michael Henderson (film director). Black and white. In English. 140 minutes.

Comment: Staged and filmed by BBC Television at the Royal Theatre in Stratford.

LET'S SING AGAIN
1936 American film with opera content

Bobby Breen plays a boy living in an orphanage who is unaware that he is the lost son of an Italian opera singer. When Carter's Traveling Theatre comes to town, he runs away with it and is befriended by Pasquale (Henry Armetta), a once-famous tenor who has lost his voice but kept the opera records he made. He teaches Breen to sing opera arias, beginning with "La donna è mobile," and the boy is a hit in the traveling show. The friendly opera diva Rosa Donelli (Vivienne Osborne) helps the pair when they go to New York. Breen's father Leon Alba (George Houston), who has been searching for his lost son, finds him for a happy ending. Audiences liked the film and Breen, so RKO made seven more Breen musicals. RKO wanted to cast Met soprano Marion Talley as Rosa Donelli but couldn't reach an agreement. Hugo Riesenfeld was music director, Don Swift and Dan Jarrett wrote the screenplay, Harry Neumann and Frank Good were the cinematographers, and Kurt Neumann directed for RKO. Black and white. 65 minutes. Video Yesteryear VHS.

LETTERS, RIDDLES AND WRITS
1991 TV opera by Nyman

Michael Nyman composed this excellent television opera to a libretto by director Jeremy Newson for the *Not Mozart* series. It's based on words by Leopold Mozart and his son Wolfgang taken from their letters to each other. The story, narrated by statues of Beethoven and Haydn, is enhanced with clever video effects by director Pat Gavin. Nyman, who appears in the opera as himself, is accused of pilfering Mozart's music. The opera was staged in London in June 1992 after its television premiere.

1991 BBC Television

English TV production: Pat Gavin (director), Michael Nyman (conductor, Michael Nyman Band).

Cast: Ute Lemper (Wolfgang Mozart), David Thomas (Leopold Mozart/Sarastro in *Die Zauberflöte*), Tony Rohr (Beethoven), Julian Glover (Haydn), Michael Nyman (himself).

Video: Connoisseur Academy (GB) VHS. Telecast November 10, 1991, on BBC 2. Color. In English. 30 minutes.

LETZTE WALZER, DER
1920 operetta by Straus

Der letzte Walzer (The Last Waltz), one of OSCAR STRAUS's most popular operettas, has been filmed five times in three languages. It tells the story of Count Dimitri's presumed last night and last waltz at a masked ball in Poland in 1910. He is to be executed the next day for having struck Prince Paul when he went to the rescue of Countess Vera. Vera, however, has other plans; she succeeds in saving his life and marrying him. The operetta, tailored to suit Fritzi Massary, premiered in Berlin in 1920 and went on to success in New York and London.

1934 Jacoby film

German feature film: Georg Jacoby (director), Max Wallner and Georg G. Webber (screenplay), Carl Drews (cinematographer), Paul Hühn (music director).

Cast: Camille Horn (Countess Vera), Ivan Petrovich (Count Dimitri), Ernst Dumcke (Prince Paul), Adele Sandrock (Countess Alexandrowna, Vera's mother), Susi Lanner (Saschinka, Vera's sister).

Black and white. In German. 90 minutes.

1936 The Last Waltz

English feature film: Gerald Barry and Leo Mittler (directors), Reginald Arkell (screenplay), Robert Gys (set designer), Warwick Films (production).

Cast: Jarmila Novotná (Countess Vera), Harry Welchman (Count Dimitri), Gerald Barry (Prince Paul), Josephine Huntley Wright (Babushka, Vera's sister), Tonie Edgar Bruce (Countess Alexandrowna).

Video: Bel Canto VHS. Black and white. In English 74 minutes.

Comment: Opera diva Jarmila Novotná played Vera in two films shot simultaneously in Paris in English and French with somewhat different casts and an altered plot.

1936 La dernière valse

French feature film: Leo Mittler (director), Paul Schiller and Reginald Arkell (screenplay), Robert Gys (set designer), Warwick Films (production).

Cast: Jarmila Novotná (Countess Vera), Jean Martinelli (Count Dimitri), Gerald Barry (Prince Paul), Armand Bernard (Old General), Josephine Huntley Wright (Babushka),

Black and white. In French. 90 minutes.

1953 Rabenalt film

German feature film: Arthur Maria Rabenalt (director), Eichberg/Carlton (production).

Cast: Eva Bartok (Countess Vera), Curt Jurgens (Count Dimitri), O. E. Hasse (Prince Paul), Christl Mardayn, Rudolf Schundler.

Black and white. In German. 93 minutes.

Comment: The plot for this version has been updated.

1953 Kraus film

German TV film: Fred Kraus (director), Bert Grund (conductor, Stuttgart Radio Symphony Orchestra), Willy Shatz (set designer), ZDF (production).

Cast: Grit van Juten (Countess Vera), Adolf Dallapozza (Count Dimitri), Marika Rökk (Countess Alexandrowna), Ivan Rebroff (Prince Paul), Fritz Tillman (Old General)

Black and white. In German. 93 minutes.

LEVANT, OSCAR
American composer (1906–1972)

Oscar Levant was a composer in addition to being a film actor, writer, wit, pianist, and promoter of George Gershwin's music. His only opera is the imaginary screen opera *Carnival*, which he composed for the 1936 film CHARLIE CHAN AT THE OPERA. His most famous film performance is in the Gershwin film *An American in Paris*, in which he acts up a neurotic storm and then plays superb piano. In the Gershwin biography *Rhapsody in Blue*, he plays himself as a friend of Gershwin and performs the title tune. His other major films include *The Band Wagon*, *The Barkleys of Broadway*, and *Romance on the High Seas*.

LEVINE, JAMES
American conductor (1943–)

The indefatigable James Levine has become America's most famous opera conductor through his Metropolitan Opera telecasts. He made his Met debut in 1971, became chief conductor in 1974, was named artistic director in 1986, and celebrated 25 years at the Met in 1996. He has helped the Met maintain its position as one of the great opera houses of the world, but he has also conducted extensively abroad. Levine is featured in the majority of the Met opera videos since 1971.

1986 James Levine: The Life in Music
Filmmaker Peter Weinberg follows the energetic conductor around the world and shows him rehearsing, conducting, and playing piano accompaniment for singers from New York to Bayreuth. Among those interviewed are Plácido Domingo, Jean-Pierre Ponnelle, Leonie Rysanek, and Lynn Harrell. Joanne Woodward is the narrator. Telecast August 11, 1986. Color. 55 minutes.

1996 James Levine's Silver Anniversary Gala
Levine's 25th anniversary at the Met was celebrated with a seven-hour all-star gala telecast live. While the singers appeared for only a few moments, the inexhaustible Levine conducted the entire marathon right down to its Wagnerian climax. The dozens of singers participating include Roberto Alagna, June Anderson, Gabriela Beňačková, Carlo Bergonzi, Grace Bumbry, Plácido Domingo, Maria Ewing, Gwyneth Jones, James King, Alfredo Kraus, Catherine Malfitano, Aprile Millo, Sherrill Milnes, James Morris, Birgit Nilsson, Jessye Norman, Samuel Ramey, Sharon Sweet, Ruth Ann Swenson, Kiri Te Kanawa, Bryn Terfel, Dawn Upshaw, Anne Sofie von Otter, and Frederica von Stade. Peter Allen narrated, and Brian Large directed the live telecast April 27, 1996. Color. English subtitles. The complete program was 420 minutes; the DG VHS is 167 minutes.

LEWIS, MARY
American soprano (1897–1941)

The beautiful Arkansas soprano Mary Lewis rose from extreme poverty to became one of the most notable Ziegfeld Follies girls. She then turned to opera, making her debut in Vienna in 1923 as Marguerite in *Faust*. In 1924 she sang the role of Mary in the premiere of Vaughan Williams's *Hugh the Drover* at Covent Garden and in 1925 starred in *The Merry Widow* in Paris. She returned to the United States with a Met contract and sang in *La bohème*, *Pagliacci*, and *Les contes d'Hoffmann*. Her Met career ended after a drunken performance as Micaëla in *Carmen* in 1930. Her film career was messy. She seems to have worked with Christie Comedies in 1919 and possibly appeared in a 1920 film called *The Ugly Duckling*. After her Met career ended, she signed with Pathé to star in a film about her life. When that didn't work out, she started work on a French Revolution film that was abandoned, probably because of her drinking. After marrying a rich man (she had been married earlier to German bass-baritone Michael Bohnen), she resumed her singing career, but mostly on radio. She died somewhat mysteriously at the age of 44 in 1941.

1927 Vitaphone films
Lewis made two Vitaphone sound films but only one was released. In the first, titled *Mary Lewis in Way Down South,* she sings songs by James Bland and Dan Emmett with backing from a male chorus. Her second Vitaphone film, started a month later, was to feature *Les contes d'Hoffmann* but it was never completed. Vitaphone sued her, claiming she was drinking on the set. Black and white. About 8 minutes.

LIBRARY OF CONGRESS

The Library of Congress in Washington, D.C., has a large collection of films and television programs, many with operatic content. They are preserved by the Motion Picture, Broadcasting and Recorded Sound Division and can be viewed by interested researchers. Some of its holdings are unique, and it is one of the few places where one can view the withdrawn Samuel Goldwyn film of *Porgy and Bess.* A partial catalog of its TV holdings is available titled *Three Decades of Television, A Catalog of Television Programs Acquired by the Library of Congress 1949–1979,* compiled by Sarah Rouse and Katharine Loughney. In 1986 the library collection increased enormously with the acquisition of 20,000 NBC Television programs.

LICITRA, SALVATORE
Swiss-born Italian tenor (1968–)

Salvatore Licitra made his American reputation overnight by substituting at the last minute for Luciano Pavarotti as Cavaradossi in the closing night Metropolitan Opera gala of *Tosca* in May 2002. *Newsday* said he "scored the most triumphant Met debut in recent memory." His debut album, not surprisingly, featured arias from *Tosca.* He made his professional debut in 1998 in Parma and his La Scala debut in 1999. He can be seen in videos of La Scala productions of TOSCA (2000) and IL TROVATORE (2000) and heard as the voice of opera tenor John Turturro in the English film THE MAN WHO CRIED.

2003 Duetto
Licitra joins fellow tenor Marcelo Álvarez in a concert in Rome with backing from the City of Prague Philharmonic Orchestra led by Daniel May. Easy on the ear and eye but more pop that opera. Color. 60 minutes. The concert was filmed and shown on PBS.

LIEBERMANN, ROLF
Swiss opera film producer (1910–1999)

Composer/administrator Rolf Liebermann, who was in charge of the Hamburg State Opera and Paris Opera at various times, was also a notable producer of opera films. Most were made during the late 1960s when he was director of the Hamburg Staatsoper, and he brought an impressive selection of them to New York for an opera film festival in 1970. Although he did not direct the films (it was usually Joachim Hess), he was the driving force behind their creation. He talks about opera films in the French documentary CINOPÉRA. See ELEKTRA (1969), FIDELIO (1969), DER FREISCHÜTZ (1968), LE NOZZE DI FIGARO (1967), DIE MEISTERSINGER VON NÜRNBERG (1969), IGOR STRAVINSKY (1968), LES CONTES D'HOFFMANN (1970), WOZZECK (1967), ZAR UND ZIMMERMANN (1968), and DIE ZAUBERFLÖTE (1971).

LIFE FOR THE TSAR, A
1836 opera by Glinka

MIKHAIL GLINKA's *A Life for the Tsar* (Zhizn' za Tsarya) is the first important Russian opera, and its strong patriotic element has ensured its continuing popularity. Yegor Rozen's libretto tells the story of the peasant Ivan Susanin, who sacrifices his life to save the Tsar from invading Poles as well as his daughter Atonida, her fiancé Sobinin, and his ward Vanya. The opera was banned in 1917, but it was revived in 1938 with a new libretto and a new title, *Ivan Susanin.* The hero in this version saves Moscow rather than the Tsar. The opera was revived in its original form after the collapse of the Soviet Union and is now available in Russian on video as written.

1992 Bolshoi Opera
Russian stage production: Nicolai Kuznetsov (director), Alexander Lazarev (conductor, Bolshoi Symphony Orchestra and Chorus), Valery Levental (set/costume designer).

Cast: Yevgeny Nesterenko (Ivan Susanin), Marina Mescheriakova (Antonida), Alexander Lomonosov (Sobinin), Elena Zaremba (Vanya), Boris Bezhko (Polish Commander).

Video: Teldec (GB) VHS. Derek Bailey (director). Taped at the Bolshoi Theater in June 1992. Color. In Russian. 175 minutes.

Early film

1911 Goncharov film
This early Russian silent film featuring highlights of the opera was directed by Vasilij Goncharov. Black and white. About 10 minutes.

LILAC DOMINO, THE

1912 operetta by Cuvillier

French composer Charles Cuvillier's biggest success as an operetta composer was premiered in Germany as *Der lila Domino,* but it found its greatest popularity in England as *The Lilac Domino.* Set in Budapest, it tells the story of a dissolute count who has gambled away his fortune. A schoolgirl, the daughter of a baron, becomes interested in him and arranges to meet him at a masked ball wearing a lilac domino mask. She eventually persuades him to change his ways. The German libretto, by Béla Jenbach and Emmerich von Gatti, was adapted for London by Adair Fitzgerald and Howard Carr and produced at the Empire Theatre by Joseph L. Sachs. It was such a success that Cuvillier's other operettas were later staged in English adaptations.

1937 The Lilac Domino

English feature film: Friedrich Zelnick (director); Basil Mason, Neil Gow, Derek Neame, and R. Hutter (screenplay); Roy Clark and Brian Langley (cinematographers); Max Schach (producer).

Cast: Michael Bartlett (Count Anatole), June Knight (Shari di Gonda), Fred Emney (Baron di Gonda), Athene Seyler (Mme. Alary), S. Z. Sakall (Sandor), Richard Dolman (Stephen).

Black and white. In English. 79 minutes.

LILY OF KILLARNEY, THE

1862 opera by Benedict

JULIUS BENEDICT's light opera, one of the big three of 19th-century Anglo-Irish light opera (with *The Bohemian Girl* and *Maritana*), is based on Dion Boucicault's play *The Colleen Bawn* as adapted by Boucicault and John Oxenford. In 19th-century Ireland, the peasant girl Eily O'Connor, known as the Colleen Bawn (i.e., fair maiden), is secretly married to aristocrat Hardress Cregan. He is being pushed to marry an heiress to solve his financial problems, and an attempt is made by one of his associates to drown the Colleen to get her out of the way. The opera's best-known airs include the tenor aria "Eily Mavourneen," the male duet "The Moon Has Raised His Lamp Above," and "Colleen Bawn." Its huge popularity in England led to its being filmed four times during the period before World War II.

1934 Elvey film

English feature film: Maurice Elvey (director), H. Fowler Mear (screenplay), Sydney Blythe (cinematographer), Twickenham Films (production).

Cast: Gina Malo (Eily O'Connor), John Garrick (Sir Patrick Cregan), Leslie Perrins (Sir James Corrigan), Dennis Hoey (Myles-na-Coppaleen), Stanley Holloway (Father O'Flynn), Sara Allgood (Mrs. O'Connor).

Video: Video Yesteryear VHS. Black and white. In English. 88 minutes.

Comment: This is more musical than opera and has extra Irish songs, but it contains the opera's most famous airs and was actually shot in Killarney. It was shown in America as *Bride of the Lake.*

Early films

1922 Tense Moments From Operas series

Betty Farquhar is the Colleen Bawn in this highlights version of the opera made for the English series *Tense Moments From Operas.* Bertram Burleigh is her husband and Booth Conway is Myles-na-Coppaleen. Challis Sanderson directed and H. B. Parkinson produced. It was presented with live music from the opera. Black and white. Silent. About 15 minutes.

1927 Cameo Operas series

Kathlyn Hillard is the Colleen Bawn with Herbert Langley as Hardress Cregan in this highlights version of the opera made for the English series *Cameo Operas.* It was screened with singers standing by the stage performing the arias. John E. Blakeley produced and H. B. Parkinson directed for Song Films. Black and white. Silent. About 18 minutes.

1929 Ridgwell film

Pamela Parr is the Colleen Bawn in this feature film of the opera made at the end of the silent era. Cecil Landreau is Hardress Cregan, Dennis Wyndham is Myles-na-Coppaleen, and Edward O'Neill is Corrigan. George Ridgwell directed for British International Pictures (BIP). Black and white. Silent. About 70 minutes.

LINCKE, PAUL

German composer (1866–1946)

Paul Lincke's music is as symbolic of Berlin as Offenbach's of Paris and Strauss's of Vienna. The song "Berliner Luft" (Berlin Air), which originated in his 1904 operetta *Berliner Luft,* is practically the theme song of the city. Lincke was the first of the famous Berlin operetta composers, starting in 1896. He is known to most Americans as the composer of the hit song "The Glow-Worm," which originated in his 1901 operetta *Lysistrata.* His best-known operetta is FRAU LUNA, an 1899 fantasy about a group of Berliners visiting the moon via balloon. It is still being staged in Berlin today.

LIND, JENNY
Swedish soprano (1820–1887)

American showman P. T. Barnum made Jenny Lind into one of the most famous singers of the 19th century with an amazing publicity campaign. The "Swedish Nightingale" made her debut at the Royal Opera in Stockholm in 1838 and was soon the most popular singer in Sweden. Voice problems in 1841 while singing *Norma* forced her to retrain with Manuel Garcia, but she then became famous all over again singing that opera along with *La sonnambula, La fille du régiment,* and *Robert le Diable.* Lind toured Europe in opera until 1849, and then Barnum boosted her to new heights of celebrity in American recitals from 1850 to 1852. She has been portrayed on film by Grace Moore, Hanna Schygulla, Françoise Rosay, Virginia Bruce, and Priscilla Gillette, among others.

1930 A Lady's Morals
Met diva Grace Moore plays Jenny Lind in this film, the first of the Hollywood show business film biographies after the coming of sound. After a successful career in Sweden, Lind loses her voice on stage during *Norma* in Italy. A composer who loves her (Reginald Denny) is blinded defending her, although later he is able to help her recover her voice. Showman P. T. Barnum (Wallace Beery) brings Lind to America and makes her into a superstar. Moore sings arias from *La fille du régiment* and *Norma* and songs by Oscar Straus. Sidney Franklin directed and Adrian designed Moore's clothes. The film, based on a novel by Dorothy Farnum titled *Jenny Lind,* was called *Jenny Lind* when it was shown in England. Black and white. In English. 75 minutes.

Jenny Lind (1930): British sheet music for Sidney Franklin's film biography starring Grace Moore as the Swedish soprano.

1930 Jenny Lind
A French version of *A Lady's Morals* was made with Grace Moore repeating her role as Jenny Lind; it was titled *Jenny Lind,* like the novel, and had a different supporting cast and director. André Berley plays P. T. Barnum, André Luguet is Lind's friend Paul, Georges Mauloy is Garcia, and Françoise Rosay is Rosatti. Arthur Robison directed. Black and white. In French. 92 minutes.

1934 The Mighty Barnum
Virginia Bruce plays Jenny Lind in this American film focusing on Barnum, played by Wallace Beery. She is shown singing "Casta diva" and other arias by Bellini and Donizetti with the actual singing done by Frances White of the Los Angeles Civic Light Opera company. Walter Lang directed for 20th Century Pictures. Black and white. 98 minutes.

1951 The Legend of Jenny Lind
Soprano Priscilla Gillette plays Jenny Lind in this Westinghouse Studio One TV production, which focuses on the relationship between the singer and Barnum, played by Thomas Mitchell. Gillette, who starred on stage in *Regina* and *The Golden Apple,* sings arias associated with Lind. Paul Nickell directed. Telecast on CBS on December 10, 1951. Black and white. 50 minutes. Video Yesteryear VHS.

1986 Barnum
German actress Hanna Schygulla, the star of many Fassbinder films, is superb as Jenny Lind opposite Burt Lancaster's Barnum in this Canadian film. He goes to Europe and mortgages his future to bring the soprano to the United States, and does this without ever hearing her sing. At her American debut Schygulla sings Lind's trademark Bellini aria "Come per me sereno" from *La sonnambula* (with the voice of soprano Jeanine Thames). Michael Norell wrote the script, Reginald Morris was cinematographer, and Lee Philips directed. Color. 94 minutes. Academy VHS.

1986 Barnum
Christina Collier plays a femme fatale Jenny Lind in this film of a London stage musical of the Barnum story and sings in both Swedish and English. Michael Crawford stars as Barnum in this circuslike production with book by Mark Bramble, music by Cy Coleman, and lyrics by Michael Stewart. Joe Layton directed the stage production and Terry Hughes directed the video. Color. 110 minutes. Waterbearer VHS.

1999 P. T. Barnum

Jayne Heitmeyer plays an elegant Jenny Lind in this A&E Television production with Beau Bridges as Barnum. She is shown on stage singing "Casta diva" after a magnificent Barnum buildup. Lionel Chetwyn wrote the screenplay, Hummie Mann composed the music, and Simon Wincer directed. Color. 200 minutes. A&E VHS.

LINDA DI CHAMOUNIX
1842 opera by Donizetti

GAETANO DONIZETTI's *Linda di Chamounix* (Linda of Chamounix) is not well known, but some critics consider it to be among the composer's finest operas. The heroine Linda, a farmer's daughter, is in love with a young painter named Carlo, who is actually the Viscount Sirval in disguise. When she thinks he is going to marry someone else, she goes mad. He doesn't get married, so she wisely recovers her sanity. The libretto by Gaetano Rossi is based on a French play.

1996 Zurich Opera

Swiss stage production: Daniel Schmid (director), Adam Fischer (conductor, Zurich Opera Orchestra and Chorus), Erich Wonder (set designer).

Cast: Edita Gruberova (Linda), Dion Van der Welt (Carlo), Cornelia Kallisch (Pierotto), Nadine Asher (Maddalena), Armando Ariostini (Antonio), László Polgár (Prefetto), Jacob Will (Marchese di Boisfleury).

Video: TDK DVD/Legato Classics VHS. Alf Bernhard-Leonardi (director). Color. In Italian with English subtitles. 164 minutes.

Early/related films

1910 Itala film

This early Italian film based on the opera was made by the Itala Film company of Turin. It was released in England in June 1910. Black and white. Silent. About 15 minutes.

1913 Linda di Chamouny

Matilde Granillo stars as Linda in this early Italian film of the opera titled *Linda di Chamouny* opposite Arnaldo Arnaldi as Carlo, Achille Voller, and Alfredo Doria. Giuseppe Gray produced it for Centauro Films of Torino. Black and white. Silent. About 30 minutes.

1921 La perla della Savoia

Nella Serravezza is Linda in this narrative film based on the libretto of the opera. Antonio Solinas is Carlo, Dillo Lombardi is Linda's father Antonio, and Decio Jacobacci is the lecherous Marquis Boisfleury. The public liked the film but critics were not enthusiastic. Luigi Ferrario directed for Eden-Ferrario Film. Black and white. Silent. About 75 minutes.

1950 The Toast of New Orleans

Kathryn Grayson, playing an opera house prima donna, sings Linda's Act I aria "O luce di quest'anima" in this film set in New Orleans at the turn of the century. See THE TOAST OF NEW ORLEANS.

LINDBERGHFLUG, DER
1929 opera by Weill

Der Lindberghflug (The Lindbergh Flight), a lesser known collaboration between BERTOLT BRECHT and KURT WEILL originally intended to be a radio opera, celebrates the flight of American aviator Charles Lindbergh. The opera is in 15 tableaux, separated by a radio commentator who reads the title of each new scene.

1994 Cologne Television

German TV production: Jean-François Jung (director), Jan Latham-König (conductor, Cologne Radio-Television Orchestra and Cologne Pro Musica Chorus), Christian Censio Savelli (set designer).

Cast: Richard Erin Samuel (Lindbergh), Peter Wallasch (narrator).

Singers: Wolfgang Schmidt, Herbert Feckler, Lorenz Minth, Christoph Scheeben.

Telecast on ARTE on October 20, 1993. Color. In German. 45 minutes.

Comment: Jung created the imagery for this television production by an innovative use of newspaper clippings, photographs, film stills, airplane models, and montage effects.

LION AND ANDROCLES, THE
1974 opera by Eaton

Roman Christian Androcles removes a thorn from a lion's paw, and the lion refuses to attack him when he is thrown into the Roman Coliseum with other Christians. John Eaton's children's opera *The Lion and Androcles,* libretto by D. Anderson and E. Walter based on a version of the Roman legend by Aeneas Silvius, was premiered at Public School 47 in Indianapolis on May 1, 1974, and then telecast on PBS by Indiana University Opera Theatre.

1974 Indiana University Opera Theatre

American TV production: Ross Allen (director), Carmon DeLeone (conductor, Indiana University Opera Theatre Orchestra and children from Public School 47), Harold F. Mack (set designer).

Cast: William Reeder, William Oberholdzer, Linda Anderson, Michael Rocchio, Signe Lando, Nelda Nelson.

Telecast June 16, 1974, on PBS. Mickey Klein (director). Color. In English. 60 minutes.

LIPP, WILMA
Austrian soprano (1925–)

Wilma Lipp, who made her debut in Vienna in 1943 as Rosina, joined the Vienna State Opera in 1945. She was popular in coloratura roles, especially as the Queen of the Night, and she sang many Mozart heroines. She played Konstanze in DIE ENTFÜHRUNG AUS DEM SERAIL in a 1954 Austrian film and was seen in the role on stage at Glyndebourne in 1957. Lipp appeared in only one other film, singing joyful Mozart in the Otto Preminger movie *The Cardinal*. Her recordings remain popular.

1963 The Cardinal
Lipp is the featured soloist with the Wiener Jugendchor in Otto Preminger's film about the life of an American Roman Catholic priest (played by Tom Tryon). The priest spends two periods of his life in Vienna, which is where he hears Lipp sing the Alleluia from the "Exsultate jubilate" motet by Mozart. Columbia Pictures. Color. 175 minutes.

LITTLE SWEEP, THE
See LET'S MAKE AN OPERA.

LITTLE WOMEN
1998 opera by Adamo

Nineteenth-century New England. Jo March has such warm relationships with sisters Meg, Beth, and Amy that she doesn't want things to change. When they do, she becomes distressed but finally accepts what has to be. Mark Adamo's two-act opera *Little Women*, libretto by the composer based on Louisa May Alcott's classic novel, was commissioned by Houston Grand Opera, which premiered it in 1998. It was so well received that it was revived by Houston in March 2000 and recorded, broadcast, and telecast.

2000 Houston Grand Opera
American stage production: Peter Webster (director), Patrick Summers (conductor, Houston Grand Opera Orchestra), Constantinos Kritikos (set/costume designer).

Cast: Stephanie Novacek (Jo), Joyce DiDonato (Meg), Stacey Tappan (Beth), Margaret Lloyd (Amy), Daniel Belcher (John Brooke), Chad Shelton (Laurie),

Kathryn Cowdrick (Mother), James Maddalena (Father), Katherine Ciesinski (Aunt Cecilia), Chen-Ye Yuan (German professor Friedrich Baer).

Telecast August 29, 2001, on PBS. Brian Large (director). Color. In English. 120 minutes.

LIVE FROM LINCOLN CENTER
PBS television series (1976–)

Technical improvements led to live telecasts of opera from Lincoln Center in 1976 under the direction of pioneer opera director Kirk Browning. The first was Douglas Moore's *The Ballad of Baby Doe*, telecast from the stage of the New York City Opera in May 1976. Live opera from Lincoln Center continues to the present time.

LIVE FROM THE MET
PBS television series (1977–)

The METROPOLITAN OPERA returned to live telecasting of its operas in March 1977, 30 years after its first experimental efforts. The first presentation was *La bohème*, with Luciano Pavarotti as Rodolfo and Kirk Browning as the genius behind the cameras. Live programs from the Met have now become a television staple, and they include not only operatic standards but premieres of new operas such as *The Ghosts of Versailles*. Brian Large has taken over as director of most of the telecasts.

LIVIETTA E TRACOLLO
1734 intermezzo by Pergolesi

The plot of this opera is delightfully absurd. Italian peasant Livietta disguises herself as a Frenchman to catch thief Tracollo, who has disguised himself as a pregnant Polish woman. He declares his love for her, but she rejects him until he comes back disguised as an astrologer and pretends to die; finally they admit their mutual attraction. Giovanni Battista Pergolesi's intermezzo *Livietta e Tracollo ou La contadina astuta*, libretto by Tommaso Mariana, premiered in Naples in 1734 between acts of the composer's "serious opera" *Adriano in Siria*. They had different casts and no musical connection, but the intermezzo was much more popular than the *opera seria*. There are only two singing roles, and much of the action is slapstick.

1996 Luna Theatre, Brussels
Belgian stage production: Ferruccio Soleri (director), Sigiswald Kuijken (conductor, La Petite Bande chamber orchestra).

Cast: Nancy Argenta (Livietta), Werner Van Mechelen (Tracollo), Marie Kuijken (Fulvia), Enrico Maggi (Faccenda).

Video: TDK DVD/Opera d'Oro and House of Opera VHS. Filmed November 23, 1996. Dirk Gryspeirt (director). Color. In Italian. 44 minutes.

LIZZIE BORDEN
1965 opera by Beeson

Lizzie Borden, daughter of a banker in Fall River, Massachusetts, is accused of killing her father and stepmother with an ax but is acquitted. Jack Beeson's opera *Lizzie Borden,* subtitled *A Family Portrait in Three Acts,* libretto by Kenward Elmslie and scenario by Richard Plant based on a famous 1892 trial in Fall River, was premiered by New York City Opera in 1965. *Lizzie Borden* has one of the most effective mad scenes in modern opera, as Lizzie unleashes her pent-up fury at the end of Act II. As in Greek tragedy, and the model for the drama seems to be *Elektra,* the actual murders occur off stage.

1967 NET Opera Theater
American TV production: James Perrin (director), Anton Coppola (conductor, Cambridge Festival orchestra).

Cast: Brenda Lewis (Lizzie Borden), Herbert Beattie (Andrew), Ellen Faull (Abigail), Ann Elgar (Margaret), Richard Krause (Rev. Harrington), Richard Fredricks (Capt. MacFarlane).

Video at the MTR. Kirk Browning (director). Telecast in January 1967. Color. In English. 115 minutes.

Comment: This is the New York City Opera cast that created the opera.

Related film

1975 The Legend of Lizzie Borden
Elizabeth Montgomery plays Lizzie in this realistic TV film of the story written by William Bast and directed by Paul Wendkos. The cast includes Ed Flanders, Finnuala Flanagan, Fritz Weaver, and Katherine Helmond. Color. 100 minutes. Video at the Library of Congress.

LLEÓ, VICENTE
Spanish composer (1870–1922)

Vicente Lleó y Balbastre, one of the best-known Spanish zarzuela composers, began composing in 1885 and completed more than 100 musical works for the stage, including operas. His greatest success and best-known zarzuela is LA CORTE DE FARAÓN (The Court of the Pharaoh), first staged in 1910. It is the only popular zarzuela with a biblical story and has been filmed twice.

LLOYD, ROBERT
English bass (1940–)

British basso Robert Lloyd became so popular as Boris Godunov that he was invited to sing the role with the Russians in St. Petersburg. Lloyd, who made his debut in 1969, joined the Royal Opera in 1972 and then sang in most of the great opera houses of the world. In some ways he assumed the mantle of Chaliapin as actor and singer, and he certainly worked with some of the world's top filmmakers, including Hans-Jurgen Syberberg for a 1982 film of PARSIFAL and André Tarkovsky for a Covent Garden production of BORIS GODUNOV (1990). He participated in the telecast celebration of the reopening of the ROYAL OPERA HOUSE (1999), and many of his performances are on video. See AIDA (1994), IL BARBIERE DI SIVIGLIA (1988), BLUEBEARD'S CASTLE (1988), LES CONTES D'HOFFMANN (1981), DON CARLO (1985), LA FANCIULLA DEL WEST (1983), FIDELIO (1991/2000), L'INCORONAZIONE DI POPPEA (1984), LOHENGRIN (1990), MESSIAH (1992), PARSIFAL (1982), IL RITORNO D'ULISSE IN PATRIA (1973), ROMÉO ET JULIETTE (1994), SIMON BOCCANEGRA (1995), and TRISTAN UND ISOLDE (1993).

1990 Six Foot Cinderella
This BBC Television film about Lloyd's career shows the breadth, depth, and especially the height of his work as an actor and a singer. One of its memorable moments is his singing simultaneously the roles of Don Giovanni, Leporello, and the Statue in the closing scene of *Don Giovanni;* this is done with multiple takes to demonstrate the dramatic possibilities of the bass voice. Color. 60 minutes.

LOCA, LA
See JUANA, LA LOCA.

LOHENGRIN
1850 opera by Wagner

RICHARD WAGNER's *Lohengrin* has been a favorite of filmmakers since 1902 so there are many screen versions of it, even one in Italian; the most praised is the one staged by filmmaker Werner Herzog. *Lohengrin* is set in Antwerp in the 10th century during the time of King Henry the Fowler. The Swan Knight Lohengrin appears to defend the honor of Elsa of Brabant, who has been accused of murdering her brother by Frederick of Telramund and his wife Ortrud. Elsa is saved and marries the knight but then breaks her promise not to ask his name and origin. The Act III "Bridal Chorus" has been popular at weddings since the 19th century and is often used in films featuring a marriage ceremony. All four available videos were directed by the omnipresent Brian Large.

1947 Calandri film

Italian feature film: Max Calandri (director), Gian Maria Cominetti and Piero Ballerini (screenplay), Giuseppe Caraccio (cinematographer).

Cast: Antonio Cassinelli (Lohengrin, sung by Giacinto Prandelli), Jacqueline Plessis (Elsa, sung by Renata Tebaldi), Inga Borg (Ortrud, sung by Elena Nicolai), Attilio Ortolani (Telramund, sung by Giuseppe Modesti), Giulio Nerii (King Henry).

Black and white. In Italian. 100 minutes.

Comment: A film for those who prefer the sound of Italian to German sung at half the length of the stage production.

1982 Bayreuth Festival

German stage production: Götz Friedrich (director), Woldemar Nelsson (conductor, Bayreuth Festival Orchestra and Chorus), Gunther Uecker (set designer), Frieda Parmeggiani (costume designer).

Cast: Peter Hofmann (Lohengrin), Karan Armstrong (Elsa), Elizabeth Connell (Ortrud), Siegfried Vogel (King Henry), Leif Roar (Telramund), Bernd Weikl (King's Herald).

Video: Philips VHS/LD. Brian Large (director). Color. In German with English subtitles. 200 minutes.

1986 Metropolitan Opera

American stage production: August Everding (director), James Levine (conductor, Metropolitan Orchestra and Chorus), Ming Cho Lee (set designer), Peter J. Hall (costume designer).

Cast: Peter Hofmann (Lohengrin), Eva Marton (Elsa), Leonie Rysanek (Ortrud), John Macurdy (King Henry), Leif Roar (Telramund), Anthony Raffell (Herald).

Video: Pioneer DVD and LD/Paramount Bel Canto VHS. Taped January 10, 1986, telecast March 26, 1986. Brian Large (director). Color. In German with English subtitles. 220 minutes.

***1989 Bayreuth Festival

German stage production: Werner Herzog (director), Peter Schneider (conductor, Bayreuth Festival Orchestra and Chorus), Henning von Gierke (set/costume designer).

Cast: Paul Frey (Lohengrin), Cheryl Studer (Elsa), Gabriele Schnaut (Ortrud), Ekkehard Wlaschiha (Telramund), Manfred Schenk (King Henry), Eike Wilm Schulte (Herald).

Video: Philips VHS/LD. Brian Large (director). Color. In German with English subtitles. 215 minutes.

Comment: Filmmaker Herzog transmits his cinematic ability to transmit intensity to this fine stage production.

1990 Vienna State Opera

Austrian stage production: Joachim Herz (production), Wolfgang Weber (staging), Claudio Abbado (conductor, Vienna State Opera Orchestra and Chorus), Rudolf and Reinhard Heinrich (set/costume designers).

Cast: Plácido Domingo (Lohengrin), Cheryl Studer (Elsa), Dunja Vejzovic (Ortrud), Robert Lloyd (King Henry), Hartmut Welker (Telramund), Georg Tichy (Herald).

Video: Image Entertainment & Arthhaus DVD/Home Vision VHS. Brian Large (director). Color. In German with English subtitles. 219 minutes.

Early/related films

1902 Lubin film
The Lubin film company of Philadelphia distributed a film of a scene from the opera in the United States in January 1902. Black and white. Silent. About 3 minutes.

1907 Messter film
Friedrich Porten directed Henny and Franz Porten as Elsa and Lohengrin in this Oskar Messter Biophon Tonbilder German sound film of a scene from the opera. The film was screened with the music synchronized on record. Black and white. In German. About 3 minutes.

1916 Deutsche Lichtspielopern film
Felix Dahn plays Lohengrin in this German feature film of the opera with Elizabeth von Endert as Elsa and Frieda Langendorff as Ortrud. It was produced by Deutsche Lichtspielopern Gesellschaft GmbH, a company founded in 1915 to produce German film operas. The screenings featured live music with singers. Black and white. Silent. About 50 minutes.

1927 The King of Kings
Cecil B. De Mille's film about the life of Jesus (played by H. B. Warner) uses motifs and situations apparently borrowed from *Lohengrin* and *Parsifal*. Black and white. In English. About 130 minutes.

1937 La canzone del cuore
Beniamino Gigli sings an aria from *Lohengrin* in this Italian/German musical about an opera singer involved with a princess. Karl Heinz Martin directed. Black and white. Lyric VHS. In German. 91 minutes.

1937 100 Men and a Girl
Deanna Durbin sneaks into a rehearsal at the Manhattan Concert Hall and watches Leopold Stokowski conduct the Prelude to Act I of *Lohengrin*. Henry Koster directed. Black and white. In English. 84 minutes.

1939 Idiot's Delight
The Prelude to Act 1 is heard on the radio in an Italian Alpine resort by millionaire Edward Arnold and his lady friend Norma Shearer. Clarence Brown directed. Black and white. 105 minutes.

1940 The Great Dictator
The Prelude to Act I of *Lohengrin* is used as musical background as Hitler clone Charlie Chaplin lifts a giant balloon of the world and sends it soaring in a famous satirical mock ballet sequence. This was Chaplin's first talkie as director and actor. Black and white. 98 minutes.

1942 La donna è mobile
In *La donna è mobile*, tenor Ferruccio Tagliavini plays a school teacher with a great voice. On a visit to Rome, he is discovered as a singer and performs arias from *La bohème*, *La sonnambula*, *Lohengrin*, and *L'elisir d'amore*. Mario Mattoli directed.. Black and white. In Italian. 78 minutes..

1944 Silenzio: si gira!
Beniamino Gigli sings an aria from *Lohengrin* in this film about an opera singer who gets a girl a role in a movie. It was shot in Rome by Carlo Campogalliani in Italian and German versions. See SILENZIO, SI GIRA!

1946 Voglio bene soltanto a te
Beniamino Gigli's film about a tenor making a movie and his relationship with a female colleague features music from *Lohengrin*. Giuseppe Fatigati directed. See VOGLIO BENE SOLTANTO A TE.

2000 Ready to Rumble
The Prelude to Act I of *Lohengrin* performed by the Vienna Philharmonic Orchestra is on the soundtrack of this film about champion wrestlers. Brian Robbins directed. Color. 106 minutes.

2001 The Wedding Planner
A film about a wedding planner (Jennifer Lopez) naturally has to feature the "Bridal Chorus" from *Lohengrin*. Adam Shankman directed. Color. 100 minutes.

2002 My Big Fat Greek Wedding
The hit film of 2002 features, not surprisingly, two wedding marches, one from *Lohengrin* and one by Mendelssohn. Color. 95 minutes.

LOLLOBRIGIDA, GINA
Italian actress (1927–)

Gina Lollobrigida is often thought of simply as an Italian cinema sex symbol ("La Lolla"), but the reality is much more interesting. She studied opera for a time, considered it as a profession, and began her career in 1946 in the opera movies L'ELISIR D'AMORE and LUCIA DI LAMMERMOOR. In the Italian film about opera singer Lina Cavalieri, LA DONNA PIÙ BELLA DEL MONDO (The Most Beautiful Woman in the World), she plays Cavalieri and sings Tosca's aria "Vissi d'arte," (it was released as a record). In the excellent 1948 film of PAGLIACCI, she is very good as Nedda, although here her singing is dubbed. In the biopic ENRICO CARUSO, LEGGENDA DI UNA VOCE (released in America as *The Young Caruso*), she is the woman Caruso loves. In Mario Costa's FOLLIE PER L'OPERA, she brings top Italian opera stars to London for a fundraising concert. She gets high praise from the experts in the 1985 French opera film documentary CINOPÉRA.

LOMBARDI ALLA PRIMA CROCIATA, I
1843 opera by Verdi

GIUSEPPE VERDI's *I Lombardi alla prima crociata* (The Lombards on the First Crusade), a complex story about family intrigues during the 11th century, ends with the Crusaders conquering the Holy Land. The complicated libretto, written by Temistocle Solera, is based on an epic poem by Tommaso Grossi. Pagano attempts to kill his brother Arvino, but he kills his father instead. To atone for his sin, he becomes a hermit in the Holy Land. Arvino's daughter Giselda falls in love with the Moslem Oronte, who is killed by the Crusaders after being baptized by the mortally wounded Pagano. The highly regarded chorus "O Signore, dal tetto natio" has patriotic similarities to *Nabucco*'s "Va pensiero."

***1984 Teatro alla Scala
Italian stage production: Gabriele Lavia (director), Gianandrea Gavazzeni (conductor, La Scala Orchestra and Chorus), Giovanni Agostinucci (set designer), Andrea Viotti (costume designer).

Cast: José Carreras (Oronte), Ghena Dimitrova (Giselda), Silvano Carroli (Pagano), Carlo Bini (Arvino), Luisa Vannini (Viclinda).

Video: Bel Canto Society/Castle/Thorn EMI VHS and Pioneer LD. Brian Large (director). Color. In Italian with English subtitles. 127 minutes.

Comment: A stirring production with colorful costumes, fine conducting, and grand singing.

1993 Metropolitan Opera

American stage production: Mark Lamos (director), James Levine (conductor, Metropolitan Opera Orchestra and Chorus), John Conklin (set designer), Dunya Ramicova (costume designer).

Cast: Luciano Pavarotti (Oronte), Samuel Ramey (Pagano), Lauren Flanigan (Giselda), Bruno Beccaria (Arvino), Imma Egida (Viclinda).

Taped December 21. 1993; telecast March 30, 1994. Brian Large (director) Color. In Italian with English subtitles. 139 minutes.

LOMBARDO, CARLO
Italian composer/librettist (1869–1959)

Carlo Lombardo created one of the first operettas about the movies, the 1914 LA SIGNORINA DEL CINEMATOGRAFO, and was involved in Italian operetta production as producer, composer, and librettist. He wrote the librettos for Pietro Mascagni's operetta Sì (1919) and Maria Costa's LA SCUGNIZZA (1922) but had even more success adapting and revising foreign stage works. His Italian version of Franz Lehár's Viennese operetta *Der Sterngucker* (The Star Gazer) was a hit as was LA DANZA DELLE LIBELLULE in 1922 after the German-language version failed. His other operetta adaptations include LA DUCHESSA DEL BAL TABARIN and MADAMA DI TEBE; both remain popular in Italy and *Duchessa* has entered the zarzuela repertory in Spain and Mexico as *Frou Frou del Tabarin.*

LONDON, GEORGE
Canadian-born American bass-baritone (1920–1985)

George London made his debut at the Hollywood Bowl in 1941 in *La traviata,* but his career did not take off until 1949 when he sang in Vienna, La Scala, and Glyndebourne. He came to the Met in 1951 as Amonasro in *Aida* and in 1960 became the first non-Russian to sing *Boris Godunov* at the Bolshoi. He was a noted Scarpia and can be seen in this role with Maria Callas on a 1956 TV show and with Renata Tebaldi in a Stuttgart State Opera production of TOSCA (1961). Much admired for his acting ability, especially in Mozart and Wagner, London went into opera management in 1968, producing notably a complete *Ring* cycle in Seattle in 1975. He made no films, but he can be seen in videos of telecasts.

1953 Metropolitan Opera Jamboree

London was one of the singers at this Met fundraising gala on April 6, 1953, at the Ritz Theater in New York. William Marshall and Marshall Diskin directed the ABC telecast. Black and white. 60 minutes. Video at the MTR.

1953–1955 Voice of Firestone

George London in Opera & Song is a compilation video of performances on four *Voice of Firestone* TV programs. He sings Varlaam's Aria from *Boris Godunov* and "Non più andrai" from *Le nozze di Figaro,* and joins Dorothy Warenskjold and Nadine Conner in duets from *Don Giovanni, Maytime,* and *Show Boat.* Black and white. 46 minutes. VAI VHS.

1956 Ed Sullivan Show

London sings Scarpia with Maria Callas as Tosca in a scene from *Tosca* staged by John Gutman on the *Ed Sullivan Show* on CBS Television November 25, 1956. Dimitri Mitropoulos conducts the Metropolitan Opera Orchestra. Black and white. 18 minutes. Video at the MTR.

1962 George London Festival

London performs arias, songs, and lieder for a TV concert in the *Festival of Performing Arts* series. Included are Leporello's Catalog Aria from *Don Giovanni* and the Death Scene from *Boris Godunov.* Telecast April 24, 1962. Black and white. 30 minutes. Video at the Library of Congress.

1964/1984 George London: A Celebration

An anthology of archival TV performances from 1964, including the *Don Giovanni* Champagne aria and an excerpt from *Boris Godunov,* and live concert performances from 1984, including an excerpt from *Die Walküre* with James King and Leonie Rysanek. Black and white and color. 127 minutes. VAI VHS.

LONG CHRISTMAS DINNER, THE
1961 opera by Hindemith

The long Christmas dinner takes 90 years as generations of the Bayard family assemble for their annual gathering in their home in the American West. Members of the family are born, marry, and die over the years as the family grows and prospers. Paul Hindemith's one-act opera *The Long Christmas Dinner,* libretto by Thornton Wilder based on his play, premiered in a German translation as *Das lange Weihnachtsmahl* in Mannheim in 1961, with Hindemith conducting. The original English version premiered at the Juilliard School in New York in 1963.

1985 HR German Television

German TV production: Andrea Meyer-Hanno (director), Rolf Reinhardt (conductor, HR Chamber Orchestra), Hessischer Rundfunk, Frankfurt (production). Cast: Mechthild Bach, Marina Sandel, Gerhard Brückel, Martin Kränzel, Manuela Mach, Cornelia Muth, Thomas Sehrbrock, Ingrid Steiner. Telecast December 24, 1985, on HR German Television. Color. In German. 60 minutes.

1986 San Francisco Opera Center

American concert production: Robert Baustian (conductor). Cast: David de Haan, Mark Delavan, Kathryn Cowdrick, Susan Patterson, Philip Skinner, Deborah Voight, Douglas Wunsch, Christiane Young. Video: Andrew Thompson VHS. Color. In English. 50 minutes.

LOOSE, EMMY
Czech soprano (1914–1987)

Emmy Loose made her debut as Blonde in DIE ENTFÜHRUNG AUS DEM SERAIL in Hanover in 1939 and can be seen in that role on video in a 1954 Vienna State Opera production. She sang with the Vienna opera house for 25 years from 1941, but she found time to visit Covent Garden and Salzburg. Loose, who was especially liked in Mozart, can be seen as Susanna in a 1954 Vienna Opera video of LE NOZZE DI FIGARO.

LOPEZ, FRANCIS
French composer (1916–1995)

Francis Lopez, the modern king of the French opérette, was by far the most popular operetta composer in France when he died in 1995; this is reflected in a great many French videos of his stage works. Despite his Gallic popularity, he remains virtually unknown in America and England. The Basque-born Lopez, who created 40 stage musicals and a thousand songs, first became popular in 1945 with *La Belle de Cadix* starring Luis Mariano. It was followed by *Andalousie* and *Le chanteur de Mexico,* both also starring Mariano. They were top box office hits as films. *La Belle de Cadix* was revived on stage in Paris in 1995 with José Todaro. Lopez created traditional, tuneful operettas with exotic settings and Spanish-style music, and the French public greatly enjoyed them. He also wrote music for more than 30 French films, including Clouzot's *Quai des orfèvres* and Bernard's *La dame aux camélias.* Many of his operettas were taped live. A partial selection is listed below.

1950 Andalousie

Luis Mariano stars as the bullfighter Juanito in this film of Lopez's 1947 operetta. After a disagreement with his girl Dolores, he goes to Mexico and become a famous matador while she dedicates herself to dance and becomes the star Estrellita. Robert Vernay directed. Black and white. In French. 94 minutes. René Chateau (France) video.

1953 La Belle de Cadix

Luis Mariano re-creates his stage role as the movie star singer Carlos in this film of Lopez's 1945 operetta. It is reset in Spain in 1953; a film company is shooting *La Belle de Cadix* and a singing partner is sought for Carlos. The gypsy Maria-Luisa (Carmen Sevilla) takes on the role. Raymond Bernard directed. Color. In French. 105 minutes. René Chateau (France) video.

1980s Les Plus Belles Opérettes de Francis Lopez

Six of the Lopez operettas were filmed on stage for French television during the early 1980s under the supervision of Lopez and are available on French videos. They are *À la Jamaique* with José Villamor, *Aventure à Monte Carlo* with Georges Guetary, *La Belle de Cadix* with José Todaro, *La Perle des Antilles* with José Villamor, *Le Vagabond tzigane* with Youri, *La Route fleurie,* and *Frénésie tzigane.* All are in color and in French. About 120 minutes each. EMI (France) VHS.

LOREN, SOPHIA
Italian actress (1934–)

Sophia Loren doesn't sing opera, but she did star in two major Italian opera films during her early movie career. In 1952 she portrayed a very beautiful Leonora in Cesare Barlacchi's film of Donizetti's LA FAVORITA, with her singing voice provided by Palmira Vitali Marini. In 1953 she had the glorious singing voice of Renata Tebaldi when she played Aida in a famous screen version of Verdi's AIDA. The film, directed by Clemente Fracassi and promoted in the United States by Sol Hurok like a theatrical event, helped make Loren world famous. In 1961 she won an Academy Award for Best Actress for her performance in *Two Women.*

LORENGAR, PILAR
Spanish soprano (1928–1996)

Pilar Lorengar, who made her U.S. debut at the San Francisco Opera as Desdemona in 1964, was hugely popular in that city and sang there regularly for 25 years. She began her career in Spain as a zarzuela singer and moved into opera in 1955. She began to sing at the Met in 1966, but the main center of her activity was the Deutsche Oper in Berlin. She is sparsely represented on video. She can be seen at Donna Elvira in a famous 1961 Deutsche Opera Berlin production of DON GIOVANNI and with seven other Spanish opera singers in the GALA LIRICA concert in Seville in 1991. She provides the voice for Violetta in a 1984 puppet version of LA TRAVIATA, and she is heard on a record of the COSÌ FAN TUTTE trio "Soave sia il vento" at a key moment in the 1971 film *Sunday Bloody Sunday*.

LORTZING, ALBERT
German composer (1801–1851)

Albert Lortzing was the leading comic opera composer of Germany during the 19th century. He began creating operas in 1828 with *Ali Pascha von Janina* and finished his last one in 1851 just before he died. In Germany his most famous comic operas are ZAR UND ZIMMERMANN, DER WAFFENSCHMIED, and *Der Wildschütz*, although the romantic tragedy UNDINE is probably the best known internationally. *Zar und Zimmermann* has been a particular favorite of German filmmakers.

LOS ANGELES

Los Angeles has been a center for opera since the 1910s, despite not having a major opera company until recently, and has staged a large number of premieres, beginning with Horatio Parker's *Fairyland* at the Hollywood Bowl in 1915. Los Angeles Opera (formerly Los Angeles Music Center Opera), founded in 1986, provides a home for major productions, with Kent Nagano as principal conductor and Plácido Domingo as artistic director. Aulis Sallilnen's KULLERVO was premiered in 1992, EL GATO MONTÉS was telecast in 1994, and Tobias Picker's *Fantastic Mr. Fox* was premiered in 1999. The UCLA Performing Arts often features operas, such as Philip Glass's MONSTERS OF GRACE, which premiered in 1998. See AMERICAN FILM INSTITUTE, ANOUSH (1999), THE CIVIL WARS, JACKSON (2002), SWEENEY TODD (1982), THE THREE TENORS (1994), and UCLA FILM AND TELEVISION ARCHIVE.

LOS ANGELES, VICTORIA DE
Spanish soprano (1923–)

Victoria de los Angeles was born in Barcelona where she made her debut in 1941 as Mimì in *La bohème*. She sang on the BBC in 1948, at Covent Garden in 1950, and at the Met in 1951. She is especially admired for her singing of lyrical roles like Mimì; many consider her recording of *La bohème* with Björling conducted by Beecham to be unsurpassed. Los Angeles has turned from opera to the concert stage, but she continues to charm audiences 50 years after she began her career.

1960s Bell Telephone Hour
Los Angeles can be seen in scenes from two operas on the *Bell Telephone Hour* TV program. She sang Cio-Cio-San with Brian Sullivan as Pinkerton in *Madama Butterfly* in the *Portraits in Music* series in 1962 (video at the MTR). She can be seen in a scene from *La bohème* on the VAI/Kultur DVD *Great Stars of Opera* with Donald Voorhees conducting the Bell Telephone Hour Orchestra.

1962 BBC Television
John Freeman talks to los Angeles about her career in the BBC Television program *Victoria de los Angeles* and she sings excerpts from *The Barber of Seville, Madame Butterfly,* and *La vida breve.* Patricia Foy directed the program telecast May 31, 1962. Black and white. 40 minutes. Print at the NFTA, London.

1967 The Glory of Spain
Los Angeles sings songs and arias by Palomin, Blas de la Cerna, Granados, and Cabeson in this tribute to the music and art of Spain filmed at Madrid's El Prado. Also performing are pianist Alicia de Larrocha and guitarist Andrés Segovia. J. Kroll directed the video. Color. 54 minutes. VAI VHS.

1968 Magnificent Victoria de los Angeles
Los Angeles sings 18 songs in this recital, including four by Ravel, three by Fauré, three by Nin, two by Toldra, "Zapateado" from Gimenez's *La Tempranica,* and Montsalvatge's "Canción de cuna par domir a un negrito." Pianist Gerald Moore introduces the selections for the recital taped by BBC TV on December 17, 1968. Color. 48 minutes. VAI VHS.

1988 Ravel
Los Angeles is one of the singers performing music by Ravel with the Montreal Symphony Orchestra and Orford String Quartet on this film about Ravel's life and music Larry Weinstein directed. Color. In English. 105 minutes.

1989 The Jubilee Recital
Los Angeles returned to the Palacido de la Musica in Barcelona on May 19, 1989, for a celebration of her 45 years as a recitalist. She performs songs by Falla, Del Vado, Mison, Pia, Esteve, Granados, Albeniz, Vives, Montsalvatge, and Mompou and concludes with an aria from *Carmen.* Manuel Garcia Morante is the pianist. Color. 90 minutes. VAI VHS.

LOS DE ARAGÓN
1927 zarzuela by Serrano

José Serrano's 1927 zarzuela *Los de Aragón* (Those People of Aragón), libretto by Juan Jose Lorente, is basically a device to show off the music and customs of the Aragón region in northeastern Spain. It takes place in the capitol city of Zaragoza in 1927; the slight story revolves around Gloria and her ex-fiancé Agustín who have returned to the city on the same day.

1940 Gloria del Moncayo

Spanish feature film: Juan Parellada (director), Antonio Calderón and Martin Herzberg (screenplay based on *Los de Aragon*), José Gaspar (cinematographer).

Cast: Eulalia Zazo (Gloria), Polita Bedros, Manuel de Diego, Jorge Greiner.

Black and white. In Spanish. 85 minutes.

LOSEY, JOSEPH
American film director (1909–1984)

Joseph Losey began his film career in the United States in 1941, but he worked mostly in England after being blacklisted in 1951. He is the cinema's equivalent of Henry James with artistic roots in both countries; one of his greatest movies was appropriately titled *The Go-Between*. His 1979 film of Mozart's DON GIOVANNI is one of the truly great opera films, unlike any other in its visual and intellectual sensibility.

LOTT, FELICITY
English soprano (1947–)

Felicity Lott began to sing with the English National Opera in 1975 and made her first appearances at Covent Garden and Glyndebourne in 1976. She sings in a wide variety of classic and modern operas but is especially noted for her Mozart and Strauss. She made her debut at the Met in 1990 as the Marschallin in *Der Rosenkavalier* and can be seen in this role on a video. See AMADEUS, LA BELLE HÉLÈNE (1999), GLYNDEBOURNE (1992), INTERMEZZO (1983), LE NOZZE DI FIGARO (1984 film), A MIDSUMMER NIGHT'S DREAM (1981), ADELINA PATTI (1977), THE RAKE'S PROGRESS (1977), DER ROSENKAVALIER (1994), and DIE ZAUBERFLÖTE (1978).

LOTTERY BRIDE, THE
1930 film operetta by Friml

RUDOLF FRIML wrote an original score for this bizarre Hollywood film operetta produced by Arthur Hammerstein, Oscar II's uncle. Jeanette MacDonald plays a woman whose love affair with John Garrick goes wrong, so she allows herself to be the prize in an Alaskan marriage lottery. She ends up as the bride-to-be of her true love's brother (Robert Chisholm), and, horrors, he is there in the same cabin in the woods. He jumps on a passing German Zeppelin to get away, but it gets lost on the ice. Jeanette sets out to rescue him, and all ends impossibly well in two-color Technicolor. The cast also includes Joe. E Brown and Zasu Pitts. Herbert Stothart originated the story, Horace Jackson wrote the screenplay, J. Kerin Brennan wrote the lyrics for the forgotten songs, Hugo Riesenfeld was music director, and Paul Stein directed the 80-minute film for ArtCinema/United Artists. This film, which has to be seen to be believed, is available on LD.

LOUISE
1900 opera by Charpentier

GUSTAVE CHARPENTIER's *Louise,* a kind of operatic love letter to the Bohemian Paris of the composer's era, revolves around young dressmaker Louise and her love affair with artist Julien. Her parents refuse to allow them to marry, so they set up house together in Montmartre. When her father becomes ill, she returns home to nurse him. After he recovers, she rejoins Julien. Her father curses the city that has robbed him of his daughter. The opera was a scandal when it premiered but today seems merely romantic. It is best known for its famous soprano aria "Depuis le jour." Charpentier was involved in the making of the 1939 film of the opera starring Grace Moore, and the role has been sung in modern recordings by Ileana Cotrubas, Beverly Sills, and Felicity Lott.

1939 Gance film

French feature film: Abel Gance (director), Eugene Bigot (music director), Roland Dorgelès (screenplay), Curt Courant and André Bac (cinematography), George Wakhévitch (set designer).

Cast: Grace Moore (Louise), Georges Thill (Julien), André Pernet (Father), Suzanne Desprès (Mother), Ginette Leclerc (Lucienne), Robert Le Vigan (Gaston).

Video: Bel Canto Society/Opera Dubs VHS/René Chateau (France) VHS. Black and white. In French. 85 minutes.

Comment: The film was produced under the supervision of the 78-year-old composer, but Moore is the film's greatest asset. It was made after her Hollywood career, and she was in peak form as singer and actress. Thill and Pernet had made a famous recording of the opera in 1935 with Ninon Vallin as Louise. The dialogue in the film is spoken.

1965 ABC Australian Television

Australian stage production: Peter Page (director), Walter Stiasny (conductor, Sydney Symphony Orchestra), Quentin Hole (set designer).

Cast: Mary O'Brien (Louise), Robert Gard (Julien), Arthur Downes (Father), Joan Milford (Mother), Gino Zancanaro (King of Fools).

Telecast June 16, 1965, on ABC Television. Color. In English. 120 minutes.

Related film

1987 Aria

Derek Jarman's episode of the British opera film ARIA features an aged opera singer taking her final curtain call and remembering the great love of her youth as "Depuis le jour" is sung by Leontyne Price. Amy Johnson is the old lady, Tilda Swinton is her younger self, and Spencer Leigh is her young man. Francesco Molinari-Pradelli conducts the RCA Italiana Orchestra Color. In French. About 10 minutes.

LOVE FOR THREE ORANGES, THE
1921 opera by Prokofiev

SERGEI PROKOFIEV's surrealistic opera *The Love for Three Oranges* (Lyubov' k tryom apel'sinam) is truly international. It was written in New York and premiered in Chicago in a French translation with its libretto based on an Italian fable by Venetian Carlo Gozzi. It revolves around the Prince of Clubs, who is dying because he is unable to laugh, but then Fata Morgana takes a pratfall. Under her spell, he seeks out three oranges that contain three princesses, one of whom will be his love. The theme for the popular radio series *The FBI in Peace and War* comes from *The Love for Three Oranges*.

1980 BBC Television

English TV production: Brian Large (director), Robin Stapleton (conductor, London Philharmonic Orchestra and the Ambrosian Opera Chorus).

Cast: Robin Leggate (Prince), Joseph Rouleau (King of Clubs), Pauline Tinsley (Fata Morgana), Alexander Oliver (Truffaldino), Dennis Wicks (Celio), Tom McConnell (Leandro), Katharine Pring (Princess Clarissa).

Video at the MTR. Color. In French with English subtitles. 130 minutes.

***1982 Glyndebourne Festival

English stage production: Frank Corsaro (director), Bernard Haitink (conductor, London Philharmonic Orchestra and Glyndebourne Festival Chorus), Maurice Sendak (set/costume designer).

Cast: Ryland Davies (Prince), Willard White (King of Clubs), Colette Alliot-Lugaz (Princess Ninetta), Nelly Morpurgo (Fata Morgana), Nuccio Condo (Princess Clarissa), Richard van Allan (Celio), Ugo Benelli

(Truffaldino), Fiona Kimm (Smeraldina), Derek Hammond-Stroud (Farfarello), John Pringle (Leandro).

Video: Home Vision VHS (titled *The Love of Three Oranges*). Rodney Greenberg (director). Color. In French with English subtitles. 120 minutes.

Comment: The real star of this extravagant production is Sendak, and his zany designs, colors, and puppets keep the eye constantly amused. Corsaro makes the *commedia dell'arte* story a play within a play staged in the middle of the French Revolution. It's outlandish fun, with acrobats, jugglers, oranges that grow princesses, animated sequences, and a giant baker.

1989 Opéra de Lyon

French stage production: Louis Erlo (director), Kent Nagano (conductor, Opéra de Lyon Orchestra), Jacques Rapp (set designer), Ferdinando Bruni (costume designer).

Cast: Jean-Luc Viala (Prince), Gabriel Bacquier (King of Clubs), Catherine Dubosc (Princess Ninetta), Michèle Lagrange (Fata Morgana), Hélène Perraguin (Princess Clarissa), Vincent Le Texier (Leandro), Gregory Reinhart (Celio), Georges Gautier (Truffaldino), Beatrice Uria-Monzon (Smeraldina), Jules Bastin (Cook).

Video: Image Entertainment and Arthaus (GB) DVD/Virgin Vision (GB) VHS/Pioneer LD. Jean-François Jung (director). Color. In French with English subtitles. 105 minutes.

LOVE ME FOREVER
1935 American film with operatic content

Grace Moore, a poor but talented soprano, gets to sing in *La bohème* at the Met opposite Michael Bartlett with the help of opera-loving gambler Leo Carrillo. *Love Me Forever* also features a mockup of the old Met and an impersonation of general manager Giulio Gatti-Casazza by Thurston Hall. In the film, heiress Moore has to sell her estate to pay off debts. She is wooed by rich Bostonian Robert Allen but doesn't fancy him. Carrillo hires her to sing in his café and, after she is a hit in *Rigoletto* (expanded to 40 voices, Hollywood-style), pays for her operatic training and arranges an audition at the Met. When he thinks she prefers her old love to him, he gambles himself into a huge debt. She finds out, pays it off with a loan, and blows him kisses after her opening night Met performance. The *La bohème* cast includes Tudor Williams as Colline, and Luis Alberni is in fine frenzied form as Luigi. Gaetano Merola conducted the operatic numbers, Jo Swerling and Sidney Buchman wrote the screenplay based on a story by Victor Schertzinger, Joseph Walker and Joseph August were the cinematographers, and Victor Schertzinger directed for Columbia Pictures. British title: *On Wings of Song*. Black and white. 90 minutes.

LOVE OF DESTINY, THE

1983 opera film pastiche by Weigl

Czech filmmaker Petr Weigl created this opera film pastiche by using well-known arias to tell an impressionistic love story. A stylish tour-de-force, it revolves around an opera singer and his memories of a dead woman he once loved. Czech tenor Peter Dvorsky plays the man, with Emilia Aasaryova as the woman, and sings arias from *Cavalleria rusticana, Tosca, Un ballo in maschera, La favorita, Manon, Madama Butterfly,* and *Lucia di Lammermoor.* The film is superbly photographed by Jiri Kadanka with the music performed by the Bratislava Symphony Orchestra led by Ondrej Lenard. Color. In French and Italian. 60 minutes. Kultur VHS.

LUBITSCH, ERNST

German-born American film director (1892–1947)

Ernst Lubitsch filmed a number of adaptations of operas and operettas in Germany and the United States. His famous cinematic "touch" extended to notable silent films of CARMEN (1918) and THE STUDENT PRINCE (1927). He filmed EIN WALZERTRAUM in 1931 as *The Smiling Lieutenant,* directed JEANETTE MACDONALD in several musicals, and made a superb 1934 English-language version of DIE LUSTIGE WITWE. Other plans didn't work out, including an ambitious *Der Rosenkavalier* and a film of Kálmán's *Kaiserin Josephine* with Grace Moore, canceled when she died in a plane crash. His last film was an adaptation of Jean Gilbert's operetta DIE FRAU IM HERMELIN (1949).

LUCIA DI LAMMERMOOR

1835 opera by Donizetti

Lucia di Lammermoor (Lucy of Lammermoor), a fixture in the modern repertory, is GAETANO DONIZETTI's finest opera, and its extraordinary sextet and Mad Scene are among the most memorable in all opera. The melodramatic libretto by Salvatore Cammarano is based on Sir Walter Scott's novel *The Bride of Lammermoor.* Lucia's brother Enrico has usurped Edgardo's estate, but Lucia and Edgardo are in love and meet secretly. Her brother persuades her to marry Arturo with the help of a forged letter, but Edgardo returns on the day of the marriage to join in the famous sextet. Lucia goes mad, kills her husband, and demonstrates her singing skills with the help of a flute. The blood and thunder plot has been popular with filmmakers, especially during the silent era, and the opera has been used for dramatic effect in several novels, most notably in Flaubert's *Madame Bovary.* The sextet has been put to odd use in a few films, including versions by alley cats and hoboes.

1946 Ballerini film

Italian feature film: Piero Ballerini (director/screenplay), Pier Giuseppe Franci (screenplay), Oliviero De Fabritiis (conductor, Rome Opera House Orchestra and Chorus), Mario Albertelli (cinematographer), Opera Film (production).

Cast: Nelly Corradi (Lucia), Mario Filippeschi (Edgardo), Afro Poli (Enrico), Italo Tajo (Raimondo), Loretta Di Lelio (Alisa), Aldo Ferracuti (Arturo), Gina Lollobrigida.

Video: Bel Canto Society/Lyric/Opera Dubs VHS. Black and white. In Italian. 95 minutes.

Comment: This was the first film ever made of the complete opera, and it shows its age but stays close to the original in text and music.

1948 First Opera Film Festival

Italian stage production: Enrico Fulchigoni (director), Angelo Questa (conductor, Rome Opera House Orchestra and Chorus), George Richfield (producer).

Cast: Anne Lollobrigida (Lucia, sung by Liliana Rossi), Zwonko Gluk (Edgardo, sung by Giacinto Prandelli), Tito Gobbi (Enrico), Giulio Tomei (Raimondo, sung by Luciano Neroni), Anna Marcangeli (Alisa), Gino Conti (Arturo, sung by Cesare Valletti).

Video: Bel Canto Society/Lyric VHS. Edmondo Cancellieri (director). Black and white. In Italian with English voice-over. 25 minutes.

Comment: Highlights version filmed on stage at the Rome Opera House with singers from La Scala and Rome. It was made for the anthology film *First Opera Film Festival.*

1964 NBC Opera Theatre

American TV production: Roger Wolf (director), Alfred Wallenstein (conductor, NBC Symphony of the Air Orchestra), Robert Wightman (set designer), Samuel Chotzinoff (producer), Anne Grossman (English adaptation).

Cast: Linda Newman (Lucia), Michael Trimbel, (Edgardo), Richard Torigi (Enrico), Chester Watson (Raimondo), Joan Caplan (Alisa), Jerold Siena (Arturo).

Telecast live January 19, 1964, on NBC. Kirk Browning (director). Black and white. In English. 100 minutes.

1967 NHK Lirica Italiana

Japanese stage production: Bruno Nofri (director), Bruno Bartoletti (conductor, NHK Lirica Italiana Orchestra and Tokyo Philharmonic Chorus), Enzo Deho (set designer).

Cast: Renata Scotto (Lucia), Carlo Bergonzi (Edgardo), Mario Zanasi (Enrico), Plinio Clabassi (Raimondo), Mirella Fiorentini (Alisa), Angelo Marchiandi (Arturo).

Video: Legato Classics VHS. Taped September 27, 1967. Color. In Italian without English subtitles. 127 minutes.

1971 Lanfranchi film

Italian feature film: Mario Lanfranchi (director), Carlo Felice Cillario (conductor, Rome Symphony Orchestra and RAI Chorus).

Cast: Anna Moffo (Lucia), Lajos Kozma (Edgardo), Giulio Fioravanti (Enrico), Paulo Washington (Raimondo), Anna Maria Segatori (Alisa), Pietro di Vietri (Arturo).

Video: VAI DVD/VHS. Color. In Italian with English subtitles. 108 minutes.

Comment: Shot on location in a 17th-century castle and its surroundings. Moffo is in fine form.

1973 Who's Afraid of Opera?

English TV film: Piers Haggard (director), Richard Bonynge (conductor, London Symphony Orchestra), Claire Merrill (screenplay), Voytek (set designer), Nathan Kroll (producer).

Cast: Joan Sutherland (Lucia), John Brecknock (Edgardo), Pieter Van Der Stolk (Enrico), Clifford Grant (Raimondo), Alicia Gamley (Alisa), Francis Egerton (Arturo), Larry Berthelson puppets.

Video: Kultur VHS. Color. In English and Italian. 30 minutes.

Comment: Highlights version for young audiences with Sutherland telling the story to puppets. Dialogue in English, arias in Italian.

1981 Bregenz Festival

Austrian stage production: Lamberto Gardelli (conductor, Vienna Symphony Orchestra and Vienna Volksoper Chorus), Maria Letizia Amadei (set/costume designer).

Cast: Katia Ricciarelli (Lucia), José Carreras (Edgardo), Leo Nucci (Enrico), John Paul Bogart (Raimondo), Waltraud Winsauer (Alisa), John Dickie (Arturo).

House of Opera/Legato Classics VHS. Color. In Italian. 125 minutes.

***1982 Metropolitan Opera

American stage production: Bruce Donnell (director), Richard Bonynge (conductor, Metropolitan Opera Orchestra and Chorus), Attilio Colonnello (set/costume designer).

Cast: Joan Sutherland (Lucia), Alfredo Kraus (Edgardo), Pablo Elvira (Enrico), Paul Plishka (Raimondo), Ariel Bybee (Alisa), Jeffrey Stamm (Arturo).

Video: Pioneer DVD and LD/Paramount VHS. Taped November 13, 1982; telecast September 28, 1983.

Kirk Browning (director). Color. In Italian with English subtitles. 128 minutes.

Comment: This role helped make Sutherland famous in 1959, and she is still a vocal wonder singing it 23 years later. The sextet and Mad Scene set the standard.

1982 New York City Opera

American stage production: Tito Capobianco (director), Judith Somogi (conductor, New York City Opera and Chorus), Marsha Louis Eck (set designer).

Cast: Gianna Rolandi (Lucia), Barry McCauley (Edgardo), Brent Ellis (Enrico), Robert Hale (Raimondo), Jane Shaulis (Alisa), David Eisler (Arturo).

Telecast April 10, 1982, on PBS. Color. In Italian with English subtitles. 179 minutes.

1983 Grand Théâtre de Genève

Swiss stage production: Pier Luigi Pizzi (director, set/costume designer), Nello Santi (conductor, Suisse Romande Orchestra and Grand Théâtre de Genève Chorus).

Cast: June Anderson (Lucia), Peter Dvorsky (Edgardo), Lajos Miller (Enrico), Agostino Ferrin (Raimondo), Adriana Stamenova (Alisa), Richard Greager (Arturo).

Video: House of Opera/Lyric VHS and Dreamlife (Japan) DVD. Pierre Matteuzzi (director). Color. In Italian. 149 minutes.

1986 Australian Opera

Australian stage production: John Copley (director), Richard Bonynge (conductor, Elizabethan Sydney Orchestra and Australian Opera Chorus).

Cast: Joan Sutherland (Lucia), Richard Greager (Edgardo), Malcolm Donnelly (Enrico), Clifford Grant (Raimondo), Patricia Price (Alisa), Sergei Baigildin (Arturo).

Video: Image Entertainment DVD/Kultur VHS. Color. In Italian with English subtitles. 145 minutes.

Comment: This is the most complete version on video, but it's not up to Sutherland's 1982 Metropolitan Opera performance.

1992 Teatro alla Scala

Italian stage production: Pier'Alli (director, set/costume designer), Stefano Ranzani (conductor, Teatro alla Scala Orchestra and Chorus).

Cast: Mariella Devia (Lucia), Vincenzo La Scola (Edgardo), Renato Bruson (Enrico), Marco Berti, Carlo Colombara, Floriana Sovilla, Ernest Cravazzi.

Video: On VHS and Japanese LD. Pier'Alli (director). Color. In Italian. 140 minutes.

Early/related films

1907 Messter film
Otto Messter's Biophon film of a scene from the opera featuring Henny Porten was screened with an aria from the opera played on a synchronized phonograph. Black and white. In Italian. About 3 minutes.

1908 Rossi film
The Rossi studio made an Italian sound film called *Lucia di Lammermoor* that featured scenes from the opera. Black and white. In Italian. About 5 minutes.

1908 Verranno a te sull'aure
The Edgardo-Lucia duet "Verranno a te sull'aure" was filmed by an Italian studio in Pisa specializing in musical sound films. The unnamed singers recorded the duet on a disc synchronized with the film. Black and white. In Italian. About 5 minutes.

1908 Ambrosio film
Italian director Ernesto Maria Pasquali made this *Lucia di Lammermoor* for the Ambrosio company in Italy in 1908. Black and white. Silent. About 10 minutes.

1909 The Bride of Lammermoor
Annette Kellerman and Maurice Costello star as Lucia and Edgardo in *The Bride of Lammermoor,* an American film based on the opera and Scott's novel. J. Stuart Blackton directed for Vitagraph. Black and white. Silent. About 8 minutes.

1911 Cinés film
Mario Caserini directed this *Lucia di Lammermoor,* based on the opera and Scott's novel, for Cinés in Turin. Aldo Sinimberghi, Maria Cleo Tarlarini, and Alberto Capozzi are the stars, and Arrigo Frusta wrote the screenplay. *The Moving Picture World* of September 14, 1912, printed a list of the opera excerpts to be played live with the film. Black and white. Silent. About 15 minutes.

1912 Cinephonograph film
Caruso is rumored to have sung the *Lucia* sextet in a legendary early Edison Cinephonograph attempt to synchronize sound and image. Caruso did make records of the sextet during this period, but the film, if it ever existed, has not been found.

1920 Tirrenia film
This *Lucia di Lammermoor,* apparently made for the Italian Tirrenia studio, was listed in contemporary journals but no further information is available.

1922 Tense Moments From Opera
Vivian Gibson plays Lucia in the English highlights film *The Bride of Lammermoor,* made for Gaumont's series *Tense Moments From Opera.* Gordon Hopkirk is Edgar, Olaf Hytten is Arturo, Frank Miller wrote the adaptation, and Challis Anderson directed. The opera music was played live with the film. Black and white. Silent. About 10 minutes.

1928 Vitaphone film
"Marion Talley, Youthful Prima Donna of the New York Metropolitan Opera" and Beniamino Gigli sing the duet "Verranno a te sull'aure" from *Lucia di Lammermoor* in this Vitaphone sound short. Black and white. In Italian. About 8 minutes.

1933 Little Women
Jo (Katharine Hepburn) hums bits from the Sextet which she had just heard at the opera house as she returns to her boarding house with Prof. Baer (Paul Lukas). George Cukor directed. Black and white. 115 minutes

1934 One Night of Love
Grace Moore's film has a delightful *Lucia di Lammermoor* sextet scene; it is set up by Spanish bass Andrés De Segurola to divert the attention of a rent-collecting landlady. Victor Schertzinger directed. Black and white. 80 minutes. Columbia VHS.

1934 Madame Bovary
Flaubert set an important scene of his novel *Madame Bovary* at a performance of *Lucia di Lammermoor* in Rouen, and Jean Renoir includes the scene in his fine film version. Black and white. In French. 101 minutes.

1935 Captain January
The sextet is performed as a trio by Shirley Temple, Guy Kibbee, and Slim Summerville in this movie about an orphan taken in by a lighthouse keeper. Black and white. In English. 78 minutes.

1936 Follow Your Heart
The *Lucia di Lammermoor* sextet is turned into a comedy number with Michael Bartlett singing to a baked ham, baritone Luis Alberni addressing a haddock, and former Met soprano Marion Talley hitting the high notes. See FOLLOW YOUR HEART.

1937 Swing It Professor
The sextet is sung by a group of hoboes sitting around a campfire in this musical comedy. Pinky Tomlin plays the music professor who stumbles on the operatic bums. Black and white. 66 minutes.

1939 Casa Lontana

Beniamino Gigli and Livia Calona are seen on stage at the end of this film singing the love duet "Verranno a te sull'aure." He has become reconciled with his wife, and all is well. See CASA LONTANA.

1941 The Flame of New Orleans

René Clair's fine film begins with *Lucia di Lammermoor* on stage at the New Orleans Opera House with Gitta Alpar and Anthony Marlowe singing Lucia and Edgardo's duet "Verranno a te sull'aure." While they perform, Marlene Dietrich baits a trap for a rich man. Black and white. 78 minutes.

1941 Andy Hardy's Private Secretary

Kathryn Grayson, playing a student hired by Mickey Rooney to sort out his mixed-up affairs, sings the Mad Scene from *Lucia* at her high school graduation. George Seitz directed for MGM. Black and white. 101 minutes. Warner Bros. VHS.

1941 Notes to You

An alley cat sets up his sheet music stand on a backyard fence and begins to sing, annoying Porky Pig, who is trying to sleep. After the cat is shot, ghost cats return singing the sextet from *Lucia di Lammermoor*. Friz Freleng directed for Warner Bros. Color. About 7 minutes. Warner Bros. VHS.

1944 Show Business

Eddie Cantor, George Murphy, Joan Davis, Constance Moore, and friends lip-synch the *Lucia* sextet in this RKO film about four friends trying to make it big in vaudeville. Edwin L. Marin directed. Black and white. 92 minutes.

1944 Gaslight

Ingrid Bergman's aunt, an opera singer whose favorite role was Lucia, has been murdered, so the Lucia-Edgardo duet "Verranno a te sull'aure" is featured on the soundtrack. Missing jewels, the reason for the murder, are found sewn into her Lucia costume. George Cukor directed. Black and white. 111 minutes.

1946 The Whale Who Wanted to Sing at the Met

Willie, the opera-singing whale with the voice of Nelson Eddy, thinks he is about to be discovered, so he auditions by singing three parts of the sextet while he fantasizes performing it at the Met. See THE WHALE WHO WANTED TO SING AT THE MET.

1948 Back Alley Oproar

Sylvester the Cat and some heavenly friends sing the sextet to the disgust of Elmer Fudd in this delightful Warner Bros. cartoon. Friz Freleng directed. Color. 7 minutes. Warner Home Video VHS.

1951 The Great Caruso

Enrico Caruso (Mario Lanza), who is extremely nervous as his wife is about to have a baby, is shown on stage at the Met singing the part of Edgardo in the *Lucia* sextet. When news of the birth of a baby girl is signaled, the news passes rapidly from singers to orchestra to stalls to loges to balcony. Dorothy Kirsten sings Lucia with Gilbert Russell as Arturo. Peter Herman Adler staged and conducted the sequence. See THE GREAT CARUSO.

1952 Because You're Mine

Mario Lanza plays an opera star drafted into the army. His buddies tease him about pulling kitchen duty and serenade him with the phrase "Renato is a potato expert" sung to the tune of the *Lucia* sextet. Alexander Hall directed. Color. 103 minutes. MGM-UA VHS.

1953 Melba

Patrice Munsel, playing opera diva Nellie Melba in this British film biography, performs in the Mad Scene from *Lucia di Lammermoor* at her Covent Garden debut. See MELBA.

1960 The Exterminating Angel

Lucia di Lammermoor is the unseen prelude to Luis Buñuel's extraordinary Mexican film *El Angel Exterminador*. A group of society folk have come from a performance of the opera to a dinner party at the Nobile mansion. Silvia (Rosa Elena Durgal), the diva who sang Lucia, and her conductor Mr. Roc (Enrique Garcia Alvarez) are among the guests. They find themselves mysteriously unable to leave. Black and white. In Spanish. 95 minutes.

1986 The Money Pit

The sextet from *Lucia di Lammermoor* is featured on the soundtrack of this romantic comedy starring Tom Hanks and Shelley Long. The singers (from a 1970 EMI recording) are Beverly Sills, Carlo Bergonzi, Piero Cappuccilli, Justino Diaz, Patricia Kern, and Adolf Dallapozza, with Thomas Schippers conducting the London Symphony Orchestra and Ambrosian Opera Chorus. Richard Benjamin directed. Color. In English. 91 minutes.

1991 Where Angels Fear to Tread

Where Angels Fear to Tread is based on a 1905 novel by E. M. Forster with a scene built around a production of

Lucia di Lammermoor in a small Italian town. An English family, led by Harriet Herriton (Judy Davis), is in Manteriano with hopes of taking her late sister's child from his Italian father. The family goes to see *Lucia* and finds the Italian audience really enjoying itself. Harriet walks out, saying this kind of enthusiasm is disgusting, and the production "not even respectable." Her brother Philip thinks it's wonderful. Charles Sturridge directed. Color. 112 minutes. New Line VHS.

1991 Madame Bovary
Claude Chabrol's film of the Flaubert novel, starring Isabelle Huppert as Madame Bovary, includes the scene where she attends *Lucia di Lammermoor* in Rouen, but the opera itself is not shown. Color. In French. 130 minutes.

1999 Lucia
Don Boyd's film intertwines the opera *Lucia di Lammermoor* with a story about a baritone staging the opera at his country house; he is putting it on to celebrate the wedding of his soprano sister to a rich American tenor. Boyd's daughter Amanda takes the role of the sister and sings Lucia with Richard Coxon as Edgardo, Mark Holland as Enrico, John Daszak as Normanno, and Andrew Greenan as Raimondo. Color. In English. 100 minutes.

1999 Man on the Moon
A recording of the *Lucia* sextet, with Alma Gluck as Lucia, is heard on the soundtrack of this Jim Carrey biopic about the comedian Andy Kaufman. Milos Forman directed. Color. 118 minutes.

1999 Bats
Montserrat Caballé, José Carreras, and the New Philharmonia Orchestra conducted by Jésus López-Cobos are heard performing excerpts from *Lucia di Lammermoor* on the soundtrack of this horror film about monster bats. Louis Morneau directed. Color. 90 minutes.

LUCREZIA BORGIA
1833 opera by Donizetti

Lucrezia Borgia was Donizetti's most popular opera during the 19th century, and it has been a star vehicle in recent times for Montserrat Caballé and Joan Sutherland. The melodramatic libretto by Felice Romani is based on a Victor Hugo play about the most famous woman of the Borgia clan. Lucrezia is married to Alfonso, but as she has already poisoned three husbands, he is afraid he may be next. When Lucrezia poisons young Orsini and his companions out of spite, she discovers that her son Gennaro is one of her victims. She tries to save him, but he rejects her and chooses to die.

1977 Australian Opera
Australian stage production: George Ogilvie (director), Richard Bonynge (conductor, Australian Opera Orchestra and Chorus).

Cast: Joan Sutherland (Lucrezia), Ronald Stevens (Gennaro), Margreta Elkins (Orsini), Robert Allman (Don Alfonso).

Video: Bel Canto Society and Home Vision VHS/Pioneer LD. John Charles (director). Color. In Italian. 138 minutes.

1980 Royal Opera
English stage production: Richard Bonynge (conductor, Royal Opera House Orchestra and Chorus), John Pascoe (set designer).

Cast: Joan Sutherland (Lucrezia), Alfredo Kraus (Gennaro), Anne Howells (Orsini), Stafford Dean (Don Alfonso), Francis Egerton (Rustighello), Paul Hudson (Gubetta).

Video: Kultur DVD/Pioneer LD. Brian Large (director). Color. In Italian with English subtitles. 157 minutes.

Related films

1910 Cines film
Maria Gasparini plays Lucrezia opposite Amleto Novelli in the Italian silent film *Lucrezia Borgia*. It was directed by Mario Caserini for the Cines Studio of Rome. Black and white. About 15 minutes.

1940 Hinrich film
Italian narrative film about Lucrezia Borgia (Isa Pola) and her circle and how she is able to deceive her husband, the Duke of Ferrara. Hans Hinrich directed. Black and white. In Italian. 76 minutes.

LUDWIG II
King of Bavaria (1845–1886)

Richard Wagner's royal patron admired the composer so much that he provided him with financial aid from the moment he became King Ludwig II in 1864, and his generous support allowed Wagner to create his most ambitious operas. The Wagner connection and the king's eccentric behavior have combined to inspire a number of film biographies. All of them, of course, use Wagner's music on the soundtrack, and most have scenes from the operas.

1922 Ludwig II
Olaf Fjord stars as Ludwig II with Eugen Freiss as Richard Wagner in this Austrian feature film biography of the monarch. It was screened with live Wagner music. Otto

Kreisler directed. Black and white. Silent. About 70 minutes.

1929 Ludwig the Second, King of Bavaria
Director William Dieterle plays Ludwig in this silent feature film shot on location in Ludwig's castles. The cast includes Max Schreck, Theodor Loos, and Hans Heinrich Von Twardowski. The German title is *Ludwig der Zweite, König von Bayern*. Black and white. About 90 minutes.

1955 Ludwig II
Helmut Kautner's romantic film about the king concentrates on his love for Elizabeth, Empress of Austria. O. W. Fischer plays Ludwig with Ruth Leuwerik as the Empress, Paul Bildt as Richard Wagner, and Erica Balque as Cosima. Wagner's music is played by the Vienna Symphony Orchestra led by Herbert von Karajan. Color. In German. 115 minutes.

1972 Ludwig, Requiem for a Virgin King
Hans-Jurgen Syberberg's eccentric approach focuses on the king as a mad virgin homosexual visionary. Harry Baer plays the king with Gerhard März as Richard Wagner I, Annette Tirier as Richard Wagner II, Ingrid Caven as Lola Montez, and Hanna Kohler as Sissi. Dietrich Lohmann was cinematographer. The German title is *Ludwig—Requiem für einem jungfräulichen König*. Color. In German. 140 minutes.

1972 Ludwig
Luchino Visconti's elaborate version of Ludwig's life, shot on location in Bavaria with authentic costumes and settings, centers around the Bavarian king's fears, fantasies, and neuroses. Helmut Berger plays Ludwig with support from Trevor Howard as Wagner, Romy Schneider as Elizabeth of Austria, Silvana Mangano as Cosima, and Gert Fröbe as Father Hoffman. Excerpts from *Lohengrin, Tannhäuser, Tristan und Isolde,* and *Siegfried* are played by the Hollywood Bowl Symphony Orchestra led by Carmen Dragon. Armando Nannuzzi is the superb cinematographer. Color. In Italian. 185 minutes.

1985 In the Ocean of Longing
Im Ozean der Sehnsucht is an impressionistic video about the life and death of King Ludwig created by Christian Rischert. Color. In German. 103 minutes.

1996 Ludwig and Richard
This is an elaborate German puppet film about the meeting between the fairy-tale king and the genius composer featuring superb art design and plenty of Wagner music. Artist Dieter Olaf Klama directed the film, which was written by Gottfried Knapp and photographed by Petrus Schloemp. It premiered at the 1996 Montreal Film Festival. Color. In German or dubbed English. 53 minutes.

LUDWIG, CHRISTA
German mezzo-soprano (1928–)

Berlin-born Christa Ludwig made her debut as Orlofsky in *Die Fledermaus* in Frankfurt, established her reputation in Vienna, and went on to sing at most of the great opera houses. She made her American debut in 1959 in Chicago and sang at the Metropolitan the same year. She was a Met regular until 1990 and sang Dido in the first U.S. production of *Les Troyens*. She can be seen on video at the Met in 1990 in the *Ring* cycle as Fricka in DAS RHEINGOLD and DIE WALKÜRE and Waltraute in GÖTTERDÄMMERUNG She participated in a 70th birthday celebration for LEONARD BERNSTEIN in 1998 and is a joy as the Old Lady in his 1989 CANDIDE. Ludwig's spiritual home was Vienna, and she sang a telecast tribute to the city in 1994. See Così FAN TUTTE (1970), FALSTAFF (1982), FIDELIO (1963), and MADAMA BUTTERFLY (1974).

1972 Brahms Recital
Ludwig sings and Leonard Bernstein accompanies on piano in this recital of songs by Brahms. Roger Englander directed the video. Color. 59 minutes.

1992 Vienna Philharmonic 150th Anniversary
Ludwig sings Mahler songs in this concert with Riccardo Muti conducting the Vienna Philharmonic at the Grosser Musikvereinssaal in Vienna. Hugo Kach directed. Color. 114 minutes. Sony VHS.

1994 Tribute to Vienna
Ludwig in concert at the Grosser Musikvereinssaal with music by Beethoven, Mahler, Schubert, Bernstein, Strauss, and Wolf. Charles Spencer plays piano; Elisabeth Birke-Malzer directed the video. Color. 77 minutes. RCA VHS.

1998 Master class with Christa Ludwig
Highlights from master classes by Ludwig at the Volkstheater in Vienna plus archival footage of Ludwig as Dorabella in *Così fan tutte* in 1970 and Leonore in *Fidelio* in 1964. Claud Villier directed the video. Color. In German. 120 minutes.

LUGO, GIUSEPPE
Italian tenor (1898–1980)

Giuseppe Lugo starred in five Italian films during the late 1930s and early 1940s, usually portraying an Italian tenor rather like himself. He began his career at the Opéra-

Comique in Paris in 1931 as Cavaradossi in *Tosca* and returned to Italy in 1936 where he had great success in Bologna in the same role. He became popular at La Scala, Rome, and other Italian opera houses and was particularly admired for his *Rigoletto* Duke. Lugo is not listed in *New Grove* but has sizable entries in Italian and German reference books. His recordings are available in the United States, and some of his films are on video.

1939 La mia canzone al vento
In *La mia canzone al vento* (My Song in the Wind), Lugo plays a famous tenor who agrees to become the prize in a charity lottery and visit the winner. When the daughter of a small-town official wins, Lugo arrives incognito to check out the situation. During the course of the film, he has the chance to sing "Quando le sere al placido" from *Luisa Miller* and other tenor arias. Guido Brignone directed. Black and white. In Italian. 82 minutes.

1940 Cantante con me
A small-town housewife becomes infatuated with tenor Lugo in *Cantante con me* (Sing With Me) and follows him to Rome to see him in *Tosca*. He sends her back to her anxious husband after singing "Ch'ella me creda" from *La Fanciulla del West,* "La donna è mobile" from *Rigoletto*, and a few other arias. Guido Brignone directed. Black and white. In Italian. 83 minutes.

1942 Miliardi, che follia!
Lugo plays a millionaire with a fine voice who hides out with a touring theater company after a kidnap attempt. His singing helps the company become a success, and he falls in love with a young woman in the troupe. Critics noted that Lugo hardly stopped singing in his films. Guido Brignone directed. Black and white. In Italian. 85 minutes.

1943 Senza una donna
Lugo plays a woman-hating duke who hides away in his castle with two other tenors. Women are not to be allowed in, but a group of stranded ballerinas gain entry and change their lives. Alfredo Guarini directed. Black and white. In Italian. 82 minutes.

1956 Il tiranno del Garda
Lugo made only one film after the war, playing the opera singer Raniero in this patriotic historical tale about an uprising in the Lake Garda area. Ignazio Ferronetti directed. Black and white. In Italian. 85 minutes.

LUHRMANN, BAZ
Australian film director (1962–)

Filmmaker Baz Luhrmann, best known for his popular movies *Moulin Rouge* and *Strictly Ballroom,* has also become known as the man who brought LA BOHÈME to Broadway. He began his stage opera career in Australia. In 1986 he wrote and directed an opera called *Lake Lost* for Australian Opera. In 1990 he staged *La bohème* for the first time, turning it into a 1950s Paris love story with a lively young cast. The Bohemians live behind a neon sign that proclaims "L'Amour," and the subtitles on the video refer to Sartre and Mary Poppins. It was revived and taped in 1993, and its success led to its acclaimed production on Broadway in 2002. Some opera aficionados think that the film *Moulin Rouge* should also be considered a modern opera, noting that Plácido Domingo is the voice of the Man in the Moon in the film.

LUISA FERNANDA
1932 zarzuela by Moreno Torroba

FEDERICO MORENO TORROBA's *Luisa Fernanda,* his most popular zarzuela, is set in Spain in the middle of the 19th century. Royalists and republicans are at each other's throats, not unlike the time when the opera premiered. Luisa Fernanda loves Royal Hussar colonel Javiar, but she is being courted by landowner Vidal. When Javiar turns his attentions to Duchess Carolina, Luisa Fernanda decides to marry republican Vidal. When the republicans win, Javiar admits his love for her, so she decides to go into exile with him.

1963 Mexican Television
Mexican TV film: Plácido Domingo (director), Max Factor company (production).

Cast: Plácido Domingo Jr., Plácido Domingo Sr., Marta Ornelas, Ernestina Garfias, Franco Inglesias.

Black and white. In Spanish. 90 minutes.

Comment: Domingo, who began his career in Mexico, filmed six zarzuelas for Max Factor in 1963.

1969 Teatro Lirico Español
Spanish TV film: Juan De Orduña (director), Federico Moreno Torroba (conductor, Orquesta Lírica Española and Cantores de Madrid), Manuel Tamayo (screenplay), Federico Larraya (cinematographer).

Singers: Dolores Pérez (Luisa Fernanda), Josefina Cubeiro (Duchess Carolina), Luis Sagi-Vela, Carlo del Monte, Manuel González, Ramón Alonso, Jesus Aguirre.

Video: Metrovideo (Spain) VHS. Shot in 35mm for RTVE Spanish Television. Juan De Orduña (director). Color. In Spanish. 96 minutes.

1982 Teatro de Colón, Bogotá

Colombia stage production: Jaime Manzur (director, set/costume designer), Jaime Leon (conductor, Colombia Symphony Orchestra and Chorus).

Cast: Zorayda Salazar (Luisa Fernanda), Antonio Blancas (Vidal), Manuel Contreras (Javiar), Beatriz Parra (Duchess Carolina).

Video: Opera Dubs VHS. Color. In Spanish. 115 minutes.

***1999 Jarvis Conservatory, Napa

American stage production: Daniel Helgot (director), Pablo Zinger (conductor), Carlo Carvajal (choreographer).

Cast: Carter Scott (Luisa Fernanda), Luis Ledesma (Vidal), Stephen Guggenheim (Javier), Susan Mello (Duchess Carolina).

Video: Jarvis Conservatory DVD/VHS. Color. Dialogue in English, singing in Spanish with English and Spanish subtitles. 103 minutes.

Comment: Finely produced, sung, and acted with good production values.

LUISA MILLER
1844 opera by Verdi

GIUSEPPE VERDI's popular early opera is set in 17th-century Tyrol. Luisa Miller and Rodolfo are in love, but his father Count Walter wants him to marry Federica so he devises a plot to separate the lovers. Luisa's father is arrested and Luisa is forced to write a letter to save him saying she loves Walter's evil henchman Wurm. The angry Rodolfo poisons Luisa and himself, but Luisa is able to tell him the truth before she dies. Rodolfo kills Wurm and defies his father with his suicide. The opera's famous tenor aria "Quando le sere al placido" is sung by Rodolfo. Salvatore Cammarano based his libretto on Schiller's play *Kabale und Liebe*.

1979 Metropolitan Opera

American stage production: Nathaniel Merrill (director), James Levine (conductor, Metropolitan Opera Orchestra and Chorus), Attilio Colonnello (set designer), Charles Caine (costume designer).

Cast: Renata Scotto (Luisa), Plácido Domingo (Rodolfo), Sherrill Milnes (Miller), Jean Kraft (Federica), Bonaldo Giaiotti (Count Walter), James Morris (Wurm).

Video at the MTR. Telecast January 20, 1979, on PBS. Kirk Browning (director). Color. In Italian with English subtitles. 150 minutes.

1979 Royal Opera House

English stage production: Filippo Sanjust (director), Lorin Maazel (conductor, Royal Opera House Orchestra and Chorus).

Cast: Katia Ricciarelli (Luisa), Plácido Domingo (Rodolfo), Renato Bruson (Miller), Gwynne Howell (Walter), Richard van Allan (Wurm).

Video: House of Opera/Lyric VHS. Telecast June 4, 1979, on BBC. Brian Large (director). Color. In Italian with English subtitles. 149 minutes.

1986 Teatro Regio, Parma

Italian stage production: Angelo Campori (conductor, Orchestra Sinfonica dell'Emilia-Romagna and Teatro Regio Chorus).

Cast: Cristina Rubin (Luisa), Carlo Bergonzi (Rodolfo), Sofia Salazar (Federica), Giancarlo Pasquetto, Michele Pertusi, Gilberto Zanellato.

Video: Bel Canto Society VHS. Color. In Italian. 152 minutes.

1988 Opéra de Lyon

French stage production: Jacques Lassale (director), Maurizio Arena (conductor, Opéra de Lyon Orchestra and Chorus and Montpellier Opera Chorus), Maurizio Balo (set/costume designer).

Cast: June Anderson (Luisa), Taro Ichihara (Rodolfo), Eduard Tumagian (Miller), Paul Plishka (Count Walter), Romuald Tesarowicz (Wurm), Susanna Anselmi (Federica).

Video: Kultur DVD/Home Vision VHS. Claus Viller (director). Color. In Italian. 150 minutes.

Early/related films

1910 Itala film

This silent *Luisa Miller,* based on the opera and the play, was made by the Itala studio of Turin and released in the United States in August 1910. Black and white. About 14 minutes.

1911 Film d'Arte Italiana film

This silent *Luisa Miller,* directed by Ugo Falena and based on the Schiller play, was shot in an early color process for Film d'Arte Italiana of Rome. Biana Lorenzoni stars as Luisa. About 15 minutes.

1939 La mia canzone al vento

Giuseppe Lugo plays a famous tenor in this Italian film and sings the aria "Quando le sere al placido" from *Luisa Miller.* Guido Brignone directed. Black and white. In Italian. 82 minutes.

LULLY, JEAN-BAPTISTE
French composer (1632–1687)

Jean-Baptiste Lully, who was born in Italy as Giovanni Battista Lulli, came to Paris at the age of 13 and became Louis XIV's court composer in 1653. He collaborated with Molière on a series of comédie-ballets including *L'amour médecin* and LE BOURGEOIS GENTILHOMME and then moved on to opera. He wrote 15 popular operas, all with librettos by Philippe Quinault, and effectively created the French opera tradition. Their *Cadmus et Hermione* (1673) is seen as the cornerstone of French opera, although ARMIDE, *Atys,* and *Thésée* seem to be the most popular in France today. Lully died, famously, from gangrene caused by hitting his foot with a stick while beating time at a concert.

1959 Pickpocket
Robert Bresson's great existential film about a Paris pickpocket uses music by Lully as the score for its soundtrack. Black and white. In French. 75 minutes.

1998 Music at the Court of Louis XIV
Documentary filmed largely at Versailles and centering around Lully and other composers. There are excerpts from Lully's opera *Armide* with Ann MacKay in the title role. Part of the series *Man and Music*. Color. 53 minutes. In English. Films for the Humanities & Sciences VHS.

2000 Le roi danse
The King Is Dancing is a lavish French film biography of the composer told in flashback as he reminisces from his deathbed. Lully (Boris Terral) becomes ballet and music master to King Louis XIV in 1653. Gérard Corbiau directed. See LE ROI DANSE.

LULU
1937/1979 opera by Berg

ALBAN BERG's opera, set in the 19th century, tells the story of femme fatale Lulu who destroys the men in her life. Her first husband, the Professor, dies of a heart attack after she is seduced by the Painter. She marries the Painter, but he kills himself after Dr. Schön describes her past. She marries Schön, but shoots him when he threatens her with a gun. She is arrested and imprisoned but escapes with the help of her lesbian lover Countess Geschwitz. She ends up as a prostitute in London where she is killed by Jack the Ripper. Berg based his libretto on Frank Wedekind's plays *Erdgeist* and *Die Büchse der Pandora,* although he was probably influenced by G. W. Pabst's 1929 silent film *Die Büchse der Pandora;* it was quite popular at the time Berg was writing the opera.

Roman Polanski based his Spoleto Festival production of the opera on the film, which stars American Louise Brooks. Teresa Stratas is among the many singers who admit being influenced by it. Acts I and II of Berg's opera (he never finished it) premiered in Zurich in 1937, two years after his death in 1935, but his widow resisted anyone completing Act III. This was arranged, after her death in 1976, by Austrian composer Friedrich Cerha, and the three-act version was premiered by Paris Opéra on May 28, 1979. This is the version usually staged today.

1979 Opéra de Paris
French stage production: Patrice Chéreau (director), Pierre Boulez (conductor, Orchestre du Theatre National de l'Opéra de Paris), Richard Peduzzi (set designer), Jacques Schmidt (costume designer).

Cast: Teresa Stratas (Lulu), Kenneth Riegel (Alwa), Toni Blankenheim (Schigolch), Franz Mazura (Schön/Jack the Ripper), Yvonne Minton (Countess Geschwitz), Robert Tear (Painter), Gerd Nienstedt.

Video: Dreamlife (Japan) DVD/VHS. Telecast in France April 15, 1979. Yvon Gérault and Bernard Sobel (directors). Color. In German. 171 minutes.

1980 Metropolitan Opera
American stage production: John Dexter (director), James Levine (conductor, Metropolitan Opera Orchestra and Chorus), Jocelyn Herbert (set designer).

Cast: Julia Migenes-Johnson (Lulu), Franz Mazura (Schön/Jack the Ripper), Kenneth Reigel (Alwa), Evelyn Lear (Countess), Frank Little (Painter), Andrew Foldi (Schigolch).

Video at the MTR. Telecast live December 20, 1980. Brian Large (director). Color. In German with English subtitles. 175 minutes.

***1996 Glyndebourne Festival
English stage production: Graham Vick (director), Andrew David (conductor, London Philharmonic Orchestra), Paul Brown (set/costume designer).

Cast: Christine Schäfer (Lulu), David Kuebler (Alwa), Norman Bailey (Schigolch), Wolfgang Schöne (Schön/Jack the Ripper), Kathryn Harries (Countess Geschwitz).

Video: House of Opera DVD and VHS/NVC Arts (GB) VHS. Taped July 1996. Humphrey Burton (director). Color. In German with English subtitles. 182 minutes.

Comment: Schäfer has been much admired in the role of Lulu.

Early/related films

1917 Antalfy film
Erna Morena plays Lulu in this silent German film loosely based on the Wedekind plays. Emil Jannings and Harry Liedtke are her costars; Alexander von Antalfy directed. Black and white. About 70 minutes.

1918 Curtiz film
Casablanca director Michael Curtiz filmed this silent *Lulu,* based on the Wedekind plays, in Budapest in 1918. Claire Lotto plays Lulu with Bela Lugosi (before he became Dracula) and Sandor Goth in supporting roles. Black and white. About 70 minutes.

1919 Csersepy film
Danish star Asta Nielsen plays Lulu in the German silent film *Die Büchse der Pandora* based on the Wedekind play. Arzan von Csersepy directed. Black and white. About 70 minutes.

1922 Jessner film
Asta Nielsen plays Lulu for the second time in the German silent film *Loulou* (aka *Erdgeist*) adapted from Wedekind's play *Erdgeist.* Albert Basserman plays Schön; Leopold Jessner directed. Black and white. About 75 minutes.

Pandora's Box (1929): Louise Brooks plays Lulu in G. W. Pabst's film of the Alban Berg opera source plays.

***1929 Pabst film
Louise Brooks stars as Lulu in G. W. Pabst's *Die Büchse der Pandora* (Pandora's Box), the classic German silent film adaptation of the Wedekind plays. In its own way, the film is as powerful as the Berg opera. Brooks, an American, gives one of the great screen performances, unsurpassed even by operatic Lulus. Fritz Kortner is

Schön, Alice Roberts is the Countess, and Gustav Diessl is Jack the Ripper. Ladislaus Vajda wrote the screenplay, and Günther Krampf was the superb cinematographer. Roman Polanski based his Spoleto production of the opera on this film. Black and white. 97 minutes. On VHS.

1962 Thiele film
Nadja Tiller is Lulu in the Austrian film *Lulu,* an adaptation of the Wedekind plays that was strongly influenced by the Pabst film. Rolf Thiele was the writer/director, and Carl de Groof composed the music. Released in America as *No Orchids for Lulu.* Black and white. In German. 88 minutes.

1979 Borowczyk film
Polish director Walerian Borowczyk wrote and directed this *Lulu,* a German-French-Italian adaptation of the plays. Anne Bennent is Lulu with support from Michèle Plácido and Jean-Jacques Delbo. Gianfranco Chiaranello wrote the music. Color. In German or French. 86 minutes.

1978 Chase film
Ronald Chase based his film *Lulu* on G. W. Pabst's film *Die Büchse der Pandora,* but he added music from the Berg opera to the soundtrack. Color. In German. 94 minutes.

1996 Klahr film
Experimental filmmaker Lewis Klahr creates a collage of stills of diva Constance Hauman in his *Lulu,* a film inspired by the Berg opera and featuring its music. Color. 3 minutes.

LUNA, LA
1978 film with opera content

Jill Clayburgh plays famous American opera soprano Caterina Silveri on tour in Italy with her teenage son Joe (Matthew Barry) in this remarkable film by BERNARDO BERTOLUCCI. The story revolves around incest, but the focus of the film is opera, including a visit to Verdi's villa, an affectionate parody of a production of *Un ballo in maschera* at the Baths of Caracalla, and scenes from *Il trovatore, La traviata,* and *Rigoletto.* The soundtrack singers include Maria Callas, Franco Corelli, Gabriella Tucci, and Robert Merrill. Carlo Verdone plays the director of the Caracalla opera with Ronaldo Bonacchi as his assistant and Alessio Vlad as the orchestra conductor. Nicola Nicoloso is Manrico in the production of *Il trovatore* with Mario Tocci as the Count di Luna. Clare Peploe wrote the screenplay with Giuseppe and Bernardo Bertolucci, and Vittorio Storaro was the cinematographer. Produced in Italy by Twentieth Century-Fox. Color. In English. 140 minutes.

LUNA, PABLO
Spanish composer (1879–1942)

Spanish composer Pablo Luna y Carné is best known for his 1910 zarzuela MOLINOS DE VIENTOS (Windmills), which is set in the flat landscapes of Holland. It became famous not only for its fine music but because it was one of the first Spanish zarzuelas to shift away from traditional settings in Spain; Luis Pascual Frutos wrote the libretto. Luna created more than 170 works for the stage, but only *Windmills* appears to have been filmed.

LUSTIGEN WEIBER VON WIEN, DIE
1909 operetta by Stolz

Robert Stolz's highly Viennese operetta *Die lustigen Weiber von Wien* (The Merry Wives of Vienna), which premiered in Vienna in 1909, is based on a libretto by Joseph Braun written originally for Johann Strauss Jr. but not used. Julius Brammer and Alfred Grünwald used it to create a new libretto that concerns lovers, romance, and various confusions on New Year's Eve in Vienna in 1875.

1931 Bolvary film
German feature film: Geza von Bolvary (director), Walter Reisch (screenplay), Willy Goldberger (cinematographer), Super Film (production).

Cast: Irene Eisinger, Willi Forst, Lee Parry, Paul Hörbiger, Evi Eva.

Black and white. In German. 106 minutes.

LUSTIGE WITWE, DIE
1905 operetta by Lehár

A *Merry Widow* craze swept the world after the premiere of *Die lustige Witwe* (The Merry Widow) in Vienna in 1905; it was staged and filmed everywhere and influenced fashion, theater, and dance. Composer FRANZ LEHÁR conducted the first English-language performance in London in 1907, and it went to New York the same year. Within three months, an American *Merry Widow* film was made, and the operetta has remained popular with filmmakers ever since. The German libretto, by Victor Léon and Leo Stein, is based on a French play by Henri Meilhac. Wealthy widow Hanna, the richest person in her small country, meets womanizing Prince Danilo in Paris, and an old romance is rekindled. Although Ambassador Zeta asks Danilo to marry her to keep her fortune in the country, Danilo doesn't want to be seen as a fortune hunter. Valencienne, the young wife of the ambas-

sador, is involved in a romantic subplot. *The Merry Widow* waltz has become an audience favorite, while Hanna's folksy "Vilja Song" is a highlight. For some reason Hanna usually gets her name changed in the film versions. Silent films about the operetta focused on the women's hats as well as the waltz.

***1934 Lubitsch film
American feature film: Ernst Lubitsch (director), Herbert Stothart (music director), Sam Raphaelson and Ernest Vaja (screenplay), Lorenz Hart (English lyrics), MGM (film studio).

Cast: Jeanette MacDonald (Sonia), Maurice Chevalier (Danilo), Edward Everett Horton (Ambassador Popoff), Una Merkel (Queen Dolores), Mina Gombelle (Marcelle).

Video: MGM-UA VHS/LD. Black and white. In English. 99 minutes.

Comment: One of the best operettas on film, well sung and most cleverly directed.

The Merry Widow (1935): Sheet music from the Ernst Lubitsch film version with Maurice Chevalier and Jeanette MacDonald.

1934 La veuve joyeuse
American feature film: Ernest Lubitsch (director), Herbert Stothart (music director), Sam Raphaelson and Ernest Vaja (screenplay), MGM (film studio).

Cast: Jeanette MacDonald (Missia), Maurice Chevalier (Danilo), Marcel Vallee (Ambassador Popoff), Danièle Parola (Queen Dolores), Fifi d'Orsay (Marcelle).

Black and white. In French. 105 minutes.

Comment: This is a French-language version of the operetta made by MGM at the same time as the above film. MacDonald and Chevalier are again the stars, but the supporting cast is different and so is the flavor of the movie.

1952 Bernhardt film
American feature film: Curtis Bernhardt (director), Sonia Levien and William Ludwig (screenplay), Jay Blackton (music director), Robert Surtees (cinematographer), Joe Pasternak (producer).

Cast: Lana Turner (Crystal, sung by Trudy Erwin), Fernando Lamas (Danilo), Una Merkel (Kitty), Richard Haydn (Baron Popoff), John Abbott (Ambassador), Thomas Gomez (King of Marshovia).

Video: MGM-UA VHS. Color. In English. 105 minutes.

Comment: Plush rewrite with Turner playing an American widow whose rich husband has just died. She is persuaded to visit his bankrupt country, where Danilo is ordered to marry her. It goes badly, so she flees to Paris where they finally sort it out with help from the famous waltz. Lamas sings most of the songs, even "Vilja."

1954 CBS Television
American TV production: Cyril Ritchard (director), Eugene Ormandy (conductor, Philadelphia Orchestra), Henry May (set designer), Omnibus (production).

Cast: Patrice Munsel (Sonia), Theodor Uppman (Danilo), Jerome Kilty (Baron Popoff), Martyn Green (Nish), James Hawthorne (Jolidon).

Video at the Library of Congress. Telecast December 26, 1954, on CBS. Seymour Robbie (director). Black and white. In English. 80 minutes.

1955 NBC Television
American TV production: Bill Hobin (director), Max Liebman (producer/director), Charles Sandford (conductor), Frederick Fox (set designer), NBC Color Special.

Cast: Anne Jeffreys (Sonia), Brian Sullivan (Danilo), Edward Everett Horton (Baron Zelta), Helena Bliss (Valencienne), Jack Russell (Lt. Nicholas), John Conte (Georges).

Telecast April 9, 1955, on NBC. Black and white. In English. 90 minutes.

1962 Jacobs film
Austrian feature film: Werner Jacobs (director).

Cast: Karin Hübner (Hanna), Peter Alexander (Danilo), Genevieve Cluny (Valencienne), Dario Moreno (Camille), Maurice Teynac (Baron).

Video: Editions Montparnasse (France) VHS. Color. In French or German. 91 minutes.

Comment: Modernized version of the operetta shot in Austria in French and German versions. In this version, Danilo sings "Vilja."

1963 Mexican Television
Mexican TV film: Plácido Domingo (director), Max Factor (production group).

Cast: Marta Ornelas (Hanna), Plácido Domingo (Danilo), Ernestina Garfias, Franco Inglesias.

Black and white. In Spanish. 85 minutes.

Comment: Domingo, who began his career in Mexico, filmed six operettas and zarzuelas for the Max Factor company in 1963. No copies are known.

1977 San Diego Opera
American stage production: Tito Capobianco (director), Theo Alcantara (conductor, San Diego Opera Orchestra), Carl Toms (set designer).

Cast: Beverly Sills (Hanna), Alan Titus (Danilo), Andrew Foldi (Baron Zeta), Glenys Fowles (Valencienne), Henry Price (Camille).

Video: House of Opera DVD/VHS. Telecast November 27, 1977, on PBS. Kirk Browning (director). Color. 120 minutes.

1988 Australian Opera
Australian stage production: Lotfi Mansouri (director), Richard Bonynge (conductor, Elizabethan Philharmonic Orchestra and Australian Opera Chorus), Kristian Fredrickson (set/costume designer), Christopher Hassall (English translation).

Cast: Joan Sutherland (Hanna), Ronald Stevens (Danilo), Ann-Marie MacDonald (Valencienne), Anson Austin (Camille), Irene Cassimatis (Olga).

Video: Kultur DVD/Home Vision VHS. Taped February 23, 1988. Virginia Lumsden (director). Color. In English. 151 minutes.

1992 La vedova allegra
Italian stage production: Sandro Massimini (director), Roberto Negri (conductor, theater orchestra), Antonio Mastromattei (set designer), Don Lurio (choreographer).

Cast: Sonia Dorigo (Anna), Sandro Massimini (Danilo), Elio Crovetto (Mirko), Tamara Trojani (Valencienne), Vincenzo De Angelis (Camillo).

Video: Ricordi (Italy) VHS. Color. In Italian. 115 minutes.

1993 Mörbisch Seefestspiele
Austrian stage production: Michael Murger (director), Konstantin Schenk (conductor, Bratislav Philharmonic Orchestra and Chorus).

Cast: Elisabeth Kales (Hanna), Peter Edelmann (Danilo), Martina Dorak, Gideon Singer.

Taurus (Germany) VHS. Kurt Pongratz (director). Color. In German. 132 minutes.

Comment: Opulent outdoor production.

1996 New York City Opera

American stage production: Robert Johanson (director/English translation), Alexander Sander (conductor, New York City Opera Orchestra), Michael Anania (set designer), Gregg Barnes (costume designer), Sharon Halley (choreographer), Albert Evans (lyrics).

Cast: Jane Thorngren (Hanna), Michael Hayes (Danilo), George S. Irving (Baron Mirko), Patricia Johnson (Valencienne), Carlo Scibelli (Camille), Robert Creighton (Njegus).

Video at the MTR. Telecast March 27, 1996. Color. In English. 180 minutes.

Comment: The telecast includes a documentary titled "What's Behind *The Merry Widow*?"

2001 San Francisco Opera

American stage production: Lotfi Mansouri (director), Erick Kunzel (conductor, San Francisco Opera Orchestra), Michael Yeargan (set designer), Lawrence Pech (choreographer), Wendy Wasserstein (English libretto), Christopher Hassall, Ted and Deena Puffer (lyrics).

Cast: Yvonne Kenny (Hanna), Bo Skovhus (Danilo), Angelika Kirchschlager (Valencienne), Gregory Turay (Camille), Elifah Cester (Njegus).

Video: Naxos/BBC Opus Arte DVD. Taped December 2001 at War Memorial Opera; telecast December 25, 2002, on PBS. Gary Halvorson (director). Color. In English. 188 minutes.

Early/related films

1907 Nordisk film

The first screen version of *The Merry Widow,* made in Sweden in 1907 by the Nordisk Company, was quite lengthy for its time. It features highlights from the operetta and was screened in theaters with the operetta music played live. Black and white. Silent. About 14 minutes.

1908 Kalem film

This enterprising film of scenes from the operetta was screened by the Kalem Studio on January 25, 1908, only three months after the New York stage premiere of the operetta on October 21, 1907. It was presented with live music and was apparently meant to show the rest of America what was happening on stage in New York. Three large numbers were pictured, including the famous waltz and Sonya singing "Vilja." The cast, which was not the stage cast, included C. Manthey, C. Davis, N. Mo-

rena, and M. Katzer. Black and white. Silent. About 15 minutes.

1908 The Merry Widow Waltz Craze

This is an American comedy film from the Edison studio about a man called Lightfoot; he can't stop himself from dancing whenever he hears the *Merry Widow* waltz. Edwin S. Porter directed the film, released April 29, 1908. Black and white. Silent. About 10 minutes.

1908 The Merry Widow Hats

Lubin comedy about the *Merry Widow* hat craze. Two young women cause trouble everywhere they go with their strange headgear; they even get thrown out of a moving picture palace. Released May 14, 1908. Black and white. Silent. About 9 minutes.

1908 The Merry Widow Hat

Vitagraph comedy film about the fashionable *Merry Widow* hat inspired by the operetta. This rival to the Lubin film was released on October 24, 1908. Black and white. Silent. About 9 minutes.

1908 La valse de la veuve joyeuse

This Pathé Frères adaptation of the operetta's hit waltz was made in France and released in the United States on November 28, 1908, as *Merry Widow Waltz*. It was screened with live music. Black and white. Silent. About 6 minutes.

1908 The Merry Widow at a Supper Party

Biograph Studio comedy film, loosely based on the operetta, shown with live music from the operetta. Arthur Marvin directed. Black and white. Silent. About 7 minutes.

1909 Brazilian Merry Widow

The Brazilian film industry made humorous adaptations of operettas during the silent era with singers standing by the screen and singing the hit tunes. One of the most successful was a "very merry" version of *The Merry Widow.* Black and white. Silent. About 10 minutes.

1910 The Merry Widow Takes Another Partner

Humorous Vitagraph film based loosely on the operetta and shown with live music from the operetta. Black and white. Silent. About 14 minutes.

1912 Reliance-Majestic film

Alma Rubens plays the widow with Wallace Reid as Danilo in this American film of the operetta made by the Reliance-Majestic company. It was screened with live music. Black and white. Silent. About 15 minutes.

1913 Solax film
Pioneer woman director Alice Guy-Blaché made a film of *The Merry Widow* for her Solax company with Marian Swayne playing the widow. Released June 21, 1913. Black and white. Silent. About 15 minutes.

1918 Curtiz film
A Hungarian feature version of the operetta titled *A Víg Özvegy,* starring Ica Lenkeffy, Frigyes Tarnay, and Emil Fenivessy, was made by Michael Curtiz in his early years in Budapest. Black and white. Silent. About 70 minutes.

1925 von Stroheim film
Mae Murray and John Gilbert star in this famous silent version of the operetta directed by Erich von Stroheim. Danilo (Gilbert) is ordered to woo rich American widow Sally (Murray), whom he had earlier jilted. Their romance is rekindled when the movie theater pianist plays the *Merry Widow* waltz on cue. Black and white. About 113 minutes.

1929 Vitaphone film
Elba Ersi sings selections from *The Merry Widow* in a Vitaphone sound short with Nat Ayres accompanying on piano. Black and white. In English. About 8 minutes.

1943 Shadow of a Doubt
Alfred Hitchcock, with the help of composer Dmitri Tiomkin, uses the *Merry Widow* waltz in a sinister way in this suspense thriller. It's the theme music of Teresa Wright's murderous uncle (Joseph Cotten), who has become known as the Merry Widow Murderer. The music gradually becomes more disturbing as it is used in crucial transitions. Black and white. 108 minutes.

1983 The Merry Widow (ballet)
This ballet adaptation of the operetta, choreographed by Ruth Page, tells the operetta story through dancers performing to Lehár's music. Patricia McBride is the Widow with Peter Martin as Danilo and Rebecca Wright as Baroness de Popoff. The Chicago Symphony Orchestra plays the music. This adaptation, which premiered at Chicago's Lyric Opera in November 1955, was telecast by Chicago's WTTW-TV on September 21, 1983. Dick Carter directed. Color. 60 minutes.

1988 The Merry Widow (ballet)
A second ballet adaptation of *The Merry Widow* was written and choreographed by Ronald Hyde and Robert Helpmann. The dancers are Karen Kain as the Widow, John Meehan, Yoko Ichino, Raymond Smith, Charles Kirby, and Jacques Gorrissen. Desmond Heeley designed the sets and costumes, Norman Campbell directed for the CBC. Color. 120 minutes.

LUSTIGEN WEIBER VON WINDSOR, DIE
1849 opera by Nicolai

Falstaff sends love letters to married women, and they get revenge in a variety of ways. *Die lustigen Weiber von Windsor,* OTTO NICOLAI's charming opera based on Shakespeare's *The Merry Wives of Windsor* as adapted by librettist Hermann Salomon Mosenthal, has almost the same story as Verdi's *Falstaff,* based on the play. Some of the characters have been given German names—for example, Mrs. Ford is Frau Fluth and Mrs. Page is Frau Reich—but there is little difference in plot. The opera is popular primarily in Germanic countries, but an American singer made an English-language film version, and Chicago Opera Theater has telecast it in English. The film *Falstaff in Vienna* pretends to explain how Nicolai came to write it.

1950 Wildhagen film
East German feature film: Georg Wildhagen (director/screenplay), Wolf von Gordon (screenplay), Walter Lehmann (producer), DEFA (production studio).

Cast: Paul Esser, (Falstaff, sung by Hans Krämer), Camilla Spira (Frau Reich, sung by Martha Mödl), Sonja Ziemann (Frau Fluth, sung by Rita Streich), Ina Halley (Anna Reich, sung by Sonja Schoener), Claus Holm (Herr Fluth, sung by Helmut Kregs), Alexander Engel (Herr Reich), Eckart Dux (Fenton).

Black and white. In German. 96 minutes.

Comment: The film was distributed in America.

***1965 Foster film
American/Yugoslav/Austrian feature film: George Tressler (director), Milan Horvath (conductor, Zagreb Symphony Orchestra), Gerd Krauss (set designer), Norman Foster (producer/English translation).

Cast: Norman Foster (Falstaff), Colette Boky (Mistress Ford), Mildred Miller (Mistress Page), Lucia Popp (Anne Page), Igor Gorin (Ford), Ernst Schütz (Fenton), Edmond Hurshell (Page).

Video: BHE VHS. Color. In English. 97 minutes.

Comment: American basso Foster, who wrote and produced this lively English-language adaptation, restored the names of the characters as they appear in the Shakespeare play. Canadian soprano Boky has a steamy bathtub scene that attracted a good deal of attention from reviewers when the film was first shown.

1978 Chicago Opera Theater
American stage production: Frank Galati (director), Robert Frisbie (Chicago Opera Theater Orchestra and Chorus), Mary Griswald (set designer).

Cast: Eugene Johnson (Falstaff), Leslie Hoffman (Mistress Ford), Charlotte Gardner (Mistress Page), Myra Cordell (Anne Page), Warren Fremling (Ford), William Martin (Fenton), Douglas Kidd (Page).

Telecast on WTTW Chicago Educational Television in 1978. Richard Carter (director). Color. In English. 60 minutes.

Comment: Shown at the National Opera Institute's TV Opera Colloquium in 1978.

Early/related films

1935 Die lustigen Weiber

Die lustigen Weiber is a German musical version of the story but with new music by Ernest Fischer and Franz Grothe. Leo Slezak plays Falstaff with Magda Schneider, Ida Wüst, and Maria Krahn as the women. Carl Hoffmann directed for Cine-Allianz. Black and white. In German. 84 minutes.

1940 Falstaff in Wien

Falstaff in Vienna is a film about composer Otto Nicolai and the creation of *Die lustigen Weiber von Windsor*. It pretends that events similar to the play happened in Nicolai's circle of friends and inspired him to write the opera. Hans Nielsen plays Nicolai; the supporting cast includes Gusti Wolf, Paul Hörbiger, and Lizzi Holtzschuh. Scenes from the opera are shown on stage with singers from the Berlin Staatsoper and Deutsches Operhaus, including Erna Berger and Carla Spletter, with the music performed by the Berlin Staatsoper Orchestra. Alois Melichar was music director, Max Wallner and Kurt Feltz wrote the screenplay, Bruno Mondi was cinematographer, and Leopold Hainisch directed for Tobis. Black and white. In German. 89 minutes. Lyric VHS.

1945 The Seventh Veil

This British melodrama about the traumatic life of a concert pianist (Ann Todd) features excerpts of classical music, including the Overture from *Die lustigen Weiber von Windsor*. Compton Bennett directed. Black and white. 94 minutes

1962 Musikalisches Rendezvous

Anthology film of excerpts from DEFA opera movies made in East Berlin with a 20-minute scene from the 1950 film of DIE LUSTIGEN WEIBER VON WINDSOR. There are also extracts from ZAR UND ZIMMERMANN, LE NOZZE DI FIGARO, and DER BETTELSTUDENT. Color. In German. 83 minutes.

LYONS/LYON

Lyons (or Lyon as the French prefer to call it), the third largest city in France, has been a center of operatic activity in France since 1687 when it began to stage operas by Lully. In recent years it has been the home of one of the most adventurous opera companies in the world. Opéra de Lyon, under the direction of Louis Erlo with American Kent Nagano as chief conductor, has created a number of impressive productions of operas new and old. They are not all to everyone's taste, but they are genuinely stimulating. See LES BRIGANDS (1989), IL CAPELLO DI PAGLIA DI FIRENZE (1999), LES CONTES D'HOFFMANN (1993), L'ELISIR D'AMORE (1996), L'ENFANT ET LES SORTILÈGES (1993), L'ÉTOILE (1986), THE LOVE FOR THREE ORANGES (1989), LUISA MILLER (1988), MADAMA BUTTERFLY (1993 film), MITRIDATE (1983), LE NOZZE DI FIGARO (1994), PELLÉAS ET MÉLISANDE (1987), RODRIGUE ET CHIMÈNE (1993), DIE SIEBEN TODSÜNDEN (1993), LES TROIS SOUHAITS (1990), LA VIE PARISIENNE (1991), and DIE ZAUBERFLÖTE (1992).

M

MAAZEL, LORIN
American conductor (1930–)

Lorin Maazel conducts the music on some of the great opera films, including Joseph Losey's DON GIOVANNI (1978), Francesco Rosi's CARMEN (1984), and Franco Zeffirelli's OTELLO (1986). He has led orchestras in New York, London, Vienna, Rome, and Berlin and conducted opera at Covent Garden, Bayreuth, La Scala, and other major opera houses. See also AIDA (1985), BAYREUTH (1960), CONDUCTORS (1994), PLÁCIDO DOMINGO (1989), L'ENFANT ET LES SORTILÈGES (1986), LA FANCIULLA DEL WEST (1991), LUISA MILLER (1979), MADAMA BUTTERFLY (1986), LA TRAVIATA (1984 film), TURANDOT (1983), and VERDI REQUIEM (1991).

MACBETH
1847 opera by Verdi

Giuseppe Verdi's opera *Macbeth,* based on the play by Shakespeare, has a libretto by Francesco Maria Piave and Andrea Maffei that follows the play fairly closely. Lady Macbeth persuades Macbeth to kill Duncan so he can become king of Scotland, but their consciences give them no peace. Lady Macbeth walks in her sleep and dies of anguish. Rebels led by Macduff kill Macbeth, and Malcolm becomes king. There are many films of the play, but only recently has the opera itself been put on film and video. Both play and opera are considered in the theater world as attracting bad luck; this superstition is exploited in the 1987 Italian horror film *Terror at the Opera,* which revolves around a disastrous production of *Macbeth.*

1953 NBC Opera Theatre
American TV production: John Bloch (director), Samuel Chotzinoff (producer), Peter Herman Adler (conductor, NBC Symphony of the Air Orchestra), William Molyneux (set designer), Giovanni Cardelli (English translation).

Cast: Warren Galjour (Macbeth), Patricia Neway (Lady Macbeth), Lee Cass (Banquo), William Böhm (Macduff), Robert Holland (Malcolm).

Video at the MTR. Telecast November 28, 1953, on NBC. Kirk Browning (director). Black and white. In English. 90 minutes.

1972 Glyndebourne Festival
English stage production: Michael Hadjimischer (director), John Pritchard (conductor, London Philharmonic Orchestra and Glyndebourne Opera Chorus), Emanuele Luzzati (set designer), Robert Bryan (lighting).

Cast: Kostas Paskalis (Macbeth), Josephine Barstow (Lady Macbeth), James Morris (Banquo), Keith Erwen (Macduff), Ian Caley (Malcolm).

Video: Opera d'Oro/VAI VHS. Dave Heather (director), Humphrey Burton (producer). Color. In Italian with English subtitles. 148 minutes.

Comment: The video looked good when shown on the large screen at London's National Film Theatre on December 27, 1994.

1987 Deutsche Oper, Berlin
German stage production: Luca Ronconi (director), Giuseppe Sinopoli (conductor, Deutsche Oper Berlin Orchestra and Chorus), Luciano Damiani (set/costume designer).

Cast: Renato Bruson (Macbeth), Mara Zampieri (Lady Macbeth), James Morris (Banquo), Dennis O'Neill (Macduff), David Griffith (Malcolm).

Video: Image Entertainment and Arthaus (GB) DVD/Bel Canto Society and Home Vision VHS. Brian Large (director). Color. In Italian with English subtitles. 150 minutes.

***1987 D'Anna film
French feature film: Claude d'Anna (director/cinematographer), Riccardo Chailly (conductor, Bologna Teatro Comunale Orchestra and Chorus), Eric Simon (art director).

Cast: Leo Nucci (Macbeth), Shirley Verrett (Lady Macbeth), John Leysen (Banquo, sung by Samuel Ramey), Philippe Volter (Macduff, sung by Veriano Luchetti), Antonio Barasorda (Malcolm).

Video: London VHS/LD. Color. In Italian with English subtitles. 134 minutes.

Comment: Shot realistically on location in Belgium at the Ardennes castle of the Crusader Godefroy de Bouillon.

1993 Savonlinna Festival
Finnish stage production: Ralf Langbacka (director), Leif Segerstam (conductor, Savonlinna Festival Orchestra), Anneli Queflander (set/costume designer).

Cast: Jorma Hynninen (Macbeth), Cynthia Makris (Lady Macbeth), Jaakko Ryhänen, Peter Lindroos, Riso Saarman.

Telecast December 5, 1993, by YLE Finnish Television. Aarno Cronvall (director). Color. In Italian. 140 minutes.

Comment: Staged in the atmospheric 16th-century Olavinlinna Castle.

***2001 Zurich Opera

Swiss stage production: David Pountney (director), Franz Welser-Möst (conductor, Zurich Opera House Orchestra and Chorus), Stefano Lazaridis (set designer), Marie-Jeanne Lecca (costume designer).

Cast: Thomas Hampson (Macbeth), Paoletta Marrocu (Lady Macbeth), Roberto Scandiuzzi (Banquo), Luis Lima (Macduff), Miroslav Christoff (Malcolm).

Video: Image/TDK (GB) DVD (includes a documentary on *Macbeth*). Thomas Grimm (director). Color. In Italian with English subtitles. 186 minutes.

Comment: Quirky but fascinating modernist production that features transvestites and riot police in key scenes and emphasizes the sexual side of the Macbeth partnership. Hampson and Marrocu are superb.

Related films

Shakespeare Films
The notable films of the play include a 1948 version, directed by and starring Orson Welles as Macbeth, and a 1971 version, directed by Roman Polanski, with Jon Finch as Macbeth.

1987 Terror at the Opera
Dario Argento's film *Terror at the Opera* is built around a Parma production of *Macbeth* with a killer prowling the corridors of an opera house. There are a number of scenes of *Macbeth* on stage at the Teatro Regio with Cristina Marsillach as Lady Macbeth. Elisabetta Norberg Schulz, Paola Leolini, Andrea Piccinni, and Michele Pertusi are the singers, accompanied by the Arturo Toscanini Symphony Orchestra of Emilia and Romagna. See TERROR AT THE OPERA.

1987 The Secret of Macbeth
Anna Raphael shot this 16mm documentary during the production of Claude d'Anna's film of *Macbeth*. It shows how the film was made and includes interviews with the principals. Color. 43 minutes.

McCORMACK, JOHN
Irish tenor (1884–1945)

John McCormack considered himself a poor actor, one of the reasons he gave for quitting the opera stage, but his films belie this and show a natural performer. The great Irish tenor, who was born in Athlone, studied in Italy and made his debut there in 1906 using a fake Italian name. He first appeared at Covent Garden in 1907 as Turiddu in *Cavalleria rusticana* and sang there until 1914. He made his Metropolitan Opera debut in 1910 as Alfredo in *La traviata* and sang in opera in the United States until 1918. After that, he devoted himself to recital tours and records. Like Caruso, he had a voice that recorded beautifully, and he is still a pleasure to hear. He starred in one rather enjoyable film and was featured in others.

1930 Song o' My Heart
McCormack is a delight in this charming musical directed by Frank Borzage. The story is mostly an excuse for the tenor to sing, everything from "Then You'll Remember Me" from *The Bohemian Girl* to "Plaisir d'Amour" and "Kitty My Love." He plays an opera singer living in a small Irish village who quit singing when he lost the woman he loved to another man. When he returns to singing for an America tour, his old love asks him to look after her children if she should die, as she fears. Spanish bass Andrés De Segurola appears in the film as a friend from La Scala days. McCormack seems at ease as a film actor, and his singing is superb. Fox. Black and white. 91 minutes. VAI VHS.

1933 The Shepherd of the Seven Hills
McCormack sings the "Panis Angelicus" in this documentary about the pope, showing the history of Rome, Vatican City, and the papacy. The medievalists sing the choral music, and Lew White plays organ. The film was sponsored by the Catholic Writers Guild of New York and the Vatican. Black and white. 60 minutes.

1937 Wings of the Morning
McCormack plays himself in the first British Technicolor feature, singing Moore's "Believe Me If All Those Endearing Young Charms," Balfe's "Killarney," and the traditional air "At the Dawning of the Day." Henry Fonda and Annabella star in a slight story about a racehorse called Wings of the Morning. Harold Schuster directed for Twentieth Century-Fox. Technicolor. 87 minutes.

1953 So This Is Love
Ray Kellogg plays McCormack in this glossy Hollywood film about soprano Grace Moore (played by Kathryn Grayson). In the film, he introduces the future diva at a recital early in her career. See SO THIS IS LOVE.

1987 Melba
Simon Burke plays McCormack in this Australian TV miniseries about soprano Nellie Melba (played by Linda Cropper). See MELBA.

2000 Nora
Karl Scully plays McCormack in this Irish film about James Joyce (Ewan McGregor) and his wife Nora (Susan Lynch). Joyce competes with McCormack in a singing competition. Pat Murphy directed. Color. 106 minutes.

McCRACKEN, JAMES

American tenor (1926–1988)

James McCracken, who won acclaim in the role of Otello, made his debut in 1952 in Central City as Rodolfo. He began at the Metropolitan in 1953 in minor roles but left for Europe in 1957 when his career seemed stymied. He sang in German in Bonn until he had built a reputation and was then invited to sing Otello in Washington, D.C., in 1960. This engagement made him famous in the role, which he then sang around the world, including at the Met. In Europe he often sang with his wife Sandra Warfield. McCracken can be seen performing in OTELLO in 1961 and 1963 videos. See AIDA (1985) and METROPOLITAN OPERA (1983).

MacDONALD, JEANETTE

American soprano (1903–1965)

Jeanette MacDonald studied with Lotte Lehmann and made her opera debut as Juliette in Gounod's *Roméo et Juliette* in Montreal in 1942. She also sang the role of Marguerite in *Faust* with the Chicago Civic Opera Company. MacDonald's stage opera performances, of course, are much less important than her film career. The Pennsylvania soprano began her career on Broadway in 1921 and made her first Paramount film, *The Love Parade,* in 1929. In 1930 she starred in a version of the operetta THE VAGABOND KING and then in a bizarre operetta film called THE LOTTERY BRIDE. She joined MGM in 1933, made a superb *Merry Widow* (DIE LUSTIGE WITWE) for Ernst Lubitsch in 1934, and then increased her popularity enormously by teaming with Nelson Eddy; it was to be the most successful singing partnership in the movies. Their operetta films are out of fashion today, but they still have many fans and are not likely to be forgotten. There are eight of them: NAUGHTY MARIETTA (1935), ROSE-MARIE (1936), MAYTIME (1937), THE GIRL OF THE GOLDEN WEST, SWEETHEARTS (1938), THE NEW MOON (1940), BITTER SWEET (1940), and I MARRIED AN ANGEL. She had equal success with Allan Jones as partner in 1937 with THE FIREFLY. Many of her films have opera numbers, and she even sang excerpts from *Madama Butterfly* in her last movie. Her other films with musical content are listed below.

1929 The Love Parade

MacDonald's first film, directed by Ernst Lubitsch, starred her opposite Maurice Chevalier in a sophisticated musical romance about a Ruritanian queen who marries a prince with a past. The song "Dream Lover" by Victor Schertzinger and Clifford Grey was a hit. Paramount. Black and white. 110 minutes.

1930 Monte Carlo

Ernst Lubitsch directed MacDonald again, this time opposite England's Jack Buchanan. She plays an impoverished countess wooed by royal Buchanan in disguise. The memorable song was "Beyond the Blue Horizon." Paramount. Black and white. 90 minutes.

1930 Oh, for a Man

MacDonald plays an opera singer who marries the man who burglarizes her apartment. This little-known film originally had strong operatic content, but most of the arias were cut when the public turned against musicals. She does get to perform the Liebestod from *Tristan und Isolde.* Fox. Black and white. 78 minutes.

1932 One Hour With You

MacDonald was teamed again with Maurice Chevalier in this musical romance about a married couple whose life is disturbed by a flirtatious woman. She made the title song a hit. George Cukor and Ernst Lubitsch directed. Black and white. 80 minutes.

1932 Love Me Tonight

One of the great film musicals and one of MacDonald's best films with innovative direction by Rouben Mamoulian and outstanding songs by Rodgers and Hart. Maurice Chevalier plays a tailor who falls in love with a princess (MacDonald); they get to sing "Lover" and "Isn't It Romantic?" Paramount. Black and white. 96 minutes.

1936 San Francisco

One of the better Hollywood epics with pretty good opera sequences. MacDonald, Clark Gable, and Spencer Tracy star in a story about an opera singer loved by a saloon keeper at the time of the 1906 earthquake. She sings arias from *Faust* and *La traviata.* See SAN FRANCISCO.

1939 Broadway Serenade

The highlight of this film is MacDonald singing Butterfly's aria "Un bel dì" in a fine sequence staged by Seymour Felix. The film revolves around the marital troubles of songwriter Lew Ayres and his wife (MacDonald). Robert Z. Leonard directed. MGM. Black and white. 114 minutes.

1941 Smilin' Through

This was the third film version of a sentimental story about romance and rivalry over two generations, based on a 1919 play. MacDonald stars opposite real-life husband Gene Raymond under the genial direction of Frank Borzage. Produced by MGM. Color. 100 minutes.

1942 Cairo

MacDonald sings a duet from *Le nozze di Figaro* with Ethel Waters in this spy mystery. She plays a movie star in Cairo whose high C eventually solves an important secret. Robert Young costars, and W. S. Van Dyke directed for MGM. Black and white. 101 minutes.

1949 The Sun Comes Up

MacDonald's last film. In an appropriate farewell, she sings (in English) her favorite aria from her favorite opera, "One Fine Day" from *Madama Butterfly*. MacDonald plays a widowed singer who has lost her son but finds happiness with orphan Claude Jarman Jr. and his dog Lassie. Richard Thorpe directed. MGM. Color. 93 minutes.

1950 Voice of Firestone

MacDonald made her sole appearance on *The Voice of Firestone* television show on November 13, 1950. As the program usually hosted opera stars, she wisely does not try to compete but sings "Will You Remember?" from *Maytime*, "Italian Street Song" from *Naughty Marietta*, and the traditional "Charlie Is My Darling." The video is titled *Jeanette MacDonald in Performance*. Black and white. 23 minutes. VAI VHS.

1992 America's Singing Sweethearts

Michael Lorentz's documentary film about the careers of MacDonald and Eddy, with clips from their films, was written by Elayne Goldstein. Jane Powell is the narrator and MacDonald's husband Gene Raymond is one of the guests. The film, produced by WTTW Chicago, was shown on PBS in 1993. Color. 57 minutes. PBS VHS and at the MTR.

McFERRIN, ROBERT
American baritone (1921–)

Robert McFerrin, the voice of Porgy in Otto Preminger's 1959 film of George Gershwin's PORGY AND BESS, was the first African-American male singer to perform at the Metropolitan Opera (Amonasro in *Aida* on January 27, 1955) and is featured in the documentary *Aida's Brothers and Sisters: Black Voices in Opera*. He created the role of voodoo priest Mamaloi in William Grant Still's opera *Troubled Island* at New York City Opera in 1949, and he was a villager in Kurt Weill's *Lost in the Stars* on Broadway in 1949. Born in Arkansas, he began his professional career with the National Negro Opera Company. His son Bobby McFerrin is a popular singer and composer. See AFRICAN-AMERICAN OPERA.

McINTYRE, DONALD
New Zealand baritone (1934–)

Donald McIntyre, one of the leading Wagnerian singers of our time, has been particularly admired for his Wotan in the *Ring* at Bayreuth. He made his debut with the Welsh National Opera in 1959 in *Nabucco* and sang regularly at Sadler's Wells. He began to appear at Covent Garden in 1967 and went to the Metropolitan in 1975 as Wotan. He has a compelling stage presence as well as a formidable voice. See CARDILLAC (1986), ELEKTRA (1980/1994), DER FLIEGENDE HOLLÄNDER (1975), MARTIN'S LIE (1964), DIE MEISTERSINGER VON NÜRNBERG (1988), DAS RHEINGOLD (1980), DER RING DES NIBELUNGEN (1980/1980 film), SIEGFRIED (1980), and DIE WALKÜRE (1980).

MACKEBEN, THEO
German composer (1879–1953)

Berliner Theo Mackeben is mostly remembered for his adaptations of other people's work. He revised Karl Millöcker's unsuccessful 1879 operetta *Gräfin Dubarry* and turned it into the international success DIE DUBARRY with opera divas Gitta Alpar and Grace Moore starring in the stage production. He was the conductor of the original stage production of DIE DREIGROSCHENOPER in Berlin, and he worked with Kurt Weill in adapting it for the 1931 film version. He worked with Max Ophuls in adapting Smetana's THE BARTERED BRIDE for a 1932 film, and he composed original music for Ophuls's film *Liebelei*. Willi Forst and Zarah Leander were among the stars who appeared in his film musicals.

MACKERRAS, CHARLES
Australian conductor (1925–)

Sir Charles Mackerras made his debut at Sadler's Wells in 1948, was a regular with the English Opera Group during the 1950s, began to conduct operas for television, and made his first appearance at Covent Garden in 1963. He was chief conductor at the Hamburg Staatsoper during the late 1960s and music director of the English National Opera for most of the 1970s, widening the repertory to include operas by Handel and Janáček. He conducted the English National Opera Orchestra for Janet Baker in MARIA STUARDA (1982) and GIULIO CESARE IN EGITTO (1984), and the Royal Opera House Orchestra for Roberto Alagna in his breakthrough performances in ROMÉO ET JULIETTE in 1994. See ALCESTE (1982 film), BILLY BUDD (1966), CARMEN (1962), THE CUNNING LITTLE VIXEN (1995), DON GIOVANNI (1991), DOWN IN THE VALLEY (1961), DIE ENTFÜHRUNG AUS DEM SERAIL (1999 film), FAUST (1975), THE GREEK PASSION (1999), DIE MEISTERSINGER VON NÜRNBERG (1988), SERSE

(1988), KIRI TE KANAWA (1991), THE TELEPHONE (1960), TOSCA (1954), THE TURN OF THE SCREW (1959), A VILLAGE ROMEO AND JULIET (1989), and ZAR UND ZIMMERMANN (1969).

MACMILLAN, JAMES
Scottish composer (1959–)

James Macmillan's opera INÉS DE CASTRO, libretto by John Clifford based on his play, created a minor scandal when it premiered in Edinburgh in 1996 with its somewhat macabre scenes. Many of Macmillan's works contain religious and political ideas, and angels have been prominent in two of his other stage productions. Macmillan is one of the more controversial members of the new generation of British composers.

MacNEIL, CORNELL
American baritone (1922–)

Cornell MacNeil made his debut in 1950 in Philadelphia by creating the role of John Sorel in Menotti's *The Consul*. He sang with the New York City Opera from 1953 to 1955 and then went on to San Francisco, Chicago, and La Scala. He made his first appearance at the Metropolitan in 1959 as Rigoletto, and he continued to sing there in a variety of roles until 1987. He is an excellent Germont in Zeffirelli's 1982 film of LA TRAVIATA and is known for his fine performances in other Verdi operas. He can be seen on video in CAVALLERIA RUSTICANA (1978), FRANCESCA DA RIMINI (1984), OTELLO (1978), AUFSTIEG UND FALL DER STADT MAHAGONNY (1979), IL TABARRO (1981), and TOSCA (1978/1985).

McTEAGUE
1992 opera by Bolcom

William Bolcom's opera was publicized as a kind of marriage between opera and cinema because it was partially based on a famous film and was cowritten and staged by film director Robert Altman. The original source was Frank Norris's realistic 1899 novel *McTeague*. It tells the story of the brutal dentist McTeague, his stingy wife Trina who wins the lottery, and the lust for gold that causes him to murder her and his best friend. The novel was the basis for Erich von Stroheim's famous, though rather grim, 1924 film *Greed*. The opera, created by Bolcom working with librettists Arnold Weinstein and Altman, premiered to good reviews at Chicago Lyric Opera in 1992.

1993 The Real McTeague
Robert Altman's TV documentary includes a number of scenes from the opera's 1992 production at Lyric Opera of Chicago. Ben Heppner is McTeague, Catherine Malfitano is wife Trina, Timothy Nolen is Marcus, Emily Golden is Maria, and Dennis Russell Davies conducts the Chicago Lyric Orchestra. The documentary compares the opera, the movie *Greed* that inspired it, and the novel on which it was based and features clips from the film and readings from the novel by Studs Terkel. Bolcom explains his ideas about the opera while Altman, who staged the opera and wrote the libretto with Arnold Weinstein, explains that opera is not really what he does. Color. In English. 60 minutes.

MADAMA BUTTERFLY
1904 opera by Puccini

Cio-Cio-San, known as Madame Butterfly, marries American naval lieutenant B. F. Pinkerton. He does not take the marriage very seriously and eventually returns to the United States. Butterfly has a child and waits three years for his return. When he does, she finds he has married an American, so she kills herself. *Madama Butterfly*, libretto by Luigi Illica and Giuseppe Giacosa, was the first of two operas GIACOMO PUCCINI based on plays by American David Belasco, this one derived from a short story by John Luther Long. The opera was a fiasco when it premiered at La Scala on February 4, 1904, with Rosina Storchio as Madama Butterfly (she was hissed and swore never to sing the role again) but was a success in a revised version staged in Brescia in May 1904 with Salomea Krusceniski. Storchio later starred in a film based on the opera (COME MORÌ BUTTERFLY) in which she kills herself during a performance, while Krusceniski was the subject of a film about her success with the opera (THE RETURN OF BUTTERFLY). The opera and its music have been featured in many fiction films; the most fascinating is probably Maria Cebotari's IL SOGNO DI BUTTERFLY, in which her cinematic life parallels her role in *Madama Butterfly*. Early films based on the opera often claimed to be derived from the play or story to avoid copyright problems.

1950 NBC Opera Theatre
American TV production: Charles Polacheck (director), Samuel Chotzinoff (producer), Peter Herman Adler (conductor, NBC Symphony of the Air Orchestra), Carl Kent (set designer).

Cast: Tamiko Kanazawa (Madama Butterfly) Davis Cunningham (Pinkerton), Conchita Gaston (Suzuki), Holger Sorenson (Sharpless), Johnny Silver (Goro).

Video at the MTR. Telecast live February 6, 1950, on NBC. Kirk Browning (director). Black and white. In English. 60 minutes.

1955 Gallone film

Italian feature: film: Carmine Gallone (director), Oliviero De Fabritiis (conductor, Rome Opera Orchestra), Claude Renoir (cinematographer), Ryotaro Mitsubayashi (set designer).

Cast: Karuo Yachigusa (Madama Butterfly, sung by Orietta Moscucci), Nicola Filacuridi (Pinkerton, sung by Giuseppe Campora), Michiko Tanaka (Suzuki, sung by Anna Maria Canali), Ferdinando Lidonni (Sharpless), Kiyoshi Takagi (Goro, sung by Paolo Caroli).

Color. In Italian. 100 minutes.

Comment: An attempt to create a realistic *Madama Butterfly* in Rome by using a Japanese designer and Japanese actors with the singing dubbed by performers from the Rome Opera. Yachigusa, who came from the Takarazuka Girls Opera Company, is very convincing as Butterfly.

1955 NBC Opera Theatre

American TV production: Samuel Chotzinoff (producer), Herbert Grossman (conductor, NBC Symphony of the Air Orchestra), Trew Hocker (set designer), Ruth and Thomas Martin (translation).

Cast: Elaine Malbin (Butterfly), Davis Cunningham (Pinkerton), Conchita Gaston (Suzuki), Warren Galjour (Sharpless), Johnny Silver (Goro).

Video at the MTR. Telecast live December 4, 1955, on NBC. Kirk Browning (director). Color. In English. 135 minutes.

1964 Indiana University Television Theater

American TV production: Ross Allen (stage director), Wolfgang Vacaro (conductor, Indiana University Opera Orchestra), Andreas Nomikos (set designer), John Gutman (English translation).

Cast: Grace Trester Jones (Madama Butterfly), Ronald Naldi (Pinkerton), Olive Fredericks (Suzuki), Richard Stilwell (Sharpless), Michael Chang (Goro).

Video at the MTR. Telecast January 16, 1965, on WFBM Educational Television. Ross Allen and Herbert Seitz (directors). Black and white. In English. 75 minutes.

***1974 Ponnelle film

German studio film: Jean-Pierre Ponnelle (director, set/costume designer), Herbert von Karajan (conductor, Vienna Philharmonic), Wolfgang Treu (cinematographer), Unitel (production).

Cast: Mirella Freni (Madama Butterfly), Plácido Domingo (Pinkerton), Christa Ludwig (Suzuki), Robert Kerns (Sharpless), Michel Sénéchal (Goro).

Video: Decca DVD/London VHS and LD. Color. In Italian with English subtitles. 144 minutes.

Comment: Ponnelle shot this superb 35mm film in a Berlin studio adding cinematic touches such as Butterfly dreaming of being with Pinkerton again. There is a highlights version in the *Great Moments* video series.

1982 New York City Opera

American stage production: Frank Corsaro (director), Christopher Keene (conductor, New York City Opera Orchestra and Chorus), Lloyd Evans (set/costume designer).

Cast: Judith Haddon (Madama Butterfly), Jerry Hadley (Pinkerton), Judith Christin (Suzuki), Alan Titus (Sharpless), James Billings (Goro).

Telecast October 20, 1982, on PBS. Kirk Browning (director). Color. In Italian with English subtitles. 145 minutes.

1983 Arena di Verona

Italian stage production: Giulio Chazalettes (director), Maurizio Arena (conductor, Arena di Verona Orchestra and Chorus), Ulisse Santicchi (set/costume designer).

Cast: Raina Kabaivanska (Madama Butterfly), Nazzareno Antinori (Pinkerton), Eleonora Jankovic (Suzuki), Lorenzo Saccomani (Sharpless), Mario Ferrara (Goro).

Video: Kultur/HBO VHS and NVC Arts (GB) DVD and VHS. Brian Large (director). Color. In Italian with English subtitles. 150 minutes.

Comment: An open-air arena like Verona isn't the ideal setting for an intimate love story like *Madama Butterfly*, but it works reasonably well on video because home viewers have close-ups and camera intimacies that the live audience doesn't.

1986 Teatro alla Scala

Italian stage production: Keita Asari (director), Lorin Maazel (conductor, La Scala Orchestra and Chorus), Ichiro Takada (set designer), Hanae Mori (costumes).

Cast: Yasuko Hayashi (Madama Butterfly), Peter Dvorsky (Pinkerton). Hak-Nam Kim (Suzuki), Giorgio Zancanaro (Sharpless), Ernesto Gavazzi (Goro).

Video: Image Entertainment DVD/Home Vision VHS/Arthaus (GB) DVD. Derek Bailey (director). Color. In Italian with English subtitles. 150 minutes.

Comment: An attempt to create an "authentic" production with Japanese soprano, stage director, set designer, and costume designer. Director Asari creates a Kabuki-like atmosphere with support from the clever sets; Butterfly's house is built from the ground up by Kabuki-style stagehands as the audience watches at the beginning of the opera. Hayashi and Dvorsky sing well, but it's pretty hard to believe in them.

1994 Metropolitan Opera

American stage production: Giancarlo del Monaco (director), Daniel Gatti (conductor, Metropolitan Opera Orchestra and Chorus), Michael Scott (set/costume designer).

Cast: Catherine Malfitano (Madama Butterfly), Richard Leech (Pinkerton), Wendy White (Suzuki), Dwayne Croft (Sharpless), Pierre Lefebvre (Goro).

Taped December 1, 1994; telecast December 27, 1995. Brian Large (director). Color. In Italian with English subtitles. 150 minutes.

***1995 Mitterrand film

French feature film: Frederic Mitterrand (director), James Conlon (music director), Philippe Welt (cinematographer), Michele Abbe-Vannier (production designer), Christian Gasc (costume designer), Daniel Toscan du Plantier (producer).

Cast: Ying Huang (Madama Butterfly), Richard Troxell (Pinkerton), Ning Liang (Suzuki), Richard Cowan (Sharpless), Jing Ma Fan (Goro).

Video: Columbia TriStar DVD/VHS. Color. In French. 135 minutes.

Comment: The opera, filmed in a traditional manner with the addition of documentary film of old Japan between Acts I and II, was shot in 35mm in a reconstruction of the city of Nagasaki as it looked in 1904 (built on a hilltop in Tunisia). The performance by 23-year-old Chinese soprano Ying Huang is heart-breaking.

Early/related films

1915 Famous Players film

Mary Pickford stars as Cho-Cho-San (so spelled) in the feature film *Madame Butterfly,* supposedly based on the 1898 source story by John Luther Long. Marshall Neilan plays Pinkerton with Olive West as Suzuki. Sidney Olcott directed for Famous Players. Black and white. Silent. About 70 minutes.

1917 Come morì Butterfly

Rosina Storchio, who created the role of Madama Butterfly, plays a famous opera singer in love with a poet in *How Butterfly Died.* When he is stolen from her by her more glamorous sister and she can no longer hope to get him back, she kills herself on stage during a performance of *Madama Butterfly.* See COME MORÌ BUTTERFLY.

1919 Harakiri

Fritz Lang was at the beginning of his career when he made the German feature film *Harakiri,* which closely resembles *Madama Butterfly.* The names of the characters are changed, but the story is the same: Lil Dagover plays a young Japanese woman who falls in love with a naval officer (Niels Prien). When he deserts her, she commits suicide. Black and white. Silent. About 87 minutes.

1932 Paramount film

Cary Grant plays Pinkerton with Sylvia Sidney as his Cho-cho-San (so spelled) in the film *Madame Butterfly* based on the novel, play, and opera. It uses Puccini's music as score, and Grant does sing a bit, but not Puccini. Marion Goring directed for Paramount. Black and white. 85 minutes.

1934 One Night of Love

Grace Moore ends this film on stage at the Metropolitan Opera portraying Cio-Cio-San in *Madama Butterfly* and singing most beautifully. See ONE NIGHT OF LOVE.

1934 The Great Ziegfeld

A soprano sings a bit of "Un bel dì" as Dennis Morgan (dubbed by Allan Jones) performs "A Pretty Girl is Like a Melody" on a gigantic revolving wedding cake in a spectacular sequence. Robert Z Leonard directed. Black and white. 176 minutes.

1937 I'll Take Romance

Grace Moore sings in the first act duet from *Madama Butterfly* in *I'll Take Romance,* her last American film. She plays an opera diva romanced by Melvyn Douglas. See I'LL TAKE ROMANCE.

1939 Il sogno di Butterfly/Premiere der Butterfly

Maria Cebotari plays a singer whose life parallels her role in *Madama Butterfly.* She falls in love with an American who leaves her pregnant. When he returns, he is with his new wife. Made in Italian and German versions. See IL SOGNO DI BUTTERFLY.

1939 First Love

Deanna Durbin sings the *Madama Butterfly* aria "Un bel dì" in English as "One Fine Day." The aria ends with her Prince Charming rescuing her in this modern version of the Cinderella story. Henry Koster directed for Universal. Black and white. 84 minutes.

1939 Broadway Serenade

The highlight of this film is Jeanette MacDonald singing "Un bel dì" in a splendid sequence staged by Seymour Felix. Robert Z. Leonard directed. MGM. Black and white. 114 minutes.

1949 The Sun Comes Up

Jeanette MacDonald's last film. In an appropriate farewell she sings her favorite aria from her favorite opera,

"Un bel dì" from *Madama Butterfly*. Richard Thorpe directed. MGM. Color. 93 minutes.

1950 The Toast of New Orleans
Mario Lanza and Kathryn Grayson are on stage as Pinkerton and Madama Butterfly in the final scene of this MGM romp. It's the culmination of their relationship, and she succumbs after he chases her around the stage. See THE TOAST OF NEW ORLEANS.

1953 Tonight We Sing
Soprano Elsa Valdine (Roberta Peters) and tenor Gregory Lawrence (voice of Jan Peerce) perform excerpts from *Madama Butterfly* in this film about impresario Sol Hurok. See TONIGHT WE SING.

1955 Interrupted Melody
Marjorie Lawrence, played by Eleanor Parker in this biopic (singing by Eileen Farrell), is shown on stage in a scene from *Madama Butterfly* in a small regional opera house. See INTERRUPTED MELODY.

1957 Ed Sullivan Show
Dorothy Kirsten as Cio-Cio-San with Mario Del Monaco as Pinkerton perform scenes from a Metropolitan Opera *Madama Butterfly* production on *The Ed Sullivan Show* on CBS Television. Black and white. About 15 minutes. Video at the MTR.

1960 Bell Telephone Hour
Victoria de los Angeles as Cio-Cio-San and Brian Sullivan as Pinkerton perform a scene from *Madama Butterfly* on *The Bell Telephone Hour* TV program. Kirk Browning directed. Black and white. About 10 minutes. Video at the MTR.

1961 My Geisha
Shirley MacLaine plays a movie star whose director husband Yves Montand goes to Japan to make a film of *Madama Butterfly* with a geisha; he does not ask her to be in it, as he wants to prove he can be successful without her. She disguises herself as a geisha for an audition and gets the starring role anyway. Selections from the opera are sung by Michiko Sunahara as Butterfly and Barry Morell as Pinkerton. Franz Waxman arranged the music, Norman Krasna wrote the script, and Jack Cardiff directed for Paramount. Color. 100 minutes. Paramount VHS.

1971 Death in Venice
Although most of the soundtrack music of this film is by Mahler, *Butterfly*'s plaintive aria "Vogliatemi bene" is also heard in Luchino Visconti's epic *Death in Venice*. Color. 130 minutes.

1980 Hopscotch
Butterfly's aria "Un bel dì" is used ironically in this amiable spy comedy while Walter Matthau works out his escape from murderous CIA pursuers. Ronald Neame directed from Brian Garfield's novel. Color. 104 minutes.

1982 The Return of Butterfly
The Return of Butterfly is a Ukrainian feature film about Salomea Kruscenìski, the singer who helped make *Madama Butterfly* a success at its second performance. See THE RETURN OF BUTTERFLY.

1987 Fatal Attraction
In this movie about a woman who refuses to take rejection as gently as Cio-Cio-San, a fondness for *Madama Butterfly* is used as an indication of cultural closeness. Glenn Close turns up the volume on a recording so she and Michael Douglas can tell each other it's their favorite opera. He should have noticed it's the death scene. The singing voices belong to Mirella Freni, Luciano Pavarotti, and Christa Ludwig. Adrian Lyne directed. Color. 119 minutes.

1987 Opera
Director Dario Argento's horror film *Opera* (U.S. title: *Terror at the Opera*) revolves around Verdi's *Macbeth* but is also features an aria from *Madama Butterfly* sung by Mirella Freni. See OPERA.

1990 Soldiers of Music
Galina Vishnevskaya, famous for performances in *Madama Butterfly* before she left the USSR with cellist husband Mstislav Rostropovich, returns with him after 16 years for a concert and sings an aria from the opera. Color. 89 minutes. Sony VHS.

1991 Butterfly: European Myth of Oriental Woman
This British TV documentary examines the way Oriental women have been portrayed on the Western stage and includes scenes from an English National Opera production of *Madama Butterfly* with Janice Cairns as Cio-Cio-San. David Henry Hwang, author of *M. Butterfly,* and Claude-Michel Schönberg, composer of *Miss Saigon,* explain their positions. Color. 60 minutes.

1991 Jennifer 8
Bruce Robinson's taut thriller features the Humming Chorus from *Madama Butterfly* on the soundtrack at a key moment. Andy Garcia plays a cop trying to keep

Uma Thurman from getting bumped off by a serial killer. Color. 127 minutes.

1993 Kiju Yoshida Meets Madama Butterfly
Documentary about Kiju Yoshida's work as director of a production of *Madama Butterfly* at the Opéra de Lyon in 1993. Michie Nakamaru sings Butterfly, Vyacheslav M. Polosov is Pinkerton, Hak-Nam Kim is Suzuki, and Richard Stillwell is Sharpless. Kent Nagano conducts the Lyons Opera Orchestra. Oliver Horn directed the documentary. Color. In French. 50 minutes.

1993 M. Butterfly
David Cronenberg's film of Henry David Hwang's play revolves around the opera *Madama Butterfly*. It tells the story of a French diplomat (Jeremy Irons) in China who falls in love with a female impersonator (John Lone), apparently because of the power of Puccini's music. See M. BUTTERFLY.

1993 Household Saints
Madama Butterfly is a running theme through this offbeat story about the odd love lives of two Italian women in New York, and it includes visions of Butterfly and Pinkerton. One character is so obsessed by the opera that he commits hara-kiri to Butterfly's suicide music. The singers are Toti Dal Monte and Beniamino Gigli with the duet "Vogliatemi bene" and Dal Monte with the aria "Un bel dì." Oliviero de Fabritiis conducts the Teatro alla Scala Orchestra. Nancy Savoca directed the film, based on a novel by Francine Prose. Color. 124 minutes.

1994 Heavenly Creatures
The Hungarian State Opera Chorus is heard on the soundtrack singing the Humming Chorus as two teenaged girls prepare for a murder. It is oddly effective. Peter Jackson directed this offbeat New Zealand film. Color. 95 minutes.

2000 Italian for Beginners
Italian opera music, including snippets of *Madama Butterfly,* is an important component of this romantic Danish film about a group of Copenhagen folk taking evening classes in Italian. Lone Scherfig directed. Color. In Danish. 112.

MADAMA DI TEBE
1918 operetta by Lombardo

Carlo Lombardo's lighthearted Italian operetta *Madama di Tebe,* set in a Paris nightclub, is a pasticcio based on Joseph Szulc's Parisian musical *Flup...!,* with bits borrowed from Charles Cuvillier's THE LILAC DOMINO and music by Jacques Offenbach, Franz Lehár, and Vincente

Lleó. It opened at the Teatro Fossati in Milan in 1918 and seems to have retained its popularity in Italy.

1992 Operette, che Passione!
Italian TV production: Sandro Massimini (director/producer), Roberto Negri (pianist), Sandro Corelli (choreographer).

Cast: Sandro Massimini, Daniela Mazzucato, Max René Cosotti.

Video: Pierluigi Pagano (director). Color. In Italian. About 20 minutes. Ricordi (Italy) VHS.

Comment: Highlights of the operetta on the Italian TV series *Operette, che Passione!* The featured songs are "Spesso a cori e picche," "Tango," "Montmartre," and "Occhio di ciel, core di gel."

MADAME POMPADOUR
1922 operetta by Fall

Operetta diva Fritzi Massary had her greatest success in LEO FALL's operetta about the love triangle of Madame Pompadour, King Louis XV, and Count René. She starred in productions in Berlin and Vienna that were considered her best stage performances. Evelyn Laye had the part in London, Wilda Bennett sang it in New York, and Paris Opéra soprano Raymonde Vécart was the Madame in Paris. This is Fall's finest operetta, comparable in quality to Offenbach's best.

1973 York film
German feature film: Eugen York (director), Wolfgang Ebert (conductor, Munich Philharmonic Orchestra and Chorus), Sergiu Singer (set designer), Accord Film (production).

Cast: Ingeborg Hallstein (Madame Pompadour), Friedrich Schoenfelder (King Louis XV), Adolf Dallapozza (Count René), Julia Migenes (Belotte), Barbara Cazpell (Madeleine).

Color. In German. 88 minutes.

Early film

1927 Herbert Wilcox film
The success of the operetta on stage in London persuaded producer E. A. Dupont and director Herbert Wilcox to turn it into a silent British film in 1927. Lillian Gish is surprisingly sexy as Madame Pompadour with Antonio Moreno as Count René and Henri Bosc as the king. Producer Dupont wrote the screenplay with Frances Marion. Black and white. About 80 minutes.

MADDALENA
1913 opera by Prokofiev

SERGEI PROKOFIEV began his opera *Maddalena* in 1913 when he was 20 but never finished it. It was finally staged in 1981 when Edward Downes completed it and conducted its premiere at Graz. It is set in 15th-century Venice. Faithless Maddalena is bored waiting for her husband Genaro to return, so she has an affair. When he arrives, she swears she has been faithful, but she goes into hiding when her lover Stenio arrives. Both men want to kill her, but she persuades them to kill each other instead.

1981 Graz Festival
Austrian film of stage production: Jorge Lavelli (stage/film director), Edward Downes (conductor, Graz Philharmonic Orchestra), Joerg Kossdorff (set designer), Peter Wolfkind (German translation).
Cast: Nancy Shade (Maddalena), Ryszard Karczykowski (Genaro), James Johnson (Stenio).
Telecast November 29, 1981, on ORF TV. Color. In German. 59 minutes.

MAESTRO DI CAPPELLA, IL
1792 intermezzo giocoso by Cimarosa

DOMENICO CIMAROSA's one-man comic opera *Il maestro di cappella* (The Music Director) is a tour de force for bass or baritone. The music director is conducting a large orchestra, but it pays little attention to his directions and keeps playing wrong notes in the wrong rhythms. He has to imitate each instrument to get the musicians to play correctly and in harmony. The opera has been telecast a number of times and is on video and CD.

1958 RAI Italian Television
Italian TV production: Vladi Orengo (director), music played by RAI Italian Television Orchestra.
Cast: Luigi Borgonovo (Music Director).
Video: Onda (Italy) VHS. Telecast September 16, 1959, on RAI. Color. In Italian. 20 minutes.

1985 ORF Austrian Television
Austrian TV production: Ernst Pichler (director), Ernst Märzendorfer (conductor, Hellbrunner Festochester).
Cast: Giuseppe Taddei (Music Director).
Video: Opera Dubs VHS. Telecast March 16, 1986, on ORF TV. Color. In Italian. 20 minutes.

***1995 Villa Medicea di Poggio a Caiano
Italian stage production: Goffredo Gori (stage director), Riccardo Cirri (conductor, Ars Cantus Orchestra), Luciano Bettarina (orchestration), Fabio Caselli (artistic director), Filmstudio Ventidue, Prato (production).
Cast: Giorgio Gatti (Music Director).
Video: Hardy Classic VHS. Silvia Scali (director). Color. In Italian. 20 minutes.

MAGGIO MUSICALE
1989 Italian film with opera content

Writer-director Ugo Gregoretti's undervalued Italian film *Maggio Musicale* (released in America as *Once Upon a Time an Opera*) revolves around a production of *La bohème* at the Florence music festival Maggio Musicale. The film is a gentle satire on Italian opera people and offbeat productions. Malcolm McDowell (dubbed by Giancarlo Giannini) plays a producer staging the Puccini opera in a very eccentric manner while he has continuing arguments with singers Shirley Verrett (Mimì) and Chris Merritt (Rodolfo), who play themselves. He befriends a 15-year-old runaway boy, who becomes his confidante; in a whimsical time twist, the runaway turns out to be the producer as the boy he was when he disappeared from the family box at La Scala in 1946 during a conventional production of *La bohème*. Cinematographer Pier Luigi Santi photographs Florence most beautifully, Ivan Stefanutti creates entertaining set designs, and Gregoretti not only satirizes himself (he is also a stage opera director) but strong-minded directors such as Franco Zeffirelli. Color. In Italian. 107 minutes.

MAGIC FLUTE, THE
See DIE ZAUBERFLÖTE.

MÁGNÁS MISKA
1916 Hungarian operetta by Szirmai

Alberto Szirmai's operetta *Mágnás Miska* (Miska the Great), libretto by Karály Bakoni with lyrics by Andor Gábor, was a big success at its premiere in Budapest in 1916. It revolves around two servants who are disguised as aristocrats, groom Miska and maid Marcsa, and their eventual pairing off as a count's daughter and her untitled lover find a way to marry. This is nearly grand operetta with splendid duets and lots of tuneful music. The operetta has been produced in Germany and Austria, but it is mainly popular in Hungary.

1948 Keleti film
Hungarian feature film: Márton Keleti (director), István Békeffy (screenplay).
Cast: Marika Németh, Miklós Gábor, Kálmán Latabár, Árpád Latabár, Ági Mészáros.
Black and white. In Hungarian. 85 minutes.

Comment: One of the most popular Hungarian films of its era, much loved for it pointed ridicule of aristocratic behavior. More than 10 million people are said to have seen the film—virtually everyone in the country at the time.

Early film

1917 Korda film
Alexander Korda, long before his great days as an English film producer, made a silent version of the operetta in Budapest soon after it was a success on stage. Black and white. About 70 minutes.

MAHLER, GUSTAV
Austrian composer (1860–1911)

Gustav Mahler wrote a number of stage works and completed Weber's *Die drei Pintos,* but there are no surviving operas by him. His operatic importance is on the performance side; he derived his primary income from conducting opera and had a major influence on opera presentation. Mahler headed the Vienna Hofoper (Staatsoper) from 1897 to 1907, directed opera orchestras in Budapest and Hamburg. and was guest conductor at the Metropolitan Opera for two years.

1974 Mahler
Ken Russell's British film biography is structured as a flashback with Mahler recalling the events of his life during a train trip with his wife Alma. Most of the high and low points of his career and music are featured. Robert Powell, who looks like the composer, plays Mahler, with Georgina Hale as Alma. Wagner's opera music is prominent, including *Die Walküre* and *Tristan und Isolde.* In one over-the-top dream sequence titled "The Convert," filmed as if it were a silent movie, Mahler is converted from Judaism by Cosima Wagner (Antonia Ellis, wearing a semi-Nazi uniform) in a symbolic Valhalla scene. After he battles a dragon like Siegfried and eats pork, the "talkies" arrive and they sing new lyrics to the "Ride of the Valkyries" music. Cosima tells him "You're no longer a Jew, boy, now you're one of us, now you're a goy, you can conduct opera." This scene is in such bad taste that it has to be seen to be believed. The music is played by the Concertgebouw Orchestra conducted by Bernard Haitink. Color. In English. 115 minutes.

MAID OF ORLEANS, THE
1881 opera by Tchaikovsky

TCHAIKOVSKY's operatic version of the story of Joan of Arc, *Orleanskaya Deva,* is based on a play by Schiller. It is his most ambitious opera and was a big success in its time, although it has almost been forgotten outside Russia. The main story is basically historic, with Joan once again the savior of France, but there is an added unhistoric love story. Joan falls in love with a Burgundian knight named Lionel, who is fighting on the English side, and their relationship becomes a central plot point. He is killed at the time the English take her prisoner.

1993 Bolshoi Opera
Russian stage production: Boris Pokrovsky (director), Alexander Lazarev (conductor, Bolshoi Opera Orchestra and Chorus), Valery Levental (set designer).
Cast: Nina Rautio (Joan of Arc), Vladimir Redkin (Lionel), Oleg Kulko (King Charles), Maria Gavrilova (Agnès Sorel), Gleb Nikolsky (Archbishop), Mikhail Krutikov (Dunois).
Video: Teldec VHS. Brian Large (director). Color. In Russian with English subtitles. 150 minutes.
Comment: This production originated at the Bolshoi in 1990 and was staged at the Metropolitan Opera in 1993 with different singers. The video was shot on stage at the Bolshoi revival in June 1993 without an audience.

MAID OF THE MOUNTAINS, THE
1916 comic opera by Fraser-Simpson

Harold Fraser-Simpson's hugely popular comic opera *The Maid of the Mountains,* libretto by Frederick Lonsdale, opened in London in 1916 with José Collins as star and ran for 1,352 performances. It tells the story of "maid of the mountain" Teresa, her love for mountain brigand Baldassare, and her rivalry with the governor's daughter. It was a must-see operetta for World War I soldiers on leave, and it remained so popular it was revived in 1972. There is even an original cast recording, one of the first ever made. *Maid*'s best-known number, a waltz called "Love Will Find a Way," begins with the first four notes of Lehár's *Merry Widow* waltz twice repeated; Joan Sutherland sings it on her album *The Golden Age of Operetta.*

1932 BIP film
English feature film: Lupino Lane (director); Douglas Furber, Frank Miller, Victor Kendall, and Edwin Greenwood (screenplay); Claude Friese-Greene and Arthur Crabtree (cinematographers); BIP (production).
Cast: Nancy Brown (Teresa), Harry Welchman (Baldassare), Betty Stockfeld (Angela), Dennis Hoey (Orsino), Albert Burdon (Tonio).
Black and white. In English. 80 minutes.
Comment: The original cast recording is better.

MAÎTRE DE MUSIQUE, LE
1988 Belgian film with opera content

Le maître de musique (The Music Teacher) is a fictional Belgian film about a famous opera singer at the turn of the century; he has just retired from the stage but wants to pass on his knowledge to someone as gifted as he was. Belgian bass-baritone José van Dam plays the teacher Joachim Dallayrac and his pupils are beautiful young Sophie (Anne Roussel) and wild young pickpocket Jean (Philippe Volter). His rigorous training of their voices and personalities is the core of the film. At the climax, they compete in a competition arranged by Dallayrac's old rival Prince Scotti (Patrick Bauchau), who was defeated by Dallayrac in a similar competition when they were young. Scotti has made arrangements for his protégé Marc Schreiber to win, but Sophie and Jean carry the day despite the supposed fix. Van Dam also sings in the film, including an aria from *Rigoletto* and a charming Giovanni-Zerlína duet with Sophie. The students, whose singing voices are dubbed by Dinah Bryant and Jérôme Pruett, are heard in duets from Verdi and Bellini and arias by Mozart and Mahler. Gérard Corbiau wrote and directed the film with loving care, and it is finely photographed by Walter van den Ende. Color. In French. 98 minutes. Orion VHS.

MAKROPOULOS CASE, THE
1926 opera by Janáček

LEOŠ JANÁČEK's opera *Věc Makropoulos* (The Makropoulos Case), based on a play by Czech playwright Karel Čapek, is the story of opera singer Emilia Marty (née Makropoulos) who has lived for more than 300 years because of a drug her father developed. As she now needs more of the drug and must get the formula to make it, she visits a law office where a relevant lawsuit is in progress. She helps settle it and gives herself to a man in return for the formula. However, she is now disillusioned by life and chooses to let herself to die.

1989 Canadian Opera
Canadian stage production: Lotfi Mansouri (director), Berislav Klobucar (conductor, Canadian Opera Company Orchestra), Leni Bauer-Ecsy (set designer).

Cast: Stephanie Sundine (Emilia Marty), Kathleen Brett (Kristina), Benoit Butet (Janek), Graham Clark (Albert Gregor), Cornelis Opthof (Jaroslav Prus), Robert Orth (Dr. Kolenatý), Richard Margison (Vítek).

Video: VAI VHS. Norman Campbell (director). Color. In Czech with English subtitles. 123 minutes.

Comment: Staged, with help from Janáček specialist Elisabeth Söderström, at the O'Keefe Center in Toronto.

***1995 Glyndebourne Festival
English stage production: Nicholas Lehnhoff (director), Andrew Davis (conductor, London Philharmonic Orchestra and Glyndebourne Festival Chorus), Tobias Hoheisel (set designer).

Cast: Anja Silja (Emilia Marty), Manuela Krisak (Kristina), Christopher Ventris (Janek), Kim Begley (Albert Gregor), Victor Braun (Prus), Andrew Shore (Kolenatý), Anthony Roden (Vítek), Robert Tear (Hauk-Šendorf).

Video: Warner Vision NVC Arts DVD/VHS. Brian Large (director). Color. In Czech with English subtitles. 95 minutes.

Comment: Powerful well-directed, well-sung production filmed without an audience so Large could have greater freedom for camera movement.

MALFITANO, CATHERINE
American soprano (1948–)

Catherine Malfitano, who made her debut in 1972 with Central City Opera, was a regular with New York City Opera from 1973 to 1979. She began to sing at the Metropolitan in 1979 and soon became a featured singer at European opera houses. She was Servilia in Ponnelle's 1980 film of LA CLEMENZA DI TITO and Tosca in a famous TOSCA telecast live from Rome in 1992. She has been especially praised for her performances in 1990 Berlin and 1995 Royal Opera productions of SALOME but also much liked for her performances in American operas, including Barber's ANTONY AND CLEOPATRA (1991), Bolcom's MCTEAGUE (1993), Menotti's THE SAINT OF BLEECKER STREET (1978), Weill's STREET SCENE (1979), Susa's TRANSFORMATIONS, and the operas of THOMAS PASATIERI (1977). See AUFSTIEG UND FALL DER STADT MAHAGONNY (1998), JAMES LEVINE (1996), MADAMA BUTTERFLY (1994), and STIFFELIO (1993).

MALIBRAN, MARIA
Spanish mezzo-soprano (1808–1836)

Maria Malibran remains one of the great myth figures of opera more than 160 years after her death, a continuing subject for movies and emulation. The myth is obviously about more than just her superb voice and notable acting ability; Malibran, who died at the age of 28 and had many love affairs in her short life, has become the embodiment of the age of Romanticism. She was the friend of many major composers of the era, including Rossini, Donizetti, Bellini, and Verdi; her sister Pauline Viardot was also a famous singer; and her father was the hugely influential teacher Manuel Garcia.

1943 Maria Malibran

Maria Cebotari stars as Malibran in this romantic Italian film biography directed by Guido Brignone. It tells the story of the singer's life from her early years through her many love affairs to her death. Cebotari is well suited for the role and sings several arias by Malibran's composer friends Rossini and Bellini. The cast includes Rossano Brazzi as Malibran's violinist lover de Beriot, Renato Cialente as her husband Ernest Malibran, Loris Gizzi as Rossini, and Roberto Bruni as Bellini. Black and white. In Italian. 92 minutes.

1943 La Malibran

Geori Boué stars as Malibran in this French film of the singer's life, written and directed by Sacha Guitry. Guitry also plays her husband Eugene Malibran, Jean Cocteau is Alfred de Musset, and Mario Podesta is Manuel Garcia. Guitry summed up Malibran's vagabond life by saying she "lived and died on tour": she was born a Spaniard in Paris, made her debut in Italy, built her career in London, married a Frenchman in New York, took a Belgian for her second husband, and died in Manchester. Black and white. In French. 95 minutes. Montparnasse (France) VHS.

1955 Un palco all'opera

Liliana Gerace plays Malibran in this Italian film that has a section devoted to her relationship with Bellini (Enrico De Melis). Siro Marcellini directed. Color. In Italian. 98 minutes.

1971 Der Tod der Maria Malibran

Werner Schroeter's experimental film *The Death of Maria Malibran* features Magdalena Montezuma as Malibran. It is a visual film to the point of wild extravagance, consisting entirely of tableaux depicting the life and death of the soprano. High fashion and decadent art meet with sometimes lurid results. There are excerpts from *Mignon*, *Le nozze di Figaro*, *Gianni Schicchi*, and *Semiramide*. The other cast members are Christine Kaufmann, Candy Darling, Ingrid Caven, and Manuela Riva. Color. In German and Italian. 104 minutes.

MAMMA
1941 film with opera content

A three-handkerchief opera movie. Opera singer Beniamino Gigli's aging mother (the legendary Emma Gramatica) prevents his wife (Carola Höhn) from eloping with another man by running through the rain while Gigli is on stage tearfully singing *Otello* with backing from the Rome Opera Orchestra. Mamma dies from the strain, but she dies happy. Gigli also sings the appropriate aria from *Rigoletto*, "La donna è mobile." The film is basically an excuse for Gigli to sing arias by Verdi and songs by Ce-

sare A. Bixio. Guido Brignone directed the film in Rome in Italian and German versions (as *Mutter*), Arturo Gallea was cinematographer, and Guido Cantini wrote the screenplay. Black and white. 82 minutes. Bel Canto Society/Opera Dubs VHS.

MAM'ZELLE NITOUCHE
1883 operetta by Hervé

This light opera, the only HERVÉ work on film, has an inventive libretto by Henri Meilhac and Albert Millaud. It tells the delightful story of a convent organist (Célestin in the convent, Floridor in the theater world) who secretly writes operettas and of a convent girl named Denise who wants to go on the stage. Denise is turned into the mysterious "Mam'zelle Nitouche" and saves the day by singing in the premiere of his operetta. An army lieutenant provides the love interest. The plot derives loosely from incidents in Hervé's own early years when he led a double life as a church organist and operetta composer and performer. The noted French actors Raimu and Fernandel have both starred in film versions of the operetta directed by the Allegret brothers Marc and Yves.

1931 Marc Allegret film

French feature film: Marc Allegret (director), Hans H. Zerlett (screenplay), Roger Hubert (cinematographer), Michael Lewin (music director).

Cast: Raimu (Célestin/Floridor), Janie Marèse (Denise/Nitouche), Jean Rousselières (Lieutenant), André Alerme (Major), Edith Méra (Corinne), Simone Simon, Edwige Feuillère.

Video: Montparnasse (France) VHS. Black and white. In French. 106 minutes.

1931 Lamac film

German feature film: Karel Lamac (director), Hans H. Zerlett (screenplay), Roger Hubert (cinematographer), Michael Lewin (music director).

Cast: Anny Ondra (Denise/Nitouche), Oskar Karlweis, Georg Alexander, Hans Junkermann.

Black and white. In German. 105 minutes.

Comment: Shot in Paris at the same time as the Allegret film with a different cast and director and retitled *Mamsell Nitouche*.

1953 Yves Allegret film

French feature film: Yves Allegret (director), Marcel Achard and Jean Aurenche (screenplay), Armand Thirard (cinematographer), George Van Parys (music director).

Cast: Fernandel (Célestin/Floridor), Pier Angeli (Denise/Nitouche), Jean Dubucourt (Major), François Guérin (Lieutenant), Michèle Cordoue (Corinne).

Video: Montparnasse (France) video. Color. In French. 90 minutes.

Early film

1912 Caserini film
This early silent Italian film of the story, also known as *Santarellina,* stars two major Italian actors of the period and was a big hit in 1912. Gigetta Morano is Denise, who becomes Mam'zelle Nitouche, Ercole Vaser is Célestin/Floridor, and Mario Bonnard is the lieutenant. Mario Caserini directed for Ambrosio film. Black and white. In Italian. About 15 minutes.

MAÑANA
1956 TV opera by Benjamin

Arthur Benjamin's *Mañana,* one of the first original TV operas in England, was composed on a commission from BBC Television. It is based on Caryl Brahms's *Under the Juniper Tree,* and Brahms wrote the libretto himself in collaboration with George Foa. Benjamin was fond of Latin American rhythms and was well known at the time for his composition "Jamaican Rumba."

1956 BBC Television
English TV production: George Foa (director), Edward Renton (conductor, Royal Philharmonic Orchestra and Glyndebourne Festival Chorus), Stephen Bund (set designer).
Cast: Frederick Sharp (Wise Man), Edith Coates (Widow), Heather Harper (Luisita), Carlos Montes (Pedro), Naida Labay-Buckingham (Conchita), Patrizia Kern (Pia), David Langford (Carlos), Ronald Lewis (José), Julian Bream (Guitar Player).
Telecast live February 1, 1956, on BBC. Black and white. In English. 73 minutes.

MANIURA, PETER
English television director(1965-)

Peter Maniura has directed the telecasts and videos of some notable new operas. His DVD of Peter Sellars's production of Adams's EL NIÑO at the Théâtre du Châtelet won the 2002 Gramophone Award. In the 1990s he directed Turnage's GREEK (1990) and the Royal Opera premiere of Birtwistle's GAWAIN (1991). He produced a fine version of the classic Purcell opera DIDO AND AENEAS (1995), and his documentary about GEORG SOLTI (1997) is the best. See CAPRICCIO (1992) and LA TRAVIATA (1994).

MANON
1884 opera by Massenet

JULES MASSENET's version of the Abbé Prévost novel *L'histoire du Chevalier des Grieux et de Manon Lescaut,* which had already provided the basis for an opera by Auber and would later become Puccini's first success, is one of the principal repertory works in French opera houses to this day. Massenet's opera, libretto by Henri Meilhac and Philippe Gille, follows the novel more closely than Puccini's but the story is the same. Convent-bound Manon Lescaut runs off with young Chevalier des Grieux, whom she meets at an inn, but she later abandons him for a rich man. After a series of complications, she dies in Des Grieux's arms. See MANON LESCAUT for the non-operatic narrative films based on the Prévost novel.

***1977 New York City Opera
American stage production: Tito Capobianco (production), Gigi Denda (stage director), Julius Rudel (conductor, New York City Opera Orchestra and Chorus), Marsha Louis Eck (set designer).
Cast: Beverly Sills (Manon Lescaut), Henry Price (Chevalier des Grieux), Richard Fredericks (Lescaut), Samuel Ramey (Count des Grieux), Robert Hale (De Brétigny).
Video: Paramount VHS. Kirk Browning (director). Color. In French with English subtitles. 152 minutes.
Comment: Historic record of one of Sills's best roles.

1983 Vienna State Opera
Austrian stage production: Jean-Pierre Ponnelle (director, set/costume designer), Adam Fischer (conductor, Vienna Staatsoper Orchestra and Chorus).
Cast: Edita Gruberova (Manon), Francisco Araiza (Chevalier des Grieux), Hans Helm (Lescaut), Pierre Tau (Count des Grieux).
Video: Lyric VHS. Brian Large (director). Color. In French. 167 minutes. On video.

Early/related films

1910 Pathé film
This Pathé *Manon,* based on the Massenet opera, stars Mlle. Regnier as Manon, M. Dehelly, and J. Perier. It was released in America in July 1910 and shown with the opera music. Black and white. Silent. About 10 minutes.

1926 UFA film
This German *Manon Lescaut,* starring Lya de Putti as Manon, is based on the Massenet opera and the Prévost novel. Vladimir Gaidarow is Des Grieux, Eduard

Rothauser is the Count, and Marlene Dietrich has a small role as Micheline. Paul Leni designed the sets, and Arthur Robison directed for UFA. The film was shown with the opera music. Black and white. Silent. About 88 minutes.

1929 Vitaphone film
Silent film actress Hope Hampton had just become a professional opera singer when she made the Vitaphone sound film *Hope Hampton in the Fourth Act of Manon*. As the titles says, she sings excerpts from Act IV of Massenet's opera accompanied by the Vitaphone Symphony Orchestra and Chorus. Hampton had made her opera debut in *Manon* with the Philadelphia Grand Opera on December 21, 1928. Black and white. In French. About 10 minutes.

1930 Call of the Flesh
Des Grieux's sad farewell "Ah! fuyez, douce image" is sung by Ramon Novarro at his opera debut in this MGM film; he thinks he has lost the woman he loves. See CALL OF THE FLESH.

1937 I'll Take Romance
Grace Moore sings the *Manon* Gavotte ("Obéissons quand leur voix appelle") in *I'll Take Romance*. She plays an opera diva romanced by Melvyn Douglas. See I'LL TAKE ROMANCE.

MANON LESCAUT (Auber)
1856 opéra-comique by Auber

DANIEL AUBER's *Manon Lescaut,* libretto by Eugène Scribe based on the novel by the Abbé Prévost, premiered in Paris in 1856, much in advance of the now better-known versions by Massenet (1884) and Puccini (1893). Scribe made many changes to the novel's story and invented new characters, but the essential plot remains the same: Manon loves young Des Grieux, but she wants to live a life of luxury so she becomes involved with a rich man. After complications, she dies in Des Grieux's arms in the deserts of Louisiana. Auber completed the opera when he was 72.

1990 Théâtre Français de la Musique
French stage production: Pierre Jourdan and David Freedman (directors), Patrick Fournillier (conductor, Orchestre de Picardie le Sinfonietta et Choeurs du Théâtre Français de la Musique).

Cast: Elisabeth Vidal (Manon), Alain Gabriel (Des Grieux), René Massis (Marquis), André Cognet (Lescaut), Brigitte Lafon (Marguerite).

Opera Classics VHS. Color. In French. 160 minutes.

MANON LESCAUT (Puccini)
1893 opera by Puccini

GIACOMO PUCCINI's first major success was based on the Abbé Prévost novel *L'histoire du Chevalier des Grieux et de Manon Lescaut,* which had already inspired operas by Auber and Massenet. His wonderful melodies and a good libretto (created with great difficulty by a team of writers including Luigi Illica, Domenico Oliva, Giuseppe Giacosa, Giulio Ricordi, Marco Prago, and Ruggero Leoncavallo) have made it the most popular of the three versions. Manon Lescaut, a young woman about to be put in a convent by her brother, meets the Chevalier des Grieux at an inn and runs away with him. She later leaves him for the rich Geronte, gets arrested as a prostitute, and is deported to Louisiana. Des Grieux goes with her, and she dies in his arms. Manon's aria "In quelle trine morbide" has become popular with sopranos.

***1980 Metropolitan Opera
American stage production: Gian Carlo Menotti (director), James Levine (conductor, Metropolitan Opera Orchestra and Chorus), Desmond Heeley (set designer).

Cast: Renata Scotto (Manon), Plácido Domingo (Des Grieux), Pablo Elvira (Lescaut), Renato Capecchi (Geronte), Philip Creech (Edmondo).

Video: Pioneer Classics DVD/Paramount VHS. Taped March 29, 1980; telecast September 27, 1980. Kirk Browning (director). Color. In Italian with English subtitles. 135 minutes.

Comment: Outstanding cast and production.

1983 Royal Opera
English stage production: Götz Friedrich (director), Giuseppe Sinopoli (conductor, Royal Opera House Orchestra and Chorus), Günther Schneider-Siemssen (set designer).

Cast: Kiri Te Kanawa (Manon), Plácido Domingo (Des Grieux), Thomas Allen (Lescaut), Forbes Robinson (Geronte), Robin Leggate (Edmondo).

Video: Warner Vision NVC Arts DVD/Castle VHS/Pioneer Artists LD. Color. Humphrey Burton (director). In Italian with English subtitles. 130 minutes.

1983/1989 Opera Stories
Charlton Heston narrates an LD highlights version of the above Royal Opera production with introductions filmed in the opera's "real" setting by Keith Cheetham in 1989. Color. In English and Italian with English subtitles. 52 minutes. Pioneer Artists LD.

1990 Gran Teatre del Liceu, Barcelona

Spanish stage production: Silvio Varviso (conductor).

Cast: Mirella Freni (Manon), Peter Dvorsky (Des Grieux), Enrique Serra.

Video: House of Opera DVD/Bel Canto Society VHS. Color. In Italian. 134 minutes.

1991 Flanders Opera

Flemish stage production: Robert Carsen (director), Silvio Varviso (conductor, Flanders Opera Symphony Chorus and Orchestra), Anthony Ward (set/costume designer).

Cast: Miriam Gauci (Manon), Antonio Ordoñez (Des Grieux), Jan Danckaert (Lescaut), Jules Bastin (Geronte), Barry Ryan (Edmondo), Herman Bekaert (Innkeeper).

Video: Image Entertainment/Arthaus (GB) DVD. Dirk Gryspeirt (director). Color. In Italian with English subtitles. 124 minutes.

Comment: Ward's minimalist stylized sets and elegant costumes create a gilded 18th-century atmosphere, and the singers are superb.

1998 Glyndebourne Festival

English stage production: Graham Vick (director), John Eliot Gardiner (conductor, London Philharmonic Orchestra and Glyndebourne Festival Chorus), Richard Hudson (set designer).

Cast: Adina Nitescu (Manon), Patrick Denniston (Des Grieux), Roberto de Candia (Lescaut), Paolo Montarsolo (Geronte), Richard Mosely-Evans (Innkeeper).

Video: House of Opera (USA)/NVC Arts (GB) VHS. Humphrey Burton (director). Color. In Italian with English subtitles. 126 minutes.

Early/related films

1908 Rossi film

Italian sound film of scenes from *Manon Lescaut*, made by the Carlo Rossi Studio and screened with the music on a synchronized phonograph. Distributed in the United States by Kleine. Black and white. In Italian. About 10 minutes.

1911 Pastrone film

Italian film diva Francesca Bertini stars as Manon in this Italian *Manon Lescaut*. It was directed by Giovanni Pastrone, later internationally known for his epic *Cabiria*. Black and white. Silent. About 12 minutes.

1911 Capellani/Napierkowska film

Stacia Napierkowska plays Manon in this French *Manon Lescaut* based on the Prévost story, directed by Albert Capellani for Pathé. Léon Bernard and Romuald Joubé add support. Black and white. Silent. About 12 minutes.

1912 Capellani/Bérangère film

Stage actress Bérangère stars as Manon in this French *Manon Lescaut* based on the opera and novel and again directed by Albert Capellani, this time for Film d'Art. M. Barry is Des Grieux and M. Barnier is Lescaut. Black and white. Silent. About 12 minutes.

1914 Cavalieri film

Italian soprano Lina Cavalieri, publicized as "the most beautiful woman in the world," starred on stage as Manon in the Puccini and Massenet operas. In the American feature film *Manon Lescaut,* she plays the role opposite her husband, French tenor Lucien Muratore, who plays Des Grieux. The film was supposedly based on the Prévost novel rather than either opera, or so they claimed for copyright reasons. Herbert Hall Winslow directed. Black and white. Silent. About 50 minutes.

1918 Gargiulo film

Tina Xeo is Manon in this Italian narrative *Manon Lescaut* based on the novel, with Giuseppe Giuffrida as Des Grieux. Mario Gargiulo directed for Flegrea Film. Black and white. Silent. About 60 minutes.

1919 Zelnik film

Lya Mara is Manon Lescaut in the German feature *Manon Lescaut* based on the novel. Friedrich Zelnik directed. Black and white. Silent. About 70 minutes.

1927 When a Man Loves

Dolores Costello stars as Manon with John Barrymore as Des Grieux in this Warner Bros. film based on the Prévost novel. The plot is somewhat altered as the studio wanted it to have a happy ending. In this version, Des Grieux starts a mutiny on the ship taking Manon to America and escapes with her in a small boat. Presumably they live happily ever after. Black and white. Silent. About 110 minutes.

1936 Sinfonie di cuori/Du bist mein Glück

Beniamino Gigli, playing an opera singer loved by a married woman, sings an aria from *Manon Lescaut* with backing from the Bavarian State Opera Orchestra and Chorus. Karl Heinz Martin directed Italian and German versions. See SINFONIE DI CUORI.

1940 Gallone film

Alida Valli stars as Manon with Vittorio De Sica as Des Grieux in this opulent Italian *Manon Lescaut*. Opera film specialist Carmine Gallone based the screenplay on the opera libretto and used Puccini's music as the film score. Italian soprano Maria Caniglia sings the Puccini arias heard on the soundtrack. Black and white. In Italian. 92 minutes.

1949 Clouzot film

Cecile Aubrey plays Manon with Michel Auclair as Des Grieux in director Henri-Georges Clouzot's harsh updated version of *Manon Lescaut,* set in post–World War II France. The desert death scene is quite powerful. Black and white. In French. 105 minutes.

1954 Gli amori di Manon Lescaut

The Loves of Manon Lescaut is an Italian film based on the novel but using the Puccini opera music as its score. Miriam Bru stars as Manon with Francesco Interlenghi as Des Grieux. Mario Costa directed. Black and white. In Italian. 95 minutes.

1986 Chalbaud film

Venezuelan television star Mayra Alejandra plays a modern Manon who runs off with her lover to a Hilton Hotel in this updated Venezuelan *Manon Lescaut.* Roman Chalbaud directed. Color. In Spanish. 112 minutes.

1986 Hannah and Her Sisters

Woody Allen's film about the complex love lives of three sisters in New York features a Metropolitan Opera performance of *Manon Lescaut*. Sam Peterson takes Diane Wiest to the opera, and the camera observes them ironically while the aria "Sola, perduta, abbandonata" is sung. Color. In English. 106 minutes.

1999 Anywhere But Here

"Sola, perduta, abbandonata" is featured on the soundtrack of this film about the relationship between a single mother (Susan Sarandon) and her teenaged daughter (Natalie Portman). Wayne Wang directed. Color. 113 minutes.

MAN WHO CRIED, THE

2000 English film with opera content

Sally Potter's Anglo-French film *The Man Who Cried* is a story about opera, Jews, and gypsies in Paris at the start of World War II. A Russian Jewish refugee (Christine Ricci) joins the chorus of an opera company in Paris in 1939, becomes involved with a gypsy (Johnny Depp) and his horse, and rooms with the beautiful but enigmatic Lily (Cate Blanchett). The company's leading tenor is

Dante Dominio (John Turturro), an Italian fascist who become involved with Lily. When the war begins, the fascist shows his true nastiness, and the opera company breaks up. Much of the film was shot at the Opéra-Comique in Paris, and there is a fair amount of opera. Italian Salvatore Licitra, who has become one of the most popular new tenors since his appearances at La Scala and the Met, provides the voice for Turturro. He sings the aria from *The Pearl Fishers* "Je crois entendre encore" three times in different contexts: first in Yiddish, then at a society reception with piano accompaniment by Katia and Marielle Labeque, and finally on the opera stage with backing from the Royal Opera House Orchestra led by Sian Edwards. Also featured are stage productions of *Tosca* (with "E lucevan le stelle") and *Il trovatore* (with "Di quella pira"). "Dido's Lament," from *Dido and Aeneas,* is featured in two scenes and sung by Czech soprano Iva Bittová. Color. In English. 100 minutes.

MAN WHO MISTOOK HIS WIFE FOR A HAT, THE

1986 opera by Nyman

MICHAEL NYMAN's chamber opera *The Man Who Mistook His Wife for a Hat* is based on a case described by Dr. Oliver Sachs in his book with that title. Christopher Rawlence's libretto follows the original closely in telling the story of a man with an unusual memory defect; he is unable to recognize familiar objects and cannot distinguish his wife from his hat. The man is a professional opera singer and is suffering from what Sacks calls "visual agnosia"; he cannot make sense of what he sees until he restores order through music. Nyman's opera relates the diagnostic journey of the neurologist who helps him. Sacks says the hero of his opera is music, that it shows "the power of music to organize, knit. and re-knit a shattered world into sense." Nyman's music, which combines popular and classical idioms, was written for baritone, soprano, and tenor. It was first heard when the opera was staged at London's Institute of Contemporary Arts in 1986.

1987 ICA film

English feature film: Michael Morris (stage director), Christopher Rawlence (film director), Michael Nyman (conductor), Institute of Contemporary Arts (production).

Cast: Emile Belcourt, Patricia Hooper, Frederick Westcott, Dr. Oliver Sachs.

Video: Films for the Humanities & Sciences VHS. Color. In English. 75 minutes.

Comment: Nyman worked with the ICA for a year to produce this film in collaboration with Rawlence and Morris. It premiered in the United States at an American Film Institute film festival in Los Angeles.

MAOMETTO II
1820 opera by Rossini

Love and loyalty become confused during the Turkish-Venetian war, culminating in the fall of Negroponte in 1476. Anna Erisso, the daughter of the governor of Negroponte, is secretly in love with a man who turns out to be Turkish leader Maometto in disguise. She tricks him into allowing her father Paolo and new husband Calbo to escape, and then kills herself. Gioachino Rossini's grandiose Italian opera *Maometto II*, libretto by Cesare della Valle based on his play *Anna Erizo*, premiered in Naples in 1820; Rossini later revised it for presentation in Paris in 1826 as the French opera *Le siége de Corinthe*.

1985 Pesaro Festival
Italian stage production: Claudio Scimone (conductor, Prague Philharmonic Orchestra and European Festival Chorus).

Cast: Samuel Ramey (Maometto), Cecilia Gasdia (Anna Erisso), Chris Merritt (Paolo Erisso), Lucia Valentini-Terrani (Calbo), William Matteuzzi (Condulmiero), Oslavia Di Credico (Selimo).

Video: Premiere Opera VHS. Color. In Italian. 180 minutes.

MARCO POLO
1995 opera by Tan Dun

Marco Polo travels from Venice to China in the 13th century and meditates on what he has seen. In the opera he is played by two people (Marco is the young traveler, Polo is his older memory), as reality mixes with surrealism and the journey becomes spiritual as well as physical. Tan Dun's complex opera *Marco Polo*, libretto by Paul Griffiths based on his novel *Myself and Marco Polo*, premiered at the Munich Biennale. The music ranges from Venetian medieval to Tibetan and Chinese and includes a double role written for a Peking Opera singer. The opera was premiered in the United States by New York City Opera in November 1997 with Tan Dun conducting.

1999 New Opera, Vienna
Austrian stage production: Erwin Piplits (director/set designer). Walter Kobéra and Peter Sommerer (conductors, Amadeus Ensemble of Vienna and New Opera of Vienna Chorus).

Cast: Serapions Ensemble of Vienna: Gisela Theisen, Lela Wiche, Ingrid Bendl, Robert Hillebrand, Alexander Kaimbacher, Michael Wilder, Joseph Garcia.

Video: B.O.A. Videofilmkunst (Germany). Color. In English. 140 minutes

MARIA DI ROHAN
1843 opera by Donizetti

An aristocratic love triangle in France during the reign of Louis XIII. Maria is secretly married to the Duke de Chevreuse who has killed Cardinal Richelieu's nephew in a duel. She asks her former lover Riccardo, Count de Chalais, to intercede to save her husband. After another duel and many complications, Riccardo dies, and Maria's husband leaves her. Gaetano Donizetti's *Maria di Rohan*, libretto by Salvatore Cammarano based on a French play, is not as well known as his other operas but has some excellent music.

1988 Festival della Valle d'Itria
Italian stage production: Filippo Crivelli (director), Massimo de Bernart (conductor, Valle d'Itria Festival Orchestra and Chorus).

Cast: Mariana Nicolesco (Maria), Paolo Conti, Giuseppe Morino.

Video: House of Opera DVD/VHS. Nikolaus Westphal (director). Telecast in Italy December 31, 1988. Color. In Italian. 105 minutes.

Comment: Staged in the Palazzo Ducale in Martina Franca for the Festival della Valle d'Itria.

MARIAGE AUX LANTERNES, LE
1857 operetta by Offenbach

Jacques Offenbach's popular one-act *Le marriage aux lanternes* (Marriage by Lantern Light), libretto by Michel Carré and Léon Battu, is a slight but charming story about a young farmer pursued by two widows who want to marry him. His uncle leaves him a "treasure" that he has to discover by lantern light; it turns out to be a pretty cousin who also has been sent to look for a treasure.

1943 Hartt Opera Workshop
American TV production: Elemer Nagy (director/set designer), Moshe Paranov (conductor, Julius Hartt School of Music Orchestra and Chorus), Truba Kaschmann (choreographer).

Cast: Students from the Julius Hartt School of Music Opera Workshop.

Telecast live in May 1943 on WRGB-TV. Robert Stone (director). Black and white. In English as *Marriage by Lantern Light*. 90 minutes.

Comment: Telecast on a double bill with Menotti's *The Old Maid and the Thief.* WRGB-TV was General Electric's pioneer station in Schenectady, New York.

MARIA GOLOVIN

1958 TV opera by Menotti

Blind veteran Donato has an affair with married Maria Golovin, a tenant in his mother's Italian villa, during World War II. When her prisoner husband returns, he is so jealous he shoots her—or so he thinks. GIAN CARLO MENOTTI's three-act opera *Maria Golovin*, libretto by the composer, was commissioned by NBC Opera Theatre. However, it was actually premiered on stage at the U.S. Pavilion at the Brussels World Fair on August 20, 1958, with Franca Duval as Maria Golovin, Richard Cross as Donato, and Patricia Neway as Donato's mother.

1959 NBC Opera Theater

American TV production: Samuel Chotzinoff (director), Peter Herman Adler (conductor, NBC Symphony of the Air Orchestra), Rouben Ter-Arutunian (set designer).

Cast: Franca Duval (Maria Golovin), Richard Cross (Donato), Ruth Kobart (Agata), Patricia Neway (Donato's Mother), Lorenzo Muti (Trottolò).

Video at the MTR. Telecast March 8, 1959, on NBC. Kirk Browning (director). Color. In English. 120 minutes.

1977 Spoleto Festival, Italy

Italian stage production: Gian Carlo Menotti (director), Christian Badea (conductor, Spoleto Festival Orchestra and Westminster Choir), Pier Luigi Samaritani (set/costume designer).

Cast: Fiorella Carmen Forti (Maria Golovin) Charles Long (Donato), Maureen Morelle (Mother), Giovanna Fioroni (Agata), Marco Biscarini (Trottolò), Giacomo Metelli (Aldo).

Telecast August 22, 1977, by RAI. Color. In English. 122 minutes.

MARIA STUARDA

1835 opera by Donizetti

GAETANO DONIZETTI's opera *Maria Stuarda* (Mary Stuart) is more creative imagination than history. Giuseppe Bartari's libretto is based on a play by Schiller that tells of a (non-historical) meeting between Mary Queen of Scots and Queen Elizabeth. This is arranged by Leicester, whom Elizabeth loves although he loves Mary. Mary responds furiously to accusations about her loyalty and ends up on the scaffold. Janet Baker has been popular in the role on stage, and her performance in the English-language version is on video. The only (partly) Italian version is a film by Petr Weigl, using the Joan Sutherland recording. There are many films telling the story in narrative form.

***1982 English National Opera

English stage production: John Copley (director), Sir Charles Mackerras (conductor, English National Opera Orchestra and Chorus), Desmond Heeley (set designer), Tom Hammond (English translation).

Cast: Janet Baker (Mary Stuart), Rosalind Plowright (Queen Elizabeth), David Rendall (Leicester), John Tomlinson (Talbot), Alan Opie (Cecil).

Video: Image Entertainment DVD and EMI/HBO/ Castle VHS. Peter Butler (director). Color. In English. 138 minutes.

2000 Weigl film

Czech feature film: Petr Weigl (director), Richard Bonynge (conductor, Bologna Teatro Communale Chorus and Orchestra).

Singers: Joan Sutherland (Maria Stuarda), Huguette Tourangeau (Elisabetta), Luciano Pavarotti (Leicester), Roger Soyer (Talbot), James Morris (Cecil), Margreta Elkins (Anna).

Video: Image Entertainment DVD. Color. In Italian and German with English subtitles. 90 minutes.

Comment: Filmed with actors miming to the 1975 Sutherland/Bonynge recording. As the Schiller source play has been added (German dialogue alternates with Italian vocals), much of the opera has been cut. Pity.

2001 Teatro Donizetti, Bergamo

Italian stage production: Francesco Esposito (director), Fabrizio Maria Carminati (conductor, Orchestra Stabile di Bergamo and Coro del Circuito Lirico Regional Lombardo), Italo Grassi (set designer).

Cast: Carmela Remigio (Maria Stuarda), Sonia Ganassi (Elisabetta), Joseph Calleja (Leicester), Riccardo Zanellato (Talbot), Cinzia Rizzone (Anna).

Video: Dynamic DVD. Marco Scalfi (director). Color. In Italian with English subtitles. 153 minutes.

Early/related films

1908 Marie Stuart

Jeanne Delvair stars in this French Pathé film made in color as *Marie Stuart* that seems to have been based on the opera libretto. Albert Capellani directed. It was distributed in America. Black and white. Silent. About 14 minutes.

1922 Mary, Queen of Scots

Cathleen Nesbitt is Mary Stuart in this English film written by Eliot Stannard and directed by Edwin Greenwood for the series *The Romance of British History*. Black and white. Silent. About 10 minutes.

1927 Maria Stuart
German feature film based on the Schiller source play with Fritz Kortner as the main star. Friedrich Feher directed and wrote it with Leopold Jessner and Anton Kuh. Black and white. Silent. About 70 minutes.

1936 Mary of Scotland
Katharine Hepburn is Mary Stuart with Florence Eldridge as Elizabeth in this U.S. film based on the play by Maxwell Anderson. John Ford directed for RKO. Black and white. 123 minutes.

1971 Mary, Queen of Scots
Vanessa Redgrave is Mary Stuart with Glenda Jackson as Queen Elizabeth in this British film written by John Hale. Charles Jarrott directed. Color. 128 minutes.

1985 Mary Stuart
German TV production of the Schiller play on which the opera is based. Heinz Schirk directed for Bavarian Television. Color. In German. 111 minutes. Inter Nationes VHS.

MARIANO, LUIS
Spanish/French tenor (1914–1970)

Luis Mariano is the equivalent of Mario Lanza for the French cinema, an operatic tenor who became a popular movie star but inspired little critical respect. His 1950s operetta films were box office hits, videos of them are still best-sellers, books about him continue to be written, and his records remain popular. Mariano was born in Spain, but he fled to France in 1936 because of the Civil War. He studied opera in Bordeaux and began his opera career as Ernesto in *Don Pasquale* in Paris in 1943. His stardom began with the operettas of FRANCIS LOPEZ. He starred on stage in Lopez's *La belle de Cadix* in 1946 and *Andalousie* in 1947 and then starred in their successful film versions. His other top box-office films include *Le chanteur de Mexique* and *Violettes imperials*. Mariano's only foreign film is a 1954 German adaptation of Lehár's DER ZAREWITSCH. He is not well known in the United States, although he appeared on *The Ed Sullivan Show* in 1951 and was the TV guest of Frank Sinatra in 1953.

1946 Histoire de chanter
Mariano plays an opera singer in his first major film. He sings on stage as the Duke in Act I of *Rigoletto* and as Alfredo in the second act of *La traviata*. Gilles Grangier directed. Black and white. In French. 88 minutes. René Chateau (France) VHS.

1950 Andalousie
Mariano is bullfighter Juanito in this film of Lopez's 1947 operetta. After a disagreement with his girlfriend, he goes to Mexico to become a matador while she dedicates herself to dance and becomes the famous Estrellita. Robert Vernay directed. Black and white. In French. 94 minutes. René Chateau (France) VHS.

1953 La Belle de Cadix
Mariano re-creates his stage role as movie star singer Carlos in this film of Lopez's 1945 operetta. It is set in Spain in 1953 where a film company is shooting *La Belle de Cadix* and a singing partner is sought. Gypsy Maria-Luisa (Carmen Sevilla) gets the role. Raymond Bernard directed. Color. In French. 105 minutes. René Chateau (France) VHS.

MARINA
1855 zarzuela by Arietta

Spanish composer EMILIO ARIETTA's *Marina*, his most popular zarzuela, was modeled on Italian opera, especially *Lucia di Lammermoor*. Francisco Camprodan's libretto tells the story of Marina, a young woman in a Catalan fishing village, and her love for ship captain Jorge. There are many problems and misunderstandings, but love wins out in the end. *Marina* has been filmed and telecast several times and remains popular.

1963 Mexican Television
Mexican TV film: Plácido Domingo (director), Max Factor Company (production).

Cast: Marta Ornelas (Marina), Plácido Domingo (Jorge), Ernestina Garfias, Franco Inglesias.

Black and white. In Spanish. 90 minutes.

Comment: Domingo, who began his career in Mexico, filmed zarzuelas for Max Factor in 1963.

1987 Asturias Opera
Spanish stage production: Joaquin Vion (director), Enrique Ricci (conductor, Asturias Symphonic Orchestra).

Cast: Aña Gonzalez (Marina), Alfredo Kraus (Jorge), Juan Pons (Roque), Alfonso Echeverria (Pascual).

Video: Lyric VHS. Taped at Campoanor Theater in Oviedo. Color. In Spanish. 118 minutes.

1996 Teatro Calderón, Madrid
Spanish stage production: José Luis Moreno (director), José A. Irasforza (conductor, Teatro Calderón Orchestra and Chorus), Julian Pérez Muñoz (set designer), Alhambra Ballet.

Cast: Milagros Poblador (Marina), Rafael Lledó (Jorge), Mario Valdivieso (Roque), Gregorio Poblador (Pascual).

Video: Metrovideo (Spain) VHS. Telecast by RTVE. José Ignado Ortega (director). Color. In Spanish. 111 minutes.

MARIONETTE
1938 film with opera content

Beniamino Gigli plays a famous tenor who returns to his Italian farm after an American tour. While riding his bicycle, he has an accident that breaks some fragile 78 rpm records. As they were meant to be the operatic accompaniment to a marionette show, he agrees to sing for the performance himself as an apology. American journalist Carla Rust hears him singing and thinks she has discovered a great peasant tenor. As he is attracted to her, he goes along with the deception and allows her to promote him. When she finds she's been deceived, she gets very upset, but all is resolved in the end. Gigli sings arias from *Rigoletto, Martha, Fra Diavolo,* and Paisiello's *Nina,* plus Italian songs by Bixio. The lifelike marionettes in the film were created by Yambo (Enrico Novelli), and one critic thought the best scene in the film was Gigli singing for the marionettes. Alois Melichar was music director; Arturo Gallea was the cinematographer; and Rudo Ritter, Walter Forster, and Otto Ernst Lubitz wrote the screenplay. Italian opera movie specialist Carmine Gallone shot the film on location in Rome and Naples in both Italian and German. The Italian version is titled *Marionette,* the German one is called *Dir gehört mein Herz.* It was shown in the United States as *My Heart Belongs to Thee.* Black and white. In Italian. 102 minutes. Bel Canto Society/Opera Dubs VHS.

MARITANA
1845 opera by Wallace

Maritana was one of the big three "Irish" operas of 19th-century England with Balfe's *The Bohemian Girl* and Benedict's *Lily of Killarney.* Composer VINCENT WALLACE was Irish, but Edward Fitzball's libretto was based on the French play *Don César de Bazan,* set in 17th-century Madrid. The plot is similar to that of Offenbach's LA PÉRICHOLE. King Charles II is attracted to gypsy Maritana, so his prime minister Don José arranges for her to marry Don Caesar in prison so she can obtain a title. *Maritana,* which was popular in London, New York, and Vienna, was staged at Sadler's Wells as late as 1931. Although it was filmed three times and stayed in the English repertory until World War II, it is no longer in fashion. There is no modern video and only a highlights recording.

Early films

1915 Don Caesar de Bazan
Alice Hollister plays Maritana in this American feature film based on the play and opera; it was shot on location at a Spanish fort in Florida by the Kalem company. Lawson Butt is Don Caesar, Robert D. Walker is King Charles, Helen Lindroth is Queen Mary Louise, and Harry Millarde is Don José. Robert G. Vignola directed. Black and white. Silent. About 60 minutes.

1922 Tense Moments From Opera
Vivian Gibson is Maritana in this English highlights film of the opera made for the series *Tense Moments From Opera.* Gordon Hopkirk is Don Caesar de Bazan and Wallace Bosco is King Charles. George Wynn directed, and H. B. Parkinson produced. Live music from the opera was played when the film was screened. Black and white. Silent. About 15 minutes.

1927 Cameo Operas
Kathlyn Hillard plays Maritana with Herbert Langley as Don Caesar in this British highlights film made for the series *Cameo Operas.* John E. Blakeley produced, and H. B. Parkinson directed for Song Films. It was shown with singers performing the arias. Black and white. Silent. About 18 minutes.

MARLOWE, ANTHONY
American tenor

Anthony Marlowe sang with the Metropolitan Opera in more than 200 performances from 1939 to 1949 but always in supporting roles. His big opera roles came in films; they were brief but memorable. In the 1941 film *The Flame of New Orleans,* he plays Edgardo opposite Gitta Alpar's Lucia in *Lucia di Lammermoor,* and they sing the duet "Verranno a te sull'aure." In the 1943 film *The Phantom of the Opera,* he is Lyonel in *Martha* at the Paris Opera and leads the magnificent quintet "Mag der Himmel" with support from Nelson Eddy as Plumkett and Tudor Williams as Tristram. He did not sing in either opera at the Met.

MARRIAGE, THE
1953 TV opera by Martinů

The Marriage, BOHUSLAV MARTINŮ's comic opera based on a play by Gogol, premiered on NBC Opera Theatre. A young man thinks he should get married so a friend finds him what he thinks is the perfect woman. A marriage broker brings the woman other suitors, but she decides to marry the young man. He then changes his mind.

1953 NBC Opera Theatre

American TV production: Samuel Chotzinoff (director), Peter Herman Adler (conductor, NBC Opera Theatre Orchestra), Otis Riggs (set designer).

Cast: Donald Gramm (Young Man); Sonia Stollin (Woman); Michael Pollock (Friend); Winifred Heidt (Marriage Broker); Andrew McKinley, Lloyd Harris, Robert Holland (Suitors); Leon Lishner (Servant).

Telecast on February 7, 1953, on NBC. John Block (director). Black and white. In English. 60 minutes.

MARRIAGE OF FIGARO, THE

See LE NOZZE DI FIGARO.

MARSCHNER, HEINRICH

German composer (1795–1861)

Heinrich Marschner was the major opera composer in Germany between Weber and Wagner. He has mostly been forgotten by the modern opera public, but some of his stage works still have admirers. He is best known for the Grand Guignol–like DER VAMPYR. As the vogue for vampires never seems to abate, it is likely to stay in the repertory. It was recently updated in a quite stylish way for British television.

MARSHALL, EVERETT

American baritone (1900–1965)

Massachusetts-born Everett Marshall studied in New York, London, and Milan but made his debut at the Teatro Massimo in Palermo in 1926 in *Il trovatore*. He began his career at the Metropolitan Opera in 1927 in *Lohengrin* and remained with the Met for four seasons. His film career began in 1930 with the operetta *Dixiana*, after which he shifted to Broadway for *George White's Scandals* in 1931 and the *Ziegfeld Follies* in 1934. He was back in Hollywood in 1935 for one more film and then turned to stage operetta, touring in standards such as *The Student Prince*.

1930 Dixiana

Marshall stars opposite Bebe Daniels in this RKO operetta film set in 1840 New Orleans. It was made by the same team that made the very successful *Rio Rita*, but this one didn't quite jell. Daniels plays circus singer Dixiana, while Marshall, who loves her, is from a wealthy Southern family. They want to marry but his family is snobbish. The film was made with two-color Technicolor sequences and songs by Harry Tierney and Anne Caldwell. Luther Reed directed. Black and white and color. 98 minutes.

1935 I Live for Love

Busby Berkeley directed this minor musical with Marshall as a singer who has a complicated relationship/rivalry with Delores Del Rio. After a series of theatrical and radio mix-ups, they get married. The songs are by Mort Dixon and Allie Wrubel. Warner Bros. Black and white. 64 minutes.

MARTHA

1847 opera by Flotow

FRIEDRICH VON FLOTOW's *Martha, oder Der Markt zur Richmond*, which used to be a popular opera at the Met and a particular favorite of Caruso's, was the first opera to be filmed on stage—a 15-minute version shot in 1898 with singers from the Castle Square Opera Company. Its fine tenor aria "Ach so fromm," its adaptation of "The Last Rose of Summer" as "Letzte Rose," and its magnificent quintet "Mag der Himmel" are still sung, but the opera is rarely staged now in the United States. Librettist W. Friedrich paints an odd Germanic view of England in 1710. As a lark, Lady Harriet and her maid Nancy attend the Richmond Market in disguise as Martha and Julia. They are hired by Lyonel and Plumkett (so spelled) who take them back to Plumkett's farm. The women escape with the help of their friend Tristran, but not before both men fall in love. Lyonel sees Lady Harriet at a royal event, but she pretends not to know him; he is devastated and calls on heaven to forgive her in "Mag der Himmel." They are finally united when Lyonel's aristocratic origins are revealed, and Harriet again pretends to be Martha. *Martha* has been filmed many times and remains popular in Germany. "Ach so fromm," usually sung in Italian as "M'apparì" by Caruso and Italian tenors, is often featured in narrative films.

1936 Martha oder Letzte Rose

German feature film: Karl Anton (director), Harald Röbbeling and Arthur Pohl (screenplay), Herbert Körner (cinematographer), Clemens Schmalstich (music director).

Cast: Helge Roswaenge (Lyonel), Carla Spletter (Lady Harriet), Fritz Kampers (Plumkett), Grethe Weiser (Nancy), Georg Alexander (Tristan).

Video: Live Opera VHS. Black and white. In German. 106 minutes.

Comment: Roswaenge was the leading tenor at the Berlin Staatsoper during this period.

1936 Martha ou les dernières rose

French feature film: Karl Anton (director), Jacques Bousquet (screenplay), Herbert Körner (cinematographer), Clemens Schmalstich (music director).

Cast: Roger Bourdin (Lionel), Sim Viva (Lady Harriet), Arthur Devere (Plumkett), Fernande Saala (Nancy), Jacques de Féraudy (Tristan).

Black and white. In French. 99 minutes.

Comment: Bourdin, a Paris Opéra-Comique baritone, is the star of this French film shot at the same time as the German film described above.

1978 Akkord film

German feature film: Arno Assmann (director), Gustav Kogel (screenplay), Horst Stein (conductor, Norddeutschen Rundfunks Orchestra and Chorus), Akkord Film (production).

Cast: Rüdiger Wohlers (Lyonel), Lucy Peacock (Lady Harriet), Nikolaus Hillebrand (Plumkett), Elisabeth Steiner (Nancy), Klaus Hirte (Tristan).

Video: House of Opera/Lyric VHS. Color. In German. 112 minutes.

Comment: A mime sequence is staged during the overture. Lucy Peacock is an American soprano.

1986 Stuttgart State Opera

German stage production: Loriot (director and set/costume designer), Wolf-Dieter Hauschild (conductor, Stuttgart Staatsoper Orchestra and Chorus).

Cast: Rüdiger Wohlers (Lyonel), Krisztina Laki (Lady Harriet), Helmut Berger-Tuna (Plumkett), Waltraud Meier (Nancy), Jörn W. Wilsing (Tristan).

Video: House of Opera DVD/Lyric and Opera Dubs VHS. Color. In German. 134 minutes.

Comment: Loriot's real name is Vicco von Bülow.

Early/related films

1898 Castle Square Opera Company

William Paley's 15-minute film *The Opera of Martha* appears to be the first opera to have been filmed on stage. Four singers from the Castle Square Opera Company were filmed in 1898 performing five scenes from the Flotow opera in costumes with sets; it was shown with singers performing from behind the screen. It premiered at the Eden Musée in New York in January 1899, was sold to Thomas Edison in July 1899, and released as an Edison film in 1900. This was a very long film for its time. Black and white. Silent.

1902 Lubin film

German-born Sigmund Lubin's Philadelphia-based Lubin Company also made a film of the very popular *Martha*. It was released in 1902, two years after the Edison film, and was meant to be screened with live music. Black and white. Silent. About 10 minutes.

1908 Pathé sound film

German film made by the Pathé company of a scene and aria from the opera. It was screened with the music played on a synchronized phonograph. Black and white. In German. About 4 minutes.

1913 Curtiz film

Casablanca director Michael Curtiz, Hungary's top director during the silent era, made a full-length version of *Martha* in Budapest in 1913. It stars Matton Ratkai, Sari Fedak, and Mihaly Varkonyi and was screened with live music. Black and white. About 40 minutes.

1916 Deutsche Lichtspielopern film

A feature-length film of *Martha* was made in Germany in 1916 by Deutsche Lichtspielopern Gesellschaft GmbH, a company founded in 1915 to produce German film operas. Screenings were accompanied by music and singing. Black and white. Silent. About 70 minutes.

1919 Delog film

The German Delog studio had a solution to the silence of early screen opera; it provided live musicians with its screen version of *Martha*. The company sent the film on tour with soloists, chorus, and orchestra. It saved money on sets and was considered an attractive novelty. Black and white. Silent. About 70 minutes.

1922 Tense Moments From Opera

Dorothy Fane plays Lady Henrietta in this British highlights version made for the series *Tense Moments From Opera*, which was screened with live music. Leslie Austin is Lyonel and James Knight is Plumkett. Gaumont. George Wynn directed. Black and white. Silent. About 12 minutes.

1923 Song-o-Reel

Walt Disney created an animated *Martha* in 1923 for his *Song-o-Reel* musical series. Black and white. About 6 minutes.

1927 Cameo Opera

Grizelda Hervey is Lady Henrietta in this highlights version made by H. B. Parkinson for the British series *Cameo Opera*. Gerald Rawlinson is Lyonel and Albergon Hicks is Plumkett. Singers stood by the screen and sang with the theater orchestra. Made for the Song Film company. Black and white. Silent. About 20 minutes.

1929 Vitaphone film with Alda

Metropolitan Opera soprano Frances Alda sings "The Last Rose of Summer" in this Vitaphone sound film released in August 1927. Black and white. In English. About 8 minutes. Bel Canto Society VHS.

1929 Vitaphone film with Martinelli
Met tenor Giovanni Martinelli sings the aria "M'apparì" from *Martha* in this Vitaphone sound film and then performs a duet from Act II with soprano Lidia Marracci. Black and white. In Italian. About 10 minutes.

1929 Metro Movietone with Kurenko
Russian-born American soprano Maria Kurenko sings the "The Last Rose of Summer" on this sound short made for the Metro Movietone series. Black and white. In English. About 8 minutes.

1930 The End of the Rainbow
The central section of this Richard Tauber film is devoted to a production of *Martha* at the Berlin Opera. He plays a Bavarian singer who becomes an opera star. The film was shot simultaneously in German as *Das Lockende Ziel*. Black and white. In English. 92 minutes. Lyric VHS.

1932 Milady's Escapade
This is an American highlights version of *Martha,* sung in English and distributed as *Milady's Escapade* by Educational Films in its *Operalogue* series. Howard Higgins directed. Black and white. 30 minutes.

1935 Stars Over Broadway
James Melton sings "M'apparì" in this film about a hotel porter with such a good voice that Pat O'Brien decides to make him an opera star. William Keighley directed. Warner Bros. Black and white. 89 minutes.

1935 Forget-Me-Not
Beniamino Gigli sings "M'apparì" while on world tour in this film about an older opera singer married to a younger woman. See FORGET-ME-NOT.

1937 When You're in Love
Beniamino Gigli is heard singing "M'apparì" on a recording in this Hollywood film with Met soprano Grace Moore. See WHEN YOU'RE IN LOVE.

1937 A Damsel in Distress
Lady Alyce's (Joan Fontaine) servant (Reginald Gardiner, dubbed by Mario Berini) sings "Ah, che a voi perdoni iddio" (the Italian version of "Mag der Himmel") in this film based on a novel by P. G. Wodehouse. He has started a betting pool about when she will marry. George Stevens directed. Black and white. 98 minutes.

1937 I'll Take Romance
Grace Moore joins in the *Martha* quintet and finale in *I'll Take Romance*. She plays an opera diva romanced by Melvyn Douglas. See I'LL TAKE ROMANCE.

1937 Die Stimme des Herzens
Beniamino Gigli sings "M'apparì" in this film about an opera singer and a princess. Karl Heinz Martin directed. Black and white. In German. 91 minutes. Lyric VHS.

1938 Marionette
Beniamino Gigli sings "M'apparì" in this Italian film about a famous tenor who performs at a marionette show as a favor. See MARIONETTE.

1939 Three Smart Girls Grow Up
Deanna Durbin sings "The Last Rose of Summer" in this movie about three sisters and their romantic attachments. Henry Koster directed for Universal. Black and white. 87 minutes.

1943 The Phantom of the Opera
The film opens with scenes from *Martha* sung in French at the Paris Opéra. Nelson Eddy (Plumkett) and chorus perform the "Porter's Song" followed by the quintet and ensemble "Mag der Himmel," led by Anthony Marlowe as Lyonel and Tudor Williams as Tristram. See THE PHANTOM OF THE OPERA.

1946 The Whale Who Wanted to Sing at the Met
Nelson Eddy sings a stirring Italian version of the "Mag der Himmel" ensemble at the end of this animated film about an operatic whale. He is shown in heaven singing "in a hundred glorious voices," all lent to him by Eddy. See THE WHALE WHO WANTED TO SING AT THE MET.

1946 Voglio bene soltanto a te
Beniamino Gigli, playing a tenor making a movie and involved with a younger woman, sings "M'apparì" once again. See VOGLIO BENE SOLTANTO A TE.

1947 This Time for Keeps
Lauritz Melchior, cast as an opera star in this Esther Williams musical, sings "M'apparì." Richard Thorpe directed. Color. 105 minutes. MGM video.

1949 House of Strangers
"M'apparì" is heard on the soundtrack of this film about opera-loving Italian-American banker Edward G. Robinson and his dysfunctional family. Joseph Mankiewicz directed for Fox. Black and white. 101 minutes.

1949 Little Women

"The Last Rose of Summer" is featured in a scene between June Allyson and Rossano Brazzi in this adaptation of the Louisa May Alcott novel. Mervyn LeRoy directed for MGM. Black and white. 121 minutes

1950 The Toast of New Orleans

Mario Lanza, a fisherman with an opera voice, sings "M'apparì" in this musical set in New Orleans. See THE TOAST OF NEW ORLEANS.

1951 The Great Caruso

The final music scenes of this biopic feature Caruso (Mario Lanza) on stage singing "M'apparì" and "The Last Rose of Summer" finale (with Dorothy Kirsten) before collapsing and dying. Caruso actually died nine months after his last opera performance, but the scene is a tear-jerking marvel. See THE GREAT CARUSO.

1979 Breaking Away

"Ach so fromm" is widely known as the Italian aria "M'apparì" because of the influence of Caruso. In this film about the ersatz Italian behavior of an Indiana boy who wants to be like his cycling heroes, it is used ironically as the "Italian" aria he sings while cycling. Peter Yates directed and Steve Tesich won an Oscar for his screenplay. Color. 100 minutes.

1982 The Grey Fox

A phonograph playing Caruso's recording of "M'apparì" keys a romantic scene in this Canadian film. Richard Farnsworth, an aging train robber in the 1910s, hears the aria and through it meets the woman of his life. Philip Borsos directed. Color. 92 minutes.

1999 Analyze This

Billy Crystal plays a psychiatrist analyzing Mafia kingpin Robert De Niro. The soundtrack includes an extract from *Martha*. Color. 103 minutes.

2002 Gangs of New York

The "Mag der Himmel" quintet is played on piano at an uptown social event attended by Horace Greeley, Boss Tweed and machine politicians as they prepare for Civil War draft riots. The irony of lyrics that ask heaven for pardon is the oblique joke of director Martin Scorsese. Color. 168 minutes.

MARTINA FRANCA

The city of Martina Franca in Puglia in the south of Italy has been the home of an enterprising summer opera festival since 1975. The Festival della Valle d'Itria, held in the open air in the courtyard of the baroque Palazzo Ducale, presents original authentic versions of often forgotten operas, usually by composers associated with the south of Italy such as Rossini and Bellini. It has presented the first performances in modern times of a number of operas that have later gone to wide success. Some have been televised and are on video, including Bellini's IL PIRATA, Donizetti's MARIA DI ROHAN, Mercadante's IL BRAVO, Paisiello's NINA, and Vivaldi's FARNACE.

MARTINELLI, GIOVANNI
Italian tenor (1885–1969)

Giovanni Martinelli sang and starred in 17 films, most of them operatic sound shorts made for Vitaphone from 1927 to 1931. He was Vitaphone's most admired and prolific artist and was featured in 15 films in four years, nearly a quarter of all their operatic films. Martinelli, who was born in 1885 in Montagnana and made his debut in Milan in 1910, sang Dick Johnson in the first La Scala production of *La fanciulla del West* in 1911 and won international fame through it. He first sang at Covent Garden in 1912 and at the Metropolitan in 1913; the Met then became the focal point of the rest of his career. He sang until 1946 in more than 900 Met performances, including tours. He made many records and continued to work into his 80s.

1927–1931 Vitaphone films

Martinelli starred in 15 musical films made for Vitaphone from 1927 to 1931, all filmed at Oscar Hammerstein's old Manhattan Opera House. A film featuring Martinelli singing "Vesti la giubba" from PAGLIACCI was screened in the first Vitaphone evening on August 6, 1926, preceding the screening of *Don Juan*. It was greatly admired and led to many more. Other films featured scenes from AIDA, CARMEN, FAUST, MARTHA, IL TROVATORE, and LA JUIVE as well as Russian, Mexican, and Italian folk songs. *Pagliacci* is on LD with *Don Juan;* scenes from *Aida, La Juive,* and *Il trovatore* are on a Bel Canto Society VHS; and most of the others survive in film archives.

1953–1955 Opera Cameos

Martinelli acted as host and introduced the singers on the DuMont TV series *Opera Cameos,* a program featuring highlight versions of famous Italian operas. See OPERA CAMEOS.

1966 Open Mind

Martinelli is one of the stars talking about the Golden Age of the Met on this NBC-TV program made after the razing of the old theater. Telecast April 17, 1966. Black and white. Video at the MTR.

1967 International Music

Martinelli is interviewed by Lord Harewood and sings an aria from *La Juive* on this BBC program made for the *International Music* series. Kenneth Gordon directed. Black and white. 70 minutes. Print at the NFTA, London.

1967 Seattle Opera

Martinelli's last stage performance at the age of 82 is shown in this brief film shot at the dress rehearsal of *Turandot* at the Seattle Opera in 1967. Martinelli is featured in the role of the Emperor. Color. 3 minutes. Print at the NFTA, London.

MARTINI, NINO
Italian tenor (1902–1976)

Nino Martini was born in Verona, site of the famous open-air opera arena, and made his debut in Treviglio in 1927 in *Rigoletto*. Jesse Lasky invited him to America in 1930 to appear in *Paramount on Parade,* after which he sang the Duke in *Rigoletto* with the Philadelphia Opera in 1932 and the Metropolitan Opera in 1933. He returned to Hollywood in the mid-1930s during the opera film boom and starred in three more films for Lasky. He continued to sing with the Met until 1946 and made his last film in England in 1948.

1930 Paramount on Parade

Martini made his film debut in Technicolor in this musical revue where he was featured in the "Song of the Gondolier" sequence singing "Torna a Surriento" on a Venice canal. Paramount. Black and white and color. 100 minutes.

1930 Moonlight and Romance

Musical short made for Paramount with Martini joining in song with Rosita Moreno. Black and white. 10 minutes. Kino VHS (in *Paramount Musical Shorts* series).

1935 Here's to Romance

Martini returned to Hollywood as an opera star and was cast in this film as a student of diva Ernestine Schumann-Heink, playing herself. She thinks he can become the greatest opera singer in the world. See HERE'S TO ROMANCE.

1936 The Gay Desperado

Martini is the singing hero of this musical Western set in Mexico with Ida Lupino as the girl and Leo Carrillo as a Mexican bandit. It begins in a cinema where Martini quells a riot with his soothing singing before being forced to join Carrillo's gang. There's a bit of *Aida*, and the hit tune is "The World Is Mine," but most of the songs are in Spanish. Rouben Mamoulian directed. Black and white. 85 minutes.

1937 Music for Madame

Martini is hired to sing "Vesti la giubbia" in clown costume at a Hollywood wedding, which is really a diversion for a robbery. If he sings again, he will go to jail. See MUSIC FOR MADAME.

1948 One Night With You

Martini pays an Italian opera/movie star stranded in a village with Patricia Roc. They end up in jail, but it works out in the end. Martini sings arias from *L'Africana* and *La traviata*. See ONE NIGHT WITH YOU.

MARTIN'S LIE
1964 church opera by Menotti

In a European church during the 16th-century religious wars, Naninga and Father Cornelius look after a group of orphans. One night Martin opens a door to a stranger who says he could be Martin's father, and Martin hides him when the sheriff arrives. Martin finally dies rather than betray the man. Gian Carlo Menotti's 50-minute church opera *Martin's Lie,* libretto by the composer, a commission from CBS Television, was first performed at Bristol Cathedral in England on June 3, 1964. The premiere production was telecast in 1965.

1964 Bristol Cathedral

English church production: Gian Carlo Menotti (director), Lawrence Leonard (conductor, English Chamber Orchestra and St. Mary Redcliffe Secondary School Chorus), Anthony Powell (set/costume designer).

Cast: Michael Wennink (Martin), Donald McIntyre (Stranger), William McAlpine (Father Cornelius), Noreen Berry (Naninga), Otakar Kraus (Sheriff), Keith Collins (Christopher), Roger Nicholas (Timothy).

Video at the MTR. Taped June 3, 1964; telecast May 30, 1965, on CBS. Kirk Browning (director). Black and white. In English. 52 minutes.

1966 San Michele Arcangelo, Perugia

Italian church production: Gian Carlo Menotti (director), Carlo Franci (conductor, Rome Opera House Orchestra and Chorus), Jürgen Henze (set/costume designer).

Cast: Lorenzo Muti, Herbert Handt, Margherita Rinaldi, Giovanna Fioroni, Lorenzo Gaetani.

Telecast by RAI TV on February 19, 1967. Black and white. In Italian. 49 minutes.

MARTINŮ, BOHUSLAV
Czech composer (1890–1959)

Bohuslav Martinů, one of the major Czech composers, spent much of his life outside his homeland so he wrote operas in English, French, and Italian as well as Czech. He was in Paris from 1923 to 1940, in the United States from 1940 to 1953, and then in France and Italy. Many of his early operas have cinematic elements, and LES TROIS SOUHAITS uses film in a central way to tell its story. THE MARRIAGE and WHAT MEN LIVE BY were written for U.S. television, while ARIANE, THE GREEK PASSION, and LES LARMES DU COUTEAU have been telecast and videotaped.

MARTON, EVA
Hungarian soprano (1943–)

Eva Marton, one of the most powerful soprano voices in opera today, is noted for her performances in Wagner and Strauss, although she is also formidable in Italian opera. Born Eva Heinrich in Budapest, she made her debut there in 1968, forged her early career in Frankfurt, and made her Metropolitan Opera debut in 1976. She has sung in most major opera houses and can be seen on video in many of her best-known roles. See ANDREA CHÉNIER (1985), ELEKTRA (1989), DIE FRAU OHNE SCHATTEN (1992), DIVAS (1993), LA GIOCONDA (1986), GLYNDEBOURNE (1994), LOHENGRIN (1986), METROPOLITAN OPERA (1983/1986), TANNHÄUSER (1982), TOSCA (1984/1986), IL TROVATORE (1988), TURANDOT (1983/1988/1993), and VERONA (1988).

1988 Eva Marton in Concert
Eva Marton performs in concert at the Budapest Convention Centre with Julius Rudel conducting the Hungarian State Orchestra. She sings arias by Verdi, Puccini, Boito, Cilea, Ponchielli, and Catalani. Color. 90 minutes. Kultur VHS/Pioneer Artists LD.

MARUXA
1914 opera by Vives

Maruxa is Spanish composer AMADEO VIVES's most successful opera, rivaling his zarzuelas in popularity. It is set in Galicia in northwest Spain, and some of the characters sing in the local Gallegan language. The shepherdess Maruxa loves the shepherd Pablo, but estate owner Rosa wants him for herself although she is engaged to Antonio. After a few misunderstandings, storms, disguises, and some folk dancing, the couples sort themselves out with help from wise Rufo. The libretto is by Luis Pascual Frutos.

1969 Teatro Lirico Español
Spanish TV film: Juan De Orduña (director), Federico Moreno Torroba (conductor, Spanish Lyric Orchestra and Madrid Chorus), Antonio Mas Guindal (screenplay), Federico Larraya (cinematographer).

Cast: Maria José Alfonso (Maruxa, sung by Dolores Perez), Ramón Pons (Pablo, sung by Luis Sagi-Vela), Mary Francis (Rosa, sung by Josefina Cubeiro), José Maria Prado (Antonio, sung by Julio Julian).

Video: Metrovideo (Spain) VHS. Shot in 35mm for RTVE Spanish Television. Juan De Orduña (director). Color. In Spanish. 80 minutes.

1979 Gran Teatre del Liceu
Spanish stage production: Diego Monio (director), Gerardo Perez Busquier (conductor, Gran Teatre del Liceu Symphonic Orchestra and Chorus).

Cast: Carmen Hernandez (Maruxa), Sergio De Sales (Pablo), Maria Uriz (Rosa), Antonio Mas Guindal (Antonio), Antonio Borras (Rufo).

Video: Opera Dubs VHS. Color. In Spanish. 116 minutes.

Early film

1923 Vorins film
French filmmaker Henry Vorins shot this silent Spanish film of the opera on location in Galicia with his wife Paulette Landais as Maruxa. The supporting cast includes Florian Rey, Asuncion Delgado, Elvira Lopez, and José Mora. Luis R. Alonso was cinematographer. The film was presented in cinemas with the opera's music played live. Black and white. In Spanish. 80 minutes.

MARY STUART
See MARIA STUARDA.

MASCAGNI, PIETRO
Italian composer (1863–1945)

Pietro Mascagni became famous overnight in 1890 with his one-act opera CAVALLERIA RUSTICANA (Rustic Chivalry). It marked the beginning of *verismo* opera and was the high point of Mascagni's career; he never again created an opera with such wide recognition and today is known almost wholly for this one opera. However, he actually wrote many others of interest, some available on video and CD, including the influential Japanese tale IRIS and the return to *verismo* AMICA, both filmed during the silent era. He also composed a pioneer film score for the 1915 Italian movie *Rapsodia Satanica,* a popular operetta called SÌ, and music for a film starring GIACOMO LAURI-VOLPI.

1915 Rapsodia Satanica

The libretto for this avant-garde film was sold as if it were written for an opera, and in some ways *Rapsodia Satanica* can be considered a "film opera." Mascagni wrote an original score for it in collaboration with scriptwriter Maria Martini and director Nino Oxilia. They described it as a "poema cinema-musical." Lyda Borelli, a major Italian cinema diva of the period, was the star opposite André Habay, with Giorgio Ricci as cinematographer. Black and white. In Italian. About 65 minutes.

1952 Melodie immortale

Pierre Cressoy plays Mascagni in this Italian film about the composer, aka *Mascagni*. It shows him being kicked out of Milan Conservatory, on tour with the Novarra company, and having success with *Cavalleria rusticana*. See MELODIE IMMORTALE.

1994 La Scala, A Documentary of Performances

This film about La Scala includes newsreel material showing Mascagni conducting the premiere of his opera *Nerone* in January 1935 with Aureliano Pertile as Nerone and Margherita Carosio as Egloge. Black and white. In Italian with English narration. 63 minutes. VIEW VHS/LD.

MASCOTTE, LA

1880 opéra-comique by Audran

French composer EDMOND AUDRAN created a number of light operas but is best known for his opéra-comique *La mascotte* (The Mascot), libretto by Henri Chivot and Alfred Duru, set in 15th-century Italy. It was staged in both London and New York only a year after its premiere in Paris. The mascot of the title is country girl Bettina who brings good luck to whoever keeps her as long as she stays a virgin. One of the most popular numbers is a farmyard duet between Bettina, who loves turkeys, and Pippo, who loves sheep. Bettina eventually becomes the good luck charm of Laurent XVIII, the Prince of Piombino, who turns her into the Comptesse de Panada; Bettina and Pippo are able to get married anyway.

1935 Mathot film

French feature film: Léon Mathot (director), Michel Lévine (music director), René Pujol (screenplay), Rene Gaveau and Paul Portier (cinematographers).

Cast: Germaine Roger (Bettina), Eric Roiné (Pippo), Lucien Baroux (Prince Laurent), Armand Dranem (Rocco), Janine Guise (Princess Fiametta), Thérèse Dorny (Dame Turlurette), René Lestelly (Prince Fritellini).

Black and white. In French. 100 minutes.

Early film

1909 Pierini film

A sound film of the Bettina/Pippo farmyard duet from *La mascotte* was screened at the Cinematografo della Borsa in Turin on January 5, 1909. The film was made with the Pierini sound-on-disc system and favorably reviewed. Black and white. In Italian. About 4 minutes.

MASKE IN BLAU

1937 operetta by Raymond

Fred Raymond, born in Vienna as Friedrich Vesely, had his biggest success with the operetta *Maske in Blau* (Mask in Blue), libretto by Heinz Hentschke, which premiered in 1937 at the Metropol Theater in Berlin and is still in that theater's repertory. It's a lavish revue-operetta, a love story set in Latin America and on the Italian Riviera. Painter Armando helps rich plantation owner Evelyne foil evil Pedro, but soubrette Juliska gets all the best songs. It has been filmed and telecast three times.

1942 Martin film

German feature film: Paul Martin (director), Walter Forster, Jo Hanns Rösler and Rolf E. Vanloo (screenplay), Stefan Eiben (cinematographer), Michael Jary (music director), Hunnia (studio).

Cast: Clara Tabody (Juliska), Wolf Albach-Retty, Hans Moser, Richard Romanowsky, Roma Bahn.

Black and white. In German. 95 minutes.

1953 Jacoby film

German feature film: Georg Jacoby (director), Röja (production).

Cast: Marika Rökk (Juliska), Paul Hubschmid, Wilfried Seyfert.

Color. In German. 100 minutes.

1972 ZDF German Television

German TV production: Herman Kugelstadt (director), Werner Schmidt-Boelche (conductor, Graunke Symphony Orchestra), Nico Kehrhahn (set designer).

Cast: Irene Mann (Juliska), Rudolf Schock (Armando Cellini), Maria Tiboldi (Evelyne), Lukas Amman (Pedro).

Telecast April 2, 1972, on ZDF. Color. In German. 90 minutes.

MASS

1971 music theater by Bernstein

Leonard Bernstein's *Mass,* "a theatre piece for singers, players, and dancers," was created for the opening of the John F. Kennedy Center for the Performing Arts in Washington, D.C., on August 8, 1971. The libretto is taken from the liturgy of the Roman Mass with secular additions by Stephen Schwartz and the composer. Alan Titus sang the role of the Celebrant at the premiere with Bernstein conducting.

1973 Vienna Konzerthaus

Austrian stage production: James Schaffer (director), John Mauceri (conductor, Yale Symphony Orchestra, Vienna Singakademie Choir), Enno Poersh (set designer).

Cast: Brian Hume, Thomas Whittemore, Yale University students.

Video at the MTR. Telecast November 11, 1973. Brian Large (director). Color. In English. 121 minutes.

1981 Kennedy Center

American stage production: Tom O'Horgan (director), John Mauceri (conductor).

Cast: Joseph Kolinski (Celebrant), Everette Govan (Boy Soloist), Stephen Bogardus, Jamie Bernstein.

Video at the MTR. Telecast September 19, 1981. Emile Ardolino (director). Color. In English. 120 minutes.

MASSARY, FRITZI

Austrian soprano (1882–1969)

Fritzi Massary, a popular Viennese singer of the early years of the 20th century, created many notable operetta roles on stage, including the Pasha's daughter in Leo Fall's DIE ROSE VON STAMBOUL in 1916, the title role in his MADAME POMPADOUR in 1922, and Manon in Oscar Strauss's EINE FRAU, DIE WEISS, WAS SIE WILL in 1932. She may also have been the first operetta star to sing in a film. At the end of 1896, Max Skladanowsky made an operetta film, probably based on *Der Vogelhändler,* with Massary and partner Josef Gianpetro. It was supposedly shown in 1896 synchronized with sound from a record, but if so, it no longer exists. Massary and Pietro were also featured in a duet in a 1903 Messter sound film that does exist.

1903 Messter film

Massary and partner Josef Gianpetro were featured in a duet on an early sound film made by German pioneer Oskar Messter. A print survives in a European film archive. Black and white. In German. About 4 minutes.

MASSENET, JULES

French composer (1842–1912)

Jules Massenet was one of the most popular French opera composers of the 19th century, but his reputation is no longer what it was. MANON and WERTHER remain in the opera house repertory, however, and there seems to be a revival of interest in his other works. More than a dozen of his operas are on CD; CENDRILLON, DON QUICHOTTE, and THAÏS have been telecast; and *Chérubin* and *Hérodiade* have been revived on stage. This is a big change from the 1950s when his operas were dismissed as dinner table music. Massenet's earlier popularity is reflected in the many silent films of his operas. He began composing operas in 1865 and continued until 1912, with *Don Quichotte* premiering when he was 70. His relationships with singers Sibyl Sanderson and Lucy Arbell are the stuff of opera legend; Sanderson is said to be one of the models for the opera-singing mistress in *Citizen Kane.*

MASSIMINI, SANDRO

Italian tenor/director (1954-)

Italian tenor and operetta master Sandro Massimini produced an enterprising Italian TV series on the history of operetta called *Operette, che Passione!* On each program he told the history and story of a classic operetta and featured musical numbers from it, sung in Italian. Highlights of these shows have been released on Ricordi videos in Italy with three operettas on each tape; they include rare works unavailable elsewhere. The operettas are L'ACQUA CHETA, DIE BAJADERE, LA DUCHESSA DEL BAL TABARIN, EVA, DIE FLEDERMAUS, GRÄFIN MARIZA, DER GRAF VON LUXEMBURG, DAS LAND DES LÄCHELNS, THE MIKADO, PAGANINI, LA REGINETTA DELLE ROSE, ROSE-MARIE, DIE ROSE VON STAMBOUL, Sî, and IM WEISSEN RÖSSL. Massimini also directed and sang in three complete operettas on stage in Italy, also available on VHS: DIE CSÁRDÁSFÜRSTIN, DIE LUSTIGE WITWE, and LA DANZA DELLE LIBELLULE.

MASTERSON, VALERIE

English soprano (1937–)

Valerie Masterson, who made her debut at Salzburg in 1963, has a delightful range of roles, from Gilbert and Sullivan to Mozart and Verdi. She was the principal soprano with the D'Oyly Carte Company from 1966 to 1970 and can be seen on video in many of these roles. The combination of a fine voice and a winning stage personality can be observed in operas produced by a wide range of companies, from the English National Opera and

Glyndebourne to Geneva and Philadelphia. See LES CONTES D'HOFFMANN (1974), DIE ENTFÜHRUNG AUS DEM SERAIL (1980), FAUST (1985), GIULIO CESARE (1984), H.M.S. PINAFORE (1974), THE MIKADO (1967/1974), MIREILLE (1981), PAGLIACCI (1974), THE PIRATES OF PENZANCE (1974), SERSE (1988), and LA TRAVIATA (1973).

MASTROCINQUE, CAMILLO
Italian film director (1901–)

Camillo Mastrocinque, who began his directing career in 1937 with a film about LA SCALA, made a number of films with opera content, including IL BARBIERE DI SIVIGLIA (1955), DON PASQUALE (1940 film), FEDORA (1942), IL MATRIMONIO SEGRETO (1943 film), PAGLIACCI (1941 film), and a biography of DONIZETTI. He also made films featuring the Italian opera singers GINO BECHI, MARIA CANIGLIA, and MARIO DEL MONACO.

MATRIMONIO SEGRETO, IL
1792 opera by Cimarosa

DOMENICO CIMAROSA composed about 60 operas but is remembered mainly for only one, the delightful *Il matrimonio segreto* (The Secret Marriage). It has always been considered one of the most enjoyable comic operas and was performed numerous times during Cimarosa's lifetime. It has also enshrined itself in opera legend for having the longest ever encore. Emperor Leopold II enjoyed it so much at its premiere that he insisted that the entire opera be repeated. And, of course, it was—all three hours of it. The story is pretty basic: rich merchant Geronimo wants to marry off his daughter Elisetta to Count Robinson, but the count prefers the second daughter Carolina, who is already secretly married to Paolino. Giovanni Bertati wrote the libretto, which is based on an English play of 1766, David Garrick and George Colman's *The Clandestine Marriage*.

***1986 Cologne Opera at Schwetzingen Festival
German stage production: Michael Hampe (director), Hilary Griffiths (conductor, Drottningholm Court Theatre Orchestra), Jan Schlubach (set designer).
Cast: Barbara Daniels (Elisetta), Georgine Resick (Carolina), Carlos Feller (Geronimo), David Kübler (Paolino), Claudio Nicolai (Count Robinson), Márta Szirmay (Aunt Fidalma).
Video: Image Entertainment DVD/Home Vision VHS/LD. Claus Viller (director). Color. In Italian with English subtitles. 140 minutes.

Related film

1943 Mastrocinque film
Italian director Camillo Mastrocinque, who made several narrative film adaptations of operas, including *Pagliacci* and *Fedora*, shot *Il matrimonio segreto* in Spain in 1943 for Appia-Safa. It was never released in Italy and may not have been completed. Laura Solari, Miguel Ligero, Franco Coop, and Nerio Bernardi were the stars.

MATZENAUER, MARGARET
Romanian-born American contralto (1881–1963)

Margaret Matzenauer was born in Romania of German parents and studied in Graz and Berlin before making her debut in Strasbourg in 1901. She came to the Metropolitan Opera in 1911 to sing Amneris in *Aida* under the direction of Arturo Toscanini, and she continued to sing there for 19 years in a wide array of roles. She also performed soprano roles, was highly praised for her acting, and was noted for having a photographic memory—being able to memorize a new role in a day. She made many recordings, but she appeared unsympathetically in only one film where she was apparently meant to embody the public stereotype of an imperious opera diva.

1936 Mr. Deeds Goes to Town
Matzenauer plays opera diva Madame Pomponi in this Frank Capra film. Gary Cooper, a small-town tuba player, inherits $30 million from an uncle and is elected chairman of a New York opera company. Matzenauer is the hostess of a fancy reception intended to introduce Deeds to the opera world and get him to continue providing a subsidy. She doesn't sing, but she looks formidable. Deeds decides opera should support itself. The film was based on Clarence Budington Kelland's short story *Opera Hat*. Produced by Columbia. Black and white. 118 minutes.

MAUREL, VICTOR
French baritone (1848–1923)

Victor Maurel, the French baritone who created the roles of Iago, Falstaff, and Tonio, was one of the first opera singers to be seen and heard in the movies. He was filmed in costume singing an aria from FALSTAFF in one early French sound film and an aria from DON GIOVANNI in another. These pioneering experimental films were shown at the Paris Exhibition in 1900. Maurel, who sang at La Scala, the Met, and Covent Garden as well as the Paris Opéra, made no other films.

MAY NIGHT

1889 opera by Rimsky-Korsakov

NIKOLAI RIMSKY-KORSAKOV's comic opera *May Night* (Maiskaya noch') is based on a story by Nikolai Gogol about a rivalry between father and son over a woman. The father, who is the village mayor, pretends to disapprove of his son Levko's love for Hanna because he wants her for himself. The son leads a group of villagers who mock his father. With the help of some water sprites, he wins his father's consent.

1953 Gorky film

Ukrainian feature film: Alexander Rou (director), K. Idayev (screenplay), Gorky Film Studios (production).

Cast: N. Losenko (Levko), T. Konukhova (Hannah), A. Khivlym (Father), G. Milliar (Village Clerk).

Color in Magicolor process. In Russian with English subtitles. 60 minutes.

Comment: The film reviewers thought Losenko sang well.

MAYTIME

1917 operetta by Romberg

SIGMUND ROMBERG's first successful operetta is based on Walter Kollo's love-over-three-generations German operetta WIE EINST IM MAI. Librettist Rida Johnson Young transmuted Bernauer and Schanzer's story into a New York tale, and Romberg wrote a new score for it. The story, however, was still a multigenerational romance, with love finally winning out after 60 years. The Romberg song "Will You Remember" (aka "Sweetheart") became popular a second time through the film with MacDonald and Eddy that was very loosely based on the operetta.

1937 MGM film

American feature film: Robert Z. Leonard (director), Noël Langley (screenplay), Oliver T. Marsh (cinematographer), Cedric Gibbons (art director), Herbert Stothart (music director), Wilhelm von Wymetal Jr. (director of operatic sequences).

Cast: Jeanette MacDonald (Miss Morrison/Marcia Mornay), Nelson Eddy (Paul Allison), John Barrymore (Nicolai).

Video: MGM-UA DVD/VHS. Black and white. 132 minutes.

Comment: The credits on the film say it is based on the Romberg *Maytime*, but not too much of the original is left. In the revised plot, elderly Miss Morrison tells a young woman about her earlier life as opera singer Marcia Mornay. In Paris she falls in love with singer Paul

Allison although she had already promised to marry jealous voice teacher Nicolai. They spend a happy Mayday together, but she won't break her promise. She marries Nicolai and becomes a famous opera singer but is reunited with Paul in New York when he is cast opposite her in a new French opera *Czaritza*. When they try to run away together, Nicolai shoots Paul. Miss Morrison finishes telling her story and dies happy knowing she will be reunited with her love. The "new" French opera was created by Stothart for the film and is based on Tchaikovsky's *Fifth Symphony*. MacDonald also sings the "Page Aria" from *Les Huguenots*, with Tudor Williams as Raoul's servant Marcel, and snippets of other opera arias in a "success montage" (with tenors Nick Angelo and Dick Dennis, bass Allan Watson, and contralto Bernice Alstock). Eddy has a delightful song about prima donnas titled "Viva l'opera" and an amazing melange of opera tunes called "Virginia Ham and Eggs" (both with lyrics by Bob Wright and Chet Forrest, music arranged by Stothart). Despite all the changes, this is actually the best of the MacDonald/Eddy musicals.

Early/related films

1923 Schulberg film

Clara Bow was at the beginning of her career when she appeared in this silent version of the Romberg operetta. She plays Alice, the girl the hero Harrison Ford marries on the rebound from Ethel Shannon. Olga Printzlau wrote the screenplay, Karl Struss was the cinematographer, Louis Gasnier directed, and B. P. Schulberg produced for Preferred Pictures. It was screened with the Romberg music. Black and white. About 80 minutes.

1927 Vitaphone film

This Vitaphone short was one of the first sound films based on an operetta. Its lengthy title says it all: John Charles Thomas, Outstanding American Baritone, and Vivienne Segal, Broadway Musical Comedy Star, Singing: Will You Remember, The Sweetheart Song from Maytime. Black and white. In English. 8 minutes.

1954 Deep in My Heart

Vic Damone and Jane Powell perform songs from *Maytime* in MGM's Sigmund Romberg biography *Deep in My Heart*. Damone sings "Road to Paradise" and they duet on "Will You Remember." Sony soundtrack CD and MGM video/DVD.

M. BUTTERFLY

1993 film with opera content

A French diplomat (Jeremy Irons) in China falls in love with a female impersonator (John Lone), apparently because of the power of Puccini's music in *Madama Butterfly*. He first sees her/him singing "Un bel dì" at a diplomatic reception and then begins to live a story parallel to the opera (the voice belongs to Michelle Couture singing with the Royal Philharmonic Orchestra led by Howard Shore). Later in the film the diplomat attends the Paris Opéra and watches Maria Teresa Uribe as Butterfly singing with the Hungarian State Opera Orchestra led by Adam Medveczky. At the end of the film, he identifies so completely with Butterfly that he kills himself while miming to a record of Mirella Freni singing Butterfly's suicide aria with the Vienna Philharmonic. Henry David Hwang's stage play *M. Butterfly,* based on a real story, was adapted for the screen by him and filmed by David Cronenberg for Warner Bros. with Peter Suschitzky as cinematographer. Color. In English. 101 minutes. Warner's VHS.

MEADER, GEORGE
American tenor (1888–1963)

Minneapolis native George Meader made his opera debut in Leipzig and had a major career in Germany before returning to America; he created the role of Scaramuccio in *Ariadne auf Naxos* in Stuttgart in 1912. He sang at the Metropolitan Opera for 11 seasons from 1921 to 1935 and also performed in operetta, including *Boccaccio* opposite Maria Jeritza in 1931. He began his Hollywood career at the age of 52, starting in 1940, and acted in 50 films between 1940 and 1952, mostly in character roles. His musical films include *Two Girls on Broadway* (1940) with Joan Blondell, *Night and Day* (1946) with Gary Grant (Meader plays a minister), *Luxury Liner* (1948) with Lauritz Melchior (he plays a secretary), *That Midnight Kiss* (1948) with Mario Lanza (as a friend), and *The Toast of New Orleans* (1950) with Lanza (as a doorman).

MEALE, RICHARD
Australian composer (1932–)

Richard Meale's opera VOSS, which was premiered by Australia Opera at the Adelaide Festival in 1986, was so well received it was issued on record, tape, CD, and VHS. Meale, born in Sydney, studied non-Western music in California, but he had no other formal musical training. His early work was fairly dissonant, but he became more melodious when he turned to opera. His second opera, *Mer de glace,* is about the Frankenstein story and its creation by Mary Shelley.

MEDIUM, THE
1946 opera by Menotti

American composer GIAN CARLO MENOTTI's chamber opera *The Medium* is one of his most popular works, with screen and stage productions around the world, including a superb film by the composer himself. It's a Grand Guignol thriller about a fake medium who feels a ghostly hand on her throat in the middle of a séance. She blames her mute assistant Toby and banishes him despite protests from her daughter Monica. When he returns secretly, she thinks he is a ghost and shoots him. The opera premiered at Columbia University in New York in 1946 with Claramae Turner as the spiritualist Madame Flora/Baba, but Marie Powers took over the role when the opera went to Broadway, where it ran for 212 performances. There have been at least four TV productions of the opera around the world, with Madame Flora sung by Marie Powers in England and France, Margaret Winkler in Australia, Elisabeth Höngen and Adelheid Schmidt in Austria, Emmy Greger in Holland, Muriel Greenspan and Beverly Evans in Italy, Maureen Forrester in Canada, and Régine Crespin in Paris. Poor-quality videos of the Forrester and Crespin telecasts exist, but only the American telecasts are listed below.

1948 NBC Television, WTZ
American TV production: Roger Englander (director), Bertha Melnic and Alison Nelson (two-piano accompaniment).

Cast: Mary Davenport (Madame Flora), Lois Hunt (Monica), Leo Coleman (Toby), Edith Evans (Mrs. Nolan), Theodora Brandon (Mrs. Gobineau), Emil Markow (Mr. Gobineau).

Telecast live October 3, 1948, from NBC station WTZ in Philadelphia. Paul Nickell (director). Black and white. In English. 60 minutes.

1948 CBS Television, Studio One
American TV production: Tony Miner (director), Alfredo Antonini (conductor, CBS Symphony Orchestra).

Cast: Marie Powers (Madame Flora), Lois Hunt (Monica), Leo Coleman (Toby), Catherine Mastice (Mrs. Nolan), Beverly Dame (Mrs. Gobineau), Joe Bell (Mr. Gobineau).

Video at the MTR. Telecast live November 15, 1948, for the CBS Studio One series. Paul Nickell (director). Black and white. In English. 60 minutes.

***1951 Menotti film
American feature film: Gian Carlo Menotti (director), Thomas Schippers (conductor, RAI Symphony Orchestra of Rome), Enzo Serafin (cinematographer), George Wakhévitch (art director).

Cast: Marie Powers (Madame Flora), Anna Maria Alberghetti (Monica), Leo Coleman (Toby), Belva Kibler (Mrs. Nolan), Beverly Dame (Mrs. Gobineau), Donald Morgan (Mr. Gobineau).

Video: VAI DVD/VHS. Black and white. In English. 84 minutes.

Comment: The only film ever made of an opera by a major composer. Menotti created an extra 20 minutes of music for the film, which he shot on location in Rome.

1959 NBC Television, Omnibus

American TV production: Gian Carlo Menotti (director), Werner Torkanowsky (conductor, NBC Symphony of the Air Orchestra), Henry May (set designer).

Cast: Claramae Turner, (Madame Flora), Lee Ventura (Monica), José Perez (Toby), Belva Kibler (Mrs. Nolan), Beverly Dame (Mrs. Gobineau), Donald Morgan (Mr. Gobineau).

Video at the MTR. Telecast live February 15, 1959, on NBC. William A. Graham (director). Black and white. In English. 60 minutes.

The Medium (1951): Fake spiritualist Madame Flora (Marie Powers) meets children in a Rome street in Menotti's film

***MEETING VENUS
1991 British film with opera content

One of the most intelligent films about opera people and opera problems. Hungarian director ISTVÁN SZABÓ tells the funny/sad story of the preparations for a multinational European live satellite TV production of *Tannhäuser* in Paris. Glenn Close plays Swedish diva soprano (KIRI TE KANAWA coached her and provided her singing voice) while Niels Arestrup is the Hungarian conductor with problems. The set is a postmodern nightmare, the dancers' union is on strike, the chorus is uncooperative, the singers are at each other's throats, and the diva is an iceberg. When a love affair somehow develops between the soprano and the married conductor, everyone finds out at once. When it seems that the opera will never be staged, there is a surprise triumphant ending. The film is fascinating in its depiction of the inside world of opera production and the egos that need to be massaged. *Meeting Venus* was filmed in Budapest in the State Opera House and in Paris. Szabó wrote the screenplay with Michael Hirst, Lajos Koltai was cinematographer, Marek Janowski was music director, Attila Kovacs was art director, and David Puttnam produced. Color. In English. 117 minutes. Warner Bros. VHS.

Meeting Venus (1991): Glenn Close and the cast of *Tannhäuser* on stage in István Szabó's operatic film.

MEFISTOFELE

1868 opera by Boito

Master librettist ARRIGO BOITO was also a fine composer, and his version of the Faust legend, based on Goethe's play, is a very different opera from Gounod's *Faust*. Instead of focusing on Marguerite, as Gounod did, Boito makes Mefistofele the center of interest and shows him betting with God that he can win Faust's soul. The ideas of Goethe are central to the opera, with the battle between good and evil always present. The story of Faust and Margherita is still important, but it is not central; there is also a remarkable bacchanalia at a Witches' Sabbath in which Helen of Troy appears. Mefistofele is one of the major operatic roles for a bass, and Samuel Ramey has been devilishly compelling in it in recent years.

***1989 San Francisco Opera

American stage production: Robert Carsen (director), Maurizio Arena (conductor, San Francisco Opera Orchestra and Chorus), Michael Levine (set designer).

Cast: Samuel Ramey (Mefistofele), Gabriela Beňačková (Margherita/Helen of Troy), Dennis O'Neill (Faust), Judith Christin (Marta), Emily Manhart (Pantalis), Daniel Harper (Wagner).

Video: Kultur, Bel Canto Society & Arthaus DVD/Home Vision VHS/Pioneer LD. Brian Large (di-

rector). Color. In Italian with English subtitles. 160 minutes.

Comment: Ramey dominates from his first appearance climbing onto the stage from the orchestra pit. The production is a visual delight with sensitive imagery, continual surprises, and bare breasts on both sexes in the bacchanalia.

1989 Genoa Opera

Italian stage production: Ken Russell (director), Edoardo Müller (conductor, Genoa Opera Orchestra and Chorus), Paul Dufficey (set/costume designer), Richard Caceres (choreographer).

Cast: Paata Burchuladze (Mephistofele), Adriana Morelli (Margherita/Helen of Troy), Ottavio Garaventa (Faust), Silvana Mazzieri (Marta), Laura Bocca (Pantalis), Fabio Armiliato (Wagner).

Pickwick (Germany) VHS. Carlo Nistri (director). Color. In Italian. 137 minutes.

Comment: Those who enjoy Russell's style and playful ideas will love his updating of the story and extravagant production, but non-admirers won't like it much.

Related films

1937 Solo per te

Beniamino Gigli is seen on stage in a scene from *Mefistofele* at the beginning of this film. He plays an opera singer married to a soprano (Maria Cebotari) with a secret past. See SOLO PER TE.

1946 The Whale Who Wanted to Sing at the Met

Willie, the opera-singing whale with the voice of Nelson Eddy, fantasizes a performance of *Mefistofele* at the Met. He breathes so much fire as the Devil that firefighters stand by to extinguish the flames. See THE WHALE WHO WANTED TO SING AT THE MET.

1949 Al diavolo la celebrità

Ferruccio Tagliavini sings a duet from the opera with wife Pia Tassinari in the Italian film *Al diavolo la celebrità* (shown in the United States as *One Night of Fame*). See FERRUCCIO TAGLIAVINI.

MEHTA, ZUBIN

Indian conductor (1936–)

Zubin Mehta, who was born in Bombay and made his debut in 1964, has become one of the most popular and best-known contemporary conductors; he led the orchestra in the first THREE TENORS concerts, the live 1992 telecast of TOSCA from Rome, the 1998 performance and telecast of TURANDOT from the Forbidden City in China, and the live 2000 telecast of LA TRAVIATA from Paris. He even conducted Andrea Bocelli's Verdi CD. Music director of the Los Angeles Philharmonic from 1978 to 1991, he was appointed music director of the Bayerische Staatsoper in Munich in 1998. See also CARMEN (1991), CARNEGIE HALL (1991), FIDELIO (1977), MOZART (1994), MOZART REQUIEM (1994), LEONTYNE PRICE (1982), BEVERLY SILLS (1980), SPOLETO (1966), TANNHÄUSER (1994), TRISTAN UND ISOLDE (1998), VERDI (2001), and VERDI REQUIEM (1980).

1967 Zubin Mehta—A Man and His Music

A *Bell Telephone Hour* profile of the conductor when he was with the Los Angeles Philharmonic Orchestra. It shows him performing at the Hollywood Bowl, explaining his ideas about music, and revealing his philosophy. Black and white. 60 minutes. Video at the MTR.

1998 Zubin Mehta: A World Full of Music

Mehta talks about his life and "musical profession" and is shown in rehearsal. Extracts from operatic and orchestral performances are included. Reiner Moritz directed. Color. 60 minutes.

MEISTERSINGER VON NÜRNBERG, DIE

1868 opera by Wagner

Die Meistersinger von Nürnberg (The Mastersingers of Nuremberg), RICHARD WAGNER'S only naturalistic opera, was inspired by the life of Hans Sachs, a 16th-century cobbler-poet and prominent member of the Mastersingers' Guild. It's set in 16th-century Nuremberg where new arrival knight Walther wants to marry Eva. Her father Pogner has decided to give her hand to the winner of a singing contest so Walther is forced to learn the complex rules of the guild. He does so with the help of Sachs and, despite strong opposition from town clerk Beckmesser, wins the contest and the woman.

1969 Hamburg State Opera

German film of stage production: Joachim Hess (film director), Leopold Lindtberg (stage director), Leopold Ludwig (conductor, Hamburg State Opera Chorus and Philharmonic Orchestra), Herbert Kirchhoff (set designer), Rolf Liebermann (producer).

Cast: Giorgio Tozzi (Sachs), Richard Cassilly (Walther), Arlene Saunders (Eva), Toni Blankenheim (Beckmesser), Ernest Wiemann (David), Gerhard Unger (Pogner), Ursula Boese (Magdalene).

Color. In German. 245 minutes.

Comment: The film, based on a Hamburg State Opera production, was shown theatrically in America.

1984 Bayreuth Festival

German stage production: Wolfgang Wagner (director/set designer), Horst Stein (conductor, Bayreuth Festival Orchestra and Chorus), Reinhard Heinrich (costume designer).

Cast: Bernd Weikl (Sachs), Siegfried Jerusalem (Walther), Mari Anne Häggander (Eva), Hermann Prey (Beckmesser), Graham Clark (David), Manfred Schenk (Pogner), Jef Vermeersch (Kothner), Marga Schiml (Magdalene).

Video: Philips VHS/LD. Brian Large (director). Color. In German with English subtitles. 269 minutes.

Comment: The story is lightly updated to the 19th century.

1988 Australian Opera

Australian stage production: Michael Hampe (director), Sir Charles Mackerras (conductor, Elizabethan Philharmonic Orchestra and Australian Opera Chorus), John Gunther (set designer), Reinhard Heinrich (costume designer).

Cast: Donald McIntyre (Sachs), Paul Frey (Walther), Helena Döse (Eva), John Pringle (Beckmesser), Christopher Dig (David), Donald Shanks (Pogner), Robert Allman (Kothner), Rosemary Gunn (Magdalene).

Video: Kultur DVD/Home Vision VHS. Peter Butler and Virginia Lumsden (directors). Color. In German with English subtitles. 277 minutes.

1995 Deutsche Staatsoper Berlin

German stage production: Götz Friedrich (director), Frübeck de Burgos (conductor, Deutsche Staatsoper Berlin Orchestra and Chorus).

Cast: Wolfgang Brendel (Sachs), Gösta Winbergh (Walther), Eva Johannson (Eva), Wilm Schulte (Beckmesser), Victor von Halem (Pogner), Uwe Peper (David), Lenus Carlson (Kothner), Ute Walther (Magdalene).

Video: Arthaus DVD/Opera d'Oro VHS. Brian Large (director). Color. In German with English subtitles. 270 minutes.

Comment: This production was first staged in 1993 but was not taped until 1995.

2001 Metropolitan Opera

American stage production: Otto Schenk (director), James Levine (conductor, Metropolitan Opera Orchestra and Chorus).

Cast: James Morris (Sachs), Ben Heppner (Walther), Karita Mattila (Eva), Hans-Joachim Ketelsen (Beckmesser), René Pape (Pogner), Matthew Polenzani (David), Jill Grove (Magdalene).

Videotaped December 8, 2001. Brian Large (director). Color. In German with English subtitles. 270 minutes.

Early/related films

1908 Pathé film
German film of a scene and aria from the opera made in 1908 by Pathé. It was screened with the music played on a synchronized phonograph. Black and white. In German. About 4 minutes.

1927 Berger film
Rudolf Rittner is Sachs in this German silent film directed by Ludwig Berger for Phoebus Film. The cast includes Maria Solveg as Eva, Gustav Fröhlich as Walther, Max Güstorff as Pogner, Julius Falkenstein, Veit Harlan, and Elsa Wagner. Black and white. About 82 minutes.

1944 Lifeboat
A lifeboat with survivors of a passenger ship that has been torpedoed pick up the captain (Walter Slezak) of the U-boat that attacked them. Black survivor Canada Lee ironically plays a German tune on his reed pipe, the Prize Song from *Die Meistersinger*. Alfred Hitchcock directed. Black and white. 96 minutes.

1957 Davy
The final scene of *The Mastersinger*s is shown on stage at the Royal Opera House, Covent Garden, in the English film *Davy*. Harry Secombe plays a Welsh comedian with a chance to become an opera singer and appears on stage as Walther. George Wakhévitch designed the opera set and the singers include Joan Sutherland as Eva (she talks about it in her autobiography *A Prima Donna's Progress*), James Pease as Sachs, and Geraint Evas as Beckmesser. Michael Relph directed the film. Color In English. 83 minutes.

1987 Hope and Glory
John Boorman uses the opera's "Dance of the Apprentices" music in an ironic way in the film *Hope and Glory* set in World War II London. A blimp is put up to protect a neighborhood from German planes, and it floats into the sky accompanied by Wagner's music as the people of the area watch. Later, it comes loose from its moorings, bounces around the houses to everyone's amusement, and is shot out of the sky by the Home Guard. Color. 118 minutes. Nelson VHS.

MELBA, NELLIE
Australian soprano (1861–1931)

Nellie Melba inspired opera composers, film writers, and chefs (peach melba and melba toast), but she is still most famous for her voice; on record it has a silvery quality unmatched by any other singer. She also created the modern concept of the opera prima donna. She was born in Melbourne as Helen Porter Mitchell, studied with Mathilde Marchesi in Paris, and made her debut in Belgium in 1887 as Gilda. The following year she sang in Paris and London and then reigned as the queen of Covent Garden until her retirement in 1926. She sang at the Met in New York from 1893 to 1910 and also at Oscar Hammerstein's Manhattan Opera House. In the later part of her career, she concentrated on the role of Mimì in *La bohème*. She made no films, but there are many films about her.

1934 Evensong
Evensong is a British film based on a roman à clef novel by Beverly Nichols—Melba's private secretary and ghost writer of her autobiography. Evelyn Laye stars as Irela, an Irish singer who becomes an opera diva and suffers when she realizes she is becoming old. Conchita Supervia plays the singer who challenges her supremacy. See EVENSONG.

Melba (1953): Sheet music for the British film biogrpahy starring Patrice Munsel as Australian soprano Nellie Melba

1953 Melba

Patrice Munsel plays Nellie Melba in this opulent British film biography that tells the story of Melba's career beginning with a performance for Queen Victoria and flashing backwards to her early years and forwards to her international success. Martita Hunt is voice teacher Mathilde Marchesi, Robert Morley is opera impresario Oscar Hammerstein, Sybil Thorndike is Queen Victoria, Dorit Welles is Adelina Patti, and John McCallum plays Charles Armstrong, the Australian she marries who cannot live with her fame. Munsel sings a wide array of arias from operas associated with Melba, including the Mad Scene from *Lucia di Lammermoor* at her Covent Garden debut, "Una voce poco fa" from *The Barber of Seville*, "Vissi d'arte" from *Tosca*, "Voi che sapete" from *Le nozze di Figaro*, "Chacun le sait" from *The Daughter of the Regiment*, the "Waltz Song" from *Roméo et Juliette*, and the Brindisi from *La traviata*. The operatic scenes were shot at Covent Garden with the Royal Opera House Orchestra. Muir Mathieson was the music director, Dennis Arunder was the operatic director, Harry Kurnitz wrote the screenplay, Ted Scaife and Arthur Ibbetson were the cinematographers, Sam Spiegel produced, and Lewis Milestone directed. Color. 113 minutes. Premiere Opera VHS.

1972 Behind the Legend

Kate Fitzpatrick plays Melba in this docu-drama created for the Australian Broadcasting Corporation TV series *Behind the Legend*. Lance Peters wrote and directed the film. Black and white. In English. 60 minutes.

1980 A Toast to Melba

Robyn Nevin plays Melba (with Roslyn Dunbar doing her singing) in this Australian TV play by Jack Hibbert telecast in August 1980. It traces the story of her career from tomboy in Australia to prima donna in Europe. Augustus Harris plays Caruso and Michael Aitkens is Melba's husband Charles Armstrong. Other actors have multiple roles, including Henri Szeps (as Thomas Beecham, Buffalo Bill, and the Mayor of Brisbane), Donald McDonald, Jane Harders, Anna Volska, and Tim Eliot. Roger Kirk designed the sets and costumes, and Alan Burke produced and directed. Color. 70 minutes.

1987 Melba

Linda Cropper plays Melba (with Yvonne Kenny doing her singing) in this Australian TV miniseries. She is shown leaving her unsympathetic husband; studying in Paris with Mathilde Marchesi; triumphing in Brussels, Paris, and London; having a passionate affair with a pretender to the French throne; and feuding with Tetrazzini and other singers. Joan Greenwood is a delight as voice teacher Mathilde Marchesi, Simon Burke plays tenor John McCormack, and Anson Austin plays Enrico Caruso. William Motzing arranged the music, Roger McDonald wrote the novel on which the miniseries was based, Andrew Lesnie and Dean Semler were the cinematographers, and Rodney Fisher directed. Telecast on PBS in the United States in 1990. Color. In English. 480 minutes.

MELCHIOR, LAURITZ
Danish-born U.S. tenor (1890–1973)

Many consider Lauritz Melchior to be the greatest heldentenor of the century. He made his debut at the Royal Opera in Copenhagen in 1913 as Silvio in *Pagliacci*, began to sing Wagner in 1918, sang in *Parsifal* at Bayreuth in 1924, and began his Metropolitan Opera career in 1926 with *Tannhäuser*. He sang at the Met until 1950 when he had disagreements with Rudolf Bing and left after 519 performances. He continued to perform until 1960 when he celebrated his 70th birthday singing the role of Siegmund on radio. Melchior starred in several films and displayed an impressive personality as well as a glorious voice. While there are no films of him in operas, he can be seen in performance in a *Voice of Firestone* video and in his movies.

1945 Thrill of a Romance

Melchior made his movie debut as Danish singer Nils Knunsen opposite Esther Williams in this mountain lodge musical. She plays a swimmer who falls in love with returning serviceman Van Johnson. Melchior sings "Vesti la giubba" from *Pagliacci*, "Please Don't Say No," and Schubert's "Serenade." Richard Thorpe directed. Color. 105 minutes. MGM-UA VHS.

1946 Two Sisters From Boston

Melchior is Metropolitan Opera tenor Olaf Ostrom in this turn-of-the-century New York musical. Kathryn Grayson pretends to be an opera singer and sneaks on stage to join him in an imaginary opera called *My Country*. He later sings an aria from *Die Meistersinger* for a recording session and teams up with Grayson for another imaginary opera called *Marie Antoinette*. See TWO SISTERS FROM BOSTON.

1947 This Time for Keeps

Melchior plays opera star Richard Harald whose son Johnnie Johnston prefers modern music and swimming star Esther Williams. Melchior sings "M'appari" from *Martha*, "La donna è mobile" from *Rigoletto*, "Ora è per sempre addio" from *Otello*, and Cole Porter's "Easy to Love." Jimmy Durante and Xaviar Cugat add to the musical mixture. Richard Thorpe directed. Color. 105 minutes. MGM-UA VHS.

1948 Luxury Liner

Melchior is opera tenor Olaf Eriksen in this delightful MGM shipboard musical with Jane Powell as the stowaway daughter of liner captain George Brent. Melchior and Marina Koshetz join in a duet from *Aida*, and Melchior sings arias from *Lohengrin* and *Die Walküre*. Also heard is the "Gavotte" from Massenet's *Manon*. Richard Whorf directed. Color. 98 minutes. MGM-UA VHS.

Danish opera tenor Lauritz Melchior plays a Danish opera tenor in the American film musical *Luxury Liner*.

1950–1951 Voice of Firestone 1

Melchior is seen in performance on *Voice of Firestone* TV programs during 1950 and 1951 on the video *Lauritz Melchior in Opera & Song*. He sings "Winterstürme" from *Die Walküre*, "Prieslied" from *Die Meistersinger*, and the "Helmsman's Song" from *The Flying Dutchman*, plus songs by Richard Strauss, Tchaikovsky, and Rodgers and Hammerstein. Howard Barlow conducts. Black and white. 45 minutes. VAI VHS.

1950–1952 Voice of Firestone 2

Melchior is seen in performance on *Voice of Firestone* TV programs during 1950, 1951, and 1952 on the video *Lauritz Melchior in Opera & Song 2*. He sings "In fernem Land" from *Lohengrin*, "Vesti la giubba" from *Pagliacci*, the "Prize Song" from *Die Meistersinger*, and "Serenade" from *The Student Prince*. Howard Barlow conducts. Black and white. 48 minutes. VAI VHS.

1953 The Stars Are Singing

In Melchior's last film he plays a former Metropolitan Opera star who befriends 15-year-old Anna Maria Alberghetti. She's an illegal immigrant and an aspiring opera singer. Melchior sings three times: once at the Met in a flashback performing "Vesta la giubba" in *Pagliacci* costume, once as Alberghetti makes him remember his singing career, and once in duet with Alberghetti. Rosemary Clooney is the main star; Norman Taurog directed. Color. 99 minutes. Paramount VHS.

1990 Melchior Centennial Tribute

Melchior would have been 100 in 1990 so Danish television devised this tribute program with excerpts and interviews. Interviewees include Esther Williams, Aage Haugland, Klaus König, Erich Leinsdorf, and Eva Johannson. Color. In Danish, English, and German. 101 minutes. Opera Dubs VHS.

MÉLIÈS, GEORGES
French film opera pioneer (1861–1938)

Georges Méliès was the first notable fiction filmmaker, a former magician who applied the tricks of his trade to the cinema and made films that still astonish. He was also the first important opera film producer, and his early adaptations of the Faust operas of Gounod and Berlioz are still a delight. Méliès played Méphistophélès in these 1903–1904 productions, and the image of him in the role has become one of the icons of early cinema. Méliès began making films in 1896, including views of the Place de l'Opéra. In 1898 he made two films based on the Faust story, a transformation film titled *Faust et Marguerite* and *Damnation de Faust*, plus a film based on the opera-inspiring legend *Guillaume Tell*. In 1899 the Paris public became interested in the Cinderella story because of the publicity around the premiere of Massenet's *Cendrillon* so Méliès made his CENDRILLON, an epic 20-scene movie of the story. In 1903 he made a famous film about a music lover, *Le Mélomane*, and the first of his two Faust opera adaptations. *Faust aux Enfers ou La Damnation de Faust*, composed of 15 scenes, is based on the Berlioz opera *La Damnation de Faust*. In 1904 Méliès made another epic Faust film (20 scenes), based on the Gounod opera *Faust*, titled *Damnation du Docteur Faust*. The same year he made his final important opera film, a "reproduction" of Rossini's opera titled *Le Barbier de Séville*. Most of Méliès's films have survived and can still be viewed with pleasure today. See IL BARBIERE DI SIVIGLIA (1904), LA DAMNATION DE FAUST (1904), and FAUST (1903).

MELODIE IMMORTALE

1952 operatic biography

Pierre Cressoy plays Italian opera composer Pietro Mascagni in this Italian film about the creator of *Cavalleria rusticana*. He gets kicked out of the Milan Conservatory after spending all his time composing *Guglielmo Ratcliffe*, tours with the Maresca operetta company, meets and marries Lina, and settles down as leader of the Cerignola Philharmonic. His wife enters his opera *Cavalleria rusticana* in the Sonzogno competition when he wants to quit after their son dies. He wins and achieves instant fame. Mario Del Monaco plays tenor Roberto Stagno, who created the role of Turiddu in *Cavalleria rusticana,* and is shown on stage in the role. Carla Del Poggio plays Mascagni's long-suffering wife Lina, and Nerio Bernardi plays music professor Del Lellis. Aldo Giordani was the cinematographer, Nino Rota adapted Mascagni's music for the screen, Giuseppe Morelli was the music director, and Ivo Pirelli, Liana Ferri, Giovanna Soria, Piero Pierotti, and Maleno Malenotti were the screenwriters. Giacomo Gentilomo directed for Lux. The film is also known as *Mascagni*. Color. In Italian. 90 minutes. Opera Dubs/Lyric VHS.

MELTON, JAMES

American tenor (1904–1961)

James Melton is probably as well known today for his films as for his opera career, although he was a member of the Metropolitan Opera from 1942 to 1950. The Georgia-born tenor studied opera at Vanderbilt and began his singing career on radio and in concert in 1927. His movie career started in 1933 with cowboy songs in a short film and took off in 1935 with *Stars Over Broadway*, which featured him singing at the Met. It must have been an inspiration because he began preparing for an opera career at this time and made his debut as Pinkerton in *Madama Butterfly* in Cincinnati in 1938. He also sang with the San Carlo and Chicago Opera companies before beginning his Met career in 1942 as Tamino. He sang a variety of roles there over the next eight years, but like many others, left with the arrival of Rudolf Bing. Melton's last film was the 1945 *Ziegfeld Follies* in which he appeared in a scene from *La traviata*. In his later years he toured the country in a production of *The Student Prince*.

1933 The Last Dogie

Melton's first film was a short in which he sang cowboy songs and performed rope tricks for his bunk mates. Black and white. 10 minutes.

1935 Stars Over Broadway

In Melton's first film he plays a hotel porter with such a good voice that Pat O'Brien decides to make him into an opera star. He auditions with "Celeste Aida" and wins approval, but O'Brien is impatient to earn money and diverts him into crooning. In the end he returns to opera and makes his debut in *Aida* at the Met. See STARS OVER BROADWAY.

1936 Sing Me a Love Song

Melton plays the heir to a department store and sings Dubin and Warren songs in this musical. He works in the store incognito to learn about its problems and is soon involved with Patricia Ellis, who works in the music department. His songs include "The Little House That Love Built" and "Shortnin' Bread." Ray Enright directed for Warner Bros. Black and white. 79 minutes.

1937 Melody for Two

Al Dubin and Harry Warren gave Melton some memorable songs to sing in this musical, including "September in the Rain." He plays a bandleader who has problems with girlfriend Patricia Ellis. She ends up competing with him in the bandleading business, but it works out after they both turn to swing music. Louis King directed for Warner Bros. Black and white. 60 minutes.

1946 Ziegfeld Follies

Melton filmed his sequence of this lavish Vincente Minnelli musical in 1944, two years before the film was released. He appears in a colorful scene from *La traviata* with soprano Marion Bell and a group of elaborately costumed dancers, and they duet on "Libiamo." The film is a heavenly dream by Florenz Ziegfeld (William Powell) about putting on a new Follies. Color. 110 minutes. MGM-UA VHS.

MENOTTI, GIAN CARLO

Italian-American composer (1911–)

Gian Carlo Menotti was the best known and most popular American opera composer/librettist of the postwar period. His operas had strong stories, were recognizably melodic, and were presented outside traditional operatic venues; they were heard on radio, staged on Broadway, composed for television, sung in cathedrals, and written for children. He was one of the first composers to write an opera for radio, THE OLD MAID AND THE THIEF (1939), and the very first to write an opera for television, AMAHL AND THE NIGHT VISITORS (1951). His success paved the way for the development of radio and TV opera. He was also the first (and still the only) composer to film his own opera, THE MEDIUM in 1951. His theatrical skills led to a contract from MGM to write film scripts, one of which became the opera THE CONSUL. Menotti was brought up in Milan but studied at the Curtis Institute in Philadelphia, and most of his professional career was in the United States. He had a close personal relationship with composer Samuel Barber (he wrote librettos for two Barber operas) and with conductor Thomas Schippers (whom he made music director of his Festival of Two Worlds in Spoleto). Ten of Menotti's operas have been filmed or telecast. Although his operas are not currently in fashion, *Amahl and the Night Visitors*, *The Medium,* and THE TELEPHONE are on commercial video and others are on alternative labels. See GOYA, JUANA LA LOCA, LABYRINTH, MARIA GOLOVIN, MARTIN'S LIE, THE SAINT OF BLEECKER STREET, and SPOLETO.

1976 Landscapes & Remembrances
Menotti's cantata for soloists, chorus, and orchestra is an autobiographical set of musical impressions ranging from his arrival in the U.S. as a teenager to his discovery of South Carolina; it was filmed when it premiered at the Performing Arts Center in Milwaukee. The soloists are Judith Blegen, Ani Yervanian, Vahan Khanzadian, and Gary Kendall. James A. Keeley conducts the Milwaukee Symphony Orchestra and Bel Canto Chorus. Filmed May 14, 1976, and telecast November 14, 1976. Color. 60 minutes. Video at the Library of Congress.

1979 Gian Carlo Menotti
The composer, shown at a rehearsal of his children's opera *Help, Help the Globolinks,* discusses his ideas about writing operas for children. University of Michigan music professor John McCollum is his interviewer. Color. 30 minutes.

1986 Gian Carlo Menotti: Musical Magician
Tom Bywaters's American documentary, made to eulogize the composer on his 75th birthday, includes scenes shot at his festivals in Spoleto and Charleston and at his estate in Scotland. Included are extracts from nine operas and interviews with Luciano Pavarotti, John Butler, Colleen Dewhurst, and Alwain Nikolais. Telecast in the PBS series *Great Performances* on November 21, 1986. Color. 90 minutes.

1998 Gian Carlo Menotti: Maestro of Two Worlds
Alexander Oppersdorff's German documentary includes interviews and archival footage from Spoleto and elsewhere. Among those appearing are Patricia Neway and Plácido Domingo, both of whom created roles in Menotti operas. Color. In German and English. 52 minutes.

2000 Music Masters: Gian Carlo Menotti
David Thomson's English documentary *Gian Carlo Menotti,* made for the BBC, allows the 89-old-composer to talk about his life from his home in Scotland. There are clips from several operas and footage from Spoleto festivals. Charles Hazlewood is the presenter. Color. In English. 50 minutes.

MERCADANTE, SAVERIO
Italian composer (1795–1870)

Saverio Mercadante, one of the most important composers in Italy during the period immediately preceding Verdi, composed more than 50 well-received operas. His fame was eclipsed by Verdi, but a few of his works were revived for the centenary of his death in 1970. His most famous operas are *Il Giuramento* (1837), *Il Bravo* (1839), *La Vestale* (1840), and *Orazi e Curiazi* (1846). All four are on CD, and IL BRAVO, telecast from Martina Franca in 1990, is on video.

MERRILL, ROBERT
American baritone (1917–)

Robert Merrill, the leading baritone at the Metropolitan Opera from 1945 to 1975, made his debut as Germont and then sang virtually all the available Italian and French baritone roles. He also sang Germont at La Fenice in 1961 and Covent Garden in 1967. He was much admired for his voice, but acting was never his strong point. Merrill's film career was short and unfortunate. Rudolf Bing fired him for going off to make a Hollywood film instead of being available for a Met tour. It was Merrill's only feature, and it was a dud. However, he made many recordings and appeared on television shows such as *The Voice of Firestone*. He remains one of the best-known American singers even today. See CARMEN (1950/1959), DON CARLO (1950), ANNA MOFFO (1963), OTELLO (1963), RIGOLETTO (1963), and LA TRAVIATA (1956).

1952 Aaron Slick From Punkin Crick
Merrill plays a city slicker who tries to fleece widow Dinah Shore down on the farm in this old-fashioned musical. The *Variety* reviewer noted that Merrill had a good voice and good screen presence but was not given a good role. His best song was the old church tune "Still Water," sung in a duet. The new songs are by Ray Evans and Jay Livingstone. Claude Binyon directed for Paramount. Released in England as *Marshmallow Moon*. Color. 95 minutes.

1953 Ed Sullivan Show
Merrill was one of the Metropolitan Opera singers performing on *The Ed Sullivan Show* on November 8, 1953. The program, telecast on CBS from the Met stage, was called *Toast to the Met*. The audience even wore black tie. Black and white. 60 minutes. Video at the MTR.

1955–1959 Robert Merrill in Opera and Song
Merrill on *The Voice of Firestone* TV series in six telecasts made from 1955 to 1959. He sings arias from *Carmen* (the "Toreador Song"), *The Barber of Seville*

("Largo al factotum"), *Pagliacci* (the Prologue), *Hamlet* (the "Drinking Song"), *The Land of Smiles* ("Yours Is My Heart Alone"), *The Red Mill* ("Every Day Is Ladies' Day"), and *Il trovatore* plus songs. Howard Barlow conducts. Black and white. 52 minutes. VAI VHS.

1955–1963 Robert Merrill in Opera and Song 2

Merrill performing in *The Voice of Firestone* telecasts from 1955 to 1963. He is seen in costume singing arias from *Faust*, *Hérodiade*, and *La traviata*, plus songs by Romberg, Kern, Youmans, and Rodgers and Hammerstein. Black and white. 55 minutes. VAI VHS.

1962–1965 Bell Telephone Hour

Merrill performs scenes from four operas with partners on *The Bell Telephone Hour* programs telecast between 1962 and 1965. They are *The Barber of Seville* with Robert Peters, *Carmen* with Regina Resnik, *La forza del destino* with Richard Tucker, and *Otello* with James McCracken. Donald Voorhees conducts the Bell Telephone Hour Orchestra. Color. 39 minutes. VAI VHS.

MERRITT, CHRIS
American tenor (1952–)

Oklahoma native Chris Merritt made his debut in Salzburg in 1978 after an apprenticeship in Santa Fe. He became a specialist in Rossini operas in Europe, and his expressive voice led to invitations to sing in many of the composer's lesser-known operas. A number of these rarely staged Rossini productions were televised and are on video. See BENVENUTO CELLINI (1987), LA BOHÈME (1990 film), LA DONNA DEL LAGO (1992), ELISABETTA, REGINA D'INGHILTERRA (1991), GUILLAUME TELL (1991), MAGGIO MUSICALE, MAOMETTO II (1986), OTELLO (Rossini, 1988), I PURITANI (1986), DER RING DES NIBELUNGEN (1999), VERDI REQUIEM (1985 film), I VESPRI SICILIANI (1990), WILLIAM TELL (1991), and ZELMIRA (1989).

1992 Rossini Bicentennial Birthday Gala

Merritt is one of the singers specializing in Rossini operas who celebrate the composer's birthday at a telecast Lincoln Center gala at Avery Fisher Hall. Roger Norrington conducts the Orchestra of St. Luke's and New York Concert Chorale. Color. In English and Italian. 159 minutes. EMI VHS/LD.

MERRY WIDOW, THE
See DIE LUSTIGE WITWE.

MERRY WIVES OF WINDSOR, THE
See DIE LUSTIGEN WEIBER VON WINDSOR.

MESSAGER, ANDRÉ
French composer (1853–1929)

André Messager was one of the last great French operetta composers; his operettas *Fortunio* and VÉRONIQUE remain popular in France, and he had great success in the 1890s with *La Basoche* and *Les p'tites Michu*. His English "romantic opera" *Monsieur Beaucaire* was a big success in London and New York in 1919, and Maggie Teyte made one of its arias ("Philomel") famous. Messager's French operas include *Madame Chrysanthème*, a predecessor of *Madama Butterfly* staged in 1893. *Véronique* has been filmed, as have his lesser-known operettas PASSIONNÉMENT, DEBURAU (based on the courtesan who inspired *La traviata*), and COUPS DE ROULIS.

MESSIAH
1742 oratorio by Handel

Messiah is GEORGE FRIDERIC HANDEL's best-liked musical work and the most popular oratorio by any composer. Composed in 1741 to an English libretto by Charles Jennens with the words taken from the Bible, it premiered in Dublin on April 13, 1742, at the Music Hall in Fishamble Street; it has been in the repertory ever since, especially at Christmas, and its Hallelujah Chorus has become the best-known single choral work. *Messiah* is featured on many videos, and its music is often used in films.

1982 Cardiff Festival of Choirs

Welsh stage production: Roger Norrington (conductor, London Baroque Players and Cardiff Polyphonic Choir).

Soloists: Norma Burrowes, Willard White, Helen Watts, Robert Tear.

Video: Kultur/Films for the Humanities VHS. Color. In English. 113 minutes.

1983 Westminster Abbey, London

English church production: Christopher Hogwood (conductor, Academy of Ancient Music and Choir of Westminster Abbey).

Soloists: Judith Nelson, Emma Kirkby, Carolyn Watkinson, Paul Elliott, David Thomas.

Video: HBO/NVC Arts (GB) VHS. Roy Tipping (director). Color. In English. 145 minutes.

Comment: Foundling Hospital Version of 1754.

1984 Pieterskerk, Leiden

Dutch church production: Stephen Cleobury (conductor, Brandenburg Consort and Choir of Kings College, Cambridge).

Soloists: Lynn Dawson, Hillary Summers, John Mark Ainsley, Alastair Miles.

Video: Image Entertainment DVD/Arthaus (GB) DVD. Dirk van Bijker (director). Color. In English. 149 minutes.

1987 Atlanta Symphony

American stage production: Robert Shaw (conductor, Atlanta Symphony Orchestra and Chamber Chorus).

Soloists: Sylvia McNair, Marietta Simpson, Jon Humphrey, William Stone.

Video: VAI VHS. Phillip Byrd (director). Color. In English. 141 minutes.

1992 Point Theatre, Dublin

Irish stage production: Neville Marriner (conductor, St.-Martin-in-the-Fields Academy Orchestra and Chorus).

Soloists: Sylvia McNair, Anne Sofie von Otter, Michael Chance, Jerry Hadley, Robert Lloyd.

Video: Philips VHS. Color. In English. 147 minutes.

Comment: Performance celebrating 250th anniversary of *Messiah* in city where oratorio was first performed. Highlights version in *Great Moments* series, Volume 3.

1998 Abbey of La Chaise Dieu

French church production: Jean-Jacques Kantorow (conductor, National Choir of Lyon and Auvergne Orchestra).

Soloists: Veronique Dietschy, Elianev Tancheff, Thomas Thomaschke, Alexander Laiter.

Video: Image Entertainment DVD. Color. In English. 58 minutes.

Related films

1962 Viridiana

Luis Buñuel features selections from *Messiah* on the soundtrack of this surrealistic film about a novice nun (Silvia Pinal) corrupted by her uncle (Fernando Rey) and his illegitimate son (Francisco Rabal). Color. In Spanish. 90 minutes.

1965 One Way Pendulum

The Hallelujah Chorus from *Messiah* is used in a delightful way in this absurdist British comedy based on a play by N. F. Simpson. Jonathan Miller, after many failures, succeeds in getting speak-your-weight scales to perform the Chorus. Peter Yates directed. Color. 90 minutes.

1999 Man on the Moon

The Hallelujah Chorus from *Messiah* is heard on the soundtrack of this Jim Carrey biopic about comedian Andy Kaufman. Milos Forman directed. Color. 118 minutes.

2000 The Ladies Man

The Hallelujah Chorus, performed by the Royal Choral Society and Royal Philharmonic Orchestra, is heard on the soundtrack of this film about a womanizing radio announcer in Chicago. Reginald Hudlin directed. Color. 84 minutes.

2001 Gabriel & Me

The Hallelujah Chorus is heard on the soundtrack of this British film about a working-class family in Newcastle and a boy who wants to become an angel after meeting Archangel Gabriel (Billy Connelly). Udayan Prasad directed. Color. 87 minutes.

MESSTER, OSKAR
German film producer (1866–1943)

Oskar Messter was a notable producer of early opera films as well as one of the great innovators of early German cinema. He perfected his Kinematography system around 1896, began experimenting with sound in 1903, and succeeded in making films of opera scenes with arias that could be synchronized with phonograph records. They lasted about 4 minutes, and Messter opened a specialist cinema in Berlin to present them. They were called *Tonbild* (the plural is *Tonbilder*), and the first one was screened in a variety program in 1903. Many notable opera and operetta stars sang for his Biophon-Tonbilder company, and many movie actors began their careers in his films, including the German silent star HENNY PORTEN. Nearly every famous opera and operetta was filmed to illustrate a recording of an aria, and they became longer toward the end of their vogue, with a 20-minute DIE FLEDERMAUS (1912) and a 35-minute CHRISTUS (1913). He ended Tonbilder production in 1913 when audiences lost interest in them. About 1,500 sound films were made in Germany during this period, more than a third of them by Messter, and quite a few survive. Messter made the first film biography of RICHARD WAGNER in 1912 and then made "Dirigengentefilm," in which famous German conductors were shown at work in a unique manner. See CONDUCTORS (1913–1917), FAUST (1907), FRA DIAVOLO (1908), DER GRAF VON LUXEMBURG (1909), LOHENGRIN (1907), LUCIA DI LAMMERMOOR (1907), FRITZI MASSARY (1903), OTELLO (1907), SALOME (1906), and LA TRAVIATA (1908).

MÉSZAROS, MÁRTA
Hungarian film director (1931–)

Márta Mészaros, one of the leading modern directors of Hungarian cinema with a strong background in documentary, is especially noted for her films, such as *Adoption* and *Nine Months,* about the situation of women. She made a fine documentary about DON PASQUALE in 1991 with American soprano Barbara Hendricks.

METROPOLITAN
1935 opera film with Tibbett

Tom (Lawrence Tibbett) begins this film by singing the baritone part of Méphistophélès to wealthy socialite soprano Anne's Marguerite (Virginia Bruce) in the *Faust* trio with accompaniment by a car radio on a country road. It turns out that he is a frustrated bit-part singer at the Metropolitan Opera, where he has waited six years for a chance, and she is an aspiring opera singer. She meets him again at the Met when diva Ghita Galin (Alice Brady) berates opera director Maselli (Orin Burke) for not choosing her for the lead and decides to form her own opera company. Tom finally gets his chance at a leading role when the man who is to sing Amonasro in *Aida* gets ill, but Maselli chooses another baritone, so Tom quits. Ghita, who fancies Tom, asks him to be artistic director of her new opera company in Philadelphia, and Tom gets her to hire Anne and former La Scala conductor Papa Perontelli (George Merion). Ghita behaves badly at rehearsals, decides to stage *The Barber of Seville* instead of *Carmen,* and jealously demands that Anne leave the company. When her voice cracks, she blames the conductor and cancels her support of the company. Tom takes over and, with a check from Anne, decides to stage a double bill of *Pagliacci* and *Cavalleria rusticana.* Tom and Anne take the leading roles, and the opening night is a big success. Tibbett sings Figaro's "Largo al Factotum" from *The Barber of Seville* as well as arias from *Carmen, Cavalleria rusticana,* and *Pagliacci,* plus "On the Road to Mandalay," a song he often performed on radio. Luis Alberni is in his usual fine frenetic form, Bess Meredyth and George Marion Jr. wrote the screenplay, Richard Day was the art director, Rudolph Maté and George Schneiderman were the cinematographers, and Richard Boleslawski directed for Twentieth Century-Fox. Black and white. 75 minutes.

METROPOLITAN OPERA

The Metropolitan Opera in New York has been America's best-known opera company for more than 100 years (since 1883) and remains one of the best in the world. It is also of great importance in the history of opera on the screen. The first American telecast of an opera by professional singers was *Pagliacci* by the Metropolitan Opera in March 1940, and the first live telecast of an opera from any theater was *Otello* from the Met in 1948. There are more videos of operas at the Met than any other opera house, and nearly every opera telecast is accessible. Many can be purchased, and others can be viewed at the Museum of Television and Radio, which mounted a large retrospective in 1986. Many fiction films with opera subjects feature scenes at or around the Met, including MOONSTRUCK, A NIGHT AT THE OPERA, METROPOLITAN, and *The Stars Are Singing;* MGM built a 500-foot-wide reproduction of the Old Met interior for the 1946 film TWO SISTERS FROM BOSTON. Most of the standard repertory operas are available as Met videos; for details see the individual operas. See also ANTONY AND CLEOPATRA (1966), MARIA CALLAS (1956), JAMES LEVINE, LAURITZ MELCHIOR (1953), LUCIANO PAVAROTTI (1999), and GIUSEPPE VERDI (2001).

1940 Metropolitan Opera Gala Concert
This was the first American television broadcast of professional opera. The Met organized the telecast from an NBC studio in Radio City on March 10, 1940, in a program called *Metropolitan Opera Gala Concert.* In the first half, singers in evening dress were featured in scenes from *Carmen* (Bruna Castagna and Licia Albanese), *La Gioconda* (Frederick Jagel), *The Barber of Seville* (Leonard Warren), and *Rigoletto* (Jagel, Castagna, Warren, and Hilde Reggiani in the Quartet). In the second half, a highlights performance of *Pagliacci* (Act I) was presented in costume with sets. Richard Bonelli sang the Prologue, Hilda Burke was Nedda, Armand Tokatyan was Canio, George Cehanovsky was Silvio, and Alessio De Paolis was Beppe. Frank St. Leger conducted the Metropolitan Opera Orchestra, Gene Hamilton was the announcer, and Met general manager Edward Johnson was master of ceremonies. There were about 1,000 television sets in the United States at this time, and the audience for the show was estimated at about 2,000. Black and white. In English, French, and Italian. 60 minutes.

1953 Metropolitan Opera Jamboree
Blanche Thebom, Richard Tucker, Salvatore Baccaloni, Licia Albanese, Mario Del Monaco, Lucini Amara, Brian Sullivan, Zinka Milanov, Roberta Peters, Eugene Conley, Leontyne Price, and George London are among the many performers at this Met fund-raising celebration simulcast on ABC television and radio. Fausto Cleva and Max Rudolf conduct the orchestra; Milton Cross, Deems

Taylor, and Howard Dietz are the masters of ceremonies; Henry Souvaine was producer; and William Marshall and Marshall Diskin directed the telecast/broadcast from the Ritz Theater in New York on April 6, 1953. Black and white. 60 minutes (the program was 90 minutes but the last half hour was on radio only). Video at the MTR.

1953 Toast to the Met
Ed Sullivan devoted his CBS show to the Met on November 8, 1953, and telecast from the opera house stage. Among the stars shown in rehearsal and singing are Risë Stevens, Richard Tucker, Hilde Gueden, Robert Merrill, Cesare Siepi, and Roberta Peters. The studio audience actually wore black tie. Black and white. 60 minutes. Video at the MTR.

1957 Ed Sullivan Show
Renata Tebaldi and Richard Tucker are the guest stars from the Metropolitan Opera on the CBS *Ed Sullivan Show* on March 10, 1957. Black and white. 60 minutes. Video at the MTR.

1966 The Met Yesterday and Tomorrow
Tribute to the old Metropolitan Opera House, which had just been razed when this program was shown. Caruso, Melba, Farrar, and Chaliapin are heard and talked about, and the guests include Richard Tucker, Wallace Harrison, and Anthony Bliss. The program ends with a discussion of the new opera house scheduled to open in September. Telecast on National Educational Television April 17, 1966. Black and white. 90 minutes. Video at the MTR.

1966 Open Mind
Lily Pons, Bidú Sayão, Lotte Lehmann, Giovanni Martinelli, and Richard Crooks talk about the Golden Age of the Metropolitan Opera after the razing of the old theater. Telecast on April 17, 1966, on NBC. Black and white. Video at the MTR.

1970 Opera with Henry Butler
Henry Butler, stage director of the Met when this film was made, talks about opera as a combination of music and theater. Included as demonstration are scenes from *La traviata* (the party scene, with Anna Moffo) and *Pagliacci*. Color. 26 minutes.

1972 Salute to Sir Rudolf Bing
Metropolitan Opera stars perform in a gala concert on April 22, 1972, to honor Rudolf Bing, retiring after 22 years as general manager. The 43 singers included Luciano Pavarotti, Joan Sutherland, Plácido Domingo, Montserrat Caballé, Roberta Peters, Birgit Nilsson, Franco Corelli, and Sherrill Milnes; the conductors included James Levine, Richard Bonynge, Francesco Moli-

nari-Pradelli, Kurt Adler, and Max Rudolf. Sydney Smith directed for CBS Television, but only one hour of the three-hour gala was telecast on April 30, 1972. 60 minutes. Video at the MTR.

1975 Danny Kaye at the Metropolitan
Danny Kaye looks behind the scenes at scenery, lighting, and special effects at the Met in this program in the series *Texaco Presents*. Beverly Sills, Robert Merrill, Rosalind Elias, Enrico Di Giuseppe, James Morris, and Judith Blegen are among those who appear. Robert Sheerer directed the CBS telecast April 27, 1972. 60 minutes. Video at the MTR.

1983 Metropolitan Opera Centennial Gala
The Met celebrated its 100th birthday October 22, 1983, with an eight-hour gala telecast featuring excerpts from 14 operas with 100 singers; seven conductors; the Met Orchestra, Chorus and Ballet; and an audience of 7,500. The participants were sopranos Kathleen Battle, Judith Blegen, Grace Bumbry, Montserrat Caballé, Ileana Cotrubas, Loretta Di Franco, Mirella Freni, Catherine Malfitano, Eva Marton, Leona Mitchell, Edda Moser, Birgit Nilsson, Roberta Peters, Leontyne Price, Katia Ricciarelli, Elisabeth Söderström, Joan Sutherland, Kiri Te Kanawa, and Anna Tomowa-Sintow; mezzo-sopranos Gail Dubinbaum, Marilyn Horne, Diane Kesling, and Frederica von Stade; tenors José Carreras, Giuliano Giannella, Plácido Domingo, Nicolai Gedda, Alfredo Kraus, William Lewis, James McCracken, Robert Nagy, Luciano Pavarotti, Dano Raffanti, and David Rendall; baritones Renato Bruson, John Darrenkamp, and Brian Schexnayder; basses Ara Berberian, Sesto Bruscantini, Nicolai Ghiaurov, Ruggero Raimondi, and Julien Robbins; and conductors Leonard Bernstein, Richard Bonynge, Thomas Fulton, James Levine, John Pritchard, David Stivender, and Jeffrey Tate. Kirk Browning directed. Color. With English subtitles. 231 minutes. Pioneer DVD and LD/Paramount VHS.

1986 Live From the Met Highlights, Volume I
This is an anthology compilation of excerpts from operas presented at the Met: *The Bartered Bride* (1978, overture conducted by James Levine), *Un ballo in maschera* (1980 with Judith Blegen and Luciano Pavarotti), *Don Carlo* (1983 with Mirella Freni and Plácido Domingo), *La bohème* (1982 with Teresa Stratas and José Carreras), *Tannhäuser* (1982 with Eva Marton), and *Lucia di Lammermoor* (1982 with Joan Sutherland). Color. 70 minutes. Pioneer DVD/Paramount VHS.

1991 Metropolitan Opera 25th Anniversary Gala
Gala celebrating the 25th anniversary of the Met's move to Lincoln Center. Luciano Pavarotti and Cheryl Studer are seen in Act III of *Rigoletto,* Plácido Domingo and

Mirella Freni appear in Act III of *Otello,* Domingo and Pavarotti sing together in a scene from *La bohème,* and other stars make guest appearances in Act II of *Die Fledermaus,* including June Anderson, Kathleen Battle, Thomas Hampson, and Frederica von Stade. James Levine conducts. Color. In English and Italian with English subtitles. 115 minutes. DG VHS.

1994 Meet the Met: Favorite Opera Scenes
Compilation of opera scenes from Met productions of Die Zauberflöte, Il trovatore, Otello, Un ballo in maschera, Aida, Ariadne auf Naxos, The Barber of Seville, Turandot, Die Fledermaus, and Götterdämmerung. Color. 101 minutes. In German and Italian with English subtitles. DG VHS/LD.

MEYERBEER, GIACOMO
French composer (1791–1864)

Giacomo Meyerbeer, born in Berlin as Jacob Meyer Beer, was the Cecil B. DeMille of 19th-century grand opera. Although German, he became the grand master of the French opera with librettist Eugène Scribe. Together they devised operas more spectacular and grandiose than anything seen on the stage before or since. His first success was the 1824 *Il crociato in Egitto,* but it was his 1931 collaboration with Scribe on *Robert le diable* that began his triumphal grand opera career at the Paris Opéra. It scandalized Paris with its dancing nuns, but the scandal, of course, attracted huge crowds. Meyerbeer afterwards collaborated with Scribe on the equally successful large-scale grand operas LES HUGUENOTS, *Le prophète,* and L'AFRICAINE. He also had success with the small-scale opéra-comique DINORAH, source of the popular "Shadow Song." Although not currently in vogue, Meyerbeer's operas continue to be staged.

MICHELENA, BEATRIZ
American film actress (1890–1942)

Beatriz Michelena, a star of the early American silent cinema, was also admired as an opera singer. She was the daughter of Spanish opera tenor Fernando Michelena and sister of Broadway musical comedy singer Vera Michelena. Beatriz was the top star of the California Motion Picture Corporation and was featured in a screen adaptation of Ambroise Thomas's opera MIGNON. When the film was first screened privately in December 1914, she sang Mignon's arias to accompany it. She was said to have been offered $5,000 to sing at the Tivoli Opera House when the film opened in 1915, but she preferred a movie career. Her other popular films include *Salomy Jane* and *Mrs. Wiggs of the Cabbage Patch,* both made in 1914. Her last film was the 1920 *The Flame of Hellgate.*

MIDSUMMER MARRIAGE, THE
1955 opera by Tippett

MICHAEL TIPPETT's first opera aroused a great deal of controversy when it premiered, mainly because of its libretto. It was considered too grand, too obscure, too mythological, and too confusing. The highly symbolic opera occurs in a clearing on top of a hill where the mysterious Mark is being rebuffed by the idealistic Jennifer whom he was supposed to wed. Meanwhile the tycoon King Fisher is looking for them to try to stop the marriage. At the end, King Fisher is killed and the marriage takes place.

1984 Thames Television
English TV production: Elijah Moshinsky (stage and TV director), David Atherton (conductor, London Sinfonietta), Peter Le Page and Jane Krall (set designers).
Cast: Philip Langridge (Mark), Lucy Shelton (Jennifer), David Wilson-Johnson (King Fisher), Patricia O'Neill (Bella), Peter Jeffes, Sarah Walker, Janet Suzman.
Telecast in 1984 on Thames TV in England. Color. In English. 155 minutes.

MIDSUMMER NIGHT'S DREAM, A
1960 opera by Britten

Shakespeare's play *A Midsummer Night's Dream* is the basis of this opera although it has been somewhat altered by composer/librettist BENJAMIN BRITTEN and co-librettist Peter Pears in order to emphasize the supernatural aspects of the story. Fairy King Oberon gets his revenge on Queen Titania by giving her a love potion that causes her to fall in love with the weaver Bottom who has been magically given an ass's head. He is in the forest with friends to rehearse the play *Pyramus and Thisbe.* Runaway lovers from the Athens court, Hermia, Lysander, Demetrius, and Helena, also get involved in bewitchery and switch affections with bewildering speed. In the end all is sorted out happily in time for the marriage celebrations of Duke Theseus and Hippolyta.

***1981 Glyndebourne Festival
English stage production: Peter Hall (director), Bernard Haitink (conductor, London Philharmonic Orchestra and Glyndebourne Festival Chorus), John Bury (set designer).
Cast: James Bowman (Oberon), Ileana Cotrubas (Titania), Cynthia Buchan (Hermia), Curt Appelgren (Bottom), Ryland Davies (Lysander), Dale Duesing (Demetrius), Felicity Lott (Helena), Robert Bryson (Quince), Andrew Gallacher (Snug), Donald Bell (Starveling), Patrick Power (Flute), Damien Nash (Puck).

Video: Home Vision/Kultur VHS. Dave Heather (director). Color. In English. 156 minutes.

FILMS OF THE SHAKESPEARE PLAY

There are several good films of the Shakespeare play, including a 1961 Czech puppet version by Jirí Trnka, a 1966 New York City Ballet version, and a 1984 experimental work by Celestino Coronado. The following are of particular interest.

1935 Reinhardt film

Max Reinhardt's lavish American film for Warner Bros., following his production of the play at the Hollywood Bowl, featured the major stars of the studio. James Cagney is Bottom, Mickey Rooney is Puck, Dick Powell is Lysander, Olivia de Havilland is Hermia, Jean Muir is Helena, Ross Alexander is Demetrius, Victor Jory is Oberon, Anita Louise is Titania, Joe E. Brown is Flute, Hugh Herbert is Snout, Ian Hunter is Theseus, and Verree Teasdale is Hippolyta. Charles Kenyon and Mary C. McCall Jr. wrote the screenplay, Erich Wolfgang Korngold composed the music, and Hal Mohr won an Oscar for cinematography. Black and white. 132 minutes.

1968 Hall film

Peter Hall, who directed the 1981 Glyndebourne production of the opera described above, directed a film of the play in 1968 with members of the Royal Shakespeare Company. It is a reasonably close version of the stage play. Judi Dench is Titania, Ian Richardson is Oberon, Ian Holm is Puck, Paul Rogers is Bottom, Diana Rigg is Helena, Helen Mirren is Hermia, David Warner is Lysander, Michael Jayston is Demetrius, Derek Godfrey is Theseus, Barbara Jefford is Hippolyta, and Bill Travers is Snout. Color. 124 minutes.

1996 Noble film

Adrian Noble's adaptation of a Royal Shakespeare Company production stars Lindsay Duncan, Alex Jennings, Desmond Barrit, Barry Lynch, Monica Dolan, Daniel Evans, Kevin Doyle, Emily Raymond, and Alfred Burke. Noble wrote the screenplay, Howard Blake composed the music, and Ian Wilson was cinematographer. Color. 105 minutes.

1999 Hoffman film

Michael Hoffman's film is quite operatic, with opera arias prominent on the soundtrack. The story is updated to the late 19th century (the lovers run away on bicycles), setting is shifted to Italy, and the film stars major movie and TV personalities. Kevin Kline is Bottom, Michelle Pfeiffer is Titania, Rupert Everett is Oberon, Stanley Tucci is Puck, Calista Flockhart is Helena, Anna Friel is Hermia, Christian Bale is Demetrius, David Strathair is

Theseus, Sophie Marceau is Hippolyta, Bill Irwin is Snout, and Sam Rockwell is Flute. The soundtrack features Renée Fleming and Marcello Giordani singing the "Brindisi" from *La traviata* and "Casta diva" from *Norma,* with Terry Davies conducting the orchestra and Terry Edwards directing the London Voices; Roberto Alagna singing "Una furtiva lagrima" from *L'elisir d'amore,* with Evelino Pidò conducting the Orchestre National de l'Opéra; and Cecilia Bartoli singing "Non più mesta" from *La Cenerentola,* with Riccardo Chailly conducting the Teatro Comunale di Bologna Orchestra and Chorus. Hoffman wrote the screenplay, Simon Boswell was music director, and Oliver Stapleton was cinematographer. Color. 130 minutes.

MIGENES, JULIA
American soprano (1949–)

Soprano Julia Migenes called herself Migenes-Johnson when she starred in Francesco Rosi's great 1984 opera film CARMEN as a mezzo-soprano and won world renown. Her opera career began in her native New York as a 3-year-old in a Metropolitan Opera production of *Madama Butterfly.* She made her adult debut in 1965 as Annina in the New York City Opera production of *The Saint of Bleecker Street* and then began to sing with the Vienna Volksoper. She returned to the Met in 1979 and has been acclaimed there and in Europe for her performances in Berg's LULU (1980) and Weill's AUFSTIEG UND FALL DER STADT MAHAGONNY (1976) and DIE DREIGROSCHENOPER (1990). She has sung in TV versions of Strauss's EINE NACHT IN VENEDIG (1973), Fall's MADAME POMPADOUR (1976), and Poulenc's LA VOIX HUMAINE (1990) and has appeared in several non-opera films and TV programs.

1985 Sherrill Milnes All-Star Gala

Migenes joins Sherrill Milnes for a concert in Berlin and duets with him on "Close as Pages in a Book" from *Up in Central Park.* Georg Mielke directed. Color. 56 minutes. VAI VHS.

1986 L'Unique

This French science-fiction film starring Migenes and Sami Frey was released in the United States with the title *Original.* Jérôme Diamant-Berger directed. Color. In French. 89 minutes.

1986 Grace Note

Migenes dreams of success as an opera singer in *Grace Note,* an episode in the TV series *Twilight Zone.* Her dying sister gives her a glimpse of her future, and she sees herself in *La traviata* at the Met. Peter Medak directed. Telecast April 4, 1986, on CBS. Color. In English. 30 minutes.

1987 Pleasure Principle

Migenes plays Dr. Rosita Estverdes in *Pleasure Principle,* an episode of the TV series *Magnum, P.I.* Telecast October 14, 1987. Color. In English. 60 minutes.

1988 Berlin Blues

Migenes plays Lola, a sultry West Berlin nightclub singer who bewitches East Berliner Keith Baxter, in this Spanish film. She also sings Susanna's aria "Deh vieni non tardar" from *Le nozze di Figaro.* Ricardo Franco directed. Color. In English. 104 minutes. Cannon VHS/LD.

1990 Plácido Grandisimo

Migenes joins Plácido Domingo in a concert in Seville for a duet from *Carmen* ("C'est toi") and sings "Summertime" from *Porgy and Bess* and "Il bel sogno de Doretta" from *La Rondine.* Eugen Kohn conducts the National Symphonic Orchestra. Juan Villaescusa directed. Color. 60 minutes. Kultur VHS.

1990 The Krays

Migenes plays Judy Garland in this British film about the infamous English gangster twins (played by Gary and Martin Kemp). Peter Medak directed. Color. 119 minutes.

1996 Orientation

Migenes, who is a member of the Church of Scientology, appears (uncredited) as an opera singer in the promotional documentary *Orientation: A Scientology Information Film.*

MIGHTY CASEY, THE

1953 opera by Schuman

Mighty Casey, Mudville's greatest baseball player, is up at bat in the state championship game against Centerville and is watched by his admiring girl Merry. The pitcher is terrified, but, incredibly, Casey strikes out. William Schuman's one-act opera *The Mighty Casey,* libretto by Jeremy Gury based on Ernest L. Thayer's much-recited 1888 poem "Casey at the Bat," premiered in Hartford in 1953. There is a large cast but no major singing roles, and Casey himself is mimed. The score is tonal and jazz-tinged with hints of 19th-century parlor songs.

1955 Omnibus, CBS Television

American TV production: Elliott Silverstein (director), Samuel Krachmalnick (conductor, CBS Television Orchestra), Henry May (set designer).

Cast: Danny Scholl (Casey), Elise Rhodes (Merry) Rufus Smith (Pitcher), Nathaniel Frey (Catcher), George Irving (Watchman), David Thomas (Umpire), Bruce Renshaw (Charlie), Robert Goss (Andy), Del

Horstmann (Red), Mark Murphy (Otis), Albert Linville (Manager).

Video at the MTR. Telecast March 6, 1955, on CBS. Ted Danielewski (director). Black and white. In English. 60 minutes.

MIGNON

1866 opera by Thomas

AMBROISE THOMAS's *Mignon,* based on Goethe's 1796 novel *Wilhelm Meister's Apprenticeship* as adapted by Jules Barbier and Michel Carré, was very popular in the early part of the century and was the subject of many silent films. Mignon is a singer with a group of traveling gypsies and is rescued by Wilhelm. Lothario, a count disguised as a wandering minstrel, is looking for his long-lost daughter. Not surprisingly, she turns out to be Mignon. The most famous aria in the opera, however, is "Je suis Titania," which is sung by Philine.

1973 Who's Afraid of Opera?

English TV film: Herbert Wise (director), Richard Bonynge (conductor, London Symphony Orchestra), George Djurkovic (set designer), Claire Merrill (screenplay), Nathan Kroll (producer).

Cast: Huguette Tourangeau (Mignon), Joan Sutherland (Philine), Ian Caley (Wilhelm Meister), Pieter Van Der Stolk (Lothario), Brian Ralph (Laertes), Gordon Wilcock (Jarno), Larry Berthelson puppets.

Video: Kultur VHS. Color. In English and French. 30 minutes.

Comment: Highlights version of an opera made for young audiences with Sutherland telling the story to puppets. Dialogue in English, singing in French.

1982 Opera Nacional, Mexico City

Mexican stage production: Carlos Diaz Dupond (director), Enrique Padron De Hueda (conductor, Teatro de Bellas Artes Orchestra and Chorus).

Cast: Estrella Ramirez (Mignon), Angelica Dorantes (Philine), Librado Alexander (Wilhelm Meister), Rogelio Vargas (Lothario), Adrian Diaz de Leon (Frederick).

Video: Lyric VHS. Manuel Yrizar (director). Color. In French with Spanish subtitles. 120 minutes.

Comment: Staged at Teatro de Bellas Artes in Mexico City.

1983 Salzburg Marionette Theater

German TV production: Matthias Kuntzsch (conductor, Munich Philharmonic), Günther Schneider-Siemssen (set designer).

Cast: Trudeliese Schmidt (Mignon), Sylvia Greenberg (Philine), Adolf Dallapozza (Wilhelm Meister), Günther Wewel (Lothario), Salzburg Marionette Theater.

Video: German Language Center VHS. Telecast on ZDF German Television. Color. In German. 60 minutes.

Comment: This highlights version of the opera mixes live singers with the Salzburg marionettes.

1992 Théâtre Français de la Musique, Compiègne

French stage production: Pierre Jourdan (director).

Cast: Lucile Vignon (Mignon), Annick Masis (Philine), Alain Gabriel (Wilhelm Meister), Christina Treguier.

Video: Dreamlife (Japan) DVD/VHS. Color. 165 minutes. In French.

Early/related films

1906 Chronographe film

A French sound film of the opera titled *Mignon* was released in 1906. An aria, probably Philine's "Je suis Titania," was reproduced using the Gaumont Chronographe sound-on-disc system. Black and white. In French. About 3 minutes.

1909 Lubin film

This American *Mignon* may also have been a singing version; the Lubin studio was marketing a sound film system in 1909 called the Lubin Synchronizer. Black and white. About 9 minutes.

1910 Cines film

This *Mignon* is an Italian film of the story produced by the Cines studio. The London *Bioscope* noted that it had "photographic quality such as only Italy can produce." Black and white. Silent. About 15 minutes.

1911 Messter film

Gertrud Runge sings the aria "Je suis Titania" from *Mignon* in this Oskar Messter sound film made for his Berlin Biophon cinema using his sound-on-disc system. Black and white. In French. About 4 minutes.

1912 Solax film

The first woman filmmaker, Alice Guy-Blaché, directed this *Mignon* for her Solax company. Marian Swayne is Mignon, Blanche Cornwall is Philine, Darwin Karr is Wilhelm Meister, and Billy Quirk is Frederick. Black and white. Silent. About 12 minutes.

1915 California film

Beatriz Michelena was highly praised for her performance as Mignon in this U.S. *Mignon* and sang her arias live at the premiere. House Peters is Wilhelm Meister, Clara Beyers is Philine, Andrew Robson is Lothario, and Will Pike is Frederick. Charles Kenyon wrote the screenplay and William Nigh directed the film in the San Francisco area for the California Motion Picture Corporation. Black and white. Silent. About 75 minutes.

1919 Flegrea film

Tina Xeo plays Mignon in this Italian feature version of *Mignon* with Franco Piersanti as Wilhelm Meister and Renée de Saint-Léger as Philine. Mario Gargiulo directed for Flegrea Film of Rome. Black and white. Silent. About 70 minutes.

1943 The Life and Death of Colonel Blimp

Michael Powell and Emeric Pressburger use Philine's aria "Je suis Titania" to help create period ambiance in this fine film. Roger Livesey plays a British Army officer in a Berlin café in 1902 on leave from the Boer War accompanied by feminist Deborah Kerr. He is there to provoke a fight about allegations of British atrocities and begins by asking the band to play the French aria. Color. 163 minutes.

1950 The Toast of New Orleans

Mignon is seen on stage in this MGM musical with Kathryn Grayson singing Philine's aria "Je suis Titania" in a production at the French Opera House in turn-of-the-century New Orleans. She plays the opera house's prima donna. See THE TOAST OF NEW ORLEANS.

1975 The Wrong Movement

Wim Wenders's German *Falsche Bewegung* (The Wrong Movement) is a loose adaptation of the Goethe source novel *Wilhelm Meisters Lehrjahre*. It stars Rudiger Vogler as Wilhelm. Color. In German. 103 minutes.

MIKADO, THE
1885 comic opera by Gilbert and Sullivan

The Mikado or The Town of Titipu is the most popular of the GILBERT AND SULLIVAN operettas. This is reflected in the large number of films, videos, and telecasts; it was first filmed in 1902, and a grandiose Technicolor version was made in 1939. While the setting is ostensibly Japan, the satire is entirely about English behavior. Nanki-Poo, the son of the Mikado, has come to the town of Titipu disguised as a minstrel to escape marrying the old maid Katisha. He falls in love with Yum-Yum, the ward of Ko-Ko, the Lord High Executioner, who is planning to marry her with the help of Pooh-Bah, who holds most of the official positions. Many of the songs are classics, including "A Wandering Minstrel" and "The Flowers That Bloom in the Spring."

1939 Schertzinger film

English feature film: Victor Schertzinger (director), Geoffrey Toye (screenplay/conductor, London Symphony Orchestra), Bernard Knowles and William Skall (cinematographers).

Cast: Martyn Green (Ko-Ko), Sydney Granville (Pooh-Bah), Kenny Baker (Nanki-Poo), Jean Colin (Yum-Yum), Constance Willis (Katisha), John Barclay (Mikado).

Video: Image Entertainment DVD/Home Vision VHS. Technicolor. In English. 91 minutes.

Comment: Schertzinger was brought to London from Hollywood to direct this lavish Technicolor film intended to be the British answer to *The Wizard of Oz*. It stars many of the best-known stars of the D'Oyly Carte Opera Company, although American Kenny Baker was imported to play Nanki-Poo. It is still enjoyable, but certainly no match for *Wizard*. It was nominated for an Oscar for its cinematography.

The Mikado (1939): Kenny Baker and Jean Colin were featured on the sheet music of Victor Schertzinger's British film.

1949 California Light Opera

American TV production: Luther Nuby (director), Bob Oakley (producer), music played by California Light Opera Orchestra.

Cast: Arthur Bradley, Phyllis Walker, Robert Kiber, John Hamilton, Mary Patrick.

Telecast January 25, 1949, on KLAC-TV. Black and white. In English. 50 minutes.

Comment: First American TV production of the operetta. This version is abridged and features only 10 singers.

1959 CBC Television

American TV production: Norman Campbell (director), Gladys Forrester (director, musical numbers), Godfrey Ridout (conductor, CBC Orchestra), Robert Lawson (set designer), Suzanne Mess (costume designer).

Cast: Eric House (Ko-Ko), Alan Crofoot (Pooh-Bah), Roma Butler (Yum-Yum), Robert Reid (Nanki-Poo), Eric Treadwell (Mikado), Irene Byatt (Katisha).

Black and white. In English. 120 minutes.

Comment: Tenor Crofoot had to have special training to sing the bass role of Pooh-Bah.

1959 NBC Television: The Ford Show

American TV production: Selwyn Touber (director), Harry Geller (conductor, NBC Television Orchestra), Danny Arnold and Howard Leeds (screenplay).

Cast: Tennessee Ernie Ford (Ko-Ko), Karen Wessler, Ken Remo, Ted Wills, Deltra Kamsler, Donna Cooke, Joanne Burgan.

Video: UCLA. Black and white. In English. 30 minutes.

Comment: "Tennessee" Ernie Ford created this somewhat hillbilly-ish version of *The Mikado* for his NBC TV series.

1960 Bell Telephone Hour

American TV production: Norman Campbell (director), Martyn Green (producer), Donald Voorhees (conductor, Bell Telephone Hour Orchestra and Norman Luboff Choir), Paul Barnes (set designer), Ray Aghayan (costume designer).

Cast: Groucho Marx (Ko-Ko), Helen Traubel (Katisha), Stanley Holloway (Pooh-Bah), Robert Rounseville (Nanki-Poo), Barbara Meister (Yum-Yum), Dennis King (Mikado).

Video at the MTR. Telecast April 14, 1960, on NBC. Color. In English. 60 minutes.

Comment: A truly amazing cast although unfortunately not available on commercial video.

1963 The Cool Mikado

American feature film: Michael Winner (director), Maurice Browning and Lew Schwartz (screenplay), Harold Baim (producer).

Cast: Frankie Howerd (Ko-Ko), Stubby Kaye (Judge Mikado), Kevin Scott (Hank Mikado), Jill Mai

Meredith (Yum-Yum), Lionel Blair (Nanki), Jacqueline Jones (Katie Shaw).

Color. In English. 81 minutes.

Comment: Modernized version of the operetta set in postwar Japan.

1967 D'Oyly Carte Opera Company

English feature film: Stuart Burge (director), Isidore Godfrey (conductor, Birmingham City Symphony Orchestra), Gerry Fisher (cinematographer), Peter Howitt (art director).

Cast: John Reed (Ko-Ko), Kenneth Sandford (Pooh-Bah), Philip Potter (Nanki-Poo), Valerie Masterson (Yum-Yum), Christine Palmer (Katisha), Donald Adams (Mikado).

Video: VAI/Opera Dubs VHS. Color. In English. 122 minutes.

Comment: This film was based on Anthony Besch's classic 1966 D'Oyly Carte Company stage production and was shot at Golders Green Hippodrome in London. It was distributed theatrically in America by Warner Bros.

1972 Gilbert & Sullivan for All series

English highlights film: Peter Seabourne (director), Peter Murray (conductor, Gilbert and Sullivan Festival Orchestra and Chorus), David Maverovitch (cinematographer), Trevor Evans (adaptation), John Seabourne (producer).

Cast: John Cartier (Ko-Ko), Lawrence Richard (Pooh-Bah), Thomas Round (Nanki-Poo), Valerie Masterson (Yum-Yum), Helen Landis (Katisha), Donald Adams (Mikado).

Video: Musical Collectables VHS. Color. In English. 50 minutes.

1982 Gilbert and Sullivan Collection series

English studio production: Michael Geliot (director), Judith De Paul (producer), Alexander Faris (conductor, London Symphony Orchestra and Ambrosian Opera Chorus), Allan Cameron (set designer), George Walker (executive producer).

Cast: William Conrad (Mikado), Clive Revill (Ko-Ko), Stafford Dean (Pooh-Bah), John Steward (Nanki-Poo), Kate Flowers (Yum-Yum), Anne Collins (Katisha).

Video: Acorn Media DVD/Pioneer LD/Braveworld (GB) VHS. Rodney Greenberg (director). Color. In English. 113 minutes.

1982 Stratford Festival

Canadian TV production: Brian Macdonald (director/choreographer), Berthold Carriere (conductor, Stratford Festival Orchestra and Chorus), Douglas McLean and Susan Benson (set/costume designer), John Banks (adaptation).

Cast: Eric Donkin (Ko-Ko), Henry Ingram (Nanki-Poo), Richard McMillan (Pooh-Bah), Marie Baron (Yum-Yum), Christina James (Katisha), Gideon Saks (Mikado).

Video: Acorn Media DVD/Home Vision and Connaisseur VHS. Norman Campbell (director). Color. In English. 150 minutes.

Comment: Updated adaptation of Stratford Festival stage production by Macdonald.

1987 English National Opera

English stage production: Jonathan Miller (director), Peter Robinson (conductor, English National Opera Orchestra and Chorus), Anthony van Laast (choreographer).

Cast: Eric Idle (Ko-Ko), Richard van Allan (Pooh-Bah), Bonaventura Bottone (Nanki-Poo), Lesley Garrett (Yum-Yum), Felicity Palmer (Katisha), Richard Angas (Mikado), Susan Bullock (Peep-Bo).

Video: HBO VHS. John Michael Phillips (director). Thames TV. Color. In English. 130 minutes.

Comment: Miller felt *The Mikado* was more English than Japanese so he shifted its locale to 1920s England and set it in a black-and-white art deco seaside resort with tap-dancing bellhops, white pianos, and silver potted palms. It was filmed at the London Coliseum using an array of period film techniques.

1987 Opera Australia

Australian stage production: Christopher Renshaw (director), Andrew Green (conductor, Elizabethan Sydney Orchestra), Carole Todd (choreographer).

Cast: Graeme Ewer (Ko-Ko), Gregory Yurisich (Pooh-Bah), Peter Cousens (Nanki-Poo), Anne Marie MacDonald (Yum-Yum), Heather Begg (Katisha), Robert Eddie (Mikado), Caroline Clack (Peep-Bo).

Video: Image Entertainment DVD. Color. In English. 162 minutes

1992 Italian TV: Operette, che Passione!

Italian TV studio production: Sandro Massimini (director/producer), Roberto Negri (pianist), Sandro Corelli (choreographer).

Cast: Sandro Massimini, Tadamici Oriè.

Video: Pierluigi Pagano (director). Color. In Italian. About 19 minutes. Ricordi (Italy) VHS.

Comment: Highlights of the operetta on the Italian TV series *Operette, che Passione!* Includes the songs "Tit Willow" and "A More Humane Mikado."

1993 D'Oyly Carte Company

English stage production film: Andrew Wickes (stage director), Virginia Mason (film director), music performed by D'Oyly Carte Company Orchestra and Chorus.

Cast: Jill Pert (Katisha), Julian Jensen, Lesley Echo Ross, Gary Montaine, Fenton Gray, Terence Sharpe, Deryck Hamon.

Video: Polygram (GB) VHS. John Michael Phillips (director). Color. In English. 120 minutes.

Comment: This new D'Oyly Carte Company production was originally staged by Andrew Wickes. It was restaged by Virginia Mason for filming at the Buxton Opera House in England.

2000 Carl Rosa Opera

English film of stage production: Eric Roberts (director), Wyn Davies (conductor, Carl Rosa Youth Orchestra and Chorus), Eva Stuart (set designer), Linda Hemming (costume designer).

Cast: Eric Roberts (Ko-Ko), Bruce Graham (Pooh-Bah), Ivan Sharpe (Nanki-Poo), Mariane Hellgren (Yum-Yum), Gillian Knight (Katisha), Donald Maxwell (Mikado), Richard Morrison (Pish-Tush), Sarah Sweeting (Pitti-Sing), Janet Cowley (Peep-Bo).

Video: Carl Rosa (GB) VHS. Color. In English 120 minutes.

Comment: An attempt by the reformed Carl Rosa Opera Company to re-create the comic opera as it was seen on opening night in 1885. It was filmed at the Hackney Empire Theatre in London using costumes and sets from the film *Topsy-Turvy*.

Early/related films

1902 Lubin film

The first film based on a Gilbert and Sullivan operetta featured a scene from *The Mikado*. It was filmed in the United States by the Lubin Company and released in January 1902. Black and white. Silent. About 3 minutes.

1904 Walterdaw film

The first sound film based on a Gilbert and Sullivan operetta used a British synchronized sound system devised by the Walterdaw Company. A scene from *The Mikado* was screened with a recording of the song pictured. Black and white. In English. About 3 minutes.

1907 Cinematophone Singing Pictures

This was an epic movie for its time with virtually all the hit songs from *The Mikado* featured on 12 reels of film with the sound provided by the Cinematophone system. Each reel carried the title of a song, such as "Tit Willow" sung by George Thorne as Ko-Ko. Other songs included "A Wandering Minstrel I," "Three Little Maids," and "The Flowers That Bloom in the Spring." John Morland directed for the Walterdaw Company. Black and white. In English. About 36 minutes.

1909 Vivaphone duet

This Vivaphone sound film shows a duet from *The Mikado* with the singing provided by a synchronized sound-on-disc system from the Hepworth Studio. Black and white. In English. About 4 minutes.

1918 Fan Fan

This oddity was actually the first complete version of *The Mikado* on film, but it is acted by children. Although retitled *Fan Fan* and with its libretto freely adapted by Bernard McConville (including renaming the characters), it was screened in cinemas with the music from the operetta. *Fan Fan* stars 7-year-old Virginia Lee Corbin as Fan Fan (i.e., Yum-Yum), Francis Carpenter as Hanki Pan (Nanki-Poo), Carmen De Rue as Lady Shoo (Katisha), Violet Radcliffe as the Chief Executioner, and Joe Singleton as the Emperor. Chester and Sidney Franklin directed for the Fox Film Corporation. These directors made five other Fox kiddie movies of this type with the same screenwriter and child actors, most based on fairy tales. Two of these films survive and are available on video, but unfortunately *Fan Fan* isn't one of them. Black and white. Silent. About 70 minutes.

1926 D'Oyly Carte film

Scenes from a 1926 D'Oyly Carte production of *The Mikado* were filmed in London for a Gaumont Mirror short film. It also shows actor Charles Ricketts in the studio. Black and white. About 10 minutes.

1937 The Girl Said No

This little-known American film contains scenes from *The Mikado* performed in a traditional manner by members of the old Gilbert and Sullivan Opera Company of New York. William Danforth, who plays the Mikado, is said to have performed it for 25 years on stage. The other Savoyards include Frank Moulan as Ko-Ko and Carita Crawford as Yum-Yum. The songs featured in the film are "A Wandering Minstrel I," "The Mikado's Song," "The Flowers That Bloom in the Spring," "Three Little Maids From School," and "The Lord High Executioner." See THE GIRL SAID NO.

1978 Foul Play

The Mikado is central to the plot of this Hollywood thriller; the Pope is to be assassinated while attending a stage performance in San Francisco. Goldie Hawn and Chevy Chase race to the theater to foil the plot while Dudley Moore is shown conducting. In Hitchcock-style cross-cutting, however, Julius Rudel is the real conductor of the music we hear while *The Mikado* scenes are performed by members of the New York City Opera. Richard McKee is Pooh-Bah, Enrico di Giuseppe is Nanki-Poo, Glenys Fowles is Yum-Yum, Kathleen Hegierski is Peep-Bo, Sandra Walker is Pitti-Sing, Jane Shaulis is

Katisha, and Thomas Jamerson is Pish-Tush. Colin Higgins directed for Paramount. Color. In English. 116 minutes.

1982 Gentlemen of Titipu
Abridged animated version of *The Mikado*. Color. In English. 27 minutes. Paragon VHS.

1999 Topsy-Turvy
The creation of *The Mikado* is central to this fine film about the partnership between Gilbert (Jim Broadbent) and Sullivan (Allan Corduner). Eight numbers from the comic opera are performed as they were on opening night. See TOPSY-TURVY.

MIKI, MINORU
Japanese composer (1930–)

Minoru Miki writes operas in Japanese in the European style for a Western-style orchestra but with Japanese themes, stories, and musical ideas. Most of his libretti are in English, and two were written by Colin Graham. Miki began in 1963 with the chamber opera *Mendori Teischu* (The Henpecked Husband), staged in Japan and Europe. Equally successful was his full-scale 1975 *Shunkin-Sho* (The Story of Shunkin), about a boy who blinds himself for the sake of love, presented at the Savonlinna Festival in Finland in 1990. His other operas include *Ada, An Actors Revenge,* based on the Kabuki drama, and *The Tale of Genji,* based on the classic novel by Lady Muraski. His only opera on video is JŌRURI, libretto by Colin Graham based on a puppet play by Monzaemon Chikamatsu. It was commissioned by Opera Theater of St. Louis, which premiered it in 1985 and reprised and taped it in Tokyo in 1988.

MILLER, JONATHAN
English director (1936–)

Jonathan Miller has directed theater, television, opera, and film and has brought a lively intelligence to each. He first became known with the Beyond the Fringe theater group and then moved on to directing Chekhov and Shakespeare on stage. He began to direct opera in 1970 and soon developed close relationships with the English National Opera and Kent Opera companies. His most famous opera productions for the ENO are a 1950s-style New York gangster version of RIGOLETTO (1982) and a 1920s-style English version of THE MIKADO (1987), both available on video. See THE BEGGAR'S OPERA (1983), LA FANCIULLA DEL WEST (1991), LE NOZZE DI FIGARO (1992/1998), TAMERLANO (2001), and DIE ZAUBERFLÖTE (2000).

MILLION, LE
1931 French film with opera content

René Clair's delightful *opéra-bouffe* film, almost a prototype for the Marx Brothers's *A Night at the Opera,* revolves around the chase after a lottery ticket. A young Parisian artist (René Lefèvre) is hounded by creditors and sells an old jacket to get money; he discovers too late that it contains a winning lottery ticket. Other people, including a gang of crooks, learn about the ticket and join the hunt for it. The jacket is eventually discovered to have been sold to the costume department at the opera. Everyone descends on the Opéra-Lyrique where an imaginary opera called *Les Bohémiens,* only vaguely related to Murger, is in progress. The stout tenor Sopranelli (Constantin Stroesco) is on stage wearing the jacket with the ticket in the pocket. While he and soprano Mme. Ravellina (Odette Talazac) sing about being alone in the forest, a large crowd watches desperately from the wings and makes furious attempts to get the lottery ticket. Two scenes from *Les Bohémiens* are seen. In the first, the duet "Alone in the Forest" is sung by Sopranelli and Ravellina with Lefèbvre and his friend Annabella hidden behind the scenery. In the second, set in a gypsy camp, the Bohemians sing about their happiness, the tenor wins a duel for his soprano's honor, and his dying rival sings to his mother. After competing groups charge on stage in a last-ditch attempt to seize the ticket, the opera ends in total chaos, but the good guys eventually win out. *Les Bohémiens* was composed by Georges van Parys with Philippe Parès and Armand Bernard. Georges Périnal and Georges Raulet were the cinematographers for the film, Lazare Meerson designed the sets, and Clair himself wrote the screenplay based on a play by George Berr and Marcel Guillemaud. Black and white. In French. 91 minutes. Video Yesteryear/Bel Canto Society VHS.

MILLO, APRILE
American soprano (1958–)

Aprile Millo studied in San Diego and began her career by singing the title role in *Aida* in Salt Lake City in 1980. In 1982 she sang at La Scala in *Ernani* and in 1984 came to the Metropolitan as Amelia in *Simon Boccanegra.* She was soon a Met favorite in a wide variety of roles and can be seen there on video as the heroine of AIDA (1989) and as Amelia in UN BALLO IN MASCHERA (1991).

1988 La Grande Notte a Verona
Millo is one of the singers in a spectacular concert celebrating the 75th anniversary of the Arena di Verona festival. Carlo Franci conducts. See VERONA.

1988 Young Toscanini

Millo provides the singing voice for Elizabeth Taylor in a stage production of *Aida* in this Franco Zeffirelli film about the conductor. See ARTURO TOSCANINI.

1991 Queens From Caracalla

Millo is one of seven singers in this concert celebrating the 50th anniversary of opera at the baths of Caracalla in Rome. Carlo Franci conducts. See SOPRANOS AND MEZZOS.

1996 James Levine's Silver Anniversary Gala

Millo is one of many the singers participating in Levine's 25th anniversary celebration at the Met. Brian Large directed the telecast. See JAMES LEVINE.

MILLÖCKER, KARL
Austrian composer (1842–1899)

Karl Millöcker, a contemporary of Strauss and Suppé in Vienna's musical golden age, was one of the major exponents of Viennese operetta at that time although his name is not well known today outside the German-speaking world. His most famous operetta, DER BETTELSTUDENT (1882), continues to be staged in Germany and is widely available on video. A revision of his *Gräfin Dubarry* (1879) renamed DIE DUBARRY was a hit on Broadway in the 1930s with Grace Moore as its star. *Gasparone* (1884), a kind of bandit romance, also has admirers.

1940 Operette

This German film, set in operetta's golden age in Imperial Vienna, is essentially a love letter to the classic Viennese operetta and its great composers. Curt Jurgens plays Millöcker, Leo Slezak is Suppé, and Edmund Schellhammer is Strauss; the film includes operetta tunes from all three. Willi Forst wrote and directed and plays the leading role. Black and white. In German. 109 minutes. Lyric VHS.

1945 Operettaklange

Operetta Tones is a German film about Millöcker and his struggles to compose his 1890 operetta *Der Arme Jonathan*. Paul Hörbiger plays the composer with Hans Holt and Margot Jahnen in supporting roles. Theo Lingen directed. Black and white. In German. 78 minutes.

MILLS, RICHARD
Australian composer (1949–)

Richard Mills, music director of the West Australian Opera since 1996, has composed two operas. THE SUMMER OF THE SEVENTEENTH DOLL (1996), based on a famous Australian play by Ray Lawler about two cane cutters and their longtime girlfriends, was premiered by the Victorian State Opera in 1996 and is on video. His second opera, *Batavia*, was staged in 2001 but does not seem to have been issued on VHS. Mills, whose audience-friendly music has gained wide acceptance in Australia, studied at the University of Queensland and the Guildhall School in London.

MILNES, SHERRILL
American baritone (1935–)

Sherrill Milnes studied with Rosa Ponselle, made his opera debut in 1960 as Masetto, and then sang in Baltimore and Milan and with the New York City Opera. His principal career, however, was with the Metropolitan Opera, where he made his debut in 1965 and sang for more than 25 years. His repertory includes most of the Verdi and Puccini baritone roles, and he created the role of Adam Brant in Marvin David Levy's *Mourning Becomes Electra*, which premiered at the Met. He is featured in a number of films and videos of operas and recitals. See AIDA (1989), ERNANI (1983), OTELLO (1979), LUCIANO PAVAROTTI (1992), SIMON BOCCANEGRA (1984), TOSCA (1976), and IL TROVATORE (1988).

1976 Sherrill Milnes: Homage to Verdi

Milnes, on a pilgrimage to Verdi's birthplace, sings Verdi arias and talks about the composer's life. He begins with "Di Provenza il mar" when he visits Villa Verdi at Sant'Agata and pays homage to Verdi's piano. He also sings arias from *La traviata*, *La forza del destino*, *I vespri siciliani*, *Attila*, *Rigoletto*, *Nabucco*, and *Macbeth* and is seen performing on stage in *Rigoletto*. Gerald Krell directed. Color. In English. 56 minutes. Kultur VHS.

1985 Sherrill Milnes All-Star Gala

Milnes in concert in Berlin; he starts on a makeshift stage with the *Pagliacci* Prologue and ends with Iago's Credo. In between he sings duets with Julia Migenes on "Close as Pages in a Book" from *Up in Central Park*, with Mirella Freni on "Pura siccome un angelo" from *La traviata*, and with Plácido Domingo on "Dio che nell'alma infondere" from *Don Carlo*. He conducts the orchestra when Peter Schreier sings "Un'aura amorosa." Georg Mielke directed. Color. 56 minutes. VAI VHS.

1986 Sherrill Milnes at Juilliard

Milnes is shown leading an opera master class at the Juilliard Institute in 1986 and giving advice to six voice students who perform arias. Color. 75 minutes. Home Vision VHS.

1992 Pavarotti Plus

Milnes joins Luciano Pavarotti as he arranges for a televised celebration with friends at Lincoln Center in 1992. See LUCIANO PAVAROTTI.

MIREILLE
1864 opera by Gounod

CHARLES GOUNOD's opera *Mireille*, with a libretto by Michel Carré based on a Provençal poem by Frédéric Mistral called *Mireio*, is set in Provence in the early 19th century. It was much discussed in its day for its agrarian setting and emphasis on class differences, but it has dropped out of the repertory. In the opera Mireille is in love with Vincent but her father is opposed to their marriage; Vincent also has a dangerous rival, the bullfighter Ourrias.

1981 Grand Théâtre de Genève

Swiss stage production: Sylvain Cambreling (conductor, Suisse Romande Orchestra and Grand Théâtre de Genève Chorus)

Cast: Valerie Masterson (Mireille), Luis Lima (Vincent), Jules Bastin, Jane Berbie.

Video: House of Opera/Opera Dubs VHS. Color. In French. 150 minutes.

Early/related films

1906 Feuillade/Guy-Blaché film

This early French *Mireille* was made by two cinema pioneers, Louis Feuillade and Alice Guy-Blaché. Black and white. Silent. About 10 minutes.

1922 Servaës film

Angéle Pornot is Mireille, Carlo Berthosa is Vincent, and Joe Hamman is Ourrias in this French silent film of the story based on the opera. It was screened with Gounod's music. Ernest Servaës directed. Black and white. About 75 minutes.

1933 Servaës/Gaveau film

Mireille Lurie is Mireille in this narrative version of the opera; the screenplay is based on the libretto and the score is based on the opera's music. Jean Brunil is Vincent, Joe Hamman is Ourrias, and Marcel Boudouresque is Ramon. René Gaveau and Ernest Servaës directed for SCEC. Black and white. In French. 75 minutes.

M IS FOR MAN, MUSIC AND MOZART
1993 TV opera by Andriessen

Dutch composer Louis Andriessen's *M Is for Man, Music and Mozart* is a British television opera written and directed by Peter Greenaway. Created for the *Not Mozart* series, it was shot in Amsterdam using a dazzling combination of song, dance, animation, and computer wizardry. The film opens with singer Astrid Seriese running through the alphabet and concentrating on the letter *M* for man. Nude dancers Kate Gowar and Karen Potisk perform rituals before a medical theater audience and then revive choreographer Ben Croft, who dances the rest of the film. Cees van Zeeland conducts the chamber orchestra. Color. 30 minutes. Connoisseur Academy (GB) VHS.

MISS CHICKEN LITTLE
1953 opera by Wilder

Miss Chicken Little is walking through the forest when an acorn falls on her head. She tells her fowl friends that the sky is falling, and they all go off to tell the king. The Fox pretends to show them the way and leads them to his foxhole. Alec Wilder's 27-minute light opera *Miss Chicken Little*, libretto by William Engvick based on the folktale, was staged in New York in November 1953 with two pianos and then orchestrated for screening on television.

1953 CBS Television, Omnibus

American TV production: Robert Saudek (director), George Bassman (CBS Television Orchestra), John Butler (choreographer), Ray Charles (choral director).

Cast: Jo Sullivan (Chicken Little), George Irving (Fox), Rosemary Kuhlmann (Goosey Loosey), Leon Lisher (Turkey Lurkey), Jim Hawthorne (Chocky Locky), Leonore Arnold (Ducky Lucky), Ruth Kobart, Eleanor Williams, Muriel Shaw, Charlotte Rae (Hens), Glen Tetley and Felisa Conde (Dancing Hens).

Telecast December 27, 1953, on CBS. Black and white. In English. 30 minutes.

MITRIDATE, RE DI PONTO
1770 opera by Mozart

Mitridate, re di Ponto (Mithridates, King of Pontus) is an *opera seria* written by MOZART when he was 14 and wanting desperately to please both singers and audience. It may not be a great opera, but it has some great music. The libretto by Vittorio Cigna-Santi is based on a play by Racine. King Mitridate has left his Black Sea country to fight the Romans. In his absence his sons Sifare and Farnace court his fiancée Aspasia. He returns having lost the war with the Romans but bringing Ismene as a bride for Farnace. He becomes suspicious of what has happened in his absence and threatens to kill them all.

1983 Opéra de Lyon

French stage production: Jean-Claude Fall (director), Theodor Guschlbauer (conductor, Opéra de Lyon Orchestra and Chorus), Gerard Didier (set/costume designer).

Cast: Rockwell Blake (Mitridate), Yvonne Kenny (Aspasia), Ashley Putnam (Sifare), Brenda Boozer (Farnace), Patricia Rozario (Ismene), Christina Papis (Marzio), Catherine Dubosc (Arbate).

Video: Polygram (France) VHS/Japanese LD. Bernard Maigrot (director). Color. In Italian. 164 minutes.

***1986 Ponnelle film

Austrian feature film: Jean-Pierre Ponnelle (director), Nikolaus Harnoncourt (conductor, Concentus Musicus Wien), Xaver Schwarzenberger (cinematographer).

Cast: Gösta Winbergh (Mitridate), Yvonne Kenny (Aspasia), Ann Murray (Sifare), Anne Gjevang (Farnace), Joan Rodgers (Ismene), Peter Straka (Marzio), Massimiliano Roncato (Arbate).

Video: London VHS/LD. Color. In Italian with English subtitles. 124 minutes.

Comment: Ponnelle filmed this inventive version of the *opera seria* at Palladio's Teatro Olimpico in Vicenza in March 1986. It is a visual and musical marvel.

1991 Royal Opera

English stage production: Graham Vick (director), Paul Daniel (conductor, Royal Opera Orchestra), Paul Brown (set designer).

Cast: Bruce Ford (Mitridate), Luba Orgonasova (Aspasia), Ann Murray (Sifare), Jochen Kowalski (Farnace), Lillian Watson (Ismene), Jacquelyn Fugell (Arbate), Justin Lavender (Marzio).

Video: Kultur DVD/Home Vision VHS/Pioneer LD. Derek Bailey (director). Color. In Italian with English subtitles. 177 minutes.

Comment: Vick and designer Brown set the opera in a formal fantasy land full of pomp and ritual akin to Japanese Kabuki. The stage production won the Olivier Award for outstanding opera achievement.

MLADA
1890 opera-ballet by Rimsky-Korsakov

Mlada is NIKOLAI RIMSKY-KORSAKOV's gigantic answer to Wagner, a spectacular opera-ballet that requires expensive production values, tricky stage effects, unusual casting, and exotic instrumentation. *Mlada* started as a collaborative project by four of the Famous Five Russian composers but was then abandoned. Rimsky-Korsakov revised Viktor Krylov's libretto many years later, refashioning Slavonic legend as Wagner had refashioned Germanic myths. The heroine Mlada is a nonsinging role for a dancer and is already dead when the opera begins. She was the fiancée of Prince Yaromir but she was murdered by rival prince Mstiovsy. His evil daughter Voislava wants Yaromir for herself. Good and evil fight it out with titanic orchestration and lavish stage effects, and even the ghost of Cleopatra enters the fray. Good wins out, more or less.

***1992 Bolshoi Opera

Russian stage production: Boris Pokrovsky (director), Alexander Lazarev (conductor, Bolshoi Symphony Orchestra and Chorus), Valery Levental (set designer), Andrei Petrov (choreographer).

Cast: Nina Ananiashvili (Princess Mlada), Oleg Kulko (Prince Yaromir), Maria Gavrilova (Princess Voislava), Gleb Nikolsky (Prince Mstivoy), Galina Borisova (Morena), Kirill Nikitin (Soul of Yaromir), Yulia Malkhassiants (Witch).

Video: Teldec VHS/LD. Barrie Gavin (director). Color. In Russian. 139 minutes.

Comment: Massive and inventive Bolshoi Opera production by Pokrovsky; he was 83 at the time.

MLLE. MODISTE
1905 comic opera by Herbert

VICTOR HERBERT's *Mlle. Modiste*, one of his most popular operettas, helped make its star Fritzi Scheff famous, primarily because of its hit song "Kiss Me Again." Herbert had earlier persuaded her to give up her career at the Metropolitan Opera to star in his operettas. Henry Blossom's libretto tells the story of Mlle. Fifi, an employee in a Parisian hat shop who becomes famous as the prima donna Madame Bellini. *Mlle. Modiste*, which has four hit songs, is still occasionally revived; there are three film versions, including one with Scheff.

1930 Kiss Me Again

American feature film: William A. Seiter (director), Paul Perez (screenplay), Lee Garmes (cinematographer), Erno Rapee (music director).

Cast: Bernice Claire (Mlle. Fifi), Walter Pidgeon (Paul de St. Cyr), Edward Everett Horton (René), June Colyer (Marie), Claude Gillingwater (Count), Judith Vosselli (Mme. Cecile).

Technicolor. In English. 76 minutes.

Comment: Enjoyable film that includes the main songs of the stage production. In England it was retitled *The Toast of the Legion*.

1951 NBC Television: Musical Comedy Time

American TV production: William Corrigan (director), Harry Sosnick (conductor, Harry Sosnick Orchestra), Robert Gundlach (set designer), Bernard Schubert (producer).

Cast: Marguerite Piazza (Mlle. Fifi), Fritzi Scheff (Etienne's mother), Brian Sullivan (Etienne), Frank McHugh (Hiram Bell), Mary Boland (Mme. Cecile).

Telecast February 5, 1951, on NBC. Black and white. In English. 60 minutes.

Comment: Scheff was 71 when she returned after 46 years to the operetta that made her famous and was able to sing "Kiss Me Again" one last time.

Silent/related films

1926 Mademoiselle Modiste

Corinne Griffith plays Mlle. Fifi in this silent feature film of the operetta that was screened in cinemas with Herbert's music. Norman Kerry is Etienne, Willard Louis is Hirman Bent, Dorothy Cumming is Marianne, and Rose Dione is Madame Claire. Robert Leonard directed. Black and white. About 70 minutes.

1933 Fifi

Warner Bros., which had the rights to the music, produced an abbreviated version of the operetta in 1933 called simply *Fifi*. Black and white. 20 minutes.

MÖDL, MARTHA
German mezzo and soprano (1912–2001)

Martha Mödl, who began her career as a mezzo-soprano, made her debut as Hansel in *Hansel and Gretel* in Remscheid in 1942 and then sang in Düsseldorf. In 1949 she joined the Hamburg State Opera as a dramatic soprano, and in 1951 she began to sing Wagnerian roles at Bayreuth. She sang the title role in *Carmen* at Covent Garden in 1950 and came to the Metropolitan Opera in 1957 in *Siegfried*. In her later years she returned to mezzo roles and continued to sing onstage into her mid-70s. See ARABELLA (1977), JULIETTA (1969), DIE LUSTIGEN WEIBER VON WINDSOR (1950), POUSSIÈRES D'AMOUR, THE QUEEN OF SPADES (1992), DIE SCHWEIGSAME FRAU (1971), and DER ZIGEUNERBARON (1975).

1984 Doppelgast in Aachen

Mödl, aged 72, talks about her opera career and is shown in scenes from Reimann's *Mélusine* and Euripides's *The*

Trojans. Peter Fuhrmann directed for WDR Television in Germany. Color. In German. 30 minutes.

MOFFO, ANNA
American soprano (1932–)

Anna Moffo was born in Pennsylvania, studied in Rome, and made her debut in Spoleto in 1955 in Don Pasquale. Her American debut came the following year in Chicago as Mimì, and she arrived at the Metropolitan Opera in 1959 as Violetta in *La traviata*. It was this role that won her acclaim for her coloratura versatility; her 1967 LA TRAVIATA video is considered by one critic as the best recording of the opera in any form. In Italy she achieved major recognition through her performance in *Madama Butterfly* on television, and she had her own Italian TV show, *The Anna Moffo Show*, during the 1960s. She appeared as a guest on many American TV shows, including *The Voice of Firestone*, *The Ed Sullivan Show*, and *The Bell Telephone Hour*. Moffo, married to director Mario Lanfranchi, starred in five opera films and a number of non-operatic features. See LA BELLE HÉLÈNE (1974), DIE CSÁRDÁSFÜRSTIN (1971), LUCIA DI LAMMERMOOR (1971), LA SERVA PADRONA (1958), and LA SONNAMBULA (1956*)*.

1950s The Ed Sullivan Show

Moffo was one of the most popular guests on *The Ed Sullivan Show*, appearing on it six times. She is one of the artists featured on the 1996 compilation video *Great Moments in Opera*. See THE ED SULLIVAN SHOW.

1958–1963 Voice of Firestone

Moffo is seen in performance on three programs of *The Voice of Firestone* TV series on the video *Anna Moffo in Opera and Song*. On September 22, 1958, she sings Musetta's Waltz and "Un bel dì" with the orchestra conducted by Howard Barlow. On January 3, 1963, she sings the "Jewel Song" from *Faust* and duets with Richard Merrill on Rodgers and Hammerstein songs, orchestra conducted by Glenn Osser. Her last appearance is on March 10, 1963, singing "Ballatella" from *Pagliacci* and two songs, orchestra led by Arthur Fiedler. Black and white. 30 minutes. VAI VHS.

1960 Austerlitz

Moffo plays Italian opera diva Josephina Grassini, a close friend of Napoleon, in Abel Gance's epic film about Napoleon and the Battle of Austerlitz. Pierre Mondy is Napoleon and the supporting cast includes Claudia Cardinale, Martine Carol, and Leslie Caron. Color. In French. 166 minutes.

Anna Moffo sings the role of Violetta in Mario Lanfranchi's 1967 film of Verdi's opera *La Traviata*.

1962–1967 Bell Telephone Hour

Moffo performs scenes from four operas with partners on *The Bell Telephone Hour* programs telecast from 1962 to 1967: *La bohème* with Richard Tucker, *Don Giovanni* with George London, *Roméo et Juliette* with Sándor Kónya, and *La traviata* with Nicolai Gedda. Donald Voorhees conducts the Bell Telephone Hour Orchestra. Color. 42 minutes. VAI VHS.

1964 The Anna Moffo Show

Moffo hosted this RAI Television show from Rome under the direction of husband Mario Lanfranchi and demonstrated charm and personality as well as a fine voice. The show usually included opera excerpts, often from *La traviata* and *Lucia di Lammermoor*. Black and white. In Italian. Each about 55 minutes.

1965 Ménage all'italiana

Moffo plays the wife of Ugo Tognazzi in this Italian comedy and sings some popular songs. The story is about a man who marries a singer but can't stop chasing other women. Franco Indovina directed. Color. In Italian. 95 minutes.

1969 Il divorzio

Moffo plays opposite Vittorio Gassman in *The Divorce*, an Italian film about a man who leaves his wife to chase younger women; he finds himself replaced by a younger man when he returns home. Romolo Girolami directed for Fair Film. Color. In Italian. 100 minutes.

1969 Una storia d'amore

Moffo stars opposite Gianni Macchia in this rather erotic Italian film released in England as *Love Me, Baby, Love Me!* She plays a woman who falls in love with a playboy while her husband is away. Color. In Italian. 100 minutes.

1970 Weekend Murders

Moffo plays opposite Eveline Stewart and Lance Percival in *Concerto per pistolo solista,* an Italian murder mystery released in the United States as *Weekend Murders*. The plot revolves around an English family's deadly quarrels. Michele Lupo directed. Color. In Italian. 98 minutes.

1970 The Adventurers

Moffo plays opera singer Dania Leonard in this potboiler and gets to sing the aria "Sempre libera" from *La traviata*. The film is based on Harold Robbins's novel about a South American republic with a revolutionary history. Lewis Gilbert directed for Avco Embassy. Color. In English. 171 minutes.

1970 La ragazza di nome Giulio

Moffo plays Lia in this Italian film, released in England as *The Girl Named Jules*. Silvia Dionisio and Gianni Macchia star; Tonino Valeri directed. Color. In Italian. 88 minutes.

1987 Aria

Julien Temple's episode of the opera film *Aria* uses recorded arias from *Rigoletto* as ironic comment about a marital mix-up; Anna Moffo is one of the featured singers. See RIGOLETTO.

MOÏSE ET PHARAON

1827 opera by Rossini

Moïse (Moses) divides the Red Sea and leads the Israelites out of Egypt, including his niece Anaï who is loved by the Pharaoh's son Aménophis. Gioachino Rossini's French grand opera *Moïse et Pharaon, ou le passage de la mer rouge* (Moses and Pharaoh, or the Crossing of the Red Sea) is based on his earlier Italian opera *Mosè in Egitto*. The new libretto by Luigi Balocchi and Etienne de Jouy has more spectacle and three new numbers.

1983 Opéra de Paris

French stage production: Luca Ronconi (director), George Prêtre (conductor, Opéra de Paris Orchestra and Chorus).

Cast: Samuel Ramey (Moïse), Cecilia Gasdia (Anaï), Shirley Verrett (Queen Sinaïde), Jean-Philippe Lafont (Pharaon), Keith Lewis (Aménophis).

Video: Premiere Opera/House of Opera VHS. Yves-André Hubert (director). Color. In Italian. 152 minutes.

MOJICA, JOSÉ
Mexican tenor (1896–1974)

José Mojica, the tenor who became a priest, was Mexico's greatest opera star before Plácido Domingo, and some still admire his films and records. He came from a very poor family, but he was able to begin an opera career in Mexico City in 1916. In 1923 he joined Chicago Opera where he sang until 1930 opposite stars such as Mary Garden and Amelita Galli-Curci. In 1930 he began to make Hollywood movies for Fox. He was promoted as a new Latin lover at the time of his first film *One Mad Kiss,* which was made in English and Spanish versions. The studio was not happy with it, however, and Mojica's other films for them were created strictly for the Spanish-speaking market. Mojica starred in 10 films for Fox between 1930 and 1934, all with musical and operatic elements. When Fox stopped producing Spanish-language films, he continued his career in Mexico and Argentina for another 15 films. He returned to the opera stage in 1940 but gave it up again when his mother died. In 1947 he entered the priesthood and became a missionary, sometimes giving concerts when he needed to raise funds. He published his autobiography *Yo, Pecador* (I, a Sinner) in 1956 as Fray José Francisco de Guadalupe Mojica O.F.M.; it was made into a popular Mexican film in 1965. His only film based on an actual opera is the 1938 *El capitan aventurero,* a version of Manuel Penella's DON GIL DE ALCALÁ. Mojica's American films are listed below plus those Mexican and Argentine films available on video.

1930 One Mad Kiss
In Mojica's first Hollywood film, a musical shot in English, he plays a Spanish outlaw in Spain who battles corrupt official Antonio Moreno and loves dance hall girl Mona Maris. Mojica wrote the title song himself. Marcel Silver directed for Fox with some added sequences by James Tinling. Black and white. 70 minutes.

1930 El precio de un beso
This is the Spanish version of *One Mad Kiss,* directed by James Tinling. The plot is the same, with Mojica besting a corrupt official and winning dance hall girl Mona Maris. Black and white. 71 minutes.

1930 Cuando el amor ríe
Mojica plays a tamer of wild horses in this Spanish remake of the 1922 Fox film *The Love Gambler.* He falls in love with Elvira (Mona Maris), the daughter of the rancher who employs him. David Howard directed. Black and white. 57 minutes. In Spanish.

1931 Hay que casar al principe
A Spanish remake of the 1927 Fox film *Paid to Love* with Mojica playing a Ruritanian prince in Paris and Conchita Montenegro as the woman he loves. He sings popular songs for which he wrote Spanish lyrics. Lewis Seiler directed for Fox. Black and white. In Spanish. 73 minutes.

1931 La ley del harem
Mojica plays an Arabian prince in *The Law of the Harem* opposite Carmen Larrabeita in this Fox remake of the 1928 film *Fazil.* It features popular songs and was directed by Lewis Seiler for Fox. Black and white. In Spanish. 77 minutes.

1931 Mi último amor
Mojica has the Warner Baxter role in this Spanish-language version of the Fox romantic comedy *Their Mad Moment.* He also wrote the Spanish song lyrics. Andrés De Segurola plays Lord Harry and Chandler Sprague directed. Black and white. In Spanish. 77 minutes.

1932 El caballero de la noche
Mojica plays English highwayman Dick Turpin opposite Mona Maris in this musical remake of the 1925 Fox film *Dick Turpin.* Andrés De Segurola has a supporting role and James Tinling directed. Fox. Black and white. In Spanish. 83 minutes.

1933 El rey de los gitanos
The King of the Gypsies features Mojica as a gypsy monarch who has an affair with a princess in disguise. The songs are gypsy-ish in style. Frank Strayer directed for Fox. Black and white. In Spanish. 82 minutes.

1933 La melodia prohibida
Mojica plays a South Sea islander in *The Forbidden Song,* a musical costarring Conchita Montenegro. Frank Strayer directed. Fox. Black and white. In Spanish. 82 minutes.

1934 La cruz y la espada
The Cross and the Sword is said to have influenced Mojica's thinking about the priesthood and religion. He plays Brother Francisco in a story about an 18th-century missionary in California. Frank Strayer directed for Fox. Black and white. In Spanish. 82 minutes.

1934 Un capitan de cosacos
In *A Cossack Captain,* Mojica is a 1910 Russian sea captain who falls in love with a woman he meets on a train. Andrés De Segurola plays a general and John Rein-

hardt directed for Fox. Black and white. In Spanish. 81 minutes.

1934 Las fronteras del amor
Mojica plays a famous opera singer in *The Frontiers of Love* and sings the *Rigoletto* aria "La donna è mobile." Most of the film takes place on a ranch and involves romance rather than opera. Frank Strayer directed for Fox. This was Mojica's last U.S. studio film. Black and white. In Spanish. 82 minutes.

1942 Melodias de las Americas
In *Melodies of the Americas,* an Argentine film musical starring Mojica, he sings modern songs created for the movie. Color. In Spanish. 82 minutes. Live Opera/Opera Dubs VHS.

1952 El portico de la gloria
The Gate of Glory is a Mexican film musical with Mojica singing popular songs. Black and white. In Spanish. 91 minutes. Opera Dubs VHS.

1965 Yo, Pecador
Yo, Pecador (I, a Sinner) is a Mexican film about the life of the tenor based on his autobiography. Much of the film is a flashback showing his film and opera career. See YO, PECADOR.

1966 Seguiré tus pasos
In Mojica's last film *Follow His Steps,* a Mexican production shot in Peru, he plays a Franciscan priest named Father José María who befriends a young boy who was named after him. Alfredo B. Crevenna directed. Color. In Spanish. 95 minutes. Opera Dubs VHS.

MOLIÈRE
French playwright/librettist (1622–1673)

Molière (born Jean-Baptiste Poquelin) is best known for his masterful plays, but he also has an important place in the development of opera. His collaborations with Lully on what came to be known as the *comèdie-ballet* began in 1661 with *Les fâcheux;* it seems to have been an accidental collusion, rather like the birth of musical comedy in America with *The Black Crook*, with Molière's play and Lully's ballet linked together because of a cast shortage. The two worked together for 10 years and even created a *tragédie-ballet*, although Lully's major operas were written by Philippe Quinault. Molière's influence continues to the present day. Richard Strauss's ARIADNE AUF NAXOS was created to be staged with Molière's LE BOURGEOIS GENTILHOMME, and the playwright is a major character in Rolf Liebermann's opera *School for Wives.*

1909 Molière
Georges Grand plays Molière in this silent film biography written by Abel Gance and directed by Léonce Perret. Gance plays the writer as a young man. Black and white. About 15 minutes.

1978 Molière
Ariane Mnouchkine's four-hour film, based on her television production, stars Philippe Caubère as Molière and Mario Gonzáles as Lully. Color. In French. 260 minutes.

2000 Le Roi Danse
Tchéky Karyo plays Molière in this lavish French film about Lully (Boris Terral) directed by Gérard Corbiau. See LE ROI DANSE.

MOLINOS DE VIENTO
1910 zarzuela by Luna

Spanish composer Pablo Luna y Carné is best known for his 1910 zarzuela *Molinos de Vientos* (Windmills) set in the flat landscapes of Holland. It became famous because it was one of the first Spanish zarzuelas to shift away from traditional settings in Spain. An English ship arrives at a small seacoast town, and the sailors compete with the local men for the affection of the local woman. Margot is loved by Romo but she fancies Captain Alberto whose real love is the sea. When he has leave, she tries to follow; Romo persuades her not to go.

1937 Pi film
Spanish feature film: Rosario Pi (director), Agustin Macasoli (cinematographer), Star Films, Barcelona (production).

Cast: Pedro Teroi, Maria Mercader, Maria Gómez, Roberto Font.

Black and white. In Spanish. 88 minutes.

1996 Teatro Calderón, Madrid
Spanish stage production: José Luis Moreno (director), José A. Irasforza (conductor, Teatro Calderón Orchestra and Chorus), Julian Perez Muñoz (set designer), Alhambra Ballet.

Cast: Rosa Martin (Margot), Mario Valdivieso (Captain Alberto), Carlos Durán (Romo), Enrique del Portal (Cabo Stock), Pepa Rosado (Sabina).

Video: Metrovideo VHS. José Ignado Ortega (director). Telecast live by RTVE. Color. In Spanish. 72 minutes.

Comment: Good basic production with excellent dance numbers by the Alhambra Ballet.

MOLL, KURT
German bass (1938–)

Kurt Moll became well known singing the bass roles in Wagner operas, but he is also impressive in Mozart, Verdi, and Strauss. He made his debut in 1961 in Aachen, joined the Hamburg Staatsoper in 1970, and was then invited to sing at opera houses from Paris to Bayreuth. He made his debut at Covent Garden in 1977 and at the Metropolitan in 1978. Many of his great Wagner and Mozart performances are on video. See DON GIOVANNI (1990), DIE ENTFÜHRUNG AUS DEM SERAIL (1987), LE NOZZE DI FIGARO (1980), PARSIFAL (1992), DAS RHEINGOLD (1989), DER ROSENKAVALIER (1982/1984/1994), DIE SCHÖPFUNG (1986), DIE SCHWEIGSAME FRAU (1971), SIEGFRIED (1989), TRISTAN UND ISOLDE (1998), DER WAFFENSCHMIED (1982), DIE WALKÜRE (1989, Met and Bavaria), WOZZECK (1972), and DIE ZAUBERFLÖTE (1983/1991, Met and Groot).

MONICELLI, MARIO
Italian film director (1915–)

Mario Monicelli, who directed an excellent film biography of ROSSINI in 1991, also created a delightful operatic comedy with an unusual use of Italian opera language. He is best known in America for his 1956 comedy *I soliti ignoti* (shown in the United States as *Big Deal on Madonna Street*) and the 1963 union film *I compagni* (The Organizer). He was nominated for Oscars for his screenplays for *The Organizer* and *Casanova '70*.

1965 Casanova '70
Monicelli has fun sending up the oddities and pretensions of Italian operatic language in this film. A Swedish woman visiting Italy arouses merriment whenever she talks because she has learned the language from listening to Italian opera and always speaks in a flowery operatic style. Marcello Mastroianni stars as a modern Casanova who is interested in women only if there is danger involved. Color. In Italian. 113 minutes.

MONIUSZKO, STANISLAW
Polish composer (1819–1872)

Stanislaw Moniuszko is the major 19th-century Polish opera composer, and his opera HALKA (1848) has become the Polish national opera; most of his work is nationalist and patriotic. He studied in Berlin and began writing operettas in 1839, the best known being *The Lottery*. *Halka* was staged as a two-act opera in 1848 and revised to four acts for its first major production in Warsaw in 1858. It made him an national celebrity and he had great success with his following operas, *The Raftsman* and *The Countess*, but THE HAUNTED MANOR (1865) was taken off the stage because of its ultra-patriotism. While Moniuszko's operas and songs remain popular in Poland, they are little known in the rest of the world. Both *Halka* and *The Haunted Manor* have been filmed and are on video and CD.

MONK, MEREDITH
American composer (1943–)

Meredith Monk is a multifaceted multimedia artist-performer whose sometimes wordless "operas" may not be traditional but are certainly theatrical. *Juice,* her 1969 "theatre cantata," is scored for 85 voices, 85 Jew's harps, and two violins. Her 1973 "opera" *Education of the Girlchild,* is for women's voices, electric organ, and piano. Her three-hour opera *Atlas,* staged by Houston Grand Opera in 1991, tells of explorer Alexandra David-Neel, whose journeys are spiritual as well as geographic. Monk also says that her 1989 film *Book of Days* is operatic.

1983 4 American Composers: Meredith Monk
Peter Greenaway shot this documentary portrait of Monk around theater performances in London. She talks about her ideas, films, music, and operas, and there are excerpts from the opera *Education of a Girlchild* and the films *Quarry* and *Ellis Island*. Monk performs with her vocal group on *Dolmen Music* and *Turtle Dreams*. Channel Four/Transatlantic Films. Color. 60 minutes. Mystic Fire VHS.

1989 Book of Days
Monk's film is a musical meditation on time and history and the connections of past and present. It is centered around a young Jewish woman in a medieval village who has visions of life during the 20th century and tries to describe them to her grandfather. She dies in a plague, but her drawings of airplanes and guns are found in our time. Black and white and color. In English. 77 minutes.

MONROE, MARILYN
American film actress (1926–1962)

Marilyn Monroe, the greatest myth figure of the modern cinema, has been transmuted from a real person into a mythical being who combines glamour with vulnerability. Excellent as she was in her best movies, such as *Some Like It Hot* and *Gentleman Prefer Blondes,* it is Monroe's persona as an innocent with sexuality that has made her mythic. She projects the image of someone who needs to be protected, and her relationships with Joe DiMaggio, Arthur Miller, and the Kennedy brothers helped bolster the legend. She has inspired countless poems, books, and paintings and two operas that have been staged.

1980 Marilyn

Italian Lorenzo Ferrero composed his Fellini-esque opera about Monroe to a libretto by Floriana Bossi and himself. Subtitled "Scenes From the Fifties, after Documents From American Life," it shows Monroe's life against the background of events of the 1950s, including the Korean War, McCarthyism, and the persecution of Wilhelm Reich during the first half of the decade, and alternative cultural heroes such as Timothy Leary, Allen Ginsberg, and Beat writers during the second. Monroe's life disintegrates and she is shown rocking a doll to sleep after taking a drug overdose. The opera premiered at the Rome Opera House on February 23, 1980.

1993 Marilyn

American Ezra Laderman composed his documentary-like opera about Monroe to a libretto by playwright Norman Rosten. It consists of scenes from her life seen as flashbacks, memories, and dreams, although it avoids naming real people. It premiered at the New York City Opera on October 6, 1993, with Kathryn Gamberoni as Monroe, Michael Rees Davis as the Senator, Ron Baker as the Psychiatrist, Philip Cokorinos as husband Rick, Susanne Marsee as Rose, Michele McBride as Vinnie, and John Lankston and Jonathan Green as Movie Moguls. Jerome Sirlin staged and designed the opera, V. Jane Suttell created the costumes, and Hal France conducted the New York City Opera Orchestra.

MONSIEUR CHOUFLEURI RESTERA CHEZ LUI LE...

1861 opérette-bouffe by Offenbach

Monsieur Choufleuri restera chez lui le... (Mr. Cauliflower Will Be at Home on...) is a delightful one-act operetta by JACQUES OFFENBACH and librettist Conte de Morny. It's the story of a man trying to break into Paris society through a musical soirée. When the singers don't appear, he and his daughter and her boyfriend impersonate them. The highlight of the operetta is a mock Italian trio called "Italia la bella."

1951 NBC Opera Theatre

American TV production: Samuel Chotzinoff (director), Peter Herman Adler (conductor, NBC Symphony of the Air Orchestra), Dino Yannopoulos (English adaptation).

Cast: Larry Weber (Offenbach), Virginia Haskins, Paul Franke, George Irving.

Video at the MTR. Kirk Browning (director). Black and white. In English. 50 minutes.

Comment: This English-language adaptation, retitled *RSVP*, was produced as if Offenbach were imagining the operetta.

MONSTERS OF GRACE

1998 screen opera by Glass and Wilson

Composer PHILIP GLASS and designer ROBERT WILSON's *Monsters of Grace*, described as a "digital opera in three dimensions," is the first opera to require 3D glasses. Three-dimensional film images range from helicopters over the Himalayas to a hand being mutilated, from a polar bear sleeping to a table with bowls and chopsticks. There is no narrative. The opera premiered at UCLA's Royce Hall in Los Angeles on April 15, 1998, with 3D computer animation as part of its visuals. The lyrics, by 13th-century Persian mystic Jelaluddin Rumi (translated by Coleman Barks), were sung by Marie Mascari, Alexandra Montano, Gregory Purnhagen, and Peter Stewart. Michael Riesman led the Philip Glass Ensemble, and the film and computer elements were created by Diana Walczak and Jeff Kleiser. Jedediah Wheeler produced.

MONTALDO, GIULIANO

Italian film/opera director (1930–)

Giuliano Montaldo, one of the best modern Italian film directors, known abroad primarily for his 1953 film *Chronicle of Poor Lovers,* has also directed a number of operas on stage. Two of his productions at Arena di Verona are on video, ATTILA (1985) and TURANDOT (1983).

MONTARSOLO, PAOLO

Italian bass (1925–)

Paolo Montarsolo, a stylish basso buffo specialist, has appeared on stage in more than 185 roles and can be seen in a number of films and videos. He was born in Portici, studied at Teatro alla Scala school, and made his debut in Bologna in 1950. In 1957 he appeared at Glyndebourne in *L'italiana in Algeri,* and in 1959 he starred in *Gianni Schicchi* at La Scala. Although he sang in Dallas in 1957, he did not reach the Metropolitan Opera until 1975 when he starred in *Don Pasquale.* Among his most popular roles are Basilio, Bartolo, Magnifico, Mustafa, Don Pasquale, and Umberto. See IL BARBIERE DI SIVIGLIA (1972), LA CENERENTOLA (1981), COSÌ FAN TUTTE (1988), L'ELISIR D'AMORE (1959), LE NOZZE DI FIGARO (1976), and LA SERVA PADRONA (1958).

MONTEMEZZI, ITALO

Italian composer (1875–1952)

Italo Montemezzi is remembered today for only one opera, the 1913 L'AMORE DEI TRE RE (The Love of Three Kings). It was a big hit at La Scala, the Met, and Covent Garden during the early years of the century and remained popular for many years, but it is currently out of fashion. Montemezzi's other major opera is the 1918 *La Nave*, based on a famous play by Gabriele D'Annunzio.

MONTEVERDI, CLAUDIO
Italian composer (1567–1643)

Claudio Monteverdi is the earliest opera composer whose work is still in the repertory. He wrote his first opera, ORFEO, in 1607, only a few years after the art form had been created, and nearly 400 years later it is still being staged. Monteverdi was born in Cremona, began his career in Mantua, and spent most of his later years in Venice where he helped make opera spectacular and grandiose. Although he wrote about 18 operas, only three survive complete. All are in the modern repertory and available on video. *Orfeo*, L'INCORONAZIONE DI POPPEA, and IL RITORNO D'ULISSE IN PATRIA received notable Zurich stage productions during the 1970s from director Jean-Pierre Ponnelle and conductor Nikolaus Harnoncourt, and these productions were later filmed..

1989 New Voices for Man
Monteverdi and the growth of opera are central to *New Voices for Man*, the third volume in the Canadian TV series *The Music of Man*. The program includes scenes from *Orfeo* and a history of the composer. Yehudi Menuhin narrates. Color. In English. 60 minutes. Home Vision VHS.

1989 Vespro della Beata Vergine
Monteverdi's life as a composer is described by John Elliot Gardiner as he travels around Venice; afterward he leads a performance of the *Vespers of the Blessed Virgin* in St. Mark's Basilica with the Monteverdi Choir, London Oratory Junior Choir, His Majesties Sagbutts and Cornetts, and the English Baroque Soloists. The soloists are sopranos Ann Monoyios and Marinella Pennicchi; countertenor Michael Chance; tenors Mark Tucker, Nigel Robson, and Sandro Naglio; and basses Bryn Terfel and Alastair Miles. Color. In English and Latin. 111 minutes. Archiv VHS.

1993 Banquet of the Senses
This is a program of Monteverdi madrigals presented like mini-operas at the palace of the Duke of Mantua where they were composed. They are performed by Anthony Rooley's Consort of Musike with sopranos Emma Kirby and Evelyn Tubb, tenors Andrew King and Joseph Cornwell, alto Mary Nichols, and bass Simon Grant. Rooley provides the commentary and directed the video, which counterpoints the singing with scenes of the palace. Color. In Italian. 60 minutes. Brilliant Classics DVD/Musica Oscura and Columns Classics VHS.

1996 Monteverdi in Mantua
A documentary about Monteverdi and the music he composed during his years with the Gonzago family in Mantua, including the opera *Orfeo*. Part of the series *Man and Music*. Color. 53 minutes. Films for the Humanities & Sciences VHS.

MONTEZUMA
1733 opera by Vivaldi

Aztec Emperor Montezuma is captured by Cortez and his Spanish troops, but he refuses to accept Christianity. A compromise is worked out, and he survives, unlike the real Montezuma, who was murdered. Antonio Vivaldi's opera *Montezuma*, libretto by Girolamo Giusti, was reconstituted by Jean-Claude Malgoire in 1992, as only the libretto had survived.

1992 Atelier Lyrique de Tourcoing
French stage production: Jean-Claude Malgoire (director and conductor, La Grande Écurie and La Chambre du Roy).
Cast: Dominique Visse (Montezuma), Nicolas Rivenq (Cortez), Danielle Borst (Mitrena), Isabelle Poulenard (Teutile), Brigitte Balleys (Ramiro), Luis Masson (Asprano).
Video: House of Opera DVD/VHS. Color. In Italian. 120 minutes.

MOONLIGHT MURDER
1936 American film with opera content

At the dress rehearsal for a Hollywood Bowl production of Verdi's *Il trovatore*, opera tenor Gino D'Acosta (Leo Carrillo) is accosted by a swami who warns that if he sings the next day, he will die. He doesn't take it seriously but he should have, especially after having been attacked by a mad composer (J. Carrol Naish), whose new opera he has ignored. Conductor Godfrey Chiltern, (H. B. Warner) also has reason to hate the tenor, who had had a affair with his wife. After D'Acosta collapses and dies on stage during the second act of *Il trovatore*, detective Steve Farrell (Chester Morris) has to find the person whodunit. The mad composer is the obvious suspect, but it turns out that poison gas was used for a misguided mercy killing. The Bowl itself got the best reviews when this low-budget mystery opened ("the best part of the film is the setting," said *Variety*). The lengthy selections from *Il trovatore* are sung by voice double Alfonso Pedroza, and the onstage opera sequences were arranged by Wilhelm von Wymetal Jr. Florence Ryerson and Edgar Allan Woolf wrote the screenplay, Charles Clarke was the cinematographer, and Edward R. Marin directed for MGM. Black and white. 80 minutes.

MOONSTRUCK
1987 American film with opera content

Moonstruck, one of the most enjoyable Hollywood films of recent years, is virtually an homage to *La bohème.* It begins in front of the Metropolitan Opera as *La bohème* billboards are put up, and from then on it focuses on different kinds of romantic love. Cher plays a young Italian-American widow who has agreed to marry the older Danny Aiello although she looks at the marriage unromantically. Then she meets his baker brother Nicolas Cage, and wham, they fall into bed. I love you, he says. Get over it, she tells him, and gives him a slap in the face. He says he won't leave her alone unless she goes to the opera with him that evening. She finally agrees, and he takes her see *La bohème* at the Met. They see part of Act III with Renata Tebaldi and Carlo Bergonzi singing and Martha Collins and John Fanning acting (the stage scenes were shot in Toronto and directed by Lotfi Mansouri). They also see Cher's father Vincent Gardenia with a woman who is not her mother, and father and daughter both realize the other is having an affair. The mother, Olympia Dukakis, is meanwhile giving good advice to John Mahoney, another older man who likes seducing young women students. Meanwhile, Feodor Chaliapin, who plays Cher's father-in-law and lives upstairs, keeps feeding his meals to his dogs. True love wins out in the end all round. Music from *La bohème* is also featured on the soundtrack, including Musetta's Waltz and Mimì's Farewell. John Patrick Shanley wrote the superb screenplay, David Watkin was the cinematographer, and Norman Jewison was the director. *Moonstruck* got six Academy Award nominations, including Best Picture, and Shanley, Cher, and Dukakis won Oscars. Color. In English. 103 minutes. On DVD and VHS.

Moonstruck (1987): Cher and Nicolas Cage at the Metropolitan Opera in Norman Jewison's Oscar-winning film.

MOORE, DOUGLAS
American composer (1893–1969)

Douglas Moore wrote 12 operas, mostly on American subjects, and was one of the chief architects of modern American opera. He had his biggest success with the 1956 Colorado silver mine romance THE BALLAD OF BABY DOE, which for a time was considered the great American opera. His other popular operas include *The Devil and Daniel Webster* (1938), based on a Stephen Vincent Benét story; and *Carrie Nation* (1966), a portrait of the ax-wielding anti-saloon campaigner. He won the Pulitzer Prize for *Giants in the Earth* (1949), based on a novel about a pioneer family in South Dakota, but it has never been popular. He also wrote music for films. *The Ballad of Baby Doe* and his delightful short "soap opera" GALLANTRY have been telecast, and *Ballad* and *Carrie Nation* have been recorded, but surprisingly there are no commercial videos of Moore's operas.

MOORE, GRACE
American soprano (1898–1947)

Glamorous Tennessee-born American opera diva Grace Moore became a major movie star at Columbia during the 1930s, and her success created a new audience for opera as well as a rush of singers to Hollywood. None of the others quite repeated her success, but the trend did ensure that many opera singers of the period can be seen on film. Moore began her career very successfully in musical comedy and operetta in New York and then went to France to study opera. She made her Metropolitan Opera debut in 1928 as Mimì in *La bohème* (it was a major social event after her Broadway success), and she was again successful, continuing to sing at the Met until 1946. Her first Hollywood films were made for MGM, a JENNY LIND biography called *A Lady's Morals* and the operetta NEW MOON, but they were not hits. After she starred on the New York stage in 1932 in a production of Millöcker's operetta DIE DUBARRY, Columbia gave her a second chance. ONE NIGHT OF LOVE was a critical and box-office hit, surprising even the studio and winning an Oscar nomination for the singer. Moore continued to make Hollywood films through the 1930s and then went to France to make a film of her favorite opera, LOUISE. She also took on Dorothy Kirsten as her protégé and published an autobiography called *You're Only Human Once.* She died in a plane crash in Denmark in 1947 while on a concert tour. Hollywood honored her with a film biography in 1953 titled *So This Is Love.*

1934 One Night of Love
Moore's best film with delightful operatic sequences including a balcony "Sempre libera," with Moore singing to a courtyard, and a *Lucia di Lammermoor* sextet, di-

verting a landlady from collecting the rent. Moore looks wonderful, acts splendidly, and sings superbly as an aspiring opera singer who ends up at the Met. See ONE NIGHT OF LOVE.

1935 Love Me Forever
Moore plays a poor but talented soprano who gets to sing in *La bohème* at the Met opposite Michael Bartlett with the help of music-loving gangster Leo Carrillo. The film features a mockup of the old Met while the *Rigoletto* quartet is expanded from four to 40 voices. See LOVE ME FOREVER.

Met soprano Grace Moore was one of the most popular opera singers in Hollywood movies in the 1930s.

1935 Broadway Highlights No. 2
Moore is one of the stars featured in this short Paramount Pictures film made by Fred Waller. Rosa Ponselle also appears. Black and white. 10 minutes.

1936 The King Steps Out
Josef von Sternberg directed Moore in this musical based on Fritz Kreisler's 1932 Vienna operetta *Sissy*. She plays Elizabeth (Sissy), daughter of the Duke of Bavaria. Moore is in terrific frothy Viennese operetta voice and gets to sing quite a lot, including the operetta's famous "Stars in My Eyes." Franchot Tone is Emperor Franz Josef, whom she marries in the end. This was a precursor of the famous Romy Schneider *Sissi* films of the 1950s. Columbia. Black and white. In English. 85 minutes.

1937 When You're in Love
Moore is an Austrian opera star who pays Cary Grant to be her husband so she can sing in America. Naturally, they fall in love by the end of the movie. Moore sings "Vissi d'arte" from *Tosca*, "Un bel dì" from *Madama Butterfly,* and the "Waltz Song" from *Roméo et Juliette*. See WHEN YOU'RE IN LOVE.

1937 I'll Take Romance
Moore's last American film. She plays an opera diva romanced by Melvyn Douglas in a plot basically about where she will sing. It has arias from *La traviata, Martha, Manon,* and *Madama Butterfly*. See I'LL TAKE ROMANCE.

1953 So This Is Love
Kathryn Grayson plays Moore in this glossy film biography that finishes on stage at the Met with Moore as Mimì in *La bohème*. Most of the film concerns Moore's early success as a Broadway star and decision to study opera. See SO THIS IS LOVE.

MORENO TORROBA, FEDERICO
Spanish composer (1891–1982)

Federico Moreno Torroba composed many operas, but he is mostly remembered for his zarzuelas, especially the 1932 LUISA FERNANDA. The Madrid-born musician was also an important newspaper critic and a much-admired conductor. At the age of 80, he conducted 13 classic zarzuelas for a major Spanish television film series called *Teatro Lirico Español*. At the age of 89 he wrote his last opera, EL POETA, on a commission from Plácido Domingo, who starred in the premiere in 1980.

MORITZ, REINER
German opera video producer (1941–)

Reiner Moritz is relatively unknown to the opera public but is one of the key people in the filming and distribution of opera on video. He is the founder of RM Arts, and it is often up to him to decide whether there will be a telecast and video of a production. Moritz, based in Munich, has been working in television for 35 years. Many of the videos in this book were created through RM Arts.

MORRIS, JAMES
American bass-baritone (1947–)

James Morris studied with Rosa Ponselle in his native Baltimore and made his debut there in 1967 in *Les contes d'Hoffmann*. He joined the Metropolitan Opera in 1970 as the king in *Aida* and then sang in many Met productions. He achieved international success in Wagner's RING, singing Wotan in the cycle in Europe and America. His imposing voice and presence make him particularly suitable in this role, and he can be seen in it on video in the 1990 Met productions of DAS RHEINGOLD, DIE WALKÜRE, and SIEGFRIED. See ANNA BOLENA (1984), BILLY BUDD (1997), LA BOHÈME (1982), LES CONTES D'HOFFMANN (1988), DON GIOVANNI (1978), FAUST (1985), LUISA MILLER (1979), MACBETH (1972/1987),

MARIA STUARDA (2000), DIE MEISTERSINGER VON NÜRNBERG (2001), METROPOLITAN OPERA (1975), MOZART (1991), and OTELLO (1995).

1996 James Levine's Silver Anniversary Gala
Morris is one of the singers participating in James Levine's 25th anniversary telecast Met gala See JAMES LEVINE.

MOSES UND ARON
1930–1957 opera by Schoenberg

As Moses and Aaron lead the Israelites out of Egypt to the Promised Land, the people despair as they wait for the Ten Commandments and erect and worship a Golden Calf while Moses is on the mountain. *Moses and Aron,* a deeply religious work, is the most often staged of ARNOLD SCHOENBERG's operas, although it has never been popular with the public. It was begun in 1930, but Schoenberg continued revising it until his death and never really finished it; a concert version premiered in Hamburg in 1954 and it was first staged in 1957. Moses is a speaking part, Aaron is a tenor, and the voice of God is six singers. Note: Aaron is called Aron in the opera, because the composer was superstitious about a title with 12 letters.

Moses und Aron (1975): Moses (Günter Reich) confronts Aron (Louis Devos) in the austere Straub/Huillet film of the opera.

1975 Straub/Huillet film
German feature film: Jean-Marie Straub and Danièle Huillet (directors/screenplay); Michael Gielen (conductor, ORF Austrian Television Orchestra and Chorus); Ugo Piccone, Saverio Diamanti, Gianni Canfarelli, Renato Berta (cinematographers); Jocken Ulrich (choreographer); Renata Morroni and Guerriono Todero (costume designers).

Cast: Günter Reich (Moses), Louis Devos (Aron), Werner Mann (Priest), Eva Csapá (Young Woman), Roger Lucas (Young Man).

Video: Opera Dubs VHS. Color. In German with English subtitles. 105 minutes.

Comment: This is one of the most demanding of all opera films and has never been popular, although it was widely shown at festivals. Straub and Huillet, who emphasize the philosophical rather than the dramatic content of the opera, shot it on location in an ancient Roman amphitheater in the south of Italy. Everything in the film is said to be authentic, even the blood, and originally they would not even allow it to be subtitled.

MOTHER OF US ALL, THE
1947 pageant opera by Thomson

Susan B. Anthony struggles to obtain rights for women during the 19th century and encounters famous people who support or oppose her work. Virgil Thomson's pageant opera *The Mother of Us All,* libretto by Gertrude Stein with scenario by Maurice Grosser, was rejected by the major New York opera companies, so its premiere was held at Columbia University. The music is tonal, tuneful, and very American, incorporating 19th-century songs, folk ballads, gospel hymns, and marches. *The Mother of Us All,* which has been revived many times, is now recognized as one of the masterpieces of American opera, but it has not been released on commercial video.

1976 Chicago Opera Theater
American stage production: Frank Galati (director), Robert Frisbie (conductor, Chicago Opera Studio Orchestra), Mary Griswold (set/costume designer), Peter Amster (choreographer).

Cast: Judith Erickson (Susan B. Anthony), Robert Orth (Virgil T.), Anne Irving (Gertrude S.), Adrienne Passen (Anne), William Martin (Jo the Loiterer), William Eichorn (President John Adams), Carol Gutknecht (Constance Fletcher), Warren Fremling (Daniel Webster), Clayton Hochhalter (Thaddeus Stevens), Steven Emanuel (Chris the Citizen), Maria Lagios (Angel More), Dalia Bach (Indiana Elliot), Vittorio Giammarrusco (Andrew Johnson), Douglas Kiddie (Anthony Comstock), Robert Heitzinger (Gloster Heming).

Telecast March 3, 1977, on Central Education Network. David Erdman (director). Color. In English. 64 minutes.

1976 Santa Fe Opera
American stage production: Peter Wood (director), Raymond Leppard (conductor, Santa Fe Opera Orchestra), Robert Indiana (set designer).

Cast: Mignon Dunn (Susan B. Anthony), Gene Ives (Virgil T.), Aviva Orvath (Gertrude S.), Ashley Putnam (Angel More), Batyah Godfrey (Anne), James Atherton (Jo the Loiterer), William Lewis (President John Adams), Helen Vanni (Constance Fletcher), Philip Booth (Daniel Webster), Douglas Perry (Thaddeus Stevens), Joseph McKee (Chris the Citizen), Linn Maxwell (Indiana Elliot), Karen Beck (Lillian Russell), Steven Loewengart (Ulysses S. Grant), David W. Fuller (Anthony Comstock), Billie Nash (Henrietta M.), Ronald Raines (Henry B.).

Telecast July 5, 1977, on PBS. David Cheshire (director). Color. In English. 90 minutes.

Related film

1986 Virgil Thomson at 90
John Huszar's documentary features Thomson talking about the origins of *The Mother of Us All* and includes photographic scenes from various productions. See VIRGIL THOMPSON.

MOVIETONE
Sound-on-film system

Movietone was the first Hollywood studio sound system using sound-on-film, as it is done today, in contrast to the Vitaphone system, which used synchronized discs. Movietone shorts were made by Fox (which developed the process), MGM, and Paramount during the period 1928 to 1930 and were meant to compete with Warner's Vitaphone shorts; several of them featured opera singers in performance. The success of this sound-on-film system led to the abandonment of the sound-on-disc system. See RICHARD BONELLI, MARIA KURENKO, TITTA RUFFO, and TITO SCHIPA.

MOZART, WOLFGANG A.
Austrian composer (1756–1791)

Wolfgang Amadeus Mozart is arguably the greatest opera composer and unquestionably the most favored by filmmakers. There are numerous screen versions of his operas and nearly as many biographies. The most impressive videos as a group are the Drottningholm Court Theatre productions in which Arnold Östman and his colleagues restore period charm to Mozart. Two of the best opera films are Ingmar Bergman's version of *The Magic Flute* (in Swedish) and Joseph Losey's *Don Giovanni* (set around Venice). Mozart's music is also used in countless non-operatic films. The biographical films, which began in 1909, are romanticized but usually interesting for their musical scenes. See LA CLEMENZA DI TITO, COSÌ FAN TUTTE, DON GIOVANNI, DIE ENTFÜHRUNG AUS DEM SERAIL, LA FINTA GIARDINIERA, IDOMENEO, MITRIDATE, MOZART AND SALIERI, MOZART REQUIEM, LE NOZZE DI FIGARO, IL RE PASTORE, DER SCHAUSPIELDIREKTOR, and DIE ZAUBERFLÖTE.

Biographical films

1909 Mozart's Last Requiem
French director Louis Feuillade's silent film *La Mort de Mozart*, released in America as *Mozart's Last Requiem*, is the first film biography of the composer. Mozart feels compelled to write a Requiem Mass as he thinks death is near, but his doctor orders him to rest. While listening to a student play violin, he has visions of scenes from *Le nozze di Figaro, Don Giovanni*, and *The Magic Flute*. He cannot resist working on his *Requiem*, and when it is finished, a group of friends visit him. They sing the *Requiem* and he dies. The film was produced by Gaumont, distributed in the United States by George Kleine, and screened with Mozart's music. Black and white. About 15 minutes. Prints survive in archives.

1921 Mozarts Leben, Lieben und Leiden
Mozart's Life, Love and Suffering is a silent feature-length Austrian film biography starring Josef Zetenius as Mozart and Dora Kaiser as Constance. The cast includes Lili Fröhlich, Alice Grobois, Käte Schindler, Paul Gerhardt, and Mizzi Trentin. Otto Kreisler and Karl Toma directed the film, which premiered at the Mozart Week celebrations in Salzburg in 1921. Black and white. About 75 minutes.

1936 Whom the Gods Love
Stephen Haggard plays Mozart in this British film biography, and Victoria Hopper is Mozart's wife. The film revolves around scenes from Mozart's life, including his wife's wooing by a prince. See WHOM THE GODS LOVE.

1939 Eine Kleine Nachtmusik
A Little Night Music is a German film based on a charming short novel by Eduard Mörike called (in English) *Mozart on the Road to Prague*. It describes an imaginary stopover the composer made in 1787 while on his way to Prague for the premiere of *Don Giovanni*. Hannes Stelzer plays Mozart with a cast that includes Christl Mardayn, Heli Finkenzeller, Gustav Waldau, and Kurt Meisel. The score consists of Mozart music arranged by Alois Melichar. Leopold Hainisch directed. Black and white. In German. 92 minutes.

1940 Melodie eterne
Eternal Melodies is an Italian film biography directed by opera film specialist Carmine Gallone and starring Gino Cervi as Mozart. Luisella Beghi is Constanze, Conchita Montenegro is Aloysia, Maria Jacobini is mother Anna Maria Mozart, Jone Salinas is sister Nannina Mozart, and

Luigi Pavese is father Leopoldo Mozart. The story revolves around Mozart's relationship with the Weber sisters from his early years to his years of great success. Mozart arias are sung on the soundtrack by Margherita Carosio; Ernest Marischka wrote the screenplay, and Achise Brizze was cinematographer. Black and white. In Italian. 99 minutes.

1942 Wen die Götter lieben
Whom the Gods Love, an Austrian film biography starring Hans Holt as Mozart, tells the story of the composer's life from the time he leaves Salzburg with the focus on his relationship with the Weber sisters. Winnie Markus plays Constanze, Irene von Meyendorff is her sister, Walter Janssen is Leopold Mozart, Curt Jurgens is Emperor Franz Josef II, and René Deltgen is Beethoven. There are several opera scenes, including *The Abduction From the Seraglio, Don Giovanni, Le nozze di Figaro,* and *The Magic Flute* (a memorable scene with Erna Berger as Queen of the Night); the music is played by the Vienna Philharmonic Orchestra conducted by Alois Melichar. There is also a nonhistorical visit by the young Beethoven to the dying Mozart. Günther Anders was the cinematographer, Eduard von Borsody wrote the screenplay based on a novel by Richard Billinger, and Karl Hartl directed for Wien Film. Also known as *Mozart.* Black and white. In German. 112 minutes. Taurus (Germany) VHS.

1948 The Mozart Story
This American adaptation of the 1942 Austrian film *Wen die Götter lieben* is almost a different film with an added framing structure featuring Salieri and Haydn; it may have been a prototype for *Amadeus* as it begins with Salieri describing the events of Mozart's life after his death. Envy has caused Salieri to oppose Mozart, but he now wants to preserve Mozart's music and reputation. There are scenes from *The Abduction From the Seraglio, Don Giovanni, Le nozze di Figaro,* and *The Magic Flute* with music performed by the Vienna Philharmonic. Karl Hartl directed the original film, which was adapted for America by George Moskov and Frank Wisbar. Hans Holt plays Mozart with Winnie Markus as Constanze, Irene von Meyendorff as her sister, Walter Janssen as Leopold, Curt Jurgens as Emperor Franz Josef II, Wilton Graff as Salieri, William Vedder as Haydn, and René Deltgen as Beethoven. Black and white. In English. 93 minutes. Opera Dubs/Video Yesteryear VHS.

1955 Reich mir die Hand, mein Leben
Reich mir die Hand, mein Leben (English title: *The Life and Loves of Mozart*) is an Austrian film starring Oskar Werner as Mozart; it was written and directed by Karl Hartl, who made the 1942 Mozart film *Wen die Götter lieben.* Mozart is shown at the end of his life composing

The Magic Flute and the *Requiem* and having a love affair with Nannina Gottlieb (Johanna Mata), who created the role of Pamina. Gertrud Kueckelman is Constanze, Nadja Tiller is Aloysia, Erich Kunz is Schikaneder, and Albin Skoda is Salieri. The singing voices of Hilde Gueden, Erika Köth, Gottlob Frick, Erich Kunz, Else Liebesberg, and Anton Dermota are heard on the soundtrack with Hans Swarowsky conducting the Vienna Philharmonic Orchestra and State Opera Chorus. Oskar Schnirch was the cinematographer. Color. In German. 100 minutes. Bel Canto Society VHS (dubbed in English).

1967 Das Leben Mozarts
The Life of Mozart is an exemplary nonfiction German film about Mozart made by Hans Conrad Fischer, a finely researched survey of the composer's life and music using original letters, documents, paintings, and even buildings. There are no reenactments, but there are photographs of places and cities associated with the composer all over Europe. Portraits of the period alternate with performances of Mozart's music by leading singers, orchestras, and conductors, including Fritz Wunderlich, Erika Köth, Maria Stader, Fiorenza Cossotto, Walter Berry, and Lotte Schädle. Black and white. In German. 140 minutes. Hänssler (Germany) VHS.

1974 Mozart: A Childhood Chronicle
Mozart: Autzeichnungen einer Jugend is an impressive German film by Klaus Kirchner depicting the composer from ages 7 to 20 as he travels around Europe by coach; the off-screen narrative is based on letters written by Mozart and his family. Pavlos Bekiaris plays Mozart at 7, Diego Crovetti plays him at 12, and Santiago Ziesmer is the composer at 20. Marianne Lowitz is Mozart's mother, Karl-Maria Schley is his father, and Ingeborg Schroeder and Nina Palmers play sister Nannerl aged 11 and 17. The soundtrack voices belong to Helen Donath, Eugenia Ratti, and Graziella Sciutti; Mozart's music is played on authentic instruments. Pitt Koch was the cinematographer. Black and white. In German with English subtitles. 224 minutes. Kino VHS/LD.

1975 Mozart in Love
American filmmaker Mark Rappaport's avant-garde Mozart biography may not resemble the standard biopic, but it is still intriguing, funny, and sometimes inspired. The composer's intense interest in the Weber sisters Aloysia and Constanze is the focus of the film, with actors in costume standing in front of backdrop projections and miming their roles. Arias from Mozart operas are the basis of the soundtrack. Color. 80 minutes.

1984 Noi tre

Noi tre (The Three of Us) is a charming Italian film by Pupi Avati about 14-year-old Mozart and the summer he spent in Bologna in 1770. Taken there by his father to prepare for an examination at the Philharmonic Institute, he stays at the country estate of a count. He becomes friends with the count's son and a girl neighbor and enjoys non-genius life so much that he tries to flunk the exam. Christopher Davidson plays Mozart, Lino Capolicchio is his father Leopoldo, Dario Parsini is the young friend, and Barbara Rebeschini is the girl. Color. In Italian. 90 minutes.

1984 Amadeus

This famous film biography of the composer was directed by Milos Forman from a superb screenplay by Peter Shaffer based on his play. Tom Hulce plays Mozart, F. Murray Abraham is Salieri, and Elizabeth Berridge is Constanze. See AMADEUS.

1985 Vergesst Mozart

Forget Mozart is a German film structured like a murder mystery and set on December 5, 1791, the day of Mozart's death. When his friends gather around his deathbed, the chief of the secret police locks them in and begins to ask questions. Everyone seems to have had a motive to kill the composer, and Mozart's connection with the Freemasons is particularly suspicious. There is even a suggestion that he might have committed slow suicide. Max Tidof plays Mozart with Armin Mueller-Stahl as police chief Pergen, Catarina Raacke as Constanze, Uwe Ochsenknecht as Schikaneder, and Winfried Glatzeder as Salieri. The film includes staged scenes from *Le nozze di Figaro,* with Juraj Hrubant as Figaro, and *The Magic Flute,* with Ondrej Malachovsky as Sarastro. Zdenek Mahler, Werner Uschkurat, and Jirina Koenig wrote the screenplay; Slavo Luther directed. Color. In German with English subtitles. 93 minutes. Facets/Water Bearer Films VHS.

1987 Mozart

Mozart's life and music as seen by writer/director Nicholas Vaszonyi. Anthony Quayle and Balint Vazsony visit Salzburg and Vienna and talk about places the composer lived; there are staged enactments of scenes from his life with lots of Mozart music. The film was made for the Canadian and Hungarian TV series *Klassix 13.* Color. In English. 55 minutes. MPI Home Entertainment VHS.

1991 Mozart on Tour

The seven-LD series *Mozart on Tour* consists of 13 documentary films about Mozart's travels in Europe and the music he composed on those trips, plus 14 piano concertos. Presented by André Previn, they were filmed in the European cities the composer visited. Volume 1 is

London: The First Journey, Volume 2 is *Mantua: Initial Steps,* Volume 3 is *Milan and Bologna: Learning by Traveling,* etc. The documentary material is from 20 to 30 minutes long and based on the letters and diaries of the Mozarts. Color. In English. Each LD is 75 minutes.

1991 Following Mozart

This German film set in Mozart's era tells the story of a group of orphan musicians living near Dresden. They have entered a competition and want to perform Mozart's piano rondo KV 382, "the one with the trill in it." It has not been published so the cleverest of the children, Trina (Maria Ferrens), follows Mozart around Germany trying to obtain a copy. Karl Heinz Lotz directed. Color. In German. 87 minutes.

1994 Mozart

Documentary about the composer made for the series *Biography* on the Arts & Entertainment cable network. The performers includes Zubin Mehta, violinist Isaac Stern, and flutist James Galway. Color. 50 minutes. Facets/A&E VHS.

1996 Mozart: Dropping the Patron

Documentary about Mozart centering around the time when he left the household of the Archbishop of Salzburg. It includes scenes from *Le nozze di Figaro.* Part of the series *Man and Music.* Color. In English. 53 minutes. Films for the Humanities & Sciences VHS.

1996 Mozart: A Genius in His Time

Documentary about Mozart and the music he composed during his last five years, including discussion about and excerpts from *Così fan tutte* and *The Magic Flute.* Part of the series *Man and Music.* Color. In English. 53 minutes. Films for the Humanities & Sciences VHS.

1996 Vienna

Documentary about Mozart and the music he composed during his years in Vienna, including an examination of his operas by Sir Peter Hall. It includes excerpts from *Così fan tutte* and *Don Giovanni.* Part of the series *Music in Time.* Color. In English. 60 minutes. Films for the Humanities & Sciences VHS.

Performance/related films

1954 Unsterblicher Mozart

The Austrian film *Unsterblicher Mozart* (Immortal Mozart) features highlight versions of three Mozart operas performed on stage by the Mozart Ensemble of the Vienna State Opera. They are *Die Entführung aus dem Serail, Don Giovanni,* and *Le nozze di Figaro.* Details under the operas. Color. In German. 95 minutes. Taurus (Germany) VHS.

1973 The Great Composers: W. A. Mozart
A basic introduction to Mozart with selections from his music performed by Nina Milkina, the London Mozart Players, and the Salzburg Puppet Theater. Part of *The Great Composers* series. Color. In English. 25 minutes. IFB VHS.

1986 Broderna Mozart
The Mozart Brothers is a Swedish fiction film by Suzanne Osten about the problems of staging *Don Giovanni*. An avant-garde director wants to stand the "old war-horse opera" on its head and create a vital new production. The singers lose their hair and their clothes, the musicians get angry, and the union is outraged. See BRODERNA MOZART.

1990 Destination: Mozart
Documentary about the Mozart–Da Ponte opera films that Peter Sellars made in Vienna. It has interviews with Sellars and cast members who talk about their ideas regarding Mozart and the operas *Così fan tutte, Don Giovanni,* and *Le nozze di Figaro.* Director Andrea Simon also includes performance extracts from the operas. Color. In English. 60 minutes. Kultur VHS.

1991 Mozart Gala
Three-hour celebration of Mozart operas at the Arena di Verona taped in August 1991 and released on three videos. Volume One (63 minutes) has arias from *Don Giovanni* and *La clemenza di Tito;* Volume Two (72 minutes) has *Così fan tutte, Idomeneo,* and *Le nozze di Figaro;* and Volume Three (63 minutes) has *Die Entführung aus dem Serail* and *The Magic Flute.* The singers are sopranos Kathleen Cassello, Katia Ricciarelli, Angela Maria Blasi, Evelyn Holzschuh, Donna Ellen, and Sona Ghazarian; mezzos Susan Quittmayer, Jutta Geister, and Ann Murray; tenors Jerry Hadley, Franz Supper, and Francisco Araiza; baritones Lucio Gallo, James Morris, and Andrea Piccinni; and bassos Yevgeny Nesterenko and Hannes Jokel. They are backed by the Linz Landestheater Chorus and the Vienna Mozart Academy Orchestra led by Theodor Guschlbauer, Johannes Wildner, and Ernst Dunschirm. Color. In Italian. 198 minutes. Castle (Germany) VHS.

1992 Mozart: The Opera Experience
Scenes from Mozart operas with commentary and introductions by Richard Baker. The excerpts of performances at the Glyndebourne Festival are from *The Abduction from the Seraglio, Così fan tutte, Don Giovanni, Idomeneo, The Magic Flute,* and *Le nozze di Figaro.* The performers include Kiri Te Kanawa, Benjamin Luxon, and Leo Goeke. Mark Gasser plays Mozart in the dramatized scenes, Bob Carruthers and Graham Holloway produced. Color. 90 minutes. Options/Cromwell VHS.

1996 For Ever Mozart
Jean-Luc Godard's self-referential fiction film about art, cinema, and Bosnia is more about Godard's ideas than Mozart's music. Madeleine Assas stars. Color. In French. 85 minutes. Facets VHS.

1997 Mozart
Documentary about Mozart's music in *The Great Composers* series features an aria from "Così fan tutte" with music played by the Moscow Symphony Orchestra led by David Palmer. Color. 26 minutes. Films for the Humanities & Sciences VHS.

1997 Great Composers: Mozart
BBC Television documentary about Mozart narrated by Kenneth Branagh, with commentary from critics and excerpts from performances of operas. Color. In English. 60 minutes.

1998 Wolfgang Amadeus Mozart
Documentary about Mozart's music with commentary by Jean and Brigitte Massin and André Tubeuf and excerpts from his operas including Wilhelm Furtwängler conducting *Don Giovanni* and Karl Böhm conducting *The Magic Flute* and *Le nozze di Figaro.* Part of the video series *Harmonics: The Innovators of Classical Music.* Color. 28 minutes. Films for the Humanities & Sciences VHS.

2001 Cecilia Bartoli Sings Mozart
Bartoli sings "Bella mia fiamme," "Resta, oh cara," "Giunse alfin al momento," and other pieces by Mozart with Nikolaus Harnoncourt conducting. Color. 60 minutes. Naxos DVD.

MOZART AND SALIERI
1898 opera by Rimsky-Korsakov

Salieri envies Mozart's divine genius and poisons him at a dinner in an inn after Mozart tells him about his *Requiem.* Alexander Pushkin's verse tragedy *Motsart i Salyeri,* which tells of Salieri's supposed murder of Mozart, is based on the same folk legend as *Amadeus.* It provided the libretto for NIKOLAI RIMSKY-KORSAKOV's chamber opera, a brilliant homage to Mozart with quotations from his operas embedded in the score. The baritone role of Salieri was created by Chaliapin, the tenor role of Mozart by Vasily Skafter, and the pianist role by Sergei Rachmaninoff.

1962 Gorikker film
> Soviet feature film: Vladimir Gorikker (director), Samuel Samosud (conductor), Vadim Mass (cinematographer), Riga Film (production studio).
> Cast: Innokenti Smoktunovsky (Mozart), Pyotry Glebov (Salieri, sung by Alexander Pirogov), A. Milbret (Blind Musician).
> Video: Corinth VHS. Black and white. In Russian with English subtitles. 47 minutes.
> Comment: Shown in the United States as *Requiem for Mozart.*

Related film

1914 Symphony of Love and Death
Alexander Geirot plays Mozart with A. Michurin as Salieri in *Simfoniya Lyubvi I Smerti,* an early Russian silent film based on the play by Pushkin that inspired the opera. Victor Tourjansky, who later made many films in exile in France and Germany, directed. Black and white. About 50 minutes.

MOZART REQUIEM
1791 Requiem Mass by Mozart

While not an opera, MOZART's *Requiem in D Minor* merits a separate entry because of its constant use in Mozart films and the many videos of it featuring major opera singers. It was his last composition, K. 626, and he was convinced that he was composing his own requiem.

1984 Herkulessaal, Munich
> German stage production: Sir Colin Davis (conductor, Bavarian Radio Symphony Orchestra and Chorus).
> Soloists: Edith Mathis, Trudeliese Schmidt, Peter Schreier, Gwynne Howell.
> Video: Image Entertainment DVD. Hugo Kach (director). RM Arts. Color. In Latin. 59 minutes.

1988 Abbey Church, Bavaria
> German church production: Leonard Bernstein (conductor, Bavarian Radio Symphony Orchestra and Chorus).
> Soloists: Marie McLaughlin, Maria Ewing, Jerry Hadley, Cornelius Hauptmann.
> Video: DG VHS. Humphrey Burton (director). Color. In Latin. 65 minutes.

1991 St. Stephen's Cathedral, Vienna
> Austrian church production: Georg Solti (conductor, Vienna Philharmonic Orchestra and Vienna State Opera Chorus).

> Soloists: Cecilia Bartoli, Arleen Auger, Vinson Cole, René Pape.
> Video: London VHS/LD. Humphrey Burton and Michael Weinmann (directors). Color. In Latin. 93 minutes.
> Comment: Mozart's funeral rites were held in this church; the video shows a Requiem Mass celebrated by Cardinal Groer on the 200th anniversary of his death, preceded by a film telling the story of the *Requiem.*

1991 Palau de la Musica Catalana, Barcelona
> Spanish stage production: John Eliot Gardiner (conductor, Monteverdi Choir and English Baroque Soloists).
> Soloists: Barbara Bonney, Anne Sofie Von Otter, Anthony Rolfe Johnson, Alastair Miles.
> Video: Philips VHS/LD. Jonathan Fuller (director). Color. In Latin. 106 minutes.
> Comment: Taped on December 5, 1991, on the 200th anniversary of Mozart's death. The video also includes Mozart's *Mass in C Minor.*

1994 City Library Ruins, Sarajevo
> International film of Bosnian production: Zubin Mehta (conductor, Sarajevo Cathedral Choir and the Sarajevo Philharmonic Orchestra), Mario Dradi and Francesco Stochino Weiss (film directors).
> Soloists: José Carreras, Ruggero Raimondi, Ildikó Komlósi, Cecilia Gasdia.
> Video: A&E VHS. Color. In Latin. 60 minutes.
> Comment: Moving, dramatic performance of the *Requiem* in Sarajevo on the site of the city's devastated historic library. The film is intercut with scenes of the siege of the city.

Related films

1909 Mozart's Last Requiem
The *Requiem* is central to Louis Feuillade's silent *La Mort de Mozart,* the first film about the composer. Mozart feels compelled to write his *Requiem* as he thinks death is near, but his doctor orders him to rest. He cannot resist working on it, however; when it is finished a group of friends visit him and sing the *Requiem* as he dies. Black and white. About 15 minutes. Prints survive.

1962 Viridiana
Luis Buñuel features selections from the *Requiem* on the soundtrack of this surrealistic film about a novice nun (Silvia Pinal) corrupted by her uncle (Fernando Rey) and his illegitimate son (Francisco Rabal). Color. In Spanish. 90 minutes. On VHS.

1984 Amadeus

The *Requiem* is featured dramatically at the end of Milos Forman's film about the composer. Mozart (Tom Hulce) has been commissioned to compose it by a mysterious masked patron (Salieri/F. Murray Abraham) and works feverishly to finish it before his death, dictating its final parts to Salieri himself. The *Requiem* extracts are performed by the Academy of St. Martin-in-the-Fields and Academy Chorus led by Sir Neville Marriner. See AMADEUS.

MUETTE DE PORTICI, LA

1828 opera by Auber

The Mute Girl of Portici is probably the only opera in which the title character can't talk, let alone sing. Fenella, the mute girl of the title, mimes her role and leaps dramatically into Mount Vesuvius at the climax of the opera. The principal singer is her brother, a Neapolitan fisherman and revolutionary named Masaniello. He leads the revolt against the Spanish but is killed by his own men at the end. DANIEL AUBER's *La muette de Portici* is considered the first grand opera and was celebrated for its revolutionary fervor during the 19th century. It has a complex French libretto by Germain Delavigne and Eugène Scribe. The early popularity of the story is attested by the number of films it inspired, but there are currently no commercial videos of the opera.

Silent/related films

1911 La muta di Portici

Mary Cléo Tarlarini stars as the mute Fenella in this Italian silent version of the opera made in Turin by Ambrosio Films. Black and white. About 10 minutes.

1916 The Dumb Girl of Portici

Dancer Anna Pavlova plays Fenella, the mute heroine of the opera, with Rupert Julien as Masaniello in this famous Universal film. The musical accompaniment, based on Auber's melodies, was arranged by Adolph Schmidt. Pioneer woman filmmaker Lois Wilson wrote and directed the film in collaboration with Phillips Smalley. Black and white. Silent. About 80 minutes.

1924 La muta di Portici

Cecyl Tryan plays the mute Fenella with Livio Pavanelli as her brother Masaniello in this Italian film based on the libretto of the opera. Telemaco Ruggeri wrote and directed it for AG Film in Rome. Black and white. Silent. About 70 minutes.

1940 La fanciulla di Portici

Mario Bonnard directed this Italian narrative film of the story titled *La fanciulla di Portici* (The Portici Girl) without the Auber music and, apparently, without the heroine being mute. Luisa Ferida plays the Portici "girl" with Carlo Ninchi as Masaniello. Black and white. In Italian. 88 minutes.

1953 La muta di Portici

Flora Mariel stars as the mute Lucia in this Italian film of the story. The reason she is mute is because she was tortured after refusing to reveal the hiding place of her brother Masaniello (Paolo Carlini). Giorgio Ansoldi directed. Black and white. In Italian. 85 minutes.

MUNSEL, PATRICE

American soprano (1925–)

Patrice Munsel was as popular for her light opera roles as for her coloratura performances. Born in Spokane, Washington, she made her debut in *Mignon* at the Metropolitan in 1943 at the age of 18, the youngest singer ever signed by the Met. She sang in a wide range of operas from *Lucia di Lammermoor* and *The Barber of Seville* to *Die Fledermaus* and *La Périchole*. Although she retired from the Met in 1957, she joined the Dallas Civic Opera in 1963 to sing in *L'incoronazione di Poppea*. She also hosted a 1950s TV variety show called *The Patrice Munsel Show* in which she sang opera arias and popular songs. Munsel is at her best in three television productions of operettas: as Marietta in an NBC production of NAUGHTY MARIETTA (1955), as Resi in an NBC production of the JOHANN STRAUSS pastiche *The Great Waltz* (1955), and as Sonia in a CBS production of *The Merry Widow* (DIE LUSTIGE WITWE/1954). She played NELLIE MELBA in a 1953 film about the Australian soprano, in which she was able to sing a number of favorite opera arias, and she sang opera on several *Voice of Firestone* TV shows, available on video.

1951/1962 Voice of Firestone

Highlights from the soprano's appearances on *The Voice of Firestone* television series in 1951 and 1962 are included on the video *Patrice Munsel in Opera & Song*. She sings arias from *Die Fledermaus, La bohème, Louise, The Daughter of the Regiment,* and *Madama Butterfly* and the songs "Home Sweet Home, "In the Still of the Night," and "I've Got You Under My Skin." Black and white. 55 minutes. VAI VHS.

MURDER AT THE OPERA

As there are a great number of murders and assassinations in operas, it is no surprise to find that a number of murder mystery movies have an operatic background. In CHARLIE CHAN AT THE OPERA, Boris Karloff is suspected of murdering a soprano on stage. In THE CLIMAX, Karloff has killed one soprano and is ready to bump off another. In FATAL LADY, opera diva Mary Ellis is accused of two murders while singing at different opera houses. In MOONLIGHT MURDER, a tenor is mysteriously murdered during a performance of *Il trovatore* at the Hollywood Bowl. In the Beniamino Gigli film SOLO PER TE, a baritone is murdered backstage during a performance of *Un ballo in maschera*. In FIND THE WITNESS, a temperamental female opera star is the murder victim. In GERALDINE FARRAR's 1918 silent film *The Turn of the Wheel,* she has to discover who really murdered the hero's wife. In THE CLOWN AT MIDNIGHT, *Pagliacci* is the opera that sets off a series of murders with the killer in a clown disguise. In TERROR AT THE OPERA, built around a production of Verdi's *Macbeth* in Parma, a mysterious killer prowls the corridors of the opera house. The most famous of opera murder mysteries are, of course, THE PHANTOM OF THE OPERA movies, in which the Phantom does in a goodly number of folks in a truly operatic manner. Opera singers HELEN TRAUBEL and ANNA MOFFO both have been featured in murder mystery movies, and Traubel published a novel titled *The Metropolitan Opera Murders* (ghostwritten by Harold Q. Masur).

MUSEUM OF TELEVISION AND RADIO

The Museum of Television and Radio (MTR), with full facilities in both New York and Los Angeles, has more than 70,000 videos for viewing, including a large number of television programs devoted to opera. It has mounted full-scale tributes to the Metropolitan Opera and Leonard Bernstein and has comprehensive holdings on many other companies and people. It also has extensive archives of historically important TV opera series such as *CBS Television Opera Theater, NBC Opera Theatre, The Voice of Firestone, The Bell Telephone Hour,* and *Cameo Operas.* It offers to anyone immediate viewing access to its tapes for a small fee.

MUSGRAVE, THEA
Scottish-born American composer (1928–)

Thea Musgrave was born in Scotland, but she moved to the United States in 1972; most of her operas have been premiered by Virginia Opera and directed by her husband, Peter Mark. She began to write her own librettos with the 1977 *Mary, Queen of Scots.* It was followed by her operatic version of Charles Dickens's A CHRISTMAS CAROL, premiered by Virginia Opera in 1979 and staged at Sadler's Wells in London in 1981 and then telecast by Granada. Her other major operas include *Harriet, the*

Woman Called Moses (1985), the story of an African-American slave, and *Simón Bolívar* (1995), about the South American liberator. Musgrave often incorporates popular music into her operas, including carols in *A Christmas Carol* and spirituals in *Harriet.*

MUSIC FOR MADAME
1937 American film with opera content

Italian tenor Nino Martini wins fame singing at the Hollywood Bowl at the climax of this enjoyable musical. He plays a naive Italian immigrant hired to sing the *Pagliacci* aria "Vesti la giubba" in clown costume at a Hollywood wedding. His singing is actually a diversion for a robbery, so he thinks that if he sings again, a famous conductor will recognize his voice and send him to jail. Instead, the conductor (Alan Mowbray in a caricature of Leopold Stokowski) thinks he is so good that he hires him to sing at the Hollywood Bowl. He is a hit and wins Joan Fontaine as well. Gertrude Purcell and Robert Harari wrote the screenplay, Joseph August was cinematographer, and John Blystone directed for RKO. Black and white. 77 minutes. Live Opera/Lyric VHS.

MUSIC IN THE AIR
1932 operetta by Kern

Bavarian villager Sieglinde and her sweetheart Karl go to Munich to get his song published but instead become involved with operetta writer Bruno Mahler and his prima donna Frieda. When Frieda walks out before the premiere of his new operetta, Sieglinde is asked to take over. She isn't good enough (this is a realistic fairy tale) so she decides to go back home and marry Karl. JEROME KERN's *Music in the Air* is a Viennese-style operetta with similarities to Kern's 1931 THE CAT AND THE FIDDLE, which also had a plot based on preparations for staging an operetta. The popular songs from the show were "I've Told Every Little Star" and "The Song Is You." Oscar Hammerstein II, Kern's collaborator on *Show Boat,* wrote the libretto and lyrics.

1934 Fox film
American feature film: Joe May (director), Billy Wilder and Howard Young (screenplay), Ernest Palmer (cinematographer), Franz Waxman (music director), Fox (production studio).

Cast: Gloria Swanson (Frieda Hotzfelt), John Boles (Bruno), Douglas Montgomery (Karl), June Lang (Sieglinde), Al Shean (Sieglinde's father), Marjorie Main (Anna).

Black and white. In English. 85 minutes.

Comment: This was the first American film for Billy Wilder. Fox reportedly hired Enrico Caruso's voice coach to help Swanson prepare for the film.

MUSIC PERFORMANCE RESEARCH CENTER, LONDON

The Music Performance Research Center (MPRC) is a London audio-video library of live public music performances that has a selection of opera videotapes. Its holdings, many quite rare, go back half a century and include unique footage such as Kirsten Flagstad and Maggie Teyte singing in *Dido and Aeneas* at the opening of the Mermaid Theatre in 1951. Donated BBC Television programs include a 1962 profile of Boris Christoff in which he sings arias from *Boris Godunov*. The MPRC, located at the Barbican Music Library, is open to the public.

MUSIC WITH ROOTS IN THE AETHER
1976 "television opera" by Ashley

American composer ROBERT ASHLEY created this unusual 14-hour "television opera" about seven contemporary musicians working in non-notational styles for the Paris Festival D'Automne. It might be better described as a video documentary. Each two-hour episode includes interview and performance against a landscape backdrop with an ensemble led by the composer. Ashley himself is the subject of one, with performances of *What She Thinks* and *Title Withdrawn* featuring Paul DeMarinis, Mimì Johnson, and Robert Sheff. The other episodes center around Philip Glass (a scene from *Einstein on the Beach*), David Behrman, Alvin Lucier, Gordon Mumma, Pauline Oliveros, and Terry Riley. The two-hour episodes were edited into one-hour television programs in 1985. Color. In English. 14 hours. Lovely Music VHS.

MUSSORGSKY, MODEST
Russian composer (1839–1881)

Modest Mussorgsky (or Musorgsky) created what many consider the greatest Russian opera, BORIS GODUNOV, as well as the popular KHOVANSHCHINA. He began composing operas in 1856 but left most of his efforts unfinished. He did complete *Boris,* but it did not become popular until it was (controversially) refashioned and smoothed out by Nikolai Rimsky-Korsakov, who also completed *Khovanshchina* after the composer's death. Mussorgsky's "Night on Bald Mountain," used to such dramatic effect in Disney's *Fantasia,* was featured by the composer in the operas MLADA and *The Fair at Sorochintsi,* both uncompleted. There are films and videos of *Boris Godunov, Khovanshchina,* and *Mlada* and an interesting Soviet film biography of the composer. (There is disagreement on the English spelling of the composer's name: the Metropolitan Opera, *The New York Times,* film credits, video

boxes, and most general encyclopedias prefer "Mussorgsky" but the *New Grove, Penguin,* and *Oxford* opera dictionaries opt for "Musorgsky.")

1948 Song of My Heart
Lewis Howard plays Mussorgsky in this much-criticized American film about Tchaikovsky. See PYOTR TCHAIKOVSKY.

1950 Mussorgsky
Alexander Borisov stars as Mussorgsky in the Soviet film biography *Mussorgsky,* a Cannes Film Festival prizewinner directed by Grigory Roshal and cowritten with A. Abramova. The story focuses on the composer's problems in getting recognition, especially for *Boris Godunov,* and includes staged sequences of the opera. Prominent in the film are the other members of the Russian musical "famous five" with A. Popov as Rimsky-Korsakov, Y. Leonidov as Borodin, V. Friendlich as Cui, and V. Balashov as Balakirev; Nikolai Cherkassov plays Mussorgsky's collaborator Stassov. The film was released theatrically in the United States. Color. In Russian. 116 minutes.

1995 Modest Mussorgsky: Towards a New Shore
A documentary film about the composer tracing his growth from Romantic to Russian original with opera excerpts, including *Boris Godunov* at the Bolshoi. Color. In English. 78 minutes. Films for the Humanities & Sciences VHS.

MUTI, RICCARDO
Italian conductor (1941–)

Riccardo Muti, chief conductor at La Scala for many years, once said that music should not be classified as entertainment but as a religious experience. Among his many notable achievements is a famous La Scala revival of Pergolesi's LO FRATE 'NNAMORATO. It is on video with many other operas presented at the Milan theater. See ATTILA (1991), COSÌ FAN TUTTE (1989), DON CARLO (1992), DON GIOVANNI (1989), LA DONNA DEL LAGO (1992), ERNANI (1982), FALSTAFF (2001), GUILLAUME TELL (1991), BARBARA HENDRICKS (1990), CHRISTA LUDWIG (1992), NABUCCO (1986), DIE SCHÖPFUNG (1990), TOSCA (2000), LA TRAVIATA (1992), IL TROVATORE (2000), I VESPRI SICILIANI (1990).

1996 La Scala 50th Anniversary Concert
Muti conducts the Teatro alla Scala Orchestra and Chorus in a concert to celebrate the 50th anniversary of the theater's restoration in 1946. Italian director Liliana Cavani filmed the concert. Color. In Italian. 100 minutes.

MY COUSIN
1918 American film with Caruso

Mario Nanni (Enrico Caruso), a poor sculptor living in New York's Little Italy, says he is the cousin of famous Italian tenor Cesare Carulli (Enrico Caruso) to impress his girlfriend Rosa (Caroline White). Rosa's father Pietro (Joseph Ricciardi) wants her to marry Robert (Henry Leone), who has a vegetable stand. Mario and Rosa see Carulli at the Met singing in *I Pagliacci,* but the singer fails to recognize his cousin. Mario is in deep trouble until Carulli learns about his troubles, visits him at his studio, and commissions a bust—from his cousin. All ends well. The film was inspired by a 1908 popular song titled "My Cousin Caruso," based on music from *Pagliacci.* It includes scenes at the Metropolitan Opera House, in Caruso's dressing room, and in Caruso's home although most of the film was shot at the Artcraft Studio on 56th Street in New York. Caruso's photogenic costar Carolina White was also an opera singer; she sang the role of Barbara in Victor Herbert's *Natoma* in Chicago. Caruso's film career never took off after this debut, but it is simply not true that it was a bad film and Caruso a bad actor. He is quite watchable and his personality shines through. Reviews were mostly favorable: *The New York Times* praised the film and said Caruso's acting was "thoroughly enjoyable," *Variety* called him a "master," and *Photoplay World* said the film was "unqualifiedly a success." But general audiences did not take to him as a film actor, and his film career never took off like Geraldine Farrar's. Margaret Turnbull wrote the screenplay, Hal Young was the cinematographer, and Edward José directed for Famous Players–Lasky. Black and white. Silent. About 65 minutes (4,710 feet). Bel Canto Society VHS (with *Caruso: A Documentary*).

MY HEART'S IN THE HIGHLANDS
1970 opera by Beeson

Fresno, California, in 1914. Young Johnny hears an old man playing "My Heart's in the Highlands" on the cornet and invites him into his somewhat eccentric household for a meal. Father Ben writes poetry and Grandmother sings Armenian songs, but they have no money for food so Johnny has to get some on credit. Jasper, the old man, turns out to be a fugitive from an old people's home. After he is taken back, the family is evicted from its home. Jack Beeson's opera *My Heart's in the Highlands,* libretto by the composer based on William Saroyan's wistful 1939 play, premiered on NET Opera on PBS in 1970. It was lengthened to 105 minutes by the composer for its stage premiere by the Center for Contemporary Opera in 1988.

1970 NET Opera

American TV production: Rhoda Levine (director), Peter Herman Adler (NET Opera Theatre Orchestra), Eldon Elder (set designer).

Cast: Gerard Harrington III (Johnny), Alan Crofoot (Ben), Spiro Malas (Mr. Kosak), Lili Chookasian (Grandmother), Ken Smith (Jasper), Michael Ferguson (Paperboy), Jack Beeson (Young Husband).

Video at the MTR. Telecast March 18, 1970, on NET Opera. Kirk Browning (director). Color. In English. 90 minutes.

My Heart Is Calling (1934): Jan Kiepura and Marta Eggerth star in Carmine Gallone's operatic English film.

MY HEART IS CALLING
1934 English film with opera content

An Italian opera company headed by Polish tenor Jan Kiepura is stranded in Monte Carlo with Hungarian soprano Marta Eggerth as a stowaway. Their relationship and his efforts to get an engagement at the Monte Carlo Opera form the basis of the story. The high point is a performance of *Tosca* on the steps of the opera house while the resident company performs the opera inside. The outside group has better singers, so the audience leaves the auditorium and comes out to hear them. Hugh Wakefield plays the absent-minded director of the Monte Carlo Opera House, Sonnie Hale is Alfonse, and Ernest Thesinger is Ferrier. Richard Benson and Sidney Gilliat wrote the screenplay, Glen MacWilliams was the cinematographer, and Carmine Gallone directed for Gaumont-British. Gallone also directed a German version titled *Mein Herz ruft nach Dir* for Cine-Allianz with a screenplay by Ernest Marischka. Black and white. 91 minutes. Opera Dubs VHS.

MYSHKIN
1973 TV opera by Eaton

JOHN EATON's television opera *Myshkin,* libretto by Patrick Creagh, is based on Dostoevsky's novel *The Idiot.* Prince Myshkin is the holy idiot of the title, a Christ-like figure subject to epileptic fits. The action is seen from Myshkin's point of view, but as he is the camera, he is never seen. The music reflects his swings between rationality and unreality and the multiple time frames of the story. The opera, composed in 1971, was premiered on television in 1973 by Indiana University Opera Theater.

1973 Indiana University Opera Theater
American TV production: Ross Allen (director), John Reeves White (conductor, Indiana University Opera Theatre Orchestra and Chorus), Andreas Nomikos (set designer).
Cast: Linda Anderson (Natasha), William Hartwell (Rogozhin), James Bert Neely (Dr. Schneider), William Oberholtzer (General Yapanchin), Anne Swedish (Marie), William Reeder (Ganya), Gregor Isaacs (Lebedev), Larry Dorminy (Totsky).
Video at the MTR. Telecast April 23, 1973, on PBS. Herbert Selt (director). Color. In English. 50 minutes.

MY SONG FOR YOU
1934 English film with opera content

Polish tenor Jan Kiepura plays Gatti, a famous Italian tenor brought to Vienna to star in a new production of *Aida.* During rehearsals, Kiepura gets to sing a fine version of "Celeste Aida" and show off his high Cs in the *Il trovatore* aria "Di quella pira." The story line revolves around a young singer in the *Aida* chorus (Aileen Marson) who charms Kiepura into giving a job to her fiancé (Emlyn Williams). When the boyfriend lets her down, her parents talk her into marrying a rich man; at the altar she changes her mind and decides to marry Kiepura instead. The supporting cast includes Sonnie Hale and Gina Malo. Austin Melford, Robert Edmunds, and Richard Benson wrote the screenplay and Maurice Elvey directed. The film was also made in a German version titled *Ein Lied für Dich* and directed by Joe May with Kiepura, Jenny Jugo, and Ida Wust. Black and white. In English or German. 89 minutes. Bel Canto Society/Live Opera VHS (English version).

MY SONG GOES AROUND THE WORLD
1934 English film with opera content

Diminutive German tenor Joseph Schmidt stars in this semiautobiographical film set in Venice. The plot is basically that he becomes a stage and radio opera star but loses his girl Nina (Charlotte Ander) to a better-looking guy (John Loder). The singing is the real story, however, and Schmidt sings a wide range of opera and popular music. He was never a stage opera singer as he was almost a dwarf and so too short to be convincing in tenor roles. Instead, he became a radio, record, and film star singing opera arias to wide acclaim. After Hitler came to power, he was no longer allowed on radio because he was Jewish. The German version of this film, *Ein Lied geht um die Welt,* was banned by the Nazis in 1937 but prints survived. Schmidt died in an internment camp in Switzerland in 1942. The English version of the film, *My Song Goes Around the World,* was written by Clifford Grey and Frank Miller and based on the German screenplay by Ernest Neubach; Reinhardt Kuntze was cinematographer and Richard Oswald directed. Black and white. 68 minutes. Bel Canto Society VHS (German version with English subtitles) and Live Opera/Lyric/Opera Dubs VHS.

N

NABUCCO
1842 opera by Verdi

Nabucco was GIUSEPPE VERDI's first great success. The Hebrew chorus "Va, pensiero" in Act III became an anthem for Italian patriots (it was sung at Verdi's funeral procession), and the opera itself was seen as a metaphor about Italy under the control of Austria. Nabucco (Nebuchadnezzar in the Bible) is the Babylonian king who orders the destruction of Jerusalem and takes the Hebrews prisoner, beginning the Babylonian captivity. The Hebrews are led by High Priest Zaccaria. Nabucco's daughters Fenena and Abigaille love the Israelite Ismaele and he loves Fenena. The libretto by Temistocle Solera is based on a play and a ballet scenario, not the Old Testament. Scenes from the successful premiere of *Nabucco* are featured in many film and video biographies of Verdi and make fascinating viewing because they are fairly authentic reproductions of the original staging at La Scala. Renato Bruson stars as Nabucco in three of the productions of the opera available on video.

1979 Paris Opéra
French stage production: Henri Ronse (director), Nello Santi (conductor, Orchestre du Theatre National de l'Opéra de Paris), Beni Montresor (set/costume designer).

Cast: Sherrill Milnes (Nabucco), Grace Bumbry (Abigaille), Ruggero Raimondi (Zaccaria), Viorica Cortez (Fenena), Carlo Cossuto (Ismaele).

Video: Dreamlife (Japan) DVD/VHS. André Flédérick (director). Color. In French. 122 minutes.

1981 Arena di Verona
Italian stage production: Renzo Giacchieri (director), Maurizio Arena (conductor, Arena di Verona Orchestra and Chorus), Luciano Minguzzi (set/costume designer).

Cast: Renato Bruson (Nabucco), Ghena Dimitrova (Abigaille), Dimiter Petkov (Zaccaria), Bruna Baglioni (Fenena), Ottavio Garaventa (Ismaele).

Video: HBO/Castle/NVC Arts (GB) VHS/Pioneer LD. Brian Large (director). Color. In Italian with English subtitles. 132 minutes.

Comment: Magnificent performance by Bruson and Dimitrova.

1986 Teatro alla Scala
Italian stage production: Robert De Simone (director), Riccardo Muti (conductor, Teatro alla Scala Orchestra and Chorus), Mauro Carosi (set designer), Odette Nicoletti (costume designer).

Cast: Renato Bruson (Nabucco), Ghena Dimitrova (Abigaille), Paata Burchuladze (Zaccaria), Raquel Pierotti (Fenena), Bruno Beccaria (Ismaele).

Video: Home Vision VHS/Japanese LD. Brian Large (director). Color. In Italian with English subtitles. 140 minutes

1998 Teatro di San Carlo
Italian stage production: Fabio Sparvoli (director), Paolo Carognani (conductor, Orchestra and Chorus of the Teatro di San Carlo).

Cast: Renato Bruson (Nabucco), Lauren Flanigan (Abigaille), Carlo Colombara (Zaccaria), Maurizio Frusoni (Ismaele), Monica Bacelli (Fenena).

Video: Image Entertainment DVD. Walter Licastro (director). Color. In Italian with English subtitles. 140 minutes.

2000 St. Margarethen Opera Festival
Austrian stage production: Wolfgang Werner (producer), Gianfranco de Bosio (director), Michael Lesky (conductor, Vienna Junge Philharmonie and Honved Ensemble Budapest), Manfred Wabo (set designer).

Cast: Walter Donati (Nabucco), Galina Kalinina (Abigaille), Alexsandro Teliga, Michael Agafonov.

Video: Beckmann DVD/W&W TV-Video (Germany) VHS. Color. In Italian with English subtitles. 100 minutes.

Comment: Nabucco arrives on horseback as spectacle dominates this production at the ancient Roman quarry of St. Margarethen in Austria in what is claimed to be "the biggest open-air stage in Europe." There is a gigantic set with hundreds of extras and seating for 3,800. You don't go to these productions for the singing.

2001 Metropolitan Opera
American stage production: Elijah Moshinsky (director), James Levine (conductor, Metropolitan Opera Orchestra and Chorus), John Napier (set designer).

Cast: Juan Pons (Nabucco), Maria Guleghina (Abigaille), Samuel Ramey (Zaccaria), Wendy White (Fenena).

Taped April 6, 2001; telecast June 5, 2002, on PBS. Brian Large (director). Color. In Italian with English subtitles. 150 minutes.

Related films

1938 Giuseppe Verdi

A re-creation of the first night of *Nabucco* is seen in this Italian film biography of the composer by Carmine Gallone. See GIUSEPPE VERDI.

1953 Verdi, King of Melody

Tito Gobbi plays baritone Giorgio Ronconi, who created the role of Nabucco, in this Italian film biography. There is a powerful re-creation of the opening night with the audience singing along with the chorus after hearing "Va, pensiero" only once. Well, it's the movies. See GIUSEPPE VERDI.

1980 Inferno

Dario Argento's hypnotic horror film concerns three evil "mother" demons. Its soundtrack features "Va, pensiero" performed by the Gaetano Riccitelli Chorus led by Fernando Previtali. Color. In Italian. 110 minutes.

1982 The Life of Verdi

The most impressive re-creation of the opening night of *Nabucco* is featured in this big-budget nine-hour docudrama about the composer directed by Renato Castellani. See GIUSEPPE VERDI.

NACHT IN VENEDIG, EINE
1883 operetta by Johann Strauss

Eine Nacht in Venedig (One Night in Venice) is one of JOHANN STRAUSS Jr.'s most popular operettas. It's set in 18th-century Venice where the Duke of Urbino is pursuing Barbara, an elderly senator's wife, although she is more interested in a young sailor. The barber Caramello organizes a trap for her, but his own girlfriend is mistakenly handed over to the duke. There's also a masked ball, pastry cook Ciboletta and her boyfriend Pappacoda, and lots of fine music. The libretto by F. Zell and Richard Genée is based on the play *Le Chateau Trompette*. *A Night in Venice* was first presented in New York in 1884 and has been staged in modern times in both America and England.

1934 Wiene film

Hungarian-German feature film: Robert Wiene (director/screenplay), Werner Bohne (cinematographer), Ladislaus Angyal (music director), Emil Kovacs (producer), Hunnia Studios, Budapest (production).

Cast: Tino Pattiera, Tina Eilers, Ludwig Stoessel, Oskar Sima, Lizzi von Balla.

Black and white. In Hungarian or German. 80 minutes.

Comment: Strong Hungarian interest in the operetta led to the first film version being shot in Budapest as *Egy éj Velencében*. Wiene made a German version at the same time.

1942 Verhoeven film

German feature film: Paul Verhoeven (director), Walter Wasserman and C. H. Diller (screenplay), Friedl Behn-Grund (cinematographer), Franz Doelle and Will Lachner (music directors), Tobis (production).

Cast: Heidemarie Hatheyer, Lizzi Waldmuller, Hans Nielsen, Harald Paulsen, Erich Ponto.

Black and white. In German. 89 minutes.

Comment: Retitled *Die Nacht in Venedig*.

1953 Wildhagen film

Austrian feature film: Georg Wildhagen (director), Rudolf Österreicher (screenplay), Nico Dostal (music director/conductor).

Cast: Hans Olden (Duke), Herman Thimig (Pappacoda), Jeanette Schultze (Annina), Peter Pasetti (Caramello), Lotte Lang (Ciboletta).

Black and white. In German. 90 minutes.

1973 Kaslík film

German feature film: Václav Kaslík (director), Bert Grund (conductor, Munich Radio-Television Orchestra and Bavarian Radio Choir).

Cast: Julia Migenes (Ciboletta), Anton de Ridder (Duke), Trudeliese Schmidt (Barbara), Sylvia Geszty (Annina), Erich Kunz (Delacqua).

Color. In German. 96 minutes.

1988 Seefestspiele Mörbisch

Austrian stage production: Robert Herzl (director), Uwe Theimer (conductor, Seefestspiele Mörbisch Chorus and Orchestra).

Cast: Giuseppe de Stefano (Duke), Karl Donch (Delacqua), Ulrike Steinsky (Annina)

Video: ORF VHS. Sylvia Dönch (director). Color. In German. 126 minutes.

Comment: Opulent large-scale outdoor Seefestspiele Mörbisch production.

NAGANO, KENT
American conductor (1951–)

Kent Nagano, principal conductor at the Opéra de Lyon in France and Los Angeles Opera, has shown a great interest in American opera. He conducted the first complete recording of Floyd's SUSANNAH in 1994, the taping of Prokofiev's THE LOVE FOR THREE ORANGES in 1989, the premiere of Adams's *The Death of Klinghoffer* in 1991, the taping of Stravinsky's THE RAKE'S PROGRESS in 1992, and the premiere of Adams's EL NIÑO in 2000. Nagano, born in California to a Japanese-American family, made his operatic debut in San Francisco in 1976. He took over the Opéra de Lyon orchestra in 1989 from John Eliot Gardiner and became principal conductor of Los Angeles Opera in 2001. See LES CONTES D'HOFFMANN (1993), MADAMA BUTTERFLY (1993 film), OWEN WINGRAVE (2001), RODRIGUE ET CHIMÈNE (1993), DIE SIEBEN TODSÜNDEN (1993), and LES TROIS SOUHAITS (1990).

NAMARA, MARGUERITE
American soprano (1888–1974)

Marguerite Namara, née Banks, made her debut in Genoa in 1908 as Marguerite in *Faust,* sang with the Boston Opera Company for a time, and then went to Broadway. In 1915 she starred opposite John Charles Thomas in Lehár's *Alone at Last.* She was with the Chicago Opera Company from 1919 to 1922 and even sang with Caruso at a musical evening. In her first film in 1920 she played opposite Rudolph Valentino. Following a European tour playing Carmen, she starred in a 1931 British film of the Bizet opera titled *Gypsy Blood.* Afterwards her film appearances were in supporting roles. See CARMEN (1931).

1920 Stolen Moments
Namara stars opposite Rudolph Valentino in this melodramatic story about a woman infatuated with a South American novelist. After a heated argument over an incriminating letter, she thinks she may have killed him. American Cinema Corp. Black and white. Silent. About 70 minutes.

1934 Thirty Day Princess
Namara is lady-in-waiting to Sylvia Sidney who has a double role as a princess and an actress who substitutes for her on a tour. Cary Grant and Edward Arnold are the men in her life. Marion Goring directed for Paramount. Black and white. 75 minutes.

1935 Peter Ibbetson
Namara plays Madame Ginghi opposite Gary Cooper and Ann Harding in this romantic fantasy based on a George du Maurier novel. Luis Buñuel called it "one of the world's ten best films" but few of critics agreed. Henry Hathaway directed for Paramount. Black and white. 85 minutes.

NANON
1877 operetta by Genée

Librettist RICHARD GENÉE, whose many masterworks include *Der Fledermaus,* was also a composer, and his biggest success was *Nanon, die Wirtin vom "goldenen Lamm"* (Nanon, the Mistress of the "Golden Lamb"). It's set in France during the time of Louis XIV where the heroine Nanon is an innkeeper in love with a drum major, actually the Marquis d'Aubigny in disguise. When he gets into trouble, she pleads with the king for his life and eventually ends up as his marquise.

1938 UFA film
German feature film: Herbert Maisch (director), Georg Zoch and Eberhard Keindorf (screenplay), Konstantin Irmen-Tschet (cinematographer), Alois Melichar (music director), UFA (production).

Cast: Erna Sack (Nanon), Dagny Servaes (Ninon), Johannes Heesters (Marquis d'Aubigny) Otto Gebuehr (Molière), Oskar Sima.

Black and white. In German. 81 minutes.

Comment: Contemporary critics praised Sack as a charming actress and splendid singer.

NAPOLI MILIONARIA
1977 opera by Rota

NINO ROTA's *Napoli milionaria* (Naples Millionaire) is a kind of operatic homage to the composer's cinema career based around scores he wrote for the movies. Eduardo De Filippo's libretto is derived from their 1950 film of the same title, and the opera includes music from that film plus Federico Fellini's *La Dolce Vita, Nights of Cabiria,* and *Toby Dammit* project; Luchino Visconti's *Rocco and His Brothers;* Sergei Bondarchuk's *Waterloo;* and Eduardo de Filippo's *Filumena Marturano.* The three-act comic opera, which describes what a Neapolitan family did to survive World War II, premiered at Spoleto in 1977. Ironically, opera critics criticized it for its cinematic melodies. It was Rota's last opera.

1977 Spoleto Festival
Italian stage production: Eduardo de Filippo (director), Bruno Bartoletti (conductor, Spoleto Festival Orchestra and Westminster Choir), Bruno Garofalo (set/costume designer).

Cast: Sylvano Pagliuca (Gennaro Jovine), Giovanna Casolla (Amalia Jovine), Mariella Devia (Maria Rosaria Jovine), Corinna Vozza (Adelaide), Renato Grimaldi (Amedeo Jovine), Angelo Nardinocchi (Federico).

Telecast on RAI Italian Television in 1977. Color. In Italian. 102 minutes.

NATIONAL FILM AND TELEVISION ARCHIVE

The National Film and Television Archive (NFTA), a part of the British Film Institute in London, is one of the largest film and television archives in the world, with a notable collection of opera films and videos. Many of its copies are unique and make the NFTA an invaluable resource center for opera film research.

NAUGHTY MARIETTA
1910 operetta by Herbert

Naughty Marietta, VICTOR HERBERT's most popular operetta, was commissioned by impresario Oscar Hammerstein for his Manhattan Opera House and his prima donna Emma Trentini, hence its fairly operatic soprano arias (she complained that her songs had too many high notes). Rida Johnson Young's libretto tells the story of Countess Marietta, who has fled to New Orleans on a ship as a *casquette* bride with a group of husband-seeking French women. She ends up falling in love with ship captain Dick Warrington, who wins her through his knowledge of a mysterious melody that haunts her, the famous "Ah! Sweet Mystery of Life." The outstanding score also includes the coloratura favorite "Italian Street Song," the melancholy "Neath the Southern Moon," and the stirring march "Tramp, Tramp, Tramp."

1935 MGM film
American feature film: W. S. Van Dyke (director); John Lee Mahin, Frances Goodrich, Albert Hackett (screenplay); William Daniels (cinematographer); Herbert Stothart (music director); Cedric Gibbons (art director).

Cast: Jeanette MacDonald (Marietta), Nelson Eddy (Captain Dick), Frank Morgan (Governor d'Annard), Elsa Lanchester (Mrs. d'Annard), Douglass Dumbrille (Prince de Namours), Cecilia Parker (Julie), Akim Tamiroff (Rudolpho).

Video: Warner Home Video and MGM-UA VHS/LD. Black and white. 106 minutes.

Comment: MacDonald and Eddy were teamed for the first time in this entertaining MGM film, and its success led to their partnership on seven more pictures. The plot is changed—MacDonald is transmuted into a French princess falling in love with American rescuer Eddy—but the essentials are the same, although only five of the original songs were retained. The film was nominated for an Oscar for Best Picture but lost to *Mutiny on the Bounty.*

1955 NBC Television
American TV production: Max Liebman and Bill Hobin (directors), Charles Sanford (conductor, NBC Orchestra), Neil Simon, Fred Saidy, Will Glickman and William Friedberg (screenplay), Frederick Fox (set designer), Max Liebman (production).

Cast: Patrice Munsel (Marietta), Alfred Drake (Captain Dick), John Conte (Etienne), Gale Sherwood (Yvonne), Don Driver (Louis), William La Massena (Rudolfo), Robert Gallagher (Ship Captain), Bambi Linn and Rod Alexander (dancers).

Video: VAI VHS (in black and white only). Telecast January 15, 1955, on NBC. Color. In English. 80 minutes.

Comment: Beautifully made, splendidly sung, and much closer to the original than the MGM film.

Related film

1974 Young Frankenstein
Mel Brooks provides an amusing variation on the haunting meaning of "Ah! Sweet Mystery of Life" in his horror movie spoof *Young Frankenstein.* Madeline Kahn sings it with ecstatic happiness in the arms of Frankenstein monster Peter Boyle. Color. 105 minutes.

NBC OPERA THEATRE
Television opera series (1949–1964)

NBC Opera Theatre presented the most important opera telecasts in the early years of American television. Producer SAMUEL CHOTZINOFF, music director PETER HERMAN ADLER, and TV director KIRK BROWNING created this unique English-language series of telecast operas. They began on February 2, 1949, with the last act of LA BOHÈME and were followed by abridged versions of THE BARBER OF SEVILLE, THE BARTERED BRIDE, and THE OLD MAID AND THE THIEF. The series officially premiered on January 14, 1950, with Kurt Weill's DOWN IN THE VALLEY, and it became famous in 1951 with the world premiere of the first television opera, Gian Carlo Menotti's AMAHL AND THE NIGHT VISITORS. Other famous productions included the American premiere of Britten's BILLY BUDD, Bernstein's TROUBLE IN TAHITI, and a mammoth production of Prokofiev's WAR AND PEACE. Among the operas Chotzinoff commissioned for the series were Martinů's THE MARRIAGE, Foss's GRIFFELKIN, Dello Joio's THE TRIAL OF ROUEN, Hollingworth's LA GRANDE BRETÈCHE, Menotti's MARIA GOLOVIN, and Kastle's DESERET. The series ended with the death of Chotzinoff in 1964. Most of its productions can be seen at the Museum of Television and Radio.

NEDBAL, OSKAR
Czechoslovak composer (1874–1930)

Oskar Nedbal is the Czechoslovakian equivalent of Franz Lehár, a composer of popular operettas with Czech and Slovak folk rhythms who found success on the Vienna stage. He composed the operettas *Die keusche Barbara* (1911), POLENBLUT (1913), and *Die schöne Saskia* (1917); the comic opera *Sedlák Jakub* (1922); and many ballets. *Polenblut,* the most successful of his operettas, was filmed in Germany in 1934 and has remained in the repertory. Nedbal, also a noted conductor, settled in Bratislava in the latter part of his life and became an important figure in Slovak music. He was director of the Bratislava Opera at the Slovak National Theater and music director of Bratislava Radio.

NEITHER
1977 monodrama by Feldman

Morton Feldman's one-hour monodrama for soprano *Neither,* composed to an 87-word, 16-line libretto by Samuel Beckett, is as close to being minimalist as opera can be. Although composed for the stage (it was premiered at the Teatro dell'Opera in Rome on May 13, 1977), it has no plot or events and, in true Beckett manner, moves very slowly indeed. The unnamed protagonist sings in the highest soprano register with little variation in pitch. *Neither* has been compared to Schoenberg's monodrama ERWARTUNG, which is also an interior monologue for soprano.

1990 HR German Television
German TV production: Barrie Gavin (director), Zoltán Peskó (conductor, Frankfurt Radio-Television Symphony Orchestra), Claire-Lise Leisegang-Holy (set designer).
Cast: Sarah Leonard (the Woman).
Telecast April 13, 1990, on HR German Television. Color. In English. 55 minutes.
Comment: The soundtrack is available on CD.

NERONE
1924 opera by Boito

ARRIGO BOITO's opera *Nerone* was unfinished at his death in 1918, a mere 56 years after he had started to work on it. Its libretto, however, had already been published and hailed as a masterwork, so the posthumous premiere of the opera conducted by Arturo Toscanini at La Scala in 1924 was reasonably successful. The opera is a large-scale portrait of Rome during the time of the Emperor Nero and contrasts good Christians with decadent pagans.

1989 Split Summer Festival
Croatian stage production: Nikša Bareza (conductor, Split Summer Festival Orchestra).
Cast: Franjo Petrušanec, David McShane, Kruno Cigoj, M. Iveljic.
Video: Opera Direct/House of Opera/Lyric/Opera Dubs VHS. Color. In Italian. 160 minutes.

Comment: Staged in an appropriate ambiance, the courtyard of the Roman Emperor Diocletian's palace, as part of the Split Summer Festival.

NESSLER, VIKTOR
Alsace composer (1841–1891)

Viktor Nessler is not a recognizable name to most opera lovers anymore as his Gothic fairy tale operas are no longer in vogue. At the turn of the century, however, he was hugely popular, and his operas DER RATTENFÄNGER VON HAMELIN (1879), a variation of the Pied Piper story, and DER TROMPETER VON SÄKKINGEN (1884), about a trumpeter who wants to marry a baron's daughter, were widely performed and translated into other languages. Their popularity resulted in them both being filmed during the early silent era.

NESTERENKO, YEVGENY
Russian bass (1938–)

Yevgeny Nesterenko has become the Russian bass of our time with a voice powerful enough to dominate even the Arena di Verona when he sings the role of Attila. He was born in Moscow, studied in Leningrad, and made his debut there in 1962. He joined the Bolshoi in 1971 and quickly became one the company's best-known performers. He has sung in most of the great opera houses, including La Scala, Vienna, Covent Garden, and the Metropolitan. Nesterenko performs many roles, but he is most admired and impressive in Russian operas. His operas on video include ALEKO (1986), ATTILA (1985), BORIS GODUNOV (1978/1987), KHOVANSHCHINA (1979), A LIFE FOR THE TSAR (1992), and PRINCE IGOR (1969).

1989 Great Gala for Armenia
Nesterenko is one of the singers at this all-star gala concert held at the Bolshoi Opera to raise money for victims of an earthquake in Armenia. Color. 120 minutes. Kultur VHS.

1989 The Phantom of the Opera
Nesterenko's recorded voice, as Méphistophélès in Gounod's *Faust,* is featured on the soundtrack of this horror film. See THE PHANTOM OF THE OPERA.

1991 Mozart Gala
Nesterenko is one of the basses performing in this three-hour celebration of Mozart operas at the Arena di Verona in August 1991. See MOZART.

NET OPERA
Educational television series (1957–1977)

NET, the National Educational Television collective network, first began to present opera programs in 1957. WGBH in Boston teamed with SARAH CALDWELL, Boston University, and the New England Conservatory of Music to present opera rarities. It started with Caldwell directing and conducting Mozart's LA FINTA GIARDINIERA and followed with Boris Goldovsky directing and conducting 1961 productions of Purcell's DIDO AND AENEAS and Ravel's L'HEURE ESPAÑOLE. In 1964 NET began a series called *This Is Opera* with the Metropolitan Guild and telecast Bartók's *Bluebeard's Castle*. In 1965 NET presented Luigi Nono's radical INTOLLERANZA 1960, the opera's only TV production, and in 1967, Jack Beeson's LIZZIE BORDEN. NET also telecast 11 operas from European television companies. In 1969 the NET Opera Company was created by PETER HERMAN ADLER and KIRK BROWNING from the ashes of the defunct NBC Opera Theatre company. This ambitious series began in October 1969 with Janáček's FROM THE HOUSE OF THE DEAD and continued with the world premiere of Beeson's MY HEART'S IN THE HIGHLANDS. After a series of operas produced by BBC and CBC, NET continued its own productions with THE ABDUCTION FROM THE SERAGLIO and THE QUEEN OF SPADES. In 1972 it successfully premiered Pasatieri's TV opera THE TRIAL OF MARY LINCOLN, but its next commissioned opera, Henze's RACHEL LA CUBANA, ran so far over budget it ended original productions. From then on, NET acted only as a presentation forum for operas by others, mostly foreign TV companies.

NEWAY, PATRICIA
American soprano (1919–)

Brooklyn-born Patricia Neway, who was gifted with an intense dramatic soprano voice, created leading roles in American operas by Gian Carlo Menotti and Carlisle Floyd. Neway made her debut in *Così fan tutte* in 1946, joined the New York City Opera in 1948, and created the role of Magda in Menotti's *The Consul* in 1950. In 1952 she began to sing with the Opéra-Comique in Paris, and in 1958 she created the role of the Mother in Menotti's *Maria Golovin* at the Brussels World Fair. In 1963 she created the role of Mollie Sinclair in Floyd's *The Sojourner and Mollie Sinclair*. She also starred in television operas and sang the role of Nettie in a TV version of *Carousel*. See THE ACCUSED (1961), CAROUSEL (1967), THE CONSUL (1951), DIALOGUES DES CARMÉLITES (1957), THE GOLDEN CHILD (1960), MACBETH (1953), MARIA GOLOVIN (1959), and THE SOJOURNER AND MOLLIE SINCLAIR (1963).

1998 Gian Carlo Menotti: Maestro of Two Worlds
Neway is one of the singers featured in Alexander Oppersdorff's documentary about Menotti. Color. In German and English. 52 minutes.

NEW MOON, THE
1927 operetta by Romberg

SIGMUND ROMBERG's tuneful operetta *The New Moon* is set in 18th-century New Orleans. A fugitive French nobleman, in the city to recruit freedom fighters, falls in love with a haughty woman. He is taken prisoner and sent back to France on the ship *New Moon,* which is captured by his men disguised as pirates. They establish a free colony on an island. The songs include "Softly as in a Morning Sunrise," "Stouthearted Men," and "Lover Come Back to Me." Oscar Hammerstein II, Laurence Schwab, and Frank Mandel wrote the lyrics and libretto.

New Moon (1931): Grace Moore and Lawrence Tibbett in Jack Conway's film of the operetta by Sigmund Romberg.

1931 Conway film
American feature film: Jack Conway (director), Sylvia Thalberg and Frank Butler (screenplay), Herbert Stothart (music director), Oliver T. Marsh (cinematographer), Cedric Gibbons (art director), MGM (production studio).

Cast: Grace Moore (Princess Tanya Strogoff), Lawrence Tibbett (Lt. Michael Petroff), Adolphe Menjou (Governor Boris Brusiloff), Roland Young (Count Strogoff), Emily Fitzroy (Countess Strogoff).

Black and white. In English. 85 minutes.

Comment: The libretto was totally changed for this movie, with the setting transposed to Russia. The couple meet on the Caspian Sea, on the ship *New Moon,* and the final scenes take place at a remote fort in the Caucasus. Moore plays a princess fought over by Tibbett and Menjou. However, it still has much of Romberg's classic score: Tibbett sings "Stouthearted Men," Moore sings "Softly as in a Morning Sunrise" and "One Kiss," and they duet on "Wanting You" and "Lover Come Back to Me."

1940 Leonard film

American feature film: Robert Z. Leonard (director), Jacques Deval and Robert Arthur (screenplay), William Daniels (cinematographer), Herbert Stothart (music director), MGM (production studio).

Cast: Jeanette MacDonald (Marianne), Nelson Eddy (Duke de Vidier/Charles), Mary Boland (Valerie), George Zucco (Vicomte Ribaud), H. B. Warner (Father Michel).

Video: Warner Home Video VHS. Black and white. In English. 105 minutes.

Comment: This film is much closer to the stage operetta than the Moore-Tibbett version and is set again in Louisiana. Eddy plays a freedom-loving aristocrat who disguises himself as a footman, MacDonald is the haughty woman he loves, and Zucco is the bad guy. Most of the famous songs are featured.

1989 New York City Opera at Wolf Trap

American stage production: Robert Johanson (director), James Coleman (New York City Opera Orchestra and Chorus), Michael Anania (set designer), David Horn (producer).

Cast: Leigh Munro (Marianne), Richard White (Robert Misson), David Rae Smith (Ribaud), Michael Cousins (Philippe), Muriel Costa-Greenspon (Clotilde), Joyce Campana (Julie).

Telecast April 7, 1989, on PBS. Kirk Browning (director). Color. In English. 150 minutes.

NEW YEAR
1989 opera by Tippett

MICHAEL TIPPETT's *New Year,* which was inspired by TV shows, is a futuristic science-fiction space-time fantasy in which a spaceship from Nowhere Tomorrow controlled by computer wizard Merlin lands in the world of Somewhere Today. Pelegrin, the ship's pilot, has been attracted by the anguished face of child psychologist Jo Ann, whose foster brother Donny is the cause of much grief. Pelegrin eventually finds Jo Ann in a crowd awaiting the New Year. The opera was co-commissioned by BBC Television but was not telecast until after it was staged by Houston Grand Opera and the Glyndebourne Festival.

1991 Glyndebourne Festival

English stage production: Peter Hall (director), Andrew Davis (conductor, London Philharmonic Orchestra and Glyndebourne Festival Chorus), Stephany Marks (producer), Bruce Macadie (set designer), Anna Buruma (costume designer).

Cast: Helen Field (Jo Ann), James Maddalena (Merlin), Kim Begley (Pelegrin), Krister St. Hill (Donny), Richetta Manager (Regan), Jane Shaulis (Nan), Mike Henry (Presenter).

Telecast September 21, 1991, on BBC. Bill T. Jones and Dennis Marks (directors). Color. In English. 105 minutes.

NEW YORK CITY OPERA
New York opera company (1944–)

The New York City Opera, started as a low-income alternative to the Met, has often outshone its richer rival in quality and adventurousness and launched many careers; soprano Beverly Sills became a major diva without singing at the Met, and conductor Julius Rudel built his reputation there. The NYCO is noted for its willingness to present new American operas, and it has premiered many of the best, beginning with William Grant Still's *Troubled Island* in 1949. Many of NYCO's American productions have been televised. The first on NBC was Menotti's THE OLD MAID AND THE THIEF in 1949, and the first on NET was Jack Beeson's LIZZIE BORDEN in 1967. The first *Live From Lincoln Center* telecast was from the New York City Opera stage in May 1976—Douglas Moore's THE BALLAD OF BABY DOE. The company even made an appearance in a feature film, performing THE MIKADO for the 1978 film *Foul Play*. See ANNA BOLENA (1985), IL BARBIERE DI SIVIGLIA (1976), LA BOHÈME (1997), CANDIDE (1986), CARMEN (1984), CAVALLERIA RUSTICANA (1992), LA CENERENTOLA (1980), THE CUNNING LITTLE VIXEN (1983), THE GOLDEN COCKEREL (1971), LUCIA DI LAMMERMOOR (1982), DIE LUSTIGE WITWE (1996), MADAMA BUTTERFLY (1982), MANON (1977), THE NEW MOON (1989), LE NOZZE DI FIGARO (1991), MARILYN MONROE (1993), PAGLIACCI (1992), PORGY AND BESS (2002), RIGOLETTO (1988), LA RONDINE (1985), THE SAINT OF BLEECKER STREET (1978), BEVERLY SILLS, STREET SCENE (1979), TOSCA (2000), LA TRAVIATA (1995), IL TURCO IN ITALIA (1978), and DIE ZAUBERFLÖTE (1987).

NEW YORK PUBLIC LIBRARY FOR THE PERFORMING ARTS

The New York Public Library for the Performing Arts (NYPL) at Lincoln Center has a division for music that houses the Rodgers and Hammerstein Archives of Recorded Sound. This archive contains a large collection of opera videos, some of which appear to be unavailable elsewhere. It also includes all of the radio broadcasts of the Metropolitan Opera and *The Bell Telephone Hour* from the 1930s to the present day.

NHK LIRICA ITALIANA
Japanese opera series (1956–1976)

From 1956 to 1976 the Tokyo television company NHK (Nippon Hoso Kyokai) brought major opera singers to Japan and filmed 35 stage productions of classic operas in Italian in Tokyo and Osaka. The sets are basic and the direction minimal, but the videos of these productions are invaluable records of top singers at their vocal peaks. They include Carlo Bergonzi, Montserrat Caballé, José Carreras, Fiorenza Cossotto, Mario Del Monaco, Plácido Domingo, Gwyneth Jones, Alfredo Kraus, Luciano Pavarotti, Renata Scotto, Giulietta Simionato, Antonietta Stella, Giuseppe Taddei, Ferruccio Tagliavini, Renata Tebaldi, and Gabriella Tucci. The quality of the images on the videos is not high and there are no English subtitles, but the sound is excellent and the music is well played by the NHK Symphony Orchestra led by Italian conductors. The first production was AIDA, staged September 29, 1956, with Antonietta Stella as Aida and Vittorio Gui as conductor. The last was SIMON BOCCANEGRA on October 2, 1976, with Piero Cappuccilli as Simon and Oliviero De Fabritiis conducting. See ADRIANA LECOUVREUR, ANDREA CHÉNIER, IL BARBIERE DI SIVIGLIA, UN BALLO IN MASCHERA, LA BOHÈME, CARMEN, CAVALLERIA RUSTICANA, DON CARLO, L'ELISIR D'AMORE, FALSTAFF, LA FANCIULLA DEL WEST, FAUST, LA FAVORITA, LUCIA DI LAMMERMOOR, MADAMA BUTTERFLY, NORMA, LE NOZZE DI FIGARO, OTELLO, PAGLIACCI, RIGOLETTO, TOSCA, LA TRAVIATA, IL TROVATORE, and TURANDOT.

NICOLAI, OTTO
German composer (1810–1849)

Otto Nicolai is known primarily for his comic opera DIE LUSTIGEN WEIBER VON WINDSOR (The Merry Wives of Windsor), which preceded Verdi's version of the Shakespeare comedy as FALSTAFF by half a century. Nicolai's earlier operas were in Italian, but he brought all his ideas together for this last opera in German. It was refused by the Vienna Hofoper, where Nicolai was music director, so he quit his post and moved to Berlin where the opera premiered. It has become a fixture of the German stage, and it is still a delight with a much-loved overture. There are a number of German films of the opera and a quite pleasant one in English. There is also a highly fictional film about Nicolai and the story behind the creation of the opera.

1940 Falstaff in Wien
Falstaff in Vienna is a German film about Nicolai and the supposed creation of *Die lustigen Weiber von Windsor*. It pretends that events similar to the play happened in Nicolai's circle of friends and that they inspired him to write the opera. Hans Nielsen plays Nicolai with support from Gusti Wolf, Paul Hörbiger, and Lizzi Holzschuh. Scenes from the opera are shown on stage with singers from the Berlin Staatsoper and Deutsches Operhaus, including Erna Berger and Carla Spletter, and the music played by the Berlin Staatsoper Orchestra. Alois Melichar was music director, Max Wallner and Kurt Feltz wrote the screenplay, Bruno Mondi was cinematographer, and Leopold Hainisch directed for Tobis. Black and white. In German. 89 minutes. Lyric VHS.

NIGHT AT THE OPERA, A
1935 American film with opera content

The funniest of all films about opera with the Marx Brothers invading the operatic world with devastating results. Their role as operatic clowns is established in the opening credits, which read "Metro-Goldwyn-Mayer presents the Marx Bros. Groucho Chico Harpo"; as their names appear, music from *Pagliacci* is heard. Groucho plays Otis P. Driftwood, a tacky promoter in Milan trying to talk Margaret Dumont into investing money in Sig Rumann's New York Opera Company. Soprano Rosa Castaldi (Kitty Carlisle) and nasty tenor Rodolfo Lassparri (Walter Woolf King) are seen on stage as Nedda and Canio in *Pagliacci* and hired to sing in New York; Carlisle, however, prefers chorus tenor Ricardo Barone (Allan Jones) as partner. Chico sells Jones to Groucho in a famous contract scene with a remarkable Sanity Clause, and they all end up as stowaways on a boat to New York. After a series of ship scenes, including an impossibly crowded stateroom routine that has become one of the icons of cinema, they reach New York where Groucho is soon fired. The Marxes don't take kindly to this (they have goodhearted reasons) and decide to sabotage the opening night of *Il trovatore*. They switch the orchestra music around, sell peanuts in the aisle as if the performance were a circus, disrupt the singing of the Anvil Chorus, knock down some of the sets, swing back and forth across the stage, and get chased back and forth and around and about. Finally they kidnap tenor Lassparri so Jones can take over the role of Manrico and become a star. Carlisle sings the part of Leonora, Olga Dane is Azucena, Luther Hoobner is Ruiz, and Rodolfo Hoyos is Count di Luna. Other singers in the film include Tandy Mackenzie, who sings "Questa o quella" from *Rigoletto,* and Alexander Giglio, who sings in the *Pagliacci* scene. Herbert Stothart was the music director, Merritt B. Gerstad was the cinematographer, Cedric Gibbons was the art director, George S. Kaufman and Morrie Ryskind wrote the script (which has been published), and Sam Wood directed for MGM. Black and white. 92 minutes. Warner Home Video DVD/VHS.

A Night at the Opera (1935): The Marx Brothers wreak havoc on *Il trovatore,* including duels in the orchestra pit

NIGHTINGALE, THE
1914 opera by Stravinsky

The Nightingale was originally created by IGOR STRAVINSKY in Russian as *Solovyei* with a libretto by the composer and Stepan Mitussov; it became known in Paris in French as *Le Rossignol.* Based on the Hans Christian Anderson fairy tale *The Emperor's Nightingale,* the opera tells how the sweet song of the nightingale conquers Death and saves the emperor's life.

1971 NET Opera
        American TV production: Kirk Browning (director), Peter Herman Adler (producer/conductor, CBC Symphony Orchestra), Allen Charles Klein (set designer), John Butler (choreographer), Robert Craft (English translation).

Cast: Reri Grist (Nightingale), Lili Chookasian (Death), Emile Renan (Emperor), Ellen Faull (Cook), Sidney Johnson (Fisherman), Herbert Beattie (Bonze)   Video at the MTR. Telecast November 22, 1971, on PBS. Kirk Browning (director). Color. In English. 45 minutes.
        Comment: NET Opera presented the opera in a program titled *Stravinsky Remembered,* which also featured an interview with Stravinsky, who had died in April 1971.

NILSSON, BIRGIT
Swedish soprano (1918–)

Birgit Nilsson, the finest Wagnerian soprano of her time, made her debut at the Royal Opera in Stockholm in 1946 as Agathe in *Der Freischütz* and then sang there in a wide variety of roles. Her international stardom began in 1954 when she sang Brünnhilde in Stockholm and Munich and began a long association with Bayreuth. She made her debut at Covent Garden in a 1957 *Ring* and went to the Met in 1959 as Isolde in TRISTAN UND ISOLDE. In addition to Wagner, she is admired for her performances in TURANDOT, TOSCA, and ELEKTRA. Nilsson, who made several appearances on *The Bell Telephone Hour,* retired in 1984. See METROPOLITAN OPERA (1972/1983), DER RING DES NIBELUNGEN (1965 film), and RUDOLF SCHOCK (1983).

1960s Bell Telephone Hour
Nilsson appeared on several *Bell Telephone Hour* television shows during the 1960s, performing scenes from *La forza del destino, Götterdämmerung, Macbeth, Tannhäuser, Tosca,* and *Turandot* and music from Handel's *Messiah* and Rossini's *Stabat Mater.* Donald Voorhees conducts the Bell Telephone Hour Orchestra. Color. 45 minutes. VAI/Kultur VHS.

1964 Opera Concert
Nilsson performs scenes from *Aida, La traviata, Tristan und Isolde,* and Weber's *Oberon* at a concert in Stockholm with the Swedish Radio Orchestra led by Stig Westerberg. Lars Egler directed the telecast on September 26, 1964. Black and white. 58 minutes.

1967 First Ladies of the Opera
Nilsson, one of four stars on a *Bell Telephone Hour* special on January 1, 1967, sings "Dich teure Halle" from *Tannhäuser* and "In questa reggia" from *Turandot.* See BELL TELEPHONE HOUR.

1968 Verdi Concert
Nilsson performs arias from Verdi operas at a concert in Stockholm including *Un ballo in maschera, La forza del Destino,* and *Macbeth* with the Swedish Radio Symphonic Orchestra led by Sergiu Celibidache. Lars Egler directed; telecast on September 5, 1968. Black and white. 56 minutes.

1979 Skyline
Nilsson appeared on the PBS arts program *Skyline* in 1979 with Beverly Sills asking questions about her career. Color. 30 minutes. Video at the NYPL.

NINA
1789 opera by Paisiello

Giovanni Paisiello's one-act opera *Nina, o sia la pazza per amore* (Nina, or the Love-mad Maid), libretto by Giovan Battista Lorenzi and Giuseppe Carpani based on a French play, has a somewhat downbeat plot for a comic opera. A count is eager for his daughter Nina to marry but dumps the first suitor, Lindoro, when a richer man comes along. Nina goes mad with despair when she

thinks Lindoro has been killed. She recovers her sanity when he turns up again for the more or less happy ending. A production of the opera at the Palazzo Ducale in Martina Franca, created for the Festival della Valle d'Itria, was televised by RAI Italian Television but is not yet on video.

2002 Zurich Opera
Swiss stage production: Cesare Lievi (director), Adam Fischer (conductor, Zurich Opera House Orchestra and Chorus).

Cast: Cecilia Bartoli (Nina), Jonas Kaufmann (Lindoro), Juliette Galstian (Susanna), László Polgár (Count), Angelo Veccia (Giorgio).

Video: Arthaus DVD. Thomas Grimm (director). Color. In English.120 minutes.

Comment: Bartoli had the opera specially revived for her but critics were not pleased with the production. DVD includes 46-minute documentary about the composer, *Paisiello: a Forgotten Genius.*

Related film

1938 Marionette
Beniamino Gigli sings Lindoro's aria from *Nina* in this Italian narrative film about a famous tenor who agrees to provide the singing voice for a marionette show. See MARIONETTE.

NIÑO, EL
2000 opera/oratorio by Adams

John Adams's multimedia nativity opera/oratorio *El Niño,* which includes dance and film, premiered at the Théâtre du Châtelet in Paris December 15, 2000, under the direction of Peter Sellars with Kent Nagano conducting. The libretto is based on biblical texts, Gnostic infancy gospels, and poems by two Latin American women writers—17th-century nun Sor Juan Ines de la Cruz and 20th-century poet Rosario Castellanos. Dawn Upshaw and Lorraine Hunt Lieberson sang the two Marys at the premiere, with Willard White as Joseph and Herod. The work was reprised in San Francisco on January 11, 2001.

2000 Théâtre du Châtelet
French stage production: Peter Sellars (director), Kent Nagano (conductor, Deutsches Symphonie Orchester Berlin, Maîtrise de Paris Children's Choir, Theatre of Voices and London Voices choruses).

Soloist: Dawn Upshaw and Lorraine Hunt Lieberson (the Marys), Willard White (Joseph/Herod), Daniel Bubeck, Brian Cummings, Steven Rickhards.

Video: Naxos/Arthaus DVD. Peter Maniura (director). Color. In English and Spanish. 147 minutes.

Comment: The DVD of Sellars's premiere production at the Théâtre du Châtelet, taped live, won the 2002 Gramophone Award. It includes a 28-minute documentary about the production.

NIXON IN CHINA
1987 opera by Adams

President Nixon, Pat Nixon, and Henry Kissinger visit Beijing in February 1972 and meet with Chairman Mao, Madame Mao, and Premier Chou En-lai. JOHN ADAMS's *Nixon in China,* libretto by Alice Goodman, one of the most publicized modern American operas, was conceived by PETER SELLARS, who wanted to stage an opera that reflected the headlines of the day; it was the first of what became known as "CNN operas." Adams, Sellers, Goodman, and choreographer Mark Morris created the opera on a commission by Houston Grand Opera, Brooklyn Academy of Music, and the Kennedy Center, and it was premiered in Houston October 22, 1987. The music is minimalist but accessible and requires strong singers; Mao is a heldentenor part while Madame Mao is a coloratura role comparable to the Queen of the Night. In June 2000 the opera was revived in London by the English National Opera and was hailed as one of the classics of modern opera.

1987 Houston Grand Opera
American stage production: Peter Sellars (director), John De Main (conductor, Houston Grand Opera Orchestra and Chorus), Mark Morris (choreographer), Adrianne Lobel (set designer), Dunya Ramicova (costume designer).

Cast: James Maddalena (Richard Nixon), Carol Ann Page (Pat Nixon), Sanford Sylvan (Chou en-Lai), John Duykers (Mao), Trudy Ellen Craney (Madame Mao), Thomas Hammons (Kissinger).

Video at the MTR. Videotaped in October/November 1987; telecast April 15, 1988. Brian Large (director). Color. In English. 180 minutes.

Comment: Walter Cronkite introduces the opera and talks about the events on which it is based; Adams is interviewed during the interval.

NOAH AND THE FLOOD
See THE FLOOD.

NONO, LUIGI
Italian composer (1924–1990)

Luigi Nono, one of the most radical modern Italian opera composers in both music and politics, considered musical theater a place to project his ideas. He completed only two operas, and rather surprisingly, one of them received its only television production in the United States. INTOLLERANZA 1960, an outcry again the intolerance shown refugees and immigrants, premiered at La Fenice in 1961 and was produced by Sarah Caldwell for NET Opera in 1965 with Beverly Sills in a leading role. Nono's other opera, *Al gran sole carico d'amore,* about the Paris Commune and the Russian Revolution, premiered in Milan in 1975 but has not been televised. Both operas, however, are on CD.

NORMA
1831 opera by Bellini

VINCENZO BELLINI's opera *Norma* is set in Gaul under the Roman occupation during the first century B.C.E. and tells the tragic story of the love affair of Druid priestess Norma and Roman proconsul Pollione. She has broken her vow of chastity for him, but he now loves temple virgin Adalgisa. The libretto by Felice Romani is based on a play by Alexandre Soumet. *Norma* contains one of the most famous soprano arias, "Casta diva," Norma's prayer for peace; it was created especially for the first Norma, Giuditta Pasta, and became a favorite of Maria Callas and Joan Sutherland.

***1974 Orange Festival
French stage production: Sandro Sequi (stage director), Giuseppe Patanè (conductor, Teatro Regio Orchestra and Chorus of Torino), Jean-Pierre Lazar (cinematographer).

Cast: Montserrat Caballé (Norma), Josephine Veasey (Adalgisa), Jon Vickers (Pollione), Agostino Ferrin (Oroveso), Marisa Ziotti (Clotilde), Gino Sinimberghi (Flavio).

Video: Bel Canto Society & Lyric VHS/DreamLife (Japan) DVD. Filmed on July 20, 1974 by Pierre Jourdan. Color. In Italian with Japanese subtitles. 161 minutes.

Comment: One of the greatest performances on film or video of Caballe, amazingly effective.

1974 Gran Teatre del Liceu
Spanish stage production: Maria Francesca Siciliani (director), Enrique Garcia Asensio (conductor, Gran Teatre del Liceu Orchestra and Chorus), Manuel Mampaso (set designer).

Cast: Montserrat Caballé (Norma), Fiorenzo Cossotto (Adalgisa), Pedro Lavirgen (Pollione), Ivo Vinco (Oroveso), Cecilia Soler (Clotilde), Antonio De Marco (Flavio).

Video: House of Opera DVD and VHS/Bel Canto Society and Lyric VHS. Ramon Diaz (director). Color. In Italian. 171 minutes.

1978 Australian Opera, Sydney

Australian stage production: Sandro Sequi (director), Richard Bonynge (conductor, Elizabethan Sydney Orchestra and Australian Opera Chorus).

Cast: Joan Sutherland (Norma), Margreta Elkins (Adalgisa), Ronald Stevens (Pollione), Clifford Grant (Oroveso), Etela Piha (Clotilde), Trevor Brown (Flavio).

Video: Arthaus Musik DVD/Kultur and Home Vision VHS. William Fitzwater (director). Color. In Italian with English subtitles. 181 minutes.

1981 Canadian Opera

Canadian stage production: Lotfi Mansouri (director), Richard Bonynge (conductor, Canadian Opera Company Orchestra and Chorus), Jose Varona (set/costume designer).

Cast: Joan Sutherland (Norma), Tatiana Troyanos (Adalgisa), Francisco Ortiz (Pollione), Justino Diaz (Oroveso), Frances Ginzer (Clotilde), Michael Shust (Flavio).

Video: VAI DVD/VHS. Norman Campbell (director). Color. In Italian with English subtitles. 150 minutes.

2001 Teatro Regio, Parma

Italian stage production: Roberto Andò (director), Fabio Biondi (conductor, Europa Galante Orchestra and Verdi Festival Chorus)

Cast: June Anderson (Norma), Daniela Barcellona (Adalgisa), Shin Young Hoon (Pollione), Ildar Abdrazakov (Oroveso), Svetlana Ignatovich (Clotilde), Leonardo Melani (Flavio).

Video: TDK DVD (two discs). Carlo Battistoni (director). Color. In Italian with English subtitles. 163 minutes.

Comment: The orchestra plays on period instruments, and Anderson is most impressive.

Early/related films

1911 Film d'Arte Italiana

Rina Agozzino-Alessio plays Norma in a silent Italian adaptation of the opera titled *La Norma* and directed by Gerolamo Lo Savio for Film d'Arte Italiana of Rome. Bianca Lorenzoni plays Adalgisa and Alfredo Robert is Pollione. The film was screened with music from the opera played live. Black and white. About 14 minutes.

1911 Vesuvio Films

Romolo Bacchini directed this competing 1911 silent Italian film version of the opera for Vesuvio Films of Naples. It was titled *Norma (Episodio della Gallia sotto il dominio di Roma Imperiale)* and also screened with

music from the opera. Black and white. About 19 minutes.

1930 A Lady's Morals

Grace Moore, playing Jenny Lind in this film biography, loses her voice on stage in Italy while singing "Casta diva." See JENNY LIND.

1939 Fascino

Italian opera soprano Iva Pacetti, who sang in Chicago in the early 1930s and was one of the leading singers at La Scala up to 1942, plays a diva who stars in *Norma*. A fire during a performance creates a panic that causes her sister to lose her voice. Ten years later the sister, now a ballerina, finds herself on stage in the same opera, and the shock brings back her voice. Singing with Pacetti in the *Norma* sequences are mezzo Gilda Alfano, tenor Renato Gigli, and bass Giuseppe Flamini. Giacinto Solito directed. Black and white. In Italian. 80 minutes.

1947 Anni difficili

Luigi Zampa's *The Difficult Years* includes a scene set in an opera house during a performance of *Norma*. Fascist officials are upset by Norma's criticism of ancient Rome in the opera and want the opera banned. Black and white. In Italian. 95 minutes.

1951 Amore di Norma

This Italian film about a love affair between a soprano (Lori Randi) and a tenor (Gino Mattera) is primarily an excuse to present excerpts from Italian operas. It also features baritone Afro Poli. Giuseppe Di Martino directed. Black and white. In Italian. 87 minutes.

1978 Fatto de sangue

Lina Wertmuller's bizarre love triangle film features the aria "Casta diva" on the soundtrack every time lawyer Marcello Mastroianni gets together with widow Sophia Loren. The full Italian title of the film is *Fatto de sangue tra due uomini a causa di una vedova* (Blood feud between two men because of a widow). In America it was titled simply *Blood Feud*. Color. In Italian. 112 minutes.

1980 Atlantic City

"Casta diva" is memorably performed by Elizabeth Harwood and the London Philharmonic in the sensual opening scene of this fine movie. Burt Lancaster watches unobserved from his window as Susan Sarandon takes a lemon bath. The aria sets the scene for their relationship in the film. Louis Malle directed this Venice Film Festival Grand Prize winner. Paramount. Color. 104 minutes. Paramount VHS.

1982 Casta diva

Eric De Kuyper's experimental Dutch film uses the *Norma* aria as a central theme although there is much other opera music on its soundtrack. Color. 110 minutes.

1987 Terror at the Opera

Dario Argento's horror film, which revolves around Verdi's *Macbeth,* also includes the aria "Casta diva" on the soundtrack, sung by Maria Callas. See TERROR AT THE OPERA.

1990 Perfectly Normal

Norma is performed in drag in a restaurant as operatic entertainment in the hilarious climax of this Canadian film. Michael Riley plays Norma to Robbie Coltrane's Pollione. See PERFECTLY NORMAL.

1992 Lorenzo's Oil

Maria Callas is heard singing "Casta diva" with the La Scala Orchestra and Chorus led by Tullio Serafin on the soundtrack of this George Miller film. The story concerns a couple (Susan Sarandon and Nick Nolte) fighting to save their child from a crippling illness. Color. 135 minutes.

1995 The Bridges of Madison County

Maria Callas is heard singing "Casta diva" on the radio at the beginning of this romantic film by Clint Eastwood. It is a prophetic moment for Italian-born housewife Meryl Streep. Tullio Serafin conducts the Teatro alla Scala Orchestra on the recording. Color. 135 minutes.

1997 Tell Me No Secrets

Maria Callas is heard on the soundtrack singing Norma's final aria "Deh! no volerli vittime" (Don't let them be victims) at the end of this thriller. Bobby Roth directed. Color. 90 minutes.

1999 A One and a Two

"Casta diva" is featured on the soundtrack of this complex film about events involving a middle-class family in present-day Taiwan. Edward Yang directed. Color. 173 minutes.

1999 A Midsummer Night's Dream

Renée Fleming is heard singing "Casta diva" on the soundtrack of this version of the Shakespeare play set in 19th-century Italy. Michael Hoffman directed. Color. 115 minutes.

2000 Brother

"Casta diva" is featured on the soundtrack of this film about a Japanese gangster who flees to Los Angeles to set up a criminal business with his brother. Takeshi Tikano directed. Color. 113 minutes.

NORMAN, JESSYE
American soprano (1945–)

Jessye Norman, who was born in Georgia and studied in U.S. universities, went to Germany to make her debut in 1969 with the Deutsche Oper in Berlin as Elisabeth in *Tannhäuser.* In 1972 she sang Aida at La Scala and Cassandra at Covent Garden. She made her U.S. debut in 1982 in Philadelphia, singing Stravinsky's Jocasta and Purcell's Dido, and gave her first performance at the Metropolitan Opera in 1983 as Cassandra in LES TROYENS (on video). Norman has a rare ability to make her voice as dramatic as it is beautiful, and her stage presence is most impressive. She is featured in several fine opera videos, including ARIADNE AUF NAXOS (1988), BLUEBEARD'S CASTLE (1989), CARMEN (1988 film), DIALOGUES DES CARMÉLITES (1987), ERWARTUNG (1989), OEDIPUS REX (1992), and VERDI REQUIEM (1982).

1986 Fanfare for Elizabeth

Norman sings "I Dreamt I Dwelt in Marble Halls" from Balfe's opera *The Bohemian Girl* at the Royal Opera House on April 21, 1986. Her performance was part of *Fanfare for Elizabeth,* a gala in honor of the queen. Color. 90 minutes. House of Opera VHS and video at the MPRC.

1987 Songs by Handel and Others

Norman sings songs by Handel, Schubert, Schumann, Brahms, and Strauss in a recital in June 1987 at the Schubertiade at the Hohenens Festival in Feld Kirch, Austria. Geoffrey Parson plays piano; Hugo Kach directed. Color. 59 minutes. Philips VHS.

1987 Karajan in Salzburg

Norman is seen in performance in *Tristan und Isolde* during the 1987 Salzburg Festival in this documentary. See HERBERT VON KARAJAN.

1988 Jessye Norman's Christmastide

Norman sings Christmas carols at Ely Cathedral with the American Boychoir, Vocal Arts Chorus, Ely Cathedral Choristers, and Bournemouth Symphony led by Robert DeCormier. Derek Jacobi introduces the concert; John Michael Phillips directed the telecast shown November 30, 1988. Color. In English. 51 minutes. Philips VHS.

1990 Spirituals in Concert

Norman teams with Kathleen Battle at Carnegie Hall for a program of spirituals. The divas, dressed in contrasting shades of blue, interact beautifully as they sing in a variety of styles. James Levine leads the orchestra and a 70-member chorus. Brian Large directed. Color. 91 minutes. DG/Cami VHS.

1991 Symphony for the Spire
Norman performs with Plácido Domingo and others at Salisbury Cathedral to raise funds to restore its spire. Richard Armstrong conducts the English Chamber Orchestra and Mike Mansfield directed. Color. 65 minutes. New Line VHS.

1991 Jessye Norman at Notre Dame
Norman gives a recital of spirituals, sacred music, and carols at Notre Dame Cathedral in December 1991 with the Notre Dame Choir and Radio France National Orchestra led by Lawrence Foster. Color. 55 minutes. Philips VHS.

1991 Jessye Norman, Singer
Documentary tracing Norman's life from her early years in Georgia through her training and international career. She describes how she developed her repertory and worked to expand her vocal capabilities. She is shown in performance around the world. Color. 74 minutes. Filmmakers Library VHS.

1996 James Levine's Silver Anniversary Gala
Norman is one of the singers participating in James Levine's 25th anniversary gala celebration at the Met. See JAMES LEVINE.

NORTON, FREDERIC
English composer (1875–1940)

Frederic Norton's CHU CHIN CHOW, one of the greatest operetta successes of the London stage, is an old-fashioned romantic tale about a slave girl and a robber based on the story of Ali Baba and the 40 Thieves. Norton, who began his musical career as an opera singer with the Carl Rosa Company, had no other major success.

NOVELLO, IVOR
English composer (1893–1951)

Ivor Novello kept the romantic operetta alive in England when his contemporaries abandoned it for jazz rhythms and musical comedy. They may have been retrograde, but they made him very popular; GLAMOROUS NIGHT (1935), THE DANCING YEARS (1939), and KING'S RHAPSODY (1949) were huge hits and were all filmed. Novello was also a notable performer on stage and film. His movies include a 1922 adaptation of Balfe's opera THE BOHEMIAN GIRL, *The White Rose* (1923), *The Rat* (1925)

and *The Lodger* (1926/1932). His music began to come back into fashion in the 21st century when he was portrayed in Robert Altman's film *Gosford Park,* where his songs delight even the servants. Novello died during the second year of the run of *King's Rhapsody* at the Theatre Royal, Drury Lane.

1975 The Music of Ivor Novello
This Canadian television tribute to Novello features performances of his songs by Mary Costa, Anna Shuttleworth, Judith Forst, and Robert Jeffrey. Richard Bonynge accompanies on piano. Color. In English. 60 minutes. Opera Dubs VHS.

2001 Gosford Park
Ivor Novello, played by Jeremy Northam, is one of the principal characters in Robert Altman's upstairs-downstairs English murder mystery. When he plays a medley of his own songs on the piano in the drawing room, all the servants leave their work to listen. Color. 136 minutes.

NOVOTNÁ, JARMILA
Czechoslovakian soprano (1907–1994)

Jarmila Novotná, who studied with legendary Czech soprano Emmy Destinn, made her debut in Prague in 1925. During the 1930s she sang regularly in Vienna and Salzburg and created the title role of Lehár's *Giuditta* at the Vienna Staatsoper in 1934. Louis B. Mayer wanted her to make musicals in Hollywood, but she turned him down and instead made films in Austria, Czechoslovakia, and Germany. Her most famous opera film of this period is Max Ophuls's classic 1932 THE BARTERED BRIDE, but she also starred in some excellent German operetta films including DER BETTELSTUDENT (1931), FRASQUITA (1934), and DER LETZTE WALZER (1936). She went to America in 1939 and was a stalwart at the Metropolitan from 1940 to 1956, noted especially for performances as Violetta in *La traviata.* She gave an outstanding nonsinging performance in the 1948 film *The Search,* had an important but unsympathetic role in *The Great Caruso* in 1951, played Orlofsky in a televised production of DIE FLEDERMAUS in 1953, and was Madame Baronska in a televised production of the JOHANN STRAUSS operetta *The Great Waltz* in 1955.

1930 Brand in der Oper
Novotná plays an opera singer in *Fire at the Opera,* a German film set in an opera house. A rich man has arranged a production to star a chorus girl he loves, but the theater burns down at the premiere. Carl Froelich directed. A French version titled *Barcarolle d'amour* was made at the same time, directed by Henry Roussell. Black and white. In German or French. 90 minutes.

1933 Song of the Lark

Novotná sings in her native language in the Czech film *Skřivánčí píseň* (released in America as *Song of the Lark*) in which she plays an opera diva who returns to her home village in southern Bohemia. A young man (Adolf Horálek) she knew as a child, now studying for the priesthood, falls in love with her, but she nobly decides to give him up to make his dying mother (Vera Ford) happy. Novotná is seen on stage in *Carmen* and also sings music by Smetana. Svatopluk Inneman, who made the Czech film of *The Bartered Bride,* directed. Black and white. In Czech. 85 minutes.

1933 Die Nacht der grossen Liebe

Novotná stars opposite Gustav Fröhlich in *The Night of Great Love,* a popular German musical with a score by Robert Stolz. The plot revolves around competition between Novotná and her teenaged daughter (Christiane Graufoff) for the love of a naval officer. Geza von Bolvary directed. Black and white. In German. 94 minutes.

1935 Der Kosak und die Nachtigall

Novotná plays an opera singer in her last German-language film, *The Cossack and the Nightingale,* an espionage tale based on a novel by Georg C. Klaren with original music by Franz Lehár. Her costars include Ivan Petrovich, Rudolf Klein-Rogge, and Fritz Imhoff. Phil Jutzi directed. Black and white. In German. 85 minutes.

1948 The Search

Novotná is superb in a nonsinging role playing a desperate mother searching for her lost son around Europe after World War II. Montgomery Clift plays an American soldier in Germany who has found the child and is looking after him. Audiences left the theaters in tears after seeing this three-handkerchief movie; it had four Oscar nominations and won for Best Screenplay. Master filmmaker Fred Zinnemann directed. Black and white. In English. 105 minutes.

1951 The Great Caruso

Novotná has a somewhat unsympathetic role in *The Great Caruso,* although she carries it off well. She plays a temperamental prima donna named Maria Selko who insults Caruso (Mario Lanza) when he first arrives at Covent Garden. See THE GREAT CARUSO.

NOYE'S FLUDDE
1958 church opera by Britten

God tells Noye (Noah) to build an ark, so he and his family do so. Animals of all kinds are brought on board, but Mrs. Noye is forced to leave her gossipy friends behind. After a terrific storm and a huge flood, the raven and the dove find dry land. God tells them all to disembark. Benjamin Britten's 50-minute "Chester miracle play," libretto by the composer, was premiered at Orford Church in Suffolk in 1958.

1964 St. George's Episcopal Church, New York

American church production: Richard Flusser (stage director), Marvin Silbersher (film director), Charles N. Henderson (conductor, CBS Orchestra), Peter Harvey (set designer).

Cast: Norman Riggins (Noye), Marie Powers (Mrs. Noye), Francis Barnard (Voice of God).

Telecast December 27, 1964, by CBS Television. Black and white. In English. 60 minutes.

Comment: Produced by CBS News and filmed at St. George's Church as a Christmas special.

NOZZE DI FIGARO, LE
1786 opera by Mozart

WOLFGANG A. MOZART's *Le nozze di Figaro* (The Marriage of Figaro) is nearly the perfect opera with memorable music, wonderful characterizations, an entertaining plot, and amazing ensembles. Lorenzo Da Ponte's delightful libretto is based on an excellent play by Beaumarchais, considered quite radical in its time, not long before the French Revolution. Figaro and Susanna make plans to marry, but they have to counter the Count's designs to bed her first. They get help from the Countess and the page Cherubino and eventually succeed after many unforeseen difficulties. The opera has been very popular with filmmakers, and quotations from it are often used in narrative movies. There are several excellent versions of the opera on video, including stage productions at Glyndebourne and Drottningholm and films by Ponnelle and Sellars.

1933 Le barbier de Séville

French feature film: Hubert Bourlon and Jean Kemm (directors), Pierre Maudru (screenplay), Marcel Lucine (cinematographer), L. Masson (conductor), Robert Gys (set designer).

Cast: Hélène Robert (Rosine), André Baugé (Figaro), Jean Galland (Almaviva), Pierre Juvenet (Bartholo), Fernand Charpin (Basile), Josette Day (Suzanne), Monique Rolland (Chérubin), Yvonne Yma (Marceline).

Video: Video Yesteryear VHS. Black and white. In French. 93 minutes.

Comment: This film combines Rossini's *The Barber of Seville* with Mozart's *Le nozze di Figaro* and tells the story and uses the music of both. There are also plot changes, for example, Rosine and Almaviva get married during the music lesson.

1948 First Opera Film Festival

Italian stage production: Enrico Fulchigoni (director), Edmondo Cancellieri (film director), Angelo Questa (conductor, Rome Opera House Orchestra and Chorus), Raffaele Gervasio (screenplay), George Richfield (producer).

Cast: Piero Biasini (Figaro), Pina Malgharini (Susanna, sung by Gianna Perea Zabia), Lidia Melasei (Countess, sung by Gabriella Gatti), Giulio Tomei (Count, sung by Luciano Neroni), Gino Conti (Bartolo, sung by Giulio Tomei), Cloe Elmo (Cherubino).

Video: Yesteryear VHS. Black and white. In Italian with English voice-over. 25 minutes.

Comment: Highlights version of the opera sung in Italian and filmed at the Rome Opera House with singers from La Scala and Rome for the anthology film *First Opera Film Festival*.

1949 Wildhagen film

German feature film: Georg Wildhagen (director), Arthur Rother (conductor, Berlin State Chamber Orchestra), Eugen Klagemann and Karl Flintzner (cinematographers), DEFA (production).

Cast: Willi Domgraf-Fassbaender (Figaro), Angelika Hauff (Susanna, sung by Erna Berger), Sabine Peters (Countess, sung by Tiana Lemnitz), Mathieu Ahlersmeyer (Count), Willi Puhlmann (Cherubino, sung by Anneliese Muller), Victor Jansen (Bartolo, sung by Eugen Fuchs), Alfred Dalthoff (Basilio, sung Paul Schmidtmann), Elsa Wagner (Marcellina, sung by Margarete Klose).

Video: Lyric VHS/Dreamlife (Japan) VHS and LD. Black and white. In German. 105 minutes.

Comment: Sung in German but with spoken dialogue. The German title is *Figaros Hochzeit*.

1954 NBC Opera Theatre

American TV production: Charles Polacheck (director), Samuel Chotzinoff (producer), Peter Herman Adler (conductor, Symphony of the Air orchestra), William Molyneux (set designer), Edward Eager (English translation).

Cast: Ralph Herbert (Figaro), Virginia Haskins (Susanna), Laurel Hurley (Countess), William Shriner (Count), Ann Crowley (Cherubino), Emile Renan (Bartolo), Ruth Kobart (Marcellina), John McCollum (Basilio), Paul Ukena (Antonio).

Video at the MTR. Telecast live in 90-minute parts on successive Saturdays in February 1954. Kirk Browning (director). Black and white. In English. 180 minutes.

1954 Vienna State Opera Mozart Ensemble

Austrian stage production: Alfred Stöger (director), Rudolf Moralt (conductor, Vienna Philharmonic).

Cast: Emmy Loose (Susanna), Erich Kunz (Figaro), Paul Schöffler (Count), Hilde Gueden (Cherubino), Hilde Zadek (Countess), Peter Klein (Basilio).

Video: Taurus (Germany) VHS. Color. In German. 30 minutes.

Comment: Highlights version of the opera included on the anthology film *Unsterblicher Mozart* (Immortal Mozart) with two other Mozart operas.

1967 Hamburg State Opera

German film of stage production: Joachim Hess (film director), Rolf Liebermann (producer), Hans Schmidt-Isserstedt (conductor, Hamburg State Opera Orchestra and Chorus), Hannes Schindler (cinematographer), Ita Maximovna (art director).

Cast: Heinz Blankenburg (Figaro), Edith Mathis (Susanna), Arlene Saunders (Countess), Tom Krause (Count), Elisabeth Steiner (Cherubino), Noël Mangin (Bartolo), Maria von Ilosvay (Marcellina), Kurt Marschner (Basilio), Natalie Usselmann (Barbarina).

Color. In German. 189 minutes.

Comment: Released theatrically in America. The German title is *Die Hochzeit des Figaro*.

***1973 Glyndebourne Festival

English stage production: Peter Hall (director), John Pritchard (conductor, London Philharmonic Orchestra and Glyndebourne Festival Chorus), John Bury (set designer).

Cast: Knut Skram (Figaro), Ileana Cotrubas (Susanna), Kiri Te Kanawa (Countess), Benjamin Luxon (Count), Frederica von Stade (Cherubino), Marius Rintzler (Bartolo), John Fryatt (Basilio), Nucci Condo (Marcellina), Elizabeth Gale (Barbarina).

Video: Opera d'Oro/VAI VHS. Dave Heather (director), Humphrey Burton (producer). Color. In Italian with English subtitles. 169 minutes.

***1976 Ponnelle film

Austrian feature film: Jean-Pierre Ponnelle (director/designer), Karl Böhm (conductor, Vienna Philharmonic Orchestra), Ernst Wild (cinematographer).

Cast: Hermann Prey (Figaro), Mirella Freni (Susanna,) Kiri Te Kanawa (Countess), Dietrich Fischer-Dieskau (Count), Maria Ewing (Cherubino), Paolo Montarsolo (Bartolo), Heather Begg (Marcellina), John van Kesteren (Basilio), Janet Perry (Barbarina).

Video: DG VHS. Color. In Italian with English subtitles. 181 minutes.

Comment: This is a virtual continuation of Ponnelle's 1972 *Barber of Seville,* shot on a sound stage with a superb cast and fine direction.

1976 Komische Opera, East Berlin

East German stage production: Walter Felsenstein (director/German translation), Rolf Reuter (conductor, Komische Oper Orchestra and Chorus).

Cast: Jozsef Dene (Figaro), Ursula Reinhardt-Kiss (Susanna), Magdalena Falewicz (Countess), Uwe Kreyssig (Count), Ute Trekel-Burckhardt (Cherubino).

Video: Dreamlife (Japan) DVD/VHS. Telecast in East Germany November 28, 1976. Georg F. Mielke (director). Color. In German. 163 minutes.

1980 Paris Opéra

French stage production: Giorgio Strehler (director), Sir Georg Solti (conductor, Paris Opéra Orchestra and Chorus), Ezio Frigerio (set/costume designer).

Cast: José van Dam (Figaro), Lucia Popp (Susanna), Gundula Janowitz (Countess), Gabriel Bacquier (Count), Frederica von Stade (Cherubino), Kurt Moll (Bartolo), Jane Berbié (Marcellina), Michel Sénéchal (Basilio), Danièle Perriers (Barbarina).

Video: House of Opera DVD/VHS. Pierre Babel (director). Color. In Italian. 177 minutes.

***1981 Drottningholm Court Theatre

Swedish stage production: Göran Järvefelt (director), Arnold Östman (conductor, Drottningholm Court Theatre Orchestra and Chorus).

Cast: Mikael Samuelsson (Figaro), Georgine Resick (Susanna), Sylvia Lindenstrand (Countess), Per-Arne Wahlgren (Count), Ann Christine Biel (Cherubino), Erik Saedén (Bartolo), Karin Mang-Habashi (Marcellina), Torbjörn Lilliequist (Basilio), Birgitta Larsson (Barbarina).

Video: Image Entertainment DVD/Philips VHS and LD. Thomas Olofsson (director). Color. In Italian with English subtitles. 179 minutes.

Comment: Delightful authentic production with period orchestra.

1985 Metropolitan Opera

American stage production: Jean-Pierre Ponnelle (director/designer), James Levine (conductor, Metropolitan Opera Orchestra and Chorus).

Cast: Ruggero Raimondi (Figaro), Kathleen Battle (Susanna), Carol Vaness (Countess), Thomas Allen (Count), Frederica von Stade (Cherubino).

Video at the MTR. Taped December 14, 1985; telecast April 23, 1986. Brian Large (director). Color. In Italian with English subtitles. 180 minutes.

***1990 Sellars film

American film: Peter Sellars (director), Craig Smith (conductor, Vienna Symphony Orchestra and Arnold Schoenberg Chorus), Adrianne Lobel (set designer), Dunya Ramicova (costume designer).

Cast: Sanford Sylvan (Figaro), Jeanne Ommerle (Susanna), Jayne West (Countess), James Maddalena (Count), Susan Larson (Cherubino), David Evitts (Bartolo), Sue Ellen Kuzma (Marcellina), Frank Kelley (Basilio), Lyn Torgove (Barbarina).

Video: London VHS/LD. Color. In Italian with English subtitles. 193 minutes.

Comment: Sellars sets his updated version of the opera, filmed in a Vienna TV studio, in the Trump Tower. Figaro is the Count's chauffeur, the Count is a very rich man who threatens the Countess with a gun, and Cherubino is quite macho in an American football uniform. It works well most of the time, and there are enjoyable references to vintage film comedy.

1991 New York City Opera

American stage production: John Copley (director), Scott Bergeson (conductor, New York City Opera Orchestra and Chorus), Carl Toms (set/costume designer).

Cast: Dean Peterson (Figaro), Maureen O'Flynn (Susanna), Elizabeth Hynes (Countess), William Stone (Count), Kathryn Gamberoni (Cherubino), Joseph McKee (Bartolo), Susanne Marsee (Marcellina), Jonathan Green (Basilio), Michele McBride (Barbarina).

Telecast September 25, 1991, in the *Live From Lincoln Center* series. Kirk Browning (director). Color. In Italian with English subtitles. 195 minutes.

1992 Vienna State Opera

Austrian stage production: Jonathan Miller (director), Claudio Abbado (conductor, Vienna State Opera Orchestra and Chorus), Peter J. Davison (set designer).

Cast: Lucio Gallo (Figaro), Marie McLaughlin (Susanna), Cheryl Studer (Countess), Ruggero Raimondi (Count), Gabrielle Sima (Cherubino), Rudolph Mazzola (Bartolo), Heinz Zednik (Basilio), Margherita Lilowa (Marcellina), Yvetta Tannebergerova (Barbarina).

Video: Sony VHS/LD. Shot in HDTV. Brian Large (director). Color. In Italian. 181 minutes.

1993 Théâtre du Châtelet, Paris

French stage production: Jean Louis Thamin (director), John Eliot Gardiner (conductor, English Baroque Soloists), Rudy Saboughi (set designer).

Cast: Bryn Terfel (Figaro), Alison Hagley (Susanna), Hillevi Martinpelto (Countess), Rodney Gilfry (Count), Pamela Helen Stephen (Cherubino), Carlos Feller (Bartolo), Francis Egerton (Basilio), Susan McCulloch (Marcellina).

Video: DG DVD/VHS/LD. Olivier Mille (director). Color. In Italian. 170 minutes.

Comment: Gardiner restructured some of the music to what he believed was Mozart's original intention for this excellent touring production.

1994 Glyndebourne Festival

English stage production: Stephen Medcalf (director), Bernard Haitink (conductor, London Philharmonic Orchestra and Glyndebourne Chorus).

Cast: Gerald Finley (Figaro), Alison Hagley (Susanna), Renée Fleming (Countess), Andreas Schmidt (Count), Marie-Ange Todorovitch (Cherubino), Manfred Rohrl (Bartolo), Wendy Hillhouse (Marcellina), Robert Tear (Basilio), Susan Gritton (Barbarina).

Video: House of Opera/NVC Arts (GB) DVD and VHS. Derek Bailey (director), Telecast May 28, 1994, in England. Color. In Italian. 189 minutes.

Comment: The first production of the rebuilt Glyndebourne Festival Theatre was, appropriately, the opera that began the Glyndebourne legend.

1994 Opéra National de Lyon

French stage production: Jean-Pierre Vincent (director), Paolo Olmi (conductor, Opéra National de Lyon Orchestra and Chorus).

Cast: Giovanni Furlanetto (Figaro), Elzbieta Szymtka (Susanna), Janice Watson (Countess), Ludovic (Count), Francesca Provvisionato (Cherubino), Rebecca Hoffmann (Barbarina), Marcello Lippi (Bartolo), Tiziana Tramonte (Marcellina), Sergio Bertocchi (Basilio).

Video: Kultur DVD/VHS. Color. In Italian with English subtitles. 193 minutes.

1995 Music Theatre London

English stage production: Nick Broadhurst (stage director/English translation), Geoff Posner (television director/TV adaptation), Tony Britten (conductor, Music Theatre London Orchestra/English translation), BBC Television (production).

Cast: Harry Burton (Figaro), Mary Lincoln (Susanna) Jan Hartley (Countess), Andrew Wadsworth (Count), Jacinta Mulcahy (Cherubino), Denis Quilley (Bartolo), Tricia George (Marcellina), Simon Butteriss (Basilio).

Video: Sony (GB) VHS. Color. In English. 180 minutes.

Comment: This BBC adaptation of Music Theater London's updated version of the opera is set in a National Trust house in the Home Counties and sung in modern English with spoken recitatives. The Count is a Tory Euro plutocrat, Susanna is a spunky Essex girl who kicks him in the groin when he gets fresh, and the Countess is an exercise fanatic.

1995 Lyon Opera

French stage production: Jean-Pierre Vincent (director), Paolo Olmi (conductor, Lyon Opera Orchestra and Chorus), Erich Wonder (set designer).

Cast: Giovanni Furlanetto (Figaro), Elzbieta Szmytka (Susanna), Janice Watson (Countess), Ludovic Tézier (Count), Marcello Lippi (Bartolo), Sergio Bertocchi (Basilio).

Video: Arthaus DVD. Mate Rabinowski (director). Color. In Italian with English subtitles. 190 minutes.

Comment: Surprisingly enjoyable, well sung and nicely staged..

1996 Zurich Opera

Swiss stage production: Jürgen Flimm (director), Nikolaus Harnoncourt (conductor, Zurich Opera House Orchestra and Chorus), Erich Wonder (set designer).

Cast: Carlos Chausson (Figaro), Isabel Rey (Susanna), Eva Mei (Countess), Rodney Gilfry (Count), Liliana Nikiteanu (Cherubino), Robert Holl (Bartolo), Elisabeth von Magnus (Marcellina), Volker Vogel (Basilio), Lisa Larsson (Barbarina).

Video: House of Opera/DK (GB) DVD and House of Opera VHS. Felix Breisach (director). Color. In Italian with English subtitles. 197 minutes.

1998 Metropolitan Opera

American stage production: Jonathan Miller (director), James Levine (conductor, Metropolitan Opera Orchestra and Chorus), Peter Davison (set designer).

Cast: Bryn Terfel (Figaro), Cecilia Bartoli (Susanna), Renée Fleming (Countess), Dwayne Croft (Count), Susanne Mentzer (Cherubino), Paul Plishka (Bartolo), Wendy White (Marcellina), Heinz Zednik (Basilio), Danielle De Niese (Barbarina).

Taped November 11, 1998; telecast December 29, 1999, on PBS. Gary Halvorson (director). Color. In Italian with English subtitles. 210 minutes.

1999 Deutsche Staatsoper Berlin

German stage production: Thomas Langhoff (director), Daniel Barenboim (conductor, Berlin Philharmonic Orchestra and Deutsche Staatsoper Chorus), Herbert Knappmüller (set designer).

Cast: René Pape (Figaro), Dorothea Röschmann (Susanna), Emily Magee (Countess), Roman Trekel (Count), Patricia Risley (Cherubino), Rosemarie Lang (Marcellina).

Arthaus DVD. Alexandre Tarta (director). Color. In Italian with English subtitles. 191 minutes.

Early/related films

1911 Cines film
Italian silent film based on the opera and the play produced by Cines Film of Rome; it screened in theaters with music from the opera. Black and white. 10 minutes.

1913 Ambrosio film
Italian silent film of the opera/play shot on location in Seville for the Ambrosio studio of Turin. Eleuterio Rodolfi is Figaro, Gigetta Morano is Rosina, Ubaldi Stefani is the Count, Ada Mantero is Cherubino, Umberto Scapellin is Bartolo, and Ernesto Vaser is Basilio. Luigi Maggi directed. The same team also made a version of *The Barber of Seville*. Black and white. 15 minutes.

1920 Mack film
German silent feature film of the opera as *Figaros Hochzeit* written and directed by Max Mack, who made several other German opera films. Critics praised its painterly images. Black and white. About 60 minutes.

1929 Figaro
Gaston Ravel wrote and directed this French film based on the Beaumarchais trilogy of Figaro plays. It takes the story from *The Barber of Seville* through *Le nozze di Figaro* to *The Guilty Mother,* in which the Countess has a child by Cherubino. E. H. Van Duren plays Figaro, Tony D'Algy is the Count, Arlette Marchal is Rosine (Rosina, the Countess), Marie Bell is Suzanne (Susanna), and Jean Weber is Chérubin (Cherubino). Black and white. In French. 76 minutes.

1932 Educational Film
Scholastic film of a rehearsal of *Le nozze di Figaro*. It shows the singers on stage in scenes from the opera with orchestra. Produced by Educational Film. Black and white. In English. 14 minutes.

1942 Cairo
Jeanette MacDonald and Ethel Waters sing a duet from *Le nozze di Figaro* in this spy mystery in which McDonald plays a movie star in Cairo. W. S. Van Dyke directed. MGM. Black and white. In English. 101 minutes.

1952 So Little Time
Doomed romance in wartime Belgium between music student Maria Schell and German officer Marius Goring. Excerpts from *Le nozze di Figaro* are featured on the soundtrack. Compton Bennett directed. Black and white. In English. 88 minutes.

1953 Melba
Patrice Munsel, who plays Nellie Melba in this opulent British film biography, sings "Voi che sapete" from *Le nozze di Figaro*. See NELLIE MELBA.

1955 On Such a Night
Sesto Bruscantini (Figaro) and Sena Jurinac (Countess) are shown performing at the Glyndebourne Festival in this famous short film by Anthony Asquith. David Knight plays an American who goes to Glyndebourne to see *Le nozze di Figaro*. Oliver Messel designed the sets, Frank North was cinematographer, and Paul Dehn wrote the script. Color. 37 minutes.

1958 The Quiet American
The overture of the opera is played during the credits of this Graham Greene thriller over a caricature of Figaro because the company that produced the film is named Figaro Productions. Joseph L. Mankiewicz directed. Color. 120 minutes.

Figaro (1929): Figaro (E. H. Van Duren) and Suzanne (Marie Bell) in French film of the trilogy of plays by Beaumarchais.

1959 Le mariage de Figaro
This French film of the Beaumarchais play uses the opera music as score. Jean Piat is Figaro, Micheline Boudet is Suzanne, Georges Descrières is the Count, Yvonne Gaudeau is the Countess, Denise Gence is Marceline, Jean Meyer is Basilio, and Michele Grellier is Chérubin. Erna Berger's singing voice is heard on the soundtrack. Jean Meyer directed the film, based on a Comédie-Française production. Color. In French. 105 minutes.

1959 The Nun's Story
Audrey Hepburn plays Cherubino's "Voi che sapete" on the piano with her father in a touching scene before she leaves for the convent. Fred Zinnemann directed. Color. 149 minutes.

1965 The Ipcress File
British intelligence agent Michael Caine (Len Deighton's Harry Palmer) meets his Albanian counterpart by a bandstand in a park to ransom a kidnapped scientist. The band plays the overture to *Marriage of Figaro,* and the Albanian comments on its delicacy. Sidney Furie directed. Color. 108 minutes.

1980 Hopscotch
Figaro's ironic martial aria "Non più andrai," sending Cherubino off to death or glory, is used ironically in this amiable spy comedy. As former spy Walter Matthau works out his escape from murderous CIA pursuers by crashing a plane, the tune is heard three times; Matthau hums the tune and Hermann Prey is heard singing it on the soundtrack. Ronald Neame directed; Brian Garfield wrote the first-class screenplay. Color. 104 minutes.

1983 Trading Places
The Overture to *Le nozze di Figaro* is appropriately featured at this beginning of this film in which street smart Eddie Murphy changes places with stockbroker Dany Ackroyd. John Landis directed. Color. 116 minutes

1984 Kaos
Italian writer Luigi Pirandello sees the ghost of his mother and hears Barbarina's aria "L'ho perduta" (I've lost it) in this Italian film by the brothers Paolo and Vittorio Taviani. She appears at his window and tells him the story of her lost innocence to this appropriate aria. Color. In Italian. 188 minutes.

1984 Amadeus
Milos Forman's Mozart biopic features scenes from *Marriage* staged by Twyla Tharpe in Prague's Tyl Theater. Miro Grisa is Figaro (sung by Samuel Ramey), Zuzana Kadlecova is Susanna (sung by Isobel Buchanan), Helena Cihelnikova is the Countess (sung by Felicity Lott), Karel Gult is the Count (sung by Richard Stilwell), Magda Celakovska is Cherubino (sung by Anne Howells), Slavena Drasilova is Barbarina (sung by Deborah Rees), Eva Senkova is Marcellina (sung by Patricia Payne), Ladislav Kretschmer is Antonio (sung by Willard White), Leos Kratochvil is Basilio (sung by Alexander Oliver), Bino Zeman is Curzio (sung by Robin Leggate), and Jaroslav Mikulin is Bartolo (sung by John Tomlinson). See AMADEUS.

1988 The Moderns
Alan Rudolph's film about American writers and artists in Paris during the 1920s includes Cherubino's aria "Voi che sapete" on the soundtrack. Color. 128 minutes.

1988 Berlin Blues
Opera mezzo Julia Migenes, playing a sultry Berlin nightclub performer, sings Susanna's aria "Deh vieni non tardar" in this Spanish film directed by Riccardo Franco. Color. 104 minutes. Cannon VHS/LD.

1989 Le Mariage de Figaro
This big-budget French film of the Beaumarchais play, shot in a chateau near Paris, follows the original closely. Roger Coggio directed. Color. In French. 171 minutes.

1993 The Last Action Hero
The acceptance of opera music in even the most commercial Hollywood films is reflected by the use of *Marriage* in *The Last Action Hero.* Arnold Schwarzenegger, playing a fictional movie hero chasing criminals in the "real" world, hears the opera overture on the radio and asks what it is. A woman tells him it is Mozart, and asks whether he likes classical music. I will, he promises. John McTiernan directed. Color. 100 minutes.

1993 L'Accompagnatrice
Barbarina's aria "L'ho perduta" is heard twice in this French film about life in Paris in 1942. The beautiful soprano Irene (Elena Safonova, sung by Laurence Monteyrol) sings it for her husband at his request, accompanied by the plain Sophie (Romane Bohringer, piano by Angeline Pondepeyre). It's repeated at an appropriate moment later in the film. Claude Miller directed. Color. In French with English subtitles. 100 minutes.

1993 Trading Places
The overture from the opera is featured on the soundtrack of this satirical comedy by John Landis. Eddie Murphy stars as a conman turned into a commodities broker. Color. 116 minutes.

1994 The Shawshank Redemption
Prisoner Tim Robbins appropriates the intercom system to let fellow inmates listen to opera—two women singing a duet—over the loudspeakers. Although the prisoners don't know what the women are singing, it's a liberating experience for Morgan Freeman and other inmates. What they hear is the duet "Che soave zeffiretto" from Act III of *Le nozze di Figaro,* sung by Edith Mathis as Susanna and Gundula Janowitz as the Countess, with the Deutsche Oper Berlin Orchestra led by Karl Böhm. Frank Darabont directed the film. Color. 142 minutes.

1996 Mozart: Overture to Le nozze di Figaro

An analysis of the overture to *Le nozze di Figaro* and how Mozart put it together; the music is played by The Scottish Chamber Orchestra led by William Conway. This is one episode in the video series *The Score: Classical Music Appreciation Through Listening.* Color. 15 minutes. Films for the Humanities & Sciences VHS.

1998 A Soldier's Daughter Never Cries

Francis Fortesque (Anthony Roth Costanzo) sings "Voi che sapete" during his music class in this film about an American writer (Kris Kristofferson) and his family living in Paris during the 1960s. James Ivory directed. Color. In English. 127 minutes.

1999 The Barber of Siberia

In Russia in 1885, soldier Oleg Menshikov plays the role of Figaro in a Military Institute production of *Le nozze di Figaro* put on for the Grand Duke. Nikita Mikhalkov directed. Color. In Russian. 180 minutes.

2000 Wild Side

Susanna's aria "Deh vieni non tardar," sung by Louise LeBrun with the Norddeutsche Philharmonic, is heard on the soundtrack of this pyschosexual thriller directed by Donald Cammell. Color. 115 minutes.

2000 Disco Pigs

The Vienna Philharmonic is heard performing music from the opera on the soundtrack of this Irish film about a couple totally obsessed with each other. Kirsten Sheridan directed. 93 minutes.

2001 The Man Who Wasn't There

Music from *Le nozze di Figaro* played by the Deutsche Opera Orchestra is featured in this film about a barber (Billy Bob Thornton) who gets involved in murder when his wife (Frances McDormand) has an affair with her boss. Joel Coen directed. Black and white. 115 minutes.

NUCCI, LEO
Italian baritone (1942–)

Leo Nucci began his career, while still a student, singing Figaro in *The Barber of Seville* at Spoleto in 1967, and it has remained one of his most popular roles. After a stint in the La Scala chorus, his real professional career began at La Fenice in 1975 in *La bohème* and at La Scala in 1976 as Figaro. He arrived at Covent Garden in 1978 and the Metropolitan in 1980, making his Met debut as Renato in *Un ballo in maschera*. Nucci is best known for his Verdi roles, and most of his videos are of Verdi operas. See UN BALLO IN MASCHERA (1991), IL BARBIERE DI SIVIGLIA (1988), I DUE FOSCARI (2000), FALSTAFF (1982),

LA FORZA DEL DESTINO (1984), LUCIA DI LAMMERMOOR (1981), MACBETH (1987), LUCIANO PAVAROTTI (1998), RIGOLETTO (1987/2001), JOAN SUTHERLAND (1987), TOSCA (2000), LA TRAVIATA (1994), IL TROVATORE (2000), VERDI (2001), VERONA (1988/1994), I VESPRI SICILIANI (1986), and IL VIAGGIO A REIMS (1984).

NYMAN, MICHAEL
English composer (1944–)

Michael Nyman, who was apparently the first to use the word "minimalism" to describe music, is best known for his film music, but he has also composed six operas. He first attracted attention with his near-operatic scores for Peter Greenaway films including *The Draughtsman's Contract* and *The Cook, The Thief, His Wife and Her Lover,* and he gained an even wider audience with his music for Jane Campion's popular film *The Piano.* Nyman's operas are all experimental in nature. The first was *The Kiss,* which he called a "video duet," created for Channel 4 television in England in 1984. More substantial are an opera about Mozart titled LETTERS, RIDDLES AND WRITS, which was televised, and an opera about a psychiatric disorder described by Dr. Oliver Sachs, THE MAN WHO MISTOOK HIS WIFE FOR A HAT, which was filmed. His major opera to date is the 2002 *Facing Goya,* about the search for the Spanish artist's skull.

O

OBERON
1826 opera by Weber

CARL MARIA VON WEBER's last opera, *Oberon, or the Elf King's Oath,* was written in English on a commission from Covent Garden to a libretto by James Robinson Planché. Elf King Oberon and Queen Titania have quarreled over whether man or woman is more inconstant and vow not to meet until they find a pair of faithful lovers. The chosen test case is Huon, who goes to Baghdad to marry the caliph's daughter Reiza. With a little help from Oberon, the pair are able to convince Titania they are faithful.

1968 Junkers film
German TV film: Herbert Junkers (director), Heinz Wallberg (conductor, Bamberger Symphony Orchestra).

Cast: René Kollo, Netta B. Ramati, Hans Putz, Ursula Schroeder-Feinen, Heinz Bosi.

Color. In German. 84 minutes.

1986 Edinburgh Festival
Scottish stage production: Frank Dunlop (director), Seiji Ozawa (conductor, Junge Deutsche Philharmonie and Edinburgh Festival Chorus), Carl Toms (set/costume designer).

Cast: Philip Langridge (Oberon), Elizabeth Connell (Rezia), Paul Frey (Huon), Benjamin Luxon (Scherasmin), LaVerne Williams (Fatima), James Robertson (Puck).

Video: Lyric VHS. Brian Large (director). Color. In English. 88 minutes.

OBERSTEIGER, DER
1894 operetta by Zeller

Carl Zeller's operetta *Der Obersteiger* (The Mine Foreman), libretto by Moritz West and Ludwig Heller, centers around Martin, the man in charge of a mining crew in a small village. Engaged to Nelly, he chases after another woman who turns out to be a countess in disguise; he ends up back with Nelly. The tenor aria known as the Obersteiger Waltz ("Sei nicht bös") has become popular with sopranos around the world, including Elizabeth Schwarzkopf and Hilde Gueden. In England it has been sung as "Don't Be Cross."

1952 Gloria film
Austrian feature film: Franz Antel (director), Jutta Bornemann, Gunther Philipp and F. Schreyvogl (screenplay), Hans Theyer (cinematographer), Hans Long (music director), Gloria Film (production).

Cast: Rudolf Carl (Martin), Waltraut Haas (Nelly), Helene Lauterböck (Countess Amalia), Hans Holt (Prince Max), Josefin Kipper (Princess Ludovika), (Wolf Albach-Retty (Andreas).

Black and white. In German. 92 minutes.

OBRAZTSOVA, ELENA
Russian mezzo-soprano (1937–)

Elena Obraztsova was born and brought up in Leningrad, but she joined the Moscow Bolshoi and made her debut there as Marina. She has performed around the world from La Scala and Covent Garden to the Metropolitan in Russian and Western operas and is especially popular in AIDA (1988), CARMEN (1979), *A Midsummer Night's Dream,* and *War and Peace.* The 1991 *Three Sopranos* concert video helped widen her reputation as did her film of CAVALLERIA RUSTICANA (1982) with Franco Zeffirelli. See SOPRANOS AND MEZZOS (1991) and VERONA (1988).

OCCASIONE FA IL LADRO, L'
1812 opera by Rossini

L'occasione fa il ladro (Opportunity Makes the Thief) is a jaunty early opera by GIOACHINO ROSSINI that has been revived on stage in recent years and is now on video and CD. It's a switched-identity farce with libertine Don Parmenione pretending to be Count Alberto to win Marquise Berenice, but she tricks him by switching identities with her maid Ernestina. In the end, the right couples get together after a lot of joyful music and good Rossini fun. The libretto by Luigi Prividali is based on a play by Eugène Scribe.

***1992 Schwetzingen Festival
German stage production: Michael Hampe (director and set designer), Gianluigi Gelmetti (conductor, Stuttgart Radio Symphony Orchestra).

Cast: Susan Patterson (Berenice), Natale de Carolis (Parmenione), Monica Bacelli (Ernestina), Stuart Kale (Eusebio), Robert Gambill (Count).

Video: Teldec VHS/LD. Claus Viller (director). Color. In Italian with English subtitles. 90 minutes.

Comment: Superbly staged and very appealing.

OEDIPUS REX
1927 opera by Stravinsky

Thebes is suffering from a plague because the murderer of Oedipus's father has not been punished. When Oedipus and his wife Jocasta realize that he is the guilty person, she hangs herself, having married him, and he blinds himself. IGOR STRAVINSKY's *Oedipus Rex,* composed in 1927 for Diaghilev's company Ballets Russes, is one of his most popular works. He wanted the libretto in a dead language to give it a timeless quality, and he wanted the characters to be masked; Jean Cocteau's libretto, based on Sophocles's version of the tragic myth, was translated into Latin by Jean Danielou.

1973 Harvard University

American stage production: Clark Santee (director), Leonard Bernstein (conductor, Boston Symphony Orchestra and Harvard Glee Club), Gene Callahan (set designer).

Cast: René Kollo (Oedipus), Tatiana Troyanos (Jocasta), Tom Krause (Creon), Ezio Flagello (Tiresias), Frank Hoffmeister (Shepherd), Michael Wager (Speaker), David Evitts (Messenger).

Video: Kultur VHS. Color. In Latin with English narration. 55 minutes.

Comment: In Volume Six of Bernstein's Harvard lecture series *The Unanswered Question.*

1984 Carré Theater, Amsterdam

Dutch stage production: Harry Wich (director/designer), Bernard Haitink (conductor, Concertgebouw Orchestra and N.O.S. Men's Choir).

Cast: Neil Rosenshein (Oedipus), Felicity Palmer (Jocasta), Claudio Desderi (Creon), Anton Scharinger (Tiresias), Justin Lavender (Shepherd), Alan Howard (Speaker), Anton Scharinger (Messenger).

Video: Home Vision VHS/LD. Hans Hulscher (director). Color. In Latin with English narration. 58 minutes.

***1992 Saito Kinen Festival, Matsumoto

Film of Japanese stage production: Julie Taymor (film/stage director), Seiji Ozawa (Saito Kinen Orchestra, Shinyu-Kai Chorus, and Tokyo Opera Singers), Bobby Bukowski (cinematographer), George Tsypin (set designer), Emi Wada (costume designer).

Cast: Philip Langridge (Oedipus, danced by Min Tanaka), Jessye Norman (Jocasta), Bryn Terfel (Creon), Harry Peters (Tiresias), Robert Swenson (Shepherd), Kayoko Shiraishi (Speaker), Michio Tatara (Messenger).

Video: Philips VHS/LD. Peter Kelb/Pat Jaffe (producers). Color. In Latin with English narration. 55 minutes.

Comment: A stunning, imaginative production, superbly sung and performed with extraordinary visual impact.

Related film

1961 Drama Into Opera: Oedipus Rex

Leonard Bernstein examines Stravinsky's opera with the help of Metropolitan Opera singers and compares it with the Sophocles play as performed by Broadway actors. Inge Borkh sings Jocasta with David Lloyd as Oedipus in excerpts from the opera, while Irene Worth plays Jocasta with Keith Michell as Oedipus in excerpts from the play. Bernstein comments on the differences between the two and conducts the New York Philharmonic on this CBS program. David Greene directed the telecast. Black and white. In English. 60 minutes. Video at the MTR.

OFFENBACH, JACQUES
German/French composer (1819–1880)

Jacques Offenbach, who popularized the operetta, was born a German but is more identified with French light opera than any other composer. He was not quite the father of the French operetta, but it was his successes that caused it to be recognized. His tuneful operettas, from *Orpheus in the Underworld* to *La Périchole,* remain popular, while his sole opera, *Les contes d'Hoffmann,* has become part of the international opera repertory. His music has been used thematically in many films, ranging from musicals such as Jean Renoir's *French Cancan* (1955) to Kenneth Branagh's romance *Peter's Friends* (1992). See BARBE-BLEUE, LA BELLE HÉLÈNE, LES BRIGANDS, LES CONTES D'HOFFMANN, LA GRANDE-DUCHESSE DE GÉROLSTEIN, LE MARRIAGE AUX LANTERNES, MONSIEUR CHOUFLEURI RESTERA CHEZ LUI LE..., ORPHÉE AUX ENFERS, LA PÉRICHOLE, and LA VIE PARISIENNE.

1949 La valse de Paris

The Paris Waltz is a romantic French film about Offenbach's relationship with his favorite singer and sometime mistress Hortense Schneider. Pierre Fresnay plays Offenbach, but the focus of the film is on Yvonne Printemps as Hortense, who sings some of Offenbach's best music; 20 songs and many stage sequences are included. Both stars are splendid, as is the re-creation of the period and opulent costumes by Dior. *Valse* was written and directed by one of the leading theater directors of the period, Marcel Achard. Black and white. In French with English subtitles. 93 minutes. Bel Canto Society VHS.

1952 Le Plaisir

Max Ophuls's omnibus film of three Guy de Maupassant short stories uses as its music themes from Offenbach operettas, arranged by Joe Hajos and Maurice Yvain. Jean Gabin heads the all-star cast. Black and white. In French. 97 minutes.

OF MEN AND MUSIC
1950 American film with opera content

This is a four-part docu-drama homage to classical music with a 20-minute segment devoted to Metropolitan Opera stars Jan Peerce and Nadine Conner. The story imagines them returning to a concert hall late at night where they put on a show in costume for the night watchman, a longtime fan. Peerce sings "O paradiso" from *L'Africaine* and Leoncavallo's "Mattinata"; Conner sings an aria from *Don Pasquale;* and they team up for the Act I duet from *Lucia di Lammermoor.* Victor Young conducts the unseen orchestra that accompanies them. The other segments of the film feature Artur Rubinstein, Jascha Heifetz, and Dimitri Mitropoulos with the New York Philharmonic. Harry Kurnitz wrote the screenplay, Irving Reis directed for Twentieth Century-Fox. Black and white. 95 minutes.

1977 Peerce, Anderson & Segovia
This 1977 compilation video includes the Jan Peerce and Nadine Conner segment of the film *Of Men and Music.* The other segments of the film feature Marian Anderson and Andrés Segovia. Black and white. 60 minutes. Kultur VHS.

OKLAHOMA!
1943 "vernacular opera" by Rodgers and Hammerstein

Composer Richard Rodgers and librettist Oscar Hammerstein's *Oklahoma!* has been called the first American vernacular opera. Like an opera it combines music, drama, and ballet in its story about a time when the state of Oklahoma was about to be born. Cowboy Curly wants to take farm girl Laurey to a box social and has problems with menacing hired hand Jud. Overly friendly Ado Annie gets doubly involved with cowboy Will and peddler Ali. *Oklahoma,* based on the play *Green Grow the Lilacs* by Lynn Riggs, premiered in 1943 with Alfred Drake as Curly, Joan Roberts as Laurey, Agnes de Mille as choreographer, and Rouben Mamoulian as director.

1955 Twentieth Century-Fox film
American feature film: Fred Zinnemann (director); Sonya Levien and William Ludwig (screenplay); Robert Surtees (cinematographer); Robert Russell Bennett, Jay Blackton, Adolph Deutsch (music directors); Twentieth Century-Fox (production).

Cast: Gordon MacRae (Curly), Shirley Jones (Laurey), Rod Steiger (Jud), Gloria Graham (Ado Annie), Charlotte Greenwood (Aunt Eller), Gene Nelson (Will).

Video: Fox DVD/VHS. Technicolor. Todd-AO. In English. 143 minutes.

Comment: Bennett, Blackton, and Deutsch won an Academy Award for the film's score; Surtees was nominated for the cinematography.

OLD DUTCH
1909 operetta by Herbert

"Old Dutch" is a nickname for a famous inventor who tries to have an incognito holiday in the Tyrol with his daughter. He runs into problems when he loses his identity papers. VICTOR HERBERT's operetta *Old Dutch,* libretto by Edgar Smith and lyrics by George V. Hobart, premiered at the Grand Opera House in Wilkes-Barre, Pennsylvania, in 1909 with Lew Fields as Old Dutch. This is one of Herbert's weaker stage works, but he recorded music from it.

1915 Shubert film
The Shubert Film Company turned *Old Dutch* into a silent film in 1915 with comedian Lew Fields reprising his stage role. Vivian Martin plays his daughter Violet, and George Hassell is the man who pretends to be Old Dutch. Frank Crane directed and wrote the screenplay. Herbert sued to block the film, but he was unsuccessful; it was screened in cinemas with his music performed live.

OLD MAID AND THE THIEF, THE
1939 opera by Menotti

Miss Todd and her servant Laetitia give shelter to the beggar Bob even after they discover that he is an escaped thief. They also rob a liquor store when he wants some gin to drink. When Miss Todd threatens to turn him over to the police, he steals her car and elopes with Laetitia. GIAN CARLO MENOTTI's opera *The Old Maid and the Thief,* commissioned by Samuel Chotzinoff for NBC, was one of the first operas composed especially for radio. It was broadcast April 22, 1939, and then put on stage by Philadelphia Opera. It has been televised at least nine times in the United States, Austria, Germany, Canada, and England.

1943 Hartt Opera Workshop
American TV production: Elemer Nagy (director), Moshe Paranov (conductor, Julius Hartt School of Music Orchestra and Chorus), Elemer Nagy (set designer), Truba Kaschmann (choreographer).

Cast: Students from the Julius Hartt School of Music Opera Workshop.

Telecast live in May 1943 on WRGB-TV. Robert Stone (director). Black and white. In English. 90 minutes.

Comment: Televised on a double bill with Offenbach's *Marriage by Lantern Light*. WRGB-TV was General Electric's pioneer station in Schenectady, New York.

1949 NBC Opera Theatre

American TV production: Gian Carlo Menotti (director), Peter Herman Adler (conductor, Symphony of the Air Orchestra), Samuel Chotzinoff (producer).

Cast: Marie Powers (Miss Todd), Norman Young (Bob), Virginia MacWatters (Laetitia), Ellen Faull (Miss Pinkerton.

Telecast live March 16, 1949, on NBC. Kirk Browning (director). Black and white. In English. 60 minutes.

Comment: Most of the television cast came from a New York City Opera production.

1954 BBC Television

English TV production: Christian Simpson (director), Stanford Robison (conductor, New London Orchestra).

Cast: Marie Powers (Miss Todd), Gwen Catley (Laetitia), Laurie Payne (Bob), Elena Danieli (Miss Pinkerton).

Telecast May 24, 1954, on BBC Television. Black and white. In English. 57 minutes.

1964 ORF Austrian Television

Austrian TV production: Otto Schenk (director), Wolfgang Rennert (conductor, Vienna Volksoper Orchestra), Gerhard Hruby (set designer).

Cast: Elisabeth Höngen (Miss Todd), Eberhard Wächter (Bob), Olive Moorefield (Laetitia), Hilde Konetzni (Miss Pinkerton).

Video: Premiere Opera VHS. Telecast June 26, 1964, on ORF Austrian Television. Black and white. In German. 60 minutes.

1972 WETA Television

American TV production: John Robbins (producer), Paul Hill (conductor, WETA-TV Orchestra), Peter Koch (set designer).

Cast: Charlotte Dixon (Miss Todd), Richard Estes (Bob), Suzanne Brock (Laetitia), Frances Bartley (Miss Pinkerton).

Telecast August 18, 1972, on PBS. David Deutsch (director). Color. In English. 60 minutes.

OLIVERO, MAGDA
Italian soprano (1910–)

Magda Olivero, who made her debut in Turin in 1933 and her Met debut as Tosca in 1975, was a favorite of composer Francesco Cilea. She became identified with the title role of his opera *Adriana Lecouvreur* in the 1950s after emerging from retirement and then sang it around the world for 30 more years, recording an aria in 1993 at the age of 83. Small wonder that she has acquired a cult following. She can be seen in full form in a 1960 Tosca and in a 1983 documentary about the opera.

1995 Magda Olivero: The Last Verismo Soprano

Compilation video of high points from Olivero's career. She is first heard singing the role of Adriana Lecouvreur in 1938, then is shown in 1993 singing the same role. The video also includes a 1960 TV show appearance with arias from *La traviata* and *Iris*, an excerpt from a 1960 film of *Tosca*, and an excerpt from *Manon Lescaut*. Color and black and white. 59 minutes. Bel Canto Society VHS.

OLOFSSON, THOMAS
Swedish TV director (1948–)

Thomas Olofsson produced and directed the videos of Mozart productions at the Drottningholm Court Theatre in Sweden conducted by Arnold Östman. While filming them with discretion and taste, he sometimes added intriguing extras. *Così fan tutte,* for example, has a charming visual prelude: while the overture is playing, the cast is seen arriving by foot, bike, and bus and changing into costume before going on stage. See AGRIPPINA (1985), ALCESTE (1998), LA CLEMENZA DI TITO (1987), COSÌ FAN TUTTE (1984), DON GIOVANNI (1987), DIE ENTFÜHRUNG AUS DEM SERAIL (1991), LA FINTA GIARDINIERA (1988), IDOMENEO (1991), LE NOZZE DI FIGARO (1981), and DIE ZAUBERFLÖTE (1989).

OMNIBUS
American television series (1952–1959)

The culturally oriented *Omnibus* series was involved with presenting opera and operetta from the start. Its first show on November 9, 1952, included scenes from THE MIKADO, the next program had scenes from THE MERRY WIDOW, and the third featured the Menotti chamber opera THE TELEPHONE. In 1953 *Omnibus* teamed with the Metropolitan Opera to present a large-scale version of DIE FLEDERMAUS in English involving more than 300 people. Next was a version of LA BOHÈME adapted from a Met production by Joseph Mankiewicz. *Omnibus* also produced operas without the help of the Met. They included Gershwin's BLUE MONDAY, Respighi's LA BELLA

DORMENTE NEL BOSCO, Schuman's THE MIGHTY CASEY, and Moore's THE BALLAD OF BABY DOE. The series, underwritten by the Ford Foundation, was seen originally on CBS and later on both ABC and CBS.

O'NEILL, DENNIS
Welsh tenor (1948–)

Dennis O'Neill, a Welsh tenor with an Irish name who began his career with the Scottish Opera, joined the English Glyndebourne Festival chorus in 1974. He was principal tenor with the South Australian Opera for two seasons and then sang with the Welsh National Opera and the Scottish Opera. He made his debut at Covent Garden in 1979 and was soon singing leading tenor roles for the Royal Opera. His career has widened to the United States and other European opera houses. See AIDA (1994), DIE FLEDERMAUS (1983), MACBETH (1987), MEFISTOFELE (1989), ADELINA PATTI (1993), DER ROSENKAVALIER (1985), KIRI TE KANAWA (1994), and VERDI (1994).

1993 Adelina Patti, Queen of Song
O'Neill plays the husband of diva Adelina Patti (June Anderson) in this English film by Chris Hunt. The music is performed by the Welsh National Opera Orchestra led by Robin Stapleton. Color. 60 minutes.

***ONE NIGHT OF LOVE
1934 American film with opera content

Met soprano Grace Moore helped fuel the surge of Hollywood opera films during the mid-1930s with this hugely successful movie and its inventive use of opera music. Movie audiences liked Moore for her personality as well as her voice; she looks wonderful, acts splendidly, and sings superbly. She plays Mary Barrett, an American who goes to Milan to study opera after failing to win a fellowship; her audition song is "One Night of Love." She impresses a courtyard full of competing musicians by singing "Follie!...follie!" over their noise and getting them to accompany her on the rest of the "Sempre libera" aria from *La traviata*. When her singing teacher Galuppi (Spanish bass Andrés De Segurola) makes a visit, he helps them divert the landlady (a former opera singer) from collecting rent by starting a sextet from *Lucia di Lammermoor* with Moore singing the tenor role; when the landlady arrives, they trick her into taking the soprano part. Giulio Monteverdi (Tullio Carminati), a top opera teacher, discovers her singing in a café and offers to make her an opera star. He has just broken off with his opera star lover Lalla (Mona Barrie), so he insists that their relationship must be strictly professional. Luis Alberni, who plays Monteverdi's rehearsal pianist, keeps her amused, but Monteverdi tyrannizes her as he trains her. They fall in love but won't admit it, and she thinks

he is still involved with Lalla. She sings "Letzte Rose" from *Martha* to quell her nervousness before going on a tour of regional theaters, and her big chance comes in Vienna, where she stars in *Carmen* and sings a splendid Habanera. After a misunderstanding about Lalla, she breaks up with Monteverdi and seizes a chance to sing *Madama Butterfly* at the Metropolitan Opera. She is unable to go on, however, until she sees him encouraging her from his usual place in the prompter's box; she then gives a magnificent performance, culminating in "Un bel di." The film was nominated for six Academy Awards, including Best Picture, Best Director, and Best Actress (Moore lost to Claudette Colbert), and it won for its score and sound. Pietro Cimini conducted the opera music, and Victor Schertzinger and Gus Kahn composed the thematic music. S. K. Lauren, James Gow, and Edmund North wrote the excellent screenplay (based on the play *Don't Fall in Love* by Dorothy Speare and Charles Beahan), Joseph Walker was the cinematographer, and Victor Schertzinger directed for Columbia Pictures. Black and white. 80 minutes. Columbia Classic VHS/LD.

One Night of Love (1935): Grace Moore tries to attract the attention of vocal coach Tullio Carminati in Schertzinger's film.

ONE NIGHT WITH YOU
1948 English film with opera content

One Night With You begins with Met tenor NINO MARTINI singing "O paradiso" over the credits. Playing an Italian opera singer traveling to Rome to make a movie, he gets stranded in a small town with Patricia Roc, who was on her to way to get married. Both have missed their trains, and as their money and papers are on the trains, they have a difficult time until they earn some food money by singing in the town square. One of the bank notes is counterfeit, however, so they end up in jail. Roc's father, fiancé, and lover come looking for her, but she prefers to escape from jail with Martini when he is freed by an opera-loving jailer. They appear to have fallen in love. Meanwhile, his clothes were found on the train by a tramp (Stanley Holloway), who puts them on and so gets mistaken for Martini when film people meet

507

him at the train station. He is made up to look like a dozen different opera characters, from Mephistopheles to Pagliacci, while the film's writers try to come up with a plot. They propose stories perilously close to *Aida* and *Il trovatore* but decide in the end to start with an aria from *La traviata*. The orchestra plays the introduction to the "Brindisi" twice, but Holloway is unable to sing a note (it is a silent role, he never speaks). Suddenly, there is a burst of glorious sound from off screen, and Martini enters belting out the aria. He takes his clothes back from Holloway, who is taken to jail, and Martini explains his romantic adventure to the film producer, who decides to use it as the story of the film. The final scene of the movie takes place in a screening room with Martini shown on the small screen singing as his girl marries another man. Roc says that is not the right ending, leaves her seat, and steps into the screen to join Martini for a happy ending. *One Night of Love* is a remake of the 1943 Italian film *Fuga a Due Voce*, which starred baritone GINO BECHI, and reprises two of the charming songs Bixio wrote for that movie. Caryl Brahms and S. J. Simon wrote the screenplay, based on Carlo Bragaglia's original story, and André Thomas was cinematographer. Terence Young, who directed the film for Two Cities, later became known for his James Bond movies. Black and white. In English. 92 minutes. Bel Canto Society/Live Opera VHS.

ON THE TOWN
1944 musical by Bernstein

Three sailors set out to discover New York during a 24-hour leave and meet three compatible women. Leonard Bernstein's Broadway musical *On The Town* is not very operatic, but it has been recorded and videotaped by opera singers in the principal roles. Betty Comden and Adolph Green wrote the lyrics and book and played the leading roles in the original production, Jerome Robbins created the choreography, and George Abbott staged it. *On the Town* grew out of Bernstein's ballet *Fancy Free*.

1949 MGM film
American feature film: Gene Kelly and Stanley Donen (directors/choreographers), Adolph Green and Betty Comden (screenplay), Harold Rosson (cinematographer), Lennie Hayton and Roger Edens (music directors).

Cast: Gene Kelly (Gabey), Frank Sinatra (Chip), Jules Munshin (Ozzie), Vera-Ellen (Ivy), Ann Miller (Claire), Betty Garrett (Hildy).

Video: MGM-UA VHS. Color. In English. 98 minutes.

Comment: Shot on location in New York. Hayton and Edens won an Oscar for the score.

1992 Barbican Hall, London
English concert production: Patricia Birch (director), Michael Tilson Thomas (conductor, London Symphony Orchestra and London Voices).

Cast: Thomas Hampson (Gabey), David Garrison (Ozzie), Kurt Ollmann (Chip), Samuel Ramey (Pitkin), Frederica von Stade (Claire), Tyne Daley (Hildy), Adolph Green and Betty Comden (narrators), Marie McLaughlin, Evelyn Lear, Cleo Laine.

Video: DG VHS/LD. Christopher Swann (director). Color. In English. 107 minutes.

OPEN-AIR OPERA

One of the pleasantest ways to watch opera in the summer is in the open air, preferably on video, as you get the best seats in the house and it is easier to see and hear the performers. Most of the major open-air opera venues in Europe issue videos of their performances. The largest and most famous is the Arena di Verona in Italy, an ancient Roman amphitheater seating 20,000 people with room for 3,000 on stage; it is famous for its gigantic sets and its *Aida* with elephants. Among its operas on video and DVD are AIDA (1966/1981), ATTILA (1985), MADAMA BUTTERFLY (1983), NABUCCO (1981), OTELLO (1982), RIGOLETTO (1981/2001), TOSCA (1984), IL TROVATORE (1985), and TURANDOT (1983). Equally spectacular is Bregenz in Austria, with a spectacular floating stage on a lake and highly imaginative sets. Among its operas on video/DVD are THE LEGEND OF THE INVISIBLE CITY OF KITEZH AND THE MAIDEN FEVRONIYA (1995), LUCIA DI LAMMERMOOR (1981), I PURITANI (1985), and LA WALLY (1990). Some of the finest productions have been staged at ancient Roman amphitheater in Orange, France, which attracts top singers. Its productions on video include AIDA (1976), ELEKTRA (1991), FIDELIO (1977), NORMA (1974), TRISTAN UND ISOLDE (1973), and IL TROVATORE (1972). The newest outdoor site is the St. Margarethen Opera Festival in an ancient Roman quarry in Austria, which claims to have "the biggest open-air stage in Europe"; its operas on video include AIDA (1997), CARMEN (1998), DIE ZAUBERFLÖTE (1999), and NABUCCO (2000). For grandiose operetta, there are large-scale productions of Strauss and Lehár classics at the Seefestspiele Mörbisch in Austria; its video releases include DIE CSÁRDÁSFÜRSTIN, IM WEISSEN RÖSSL, DIE LUSTIGE WITWE, EINE NACHT IN VENEDIG, and DER ZIGEUNERBARON. The major open-air summer venue in the United States is the Santa Fe Opera in New Mexico; it does not issue videos but there have been telecasts of several productions, including THE MOTHER OF US ALL and EMMELINE (1996).

OPERA

See TERROR AT THE OPERA.

OPERA CAMEOS
American television series (1950–1955)

Opera Cameos presented 30-minute highlight versions of famous operas in their original languages (mostly Italian) on U.S. television. They usually featured three or four arias or duets performed by well-known singers, sometimes from the Metropolitan; they included Mario Del Monaco, Regina Resnik, Ettore Bastianini, Irene Fratiza, Brenda Lewis, Martial Singher, Rina Telli, and Beverly Sills (just beginning her career and singing *Thaïs* and *La traviata*) The series, which originated on the New York station WPIX-TV in 1950, was presented on the DuMont Network from its New York station WABD from November 8, 1953, to January 8, 1955. The operas were introduced and their plots explained, first by Hugh La Rue or H. E. Currier and then by Giovanni Martinelli on DuMont. They were produced by Carlo Vinti and written by Joseph Vinti, with Giuseppe Bamboschek and Salvatore Dell'Isola conducting the Opera Cameos Orchestra. The programs were sponsored by Progresso Quality Foods and Gallo Wines, and there was usually a commercial after every number. The potted operas presented included CAVALLERIA RUSTICANA (1952), LA FORZA DEL DESTINO (1951), PAGLIACCI (1953), RIGOLETTO (1951/1952), THAÏS (1954), and LA TRAVIATA (1953/1954).

OPERA HOUSES

Quite a number of films and TV programs, both fiction and nonfiction, are devoted to the history and achievements of the world's great opera houses. The most interesting and most numerous are those about LA SCALA, which has had so many notable premieres. There are also fascinating films about La Fenice in VENICE, ROYAL OPERA in London, GLYNDEBOURNE in England, METROPOLITAN OPERA in New York, SAN FRANCISCO OPERA in California, Opéra Bastille in PARIS, BOLSHOI OPERA in Moscow, KIROV OPERA in St. Petersburg, Teatro Royale in ROME, DROTTNINGHOLM COURT THEATRE in Sweden, BAYREUTH Festspielhaus in Germany, SALZBURG Festspielhaus in Austria, opera houses in BERLIN and VIENNA, and the ZURICH Operhaus.

OPERA IMAGINAIRE
1993 animated opera anthology

A splendid compendium of 12 animated films based around arias and created by modern European animators. *Carmen* by Christophe Vallaux and Pascal Roulin illustrates "Avec la garde montante" sung by Les Petits Chanteurs à la Crois de Bois. *Cinderella* by Stephen Palmer has "Questa è un nodo avviluppato" sung by Giulietta Simionato, Paolo Montarsolo, Dora Carral, Giovanni Foiani, and Miti Truccato Pace. *Faust* by Hilary Audus has "Le veau d'or" sung by Nicolai Ghiaurov. *Lakmé* by Pascal Roulin depicts "Viens Malika" sung by Mady Mesplé and Danielle Millet. *Madama Butterfly* by Jonathan Hills illustrates "Un bel dì" sung by Felicia Weathers. *The Magic Flute* by Raimund Krumme has "Du also bist mein Bräutigam?" sung by Lucia Popp. *Le nozze di Figaro* by Pascal Roulin portrays "Voi che sapete" sung by Suzanne Danco. *Pagliacci* by Ken Lidster depicts "Vesti la giubba" sung by Franco Corelli. *The Pearl Fishers* by Jimmy T. Murakami has "Au fond du temple saint" sung by Nicolai Gedda and Ernest Blanc. *Rigoletto* by Monique Renault has "La donna è mobile" sung by Nicolai Gedda. *Tosca* by Jose Abel illustrates "E lucevan le stelle" sung by Carlo Bergonzi. *La traviata* by Guionne Leroy depicts the "Gypsy Chorus" sung by the Santa Cecilia Academy Choir. Sue, Sarah, and Tess Malinson produced the films for Pascavision. They were commissioned by the Arts Council of Great Britain. Color. 52 minutes. Miramar VHS.

OPERALOGUE
1932 opera film series

The *Operalogue* short film series condensed opera stories to about 20 minutes and featured only the musical highlights. They were made in 1932 for Educational Films by Howard Higgins and Lew Seller, and the operas were usually given new titles; CARMEN became *The Idol of Seville*, CAVALLERIA RUSTICANA was turned into *Vendetta*, and MARTHA was promoted as *Milady's Escape*.

OPERA NORTH
English opera company

Opera North is a British opera company based in Leeds and founded in 1977 as the English National Opera North. Renamed Opera North in 1981, it has been highly innovative and very popular with operagoers in the north of England. Its operas on video include BAA BAA BLACK SHEEP and GLORIANA.

1992 Harry Enfield's Guide to Opera
Opera North is central to this six-part English TV series intended as a beginner's guide to opera. Paul Daniel of Opera North acts as Harry Enfield's guide, and the illustrative opera scenes are performed by the Opera North company. Program One is about how a person becomes interested in opera, Two is concerned with plots, Three focuses on the voice, Four deals with Italian opera, Five features opera stars, and Six concerns the Opera North company itself. There are interviews with Plácido Do-

mingo, José Carreras, Joan Sutherland. and June Anderson, plus films showing Enrico Caruso, Maria Callas, and Mario Lanza. The opera scenes staged by Opera North are from *La bohème, Carmen, Don Giovanni, Gianni Schicchi, Madama Butterfly, Le nozze di Figaro, Nabucco, The Pearl Fishers, Rigoletto, Tosca, La traviata,* and *Turandot.* The singers include Cheryl Barker, David Maxwell Anderson, Linda Kitchen, Claire Powell, Edmund Barham, Anne Dawson, Donald Maxwell, Robert Hayward, John Connell, Janice Cairns, Keith Latham, Joan Rodgers, and Anthony Michaels-Moore. The opera extracts were staged by Jonathan Alver and the music played by the English Northern Philharmonia conducted by Paul Daniel. The series was written by Paul Whitehouse, produced by Douglas Rae, and directed by Robin Lough. The video is a condensed version of the TV series. Color. 70 minutes. PMI (GB) VHS.

OPERA ON CD-ROM

Quite a number of operas are available on CD-ROM, most with sound and image in addition to searchable data. Most major libraries now have CD-ROM indexes of opera and music publications. Whether the CD-ROM format for opera will become widely popular is not clear, but it has already proved useful and informative.

A Magyar opera
This Hungarian CD-ROM is a comprehensive overview of three centuries of Hungarian opera history with 30 minutes of video and 55 minutes of audio, plus illustrations and text. It describes about 800 operas, including all those of Hungarian origin, and has portraits of some 3,000 personalities. It's available on the Internet from Arts Harmony or from the Opera Shop in Budapest.

Annals of the Metropolitan Opera
There are no visuals on this CD-ROM, but it is a useful research tool. Subtitled *Complete Chronicle of Performances and Artists, Performances and Artists 1883–2000,* it provides the same information as the book editions but in a more searchable format. Unfortunately, the current design is clunky and not as user friendly as it should be. DiscEdition published by the Metropolitan Opera Guild in 2001.

The Audio Encyclopedia
Mike Richter has created a series of invaluable CD-ROMs containing audio versions of operas titled collectively *The Audio Encyclopedia.* They include sound, text, and image, although not video, and each contains an enormous amount of hard-to-find material. *From Which We Came,* for example, features the first opera sets, including 20 complete operas recorded from 1907 to 1927; two series of excerpts from the *Ring;* acts from three

Wagner operas; four Gilbert and Sullivan operettas recorded from 1918 to 1924; and five excerpts form German operas recorded from 1927 to 1930. Each opera is headed by a poster or illustration with notes. Other CDs feature operas by Meyerbeer, Strauss, and Wagner and selections of operas from Bayreuth, Germany, Russia, Bulgaria, Paris, and Munich plus CDs devoted to Italian baritones, Germanic tenors, Jewish singers, British Empire male singers, and Callas master classes. These CD-ROMs are available at very low prices from the House of Opera and Premiere Opera Web sites and some dealers.

The Art of Singing
This entertaining and informative CD-ROM centers around an imaginary Academy of Music through which you travel via mouse clicks. In the concert hall there are 56 minutes of music, texts, translations, and information about the performers. You can visit Joan Sutherland's or John Tomlinson's dressing room and learn about their repertory, drop in on the canteen and hear operatic anecdotes, and even play cards in the porter's lodge. The CD was written and directed by Wilf Judd and Felicity Hayes-McCoy and produced by Ben Whittam Smith. Notting Hill, London. 1996.

BBC Music Magazine
BBC Music Magazine issues a CD with each print issue that, in addition to music, includes a multimedia CD-ROM Extra Program for Windows. It features background on the music on the CD, which is often operatic. The CD-ROM material is produced by Strange Software Ltd.

Champions der Oper
This German CD-ROM containing information about major opera singers was published in 1998 and is available on the Internet. Not viewed.

Encarta Encyclopedia
The Microsoft multimedia encyclopedia *Encarta* is strong on video and audio excerpts and includes a number of opera entries with sound and image. Aside from the main opera entry, there are biographies of composers and opera singers with photographs and posters, audio excerpts from selected operas, and snippets of arias performed by singers from Enrico Caruso to Marian Anderson. Microsoft Corporation.

Die großen Opern
The Great Operas is a German multimedia dictionary of opera available for Windows and Macintosh from Hörzu-Software. Not viewed.

Reclams Opern

German CD-ROM with information about operas, composers, singers, opera houses, and opera history with photos, libretto excerpts, and music. With accompanying booklet. Published in 1997 by Von Rolf Fath. For Windows. Not viewed.

The Ring Disc

The Ring Disc includes an audio version of the complete four-opera ring cycle with libretto in German with English translation, piano-vocal score, and running commentary; more than 14 hours of music; and 100 essays. This amazing aid to serious study of the *Ring* was published by The Media Café in 1997.

The Viking Opera Guide

This excellent 1993 reference book (transformed in 2001 into *The New Penguin Opera Guide*) was also issued on a CD-ROM. In addition to the primary information on operas and their composers, it has 300 pictures of operas and composers, three hours of audio excerpts, indexes, timelines, maps, pronunciation guides, glossary, bibliography, and full search capabilities *The Viking Opera Guide* was edited by Amanda Holden with Nicholas Kenyon and Stephen Walsh. Penguin Books.

OPERAS ABOUT MOVIES AND STARS

Operas and operettas about movies and movie stars date back to the early days of silent cinema. Cinema-themed operettas were popular in Berlin, London, New York, and Rome during the 1910s, but most of them have not been filmed or televised. The best-known movie-themed operas are recent American works dealing with the mythical Hollywood stars MARILYN MONROE and Rudolph Valentino (THE DREAM OF VALENTINO). The more generic cinema operettas/operas are listed below.

1912 Filmzauber

German composer Walter Kollo's *Filmzauber* (Film Magic), the first operetta with cinema as its subject, premiered in Berlin in 1912 and was staged in London and New York in 1913 as *The Girl on the Film*. The story concerns a film company making a movie about Napoleon in a village where a girl pretends to be a boy to get a role. See FILMZAUBER.

1913 Die Kinokönigen

German composer Jean Gilbert's *Die Kinokönigen* (The Cinema Queen), the second operetta about the movies, opened in Berlin in 1913; it reached London in 1914 as *The Cinema Star* and New York in 1914 as *The Queen of the Movies*. The "queen" is an actress who pretends to be a princess to trick a man into being in a film. See DIE KINOKÖNIGEN.

1913 Der Kinotopponkel

Herman Höfert wrote the music for the German movie-oriented operetta *Der Kinotopponkel* (literally, The Movie Deal Uncle) using a libretto by Georg Schade. It premiered in Berlin on December 17, 1913.

1914 La signorina del cinematografo

Carlo Lombardo created *La signorina del cinematografo* (The Movie Girl), an Italian operetta about a movie diva, by drastically adapting Carlo Weinberger's 1896 Austrian operetta *Der Schmetterling*. It was a hit in its new cinematic form, and its libretto was published in a popular edition. See LA SIGNORINA DEL CINEMATOGRAFO.

1920 Der Filmstern

Der Filmstern (The Film Star) is an Austrian operetta with a cinematic plot by Fritz Lehner and Willi Stick. It was first staged in Vienna on July 22, 1920.

1928 Les trois souhaits

Bohuslav Martinů's *Les trois souhaits* (The Three Wishes) is an opera that has cinema central to its story. It opens in a movie studio where a fairy-tale film titled *Les trois souhaits* is being screened. A fairy grants three wishes to a young couple, and they are seen being fulfilled on a movie screen. See LES TROIS SOUHAITS.

1963 Il pianista del Globe

Italian composer Sergio Cafaro's *Il pianista del Globe* (The Globe Pianist) is a light opera dedicated to the music of the silent movie era. Mario Verdone, who wrote the libretto, was a leading Italian film historian and documentarian with a particular interest in silent films and their music. *Il pianista del Globe* revolves around a piano player who accompanies silent films in Italy during the early years of the century.

OPERAS AS MOVIES

The usual work described as a "movie opera" is an imaginary opera whose highlights are created and staged as part of the plot of a film about opera singers. They are described under the entry IMAGINARY OPERAS IN FILMS. The genuine "movie opera" is quite rare although a few have been composed and are listed below.

1915 Rapsodia Satanica

Cavalleria rusticana composer Pietro Mascagni wrote the score for *Rapsodia Satanica* (Satanic Rhapsody), a silent avant-garde film whose screenplay was sold as the "libretto dell'opera." Mascagni, who called it a "poema cinema-musical," created it in collaboration with writer Maria Martini, cinematographer Giorgio Ricci, and director Nino Oxilia. Lyda Borelli, a major diva of the Italian silent cinema, was the main star with André Habay as her male partner. Mascagni's music was played live by the cinema orchestras in the theaters. Black and white. About 70 minutes.

1922 Jenseits des Stromes

Jenseits des Stromes (The Other Side of the River), said to be the first opera written expressly for the movies, was the work of Berlin opera composer Ferdinand Hummel (1855–1928). He wrote seven operas for the stage, the most famous being the 1893 *Mara*, but they are now all forgotten, as is his film opera. Composed for singers and orchestra during the silent cinema era, it had its score literally on the screen. A strip of musical notation ran from left to right at the bottom of the image on screen as the picture progressed to provide guidance to singers and orchestra in the theaters showing the film. Apparently not many did as the film made hardly a ripple in movie history.

1930 Zwei Kravaten

Zwei Kravaten (Two Ties) was described by *Variety* when it opened in America as an "attempt to create a film opera in the modern music sense of opera, something musically along the lines of Krenek's *Jonny spielt auf*, but strictly intended for filming." Metropolitan Opera bass-baritone Michael Bohnen does all the singing in this musical satire set in America. It revolves around a waiter (Bohnen) and his adventures after he exchanges his white tie for a gentleman criminal's black tie as part of an escape ruse. Olga Tschechowa plays the millionaire who sets him on his adventurous way. The music was composed by Mischa Spoliansky, with words and screenplay by Ladislaus Vajda, based on a novel by Georg Kaiser. Nikolaus Farkas was the cinematographer, and Felix Basch and Richard Weichert codirected. The film was shown in America in 1932. Black and white. In German. 86 minutes.

1936 The Robber Symphony

This British film also claimed to be the first opera specially created for the screen. It was written, composed, and directed by Austrian Friedrich Feher and has some similarities to *The Threepenny Opera*. It tells the story of a group of robber musicians and their search for a treasure hidden in a piano. There is no dialogue. Magda Sonja is the mother, Françoise Rosay is the fortuneteller, Hans Feher is Giannino, George Graves is the grandfather, Webster Booth is the singer, and Oscar Ashe is the chief of police. Feher conducted the London Symphony Or-

chestra. The film was produced by Concordia Films. Black and white. 105 minutes.

1971 La cireuse electrique

La cireuse electrique (The Electric Waxer), described by director Jean Renoir as "a little opera," is the second of four episodes in his last film *Le Petit théâtre de Jean Renoir*. It's the satirical story of a woman (Marguerite Cassan), who has a great love for her electric floor-waxing machine and sings about her affection for it. Renoir wrote the words, Joseph Kosma composed the music. Color. In French. 100 minutes.

1983 The Love of Destiny

Petr Weigl, the Czech director known for his beautifully photographed opera films, wrote and directed this opera film pastiche. It uses arias from seven operas to tell the impressionistic story of a man's relationship with a mysterious woman. Peter Dvorsky, who plays the man, sings arias from *Cavalleria rusticana, Tosca, Un ballo in maschera, La favorita, Manon, Madama Butterfly,* and *Lucia di Lammermoor.* Emilia Aasaryova plays the enigmatic woman he loves. The film was photographed by Jiri Kadamka and the music played by the Bratislava Symphony Orchestra. Bratislava Television. Color. In French and Italian. 60 minutes. Kultur VHS.

OPERAS BASED ON MOVIES

Basing operas and stage musicals on movies and their screenplays has become a popular idea in recent years and appears to have growing interest for modern composers. Most of the following operas have entries with more complete descriptions.

The earliest opera based on a movie scenario is the 1921 LA FORFAITURE by Claude Erlanger, derived from the 1915 American film *The Cheat*.

Philip Glass composed his operas ORPHÉE and LA BELLE ET LE BÊTE to the screenplays of Jean Cocteau films; *Belle* is sung while the movie is projected.

Swiss composer Mathias Ruegg also wrote an opera based on *La Belle et le Bête,* but he used slide projection for his images.

Vaclav Kaslik created an opera based on the screenplay of Fellini's film LA STRADA.

Polly Pen composed an opera based on Abraham Room's Soviet silent film BED AND SOFA.

Harrison Birtwistle was inspired by the RKO monster movie *King Kong* to compose his opera THE SECOND MRS. KONG.

William Bolcom's MCTEAGUE is based on Erich Von Stroheim's film *Greed* and the source novel by Frank Norris.

Malcolm Williamson's opera *Our Man in Havana* is based on the Graham Greene novel, but the libretto is by screenwriter Sidney Gilliat; he was undoubtedly influenced by the famous 1959 film that preceded it.

Conrad Susa's opera THE DANGEROUS LIAISONS is based on an epistolary French novel, but it was influenced by the films that preceded it.

Dominick Argento, who composed the movie opera THE DREAM OF VALENTINO, plans to use the screenplay of Luchino Visconti's film *The Leopard* as a libretto.

OPERA STARS IN CONCERT
1991 Spanish opera concert video series

Ruggero Raimondi, Alfredo Kraus, Katia Ricciarelli, Paolo Coni, and Lucia Valentini-Terrani are the stars of colorful concerts filmed in Madrid, at the Plaza de Toros Monumental, and in Barcelona and released in three volumes. On the first in Madrid Raimondi sings "Vieni la mia vendetta" from *Lucrezia Borgia* and duets with Coni on "Il rival salvar tu dei" from *I puritani,* and joins Kraus and Ricciarelli on the final trio from *Faust.* Ricciarelli sings Tosca's "Vissi d'arte" and joins Valentini-Terrani in a duet from *Les contes d'Hoffmann,* Kraus sings "Lunge da lei" from *La traviata,* and Coni sings an aria from *Don Carlos.* In the second video in Madrid, Raimondi and Ricciarelli sing a duet from *Lucrezia Borgia,* while Kraus sings "Una furtiva lagrima" and starts the quartet from *Rigoletto* joined by Valentini-Terrani, Coni, and Ricciarelli. Ricciarelli sings "O mio babbino caro," Coni sings "Eri tu," Raimondi sings "La calunnia," Kraus sings Federico's lament from Cilea's *L'Arlesiana,* and Valentina-Terrani closes with an aria from *Carmen.* Gian Paolo Sanzogno conducts the Madrid Symphony Orchestra. In the third video, taped live in Barcelona, Kraus and Coni are joined by Renata Scott, Melanie Holliday, Ramón Vargas, and Gail Gilmore in a separate concert of opera arias. Color. In Italian and French. Madrid videos, 60 minutes each; Barcelona video, 80 minutes. Kultur VHS.

OPERA STORIES
1989 laser disc opera highlights series

Charlton Heston introduces operas from the locations of their stories, followed by highlights from videos of productions at Covent Garden, La Scala, and Verona. He narrates from Egypt for AIDA (1981, Arena di Verona production), Paris for ANDREA CHÉNIER (1985, Royal Opera), Paris for LA BOHÈME (1985, Royal Opera), Spain for ERNANI (1982, La Scala), London for FALSTAFF (1982, Royal Opera), Vienna for DIE FLEDERMAUS (1983, Royal Opera), Paris for MANON LESCAUT (1983, Royal Opera), Jerusalem for OTELLO (1982, Arena di Verona), Rome for TOSCA (1984, Arena di Verona), and Spain for IL TROVATORE (1985, Arena di Verona). Heston's informative introductions were written by Gerald Sinstadt and

filmed by Keith Cheetham in 1989. Color. English subtitles. Each 50 minutes. Pioneer Artists LD.

OPERA TELECASTS

Most of the operas on video derive from telecasts by TV companies of staged operas and studio productions. In Italy they are mainly on RAI; in England on BBC and Channel 4; in Finland on YLE; in Australia on ABC; in the United States on ABC, Bravo, CBS, NBC, NET, and PBS; and in Germany on a wide range of stations from Bavaria to ZDF. Unfortunately, not all of these telecasts are issued on commercial videos, but some alternative companies record telecasts and make them available to enthusiasts when no one else does. As most of the commercial videos come from a small number of opera houses, it is often only through alternative videos that one can experience operas from the lesser known opera venues and smaller companies and view less popular operas. Most of the alternative companies now have their own Web sites.

OPERAVOX
1995 animated operas

Operavox is a program of six operas in animated form created through a collaboration by BBC, S4C, and British and Moscow animation studios. The Welsh National Opera Orchestra plays the adapted scores for these films, made with budgets of around $800,000 and Christopher Grace as executive producer. The 27-minute films of IL BARBIERE DI SIVIGLIA, CARMEN, DAS RHEINGOLD, RIGOLETTO, TURANDOT, and DIE ZAUBERFLÖTE use different animation techniques but the critics liked them all. Color. Total running time, 184 minutes. Image Entertainment DVD.

OPERA VS. JAZZ
1953 American TV series

Opera vs. Jazz was a half-hour American television series on the ABC network that presented contrasting selections from opera and jazz. Jan Peerce and Alan Dale were regular performers, Nancy Kenyon was the moderator, Fred Heider produced the series, and Charles Dubin directed. The series aired from May to September in 1953. (There is a segment titled *Opera vs. Jazz* in the 1939 JUDY GARLAND film *Babes in Arms,* but there seems to be no connection).

OPERETTA

The operetta, or "little opera," which originated in France, is usually light, tuneful, and operatic with spoken dialogue and a happy ending. The musical comedy, which replaced it in the United States, does not necessarily have connections to opera, as it grew out of popular music, ragtime, and jazz. Librettist Oscar Hammerstein, who wrote both, is the link between the two genres. His musical masterpieces SHOW BOAT and OKLAHOMA are clearly related to operetta, although they are so different from DER FLEDERMAUS that they must be considered another species. For the purposes of this book, modern U.S. and British stage musicals are not considered operettas unless they were deliberately created in the old-fashioned Continental style. Modern French "opérettes" and Central European "operette" are usually included, even though they are also quite different from their 19th-century predecessors. For the Spanish equivalent, see ZARZUELA.

France
The light operas of DANIEL AUBER and ADOLPHE ADAM were transmuted into operettas in France during the 1850s when JACQUES OFFENBACH defined the genre. HERVÉ, CHARLES LECOCQ, and ANDRÉ MESSAGER created other operettas that are still in the French repertory. The form was revitalized during the 1920s by HENRI CHRISTINÉ and REYNALDO HAHN and popularized by FRANCIS LOPEZ during the 1940s. Most of the films and videos of French operettas are, not surprisingly, French. Offenbach remains popular with opera companies, but Lopez has the greatest number of videos. See EDMOND AUDRAN, LOUIS GANNE, FERDINAND HÉROLD, YVONNE PRINTEMPS, and VICTOR ROGER.

Central Europe
FRANZ VON SUPPÉ is said to have written the first Viennese operetta in 1860, but it was JOHANN STRAUSS who made Vienna and the waltz synonymous with operetta. CARL ZELLER and RICHARD HEUBERGER followed in the 1890s, while FRANZ LEHÁR, EMMERICH KÁLMÁN, and OSCAR STRAUS gave the genre new impetus in the new century. The center of gravity shifted to Germany during the 1920s with a strong contribution from Hungarian composers. Nearly all the major German-language operettas have been filmed in Germany or Austria, and most are on video. See PAUL ABRAHAM, RALPH BENATZKY, LEO FALL, JEAN GILBERT, GEORG JARNO, WALTER KOLLO, PAUL LINCKE, KARL MILLÖCKER, OSKAR NEDBAL, FRED RAYMOND, FRANZ SCHUBERT, ROBERT STOLZ, and KARL MICHAEL ZIEHRER.

England
The English light operas of the early 19th century are no longer as visible as they once were, but there is great charm in the works of MICHAEL BALFE, JULIUS BENEDICT, and VINCENT WALLACE, and they inspired several films. However, comic opera composers GILBERT AND SULLIVAN remain popular, and nearly all of their operettas are on video. Most of the English stage composers of the 20th century wrote what they liked to call "musical comedy," although HAROLD FRASER-SIMSON, FREDERIC NORTON, IVOR NOVELLO, and NOËL COWARD created throwbacks to the old operetta style.

United States
The operetta was brought to the United States in its Viennese form by European-born composers who created superb additions to the genre. The earliest U.S. operetta of note is REGINALD DE KOVEN's *Robin Hood*, but it was VICTOR HERBERT who made the American operetta into a major force. He was followed by the equally tuneful SIGMUND ROMBERG and RUDOLF FRIML. GEORGE GERSHWIN and HARRY TIERNEY experimented with traditional operetta, and LEONARD BERNSTEIN also paid homage to the genre. Although some critics consider the musicals of JEROME KERN, Gershwin, and RICHARD RODGERS to be operettas, it can be argued that they created a new American genre. The major period of filming traditional operettas in Hollywood was at the beginning of sound.

Italy
The light comic opera was created in Italy, but the operetta as a separate form never really took root there. However, there are a few Italian operettas, mostly dating from the early 20th century, and some were written by major opera composers, including Puccini (LA RONDINE), Mascagni (SÌ), and Leoncavallo (LA REGINETTA DELLE ROSE). However, most Italian operettas were created by lesser-known composers, most notably MARIO COSTA, CARLO LOMBARDO, and GIUSEPPE PIETRI.

OPERETTE
1940 film about operetta by Forst

This Austrian musical is essentially a love letter to the classic Viennese operetta. Set in operetta's golden age in Imperial Vienna, it features operetta tunes from the three composers who appear in the film: Franz von Suppé (played by Leo Slezak), Johann Strauss Jr. (played by Edmund Schellhammer), and Karl Millöcker (played by Curt Jurgens). Willi Forst, who wrote and directed this homage, has the main connective role as Franz Jauner. Willy Schmidt-Gentner, who arranged the operetta melodies, conducted the Vienna Philharmonic and Vienna State Opera Chorus, and Hans Schneeberger was the cinematographer. The film was distributed theatrically in the United States after the war. Black and white. In German. 109 minutes. Lyric VHS.

OPERNBALL, DER
1898 operetta by Heuberger

Der Opernball (The Opera Ball) is the most famous operetta by Austrian composer RICHARD HEUBERGER, and it continues to be revived in its native Vienna. The libretto, by Victor Léon and Heinrich von Waldberg, is based on the play *Les Dominos Roses* by Alfred Hennequin and Alfred Delacour. The plot is similar to that of *Die Fledermaus,* with the principal characters attending a masked ball in Paris wearing pink dominos. The men in the story have been set up by the wives in a test of fidelity, and the confusion gets pretty tricky at times. The most famous tune is the waltz "Geh'n wir in's Chambre séparée," which has become a staple of operetta singers; Joan Sutherland includes it on her album *The Golden Age of Operetta. The Opera Ball* was first staged in New York in 1912 with Marie Cahill as its star. It has been filmed several times.

1939 Bolvary film
German feature film: Geza von Bolvary (director), Ernst Marischka (screenplay), Willy Winterstein (cinematographer), Peter Kreuder (music director).
Cast: Marte Harell (Elisabeth), Paul Hörbiger (Georg), Will Dohm (Paul), Hans Moser (Anton), Theo Lingen (Philipp), Heli Finkenzeller.
Video: Lyric VHS. Black and white. In German. 93 minutes.

1956 Marischka film
Austrian feature film: Ernst Marischka (director), Bruno Mondi (cinematographer).
Cast: Sonja Ziemann (Helene), Josef Meinrad (Paul), Johannes Heesters (George), Herta Feilder (Elisabeth), Hans Moser, Rudolf Vogel, Fita Benkhoff.
Black and white. In German. 92 minutes.
Comment: The setting of the ball is transferred from Paris to Vienna.

1971 York film
German feature film: Eugen York (stage and film director), Willy Mattes (conductor, Kurt Graunke Symphony Orchestra).
Cast: Harald Serafin (Paul Aubier), Maurice Besançon (George Duménil), Helen Mané (Angèle Aubier), Maria Tiboldi (Marguerite Duménil), Ernst Stankowsky (Toulouse-Lautrec).
Color. In German. 100 minutes.

OPHULS, MAX
German-born film director (1902–1957)

Max Ophuls was born in Germany, but he spent most of his life as a vagabond making films in different countries. His early German and French films are great, his middle-period U.S. films are superb, and his final French films are masterpieces; no one has ever used the camera as fluidly as Ophuls. There are many opera connections in his films, and often their structure is operatic. *Die verkaufte Braut* (1932) is a German version of Smetana's Czech opera THE BARTERED BRIDE, and one of the best films of the genre. LA SIGNORA DI TUTTI (1934) centers around an IMAGINARY OPERA that helps bring about a love affair. *Letter From an Unknown Woman* (1948) reaches its climax at a performance of DIE ZAUBERFLÖTE at the Vienna Opera House. *Yoshiwara* (1937) has a *Madama Butterfly*–type plot, but the opera at its center is FIDELIO. *Le Plaisir* (1952) is influenced by OFFENBACH and features his music. The plot of *Madame de...* (1951) revolves around a pair of earrings supposedly lost at an opera house and features musical themes from LES HUGUENOTS. WERTHER (1938) is derived from the source novel of the Massenet opera. OSCAR STRAUS, the creator of *The Chocolate Soldier,* composed the famous theme for *La Ronde* (1950).

ORATORIO
Religious musical drama

The oratorio and the opera are closely related and originated at almost the same time around 1600. An oratorio, in essence, is a religious opera; it has a story and vocal parts for soloists and ensembles even though it is usually presented without scenery, costumes, or theatrical movement. Some modern oratorios, such as Stravinsky's OEDIPUS REX, are not even traditionally religious, so it is not always easy to distinguish between the genres. Handel's Italian oratorios do not seem all that different from his Italian operas, and some have been staged like operas. A few operatic oratorios have entries in this book. See BELSHAZZAR, CARMINA BURANA, ISRAEL IN EGYPT, JEANNE D'ARC AU BÛCHER, MESSIAH, EL NIÑO, SCHÖPFUNG, THEODORA, and WAR REQUIEM.

ORDUÑA, JUAN DE
Spanish film director (1907–1973)

Juan de Orduña y Fernández-Shaw began his film career as an actor starring in zarzuela films during the 1920s, including LA REVOLTOSA and EL REY QUE RABIÓ. He began to direct in 1943 and soon became one of the most commercially successful modern Spanish directors. His biggest commercial hit was *El último cuplé* starring Sara Montiel. Toward the end of his career, he returned to the zarzuela film; from 1967 to 1969 he directed a series of 35mm versions of classic zarzuelas for Spanish television. See EL BARBERILLO DE LAVAPIÉS, BOHEMIOS, LA CANCIÓN DEL OLVIDÓ, EL CASERÍO, GIGANTES Y CABEZUDOS, LAS GOLONDRINAS, EL HUÉSPED DEL SEVILLANO, LUISA FERNANDA, MARUXA, LA REVOLTOSA, EL REY QUE RABIÓ, and LOS SOBRINOS DEL CAPITÁN GRANT.

ORFEO
1607 opera by Monteverdi

CLAUDIO MONTEVERDI's *Orfeo* is the earliest opera still regularly performed and the earliest available on video. Monteverdi's version of the myth of Orpheus and Eurydice (Orfeo and Euridice in Italian), libretto by Alessandro Striggio, retells in elaborate form the legend of the musician who can charm Death but still lose the woman he loves. The opera has a number of singing roles in addition to Orpheus and Eurydice, including Charon, Pluto, Apollo, and Proserpina.

1971 RAI Italian Television
Italian TV production: Raymond Rouleau (director), Nino Sanzogno (conductor, Milan RAI Television Orchestra and Chorus).
Cast: Lajos Kozma (Orfeo), Nicoletta Panni (Euridice), Valeria Mariconda, Nicola Zaccaria, Gloria Lane.
Telecast on RAI Italian Television on January 13, 1968, and then on NET Opera Theater in February 1971. Fernanda Turvani (director). Black and white. In Italian with English subtitles. 60 minutes.
Comment: The opera is staged as if were a Renaissance entertainment for a wealthy patron.

***1978 Ponnelle film
Austrian film: Jean-Pierre Ponnelle (director/screenplay), Nikolaus Harnoncourt (conductor, Monteverdi Ensemble and Chorus of the Zurich Opera House), Wolfgang Treu (cinematographer), Gerd Janka (set designer), Pet Halmen (costume designer).
Cast: Philippe Huttenlocher (Orfeo), Dietlinde Turban (Euridice), Trudeliese Schmidt (Music/Hope), Roland Hermann (Apollo), Glenys Linos (Messenger/Proserpina), Werner Gröschel (Pluto), Hans Franzen (Charon).
Video: London VHS/LD. Color. In Italian with English subtitles. 102 minutes.
Comment: Filmed as an opera being performed for a period audience with singers, players, and audience intermingling in a theatrically effective manner. The film grew out of a famous cycle of the Monteverdi operas at the Zurich Opera House, and it has nearly the same cast as the stage production.

1985 Goretta film
Swiss feature film: Claude Goretta (director), Michel Corboz (conductor, Lyons Opera Orchestra and Chapelle Royalle Vocal Ensemble), Jacques Bufnoir (set designer), Gabriella Pescucci (costume designer).
Cast: Gino Quilico (Orfeo), Audrey Michael (Euridice), Eric Tappy (Apollo), Colette Alliot-Lugaz (Music), Carolyn Watkinson (Messenger), Danielle Borst (Proserpina), Frangiskos Voutsinos (Pluto), Filippo Da Garra (Charon).
Color. In Italian. 92 minutes.
Comment: Goretta, a Swiss filmmaker known for *The Lacemaker*, premiered his film at the 1985 Venice Film Festival where some critics objected to its stylized sets and lack of naturalism but most liked its sensitive direction, good acting, and excellent singing.

2002 Gran Teatre del Liceu
Spanish stage production Gilbert Deflo (director), Jordi Savall (conductor, Le Concert des Nations and La Capella Reial de Catalunya), William Orlandi (set designer), Anna Casas (choreographer).
Cast: Furio Zanasi (Orfeo), Arianna Savall (Euridice), Montserrat Figueras (Music), Sara Mingardo (Messenger), Cécile van de Sant (Hope), Fulvio Bettini (Apollo), Adriana Fernández (Proserpina), Daniel Carnovich (Pluto) Antonio Abete (Charon).
Video: BBC Opus Arte DVD. Taped January 31, 2002. Brian Large (director). Color. In Italian with English subtitles. 140 minutes.
Comment: Not great singers but a superb production with interesting use of mirrors, and as a plus, the DVD includes film shot in the Palazzo Ducale in Mantua, where the opera premiered.

Related film

1997 The Golden Age
Documentary about the music created during the reign of Queen Elizabeth I and featuring music by Byrd, Purcell, Monteverdi, and Lully. It includes scenes from *Orfeo* performed by the Zurich Opera. Part of the series *Music in Time*. Color. In English. 60 minutes. Films for the Humanities & Sciences VHS.

ORFEO ED EURIDICE
1762 opera by Gluck

CHRISTOPH WILLIBALD GLUCK's version of the Orpheus and Eurydice myth was the first of his so-called simplified "reform" operas. Ranieri de' Calzabigi wrote the original libretto in Italian as *Orfeo ed Euridice*, and Pierre Louis Moline later revised it in French as *Orphée et Eurydice*. The story is the traditional version with Orpheus rescuing his dead wife from Hades by his music but losing her when he looks back. It has a smaller cast than the Monteverdi opera of the same myth with only three singers. Orfeo is a contralto role, and Euridice and Amore are both sopranos.

***1982 Glyndebourne Festival

English stage production: Peter Hall (director), Raymond Leppard (conductor, London Philharmonic Orchestra.), John Bury (set designer).

Cast: Janet Baker (Orfeo), Elisabeth Speiser (Euridice), Elizabeth Gale (Amore).

Video: Bel Canto Society/Home Vision VHS and Pioneer Artists LD. Rodney Greenberg (director). Color. In Italian with English subtitles. 135 minutes.

Comment: An elegant neoclassic production that breaks out of the stage in the final scene with a celebration spilling into the stalls and balconies. Baker chose this work as her farewell to the opera stage, and she is at her best.

1985 Gaál film

Hungarian feature film: István Gaál (director), Tamás Vásári (conductor, Franz Liszt Chamber Orchestra and Hungarian Radio and Television Chorus), Sandor Sara and Sandor Kurucz (cinematographers), Tamas Zanko (set designer), Judith Gombar (costume designer).

Cast: Sándor Téri (Orfeo, sung by Lajos Miller, Eniko Eszenyi (Euridice, sung by Maddalena Bonifaccio), Ákos Sebestyén (Amore, sung by Veronika Kincses).

Color. In Italian. 95 minutes.

Comment: Gaál, one of Hungary's best filmmakers, premiered his cinematic version of the opera at the Venice Film Festival. He shot it in natural settings but was still able to create a rather dreamlike atmosphere. The Hungarian title is *Orfeusz es Eurydike*.

1987 DDR/ORF Television

East German/Austrian television production: Jörg Scheffel (director), Max Pommer (conductor, Leipzig Rundfunk Symphony Orchestra and Chorus), Cornelia Halle (set designer).

Cast: Murray Dickie (Orfeo), Patricia Wise (Euridice), Birgit Fandrey (Amore).

Video: Dreamlife (Japan) DVD/VHS/LD. Georg F. Mielke (director). Telecast in Austria October 18, 1987. Color. In German. 90 minutes.

***1991 Royal Opera

English stage production: Harry Kupfer (director), Harmut Haenchen (conductor, Royal Opera House Orchestra and Chorus), Hans Schavernoch (set designer).

Cast: Jochen Kowalski (Orfeo), Gillian Webster (Euridice), Jeremy Budd (Amore).

Video: Kultur DVD/Home Vision VHS/Pioneer Artists LD. Hans Hulscher (director). Color. In Italian with English subtitles. 80 minutes.

Comment: In this modernized version, Orfeo wears a leather jacket and jeans, charms the beasts of the city, watches Eurydice die in a street accident, and goes to a hospital as Hades to trying to bring her back. The sets are impressive with projected imagery on revolving screens and mirrors reflecting performers, musicians, and, finally, the audience. The production was conceived for the Berlin Komische Opera and won the Olivier Award for Outstanding Achievement in Opera when it was staged in London.

1998 Drottningholm Court Theatre

Swedish stage production: Göran Järvefelt (director), Arnold Östman (conductor, Drottningholm Court Theatre Orchestra and Chorus).

Cast: Ann-Christine Biel (Orfeo), Maya Boog (Euridice), Kerrsti Avemo (Amore).

Video: Naxos DVD. Thomas Olofsson (director). Color. In Italian with English subtitles. 67 minutes.

1999 Théâtre du Châtelet, Paris

French stage production: Robert Wilson (director/designer), John Eliot Gardiner (conductor, Orchestre Revolutionnaire et Romantique and Monteverdi Chorus),

Cast: Magdalena Kozena, Madeline Bender, Patricia Petibon.

Video: Arthaus (GB) DVD. Brian Large (director). Color. 100 minutes. In French with English subtitles.

Early/related films

1906 Royal Danish Ballet

When Gluck revised the opera for France, he added a ballet in the second act. This early film shows the ballet performed by the Royal Danish Ballet in 1906 for the silent camera. The soloists are Valborg Borchsenius, Ellen Price, Elisabeth Beck, and Anna Agerhold. Black and white. About 10 minutes. Print survives in the Danish film archive.

1949 Orphée

Jean Cocteau's superb film version of the Orpheus and Eurydice legend pays homage to Gluck by occasionally quoting music from the opera. Jean Marais plays Orpheus with Maria Déa as Eurydice. Black and white. In French. 112 minutes.

1968 Hot Millions.
The "Dance of the Blessed Spirits" from the opera is played on the flute by Maggie Smith while Peter Ustinov listens seated at an antique keyboard. He is so impressed that romance blossoms. Eric Till directed. Color. 105 minutes.

1976 The Innocent
L'Innocente, Luchino Visconti's last film, has an ironic use of the aria "Che farò senza Euridice?" (What will I do without Eurydice?). The story concerns an aristocrat who neglects his beautiful wife; when she becomes interested in someone else, he falls in love with her again. Color. In Italian. 125 minutes.

1999 Janice Beard 45 WPM
Music from *Orfeo ed Euridice* in featured in this British film about a Scottish woman trying to cure her agoraphobic mother. Clare Kilner directed. Color. 93 minutes.

2001 Heartbreakers
Violinist Arturo Delmoni and pianist Meg Bachman Vas perform music from the opera in this film about a mother-daughter confidence team. David Mirkin directed. Color. 123 minutes.

ORFF, CARL
German composer (1895–1982)

Carl Orff, who studied opera intensely as a young man, wrote many stage works, although few are in the traditional sense. His influence on modern composers such as the minimalists, however, is now becoming evident. His operas include *Antigonae* and *Oedipus der Tyran,* which are on CD, and the earlier and more popular *Der Mond* and *Die Kluge.* Orff's best-known stage work, and the most often recorded and videotaped, is his "staged cantata" CARMINA BURANA. It may not be an opera in the usual sense, but it is one of the works that has helped alter modern ideas about what opera can be.

ORLANDO FURIOSO
1727 opera by Vivaldi

ANTONIO VIVALDI's Venetian opera, libretto by Grazio Braccioli, is loosely based on Ludovico Ariosto's epic poem *Orlando Furioso.* It centers around the crusader knight Orlando (Roland in English) who has fallen in love with a woman named Angelica. She, however, loves and marries Medoro, and this drives Orlando mad. Meanwhile, the sorceress Alcina has bewitched the knight Ruggiero, who is eventually saved by his fiancée Bradamante. The plot is somewhat complicated and

confusing, with strange mixtures of lovers and magic, but then so is the source poem.

1978 Teatro Filarmonico, Verona
Italian stage production: Pier Luigi Pizzi (director/set designer), Claudio Scimone (conductor, I Solisti Veneti and Chorus).
Cast: Marilyn Horne (Orlando), Nicola Zaccaria (Astolfo), James Bowman, Dano Raffanti, Anastasia Tomaszewska Schepis.
Video: House of Opera DVD/VHS. Color. In Italian. 130 minutes.
Comment: This was the first modern public production of the opera although Scimone had recorded it in 1977 with Horne and Vittoria de los Angeles.

1989 San Francisco Opera
American stage production: Pier Luigi Pizzi (director/set designer), Randall Behr (conductor, San Francisco Opera Orchestra and Chorus), Jennifer Green (costume designer).
Cast: Marilyn Horne (Orlando), Susan Patterson (Angelica), Kathleen Kuhlmann (Alcina), Jeffrey Gall (Ruggiero), Sandra Walker (Bradamante), William Matteuzzi (Medoro), Kevin Langan (Astolfo).
Video: Image Entertainment and Arthaus (GB) DVD/Kultur and Home Vision VHS/Pioneer LD. Brian Large (director). Color. In Italian with English subtitles. 130 minutes.

ORMANDY, EUGENE
Hungarian-born American conductor (1899–1985)

Eugene Ormandy came to the United States in 1921 and made his debut as a conductor in 1924. Most of his career was with the Minneapolis and Philadelphia orchestras. He began his operatic career by conducting DIE FLEDERMAUS at the Metropolitan Opera House in 1950. It was such a hit that it was restaged as a television special in 1953 and gained even wider acclaim. The following year he conducted the Philadelphia Orchestra for a CBS production of *The Merry Widow* (DIE LUSTIGE WITWE) with Patrice Munsel. It was again a success; both operettas are on video and stand up well. There are many recordings of Ormandy conducting operas, but no videos.

ORPHÉE
1993 screen opera by Glass

PHILIP GLASS took his libretto for this opera directly from the screenplay of the 1949 French film *Orphée* written and directed by Jean Cocteau. The film is a surrealistic modern version of the Orpheus myth set in Paris. Death is a princess who falls in love with the poet Orpheus and helps him go to Hell to retrieve his lost love Eurydice. Francesca Zambello directed the first production of the Glass opera at the American Repertory Theater in Cambridge, Massachusetts, with moveable sets by Robert Israel. Eugene Perry was Orpheus, Lynn Torgove was Eurydice, and Wendy Hill was the Princess. Martin Goldray conducted the Philip Glass Ensemble.

ORPHÉE AUX ENFERS
1858 opéra-bouffe by Offenbach

JACQUES OFFENBACH gave Paris and the world the music for the cancan dance in his delightful *Orphée aux enfers* (Orpheus in the Underworld), a satire based on the legend of Orpheus and Eurydice and the Olympian gods. It's one of the best Offenbach operettas, a remarkable send-up of serious Gluck-style operas and a tuneful delight to boot. Orpheus and Eurydice are bored with each other and have other lovers. When Eurydice goes to the Underworld, Public Opinion forces Orpheus to go after her, although he is clearly not interested and Eurydice was quite happy to get away. Jupiter, Pluto, and other gods get involved, and Jupiter turns into a fly and sings a fly aria to seduce Eurydice. The *galop infernal,* the cancan dance music, comes at the end of the opera with all the gods and gods joining in the fun. It was called an "immoral dance" by Khrushchev when he visited the set of the Hollywood film *Can-Can* in 1959. The operetta is usually produced in translation outside France, in English in England and America, in German in Germany, etc.

1962 Sadler's Wells Theatre
English stage production: Wendy Toye (director), Alexander Faris (conductor, Sadler's Wells Orchestra and Chorus).

Cast: Kevin Miller (Orpheus), June Bronhill (Eurydice), Eric Shilling (Jupiter), Anna Pollak (Calliope), Heather Begg, Jon Weaving, Sophie Trant.

Filmed for Granada Television in England and telecast in the United States on NET. Douglas Terry (director). Black and white. In English. 90 minutes.

1968 Hamburg State Opera
German film of stage production: Joachim Hess (director), Rolf Liebermann (producer), Marek Janowski (conductor, Hamburg State Opera Orchestra and Chorus), Bernard Dayde (set/costume designer), Günther Fleckenstein, Victor Reinshagen, Joachim Hess (German adaptation as *Orpheus in der Unterwelt*).

Cast: Karl Marschner (Orpheus), Elisabeth Steiner (Eurydice), Toni Blankenheim (Jupiter), Inge Meysel (Juno), Peter Haage (Mercury), William Workman (Pluto), Heinz Kruse (Cupid).

Telecast in Germany. Igor Luther (director). Color. In German. 106 minutes.

***1983 George Walker film
English studio production: Christopher Renshaw (director), Judith De Paul (producer), Alexander Faris (conductor, London Symphony Orchestra and Ambrosian Opera Chorus), Allan Cameron (set designer), George Walker (executive producer).

Cast: Alexander Oliver (Orpheus), Lillian Watson (Eurydice), Dennis Quilley (Napoleon/Jupiter), Honor Blackman (Empress/Juno), Christopher Gable (Mercury), Emile Belcourt (Pluto), Elizabeth Gale (Cupid), Pauline Tinsley (Public Opinion), Felicity Palmer (Venus), Isobel Buchanan (Diana).

Video: Lyric VHS. Derek Bailey (director). Color. In English. 90 minutes.

Comment: Presented as if the operetta is being seen by Emperor Napoleon III and his empress in a private theater in 1865. The conductor wears makeup to look like Offenbach.

1997 Théâtre de la Monnaie
Belgian stage production: Herbert Wernicke (director, set/costume designer), Patrick Davin (conductor, Théâtre de la Monnaie Orchestra and Chorus), Andrew George and Sylvia Printemps (choreographers), ZDF/BRTN (production).

Cast: Alexandru Badea (Orpheus), Elisabeth Vidal (Eurydice), Dale Duesing (Jupiter), Jacqueline van Quaille (Juno), Franck Cassard (Mercury), Reinaldo Macias (Pluto/Aristeus), Marie-Noëlle de Callatay (Cupid), Désirée Meiser (Public Opinion), André Jung (John Styx), Michele Patzakis (Venus), Sonja Theodoridou (Diana), Laurence Misonne (Minerva), Thomas Stache (Cerberus).

Video: Image Entertainment/Arthaus Musik (GB) DVD. Dirk Gryspeirt (director). Color. In French with English subtitles. 120 minutes.

Comment: Some critics disliked this production set in a turn-of-the-century Brussels café with the gods turned into society folk, but it is certainly original.

Related films

Cancan music from the operetta is used in many films about Paris; a select few are listed below.

1898 Can Can
This French film, distributed in America by the Lubin Company, was the first to use the music even though it did not have a soundtrack; the music was played live when it was screened. Lubin's description of the film to potential renters needs to be quoted in full: "You are not often afforded the privilege of viewing a real French can-can and this film is therefore bound to score a success. Mlle. Fraidora, the celebrated French can-can dancer, is shown in all her glory dancing her favorite dance as only she can do it. And it is not necessary to go into detail as

all who have seen her pronounce her to be an artist in her line. Take this film with you to please the bald-heads. Very warm." Black and white. Silent. About 1 minute.

1909 Orfeus I Underjorden
Oscar Bergstrom sings John Styx's air "Nar jag var prins utav Arkadien" (Quand j'étai roi de Boétie) in this early Swedish sound film. Charles Magnusson directed for Svenska Biografteatern using the Biophon sound system. Black and white. In Swedish. About 4 minutes.

1959 Can-Can
This is the most famous cancan film, the one that offended Soviet premier Nikita Khrushchev when he visited its set in Hollywood. It revolves around an attempt to ban the dance in Paris during the 1890s. Shirley MacLaine and Juliet Prowse lead the dancing; Walter Lang directed. Color. 131 minutes.

1997 Titanic
A string quartet bravely plays the Can-Can as Leonardo DiCaprio and Kate Winslet fight their way up the sinking doomed ship. The film won eleven Oscars for director James Cameron. Color. 194 minutes

1999 Music of the Heart
Meryl Streep plays a music teacher in an East Harlem high school who gets her students to like classical music. The cancan music, arranged by Mason Daring, is performed by the Young Musicians Foundation. Wes Craven directed. Color. 124 minutes.

ORPHÉE ET EURYDICE
See ORFEO ED EURIDICE.

OSTEN, SUZANNE
Swedish film director (1944 -)

Susanne Osten, one of the best Swedish filmmakers, had international success with her 1986 film *Broderna Mozart* (shown in America as *The Mozart Brothers*), which dealt with the problems of staging DON GIOVANNI. The influence of the Marx Brothers and *A Night at the Opera* is evident, but there is genuine empathy with Mozart. The film tells the story of a director who wants to stand the "old war-horse opera" on its head and create a vital new production. Her 1996 film *Carmen's Revenge*, despite its title, does not have operatic content.

ÖSTMAN, ARNOLD
Swedish conductor (1939–)

Arnold Östman made Mozart operas into a new and delightful experience with his authentic period performances at the Drottningholm Court Theatre in Sweden where the operas were presented with the orchestra in period costume playing period instruments. Östman became music director of the theater in 1979, and his recordings and videos of operas by Mozart and other early composers have been highly acclaimed. He has now left Drottningholm, but he left a remarkable legacy of videos from there and the Schwetzingen Festival. See AGRIPPINA (1985), ALCESTE (1998), LA CLEMENZA DI TITO (1987), COSÌ FAN TUTTE (1984), DON GIOVANNI (1987), LA DONNA DEL LAGO (1990), DIE ENTFÜHRUNG AUS DEM SERAIL (1991), FALSTAFF (Salieri, 1995), LA FINTA GIARDINIERA (1988), IDOMENEO (1991), LE NOZZE DI FIGARO (1981), ORFEO ED EURIDICE (1998), and DIE ZAUBERFLÖTE (1989).

OTELLO (Rossini)
1816 opera by Rossini

GIOACHINO ROSSINI's opera of Shakespeare's *Othello*, composed to a libretto by Francesco Beria di Salsa, was quite popular during the 19th century, but it is less well known today because it has been replaced in the repertory by the Boito/Verdi masterpiece. Rossini's version, which does not follow the play as closely as Verdi's, is set in the Venetian first act of the Shakespeare play with Desdemona engaged to Rodrigo but in love with Otello. After being made jealous by Iago and fighting a duel, Otello is banished and returns secretly to kill Desdemona. Iago and Otello both commit suicide at the end of the opera.

1988 Pesaro Festival
Italian stage production: Pier Luigi Pizzi (director/designer), John Pritchard (conductor, RAI Symphony Orchestra of Torino).

Cast: Chris Merritt (Otello), June Anderson (Desdemona), Enzo di Cesare (Iago), Rockwell Blake (Rodrigo), Raquel Pierotti (Emilia).

Video: House of Opera DVD/VHS. Ilio Catani (director). Color. In Italian. 184 minutes.

OTELLO (Verdi)
1887 opera by Verdi

GIUSEPPE VERDI had not written a new opera for 16 years when he was cajoled back into composing by poet-composer Arrigo Boito. Boito's *Otello* is one of the great opera librettos; although there are many changes (the Venetian first act is eliminated), the basic story is not altered and the emotional effect is as strong as the play. Military leader Otello is married to beautiful Desdemona but is made jealous of her by Iago. He becomes enraged, strangles her, and kills himself. Iago's "Credo" is one of the great pieces of operatic dramatic writing, and Desdemona's "Willow Song" is one of the most moving of arias.

1948 Metropolitan Opera

American stage production: Herbert Graf (director), Fritz Busch (conductor, Metropolitan Opera Orchestra and Chorus), Donald Oenslager (set designer).

Cast: Ramón Vinay (Otello), Licia Albanese (Desdemona), Leonard Warren (Iago), Martha Lipton (Emilia), John Garris (Cassio), Thomas Hayward (Roderigo).

Telecast November 29, 1948, on CBS. Burke Crotty (director). Black and white. In Italian. 210 minutes.

Comment: This was the first complete opera to be televised live; it opened the 1948–1949 season at the Metropolitan Opera. Sponsor Texaco paid an extra $20,000 for the rehearsals for the telecast, which reached an estimated 500,000 TV sets. Milton Cross introduced the acts and explained the action, as there were no subtitles.

1958 Enriquez film

Italian TV film: Franco Enriquez (director), Tullio Serafin (conductor, Milan RAI Orchestra and Chorus), Mariano Mercuri (set designer).

Cast: Mario Del Monaco (Otello), Rosanna Carteri (Desdemona), Renato Capecchi (Iago), Luisella Ciaffi (Emilia), Gino Mattera (Cassio), Athos Cesarini (Roderigo).

Video: Hardy Classics DVD/Bel Canto Society VHS. Black and white. In Italian. 136 minutes.

Comment: They didn't want subtlety in the early RAI productions aimed at the widest audience with pop song style close-ups. All the same, Del Monaco has rarely been more powerful and impressive.

1959 NHK Lirica Italiana

Japanese stage production: Bruno Nofri (director), Alberto Erede (conductor, NHK Radio Symphony Orchestra and Nikikai and Fujiwara Opera Chorus), Camillo Pallavincini (set designer).

Cast: Mario Del Monaco (Otello), Gabriella Tucci (Desdemona), Tito Gobbi (Iago), Anna Di Stasio (Emilio), Mariano Caruso (Cassio), Gabriele de Julis (Roderigo).

Video: Bel Canto Society VHS. Filmed live in Tokyo on February 4, 1959. Black and white. In Italian. 126 minutes.

1959 BBC Television

English TV film: Rudolph Cartier (director), Brykan Balkwill (conductor, Royal Philharmonic Orchestra and Glyndebourne Festival Chorus), Clifford Hatts (set designer).

Cast: Charles Holland (Otello), Heidi Krall (Desdemona), Ronald Lewis (Iago), Barbara Howitt (Emilia), John Ford (Cassio), John Kentish (Roderigo).

Telecast October 1, 1959, on BBC. Black and white. In English. 123 minutes. Film preserved at the NFTA, London.

1961 Zurich Stadttheater

Swiss stage production: Herbert Graf (director), Nello Santi (conductor, Zurich Stadttheater Orchestra and Chorus), Max Rothlisberger (set/costume designer), SRG (production).

Cast: James McCracken (Otello), Maria van Dongen (Desdemona), Rudolf Knoll (Iago), Mary Davenport (Emilia), Robert Thomas (Cassio), Leonhard Päckl (Roderigo).

Telecast in 1961 by SRG Swiss Television. Black and white. In Italian. 150 minutes.

Comment: This popular production helped make McCracken one of the top Otellos of his time. The Stadttheater became the Opernhaus in 1964.

1963 Voice of Firestone

American TV highlights production: Harry John Brown (conductor, Voice of Firestone orchestra).

Cast: James McCracken (Otello), Gabriella Tucci (Desdemona), Robert Merrill (Iago).

Video: VAI VHS titled *A Firestone Verdi Festival*. Telecast March 3, 1963. Black and white. In Italian with English introductions. 22 minutes.

Comment: Fully staged with costumes, sets, and extras.

1969 Komischer Oper Berlin

East German film: Walter Felsenstein (director), Kurt Masur (conductor, Komischer Oper Berlin Orchestra and Chorus), Otto Merz and Hans-Jurgen Reinecke (cinematographers), Alfred Tolle (set designer), DEFA (production).

Cast: Hans Nöcker (Otello), Christa Noack–Von Kamptz (Desdemona), Vladimir Bauer (Iago), Hanna Schmook (Emilia), Hans-Otto Ragge (Cassio), Peter Seuffert (Roderigo).

Video: VIEW VHS. Color. In German. 121 minutes.

Comment: Felsenstein seems to have been influenced in his movie-making style by Eisenstein and Pudovkin.

1974 Karajan film

German TV film: Roger Benamou (director), Herbert von Karajan (producer/conductor, Berlin Philharmonic and Deutsche Oper Berlin Chorus).

Cast: Jon Vickers (Otello), Mirella Freni (Desdemona), Peter Glossop (Iago), Stefania Malagu (Emilia), Cassio (Aldo Bottion), Michel Sénéchal (Roderigo).

Video: DG DVD/VHS. Color. In Italian with English subtitles. 145 minutes.

1976 Teatro alla Scala

Italian stage production: Franco Zeffirelli (director, set/costume designer), Carlos Kleiber (conductor, Teatro alla Scala Orchestra and Chorus).

Cast: Plácido Domingo (Otello), Mirella Freni (Desdemona), Piero Cappuccilli (Iago).

Video: House of Opera DVD and VHS/Bel Canto Society VHS. Taped live December 7, 1976. Color. In Italian. 143 minutes.

1978 Metropolitan Opera

American stage production: Franco Zeffirelli (director/designer), Fabrizio Melano (staging), James Levine (conductor, Metropolitan Opera Orchestra and Chorus).

Cast: Jon Vickers (Otello), Renata Scotto (Desdemona), Cornell MacNeil (Iago), Jean Kraft (Emilia), Raymond Gibbs (Cassio), Andrea Velis (Roderigo).

Video at the MTR. Telecast live September 25, 1978. Kirk Browning (director). Color. In Italian with English subtitles. 140 minutes.

1979 Metropolitan Opera

American stage production: Franco Zeffirelli (director/designer), Fabrizio Melano (staging), Michelangelo Veltri (conductor, Metropolitan Opera Orchestra and Chorus).

Cast: Plácido Domingo (Otello), Gilda Cruz-Romo (Desdemona), Sherrill Milnes (Iago), Shirley Love (Emilia), Giuliano Ciannella (Cassio), Charles Anthony (Roderigo).

Video at the MTR. Telecast live September 24, 1979. Kirk Browning (director). Color. In Italian with English subtitles. 140 minutes.

1982 Arena di Verona

Italian stage production: Gianfranco de Bosio (director), Zoltan Pesko (conductor, Arena di Verona Orchestra and Chorus), Vittorio Rossi (set/costume designer).

Cast: Vladimir Atlantov (Otello), Kiri Te Kanawa (Desdemona), Piero Cappuccilli (Iago), Flora Rafanelli (Emilia), Antonio Bevacqua (Cassio), Gianfranco Manganotti (Roderigo).

Video: HBO/Castle VHS/Pioneer LD/NVC Arts (GB) VHS. Preben Montell (director). Color. In Italian with English subtitles. 145 minutes.

1982/1989 Opera Stories

Highlights LD version of the above production narrated by Charlton Heston; framing new material shot in Jerusalem in 1989 by Keith Cheetham. Color. In English and Italian with English subtitles. 52 minutes. Pioneer Artists LD.

1986 Zeffirelli film

Italian feature film: Franco Zeffirelli (director/designer), Lorin Maazel (conductor, La Scala Orchestra and Chorus), Ennio Guarnieri (cinematographer), Anna Anni and Maurizio Millenotti (costume designers).

Cast: Plácido Domingo (Otello), Katia Ricciarelli (Desdemona), Justino Diaz (Iago), Petra Malakova (Emilia), Umberto Barberini (Cassio, sung by Ezio Di Cesare), Sergio Nicolai (Roderigo).

Video: Kultur/Cannon VHS. 123 minutes. Color. In Italian with English subtitles.

Comment: Zeffirelli was criticized by those who insist an opera be filmed exactly as it was written as he cut it considerably, including Desdemona's "Willow Song." All the same, Zeffirelli created a beautiful film, extraordinarily well photographed. The opening storm is a powerhouse, the cast is outstanding, the sets are impressive, and the costumes were nominated for an Oscar.

Otello (1986): Otello (Plácido Domingo) after killing Desdemona (Katia Ricciarelli) in Zeffirelli's film.

1992 Royal Opera House

English stage production: Elijah Moshinsky (director), Sir Georg Solti (conductor, Royal Opera House Orchestra and Chorus).

Cast: Plácido Domingo (Otello), Kiri Te Kanawa (Desdemona), Sergei Leiferkus (Iago), Claire Powell (Emilia), Robin Leggate (Cassio), Ramon Remedios (Roderigo).

Video: Kultur DVD/Home Vision VHS/Pioneer LD. Brian Large (director). Color. 146 minutes.

1995 Metropolitan Opera

American stage production: Elijah Moshinsky (director), James Levine (conductor, Metropolitan Opera Orchestra and Chorus), Michael Yeargan (set designer), Peter Hall (costume designer).

Cast: Plácido Domingo (Otello), Renée Fleming (Desdemona), James Morris (Iago), Jane Bunnell (Emilia), Richard Croft (Cassio), Charles Anthony (Rodrigo).

Taped October 13, 1995; telecast January 31, 1996. Brian Large (director). Color. In Italian with English subtitles. 150 minutes.

2001 Berlin State Opera

German stage production: Jürgen Flimm (director), Daniel Barenboim (conductor, Berlin Staatsoper Orchestra and Berlin Staatskapelle), George Tsypin (set designer).

Cast: Christian Franz (Otello), Emily Magee (Desdemona), Valery Alexeyev (Iago), Katharina Kammerloher (Emilia), Stephan Rügamer (Cassio).

Video: Arthaus Musik DVD. Alexandre Tarta (director). Color. In Italian with English subtitles. 157 minutes.

Comment: Modernized version with three-level ship-like set and most of the cast in modern naval uniforms. The singing is OK but the concept isn't.

***2001 Teatro alla Scala

Italian stage production: Graham Vick (director), Riccardo Muti (conductor, La Scala Orchestra, Chorus and Children's Choir and Giuseppe Verdi Conservatory Children's Choir), Ezio Frigero (set designer), Franca Squarciapino (costume designer).

Cast: Plácido Domingo (Otello), Barbara Frittoli (Desdemona), Leo Nucci (Iago), Rossana Rinaldi (Emilia), Cesare Catani (Cassio).

Video: TDK DVD. Taped December 2002. Carlo Battistoni (director). Color. In Italian with English subtitles. 140 minutes.

Comment: Considered the best DVD of the opera, well sung, staged and conducted.

2002 St. Margarethen Opera Festival

Austrian stage production: Wolfgang Werner (producer), Robert Herzl (director), Anton Guadagno (conductor, Stagione d'Opera Italiana Orchestra and Chorus), Manfred Wabo (set designer).

Video: W&W TV-Video (Germany) VHS. Color. In Italian with introduction in German. 150 minutes.

Comment: Spectacle dominates this abridged production filmed at the ancient Roman quarry of St. Margarethen in Austria, "the biggest open-air stage in Europe" with seating for 3,800. Marcel Prawny gives a talk about the opera in German before the curtain.

Early/related films

Films of the Shakespeare play

There are a many films of the play *Othello* from the silent era onward. The best are the 1952 version directed by and starring Orson Welles, and the 1965 version starring Laurence Olivier and directed by Stuart Burge.

1905/1907 Tamagno films

Francisco Tamagno, who created the role of Otello in 1887, was featured in two screenings in Italy of sound films of the opera. On November 13, 1905, he was seen and heard in a film presented at the Gran Salon Excelsior in Rome. In January 1907 he was seen and heard in a film of a scene from Act IV of the opera at the Politeama Carboni in Cagliari. Black and white. In Italian. About 5 minutes. The films appear to be lost.

1907 The Death of Otello

Henny Porten plays Desdemona with her father Franz as Otello and her sister Rosa as Emilia in this early German sound film; Verdi's music was played on a synchronized record. Franz Porten directed in a Berlin studio using Oskar Messter's sound system. Black and white. In German. About 4 minutes.

1913 Bianco contro Negro

Ernesto Maria Pasquali made this Italian sound film of the Otello story in 1913 using Verdi's opera music. In *Bianco contro Negro* (White Against Black), Alberto Capozzi plays Otello with Mary Cleo Tarlarini as Desdemona. Pasquali Films. Black and white. In Italian. About 45 minutes.

1930 Vitaphone film with Alda

Metropolitan Opera soprano Frances Alda sings the "Ave Maria" aria from *Otello* in costume in this Vitaphone sound short. Black and white. About 8 minutes. Bel Canto Society VHS.

1930 Ruffo Sings Iago's Credo
This early sound film, made by the MGM studio, features Italian baritone Titta Ruffo singing Iago's "Credo" on a set in costume with orchestra. Black and white. In Italian. About 8 minutes.

1941 Mamma
Beniamino Gigli plays an opera singer whose aging mother (Emma Gramatica) prevents his wife from leaving him after running through the rain, while he is on stage tearfully singing *Otello* with backing from the Rome Opera Orchestra. See MAMMA.

1947 This Time for Keeps
Lauritz Melchior plays an opera star in this musical and sings an aria from *Otello*. Richard Thorpe directed. Color. 105 minutes. MGM-UA VHS.

1956 Serenade
Mario Lanza as Otello and Licia Albanese as Desdemona join voices for the duet "Dio ti giocondi, o sposo" on the stage of the Metropolitan Opera in this film about an opera singer with emotional problems. It does not go well, and he leaves the stage. See SERENADE.

1970 Terre em Transe
The overture from *Otello* is featured in the Brazilian film *Terre em Transe* directed by Glauber Rocha. The plot revolves around a political murder. Color. In Portuguese with English subtitles. 110 minutes.

1979 Domingo: Make-up for Otello
This PBS documentary shows Plácido Domingo's preparations for the 1979 Metropolitan Opera production of *Otello*. Telecast on September 24, 1979, with the opera. Color. 55 minutes. Video at the MTR.

1994 Domingo at Verona
Plácido Domingo celebrated 25 years of appearances at the Arena di Verona with a televised program of staged opera scenes. It included Act I of *Otello* with Domingo as Otello and Daniela Dessi as Desdemona. Nello Santi conducted the Arena di Verona Orchestra. Color. 90 minutes.

1999 8½ Women
Peter Greenaway's bizarre film revolves around 8½ pachinko parlors in Tokyo and 8½ women in a Geneva bordello. Vladimir Bogachov is heard on the soundtrack singing an aria from *Otello* with the Royal Concertgebouw Orchestra led by Richard Chailly. Color. In English. 120 minutes.

2001 O
Shakespeare's *Otello* retold as a American high school melodrama with Otello as a star basketball player, the Duke as his coach, and Desdemona as the coach's daughter. The Paris Opera Boys Choir performs the "Ave Maria" from the opera. Tim Blake Nelson directed. Color. 94 minutes.

OTTER, ANNE SOFIE VON
Swedish mezzo-soprano (1955–)

Anne Sofie von Otter, who was born in Stockholm, began her professional career in Basle in 1983 as Alcina in Haydn's *Orlando Paladino* and sang there and at Aix-en-Provence for the next two years. She made her Covent Garden debut in 1985 as Cherubino and reached the Metropolitan in 1988 in the same role. Her career is truly international, and she has become noted for her trouser roles, especially as Cherubino, Sextus, and the Composer. Her first CARMEN, at the Glyndebourne Festival in 2002, attracted a good deal of attention and is on DVD. See ALCESTE (1999), La DAMNATION DE FAUST (1989), JAMES LEVINE (1996), MESSIAH (1992), MOZART REQUIEM (1991), and DER ROSENKAVALIER (1994).

OTTONE, RE DI GERMANIA
1723 opera by Handel

George Frideric Handel's opera *Ottone, re di Germania*, libretto by Nicol Francesco Haym, is based on incidents in the life of Western Holy Roman Emperor Otto II and his marriage in Rome in 972 to Princess Theophano of the Eastern Roman Empire. It premiered at the Royal Academy in London with castrato Senesina as Ottone (Otto), soprano Francesca Cuzzona as Teofane (Theophano), and castrato Berenstadt as Adelberto (Archbishop Adelbert of Prague). The opera has been recorded but is not currently on video.

2000 Le Goût des autres
This French film about an industrialist in love with an actress features Kathleen Ferrier on the soundtrack singing the aria "Spring Is Coming" from the opera. Gerald Moore accompanies her on piano on the recording made in 1945. Agnès Jaoui directed the film. Color. In French. 112 minutes.

OVERTURE TO GLORY
1940 American Yiddish film with opera content

Moishe Oysher plays a cantor who become involved in singing opera in this American Yiddish film. He is befriended by Polish composer Stanislaw Moniuszko, who hears him sing in a synagogue in Vilna and asks him to take the role of Jontek in *Halka* at the Warsaw Opera. Although the local rabbi opposes his leaving, the cantor agrees and is seen on stage performing Jontek's most famous aria. Although he is a success, he feels he should return home. He arrives at the Vilna synagogue on Yom Kippur, sings the Kol Nidre, and dies at the altar. The film is based on the legend of the Vilna Balabessel, as told in Mark Arnshteyn's play *Der Vilner Balabesl*. Larry Williams and Don Malkames were the cinematographers, and Max Nosseck wrote and directed the film, whose Yiddish title is *Der Vilner Shtot Khazn*. Black and white. 84 minutes.

OWEN WINGRAVE
1971 TV opera by Britten

BENJAMIN BRITTEN's *Owen Wingrave*, which was commissioned by BBC Television and produced with TV techniques, is one of the most notable operas written for the small screen. Myfanwy Piper's libretto is based on a ghost story by Henry James about a pacifist in 19th-century England. When he refuses to join the army, his military-oriented family shuns him, and his fiancée Kate accuses him of cowardice.

1971 BBC Television
British TV film: Colin Graham (director), John Culshaw (producer), Benjamin Britten (conductor, English Chamber Orchestra and Wandsworth School Boys' Choir).
Cast: Benjamin Luxon (Owen Wingrave), Peter Pears (General Sir Philip Wingrave), Sylvia Fisher (Miss Wingrave), Janet Baker (Kate), John Shirley-Quirk (Coyle), Heather Harper (Mrs. Coyle), Jennifer Vyvyan (Mrs. Julian).
Premiere Opera VHS. Telecast May 16, 1971, on BBC in England and NET in the United States. Brian Large (director). Color. In English. 110 minutes.
Comment: This was the world premiere performance and the soundtrack is on CD.

2001 Channel 4 Television
British TV film: Margaret Williams (director), Kent Nagano (conductor).
Cast: Gerald Finley (Owen Wingrave), Martyn Hill (General Sir Philip Wingrave), Charlotte Hellekant (Kate), Josephine Barstow (Miss Wingrave), Peter Savidge (Coyle), Anne Dawson (Mrs. Coyle), Elizabeth Gale (Mrs. Julian).
Telecast July 28, 2001, on Channel 4 in England. Color. In English. 111 minutes.
Comment. The time of the opera was updated to 1958, and the film was shot on location in Gloucestershire, Woolwich, and London with the performers singing to a prerecorded orchestral soundtrack.

OZAWA, SEIJI
Chinese-born American conductor (1935–)

Seiji Ozawa studied in Tokyo, won a number of international competitions, and then began to work with Herbert von Karajan and Leonard Bernstein. The first opera he conducted was *Così fan tutte* at Salzburg in 1969, and one of the most famous was *Eugene Onegin* at Covent Garden in 1974, repeated at the Vienna State Opera in 1988. He has recorded several operas with Jessye Norman, including CARMEN (there is a 1998 film about the recording session), and he conducted her 1992 OEDIPUS REX filmed in Japan with Philip Langridge. See also BEÁTRICE ET BÉNÉDICT (1979), CARMINA BURANA (1989), DVORÁK (1993), JEANNE D'ARC AU BÙCHER (1993), OBERON (1986), PETER GRIMES (1997 film), THE QUEEN OF SPADES (1992), and TOSCA (1991).

1985 Ozawa
Ozawa talks about Karajan, Bernstein, and his Japanese teacher Professor Saitoh, all of whom helped him rise to prominence. He is shown at work and home discussing his ideas with Jessye Norman, Edith Wiens, Rudolf Serkin, and Yo-Yo Ma. David and Albert Maysles, Susan Froemke, and Deborah Dickson made the film. Color. 60 minutes. CAMI VHS.

1997 A Tale of Tanglewood: Peter Grimes Reborn
Barbara Willis Sweete's documentary centers around Ozawa and his role as music director of the Boston Symphony Orchestra. It was made for the Canadian company Rhombus Media. Color. In English. 60 minutes.

P

PAGANINI
1925 operetta by Lehár

Paganini, one of FRANZ LEHÁR's most melodious operettas, tells the story of the reputed greatest violin player of all time, Nicolo Paganini. The story revolves around his legendary love affair with Maria Anna Luisa, Princess of Lucca and sister of Napoleon. *Paganini* was not a success when it premiered in Vienna, but it was a triumph when Richard Tauber sang it in Berlin in 1926 opposite soprano Vera Schwarz. Tauber also presented it in London in 1937. The operetta's most popular song is Paganini's explanation of his success with women, "Gern hab' ich die Frau'n geküsst (Girls Were Made to Love and Kiss).

1934 Emo film
German feature film: E. W. Emo (director), Georg Zoch (screenplay), Ewald Daub (cinematographer).

Cast: Ivan Petrovich (Paganini), Eliza Illiard (Princess Maria Anna Luisa), Theo Lingen, Rudolf Klein-Rogge, Veit Harlan.

Black and white. In German. 85 minutes.

1972 York film
German TV film: Eugen York (director), Wolfgang Ebert (conductor, Kurt Graunke Symphony Orchestra), Gerd Staub (set designer).

Cast: Antonio Theba (Paganini), Teresa Stratas (Princess Maria Anna Luisa), Johannes Heesters (Prince Felice), Peter Kraus (Marchese Pimpinelli), Dagmar Koller (Bella Giretti).

Color. In German. 108 minutes.

1992 Italian TV: Operette, che Passione!
Italian TV studio production: Sandro Massimini (director/producer/host), Roberto Negri (pianist), Sandro Corelli (choreographer).

Cast: Sandro Massimini, Sara Dilena, Tadamici Oriè.

Video: Pierluigi Pagano (director). Color. In Italian. About 19 minutes. Ricordi (Italy) VHS.

Comment: Highlights of the operetta on the Italian TV series *Operette, che Passione!* Songs include "Se le donne vo baciar," "Bel ciela azzurro dell'Italia mia," and "Oh dolce malia."

Silent film

1926 Rahn film
Eduard Von Winterstein plays Paganini in this silent German film of the operetta titled *Gern hab' ich die Frau'n geküsst,* after the hit song. It was directed by Bruno Rahn and screened with live music. Black and white. About 70 minutes.

PAGLIACCI
1892 opera by Leoncavallo

A group of traveling players arrive in the Calabrian village of Montalto where a drama of jealousy is played out like a Greek tragedy. Canio murders his wife Nedda and her lover Silvio during a *commedia dell'arte* performance after they are betrayed by Tonio. Canio's arioso "Vesti la giubba," sung as he puts on his clown costume, is one of the most popular tenor arias. Composer-librettist RUGGERO LEONCAVALLO's *Pagliacci,* first staged in Milan in 1892, made him instantly famous. Unfortunately, he was never to have another comparable success, and it is his only opera in the standard repertory. It is not only one of the most popular operas of all time, it is also one of the most filmed and videotaped. Efforts to film it have been made since the beginnings of cinema and television, often using pioneering sound systems. It was the first opera to be filmed complete with sound and the first opera televised in America. Its music is used with striking effect in many non-opera films, and the image of Canio in his clown costume has become one of the iconic images of opera.

1931 San Carlo Grand Opera
American film of stage production: Joe W. Coffman (director), Carlo Peroni (conductor, San Carlo Symphony Orchestra), Al Wilson (cinematographer), Fortuno Gallo (producer).

Cast: Fernando Bertini (Canio), Alba Novella (Nedda), Mario Valle (Tonio), Giuseppe Interranti (Silvio), Francesco Curci (Beppe).

Black and white. In Italian. 80 minutes.

Comment: This is the first sound film of a full opera; its credits claim it is the "world's first sound picture of a grand opera." It was filmed as a stage production on Long Island by Italian-Americans of the San Carlo Grand Opera Company. Critics thought the singing was fine but the film crudely made. It has survived and can still be viewed.

1936 Tauber film

English feature film: Karl Grune (director), Albert Coates (conductor), Hans Eisler (music director), Otto Kanturek (cinematographer), Monckton Hoffe and Roger Burford (English adaptation), John Drinkwater (English lyrics).

Cast: Richard Tauber (Canio), Steffi Duna (Nedda), Diana Napier (Trina), Arthur Margetson (Tonio), Esmond Knight (Silvio), Jerry Verne (Beppe).

Video: House of Opera DVD and Bel Canto Society/Video Yesteryear VHS. Black and white (two of the scenes were shot in a color process called Chemicolor). In English. 92 minutes.

Comment: This is a film for people who want to hear Tauber sing; he plays Canio but he also sings Tonio's Prologue and the music written for Silvio and Beppe. It was titled *Pagliacci* in England but released in America as *A Clown Must Laugh.*

1938 BBC Television

British TV production: D. H. Munro (director), Robert Ainsworth (conductor, BBC Orchestra and Covent Garden English Opera Chorus), Percy Cornish (set designer).

Cast: Frank Sale (Canio), Hella Toros (Nedda), Dennis Noble (Tonio), Morgan Davies (Silvio), John Fullard (Beppe).

Telecast live October 5, 1938, by the fledgling BBC. Vladimir Rosing (director). Black and white. In English. 66 minutes.

1940 Metropolitan Opera

American TV production (Act I): Frank St. Leger (conductor, Metropolitan Opera Orchestra).

Cast: Armand Tokatyan (Canio), Hilda Burke (Nedda), Richard Bonelli (Tonio), George Cehanovsky (Silvio), Alessio De Paolis (Beppe).

Black and white. In Italian. 60 minutes.

Comment: The first American television telecast of an opera by professional singers. Act I of the opera was presented live by the Met, with sets and costumes, in an NBC studio in Radio City on March 10, 1940. Gene Hamilton was the announcer; Met general manager Edward Johnson acted as master of ceremonies. The opera was half of a gala concert.

1948 Costa film

Italian feature film: Mario Costa (director); Giuseppe Morelli (conductor, Rome Opera House Orchestra and Chorus); Anton Giulio Majano, Carlo Castelli, Mario Costa (screenplay); Mario Bava (cinematographer).

Cast: Tito Gobbi (Tonio/Silvio), Gina Lollobrigida (Nedda, sung by Onelia Fineschi), Afro Poli (Canio, sung by Galliano Masini), Filippo Morucci (Arlecchio/Beppe, sung by Gino Sinimberghi).

Video: House of Opera DVD/Bel Canto Society VHS. Black and white. In Italian with English subtitles. 68 minutes.

Comment: The film begins with Leoncavallo talking to the audience and composing the opera on the piano. Gobbi is then seen on stage at La Scala singing the Prologue. After that, the opera proper begins in naturalistic settings. The film is well acted, directed, and photographed and has memorable lighting effects. It was called *I Pagliacci (Amore tragico)* in Italy, but it was released in America as *Love of a Clown,* with an added introduction written by Sinclair Lewis.

1951 NBC Opera Theatre

American TV production: Charles Polacheck (director), Samuel Chotzinoff (producer), Peter Herman Adler (NBC Opera Theatre Orchestra and Chorus), Liz Gillelan (set designer), Townsend Brewster (English translation).

Cast: Joseph Mordino (Canio), Elaine Malbin (Nedda), Paul Ukena (Tonio), Jack Russell (Silvio), Paul Franke (Beppe), Thomas L. Thomas (Prologue).

Video: Live Opera Heaven VHS and video at the MTR. Telecast live October 4, 1951. Kirk Browning (director). Black and white. In English. 70 minutes.

1953 Opera Cameos

American TV production: Fausto Bozza (director), Salvatore Dell'Isola (orchestra conductor), Joseph Vinti (screenplay), Carlo Vinti (producer).

Cast: Mario Del Monaco (Canio), Mildred Ellar (Nedda), Paolo Silveri (Tonio).

Video: Lyric VHS. Louis Ames (director). Black and white. In Italian. 28 minutes.

Comment: Abridged highlights version made for the *Opera Cameos* TV series and shown on the DuMont television network.

***1954 Enriquez film

Italian TV film: Franco Enriquez (director), Alfredo Simonetto (conductor, Milan RAI Orchestra and Chorus).

Cast: Franco Corelli (Canio), Mafalda Micheluzzi (Nedda), Tito Gobbi (Tonio), Lino Puglisi (Silvio), Mario Carlin (Beppe).

Legato Classics VHS. Black and white. In Italian. 74 minutes.

Comment: Corelli is at her best, and many critics think that this is still the best Pagliacci on video, despite its technical flaws.

1955 Canadian Television

Canadian TV production: Otto-Werner Mueller (conductor, Montreal Radio-Canada Orchestra).

Cast: Jon Vickers (Canio), Eva Likova (Nedda), Robert Savoie (Tonio), Louis Quilico (Silvio), Pierre Boutet (Beppe).

Video: VAI VHS. Telecast November 3, 1955, on CBC. Black and white. In Italian with English subtitles. 58 minutes.

Comment: Vickers was at the beginning of his career when he played Canio in this abridged Canadian TV production; it was a role often associated with him in later years.

1961 NHK Lirica Italiana

Japanese stage production: Bruno Nofri (director), Giuseppe Morelli (conductor, NHK Radio Symphony Orchestra and Nikikai and Fujiwara Opera Chorus), Cesare Mario Cristini (set designer).

Cast: Mario Del Monaco (Canio), Gabriella Tucci (Nedda), Aldo Protti (Tonio), Attilio D'Orazi (Silvio), Antonio Pirino (Beppe).

Video: VAI VHS/Japanese LD. Black and white. In Italian with English subtitles. 75 minutes.

Comment: Del Monaco is at his belting tenor best, and the audience loves it. Filmed live in Tokyo on October 25, 1961, for the NHK series *Lirica Italiana*.

1968 Teatro alla Scala

Italian studio film: Paul Hagar (director), Herbert von Karajan (producer/conductor, Teatro alla Scala Orchestra and Chorus), George Wakhévitch (set/costume designer).

Cast: Jon Vickers (Canio), Raina Kabaivanska (Nedda), Peter Glossop (Tonio), Rolando Panerai (Silvio), Sergio Lorenzi (Beppe).

Video: London VHS/LD. Color. In Italian. 79 minutes.

Comment: This film, shot in a studio with four cameras, is based on a Teatro alla Scala production. Like many of von Karajan's studio films, it feels a bit embalmed. It was shown theatrically in America.

1974 Focus on Opera

English TV film: Peter Seabourne (director), John J. Davies (conductor, Classical Orchestra), Peter Murray (screenplay), Chatsworth Film (production).

Cast: Kenneth Woollam (Canio), Valerie Masterson (Nedda), Malcolm Rivers (Tonio), Michael Wakeham (Silvio), David Young (Beppe).

Color. In English. 61 minutes.

Comment: Abridged version filmed at Knebworth House in England for the series *Focus on Opera*. Distributed on 16mm film in America.

1978 Metropolitan Opera

American stage production: Franco Zeffirelli (director, set/costume designer), Fabrizio Melano (staging), James Levine (conductor, Metropolitan Opera Orchestra and Chorus).

Cast: Plácido Domingo (Canio), Teresa Stratas (Nedda), Sherrill Milnes (Tonio), Allan Monk (Silvio), James Atherton (Beppe).

Video at the MTR. Telecast live on April 5, 1978. Kirk Browning (director). Color. In Italian. 72 minutes.

1982 Zeffirelli film

Italian feature film: Franco Zeffirelli (director), Georges Prêtre (conductor, Teatro alla Scala Orchestra and Chorus), Nino Cristiani and Armando Nannuzzi (cinematographers), Gianni Quaranta (set designer), Anna Anni (costume designer).

Cast: Plácido Domingo (Canio), Teresa Stratas (Nedda), Juan Pons (Tonio), Alberto Rinaldi (Silvio), Florindo Andreolli (Beppe).

Video: Decca and Philips DVD/VHS/LD. Color. In Italian with English subtitles. 72 minutes.

Comment: Zeffirelli shifts the period of the story to the 1930s for his film version and gives it a Fellini-esque look with the help of his designers. Based on his La Scala production, it was shot on a sound stage with a few scenes filmed on location. It won an Emmy Award after being telecast on PBS in 1984; the TV presentation included an introduction by Domingo shot in the Calabrian village of Montalto where the opera takes place.

1992 New York City Opera

American stage production: Jonathan Eaton (director), Steven Sloane (conductor, New York Opera Orchestra and Chorus), Paul Short (set designer), Eduardo V. Sicango (costume designer).

Cast: Antonio Barasorda (Canio), Gwynne Geyer (Nedda), Sigmund Cowan (Tonio), Eugene Perry (Silvio), Peter Blanchet (Beppe).

Video at the MTR. Telecast September 20, 1992. Kirk Browning (director). Color. In Italian. 70 minutes.

Comment: The locale of the opera is transposed from Calabria to an Italian immigrant neighborhood in New York City in the late 19th century.

1994 Metropolitan Opera

American stage production: Franco Zeffirelli (director, set/costume designer), Fabrizio Melano (staging), James Levine (conductor, Metropolitan Opera Orchestra and Chorus).

Cast: Luciano Pavarotti (Canio), Teresa Stratas (Nedda), Juan Pons (Tonio), Dwayne Croft (Silvio), Kenn Chester (Beppe).

Video: DG VHS. Taped September 26, 1994; telecast December 18, 1994. Brian Large (director). Color. In Italian with English subtitles. 70 minutes.

1998 Teatro Alighieri, Ravenna

Italian stage production: Liliana Cavani (director), Riccardo Muti (conductor, Teatro Alighieri Orchestra and Chorus).

Cast: Plácido Domingo (Canio), Svetla Vassileva (Nedda), Juan Pons (Tonio).

Video: Video Opera House VHS. Taped July 19, 1998; telecast February 7, 1999, on RAI. Color. In Italian. 72 minutes.

Early/related films

1905 Caruso film

On November 13, 1905, Enrico Caruso was featured singing in a sound film of *Pagliacci* at the Gran Salon Excelsior in Rome. As the information about the film is from contemporary advertisements, it could be that another actor appeared on screen miming to his recording. The film apparently does not survive. Black and white. In Italian. About 4 minutes.

1907 Ambrosio film

Italian film featuring scenes from the opera directed by Luigi Maggi, who also plays Canio with Mirra Principi as Nedda and Arthur Ambrosio as Silvio. Produced by the Ambrosio Company of Turin. Black and white. Silent. About 5 minutes.

1907 Messter film

German sound film of the Prologue, sung by Sigmund Lieban, made with Oskar Messter's Biophon system of disc synchronization. It was screened in 1907 but may have been filmed as early as 1903. Black and white. In Italian. About 4 minutes.

1908 Bioscop film

German sound film of the Nedda-Silvio duet, "Silvio! a quest'ora," first shown in 1908, was made by the Deutsche Bioscop company using their synchronized sound-on-disc system. Black and white. In Italian. About 5 minutes.

1909 Lubin film

American sound film of a scene from the opera made by the Lubin studio with the Lubin Synchronizer system. Black and white. In Italian. About 4 minutes.

1913 Vi-T-Ascope film

This three-reel *Pagliacci* film is described by the *Guinness Book of Records* as the first complete opera to be filmed in America. It was produced by the Vi-T-Ascope Company in 1913 using the Vi-T-Phone sound system. Black and white. In Italian. About 45 minutes.

1914 Webb's Electric Pictures

An abridged version of *Pagliacci* using George Webb's sound-on-film system was shown in May 1914 at the Fulton Theater in New York. Pilade Sinagra sang Canio, Elly Barnato was Nedda, and W. Rossini was Tonio. Black and white. In Italian. About 30 minutes.

1914 Messter films

Two German sound films of arias from the opera, made by Oskar Messter's Biophon-Tonbilder company, were released in 1914. Emil Lieben sings the Prologue on one and Canio's Lament ("Vesti la giubba") on the other. Black and white. In Italian. Each about 4 minutes.

1914 Oswald film

Olaf Fons stars as Canio in this German film of scenes from *Pagliacci* (titled *Lache Bajazzo*) directed by Richard Oswald. Black and white. Silent. About 15 minutes.

1915 Leoncavallo film

Ruggero Leoncavallo helped make this Italian silent feature film based on his opera, choosing the actors and designing the production. Achille Vitti plays Canio, Bianca Virginia Camagni is Nedda, Umberto Zanuccoli is Tonio, Annibale Nichi is Silvio, and Paolo Colaci is Beppe. Francesco Bertolini directed for the Mediolanum Film of Milan. It was screened with Leoncavallo's music played live. Black and white. About 65 minutes.

1917 Caruso film

Enrico Caruso turned up in person at the Cohan and Harris Theatre in New York on January 14, 1917, for the premiere of this sound film made by Webb's Singing Pictures. While actors appeared on screen in scenes from *Pagliacci*, Caruso's voice was heard singing the arias on loudspeakers connected to synchronized records. Black and white. In Italian. About 10 minutes.

1918 Guazzoni film

The Italian feature film *I Pagliaccio*, starring Amleto Novelli and Elena Sangro, uses the opera libretto as its screenplay. Enrico Guazzoni directed. The film was screened with the opera music played live. Black and white. Silent. About 70 minutes.

1923 I'Pagliacci
Adelqui Millar plays Canio opposite Lilian Hall-Davis as Nedda in this British feature film based on the opera, but with the plot altered. Campbell Gullan is Tonio, Frank Dane is Silvio, and George B. Samuelson and Walter Summers directed. The film was screened with live music from the opera. Black and white. Silent. About 70 minutes.

1926 Vitaphone film with Martinelli
Met tenor Giovanni Martinelli sings "Vesti la giubba" on stage in costume with orchestra in this Vitaphone sound film. It was presented before *Don Juan* in the first Vitaphone sound program on August 6, 1926, and was a huge hit. Black and white. In Italian. 7 minutes.

1927 Vitaphone film with Thomas
John Charles Thomas sings the Prologue to *Pagliacci* on stage in costume in this Vitaphone sound film. He is accompanied by the Vitaphone Symphony Orchestra. Black and white. In Italian. 8 minutes.

1927 Vitaphone film with Barclay
The full title of this Vitaphone short film is John Barclay Offering Impersonations of Famous Characters Singing the Prologue From Pagliacci (and others). Black and white. In Italian. 10 minutes.

1928 Fox film with Bonelli
Richard Bonelli sings the Prologue in this opera short made for the Fox studio music series *Movietone Numbers*. Black and white. In Italian. 8 minutes.

1928 The Singing Fool
Al Jolson, heartbroken over the death of his little "Sonny Boy," emulates the protagonist of *Pagliacci* and puts on blackface makeup to the music of "Vesti la giubba." Audiences loved the overt sentimentality, and the film became a big success. Lloyd Bacon directed. Black and white. In English. 110 minutes.

1929 Electrocord film
Sound film of the aria "Vesti la giubba" made for the Electrocord Films series featuring opera arias and songs. Black and white. In Italian. About 7 minutes.

1930 Call of the Flesh
Ramon Novarro sings "Vesti la giubba" in this early Technicolor musical about a dancer turned opera singer. Charles Brabin directed. Color. In English. 89 minutes.

1935 A Night at the Opera
Music from *Pagliacci* is used to establish the Marx Brothers as operatic clowns in the credits of this film. As their names appear on screen, music from *Pagliacci* is played. There is a staged production of *Pagliacci* in Milan at the beginning of the film with Kitty Carlisle as Nedda and nasty tenor Walter Woolf King as Canio. See A NIGHT AT THE OPERA.

1938 Kentucky Moonshine
Tony Martin sings the Prologue to Pagliacci in this Twentieth Century-Fox film; he plays a radio singer mixed up with the Ritz Brothers. David Butler directed. Black and white. 85 minutes.

1939 Casa Lontana
A sad Beniamino Gigli sings the aria "Vesti la giubba" in this film about an opera singer whose ballerina wife leaves him for another man. See CASA LONTANA.

1941 Ridi, Pagliaccio!
Despite the title, this is not a film of the opera story but it does feature the opera's music on the soundtrack. Camillo Mastrocinque directed this modern story about a sad love affair involving Fosco Giachetti and Laura Solari. Black and white. In Italian. 90 minutes.

1943 Ridi, Pagliaccio/Lache Bajazzo
These are the titles of American videos of a 1943 film made in Italian and German purporting to tell how Leoncavallo's opera *Pagliacci* originated. It stars Beniamino Gigli as an opera singer who plays Canio in the first production. See RIDI, PAGLIACCIO.

1946 The Whale Who Wanted to Sing at the Met
Willie, the opera-singing whale with the voice of Nelson Eddy, fantasizes a performance of *Pagliacci* at the Met. He performs in clown costume, and his tears flood the auditorium as he sings "Vesti la giubba." See THE WHALE WHO WANTED TO SING AT THE MET.

1951 The Great Caruso
Enrico Caruso (Mario Lanza) is shown on stage at a bond-raising concert singing and sobbing "Vesti la giubba" with real emotion; the woman he loves has not come to the concert as she promised. See THE GREAT CARUSO.

1951 Two Tickets to Broadway
Tony Martin performs the Prologue in this RKO film about a singer trying to get onto the Bob Crosby TV show. James V. Kern directed. Color. 106 minutes.

1987 The Untouchables

A scene from *Pagliacci* is used as a harsh ironic counterpoint in this G-men vs. the Mafia movie directed by Brian De Palma. Al Capone (Robert De Niro) is shown at the opera shedding a tear for the clown on stage as Mario Del Monaco sings "Vesti la giubba." At the same time, in crosscut scenes, incorruptible policeman Sean Connery is ambushed and killed by Capone's men. Color. 119 minutes.

1987 Aria

Bill Bryden's segment of the British opera film *Aria* features John Hurt in *Pagliacci*. He enters an opera house, makes up as a clown, has a vision of a girl he once loved (Sophie Ward), mimes to Enrico Caruso singing "Vesti la giubba," and dies on stage. Bryden shot the scenes in Cremona. See ARIA.

1998 The Clown at Midnight

Horror film set in an old opera house in which the clown Pagliacci murders a group of teenagers. Music from the opera is performed by the Slovak Philharmonic Choir and Czechoslovak Radio Symphony Orchestra of Bratislava. See THE CLOWN AT MIDNIGHT.

1998 Urban Ghost Story

The aria "Vesti la giubba" is heard on the soundtrack of this British film about a Glasgow tower block that appears to be haunted. Genevieve Jollife directed. Color. 88 minutes.

PAGLIUGHI, LINA
Italian-American soprano (1907–1980)

Lina Pagliughi was born in New York but made her career in Italy where she was the leading light soprano after Toti dal Monte retired. She sang on stage from 1927 to 1957 and was a mainstay at La Scala and Rome although she also sang at Covent Garden. She made many excellent recordings for RAI, released on Cetra, but had only a tiny movie career. She can be seen singing Gilda in Germany in a 1931 film, provides the singing voice for one of the opera singers in the 1943 Italian film *La Primadonna* set in the TEATRO ALLA SCALA, and provides the voice of Gilda opposite Tito Gobbi in the 1947 film of RIGOLETTO. She also dubbed the voice of Snow White in the Italian version of the Disney film *Snow White and the Seven Dwarfs*.

1931 Lina Pagliughi sings "Caro nome"

Pagliughi plays Gilda in *Rigoletto* and sings the aria "Caro nome" on a small studio stage in Berlin in 1931. She is accompanied by Arturo Lucon and the Berlin Philharmonic Orchestra. This scene, from a 1931 German film, is included in the video *Legends of Opera*. Black and white. About 5 minutes. Legato Classics VHS.

PAINTER, ELEANOR
American soprano (1886–1947)

Eleanor Painter made her opera debut in Nuremberg in 1913, but she was really best known for her performances in operettas. She created Victor Herbert's Princess in *Princess Pat* in 1915 and was the star of such Broadway musical shows as *The Lilac Domino, Gloriana, The Last Waltz,* and *The Chiffon Girl*. She was married to opera singer Louis Graveure.

1929 Eleanor Painter, The Lyric Soprano

Painter's only film is a sound short made for Vitaphone titled *Eleanor Painter, The Lyric Soprano*. She sings the "Habanera" from *Carmen*, "Love Is Best of All" from Herbert's *Princess Pat* (which she introduced on stage), and the Irving Berlin song "How About Me?" Black and white. About 10 minutes.

PAISIELLO, GIOVANNI
Italian composer (1740–1816)

Giovanni Paisiello was one of the most successful opera composers of his era, but his reputation has faded with time, partially because two of his most famous operas have been overshadowed by versions by other composers. His 1781 *La serva Padrona* was never able to compete with Pergolesi's earlier opera using the same libretto. More famously, his 1782 IL BARBIERE DI SIVIGLIA dropped out of the repertory after Rossini created his version in 1816. It is on video, however, and is still quite enjoyable. Paisiello's other opera of note is NINA, which has been telecast and recorded.

PAL, GEORGE
American producer (1908–1980)

Hungarian-born George Pal, who produced 42 Puppetoons films for Paramount using animated puppets, featured music by Johann Strauss in two of them. The first was the 1943 *Mr. Strauss Takes a Walk* with Strauss strolling around to his own tunes. The second, also in 1943, was *Bravo, Mr. Strauss* in which a statue of the composer comes to life when the Screwball Army (i.e., the Nazis) starts to destroy the Vienna Woods. He leads them into the Danube River, like the Pied Piper, by playing his violin. Pal later became famous for his special effects science-fiction movies.

PALACE, THE
1995 opera by Sallinen

Finnish composer AULIS SALLINEN's *The Palace*, a satire about political power and its effect on those who have it, premiered at the Savonlinna Festival in 1995. Irene Dische and Hans Magnus Enzenberger's libretto was inspired by Ryszard Kzpuscinski's book about the downfall of Haile Selassie of Ethiopia, *The Emperor,* and by Mozart's *Die Entführung aus dem Serail.*

1995 Savonlinna Festival
Finnish stage production: Kalle Holmberg (director), Okko Kamu (conductor, Savonlinna Festival Orchestra and Chorus).

Cast: Veijo Varpio (King), Jaana Mantyne (Queen), Tom Krause, Sauli Tilikainen, Jorma Silvasti, Ritva-Liisa Korhonen.

Telecast in Finland in 1995. Aarno Cronvall (director). Color. 130 minutes.

PALERMO

Palermo's Teatro Massimo, which dates from 1897 and is one of the largest opera houses in the world, was the scene of Enrico Caruso's earliest success, as referenced at the end of the 1951 film ENRICO CARUSO, LEGGENDA DI UNA VOCE. The opera house is also featured prominently in the 1990 Francis Ford Coppola film *The Godfather Part III* (a production of CAVALLERIA RUSTICANA is key to the plot), in the 1939 Beniamino Gigli film CASA LONTANA (with scenes from Zandonai's opera *Giulietta e Romeo*), and the 1991 Roberto Benigni comedy *Johnny Stecchino* (he is mistaken for a Mafia boss and empties the theater of its patrons). There are Teatro Massimo opera videos of FEDORA (1998), ZAZÀ (1995), and DER ROSENKAVALIER (1997) and a Bellini Conservatory video of BEATRICE DI TENDA (2000). American baritone Marshall Everett made his debut at the Teatro Massimo in Palermo in 1926 in *Il trovatore*. Verdi's opera I VESPRI SICILIANI, about the famous Sicilian Vespers uprising in 1282, takes places in Palermo.

PALIASHVILI, ZAKHARY
Georgian composer (1871–1933)

Zakhary Petrovich Paliashvili is considered the father of Georgian opera, and the opera theater in the Georgian capital Tbilisi is named for him. After helping to create awareness of Georgian folk music, he composed three operas. *Abesalom da Eteri* (Absalom and Etery), based on an ancient Georgian legend and incorporating Georgian folk tunes, was a huge success at its 1919 premiere. DAISI (Twilight), which premiered in 1923, was equally successful and became the first opera ever staged in

Georgia and the first to be filmed. It is based on a patriotic folk legend about two men competing for a woman when the country is being attacked by a foreign power. His third and final opera was *Latavra,* first performed in 1928.

PALMER, FELICITY
English soprano/mezzo (1944–)

Felicity Palmer, who made her operatic debut as Dido with Kent Opera in 1971, has been a regular performer at the English National Opera, singing Pamina, Donna Elvira, and Katisha in a famous Jonathan Miller production of THE MIKADO (1987). She has sung in Houston and Chicago and, in recent years, has taken on mezzo roles, including Kabanicha in *Katya Kabanova.* She has a strong stage presence as is shown in her many excellent videos. See ALBERT HERRING (1985), KATYA KABANOVA (1988), OEDIPUS REX (1984), ORPHÉE AUX ENFERS (1983), and THE QUEEN OF SPADES (1992).

PALMER, TONY
English film director (1935–)

Tony Palmer has been directing musical documentaries and films since the 1960s and has devoted a good deal of time to opera. His biggest work by far is a epic nine-hour film biography of RICHARD WAGNER (1983), but he has also filmed operas, including Britten's DEATH IN VENICE (1981) and PARSIFAL (1999 film). His informative films on composers and singers are of real value. See HECTOR BERLIOZ (1992), BENJAMIN BRITTEN (1967/1980), MARIA CALLAS (1987), GEORGE FRIDERIC HANDEL (1985), ANDRÉ PREVIN (2001), GIACOMO PUCCINI (1984), HENRY PURCELL (1995), PETER SELLARS (1995), DIMITRI SHOSTAKOVICH (1987), IGOR STRAVINSKY (1982), and WILLIAM WALTON (1981).

PANNELL, RAYMOND
Canadian opera composer (1935–)

Raymond Pannell, one of the most successful modern Canadian opera composers, has been involved with a number of opera companies. His major stage work, *The Luck of Ginger Coffey* (1967), based on the novel by Brian Moore, was commissioned by the Canadian Opera Company for Canada's centenary celebrations. His TV opera ABERFAN (1977), commissioned by CBC Television, won the Salzburg Opera Prize.

PAPPANO, ANTONIO
English-born American conductor (1961–)

Antonio Pappano became music director of the Royal Opera in London in September 2002 after a highly successful career as music director of the Théâtre Royal de la Monnaie in Brussels. Pappano was born in London of Italian parents but was brought up in the United States. His operas on video include a 1996 Théâtre du Châtelet production of DON CARLOS, with Robert Alagna, and a 2001 film of TOSCA, with Alagna and his wife Angela Gheorghiu.

2000 Antonio Pappano
János Darvas's documentary about the conductor shows him at rehearsals and performances of *Falstaff* in Florence, *Lohengrin* in Bayreuth, and *Lady Macbeth of the Mtsensk District* in Brussels. Pappano talks about his career and explains his musical ideas. Color. 59 minutes.

2002 Il maestro Pappano
This excellent biography follows the director from his childhood in London to his teenage years in Connecticut through his years at La Monnaie and on to London. Pappano talks about his emergence as a conductor in Norway after years as an accompanist, and he is shown at work preparing operas in Brussels and rehearsing the *Verdi Requiem*. Pierre Barré and Thierry Loreau filmed it for BBC and La Monnaie. Color. 76 minutes.

"PARALLEL" OPERA FILMS

The "parallel" opera film is a film in which a contemporary story parallels the plot of an opera around which the film is centered. They are usually based on the most popular Italian repertory operas and feature notable singers performing highlights from the opera. The first major success was the 1937 Austrian film ZAUBER DE BOHÈME starring Marta Eggerth and Jan Kiepura, based around *La bohème;* it was so popular it was remade in English in 1947 with the same stars as HER WONDERFUL LIE. Equally popular was the 1939 Italian-German film IL SOGNO DI BUTTERFLY starring Maria Cebotari based around *Madama Butterfly*. Its success led to a 1940 film starring Cebotari based around *La traviata* (AMAMI, ALFREDO!). The 1942 Beniamino Gigli film VERTIGINE has parallels with both *Adrian Lecouvreur* and *La bohème*. The 1946 film *Davanti a lui tremava tutta Roma* with Anna Magnani and Tito Gobbi parallels events in TOSCA. The genre has continued to the present day. Modern variations include M. BUTTERFLY (1993, based around *Madama Butterfly*), BABEL OPERA (1985, based around *Don Giovanni*), and *Don Juan, Karl-Liebknect-Strasse 78* (1980, based around *Don Giovanni*). Cole Porter's *Kiss Me Kate* features a parallel story based

around THE TAMING OF THE SHREW, but in this case the music is original.

PARIS

Paris opera houses go back many centuries, but the main theaters today are the Paris Opéra (Palais Garnier, 1875), now the home of both ballet and opera; the $300 million Opéra Bastille (1990), which has four theaters; the Opéra-Comique (Salle Favart, 1898), which presents light opera; and the Châtelet Theater (taken over by the city in 1980 and renamed Théâtre Musical de Paris), site of many fine Mozart productions. The first live telecast from the Paris Opéra was the Maria Callas gala evening on December 19, 1958, which is on video. There are videos of telecasts from all the theaters, although not nearly as many as there could be. The Paris Opéra archive has tapes of more than 900 operas and ballets telecast since 1971. Most were televised only once and never released on video, but there are now plans to make them more available. Quite a number are currently available from alternative video companies. See ALCESTE (1999), IL BARBIERE DI SIVIGLIA (1947), LA BELLE HÉLÈNE (1999), LES BORÉADES (1987), BORIS GODUNOV (1980), MARIA CALLAS (1958), CARMEN (1980), COSÌ FAN TUTTE (1992), THE CUNNING LITTLE VIXEN (1995), DARDANUS (1980), DON CARLOS (1996), DIE ENTFÜHRUNG AUS DEM SERAIL (1991), FAUST (1975), LA GRANDE-DUCHESSE DE GÉROLSTEIN (1981), HAMLET (2000), L'ITALIANA IN ALGERI (1998), NABUCCO (1979), EL NIÑO (2000), LE NOZZE DI FIGARO (1980/1993), MADO ROBIN, ORFEO ED EURIDICE (1999), ROMÉO ET JULIETTE (1982), TOSCA (1991), and VÉRONIQUE (1979).

Phantom of the Opera films
Gaston Leroux's 1911 novel *Le Fantôme de l'Opéra,* set at the Palais Garnier, has been popular with filmmakers since the 1925 Lon Chaney movie made it world famous. It has not, however, aroused the interest of French filmmakers, and none of the films was actually shot at the Palais Garnier. See THE PHANTOM OF THE OPERA.

1983 Naissance d'un opéra à la Bastille
French filmmaker François Reichenbach made this short film, the first of a number of documentaries about the creation of the new Parisian opera house. Color. In French. 20 minutes.

1989 La nuit d'avant le jour
Concert in honor of the new Bastille Opera House featuring Plácido Domingo, June Anderson, Teresa Berganza, Barbara Hendricks, Ruggero Raimondi, Alfredo Kraus, Martine Dupuy, Alain Fondary, and Jean-Philippe Lafont. Georges Prêtre leads the orchestra. Color. In French. 90 minutes. Lyric VHS.

1990 L'Opéra Bastille

Jean-François Roudot made this French documentary film about the new opera house. Color. In French. 54 minutes.

1991 Histoires d'Opéra

Opéra Bastille opened in March 1990 to controversy over prices, standards, and staff. Robin Lough and Cathie Levy's film shows the opera house during preparations for Andrei Konchalovsky's staging of *The Queen of Spades* and Graham Vick's staging of Berio's *Un re in Ascolto*. There is comment about the pluses and minuses of the opera house, and music director Myung-Whung Chung discusses criticisms leveled at him. Color. With English narration. 59 minutes. On VHS.

PARSIFAL

1882 opera by Wagner

RICHARD WAGNER's most religious (and most pretentious) opera was meant to be performed only at Bayreuth; Hitler felt it was a close reflection of his philosophy. The opera story is a variation on the Grail legend, with Parsifal, the "holy fool" knight, sent to get the Holy Spear back from the evil sorcerer Klingsor. The spear will cure the wounded King Amfortas, but it is guarded by the irresistible enchantress Kundry and her euphemistically named "flower maidens." Thomas Edison made an "epic film" of it in 1904 during a copyright controversy, and Hans-Jurgen Syberberg made a 1982 film of it that some critics consider "wacky."

1981 Bayreuth Festival

German stage production: Wolfgang Wagner (director/set designer), Horst Stein (conductor, Bayreuth Festival Orchestra and Chorus), Reinhard Heinrich (costume designer).

Cast: Siegfried Jerusalem (Parsifal), Eva Randova (Kundry), Bernd Weikl (Amfortas), Matti Salminen (Titurel), Hans Sotin (Gurnemanz), Leif Roar (Klingsor).

Video: Philips VHS/LD. Brian Large (director). Color. In German with English subtitles. 233 minutes.

1982 Syberberg film

German feature film: Hans-Jurgen Syberberg (director), Armin Jordan (conductor, Monte Carlo Philharmonic Orchestra and Prague Philharmonic Chorus), Igor Luther (cinematographer), Werner Achmann (set designer), Veronicka Dorn and Hella Wolter (costume designers), Gaumont (production).

Cast: Michael Kutter and Karen Krick (Parsifal 1 and 2, sung by Reiner Goldberg), Edith Clever (Kundry, sung by Yvonne Minton), Armin Jordan (Amfortas, sung by Wolfgang Schöne), Robert Lloyd (Gurnemanz),

Martin Sperr (Titurel, sung by Hans Tschammer), Aage Haugland (Klingsor).

Video: Corinth Films/Image Entertainment DVD and Kultur VHS. Color. In German with English subtitles. 255 minutes.

Comment: Syberberg's inventive but controversial film (the background rocks are modeled after Wagner's death mask) features three people as Parsifal: Goldberg sings the role while Kutter and Krick play him/her on screen. Not a film for everyone's taste but truly fascinating.

1992 Metropolitan Opera

American stage production: Otto Schenk (director), Phoebe Berkowitz (stage director), James Levine (conductor, Metropolitan Opera Orchestra and Chorus), Günther Schneider-Siemssen (set designer), Rolf Langenfass (costume designer).

Cast: Siegfried Jerusalem (Parsifal), Waltraud Meier (Kundry), Bernd Weikl (Amfortas), Kurt Moll (Gurnemanz), Jan-Hendrik Rootering (Titurel), Franz Mazura (Klingsor),

Video: DG DVD/VHS/LD. Brian Large (director). Taped March 28, 1992; telecast April 7, 1993. Color. In German with English subtitles. 266 minutes.

***1992 Staatsoper Unter den Linden

German stage production: Harry Kupfer (director), Daniel Barenboim (conductor, Deutsche Staatskapelle Berlin and Chor der Deutschen Staatsoper Berlin), Hans Schavernoch (set designer), Christine Stromberg (costume designer).

Cast: Poul Elming (Parsifal), Waltraud Meier (Kundry), Falk Struckmann (Amfortas), John Tomlinson (Gurnemanz), Fritz Hübner (Titurel), Gunter von Kannen (Klingsor).

Video: Teldec DVD/VHS/LD. Telecast November 1, 1992. Hals Hulscher (director). Color. In German with English subtitles. 244 minutes.

Comment: In this ultra modernist production, the story takes place in a kind of steel bank vault and the flower maidens are images on video screens. Despite this, it is very well done, finely acted and sung, and superbly conducted.

Early/related films

1904 Edison film

This *Parsifal* is an important early opera film that helped establish the right of authors to their work. When Wagner's opera opened in 1903 at the Metropolitan in New York, despite hostility from Bayreuth, it attracted a lot of newspaper attention. The Edison studio and director Edwin S. Porter decided to turn it into a costly and ambitious epic in eight episodes using elaborate sets by H.

Merry; Robert Whittier played Parsifal, and Adelaide Fitz-Allen was Kundry. The film was to be screened with recordings of the Wagner music, but a copyright lawsuit hurt its release and it was not widely shown. The film, however, survived in the paper print collection of the Library of Congress. Black and white. Silent. About 20 minutes. Prints at the NFTA and Library of Congress.

1912 Ambrosio film

Mario Caserini directed this epic Italian *Parsifal* for the Ambrosio Company of Turin. Vitale De Stefano plays Parsifal, Mario Bonnard is Amfortas, Mary Cleo Tarlarini is Kundry, Maria Gasperini is Parsifal's mother, and Antonio Gristanti is the Bishop. Alberto Capozzi and Arrigo Frusta wrote the screenplay. The film was advertised as having more than 500 extras with costumes borrowed from La Scala. Black and white. Silent. About 60 minutes.

1927 The King of Kings

Cecil B. DeMille's film about the life of Jesus, played by H. B. Warner, borrows motifs from *Lohengrin* and *Parsifal.* Black and white. Silent. About 130 minutes.

1952 Tcherina film

Russian dancer Ludmilla Tcherina stars as Kundry with Gustavo Rojo as Parsifal in the Spanish film *Parsifal,* inspired by the opera and directed by Daniel Mangrané and C. Serrano de Osma. The cast includes Carlo Tamberlani as Klingsor, Felix de Pomes, and Alfonso Estela. Black and white. In Spanish. 95 minutes.

1963 To Parsifal

American experimental filmmaker Bruce Baillie's tribute to the opera is a visual hymn set to the overture of the opera. Color. 16 minutes.

1999 Palmer film

Tony Palmer's documentary *Parsifal,* filmed on location in Bayreuth and St. Petersburg, is hosted by Plácido Domingo who performs in excerpts from the opera. The other performers are Violeta Urmana, Matti Salminen, and Nikolai Putilin; Valery Gergiev conducts the Kirov Orchestra and Choir. Mike Bluett produced. Color. In English. 90 minutes. Kultur DVD/VHS.

PASATIERI, THOMAS
American composer (1945–)

Thomas Pasatieri has had considerable success with his neo-romantic, melodic operas; the two most successful— *The Seagull* (1974) and *The Three Sisters* (1979)—were based on Chekhov plays, but neither is on video. THE TRIAL OF MARY LINCOLN, a harrowing portrait of President Lincoln's widow on trial for her sanity, was telecast in 1972.

1977 The Operas of Thomas Pasatieri

This CBS *Camera Three* television program features the composer and singers in conversation and performance of scenes from three operas. Catherine Malfitano, Brent Ellis, and Elaine Bonazzi perform the "Carriage Scene" from *Washington Square;* Joanna Simon sings the "Cradle Song" from *The Black Widow;* and Ellis and Bonazzi duet on "Nina's Good-bye to Constantin" from *The Seagull.* Roger Englander directed. Color. In English. 30 minutes. Video at the MTR and New York State Education Department.

PASINI, LAURA
Italian soprano (1894–1942)

Laura Pasini made her debut in Milan in 1921 and was a Teatro alla Scala favorite from 1923 on, mainly in coloratura roles. She was particularly admired as the Queen of the Night in *The Magic Flute* and as the heroines of Rossini's *La Cenerentola* and *L'italiana in Algeri.* She made two Italian opera films. In the 1932 composer biography PERGOLESI, she sings the role of the wily servant Serpina in scenes from LA SERVA PADRONA. In *La cantante dell'opera* she appears in several opera scenes.

1932 La cantante dell'opera

The Italian film *The Opera Singer* features soprano Pasini with La Scala tenor colleague Alessio De Paolis in a number of opera scenes. The story revolves around a young opera singer in Venice and her involvement with a man pretending to be an American. Nunzio Malasomma directed. Black and white. In Italian. 90 minutes.

PASSIONNÉMENT
1926 operetta by Messager

André Messager's operetta *Passionnément* (Passionately), libretto by Maurice Hennequin and Albert Willemetz, centers around an American millionaire and his wife. Wealthy William Stevenson goes to France to try to cheat gambler Robert Perceval out of some oil land. As he is jealous of his pretty young wife, he insists that she wear a wig and pretend to be old. It doesn't work, and she falls in love with Perceval and reveals all. Her husband discovers the joys of champagne and ends up with the sexy Julia.

1932 Paramount film

French feature film: René Guissart (director), René Guissart and Jean Boyer (screenplay), Paramount (production company).

Cast: René Koval (William Stevenson), Florelle (Ketty Stevenson), Fernand Gravey (Robert Perceval), Davia (Julia), Danielle Brégis (Hélène Le Barrois), Louis Baron (Le Barrois).

Black and white. In French. 80 minutes.

PAS SUR LA BOUCHE
1925 operetta by Yvain

Maurice Yvain's French operetta *Pas sur la bouche* (Not on the Mouth), libretto by André Barde, was a major success when it opened in Paris in 1925; it was staged in London the following year as *Just a Kiss*. The plot is as gossamer light as the tuneful music. Gilberte is happily married to George, but she has never told him that she was once wed to an American named Eric. When Eric turns up and tries to renew the relationship, she has to exploit his weakness; he won't allow anyone to kiss him on the mouth. Her friend Mlle. Poumaillac agrees to help out.

1931 Luna film
French feature film: Nicolas Rimsky and Nicolas Evreimof (directors), André Barde (screenplay), Nicolas Roudakoff and Georges Raulet (cinematographers), Luna Film (production).

Cast: Mireille Perry (Gilberte), Jacques Grétillat (Georges), Nicolas Rimsky (Eric), Alice Tissot (Mlle. Poumaillac), Jeanne Marney (Huguette).

Black and white. In French. 80 minutes.

PASTERNAK, JOE
Hungarian-born American film producer (1901–1991)

Josef Pasternak began his career as a film producer in Budapest and Berlin. After emigrating to the United States, he became one of the top producers at the Universal and MGM studios, usually of movies with opera content. His pictures featured such stars as DEANNA DURBIN, MARIO LANZA, KATHRYN GRAYSON, ANNA MARIA ALBERGHETTI, LAURITZ MELCHIOR, and JANE POWELL. Pasternak, who was involved with more than 100 movies between 1929 and 1968, produced films of the operettas *Spring Parade* (FRÜHJAHRSPARADE), *The Merry Widow* (DIE LUSTIGE WITWE), and THE STUDENT PRINCE. He even built a reproduction of the old Met for his 1946 film TWO SISTERS FROM BOSTON.

PATANÈ, GIUSEPPE
Italian conductor (1932–1989)

Giuseppe Patanè was reputed to have an exceptional operatic memory (his father Franco was also an opera conductor), and was said to know the scores of more than 200 operas. He was born in Naples and made his debut there in 1951 conducting, without a score, *La traviata*. After working in Italy and Germany, he made his American debut in San Francisco in 1967 and began to conduct at the Met in 1975. He was a regular at the Met and Covent Garden for many years. His operas on video include UN BALLO IN MASCHERA (1980), LA FORZA DEL DESTINO (1978), NORMA (1974), LA TRAVIATA (1968), and IL TURCO IN ITALIA (1978).

PATIENCE
1881 comic opera by Gilbert and Sullivan

Patience or Bunthorne's Bride is a delightful spoof of Oscar Wilde, the aesthetes, and the Pre-Raphaelite movement. It is one of W. S. Gilbert's cleverest librettos, and its famous song about faking the esthetic game, "If you're anxious for to shine," is just as relevant today as when it was written. The story centers around the Oscar Wilde–type character Reginald Bunthorne and the 20 maidens who swoon over him to the annoyance of the Guards of the Dragoons, who used to enjoy their favors. Reginald, however, loves the milkmaid Patience, who knows nothing about estheticism; she is also loved by her childhood sweetheart Archibald Grosvenor. *Patience* was the first GILBERT AND SULLIVAN operetta performed at the Savoy Theater.

1982 Gilbert and Sullivan Collection series
English studio production: John Cox (director), Judith De Paul (producer), Alexander Faris (conductor, London Symphony Orchestra and Ambrosian Opera Chorus), Allan Cameron (set designer), George Walker (executive producer).

Cast: Derek Hammond-Stroud (Reginald Bunthorne), Sandra Dugdale (Patience), John Fryatt (Archibald Grosvenor), Donald Adams (Colonel Calverley), Terry Jenkins (Duke of Dunstable), Roderick Kennedy (Major Murgatroyd), Anne Collins (Lady Jane), Shelagh Squires (Lady Saphir).

Video: Opera World/Braveworld (GB) VHS. Dave Heather (director). Color. In English. 117 minutes.

Related film

1937 The Girl Said No
This little-known American film contains scenes from Gilbert and Sullivan operettas performed in a traditional manner by members of the old Gilbert and Sullivan Opera Company of New York. It includes the song "The Magnet and the Churn" from *Patience*. See THE GIRL SAID NO.

PATTI, ADELINA
Italian soprano (1843–1919)

Adelina Patti was born in Madrid of Italian parentage but was brought up in New York City as a child prodigy able to sing "Casta diva" at the age of 7. She made her professional debut at 16 in *Lucia di Lammermoor* at the New York Academy of Music and sang 14 other roles the same year. She made her Covent Garden debut in 1861 as Amina in *La sonnambula,* was the first Aida at Covent Garden, and continued singing on stage around the globe until the turn of the century. Her records are still admired as she seemed to have kept the purity of her voice into her final years. She made no films but is played by other sopranos in several.

Adelina Patti wore fancy hats at the height of her fame in the late 19th century.

1945 Pink String and Sealing Wax
English soprano Margaret Ritchie plays Patti on tour in this Ealing film set in Brighton in 1880 and sings the delightful "Hush, Every Breeze," which she later recorded. The film is the story of a publican's wife and her plot to poison her husband. Robert Hamer directed. Black and white. In English. 89 minutes.

1953 Melba
Dorit Welles plays Patti in this British film about the life of Nellie Melba. See MELBA.

1959 Gayarre
Lina Huarte plays Patti in this Spanish film about the 19th-century tenor Julián Gayarre with Alfredo Kraus as Gayarre. Domingo Viladomat directed. Color. In Spanish. 90 minutes. Bel Canto/Opera Dubs VHS.

1977 Anna Karenina
The voice of Patti, impersonated by Felicity Lott, is heard in this BBC Television miniseries version of the Tolstoy novel. Basil Coleman directed. Color. In English. 500 minutes.

1993 Adelina Patti, Queen of Song
June Anderson plays Patti and sings arias associated with her in this English film by Chris Hunt. The focus is on a concert performance in her home theater in Wales, but she is also pictured at Covent Garden and traveling with her jewel collection and bodyguards. Dennis O'Neill plays her husband. The music is performed by the Welsh National Opera Orchestra conducted by Robin Stapleton. Color. In English. 60 minutes.

PAVAROTTI, LUCIANO
Italian tenor (1935–)

If one can measure popularity by videos, films, TV appearances, and recordings, Luciano Pavarotti is one of the most popular opera singers of the century. The Modena tenor is certainly the most recognizable opera personality of our time, confirmed by his World Cup success singing its theme "Nessun dorma" and the THREE TENORS concert series. There has not been a phenomenon like Pavarotti—the opera singer as pop icon—since Caruso, and his clutched white handkerchief has become world famous. Pavarotti, who has remained within the Italian repertoire, made his debut in 1961 as Rodolfo in Reggio Emilia, went to Covent Garden in 1963 in the same role, and first won fame touring with Joan Sutherland in Australia. He went at the Metropolitan in 1968 as Rodolfo and quickly became one of the Met's most popular performers. He can be seen on video in many operas, recitals, and concerts and one unsuccessful Hollywood film. See AIDA (1981/1985/1987 film), ANDREA CHÉNIER (1996), UN BALLO IN MASCHERA (1980/1987/1991), LA BOHÈME (1977/1983/1986/1989), JOSÉ CARRERAS (1992), ENRICO CARUSO (1998), DON CARLO (1992), L'ELISIR D'AMORE (1981/1991), ERNANI (1983), DIE FLEDERMAUS (1990), LA GIOCONDA (1980/1980 film), MARILYN HORNE (1981), IDOMENEO (1982), I LOMBARDI (1993), MADAMA BUTTERFLY (1987 film), MARIA STUARDA (2000), GIAN CARLO MENOTTI (1986), METROPOLITAN OPERA (1972/1983/1986/1991), PAGLIACCI (1994), RIGOLETTO (1981/1983/2000 film), DER ROSENKAVALIER (1982), JOAN SUTHERLAND (1987/1993), SYDNEY (1984), TENORS (2000), TOSCA (1978/1993), IL TROVATORE (1988), TURANDOT (1987 film), GIUSEPPE VERDI (1998), VERDI REQUIEM (1967/1991/1996), and VERONA (1994).

1978 Christmas with Luciano Pavarotti
Pavarotti performs Christmas classics at a recital in Montreal's Notre Dame Cathedral on September 22, 1978, with the Petits Chanteurs du Mont-Royal and the Disciples de Massenet. Franz-Paul Decker conducts the Montreal Symphony Orchestra. Color. 60 minutes. Video Treasures VHS.

1979 Opera Master Class at Juilliard

There are several films of Pavarotti giving master classes and sharing his knowledge with singers at the Juilliard School. The most accessible is this video by Nathan Kroll, which has commercial distribution. Pavarotti sings "Per la gloria d'adorarvi" from Bononcini's *Griselda*, and critiques six students as they sing. John Wustman is the accompanist. Color. 60 minutes. Kultur VHS.

1982 Yes, Giorgio

Pavarotti's sole attempt at Hollywood fame is an entertaining but plotless, old-fashioned story about a famous opera singer (Pavarotti) and his light-hearted affair with a doctor (Kathryn Harrold). It was a resounding commercial failure, despite pretty cinematography, rather good singing by Pavarotti (including "Nessun dorma," of course), and deft direction by master filmmaker Franklin J. Schaffner. The film was an attempt to make Pavarotti into a new Mario Lanza, but it was a misjudgment. Color. 110 minutes.

1982 Pavarotti & Friends

This ABC-TV program about Pavarotti shows him at home in Modena, talking with Jacqueline Bissett, meeting friends in Hollywood, singing in church, and paying tribute to Caruso. Dwight Hemion and Gary Smith directed. Color. 60 minutes.

1982 Pavarotti In London

Pavarotti is in good form at this concert at the Royal Albert Hall in London April 13, 1982. The program opens with Pavarotti singing "Recondita armonia" and includes music by Verdi, Donizetti, Cilea, and de Curtis. Rodney Greenberg directed for the BBC. Color. 78 minutes. Sony VHS.

1984 Pavarotti in Recital/A Pavarotti Valentine

Pavarotti performs love songs by art song master Tosti and arias by Gluck, Verdi, Donizetti, Puccini, Bononcini, Bizet, and Caldara at the Teatro Petruzzelli in Bari on February 14, 1984. Leone Magiera accompanies on piano. Color. 78 minutes. VAI DVD (as *Pavarotti in Recital*) and VAI VHS as *A Pavarotti Valentine*.

1984 Pavarotti

Pavarotti at the Riviera Hotel in Las Vegas singing arias from *La traviata, L'elisir d'amore, Un ballo in maschera, Werther, La Gioconda, La bohème,* and, of course, *Turandot* ("Nessun dorma"). Emerson Buckley conducts the Las Vegas Symphony Orchestra. Stan Harris directed. Color. 77 minutes. USA Home VHS.

1986 Luciano Pavarotti Gala Concert

Pavarotti in concert at Olympia Hall in Munich singing arias from operas by Verdi, Cilea, Giordano, Leoncavallo, and Puccini. Emerson Buckley conducts the Munich Radio Orchestra and Karlheinz Hundorf directed. Color. 60 minutes. Kultur VHS.

1986 Distant Harmony: Pavarotti in China

Pavarotti on a visit to China in June 1986 visits schools, dines in restaurants, tries out Chinese opera gear, and sings a good deal, including arias from *Rigoletto, La bohème, Turandot, Pagliacci,* and *L'Arlesiana.* Dewitt Sage directed. Color. 85 minutes. Pacific Arts VHS.

1986 Pavarotti in Concert in China

Pavarotti performs at Exhibition Hall in Beijing during his 1986 tour of China and sings music by Verdi, Giordano, and Puccini plus "O Sole Mio." Emerson Buckley conducts the Genoa Municipal Opera Orchestra. Color. 96 minutes. Kultur VHS.

1988 Pavarotti and Levine in Recital

Pavarotti in recital at the Metropolitan Opera sings music by Mozart, Verdi, Rossini, Bellini, Massenet, Respighi, Flotow, and Mascagni with James Levine playing piano. Brian Large directed. Color. 71 minutes. London VHS/LD.

1988 The Fortunate Pilgrim

Pavarotti sings an aria on the soundtrack of the American TV film *The Fortunate Pilgrim* based on a novel by Mario Puzo. Stuart Cooper directed. Color. 250 minutes. On VHS.

1989 Dal Vivo

Pavarotti gives a recital at the Gran Teatre del Liceu in Barcelona on June 8, 1989, with Leone Magiera on piano. Color. 60 minutes. Revelation DVD.

1989 Pavarotti: Concert at Olympia Hall, Munich

Pavarotti performs in concert before an enthusiastic audience at the Olympia Hall in Munich. Color. 58 minutes. On DVD.

1990 Luciano Pavarotti: The Event

The World Cup Celebration Concert features the tenor at Milan's Palatrussardi Hall singing for the 1990 World Cup players with an audience of 10,000. He sings music by Donizetti, Mozart, Verdi, Puccini, Massenet, Leoncavallo, and Mascagni, plus six encores. Leone Magiera conducts the Bologna Chamber Orchestra. Pier Quinto Cariaggi directed. Color. 88 minutes. MCA Universal DVD/VHS.

1991 Pavarotti 30th Anniversary Concert

Pavarotti, who made his stage debut in 1961 in *La bohème* in Reggio Emilia, returned for a 30th anniversary concert on April 29, 1991. The program includes selections from *La bohème, Tosca, Don Giovanni, Lucia di Lammermoor, Il trovatore, La forza del destino, La favorita, L'Arlesiana,* and *L'elisir d'amore.* Joining him are Raina Kabaivanska, June Anderson, Piero Cappuccilli, Shirley Verrett, Paolo Coni, Enzo Dara, and Giuseppe Sabbatini. The Bologna Teatro Comunale Orchestra is led by Leone Magiera and Maurizio Benini. Color. 104 minutes. London VHS/LD.

1991 Pavarotti in Hyde Park

Pavarotti gives an impressive open-air recital in Hyde Park, London, on July 30, 1991, with a massive crowd and good English rain. He sings a selection of arias from Verdi, Puccini, Mascagni, Leoncavallo, Meyerbeer, and Massenet. Leone Magiera leads the Philharmonia Orchestra and Chorus. Christopher Swann directed. Color. 99 minutes. London VHS. (Highlights version in the *Great Moments* video series.)

1992 Pavarotti and Friends

A concert in Pavarotti's hometown of Modena for a local charity. The tenor's performing friends include Sting, Suzanne Vega, and the Neville Brothers. Color. 60 minutes. On VHS.

1992 Pavarotti & the Italian Tenor

Joshua Waletzky's documentary tries to show how Italy nurtures its tenors. Pavarotti listens to records and talks about the tenors who have most influenced him: Caruso, Gigli, Schipa, and Di Stefano. The film includes performances, interviews with teachers and friends, and a radio broadcast by his father. Telecast in the *Great Performances* series November 20, 1992. Color. 58 minutes. London VHS.

1992 Luciano Pavarotti

Portrait of the tenor made for the Italian opera singer series *I Grandi della Lirica.* Color. In Italian. 60 minutes. Center (Italy) VHS.

1993 Pavarotti in Paris

Open-air recital at the Champs de Mars in Paris before an audience of 50,000. The program includes music by Puccini, Rossini, Verdi, and Leoncavallo. Elliott Forest is host. Color. 60 minutes. On VHS.

1993 Pavarotti in Central Park

Recital before an enthusiastic crowd in New York's Central Park in June 1993 with music by Verdi, Puccini, Leoncavallo, and Rossini. The concert was shown on PBS August 10, 1993. Color. 60 minutes.

1993 Pavarotti: My Heart's Delight

Pavarotti is joined by Nuccia Focile for a recital in Modena, and they perform arias and songs by Verdi, Puccini, and others. Maurizio Benini conducts the Royal Philharmonic Orchestra. Color. In Italian. 60 minutes. On VHS.

1994 Pavarotti in Confidence

Peter Ustinov visits Pavarotti in Pesaro and they discuss the tenor's life and career. Pavarotti sings arias by Verdi and Puccini, and there are excerpts from performances of *Rigoletto, Turandot,* and *Madama Butterfly.* Color. 50 minutes. Kultur VHS.

1994 Pavarotti Plus in London

Charity concert for the Red Cross by Pavarotti and others at the Royal Albert Hall in May 1994. The singers include Dwayne Croft, Natalie Dessay, Elero D'Artenga, and Dolora Zajick. Color. 80 minutes. Decca (GB) VHS.

1995 Pavarotti: My World

Survey of Pavarotti's career created for his 60th birthday, basically a "greatest hits" compilation with memorable moments from concerts in Paris, Miami, London, Modena, Beijing, and the Three Tenors events. David Horn directed. Televised in December 1995. Color. 90 minutes.

1995-2001 Charity Telecasts

Pavarotti and friends performed in a number of telecasts to raise money for worthy international causes. The first was a concert in Modena in September 1995 titled *Pavarotti & Friends: Together for the Children of Bosnia.* The friends include the Chieftains, Michael Bolton, Meat Loaf, and Brian Eno. In 1996 the telecast was to raise funds to help war children, in 1998 for the children of Liberia, in 1999 for Guatemala and Kosovo, in 2000 for Cambodia and Tibet, and in 2002 for Afghanistan. The telecasts were 60 minutes and in color

1996 Pavarotti in Miami Beach

Pavarotti in a Miami Beach seaside recital with soprano Cynthia Lawrence, back-up chorus, and orchestra in a program of music by Puccini, Verdi, Mascagni, and other Pavarotti favorites. The crowd is enthusiastic. Telecast on PBS. Color. 60 minutes.

1996 Pavarotti-Abbado Concert at Ferrara
Pavarotti in performance in Ferrara with Claudio Abbado conducting. Manuela Crivelli directed for Italian television. Color. In Italian. 90 minutes.

1998 Luciano Pavarotti 30th Anniversary Gala
The Metropolitan Opera celebrates Pavarotti's 30th anniversary with the Met by presenting acts from three operas associated with him: *L'elisir d'amore* (Act II) features Pavarotti as Nemorino with Ruth Ann Swenson as Adina, Leo Nucci as Dulcamara, Roberto De Candia as Belcore, and Yvonne Gonzales as Gianetta. *La bohème* (Act III) has Pavarotti as Rodolfo with Daniela Dessì as Mimì, Aïnhoa Arteta as Musetta, and Dwayne Croft as Marcello. *Aida* (Act IV) has Pavarotti as Radames, Maria Guleghina as Aida, Dolora Zajick as Amneris, and Paul Plishka as Ramfis. James Levine conducted the Metropolitan Opera and Chorus, while Brian Large directed the program taped November 22, 1998, and telecast March 31, 1999, on PBS. Color. In Italian with English subtitles. 180 minutes.2001 Kennedy Center Honors
Pavarotti was one of the Kennedy Center honorees in 2001 and watched a tribute to his career in this telecast of the event. Color. In English. 120 minutes.

PEARS, PETER
English tenor (1910–1986)

Sir Peter Pears, Benjamin Britten's life partner and collaborator, created the leading roles in most of Britten's major operas from *Peter Grimes* to *Death in Venice*. He was also co-librettist on A MIDSUMMER NIGHT'S DREAM. See BILLY BUDD (1966), BENJAMIN BRITTEN (1963/1966/1967/1976/1980), CURLEW RIVER, GLORIANA, IDOMENEO (1966), OWEN WINGRAVE (1971), PETER GRIMES (1969), and WAR REQUIEM (1988).

1975 Doria
Peter Pears was 65 when he was filmed at the Bergen Festival singing this poem by Ezra Pound. It was set to music at his request by composer Arne Nordheim. NRK. Color. 20 minutes.

PÊCHEURS DE PERLES, LES
1863 opera by Bizet

Les pêcheurs de perles (The Pearl Fishers), set in ancient Ceylon, tells the story of the friendship of tribal chief Zurga and fisherman Nadir and their rivalry over the priestess Leila. The second opera by GEORGES BIZET to be staged, it was written on commission to a libretto by Eugene and Michel Corman. Like *Carmen,* it was originally an opéra-comique with spoken dialogue, later changed to recitative. A number of films have featured the famous tenor-baritone friendship duet "Au fond du temple saint," but the complete opera is badly represented on video.

Videos
There appear to be only three videos of the complete opera from alternative video companies, none originating at major opera houses with notable singers. Premiere Opera has a 1993 production telecast in Amsterdam while House of Opera has productions telecast in Chile and Argentina with local singers.

Early/related films

1928 Vitaphone film with Gigli/De Luca
Beniamino Gigli and Giuseppe De Luca perform the duet "Au fond du temple saint" in Italian on this early sound film made by the Vitaphone Company. Considered one of the best performances of the duet, it has also been released on CD. Black and white. In Italian. About 8 minutes.

1981 Gallipoli
Peter Weir's film about idealistic Australian soldiers in World War I features the friendship duet as an emotional highlight. On the night before an attack, in which the commanding major knows he and many of his men are likely to be killed, he sits alone drinking champagne and listening to a recording of "Au fond du temple saint." The singers are Léopold Simoneau and René Bianco with the Lamoureux Orchestra of Paris led by Jean Fournet. Color. 110 minutes.

1993 Opera Imaginaire
This English compilation includes an animated film by Jimmy Murakami illustrating "Au fond du temple saint." The duet is sung by Nicolai Gedda and Ernest Blanc with the Paris Opéra-Comique Orchestra led by Paul Dervaux. See OPERA IMAGINAIRE.

1994 Little Women
Friedrich (Gabriel Byrne) translates the French for Jo (Winona Ryder) as they watch the opera from free seats up among the scenery in this fine adaptation of the Louisa May Alcott novel. Barbara Hendricks (Leila) and John Aler (Nadir) sing the duet "Leïla! Leïla! Dieu puissant" from Act II accompanied by the Orchestra du Capitole du Toulouse led by Michel Plasson. The actors seen on stage in the opera are Kate Robbins and David Adams. Color. 118 minutes.

1999 Whatever

American tenor John Aler is heard on the soundtrack of this French film singing an aria from the opera with the Toulouse Capitole Orchestra. Philip Harel directed and starred in this film about a lonely Parisian. Color. 120 minutes.

2000 The Man Who Cried

Sally Potter's Anglo-French film about Jews and opera in Paris just before World War II features *The Pearl Fishers* aria "Je crois entendre encore" three times. Salvatore Licitra, dubbing for the film's opera star John Turturro, sings it first in Yiddish, then at a society reception with pianists Katia and Marielle Labeque, and finally on the opera stage with backing from the Royal Opera House Orchestra. See THE MAN WHO CRIED.

2001 Laissez-passer

Bertrand Tavernier's fascinating French film about the meaning of collaboration during World War II features the aria "Je crois entendre encore" on the soundtrack. Color. In French. 165 minutes.

PEERCE, JAN
American tenor (1904–1984)

Jan Peerce was one of the Met's top attractions for more than 25 years, but he began his singing career at Radio City Music Hall during the 1930s, performing for nine years on radio. Then he decided to try opera; he made his stage debut in Baltimore in 1939 and his Met debut in 1941 as Alfredo in *La traviata*. He was the first American to sing at the Bolshoi Opera after the war and, after leaving the Met, became a Broadway musical star playing Tevye in *Fiddler on the Roof*. Peerce was featured in a number of films, but he never really had a Hollywood career although he was a regular on television. See OF MEN AND MUSIC.

1943 Keep 'em Rolling

Peerce sings a patriotic song by Richard Rodgers and Lorenz Hart in this wartime propaganda film, encouraging factory workers and defense bond buyers to keep them rolling. Black and white. In English. 8 minutes. Video Yesteryear VHS.

1944 Hymn of Nations

Peerce is featured in this Office of War Information film with Arturo Toscanini conducting the NBC Symphony Orchestra; he sings the tenor solo with the Westminster Choir on the "Hymn of Nations." Alexander Hammid directed. Black and white. 28 minutes. Video Yesteryear VHS.

1947 Carnegie Hall

Peerce sings "O Sole Mio" in this pleasant film that is primarily a fiction framework for a series of numbers by classical stars of the period. See CARNEGIE HALL.

1947 Something in the Wind

Peerce teams with Deanna Durbin to sing the "Miserere" from *Il trovatore* in this light comedy. She's a singing disc jockey and he's an opera singer, but their voices match quite well. Irving Pichel directed. Black and white. 89 minutes.

1950 Jan Peerce in Opera and Song

On the January 9, 1950, *Voice of Firestone* television program, Peerce sings arias by Leoncavallo ("Vesti la giubba") and Victor Herbert ("Thine Alone") and songs by Rossini and Rodgers and Hammerstein. Howard Barlow conducts. Black and white. 25 minutes. VAI VHS.

1950 Your Show of Shows

Peerce was a singing guest host on this Sid Caesar and Imogene Coca television program on May 22, 1952. Black and white. 90 minutes.

1953 Tonight We Sing

Peerce is the voice of Gregory Lawrence in this multistar film about the career of impresario Sol Hurok. See TONIGHT WE SING.

1953 Opera vs. Jazz

Peerce was one of the regular performers on this ABC television series contrasting selections from opera and jazz. See OPERA VS. JAZZ.

1956 Producers' Showcase

Peerce sings "Vesti la giubba" from *Pagliacci* in this operatic all-star TV program produced by Sol Hurok. See PRODUCERS' SHOWCASE.

1969 Goodbye, Columbus

Peerce's son Larry directed his father in this Hollywood film based on Phillip Roth's novel about a suburban Jewish family. Peerce has a cameo role at the wedding. Color. 105 minutes.

1992 If I Were a Rich Man

Documentary about the tenor narrated by Isaac Stern, with interesting film clips: Peerce is shown singing arias from *La traviata, Rigoletto, Tosca,* and *Eugene Onegin;* performing with Toscanini in the film *Hymn to the Nations;* being interviewed by Edward R. Murrow on *Person to Person;* touring in the USSR in 1956; and starring on Broadway in *Fiddler on the Roof.* Peter Rosen directed. Black and white and color. 59 minutes. Bel Canto Society/Proscenium VHS.

PELLÉAS ET MÉLISANDE
1902 opera by Debussy

Pelléas and Mélisande, one of the most popular operas of the 20th century, is the only one that composer CLAUDE DEBUSSY actually finished. Using a play by Maurice Maeterlinck as libretto, it tells a highly romantic story in an obscurist symbolist manner. Mélisande is a mysterious woman of unknown origin married to Golaud, grandson of King Arkel. Golaud becomes jealous when his half-brother Pelléas and Mélisande fall in love. He kills Pelléas, and Mélisande dies in childbirth. The opera is full of hard-to-explain poetic symbols from deep wells and tall towers to lost rings and long flowing hair. It premiered in Paris with Mary Garden as Mélisande, and her performance helped make it famous. Maeterlinck, however, had wanted the part for his wife Georgette Leblanc and quarreled with Debussy over this.

1954 NBC Opera Theatre
American TV production: John Black (director), Samuel Chotzinoff (producer), Jean Morel (conductor, NBC Opera Theatre Orchestra and Chorus), William Molyneux (set designer), John Boxer (costume designer).

Cast: Virginia Haskins (Mélisande), Davis Cunningham (Pelléas), Carlton Gaud (Golaud), Lee Cass (Arkel), Mary Davenport (Geneviève), Bill McIver (Yniold).

Video at the MTR. Telecast live April 10, 1954. Kirk Browning (director). Black and white. In English. 90 minutes.

Comment: The opera was abridged for this TV production.

1987 Opéra de Lyon
French stage production: Pierre Strosser (director/set designer), John Eliot Gardiner (conductor, Opéra de Lyon Orchestra and Chorus), Patrice Cauchetier (costume designer).

Cast: Colette Alliot-Lugaz (Mélisande), François Le Roux (Pelléas), José van Dam (Golaud), Roger Soyer (Arkel), Jocelyne Taillon (Geneviève), François Golfier (Yniold).

Video: Arthaus DVD/Kultur VHS. Jean-François Jung (director). Color. In French with English subtitles. 137 minutes.

Comment: Strosser sets the opera in an Edwardian living room, so there is no well, ring, or tower. The singing and the playing are wonderful, but many critics disliked the production.

***1992 Welsh National Opera
Welsh stage production: Peter Stein (director), Pierre Boulez (conductor, Welsh National Opera Orchestra and Chorus), Karl-Ernst Herrmann (set designer), Moidele Bickel (costume designer).

Cast: Alison Hagley (Mélisande), Neil Archer (Pelléas), Donald Maxwell (Golaud), Kenneth Cox (Arkel), Penelope Walker (Geneviève), Samuel Burkey (Yniold).

Video: DG DVD/VHS/LD. Peter Stein (director). Color. In French with English subtitles. 158 minutes.

Comment: Inventive, often magical production filmed in HDTV in studio conditions at the New Theater, Cardiff, in March 1992.

1999 Glyndebourne Festival
English stage production: Graham Vick (director), Sir Andrew Davis (conductor, London Philharmonic Orchestra and Glyndebourne Festival Chorus), Paul Brown (set designer).

Cast: Christine Oelze (Mélisande), Richard Croft (Pelléas), John Tomlinson (Golaud), Gwynne Howell (Arkel), Jean Rigby (Geneviève).

Video: House of Opera DVD/VHS.

Telecast June 6, 1999, on Channel 4. Humphrey Burton (director). Color. In French with English subtitles. 165 minutes.

Early films

1913 Universal film
Constance Crawley plays Mélisande with Arthur Maude as Pelléas in this early American feature film of the Maeterlinck play. It was directed by S. MacDonald and scripted by Harrison Del Ruth for the Bison division of Universal Studios. Black and white. Silent. About 45 minutes.

1915 Leblanc film
This historic French movie is based on the source play and stars Maeterlinck's wife Georgette Leblanc as Mélisande. While she didn't get to sing in the opera, she did get to play the role on screen with Debussy's music used as live accompaniment. Gustave Labruyere directed for the Eclair Company. Black and white. Silent. About 70 minutes. Print survives in Romanian film archive.

PENDERECKI, KRZYSZTOF
Polish composer (1933–)

Krzysztof Penderecki's most famous opera, THE DEVILS OF LOUDUN (1969), is the story of a priest and a group of nuns in 17th-century Loudun. The composer based his libretto on Erich Fried's German translation of an English play by John Whiting, a dramatization of a book by Aldous Huxley. The opera has been quite popular, televised and produced around the world, possibly because erotic fantasies in a religious setting with blasphemy for spice can count on audiences even if the music is difficult. Another of Penderecki's operas uses as libretto a screenplay for a film that was never made. *Paradise Lost* (1978), based on Milton's epic poem, was created by English playwright Christopher Fry. It premiered in Chicago in 1978, but it is not on video.

PENELLA, MANUEL
Spanish composer (1880–1939)

Manuel Penella composed a world-famous piece of music for a Spanish opera in 1916, but it is rarely associated with the opera. This was a pasodoble composed for his opera EL GATO MONTÉS, which has become the theme music of the Spanish bullfight. One of the characters in the opera, set in Seville, is a toreador. Plácido Domingo has promoted *El Gato Montés* strongly in recent years, including a televised Los Angeles stage production, a complete recording, and an excerpt in a video about Seville. Penella's other major opera is DON GIL DE ALCALÁ, about a soldier rescuing a convent girl from an evil nobleman. It was made into a Mexican film starring tenor José Mojica.

PEPUSCH, JOHANN
German-born English composer (1667–1752)

Johann Pepusch is probably the only opera composer who is less well known than his librettist. He compiled the songs and wrote the overture for Gay's THE BEGGAR'S OPERA, which changed the face of English theater. He also worked with Gay on another ballad opera, *Polly,* but it got banned. His original operas, like the 1716 *The Death of Dido,* were successful in their time but have been forgotten.

PERFECT LIVES
1980 TV opera by Ashley

ROBERT ASHLEY's three-hour TV opera *Perfect Lives,* created for The Kitchen in New York, consists of seven 30-minute episodes: The Park, The Supermarket, The Bank, The Bar, The Living Room, The Church, and The Backyard. It is set in a midwestern town where the characters propose to "borrow" money from a bank for a day and return it the next. Ashley is the Narrator; "Blue" Gene Tyranny is Buddy, the World's Greatest Piano Player; Jill Kroesen is Isolde; and David Van Tieghem is D, the Captain of the Football Team. The opera is full of imaginative techniques with orchestral tracks and video imagery created by John Sanborn. Ashley says television should feature reviewable works of art to be seen again and again. Peter Gordon produced the music and Sanborn directed the video. Color. In English. 182 minutes. Lovely Music VHS.

1984 Music Word Fire
Music Word Fire and I Would Do It Again: The Lessons is a 1984 video of variations on the theme song from Episode Three of *Perfect Lives.* It contains seven-minute portraits of the characters Isolde, NoZhay, Buddy, and Donnie. Color. In English. 28 minutes. Lovely Music VHS.

PERFECTLY NORMAL
1990 Canadian film with opera content

Opera music permeates this quirky Canadian film in which even the beer bottles on a conveyer belt in a factory move to Verdi music. Robbie Coltrane plays an inventive conman who loves opera so much he wants to open an operatic restaurant, to be called La Traviata, where he can perform in opera with friends. His friend/victim Michael Riley, who works in a brewery and plays on its hockey team, is dragged into the scheme for his remarkable falsetto, his money, and his mother's dresses. The opening night of the restaurant features a mini-production of *Norma* with Coltrane as Pollione and Riley as Norma. When the big hockey game ends up on the same night, Riley has to dash between venues and costumes. There is a lot of other opera music in the film, including excerpts from *La traviata* with Peter Chin, Sean Hewitt, and Dianne Heatherington as well as *Il trovatore, Tosca, Manon Lescaut,* and *Salome.* Eugene Lipinski and Paul Quarrington wrote the lovably eccentric screenplay, Alain Dostie was the creative cinematographer, Richard Gregoire arranged and conducted the music, and Yves Simoneau directed. Color. In English. 105 minutes. Academy VHS.

PERGOLESI, GIOVANNI
Italian composer (1710–1736)

Giovanni Battista Pergolesi died young, barely 26, but in his few short years he helped change opera history. His intermezzo LA SERVA PADRONA (1733) brought him posthumous fame when it came to be considered the model for *opera buffa* and helped create the famous "Guerre des Bouffons" in Paris in 1752. Pergolesi, who was born in Jesi, studied in Naples and had his first real success with his full-length Neapolitan comic opera LO FRATE 'NNAMORATO (1732), recently revived at La Scala and on video. His entertaining intermezzo LIVIETTA ET TRACOLLO (1734), widely performed after its Naples premiere, is also on video. His best-known work after his operas is his *Stabat mater*, composed just before he died in a monastery in Pozzuoli near Naples. It is featured in all the films about him.

1912 Pergolesi

Pergolesi falls in love with young aristocrat Maria in Naples; they plan to wed, but her brother insists she marry a rich man. Unable to accept this, she becomes a nun and asks Pergolesi to play the organ as she takes the veil. He plays his *Stabat mater* and dies a little while later. The film was made by La Milanese company of Milan and Pathé Frères of Paris. Black and white. Silent. About 15 minutes.

1932 Pergolesi

Romantic Italian film biography set in 1736, the year of the composer's death. Pergolesi falls in love with a noble woman, but her brother opposes the relationship and locks her up in his castle. The composer becomes ill and dies in the monastery in Pozzuoli to music of *Stabat mater*. Elio Steiner plays Pergolesi and Dria Paola is the woman he loves. The film features excerpts from *La Serva Padrona*, sung by La Scala singers Laura Pasini and Vincenzo Bettoni, with Pergolesi's music arranged by Vittorio Gui and conducted by Francesco Previtali. Gian Bistolfi wrote the screenplay and Guido Brignone directed. (The French version is called *Les Amours de Pergolèse*.) Black and white. In Italian. 80 minutes.

1997 Giro de lune tra terra e mare

Pergolesi, played by Lucio De Cicco in this odd time-fractured film, dies in his monastery in Pozzuoli with his *Stabat mater* on the soundtrack. It seems that the many earthquakes in the area have caused a time jumble, mixing past and present events. These include scenes from ancient Roman times involving Agrippina, Nero, the Cumean Sibyl, and a Christian martyr. Giuseppe M. Gaudino wrote and directed. Color. In Italian. 100 minutes.

PÉRICHOLE, LA

1868 opéra-bouffe by Offenbach

JACQUES OFFENBACH's operetta *La Périchole*, which is romantic rather than satirical, tells the story of the 18th-century Peruvian street singers La Périchole and Piquillo; they want to marry but are too poor to afford a license. When love-stricken Viceroy Don Andrès offers La Périchole a position at court and she accepts out of hunger, she is obliged to marry for the sake of protocol. A bogus marriage is secretly arranged, but the chosen groom is Piquillo, who is too drunk to know what is happening. After the usual complications, true love wins out. Henri Meilhac and Ludovic Halévy's libretto is based on a play by Prosper Mérimée inspired by a real Peruvian actress

who became the mistress of the Viceroy. Jean Renoir starred Anna Magnani in a film based on the same story.

1958 Metropolitan Opera on Omnibus

American TV production: Cyril Ritchard and Richard Dunlap (directors), Jean Morel (conductor, Metropolitan Opera Orchestra and Chorus), Rolf Gérard (set designer), Maurice Valency (English translation).

Cast: Laurel Hurley (La Périchole), Theodor Uppman (Piquillo), Cyril Ritchard (Viceroy), Alessio de Paolis (Prisoner), Osia Hawkin (Don Pedro), Paul Franke (Panatellas).

Video at the MTR, film at the Library of Congress. Telecast live January 26, 1958, on NBC. Black and white. In English. 90 minutes.

1973 Who's Afraid of Opera?

English TV film: Piers Haggard (director), Richard Bonynge (conductor, London Symphony Orchestra), George Djurkovic (set designer), Claire Merrill (screenplay), Nathan Kroll (producer).

Cast: Joan Sutherland (La Périchole), Pieter Van Der Stolk (Piquillo), Francis Egerton (Viceroy), John Fryatt (Don Pedro), Gordon Wilcock (Panatellas), Larry Berthelson (puppets)

Video: Kultur VHS. Color. In English and French. 30 minutes.

Comment: Highlights version made for young audiences with Sutherland telling the story to puppets. Dialogue in English, arias in French.

1982 Grand Théâtre de Genève

Swiss stage production: Jérôme Savary (director), Marc Soustrot (conductor, Suisse Romande Orchestra and Grand Théâtre de Genève Chorus), Michel Lebois (set designer).

Cast: Maria Ewing (La Périchole), Neil Rosenshein (Piquillo), Gabriel Bacquier (Viceroy), Paolo Martinelli (Don Pedro), Ricardo Cassinelli (Panatellas).

Video: House of Opera DVD/VHS. Telecast December 29, 1982, by Television Suisse Romande. Jean Boven (director). Color. In French. 141 minutes.

Related films

1952 The Golden Coach

Jean Renoir's classic film *Le Carosse d'or/La Corrozza d'oro* is based on the same Mérimée play as the opera. Anna Magnani plays an actress in a touring *commedia dell'arte* troupe in 18th-century Peru who is pursued by three lovers, including the Viceroy. Renoir said he was inspired to make the film while listening to Vivaldi, so he uses his music rather than Offenbach's on the soundtrack. The film, shot in Italy, was released in America in an

English version as *The Golden Coach*. Color. In English, French, or Italian. 101 minutes.

1972 Ludwig

Luchino Visconti's elaborate biographical film about Bavarian King Ludwig II (played by Helmut Berger) features mostly music by Wagner, but it also includes the overture to *La Périchole*. The music is played by the Hollywood Bowl Symphony Orchestra conducted by Carmen Dragon. Color. In Italian. 185 minutes.

PEROJO, BENITO
Spanish film director (1893–1974)

Benito Perojo, who began working in the cinema in 1913 and continued for another 60 years, was especially noted for making film musicals based on zarzuelas, operettas, and operas. The most successful was his 1935 version of Bretón's zarzuela LA VERBENA DE LA PALOMA, which he remade in 1963, but he also produced films of Granados's GOYESCAS, Gilbert's DIE KEUSCHE SUSANNE, Vives's DOÑA FRANCISQUITA, and Spanish versions of IL BARBIERE DI SIVIGLIA in 1938 and CARMEN in 1959.

PETER GRIMES
1945 opera by Britten

BENJAMIN BRITTEN's *Peter Grimes*, the first British opera to win international acclaim in the modern era, was voted favorite opera of the 20th century by readers of *BBC Magazine* in 2000. Based on George Crabbe's narrative poem *The Borough*, it concerns a Suffolk fisherman whose apprentice is lost at sea. The village is full of suspicion, and when a second boy dies, Grimes is driven to commit suicide. The libretto by George Slater changes Grimes from an evil man to a person victimized by his weaknesses and society. At the end it is unclear whether he is to be blamed or pitied for what has happened. Peter Pears created the role of Grimes.

1969 Aldeburgh Festival

English stage production: Benjamin Britten (conductor, Aldeburgh Festival Orchestra and Ambrosian Opera Chorus).

Cast: Peter Pears (Peter Grimes), Heather Harper (Ellen Orford), Elizabeth Bainbridge (Auntie), Ann Robson (Mrs. Sedley), Owen Brannigan (Swallow), Robert Tear (Rev. Adams).

Telecast November 2, 1969, on BBC and NET. Brian Large (director). Color. In English. 148 minutes.

Comment: The first telecast of the opera was from The Maltings, Snape, near the historical setting of the opera. It was a collaboration between NET in the United States, BBC in England, and CBC in Canada.

1981 Royal Opera House

English stage production: Elijah Moshinsky (director), Colin Davis (conductor, Royal Opera House Orchestra and Chorus), Timothy O'Brien and Tazeena Firth (set designer).

Cast: Jon Vickers (Peter Grimes), Heather Harper (Ellen Orford), Norman Bailey (Capt. Balstrode), Elizabeth Bainbridge (Auntie), Patricia Payne (Mrs. Sedley), Marilyn Hill Smith and Anne Pashley (Auntie's nieces), Andrew Wilson (Boy), John Dobson (Bob Boles).

Video: Warner Vision NVC Arts DVD & VHS/HBO VHS. Taped June 30, 1981. John Vernon (director). Color. In English. 150 minutes.

***1994 English National Opera

English stage production: Tim Albery (director), David Atherton (conductor, English National Opera Orchestra and Chorus), Hildegard Bechtler (set designer).

Cast: Philip Langridge (Peter Grimes), Janice Cairns (Ellen Orford), Alan Opie (Capt. Balstrode), Susan Gorton (Mrs. Sedley), Ann Howard (Auntie), Edward Byles (Rector), Alan Woodrow (Bob Boles), Robert Poulton (Ned Keene).

Video: Arthaus DVD & London/Philips VHS. Barry Gavin (director). Color. 144 minutes.

Related film

1997 A Tale of Tanglewood: Peter Grimes Reborn

Barbara Willis Sweete's documentary about a production of *Peter Grimes* at Tanglewood centers around Boston Symphony Orchestra music director Seiji Ozawa. It was made for the Canadian company Rhombus Media. Color. In English. 60 minutes.

PETERS, ROBERTA
American soprano (1930–)

Roberta Peters became an overnight star at the Metropolitan Opera singing the role of Zerlina in *Don Giovanni* as a last-minute substitute for Nadine Conner. She went on to even greater success with brilliant performances in coloratura roles. Peters, who had had no stage experience, was signed by the Met at age 19 to sing the Queen of the Night. She stayed with the company for 34 years, singing in 22 operas. She was especially noted for her Rosina, Lucia, and Gilda, and critics ranked her voice with those of Lily Pons and Amelita Galli-Curci. Peters can be seen on three videos of *Voice of Firestone* telecasts, including a 1963 version of ROMÉO ET JULIETTE, and several films and TV shows.

1952–1957 Roberta Peters in Opera and Song

Peters is shown in four appearances on the TV series *The Voice of Firestone*. On August 4, 1952, she sings the Queen of the Night aria "Der Hölle Rache." On November 15, 1954, she sings "Sempre libera," "I Dreamt I Dwelt in Marble Halls," and "Indian Love Call." On September 20, 1957, she sings the "Bell Song," "Stranger in Paradise," and "Song of India." On November 25, 1957, she sings "Ardon gl'incensi" from *Lucia di Lammermoor*. Black and white. 50 minutes. VAI VHS.

1952–1959 Roberta Peters in Opera and Song 2

The second volume of appearances by Peters on *The Voice of Firestone* TV show. She sings songs and arias from *Don Giovanni, Les contes d'Hoffmann, Rigoletto,* and *Naughty Marietta* plus "Greensleeves" and "One Night of Love." Black and white. 55 minutes. VAI VHS.

1953 Tonight We Sing

Peters plays diva Elsa Valdine (a composite of famous sopranos) and sings Violetta's aria "Sempre libera" in this film about impresario Sol Hurok and the musicians he promoted. See TONIGHT WE SING.

1956 Producers' Showcase

Peters sings Olympia's aria "Les oiseaux" from *Les contes d'Hoffmann* on this all-star television opera festival produced by Sol Hurok. See PRODUCERS' SHOWCASE.

1962 Jack Does Opera

Peters plays herself as an opera singer involved with Jack Benny on an episode of *The Jack Benny Show* telecast July 1, 1962. Black and white. 30 minutes.

1983 Metropolitan Opera Centennial Gala

Peters is one of the singers as the Met celebrates its 100th birthday October 22, 1983, with an eight-hour gala telecast. See METROPOLITAN OPERA.

1995 City Hall

Peters plays Nettie Anselmo in this political thriller about a New York City scandal. Al Pacino plays the mayor. Harold Becker directed. Color. In English. 111 minutes.

PETROVICS, EMIL

Hungarian composer (1930–)

Emil Petrovics became one of the leading lights of postwar Hungarian opera after the success of his one-act C'EST LA GUERRE, which has been compared to Berg's *Wozzeck*. It has been recorded and televised. His other operas include *Lysistrata* (1962), based on the Aristo-

phanes play, and *Crime and Punishment* (1969), based on the Dostoevsky novel.

PHANTOM OF THE OPERA, THE

Film series based on Leroux novel

Gaston Leroux's 1911 novel *Le Fantôme de l'Opéra* has been popular with filmmakers since the 1925 Lon Chaney movie made it famous. The story, a variation of the Faust legend, uses Gounod's *Faust* as a plot device. A mad composer who lives in the cellars of the Paris Opera House (Palais Garnier) teaches a young soprano to sing and then advances her career with acts of terror. She, in a sense, sells him her soul for the sake of her opera career. The many films based on the book are of interest operatically for their opera house settings and opera scenes. *Faust* is central to most, with the implication that the Phantom is playing Mephistopheles to his Faustian protégé Christine. The 1943 Nelson Eddy version, however, revolves around imaginary operas, and in others, the locale is shifted to London and Budapest. The novel has also spawned stage musicals and spin-off movies. Leroux (1868–1927) was a major French mystery writer, and many of his stories have been made into French films but, surprisingly, not *Phantom*.

1925 Julian film

The first, and still most famous, film of the novel. Lon Chaney plays disfigured composer Erik, the Phantom who lives in the cellars of the Paris Opera House. He is in love with understudy soprano Christine Daaé (Mary Philbin) and makes her a star by forcing diva Carlotta (Virginia Pearson) to stop singing Marguerite in *Faust*. Edward Cecil plays Faust, John Miljan is Valentin, and Alexander Bevani is Méphistophélès. The film was reissued with sound in 1929 with the Gounod arias. Elliot J. Clawson wrote the screenplay, Charles van Enger was the cinematographer, and Rupert Julian directed. Universal. Two-color Technicolor and black and white. 79 minutes. Milestone DVD with two versions(1925 & 1930), commentary and interviews. The film is also available on VHS and LD.

1943 Lubin film

Nelson Eddy stars opposite soprano Susanna Foster in this operatic version of the Gaston Leroux tale. Foster plays the Paris Opera soprano Christine loved by Phantom Claude Rains, Eddy is her singing partner, and Jane Farrar is the diva she replaces. The film opens with Eddy on stage as Plumkett singing "The Porter's Song" ("Lasst mich euch fragen") from Act II of Flotow's *Martha* in a French translation by Wilhelm von Wymetal Jr., who staged the opera sequences. Next we see tenor Anthony Marlowe as Lyonel leading the third act quintet "Mag der Himmel" with help from bass Tudor Williams as Tristram and the ensemble. *Martha* is the only genuine opera in the movie, but composer Edward Ward created two imaginary ones, both elaborately staged. *Amour et Gloire,* a French opera, is based on themes by Chopin with French lyrics written by Wilhelm von Wymetal Jr. *Le Prince de Caucasie,* a Russian opera, is based on Tchaikovsky's Fourth Symphony with English libretto by George Waggner and Russian translation by Max Rabinowitz. Samuel Hoffenstein and Eric Taylor wrote the screenplay, Hal Mohr was the cinematographer, and Arthur Lubin directed the film. *Phantom* won Academy Awards for cinematography and art direction. Color. 92 minutes. MCA Universal VHS.

The Phantom of the Opera (1943): The Phantom (Claude Rains) confronts his protégée (Susanna Foster) in this film of the novel.

1955 El fantasma de la operetta
The Argentine film *El fantasma de la operetta* is a spoof on *Phantom* and similar horror films. Amelita Vargas and Alfredo Barbieristar; Enrique Carreras directed. Black and white. In Spanish. 70 minutes.

1960 El fantasma de la operetta
This Mexican adaptation of the novel titled *El fantasma de la operetta* has a multitude of opera phantoms. Tin-Tan and Ana Luisa Peluffo star; Fernando Cortes directed. Color. In Spanish. 90 minutes.

1961 Il mostro dell'opera
Il mostro dell'opera is a low-budget Italian variation on the story written and directed by Renato Polselli. Barbara Howard, Marco Mariani, Giuseppe Addobati, and Alberto Archetti star. Color. In Italian. 85 minutes.

1962 Fisher film
The imaginary opera *Saint Joan,* supposedly composed by the Phantom, is the centerpiece of this Hammer film directed by horror master Terence Fisher. Lord Ambrose D'Arcy (Michael Gough) pretends he composed the op-

era and gets it staged. Herbert Lom plays the Phantom with Heather Sears as the singer Christine whom he teaches to sing his opera. The Phantom is depicted here as a sympathetic character who dies to save Christine's life when a chandelier falls. The imaginary *Saint Joan* opera in the film was composed and conducted by Edwin Astley. Producer Anthony Hinds wrote the screenplay (as John Elder), and Arthur Grant was cinematographer. Color. In English. 84 minutes.

1983 Markowitz film
Maximilian Schell plays the Phantom in this impressive TV film of the novel made and set in Budapest with a British/Hungarian cast and crew. The Phantom is a Hungarian musician called Sandor Korvin who orchestrates the stardom of soprano Maria Gianelli (Jane Seymour) because she looks like his deceased opera singer wife. The central opera is again *Faust* with Pal Kovacs as Faust and Ferenc Begalyi as Méphistophélès. Michael York plays an opera producer who loves Maria, and Diana Quick is prima donna Brigida Bianchi. Sherman Yellen wrote the screenplay, Larry Pizer was cinematographer, and Robert Markowitz directed. Color. 100 minutes.

1987 Terror at the Opera
Dario Argento's Italian film *Opera* (released in America as *Terror at the Opera*) is a variation of *The Phantom of the Opera* built around a production of Verdi's *Macbeth* in Parma. The plot is close to that of *Phantom* with a mysterious figure prowling the secret corridors of the opera house, furthering the career of a young soprano and killing those involved with her. See TERROR AT THE OPERA.

1989 Little film
Horror star Robert Englund plays the Phantom in this handsome, but rather gory, film set at Covent Garden in London. The central opera is again *Faust,* but there is also an aria from the Phantom's lost opera *Don Juan Triumphant,* which is described in Leroux's novel. Jill Schoelen plays soprano Christine, who starts off in contemporary New York and ends up in 19th-century London understudying and replacing diva Carlotta (Stephanie Lawrence) in *Faust.* Her stardom arrives after she sings the "Jewel Song" to a standing ovation. The *Faust* music comes from a recording with Colin Davis conducting the Bavarian Radio Symphony Orchestra; Faust is Francisco Araiza, Méphistophélès is Yevgeny Nesterenko, and Marguerite is sung by Kiri Te Kanawa. Misha Segal composed and conducted the film score, and Adras Miko directed the opera extracts. Duke Sandefur and Gerry O'Hara wrote the screenplay, Elemer Ragalyi was the cinematographer, and Dwight H. Little directed. Color. 90 minutes.

1990 Richardson film

Burt Lancaster is the Paris Opera House general manager and protective father of the Phantom (Charles Dance) in this elaborate television variation of *The Phantom* devised by playwright Arthur Kopit. Things start to go wrong when villain Ian Richardson takes over the opera house so his wife Andrea Ferreol can be the prima donna. Teri Polo plays the singer Christine who gets singing lessons from the Phantom, with Michele LaGrange providing her singing voice. Helia T'hezan sings for Ferreol and Gerard Carino sings for the Phantom. John Addison arranged the music; Tony Richardson directed. Color. 189 minutes. Image Entertainment DVD.

1998 Il fantasma dell'opera

Italian director Dario Argento's horrific version of *The Phantom of the Opera* stars Julian Sands as the Phantom with Asia Argento as his Christine (sung by Raffaella Milanesi). Nadia Rinaldi plays Carlotta, the prima donna she replaces. This version, shot in the opera house in Budapest, also features music from *Faust*, *Carmen* ("Habanera"), *Lakmé* ("Bell Song"), and *Romeo e Giulietta*. Ennio Morricone conducted the orchestra and composed the original music. Color. 99 minutes. On DVD and VHS.

PHI-PHI
1918 operetta by Christiné

HENRI CHRISTINÉ's tuneful French operetta *Phi-Phi,* libretto by Albert Willemetz and Francis Solar, is set in ancient Greece. It tells the story of the sculptor Phidias (known as Phi-Phi), the model/courtesan Aspasie, the sculptor's jealous wife Théodora, and her paramour Prince Ardimedon. The operetta even tells how Venus de Milo lost her arms.

1927 Pallu film

Phi-Phi was made into a French silent film in 1927 with Georges Gautier as Phidias, Irène Wells as Aspasie, Rita Jolivet as Théodora, and Gaston Norès as Ardimedon. Georges Pallu directed. The film was presented in cinemas with live music from the operetta. Black and white. In French. About 80 minutes.

PICKWICK
1936 opera by Coates

This relatively obscure English opera by ALBERT COATES has a secure niche in the history of music as it was the first televised opera. It was presented on BBC Television on November 13, 1936, 10 days before it had its premiere at Covent Garden. Twenty-five minutes of scenes from the opera were shown in a "special adaptation for televi-sion" devised by Dallas Bower. Two orchestral interludes from the opera, *Pickwick Scherzo* and *Cricket Fugue,* achieved a certainly popularity in England, but Coates's best-known piece of music is the stirring March from the 1954 film *The Dambusters.*

1936 BBC Television

British television production: Dallas Bower (director), Albert Coates (conductor, BBC Television Orchestra).

Cast: William Parsons (Mr. Pickwick), Dennis Noble (Sam Weller).

Telecast on November 13, 1936, on BBC TV. Black and white. In English. 25 minutes.

PIETRA DEL PARAGONE, LA
1812 opera by Rossini

GIOACHINO ROSSINI's comic opera *La pietra del paragone* (The Touchstone), libretto by Luigi Romanelli, is a kind of house party where everyone plays mind games to see what people really feel about each other. The wealthy Count Asdrubale, who is giving the party, pretends he is suddenly bankrupt and disguises himself as a Turk. Clarice, Aspasia, and Fulvia, who all want to marry him, get upset, but Clarice and poet Giocondo rally to him. Clarice then tests his love for her by pretending to be her brother Lucina come to take her away. All ends more or less well.

1965 Glyndebourne Festival

English stage production: Günther Rennert (director), John Pritchard (conductor, London Philharmonic Orchestra and Glyndebourne Festival Chorus), Osbert Lancaster (set designer).

Cast: Ugo Trama (Asdrubale), Josephine Veasey (Clarice), Umberto Grilli (Giocondo), Anna Reynolds (Aspasia), Alberta Valentini (Fulvia).

Telecast September 9, 1965, on BBC. John Vernon (director). Black and white. In Italian. 116 minutes.

PIETRI, GIUSEPPE
Italian composer (1886–1946)

Giuseppe Pietri wrote six operas but is better known as the leading Italian operetta composer of the early 20th century. His opera career began in 1910 with *Calendimaggio,* and he had his greatest success in 1934 with *Maristella,* which premiered with Beniamino Gigli in the leading role. Success with operetta began in 1915 with the charming *Addio Giovinezza,* based on a famous stage play that has been filmed four times. Pietri's biggest operetta success was the 1920 L'ACQUA CHETA, based on a stage play by Augusto Novelli about sisters and their trouble with men.

PINZA, EZIO
Italian-born American bass (1892–1957)

Rome native Ezio Pinza was a major star at La Scala in Milan, but it was the Metropolitan Opera in New York that made him internationally famous. He appeared there in 22 consecutive seasons beginning in 1926; he starred in 878 performances and was particularly noted for his Figaro and Don Giovanni. He left the Met at the age of 56 and became a major Broadway star, appearing in *South Pacific* in 1949 and *Fanny* in 1954. He starred in two TV series in the early 1950s, the *Ezio Pinza Show* and the sitcom *Bonino,* in which he portrayed a music-loving widower. He also had a Hollywood career, but he was not given many good films and was never filmed in a complete opera.

1947 Rehearsal
Pinza and Blanche Thebom star in this documentary about the *Bell Telephone Hour* radio show. Pinza sings Tosti's "L'Ultima Canzone" and joins Thebom in a duet on "Là ci darem la mano" from *Don Giovanni.* See BELL TELEPHONE HOUR.

1947 Carnegie Hall
Pinza performs arias from *Don Giovanni* and *Simon Boccanegra* in this pleasant film, basically a fiction framework for a series of numbers by classical stars. See CARNEGIE HALL.

1951 Mr. Imperium
Pinza is a prince who becomes a king in this MGM musical romance. Lana Turner is the movie star he loves and has to leave for the good of his country. The film is stilted but has a certain charm, especially in the scene on a Hollywood set built to resemble their original meeting place. Pinza and Turner both sing but not memorably. Don Hartman directed. Color. 87 minutes.

1951 Strictly Dishonorable
Pinza plays an opera star who dallies with Janet Leigh and marries her to save her reputation. In the film he appears on stage in an opera written by Mario Castelnuovo-Tedesco, performs the aria "Le veau d'or" from *Faust,* and sings two pop songs. The film, based on a Preston Sturges play that was more daringly filmed in 1931, was scripted and directed by Melvin Frank and Norman Panama for MGM. Black and white. 86 minutes.

1953 Tonight We Sing
Pinza impersonates Russian bass Feodor Chaliapin in this film about impresario Sol Hurok and sings arias from *Faust* and *Boris Godunov.* See TONIGHT WE SING.

1954 Tribute to Rodgers and Hammerstein
Pinza appears on this General Foods Anniversary Show TV tribute to the creators of the musical *South Pacific* and re-creates one of his scenes from it. Black and white. 60 minutes.

1995 Six Great Basses
Compilation of performances by noted basses. Pinza is shown singing the *Don Giovanni* duet "Là ci darem la mano" with Blanche Thebom from the 1947 film *Rehearsal.* See BARITONES AND BASSES.

PIQUE DAME
See THE QUEEN OF SPADES.

PIRATA, IL
1827 opera by Bellini

VINCENZO BELLINI's *Il pirata* (The Pirate) is an operatic love triangle set against the complicated politics of 13th-century Sicily. Count Gualtiero and Duke Ernesto, on opposite sides in the war for the throne, both love Imogene. After Gualtiero's side loses, he becomes a pirate, and Ernesto forces Imogene to marry him. When Gualtiero returns, Imogene won't abandon her husband and child, and Gualtiero kills Ernesto in a duel. Felice Romani wrote the libretto based on a French play derived from an English novel. There are famous recordings of Maria Callas and Montserrat Caballé in the opera but neither is on video.

1987 Festival della Valle d'Itria
Italian stage production: Italo Nunziata (director), Alberto Zedda (conductor, Orchestra Internazionale d'Italia and Teatro Petruzzelli Chorus), Carlo Sala (set/costume designer).

Cast: Lucia Aliberti (Imogene), Giuseppe Morino (Gualtiero), Giorgio Surjan (Ernesto), Adriana Molina (Adele), Pietro Spagnoli (Goffredo), Michele Farruggia (Itulbo).

Video: Bel Canto Society VHS. Telecast August 12, 1991, on RAI Italian Television. Tonino delle Colle (director). Color. In Italian. 160 minutes.

Comment: Staged in the Palazzo Ducale in Martina Franca.

PIRATES OF PENZANCE, THE

1879 comic opera by Gilbert and Sullivan

The very British GILBERT AND SULLIVAN operetta *The Pirates of Penzance or The Slave of Duty* is the source of the very American song "Hail, Hail, the Gang's All Here," but in the operetta it is sung as "Come Friends Who Plough the Sea." The story is wonderfully ridiculous. Frederic has been apprenticed to the pirates of Penzance by his nursemaid Ruth who misunderstood the word "pilot." The pirates are really quite soft-hearted and especially partial to orphans. Frederic falls in love with Mabel, one of the many daughters of Major General Stanley, who also happens to be an orphan. A band of policemen led by a tough sergeant arrive to combat the pirates, but all works out delightfully well. Mabel's popular "Poor Wandering One" is virtually a coloratura aria and a real test for the soprano in the role. The popularity of the operetta is reflected in the large number of films and videos.

1939 NBC Television

NBC experimented with the new medium of television by presenting excerpts from *The Pirates of Penzance* in June 1939. There weren't many viewers as a TV set cost a small fortune at the time (around $800) and programming was limited to a few hours a week.

1955 D'Oyly Carte Opera on Omnibus

American TV studio highlights production: Bridget D'Oyly Carte (director), Isadore Godfrey (conductor, orchestra), Henry May (set designer).

Cast: Joy Mornay, Joyce Wright, Neville Griffiths.

Videos at the MTR and Library of Congress. Telecast November 13, 1955, on CBS. Charles S. Dubin (director). Black and white. In English. 35 minutes.

1972 Gilbert & Sullivan for All series

English highlights film: Peter Seabourne (director), Peter Murray (conductor, Gilbert and Sullivan Festival Orchestra and Chorus), David Maverovitch (cinematographer), Trevor Evans (adaptation), John Seabourne (producer).

Cast: Donald Adams (Pirate King), Valerie Masterson (Mabel), Thomas Round (Frederic), Helen Landis (Ruth), John Cartier (Major-General), Lawrence Richard (Police Sergeant).

Video: Musical Collectables VHS. Color. In English. 50 minutes.

1982 Gilbert and Sullivan Collection series

English studio production: Michael Geliot (director), Judith De Paul (producer), Alexander Faris (conductor, London Symphony Orchestra and Ambrosian Opera Chorus), Allan Cameron (set designer), George Walker (executive producer).

Cast: Peter Allen (Pirate King), Keith Michell (Major General), Janis Kelly (Mabel), Gillian Knight (Ruth), Alexander Oliver (Frederic), Paul Hudson (Police Sergeant).

Video: CBS Fox VHS/Pioneer LD/Opera World and Braveworld (GB) VHS. Rodney Greenberg (director). Color. In English. 112 minutes.

1982 Universal film

American feature film: Joseph Papp (stage director), Wilford Leach (film director), William Elliott (conductor), Peter Howitt (set designer), Graviela Daniele (choreographer), Universal Pictures (production).

Cast: Kevin Kline (Pirate King), Linda Ronstadt (Mabel), Angela Lansbury (Ruth), Rex Smith (Frederic), George Rose (Major-General), Tony Azito (Police Sergeant).

Video: Image Entertainment DVD and VHS/MCA VHS and LD. Color. In English. 112 minutes.

1985 Stratford Festival

Canadian TV production: Brian Macdonald (director/choreographer), Berthold Carriere (conductor, Stratford Festival Orchestra and Chorus), Douglas McLean and Susan Benson (set/costume designers).

Cast: Brent Carver (Pirate King), Jeff Hyslop (Frederic), Caralyn Tomlin (Mabel), Ruth Galloway (Pat), Douglas Chamberlain (Major General), Wendy Abbot (Blue Stocking), Stephen Beamis (Police Sergeant).

Video: Connoisseur VHS. Telecast December 29, 1985, on CBC. Norman Campbell (director). Color. In English. 130 minutes.

Comment: Adaptation of Stratford Festival stage production by Macdonald.

Related films

1937 The Girl Said No

This little-known American film contains scenes from Gilbert and Sullivan operettas performed in a traditional manner by members of the old Gilbert and Sullivan Opera Company of New York. It includes "A Policeman's Lot Is Not a Happy One" from *The Pirates of Penzance*. See THE GIRL SAID NO.

1976 Graber film

English animator Sheila Graber made an animated cartoon version of one of the best-known comic songs of the operetta. She called it, after the song, *I Am the Very*

Model of a Modern Major General. Color. In English. 4 minutes.

2002 Kate and Leopold
Duke Leopold (Hugh Jackson) travels through time from the Gilbert and Sullivan era to the modern day where he meets and falls in love with Kate (Meg Ryan). Naturally, the soundtrack includes the *Penzance* aria "I Am the Very Model of a Modern Major General." James Mangold directed. Color. In English. 118 minutes.

PIROGOV, ALEXANDER
Russian bass (1899–1964)

Alexander Pirogov, one of the finest Russian bass singers of the century and brother of the equally talented Grigory, made his debut in Moscow in 1922. He spent most of his career at the Bolshoi but luckily was captured on film by Soviet filmmaker Vera Stroyeva in two of his best roles, as Igor in PRINCE IGOR (1951, in two versions) and as Boris in BORIS GODUNOV (1954). He is the voice of Salieri in a 1966 film of Rimsky-Korsakov's MOZART AND SALIERI, and he can be seen in a Soviet film in the 1940s singing Méphistophélès's "Serenade" from FAUST.

PLISHKA, PAUL
American bass (1941–)

Paul Plishka has been a mainstay of the Metropolitan Opera since 1967, and if he doesn't have the renown of a Pavarotti, he has the enduring admiration of all who love opera. One of the most reliable of performers, he often gets better notices than the stars. He is best known for his Verdi interpretations and is a notable Falstaff and a fine Leporello. While his career has been centered around the Met, he has also sung at La Scala, Berlin, Munich, Chicago, and San Francisco. His work is well represented on video. See AUFSTIEG UND FALL DER STADT MAHAGONNY (1979), LA BOHÈME (1977), BORIS GODUNOV (1989), LA CENERENTOLA (1981), DON CARLOS (1980), FALSTAFF (1992), LUCIA DI LAMMERMOOR (1982), LUISA MILLER (1988), LE NOZZE DI FIGARO (1998), LUCIANO PAVAROTTI (1998), SIMON BOCCANEGRA (1984), STIFFELIO (1993), LES TROYENS (1983), TURANDOT (1987), and VERDI REQUIEM (1991).

POETA, EL
1980 opera by Moreno Torroba

Spanish composer FEDERICO MORENO TORROBA began his career in opera, built a reputation with zarzuelas (most notably LUISA FERNANDA), and returned to opera at the end of his life. Plácido Domingo commissioned his opera *El Poeta* (The Poet) and played the leading role when it premiered in Madrid. José Mendez Herrara's libretto is based on an episode in the life of 19th-century Spanish poet José Ignacio de Espronceda, a freedom-loving patriot who was exiled during the reign of King Ferdinand VII. The plot revolves around his relationship with two women, Teresa Mancha and Carmen Osario, with one killing the other out of jealousy.

1980 Teatro de la Zarzuela, Madrid
Spanish stage production: Rafel Perez Sierra (director), Luis Antonio García Novarro (conductor, Spanish National Orchestra), Gustavo Torner (set designer). Cast: Plácido Domingo (José Ignacio de Espronceda), Carmen Bustamente (Teresa Manca), Angeles Gulin (Carmen Osario).

Video: House of Opera/Opera Dubs/Lyric VHS. Color. In Spanish. 137 minutes.

POLANSKI, ROMAN
Polish film director (1933–)

Roman Polanski became famous in 1962 with his first Polish feature film, *Knife in the Water.* He became even better known after moving to the United States and making *Rosemary's Baby* and *Chinatown.* Polanski began to direct opera on stage in 1974 with LULU at the Festival of Two Worlds in Spoleto. He based his production of the Berg opera on the Pabst film of the story, *Pandora's Box.* Polanski has also staged *Rigoletto* in Munich and *Les contes d'Hoffmann* in Paris. In 1981 he returned to Poland to produce Peter Shaffer's play *Amadeus* on stage. His 2002 film *The Pianist* has been a critical favorite.

POLENBLUT
1913 operetta by Nedbal

OSKAR NEDBAL's popular operetta *Polenblut* (Polish Blood) is a kind of Polish counterpart to the patriotic Viennese operetta *Wiener Blut.* Set in Russian-occupied Poland at the beginning of the century, it is flavored with mazurkas and polonaises. Leo Stein's libretto tells the story of Hélena, a high-spirited young woman who wins the love of a high-living count who had first spurned her for not being an aristocrat. It was presented in America in 1915 as *The Peasant Girl* with Emma Trentini in the starring role and new songs by Rudolf Friml. *Polenblut* has remained in the operetta repertory in Central Europe.

1934 Lamac film
Czech/German film: Karel Lamac (director), Václav Wasserman and Peter Ort (screenplay), Otto Keller and Otto Martini (cinematographers).

Cast: Anny Ondra (Héléna), Hans Moser (Héléna's father in German version), Theodore Pistak (Héléna's father in Czech version), Ivan Petrovich (German Count), Stefan Hoza (Czech Count).

Black and white. In Czech or German. 87 minutes.

Comment: The film was shot in Prague in Czech and German versions with Ondra starring in both but with slightly different supporting casts. The Czech title is *Polská Krev.*

1966 ZDF German Television

German TV production: Wolfgang Liebeneiner (director), Wolfgang Ebert (conductor, Nürnberg Symphony Orchestra and Chorus), Maleen Pacha (set designer).

Cast: Ina Dressel (Héléna), Günther George (Count), Hans Joachim Worrigen (Héléna's father).

Telecast May 29, 1966, on ZDF German Television. Color. In German. 100 minutes.

POLI, AFRO
Italian baritone (1902–1988)

Pisa-born baritone Afro Poli, who recorded with Tito Schipa and sang on stage with Ferruccio Tagliavini, had important roles in a number of Italian opera films of the 1950s and 1960s. First was the 1948 *Lucia di Lammermoor* with Nelly Corradi, in which he plays Lord Ashton; it was followed by six others, including the Sophia Loren *Aida.* He also acted in non-operatic films such as Steve Reeves's 1957 *Hercules.* See AIDA (1953), LA CENERENTOLA (1948), LUCIA DI LAMMERMOOR (1948), NORMA (1950 film), PAGLIACCI (1948), TOSCA (1956), and LA TRAVIATA (1966).

PONCHIELLI, AMILCARE
Italian composer (1834–1886)

Amilcare Ponchielli wrote many operas, including one based on the famous Italian novel *I Promessi Sposi,* but he is remembered today for only one, the truly grand LA GIOCONDA. Even those who have never seen the opera know some of its music, including the famous "The Dance of the Hours" featured so cleverly in Disney's *Fantasia.* The masterful libretto is by the multitalented Arrigo Boito. Ponchielli was married to soprano Teresina Brambilla, whose descendants include Tullio Carminati, Grace Moore's costar in the popular opera film ONE NIGHT OF LOVE.

PONNELLE, JEAN-PIERRE
French director/designer (1932–1988)

Jean-Pierre Ponnelle, who has been called the "father of the opera film," directed 16 opera films and is one of the major auteurs in the genre, although he is not usually listed in film reference books. Like Franco Zeffirelli, he was a designer and director for both film and theater and his theater productions were usually the basis of his films, most notably the Monteverdi cycle. They were shot on 35mm and are as exciting visually as they are musically; some had theatrical release, although they were made primarily for television. Ponnelle began his career in Germany in 1952, made his U.S. debut designing sets for the San Francisco Opera in 1958, and began to direct on stage in 1962. He died tragically young from an accidental fall into an orchestra pit while producing *Carmen* in Tel Aviv. Most of his films are available on video, and his Figaro and Monteverdi operas are especially popular. See ARIADNE AUF NAXOS (1988), IL BARBIERE DI SIVIGLIA (1972), CARDILLAC (1986), CARMINA BURANA (1975), LA CENERENTOLA (1981), LA CLEMENZA DI TITO (1980), COSÌ FAN TUTTE (1988), FALSTAFF (1976), IDOMENEO (1982), L'INCORONAZIONE DI POPPEA (1979), INTERMEZZO (1963), L'ITALIANA IN ALGERI (1986), JAMES LEVINE (1986), MADAMA BUTTERFLY (1974), MANON (1983), MITRIDATE (1986), LE NOZZE DI FIGARO (1976/1985), ORFEO (1978), RIGOLETTO (1983), IL RITORNO D'ULISSE IN PATRIA (1980), SEVILLE (1982), TRISTAN UND ISOLDE (1983), and DIE ZAUBERFLÖTE (1982).

1986 Jean-Pierre Ponnelle or The Warpath
German television documentary about Ponnelle by Brigitte Carreau showing the director at work. Color. In German. 54 minutes.

PONS, LILY
French/American soprano (1898–1976)

Lily Pons was the top female opera star in Hollywood during the 1930s, after Grace Moore, and one of the finest coloratura sopranos in the world. She was born near Cannes, began to sing in operetta in 1917, and made her operatic debut in 1927 in *Lakmé* with Reynaldo Hahn conducting in Mulhouse. Despite her petite size (5 feet high and barely 98 pounds), she made a sensational debut at the Metropolitan Opera on January 1, 1931, as Lucia in *Lucia di Lammermoor.* She continued to sing there for another 30 years (29 seasons). Pons made three reasonable films with good directors in Hollywood during the 1930s but then gave up on the movies. She was married to conductor André Kostelanetz from 1938 to 1958 and gave her farewell performance at the Met as Lucia on December 4, 1960. Her last stage performance was in

Fort Worth where she opened the opera season, again as Lucia.

1935 I Dream Too Much
Pons made her film debut opposite Henry Fonda in this enjoyable RKO picture, and her delightful personality comes through well in her portrayal of an opera singer married to an aspiring composer. She sings her signature aria "Bell Song," "Caro nome," and songs by Jerome Kern and Dorothy Fields. See I DREAM TOO MUCH.

1936 That Girl From Paris
Pons's second RKO film featured her as a Parisian opera star who runs away from an arranged marriage. She ends up in the United States as an illegal immigrant involved in romantic mix-ups with jazz musician Gene Raymond. She sings "Una voce poco fa" from *The Barber of Seville,* a Strauss waltz, a tarantella. and songs by Arthur Schwartz and Edward Heyman. Lucille Ball plays a jealous friend, André Kostelanetz conducted the orchestra, and Leigh Jason directed the film. Black and white. 102 minutes. RKO/Turner VHS.

Lily Pons tootles along with jazz musician Gene Raymond in *That Girl From Paris* (1936).

1937 Hitting a New High
In her last Hollywood film, Pons plays a French jazz singer who wants to switch to opera. She becomes involved in a complicated ruse posing as a Bird Girl to deceive millionaire Edward Everett Horton. Her opera arias include the mad scene from *Lucia di Lammermoor* and "Je suis Titania" from *Mignon*. There are also songs by James McHugh and Harold Adamson. Pons left Hollywood complaining that there was comic business in the film even when she was singing. Raoul Walsh directed for RKO. Black and white. 80 minutes.

1950 Moments in Music
Pons is one of the musicians shown briefly in this short film about the different kinds of music enjoyed by moviegoers. Color and black and white. 10 minutes.

1956 The Bob Hope Show
Pons was guest star on *The Bob Hope Show* on NBC television on October 24, 1956. Black and white. 30 minutes.

1966 Open Mind
Pons and other singers talk about the Golden Age of the Met on this NBC television program. See METROPOLITAN OPERA.

1973 Lily Pons
American documentary about Pons made when she was 75. She talks about her life in music and the film follows her as she visits places associated with her career. Telecast on February 21, 1973. Color. 60 minutes. Video at the Library of Congress.

1976 The Front
Pons is shown with President Eisenhower and his wife in a newsreel in this film about blacklisted writers. Martin Ritt directed. Color and black and white. 95 minutes.

PONSELLE, ROSA
American soprano (1897–1981)

Rosa Ponselle's life sounds like a fairy tale. With no previous experience on an opera stage, this untrained vaudeville singer made her debut at the Metropolitan Opera at the age of 21 opposite Enrico Caruso in *La forza del destino*. She was immediately acclaimed as a vocal miracle with a voice of pure gold and an actress of great ability. Ponselle was a Met favorite from her debut in 1918 until her retirement in 1937. Her records are still admired, but she made no feature films, although she did test for one.

1935 Broadway Highlights No. 2
Ponselle is one of the stars featured in this short film made by Fred Waller for Paramount Pictures in 1935. Grace Moore also appears. Black and white. 10 minutes.

1936 Carmen screen tests

Ponselle, who began to sing the mezzo role of Carmen in the last two years of her stage career, was tested for the role for a Hollywood movie. In MGM screen tests, dated October 12, 1936, she talks about her love for *La traviata,* her interest in seeing Greta Garbo in the film of the story, and the difficulty of singing *Norma.* She is shown in costume singing the "Habanera" and the "Chanson bohémienne" and looks and sounds splendid. She felt these tests of *Carmen* were among the best recordings she made. The tests are on the video *Legends of Opera.* Black and white. About 4 minutes. Legato Classics VHS.

1977 Metropolitan Opera

The Met celebrated Ponselle's 80th birthday with a tribute to her during the interval of the 1977 telecast of LUISA MILLER. She was interviewed at her home in the Villa Pace for the program, and her screen tests were shown. Color and black and white. 10 minutes.

POPP, LUCIA

Czech-born Austrian soprano (1939–1993)

Lucia Popp, who died tragically young at age 54 of a brain tumor, made her debut in 1963 in Bratislava as the Queen of the Night. She then moved to the Vienna Staatsoper, the opera house where she sang regularly for the rest of her life. She was a regular at the Salzburg Festival and went to the Met in 1967 as the Queen of the Night. Her specialties were Mozart and Strauss. Popp made a large number of recordings and can be seen in fine form on many videos. See THE BARTERED BRIDE (1982), CARMINA BURANA (1976), FIDELIO (1968/1978), HÄNSEL UND GRETEL (1984), DIE LUSTIGEN WEIBER VON WINDSOR (1965), LE NOZZE DI FIGARO (1980), DER ROSENKAVALIER (1979), SCHÖPFUNG (1986/1990), UNDINE (1969), ZAR UND ZIMMERMANN (1969/1976), and DIE ZAUBERFLÖTE (1983).

1984 OperaFest

Popp is one of the performers at a gala concert at the Zurich Operhaus on December 1, 1984. See ZURICH.

1986 Fanfare for Elizabeth

Royal Opera House concert in honor of Queen Elizabeth; Popp and Plácido Domingo perform in scenes from *La traviata* and *Don Giovanni.* See ROYAL OPERA HOUSE.

1993 Philadelphia

This film, about a gay lawyer with AIDS (Tom Hanks), features Popp on the soundtrack singing Idamante's aria "Non temer, amato bene" accompanied by the Vienna State Opera Orchestra led by John Pritchard. Color. 119 minutes.

1993 Opera Imaginaire

Popp is a featured singer on an animated film in this compendium. Raimund Krumme animates her version of "Du also bist mein Bräutigam?" from *The Magic Flute.* Color. 52 minutes. See OPERA IMAGINAIRE.

1999 Bicentennial Man

Popp is featured singing the "Song to the Moon" from *Rusalka* on the soundtrack of this film about an immortal android (Robin Williams) who wants to be a mortal human. Chris Columbus directed. Color. 130 minutes.

PORGY AND BESS

1935 opera by Gershwin

GEORGE GERSHWIN's *Porgy and Bess,* now recognized as the major American opera, has been staged in most of the major opera houses of the world, even the Met. It took a long time for it to gain respect from the opera world because it was first presented on Broadway and was considered too popular to be high art. There was also the question of whether a trio of white men could write an African-American opera, a question that is now irrelevant as the opera has created its own universality. DuBose Heyward wrote the libretto based on his 1925 novel about people he observed in South Carolina, Ira Gershwin helped with the superb lyrics, and George Gershwin composed music for their words that is likely to live as long as anything by Mozart or Verdi. The unforgettable arias of what Gershwin called a "folk opera" include "Summertime," "It Ain't Necessarily So," and "I Got Plenty of Nothin'." The opera is set in an African-American ghetto in Charleston called Catfish Row. The crippled Porgy becomes involved with the beautiful Bess after her protector Crown goes to jail, but she eventually runs away with the gambler Sportin' Life. The opera arrived on Broadway in October 1935 with Todd Duncan as Porgy, Anne Brown as Bess, and John W. Bubbles as Sportin' Life. It was staged at New York City Opera in 1962, but it did not reach the Met until 1985, 50 years after its premiere.

1959 Goldwyn film

American feature film: Otto Preminger (director), N. Richard Nash (screenplay), Leon Shamroy (cinematographer), André Previn (music supervisor/conductor), Ken Darby (music arrangements), Samuel Goldwyn (producer).

Cast: Sidney Poitier (Porgy, sung by Robert McFerrin), Dorothy Dandridge (Bess, sung by Adele Addison), Sammy Davis Jr. (Sportin' Life), Pearl Bailey (Maria), Diahann Carroll (Clara, sung by Loulie Jean

Norman), Brock Peters (Crown), Ruth Attaway (Serena, sung by Inez Matthews), Maya Angelou (dancer).

Color. In English. 146 minutes.

Comment: *The New York Times* listed this as one of the Ten Best Films of the Year, and Ira Gershwin said he liked it, but it was not a box office success. It was the final and most expensive film of producer Samuel Goldwyn and was nominated for four Academy Awards. It won Oscars for Best Scoring (Previn and Darby), Best Costume Design (Irene Sharaff), and Best Sound Recording (Gordon Sawyer). It also won a Grammy for best soundtrack of the year. There was a go od deal of controversy about the film which is currently withdrawn from circulation by the Gershwin estate and is not on video; it can be viewed by scholars at the Library of Congress, and it surfaces occasionally at film festivals.

Porgy and Bess (1959): Porgy (Sidney Poitier) just after killing Crown (Brock Peters) in Otto Preminger's film.

1992 Glyndebourne Festival film

English studio film: Trevor Nunn (director), Simon Rattle (conductor, London Philharmonic Orchestra and Glyndebourne Festival Chorus), John Gunter (set designer).

Cast: Willard White (Porgy), Cynthia Haymon (Bess), Damon Evans (Sportin' Life), Gregg Baker (Crown), Cynthia Clarey (Serena), Marietta Simpson (Maria), Paula Ingram (Clara, sung by Harolyn Blackwell), Bruce Hubbard (Jake).

Video: EMI Classics DVD/VHS/LD. Greg Smith (director). Color. In English. 184 minutes.

Comment: The cast is from Nunn's Covent Garden revival, but it is essentially the same as his 1986 Glyndebourne Festival production and it uses as its soundtrack the 1988 Glyndebourne Festival cast recording. It was filmed in Shepperton Studios.

2002 New York City Opera

American stage production: Tazewell Thomson (director), John DeMain (conductor, New York City Op-era Orchestra and Chorus), Douglas Schmidt (set designer).

Cast: Alvy Powell (Porgy), Marquita Lister (Bess), Dwayne Clark (Sportin' Life), Angela Simpson (Serena), Timothy Robert Blevins (Crown), Sabrina Elayne Carten (Maria), Adina Aaron (Clara), David Aron Damane (Jake).

Telecast live March 20, 2002, on PBS. Kirk Browning (director). Color. In English. 180 minutes.

Related films

1945 Rhapsody in Blue

Anne Brown, who created the role, plays Bess in the *Porgy and Bess* sequence of the 1945 film *Rhapsody in Blue* and sings "Summertime." William Gillespie plays Porgy with Robert Johnson as Sportin' Life. Irving Rapper directed for Warner Bros. Black and white. 139 minutes.

1998 Porgy and Bess: An American Voice

Documentary about the history of the opera since its premiere. Todd Duncan and Anne Brown, who created the title roles, are featured with Leontyne Price, William Warfield, Grace Bumbry, Cab Calloway, Diahann Carroll, and Willard White. Ruby Dee narrates, Gloria Naylor and Ed Apfel wrote the script, and James A. Standifer produced the documentary telecast February 4, 1998, on PBS in the *Great Performances* series. Color. 60 minutes. PBS VHS.

PORPORA, NICOLA
Italian composer (1686–1768)

Nicola Porpora, a strong rival to Handel during his heyday, is said to have composed more than 50 operas in the *opera seria* mode, five of them in London. He was also a famous teacher, with Haydn and Farinelli among his more notable pupils. His operas emphasized vocal virtuosity and were popular with castratos because of this. Examples of his work can be seen on stage in the film FARINELLI, including the aria "Alto Giove" from his opera *Polifemo*.

PORTEN, HENNY
German film actress (1888–1960)

Henny Porten, Germany's first important film star, was the daughter of an opera singer, and she played the heroine in many early German opera sound films. She usually worked with Oskar Messter, who developed a synchronization process for his Biophon-Theater using phonograph records of opera arias; her first such "tonbilder" (sound-picture) was made in 1906. Porten's father Franz directed and often acted in the films, usually shot in a Berlin studio. Porten also starred in the 1921 feature *Die Geier-Wally,* based on the source story of Catalani's opera LA WALLY, and a 1927 adaptation of Donizetti's DON PASQUALE. It's not known exactly how many of these miniature opera films she made, but it may have been as many as 40; most have not survived. Those with entries in this book are DER BETTELSTUDENT (1907), FAUST (1908), DER FREISCHÜTZ (1908), LOHENGRIN (1907), LUCIA DI LAMMERMOOR (1907), OTELLO (1907), TANNHÄUSER (1908), DER TROMPETER VON SÄKKINGEN (1908), and IL TROVATORE (1908).

Henny Porten Germany's first major movie star, appeared in many early opera films

POSFORD, GEORGE
English composer (1906–1976)

George Posford had his first real success as a composer when he teamed with librettist Eric Maschwitz to create the radio operetta *Good Night Vienna.* When the broadcast got delayed, it was transmuted into a hit film starring Jack Buchanan and Anna Neagle. Posford's major stage success was the long-running operetta BALALAIKA (1936), which was made into an MGM film in 1939 with Nelson Eddy. Joan Sutherland has recorded its most popular song, "At the Balalaika."

POSTILLON DE LONJUMEAU, LE
1844 opera by Adam

ADOLPHE ADAM's French opera *Le postillon de Lonjumeau* (The Coachman From Longjumeau) is the tuneful story of coachman Chapelou, who abandons his bride Madeleine on their wedding night when he is taken off to sing at the Paris Opera. Ten years later, when they are re-united, he is famous as the opera divo Saint Phar and she is rich as Madame Latour. This is Adam's most popular opera, especially in German-speaking countries where tenors favor the role of Chapelou to show off their high Ds. The opera is somewhat of a parody of operatic mannerisms. Adolphe de Leuven and Léon-Lévy Brunswick wrote the satirical libretto. (Note: "Longjumeau" is the English name for the town known in French and German as "Lonjumeau.")

1936 Lamac film
Austrian feature film: Carl Lamac (director), Anton Profes (conductor), Eduard Hoesch (cinematographer), Atlantis film (production)
Cast: Willy Eichberger (Chapelou), Rose Stradner (Madeleine), Alfred Neugebauer (King Louis XV), Leo Slezak (Count de Latour), Thekla Ahrens (Mme. de Pompadour).
Video: Lyric VHS. Black and white. In German. 91 minutes.
Comment: Good entertainment, if not quite the opera as written, played as much for comedy as musical values. Shown in America as *King Smiles—Paris Laughs.*

1989 Grand Théâtre de Genève
Swiss stage production: Nina Companeez (director), Patrick Fournillier (conductor, Orchestre de la Suisse Romance and Grand Théâtre de Genève Chorus), Thierry Bosquet (set/costume designer).
Cast: Jorge López-Yanez, Donna Brown, Jorge Anton, Ewa Malas-Godlewska, Maurice Sieyes, René Massis.
Video: House of Opera/Lyric VHS. Michel Dami (director). Color. In French. 130 minutes.

POTENZA DELLA MUSICA, LA
1549 musical interludes by various composers

La potenza della musica (The Power of Music) is a collection of Italian musical interludes *(intermedi)* performed in Florence before the official birth of opera in 1599. Some critics consider them to be virtually miniature operas, devised by Count Giovanni de' Bardi to be presented with Girolamo Bargagli's comedy *La pellegrina* at a Medici wedding. Bardi was a central figure in the Camerata, with composers Jacopo Peri and Giulio Caccini, who wrote some of the music for this event. The other composers were Luca Marenzio, Cristofano Malvezzi, and Emile de' Cavaliere. The collection was filmed as a set of mini-operas by Thames Television in London as *Una Stravaganza dei Medici.*

1989 Una Stravaganza dei Medici

    English TV production: Andrew Parrott (conductor, Taverner Consort and Players), Thames Television (producer).

    Cast: Tessa Bonner, Emma Kirkby, Emily Van Evera, Nigel Rogers.

    Video: EMI (GB) VHS/LD. Color. In Italian. 71 minutes.

POTTER, SALLY
English film director (1949–)

English filmmaker Sally Potter is best known for her films *Orlando* (1992), a remarkable adaptation of the Virginia Woolf novel, and *The Tango Lesson* (1997), a postmodern film in which the director herself becomes obsessed by the dance. Her first film was THRILLER (1979), a fascinating feminist examination of the role of victim that Mimì is forced to play in Puccini's *La bohème*. Her film THE MAN WHO CRIED (2000) revolves around a group of people working at the Paris Opéra during World War II.

POULENC, FRANCIS
French composer (1899–1963)

Francis Poulenc, one of the influential avant-garde group Les Six, came to opera late in his career and wrote only three operas. The first, the surrealistic 1947 *Les mamelles de Terésias,* was based on a play by Apollinaire. It was followed by the powerful and strongly religious 1948 DIALOGUES DES CARMÉLITES, an opera based on a screenplay for a film. His last work, the 1958 LA VOIX HUMAINE, is a hugely effective monodrama composed for Denise Duval.

POUNTNEY, DAVID
English director (1947–)

David Pountney, who began directing while still at Cambridge, made his debut at Wexford in 1972, staged Macbeth for the Houston Grand Opera in 1973, and attracted world attention with the Netherlands Opera premiere of Philip Glass's SATYAGRAHA in 1980. He also staged Glass's *The Voyage* at the Met in 1992. Pountney was in charge of production at the Scottish Opera from 1975 to 1980 and English National Opera from 1982 to 1993. His productions are idiosyncratic but always thoughtful. See THE FAIRY QUEEN (1995), MACBETH (2001), RUSALKA (1986), and STREET SCENE (1992).

POUSSIÈRES D'AMOUR
1996 opera film by Schroeter

German director WERNER SCHROETER's film *Poussières d'amour,* known in English as both *Love's Debris* and *Tears of Love,* is a fascinating examination of opera singing and the emotions the opera voice creates. The film begins with a quote from Roland Barthes asking "Why and how do opera singers find the emotion in their voices?" Schroeter, who has long been obsessed with opera, attempts to find out by inviting a number of singers to the 13th-century abbey of Roymaunt in France and working with them on presenting an aria of their choice. The singers include Martha Mödl, Anita Cerquetti, Rita Gorr, Trudeliese Schmidt, Katherine Ciesinski, Kristine Ciesinski, Laurence Dale, Jenny Drivala, Gail Gilmore, and Sergei Larin. The arias chosen come from a range of operas, with Mödl and Gorr both singing an aria from *The Queen of Spades.* The central figure in the film is Cerquetti with a particularly moving scene when Schroeter plays her recording of "Casta diva." The singers are accompanied on piano by Elizabeth Cooper and are interviewed about their singing by, among others, actresses Isabelle Huppert (Mödl) and Carole Bouquet (Cerquetti). The film is dedicated "to Maria Callas and all the others." Elfi Mikesch was the cinematographer. In German, French, Italian, Russian, and English. 120 minutes.

POWDER HER FACE
1995 chamber opera by Adès

Margaret, the Duchess of Argyll, reviews her life from her decadent marriages to her present penniless state in a luxury hotel. Thomas Adès's opera *Powder her Face,* libretto by Philip Henscher, is based on the life of Margaret, Duchess of Argyll, who gained notoriety during a scandalous divorce case in 1963. It premiered at the Cheltenham Festival in 1995, attracting popular attention for a fellatio scene and critical attention for the brilliance of its music. It made the composer famous, and there were soon follow-up productions around the world. The opera uses four singers for multiple roles; a "heldensoubrette" plays all the female parts, except the duchess, while a tenor and basso play the male roles.

2000 Aldeburgh Festival

    English TV film: David Alden (director), Thomas Adès (conductor, Birmingham Contemporary Music Group).

    Cast: Mary Plazas (Duchess), Heather Buck (maid, reporter, Duke's mistress), Daniel Norman (waiter, electrician, gigolo), Graeme Broadbent (Duke, judge, hotel manager).

Telecast December 25, 2000, on Channel 4 in England. Color. In English. 90 minutes.

Comment: Alden's bawdy film of the opera is based on his 1999 production at the Aldeburgh festival. The singers perform live to a prerecorded playback track.

POWELL, JANE

American film soprano (1929–)

Jane Powell was MGM's answer to Deanna Durbin during the 1940s, a precocious teenaged heroine with a high soprano voice who occasionally dabbled in opera or operetta. Her Hollywood career began in 1943 when she won a contest with an aria from *Carmen* and was signed to a movie contract. She sang classical music in her first film, the 1944 *Song of the Open Road*, and was taken up by Joe Pasternak who had been Durbin's producer. In 1948 she was featured with Jeanette MacDonald in *Three Daring Daughters*, a remake of Durbin's *Three Smart Girls*. Later that year she teamed up with Metropolitan Opera tenor Lauritz Melchior in *Luxury Liner*. In 1951 she was paired with Fred Astaire in *Royal Wedding*. Her best film year was 1954. She starred opposite Howard Keel in the outstanding *Seven Brides for Seven Brothers*, sang an opera aria in *Athena*, and was a guest star in the Sigmund Romberg biography *Deep in My Heart*. Her film career faded during the late 1950s when the Hollywood musical died, but she continued to work on stage and in television.

1948 Luxury Liner
Powell plays the stowaway daughter of liner captain George Brent in this delightful MGM shipboard musical. She is an aspiring opera singer and admirer of Olaf Erickson (Met tenor Lauritz Melchior) whom she has seen in *Aida*. She stows away to be near him, and he finally asks her to sing a duet with him. Richard Whorf directed. Color. 98 minutes. MGM-UA VHS.

1954 Athena
Powell plays Athena and sings the aria "Chacun le sait" from Donizetti's *The Daughter of the Regiment* in this musical about health fads. She was teamed with Vic Damone, Debbie Reynolds, and Edmund Purdom. Richard Thorpe directed. Color. 96 minutes.

1954 Deep in My Heart
Powell is one of the guest singers in this lively film biography of operetta composer Sigmund Romberg, played by José Ferrer. She and Vic Damone sing one of Romberg's most famous songs, "Will You Remember." Stanley Donen directed. Color. 132 minutes. MGM-UA VHS and LD.

POWELL, MICHAEL

English film director (1905–1990)

Michael Powell, one of the major British filmmakers, is best known for his ballet film *The Red Shoes* (1948) made with his collaborator Emeric Pressburger. They also produced two fine opera films, *The Tales of Hoffmann* and *O Rosalinda!*, a modern version of *Die Fledermaus*. Powell also directed a 1964 television film of Bartók's BLUEBEARD'S CASTLE. Powell used opera on the soundtrack of some of his non-operatic films, most notably *Mignon* in *The Life and Death of Colonel Blimp*. See DIE FLEDERMAUS (1955), MIGNON (1943 film), and LES CONTES D'HOFFMANN (1951).

POWERS, MARIE

American contralto (1910–1973)

Marie Powers, whose career was closely associated with operas by Gian Carlo Menotti, began her American career touring with the San Carlo Opera Company during the 1940s in *Aida* and *Un ballo in maschera*. In 1947 she sang Madame Flora in the Broadway production of Menotti's *The Medium* and in 1948 sang the role in London. She starred in Menotti's *The Old Maid and the Thief* at New York City Opera in 1948, and she created the role of the Mother in Menotti's *The Consul* in 1950. In the 1950s she sang at the Paris Opéra as Fricka and Mistress Quickly. She was a powerful singing actress, as can be seen in her superb performance as Madame Flora in Menotti's great 1951 film of *The Medium*. See THE MEDIUM (1948/1951), NOYE'S FLUDDE (1964), and THE OLD MAID AND THE THIEF (1949).

1950 Give Us Our Dream
Powers plays Jessamine, an ex-opera star who thinks she is still performing at La Scala, in this *Studio One* play on CBS television. She is helped by neighbor Lily (Josephine Hall). Paul Nickell directed. Black and white. 60 minutes. Video at the MTR.

1954 The Brain Machine
Powers plays Zydereen in this episode of the *Flash Gordon* television series. Black and white. 30 minutes.

PREMINGER, OTTO

Austrian/American director (1906–1986)

Otto Preminger, who began directing films during the 1930s, made his breakthrough in 1944 with *Laura*. He made three films with operatic content. His 1954 Bizet-derived *Carmen Jones* is undervalued but still impressive; his 1959 film of Gershwin's *Porgy and Bess* remains controversial and has been kept out of circulation;

and his 1963 *The Cardinal* features Austrian soprano Wilma Lipp. See CARMEN (1954), WILMA LIPP (1963), and PORGY AND BESS (1959).

PREVIN, ANDRÉ
American composer/conductor (1929–)

Composer/conductor/pianist André Previn, a musical master-of-all-trades, added opera to his repertory in 1998 when A STREETCAR NAMED DESIRE, libretto by Philip Littell based on the play by Tennessee Williams, was premiered by San Francisco Opera. Previn, born in Berlin, moved to California as a child and studied composing with Mario Castelnuovo-Tedesco and conducting with Pierre Monteux. Although *Streetcar* was his first opera, he had already written a number of music theater works including the musicals *Coco* (1969) and *The Good Companions* (1974). He conducted the orchestra for the 1959 film of PORGY AND BESS and shared an Oscar for scoring it. He was knighted in 1996 and was a Kennedy Center honoree in 1998.

2000 André Previn: The Kindness of Strangers
Tony Palmer's documentary film about Previn and his musical career was produced in connection with the production of *A Streetcar Named Desire*. Color. In English. 90 minutes. Arthaus DVD.

PREY, HERMANN
German baritone (1929–1998)

Berlin-born Hermann Prey made his debut in Wiesbaden in 1952 and became internationally popular during the 1960s, especially in Mozart operas. He has a most engaging personality as singer and actor, and this can be seen in his many videos. He is particularly notable as Figaro in the Ponnelle film versions of *The Barber of Seville* and *Le nozze di Figaro*. See IL BARBIERE DI SIVIGLIA (1959/1972), CARMINA BURANA (1975), COSÌ FAN TUTTE (1970), EUGENE ONEGIN (1962/1968), DIE FLEDERMAUS (1983), HÄNSEL UND GRETEL (1981), INTERMEZZO (1963), DIE MEISTERSINGER VON NÜRNBERG (1984), LE NOZZE DI FIGARO (1976), IL TURCO IN ITALIA (1971), UNDINE (1969), DER WILDSCHÜTZ (1973), ZAR UND ZIMMERMANN (1976), and DIE ZAUBERFLÖTE (1975 film).

1980 Hopscotch
Prey sings Figaro's ironic martial aria "Non più andrai" on the soundtrack of this amiable spy comedy as Walter Matthau works out his escape from murderous pursuers. Ronald Neame directed. Color. 104 minutes.

1989 Great Gala for Armenia
Prey is one of the performers at a gala concert held at the Bolshoi Opera in 1989 to raise money for victims of an earthquake in Armenia. See BOLSHOI.

PRICE, LEONTYNE
American soprano (1927–)

Leontyne Price, the preeminent Verdi soprano in America for many years, can be seen and heard in fine form performing in Verdi operas on video. She was born in Mississippi, studied at Juilliard, and made her debut in 1952 on Broadway singing St. Cecilia in Barber's *Four Saints in Three Acts*. The following year she played Bess in the Gershwin opera at the Ziegfeld Theatre. She made her opera house debut in San Francisco in 1957 as Madame Lidoine in *Dialogue des Carmelites*. She was Aida at Covent Garden in 1958 and La Scala in 1960, and she reached the Met in 1961 as Leonora in *Il trovatore*. She sang a wide series of roles at the Met, including Butterfly, Tosca, and Pamina and was Samuel Barber's Cleopatra in the premiere of *Antony and Cleopatra,* which opened the new Met. Price retired from the stage in 1985 after singing *Aida* at the Met. See AFRICAN-AMERICAN OPERA, AIDA (1958 film/1962 film/1985), ANTONY AND CLEOPATRA (1966 film), THE ART OF SINGING, CARNEGIE HALL (1991), DIALOGUES DES CARMÉLITES (1957), DON GIOVANNI (1960), THE ED SULLIVAN SHOW (1996), LA FORZA DEL DESTINO (1984), LOUISE (1987 film), METROPOLITAN OPERA (1953/1983), PORGY AND BESS (1998 film), WERNER SCHROETER (1986), TOSCA (1955), VERDI REQUIEM (1967), THE VOICE OF FIRESTONE (1950–1963), and DIE ZAUBERFLÖTE (1956).

1963–1967 Bell Telephone Hour
Video of the appearances Price made on *The Bell Telephone Hour* TV program between 1963 and 1967, performing arias from *Adriana Lecouvreur, Aida, La forza del destino,* and *Il trovatore.* Donald Voorhees conducts the Bell Telephone House Orchestra. Color. 32 minutes. VAI VHS.

1967 First Ladies of the Opera
Price appeared on this *Bell Telephone Hour* special on January 1, 1967, talking with Donald Voorhees and singing "Io son l'umile ancella" from *Adriana Lecouvreur* and "Pace, pace, mio Dio" from *La forza del destino.* See BELL TELEPHONE HOUR.

1980 Beverly Sills Farewell
Price is one of the guests at this all-star farewell party for Beverly Sills held at the New York City Opera. The setting is Act II of *Die Fledermaus* with Kitty Carlisle as Prince Orlofsky. See BEVERLY SILLS.

1980 Kennedy Center Honors

Price was a Kennedy Center honoree in 1980 and is shown watching a tribute to her career in this telecast of the event. Color. In English. 120 minutes.

1982 Leontyne Price with Zubin Mehta

Price performs at Avery Fisher Hall with Zubin Mehta conducting the New York Philharmonic Orchestra at the opening of the orchestra's 141st season. She sings arias from operas by Mozart ("Come scoglio" from *Così fan tutte*), Verdi ("Willow Song" and "Ave Maria" from *Otello*), and Strauss (final scene from *Salome*). The video, titled *Zubin Mehta, Leontyne Price,* was taped September 15, 1982. Color. 152 minutes. Paramount VHS.

1983 Leontyne Price in Montreal

Price gives a concert in Montreal with the Montreal Symphony Orchestra; the program includes arias by Mozart, Verdi, Gershwin, and Puccini. Evelyne Robidas filmed it for Canadian TV. Color. 60 minutes.

1983 Leontyne Price Sings Noël

Price gives a Christmas concert at Notre Dame Cathedral in Montreal and sings a range of carols with the Montreal Symphony Orchestra led by Charles Dutoit. Telecast by CBS December 18, 1983. Color. In English. 58 minutes. CBC video.

1987 Aria

Price is the most popular singer on the soundtrack of this episodic English opera film, heard singing in three operas. See ARIA, UN BALLO IN MASCHERA, LA FORZA DEL DESTINO, and TRISTAN UND ISOLDE.

1999 Magnolia

Price is heard singing the "Habanera" from *Carmen* on the soundtrack of this film about some odd people who live in Los Angeles. See CARMEN.

PRINCE IGOR

1890 opera by Borodin

This superb Russian opera by ALEXANDER BORODIN also provided the music for the popular pastiche operetta KISMET. *Prince Igor* (Kniaz Igor) revolves around the conflict between the Russians, led by Prince Igor, and the powerful Polovsti of Central Asia, who invaded Russia in the 12th century. While Igor is a prisoner of the Polovsti, his son falls in love with the daughter of the enemy Khan. Borodin based his libretto on a 12th-century epic poem. The music of the Polovtsian dances from the opera has become especially well-known. The opera was not fin-

ished when the composer died in 1887 but was completed by Rimsky-Korsakov and Glazunov.

1951 Bolshoi Opera

Russian highlights stage production: Vera Stroyeva (film director).

Cast: Alexander Pirogov (Prince Igor), Yevgeniya Smolenskaya (wife), Maxim Mikhailov (Khan Konchak), Olga Lepeshinskaya (Polovtsian dancer).

Black and white. In Russian. 45 minutes.

Comment: Condensed version of the opera filmed at the Bolshoi and used in film *Bolshoi Koncert*.

1969 Tikhomirov film

Soviet feature film: Roman Tikhomirov (director/screenplay), Isaak Glikman (screenplay), Gennady Provatorov (conductor, Kirov Theater Orchestra and Chorus), Mikhail Fokine (choreographer), Lenfilm (production studio).

Cast: Boris Khmelnitsky (Prince Igor, sung by Vladimir Kiniayev), Bimbolat Vatayev (Khan Konchak, sung by Yevgeny Nesterenko), Nelly Pshennaya (Princess Yaroslavna, sung by Tamara Milashkina), Boris Takarev (Vladimir, sung by Virgilius Noreika), Invetta Murgoyev (Konchakovna, sung by Irina Bogacheva).

Video: Corinth VHS/LD. Color. In Russian with English subtitles. 105 minutes.

Comment: Tikhomirov filmed this abridged widescreen version of the opera on location on the steppes with the actors dubbed by Kirov Opera singers. Many of the arias are presented naturally as interior monologues. Fokine's choreography of the Polovtsian dances was widely praised.

Prince Igor (Boris Khmelnitsky) and Princess Yaroslavna (Nelly Pshennaya) in Tikhomirov's film

1990 Royal Opera House

English stage production: Andrei Serban (director), Bernard Haitink (conductor, Royal Opera Orchestra and Chorus), Liviu Ciulei (set designer), Christopher Newton (adaptation of Fokine's choreography).

Cast: Sergei Leiferkus (Prince Igor), Anna Tomowa-Sintow (Princess Yaroslavna), Alexei Steblianko (Vladimir), Paata Burchuladze (Khan Konchak), Elena Zaremba (Konchakovna), Nicola Ghiuselev (Vladimir), Francis Egerton (Eroshka), Eric Garrett (Skula), Robin Leggate (Ovlur).

Video: London VHS/LD. Humphrey Burton (director). Color. In Russian with English subtitles. 194 minutes.

Related film

1955 Fire Maidens from Outer Space

The Polovtsian dances from *Prince Igor* provide seductive music for the lightly clad Fire Maidens of this unusual low-budget British science fiction movie. The maidens' exotic dance to Borodin's music has helped make this really bad space opera a cult classic. Cy Roth directed. Black and white. 80 minutes.

PRINCESS IDA

1884 comic opera by Gilbert and Sullivan

Princess Ida or Castle Adamant is a satire on the women's movement of the late 19th century. Princess Ida, the daughter of King Gama, is head of a women's university at Castle Adamant to which men are denied access. As a child she was betrothed to Hilarion, son of King Hildebrand. He and his friends disguise themselves as women and become students. After some tomfoolery and war, Ida and Hilarion finally get together. The opera, written in blank verse, has never been among the most popular GILBERT AND SULLIVAN operettas, although it is quite entertaining. Ken Russell staged a bizarre version of it at the English National Opera in 1994.

1982 Gilbert and Sullivan Collection series

English studio production: Terry Gilbert (director), Judith De Paul (producer), Alexander Faris (conductor, London Symphony Orchestra and Ambrosian Opera Chorus), Allan Cameron (set designer), George Walker (executive producer).

Cast: Nan Christie (Princess Ida), Laurence Dale (Hilarion), Frank Gorshin (King Gama), Neil Howlett (King Hildebrand), Anne Collins (Lady Blanche), Bernard Dickerson (Cyril), Richard Jackson (Florian).

Video: Braveworld (GB) VHS. Dave Heather (director). Color. In English. 117 minutes.

Related film

1999 Topsy-Turvy

The relatively unsuccessful premiere of *Princess Ida* in London in 1884 is featured at the beginning of this Mike Leigh film about the difficult relationship between Gilbert (Jim Broadbent) and Sullivan (Allan Corduner). The Overture and "If You Give Me Your Attention" are performed with Carl Davis conducting. See TOPSY-TURVY.

PRINTEMPS, YVONNE
French soprano (1894–1977)

Yvonne Printemps, the French soprano best known for her stage operettas and films, is very popular with opera enthusiasts. *Opera* magazine devoted an article to her centennial in 1994 and the *New Grove* laments that she never sang the roles of Manon and Louise. Her wonderful voice and charm can be experienced on video, most notably in the 1938 film of the Oscar Straus operetta TROIS VALSES. Yvonne (née Wigniole) acquired the nickname "Printemps" (springtime) as an ingenue. She rose to fame with Sacha Guitry, whom she married, and many composers wrote operettas especially for her. Her most famous stage appearances were in Reynaldo Hahn's *Mozart,* Noël Coward's *Conversation Piece,* and Straus's *Mariette* and *Trois valses.* Her second husband was Pierre Fresnay, who usually appeared on stage and screen with her. Printemps can also be seen as JACQUES OFFENBACH's favorite singer Hortense Schneider in the 1949 film *La valse de Paris.* See ADRIANA LECOUVREUR (1938 film) and REYNALDO HAHN.

Glamorous French film and stage star Yvonne Printemps is popular with opera enthusiasts.

1934 La dame aux camélias
Printemps plays Parisian courtesan Marguerite Gautier, whose life provided the basis for Verdi's opera *La traviata.* Printemps does not sing Verdi, however, but

music written for her by Reynaldo Hahn. Pierre Fresnay plays her lover Armand. Fernand Rivers directed under the supervision of Abel Gance. Black and white. In French. 118 minutes.

1939 Le duel
Printemps was directed by husband Pierre Fresnay in this film about a widow wrongly persuaded to enter a convent rather than marry. Black and white. In French. 84 minutes.

1943 Je suis avec toi
Printemps plays a wife who has doubts about the fidelity of her husband Pierre Fresnay. She pretends to be another woman and seduces him. Henri Decoin directed. Black and white. In French. 95 minutes.

1947 Les condamnés
Printemps plays a woman married to Pierre Fresnay who dies suspiciously after she falls in love with another man. Georges Lacambe directed. Black and white. In French. 100 minutes.

1951 Le voyage en Amérique
Printemps's last film includes a song written for her by Poulenc. She and Pierre Fresnay are a married couple in a French village who go to visit their daughter in America. Henri Lavorel directed. Black and white. In French. 91 minutes.

PRINZ VON HOMBURG, DER
1960 opera by Henze

Hans Werner Henze's opera *Der Prinz von Homburg* (The Prince of Homburg), libretto by Ingeborg Bachmann based on the play by Heinrich von Kleist, was suggested to him by Italian film/opera director Luchino Visconti. It contrasts the ideas of an aristocratic dreamer (Prince Friedrich) with the militaristic world in which he lives. His love for and relationship with Princess Natalie is central to the story with the Prince condemned to death for disobeying orders and the Princess determined to save him at any cost.

1994 Cuvillies Theatre, Munich
German stage production: Nikolaus Lehnhoff (director), Wolfgang Sawallisch (conductor, Bavarian State Orchestra), Gottfried Pilz (set designer).
Cast: Francois Le Roux (Prince Friedrich von Homburg), Mari Anne Häggander (Princess Natalie), William Cochran (Elector), Helga Dernesch (Elector's Wife), Claes-Håkon Ahnsjö (Count Hohenzollern), Hans Günter Nöcker (Dörfling).

Video: Arthaus DVD. Eckhart Schmidt (director). Color. In German with English subtitles. 105 minutes.

PRITCHARD, JOHN
English conductor (1921–1989)

Sir John Pritchard made his debut at Glyndebourne in 1951 with *Don Giovanni.* He remained associated with the festival for many years, and a number of his productions there were telecast and are on video, most notably his famous IDOMENEO (1974/1993 film). He also conducted at the Royal Opera, the Met, and other major operas houses, including especially Cologne, la Monnaie, and San Francisco. See Così FAN TUTTE (1975), DIDO AND AENEAS (1966), FALSTAFF (1976), MACBETH (1972), METROPOLITAN OPERA (1983), LE NOZZE DI FIGARO (1973), OTELLO (Rossini, 1988), and LA PIETRA DEL PARAGONE (1965).

PRODUCERS' SHOWCASE
1956 operatic television program

Sol Hurok produced this all-star television show showcasing major opera singers of the era. Leonard Warren sings the Prologue from *Pagliacci*, Zinka Milankov sings "Vissi d'arte" from *Tosca*, Roberta Peters sings Olympia's aria "Les oiseaux" from *Les contes d'Hoffmann*, Jan Peerce sings "Vesti la giubba" from *Pagliacci*, Marian Anderson sings spirituals, Blanche Thebom and Mildred Miller sing the Barcarolle duet from *Tales of Hoffmann*, and Risë Steven sings the Card Aria from *Carmen*. Max Rudolf conducted the orchestra, Herbert Graf directed the staging, and Kirk Browning directed the telecast on January 30, 1956. Black and white. 60 minutes. Video at the MTR.

PROKOFIEV, SERGEI
Russian composer (1891–1953)

Sergei Prokofiev is as important musically for film as for opera. He wrote some of the most powerful and influential film scores of all time for director SERGEI EISENSTEIN, and it has been argued that his music for IVAN THE TERRIBLE and *Alexander Nevsky* is operatic in effect and style, that these are effectively "opera films." His music for the film *Lieutenant Kije* is well known through an orchestral suite, and he also composed music for the popular 1936 film THE QUEEN OF SPADES. Prokofiev created a number of important stage operas that have been translated to the screen. The extraordinary THE LOVE FOR THREE ORANGES was written in the United States on commission and had its world premiere in Chicago. His epic opera WAR AND PEACE was given its American premiere on NBC television, and he appears as a character in the American movie version of the novel. His other popular operas include BETROTHAL IN A MONASTERY, THE GAMBLER, and THE FIERY ANGEL.

1956 War and Peace
Alberto Lolli plays Prokofiev in this American film of the novel directed by King Vidor and starring Henry Fonda and Audrey Hepburn. Color. In English. 208 minutes.

1961 Portrait of a Soviet Composer
Ken Russell's first biography for television was this portrait of Prokofiev. With this film, Russell began to experiment with editing film images to music, mostly newsreel footage in this case. Stills and stock footage are used as well as new material, but the BBC would not allow Russell to use an actor to portray the composer. Telecast June 18, 1961. Black and white. In English. 30 minutes.

1993 Prokofiev: The Prodigal Son
Portrait of the composer including performances of his works, archival footage, biographical reenactments, and stills. Color. In English. 92 minutes. Films for the Humanities & Sciences VHS.

1993 Peter and the Wolf: A Prokofiev Fantasy
Roy Hudd plays Prokofiev in this puppet version of the composer's famous symphonic tale for children. Sting narrates the story performed by Spitting Image Puppets, and Claudio Abbado conducts the Chamber Orchestra of Europe. Christopher Swann directed. Color. In English. 52 minutes.

PROMPTER, THE
1999 Norwegian film with opera content

In the romantic comedy *The Prompter* (*Sufflosen* in Norwegian), a woman prompter (Hege Schøyen) is rehearsing a production of *Aida* at the Norwegian National Opera, and her real life seems to be reflected in the opera story. She is about to marry a divorced doctor (Seven Nordin) who is very controlling and even wants to chose her wedding dress. When she moves her own things into his house, they are put away in the basement. He doesn't like her working at night at opera rehearsals, and he never visits her at the theater. The marriage is starting to fall apart when she meets a friendly good-humored Swedish tuba player (Philip Zandén), but she resists involvement. She also has a lot of problems with the soprano singing Aida (Liv Gunhild Tandberg), who can't seem to learn her lines properly or pronounce Italian words correctly. Things come to a head when the doctor's ex-wife has an accident, and he moves her back into the house in a wheelchair. At the opening night of Aida, the soprano stumbles so badly that the prompter crawls out of her prompter's box to assail her. She then leaves the opera house followed by the tuba player, and they walk off together into who knows what future. Radames is played by Richard Edgar-Wilson and Anne-Lise Bernsten is Amneris with Carlo Barsotti as the Italian stage director. Harald Gunnar Paalgard was the cinematographer, and Hilde Heier wrote and directed the film. *The Prompter* has won several awards at film festivals. Color. In Norwegian with English subtitles. 96 minutes. Universal Laser & Video DVD.

PUCCINI, GIACOMO
Italian composer (1858–1924)

Filmmakers love to use Puccini's music in their movies, presumably because there are few more evocative and memorable melodies. Songwriters for the first half of the century, including many in Hollywood, made Puccini their role model, and his operas were filmed even during the early silent era. Puccini, who was born in Lucca into a musical family and studied with composer Amilcare Ponchielli, had success with his first opera, LE VILLI, which premiered at La Scala in 1884. His second opera, the 1889 *Edgar,* was a failure, but the 1893 MANON LESCAUT made him famous. LA BOHÈME in 1896 and TOSCA in 1900 won Puccini international acclaim, and they remain among the most popular operas ever composed. Equally popular is MADAMA BUTTERFLY although it was badly received when it premiered in 1904 and was not a success until Puccini revised it. LA FANCIULLA DEL WEST, which premiered at the Met in 1910, has never had the popularity of the big three. Puccini's 1917 light opera LA RONDINE is rarely staged today but the 1918 trilogy IL TRITTICO remains popular. Puccini's last opera TURANDOT, premiered after he died in 1924, has also become an audience favorite.

1952 Puccini
Gabriele Ferzetti plays Puccini in Carmine Gallone's Italian feature film *Puccini*. Marta Toren is his wife Elvira, Carlo Duse is librettist/composer Arrigo Boito, Oscar Andreani is librettist Giuseppe Giacosa, and René Clermont is librettist Luigi Illica. The film, which includes many opera scenes, features Nelly Corradi in *Madama Butterfly,* Gino Sinimberghi in *La bohème* and *Manon Lescaut,* and the voices of Beniamino Gigli, Giulio Neri, Antonietta Stella, Rosanna Carteri, Dino Lo Patto, Dea Koronoff, and Gino Penno. The original American release title was *Two Hearts Have I* but it is now called simply *Puccini*. Color. In Italian. 98 minutes. Bel Canto Society VHS (in dubbed English)/Opera Dubs VHS.

1954 Casa Ricordi
Puccini (Gabriele Ferzetti) is inspired to write *La bohème* by a girl he meets in a shop, but she dies of TB before the premiere at which Renata Tebaldi sings Mimì's deathbed aria. At least that is what it says in this film about the Ricordi opera publishing firm. See RICORDI.

1984 Puccini
Tony Palmer's British film, which stars Robert Stephens as Puccini, centers around a famous scandal that affected his career. His wife accused a maid of having an affair with the composer, and the girl, who was innocent and a virgin, killed herself. Virginia McKenna is Elvira Puccini, Judith Howarth is the maid, Rupert Graves is Puccini's son, and Ronald Pickup is Giulio Ricordi. The film, written by Charles Wood, is intercut with rehearsal scenes of a Scottish Opera production of *Turandot* directed by Palmer with Judith Howart and Ashley Putnam. Color. In English. 113 minutes. Home Vision VHS.

1987 La famiglia Ricordi
Massimo Ghini plays Puccini in this four-part TV miniseries about the Italian opera publishing family. See RICORDI.

1989 Opera Favorites by Puccini
Compilation video featuring scenes from Puccini operas at the Royal Opera House and the Arena di Verona. The London operas are *La bohème* with Ileana Cotrubas and *Manon Lescaut* with Kiri Te Kanawa. The Verona operas are *Tosca* with Eva Marton, *Madama Butterfly* with Raina Kabaivanska, and *Turandot* with Ghena Dimitrova. Color. In Italian with English subtitles. 59 minutes. HBO VHS.

1996 Famous Composers: Giacomo Puccini
Documentary about the life and music of the composer featuring excerpts from his works. Color. 30 minutes. Kultur VHS.

1997 Great Composers: Puccini
BBC documentary about the composer produced by Alan Sievewright and directed by Chris Hunt as a segment of the seven-composer series *Great Composers*. It follows him from childhood to fame, from first opera to obsession with librettos. It includes opera extracts conducted by Richard Buckley with Julia Migenes as Tosca and Manon Lescaut, Leontina Vaduva as Mimì and Madama Butterfly, and José Cura as their tenor partner. Kenneth Branagh narrates. Color. In English. 59 minutes. Warner (GB) DVD (with biographies of Tchaikovsky and Mahler).

1999 The Annihilation of Fish
Poinsettia (Lynn Redgrave) claims to be having a torrid affair with Puccini, even though he's been dead for 75 years. She insists on singing arias from his operas, loudly, often, and out of key. When she meets the equally imaginative Fish (James Earl Jones), who's been wrestling with an imaginary demon for many years, it's love at, well, second sight. Charles Burnett directed. Color. In English. 90 minutes.

PUNCH AND JUDY
1968 opera by Birtwistle

HARRISON BIRTWISTLE's riddles-and-rituals work *Punch and Judy* is not an opera for children but a stylized drama for adults that uses the famous puppet show as departure point. Stephen Pruslin's libretto has Punch killing people every season and then going in search of Pretty Polly: in the summer he kills Judy and the baby, in the autumn the doctor and the lawyer, in the winter his nemesis Choregos, and in the spring the hangman Jack Ketch. The opera premiered at the Aldeburgh Festival in 1968 and was revived very successfully by the Opera Factory in London in 1982. The music is said to be modeled on Bach's *St. Matthew Passion*.

1984 Opera Factory, London
English stage production: David Freeman (director), Daniel Paul (conductor, Opera Factory Ensemble), Belinda Scarlett (costume designer).
Cast: Titus Graham, Omar Ebrahim, Hilary Western, Marie Angel, Nigel Robson, Roger Bryson.
Video at the NFTA, London. Telecast September 12, 1984, on Channel 4. Derek Bailey (director). Color. In English. 103 minutes.

Related film

1980 Griffiths/Quay brothers puppet film
Birtwistle's opera provides the basis for this powerful puppet film founded on the traditional Punch and Judy show. It was created for the Arts Council by Keith Griffiths in collaboration with brothers Timothy and Stephen Quay. Birtwistle's music is played by the London Sinfonietta conducted by David Atherton. Color. 12 minutes.

PUPPET OPERAS

Quite a number of operas have been created for puppets and marionettes, and also a number of videos are available with puppets starring in repertory operas. Puppet operas, which are not necessarily for children, have a long and interesting history, including such modern operas as Respighi's LA BELLA DORMENTE NEL BOSCO,

Falla's EL RETABLO DE MAESE PEDRO, Satie's GENEVIÈVE DE BRABANT, and Birtwistle's PUNCH AND JUDY. Opera puppet companies presenting repertory operas to live audiences exist in several cities around the world, and some have put their work on video. The best known is probably the SALZBURG MARIONETTE THEATRE in Austria, which has issued videos of Mozart operas with introductions by Peter Ustinov. The Düsseldorf Puppet Theatre telecast six operas in 1990 in a series titled *Tales From the Puppet Opera,* including *The Magic Flute.* Created especially for TV and video were Joan Sutherland's series *Who's Afraid of Opera?* (eight operas with Sutherland singing the principal roles), *The Maestro's Company* series (puppets performing four operas), and TV personality Shari Lewis presenting opera scenes with hand puppets (see below for details on these). There is also a full-length 1954 feature film of HÄNSEL UND GRETEL featuring electronic puppets.

1947 Largo al Factotum
Fernando Cerchio's Italian puppet film dramatizes Figaro's aria "Largo al factotum" from *The Barber of Seville.* Black and white. 7 minutes.

1950 Magie di Figaro
Figaro's Magic is an Italian marionette film by Franco Cagnoli based on Rossini's *The Barber of Seville.* Color. 9 minutes.

1972–1973 Who's Afraid of Opera?
Joan Sutherland stars in eight 30-minute highlight versions of operas intended for young audiences, including operas she did not perform on stage such as Offenbach's LA PÉRICHOLE and Thomas's MIGNON. Sutherland tells the story of the opera to three puppets and performs the principal role on a small stage with supporting singers. The dialogue is in English, but the arias are sung in their original languages. The other operas in the series are IL BARBIERE DI SIVIGLIA, FAUST, LA FILLE DU RÉGIMENT, LUCIA DI LAMMERMOOR, RIGOLETTO, and LA TRAVIATA. The music is played by the London Symphony Orchestra conducted by Richard Bonynge with sets designed by George Djurkovic. The puppets were created by Larry Berthelson and the screenplays written by Claire Merrill. The series was devised and produced by Nathan Kroll. Color. Each opera is about 30 minutes. Kultur VHS.

1984 Maestro's Company Puppets
The Australian Maestro's Company taped highlights versions of four operas with puppets who sing with the recorded voices of major opera singers. The story involves two children who discover the puppets rehearsing their operas under an old theater and get to watch. The dialogue is in English, but the arias are sung in Italian. William Fitzwater directed, and Jim George produced the videos for the series created by Marcia Hatfield. The operas are IL BARBIERE DI SIVIGLIA, HÄNSEL UND GRETEL, RIGOLETTO, and LA TRAVIATA.

1984 Kooky Classics: Shari Lewis
Children's TV star Shari Lewis features operas and classical music in this video in which she appears with her hand puppets Lamb Chop, Hush Puppy, Charley Horse, et al. There is music from *Le nozze di Figaro* and *William Tell* and a version of *Carmen* with Lewis playing all the roles. Larry Granger conducts the orchestra. Color. In English. 55 minutes. MGM-UA VHS.

PURCELL, HENRY
English composer (1658–1695)

Henry Purcell is considered the most important English opera composer before the 20th century although this is hardly fair to the comic and light opera masters such as Sullivan, Balfe, Benedict, and Wallace. His DIDO AND AENEAS (1689), considered the first British opera, has risen in popularity in recent years and is now on video. His other musical stage works, such as THE FAIRY QUEEN, THE INDIAN QUEEN, and *King Arthur,* are usually described as "semi-operas," that is, plays with substantial musical segments. His dramatic biblical work SAUL AND THE WITCH OF ENDOR has also been staged.

1995 England, My England
Michael Ball stars as Purcell in Tony Palmer's postmodern film about Purcell written by John Osborne and Charles Wood. Simon Callow plays both King Charles II and the actor who is portraying him who wants to find out more. Robert Stephens plays Purcell's librettist John Dryden, and there are opera scenes with John Eliot Gardiner conducting. Color. In English. 90 minutes. Warner Classics (GB) VHS.

PURITANI, I
1835 opera by Bellini

VINCENZO BELLINI's last opera *I puritani* (The Puritans), libretto by Carlo Pepoli, is a tragic love story set in Plymouth, England, during the English Civil War. Elvira, daughter of Puritan governor-general Gualtiero, is abandoned at the altar by Arturo when duty forces him to leave her to save the queen's life. Elvira feels betrayed and goes famously mad in one of the most difficult mad scenes in opera. The opera was made popular again in recent years in productions starring Maria Callas and Joan Sutherland, but Callas was never filmed in the role.

1985 Australian Opera

Australian stage production: Robert Helpmann (director), Richard Bonynge (conductor, Elizabethan Sydney Orchestra and Australian Opera Chorus).

Cast: Joan Sutherland (Elvira), Anson Austin (Arturo), Donald Shanks (Giorgio), Michael Lewis (Riccardo), Rosemary Gunn (Enrichetta).

Video: House of Opera/Lyric DVD/VHS. Color. In Italian. 155 minutes.

1985 Bregenz Festival

Austrian stage production: Gilbert Deflo (director), Gianfranco Masina (conductor, Vienna Symphony and Vienna Volksoper and Bregenz Festival Chorus), Carlo Tommasi (set/costume designer).

Cast: Edita Gruberova (Elvira), Salvatore Fisichella (Arturo), Giorgio Zancanaro (Riccardo), Dimitri Kavrakos (Giorgio), Mariana Cioromila (Enrichetta), Carlo Del Bosco (Gualtiero).

Video: Premiere Opera VHS. Franz Kabelka (director). Color. In Italian. 155 minutes.

1986 Teatro Petruzzelli, Bari

Italian stage production: Pier Luigi Pizzi (director, set/costume designer), Gabriele Ferro (conductor, Orchestra Sinfonica Siciliana and Teatro Petruzzelli Chorus).

Cast: Katia Ricciarelli (Elvira), Chris Merritt (Arturo), Robert Scandiuzzi (Giorgio), Ambrogio Riva (Gualtiero), Eleonora Jankovic (Enrichetta).

Video: Lyric/Opera Dubs VHS. Telecast September 4, 1986. Renato Zanetto (director). Color. In Italian. 166 minutes.

Related films

1908 Cinemafono Pagliej

CINEMAFONO PAGLIEJ, an Italian sound-on-disc company specializing in opera films, screened a film titled *I puritani* on April 19, 1908, in Pisa; it featured the duet "Suoni la tromba." Black and white. In Italian. About 5 minutes.

1933 La canzone del sole

Italian tenor Giacomo Lauri-Volpi sings Arturo's cavatina "A te, o cara, amor talora" from *I puritani* on stage at a formal concert at the beginning of this fiction film. See LA CANZONE DEL SOLE.

1987 The Dead

John Huston's adaptation of James Joyce's tale about a Dublin party features Elvira's aria "Son vergin vezzosa." It is sung in English as "Arrayed for the Bridal" by elderly Aunt Julia (Cathleen Delany) over a montage of mementos of her life. Color. 83 minutes.

1982 Fitzcarraldo

Werner Herzog's film *Fitzcarraldo* ends with a whimsical production of *I puritani* with orchestra and singers positioned on a Brazilian river boat. Isabel Jimenez de Cisneros is Elvira and Liborio Simonella is Arturo with the music performed by the Lima Repertory Symphony Orchestra. See FITZCARRALDO.

PUTNAM, ASHLEY
American soprano (1952–)

Ashley Putnam, who began her career in 1976 singing Lucia in Norfolk, has continued to be a standout in *bel canto* operas, but she is also known for her performances in modern works, including Moore's THE MOTHER OF US ALL (1976), Musgrave's *Mary, Queen of Scots* (1978), Weill's STREET SCENE (1994), and Thomson's FOUR SAINTS IN THREE ACTS (1996). Putnam made her first appearance in Europe in 1978 singing Musetta at Glyndebourne and can be seen on two Glyndebourne Festival videos, ARABELLA (1984) and LA CLEMENZA DI TITO (1991), and an Opéra de Lyon production of MITRIDATE (1983). She sings in the DON GIOVANNI sections of the Belgian film *Babel Opera* (1985) and the TURANDOT sections of the English film *Puccini* (1984). She made her belated debut at the Met in 1991 as Marguerite in Faust.

Q

QUEEN OF FRUIT
1993 TV opera by Scherrer

Millicent's fruiterer husband is about to be crowned King of Fruit. He engages in a duel with her lover, a taxidermist, in which the weapons are pieces of fruit and dead birds. She has to decide who wins. The English TV opera *Queen of Fruit* was written, composed, and directed by Swiss-born Dominik Scherrer while he was a film student at the London College of Printing, with help from Channel 4 television. He had already made a number of experimental films, but this was his first go at opera.

1993 Scherrer film
English TV film: Dominik Scherrer (director/screenplay), music performed by the Béla Bartók Chamber Orchestra of Budapest.

Cast: Lena Lovich (Millicent), Simon Packham (Husband), Martin Turner (Lover).

Telecast June 10, 1993, on Channel 4. Color. In English. 20 minutes.

QUEEN OF SPADES, THE
1890 opera by Tchaikovsky

Hermann loves Lisa, but he is a soldier without money while she is engaged to a prince. When he tries to force the Old Countess, Lisa's grandmother, to tell him her secret for winning at cards, he frightens her to death; however, she returns as a ghost and gives him the secret. He becomes obsessed with gambling, causes Lisa to drown herself, and loses all his money when the Queen of Spades turns up instead of the expected Ace. PYOTR TCHAIKOVSKY's brother Modest wrote most of the libretto for his popular ghost story opera based on Pushkin's novella *Pikovaya Dama* (The Queen of Spades). Most of the film and TV versions of the opera are abridgments of the stage opera running time of around 165 minutes. The opera is sometimes referred to by its French title as *Pique Dame*.

1952 NBC Opera Theatre
American TV production: Charles Polacheck (director), Samuel Chotzinoff (producer), Peter Herman Adler (conductor, NBC Opera Theatre Orchestra and Chorus), Carl Kent (set designer), Jean Karsavina (English translation).

Cast: David Poleri (Hermann), Margarita Zambarana (Lisa), Winifred Heidt (Countess), Ralph Herbert (Tomsky), Guy Tano (Doctor-Narrator).

Video at the MTR. Kirk Browning (director). Black and white. In English. 60 minutes.

Comment: Heavily abridged English version in a revised format with the story told in flashbacks.

1960 Tikhomirov film
Soviet feature film: Roman Tikhomirov (director/screenplay), Georgi and Sergei Vasilyev (screenplay), Yevgeny Shapiro (cinematographer), Yevgeny Svetlanov (conductor, Bolshoi Theater Orchestra and Choir).

Cast: Oleg Strizhenov (Hermann, sung by Zurab Andzhaparidze), Olga Krasina (Lisa, sung by Tamara Milashkina), Yelena Polevitskaya (Countess, sung by Sofia Preobrazhenskaya), Vadim Medvedev (Tomsky, sung by Vadim Nechipaylo), V. Kulik (Yeletsky, sung by Evgeny Kibkalo), Olga Krasina (Pauline, sung by Larissa Avdeeva).

Video: Corinth VHS/LD. Color. In Russian with English subtitles. 105 minutes.

Comment: Much abridged but still enjoyable film version splendidly shot on location with the actors dubbed by Bolshoi Opera singers.

1971 NET Opera
American TV production: Kirk Browning (director), Peter Herman Adler (conductor, Boston Symphony Orchestra), Francis Mahard (set designer).

Cast: Vahan Khanzadian (Hermann), Evelyn Mandac (Lisa), Jennie Tourel (Countess), John Reardon (Tomsky), Mary Lou Falcone (Masha), James Fleetwood (Surin), Jack Trussel (Narumov).

Video: House of Opera VHS. Telecast February 28, 1971, on PBS. Kirk Browning (director). Color. In English. 90 minutes.

Comment: Much abridged TV adaptation but interesting cast and production.

1983 Bolshoi Opera
Russian stage production: Boris Pokrovsky (director), Yuri Simonov (conductor, Bolshoi Opera Orchestra and Chorus).

Cast: Vladimir Atlantov (Hermann), Tamara Milashkina (Lisa), Elena Obraztsova (Countess), Yuri Mazurok (Yeletsky), Yuri Grigoriev (Tomsky), Ludmila Semtschuk (Pauline).

Video: Bel Canto Society/Kultur VHS. A. Barannikov (director). Color. In Russian with English subtitles. 174 minutes.

1992 Vienna State Opera

Austrian stage production: Seiji Ozawa (conductor, Veinna State Opera Orchestra and Chorus).

Cast: Vladimir Atlantov (Hermann), Mirella Freni (Lisa), Martha Mödl (Countess), Vladimir Chernov (Yeletsky), Sergei Leiferkus (Tomsky), Vesselina Kasarova (Pauline).

Video: Bel Canto Society VHS. Color. In Russian with English subtitles. 172 minutes.

***1992 Kirov Opera

Russian stage production: Yuri Temirkanov (director), Valery Gergiev (conductor, Kirov Opera Orchestra and Chorus), Igor Ivanov (set designer).

Cast: Gegam Gregoriam (Hermann), Maria Guleghina (Lisa), Ludmilla Filatova (Countess), Olga Borodina (Pauline), Sergei Leiferkus (Count Tomsky), Alexander Gergalov (Prince Yeletsky).

Video: Philips DVD/VHS/LD. Brian Large (director). Color. In Russian. 180 minutes.

Comment: An outstanding Russian production, finely conducted, played, sung, and staged.

***1992 Glyndebourne Festival

English stage production: Graham Vick (director), Sir Andrew Davis (conductor, London Philharmonic Orchestra and Glyndebourne Chorus), Richard Hudson (set/costume designer).

Cast: Yuri Marusin (Hermann), Nancy Gustafson (Lisa), Felicity Palmer (Countess), Sergei Leiferkus (Tomsky), Dimitri Kharitonov (Yeletsky), Marie-Ange Todorovitch Pauline).

Video: Image Entertainment/Arthaus (GB) DVD/Home Vision VHS. Peter Maniura (director). Color. In Russian with English subtitles. 168 minutes.

Comment: An outstanding English production, finely conducted, played, sung, and staged.

1999 Metropolitan Opera

American stage production: Elijah Moshinsky (director), Valery Gergiev (conductor, Metropolitan Opera Orchestra and Chorus), Mark Thompson (set/costume designer).

Cast: Plácido Domingo (Hermann), Galina Gorchakova (Lisa), Elizabeth Söderström (Countess), Dmitri Hvorostovsky (Yeletsky), Nikolai Putilin (Tomsky), Olga Borodina (Pauline).

Taped April 15, 1999; telecast September 8, 1999, on PBS. Brian Large (director). Color. In Russian with English subtitles. 180 minutes.

Comment: Domingo sings the role of Hermann in Russian for the first time with a mostly Russian cast and Russian conductor

Early/related films

1906 Gaumont film

Pique Dame is a French sound film made for the Gaumont Phonoscènes series and shown with a synchronized aria on a recording. Alice Guy-Blaché directed. Black and white. About 3 minutes.

1910 Cardynin film

Pikovaya Dama is a Russian narrative film based on the Pushkin story and the libretto of the opera. P. Birjukov plays Herman, A. Goncharova is Lisa, and Petr Cardynin directed. Black and white. Silent. About 15 minutes.

1910 Deutsche Bioscop film

German narrative film of the Pushkin story made by the Deutsche Bioscop Company. Black and white. Silent. About 15 minutes.

1911 Cines film

Italian silent film of the Pushkin story made for the Cines studio and screened with the opera music played live. Black and white. Silent. About 12 minutes.

1913 Celio film

Leda Gys and Hesperia star in this Italian film version of the Pushkin story made for the Celio studio and shown with the opera music played live. Black and white. Silent. About 15 minutes.

1916 Protazanov film

This famous Russian silent film, directed by Yakov Protazanov, was based on the Pushkin story but it was shown in theaters with the opera music. Ivan Mozhukhin is Hermann, Vera Orlova is Lisa, E. Shebujeva is the Old Countess, Tamara Duvan is the young Countess, and P. Pavlov is her husband. The film has recently been restored. Black and white. About 63 minutes.

1922 Fejos film

Hungarian narrative feature film version of the Pushkin story written and directed by Pal Fejos. Black and white. Silent. About 70 minutes.

1925 Fraser film

American feature film of the Pushkin story directed by Harry Fraser and starring Gordon Clifford and Charlotte Pierce. Black and white. Silent. About 70 minutes.

1927 Rasumny film

German feature film version of the story titled *Pique Dame, Das Geheimnis der Alten Grafin*. It was directed by Alexander Rasumny and starred Rudolf Forster and Jenny Jugo. Black and white. Silent. About 70 minutes.

1936 Romm film
Unfinished Soviet film of the story directed by Mikhail Romm. Sergei Prokofiev wrote a score for it in 24 scenes, 20 of which he orchestrated. When the film was abandoned in 1938 for political reasons, Prokofiev saved the lyrical theme he had composed for Lisa and used it as the slow movement of his Fifth Symphony.

1937 Ozep film
La dame de pique is a famous French film based on the Pushkin story and directed by Fedor Ozep. Pierre Blanchar plays Hermann, Madeleine Ozeray is Lisa, and Marguerite Moreno is the Old Countess. Black and white. In French. 100 minutes.

1949 Dickinson film
The Queen of Spades is an excellent British film version of the Pushkin story directed by Thorold Dickinson. Anton Walbrook plays Hermann, Yvonne Mitchell is Lisa, and Edith Evans is the Old Countess. Black and white. In English. 95 minutes.

1966 Keigel film
French film of the Pushkin story directed by Leonard Keigel. Michael Subor is Hermann, Simone Bach is Lisa, and Dita Parlo is the Old Countess. Color. In French. 92 minutes.

1970 Tchaikovsky
This stolid Soviet biography includes a staged scene from *The Queen of Spades*. Innokenti Smoktunovsky plays Tchaikovsky. See PYOTR TCHAIKOVSKY.

1972 Morgenstern film
Polish TV film of the story titled *Dama Pikowa* directed by Janusz Morgenstern. Jan Englert and Halina Mikolajska star. Color. In Polish. 90 minutes.

QUESTIONS OF ABRAHAM, THE
1973 TV opera by Laderman

Abraham, founder of the Hebrew people, was said to have lived to the age of 175 and had many questions and doubts toward the end of his life. Ezra Laderman's television opera *The Questions of Abraham*, libretto by Joseph Darion based on the life of the biblical patriarch, was commissioned and premiered by CBS with a cast that included mezzo-soprano Hilda Harris. It was telecast in color by CBS Television on September 30, 1973. Color. In English. 50 minutes.

QUIET PLACE, A
1983 opera by Bernstein

LEONARD BERNSTEIN's opera A Quiet Place, libretto by Stephen Wadsworth, is a sequel to his 1952 TROUBLE IN TAHITI and incorporates the earlier opera. The members of a dysfunctional American family meet for the first time in 20 years at the funeral of wife/mother Dinah who has died in a car accident. Husband Sam, son Junior, daughter Dede, and son-in-law François remember events about her and each other. The next morning they meet in her garden, her "quiet place," and effect a reconciliation.

1986 Vienna State Opera
Austrian stage production: Stephen Wadsworth (director), Leonard Bernstein (conductor, ORF Austrian Radio/Television Symphony Orchestra).
Cast: Chester Ludgin (Old Sam), Edward Crafts (Young Sam), Wendy White (Dinah), Beverly Morgan (Dede), Peter Kazaras (François), John Brandstetter (Junior), Theodor Uppman (Bill), Jean Craft (Susie), John Kuether (Doc), Clarity James (Mrs. Doc), Louise Edeiken, Mark Thomsen, Kurt Ollmann (Chorus Trio).
Video: Custom Opera VHS. Hugo Käch (director). Telecast April 12, 1986. Color. In English. 163 minutes.

QUILICO, GINO
Canadian baritone (1955–)

Gino Quilico, son of baritone Louis Quilico, made his debut at Toronto's Macmillan Theatre in June 1977 as Mr. Gobineau in *The Medium* and reprised the role in 1978 on Canadian television. He made his first appearance in Paris in 1980, sang at Covent Garden in 1983, and went to the Metropolitan in 1987. He can be seen on several videos, most notably as Figaro in two operas, in THE BARBER OF SEVILLE (1988) opposite Cecilia Bartoli, and in THE GHOSTS OF VERSAILLES (1992) opposite Teresa Stratas. See LA BOHÈME (1988/1989), CARMEN (1991), LA CENERENTOLA (1988), DON PASQUALE (1991), FAUST (1985), ORFEO (1985), and ROMÉO ET JULIETTE (1982).

QUILICO, LOUIS
Canadian baritone (1929–)

Louis Quilico, father of baritone Gino Quilico, studied in Rome and New York and made his debut with New York City Opera in 1951. He sang at Covent Garden in 1961 and went to the Met in 1972 as Golaud in *Pelléas and Mélisande*. He became a Met regular and an important member of the Canadian Opera Company. His operas on video include UN BALLO IN MASCHERA (1980), LA

CENERENTOLA (1979), DON CARLO (1983), PAGLIACCI (1955), and RIGOLETTO (1981).

1954–1956 Vickers Sings Verdi and Puccini
Quilico sings with Vickers on this highlights video that features excerpts from operas presented on Canadian television. See JON VICKERS.

1965 Renata Tebaldi and Louis Quilico Concert
Quilico and Tebaldi join forces in a Canadian TV concert. Quilico sings the finale of *Il Tabarro,* Tebaldi sings "O mio babbino caro" from *Gianni Schicchi,* and they sing together in the finale of Act II of *Tosca.* Ernesto Barbini conducts the CBC Festival Orchestra. Color. 30 minutes. VAI VHS.

R

RABBIT OF SEVILLE, THE
1950 animated film with opera content

Bugs Bunny has a grand time to Rossini's music from *The Barber of Seville,* including the Overture and "Largo al factotum," in one of the great opera cartoons. The film begins with hunter Elmer Fudd chasing Bugs across the stage of the Hollywood Bowl as the orchestra tunes up for the opera. When the curtain goes up, Bugs is dressed as a barber, and Elmer realizes that he is the customer. Bugs sings to Elmer to the tune of the *Barber* Overture ("Let me cut your mop") as he shaves him, plays games with his bald head, and uses Figaro Fertilizer to grow flowers on it. This is too much for Elmer, and they have a John Woo–style face-off with bigger and bigger axes and guns. It ends happily when Bugs offers Elmer flowers and a ring, and they get married. Chuck Jones directed this fine entertainment, Michael Maltese wrote the delightful script, Mel Blanc provided the voices, and Carl Stalling arranged and conducted the music. Warner Bros. Color. 7 minutes.

RABENALT, ARTHUR MARIA
Austrian film director (1905–)

Vienna-born Arthur Maria Rabenalt, who had a great love of operetta and even wrote a history of German operettas on film and TV, was an important stage director as well as a filmmaker. He began making films in 1934 and directed more than 50, many based on popular operettas with stars such as Teresa Stratas. Several were shot in German and French versions. His operetta films include DIE FÖRSTER-CHRISTL (1952), EINE FRAU, DIE WEISS, WAS SIE WILL (1957), DAS LAND DES LÄCHELNS (1973), DER LETZTE WALZER (1953), DER VOGELHÄNDLER (1953), DER ZAREWITSCH (1954/1973), and DER ZIGEUNERBARON (1954/1975). Rabenalt also made films with bass-baritone MICHAEL BOHNEN (1940), tenor LEO SLEZAK (1936), and tenor FERRUCCIO TAGLIAVINI (1959).

RACHEL LA CUBANA
1974 TV opera by Henze

HANS WERNER HENZE's TV opera is a Brecht/Weill–like 12-tone memory piece, the reminiscences of a Cuban cabaret singer during the last days of the Battista regime. Rachel is portrayed by two women (only young Rachel sings), and all three lovers are played by the same baritone. The opera was commissioned by producer Peter Herman Adler for NET Opera on National Educational Television, but its production costs grew to $505,000, four times its budget. This huge deficit caused the demise of the opera series, and director Kirk Browning quit the series because of problems associated with it. The German title is *La Cubana, oder Ein Leben für die Kunst.*

1974 NET Opera
American TV production: Kirk Browning (director), Peter Herman Adler (producer), Hans Werner Henze (conductor, NET Opera Orchestra), Rouben Ter-Arutunian (set/costume designer).

Cast: Lee Venora (Young Rachel), Lili Darvas (Old Rachel), Alan Titus (Eusebio/Paco/Federico), Susanne Marsee (Lucile/Rosita), Olympia Dukakis (Ofelia), Ronald Young (Yarini/Alberto), Robert Rounseville, Alan Crofoot.

Video at the MTR. Telecast March 4, 1974. Color. In English. 90 minutes.

RACHMANINOFF, SERGEI
Russian composer/pianist/conductor (1873–1943)

Sergei Rachmaninoff (or Rakhmaninov) died in Beverly Hills, which seems appropriate as his music had had a great influence on Hollywood film scores. While he is better known for piano and orchestra compositions, his very first opera, ALEKO, written when he was only 19, was produced at the Bolshoi. It became a popular success when Chaliapin sang the title role in St. Petersburg, and it is still in the Russian repertory; it is his only opera on video. However, he also created the role of the pianist in Rimsky-Korsakov's opera MOZART AND SALIERI in 1898. In addition, Rachmaninoff conducted the premieres of many Russian operas at the Bolshoi.

RAIMONDI, RUGGERO
Italian bass-baritone (1941–)

Ruggero Raimondi is known to moviegoers as the star of two of the finest opera films, the irresistible Don in Joseph Losey's DON GIOVANNI (1978) and the full-of-himself bullfighter Escamillo in Francesco Rosi's CARMEN (1984). He also won praise for his Scarpia in the *Live From Rome* TV TOSCA (1992) and for his Boris in the Polish film of BORIS GODUNOV (1989). As his films demonstrate, he has a strong screen presence as well as a fine resonant voice. Raimondi, who was born in Bologna, made his debut at Spoleto in 1964 as Colline in *La bohème*. He soon began to sing at La Scala, acquired international fame in 1969 as Don Giovanni at Glyndebourne, and went to the Met in 1970 in *Ernani*. Raimondi, who is also noted for his fine performances as Don Quixote and Méphistophélès, is featured on a large number of opera videos. See BORIS GODUNOV (1980), CARMEN (1980/La Scala 1984), CINÉPÉRA, JOSÉ CARRERAS (1991), DON GIOVANNI (1992), ERNANI (1983), LA FAVORITA (1971), GLYNDEBOURNE (1992), MOZART REQUIEM (1994), LE NOZZE DI FIGARO (1985/1992), METROPOLITAN OPERA (1983), MOZART REQUIEM (1994), NABUCCO (1979), OPERA STARS IN CONCERT, PARIS (1989), GIOACHINO ROSSINI (1985), TOSCA (2001), GIUSEPPE VERDI (2001), VERDI REQUIEM (1970/1982), VERONA (1988), SHIRLEY VERRETT (1985), IL VIAGGIO A REIMS (1984/1988), and VIENNA (1993).

1991 Ruggero Raimondi
French film about Raimondi showing him on stage at opera houses, talking about his career, and interacting with directors and conductors. In his native Bologna he is seen rehearsing *Don Carlo* with conductor Myung Whun Ching. At the Rome Opera, he sings the title role in Rossini's *Moses in Egypt* under the direction of Pier Luigi Pizzi. In Paris, he sings Massenet's *Don Quichotte* with Piero Faggioni directing and Georges Prêtre conducting. He goes to Washington to sing the title role in *Boris Godunov* with Mstislav Rostropovich conducting and is seen as Don Giovanni in Nancy in a production he directed. Color. 50 minutes.

RAISA, ROSA
Polish-American soprano (1893–1963)

Rosa Raisa, one of the great dramatic sopranos of the century, created the role of Turandot in Puccini's last opera and the role of Asteria in Boito's *Nerone*. She was born in Poland, began her career in Italy in 1913, became a featured singer at La Scala and Covent Garden, and became a regular on the Chicago opera scene from 1916 to 1936. When she retired in 1937, she opened a singing school in Chicago with her husband, baritone Giacomo Rimini. Raisa made only three short films.

1927/1928 Vitaphone films
"Mme. Rosa Raisa" was featured on three Vitaphone sound films made in 1927 and 1928. In the first, filmed in June 1927, she performs excerpts from Act IV of *Il trovatore* with husband Giacomo Rimini, who was singing with her at Chicago Opera at the time. In the second, made in May 1928, she sings art songs by Tosti and Schindler. In the third, filmed in June 1928, she sings

"Plaisir d'amour" and "La Paloma." Black and white. In Italian. Each about 8 minutes. Bel Canto Society VHS.

RAJAH'S DIAMOND, THE
1979 TV opera by Hoddinott

Alun Hoddinott's TV opera *The Rajah's Diamond*, libretto by Myfanwy Piper, is based on a story sequence by Robert Louis Stevenson. The Rajah of Kashgar has given English Major-General Sir Thomas Vandeleur an extremely valuable diamond. It has made him rich and famous and won him a beautiful wife, but it has also caused enormous problems. The opera, a 50th birthday commission from BBC Television, was created for Welsh baritone Geraint Evans.

1979 BBC Wales Television
Welsh television production: Basil Coleman (stage director), Robin Stapleton (conductor, BBC Wales Symphony Orchestra), Peter Phillips (set designer).
Cast: Geraint Evans (General Vandeleur), Geoffrey Chard (Prince Florizel), Ken Bowen (Rolles), Myron Burnett (Scrymgeour), David Hillman (Rolles's friend), Susanna Ross (Rose).
Telecast November 24, 1979, on BBC Wales Television. J. Mervyn Williams (director). Color. In English. 80 minutes.

RAKE'S PROGRESS, THE
1951 opera by Stravinsky

IGOR STRAVINSKY was inspired to write this unusual opera while visiting an exhibition of Hogarth drawings in Chicago that included the 1735 series *A Rake's Progress*. The libretto for *The Rake's Progress*, by W. H. Auden and Chester Kallman, keeps the 18th-century English setting of the original and the character of the rake, but the story is mostly original. Nick Shadow tells Tom Rakewell he has inherited a fortune, takes him away from his true love Anne, and leads him down the road of vice and ruin. He even persuades him to marry a bearded woman and invest in a machine that makes bread out of stones. Nick turns out to be the Devil, and he takes Tom's sanity when he can't win his soul, so Tom ends up in the Bedlam madhouse.

***1977 Glyndebourne Festival
English stage production: John Cox (director), Bernard Haitink (conductor, London Philharmonic Orchestra and Glyndebourne Festival Chorus), David Hockney (set designer).
Cast: Leo Goeke (Tom Rakewell), Samuel Ramey (Nick Shadow), Felicity Lott (Anne Trulove).

Rosalind Elias (Baba the Turk), Richard van Allan (Trulove), Nuala Willis (Mother Goose).

Video: VAI/Opera d'Oro VHS. Dave Heather (director). Color. In English. 146 minutes.

Comment: This production, which became famous for its colorful Hogarthian set designs by David Hockney, is also finely sung, played, and directed.

1982 Maggio Musicale

Italian stage production: Ken Russell (director), Derek Jarman (set/costume designer), Riccardo Chailly (conductor, Maggio Musicale Fiorentino Orchestra).

Cast: Gösta Winbergh (Tom Rakewell), Istvan Gati (Nick Shadow), Cecilia Gasdia (Anne), Carlo Del Bosco (Trulove), Michael Aspinall (Mother Goose).

Video: Opera Dubs VHS. Ken Russell (director). Color. In English. 148 minutes.

Comment: Two noted English filmmakers combined their talents to create this lively production at the Teatro della Pergola in Florence.

1992 Aix-en-Provence Festival

French stage production: Alfredo Arias (director), Kent Nagano (conductor, Lyons Opera Orchestra and Aix-en-Provence Festival Choir), Robert Plate (set designer), Françoise Tournafond (costume designer).

Cast: Jerry Hadley (Tom Rakewell), Samuel Ramey (Nick Shadow), Dawn Upshaw (Anne Trulove), Victoria Vergara (Baba the Turk), John Macurdy (Steven Cole).

Telecast in France in 1992. Yves-André Hubert (director). Color. In English. 150 minutes.

1995 Aby film

Swedish feature film: Inger Aby (director), Esa-Pekka Salonen (conductor, Swedish Radio Symphony Orchestra and Chorus), Gunnar Kallstrom (cinematographer).

Cast: Greg Fedderly (Tom Rakewell), Barbara Hendricks (Anne Trulove), Håkan Hagegård (Nick Shadow), Brian Asawa (Baba, the Turk), Erik Saedén (Trulove), Gunilla Söderström (Mother Goose).

Video: NVC Arts (GB) VHS. Telecast in the United States. Color. In English. 150 minutes.

Comment: Aby modeled his film on a stage production by Ingmar Bergman. A countertenor sings the role of Baba the Turk.

1996 Salzburg Festival

Austrian stage production: Peter Mussbach (director), Sylvain Cambreling (conductor, Camerata Academica and Vienna State Opera Chorus), Jörg Immendorff (set/costume designer).

Cast: Jerry Hadley (Tom Rakewell), Monte Pederson (Nick Shadow), Dawn Upshaw (Anne Trulove),

Jane Henschel (Baba the Turk), Jonathan Best (Trulove), Linda Ormiston (Mother Goose).

Image Entertainment DVD/Arthaus (GB) DVD/ House of Opera VHS. Brian Large (director). Color. In English. 156 minutes.

Related film

1945 Gilliat film

Sidney Gilliat and Frank Launder's film *The Rake's Progress* is only very loosely based to the Hogarth source drawings. This version of the rake's life takes place in the 1930s with Rex Harrison as the ne'er-do-well misbehaving with everyone. Black and white. 124 minutes.

RAMEAU, JEAN-PHILIPPE
French composer (1683–1764)

Jean-Philippe Rameau's international reputation as an opera composer, which has been pretty weak because his operas were so rarely performed outside France, has started to rise again. A much acclaimed traveling production of *Platée* allowed many critics to see why he was the leading composer in France during the 18th century. See LES BORÉADES.

RAMEY, SAMUEL
American bass (1942–)

Samuel Ramey, one of the most popular bassos in the world, made his debut with New York City Opera in 1973 and worked with that company for a number of years. He sang Don Giovanni, Don Quichotte, Méphistophélès, and the villains in *Tales of Hoffmann* with NYCO, and he can be seen on video singing Basilio with Beverly Sills in THE BARBER OF SEVILLE (1976) and the Count des Grieux with Sills in MANON (1977). Ramey made his first appearance at Glyndebourne in 1977, at La Scala in 1981, at Covent Garden in 1982, and at the Met in 1984 in *Rinaldo*. Ramey is well known for his performances in Verdi and Rossini operas, but his range is quite wide. He is well represented on video, including an outstanding performance in Boito's MEFISTOFELE (1989) in San Francisco and a fine performance as Figaro in the Mozart biopic AMADEUS. See ATTILA (1987/1991), BLUEBEARD'S CASTLE (1989), BORIS GODUNOV (1993), CARMEN (1987), CARNEGIE HALL (1991), DON CARLO (1992), DON GIOVANNI (1987/1990), DON QUICHOTTE (2000), HERBERT VON KARAJAN (1987), JAMES LEVINE (1996), I LOMBARDI ALLA PRIMA CROCIATA (1993), MACBETH (1987), MAOMETTO II (1986), MOÏSE ET PHARAON (1983), NABUCCO (2001), ON THE TOWN (1992), THE RAKE'S PROGRESS (1977/1992), GIOACHINO ROSSINI (1985/1992), DIE SCHÖPFUNG (1990), SEMIRAMIDE (1980/1990), VERDI REQUIEM (1985 film),

RAPE OF LUCRETIA, THE
1946 opera by Britten

Lucretia is the most virtuous wife in the city of Rome during the time of the Etruscan kings. This arouses the envy and animosity of Tarquinius, son of the king, who goes to her house at night and rapes her. She confesses her shame to her husband Collatinus and then kills herself. Bernard Britten's chamber opera *The Rape of Lucretia,* libretto by Ronald Duncan based on a French play by André Obey, is a retelling of a legend told by Livy; it also is the subject of a poem of Shakespeare. The rape was supposedly the cause of expulsion of the Tarquin kings from Rome. Reflecting its classical antecedents, the opera features male and female choruses who comment on the action.

1987 Glyndebourne Festival
English stage production: Graham Vick (director), Lionel Friend (conductor, English National Opera Orchestra and Chorus), Russell Craig (set designer), Howard King (lighting designer).
Cast: Jean Rigby (Lucretia), Russell Smythe (Tarquinius), Richard van Allan (Collatinus), Anthony Rolfe Johnson (Male Chorus), Kathryn Harries (Female Chorus), Alan Opie (Junius), Cathryn Pope (Lucia), Anne-Marie Owens (Bianca).
Video: House of Opera DVD/VHS, Michael Simpson (director). Color. In English. 108 minutes.

RAPSODIA SATANICA
1915 "film opera" by Mascagni

Italian composer Pietro Mascagni wrote an original score for this avant-garde film that has been called a "film opera," and certainly its screenplay was sold like an opera libretto. Mascagni created *Rapsodia satanica* (Satanic Rhapsody) with writers Alfa (Alberto Fassini) and Fausto Maria Martini and director Nino Oxilia, who described it as a "poema cinema-musical." Mascagni's music was played live when the film was shown. The plot is modeled on the story of Faust. The elderly Countess Alba (Lydia Borelli) becomes young again with the help of Mephisto (Ugo Bazzini), but she has to agree to give up love forever. When she falls in love with a young man named Tristano (Andrea Habay), she becomes old again and kills herself. Giorgio Ricci was the cinematographer for the Cines Studio of Rome. Black and white. Silent. About 70 minutes.

RATTENFÄNGER VON HAMELN, DER
1879 opera by Nessler

Viktor Nessler's operatic version of the Pied Piper legend, *Der Rattenfänger von Hameln* (The Ratcatcher of Hamelin), libretto by Friedrich Hofman, is based on a popular poetic romance by Julius Woolf. The story is essentially the same. A piper is hired to rid the town of Hamelin of rats and he pipes them into a river. The city fathers refuse to pay, saying he has also bewitched the mayor's daughter. She drowns herself and he pipes the children out of town and out of sight forever.

1916 Wegener film
Paul Wegener directed this German feature film, which uses the opera libretto as screenplay. He also stars as the wandering piper with support from Lydia Salmonova and Wilhelm Diegelmann. The Union Company produced the film, which was screened with Nessler's music played live. Black and white. Silent. 60 minutes

RATTLE, SIMON
English conductor (1955–)

Liverpool-born Simon Rattle, who has become one of the most admired English conductors on the international circuit, made his debut at Glyndebourne in 1977, at the English National Opera in 1985, and at Covent Garden in 1990. His works on video include a Glyndebourne L'ENFANT ET LES SORTILÈGES (1987) and a superb film of PORGY AND BESS (1992), based on a Glyndebourne production. See also JOHN ADAMS (1998).

RAUTAVAARA, EINOJUHANI
Finnish composer (1928–)

Einojuhani Rautavaara is one of the new composers who have vitalized modern opera in Finland. His first opera, KAIVOS, composed after studying in America and Italy, is a 12-tone examination of liberty and state control; it was inspired by the Hungarian uprising against the Soviets in 1956. After an opera about Apollo, he began to create operas with Finnish backgrounds, including two with ideas derived from the *Kalevala* and one about the first bishop of Finland. In 1997 he created a charming listener-friendly Christmas opera for television based on an American story, O. Henry's THE GIFT OF THE MAGI.

RAVEL, MAURICE
French composer (1875–1937)

Maurice Ravel is best known for music outside the operatic genre but he did write two successful one-act operas.

L'HEURE ESPAGNOLE (1911) tells the amusing story of a clock maker's wife who has to cope with three possible lovers when her husband goes away for a day. L'ENFANT ET LES SORTILÈGES (1925) is the tale of an angry child sent to his room for misbehavior. Both are on video with delightful sets by Maurice Sendak.

1988 Ravel
Larry Weinstein's Canadian film about Ravel's life and music includes archival and home movie footage, interviews, photographs, letters, and performances. Among the performed are Victoria de los Angeles, Jean-Phillipe Collard, Augustin Dumay, Alicia de Larrocha, Charles Dutoit, the Montreal Symphony Orchestra, and the Orford String Quartet. Len Gilday was the cinematographer. Color. In English. 105 minutes.

RAYMOND, FRED
Austrian composer (1900–1954)

Viennese-born bank clerk Friedrich Vesely changed his name to "Fred Raymond" and this supposedly helped him become one of Germany's most popular operetta composers. His biggest success was MASKE IN BLAU, a lavish revue-operetta about a painter and his love, which premiered in 1937 at the Metropol Theater in Berlin and is still in that theater's repertory. Also still popular is *Salzburger Nockerln,* which has equally attractive songs.

RED MILL, THE
1906 operetta by Herbert

Americans Kid Conner and Con Kidder are stranded in Holland and work at the Red Mill Inn to pay off their debts. They help the burgomaster's daughter Gretchen to marry the soldier she loves, while Con woos the innkeeper's daughter Tina. Victor Herbert's tuneful operetta *The Red Mill,* book by Henry Blossom, was written as a vehicle for comedians Fred Stone and David Montgomery, but it is really remembered for its wonderful songs, including "The Streets of New York" and "Every Day Is Ladies Day With Me."

1958 CBS Television
American TV production: Delbert Mann (director), Fred Coe (producer), Robert Alan Arthur (adaptation), Don Walker (music director), Robert Tyler Lee (set designer).

Cast: Shirley Jones (Gretchen Van Damm), Donald O'Connor (Johnny Shaw), Mike Nichols (Rod Carter), Elaine May (Candy Carter), Elaine Stritch (Mayor Jan Van Borkem), Harpo Marx and Evelyn Rudie (Narrators).

Video at the MTR. Telecast April 19, 1958, on CBS. Color. In English. 90 minutes.

Comment: The operetta, presented as a DuPont Show of the Month, was updated and set in the Brussels World Fair. This was one of the first TV productions to be recorded on videotape.

Early film

1927 MGM film
William Randolph Hurst bought the rights in *The Red Mill* for his mistress Marion Davies and produced this lavish film version for MGM through his Cosmopolitan Company. Davies plays the Cinderella-like Tina, Owen Moore is the American Dennis who falls in love with her, and Louise Fazenda is Gretchen. Blacklisted comedian Fatty Arbuckle directed under the pseudonym William Goodrich from a screenplay by Frances Marion. The music was played live with the film, but critics and audiences were not impressed. Black and white. Silent. About 70 minutes.

REGINA DELLA SCALA
1937 Italian film with opera content

Regina della Scala (Queen of La Scala) is an Italian fiction film presumably designed to glorify the Milan opera house Teatro all Scala, and much of it was shot on location in the theater. *Regina della Scala,* in the film plot, is an opera by a young composer that is to be sung at La Scala by his prima donna lover (Margherita Carosio). The director of La Scala tells the composer about the difficulties the architect Premarin had when he designed the theater and the problems Verdi faced when audiences booed his opera *Un giorno di regno.* The film features excerpts from operas by Mascagni, Salieri, Pergolesi, Rossini, Donizetti, Puccini, and Verdi, and there are personal appearances by composer Mascagni, tenor Galliano Masini, and a number of Milan aristocrats. Franco Ghione conducted the music, Vaclav Vich was cinematographer, and Guido Salvini and Camillo Mastrocinque wrote and directed. Black and white. In Italian. 88 minutes.

REGINETTA DELLE ROSE, LA
1912 operetta by Leoncavallo

RUGGERO LEONCAVALLO is best known for his opera *Pagliacci,* but he also tried his hand at lighter fare. His charming 1912 operetta *La reginetta delle rose* (The Little Queen of the Roses), libretto by Giovacchino Forzano, was quite popular in Italy and France for a time. Max, crown prince of a Ruritanian country, falls in love while in London with a lovely flower seller named Lilian and wants to take "reginetta delle rose" in his country.

When the queen orders Lilian arrested at the border, the people revolt and depose her; Max becomes the king and Lilian is his "little queen."

1992 Operette, che Passione!

Italian TV production: Sandro Massimini (director/producer), Roberto Negri (pianist), Sandro Corelli (choreographer).

Cast: Sandro Massimini, Sara Dilena, Max René Cosotti.

Video: Pierluigi Pagano (director). Color. In Italian. About 19 minutes. Ricordi (Italy) VHS.

Comment: Highlights of the operetta on the Italian TV series *Operette, che Passione!* Included are the ballet "Gavotta," the aria "Il valzer delle rose," and the duet "Tutte rose i tuoi capelli d'or."

Early film

1915 Musical Film Company

Luigi Sapelli (Caramba) directed this feature film version of the operetta soon after its success on stage, and it was shown in cinemas with Leoncavallo's music played live. Ester Soarez is Lilian, Luigi Hornac is Max, and Mrs. Cicogna is the queen. Renzi Sonzogno, owner of the Musical Film Company in Milan, also produced a film of *Pagliacci* in 1915. Black and white. Silent. About 70 minutes.

REICH, STEVE
American composer(1936–)

Steve Reich, one of the leading composers of the American minimalist movement and a major influence on Philip Glass, does not write traditional operas but what he describes as "documentary music video theater." THE CAVE (1993) was a collaboration with his wife, video artist Beryl Korot, using video screens to tell a powerful story about the underpinnings of the Middle East conflict; the screens provide text as well as images. They followed in 1998 with HINDENBURG, an audiovisual portrait of the German zeppelin that caught fire and crashed in 1937. In 2002 they premiered THREE TALES at the Spoleto Festival USA; concerned with problems resulting from the growth of technology. it includes the multimedia operas *Bikini, Dolly,* and *Hindenberg.*

REINIGER, LOTTE
German animator (1899–1981)

Lotte Reiniger, one of the great pioneers of animated film, became famous for her silhouette films, especially for the animated feature *The Adventures of Prince Achmed* (1926). Many of her films were based around music

and opera. In 1930 she made *Ten Minutes of Mozart* in Germany. In 1933 she created an acclaimed silhouette version of CARMEN in Italy. In 1935 she designed a *Papageno* that focused on the bird catcher from DIE ZAUBERFLÖTE. In 1940, back in Italy, she made a version of Donizetti's *L'elisir d'amore* but was not able to complete it because of the war. Later, after moving to England, she made films of HÄNSEL UND GRETEL (1954), LA BELLE HÉLÈNE (1957), and DIE ENTFÜHRUNG AUS DEM SERAIL (1958).

RENOIR, JEAN
French film director (1894–1979)

Jean Renoir, one of the all-time great filmmakers, directed one opera film, created a mini-opera in another, and referenced opera in many more. His opera film, TOSCA (1941), was finished by another director when he had to abandon it because of the start of the war. In *La Grande Illusion* (1937), he features an aria from FAUST as a signal by prisoners in a military camp. In *Madame Bovary* (1934), he uses music from LUCIA DI LAMMERMOOR in a key scene. In *The Rules of the Game* (1939), he features music from *Die Fledermaus*. He directed most of a Deanna Durbin film, *The Amazing Mrs. Holiday* (1943), in which she sings "Vissi d'arte" from *Tosca*. Kurt Weill wrote the music for his patriotic short film *Salute to France* (1944). His 1952 *The Golden Coach* is based on the same story as Offenbach's LA PÉRICHOLE, and his 1955 *French Can Can* uses Offenbach's dance music. His last film, the 1969 *Le Petit Théâtre par Jean Renoir,* features a very unusual "little opera."

1969 La Cireuse Electrique

La Cireuse Electrique (The Electric Waxer), described by Renoir as "a little opera," is the second of four episodes in his last film, *Le Petit Théâtre par Jean Renoir.* It's the satirical story of a woman (Marguerite Cassan) who has a great love for an electric floor-waxing machine and likes to sing about it. Renoir wrote the words; Joseph Kosma wrote the music. Color. In French. Episode, about 20 minutes; full feature, 100 minutes.

RE PASTORE, IL
1775 opera by Mozart

Mozart composed *Il re pastore* (The Shepherd King), a charming chamber opera or "serenata," when he was 19 to a libretto by Metastasio (it had first been set in 1751 by Giuseppe Bonno). Mozart's version has lovely music despite the somewhat conventional plot. Alessandro (Alexander the Great) discovers that Aminta, the shepherd, is really the rightful heir to the throne of Sidon and so insists that he should marry the ex-tyrant's daughter

Tamiri. The couple object to this arrangement, however, as Aminta loves Elisa and Tamiri loves Agenore. It gets sorted out.

1989 Salzburg Landestheater
Austrian stage production: John Cox (director), Neville Marriner (conductor, Academy of St. Martin in the Fields), Elisabeth Dalton (set/costume designer).
Cast: Jerry Hadley (Alessandro), Angela Maria Blasi (Aminta), Sylvia McNair (Elisa), Iris Vermillion (Tamiri), Claes H. Ahnsjö (Agenore).
Video: Philips VHS. Brian Large (director). Color. In Italian with English subtitles. 116 minutes.
Comment: Cox stages the opera like a series of concentric boxes. On the theater stage an 18th-century audience, in costume in a stately room, watches the opera performed on a platform.

RESNIK, REGINA
American soprano/mezzo-soprano (1922–)

New Yorker Regina Resnik, who made her debut as a soprano as Lady Macbeth with New York's New Opera Company in 1942, sang with the Met for 30 seasons between 1944 and 1984 in a wide range of Italian and German operas. She switched from soprano to mezzo roles in the early 1950s. One of her most notable achievements was the creation of the role of the baroness in Samuel Barber's opera *Vanessa*, which unfortunately is not on video. A fine actress as well as a splendid singer, she is not well represented on screen. She also directed opera on stage. See THE BEAR (1970), BELL TELEPHONE HOUR (1959–1966), CARMEN (1972 film/1983 film), ELEKTRA (1969), ROBERT MERRILL (1962–1965), and SOPRANOS AND MEZZOS (1991).

1960s Stars of Bel Canto
A Belgian TV compilation of studio appearances by nine singers in the 1960s, including Resnik. RTBF, Radiotélévision Belge Française. Black and white. 60 minutes.

RESPIGHI, OTTORINO
Italian composer. (1879–1936)

Ottorino Respighi is not well known as an opera composer as his continuing reputation rests mostly on tone poems such as *The Fountains of Rome*. However, he wrote a number of operas, including the relatively popular LA BELLA DORMENTE NEL BOSCO (Sleeping Beauty in the Woods). It never entered the standard repertory but has had success around the world in a different way; it was written for Vittorio Podrecca's puppet theater and is performed by puppets. The libretto by Gian Bistolfi follows the outlines of the Perrault fairy tale.

RETABLO DE MAESE PEDRO, EL
1923 opera by Falla

MANUEL DE FALLA's one-act chamber opera *El retablo de maese Pedro* (Master Peter's Puppet Show), based on an episode in Cervantes's *Don Quixote*, was created for a princess for performance at her home. In the opera a puppet show is being performed by Master Peter and his narrator boy assistant in the courtyard of a Spanish inn. They are interrupted by Don Quixote, who is watching from the audience and believes that the story about the conflict between Crusaders and Moors is real. When the Moors chase the Christian lovers, he "rescues" them by wrecking the puppet show with his sword. Afterwards he explains it was his duty as a knight errant.

1938 BBC Television
English TV production: Anthony Tudor (director), Hyam Greenbaum (conductor, BBC Television Orchestra), Malcolm Baker-Smith (set designer).
Cast: Frederick Sharp (Don Quixote), Perry Jones (Master Pedro), Jane Connard (Boy Narrator), Hogarth Puppets.
Telecast live May 29, 1938, on BBC. Dallas Bower (director). Black and white. In English. 26 minutes.

***1990 Opera Atelier
Canadian film: Larry Weinstein (director), Charles Dutoit (conductor, Montreal Symphony Orchestra), Gerard Gauci (set designer), Dora Rust D'Eye (costume designer).
Cast: Justino Diaz (Don Quixote), Juan Cabero (Master Pedro), Xavier Cabero (Boy Narrator), Opera Atelier puppets.
Video: London VHS/LD. Color. In Spanish with English subtitles. 30 minutes.
Comment: The puppets really seem to come alive in this splendid film through clever cross-cutting with the human participants.

RETURN OF BUTTERFLY, THE
1982 film with opera content

Elena Safonova stars as SALOMEA KRUSCENISKI in *The Return of Butterfly* (Vozrastchenié Batterflai), a Soviet/Ukrainian film about the famous Ukrainian soprano. It begins with the singer aged 80 telling the audience about her early life and remembering scenes from it, especially her triumph in Brescia in the revised second production of *Madama Butterfly*. Her life from childhood to international fame is presented with arias by Puccini, Mascagni, Strauss, and Wagner as well as Ukrainian and Italian folk songs. As an outspoken Ukrainian patriot, she became unpopular in Russia, so after 1903 she sang mostly in Italy and was the first to sing Salome and Elektra at La Scala. The supporting cast includes Ivan Mikolaichuk, Ivan Gavriliuk, and Galina Zolotareva. Valerie Vrublevskaya wrote the screenplay, Gennadi Engstrem was the cinematographer, and Oleg Fialko directed the film for the Dovzhenko Film Studio. Color. In Ukrainian. 90 minutes. Dovzhenko VHS.

REVOLTOSA, LA
1897 zarzuela by Chapí

RUPERTO CHAPÍ's popular zarzuela *La revoltosa* (The Troublemaker) centers around Mari-Pepa, a flirtatious woman in a Madrid apartment block who dazzles the husbands of the other women living there. In revenge the wives send the husbands fake rendezvous notes and trap them in an embarrassing scene. This causes Felipe, the single man Mari-Pepa has never been able to snare, to get jealous and allows the story to end in a romance. Carlos Fernández Shaw and J. Lopez Silva wrote the libretto.

1949 Morales film
Spanish feature film: José Diaz Morales (director), Intercontinental Films (production).
Cast: Carmen Sevilla (Mari-Pepa), Tony Leblanc (Felipe), Maria Bru, Tomás Blanco, Mario Berriatua, Maria de Los Angeles Morales.
Video: Divisa (Spain) VHS. Black and white. In Spanish. 109 minutes.

1963 Morales film
Spanish feature film: José Diaz Morales (director), Francisco Marin (cinematographer).
Cast: Teresa Locke (Mari-Pepa) German Cobos (Felipe), Eulalia Soldevilla, Amalia Rodriguez, Matilde Muñoz Sampedro, Julia Pachelo.
Color. In Spanish. 95 minutes.

1968 Teatro Lirico Español
Spanish TV film: Juan De Orduña (director), Federico Moreno Torroba (conductor, Spanish Lyric Orchestra and Madrid Chorus), Manuel Tamayo (screenplay), Federico Larraya (cinematographer).
Cast: Elisa Ramirez (Mari-Pepa, sung by Isabel Rivas), José Moreno (Felipe, sung by Luis Sagi-Vela), José Sacristán, Maria Carmen Ramirez, Luis Frutos, Antonio Casal, Marisa Paredes, María Luisa Ponte.
Video: Metrovideo (Spain) VHS. Shot in 35mm for RTVE Spanish Television. Juan De Orduña (director). Color. In Spanish. 75 minutes.

***1999 Jarvis Conservatory, Napa
American stage production: Daniel Helfgot (director), Philip J. Bauman (conductor, Jarvis Conservatory

Orchestra), Peter Crompton (set designer), Carlos Carvajal (choreographer), William Jarvis (producer/translator).
Cast: Camille Zamora (Mari-Pepa), Diego Garcia (Felipe), Gisella Monclova (Soledad), Celia Green (Gorgonia).
Video: Jarvis Conservatory VHS. Color. Dialogue in English, singing in Spanish with English subtitles. 58 minutes.

Early film

1925 Rey film
Florián Rey's silent Spanish film of the zarzuela concentrates on the relationship between Mari-Pepa (Josefina Tapias) and Felipe (Juan De Orduña) with a supporting cast that includes José Moncayo and Ceferino Barrajon. The film was screened with music played lived. Black and white. About 85 minutes.

REY QUE RABIÓ, EL
1891 zarzuela by Chapí

RUPERTO CHAPÍ's charming zarzuela *El rey que rabió* (The King Who Was Rabid) is a comedy about a young king (soprano role) who wanders around his country dressed like a shepherd to see what is actually going on. His general (baritone) accompanies him, also in disguise. The king falls in love with Rosa, an innkeeper's daughter, and they run off together. Her boyfriend Jeremías, who is mistaken for the king, gets bitten by a rabid dog, hence the title.

1939 Buchs film
Spanish feature film: José Buchs (director/screenplay), Agustin Macasoli and Alfonso Nieva (cinematographers).
Cast: Raquel Rodrigo (King), Luis Peña, Juan Bonate, Luis Heridia.
Black and white. In Spanish. 93 minutes.

1968 Teatro Lirico Español
Spanish TV film: Juan De Orduña (director), Federico Moreno Torroba (conductor, Spanish Lyric Orchestra and Madrid Chorus), Manuel Tamayo (screenplay), Federico Larraya (cinematography).
Cast: Josefina Cubeiro (King), Luis Sagi-Vela, Rosa Sarmiento, Manuel Gonzalez, Ramon Alonso, Jesus Aguirre.
Video: Metrovideo (Spain) VHS. Shot in 35mm for RTVE Spanish Television. Juan De Orduña (director). Color. In Spanish. 96 minutes.

Early film

1929 Buchs film
Amelia Muñoz stars as the king in this silent version of the zarzuela written and directed by José Buchs. The supporting cast includes Juan De Orduña, José Montenegro, and Pedro Barreto with Agustin Macasoli as cinematographer. It was screened with music from the zarzuela. Buchs also made a sound version of the zarzuela. Black and white. About 90 minutes.

REY, FLORIÁN
Spanish film director (1894–1962)

Florián Rey began his film career in the early 1920s as an actor in zarzuelas such as LA VERBENA DE LA PALOMA (1921), MARUXA (1923), and *La chavala*. He turned director in 1925 with the zarzuela film LA REVOLTOSA followed by GIGANTES Y CABEZUDOS; he won wide acclaim for his realistic *La aldea maldita* in 1929. Rey discovered and married Imperio Argentina, the top Spanish female film star of the 1930s, and featured her in 15 of his films; their biggest success was *Morena Clara* (1936). He made a version of CARMEN with her in 1938 titled *Carmen la de Triana*.

RHEINGOLD, DAS
1869 opera by Wagner

Das Rheingold (The Rhine Gold) is the first opera in RICHARD WAGNER's epic tetralogy DER RING DES NIBELUNGEN. Alberich, a member of the dwarf race of Nibelungs, steals the Rhine Maidens' magic gold and creates a ring that can make its wearer master of the world. Wotan, chief of the gods, tricks it away from Alberich so the dwarf puts a terrible curse on it. Wotan is forced to give the ring to the giants Fafner and Fasolt as part of their payment for building Valhalla and freeing the goddess Freia. Fafner kills Fasolt and keeps the gold for himself. The curse has begun to take effect. The gods enter Valhalla.

1978 Karajan film
German studio film: Herbert von Karajan (director/conductor, Berlin Philharmonic Orchestra), Georges Wakhévitch (set/costume designer).

Cast: Thomas Stewart (Wotan), Brigitte Fassbaender (Fricka), Zoltan Kelemen (Alberich), Peter Schreier (Loge), Gerhard Stolze (Mime), Jeannine Altmeyer (Freia), Louis Hendrix (Fafner), Gerd Nienstedt (Fasolt, sung by Karl Ridderbusch), Birgit Finnila (Erda), Herman Esser (Froh), Vladimir De Kanel (Donner, sung by Leif Roar), Eva Randova, Edda Moser, and Liselotte Rebmann (Rhine Maidens).

Video: DG VHS. Ernst Wild (director). Color. In German. 145 minutes.

Comment: Von Karajan shot his film in a Munich film studio using a soundtrack he recorded in 1974 at the Salzburg Festival.

1980 Bayreuth Festival
German stage production: Patrice Chéreau (director), Pierre Boulez (conductor, Bayreuth Festival Orchestra and Chorus), Richard Peduzzi (set designer), Jacques Schmidt (costume designer).

Cast: Donald McIntyre (Wotan), Hanna Schwarz (Fricka), Hermann Becht (Alberich), Siegfried Jerusalem (Froh), Martin Egel (Donner), Helmut Pampuch (Mime), Carmen Reppel (Freia), Matti Salminen (Fasolt), Heinz Zednik (Loge), Fritz Hübner (Fafner), Gisella Monclova (Erda), Norma Sharp, Ilse Gramatzki, and Marga Schiml (Rhine Maidens).

Video: Philips DVD/VHS/LD. Brian Large (director). Color. In German with English subtitles. 163 minutes.

Comment: Controversial 1976 Bayreuth Festival centenary production taped four years after its premiere. Chéreau sets the story in the 19th century where the Rhine Maidens are whores cavorting around a hydroelectric dam and the gods wear aristocratic Victorian dress.

1989 Bavarian State Opera
German stage production: Nikolaus Lehnhoff (director), Wolfgang Sawallisch (conductor, Bavarian State Opera Orchestra and Chorus), Erich Wonder (set designer), Frieda Parmeggiani (costume designer).

Cast: Robert Hale (Wotan), Marjana Lipovsek (Fricka), Nancy Gustafson (Freia), Ekkehard Wlaschiha (Alberich), Floria Cerny (Donner), Robert Tear (Loge), Helmut Pampuch (Mime), Joseph Hopferwieser (Froh), Jan-Hendrik Rootering (Fasolt), Kurt Moll (Fafner), Hans Schwarz (Erda), Julie Kaufmann, Angela Maria Blasi and Birgit Calm (Rhine Maidens).

Video: EMI VHS. Shokichi Amano (director). Color. In German with English subtitles. 160 minutes.

***1990 Metropolitan Opera
American stage production: Otto Schenk (director), James Levine (conductor, Metropolitan Opera Orchestra and Chorus), Günther Schneider-Siemssen (set designer), Rolf Langenfass (costume designer).

Cast: James Morris (Wotan), Christa Ludwig (Fricka), Ekkehard Wlaschiha (Alberich), Siegfried Jerusalem (Loge), Matti Salminen (Fafner), Mari Anne Haggander (Freia), Alan Held (Donner), Mark Baker (Froh), Heinz Zednik (Mime), Jan-Hendrik Rootering (Fasolt), Birgitta Svendén (Erda), Kaaren Erickson, Diane Kesling, and Meredith Parson (Rhine Maidens).

Video: DG DVD/VHS/LD. Taped April 23, 1990; telecast June 18, 1990. Brian Large (director). Color. In German with English subtitles. 162 minutes.

Comment: Traditional production as Wagner might have done it with outstanding vocal and orchestral performances.

1991 Bayreuth Festival

German stage production: Harry Kupfer (director), Daniel Barenboim (conductor, Bayreuth Festival Orchestra and Chorus), Hans Schavernoch (set designer), Reinhard Heinrich (costume designer).

Cast: John Tomlinson (Wotan), Linda Finnie (Fricka), Bodo Brinkmann (Donner), Graham Clark (Loge), Kurt Schreibmayer (Froh), Eva Johannson (Freia), Helmut Pampuch (Mime), Günther von Kannen (Alberich), Philip Kang (Fafner), Matthias Hölle (Fasolt), Birgitta Svendén (Erda), Hilde Leidland, Annette Küttenbaum, and Jane Turner (Rhine Maidens).

Video: Teldec VHS/LD. Horant H. Hohlfeld (director). Color. In German with English subtitles. 153 minutes.

1996 Jutland Opera

Danish stage production: Klaus Hoffmeyer (director), Tamás Vetö (conductor, Aarhus Symphony Orchestra), Lars Juhl (set/costume designer).

Cast: Lars Waage (Wotan), Jørgen Klint (Alberich), Lennart Stregaaro, Marianne Eklöf, Iréne Theorin, Hans Jorgen Laursen, Steffen Milling, Jesper Brun-Jensen.

Video: Musikhuset Aarhus (Denmark) VHS. Telecast on Danmarks Radio, Copenhagen. Thomas Grimm (director). Color. In German. 150 minutes.

Related films

1978 Rheingold

Director Niklaus Schilling sets his metaphorical German film on the Rheingold luxury train traveling along the Rhine River and uses as background Wagner's music and Rhinegold legends. The symbolic plot is a murder mystery involving a diplomat, his wife, and her lover. Color. In German. 91 minutes.

1979 Nosferatu the Vampyre

Director Werner Herzog uses the music of the *Rheingold* Prelude to emphasize the unworldly character of the story in his vampire film *Nosferatu Phantom der Nacht*. Klaus Kinski plays Nosferatu. This is a modern version of the classic 1922 film by F. W. Murnau. Color. In German. 107 minutes.

1995 Operavox Animated Opera

An animated version of *Rheingold* was produced for the Operavox series with the Welsh National Opera Orchestra playing the music. David Seaman was music editor, John Cary produced, and Graham Ralph directed. Color. 27 minutes.

RICCI, LUIGI AND FEDERICO
19th-century Italian composers

The Neapolitan brothers Luigi (1805–1859) and Federico (1809–1877) Ricci wrote many operas on their own, but they are remembered primarily for their collaboration on their delightful comedy CRISPINO E LA COMARE (Crispino and the Fairy). After its premiere in Venice in 1850, it became one of the most popular comic operas of the 19th century. Luigi is also remembered for his scandalous ménage à trois with Fanny and Lidia Stolz, the twin sisters of the opera singer Teresa Stolz. He fell in love with both, lived with both, wrote an opera for both, had children by both, and married one without giving up the other. Federico had a less interesting personal life but is considered the better composer.

RICCIARDO E ZORAIDE
1818 opera by Rossini

This lesser known opera by GIOACHINO ROSSINI has a libretto by Francesco Berio de Salsa, who also wrote the book for Rossini's *Otello*. Based on an epic poem by Forteguerri, it tells a complicated story about a love affair between Crusader knight Ricciardo and Asian princess Zoraide. The music is splendid, however, and there is a happy ending.

1990 Pesaro Festival

Italian stage production: Luca Ronconi (director), Riccardo Chailly (conductor, Bologna Teatro Communale Orchestra and Prague Philharmonic Chorus), Gae Aulenti (set designer).

Cast: June Anderson (Zoraide), William Matteuzzi (Ricciardo), Gloria Scalchi (Zomira), Bruce Ford (Agorante).

Video: House of Opera/Lyric VHS. Manuela Crivelli (director). Color. In Italian. 141 minutes.

Comment: This Pesaro Festival production was apparently the first since the 19th century.

RICCIARELLI, KATIA
Italian soprano (1946–)

Katia Ricciarelli made her debut in Mantua in 1969 as Mimì, began to sing at La Scala in 1973, made her first appearance in America in 1972 in Verdi's *I Due Foscari* in Chicago, and went to the Met in 1975 as Mimì. She has a wide repertory but is best known for her work in Italian *bel canto* operas. Ricciarelli has an appealing screen presence that matches her warm voice, as is evident in her fine performance as Desdemona in Franco Zeffirelli's film of OTELLO (1986). See AMICA, UN BALLO IN MASCHERA (1975/1980), I CAPULETI ED I MONTECCHI (1991), CARMEN (1980), PLÁCIDO DOMINGO (1984), FALSTAFF (1982), JÉRUSALEM (1986), LUCIA DI LAMMERMOOR (1981), LUISA MILLER (1979), METROPOLITAN OPERA (1983), WOLFGANG A. MOZART (1991), OPERA STARS IN CONCERT, I PURITANI (1986), SIMON BOCCANEGRA (1976), SOPRANOS AND MEZZOS (1990/1991), TANCREDI (1981), and TURANDOT (1983).

1983 Metropolitan Opera Centennial Gala
Ricciarelli was one of those participating when the Met celebrated its 100th birthday October 22, 1983, with an eight-hour telecast. See METROPOLITAN OPERA.

1984 Ricciarelli and Carreras in Concert
Ricciarelli and José Carreras in concert includes a duet from *Aida* and music from *Adriana Lecouvreur, L'Arlesiana, Le Cid, Il corsaro, Poliuto, La traviata,* and *La Wally.* Bruno Amaducci conducts. Color. 66 minutes. Bel Canto Society VHS.

1991 José Carreras and Friends
An evening of arias, duets, and songs with Carreras and friends, including Ricciarelli, accompanied by the London Arts Orchestra led by Jacques Delacôte. Color. 60 minutes. On VHS.

RICORDI
Italian opera publishing firm

Ricordi is probably the most important publishing firm ever associated with opera, as it was the exclusive publisher for most of the great Italian opera composers of the 19th century, including Rossini, Bellini, Donizetti, Verdi, and Puccini. Founded in Milan in 1808 by violinist Giovanni Ricordi, it continues to be run by members of the family to the present day. Its history is shown in two fascinating Italian films.

1954 Casa Ricordi
This is a grand Hollywood-on-the-Tiber opera film, the romanticized story of the publishing house, with an all-star cast of Italian singers re-creating and inventing operatic history under the direction of Carmine Gallone. The film traces the history of 19th-century Italian opera through tales about its greatest composers. First there is Rossini (Roland Alexandre) having a tempestuous love affair while writing *The Barber of Seville,* after which

Tito Gobbi and Giulio Neri sing scenes from it. Then we see Donizetti (Marcello Mastroianni) taming a temperamental diva during rehearsals of *L'elisir d'amore.* Bellini (Maurice Ronet) dies as *I puritani* is being premiered. Verdi makes a comeback with *Otello,* and Mario Del Monaco sings the final scene impersonating Francesco Tamagno, the tenor who created the role. Puccini (Gabriele Ferzetti) is inspired to write *La bohème* by a girl he meets in a shop, but she dies of tuberculosis before the premiere, during which Renata Tebaldi sings Mimì's last aria. Other featured singers include Giulietta Simionato, Gianni Poggi, Giulio Neri, and Italo Tajo. The actors include Paolo Stoppa as the founder of the Ricordi firm, Marta Toren, Nadia Gray, and Micheline Presle. *The New York Times* critic loved this movie. Color. In Italian. 120 minutes. House of Opera/Premiere Opera/Opera Dubs/ Lyric VHS.

1995 La Famiglia Ricordi
Mauro Bolognini's four-part TV film *The Ricordi Family* traces the history of the publishing firm from 1808, when Giovanni Ricordi founded it, to the 1920s. It includes a full-scale history of Italian opera during the 19th century and features Luca Barbareschi as Rossini, Kim Rossi Stuart as Bellini, Alessandro Gasmann as Donizetti, Mariano Rigillo as Verdi, Massimo Ghini as Puccini, Anna Kanakis as Maria Malibran, and Melba Ruffo as Giuditta Turina. Aldo Buti designed the costumes, Camillo Bazzoni photographed the film, and Marco Boemi conducted the music. Color. In Italian. 240 minutes.

RIDERS TO THE SEA
1937 opera by Vaughan Williams

RALPH VAUGHAN WILLIAMS's one-act opera uses as libretto the exact text of John Millington Synge's powerful 1904 Irish play *Riders to the Sea.* The story takes place in the Aran Islands off the west coast of Ireland where Maurya has lost her husband and four of her sons to the sea. Her daughters Nora and Cathleen identify clothes taken from a drowned man as belonging to the missing son, their brother Michael. The last son Bartley leaves to take horses to Galway and drowns. Maurya sings mournfully that the sea can hurt her no more.

1990 RTE Irish Television
Irish TV production: Louis Lentin (director), Bryden Thomson (conductor, Radio Telefis Eireann Concert Orchestra and Chamber Choir), Jay Clements (set designer). Cast: Sarah Walker (Maurya), Yvonne Brennan (Cathleen), Kathleen Tynan (Nora), Hugh Mackey (Bartley), Martin Murphey as author J. M. Synge in the prologue).

Video: Opera Dubs VHS. Louis Lentin (director). Color. In English. 45 minutes.

RIDIN' THE CHEROKEE TRAIL
1941 cowboy film with opera content

This cheap Monogram B-Western contains what is probably the most bizarre use of opera music in all cinema, transmuting arias from *Rigoletto* and *Carmen* into cowboy songs. Craven, the slick, sophisticated villain of the film, runs an outlaw empire in the Cherokee Strip at the turn of the century and is an opera enthusiast. He plays Caruso's version of "La donna è mobile" on a wind-up cylinder phonograph to demonstrate good music to hero Tex Ritter. Tex, however, claims that the aria is actually a cowboy song about Ol' Pete the Bandit. He strums Verdi's melody on his guitar and sings "Ol' Pete the Bandit-o/Held up the sheriff-o..." etc. He claims the "galoot Rigoletto" stole the tune from the cowboys. The astonished Craven then plays the "Toreador Song" from *Carmen* on the piano and asks Tex what he thinks of it. Tex tells him that it is actually another song about Pete the Bandit that he himself composed. He then sings an amazing cowboy-style song to the Bizet music beginning "Ol' Pete the Bandit/Robbed the country store/Smashed in the window/Tore down the door." Opera connoisseur Craven breaks out laughing and congratulates Tex on his inventiveness. All this happens in the middle of a perfectly ordinary cheapo cowboy movie about Texas Rangers trying to lure a bad guy over a border. Ritter, who sang on Broadway early in his career, presumably filmed the sequence tongue-in-cheek with the help of writer Edmund Kelso and director Spencer C. Bennett. Critics never took notice of this odd joke, and B-Western audiences simply laughed at the hokum. It has to be seen to be believed. Black and white. 62 minutes. Hollywood Nostalgia VHS.

RIDI, PAGLIACCIO
1943 film with opera content

Ridi, Pagliaccio or *Lache Bajazzo* (Laugh, Clown) are the American video titles of an Italian-German fiction film purporting to tell how Ruggero Leoncavallo's opera PAGLIACCI originated. Leoncavallo claimed that the story was based on a real incident that happened in the Calabrian village of Montalto during the 1860s. In the film, the "real" Canio (Paul Hörbiger) is a clown who killed his wife and her lover and has been let out of jail after 20 years. He seeks out his daughter Giulia (Alida Valli), who has been raised as an aristocrat, to ask forgiveness. When he is not allowed to see her, he tells his story to Leoncavallo (Carlo Romano), who writes the opera based on his story. Beniamino Gigli plays a (fictional) opera singer named Morelli who sings the role of Canio

in the supposed premiere with Adriana Perris as Nedda, Leone Paci as Tonio, Mario Borriello as Silvio, and Adelio Zagonara as Beppe. The real Canio, after watching the opera, disappears to the music of "Vesti la giubba" with its famous phrase "ridi, Pagliaccio." The great value of the film is Gigli in peak form. It opens with him singing the Prologue and even has snippets from other operas, including "Prendi, l'anel ti dono" from *La sonnambula*. The film was shot in Berlin with Leopold Hainisch directing it in German as *Lache Bajazzo* and Giuseppe Fatigati directing it in Italian as *I Pagliacci*. In the German version, Monika Burg has the Alida Valli role, Heinz Moog is Leoncavallo, and Hans Hotter sings the Prologue. Harald Bratt and Gesare Giulio Viola wrote the German and Italian screenplays, Fritz Arno Wagner and Erich Nitzschmann were the cinematographers, and Willy Schmidt-Gentner was music director. Black and white. In Italian or German. 85 minutes. House of Opera DVD/Bel Canto Society VHS (as *Ridi, Pagliaccio* in Italian with English subtitles and as *Lache Bajazzo* in German without subtitles).

RIGOLETTO
1851 opera by Verdi

Rigoletto, the first opera by GIUSEPPE VERDI to become internationally popular, has been a favorite of filmmakers since the earliest days of cinema. Francesco Maria Piave's libretto is based on Victor Hugo's play *Le roi s'amuse* but with the setting shifted to Mantua and the king transformed into a duke. Rigoletto, the hunchback jester, is cursed by a man whose daughter has been dishonored by the duke. The curse is fulfilled when the duke seduces Rigoletto's daughter Gilda. Rigoletto pays to have the duke killed by the criminal Sparafucile when he visits Maddalena at an inn, but the scheme backfires and results in the death of Gilda. Besides the famous Quartet with the duke, Gilda, Sparafucile, and Maddalena, the opera contains such popular arias as the duke's "La donna è mobile" and Gilda's "Caro nome." There is a wide choice of videos of the opera, and music from the opera is often used in fiction films.

1931–1981 Rigoletto Collection
This is a compilation of excerpts from 50 years of *Rigoletto* on screen. The rarest excerpts are from a 1931 German film featuring four Italian singers: soprano Lina Pagliughi, her husband tenor Primo Montanari, baritone Carlo Galeffi, and mezzo Maria Castagna-Fullin. They each sing arias and join for the Quartet accompanied by Arturo Lucon and the Berlin Philharmonic. The other films excerpted on the anthology (all described below) are a Rome Opera film of *Rigoletto* (1947), the biographic film *Verdi, King of Melody* (1953), and an Arena di Verona video of *Rigoletto* (1981). Black and white and color. In Italian. Japanese VHS/LD.

1947 Rome Opera

Italian film of stage production: Carmine Gallone (director), Tullio Serafin (conductor, Rome Opera House Orchestra and Chorus), Anchise Brizzi (cinematographer), Excelsa Film (production).

Cast: Tito Gobbi (Rigoletto), Mario Filippeschi (Duke), Marcella Gavoni (Gilda, sung by Lina Pagliughi), Giulio Neri (Sparafucile), Anna Maria Canali (Maddalena).

Video: Bel Canto Society/Lyric/Multimedia (Italy) VHS. Black and white. In Italian. 98 minutes.

Comment: Critic Stephen Stroff considers this the best recording of the opera in any form. It was filmed at the Rome Opera House without an audience with the singers miming to their own voices. Gobbi and Serafin are in marvelous form.

1951 Opera Cameos

American TV highlights production: Lou Ames (director), Carlo Vinti (producer), Salvatore Dell'Isola (conductor, Opera Cameos Orchestra), Joseph Vinti (screenplay), H. E. Currier and Jettie Preminger (narrators)

Cast: Giuseppe Valdengo (Rigoletto), Costanzo Gero (Duke), Nina Alba (Gilda), Carlo Tomanelli (Sparafucile), Joan Bishop (Maddalena).

Video at the MTR. Telecast live November 25, 1951, on WPIX-TV in New York. Black and white. In Italian. 30 minutes.

1952 Opera Cameos

American TV highlights production: Carlo Vinti (director), Giuseppe Bamboschek (conductor, Opera Cameos Orchestra), Joseph Vinti (screenplay).

Cast: Robert Weede (Rigoletto), Salvatore Puma (Duke), Irene Fratiza (Gilda).

Video at the MTR. Telecast live December 14, 1952, on WPIX-TV in New York. Black and white. In Italian. 30 minutes.

1954 Rigoletto e la sua tragedia

Italian feature film: Flavio Calzavara (director), Adalberto Albertini (cinematographer), Oliviero De Fabritiis (conductor, Rome Opera Orchestra and Chorus).

Cast: Aldo Silvani (Rigoletto, sung by Tito Gobbi), Gerard Landry (Duke, sung by Mario Del Monaco), Janet Vidor (Gilda, sung by Giuseppina Arnaldi), Cesare Polacco (Sparafucile), Franca Tamantini (Maddalena).

Video: VIEW/Video Yesteryear VHS. Color. Arias in Italian, dialogue in dubbed English. 90 minutes.

1958 NBC Opera Theatre

American TV production: Samuel Chotzinoff (director), Jean Morel (conductor, NBC Symphony of the Air Orchestra and NBC Opera Theatre Chorus), Otis Riggs (set designer), Peter Herman Adler (artistic director), Joseph Machlis (English adaptation).

Cast: Igor Gorin (Rigoletto), Oreste Kirkup (Duke), Dorothy Coulter (Gilda), Joshua Hecht (Sparafucile), Gloria Lane (Maddalena).

Video: House of Opera DVD/VHS. Telecast February 16, 1958. Kirk Browning (director). Color. In English. 120 minutes.

1963 Voice of Firestone

American TV highlights production: Emerson Buckley (conductor, Voice of Firestone Orchestra).

Cast: Richard Tucker (Duke), Robert Merrill (Rigoletto), Anneliese Rothenberger (Gilda).

Video: VAI VHS titled *A Firestone Verdi Festival*. Telecast March 3, 1963. Black and white. In Italian with English introductions. 15 minutes.

1973 Who's Afraid of Opera?

English TV film: Herbert Wise (director), Richard Bonynge (conductor, London Symphony Orchestra), Claire Merrill (screenplay), George Djurkovic (set designer).

Cast: Joan Sutherland (Gilda), Pieter Van Der Stolk (Rigoletto), André Turp (Duke), Nelson Taylor (Sparafucile), Huguette Tourangeau (Maddalena), Larry Berthelson puppets.

Video: Kultur VHS. Color. In English and Italian. 30 minutes.

Comment: Highlights version for young audiences with Sutherland telling the story to puppets. Dialogue in English, arias in Italian.

1974 Focus on Opera

English highlights TV film: Peter Seabourne (director), John J. Davies (conductor, The Classical Orchestra), Peter Murray (screenplay).

Cast: Malcolm Rivers (Rigoletto), John Brecknock (Duke), Lillian Watson (Gilda), Thomas Lawlor (Sparafucile), Antonia Butler (Maddalena).

Color. In English. 54 minutes.

Comment: Abridged English-language version filmed at Knebworth House in Hertfordshire.

1977 Metropolitan Opera

American stage production: John Dexter (director), James Levine (conductor, Metropolitan Opera Orchestra and Chorus), Tanya Moiseiwitsch (set designer).

Cast: Cornell MacNeil (Rigoletto), Plácido Domingo (Duke), Ileana Cotrubas (Gilda), Justino Diaz (Sparafucile), Isola Jones (Maddalena).

Video at the MTR. Telecast live November 7, 1977. Kirk Browning (director). Color. In Italian with English subtitles. 120 minutes.

1981 Arena di Verona

Italian stage production: Carlo Lizzani (director), Donato Renzetti (conductor, Arena di Verona Orchestra and Chorus), Carlo Savi (set designer).

Cast: Garbis Boyagian (Rigoletto), Vincenzo Bello (Duke), Alida Ferrarini (Gilda), Antonio Zerbini (Sparafucile), Franca Mattiuci (Maddalena).

Video: House of Opera DVD/Mastervision/Applause VHS, Brian Large (director). Color. In Italian. 115 minutes.

Comment: Mammoth sets but a fairly traditional production by one of the best Italian filmmakers.

1981 Metropolitan Opera

American stage production: John Dexter (director), James Levine (conductor, Metropolitan Opera Orchestra and Chorus), Tanya Moiseiwitsch (set designer).

Cast: Louis Quilico (Rigoletto), Luciano Pavarotti (Duke), Christiane Eda-Pierre (Gilda), Ara Berberian (Sparafucile), Isola Jones (Maddalena).

Video at the MTR. Taped December 15, 1981; telecast December 16, 1981. Brian Large (director). Color. In Italian with English subtitles. 120 minutes.

***1982 English National Opera

English TV production: Jonathan Miller (director), Mark Elder (conductor, English National Opera Orchestra and Chorus), Patrick Robertson and Rosemary Vercoe (set/costume designers), James Fenton (English translation).

Cast: John Rawnsley (Rigoletto), Arthur Davies (Duke), Marie McLaughlin (Gilda), John Tomlinson (Sparafucile), Jean Rigby (Maddalena).

Video: HBO VHS. John Michael Phillips (director). Color. In English. 140 minutes.

Comment: Famous production updated to mob-controlled New York's Little Italy in the 1950s with the duke transmuted into a Mafia boss.

1983 Ponnelle film

Austrian feature film: Jean-Pierre Ponnelle (director), Riccardo Chailly (conductor, Vienna Philharmonic Orchestra and Vienna State Opera Chorus) Pasqualino De Santis (cinematographer), Gianni Quaranta (set designer).

Cast: Ingvar Wixell (Rigoletto), Luciano Pavarotti (Duke), Edita Gruberova (Gilda), Ferruccio Furlanetto (Sparafucile), Victoria Vergara (Maddalena), Kathleen Kuhlmann (Countess Ceprano), Fedora Barbieri (Giovanna).

Decca-London DVD/VHS. Color. In Italian with English subtitles. 116 minutes. (Highlights version in *Great Moments* VHS series as Volume 8).

Comment: Shot on location at the supposed sites of the story in Mantua. The film won an Emmy Award in 1985 when it was shown on U.S. television.

1987 Teatro Regio, Parma

Italian stage production: Pier Luigi Samaritani (director, set/costume designer), Angelo Campori (conductor, Orchestra Sinfonica dell'Emilia-Romagna and Teatro Regio Chorus).

Cast: Leo Nucci (Rigoletto), Alfredo Kraus (Duke), Luciana Serra (Gilda), Michele Pertusi (Sparafucile), Ambra Vespasiani (Maddalena).

Video: Hardy Classics/House of Opera DVD and Bel Canto Society VHS. Color. In Italian. 138 minutes.

1988 New York City Opera

American stage production: Tito Capobianco (director), Elio Boncompagni (conductor, New York City Opera Orchestra and Chorus), Carl Toms (set designer).

Cast: Brent Ellis (Rigoletto), Richard Leech (Duke), Faith Esham (Gilda), Mark S. Doss (Sparafucile), Susanne Marsee (Maddalena).

Telecast September 21, 1988. Kirk Browning (director). Color. In Italian. 180 minutes.

***2000 Royal Opera

English stage production: David McVicar (director), Sir Edward Downes (conductor, Royal Opera House Orchestra and Chorus), Michael Vale (set designer), Tanya McCallin (costume designer).

Cast: Paulo Gavanelli (Rigoletto), Marcelo Álvarez (Duke), Christine Schäfer (Gilda), Eric Halfvarson (Sparafucile), Graciela Araya (Maddalena).

Video: Naxos/BBC Opus Arte DVD. Color. In Italian with English subtitles. 169 minutes

Comment: This is an X-rated version of the opera with full-frontal nudity and sex scenes, but it is extremely effective. The DVD has an interview with McVicar explaining his ideas plus a Verdi documentary.

2001 Arena di Verona

Italian stage production: Charles Roubaud (director), Marcello Viotti (conductor, Arena di Verona Orchestra and Chorus).

Cast: Leo Nucci (Rigoletto), Aquiles Machado (Duke), Inva Muler (Gilda), Mario Luperi (Sparafucile), Sarah M'Punga (Maddalena).

Video: TDK DVD. Color. In Italian with English subtitles. 134 minutes.

Comment: The giant Arena is not the best place for this opera, which requires intimacy rather than spectacle.

Early/related films

1906/1908 Cinemafono Pagliej sound films
CINEMAFONO PAGLIEJ, an Italian sound-on-disc company specializing in opera films, screened a film featuring an aria from *Rigoletto* at the Sala Umberto I in Rome from May 19 to July 30, 1906. The company showed a *Rigoletto* film featuring Titta Ruffo in Pisa on March 28, 1908, and a film featuring the *Rigoletto* duet "Sì, vendetta!" in Rome on May 19, 1908. The films do not appear to have survived.

1908 Deutsche Bioscop sound films
The German Deutsche Bioscop Company made two sound films of music from *Rigoletto*, one with the Quartet and the other with the aria "Ach wie so trügerisch" sung by Alberti Werner. The films were screened with a synchronized recording. Black and white. In German. Each about 4 minutes. Prints in German archive.

1908 Ambrosio film
The Italian film *Rigoletto* featuring scenes from the opera was releaded the Ambrosio studio of Turin in 1908. It was photographed and directed by the industrious Giovanni Vitrotti, who made hundreds of films from 1905 to 1954. Black and white. Silent. About 9 minutes.

1909 A Fool's Revenge
A Fool's Revenge, directed by D. W. Griffith for the American Biograph Company, is based on the Verdi opera and Hugo play. Charles Inslee is Rigoletto, Owen Moore, is the Duke, and Marion Leonard is Gilda. It was screened with Verdi's music. Black and white. Silent. About 14 minutes.

1909 The Duke's Jester or A Fool's Revenge
The Duke's Jester or A Fool's Revenge, directed by J. Stuart Blackton for the American Vitagraph Company, is based on the Verdi opera and Hugo play. Maurice Costello and William Humphrey are the stars. It was screened with Verdi's music. Black and white. Silent. About 14 minutes.

1909 Film d'Art film
French film directed by André Calmettes for the Film d'Art Company in Paris titled *Rigoletto* and based on the Verdi opera. Paul Mounet and Rolla Norman star. Black and white. Silent. About 15 minutes.

1909 Le roi s'amuse
Albert Capellani's Pathé film is based on the Hugo play, but it was released in America with the title *Rigoletto* and screened with Verdi's opera music. Paul Capellani plays the hunchback, Marcelle Geniat is his daughter, and Henri Sylvain is the king. Twenty scenes. Black and white. Silent. About 14 minutes.

1909 Itala sound films
Itala Film of Torino released two sound-on-disc films in 1909 of arias from *Rigoletto*, "Miei signori" and "Piangi fanciullo." Black and white. Each about 3 minutes.

1910 Film d'Arte Italiana film
Italian film based on the opera written and directed by Gerolamo Lo Slavio and Ugo Falena for the Film d'Arte Italiana Company in Rome. Ferruccio Garavaglia and Vittoria Lepanto star. Black and white. Silent. About 12 minutes.

1917 Webb's Singing Pictures
Enrico Caruso turned up in person at the Cohan and Harris Theatre in New York on January 14, 1917, for this early attempt at sound cinema by George Webb and his Singing Pictures Company. Caruso's voice was heard singing the aria "La donna è mobile" over loudspeakers in the auditorium while a costumed actor on screen mimed the words; a Caruso record provided the soundtrack. Black and white. In Italian. About 5 minutes.

1918 Kolm/Fleck film
Austrian feature film based on the play and opera and directed by Luise Kolm and Jacob Fleck. Hermann Benke is Rigoletto, Liane Haid is Gilda, and Wilhelm Klitsch is the ding. It was shown in Germany as both *Rigoletto* and *Der König amüsiert sich*, but always with Verdi's music. Black and white. Silent. About 60 minutes.

1922 Tense Moments From Opera
A. B. Imeson is Rigoletto, Clive Brook is the duke, and Gwyn Richmond is Gilda in this English film of scenes from the opera made for the series *Tense Moments From Opera*. It was screened with live music from the opera. George Wynn directed; H. B. Parkinson produced. Black and white. Silent. About 12 minutes.

1926 British Phonofilm
The Guinness Book of Records considers this film of Act II of *Rigoletto* to be the first sound-on-film operatic production. It was made in England in 1926 and produced with the De Forest Phonofilm sound process. Black and white. In Italian. 30 minutes

1926 Vitaphone with Talley
"Marion Talley, Youthful Prima Donna of the New York Metropolitan Opera" sings Gilda's "Caro nome" in this famous Vitaphone sound short. It premiered with the first sound feature *Don Juan* on August 26, 1926, but her performance was not much liked. Black and white. In Italian. 7 minutes. On VHS and LD.

1927 Cameo Operas
Herbert Langley is Rigoletto and Mme. Karina is Gilda in this English film of scenes from the opera directed by H. B. Parkinson for the *Cameo Opera* series. Offstage singers performed the arias when the film was screened. Black and white. Silent. 20 minutes.

1927 Vitaphone Quartet
Beniamino Gigli is the duke with Marion Talley as Gilda, Jeanne Gordon as Maddalena, and Giuseppe De Luca as Rigoletto in this sound film of the *Rigoletto* Quartet made by the Vitaphone Company. It was shot in the Manhattan Opera House with the Vitaphone Symphony Orchestra. Black and white. In Italian. About 9 minutes. On VHS.

1927 Vitaphone with Hackett
Charles Hackett, the "leading tenor of the Chicago Civic Opera Co," performs "Questa o quella" and "La donna è mobile" in Italian in costume on this Vitaphone sound film. The arias were recorded in the old Manhattan Opera House with the Vitaphone Symphony Orchestra. Black and white. About 9 minutes. On VHS.

1930 Call of the Flesh
"Questa o quella" is sung by Ramon Novarro in this early Technicolor musical about a café singer who turns to opera. See CALL OF THE FLESH.

1934 Las fronteras del amor
José Mojica plays an opera singer in *Frontiers of Love* and sings the Rigoletto aria "La donna è mobile." Most of the film takes place on a ranch. Frank Strayer directed for Fox. Black and white. In Spanish. 82 minutes.

1935 I Dream Too Much
Lily Pons plays a young opera singer who sings "Caro nome" during her music lesson with her uncle. Inspired by it, she slips off to meet and fall in love with aspiring composer Henry Fonda. John Cromwell directed. Black and white. 95 minutes.

1935 Broadway Gondolier
Taxi driver Dick Powell sings "La donna è mobile" and is discovered and promoted by some music critics. When his radio career doesn't work out, he ends up in Venice as a singing gondolier. The film also features an excerpt from the Quartet. Lloyd Bacon directed. Black and white. 98 minutes.

1935 Forget-Me-Not
Beniamino Gigli sings "La donna è mobile" while on a world tour in this film about an older opera singer married to a younger woman. See FORGET-ME-NOT.

1938 Giuseppe Verdi
Beniamino Gigli plays tenor Raffaele Mirate, who created the role of the duke, in this film about the composer. He is seen practicing "La donna è mobile" with Verdi (Fosco Giachetti) in a gondola in Venice before the premiere. See GIUSEPPE VERDI.

1938 Marionette
Beniamino Gigli sings "La donna è mobile" in this Italian film about a famous opera tenor who performs with a marionette show as a favor. See MARIONETTE.

1941 Il re si diverte
Il re si diverte, shown in the United States as *The King's Jester*, is an Italian narrative film based on the Hugo play but using Verdi's music as score. Michel Simon is Rigoletto, Rossano Brazzi is King François I, and Maria Mercader is Gilda. The arias are sung by Ferruccio Tagliavini and Toti dal Monte, although only "La donna è mobile" is heard complete. Mario Bonnard directed. Black and white. In Italian. 92 minutes.

1941 Mamma
Beniamino Gigli plays an opera star whose wife is planning to leave him so, of course, he has to sing "La donna è mobile." See MAMMA.

1941 Ridin' the Cherokee Trail
This Tex Ritter B-Western contains what is surely the most bizarre version of "La donna è mobile" in the cinema. See RIDIN' THE CHEROKEE TRAIL.

1943 Crazy House
The *Rigoletto* Quartet is turned into "The Rigoletto Blues" in this absurdist Olson and Johnson comedy set in a film studio and directed by Edward Kline. Black and white. 80 minutes.

1944 Silenzio, si gira!
Beniamino Gigli plays an opera singer who gets a girl a role in his movie but finds she prefers a younger man. Naturally, he has to sing "La donna è mobile." See SILENZIO, SI GIRA!

1944 Leningrad Opera Company
Soviet short film of excerpts from *Rigoletto* performed by the Leningrad Opera Company. It was distributed theatrically in the United States in 1944. Black and white. In Russian and Italian. About 10 minutes.

1947 This Time for Keeps
Lauritz Melchior plays an opera star in this MGM musical and has a chance to sing "La donna è mobile." Richard Thorpe directed. Color. 105 minutes. MGM-UA VHS.

1948 A Song Is Born
The *Rigoletto* Quartet is featured in this Danny Kaye movie about a encyclopedia editor who has to learn about jazz. Howard Hawks directed this remake of his *Ball of Fire*. Color. 111 minutes.

1949 House of Strangers
"La donna è mobile" is heard on the soundtrack of this film about opera-loving Italian-American banker Edward G. Robinson and his dysfunctional family. Joseph Mankiewicz directed for Fox. Black and white. 101 minutes.

1949 Song of Surrender
Wanda Hendrix plays a recording of Enrico Caruso singing "La donna è mobile" in 1906 and the music becomes central to the plot. See SONG OF SURRENDER.

1951 The Great Caruso
Two scenes from *Rigoletto* are featured in this romantic biography. Enrico Caruso (Mario Lanza) has a row with a prima donna (Jarmila Novotná) before his debut at Covent Garden but triumphs onstage singing "La donna è mobile." Later on tour he sings in the Quartet in Berlin with Olive Mae Beach as Gilda. See THE GREAT CARUSO.

1951 Golden Girl
"La donna è mobile" is featured in this biopic about 19th-century entertainer Lotta Crabtree (Mitzi Gaynor). Lloyd Bacon directed. 108 minutes.

1952 The Importance of Being Earnest
Ernest (Michael Redgrave) sings "La donna è mobile" in his Albany bath as servants pour water over him. He sings it again on his way to meet the woman he loves and overhears Algernon (Michael Denison) singing the same aria. Denison is told by his valet (Walter Hudd) to pretend not to have heard. Anthony Asquith directed this fine adaptation of Oscar Wilde's play. Color. 95 minutes. On VHS.

1952 Because You're Mine
Mario Lanza sings the "Addio…speranza ed anima" cabaletto from *Rigoletto* in this film about an opera star drafted into the army. Alexander Hall directed. Color. 103 minutes. MGM-UA VHS.

1953 Melba
Patrice Munsel plays opera diva Nellie Melba in this British film biography and sings "Caro nome." Lewis Milestone directed. Color. 113 minutes.

1970 La strategia del ragno
Bernardo Bertolucci's superb film *The Spider's Stratagem*, based on a Borges story, revolves around a plot to kill Mussolini during a performance of *Rigoletto* in the opera house in a provincial city. The son of the town's hero returns after many years to find out what really happened. His father, who had betrayed the plan, arranged his own operatic assassination to create a martyr hero and was killed in the opera house during the opera. Giulio Brogi and Alida Valli star. Color. In Italian. 98 minutes. On VHS.

1984 Maestro's Company puppets
The Australian Maestro's Company presents scenes from the opera for children with puppets dubbed by opera singers. The *Rigoletto* voices belong to Joan Sutherland, Cesare Siepi, Renato Cioni, Cornell MacNeil, and Stefania Malagu. Nino Sanzogno conducts the Santa Cecilia Academy Orchestra and Chorus; William Fitzwater directed the film. Color. Dialogue in English, arias in Italian. 30 minutes. VAI VHS.

1987 Aria
Julien Temple's episode of the film *Aria* uses arias from *Rigoletto* as ironic comment. A husband and wife sneak off separately for sexual dalliance and accidentally end up at the same place, the Madonna Inn in San Luis Obispo. Buck Henry, Anita Morris, Beverly D'Angelo, and Gary Kasper are the foursome with Alfredo Kraus, Robert Merrill, and Anna Moffo as the singers. Sir Georg Solti conducts the RCA Italiana Orchestra. Color. In Italian. About 10 minutes. See ARIA.

1987 Wall Street
The duke's aria "Questa o quella" is heard on the soundtrack of Oliver Stone's film while ambitious young broker Charlie Sheen is having dinner with Daryl Hannah. Color. 124 minutes.

1992 Honeymoon in Vegas
James Caan plays a gambler who wins Nicolas Cage's fiancée Sarah Jessica Parker in a rigged poker game in this

film. The soundtrack features the aria "La donna è mobile." Andrew Bergman directed. Color. 95 minutes.

1995 Rigoletto
This musical fairy tale was inspired by the opera, but it does not use Verdi's music and the story is not the same. The deformed Rigoletto character (Ribaldi) is played by Los Angles Civic Opera veteran Joseph Paur. He befriends singer Bonnie (Ivey Lloyd) in a beauty-and-the-beast story. Leo Paur directed. Color. 98 minutes.

1995 Operavox animated opera
The British animation studio Bare Boards created an animated version of *Rigoletto* for the British Operavox series with the music performed by the Welsh National Opera Orchestra. Wyn Davies was music editor. Color. 27 minutes.

1999 The Barber of Siberia
Director Nikita Mikhalkov features Gilda's aria "Caro nome" in this film set in Russia in 1885. Oleg Menshikov plays a soldier who is involved with Julia Ormond. Color. In Russian. 180 minutes.

1999 Analyze This
Music from *Rigoletto* is featured in this film about a mobster (Robert De Niro) who needs help from a psychiatrist (Billy Crystal). Harold Ramis directed. Color. 103 minutes.

2000 The Family Man
Two versions of "La donna è mobile" are heard in this film about a banker (Nicolas Cage) who discovers the joys of family life. The first time it is sung by Luciano Pavarotti with the London Symphony Orchestra, the second time by Alfredo Kraus with the RCA Italiana Opera Orchestra and Chorus. Brett Ratner directed. Color. 125 minutes.

2000 Le goût des autres
This popular French film about an industrialist in love with an actress features two numbers from *Rigoletto*: soprano Edita Gruberova sings "Caro nome" with the Santa Cecilia National Orchestra and Chorus led by Giuseppe Sinopoli, and baritone Edward Tumagian and soprano Alida Ferrarini perform a duet with the Slovakian Radio Symphony Orchestra and Chorus. Agnès Jaoui directed. Color. 112 minutes.

RIMINI, GIACOMO
Italian baritone (1887–1952)

Giacomo Rimini sang with his wife Rosa Raisa in the premiere of Puccini's *Turandot* in 1926; she was Turandot and he was Pong. Rimini, who was born in Italy in 1887, made his debut in 1910 singing Albert in *Werther* and sang Falstaff in 1915 for Arturo Toscanini in Milan. He sang regularly with his wife in Chicago, and they opened a singing school there in 1937. He left one film that shows his vocal and acting ability.

1927 Vitaphone film
"Giacomo Rimini, Baritone, of the Chicago Opera Company" is featured with "Rosa Raisa, Soprano" in this Vitaphone film made in 1927 at the old Manhattan Opera House in New York. The film features excerpts from Act IV of *Il trovatore*. Black and white. About 8 minutes. Bel Canto Society VHS.

RIMSKY-KORSAKOV, NIKOLAI
Russian composer (1844–1908)

Nikolai Rimsky-Korsakov concentrated on works for orchestra during the 1880s but seeing Wagner's *Ring* made him want to focus on operas. He wrote 15, beginning with *The Maid of Pskov* (IVAN THE TERRIBLE) in 1873, most of them based on Russian folklore and legend with fantasy elements and memorable melodies. The popular "Flight of the Bumble Bee," for example, comes from his opera THE TALE OF TSAR SALTAN. He also helped build the Mozart poisoning legend through his opera MOZART AND SALIERI. Rimsky-Korsakov was a superb arranger and took it upon himself to complete many of his colleagues' unfinished operas, not without controversy. See also THE GOLDEN COCKEREL, MAY NIGHT, MLADA, THE LEGEND OF THE INVISIBLE CITY OF KITEZH, SADKO, and THE TSAR'S BRIDE.

1947 Song of Scheherazade
Jean-Pierre Aumont plays Rimsky-Korsakov in this kitsch American film; it's poor biography but highly enjoyable for its garish awfulness. It's set in 1865 when naval cadet Lt. Nikolai Rimsky-Korsakov falls in love with dance hall girl Yvonne De Carlo, who inspires him to write his greatest music. Opera tenor Charles Kullman plays Dr. Klin, the physician of the Russian Navy ship on which the composer is traveling, and he does all the singing in the film, even the soprano aria "Hymn to the Sun" from *The Golden Cockerel*. Walter Reisch directed for Universal with musical direction from Miklos Rozsa. Color. 107 minutes.

1948 Song of My Heart

David Leonard plays Rimsky-Korsakov in this much-disliked American film about Tchaikovsky. See PYOTR TCHAIKOVSKY.

1952 Rimsky-Korsakov

Grigori Belov plays the composer in this lavish if somewhat stolid Soviet film biography. Nikolai Cherkassov plays Stassov and basso Alexander Ognivtsev has the singing role of Chaliapin. There are excerpts from *The Snow Maiden* (with Ognivtsev and L. Grisasenko), *Sadko, The Tale of Tsar Saltan,* and *The Golden Cockerel,* all specially staged for the film by the Kirov Opera with Boris Khaikin leading the Kirov Opera Orchestra. Grigory Roshal and Gennadi Kazansky directed the film from a screenplay by Roshal and A. Abramova. Color. In Russian. 113 minutes.

RINALDO
1711 opera by Handel

GEORGE FRIDERIC HANDEL'S *Rinaldo* was the first Italian opera created for the English stage and the first opera Handel composed for London. It was a big success and began the rage for Handel operas in Italian. Giacomo Rossi's libretto is based on Tarquato Tasso's 1575 epic poem about the First Crusade, *Gerusalemme Liberata,* and revolves around Crusade hero Rinaldo and his loves and adventures. The famous castrato Nicolini portrayed him at the London premiere.

2001 Prinzregententheater, Munich

German stage production: David Alden (director), Harry Bicket (conductor, Bavarian State Orchestra).

Cast: David Daniels (Rinaldo), David Walker (Goffredo), Deborah York (Almirenaë, Noemi Nadelmann (Armida), Egil Silins (Argante).

Video: Arthaus DVD. Brian Large (director). In Italian with English subtitles. Color. 217 minutes.

Comment: Alden updates the action with the some of cast wearing trenchcoats and the Crusader Geoffrey transformed into a television evangelist. The DVD includes an informative documentary by Reiner E. Moritz, *Handel the Entertainer,* with comments from Alden, Bicket and Nicholas Hytner.

Early/related films

1911 La Gerusalemme liberata

Emilio Ghione plays Rinaldo in this Italian silent film of the Tasso epic that was the basis for Handel's opera. Amleto Novelli plays Tancredi, Fernanda Negri-Pouget is Armida, and Gianna Terribili-Gonzales is Clorinda. Enrico Guazzoni spent five months directing this epic for Cines with a cast of more than 800. It was shown in the United States as *The Crusaders or Jerusalem Delivered* and promoted as the "most magnificent production in the history of motion pictures." Black and white. About 60 minutes.

1985 Honor, Profit and Pleasure

Anna Ambrose's film about Handel features excerpts from a beautifully reconstructed performance of *Rinaldo,* created with a feeling for period and performance style. About 5 minutes of the opera are shown at the beginning of the movie with authentic sets and special effects. James Bowman impersonates Nicolini singing Rinaldo's aria "Cara sposa" with support from Nicola Jenkin and Liz Anderson. Simon Callow plays Handel and Alan Devlin plays Handel's friend James Quin, who narrates the film. Nicholas Kraemer was the musical director, and Peter Luke was the coscripter. Color. 70 minutes. Films for the Humanities VHS.

2000 The Monkey's Mask

Yvonne Kenny sings Almirena's aria "Lascia ch'io pianga" with the Australian Brandenburg Orchestra on the soundtrack of this Australian film about the disappearance of a student poet in Sydney. Samantha Lang directed. Color. 93 minutes.

2001 L.I.E.

"Lascia ch'io pianga" from *Rinaldo* is sung by the Vienna Boy Choir at the end of this coming-of-age film, as the adolescent protagonist enters a prison to see his father. Michael Cuesto directed. (L.I.E. = Long Island Expressway.) Color. 87 minutes.

RING DES NIBELUNGEN, DER
1876 opera tetralogy by Wagner

RICHARD WAGNER'S *Der Ring des Nibelungen* (The Ring of the Nibelung) is the longest and most complex work in opera, an heroic fantasy of great power. The Nibelungs are mythological German dwarves, and the ring is a magic ring of ultimate power. The four operas, DAS RHEINGOLD, DIE WALKÜRE, SIEGFRIED, and GÖTTERDÄMMERUNG, were first staged as a group at Bayreuth in August 1876. Each opera is complete in itself, but together they tell a multigenerational saga of greed, curses, love, incest, betrayal, and heroism among the ancient Norse gods and heroes. The story begins when the Nibelung Alberich steals magic gold from the Rhine Maidens and creates the ring and a magic helmet called the Tarnhelm. It ends with the destruction of Valhalla and the retrieval of the gold by the Rhine Maidens. There are five complete versions of the *Ring* cycle on video and a sixth that has been telecast; all are worthwhile although none is a clear-cut favorite. The Met version seems to be closest to what Wagner imagined.

1979/1980 Bayreuth Festival
Conductor Pierre Boulez and director Brian Large created the first complete version of the tetralogy on film or video, Patrice Chéreau's once controversial 1976 Bayreuth Festival production (filmed in 1979 and 1980) was televised worldwide. Chéreau sets the operas in the 19th century with the Rhine Maidens on a hydroelectric dam and the costumes ranging from medieval to Victorian. The casts include Donald McIntyre as Wotan, Peter Hofmann as Siegmund, and Gwyneth Jones as Brünnhilde. The box set contains a film called *The Making of the Ring*. Color. In German with English subtitles. 832 minutes. Philips DVD/VHS/LD.

1989 Bavarian State Opera
Wolfgang Sawallisch was the conductor of the second complete tetralogy taped in Munich with the Bavarian State Opera. It is a rather science fiction–like production staged by Nikolaus Lehnhoff. The casts include Robert Hale as Wotan, Hildegard Behrens as Brünnhilde, and René Kollo as Siegfried. EMI VHS/Japanese LD.

***1990 Metropolitan Opera
James Levine conducted the third complete taped tetralogy for the Met—a solid, traditional production by Otto Schenk with naturalistic sets and costumes by Günther Schneider-Siemssen. The casts include James Morris as Wotan, Hildegard Behrens as Brünnhilde, and Siegfried Jerusalem as Siegfried. It was directed for video by Brian Large and telecast on PBS over four nights in June 1990, at 17 hours the longest opera telecast in American TV history. DG DVD/VHS/LD.

1991 Bayreuth Festival
Daniel Barenboim conducted the fourth complete tetralogy from the Bayreuth Festival, a modernist technological production by Harry Kupfer staged in 1988 and filmed in 1991. Hans Schavernoch created the austere minimalist sets. The casts include John Tomlinson as Wotan, Anne Evans as Brünnhilde, and Poul Elming as Siegfried. The series was directed for video by Horant H. Hohlfeld. Teldec VHS/LD.

1996 Jutland Opera
Denmark's Jutland Opera's all-Scandinavian cast *Ring*, staged by Klaus Hoffmeyer with sets and costumes by Lars Juhl, was telecast in 1996 by Danmarks Radio, Copenhagen, from the Musikhuset in Aarhus. Lars Waage sang Wotan with Lisbeth Balslev as Brünnhilde, Stig Anderson is Siegfried, Jørgen Klint as Alberich, Aage Haugland as Hunding and Hagen, Poul Elming as Sieg-mund, and Tina Kiberg as Sieglinde. Tamás Vetö conducted *Rheingold* and *Siegfried* while Francesco Cristofoli conducted *Walküre* and *Götterdämmerung*. Thomas Grimm directed the videos. Musikhuset Aarhus VHS.

1999 Netherlands Opera
Harmut Haenchen conducted the complete *Ring* cycle at the Netherlands Opera in 1999 in a production by Pierre Audi, telecast with the orchestra on the stage. The cast included Wolfgang Göbbel, Jeannine Altmeyer, John Bröcheler, Henk Smit, Graham Clark, Chris Merritt, Anne Gjevang, John Keyes, and Wolfgang Schöne. Haenchen led the Nederlands Philharmonic Orchestra and Opera Chorus. Misjel Vermeiren and Hans Hulscher directed the telecasts in Holland in December 1999.

Early/related films

1910 I Nibelungi
Italian film inspired by the Wagner epic and screened with the opera music. Mario Bernacchi wrote and directed it for the Milano Film Company. Although it was only a third of an hour long, it was promoted as the "dramatic story of the Wagnerian tetralogy." Black and white. Silent. About 20 minutes.

1912 L'epopea dei Nibelunghi
Alberto Capozzi, Franz Sala, and Antonietta Calderari star in this Italian film of the Nibelungen legend directed by Mario Caserini for the Cines Company of Rome. Written by Arrigo Frusta and Alberto Capozzi, it is also known as *Siegfried*. Black and white. Silent. About 14 minutes.

1924 Die Nibelungen
The most famous non-operatic version of the story was created by German director Fritz Lang and his scriptwriter wife Thea Von Harbou. It is based on the original 13th-century epic poem and differs considerably from the Wagner operas, but it features a truly great dragon. Paul Richter plays Siegfried, Margarete Schön is Kriemhild, Hanna Ralph is Brünnhilde, and Rudolph Klein-Rogge is Attila. The film was made in two parts, *Siegfried* and *Kriemhild's Revenge,* and released with music by Gottfried Huppertz played live. Black and white. Silent. 249 minutes.

1927 The Ring
This very abbreviated *Ring,* made for the English series *Cameo Opera,* was reportedly based on all the Wagner operas. H. H. Parkinson directed and John E. Blakely produced. The film was silent, but it was screened with live orchestra and singers. Black and white. About 22 minutes.

1952 Operation: Rabbit

Bugs Bunny meets Wiley E. Coyote in this superb cartoon filled with music from the *Ring* operas, including Siegfried's theme and the music for the trip to Alberich's cave in *Rheingold*. Carl Stalling arranged the music, Michael Maltese wrote the script, and Chuck Jones directed. Color. 7 minutes.

1957 La leggenda dei Nibelunghi

Italian film based on the Nibelungen legend directed by Giacomo Gentilomo. Sebastian Fischer plays Sigfrido (i.e., Siegfried), Ilaria Occhini is Crimilde, and Katharina Mayberg is Brunilde. The film borrows music from Wagner's *Siegfried* and *Götterdämmerung*. Also known as *Sigfrido*. Color. In Italian. 95 minutes.

1957 What's Opera, Doc?

Chuck Jones's animated film for Warner Bros. is a brilliant pastiche of the *Ring*. Elmer Fudd plays Siegfried hunting down Bugs Bunny while singing, to the Valkyries' music, "Kill da wabbit, kill da wabbit." Bugs disguises himself as Brünnhilde and they try a love duet. See WHAT'S OPERA, DOC?

1965 The Golden Ring

Humphrey Burton's *The Golden Ring: The Making of Solti's "Ring"* is a BBC film about the creation of the classic Decca recording with Georg Solti conducting the Vienna Philharmonic. It focuses primarily on the recording of *Götterdämmerung* in 1964, and Burton brilliantly immerses the viewer in the task alongside record producer John Culshaw. The singers are Birgit Nilsson as Brünnhilde, Wolfgang Windgassen as Siegfried, Gottlob Frick as Hagen, Claire Watson as Gutrune, and Dietrich Fischer-Dieskau as Gunther. The Solti recording of the *Ring* is now available on CD. Black and white. In English. Decca DVD (157 minutes with recording excerpts) or London VHS and LD (87 minutes).

1966 Die Nibelungen

Spectacular modern German narrative version of the story modeled on the 13th-century saga and the Fritz Lang film. Uwe Beyer is Siegfried, Karin Dor is Brünnhilde, Maria Marlow is Kriemhild, and Herbert Lom is Attila. It was released in the United States as *Whom the Gods Wish to Destroy*. Harald Reinl directed. Color. In German. 195 minutes.

1980 The Making of the Ring

Peter Wienberg's informative documentary about the filming of the Bayreuth *Ring* in 1980 features Friedlind Wagner, Wolfgang Wagner, Patrice Chéreau, Pierre Boulez, Gwyneth Jones, Donald McIntyre, and Brian Large. Written by John Ardoin and narrated by George Grizzard, it is included with the video of *Die Walküre*. Color. In English and German with English subtitles. About 59 minutes. Philips DVD/VHS/LD.

1990 Scenes from the Ring at the Met

Compilation of scenes from the four videos of the Metropolitan Opera's 1990 *Ring* cycle. The tetralogy was produced by Otto Schenk and conducted by James Levine. Color. 90 minutes. DG VHS.

1992 Valhalla

Goofy but affectionate American film comedy built around the *Ring* cycle. The sons of an ailing opera buff stage a bargain basement lip-synched version of the four operas in his house, using whomever and whatever they can get to help. The biker chick who plays Brünnhilde thinks of it as a musical version of *Conan the Barbarian*, while the muscular surfer who plays Siegfried thinks he is catching musical waves. Jonathan D. Grift wrote and directed this odd Wagnerian homage. Color. In English. 87 minutes.

RIO RITA

1927 operetta by Tierney

HARRY TIERNEY wrote this traditional-style operetta at the direct request of Broadway showman Florenz Ziegfeld, and it turned out to be a surprise hit on stage and screen. Joseph McCarthy wrote the lyrics and Guy Bolton and Fred Thompson wrote the book for this variation on the who-is-the-bandit theme. A Texas Ranger chases a masked outlaw, known as Kinkajou, and falls in love with Rio Rita, who might be the bandit's sister. The most popular songs were the title tune and the stirring "March of the Rangers."

1929 RKO film

American feature film: Luther Reed (director/screenplay), Robert Kurrle and Lloyd Knechtel (cinematographers), Victor Baravalle (music director), RKO (studio).

Cast: Bebe Daniel (Rita), John Boles (Capt. Jim Stewart), Don Alvarado (Roberto Ferguson), Bert Wheeler (Chick Bean), Robert Woolsey (Ed Lovett).

Black and white and some color. In English. 135 minutes.

Comment: Advertised as "The Radio Pictures Screen Operetta," and a major hit, this film helped create an operetta boom at the beginning of the sound era.

1942 MGM film

American feature film: S. Sylvan Simon (director), Richard Connell and Gladys Lehman (screenplay), George Folsey (cinematographer), Herbert Stothart (music director), MGM (studio).

Cast: Kathryn Grayson (Rita), John Carroll (Ricardo), Bud Abbott (Doc), Lou Costello (Wishy).

Black and white. In English. 91 minutes.

Comment: Risë Stevens was considered for the role of Rita in this modernized version of the operetta that reflects its wartime production; there are Nazis in disguise on a Western ranch. As a musical bonus, Grayson sings the "Shadow Song" from *Dinorah.*

1950 NBC Television

American TV production: William Corrigan (director), Harry Sosnick (conductor, Harry Sosnick Orchestra), Kevin Johnson (choreographer).

Cast: Patricia Morison (Rita), John Tyers (Capt. Jim Stewart), Bert Wheeler (Chick Bean), Hal LeRoy (Ed Lovett), Donald Buka (Roberto).

Telecast November 13, 1950, on NBC's *Musical Comedy Time.* Black and white. In English. 60 minutes.

RISE AND FALL OF THE CITY OF MAHAGONNY

See AUFSTIEG UND FALL DER STADT MAHAGONNY.

RITCHIE, MARGARET
English soprano (1903–1969)

Margaret Ritchie created roles in three important English operas: Vaughan Williams's *The Poisoned Kiss,* Britten's THE RAPE OF LUCRETIA (Lucia), and Britten's ALBERT HERRING (Miss Wordsworth). Her most famous recording is a fine version of James Hook's song "Hush, Every Breeze" included in the collection *The Record of Singing;* she had originally sung it in a film.

1945 Pink String and Sealing Wax

Ritchie plays soprano Adelina Patti in this Ealing film set in Brighton in 1880. As Patti, she sings James Hook's song "Hush, Every Breeze," which was so popular that she recorded it in 1948. The film is the story of a publican's wife who plots to poison her husband. Robert Hamer directed. Black and white. 89 minutes.

RITORNO
1940 Italian-German film with opera content

BENIAMINO GIGLI plays an opera tenor named Beniamino Gigli who is asked to sing the role of Ulysses in a new opera *Penelope,* based on the Greek legend of the most faithful wife in history. The request comes from Marte Harell, who wants to sing Penelope (actual singing by Mafalda Favero) as the opera was composed for her by her Italian boyfriend Rossano Brazzi. The scenes from this imaginary opera were created by opera composer Riccardo Zandonai, best known for FRANCESCO DA RIMINI. The film also has a scene from *La bohème.* Geza Von Bolvary directed; J. B. Malina, Georg C. Klaren, and Richard Billinger wrote the screenplay; and the film was made in Berlin in Italian and German versions. The German film, titled *Traummusik,* has the same cast. In Italy the film is also known as *Melodie di sogno.* Black and white. 80 minutes. In German or Italian. Bel Canto/Opera Dubs VHS.

RITORNO D'ULISSE IN PATRIA, IL
1640 opera by Monteverdi

CLAUDIO MONTEVERDI's Venetian opera *Il ritorno d'Ulisse in patria* (The Return of Ulysses to his Homeland) tells of the final adventure of the hero of the *Odyssey.* The weary traveler returns home after 20 years disguised as a beggar to see what has occurred in his absence. Penelope is still faithful, but she is under siege from ardent suitors, and his son Telemaco (Telemachus) is not strong enough to take control. Ulysses destroys the suitors in an extraordinary scene during which his mighty bow becomes a test of strength. The libretto by Giacomo Badoara keeps fairly close to Homer.

***1973 Glyndebourne Festival

English stage production: Peter Hall (director), Raymond Leppard (conductor, London Philharmonic and Glyndebourne Festival Chorus), John Bury (set designer).

Cast: Benjamin Luxon (Ulisse), Janet Baker (Penelope), Richard Lewis (Eumete/Eumaeus), Ian Caley (Telemaco), Anne Howells (Minerva), Robert Lloyd (Nettuno/Neptune), Brian Burrows (Giove/Jupiter), Ugo Trama (Antinoo).

Video: Opera d'Oro/VAI VHS. Dave Heather (director). Color. In Italian with English subtitles. 152 minutes.

Comment: Slightly abridged but excellent production with Luxon and Baker in marvelous form.

1980 Ponnelle film

Swiss feature film: Jean-Pierre Ponnelle (director), Nikolaus Harnoncourt (conductor, Monteverdi Ensemble of the Zurich Opera House), Wolfgang Treu (cinematographer), Gerd Janka (set designer), Pet Halmen (costume designer).

Cast: Werner Hollweg (Ulisse), Trudeliese Schmidt (Penelope), Francisco Araiza (Telemaco), Simon Estes (Antinoo), Paul Esswood (Anfinomo), Philippe Huttenlocher (Eumete), Janet Perry (Melanto).

Color. In Italian with English subtitles. 154 minutes.

Comment: This outstanding film grew out of a cycle of the Monteverdi operas produced by Ponnelle and Harnoncourt at the Zurich Opera House.

1985 Salzburg Festival

Austrian stage production: Michael Hampe (director), Jeffrey Tate (conductor, ORF Symphony Orchestra and Tölzer Boys Choir), Mauro Pagano (set/costume designer), Hans Werner Henze (adaptation).

Cast: Thomas Allen (Ulysses), Kathleen Kuhlmann (Penelope), Robert Tear (Eumete), Alejandro Ramirez (Telemachus), Delores Ziegler (Minerva), Manfred Schenk (Nettuno), James King (Giove), Harald Stamm (Antinoo), Curtis Rayam (Iro).

Video: Image Entertainment DVD/Home Vision VHS/Pioneer LD. Claus Viller (director). Color. In Italian with English subtitles. 187 minutes.

2002 Zurich Opera

Swiss stage production: Klaus-Michael Grüber (director), Nikolaus Harnoncourt (conductor, Orchestra La Scintilla of the Opernhaus Zürich).

Cast: Dietrich Henschel (Ulysses), Vesselina Kasarova (Penelope), Isabel Rey (Minerva), Pavel Daniluk (Neptune), Rudolf Schasching (Iro), Anton Scharinger (Jupiter).

Video: Arthaus Musik DVD. Felix Breisach (director). Color. In Italian with English subtitles. 155 minutes.

Comment: Gruber uses puppets for the suitors with a simple, effective set and first-class singers.

ROBERTO DEVEREUX

1837 opera by Donizetti

Robert Devereux is the Earl of Essex, whom Queen Elizabeth I loved but sentenced to death anyway. GAETANO DONIZETTI's opera *Roberto Devereux*, composed to a libretto by Salvatore Cammarano, is based on a French play and is more about the queen than Essex. Elizabeth loves Devereux, but he prefers Sara, the Duchess of Nottingham, and the duke is suspicious. When Devereux is accused of treason, Elizabeth sentences him to death out of spite and then cannot reprieve him in time. The opera is known in our time mostly through productions starring Montserrat Caballé and Beverly Sills. The stormy relationship between Elizabeth and Essex was also the basis of a famous and influential Hollywood film.

1975 Wolf Trap Farm Park

American stage production: Tito Capobianco (director), Julius Rudel (conductor, Filene Center Orchestra and Wolf Trap Company Chorus), Ming Cho Lee (set designer).

Cast: Beverly Sills (Elisabetta/Queen Elizabeth), John Alexander (Devereux), Susanne Marsee (Sara), Richard Fredricks (Nottingham), John Lankston (Lord Cecil), David Rae Smith (Gualitero/Walter Raleigh).

Video: VAI DVD/VHS. Kirk Browning (director). Color. In Italian with English subtitles. 145 minutes.

Comment: Sills had one of her greatest successes in this role and had perfected her characterization for five years when the Wolf Trap production was telecast.

1977 Aix-en-Provence Festival

French stage production: Julius Rudel (conductor, Aix-en-Provence Festival Orchestra and Chorus).

Cast: Montserrat Caballé (Queen Elizabeth), José Carreras (Devereux), Janet Coster (Sara), Franco Bordoni (Nottingham).

Video: House of Opera/Lyric VHS. Color. In Italian. 140 minutes.

1998 Teatro San Carlo, Naples

Italian stage production: Alain Guingal (conductor, San Carlo Opera House Orchestra and Chorus).

Cast: Alexandrina Pendatchanska (Queen Elizabeth), Giuseppe Sabbatini (Devereux), Ildikó Komlósi (Sarah), Roberto Servile (Nottingham).

Video: Image Entertainment DVD. Alberto Fassini (director). Color. In Italian with English subtitles. 136 minutes.

Related film

1939 The Private Lives of Elizabeth and Essex

This enjoyable and colorful film, starring Bette Davis as Elizabeth and Errol Flynn as Devereux/Essex, is based on the Maxwell Anderson play *Elizabeth the Queen*. It has had considerable influence on productions of the opera. Beverly Sills is said to have modeled her performance on Davis's, and set designs for a Met production were based on those created for the film. Michael Curtiz directed the film for Warner Bros. Color. 106 minutes.

ROBESON, PAUL

American bass (1898–1976)

African-American Paul Robeson was not able to become a professional opera singer because of the racial bigotry of his time, and it was a sad loss for American opera. Like his gifted female counterpart Marian Anderson, he settled for a concert career. He once commented that the only place he could sing opera was in the bathroom, and he recorded only one opera aria, the Prayer from *Boris*

Godunov. He was George Gershwin's first choice for Porgy, but he had to turn the role down because of other commitments. He plays Joe in the fine 1936 film version of SHOW BOAT, and his performance of the bass aria *Ol' Man River* is the highlight of the movie. His first film was the 1925 *Body and Soul* followed in 1933 by a version of Eugene O'Neill's *The Emperor Jones,* in which he had starred on stage. His other movies include *Sanders of the River* (1935), *Song of Freedom* (1936), *King Solomon's Mines* (1937), *Jerico* (1937), and *Proud Valley* (1940). Most of his films are available on video from the Bel Canto Society and other distributors.

ROBIN, MADO
French soprano (1918–1960)

Coloratura Mado Robin was much admired in France, but she remains relatively little known in America. Robin was noted for her vocal agility and extremely high range while singing roles such as Lucia, Lakmé, and Stravinsky's Nightingale. She made her debut in Paris in 1945, gained popular fame as Gilda and Rosina, and was seen as Lucia and Gilda in San Francisco in 1954. She died young of cancer, but she left film and television records of many performances.

1985 Mado Robin, Highest Voice in the World
Robin is shown in performance on the Opéra-Comique stage and on television singing coloratura arias (including the "Bell Song" from *Lakmé*) in this French TV documentary by Ariane Adriani. Arias associated with her career are performed by guest sopranos Christine Barbaux, Michele Langrande, and Ghyslaine Raphanel. Color. In French. 60 minutes. House of Opera/Lyric VHS.

1992 Mado Robin Live!
Robin's coloratura range is evident in this fascinating compilation. She is seen in the *Lucia di Lammermoor* Mad Scene with a B-flat above high C, in *Hamlet* with an F-sharp, and in *Mireille* with a G. The selections, which also include *Lakmé, Rigoletto,* and *The Barber of Seville,* come from kinescopes of French television appearances. Black and white. 24 minutes. Bel Canto VHS.

ROBSON, CHRISTOPHER
English countertenor (1953–)

Christopher Robson made his debut in Birmingham in the opera *Sosarme* after studying with countertenor Paul Esswood. He sings in both modern and baroque opera and has had considerable success in operas by Handel. He was especially liked as Arsamene in SERSE (1988) and Polinesso in ARIODANTE (1996) at the English National Opera, and he joins Claron McFadden in a duet from *So-*

sarme in a 1996 film of HANDEL arias set in modern London. He was also very impressive in the title role of Glass's AKHNATEN in Houston in 1984.

RODELINDA
1725 opera by Handel

During a dynastic war between brothers over the kingdom of Lombardy, Rodelinda mourns her supposedly dead husband Bertarido, who has actually fled safely to Hungary. After many trials and tribulations, he returns to rescue her from the villainous Garibaldo. Georg Frideric Handel's opera *Rodelinda, regina de' longobardi,* libretto by Nicola Francesco Haym based on incidents in Lombard history, premiered at the King's Theatre, Haymarket, on February 13, 1725. It was not produced in America until 1931.

1998 Glyndebourne Festival
English TV production: Jean-Marie Villegier (director), William Christie (conductor, Orchestra of the Age of Enlightenment).

Cast: Anna Caterina Antonacci (Rodelinda), Andreas Scholl (Bertarido), Umberto Chiummo (Garibaldo), Louise Winter (Edwige), Kurt Streit (Grimoaldo), Artur Stefanowicz (Unulfo).

Video: NVC Arts (GB) VHS. Telecast June 27, 1998, on Channel 4. Humphrey Burton (director). Color. In Italian with English subtitles. 200 minutes.

Comment: In an attempt to give it modern relevance, Villegier updates the opera to a modern fascist-like state during the 1920s.

RODGERS, RICHARD
American composer (1902–1979)

Richard Rodgers was, in his time, the composer whose work represented the best of his country's musical theater. He was a major force in American music for 50 years, the first half (1918 to 1943) in a magnificent collaboration with librettist/lyricist LORENZ HART culminating in the masterpiece *Pal Joey,* the second half in an equally notable collaboration with OSCAR HAMMERSTEIN II beginning with "the first American vernacular opera" OKLAHOMA! Rodgers and Hart started off with an "American jazz opera" in their first successful stage show, *The Joy Spreaders,* but it was not popular and they did not venture down that road again. Instead, they simply created some of the finest songs and musicals of the American stage. After Hart died, Rodgers formed a partnership with Hammerstein and forged a new genre of American operetta music. After *Oklahoma!,* they created the classics CAROUSEL, SOUTH PACIFIC, THE KING AND I, and THE SOUND OF MUSIC. A fair amount of operatic singing is featured in these shows, and there is usually an operatic mezzo-soprano. *South Pacific* was created for opera bass Ezio Pinza, Helen Traubel starred in *Pipe Dream,* and *Carousel* has an operatic soliloquy. Many of Rodgers's operettas have been recorded by opera singers and have begun to enter the opera house repertory. The Rodgers & Hammerstein Archive of Recorded Sound at the New York Public Library for the Performing Arts at Lincoln Center is an invaluable research center.

1948 Words and Music
Tom Drake plays Rodgers with Mickey Rooney as Hart in this musical biography. The film is not much, but there are impressive musical numbers by Lena Horne, Judy Garland, Perry Como, Gene Kelly, and Cyd Charisse. Norman Taurog directed for MGM. Color. 119 minutes.

RODRIGUE ET CHIMÈNE
1892 opera by Debussy

CLAUDE DEBUSSY did not finish the heroic opera *Rodrigue et Chimène,* so it was not staged during his lifetime; however, it was eventually premiered in extract form at the Bibliothèque Nationale in 1987. It's a version of the story of the Spanish knight El Cid composed to a libretto by Catulle Mendès. Rodrigue, the Cid, is in love with Chimène, the daughter of Don Gomez who has insulted Rodrigue's father. Rodrigue sets out to win her love even though he knows he will have to avenge his father. The story is also the basis of Massenet's 1885 opera LE CID.

1993 Opéra de Lyon
French stage production: Kent Nagano (conductor, Opéra de Lyon Orchestra and Chorus), Richard Langham Smith (re-creation), Edison Denisov (orchestration).

Cast: Laurence Dale (Rodrigue), Donna Brown (Chimène), José van Dam (Don Diègue), Hélène Jossoud (Inez), Jules Bastin (Don Gomez).

Video: On VHS/LD. Color. In French. 109 minutes.

Comment: First staged performance of the Debussy opera in complete form.

ROEG, NICOLAS
English film director (1928–)

Nicolas Roeg, who began his cinema career as a cinematographer, switched to directing with the controversial 1970 film *Performance.* The films that followed, *Walkabout* and *Don't Look Now,* were more popular, but *Bad Timing* was again the center of controversy. Roeg directed the excellent UN BALLO IN MASCHERA episode of the 1987 English opera film ARIA featuring his wife Theresa Russell. He also features opera on the sound-

tracks of other films, including the LA TRAVIATA Brindisi in his 1973 Venice film *Don't Look Now.*

ROGER, VICTOR
French composer (1853–1904)

Victor Roger created some 30 operettas during the latter part of the 19th century, more or less in the style of Offenbach and Lecocq, and they were staged in Paris with the major stars of the time. Most are forgotten today, even in France, except for *Joséphine vendue par ses soeurs* (1886), in which the biblical Joseph is turned into a woman in a parody of Méhul's grand opera *Joseph,* and the LES VINGT-HUIT JOURS DE CLAIRETTE (1892), which was filmed.

ROI DANSE, LE
2000 French film biography of Lully

Director Gérard Corbiau, who earlier made the operatic films LE MAÎTRE DU MUSIQUE and FARINELLI, tells the story of the founder of French opera, Jean-Baptiste Lully. *Le roi danse* (known as *The King Is Dancing* in English) is structured as a flashback as Lully (Boris Terral) reminisces from his deathbed while dying of gangrene from a self-inflicted foot injury. He becomes ballet and music master to the Sun King Louis XIV (Benoît Magimel) in 1653, despite opposition from the Queen Mother, Anne of Austria (Colette Emmanuelle), and he grows in favor as his music calms the king's fevers. Soon he is writing ballets for the king, who likes to dance to them, and enjoying a fruitful collaboration with Molière (Tchéky Karyo). When rival Cambert has success with his opera *Pomone* in 1671, Lully decides that opera will be the future, and he persuades the king to give him all rights to the genre. The music used in the film, almost entirely by Lully, is performed by the Musica Antique Köln, led by Reinhard Goebel, and the Ex Tempore Choir, led by Florian Heyerick. Music and staged scenes of ARMIDE, *Atys,* and other Lully operas are included. The screenplay by Eva de Castro, Andrée Corbiau and the director is based on Philippe Beaussant's book *Lully ou le musicien du soleil.* Gérard Simon was the cinematographer. Color. In French. 114 minutes. Remstar DVD.

ROMANCE IN THE DARK
1938 American film with opera content

Met contralto Gladys Swarthout stars in this operatic film set in Hungry, which features her singing the "Berceuse" from the Benjamin Godard opera *Jocelyn,* the "Habanera" from *Carmen,* the "Song of India" from *Sadko,* and a duet from *Don Giovanni.* She plays Ilona Boros, a young singer with operatic aspirations. When her small town music school graduation is attended by opera baritone Tony Kovach (John Boles) and his manager Zoltan Jason (John Barrymore), she decides to follow them to Budapest for an audition. They are too busy chasing beautiful Countess Monica Foldessy (Claire Dodd), but Tony's butler Fritz (Fritz Feld) hires her to be a maid. She finally auditions for Tony while he is sleeping. It's a failure but he decides to use her to lure Jason away from the countess. Ilona pretends to be an Egyptian princess, and Jason falls for her and gets her a booking at the Budapest opera. In the meantime Tony realizes he is love with her, not the countess. Ilona's debut is widely publicized and the performance is sold out, but a gossip columnist learns that she is a fake princess. The news is circulated at the performance, and the audience boos her and throw fruit. She confesses to the fraud and tries to continue, but she has great difficulty until Tony joins her on stage to sing "La ci darem la mano." The audience cheers. Frank Partos and Anne Morrison Chapin wrote the screenplay based on Hermann Bahr's German play *Die Gelbe Nachtigall* (The Yellow Nightingale). Frank Chapman was vocal director, William C. Mellor was the cinematographer, and H. C. Potter directed for Paramount. Black and white. 80 minutes.

ROMBERG, SIGMUND
Hungarian-born American composer (1887–1951)

Sigmund Romberg, who was born in Hungary and began his studies in Vienna with operetta composer Richard Heuberger, moved to New York in 1909, and his composing career was entirely American. Like colleagues Victor Herbert and Rudolf Friml, he grafted the middle-European tradition of operetta onto the American theater. Romberg wrote more than 60 theater shows, including the popular trio of THE STUDENT PRINCE, THE DESERT SONG, AND THE NEW MOON; songs from these shows are still being recorded. Romberg's stage career continued right into the 1940s with the hit show UP IN CENTRAL PARK. In addition to many films of stage operettas, he also created a number of original film operettas. See DAS DREIMÄDERLHAUS (Blossom Time), THE GIRL OF THE GOLDEN WEST, and MAYTIME.

1930 Viennese Nights
Viennese Nights, book by Oscar Hammerstein II, is the best of several operettas that Romberg wrote directly for the screen. Set in Vienna and New York, it tells of a bittersweet romance that finally comes right for Vivienne Segal and Alexander Gray. The best-known song is "You Will Remember Vienna." Alan Crosland directed the film in two-color Technicolor for Warner Bros. 99 minutes.

1954 Deep in My Heart
José Ferrer plays Romberg in this lively film biography that traces his operetta career from the early years. The

singers include Met soprano Helen Traubel, Rosemary Clooney, Gene Kelly, Jane Powell, and Howard Keel. See DEEP IN MY HEART.

ROME

The main opera houses in Rome are the Teatro dell'Opera and the open-air Baths of Caracalla in the summer. The Rome Opera House, built in 1880 as the Teatro Costanzi, was the Royal Opera House until the country became a republic after World War II. For a period it was a genuine rival of La Scala. Several operas were filmed there during the late 1940s; it has been featured in fiction films such as Mario Lanza's FOR THE FIRST TIME (1959); and there are videos of stage productions such as IRIS (1985) and TOSCA (1993). The Live From Rome telecast of TOSCA in 1992 attracted a world audience and is on DVD. There is no video of an opera at the 6,000-seat Baths of Caracalla, but it is the site of the 1990 THREE TENORS concert and a 1991 soprano concert, both on video. A Caracalla production is affectionately parodied in Bertolucci's film LA LUNA, and part of Ponnelle's 1980 film of LA CLEMENZA DI TITO was shot there. See AMELIA AL BALLO (1957), IL BARBIERE DI SIVIGLIA (1946/1948), CARMEN (1948), LA CLEMENZA DE TITO (1980), DON PASQUALE (1948), FRA DIAVOLO (1948), GUILLAUME TELL (1948), MARIO LANZA (1958), LUCIA DI LAMMERMOOR (1948), LE NOZZE DI FIGARO (1948), RIGOLETTO (1947), SOPRANOS AND MEZZOS (1991), TOSCA (1946 film/1993), and GIUSEPPE VERDI (1938).

1942 Una notte dopo l'opera
Una notte dopo l'opera (One Night after the Opera) is an Italian fiction film shot in and around what was then the Teatro Reale dell'Opera, the Royal Opera House. It tells the story of Anna, the prima ballerina at the opera house, and her love affair with the conductor Paolo Marini. Beatrice Mancini plays Anna and Mino Doro is Paolo. Arnold Foresti wrote the screenplay and Nicola Manzari and Nicola Fausto Neroni directed for Rex Film. Black and white. In Italian. 85 minutes.

1943 In due si soffre meglio
Dedi Montano stars as a young woman with a voice who ends up singing at the Teatro Reale dell'Opera with the help of a rich industrialist. She sings bits from operas by Puccini, including *Madama Butterfly,* and Rossini. Nunzio Malasomma directed. Black and white. In Italian. 90 minutes.

1948 First Opera Film Festival
This film features highlight versions of five operas staged at the Rome Opera House in 1948: CARMEN, DON PASQUALE, FRA DIAVOLO, GUILLAUME TELL, and LE NOZZE DI FIGARO. Most roles are played by actors and

dubbed by singers such as Tito Gobbi, Cloe Elmo, and Piero Biasini. Olin Downes introduces the operas, and Angelo Questa conducts the Rome Opera House Orchestra. George Richfield produced the film, released in the United States by Classic Pictures. Black and white. In Italian. 90 minutes.

1955 Un palco all'opera

A retired orchestra conductor overhears a lovers' quarrel between the director and the prima ballerina at the Teatro dell'Opera and tells them stories about the love lives and problems of Bellini (with Maria Malibran), Donizetti (with married Luisa), and Rossini (with Isabella Colbran). The film is basically an excuse for presenting excerpts from the operas. Enrico De Melis plays Bellini, Eduardo De Santis is Donizetti, Augusto Di Giovanni is Rossini, Liliana Gerace is Maria Malibran, Elena Kleus is Luisa, and Eugenia Bonino is Isabella. Siro Marcellini directed. Color. In Italian. 98 minutes.

ROMÉO ET JULIETTE
1867 opera by Gounod

Roméo et Juliette (Romeo and Juliet) is CHARLES GOUNOD's French version of Shakespeare's tragic romance as adapted by librettists Jules Barbier and Michel Carré. It follows the play fairly closely and has become the most popular of the operatic adaptations of the story; Juliet's Act I "Waltz Song" is particularly admired. Despite its early success (*Faust* and *Roméo et Juliette* were said to be the most popular operas in the world at the beginning of the 20th century), it has not remained in the Anglo repertory. However, interest in it has revived since Roberto Alagna starred in a Covent Garden production and filmed it with wife Angela Gheorghiu.

1963 Voice of Firestone

American TV highlights production: Wilfrid Pelletier (conductor, Voice of Firestone Orchestra).

Cast: Nicolai Gedda (Roméo), Roberta Peters (Juliette), William Walker (Mercutio).

Video: VAI VHS as *Firestone French Opera Gala*. Telecast February 10, 1963. Black and white. In French with English introductions. 22 minutes.

1982 Paris Opéra

French stage production: Georges Lavaudant (director), Alain Lombard (conductor, Opéra de Paris Orchestra and Chorus), Jean-Pierre Vergier (set/costume designer).

Cast: Neil Shicoff (Roméo), Barbara Hendricks (Juliette), Gino Quilico (Mercutio), Robert Dumé (Tybalt), Yves Bisson (Capulet), Marie McLaughlin (Stéphano), Anna Ringart (Gertrude).

Video: House of Opera/Lyric VHS. Yves-André Hubert (director). Color. In French. 139 minutes.

Comment: Hendricks's Paris Opéra debut

1985 Teatro Regio, Parma

Italian stage production: Beppe De Tomasi (director, set/costume designer), Alain Guingal (conductor, Orchestra Sinfonica dell'Emilia-Romagna and Teatro Regio Chorus).

Cast: Alfredo Kraus (Roméo) Faye Robinson (Juliette), Roberto Coviello (Mercutio), Gianfranco Manganotti (Tybalt), Lucetta Bizzi (Stéphano), Ambra Vespasiani (Gertrude), Marcello Crisman (Paris), Franco Federici (Capulet), Boris Martinovich (Frère Laurent).

Video: House of Opera DVD/Bel Canto Society VHS. Color. In French. 160 minutes.

1994 Royal Opera

English stage production: Nicolas Joel (director), Charles Mackerras (conductor, Royal Opera House Orchestra and Chorus), Carlo Tommasi (set designer).

Cast: Roberto Alagna (Roméo), Leontina Vaduva (Juliette), François le Roux (Mercutio), Paul Charles Clarke (Tybalt), Peter Sidhom (Capulet), Anna Maria Panzarella (Stéphano), Robert Lloyd (Frère Laurent).

Video: Kultur and Bel Canto Society DVD and VHS/Home Vision VHS/Pioneer LD. Brian Large (director). Color. In French with English subtitles. 171 minutes.

Comment: Alagna was hailed as a major new tenor after his success in this fine production.

2002 Sweete film

English TV film: Barbara Willis Sweete (film director), Anton Guadagno (conductor, Czech Philharmonic Chamber Orchestra), Tony Miller (cinematographer), Donna Feore (stage director/choreographer), Karel Vacek (art director).

Cast: Roberto Alagna (Roméo), Angela Gheorghiu (Juliette), Tito Beltrán (Tybalt), Pavel Novák (Mercutio, sung by Vratislav Kříž), Jan Šváb (Capulet, sung by Aleš Hendrych), Daniel Lipnik (Frère Laurent, sung by František Zahradíček).

Video: Arthaus DVD. Color. In French with English subtitles. 75 minutes.

Comment: Drastically abridged film version shot on location in a Czech castle with prerecorded soundtrack. Critics were dismayed at the cuts, which include the character of the nurse.

Early/related films

Shakespeare Films
Most of the many films of the story, which date back to the earliest days of silent cinema, are based on the Shakespeare play rather than the opera. The most famous versions are George Cukor's 1936 MGM film with Leslie Howard and Norma Shearer as not-very-young lovers; Renato Castellani's stolid 1954 version with Laurence Harvey and Susan Shentall; Franco Zeffirelli's youth-oriented 1968 film with Leonard Whiting (age 17) and Olivia Hussey (age 15); and Baz Luhrmann's amazing updated rock music version with Leonardo DiCaprio and Claire Danes.

1900 Cossira film
Emile Cossira, who sang Roméo at Covent Garden and the Paris Opéra, is the star of the first sound opera film, presented June 8, 1900, at the Phono-Cinéma-Théâtre at the Paris Exhibition with synchronized phonographic cylinder. Cossira is seen and heard singing an aria from *Roméo et Juliette,* probably "Ah! Lève-toi soleil," in a film made by Clément Maurice. Films of *Falstaff* and *Don Giovanni* with arias sung by Victor Maurel were also on the program and share first honors, but they were not advertised on the poster. Black and white. In French. About 3 minutes.

1909 Tetrazzini film
Luisa Tetrazzini sang Juliet in the German sound film *Roméo und Julia,* made in 1909 by Deutsche Vitascope and featuring Juliet's "Waltz Song." Black and white. In Italian. About 4 minutes.

1915 Metro film
This famous Metro studio *Romeo and Juliet* is based on Shakespeare, not the opera, but Gounod's music accompanied it when it was shown in theaters; a special score based on the opera airs was compiled for cinema orchestras. Francis X. Bushman plays Romeo with his wife Beverly Bayne as Juliet. They're not exactly young lovers, but they were major romantic stars at the time and the film was a big success. John W. Noble directed. Black and white. Silent. About 80 minutes.

1927 Vitaphone film
This Vitaphone sound film features Charles Hackett and Rosa Low of the Chicago Opera singing from "C'est la! Salut! Tombeau" to the end of the opera, accompanied by the Vitaphone Symphony Orchestra. Black and white. In French. About 10 minutes.

1927 De Forest Phonofilm
Czech tenor Otakar Marák and his soprano wife Marie Cavan (aka Mary Cavanova) are Roméo and Juliette in this early British sound film made with the De Forest Phonofilm system. Black and white. About 7 minutes. Print without sound at the NFTA.

1931 The Great Lover
Juliette's "Waltz Song" is sung at an opera dinner by Irene Dunne, a young soprano taken up by baritone Adolphe Menjou, who is giving her a chance to sing at the Met. Ironically, Dunne did want to be an opera singer but was rejected by the Met. Harry Beaumont directed. Black and white. 79 minutes.

1936 Rose Marie
Jeanette MacDonald sings music from *Roméo et Juliette* in this MGM film based on a Rudolf Friml operetta. She plays an opera star and is on stage at the beginning of the film in the opera singing Juliette's "Waltz Song" and other snippets. W. S. Van Dyke directed. Black and white. 110 minutes. MGM-UA VHS/LD.

1938 That Certain Age
Deanna Durbin gets a crush on Melvyn Douglas and sings "Daydreams," an English version of Juliette's "Waltz Song." Edward Ludwig directed. Universal. Black and white. 95 minutes.

1953 Melba
Patrice Munsel plays Nellie Melba in this opulent British film biography and sings Juliette's "Waltz Song." See NELLIE MELBA.

RONDINE, LA
1917 opera by Puccini

La rondine (The Swallow) was GIACOMO PUCCINI's attempt at writing an operetta/light opera for Vienna, but because of the war, it had to premiere in neutral Monte Carlo. Light opera turned out to be more difficult than Puccini envisioned, and he revised the opera considerably for later productions, but it has never been popular. Giuseppe Adami's libretto tells the story of Magda, the mistress of the banker Rambaldo, who has a bittersweet love affair with young Ruggero.

1970 CBC Canadian Television
Canadian TV film: Norman Campbell (director), Brian Priestman (conductor, CBC Orchestra and Chorus).

Cast: Teresa Stratas (Magda), Cornelis Opthof (Rambaldo), Anastasios Vrenios, Barbara Shuttleworth, John Edward Walker.

Video: Lyric VHS. Telecast in the United States in May 1972. Color. In English. 90 minutes.

1985 New York City Opera

American stage production: Lotfi Mansouri (director), Alessandro Siciliani (conductor, New York City Opera Orchestra and Chorus), Ralph Funicello (set designer).

Cast: Elizabeth Knighton (Magda), Jon Garrison (Ruggero), Richard McKee (Rambaldo), Claudette Peterson (Lisette), David Eisler (Prunier).

Telecast October 30, 1985, on PBS with introduction by Beverly Sills in the series *Live From Lincoln Center*. Kirk Browning (director). Color. In Italian with English subtitles. 165 minutes.

1988 Puccini Festival, Torre del Lago

Italian stage production: Pier Luigi Urbini (conductor).

Cast: Elena Mauri-Nunziata (Magda), Vincenzo Bello (Ruggero), Lucio Bizzi (Rambaldo).

Video: Opera Dubs VHS. Color. In Italian. 90 minutes.

Comment: It was in this village in Tuscany that Puccini composed most of his operas.

1998 Washington Opera

American stage production: Marta Domingo (director), Emmanuel Villaume (conductor, Washington Opera Orchestra and Chorus), Michael Scott (set/costume designer).

Cast: Aïnhoa Arteta (Magda), Marcus Haddock (Ruggero), William Parcher (Rambaldo), Richard Troxell (Prunier), Inva Mula (Lisette), Angela Turner Wilson (Yvette), Kathleen Segar (Bianca).

Taped at the Kennedy Center in March 1998; telecast December 13, 1999, on PBS. Brian Large (director). Color. In Italian with English subtitles. 90 minutes.

Related film

1985 A Room With a View

Kiri Te Kanawa sings the aria "Che il bel sogno di Doretta" from *La rondine* on the soundtrack as confused young Helena Bonham Carter gets kissed by Julian Sands. The aria, not surprisingly, concerns a young girl awakening to love through a kiss. James Ivory directed this adaptation of an E. M. Forster novel set in the Florence of yesteryear. Color. 115 minutes.

ROSA: DEATH OF A COMPOSER
1994 opera by Andriessen

Louis Andriessen and librettist/director Peter Greenaway attracted international attention for this innovative opera when it was premiered by the Netherlands Opera in Amsterdam in 1994. *Rosa: The Death of a Composer* (originally reviewed as *Rosa: A Horse Opera*) is the story of composer Juan Manuel de Rosa who lives in an abattoir in Uruguay and writes scores for Hollywood Westerns. He loves his horse more than his fiancée Esmeralda, so she tries to turn herself into a horse to get him to love her and spends much of the opera in the nude. Eventually, he and his horse are killed by cowboys firing from a Western movie. As the opera ends, the Index Singer, seated in a box in the theater, recites and defines the words used in the opera. Greenaway uses many cinematic techniques in the production, including three levels of screens on stage, and critics praised his imaginative stagecraft. The opera was revived by the Netherlands Opera in 1998 and filmed with the original cast.

1998 Netherlands Opera

Dutch stage production: Peter Greenaway (director), Saskia Boddeke (stage director), Reinbert de Leeuw (conductor, Asko and Schoenberg Ensembles and Netherlands Opera Chorus), Steven Scott (set designer).

Cast: Lyndon Terracini (Rosa), Marie Angel (Esmeralda/Second Singer/Blonde), Miranda van Kralingen (Madame de Vries/Investigatrix/Texas Whore/First Singer), Christopher Gillett and Rogers Smeets (Gigolos/Cowboys), Phyllis Blanford (Index Singer).

Color. In English. 90 minutes.

Comment: Greenaway shot the video with Reinier van Brummelen as cameraman in July 1998 at the Musiektheater in Amsterdam. It premiered at the Venice Film Festival on September 5, 1999.

ROSE-MARIE
1924 operetta by Friml and Stothart

Rose-Marie was a worldwide success for composers RUDOLF FRIML and HERBERT STOTHART. Its greatest attraction was a spectacular "Totem Tom-Tom" number, featuring a hundred dancers dressed as totem poles, and its most famous tune was the still popular "Indian Love Call." Otto Harbach and Oscar Hammerstein II wrote the libretto. Rose-Marie (she loses her hyphen in most of the movies) is a Canadian woman in love with outlaw trapper Jim Kenyon, who is being pursued on a murder charge by Royal Canadian Mounted Policeman Sergeant Malone. The operetta has been filmed three times with considerably altered plots.

1928 Hubbard film

American feature film: Lucien Hubbard (director/screenplay), John Arnold (screenplay), Herbert Stothart (music director), MGM (studio).

Cast: Joan Crawford (Rose-Marie), James Murray (Jim Kenyon), House Peters (Sergeant Malone).

Black and white. In English. 90 minutes.

Comment: The film has the Friml/Stothart score but there is no singing.

1936 Van Dyke film

American feature film: W. S. Van Dyke (director), Herbert Stothart (music director), Frances Goodrich, Albert Hackett and Alice Duer Miller (screenplay), William Daniels (cinematographer), Wilhelm von Wymetal Jr. (director, operatic scenes), MGM (studio).

Cast: Jeanette MacDonald (Marie de Flor/Rose Marie), Nelson Eddy (Sgt. Bruce), James Stewart (John Flower), Alan Mowbray (Premiere), David Niven (Teddy), Una O'Connor (Anna), Allan Jones (Roméo and Cavaradossi in opera scenes).

Video: MGM-UA VHS/LD. Black and white. 110 minutes.

Comment: Heavily revised version filmed on location at Lake Tahoe. MacDonald plays an opera singer searching the Northwest for her fugitive brother (Stewart) sought by a Mountie (Eddy). "Totem Tom-Tom" and "Indian Love Call" are retained, but many stage songs are dropped. Scenes from *Tosca* and *Roméo et Juliette* are added for MacDonald.

1954 LeRoy film

American feature film: Mervyn LeRoy (director), Busby Berkeley (choreographer), Ronald Millar (screenplay), Paul C. Vogel (cinematographer, CinemaScope), Edmund B. Willis (set designer), MGM (studio).

Cast: Ann Blyth (Rose-Marie), Howard Keel (Sgt. Malone), Fernando Lamas, Bert Lahr, Marjorie Main.

Video: MGM-UA VHS. Color. In English. 115 minutes.

Comment: More faithful to the plot than the 1936 film but not as much fun.

1992 Operette, che Passione!

Italian TV studio production: Sandro Massimini (director/producer), Roberto Negri (pianist), Sandro Corelli (choreographer).

Cast: Sandro Massimini, Sonia Dorigo, Max René Cosotti.

Video: Pierluigi Pagano (director). Color. In Italian. About 19 minutes. Ricordi (Italy) VHS.

Comment: Highlights of the operetta on the Italian TV series *Operette, che Passione!* Featured songs include "Rose-Marie," "Indian Love Call," and "Pretty Things" plus a film clip of the totem dance.

Related film

1999 Man on the Moon

Jim Carrey sings "Rose Marie" in this biopic about the strange comedian Andy Kaufman. Milos Forman directed. Color. 118 minutes. On VHS.

ROSENKAVALIER, DER
1911 opera by Richard Strauss

Der Rosenkavalier (The Rose Knight), RICHARD STRAUSS's most popular opera, has an outstanding libretto by Hugo von Hofmannsthal. It's set in Vienna during the reign of the Empress Maria Theresa where the no-longer-young Marschallin has been having an affair with young Octavian (soprano trouser role). He is sent as Rose Knight, an aristocratic marital emissary, to young Sophie whom boorish Baron Ochs intends to wed. Octavian and Sophie fall in love at first sight, Ochs is humiliated, and the Marschallin accepts the loss of her lover with good grace. The Act III soprano trio is particularly famous, and there are many fine waltz tunes. The opera has been popular with filmmakers, and Strauss himself helped created a silent version.

1926 Strauss film

Austrian silent film: Robert Wiene (director), Richard Strauss (conductor, Vienna and London premiere orchestras), Hugo von Hofmannsthal (screenplay), Alfred Roller (set designer), Pan Film (production).

Cast: Huguette Duflos (Marschallin), Jacques Catelain (Octavian), Elly Felisie Bergen (Sophie), Michael Bohnen (Baron Ochs), Paul Hartmann (Field Marshall), Carl Forest (Faninal).

Black and white. Silent with German intertitles. About 110 minutes.

Comment: Strauss composed a new march and arranged the music for this film while Hofmannsthal wrote new battle and masked ball scenes, eliminated the inn scene, and devised a new ending reconciling the Marschallin and the Field Marshall. A restored print was shown at Avery Fisher Hall in 1993 with the music played by the American Symphony Orchestra led by Leon Botstein.

1949 Metropolitan Opera

American stage production: Herbert Graf (director), Fritz Reiner (conductor, Metropolitan Opera Orchestra and Chorus), Hans Kautsky (set designer).

Cast: Eleanor Steber (Marschallin), Risë Stevens (Octavian), Erna Berger (Sophie), Emanuel List

(Baron Ochs), Giuseppe Di Stefano (Italian Singer), Peter Klein (Valzacchi), Hugh Thompson (Faninal).

Telecast live November 21, 1949. Burke Crotty (director). Black and white. In German with English introductions. 240 minutes.

Comment: Pioneering telecast of the opening night of the 1949–1950 Met season seen on ABC in six cities. The program included comments from patrons and backstage interviews. No known copy.

1953 NBC Opera Theatre

American TV production: Samuel Chotzinoff (producer/director), Peter Herman Adler (conductor, NBC Symphony of the Air Orchestra and Chorus), William Molyneux (set designer), John Gutman (English translation).

Cast: Wilma Spence (Marschallin), Frances Bible (Octavian), Virginia Haskins (Sophie), Ralph Herbert (Baron Ochs), Andrew McKinley (Valzacchi), Manfred Hecht (Faninal), Robert Marshall (Italian Singer).

Video at the MTR. Telecast live in two parts on April 25 and May 3, 1953. Kirk Browning (director). Black and white. In English. 150 minutes.

1960 Salzburg Festival

English film of Austrian stage production: Paul Czinner (film director), Rudolf Hartmann (stage director), Herbert von Karajan (conductor, Mozarteum Orchestra, Vienna Philharmonic Orchestra, and Vienna State Opera Chorus), S. D. Onions (cinematographer), Teo Otto (set designer), Erni Kniepert (costume designer), Rank Organization (production).

Cast: Elisabeth Schwarzkopf (Marschallin), Sena Jurinac (Octavian), Anneliese Rothenberger (Sophie), Otto Edelmann (Baron Ochs), Erich Kunz (Faninal), Renato Ercolani (Valzacchi), Giuseppe Zampieri (Italian Singer).

Video: Kultur/VAI VHS. Color. In German with English subtitles. 192 minutes.

Comment: The film was shot at the Salzburg Festival in 1960 but it was not premiered until July 1962. The film begins with cards that explain the action while Karajan is conducting the overture. The soundtrack was recorded by the singers who lip-synched for the film.

1979 Bavarian State Opera

German stage production: Otto Schenk (director), Carlos Kleiber (conductor, Bavarian State Opera Orchestra and Chorus), Jürgen Rose (set/costume designer).

Cast: Gwyneth Jones (Marschallin), Brigitte Fassbaender (Octavian), Lucia Popp (Sophie), Manfred Jungwirth (Baron Ochs), Francisco Araiza (Italian Singer), David Thaw (Valzacchi), Benno Kusche (Faninal).

Video: DG VHS/LD. Telecast December 8, 1980, by PBS in the *Great Performances* series. Karlheinz Hundorf (director). Color. In German with English subtitles. 186 minutes.

1982 Metropolitan Opera

American stage production: Nathaniel Merrill (production), Bruce Donnell (stage director), James Levine (conductor, Metropolitan Opera Orchestra and Chorus), Robert O'Hearn (set/costume designer).

Cast: Kiri Te Kanawa (Marschallin), Tatiana Troyanos (Octavian), Judith Blegen (Sophie), Luciano Pavarotti (Italian Singer), Kurt Moll (Baron Ochs), Joseph Frank (Valzacchi), Derek Hammond-Stroud (Faninal).

Video at the MTR. Telecast live October 7, 1982; telecast a second time March 22, 2000. Kirk Browning (director). Color. In German with English subtitles. 200 minutes.

1984 Salzburg Festival

Austrian stage production: Herbert von Karajan (director/conductor, Vienna Philharmonic Orchestra and Vienna State Opera Chorus), Teo Otto (set designer).

Cast: Anna Tomowa-Sintow (Marschallin), Agnes Baltsa (Octavian), Janet Perry (Sophie), Kurt Moll (Baron Ochs), Gottfried Hornik (Faninal), Heinz Zednik (Valzacchi), Vinson Cole (Italian Singer).

Video: Sony Classic DVD/VHS/LD. Hugo Kach (director). Color. In German. 196 minutes.

1985 Royal Opera

English stage production: John Schlesinger (director), Georg Solti (conductor, Royal Opera House Orchestra and Chorus), William Dudley (set designer), Maria Bjoernson (costume designer).

Cast: Kiri Te Kanawa (Marschallin), Anne Howells (Octavian), Barbara Bonney (Sophie), Aage Haugland (Baron Ochs), Robert Tear (Valzacchi), Jonathan Summers (Faninal), Dennis O'Neill (Italian Singer).

Home Vision/NVC Arts (GB) VHS and Pioneer Artists LD. Brian Large (director). Color. In German with English subtitles. 204 minutes.

Comment: Film director Schlesinger uses his cinematic expertise to make the characterizations as important as the singing and the music.

1994 Vienna State Opera

Austrian stage production: Otto Schenk (director), Carlos Kleiber (conductor, Vienna State Opera Orchestra and Chorus).

Cast: Felicity Lott (Marschallin), Anne Sofie von Otter (Octavian), Barbara Bonney (Sophie), Kurt Moll (Baron Ochs), Gottfried Hornik (Faninal), Heinz Zednik (Valzacchi), Keith Ikaia-Purdy (Italian Singer).

Video: DG DVD/VHS/LD. Horant H. Hohlfeld (director). Color. In German with English subtitles. 193 minutes.

1997 Teatro Massimo, Palermo
Italian stage production: Pier Luigi Pizzi (director, set/costume designer), John Neschling (conductor, Teatro Massimo Orchestra and Chorus).

Cast: Elizabeth Whitehouse (Marschallin), Ildiko Komlosi (Octavian), Desiree Rancatore (Sophie), Daniel Lewis Williams (Baron Ochs), Pietro Ballo (Italian Singer), David Pittman-Jennings (Faninal).

Video: Image Entertainment DVD. Elisabetta Brusa (director). Color. In German with English subtitles. 190 minutes.

Early/related films

1910 Messter film
This early German sound film featuring an aria from the opera was made by Oskar Messter for his cinema in Berlin. The film was shown with a synchronized phonograph record. Black and white. In German. About 3 minutes. Print in German archive.

1956 Serenade
Mario Lanza sings the Italian singer's aria "Di rigori armato il seno" with Ray Heindorf and his orchestra in this film about an opera singer with emotional problems. See SERENADE.

1992 Berlin Philharmonic Trio
Renée Fleming is the Marschallin, Frederica von Stade is Octavian, and Kathleen Battle is Sophie in this concert performance of the Trio and Act III finale with Andreas Schmidt as Faninal. The performance is the conclusion of a New Year's concert by the Berlin Philharmonic conducted by Claudio Abbado. The video is called *Richard Strauss Gala*. Color. In German. 77 minutes. Sony Classical VHS.

ROSE VON STAMBOUL, DIE
1916 operetta by Fall

The Pasha's daughter Kondja Gül has been educated in Europe; she has modern ideas about the role of women in Turkey so she resists marrying Achmed Bey. However, he is secretly one of the chief supporters of women's rights. Austrian soprano Fritzi Massary starred in the Berlin premiere of LEO FALL's *The Rose of Stamboul* in 1916 and reprised her role in a silent film made three years later. The operetta, written by Julius Brammer and Alfred Grünwald, was a major hit in German-speaking countries, where it remains popular. It went to New York in 1922 with new songs by Sigmund Romberg but did not catch on in the United States. Tenor arias from the operetta have been recorded by Fritz Wunderlich and Rudolf Schock.

1919 Massary film
The first film of the operetta featured its great stage exponent Fritzi Massary reprising her role as Kondja Gül, the beautiful but rebellious daughter of the Pasha. Unfortunately, as the film was made during the silent era, Massary could not be heard singing her hit songs. The film was shown in theaters with the operetta music performed live. Black and white. About 70 minutes.

1953 Anton film
German feature film: Karl Anton (director), Walter Forster and Joachim Wedekind (screenplay), Karl Lob (cinematographer), Willy Schmidt-Gentner (music director).

Cast: Inge Egger (Kondja Gül, sung by Ursula Ackermann), Albert Lieven (Achmed Bey, sung by Herbert Ernst Groh), Paul Hörbiger (Kemel Pascha), Hans Richter (Fridolin Müller), Laya Raki.

Black and white. In German. 100 minutes.

1992 Operette, che Passione!
Italian TV studio production: Sandro Massimini (director/producer), Roberto Negri (pianist), Sandro Corelli (choreographer).

Cast: Sandro Massimini, Sara Dilena, Max René Cosotti.

Video: Pierluigi Pagano (director). Color. In Italian. About 19 minutes. Ricordi (Italy) VHS.

Comment: Highlights of the operetta on the Italian TV series *Operette, che Passione!* The featured songs are "Oh Rosa di Stambul," "Chiamami Pussy Orsù," and "Lilly del Trianon."

ROSHAL, GRIGORY
Russian film director (1899–?)

Grigory Roshal, who began working in the cinema in 1926, is best known for his Dostoevsky adaptation *St. Petersburg Nights,* made in 1934 in collaboration with his director wife Vera Stroyeva. Like her, he turned to opera films during the 1950s. He directed a fine film version of Rachmaninoff's ALEKO in 1954 and filmed biographies of MODEST MUSSORGSKY and NIKOLAI RIMSKY-KORSAKOV, both with opera sequences.

ROSI, FRANCESCO
Italian film director (1922–)

Francesco Rosi, who began his cinema career as assistant to opera-oriented Luchino Visconti, created one of the truly great opera films. Unlike other opera films, his neorealistic 1984 CARMEN breathes the same air as a naturalistic movie. Rosi had a great understanding of the background, having already made the superb bullfighting movie *The Moment of Truth*. As he was able to use Bizet's original spoken dialogue, his film of *Carmen* is probably as close as an opera movie can come to being totally cinematic.

ROSS, HERBERT
American film director (1927–)

Herbert Ross began his film career in the opera genre by working with Otto Preminger and choreographing CARMEN JONES. Some of his most popular films were musicals, including *Funny Girl* and *Funny Lady* with Barbra Streisand, and *The Turning Point* with Shirley MacLaine, but they are not operatic. Ross returned to opera in 1993 when he directed a stage production of *La bohème* for the Los Angeles Music Center Opera.

ROSSELLINI, RENZO
Italian composer (1908–1982)

Film composer Renzo Rossellini saw Gian Carlo Menotti's opera *The Saint of Bleecker Street* in Italy in 1955 and it made him interested in writing traditional romantic operas. Renzo was the brother of filmmaker Roberto Rossellini and wrote the scores for most of his great films. He also wrote the screen opera *La campane*, conducted the orchestra for the popular 1953 film of AIDA starring Sophia, Loren, and worked as artistic director of the Monte Carlo Opera during the 1970s.

1959 Le campane
Rossellini wrote both words and music for *Le campane* (The Bells), a short romantic opera commissioned by Italian television. It was telecast by the Italian TV network RAI from Milan on May 9, 1959. Black and white. In Italian.

ROSSELLINI, ROBERTO
Italian film director (1906–1977)

Roberto Rossellini, one of the most important filmmakers in the history of the cinema, was hugely influential on both Italian neorealism and the French *nouvelle vague*. His 1945 film *Roma città aperta* launched neorealism and modern Italian cinema, and his 1953 *Viaggio in Italia* became a role model for Jean-Luc Godard and his French colleagues. Two of Rossellini's films have an operatic connection. He filmed his stage production of Honegger's JEANNE D'ARC AU BÛCHER in 1954 with Ingrid Bergman as Joan, and he filmed Cocteau's play LA VOIX HUMAINE in 1947 with Anna Magnani before Poulenc turned it into an opera.

ROSSINI, GIOACHINO
Italian composer (1792–1868)

Gioachino (or Gioacchino) Rossini has been a favorite of filmmakers since the earliest days of cinema, primarily because of *The Barber of Seville*. His personal popularity is reflected as early as 1898 when Italy's first filmmaker, Leopoldo Fregoli, made a movie in which he impersonated Rossini conducting his music. There are two full film biographies, and he often appears as a character in films about other composers. The 200th anniversary of Rossini's birth in 1992 was the stimulus for many new stage productions and subsequent videos of his rarer operas. Rossini was born in Pesaro, which now holds an opera festival in his honor, and was a success almost at once. He composed all of his operas in an amazing 19-year burst of creativity from 1810 to 1829 and then stopped. He lived another 39 years after finishing *William Tell*, but he never wrote another opera. See IL BARBIERE DI SIVIGLIA, LA CAMBIALE DI MATRIMONIO, LA CENERENTOLA, LE COMTE ORY, LA DONNA DEL LAGO, ELISABETTA REGINA D'INGHILTERRA, LA GAZZA LADRA, GUILLAUME TELL, L'ITALIANA IN ALGERI, MAOMETTO II, MOÏSE ET PHARAON, L'OCCASIONE FA IL LADRO, OTELLO, LA PIETRA DEL PARAGONE, RICCIARDO E ZORAIDE, LA SCALA DI SETA, SEMIRAMIDE, IL SIGNOR BRUSCHINO, TANCREDI, IL TURCO IN ITALIA, IL VIAGGIO A REIMS, and ZELMIRA.

1935 The Divine Spark
Edmund Breon plays Rossini in this English version of an Italian film about rival composer Vincenzo Bellini. See VINCENZO BELLINI.

1935 Casta diva
Achille Majeroni plays Rossini in the Italian version of the above film about Bellini. See VINCENZO BELLINI.

1943 Rossini
Nino Besozzi plays the composer in this Italian film covering Rossini's life from 1815 to 1829. It features claques, controversies, and his marriage to Isabella Colbran (Paola Barbara) as it follows him from Naples to Rome to Paris where it ends as he starts to compose *William Tell*. One of the highlights is Rossini's meeting with Beethoven in Vienna in 1822. There is a good deal of staged opera in the film, including excerpts from *The*

Barber of Seville, Otello, and *Moses.* The singers include Enzo De Muro Lomanto as Almaviva, Gianna Pederzini as Rosina, Mariano Stabile as Figaro, Tancredi Pasero as Don Basilio (a memorable performance of "Calunnia"), Vito De Taranto as Don Bartolo, Piero Pauli as Otello, and Gabriella Gatti as Desdemona. Vittorio Gui conducts the orchestra and Mario Bonnard directed the film. Black and white. In Italian with English subtitles. 94 minutes. Bel Canto Society/Lyric VHS.

1954 Casa Ricordi
Rossini, played by Roland Alexandre, has a tempestuous love affair while writing *The Barber of Seville,* after which Tito Gobbi and Giulio Neri sing in its premiere. At least that's what happens in this film about the Ricordi publishing firm. See RICORDI.

1955 Un palco all'opera
Augusto Di Giovanni plays Rossini in this Italian film, which has a section about the premiere of *Barbiere* and the composer's relationship with Isabella Colbran. Siro Marcellini directed. Color. In Italian. 98 minutes.

1985 Homage to Rossini
A TV tribute to Rossini with Paul Brooke impersonating the composer and Claudio Abbado conducting his music. The singers include Francizo Araiza, Montserrat Caballé, Marilyn Horne, Ruggero Raimondi, and Samuel Ramey. Color. 50 minutes.

1987 La Famiglia Ricordi
Luca Barbareschi plays Rossini in this four-part TV miniseries about the Italian opera publishing family. See RICORDI.

1988 Gioacchino Rossini
Solid informative Italian documentary about the composer, directed by Giuseppe Ferrara. Color. In Italian. 58 minutes. Mastervideo (Italy) VHS.

1991 Rossini! Rossini!
Mario Monicelli's Italian film, starring Philippe Noiret as Rossini, was shot on location at sites associated with the composer. It begins with him as an old man in a villa in Passy reminiscing about his rise to operatic fame. Sergio Castellitto plays Rossini as a youth, and the women in his life are portrayed by Jacqueline Bisset and Sabine Azema. Franco Di Giacomo was cinematographer, and Monicelli wrote the screenplay with Suso Cecci D'Amico, Bruno Cagli, and Nicola Badalucco. Color. In Italian or French. 90 minutes.

1992 Rossini Bicentennial Gala
Rossini's birthday is celebrated at a Lincoln Center gala at Avery Fisher Hall by singers specializing in his operas, including Marilyn Horne, Frederica von Stade, Rockwell Blake, Chris Merritt, Thomas Hampson, Samuel Ramey, Kathleen Kuhlmann, and Deborah Voigt. Roger Norrington conducts the Orchestra of St. Luke's and Concert Chorale of New York. In addition to the usual *Barber* and *Cinderella,* there are selections from *Zelmira, Il viaggio a Reims, Le siège de Corinthe, Bianca e Falliero,* and *Guillaume Tell.* Color. In English and Italian. 159 minutes. EMI VHS/LD.

1996 Rossini's Ghost
Joe Dimambro plays Rossini in this pleasant Canadian television film made for young people as an introduction to Rossini's music. David Devine directed, one of a series about classical composers shot in the Czech Republic. Shown on HBO in its Composers Series. Color. 52 minutes. Sony Classical VHS.

ROTA, NINO
Italian composer (1911–1979)

Nino Rota is better known for his film music than for his operas, but there is actually considerable overlap. His 1977 stage opera NAPOLI MILIONARIA is based on a film and features music from such Rota movies as *La Dolce Vita, Nights of Cabiria, Waterloo,* and *Rocco and His Brothers.* His most popular stage opera is the delightful 1955 IL CAPELLO DI PAGLIA DI FIRENZE, which has been telecast. He also composed an imaginary opera for the 1950 English film THE GLASS MOUNTAIN, and its theme music became well known in England. Rota, who was born in Milan, was a child prodigy and composed his first opera at the age of 15. He began to compose for films in 1933, starting with *Treno popolare,* and he created memorable music for films by Fellini, Visconti, Zeffirelli, Wertmuller, Bondarchuk, and Coppola. His haunting music for LA STRADA has been turned into a La Scala ballet, and the movie was the basis of a Czech opera in 1982. Some of Rota's operas have been staged in the United States.

ROTHENBERGER, ANNELIESE
German soprano (1924–)

Anneliese Rothenberger is well known for her recordings of operetta, but her stage career in primarily in opera. She made her debut in 1943, sang with the Hamburg State Opera from 1946 to 1973, and then began to be seen at Salzburg, Munich, Glyndebourne, and the Met. She plays a range of heroines, from Gilda, Susanna, and Musetta to Sophie, Lulu, and Adele, and she created the title role in Sutermeister's *Madame Bovary* in 1967. She can be enjoyed on video as Adele in Michael Powell's 1955 film of DIE FLEDERMAUS, as Sophie in Paul Czinner's 1960 film of DER ROSENKAVALIER, as Zdenka in ARABELLA (1960), and as Gilda in RIGOLETTO (1963).

1960 Marchenland Operette
Fairyland Operetta is a German television potpourri of scenes from operettas starring Rothenberger. They include Strauss's *Wienerblut*, Lehár's *Der Graf von Luxemburg*, Millöcker's *Dubarry*, Nico Dostal's *Hungarian Wedding*, and Fred Raymond's *Maske in Blau*. The other singers are Per Grunden, Rosl Schwaiger, Ferry Gruber, and Luise Crame. Werner Schmidt-Boelcke conducts the Bavarian Radio Orchestra and Hermann Lanske directed. Black and white. In German. 90 minutes.

1970 Anneliese Rothenberger gibt sich die Ehre
Anneliese Rothenberger Honors Herself is a German TV program featuring arias associated with the soprano. It includes an excerpt from a ZDF film of *Madama Butterfly* and arias from *La bohème, Gianni Schicchi, Pagliacci, Rusalka, Zigeunerliebe,* and the film *Zwei Herzen im Dreivierteltakt.* Color. In German. 60 minutes.

ROTHSCHILD'S VIOLIN
1997 French film of Russian opera

Edgardo Cozarinsky's film *Rothschild's Violin* is the dramatic story of a banned Russian opera created by Soviet Jewish composer Benjamin Fleischmann and completed by Dimitri Shostakovich. Adapted from a Chekhov story, the one-act opera, which is seen complete in the film, was unfinished when Fleischmann died during the defense of Leningrad in 1941. Shostakovich completed and orchestrated it, but it was suppressed as a Jewish work until 1968 when it was staged for the first time. It was banned the next day. The opera takes place in a Jewish shtetl where violinist and coffin maker Bronza is unhappy because the old people in the village never seem to die and give him work. When his wife dies, his life is suddenly empty, so he tries to atone for his past behavior by giving his precious violin to Rothschild, the poorest man in the village. Rothschild begins immediately to play wonderful new melodies. Hungarian actors portray the characters in the opera on screen with their singing dubbed by Russians from a recording featuring Sergei Leiferkus and Konstantin Pluzhnikov with Gennadi Rozhdestvensky conducting the Rotterdam Philharmonic Orchestra. Newsreel footage of Nazi and Stalinist rallies is intercut with the narrative, and Shostakovich himself speaks the final works of the film, suggesting that only music can create a monument for the forgotten dead. Color and black and white. In Russian with English subtitles. 101 minutes.

ROUNSEVILLE, ROBERT
American tenor (1914–1974)

New York Opera tenor Robert Rounseville appeared regularly on NBC and CBS television opera productions during the 1950s, but he is probably best known today for his two films. He portrays Hoffmann in the 1951 Powell and Pressburger film version of LES CONTES D'HOFFMANN and he is Mr. Snow in the 1956 movie of CAROUSEL opposite Barbara Ruick as Carrie. See CARMEN (1950/1953), DIALOGUES DES CARMÉLITES (1957), FROM THE HOUSE OF THE DEAD (1969), THE MIKADO (1960), RACHEL LA CUBANA (1974), and ELEANOR STEBER (1950–1954).

ROYAL OPERA HOUSE
Covent Garden theater (1892–)

Opera has been performed at Covent Garden in London for the past 250 years, although the buildings have changed over the years. The present 19th-century edifice became the Royal Opera House in 1892, and it has been one of the major centers of world opera for the past century. The first live opera telecast from Covent Garden was shown by the BBC in 1988, but union disagreements prevented continuing television presentations for some years. There are now regular telecasts and many videos of Covent Garden operas. See AIDA (1994), ANDREA CHÉNIER (1985), LA BOHÈME (1982), MARIA CALLAS (1962), CARMEN (1991), LA CENERENTOLA (2000), A CHRISTMAS CAROL (1982), LES CONTES D'HOFFMANN (1981), DON CARLO (1985), DIE ENTFÜHRUNG AUS DEM SERAIL (1987), FALSTAFF (1982/1999), LA FANCIULLA DEL WEST (1983), FIDELIO (1991), DIE FLEDERMAUS (1983/1990), GAWAIN (1991), ANGELA GHEORGHIU (2001), KIROV OPERA HOUSE (1992), LUCREZIA BORGIA (1980), LUISA MILLER (1979), MANON LESCAUT (1983), MITRIDATE RE DI PONTO (1991), NELLIE MELBA (1953), ORFEO ED EURIDICE (1991), OTELLO (1992), ADELINA PATTI (1993), PETER GRIMES (1981), PRINCE IGOR (1990), RIGOLETTO (2000), ROMÉO ET JULIETTE (1994), DER ROSENKAVALIER (1985), SALOME (1992/1995), SAMSON ET DALILA (1981), SIMON BOCCANEGRA (1991), STIFFELIO (1993), TCHAIKOVSKY (1993), KIRI TE KANAWA (1978), TOSCA (1964/1979), and LA TRAVIATA (1994).

1979 Prince Charles Backstage at Covent Garden
Prince Charles launched a fund-raising campaign for the Royal Opera House with this film; he narrates it and is seen backstage during rehearsals and productions of *L'Africaine* and *Die Zauberflöte.* Grace Bumbry, Dame Joan Sutherland, and Plácido Domingo discuss the inadequacies of the building, and Colin Davis rehearses the orchestra in the bar. Drummond Challis directed. Color. 34 minutes.

1986 Fanfare for Elizabeth

The Royal Opera House organized a televised gala concert in honor of Queen Elizabeth on April 21, 1986, with fully staged scenes from the following: *La traviata* with Lucia Popp and Plácido Domingo in the "Libiamo" scene; *Der Rosenkavalier* with Yvonne Kenny and Ann Murray in the Rose presentation scene; *The Bohemian Girl* with Jessye Norman singing "I Dreamt I Dwelt in Marble Halls"; *Tosca* with Domingo singing "E lucevan le stelle"; *Don Giovanni* with Popp and Thomas Allen singing "Là ci darem la mano"; *Turandot* with Gwyneth Jones singing a duet with Giuseppe Giacomini; and *Treemonisha* with Jessye Norman, Lisa Casteen, and chorus singing "Marching Onward." Edward Downes conducts the Royal Opera House Orchestra. Color. 90 minutes. House of Opera/Lyric VHS and video at the MPRC in London.

1995 The House

The ultimate opera house documentary—a six-part BBC Television film showing the inner workings of the Royal Opera House in all its glories, and problems. Director Michael Waldman's cameras filmed from October 1993 to June 1994, and the edited six hours are the most candid film portrait ever of a major opera institution. See THE HOUSE.

1996 Gold and Silver Gala

Gala concert with top singers celebrating the 50th anniversary of the postwar opera company at Covent Garden and the 25th anniversary of Plácido Domingo's first appearance. The other singers include Robert Alagna, Angela Gheorghiu, Dwayne Croft, Leontina Vaduva, and Verónica Villarroel. Color. 100 minutes. Covent Garden Pioneer DVD.

1999 Opening Celebration

The Royal Opera House reopened on December 1, 1999, with a gala celebration after closing for refurbishment. The evening begins with the overture to Weber's *Oberon* and includes scenes form *Die Walküre* and *Fidelio* plus ballet performances. Plácido Domingo and Robert Lloyd are among the guests singers, with Bernard Haitink and Anthony Twiner as conductors. Color. 90 minutes. BBC VHS.

RUDDIGORE

1887 comic opera by Gilbert and Sullivan

Ruddigore or The Witch's Curse was not a success when it premiered, but over the years it has become one of the more popular Gilbert and Sullivan operettas. It's a burlesque Gothic melodrama with a witch's curse forcing the baronets of the Murgatroyd family to commit a crime every day. Ruthven flees the curse and lives as the simple farmer Robin, while his brother Despard succeeds to the title and its curse. Robin loves the maid Rose and asks his foster brother Richard to help in wooing her, but Richard also falls in love with her. After many fine songs, the curse is foiled and all the problems are sorted out.

1967 Batchelor film

English animated feature film: Joy Batchelor (producer/director), James Walker (conductor, Royal Philharmonic Orchestra), John Cooper (designer), Halas and Batchelor (studio).

Singers: John Reed, Ann Hood, David Palmer, Peggy Ann Jones, Donald Adams, Kenneth Sandford.

Color. In English. 55 minutes.

Comment: The film follows the operetta plot closely, even though it is abridged. The singers are all members of the D'Oyly Carte Opera Company.

1972 Gilbert & Sullivan for All series

English highlights film: Peter Seabourne (director), Peter Murray (conductor, Gilbert and Sullivan Festival Orchestra and Chorus), David Maverovitch (cinematographer), Trevor Evans (adaptation), John Seabourne (producer).

Cast: John Cartier (Ruthven/Robin) Gillian Humphreys (Rose), Thomas Round (Richard), Helen Landis (Hannah), Lawrence Richard (Despard), Ann Hood (Mad Margaret), Donald Adams (Roderick).

Video: Musical Collectables VHS. (Originally released as part of the *World of Gilbert and Sullivan* series). Color. In English. 50 minutes.

1982 Gilbert and Sullivan Collection series

English studio production: Christopher Renshaw (director), Judith De Paul (producer), Alexander Faris (conductor, London Symphony Orchestra and Ambrosian Opera Chorus), Allan Cameron (set designer), George Walker (executive producer).

Cast: Vincent Price (Despard), Keith Michell (Robin), Sandra Dugdale (Rose), Donald Adams (Roderick), Ann Howard (Margaret), John Treleaven (Richard), Paul Hudson (Adam), Johanna Peters (Hannah).

Video: CBS Fox/Braveworld (GB) VHS. Barrie Gavin (director). Color. In English. 112 minutes.

RUDEL, JULIUS

Austrian-born American conductor (1921–)

Julius Rudel emigrated to America at the age of 17, joined the New York City Opera in 1943, was its artistic director from 1957 to 1979, and was closely associated with Beverly Sills. He was named music director of Wolf Trap Park when its performing arts center opened in 1971. His work in television includes Ottorino Respighi's

LA BELLA DORMENTE NEL BOSCO (1954), John Strauss's THE ACCUSED (1961), and Carlisle Floyd's THE SOJOURNER AND MOLLIE SINCLAIR (1963). See ANDREA CHÉNIER (1985), THE GOLDEN COCKEREL (1971), MANON LESCAUT (1977), EVA MARTON (1988), THE MIKADO (1978 film), ROBERTO DEVEREUX (1975/1977), SALOME (1979), SAMSON ET DALILA (1980), BEVERLY SILLS (1980), LA TRAVIATA (1976), IL TURCO IN ITALIAN (1978), FREDERICA VON STADE (1987), and WOLF TRAP PARK.

RUFFO, TITTA
Italian baritone (1877–1953)

Maestro Tullio Serafin described baritone Titta Ruffo as one of the three singing miracles of the century (the others being Enrico Caruso and Rosa Ponselle). Ruffo (born Ruffo Cafiero Titta) made his debut in Rome in 1898 and then had a famous dispute with Melba at Covent Garden in 1903; it helped make him world famous. He began to sing in Philadelphia in 1912 and was a regular in that city and in Chicago until 1926. He made his debut at the Met in 1922 and sang there for eight seasons as Figaro, Carlo, Amonasro, and Tonio. Ruffo is credited with changing the way baritones sang 19th-century opera. He can be seen in performance in three short films.

1906/1908 Cinemafono Pagliej
CINEMAFONO PAGLIEJ, an Italian sound-on-disc company specializing in opera films, screened a film with an aria from *Rigoletto* sung by Ruffo at the Sala Umberto I in Rome from May 19 to July 30, 1906. The company presented the same film at the Politeama Pisana in Pisa on March 28, 1908. Black and white. In Italian. About 4 minutes.

1929/1930 Metro Movietone Acts
Ruffo made three opera films for MGM in 1929 and 1930. On the first he performs Nelusko's invocation from Meyerbeer's *L'Africaine,* "Adamastor, re dell'onde profonde." On the second he sings Figaro's "Largo al Factotum" from *The Barber of Seville.* On the third he sings Iago's "Credo" from *Otello.* The soundtracks of the Rossini and Verdi films have been issued as records. Black and white. In Italian. Each about 8 minutes.

RUSALKA
1901 opera by Dvořák

Rusalka has become ANTONÍN DVOŘÁK's most popular opera and eclipsed Dargomizhsky's Russian opera based on the same legend. Rusalka, a water spirit, falls in love with a prince and becomes human for his sake with the help of the witch Ježibaba. As she has to become mute to do this, she cannot explain her love and origin. Their re-

lationship ends tragically with his death through a fatal kiss. Jaroslav Kvapil's libretto is based on Friedrich Fouqué's play *Udine.* The opera's "Song to the Moon" has become a recital favorite.

1962 Kaslík TV film
Czech television film: Václav Kaslík (director/conductor, Prague National Theater Orchestra and Chorus), Jan Stallich (cinematographer), Jiri Nemecek (choreographer).
Cast: Jana Andrsova (Rusalka, sung by Milada Šubrtová), Vladimir Raz (Prince, sung by Zdenek Svelela), Ivanova Mixova.
Color. In Czech. 120 minutes.

1978 Weigl film
Czech/German feature film: Petr Weigl (director), Marek Janowski (conductor, Bavarian Symphony Orchestra),
Cast: Magda Vasaryova (Rusalka, sung by Gabriela Beňačková in Czech and Lilian Sukis in German), Milan Knazko (Prince, sung by Peter Dvorsky in Czech and Peter Hofman in German), Jaroslava Adamová (Ježibaba, sung by Libuse Marova in Czech and by Rose Wagemann in German).
Color. In Czech or German. 124 minutes.
Comment: Two versions were made at the same time with the actors dubbed by Czech singers in one and by German singers in the other.

***1986 English National Opera
English stage production: David Pountney (director), Mark Elder (conductor, English National Opera Orchestra and Chorus), Stefanos Lazaridis (set designer), Rodney Milnes (English translation).
Cast: Eilene Hannan (Rusalka), John Treleaven (Prince), Ann Howard (Ježibaba), Rodney Macann (Water Spirit), Fiona Kimm (Kitchen Boy), Phyllis Cannan (Foreign Princess).
Video: Kultur/Home Vision VHS. Derek Bailey (director). Color. In English. 160 minutes.
Comment: Pountney turns the story into a fable about a young Victorian woman's journey to adulthood, making her underwater home into a playroom with dreamlike sets.

Early/related films

1910 Goncharov film
Vasilij Goncharov directed this Russian silent film of the Rusalka legend with Aleksandra Goncharova as Rusalka and V. Stepanov as the Prince. Black and white. In Russian. About 12 minutes. Print in Russian archive.

1989 Driving Miss Daisy
It is spring in Atlanta in 1949 when Miss Daisy (Jessica Tandy) listens to "Song to the Moon" on the radio, sung by Gabriela Benacková with the Czech Philharmonic Orchestra. The water spirit tells of her need for love, and Miss Daisy decides to be nice to her driver Hoke Colburn (Morgan Freeman). Bruce Beresford's fine film about the relationship between an African-American chauffeur and an elderly white woman won the Academy Award for Best Picture. Color. 99 minutes. Warner VHS.

1993 Dvořák in Prague
Frederica von Stade sings the "Song to the Moon" in this tribute to Dvořák held at Smetana Hall in Prague. Seiji Ozawa conducts the Boston Symphony Orchestra. Brian Large directed. Color. 90 minutes. Sony VHS.

1999 Bicentennial Man
Lucia Popp performs the "Song to the Moon" on the soundtrack of this film about an immortal android (Robin Williams) who wants to become a human being. Chris Columbus directed. Color. 130 minutes.

RUSLAN AND LYUDMILA
1842 opera by Glinka

Mikhail Glinka's *Ruslan and Lyudmila,* the first authentically Russian opera, was considered revolutionary in its time. Based on a poem by Pushkin, it's a magical fairy tale about a princess (Lyudmila) and a warrior (Ruslan) who fall in love. Lyudmila is kidnapped by the dwarf Chernomor on the eve of their marriage so Ruslan sets out to rescue her. He succeeds after many adventures, including battles with sorcerers and witches. The music composed around the character of Chernomor is especially famous, ironically, as it is a nonsinging role.

1995 Kirov Opera
Russian stage production: Lotfi Mansouri (director), Valery Gergiev (conductor, Kirov Opera Orchestra and Chorus), Alexander Golovin (set/costume design based on pre-Revolutionary designs).
Cast: Anna Netrebko (Lyudmila), Vladimir Ognovenko (Ruslan), Galina Gorchakova (Gorislava), Larissa Diadkova (Ratmir), Mikhail Kit (King Svetozar), Yuri Marusin (Bayan), Konstantin Plushinikova (Finn), Gennadi Bezzubenko (Farlaf).
Video: Philips DVD/VHS. Hans Hulscher (director). Color. In Russian with English subtitles. 287 minutes.
Comment: Uncut version of the complete opera, co-produced with San Francisco Opera.

Related films

1915 Starewicz film
There are two Soviet feature films titled *Ruslan and Lyudmila,* both based on the Pushkin poem. The first was a 1915 silent film written, photographed, and directed by animation master Wladyslaw Starewicz. It stars Ivan Mozhukhin, S. Goslavskaya, A. Bibikov, and E. Pukhalsky. Black and white. About 55 minutes.

1974 Ptouchko film
This opulent but charming epic-length film of the Pushkin poem was made by Alexandre Ptouchko, who also filmed Rimsky-Korsakov operas. Natala Petrova plays Lyudmila and Valeri Kosinets is Ruslan, with support from Vladimir Fiodorov, Maria Kapniste-Serko, and Andrei Abrikossov. The special effects, sets, and costumes are outstanding, as is the cinematography by Igor Guelein and Valentine Zakharov. The film's score is by Tikon Khrennikov. Color. In Russian. 225 minutes.

RUSSELL, ANNA
British-born Canadian soprano (1911–)

Anna Russell has been the diva of opera parody for nearly 60 years and is still a delight on record and video. She began her satirical career in Canada in 1942, made her New York debut at Carnegie Recital Hall in 1947, and reached Broadway in 1953 in *Anna Russell's Little Show.* Among her memorable creations are an explanation of how to become a singer, an examination of the *Ring* tetralogy, and a dissection of a modern opera that begins with her entering an Automat. She has also sung roles in repertory operas. She was the witch in a New York City Opera English-language production of Humperdinck's HÄNSEL UND GRETEL in 1954 and the Duchess of Crakentorp in a Canadian Opera Company production of *The Daughter of the Regiment* in 1977.

1976 Anna Russell: Clown Princess of Comedy
Russell performs three of her opera routines and confesses all in a candid interview in these performances taken from the CBC archives. She even explains how her voice dropped to baritone while she was singing in the bathtub with a Lawrence Tibbett recording. Color. 47 minute. VAI VHS.

1984 Anna Russell: The (First) Farewell Concert
Russell is in fine form in this concert for an appreciative audience at the Baltimore Museum of Art. Highlights include her deconstruction of the *Ring* cycle: "If you know the chord of E-flat major, you know the prelude to *Rheingold,*" she explains. She tells how to create a Gilbert and Sullivan operetta, explains how to become an

opera singer, praises pink chiffon, and reminisces about wind instruments she has known. Robert Rosenberger accompanies on piano; Phillip Byrd directed the video. Color. 85 minutes. VAI DVD/VHS.

RUSSELL, KEN
English film director (1927–)

Ken Russell says that opera is the "last believable religion." This provocative but always stimulating filmmaker, who has made a number of fascinating screen biographies of opera composers, has also directed stage operas that are available on video. He began his career in 1959 with the *Monitor* arts program on BBC, and his first film of operatic interest—about Prokofiev—was *Portrait of a Soviet Composer* (1961). It was followed in 1962 by *Lotte Lenya Sings Kurt Weill* and an immensely popular *Elgar*, now on DVD. His other TV composer films include *Bartók, The Debussy Film, Song of Summer* (about Delius), and *The Dance of the Seven Veils: A Comic Strip in Seven Episodes on the Life of Richard Strauss*. His Tchaikovsky movie biography *The Music Lovers* aroused a good deal of controversy, but then so did his extravagant TURANDOT episode of *Aria* in 1987 and his dazzling *Salome's Last Dance*. Russell began directing opera on stage in 1982 in Florence with THE RAKE'S PROGRESS and has since worked in opera houses in London, Geneva, Spoleto, Lyons, Macerata, and Genoa where he staged Boito's MEFISTOFELE in 1989. See also BÉLA BARTÓK (1964), CLAUDE DEBUSSY (1965), FREDERICK DELIUS (1968), THE DEVILS OF LOUDUN (1970 film), GUSTAV MAHLER (1974), SERGEI PROKOFIEV (1961), SALOME (1998 film), RICHARD STRAUSS (1970), PYOTR TCHAIKOVSKY (1971), RALPH VAUGHAN WILLIAMS (1984), RICHARD WAGNER (1975), and KURT WEILL (1964).

1962 Elgar
Russell's *Elgar,* made for BBC Television, is still Russell's best music film, a nearly perfect marriage of music and image with superb cinematography by Ken Higgens and clever editing by Allan Tyrer. The DVD includes additional historical material. Black and white. In English. 71 minutes. British Film Institute DVD.

1987 Ken Russell's ABC of British Music
Ken Russell celebrates his love of British composers with this idiosyncratic but enjoyable TV guide to the best and worst of British music. It is organized on alphabetic principles with each letter standing for several composers or items, many of which are operatic. Color. In English. 78 minutes. On VHS.

RUSSELL, LILLIAN
American soprano (1861–1922)

Lillian Russell, who was known as the "Queen of Light Opera" during the 1890s, remains a legend a century after her glory days as her colorful personality continues to be celebrated in books and films. Russell, born Helen Leonard in Iowa, studied with Leopold Damrosch and became the Queen of Broadway with the help of Tony Pastor. She made her debut in *H.M.S. Pinafore* in 1879, starred in other Gilbert and Sullivan works, and was a hit in the Offenbach operettas *The Brigands* and *The Grand Duchess*. She apparently combined a wonderful voice with incredible charm and a great many feathered hats. She can be heard in recordings singing her signature tune "Come Down, Ma Evenin' Star." She starred in two early silent films, is the subject of a movie biography starring Alice Faye, and appears as a character in several others.

Lillian Russell, "Queen of Light Opera" during the 1890s, has become a cinematic legend.

1906 Lillian Russell
Russell appears in person in this Biograph film about her shot by F. A. Dobson in October 1906. Black and white. About 2 minutes. Print survives in an American archive.

1915 Wildfire
Russell reprises the role she created on Broadway in the play *Wildfire*. She plays Henrietta Barrington in a story centering around a horse named Wildfire with Lionel Barrymore and Glen Moore adding support. George Hobart and George Broadhurst wrote the play, which was filmed straight by Edward Middleton for World Film. Black and white. About 70 minutes.

1934 David Harem
Russell is portrayed by Ruth Gillette in this Will Rogers film about a racehorse that likes music. James Cruze directed. Black and white. 82 minutes.

1935 Diamond Jim

Russell, played by Binnie Barnes, is a close friend of Diamond Jim Brady (Edward Arnold) in this film about the colorful industrialist. Edward Sutherland directed. Black and white. 90 minutes.

1936 The Great Ziegfeld

Russell is portrayed by Ruth Gillette for a second time in this lavish film biography of showman Florenz Ziegfeld (William Powell). Robert Z. Leonard directed. Black and white. 170 minutes.

1936 The Gentleman From Louisiana

Russell (Ruth Gillette again), as a friend of Diamond Jim Brady (Charles Wilson), is seen briefly in this film about a racehorse trainer (Eddie Quillan). Irving Pichel directed. Black and white. 67 minutes.

1940 Lillian Russell

Alice Faye plays Russell in this lavish biography that shows her rise to stardom with the help of Tony Pastor and appearances in Gilbert and Sullivan operettas. Faye performs songs associated with Russell, including her signature tune "Come Down, Ma Evenin' Star." Leo Carrillo plays Tony Pastor, Nigel Bruce is William S. Gilbert, and Claude Allister is Arthur Sullivan. The men in her life are Henry Fonda, Don Ameche, and Edward Arnold as Diamond Jim Brady. Irving Cummings directed for Twentieth Century Fox. Black and white. 127 minutes.

1944 Bowery to Broadway

Russell, portrayed by Louise Allbritton, performs "Under the Bamboo Tree" in a Bowery beer garden run by Donald Cook. Charles Lamont directed. Black and white. 91 minutes.

1947 My Wild Irish Rose

Russell (Andrea King) encourages songwriter Chauncey Olcott (Dennis Morgan) and performs her signature tune "Come Down, Ma Evenin' Star" in this biopic about Olcott. David Butler directed. Black and white. 98 minutes.

RYSANEK, LEONIE

Austrian soprano (1926–1998)

Leonie Rysanek, who began her opera career in Innsbruck in 1949, first won fame singing Sieglinde in Bayreuth in 1951. She became a Munich Opera regular, made her American debut in 1956 in San Francisco, and came to the Met famously in 1959 as Lady Macbeth, replacing Maria Callas. She had an active career in Vienna and New York for nearly 40 years and can be seen on video (successively) as Chrysothemis, Elektra, and Klytem-

nästra in ELEKTRA (1980/1981/1991); as Ortrud in LOHENGRIN (1986); as Herodias in SALOME (1990); and as TOSCA in the 1983 documentary *I Live for Art.* See JAMES LEVINE (1986), GEORGE LONDON (1964), and DIE WALKÜRE (1977/1989 films).

S

SACK, ERNA
German soprano (1898–1972)

Berlin coloratura Erna Sack made her debut at the Berlin Staatsoper in 1928 and joined the Dresden Opera in 1933. She had a strong association with composer Richard Strauss, created Isotta in *Die Schweigsame Frau* for him, and sang Zerbinetta under his direction at Covent Garden. She also toured America during the 1930s and after the war. Sack made two German musical movies in the mid-1930s, including a version of Richard Genée's operetta NANON (1938). Her looks, personality, acting, and voice charmed the film critics.

1936 Blumen aus Nizza
Flowers From Nice is an appealing musical set in the south of France. Sack plays a gifted soprano who can sing above high C with no difficulty but can't get recognition for it. In order to attract attention, she hires a count (Karl Schönbock) to fake his suicide as a publicity stunt. She performs several arias in the film plus songs by D. V. Buday and Willy Schmidt-Gentner. Her costars are Friedl Czepa, Jane Tilden, and Paul Kemp. Max Wallner wrote the screenplay and Augusto Genina directed for Gloria Film. The film was distributed in the United States. Black and white. In German. 82 minutes.

SADKO
1898 opera by Rimsky-Korsakov

NIKOLAI RIMSKY-KORSAKOV's *Sadko* is an adaptation of a Russian folktale about a legendary merchant whose singing wins the heart of the Ocean King's daughter. It takes place simultaneously in the realistic merchant world of Novgorod and the fantasy land of an underwater kingdom. Sadko alone is able to exist in both realms, and his travels and adventures are the story of the opera. The opera's best-known melody in the West is the "Song of India," which is sung to Sadko by an Indian merchant describing his homeland. Russian audiences, however, seem to prefer the song by the Viking merchant.

1994 Kirov Opera
Russian stage production: Alexei Stepaniuk (director), Valery Gergiev (conductor, Kirov Opera Orchestra and Chorus), Vitslav Opunke (set designer), Oleg Ignatiev (choreographer).

Cast: Vladimir Galuzin (Sadko), Marianna Tarasova (Lyubava), Valentina Tsidipova (Volkova), Sergei Alexashkin (Sea King), Larissa Diadkova (Nezhata), Gegam Gregoriam (Indian merchant), Alexander Gergalov (Venetian merchant), Bulat Minjelkiev (Viking merchant)

Video: Philips VHS/LD. Brian Large (director). Color. In Russian. 175 minutes.

Related films

1927 Vitaphone film
Chicago Opera tenor Charles Hackett sings the "Song of India" from *Sadko* in this early sound film made by the Vitaphone Company. Black and white. 8 minutes.

1952 Ptushko film
Alexander Ptushko, one of the world's great fantasy filmmakers, aimed for magnificence in this dazzling Mosfilm Studio adaptation of the story, which uses Rimsky-Korsakov's music as its score. In this version, written by K. Isayev, Sadko sails around the world looking for a magic bird before ending up in the undersea kingdom. Serge Stolyarov is Sadko and Anna Larionava is Lyubava with Olga Vikland, Sergei Kayukov, Nicolai Troyanofsky, and Boris Surovtsev in support. Color. In Russian. 88 minutes.

1975 Marionette film
Vadim Kourtchevski directed an adaptation of the fantasy as a Soviet marionette film. Soyouz Multfilm. Color. In Russian.

SAFINA, ALESSANDRO
Italian tenor (1968–)

Siena-born Alessandro Safina has become famous as an "opera crossover" singer through recitals and TV appearances at which he performs arias from popular operas such as *The Barber of Seville* and *La traviata*. He became better known in America in September 2001 when PBS telecast his Taormina amphitheater concert as a pledge drive special. He has appeared on stage in Italy in *La bohème, Eugene Onegin,* and *The Merry Widow.*

SAGI-VELA, LUIS
Spanish baritone (1914–)

Luis Sagi-Vela, one of the leading Spanish singers of zarzuela and light opera, is the son of baritone Emilio Sagi-Barba and soprano Luisa Vela. He made his stage debut in 1932 and had a notable film career. During the 1960s he sang starring roles in a series of zarzuelas produced for Spanish TV, which were also issued on VHS and LP. See EL BARBERILLO DE LAVAPIÉS (1968), EL CASERÍO (1969), EL HUÉSPED DEL SEVILLANO (1939), LUISA FERNANDA (1968), MARUXA (1969), LA REVOLTOSA (1968), and EL REY QUE RABIÓ (1968).

SAINT OF BLEECKER STREET, THE
1954 opera by Menotti

GIAN CARLO MENOTTI's opera *The Saint of Bleecker Street* ran on Broadway for 92 performances and won the composer/librettist the New York Drama Circle Critic's Award and his second Pulitzer Prize. It is set in the Bleecker Street area in New York where the saintly but very sick Annina has been having visions and is being besieged to perform miracles. She wants to become a nun, but her brother Michele is strongly opposed. When his mistress Desideria accuses him of loving his sister rather too much, he becomes so angry he kills her. He goes on the run and Annina meets him secretly in a subway station. She becomes a nun on her deathbed. The opera features a large cast, chorus, and orchestra in the manner of a traditional Italian opera.

1955 CBS Television
American TV production (Act II only): Gian Carlo Menotti (director), Thomas Schippers (conductor, CBS Orchestra), Chandler Cowes (producer), Ed Sullivan (host).

Cast: Virginia Copeland (Annina), David Poleri (Michele), Gloria Lane (Desideria), Leon Lishner (Don Marco), Maria di Gerlando Carmela), David Aiken (Salvatore), Catherine Akos (Assunta), Maria Marlo (Maria Corona), Ernesto Gonzalez (Maria's son), Lucy Beque (Concettina).

Telecast live January 16, 1955, on *The Ed Sullivan Show* on CBS Television. Black and white. In English. 40 minutes.

Comment: The Broadway cast staged the wedding sequence from Act II for the show.

1955 NBC Opera Theatre
American TV production: Samuel Chotzinoff (producer), Samuel Krachmalnick (conductor, NBC Symphony of the Air Orchestra and NBC Opera Theatre Chorus), Trew Hocker (set designer), Peter Herman Adler (artistic director).

Cast: Virginia Copeland (Annina), Richard Cassilly (Michele), Leon Lishner (Don Marco), Rosemary Kuhlmann (Desideria), Maria di Gerlando (Carmela), David Aiken (Salvatore), Mignon Dunn (Assunta).

Video at the MTR; 16mm telecine film at the NFTA. Telecast live May 15, 1955, on NBC. Kirk Browning (director). Black and white. In English. 90 minutes.

1956 BBC Television
English TV production: Rudolph Cartier (director), Thomas Schippers (conductor, London Symphony Orchestra and BBC Chorus), Stephen Taylor (set/costume designer).

Cast: Virginia Copeland (Annina), Raymond Nilsson (Michele), Rosalind Elias (Desideria), Jess Walters (Don Marco), June Bronhill (Carmela), Janet Howe (Assunta), Ronald Evans (Salvatore).

Telecast live October 4, 1956, on BBC. Black and white. In English. 90 minutes.

1978 New York City Opera
American stage production: Francis Rizzo (director), Carl Stewart Kellogg (conductor, New York City Opera Orchestra and Chorus), Beeb Salzer (set designer).

Cast: Catherine Malfitano (Annina), Enrico di Giuseppe (Michele), Sandra Walker (Desideria), Irwin Densen (Don Marco), Diana Soviero (Carmela), Jane Shaulis (Assunta), William Ledbetter (Salvatore).

Video at the MTR. Telecast April 19, 1978, in the series *Live From Lincoln Center*. Kirk Browning (director). Color. In English. 100 minutes.

Comment: Beverly Sills interviews Menotti and Malfitano during the intermission.

1986 Spoleto Festival
Italian stage production: Gian Carlo Menotti (director), Tzimon Barto (conductor, Spoleto Festival Orchestra and Westminster Choir), Pasquale Grossi (set/costume designer).

Cast: Adriana Morelli (Annina), Richard Burke (Michele), Adriana Cicogna (Desideria), Gabriele Monici (Don Marco), Antonia Brown (Carmela), Giorgio Gatti (Salvatore), Graziella Biondini (Assunta).

Telecast August 7, 1986, by RAI Italian Television. Fernando Turvani (director). Color. In English. 130 minutes.

Related film

1986 Spoleto Festival USA
The wedding party fight scene, from Menotti's production at the 1986 Spoleto Festival USA, is shown on a German television program with an interview with Menotti. Color. About 10 minutes. Video at the NYPL.

SAINT-SAËNS, CAMILLE
French composer (1835–1921)

Camille Saint-Saëns was the first composer to write an original score for a film, and his score for the 1908 French movie *L'Assassinat du Duc de Guise* helped movies gain stature as an art form. He was also, of course, a major opera composer. The best known of his 12 operas, and the only one still in the international repertory is the popular biblical epic SAMSON ET DALILA. The other opera that continues to be staged is HENRY VIII, which deals with the English king's split with the Catholic Church.

1974 Effie Briest
All the music in R. W. Fassbinder's popular German film *Effie Briest* is based on themes taken from compositions by Saint-Saëns. Hanna Schygulla stars as the unhappy young heroine of this adaptation of a famous novel by Theodor Fontane. Color. In German. 141 minutes.

SALIERI, ANTONIO
Italian composer (1750–1825)

Antonio Salieri, Mozart's arch-rival in Vienna, has begun to return to fashion, partially as a result of the film *Amadeus*. His operas are now being staged and televised and are available on DVD and CD, and several new books have been written about him. Salieri's operas may not rival Mozart's, but they still have real quality. The most popular is TARARE, originally a French opera with a libretto by Beaumarchais, but better known in its Italian version as *Axur* with a new libretto by Lorenzo Da Ponte. Also popular is Salieri's FALSTAFF, a version of *The Merry Wives of Windsor,* one of the first operas based on a Shakespeare play. Of interest is *Prima la musica e poi le parole,* which premiered with Mozart's *Der Schauspieldirektor.* There are no film biographies of Salieri, but he is a character in many of the films about Mozart. There is also a Rimsky-Korsakov opera about their rivalry, MOZART AND SALIERI, which helped spread the rumor that he poisoned Mozart.

1948 The Mozart Story
This American adaptation of the 1942 Austrian film *Wen die Götter lieben* has a framing structure featuring Wilton Graff as Salieri. It may have been a prototype for *Amadeus* as it begins with Salieri describing the events of the composer's life after his death. See MOZART.

1955 Reich mir die Hand, mein Leben
Albin Skoda plays Salieri in *The Life and Loves of Mozart,* an Austrian film starring Oskar Werner as Mozart at the end of his life. See MOZART.

1984 Amadeus
Salieri is portrayed by F. Murray Abraham in this famous film biography of Mozart in which he tells the story of Mozart's musical achievements. Ironically, he won the Best Actor Oscar, besting the actor playing Mozart, Tom Hulce. See AMADEUS.

1985 Mostly Mozart Meets Salieri
Salieri and Mozart are compared and contrasted in this fascinating concert. Arias, overtures, and concertos by each are performed by soprano Elly Ameling, pianist Horacio Gutiérrez, and the Mostly Mozart Festival Orchestra led by Gerard Schwarz. Patrick Watson is narrator. Telecast July 10, 1985. Color. 120 minutes.

1985 Vergesst Mozart
Winfried Glatzeder plays Salieri in *Forget Mozart,* a German film structured like a murder mystery and set on December 5, 1791, the day of Mozart's death. The chief of police is suspicious and begins to ask questions about who had a motive to kill the composer. See MOZART.

SALLINEN, AULIS
Finnish composer (1935–)

Aulis Sallinen, one of the best-known modern Finnish composers, premiered his opera *Kullervo* at the Los Angeles Music Center in 1992 when the new Finnish National Opera House opening was delayed. His opera THE PALACE, inspired by the downfall of Haile Selassie of Ethiopia, has been telecast in Finland. His other operas of note include *The Horseman* (1975), *The Red Line* (1975), and *The King Goes Forth to France* (1984), staged at Covent Garden in 1987. Sallinen's operas are nationalist and enigmatic, but quite accessible.

1992 Aulis Sallinen—Man, Music, Nature
Brad Oldenburg's documentary about the composer includes extracts from his historical operas *The Horseman* and *The Red Line* and excerpts from other compositions. Sallinen talks about himself and his ideas, and there are comments from Arto Noras, Mstislav Rostropovich, James de Priest, and David Harrington. Distributed by Amaya. Color. With English narration. 56 minutes.

SALOME
1905 opera by Richard Strauss

The Salome craze caused by the Oscar Wilde play and the RICHARD STRAUSS opera is reflected in the exceptionally large number of early films based on the story. The opera's popularity was as much due to its sexual connotations as to its intense drama and powerful music, and there were many scandals revolving around the Dance of the Seven Veils. Times have greatly changed; Maria Ewing and Catherine Malfitano both went nude in their performances without controversy. Strauss wrote the libretto based on Hedwig Lachmann's German translation of the play, and it follows Wilde's text quite closely. The story is close to that in the Bible, but the character of Salome is much more developed, and the conflict is between religious zeal and sexual obsession. Beautiful young Salome, daughter of Herodias and stepdaughter of King Herod, is angered that holy man Jokanaan (John the Baptist) ignores her allure. She performs an erotic dance for Herod, who is lusting after her, and demands John's head as her reward. When she gets it and smothers it in kisses, Herod is horrified and has her killed.

1954 NBC Opera Theatre

American TV production: Samuel Chotzinoff (producer/director), Peter Herman Adler (conductor, NBC Symphony of the Air Orchestra), William Molyneux (set designer), John Butler (choreographer), Charles Polacheck (English translation).

Cast: Elaine Malbin (Salome, dancing by Carmen Guttierez), John Cassavetes (Jokanaan, sung by Norman Atkins), Andrew McKinley (Herod), Lorna Sidney (Herodias), Davis Cunningham (Narraboth), Sal Mineo (Page, sung by Carol Jones).

Video at the MTR. Telecast live on May 8, 1954. Kirk Browning (director). Black and white. In English. 90 minutes.

1974 Friedrich film

Austrian feature film: Götz Friedrich (director), Karl Böhm (conductor, Vienna Philharmonic Orchestra), Gerd Staub (set designer), Robert Cohan (choreographer).

Cast: Teresa Stratas (Salome), Bernd Weikl (Jokanaan), Hans Beirer (Herod), Astrid Varnay (Herodias), Wieslaw Ochman (Narraboth), Hanna Schwarz (Page).

Video: DG VHS/LD. Color. In German with English subtitles. 112 minutes.

Comment: Stratas never sang Salome on stage, but she is wonderfully effective in this film shot in a studio with sets in the Hollywood biblical style.

1979 Teatro de la Zarzuela, Madrid

Spanish stage production: Julius Rudel (conductor, Teatro de la Zarzuela Orchestra).

Cast: Montserrat Caballé (Salome), Norman Bailey (Jokanaan), Josephine Veasey (Herodias).

Video: House of Opera DVD and VHS/Legato Classics VHS. Color. In German. 92 minutes.

1990 Deutsche Oper Berlin

German stage production: Petr Weigl (director), Giuseppe Sinopoli (conductor, Deutsche Oper Berlin Orchestra and Chorus), Josef Svoboda (set designer), Bernd Schindowski (choreographer).

Cast: Catherine Malfitano (Salome), Simon Estes (Jokanaan), Leonie Rysanek (Herodias), Horst Hiestermann (Herod), Clemens Bieber (Narraboth), Camille Capasso (Page).

Video: Teldec VHS. Telecast in Germany September 30, 1990. Brian Large (director). Color. In German with English subtitles. 109 minutes.

Comment: Malfitano is strong and intense as Salome, and defiantly nude at the end of her dance.

1992 Royal Opera

English stage production: Peter Hall (director), Sir Edward Downes (conductor, Royal Opera Orchestra), John Burry (set/lighting designer), Elizabeth Keen (choreographer).

Cast: Maria Ewing (Salome), Michael Devlin (Jokanaan), Kenneth Riegel (Herod), Gillian Knight (Herodias), Robin Leggate (Narraboth), Fiona Kimm (Page).

Video: Kultur and Bel Canto DVD/Home Vision VHS/Pioneer LD. Derek Bailey (director). Color. In German with English subtitles. 108 minutes.

Comment: Ewing matches Malfitano by going nude at the end of her disturbing dance.

1994 Netherlands Opera

Dutch stage production: Harry Kupfer (director), Edo de Waart (conductor, Amsterdam Radio Philharmonic Orchestra), Wilfried Werz (set/costume designer).

Cast: Josephine Barstow (Salome), John Bröcheler (Jokanaan), Günter Newmann (Herod), Isolde Elchlepp (Herodias), Adrian Thompson (Narraboth), Birgit Calm (Page).

Video: House of Opera DVD and VHS/Legato Classics VHS. Jellie Dekker (director). Color. In German with Dutch subtitles. 105 minutes.

1995 Royal Opera

English stage production: Luc Bondy (director), Christoph von Dohnányi (conductor, Royal Opera House Orchestra and Chorus), Erich Wonder (set designer).

Cast: Catherine Malfitano (Salome), Bryn Terfel (Jokanaan), Anja Silja (Herodias), Kenneth Riegel (Herod), Robert Gambill (Narraboth), Ruby Philogene (Page).

Video: London/Teldec VHS. Hans Hulscher (director). Color. In German with English subtitles. 109 minutes.

Early/related films

1906 Salome's Dance

German film pioneer Oskar Messter shot the film *Salome's Dance* with Adorée Villany Messter as Salome. Based on the Wilde play, it concentrates on the dance and the request for the head of John the Baptist. It was made with synchronized sound on a recording. Black and white. 3 minutes.

1907 Biograph film

D. W. Griffith's great cameraman Billy Bitzer photographed this *Salome* in the New York studio of the American Mutoscope and Biograph Company. Black and white. Silent. About 7 minutes.

1908 Salome, or the Dance of the Seven Veils

Florence Lawrence, the first movie actress to be publicized by name, stars as Salome with Maurice Costello as John the Baptist in the Vitagraph studio film *Salome, or the Dance of the Seven Veils*. The plot is close to that of the opera. Black and white. Silent. About 10 minutes.

1908 Salome: The Dance of the Seven Veils

This is the Salome story as retold by Vitagraph's main competitor, the Lubin studio. It uses the very similar title of *Salome: The Dance of the Seven Veils*. Black and white. Silent. About 10 minutes.

1908 The Great Salome Dance

This is a British film of a dancer (Salome) who kisses a severed head (John the Baptist) and then faints. Walter Tyler directed. Black and white. Silent. About 4 minutes.

1908 Gaumont film

French film companies were also willing to cash in on the Salome craze. This *Salome* was made by Gaumont and released in America by Kleine. Black and white. Silent. About 9 minutes.

1908 The Saloon Dance

Two tramps find tickets for the opera and go to see *Salome*. They are so impressed that they steal female costumes so they can earn money imitating what they call the "Saloon Dance." Made by the Lubin studio. Black and white. Silent. About 10 minutes.

1908 Salome and the Devil to Pay

A young man's family is shocked when he admits he has seen *Salome*, but they all slip off later to see it for themselves. Made for the Lubin studio. Black and white. Silent. About 9 minutes.

1909 Pathé film

Stacia Napierkowska stars as Salome with Paul Capellani as John the Baptist in this French *Salome* directed by Albert Capellani for Pathé. Black and white. Silent. About 10 minutes.

1909 The Salome Craze

This American film about the obsession with *Salome* was made by the Phoenix Film Company. Black and white. Silent. About 8 minutes.

1909 The Salome Dance Music

British sound film featuring the Dance of the Seven Veils screened in synchronization with a recording of the dance music. It was produced by Warwick Cinephone Films. Black and white. About 4 minutes.

1909 Salome Mad

British film about a man chasing a *Salome* poster into the sea. A. E. Coleby directed it for Cricks & Martin. Black and white. Silent. About 6 minutes.

1909 Salome Mad

British film about a man obsessed by the *Salome* dance. Theo Bouwmeester directed for the Hepworth studio. Black and white. Silent. About 7 minutes.

1910 Film d'Arte Italiana film

Vittorio Lepanto plays Salome in this Italian film with Ciro Gavani as John the Baptist, Laura Orette as Herodias, and Achille Vitti as Herod. Ugo Falena directed with a screenplay based on the play. Tinted color. Silent. 15 minutes.

1913 European film

Suzanne de Laarboy stars as Salome in this feature-length *Salome*, an Italian version of the opera story. When Salome did her famous dance, the Strauss music was played live in the theater. Produced by the European Feature Film Company of Turin. Black and white. Silent. About 40 minutes.

1915 La danza di Salomè

Italian comedy film about Salome's Dance of the Seven Veils starring Belgian dancer Féline Werbist. Eleutaria Rodolfo directed. Black and white. Silent. About 40 minutes.

1918 Fox film

Theda Bara, the famous vamp of the silent cinema, plays Salome in the Fox spectacular *Salome*, with Albert Roscoe as John the Baptist and G. Raymond Nye as King Herod. Contemporary critics were quick to note the scantiness of Bara's costumes. The plot is about the same as that of the opera. J. Gordon Edwards directed. Black and white. Silent. About 90 minutes. This is a lost film.

1922 Nazimova film
Alla Nazimova plays Salome in this famous American film of the Wilde play, with Nigel De Brulier as Jokanaan, Mitchell Lewis as King Herod, and Rose Diane as Herodias. Natasha Rambova created the exotic sets and costumes based on designs by Aubrey Beardsley, and Charles Bryant directed for Nazimova Productions. Black and white. Silent. About 80 minutes. On VHS.

1923 Strauss' Salome
Diana Allen plays Salome in this version of the story advertised as *Strauss' Salome.* The Strauss it refers to is not the German composer but the U.S. producer/director Malcolm Strauss. Vincent Coleman plays Herod with Christine Winthrop as Herodias. Black and white. Silent. About 75 minutes.

1945 Salome, Where She Danced
Yvonne De Carlo became a star on the strength of her torrid dancing in the film *Salome, Where She Danced,* one of the all-time delightfully bad movies. She plays a 19th-century dancer-spy who comes to the American West and gets a town named after her. There is no music by Richard Strauss but there is a little by Johann, plus selections from Balfe's opera *The Bohemian Girl.* Laurence Stallings wrote the screenplay, and Charles Lamont directed for Universal. Color. In English. 90 minutes. On VHS.

1953 Columbia film
Rita Hayworth is the star of this *Salome,* a really romantic Hollywood revisionist version of the story in which Salome wants to save John. Alan Badel is John the Baptist, Charles Laughton is King Herod, and Judith Anderson is Herodias. The plot is similar to that of the opera and the Dance of the Seven Veils is prominent, but the Strauss connection is slim. The music is by Daniel Amfitheatrof and George Duning. William Dieterle directed for Columbia Pictures. Color. In English. 102 minutes. On VHS.

1953 The Man Between
Carol Reed's fine British thriller *The Man Between* has a key sequence in which James Mason and Claire Bloom attend a production of *Salome* at the East Berlin Staatsoper. Bulgarian soprano Ljuba Welitsch sings the role of Salome and is shown in her final scene as the couple slip away to try to escape to the West. Black and white. In English. 101 minutes.

1972 Bene film
Donyale Luna stars as Salome in this bizarre, experimental, and generally over-the-top film of the Oscar Wilde play by Italian director Carmelo Bene. Color. In Italian. 77 minutes.

1986 D'Anna film
French writer-director Claude D'Anna based his Salome film on the Strauss opera and the Wilde play, but he set it in vaguely modern times. Jo Champa is Salome, Fabrizio Bentivoglio is Jokanaan, Tomas Milian is Herod, and Pamela Salem is Herodias. Color. In English or French. 95 minutes.

1988 Salome's Last Dance
British director Ken Russell was denied use of the Strauss music for *Salome's Last Dance,* an excellent film of the Oscar Wilde play set in an 1892 brothel with Wilde himself as observer. Imogen Millais-Scott plays Salome, but Doug Howes performs the Dance of the Seven Veils. Glenda Jackson is Herodias, Stratford Johns is Herod, Douglas Hodge is John the Baptist, and Nicholas Grace is Wilde. Color. In English. 89 minutes.

1998 A Soldier's Daughter Never Cries
A spoof of a production of *Salome* at its kitschy extreme is featured in this film about an American writer and his family living in Paris during the 1960s. His daughter Channe (Leelee Sobieski) is taken to see an avant-garde production of *Salome.* The cast loll around on bright inflatable plastic chairs, Salome nearly makes a meal of John's severed head, and Herodias sniffs cocaine and shoots up. When Herod orders Salome killed, Herodias stabs her in the neck with a giant syringe. Salome's singing is by Hildegarde Behrens, from a 1977 recording with the Vienna Philharmonic led by Herbert von Karajan. James Ivory directed the film. Color. In English. 127 minutes.

2002 Salome
Carlo Saura's flamenco dance version of the story stars Aida Gomez as Aida, Javier Toca as John the Baptist, Paco Mora as Herod, and Carmen Villena as Herodias. Roque Banos composed the music and Gomez created the choreography with José Antonio. Color. In Spanish. 86 minutes.

SALTIMBANQUES, LES
1899 opéra-comique by Ganne

French composer LOUIS GANNE's best-known stage work is *Les Saltimbanques* (The Traveling Players or, literally, The Tumblers), a romantic operetta about a group of performers in a small traveling circus. It has pleasant tunes, colorful circus stage effects, and a clever libretto by Maurice Ordonneau. The plot revolves around Suzanne, foster daughter of the circus owner Malicorne, strongman Grand Pingouin, beautiful tightrope walker Marion, and sad clown Paillasse who loves little Suzanne. Her love for the soldier André creates a conflict, so she runs away from the circus and finds her real, and quite wealthy, parents. There is a good French CD version with Mady Mesplé as Suzanne.

1930 Nero film

German/French/Italian film: Jaquelux and Robert Land (directors), Herbert Brown (screenplay), Willy Goldberger (cinematographer), Albert Lauzin (producer), Nero Film (production).

Cast: Käthe von Nagy (Suzanne), Nicolas Coline (Paillasse), Louis Ralph (Malicorne), Max Henson (André), Suzanne Gouts (Marion).

Black and white. In German, French, or Italian. 88 minutes.

Comment: Shot simultaneously in three languages in Germany. The French title is *Les Saltimbanques,* the German title is *Gaukler,* and the Italian title is *I Saltimbanchi.*

SALZBURG

Mozart's hometown has a long history of opera performance going back to 1618, but the famous Salzburg Festival itself dates only from 1922 when the Grosses Festspielhaus opened. One of the earliest major opera films of a stage production—Paul Czinner's pioneering 1954 DON GIOVANNI—was shot at Salzburg. It was followed in 1960 with his equally famous DER ROSENKAVALIER. Although it is almost impossible to go to an opera at the festival without booking expensive tickets months in advance, it is fairly easy to visit the festival on video. There is a particularly wide range of choice as Herbert von Karajan, who ran the festival for many years, filmed nearly every opera he produced there. See AUFSTIEG UND FALL DER STADT MAHAGONNY (1998), CAPRICCIO (1990), CARMEN (1967), JOSÉ CARRERAS (1985), LA CENERENTOLA (1988), LA DAMNATION DI FAUST (1999), DON CARLO (1986), DON GIOVANNI (1954/1987), DIE ENTFÜHRUNG AUS DEM SERAIL (1989/1971 film), FALSTAFF (1982), DIE FRAU OHNE SCHATTEN (1992), FROM THE HOUSE OF THE DEAD (1993), HERBERT VON KARAJAN (1987/1995), KATYA KABANOVA (1998), THE RAKE'S PROGRESS (1996), IL RE PASTORE (1989), IL RITORNO D'ULISSE IN PATRIA (1985), DER ROSENKAVALIER (1960/1984), SALZBURG MARIONETTE THEATRE, DER SCHAUSPIELDIREKTOR (1980), DIE SCHÖNE GALATHÉE (1967), DIE SCHÖPFUNG (1990), LES TROYENS (2000), VERDI REQUIEM (1982), and DIE ZAUBERFLÖTE (1975 film/1982).

1931 Salzburg, City of Mozart

This early film about Salzburg is of particular interest as it shows opera scenes at the festival as well as Salzburg sights. Rosette Anday is seen in *Orpheus and Eurydice* with Bruno Walter conducting, and Richard Mayr is shown in *Die Zauberflöte* with Clemens Krauss conducting the Vienna Philharmonic Orchestra. The film was made by Selenophon Talking Pictures. Black and white. 10 minutes. Print at NFTA, London.

1944 Musik in Salzburg

This is a romantic German fiction film set in Salzburg during the period of the Festival with Lil Dagover, Willy Birgel, and Hans Nielsen in the leading roles. Herbert Maisch directed. Black and white. In German. 103 minutes.

1956 Salzburg Pilgrimage

A respectful film about the city and its opera festival made by opera film pioneer Paul Czinner, who shot *Don Giovanni* on stage there in 1954. Black and white. In English. 20 minutes.

SALZBURG MARIONETTE THEATER

The Marionettetheater Salzburg (Salzburg Marionette Theater) specializes in shortened puppet versions of opera and operetta using notable recordings as the singing voices. A few of them are now available on DVD and VHS in English, German, or French in NTSC and PAL formats. Some are quite rare, such as Lortzing's DER WAFFENSCHMIED (1982) and Thomas's MIGNON (1983), but the focus is on the operas of Mozart, including versions of DIE ENTFÜHRUNG AUS DEM SERIAL (1984), *Così fan tutte, Don Giovanni, Die Zauberflöte,* and *Le nozze di Figaro.* Most have introductions by Peter Ustinov.

SAMSON ET DALILA
1877 opera by Saint-Saëns

CAMILLE SAINT-SAËNS's biblical opera *Samson et Dalila* (Samson and Delilah) is probably best known for its soprano aria "Mon coeur s'ouvre à ta voix," which is often featured in recitals and movies. Ferdinand Lemaire based the libretto on the story as told in the Book of Judges in the Bible. Strongman Hebrew warrior Samson leads a revolt against the Philistines but is seduced by beautiful Philistine spy Delilah, who discovers that the secret of his strength is in his hair. After it is cut off, he becomes weak and is taken prisoner. At the end, God gives him the strength to pull down his captors' temple.

1980 San Francisco Opera

American stage production: Nicolas Joel (director), John Goberman (producer), Julius Rudel (conductor, San Francisco Opera Orchestra and Chorus), Douglas Schmidt (set designer), Carrie Robbins (costume designer).

Cast: Shirley Verrett (Dalila), Plácido Domingo (Samson), Wolfgang Brendel (High Priest of Dagon), Arnold Voketaitis (Abimélech), Kevin Langan (Old Hebrew).

Video: Kultur/Bel Canto Society/Arthaus (GB) DVD, Home Vision VHS, and Pioneer LD. Taped October 24, 1980. Kirk Browning (director). Color. In French with English subtitles. 111 minutes.

1981 Royal Opera

English stage production: Elijah Moshinsky (director), Colin Davis (conductor, Royal Opera House Orchestra and Chorus), Sidney Nolan (set/costume designer).

Cast: Shirley Verrett (Dalila), Jon Vickers (Samson), Jonathan Summers (High Priest of Dagon), John Tomlinson (Abimélech), Gwynne Howell (Old Hebrew).

Video: HBO VHS. Taped October 15, 1981. John Vernon (director). Color. In French with English subtitles. 135 minutes.

1998 Metropolitan Opera

American stage production: Elijah Moshinsky (director), James Levine (conductor, Metropolitan Opera Orchestra and Chorus), Richard Hudson (set/costume designer).

Cast: Olga Borodina (Dalila), Plácido Domingo (Samson), Sergei Leiferkus (High Priest of Dagon), Richard Paul Fink (Abimélech), René Pape (Old Hebrew).

Telecast live September 28, 1998, on PBS. Brian Large (director). Color. In French with English subtitles. 180 minutes.

Comment: Hudson, who designed the much-praised sets for *The Lion King,* created colorful new sets and costumes for this fine production.

Early/related films

1902 Pathé film

Ferdinand Zecca's French film *Samson et Dalila* was inspired by the opera and screened with its music played live. It was produced by Pathé in France and distributed in the United States in 1904 by Edison. Black and white. Silent. About 3 minutes.

1907 Capellani film

Albert Capellani Italian film inspired by the opera and screened with its music played live. Black and white. Silent. About 7 minutes. Print in NFTA, London.

1910 Samson's Betrayal

This French film, inspired by the opera and screened with its music, was made by the Gaumont studio and distributed in the United States by Kleine. It was titled *Samson et Dalila* in France and *Samson's Betrayal* in the United States. Black and white. About 8 minutes.

1922 Tense Moments From Opera series

Valia plays Dalila with M. D. Waxman as Samson in this British highlights film of the opera screened with Saint-Saëns's music. It was produced by H. B. Parkinson, written by Frank Miller, and directed by Edwin J. Collins for the series *Tense Moments From Opera.* Black and white. Silent. About 12 minutes.

1922 Samson and Delilah: Story of an Opera Singer

Samson und Delila is an Austrian feature film about an opera singer who has been picked to sing the role of Delilah. She seeks out a Jewish scholar to tell her the story of Samson and Delilah and is then able to relate the biblical story to her own career—a kind of parallel story with the opera. Maria Corda plays the prima donna and Delilah, Alfredo Galoar is Samson, and Franz Herterich is Khan. Alexander Korda directed. The U.S. release title was *Samson and Delilah: Story of an Opera Singer.* Black and white. Silent. About 70 minutes.

1927 Cameo Operas series

William Anderson plays Samson in this film of scenes from the opera made by H. B. Parkinson for the British *Cameo Opera* series. The film was shown with singers off stage performing the arias. Black and white. Silent. 20 minutes.

1947 Carnegie Hall

Risë Stevens sings "Mon coeur s'ouvre à ta voix" in this film celebrating the concert hall and its singers. See CARNEGIE HALL.

1949 DeMille film

Cecil B. DeMille's epic sin-and-sandals film *Samson and Delilah* stars Hedy Lamarr as Delilah and Victor Mature as Samson with music provided by Victor Young. The story is more or less the same as that of the opera, but the film has more spectacular sets and more garish colors. Color. In English. 128 minutes.

1955 Interrupted Melody

Australian opera diva Marjorie Lawrence (Eleanor Parker) makes her debut in Paris in *Samson et Dalila* and is seen on stage singing "Mon coeur s'ouvre à ta voix" (in real life she never sang this mezzo role). A few years later, after she has been felled by polio, she forces herself to crawl across a room to knock over a phonograph playing her recording of the aria. Husband Glenn Ford set up the situation to force her to move unaided and begin her recovery. The voice heard on the record belongs to Eileen Farrell (in real life Lawrence never recorded it). See INTERRUPTED MELODY.

1957 The Lady From Philadelphia

Edward R. Murrow's film about Marian Anderson's goodwill tour of Southeast Asia for the State Department, shown on his CBS Television program *See it Now*, features Anderson singing "Mon coeur s'ouvre à ta voix" with the Bombay Symphony Orchestra. The soundtrack is on an LP. Black and white. 60 minutes. Video at the MTR.

1984 Phillips film

Lee Phillips directed this remake of DeMille's *Samson and Delilah* with Victor Mature now cast as Samson's father. Antony Hamilton plays Samson and Belinda Bauer is Delilah with a new script by John Gay, new music by Maurice Jarre, and a starry supporting cast. Color. 100 minutes.

1987 Slamdance

Director Wayne Wang features the aria "Mon coeur s'ouvre à ta voix" (in an English translation as "My heart opens at thy voice") in a key scene about betrayal at the end of this psychological crime drama. It's sung by Billy Bizeau with backing by Richard Thompson, Alex Acuna, Jerry Scheff, Jim Keltner, and Mitchell Froom. Color. In English. 101 minutes.

1995 The Bridges of Madison County

Maria Callas is heard on the radio singing "Mon coeur s'ouvre à ta voix" in an appropriate moment for housewife Meryl Streep in this romantic film directed by Clint Eastwood. The Callas recording was made with the French National Radio Orchestra led by Georges Prêtre. Color. In English. 135 minutes.

SAN FRANCISCO

1936 American film with opera content

One of the better Hollywood epics with charismatic stars, a memorable earthquake, and entertaining opera sequences. It takes places in San Francisco in 1906. Out-of-work and starving Jeanette MacDonald is hired by saloon keeper Clark Gable to sing at his Paradise Café. The owner of the Tivoli Opera House (Jack Holt) hears her and invites her to sing opera there, but Gable won't allow it. When she goes anyway, he tries to stop her but repents after he sees her on stage in Gounod's *Faust*. Gable's boyhood priest friend Spencer Tracy convinces McDonald that Gable will eventually reform, and this is brought about by the earthquake. The pair end up together singing "Glory, Glory Hallelujah" as the film ends. The *Faust* sequence, staged by Wilhelm von Wymetal Jr., features McDonald as Marguerite with Tandy MacKenzie as Faust and Tudor Williams as Méphistophélès. MacDonald sings "The Jewel Song," part of the duet "Il se fait tard" with MacKenzie, and the prayer aria "Anges purs" with MacKenzie and Williams. There is also a bit of the Soldiers Chorus. In another scene McDonald is shown on stage in *La traviata* singing "Sempre libera" with MacKenzie. Herbert Stothart was the conductor and music director, Anita Loos wrote the screenplay, Oliver T. Marsh was cinematographer, Cedric Gibbons was art director, and W. S. Van Dyke directed for MGM. Black and white. In English. 115 minutes. MGM-UA VHS.

SAN FRANCISCO OPERA

The first opera was presented in San Francisco in 1851, and the city has been enthusiastic about opera ever since. The present building, the War Memorial Opera House, dates from 1932 and has recently been restored. San Francisco Opera has been among the most adventurous opera companies in America in recent years, with premieres of American operas such as Susa's THE DANGEROUS LIAISONS, Previn's A STREETCAR NAMED DESIRE, and Heggie's *Dead Man Walking*. See L'AFRICAINE (1988), LA BOHÈME (1989), CAPRICCIO (1993), LA GIOCONDA (1980), MEFISTOFELE (1989), ORLANDO FURIOSO (1990), SAMSON ET DALILA (1980), and TURANDOT (1993).

1964 The Roving Boys at the Opera

Cartoonist Bill Bates and disc jockeys Don Sherwood and Carter B. Smith attend the opening night of the San Francisco Opera season in 1964 and poke fun at the things they see. Bates created a hundred sketches for this popular telecast on KGO-TV. Black and white. 30 minutes.

1991 In the Shadow of the Stars

Superb Academy Award–winning documentary about the people who make up the chorus of the San Francisco Opera Company and swell the crowds on stage. The filmmakers allow them to explain the drive that makes them want to participate and the sacrifices they make to be in the chorus. As one chorus member explains, "all of us are stars." The yearning to take center stage is obvious, and sometimes the dreams are fulfilled. There are scenes of rehearsals and productions including *L'Africaine, La bohème, La Gioconda, Macbeth, Die Meistersinger, Parsifal,* and *Il trovatore.* Irving Saraf and Allie Light directed and edited the film with genuine humanity. Color. 93 minutes. Kultur DVD.

1997 San Francisco Opera Gala Celebration
The opera company celebrates the reopening of the renovated War Memorial Opera House on September 5, 1997, with performances and archival film. Beverly Sills and Derek Jacobi host this *Great Performances* telecast with Donald Runnicles conducting the San Francisco Opera Orchestra and Chorus. The all-star cast of singers includes Plácido Domingo and Frederica von Stade. Brian Large directed. Color and black and white. In English. 90 minutes.

SATIE, ERIC
French composer (1866–1925)

Eric Satie is probably best known for his ballet *Parade,* but he also created two notable operas. The first was the brief marionette opera GENEVIÈVE DE BRABANT, composed in 1899 for piano and singers and orchestrated and staged after his death. His major opera was the 1920 *Socrate,* based on Plato's dialogues, famously staged in Hartford, Connecticut, in 1936. Satie was very influential on opera composers such as Virgil Thomson and Ned Rorem.

SATYAGRAHA
1980 opera by Glass

This is an opera about Mahatma Gandhi while he was living in South Africa from 1893 to 1914 and fighting to repeal the Black Act. He meets his past as Leo Tolstoy, his present as Rabindranath Tagore, and his future as Martin Luther King Jr. PHILIP GLASS's opera *Satyagraha,* libretto by Constance De Jong in English and Sanskrit, was premiered in Rotterdam by the Netherlands Opera in 1980 in a production by David Pountney. The title comes from the Sanskrit words *sat* (truth) and *graha* (firmness), a concept the Gandhi coined to describe his passive resistance movement. The opera incorporates elements from Indian mythological epics.

1983 Stuttgart State Opera
German stage production: Achim Freyer (director, set/costume designer), Dennis Russell Davies (conductor, Staatsoper Stuttgart Orchestra and Chorus).

Cast: Leo Goeke (Gandhi 1), Ralf Harster (Gandhi 2), Helmut Danniger (Gandhi 3), Inga Nielsen (Gandhi's secretary Schlesen), Elke Estlinbaum (Gan-

dhi's wife Kasturbai), Wolfgang Probst and Kimmo Lappalainen (Gandhi's European aides), Daniel Bonilla and Melinda Liebermann (Gandhi's Indian aides), Helga Merkl-Freivogel (Mrs. Alexander), Karl-Friedrich Dürr (Krishna), Helmut Holzapfel (Arjuna), George Greiwe (Tolstoy/Tagore).

Image Entertainment/Arthaus (GB) DVD. Hugo Käch (director). Color. In English and Sanskrit with English subtitles. 166 minutes.

Related film

1981 A Composer's Notes: Philip Glass
Achim Freyer's 1981 production of *Satyagraha* for Stuttgart State Opera is shown in excerpts in this documentary by Michael Blackwood, although most of the film is devoted to *Akhnaten.* Color. 87 minutes. VAI VHS.

SAUL AND THE WITCH OF ENDOR
1693 biblical drama by Purcell

Henry Purcell's biblical drama *Saul and the Witch of Endor* is not considered one of the composer's semi-operas, but it is a dramatic musical story and has been staged. It is based on an episode in the biblical book 1 Samuel and features three singers. Hebrew King Saul is deeply worried about an upcoming battle with the Philistines. He goes in disguise to a medium, the Witch of Endor, and asks her to summon the spirit of the late prophet Samuel. She does so, and Samuel informs him he will lose the battle and be killed.

1959 CBS Television
American TV production: John Desmond (director), Arnold Gamson (conductor, CBS Chamber Ensemble).

Cast: Loren Driscoll (King Saul), Eleanor Ross (Witch of Endor), Chester Watson (Prophet Samuel).

Telecast June 7, 1959, on the *Camera Three* program on CBS. John Desmond (director). Black and white. In English. 30 minutes.

SAWALLISCH, WOLFGANG
German conductor (1923–)

Wolfgang Sawallisch, who was born in Munich and made his conducting debut there in 1947, has been closely associated with the Bavarian State Opera in Munich since 1971. Sawallisch is noted for his Wagner and Strauss productions (his complete RING DES NIBELUNGEN cycle is on video), but he can also be seen conducting a Mozart and a Hindemith opera. See BAYREUTH (1960), CARDILLAC (1986), DER FLIEGENDE HOLLÄNDER (1975/1991),

GÖTTERDÄMMERUNG (1989), DAS RHEINGOLD (1989), DIE SCHWEIGSAME FRAU (1971), SIEGFRIED (1989), DIE WALKÜRE (1989), and DIE ZAUBERFLÖTE (1983).

SAYÃO, BIDÚ
Brazilian soprano (1902–1999)

Bidú Sayão, who was born in Rio de Janeiro, studied in Nice with Jean de Reszke and returned to Rio for her debut at the Teatro Municipal in 1926. By the early 1930s she was performing in major theaters in Paris and Italy, but her greatest success was at the Metropolitan Opera in 1937 in Massenet's *Manon;* it launched an American career that lasted through 1952. She was heard in a wide variety of roles at the Met, but especially as Mozart's Susanna and Zerlina. Sayão retired from the stage in 1958, but her silvery charm can still be experienced on video.

1951/1952 Bidú Sayão in Opera and Song
Highlights of appearances by the soprano on the *Voice of Firestone* TV series in 1951 and 1952. She performs the "Gavotte" from Massenet's *Manon,* "Un bel dì" from Puccini's *Madama Butterfly,* and "O mio babbino caro" from Puccini's *Gianni Schicchi,* plus songs by Arditi, Hahn, Sandoval, Padilla, and Coward. Howard Barlow leads the Voice of Firestone Orchestra. Black and white. 45 minutes. VAI VHS.

1966 Open Mind
Sayão is one of the singers who talks about the Golden Age of the Metropolitan Opera on this telecast after the razing of the old Met theater. See METROPOLITAN OPERA.

1985 Toscanini: The Maestro
Sayão is one of those interviewed in Peter Rosen's outstanding film about Toscanini, who often conducted her operas. See ARTURO TOSCANINI.

SCALA DI SETA, LA
1812 opera by Rossini

La scala di seta (The Silk Ladder), a romantic farce with a famous overture and a libretto by Giuseppe Maria Foppa, is the second of three early one-act comedies that GIOACHINO ROSSINI premiered in Venice. Like the others, it is concerned with a young woman being urged to marry against her will. In this case Giulia (coloratura soprano) is already secretly married to Dorvil, and he uses the silk ladder to climb up to her room. To block a plan by her guardian Dormant to marry her to Blansac, she sets up her cousin Lucilla to marry him instead. Dormant has to accept a changed situation.

1989 Schwetzingen Festival
German stage production: Michael Hampe (director/designer), Gianluigi Gelmetti (conductor, Stuttgart Radio Symphony Orchestra), Harmut Warnecke (set designer), Chiara Donato (costume designer). Cast: Luciana Serra (Giulia), David Kuebler (Dorvil), Alessandro Corbelli (Germano), Alberto Rinaldi (Blansac), Jane Bunnell (Lucilla), David Griffith (Dormont). Video: Teldec VHS/LD. Claus Viller (director). Color. In Italian with English subtitles. 100 minutes (includes documentary *Schwetzingen Portrait*).

Related film

2000 The Family Man
The Overture to *La scala di seta* is featured on the soundtrack of this U.S. film about a banker (Nicolas Cage) who discovers the joys of family life in an alternate universe. Brett Ratner directed. Color. 125 minutes.

SCARLATTI, DOMENICO
Italian composer (1685–1757)

Domenico Scarlatti is best known for his keyboard sonatas, but he also wrote a dozen operas that were popular in Rome during his time. They include seven composed for the dowager Queen of Poland Maria Casimira, who lived in Rome and built her own opera theater. Scarlatti's comic masterpiece is the intermezzo buffa LA DIRINDINA, which is still being staged today, but his mythological "drama per musica" *Tetide in Sciro* (Thetis on Scyros) is also receiving renewed interest.

SCHAUSPIELDIREKTOR, DER
1786 opera by Mozart

Der Schauspieldirektor (The Impresario) is a delightful one-act comic singspiel (i.e., the dialogue is spoken) in German about the rivalry of prima donnas. MOZART wrote it for an Imperial social event to a libretto by Gottlieb Stephanie Jr. An impresario is hiring performers for an engagement in Salzburg. Sopranos Mme. Herz and Mlle. Silberklang audition with very different styles of arias, and both are hired. They argue over who will be the prima donna while the tenor Monsieur Vogelsang tries to keep the peace. The roles were written for Aloysia Weber, who specialized in singing German opera with sentiment, and Catarina Cavalieri, who specialized in singing Italian opera with brilliance. It is usually performed in the United States and England in English as *The Impresario* and is often modernized.

1938 Paul Nipkow Sender Television

German TV film: Leopold Hainisch (director), Walter Kolle (conductor, television orchestra), Heinz Monnier (set designer).

Cast: Mara Jankisch (Mme. Herz), Melitta Kiefer (Mlle. Silberklang), Eugen Bodart (Monsieur Vogelsang), A. Münch (Impresario).

Telecast December 20, 1938. Black and white. In German. 50 minutes

Comment: This was the first opera shown on television in Germany, and it was repeated eight times.

1961 CBS Camera Three

American TV production: John Desmond (director), Arnold Gamson (conductor, CBS Orchestra), Clair Roskam and Joseph Hurley (English translation).

Cast: Jacquelyne Moody (Mme. Heartmelt), Eleanor Steber (Mlle. Warblewell), John Kuhn (Impresario).

Videos at the MTR and NYPL. Black and white. In English. 30 minutes.

Comment: Updated to the present time with a simple set consisting of a piano and a desk.

1980 BBC Television

English TV production: Francis Coleman (director/English adaptation with Kenneth Corden), Vilem Tausky (conductor, English Chamber Orchestra).

Cast: Nan Christie (Elisabeth Herzkoph), Patricia Wise (Beverly Silvertone), Giuseppe Di Stefano (Luciano Buffarotti), Patrick Cargill (Impresario Rudolph Bang).

Video: House of Opera/Lyric/Opera Dubs VHS. Kenneth Corden (director). Color. In English with some arias in German. 60 minutes.

Comment: In this updated English-language version, the Nemesis Opera Company wants to present a Mozart opera with two star sopranos for a TV film. After many problems, they stage the opera *Der Schauspieldirektor*.

1980 Schlosstheater, Salzburg

Austrian stage production: Federik Mirdita (director), Friedmann Layder (conductor, ORF Austrian Television Orchestra), Georg Schmid (set designer).

Cast: Zdzislawa Donat (Mme. Herz), Gudrun Seiber (Mlle Silberklang), Peter Drahosch (Pertini), Carl Dönch (Impresario).

Video: Lyric VHS. Telecast December 7, 1980, on ORF Austrian Television. Miroslav Svoboda (director). Color. In German. 81 minutes.

1990 Mostly Mozart Festival

American concert production: Gerald Schwarz (conductor, Mostly Mozart Festival Orchestra).

Cast: Francis Ginsberg (Mme. Herz), Sally Wolf (Mlle. Silberklang), Vinson Cole (Vogelsang), Werner Klemperer (Impresario).

Telecast July 11, 1990, in the series *Live From Lincoln Center* on PBS. Kirk Browning (director). Color. 118 minutes.

1991 Mozart at Buckingham Palace

English stage production: Sir Colin Davis (conductor, English Chamber Orchestra).

Cast: Yvonne Kenny (Mme. Herz), Ann Howard (Mlle. Silberklang), Barry Banks (Vogelsang), Mathew Best (Impresario), Peter Shaffer (Narrator).

Video: EMI VHS/Dreamlife LD. Telecast by Thames Television. Color. In English. 60 minutes.

SCHEFF, FRITZI
Austrian-born American soprano (1879–1954)

Fritzi Scheff, who was known as the "little devil of grand opera" at the height of her Broadway fame, created the role of Fifi in Victor Herbert's 1905 operetta MLLE. MODISTE and is remembered for her performance of its hit "Kiss Me Again." Scheff, who was born in Vienna, made her debut in 1897 in Frankfurt as Juliette in the Gounod opera. She moved to the United States in 1900 and sang Musetta in *La bohème* and Marzelline in *Fidelio* at the Met. After three years and 141 Met performances, she switched to light opera. Her only film came in 1915 when she starred in a movie version of her Broadway stage success *Pretty Mrs. Smith*. In 1951 she appeared in a television production of *Mlle. Modiste* as Etienne's mother and sang "Kiss Me Again" one last time.

1915 Pretty Mrs. Smith

Straightforward film adaptation of Scheff's Broadway stage success, *Pretty Mrs. Smith* was written by Oliver Morosco and Elmer Harris. Scheff plays Mrs. Drucilla Smith, a two-time widow who has married three men named Smith. She then finds that her first two supposedly deceased husbands are still alive, and she is a trigamist. It gets happily sorted out. The film, produced by Morosco's own company, was directed by Hobart Bosworth for Paramount. Black and white. Silent. About 70 minutes.

SCHERTZINGER, VICTOR
American film director (1880–1941)

Victor Schertzinger, a composer and songwriter as well as an excellent film director, wrote one of the first original film scores for the 1916 Thomas Ince movie *Civilization*. His 1934 Grace Moore film ONE NIGHT OF LOVE helped create the Hollywood opera film boom of the

1930s and was followed by another fine Moore picture, LOVE ME FOREVER (1935). He wrote the songs for the amazing Marian Talley opera film FOLLOW YOUR HEART (1936), and his 1939 film of THE MIKADO was the first complete Gilbert and Sullivan operetta to reach the screen.

SCHICKELE, PETER
American composer (1935–)

Musical jester/satirist Peter Schickele has a split personality. As Schickele, he is the host of a popular classical music program. As P.D.Q. Bach, he is a famous composer/librettist who creates brilliant parodies of baroque and classical music, including operas. His first opera was *The Stoned Guest* (a "half-act opera") presented in Carnegie Hall in 1967. The only one on video is the Mozartian pastiche THE ABDUCTION OF FIGARO, staged in Minneapolis in 1984. The others include *Hansel & Gretel & Ted & Alice* ("opera in one unnatural act for bargain countertenor and beriberitone"), *A Little Nightmare Music,* and *Prelude to Einstein on the Fritz.* Schickele, who studied at Swarthmore, Juilliard, and Aspen, has composed more than 100 musical works.

SCHIPA, TITO
Italian tenor (1889–1965)

Tito Schipa, one of the finest tenors of the 20th century, made his debut in 1910 in the mosquito-ridden provincial town of Vercelli. In 1915 he began to sing at La Scala, and in 1917 he created the role of Ruggero in Puccini's operetta *La Rondine* in Monte Carlo. He sang in Chicago during the 1920s and at the Metropolitan during the 1930s, but he still continued to perform at La Scala. Schipa specialized in the lighter lyrical Italian roles, but he was also known for singing in French operas, such as *Manon* and *Werther.* He began to make films in Italy in 1932 and had a major success with *Vivere* in 1936.

1929/1930 Paramount Operatic Selections
Schipa made two films for Paramount Movietone at the Astoria Studio in New York in 1929 and 1930. In one he appears in costume singing "M'apparì" from Flotow's *Martha;* in the other he sings "Princesita." *Paramount Operatic Selections* was the studio's equivalent of the Vitaphone opera films of Warner Bros. Black and white. In Italian. About 8 minutes each.

1929 RCA Photophone
Schipa sings "Un furtiva lagrima" from *L'elisir d'amore* plus the songs "El Gaucho" and "I Shall Return" in this sound short made for RCA Photophone. Black and white. In Italian and English. About 8 minutes each.

1932 I Sing for You Alone
In Schipa's first feature film, made in three languages, he plays a tenor who has a great voice but crippling stage fright. He allows his voice to be used by a friend who becomes famous. See I SING FOR YOU ALONE.

1936 Vivere
In Schipa's biggest film success, he plays a nightclub singer who becomes an opera star with the motto "Vivere," the title of his favorite song. His daughter Caterina Boratto marries a man he doesn't like, but after a time, they become reconciled. See VIVERE.

1938 Chi è più felice di me!
Vivere was such a big hit that the producers reunited Schipa and Boratto for this sequel *Who Is Happier Than Me?* Schipa plays a Don Juan middle-aged opera tenor who has an affair with a young woman. She bears his child secretly while he is away, but when he finds out, he marries her and they live happily ever after. The film is a three-handkerchief weepie with songs such as "Bimbo mio" and arias from *Andrea Chénier.* Black and white. In Italian. 86 minutes.

1938 Terra di fuoco/Terre de feu
In the Italian-French film *Land of Fire,* Schipa plays a jealous Italian tenor who kills a presumed rival. His wife lies and says she was unfaithful so he will get a short prison sentence. When he is released, he discovers her innocence and begins his opera career again. Schipa's performances in the film include an aria from Massenet's *Werther.* The other cast members are Mireille Balin, Jean Servais, and Marie Glory. Giorgio Ferroni directed the Italian version titled *Terra di fuoco* and Marcel L'Herbier directed the French version titled *Terre de feu.* Black and white. In Italian or French. 92 minutes.

1943 In cerca di felicità
In Search of Happiness stars Schipa as an opera singer who adopts a young woman who reminds him of his daughter. However, he disapproves of the young singer whom she loves, and this causes many problems. The cast includes Helen Luber, Alberto Rabagliati, and Lucia D'Alberti. Giacomo Gentilomo directed. Black and white. In Italian. 82 minutes.

1946 Il cavaliere del sogno
Schipa plays Gilbert Duprez, the French tenor who created the role of Edgardo in *Lucia di Lammermoor,* in this Italian film about composer Gaetano Donizetti. He also sings excerpts from *L'elisir d'amore* and *Don Pasquale.* See IL CAVALIERE DEL SOGNO.

1948 Follie per l'opera

Mad About Opera is a romantic film about the Italian community in London, which organizes a concert with Italian opera stars to raise funds to rebuild a church. Schipa is one of the stars. See FOLLIE PER L'OPERA.

1950 Una voce nel tuo cuore

The singing of Schipa, Beniamino Gigli, and Gino Bechi make the musical *A Voice in Your Heart* almost memorable. They play themselves as opera singers, and their operatic sequences are the best thing in the film. Vittorio Gassman stars as a war correspondent who loves a nightclub performer who wants to be an opera singer. Alberto D'Aversa directed. Black and white. In Italian. 98 minutes.

1951 I misteri di Venezia

Schipa's last film, *The Mysteries of Venice*, is a crime melodrama. He supports Virginia Belmont and Renato Valente in a complicated story about love, despair, and smuggling. Ignazio Ferronetti directed. Black and white. In Italian. 85 minutes.

SCHIPPERS, THOMAS
American conductor (1930–1977)

Thomas Schippers, who made his conducting debut in 1948 in New York with the Lemonade Opera Company, began a long collaboration with GIAN CARLO MENOTTI in 1949 when he took over conducting *The Consul*. In 1951 he conducted two of Menotti's greatest screen successes, the TV opera AMAHL AND THE NIGHT VISITORS and the feature film THE MEDIUM. He was also, for a time, music director of Menotti's Festival of Two Worlds at Spoleto. Schippers began to conduct at the Met in 1955, and he was the conductor chosen to lead the orchestra at the Met's reopening in 1966 with Barber's ANTONY AND CLEOPATRA.

SCHLESINGER, JOHN
English film/opera director (1926–2003)

John Schlesinger, who won an Academy Award for *Midnight Cowboy* and acclaim for such films as *Darling* and *Far From the Madding Crowd*, directs stage operas as well as films. He began at Covent Garden in 1980 with LES CONTES D'HOFFMANN and followed in 1984 with DER ROSENKAVALIER, both on video. In 1989, he won wide praise for a spectacular *Un ballo in maschera* at the Salzburg Festival. He also features opera extracts in his films, most notably in *Sunday Bloody Sunday* (1971), which contains a brilliant use of the COSÌ FAN TUTTE trio "Soave sia il vento." In addition, he has directed opera

documentaries for BBC Television and had a small role in Michael Powell's film of *Die Fledermaus*.

1959/1960 Operatic TV films

John Schlesinger directed 24 films for the British BBC Television series *Tonight* and *Monitor*. They included two opera-connected films made for *Monitor—Benjamin Britten*, screened in 1959, and *The Italian Opera*, screened in 1960.

SCHMID, DANIEL
Swiss film director (1941–)

Daniel Schmid, whose films include *Tonight or Never* and *Shadow of Angels*, also directs operas on stage. In his 1974 film *La Paloma* he has Ingrid Caven and Peter Kern perform a duet from a German operetta in an Alpine landscape. In 1984 he made the documentary *Tosca's Kiss*, a portrait of CASA VERDI, a retirement home for opera singers in Milan. He began to produce operas on stage in Switzerland the same year, starting with Offenbach's *Barbe-Bleue* and Berg's *Lulu* in Geneva. His operas on video include Rossini's GUILLAUME TELL (1987) and Donizetti's LINDA DI CHAMOUNIX (1996).

SCHMIDT, ANDREAS
German baritone (1947–)

Andreas Schmidt, who studied with Dietrich Fischer-Dieskau and made his debut in 1970, has become one of the more sought-after baritones in the world. He has a preference for Mozart as can be seen in his videos, which include DIE ZAUBERFLÖTE at the Metropolitan in 1991 and LE NOZZE DI FIGARO at Glyndebourne in 1994. See CAPRICCIO (1990), DER ROSENKAVALIER (1992 film), and FRANZ SCHUBERT (1988).

SCHMIDT, JOSEF
Romanian tenor (1904–1942)

Joseph Schmidt never became an opera star because he was almost a dwarf and too short to be convincing on stage in tenor roles. Instead, he became a German radio and recording star singing opera arias to wide acclaim. After Hitler came to power, he was no longer allowed on Berlin radio because he was Jewish. Schmidt, who was born in Bucovina in Romania, studied in Vienna and appeared in concerts around the world, including at Carnegie Hall. He died in an internment camp in Switzerland. Schmidt starred in several German films and remains popular today because of his movies and recordings. In most of his films he becomes a singing star but loses the woman he loves.

1931 Der Liebesexpress

Schmidt's first film, *The Love Express,* is a slight musical comedy in which he is only a featured singer, third billed after Georg Alexander and Dina Gralla. Robert Wiene directed. Black and white. In German. 84 minutes.

1932 Gehetzte Menschen

Schmidt is a featured performer in this crime drama starring Maga Sonja and Hans Feher set in the south of France. Friedrich Feher directed. Black and white. In German. 92 minutes.

1933 My Song Goes Around the World

Schmidt becomes a singing star in this film, but he loses his girl to a better-looking guy after he sings a wide range of opera and popular music. The German-language version of this film was banned by the Nazis in 1937. See MY SONG GOES AROUND THE WORLD.

1934 Ein Stern fällt vom Himmel

A Star Fell From Heaven is an Austrian musical made in Vienna after Schmidt had to leave Germany. He plays a music student who dubs the voice of a movie tenor (Egon von Jordan) and loses the woman he loves because of it. An English version was released in 1936. Black and white. In German. 80 minutes.

1934 Wenn du jung bist, gehört dir die Welt

Austrian musical made in Vienna with Schmidt in his usual role as a singer who is unlucky in love. Frieda Richard plays his mother, Artur Preuss is the competing tenor, Lililane Dietz is the girl, and S. Z. Sakall adds his genial personality. Hans May wrote the music and Richard Oswald and Henry Oebels-Oebström directed. Black and white. In German. 89 minutes.

1936 A Star Fell From Heaven

This is British version of *Ein Stern fällt vom Himmel,* also made in Vienna. Schmidt plays a singer who dubs the voice of a movie star. See A STAR FELL FROM HEAVEN.

1936 Heut' ist der schönste Tag in meinem Leben

Today Is the Most Beautiful Day in My Life is an Austrian musical with Schmidt in twin roles as brothers Beppo and Tonio Forti. They both love and lose the same woman. The supporting cast includes Felix Bressart, Otto Wallburg, Lisl Kinast, and Lizzi Natzler. Hans May wrote the music and Richard Oswald directed for Globe Film. Black and white. In German. 80 minutes.

SCHMIDT, TRUDELIESE
German mezzo-soprano (1941–)

Trudeliese Schmidt, who made her debut in 1965, joined Düsseldorf Opera in 1967 and specialized in trouser roles. She sang at Covent Garden as Cherubino in 1974, at Bayreuth in 1975 in the *Ring* cycle, and at Glyndebourne in 1976 as Dorabella. She is featured in all three of the Monteverdi opera films created by Jean-Pierre Ponnelle, as Music in ORFEO in 1978, as Octavia in L'INCORONAZIONE DI POPPEA in 1979, and as Penelope in IL RITORNO D'ULISSE IN PATRIA in 1980. She is one of the singers featured in Werner Schroeter's film POUSSIÈRES D'AMOUR about how opera singers sing. See ARIADNE AUF NAXOS (1978/1988), DER BARBIER VON BAGDAD (1974), FALSTAFF (1982), MIGNON (1983), MOZART REQUIEM (1984), EINE NACHT IN VENEDIG (1973), and VERDI REQUIEM (1990).

SCHOCK, RUDOLF
German tenor (1915–1986)

Rudolf Schock was acclaimed as the successor to Richard Tauber in post–World War II Germany and was one of the most popular tenors in Europe in his time. He began his career in Duisburg at the age of 18, sang with Hamburg Staatsoper from 1947 to 1956 in roles such as Lohengrin and Florestan, and Covent Garden in 1949 as Rodolfo, Alfredo, and Tamino. His wider popularity came from operettas and movies. He starred in a number of films based on Lehár operettas, as Tauber had before him, and he portrayed Tauber in the film *The Richard Tauber Story.* See DAS DREIMÄDERLHAUS (1958), GIUDITTA (1970), GRÄFIN MARIZA (1958), EMMERICH KÁLMÁN (1958), MASKE IN BLAU (1972), SCHÖN IST DIE WELT (1954), RICHARD TAUBER (1953), TIEFLAND (1963), and DIE ZIRKUSPRINZESSIN (1969).

1955 Der Fröhliche Wanderer

Schock plays the director of a small town's children's choir in *The Happy Wanderer,* a pleasant rural musical. His costars are Elma Karlowa and Waltraud Haas. Hans Quest directed. Color. In German. 100 minutes.

1956 Die Stimme der Sehnsucht

Schock is an opera tenor with a marriage problem in the German film *The Voice of Yearning.* It is finally sorted out by an orphan. Christine Kaufmann and Waltraud Haas are his costars. Thomas Engel directed. Color. In German. 89 minutes.

1983 Rudolf Schock Gala

German television gala in honor of the singer. The participants include Birgit Nilsson, René Kollo, Erika Köth,

Renate Holm, and Ludwig Baumann. Color. In German. 60 minutes. Lyric VHS.

SCHOENBERG, ARNOLD
Austrian-born American composer (1874–1951)

Arnold Schoenberg is probably the most influential composer of the century, for good or for bad, as his ideas were noted by all those who came after him. He virtually invented atonality and 12-tone serial music, and his early compositions caused riots among listeners. Ironically, the composer spent the last 17 years of his life in Hollywood, a place not noted for its avant-garde taste. MGM chief Irving Thalberg asked him to compose the score for the 1937 *The Good Earth,* and he agreed to do it for $50,000 if the studio would agree not to change a single note. Thalberg balked and gave the task to another composer, and Schoenberg's Hollywood career ended. However, several notable film composers became his pupils in Hollywood, including David Raksin and Leonard Rosenman. Schoenberg's operas are becoming more popular today, with the Met even daring to present ERWARTUNG on television. However, MOSES UND ARON is the only Schoenberg opera currently available on commercial video.

1989 My War Years: Arnold Schoenberg
A film about Schoenberg's life from 1906 to 1923 when he was transforming the language of music. Director Niv Fichman uses home movies, archival footage, interviews, and performances to tell the story. The performers include Marianne Pousseur, Stefan Vladar, Arleen Auger, Pierre Boulez, Michael Tilson Thomas, the London Symphony Orchestra, and the Schoenberg Quartet. There are comments from Anton Webern, Alban Berg, Alma Mahler, and Wassily Kandinsky. Color. In English. 83 minutes.

1998 Arnold Schoenberg
Musicologists David Rosen and Michel Fischer discuss Schoenberg's musical development with excerpts from several historic performances, including *Moses und Aron* with Pierre Boulez conducting. Part of series *Harmonics: The Innovators of Classical Music.* Color. In English. 28 minutes. Films for the Humanities & Sciences VHS.

SCHÖN IST DIE WELT
1930 operetta by Lehár

Opera stars Gitta Alpar and Richard Tauber had the leading roles in FRANZ LEHÁR's German operetta *Schön ist die Welt* (The World Is Beautiful) when it premiered in 1930 at the Berlin Metropol. It's a revision of his 1914 mountain operetta *Endlich allein* about a love affair on

the Jungfrau. Penniless Crown Prince Georg and wealthy Princess Elizabeth climb a mountain together and fall in love without knowing their true identities. Fritz Löhner-Beda and Ludwig Herzer wrote the libretto, the sets were spectacular, and the title song was a hit, but the operetta never entered the repertory. The earlier version was staged in New York in 1915 as *Alone at Last* with Marguerite Namara and John Charles Thomas in the leading roles.

1954 Bolvary film
German feature film: Geza von Bolvary (director), Astra (production).
Cast: Rudolf Schock (Georg), Renate Holm (Elisabeth), Mady Rahl.
Color. In German. 87 minutes.
Comment: In this updated version Schock is a famous singer and Holm is an aspiring vocalist whom he at first rejects. The duo also recorded highlights from the operetta.

SCHÖNE GALATHÉE, DIE
1865 operetta by Suppé

Die schöne Galathée (The Beautiful Galathea) is a comic operetta by FRANZ VON SUPPÉ retelling the story of sculptor Pygmalion and his statue of beautiful Galatea that comes to life. According to Leopold Kohl von Kohlnegg's libretto, modeled after an earlier French *Galathée,* she is not quite so charming once she becomes human. She eats and drinks too much, starts to flirt with Ganymede, demands jewels, and carries on rather like a spoiled woman.

1967 Salzburg Festival
German stage production: Walter Giller (director), Paul Angerer (conductor, Salzburg Mozarteum Orchestra).
Cast: Anneliese Hückl (Galathée), Peter Luipold, Kurt Strauss, Kurt Hansen.
Video: House of Opera/Lyric VHS. Black and white. In German. 80 minutes.

SCHÖPFUNG, DIE
1878 oratorio by Haydn

JOSEF HAYDN was a good opera composer, but his best-known stage work is an oratorio; *Die Schöpfung* (The Creation) is a superb demonstration of his writing for voice. Based on Milton's epic poem *Paradise Lost* as adapted by Gottfried van Swieten, it tells the story of the creation and of Adam and Eve. Several excellent versions are on video, most of them filmed magnificently in cathedrals.

1986 Munich Cathedral

German concert production: Humphrey Burton (director), Leonard Bernstein (conductor, Bavarian Radio Symphony Orchestra and Chorus).

Soloists: Judith Blegen (Gabriel), Thomas Moser (Uriel), Kurt Moll (Raphael), Lucia Popp (Eve), Kurt Ollmann (Adam).

Video: DG DVD/VHS. Humphrey Burton (director). Color. In German. 120 minutes.

1990 Gloucester Cathedral

English concert production: Chris Hunt (director), Christopher Hogwood (conductor, Choir of New College, Oxford, and Academy of Ancient Music).

Soloists: Emma Kirkby, Anthony Rolfe Johnson, Michael George.

Video: Decca VHS. Chris Hunt (director). Color. In German. 105 minutes.

Comment: Hunt intercuts the performance with creation images from paintings and nature.

1990 Chartres Cathedral

French concert production: Georges Bessonnet (director), Amaury du Closel (conductor, Chambord Sinfonietta and Versailles Choir).

Soloists: Brigitte Lafoix, Douglas Nasrudel, Michel Piquemal.

Video: Image Entertainment DVD. Color. In German. 115 minutes.

1990 Salzburg Festival

Austrian stage production: Franz Kabelka (director), Riccardo Muti (conductor, Vienna Philharmonic and Vienna State Opera Chorus).

Soloists: Lucia Popp (Gabriel/Eve), Samuel Ramey (Raphael), Olaf Bar (Adam), Francisco Araiza (Uriel), Iris Vermillion.

Video: Image Entertainment DVD/Sony VHS and LD. Color. In German. 120 minutes.

1992 Church of the Jesuits, Lucerne

Swiss concert production: Peter Schreier (conductor, Scottish Chamber Orchestra and Lucerne Festival Choir).

Soloists: Edith Mathis, Christoph Pregardien, René Pape.

Video: Arthaus Musik DVD. Elisabeth Birke-Malzer (director). Color. In German. 109 minutes.

SCHORM, EVALD
Czech film director (1931–1988)

Evald Schorm, whose best-known film is *Everyday Courage* (1964), was an opera singer before turning to filmmaking, so it was natural for him to feature opera in his movies. *Five Girls to Deal With* (1967), for example, centers around some very romantic girls attending Weber's DER FREISCHÜTZ every night in a provincial opera house. After the Soviet invasion of Czechoslovakia in 1968, Schorm said he could no longer direct the films he wanted so he turned to producing opera on stage.

SCHREIER, PETER
German tenor/conductor (1935–)

Peter Schreier made his debut in 1961 in Dresden and soon became a leading tenor at Berlin Staatsoper. He made his first appearance at the Metropolitan in 1967 as Tamino in *Die Zauberflöte* and quickly became known around the world for his performances in Mozart operas. He can be seen on video in the role in a 1982 Salzburg production of DIE ZAUBERFLÖTE and heard in a 1991 animated version. In 1967 he was filmed making a recording of DON GIOVANNI and in 1984 in a German stage production of the MOZART REQUIEM. He can also be seen as Loge in a 1978 Herbert von Karajan film of DAS RHEINGOLD. In 1971 he began a parallel career as conductor; he can be seen leading orchestras on videos of GIULIO CESARE in 1977 and DIE SCHÖPFUNG in 1992.

1972 Peter Schreier Recital

Schreier in recital in 1972 with Rudolf Buchbinder accompanying him on piano. The program consists of songs by Mozart, Beethoven, Schubert, Brahms, Schumann, and Prokofiev. Hugo Kach directed. Color. 64 minutes.

1976 Gala Unter den Linden

Schreier is one of the stars performing in this East German film celebrating the Staatsoper Unter den Linden opera house. See BERLIN.

1985 Sherrill Milnes All-Star Gala

Sherrill Milnes conducts the orchestra while Schreier sings Ferrando's aria "Un'aura amorosa" in a Berlin concert. See SHERRILL MILNES.

SCHROETER, WERNER
German film director (1945–)

Werner Schroeter is an extravagant German filmmaker who has been obsessed with opera since beginning his career in 1968 with amateur movies of MARIA CALLAS. Opera music appears regularly on the soundtracks of his films and is often central to them. His early shorts include *Callas Walking Lucia, Maria Callas Sings,* and *Maria Callas Portrait.* EIKA KATAPPA (1969) is an opera celebration with dozens of operas mixed in a frenzied manner. The innovative SALOME (1972) mixes music by

Donizetti and Wagner with that of Strauss. His *Macbeth* (1972) crosses Shakespeare with Verdi. Schroeter celebrates the glories of the famous 19th-century soprano MARIA MALIBRAN in *The Death of Maria Malibran* (1971), and he features more opera excerpts in *Willow Springs, The Black Angel,* and *Goldflocken. Der Rosenkönig* (1986), an homage to his dying star Magdalena Montezuma, features music from a large number of operas. POUSSIÈRES D'AMOUR (1996) is devoted to finding out how an opera singer creates an aria and involves the participation of Martha Mödl, Anita Cerquetti, Rita Gorr, and Trudeliese Schmidt. Schroeter staged opera sequences for Werner Herzog's film FITZCARRALDO and began to direct opera on stage himself in 1979 with *Lohengrin* at the Kassel Opera House. His production of TOSCA at the Paris Opéra was telecast in 1994.

1973 Willow Springs
This experimental film, shot in Willow Springs in the Mojave desert, features music from *Mignon, Die Fledermaus, Carmen, Samson et Dalila, Faust,* and *Mefistofele.* Color. In English and German. 79 minutes.

1973 The Black Angel
This Schroeter film features music by Bizet, Giordano, and Offenbach, including bits of *Les contes d'Hoffmann.* Color. In German. 71 minutes.

1975 Goldflocken
The singers featured in this film include Emma Calvé and Conchita Supervia with music from operas by Bizet, Dvořák, Mozart, Rossini, and Verdi. Color. In French and German. 163 minutes.

1986 Der Rosenkönig
Magdalena Montezuma, who starred in *Eika Katappa,* cowrote and starred in this extravaganza as her final testament (she was dying of cancer at the time). It includes music from *Agnese di Hohenstaufen, Aida, Casanova, Louise, Otello, Tosca, La traviata, Il trovatore,* and *Zaïde.* The singing voices belong to Maria Callas, Beverly Sills, Franco Corelli, Elisabeth Schwarzkopf, and Leontyne Price. The cast includes Karine Fallenstein, Mustafa Djadjam, and Antonio Orlando. Color. In German, Portuguese, Italian, Spanish, French, English, and Arabic. 110 minutes.

SCHUBERT, FRANZ
Austrian composer (1797–1828)

Franz Schubert wrote 14 operas but none was successful, possibly because of weak librettos. The only one staged during his lifetime was the 1820 *Die Zwillingsbrüder.* However, his last and possibly best opera, the 1823

FIERRABRAS, was revived with great success in Vienna in 1988. Ironically, Schubert's music has been enormously popular on stage in another vocal format. The 1916 Viennese pastiche operetta DAS DREIMÄDERLHAUS, a fictional tale about the composer's love for a young woman, is totally derived from Schubert melodies. It has become one of the most popular operettas in the world with an English version starring Richard Tauber and an American version called *Blossom Time* arranged by Sigmund Romberg. Schubert's love life has also been a favorite film subject.

1934 The Unfinished Symphony
Romantic film about Franz Schubert (Hans Jaray) and his love for Caroline Esterhazy (Marta Eggerth). As she is the daughter of a count who hired Schubert to give music lessons and doesn't approve of this love affair, he gets sent back to Vienna. He doesn't return until her wedding to another man when Eggerth sings Schubert's "Ave Maria." This is the English version of an Austrian film made in 1933 in German as *Schuberts Unvollendete Symphonie.* Willi Forst directed both. Black and white. In English. 90 minutes.

1939 Sérénade
Schubert (Bernard Lancret) has a bittersweet love affair with an English dancer (Lilian Harvey) in this highly romantic French film. It is told to Schubert's music as arranged by Paul Abraham. Jean Boyer directed. Black and white. In French. 90 minutes.

1941 The Melody Master/New Wine
Hollywood's romantic version of the composer's life stars Alan Curtis as Schubert with Ilona Massey as Anna, the love of his life. He meets her on a Hungarian estate and takes her with him to Vienna after a countess (Binnie Barnes) fires her for defending his music. Her faith in him leads to a visit to Beethoven (Albert Basserman), who calls Schubert a genius after reading his symphony. Beethoven dies before he can help, so Schubert decides to give up composing and get a job so he can marry Anna. She won't allow this and goes back to Hungary saying that if he gave up his music, he would hate her. Schubert sits down and writes his famous "Ave Maria." Reinhold Schunzel directed the film, originally titled *New Wine* and shown in England as *The Great Awakening.* Black and white. In English. 89 minutes. Video Yesteryear VHS.

1948 La belle meunière
Tino Rossi plays Schubert in this charming French film directed by Marcel Pagnol. Based on the composer's famous song cycle *Die schöne Müllerin,* it imagines that he has a love affair with a miller's daughter (Jacqueline

Pagnol) who inspired the music. Color. In French. 120 minutes.

1955 Schubert
Schubert is played by Claude Laydu in this romantic Italian film biography of the composer. Gino Bechi plays baritone Johann Vogl, Schubert's friend and ideal interpreter, while Lucia Bosé and Marina Vlady are the women in his life. Glauco Pellegrini directed. Also known as *Sinfonia d'Amore*. Color. In Italian or French. 100 minutes.

1988 Franz Peter Schubert
Documentary film by Christopher Nupen about Schubert's life and music, subtitled *The Greatest Love & the Greatest Sorrow*. Andreas Schmidt sings Schubert's lieder, and Wolfgang Sawallisch conducts the Bavarian Symphony Orchestra. Color. 60 minutes. Teldec VHS.

1989 Schubert: Klassix 13
Anthony Quayle and Balint Vaszonyi visit Schubert's "garage," where he composed many of his best works, in this potted film biography. Scenes from Schubert's life in Vienna are filmed at authentic locations, including one depicting a night gathering of 19th-century students. Klassix 13 series. Color. 60 minutes. MPI Home Entertainment VHS.

SCHUMAN, WILLIAM
American composer (1910–1992)

William Schuman won the first Pulitzer Prize in music in 1943 for *A Free Song*. His first and most famous opera is the highly entertaining one-act THE MIGHTY CASEY (1953), based on the famous baseball poem by Ernest L. Thayer; it has been presented on America television. Schuman's second opera was the 1989 *A Question of Taste,* based on a Roald Dahl story about a man who bets his daughter in a wine-tasting contest.

SCHUMANN-HEINK, ERNESTINE
Austrian-born American contralto (1861–1936)

Ernestine Schumann-Heink, who took her last names from her first two husbands, sang professionally from the age of 17 to the age of 74. She made her debut in *Il trovatore* in Dresden in 1878, reached the Met in 1898, was much admired in Wagner operas, and had a long association with Bayreuth. She created the role of Clytemnestra in Strauss's *Elektra* in Dresden in 1909, but it was her concert tours that made her a singing legend. She gave her final performance at the Met in 1932 at the age of 70 singing Erda in *Siegfried*. She wanted to make movies and many were planned, but she was able to appear in only one Hollywood feature and three shorts. Deanna Durbin was hired to portray her as a girl in a film biography, but Schumann-Heink died before it could be made.

1927 Vitaphone films
She was billed as "Mme. Ernestine Schumann-Heink, Contralto" when she made three sound shorts for Vitaphone in New York in 1927. In the first she sings "By the Waters of Minnetonka," Arditi's "Leggero Invisible," and Reimann's "Spinnerliedchen." The second has "Danny Boy," "The Rosary," and "Stille Nacht, heilige Nacht." The third includes Schubert's "Der Erlkönig," "Trees," and "Pirate Dreams." Josefin H. Vollmer plays the piano accompaniment. Black and white. Each about 7 minutes. Bel Canto Society VHS.

1935 Here's to Romance
Schumann-Heink appears in her only feature film as Nino Martini's singing teacher and sings Brahms's "Wiegenlied" ("Cradle Song"), one of her favorite songs. The film plot revolves around Martini's relationship with a rich woman (Genevieve Tobin), who becomes his patron. Alfred E. Green directed for Twentieth Century-Fox. Black and white. 83 minutes.

SCHWARZKOPF, ELISABETH
German soprano (1915–)

Elisabeth Schwarzkopf, one of the great singers of the postwar period, began her career with the Berlin Städtische Oper in 1938 as a flower maiden. She became a pupil of Maria Ivogün, and then Karl Böhm invited her to join the Vienna Staatsoper, where she gained her international reputation. Her status grew while she was at Covent Garden for five seasons from 1947, singing major roles in English. She was a featured performer at the Salzburg Festival from 1947 to 1964 and appeared there in one of the major opera films, Paul Czinner's influential 1960 DER ROSENKAVALIER. Her superb recordings of her major roles, made with her EMI record producer husband Walter Legge, ensure that her reputation will remain high. She retired from the stage in 1972 after a final *Rosenkavalier* in Brussels. Her relationship with the Nazi Party during World War II, however, became a subject of debate in 1996 when it was discussed in a biography by Alan Jefferson; she appeared in several German films that were banned as propaganda after the war. See JOHANN SEBASTIAN BACH (1950), WERNER SCHROETER (1986), SOPRANOS AND MEZZOS (1995), and TRILBY (1954).

1939 Drei Unteroffiziere
Schwarzkopf is seen in the role of Carmen singing in German opposite Günther Treptow as José in a theater production of *Carmen* in *Drei Unteroffiziere* (Three NCOs). A soldier and his girlfriend attend the opera, and

music from *Carmen* becomes the leitmotif of their love story. As the story is about soldiers, the Allies considered the film propagandistic and banned it after the war. Ironically, Werner Hochbaum was actually a director of genuine discernment, and the Nazis never let him work again after this film. Albert Hehn plays the soldier who goes to see Schwarzkopf in *Carmen*, and Ruth Hellberg plays his girlfriend. Black and white. In German. 92 minutes.

1943 Nacht ohne Abschied
Schwarzkopf appears as Violetta in a stage production of *La traviata* opposite tenor Peter Anders in a scene of the film *Nacht ohne Abschied* (Night Without Parting). This was also considered a propaganda film and was banned by the Allies after World War II. Anna Damman and Karl Ludwig Diehl are the stars, and Erich Waschneck directed. Black and white. In German. 77 minutes.

1944 Der Verteidiger hat das Wort
Schwarzkopf has a small role singing "Mona" in an elegant living room at a party in the crime thriller *Der Verteidiger hat das Wort* (The Defender Has the Last Word). Heinrich George stars in the film, which Werner Klingler directed. Black and white. In German. 87 minutes.

1960 Elisabeth Schwarzkopf Recital
Schwarzkopf gives a recital for a Canadian television program, accompanied by pianist George Reeves. The recital includes works by Schubert, Schumann, Wolf, and Martini. Radio-Canada. Black and white. 30 minutes.

1980 Master Class with Elisabeth Schwarzkopf
Schwarzkopf works with young singers as she leads a master class in New York City in this video produced by Eve Ruggieri and directed by Ariane Adriani. Color. 60 minutes. Video at the NYPL.

1988 Elisabeth Schwarzkopf: A Portrait
Schwarzkopf is interviewed about her career in this English documentary and is seen performing arias by Mozart and Strauss. Alan Benson directed for London Weekend Television. Color. 55 minutes.

1990 Schwarzkopf Master Classes
Schwarzkopf gives two master classes in 1990. In the first she works with student Tinuke Olafimihan on Mozart in a video directed by Ariane Adriani. 58 minutes. In the second she works with student Robert Brooks on Schubert. Color. 66 minutes.

1995 Elisabeth Schwarzkopf: A Self-Portrait
Schwarzkopf narrates this documentary by Gérald Caillat about her life and career. It includes film of her performing in many roles associated with her as well as scenes from films she made in Germany during the war. She comments about developments in her career and her way of singing. Opera excerpts include *Carmen, Le nozze di Figaro, Don Giovanni,* and *Der Rosenkavalier.* Black and white and color. 57 minutes. EMI Classics DVD and VHS.

SCHWARZWALDMÄDEL
1917 operetta by Jessel

Schwarzwaldmädel (Black Forest Maiden), a lively country-style operetta by LÉON JESSEL, premiered at the Komische Oper in Berlin in 1917 and has been popular ever since, no thanks to the Nazis, who tortured and killed its Jewish composer. August Niedhart's libretto tells of a series of complicated romantic entanglements in a town in the heart of the Black Forest. A number of young women in the operetta have to wear folksy peasant costumes before they can win the fellows they fancy. The central character of the operetta is cathedral music master Blasius Römer, father of Hannele. He is interested in Bärbele, but she wants Hans while Malwine gets Richard and Lorle gets Theobald.

1933 Zoch film
German feature film: Georg Zoch (director), Franz Rauch (screenplay), Ewald Daub and Georg Bruckbauer (cinematographers), Fritz Wenneis (music director), Ariel Film (production).

Cast: Hans Söhnker, Maria Beling, Walter Janssen, Kurt von Ruffin, Lotte Lorring, Eugen Rex.

Black and white. In German. 89 minutes.

Comment: This German film of what was soon to be called a "Jewish" operetta was made just before the Nazis took over.

1950 Deppe film
German feature film: Hans Deppe (director), B. E. Lüthge (screenplay), Frank Fox (music director), Kurt Schulz (cinematographer), Berolina Film (production).

Cast: Paul Hörbiger (Blasius Römer), Sonja Ziemann (Bärbele), Lucie Englisch (Lorle), Gretl Schorg (Malwine), Rudolf Prack (Hans).

Color. In German. 100 minutes.

Comment: This adaptation of the operetta was the first color film to be made in postwar Germany.

1973 ZDF German Television
German TV film: Wolfgang Liebeneiner (director), Bernhard Stimmler (Bavarian Radio-Television

Symphony Orchestra, Munich), Maleen Pacha (set/costume designer).

Cast: Wolfgang Windgassen (Blasius Römer), Janet Perry (Bärbele), Ulla Keller (Hannele), Rut Rex (Malwine), Kristine Schober (Lorle), Dick Laan (Hans).

Telecast December 15, 1973, on ZDF German Television. Color. In German. 100 minutes.

Early films

1920 Wellin film
Uschi Elleot stars in this silent version of the operetta directed by Arthur Wellin for Luna Films. Black and white. About 70 minutes.

1929 Janson film
Viktor Janson directed this version of the operetta starring Käthe Haack, Fred Louis Lerch, Walter Janssen, Georg Alexander, and Olga Limburg. Black and white. About 80 minutes.

SCHWEIGSAME FRAU, DIE
1935 comic opera by Richard Strauss

Opera singers Aminta and Henry devise a stratagem to get approval of their marriage from his grouchy uncle, an admiral who can't stand noise. Aminta impersonates a timid silent woman, pretends to marry him, and then turns into a noisy shrew. Richard Strauss's comic opera *Die schweigsame Frau* (The Silent Woman), libretto by Stefan Zweig, is based on a play by Ben Jonson set in London in 1780 and has similarities to Donizetti's *Don Pasquale*. Zweig was Jewish and the opera was banned in Germany after its first four performances.

1971 Bavarian State Opera
German stage production: Günther Rennert (director), Wolfgang Sawallisch (conductor, Bavarian State Opera Orchestra and Chorus), Rudolf Heinrich (set/costume designer).

Cast: Reri Grist (Aminta), Kurt Moll (Sir Morosus), Donald Grobe (Henry Morosus) Barry McDaniel (Barber), Martha Mödl (Housekeeper), Lotte Schädle (Isotta), Glenys Loulis (Carlotta), Benno Kusche (Vanuzzi), Max Pröbstl (Farallo).

Video: House of Opera/Legato Classics VHS. Horst Wimmer (director). Color. In German. 132 minutes.

SCHWETZINGEN FESTIVAL
German opera festival (1952–)

The Rococo Schlosstheater in the small town of Schwetzingen, built in 1752, is the only surviving German chamber opera theater of its kind. It has been the site of a spring opera festival since 1952 and has become noted for its revivals of classical and baroque opera. It is certainly a charming place to visit on video, and there are quite a number available as the festival is sponsored by Süddeutscher Television. See AGRIPPINA (1985), IL BARBIERE DI SIVIGLIA (1988), LA CAMBIALE DI MATRIMONIO (1989), LE CINESI (1987), ECHO ET NARCISSE (1987), FALSTAFF (Salieri) (1995), L'INCORONAZIONE DI POPPEA (1993), L'ITALIANA IN ALGERI (1987), IL MATRIMONIO SEGRETO (1986), L'OCCASIONE FA IL LADRO (1992), LA SCALA DI SETA (1989), IL SIGNOR BRUSCHINO (1989), TANCREDI (1992), TARARE (1993), and THE TURN OF THE SCREW (1990).

SCORSESE, MARTIN
American film director (1942–)

Italian-American Martin Scorsese, one of the most impressive American directors to emerge during the 1970s and known for films such as *Taxi Driver, Raging Bull,* and *Gangs of New York,* has used Italian opera in many of his films. *Mean Streets* (1973) features Giuseppe Di Stefano singing on the soundtrack. *Raging Bull* (1980) uses excerpts from three Mascagni operas: *Cavalleria rusticana, Guglielmo Ratcliff,* and *Silvano. The Color of Money* (1985) has "Va pensiero" from *Nabucco. Life Lessons* (1989), Scorsese's episode in *New York Stories,* features Mario Del Monaco singing "Nessun dorma" from TURANDOT. *Goodfellas* (1990) features Giuseppe Di Stefano again on the soundtrack. *Cape Fear* (1991) has an aria from *Lucia di Lammermoor. The Age of Innocence* (1993) begins at a stage production of FAUST in the 1870s, and the plot unfolds as the actors in the film watch Faust and Marguerite in Act III. In the film *Pavlova* (1984) directed by Emil Lotianou, Scorsese plays Metropolitan Opera general manager Giulio Gatti-Casazza.

SCOTTO, RENATA
Italian soprano (1933–)

Renata Scotto made her debut in 1952 at the age of 19 in Savona, sang in *La Wally* at La Scala in 1955, and began to perform in London in 1957. She came to the United States in 1960 to sing Mimì in Chicago and made regular appearances at the Met from 1965 to 1987. Scotto, who sings a wide range of roles, is noted for the emotion she can convey in her singing. The *Washington Post* once called her the "greatest singing actress in the world." She has also begun to direct, and her production of LA TRAVIATA for New York City Opera was telecast in 1995. Scotto can be seen in performance in many videos. See LA BOHÈME (1977/1982), DON CARLO (1980), FAUST (1973), FRANCESCA DA RIMINI (1984), GIANNI SCHICCHI (1981), LA GIOCONDA (1980), LUCIA DI LAMMERMOOR

(1967), LUISA MILLER (1979), MANON LESCAUT (1980), OTELLO (1978), SOPRANOS AND MEZZOS (1991/1991), SUOR ANGELICA (1981), IL TABARRO (1981), LA TRAVIATA (1973), IL TRITTICO (1981), and WERTHER (1987).

1984 Renata Scotto in Japan
Scotto in recital at the NHK Auditorium in Tokyo September 2, 1984. She sings "Lascia ch'io pianga" from *Rinaldo*, "Tu che le vanità" from *Don Carlo*, "Sole e amore" and "Nel villagio d'Edgar" from *Edgar*, "Senti, bambino" from *Zanetto*, "Vissi d'arte" from *Tosca*, and "Tu? Tu? Piccolo Iddio!" from *Madama Butterfly*, plus songs by Verdi, Rossini, Scarlatti, Respighi, Liszt, and Mascagni. Thomas Fulton is the pianist. Color. 99 minutes. VAI VHS.

1986 Renata Scotto in Canada
Scotto performs arias from *Don Carlo, Gianni Schicchi, Macbeth, Otello, Tosca,* and *La Wally* in this concert at the Cathédrale de Joliette during the Lanaudière Festival. Raffi Armenian conducts the Orchestre Symphonique de Québec. Color. 58 minutes. VAI VHS.

1991 Renata Scotto in Hungary
Scotto in recital at the Franz Liszt Music Academy in Budapest. The centerpiece is *Les Nuits d'Été* by Berlioz, but the recital also includes arias from *Giulio Cesare, La clemenza di Tito, Manon, La Wally, Carmen, Gianni Schicchi,* and *Adriana Lecouvreur.* She is accompanied by the Budapest Symphony Orchestra led by Ervin Lukacs. Color. 86 minutes. VAI VHS.

1994 Renata Scotto at the Vatican
Scotto is the operatic star of this Vatican Christmas concert arranged by RAI TV. Vladimir Spivacov leads the St. Cecilia Academy Symphony Orchestra. Color. 90 minutes.

SCUGNIZZA
1922 operetta by Costa

Mario Costa's *Scugnizza* is a lighthearted romantic operetta about a millionaire named Toby, his daughter Gaby, and his secretary Chic. The millionaire visits a small Italian town and falls for the local girl Salomè. "Scugnizza" is a Neapolitan term for a female street urchin. This was Costa's biggest success as an operetta composer, and it remains popular.

1992 Operette, che Passione!
Italian TV studio production: Sandro Massimini (director/producer), Roberto Negri (pianist), Sandro Corelli (choreographer).

Cast: Sandro Massimini, Daniel Mazzucato, Max René Cosotti.

Video: Pierluigi Pagano (director). Color. In Italian. About 19 minutes. Ricordi (Italy) VHS.

Comment: Highlights of the operetta on the TV series *Operette, che Passione!* Includes songs "Napoletana," "Bada Salomè," "Salomè, un rondine non fa primavera," and "Vedo un cielo tutto azzurro."

SEABOURNE, PETER
English opera film director(1930-)

Peter Seabourne made 14 TV films during 1974, highlights versions of operas and operettas from *La traviata* to Gilbert and Sullivan adaptations. They may not be on the highest level of operatic film, but they are all enjoyable and quite a few are on VHS. See (all 1974) IL BARBIERE DI SIVIGLIA, LES CONTES D'HOFFMANN, THE GONDOLIERS, H.M.S. PINAFORE, IOLANTHE, THE MIKADO, PAGLIACCI, THE PIRATES OF PENZANCE, RIGOLETTO, RUDDIGORE, LA TRAVIATA, TRIAL BY JURY, and THE YEOMEN OF THE GUARD.

SECOND HURRICANE, THE
1937 opera by Copland

AARON COPLAND's first opera was staged by Orson Welles, who arranged its premiere before he went to Hollywood. Intended as a "play opera" for high school students, poet Edwin Denby's libretto concerns the adventures of six high school students who volunteer to help an aviator take supplies to an area hit by a hurricane and end up stranded on a hill. The story revolves around how Butch, Fat, Queenie, and the others learn to cooperate. Leonard Bernstein helped bring the opera back to prominence when he telecast and recorded it in 1960.

1960 Carnegie Hall
American concert production: Leonard Bernstein (conductor, New York Philharmonic Orchestra and New York City High School of Performing Arts Chorus).

Cast: Leonard Bernstein (narrator), students from New York City High School of Performing Arts (soloists are Marion Cowings, Julian Liss, Julie Makis, Omega Melbourne, John Richardson, Steven Wertheimer, Lawrence Willis).

Video at the MTR. Telecast April 24, 1960, in the CBS series *Young People's Concerts.* Roger Englander (director). Black and white. In English. 60 minutes.

SECOND MRS. KONG, THE

1994 screen opera by Birtwistle

HARRISON BIRTWISTLE's opera *The Second Mrs. Kong,* libretto by Russell Hoban, updates the story of King Kong and mixes in computers, paintings, and mythological beings such as Orpheus and the Sphinx. Birtwistle and Hoban are reportedly great admirers of the 1933 RKO movie *King Kong,* but they have not tried to retell the film story. Their alternate version features Pearl (from Vermeer's painting "Girl With a Pearl Earring") as the love object equivalent of Fay Wray. Kong and Pearl communicate via computer but finally realize that their love is not possible as they are creations of the artistic imagination and will never be able to meet. The opera includes excerpts from the films *King Kong, Brief Encounter,* and *Night Mail.*

1995 Glyndebourne Festival

English stage production: Tom Cairns (director), Elgar Howarth (conductor, London Philharmonic Orchestra and Glyndebourne Festival Chorus), Aletta Collins and Tom Cairns (set designers), Wolfgang Göbbel (lighting designer).

Cast: Philip Langridge (King Kong), Helen Field (Pearl), Michael Change (Orpheus), Nuala Willis (Madame Lena), Stephen Page (Anubis), Omar Ebrahim (Vermeer).

Color. In English. 118 minutes.

SEEFESTSPIELE MÖRBISCH

Austrian operetta festival

Seefestspiele Mörbisch is a popular Austrian operetta festival that stages lavish outdoor productions of classical operettas in the summer, most of which are televised and issued on video. The festival, directed by Harald Serafin, is held on the shore of Neudiedler Lake about 40 miles from Vienna. The Seefestspiele Mörbisch productions with entries in this book are DIE CSÁRDÁSFÜRSTIN, IM WEISSEN RÖSSL, DIE LUSTIGE WITWE, EINE NACHT IN VENEDIG, and DER ZIGEUNERBARON.

SEGUROLA, ANDRÉS DE

Spanish bass (1874–1953)

Andrés de Segurola, who was born in Valencia, made his debut in Barcelona in 1895 and sang in Madrid, Lisbon, and Milan before going to the Metropolitan Opera in 1902. He created Jake in *La fanciulla del West* opposite Enrico Caruso in 1910 and continued to sing at the Met until 1913. His movie career began in 1927 when Gloria Swanson invited him to Hollywood to play an opera impresario in *The Love of Sunya.* In 1928 he appeared in five more films, including *Glorious Betsy* with fellow Met singer Pasquale Amato. He had character roles in many other Hollywood films, including those made in Spanish with tenor JOSÉ MOJICA. He also began to coach movie singers. Deanna Durbin was his most prominent pupil; he was given screen credit as vocal instructor on her films, and he wrote the introduction for her souvenir songbook of opera arias. Only his films with some opera content are listed below.

1927 The Love of Sunya

Segurola plays opera impresario De Salvo who pushes Gloria Swanson to become a singer. She opts instead to marry her first love, John Boles. Albert Parker directed. Black and white. Silent. About 85 minutes.

1928 Glorious Betsy

Segurola sings a stirring "La Marseillaise" in this tall tale about Napoleon's younger brother falling in love with an American named Betsy. Fellow Met singer Pasquale Amato plays Napoleon in this patriotic part-talkie. Dolores Costello, Conrad Nagel, and Betty Blythe star and Alan Crosland directed. Black and white. In English. 80 minutes.

1930 Song o' My Heart

Segurola plays Guido, a former opera stage colleague of John McCormack, in this charming musical directed by Frank Borzage. Segurola reminds McCormack of their days together at La Scala when they meet in a New York impresario's office. Fox. Black and white. In English. 91 minutes. VAI VHS.

1934 One Night of Love

Segurola is Grace Moore's voice teacher in Milan before she meets Tullio Carminati, who makes her a star. There is a delightful scene in her apartment when he instigates a *Lucia di Lammermoor* sextet to divert Moore's landlady, a former opera colleague, from collecting the rent. He sings the bass role and entices the landlady to sing the soprano part. See ONE NIGHT OF LOVE.

1935 Public Opinion

Segurola plays opera singer Enrico Martinelli in this film about an opera star (Lois Wilson) whose career causes her marriage to break up. Frank R. Strayer directed. Black and white. 70 minutes.

SELLARS, PETER

American opera director (1957–)

Peter Sellars has been the leading American exponent of modernized nontraditional opera staging since the early 1980s. He transposed *Pelléas et Mélisande* to modern Malibu, *Le nozze di Figaro* to the Trump Tower, *Così fan tutte* to Despina's Diner, *Don Giovanni* to the back streets of Harlem, and *Giulio Cesare* to the Cairo Hilton. He has been admired by many and excoriated by others (his Glyndebourne *Magic Flute* was the first ever booed at that festival), but his productions have certainly been innovative and thought-provoking. His collaborations with composer John Adams on the operas NIXON IN CHINA, *The Death of Klinghoffer,* and EL NIÑO have been greatly admired. Much of his work is available on video, and there is a documentary about his Da Ponte/Mozart opera films. See COSÌ FAN TUTTE (1989), DON GIOVANNI (1990), GIULIO CESARE (1990), LE NOZZE DI FIGARO (1990), THE SEVEN DEADLY SINS (1993), and THEODORA (1996).

1990 Destination: Mozart
Subtitled *A Night at the Opera With Peter Sellars,* this is a documentary about the modernized Mozart–Da Ponte opera films Sellars made in Vienna. Cast members talk about their ideas regarding Mozart and the operas *Così fan tutte, Don Giovanni,* and *Le nozze di Figaro,* and performance excerpts are shown. Andrea Simon directed. Color. In English. 60 minutes. Kultur VHS.

1990 A Mind for Music with Peter Sellars
Bill Moyers talks to Sellars on his PBS series *A World of Ideas.* Sellars discusses his ideas about staging Mozart and Shakespeare, with excerpts from his Mozart productions and *Nixon in China.* Leslie Clark directed. Color. 56 minutes. PBS video.

1995 A Short Film About Loving
Tony Palmer's film insists that Sellars does not set out to be controversial but simply wants to make his productions relevant to modern society. He is interviewed in Paris, Edinburgh, and Salzburg and is seen in rehearsal and organizing the Los Angeles Festival. There are excerpts from *Così fan tutte, Don Giovanni,* and *Giulio Cesare.* Color. 60 minutes.

SEMIRAMIDE
1823 opera by Rossini

GIOACHINO ROSSINI's last Italian opera, libretto by Gaetano Rossi based on Voltaire's play *Sémiramis,* is set in ancient Babylon. Queen Semiramide has murdered her husband Nino with the help of her lover Assur, but she is now interested in giving her favors to the soldier Arsace. To her annoyance he prefers the princess Azema. When she finds out that he is actually her own son, she tries to protect him from Assur and is killed. Arsace becomes king.

1980 Aix-en-Provence Festival
French stage production: Pier Luigi Pizzi (director/set designer), Jesús López-Cobos (conductor, Scottish Chamber Orchestra and Festival Chorus).

Cast: Montserrat Caballé (Semiramide) Marilyn Horne (Arsace), Samuel Ramey (Assur), Francisco Araiza (Idreno).

Lyric VHS and video at the NYPL. Telecast by Antenne 2 in France. Color. In Italian. 204 minutes.

Comment: An hour of the opera as it was staged in Aix, mostly recitative, was cut when the film was televised.

1986 Australian Opera
Australian stage production: John Copley (director), Richard Bonynge (conductor, Elizabethan Sydney Orchestra and Australian Opera Chorus).

Cast: Joan Sutherland (Semiramide), Marilyn Horne (Arsace).

Video: Sony VHS. John Widdicombe (director). Color. In Italian with English subtitles. 205 minutes.

1990 Metropolitan Opera
American stage production: John Copley (director), James Conlon (conductor, Metropolitan Opera Orchestra and Chorus), John Conklin (set designer), Michael Stennet (costume designer).

Cast: June Anderson (Semiramide), Marilyn Horne (Arsace), Samuel Ramey (Assur), Stanford Olsen (Idreno), John Cheek (Oroe), Young Ok Shin (Azema), Michael Forest (Mitrane), Jeffrey Wells (Ghost of Nino).

Video: Image Entertainment and Arthaus (GB) DVD/Kultur VHS. Taped December 22, 1990; telecast October 16, 1991. Brian Large (director). Color. In Italian with English subtitles. 220 minutes.

Comment: Lavish production with eye-catching sets and costumes and a strong cast.

Early/related films

1909 Pathé film
The French film *Sémiramis* is based on the Voltaire source play and the opera with Stacia Napierkowska as Sémiramis and Paul Capellani as Arsace. Albert Capellani directed for Pathé. Black and white. Silent. About 10 minutes. Print at the NFTA, London.

1948 Unfaithfully Yours
Orchestra conductor Rex Harrison, convinced that his wife Linda Darnell is betraying him, imagines her murder while conducting the overture to *Semiramide.* Preston Sturges directed the film. Black and white. 105 minutes.

SENDAK, MAURICE
American designer/librettist (1928–)

American author and illustrator Maurice Sendak began writing children's books in 1956, and the 1963 WHERE THE WILD THINGS ARE made him well-known. It also became the basis of a delightful opera in 1980 in collaboration with English composer Oliver Knussen. His subsequent children's book HIGGLETY PIGGLETY POP! was made into an opera by the same team in 1985. Sendak designed wondrous sets and costumes for both of his operas, as well as for THE CUNNING LITTLE VIXEN (1983), L'ENFANT ET LES SORTILÈGES (1987), HÄNSEL UND GRETEL (1997/1998), L'HEURE ESPAGNOLE (1987), and THE LOVE FOR THREE ORANGES (1982).

1966 Maurice Sendak
American film about the artist that takes the form of an informal visit to his studio apartment in New York. He talks about music, art, and the ideas that have influenced him. Produced and distributed by Weston Woods. Color. In English. 14 minutes.

1987 Maurice Sendak: "Mon Cher Papa"
The "cher papa" of the title is Mozart, whom Sendak adopted as his father and creative mentor after the death of his father in 1972. He talks about his ideas for set design for operas; he considers it as illustration on a grand scale. Telecast August 31, 1987. Color. In English. 60 minutes.

SERAFIN, TULLIO
Italian conductor (1878–1968)

Tullio Serafin was one of the most influential conductors of the modern era in both Italy and the United States. While he was at the Metropolitan Opera from 1924 to 1934, he conducted the premieres of a number of American operas, including HOWARD HANSON's *Merry Mount,* and helped advance the career of ROSA PONSELLE. Back in Europe after World War II, he worked with MARIA CALLAS and JOAN SUTHERLAND and helped them to achieve greatness. He can be seen in three opera videos: AIDA (1963) with Leyla Gencer, RIGOLETTO (1947) with Tito Gobbi, and OTELLO (1958) with Mario Del Monaco. His recordings of operas with Callas have been featured in several films, most notably *Philadelphia* with the aria "La mamma morta" from ANDREA CHENIER (1993), and *The Bridges of Madison County* and other Hollywood films with "Casta diva" from NORMA (1992/1995/1997).

SERENADE
1956 American film with opera content

Mario Lanza plays Damon Vincenti, an opera singer with emotional problems, in this adaptation of James M. Cain's novel *Serenade.* He's the protégé of rich socialite Kendall Hale (Joan Fontaine) who helps him become a success after she finds him singing in a vineyard. When she loses interest and finds another lover, he becomes unbalanced. When she doesn't come to the Metropolitan Opera to see his debut as the lead in *Otello,* he walks off stage in despair (Licia Albanese is his baffled Desdemona while they are singing the duet "Dio ti giocondi, o sposo"). His career immediately goes into a tailspin and an attempt to sing at Mexico City Opera leads to his losing his voice completely. Juana Montes (Sarita Montiel), the daughter of a famous Mexican bullfighter, takes him in hand, marries him, and restores his "manhood." He makes a comeback in San Francisco and returns to New York in triumph. The film allows Lanza to sing music from *La bohème* ("O soave fanciulla" with Jean Fenn as Mimì), *Il trovatore* ("Di quella pira"), *Der Rosenkavalier* (the Italian singer's aria "Di rigori armato il seno"), *L'Africana* ("O paradiso"), *L'Arlesiana* ("È la solita storia di pastore"), and *Turandot* ("Nessun dorma"). Music director Ray Heindorf conducts the orchestra, and Jacob Gimpel plays the piano accompaniment. The Carmen myth is central to novel and film. The Lanza character's favorite opera is *Carmen,* his destructive Carmen is the socialite, and his Escamillo is the Mexican woman who fights figurative bulls and almost kills Carmen. The book is more resonant than the film, but director Anthony Mann keeps it interesting. Ivan Goff, Ben Roberts,· and John Twist wrote the screenplay, and Peverell Marley photographed it for Warner Bros. Color. 121 minutes. Warner Bros. DVD/VHS.

SERRANO, JOSÉ
Spanish composer (1873–1941)

José Serrano, who was one of the leading composers of zarzuelas at the beginning of the 20th century, wrote more than 50 of them, all richly melodic and often featuring regional music. LA DOLOROSA is usually considered his finest work, but LA ALEGRÍA DEL BATALLÓN, LOS CLAVELES, LOS DE ARAGON, and LA CANCIÓN DEL OLVIDÓ are also popular. There are Spanish films of five of his zarzuelas, two directed by French master Jean Grémillon.

SERSE
1738 opera by Handel
GEORGE FRIDERIC HANDEL's splendid opera *Serse* (*Xerxes* in English) is most famous for a delightful hymn of love to a plane tree. "Ombra mai fu" has, through the

vagaries of time, been transmuted into the rather somber piece of music now known as Handel's Largo. The opera, set in ancient Persia, concerns King Xerxes's efforts to win Romilda, who loves his brother Arsamene. Xerxes, who already has a wife, finally contents himself with Romilda's sister Atalanta. Handel's anonymous libretto is based on a 1694 Italian libretto by Silvio Stampiglia called *Il Xerse*. Odd as it may seem, the historical King Xerxes really did revere a plane tree.

***1988 English National Opera

English stage production: Nicholas Hytner (director/English translation), Sir Charles Mackerras (conductor, English National Opera Orchestra and Chorus), David Fielding (set designer).

Cast: Ann Murray (Xerxes), Valerie Masterson (Romilda), Christopher Robson (Arsamene), Jean Rigby (Amastris), Lesley Garrett (Atalanta), Christopher Booth-Jones (Elviro), Rodney Macann (Ariodates).

Video: Image Entertainment/Arthaus (GB) DVD and Kultur/Home Vision VHS. John Michael Phillips (director). Color. In English. 187 minutes.

Comment: The original stage production won the Olivier Opera Award in England.

Related films

1988 Dangerous Liaisons

Stephen Frears's film *Dangerous Liaisons* features the Largo ("Ombra mai fu") from *Serse* on the soundtrack as aristocrats John Malkovich and Glenn Close plan seductions. Color. In English. 120 minutes.

2001 Invincible

Werner Herzog's film *Invincible,* the story of a Samson-like Jewish strongman in 1930s Poland and Germany, features the aria "Ombra mai fu" on the soundtrack. Color. In German. 132 minutes.

SERVA PADRONA, LA

1733 opera by Pergolesi

La serva padrona (The Maid Mistress), a seemingly throwaway comic intermezzo composed as the interlude in the middle of GIOVANNI PERGOLESI's "serious" opera *Il prigionier superbo,* turned out ironically to be one of the most influential operas of all time. It became the model for *opera buffa,* the focus of the "guerre des bouffons" in Paris in 1752, and the first opera to be televised in its entirety. *The Guinness Book of Records* also says it was the first complete opera to be filmed with sound, but this appears to be untrue. *La serva padrona,* adapted by Gennarantonio Federico from a play, tells the story of the maid Serpina and how she tricks her master Uberto into

marrying her by pretending to go off with another man. It's a chamber opera for two singers, a bass and a soprano, plus a silent servant called Vespone.

1934 Lirica Film

Italian feature film: Giorgio Mannini (director), Amleto Palermi (screenplay), Giovanni Vitrotti (cinematographer), Lirica Film (production).

Cast: Bruna Dragoni (Serpina), Vincenzo Bettoni (Uberto), Carlo Lombardi, Enrica Mayers, Arturo Falconi.

Black and white. In Italian. 62 minutes.

Comment: *The Guinness Book of Records* says this was the first complete sound opera film although it was actually preceded by a 1931 American film of *Pagliacci.* It is still impressive, however, and was one of the first Italian sound films, although it had a very limited release.

1937 BBC Television

English TV production: Stephen Thomas (director), Hyam Greenbaum (conductor, BBC Television Orchestra), Cecil Gray (English translation).

Cast: Tessa Deane (Serpina), Arnold Matteras (Uberto), H. D. C. Pepler (Vespone).

Telecast live September 23, 1937, on BBC. Black and white. In English. 35 minutes.

Comment: Even though it was abridged, this was the first opera televised in its entirety, an historic telecast made by fledgling BBC Television from Alexander Palace in London. There weren't many receivers, but it was a good start.

1950 BBC Television

English TV production: George R. Foa (director/English translation), Eric Robinson (conductor, BBC Television Orchestra), Richard Greenough (set designer).

Cast: Rose Hill (Serpina), Martin Lawrence (Uberto), Alain Reid (Vespone).

Telecast live May 19, 1950. Black and white. In English. 65 minutes.

1958 RAI Italian Television

Italian TV film: Mario Lanfranchi (director), Franco Ferrara (conductor, Rome Philharmonic Orchestra), Attilio Glorioso (set designer).

Cast: Anna Moffo (Serpina), Paolo Montarsolo (Umberto), Giancarlo Cobelli (Vespone).

Video: VIEW VHS. Telecast November 24, 1962, on RAI. Black and white. In Italian. 59 minutes.

Comment: Both singers were in peak form, and the video from a 35mm film is most enjoyable.

1996 Luna Theater, Brussels

Belgian stage production: Ferruccio Soleri (director), Sigiswald Kuijken (conductor, La Petite Bande chamber orchestra).

Cast: Patricia Bicciré (Serpina), Donato di Stefano (Umberto), Enrico Maggi (Vespone).

Video: TDK (GB) DVD/Opera d'Oro VHS. Filmed November 23, 1996. Dirk Gryspeirt (director). Color. In Italian. 45 minutes.

Related film

1932 Pergolesi

La Scala soprano Laura Pasini plays Serpina opposite Vincenzo Bettoni as Umberto in scenes from *La serva padrona* in this Italian film about the composer. Francesco Previtali conducts the orchestra. See PERGOLESI.

SEVEN DEADLY SINS, THE

See SIEBEN TODSÜNDEN, DIE.

SEVILLE

Seville (Sevilla in Spanish, Siviglia in Italian) has a long opera tradition, but it is most well-known operatically as the setting of such famous operas as *Carmen, Il barbiere di Siviglia, Le nozze di Figaro, Don Giovanni, Fidelio,* and *El gato montés.*

1982 Hommage a Sevilla

Domingo sings arias in their Seville setting in Jean-Pierre Ponnelle's film about the city and its place in opera history. Don Giovanni boasts of his conquests from the Giralda tower, Figaro and Almaviva duet in the Barrio Santa Cruz, and Florestan sings his aria in the Roman ruins in Italica. There are two duets in the Maestranza Bullring, one from *Carmen* with Victoria Vergara, the other from Penella's *El gato montés* with Virginia Alonzo. James Levine leads the Vienna Symphony Orchestra. Color. In English. 60 minutes. DG VHS.

1991 Gala Lirica

A group of major Spanish opera singers—Giacomo Aragall, Teresa Berganza, Montserrat Caballé, José Carreras, Plácido Domingo, Alfredo Kraus, Pilar Lorengar, Pedro Lavirgen, and Juan Pons—inaugurate the Gran Teatro de la Maestranza in Seville. Aragall sings "E lucevan le stelle," Berganza sings "Tu che accendi" from *Tancredi* and arias from *Carmen,* Caballé sings "Pleurez, pleurez mes yeux" from *Le Cid,* Carreras sings "No puede ser" from Sorozabal's *La tabernera del puerto,* Domingo performs an aria from *Macbeth* and a duet from *La forza del destino* with Pons, Kraus sings arias from *Daughter of the Regiment* and *Rigoletto,* Lorengar sings arias from *La Wally* and *El barberillo de Lavapiés,* Lavirgen sings an aria from *Alma de Dios,* and Pons sings an aria from *Rigoletto.* The group ends with the *La traviata* "Libiamo" toasting the new theater. Color. In Spanish and Italian. 72 minutes. RCA Victor VHS.

SHAKESPEARE AS OPERA

William Shakespeare's plays have been a major source of librettos for opera composers; *The New Grove Dictionary of Opera* lists 270 operas based on his plays, most of them fairly obscure. The best librettos are probably the two written by Arrigo Boito for Verdi, OTELLO (1887) and FALSTAFF (1893), both well represented on video. Also still quite popular and on video are Verdi's MACBETH (1847), Britten's A MIDSUMMER NIGHT'S DREAM (1960), and Gounod's ROMÉO ET JULIETTE (1867). Nicolai's DIE LUSTIGEN WEIBER VON WINDSOR (1849), based on *The Merry Wives of Windsor,* continues to be performed and telecast in German-speaking countries, and interest in Thomas's HAMLET (1868) is reviving. There are no American Shakespeare operas on video, although two have been telecast: Samuel Barber's ANTONY AND CLEOPATRA (1966) and Vittorio Giannini's THE TAMING OF THE SHREW (1953). There are also worthwhile American versions of *The Tempest* by John Eaton and Lee Hoiby and *The Winter's Tale* by John Harbison, but they do not exist in screen versions. The other Shakespeare operas with entries in this book are BEÁTRICE ET BÉNÉDICT (based on *Much Ado About Nothing*), I CAPULETI ED I MONTECCHI (based on *Romeo and Juliet*), THE FAIRY QUEEN (based on *A Midsummer Night's Dream*), FALSTAFF (Salieri opera based on *The Merry Wives of Windsor*), and OTELLO (opera by Rossini). The most complete source of information about Shakespeare operas is *Shakespeare and Opera* by Gary Schmidgall. Shakespeare operas were also filmed during the silent era, but it is not always possible to tell whether the film is based on the opera libretto or the play; the authority for this is Robert Hamilton Ball, whose *Shakespeare on Silent Film* is an invaluable resource. This is not a problem with the earliest sound films. The first opera films screened with sound and image were presented at the Phono-Cinéma-Théâtre at the Paris Exhibition on June 8, 1900; Victor Maurel sang in a scene from *Falstaff,* and Emile Cossira sang in a scene from *Roméo et Juliette.* There were short German sound films of *Otello* in 1907 with Henny Porten, *Roméo et Juliette* in 1909 with Luisa Tetrazzini, and *Die Lustigen Weiber von Windsor* in 1916.

SHOSTAKOVICH, DIMITRI
Russian composer (1906–1975)

Dimitri Shostakovich was famous by the age of 20 after the success of his first symphony and his first opera *The Nose*, but he then had to tone down his experimental style; the political climate was changing. His second opera, LADY MACBETH OF THE MTSENSK DISTRICT, nearly destroyed his career. Stalin attended a performance and didn't like it, so Shostakovich was attacked in *Pravda*. It was the beginning of the Terror. The opera was withdrawn, and it did not reappear until after Stalin's death in 1962, when the composer produced a revised version titled *Katerina Ismailova*. In the intervening period, he had composed symphonic works and stayed away from the stage. Both versions of the opera are now on video. Shostakovich also had problems with Jewish composer Benjamin Fleischmann's opera ROTHSCHILD'S VIOLIN, which he completed; it was banned as soon as it was staged in 1968. It now exists, however, in a fine screen version.

1987 Testimony
Tony Palmer directed this epic biography of the composer with Ben Kingsley giving a powerful performance as Shostakovich. David Rudkin wrote the script, basing it on a book by Solomon Vokov derived from the composer's memoirs, and the film is as much about his political problems as about his music. Nic Knowland, the cinematographer, shot most of the film in black and white and CinemaScope. In English. 157 minutes.

SHOW BOAT
1927 operatic American musical by Kern

Jerome Kern's *Show Boat*, which virtually created the integrated modern American musical, has entered the opera house repertory. New York City Opera staged it in 1954, Houston Grand Opera mounted an impressive production in 1983, and Frederica von Stade, Teresa Stratas, and Jerry Hadley recorded it in operatic style in 1988. Based on a novel by Edna Ferber and composed to a fine libretto by Oscar Hammerstein II, *Show Boat* tells of the loves and woes of a group of people on a turn-of-the-century Mississippi river boat. Magnolia Hawks, the daughter of showboat owner Capt. Andy, falls in love with gambler Gaylord Ravenal after they sing "Make Believe." Singer Julie La Verne runs into race prejudice after she sings "Can't Help Lovin' Dat Man." Stevedore Joe sums up the problems of being black in Mississippi in the bass aria "Ol' Man River." The musical has been filmed four times, and there is an LD set of all four versions. Miles Kreuger's *Show Boat: The Story of a Classic American Musical* is the definitive source book.

1929 Universal film
American feature film: Harry Pollard (director), Tom Reed and Charles Kenyon (screenplay), Gilbert Warrenton (cinematographer).

Cast: Laura La Plante (Magnolia), Joseph Schildkraut (Ravenal), Alma Rubens (Julie), Stepin Fetchit (Joe).

Video: MGM-UA LD. Black and white. In English. 85 minutes.

Comment: This film, based on the novel rather than the musical, was intended to be a silent movie. After the success of the musical, Universal acquired rights and added an 18-minute sound prologue featuring songs by members of the New York stage cast, including Jules Bledsoe and Helen Morgan. The film has been restored and is on LD, but without the prologue.

1936 Universal film
American feature film: James Whale (director), Oscar Hammerstein (screenplay), Victor Baravelle (conductor/music director), John Mescall (cinematographer).

Cast: Irene Dunne (Magnolia), Allan Jones (Gaylord), Helen Morgan (Julie), Paul Robeson (Joe), Hattie McDaniel (Queenie), Charles Winninger (Capt. Andy), Helen Westley (Parthy), Sammy White (Frank).

Video: On VHS and LD. Black and white. In English. 113 minutes.

Comment: Many critics consider this the best film version. Robeson, the original choice as Joe for the American stage version, had earlier played the role in a London stage production.

1946 Till the Clouds Roll By
American highlights version on film: Richard Whorf and Vincente Minnelli (directors), Jean Holloway, George Wells and Myles Connelly (screenplay), Harry Stradling and George J. Folsey (cinematographers), Lennie Hayton (music director).

Cast: Kathryn Grayson (Magnolia), Tony Martin (Ravenal), Lena Horne (Julie), Caleb Peterson (Joe), Frank Sinatra, Virginia O'Brien.

Video: MGM DVD/VHS/LD. Color. In English. 137 minutes.

Comment: MGM's romanticized biography of Jerome Kern contains a staged highlights version of *Show Boat*. Grayson and Martin sing "Make Believe," Horne sings "Can't Help Loving That Man," Sinatra sings "Ol' Man River," and O'Brien sings "Life Upon the Wicked Stage."

1951 MGM film
American feature film: George Sidney (director), John Lee Mahin (screenplay), Charles Rosher (cinematographer), Adolf Deutsch (music director/conductor, MGM Studio Orchestra).

Cast: Kathryn Grayson (Magnolia), Howard Keel (Ravenal), Ava Gardner (Julie, sung by Annette Warren), William Warfield (Joe), Joe E. Brown (Capt. Andy), Agnes Moorehead (Parthy), Gower Champion (Frank), Marge Champion (Elly).

Video: MGM DVD/VHS/LD. Color. In English. 107 minutes.

SÍ
1919 operetta by Mascagni

PIETRO MASCAGNI is best known for his *verismo* opera *Cavalleria rusticana*, but he also tried his hand at lighter stage works, including operettas. *Sí*, libretto by Carlo Lombardo and A. Franci, tells the bittersweet story of a showgirl who can never say "no," only "sí," and the marital problems this leads to. The operetta opened at the Quirino Theatre in Rome in 1919 and was well received, helping Mascagni to regain favor with the Italian public, which had been losing faith in him.

1992 Operette, che Passione!
Italian TV studio production: Sandro Massimini (director/producer), Roberto Negri (pianist), Sandro Corelli (choreographer).

Cast: Sandro Massimini, Sonia Dorigo, Max René Cosotti.

Video: Ricordi (Italy) VHS. Pierluigi Pagano (director). Color. In Italian. About 19 minutes.

Comment: Highlights of the operetta featured on the TV series *Operette, che Passione!* The featured songs are "Sì! Sì!," "Romanza del Sì," and "Bimbe la luce elettrica rimpiazza il sol."

SIEBEN TODSÜNDEN, DIE
1933 opera-ballet by Weill

KURT WEILL's *Die sieben Todsünden* (The Seven Deadly Sins), composed in Paris to a libretto by BERTOLT BRECHT, is a "singing ballet," the story of twin sisters named Anna I and II. Anna I, who tells us she is "practical," sings her role. Anna II, who is "beautiful," dances hers. As the sisters travel to seven cities to earn money to buy a house in Louisiana, they encounter the seven deadly sins and turn morality on its head. Each of the sins has its own musical sequence. Anna I was first sung by Lotte Lenya, and Anna II was first danced by Tilly Losch.

1993 Opéra de Lyon
French studio production: Peter Sellars (director), Kent Nagano (conductor, Opéra de Lyon Orchestra), Donald Byrd (choreographer), Dunya Ramicova (costume designer).

Cast: Teresa Stratas (Anna I), Norma Kimball (Anna II), Peter Rose (Mother), Howard Haskin (Father), Frank Kelley (First Son), Herbert Perry (Second Son).

Video: London VHS/Pioneer LD. Peter Sellars (director). HDTV. Color. In German with English subtitles. 47 minutes.

Comment: The film alternates between studio scenes and scenes of present-day America.

SIEGFRIED
1876 opera by Wagner

Siegfried is the third opera in RICHARD WAGNER's epic DER RING DES NIBELUNGEN tetralogy. Siegfried, the son of Siegmund and Sieglinde, is reared by Alberich's brother Mime, who wants him to regain the gold and the ring. Siegfried reforges the heroic sword Nothung and uses it to kill the giant Fafner, who has become a dragon. The Forest Bird then leads him to the Valkyries' Rock. Wotan, in his disguise as the Wanderer, tries to stop him, but Siegfried breaks his spear and awakens Brünnhilde from her long sleep.

1980 Bayreuth Festival
German stage production: Patrice Chéreau (director), Pierre Boulez (conductor, Bayreuth Festival Orchestra and Chorus), Richard Peduzzi (set designer), Jacques Schmidt (costume designer).

Cast: Manfred Jung (Siegfried), Donald McIntyre (Wotan), Heinz Zednik (Mime), Gwyneth Jones (Brünnhilde), Hermann Becht (Alberich), Fritz Hübner (Fafner), Ortrun Wenkel (Erda), Norma Sharp (Forest Bird).

Video: Philips DVD/VHS/LD. Brian Large (director). Color. In German with English subtitles. 226 minutes.

Comment: Bayreuth Festival centenary production set in the 19th century, first staged in 1976.

1989 Bavarian State Opera
German stage production: Nikolaus Lehnhoff (director), Wolfgang Sawallisch (conductor, Bavarian State Opera Orchestra and Chorus), Erich Wonder (set designer).

Cast: René Kollo (Siegfried), Robert Hale (Wotan), Helmut Pampuch (Mime), Hildegard Behrens (Brünnhilde), Ekkehard Wlaschiha (Alberich), Kurt Moll (Fafner), Hanna Schwarz (Erda), Julie Kaufmann (Forest Bird).

Video: EMI VHS/Japanese LD. Shokichi Amano (director). Color. In German with English subtitles. 230 minutes.

***1990 Metropolitan Opera

American stage production: Otto Schenk (director), James Levine (conductor, Metropolitan Opera Orchestra and Chorus), Günther Schneider-Siemssen (set designer), Rolf Langenfass (costume designer).

Cast: Siegfried Jerusalem (Siegfried), James Morris (Wotan), Heinz Zednik (Mime), Hildegard Behrens (Brünnhilde), Ekkehard Wlaschiha (Alberich), Matti Salminen (Fafner), Birgitta Svendén (Erda), Dawn Upshaw (Forest Bird).

Video: DG DVD/VHS/LD. Taped April 26, 1990; telecast June 20, 1990. Brian Large (director). Color. In German with English subtitles. 252 minutes.

Comment: The most traditional and most convincing of the *Ring* versions on video.

1992 Bayreuth Festival

German stage production: Harry Kupfer (director), Daniel Barenboim (conductor, Bayreuth Festival Orchestra and Chorus), Hans Schavernoch (set designer).

Cast: Siegfried Jerusalem (Siegfried), Helmut Pampuch (Mime), John Tomlinson (Wotan), Anne Evans (Brünnhilde), Gunter von Kannen (Alberich), Philip Kang (Fafner), Birgitta Svendén (Erda).

Video: Teldec VHS/LD. Horant H. Hohlfeld (director). Color. In German with English subtitles. 230 minutes.

1996 Jutland Opera

Danish stage production: Klaus Hoffmeyer (director), Tamás Vetö (conductor, Aarhus Symphony Orchestra), Lars Juhl (set/costume designer).

Cast: Stig Anderson (Siegfried), Lisbeth Balslev (Brünnhilde), Lars Waage (Wotan).

Video: Musikhuset Aarhus (Denmark) VHS. Telecast on Danmarks Radio, Copenhagen. Thomas Grimm (director). Color. In German. 231 minutes.

Early/related films

1905 Nothung film

German sound film of the scene in the opera when Siegfried forges his sword Nothung. It was screened with a synchronized phonograph record. Black and white. About 2 minutes. Print at the NFTA.

1912 Ambrosio film

Mario Caserini directed this Italian *Siegfried* for the Ambrosio Film Company of Turin. Alberto Capozzi and Mary Cleo Tarlarini are the stars; Arrigo Frusta wrote the screenplay. Black and white. Silent. About 14 minutes.

1930 L'Âge d'or

Spanish director Luis Buñuel was obsessed with Wagner's operas and used their music in many of his films. He features the "Forest Murmurs" from *Siegfried* on the soundtrack of *L'Âge d'or*. Black and white. In French. 60 minutes.

1957 Sigfrido

Italian narrative film based on the German epic *The Nibelungenlied*. It uses Wagner's music as score, although the epic story differs from Wagner's version; for instance, Sigfrido (Siegfried) loves Kriemhild, not Brünnhilde. Sebastian Fischer is Sigfrido, with Ilaria Occhini as Crimilde, Katharine Mayber as Brunilde, Rolf Tasna as Hagen, and Giorgio Constantini as Gunther. Giacomo Gentilomo directed. Color. In Italian. 98 minutes.

1998 L'ennui

"Siegfried's Idyll," performed by the Liszt Chamber Orchestra led by Ernest Lukas, is on the soundtrack of this French film about an obsessive sexual relationship. Cédric Kahn directed. Color. In French. 122 minutes.

SIEPI, CESARE
Italian bass (1923–)

Cesare Siepi was particularly admired for his performances as Don Giovanni and Figaro in the Mozart operas. The Milan-born singer, who made his debut in 1941, began to sing at La Scala in 1946 and at Covent Garden in 1950. His place in opera film history was secured when he sang the role of the Don in the pioneer Salzburg Festival film of DON GIOVANNI in 1954. Siepi also starred in the Broadway musicals *Bravo, Giovanni* (1962) and *Carmelina* (1979). See AIDA (1988), BARITONES AND BASSES (1995), DON CARLO (1950), DON GIOVANNI (1954/1960), FAUST (1963 film/1965 film), JÉRUSALEM (1986), and RIGOLETTO (1984 film).

1953 Toast to the Met

Siepi was one of the stars shown in rehearsal when Ed Sullivan devoted his CBS show to the Met on November 8, 1953, and telecast it from the opera house stage. See METROPOLITAN OPERA.

1963 Legends of Opera

Siepi was filmed on stage for a RAI Italian Television concert in 1963, and his performance of Figaro's aria "Aprite un po' quegli occhi" from *Le nozze di Figaro* is on the video *Legends of Opera*. Black and white. 4 minutes. Legato Classics VHS.

1985 Freni and Siepi Concert

Siepi joins Mirella Freni in an Italian concert of favorite arias, with selections from *Don Carlo, Gianni Schicchi, Mefistofele, Philemon et Baucis, Simon Boccanegra,* and *Tosca.* Bruno Amaducci conducts. Color. 48 minutes. Bel Canto Society VHS.

SIGNORA DI TUTTI, LA

1934 Italian film with opera content

An imaginary opera is an important component of MAX OPHULS's Italian film *La signora di tutti* (Everybody's Woman). Film star Gaby Doriot (Isa Miranda), who has been a disaster for the men in her life, has tried to kill herself. In the hospital she remembers events from her past, including being taken to La Scala by a married man (Memo Benassi) as a young woman. She listens enthralled afterwards as he describes the plot in detail to his bedridden wife (Tatiana Pavlova), and their illicit love is born during the telling. On the following night, as the opera is playing on the radio, Miranda and Benassi embrace in the garden. The wife is suspicious, sets out to look for them, and dies when her wheelchair falls down the stairs. Miranda later imagines that she hears this music even when it is not playing. The opera is about a young officer who is magically healed by a woman after he is shot. She becomes his lover and goes on a military campaign with him, but the emperor takes the woman away from him. The officer ends up insane in prison. The opera's music was written by Daniel Amfitheatrof, who began his professional career at La Scala. The film also includes Nelly Corradi as Miranda's sister, Mario Ferrari as a film producer, and Giulia Puccini as a singing teacher. Ubaldo Arata was the cinematographer, and Ophuls wrote the screenplay with Hans Wilheim and Kurt Alexander based on a novel by Salvator Gotta. Black and white. In Italian with English subtitles. 89 minutes. Connoisseur VHS.

SIGNOR BRUSCHINO, IL

1813 opera by Rossini

Il Signor Bruschino (Mr. Bruschino) was the last of GIOACHINO ROSSINI's early romantic one-act farces. The libretto by Giuseppe Maria Foppa, based on a French play, centers around Sofia who is being married off by her guardian Gaudenzio to the son of Signor Bruschino. Her lover Florville disguises himself as young Bruschino and marries her instead. He is helped by Signor Bruschino, who has complicated identity problems.

1988 Pesaro Festival

Italian stage production: Roberto de Simone (director), Donato Renzetti (conductor, Turin RAI Symphonic Orchestra), Enrico Job (set/costume designer).

Cast: Mariella Devia (Sofia), Dalmacio Gonzalez (Florville), Enzo Dara (Gaudenzio), Alberto Rinaldi (Signor Bruschino), Eugenio Favano (Bruschino's son).

Video: House of Opera/Lyric VHS. Claudio Codilupi and Luciana Ceci Mascola (directors). Color. In Italian. 95 minutes.

1989 Schwetzingen Festival

German stage production: Michael Hampe (director), Gianluigi Gelmetti (conductor, Stuttgart Radio Symphony Orchestra), Carlo Tommasi (set designer), Carlo Diappi (costume designer).

Cast: Amelia Felle (Sofia), David Kuebler (Florville), Alexander Corbelli (Gaudenzio), Alberto Rinaldi (Signor Bruschino), Carlos Feller (Filiberto), Vitto Gobbi (Bruschino's son), Janice Hall (Marianna).

Video: Teldec VHS/LD. Claus Viller (director). Color. In Italian with English subtitles. 85 minutes.

SIGNORINA DEL CINEMATOGRAFO, LA

1914 screen operetta by Lombardo

Italian composer Carlo Lombardo created *La signorina del cinematografo* (The Movie Girl), an Italian operetta about a movie queen, at a time when Italy was one of the film centers of the world with internationally popular female movie stars. He based it on an 1896 Austrian operetta titled *Der Schmetterling* (The Butterfly) composed by Carlo Weinberger and written by A. M. Willner and Bernhard Buchbinder. As with his other adaptations, Lombardo completely revised the plot and libretto. It was a hit in its new cinematic form, and its libretto was published in a popular edition, but it has not been revived nor recorded.

SILENT FILMS ABOUT OPERA

Films during the silent era from 1896 to 1927 often featured opera and opera singers as a central plot theme because the opera diva was considered the most glamorous of women and opera symbolized culture. The music from operas shown in the films was usually played live by the theater orchestra or on a piano. Silent films directly related to individual operas are listed under those operas; the more generic opera films are described below. See also the film series THE GREAT LOVER, THE PHANTOM OF THE OPERA, and TRILBY.

1909 Le ténor fait des conquêtes

The Tenor Makes Conquests is a French comedy starring Gabriel Moreau as an irresistible tenor looking for women admirers. Produced for Pathé. Black and white. Silent. About 7 minutes.

1914 Grand Opera in Rubeville
Richard Tucker (not the famous tenor) and Herbert Prior star in this Edison two-reel comedy written and directed by Ashley Miller for the Edison Studio. Black and white. Silent. About 25 minutes.

1915 The Opera Singer's Romance
Gale Henry plays a famous opera prima donna opposite William Franey in this Joker Studio romance. Allen Curtis directed. Black and white. Silent. About 60 minutes.

1915 What Happened to Father
Frank Daniels plays a man who writes a comic opera to make money and then has to sing the leading role. C. Jay Williams directed this comedy for Vitagraph. Black and white. Silent. About 60 minutes.

1916 The Prima Donna's Husband
Kathryn Browne-Decker plays an opera prima donna whose husband kills a man he believes is her lover. Julius Steger and Joseph Golden directed this melodrama for Triumph Film. Black and white. Silent. About 60 minutes.

1916 The Yellow Passport
Clara Kimball Young plays a famous opera singer falsely accused of having once been a prostitute. Edwin August directed this melodrama for World Film. Black and white. Silent. About 60 minutes.

1916 Two Seats at the Opera
William Garwood stars in this comedy short made for the IMP Company, with a supporting cast of William Welsh, Inez Marcel, Edwina Martin, and William J. Dyer. Black and white. Silent. About 12 minutes.

1917 The Master Passion
Mabel Trunnelle, obsessed with becoming an opera singer, abandons her husband and child to go to Paris to become famous. Richard Ridgely directed for Edison. Black and white. Silent. About 65 minutes.

1917 The Snarl
Bessie Barriscale plays twin sisters, one of whom is a famous opera singer. After she is hurt in an accident, she has to sing behind a curtain while her twin mimes her role on stage. Raymond West directed for Triangle. Black and white. Silent. About 65 minutes.

1918 Das Leben einer Primadonna
Anetta Melton plays an opera prima donna with emotional problems in *The Life of a Prima Donna*, an Austrian film directed by Franz Köhler and written by Melton. Black and white. Silent. About 50 minutes.

1919 Heartsease
Tom Moore plays a composer who writes an opera called *Heartsease* and dedicates it to Helene Chadwick. Harry Beaumont directed for Goldwyn Pictures. Black and white. Silent. About 70 minutes.

1920 Greater Than Fame
Elaine Hammerstein plays an opera singer who becomes famous when composer Walter McGrail writes an opera for her. Alan Crosland directed for Selznick. Black and white. Silent. About 70 minutes.

1920 Out of the Storm
Margaret Hill plays a nightclub singer who becomes an opera star with help from an admirer who turns out to be a criminal. William Parke directed for Goldwyn. Black and white. Silent. About 70 minutes.

1920 Once to Every Woman
Dorothy Phillips becomes an opera star with the help of an Italian admirer who eventually shoots her out of jealousy. Allen Houlbar directed for Universal. Black and white. Silent. About 80 minutes.

1922 How Women Love
Betty Blythe borrows money to study to become an opera singer and tries to pay off her backer with stolen rubies. Kenneth Webb directed for B. B. Productions. Black and white. Silent. About 75 minutes.

1926 The Torrent
Greta Garbo plays a famous opera diva who has an unhappy relationship with Spanish aristocrat Ricardo Cortez. Monta Bell directed this famous film for MGM. Black and white. Silent. About 80 minutes.

SILENT FILMS OF OPERAS

Interest in opera was so intense during the early part of the century that silent films of operas became surprisingly common. Most of the operas popular at the time were filmed and presented with live music when screened—a piano in small towns, orchestras in cities. There were also many early films made to be shown with synchronized records, mostly of individual arias. The first silent film of an opera was a 2-minute version of Donizetti's THE DAUGHTER OF THE REGIMENT shot in July 1898 at a New York City studio. The first film of an actual opera was William Paley's 15-minute *The Opera of Martha*, also shot in 1898 and screened at the Eden Musée in New

York in January 1899. The Edison Studio made a version of PARSIFAL in 1904, a 22-minute epic shot at the time of the New York stage production. Opera stars such as GERALDINE FARRAR, ENRICO CARUSO, and MARY GARDEN were often featured in silent operatic films, and Farrar became a genuine movie star. The most important silent film of an opera is the 1926 version of Richard Strauss's DER ROSENKAVALIER, for which composer and librettist wrote new music and scenes; it was recently restored and screened with live music. The most interesting film cinematically is King Vidor's version of LA BOHÈME with Lillian Gish as Mimì. See also FIRST OPERA FILMS.

SILENZIO, SI GIRA!
1944 Italian film with opera content

Italian opera tenor Beniamino Gigli plays a famous opera singer in *Silenzio, si gira!* (Silence, We're Filming!). As he is no longer a young man, he hopes to win a woman he fancies (Mariella Lotti) by getting her a role in his current film. When he finds out that she prefers a younger actor (Rossano Brazzi), he becomes petulant and abandons the film out of spite. However, his secretary finds a double (a petty thief, also played by Gigli), and filming continues without the temperamental star. When he finds this out, he comes to his senses and returns to the set. Gigli sings arias from *Rigoletto* ("La donna è mobile"), *Lohengrin*, and other operas. Cesare Zavattini, one of the creators of Italian neorealism, was co-screenwriter with Mario Brancacci and Vittorio Nono Novarese. Leonida Barboni was the cinematographer, and Carlo Campogalliani directed the film in Rome in Italian and German versions for Itala Film. The German title is *Achtung Aufnahme*. Black and white. 86 minutes. Bel Canto/Lyric VHS.

SILJA, ANJA
German soprano (1940–)

Berliner Anja Silja became a major presence at Bayreuth during the 1960s when she was associated with Wieland Wagner, who engaged her to sing the roles of Senta, Elsa, Eva, Elisabeth, Freia, and Venus. Silja, who had made her debut in 1955 as Rosina at Brunswick, first went to London in 1963 to sing *Fidelio* with the Frankfurt Opera at Sadler's Wells and sang with the Royal Opera during the 1990s. Her American career began in Chicago as Senta, and she reached the Met in 1971 in *Fidelio* and *Salome*. Silja has a magnetic stage personality as well as a fine voice, as can be seen on her videos. See BAYREUTH (1960), JENŮFA (1989), FIDELIO (1968), THE MAKROPOULOS CASE (1995), and SALOME (1995).

SILLS, BEVERLY
American soprano (1929–)

Her nickname "Bubbles" is an indication of the personality of this extraordinary singer who became an American diva at NEW YORK CITY OPERA. Sills, who was born Belle Miriam Silverman in Brooklyn, made her debut in 1947 in the Lehár operetta *Frasquita* at the Philadelphia Civic Opera. She appeared on the New York TV series OPERA CAMEOS during the early 1950s, joined the NYCO in 1955, soon became its prima donna, and gained wide recognition for her singing and personality. She sang at La Scala, Vienna, and Covent Garden during the 1960s, and she made a token Met appearance in 1975. She was general director of the NYCO from 1979 to 1989 and then headed the entire Lincoln Center arts complex. Her videos are almost as enjoyable for her sense of fun as for her exceptional voice. See THE BALLAD OF BABY DOE (1962), IL BARBIERE DI SIVIGLIA (1976), LEONARD BERNSTEIN (1988), ENRICO CARUSO (1998), DON PASQUALE (1979), ED SULLIVAN SHOW (1996), DIE LUSTIGE WITWE (1977), LA FILLE DU RÉGIMENT (1974), THE GOLDEN COCKEREL (1971), INTOLLERANZA 1960 (1965), JUANA LA LOCA (1979), LUCIA DI LAMMERMOOR (1986 film), MANON (1977), METROPOLITAN OPERA (1975), BIRGIT NILSSON (1979), ROBERTO DEVEREUX (1975), SAN FRANCISCO (1997), WERNER SCHROETER (1986), THAIS (1954), LA TRAVIATA (1954/1976), and IL TURCO IN ITALIA (1978).

1936 Uncle Sol Solves It
This, unfortunately, is Sills's only film, and it was made in New York when she was only 7 years old. She had begun to appear on radio at the age of 4 on *Uncle Bob's Rainbow Hour* on station WOR, and that led to this short film made for Twentieth Century-Fox. Black and white. 10 minutes.

1974 Johnny Carson Show
Sills plays Jeanette MacDonald to Johnny Carson's Nelson Eddy on the *Johnny Carson Show*. He dressed in a Mountie costume so they could sing the "Indian Love Song" together. Color. 60 minutes.

1976 Sills and Burnett at the Met
Sills and Carol Burnett sing and dance on the Metropolitan Opera stage beginning with the duet "Only an Octave Apart." Sills sings arias and popular songs and joins Burnett in an opera spoof. Dave Powers directed. Telecast November 25, 1976. Color. 50 minutes. Video at the MTR.

1976 Lifestyles With Beverly Sills
Sills made her debut as a talk show host with this program in October 1976. Her guests included Melba Moore, Phyllis Diller, and Tammy Grimes. Color. 60 minutes.

1978 Beverly & Friends
Sills, who hosted this TV show, seems to enjoy herself talking to stars. She sang, danced, and welcomed guests Burt Lancaster, Lily Tomlin, and Joan Rivers. Telecast December 6, 1978. Color. 90 minutes.

1979 Muppet Show
Sills joins Miss Piggy, Kermit, and the rest of the muppets in an amazing production of the porcine opera *Pigoletto.* She also gets to sing "When It's Roundup Time in Texas." Color. 30 minutes.

1980 Beverly Sills Farewell
An all-star farewell party for Sills held at New York City Opera October 27, 1980. The setting is Act II of *Die Fledermaus* with Kitty Carlisle as party-giver Prince Orlofsky. The guests include Plácido Domingo, Sherrill Milnes, Leontyne Price, Renata Scotto, Zubin Mehta, and Ethel Merman. Sills closes the party with a duet with Carol Burnett. Julius Rudel conducts. Telecast January 5, 1981, as a Lincoln Center special. Color. 60 minutes. Video at the NYPL.

1985 Kennedy Center Honors
Sills is one of the honorees on this Kennedy Center Honors program in December 1985. Sherrill Milnes and Carol Burnett salute her in a duet. Telecast December 27, 1985. Color. 120 minutes.

SIMIONATO, GIULIETTA
Italian mezzo-soprano (1910–)

Giulietta Simionato, who retired in 1966, was one of the most attractive personalities to emerge from Italy after World War II; her coloratura was vivacious and her acting charming. She began to sing at La Scala in 1939 and was invited to sing in London and New York during the 1950s. She made a few films, mostly just as a voice, but she can be seen on stage in person in the 1954 film *Casa Ricordi,* and she is interviewed in the 1998 film *Opera Fanatic* about Italian divas. See AIDA (1956/1961/1963), IL BARBIERE DI SIVIGLIA (1955), BELL TELEPHONE HOUR (1959–1966), CAVALLERIA RUSTICANA (1961/1963 film), OPERA IMAGINAIRE (1993), RICORDI (1954), SOPRANOS AND MEZZOS (1998), and IL TROVATORE (1964 film).

SIMON BOCCANEGRA
1857 opera by Verdi

The plot of this opera by GIUSEPPE VERDI is as complicated as that of *Il trovatore,* probably because it is based on a melodrama by the same overheated Spanish author, Antonio García Gutiérrez. *Simon Boccanegra* is set in 14th-century Genoa. Simon, a plebeian seaman, has become the Doge of Genoa. Many years before, he loved the daughter of his patrician enemy Fiesco, and they had a daughter named Maria who disappeared. She was brought up by Fiesco, who thinks she is an orphan named Amelia. Plebeian Paolo wants to marry her, but she loves patrician Gabriele. Francesco Maria Piave's libretto was revised by Arrigo Boito in his first collaboration with Verdi. The opera is noted for its duets, especially those between father and daughter.

1976 NHK Lirica Italiana
Japanese stage production: Oliviero De Fabritiis (conductor, NHK Symphony Orchestra and Chorus of Lyric Opera of Nikikai and Fujiwara).
Cast: Piero Cappuccilli (Simon Boccanegra), Katia Ricciarelli (Maria/Amelia), Nicolai Ghiaurov (Jacopo Fiesco), Giorgio Merighi (Gabriele Adorno), Lorenzo Saccomani (Paolo Albiani).
Filmed September 23, 1966, in Tokyo for Japanese TV. Black and white. In Italian with English subtitles. 163 minutes.
Comment: This was the last production telecast in the invaluable NHK series, but it is not currently on VHS.

1978 Paris Opéra
French stage production: Giorgio Strehler (director), Claudio Abbado (conductor, Paris Opéra Orchestra and Chorus), Ezio Frigerio (set designer).
Cast: Piero Cappuccilli (Simon Boccanegra), Mirella Freni (Maria/Amelia), Nicolai Ghiaurov (Fiesco).
Video: Lyric VHS/Dreamlife (Japan) DVD. Telecast December 3, 1978, in France. André Flédérick (director). Color. In Italian. 141 minutes.

1984 Metropolitan Opera
American stage production: Tito Capobianco (director), James Levine (conductor, Metropolitan Opera Orchestra and Chorus).
Cast: Sherrill Milnes (Simon Boccanegra) Anna Tomowa-Sintow (Maria/Amelia), Paul Plishka (Fiesco), Vasile Moldoveanu (Gabriele), Richard J. Clark (Paolo), Lady-in-Waiting (Dawn Upshaw).
Video: Pioneer DVD/LD and Paramount VHS. Taped December 29, 1984; telecast April 17, 1985. Brian Large (director). Color. In Italian with English subtitles. 153 minutes.

1991 Royal Opera House

English stage production: Elijah Moshinsky (director), Sir Georg Solti (conductor, Royal Opera House Orchestra and Chorus), Michael Yeargan (set designer), Peter J. Hall (costumes).

Cast: Alexandru Agache (Simon Boccanegra), Kiri Te Kanawa (Maria/Amelia), Roberto Scandiuzzi (Fiesco), Michael Sylvester (Gabriele), Alan Opie (Paolo).

London VHS. Brian Large (director). Color. In Italian with English subtitles. 135 minutes.

1995 Metropolitan Opera

American stage production: Giancarlo del Monaco (director), James Levine (conductor, Metropolitan Opera Orchestra and Chorus), Michael Scott (set/costume designer).

Cast: Vladimir Chernov (Simon Boccanegra), Kiri Te Kanawa (Amelia/Maria), Robert Lloyd (Fiesco), Plácido Domingo (Gabriele), Bruno Pola (Paolo).

Video: DG DVD/VHS/LD. Taped January 26, 1995; telecast April 26, 1995. Brian Large (director). Color. In Italian with English subtitles. 152 minutes.

Comment: Chernov is wonderful, but the production is less than inspiring.

SIMPLICIUS
1887 operetta by Johann Strauss II

JOHANN STRAUSS II'S operetta *Simplicius*, libretto by Victor Leon based on the famous anti-war novel by Johann Grimmelshausen, has never been popular. It was revived by Zurich Opera to mark the centenary of the death of the composer. The complicated story takes places during the Thirty Years' War of 1618-1648 and revolves around the simple peasant Simplicius and his adventures in love and war. It is meant to be satirical.

2002 Zurich Opera

Swiss stage production: David Pountney (director), Franz Welser-Möst (conductor, Zurich Opera House Chorus and Orchestra).

Cast: Martin Zysset (Simplicius), Martina Jankova (Tilly), Elizabeth Magnuson (Hildegarde), Louise Martini (Schnapslotte), Piotr Beczala (Armin), Michale Volle (Hermit).

Video: Arthaus DVD. Thomas Grimm (director). Color. In German with English subtitles. 132 minutes.

SINFONIE DI CUORI
1936 Italian-German film with opera content

Italian tenor Beniamino Gigli stars opposite Isa Miranda in this melodramatic musical. She plays the wife of a Munich music teacher (Josef Sieber) who taught Gigli to be a singer. When she falls in love with Gigli, the angry husband takes their little girl off to America. Fifteen years later mother and daughter are reunited. She has become an opera ballerina and, like her mother, has fallen in love with a tenor (Eric Helgar). Miranda plays both mother and daughter. Gigli is seen on stage in *Aida* and sings "E lucevan le stelle" from *Tosca* and "Donna non vidi mai" from *Manon Lescaut* with the Bavarian State Opera Orchestra and Chorus led by Giuseppe Becce. Karl Heinz Martin directed the film in two languages, in Italian as *Sinfonia di Cuori* and in German as *Du bist mein Glück.* Franz Hoch was cinematographer, and Walter Wassermann and C. H. Diller wrote the screenplay. Shown in the United States as *Thou Art My Joy.* Black and white. 95 minutes. Bel Canto Society/House of Opera/Lyric VHS.

SINIMBERGHI, GINO
Italian tenor (1913–1997)

Gino Sinimberghi learned his craft in his native Rome, but he spent the early years of his career, from 1937 to 1944, singing with the Berlin Staatsoper. After he returned to Italy, he was a fixture at the major opera houses until 1968. One of his finest moments was singing Ismaele opposite Maria Callas in *Nabucco* at San Carlo in 1949. He appeared in a number of Italian opera films during the 1940s and 1950s as both singer and actor. See LINA CAVALIERI (1955), L'ELISIR D'AMORE (1947), LA FAVORITA (1952), LA FORZA DEL DESTINO (1949), NORMA (1974), PAGLIACCI (1948), GIACOMO PUCCINI (1952), LA SONNAMBULA (1949), TOSCA (1946 film), and IL TROVATORE (1949).

63: DREAM PALACE
1990 opera by Bose

Hans-Jurgen von Bose's opera *63: Dream Palace,* libretto in English by the composer based on James Purdy's American novel, tells what happens when 19-year-old Fenton goes to Chicago with his 8-year-old brother Claire. The opera incorporates rock, jazz, and pop music in its score. It premiered at the Munich Biennale in 1990 and has been reprised a number of times in Europe.

1990 Munich Biennale

German stage production: Jonathan Moore (director), Alicia Mounk (conductor, Frankfurt Modern Ensemble and Munich Chorus), David Blight (set/costume designer).

Cast: Philip Sheffield (Fenton), Barry Flutter (Claire), Eileen Hulse (Bella Mamma), Omar Ebrahim (Parkhurst), Patricia Bardon (Grainger).

Telecast May 19, 1990, on Bavarian Television. Georg Wübbolt (director). Color. In English. 140 minutes.

SKLADANOWSKY, MAX
German film pioneer (1863–1939)

Max Skladanowsky occupies a position in German cinema similar to that of Edison in the United States and Lumière in France—one of the very earliest filmmakers. He gave a public performance of moving pictures at the Berlin Wintergarten in a variety program on February 1, 1895. At the end of 1896, he is believed to have shown the first sound film that featured music from an operetta. Viennese operetta singer Fritzi Massary and her comic partner Josef Gianpietro appeared in a scene from an unknown operetta, probably *Der Vogelhändler* or *Der Bettelstudent*. The film, played with synchronized records, has not survived although Massary made many early recordings for the Berliner record company.

SLEZAK, LEO
Austrian-Czech tenor (1873–1946)

Leo Slezak was as popular with other singers as he was with audiences and was widely liked for his sense of humor. After he left the opera stage in 1932, he appeared in more than 40 German films. Slezak, who was born in Moravia, made his opera debut in the title role of *Lohengrin* in 1896 and became forever associated with the opera when he missed his Lohengrin swan entrance at a performance and asked, "What time is the next swan?" He was hugely popular in Vienna, sang 10 roles with the Metropolitan Opera from 1909 to 1912, and became one of the leading Otellos of his era. Listed below is a selection of his films with a musical element. See CLOCLO (1935), MARTA EGGERTH (1932/1935), GASPARONE (1937), MARIA JERITZA (1933), DIE LUSTIGEN WEIBER VON WINDSOR (1935 film), OPERETTE (1940), LE POSTILLON DE LONJUMEAU (1936), and DER VOGELHÄNDLER (1940).

1934 Rendezvous in Wien
Slezak plays an Austrian publisher with a charming daughter in the musical comedy *Rendezvous in Vienna,* the story of a romance between a poor composer and a tourist guide. Viktor Janson directed. Black and white. In German. 87 minutes.

1936 Das Frauenparadies
The Woman Parade is a Robert Stolz operetta set in the world of high fashion with Slezak, Hortense Raky, and Ivan Petrovich. Operetta specialist Arthur Maria Rabenalt directed. Black and white. In German. 83 minutes.

1937 Liebe im Dreivierteltakt
Slezak is one of several stars in *Love in Waltz Time,* a Robert Stolz musical made in Czechoslovakia and Austria. Hubert Marischka directed. It was released in the United States. Black and white. In German. 94 minutes.

1938 Die 4 Gesellen
Ingrid Bergman is the star of the German film *The Four Companions,* her 10th as an emerging movie diva. Slezak and Sabine Peters lend support in a story set in Berlin. Carl Froelich directed from a play by Jochen Huth. Black and white. In German. 94 minutes.

1943 Münchausen
Slezak is one of many stars in this lavish color film fantasy about the tale-telling Baron Münchausen. It was made during the worst days of the war in Germany but still charms audiences today. Josef von Baky directed. Color. In German. 110 minutes.

SLEZAK, WALTER
Austrian-born American actor (1902–1983)

Walter Slezak appeared on stage at the Metropolitan Opera in 1957 in Johann Strauss's *The Gypsy Baron.* Although he was primarily a film and stage actor, he did occasionally sing at the Met and other opera houses. Born in Vienna, the son of tenor Leo Slezak, he was discovered by Michael Curtiz, who cast him in his 1922 Austrian film *Sodom and Gomorrah.* He went on to play romantic leads on stage and film, made his Broadway debut in 1931, and started a Hollywood career in 1942 appearing in more than 30 films, including *Lifeboat* (1944), *The Pirate* (1948), *The Inspector General* (1949), and *Call Me Madame* (1953). In 1955 he won a Tony Award for singing on Broadway in *Fanny,* and two years later he was singing at the Met.

SLY
1927 opera by Wolf-Ferrari

Drunken poet and dreamer Christopher Sly is the victim of a cruel hoax by the wealthy Earl of Westmore. He is made to believe that he has just recovered his memory after 10 years, is the lord of a castle, and is married to Dolly (she's actually the earl's mistress). When Sly becomes aware of the hoax, he kills himself. Ermanno Wolf-Ferrari's tragic *Sly, ovvero la leggenda del dormiente risvegliato* (Sly, or the Legend of the Wakened Sleeper) is based on the prologue to Shakespeare's *The Taming of the Shrew.* Out of the repertory for many years, it has recently been revived by José Carreras, who has recorded it and starred in several stage productions.

2000 Gran Teatre del Liceu, Barcelona

Spanish stage production: Hans Hollman (director), David Giménez (conductor, Gran Teatre del Liceu Symphonic Orchestra and Chorus).

Cast: José Carreras (Sly), Isabelle Kabatu (Dolly), Sherrill Milnes (Earl of Westmore).

Video: Premiere Opera VHS. Color. In Italian. 120 minutes.

SMETANA, BEDŘICH
Czech composer (1824–1884)

Bedřich Smetana, the major Czech opera composer of the 19th century, is known abroad mostly for his 1866 opera THE BARTERED BRIDE, but he composed seven others and they helped establish the pattern for nationalist opera in his country. The best known is the patriotic DALIBOR of 1868, which has striking similarities to *Fidelio*. Other Smetana operas available on CD include *Libuše* and *The Two Widows. The Bartered Bride,* however, remains his greatest achievement and for many years was the only Czech opera staged abroad.

1954 From My Life
Karel Hoger plays Smetana in *Z Meho Zivota*, a Czech film adapted from Jiri Maranek's novel *The Song of the Heroic Life*. It portrays Smetana's life in the context of the history of his period and includes a good deal of the music from his operas. The other actors include Zdenka Prochazkova, Ludmila Vendolova, Jaromir Spal, and Bedřich Karen. Vaclav Krska, who filmed Smetana's opera *Dalibor,* wrote the screenplay and directed the film. Color. In Czech. 91 minutes.

SNOW MAIDEN, THE
1882 opera by Rimsky-Korsakov

The Snow Maiden (Snegurochka), described as a "spring fairy tale," is one of the most charming of NIKOLAI RIMSKY-KORSAKOV's 15 operas. He based the libretto on a play by Alexander Ostrovsky that derives from a Russian folktale. The Snow Maiden is the daughter of Father Frost and Mother Spring. She is beautiful and sympathetic, but her heart is made of ice; she will die if she falls in love because her heart will melt. She first falls in love with Lell, who rejects her, so she agrees to marry Mizgir. Her heart is warmed and melts.

1952 Ivanov-Vano film
Russian animated feature: Ivan Ivanov-Vano (director), Bolshoi Opera Orchestra and Chorus (music), Soyuzmult Film (studio).

Cast: Singers from the Bolshoi Opera.

Color. In Russian. 67 minutes.

Comment: In this animated version of the opera, the cold and passionless Snow Maiden falls in love after her mother Spring gives her a magic gift. She is eventually melted by the Sun, who hates Frost.

Silent/related films

1914 Starewicz film
Wladyslaw Starewicz's silent Russian version of the story, based on the fable and a Gogol story, was screened in theaters with the Rimsky-Korsakov music played live. Black and white. About 30 minutes.

1953 Mood Contrasts
Experimental filmmaker Mary Ellen Bute created this abstract film as a visual interpretation of Rimsky-Korsakov opera music. "The Dance of the Tumblers" from *The Snow Maiden* is contrasted to the "Hymn to the Sun" from *The Golden Cockerel*. Color. 7 minutes.

SOBRINOS DEL CAPITÁN GRANT, LOS
1877 zarzuela by Caballero

Spanish composer MANUEL FERNÁNDEZ CABALLERO, best known for the zarzuela *Gigantes y cabezudos,* also had a big success with his zarzuela *Los sobrinos del capitán Grant* (The Nephews of Captain Grant). The libretto by Miguel Ramos Carrión is based on a Jules Verne novel, and the plot is wonderfully fantastic. Lt. Mochila sets out to rescue Capt. Grant after finding an SOS in a fish; it offers a large reward if he will come to his rescue. Accompanied by Soledad, Sir Cyron, and other hangers-on, he travels to Chile, Argentina, and Australia and finally succeeds after many bizarre adventures.

1968 Teatro Lirico Español
Spanish TV film: Juan De Orduña (director), Federico Moreno Torroba (conductor, Spanish Lyric Orchestra and Madrid Chorus), Manuel Tamayo (screenplay), Federico Larraya (cinematographer).

Cast: Josefina Cubeiro, Mari Carmen Ramirez, Vicente Sardinero, Andres Garcia Marti.

Video: Metrovideo (Spain) VHS. Shot in 35mm for RTVE Spanish Television. Juan De Orduña (director). Color. In Spanish. 92 minutes.

SOGNO DI BUTTERFLY, IL
1939 film with opera content

Opera diva Maria Cebotari, who had sung the role of Cio-Cio-San on stage, stars in *Il sogno di Butterfly* (Butterfly's Dream) as Rosa Belloni, a singer whose life parallels her role in *Madama Butterfly*. She falls in love with American musician Henry Peters (Fosco Giachetti), who goes off to America not knowing that she pregnant. When he returns four years later, now rich and famous, he visits her as she is about to go on stage in *Madama Butterfly*. He is with his American wife (Germana Paolieri). Unlike her operatic counterpart, Belloni does not kill herself but decides instead to dedicate her life to her young son. The other singers include Tito Gobbi, Palmira Vidali Marini, and Alfredo De Lidda. Ernst Marischka wrote the story, Guido Cantini wrote the screenplay, Anchise Brizzi was the cinematographer and Luigi Ricci arranged Puccini's music and conducted the orchestra. Carmine Gallone directed two versions of the film for Grandi Film Storici, one in Italian titled *Il sogno di Butterfly*, one in German called *Premiere der Butterfly*. The English release title was *The Butterfly Dream*. Black and white. In Italian. 95 minutes. Opera Dubs VHS.

SOJOURNER AND MOLLIE SINCLAIR, THE
1963 opera by Floyd

"Sojourner" Dougald MacDougald is a 60-year-old Scottish clan chieftain trying to maintain loyalty to England in East Carolina at the time of the American Revolution. When the British blockade Wilmington harbor, Mollie Sinclair leads a protest march and persuades the sojourner to join the revolution. Carlisle Floyd's one-act comic opera *The Sojourner and Mollie Sinclair*, libretto by the composer, was commissioned for the Carolina Tercentenary for television but premiered on stage at East Carolina College in Raleigh, North Carolina.

1963 East Carolina College
American stage production: Edgar R. Loessin (director), Gene Strassler (producer), Julius Rudel (conductor, East Carolina School of Music Orchestra and Chorus), Clive L. Hewitt (set/costume designer), Betsy Rose Griffith (choreographer).

Cast: Norman Treigle (Dougald MacDougald), Patricia Neway (Mollie Sinclair), Alison Herne Moss (Jenny MacDougald), William Newberry (Lachlan Sinclair), Jerold Teachey (Spokesman).

Taped December 2, 1963; telecast December 15, 1963, on North Carolina Educational Television. Clive L. Hewitt (director). Black and white. In English. 57 minutes.

Comment: The video appears to have been lost, but the soundtrack has survived and is on CD.

SOLDATEN, DIE
1965 opera by Zimmermann

BERND ALOIS ZIMMERMANN's controversial large-scale opera *Die Soldaten* (The Soldiers) uses film as an integral part of the production and features projection of scenes on three screens on the stage. Zimmermann wrote the antimilitaristic libretto himself, basing it on a 1776 play by Jakob Lenz. It tell a sad story of ruined innocence. Marie is engaged to the draper Stolzius but is seduced and humiliated by army officer Desportes. He later gives her to his servant, who rapes her; she ends up a whore and a beggar. *Die Soldaten,* which requires a large orchestra, incorporates several types of popular music in its score, from dance rhythms and jazz to electronic sound.

1989 Stuttgart Staatstheater
German stage production: Harry Kupfer (director), Bernhard Kontarsky (conductor, Stuttgart State Opera Orchestra and Chorus), Wolfgang Münzer (set/costume designer).

Cast: Nancy Shade (Marie), William Cochran (Desportes), Michael Ebbecke (Stolzius), Mark Munkittrick (Wesener), Milagro Vargas (Charlotte), Grace Hoffmann (Marie's grandmother).

Video: Arthaus (GB) DVD/Home Vision VHS. Hans Hulscher (director). Color. In German with English subtitles. 111 minutes.

SOLDIER'S TALE, THE
See L'HISTOIRE DU SOLDAT.

SOLO PER TE
1937 Italian film with opera content

In *Solo per te* (Only for You), Beniamino Gigli plays Ettore Vanni an opera singer married to a soprano (Maria Cebotari) with a secret past. That past catches up with her when baritone Michael Bohnen joins their opera company; he had seduced her before she met Gigli and she had a child. When he tries to start their affair again, she is afraid to tell her husband about it. One evening the baritone is found dead in the theater, and the wife is arrested for the crime. She turns out be innocent, however, as the real killer later confesses. The film begins with Gigli on stage in Boito's *Mefistofele*, spotlights a scene from *Andrea Chénier*, includes a sequence in which Gigli sings a duet with himself as both Don Giovanni and Zerlina in "Là ci darem la mano," and features the backstage murder during *Un ballo in maschera*. Carmine Gallone directed Italian and German versions of the film for Itala Film: the Italian version is *Solo per te,* and the German version is titled *Mutterlied*. Aldo De Benedetti wrote the Italian screenplay, Massimo Terzano was the cinematographer, and Alois Melichar was music director. Black and white. 86 minutes. In Italian or German. Bel Canto Society (in Italian with English subtitles) VHS.

SOLTI, GEORG
Hungarian/English conductor (1912–1997)

Sir Georg Solti, music director of Covent Garden from 1961 to 1971, helped it become one of the great opera houses of the world. He conducted his first opera in Budapest in 1938, but as he was Jewish, he thought it prudent to move to Switzerland after the arrival of the German Army. In the postwar period, he ran the Bavarian State Opera for six years and helped create its international reputation. He made his American debut with San Francisco Opera in 1953, made his first visit to the Metropolitan Opera in 1960, and helped raise the profile of the Chicago Symphony from 1969 on. Solti conducted the first complete recording of the *Ring* cycle, and there is a fascinating film showing how it was done. There are also documentaries about his career. See ARABELLA (1977), LUDWIG VAN BEETHOVEN (1994 film), BLUEBEARD'S CASTLE (1980), CONDUCTORS (1994), LA DAMNATION DE FAUST (1989), DIE ENTFÜHRUNG AUS DEM SERAIL (1987), EUGENE ONEGIN (1988), FALSTAFF (1979), DIE FRAU OHNE SCHATTEN (1992), HÄNSEL UND GRETEL (1981), MOZART REQUIEM (1991), LE NOZZE DI FIGARO (1980), OTELLO (1992), RIGOLETTO (1987 film), DER ROSENKAVALIER (1985), SIMON BOCCANEGRA (1991), RICHARD STRAUSS (1984), LA TRAVIATA (1994), and RICHARD WAGNER (1983/1998).

1965 The Golden Ring
Humphrey Burton's *The Golden Ring: The Making of Solti's "Ring"* is a BBC film about the creation of the classic Decca recording by Solti with the Vienna Philharmonic. See DER RING DES NIBELUNGEN.

1977 Solti Conducts Wagner
Solti leads the Chicago Symphony Orchestra in music from *The Flying Dutchman, Die Meistersinger, Tannhäuser,* and *Tristan und Isolde.* Telecast in the *Great Performances* series on March 1, 1977. Color. 60 minutes. Video at the Library of Congress.

1978 Portrait of Solti
Portrait of Solti is an excellent documentary about the conductor's life and musical career. It includes grim newsreel of German tanks rolling into his native Hungary at the beginning of World War II, the moment he decided to move elsewhere. The trio "Soave sia il vento" is heard on the soundtrack as ironic commentary. Among those interviewed are Hildegard Behrens, Wolfgang Wagner, and Isaac Stern. Valerie Pitts directed. Color and black and white. 73 minutes.

1979 Apocalypse Now
This is the most famous use of music conducted by Solti in a feature film. His Vienna Philharmonic recording of "The Ride of the Valkyries" from *Die Walküre* is heard in all its glory on the soundtrack as Robert Duvall leads a mad helicopter charge on the Vietcong. Francis Ford Coppola directed. Color. 150 minutes. Paramount VHS.

1990 The Maestro and the Diva
Solti was known for his love of the music of Richard Strauss, and he proves the ideal conductor for Kiri Te Kanawa at this Strauss concert in Manchester, England. He leads the BBC Philharmonic Orchestra, and the selections include the "Four Last Songs." Humphrey Burton directed the telecast. Color. 118 minutes.

1992 Sir Georg Solti
An English television salute to the conductor on his 80th birthday, made by the South Bank Show. It includes footage of his return to his native Hungary after 50 years. Color. 60 minutes.

1997 Georg Solti: The Making of a Maestro
Peter Maniura's documentary, finished just before the conductor's death at the age of 84, follows his career from his earliest years with personal and performance footage filmed in Budapest, Bavaria, London, and Chicago. Elijah Moshinsky and Peter Hall are among those interviewed. Made for the *Omnibus* TV series. Black and white and color. 93 minutes. Films for the Humanities & Sciences VHS/Arthaus (GB) DVD.

SONDHEIM, STEPHEN
American composer (1930–)

Stephen Sondheim has blurred the distinction between opera and musical by creating ambitious Broadway musicals of operatic scope and content. He insists that they should not be called Broadway operas, although many have been embraced by opera lovers; despite his protest, those staged in opera houses with screen versions are given entries in this book. The most operatic is the macabre SWEENEY TODD (1979), about a barber who turns people into meat pies. It features recurring motifs and complex ensembles, and has been staged by New York City Opera, Houston Grand Opera, Opera North in Leeds, and Finnish Opera. A LITTLE NIGHT MUSIC (1973), a classical waltz-based operetta in all but name, is based on an Ingmar Bergman movie about a weekend house party; it was filmed in 1973 and staged by New York City Opera in 1990. PASSION (1994), based on a film by Ettore Scola about love as obsession, was described by one admirer as the most important modern American opera. Leonard Bernstein's "American opera" WEST SIDE STORY (1957), a modern variation on the Romeo and Juliet story, features superb lyrics written by Sondheim at the beginning of his Broadway career; it has been recorded and staged with opera singers. Sondheim, a native New Yorker, learned his trade from two very different mentors, Oscar Hammerstein II and Milton Babbitt. He started out writing for television and then made his reputation writing the lyrics for *West Side Story* and *Gypsy*. His first solo show as composer and lyricist was *A Funny Thing Happened on the Way to the Forum* (1962), followed by *Anyone Can Whistle* (1964). His later shows, all stretching the boundaries of music theater, include *Company* (1970), *Follies* (1971), *Pacific Overtures* (1976), *Merrily We Roll Along* (1981), *Sunday in the Park With George* (1984), *Into the Woods* (1989), and *Assassins* (1991).

SONG OF SURRENDER
1949 American film with opera content

Enrico Caruso is the unseen but often heard focus of this film set in a small New England town in 1906. Wanda Hendrix, the young wife of puritanical Claude Raines, buys a newfangled gramophone at an auction, but the townspeople scorn it as the instrument of the devil. It comes with recordings of Caruso singing opera arias, and she immediately falls in love with his voice and opera music. When her husband forbids her to keep the gramophone, she gives it to a friend and listens to the recordings at night on a hilltop. One night a young lawyer (MacDonald Carey) hears the music, visits her, and they fall in love. The village deacon (Henry Hull) tells her husband that a shameless heathen has been singing on a hill every night, and he threatens to destroy the gramophone with an ax. When Carey sends her another Caruso recording, Raines smashes it and denounces her in church. She leaves him, and he has a mental breakdown. When she returns to the house, she finds him in a delirium listening to Caruso records and calling her name. She takes care of him until he dies, and she can be again with Carey. The Caruso recordings featured in the film are "Una furtiva lagrima" from Donizetti's *L'elisir d'amore*, "O paradiso" from Meyerbeer's *L'Africaine*, "La donna è mobile" from Verdi's *Rigoletto*, and Edoardo di Capua's song "O sole mio." Richard Maibaum wrote the screenplay, Daniel L. Fapp was the cinematographer, and Mitchell Leisen directed for Paramount. Black and white. 93 minutes.

SONG OF THE FLAME
1925 "romantic opera" by Gershwin and Stothart

Although advertised as a "romantic opera" when it opened on Broadway, this is actually GEORGE GERSHWIN's only Viennese-style operetta. It was a collaboration with composer Herbert Stothart and writers Otto Harbach and Oscar Hammerstein II, all of whom knew the genre well. The plot is an operetta-style story about the Russian Revolution that appears to have been modeled on the story of Zorro. A Russian woman disguises herself as The Flame and sings to incite the downtrodden to rebel against the Czarist government. Handsome Prince Volodya falls in love with her in this disguise; after the revolution turns sour, they find happiness together in Paris. Konstantin is a revolutionary who turns into the bad guy, and Natasha is The Flame's rival.

1930 First National film
American feature film: Alan Crosland (director), Gordon Rigby (screenplay), Leo Forbstein (music conductor/director), Lee Garmes (cinematographer), First National (studio).
Cast: Bernice Claire (Aniuta, The Flame), Alexander Gray (Prince Volodya), Alice Gentle (Natasha), Noah Beery (Konstantin), Bert Roach (Count Boris).
Technicolor. In English. 89 minutes.
Comment: This is believed to be a lost film.

1934 The Flame Song
American short film: Vitaphone abridged version of the operetta with four songs.
Cast: Bernice Claire (Aniuta, The Flame), J. Harold Murray (Prince Volodya).
Black and white. In English 20 minutes.

SONNAMBULA, LA
1831 opera by Bellini

Sleepwalking seems an unlikely subject for an opera today, but it was a common literary theme at the time VINCENZO BELLINI composed *La sonnambula* (The Sleepwalker). The libretto by Felice Romani, based on a Scribe play, tells of a charming, if somewhat naïve, young woman named Amina who sleepwalks into, and spends the night in, a man's room at an inn. It causes a scandal, and she almost loses her fiancé Elvino because of it. Amina's music, which has a lot of vocal pyrotechnics, has been a favorite of agile sopranos such as Maria Callas and Joan Sutherland. There are many silent films titled *The Somnambulist* but none inspired by the opera.

1949 Barlacchi film
Italian feature film: Cesare Barlacchi (director), Graziano Mucci (conductor, Rome Opera House Orchestra), Carlo Carlini (cinematographer), Lessicum Films (production).
Cast: Paola Bertini (Amina, sung by Fiorella Ortis), Gino Sinimberghi (Elvino, sung by Licinio Francardi), Alfredo Colella (Count Rodolfo), Franca Tamantini, Rosetta Riscica, Maruzio Lolli.

Video: VIEW/Lyric/Opera Dubs VHS. Black and white. In Italian with off-screen narration. 85 minutes.

1956 Lanfranchi film

Italian TV film: Mario Lanfranchi (director), Bruno Bartoletti (conductor, RAI Milan Orchestra and Chorus), Luca Crippa (set designer).

Cast: Anna Moffo (Amina), Danilo Vega (Elvino), Plinio Clabassi (Rodolfo), Gianna Galli (Lisa), Anne Maria Anelli (Teresa), Guido Massini, Giuseppe Nessi.

Video: VAI DVD/VIEW VHS. Black and white. In Italian. 122 minutes.

Related films

1942 La sonnambula

Bellini's love affair with a sleepwalker inspired *La sonnambula*. Anyway, that's what this Italian film claims, and the music is certainly by Bellini. It's loosely based on the relationship between Bellini and Giuditta Turina, the most famous of his lovers. It takes place at Lake Como where the composer was recovering from an illness in 1830, the year before the premiere of the opera. Roberto Villa plays Bellini, Germana Paolieri is Giuditta Turina, and Anita Farra is Giuditta Pasta, the singer who created Amina on stage. Piero Ballerini directed. Black and white. In Italian. 88 minutes.

1942 La donna è mobile

In *La donna è mobile*, tenor Ferruccio Tagliavini plays a school teacher with a great voice. On a visit to Rome, he is discovered as a singer and performs arias from *La bohème*, *La sonnambula*, *Lohengrin*, and *L'elisir d'amore*. Mario Mattoli directed.. Black and white. In Italian. 78 minutes.

1948 La terra trema

Luchino Visconti's epic film about the life of a poor Sicilian fisherman features Amina's disbelieving aria "Ah! Non credea mirarti" during a scene in which a large school of fish appear jumping up as a group. Black and white. In Italian. 160 minutes.

1962 The Leopard

Luchino Visconti obviously liked *La sonnambula* as he featured another appropriate aria from it in his epic film *Il Gattopardo*. It is also set in Sicily, but this time centers around a rich aristocrat, played by Burt Lancaster. The aria is "Vi ravvisco, o luoghi ameni," sung in the opera by Count Rudolfo as he reminiscences nostalgically about the good old days. Color. In Italian. 205 minutes.

SOPRANOS AND MEZZOS

There are a number of worthwhile films and videos about the great female singers and divas of today and yesterday, mostly sopranos but also mezzos and contraltos. In addition to those listed below, there are documentaries about those who sang in TOSCA *(I Live for Art)* and AIDA *(The Aida File)* and a remarkable gathering of great female singers on THE BELL TELEPHONE HOUR *(First Ladies of the Opera)*. One of the more popular fiction films centering on an opera singer is called DIVA.

1987 Le cinéma des divas

The Cinema of Divas is a compilation created from scenes in opera films featuring divas. It was put together for the Cannes Film Festival in 1987 when the festival mounted a series called *Cinéma & Opéra*. Color and black and white. 90 minutes.

1990 Donne e dive

Women and Divas is an Italian TV program showcasing three top women singers performing in Bologna in 1990: mezzo-soprano Marilyn Horne and sopranos Katia Ricciarelli and Daniela Dessi. Valery Gergiev conducts. Color. In Italian. 60 minutes. Lyric VHS.

1991 The Three Sopranos

Not to be bested by mere tenors, three sopranos (Renata Scotto, Ileana Cotrubas, and Elena Obraztsova) got together for their own concert at the Roman Amphitheater in Syracuse in Sicily in 1991. They sing arias and ensembles from *Pagliacci*, *Le villi*, *Samson et Dalila*, *La bohème*, *Un ballo in maschera*, *Les contes d'Hoffmann*, *Gianni Schicchi*, *Carmen*, *Der Fledermaus*, and *Aida*. Armando Krieger conducts the Czech Symphony Orchestra. Color. 67 minutes. Kultur VHS/Pioneer LD.

1991 Primadonna Belcanto Italiano

Eight Italian sopranos perform in the open air in St. Mark's Square in Venice on June 24, 1991. The setting is marvelous and the singing enjoyable. Regina Resnik introduces the divas. Renata Scotto sings "Bondi, cara Venezia" from *Il campiello*, Raina Kabaivanska sings "Io son l'umile ancella" from *Adriana Lecouvreur*, Daniela Dessi sings "Tu, che le vanità" from *Don Carlo*, Mariella Devia sings "Ardon gl'incensi" from *Lucia di Lammermoor*, Cecilia Gasdia sings "Al dolce guidami castel natio" from *Anna Bolena*, Katia Ricciarelli sings "Ebben...ne andrò lontana" from *La Wally*, Luciana Serra sings "Der Hölle Rache" from *Die Zauberflöte*, Lucia Valentini-Terrani sings "Les tringles des sistres tintaient" from *Carmen*, and all eight join voices on the Barcarolle from *Les contes d'Hoffmann*. Massimo Manni directed. Color. In Italian. 80 minutes. Ricordi (Italy)/ Lyric VHS.

1991 Queens From Caracalla

A gala concert of women opera singers arranged to mark the 50th anniversary of the opening of the 6,000-seat theater at the Baths of Caracalla in Rome. They include Marilyn Horne, Eva Marton, Cecilia Gasdia, Aprile Millo, Lucia Aliberti, Giusi Devinu, and Mariella Devia. Carlo Franci conducts the Rome Opera House Orchestra. Luigi Bonori directed the video. Color. 112 minutes. Lyric VHS.

1994 Restless in Thought, Disturbed in Mind

Mary Jane Walsh's documentary traces the history of women in opera. As female singers were not allowed by the Church, it was not until opera became an important art form that they could achieve status by singing. The film begins with Hildegard of Bingen and traces operatic women to the present. It examines the mad song, the lament, virtuosity, the diva, and why opera composers are fascinated by fallen women. Composer Judith Weir, director Francesca Zambello, and John Rosselli provide commentary while Emma Kirkby and Jane Manning perform staged sequences. Telecast on Channel 4 in England. Color. 60 minutes.

1995 Where Have All the Divas Gone?

Elijah Moshinsky investigates the phenomenon of the diva for the British TV series *Omnibus*, shown in England as *Where Have All the Divas Gone?* and in America simply as *Divas*. Moshinsky believes that the days of great divas are over because the toll on the personal lives of female singers is becoming too great. Appearing are Birgit Nilsson, Kiri Te Kanawa, Jessye Norman, Elisabeth Schwarzkopf, Dennis Marks, Jeremy Isaacs, and Kathleen Battle's chauffeur. Color. 60 minutes.

1998 Opera Fanatic: Stefan and the Divas

Stefan Zuckerman interviews 10 leading Italian sopranos and mezzos of the 1950s and 1960s in Italy in a fascinating documentary by Jan Schmidt-Garre. They are Iris Adami Corradetti, Fedora Barbieri, Anita Cerquetti, Gina Cigna (96 at the time), Gigliola Frazzoni, Carla Gavazzi, Leyla Gencer (Turkish-born, the only non-Italian), Magda Olivero, Marcella Pogge, and Giulietta Simionato. They discuss their work and demonstrate their techniques with performance footage. Color and black and white. In English and Italian with subtitles. 93 minutes. Bel Canto Society VHS.

SORCERER, THE

1877 comic opera by Gilbert and Sullivan

The Sorcerer or The Elixir of Love is one of the most entertaining of the GILBERT AND SULLIVAN operettas and has some of their most delightful patter songs. It tells the story of the sorcerer John Wellington Wells and a love

potion that goes wrong. Alexis and Aline are betrothed, Dr. Daly loves Aline, Constance is attracted to Dr. Daly, and Lady Sangazure has feelings about Sir Marmaduke. The elixir of love makes everyone fall for the wrong person, but sorcerer Wells is finally able to sort it all out in the end. His song "My Name Is John Wellington Wells" is deservedly famous.

1982 Gilbert and Sullivan Collection series

English studio production: Stephen Pimlott (director), Judith De Paul (producer), Alexander Faris (conductor, London Symphony Orchestra and Ambrosian Opera Chorus), Allan Cameron (set designer), George Walker (executive producer).

Cast: Clive Revill (John Wellington Wells), Nan Christie (Aline), David Kernan (Dr. Daly), Donald Adams (Sir Marmaduke Pointdexter), Alexander Oliver (Alexis), Nuala Willis (Lady Sangazure.)

Video: Pioneer LD/Braveworld (GB) VHS. Dave Heather (director). Color. In English. 119 minutes.

Related film

1999 Topsy-Turvy

Two numbers from *The Sorcerer* are featured in this Mike Leigh film about the relationship between Gilbert and Sullivan, "But Soft...Why, Where Be Oi?" and "Incantation." See TOPSY-TURVY.

SORCERESS, THE

1993 pastiche opera by Handel and Sweete

The Sorceress originated as an idea by Kiri Te Kanawa and Christopher Hogwood who wanted to make a video of HANDEL arias for the Rhombus Company. Barbara Willis Sweete suggested the idea of a pastiche opera rather than a concert and stitched together pieces of six Handel operas to create the new work. For the plot she inverted the story of ALCINA so the enchantress falls in love with the mortal knight Ruggiero who is betrothed to Bradamante. The opera has only one singing role, Alcina; the other characters only dance or mime. She sings seven Handel arias, including "Ombre pallide" from *Alcina,* "V'adoro pupille" from *Giulio Cesare,* and "Bel piacere" from *Agrippina.*

1993 Sweete film

Canadian film: Barbara Willis Sweete (director), Christopher Hogwood (conductor, Academy of Ancient Music), Jeannette Zingg and Ed Wubbe (choreographers), Rhombus (production).

Cast: Kiri Te Kanawa (Alcina), Andrew Kelley (Ruggiero), Jeannette Zingg (Bradamante), Scapino Ballet of Rotterdam, Opera Atelier of Toronto.

Video: Philips VHS. Color. In English and Italian. 51 minutes.

SO THIS IS LOVE
1953 American film with opera content

Kathryn Grayson plays Metropolitan Opera soprano Grace Moore in this glossy film biography that begins and finishes at the Metropolitan Opera. It opens with her arriving at the Met for her debut as Mimì in *La bohème* and remembering her first visit, when she wished she could get closer to the stage. The rest of the film is flashback starting with her childhood dreams. On a school visit to Washington, she meets Mary Garden (Mabel Albertson) and sings her the "Waltz Song" from *Roméo et Juliette*. Garden encourages her. A year later she is a guest singer at a John McCormack (Ray Kellogg) recital, but her performance is interrupted by news of the end of World War I. She begins to work in musical comedy and is a hit with the "Kiss Waltz" in a nightclub, but then she loses her voice. She regains it after six months with the help of Dr. P. Mario Marafioti (Fortunio Bonanova), who starts her road to recovery with "Voi che sapete" from *Le nozze di Figaro*. She returns to musical comedy and becomes a Broadway star. However, she still dreams of singing opera so when she meets Mary Garden again with Met director Otto Kahn (Roy Gordon), she decides to audition for the Met. Kahn and Met general manager Giulio Gatti-Casazza (Mario Siletti) like her voice but tell her it is not quite right for opera. She goes to France with Garden to study and returns two years later to make her Met debut in *La bohème*. After she sings "Mi chiamano Mimì," she gets a standing ovation. John Monks Jr. wrote the screenplay based on Moore's 1944 autobiography *You're Only Human Once*, LeRoy Prinz staged and directed the musical numbers, Ray Heindorf conducted the music, and Gordon Douglas directed for Warner Bros. Aka *The Grace Moore Story*. Technicolor. In English. 101 minutes.

SOUND OF MUSIC, THE
1959 "American operetta" by Rodgers and Hammerstein

RICHARD RODGERS and OSCAR HAMMERSTEIN's "American operetta" *The Sound of Music* has become popular with opera singers and may enter the opera repertory. Set in Austria in 1938, it tells the story of novice Maria sent by the abbess of her convent to be governess to the seven children of wealthy landowner Capt. Von Trapp. She teaches the children to sing and marries their father, but they have to flee the country when the Nazis arrive. Howard Lindsay and Russell Crouse's libretto, with lyrics by Hammerstein, is based on Maria Von Trapp's autobiography *The Trapp Family Singers*.

1965 Twentieth Century-Fox film
American feature film: Robert Wise (director), Ernest Lehman (screenplay), Ted McCord (cinematographer), Irwin Costal (music director), Twentieth Century-Fox (studio).

Cast: Julie Andrews (Maria), Christopher Plummer (Capt. Von Trapp, sung by Bill Lee), Peggy Wood (Abbess, sung by Margery McKay), Charmian Carr (Liesl), Eleanor Parker (Elsa).

Video: Twentieth Century-Fox DVD/VHS. Color. In English. 172 minutes.

Comment: The hugely popular film won five Oscars, including Best Picture and Best Director. The opening mountaintop sequence has become a cinematic icon.

SOUTH PACIFIC
1949 "American operetta" by Rodgers and Hammerstein

It may not be an opera but Metropolitan Opera basses have sung the lead of this RICHARD RODGERS and OSCAR HAMMERSTEIN II musical on stage and on film, and it has been performed in concert by Kiri Te Kanawa and José Carreras. Ezio Pinza played French planter Emile de Becque in the original Broadway production, and Giorgio Tozzi sang the role in the film version and the 1967 Lincoln Center stage production. The book of *South Pacific*, written by Hammerstein in collaboration with Joshua Logan, is based on stories in James Michener's *Tales of the South Pacific*. It centers around two cross-cultural love affairs, an eventually happy one between de Becque and nurse Nellie Forbush, and a tragic one between Lt. Joe Cable and Polynesian Liat.

1958 Twentieth Century-Fox film
American feature film: Joshua Logan (director), Paul Osborn (screenplay), Leon Shamroy (cinematographer, in Todd AO), Alfred Newman (conductor/music director), LeRoy Prinz (choreographer), Magna Theatre Corporation/Twentieth Century-Fox (production).

Cast: Rossano Brazzi (Emile de Becque), sung by Giorgio Tozzi), Mitzi Gaynor (Nellie Forbush), John Kerr (Lt. Cable, sung by Bill Lee), France Nuyen (Liat), Juanita Hall (Bloody Mary, sung by Muriel Smith), Ray Walston (Luther).

Video: Twentieth Century-Fox DVD/VHS. Color. In English. 151 minutes.

Comment: Logan, who directed the musical on Broadway, shot much of the film in Kauai and the Fiji Islands. Unfortunately, it still looks studio-made and surprisingly garish.

1986 South Pacific: The London Sessions
English concert performance: Jonathan Tunich (conductor, London Symphony Orchestra).

Cast: José Carreras (Emile de Becque), Kiri Te Kanawa (Nellie Forbush), Sarah Vaughan (Bloody Mary), Mandy Patinkin (Lt. Cable).

Video: Twentieth Century-Fox VHS. Color. In English. 60 minutes.

Comment: This production has few admirers. Carreras sings the bass role of de Beque with the music transposed up, and Te Kanawa sings Forbush with skill but not much character.

2001 Disney TV film

American TV film: Richard Pearce (director), Lawrence D. Cohen (screenplay), Stephen F. Windon (cinematographer), Walt Disney (studio).

Cast: Rade Sherbedgia (Emile de Becque), Glenn Close (Nellie Forbush), Harry Connick Jr. (Lt. Cable), Lori Tan Chinn (Bloody Mary), Natalie Mendoza (Liat), Robert Pastorelli (Billis).

Video: Buena Vista DVD/VHS. Color. In English. 129 minutes.

Comment: Heavily adapted version filmed in Australia.

SPOLETO

The Festival dei Due Mondi (Festival of Two Worlds) was created by Gian Carlo Menotti in the small town of Spoleto, Italy, in 1958, and expanded in 1977 to include a counterpart in Charleston, North Carolina. It takes place annually in June and July and often revolves around new opera productions. Luchino Visconti staged important productions at the festival, and its artistic directors have included Thomas Schippers and Romolo Valli. The American version is no longer connected with Menotti, but the Italian festival is still held under his supervision.

1959 Ed Sullivan in Spoleto

Ed Sullivan hosted a program from the Festival of Two Worlds in July 1959 with interviews with Menotti and participants and scenes from productions. Eileen Farrell sings "Pace, pace, mio Dio" from *La forza del destino* and joins Louis Armstrong's band to sing "On the Sunny Side of the Street". Bob Precht directed. Black and white. 60 minutes. Video at the MTR.

1966 Festival of Two Worlds

Bell Telephone Hour TV special shot at the Festival of Two Worlds in Italy. Menotti explains his ideas about the festival and philosophizes about the arts. The musical excerpts include a scene from *Pelléas et Mélisande* with Shirley Verrett, Judith Blegen, and John Reardon. Thomas Schippers, Zubin Mehta, and Sviatoslav Richter make appearances. Robert Drew directed. Color. In English. 60 minutes.

1983 Festival! Spoleto, USA

A survey of events held during Menotti's seventh annual festival in Charleston. There are scenes from his production of Samuel Barber's *Antony and Cleopatra*, chamber music selections, bits of jazz, and views of sculptures. Kirk Browning directed the telecast on June 27, 1983. Color. 60 minutes.

SPONTINI, GASPARE
Italian composer (1774–1851)

Although Gaspare Spontini was an Italian composer, he made his reputation in France through the patronage of the Empress Josephine. His grand opera *La vestale* (1807) was his biggest success and was very popular during most of the 19th century. It was said to be a major influence on Berlioz and Wagner. Many of Spontini's operas are on CD, including *La vestale* and *Olympie,* but they are not often found on video in the stage repertory. The only one currently on video is his 1829 Italian historical opera AGNESE DI HOHENSTAUFEN, which was staged in Rome with Montserrat Caballé and telecast.

STAR FELL FROM HEAVEN, A
1936 English film with opera content

Diminutive German tenor Josef Schmidt plays a singer who dubs the voice of a movie star who has lost his voice. He sings opera arias and popular songs and is a big hit, although his identity is not at first revealed. The truth comes out at the premiere of the film, however, and Schmidt is recognized as the real star. The plot is not all that different from *Singin' in the Rain* except that Schmidt loses the woman he loves (Florine McKinney) to the movie star. The supporting cast includes Billy Milton, George Graves, and W. H. Berry. Ronald Neame was cinematographer; Marjorie Deans, Val Guest, Dudley Leslie, Jack Davies, Gerald Elliott, and Geoffrey Kerr wrote the screenplay; and Paul Merzbach directed. The film was shot in Vienna after Josef Schmidt had to leave Germany because he was Jewish. It was also made in a German-language version, *Ein Stern fällt vom Himmel,* with Max Neufeld directing. That version was banned in Germany. Black and white. 70 minutes. Bel Canto Society VHS (in German with English subtitles).

STARS OVER BROADWAY
1935 American film with opera content

James Melton plays a hotel porter with such a good voice that manager Pat O'Brien decides to make him into an opera star. After training, he auditions at the Met with "Celeste Aida" and wins approval. O'Brien, however, is impatient to earn money, so he diverts him into crooning in clubs and on radio. In the end, Melton returns to opera and makes his debut at the Met in *Aida*. He also sings "M'apparì" from *Martha* and popular songs. His singing costar in the film is Jane Froman, who, like him, had become popular on radio. After this film, Melton began to study opera seriously and made his real-life debut at the Met in 1942 as Tamino. Ray Heindorf was music director of the film, Busby Berkeley and Bobby Connolly directed the music numbers, Jerry Wald and Julius J. Epstein wrote the screenplay, George Barnes was cinematographer, and William Keighley directed for Warner Bros. Black and white. 89 minutes.

STEBER, ELEANOR
American soprano (1916–1990)

Eleanor Steber was one of the pillars of the Metropolitan Opera when she sang there from 1940 to 1966. She began her career at the Met as Sophie in *Der Rosenkavalier*, was much admired in Mozart, starred in the American premiere of several operas, and created the title role in Samuel Barber's *Vanessa*. In later years she also sang in musical comedy. Steber was one of the most popular stars on *The Voice of Firestone* TV series and appeared on it 36 times; she is featured in six Firestone videos, including one with Leonard Warren. Steber is undervalued today, but her status as one of the great American sopranos is evident on the small screen. See DER ROSENKAVALIER (1949), DER SCHAUSPIELDIREKTOR (1961), and LEONARD WARREN (1949).

1950–1954 Eleanor Steber in Opera & Oratorio
One of six videos featuring Steber on The Voice of Firestone television series. She sings arias from Le nozze di Figaro, Manon, La bohème, Otello, Lohengrin, Pagliacci, La traviata, and Tosca plus music from Handel's Messiah and Rossini's Stabat Mater. Black and white. 65 minutes. VAI VHS.

1949–1952 Eleanor Steber in Opera & Song
The second of *The Voice of Firestone* Steber videos features selections from *Louise, Naughty Marietta, Le nozze di Figaro* ("Dove sono" and "Porgi amor"), and *La forza del destino* plus songs by Rodgers and Hammerstein, Herbert, Weill, and Porter. Black and white. 50 minutes. VAI VHS.

1950–1954 Eleanor Steber in Opera & Song 2
The third selection of Steber appearances on The Voice of Firestone television series. She sings arias from Ernani, Madama Butterfly, Die Fledermaus, Porgy and Bess, and The Chocolate Soldier. There are also ensembles from Rigoletto, Faust, and Lucia di Lammermoor with Risë Stevens, Jerome Hines, Thomas L. Thomas, Brian Sullivan, and Robert Rounseville. Black and white. 50 minutes. VAI VHS.

1950–1952 Eleanor Steber Sings Love Songs
The fourth *Voice of Firestone* selection of Steber appearances on the TV program features her in popular love songs composed by Kern, Rodgers and Hammerstein, Porter, Herbert, Coward, and Oscar Straus. Black and white. 55 minutes. VAI VHS.

1950–1957 Christmas with Eleanor Steber
This seasonal video features highlights from three of Steber's *Voice of Firestone* Christmas telecasts. She sings "Silent Night," "White Christmas," "The First Noël," "Deck the Halls," "Joy to the World," and Mozart's *Alleluia*. Howard Barlow and Wilfrid Pelletier conduct. Black and white. 30 minutes. VAI VHS.

STEIN, GERTRUDE
American librettist/playwright/poet (1874–1946)

Gertrude Stein was muse to generations of artists, musicians, and writers from her home in Paris and contributed mightily to the growth of American opera with her librettos. The most famous is FOUR SAINTS IN THREE ACTS (1934), one of the foundations of modern American opera, created in collaboration with composer Virgil Thomson. Stein's second libretto for Thomson, THE MOTHER OF US ALL (1947), is a pageant opera revolving around 19th-century American feminist leader Susan B. Anthony. Both operas are beginning to enter the repertory. Stein was the center of an artistic salon in Paris with her lifetime companion Alice B. Toklas. Her influence on writers and artists was as important as her involvement in music and opera. Many of her plays have been used as opera librettos by modern composers.

1970 Gertrude Stein: When This You See, Remember Me
"When this you see, remember me" is a line sung by the chorus in the final scene of *Four Saints in Three Acts*. Perry Miller Adato's excellent documentary film traces Stein's life and career from her childhood in California to her glory days in Paris and explores her position as writer, librettist, and muse to Picasso, Cocteau, Eliot, Hemingway, and others. The important role of her life companion Alice B. Toklas is amply demonstrated. Virgil Thomson, interviewed in Stein's French country house, talks about their fruitful collaboration. Color. 89 minutes. Meridian VHS.

STEVENS, RISË
American mezzo-soprano (1913–)

Risë Stevens sang *Carmen* 124 times with the Metropolitan Opera, so it's not surprising that an aria from it turns up in all of her movies, but it was her *Carmen* aria in *Going My Way* that identified her with the role before she sang it on an American stage. Stevens, who was born in New York City, studied at Juilliard and in Europe before making her debut in Prague in 1936. She became a Met singer in 1938 and appeared there regularly until 1961. She made her farewell to opera in 1961 in *Carmen*, sang in *The King and I* at Lincoln Center in 1964, and then joined the management side of the Met. Stevens made only a few movies, but *Going My Way* was so popular it made her a cultural icon. She was by far the most popular guest on *The Voice of Firestone* television series, performing on it 47 times. See CARMEN (1952), THE CHOCOLATE SOLDIER (1941/1955), HÄNSEL UND GRETEL (1958), SOL HUROK (1956), DER ROSENKAVALIER (1949), and ELEANOR STEBER (1950).

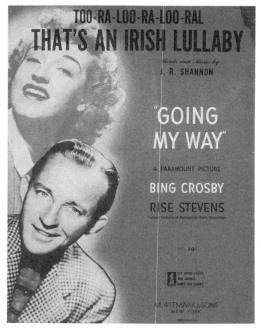

Risë Stevens's first public performance as Carmen was in the 1945 film *Going My Way*. Sheet music shows her and Crosby.

1944 Going My Way

Bing Crosby, playing a priest who needs to raise money for his church, goes to the Metropolitan Opera to ask for help from old friend Genevieve Linden (Risë Stevens). He watches from backstage as she sings the "Habanera" from *Carmen*, after which she agrees to take Crosby's choir (played by the Robert Mitchell Boys' Choir) on tour to raise the needed funds. It was Stevens's husband's idea that she should sing an aria from *Carmen* in the film, although she had not yet appeared in it on the American stage. She also sings Schubert's "Ave Maria" and the title song in duet with Crosby. *Going My Way* won seven Os-

cars, including Best Picture. Leo McCarey wrote and directed it for Paramount. Black and white. In English. 126 minutes. Paramount VHS.

1947 Carnegie Hall

Stevens is one of the stars of this pleasant musical that is basically just a fiction framework for performances by classical musicians. She sings arias from *Carmen* and *Samson et Dalila*. See CARNEGIE HALL.

1951/1954 Risë Stevens in Opera & Song

The first Stevens video from *The Voice of Firestone* television series is taken from programs telecast in 1951 and 1954. She sings three arias from *Carmen* plus songs by Schumann, Schubert, Berlin, Kern, and others. Black and white. 45 minutes. VAI VHS.

1951–1962 Risë Stevens in Opera & Song 2

The second video from *The Voice of Firestone* TV series features Stevens in performances telecast over 11 years from 1951 to 1962. She sings arias from *Samson et Dalila*, *Le nozze di Figaro,* and *Carmen* and songs by Debussy, Rachmaninoff, Stolz, Herbert, and Rodgers and Hammerstein. Black and white. 50 minutes. VAI VHS.

1953 Toast to the Met

Ed Sullivan devoted his CBS show to the Met on November 8, 1953, telecasting from the opera house stage. Stevens is one of the stars shown in rehearsal and performance. See METROPOLITAN OPERA.

1956 Producers' Showcase

Stevens sings the Card Aria from *Carmen* in this all-star television festival of opera singers produced by impresario Sol Hurok. See PRODUCERS' SHOWCASE.

STIFFELIO
1850 opera by Verdi

GIUSEPPE VERDI's *Stiffelio*, libretto by Francesco Maria Piave based on a French play, is a tale about adultery in a religious community in 19th-century Austria. Stiffelio is a devout minister whose wife Lina has been having an affair with a libertine nobleman named Raffaele. When her father Stankar discovers this, he challenges Raffaele to a duel. Stiffelio stops the duel but learns of his wife's unfaithfulness and has to confront her. Raffaele is killed by Stankar, but in a church service the minister and his congregation voice forgiveness for all.

1993 Royal Opera

English stage production: Elijah Moshinsky (director), Edward Downes (conductor, Royal Opera

House Orchestra and Chorus), Michael Yeargan (set designer), Peter J. Hall (costume designer).

Cast: José Carreras (Stiffelio), Catherine Malfitano (Lina), Gregory Yurisich (Stankar), Robin Leggate (Raffaele), Gwynne Howell (Jorg).

Video: Kultur and Bel Canto Society DVD/Home Vision VHS/Pioneer LD. Brian Large (director). Color. In Italian with English subtitles. 123 minutes.

Comment: The setting is changed to a 19th-century American frontier community in Nebraska, with sets and costumes inspired by John Ford films.

1993 Metropolitan Opera

American stage production: Giancarlo Del Monaco (director), James Levine (conductor, Metropolitan Opera Orchestra and Chorus), Michael Scott (set/costume designer).

Cast: Plácido Domingo (Stiffelio), Sharon Sweet (Lina), Vladimir Chernov (Stankar), Peter Ribert (Raffaele), Paul Plishka (Jorg).

DG VHS/LD. Taped November 13, 1993; telecast December 27, 1993. Brian Large (director). Color. In Italian with English subtitles. 130 minutes.

STILL, WILLIAM GRANT
American composer (1895–1978)

William Grant Still was the first African-American opera composer to win wide recognition, and his *Troubled Island* was the first African-American opera to be staged by a major company. Still studied at Oberlin, worked with Paul Whiteman, and first became known for his 1930 *Afro-American Symphony*. He began to compose operas in collaboration with librettist Verna Arvey, whom he later married. Three of his operas were staged in his lifetime: *Troubled Island* was produced at New York City Opera in 1949, *Highway No. 1 USA* was presented in Florida in 1963, and *A Bayou Legend* was produced in Mississippi in 1974. Opera South's production of A BAYOU LEGEND was telecast by Opera South in 1981, and *Minette Fontaine* was staged in Louisiana in 1985.

STOCKHAUSEN, KARLHEINZ
German composer (1928–)

Karlheinz Stockhausen, a leading figure of the modern German avant-garde, did not begin to compose opera until 1977 when he started an ambitious cycle of seven operas. They have the collective title of *Licht: Die sieben Tage der Woche* (Light: The Seven Days of the Week). *Donnerstag aus Licht* (Thursday From Light) has been telecast in England and Italy and there is a video about *Monday*.

1988 Montag aus Light

Thomas Letocha and Henning Lohner's film is a documentary about the staging of Stockhausen's opera *Monday From Light* at La Scala in Milan in May 1988. It shows how the production was set up and how Stockhausen supervised the work of director Michael Bodanov. Scenes from the premiere are included. Color. In English or German. 28 minutes. Inter Nationes VHS.

STOLZ, ROBERT
Austrian composer (1880–1975)

Robert Stolz, great nephew of Verdi's soprano friend Theresa Stolz, was the last purveyor of the traditional Viennese operetta style. He described himself as "the last of the waltz kings" and composed in a style long out of fashion in much of the world. His popularity, however, remained high in German-speaking countries, where he was also a celebrity conductor. Stolz was music director of Vienna's Theater an der Wien in the golden age of operetta, and he conducted the premieres of works by Lehár, Kálmán, Straus, and Fall. He himself wrote more than 65 stage operettas and a number of film operettas. His 1909 operetta DIE LUSTIGEN WEIBER VON WIEN was made into a German film in 1931, and he was also an important contributor to the operetta *The White Horse Inn* (IM WEISSEN RÖSSL). His most popular operettas, however, originated as films. The 1930 ZWEI HERZEN IN DREIVIERTELTAKT (Two Hearts in 3/4 Time), starring opera soprano Irene Eisinger, was a huge international success; he later turned it into a stage operetta. His 1934 FRÜHJAHRSPARADE, the basis of the Deanna Durbin film *Spring Parade*, was also transmuted into a stage operetta. Stolz worked in the United States from 1940 to 1946 where he composed songs and for films and staged two Broadway operettas. His operettas continue to be telecast in Austria, and his 1955 film operetta *Die Deutschmeister* with Romy Schneider remains popular on video.

1967 Mein Leben, Meine Lieder: Robert Stolz

My Life, My Songs: Robert Stolz is an Austrian TV tribute to the grand old man of Viennese operetta, a lavish full-scale portrait tracing his career with music, singers and dancers, clips from films, and interviews with Stolz and his wife. His famous waltz "Two Hearts in Three-Quarter Time" is used as the theme music. Martin Jente produced, and Alexis Neve directed. Color. In German. 105 minutes.

1990 Robert Stolz Gala

Viennese television tribute to the music of Stolz with top singers presenting his best-known melodies. The performers include Marta Eggerth, Nicolai Gedda, Andrea Huber, Ulrike Steinsky, Michael Helteau, and Frank Odjidja. Siegried Koehler conducts the orchestra. Color. In German. 60 minutes. Lyric VHS.

STONE GUEST, THE
1872 opera by Dargomizhsky

ALEXANDER DARGOMIZHSKY's opera *Kamenyi Gost* (The Stone Guest) is a variation on the Don Giovanni story. An Alexander Pushkin poem, inspired by the first production of Mozart's *Don Giovanni* in St. Petersburg, is used as the libretto. Don Giovanni is banished for killing the Commander, but he returns with Leporello under an assumed name to see the actress Laura. He falls in love with Donna Anna, the Commander's widow, whom he meets in the cemetery in front of the Commander's statue. The statue is invited to Anna's house where it seizes the Don and takes him to Hell. *The Stone Guest* is Dargomizhsky's best-known opera, although it is rarely staged in the West.

1967 Atlantov film
Russian feature film: Vladimir Gorikker (director and screenplay) Andrei Donatov (screenplay), Leonid Kosmatov (cinematographer), Boris Khaikin (conductor).
Cast: Vladimir Atlantov (Don Giovanni), Irina Pechernikova (Donna Anna, sung by Tamara Milashkina), Yevgeny Lebedev (Leporello, sung by Alexander Vedernikov), Larissa Trembovelskaya (Laura, sung by Tamara Sinyavskaya), Arthur Eisen (Monk).
Video: House of Opera DVD and VHS/Lyric and Opera Dubs VHS. Color. In Russian. 83 minutes.

STORCHIO, ROSINA
Italian soprano (1872–1945)

Rosina Storchio created the role of Madama Butterfly at Teatro alla Scala on February 17, 1904, but it was a disaster. The opera was hissed, and she vowed never to sing the role again. Puccini revised the opera and it became a success, but without Storchio. The Venice-born soprano, who also created roles in operas by Leoncavallo (*La bohème* and *Zazà*), Giordano (*Siberia*), and Mascagni (*Lodoletta*), was one of the most popular singers of her time, singing around the world, including New York and Chicago. She sang the revised *Madama Butterfly* only once, in Rome in 1920, but she also acted in a film featuring the opera.

1917 Come morì Butterfly
Storchio plays a famous opera singer in love with a poet in the Italian film *How Butterfly Died.* When he is stolen from her by her glamorous sister, she kills herself on stage during a performance of *Madama Butterfly.* See COME MORÌ BUTTERFLY.

STOTHART, HERBERT
American composer (1895–1949)

Herbert Stothart is not as well known as he should be, considering the important contributions he made to stage operettas and Hollywood film music. He collaborated with George Gershwin on the operetta SONG OF THE FLAME, with Emmerich Kálmán on the operetta GOLDEN DAWN, and with Rudolf Friml on the operetta ROSE-MARIE. He was also music director of the 1936 film version of Rose-Marie, to which he added bits of *Tosca* and *Roméo et Juliette*. He wrote songs for the Franz Lehár operetta film THE ROGUE SONG (1930), based on ZIGEUNERLIEBE, and adapted Lehár's music for Lubitsch's film of THE MERRY WIDOW (1934). He adapted music from *Il trovatore* and *Pagliacci* for A NIGHT AT THE OPERA (1935), and he arranged a stage production of EUGENE ONEGIN in *Anna Karenina* (1935). He was music director on the opera-oriented *San Francisco* (1936), and he worked on all the JEANETTE MACDONALD and NELSON EDDY operetta films. He composed an imaginary opera called *Czarita* for MAYTIME (1937). His score for *Camille* (1937) is based entirely on themes from LA TRAVIATA. He was nominated for 12 Oscars for scoring films and won for *The Wizard of Oz.* See THE CHOCOLATE SOLDIER (1941), LA FANCIULLA DEL WEST (1938 film), THE FIREFLY (1937), THE NEW MOON (1940), and SWEETHEARTS (1938).

STRADA, LA
1982 screen opera by Kaslík

Czech composer VÁCLAV KASLÍK based his opera *La Strada* on Federico Fellini's 1954 Academy Award–winning Italian film *La Strada* starring Anthony Quinn as a brutal strongman and Giulietta Masina as simple-minded Gelsomina. Kaslík's opera casts Zampano as a bass-baritone and Gelsomina as a soprano. The opera, which has spoken dialogue like a singspiel, was first staged in Prague in 1982 but does not appear to have been filmed or televised. The film screenplay, also nominated for an Oscar, was written by Fellini in collaboration with Tullio Pinelli and Ennio Flaiano. The *La Strada* film was also the inspiration for an 1969 Broadway musical composed by Lionel Bart.

STRATAS, TERESA
Canadian soprano (1938–)
Teresa Stratas, one of the finest singing actresses of our time, was born Anastasia Stratakis in Canada of Greek parents. She made her debut in 1958 in Toronto with the

Canadian Opera in the role of Mimì and sang at the Met the following year in a small role in *Manon*. She was soon a regular at the Met and at opera houses in Europe. Stratas created the role of Marie Antoinette in THE GHOSTS OF VERSAILLES at the Met in 1991, and she celebrated 35 years on the Met stage when she opened the 1994–1995 season. Stratas began making films as early as 1961, including some excellent operettas. Her acting ability is notable in Zeffirelli's films of LA TRAVIATA (1982) and PAGLIACCI (1982), Friedrich's film of SALOME (1974), and Brown's film of AMAHL AND THE NIGHT VISITORS (1978). She has also been popular singing KURT WEILL, starring in productions of AUFSTIEG UND FALL DER STADT MAHAGONNY (1979) and DIE SIEBEN TODSÜNDEN (1993). See THE BARTERED BRIDE (1975/1978), BELL TELEPHONE HOUR (1959–1966), LA BOHÈME (1982), COSÌ FAN TUTTE (1988), EUGENE ONEGIN (1968), GIUDITTA (1970), THE KAISER VON ATLANTIS (1978), LULU (1979), METROPOLITAN OPERA (1986), PAGANINI (1972), PAGLIACCI (1978/1994), LA RONDINE (1970), IL TABARRO (1994), and DER ZAREWITSCH (1973).

1961 The Canadians

Teresa Stratas's first movie was this American-style Canadian Western. The plot is basically pitting the Mounties against the Sioux. Robert Ryan and John Dehner are the stars, and Burt Kennedy directed. Color. 85 minutes.

1983 Stratosphere: A Portrait of Teresa Stratas

In Harry Rasky's documentary film, Stratas talks candidly about her early life in Toronto, her ties to her Crete heritage, and her rise to success. There is archival footage of rehearsals with Franco Zeffirelli at the Met and clips from performances of *Salome, Der Zarewitsch,* and *La bohème*. Stratas's quality as singer and actress is amply demonstrated. CBC. Color. In English. 90 minutes. Kultur VHS.

1995 Under the Piano

Stratas plays Regina Basilio, a faded but still vain and ambitious former opera singer who refuses to acknowledge that her autistic daughter (Megan Follows) has exceptional musical talent. Amanda Plummer plays her protective older sister. It is not a very sympathetic role for Stratas, but she does it well. Stefan Scaini directed. Color. 92 minutes. Sullivan VHS.

STRAUS, OSCAR

Austrian composer (1870–1954)

Oscar Straus wrote cheerful, enjoyable operettas in the Viennese style that remain surprisingly popular. They have also attracted great interest from opera singers, although most of them have not entered the opera house

repertory. Straus was born in Vienna and wrote his operettas in German, but he had some of his biggest successes in translations in other countries. *Der Tapfere Soldat,* based on Shaw's play *Arms and the Man,* was not very successful in Europe, but it was a major hit in New York in its English-language version as THE CHOCOLATE SOLDIER. *Drei Wälzer* had its greatest success in Paris in its French incarnation as TROIS VALSES. HOCHZEIT IN HOLLYWOOD was the first European operetta to be made into a sound film in Hollywood and was a hit as *Married in Hollywood*. EIN FRAU, DI WEISS, WAS SIE WILL was popular on stage in London as *Mother of Pearl*. Straus, who settled in Hollywood for a time, also composed music for films and had a surprise hit at the age of 80 with his theme tune for the 1950 film *La ronde*. See DER LETZTE WALZER, RICHARD TAUBER (1936), and EIN WALZERTRAUM.

1950 La ronde

Straus gained renewed fame around the world with his memorable theme music for this superb Max Ophuls film. Based on an Arthur Schnitzler play, it's a cynical story about the way love (or sex) goes around in a circle. The all-star cast includes Anton Walbrook (who plays many roles and sings the theme tune), Isa Miranda, and Simone Signoret. Straus wrote the music when he was 80. Black and white. In French. 97 minutes.

STRAUSS, JOHANN

Austrian composer (1825–1899)

Waltz King Johann Strauss Jr. is also the king of Viennese operetta, and his DIE FLEDERMAUS is now welcome in most of the great opera houses of the world. There are few more enjoyable experiences than a really good *Fledermaus*, especially with the accepted practice of stars appearing as guests in the Act II party scene. Equally admirable, although not as well known, are DER ZIGEUNERBARON, which became a role model for operetta writers, and the Venetian entertainment EINE NACHT IN VENEDIG. Strauss, who wrote 16 operettas, essentially established the form of the Viennese operetta. There is also a pastiche operetta of Strauss melodies, the popular WIENER BLUT. Strauss and his father, who together created the waltz as we know it, have been the subject of many films; the major ones are listed below. None can be described as genuine biography, but they are usually quite entertaining. See OPERETTE and TROIS VALSES.

1925 Ein Walzer vom Strauss

A Waltz From Strauss is an Austrian film, the first film biography of the Waltz King. Johann Strauss, nephew of the composer, plays his uncle in the film. He also conducted the orchestra that played Strauss music at the film's premieres in Vienna and London. Max Neufeld directed and Otto Kreisler supervised for Helios Film. Black and white. Silent. About 70 minutes.

1929 Heut spielt der Strauss
Strauss, the Waltz King is a German film starring Imre Raday as Strauss. The plot is based around the rivalry between father and son and the eventual triumph of young Strauss; this was to become the basic plot of most Strauss film biographies. The cast includes Alfred Abel as Strauss Sr., Hermione Sterler, and Lillian Ellis. Robert Wiene wrote the screenplay and Conrad Wiene directed. Black and white. 84 minutes.

1930 Der Walzerkönig
The Waltz King is a German film biography starring Hans Stuwe as Strauss with a supporting cast Claire Rommer, Ida Wust, and Viktor Janson. Manfred Noa directed. Black and white. In German. 88 minutes.

1931 A Waltz From Strauss
Gustav Frölich plays Strauss in the German film *So Lang noch ein Walzer vom Strauss Erklingt,* known in English as *A Waltz From Strauss.* Hans Junkermann is father Strauss attempting to stop his son from following in his waltzing footsteps; Julia Serda is mother Strauss; and Maria Paudler as the young sweetheart. Conrad Wiene directed. Black and white. In German. 88 minutes.

1932 Johann Strauss, Hofballmusikdirektor
German film starring bass-baritone Michael Bohnen as Strauss with a score based on waltzes such as "Wiener Blut." The cast includes Gretl Theimer, Lee Parry, and Paul Hörbiger. Conrad Wiene directed. The film was released in America as *Wiener Blut.* Black and white. In German. 99 minutes.

1934 Waltzes From Vienna
Esmond Knight plays Strauss in Alfred Hitchcock's film of a 1931 London stage musical. It is based on the 1930 Vienna pastiche operetta *Walzer aus Wien,* created by Erich Wolfgang Korngold before he went to Hollywood. It tells the traditional story of a father-son musical feud, with young Strauss being helped to fame by Resi (Jessie Mathews) and Countess Baranskaja (Fay Compton). It was shown in America as *Strauss's Great Waltz.* Gaumont-British. Black and white. In English. 81 minutes.

1938 The Great Waltz
The London stage musical *Waltzes From Vienna* came to Broadway in 1934 in a revision by Moss Hart called *The Great Waltz.* MGM turned it into a film in 1938 with Fernand Gravet as Strauss, Polish soprano Miliza Korjus as Imperial Opera star Carla Donner, and tenor George Houston as Imperial Opera star Fritz Schiller. Strauss loves Korjus but marries sweetheart Luise Rainer on the rebound. Korjus sings the waltz that gets Strauss a publisher and persuades him to write an operetta, but faithful wife Rainer wins out in the end. Julien Duvivier directed the lavish film, which won an Academy Award for its waltzing cinematography by Joseph Ruttenberg. Korjus was nominated for Best Supporting Actress, but it was her only Hollywood movie. Black and white. In English. 100 minutes.

1938 Unsterbliche Melodien
The romantic Austrian film *Unsterbliche Melodien* (Immortal Melodies) stars Alfred Jerger as Strauss in a story with plenty of room for waltzes and love interest. Lizzi Holzschuh and Maria Paudler play the women who love him, and the music is performed by the Vienna Philharmonic. Helen Moja wrote the screenplay; Heinz Paul directed. Black and white. In German. 90 minutes.

1953 Johann Mouse
This is a delightful Tom and Jerry cartoon about a musical mouse who lives in the house of Johann Strauss and is as fond of waltzes as the composer. It deservedly won the Best Cartoon Oscar for Hanna-Barbera in 1953. Color. 7 minutes.

1954 Ewiger Walzer
Ewiger Walzer (Eternal Waltz) is a romantic film about Strauss and his love life with Bernhard Wicki playing the composer. Much of it is concerned with his affair with singer Henriette Treffz (Hilde Krahl), but there are quite good re-creations of his operas on stage, including his rarely seen first attempt, *Indigo.* Annemarie Düringer is Adele, Friedl Loor is Maria Geistinger, Gert Frobe is Gawrinoff, and Arnulf Schröder is Jacques Offenbach. Paul Verhoeven directed. Color. In German. 99 minutes. Video Yesteryear/Toppic (Germany) VHS.

1955 The Great Waltz
Patrice Munsel stars as Resi with Jarmila Novotná as Madame Baronska in this excellent television production of the musical. Keith Andes is Strauss, Henry Sharp is his father, and Bert Lahr is Hans Ebesteder. Max Liebman produced, Frederick Fox designed the sets, and Charles Sanford was the music director. Telecast November 5, 1955, on NBC. Black and white. In English. 79 minutes. VAI VHS.

1961 Wien Tanzt
Vienna Waltzes is an Austrian film about the rise to fame of Johann Strauss the father with Anton Walbrook playing the waltz composer. It includes the traditional rivalry and reconciliation with his son, and there is music by

660

both Strausses. Emile Edwin Reinert directed. Black and white. In German. 90 minutes.

1963 The Waltz King
Kerwin Mathews is Strauss, Senta Berger is his love Jetty Treffz, and Brian Aherne as his father in this romantic Disney film directed by Steve Previn. It was shot in Germany and first shown in America on television. Color. In English. 95 minutes.

1972 The Great Waltz
Horst Bucholz plays Strauss in the second MGM version of the story. Opera diva Mary Costa, who plays Jetty Treffz, does most of the singing and encourages Strauss to write operettas. Nigel Patrick is Strauss Sr., and Rossano Brazzi is a jealous Baron. Andrew Stone directed. Color. In English. 134 minutes. Opera Dubs/Premiere Opera VHS.

1972 The Strauss Family
A grand old-style television miniseries from England devoted to the lives, ladies, rivals, and conflicts of the Strauss dynasty. Eric Woofe is Johann Sr., Stuart Wilson is Johann Jr., Nicolas Simmonds is Josef Strauss, Derek Jacobi is Josef Lanner, Anne Stallybrass is Anna, Barbara Ferris is Emilie, Margaret Whiting is Hetti, and Georgina Hale is Lili. David Reid produced, Anthony Skene wrote the screenplay, and David Giles directed for ATV, Birmingham. The music is played by the London Symphony Orchestra conducted by Cyril Ornadel. Color. In English. 450 minutes.

1987 Johann Strauss: Der König ohne Krone
Johann Strauss: King Without a Crown is an Austrian movie telling the life of Johann Jr. in flashback as imagined in a book written by Frédéric Morton. The film revolves around his music, but it focuses on his love affairs with Olga in Moscow, Yvonne in Paris, Marie in Vienna, and true love Adele. Oliver Tobias plays Strauss with Zsa Zsa Gabor as his aunt Amalie. Franz Antel directed. Color. In German. 124 minutes.

1996 Strauss: The King of Three-Quarter Time
Michael Riley plays Strauss in this Canadian film aimed at young television viewers. Like the others in the *Composers Series* made by Devine Entertainment, it was shot in the Czech Republic and features a young person as a friend of the composer, in this case Derek Senft. The main musical theme is "Tales From the Vienna Woods." David Devine directed. Color. In English. 50 minutes. Sony Classical VHS.

STRAUSS, RICHARD
German composer (1864–1949)

Richard Strauss is the most successful 20th-century opera composer in terms of critical appreciation and audience acceptance. Of the 15 operas he composed, 10 have found a place in the international repertory and nine are on commercial video. Strauss (who is not related to Johann) acquired operatic fame and notoriety in 1905 through his scandal-creating version of Oscar Wilde's infamous play SALOME, and there were a large number of early film versions to help spread the scandal. His collaboration with playwright Hugo von Hofmannsthal began with ELECTRA (1909) and resulted in some of the most popular and adventurous operas of the century, including the neo-Mozartian DER ROSENKAVALIER and the neo-classic ARIADNE AUF NAXOS. Strauss's work is well represented on video. See ARABELLA, CAPRICCIO, DIE SCHWEIGSAME FRAU, DIE FRAU OHNE SCHATTEN, and INTERMEZZO.

1970 The Dance of the Seven Veils
Ken Russell's controversial film, subtitled *A Comic Strip in Seven Episodes About Richard Strauss,* was made for the BBC TV series *Omnibus*. It's based on a book by American George Marek that stresses the composer's relationship with the Nazis during World War II. Christopher Gable, Judith Paris, and Vladek Sheybal are the principal actors, with Imogen Claire as Salome. When the film was telecast February 15, 1970, it caused such controversy that another program favorable to Strauss was presented as a balance. Strauss's son threatened to sue Russell over the "slanderous" portrayal of his father, and the film was not shown again.

1984 Richard Strauss Remembered
Film portrait of the composer as seen through the eyes of his family and friends. Peter Adam filmed it where Strauss lived and performed and uses his letters and diaries as narration. There are photographs and extracts from operas, archival films, and home movies. The interviewees include Sir John Gielgud, Frank Finlay, Sir Georg Solti, and Herbert von Karajan. Blackford Carrington produced for BBC TV. Color. In English. 120 minutes.

1989 Richard Strauss: Between Romanticism and Resignation
Documentary about the last 15 years of the composer's life, including archival footage and home movie material. Color. In English. 58 minutes. Films for the Humanities & Sciences VHS.

1996 Famous Composers: Richard Strauss
Short documentary about the life and music of the composer featuring excerpts from his works. Color. 30 minutes. Kultur VHS.

STRAVINSKY, IGOR
Russian-born composer (1882–1971)

Igor Stravinsky composed unusual operas that broke the boundaries of what operas were expected to be, and through them he influenced postmodern American opera composers such as Robert Ashley. Many of his theater pieces are nontraditional halfway operas. L'HISTOIRE DU SOLDAT, for example, can be seen as an acted/narrated ballet-opera, while OEDIPUS REX is an oratorio-opera. His major opera, THE RAKE'S PROGRESS, is virtually an old-fashioned number opera based on a series of Hogarth drawings. THE NIGHTINGALE is based on a Hans Christian Anderson fairy tale, but it is not a tale for children. All of his operas are full of ritual and magic, with new ideas derived from his revolutionary ballets. His internationalism is important because as he moved across borders he introduced Russian rhythms to Western Europe and America. He composed specifically for the screen when he created the 1962 television opera THE FLOOD, and his music has been used to great effect in films such as *Fantasia* and *La Belle Noiseuse*.

1958 Igor Stravinsky
This NBC Television film of an interview with the composer was made available for use in the university *Wisdom Series*. Black and white. In English. 30 minutes.

1965 Stravinsky
An informal biography of the composer made by Roman Kroiter and Wolf Koenig for the National Film Board of Canada. Black and white. In English. 50 minutes.

1965 Stravinsky
Film profile of Stravinsky conducting, visiting fellow artists, and working on a project with choreographer George Balanchine. Charles Kuralt narrates. Black and white. In English. 43 minutes. Carousel VHS.

1966 Stravinsky
Personal portrait of the composer as he reminiscences about the past and makes plans for the future, plus excerpts from his works. Made for a CBS News special and telecast May 3, 1966. Black and white. In English. 60 minutes. Video at the Library of Congress.

1968 A Stravinsky Portrait
Stravinsky is seen with wife and friends at his Beverly Hills home, conducting the West German Symphony Orchestra, discussing his work with colleagues, and being interviewed. Pierre Boulez, George Balanchine, and Christopher Isherwood are among those who participate. Richard Leacock directed, photographed, and edited the film with help from Rolf Liebermann. Black and white. In English. 57 minutes. On VHS.

1982 "Once, at a border..." Aspects of Stravinsky
Tony Palmer's 100th anniversary film about Stravinsky was shown on television in three segments. Part One tells of the composer's life and career in Russia, Part Two is set in Western Europe, and Part Three shows his life in America. Includes documents, photographs, and extracts from films and musical performances, plus appearances by Robert Craft, Marie Rambert, George Balanchine, and Nadia Boulanger. The London Sinfonietta plays most of the music. Made for London Weekend Television. Color and black and white. In English. 166 minutes. Kultur VHS.

1982 America Celebrates Stravinsky
Concert at the National Cathedral in Washington celebrating the 100th anniversary of the composer's birth with Leonard Bernstein and Michael Tilson Thomas conducting the National Symphony Orchestra. The program included an excerpt from a film showing Stravinsky conducting. Humphrey Burton directed. Color. In English. 90 minutes.

STREETCAR NAMED DESIRE, A
1998 opera by Previn

Faded Southern belle Blanche DuBois comes to stay with her sister Stella in New Orleans but has problems coping with Stella's brutish husband Stanley Kowalski. She almost persuades his friend Mitch to marry her, but he rejects her after Stanley finds out about Blanche's past. While Stella is in the hospital having a baby, Stanley rapes Blanche and destroys her faint hold on reality. André Previn's opera *A Streetcar Named Desire*, libretto by Philip Littell based on the play by Tennessee Williams, was commissioned by San Francisco Opera, which premiered it September 19, 1998. The opera received mixed reviews but was generally praised for its faithfulness to the play and fine performances.

1998 San Francisco Opera
American stage production: Colin Graham (director), André Previn (conductor, San Francisco Opera Orchestra), Michael Yeargan (set designer).
Cast: Renée Fleming (Blanche Dubois), Rodney Gilfry (Stanley Kowalski), Elizabeth Futral (Stella), Anthony Dean Griffey (Mitch), Judith Forst (Eunice), Josepha Gayer (Flower Seller), Matthew Lord (Steve).

Video: Image Entertainment/Arthaus (GB) DVD/ Kultur VHS. Telecast December 30, 1998. Kirk Browning (director). Color. In English. 166 minutes.

STREET SCENE
1946 "American opera" by Weill

KURT WEILL considered his "American opera" *Street Scene* to be his masterpiece. Based on a Pulitzer Prize–winning play by Elmer Rice, it tells the story of 24 hours in the life of a group of people in a Manhattan tenement on a sweltering summer day. The loose plot revolves around Anna Maurrant, who is eventually killed by her jealous husband Frank, and their daughter Rose, who is loved by Sam Kaplan. Rice wrote the libretto in collaboration with poet Langston Hughes, who wrote the lyrics. The opera, which premiered in Philadelphia in 1946, was revived by New York City Opera in 1959 and continues to be staged, with recent productions by Scottish Opera, English National Opera, Houston Grand Opera, and Chicago Lyric Opera.

1979 New York City Opera
American stage production: Jack O'Brien (director), John Mauceri (conductor, New York City Opera Orchestra and Chorus), Paul Sylbert (set designer), Nancy Potts (costume designer).

Cast: Catherine Malfitano (Rose Maurrant), Eileen Schauler (Anna Maurrant), William Chapman (Frank Maurrant), Harlan Foss (Harry Easter), Alan Kays (Sam Kaplan).

Telecast October 27, 1979, in the series *Live From Lincoln Center*. Kirk Browning (director). Color. In English. 180 minutes.

Comment: Beverly Sills interviewed Lotte Lenya during the intermission.

1992 English National Opera
English stage production: Nicolette Molnár (director, based on the Scottish Opera production by David Pountney), James Holmes (conductor, English National Opera Orchestra and Chorus), David Fielding (set designer).

Cast: Lesley Garrett (Rose Maurrant), Janice Cairns (Anna Maurrant), Mark Richardson (Frank Maurrant), Kevin Anderson (Sam Kaplan), Terry Jenkins (Abraham Kaplan), Richard Halton (Harry Easter), Sheila Squires (Olga Olsen), Arwel Huw Morgan (Mr. Olsen), Meriel Dickinson (Emma Jones).

Video: Live Opera VHS. Telecast January 1, 1993, on BBC. Barrie Gavin (director). Color. In English. 140 minutes.

1994 Houston Grand Opera
American stage production: Francesca Zambello (director), James Holmes (conductor, Rhineland Palatinate State Philharmonic Orchestra and Ludwigshafen Theatre Chorus), Adrianne Lobel (set designer), Manfred Bödefeld (cinematographer).

Cast: Ashley Putnam (Anna Maurrant), Teri Hansen (Rose Maurrant), Marc Embree (Frank Maurrant), Kip Wilborn (Sam Kaplan), Michael Scarborough (Harry Easter), David Rae Smith (Abraham Kaplan), Wendy Hill (Mrs. Fiorentino), Anthony Mee (Lippo Fiorentino), Janice Felty (Emma Jones), Heidi Eisenberg (Olga Olsen), John Kuether (Olsen), Dean Anthony (Buchanan), Claudia Ashley and Muriel Costa-Greenspon (Nursemaids), Anita Vidovic (Mae Jones).

Video: Image Entertainment/Arthaus (GB) DVD. Taped December 1994. José Montes-Baquer (director). Color. In English. 142 minutes.

Comment: This production, first staged in Houston in January 1994, was presented in Berlin in partnership with Theater im Pfalzbau and Theatre des Westerns and filmed in Ludwigshafen.

Related film

1931 Elmer Rice play
Elmer Rice's play, which is essentially the libretto of the opera, was filmed in 1931 in an adaptation written by Rice. Sylvia Sidney plays Rose Maurrant, Estelle Taylor is Anna Maurrant, David Landau is Frank Maurrant, William Collier Jr. is Sam Kaplan, Max Montor is Abe Kaplan, Louis Natheaux is Harry Easter, and Beulah Bondi is Emma Jones. King Vidor directed the film for Samuel Goldwyn. Black and white. In English. 80 minutes.

STREHLER, GIORGIO
Italian opera director (1921–)

Stage director Giorgio Strehler, famous for his influential theater productions with Piccolo Teatro of Milan, was also a major opera producer at La Scala, Salzburg, and Paris. After beginning in 1947 with *La traviata,* he staged widely admired productions of *The Threepenny Opera, Simon Boccanegra, Die Entführung aus dem Serail, Macbeth, Cavalleria rusticana,* and *Die Zauberflöte.* Although he did not make any opera films, there are videos of some of his stage productions. See CAVALLERIA RUSTICANA (1968), DIE DREIGROSCHENOPER (1972), DIE ENTFÜHRUNG AUS DEM SERAIL (1984), LE NOZZE DI FIGARO (1980), SIMON BOCCANEGRA (1978), and DER ZAUBERFLÖTE (1975 film).

1971 Giorgio Strehler Rehearses

Strehler is shown at work rehearsing and staging *Die Entführung aus dem Serail,* a famous production he originally created for the Salzburg Festival in 1965. It was influential for its radical *commedia dell'arte* ideas and shadow silhouettes. Norbert Beilharz directed for SDR German Television. Color. In German. 60 minutes.

STRICTLY DISHONORABLE

American films with opera content

Preston Sturges's 1929 play *Strictly Dishonorable,* the story of an operatic Don Juan with strictly dishonorable intentions, has been filmed twice, but not by Sturges. A young Southern woman breaks her engagement and stays in his apartment overnight. She says she cannot go back to her family because her reputation is ruined, so he agrees to marry her.

1931 Universal film

Paul Lukas plays opera singer Tino Caraffo with Sidney Fox as Isabelle Parry, the woman who gets him to marry her. Gladys Lehman wrote the screenplay, and John M. Stahl directed for Universal. Black and white. In English. 91 minutes.

1951 MGM film

Ezio Pinza plays the operatic Don Juan with Janet Leigh as the innocent lass who falls in love with him. Mario Castelnuovo-Tedesco created an imaginary opera for the film, and Pinza gets to belt out its bass aria "Il Ritorno de Cesare" with Leigh on stage as his sword bearer. Melvin Frank and Norman Panama wrote and directed the film for MGM with Ray June as cinematographer. Black and white. In English. 94 minutes.

STROYEVA, VERA

Russian opera film director (1903–?)

Vera Stroyeva, born in Kiev, which is now in the Ukraine, was a leading figure in Soviet cinema from 1927, writing, directing, and often collaborating with her director husband Grigori Roshal. During the 1950s she turned to opera and dance films. After her 1951 BOLSHOI OPERA concert film, she made two of the most cinematic movies in the genre, both based on Mussorgsky operas: BORIS GODUNOV (1954) and KHOVANSHCHINA (1959).

Strictly Dishonorable (1951): Ezio Pinza plays an operatic Don Juan opposite Janet Leigh in this film of Preston Sturges's play.

STUDENT PRINCE, THE
1924 operetta by Romberg

The highly romantic story of German Prince Karl-Franz, heir to the throne of Karlsberg, and his bittersweet romance with an innkeeper's daughter, Kathie, while attending the university in Heidelberg. In the end they know that it is his duty to marry Princess Margaret. SIGMUND ROMBERG's enduring operetta *The Student Prince in Heidelberg*, libretto by Dorothy Donnelly, is based on a play by Rudolf Bleichman called *Old Heidelberg* that had been staged in New York in 1903. This was a translation of his German play, *Alt Heidelberg*, derived from a romantic novel by Wilhelm Meyer-Forster. Many of the songs in Romberg's operetta, such as the near-operatic "Serenade," "Deep in My Heart," and "The Drinking Song," have been recorded by opera singers. One song, however, was borrowed from the original play—the medieval Latin student drinking song "Gaudeamus igitur."

1954 MGM film
American feature film: Richard Thorpe, (director), Sonia Levien and William Ludwig (screenplay), Paul Vogel (cinematographer), George Stoll (music director).

Cast: Edmund Purdom (Prince Karl, sung by Mario Lanza), Ann Blyth (Kathie), Louis Calhern (King of Karlsberg), S. Z. Sakall (Joseph Ruder), Edmund Gwenn (Prof. Juttner), Betta St. John (Princess Johanna).

Video: MGM-UA VHS. Color. In English. 107 minutes.

Comment: Lanza had already recorded the soundtrack when he quit MGM, so the studio hired Purdom to replace him on screen and dubbed in the songs. The voice alone was enough to make the film a box-office hit.

1994 Abilene Opera
American stage production: Wyatt Hester (director), Richard Burke (conductor, Abilene Opera Orchestra), Ted Starnes (set designer).

Cast: Kelly Neil (Prince Karl-Franz), Jane Guitar (Kathie), Wendy Mitchell-Humphrey (Gretchen), David Lawrence (Detlef), Andrew LeBlanc (Dr. Engel), Amy James (Grand Duchess), Lanie Westman (Princess Margaret).

Video: Premiere Opera VHS. Taped July 22, 1994, at the Paramount Theater in Abilene, Texas. Color. In English. 105 minutes.

Comment: This is the only video of the operetta on stage, but it's a rather amateurish production.

Silent/related films

1909 Old Heidelberg
This *Old Heidelberg* is an American film made by the Essanay studio and based on the source play. Black and white. Silent. 15 minutes

1915 Old Heidelberg
Wallace Reid plays the student prince in *Old Heidelberg*, an American feature film based on the source play. Dorothy Gish is Kathie with Eric Von Stroheim as Lutz and Karl Formes Jr. as Dr. Juttner. D. W. Griffith supervised, and John Emerson directed and wrote the screenplay for Triangle Film. Black and white. Silent. About 70 minutes.

1923 Alt-Heidelberg
Paul Hartmann plays the student prince in *Alt-Heidelberg*, a German silent film based on the source novel and play and directed by Hans Behrendt. Werner Krauss has a supporting role. Black and white. In German. About 70 minutes.

1927 The Student Prince in Old Heidelberg
Ernst Lubitsch's silent version of the play and operetta, *The Student Prince in Old Heidelberg*, is outstanding even without the songs, but as a visual rather than a vocal masterpiece. It credits the operetta but was shown with a new score by David Mendoza and William Axt. Lubitsch expanded the story to include the early years of the prince before he goes to the university. Ramon Novarro plays Prince Karl with Norma Shearer as Kathie. Hans Kraly wrote the screenplay, and John Mescall photographed it for MGM. The video has an orchestral soundtrack. Black and white. 107 minutes. MGM-UA VHS.

1959 Alt-Heidelberg
Christian Wolff plays the prince in this *Alt-Heidelberg*, a German film based on the source play. Christian Wolff, Sabine Sinjen, and Gert Grobe are the main actors; Ernst Marischka directed. Color. In German. 105 minutes.

STUDER, CHERYL
American soprano (1955–)

Cheryl Studer was born in Michigan but studied in Vienna and made her debut in Munich in 1980. She was soon recognized as one of the finest sopranos of her generation and has now sung in most of the major opera houses in Europe and America in a range of roles from Verdi to Wagner. Much of her work is on video. See AIDA (1994), ATTILA (1991), MONTSERRAT CABALLÉ (1993), ELEKTRA (1989), DIE FRAU OHNE SCHATTEN

(1992), GUILLAUME TELL (1991), LOHENGRIN (1989/
1990), METROPOLITAN OPERA (1991), LE NOZZE DI
FIGARO (1992), TANNHÄUSER (1990), and I VESPRI SI-
CILIANI (1990).

STURRIDGE, CHARLES
English film director (1951–)

Charles Sturridge is best known internationally for his
Evelyn Waugh adaptations, the television series *Brides-
head Revisited,* and the film *A Handful of Dust.* Operatically he directed the black-and-white LA FORZA DEL
DESTINO (1987) episode of the collective film ARIA, and
he featured an excellent opera scene built around LUCIA
DI LAMMERMOOR (1991) in his adaptation of E. M. Forster's *Where Angels Fear to Tread.*

SULLIVAN, ARTHUR
See GILBERT AND SULLIVAN.

SUMMER AND SMOKE
1971 opera by Hoiby

Composer LEE HOIBY and librettist Lanford Wilson's
Summer and Smoke is based on a play by Tennessee
Williams. It tells the story of the sexually repressed
Southern minister's daughter Alma Winemiller who is
unable to admit her love for Dr. John Buchanan until it is
too late. The title comes from the description of Alma as
"suffocated in smoke from something on fire inside her."
The opera, the first based on a Williams play, was commissioned and premiered by St. Paul Opera in 1971 with
Mary Jane Peil as Alma, John Reardon as Dr. Buchanan,
and Alan Titus as the Traveling Salesman.

1982 Chicago Opera Theater
American stage production: Kirk Browning (di-
rector), Robert Frisbie (Chicago Opera Theater Orches-
tra).
Cast: Mary Beth Peil (Alma), Robert Orth
(John Buchanan), Joyce Carter (Rosa), Diane Barclay
(Nellie), Clayton Hochhalter (Roger), Paul Kiesgen
(Winemiller), Charlotte Gardner (Mrs. Winemiller).
Video at the NYPL. Telecast June 23, 1982, on
PBS. Color. In English. 120 minutes.
Comment: The telecast was based on a 1980
Chicago Opera Theatre production, but Browning
brought the company into a studio to maintain the claus-
trophobic Williams atmosphere.

Related film

1961 Paramount film
Geraldine Page stars as Alma opposite Laurence Harvey
as Buchanan in this *Summer and Smoke,* a somewhat
overheated screen version of the Tennessee Williams
play. Elmer Bernstein wrote the music, and Peter
Glenville directed the film. Color. In English. 118 minutes.

SUMMER OF THE SEVENTEENTH DOLL, THE
1996 opera by Mills

Every summer for 17 years Queensland sugarcane cutters
Barney and Roo have paid a summer visit to women
friends in Melbourne bringing a kewpie doll as a present.
The 17th summer in 1953 changes everything. RICHARD
MILLS's opera *The Summer of the Seventeenth Doll,* libretto by Peter Godsworth based on an influential play by
Ray Lawler, premiered in Melbourne in 1996. Mills
composes in an accessible and melodious style with arias,
ensembles, and even a showcase for a coloratura soprano.

1997 Victorian State Opera
Australian stage production: Richard Wherrett
(director), Richard Mills (conductor, State Orchestra of
Victoria), Brian Thomson (set designer).
Cast: Barry Ryan (Barney), Gary Rowley
(Roo), Elizabeth Campbell (Pearl), Gillian Sullivan
(Oliver), Natalie Jones (Bubba), Eilene Hannan (Emma),
Nicholas Todorovic (Johnnie Dowd).
Video: ABC Video Arts (Australia) VHS. Peter
Butler (director). Color. In English. 143 minutes.
Comment: The opera was videotaped at the
Playhouse at the Victorian Arts Centre, Melbourne.

Related film

1959 Norman film
Heavy-handed Australian/American film of the Ray
Lawler source play. Ernest Borgnine and John Mills are
the cane-cutters, with Angela Lansbury and Anne Baxter
as their women friends. Leslie Norman directed. Black
and white. In English. 94 minutes.

SUOR ANGELICA
1918 one-act opera by Puccini

Suor Angelica (Sister Angelica) is the second opera in
GIACOMO PUCCINI's triple-bill *Il Trittico,* which premiered at the Metropolitan Opera in 1918. The libretto,
by Gioacchino Forzano, tells the story of Sister Angelica,

a nun in 17th-century Tuscany who has been forced by her aristocratic family to give up her illegitimate child and enter a convent. Her aunt, a princess, comes to tell her that the child is dead and ask her to give up her inheritance. Sister Angelica takes poison, but the Madonna appears with the child to show her forgiveness. All the roles in the opera are for women.

1953 NBC Opera Theatre

American TV production: Samuel Chotzinoff, (director), Peter Herman Adler (conductor, Symphony of the Air Orchestra and NBC Opera Theatre Chorus), William Molyneux (set designer), Townsend Brewster (English translation).

Cast: Elaine Malbin (Sister Angelica), Winifred Heidt (Princess), Virginia Viney (Abbess).

Video at the MTR. Telecast live March 7, 1953. Kirk Browning (director). Black and white. In English. 60 minutes.

1954 NBC Opera Theatre

American TV production: Samuel Chotzinoff (director), Peter Herman Adler (conductor, Symphony of the Air Orchestra and NBC Opera Theatre Chorus), William Molyneux (set designer), Townsend Brewster (English translation).

Cast: Elaine Malbin (Sister Angelica), Shannon Boblin (Princess), Mary Kreste (Abbess).

Video at the MTR. Telecast live December 5, 1954. Kirk Browning (director). Black and white. In English. 60 minutes.

1981 Metropolitan Opera

American stage production: Fabrizio Melano (director), James Levine (conductor, Metropolitan Orchestra and Chorus), David Reppa (set designer).

Cast: Renata Scotto (Sister Angelica), Jocelyne Taillon (Princess), Jean Kraft (Abbess).

Video at the MTR. Telecast live November 14, 1981, as part of *Il Trittico*. Kirk Browning (director). Color. In Italian with English subtitles. 55 minutes.

1983 Teatro alla Scala

Italian stage production: Sylvano Bussotti (director), Gianandrea Gavazzeni (conductor, Teatro alla Scala Orchestra and Chorus), Michele Canzoneri (set/costume designer).

Cast: Rosalind Plowright (Suor Angelica), Dunja Vejzović (Princess), Maria Grazia Allegri (Abbess).

Home Vision VHS/Pioneer LD (with *Il Trittico*). Brian Large (director). Color. In Italian with English subtitles. 55 minutes.

SUPERVIA, CONCHITA
Spanish mezzo-soprano (1895–1936)

Conchita Supervia was renowned for her vivacious personality and famous for singing Carmen and Rosina. She was born in Barcelona, but she began her stage career with a Spanish company in Argentina. She sang Octavian in *Der Rosenkavalier* in Rome in 1911, made her U.S. debut in Chicago in 1915, and became a regular at La Scala during the 1920s. Her greatest fame came in the last decade of her life. She was living in London and singing at Covent Garden in 1934 when she appeared in her only film, *Evensong*. She died tragically in childbirth in 1936 but left a notable recording legacy.

1934 Evensong

Evensong is a British film based on the life of Melba. Evelyn Laye plays Melba/Irela, while Supervia is Baba L'Etoile, a new singer who challenges her stardom. Supervia performs the role of Musetta in *La bohème* and is shown on stage singing the aria "Quando me'n vo' soletta," and outshining Mimì. See EVENSONG.

SUPPÉ, FRANZ VON
Austrian composer (1819–1895)

Franz von Suppé is the father of the Viennese operetta and the predecessor of Strauss, although he is known today primarily for his overtures. Admirers of the *Light Cavalry* and *Poet and Peasant* overtures are often surprised to learn that they came from operettas staged in 1846 and 1866. Suppé, who began writing for the stage in 1841, was also an opera singer and conductor. His most popular operettas, and the best remembered, are DIE SCHÖNE GALATHÉE, *Fatinitza*, and BOCCACCIO. The diminished popularity of his operettas is reflected in a scarcity of videos. See also OPERETTE.

SUSA, CONRAD
American composer (1935–)

Conrad Susa has composed four operas and more than 100 scores for film, theater, and television. His first opera, TRANSFORMATIONS (1973), is a setting of poems from a book by Anne Sexton which she retells Grimm fairy tales. *Black River* (1975) is based on Michael Lesy's powerful book *Wisconsin Death Trip*. More traditional is *The Love of Don Perlimpli* (1984), adapted from a play by Lorca and inspired by the music of Scarlatti. Susa's major achievement is THE DANGEROUS LIAISONS, based on the epistolary novel by Pierre Choderlos de Laclos, which premiered at San Francisco Opera in 1994.

SUSANNAH

1955 opera by Floyd

CARLISLE FLOYD's opera has claims to being the most performed and most popular American opera. There have been an estimated 200 productions since 1956, including four at New York City Opera, one at Chicago Lyric, and one at the Met. Floyd's libretto is based on the biblical story of Susanna and the Elders but transposed to the mountains of Tennessee. After being condemned by church elders, who caught Susannah bathing nude, she is betrayed by her friend Little Bat and seduced by the preacher Olin Blitch. When her brother Sam find this out, he shoots Blitch. The opera has memorable square dance music, hymns, and folk songs, but they were actually composed by Floyd. A CD version has been recorded in France by Lyons Opera with Cheryl Studer as Susannah and Samuel Ramey as Blitch, but there is no commercial video.

1979 Indiana Opera Theater

American stage production: Allan Ross (director), Brian Falkwill (conductor, Indiana Opera Theater Orchestra), David Higgins (set designer).

Cast: Jean Herzberg (Susannah), William Parcher (Olin Blitch), Jon Fay (Sam), Neil Jones (Little Bat).

Video at the MTR. Telecast November 17, 1979. Mickey Klein (director). Color. In English 90 minutes.

1986 Chicago Opera Theater

American stage production: N. Larsen (conductor, Chicago Opera Theater Orchestra).

Cast: Mary Ellen (Susannah), Gerhard Stolze (Sam).

Opera Dubs VHS. Black and white. In English. 86 minutes.

Comment: Low-quality nonprofessional tape of Chicago Opera Theater production shot from a balcony at a staged rehearsal.

SUTHERLAND, JOAN

Australian soprano (1926–)

Dame Joan Sutherland has an extraordinarily beautiful voice that is especially well suited for *bel canto* roles, but she is a delight in almost everything. She was born in Sydney, made her debut in Australia in 1947 as Purcell's Dido, and made her Covent Garden debut in 1952 as First Lady in *Die Zauberflöte*. She married conductor Richard Bonynge in 1954, and together they developed the *bel canto* repertoire that culminated in her 1959 Covent Garden *Lucia di Lammermoor*. After Italian critics dubbed her "La Stupenda," she took her Lucia to Paris, La Scala, and the Met and quickly became the reigning opera diva. She retired from the stage in 1990 but left a formidable legacy of recordings and videos. See ADRIANA LECOUVREUR (1984), ANNA BOLENA (1984/1985), BELL TELEPHONE HOUR (1967/1968), DIALOGUES DES CARMÉLITES (1985), DON GIOVANNI (1978), FAUST (1973), LA FILLE DU RÉGIMENT (1972/1986), DIE FLEDERMAUS (1982/1990), MARILYN HORNE (1981/1985), LES HUGUENOTS (1990), LAKMÉ (1976/1976/1987 film), LUCIA DI LAMMERMOOR (1973/1982/1986), LUCREZIA BORGIA (1977/1980), DIE LUSTIGE WITWE (1988), MARIA STUARDA (2000), METROPOLITAN OPERA (1972/1983/1986), MIGNON (1973), NORMA (1978/1981), LE NOZZE DI FIGARO (1972), LA PÉRICHOLE, (1973), I PURITANI (1985), RIGOLETTO (1973), SEMIRAMIDE (1986), LA TRAVIATA (1973), and IL TROVATORE (1983).

1961–1968 Bell Telephone Hour

Sutherland's 13 appearances on the NBC television program *The Bell Telephone Hour* from 1961 to 1968, mostly in color, are available on DVD and VHS. VHS Volume One has arias and scenes from *Crispino e la Comare*, *Ernani*, *Hamlet* (the Mad Scene in black and white), *Lakmé*, *Norma*, *I puritani*, and *Rigoletto* (the quartet with Gedda, Gobbi, and Miller). Volume Two has arias and scenes from *Lucia di Lammermoor* (the sextet with Gedda, Gobbi, Hines, Miller, and Anthony), *Otello* (the "Willow Song" in black and white), *La sonnambula*, *Tosca*, and *La traviata*. Donald Voorhees conducts the Bell Telephone Hour Orchestra. Color. 102 minutes VAI DVD/VHS.

1963 Voice of Firestone

Sutherland is in fine form on a *Voice of Firestone* TV show on April 21, 1963. She sings the arias "The Soldier Tir'd" from Arne's *Artaxerxes;* "Bel raggio lusinghieri" from Rossini's *Semiramide*, "Donde lieta usci" from *La bohème*, and "O beau pays" from *Les Huguenots*. Richard Bonynge conducts. Black and white. In English. 26 minutes. VAI VHS is titled *Presenting Joan Sutherland*/Bel Canto Society VHS is titled *Joan Sutherland: Bel Canto Showcase*.

1963 Joan Sutherland Show

Sutherland performs arias from *Les Huguenots*, *La traviata*, and *Lucia di Lammermoor* and is joined on a duet by Margreta Elkins in this Australian show. Michael Denison introduces the music, and Richard Bonynge conducts the London Symphony Orchestra. Peter Bernardos directed. Black and white. 60 minutes. Video at the MTR and film at the NFTA.

1963 Joan Sutherland: The Age of Bel Canto

Sutherland is superb in this Canadian television program performing staged versions of *bel canto* numbers by Bellini, Donizetti, Rossini, and Verdi. She sings arias from *I puritani, Semiramide, Crispino e la comare,* and *La traviata* and duets from *La sonnambula* and *Don Pasquale* with Richard Conrad. Vancouver Opera artistic director Irving Guttman staged the numbers, Murray Laufer designed the sets, Suzanne Mess and Piero Tosi created the costumes, and Richard Bonynge conducted the CBC Toronto Radio-Canada Orchestra. Franz Krae-mer directed the CBC telecast December 11, 1963. Color. 50 minutes. VAI VHS.

1965 An Hour With Joan Sutherland
Sutherland sings arias by Handel, Paisiello, and Rossini plus Benedict's "The Gypsy and the Bird" and joins in a duet from *Semiramide* with Marilyn Horne and a duet from *I puritani* with John Alexander. Terry McEwen talks to her and her husband about her career. Kirk Browning directed. Black and white. 60 minutes. Video at the MTR.

1969 Joan Sutherland in Concert
Sutherland in recital at the Macmillan Theatre at the University of Toronto on February 12, 1969, with Richard Bonynge playing piano. An adoring crowd helps make this one of the most enjoyable Sutherland videos, with selections from Balfe, Bononcini, Handel, Massenet, and others. Color. 60 minutes. VAI VHS.

1972/1973 Who's Afraid of Opera?
Sutherland stars in highlight versions of operas for young audiences, telling the story to puppets and performing the leading roles. The operas are IL BARBIERE DI SIVIGLIA, LA FILLE DU REGIMENT, FAUST, LUCIA DI LAMMERMOOR, MIGNON, LA PÉRICHOLE, RIGOLETTO, and LA TRAVIATA. George Djurkovic designed the sets, and Richard Bonynge conducts the London Symphony Orchestra. Color. Each 30 minutes. Kultur VHS.

1979 Joan Sutherland: A Life on the Move
Brian Adams, who spent a year following Sutherland around the world for this documentary, traces her career from early years in Sydney through success in London to international stardom. She is seen in rehearsal and performance at the Met and other opera houses. It was made for Australian television and telecast in August 1979. Color. In English. 80 minutes.

1982 Joan Sutherland in Concert
Sutherland in concert at the Perth Concert Hall in Australia on March 9, 1982. She performs arias from *La traviata, Alcina, La petite Bohémienne, Semiramide,* and *Les Huguenots,* plus songs. Richard Bonynge accompanies her and Philip Booth directed the telecast. Color. 49 minutes. Kultur VHS.

1986 A Gala Concert
Joan Sutherland and Marilyn Horne in concert at the Sydney Opera House in 1986. They sing arias and duets from *Norma, Semiramide, Lakmé,* and *The Tales of Hoffmann.* Richard Bonynge conducts the Elizabethan Sydney Orchestra. John Widdicombe directed. Color. 141 minutes. Arthaus DVD.

1987 An Evening With Sutherland & Pavarotti
Sutherland and Luciano Pavarotti in staged scenes from three operas at a Metropolitan Opera gala. *La traviata* (Act II), with Leo Nucci as Germont, was staged by David Kneuss. The scene from *Lucia di Lammermoor,* with Ariel Bybee as Alisa and Julien Robbins as Raimondo, was also staged by Kneuss. *Rigoletto* (Act III), with Leo Nucci as Rigoletto, Isola Jones as Maddalena and Ferruccio Furlanetto as Sparafucile, was staged by David Sell. Richard Bonynge conducts the Metropolitan Opera Orchestra. Kirk Browning directed the video taped January 11, 1987, and telecast March 4 as *The Sutherland/Pavarotti Anniversary Gala.* Color. In Italian with English subtitles. 115 minutes. DG VHS/LD.

1991 La Stupenda: A Portrait of Dame Joan Sutherland
This is the best screen biography of Sutherland, intelligently written and directed by Derek Bailey and finely narrated by Humphrey Burton. It traces Sutherland's career from its beginnings to her rise to stardom with many performance extracts, including her splendid *Lucia di Lammermoor.* Sutherland and Richard Bonynge talk about her career, and there are informative interviews with Franco Zeffirelli and other associates. Color. 88 minutes. London VHS.

1993 The Essential Sutherland
Anthology of highlights from 12 Sutherland operas filmed at the Sydney Opera House by the Australian Broadcasting Corporation, plus a scene with Marilyn Horne and Luciano Pavarotti in *Die Fledermaus* at Covent Garden. The operas are *Norma, Lucia di Lammermoor, Lucrezia Borgia, The Daughter of the Regiment, Lakmé, Adriana Lecouvreur, Semiramide, La traviata, Il trovatore, The Merry Widow, Dialogues des Carmélites,* and *Les Huguenots.* The excerpts are introduced by Sutherland and Richard Bonynge. Color. 116 minutes. On VHS.

1995 Dave and Dad on our Selection
Sutherland plays Mother Rudd with Leo McKern as her husband in this fiction film based on Steele Rudd's stories of his family's hard life on their "selection" (farm) in Queensland. George Whaley wrote and directed Sutherland's first film as a nonsinging actress, and she received

warm reviews as the tower-of-strength mother around whom the family revolves. Color. 105 minutes.

SWANN, CHRISTOPHER
English TV opera director(1950-)

Christopher Swann has directed a large number of telecasts and videos of operas from Glyndebourne as well as films about Glyndebourne's history. He has also directed videos of operas at Teatro alla Scala and concert stagings of Bernstein musicals in London. See ATTILA (1991), GLYNDEBOURNE (1992/1994), HIGGLETY PIGGLETY POP! (1985), IDOMENEO (1983), ON THE TOWN (1992), LUCIANO PAVAROTTI (1991), I VESPRI SICILIANI (1990), WEST SIDE STORY (1985), and WHERE THE WILD THINGS ARE (1985).

SWARTHOUT, GLADYS
American mezzo-soprano (1904–1969)

Gladys Swarthout made her debut with the Chicago Civic Opera in 1924 in *Tosca* but only as the offstage shepherd boy. However, by 1929 she was singing the lead in *La Gioconda* at the Metropolitan Opera, and she continued to appear there until 1945. Her most famous roles were Carmen and Mignon, but she also sang in the premiere of Howard Hanson's neglected opera *Merry Mount*. In 1950 she starred in a CBS Television production of CARMEN and then, after a period on the concert circuit, retired to Florence in 1954. Swarthout starred in five movies for Paramount in the 1930s during the cinema opera boom. None of them used her talent properly, and they were probably not helpful to her opera career. However, because of them, she can still be seen performing today in her prime. She published her autobiography *Come Soon, Tomorrow* in 1945.

1935 Rose of the Rancho
Swarthout's first film was a musical Western with John Boles set in California in 1852. It's a variation on *The Mark of Zorro* with Swarthout as the masked mystery person who leads the ranchers against the villains. She sings to alert her followers to assemble and even dances on Boles's sombrero. Justice and true love triumph in the end. Marion Gering directed for Paramount. Black and white. 85 minutes.

1936 Give Us This Night
Swarthout stars opposite Jan Kiepura in this operatic story, her best film. She refuses to work with a tenor who sings badly at rehearsals of a new opera, so Kiepura joins her in the premiere of Korngold's *Romeo and Juliet*. See GIVE US THIS NIGHT.

Gladys Swarthout and John Boles in *Rose of the Rancho* (1937)

1937 Champagne Waltz
Swarthout plays a Strauss named Elsa in this film set in Vienna that revolves around the rivalry between the Vienna Waltz Palace and a jazz club next door. Swarthout is romanced by jazzman Fred MacMurray, and together they imagine the waltz palace in its heyday when the "Blue Danube Waltz" was first played. Despite the title, the film doesn't have much fizz. Edward Sutherland directed for Paramount. Black and white. 87 minutes.

1938 Romance in the Dark
Swarthout plays a naïve singer used by John Boles to distract a rival. She sings the "Berceuse" from Godard's *Jocelyn*, the "Habanera" from *Carmen*, the "Song of India" from *Sadko*, and a duet from *Don Giovanni* with Boles. See ROMANCE IN THE DARK.

1939 Ambush
In Swarthout's last film, a low-budget crime picture, she has a dramatic nonsinging role as the innocent sister of a man who joins a gang of bank robbers. She is taken hostage but rescued by truck driver Lloyd Nolan. Kurt Neumann directed for Paramount. Black and white. 60 minutes.

SWEENEY TODD
1979 Broadway opera by Sondheim

Crazed 19th-century London barber Sweeney Todd seeks revenge on evil Judge Turpin who unjustly imprisoned him, ravished his wife, and stole his daughter Johanna. With the help of Mrs. Lovett, he turns customers into meat pies. Stephen Sondheim's *Sweeney Todd, the Demon Barber of Fleet Street,* libretto by Hugh Wheeler based on Christopher Bond's 1973 play, lyrics by the composer, opened in New York in 1979 with Len Cariou as Sweeney Todd and Angela Lansbury as Mrs. Lovett. It won eight Tony Awards, including Best Musical. The score is near operatic, with three-quarters of it sung, and there is a strong use of recurring motifs and complex ensembles. *Sweeney Todd* has begun to enter the opera repertory with presentations by New York City Opera in 1984, Opera North in Leeds in 1998, and Finnish National Opera in 1998.

1982 Dorothy Chandler Pavilion, Los Angeles

American stage production: Terry Hughes (director), Paul Gemignani (conductor), Eugene Lee (set designer).

Cast: George Hearn (Sweeney Todd), Angela Lansbury (Mrs. Lovett), Edmund Lyndeck (Judge Turpin), Betsy Joslyn (Johanna), Chris Groenendaal (Anthony), Calvin Remsberg (The Beadle), Ken Jennings (Tobias), Sara Woods (Beggar Woman).

Video: RKO VHS. Telecast September 12, 1982. Color. In English. 140 minutes

2001 Davies Symphony Hall, San Francisco

American semistaged concert production: Lonny Price (director), Rob Fisher (conductor, San Francisco Symphony and Chorus).

Cast: George Hearn (Sweeney Todd), Patti LuPone (Mrs. Lovett), Timothy Nolen (Judge Turpin), Lisa Vroman (Johanna), Davis Gaines (Sailor), Neal Patrick Harris (Tobias).

Telecast October 25, 2001, on PBS. Color. In English. 139 minutes.

Related film

2002 Tomorrow La Scala!

Fiction film about a small English opera company presenting *Sweeney Todd* in the maximum-security wing of a prison and putting lifers in the chorus line. Jessica Stevenson plays the director of the opera; Francesca Joseph directed the film. Color. In English. 108 minutes.

SWEETE, BARBARA WILLIS
Canadian opera film director (1955-)

Barbara Willis Sweet has directed more than 25 films for her Toronto company Rhombus Media, mostly about music and dance, including five with opera content. They are remarkably innovative, but they have not always been well received by critics. The first operatic film was the 1993 Handel pastiche opera THE SORCERESS, which she created for Kiri Te Kanawa by stitching together arias from six operas. The best-liked was her 1995 dance/opera version of Purcell's DIDO AND AENEAS with Mark Morris as choreographer/dancer. The most straightforward was her 1997 documentary *A Tale of Tanglewood: Peter Grimes Reborn.* The most unusual was her idiosyncratic 2000 film DON GIOVANNI: LEPORELLO'S REVENGE, in which she tries to improve on Mozart and da Ponte's version of the story. The most controversial was her 2002 film of Gounod's ROMÉO ET JULIETTE, with Roberto Alagna and Angela Gheorghiu, in which she trimmed nearly two hours off the original.

SWEETHEARTS
1913 operetta by Herbert

VICTOR HERBERT's popular operetta *Sweethearts* has a Ruritanian-type plot about a young woman named Sylvia who works in a laundry in Belgium. She is really a princess, however, and so she finally wins a prince. The book is by Harry B. Smith and Fred de Grésac with lyrics by Robert B. Smith. The "Sweethearts Waltz" and "Pretty as a Picture" are the best-known songs.

1938 MGM film

American feature film: W. S. Van Dyke (director), Dorothy Parker and Alan Campbell (screenplay), Oliver Marsh (cinematographer), Cedric Gibbons (art director).

Cast: Jeanette MacDonald (Gwen Marlowe), Nelson Eddy (Ernest Lane), Frank Morgan (Felix Lehman), Ray Bolger (Hans), Mischa Auer (Lee Kronk).

Video: MGM VHS/LD. Color. In English. 114 minutes.

Comment: The plot is entirely new. MacDonald and Eddy play a married couple starring in a longrunning stage production of the operetta *Sweethearts.* Their producer (Morgan) manipulates them into a quarrel because he is afraid they are going to Hollywood, and this causes them to split for a time. This was MGM's first three-strip Technicolor film, and cinematographer Marsh won an Oscar for his colorful work.

Related film

1951 The Great Caruso

Dorothy Kirsten, playing Enrico Caruso's Met stage partner, is shown singing "Sweethearts" at the home of his wife-to-be while he pines for her at a distant concert. See THE GREAT CARUSO.

SWEETHEARTS ON PARADE
1953 American film with opera content

Sweethearts on Parade, a low-budget Republic musical set in 19th-century Indiana, features several operatic arias. Kathleen (Lucille Norman) plays Aline in a production of Balfe's *The Bohemian Girl* and marries fellow performer Cam (Ray Middleton); he has the role of Thaddeus and sings "Then You'll Remember Me." After they have a daughter Sylvia (Eileen Christy), Cam is unfaithful, so Kathleen leaves him and settles in Kokomo. Many years later a traveling medicine show run by Cam arrives in town, and Sylvia becomes involved with a man in the show (Bill Shirley). When she sings an aria she learned from her mother, Cam is upset and sends her home. When Sylvia learns that Cam is her father, she decides to join the traveling show with her mother Kathleen, who still loves Cam. The opera arias featured in the film include Lucia's "Regnava nel silencio" from *Lucia di Lammermoor*, Lionel's "Ach, so fromm" from *Martha* sung in English, and Amina's "Ah! non giunge uman pensiero" from *La sonnambula*. Robert Armbruster arranged the music, Houston Branch wrote the screenplay, Reggie Lanning was the cinematographer, and Allan Dwan directed for Republic Pictures. Trucolor. In English. 90 minutes.

SWING, THE
1956 TV opera by Kastle

A young bride-to-be doesn't know whether to be happy or sad on her wedding day. Her father pushes her back and forth in the family swing to calm her fears, as he had when she was a child. Her mother comes out, and they go to the wedding. Leonard Kastle's brief but poignant TV opera *The Swing*, libretto by the composer, was commissioned for the NBC women's program *The Home Show*.

1956 NBC Television
American TV production: Garth Dietrick (director), Norman Paris (conductor, NBC Opera Theatre Orchestra), Lewis Ames (producer), Arlene Dahl (host of show).
Cast: Norman Atkins (father), Edith Gordon (daughter), Marguerite Lewis (mother).
Telecast June 11, 1956, on *The Home Show* on NBC. Black and white. In English. 15 minutes.

SYBERBERG, HANS JÜRGEN
German film director (1935–)

Hans Jürgen Syberberg, who has made notable films about Hitler and Karl May, directed one of the most controversial modern opera films, a highly symbolic but very beautiful 1982 PARSIFAL. He has also made films that feature Richard Wagner, including the fictional *Ludwig, Requiem for a Virgin King* and the documentary *The Confessions of Winifred Wagner.* See LUDWIG II (1972) and RICHARD WAGNER (1975).

SYDNEY

Joan Sutherland and Australian Opera videos have made the beauty of the Sydney Opera House recognizable to the rest of the world, even to those who never heard of the controversy over its construction. It soars out over Sydney Harbor at the beginning of each Australian Opera video. There are also fascinating documentaries about the opera house itself. See ABC TELEVISION (Australia), ADRIANA LECOUVREUR (1984), LA BOHÈME (1993), COSÌ FAN TUTTE (1990), DIE CSÁRDÁSFÜRSTIN (1990), LA FILLE DU RÉGIMENT (1986), DIALOGUES DES CARMÉLITES (1985), DIE FLEDERMAUS (1982), THE GONDOLIERS (1989), LES HUGUENOTS (1990), LAKMÉ (1976), LUCIA DI LAMMERMOOR (1986), LUCREZIA BORGIA (1977), DIE MEISTERSINGER VON NÜRNBERG (1988), NORMA (1978), I PURITANI (1985), SEMIRAMIDE (1986), JOAN SUTHERLAND (1985/1993), TOSCA (1986), IL TROVATORE (1983), VOSS (1987), WAR AND PEACE (1973), and DIE ZAUBERFLÖTE (1986).

1973 The Fifth Façade
Danish architect Jörn Utzon provides the commentary for this film and notes that "one could not design a building for such an exposed position without paying attention to the roof—one must have a fifth façade." All the façades are shown during the construction and opening of the opera house. Also seen are rehearsals by the Sydney Symphony Orchestra and scenes from productions of *War and Peace* and *The Threepenny Opera*. Color. 28 minutes.

1984 As Frozen Music
Lively documentary about the Sydney Opera House and how it moved from being controversial to being a performing arts center. Featured in interviews are Joan Sutherland, Luciano Pavarotti, and Janet Baker, and there are extracts from operas and plays. Produced, directed, and edited by John Davy Tristram and I. James Wilson for Juniper Film. Color. In English. 55 minutes. Brighton VHS.

1997 Celebration! 40 Years of Australian Opera
Australian television documentary celebrating 40 years of Australian Opera and ABC Television. It includes archival materials, interviews, and a farewell tribute to Joan Sutherland. Peter Butler wrote and directed it for ABC Television. Color and black and white. In English. 89 minutes.

SYLVA, MARGUERITA
Belgian/American soprano (1875–1957)

Marguerita Sylva, who sang the role of Carmen more than 600 times on stages around the world, was compared to Calvé, who sang the role more than 1,000 times. In 1916 she made an Italian film of the opera to showcase her interpretation. Sylva was born in Brussels with the plain name of Smith (her father was English). She became a protégé of William S. Gilbert at the age of 17, and he changed her name and helped her make her London debut in *Carmen* in 1892. She later sang in Paris, Berlin, Vienna, New York, and other U.S. cities. She starred in Victor's Herbert's operetta THE FORTUNE TELLER on Broadway in 1898 and in several films. Her last stage role was *Three Waltzes* on Broadway in 1937. She began to take small roles in Hollywood films during the 1940s, including some classic movies. Most of her recordings were destroyed in a 1914 fire, which may explain why she is not as well remembered as other singers of her time.

1916 Carmen
Sylva shows off her style of playing the tempestuous gypsy in the Italian film *Carmen,* made for the Cines Studio in Rome. Critics praised the intensity of her performance. The supporting cast includes André Habay as Don José, Juan Rovira as Escamillo, Cecile Tryan as Frasquita, and Suzanne Arduini. Giovanni Doria and August Turchi directed for Cines. Black and white. Silent. About 75 minutes.

1920 The Honey Bee
Sylva plays a woman who falls in love with a married man and flees to Paris where she becomes involved with a boxer. Sylva's costars were Thomas Holding and Nigel Barrie. Rupert Julian directed and wrote the screenplay based on a novel by Samuel Merwin. American Film Company. Black and white. Silent. About 75 minutes.

1941 They Dare Not Leave
Sylva plays Countess Marlik in this film about Austrian patriots during World War II. James Whale directed for Columbia. Black and white. 75 minutes.

1943 The Leopard Man
Sylva is Marta in this Val Lewton thriller based on a Cornell Woolrich novel directed by Jacques Tourneur. The story concerns a town terrified of a killer leopard. RKO. Black and white. In English. 66 minutes.

1943 The Seventh Victim
Sylva is restaurant owner Mrs. Romarci in this Val Lewton thriller directed by Mark Robson. Kim Hunter plays a woman involved with devil worship. RKO. Black and white. 71 minutes.

1944 The Conspirators
Sylva has a small role in this World War II spy film starring Hedy Lamarr and Sydney Greenstreet. Jean Negulesco directed. Black and white. 100 minutes.

1944 To Have and Have Not
Sylva is a nightclub cashier in this famous movie in which Humphrey Bogart first met Lauren Bacall. He's a tough guy in Martinique in 1940 involved in the French Resistance. Howard Hawks directed. Black and white. 100 minutes.

1945 The Gay Señorita
Sylva plays matriarch Dona Maria Sandoval who wants to build a street to spotlight Latin American culture. Arthur Dreifuss directed. Columbia. Black and white. In English. 70 minutes.

1945 Her Highness and the Bellboy
Sylva has a small role as a diplomat's wife in this romantic comedy starring Hedy Lamarr. Richard Thorpe directed for MGM. Black and white. 108 minutes.

SZABÓ, ISTVÁN
Hungarian film director (1938–)

István Szabó, who won an Academy Award for his 1981 film *Mephisto,* began making films in Hungary in 1960 and gained international success with *Love Film* and *25 Fireman's Street.* His opera film MEETING VENUS is one of the best screen portrayals of the problems of producing an opera. Szabó also directs opera on stage, and *Meeting Venus* is said to be partially autobiographical.

SZIRMAI, ALBERT
Hungarian composer (1880–1967)

Albert Szirmai (or Sirmay) was one of a group of composers, including Emmerich Kálmán and Viktor Jacobi, who made Hungarian operettas famous during the early years of the century. He had a major success with his 1907 operetta *The Yellow Domino* and continued to compose in the genre until 1964. His biggest hit was the 1916 Hungarian operetta MÁGNÁS MISKA (Miska the Great), which has been filmed three times. Szirmai was also one of the collaborators on a notable 1913 London operetta about the movies called *The Girl on the Film,* adapted from the German FILMZAUBER. He moved to New York in 1926 where he worked with Broadway composers as music editor for Chappell.

T

TABARRO, IL

1918 opera by Puccini

Il tabarro (The Cloak) is the first part of GIACOMO PUCCINI'S trilogy *Il trittico*, which premiered at the Metropolitan Opera in 1918. It's a harsh, realistic story about a tragic love triangle. Seine River barge captain Michele finds out that his wife Giorgetta is being unfaithful and kills her lover Luigi. He wraps the body in his cloak and gives it to his wife. The libretto by Giuseppe Adami is based on Didier Gold's play *La houppelande.*

1950 BBC Television

English TV production: John Lanchbery (conductor, BBC Television Orchestra).

Cast: John Hargreaves (Michele), Jennifer Vyvyan (Giorgetta), Arthur Serven (Luigi), Gertrude Holt (Frugola), Craig Sinkinson (Tinca).

Telecast live December 7, 1950. Black and white. In English. 50 minutes.

1952 NBC Opera Theatre

American TV production: Hans Busch (director), Samuel Chotzinoff (producer), Peter Herman Adler (conductor, NBC Opera Theatre Orchestra), Carl Kent (set designer), Townsend Brewster (English translation).

Cast: Robert Weede (Michele), Elaine Malbin (Giorgetta), Davis Cunningham (Luigi), Margery Mayer (Babila), Kenneth Smith (Todo).

Video at the MTR. Telecast live February 14, 1952. Kirk Browning (director). Black and white. In English. 52 minutes.

1981 Metropolitan Opera

American stage production: Fabrizio Melano (director), James Levine (conductor, Metropolitan Opera Orchestra and Chorus), David Reppa (set/costume designer).

Cast: Cornell MacNeil (Michele), Renata Scotto (Giorgetta), Vasile Moldoveanu (Luigi) Bianca Berini (Frugola), Charles Anthony (Tinca), Italo Tajo (Talpa).

Video at the MTR. Telecast live November 14, 1981, as part of *Il trittico.* Kirk Browning (director). Color. In Italian with English subtitles. 51 minutes.

1983 Teatro alla Scala

Italian stage production: Silvano Bussoti (director), Gianandrea Gavazzeni (conductor, Teatro alla Scala Orchestra and Chorus), Silvia Lelli, Roberto Masotti, Luciano Moarinie (set/costume designers).

Cast: Piero Cappuccilli (Michele), Sylvia Sass (Giorgetta), Nicola Martinucci (Luigi), Eleanora Jankovic (Frugola), Sergio Bertocchi (Tinca).

Home Vision VHS (with *Il trittico*). Brian Large (director). Color. In Italian with English subtitles. 51 minutes.

1994 Metropolitan Opera

American stage production: Fabrizio Melano (director), James Levine (conductor, Metropolitan Opera Orchestra and Chorus), David Reppa (set/costume designer).

Cast: Juan Pons (Michele), Teresa Stratas (Giorgetta), Plácido Domingo (Luigi), Florence Quivar (Frugola), Charles Anthony (Tinca).

Video: DG VHS. Taped September 26, 1994; telecast December 18, 1994, with *Pagliacci*. Brian Large (director). Color. In Italian with English subtitles. 52 minutes.

TADDEI, GIUSEPPE

Italian baritone (1916–)

Giuseppe Taddei made his debut in Rome in 1936 and sang there regularly until World War II. During the postwar period, he sang in Vienna, London, Salzburg, and La Scala and began to specialize in Mozart. He sang at Covent Garden and in the United States during the 1950s and has been particularly popular in comic roles such as Verdi's Falstaff and Pergolesi's Music Master. See ANDREA CHÉNIER (1955), DON GIOVANNI (1954), L'ELISIR D'AMORE (1954), FALSTAFF (1982), IL MAESTRO DI CAPELLA (1987), and TOSCA (1983 film).

1956 Giuseppe Taddei in Tokyo

Taddei is shown on stage in Tokyo in two of his favorite roles in the compilation video *Legends of Opera*. As Falstaff he sings "Quand'ero paggio" opposite Orietta Moscucci. As Figaro in *Le nozze di Figaro*, he sings "Non più andrai." Black and white. In Italian. 8 minutes. Legato Classics VHS.

TAGLIAVINI, FERRUCCIO
Italian tenor (1913–1995)

Ferruccio Tagliavini, one of the great Italian postwar tenors, was a regular at the Metropolitan Opera from 1947 to 1954. He made his debut in Florence in 1938, sang widely in Italy during the war, and had a strong international career from 1947 to 1965 when he retired from the stage. He also had a small but memorable film career. He began singing, though not acting, in the 1941 film TOSCA and made his first screen appearance with Tito Gobbi in the 1946 IL BARBIERE DI SIVIGLIA. It opened in New York while he was having great success at the Met, so it was promoted as a Tagliavini film. In addition to his films, he can be seen in fine form on *Voice of Firestone* television shows and a documentary about La Scala. See L'ELISIR D'AMORE (1941 film/1959), RIGOLETTO (1941 film), and TEATRO ALLA SCALA (1994).

1941 Voglio vivere così
Voglio vivere così, Tagliavini's first film as an actor, is primarily an excuse for letting him sing and gets its title from the name of one of his songs. He plays a man from the country who thinks he has been given an opera audition. It's a joke, but he is still able to get a job with the opera theater as a stagehand. When he has to step in to replace the tenor, he becomes a star. Tagliavini's singing is splendid even if the film is a bit creaky. Mario Mattoli wrote and directed. Black and white. In Italian. 83 minutes.

1942 La donna è mobile
In *La donna è mobile* (released in America as *The Lady Is Fickle*), Tagliavini plays a schoolteacher with a great voice. On a visit to Rome, he is discovered as a singer but loses his fiancée. After singing arias from *La bohème, La sonnambula, Lohengrin*, and *L'elisir d'amore*, he gets his girl back. Mario Mattoli directed the screenplay by Mario Monicelli and Steno. Black and white. In Italian. 78 minutes.

1944 Ho tanta voglia di cantare!
In *Ho tanta voglia di cantare!* (shown in America as *Anything for a Song*), Tagliavini plays a man who would rather sing than eat, despite his father's opposition. The sound and photography are poor, but this is not surprising as it was one of the few Italian films made in the chaos after Mussolini's downfall on July 25, 1943. Mario Monicelli directed. Black and white. In Italian. 80 minutes.

1949 Al diavolo la celebrità
Al diavolo la celebrità (shown in America as *One Night of Fame*) is a comedy fantasy about a man who accidentally invokes the devil and is forced to become famous people like Tagliavini, who plays a tenor. Tagliavini's wife Pia Tassinari joins him for a duet from Boito's *Mefistofele*. Mario Monicelli cowrote the screenplay with Steno and codirected it with Stefano Vanzina. Black and white. In Italian. 91 minutes. Opera Dubs/Lyric VHS.

1950 I cadetti di Guascogna
Ugo Tognazzi made his debut opposite Tagliavini and Walter Chiari in *The Cadets of Guascogna*, a "let's-put-on-a-show" comedy. Tagliavini sings "Una furtiva lagrima," a Rossini tarantella, and "Santa Lucia" as a group of army draftees hold a fund-raising show for stranded actors. Mario Mattoli directed for Excelsa Film. Black and white. In Italian. 90 minutes.

1950–1954 Tagliavini in Opera & Song Vol. 1
Tagliavini in performances on *The Voice of Firestone* television programs between 1950 and 1954. He sings arias from *Tosca, La bohème, Martha, L'elisir d'amore*, and *Rigoletto* and songs by Leoncavallo, Tchaikovsky, Schubert, di Capua, Tosti, and de Curtis. Black and white. 50 minutes. VAI VHS.

1951 Anema e core
Tagliavini plays a singer discovered by crooks who become his managers, but they are stymied by his inability to sing in public. The supporting cast includes Nino Manfredi, Dorian Gray, and Mario Riva. The title comes from a famous Neapolitan song. Mario Mattoli directed for Excelsa Film. Color. In Italian. 86 minutes. Premiere Opera/Opera Dubs VHS.

1952–1955 Tagliavini in Opera and Song Vol. 2
Tagliavini in performance on *The Voice of Firestone* television programs from 1952 to 1955. He sings arias and duets (with Margaret Broderson and Frances Wyatt) from *Carmen, Martha, Il trovatore*, and *La traviata*, plus songs by Rossini, di Capua, and d'Esposito. Black and white. 30 minutes. VAI VHS.

1959 Vento di Primavera
Tagliavini plays a famous Italian tenor in *Spring Wind*, a virtual remake of Gigli's first film *Forget-Me-Not*. He marries a German woman (Sabine Bethmann) who is on the rebound from a love affair and almost loses her when she meets up with her first love again. Giulio Del Torre directed the Italian version, and Arthur Maria Rabenalt directed the German version titled *Vergiss mein nicht* (like the Gigli film). Cineitalia-Trio Film. Color. 103 minutes.

1993 Ferruccio Tagliavini—L'Uomo, la voce

Ferruccio Tagliavini—The Man, the Voice, an Italian documentary celebrating the tenor, was produced in his native Reggio Emilia and published with a book devoted to his career and films. There are scenes at the Reggio Emilia theater where his career began, excerpts from *Voice of Firestone* telecasts, and interviews. Umberto Bonafini directed. Color and black and white. In Italian. 60 minutes. Magis Books (Italy) VHS.

TAJO, ITALO
Italian bass (1915–1993)

Italo Tajo made his debut in 1935 in Turin and was still singing on stage in 1991. His early career was at the Rome Opera and La Scala, but later he became a regular at Covent Garden, San Francisco, and the Met. He made his Met debut in 1948 as Don Basilio in *The Barber of Seville* and became noted there for his buffo roles. He also appeared on Broadway, taking over the lead in *The Most Happy Fella* from Robert Weede. Tajo helped create the opera department at the University of Cincinnati and was active teaching there. His longevity is evident in his screen career. He can be seen in films of operas made in Italy during the 1940s and videos of operas made in the United States during the 1980s. See IL BARBIERE DI SIVIGLIA (1946), LA BOHÈME (1977/1982/1989), DON GIOVANNI (1947/1954), DON PASQUALE (1955), L'ELISIR D'AMORE (1947), FAUST (1949), LUCIA DI LAMMERMOOR (1946), RICORDI (1954), IL TABARRO (1981), and TOSCA (1985).

TAKE MY LIFE
1947 English film with opera content

Greta Gynt plays an opera singer married to Hugh Williams in the 1947 British suspense film *Take My Life*. She has to prove that he did not murder old girlfriend Rosalie Crutchley and is finally able to find the real murderer with the help of music. Gynt is seen on stage performing an imaginary opera aria created for the film by composer William Alwyn; the singing voice belongs to Victoria Sladen. A recent CD of music by Alwyn features a new version sung by Susan Bullock. Ronald Neame directed the film, Guy Green photographed it, and Winston Graham, Valerie Taylor, and Margaret Kennedy wrote the screenplay. Made for Cineguild. Black and white. 79 minutes.

TALE OF TSAR SALTAN, THE
1900 opera by Rimsky-Korsakov

The full name of NIKOLAI RIMSKY-KORSAKOV's imaginative fantasy opera is *The Tale of Tsar Saltan, of his Son the Famous and Mighty Hero Prince Guidon Saltano-*

vich, and of the Beautiful Swan Princess. It tells the story of Tsar Saltan who marries Militrissa, the youngest of three sisters, and what happens to their son Prince Guidon after his exile to an island with the Swan Princess. The princess changes the prince into a bumble bee (the popular "Flight of the Bumble Bee" music) so he can spy on his family back home. Librettist Vladimir Bielsky took the story from Pushkin. The Russian title is *Skazka o Tsare Saltane.*

1978 Dresden State Opera

East German stage production: Harry Kupfer (director), Siegfried Kurz (conductor, Dresden State Opera Orchestra and Chorus), Peter Sykora (set/costume designer).

Cast: Rolf Wollard (Tsar), Lidija Rushizkaja (Militrissa), Stephan Spiewok (Prince Guidon), Ilse Ludwig (Swan Princess), Barbara Hoene (Barbaricha), Elenore Elstermann and Barbara Gubisch (Militrissa's sisters).

Video: VIEW/House of Opera VHS. Annelies Thomas (director). Color. In German. 98 minutes.

Comment: Imaginative and entertaining.

Related film

1966 Ptushko film

Soviet director Alexander Ptushko's *The Tale of Tsar Saltan* is a large-scale fantasy based on the Pushkin story with Rimsky-Korsakov's music used as score. Larissa Golubkina, Oksana Ryabinkina, and Olga Vikland are the main actors, with Igor Gelein and Valentin Zakharov as cinematographers. This was Ptushko's last film, but it never seems to have been released in the West. Made for Mosfilm Studios. Color. In Russian. 85 minutes.

TALE OF TWO CITIES
1951 opera by Benjamin

The French Revolution as seen through the prism of a cross-Channel love story and a noble sacrifice. Arthur Benjamin's *Tale of Two Cities,* an operatic adaptation of the Charles Dickens novel *A Tale of Two Cities,* was one of four winning operas in the 1951 Festival of Britain Opera Competition. Composed to a libretto by Cedric Cliffe with strong choral numbers, it premiered on BBC Radio's Third Program on April 17, 1953, and was repeated twice. It was staged by the New Opera Company at Sadler's Wells in 1957 and adapted for television and telecast by BBC in 1958.

1958 BBC Television

British TV production: Rudolph Cartier (director), Leon Lovett (conductor, Royal Philharmonic Orchestra and New Opera Chorus), Norman James (set designer).

Cast: John Cameron (Sidney Carton), Geoffrey Clifton Young (Charles Darnay), Heather Harper (Lucie Manette), Heddle Nash (Dr. Manette), Michael Langdon (Marquis de St. Evremonde), Amy Shuard (Madame Defarge), Janet Howe (Miss Pross).

Telecast live December 2, 1958. Rudolph Cartier (director). Black and white. In English. 113 minutes.

TALES OF HOFFMANN, THE

See Les Contes d'Hoffmann.

TALLEY, MARION

American soprano (1907–1983)

Missouri-born Marion Talley was a child prodigy, a brilliant coloratura soprano whose overly quick rise to stardom probably ruined a promising career. She was only 15 when excitement over her performance as Mignon in an amateur production led to a much-publicized audition at the Met. It was impossible for her to live up to hyped expectations so her debut at the Met in 1926 as Gilda in *Rigoletto* was inevitably a letdown. However, she continued to sing at the Met in important roles until 1929 when, more or less burned out, she retired from opera. She later attempted a comeback, but it was not successful. The publicity around her Met debut was such that she was invited to star in three of the first Vitaphone opera shorts. In 1936 she was signed by Republic Pictures in an attempt to create prestige for the studio with a classy operatic film. It was not a success and her movie career ended.

1926/1928 Vitaphone films
She was billed as "Marion Talley, Youthful Prima Donna of the New York Metropolitan Opera" when she starred in three Vitaphone sound shorts, two with tenor Beniamino Gigli. In the first, which premiered with the feature *Don Juan* in 1926, she sings Gilda's "Caro nome" from *Rigoletto*. In 1927 and 1928 she made her films with Gigli. In one she sings Gilda in the *Rigoletto* Quartet with Gigli, Giuseppe De Luca, and Jeanne Gordon. In the other she sings Lucia opposite Gigli in the *Lucia di Lammermoor* duet "Verranno a te sull'aura." Black and white. About 8 minutes each.

1936 Follow Your Heart
This was a down-home, tongue-in-cheek Republic Pictures opera film for the folks. Talley plays a farm girl with an operatic voice who sings one aria in a cellar poking a furnace and another in a haymow. Despite all this, she sings rather well. See Follow Your Heart.

TAMAGNO, FRANCISCO

Italian tenor (1850–1905)

Francisco Tamagno, who created the role of Verdi's Otello at Teatro alla Scala in 1887, was known internationally for his interpretation of the role, including performances in London, Chicago, and the Met. Although he was popular in other roles, he is remembered as Otello.

1905/1907 Otello films
Tamagno was featured in two screenings of sound films of *Otello*. On November 13, 1905, he sang in a film featuring a scene from the opera presented at the Gran Salon Excelsior in Rome. In January 1907 he sang in a film of a scene from Act IV of the opera shown at the Politeama Carboni in Cagliari. As the information about these films is from contemporary advertisements, it could be that other actors appeared on screen miming to his recordings. The films do not survive, and the Italian company that made them is not known.

TAMERLANO

1724 opera by Handel

George Frideric Handel's *Tamerlano,* libretto by Nicola Haym, is based on several plays about the Eastern military genius Tamerlane but not Marlowe's. Asteria, in Tamerlano's prison with her father Bajazet, agrees to marry the tyrant if he will free her father. She plans to murder him after the wedding, but her father commits suicide before the wedding. Tamerlano relents and marries Irene instead.

2001 Halle Handel Festival
German stage production: Jonathan Miller (director), Trevor Pinnock (conductor, The English Concert), Judy Levin (costume designer).

Cast: Monica Bacelli (Tamerlano), Elizabeth Norberg-Schulz (Asteria), Thomas Randle (Bajazet), Anna Bonitatibus (Irene).

Video: Arthaus DVD. Helga Dubnyicsek (director). Color. In Italian with English subtitles. The opera itself is 192 minutes, the DVD is 323 minutes with extras.

Comment: Nicely sung and directed production filmed at the Goethe Theatre at Bad Lauchstad. The DVD includes documentary on Halle where Handel was born, history of the festival, and related material.

TAMING OF THE SHREW, THE

1953 opera by Giannini

Clever wealth-seeking adventurer Petruchio marries and tames shrewish Katherina in medieval Italy. Vittorio

GIANNINI's most popular opera is based on Shakespeare's *The Taming of the Shrew* as adapted by Dorothy Fee and the composer. It premiered in a concert version in Cincinnati in 1953 and was first performed by regional groups. It attracted national attention after it was given a large-scale production on NBC Opera Theatre in 1954 and staged by New York City Opera in 1958.

1954 NBC Opera Theatre

American TV production: Charles Polacheck (director), Samuel Chotzinoff (producer), Peter Herman Adler (conductor, NBC Symphony of the Air Orchestra), William Molyneux (set designer), John Boxer (costumes).

Cast: John Raitt (Petruchio), Susan Yager (Katherina), Sonia Stollin (Bianca), John Alexander (Lucentio), Donald Gramm (Hortensio), Leon Lishner (Baptista), Emile Renan (Biondello).

Video at the MTR. Telecast live March 13, 1954, on NBC. Kirk Browning (director). Color. In English. 90 minutes.

Related films

Shakespeare play
Shakespeare's play has been filmed twice by famous acting couples. The static 1929 version, starring Mary Pickford and Douglas Fairbanks as the battling pair, was directed by Sam Taylor. The more cinematic 1967 film, starring Elizabeth Taylor and Richard Burton, was directed by Franco Zeffirelli.

1953 Kiss Me Kate
Cole Porter's 1948 stage musical based on *The Taming of the Shrew* was filmed in 1953, the same year Giannini's opera version was first staged. Porter tells a double story, paralleling the play with a backstage plot and using actual lines from the play to begin songs such as "I've Come to Wive it Wealthily in Padua" and "Were Thine That Special Face." Kathryn Grayson and Howard Keel play the shrew and her tamer in this MGM film directed by George Sidney. Color. 109 minutes. MGM-UA VHS.

TANCREDI
1813 opera by Rossini

GIOACHINO ROSSINI's biggest success before *The Barber of Seville* was this *opera seria* set in Syracuse in 1005, the legendary age of the heroic Christian knight Tancredi and the conflict between Christians and Saracens. Tancredi loves Amenaide, who refuses to marry Orbazzano, who seeks revenge by false accusations. Tancredi fights as her champion and defeats the Saracens. The libretto by

Gaetano Rossi is based on Voltaire's *Tancrède,* which was derived from Tasso's epic *Gerusalemme Liberata.*

1981 Aix-en-Provence Festival
French stage production: Ralf Weikert (conductor, Scottish Chamber Orchestra).

Cast: Marilyn Horne (Tancredi), Katia Ricciarelli (Amenaide), Magali Damonte, Sonia Rigoghossian, Dalmacio Gonzales, Nicola Zaccaria.

Video: House of Opera/Lyric VHS. Color. In Italian. 160 minutes.

1992 Schwetzingen Festival
German stage production: Pier Luigi Pizzi (director, set/costume designer), Gianluigi Gelmetti (conductor, Stuttgart Radio Symphony Orchestra and South German Radio Chorus).

Cast: Bernadette Manca di Nissi (Tancredi), Maria Bayo (Amenaide), Ildebrando d'Arcangelo (Orbazzano), Raúl Giménez (Argirio), Katarzyna Bak (Isaura), Maria Pia Piscetelli (Roggiero).

Video: Arthaus (GB) DVD and RCA VHS/LD. Claus Viller (director). Color. In Italian with English subtitles. 166 minutes.

Related film

1911 La Gerusalemme liberata
Amleto Novelli plays Tancredi in this four-reel Italian epic based on the Tasso poem that was the basis of Rossini's opera. Emilio Ghione is Rinaldo, Fernando Negri-Pouget is Armida, and Gianna Terribili-Gonzales is Clorinda. Director Enrico Guazzoni spent five months making the film for Cines with a cast of more than 800. Released in the United States as *The Crusaders or Jerusalem Delivered.* Black and white. About 60 minutes.

TAN DUN
Chinese-born American composer (1957–)

Tan Dun was born in China but moved to New York as a young man to study and compose. His MARCO POLO, presented in Munich in 1996 and New York in 1997, won praise as a successful attempt to combine Eastern and Western music and led to a commission to create an opera for the Met. He also composed music for the 16th-century Chinese opera *Peony Pavilion* when it was staged in Europe and the United States by Peter Sellars in 1998; he described it as a combination of Gregorian chant, rock 'n' roll, and ancient Chinese opera. His *Ghost Opera,* performed around the world by the Kronos Quartet, is not really an opera, although it is based on Chinese "spirit operas." Tan reached his largest audience ever with his score for Ang Lee's popular 2000 film *Crouching Tiger, Hidden Dragon.*

TANNHÄUSER
1845 opera by Wagner

Tannhäuser und der Sängerkrieg auf Wartburg (Tannhäuser and the Wartburg Song Contest) is RICHARD WAGNER's examination of redemption through love. The minstrel knight Tannhäuser has been living a life of pure pleasure in Venusburg after being seduced by Venus, but he is enabled to return home to Thuringia after he calls on the Virgin Mary for help. He tries to win the hand of Elisabeth in a minstrel singing contest but fails when he reveals his past in his song. He is sent on a pilgrimage to Rome to get absolution from the Pope but returns without it. Elisabeth dies of a broken heart, but her self-sacrificing love redeems him at the last moment before he also dies. The "Pilgrims' Chorus" and Wolfram's "Hymn to the Evening Star" are popular numbers from the opera.

1978 Bayreuth Festival
German stage production: Götz Friedrich (director), Colin Davis (conductor, Bayreuth Festival Orchestra and Chorus), Jürgen Rose (set/costume designer), John Neumeier (choreographer).

Cast: Spas Wenkoff (Tannhäuser), Gwyneth Jones (Elisabeth/Venus), Hans Sotin (Landgrave Hermann), Bernd Weikl (Wolfram), Franz Mazura (Biterolf), Klaus Brettschneider (Young Shepherd), Robert Schunk (Walther).

Video: Philips VHS/LD. Thomas Olofsson (director). Color. In German with English subtitles. 190 minutes.

Comment: This was the first opera to be filmed at Bayreuth, and it stands up very well.

***1982 Metropolitan Opera
American stage production: Otto Schenk (director), James Levine (conductor, Metropolitan Opera Orchestra and Chorus), Günther Schneider-Siemssen (set designer), Patricia Zipprodt (costume designer), Norbert Vesak (choreographer).

Cast: Richard Cassilly (Tannhäuser), Eva Marton (Elisabeth), Tatiana Troyanos (Venus), John Macurdy (Landgrave Hermann), Bernd Weikl (Wolfram), Richard J. Clark (Biterolf), Bill Blaber (Young Shepherd), Robert Nagy (Walther).

Video: Pioneer DVD/LD and Paramount VHS. Taped December 20, 1982; telecast March 23, 1983. Brian Large (director). Color. In German with English subtitles. 176 minutes.

Comment: Traditional but exceptionally well done with Levine and the Met Orchestra at their best.

1990 Bayreuth Festival
German stage production: Wolfgang Wagner (director/set designer), Giuseppe Sinopoli (conductor, Bayreuth Festival Orchestra and Chorus), Reinhard Heinrich (costume designer), Ivan Marko (choreographer).

Cast: Richard Versalle (Tannhäuser), Cheryl Studer (Elisabeth), Ruthild Engert-Ely (Venus), Hans Sotin (Landgrave Hermann), Wolfgang Brendel (Wolfram), Siegfried Vogel (Biterolf), William Pell (Walther).

Video: Philips VHS/LD. Brian Large (director). Color. In German with English subtitles. 187 minutes.

Comment: Not at good as the early Bayreuth video.

1994 Bavarian State Opera
German stage production: David Alden (director), Zubin Mehta (conductor, Bavarian State Opera Orchestra and Chorus), Rony Toren (set designer), Buki Schiff (costume designer).

Cast: René Kollo (Tannhäuser), Nadine Secunde (Elisabeth), Waltraud Meier (Venus), Jan-Hendrik Rootering (Landgrave Hermann), Bernd Weikl (Wolfram), Ekkehard Wlaschiha (Biterolf).

Video: Image Entertainment/Arthaus (GB) DVD and Pioneer LD. Brian Large (director). Color. In German with English subtitles. 201 minutes.

Comment: Modernized and innovative but controversial production created for the Munich Opera Festival. The much-discussed sets include the giant letters GERMANIA NOSTRA as backdrop.

1998 San Carlo Opera, Naples
Italian stage production: Werner Herzog (director), Gustav Kahn (conductor, Teatro di San Carlo Opera Orchestra and Chorus).

Cast: Alan Woodrow (Tannhäuser), Gertrud Ottenthal (Elisabeth), Marianna Pentcheva (Venus), Ludwig Baumann (Wolfram), Andrea Silvestrelli (Hermann), Nikolov Bojidar (Walther), Ivan Konsulov (Biterolf).

Video: Image Entertainment DVD/Pioneer LD. Fabio Sparvoli (director). Color. In German with English subtitles. 186 minutes.

Early/related films

1908 Messter film
Henny Porten, Germany's first important film star, plays Elisabeth in this German Biophon sound film using a record of an´aria from the opera as soundtrack. Porten's father Franz, a former opera singer, directed the film in a Berlin studio using Oskar Messter's synchronization process. Black and white. In German. About 3 minutes.

1913 Thanhouser Studio film
James Cruze, later a major director, plays Tannhäuser with Marguerite Snow as Elisabeth in *Tannhäuser*, a film of the opera made by the American Thanhouser Studio. Florence La Badie is Venus, William Russell is Wolfram, and Lucius J. Henderson directed. The film was screened with the opera music played live. Black and white. Silent. About 35 minutes.

1938 Symphonic Films
Friedrich Feher conducts orchestral music from the opera for a one-reel film titled *Tannhäuser* made for the Symphonic Films Company. Black and white. 10 minutes.

1941 The Lady Eve
The "Pilgrims' Chorus" from *Tannhäuser* is heard on the soundtrack as Henry Fonda and Barbara Stanwyck begin their brief honeymoon in the sleeping car of a train. Preston Sturges directed. Black and white. 105 minutes.

1941 The Chocolate Soldier
Mezzo soprano Rise Stevens sings some of the *Tannhäuser* baritone aria "O du mein holder Abendstern" to the annoyment of her baritone husband Nelson Eddy in this rather odd adaptation of the Oscar Straus operetta. Roy Del Ruth directed. Black and white. 102 minutes.

1946 Voglio bene soltanto a te
Beniamino Gigli plays a tenor making a movie in this film, which features music from *Tannhäuser*. Giuseppe Fatigati directed. Black and white. In Italian. 80 minutes. Lyric/Opera Dubs VHS.

1948 Unfaithfully Yours
Orchestra conductor Rex Harrison, convinced the his wife Linda Darnell is betraying him, imagines how to forgive her while conducting the "Pilgrims' Chorus" from *Tannhäuser*. Preston Sturges directed. Black and white. 105 minutes.

1974 Butley
Simon Gray's 1971 stage play *Butley* and the 1974 film based on it both open with the *Tannhäuser* overture. Teacher Alan Bates is trying to listen to a recording of it while mulling over his love problems. Harold Pinter directed. Color. 127 minutes.

1982 The Night of the Shooting Stars
A retreating German soldier, singing Wolfram's "Hymn to the Evening Star" ("O du mein holder Abendstern"), is watched by villagers as he hurries ahead of the liberating U.S. Army at the end of World War II. Paolo and Vittorio Taviani feature this star theme in their film *La notte di San Lorenzo*, a harsh but poetic portrayal of the end of war in Tuscany, shown in the United States as *The Night of the Shooting Stars*. Color. In Italian with English subtitles. 107 minutes.

1991 Meeting Venus
István Szabó's bittersweet film centers around a major TV production of *Tannhäuser* in Paris. Glenn Close plays the soprano (voice of Kiri Te Kanawa) and Niels Arestrup is the conductor. See MEETING VENUS.

1997 Absolute Power
Director Clint Eastwood features an extract from *Tannhäuser* in this thriller in which he plays a thief who witnesses a U.S. president kill a woman. Color. 120 minutes.

TAPFERE SOLDAT, DER
See CHOCOLATE SOLDIER, THE.

TARARE
1787 opera by Salieri

Mozart's rival ANTONIO SALIERI joined forces with Beaumarchais, the author of *Le nozze di Figaro*, for a revolutionary French opera in which a king is deposed; it premiered just two years before the French Revolution. King Atar is jealous of his general Tarare so he burns his house, kidnaps his wife Astasie, and then condemns them to be burned alive. The people rise up against Atar, he is deposed by the eunuch Calpigi and his soldiers, and Tarare is crowned king. The opera was heavily revised for Italy by Salieri and librettist Lorenzo da Ponte and turned into the opera *Axur, rè d'Ormus*.

1988 Schwetzingen Festival
German stage production: Jean-Louis Martinoty (director), Jean-Claude Malgoire (conductor, Die Deutschen Händersolisten), Heniz Balthese (set designer), Daniel Ogier (costume designer).
Cast: Howard Crook, Jean-Philippe Lafont, Gabriele Rossmanith, Anna Caleb, Klaus Kirchner, Eberhard Lorenz.
Telecast by SDR German Television, Stuttgart. Claus Viller (director). Color. In French. 184 minutes.

TARKOVSKY, ANDREI
Russian film/opera director (1932–1986)

Andrei Tarkovsky, known for such powerful metaphysical movies as *Andrei Rublev, Solaris, The Mirror*, and *Stalker*, moved into stage opera direction toward the end of his life while in exile from the USSR. His masterful and hugely effective BORIS GODUNOV, first staged at

Covent Garden in 1983, was restaged and videotaped at the Kirov Opera in 1990.

TAUBER, RICHARD
Austrian tenor (1892–1948)

Richard Tauber, one of the leading tenors of the prewar period in Mozart operas, made his debut in 1913 in *Die Zauberflöte* and sang with Dresden Opera for many years. In the second part of his career, he began to sing in the operettas of Franz Lehár and helped revive that composer's career. In 1931 he brought Lehár's *The Land of Smiles* to London and, through it, became a popular star in England. In 1933, when Hitler came to power, Tauber moved permanently to London where he continued to appear in both opera and operetta. Although never notable as an actor, he was able to develop a major film career in Germany and England through his singing. See DAS LAND DES LÄCHELNS (1932) and PAGLIACCI (1936).

Richard Tauber

1923 Achtung! Aufnahme!
Tauber made this German promotional film to help sell his recordings. It is silent but his records were meant to be played with it. Black and white. 5 minutes. Print at the NFTA.

1929 Ich küsse ihre Hand, Madame
Tauber performs (voice only) the title song of *I Kiss Your Hand, Madame,* the first German sound film, and his song helped make it an international hit. The stars of the film are Marlene Dietrich and Harry Liedtke, who is the one singing on screen with Tauber's voice. Robert Land directed. Black and white. In German. 72 minutes.

1930 Ich glaub' nie mehr an eine Frau
In Tauber's first film as an actor, he plays a wise old sailor who sings popular tunes by Paul Dessau and helps a young friend win music hall girl Maria Solveg. Max

Reichmann directed. It was released in America as *Never Trust a Woman.* Black and white. In German. 96 minutes. Opera Dubs VHS.

1930 The End of the Rainbow
Tauber plays a Bavarian singer who becomes an opera star in Berlin where he stars in a production of *Martha* at the Berlin Opera. The other actors include Sophie Pagay, Lucie English, and Oscar Sima. Tauber made the film in English and German for his own company with Max Reichmann directing. The German version is titled *Das lockende Ziel.* Black and white. In English or German. 92 minutes. House of Opera/Lyric VHS (in German).

1931 Die grosse Attraktion
In the German film *The Big Attraction,* Tauber sings songs by Franz Lehár (including a tango called "Tauber-Lied"), by Bronislaw Kaper (a fox-trot called "Du warst mir ein Roman"), by Paul Dessau, and Franz Grothe. The cast includes Margiol Lion, Marianne Winkelstern, and Teddy Bill. This was Tauber's last film for his company. Max Reichmann directed. Black and white. In German. 85 minutes.

1932 Melodie der Liebe
In the German film *Melody of Love,* Tauber plays an opera star who falls in love with a gold digger (Alice Treff). When he finds that she is only interested in his money, he is heartbroken until Lien Deyers consoles him. Tauber sings opera arias and popular songs. Georg Jacoby directed. Black and white. In German. 100 minutes.

1934 Blossom Time
Tauber plays Franz Schubert in this excellent British musical about the life of the composer derived from the pastiche operetta *Das Dreimäderlhaus.* He loses the girl he loves to a count even though he sings beautifully. See DAS DREIMÄDERLHAUS.

1935 Heart's Desire
Tauber plays a Viennese beer garden singer who is brought to London by Leonora Corbett to play a gondolier in Carl Harbord's opera *Venetian Moon* (an imaginary opera created by Edward Lockton and Rudolph Sieczynski). Unfortunately, he loses her to the composer and has to go back to his Viennese sweetheart, Kathleen Kelly. The song "Vienna, City of My Dreams" became a hit through this English film, which also features Tauber's wife Diana Napier. Clifford Grey and Jack Davies wrote the screenplay, Jack Cox was the cinematographer, and Paul L. Stein directed for BIP. Black and white. 82 minutes. Bel Canto Society/Video Yesteryear VHS.

1936 Land Without Music/Forbidden Music

A practical princess bans music in a bankrupt Ruritanian country so its obsessively musical people can concentrate on making money. Tauber leads a revolution so people can get music back; he also wins the princess. See LAND WITHOUT MUSIC.

1945 Waltz Time

Tauber plays a shepherd in this English film telling how the waltz invaded Imperial Vienna. Empress Maria (Carol Raye) wants to marry one of her officers (Peter Graves), who is caught in a flirtation with Patricia Medina. Tauber sings "Break of Day," and Webster Booth and Anne Ziegler sing operetta-like music by Hans May. Paul L. Stein directed for British National. Black and white. 100 minutes. Bel Canto Society VHS.

1946 Lisbon Story

Tauber has a supporting role in his last feature, set in wartime Lisbon. Intelligence officer David Farrar uses his French actress fiancée Patricia Burke to foil Nazi Walter Rilla. Paul L. Stein directed for British National. Black and white. 103 minutes. Opera Dubs VHS.

1953 The Richard Tauber Story

Rudolf Schock plays Tauber in *Du bist die Welt für mich,* an Austrian film biography released in America as *The Richard Tauber Story.* The plot revolves around the tenor's love for a ballerina who quits the stage because of a bad heart. Ernst Marischka wrote and directed. Black and white. In German. 100 minutes. Opera Dubs VHS.

1958 Richard Tauber

John Hendrik narrates this German TV film about the singer's career, including information about his collaboration with Lehár. It includes excerpts from a home movie Tauber made while touring the United States plus newsreel and other archival film. Made for SFB Television. Black and white. In German. 30 minutes.

1971 This Was Richard Tauber

Charles Castle's film biography traces the history of the tenor's career over 30 years and includes excerpts from Tauber's feature films plus films of stage shows, public appearances, and tributes. The film, made with the help of Tauber's widow Diana Napier, concentrated on his singing. The soundtrack was released on an LP. Color. In English. 90 minutes.

TAVIANI, VITTORIO AND PAOLO

Italian film directors

The brothers Vittorio (1929–) and Paolo (1931–) Taviani, who have had international success with movies such as *Padre Padrone* and *Allonsafan,* say their childhood was full of live concerts and this is why music is a major component of their films. *The Night of the Shooting Stars* and *Kaos* both feature music from operas. See LE NOZZE DI FIGARO (1984 film) and TANNHÄUSER (1982 film).

TAXI DI NOTTE

1950 Italian film with opera content

Italian tenor Beniamino Gigli is at his amiable best in *Taxi di notte* (Night Taxi), a charming film about a taxi driver who sings opera for his customers to make extra tips. The story takes place within a 48-hour period in Rome during which time Gigli has the chance to sing Donizetti and Leoncavallo arias and Italian folk songs. He also gets an offer to sing opera in America, but it doesn't work out. The plot revolves around a baby abandoned in the taxi and the desperate search for the parents. Alberto Domenico Savino was music director, Aldo Giordani was cinematographer, Aldo De Benedetti wrote the screenplay based on a newspaper article by Bruno D'Agostini, and opera film specialist Carmine Gallone directed. Released in America as *The Singing Taxi Driver.* Black and white. In Italian. 100 minutes. Bel Canto Society/Opera Dubs VHS.

TCHAIKOVSKY, PYOTR

Russian composer (1840–1893)

Pyotr Ilyich Tchaikovsky devoted much of his time to composing opera, although he is probably better known for his piano and orchestral works. His most popular operas, EUGENE ONEGIN (1879) and THE QUEEN OF SPADES (1890), have become part of the international repertory and are available in multiple film and video versions. Tchaikovsky's first opera was *Voyevoda,* which premiered in 1868; the last was IOLANTA, first staged in 1891. There is also a video of his 1881 Joan of Arc opera THE MAID OF ORLEANS. Tchaikovsky's personal life has provided the basis for a number of not very enlightening films. Although he was homosexual, he jumped into a bad marriage that nearly drove him to suicide. It is worth noting that, in his lifetime, he was Russia's only full-time professional composer and that this was possible only because he had a rich patroness.

1948 Song of My Heart

Frank Sundstrom plays Tchaikovsky in this American film written and directed by Benjamin Glazer. Its basic plot is that Tchaikovsky is tormented because he can't marry a princess. Why? Because Production Code boss Joseph I. Breen warned the director about "the necessity of handling all situations very carefully in view of the fact that Tchaikovsky was a sex pervert...any emphasis on the fact that he led a 'womanless life' would be highly objectionable." This is only one of the reasons that critics and audiences profoundly disliked the film. David Leonard plays Rimsky-Korsakov, Lewis Howard is Mussorgsky, Robert Barron is Borodin, William Ruhl is Cui, and Jose Iturbi plays piano. Allied Artists. Black and white. In English. 92 minutes.

1959 Tchaikovsky
Respectful Soviet documentary about the composer produced by the Central Documentary Film Studio of Moscow. It follows his life and career from childhood through his adult life and has many musical excerpts. Pianists Sviatoslav Richter and Van Cliburn are among the performers. Color. In Russian. 50 minutes.

1964 The Peter Tchaikovsky Story
This is a pretty bland Disney documentary about the composer (no sexual content) focusing on his successes, failures, loves, and hates. Color. In English. 30 minutes.

1970 Tchaikovsky
Innokenti Smoktunovsky plays Tchaikovsky in *Krasnaya Palatka*, a stolid 70mm Soviet biography directed by Igor Talankin. The composer is treated reverently as his life and career is depicted from youth to death at the age of 53. Dimitri Tiomkin arranged the music, which includes excerpts from *Eugene Onegin* and *The Queen of Spades*. Vladimir Atlantov, Irina Arkhipova, Galina Oleinitchenko, Lev Vlasenko, and Valentina Levko are among the singers. Budimir Metalnikov, Yuri Naghibin, and Igor Talankin wrote the screenplay, and Margarita Pilikhina was the cinematographer. MGM-Mosfilm. Color. In Russian. 108 minutes.

1971 The Music Lovers
Director Ken Russell obviously relishes the music, but his vision of Tchaikovsky is more likely to dismay than enlighten. Richard Chamberlain plays Tchaikovsky with Glenda Jackson as his wife Nina. Like the curate's egg, the film is good in parts, but the bad parts are pretty rotten. The opera selections include the "Letter Song" from *Eugene Onegin* sung by April Cantelo and "Porgi Amor" from *Le nozze di Figaro*. Melvyn Bragg wrote the screenplay, based on the book *Beloved Friend* by Catherine Drinker Bowen and Barbara von Meck, and Douglas Slocombe was cinematographer. Color. In English. 122 minutes.

1986 Tchaikovsky
Vladimir Ashkenazy plays Tchaikovsky in two linked British films by writer/director Christopher Nupen. *Tchaikovsky's Women* tells the story of his life and career up to the time of his marriage and the opera *Eugene Onegin*. *Fate* is concerned with his life and musical ideas through *Manfred* and the Fifth and Sixth Symphonies. The music is played by the Swedish Radio Symphony Orchestra. Allegro Films. Color. In English. 120 minutes. Teldec VHS.

1993 A Gala for Tchaikovsky
Gala program at the Royal Opera House, Covent Garden, celebrating the 100th anniversary of the death of the composer. Plácido Domingo sings Lensky's aria from *Eugene Onegin*, Dmitri Hvorostovsky sings arias from *Sadko* and *The Queen of Spades*, Anna Tomowa-Sintow sings Lisa's aria from *The Queen of Spades*, Paata Burchuladze sings arias from *Iolanta* and Rimsky-Korsakov's *Sadko*, and Sergei Leiferkus sings an aria from Rachmaninoff's *Aleko*, a favorite of Tchaikovsky's. Kiri Te Kanawa sneaks in Puccini and sings Musetta's waltz from *La bohème*. The evening includes ballet as well as opera with the music performed by the Royal Opera House Orchestra conducted by Bernard Haitink and Valery Gergiev. Color. 90 minutes. Pioneer LD.

1996 Music for a Nation
Documentary about the music created in Russia at the end of the 19th century, with the focus on Tchaikovsky, including excerpts from *Eugene Onegin*. The film is part of the series *Man and Music*. Color. 53 minutes. Films for the Humanities & Sciences VHS.

1997 Tchaikovsky
Portrait of the composer and his music from his early years to his death in 1893 with excerpts from his works performed by the Moscow Symphony Orchestra led by David Palmer. This is part of the series *The Great Composers*. Color. In English. 26 minutes. Films for the Humanities & Sciences VHS.

1997 Great Composers: Tchaikovsky
BBC documentary about the composer produced by Simon Broughton as a segment of the seven-composer series *Great Composers*. It follows him from childhood to fame, from first opera to success, and includes opera extracts, comments from a tram driver, and other musical experts. Among those participating are Yuri Temirkanov, Valery Gergiev, and Evgeny Kissin. Kenneth Branagh narrates. Color. In English. 59 minutes. Warner (GB) DVD (with biographies of Puccini and Mahler).

2000 Great Composers
A DVD anthology with BBC TV biographies of three composers—Tchaikovsky, Puccini, and Mahler—all narrated by Kenneth Branagh. Color. In English. 177 minutes. Warner (GB) DVD.

TEATRO ALLA SCALA
Milan opera house

Teatro alla Scala in Milan, Italy's most famous opera house, has played an important role in the development of Italian opera, including premieres of operas by Rossini, Bellini, Donizetti, Verdi, and Puccini. It opened in 1778 was partially destroyed during World War II; it was rebuilt and reopened in 1946. It is extremely well represented on video, most of which begin by showing the theater from the square in front of it, although Jean-Pierre Ponnelle's film of *La Cenerentola* prowls around the lobby during the overture. The opera house has also been featured in many fiction films and documentaries. See ADRIANA LECOUVREUR (1989), AIDA (1985), ANDREA CHÉNIER (1985), ATTILA (1991), CARMEN (1984), LA CENERENTOLA (1981), COSÌ FAN TUTTE (1989), DON CARLO (1992), DON GIOVANNI (1989), LA DONNA DEL LAGO (1992), I DUE FOSCARI (1990), ERNANI (1982), LA FANCIULLA DEL WEST (1991), FEDORA (1993), LA FORZA DEL DESTINO (1978), LO FRATE 'NNAMORATO (1990), GIANNI SCHICCHI (1983), GUILLAUME TELL (1991), I LOMBARDI ALLA PRIMA CROCIATA (1984), LUCIA DI LAMMERMOOR (1992), MADAMA BUTTERFLY (1986), NABUCCO (1986), OTELLO (1976), PAGLIACCI (1968), SUOR ANGELICA (1983), LA TRAVIATA (1992), IL TABARRO (1983), TOSCA (2000), IL TRITTICO (1983), IL TROVATORE (2000), VERDI REQUIEM (1967), and I VESPRI SICILIANI (1990).

1937 Regina Della Scala
Regina della Scala (Queen of La Scala) is an Italian feature film designed to glorify the opera house, and much of it was shot on location in the theater. *Regina della Scala* is the name of an opera by a young composer that is to be sung at the opera house by his prima donna lover. The director of La Scala tells the composer of the difficulties that architect Piermarini had when he designed the theater and the problems Verdi faced when audiences booed his opera *Un Giorno di Regno*. Guido Salvini and Camillo Mastrocinque wrote and directed the film. Black and white. In Italian. 88 minutes.

1943 La Primadonna
Two sopranos become deadly rivals at La Scala in the early 19th century in this Italian feature film based on a novel by Filippo Sacchi. A young singer who substitutes for a prima donna is such a success that the older woman decides to kill her. Anneliese Uhlig plays the prima donna (sung by Maria Caniglia) with Maria Mercader as the young singer (sung by Lina Pagliughi). Ivo Perelli directed. Black and white. In Italian. 88 minutes.

1939 Retroscena
An Italian baritone pretends to be a Polish singer for his second appearance at his La Scala debut after he is attacked by a jealous critic in his debut in his own name. When the critic praises his performance, he reveals his identify in revenge; he also wins the woman he loves. Filippo Romito plays the baritone. Alessandro Blasetti directed. Black and white. In Italian. 100 minutes.

1990 The House of Magical Sounds
A boy is impressed by what he hears at La Scala and determines to make music the center of his life in this film based on an autobiographical novel by conductor Claudio Abbado, directed by Daniele Abbado. It includes music by Mozart, Beethoven, Debussy, and Schubert performed by the Youth Orchestra of United Europe led by Abbado. Raul Julia narrates. Color. In English. 60 minutes. Sony VHS.

1994 La Scala: A Documentary of Performances
This fascinating history of La Scala, and those who have sung there, includes scenes of Mascagni conducting the premiere of *Nerone,* images of the devastated theater after being bombed during World War II, and scenes of rehearsals and opening nights. Mario Del Monaco, Tito Schipa, Tito Gobbi, Ferruccio Tagliavini, and Arturo Toscanini are among those seen in performance in operas by Verdi, Puccini, Rossini, and Bellini. The older opera scenes were taken from the Italian movies *Al diavolo la celebrità,* LA DONNA PIÙ BELLA DEL MONDO, FOLLIE PER L'OPERA, GIUSEPPE VERDI, and MELODIE IMMORTALE. Color and black and white. English narration. 63 minutes. VIEW VHS.

1996 La Scala 50th Anniversary Concert
Teatro alla Scala celebrated the 50th anniversary of its restoration in 1946 with a concert conducted by Riccardo Muti and filmed by Italian director Liliana Cavani. Color. In Italian. 100 minutes.

2002 Tomorrow La Scala!
A group of English opera singers have hopes of getting to Teatro alla Scala, but for the moment their venue for presenting an opera is a prison. Francesca Joseph directed this fiction film. Color. In English. 108 minutes.

TEBALDI, RENATA
Italian soprano (1922–)

Renata Tebaldi was born in Pesaro, studied in Parma, and made her debut in *Mefistofele* in 1944 in the small town of Rovigo. She was soon a regular at La Scala and was one of those on stage when it reopened in 1946 with Toscanini conducting. She first sang in England and America in 1950, joined the Metropolitan Opera in 1955, and remained there until 1973. As her records and videos show, she had one of the most beautiful voices of her time, and her reputation remains high. She was noted for her glorious performances as Mimì, and her voice was used on the soundtrack of the romantic 1987 film MOONSTRUCK. She provided the singing voice for Sophia Loren in the famous 1953 film of AIDA and participated in excellent documentaries about *Aida* (1987) and TOSCA (1983). See ANDREA CHÉNIER (1961), BELL TELEPHONE HOUR (1967), LA BOHÈME (1987 film), LA FORZA DEL DESTINO (1958), LOHENGRIN (1947), METROPOLITAN OPERA (1957), OTELLO (1962), RICORDI (1954), and TOSCA (1961).

1957 Ed Sullivan Show
Tebaldi and Richard Tucker are the guest stars from the Met on the CBS *Ed Sullivan Show* March 10, 1957. Black and white. 60 minutes. Video at the MTR.

1958 Tebaldi rehearses La bohème
Tebaldi is shown rehearsing the aria "Sono andati" from *La bohème* with a pianist in 1958. The film of the scene is included in the video *Legends of Opera*. Black and white. 2 minutes. Legato Classics VHS.

1959 Voice of Firestone
Tebaldi is seen in fine form in her performances on *The Voice of Firestone* TV program on February 2, 1959. She sings three arias from Puccini operas: "Un bel dì" from *Madama Butterfly*, "Vissi d'arte" from *Tosca*, and "Donde lieta uscì" from *La bohème*. Black and white. 35 minutes. VAI VHS titled *Renata Tebaldi & Franco Corelli*.

1959–1967 Bell Telephone Hour
This compilation of Tebaldi's appearances on this NBC television program from 1959 to 1967 includes arias and scenes from *Adriana Lecouvreur, Cavalleria rusticana, La Gioconda, Madama Butterfly,* and *Tosca.* Donald Voorhees conducts The Bell Telephone Hour Orchestra. Color. 30 minutes. VAI VHS.

1965 Renata Tebaldi and Louis Quilico Concert
Tebaldi and Quilico team for a 1965 Italian concert on CBC in Canada. Tebaldi sings "O mio babbino caro" from *Gianni Schicchi,* Quilico sings the finale of *Il tabarro,* and they join forces for the finale of Act II of *Tosca.* Ernesto Barbini conducts the CBC Festival Orchestra. Color. 30 minutes. VAI VHS.

1983 Tebaldi: la voce d'angelo
Tebaldi's musical career is the focus of this TV documentary that includes archival film of the young Tebaldi,

interviews, and excerpts from *Adriana Lecouvreur, Aida, Andrea Chénier, Madama Butterfly, Manon Lescaut, Otello,* and *Tosca.* The film was made for the Antenne 2 *Musiques au coeur* series. Black and white. In French and Italian. 70 minutes.

1995 Renata Tebaldi Live!
Compilation video of Tebaldi during the 1950s and 1960s, including a televised 1959 concert. She is seen in excerpts from *Adriana Lecouvreur, Aida, Gianni Schicchi, Madama Butterfly, Manon Lescaut,* and *Otello.* Black and white. 25 minutes. Bel Canto Society VHS.

TE KANAWA, KIRI
New Zealand soprano (1944–)

Dame Kiri Te Kanawa began her career in New Zealand, but it was her singing Elena in *La donna del lago* at the Camden Festival in England in 1969 that began her rise to stardom. In 1971 she sang the Countess in *Le nozze di Figaro* at Covent Garden, and international recognition came quickly. She made her triumphant Metropolitan Opera debut in 1974 as Desdemona. Te Kanawa's voice, beauty, and dignity have made her one of the most popular singers in the world today. Joseph Losey's 1978 DON GIOVANNI is probably her best film, but she is also a major contributor to the excellent 1991 opera film MEETING VENUS, supplying the singing voice for Glenn Close. There are many videos of her stage performances, and most of them are splendid. See ANTHOLOGIES (1988/1992), ARABELLA (1994), CAPRICCIO (1992), CITIZEN KANE, PLÁCIDO DOMINGO (1984), DIE FLEDERMAUS (1983/1986), MANON LESCAUT (1983), LE NOZZE DI FIGARO (1973/1976), METROPOLITAN OPERA (1983), OTELLO (1982/1992), DER ROSENKAVALIER (1982/1985), SIMON BOCCANEGRA (1991/1995), GEORG SOLTI (1990), SOPRANOS AND MEZZOS (1995), THE SORCERESS (1993), SOUTH PACIFIC (1986), TOSCA (1983 film/1991), VERONA (1990), and WEST SIDE STORY (1984 film).

1964 Runaway
Te Kanawa, an unknown at the time, has a small role as Isobel Wharewera in this low-budget film about a runaway boy in New Zealand. John O'Shea directed. Black and white and color. In English. 85 minutes.

1966 Don't Let It Get You
Te Kanawa was still an unknown singer when she appeared in this New Zealand movie with eighth billing. *Variety* reviewed the film but didn't mention Te Kanawa. The film, a tourist musical set in a New Zealand resort, centers around a drummer looking for a job. Most of the singing is by Maori Howard Morrison. John O'Shea directed for Pacific Films. Black and white. 80 minutes.

1978 Kiri Te Kanawa: Royal Gala Concert

Te Kanawa's first recital at the Royal Opera House, Covent Garden. She looks stunning and sings beautifully accompanied by pianist Richard Amner. The program has songs by Strauss, Schubert, Schumann, Wolf, Fauré, Duparc, Walton, and Dvořák. Richard Baker introduces the songs; David Heather directed the video December 3, 1978. Color. 60 minutes. Kultur VHS.

1985 Kiri Te Kanawa at Christmas

Te Kanawa celebrates Christmas with a concert at the Barbican Hall in London joined by conductor Carl Davis and a hundred musicians and singers from the Philharmonia Orchestra and Tallis Chamber Choir. She sings 11 Christmas songs, including "White Christmas." Brian Kay is TV presenter. Color. 50 minutes. VIEW VHS.

1987 An Evening With Kiri Te Kanawa

Te Kanawa concert at the Royal Albert Hall in London. In the first half she sings arias from *Die Zauberflöte, Le nozze di Figaro, Faust, Louise, Tosca,* and *La rondine.* In the second half she sings the role of Eliza Doolittle in a concert version of *My Fair Lady* with Jeremy Irons as Henry Higgins and Warren Mitchell as Eliza's father. John Mauceri leads the London Symphony Orchestra; Yvonne Littlewood directed the video. Color. 108 minutes. London VHS/LD (highlights version in the *Great Moments* VHS series as Vol. 9).

1989 Canteloube: Chants d'Auvergne

Te Kanawa sings Joseph Canteloube's famous *Songs of the Auvergne* in a concert with backing from the English Chamber Orchestra conducted by Jeffrey Tate. Peter Bartlett directed. Color. 52 minutes. London VHS.

1989 Kiri in Concert

Te Kanawa in concert at the Barbican in London on April 29, 1989, with Carl Davis leading the Royal Philharmonic Orchestra. Highlights include the Countess's arias from *Le nozze di Figaro,* "O mio babbino caro" from *Gianni Schicchi,* and "Pace, pace, mio dio" from *La forza del destino.* She also sings music by Wolf-Ferrari, Charpentier, Puccini, Canteloube, Herbert, Gershwin, and Rodgers and Hammerstein. Hefin Owen directed. Color. 100 minutes. EMI Classics VHS.

1990 Kiri Concert Special

Two 1990 concerts by Te Kanawa filmed for London Weekend Television's *South Bank Show* were combined to create this video. In the first she sings at an open-air concert in Wellington in New Zealand. In the second she performs at the Royal Naval College chapel in Greenwich. Color. 60 minutes. Polygram (GB) VHS.

1991 Kiri Sings Mozart

Te Kanawa sings at St. David's Hall with the Welsh National Opera Orchestra led by Sir Charles Mackerras. The concert includes arias from *Don Giovanni, Die Zauberflöte,* and *La clemenza di Tito.* Color. 90 minutes. On VHS.

1991 Together...Kiri & André on Broadway

Documentary about the making of Te Kanawa's jazz album *Sidetracks.* André Previn plays piano and works with her as she learns how to swing in a jazz manner with help from bassist Ray Brown and guitarist Mundell Lowe. Songs include "It Could Happen to You" and "Honeysuckle Rose." Robin Lough directed. Color. 52 minutes. Philips VHS.

1991 Kiri Te Kanawa

London Weekend Television *South Bank Show* documentary about Te Kanawa in which she talks about her life, roles, future, and preparations for singing the Countess in *Capriccio.* She sings Mozart, Strauss, Handel, Gershwin, and Maori songs, and there is a touching scene of her in New Zealand singing "Now Is the Hour" as she remembers leaving hernative country years before to the same song. Melvyn Bragg narrates; Nigel Wattis directed. Color. Arthaus (GB) DVD (157 minutes with highlights from three concerts)/Kultur VHS (107 minutes).

1991 Nobel Jubilee Concert

Te Kanawa gives a concert in Stockholm to celebrate the 90th anniversary of the Nobel Prize. She is partnered with Georg Solti in a program that is mostly Mozart. Color. 86 minutes. Kultur VHS.

1994 Kiri: Her Greatest Hits Live

Te Kanawa celebrates her 50th birthday with a concert at the Royal Albert Hall, March 13, 1994, with the London Symphony Orchestra led by Stephen Barlow. She sings Korngold's "Salammbô" aria from *Citizen Kane,* "Porgi amor," "Art Is Calling for Me" from *The Enchantress,* "Depuis le jour," and songs by Rodgers and Hammerstein and Lloyd Weber. Dennis O'Neill teams with her for duets from *La bohème,* a Maori choir joins her for music from her own country, and André Previn conducts her in a Strauss song and a Mozart aria. Color. 90 minutes. London VHS/LD.

1994 Christmas With Kiri Te Kanawa

Te Kanawa gives a carol concert at Coventry Cathedral in December 1994 with baritone Michael George, trumpeter Jouko Harjanne, and the choirs of Coventry and Lichfield cathedrals. Robin Stapleton conducts the BBC Philharmonic Orchestra. Color. 70 minutes. NVC Arts (USA) and Teldec (GB) VHS.

1997 Kiri Te Kanawa: Opera in the Outback

Te Kanawa sings a selection of arias and songs in a concert at the Yalkarinha Gorge in the South Australian Flinders Ranges. She is joined by the Adnyamathanka Women's Choir for the first performance of the "Warrioota Song." Robin Stapleton conducts the Adelaide Symphony Orchestra and Virginia Lumsden directed the video on September 20, 1997. Color. 84 minutes. Image Entertainment DVD/Quantum Leap (GB) video.

2000 Kiri Te Kanawa: Home and Afar

Te Kanawa returns home to New Zealand in this documentary and performs everything from Gershwin to Puccini in three locations. Back in England, she sings at the Royal Navy College Chapel in London. Color. 57 minutes. Image Entertainment DVD.

TELEPHONE, THE

1947 opera by Menotti

GIAN CARLO MENOTTI's one-act comic opera *The Telephone or L'amour à trois* (The Eternal Triangle), a slight but enjoyable entertainment, was composed as a curtain raiser for *The Medium* on Broadway. Ben is trying to propose to Lucy, but he is always being interrupted by her taking telephone calls. He eventually solves the problem by leaving the house and phoning in his proposal. The opera has been telecast more than 20 times around the world from Hungary to Australia. American and British TV productions are listed below.

1948 NBC Television

American TV production: Paul Nickell (director), Roger Englander (producer), Maricarol Hanson (pianist), W. C. Smith (set designer).

Cast: Barbara Cooper (Lucy), David Daniels (Ben).

Telecast live May 28, 1948, from NBC's Philadelphia station WPTZ. Black and white. In English. 24 minutes.

Comment: One of the first operas on network television. The singers were students at the Curtis Institute of Music.

1951 BBC Television

English TV production: Christian Simpson (director), Antony Hopkins (conductor, BBC Television Orchestra), Stephen Bund (set designer).

Cast: Elizabeth Boyd (Lucy), Eric Shilling (Ben).

Telecast June 12, 1951, on BBC. Black and white. In English. 25 minutes.

1952 Omnibus, CBS Television

American TV production: Andrew McCullough (director), Emmanuel Balaban (conductor, CBS Orchestra).

Cast: Edith Gordon (Lucy), Andrew Cainey (Ben).

Telecast live November 16, 1952. Black and white. In English. 25 minutes.

1960 BBC Television

English TV production: Walter Todds (director), Charles Mackerras (conductor, Goldsborough Orchestra), Malcolm Goulding (set/costumes designer).

Cast: Stephanie Voss (Lucy), Bill Newman (Ben).

Telecast October 16, 1960, on BBC. Black and white. In English. 25 minutes.

***1992 BBC Television, Scotland

Scottish TV production: Mike Newman (director), José Serebrier (conductor, Scottish Chamber Orchestra).

Cast: Carole Farley (Lucy), Russell Smythe (Ben).

Video: PolyGram VHS/London LD. Color. In English. 23 minutes.

Comment: Superbly sung and acted, brilliantly directed, Menotti at his best.

TELEVISION OPERAS

Operas have been composed especially for television for more than half a century. The first was Gian Carlo Menotti's AMAHL AND THE NIGHT VISITORS, commissioned by NBC and telecast in 1951. It was so popular that it led to many further commissions for TV operas in the United States and Europe. The first BBC TV opera was Richard Arnell's *Love in Transit,* telecast in 1955, followed by Arthur Benjamin's *Mañana,* telecast February 1, 1956. Television operas tend to be relatively short, with small casts and strong stories. Listed below are some of the better-known works, including electronic "television operas." See composer and individual opera entries for details.

1951—Menotti: Amahl and the Night Visitors (NBC)
1953—Martinů: *The Marriage* (NBC)
1953—Martinů: *What Men Live By* (NBC)
1954—Herrmann: *A Christmas Carol* (CBS)
1954—Copland: The Tender Land
1955—Arnell: *Love in Transit* (BBC)
1955—Foss: *Griffelkin* (NBC)
1955—Herrmann: *A Child Is Born* (CBS)
1956—Benjamin: *Mañana* (BBC)
1957—Hollingsworth: *La grande Bretèche* (NBC)
1958—Menotti: *Maria Golovin* (NBC)

1959—Rossellini: *Le campane* (RAI)
1960—Bliss: Tobias and the Angel (BBC)
1962—Coleman: *Christmas Carol* (BBC)
1962—Stravinsky: *The Flood* (CBS)
1962—Tate: *Dark Pilgrimage* (BBC)
1963—Menotti: *Labyrinth* (NBC)
1963—Rautavaara: *Kaivos* (Finland)
1965—Bucci: *The Hero* (PBS)
1967—Laderman: The Trials of Galileo (CBS)
1971—Britten: *Owen Wingrave* (BBC)
1972—Pasatieri: The Trial of Mary Lincoln (NET)
1973—Eaton: *Myshkin* (PBS)
1973—Laderman: The Questions of Abraham (CBS)
1976—Ashley: Music With Roots in the Aether
1976—Hoddinott: *Murder the Magician* (C4)
1977—Pannell: *Aberfan* (CBC)
1980—Ashley: *Perfect Lives* (The Kitchen)
1987—Kortekangas: *Grand Hotel* (YLE)
1991—Nyman: Letters, Riddles and Writs (BBC)
1993—Andriessen: M Is for Man, Music & Mozart (C4)
1994—Copeland: *Horse Opera* (C4)
1994—Moore: *Camera* (C4)
1995—Barry: The Triumph of Beauty and Deceit (C4)
1995—Torke: *King of Hearts* (C4)
1995—Westbrook: *Good Friday 1663* (C4)
1997—Rautavaara: *The Gift of the Magi* (YLE)
1999—Ashley: *Dust* (The Kitchen)
2002—Dove: When She Died: Death of a Princess (C4)

TELL ME TONIGHT
1932 film with opera content

Polish tenor Jan Kiepura plays an Italian tenor in Switzerland who changes places with a fugitive and falls in love with the daughter of a mayor (Magda Schneider). In the course of the film, he has the chance to sing arias from *La bohème, Rigoletto, La traviata,* and *Martha* and songs by Mischa Spoliansky. John Orton wrote the screenplay, Fritz Arno Wagner and Willi Goldberger were the cinematographers, and Anatole Litvak directed for Gaumont-British. The film was shot in Germany, and the German version, also directed by Litvak, is titled *Das Lied einer Nacht.* It was released in America as *Be Mine Tonight.* Black and white. In English. 91 minutes. On VHS.

TEMPESTAD, LA
1882 zarzuela by Chapí

La tempestad (The Storm) is one of Spanish composer RUPERTO CHAPÍ's most popular zarzuelas. Simon, an innkeeper in a Breton coastal village, has raised orphan Angela whose father was murdered during a storm. She is in love with the fisherman Roberto (a soprano role), but Simon opposes their marriage. Simon accuses the rich

Beltran of being the murderer but eventually has to admit that he is the guilty one.

1943 Rivera film
Spanish feature film: Javier Rivera (director), Manuel Beringola (cinematographer), Cepilsa Madrid (production company).
Cast: Maria Luisa Gerona, Rufino Ingles, Julia Lajos, Manuel Arbo.
Black and white. In Spanish. 91 minutes.

TENDER LAND, THE
1954 opera by Copland

Laurie, who has grown up on a farm in the Midwest during the 1930s, longs to escape to a wider world despite the kindness of Ma and Grandpa Moss. She falls in love with a drifter and asks him to elope with her. When he refuses, she decides to go off on her own. Aaron Copland's opera The Tender Land, libretto by Horace Everett (pseudonym of Eric Johns), was inspired by photographs by Walker Evans in James Agee's *Let Us Now Praise Famous Men.* It was commissioned as a television opera by Rodgers and Hammerstein, but NBC turned it down so Copland adapted it for the stage. It premiered at New York City Opera in 1954.

1978 Michigan Opera Theater
American stage production: Michael Montel (director), Aaron Copland (conductor, Midland Festival Orchestra and Michigan Opera Theater Chorus), Robert Joel Schwartz (set designer), Eugene Loring (choreographer).
Cast: Karen Hunt (Laurie), Frances Bible (Ma Moss), George Gaynes (Grandpa Moss), John Sandor (Martin), Charles Row (Top), Kim Harper and William Nolte take small roles.
Video: House of Opera DVD/VHS. Telecast August 28, 1979, by WCMU/WCML on PBS. Clark Santee (director). Color. In English. 120 minutes.

TENORS

Tenors are currently the darlings of the opera world, as the success of THE THREE TENORS concert series amply demonstrates. But tenor adulation actually goes back to Caruso and the emergence during the 19th century of the tenor hero. Videos that feature more than one tenor are described below; those about one singer are listed under individual names.

1990 Concerto di Tenori
The *Concerto di Tenori* (Concert of Tenors) is a Gigli memorial event featuring 14 tenors singing at the Arena

di Verona. Carlo Bergonzi begins the program singing "Una furtiva lagrima" and closes it with "O paradiso." The other tenors are Piero Ballo, Franco Bonisolli, Alberto Cupido, Peter Dvorsky, Salvatore Fisichella, Emil Ivanov, Mario Malagnini, Gianfranco Pastine, Vincenzo Scuderi, José Sempere, Anatoly Solovianenko, Giorgio Tieppo, and Nunzio Todisco. Anton Guadagno conducts the Arena di Verona Orchestra. Color. In Italian. 173 minutes. Lyric/Multigram (Italy) VHS.

1996 Bel Canto: The Tenors of the 78 Era
Superb historical series about 12 top tenors of the past created for German television by Jan Schmidt-Garre and Marieke Schroeder. Each section about a tenor is 30 minutes long, with three on each of four videos. There is ample archival footage from films and newsreels, and colleagues, relatives, and critics discuss the tenors' art. Volume One features Enrico Caruso, Beniamino Gigli, and Tito Schipa; Volume Two has Richard Tauber, Leo Slezak, and Joseph Schmidt; Volume Three has Jussi Björling, Lauritz Melchior, and Helge Rosvaenge; Volume Four has Georges Thill, Ivan Kozlovsky, and a program about the gramophone replacing a John McCormack episode not licensed for America. Black and white and color. The discussions are in English or are subtitled. 360 minutes. Bel Canto Society VHS.

1997 Ten Tenors: A Treasury of Rare Footage
Bel Canto Society compilation video featuring 10 great tenors of the past in scenes from their films and stage productions. The tenors are Carlo Bergonzi, Franco Corelli, Beniamino Gigli, Jan Kiepura, Giacomo Lauri-Volpi, Nino Martini, John McCormack, Alfred Piccaver, Tito Schipa, and Ferruccio Tagliavini. The excerpts are taken from films and videos dating from 1932 to the 1960s. Black and white and color. 60 minutes. Bel Canto Society VHS.

1997 Great Tenors, Vol. 2
A second Bel Canto Society compilation video with more tenors in scenes from mainly more modern films and stage productions. The tenors here are Carlo Bergonzi, Jussi Björling, Franco Corelli, Giuseppe Di Stefano, Nicolai Gedda, Alfredo Kraus, Veriano Luchetti, Alain Vanzo, and Fritz Wunderlich. Black and white and color. 55 minutes. Bel Canto Society VHS.

1997 Great Tenor Performances
Compilation video of scenes from operas featuring notable tenors including the big three, Luciano Pavarotti (Aida), Plácido Domingo (La fanciulla del West), and José Carreras (I Lombardi). Also performing are Robert Alagna (Don Carlos), Jon Vickers (Samson et Dalila), Nicola Martinucci (Turandot), Franco Bonisolli, and

John Mark Ainsley. Color. English subtitles. 90 minutes. Warner (GB) DVD.

1998 The Original Three Tenors
Richard Fawkes's documentary for BBC Television looks at three great tenors of an earlier era: Enrico Caruso, Beniamino Gigli, and Jussi Björling. Soprano Mary Ellis, then 98 years old and the last person alive at the time who had sung with Caruso, is one of the interviewees. Nigel Douglas provides informed commentary. Color & black and white. 50 minutes.

TENSE MOMENTS FROM OPERA
1922 English opera film series

Harry B. Parkinson produced this series of short opera films in 1922 for Master-British Exhibitors/Gaumont. It seems to have been an attempt to be cultural and popular at the same time. The operas were filmed in abridged versions with well-known stage players and had formats similar to the company's other series, *Tense Moments From Great Plays* and *Tense Moments With Great Authors*. The directors included George Wynn, Challis Sanderson, and Edwin J. Collins. The operas chosen for the series are a reflection of their relative popularity at the time. See (all 1922) CARMEN, DON GIOVANNI, FAUST, FRA DIAVOLO, THE LILY OF KILLARNEY, LUCIA DI LAMMERMOOR, MARITANA, MARTHA, RIGOLETTO, SAMSON ET DALILA, LA TRAVIATA, and IL TROVATORE.

TEREZIN OPERAS

Several operas have been revived in recent years because of interest in the Jewish composers Viktor Ullmann and Hans Krása, whose work was composed or staged in the World War II Terezin (Theresienstadt) concentration camp outside Prague. Two operas have been filmed and have entries in this book. See BRUNDIBÁR and DER KAISER VON ATLANTIS.

1994 The Music of Terezin
Simon Broughton's documentary film about the music and musicians of Terezin features excerpts from Ullmann and Krása operas. Included are scenes of the original Terezin production of *Brundibár,* filmed by camp officials for a Nazi propaganda film, and staged scenes of *The Emperor of Atlantis.* Color. In English. 30 minutes.

TERFEL, BRYN
Welsh baritone (1965–)

Bryn Terfel, who made his debut in 1990 in *Così fan tutte* with the Welsh National Opera, has rapidly become one of the most acclaimed modern singers, nearly rivaling Cecilia Bartoli in publicity when he made his first appearance at the Met. He has been particularly admired for his Figaro in *Le nozze di Figaro,* which he has sung widely and is on video in a Paris production. See LA DAMNATION DE FAUST (1998), DON GIOVANNI (2000), FALSTAFF (1999), DIE FRAU OHNE SCHATTEN (1992), JAMES LEVINE (1996), CLAUDIO MONTEVERDI (1989), LE NOZZE DI FIGARO (1993/1998), OEDIPUS REX (1992), and SALOME (1995).

1995 The Last Night of the Proms
Terfel is the featured singer in a performance of Walton's *Belshazzar's Feast* performed in the first half of this Proms concert in London. Andrew Davis conducts the BBC Symphony Orchestra and Chorus. Color. 60 minutes. Teldec VHS.

1998 Lesley Garrett Tonight
In the first of these BBC-TV programs, Terfel and Garrett perform numbers from *Porgy and Bess.* Peter Robinson conducts the BBC Concert Orchestra; Mike Leggett directed. Color. In English. 60 minutes.

1999 Cecilia & Bryn at Glyndebourne
Terfel and Cecilia Bartoli perform scenes from *The Barber of Seville, Don Giovanni, L'elisir d'amore,* and *Le nozze di Figaro* at the Glyndebourne Festival in 1999. Myung-Whung Chung conducts the London Philharmonic Orchestra. Brian Large directed. Opus Arte (GB) DVD.

2000 Christmas Glory From Westminster Abbey
Terfel sings in a Christmas program at Westminster Abbey with blind tenor Andrea Bocelli and teen soprano Charlotte Church, backed by the Westminster Abbey Choir and City of London Sinfonia. Color. 60 minutes. On DVD/VHS.

TERROR AT THE OPERA
1987 Italian film with opera content

Dario Argento's Italian film *Terror at the Opera* is built around a Parma production of Verdi's *Macbeth,* traditionally a bad luck play and opera. The plot is similar to that of *The Phantom of the Opera.* A mysterious hooded figure is prowling the secret corridors of the opera house, furthering the career of a young soprano (Cristina Marsillach) and killing those involved with her. There are a number of scenes of the opera on stage at the Teatro Regio, with Marsillach as Lady Macbeth. The voices belong to Elisabetta Norberg Schulz, Paola Leolini, Andrea Piccinni, and Michele Pertusi, with the music played by the Arturo Toscanini Symphony Orchestra of Emilia and Romagna. The soundtrack also features arias from *Norma*

and *Madama Butterfly* sung by Maria Callas and Mirella Freni. *Terror at the Opera* is the U.S. release title. In Italy the film is called simply *Opera.* Color. In Italian with English subtitles. 90 minutes. South Gate DVD and VHS.

TERRY, PAUL
Animated film producer (1887–1971)

Paul Terry and his Terrytoons were a staple in the Hollywood animated cartoon world from the 1910s to the 1950s. Among his more famous cartoon characters are the Heckle and Jeckle magpies and Mighty Mouse. Some of his cartoons had operatic content.

1935 Opera Night
A night at the opera cartoon style in this Terrytoons Studio film directed by Paul Terry and Frank Moser. Black and white. 7 minutes.

1944 Carmen's Veranda
A veritable hodgepodge of opera music is used in this Terrytoon about gallant knight Gandy Goose, who rescues a fair damsel from a castle. There's a bit of Rossini, a little Gilbert and Sullivan, and a touch of Bizet. Color. 7 minutes.

1952 Off to the Opera
Classic operatic cartoon about the argumentative magpies Heckle and Jeckle made at the Terrytoons Studio. Heckle speaks with a New York accent and attitude, Jeckle with a British one. Connie Rasinski directed. Color. 7 minutes.

TETRAZZINI, LUISA
Italian soprano (1871–1940)

Luisa Tetrazzini was a hugely popular opera soprano during the first third of the 20th century and one of the most dazzling singers ever to make records. After she made her debut in 1890, she was acclaimed at the major opera houses for the beauty of her voice and technical agility. Her popularity was so high that the 1909 Ziegfeld Follies featured a song called "I'm After Madame Tetrazzini's Job." She made many recordings, which are still admired today, but unfortunately does not seem to have been interested in the cinema.

1909 Romeo und Julia
This lost early sound film was made in Germany in 1909 by Deutsche Vitascope with the images synchronized to a recording. Tetrazzini sang the "Waltz Song" from the Gounod opera *Roméo et Juliette* on the recording, but

there is no evidence that she appeared in the film. Black and white. In German. About 5 minutes.

1932 Tetrazzini Listens to Caruso
Tetrazzini listens to a Caruso recording of "M'apparì" from *Martha* and then joins him in song. Her voice may not be what it once was (she was 63 at the time), but the scene is an historic wonder. It is included in several videos, but notably on *Legends of Opera*. Black and white. 2 minutes. Legato Classics VHS.

TEYTE, MAGGIE
English soprano (1888–1976)

Maggie Teyte began her career singing Mozart with Jean de Reszke in Paris in 1906. She sang around the world from London to Chicago and was once partnered with Mary Garden, whom she had succeeded in Paris in the role of Mélisande. She can be seen on film with Kirsten Flagstad in scenes from a famous 1951 production of DIDO AND AENEAS in London.

THAÏS
1894 opera by Massenet

Thaïs is a fourth-century courtesan rescued from evil ways by a monk who falls in love with her. They both die, of course, but not before they sing some fine music. JULES MASSENET's opera is not well known today, except for its contribution to the violin repertory; the Méditation between Act II and III has acquired a life of its own. The opera was written for American soprano Sibyl Sanderson, Massenet's mistress at the time and one of the prototypes for the opera singer/mistress in *Citizen Kane*. It's based on a once scandalous Anatole France novel adapted by librettist Louis Gallet. The opera itself has been the cause of scandal more than once. In the 1894 premiere, Sanderson "accidentally" exposed her breasts. In the 1973 New Orleans production, Carol Neblett became the first opera singer to appear full-frontally nude on stage. *Thaïs* has been out of vogue, but it may be coming back into fashion; Renée Fleming sang Thaïs in a recent Chicago production. (In the novel the monk is Paphnuce, but his name was changed to Athanaël for the opera.)

1954 Opera Cameos
American highlights film: Carlo Vinti (director), Joseph Vinti (screenplay), Giuseppe Bamboschek (conductor, Opera Cameos Orchestra).

Cast: Beverly Sills (Thaïs), Martial Singher (Athanaël), Giovanni Martinelli (introduction).

Telecast on the DuMont TV network. Black and white. In French. 30 minutes.

1985 École de Bordeaux
French stage production: Jacques Bourgeois (director), Jacques Pernoo (conductor, Orchestra Musical de Chambre d'Aquitaine), Alain Gaucher (set/costume designer).

Cast: Lysiane Leonard (Thaïs), Philippe Rouillon (Athanaël), Christian Papys (Nicias).

Video: House of Opera/Lyric VHS. Telecast February 22, 1986, by FR3. Patrice Bellot (director). Color. In French. 90 minutes.

Comment: This abridged, experimental production was staged at a French regional school.

Early/related films

1911 Feuillade film
French film based on the opera directed by Louis Feuillade for Gaumont. It was successfully released in America, although *The New York Dramatic Mirror* commented adversely on the operatic style of acting. Black and white. Silent. About 10 minutes.

1914 Crawley-Maude film
Constance Crawley stars as Thaïs with Arthur Maude as Paphnuce and George Gebhard as Nicias in this American film produced and directed by Crawley and Maude. It's based on the Anatole France novel rather than the opera, or so its copyright-conscious producers claimed. Black and white. Silent. About 60 minutes.

1916 Novissima film
Anton Giulio Bragaglia, a major exponent of the Futurist art movement, used Futurist designs in this Italian film based on the opera made for his Novissima Film Company. Black and white. Silent. About 60 minutes. A print survives.

1917 Goldwyn film
Opera diva Mary Garden plays Thaïs in her famous debut film. She had starred in the opera in Paris and at the Manhattan Opera House, and it was hoped that her reputation would make the film popular. It didn't, even though Garden is quite photogenic. The problem is that the film is shot in operatic poses in a stilted stage-acting style, and audiences were not impressed. Hamilton Revelle is Paphnutius (Athanaël), Charles Trowbridge is Nicias, Crawford Kent is Lollius, Lionel Adams is Cynius, and Alice Chapin is the Mother Superior. Edfrid Bingham wrote the screenplay, David Abel was the cinematographer, and Frank H. Crane and Hugo Ballin directed the film, shot at the Goldwyn Studios in Fort Lee, New Jersey. Black and white. Silent. About 75 minutes.

1919 The World and Its Women

Geraldine Farrar, playing a famous opera singer, is seen onstage in a scene from *Thaïs* in this Goldwyn Pictures film. Offstage she is in love with a Russian prince (Lou Tellegen), who rescues her from the Bolshevists. Frank Lloyd directed. Black and white. Silent. About 80 minutes.

1921 Stardust

Opera-singer-to-be Hope Hampton stars in this film based on a Fannie Hurst novel. It's the story of a young soprano from Iowa who goes to New York and becomes famous singing in *Thaïs*. The opera scene was accompanied by the Massenet music in theaters. Hobart Henley directed for First National Pictures. Black and white. Silent. About 80 minutes.

1937 Women of Glamour

Virginia Bruce plays a modern gold digger/lady of leisure in this Columbia film who is taken to see an opera by Melvyn Douglas. Naturally, the opera has to be *Thaïs*. Gordon Wiles directed. Black and white. 72 minutes.

1939 Golden Boy

The Méditation from *Thaïs* is played by violinist-turned-boxer William Holden on a violin given to him by his father. Rouben Mamoulian directed. Black and white. 99 minutes.

1993 L'Accompagnatrice

The French film *The Accompanist* is the story of a beautiful singer and her plain-Jane accompanist in Paris in 1942. Soprano Irene (Elena Safonova, sung by Laurence Monteyrol) uses as her signature tune the "Mirror Aria" from *Thaïs* ("Dis-moi que je suis belle et que je serai belle éternellement," which translates as "Tell me that I am beautiful and that I will be beautiful forever"). Pianist Sophie (Romane Bohringer, piano played by Angeline Pondepeyre) is her accompanist. Claude Miller directed. Color. In French with English subtitles. 100 minutes.

1994 Angie

The "Mirror Aria" from *Thaïs* is featured in this movie about a strong-willed Italian-American woman (Geena Davis) who finds that life may not be quite what she planned. Martha Coolidge directed. Color. In English. 107 minutes.

THAT MIDNIGHT KISS

1949 American film with opera content

Mario Lanza made his debut in this film playing a Philadelphia truck driver with a great but untrained voice who links up with heiress and would-be opera singer Kathryn Grayson. With a little help from Ethel Barrymore and José Iturbi, they make their opera debut in an opera called *The Princess*, which Charles Previn cobbled together with themes from Tchaikovsky's Fifth Symphony. Lanza also sings "Celeste Aida" from *Aida* and "Una furtiva lagrima" from *L'elisir d'amore*, and Grayson sings "Caro nome" from *Rigoletto*. There are also excerpts from *Lucia di Lammermoor*, *Cavalleria rusticana*, and *Semiramide*. Thomas Gomez plays a competing tenor, a nicely egotistical Italian named Guido Russino Betelli. Bruce Manning and Tamara Hovey wrote the screenplay, Robert Surtees was the cinematographer, and Norman Taurog directed for MGM. Color. 96 minutes. MGM-UA VHS.

THEBOM, BLANCHE

American mezzo-soprano (1918–)

Pennsylvania-born Blanche Thebom, who studied with opera divas Margaret Matzenauer and Edyth Walker, began her opera career with the Metropolitan on tour. She made her New York debut with the company in 1944 as Fricka in *Die Walküre* and stayed with the Met until 1967. She also sang at Covent Garden and Glyndebourne, where she was noted for her Dorabella and Carmen. Thebom appears briefly in opera sequences in Hollywood films and in a documentary, but her best screen singing was on television; she was a frequent guest on *The Voice of Firestone* TV series, and there is a fine video of highlights from these programs. See also BELL TELEPHONE HOUR (1947), THE GREAT CARUSO, SOL HUROK (1956), and METROPOLITAN OPERA (1953).

1944 Irish Eyes Are Smiling

Thebom appears in this tuneful biography of songwriter Ernest R. Ball with Leonard Warren, and both sing his songs. Dick Haymes stars as Ball opposite June Haver. Gregory Ratoff directed for Twentieth Century-Fox. Color. 90 minutes.

1950–1959 The Voice of Firestone

Thebom appeared on *The Voice of Firestone* television series 36 times when she was a Metropolitan Opera star. The video *Blanche Thebom in Opera & Song* shows highlights from three appearances with performances in operas and musicals. She is shown singing arias from *Samson et Dalila* and *Il trovatore* and songs from *My Fair Lady* and *A Connecticut Yankee*. Black and white. 28 minutes. VAI VHS.

THEODORA

1750 oratorio by Handel

GEORGE FRIDERIC HANDEL's oratorio *Theodora,* libretto by T. Morell, is set in fourth-century Roman Antioch in Asia Minor. A Christian princess refuses to make an offering to the Roman gods in the emperor's honor. Valens, the Roman emperor of the East, orders her to be thrown into prison and given to the soldiers for their amusement. Didymus, a Roman soldier, sneaks into her cell and allows her to escape wearing his clothes. They both die heroic deaths as martyrs.

1996 Glyndebourne Festival
   English stage production: Peter Sellars (director), William Christie (conductor, Orchestra of the Age of Enlightenment).
   Cast: Dawn Upshaw (Theodora), David Daniels (Didymus), Frode Olsen (Valens), Richard Croft (Septimius), Lorraine Hunt (Irene).
   Video: Kultur DVD and VHS/NVC Arts (GB) VHS. Peter Sellars (director). Color. In English but there are also English subtitles. 206 minutes.
   Comment: Sellars's updated version of the story is set in modern America in a state that allows killing by lethal injection.

THESPIS

1871 operetta by Gilbert and Sullivan

Thespis or The Gods Grown Old, the first collaboration between William S. Gilbert and Arthur Sullivan, opened at the Gaiety Theater December 26, 1871. It was modeled on Offenbach's *Orpheus in Hell,* with humans exchanging jobs with bored gods. It was successful but not a hit. The libretto has survived, but most of the original music was lost or destroyed by Sullivan. See GILBERT AND SULLIVAN.

1989 Connecticut Gilbert & Sullivan Society
Thespis, the "lost opera," was staged in 1989 in a reconstructed version created by the Connecticut Gilbert and Sullivan Society. It was said to be the only performance of *Thespis* in the 20th century and was taped for distribution by the society. Color. In English. 110 minutes. Gilbert and Sullivan Society VHS.

THIRTEEN CLOCKS, THE

1953 TV musical by Bucci

A cold evil duke has frozen time, but his niece Princess Saralina remains warm. Suitors for her hand are given impossible tasks and slain when they fail. Prince Zorn, with the help of the Golux, fulfills the tasks and wins the princess. The duke is left in the hands of the horrible Todal. MARK BUCCI's *The Thirteen Clocks,* libretto by the composer with help from Fred Sadoff and John Crilly, is based on the 1944 fable by James Thurber. It premiered on ABC Television in 1953 with Met soprano Roberta Peters as the princess. Bucci has written a number of operas, including *Tale for a Deaf Ear* presented at New York City Opera in 1958.

1953 ABC Television
   American TV production: Donald Richardson and Ralph Nelson (directors), Henry Brodkin (producer), Al Lehman (costumes), Fred Stover (set designer).
   Cast: Roberta Peters (Princess), John Raitt (Prince), Basil Rathbone (Duke), Cedric Hardwick (Golux).
   Telecast December 29, 1953, on the *Motorola TV Hour* on ABC Television. Black and white. In English. 60 minutes.

THOMAS, AMBROISE

French composer (1811–1896)

Ambroise Thomas was a very popular composer at the turn of the century when his operas HAMLET and MIGNON were part of the standard repertory. Arias from these two operas are often found on phonograph records of this earlier era, but both fell out of fashion for many years. However, they are now being staged again and are available on commercial CDs and alternative videos. Modern operatic Hamlets include Thomas Hampson, Sherrill Milnes, Bo Skovhus, and Thomas Allen, all of whom have starred in telecasts of the opera. It is likely that Thomas and his operas will return to the repertory.

THOMAS, JOHN CHARLES

American baritone (1891–1960)

John Charles Thomas, who began his singing career in Broadway operettas and Gilbert and Sullivan, sang opposite Marguerite Namara in Franz Lehár's operetta *Alone at Last* in 1915 and made his opera debut in 1924 as Amonasro in *Aida* at Washington Opera. He made his first appearance in Europe in Brussels and went on to sing in Berlin and Vienna and at Covent Garden. He went back to the United States in 1930, sang in operas in San Francisco and Chicago, and made his debut with the Metropolitan in 1934 as Germont in *La traviata.* He sang at the Met until 1943 and also became an NBC radio singing star.

1923 Under the Red Robe
Thomas sang the Prologue to *Pagliacci* on stage at the premiere of this epic silent film in which he plays a fa-

mous duelist. Thomas is ordered to catch a suspected traitor by Cardinal Richelieu (Robert Mantell) and does so but then falls in love with the captive's sister (Alma Rubens). Alan Crosland directed for Goldwyn-Cosmopolitan. Black and white. About 100 minutes.

1927 Vitaphone films
"John Charles Thomas, Outstanding American Baritone," as he was billed, made three Vitaphone sound shorts in 1927. In the first he sings the Prologue to *Pagliacci* and in the second the songs "Danny Deever" and "In the Gloaming." In the third Vitaphone film, he teams with musical comedy soprano Vivienne Segal in Sigmund Romberg's "Will You Remember" from *Maytime*. Black and white. Each about 8 minutes.

THOMSON, VIRGIL
American composer (1896–1989)

Virgil Thomson composed only three operas, but the two created with Gertrude Stein as librettist are among the most influential of all American operas. The first was the amazing FOUR SAINTS IN THREE ACTS (1934), a nonnarrative opera with memorable poetry, cellophane scenery, and an all-black cast. The second was THE MOTHER OF US ALL (1947), a pageant opera based on Susan B. Anthony and the struggle for women's suffrage. Thomson's last opera was *Lord Byron* (1972), libretto by Jack Larson about the British poet; it was composed for the Met but never staged there. Thomson's operas are not on video, although there are scenes from them on documentaries about Thomson and Stein, and both have been televised.

1936–1964 Thomson films
Thomson is one of the great film music composers, although his output was small and mostly written for documentaries. The best are probably for Pare Lorentz's *The Plow That Broke the Plains* (1936) and *The River* (1937) and Robert Flaherty's *Louisiana Story* (1948). He also collaborated with Marc Blitzstein on the music for Joris Ivens's classic *Spanish Earth* (1937). Thomson's only fiction film was John Cromwell's *The Goddess* (1958), but he composed music for Peter Brook's TV production of *King Lear* with Orson Welles. In addition, he wrote music for the documentaries *Tuesday in November* (1948), made for the U.S. government; *Power Among Men* (1959), made for the United Nations; and *Voyage to America* (1964), made for the New York World's Fair.

1970 Gertrude Stein: When This You See Remember Me
In Perry Miller Adato's documentary about poet/librettist Gertrude Stein, Thomson is shown at Stein's country house in France talking about *Four Saints in Three Acts*.

He plays piano and rehearses Edward J. Pierson, Claudia Lindsey, and Betty Allen in excerpts from the opera. Color. 89 minutes. Meridian VHS.

1974 Day at Night: Virgil Thomson
James Day talks to Thomson about his life and music in this television show directed by Bob Hankal. Color. 29 minutes. Video at the MTR.

1986 Virgil Thomson at 90
John Huszar's fine film tribute to the composer is primarily about his music, but it gives ample biographical background. Thomson sets the tone and guides the film along its way by talking about his film scores and his friendships with Picasso and Gertrude Stein and Alice B. Toklas. There are filmed scenes of the original 1934 "cellophane" production of *Four Saints in Three Acts* and bits of *The Mother of Us All* and *Lord Byron*. Librettist Jack Larson talks about working with Thomson on *Byron*, mezzo Betty Allen sings lines from *Four Saints* and Stein's poem "Susie Asado," and there is an excerpt from the ballet *Filling Station*. The film was telecast December 30, 1980, as *Virgil Thomson: Composer* and on November 30, 1986, in an updated version as *Virgil Thomson at 90*. Color. 60 minutes. FilmAmerica VHS.

THREEPENNY OPERA, THE
See DREIGROSCHENOPER, DIE.

THREE TALES
2002 screen operas by Reich and Korot

This is an operatic examination of three historically significant events of the 20th century that arose through the growth of technology. Steve Reich's 60-minute multimedia screen opera *Three Tales*, libretto by the composer with video artist Beryl Korot, premiered at the Spoleto Festival USA in 2002. Described by Reich as "documentary music video theater," it was presented in an abandoned theater in downtown Charleston with 16 musicians and singers. Videos in the auditorium showed historical film footage, interviews, photographs, and text. Nick Mangano directed, and Brad Lubman was conductor. The three operas are HINDENBERG, *Bikini* and *Dolly*. *Bikini* is concerned with the Pacific atoll used as an atomic testing ground while *Dolly* uses the cloning of that famous sheep to examine the future of such experiments.

2002 Spoleto Festival
The three operas are featured on DVD performed by the Steve Reich Ensemble with Synergy Vocals. The DVD includes an interview with Reich and Korton plus a CD version. Color. 60 minutes. Nonesuch DVD.

THREE TENORS, THE

Opera concert series

The Three Tenors concerts are among the most popular opera events ever organized, and the televised shows, records, and videos have been runaway successes. The first concert sold more than 9 million copies on audio and video after many millions watched it on TV from Rome in 1990 before the World Cup. It was equally successful in 1994 in Los Angeles and in 1998 in Paris. It may not be great opera, but it is certainly great show business. José Carreras, Plácido Domingo, and Luciano Pavarotti are the three stars, but conductor Zubin Mehta, organizer Tibor Rudas, and video director Brian Large deserve a lot of credit.

1990 The Three Tenors in Rome

The most popular opera video and CD ever released was taped July 7, 1990, at the Baths of Caracalla in Rome on the night before the World Cup final. There are 16 numbers, mostly solos such as Pavarotti's famous version of "Nessun dorma," which was used as the World Cup theme. The *Turandot* aria is sung again by the trio as an encore, along with "O sole mio." Zubin Mehta conducts the Rome Opera and Florence Maggio Musicale Orchestras. Brian Large directed the video. (It was not called *The Three Tenors* on its original VHS release but was usually referred to by that name; the actual title was *Carreras Domingo Pavarotti in Concert*. On DVD it is now the *Original Three Tenors Concert*). Color. 86 minutes. Universal London DVD/VHS.

1990 The Three Tenors Encore

The first sequel in opera video history, *The Three Tenors Encore* was released because of continuing interest in the original concert video. It goes behind the scenes of the taping of the original event, shows how it was set up, includes interviews with the tenors, features more singing, and describes the evening from a different viewpoint. There are also splendid scenes of the Baths of Caracalla. Derek Jacobi narrates. Color. 57 minutes. New Line DVD/VHS.

1994 The Three Tenors in Los Angeles

The success of the Rome concert guaranteed the success of this follow-up concert in Los Angeles on July 16, 1994, and the hype was even greater. Despite efforts to make the concert as populist as possible, it is an enjoyable event vocally and visually. Where else can you see Frank Sinatra acknowledging someone else singing "My Way"? Some of the selections are hardly common fare, with Carreras performing an aria from Massenet's *Le Cid,* Domingo from *Luisa Miller,* and Pavarotti from *Werther.* Zubin Mehta conducts and seems to enjoy the evening as much as the tenors. William Cosel directed

the video. Color. In English. 89 minutes. Warner Music DVD/Teldec VHS and LD.

1994 The Making of the Three Tenors

This backstage documentary about the Los Angeles Three Tenors concert, with commentary by Roger Moore, was rushed out soon after the concert video was released. Sets for the show are shown being built in Hungary and flown to Los Angeles, Lalo Schifrin talks about the repertoire, the tenors are shown relaxing in Monte Carlo, and the final dress rehearsal is filmed. Tibor Rudas created and produced the film directed in Los Angeles by David Dinkins Jr. Color. 62 minutes. Warner VHS.

1998 The Three Tenors in Paris

The triple-threat tenor combination of Carreras, Domingo, and Pavarotti was a hit once again when they gave their popular show in Paris on July 10, 1998, at the foot of the Eiffel Tower with more or less the same format. James Levine conducted the Orchestre de Paris, and Tibor Rudas created and produced the film. Brian Large directed. Telecast in the United States by PBS on July 11, 1998. Color. 85 minutes. WEA DVD/VHS.

1999 The Three Tenors Christmas

The popular three tenor combination was taped giving a Christmas concert in Vienna in December 1999 and singing appropriate songs of the season, mostly in English and including "Amazing Grace." Brian Large directed. Color. 60 minutes. Sony Classical DVD/VHS.

THRILLER

1979 film with opera content

Sally Potter's provocative feminist film *Thriller* examines the role Mimì plays in the opera *La bohème* and reconstructs her death as possibly murder. A reincarnation of Mimì (Colette Laffont) looks at herself in the mirror and asks what would have happened if she had been the subject of the story rather than its object. She challenges her image in the mirror and the representation of women in opera as victims. Using photographs of productions of *La bohème* at the Royal Opera House, she looks at possible ways Mimi might have died, helped by voice-overs and even *Psycho* shower music. Mimi finds that, for narrative reasons, she had to be "young, single, and vulnerable" in the opera, and she lays a charge of murder again fictional representations of woman. The other actors in the film are Rose English as Musetta/Mimì with Tony Cacon and Vincent Meehan as Bohemian artists. The voices heard on the soundtrack are Licia Albanese as Mimì, Tatiana Menotti as Musetta, and Beniamino Gigli as Rodolfo. Potter, who wrote, directed, photographed, and edited this 33-minute color film, is best known for the features

Orlando and THE MAN WHO CRIED, which is set at the Paris Opéra.

THROUGH ROSES
1980 American opera by Neikrug

American composer Mark Niekrug's one-character chamber opera *Through Roses* is the story of a Jewish violinist who survived the German extermination camps by playing music as other prisoners walk to the gas chambers. He now finds that the music of Bach and Beethoven he once loved has become strangely distorted and discordant. The opera, based on a true story, premiered at the National Theatre in London in 1980 and has since been performed around the world.

1997 Flimm film
German feature film: Jurgen Flimm (director), Pinchas Zukerman (violinist), David Watkin (cinematographer), Philip Traugott (producer).
Cast: Maximilian Schell.
Color. In English. 80 minutes.

TIBBETT, LAWRENCE
American baritone (1896–1960)

Lawrence Tibbett occupies a special place in the history of screen opera as the first opera singer to became a Hollywood movie star during the sound era and help break down prejudices against opera as being elitist. He was born in Bakersfield, grew up in Los Angeles, began his career as a member of a light opera company, made his debut as Amonasro in *Aida* at the Hollywood Bowl in 1923, and began singing at the Met the same year. His performance as Ford in *Falstaff* in 1925 made him a major star, and he also won acclaim for his acting. His film career began in 1930 with *The Rogue Song*, an adaptation of Franz Lehár's operetta ZIGEUNERLIEBE. Next was an adaptation of Romberg's THE NEW MOON with Grace Moore, but the combination didn't spark, and the film didn't sparkle. Two more films were less than hits, so he went back to opera and into radio. He returned to Hollywood in the mid-1930s for two more films, but they were only minor successes so he quit moviemaking for good. By the 1940s he had become so well known to the general public that he was able to substitute for Frank Sinatra on the radio show *Your Hit Parade*. He left the Met in 1950 after disagreements with Rudolf Bing.

1931 The Cuban Love Song
Tibbett plays a fun-loving marine who goes to Cuba so he can sing the hit songs "The Peanut Vendor" and "The Cuban Love Song" and gets entangled with hot-tempered peanut vendor Lupe Velez. He got excellent reviews for his singing and acting, and the film itself was reasonably popular. Tibbett's comic sidekicks in the film are Ernest Torrence and Jimmy Durante. W. S. Van Dyke directed for MGM. Black and white. 80 minutes.

Lawrence Tibbett starred opposite Lupe Velez in his first film, *The Cuban Love Song* (1931).

1931 The Prodigal
Tibbett plays an aristocratic hobo alongside Roland Young and Cliff Edwards and sings Straus's "Life Is a Dream," Youmans's "Without a Song," and Bishop's "Home Sweet Home." When he finally does return home, he falls in love with his brother's wife. Being a good chap, he does the right thing, gives her up, and goes back to being a hobo. Harry Pollard directed for MGM. Aka *The Southerner*. Black and white. 76 minutes.

1935 Metropolitan
Tibbett returned to moviemaking with this big-budget opera film playing a spear bearer at the Metropolitan Opera. A wealthy diva forms a rival opera company and hires Tibbett, who sings arias from *The Barber of Seville*, *Carmen*, *Cavalleria rusticana*, and *Pagliacci*. See METROPOLITAN.

1936 Under Your Spell
Tibbett plays an opera star fed up with his manager's publicity stunts, and most of the complicated story is about his romance with a Chicago socialite; however, he does have a chance to sing arias from *The Barber of Seville* and *Faust*. Otto Preminger directed, his first American movie, with a script adapted from José Mo-

jica's Spanish-language Fox film *Las fronteras del amor.* MGM. Black and white. 63 minutes.

1991 Bugsy

Tibbett is played by actor Joe Baker in this gangster movie. Crime boss Bugsy Siegel (Warren Beatty) sees Tibbett's house in Beverly Hills, stops to say how much he admired him in *Rigoletto* the year before, and then forces the singer to sell him the house. It is in this scene that Warren makes his famous diatribe against being called "Bugsy." James Toback wrote the screenplay; Barry Levinson directed for TriStar. Color. 135 minutes.

TIEFLAND
1903 opera by d'Albert

EUGEN D'ALBERT's *Tiefland,* libretto by Rudolf Lothar based on the play *Terra baixa* by Catalan author Angel Guimera, is a story of sexual slavery. Marta is the mistress of the landowner Sebastiano, but he wants to marry someone else. He arranges for her to wed the shepherd Pedro, who does not know of her past. The opera, still popular in Europe, was a favorite in Germany between the wars and was one of the operas that helped launch the careers of Kirsten Flagstad and Maria Callas. *Tiefland,* sometimes known in English as *The Lowlands* or *Marta of the Lowlands,* was staged at the Met in 1908 but did not stay in the American repertory. It was quite well received when Washington Opera revived it in 1995.

1963 Accord film

German feature film: Werner Kelch (director), Hans Zanotelli (conductor, RIAS Kammerchor and Berliner Symphoniker), Karl Schneider (set designer), Accord (production).

Cast: Isabel Strauss (Marta), Rudolf Schock (Pedro), Gerd Feldhoff (Sebastiano), Ivan Sardi (Tommaso), Ernst Krukowski (Moruccio), Karl-Ernst Mercker (Nando), Angelika Fischer (Nuri), Margarete Klose (Rosalia), Martha Musial (Pepa), Alice Oelke (Antonia).

Color. In German. 129 minutes.

Comment: The soundtrack of the film is on a CD.

Early/related films

1914 Famous Players film

Opera singer Bertha Kalich plays Marta in *Marta of the Lowlands,* an American silent film of the source play. It was screened with music from the opera. J. Searle Dawley directed for Famous Players. Black and white. In English. About 70 minutes.

1918 Wiener Kunstfilm

Marie Marchal plays Marta opposite Wilhelm Klitsch and Anton Edthofer in this *Tiefland,* an Austrian silent film based on the source play. It was screened with music from the opera. Rudolf Lothar directed for Wiener Kunstfilm. Black and white. In German. About 80 minutes.

1922 Licho film

Lil Dagover plays Marta in this *Tiefland,* a German silent film of the opera made with the composer's cooperation and screened with live music. Also in the cast are opera bass-baritone Michael Bohnen, director-to-be Wilhelm Dieterle, Ilka Grüning, and Ida Perry. A. E. Licho produced and directed, and Karl Freund was cinematographer. Black and white. In German. About 75 minutes.

1954 Riefenstahl film

Leni Riefenstahl directed this famous *Tiefland,* a narrative film based on the opera libretto and using the opera music as score. The notorious cinematic genius, who made *Triumph of the Will* and *Olympiad,* started this film in 1940 but didn't finish it until 1954. She herself plays Marta with support from Academy Award–winning actress Luise Rainer, Franz Eichberger, and Maria Koppenhofer. Albert Benitz was her cinematographer. Black and white. In German. 95 minutes. On VHS.

TIERNEY, HARRY
American composer (1890–1965)

Harry Tierney, primarily a composer of music for Broadway shows and revues, had his most enduring success with the splendid 1919 musical comedy *Irene.* At the request of Florenz Ziegfeld, he wrote an old-fashioned traditional operetta, the 1927 RIO RITA, which was a spectacular hit on stage and screen. It has some quite pleasant tunes and has been filmed twice.

TIKHOMIROV, ROMAN
Russian film director (1915–1984)

Roman Tikhomirov, a Leningrad stage director turned filmmaker, transmuted three Russian operas into quite cinematic films. He shot them on location in memorable landscapes with good actors whose singing voices were provided by first-class singers. Tikhomirov adapted the operas to the screen with many changes and abridgments but with a real feeling for the essence of the operas. See EUGENE ONEGIN (1958), PRINCE IGOR (1969), and THE QUEEN OF SPADES (1960).

TIPPETT, MICHAEL
English composer (1905–1998)

Sir Michael Tippett has never been really popular in America, but he helped restore British opera to a position of prestige in postwar England and his work had wide influence. He wrote his own librettos, which became famous for their complicated literary and cultural allusions. His major postwar operas have been telecast, including THE MIDSUMMER MARRIAGE (1955), KING PRIAM (1962), THE KNOT GARDEN, and NEW YEAR (1989), but only *King Priam* is on a commercial video.

1975 Camera Three
This *Camera Three* program, titled *A Composer for Our Time: Michael Tippett,* is moderated by Andrew Porter. Tippett talks about his life and work, and selections from his compositions are played. John Musill produced and directed. Telecast February 23, 1975. Color. 30 minutes. Video at the MTR.

1985 Sir Michael Tippett: A Musical Biography
A *South Bank Show* profile made for London Weekend Television. Tippett talks about his operas, and there are scenes from his opera *The Midsummer Marriage* performed by members of the Welsh National Opera with Richard Armstrong conducting. The singers are Raimund Herincx, Mary Davies, Mark Hamilton, Maureen Guy, and Peter Massochi. Alan Benson directed the film. Color. 85 minutes. Video at the MTR.

TITUS, ALAN
American baritone (1945–)

Alan Titus, who has had a major international career in Mozart, Rossini, and Puccini operas, also participated in the premieres of several important U.S. operas. He helped create Lee Hoiby's SUMMER AND SMOKE in St. Paul in 1971, Leonard Bernstein's MASS in Washington in 1971, Thomas Pasatieri's THE TRIAL OF MARY LINCOLN on TV in 1972, Hans Werner Henze's RACHEL LA CUBANA on TV in 1974, Carlisle Floyd's *Bilby's Doll* in Houston in 1976, and Dominick Argento's *Miss Havisham's Fire* in New York in 1979. Titus was born in New York, brought up in Denver, and trained at Juilliard. See IL BARBIERE DI SIVIGLIA, (1976), LA CENERENTOLA (1980), IL DUCA D'ALBA (1992), DER LUSTIGE WITWE (1977), MADAMA BUTTERFLY (1982), and IL TURCO IN ITALIA (1978).

TOAST OF NEW ORLEANS, THE
1950 American film with opera content

Mario Lanza plays a Louisiana fisherman who becomes an opera star with tutoring from Kathryn Grayson and David Niven in this enjoyable film set in turn-of-the-century New Orleans. Grayson is the prima donna of the French opera house, so naturally she and Lanza have to fall in love. Grayson sings Linda's aria "O luce di quest'anima" from Donizetti's *Linda di Chamounix* and Philine's aria "Je suis Titania" from *Mignon.* Lanza sings "O paradiso" from *L'Africaine,* the "Flower Song" from *Carmen,* "M'apparì" from *Martha,* and the Brindisi from *La traviata.* As their love affair begins, they perform the seduction duet "Là ci darem la mano" from *Don Giovanni.* The film ends with an extended scene from *Madama Butterfly* in which Lanza chases Grayson around the stage. Lanza also sings "Be My Love," which became his biggest hit—so much for Verdi and Bizet. Niven doesn't sing as he's the director of the opera house, but he adds a good deal of class to the film. Johnny Green conducted the opera numbers, Sy Gomberg and George Wells wrote the screenplay, William Snyder was the cinematographer, Joe Pasternak produced, and Norman Taurog directed for MGM. Color. 97 minutes. MGM-UA VHS.

TOBIAS AND THE ANGEL
1960 TV opera by Bliss

Sir ARTHUR BLISS's television opera *Tobias and the Angel,* libretto by Christopher Hassall, tells the apocryphal story of Tobias, who hires the angel Azarias as his servant. The angel helps him conquer the devil, who possesses beautiful Sara, fight some monsters, and restore eyesight to his blind father Tobit. Commissioned by BBC Television and telecast in 1960, it won the Salzburg TV Opera Prize that year.

1960 BBC Television
English TV production: Rudolph Cartier (director), Norman del Mar (conductor, London Symphony Orchestra), Clifford Hatts (set designer).

Cast: John Ford (Tobias), Elaine Malbin (Sara), Ronald Lewis (Azarias), J. Walters (Tobit).

Telecast in May 1960 on BBC. Black and white. In English. 80 minutes.

TONIGHT WE SING
1953 American film with opera content

Russian-born American impresario Sol Hurok, who helped popularize classical music in America by promoting singers such as Feodor Chaliapin, Jan Peerce, Roberta Peters, Victoria de Los Angeles, Marian Anderson, and Leonard Warren, is romanticized in this highly fictional music extravaganza. The film, based on Hurok and Ruth Goode's book *Impresario,* stars David Wayne as Hurok (he did not want to seem Jewish) and Anne Bancroft as his wife Emma. Ezio Pinza plays Chaliapin and sings the Coronation and Death Scenes from *Boris Godunov* and Act III trio from *Faust*. (Chaliapin's family reportedly objected strongly to his portrayal in the film.) Roberta Peters plays the fictional soprano Elsa Valdine and sings "Sempre libera" from *La traviata,* the "Jewel Song" from *Faust,* and the love duet from *Madama Butterfly*. Jan Peerce, heard but not seen as the voice of fictional tenor Gregory Lawrence (played onscreen by Byron Palmer), joins Peters in *La traviata* and *Madama Butterfly* and Pinza and Peters in the *Faust* trio. Tamara Toumanova plays dancer Anna Pavlova, and Alfred Newman conducts the Twentieth Century-Fox Symphony Orchestra and Chorus. Ruth Goode wrote the screenplay, based on her book, and Mitchell Leisen directed for Twentieth Century-Fox. Color. In English. 109 minutes. Premiere Opera VHS.

TOPSY-TURVY
1999 film about Gilbert and Sullivan

The creation of *The Mikado* is central to this superb Mike Leigh film about the difficult relationship between poet/librettist William S. Gilbert (Jim Broadbent) and composer Arthur Sullivan (Allan Corduner). Their personalities are like chalk and cheese. Gilbert is an emotionless, unfeeling military type unable to relate to his sad wife (Leslie Manville) and slightly mad father (Charles Simon). Sullivan is a pleasure-loving sophisticate who enjoys female company and wants to write serious opera instead of the "topsy-turvy" world envisioned in Gilbert's librettos. The other central character is Richard D'Oyly Carte (Ron Cook), the producer who built the Savoy Theatre for the duo's operetta. He is unable to get them together after a quarrel, but this is finally achieved by Gilbert's wife, who forces him to see a Japanese exhibition that inspires *The Mikado*. The film begins with the premiere of their relatively unpopular *Princess Ida* in 1884 and ends with the triumph of *The Mikado* in 1885, and also includes music from *The Sorcerer* and *The Yeomen of the Guard*. A large part of *The Mikado*—eight numbers in all—is shown in rehearsal and production with Savoy cast members. Timothy Spall is Richard Temple, Martin Savage is George Grossmith, Kevin McKidd is Lely, Shirley Henderson is Leonora Braham, and Dorothy Atkinson is Jessie Bond. Wendy Nottingham is D'Oyly Carte's business manager Helen Lenoir, and Eleanor David is Fanny Ronalds. The re-creation of the period is outstanding, through the efforts of production designer Eve Stuart, costume designer Linda Hemming, and make-up artist Christine Bundell; Hemming and Bundell won Academy Awards for their work. The music is splendidly performed with Carl Davis as conductor and Cary Yershon as music director. Leigh himself wrote the screenplay, and Dick Pope was his superb cinematographer. Color. In English. 160 minutes. USA Home Entertainment DVD/VHS.

TORROBA MORENO, FEDERICO
See MORENO TORROBA, FEDERICO.

TOSCA
1900 opera by Puccini

GIACOMO PUCCINI's *Tosca,* one of the great opera melodramas, is set in Rome about 1800 in three famous buildings that still stand: the Church of Sant'Andrea della Valle, the Farnese Palace, and the Castel Sant'Angelo. Opera singer Floria Tosca loves painter Mario Cavaradossi and is lusted after by police chief Baron Scarpia. When Cavaradossi is arrested for revolutionary activity, Tosca agrees to submit to Scarpia to save his life. After Scarpia arranges a fake execution, she stabs him to death. The fake execution, however, turns out to be real, and Cavaradossi is killed. Tosca flees from the police and leaps to her death from the top of the castle. Giuseppe Giacosa and Luigi Illica's libretto is based on Victorien Sardou's play *La Tosca*. The story has been very popular with filmmakers.

1954 BBC Television
English TV production: George R. Foa (director), Charles Mackerras (conductor, London Symphony Orchestra).
Cast: Victoria Elliott (Tosca), Kenneth Neate (Cavaradossi), Roderick Jones (Scarpia).
Telecast live May 18, 1954, on BBC. Black and white. In Italian. 105 minutes.

1955 NBC Opera Theatre
American TV production: Samuel Chotzinoff (director/producer), Peter Herman Adler (conductor, Symphony of the Air Orchestra and NBC Opera Theatre Chorus), William Molyneux (set designer), John Gutman (English translation).
Cast: Leontyne Price (Tosca), David Poleri (Cavaradossi), Josh Wheeler (Scarpia).
Video at the MTR. Telecast live January 23, 1955, on NBC. Kirk Browning (director). Black and white. In English. 120 minutes.
Comment: This historic production was a breakthrough for Price in her first major opera role, although some racist Southern TV stations refused to air it. An abridged 78-minute audio version is on CD (Legato Classics).

1955 Blasi TV film
Italian television film: Silverio Blasi (director), Antonio Votti (conductor, Milan RAI Orchestra and Chorus).
Cast Renata Heredia (Tosca), Franco Corelli (Cavaradossi), Carlo Tagliabue (Scarpia).

Video: Bel Canto Society VHS. Telecast in 1955. Black and white. In Italian. 113 minutes.

1956 Gallone film

Italian feature film: Carmine Gallone (director), Oliviero De Fabritiis (conductor, Teatro dell'Opera Orchestra and Chorus), Giuseppe Rotunno (cinematographer), Guido Fiorini (set designer).

Cast: Franca Duval (Tosca, sung by Maria Caniglia), Franco Corelli (Cavaradossi), Afro Poli (Scarpia, sung by Giangiacomo Guelfi).

Video: Bel Canto Society/House of Opera/Lyric VHS. Color. CinemaScope. In Italian. 111 minutes.

Comment: Opera film specialist Gallone shot this film on location in Rome at the sites specified in each act and does a good job of capturing the feeling of the city.

1956 CBS Television: Ed Sullivan Show

American TV production (Act II scene): John Gutman (director), Dimitri Mitropoulos (conductor, Metropolitan Opera Orchestra).

Cast: Maria Callas (Tosca), George London (Scarpia).

Video: Kultur DVD/Consumer Video VHS (in the compilation *Great Moments in Opera*) and video at the MTR. Telecast November 25, 1956, on CBS. Black and white. In Italian. 18 minutes.

Comment: Callas made her television debut with this performance on *The Ed Sullivan Show.*

1958 Théâtre National de l'Opéra

French stage production (Act II only): Roger Benamou (director), Georges Sebastian (conductor, Théâtre National de l'Opéra Orchestra).

Cast: Maria Callas (Tosca), Tito Gobbi (Scarpia).

Tosca (1956): Tosca (Franca Duval) prepares to jump off the top of Castel Sant'Angelo in Carmine Gallone's film.

Video: EMI Classics DVD/VHS/Pioneer LD as *Maria Callas Debuts at Paris.* Telecast December 19, 1958. Black and white. In Italian. About 40 minutes.

Comment: Staged as part of a Callas concert at the Théâtre National de l'Opéra in Paris.

1960 Lanfranchi film

Italian TV film: Mario Lanfranchi (director), Fulvio Vernizzi (conductor, RAI Milan Orchestra).

Cast: Magda Olivero (Tosca), Alvinio Misciano (Cavaradossi), Giulio Fioravanti (Scarpia).

Video: House of Opera/Legato Classic VHS. Black and white. In Italian. 120 minutes.

Comment: This is the only film of Olivero in a complete role. She made her debut at the Met in this role 15 years later at the age of 65.

1961 Stuttgart State Opera

German stage production: Werner Dobbertin (director), Franco Patanè (conductor, Stuttgart Staatsoper Orchestra and Chorus), Max Fritzsch (set designer).

Cast: Renata Tebaldi (Tosca), Eugene Tobin (Cavaradossi), George London (Scarpia).

Video: VAI DVD/VHS. Telecast June 3, 1961. Korbinian Koberte (director). Black and white. In Italian. 126 minutes.

Comment: This is the only commercial video of Tebaldi in one of her favorite roles; it was the first international opera telecast, transmitted to a consortium of European TV stations.

1961 NHK Lirica Italiana

Japanese stage production: Arturo Basile (conductor, NHK Symphony Orchestra and Chorus).

Cast: Renata Tebaldi (Tosca), Gianni Poggi (Cavaradossi), Gian Giacomo Guelfi (Scarpia).

Video: House of Opera/Lyric VHS. Taped live in Tokyo October 11, 1961, for NHK's *Lirica Italiana* series. Black and white. In Italian with English subtitles. 124 minutes.

1964 Royal Opera

English stage production (Act II only): Franco Zeffirelli (director), Carlo Felice Cillario (conductor, Royal Opera House Orchestra and Chorus), Tom Lingwood (set designer).

Cast: Maria Callas (Tosca), Renato Cioni (Cavaradossi), Tito Gobbi (Scarpia).

Video: EMI Classics VHS. Telecast live February 9, 1964, by Associated Television. Bill Ward (director). Black and white. In Italian. 41 minutes.

Comment: This is the only visual record of Callas on stage in an actual performance of an opera.

1976 de Bosio Film

Italian feature film: Gianfranco de Bosio (director), Bruno Bartoletti (conductor, New Philharmonia Orchestra and Ambrosian Singers), Giancarlo Pucci (set/costume designer).

Cast: Raina Kabaivanska (Tosca), Plácido Domingo (Cavaradossi), Sherrill Milnes (Scarpia).

Video: Decca DVD/London VHS. Color. In Italian with English subtitles. 116 minutes.

Comment: Filmed on location in Rome with the first act at the Church of Sant'Andrea della Valle and third act at the Castel Sant'Angelo. The Palazzo Farnese, site of the second act, could not be used, so a substitute palace was used. Domingo's 10-year-old son Pláci plays the Shepherd Boy.

1978 Metropolitan Opera

American stage production: Tito Gobbi (director), James Conlon (conductor, Metropolitan Opera Orchestra and Chorus), Rudolf Heinrich (set designer).

Cast: Shirley Verrett (Tosca), Luciano Pavarotti (Cavaradossi), Cornell MacNeil (Scarpia).

Video at the MTR. Telecast live December 19, 1978. Kirk Browning (director). Color. In Italian with English subtitles. 124 minutes.

Comment: Gobbi as director rather than singer.

1979 Royal Opera in Tokyo

English touring stage production: Anthony Craxton (director), Colin Davis (conductor, Royal Opera House Orchestra and Chorus).

Cast: Montserrat Caballé (Tosca), José Carreras (Cavaradossi), Ingvar Wixell (Scarpia).

Video: Bel Canto Society/House of Opera VHS. Taped by BBC Television. Color. In Italian with English subtitles. 125 minutes.

1979 Nice Opéra

French stage production: Jésus Etcheverry (conductor, Nice Opéra Orchestra and Chorus).

Cast: Montserrat Caballé (Tosca), José Carreras (Cavaradossi), Juan Pons (Scarpia).

Video: House of Opera/Premiere Opera VHS. Color. In Italian with French subtitles. 109 minutes.

1984 Arena di Verona

Italian stage production: Sylvano Bussotti (director), Daniel Oren (conductor, Arena di Verona Orchestra and Chorus), Fiorenzo Giorgi (set/costume designer).

Cast: Eva Marton (Tosca), Giacomo Aragall (Cavaradossi), Ingvar Wixell (Scarpia).

Video: HBO/Castle Opera/NVC Arts (GB) VHS. Brian Large (director). Color. In Italian with English subtitles. 126 minutes.

Comment: The singers are good but the giant sets tend to dominate; nonetheless, video director Large is mostly able to bring a sense of intimacy to the home viewer.

1984 Opera Stories
Highlights version of above production with narration by Charlton Heston speaking from Rome. Framing material shot in 1989 by Keith Cheetham. Color. In English and Italian with subtitles. 52 minutes. Pioneer Artists LD.

***1985 Metropolitan Opera
American stage production: Franco Zeffirelli (director/set designer), Giuseppe Sinopoli (conductor, Metropolitan Opera Orchestra and Chorus).

Cast: Hildegard Behrens (Tosca), Plácido Domingo (Cavaradossi), Cornell MacNeil (Scarpia).

Pioneer Classics DVD/LD and Paramount VHS. Telecast live March 27, 1985. Kirk Browning (director). Color. In Italian with English subtitles. 127 minutes.

Comment: Browning won an Emmy Award for the telecast of this awe-inspiring production staged by Zeffirelli in a grandiose manner with grand singing.

1986 Australian Opera
Australian stage production: John Copley (director), Alberto Erede (conductor, Elizabethan Sydney Orchestra and Australian Opera Chorus), Allan Lees (set designer).

Cast: Eva Marton (Tosca), Lamberto Furlan (Cavaradossi), John Shaw (Scarpia).

Video: Kultur DVD/VHS. Peter Butler (director). Color. In Italian with English subtitles. 123 minutes.

1991 Paris Opéra
French stage production: Jean-Claude Auvray (director), Seiji Ozawa (conductor, Opéra de Paris Orchestra and Chorus).

Cast: Kiri Te Kanawa (Tosca), Ernest Veronelli (Cavaradossi), Ingvar Wixell (Scarpia).

Dreamlife (Japan) DVD/VHS/LD. Dirk Sanders (director). Color. In Italian. 128 minutes.

1992 Tosca Live From Rome
Italian feature film: Giuseppe Patroni Griffi (director), Vittorio Storaro (cinematographer), Zubin Mehta (conductor, RAI Symphony Orchestra of Rome), Andrea Andermann (producer).

Cast: Catherine Malfitano (Tosca), Plácido Domingo (Cavaradossi), Ruggero Raimondi (Scarpia).

Teldec DVD/VHS/LD. Brian Large (director). Color. In Italian with English subtitles. 115 minutes.

Comment: Filmed at the sites of the three acts of the opera at the times specified in the libretto and broadcast live in Europe on July 11 and 12, 1992. Act I was filmed at Sant'Andrea Church at noon, Act II at the Farnese Palace at sunset, and Act III at the Castel Sant'Angelo at dawn the next day. It's a terrific spectacle.

1993 Rome Opera
Italian stage production: Mauro Bolognini (director), Daniel Oren (conductor, Rome Opera Orchestra and Chorus), Mario Ceroli, Enzo Cucchi, Gianfranco Fini (set designers).

Cast: Raina Kabaivanska (Tosca), Luciano Pavarotti (Cavaradossi), Ingmar Wixell (Scarpia).

Video: RCA VHS/LD. Mauro Bolognini (director). Color. In Italian with English subtitles. 137 minutes.

1994 Opéra National de Paris
French stage production: Werner Schroeter (director), Michelangelo Veltri (conductor, Opéra National de Paris Orchestra and Chorus), Alberte Barsecq (set/costume designer).

Cast: Carol Vaness (Tosca), Plácido Domingo (Cavaradossi), Sergei Leiferkus (Scarpia).

Telecast in 1994 in France. Pierre Cavassilas (director). Color. In Italian. 125 minutes.

2000 New York City Opera
American stage production: Mark Lamos (director), George Manahan (conductor, New York City Opera Orchestra and Chorus), Michael Yeargan (set designer).

Cast: Amy Johnson (Tosca), Alfredo Portilla (Cavaradossi), Mark Delevan (Scarpia).

Telecast March 29, 2000, on PBS. Kirk Browning (director). Color. In Italian with English subtitles. 127 minutes.

2000 Arena della Vittoria, Bari
Italian stage production: Enrico Castiglione (director), Pier Giorgio Morandi (conductor, Orchestra Sinfonica Siciliana and Teatro Petruzzelli Chorus).

Cast: Francesca Patanè (Tosca), José Cura (Cavaradossi), Renato Brusan (Scarpia).

Video: Kultur DVD/House of Opera DVD and VHS. Color. In Italian. 126 minutes.

2000 Teatro alla Scala
Italian stage production: Luca Ronconi (director), Riccardo Muti (conductor, Teatro alla Scala Orchestra and Chorus), Margherita Palli (set designer).

Cast: Maria Guleghina (Tosca), Salvatore Licitra (Cavaradossi), Leo Nucci (Scarpia).

Video: TDK/Premiere Opera DVD. Pierre Cavasillas (director). Color. In Italian. 121 minutes.

2001 Jacquot film
French feature film: Benoit Jacquot (director/screenplay), Antonio Pappano (conductor, Royal Opera House Orchestra and Chorus and Tiffin Boys Choir), Romain Winding (cinematographer), Sylvain Chauvelot (art director), Daniel Toscan du Plantier (producer).

Cast: Angela Gheorghiu (Tosca), Roberto Alagna (Cavaradossi), Ruggero Raimondi (Scarpia).

Video: BBC Opus Arte DVD. Color & black and white. In Italian with English subtitles. 141 minutes.

Comment: The singers perform to a prerecorded soundtrack, and there are intercut black-and-white scenes of the recording session. Reviews were decidedly mixed.

Early/related films

1908 The Queen's Love
This silent Danish color film, titled *La Tosca* in Europe, was released in America as *The Queen's Love*. It was supposedly based on the Sardou play rather than the opera. Viggo Larsen directed for Nordisk Films. Silent. About 7 minutes.

1908 Bernhardt film
Victorien Sardou wrote the play *La Tosca* for Sarah Bernhardt, and she was filmed in scenes from it by French director André Calmettes. It was presented in the United States by Universal in October 1912. Black and white. Silent. About 12 minutes.

1910 Sorel film
Cécile Sorel plays Tosca in this French film based on the Sardou play with Alexandre Mosnier as Cavaradossi and Charles Le Bargy as Scarpia. It was screened with Puccini's music. André Calmettes and Ferdinand Zecca directed for Film d'Art/Pathé. Black and white. Silent. About 15 minutes.

1915 The Song of Hate
Betty Ansen plays Floria Tosca in this U.S. film based on the Sardou play with Arthur Hoops as Scarpia. Rex Ingram wrote the screenplay, and J. Gordon Edwards directed for Fox. Black and white. About 70 minutes.

1916 The Chalice of Sorrow
This is the plot of *Tosca* transposed to Mexico. Cleo Madison plays American opera singer Lorelei in Mexico lusted after by provincial governor Francisco De Sarpina (Wedgewood Nowell). As she prefers her fiancé Marion Leslie (Charles Cummings), Sarpina has him arrested and orders him executed, unless Lorelei spends the night with him. She agrees, but then stabs him and goes to rescue Marion with exit passports. It's too late; Marion has already been executed. Rex Ingram wrote and directed for Bluebird Film. Black and white. Silent. About 70 minutes.

1918 Famous Players-Lasky film
Pauline Frederick plays Tosca in *La Tosca*, an American adaptation of the Sardou play, with Frank Losee as Scarpia and Jules Raucourt as Cavaradossi. Edward José directed for Famous Players–Lasky. Black and white. Silent. About 70 minutes.

1918 Itala film
Francesca Bertini, Italy's top movie star during this period, plays Tosca in *La Tosca*, an Italian film based on the Sardou play. Gustavo Serena directed for Itala Film. Black and white. Silent. About 70 minutes.

1919 Magnussen film
Ebba Thomsen stars as Tosca in the Danish silent feature film *Tosca* directed by Fritz Magnussen. Black and white. About 80 minutes.

1934 My Heart Is Calling
Jan Kiepura's opera company gives an open-air performance of *Tosca* on the steps of the Monte Carlo Opera House in competition with the resident company performing the opera inside. The outsiders are better, so the audience leaves the theater. See MY HEART IS CALLING.

1934 Enter Madame
Nina Koshetz sings Tosca's aria "Vissi d'arte" for Elissa Landi in this film about a glamorous opera singer married to millionaire Cary Grant. See ENTER MADAME.

1936 Rose-Marie
Jeanette MacDonald, playing an opera diva, is shown singing in the finale of Act III of *Tosca* with Allan Jones in this MGM version of the Friml musical. See ROSE-MARIE.

1936 Sinfonia di Cuori
Beniamino Gigli, an opera singer loved by a married woman, sings "E lucevan le stelle" from *Tosca* with backing from the Bavarian State Opera Orchestra and Chorus. See SINFONIE DI CUORI.

1937 Stark Herzen

This is a lost film about a production of *Tosca* during a Communist uprising in Hungary in 1918. Maria Cebotari plays the actress who sings the role of Tosca with a cast including Gustav Diesl and René Deltgen. Herbert Maisch directed the film, which was banned and apparently no longer exists. UFA. Black and white. In German. 79 minutes.

1941 Tosca

This famous Italian film, which features music and arias from the opera and has a screenplay based on the opera, is a truly international production. Spain's Imperio Argentina plays Tosca (sung by Mafalda Favero), Italy's Rossano Brazzi is Cavaradossi (sung by Ferruccio Tagliavini), and France's Michel Simon is Scarpia. Its internationalism was complicated by World War II. France's Jean Renoir was the writer/director, with Italy's Luchino Visconti as his assistant, but Renoir had to leave when the war began so the film was finished by Carlo Koch. It was released in the United States in 1947—with the title *The Story of Tosca*—as a Tagliavini movie because of his success at the Met. Scalera Film. Black and white. In Italian. 105 minutes. On VHS.

1943 The Amazing Mrs. Holliday

Deanna Durbin sings Tosca's aria "Vissi d'arte" during this film about a missionary and Chinese orphans. Jean Renoir directed most of the movie, but Bruce Manning finished it. Universal. Black and white. 96 minutes.

1946 Davanti a lui tremava tutta Roma

Tito Gobbi is a superb Scarpia in scenes from a 1944 production of *Tosca* at the Rome Opera House in this film set during the German occupation. *Davanti a lui tremava tutta Roma* gets its title from a line in the libretto about Scarpia, "Before him all Rome trembled." Anna Magnani plays an opera diva starring in *Tosca* whose life parallels the opera plot. Her lover, the tenor Franco (Gino Sinimberghi), rescues an English aviator, and the police become suspicious. On stage Elisabetta Barbato is the singing voice of Tosca, Sinimberghi sings Cavaradossi, and Gobbi sing Scarpia, with Luigi Ricci conducting the Rome Opera House Orchestra. Carmine Gallone directed for Excelsa Film. Black and white. In Italian with English subtitles. 110 minutes.

1951 The Great Caruso

Enrico Caruso (Mario Lanza) is seen on stage singing "È lucevan le stelle" in a production of *Tosca* in Madrid in this American biopic. See THE GREAT CARUSO.

1953 Melba

Patrice Munsel, playing Nellie Melba in this opulent British film biography, sings Tosca's aria "Vissi d'arte." See NELLIE MELBA.

1973 Magni film

Monica Vitti plays Tosca in *La Tosca,* an Italian film of the Sardou play with Puccini's music featured on the soundtrack. Luigi Proietti is Cavaradossi, Vittorio Gassman is Scarpia, and Luigi Magni wrote the screenplay and directed for Titanus. Color. In Italian. 100 minutes.

1973 Serpico

Al Pacino plays Frank Serpico, an Italian-American cop who likes opera. When he puts a recording of Cavaradossi's aria "È lucevan le stelle" on his phonograph and listens to it in his backyard, the woman next door asks whether it is Björling. He says it is di Stefano, but they become friends anyway. Sidney Lumet directed. Color. 130 minutes.

1983 I Live for Art

This fine documentary, about *Tosca* and the sopranos who have sung the role, takes its title from Tosca's aria "Vissi d'arte." Among the many Toscas interviewed and heard singing are Licia Albanese, Grace Bumbry, Montserrat Caballé, Gina Cigna, Régine Crespin, Dorothy Kirsten, Zinka Milanov, Birgit Nilsson, Magda Olivero, Leonie Rysanek, Renata Tebaldi, Kiri Te Kanawa, Eva Turner, Galina Vishnevskaya, and Ljuba Welitsch. Maria Callas and Maria Jeritza are also seen and discussed. The film, hosted by Robert Merrill, was written by Raymond Vanover, produced by Joseph Wishy, and directed by Muriel Balash. Color. In English. 91 minutes. Kultur VHS.

1983 Kabaivanska film

Raina Kabaivanska sings the role of Tosca in Act II of the opera opposite Giuseppe Taddei as Scarpia in this Bulgarian television film. Color. In Italian. 30 minutes. On VHS.

1992 The Last Mile

Bernadette Peters plays a young Met soprano in this teleplay written by Terrence McNally. She is waiting nervously in her dressing room before her debut as Tosca. The story begins with the opening chords of *Tosca* and ends 13 minutes later with Tosca's offstage cries of "Mario, Mario." It was written for the 20th anniversary celebration of the *Great Performances* series and telecast October 9, 1992. Color. 13 minutes.

1993 Household Saints
Tosca's aria "Vissi d'arte," sung by Maria Caniglia, is heard on the soundtrack of this offbeat story about the saintly lives of two Italian women in New York. Nancy Savoca directed the film, based on a novel by Francine Prose. Color. 124 minutes.

1994 Heavenly Creatures
Peter Dvorsky is heard singing Cavaradossi's aria "È lucevan le stelle" in this New Zealand film set in the early 1950s. However, the tenor who dominates the film is Mario Lanza. Color. 95 minutes.

1997 Hoodlum
Bill Duke's film about gangsters in Harlem during the 1930s, modeled on Coppola's *Godfather* films, includes a climactic shoot-out to music from *Tosca.* Color. 130 minutes.

2000 The Man Who Cried
Sally Potter's film about Jews and opera in Paris during World War II features "È lucevan le stelle" sung by John Turturro (dubbed by Italian tenor Salvatore Licitra) with backing from the Royal Opera House Orchestra led by Sian Edwards. See THE MAN WHO CRIED.

2000 Italian for Beginners
Italian opera music, including snippets from *Tosca,* is an important mood component of this Danish film about a group of Copenhageners taking evening classes in Italian. Lone Scherfig directed. Color. In Danish. 112 minutes.

2000 Tosca: A Tale of Love and Torture
Trevor Graham's documentary about Opera Australia's production of *Tosca* in the of winter 2000 is a close-up portrait of three weeks of rehearsals and the opening night. Joan Carden is Tosca, Cathy Dadd is the opera director, and Roderick Brydon is the conductor. Patricia Lovell produced the film. Color. 85 minutes. Film Australia VHS.

TOSCAN DU PLANTIER, DANIEL
French film producer (1941–2003)

Daniel Toscan du Plantier, a French film producer who once headed the Gaumont film company in Paris, produced a number of opera films with major directors who had no previous experience of opera. By so doing he gave the cinema some of the best opera films ever made. They include Joseph Losey's DON GIOVANNI (1978), Francesco Rosi's CARMEN (1984), Luigi Comencini's LA BOHÈME (1988), Frederic Mitterand's MADAMA BUTTERFLY (1995), and Benoit Jacquot's TOSCA (2001). He

can be seen talking about his work in the 1985 TV documentary CINOPÉRA.

TOSCANINI, ARTURO
Italian conductor (1867–1957)

Arturo Toscanini, one of the legends of modern music, began to conduct opera in 1886 at the age of 19. He was a major influence on La Scala, the Metropolitan, Bayreuth, Salzburg, and the NBC Symphony. The Parma-born conductor, who was a valiant fighter for proper opera staging and presentation, was also a strong voice of protest in the fascist years of Italy and Germany. In his final years, he was no longer simply a famous conductor; he was the symbol of classical music—he was *the* conductor. See AIDA (1949) and CONDUCTORS (1995).

1944 Toscanini: Hymn of the Nations
Avant-garde filmmaker Alexander Hammid directed this Oscar-nominated documentary that shows Toscanini leading the NBC Symphony Orchestra in December 1943. He conducts the overture to Verdi's *La forza del destino* and the *Hymn of Nations,* with Met tenor Jan Peerce and the Westminster Choir. May Sarton wrote the film for the Office of War Information. Black and white. 28 minutes. RCA/Video Yesteryear VHS.

1948–1952 Toscanini: The Television Concerts
Nine concerts with Toscanini conducting the NBC Symphony Orchestra have been released on VHS and LD. One is devoted to Wagner and another to a 1949 concert performance of AIDA. They were made from black and white kinescopes.

1985 Toscanini: the Maestro
Peter Rosen's outstanding film about the conductor, hosted by James Levine, includes home movies, archival film, and interviews. Herva Nelli, Jarmila Novotná, Robert Merrill, Bidú Sayão, and Licia Albanese are among those interviewed, and former members of the NBC Symphony Orchestra recall his genius. Color. 74 minutes. RCA Victor VHS/LD and Films for the Humanities & Sciences VHS.

1988 Young Toscanini
Franco Zeffirelli's $14 million Italian film biography *Il giovane Toscanini* stars C. Thomas Howell as the young Toscanini and Elizabeth Taylor as diva Nadina Bulichioff. It was not well received at its Venice Festival premiere, and it has been little seen since. It begins with Toscanini auditioning for La Scala in 1883 and is mainly concerned with the conductor's success in Brazil. The high point of the film is Taylor as Aida (sung by Aprile Millo), which has to be seen to be believed. Carlo Ber-

gonzi appears in the film playing Bertini. William H. Stadiem wrote the screenplay. Color. In Italian. 110 minutes.

TOTE STADT, DIE
1920 opera by Korngold

ERICH WOLFGANG KORNGOLD's opera *Die tote Stadt* (The Dead City) is a symbolist dream tale set in Bruges at the end of the 19th century. The libretto, by Korngold and his father Julius, was based on Georges Rodenbuch's novel *Bruges la morte*. Paul is obsessed by his love for his dead wife Marie. In his dreams a dancer named Marietta becomes confused with his wife, and he imagines her seduction. Afterwards he feels disloyal and strangles her with a lock of Maria's hair. When he wakes from the dream, Paul decides to leave the city of death.

1983 Berlin Deutsche Oper
German stage production: Götz Friedrich (director), Heinrich Hollreiser (conductor, Berlin Deutsche Oper Orchestra), Jean-Pierre Liégeois (choreographer).
Cast: James King (Paul), Karen Armstrong (Marie/Marietta), William Murray (Frank), Margit Neubauer (Brigitta), Sylvia Greenberg (Juliette).
Video: Opera Dubs VHS/Japanese LD. Brian Large (director). Color. In German. 120 minutes.

2001 Opéra National du Rhin
German stage production: Inga Levant (director), Jan Latham-Koenig (conductor, Strasbourg Philharmonic Orchestra and Rhine Opera Chorus).
Cast: Torsten Kerl (Paul), Angela Denoke (Marie/Marietta), Yuri Batukov (Frank), Birgitta Svendén (Brigitta), Barbara Baier (Juliette), Stephan Genz (Fritz), Julia Oesch (Lucienne).
Video: Arthaus DVD. Don Kent (director). Color. In German with English subtitles. 145 minutes.
Comment: Updated modernist production with many cinematic allusions, presumably because of Korngold's Hollywood career, including Marietta's standing over a grating and having her dress blown upward like Marilyn Monroe.

Related films

1987 Aria
Australian director Bruce Beresford based his episode of the film *Aria* around the duet known as "Marietta's Song." A man (Peter Birch) and a woman (Elizabeth Hurley) share their love to the haunting "Glück, das mir verblieb." The singers are Carol Neblett and René Kollo with the music played by the Munich Radio Orchestra conducted by Erich Leinsdorf. Beresford shot the film on location in Belgium. Color. 89 minutes. Academy DVD/VHS/LD.

1998 Marietta's Lied
Animated collage set to "Marietta's Song" featuring cutouts of German cabaret performers of the 1930s. It tells the story of the emigration of German composers to Los Angeles during the Nazi era, including composer Korngold. Color. 4 minutes.

TOZZI, GIORGIO
American bass (1923–)

Giorgio Tozzi was born in Chicago, where he studied with Rosa Raisa and Giacomo Rimini. He made his American debut on Broadway in 1948 in *The Rape of Lucretia*, his La Scala debut in 1953 in *La Wally*, and his Met debut in 1955 in *La Gioconda*. He created the role of the doctor in Samuel Barber's *Vanessa* at the Met in 1958, and he joined Joan Sutherland and Franco Corelli in the revival of *Les Huguenots* at La Scala in 1962. His most popular roles have been Boris Godunov and Philip II. He also sang in musical comedy and had a small Hollywood career. See AMAHL AND THE NIGHT VISITORS (1978) and DIE MEISTERSINGER VON NÜRNBERG (1969).

1958 South Pacific
Tozzi sings the role of Emile de Beque, dubbing for Rossano Brazzi, who plays the role on screen. See SOUTH PACIFIC.

1973 Shamus
Tozzi got good notices for his performance as Il Dottore, a smooth gangster gourmet who dines with the police and gives away underworld secrets. Burt Reynolds stars as a private detective. Buzz Kulik directed for Columbia. Color. 106 minutes.

1975 One of Our Own
Tozzi has a supporting role in this movie in which George Peppard plays an administrator solving a hospital's problems. Richard C. Sarafian directed. Color. 100 minutes.

1979 Torn Between Two Lovers
Tozzi has a small role in this romantic TV movie about married Lee Remick having an affair with George Peppard. Delbert Mann directed. Color. 100 minutes.

TRANSFORMATIONS

1973 opera by Susa

Confessional poet Anne Sexton examines her life through disturbing retellings of Grimm fairy tales, including *Snow White and the Seven Dwarfs* (difficult relationship with mother) and *The Sleeping Beauty* (incest with father). Conrad Susa's opera *Transformations,* libretto by the composer based on Sexton's poems of the fairy tales, was premiered by Minnesota Opera in Minneapolis in 1973 with Catherine Malfitano as the princess. Susa references popular musical styles of the 1940s and 1950s, from Bing Crosby to Perez Prado, in the work that has become one of the most frequently performed modern American operas.

1978 Minnesota Opera

American stage production: H. Wesley Balk (director), Philip Brunelle (conductor, Minnesota Opera Orchestra), Robert Israel (set/costume designer).

Cast: Barbara Brandt (Anne Sexton/Witch), Marsha Hunter (Princess), Janis Hardy (Good Fairy), Michael Riley (King), Vern Sutton (Wizard), William Wahman (Prince).

Telecast August 14, 1978, on PBS. Lynwood King (director). Color. In English. 90 minutes.

Comment: Sexton, one of the most popular modern American poets, committed suicide three years after writing *Transformations.* The video of the Minnesota production was featured at a TV Opera Colloquium in 1978, sponsored by the National Opera Institute.

TRAUBEL, HELEN

American soprano (1898–1972)

Helen Traubel, the foremost American Wagnerian of her time, had personality and grandeur on top of her remarkable voice. She began her career in 1923 in concerts and did not make her opera debut until 1937 when she sang at the Met in the premiere of Walter Damrosch's *The Man Without a Country.* In 1939 she sang the role of Sieglinde in *Die Walküre* and her Wagnerian career began. She was a major star at the Met until 1953 when she left after a disagreement with Rudolf Bing. She continued her career in television, concerts, and nightclubs; starred on Broadway in the Rodgers and Hammerstein musical *Pipe Dream;* and appeared in three films. One of her most unusual performances was as Katisha opposite Groucho Marx as Ko-Ko in a 1960 TV version of THE MIKADO. She also published a popular mystery novel titled *The Metropolitan Opera Murders,* ghostwritten by Harold Q. Masur.

1950 Helen Traubel in Opera and Song

Traubel made two appearances on *The Voice of Firestone* television show in 1950. She sings arias from *Die Walküre* ("Du bist der Lenz" and "Ho-jo-to-ho") and the songs "Deep River," "Vienna, City of My Dreams," "I Love Thee," "Loch Lomond," "The World Is Waiting for the Sunrise," and "Wish You Were Here." Black and white. 27 minutes. VAI VHS.

1954 Deep in My Heart

In this biopic, Traubel plays a jolly woman who runs a restaurant where Victor Herbert's career begins. She gets to sing "You Will Remember Vienna," "Auf Wiedersehn," "Softly as in a Morning Sunrise," and "Stouthearted Men." See DEEP IN MY HEART.

1961 The Ladies' Man

Traubel stars opposite Jerry Lewis in this silly but rather fun comedy directed by Lewis. She's an ex–opera star called Welenmelon and runs a boarding house for career women. He's a girl-shy incompetent handyman who eventually becomes a ladies' man. Paramount. Color. 106 minutes.

1967 Gunn

Traubel is nightclub operator Mother in this film based on the Peter Gunn TV mystery series. Her waterfront club has been forced to pay protection money, as Gunn (Craig Stevens) discovers when he begins to investigate a murder. Blake Edwards directed. Paramount. Color. 94 minutes.

TRAVIATA, LA

1853 opera by Verdi

The story of *La traviata* has been very popular with filmmakers, although many of the films are based on the source novel and play *La dame aux camélias* by Alexandre Dumas. Dumas modeled his heroine on courtesan Alphonsine Plessis, whose Paris grave has become a tourist site. In the Dumas play this glamorous lady of easy virtue is called Marguerite Gautier, but in the opera GIUSEPPE VERDI and librettist Francesco Maria Piave call her Violetta. Despite the name change, the stage, opera, and screen stories are essentially the same. Violetta falls in love with young Alfredo Germont and gives up her hedonistic life to live with him although she knows she is dying of tuberculosis. Alfredo's father persuades her to break up with his son for the good of his family and his sister. The lovers are reconciled at her deathbed, but it is too late. Violetta/Marguerite has been portrayed on screen nearly as often as Carmen.

1947 La signora delle camelie

Italian feature film: Carmine Gallone (director), Giuseppe Morelli (conductor, Rome Opera Orchestra and Chorus).

Cast: Nelly Corradi (Violetta, sung by Onelia Fineschi), Gino Mattera (Alfredo), Manfredi Polverosi (Germont, sung by Tito Gobbi).

Black and white. In Italian. 84 minutes.

Comment: The film begins with Verdi and Dumas standing beside the grave of the Parisian courtesan who inspired the story and talking about her life and loves. The rest of the film is the opera. It was released in America as *The Lost One.*

1950 CBS Opera Television Theater

American TV production: Herbert Graf (director), Fausto Cleva (conductor, CBS Opera Television Orchestra), Richard Rychtarik (set designer), Henry Souvaine (producer), George Meade (English translation).

Cast: Elaine Malbin (Violetta), Brooks McCormack (Alfredo), Lawrence Tibbett (Germont).

Video at the MTR. Telecast March 12, 1950. Byron Paul (director). Black and white. In English. 95 minutes.

1953 Vinti film

Italian highlights film: Carlo Vinti (director), Marion Rhodes (producer), Anthony Stivanello (stage director), Joseph Vinti (screenplay), Giuseppe Bamboschek (conductor, Opera Cameos Orchestra and Chorus), Jon Ericson (narrator).

Cast: Lucia Evangelista (Violetta), Giulio Gari (Alfredo), Frank Valentino (Germont).

Video: Lyric/Video Yesteryear VHS. Color. In Italian. 53 minutes.

Comment: Shown theatrically in December 1953 with *Cavalleria rusticana* and later telecast in the *Opera Cameos* series.

1954 Enriquez film

Italian TV film: Franco Enriquez (director), Nino Sazogna (conductor, RAI Milan Orchestra and Chorus), Enrico Tovaglieri (set/costume designer).

Cast: Rosanna Carteri (Violetta), Nicola Filacurida (Alfredo), Carlo Tagliabue (Germont).

Video: Bel Canto Society VHS. Telecast December 22, 1954, on RAI. Black and white. In Italian. 116 minutes.

1954 Opera Cameos

American TV production: Carlo Vinti (director), Joseph Vinti (screenplay), Giuseppe Bamboschek (conductor, Opera Cameos Orchestra).

Cast: Beverly Sills (Violetta), John Drury (Alfredo), Frank Valentino (Germont), Giovanni Martinelli (introductions).

Video at the MTR. Telecast live November 17, 1954, on the DuMont Network from New York. Black and white. In Italian. 30 minutes.

1956 Voice of Firestone

American highlights TV production: Howard Barlow (Voice of Firestone Orchestra).

Cast: Elaine Malbin (Violetta), Richard Tucker (Alfredo), Russell Hammar (Germont).

Video: VAI VHS as *Firestone Verdi Festival.* Telecast January 3, 1956. Black and white. In Italian with English introductions. 14 minutes.

1957 NBC Opera Theatre

American TV production: Samuel Chotzinoff (producer/director), Peter Herman Adler (conductor, Symphony of the Air Orchestra and NBC Opera Theatre Chorus), Ed Wittstein (set/costume designer), Joseph Machlis (English translation).

Cast: Elaine Malbin (Violetta), John Alexander (Alfredo), Igor Gorin (Germont).

Video: House of Opera/Lyric VHS. Telecast live April 21, 1957. Kirk Browning (director). Color. In English. 120 minutes.

***1968 Lanfranchi film

Italian TV film: Mario Lanfranchi (director), Giuseppe Patanè (conductor, Orchestra and Chorus of Rome Opera House), Maurizio Monteverde (set/costume designer).

Cast: Anna Moffo (Violetta), Franco Bonisolli (Alfredo), Gino Bechi (Germont).

Video: VAI VHS. Color. In Italian with English plot summaries. 113 minutes.

Comment: Visually opulent and vocally splendid film that one critic felt was the best performance of the opera in any form. Moffo is in peak form, Bechi is superb, and Lanfranchi's direction is spot on..

1973 Focus on Opera

English highlights film: Peter Seabourne (director), John J. Davies (conductor, The Classical Orchestra), Peter Murray (English translation).

Cast: Valerie Masterson (Violetta), Kenneth Woollam (Alfredo), Michael Wakeham (Germont).

Color. In English. 57 minutes.

Comment: Filmed at Knebworth House in Hertfordshire for the series *Focus on Opera.* Distributed in America on 16mm.

1973 Who's Afraid of Opera?

English highlights TV film: Ted Kotcheff (director), Richard Bonynge (conductor, London Symphony Orchestra), George Djurkovic (set designer), Claire Merrill (screenplay), Nathan Kroll (producer).

Cast: Joan Sutherland (Violetta), Ian Caley (Alfredo), Pieter Van Der Stolk (Germont), Larry Berthelson puppets.

Video: Kultur VHS. Color. In English and Italian. 30 minutes.

Comment: Highlights version of the opera made for young audiences with Sutherland telling the story to puppets. The dialogue is in English, the arias in Italian.

1973 NHK Lirica Italiana

Japanese film of stage production: Bruno Nofri (director), Nino Verchi (conductor, NHK Symphony Orchestra and Nikikai Opera Chorus).

Cast: Renata Scotto (Violetta), José Carreras (Alfredo), Sesto Bruscantini (Germont),.

Video: House of Opera/Lyric VHS. Filmed at Metropolitan Hall, Tokyo, September 9, 1973. Color. In Italian with Japanese subtitles. 128 minutes.

1973 BBC Television

English TV production: Cedric Messina (director), Alexander Gibson (conductor, New Philharmonia Orchestra and BBC Chorus).

Cast: Elizabeth Harwood (Violetta), John Brecknock (Alfredo), Norman Bailey (Germont).

Harwood Memorial Trust DVD. Telecast December 29, 1974. Brian Large (director). Color. In English. 120 minutes.

Comment: The video was released to raise money for a scholarship for a young British opera singer.

1976 Wolf Trap Festival

American stage production: Tito Capobianco (director), Julius Rudel (conductor, Filene Center Orchestra and Wolf Trap Company Chorus), Carl Toms (set/costume designer).

Cast: Beverly Sills (Violetta), Henry Price (Alfredo), Richard Fredricks (Germont).

Video: VAI DVD/VHS. Kirk Browning (director). Color. In Italian with English subtitles. 135 minutes.

1981 Metropolitan Opera

American stage production: Colin Graham (director), James Levine (conductor, Metropolitan Opera Orchestra and Chorus), Tanya Moiseiwitsch (set designer).

Cast: Ileana Cotrubas (Violetta), Plácido Domingo (Alfredo), Cornell MacNeil (Germont).

Video at the MTR. Taped March 28, 1981; telecast September 30, 1981. Brian Large (director). Color. In Italian with English subtitles. 140 minutes.

***1982 Zeffirelli film

Italian feature film: Franco Zeffirelli (director/designer/screenplay), James Levine (conductor, Metropolitan Opera Orchestra and Chorus), Ennio Guarnieri (cinematographer), Piero Tosi (costume designer), Alberto Testa (choreographer).

Cast: Teresa Stratas (Violetta), Plácido Domingo (Alfredo), Cornell MacNeil (Germont).

Video: Universal DVD/MCA VHS. Color. In Italian with English subtitles. 105 minutes.

Comment: Stratas is an utterly believable and heart-breaking Violetta in this great opera film, Zeffirelli's finest achievement in the genre. He uses a clever conceit to frame the story, imagining the opera as a feverish memory by Violetta while she is dying. There are cinematic devices to keep the narrative flowing, including complex flashbacks and camera movements. The bravura rococo style is exactly in keeping with Violetta's romantic memories. The opera is slightly abridged.

Plácido Domingo and Teresa Stratas in Zeffirelli's 1982 film.

***1987 Glyndebourne Festival

English stage production: Peter Hall (director), Bernard Haitink (conductor, London Philharmonic Orchestra and Glyndebourne Festival Chorus), John Gunter (set/costume designer).

Cast: Marie McLaughlin (Violetta), Walter MacNeil (Alfredo), Brent Ellis (Germont).

Video: Arthaus DVD/Home Vision VHS. Peter Hall (director); Derek Bailey (producer). Color. In Italian with English subtitles. 135 minutes.

Comment: This superb video is the best that exists of a stage performance of the opera. It was filmed live but without an audience to allow more effective camera movement.

1992 Teatro alla Scala

Italian stage production: Liliana Cavani (director), Riccardo Muti (conductor, Teatro alla Scala Orchestra and Chorus), Dante Ferretti (set designer), Gabrielle Pescutti (costume designer).

Cast: Tiziana Fabbricini (Violetta), Roberto Alagna (Alfredo), Paolo Coni (Germont).

Sony VHS/LD. Liliana Cavani (director). Color. In Italian with English subtitles. 148 minutes.

Comment: Fine production, with singers who can act. As it was shot in HDTV, it has the gloss of a 35mm film.

1992 Teatro La Fenice

Italian stage production: Pier Luigi Pizzi (director, set/costume designer), Carlo Rizzi (conductor, Teatro La Fenice Orchestra and Chorus).

Cast: Edita Gruberova (Violetta), Neil Shicoff (Alfredo), Giorgio Zancanaro (Germont).

Video: NVC Arts (GB) DVD/Teldec VHS and LD. Taped in December 1992. Derek Bailey (director). Color. In Italian. 130 minutes.

1994 Royal Opera House

English stage production: Richard Eyre (director), Sir Georg Solti (conductor, Royal Opera House Orchestra and Chorus), Bob Crowley (set designer).

Cast: Angela Gheorghiu (Violetta), Frank Lopardo (Alfredo), Leo Nucci (Germont).

Video: London/Decca DVD and VHS. Telecast in December 1994 on BBC. Peter Maniura and Humphrey Burton (directors). Color. In Italian with English subtitles. 135 minutes.

Comment: Gheorghiu was 29 when she was acclaimed for this performance, her first *La traviata*. The English critics adored it.

1995 New York City Opera

American stage production: Renata Scotto (director), Yves Abel (conductor, New York City Opera Orchestra and Chorus), Thierry Bosquet (set/costume designer), Sherrill Milnes (host, backstage program).

Cast: Janice Woods (Violetta), Stephen Mark Brown (Alfredo), Louis Otey (Germont).

Telecast March 28, 1995, in the series *Live From Lincoln Center*. Kirk Browning (director). Color. In Italian with English subtitles. 175 minutes.

2000 La traviata From Paris

Live Paris TV production: Giuseppe Patroni-Griffi (director), Zubin Mehta (conductor, RAI National Symphony Orchestra and Solisti Cantori), Vittorio Storaro (cinematographer), Andrea Andermann (producer).

Cast: Eteri Gvazava (Violetta), José Cura (Alfredo), Rolando Panerai (Germont), Raphaëlle Farman (Flora), Nicolas Rivenq (Baron).

Telecast live in Europe June 3 and 4, 2000; shown on PBS in the United States in August 2000. Giuseppe Patroni-Griffi (director). Color. In Italian with English subtitles. 170 minutes.

Comment: Telecast live from Paris locations at the time of the action in the opera: Act I from the 18th-century Hotel de Boisgelin, Act II from the hamlet built for Marie Antoinette in the Parc de Versailles with the finale in the Petit Palais, and Act III from an apartment on the Île Saint-Louis with a view of Notre Dame. Each performer carried radio microphones and could follow the conductor on TV monitors while Mehta watched them on his monitors. Highlights from the telecast are on CD. Gvazava is a Siberian soprano discovered by producer Andermann, who conceived the project.

2002 Teatro Verdi, Busseto

Italian stage production: Frnaco Zeffirelli (director/designer), Placido Domingo (conductor, Arturo Toscanini Foundation Orchestra and Chorus).

Cast: Stefania Bonfadelli (Violetta), Scott Piper (Alfredo), Renato Bruson (Germont), Annely Peebo (Flora), Ezio Maria Tisi (Baron).

Video: TDK DVD. Fausto Dall'Olio (director). Color. In Italian with English subtitles. 205 minutes.

Comment: The DVD includes interviews with cast and crew and sequences showing places in Busseto itself, Verdi's hometown.

Early/related films

The role of Violetta-Marguerite is one of the most popular females roles in the history of the cinema. Although many of the early silent films claimed to be based on the Dumas story rather than the opera, this was to avoid paying copyright fees; they were usually screened with music from the opera.

1906/1908 Cinemafono Pagliej

CINEMAFONO PAGLIEJ, an Italian sound-on-disc company specializing in opera films, screened films featuring arias from *La traviata* ("De' miei bollenti spiriti" and "Addio, del passato") at the Sala Umberto I in Rome from May 19 to July 30, 1906. On April 19, 1908, a screening in Pisa featured a film with a scene from *La traviata*. The films are apparently lost. Black and white. In Italian.

1907 Kamieladamen
Oda Alstrup stars as Marguerite in *Kamieladamen,* a Danish film of the Dumas/Verdi story released in the United States as *The Lady With the Camellias.* Viggo Larsen directed for Nordisk Films. Black and white. Silent. About 14 minutes.

1908 Messter sound film
This German film of an aria from the opera was screened with the music played on a synchronized phonograph. Oskar Messter produced a number of films of this kind in Berlin. Black and white. In Italian. About 4 minutes.

1909 La signora delle camelie
Vittoria Lepanto stars as Marguerite in *La signora delle camelie,* an Italian film based on the Dumas novel but screened with music from the opera. Ugo Falena directed for Film d'Arte Italiana. Black and white. Silent. About 14 minutes. A print survives.

1909 Itala sound film
Itala Film of Torino released in 1909 a sound-on-disc film of an aria from La Traviata titled "De'miei bollenti spiriti." Black and white. About 4 minutes.

1911 La dame aux camélias
Stage immortal Sarah Bernhardt (then aged 67) stars as Marguerite in *La dame aux camélias,* a French adaptation of the Dumas play. This was one of the most famous early silent films, and it was usually screened with the Verdi music. André Calmettes and Henry Pouctal directed. Black and white. About 12 minutes. Prints survive.

1912 Camille
Gertrude Shipman stars as Marguerite in *Camille,* an American film version of the Dumas play made for the Champion Film Company and directed by Herbert Brenon. Black and white. Silent. About 15 minutes.

1915 La signora delle camelie
Francesca Bertini, Italy's top movie diva at the time, portrays Marguerite in *La signora delle camelie,* an Italian film based on the Dumas play. Gustavo Serena directed for Caesar Film. Black and white. Silent. About 67 minutes.

1915 La signora delle camelie
Italian diva Hesperia stars as Marguerite in this *La signora delle camelie,* a rival 1915 Italian film of the Dumas play. Her husband Baldassare Negroni directed for Tiber Film. Hesperia's real name was Olga Mabelli and Marguerite was her most famous role. Black and white. Silent. About 70 minutes.

1915 Camille
Clara Kimball Young stars as Marguerite in *Camille,* an American film based on the Dumas play. Albert Capellani directed for the World Film Corp. Black and white. Silent. About 70 minutes.

1917 Camille
Theda Bara stars as Marguerite in this *Camille,* an American film based on the Dumas play. J. Gordon Edwards directed for the Fox Film Corp. Black and white. Silent. About 70 minutes.

1917 Die Kameliendame
Erna Morena is Marguerite in *Die Kameliendame,* a German film of the Dumas play. Paul Leni, who later went to Hollywood, directed and designed the sets and costumes. Black and white. Silent. About 70 minutes.

1921 Camille
Alla Nazimova plays Marguerite in *Camille* with newcomer Rudolph Valentino as her young lover in this American film of the Dumas play. Ray C. Smallwood directed for Metro. Black and white. About 75 minutes.

1921 Arme Violetta
Pola Negri stars as Violetta in the German film *Arme Violetta* directed by Paul Ludwig Stein. Black and white. Silent. About 80 minutes.

1922 Tense Moments From Operas
Thelma Murray is Violetta with Clive Brook as Alfredo in this British film of the Verdi opera made for the series *Tense Moments From Operas.* H. B. Parkinson produced and George Wynn directed. The music of the opera was played live with the film. Black and white. Silent. About 12 minutes.

1925 Damen med Kameliorna
Swedish actress Tora Teje stars as Marguerite in *Damen med Kameliorna,* a Swedish film based on the Dumas play. Olof Molander directed. About 75 minutes.

1927 Camille
Norma Talmadge stars as Marguerite in *Camille,* an American film based on the Dumas play. Fred Niblo directed for First National. Black and white. Silent. About 90 minutes.

1927 Cameo Opera
Peggy Carlisle is Violetta, Anthony Ireland is Alfredo, and Booth Conway is Baron Douphol in this English film of scenes from the opera. H. B. Parkinson directed for the *Cameo Opera* series. It was screened with singers on stage performing the arias. Black and white. Silent. 20 minutes.

1932 Die—oder Keine
In the German film *Die—oder Keine*, Gita Alpar is a prima donna appearing in a production of *La traviata*, an opera in which she had been popular on the Berlin stage. Gustav Fröhlich directed. It was distributed in the United States as *She or Nobody*. Black and white. In German. 92 minutes.

1934 La dame aux camélias
Yvonne Printemps stars as Marguerite in *La dame aux camélias*, a French film based on the Dumas novel. Abel Gance supervised and Fernand Rivers directed. Black and white. In French. 118 minutes.

1934 Evensong
Evelyn Laye enchants an Austrian archduke while portraying Violetta on stage in the "Libiamo" party scene in this film inspired by Melba's career. He throws her jewels in a flower bouquet. See EVENSONG.

1936 Ave Maria
Beniamino Gigli (Alfredo) and Erna Berger (Violetta) are seen on stage in *La traviata* in the Act I duet "Un di felice" and the Act III scene in which he throws money at her. Alois Melichar conducts the Berlin State Opera Orchestra and Cathedral Boys Choir. A nightclub singer in the audience identifies with Violetta. See AVE MARIA.

1936 Camille
Herbert Stothart's score for George Cukor's *Camille* was created from themes from Verdi's *La traviata*. Greta Garbo plays Marguerite opposite Robert Taylor in this MGM film based on the Dumas novel and play. Black and white. 108 minutes.

1936 San Francisco
Jeanette MacDonald impresses Clark Gable by singing "Sempre libera" from *La traviata* in this film culminating in an earthquake. See SAN FRANCISCO.

1937 100 Men and a Girl
Deanna Durbin sings "Libiamo" in this film about the precocious daughter of a musician. Her costar is conductor Leopold Stokowski. Henry Koster directed for Universal. Black and white. 83 minutes.

1937 I'll Take Romance
Grace Moore, playing an opera diva romanced by Melvyn Douglas, is seen on stage in New York as Violetta in the "Libiamo" sequence from Act I of *La traviata*. See I'LL TAKE ROMANCE.

1937 Women of Glamour
Armanda Chirot sings Violetta's "Sempre libera" on stage in a production of the opera in this American film. Virginia Bruce plays an equivalent modern gold digger. Gordon Wiles directed for Columbia. Black and white. 72 minutes.

1938 The Goldwyn Follies
Helen Jepson sings Violetta opposite Charles Kullman's Alfredo on stage in *La traviata* in the "Libiamo" and "Sempre libera" scenes. Jepson plays an opera singer hired by producer Adolphe Menjou in this Goldwyn musical. George Marshall directed. Black and white. 120 minutes.

1940 Amami, Alfredo!
Maria Cebotari plays a singer who persuades La Scala to present an opera by her fiancé, but the illness that struck down the heroine of *La traviata* threatens her. Luckily, it's a bad diagnosis and she really isn't sick, so there's a happy ending after a good deal of Verdi music. See AMAMI, ALFREDO!

1941 Sis Hopkins
Hillbilly student Judy Canova shows off to her snooty college schoolmates by singing the aria "Sempre libera" in Italian with an orchestra at a college function. Joseph Santley directed for Republic Pictures. Black and white. 89 minutes.

1941 They Meet Again
Violetta's aria "Ah fors'è lui" (Ah perhaps it's him) is featured in this *Dr. Christian* series film starring Jean Hersholt. He is trying to prove the innocence of a bank teller. Earle C. Kenton directed. Black and white. 67 minutes.

1942 Get Hep to Love
Child singing prodigy Gloria Jean sings the aria "Sempre libera" in this film about a young girl who wants to be a normal teenager. Charles Lamont directed for Universal. Black and white. 77 minutes.

1943 Thousands Cheer
Kathryn Grayson sings Violetta's aria "Sempre libera" in this variety film in which she is the love interest of army

private Gene Kelly. George Sidney directed. Black and white. 126 minutes.

1944 La dama de las camelias
Lina Montes plays Marguerite in *La dama de las camelias*, a Mexican film based on the Dumas novel. Gabriel Soria directed. Black and white. In Spanish. 115 minutes.

1945 The Lost Weekend
Writer/director Billy Wilder offers an ironic reason why alcoholics should avoid *La traviata*. Ray Milland flees his seat at the Metropolitan Opera as the "Libiamo" drinking song reminds him of the bottle he has hidden in his coat in the cloakroom. He then has to sit out the opera waiting for Jane Wyman, the woman whose coat has been mixed up with his. The bottle gets broken, but he wins the woman. John Garris and Theodora Lynch are the singers in the "Libiamo" sequence, performing with the San Francisco Opera. Black and white. 101 minutes.

1950 The Toast of New Orleans
Maria Lanza sings "Libiamo" in this film about a Louisiana fisherman who becomes an opera star in turn-of-the-century New Orleans. See THE TOAST OF NEW ORLEANS.

1952 La dame aux camélias
Micheline Presle plays Marguerite in *La dame aux camélias*, a French film based on the Dumas novel. Raymond Bernard directed. Color. In French. 111 minutes.

1953 Melba
Patrice Munsel, playing opera diva Nellie Melba in this British film biography, sings an aria from *La traviata*. See MELBA.

1953 Tonight We Sing
Soprano Elsa Valdine (Roberta Peters) and tenor Gregory Lawrence (voice of Jan Peerce) perform excerpts from *La traviata* in this film about impresario Sol Hurok. See TONIGHT WE SING.

1953 Camelia, passion sauvage
Maria Felix plays Camelia in *Camelia, passion sauvage*, a Mexican film of the story based on the Dumas novel. Roberto Gavaldon directed. Black and white. In Spanish. 89 minutes.

1953 Traviata 53
Barbara Laage plays the heroine in *Traviata 53*, a modernized Italian adaptation of the Dumas/Verdi story. Vittorio Cottafavi directed. Black and white. In Italian. 92 minutes.

1962 La bella Lola
Sarita Montiel stars as Marguerite, aka Lola, in *La bella Lola*, a Spanish film of the Dumas story directed by Alfonso Balcazar. Black and white. In Spanish. 88 minutes.

1965 I pugni in tasca
Marco Bellochio's powerful Italian film *Fists in the Pocket* uses Violetta's aria "Sempre libera" to emphasize the mental agony of star Lou Castel. Black and white. In Italian. 113 minutes.

1966 Trans-Europ-Expres
Alain Robbe-Grillet's postmodernist film uses excerpts from *La traviata* as most of its score. Michael Fano arranged the opera music, performed by the Prima Symphony Orchestra. Color. In French. 90 minutes.

1970 Camille 2000
Radley Metzer transfers the Dumas story to contemporary Rome with Danielle Gaubert as Margherita Gautier and Nino Castelnuovo as Armand Duval. It's a bit more nude than usual. Color. In Italian. 104 minutes.

1972 The Seduction of Mimi
Violetta's aria "Sempre libera" is heard on the soundtrack of this Italian film as metal worker Giancarlo Giannini rescues outspokenm Marxist Mariangela Melato from right-wing attackers on a busy Turin street. He says he's called Mimì, she says why not Lucia. Lina Wertmuller directed. Color. 89 minutes in American version, 121 minutes in Italian version as *Mimì metallurgiico ferito nel l'onore*.

1973 Don't Look Now
Nicolas Roeg features the Brindisi drinking song on the soundtrack of this erotic Daphne Du Maurier thriller set in Venice. Julie Christie and Donald Sutherland star. Color. In English. 110 minutes.

1982 La vera storia della signora dalle camelie
Isabelle Huppert plays Marguerite in *The True Story of the Lady of the Camelias*, an Italian film based on the life of courtesan Alphonsine Plessis, the woman who inspired the Dumas novel. Mauro Bolognini directed. Color. In Italian. 92 minutes.

1984 Maestro's Company Puppets
Scenes from *La traviata* are performed by puppets rehearsing under an old theater. The voices belong to Pilar Lorengar as Violetta, Giacomo Aragall as Alfredo, and Dietrich Fischer-Dieskau as Germont. Lorin Maazel conducts the Berlin Deutsche Oper Orchestra. The puppets belong to the Australian Maestro's Company, and Wil-

liam Fitzwater directed the video. Color. Dialogue in English, arias in Italian. 30 minutes. VAI VHS.

1984 The Lady of the Camelias
Greta Scacchi plays Marguerite in *The Lady of the Camelias,* a British television film based on the Dumas novel and directed by Desmond Davis. Color. In English. 100 minutes.

1986 Grace Note
In this *Twilight Zone* TV series episode, a woman who wants to be opera singer (Julia Migenes) is given a glimpse of the future by her dying sister and sees herself in *La traviata* at the Met. Peter Medak directed for CBS. Color. 30 minutes.

1987 Terror at the Opera
Dario Argento's operatic horror film features an aria from *La traviata* on the soundtrack. See TERROR AT THE OPERA.

1989 The Europeans
The *La traviata* waltz is featured ironically at a ball in this splendid adaptation of the Henry James novel. James Ivory directed; Ismail Merchant produced. Color. 90 minutes.

1990 Pretty Woman
Verdi's pretty 19th-century courtesan strikes a responsive chord in a pretty 20th-century prostitute when Hollywood streetwalker Julia Roberts is taken to San Francisco's War Memorial Opera House by millionaire Richard Gere. He wants to observe her response to opera, telling her that the first time one sees opera is very important. He says one falls in love with it at once or it never becomes a part of one's soul; Roberts naturally loves it. On the stage are Karin Calabro singing Violetta with Bruce Eckstut as her Alfredo. Thomas Pasatieri arranged and conducted the opera; Garry Marshall directed the film. Color. 117 minutes.

1994 The Adventures of Priscilla, Queen of the Desert
A drag queen in an elaborate silvery costume on top of a pink bus on a highway in the Australian outback mimes to Violetta's aria "E strano!...Ah fors'è lui." This is one of the odder opera scenes in modern cinema but seems perfectly justified in the context of a film about drag queens driving to the center of Australia. The voice belongs to Joan Carden backed by the Sydney Symphony Orchestra. Stephan Elliot wrote and directed the film. Color. 103 minutes.

2001 Rat Race
Carlo Del Monte and Victoria de los Angeles are heard on the soundtrack of this film singing the "Libiamo" with the Rome Opera House Orchestra and Chorus. The story concerns a group of Los Vegas gamblers trying to win $2 million. Jerry Zucker directed. Color. 111 minutes.

TREEMONISHA
1911 opera by Joplin

SCOTT JOPLIN's ragtime opera *Treemonisha* is the sleeping beauty of American music, forgotten for more than 50 years after its 1915 premiere. The premiere was a sad affair, paid for by the composer himself and staged in Harlem with only a piano. The opera was judged a dismal failure, and Joplin went crazy with disappointment, later dying in an asylum. *Treemonisha* finally won deserved acclaim when it was revived in 1972 and recorded and telecast; Joplin was awarded a posthumous Pulitzer Prize. The memorable final ensemble of the opera, "A Real Slow Drag," with its refrain "Marching Onward," has become popular in its own right. The story takes place on an abandoned Arkansas plantation in 1884. Treemonisha helps her people, who are former slaves, fight exploitative evil magicians, who try to control them. She is kidnapped but rescued by Remus, and all ends in forgiveness and fine music.

1982 Houston Grand Opera
American stage production: Frank Corsaro (director), John DeMain (conductor, Houston Grand Opera Orchestra and Chorus), Günther Schuller (arranger, orchestration), Franco Colavecchia (set/costume designer), Mabel Robinson (choreographer).

Cast: Carmen Balthrop (Treemonisha), Curtis Rayam (Remus), Obba Babatunde (Zodzetrick), Delores Ivory (Monisha), Dorceal Duckens (Ned), Kenn Hicks (Andy), Cora Johnson (Lucy).

Video: Kultur VHS. Sid Smith (director). Color. In English. 86 minutes.

Comment: Houston's colorful production of *Treemonisha* in 1975 was a well-deserved success, and the revival is effectively captured on video.

Related films

1977 Scott Joplin
Treemonisha is central to this film biography of Joplin, played by Billy Dee Williams. He abandons everything else to complete it but then can't get the money to have it staged in New York. A rehearsal of the "Marching Onward" number is shown with four amateur singers, a piano, and a desperate composer. A final voice-over in the film explains that the opera was not staged in 1974 but then won the Pulitzer Prize. Christopher Knopf wrote the

screenplay and Jeremy Paul Kagan directed. Color. 96 minutes.

1986 Royal Opera House
Jessye Norman, Lisa Casteen, and company sing the ensemble "A Real Slow Drag" and "Marching Onward" in a staged scene at the Royal Opera House on April 21, 1986. It was presented during a gala telecast in honor of the queen. Edward Downes conducts the Royal Opera House Orchestra. Color. 90 minutes. Lyric VHS and video at the MPRC.

TRIAL AT ROUEN, THE
1956 opera by Dello Joio

Norman Dello Joio's opera about the Maid of Orleans has had three incarnations. The first version was staged at Sarah Lawrence College in 1950 as *The Trial of Joan*. Dello Joio then wrote a new libretto and score for NBC Opera Theatre, and this opera was telecast in 1956 as *The Trial at Rouen*. When he revised it for the third time for the stage, it became *The Trial of St. Joan* and was produced by New York City Opera in 1959, when it won the New York Music Critics Circle Award. The story focuses on Joan's trial at Rouen in 1431. In the first part sympathetic Friar Julien urges Joan to submit to authority, and Bishop Cauchon seems intent on destroying her. In the second part, she is tried and condemned to death.

1956 NBC Opera Theatre
American TV production: Samuel Chotzinoff (director/producer), Peter Herman Adler (conductor, Symphony of the Air Orchestra), Trew Hocker (set designer), Noël Polacheck (costume designer).

Cast: Elaine Malbin (Joan), Hugh Thompson (Bishop Cauchon), Chester Watson (Friar Julien), Paul Ukena, Loren Driscoll, Carole O'Hara, R. W. Barry.

Telecast April 8, 1956, on NBC. Kirk Browning (director). Black and white. In English. 90 minutes.

TRIAL BY JURY
1875 comic opera by Gilbert and Sullivan

Trial by Jury, a satire on the English court system, was the first successful collaboration between William S. Gilbert and Arthur Sullivan and is the shortest of their operettas. It takes place in a courtroom where a judge is called upon to decide a breach of promise action. Angelina is suing Edwin and arrives with her bridesmaids ready for a wedding. In the end, the judge decides he wants to marry her himself.

1950 CBS Television
American TV production: Marc Daniel (director), CBS Orchestra, William Gaxton (host).

Cast: Ralph Riggs (Judge), Patricia Morison (Angelina), Donald Clark (Edwin.)

Telecast November 30, 1950, on the *Airflyte Theater* program. Black and white. In English. 30 minutes.

1953 CBS Television
American TV production: William Spier (director), CBS Orchestra, Henry May (set designer).

Cast: Martyn Green (Judge), Arlyne Frank (Angelina), Davis Cunningham (Edwin).

Videos at the MTR and Library of Congress. Telecast April 19, 1953, on the *Omnibus* program. Andrew McCullough (director). Black and white. In English. 25 minutes.

1972 Gilbert & Sullivan for All series
English studio film: Peter Seabourne (director), Peter Murray (conductor, Gilbert and Sullivan Festival Orchestra and Chorus), David Maverovitch (cinematographer), Trevor Evans (adaptation), John Seabourne (producer).

Cast: Lawrence Richard (Judge), Gillian Humphreys (Angelina), Thomas Round (Edwin), Michael Wakeham (Angelina's Counsel).

Video: Musical Collectables VHS. Color. In English. 50 minutes.

1982 Gilbert and Sullivan Collection series
English studio production: Wendy Toye (director), Judith De Paul (producer), Alexander Faris (conductor, London Symphony Orchestra and Ambrosian Opera Chorus), Allan Cameron (set designer), George Walker (executive producer).

Cast: Frankie Howerd (Judge), Kate Flowers (Angelina), Ryland Davies (Edwin), Anna Dawson (Ann Other), Tom McDonnell (Angelina's Counsel).

Video: Braveworld (GB) VHS. Derek Bailey (director). Color. In English. 40 minutes.

TRIAL OF MARY LINCOLN, THE
1972 TV opera by Pasatieri

President Lincoln's widow Mary is put on trial for her sanity. Her son Robert says her behavior is so peculiar that she should be committed to an asylum—but does he have an ulterior motive? American composer THOMAS PASATIERI composed seven operas before creating this notable television opera with librettist Anne Howard Bailey. They tailored the opera specifically for TV, with flashbacks, voice-overs, and other screen techniques. It premiered on NET Opera Theater.

1972 NET Opera Theater

American TV production: Kirk Browning (director), Peter Herman Adler (conductor, Boston Symphony Orchestra), William Ritman (set designer).

Cast: Elaine Bonazzi (Mary Lincoln), Wayne Turnage (Robert Lincoln), Carole Bogard (Elizabeth Edwards, Mary's sister), Chester Watson (Leonard Swett), Louise Parker (Mary's dressmaker friend), Julian Patrick (Lincoln's clerk), Alan Titus, Lizabeth Pritchett, Robert Owen Jones.

Video at the MTR. Telecast February 14, 1972. Kirk Browning (director). Color. In English. 59 minutes.

Comment: The telecast won an Emmy Award and the Salzburg TV Opera Prize. Critics particularly liked Bonazzi's "Abraham Lincoln" aria and her duet with her sister.

TRIALS OF GALILEO, THE
1967 TV opera by Laderman

The Catholic Church forces the 17th-century astronomer Galileo to recant his heretical ideas. Cardinals Bellarmine and Barberini defend him at first, but when Barberini becomes Pope Urban VIII, Galileo is tortured and imprisoned. American composer EZRA LADERMAN wrote the television opera *The Trials of Galileo,* libretto by Joseph Darion, on commission from CBS. It was staged in a revised version in 1979 as *Galileo Galilei.*

1967 CBS Television

American TV production: Bruce Minnix (director), Alfredo Antonini (conductor, CBS Orchestra and Camerata Singers).

Cast: Ara Berberian (Galileo), David Clatworthy (Cardinal Bellarmine), Ray de Voll (Interrogator), Joanna Simon (Friend), Fred Mayer, Vahan Khanzadian.

Video at the MTR. Telecast May 14, 1967, on CBS. Color. In English. 75 minutes.

Comment: The opera was taped at the Riverside Church in New York City and presented as an oratorio in the series *Look Up and Live.*

TRILBY
Film series with opera content

Trilby O'Farrell is the tragic heroine of George du Maurier's 1894 novel *Trilby,* the story of an artist's model who becomes a famous singer. She does this under the sinister hypnotic influence of Svengali, a Hungarian musician, who makes her into one of the great singers of Europe. She sings opera arias in controlled concerts but never appears in actual operas; Elisabeth Schwarzkopf provided her singing voice in a 1954 film. When Svengali dies, Trilby loses her voice and dies. Little Billee, the artist who loves her, dies soon after. The novel, which

became a play in 1895, has been enormously popular with filmmakers. The Trilby-Svengali myth is a powerful one, and has been seen as a metaphor for the harsh training of opera singers, molded into something strange and distant. Du Maurier is said to have modeled Trilby on the English contralto Clara Butt, who was a Royal College of Music student in 1893 and had just won acclaim singing in *Orphée et Eurydice* at the Lyceum Theater in London.

1896 Trilby Burlesque
The popularity of the play in London is reflected in its instant appearance on film in April 1896. This R. W. Paul film simply shows dancing girls from the play at the Alhambra Theatre in London. Black and white. Silent. About 1 minute.

1896 Trilby and Little Billee
The popularity in America of the play led to this Biograph film being shot in September 1896. It shows a studio scene with Trilby and Little Billee. Black and white. Silent. About 1 minute.

1898 Ella Lola, a la Trilby
This adaptation of the story, starring Ella Lola and featuring Trilby dancing, was filmed by the America Edison Company. Black and white. Silent. About 2 minutes.

1908 Trilby
The popularity of the story soon spread across Europe. Danish actress Oda Alstrup plays Trilby in this Danish film of the Du Maurier story. Black and white. Silent. About 10 minutes.

1914 Trilby
Viva Birkett plays Trilby with Sir Herbert Tree as Svengali and Ion Swinley as Little Billee in this English feature film of the story. Harold Shaw directed. Black and white. Silent. About 60 minutes.

1915 Trilby
Clara Kimball Young plays Trilby with Wilton Lackaye as Svengali and Chester Barnett as Billie in this American feature film. Maurice Tourneur directed for Equitable Pictures. Black and white. Silent. About 70 minutes.

1922 Tense Moments With Great Authors series
Phyllis Neilson-Terry plays Trilby with Charles Garry as Svengali in this English film made for the series *Tense Moments With Great Authors.* H. B. Parkinson directed. Black and white. Silent. About 15 minutes.

1923 Trilby

Andrée Lafayette plays Trilby with Arthur Edmund Carew as Svengali and Creighton Hale as Little Billee in this American feature film made for First National. James Young directed. Black and white. Silent. About 85 minutes.

1927 Svengali

Anita Dorris stars as Trilby with Paul Wagener as Svengali in this German feature film. Gennaro Righelli directed. Black and white. Silent. About 80 minutes.

1931 Svengali

This is the most famous film of the book, with superb performances by Marian Marsh as Trilby, John Barrymore as Svengali, Bramwell Fletcher as Little Billee, and Luis Alberni as Svengali's flatmate Gecko. The sets by Anton Grot are a delight. Archie Mayo directed for Warner Bros. Black and white. In English. 79 minutes.

1954 Svengali

Elisabeth Schwarzkopf supplies Trilby's singing voice in this English film. At the end of the film she sings the aria "Libera me," written for her for the movie by William Alwyn. Hildegarde Neff plays Trilby with Donald Wolfit as Svengali. Noël Langley directed for MGM. Color. 82 minutes.

1983 Svengali

Operatic singing is left behind in this modern *Svengali* set in the rock music world. Jodie Foster is the singer Trilby with Peter O'Toole is her over-the-top Svengali. Anthony Harvey directed. Color. 100 minutes.

TRISTAN UND ISOLDE
1865 opera by Wagner

The Celtic legend of Tristan and Isolde originated in the mists of time, but RICHARD WAGNER based his libretto for *Tristan und Isolde* on a 13th-century German version by Gottfried von Strassburg. Tristan is sent to Ireland by King Mark of Cornwall to collect Mark's bride Isolde. Unfortunately, they had met earlier and are secretly in love. When they try to take poison to avoid betrayal or suffering, Isolde's attendant Brangäne substitutes a love potion, and passion overwhelms them. Mark discovers the betrayal, and both lovers die. The famous Liebestod is one of the best-known melodies in opera and is often used as musical comment in films.

1967 Osaka World Fair

Japanese stage production: Wieland Wagner (director/designer), Pierre Boulez (conductor, Osaka Festival Orchestra and Chorus).

Cast: Birgit Nilsson (Isolde), Wolfgang Windgassen (Tristan), Hans Hotter (King Mark), Hertha Töpper (Brangäne), Hans Andersson (Kurwenal).

Video: Bel Canto Society/Legato Classics VHS. Taped April 10, 1967. Black and white. In German. 206 minutes.

Comment: Wieland Wagner designed and directed this production for Bayreuth before taking it to Japan.

***1973 Orange Festival

French stage production: Nikolaus Lehnhoff (stage director), Pierre Jourdan (film director), Karl Böhm (conductor, Orchestre National de RTF and London New Philharmonic Choir), Jean-Pierre Lazar (cinematographer).

Cast: Birgit Nilsson (Isolde), Jon Vickers (Tristan), Bengt Rundgren (King Mark), Ruth Hesse (Brangäne), Walter Berry (Kurwenal).

Video: Kultur DVD/Lyric VHS/Dreamlife LD. Color. In German. 212 minutes.

Comment: Magnificent outdoor production filmed live July 7, 1973, at the Roman amphitheater in Orange. Some consider this video to be the finest performance of the opera in any format.

1976 L'Opéra du Québec

Canadian TV highlights production: Franz-Paul Decker (conductor, Montreal Symphony and Chorus of Opéra du Québec).

Cast: Roberta Knie (Isolde), Jon Vickers (Tristan), William Wilderman (King Mark), Maureen Forrester (Brangäne), Victor Braun (Kurwenal).

Video: VAI VHS. Color. In German with English narration. 88 minutes.

Comment: The video features seven extended scenes from the opera, plus background on Wagner, Vickers, and the opera.

***1983 Bayreuth Festival

German stage production: Jean-Pierre Ponnelle (director/designer), Daniel Barenboim (conductor, Bayreuth Festival Orchestra and Chorus).

Cast: Johanna Meier (Isolde), René Kollo (Tristan), Matti Salminen (King Mark), Hanna Schwarz (Brangäne), Hermann Becht (Kurwenal).

Video: Philips VHS/LD. Color. In German with English subtitles. 245 minutes.

Comment: Ponnelle makes the opera visually interesting, the singers are effective, and Barenboim shows his sympathy for the music.

1993 Deutsche Oper Berlin

German stage production in Tokyo: Götz Friedrich (director), Jirí Kout (conductor, Deutsche Opera Berlin Orchestra and Chorus), Günther Schneider-Siemssen (set designer).

Cast: Gwyneth Jones (Isolde), René Kollo (Tristan), Robert Lloyd (King Mark), Hanna Schwarz (Brangäne), Peter Edelmann (Kurwenal),.

Video: TDK DVD/Opera d'Oro VHS/Pioneer LD. Shuji Fujii (director). Color. In German. 235 minutes.

1998 Bavarian State Opera

German stage production: Peter Konwitschny (director), Zubin Mehta (conductor, Bavarian State Opera Orchestra and Chorus).

Cast: Waltraud Meier (Isolde), Jon Frederic West (Tristan), Kurt Moll (King Mark), Marjana Lipovsek (Brangäne), Bernd Weikl (Kurwenal).

Video: Image Entertainment (USA) and Arthaus (GB) DVD. Brian Large (director). Color. In German with English subtitles. 241 minutes.

Comment: Ultramodern production created for the Munich Opera Festival; the first act is set on an ocean liner.

1999 Metropolitan Opera

American stage production: Dieter Dorn (director), James Levine (conductor, Metropolitan Opera Orchestra and Chorus), Jürgen Rose (set/costume designer).

Cast: Jane Eaglen (Isolde), Ben Heppner (Tristan), René Pape (King Mark), Katarina Dalayman (Brangäne), Monte Pederson (Kurwenal).

Videotaped December 18, 1999; telecast March 21, 2001. Brian Large (director). Color. In German with English subtitles. 255 minutes.

Early/related films

1909 Tristan et Yseult

Paul Capellani is Tristan with Stacia Napierkowska as Isolde in this French film directed by Albert Capellani for Pathé. It was based on the opera and was screened with Wagner's music. Black and white. Silent. About 10 minutes.

1911 Tristano e Isotta

Italian movie diva Francesca Bertini is Isolde in this Italian film of the opera shown in theaters with Wagner's music. Giovanni Pezzinga plays Tristan, Serafino Mastracchio is King Marc, and Ugo Falena directed for Film d'Arte Italiana of Rome and Pathé Frères of Paris. Color and black and white. Silent. About 25 minutes.

1928 Un chien andalou

Spanish filmmaker Luis Buñuel was obsessed with *Tristan und Isolde* and featured music from it in three of his films. *Un chien andalou* is a silent film but it was usually screened accompanied by a gramophone record of music from the opera. When a sound version was made in 1960, the music of *Tristan und Isolde* was used on the soundtrack. Black and white. 17 minutes.

1930 L'age d'or

Luis Buñuel's masterpiece, as startling today as when it was made, features music from *Tristan und Isolde*. An orchestra conducted by an aged bearded man is shown tuning up and playing the Liebestod. The orchestra's playing is crosscut with an erotic scene of a man and a woman in a garden. As they become passionate, the woman talks of murdering their children and blood appears on the man's face. The music stops after the conductor throws away his baton, goes to the couple, and kisses the woman. Black and white. In French. 62 minutes.

1942 Now Voyager

Paul Henried gives a chaste kiss to a sleeping Bette Davis while they're stranded in a cabin on Sugarloaf Mountain outside Rio di Janeiro, and soundtrack composer Max Steiner underscores this decisive "night of love" moment with a quotation from *Tristan und Isolde*. Steiner won an Oscar for his superb score. Irving Rapper directed. Black and white. 117 minutes.

1943 Battle for Music

British film about the problems of the London Philharmonic Orchestra during World War II with extracts from *Tristan und Isolde*. Among the conductors in the film are Sir Adrian Boult, Warwick Braithwaite, and Sir Malcolm Sargent. Donald Taylor directed for Strand Films. Black and white. In English. 87 minutes.

1946 Humoresque

Ambitious violinist John Garfield is performing the Liebestod music from *Tristan und Isolde* as the film cuts to Joan Crawford, who loves him, walking melodramatically into the Atlantic Ocean to drown herself. The music was recorded for the film by Isaac Stern. Jean Negulesco directed. Black and white. 125 minutes.

1946 The Whale Who Wanted to Sing at the Met

Willie, the opera-singing whale with the voice of Nelson Eddy, fantasizes a performance in *Tristan* at the Met and nearly blows his Isolde away with the wind he creates singing. See THE WHALE WHO WANTED TO SING AT THE MET.

1953 Wuthering Heights

Abismos de pasión, Luis Buñuel's Mexican adaptation of *Wuthering Heights*, uses themes from *Tristan und Isolde* as its music soundtrack. Buñuel intended to feature the opera music only in the climax of the film, but he ended up with 50 minutes of Wagner. Raul Lavista conducted the Philharmonic Society Orchestra. Black and white. In Spanish with English subtitles. 90 minutes.

1953 The Blue Gardenia

Fritz Lang uses the Liebestod music to indicate that a crime being reconstructed was committed in the name of love. Anne Baxter and Raymond Burr star in this film noir murder mystery. Black and white. 90 minutes.

1955 Interrupted Melody

Marjorie Lawrence, played by Eleanor Parker (singing by Eileen Farrell), collapses on stage during a rehearsal of *Tristan und Isolde* in a South American opera house. After King Mark (Tudor Williams) sings, she begins the Liebestod but collapses after a few difficult moments. It turns out that she has polio, but she fights back and returns to the Met in the same opera. This time she sings the Liebestod seated up to the end, when she stands and collapses onto Tristan. The Met audience gives her a standing ovation. See INTERRUPTED MELODY.

1957 Love in the Afternoon

Millionaire Gary Cooper attends the opera in Paris and is observed listening to the Prelude to *Tristan und Isolde* by lovestruck Audrey Hepburn. Billy Wilder directed. Black and white. 130 minutes.

1958 The Brain Eaters

Among the many pieces of classical music (mis)used in this cheap horror film are bits of *Tristan und Isolde*. Tom Jonson is named as composer, but the piece titled "Up the Hatch" is actually the Prelude to Act III of *Tristan*. Bruno Ve Sota directed. Black and white. 60 minutes.

1965 The Loved One

Tony Richardson's satirical film about a Hollywood cemetery has a scene in which loudspeakers play music appropriate for those living in the area. For poets, the music is from *Tristan und Isolde*. Black and white. 116 minutes.

1973 Tristan et Iseult

Writer/director Yvan Lagrange's mannered but visually fascinating French film is based on the legend, but it has an operatic musical background. Lagrange himself plays Tristan with Claire Wauthion as his Isolde. Color. In French. 80 minutes.

1974 Mahler

Carol Mudie sings the Liebestod on the soundtrack during a symbolic scene in Ken Russell's film about Mahler. Alma Mahler (Georgina Hale) buries the manuscript of her rejected song as the music plays. Color. In English. 115 minutes.

1975 Visualization

Ron Hays attempts to use video art to visualize music from the opera. He calls his piece *A Visualization of an Experience with Music—The Prelude and Liebestod From Tristan und Isolde by Richard Wagner*. Color. 20 minutes. Video at the Library of Congress.

1975 Black Moon

Louis Malle's futuristic fantasy uses the Prelude and "Death of Isolde" music to create a surrealistic atmosphere while men and women engage in deadly combat. Color. In French. 101 minutes.

1979 Tristan and Isolde

Richard Burton plays Tristan with Kate Mulgrew as Isolde in this version of the legend shot in Ireland. Cyril Cusack, Nicholas Clay, and Geraldine Fitzgerald lend support; Tom Donovan directed. Aka *Lovespell*. Color. 91 minutes.

1987 Aria

Franc Roddam uses the Liebestod as the basis of his episode of the opera film *Aria*. Lovers Bridget Fonda and James Mathers spend an amorous night in a Las Vegas hotel and then kill themselves. The singer is Leontyne Price with the Philharmonia Orchestra led by Henry Lewis. See ARIA.

1990 Reversal of Fortune

Law professor Alan Dershowitz (Ron Silver) goes to interview suspected wife murderer Claus von Bülow (Jeremy Irons) and discovers him enjoying the love and death Liebestod theme. Eva Marton is the singer with the London Philharmonic. Barbet Schroeder directed. Color. 120 minutes.

1999 Ivansxtc

Excerpts from *Tristan und Isolde* are played by Elmo Weber on this updated Hollywood version of Tolstoy's novella *The Death of Ivan Ilyich*. Danny Huston plays Ivan; Bernard rose directed. Color. In English. 93 minutes.

2000 Shadow of the Vampire

The Overture to *Tristan und Isolde* is featured in this film about director F. W. Murnau (John Malkovich) during the time he was making *Nosferatu,* the first Dracula movie. Max Schreck (Willem Dafoe), who plays Nosferatu, turns out to be a real vampire. E. Elias Merhige directed. Color. 91 minutes.

2001 The Pornographer
The Liebestod, performed by the Dresden Staatskapelle, is featured on the soundtrack of this French film about a maker of pornographic films. Bertrand Bonello directed. Color. 100 minutes

TRITTICO, IL
1918 one-act operas by Puccini

Il trittico (The Triptych) is the collective name for a triple bill of one-act operas by GIACOMO PUCCINI that premiered at the Metropolitan Opera in New York in 1918. For details on the individual operas, see GIANNI SCHICCHI, SUOR ANGELICA, and IL TABARRO.

1981 Metropolitan Opera
Renata Scotto stars in all three operas with casts including Cornell MacNeil, Jean Kraft, and Gabriel Bacquier. The operas were produced by Fabrizio Melano with set designs by David Reppa and James Levine conducting the Metropolitan Orchestra. Kirk Browning directed the telecast on November 14, 1981. Color. In Italian with English subtitles. Video at the MTR.

1983 Teatro alla Scala
Sylvano Bussoti's La Scala production features Sylvia Sass, Piero Cappuccilli, and Nicola Martinucci in *Il tabarro;* Rosalind Plowright and Dunja Vejzovic in *Suor Angelica;* and Juan Pons and Cecilia Gasdia in *Gianni Schicchi.* Gianandrea Gavazzeni conducts the La Scala Orchestra and chorus; Brian Large directed the video. Color. In Italian with English subtitles. 150 minutes. Home Vision VHS.

TRIUMPH OF BEAUTY AND DECEIT, THE
1995 TV opera by Barry

The Triumph of Beauty and Deceit is an English television opera based on Handel's oratorio *The Triumph of Time and Truth,* which had a libretto by Benedetto Pamphili. The new opera, composed by Gerald Barry to a libretto by Meredith Oakes, is set in the Court of Pleasure and revolves around a struggle for the possession of Beauty. Beauty is a tenor, Deceit is a baritone, Pleasure and Truth are countertenors, and Time is a bass. The opera, commissioned by Channel 4 and telecast in 1995, has not been released on a commercial video but its soundtrack is on CD.

1995 Channel 4 Television
English TV production: Mary Jane Walsh (director), Diego Masson (conductor, Composers Ensemble).

Cast: Richard Edgar-Wilson (Beauty), Adrian Clarke (Deceit), Nicholas Clapton (Pleasure), Denis Lakey (Truth), Stephen Richardson (Time).

Telecast March 5, 1995, on Channel 4. Donald Taylor Black (director). Color. In English. 51 minutes.

TROIS SOUHAITS, LES
1928 screen opera by Martinů

Czech composer BOHUSLAV MARTINŮ's *Les trois souhaits* (The Three Wishes) begins in a movie studio where a fairy-tale film titled *The Three Wishes* is being screened. The fairy Nulle grants the wishes of riches, youth, and love to the couple Nina and Arthur, and their wishes are seen being fulfilled in the following acts in dreamlike films. Georges Ribemont-Dessaignes wrote the French libretto and Martinů completed the opera in 1928, but it was not staged until 1971. It has been telecast and released on video in France.

1990 Opéra de Lyon
French stage production: Louis Erlo and Alain Maratrat (directors), Kent Nagano (conductor, Opéra de Lyon Orchestra and Chorus), Jacques Rapp (set designer).

Cast: Valerie Chevalier (Nina/Indolende), Gilles Cachemaille (Arthur/M. Juste), Hélène Perraguin (Nulle), Christian Papis (Serge/Adolphe), Valerie Millot (Eblouie), Jocelyne Taillon (Adélaïde), Jules Bastin (Captain), Georges Gautier (Director), Beatrice Uria-Monzon (Dinah), Riccardo Cassinelli (Argentine singer).

Video: Polygram (France) VHS. Taped in October 1990. Color. In French. 101 minutes.

TROIS VALSES
1935 operetta by Straus

OSCAR STRAUS composed the operetta *Drei Wälzer* (Three Waltzes), best known in French as *Trois valses,* with help from his predecessors Johann Strauss Sr. and Jr. He created the music for this bittersweet story using tunes by Strauss Sr. for the first act, which is set in 1865; by Strauss Jr. for the second act, set in 1900; and by himself for the third act, set in 1935. Paul Knepler and Armin Robinson's libretto takes place over three generations, with the central character played by the same singer. She is a ballet dancer in the first act, her operetta-star daughter in the second, and her film-star granddaughter in the third. In each, the woman has to decide between her career and her love for a man (again the same singer), who is also a direct descendent. The operetta, which premiered in 1935 in Zurich in German, became famous in its 1937 French version with Yvonne Printemps and Pierre Fresnay. It was filmed with the same cast.

1938 Berger film

French feature film: Ludwig Berger (director); Leopold Marchant and Albert Willemetz (screenplay); Eugen Schüfftan, Paul Portier (cinematographers); Cadou (music director).

Cast: Yvonne Printemps (Fanny/Yvette/Irène Grandpré), Pierre Fresnay (Octave/Philippe/Gérard de Chalencey).

Video: Bel Canto Society/Opera Dubs VHS. Black and white. In French with English subtitles. 101 minutes.

Comment: The years are shifted, as they were on the Paris stage, to 1867, 1900, and 1937 to coincide with three World Fairs. The screenplay is by the writers who created the Paris stage adaptation.

TROMPETER VON SÄKKINGEN, DER
1884 opera by Nessler

A baron learns that his trumpeter wants to marry his daughter so he banishes him. When peasants rebel against the baron, the trumpeter returns with troops and saves the baron's bacon. It turns out that he is actually of noble birth so he can marry the daughter after all. *Der Trompeter von Säkkingen* (The Säkkingen Trumpeter), Viktor Nessler's 1884 opera based on a romantic poem by J. V. von Scheffel, was so popular in its time that it was staged in Germany more than 500 times after its Leipzig premiere and then went on London and New York. The opera is on CD, with Herman Prey singing the role of the trumpeter, but there is no modern video.

1908 Messter film

Henny Porten, Germany's first film star, is featured as the trumpeter's love in this 1908 Messter sound film depicting an aria and scene from the opera. Porten's father Franz, a former opera singer, directed the film shot in a Berlin studio with Oskar Messter's synchronization process. Black and white. In German. 4 minutes.

TROUBLE IN TAHITI
1952 opera by Bernstein

Dinah and Sam are stuck in a loveless marriage in a boring suburban home. He goes off to work and the gym; she goes off to see a movie called *Trouble in Tahiti*. A Greek chorus–like jazz trio comments on the events of the day. LEONARD BERNSTEIN wrote both music and libretto for this surprisingly entertaining study in alienation

that premiered at Brandeis University in 1952. Particularly fine is a satirical aria by Dinah in which she describes the Hollywood South Seas sarong-and-volcano movie of the title. The opera was incorporated by Bernstein into his 1983 opera A QUIET PLACE as a flashback after the death of Dinah. There have been several international TV productions; the American and British ones are listed below, including two on video.

1952 NBC Opera Theatre

American TV production: Charles Polacheck (director), Samuel Chotzinoff (producer), Leonard Bernstein (conductor, NBC Opera Orchestra), William Riva (set designer).

Cast: Beverly Wolff (Dinah); David Atkinson (Sam); Constance Brigham, Robert Kole, William Harder (Trio).

Video at the MTR. Telecast live November 16, 1952. Kirk Browning (director). Black and white. In English. 43 minutes.

1968 BBC Television

English TV production: Bill Hays (director), David Lloyd-Jones (conductor, BBC Television Orchestra).

Cast: Joyce Blackham (Dinah); Raimund Herincx (Sam); Marion Davies, Nicholas Curtis, Neilson Taylor (Trio).

Telecast March 17, 1968. Color. In English. 42 minutes.

***1973 London Weekend Television

English TV production: David Griffiths (director), Leonard Bernstein (conductor, London Symphonic Wind Band), Eileen Diss (production designer), Pat Gavin (graphic sequences).

Cast: Nancy Williams (Dinah); Julian Patrick (Sam); Antonia Butler, Michael Clark, Mark Brown (Trio).

Video: Kultur VHS. Bill Hays (director). Color. In English. 45 minutes.

Comment: The singers perform in front of cleverly drawn and animated sets.

1994 Cabrillo Music Festival

American stage production: Marin Alsop (conductor, Concordia Symphony).

Cast: Judy Kaye (Dinah), William Sharp (Sam). Telecast on Bravo in 1994. Color. In English. 30 minutes.

Comment: This abridged version was taped for its television screening at the Cabrillo Music Festival in Santa Cruz, California.

2001 BBC Wales Television

Welsh TV production: Tom Cairns (director), Paul Daniel (conductor, BBC Wales Orchestra), Amir Hosseinpour (choreographer), Fiona Morris (producer).

Cast: Stephanie Novacek (Dinah), Karl Daymond (Sam), Tom Randle (Gardener), Toby Stafford-Alle (Milkman), Mary Hagerty (Woman).

Video: BBC Opus Arte/Naxos DVD. Telecast December 26, 2001, on BBC. Color. In English. 75 minutes.

Comment: Period archival footage is intercut with the opera sequences.

TROVATORE, IL
1853 opera by Verdi

GIUSEPPE VERDI's *Il trovatore* (The Troubadour) has one of the most complicated plots in opera, and also some of the best music, including the famous Anvil and Soldier Choruses and the great tenor aria "Di quella pira." Manrico is the troubadour of the title, a rebel leader in 15th-century Spain, whose archenemy Count di Luna leads the king's army. Both love Leonora, but she prefers Manrico. Manrico's mother, the gypsy Azucena, is taken prisoner by Luna, and Manrico is captured when he tries to rescue her. Leonora offers herself to Luna if he will free Manrico but takes poison after he agrees. When Luna finds he has been tricked, he executes Manrico anyway. Azucena reveals that Manrico was not her son but Luna's long-lost brother. Salvatore Cammarano's libretto is based on an overheated Spanish play by Antonio García Gutiérrez.

1949 Gallone film

Italian feature film: Carmine Gallone (director); Mario Corsi, Tullio Cavaz, Ottavio Poggi (screenplay); Gabriele Santini (conductor, Rome Opera House Orchestra and Chorus); Aldo Giordani (cinematographer).

Cast: Gino Sinimberghi (Manrico, sung by Antonio Salvarezza), Vittorina Colonnello (Leonora, sung by Franca Sacchi), Gianna Pederzini (Azucena), Enzo Mascherini (Count di Luna) Cesare Polacco (Ferrando, sung by Enrico Formichi).

Video: Bel Canto Society/Lyric VHS. Black and white. In Italian. 105 minutes.

***1957 Fino film

Italian TV film: Claudio Fino (director), Fernando Previtali (conductor, RAI Orchestra and Chorus), Enrico Tovaglieri (set/costume designer).

Cast: Mario Del Monaco (Manrico), Leyla Gencer (Leonora), Fedora Barbieri (Azucena), Ettore Bastianini (Count di Luna), Plinio Clabassi (Ferrando).

Video: Hardy Classics DVD/Bel Canto Society VHS. Black and white. In Italian. 124 minutes.

Comment: Cardboard sets and grainy black-and-white video but critic Stephen Stroff rated this as the best recording ever of the opera. Del Monaco and the other singers are superb.

1972 Orange Festival

French stage production: Charles Hamilton (stage director), Pierre Jourdan (film director), Reynald Giovanetti (conductor, ORTF Orchestra and Chorus).

Cast: Ludovic Spiess (Manrico), Montserrat Caballé (Leonora), Irina Arkhipova (Azucena), Peter Glossop (Count di Luna).

Video: House of Opera/Lyric VHS. Color. In Italian. 205 minutes.

1978 Vienna State Opera

Austrian stage production: Herbert von Karajan (director/conductor, Vienna Staatsoper Orchestra and Chorus), Teo Otto (set designer).

Cast: Plácido Domingo (Manrico), Raina Kabaivanska (Leonora), Fiorenza Cossotto (Azucena), Pietro Cappuccilli (Count di Luna), José van Dam (Ferrando).

Video: Bel Canto Society VHS. Gunter Schneider-Siemssen (director). Color. In Italian. 155 minutes.

1983 Australian Opera

Australian stage production: Elijah Moshinsky (director), Richard Bonynge (conductor, Elizabethan Sydney Orchestra and Australian Opera Chorus), Sidney Nolan (sets), Luciana Arrighi (costume designer).

Cast: Kenneth Collins (Manrico), Joan Sutherland (Leonora), Lauris Elms (Azucena), Jonathan Summers (Count di Luna), Donald Shanks (Ferrando).

Video: Image Entertainment/Arthaus (GB) DVD and Sony VHS. Taped live July 2, 1983. Riccardo Pellizzeri (director). Color. In Italian with English subtitles. 138 minutes.

Comment: Sutherland is extraordinary even if the production isn't.

1985 Arena di Verona

Italian stage production: Giuseppe Patroni Griffi (director), Reynald Giovanetti (conductor, Arena di Verona Orchestra and Chorus), Mario Ceroli (set designer), Gabriella Pescucci (costume designer).

Cast: Franco Bonisolli (Manrico), Rosalind Plowright (Leonora), Fiorenza Cossotto (Azucena), Giorgio Zancanaro (Count di Luna), Paolo Washington (Ferrando).

Video: Home Vision/Castle/NVC Arts (GB) VHS and Pioneer LD. Brian Large (director). Color. In Italian with English subtitles. 150 minutes.

1985/1989 Opera Stories

Highlights version of the 1985 Verona production above with Charlton Heston setting the scene from Spain and describing the opera. Framing material was shot in 1989 by Keith Cheetham. Color. 52 minutes. Pioneer Artists LD.

***1988 Metropolitan Opera

American stage production: Fabrizio Melano (director), James Levine (conductor, Metropolitan Opera Orchestra and Chorus), Ezio Frigerio (set designer), Franca Squarciapino (costume designer).

Cast: Luciano Pavarotti (Manrico), Eva Marton (Leonora) Dolora Zajick (Azucena), Sherrill Milnes (Count di Luna), Jeffrey Wells (Ferrando).

Video: DG DVD/VHS/LD. Taped October 15, 1988; telecast October 21, 1988. Brian Large (director). Color. In Italian with English subtitles. 139 minutes.

Comment: Pavarotti carries the day.

2000 Teatro alla Scala

Italian stage production: Riccardo Muti (conductor, Teatro alla Scala Orchestra and Chorus).

Cast: Salvatore Licitra (Manrico), Barbara Frittoli (Leonora), Violetta Urmano (Azucena), Leo Nucci (Count di Luna).

Video: House of Opera/Premiere Opera DVD/VHS. Taped in December 2000. Color. In Italian. 138 minutes.

2002 Royal Opera House

English stage production: Elijah Moshinsky (director), Carlo Rizzi (conductor, Royal Opera House Orchestra and Chorus), Dante Ferretti (set designer).

Cast: José Cura (Manrico), Veronica Villarroel (Leonora), Yvonne Naef (Azucena), Dmitri Hvorostovsky (Count di Luna).

Video: BBC Opus Arte DVD. Taped in May 2002. Brian Large (director). Color. In Italian. 172 minutes.

Early/related films

The popularity of the opera's music is reflected in an unusually large number of early sound films.

1897 The Troubadour

A short silent film titled *The Troubadour* was made by the American Mutoscope Company and released in June 1897. The plot is not known. About 1 minute.

1906 Royal Danish Ballet

The Gypsy Dance from *Il trovatore* is performed by the Royal Danish Ballet in this early Danish film with Val-borg Borchsenius as soloist. Black and white. Silent. About 4 minutes. A print survives.

1906 The Troubadour

A French silent film made by Pathé Frères was distributed in America in 1906 as *The Troubadour*. Black and white. Silent. About 3 minutes.

1906 Chronophone sound films

Two sound films of arias from *Il trovatore* were made in England in 1906 with the Chronophone system. Edith Albord and Frank Rowe are pictured singing the "Miserere" and "Home to Our Mountains," the English version of "Ai nostri monti." Arthur Gilbert directed. Black and white. Each about 3 minutes.

1906/1908 Cinemafono Pagliej sound films

CINEMAFONO PAGLIEJ, an Italian sound-on-disc company specializing in opera films, screened films featuring arias, duets, and trios from *Il trovatore* at the Sala Umberto I in Rome from May 19 to July 30, 1906. On March 1, 1908, a screening at the Teatro Goldoni in Livorno featured soprano Teresina Burzio and baritone Magini-Coletti in the duet "Mira d'acerbe lacrime" from *Il trovatore*, and the couple appeared in person after the show to thank the public. On April 19, 1908, a screening in Pisa featured "Stride la vampa" and "Di quella pira" from *Il trovatore*. The films apparently no longer exist.

1908 Fonoteatro Pineschi sound film

The Italian Fonoteatro Pineschi company released a sound film in Rome in September 1908 as a major theatrical event. It featured the important numbers from *Il trovatore* performed by a variety of singers, including soprano Albani, contralto Alboni, tenor Delfini, baritone Mancini, bass Besi and La Scala Opera House chorus. The sound-on-disc event was highly praised by critics and was authorized by Ricordi. Black and white. Running time not known but substantial

1908 Messter sound film

Henny Porten, Germany's first film star, played Leonora in a German sound film illustrating an area from *Il trovatore*. Porten's father Franz, a former opera singer, directed it, using Oskar Messter's synchronization system. Black and white. In German. About 5 minutes.

1908 Bioscop sound films

Two German sound films made by the German Deutsch Bioscop Company of scenes from *Il trovatore*. One shows the Azucena trio, the other the "Miserere." Black and white. In German. Each about 4 minutes. Both films survive in a German film archive.

1909 Pathé film

French film made by Albert Capellani for Pathé and starring Paul Capellani and Stacia Napierkowska. It had some scenes in color and was released in the United States in 1910 as *The Troubadour* to favorable reviews. Silent. About 12 minutes.

1909 Pierini film

This Italian sound film of the Azucena/Manrico duet "Ai nostri monti" from *Il trovatore* was screened at the Cinematografo della Borsa in Turin on January 5, 1909. It was made with the Pierini sound-on-disc system and favorably reviewed. Black and white. In Italian. About 4 minutes.

1909 Lubin film

American film of scenes from the opera made by the Lubin Company for their Verdi series. Black and white. Silent. About 10 minutes.

1909 Film d'Arte Italiana film

Francesca Bertini stars as Leonora in the Italian silent film *Il trovatore* based on the Verdi opera and directed by Ugo Falena for Film d'Arte Italiana of Rome. Black and white. About 10 minutes.

1909 Itala sound films

Itala Film of Turin released two sound films of arias from *Il trovatore* in August 1909, "Di quella pira" and "Questa donna conoscete." The moving picture images were synchoronized with a sound-on-disc system. Black and white. Each about 3 minutes.

1910 Animatophone film

British sound film with arias from *Il trovatore* synchronized with records made by David Barnett for the Animatophone Company. Black and white. In Italian. About 12 minutes.

1911 Il Trovatore: "Stride la vampa"

Italian sound film featuring the aria "Stride la vampa." It was made by Itala Film of Turin, which specialized in the genre. Black and white. In Italian. About 4 minutes.

1914 Centaur film

Agnes Mapes plays Azucena in the feature-length American film *Il trovatore* based on the Verdi opera and the play. The cast also includes Julia Hurley, Jean Thrall, and Frank Holland. Charles Simone wrote and directed the film for Centaur Film. Black and white. Silent. About 70 minutes.

1922 Tense Moments From Opera

Bertram Burleigh is Manrico, Lillian Douglas is Leonora, Cyril Dane is Count di Luna, and Ada Grier is Azucena in this British silent film made for the series *Tense Moments From Opera*. It was presented with live singers. Edwin J. Collins directed. Black and white. About 10 minutes.

1927 Cameo Operas

British highlights film made by A. E. Coleby for John E. Blakeley's *Song Films* series. The music accompanying the opera scenes was played by the theater orchestra. Black and white. Silent. About 18 minutes.

1927 Vitaphone film with Raisa and Rimini

Rosa Raisa and Giacomo Rimini, both then with the Chicago Opera, sing selections from Act IV of *Il trovatore* in this Vitaphone sound film. Black and white. In Italian. About 8 minutes.

1930 Vitaphone film with Martinelli

Giovanni Martinelli sings selections from *Il trovatore* in this Vitaphone sound film, including "Ah! si ben mio" and "Di quella pira," assisted by soprano Livia Marraci and accompanied by the Vitaphone Symphony Orchestra. Black and white. In Italian. About 9 minutes.

1934 Enter Madame

"The Anvil Chorus" and "Miserere" are featured in this film about a glamorous opera singer (Elissa Landi) who marries a millionaire (Cary Grant). See ENTER MADAME.

1935 Forget-Me-Not

Music from *Il trovatore* is featured in this Beniamino Gigli film about an older opera singer married to a younger woman. See FORGET-ME-NOT.

1935 A Night at the Opera

A production of *Il trovatore* at the Met is central to this Marx Brothers comedy. Chico and Harpo mess up the music, Groucho sells peanuts, the Anvil Chorus is guyed, Harpo swings across the stage, Manrico (Walter Woolf King) is kidnapped, and Allan Jones takes his place on stage. Kitty Carlisle is Leonora, Olga Dane is Azucena, Luther Hoobner is Ruiz, and Rodolfo Hoyos is Count di Luna. See A NIGHT AT THE OPERA.

1935 El cantante de Napoles

Enrico Caruso Jr. sings "Di quella pira" in this American Spanish-language film loosely based on the life of his father. Howard Bretherton directed. Black and white. 77 minutes.

1936 Ave Maria
Beniamino Gigli sings "De quella pira" from *Il trovatore* in a formal concert at the beginning of this Italian film. See AVE MARIA.

1936 Moonlight Murder
A tenor is killed at the Hollywood Bowl during a performance of *Il trovatore* in this murder mystery. Leo Carrillo plays the tenor with his singing by Alfonso Pedroza. See MOONLIGHT MURDER.

1944 The Anvil Chorus Girl
This is a Popeye cartoon featuring "The Anvil Chorus" as its focal point. The girl of the title creates the anvil music wherever she goes. I. Sparber directed for Paramount. Color. 7 minutes.

1947 Something in the Wind
Met tenor Jan Peerce and Deanna Durbin join voices in the *Il trovatore* "Miserere" rather appropriately as they are both in jail. Irving Pichel directed for Universal. Black and white. 89 minutes.

1948 A Song Is Born
"The Anvil Chorus" is featured in a novel way in this Danny Kaye movie about a group of encyclopedia writers. Showgirl Virginia Mayo teaches them to sing the chorus using words taken from *The Racing News*. Howard Hawks directed this remake of his film *Ball of Fire*. Color. 111 minutes.

1951 The Great Caruso
Enrico Caruso (Mario Lanza) is shown on the Paris Opéra stage in prison singing the *Il trovatore* "Miserere" in this romantic biopic. See THE GREAT CARUSO.

1954 Senso
Luchino Visconti's film opens with a production of *Il trovatore* at La Fenice Theater in Venice in 1866 when Austria controlled the city. When the tenor steps down stage and begins to sing "Di quella pira," the Venetians perceive it as a patriotic statement, triggering an avalanche of revolutionary leaflets and a riot. Color. In Italian. 115 minutes.

1955 Interrupted Melody
Opera diva Marjorie Lawrence, played by Eleanor Parker in this film biography (singing by Eileen Farrell) is seen as Leonora in the final trio on a stage in Ravenna. See INTERRUPTED MELODY.

1956 Serenade
Mario Lanza sings "Di quella pira" with Ray Heindorf and his orchestra in this film about an opera singer with emotional problems. See SERENADE.

1964 Gwyneth Jones on the BBC
Welsh soprano Gwyneth Jones stars as Leonora in this BBC highlights production of the opera. She is supported by Italian tenor Bruno Prevedi, Italian mezzo Giulietta Simionato, and English baritone Peter Glossop. Black and white. In Italian. 66 minutes. Print at the NFTA in London.

1993 Heart and Souls
Franco Corelli, Gabriella Tucci, and Angelo Mercuriali perform "Ah! si, ben mio, coll'essere...Di quella pira." on the sound track of this Hollywood fantasy film. Thomas Schippers conducts the Rome Opera House Orchestra, and Ron Underwood directed the film. Color. 104 minutes.

2000 The Man Who Cried
Sally Potter's film about an opera company in Paris features "Di quella pira" performed by John Turturro (singing by Italian tenor Salvatore Licitra) with backing from the Royal Opera House Orchestra and Chorus led by Sian Edwards. See THE MAN WHO CRIED.

2001 Me Without You
Leonora's aria "Tacea la notte placida" is featured on the soundtrack of this British film about the evolving relationship between two London women. Sandra Golbacher directed. Color. 107 minutes.

TROYANOS, TATIANA
American mezzo-soprano (1938–1993)

Tatiana Troyanos, whose untimely death at the age of 54 robbed opera of a fine artist, was notable for her warmth and emotion as well as the range of her roles. She was born in a New York tenement, worked as a secretary while studying at Juilliard, and endured two years as a chorus nun in *The Sound of Music* before breaking into opera. She made her debut in 1963 at New York City Opera and then moved to Hamburg where she sang for 10 years. Her breakthrough was her 1969 Royal Opera Octavian, a role she repeated in her debut at the Met in 1976. She created the main role in Penderecki's THE DEVILS OF LOUDUN in 1969 and the role of Isabella in Glass's *The Voyage* in 1992. She was much admired in trouser roles and can be seen on video in a number of them. See ARIADNE AUF NAXOS (1988), CAPRICCIO (1992), CAVALLERIA RUSTICANA (1978), LA CLEMENZA DI TITO (1980), LES CONTES D'HOFFMANN (1988), DON

CARLO (1980), DIE FLEDERMAUS (1986), NORMA (1981), OEDIPUS REX (1973), DER ROSENKAVALIER (1982), TANNHÄUSER (1982), LES TROYENS (1983), and WEST SIDE STORY (1983 film).

TROYENS, LES
1863 opera by Berlioz

Les Troyens (The Trojans) is HECTOR BERLIOZ's grand *opéra maudit,* never staged complete in his lifetime. Acts III, IV, and V were presented in 1863, but the complete five-act opera was not produced until 1890. The libretto, by the composer, is based on Virgil's *Aeneid,* which Berlioz greatly admired. The first half of the opera is set in Troy and focuses on the story of Cassandra, Aeneas, and the Trojan Horse; the second is set in Carthage where Aeneas has taken refuge with Queen Dido. The problems Berlioz had with the opera are explored in Tony Palmer's informative film *I, Berlioz.*

***1983 Metropolitan Opera
American stage production: Fabrizio Melano (director), James Levine (conductor, Metropolitan Opera Orchestra and Chorus), Peter Wexler (set/costume designer).

Cast: Jessye Norman (Cassandre/Cassandra), Tatiana Troyanos (Didon/Dido), Plácido Domingo (Enée/Aeneas), Allan Monk (Chorèbe), Paul Plishka (Narbal), Barbara Conrad (Hécube/Hecuba), John Macurdy (Priam), Jocelyn Tailon (Anna), Douglas Ahlsted (Iopas), Philip Creech (Hylas), Claudia Catania (Ascagne), Robert Nagy (Helenus).

Video: Pioneer DVD/Paramount VHS/Pioneer LD. Taped October 8, 1983; telecast March 28, 1984. Brian Large (director). Color. In French with English subtitles. 253 minutes.

Comment: Impressive production, fine singers.

2000 Salzburg Festival
Austrian stage production: Herbert Wernicke (director, set/costume designer), Sylvain Cambreling (conductor, Orchestre de Paris, Salzburg Chamber Philharmonic, Vienna State Opera Chorus, Tolz Boys' Choir, and Bratislava Philharmonic Choir).

Cast: Deborah Polaski (Dido/Cassandra), Jon Villars (Aeneas), Robert Lloyd (Narbal), Russell Braun (Chorebus), Tigran Martirossian (Pantheus), Gaële le Roi (Ascanius), Ilya Levinskyk (Iopas), Yvonne Naef (Anna), Toby Spence (Hylas).

Video: ArtHaus DVD. Alexandre Tarta (director). Color. In French with English subtitles. 257 minutes.

Comment: Minimal sets with most of the cast wearing black; the Trojans have red gloves and the Carthaginians have blue ones. Critics were not impressed.

Related film

1992 I, Berlioz
Tony Palmer's film *I, Berlioz,* which centers around the difficulties Berlioz had in creating the opera, contains sizable extracts from *Les Troyens* as staged by the Zurich Opera House. Agnes Habereder is Cassandra, Ludmilla Schemtschuk is Dido, Giorgio Lamberti is Aeneas, and Vesselina Kasarova is Anna. Ralf Weikert conducts the Zurich Opera Orchestra and Chorus. The opera is sung in French with English subtitles. Color. In English. 90 minutes.

TSAR'S BRIDE, THE
1899 opera by Rimsky-Korsakov

The unhappy bride of NIKOLAI RIMSKY-KORSAKOV's opera *Tsarskaya nevesta* (The Tsar's Bride) is Marfa, who has been chosen to be the bride of Tsar Ivan the Terrible. She is in love with Lykov but is lusted after by Gryaznoy, which causes his jealous mistress Lyubasha to poison her. Lykov is blamed and executed, while Lyubasha is murdered by Gryaznoy. Meanwhile poor Marfa goes mad. The story is gloomy but the music is splendid. The libretto is based on a play by Lev Mey.

1965 Gorikker film
Soviet feature film: Vladimir Gorikker (director), Andrei Donativ and Gorikker (screenplay), Vadim Mass (cinematographer), Yevgeny Svetlanov (conductor, Bolshoi Theater Orchestra and Choir), G. Balodis (art director).

Cast: Raissa Nedashkovskaya (Marfa, sung by Galina Oleinichenko), Natalya Rudnaya (Lyubasha, sung by Larissa Avdeyeva), Otar Koberidze (Gryaznoy, sung by Yevgeny Kibkalo), Victor Nuzhny (Lykov, sung by Evgeny Raikov), Pyotr Glebov (Tsar Ivan the Terrible).

Video: Kultur/Corinth VHS. Black and white. In Russian with English subtitles. 97 minutes.

Comment: Gorikker filmed this beautiful, though heavily abridged, version of the opera on location in Latvia and seems to have been influenced by Eisenstein's film about the same Tsar.

TUCKER, RICHARD
American tenor (1913–1975)

Richard Tucker made his debut in *La traviata* in 1943 with the Salmaggi Opera in New York and reached the Met in 1945 in *La Gioconda.* In 1947 he sang in *La Gioconda* at the Arena di Verona with Maria Callas, when she made her Italian debut. Although he performed in many opera houses, the Met remained his center; he sang there for three decades in more than 700 performances and was always an audience favorite. His screen opera debut was singing Radames in a Toscanini telecast of AIDA in 1949, which is on video. Unfortunately, it's his only complete opera on video, but he can be seen in excerpts from FAUST and RIGOLETTO on *The Voice of Firestone* TV series in 1963, in Act IV of a Met telecast of CARMEN in 1952, and in METROPOLITAN OPERA TV programs in 1953, 1957, and 1966. Tucker is remembered every year on television at a gala honoring the Richard Tucker Award winner.

1949 Song of Surrender
In Tucker's only Hollywood film, he is heard but not seen singing Schubert's "Ständchen." The film, set at the turn of the century, stars Wanda Hendrix as a woman who loves Caruso records. Mitchell Leisen directed. Black and white. 93 minutes.

1957–1963 Richard Tucker in Opera & Song
Tucker in performance on *The Voice of Firestone* television programs from 1957 to 1963. He sings arias from *Aida, Carmen, Pagliacci,* and *Rigoletto* plus songs by Leoncavallo, Victor Herbert, and Jerome Kern. Black and white. 40 minutes. VAI VHS.

1958 Lisa Della Casa in Opera & Song
Tucker joins soprano Lisa Della Casa on *The Voice of Firestone* television show telecast September 22, 1958. He sings the aria "E lucevan le stelle" from *Tosca* and duets with the soprano on "O soave fanciulla" from *La bohème.* Black and white. 30 minutes.

1961–1966 Bell Telephone Hour
Tucker performs scenes from four operas with partners on *The Bell Telephone Hour* from 1961 to 1966: *La bohème* with Anna Moffo, *La forza del destino* with Robert Merrill, *Madama Butterfly* with Gabriella Tucci, and *Pagliacci* with Lucine Amara. Donald Voorhees conducts the Bell Telephone Hour Orchestra. Color. 36 minutes. VAI VHS.

1970 "Cielo e mar"
Tucker sings the aria "Cielo e mar" from *La Gioconda* on stage in a 1970 telecast. It's included on the video *Legends of Opera.* Black and white. In Italian. 5 minutes. Legato Classics VHS.

1994 The Legacy of Richard Tucker
Compilation video from the Richard Tucker Foundation archives with arias from *Turandot, Pagliacci,* and *Aida* and duets with Renata Tebaldi from *Manon Lescaut.* Produced by D'Alessio Productions. Color and black and white. 30 minutes.

TURANDOT
1926 opera by Puccini

Turandot was GIACOMO PUCCINI's last opera and some critics consider it his best. Its tenor aria, "Nessun dorma," sung by Prince Calaf, has been a part of popular culture since Luciano Pavarotti's version was used as the theme song of the 1990 World Cup. The opera libretto, by Renato Simoni and Giuseppe Adami, is derived from a Chinese fairy tale by Carlo Gozzi: cold-hearted Princess Turandot beheads any man who tries to win her and fails. Prince Calaf succeeds in thawing her out, but not before slave girl Liù has sacrificed herself to avoid betraying him. Puccini died before finishing the opera, and it was completed by Franco Alfano from his notes. The aria "Nessun dorma" has been inserted into a number of Hollywood movies.

1958 Lanfranchi film
Italian TV film: Mario Lanfranchi (director), Fernando Previtali (conductor, Milan RAI Orchestra and Chorus), Attilio Colonnello (set designer).
Cast: Lucille Udovick (Turandot), Franco Corelli (Calaf), Renata Mattioli (Liù), Plinio Clabassi (Timur).
Video: Bel Canto Society/Lyric VHS. Black and white. In Italian. 114 minutes.
Comment: Corelli was in peak form when this film was made, and his singing is memorable, although the video shows its age badly.

1969 Wallman film
Italian TV film: Margarita Wallman (director), Georges Prêtre (conductor, Torino RAI Orchestra and Chorus), Eugenio Guglielminetti (set/costume designer).
Cast: Birgit Nilsson (Turandot), Gianfranco Cecchele (Calaf), Gabriella Tucci (Liù), Boris Carmeli (Timur).
Video: House of Opera/Lyric VHS. Black and white. In Italian. 124 minutes.

1983 Arena di Verona
Italian stage production: Giuliano Montaldo (director), Maurizio Arena (conductor, Arena di Verona Orchestra and Chorus), Luciano Rucceri (set designer), Nana Cecchi (costume designer).
Cast: Ghena Dimitrova (Turandot), Nicola Martinucci (Calaf), Cecilia Gasdia (Liù), Ivo Vinco (Timur).
Video: HBO and NVC Arts (GB) VHS/Pioneer Artists LD. Brian Large (director). Color. In Italian with English subtitles. 116 minutes.
Comment: Dimitrova is a dominating Turandot and easily holds her own against the gigantic sets in this colorful staging by filmmaker Montaldo.

1983 Vienna State Opera

Austrian stage production: Hal Prince (director), Lorin Maazel (conductor, Vienna State Opera Orchestra and Chorus and Vienna Boys Choir), Tazeena Firth and Timothy O'Brien (set/costume designers).

Cast: Eva Marton (Turandot), José Carreras (Calaf), Katia Ricciarelli (Liù), John Paul Bogart (Timur).

Video: MGM-UA Home Video VHS. Color. In Italian with English subtitles. 138 minutes.

Comment: Innovative dreamlike production by Broadway's Hal Prince with a strong cast, intriguing direction, and surprising modernist sets.

***1987 Metropolitan Opera

American stage production: Franco Zeffirelli (director/set designer), James Levine (conductor, Metropolitan Opera Orchestra and Chorus), Dada Saligieri (costume designer).

Cast: Eva Marton (Turandot), Plácido Domingo (Calaf), Leona Mitchell (Liù), Paul Plishka (Timur).

Video: DG VHS. Taped April 4, 1987; telecast January 27, 1988. Color. In Italian with English subtitles. 134 minutes.

Comment: Spectacular production with opulent costumes and sets almost as impressive as the singers, but conductor Levine keeps the music as relevant as the scenery.

***1993 San Francisco Opera

American stage production: Peter McClintock (director), Donald Runnicles (conductor, San Francisco Opera Orchestra), David Hockney (set designer), Ian Falconer (costume designer).

Cast: Eva Marton (Turandot), Michael Sylvester (Calaf), Lucia Mazzaria (Liù), Kevin Langan (Timur).

Video: Image Entertainment and Arthaus (GB) DVD/Kultur and Home Vision VHS/Pioneer LD. Brian Large (director). Color. In Italian with English subtitles. 124 minutes.

Comment: This is a production where you could go out happily whistling the sets. Hockney's colorful designs dominate the stage with their brightness and zigzag angles, and they work well with the costumes and performances.

1998 Turandot at the Forbidden City

Chinese stage production: Zhang Yimou (director), Zubin Mehta (conductor, Maggio Musical Fiorentino Orchestra and Voci Bianche Chorus), Gao Guang Jian (set designer), Zen Li (costume designer).

Cast: Giovanna Casolla (Turandot), Sergei Larin (Calaf), Barbara Frittoli (Liù), Carlo Colombara (Timur).

Video: BMG DVD. Taped September 1998; telecast in the United States June 9, 1999. Hugo Kach (director). Color. In Italian with English subtitles. 122 minutes.

Comment: The most spectacular *Turandot* production ever, staged by Chinese film director Zhang Yimou in the Forbidden City in front of the Ming Dynasty Palace with a cast of thousands. A cross-cultural extravaganza, it was telecast around the world, but it looks and sounds much better on the DVD, which includes a documentary about the production.

2002 Salzburg Festival

Austrian production: David Pountney (director), Valery Gergiev (conductor, Vienna Philharmonic Orchestra, Vienna State Opera Chorus and Tölz Boys Chorus), Johan Engels (set designer), Marie-Janne Lecca (costume designer).

Cast: Gabriele Schnaut (Turandot), Johan Botha (Calaf), Christina Gallardo-Domâs (Liù), Paata Burchuladze (Timur), Robert Tear (Emperor).

Video: TDK DVD. Brian Large (director). Color. In Italian with English subtitles. 141 minutes.

Comment: Extragant production using the controversial ending devised by Luciano Berio in place of that created by Alfano.

Early/related films

1934 Prinzessin Turandot

Light musical version of the Turandot story written by Thea von Harbou and based on the opera and Gozzi play. Käthe von Nagy plays Turandot with Willy Fritsch as Calaf in the German version and Pierre Blanchar as Calaf in the French. Gerhard Lamprecht directed the film in German as *Prinzessin Turandot* and in French as *Turandot, Princesse de Chine*. Black and white. 83 minutes.

1936 Opernring

Jan Kiepura plays a singing taxi driver who becomes a successful opera tenor and sings in *Turandot* at the Vienna State Opera. Carmine Gallone directed this Austrian film. The English title is *Thank You, Madame*. Black and white. In German. 91 minutes.

1943 His Butler's Sister

Deanna Durbin sings the tenor aria "Nessun dorma" from *Turandot* in English at a butler's ball in this charming film about a girl and a composer. Frank Borzage directed. Universal. Black and white. 94 minutes.

1956 Serenade

Mario Lanza sings "Nessun dorma" with Ray Heindorf and orchestra in this film about an opera singer with emotional problems. See SERENADE.

1967 Martinelli at Seattle Opera

Tenor Giovanni Martinelli's last stage performance at the age of 82 is seen in this film, shot at the dress rehearsal of *Turandot* at Seattle Opera in 1967. He plays the emperor. Color. 3 minutes. Print at the NFTA, London.

1974 Gianini/Luzzati cartoon

The opera-oriented Italian animation team of Giulio Gianini and Emmanuele Luzzati created this *Turandot*, an animated cartoon based on the Puccini opera. Color. 8 minutes.

1984 The Killing Fields

"Nessun dorma" is sung by Franco Corelli in ironic counterpoint during a key scene of this film about the horrors of war in Cambodia. Sam Waterson wonders whether his Cambodian assistant is still alive while Corelli sings on the stereo that his secret cannot be known. When Richard Nixon declaims about Cambodia on TV, Corelli sings that he will certainly conquer. Roland Joffe directed. Color. 141 minutes.

1984 Puccini

Tony Palmer's film about Puccini is intercut with rehearsal scenes of a Scottish Opera production of *Turandot* with Ashley Putnam and Judith Howart. Color. In English. 113 minutes. Home Vision VHS.

1987 Aria

Ken Russell's *Turandot* episode in the opera film ARIA is a visually spectacular, surrealistic interpretation of "Nessun dorma." Linzi Drew dreams that she is being adorned with dazzling jewels, although she is actually having visions on an operating table after a car accident. The singer is Jussi Björling with the Rome Opera House Orchestra led by Erich Leinsdorf. Color. In Italian. Color. About 10 minutes.

1987 The Witches of Eastwick

Luciano Pavarotti is heard singing "Nessun dorma" on the soundtrack at an apt moment in this Jack Nicholson-as-the-Devil film directed by George Miller. Color. 118 minutes.

1989 New York Stories

Martin Scorsese's episode of the omnibus film *New York Stories,* titled "Life Lessons," focuses on a New York painter and his girlfriend. Mario Del Monaco is heard singing "Nessun dorma" on the stereo. Color. 129 minutes.

1992 Over the Hill

Peter Dvorsky is heard singing "Nessun dorma" as characters in this romantic Australian comedy pass a sleepless night. Olympia Dukakis plays a woman looking for herself in the Australian outback. George Miller directed. Color. 99 minutes.

1995 Operavox

The Welsh animation studio Cartwn Cymru created an animated version of *Turandot* for the British Operavox series with the music performed by the Welsh National Opera Orchestra. Wyn Davies was music editor; Gary Hurst directed. Color. 27 minutes.

2000 The Turandot Project

Allan Miller's documentary observes director Zhang Yimou and conductor Zubin Mehta during the huge cross-cultural production of *Turandot* in Beijing's Forbidden City. Color. 85 minutes.

2001 Very Annie-Mary

Jonathan Pryce belts out the aria "Nessun dorma" in this Welsh film about a young woman denied a musical career. See VERY ANNIE-MARY.

2002 The Sum of All Fears

"Nessun dorma," sung by Brian Sledge, is featured on the soundtrack of this Tom Clancy thriller. Ben Affleck plays Jack Ryan; Phil Alden Robinson directed. Color. In English. 123 minutes.

TURCO IN ITALIA, IL
1814 opera by Rossini

GIOACHINO ROSSINI's comic opera *Il turco in Italia* (The Turk in Italy), libretto by Felice Romani, followed the popular *L'italiana in Algeri* and has a kind of reverse emphasis of location and amorous intrigue. The setting is Naples. The Turk of the title is Selim, who is fancied by Zaide but attracted to Fiorilla, who is married to Geronio but has Narciso as her lover. Meanwhile, poet Prosdocimo, who is looking for comic characters, finds a goodly number.

1971 Enriquez film

German TV film: Franco Enriquez (director), Giuseppe Patane (conductor, Berlin Radio Symphony Orchestra and RIAS Chorus), Karl Wägele (set designer), Bavaria Film (production).

Cast: Ingeborg Hallstein (Fiorilla), Barry McDaniel (Selim), Hermann Prey (Prosdocimo), Rohangiz Yachkmi (Zaide), Adolf Dallapozza (Narciso), Oskar Czerwenka (Geronio).

Telecast May 30, 1971, on ZDF. Color. In German. 109 minutes.

1978 New York City Opera

American stage production: Tito Capobianco (director), Julius Rudel (conductor, New York City Opera Orchestra and Chorus), Andrew Porter (English translation).

Cast: Beverly Sills (Fiorilla), Donald Gramm (Selim), Alan Titus (Prosdocimo), Susanne Marsee (Zaide), James Billings (Geronio), Jonathan Green (Albazar), Henry Price (Narciso).

Video at the New York Public Library. Telecast October 4, 1978. Kirk Browning (director). Color. In English. 178 minutes.

Comment: The opera is sung in English as *The Turk in Italy*.

TURNAGE, MARK-ANTHONY
English composer (1960–)

Mark-Anthony Turnage studied with Oliver Knussen and John Lambert and then worked with Hans Werner Henze at Tanglewood. Henze commissioned Turnage's opera GREEK for the Munich Biennale, where it was premiered in 1988 and later staged successfully in Edinburgh and London. His second major opera, *The Silver Tassie*, based on the Irish play by Sean O'Casey, was premiered in London in 2000. Turnage composes in a modern idiom that includes influences from rock and jazz to Britten and Stravinsky.

TURNER, CLARAMAE
American contralto (1920–)

Claramae Turner began her career in the chorus of the San Francisco Opera and gradually moved into major roles. Gian Carlo Menotti picked her to create the title role in *The Medium* at Columbia University in 1946, and she made her debut at the Metropolitan Opera the same year in *Faust*. She stayed with the Met for four years and then sang around the United States and Europe, including in the premiere of Aaron Copland's *The Tender Land*. She was the Witch in a 1950 NBC Opera Theatre production of HÄNSEL UND GRETEL, had the role of Nettie in the 1956 film version of Rodgers and Hammerstein's CAROUSEL, and re-created her Madame Flora in THE MEDIUM for NBC Television in 1959.

TURNER, EVA
English soprano (1892–1990)

Eva Turner made her debut in 1916 as a page in *Tannhäuser* with the Carl Rosa Company and sang with them for eight years. In 1924 she was Freia in *Das Rheingold* at La Scala and began her rise to stardom in the roles of Aida, Leonora, and, most importantly, Turandot. She was associated with the Ice Princess role for the rest of her life, and many thought her its ideal singer. Although Turner was one of the major dramatic sopranos of the world during the 1930s and 1940s, she did not appear in any films. However, she can be seen talking about and performing TOSCA in the 1983 documentary *I Live for Art* and talking about and performing AIDA in the 1987 documentary *The Aida File*.

TURN OF THE SCREW, THE
1954 opera by Britten

BENJAMIN BRITTEN's musical adaptation of Henry James's gothic ghost story *The Turn of the Screw*, libretto by Myganwy Piper, concerns a supernatural war over two young children. Their governess struggles to rescue them from the malign influence of the dead servants Peter Quint and Miss Jessel. She succeeds in wresting the girl Flora away with the help of the housekeeper Mrs. Grose, but the boy Miles dies in the battle for his soul.

1959 Associated-Rediffusion Television

English TV production: Peter Morley (director), Charles Mackerras (conductor, English Opera Group Orchestra), John Piper (set designer), Associated-Rediffusion (production).

Cast: Jennifer Vyvyan (Governess), Raymond Nilsson (Peter Quint/Prologue), Arda Mandikian (Miss Jessel), Judith Pierce (Mrs. Grose), Tom Bevan (Miles), Janette Miller (Flora).

Telecast December 25, 1959, on ITV. Black and white. In English. 120 minutes.

Comment: Vyvyan created the role of the Governess in the stage production.

***1982 Weigl film

Czech feature film: Petr Weigl (director), Colin Davis (conductor, Royal Opera House Orchestra and Chorus), Miloš Červinka (set designer), Milan Čorba (costume designer), Unitel (production).

Cast: Magdalena Vásáryová (Governess, sung by Helen Donath), Juraj Kukura (Peter Quint, sung by Robert Tear), Emilia Vásáryová (Miss Jessel, sung by Heather Harper), Dana Medřická (Mrs. Grose, sung by Ava June), Michael Gulyas (Miles, sung by Michael Ginn), Beata Blažičková (Flora, sung by Lillian Watson), Philip Langridge (Prologue).

Video: Philips VHS. Color. In English. 116 minutes.

Comment: Weigl shot the film on a country estate in Czechoslovakia with actors miming to the recorded voices of English singers. The film looks a bit over pretty but is still effective.

1990 Schwetzingen Festival

German stage production: Michael Hampe (director), Steuart Bedford (conductor, Stuttgart Radio Symphony Orchestra and Chorus), John Gunter (set/costume designer).

Cast: Helen Field (Governess), Richard Greager (Peter Quint), Samuel Linay (Miles), Machiko Obata (Flora), Menai Davies (Mrs. Grose), Phyllis Cannan (Miss Jessel).

Video: Arthaus DVD. Claus Viller (director). Color. In English. 108 minutes.

Comment: An excellent cast but an unexciting production.

1994 Scottish Opera

Scottish stage production: David Leveux (director), Timothy Lole (conductor, Scottish Opera Orchestra and Chorus).

Cast: Anne William-King (Governess), Philip Salmon (Peter Quint), Louisa Kennedy-Richardson (Miss Jessel), Menai Davies (Mrs. Grose), Colin McLean (Miles), Paula Bishop (Flora).

Telecast in 1994 by BBC Scotland. Mike Newman (director). Color. In English. 118 minutes.

Comment: Originally staged in Glasgow's Tramway.

TWO SISTERS FROM BOSTON
1946 American film with opera content

In *Two Sisters From Boston,* set in New York in 1903, Lauritz Melchior plays a Met tenor who becomes involved with aspiring singer Kathryn Grayson. She has been singing at Jimmy Durante's beer garden (where she is known as High-Note Susie), but her socialite parents think she is singing in opera. When they come to town, she sneaks on stage during an opera starring Melchior to prove it (it's an imaginary one created for the film using music by Liszt). By the end of the movie, Grayson succeeds in really getting invited to sing with him. They appear together in *Marie Antoinette,* an imaginary opera based on music by Mendelssohn; he plays King Louis XIV to her Marie, and they are surrounded by hundreds of extras on an elaborate set. MGM reportedly built a 500-foot-wide reproduction of the Old Met interior for the film. Met soprano Nina Koshetz plays an innkeeper's daughter in the film. Charles Previn arranged the music and wrote the imaginary operas, Myles Connolly wrote the screenplay, Robert Surtees was the cinematographer, Joseph Pasterak produced, and Henry Koster directed. Black and white. 112 minutes. MGM-UA VHS.

U

UCLA FILM AND TELEVISION ARCHIVE

The UCLA Film and Television Archive in Los Angeles has one of the largest collections of film and television material in the United States. It has excellent research facilities, and its holdings include not only opera films but many television programs with operatic content. Its comprehensive Hallmark collection is especially notable. It presents an annual preservation festival, which often includes films of operatic interest.

UKRAINIAN OPERA

Ukrainian national opera began to take shape in the 19th century with Semyon Gulak-Artemovsky's comic opera *Cossacks Beyond the Danube* and developed while the country was still part of the Russian Empire and Soviet Union. The composer Mykola Lysenko is credited with creating the model for Ukrainian grand opera with his *Taras Bulba* in 1891. There are several Ukrainian opera singers of note, and there is a feature film about the great interpreter of *Madama Butterfly* SALOMEA KRUSCENISKI. Ukrainian composer Oles Semenovich Chishko wrote an opera inspired by Eisenstein's famous Potemkin film. See BORIS GODUNOV (1953 film), IGOR GORIN, SERGEI EISENSTEIN, MAY NIGHT (1953), NINA KOSHETZ, and THE RETURN OF BUTTERFLY.

1944 Cossacks Beyond the Danube
Soviet compilation of excerpts from Gulak-Artemovsky's comic opera *Cossacks Beyond the Danube*. The story concerns Ukrainians forced to take refuge in Turkey by Catherine the Great and the efforts of the refugees to return home. Artkino. In Russian. 30 minutes.

1953 Stars of the Ukraine
Stars of the Ukraine is a two-part Soviet film in Magi-Color promoting the glories of Ukrainian composers and singers. Part One is a 52-minute version of the opera *May Night,* which is based on a story by Ukrainian writer Nicolai Gogol. Part Two is the 74-minute *Ukrainian Concert Hall* featuring singers and dancers at the Shevchenko State Opera House. Ukrainian basso Boris Gmirya (Borys Hmyrya in Ukrainian) is the star of the concert, and his aria from *Boris Godunov* is a highlight. Mikhail Romensky, Lydia Rudenko, and Dimitri Gnatok appear in scenes from Lyksenko's opera *Taras Bulba,* and Ivan Patorchinsky and Maria Litvinenko perform in Gulak-Artemovsky's opera *Cossacks Beyond the Danube.* Boris Barnett directed the film, which features the Dumka State Academy Choir and Shevchenko State Opera Orchestra, Chorus, and Ballet. Color. In Russian and Ukrainian with English subtitles. 126 minutes.

ULLMANN, VIKTOR
Austro-Czech composer (1898–1944)

Jewish composer Viktor Ullmann, who died at Auschwitz, is remembered today primarily because of an opera he created in 1943 in the Terezin (Theresienstadt) concentration camp with librettist Peter Kien. They wrote DER KAISER VON ATLANTIS (The Emperor of Atlantis) on the back of SS deportation forms and were able to hold rehearsals of it, but they were sent to Auschwitz before they could stage it. The opera, the harrowing story of a ruler who kills so many people that even Death objects, survived the war and premiered in Amsterdam in 1975. Ullmann composed earlier operas, but none with the intensity of his last.

UNDER THE ARBOR
1992 opera by Greenleaf

In 1943 in a rural community in Alabama by the Chattahoochee River, teenaged cousins Hallie and Robert fall in love against a background of religion, guilt, and voodoo. Robert Greenleaf's opera *Under the Arbor,* libretto by Marian Motley Carcache based on her story, premiered in 1992 in Birmingham, Alabama. The music is traditional in style, somewhat reminiscent of Copland's *The Tender Land.*

1993 Opera Alabama
American stage production: David Gately (director), Bob Cooley (producer), Paul Polivnick (conductor, Alabama Symphony Orchestra), Charles Caldwell (set designer).

Cast: Sunny Joy Langton (Hallie), Mark Calkins (Robert), Carmen Balthrop (Annie), Vanessa Ayers (Duck), Ruby Hinds (Madame Queen), Tichina Vaughn (Mattie), Claudia Cummings (Miss Nell), Bruce Hall (Papa Brown).

Video: Kultur VHS. Telecast January 21, 1994, on PBS. Bruce Kuerten (director) Color. In English. 112 minutes.

UNDINE
1845 opera by Lortzing

ALBERT LORTZING's most popular opera, based on a story by Fouqué, is a fairy tale about the water nymph Undine. She falls in love with the knight Hugo von Ringstetten and goes to his court to be with him. When he is unfaithful to her, she returns to the sea, but she takes him back in the end. The same tale provided the basis for an opera by E. T. A. Hoffmann. The story was quite popular during the silent cinema era.

1969 Stuttgart State Opera
German stage production: Herbert Junkers (director), Hans Zanotelli (conductor, Württembergisches Staatstheater Orchestra), Hein Heckroth (set designer).

Cast: Lucia Popp (Undine), Horst Hoffman (Hugo), Herman Prey (Kühleborn), Ruth-Marget Putz (Bertalda), Fritz Ollendorf (Hans), Harald Axtner (Veit).

Telecast November 23, 1969, on ZDF German Television. Color. In German. 108 minutes.

Silent films

1912 Thanhauser film
Florence LaBadie stars as Undine in this American film of the story made for the Thanhauser studio. It follows the plot of the Lortzing opera quite closely. Theodore Marston directed. Black and white. About 30 minutes.

1916 Bluebird film
Ida Schnall, a champion swimmer, was chosen to star as Undine in this movie of the story because of her swimming ability as well as her beauty. It was filmed on location in the Santa Catalina area. Henry Otto directed for Bluebird Pictures. Black and white. About 65 minutes.

1919 Delog film
The German Delog Company produced a film of the opera that required live singers and orchestra. The company sent the film (this was one of four it made) on tour with soloists, chorus, and orchestra. Presumably, it saved money on sets and was popular as a novelty in smaller cities. Black and white. About 70 minutes.

UP IN CENTRAL PARK
1945 operetta by Romberg

SIGMUND ROMBERG's vintage New York operetta *Up in Central Park* was a comeback for the composer and his old-fashioned style of traditional operetta. Dorothy Fields's book and lyrics brought the Courier and Ives Manhattan of the 1870s back to life, including a Courier and Ives skating ballet, in a story about Boss Tweed and Tammany Hall graft. Rosie Moore, the daughter of a Tweed crony, falls in love with crusading newspaper reporter John Matthew, and they sing the hit song "Close as the Pages in a Book."

1948 Universal film
American feature film: William Seiter (director), Karl Tunberg (screenplay), Milton Krasner (cinematographer), Howard Bay (production designer), Johnny Green (music director/conductor), Universal Pictures (studio).

Cast: Deanna Durbin (Rosie Moore), Dick Haymes (John Matthews), Vincent Price (Boss Tweed), Albert Sharp (Timothy Moore),Tom Powers (Rogan).

Black and white. In English. 88 minutes.

Comment: Durbin sings most of the songs plus "Pace, pace, mio dio" from *La forza del destino*.

UPPMAN, THEODOR
American baritone (1920–)

Theodor Uppman created the role of Billy Budd in Benjamin Britten's opera at Covent Garden in 1951 and was also featured in premieres of operas by Floyd, Hermann, Villa-Lobos, and Pasatieri. He began his career in 1947 in his native California singing Pelléas with Maggie Teyte as his Mélisande at San Francisco. It was such a success that he was invited to repeat the role at the Met. His light baritone was much admired in its time, and he soon became internationally popular. See BELL TELEPHONE HOUR (1959–1966), BILLY BUDD (1952), A CHILD IS BORN (1955), DIE LUSTIGE WITWE (1954), LA PÉRICHOLE (1958), and A QUIET PLACE (1986).

USANDIZAGA, JOSÉ MARIA
Basque composer (1887–1915)

José Maria Usandizaga, one of the best-known Basque composers, is particularly popular in Spain for his 1914 zarzuela LAS GOLONDRINAS (The Swallows). Usandizaga, who was born in San Sebastian, studied in Paris before returning to his Basque homeland to write an opera in the Basque language, *Mendi Mendiyan* (High in the Mountains); it premiered in Bilbao in 1910 and was produced in other cities. *Las Golondrinas* won him national fame after its production in Madrid in 1914, but he died of tuberculosis in 1915 before completing more operas.

V

VAGABOND KING, THE
1925 operetta by Friml

RUDOLF FRIML's last major stage operetta was based on Justin McCarthy's play *If I Were King,* a romantic tale about the French poet/rogue François Villon during the reign of King Henry XI. The libretto by Brian Hooker and W. H. Post concentrates on his romances with his free-living companion Huguette and Lady Katherine de Vaucelles. The stage production starred Dennis King, a fine singer and a trained Shakespearean actor. The score, one of Friml's best, includes such memorable songs as "Only a Rose" and the "Huguette Waltz."

1930 Berger film
     American feature film: Ludwig Berger (director), Herman J. Mankiewicz (screenplay), Henry Gerrard and Ray Rennahan (cinematographers), Hans Dreier (set designer), Paramount (studio).
     Cast: Dennis King (François Villon), Jeanette MacDonald (Lady Katherine), Lillian Roth (Huguette), O. P. Heggie (King Louis XI), Warner Oland (Thibault).
     Video: Premiere Opera VHS in black and white; two-color Technicolor print at UCLA Film Archive. In English. 104 minutes.
     Comment: The film was well reviewed but not popular and seems quite static for a Berger film.

1956 Curtiz film
     American feature film: Michael Curtiz (director), Ken Englund and Noel Langley (screenplay), Robert Burks (cinematographer, in VistaVision), Paramount (studio).
     Cast: Oreste (François Villon), Kathryn Grayson (Lady Katherine), Rita Moreno (Huguette), Walter Hampden (King Louis XI), Leslie Nielsen (Thibault).
     Video: Paramount VHS. Color. In English. 88 minutes.
     Comment: A somewhat dull movie. Maltese tenor Oreste (Kirkop) was promoted by Paramount as a new Mario Lanza, but he wasn't; this was his only movie. He sings well enough, but his screen personality is not enough to carry a film.

The Vagabond King (1930): Warner Oland and Jeanette MacDonald in Ludwig Berger's film of the operetta.

VAMPYR, DER
1828 opera by Marschner

HEINRICH MARSCHNER's opera *Der Vampyr,* libretto by Wilhelm Wohlbrück, is based on the famous story by Byron's doctor John Polidori that began the 19th-century vampire craze. It premiered in Leipzig in 1828 and has remained popular, possibly because the vampire vogue never went away. The opera focuses on vampire Lord Ruthven; he has to sacrifice three brides in one day or be sent to Hell. He succeeds with the first two, but he is foiled when he tries to marry Davenant's daughter.

1992 The Vampyr: A Soap Opera
     English TV film: Nigel Finch (director), David Parris (conductor, BBC Philharmonic Orchestra and Britten Singers), Charles Hart (screenplay), Janet Street-Porter (producer), Jim Grant (set designer), BBC (production).
     Cast: Omar Ebrahim (Ripley, the Vampyr), Richard van Allan (Davenant), Fiona O'Neill (Miranda), Willemijn Van Gent (Ginny), Philip Salmon (Alex), Colenton Freeman (George), Sally-Ann Shepherdson (Emma), Robert Stephens (narrator).
     Video: CBS Fox VHS Color. In English. 115 minutes.

Comment: Modernized film version set in present-day London. The vampire Riley, awakened after a 200-year sleep, has become a successful businessman, but he has to kill three women in three days or perish. The killings are quite nasty, but then so are the seductions, and there is a good deal of nudity. The singing, set designs, costumes, cinematography, and acting are top notch. The film, originally screened on BBC Television between Christmas and New Year 1992 in 15-minute segments like a soap opera, won the Prix Italia for Music.

VAN DAM, JOSÉ
Belgium bass-baritone (1940–)

José van Dam, a superb actor as well as singer, has been featured in three opera films, including two versions of *Don Giovanni.* He was born in Brussels, made his debut in Liège in 1960, and sang minor roles in Paris for five years. His career took off in the late 1960s when he sang Figaro and Leporello with Deutsche Oper in Berlin. He performed at Covent Garden in 1973 and at the Met in 1975, but the Théâtre de la Monnaie in Brussels is his main focus. He was Leporello in Joseph Losey's great film of DON GIOVANNI (1978), and he played the Don in the stage opera in the Belgium film BABEL OPERA (1985). His fine performance as a singing teacher in the Belgian film LE MAÎTRE DE MUSIQUE (1988) gained him international admiration. See LES CONTES D'HOFFMANN (1993), LA DAMNATION DE FAUST (1989), DON CARLOS (1996), HAMLET (2001), and PELLÉAS ET MÉLISANDE (1987).

1990 Music Lessons with José van Dam
Van Dam, who intends to be a voice teacher when he retires and played the role of one in the film *The Music Master,* was filmed in this two-part music lesson in 1990. The first part, "The Construction of a Voice," shot in Liège, shows the training required to prepare a voice for a performance. The second part, "The Construction of a Role," was shot in Lyon and shows van Dam giving advice to singers on the interpretations of their roles. Jean-François Jung directed. Color. 114 minutes.

VANESSA
1958 opera by Barber

Vanessa has been waiting 20 years on her isolated northern estate for the return of her lover. Anatol, the man who finally comes, turns out to be her lover's son and a fortune hunter. He is attracted to her niece Erika and seduces her, but he goes away with Vanessa. SAMUEL BARBER's *Vanessa,* once praised as the finest opera written by an American, won the Pulitzer Prize for Music. Librettist Gian Carlo Menotti said he was inspired by the stories of Isak Dinesen, although the opera plot is not based on any particular tale. *Vanessa* premiered at the Metropolitan Opera January 15, 1958.

1978 Spoleto Festival, USA
American stage production: Gian Carlo Menotti (director), Christopher Keene (conductor, Spoleto Festival Orchestra), Pasquale Grossi (set/costume designer).

Cast: Johanna Meier (Vanessa), Henry Price (Anatol), Katherine Ciesinski (Erika), Alice Garrott (Old Baroness), Irwin Densen (Doctor), William Bender (Nicholas).

Video: Premiere Opera/Lyric VHS and video at the New York Public Library. Telecast January 31, 1979, on PBS in the *Great Performances* series. Kirk Browning (director).Color. In English. 119 minutes.

VARADY, JULIA
Romanian soprano (1941–)

Julia Varady was born in Romania and studied in Bucharest, but she began her career in Germany. She first became noted in Mozart and then expanded her repertory to Verdi, Puccini, Wagner, Offenbach, and Bartók. She has since become one of the most sought-after sopranos and is particularly liked as Donna Elvira. She married Dietrich Fischer-Dieskau in 1978. See DON GIOVANNI (1978/1987), DER FLIEGENDE HOLLÄNDER (1991), HERBERT VON KARAJAN (1987), and DIE WALKÜRE (1989).

1998 Julia Varady: Song of Passion
Bruna Monsaingeon's documentary about Varady examines her art and career and finishes with a 26-minute recital. There are extracts from operas by Mozart, Verdi, Wagner, Tchaikovsky, Puccini, and Richard Strauss. Viktoria Postnikova plays piano in the recital. Telecast in Germany in February 1999. Color. In German. 81 minutes.

VARGAS, RAMÓN
Mexican tenor (1960–)

Ramón Vargas, one of the fast-rising new tenors, became known in America when he made his debut at the Met by replacing Luciano Pavarotti as Edgardo in *Lucia di Lammermoor* in 1992. He first attracted attention in Italy when he won the Caruso Competition in 1986. He has now appeared in more than 50 roles on stage in major opera houses and won wide praise for his CD of Verdi operas. He played the Prince to Cecilia Bartoli's Cinderella at the Met in 1997 in Rossini's LA CENERENTOLA. Werther is one of his favorite roles, and he has telecast the Massenet opera in Mexico. See OPERA STARS IN CONCERT (1991).

VAUGHAN WILLIAMS, RALPH
English composer (1872–1958)

Ralph Vaughan Williams, one of the pioneers of modern English opera, wrote six very British operas during his long career, all based on British authors and folk song. The best known are *Hugh the Drover* (1924) and *The Pilgrim's Progress* (1951), but the most interesting may be the 1937 RIDERS TO THE SEA, a word-for-word setting of John Millington Synge's great Irish tragedy. Vaughan Williams also wrote music for several British films, including *The 49th Parallel, Coastal Command,* and *Scott of the Antarctic.*

1984 Ralph Vaughan Williams
This tribute to Vaughan Williams by music film specialist Ken Russell tells the story of the "quiet" composer through his music with stories and anecdotes from his widow Ursula and colleagues. It begins in Cornwall with the composer's *The Sea,* goes to a village green for the *Pastoral Symphony,* travels to the Antarctic for the *Seventh Symphony,* and winds up on Salisbury Plain for the *Ninth Symphony.* Telecast April 8, 1984, on the *South Bank Show.* Color. 55 minutes.

VENICE

The Gran Teatro La Fenice in Venice, constructed in 1792 and considered one of the most beautiful opera houses in the world, was devastated by a fire in 1996 but is to be rebuilt exactly as it was. La Fenice has been the site of 179 opera premieres, including Verdi's RIGOLETTO and LA TRAVIATA, Stravinsky's THE RAKE'S PROGRESS, and notable works by Paisiello, Cimarosa, Rossini, Bellini, and Donizetti. It can be experienced historically as it looked during the 19th century in Verdi film biographies, Visconti's film *Senso,* and the Venetian documentary *Sull'ali dorate.* There are splendid tours of the city in videos about MONTEVERDI, WAGNER, and VERDI; fine views of the city in Visconti's film DEATH IN VENICE; and even a video of sopranos giving a recital in St. Mark's Square in 1991 (See SOPRANOS AND MEZZOS). Operas actually set in Venice include Britten's DEATH IN VENICE, Ponchielli's LA GIOCONDA, and Gilbert and Sullivan's THE GONDOLIERS. Videos of performances at La Fenice include ATTILA (1987), CECILIA BARTOLI (1992), I CAPULETI ED I MONTECCHI (1991), and LA TRAVIATA (1992).

1995 Five Centuries of Music in Venice
Five-part five-hour series about the musical history of Venice by H. C. Robbins Landon, with excerpts from operas and other music composed in Venice. The individual programs are titled "Venice and the Gabrielis," "The World of Claudio Monteverdi," "Venice and Vivaldi," "Verdi and Venetian Theatre," and "20th Century Music in Venice." Color. In English. Each part is 60 minutes. Films for the Humanities & Sciences VHS.

1996 Sull'ali dorate
Virgilio Boccardi's documentary *On Golden Wings* was made to celebrate the bicentenary of La Fenice and traces the history of the opera house from 1792 to 1996. There are excerpts from operas performed on stage, drawings, and set designs of older performances as well as a description of the great fire of 1836 which, like the modern one, destroyed the building. Color. In English and Italian versions. 47 minutes. La Fenice VHS.

VERBENA DE LA PALOMA, LA
1894 zarzuela by Bretón

TOMÁS BRETÓN's *La verbena de la paloma* (The Festival of the Dove), one of the most popular Spanish zarzuelas, is set in a working-class area of Madrid in 1893 as the inhabitants prepare for a street fair held on the saint's day of the Virgin of the Dove. Julian loves Susana, but she doesn't seem to be interested in him. When the old chemist Don Hilarion takes her out to a dance hall, Julian's jealousy causes a fight, and the police are called. The role of Don Hilarion is a favorite for comic tenors. The popularity of the zarzuela has led to three films and a cinematic homage by Pedro Almodovar.

1935 Perojo film
Spanish feature film: Benito Perojo (director/screenplay), Fred Mendel (cinematographer), Cifesa (production).

Cast: Raquel Rodrigo (Susana), Roberto Rey (Julian), Miguel Ligero (Don Hilarion), Charito Leonis (Casta), Dolores Cortes (Aunt Antonia), Selica Perez Carpios (Señora Rita).

Video: Divisa Ediciónes (Spain) VHS. Black and white. In Spanish. 69 minutes.

Comment: This film, which was distributed in the United States, is considered one of the best in the genre.

1963 Heredia film
Spanish feature film: Jose Luis Sáenz de Heredia (director/screenplay), Benito Perojo (producer).

Cast: Conchita Velasco (Susana), Miguel Ligero (Don Hilarion), Irán Eory, Vicente Parr, Mercedes Vecino.

Color. In Spanish. 75 minutes.

Comment: Ligero is again featured as Don Hilarion, a role he often performed on stage.

***1999 Jarvis Conservatory

American stage production: Daniel Helfgot (director), Philip J. Bauman (conductor, Jarvis Conservatory Orchestra), Peter Crompton (set designer), Carlos Carvajal (choreographer), William Jarvis (producer/translator).

Video: Jarvis Conservatory VHS. Color. Dialogue in English; singing in Spanish with English and Spanish subtitles. 64 minutes.

Comment: Finely produced, sung, and acted with good production values.

Silent/related films

1921 Buchs film

José Buchs wrote and directed this popular film that helped launch the zarzuela as a cinematic genre. Although made during the silent era, it was not silent. The composer arranged his music to accompany the film, and he conducted the orchestra when it premiered. The film stars Elisa Ruiz Romero as Susana, Julia Lozano, Florian Rey, and Jose Montenegro. Juan Sola was the cinematographer. Black and white. About 67 minutes.

1980 Almodovar film

There is an inverted homage to *La verbena* in Pedro Almodovar's film *Pepi, Luci, Bom y otros chicas del Montón.* Pepi's punk rock group friends dress up like characters from *Verbena* and sing songs from the zarzuela as they go after a policeman who raped Pepi. Color. In Spanish. 85 minutes.

VERDI, GIUSEPPE

Italian composer (1813–1901)

Giuseppe Verdi has become synonymous with Italian opera, which he dominated for half a century; happily, most of his operas are available on film and video. There are also interesting film biographies with fascinating reconstructions of original productions as well as films about the RICORDI publishing firm featuring his operas. Verdi wrote his first opera in 1836, became successful with NABUCCO in 1842, and then became world famous with RIGOLETTO, IL TROVATORE, LA TRAVIATA, UN BALLO IN MASCHERA, LA FORZA DEL DESTINO, and AIDA. Instead of fading away, he finished strongly with OTELLO and FALSTAFF. When he died, he was an Italian national hero.

He still is. See ATTILA, UN BALLO IN MASCHERA, DON CARLOS, I DUE FOSCARI, ERNANI, GIOVANNA D'ARCO, JÉRUSALEM, I LOMBARDI ALLA PRIMA CROCIATA, LUISA MILLER, MACBETH, SIMON BOCCANEGRA, STIFFELIO, VERDI REQUIEM, and I VESPRI SICILIANI.

Biographical films

1898 Maestri di musica

Leopoldo Fregoli, the first Italian filmmaker, was a quick-change variety illusionist who transformed himself into famous people. With his film *Maestri di musica,* he impersonated Verdi conducting an opera as he stood by the screen singing and talking in synchronization with it. Black and white. Silent. About 6 minutes.

1901 Funerale di Giuseppe Verdi a Milano

One of the first Italian nonfiction films, *Giuseppe Verdi's Funeral in Milan,* was shot during Verdi's funeral and screened in Italy in March 1901. It was made by pioneer filmmaker Italo Pacchioni. Some segments of the film survive. Black and white. Silent. About 3 minutes.

1913 Giuseppe Verdi nella vita e nella gloria

Paolo Rosmino stars as Verdi in *Giuseppe Verdi in His Life and Glory,* an Italian film biography written and directed by Count Giuseppe de Luguoro-Presicce for Milano Film. Black and white. Silent. About 30 minutes.

1931 Verdi

This "sketch with music" about the composer was made by James J. Fitzpatrick, the famous travelogue creator. It features an excerpt from *Aida.* Black and white. In English. 10 minutes.

1938 Giuseppe Verdi

Fosco Giachetti plays Verdi in this epic Italian film directed by Carmine Gallone. Germana Paolieri is first wife Margherita Barezzi, Gaby Morlay is second wife Giuseppina Strepponi, and Maria Cebotari is Theresa Stolz, the soprano who was Verdi's love interest in later life. Beniamino Gigli plays tenor Raffaele Mirate, who created the role of the Duke in *Rigoletto,* and is seen practicing "La donna è mobile" with Verdi in a gondola before the premiere. Most of the people in Verdi's life and career appear in the film, from his family to Donizetti, Rossini, and Victor Hugo. The opera scenes were shot on stage at the Rome Royal Opera House, and the film ends with the premiere of *Aida.* The singers include Tito Gobbi, Pia Tassinari, Gabriella Gatti, and Apollo Granforte. Black and white. In Italian. 110 minutes. House of Opera VHS.

1948 Luoghi Verdiani
Luciano Emmer, who made nonfiction films during the 1940s before turning to features, was known for his fine studies of artists. His documentary *Luoghi Verdiani* (Verdi Places) is an evocation of the composer through places in Rome featured in his operas. Black and white. In Italian. 30 minutes.

1953 Giuseppe Verdi
Pierre Cressoy plays Verdi in this Italian film biography shown in America as *Verdi: The King of Melody*. Mario Del Monaco plays tenor Francesco Tamagno, who created the role of Otello, and Tito Gobbi plays baritone Giorgio Ronconi, who created the role of Nabucco. They are featured, with singers Orietta Moscucci and Vito de Taranto, in scenes from *Aida, Ernani, Falstaff, Nabucco, Otello, Rigoletto, La traviata,* and *Il trovatore*. Gaby André plays Giuseppina Strepponi, Emilio Cigoli is Donizetti, and Loris Gizzi is Rossini. Raffaello Matarazzo directed. Color. Arias in Italian, dialogue in dubbed English. 117 minutes. VIEW/House of Opera VHS.

1982 The Life of Verdi
Ronald Pickup stars as Verdi in this nine-hour Italian TV docu-drama, a comprehensive biography from birth to death with documentary-style English narration and reconstructed episodes of Verdi's life. Most of the film was shot on location, and there is a real feeling of place in the re-creations of 19th-century Milan and Venice. There are also many scenes from operas staged in period style. Mara Zampieri sings roles introduced by Teresa Stolz, but most of the excerpts are based on Fonit-Cetra recordings. Carla Fracci plays Giuseppina Strepponi, Roman Vlad was music director, and Renato Castellani wrote the screenplay and directed the film. The version shown on PBS and Bravo and available on video in America is in English. The Italian version is called simply *Verdi*. Color. 10 hours. Kultur VHS (four tapes).

1994 The Life of Verdi
English TV documentary about Verdi by Barrie Gavin filmed in Busseto, Parma, Venice, Milan, and Genoa with staged opera extracts intercut with the biographical material. Conductor Mark Elder, who provides the commentary, selected the opera extracts filmed in a studio with casts that include Edmund Barham, Josephine Barstow, Dennis O'Neill, Jonathan Summers, Richard Van Allen, and Willard White. The featured operas are *Attila, Don Carlo, Falstaff, La forza del destino, Luisa Miller, Macbeth, Nabucco, Otello, Rigoletto, Simon Boccanegra,* and *La traviata*. Telecast on BBC Television in two parts August 27 and September 3, 1994. Color. In English. 120 minutes.

1996 Famous Composers: Giuseppe Verdi
Video documentary about the life of the composer featuring excerpts from his works. Color. In English. 30 minutes. Kultur VHS.

Performance/related films

1956–1963 Firestone Verdi Festival
Highlights from Verdi operas featured on *The Voice of Firestone* television series. LA TRAVIATA (1956), AIDA (1962), RIGOLETTO (1963), and OTELLO (1963) are performed in costume by leading opera singers of the period (see details under individual operas). Black and white. In Italian with English introductions. 60 minutes. VAI VHS.

1976 Sherrill Milnes: Homage to Verdi
Sherrill Milnes goes on pilgrimage to Verdi's birthplace and sings Verdi arias as he tells of the composer's life. He begins with "Di Provenza il mar" as he visits Villa Verdi at Sant'Agata and pays homage to Verdi's piano. He also sings arias from *La traviata, La forza del destino, I vespri siciliani, Attila, Rigoletto, Nabucco,* and *Macbeth* and is seen rehearsing/performing *Rigoletto*. Gerald Krell produced and directed the film. Color. In English. 56 minutes. Kultur VHS.

1976 Novecento
Bernardo Bertolucci's epic movie *1900* is virtually a tribute to Verdi. Stars Robert De Niro and Gérard Depardieu are born on the day the composer dies in 1901, Italian history over the century is seen across families in Verdi's Emilia-Romagna region, Verdi's music is featured on the soundtrack, and there is even a hunchback clown named Rigoletto. Color. In Italian. 320 minutes. On VHS.

1987 Little Dorritt
Christine Edzard's six-hour film of Charles Dickens's novel uses music from Verdi operas as its complete score. The music was arranged and conducted by Michael Sanvoisin with soloists Pat Halling, F. Gabarro, and Jack Brynmer. Color. 357 minutes. Cannon VHS.

1989 Opera Favorites by Verdi
Compilation video of scenes from six Verdi operas. Seen at Verona are *Aida* with Maria Chiara, *Nabucco* with Ghena Dimitrova, *I Lombardi* with José Carreras, and *Otello* with Vladimir Atlantov. Seen at La Scala is *Ernani* with Mirella Freni. Seen at Covent Garden is *Falstaff* with Renato Bruson. Color. In Italian with English subtitles. 54 minutes. HBO VHS.

1997 Verdi and Venetian Theatre

This is part of the video series *Five Centuries of Music in Venice*. It shows Verdi's connections with Venice, as well as those of Rossini and Wagner, and features performances at La Fenice. Color. 52 minutes. Films for the Humanities & Sciences VHS.

1998 Giuseppe Verdi

Documentary about Verdi operas with commentary from Luchino Visconti and Gérard Mortier. Luciano Pavarotti sings an aria from *Rigoletto*, Sir George Solti conducts *Falstaff*, and Herbert von Karajan conducts *Otello*. There are also selections from *Aida, Don Carlo, Macbeth, Nabucco*, and *La traviata*. Part of the video series *Harmonics: The Innovators of Classical Music*. Color. 28 minutes. Films for the Humanities & Sciences VHS.

2001 Verdi Gala

This is a video of a concert in honor of the Verdi centennial staged at the Teatro Padiglione Palacassa in Parma on March 11, 2001. The program, which begins and ends with the *Nabucco* slave chorus, includes excerpts from *Aida, Un ballo in maschera, Il corsaro, Don Carlo, Falstaff, La forza del destino, Jérusalem, Otello, Rigoletto, La traviata*, and *Il trovatore*. The singers include Marcelo Álvarez, José Carreras, José Cura, Daniela Dessi, Mariella Devia, Luciana D'Intino, Plácido Domingo, Gianluca Floris, Barbara Frittoli, Konstantin Gorny, Elisabète Matos, Leo Nucci, Ruggiero Raimondi, Rossano Rinaldi, Cinzia Rizzone, Gloria Scalchi, and Riccardo Zanellato. Zubin Mehta conducts the Florence Maggio Musicale Orchestra and Verdi Festival Chorus. Color. 182 minutes. TDK DVD.

2001 The Met Celebrates Verdi

The Metropolitan Opera concluded its year of Verdi centennial celebrations with a televised compilation of highlights from Met telecasts of eight Verdi operas. James Levine was host. Color. Excerpts in Italian with English subtitles. 120 minutes. Telecast by PBS in two parts on May 30 and December 27, 2001.

2001 A Passion for Verdi

London concert celebrating the Verdi centennial with tenor José Cura and soprano Daniela Dessi and the London Symphony Orchestra conducted by Giorgio Morandi. Color. In English. 60 minutes.

VERDI REQUIEM
1874 mass by Verdi

Verdi's *Messa da Requiem*, written to honor the poet-patriot Alessandro Manzoni, is considered by some critics to be Verdi's best opera. It is usually performed by opera singers, and church officials have criticized it for being too "theatrical." It premiered at Milan's San Marco Church on May 22, 1874, and was reprised three days later at the La Scala Opera House, where it received the applause that was not allowed in church. Most of the videos of *Requiem* feature major opera singers.

***1967 Teatro alla Scala

Filmed Italian stage production: Henri-Georges Clouzot (director), Herbert von Karajan (conductor, Teatro alla Scala Orchestra and Chorus).

Soloists: Leontyne Price, Luciano Pavarotti, Fiorenza Cossotto, Nicolai Ghiaurov.

Video: DG DVD/VHS/LD. Color. In Latin. 85 minutes.

Comment: Clouzot filmed this performance at La Scala in January 1967 without an audience. The singers are outstanding, the conducting is first class, and Clouzot is a marvel as he demonstrates how a filmmaker of genius can make even a static Mass visually interesting and exciting. His choice of shots, cuts, camera movements, and close-ups makes this both a cinematic and a musical experience.

1970 St. Paul's Cathedral

English church production: Leonard Bernstein (conductor, London Symphony Orchestra and Chorus).

Soloists: Plácido Domingo, Ruggero Raimondi.

Video: Kultur VHS. Color. In Latin. 97 minutes.

1980 Lincoln Center

American concert production: Zubin Mehta (conductor, New York Philharmonic and Chorus).

Soloists: Montserrat Caballé, Bianca Berini, Michael Svetlev, Martti Talvela.

Telecast October 22, 1980, in the *Live From Lincoln Center* series on PBS. Color. In Latin. 90 minutes.

1982 Edinburgh Festival

Scottish concert production: Claudio Abbado (conductor, London Symphony Orchestra and Edinburgh Festival Choir).

Soloists: Jessye Norman, José Carreras, Margaret Price, Ruggero Raimondi.

Video: Image Entertainment DVD/Kultur and HBO VHS. Color. In Latin. 82 minutes.

Comment: Taped at Usher Hall in Edinburgh with an introduction by John Drummond.

1982 Salzburg Festival

Austrian stage production: Herbert von Karajan (conductor, Vienna Philharmonic Orchestra, Vienna State Opera Choir, and Sofia National Opera Choir).

Soloists: Anna Tomowa-Sintow, Agnes Baltsa, José Carreras. José van Dam.

Video: Sony DVD. Color. In Latin. 111 minutes.

1990 Frankfurt Opera

German stage production: Enoch zu Guttenberg (conductor, European Symphony Orchestra and Neubeuren Choral Society).

Soloists: Pamela Coburn, Trudeliese Schmidt, Vinson Cole, Kurt Rydl.

Video: Pioneer DVD. Color. In Latin. 90 minutes.

1991 Moscow Theater

Russian stage production: Lorin Maazel (conductor, Moscow Philharmonic Orchestra and World Festival Choir).

Soloists: Luciano Pavarotti, Sharon Sweet, Dolora Zajick, Paul Plishka.

Multigram (Italy) LD. Color. In Latin. 96 minutes.

1996 Naples Sports Stadium

Italian concert production: Daniel Oren (conductor, San Carlo Opera Orchestra and Chorus).

Soloists: Luciano Pavarotti, Carlo Colombara, Dolora Zajick, Kallen Esperian.

Video: Image Entertainment DVD. Color. In Latin. 86 minutes.

1997 Royal Albert Hall

English concert production: Sir Colin David (conductor, London Symphony Orchestra, London Symphony Chorus, and London Voices).

Soloists: Michele Crider, Olga Borodina, René Pape, Frank Lopardo.

Telecast September 12, 1997, by BBC. Rodney Greenberg (director). Color. In Latin. 85 minutes.

Comment: Sir Georg Solti was to have conducted but died six days before the performance, which was dedicated to him.

2001 Berlin Philharmonie

German concert production: Claudio Abbado (conductor, Berlin Philharmonic Orchestra, Swedish Radio Chorus, and Eric Ericson Chamber Choir).

Soloists: Angela Gheorghiu, Roberta Alagna, Daniela Barcellona, Julian Konstantinov.

Video: EMI DVD. Color. In Latin. 89 minutes.

VERNON, JOHN
British TV opera director (1940-)

John Vernon directed a number of operas for television in England and Austria, and many are available on video, including productions from Glyndebourne, Covent Garden, and Vienna. See ARABELLA (1984), ARIADNE AUF NAXOS (1978), UN BALLO IN MASCHERA (1975), LA CENERENTOLA (1983), DIDO AND AENEAS (1966), LA FANCIULLA DEL WEST (1983), PETER GRIMES (1981), LA PIETRA DEL PARAGONE (1965), and SAMSON ET DALILA (1981).

VERONA

The Arena di Verona is the home of truly grand spectacle, where elephants on stage look natural and videos provide the best seats in the house. The Arena, an ancient Roman amphitheater seating 20,000 people with room for 3,000 on stage, began to present opera on a regular basis in 1913. It specializes in grand operas such as *Aida* and *Nabucco*, but it also presents some more intimate works. It can be seen as it looked in 1933 in the Giacomo Lauri-Volpi film LA CANZONE DEL SOLE, which features a production of *Les Huguenots*. It has also been the site of several gala recitals. The city also has the smaller Teatro Filarmonico, where Vivaldi's ORLANDO FURIOSO was staged and telecast in 1978. For opera performances at the Arena di Verona, see AIDA (1966/1981), ATTILA (1985), PLÁCIDO DOMINGO (1994), MADAMA BUTTERFLY (1983), MOZART (1991), NABUCCO (1981), OTELLO (1982), RIGOLETTO (1981/2001), TENORS (1990), TOSCA (1984), IL TROVATORE (1985), and TURANDOT (1983).

1988 La grande notte a Verona

The Big Night in Verona is a spectacular concert celebrating the 75th anniversary of opera at the Arena di Verona and featuring 23 singers with arias from 20 operas. The singers are Leo Nucci, Ghena Dimitrova, Peter Dvorsky, Sona Ghazarian, Giacomo Aragall, Ruggero Raimondi, Elena Obraztsova, Ferruccio Furlanetto, Natalia Troitskaya, Luca Canonici, Montserrat Caballé, Plácido Domingo, Samuel Ramey, Aprile Millo, Vincenzo La Scola, Mara Zampieri, René Kollo, Silvano Carroli, Eva Marton, Juan Pons, Antonio Ordoñez, Ileana Cotrubas, and José Carreras. Carreras helped organize the concert as a benefit, and he closes the evening with "Granada." Jose Collado and Carlo Franci conducted the Madrid Symphony Orchestra, and Karlheinz Hundorf directed the video. Color. 122 minutes. Kultur VHS.

1990 Highlights from Arena di Verona

Compilation video of scenes from Verona productions of *Tosca, Turandot, Otello,* and *Il trovatore.* The singers include Kiri Te Kanawa, Vladimir Atlantov, Franco

Bonisolli, Piero Cappuccilli, Ghena Dimitrova, Cecilia Gasdia, Nicola Martinucci, Rosalind Plowright, Ivo Vinco, and Ingvar Wixell. Color. 60 minutes. Kultur VHS.

1994 Pavarotti's 25th Anniversary

Plácido Domingo celebrated 25 years of appearances at the Arena di Verona with a program of staged opera scenes. Joining him in scenes from *Otello, Aida,* and *La bohème* are Daniela Dessi, Leo Nucci, and Cecilia Gasdia. Nello Santi conducts the Arena di Verona Orchestra. SACIS. Color. 90 minutes.

VÉRONIQUE
1898 opéra-comique by Messager

ANDRÉ MESSAGER's light opera, which revolves around a case of fake identity, is set in 1840 Paris and features the memorable duets known as the "Donkey Song" and the "Swing Song." Wealthy Hélène de Solanges pretends to be shopgirl Véronique to get revenge on playboy Viscount Florestan, whom she had expected to marry. She is angry because she discovered he was having a dalliance with a married woman. He falls in love with Véronique and wants to give up his rich bride-to-be, not realizing that they are the same person. It works out in the end. The libretto is by Albert Vanloo and Georges Duval.

1949 Vernay film

French feature film: Robert Vernay (director), Claude-André Puget and Jean Ferry (screenplay), Louis Beydts (music director).

Cast: Marina Hotine (Véronique/Hélène), Jean Desailly (Florestan), Giselle Pascal (Estelle), Mila Parély (Agathe), Jean Marchat (Baron), Pierre Bertin (Coquenard).

Black and white. In French. 100 minutes.

1979 Paris Opéra-Comique

French stage production: Jean Laurent Cochet (director), Pierre Dervaux (conductor, Théâtre National de l'Opéra Orchestra and Chorus), François de la Motte (set designer), Rosine Delamare (costume designer).

Cast: Daniele Chlostowa (Véronique/Hélène), François le Roux (Florestan), Michel Roux (Coquenard), Annick Dutertre (Agathe), Odette Laure (Ermerance).

Video: Lyric VHS. Yvon Gerault (director). Color. In French. 110 minutes.

VERRETT, SHIRLEY
American mezzo/soprano (1931–)

Shirley Verrett, whose most famous role is Carmen, prepared for her career studying in Los Angeles and at Juil-

liard. She made her debut in Yellow Springs, Ohio, in 1957 as Lucretia in Britten's *The Rape of Lucretia* and went to the New York City Opera in 1958 as Irina in Weill's *Lost in the Stars.* Unusual roles continued in Europe where she made her debut in Hamburg in Nabokov's *Rasputin's End.* She first sang *Carmen* in 1962 in Spoleto and then repeated the role at the Bolshoi, La Scala (televised and on DVD), New York City Opera, the Met, and Covent Garden. Afterwards she began to widen her range at the Met moving up to soprano roles such as Norma, Tosca, and Aida. Verrett has a memorable voice and a strong stage presence, as can be seen in her videos. See L'AFRICAINE (1988), AFRICAN-AMERICAN OPERA (2000), LA BOHÈME (1990 film), CARMEN (1984), ENRICO CARUSO (1994), CAVALLERIA RUSTICANA (1990), PLÁCIDO DOMINGO (1989), MACBETH (1987), MAGGIO MUSICALE (1989), MOÏSE ET PHARAON (1983), LUCIANO PAVAROTTI (1991), SAMSON ET DALILA (1980/1981), SPOLETO (1966), and TOSCA (1978).

1985 Shirley Verrett

Herbert Chappell's excellent documentary, subtitled *A Film Biography of the Black Diva,* shows the singer's life over the course of a year and includes many performance extracts. She is seen as Carmen at La Scala, Tosca in Verona, Dalila at the Royal Opera House, and Iphigenia at the Paris Opéra, singing with Plácido Domingo, Ruggero Raimondi, Jon Vickers, and Piero Faggioni. She also performs blues and spirituals, talks about her upbringing in the South, and explains her ideas about singing. NVC Arts. Color. 60 minutes. Kultur VHS.

1992 Songs of Freedom

Verrett is joined by guitarist John Williams and the Boston Pops Orchestra in a concert in tribute to the civil rights movement. There are also appearances by folksinger Odetta and the Boys Choir of Harlem. Telecast in February 1992 on PBS. Color. 60 minutes.

VERTIGINE
1942 Italian film with opera content

In *Vertigine* (Vertigo), Beniamino Gigli plays the "most famous tenor in the world" (a newspaper headline tells us so). His sickly daughter (Ruth Hellberg) is involved with an unworthy man (Herbert Wilk), and her life seems to parallel the plots of operas in which Gigli appears. When he is on stage at La Fenice as Maurizio in *Adriana Lecouvreur,* she is symbolically poisoned by her fiancé's jealous former lover via a phone call from the opera house. When he is on stage at the Rome Opera as Rodolfo in *La bohème,* she leaves the theater during Act III to take money to her fiancé to save him from prison for gambling debts. The strain is too much for her weak heart, and she collapses in front of her home. Her deathbed scene with her repentant lover is intercut with that of Mimì (Livia Caloni) on stage at the opera with Gigli, Tatiana Menotti (Musetta), Tito Gobbi (Marcello), and Gino Conti (Colline). Gigli, however, is able to get home in time for her final moments and is comforted by his sister (Emma Gramatica). The film also features an aria from *Die Walküre,* sung by Gigli in Italian, and scenic views of Venice, Rome, and San Remo. Guido Brignone directed the film in Italian and German versions with the same cast; the German film is called *Tragödie einer Liebe.* Guido Cantini wrote the screenplay, Günther Arko was the cinematographer, and Luigi Ricci conducted the music. Black and white. 88 minutes. House of Opera/Opera Dubs VHS.

VERY ANNIE-MARY
2001 Welsh film with opera content

Annie-Mary's father (Jonathan Pryce) drives his baker's truck around the Welsh valleys wearing a Pavarotti mask and belting out "Nessun dorma" over its loudspeakers. He is known as the "Voice of the Valleys," though his daughter Annie-Mary (Rachel Griffiths) is actually a better singer. When she was 16, she was offered a scholarship to study opera in Milan, but she had to turn it down because of her mother's illness. She still dreams of a musical career, so when her father has a stroke, she grabs the chance. Next thing you know she is also singing Puccini from the bakery truck loudspeakers, although her aria is ironically "O mio babbino caro." Barry Ackroyd photographed the film written and directed by Sara Sugerman for Film Four. Color. In English. 104 minutes.

VESPRI SICILIANI, I
1855 opera by Verdi

The Sicilian Vespers was a 1282 uprising in which Sicilian revolutionaries massacred French overlords in Palermo. *Les vêpres siciliennes* was GIUSEPPE VERDI's first French grand opera, but it is usually sung in Italian as *I vespri siciliani.* In the opera, Sicilian patriot Arrigo is the son of hated French governor Guido di Monforte, although he is involved with rebel Giovanni da Procida and Duchess Elena. He is accused of betrayal when he saves his father from an assassination but then gets a pardon for the conspirators. He is allowed to marry Elena, but the rebels use the wedding as the signal to launch the massacre.

1986 Teatro Communale, Bologna
Italian stage production: Luca Ronconi (director), Riccardo Chailly (conductor, Teatro Communale di Bologna Orchestra and Chorus), Pasquale Grossi (set/costume designer).

Cast: Veriano Luchetti (Arrigo), Susan Dunn (Duchess Elena), Leo Nucci (Guido di Monforte), Bonaldo Giaiotti (Giovanni da Procida).
Video: Home Vision VHS. Luca Ronconi (director). Color. In Italian with English subtitles. 155 minutes.

1990 Teatro alla Scala
Italian stage production: Pier Luigi Pizzi (director, set/costume designer), Riccardo Muti (conductor, Teatro alla Scala Orchestra and Chorus).
Cast: Chris Merritt (Arrigo), Cheryl Studer (Duchess Elena), Giorgio Zancanaro (Guido di Monforte), Ferruccio Furlanetto (Giovanni da Procida).
Video: Image Entertainment DVD/Home Vision VHS. Christopher Swann (director). Color. In Italian with English subtitles. 210 minutes.
Comment: This production includes the third act Ballet of the Four Seasons, danced by Carla Fracci and Wayne Eagling.

Related film

1949 Vespro Siciliana
Italian narrative film about the events surrounding the Sicilian Vespers with Clara Calamai as Elena and Roldano Lupi as Procida. Giorgio Pàstinia wrote and directed it. Color. In Italian. 95 minutes.

VETTER AUS DINGSDA, DER
1912 operetta by Künneke

A stranger is invited into a Dutch country house by romantic young Julia who believes he is the cousin she has been waiting to marry. He isn't. Soon, there are complications. EDWARD KÜNNEKE's Berlin operetta *Der Vetter aus Dingsda* (The Cousin From Nowhere), libretto by Herman Haller and "Rideamus," is his most successful stage work and is still in the German repertory. It was staged in London as *The Cousin From Nowhere* and in New York as *Caroline,* and it was revived in the United States in 2002 by Ohio Light Opera as *The Cousin From Batavia.*

1934 Zoch film
German feature film: Georg Zoch (director/screenplay), Bruno Monid (cinematographer), Franz Marszalek (music director), Victor Klein Film (production).
Cast: Lien Deyers (Julia), Lizzi Holzschuh, Walter von Lennep, Rudolf Platte.
Black and white. In German. 74 minutes.

1953 Anton film

German feature film: Karl Anton (director), Central-Europa (production group).

Cast: Vera Molnar (Julia), Gerhard Riedmann, Joachim Brenneck, Ina Halley, Grethe Weiser.

Black and white. In German. 95 minutes.

VIAGGIO A REIMS, IL
1825 opera by Rossini

Il viaggio a Reims (The Voyage to Rheims) never actually happens in this delightful comic opera by GIOACHINO ROSSINI. A group of aristocrats from all over Europe stop at the Golden Lily Hotel on their way to the coronation of Charles X in Paris, but a lack of horses keeps them from traveling on. They wile away the time with stories and songs and, although there is not much plot, there are 10 starring roles and lots of good humor about national characteristics. The opera was virtually unstaged for 100 years, but it was successfully revived in Pesaro in 1984 with a remarkable all-star cast and seems to have returned to the repertory.

1984 Pesaro Festival

Italian stage production: Luca Ronconi (director), Claudio Abbado (conductor, Pesaro Chamber Orchestra and Chorus).

Cast: Katia Ricciarelli (Madama Cortese), Cecilia Gasdia (Corinna), Lella Cuberli (Contessa di Folleville), Lucia Valentini-Terrani (Marchesa Melibea), Samuel Ramey (Lord Sidney), Ruggero Raimondi (Don Profondo), Francisco Araiza (Conte di Libenskof), Edoardo Giménez (Cavalier Belfiore), Enzo Dara (Barone di Trombonok), Leo Nucci (Don Alvaro).

Video: House of Opera DVD/VHS. Taped at the Pesaro Festival on August 25, 1984. Color. In Italian. 180 minutes.

1988 Vienna State Opera

Austrian stage production: Luca Ronconi (director), Claudio Abbado (conductor, Vienna State Opera Orchestra and Chorus).

Cast: Montserrat Caballé (Madama Cortese), Cecilia Gasdia (Corinna), Lella Cuberli (Contessa di Folleville), Lucia Valentini-Terrani (Marchesa Melibea), Ferruccio Furlanetto (Lord Sidney), Ruggero Raimondi (Don Profondo), Enzo Dara (Barone di Trombonok) Chris Merritt (Conte di Libenskof), Frank Lopardo (Cavalier Belfiore. Telecast February 7, 1988, on ORF in Austria. Brian Large (director). Color. In Italian. 165 minutes.

Related films

1988 Backstage at Il viaggio a Reims

A visit backstage at the Vienna State Opera during the presentation of the opera in 1988. Conductor Claudio Abbado and soprano Montserrat Caballé are among those interviewed by director Michael Fischer-Ledinice. Color. In German. 30 minutes.

1994 Clear and Present Danger

Music from *Il viaggio a Reims,* performed by the Plovdiv Philharmonic Orchestra, is featured on the soundtrack of this thriller about skullduggery in the CIA. Phillip Noyce directed. Color. 101 minutes.

VICK, GRAHAM
English director (1953–)

Graham Vick, one of the more radical and provocative stage directors working today, began with the Scottish Opera in 1984, joined the Birmingham Touring Opera in 1987, and quickly became known throughout Europe for his innovative productions. His 1984 *Madama Butterfly* at the English National Opera created a lot of discussion about its political viewpoint. His 1989 Royal Opera production of Berio's *Un re in ascolto* was staged as if it were a knockabout rehearsal at the Royal Opera. His operas on video include EUGENE ONEGIN (1994), FALSTAFF (1999), LULU (1996), MANON LESCAUT (1998), MITRIDATE (1991), PELLÉAS ET MÉLISANDE (1999), THE RAPE OF LUCRETIA (1987), and WAR AND PEACE (1991).

VICKERS, JON
Canadian tenor (1926–)

Jon Vickers made his stage debut in Toronto in 1954 and began almost at once to sing in televised operas, many now on video. He made his first appearance at Covent Garden in 1957 in *Un ballo in maschera* and then played Don Carlos in a famous production of the Verdi opera by Luchino Visconti. He sang in Dallas with Maria Callas in *Medea* and reached the Metropolitan Opera in 1960 as Canio in *Pagliacci,* one of his great roles. Vickers sang at the Met for more than 25 years and became one of its most popular performers. See THE BARTERED BRIDE (1978), CARMEN (1967), FIDELIO (1977), NORMA (1974), OTELLO (1974/1978), PAGLIACCI (1955/1968), PETER GRIMES (1981), SAMSON ET DALILA (1981), and TRISTAN UND ISOLDE (1973/1976).

1955–1956 Vickers Sings Verdi and Puccini

Highlights video with excerpts from three operas featuring Vickers presented on Canadian television in the 1950s: *Tosca* (May 25, 1955), *Il trovatore* (January 5,

1956), and *Manon Lescaut* (December 30, 1956). Lending support are Eva Likova, Mary Simmons, Louis Quilico, and the Montreal Radio Canada Orchestra under the direction of Jean Deslauriers and Ernest Barbini. CBC. Black and white. 80 minutes. VAI VHS.

1962–1964 Bell Telephone Hour
The video anthology *Corelli—Di Stefano—Vickers* showcases the three tenors as they appeared on *The Bell Telephone Hour* television show. Vickers sings the *Aida* Radames-Amneris duet "Già I sacerdoti adunansi" with Giulietta Simionato. Donald Voorhees conducts the Bell Telephone Hour Orchestra. Color. 36 minutes. VAI VHS.

1965 Karl Böhm & Jon Vickers in Concert
This is a record of a Toronto concert taped October 10, 1965. Vickers performs Siegmund's monologue and "Wintersturme" from *Die Walküre*, and Florestan's dungeon scene from *Fidelio*. Böhm conducts the overture to *Die Meistersinger* and other works. Black and white. 60 minutes. VAI VHS.

1974 Jon Vickers—A Man and His Music
This CBS Vancouver tribute mixes interviews, home sequences, rehearsals, and performance footage. Included are scenes of *Pagliacci* and *Fidelio* at Covent Garden, *Tristan und Isolde* with Birgit Nilsson at Orange, *Peter Grimes* at the Met, and *Otello* at Opéra du Quebec. Dick Bocking produced. Black and white and color. 90 minutes.

1984 Jon Vickers: Four Operatic Portraits
Vickers, in costume, performs scenes from four operas— *Fidelio, Otello, Peter Grimes,* and *Samson*—at a 1984 concert at the National Arts Center in Ottawa. The DVD includes the finale of *Die Walküre* in a 1969 concert with soprano Irene Lensky. Patrick Watson introduces selections, Franz-Paul Decker conducts the Montreal Symphony Orchestra, John Gemmill produced, and Paddy Samson directed the original CBC telecast December 6, 1984. Color. 60 minutes. VAI DVD/VHS.

VIDÉOTHÈQUES IN FRANCE

The vidéothèques in Paris and other cities in France are the Gallic equivalents of the Museum of Television and Radio in New York and Los Angeles. They allow visitors to view videos privately or on large screens, and they have many operas in their collections. The Vidéothèque International d'Art Lyrique et de Music in Aix-en-Provence has opera videos that are not commercially available, notably those from the Aix-en-Provence Festival, Marseilles Opera, and Opéra de Lyon. Like the

MTR, it has individual viewing booths. Admission is free. The Vidéothèque de Paris also has a large collection of opera videos, but its videos are shown on large screens, usually with discussions. It sometimes has weekends devoted to opera.

VIENNA

Vienna, the city of Mozart and the waltz, is a very musical town and has a long musical history. Its two principal opera houses, the world-famous Vienna State Opera (Staatsoper) and the delightful Volksoper, plus other beautiful venues and festival events, can be experienced on video. The Vienna City Hall is also used for concerts that include opera singers. Many operas, operettas, and operatic films are set in the city, including the frothy operetta film CONGRESS DANCES. See ANDREA CHÉNIER (1991), ARABELLA (1977), ARIADNE AUF NAXOS (1978), THE BARTERED BRIDE (1982), CARMEN (1979), THE CONSUL (1963), DON GIOVANNI (1954), ELEKTRA (1989), DIE ENTFÜHRUNG AUS DEM SERAIL (1954), FIDELIO (1978), FIERRABRAS (1988), DIE FLEDERMAUS (1972), GASPARONE (1983), LA GIOCONDA (1986), KHOVANSHCHINA (1989), LOHENGRIN (1990), CHRISTA LUDWIG (1992/1994), MANON (1983), MARCO POLO (1999), MASS (1971), MOZART REQUIEM (1991), LE NOZZE DI FIGARO (1954/1992), THE QUEEN OF SPADES (1992), A QUIET PLACE (1986), DER ROSENKAVALIER (1994), IL TROVATORE (1978), TURANDOT (1983), IL VIAGGIO A REIMS (1988), and WOZZECK (1987).

1991 Vienna New Year's Day Celebration
Carlos Kleiber conducts the Vienna Philharmonic's 150th anniversary celebration with the focus on Viennese operetta. José Carreras sings Lehár's "Dein is mein ganzes Herz" with Plácido Domingo conducting, and there is film of Richard Tauber singing "Vienna, City of My Dreams." Color. In German. 60 minutes.

1992 Christmas in Vienna
José Carreras and Plácido Domingo are the stars of this Christmas concert telecast from Vienna City Hall. Vjekoslav Sutej conducts the Vienna Symphony Orchestra. Christopher Swann directed. Color. 87 minutes. Sony VHS.

1993 Christmas Time in Vienna
Ruggero Raimondi, Plácido Domingo, and Dionne Warwick star in this Christmas concert telecast from Vienna City Hall. Vjekoslav Sutej conducts the Vienna Symphony Orchestra and Mozart Boys Choir. RAI. Color. 77 minutes.

1994 125 Years of the Vienna State Opera

Austrian documentary about the Vienna State Opera celebrating its 125th birthday with vintage excerpts of past performers, including Kiepura, Piccaver, and many others. Color. In German. 60 minutes. House of Opera VHS.

1994 Christmas Concert in Vienna

Plácido Domingo, Charles Aznavour, and Sissel Kyrkjeboe star in this Christmas concert telecast from the Vienna City Hall. Vjekoslav Sutej conducts the Vienna Symphony Orchestra. RAI TV. Color. 90 minutes.

VIE PARISIENNE, LA
1866 opéra-bouffe by Offenbach

JACQUES OFFENBACH's operetta *La vie parisienne* (Parisian Life), set in Paris in 1867, is a lively satirical farce on morals of the Second Empire by librettists Henri Meilhac and Ludovic Halévy. Men-about-town Gardefeu and Bobinet each think Métella is his mistress; when she spurns them both, they decide to seduce a tourist coming to Paris for the 1867 World Exhibition. A Swedish baron and his beautiful wife are tricked into believing that Raoul's house is a hotel so Gardefeu can seduce the baroness. His pretty glove-maker friend Gabrielle helps out, and she ends up with a Brazilian millionaire. The baron, who had arranged to meet Métella, becomes interested in the maid Pauline but ends up with his wife in disguise.

1935 Siodmak English film

English feature film titled *Parisienne Life*: Robert Siodmak (director), Emmerich Pressburger, Michel Carré and Benno Vigny (screenplay), Armand Thirard (cinematographer), Maurice Jaubert (music director).

Cast: Max Dearly (Mendoza), Conchita Montenegro (Helenita), Neil Hamilton, Eva Moore, Austin Trevor, Gertrude Goodner.

Black and white. In English. 95 minutes.

Comment: Heavily rewritten version of the operetta filmed in English and French (see below). In this variant, Brazilian millionaire Mendoza is the central character and is returning to Paris with his granddaughter Helenita after a 35-year absence. He soon meets up with his former mistress, the star of a 1900 production of Offenbach's *La vie parisienne*.

1935 Siodmak French film

French feature film titled *La vie parisienne*: Robert Siodmak (director), Michel Carré and Benno Vigny (screenplay), Maurice Jaubert (music director), Armand Thirard (cinematographer).

Cast: Max Dearly (Mendoza), Conchita Montenegro (Helenita), Georges Rigaud, Marcelle Praince, Austin Trevor, Germaine Aussey.

Black and white. In French. 95 minutes.

Comment: Filmed at the same time as the English film above with the same plot and a slightly different cast.

1977 Christian-Jaque film

French feature film: Christian-Jaque (director), Jacques Emmanuel (screenplay), Michel Carré (cinematographer).

Cast: Bernard Alane (Gardefeu), Jacques Balutin (Urbain), Jean-Pierre Darras (Baron), Martine Sarcey (Baroness), Georges Aminel (Brazilian), Evelyn Buyle (Gabrielle), Danvy Saval (Pauline).

Color. In French. 100 minutes.

1991 Opéra de Lyon

French stage production: Alain Francon (director), Jean-Yves Ossonce (conductor, Opéra National de Lyon Orchestra), Carlo Tommasi (set designer).

Cast: Jean-François Sivadier (Gardefeu), Jacques Verzier (Bobinet), Hélène Delavault (Métella), Jean-Yves Chateleais (Baron), Claire Wauthion (Baroness), Isabelle Mazin (Gabrielle), Pierre-François Pistorio (Brazilian), Nathaline Joly (Pauline).

Video: Kultur and Arthaus (GB) DVD/Kultur and Home Vision VHS/Pioneer LD. Pierre Cavassilas (director). Color. In French with English subtitles. 159 minutes.

Comment: Stylized and lively, although not exactly comic.

VIKTORIA UND IHR HUSAR
1930 operetta by Abraham

Viktoria und ihr Husar (Victoria and Her Hussar) is the most popular operetta by the Hungarian composer PAUL ABRAHAM. Hungarian Countess Viktoria believes her beloved Hussar husband Koltay died in World War I. She marries American ambassador John Cunlight but then discovers that her first husband is still alive. The ambassador realizes she still loves her Hussar and arranges to give her up. The plot resembles a travelogue as it moves around the world from Siberia, Tokyo, and St. Petersburg to Hungary. After premiering in Budapest, the operetta was a hit in Vienna, Berlin, Montreal, and London.

1931 Oswald film

German feature film: Richard Oswald (director), Robert Liebmann (screenplay), Reimar Kuntze (cinematographer), Rolf Jacobi (music director), Roto film (production).

Cast: Michael Bohnen, Friedel Schuster, Ivan Petrovitch, Gretl Theimer, Ernst Verebes, Willi Stettner.

Black and white. In German. 96 minutes.

1954 Schündler film
German feature film: Rudolf Schündler (director), Allfram/Sonor (production).

Cast: Eva Bartok (Viktoria), Frank Felder, Rudolf Forster.

Black and white. In German. 95 minutes.

1992 Operette, che Passione!
Italian TV production: Sandro Massimini (director/producer), Roberto Negri (pianist), Sandro Corelli (choreographer).

Cast: Sandro Massimini, Sara Dilena, Max René Cosotti.

Video: Ricordi (Italy) VHS. Pierluigi Pagano (director). Color. In Italian. About 19 minutes.

Comment: Highlights of the operetta in Italian as *Vittoria e il suo Ussaro* on the TV series *Operette, che Passione!* Featured songs are "Oh Mister Brown," "Toujours l'amour," and "Tangolita."

VILLAGE ROMEO AND JULIET, A
1907 opera by Delius

FREDERICK DELIUS's opera *A Village Romeo and Juliet*, libretto by the composer, is in English, but his libretto is based on a story by Gottfried Keller set in Switzerland, and the premiere was in Berlin in a German translation. Sali and Vreli are the children of neighboring farmers Manz and Marti, who are engaged in a bitter feud over land. When the children grow up and fall in love, they become outcasts from their families. They are encouraged by the mysterious Dark Fiddler to elope and end up fleeing down the river on a boat that they decide to sink.

***1989 Weigl Film
Czech feature film: Petr Weigl (director/screenplay), Charles Mackerras (conductor, ORF Symphony Orchestra and Arnold Schönberg Choir), Jaroslav Kucera (cinematographer), Karel Lier (production designer).

Cast: Thomas Hampson (Dark Fiddler), Michal Dlouhy (Sali, sung by Arthur Davies), Dana Moravkova (Vreli, sung by Helen Field), Leopold Haverl (Manz, sung by Barry Mora), Pavel Mikulik (Marti, sung by Stafford Dean), Jan Kalous (Sali as child, sung by Samuel Linay), Katerina Svobodova (Vreli as child, sung by Pamela Mildenhall).

Video: London VHS/LD. Color. In English. 113 minutes.

Comment: A beautiful and effective film shot on location in Czechoslovakia with everyone but Hampson miming to a recording.

VILLARROEL, VERONICA
Chilean soprano (1962–)

Veronica Villarroel, a frequent partner for Plácido Domingo, made her debut at the Met in 1991 as Mimì in *La bohème* and played Nedda in *Pagliacci* on the Met season opening night in 1999. She began her singing career in Santiago, was discovered there by Renata Scotto, studied at Juilliard, and first attracted world attention singing Fiordiligi at the Teatro Liceu in Barcelona in 1990. Her debut at the Royal Opera in 1996 in the Verdi opera gained her comparison to Ileana Cotrubas, who also sang the role. Villarroel can be seen on video with Domingo in IL GUARANY (1994) and EL GATO MONTÉS (1994), and she has recorded both with him. She sings Leonora opposite José Cura in a Royal Opera production of IL TROVATORE (2002), which was televised and is on DVD.

VILLER, CLAUS
TV opera director (1961-)

Claus Viller has directed a number of important operas for television in Austria, France, and Germany that are available on video. They include major productions from the Salzburg and Schwetzingen festivals, including Cecilia Bartoli's breakthrough appearance in IL BARBIERE DI SIVIGLIA (1988) and two operas by Salieri. See LA CENERENTOLA (1988), LE CINESE (1987), DON GIOVANNI (1987), ECHO ET NARCISSE (1987), FALSTAFF (Salieri, 1995), L'ITALIANA IN ALGERI, (1987), LUISA MILLER (1988), IL MATRIMONIO SEGRETO (1986), L'OCCASIONE FA IL LADRO (1992), IL RITORNO D'ULISSE IN PATRIA (1985), LA SCALA DI SETA (1989), IL SIGNOR BRUSCHINO (1989), TANCREDI (1992), and TARARE (1988).

VILLI, LE
1884 opera by Puccini

Le villi (The Willis) was GIACOMO PUCCINI's first opera and was successful enough to encourage the young composer to make opera his career. The "villi" of the title are the ghosts of abandoned women who return to haunt untrue lovers and dance them to death. Anna is engaged to Roberto, but he leaves her to collect an inheritance and never returns. She dies of grief, and her ghost is called back by her vengeful father. Roberto believes that she is alive, but she and other villi force him to dance until he dies of exhaustion. The libretto by Ferdinando Fontana is based on the same legend as the ballet *Giselle*. *Le villi* has not become a part of the repertory and is rarely staged, but it is on CD and video.

1986 Tokyo television
> Japanese television production: Music performed by unknown orchestra.
> Cast: Ms. Yamagi (Anna), Mr. Atsuma (Roberto).
> Video: Opera Dubs VHS. Color. In Italian. 75 minutes.

VINAY, RAMÓN
Chilean tenor/baritone (1911–1996)

Ramón Vinay, who began his opera career in Mexico in 1931 as a baritone, shifted to tenor roles in 1943. He went to New York as Don José in *Carmen* and sang at the Metropolitan for 17 seasons between 1946 to 1966. He was especially popular for his portrayal of *Otello;* he inaugurated seasons with the opera at La Scala in 1947 and at the Met in 1948, and he recorded the role with Toscanini. Vinay began to sing Wagner roles at Bayreuth during the 1950s and resumed singing baritone parts in 1962. See OTELLO (1948).

VINGT-HUIT JOURS DE CLAIRETTE, LES
1892 operetta by Roger

VICTOR ROGER composed more than 30 operettas, but *Les vingt-huit jours de Clairette* (Clairette's 28 Days) is his most popular work by far and has been filmed several times. The "28 days" of the title is the military service requirement of the time. Clairette spends them disguised as a soldier through a series of mix-ups. She is trying to prevent her husband Vivarel from being seduced by his former mistress, Bérénice, who doesn't know he is now married. An English version titled *Trooper Clairette* was staged in London in 1892, and an American one called *The Little Trooper* was produced in New York in 1894.

1933 Hugon film
> French feature film: André Hugon (director), Paul Fékété (screenplay), Marc Bujard (cinematographer), Robert-Jules Garnier (art director), Gaumont (production company).
> Cast: Mireille (Clairette), Jean Guise (Bérénice), Armand Bernard (Michonnet), Berval (Vivarel), Robert Hasti (Captain).
> Black and white. In French. 98 minutes.

Early films

1902 De 28 Dagen van Clairette
One of the early Dutch sound films was an aria from the operetta titled *De 28 Dagen van Clairette*. It was screened in the Netherlands in September 1902 at Alber's Electro Talking Bioscope, fresh from France where the operetta had been a recent success. Black and white. In Dutch. 3 minutes.

1927 I 28 giorni de Claretta
Italian director Eugenio Perego wrote and directed *I 28 giorni de Claretta,* a full-length silent version of the operetta. Italian silent movie diva Leda Gys stars as Clairette opposite Silvio Orsini. Pittaluga Film produced. Black and white. About 75 minutes.

VISCONTI, LUCHINO
Italian opera/film director (1906–1976)

Luchino Visconti occupies a unique position as a major figure in both opera and cinema. His influence on opera production was enormous, especially in restoring quality staging and through working with Maria Callas. He never made a film of an opera, but he featured opera scenes and music in many of his films, and his filmmaking style has been called "operatic realism." He claimed that the operatic connection began at birth, as he was born in Milan as the curtain went up at La Scala. His cinema career began in 1940, assisting Jean Renoir with TOSCA. He directed his first film, *Ossessione,* in 1942 and followed it with the visually operatic *La terra trema.* His *Bellissima* (1951) uses music from Donizetti's L'ELISIR D'AMORE in a most creative manner. *Senso* (1954) begins in Venice's La Fenice Opera House with a striking production of IL TROVATORE. *The Leopard* (1963) has many operatic elements in its account of an aristocratic Sicilian family faced with political changes. *The Damned* (1969) combines opera and politics in a Wagnerian account of the fall of a German industrial family. *Death in Venice* (1971) makes an interesting contrast to the Britten opera, especially through its use of Mahler's music. *Ludwig* (1973) returns to Wagner in a colorful rendition of the life of the Bavarian king. *L'innocente* (1976) features an aria by Gluck. See LUDWIG II (1973), MADAMA BUTTERFLY (1971), and ORFEO ED EURIDICE (1976).

VISHNEVSKAYA, GALINA
Russian soprano (1926–)

Galina Vishnevskaya's autobiography is a portrait of an era as well as a strong-minded singer. Vishnevskaya lived through the horrors of the siege of Leningrad and the madness of Stalin, as well as the politics of the Bolshoi Opera. She joined the Bolshoi in 1952 and became famous for her portrayals of Tatyana in *Eugene Onegin* and Leonore in *Fidelio.* She created the role of Katherina in Shebalin's *The Taming of the Shrew* in 1957 and Natasha in Prokofiev's *War and Peace.* She sang at the Met in 1961 as Aida and Butterfly and at Covent Garden in 1962 as Aida. She left the USSR in 1974 in political exile with her husband Mstislav Rostropovich and moved to the United States. She stars in one Soviet opera film, is a featured singer in others, and is one of the sopranos highlighted in a documentary about *Tosca*. Her return visit to the USSR with her husband is also on film. Her 1984 autobiography, *Galina: A Russian Story*, became the basis of Marcel Landowski's 1996 opera *Galina*. In 2002 she opened an opera school in Moscow—the Galina Vishnevskaya Center for Opera Singing. See BOLSHOI OPERA (1999), BORIS GODUNOV (1989), EUGENE ONEGIN (1958), LADY MACBETH OF THE MTSENSK DISTRICT (1966/1999), TOSCA (1983 film), and WAR REQUIEM (1988).

1990 Soldiers of Music

Vishnevskaya and cellist husband Mstislav Rostropovich return to Moscow after 16 years of exile. The film follows them as they meet friends, visit places where they lived or worked, and remember the old days. Vishnevskaya passes by the Bolshoi Opera but refuses to enter the building. The film includes a concert at which Vishnevskaya sings an aria from *Madama Butterfly* and a song by Tchaikovsky. The filmmakers are Susan Froemke, Peter Gelb, Albert Maysles, and Bob Eisenhardt. Color. In English. 89 minutes. Sony VHS.

VITAPHONE OPERA FILMS
Early sound opera films (1926–1930)

The Vitaphone Corporation, the sound-on-disc system that Warner Bros. used to launch the sound era in the cinema, made a first step toward what was described as "movie grand opera" when it signed a contract with the Metropolitan Opera Company in June 1926. The contract gave them the exclusive right to engage Met artists for its films. At the same time the company leased Oscar Hammerstein's old Manhattan Opera House to film its productions. *The New York Times* predicted a great future for the system, commenting that "if the plans of the corporation work as expected, Main Street will no longer have to journey to Broadway to hear grand opera. The 'movie grand opera' will be brought to Main Street." The first three opera films were shown August 6, 1926, preceding the John Barrymore *Don Juan,* and featured Giovanni Martinelli, Marion Talley, and Anna Case. The Vitaphone films were usually one reel and ran from 4 to 10 minutes. William Sharman, who has written a definitive study of these films, lists 64 films of opera content made from 1926 to 1930. Most have survived, and Sir Paul Getty has funded the restoration of many of them. Roy Liebman's book *Vitaphone Films* (2002/McFarland) is a catalog of all the Vitaphone shorts and features. See FRANCES ALDA, PASQUALE AMATO, JOHN BARCLAY, ANNA CASE, GIUSEPPE DE LUCA, ADAM DIDUR, BENIAMINO GIGLI, CHARLES HACKETT, HOPE HAMPTON, MARY LEWIS, GIOVANNI MARTINELLI, ELEANOR PAINTER,

ROSA RAISA, GIACOMO RIMINI, ERNESTINE SCHUMANN-HEINK, MARION TALLEY, and JOHN CHARLES THOMAS.

1928 Between the Acts of the Opera

Willie and Eugene Howard imitate top opera stars in the Vitaphone comedy *Between the Acts of the Opera*. Black and white. About 7 minutes.

VIVALDI, ANTONIO
Italian composer (1678–1741)

Antonio Vivaldi is best known for concertos and violin music, but he made notable contributions to opera in his native Venice, and his operas may be coming back into vogue. Revival of interest began in Verona in 1978 when Pier Luigi Pizzi produced ORLANDO FURIOSO for the first time in the modern era; it was also staged in San Francisco in 1989, and both versions are on video. Cecilia Bartoli has also helped renew interest in Vivaldi operas through concerts and recordings of their arias. Vivaldi's first was produced in 1713, and he composed 44 more over the years, 16 of which survive. He worked in the *opera seria* style of the period, with ancient history and mythology as his subject; they are not strong on drama, but they are a delight to hear. The other Vivaldi operas on video are FARNACE and MONTEZUMA.

1987 Vivaldi

Biographical docu-drama shot on location in Venice with excerpts from operas and other works by Vivaldi. Violinist Corey Cerovsek plays Vivaldi as a young man, and violinist Steven Staryk plays him as an adult. Color. In English. 105 minutes. Films for the Humanities & Sciences VHS.

1993 Vivaldi

Lina Wertmuller made this Italian television biopic retracing Vivaldi's life and musical development; it includes excerpts from operas and *Juditha Triumphans*. Color. 55 minutes. Films for the Humanities & Sciences VHS.

1997 Vivaldi

Portrait of the composer with excerpts from his works played by the Moscow Symphony Orchestra led by David Palmer. Part of *The Great Composers* series. Color. In English. 25 minutes. Films for the Humanities & Sciences VHS.

1999 Bartoli on Vivaldi

Cecilia Bartoli discovers Vivaldi and his neglected operas in this fine documentary and records some of their arias. The music is performed by Il Giardino Armonico led by Giovanni Antonini. Melissa Raines shot the film for the *South Bank Show,* and it was telecast in October 1999. Color. In English and Italian. 60 minutes.

2000 Viva Vivaldi
Cecilia Bartoli performs arias from Vivaldi operas, the oratorio from *Juditha Triumphans,* and his *Gloria* at a recital at the Théâtre des Champs-Élysées in Paris in September 2000. The operas are *L'Olimpiade, Tito Manilo, Ottone in Villa, Farnace, Bajazet,* and *La fida ninfa.* The music is played by Il Giardino Armonico led by Giovanni Antonini. Color. 106 minutes Arthaus DVD.

Sheet music for Italian film *Vivere* (1937).

VIVERE
1937 film with opera content

Vivere (Live, i.e., Enjoy Living) was Italian opera tenor Tito Schipa's biggest film success. He plays a nightclub singer who becomes an opera star with the motto "Vivere," the title of his favorite song and his motto for his fast-paced lifestyle (the song was a huge popular hit). His daughter Paola (Caterina Boratto) marries a man he doesn't like (Nino Besozzi), but after a period of misery apart they become reconciled so he can sing the touching "Torna piccina mia" to her over the telephone. He also gets to sing arias by Cilea, Donizetti, and Scarlatti. Boratto is probably best known today for her role as the mystery woman in Fellini's *8½.* Otello Martelli was cinematographer, Amlato Palmieri wrote the screenplay, and Guido Brignone directed the film. Black and white. In Italian. 88 minutes.

VIVES, AMADEO
Spanish composer (1871–1932)

Amadeo Vives wrote more than 100 works for the stage, but his biggest successes were his zarzuelas. The delightful BOHEMIOS is a Spanish interpretation of Bohemian life in Paris, very different from Puccini's *La bohème* although based on the same book. The tune-filled DOÑA FRANCISQUITA is an updated version of a play by Lope de Vega. Both have been filmed many times. There is also a Spanish film of his lesser known Valencian zarzuela *Entre barracas.* Vives's best-known opera is MARUXA (1914), set in Galicia and sung in the language of the region. His operetta *La generala,* a Ruritanian satire set in England, is also still popular.

VOGELHÄNDLER, DER
1891 operetta by Zeller

CARL ZELLER's charming and tuneful operetta *Der Vogelhändler* (The Bird Seller), a story about rustic folk mixing with nobility in 18th-century Rhineland, features a princess in disguise and a man who pretends to be a prince. It also has two famous songs that have helped make the roles of Adam, the bird seller, and Christel, the postmistress, popular with singers; the one about roses in the Tyrol titled "Rosen in Tirol" has almost become a folk tune. Moritz West and Ludwig Held based their libretto on a French play.

1935 Emo film
German feature film: E. W. Emo (director); Max Wallner, M. West, L. Held (screenplay); Edward Daug (cinematographer); Fritz Wenneis (music director); Majestic Film (production).

Cast: Maria Andergast (Christel), Wolf-Albach Retty (Adam), Lil Dagover (Princess), Georg Alexander (Stanislaus), Hans Zesch-Ballot (Prince).

Black and white. In German. 80 minutes.

1940 Bolvary film
German feature film: Geza von Bolvary (director), Ernst Marischka (screenplay), Willy Winterstein (cinematographer), Franz Grothe (music director), Terra Film (production).

Cast: Marte Harell (Christel), Johannes Heesters (Adam), Hans Moser, Leo Slezak, Theo Lingen.

Video: UFA Klassiker (Germany) VHS. Black and white. In German. 97 minutes.

Comment: The film was titled *Rosen in Tirol* after the operetta's most famous song.

1953 Rabenalt film
German feature film: Arthur Maria Rabenalt (director), Berolina Film (production).
Cast: Ilse Werner (Christel), Gerhard Riedmann (Adam), Eva Probst, Ernie Mangold, Sybill Verden and Gert Reinhold (dancers).
Color. In German. 92 minutes.

1962 Cziffra film
German feature film: Geza von Cziffra (director/screenplay), Hagen Galatis and Kurt Feltz (music directors), Willy Winterstein (cinematographer), Divina Film (production).
Cast: Conny Froboess (Christel), Albert Reuprecht (Adam), Peter Weck (Stanislaus), Maria Sebaldt (Princess), Georg Thomalla (Prince), Rudolf Vogel (Weps), Rudolf Platte (Weckerli), Alice and Ellen Kessler (dancers).
Video: Taurus/German Language Video Center VHS. Color. In German. 88 minutes.

VOGLIO BENE SOLTANTO A TE
1946 Italian opera film

Voglio bene soltanto a te (I Want Only You) was Italian tenor Beniamino Gigli's first movie after World War II. He plays a tenor making a movie in Rome who fancies his female costar, Greta Gonda. Unfortunately, she spreads her favors around a bit, so he gets jealous and quits the film. After a while, he returns because the film crew cannot get other work, and this softens his lady-love's heart. The film includes music from *L'Africana, L'elisir d'amore, La favorita, Lohengrin, Martha, Tannhäuser,* and *Die Walküre,* plus clips from Gigli's 1940 film *Mamma.* Giovanni Pucci was the cinematographer, Guido Brignone wrote the screenplay based on the title song, and Giuseppe Fatigati directed for Itala Film. Black and white. In Italian. 80 minutes. Lyric/Opera Dubs VHS.

VOICE OF FIRESTONE, THE
American television opera series (1949–1963)

The Voice of Firestone was a prestigious television series, as it featured the top opera singers of its time in performance, most of them stars of the Metropolitan Opera. The program began as a radio show in 1928 and moved to television in 1949. It continued as a weekly show on NBC until 1954, when it was moved to ABC because of ratings problems. Kinescopes of these programs are a treasure trove of performances by top singers. Forty-one selections from the kinescopes, owned by the New England Conservatory of Music, have been issued on VAI VHS. Most focus on one singer, but there are also compilations devoted to sopranos, tenors, Verdi, and

French opera. Risë Stevens was the most popular artist on the program (47 appearances), followed by Eleanor Steber. The videos, all in black and white, begin and end with theme tunes written by Idabelle Firestone. The Voice of Firestone orchestra is usually conducted by Howard Barlow. For details, see LICIA ALBANESE, JUSSI BJÖRLING, NADINE CONNER, FRANCO CORELLI, LISA DELLA CASA, IGOR GORIN, JEROME HINES, DOROTHY KIRSTEN, GEORGE LONDON, JAMES MCCRACKEN, JEANETTE MACDONALD, LAURITZ MELCHIOR, ROBERT MERRILL, ANNA MOFFO, PATRICE MUNSEL, JAN PEERCE, ROBERTA PETERS, BIDÚ SAYÃO, ELEANOR STEBER, RISË STEVENS, JOAN SUTHERLAND, FERRUCCIO TAGLIAVINI, RENATA TEBALDI, BLANCHE THEBOM, HELEN TRAUBEL, RICHARD TUCKER, GIUSEPPE VERDI, and LEONARD WARREN.

1950–1963 The Great Sopranos
Compilation of highlights from *Voice of Firestone* programs with famous sopranos including Licia Albanese, Jeanette MacDonald, Anna Moffo, Patrice Munsel, Birgit Nilsson, Roberta Peters, Leontyne Price, Bidú Sayão, Eleanor Steber, Joan Sutherland, Renata Tebaldi, and Helen Traubel. Black and white. 58 minutes. VAI VHS.

1950–1963 The Great Tenors
Compilation of highlights from *Voice of Firestone* programs with famous tenors, including Jussi Björling, Franco Corelli, Nicolai Gedda, James McCracken, Lauritz Melchior, Jan Peerce, Ferruccio Tagliavini, Jess Thomas, and Richard Tucker. Black and white. 58 minutes. VAI VHS.

1959–1963 French Opera Gala
Highlights from French operas presented on *The Voice of Firestone* television shows. They are CARMEN with Robert Merrill, FAUST with Richard Tucker, and ROMÉO ET JULIETTE with Roberta Peters. For details, see entries under the opera. Black and white. In French with English introductions. 65 minutes. VAI VHS.

VOICES OF LIGHT
1994 film opera by Einhorn

American composer Richard Einhorn's opera/oratorio *Voices of Light* was created to be shown in synchronization with Carl Dreyer's 1928 silent film *La Passion de Jeanne d'Arc.* It is scored for orchestra, chorus, and four soloists, with the voice of Joan sung by two singers. The libretto is derived from writings by Joan and medieval mystics. Dreyer's film, among the most intensively powerful ever made, stars Falconetti as Joan in a screenplay based on transcripts of her trial. Einhorn's film opera premiered in Northampton, Massachusetts, in 1994 and was presented in the Hollywood Bowl in Los Angeles in

1995. Criterion DVD. Black and white. In English. 75 minutes.

VOIX HUMAINE, LA
1959 monodrama by Poulenc

Jean Cocteau's 1928 play *La voix humaine* (The Human Voice) enjoyed success on stage, radio, and film before it became an opera. FRANCIS POULENC, who used the play unchanged as libretto for his opera, composed it as a vehicle for soprano Denise Duval. It's a one-woman, one-act, one-set tour de force. A woman takes an overdose of pills and then calls her lover on the phone. She knows he is with another woman, but she cajoles, lies, begs, and pleads for his love.

1979 PBS Television
American TV production: Barbara Karp (director), Dino Anagnost (conductor, American Symphony Orchestra).
Cast: Karan Armstrong.
Telecast November 28, 1979, on PBS. Color. In English. 60 minutes.
Comment: Shown in the *Great Performances* series after a screening of the Cocteau play starring Liv Ullmann.

1990 Théâtre du Châtelet
French TV production: Alain Francon (director), Serge Baudo (conductor, Ensemble Orchestral de Paris), Yannis Kokkos (set/costume designer).
Cast: Gwyneth Jones.
Telecast April 12, 1990, on La Sept. Hugo Santiago (director). Color. In French. 57 minutes.

1990 Bavarian Television
German TV film: Peter Medak (stage/film director), Georges Prêtre (conductor, Orchestre National de France), Nicolas Dvigoubsky (set designer).
Cast: Julia Migenes.
Telecast April 4, 1991, on Bavarian Television, Munich. Color. In French. 50 minutes.

***1992 BBC Scotland
Scottish TV film: Mike Newman (director), José Serebrier (conductor, Scottish Chamber Orchestra), Iain McDonald (set designer), David Beeton (costume designer).
Cast: Carole Farley.
Video: London VHS/LD. Color. In French with English subtitles. 42 minutes.
Comment: Farley sings and acts superbly and always retains our sympathy in this excellent film.

Related films

1947 Rossellini film
Italian actress Anna Magnani stars as the woman on the phone in *La voce umana,* a film of the Cocteau play directed by Roberto Rossellini. Magnani won Italy's Best Actress award for her performance. It is half of the feature film *Amore.* Black and white. In Italian. 50 minutes.

1978 Quintero video
Swedish actress Liv Ullmann is the woman in this production of the play in English by José Quintero. It was staged in Australia as part of a one-woman tour, videotaped by Quintero in 1978, and telecast in 1979 on the PBS series *Great Performances* with the opera. Color. In English. 50 minutes.

VON STADE, FREDERICA
American mezzo-soprano (1945–)

Frederica von Stade, one of the most admired singers of her generation, has created a number of roles in modern operas. Born in New Jersey, she studied in New York and made her debut at the Met in 1970 as Third Boy in *Die Zauberflöte.* She built a reputation in Europe in 1973 in Paris and Glyndebourne singing Cherubino in *Le nozze di Figaro,* a performance that is on video from Glyndebourne, Paris, and the Met. She is much liked for her other trouser roles as well, including Octavian, Sesto, the Composer, and Hansel, but is equally splendid as Cinderella in Massenet's CENDRILLON (1979/1982) and Rossini's LA CENERENTOLA (1981). Among the roles she has created are Merteuil in Susa's THE DANGEROUS LIAISONS (1994), Tina in Argento's THE ASPERN PAPERS (1988), Maria in Villa-Lobos's *Yerma,* and Nina in Pasatieri's *The Seagull.* See LEONARD BERNSTEIN (1988/1994), CARNEGIE HALL (1991/1998), ANTONÍN DVOŘÁK (1993), SIMON ESTES (1990), GEORGE GERSHWIN (1998), GLYNDEBOURNE (1992), HÄNSEL UND GRETEL (1982) IDOMENEO (1982), JAMES LEVINE (1996), METROPOLITAN OPERA (1983/1991), LE NOZZE DI FIGARO (1973/1980/1985), ON THE TOWN (1992), DER ROSENKAVALIER (1992 film), GIOACHINO ROSSINI (1992), SAN FRANCISCO (1997), and WERTHER (1986 film).

1987 Christmas with Flicka
Von Stade has had the nickname of Flicka since childhood. In this video she celebrates Christmas in the Alpine village of St. Wolfgang with children, townspeople, conductor Julius Rudel, Melba Moore, and Rex Smith. She sings 18 seasonal airs, from "O Tannenbaum" and "Deck the Halls" to "Rise Up Shepherd and Follow," plus music by Handel and Mozart. Color. 58 minutes. VIEW VHS.

1990 Flicka and Friends

Von Stade is joined by bass Samuel Ramey and tenor Jerry Hadley in a program of music by Donizetti, Gounod, Kern, Massenet, Meyerbeer, Mozart, and Rossini. Henry Lewis conducts the Orchestra of St. Luke's and New York Concert Singers. Telecast April 18, 1990. Color. 150 minutes.

VOSS

1986 Australian opera by Meale

Australia in 1845. Johann Voss, who wants to be the first European to cross Australia, leads an expedition into the interior. In Sydney his spiritual soul mate Laura Trevelyan, whose uncle is the sponsor of the expedition, communicates with him mentally and by letter. The expedition ends in disaster. RICHARD MEALE's opera *Voss,* libretto by David Malouf based on the 1957 novel by Patrick White, was premiered on March 1, 1986, by Australian Opera at the Adelaide Festival. Geoffrey Chard sang the role of Voss, Marilyn Richardson was Laura, Jim Sharman directed, and Stuart Challender conducted the Sydney Symphony Orchestra. Meale's score is traditional and melodious, with frequent use of 19th-century Australian tunes.

1987 Australian Opera

Australian stage production: Jim Sharman (director), Stuart Challender (conductor, State Orchestra of Victoria), Brian Thomson (set designer).

Cast: Geoffrey Chard (Voss), Marilyn Richardson (Laura), Robert Gard (Frank Le Mesurier), Clifford Grant (Mr. Bonner), Heather Begg (Mrs. Bonner), John Pringle (Palfreyman), Anne-Maree McDonald (Belle Bonner), Paul Ferris (Lt. Tom Radclyffe), Harry Robarts (Gregory), Robert Eddie (Judd).

Video: Premiere/ABC Video Arts (Australia) VHS. Telecast on ABC. Peter Butler (director). Color. In English. 110 minutes.

W

WAFFENSCHMIED, DER
1846 comic opera by Lortzing

Albert Lortzing's 1846 comic opera *Der Waffenschmied* (The Armorer) is set in the city of Worms in the 16th century. Count Liebenau loves Marie, the daughter of Hans Stadinger, but he disapproves of aristocrats. The count disguises himself as a commoner and goes to work for him as the armorer Konrad. After many problems, all ends happily.

1982 Salzburg Marionette Theatre
Austrian puppet production: Karlheinz Hundorf (director), Peter Schneider (conductor, Stuttgart Symphony Orchestra), Günther Schneider-Siemssen (set designer).

Cast: Kurt Moll (Hans Stadinger), Monika Schmitt (Marie), Ludwig Baumann (Count Liebenau).

Telecast November 21, 1982, on ORF Austrian Television. Color. In German. 60 minutes.

Comment: The Marionettetheater Salzburg specializes in shortened versions of operas and operettas. Many are available on DVD, with introductions by Peter Ustinov.

Early film

1919 Delog Company
The German Delog Company filmed the opera in 1919 and sent it on tour with soloists, chorus, and a small orchestra. This was seen as a way of bringing opera to small towns at low cost without building sets. Black and white. Silent. About 70 minutes.

WAGNER, RICHARD
German composer (1813–1883)

Richard Wagner is one of the most important and, at the same time, one of the most controversial figures in music history. He influenced almost everyone, but it is sometimes difficult to separate his music from his ideas and the admiration he inspired in people such as Hitler. Wagner wrote his own librettos and composed operas that admirers claim are the ultimate opera experience; de-

tractors say they are overblown. He began creating operas in 1832, and his musical genius quickly became evident with DER FLIEGENDE HOLLÄNDER, TANNHÄUSER, and LOHENGRIN. As his ideas about unified music drama developed, he turned to pre-Christian Teutonic myth and wrote the longest and most complex work in opera, DER RING DES NIBELUNGEN, which consists of four operas with a continuous narrative: DAS RHEINGOLD, DIE WALKÜRE, SIEGFRIED, and GÖTTERDÄMMERUNG. Wagner thought so highly of them that he built an opera house in BAYREUTH to stage them; his last and most pretentious opera, PARSIFAL, was meant to be presented nowhere else. His other major operas, all on video, are DIE MEISTERSINGER VON NÜRNBERG and TRISTAN UND ISOLDE. Wagner's life has inspired numerous film biographies since the early days of cinema, and he figures prominently in films about his patron King LUDWIG II. Among those who have played him on screen are Richard Burton, Trevor Howard, and Alan Badel. His music is often used for atmospheric effect in non-operatic films, including such classics as *L'age d'or*, *Dracula*, and *Apocalypse Now*.

1913 Richard Wagner
Italian composer Giuseppe Becce stars as Wagner in this feature-length German film produced by Oskar Messter. The movie reached New York in November 1913 as *The Life of Richard Wagner*. Carl Froelich, who directed it, continued to work in German cinema until 1951. As well as acting, Becce also scored the Wagner music that was performed with the film, the first score specially created for a German film. He became an important film music composer and wrote influential books about music and silent cinema. Black and white. Silent. About 60 minutes.

1925 Wagner
One-reel silent movie about Wagner's life and career made for the series *British Music Masters*. It features a number of scenes from the operas, and they were screened with Wagner's music played by a small orchestra. Black and white. Silent. About 10 minutes.

1956 Magic Fire
Alan Badel plays Wagner in this Hollywood-style biography filmed on location in Germany. It was based on a novel by Bertita Harding and describes Wagner's life from age 21 to his death. Yvonne De Carlo is first wife Minna, Rita Gam is Cosima, Carlos Thompson is Franz Liszt, and Valentina Cortese is his patroness Mathilde. The opera scenes were staged in Munich by Rudolf Hartmann with the Bavarian State Opera and Alois Melichar conducting. Erich Wolfgang Korngold, who plays conductor Hans Richter in the film, arranged and conducted the rest of the music ("to protect Wagner," he claimed), including condensing the music of the *Ring* to

3 minutes. Novelist Harding, E. A. Dupont, and David Chantler wrote the screenplay, Ernest Haller was cinematographer, and Wilhelm Dieterle directed for Republic Pictures. Color. 94 minutes.

1960 Song Without End
Lyndon March plays Wagner in this romantic Hollywood biography of composer Franz Liszt. (played by Dirk Bogarde). Charles Vidor and George Cukor directed. Color. 141 minutes

1975 The Confessions of Winifred Wagner
Hans-Jürgen Syberberg's film about Winifred Wagner, the 78-year-old English-born widow of Wagner's son Siegfried, is fascinating as an exploration of the Wagner-Hitler connection. Hitler attended more than 100 performances at Bayreuth, which he helped finance while Winifred administered it from 1931 to 1945. Hitler considered *Parsifal* a mirror of his own philosophy and made annual visits to Wagner's house Wahnfried. The film was shown in America and England as *The Confessions of Winifred Wagner;* the German title is *Winifred Wagner und die Geschichte des Hauses Wahnfried 1914–1975.* Color. In German. 105 minutes.

1975 Lisztomania
Paul Nicholas plays Wagner in this extravagant Ken Russell biopic. Veronica Quilligan is Cosima and Roger Daltrey has the role of Liszt. Color. In English. 105 minutes.

1982 Wagner and Venice
Orson Welles narrates this documentary about Wagner's visits to Venice from 1858 to 1883 by using the composer's letters and poems as text. Wagner wrote much of *Tristan und Isolde* in Venice. The film includes a sequence built around Siegfried's Funeral March, with the orchestra on a boat on the Grand Canal. Petr Ruttner wrote and directed. Color. 43 minutes. Italtoons VHS.

1983 Wagner
Richard Burton plays Wagner in Tony Palmer's epic film written by playwright Charles Wood. The nine-hour movie was shot on location in 200 sites in six countries, including Ludwig's castles and Wagner's residences. Vanessa Redgrave is Cosima, Gemma Craven is Minna, Lászlo Gálffi is Ludwig II, and the starry supporting cast includes Laurence Olivier, John Gielgud, Ralph Richardson, Cyril Cusack, Franco Nero, Marthe Keller, Ronald Pickup, William Walton, Joan Plowright, and Arthur Lowe. Vittorio Storaro was the indefatigable cinematographer, and Sir Georg Solti conducted the music. Color. 300 minutes as a feature film, 540 minutes on video. Kultur VHS (four cassettes).

1984 Richard Wagner: The Man & His Music
This biography of Wagner is combined with a mini-guide to the *Ring* cycle. It explains Wagner's development as an opera composer; shows his relationship with family, friends, and King Ludwig; and discusses the influence of his stay in Venice. Color. 58 minutes. On VHS.

1987 Richard and Cosima
Otto Sander is Wagner and Tatja Seibt is Cosima in Peter Patzak's Austrian film that treats their love story as a romantic drama that turns into a tragic myth. Reinhard Baumgartner wrote the screenplay, and Anton Peschke was the cinematographer. The soundtrack music is played by the SWF Symphony Orchestra conducted by Pierre Boulez and Erich Leinsdorf. Color. In German. 108 minutes.

1988 Wagner Concert in Leipzig
A concert of overtures and vocal music from Wagner operas held at the new Leipzig Gewandhaus and conducted by Kurt Masur. Theo Adam sings excerpts from *Die Meistersinger,* and Karan Armstrong sings the Liebestod from *Tristan und Isolde.* Color. In German. 90 minutes. Kultur VHS.

1996 Famous Composers: Richard Wagner
Documentary about the life and music of the composer featuring excerpts from his works. Color. 30 minutes. Kultur VHS.

1997 Great Composers: Wagner
BBC Television documentary about Wagner narrated by Kenneth Branagh, with commentary from critics and excerpts from performances of 10 operas. Color. In English. 60 minutes. Warner Music/NVC Arts DVD.

1998 Richard Wagner
An examination of Wagner's operas and the events in his life that inspired them. There are brief excerpts from *The Flying Dutchman, Lohengrin, Tristan und Isolde, Parsifal, Tännhauser* (Sir George Solti conducting), and the *Ring* cycle (Pierre Boulez conducting). Part of the series *Harmonics: The Innovators of Classical Music.* Color. In English. 28 minutes. Films for the Humanities & Sciences VHS.

WALKÜRE, DIE
1870 opera by Wagner

Die Walküre (The Valkyrie) is the second opera in RICHARD WAGNER's epic tetralogy *Der Ring des Nibelungen.* Siegmund and Sieglinde, mortals who are the children of Wotan, do not know they are brother and sister. They fall in love and he forges the sword Nothung.

When her husband Hunding and Siegmund fight, the Valkyrie Brünnhilde sides with her siblings against her father Wotan. Wotan kills Siegmund by shattering the sword and punishes Brünnhilde by putting her to sleep in a circle of fire. The "Ride of the Valkyries" music, the prelude to Act III, is often used in non-operatic movies.

1980 Bayreuth Festival

German stage production: Patrice Chéreau (director), Pierre Boulez (conductor, Bayreuth Festival Orchestra and Chorus), Richard Peduzzi (set designer), Jacques Schmidt (costumes).

Cast: Gwyneth Jones (Brünnhilde), Peter Hofmann (Siegmund), Jeannine Altmeyer (Sieglinde), Donald McIntyre (Wotan), Matti Salminen (Hunding), Hanna Schwarz (Fricka).

Video: Philips DVD/VHS/LD. Brian Large (director). Color. In German with English subtitles. 216 minutes.

Comment: This is a reprise of the 1976 Bayreuth Festival centenary production, with the action apparently set in the 19th century.

1989 Bavarian State Opera

German stage production: Nikolaus Lehnhoff (director), Wolfgang Sawallisch (conductor, Bavarian State Opera Orchestra and Chorus), Erich Wonder (set designer).

Cast: Hildegard Behrens (Brünnhilde), Robert Schunk (Siegmund), Julia Varady (Sieglinde), Robert Hale (Wotan), Kurt Moll (Hunding), Marjana Lipovsek (Fricka).

Video: EMI VHS/Dreamlife (Japan) LD. Shokichi Amano (director). Color. In German with English subtitles. 235 minutes.

Comment: This is a highly modernist production with symbolic high-tech sets.

***1989 Metropolitan Opera

American stage production: Otto Schenk (director), James Levine (conductor, Metropolitan Opera Orchestra and Chorus) Günther Schneider-Siemssen (set designer), Rolf Langenfass (costume designer).

Cast: Hildegard Behrens (Brünnhilde), Gary Lakes (Siegmund), Jessye Norman (Sieglinde), James Morris (Wotan), Kurt Moll (Hunding), Christa Ludwig (Fricka).

Video: DG DVD/VHS/LD. Taped April 8, 1989; telecast June 19, 1990. Brian Large (director). Color. In German with English subtitles. 244 minutes.

Comment: This is a traditional production with naturalistic sets, probably the nearest on video to what Wagner would have staged.

1989 Leonie Rysanek in Act I

Leonie Rysanek sings Sieglinde in a Madrid concert performance of Act I opposite Siegfried Jerusalem and Philip Kang. Arpád Joó conducts. Color. In German. 71 minutes. Lyric VHS.

1991 Bayreuth Festival

German stage production: Harry Kupfer (director), Daniel Barenboim (conductor, Bayreuth Festival Orchestra and Chorus), Hans Schavernoch (set designer), Reinhard Heinrich (costume designer).

Cast: Anne Evans (Brünnhilde), Poul Elming (Siegmund), Nadine Secunde (Sieglinde), John Tomlinson (Wotan), Matthias Hölle (Hunding), Linda Finnie (Fricka).

Video: Teldec VHS/LD. Horant H. Hohlfeld (director). Color. In German with English subtitles. 233 minutes.

Comment: This is a modernist production with minimalist sets.

1996 Jutland Opera

Danish stage production: Klaus Hoffmeyer (director), Francesco Cristofoli (conductor, Aarhus Symphony Orchestra), Lars Juhl (set/costume designer).

Cast: Poul Elming (Siegmund), Tina Kiberg (Sieglinde), Lars Waage (Wotan), Lisbeth Balslev (Brünnhilde), Aage Haugland (Hunding), Sylvia Lindenstrand.

Video: Musikhuset Aarhus (Denmark) VHS. Telecast on Danmarks Radio, Copenhagen. Thomas Grimm (director). Color. In German. 231 minutes.

Comment: For those who prefer an all-Danish cast.

Early/related films

1915 The Birth of a Nation

D. W. Griffith compiled a potpourri of 19th-century classics as the score for his silent epic, including "The Ride of the Valkyries," played when the Ku Klux Klan rides. Videos that use the original score will include the Wagner music. Black and white. 159 minutes. On DVD and VHS.

1936 The Big Broadcast of 1938

Met soprano Kirsten Flagstad sings Brünnhilde's battle cry "Ho-jo-to-ho!" with the Metropolitan Opera Orchestra under the baton of Wilfrid Pelletier. Flagstad's scene for the film, one of many unconnected numbers, was shot at the Eastern Service Studios at Astoria, Long Island. It was her only film. Mitchell Leisen directed for Paramount. Black and white. In English. 100 minutes.

1942 Three Hearts for Julia
"The Ride of the Valkyries" is featured during a rehearsal by an all-women orchestra while first violinist Julia (Ann Sothern) is breaking up with her husband Jeff (Melvyn Douglas). Richard Thorpe directed for MGM. Black and white. 89 minutes.

1946 Voglio bene soltanto a te
Beniamino Gigli plays a tenor making a movie who fancies a costar who prefers a younger man. The film soundtrack includes music from *Die Walküre*. See VOGLIO BENE SOLTANTO A TE.

1970 The Clowns
Federico Fellini features "The Ride of the Valkyries" music ironically on the soundtrack in this brilliant semi-documentary about the world of clowns. Color. In Italian. 93 minutes.

1974 Mahler
One of the most bizarre uses of "The Ride of the Valkyries" in cinema occurs in Ken Russell's weird biography of composer Gustav Mahler. Russell wrote new English lyrics to the melody, and they are sung by Mahler (Robert Powell) and Cosima Wagner (Antonia Ellis) in a symbolic Valhalla scene. The scene is meant to show the composer converting from Judaism to Christianity to further his career. Cosima tells him "You're no longer a Jew, boy, now you're one of us, now you're a goy, you can conduct opera." This scene is in such bad taste that it has to be seen to be believed. Color. In English. 115 minutes. Thorn EMI VHS.

1977 That Obscure Object of Desire
The duet from *Die Walküre* by twins Siegmund and Sieglinde is featured in the final moments of *Cet obscur objet du désir,* a satirical film by Luis Buñuel about sexual obsession. Fernando Rey is an old man obsessed with young Conchita, portrayed by Carol Bouquet and Angela Molina. At the end of the film, a loudspeaker in a Madrid shopping mall gives news about terrorist activity and then plays the duet. As Siegmund explains that at last he knows what has captured his heart, Rey watches a woman sewing threads of fate in a window. A few seconds later a bomb blows up the shopping mall. The duet is sung by James King and Leonie Rysanek with Karl Böhm conducting. Color. In French. 100 minutes. Embassy VHS.

1979 Apocalypse Now
Francis Ford Coppola made memorable and effective use of music from *Die Walküre* in his film *Apocalypse Now.* Air Cavalry Colonel Robert Duvall leads a noisy helicopter charge on the Vietcong by blasting them with "The Ride of the Valkyries" as well as guns and rockets.

The music is played by the Vienna Philharmonic led by Georg Solti. Color. In English. 150 minutes. Paramount VHS.

1997 L. A. Confidential
The Magic Fire music is, rather appropriately, heard on a TV set as a tough Los Angeles cop (Russell Crowe) breaks into a house to rescue a kidnapped woman and slay the dragon-like thug holding her. Curtis Hanson directed. Color. 136 minutes.

2001 Freddy Got Fingered
The Vienna Philharmonic plays "The Ride of the Valkyries" on the soundtrack of this film starring and directed by comic Tom Green. It is considered one of the truly bad movies of the new millennium. Color. In English. 86 minutes.

2001 Super Troopers
Another really bad American comedy trying to find a laugh by using "The Ride of the Valkyries" on the soundtrack. This recording is by the St. Petersburg Symphony Orchestra. Jay Shandrasekhar directed. Color. 100 minutes.

WALLACE, VINCENT
Irish composer (1812–1865)

Vincent Wallace, one of the major British opera composers of the 19th century, became internationally famous for his 1845 MARITANA about a king infatuated with a gypsy. It was such an enormous hit that it influenced many other composers, including even Bizet on *Carmen.* Wallace, who was born in Waterford, was one of the big three Irish composers' with Balfe and Benedict. Like them, he was a one-opera wonder and was never able to repeat this success, although he wrote five more operas. *Maritana* has been filmed three times.

WALLY, LA
1892 opera by Catalani

Italian composer ALFREDO CATALANI is remembered primarily for his wonderful opera *La Wally,* a kind of mountain Romeo and Juliet story with superb music. The Wally of the title is a young woman in a small Tyrolean village in the early 19th century who has an ill-fated love affair with Hagenbach, the son of a family enemy. The libretto by Puccini collaborator Luigi Illica has resemblances to *La bohème* and *Tosca* but is actually based on a story by Wilhelmine von Hillern called "Die Geyer-Wally." The movie-going public became aware of the glories of Catalani's opera in 1981 when the French film *Diva* used its most famous aria as a plot point.

756

1931 Brignone film

Italian feature film: Guido Brignone (director), Gian Bistolfi (screenplay), Ubaldo Arata (cinematographer), Pietro Sassòli (music director), Cines (production).

Cast: Germana Paolieri (Wally, arias sung by Giannina Arangi-Lombardi), Carlo Ninchi (Hagenbach), Achille Majeroni (Stromminger), Isa Pola (Afra), Renzo Ricci (Gellner), Gino Sabbatini (Walter).

Black and white. In Italian. 85 minutes.

Comment: Brignone's film is based on Illica's libretto for *La Wally* and uses Catalani's music as score, but it retains only a couple of arias. The Alpine scenes and scenery were much admired by contemporary critics.

1990 Bregenz Festival

Austrian stage production: Tim Albery (director), Pinchas Steinberg (conductor, Vienna Symphony Orchestra, Vienna Volksoper Choir, Sofia Kammerchor and Bregenz Festival Choir).

Cast: Mara Zampieri (Wally), Norman Bailey (Stromminger), Michael Sylvester (Hagenbach), David Malis (Gellner), Liliana Niehiteanu (Afra), Ildiko Raimondi (Walter).

Video: House of Opera DVD and VHS/Lyric VHS. Hugo Kach (director). Color. In Italian. 121 minutes.

Comment: This is an updated modernized production.

Related films

1921 Die Geierwally

Silent cinema star Henny Porten plays Wally in this German silent film based on the source novel by Wilhelmine von Hillern. E. A. Dupont wrote and directed it. Black and white. About 75 minutes.

1940 Die Geierwally

Heidemarie Hatheyer plays Wally in this German film directed by Hans Steinhoff and based on the source novel. Black and white. In German. 97 minutes.

1956 Die Geierwally

Barbara Rutting stars as Wally in this German film based on the source novel directed by Franz Cap. Black and white. In German. 90 minutes

1981 Diva

This stylish French thriller uses the *La Wally* soprano aria "Ebben...ne andrò lontana" as a central plot point. African-American diva Wilhelmenia Wiggins Fernandez refuses to make recordings, so a fanatic admirer tapes her in concert. The tape gets mixed up with one containing evidence of a crime ring. The film made the aria, composer, and singer well known in cinephile circles. Jean-Jacques Beineix, who directed from a crime novel by Delacorta, was reportedly inspired to make the film after seeing Jessye Norman in recital in Bordeaux. Color. In French with English subtitles. 117 minutes. MGM-UA Video.

1986 Dangerously Close

The aria "Ebben...ne andrò lontana" is heard three times on the soundtrack of this film about fascist-style students who like to bully those who don't fit in with their ideas. John Stockwell and J. Eddie Peck are the stars, Albert Pyun directed. Color. In English. 95 minutes.

1987 Someone to Watch Over Me

Wilhelmenia Wiggins Fernandez again sings "Ebben...ne andrò lontana," but this time only on the soundtrack. She is supported by the London Symphony Orchestra conducted by Vladimir Cosma. Ridley Scott directed this stylish thriller about a cop (Tom Berenger) assigned to protect a murder witness (Lorraine Bracco). Color. 106 minutes.

1988 Die Geierwally

Samy Orgen stars as Wally in this musical filmed as a comic parody of a mountain love affair. Walter Bockmayer directed. Color. In German. 93 minutes.

1993 Philadelphia

A recording of Maria Callas singing "Ebben...ne andrò lontana" is heard in this film about a lawyer dying of AIDS, played by Tom Hanks. Jonathan Demme directed for TriStar. Color. 119 minutes. On VHS.

1995 Crimson Tide

Miriam Gauci is heard singing "Ebben...ne andrò lontana" with the BRT Philharmonic Orchestra on the soundtrack of this hi-tech thriller set on a nuclear submarine. Denzel Washington and Gene Hackman are the stars; Tony Scott directed. Color. 116 minutes.

2000 The Contender

Miriam Gauci is heard singing "Ebben...ne andrò lontana" with the BRT Philharmonic Orchestra (again) on the soundtrack of this film about a woman senator (Joan Allen) who is nominated for vice president. Rod Lurie directed. Color. 126 minutes.

WALSKA, GANNA
Polish soprano (1891–1984)

Ganna Walska was probably the prototype for the cinema's greatest operatic failure, Susan Alexander in Orson

Welles's *Citizen Kane*. Walska wasn't very talented, but she was hugely ambitious with a rich New York husband and a powerful friend, Chicago newspaper magnate Harold McCormick. He hired Met diva Frances Alda to develop what there was of her voice, and he arranged for her to star in Leoncavallo's opera *Zazà* with the Chicago Opera Company, of which he was the major funder. Like Alexander, Walska had a disastrous experience and fled the city before the opening night. Welles is said to have kept copious notes on the Walska story. Walska, whose real name was Leszcynska, made her singing debut as Sonia in *The Merry Widow* in Kiev. In New York she appeared in Hervè's operetta *Man'zelle Nitouche* in 1915 and acted in one film. She also wrote an autobiography called *Always Room at the Top*. After a recital at Carnegie Hall in 1929, *New York Times* critic Olin Downes commented that she had "leaped for glory before it was sensible or prudent to do so." During a performance of the opera *Fedora* in Havana, she went so far off key that the audience pelted her with vegetables. It didn't seem to faze Walska. She went through six husbands, mostly rich, during her long life, and finally ended up in Montecito, California, as a very wealthy gardener. Her legacy is a horticultural folly called Lotusland filled with hundreds of exotic plants; it can still be visited.

1916 Child of Destiny
Walska gets only second billing in this Columbia/Metro film directed by William Nigh, but she does get to be listed in the credits as "Madama Ganna Walska." She plays Constance, an unfaithful woman who has been divorced and is now the rival of the heroine Irene Fenwich. She is quite remorseful at the end of the film and commits suicide. Black and white. In English. About 70 minutes.

WALTER, BRUNO
German conductor (1876–1962)

Bruno Walter, who made his conducting debut with Lortzing's *Der Waffenschmied* in 1894 in Cologne, is known as a champion of Mahler but also is associated with opera composer Hans Pfitzner. After the Nazis took over in Germany, he moved to Austria, then France, and finally the United States. After the war he decided to remain in the States but made visits to Salzburg, Edinburgh, Vienna, and other opera houses. There is no film of him conducting a complete opera, but he can be seen conducting in several videos. See CARNEGIE HALL (1947), CONDUCTORS (1993/1994/1995), and SALZBURG (1931).

WALTON, WILLIAM
British composer (1902–1983)

Although Sir William Walton loved Italian opera intensely, he composed only two operas. Walton's principal connection with the screen is as a composer for the cinema, most notably for Laurence Olivier's Shakespeare films. *Troilus and Cressida* was composed in 1954 after Walton wrote the score for Olivier's film of *Hamlet,* and there are said to be many influences from it, noticeably in similarities between Ophelia's and Cressida's music. There is an excerpt from it in the Walton documentary *At the Haunted End of the Day* but no complete video. He composed the genial opera THE BEAR, based on a famous Chekhov story, in 1965, and it has been telecast twice but is not on video.

1935–1972 British films
Walton began composing for the movies in 1935 with Elizabeth Bergner's *Escape Me Never,* directed by her husband Paul Czinner. This was followed in 1936 with Czinner's Shakespeare adaptation *As You Like It* with Bergner and Laurence Olivier. In 1938 he wrote the score for Czinner's *A Stolen Life* and in 1941 for Gabriel Pascal's *Major Barbara* and Charles Frend's *The Foreman Went to France.* In 1942 he created the music for Thorold Dickinson's *Next of Kin,* Alberto Cavalcanti's *Went the Day Well?,* and (notably) for Leslie Howard's *First of the Few* with its famous Spitfire "Prelude and Fugue." In 1944 he began his collaboration with Laurence Olivier on the Shakespeare epics *Henry V, Hamlet,* and *Richard III.* Their partnership has been compared in greatness to that between Eisenstein and Prokofiev. Walton's final screen scores were for Guy Hamilton's *Battle of Britain* (1969) and Olivier's *Three Sisters* (1972).

1981 At the Haunted End of the Day
Tony Palmer's fine film traces the life and career of Walton with commentary by Walton and his wife. There are 20 musical excerpts, including Yvonne Kenny in a scene from *Troilus and Cressida* (the film's title comes from an aria in the opera), plus Shakespeare film scores, other Walton movies, and the Coronation Ode "Crown Imperial." Among those appearing are Julian Bream, Ralph Kirschbum, Yehudi Menuhin, Sacheverell Sitwell, and Laurence Olivier. The film won the Prix Italia. Color. 100 minutes. Decca DVD/Kultur VHS.

WALZERTRAUM, EIN
1907 operetta by Straus

Ein Walzertraum (The Waltz Dream) contains one of the most popular waltzes OSCAR STRAUS ever wrote: the dreamy and memorable "Leise, ganze leise." The operetta itself was his first international hit and played in most of the world capitols. It has a bittersweet romance at its center. Viennese Lieutenant Niki marries Princess Helene. On their wedding night he slips off to a restaurant and meets and is fascinated by charming Franzi, who leads a female orchestra. Eventually, he finds it better to accept wife and duty. Felix Dörmann and Leopold Jacobson wrote the libretto.

1931 The Smiling Lieutenant

American feature film: Ernst Lubitsch (director), Ernest Vajda and Samson Raphaelson (screenplay), George Folsey (cinematographer), Adolph Deutsch (music director).

Cast: Maurice Chevalier (Lt. Niki), Claudette Colbert (Franzi), Miriam Hopkins (Princess Anna), Charlie Ruggles (Max), George Barbier (King).

Black and white. In English. 88 minutes.

Comment: The plot is altered, with Niki and Franzi having a full-fledged affair before the marriage, and contains a song with an unusual piece of advice from a mistress to a wife, "Jazz Up Your Lingerie." The film was believed lost until a print was found in Denmark in 1950. *The New York Times* listed it as one of the Ten Best Films of the year, and it was nominated for an Academy Award as Best Picture.

1960 Wilhelm film

German TV film: Kurt Wilhelm (director), music performed by Cologne Radio-Television Orchestra and Choir.

Cast: Hans von Borsody (Lt. Niki, sung by Fritz Wunderlich), Heidi Bruehl (Princess Helene, sung by Luise Cramer), Waltraud Haas, Cissy Kramer, Hans Timmerdings, Balduin Baas.

Telecast May 23, 1960, by NWRV, Cologne. Black and white. In German. 135 minutes.

1969 Kraus film

German TV film: Fred Kraus (director), Franz Allers (conductor, Graunke Symphony Orchestra and Bavarian Television Chorus), Wazlaw Orlikowsky (set designer).

Cast: Wolfgang Siesz (Lt. Niki), Margit Schramm (Princess Helene), Herta Staal (Franzi).

Telecast November 30, 1969, on ZDF German Television. Color. In German. 105 minutes.

Early/silent films

1907 Ein Walzertraum

This is considered the first Austrian fiction film. It shows a scene from the operetta at its premiere at the Carl Theater in Vienna on March 2, 1907. Black and white. Silent. About 4 minutes.

1908 Piccolo Duet

Fritz Werner performs the Franzi-Lothar violin and piccolo "Piccolo Duet" in this German Deutsche Bioscop sound film. It was screened with the music played on a synchronized phonograph. Black and white. In German. About 5 minutes. Print in German archive.

1925 Berger film

Ludwig Berger, the master of the waltz film, made this light romantic version of the Straus operetta toward the end of the silent era. Mady Christians takes the role of the princess who doesn't know what to expect from new Hussar husband Willy Fritsch. The cast includes Xenia Desni, Lydia Potechina, Hermann Picha, and Julius Falkenstein. It was screened with the music played live and shown in Germany as *Ein Walzertraum* and in America as *The Waltz Dream*. Black and white. Silent. About 83 minutes.

WAR AND PEACE
1946 opera by Prokofiev

Sergei Prokofiev shaped Tolstoy's sprawling novel *Voyna i Mir* into an opera libretto in collaboration with his companion Mira Mendelson. It doesn't encompass the whole novel, but it does contain big chunks of it with 13 peace and war scenes and most of the important characters. It is by far the most ambitious of Prokofiev's operas and possibly his greatest achievement. It was composed during 1941–1942 and had its first real production in 1946, but the final version was not presented until 1959. The U.S. premiere took place on television in 1957.

1957 NBC Opera Theatre

American TV production: Samuel Chotzinoff (director/producer), Peter Herman Adler (conductor, Symphony of the Air Orchestra and American Concert Choir), Otis Riggs (set designer), Guy Kent (costume designer), Joseph Machlis (English translation).

Cast: Helen Scott (Natasha), Morley Meredith (Andrei), David Lloyd (Pierre), Beatrice Krebs (Maria), Kenneth Smith (Kutuzov), Gloria Lane (Helena), Linda McNaughton (Sonya), Davis Cunningham (Anatol), Chester Watson (Rostov), Leon Lishner (Napoleon), Alice Howland (Maria), Michael Kermoyan (Dolokhov),

Video at the MTR. Telecast January 13, 1957. Kirk Browning (director). Color. In English. 150 minutes.

Comment: This grandiose production was the U.S. premiere of the opera. It required a cast of 90 singers, a 63-piece orchestra, and three studios, and it cost a whopping $160,000.

1973 Australian Opera

Australian stage production: Sam Wanamaker (director), Sir Edward Downes (conductor, Elizabethan Sydney Orchestra and Australian Opera Chorus).

Cast: Eilene Hannan (Natasha), Tom McDonnell (Andrei), Robert Gard (Pierre), John Shaw, Rosina Raisbeck, Stephen Dickson.

Video: House of Opera DVD/VHS. Color. In English. 255 minutes.

Comment: This was the first opera performance at the new Sydney Opera House, September 28, 1973.

1990 Seattle Opera

American stage production: Francesca Zambello (director), Mark Ermler (conductor, Seattle Opera Orchestra and Chorus), John Conklin (set designer). Bruno Schwengel (costume designer).

Cast: Sheri Greenawald (Natasha), Vladimir Chernov (Andrei), Peter Kazaras (Pierre), Victoria Vergara (Hélène), Stella Zambalis (Sonya), James Hoback (Anatol), Nikolai Okhotnikov (Kutuzov), Julian Patrick (Napoleon), Alexander Morozov (Dolokhov).

Videotaped on HDTV. Color. In Russian. 260 minutes.

Comment: This spectacular production cost $2 million. The high-definition videotape has been shown in cinemas but is not available on commercial video.

***1991 Kirov Opera

Russian stage production: Graham Vick (director), Valery Gergiev (conductor, Kirov Opera Orchestra and Chorus), Timothy O'Brien (set designer), Valentina Komolova (costume designer).

Cast: Yelena Prokina (Natasha), Alexander Gergalov (Andrei), Gegam Gregoriam (Pierre), Olga Borodina (Hélène), Svetlana Volkova (Sonya), Yuri Marusin (Anatol), Nikolai Okhotnikov (Kutuzov), Vassily Gerelo (Napoleon), Irina Bogacheva (Maria), Sergei Alexashkin (Rostov), Alexandr Morozov (Dolokhov), Mikhail Kit (Denisov).

Video: Philips DVD/VHS/LD. Humphrey Burton (director). Color. In Russian with English subtitles. 248 minutes.

Comment: Magnificent production taped at the Maryinsky Theater in St. Petersburg with great singers and a superb orchestra.

2000 Paris Opéra

French stage production: Francesca Zambello (director), Gary Bertini (conductor, Paris Opéra Orchestra and Chorus), John Macfarlane (set designer), Valentina Komolova (costume designer).

Cast: Olga Guryakova (Natasha), Nathan Gunn (Andrei), Robert Brubaker (Pierre), Anatoli Kotcherga (Kutuzov).

Video: TDK DVD. François Roussillon (director). Color. In Russian with English subtitles. 289 minutes.

Comment: Spectacular production superbly photographed and finely sung. Includes 79-minute documentary about the staging.

WARNER BROS. CARTOONS
Animated opera films

The animation geniuses at the Warner Bros. studios were more than a match for their colleagues at Disney in creating great and stylish cartoons with opera music. The magnificent WHAT'S OPERA, DOC? and the delightful THE RABBIT OF SEVILLE were created by director CHUCK JONES and writer Michael Maltese, while Tex Avery and Friz Freleng were making other memorable films.

1941 Notes to You

An alley cat sets up a sheet music stand on a backyard fence and begins Figaro's aria "Largo al factotum" from *The Barber of Seville* to the annoyance of Porky Pig, who is trying to sleep. After the cat gets shot, ghost cats return singing the sextet from *Lucia di Lammermoor*. Michael Maltese wrote the story, Carl Stalling conducted the music, and Friz Freleng directed. Color. About 7 minutes.

1948 Back Alley Oproar

In this brilliant remake of *Notes to You*, Sylvester is the cat and Elmer Fudd is the one trying to sleep as the feline tries out his Figaro aria. After much music, the film ends in an explosion of dynamite and a heavenly sextet from *Lucia di Lammermoor*. Friz Freleng again directed. Color. 7 minutes.

1952 The Magical Maestro

Tex Avery's classic cartoon features the Great Poochini in a story about a man trying to sing an aria from *The Barber of Seville*. A magician transforms the opera singer in and out of outlandish costumes as he desperately tries to keep singing. Color. 7 minutes.

WARREN, LEONARD
American baritone (1911–1960)

Leonard Warren virtually lived and died at the Metropolitan Opera. He began his career by winning a Met competition in 1938 and made his debut there in 1939 in a small role in *Simon Boccanegra*. In 1940 he sang with the Met in the first U.S. opera telecast, and in 1948 he sang Iago in OTELLO in the first live telecast of an opera from the stage. He sang at the Met for 21 years and died on stage singing Don Carlo in *La forza del destino*. He can be seen in performance in videos of Met telecasts, in a Hollywood film, and in *The Voice of Firestone* TV shows. See SOL HUROK (1956) and METROPOLITAN OPERA (1940/1948).

1944 Irish Eyes Are Smiling
Leonard Warren and Blanche Thebom play turn-of-the-century opera singers using their own names in this musical about songwriter Ernest R. Ball. Dick Haymes plays Ball; Gregory Ratoff directed. Twentieth Century-Fox. Color. 90 minutes.

1949–1953 Leonard Warren in Opera and Song
Compilation of performances by the baritone on *The Voice of Firestone* television shows. Warren sings the "Toreador Song" from *Carmen* November 7, 1949; "Eri tu" from *Un ballo in maschera* June 2, 1952; and an aria from *Faust* August 24, 1953. Howard Barlow conducts the Voice of Firestone Orchestra. Black and white. 45 minutes. VAI VHS.

1949 Leonard Warren in Opera and Song 2
Eleanor Steber joins Warren on this video of highlights from 1949 *Voice of Firestone* telecasts. On November 7, he sings "On the Road to Mandalay" and on December 5 "Largo al factotum" from *The Barber of Seville* and Huhn's "Invictus." Steber sings "Vissi d'arte" from *Tosca* and "My Hero" from *The Chocolate Soldier* and joins Warren in duet on "Will You Remember" from *Maytime*. Black and white. 27 minutes. VAI VHS.

WAR REQUIEM
1988 oratorio by Britten

Benjamin Britten's pacifist oratorio *War Requiem*, inspired by the poems of Wilfred Owen, was created for the reopening of Coventry Cathedral in 1962; it had been destroyed in an air raid during World War II. The oratorio mixes Owen's poems with traditional Latin texts. The premiere at Coventry featured German, Russian, and English soloists.

1988 Jarman film
English feature film: Derek Jarman (director), Benjamin Britten (conductor, London Symphony Orchestra and London Symphony Chorus), Richard Greatrex (cinematographer), Don Boyd (producer).
Soloists: Galina Vishnevskaya, Peter Pears, Dietrich Fischer-Dieskau.
Actors: Laurence Olivier (Old Soldier), Nathaniel Parker (Wilfred Owen), Tilda Swinton (Nurse), Patricia Hayes (Mother).
Video: Mystic Fire VHS. Color. In English. 93 minutes.

Comment: *War Requiem* is not an opera, but it nearly becomes one in this brilliant film. Jarman shot it at Darenth Park Hospital as a story remembered by an old soldier, and he uses Owen's experiences in World War I as the narrative framework for Britten's 1963 recording.

1992 Lübeck Marienkirche
German concert film: Barrie Gavin (director), John Eliot Gardiner (conductor, Tölz Boys Choir, Monteverdi Choir, and North German Radio Chorus and Symphony Orchestra).
Soloists: Luba Orgonasova, Anthony Rolfe Johnson, Bo Skovhus.
Video: DG VHS/LD. Color. In English. 87 minutes.
Comment: This performance was held to commemorate the restoration of the war-bombed Lübeck Marienkirche in August 1992. Gavin uses a damaged bell from the church as a connecting symbol on the video.

WATSON, RUSSELL
English tenor (1967–)

Russell Watson has become one of the most popular "opera" singers in England through recitals and recordings, although he is self-taught and has yet to sing on the opera stage. His 2000 debut album *The Voice* topped the British classical charts and reached No. 13 in the pop charts. He made his operatic reputation on the pub circuit after a request to sing Pavarotti's "nesty doormat." He went home, taught himself to sing "Nessun dorma," and became famous. He has already issued two CDs and two DVDs.

2001 Russell Watson—The Voice Live
The highlight of this recital is "Nessun dorma" with an explosion of fireworks before his encore in the open-air arena in Leeds Millennium Square. Color. 75 minutes. Universal Pictures (GB) DVD.

2002 Russell Watson—Live in New Zealand
More operatic and popular music performed by Watson at a recital in New Zealand. Color. 91 minutes. Universal Pictures (GB) DVD.

WEBB'S SINGING PICTURES
Early opera sound films

George Webb was a Baltimore entrepreneur who tried to present opera on screen with synchronized sound. His first program in May 1914, using a primitive sound-on-film system, included an abridged *Pagliacci*. Later presentations with sound-on-disc systems were called Webb's Singing Pictures. On January 14, 1917, Enrico Caruso turned up in person at the Cohan and Harris Theatre in New York for the premiere of a film in which he was the featured singer. The onscreen actors performed scenes from *Pagliacci* and *Rigoletto* while the voice of Caruso was heard on loudspeakers singing the arias. The second item was a scene of *Carmen* starring Met baritone Giuseppe Campanari as Escamillo. He was shown singing the "Toreador Song" with Marie Conesa as Carmen, Salvatore Giordano, and Léon Rothier. Webb repeated this program at Westminster Cathedral Hall in London in 1921. Rothier, a Metropolitan Opera bass famous for his portrayal of Méphistophélès, reportedly made a film of *Faust* for Webb.

WEBER, CARL MARIA VON
German composer (1786–1826)

Carl Maria von Weber's DER FREISCHÜTZ, the most popular German opera during the first half of the 19th century, seemed to embody the ideas of Germanic romanticism, especially the mysterious Wolf Glen scene. Weber, who played a key role in the development of German Romantic opera, composed other successful operas such as OBERON, *Abu Hassan,* and *Euryanthe,* but *Der Freischütz* remains by far his most performed opera.

1934 Der Weg Carl Maria von Webers
Carl Maria von Weber's Way, a romantic German film about the composer, is a love story set in Dresden with Weber's music used as score. German baritone Willi Domgraf-Fassbänder stars with support from Eliza Illiard, Margo Kochlin, Ernst Rotmund, and Else Botticher. Rudolf van der Noss directed. Black and white. In German. 73 minutes.

WEIGL, PETR
Czech filmmaker (1938–)

Petr Weigl, born in Brno and brought up in Prague, learned his film craft at the national FAMU film school. He began making films in 1964 and has now directed more than 50, including many based on operas or opera subjects. He has also directed opera on stage and won Emmy Awards for his TV work. Weigl's filmed operas are impressive, although they tend to be overly beautiful as he shoots them in lovely outdoor Czech locations with actors miming to the opera. Many opera purists dislike them heartily as they are usually much shorter than the stage versions. His opera films, all shot to preexistent recordings, include EUGENE ONEGIN (1988), LADY MACBETH OF THE MTSENSK DISTRICT (1999), MARIA STUARDA (2000), RUSALKA (1978), SALOME (1990), THE TURN OF THE SCREW (1982), A VILLAGE ROMEO AND JULIET (1989), and WERTHER (1985). He also created an opera film pastiche called THE LOVE OF DESTINY (1983)

starring Czech tenor Peter Dvorsky. His productions of operas on stage include *La traviata* at the National Theatre in Prague and SALOME (1990) at the Deutsche Oper in Berlin, with Catherine Malfitano.

WEIKL, BERND
Austrian baritone (1942–)

Bernd Weikl, who made his operatic debut in 1968, has a repertory of more than 100 roles in Italian and German operas, but he is best known for his performances in works by Wagner and Strauss. His performances as Hans Sachs in *Die Meistersinger* are much admired for both their acting and their singing. See ARABELLA (1977), EUGENE ONEGIN (1988), LOHENGRIN (1982), DIE MEISTERSINGER VON NÜRNBERG (1984), PARSIFAL (1981/1992), SALOME (1974), TANNHÄUSER (1978/1982/1994), and TRISTAN UND ISOLDE (1998).

WEILL, KURT
German/American composer (1900–1950)

Kurt Weill straddles the worlds of opera and musical with popular operas and serious musicals. The early Berlin part of his career used to be considered serious and the part in New York less so, but in this postmodern age it is harder to compartmentalize his musical genius. He is a major stage composer however his music is described, and his 1946 STREET SCENE is now recognized as one of the great American operas. Weill became famous in Berlin during the late 1920s collaborating with BERTOLT BRECHT on DIE DREIGROSCHENOPER (The Threepenny Opera), DER LINDBERGHFLUG, HAPPY END, and AUFSTIEG UND FALL DER STADT MAHAGONNY. After he left Nazi Germany for Paris, he collaborated with Brecht for the last time on the ballet-opera DIE SIEBEN TODSÜNDEN. After moving to the United States he presented the epic THE ETERNAL ROAD at the Manhattan Opera House in 1937. He was soon successful on Broadway with musicals such as *Knickerbocker Holiday, Lady in the Dark,* and *One Touch of Venus.* He had great success with the folk opera DOWN IN THE VALLEY, originally created for radio, and he won acclaim with the musical tragedy *Lost in the Stars.* Weill died at the age of 50 before his full potential could be realized and before MARC BLITZSTEIN revitalized his reputation with a popular revival of *The Threepenny Opera* in New York in 1954.

Musicals

1944/1955 Lady in the Dark
The 1944 film of Weill's 1941 stage musical, lyrics by Ira Gershwin and book by Moss Hart, eliminates most of Weill's music. Ginger Rogers plays a woman who undergoes psychoanalysis. Mitchell Leisen directed. Color.

100 minutes. Max Liebman's 1955 television production keeps closer to the original, with Ann Sothern as Liza. Color. 84 minutes. Video at the MTR.

1944 Knickerbocker Holiday
Only three Weill songs survive in this poor film of his 1938 musical. Maxwell Anderson wrote the book for this satire set in old Dutch New York. Nelson Eddy and Charles Coburn star; Harry Brown directed. Black and white. 85 minutes.

1945 Where Do We Go From Here?
Kurt Weill created a 12-minute comic opera with librettist Ira Gershwin for this time-travel film. It's sung on Columbus's mutinous ship just before land is sighted. See WHERE DO WE GO FROM HERE?

1948 One Touch of Venus
Ava Gardner stars as a statue that comes to life in this poor film of Weill's 1943 stage musical, with book and lyrics by S. J. Perelman and Ogden Nash. William A. Seiter directed. Black and white. 81 minutes.

1974 Lost in the Stars
Weill's 1949 stage musical was based on Alan Paton's novel *Cry, the Beloved Country* with book by Maxwell Anderson. It tells a tragic tale about racial prejudice in South Africa. The American Film Theatre production stars Brock Peters and Melba Moore. Daniel Mann directed. Color. 114 minutes.

Tributes

1964 Lotte Lenya Sings Kurt Weill
Lotte Lenya performs Weill songs for the British *Monitor* TV program. Ken Russell and Humphrey Burton directed the 60-minute program telecast September 10, 1962. Black and white. 60 minutes.

1964 Broadway Years of Kurt Weill
Lotte Lenya performs songs from *One Touch of Venus, Lady in the Dark, Knickerbocker Holiday, Street Scene,* and *The Firebrand of Florence* on a *Camera Three* program directed by Jack Landau. It was telecast on WCBS October 28, 1964. Video at the MTR.

1992 Ute Lemper Sings Kurt Weill
Ute Lemper performs songs from *Die Dreigroschenoper, One Touch of Venus, Lady in the Dark,* and other Weill stage works at Les Bouffes du Nord in Paris. Jeff Cohen plays piano. Jean-Pierre Barizien directed. Color. In English, German, and French. 100 minutes. London VHS.

1994 Kurt Weill in America
Barrie Gavin directed this television documentary about Weill's American years for German television. Color. In German. 60 minutes.

1994 Music of Kurt Weill: September Songs
A Canadian tribute to Weill set in a warehouse with singers Teresa Stratas, Stan Ridgeway, Betty Carter, Elvis Costello, Charlie Haden, and Lou Reed. Lotte Lenya and Weill are seen in archival film. Larry Weinstein directed for Rhombus Media and ZDF Television. Color. Telecast on PBS. On VHS.

1995 Lotte Lenya: An Invented Life
Lenya: ein Erfundenes Leben is a German documentary about Lenya that concentrates on her relationship with Weill. Barrie Gavin directed for Hessian Television. Color. In German. 60 minutes.

2001 Kurt Weill
Respectful documentary by Sven Düfer with footage of a 1932 performance of *Der Jasager* in Paris, scenes from *The Eternal Road,* and film of Weill and Brecht at the time of *Die Dreigroschenoper.* Pop star Milva sings "Mastrosen-Tango," Kathrin Angerer sings "Surabaya Johnny," Kaja Plessing sings "Youkali," Jocelyn B. Smith sings "Lost in the Stars," and Udo Lindenberg sings "Moritat." Made for SFB. Color. In German. 97 minutes.

WEIR, JUDITH
Scottish composer (1954–)

Judith Weir, who writes her own librettos, has become one of the most successful modern composers and seems to have little trouble in getting her operas produced. Her 13-minute *King Harald's Saga* (1979), described as a "grand opera in three acts for solo soprano," is popular on CD, possibly because the soprano has to sing the role of the entire Norwegian Army as well as eight other parts. Weir's first full-length opera was the 1987 *A Night at the Chinese Opera.* She has also written operas for television. Her opera BLOND ECKBERT was telecast in England in 1995.

1988 Missa Del Cid
Weir takes a cool look at violence in brief operatic form. The libretto combines a deadpan reading of the heroic actions of the medieval Spanish knight El Cid with a modern Mass. Telecast in England in 1988. Color. 30 minutes.

1991 Scipio's Dream

This is Weir's revamping of Mozart's 1771 *Il Sogno di Scipione,* created for the Mozart centennial. It was commissioned for and telecast by BBC. Color. 40 minutes.

WEIR, PETER
Australian film director (1944–)

Peter Weir, known for Australian films such as *Picnic at Hanging Rock* and *Gallipoli* and U.S. films such as *Witness* and *Dead Poet's Society,* sometimes features opera and opera singers on his soundtracks. In *Gallipoli* (1981), there is a fine use of the friendship duet "Au fond du temple saint" from Bizet's LES PÊCHEURS DE PERLES. A major plays its knowing that he and most of his men will die in battle the next day. In *The Year of Living Dangerously,* Kiri Te Kanawa sings "September" from the *Four Last Songs* by Richard Strauss.

WELITSCH, LJUBA
Bulgarian soprano (1913–1996)

Ljuba Welitsch made her debut at the Sofia Opera in 1936, started her career in Germany, and joined the Vienna State Opera in 1946 where she became especially popular as Tosca and Salome. After appearances in *Salome* at the Met and Covent Garden, she was hailed as one of the great voices of the world. When she retired from the stage because of voice problems, she began to act in film and television in Europe, mostly in character and supporting roles. She was featured in more than 75 films and 45 television shows; a sampling is listed below. She played Princess Bozeno is a 1973 film of Kálmán's operetta GRÄFIN MARIZA, and she talks about her career in the 1983 TOSCA documentary *I Live for Art.*

1953 The Man Between

Welitsch is seen on stage as Salome in the final scene of the opera in this British spy film. James Mason and Claire Bloom attend a production of *Salome* at the East Berlin Staatsoper at the height of the Cold War and try to slip away to escape to the West. Carol Reed directed. Black and white. 101 minutes.

1960 Schlussakkord

Welitsch and Mario Del Monaco play opera singers in *Schlussakkord* (Final Resolution), a German/Italian film revolving around the premiere of an opera in Salzburg. There are the usual operatic problems of love, suspicion, jealousy, and hate. Eleanora Rossi-Drago, Victor de Kowa, and Christian Wolff star; Wolfgang Liebeneiner directed. Black and white. In German. 102 minutes. Lyric/Opera Dubs VHS.

1961 Julia, du bist zauberhaft

Welitsch plays Dolly de Fries in this French/Austrian adaptation of Somerset Maugham's novel *Theatre.* Lilli Palmer stars as a theatrical grande dame who falls in love with Jean Sorel. Alfred Weidemann directed. The English title is *Adorable Julia.* Color. In French or German. 97 minutes.

1962 Arms and the Man

Welitsch is a matronly operatic Katherina in this German adaptation of George Bernard Shaw's antiwar play. Liselotte Pulver plays her daughter Raina, who is charmed by chocolate soldier Bluntschli (O. W. Fischer). Franz Peter Wirth directed. Black and white. In German. 96 minutes.

1989 Portrait of Ljuba Welitsch

Welitsch was 75 and still lively when this documentary was made. The focus is on her portrayal of Salome, and she talks about different productions. There is a brief scene of her performing the Dance of the Seven Veils. Jordan Djoumaliev directed for Bulgarian television. Color. In Bulgarian. 70 minutes.

WELLES, ORSON
American theater/film director (1915–1985)

Orson Welles made his stage debut in an opera; he was 3 years old when he appeared as Cio-Cio-San's child in *Madama Butterfly* with Claudia Muzio as his mother. The child, of course, is aptly named Trouble. Welles, who once described himself as starting at the top and working his way down, was strongly involved with progressive American opera in his early theater days. He directed premieres of two radical operas in 1937. The first, in April, was only a populist production by a New York City school, but as the composer was Aaron Copland and THE SECOND HURRICANE was his first opera, it was an important debut. In June, Welles staged one of the most famous opera debuts in U.S. history: Marc Blitzstein's THE CRADLE WILL ROCK. The opera was considered too left-wing by conservative politicians, so the theater where it was to premiere was padlocked. Welles quickly found another theater, led the cast and audience to it, and staged the opera without scenery or orchestra. The actors sang from their seats (their union said they couldn't go on stage), and the composer played his music on a piano. It was a triumph. The premiere is depicted in Tim Robbins's 1999 film *Cradle Will Rock* with Angus Macfadyen playing Welles. When Welles left New York for Hollywood to make his classic film CITIZEN KANE, he took composer Bernard Hermann with him and had him create the imaginary opera *Salammbô.*

WERNICKE, HERBERT

German opera director (1946–2002)

Herbert Wernicke studied in Munich and made his directorial debut in 1978 with a production of *Belshazzar* in Darmstadt. He specialized in baroque operas, such as Lully's *Alceste* and Rameau's *Hippolyte et Aricie;* he staged *Calisto* at the Théâtre de la Monnaie in Brussels and *Orfeo* at the Salzburg Festival. He also had success with modern operas, including *Moses und Aaron* in Paris. A number of his productions were controversial, including his *Les Troyens,* but they were all thought provoking. See LE CINESE (1987), ECHO ET NARCISSE (1987), FALSTAFF (2001), CHRISTOPH GLUCK (1988), ORPHÉE AUX ENFERS (1997), and LES TROYENS (2000).

WERRENRATH, REINALD

American baritone (1883–1953)

Metropolitan Opera baritone Reinald Werrenrath, who was born in Brooklyn, was the son of a Danish tenor. He made his concert debut in 1907 and had a successful concert career for many years. He made his stage debut at the Met in 1919 as Silvio in *Pagliacci* and sang with the company until 1921. He was a popular recording artist for Victor in opera and operetta.

1928 Vitaphone film

Werrenrath is featured on a Vitaphone sound film in 1928 singing "Duna" and "On the Road to Mandalay." Black and white. In English. About 8 minutes.

WERTHER

1892 opera by Massenet

JULES MASSENET's *Werther,* an operatic adaptation of Goethe's highly romantic novel *Die Leiden des jungen Werther* (The Sorrows of Young Werther), is currently his most popular and widely recorded opera. The story takes place in Frankfurt in 1772. Werther and Charlotte are in love, but she is already engaged to Albert. When Werther goes away for a time, Charlotte marries Albert. When Werther returns and discovers what has happened, he kills himself. The libretto is by Edouard Blaud, Paul Milliet, and Georges Hartmann. There is also a modern opera based on the novel, Hans-Jürgen von Bose's 1986 DIE LEIDEN DES JUNGEN WERTHER.

1985 Weigl film

Czech feature film: Petr Weigl (director), Libor Pešek (conductor, Prague Radio Symphony Orchestra).

Cast: Peter Dvorsky (Werther), Brigitte Fassbaender (Charlotte), Michal Dočolomanský (Albert, sung by Hans Helm), Magdalena Vásáryová (Sophie, sung by Magdaléna Hajóssyová).

Video: Image Entertainment DVD/European Video VHS. Color. In French. 110 minutes.

Comment: Weigl shot the opera outdoors in ravishing locations, which tend to make it look almost too romantic and beautiful.

1987 Gran Teatre del Liceu

Spanish stage production: Giuseppe De Tomasi (director), Alain Guingal (conductor, Orchestra Sinfonica of the Gran Theatre del Liceu and Coro de Nais de l'Escola Pia Lames), Ferruccio Villagrossi (set designer).

Cast: Alfredo Kraus (Werther), Renata Scotto (Charlotte), Vincente Sardinero (Albert), Maria Angeles Peters (Sophie).

Video: Bel Canto Society VHS. Color. In French. 146 minutes.

1991 Alfredo Kraus: My Favorite Opera

Portuguese highlights stage production: Paolo Trevis (stage director), Bernhard Sinkel (film director), Gianpaolo Sanzogno (conductor, Teatro Nacional de Sao Carlos Orchestra and Chorus), Ferruccio Villagrossi (set designer).

Cast: Alfredo Kraus (Werther), Ileana Cotrubas (Charlotte), Elsa Saque (Sophie), J. Vaz de Carvalho (Albert).

Video: Kultur VHS. Color. In English and French. 60 minutes.

Comment: Kraus is shown preparing and singing *Werther* at Lisbon's Teatro Nacional de Sao Carlos in this documentary in the series *My Favorite Opera.* About 30 minutes of scenes from the stage production are presented in narrative order.

Early/related films

1910 Film d'Art film

The opera was the inspiration for the French silent film *Werther,* which stars André Brule as Werther and Mlle. Dulac as Charlotte. It was produced by the Film d'Art Company and screened with Massenet's music. Black and white. About 10 minutes.

1938 Werther or Le roman de Werther

Max Ophuls directed this excellent French film version of the Goethe novel, but he uses music by Mozart, Grétry, Bach, and Beethoven rather than Massenet. Pierre-Richard Willm plays Werther with Annie Vernay as Charlotte. Black and white. In French. 85 minutes.

1976 Die Leiden des jungen Werthers
Egon Gunther directed this East German version of the Goethe novel starring Hans-Jürgen Wolf as Werther. The music here is by Mozart and Siegfried Matthus. Color. In German. 91 minutes.

1986 Werther
Spanish filmmaker Pilar Miro's *Werther* uses music from Massenet's opera as its score, but the story is updated and reset in contemporary Spain. Eusebio Poncela plays Werther, and the singers are José Carreras and Frederica von Stade. Colin Davis conducts the Royal Opera House Orchestra. Color. In Spanish. 110 minutes.

1992 Le jeune Werther
Massenet's music is the basic soundtrack of this French film, loosely derived from Goethe's novel. It's set in a contemporary French school where a group of 14-year-olds try to discover why a friend has committed suicide. Philippe Sarde arranged the music; Jacques Doillon directed the film. Color. In French. 94 minutes.

WEST SIDE STORY
1957 "American opera" by Bernstein

LEONARD BERNSTEIN's *West Side Story* has the structure of a Broadway musical but has been called an "American opera" because of its symphonic writing, vocal requirements, and tragic libretto. It has certainly been sung by opera singers and may well enter the opera house repertory. The libretto by Arthur Laurents updates Shakespeare's play *Romeo and Juliet* to New York City during the 1950s. The rival families are now youth gangs, with the Italian Jets led by Riff and the Puerto Rican Sharks led by Bernardo. Tony, who is Riff's best friend, and Maria, who is Bernardo's sister, fall in love and the star-crossed tragedy begins. The superb lyrics were written by Stephen Sondheim, and the brilliant choreography was created by Jerome Robbins.

1961 Robbins/Wise film
American feature film: Jerome Robbins and Robert Wise (directors), Jerome Robbins (choreographer), Ernest Lehman (screenplay), Daniel Fapp (cinematographer), Johnny Green and Saul Chaplin (music directors), Boris Leven (art director).
Cast: Natalie Wood (Maria, sung by Marni Nixon), Richard Beymer (Tony, sung by Jim Bryant), Rita Moreno (Anita), Russ Tamblyn (Riff), George Chakiris (Bernardo).
Video: On VHS and DVD Color. In English. 155 minutes.
Comment: This electrifying cinematic version of *West Side Story* won 10 Academy Awards, including Best Picture, Best Director, Best Cinematographer, and Best Art Director. Robbins, who directed the stage show, created the amazing dance sequences but was replaced by Wise after three weeks of filming.

Related film

1984 West Side Story: The Making of the Recording
A fascinating documentary about opera singers making a recording of *West Side Story* with Leonard Bernstein. Kiri Te Kanawa sings Maria, José Carreras is Tony, Tatiana Troyanos is Anita, and Kurt Ollmann is Riff. Te Kanawa sings well, Carreras has problems with his accent, Troyanos sounds too old for the role, and Bernstein enjoys even the problems as this was the first time he had conducted his "American opera." The film was photographed by John Else, produced by Humphrey Burton, and directed by Christopher Swann. Color. 89 minutes. DG DVD/VHS.

WHALE WHO WANTED TO SING AT THE MET, THE
1946 animated film with opera content

Nelson Eddy is superb as the multiple voices of an operatic whale, and the artwork of this animated classic is as grand as grand opera. Willie, who dreams of singing at the Metropolitan Opera, has three voices and can sing bass, baritone, and tenor at the same time. When he arouses international attention by entertaining ships at sea, Met impresario Tetti-Tatti imagines he has swallowed an opera singer, so he sails off to rescue him. Meanwhile, the whale imagines that he is about to be discovered, so he auditions with Figaro's aria "Largo al Factotum" from *The Barber of Seville* and the sextet from *Lucia di Lammermoor*. He then fantasizes performances at the Metropolitan as a cavalier in *Lucia*, as a crying clown in *Pagliacci* (the audience needs umbrellas), as Tristan singing the "Love Duet" to a diminutive Isolde in the Wagner opera, and as a fire-breathing devil in *Mefistofele* (firemen are standing by). He is harpooned while performing Boito's ominous music and ends up in heaven singing the great "May Heaven Grant You Pardon" ("Mag der Himmel") ensemble from *Martha*. The narrator points out that he can now sing "in a hundred voices, each more golden than the one before." He also sings in Italian, which is apparently the preferred language of heaven. Eddy is the narrator and all the other voices in the film, and is hugely impressive. *Whale* is based on a story by Irvin Graham, adapted by Richmond Kelsey and T. Hee, and Clyde Geronimi and Hamilton Luske directed the film, originally released as part of the feature *Make Mine Music*. It is also on video as *Willie, The Operatic Whale*. Color. 12 minutes. Walt Disney VHS.

WHAT MEN LIVE BY

1953 TV opera by Martinů

An angel, who is being punished by God, is forced to live on Earth with a poor peasant shoemaker until he learns three great truths about what men live by. Bohuslav Martinů's 55-minute television opera *What Men Live By*, libretto in English by the composer based on a famous 1881 short story by Leo Tolstoy, premiered on television in New York on CBS in May 1953. It has also been staged.

WHAT'S OPERA, DOC?

1957 animated film with opera content

What's Opera, Doc?, voted the greatest cartoon of all time in a poll of people working in the animation field, is also one of the most enjoyable opera films. Director Chuck Jones and writer Michael Maltese somehow compress 14 hours of Wagner's *Der Ring des Nibelungen* into six action-packed minutes with such awe-inspiring artistry that even Picasso admired it. Elmer Fudd in Teutonic helmet hunts Bugs Bunny singing "Kill da wabbit, kill da wabbit" to the "Ride of the Valkyries" music. Bugs puts on a wig and disguises himself as Brünnhilde, so Elmer falls in love with him. They dance and sing a love duet titled "Return My Love" until Bugs loses his disguise and Elmer gets over-the-top angry. He conjures up a howling wind and throws a lightning bolt that destroys the rabbit. As Elmer mourns his death, Bugs turns to the audience and asks, "What did you expect in an opera, a happy ending?" The film is a visual masterpiece with a unique and memorable color scheme. Mel Blanc provides the voices, Maurice Noble created the layouts, and Milt Franklyn conducted the music. Jones said this was the most difficult film he ever made. It was also the best. Warner Bros. Color. 6 minutes.

WHEN SHE DIED: DEATH OF A PRINCESS

2002 TV opera by Dove

Jonathan Dove's television opera *When She Died: Death of a Princess*, libretto by David Harsent, is not so much about Princess Diana as about public reaction to her untimely death. Filmed in and around London, it focuses on seven people: a working-class couple named Doris and Dennis, who feel they knew her; a mentally disturbed young woman named Annie, who can't have children and who is watched over by her worried husband and sister; a man with a mad belief that the princess secretly loved him; and a homeless man who comments on events like a Greek chorus. They all watch the car crash on television and join the crowd in Kensington Gardens the night before the funeral. Intercut with the live action are images of Princess Diana on television. The opera was commissioned by Jan Younghusband for Channel 4 in England and Trio in the United States.

2002 Edwards film

English TV film: Rupert Edwards (director), Paul Sommers (producer), Brad Cohen (conductor, Birmingham Contemporary Music Group and Pegasus Choir), Indie Tiger Aspect Productions (production).

Cast: Willard White (Homeless Man), Nuala Willis (Doris), Linda Richardson (Annie), Philippa Lay, Anne Mason.

Telecast August 25, 2002, on Channel 4 in England and August 30, 2002, on Trio in the United States. Color. In English. 60 minutes.

WHEN YOU'RE IN LOVE

1937 American film with opera content

Met diva Grace Moore plays Louise Fuller, an Austrian opera singer working in the United States who is forced to go to Mexico when her visa expires. She meets penniless artist Cary Grant in Mexico, and he agrees to become her husband of convenience so she can sing in the United States. Naturally, after many complications, they fall in love and decide not to get a divorce. Thomas Mitchell plays Moore's opera publicist Hank Miller, and Luis Alberni plays a frenetic character called Serge Vilnikoff. Moore sings "Vissi d'arte" from *Tosca* with Emery D'Arcy as her Scarpia, "Un bel dì" from *Madama Butterfly,* and the "Waltz Song" from Gounod's *Roméo et Juliette,* plus a delightful "Minnie the Moocher" in homage to Cab Calloway. Beniamino Gigli is heard singing "M'apparì" on a phonograph record. Joseph Walker was the cinematographer, Alfred Newman was music director, and Robert Riskin wrote and directed the film for Columbia Pictures. The film was shown in England as *For You Alone*. Black and white. In English. 104 minutes.

WHERE DO WE GO FROM HERE?

1945 American film with opera content

In *Where Do We Go From Here?* Fred MacMurray plays a man with a genie (Gene Sheldon) who lets him to travel backwards into American history. On one trip he ends up on Columbus's mutinous ship just before land is sighted where he becomes involved in a miniature comic opera. Benito (Carlos Ramirez) sings about the mutiny, saying the world is flat; Columbus (Fortunio Bonanova) defends his voyage for the queen saying the world is round; and time traveler Bill Morgan (Fred MacMurray) tells the crew what they are about to discover. Kurt Weill wrote the music and Ira Gershwin wrote the words for this odd little Columbus opera. The other time-travel trips are to Valley Forge in 1776 and Manhattan in the 1600s, but there are no more mini-operas. MacMurray's love interests in the film, Joan Leslie and June Haver, appear in various guises in the past. Morrie Ryskind wrote the screenplay, Leon Shamroy was the cinematographer, David Raksin was the music director, and Gregory Ratoff directed the film for Twentieth Century-Fox. Color. In English. 78 minutes.

WHERE THE WILD THINGS ARE
1980 opera by Sendak and Knussen

American illustrator-author MAURICE SENDAK's popular children's book *Where the Wild Things Are* (1963) was turned into a fantasy opera by its author and English composer OLIVER KNUSSEN. It premiered in Brussels in 1980, but the definitive Glyndebourne version was not presented until 1984. It tells the story of Max, a rather naughty 6-year-old boy who is sent to bed without supper. He imagines a journey to the land of the Wild Things, where he becomes king and has a grand old time before having to flee back home.

1985 Glyndebourne Festival
English stage production: Frank Corsaro (director/co-choreographer), Jonathan Wolken (co-choreographer), Oliver Knussen (conductor, London Sinfonietta), Maurice Sendak (set/costume designer).
Cast: Karen Beardsley (Max), Mary King (Mama), Jenny Weston (Tzippy, sung by Mary King), Perry Davey (Moishe, sung by Hugh Hetherington), Cengiz Saner (Bruno, sung by Jeremy Munro), Brian Andro (Emile, sung by Stephen Rhys-Williams), Bernard Bennet (Bernard, sung by Andrew Gallacher), Mike Gallant (Goat, sung by Hugh Hetherington)
Video: Teldec/Home Vision VHS/LD. Christopher Swann (director). Color. In English. 40 minutes.
Comment: Sendak is really the star of this production with imaginative characters, costumes, and sets that appeal equally to children and adults.

WHITE HORSE INN
See IM WEISSEN RÖSSL.

WHOM THE GODS LOVE
1936 British film about Mozart

This British film, publicized as "the original story of Mozart and his wife," features scenes of their life together, culminating in the recognition of the composer's genius just before his death. Constance Weber Mozart (played by Victoria Hopper, the film director's wife) is as central to the story as Mozart (Stephen Haggard), as she remains faithful to him, despite heavy adulation from Prince Lopkonitz (John Loder). Most of the extended Mozart/Weber family appear in the film, including Hubert Harben as father Leopold Mozart, Jean Cadell as Mozart's mother, Liane Haid as Mozart's first love Aloysia Weber (Constance's sister), Richard Goolden as the girls's father, Muriel George as their mother, and Leueen Magrath as their brother. Also in the film are George Curzon as librettist Lorenzo Da Ponte, Frederick Leister as the emperor, Marie Lohr as the empress, and Lawrence Hanray as the archbishop. Scenes from *Le nozze di Figaro* and *Die Zauberflöte* are staged by Bernhard Baumgartner, with sets and costumes by Ernst Stern and Sir Thomas Beecham conducting the London Philharmonic Orchestra. Margaret Kennedy wrote the screenplay, Jan Stallich was the cinematographer, and Basil Dean directed for ATP. The film was reissued in 1949 with the simple title *Mozart*. Black and white. In English. 82 minutes. Video Yesteryear VHS.

WHO'S AFRAID OF OPERA?
1972–1973 puppet opera series

The *Who's Afraid of Opera* series consists of eight operas with Joan Sutherland singing the principal roles in the language of the opera and explaining the story to puppets in English. They are intended to introduce opera to children but are enjoyable for adults as well. Nathan Kroll devised and produced the series in 1972–1973 with the Larry Berthelson Puppeteers. The screenplays are by Claire Merrill (who abridged each opera to 30 minutes), the music is performed by the London Symphony Orchestra conducted by Richard Bonynge, and the three puppets are voiced by Larry Berthelson (Billy), Danny Seagren (Rudi), and Rod Young (Sir William). The directors are Ted Kotcheff, Herbert Wise, and Piers Haggard; the set designers are George Djurkovic and Voytek. The eight operas, on four Kultur videos, are IL BARBIERE DI SIVIGLIA, FAUST, LUCIA DI LAMMERMOOR, MIGNON, LA FILLE DU RÉGIMENT, LA PÉRICHOLE, RIGOLETTO, and LA TRAVIATA.

WIE EINST IM MAI
1913 operetta by Kollo and Bredschneider

WALTER KOLLO and Willy Bredschneider's tuneful 1913 German operetta *Wie einst im Mai* (Once Upon a Time in May) provided the basis for Sigmund Romberg's hit MAYTIME, although it is hardly known today outside Germany. Rudolf Bernauer and Rudolf Schanzer's libretto tells the bittersweet story of love across three generations as Ottilie and Fritz meet and part three times over the years from 1838 to 1913. *Wie einst im Mai* was a big hit on stage in Berlin and continues to be presented there. It was filmed in 1926 and 1937, and a 1966 Berlin stage production starred opera tenor René Kollo, the composer's grandson. Meanwhile, back in the United

States, Romberg composed a completely new score for his version, and librettist Rida Johnson Young transmuted the story into a New York tale. *Maytime* was such a success it overshadowed the original in America and England.

1937 Ariel film

German feature film: Richard Schneider-Edenkoben (director), Kurt Heynicke (screenplay), Willy Winterstein (cinematographer), Ernst Erich Budter (music director), Ariel Films (production).

Cast: Charlotte Ander (Ottilie), Paul Klinger (Fritz), Otto Wernicke, Ilse Fürstenberg, Robert Dorsay.

Black and white. In German. 91 minutes.

Comment: The time period of the film was reset to 1900, 1913, and 1937.

1978 Theater des Westerns, Berlin

German stage production: Karl Vibach (director), Paul Kuhn (conductor, SFB Berlin Big Band and Lübeck Hansestadt Orchestra), Michael Goden (set designer).

Cast: Sylvie Anders (Ottilie), Hans-George Panczak (Fritz), Harry Wüstenhagen (Stanislaus), Rainer Luxen (Cicero), Isy Orén (Juliette), Peter Zeiller (Harry).

Telecast January 27, 1978, on ARD German Television. Color. In German. 87 minutes.

Silent film

1926 Wolff film

German silent version of the operetta shot in Berlin and starring Trude Hesterberg and Camilla Spira. It was shown in cinemas with music from the operetta played live. Willi Wolff directed. Black and white. About 80 minutes.

WIENER BLUT
1899 operetta by Strauss and Müller

Wiener Blut (Viennese Blood) is not exactly an operetta by JOHANN STRAUSS Jr., even though he composed its music, but rather it is a *pasticcio*—a mosaic of preexisting melodies. Strauss had wanted to rearrange some older compositions to fit a libretto written by Viktor Leon and Leo Stein, but he was too ill to work. He agreed to let Adolf Müller do the arrangements in his place but died before it was completed. Like the 1931 film *Congress Dances*, it is set at the Congress of Vienna in 1815 where everybody apparently had a very good time. Count Zedlau is trying to hide his relationship with his mistress Franzi from his wife Gabriele, who has unexpectedly turned up, but he is also creating a new friendship with dress fitter Pepi. Most of the action revolves around various confusions with these women. All is sorted out at the end, and their various misbehaviors are blamed on the powers of ardent "Viennese blood."

1942 Forst film

Austrian feature film: Willy Forst (director), Ernest Marischka and Axel Eggebrecht (screenplay), Jan Stallich (cinematographer), Willy Schmidt-Gentner (music director), Forst Film (production).

Cast: Willy Fritsch (Count Zedlau), Maria Holst (Countess Gabriele), Doris Kreysler (Franzi), Hans Moser (Count's Valet), Theo Lingen (Jean).

Black and white. In German. 104 minutes.

Comment: This lavish production was not released in the United States until 1951.

1971 Lanske film

Austrian feature film: Herman Lanske (director), Anton Paulik (conductor, Kurt Graunke Symphony Orchestra and Munich Kammerchor), Roert Hofer-Ach (set designer).

Cast: René Kollo (Count Zedlau), Ingeborg Hallstein (Countess Gabriele), Dagmar Koller (Franzi), Helga Papouschek (Pepi).

Video: Taurus (Germany) VHS. Color. In German. 103 minutes.

WIFE, HUSBAND AND FRIEND
1939 film with opera content

A woman with not much talent tries to become an opera singer, but ironically it is her businessman husband who has a genuine operatic voice. Loretta Young plays the wannabe singer, Warner Baxter is the husband with talent, and Binnie Barnes is the opera diva who discovers he can sing. She tries to launch him on an operatic career, but his debut is a debacle. *Wife, Husband and Friend*, directed by Gregory Ratoff and written by Nunnally Johnson, is based on James Cain's story *Career in C Major*, filmed again in 1949 as *Everybody Does It*. Nina Koshetz provides the singing voice for Barnes, Emery Darcy sings for Baxter, T. Chavrova sings for Young, and Tudor Williams is seen on stage as Wotan. The imaginary opera *Arlesiana*, which is staged in the film, was composed by Sam Pokrass to a libretto by Armando Hauser. Vladimir Bakaltinoff conducts the music, and Ernest Palmer was the cinematographer. Twentieth Century-Fox. Black and white. 75 minutes.

WILDER, ALEC
American composer (1907–1980)

Songwriter Alec Wilder, who turned to opera in 1946, composed 13 operas/music theater works with three librettists, and his song/jazz background encouraged him to make them melodious and singer-friendly. Wilder's third librettist partner was William Engvick, with whom he created three operas. Their "musical fable" MISS CHICKEN LITTLE, in which Fox takes advantage of fowl gullibility, was telecast by CBS in 1953. Wilder's 1972 book *American Popular Song* is one of the definitive studies of the genre.

WILDHAGEN, GEORG
German film director(1920-)

German filmmaker Georg Wildhagen directed three opera films of note, and his version of *Le nozze di Figaro* in German was one of the first German opera films of importance during the postwar period. See LE NOZZE DI FIGARO (1949), DIE LUSTIGEN WEIBER VON WINDSOR (1950), and EINE NACHT IN VENEDIG (1953).

WILDSCHÜTZ, DER
1842 comic opera by Lortzing

An operatic comedy of disguises and melodic confusion. Schoolmaster Baculus, who has just gotten engaged to Gretchen, is accused of poaching by Count Eberbach. Gretchen wants to intercede, but Baculus won't allow it, so a visiting student offers to impersonate her. The "student" is really the count's sister, who wants to visit her brother in disguise and check out a baron he wants her to marry. After multiple mix-ups, all is happily sorted out. Albert Lortzing's *Der Wildschütz, oder Die Stimme der Natur* (The Poacher, or The Voice of Nature), libretto by the composer based on a play by August von Kotzebue, was an immediate success after its Leipzig premiere. It has remained so in Germany to the present day and is considered the composer's comic masterpiece.

1973 Bavaria Film
German television film: Axel Corti (director), Ferdinand Leitner (conductor, Bavarian Television Symphony Orchestra and Chorus), Gerd Krauss (set designer), Bavaria Film (production).

Cast: Hermann Prey (Count), Gerti Zeumer (Count's Sister) Walter Berry (Baculus), Werner Krenn (Baron), Charlotte Berthold (Countess), Hugo Gottschlich (Count's Steward), Elke Schary (Gretchen), Daphne Evangelatos (Nanette).

Color. In German. 112 minutes.

WILLIAMS, TUDOR
English-born American singer/actor (1896–1971)

Tudor Williams had small operatic roles as a bass in a number of Hollywood films from the 1930s to the 1950s, much of the time uncredited. He plays Colline in *La bohème* opposite Grace Moore in LOVE ME FOREVER; Méphistophélès in *Faust* opposite Jeanette MacDonald in SAN FRANCISCO; the servant Marcel who introduces MacDonald in *Les Huguenots* in MAYTIME; Wotan in an opera scene in WIFE, HUSBAND AND FRIEND; and Tristram in *Martha* opposite Nelson Eddy in the 1943 THE PHANTOM OF THE OPERA. His finest moment may be as King Mark in *Tristan und Isolde* in the Marjorie Lawrence biopic INTERRUPTED MELODY. Williams is chorus master for Korngold's imaginary opera *Salammbô* in CITIZEN KANE, major domo in Mary Ellis's *Fatal Lady,* a singer in the musicals RIO RITA and *Rosalie,* leader of a male chorus in *Winter Carnival,* and singer/arranger for *How Green Was My Valley.*

WILLIAM TELL
See GUILLAUME TELL.

WILLIE STARK
1981 opera by Floyd

Populist Southern governor Willie Stark is about to be impeached by Judge Burden, but Stark's idealist lawyer son Jack confronts the judge over past misdeeds and the judge kills himself. When Willie steals Jack's fiancée Ann, however, Jack shoots him. Carlisle Floyd's opera *Willie Stark,* libretto by the composer based on Robert Penn Warren's Pulitzer Prize–winning novel *All The King's Men,* was commissioned by Houston Grand Opera. Floyd has specialized in operas with American settings such as SUSANNAH and *Of Mice and Men,* but none is more American than *Willie Stark,* based on the life of Louisiana Governor Huey Long. Like the Hollywood film based on the novel, it portrays the rise and fall of one of the most corrupt and yet charismatic populist politicians in U.S. history. The music has strong influences from jazz and folk song, but it maintains an operatic framework with arias and ensembles.

1981 Houston Grand Opera
American stage production: Hal Prince (director), John DeMain (conductor, Houston Grand Opera Orchestra), Eugene Lee (set designer).

Cast: Timothy Nolen (Willie Stark), Alan Kay (Jack), Jan Curtiz (Sadie), Julia Conwell (Ann), David Busby (Duffy), Robert Moulson (Sugar Boy), Don Garret (Judge Burden).

Video at the MTR. Brian Large (director). Color. In English. 120 minutes.

Comment: Large taped the opera without an audience so he could place his cameras in the auditorium and on stage. Critics said it was magnificent screen opera.

Related films

1949 All the King's Men
Broderick Crawford stars as Willie Stark in this superb Academy Award–winning film of the Robert Penn Warren novel written and directed by Robert Rossen. It makes an enriching counterpoint to Floyd's musical adaptation of the story. Black and white. 109 minutes.

1995 Kingfish: A Story of Huey P. Long
Thomas Schlamme directed this film telling the undisguised story of the Kingfish, Huey P. Long, portrayed by John Goodman. Paul Monoash wrote the screenplay for Turner Pictures for television. Color. 110 minutes.

WILSON, ROBERT
American director/designer/playwright (1941–)

Robert Wilson conceived, designed, and staged EINSTEIN ON THE BEACH with composer PHILIP GLASS, and they premiered it at the Avignon Theatre Festival in 1976. It helped make them both famous. They also collaborated on the 12-hour THE CIVIL WARS for the 1984 Los Angeles Olympics art festival, but it became too expensive to stage. Their digital film opera MONSTERS OF GRACE was unveiled in 1998 in Los Angeles. Wilson, one of the great visionaries of modern theater, often calls his unusual stage productions "operas," but he also directs traditional operas. His productions of the Gluck classics ALCESTE and ORFEO ED EURIDICE at the Théâtre du Châtelet in Paris in 1999 were widely praised, and both are on DVD. His minimalist production of *Aida* at Covent Garden in 2003, however, was booed by the audience and savaged by critics; it sold out.

WINDGASSEN, WOLFGANG
German tenor (1914–1974)

Wolfgang Windgassen, who sang at the Met in 1957 as Siegmund in *Die Walküre,* was one of the great Wagner tenors and a regular at Bayreuth for 20 years. He can be seen in two opera videos. In TRISTAN UND ISOLDE (1967) he is Tristan, one of his great roles, opposite Birgit Nilsson; in the other he plays Prince Orlofsky in the Strauss operetta DIE FLEDERMAUS (1972). He starred in a 1973 telecast of Jessel's operetta SCHWARZWALDMÄDEL, and he sings Siegfried in a documentary about recording DER RING DES NIBELUNGEN (1965 film).

WINDHEIM, MAREK
Polish/American tenor/actor (1895–1960)

Marek Windheim began his career in Vienna in 1914, went to America from Poland in 1926, joined the Metropolitan Opera in 1928, and stayed with the company until 1936. Windheim was only 5 feet tall but he sang a wide range of roles at the Met, including the Lamplighter in *Manon Lescaut,* Walther in *Tannhäuser,* and the dwarf in *Siegfried.* He began to appear in films in 1937 and played character parts in dozens of films, including *Hitting a New High* with Lily Pons, *Ninotchka* with Greta Garbo, and *Mrs. Miniver* with Greer Garson. His other films include *Something to Sing About* in 1937, *Bringing Up Baby* and *Say It in French* in 1938, *On Your Toes* in 1939, *Play Girl* and *Escape* in 1940, *Too Many Blondes* and *Marry the Boss's Daughter* in 1941, *Madame Curie* and *Mission to Moscow* in 1943, *Mrs. Parkington* and *In Our Time* in 1944, *A Royal Scandal* in 1945, and *The Razor's Edge* and *Two Smart People* in 1946.

WLASCHIHA, EKKEHARD
German baritone (1938–)

Ekkehard Wlaschiha, one of the most popular Wagnerian singers, is featured on a number of videos. He made his debut in East Germany in 1961 in *Die lustigen Weiber von Windsor* and then began to sing regularly in Leipzig and Dresden. He made his first Bayreuth appearance in 1986 and has now sung around the world from the Met to Covent Garden, mostly in German operas. In addition to the operas listed below, he was featured as Don Pizarro in a Leningrad TV film of *Fidelio.* See DER FREISCHÜTZ (1985), GÖTTERDÄMMERUNG (1989/1990), LOHENGRIN (1989), DAS RHEINGOLD (1989/1990), SIEGFRIED (1989/1990), and TANNHÄUSER (1994).

WO DIE LERCHE SINGT
1918 operetta by Lehár

Wo die Lerche singt (Where the Lark Sings) is a folksy Hungarian operetta by Franz Lehár. It premiered in Budapest in January 1918 as *A pacsirta* (The Lark) and after revisions by librettists A. M. Willner and Heinz Reichert went to Vienna in March as *Wo die Lerche singt.* It was such a hit with the Viennese that it held the stage for 415 performances and went to New York in 1920. It tells the story of the love between city artist Sandor and village maiden Margit, who sings like a lark. They fall in love and he takes her to the city, where his painting of her makes him famous. His old flame, however, the actress Vilma, comes between them, and the lark decides to return to her village.

1936 Hunnia film
Hungarian/German feature film: Karel Lamac (director), Geza von Cziffra (screenplay), Werner Brandes (cinematographer), Franz Grothe (music director), Hunnia Studio, Budapest (production).

Cast: Marta Eggerth (Margit), Hans Söhnker (Sandor), Lucie Englisch (Vilma), Fritz Imhoff, Rudolf Carl.

Black and white. In Hungarian or German. 95 minutes.

Silent film

1918 Marischka film
The popularity of the Lehár operetta led to a film version the same year as the Vienna stage premiere. Hubert Marischka wrote, directed, and starred in the film based on the production at Theater an der Wien. Luise Kartousch plays Margit (as she had on stage), Marischka is the painter Sandor, Ernst Tautenhayn is the farmer Török (also from the stage production), Marietta Weber is Vilma, and Gustav Siege is the Baron. Lehár's music was played live with the film. Black and white. Silent. About 80 minutes.

WOLF TRAP PARK

Wolf Trap Park in Vienna, Virginia, near Washington, D.C., was opened as a performing arts center in 1971. Julius Rudel was named music director, the Wolf Trap Opera Company was organized, and a number of notable singers made their debut there. Operas were telecast from the Filene Center Auditorium, an amphitheater seating 6,800, with the involvement of the Washington Education Telecommunication Association (WETA). Four of them starred Beverly Sills, and three are available on commercial videos. See LA FILLE DU RÉGIMENT (1974), THE NEW MOON (1989), ROBERTO DEVEREUX (1975), and LA TRAVIATA (1976).

WONDER MAN
1945 American film with opera content

An imaginary opera was created for Danny Kaye for the 1945 Goldwyn movie *Wonder Man*. Kaye, who plays identical twins, takes the place of his murdered brother to testify against the gangsters who killed him. He need to give information to the district attorney, who is attending an operas, but the gangsters are in hot pursuit. He escapes onto the opera stage where he sings his testimony to the DA as an opera aria. Sylvia Fine created the words and music for this bizarre opera sequence which is titled simply "Opera Number." The opera singers on stage with Kaye are Noël Cravat, Nick Thompson, Nino Pipitone, and Baldo Minuti. Luis Alberni is the frenetic prompter, Aldo Franchetti is the worried opera orchestra conductor, and Virginia Mayo and Vera-Ellen play the women in Kaye's double life. Ray Heindorf orchestrated and conducted the music, Don Hartman and Mel Shavelson wrote the screenplay, Victor Milner and William Snyder were the cinematographers, and H. Bruce Humberstone directed. Color. 96 minutes.

WORST OPERA ON FILM

The films with the worst use of opera music are a cheap B-Western and an expensive Mahler biopic. In the low-budget 1941 Monogram film RIDIN' THE CHEROKEE TRAIL, arias from *Rigoletto* and *Carmen* are transmuted into cowboy songs by Tex Ritter, and they are truly awe-inspiring in their awfulness. The villain is an opera enthusiast who plays Caruso's version of "La donna è mobile" on a wind-up phonograph. Ritter claims the aria is really a cowboy song about Ol' Pete the Bandit that the "galoot Rigoletto" stole from the cowboys. The "Toreador Song," it turns out, is also a song by Pete the Bandit. What B-Western audiences thought of this strange sequence is hard to imagine. However, it is not nearly as awful as the "Ride of the Valkyries" sequence in Ken Russell's *Mahler*. Ritter is weird but funny; Russell is bizarre and excruciating. In an over-the-top dream sequence titled "The Convert," Mahler (Robert Powell) and Cosima Wagner (Antonia Ellis) sing weird new lyrics to the Valkyries's music in Valhalla as he converts from Judaism. It has lines such as "You're no longer a Jew boy, now you're one of us, now you're a goy, you can conduct opera." It is hard to imagine an opera sequence in worse taste. See GUSTAV MAHLER (1974).

WORST OPERETTA ON FILM

Two operetta films made in Hollywood at the beginning of the sound era are the top contenders for worst operetta on film. Rudolf Friml's 1930 film operetta THE LOTTERY BRIDE stars Jeanette MacDonald as the prize in an Alaskan marriage lottery. She is won by a man she once loved and is trying to forget (no coincidence is to unlikely for this film). He doesn't look at her photo but gives his winning ticket to his brother. When Jeanette arrives and he sees what has happened, he leaps on a passing German Zeppelin and heads north to forget his sorrows. The blimp gets lost in the frozen Arctic, and Jeanette has to rescue him. It's a pretty bad movie, but it does keep you wondering what might happen next. Even worse is GOLDEN DAWN, a 1930 film based on an operetta by Emmerich Kálmán that features Viennese music sung in blackface in Africa in a World War I prison camp. The hit song is the overseer's ode to his whip. As critic Lucius Beebe noted in a *Herald-Tribune* review, "Reason totters at the thought that any one could have conceived in seriousness such a definitive catalogue of vulgarity, witlessness, and utterly pathetic and preposterous nonsense." And that's putting it mildly.

WOZZECK

1925 opera by Berg

Alban Berg's powerful opera is based on the play *Woyzeck* by George Büchner. Despite its 19th-century source, the opera seems very modern in its concern with a person brutalized by society. Wozzeck is a soldier who senses mysterious forces he does not understand. His captain uses him as a barber and his doctor uses him as an experimental guinea pig, while his woman Marie has begun a dalliance with the drum major. His visions increase until eventually he kills Marie. Berg was influenced by movies in his libretto and uses cinematic rather than theatrical time flow for the action.

1967 Hess film

German film of stage production: Joachim Hess (film director), Rolf Liebermann (stage director), Günther Rennert (Hamburg Opera producer), Bruno Maderna (conductor, Hamburg Philharmonic Orchestra), Peter Hassenstein (cinematographer), Herbert Kirchhoff (set designer).

Cast: Toni Blankenheim (Wozzeck), Sena Jurinac (Marie), Richard Cassilly (Drum Major), Peter Haage (Andres), Gerhard Unger (Captain), Hans Sotin (Doctor).

Color. In German. 103 minutes.

***1987 Vienna State Opera

Austrian stage production: Adolf Dresen (director), Claudio Abbado (conductor, Vienna State Opera Orchestra and Chorus), Herbert Kapplmüller (set/costume designer).

Cast: Franz Grundheber (Wozzeck), Hildegard Behrens (Marie), Walter Raffeiner (Drum Major), Philip Langridge (Andres), Heinz Zednik (Captain), Aage Haugland (Doctor).

Video: Image Entertainment and Arthaus (GB) DVD/Kultur and Home Vision VHS/Pioneer LD. Brian Large (director). Color. In German with English subtitles. 97 minutes.

Comment: Very impressive, with superb singers, fine production, and sensitive conducting.

1994 Berlin State Opera

German stage production: Patrice Chéreau (director), Daniel Barenboim (conductor, Berlin Staatskapelle and Chorus of the Deutsche Oper, Berlin).

Cast: Franz Grundheber (Wozzeck), Waltraud Meier (Marie), Mark Baker (Drum Major), Endrik Wottrich (Andres), Graham Clark (Captain), Günter von Kannen (Doctor).

Video: Teldec/NVC Arts (GB) VHS. Color. In German with English subtitles. 100 minutes.

2001 Metropolitan Opera

American stage production: Mark Lamos (director), James Levine (conductor, Metropolitan Opera Orchestra and Chorus), Robert Israel (set designer).

Cast: Fall Struckmann (Wozzeck), Katarina Dalayman (Marie), Wolfgang Neumann (Drum Major), John Horton Murray (Andres), Graham Clark (Captain), Michael Devlin (Doctor).

Taped October 6, 2001. Brian Large (director). Color. In German with English subtitles. 102 minutes.

Related films

1947 Klaren film

Kurt Meisel stars as Wozzeck with Helga Zülch as Marie in this East German film adaptation of the source Büchner play directed by Georg C. Klaren. It does not use Berg's music. Black and white. In German. 101 minutes.

1979 Herzog Film

Werner Herzog's claustrophobic film adaptation of the Büchner play *Woyzeck* stars Klaus Kinski as Wozzeck and Eva Mattes as Marie. A brilliant transposition of play to screen, it deserves comparison with the opera. Josef Bierbichler is the drum major, Willy Semmelrogge is the doctor, Paul Burien is Andres, and Wolfgang Reichmann is the captain. Color. In German. 81 minutes.

1994 Szasz film

Janos Szasz wrote and directed this bleak but beautiful Hungarian adaptation of the Büchner play, reset in a grimy railway yard. Woyzeck is portrayed as a railway worker humiliated by his boss and rejected by his wife Maria, who prefers a policeman. Eventually, he goes over the edge. Black and white. In Hungarian. 94 minutes.

WUNDERLICH, FRITZ

Austrian tenor (1930–1966)

Fritz Wunderlich, who died young in an accident, was Germany's top lyric tenor during his short career, equally adept at opera and operetta. He made his debut in Stuttgart in 1955 as Tamino in *Die Zauberflöte,* joined the Munich Opera in 1960, and sang with the Vienna State Opera from 1962. He was noted for the sweetness and melodiousness of his voice and was especially admired in Mozart. His records remain popular. See IL BARBIERE DI SIVIGLIA (1959), EUGENE ONEGIN (1965), WOLFGANG A. MOZART (1967), and EIN WALZERTRAUM (1960).

1990 Fritz Wunderlich: Portrait of a Singer

German TV documentary about the singer and his career, written and directed by Manfred Deide. Color. In German. 30 minutes. Video at New York Public Library.

X

XERXES
See Serse.

Y

YEOMAN OF THE GUARD, THE
1888 comic opera by Gilbert and Sullivan

The Tower of London in the 16th century. Colonel Fairfax wants to get married before he is executed to keep his wealth from going to crooked relatives. Strolling player Elsie agrees to become his blindfolded bride so she can inherit it; Jack Point, her frustrated partner, reluctantly agrees. Sgt. Meryll, of the Yeomen of the Guard, and his daughter Phoebe help Fairfax escape. He pretends to be Phoebe's brother, Leonard, and woos and wins Elsie. When Fairfax is reprieved, he reveals that he is the one she married when blindfolded. Jack Point is broken-hearted. Sir Arthur Sullivan's *The Yeomen of the Guard, or The Merryman and His Maid,* libretto by W. S. Gilbert, comes the closest of the Savoy operas to being a "serious" opera. It has been compared in plot to Wallace's *Maritana.*

1957 Hallmark Hall of Fame
American TV production: George Schaefer (director), Franz Allers (conductor, NBC Orchestra), Paul Barnes (set designer), William Nichols (screenplay).

Cast: Alfred Drake (Jack Point), Barbara Cook (Elsie), Bill Hayes (Col. Fairfax), Celeste Holm (Phoebe), Henry Calvin (Wilfred), Muriel O'Malley (Dame Carruthers), Robert Wright (Sir Richard), Norman Atkins (Sgt. Meryll).

Video at UCLA. Telecast live April 10, 1957, on NBC. Color. In English. 90 minutes.

1970 Doreman film
English feature film: Stanley Doreman (director), David Lloyd-Jones (conductor, New World Philharmonic Orchestra), Peter Rice (costume designer).

Cast: Tommy Steele (Jack Point), Laureen Livingstone (Elsie), Terry Jenkins (Col. Fairfax), Della Jones (Phoebe), Dennis Wicks (Wilfred), Anne Collins (Dame Carruthers), Tom McDonnell (Sir Richard), Paul Hudson (Sgt. Meryll).

Video: Magnetic VHS. Color. In English. 105 minutes.

Comment: The film was shot on location at the Tower of London and was based on a production staged there by Anthony Besch.

1972 Gilbert & Sullivan for All series
English highlights film: Peter Seabourne (director), Peter Murray (conductor, Gilbert and Sullivan Festival Orchestra and Chorus), David Maverovitch (cinematographer), Trevor Evans (adaptation), John Seabourne (producer).

Cast: John Cartier (Jack Point), Valerie Masterson (Elsie), Thomas Round (Col. Fairfax), Sylvia Eaves (Phoebe), Lawrence Richard (Wilfred), Helen Landis (Dame Carruthers), Michael Wakeham (Sir Richard), Donald Adams (Sgt. Meryll).

Video: Musical Collectables VHS. Color. In English. 50 minutes.

Comment: Previously released as part of the *World of Gilbert and Sullivan* series.

1982 Gilbert and Sullivan Collection series
English studio production: Anthony Besch (director), Judith De Paul (producer), Alexander Faris (conductor, London Symphony Orchestra and Ambrosian Opera Chorus), Allan Cameron (set designer), George Walker (executive producer).

Cast: Joel Grey (Jack Point), Elizabeth Gale (Elsie), David Hillman (Col. Fairfax), Claire Powell (Phoebe), Alfred Marks (Wilfred), Geoffrey Chard (Sgt. Meryll), Elizabeth Bainbridge (Dame Carruthers), Peter Savidge (Sir Richard).

Video: Opera World/Braveworld (GB) VHS/Pioneer LD. Dave Heather (director). Color. In English. 119 minutes.

Early/related films

1907 Cinematophone Singing Pictures
British sound film of the final scene of Act I. John Morland directed the film, titled *Great Finale,* for Cinematophone Singing Pictures. Black and white. In English. 3 minutes.

1999 Topsy-Turvy
The overture to *The Yeomen of the Guard* is featured in this film about the relationship between Gilbert (Jim Broadbent) and Sullivan (Allan Corduner). See TOPSY-TURVY.

YO, PECADOR
1965 Mexican film biography of Mojica

Yo, Pecador (I, a Sinner), a narrative film about the life of the Mexican tenor José Mojica, is based on the tenor's best-selling autobiography. Mojica went from being a major opera star, singing at the Chicago Opera during the 1920s with Mary Garden and Amelita Galli-Curci, to being a Hollywood movie star during the 1930s. He made 10 films for Fox during the early 1930s, all but one in

Spanish, and another 15 in Mexico and Argentina. He gave up opera when his mother died and became a Franciscan friar in 1947. Much of the film is a flashback showing his film and opera career in the United States, with excerpts from *Rigoletto, Il trovatore, Madama Butterfly, La bohème, La favorita, Lucia di Lammermoor, L'elisir d'amore,* and *Faust.* Pedro Geraldo plays Mojica onscreen but the singing is by Mojica. Alfonso Corona Blake directed. Color. In Spanish. 90 minutes. Video Latino VHS.

YVAIN, MAURICE
French composer (1891–1965)

Maurice Yvain, who wrote film music as well as operettas and musical comedies, is probably most famous in America for the song "Mon Homme," which he created for Mistinguett. It was presented in the *Ziegfeld Follies of 1922* as "My Man," and it became Fanny Brice's theme song. Yvain's most popular stage works were the three operettas in his "Bouche" series; PASS SUR LA BOUCHE was filmed in 1925. Among Yvain's many original film scores were the 1936 Julien Duvivier classic *La belle équipe* and the 1939 Pierre Fresnay movie *Le duel* with Yvonne Printemps.

Z

ZAMPA
1831 opéra-comique by Hérold

Zampa is a pirate who tries to steal his brother's bride-to-be. Like Don Giovanni, he is destroyed by a statue, a marble one of Alice, a woman he had seduced and abandoned. FERDINAND HÉROLD's *Zampa, ou La fiancée de marbre* (Zampa, or the Marble Fiancée) was a highly popular opera and repertory regular in the 19th century, but it is now known mostly for its overture and through vintage recordings. The libretto is by Mélesville (Anne-Honoré-Joseph Duveyrier). There is no complete version of the opera on film or video.

1930 Menzies film
William Cameron Menzies, art director and designer of films such as *Things to Come,* made a series of brilliant musical short films in the early days of sound. His abbreviated but imaginative visualization of *Zampa* was popular in 16mm rental catalogs until the coming of video. Tinted black and white. 10 minutes.

1935 The Band Concert
Mickey Mouse conducts an animated band in the park in his first color film, and the audience cheers him after a performance of selections from *Zampa.* Wilfred Jackson directed. Color. 7 minutes.

ZANDONAI, RICCARDO
Italian composer (1883–1944)

Riccardo Zandonai was considered a possible successor to Puccini by the Ricordi publishing firm after his success in 1908 with the Dickens adaptation *Il Grillo del Focolare* (The Cricket on the Hearth). Zandonai also found admirers for his Spanish-flavored gypsy opera *Conchita* and his Shakespeare adaptation GIULIETTA E ROMEO. Today he is known primarily for his 1914 opera FRANCESCA DA RIMINI, the tragic story of the lovers immortalized in Dante's *Divine Comedy.* Zandonai also composed music for several operatic films, including CASA LONTANA (1939), AMAMI, ALFREDO! (1940), and RITORNO (1940) for which he created an imaginary opera called *Penelope.*

ZAR UND ZIMMERMANN
1837 comic opera by Lortzing

ALBERT LORTZING's *Zar und Zimmermann* (The Tsar and the Carpenter) is a tuneful comic opera based on a legend about Tsar Peter I of Russia, known as Peter the Great. He was said to have worked in disguise in Holland in 1698 to learn shipbuilding skills that he could not learn at home. While there, he befriends a carpenter named Peter, who is in love with Burgomaster Van Bett's daughter Marie. Young Peter is wrongly identified as the Tsar and feted by local ambassadors and assorted fools, but all is sorted out in the end with the help of the real Tsar. The libretto is by the composer. The opera remains popular in the German-speaking world but has not been much seen in America since its New York premiere in 1851.

1956 DEFA film
East German feature film: Hans Müller (director), Arthur Kuhnert (screenplay). Hans Löwlein (conductor, DEFA Orchestra), DEFA (production).

Cast: Bert Fortell (Tsar, sung by Josef Metternich), Lore Frisch (Marie, sung by Ingeborg Wenglor), Gunther Haach (Peter, sung by Gerhard Unger), Willy Kleinau (Van Bett, sung by Heinrich Pflanzl).

Color. In German. 101 minutes.

Comment: Highlights are featured in the DEFA anthology film *Musikalisches Rendezvous* (1962).

1969 Polyphon film
West German feature film: Joachim Hess (director), Rolf Liebermann (stage director), Charles Mackerras (conductor, Hamburg Philharmonic Orchestra and Hamburg State Opera Chorus) Herbert Kirchhoff (set designer), Polyphon Film (production).

Cast: Raymond Wolansky (Tsar), Lucia Popp (Marie), Peter Haage (Peter), Hans Sotin (Van Bett), Ursula Boese (Widow Browe), Horst Wilhelm (Chateauneuf).

Color. In German. 137 minutes.

Comment: Based on a Hamburg State Opera stage production. Shown theatrically in the United States.

1976 Corti film
German TV film: Axel Corti (director), Heinz Wallberg (conductor, Munich Radio-TV Orchestra and Bavarian Chorus), Xaver Schwarzenberger and Sepp Vavra (cinematographers), Bernd Müller and Jörg Neumann (set designers).

Cast: Hermann Prey (Tsar), Lucia Popp (Marie), Adalbert Kraus (Peter), Karl Ridderbusch (Van Bett), Werner Krenn (Chateauneuf), Alexander Malta (General Lefort), Helmut Berger-Tuna (Lord Syndham)

Video: House of Opera/Lyric VHS. Color. In German. 102 minutes.

ZAREWITSCH, DER

1927 operetta by Lehár

Der Zarewitsch (The Crown Prince) tells the bittersweet story of a Russian crown prince who thinks he dislikes women. When he is tricked into falling in love with a dancer named Sonja, however, he abandons his royal life and goes off to live with her in Italy. When he inherits the crown, duty gets the better of him so he gives her up and returns home. FRANZ LEHÁR's *Der Zarewitsch,* which premiered in Berlin with Richard Tauber in the leading role, is still popular in Germany. Bela Jenbach and Heinz Reichert's libretto is based on a play by Gabriela Zapolska.

1933 Janson film

German feature film: Viktor Janson (director), George Zoch (screenplay), Karl Puth and Bruno Timm (cinematographers), Alfred Strass (music director).

Cast: Hans Söhnker (Prince), Marta Eggerth (Sonja), Ery Bos, Paul Otto, Georg Alexander, Ida Wüst.

Black and white. In German. 85 minutes.

Comment: A French version was made at the same time with a different cast (see below).

1933 Janson/Bernard-Derosne film

French feature film: Jean Bernard-Derosne and Victor Janson (directors), Robert Lorette and George Zoch (screenplay), Karl Puth and Bruno Timm (cinematographers), Alfred Strass (music director).

Cast: George Rigaud (Prince), Marie Glory (Monique), Gaston Jacquet (Grand Duke), Germaine Aussey (Princess Dorotheá), Felix Oudart (General), Maurice Escande (Count Symoff).

Black and white. In French. 85 minutes.

Comment: Made at the same time as the German film above and titled *Son Altesse Impériale*

1954 Le Tzarewitch

French feature film: Arthur Maria Rabenalt (director), Roger Richebé and Pierre Gaspard-Huit (screenplay), Bert Grund (music director), CCC Films (production).

Cast: Luis Mariano (Prince), Sonja Ziemann (Sonja), Ivan Petrovich (Grand Duke), Maria Sebaldt (Mascha), Hans Richter.

Video: René Chateau (France) VHS. Color. In French. 95 minutes.

Comment: The operetta is performed inside a framing story. Mariano plays a tenor singing the prince in a stage production of the operetta, and Ziemann is the ballerina who loves him. After a fall, she dreams the operetta until all ends happily. The film was made in French and German versions and shown in France as *Le Tzarewitch* and in the United States and Germany as *Der Zarewitsch.*

***1973 Rabenalt film

German TV film: Arthur Maria Rabenalt (director), Willy Mattes (conductor, Kurt Graunke Symphony Orchestra), Otto Pischinger (set designer), Unitel (production company).

Cast: Wieslaw Ochman (Prince), Teresa Stratas (Sonja), Harald Juhnke (Ivan), Birke Bruck (Mascha), Paul Esser (Grand Duke), Lukas Amman (Prime Minister).

Video: Taurus (Germany) VHS. Color. In German. 92 minutes.

Comment: Rabenalt's second film of the operetta was lavishly made with Stratas at her peak in voice and charm. It won warm praise from German critics.

Silent film

1929 Fleck film

Ivan Petrovich plays the crown prince in this silent German film that was screened with live music from the operetta. Mariette Millner is his Sonja and the supporting cast includes Paul Otto, Albert Steinrück, and John Hamilton. Jacob and Louise Fleck directed. Black and white. In German. About 80 minutes.

ZARZUELA

A zarzuela—the counterpart of the operetta of central Europe—is a Spanish light opera with spoken dialogue, but it is based on Spanish dance rhythms rather than the waltzes and czardas of Austria and Hungary. Zarzuelas are normally set in Spain and reflect aspects of regional culture, from the street life of Madrid to the country life of Galicia. Their importance in Spanish cultural life is indicated by the many films based on them. Spanish critic J. F. Aranda felt that the best classic films of zarzuelas were Benito Perojo's LA VERBENA DE LA PALOMA (1935) and Jean Grémillon's LA DOLOROSA (1934). The best modern productions on video are those made at the JARVIS CONSERVATORY in California since 1995 and those directed by JUAN DE ORDUÑA for Spanish television during the 1960s. Spanish opera singers usually include zarzuela arias in their recitals; PLÁCIDO DOMINGO, who made zarzuela films early in his career, produced EL GATO MONTES on stage in Los Angeles and got it shown on national television. One of the best descriptions of the zarzuela genre is in James A. Michener's fine book *Iberia.* For details about other zarzuelas, see the entries on composers EMILIO ARRIETA, FRANCISCO BARBIERI, TOMÁS BRETÓN, MANUEL FERNÁNDEZ CABALLERO, RUPERTO CHAPÍ, FEDERICO CHUECA, ENRIQUE GRANADOS, JACINTO GUERRERO, JESUS GURIDI, VICENTE LLEÓ, MANUEL PENELLA, JOSÉ SERRANO, FEDERICO MORENO TORROBA, JOSÉ MARÍA USANDIZAGA, and AMADEO VIVES.

1991 Zarzuela Royal Gala Concert

Plácido Domingo is the main singer in this zarzuela concert staged in the National Music Auditorium in Madrid in the presence of the Spanish king. Noted zarzuela singers—including Guadalupe Sanchez, Teresa Verderam, and Paloma Perez Inigo—join Domingo in performances of music by Chapi, Chueca, Giménez, Guerrero, Serrano, Sorozabal, Torroba, and Vives, with support from the Ballet Español and the Madrid Symphonic Orchestra. Enriques Garcia Asensio directed the telecast. Color. 69 minutes. Kultur VHS.

ZAUBER DE BOHÈME

1937 Austrian film with opera content

Zauber de Bohème (The Charm of *La bohème*) is a "parallel" style film in which what happens to the characters in *La bohème* is reflected in the lives of the people who sing the roles in the opera. Hungarian soprano Marta Eggerth stars as Denise with Polish tenor Jan Kiepura as the man she loves. They are opera singers who want to sing together and perform Puccini arias and Robert Stolz songs. When Eggerth learns she will soon die of an incurable illness, she goes nobly away so he can have a career without worrying about her. They become famous separately and finally appear on stage together in *La bohème*. At the end of the opera, she dies on cue, like Mimì. The film was written by Ernst Marischka, photographed by Franz Planer, and directed by Geza von Bolvary. Black and white. In German with English subtitles. 97 minutes. Bel Canto Society/Live Opera/Lyric VHS.

ZAUBERFLÖTE, DIE

1791 opera by Mozart

Die Zauberflöte (The Magic Flute) is the most magical of WOLFGANG A. MOZART's operas, mixing Masonic rituals and populist entertainment in an educational fairy tale. A queen asks a prince to rescue a princess from an evil wizard. She provides him with a magic flute and a birdman assistant with magic bells. But things are not what they first seem, and he has many adventures while learning the truth and winning the princess. This singspiel (it has spoken dialogue) was commissioned by Emanuel Schikaneder, who wrote the libretto and created the role of Papageno. It contains some of Mozart's greatest music. *The Magic Flute* was rarely filmed during the silent era (it was less popular then) but is a favorite of modern filmmakers, so there is a choice of excellent videos.

1956 NBC Opera Theatre

American TV production: George Balanchine (director/choreographer), Samuel Chotzinoff (producer), Peter Herman Adler (conductor, Symphony of the Air

Orchestra), W. H. Auden and Chester Kallman (English-language adaptation), Rouben Ter-Arutunian (set and costume designer).

Cast: William Lewis (Tamino), Leontyne Price (Pamina), John Reardon (Papageno), Adelaide Bishop (Papagena), Laurel Hurley (Queen of the Night), Yi Kwe Sze (Sarastro), Andrew McKinley (Monostatos), Frances Paige, Joan Moynagh, Helen Vanni (Three Ladies).

Video at the MTR. Telecast live January 15, 1956. Kirk Browning (director). Black and white. In English. 120 minutes.

1971 Polyphon film

German feature film: Joachim Hess (director), Peter Ustinov (screenplay), Gero Erhardt (cinematographer), Horst Stein (Hamburg State Opera Orchestra and Chorus), Rolf Liebermann (producer), Polyphon Film (production company).

Cast: Nicolai Gedda (Tamino), Edith Mathis (Pamina), William Workman (Papageno), Carol Malone (Papagena), Cristina Deutekom (Queen of the Night), Hans Sotin (Sarastro), Dietrich Fischer-Dieskau (Speaker).

Color. In German. 154 minutes.

Comment: The film was shot in a studio, but it was based on a Hamburg State Opera stage production.

The Three Ladies and Tamino in Bergman's film of the opera.

***1973 Bergman film

Swedish feature film: Ingmar Bergman (director/screenplay), Sven Nykvist (cinematographer), Eric Ericson (conductor, Swedish State Broadcasting Network Symphony and Chorus) Donya Feuer (choreographer).

Cast: Joseph Köstlinger (Tamino); Irma Urrila (Pamina); Håkan Hagegård (Papageno); Elisabeth Erikson (Papagena); Birgit Nordin (Queen of the Night); Ulrik Cold (Sarastro); Ragnar Ulgung (Monostatos); Britt-Marie Aruhn, Birgitta Smiding, Kirsten Vaupel (Three Ladies); Urban Malberg, Erland von Haijne, Ansgar Krook (Three Boys); Erik Saeden (Speaker).

Video: Criterion DVD/Home Vision and Paramount VHS. Color. In Swedish as *Trollflöjten* with English subtitles. 135 minutes.

Comment: One of the great opera films and one of the most enjoyable; it hardly seems to matter that it is sung in Swedish by relative unknowns. Bergman filmed it as an opera in performance in a mock-up of the 18th-century Drottningholm Court Theatre. He shows the audience, focuses on a girl's wonder at seeing the opera, and then presents the opera beautifully staged and filmed. At intermission, the camera observes the singers backstage. During the opera, lines of the libretto occasionally descend from the heavens so the trios can sing them in a charming manner. Indeed, almost everyone is charming in the film, which suggests that Pamina is the daughter of Sarastro and the Queen of the Night. Hagegård became known internationally through this film.

1976 Leipzig Opera

East German stage production: Joachim Herz (director), Gert Bahner (conductor, Leipzig Gewandhaus Orchestra), Rudolf Heinrich (set/costume designer), Marion Schurath (choreographer).

Cast: Horst Gebhardt (Tamino); Magdalena Falewicz (Pamina); Dieter Scholz (Papageno); Heidrun Halk (Papagena); Inge Uibel (Queen of the Night); Herman Christian Polster (Sarastro); Gutfried Speck (Monostatos); Jitka Kovarikova, Anne-Kristin Paul, Gertrud Lahusen-Oertel (Three Ladies); Gerhild Muller, Renate Schneeweiss, Heike Syhre (Three Boys); Rainer Lüdeke, Hans-Peter Schwarzbach (Speakers).

Video: VIEW DVD/VHS (DVD has Mozart biography). Georg F. Mielke (director). Color. In German. 156 minutes.

1976 The Magic Flute Story: An Opera Fantasy

Abridged version for children of the Leipzig Opera production described above with added English-language narration. Color. In German. 42 minutes. VIEW DVD/VHS.

1978 Glyndebourne Festival

English stage production: John Cox (director), Bernard Haitink (conductor, London Philharmonic Orchestra and Glyndebourne Festival Chorus), David Hockney (set designer).

Cast: Leo Goeke (Tamino); Felicity Lott (Pamina); Benjamin Luxon (Papageno); Elizabeth Conquet (Papagena); May Sandoz (Queen of the Night); Thomas Thomaschke (Sarastro); John Fryatt (Monostatos); Willard White (Speaker); Teresa Cahill, Patricia Parker, Fiona Kimm (Three Ladies); Kate Flowers, Lindway John, Elizabeth Stokes (Three Boys).

Video: VAI/Opera d'Oro VHS. Dave Heather (director). Color. In German with English subtitles. 164 minutes.

Comment: Hockney's superb set designs are a major attraction of this production.

1982 Salzburg Festival

Austrian stage production: Jean-Pierre Ponnelle (director, set/costume designer), James Levine (conductor, Vienna Philharmonic and Vienna State Opera Chorus).

Cast: Peter Schreier (Tamino), Ileana Cotrubas (Pamina), Christian Boesch (Papageno), Gudrun Seiber (Papagena), Edita Gruberova (Queen of the Night), Martti Talvela (Sarastro), Walter Berry (Speaker), Edda Moser, Ann Murray, Ingrid Mayr (Three Ladies).

Video: House of Opera VHS. Telecast August 28, 1982, on ORF Austrian Television. Color. In German. 190 minutes.

Comment: One critic rated this outstanding production from the Salzburg Festival as best of all the video operas.

1983 Bavarian State Opera

German stage production: August Everding (director and designer), Wolfgang Sawallisch (conductor, Bavarian State Opera Orchestra and Chorus), Jürgen Rose (set designer).

Cast: Francisco Araiza (Tamino); Lucia Popp (Pamina); Wolfgang Brendel (Papageno); Edita Gruberova (Queen of the Night); Kurt Moll (Sarastro); Gudrun Sieber (Papagena); Norbert Orth (Monostatos); Pamela Coburn, Daphne Evangelatos, Cornelia Wulkopf (Three Ladies); Cedric Rossdeutscher, Christina Immler, Stefan Bandemehr (Three Boys); Jan-Hendrik Rootering (Speaker).

Video: Philips VHS/LD. Peter Windgassen (director). Color. In German with English subtitles. 160 minutes.

Comment: A highlights version is available in the *Great Moments* series as Volume 4.

1986 Australian Opera

Australian stage production: Göran Järvefelt (director), Richard Bonynge (conductor, Elizabethan Sydney Orchestra and Australian Opera Chorus).

Cast: Gran Wilson (Tamino); Yvonne Kenny (Pamina); John Fulford (Papageno); Peta Blyth (Papagena); Christa Leahmann (Queen of the Night); Donald Shanks (Sarastro); Graeme Ewer (Monostatos); Nicola Ferner-White, Patricia Price, Rosemary Gunn (Three Ladies); Anthony Phipps, Andrew Wentzel, Cameron Phipps (Three Boys); John Pringle (Speaker).

Video: Kultur VHS. Color. In English 160 minutes.

1987 National Arts Centre, Ottawa

Canadian stage production: John Thomson (director), Mario Bernardi (conductor, National Arts Center of Canada Orchestra), Peter Rice (set/costume designer).

Cast: David Rendall (Tamino); Patricia Wells (Pamina); David Holloway (Papageno); Nancy Hermiston (Papagena); Rita Shane (Queen of the Night); Don Garrard (Sarastro); Alan Crofoot (Monostatos); Barbara Collier, Diane Loeb, Janet Stubbs (Three Ladies); John Griffith, John Maxwell, Kevin Branshell (Three Boys).

Video: CBC VHS. John Thomson (director). Color. In English. 160 minutes.

1987 New York City Opera

American stage production: Lotfi Mansouri (director), Sergiu Comissiona (conductor, New York City Opera Orchestra and Chorus), Thierry Bosquet (set/costume designer), Beverly Sills (host).

Cast: Jon Garrison (Tamino), Faith Esham (Pamina), Stephen Dickson (Papageno), Rachel Rosales (Queen of the Night), Gregory Stapp (Sarastro).

Telecast October 14, 1987, on PBS. Kirk Browning (director). Color. In German with English subtitles. 195 minutes.

***1989 Drottningholm Court Theatre

Swedish stage production: Göran Järvefelt (director), Arnold Östman (conductor, Drottningholm Court Theatre Orchestra and Chorus), Carl Friedrich Oberle (set/costume designer).

Cast: Stefan Dahlberg (Tamino); Ann Christine Biel (Pamina); Mikael Samuelson (Papageno); Birgitta Larsson (Papagena); Birgit Louise Frandsen (Queen of the Night); Laszlo Polgar (Sarastro); Magnus Kyhle (Monostatos); Anita Soldh, Linnea Sallay, Inger Blom (Three Ladies); Elisabeth Berg, Ann-Christine Larsson, Anna Tomson (Three Boys); Petteri Salomaa (Speaker).

Video: Image Entertainment DVD/Philips VHS/LD. Thomas Olofsson (director). Color. In German with English subtitles. 165 minutes.

Comment: A most enjoyable production with Östman leading the orchestra in period costume with authentic instruments in a lovely intimate, ancient theater.

1991 Metropolitan Opera

American stage production: John Cox (director, staging by Gus Mostart), James Levine (conductor, Metropolitan Opera Orchestra and Chorus), David Hockney (set/costume designer).

Cast: Francisco Araiza (Tamino); Kathleen Battle (Pamina); Manfred Hemm (Papageno); Barbara Kilduff (Papagena); Luciana Serra (Queen of the Night); Kurt Moll (Sarastro); Heinz Zednik (Monostatos); Juliana Gondek, Mimì Lerner, Judith Christin (Three Ladies); Ted Huffman, Benjamin Schott, Per-Christian Brevig (Three Boys); Andreas Schmidt (Speaker).

Video: DG DVD/VHS. Taped February 9, 1991; telecast June 19, 1991. Brian Large (director). Color. In German with English subtitles. 169 minutes.

Comment: Hockney's designs are once again a major attraction.

1991 Groot film

Dutch animation film: Colin Davis (conductor, Dresden State Orchestra and Leipzig Chorus).

Voices: Peter Schreier (Tamino); Margaret Price (Pamina); Mikael Melbye (Papageno); Maria Venuti (Papagena); Luciana Serra (Queen of the Night); Kurt Moll (Sarastro); Robert Tear (Monostatos); Marie McLaughlin, Ann Murray, Hanna Schwarz (Three Ladies); Theo Adam (Speaker).

Color. In Italian. 160 minutes.

Comment: This animated film version of the opera features chalk pictures that move around on a blackboard with a Colin Davis recording as its soundtrack.

1992 ...une petite flûte enchantée

French stage production: Louis Erlo and Myriam Tanant (directors), Claire Gibault (conductor, Opéra de Lyon Orchestra and Chorus), Montserrat Casanova (set/costume designer).

Cast: Jean Delescluse (Tamino), Virginie Pochon (Pamina), Christophe Lacassagne (Papageno), Cyrille Gerstenhaber (Papagena), Isabelle Sabrié (Queen of the Night), Frederic Caton (Sarastro), Caroline Pelon, Pomone Epoméo, Francine André (Three Ladies).

Video: Imalyre (France) VHS. Pierre Cavassilas (director). Color. In French. 117 minutes.

Comment: *A Little Magic Flute* is an experimental production devised by Erlo, Gibault, and Tanant for Opéra de Lyon's Atelier Lyrique (Opera Workshop). It is simplified, shortened, and modernized (the three ladies shoot the dragon with pistols) and sung by relative unknowns.

***1992 Ludwigsburg Festival

German stage production: Axel Manthey (director), Wolfgang Gönnerwein (conductor, Ludwigsburg Festival Orchestra and Chorus).

Cast: Deon van der Walt (Tamino); Ulrike Sonntag (Pamina); Thomas Mohr (Papageno); Patricia Rozario (Papagena); Andrea Frei (Queen of the Night); Cornelius Hauptmann (Sarastro); Kevin Connors (Monostatos); Elizabeth Whitehouse, Helen Schneiderman, Renée Morloc (Three Ladies); Sebastian Holecek (Speaker).

Video: Arthaus DVD. Ruth Kärch (director). Color. In German with English subtitles. 147 minutes.

Comment: Critically acclaimed production created for the Ludwigsburger Schlossfestspiele in its home in an 18th-century royal palace.

1995 Amsterdam Concertgebouw
Dutch semistaged concert production: Stephen Medcalf (director), John Eliot Gardiner (conductor, English Baroque Soloists and Monteverdi Choir).

Cast: Michel Schade (Tamino), Christiane Oelze (Pamina), Gerald Finley (Papageno), Constanze Backes (Papagena), Cynthia Sieden (Queen of the Night), Harry Peeters (Sarastro), Uwe Peper (Monostatos), Susan Roberts, Carola Guber, Maria Jonas (Three Ladies).

Video: DG VHS/LD. Pim Marks (director). Color. In German with English subtitles. 160 minutes.

1998 Zirkus um Zauberflöte
German film of circus production: Percy Adlon (film director), George Tabori (stage director), Christoph Hagel (conductor, Hans von Bülow Chamber Orchestra), Bernhard Paul (choreographer).

Cast: Dmitri Artemieve (Tamino, sung by Lynton Atkinson), Elena Mazgalevskaia (Pamina, sung by Marina Rüping), Diana Gilchrist, Gitte Haenning, Andre Eisermann, Andreas Kohn.

Telecast on ZDF German Television. Color. In German. 88 minutes.

Comment: Adlon shot his film *The Magic Flute at the Circus* at the Roncalli Circus in Berlin. It features trapeze artists performing the roles in parallel with singers performing on the ground. Does it work? Well, it is certainly different.

1999 St. Margarethen Opera Festival
Austrian stage production: Wolfgang Werner (producer), Robert Herzl (director), Giorgio Croci (conductor, Stagione d'Opera Italiana Orchestra and Chorus), Manfred Wabo (set designer).

Video: W&W TV-Video (Germany) VHS. Color. In Italian with introduction in German. 90 minutes.

Comment: Spectacle dominates this abridged production filmed at the ancient Roman quarry of St. Margarethen in Austria, "the biggest open-air stage in Europe" with seating for 3,800. There are two fire-breathing dragons in the opening scene and hundreds of extras on stage.

2000 Zurich Opera
Swiss stage production: Jonathan Miller (director), Franz Welser-Möst (conductor, Zurich Opera House Orchestra and Chorus), Philip Prowse (set designer).

Cast: Piotr Beczala (Tamino), Malin Hartelius (Pamina), Anton Scharinger (Papageno), Julius Neumann (Papagena), Elena Mosuc (Queen of the Night), Matti

Salminen (Sarastro), Volker Vogel (Monostatos), Martina Janková, Irène Friedli, Ursula Ferri (Three Ladies).

Video: TDK (GB) DVD. Color. In German with English subtitles. 151 minutes.

Comment: Modernist, intellectual, and strongly symbolic Masonic version with Tamino falling asleep in the Bibliothèque Nationale in Paris and dreaming the opera. Miller originated his rational, as opposed to magical, production at Scottish Opera and English National Opera in 1999.

2003 Royal Opera
English stage production: David McVicar (director), Colin Davis (conductor, Royal Opera House Orchestra and Chorus).

Cast: Will Hartmann (Tamino), Dorothea Röschmann (Pamina), Simon Keenlyside (Papageno), Kathleen Tynan (Papagena), Diana Damrau (Queen of the Night), Franz-Josef Selig (Sarastro), Volker Vogel (Monostatos), Gillian Webster, Christine Rice, Yvonne Howard (Three Ladies).

Video: BBC/Opus Arte DVD. Taped January 27, 2003. Sue Judd (director). Color. In German with English subtitles. 185 minutes.

Comment: British critics were highly impressed with both the stage production and the DVD.

Early/related films

1906 La flûte enchantée
A French film produced by Pathé titled *La Flûte Enchantée* was released in America in December 1906. Black and white. Silent. About 5 minutes.

1908 The Magic Flute
The American film *The Magic Flute* was distributed in the United States in November 1908. Black and white. Silent. About 7 minutes.

1919 Die Zauberflöte
German director Max Mack produced this feature-length film of *Die Zauberflöte* in 1919. Black and white. Silent. About 70 minutes.

1935 Papageno
German animation pioneer Lotte Reiniger's silhouette film revolves around the birdcatcher from *The Magic Flute*. Black and white. 8 minutes.

1946 La flûte magique
Music from *The Magic Flute* is used in this animated film by French master Paul Grimault. Roger Leenhardt wrote the script. Color. 11 minutes.

1948 Letter From an Unknown Woman
This fine film reaches its climax at a performance of *The Magic Flute*, sung in Italian, at the Vienna Opera House. Joan Fontaine sees her lover Louis Jourdan for the first time in 10 years as her husband watches. Max Ophuls directed. Black and white. 86 minutes.

1967 Hour of the Wolf
Ingmar Bergman's film *Vargtimmen* (Hour of the Wolf) has several references to *The Magic Flute*. Moody artist Max von Sydow and wife Liv Ullmann live on a lonely island where he is beginning to encounter strange demons, perhaps in his mind, and one is a birdman he thinks is related to Papageno. A rich man invites him to dinner in his castle and displays a toy theater in which a tiny but seemingly real Tamino (Folke Sundquist) performs the aria "O ew'ge Nacht!" They talk about the meaning of the words "O eternal night! When will it end?" Color. In Swedish. 80 minutes.

1974 Night Porter
There is a memorable use of the Pamina-Papageno duet "Bei Männern" in the opera scene in this strange Liliana Cavani film. It tells the story of an opera conductor's wife (Charlotte Rampling) who meets up with the SS officer (Dirk Bogarde) who sexually abused her in a concentration camp. Color. In English. 115 minutes.

1975 Gute Nacht, du fasche Welt
German documentary film showing rehearsals for a 1975 production of *Die Zauberflöte* at the Salzburg Festival, directed by Giorgio Strehler. The title refers to Papageno's suicidal line "Goodbye, cruel world" near the end of the opera when he thinks he has lost his Papagena. The opera stars Edith Mathis, René Kollo, Hermann Prey, and Reri Grist. Norbert Beilharz directed the film for SDR Television. Color. In German. 43 minutes.

1977 Mozart by Ingmar Bergman
German TV documentary about the creation of Ingmar Bergman's 1975 film of *The Magic Flute*. Made for WDR Television. Color. In German. 60 minutes.

1977 The Magic Flute
Inventive cartoon version of the Mozart opera by Italian masters of opera animation Giulio Gianini and Emmanuele Luzzati. Color. 25 minutes.

1984 Amadeus
Milos Forman's Mozart biopic describes the genesis of *The Magic Flute* and shows Mozart's (Tom Hulce) relationship with showman/librettist Emanuel Schikaneder (Simon Callow). Callow is seen on stage creating the role of Papageno (sung by Brian Kay) with Lisabeth Bartless as Papagena (sung by Gillian Fisher).

There is a striking scene showing the arrival of Milada Cechalova as the Queen of the Night singing "Die Hölle Rache," with the singing done by June Anderson. See AMADEUS.

1991 Papageno
Papageno is British animator Sarah Roper's tribute to the birdman of *The Magic Flute*. Color. 7 minutes.

1994 The Magic Flute
Mark Hamill is the voice of Tamino in this animated film for children based on the opera but with very little of the opera music used. Michael York is Sarastro, Samantha Eggar is Queen of the Night, Joely Fisher is Pamina, and Jerry Houser is Papageno. Rony Myrick and Marlene Robinson directed. Color. In English. 60 minutes.

1995 Operavox
The Russian animation studio Christmas Films created an animated version of *The Magic Flute* for the British Operavox series. The Welsh National Opera Orchestra plays a specially recorded score. David Seaman was music editor. Color. 27 minutes.

1998 In All Innocence
The Rias Symphonie Orchester of Berlin led by Ferenc Fricsay performs music from *Die Zauberflöte* on the soundtrack of this French film, based on a novel by Georges Simenon. Pierre Jolivet directed. Color. 101 minutes.

1999 24 Hours in London
Pamina's haunting aria "Ach, ich fühl's" is on the soundtrack of this British gangster film revolving around a turf war started by an American woman. Alexander Finbow directed. Color. 95 minutes.

2000 Miss Congeniality
The Queen of the Night's aria "Der Hölle Rache" is featured on the soundtrack of this thriller about an FBI agent (Sandra Bullock) who enters a beauty contest to trap a killer. Awet Andemicael is the singer; Donald Petrie directed. Color. 110 minutes.

2002 Sweet Sixteen
Helen Kwon and the Failoni Orchestra of Budapest perform the music for the arrival of the Queen of the Night in this Ken Loach film about a teenaged thug in Greenock, Scotland. Color. 105 minutes.

ZAZÀ
1900 opera by Leoncavallo

Parisian music hall star Zazà is in love with Milo Dufresne, but she does not know he is already married. She is ready to give up her career for him, but when she finds out the deception, she decides to forget him. Ruggero Leoncavallo's opera *Zazà,* once one of the most popular operas in the repertory and a favorite of sopranos such as Geraldine Farrar, has dropped out of fashion. A disastrous Chicago Opera production of this opera starring off-key soprano Ganne Walska was one of the inspirations for Orson Welles's film *Citizen Kane.*

1995 Teatro Massimo, Palermo
Italian stage production: Filippo Crivelli (director), Gianandrea Gavazzeni (conductor, Teatro Massimo Orchestra and Chorus), Danilo Donati (set/costume designer).

Cast: Denia Gavezzini Mazzola (Zazà), Luca Canonici (Milo Dufresne), Donatella Lombardi (Floriana), Viorica Cortez (Anaide), Stefano Antonucci (Cascart), Armando Gabba (Bussy).

Video: Premiere Opera/House of Opera VHS. Color. In Italian. 105 minutes.

ZEFFIRELLI, FRANCO
Italian film/opera director (1923–)

Franco Zeffirelli is equally well known in the worlds of film, theater, and opera with success in all three as director and designer. He first became known for his revolutionary Shakespeare stage productions and for helping guide Maria Callas to some of her greatest performances. His best opera film is his LA TRAVIATA (1982) with Teresa Stratas, based on a thought-provoking stage production, but there are many admirers of his other opera productions on video, especially his intimate 2001 AIDA. Zeffirelli began as an assistant to Luchino Visconti, a director also at home in opera and cinema. His first opera film was LA BOHÈME in 1965, but he did not direct it and it was only a mild success. He won wider acclaim for his Shakespeare films *The Taming of the Shrew* (1967), with Richard Burton and Elizabeth Taylor, and his youthful *Romeo and Juliet* (1968), modeled on his stage production. Zeffirelli's theatrical productions, like his films, are usually lavish, with sumptuous sets and costumes. They have been greatly admired at the Metropolitan Opera, so much so that one sponsor gives money earmarked only for his productions. He can be seen at work as a stage director in documentary videos about Maria Callas and Teresa Stratas. He has also written librettos, including one for Samuel Barber's opera ANTONY AND CLEOPATRA (1966 film). His unusual name derives from a Mozart opera. He says: "I was registered as the son of NN...being an illegitimate son I could not take my father's name. Illegitimate children were allocated a letter in alphabetical order. When my turn came along, I was allocated Z. Since my mother loved Mozart's aria 'Zeffiretti lusinghieri,' she named me Zeffiretti, but the clerk wrote Zeffirelli, forgetting to cross the t's, hence my name. Probably the only one in the world." See LA BOHÈME (1982), MARIA CALLAS (1964/1978/1987/2002), CARMEN (1979/1997), CAVALLERIA RUSTICANA (1978/1982), CINOPÉRA (1985), DON CARLO (1992), DON GIOVANNI (1990/2000), FALSTAFF (1992), OTELLO (1976/1978/ 1979/1986), PAGLIACCI (1978/1982/1994), JOAN SUTHERLAND (1991), TERESA STRATAS (1983), TOSCA (1964/1985), ARTURO TOSCANINI (1988), and TURANDOT (1987).

1973 Franco Zeffirelli: A Florentine Artist
This British documentary by Reginald Mills was filmed while Zeffirelli was making the film *Brother Sun, Sister Moon.* It shows his care in choosing locations and costumes and how he works with actors. Color. In English. 51 minutes.

Franco Zeffirelli gives instructions to Maria Callas.

ZELLER, CARL
Austrian composer (1842–1898)

Carl Zeller began writing operettas in 1880 and had his first major success in 1891 with the charming DER VOGELHÄNDLER (The Bird Seller). Some of its tunes have become world favorites, including the rose-drenched "Schenkt man sich Rosen in Tirol." The operetta is particularly popular in German-speaking countries, but there was a London production in 1947 conducted by Richard Tauber. Zeller's 1894 operetta DER OBERSTEIGER (The Mine Foreman) is also still popular in Germany, and its waltz has became internationally popular with sopranos.

ZELMIRA

1822 opera by Rossini

Zelmira is the daughter of Polidoro, king of the island kingdom of Lesbos in ancient Greece, and is happily married to Trojan Prince Ilo. After a series of calamities following the takeover of the kingdom by the evil Antenore, during which she hides Polidoro, justice and order are restored. GIOACHINO ROSSINI's melodious opera *Zelmira*, libretto by Andrea Tottola based on a play by Dormont de Belloy, premiered in Naples at the Teatro San Carlo. It was his last Neapolitan opera.

1989 Teatro dell'Opera, Rome

Italian stage production: Evelino Pidò (conductor, Teatro dell'Opera Orchestra and Chorus).

Cast: Cecilia Gasdia (Zelmira), Rockwell Blake (Prince Ilo), Chris Merritt (Antenore), Simone Alaimo (Polidoro), Gloria Scalchi (Emma), Robert Servile (Leucippo), Tullio Pane (Eacide).

Video: Premiere Opera VHS. Color. In Italian. 150 minutes.

Comment: Gasdia and Blake have also recorded the opera.

ZIEHRER, KARL MICHAEL

Austrian composer (1843–1922)

Karl Michael Ziehrer is more famous for composing waltzes than operettas, but he actually wrote 22 of them. The best known is the 1899 DIE LANDSTREICHER, the story of a couple of artful vagabonds that has been filmed. Ziehrer was a competitor of Strauss in the composition of traditional Viennese waltzes, and he had a big success with the *Wiener Mädeln* (Vienna Maidens) waltz. He was also a popular bandmaster and took his band to the Chicago World's Fair in 1893.

1945 Wiener Mädeln

The film *Vienna Maidens* concerns Ziehrer's rivalry and competition with Johann Strauss for attention as a waltz composer; it climaxes with the composition and success of the famous waltz. Willi Forst, who stars as the composer, directed this Agfacolor film in Vienna and Prague. Dora Komar and Hans Moser lend support. In German. 101 minutes.

ZIGEUNERBARON, DER

1885 operetta by Johann Strauss

Der Zigeunerbaron (The Gypsy Baron), considered the best JOHANN STRAUSS operetta after *Die Fledermaus*, became a model for later operetta writers. The complicated story focuses on aristocrat Sandor Barinkay, who returns from exile to claim his land. The pig farmer Zsupan wants him to marry his daughter Arsena, but Sandor prefers the gypsy Saffi. The libretto by Ignatz Schnitzer is based on the Hungarian story *Sáffi* by Mór Jókai. The operetta has remained popular in Germany and France and has been filmed several times.

1935 Hartl film

German feature films: Kart Hartl (director); Vineta Klinger, Walter Supper, Tibor Jost (screenplay); Günther Rittau and Otto Baecker (cinematographers); Alois Melichar (music director); UFA (production).

Cast: Adolf Wöhlbrück (Sandor), Hansi Knoteck (Saffi), Fritz Kampers (Zsupan), Gina Falckenberg (Arsena), Edwin Jürgensen (Homonay).

Black and white. In German. 105 minutes.

Comment: German and French versions were shot simultaneously (see below). Wöhlbruck later changed his name and became Anton Walbrook.

1935 Chomette film

French feature film: Henri Chomette (director); Vineta Klinger, Walter Supper, Tibor Jost (screenplay); Günther Rittau and Otto Baecker (cinematographers); Alois Melichar (music director); UFA (production).

Cast: Adolf Wöhlbrück (Sandor), Jacqueline Francell (Saffi), Daniele Parola (Arsena), Gabriel Gabrio (Zsupan), Henri Bosc (Homonay).

Black and white. In French. 105 minutes.

Comment: The French film of the operetta is called *Le baron tzigane*.

1954 Rabenalt German film

German feature film: Arthur Maria Rabenalt (director), Belgrade State Opera Ballet (dancers), Herzog Film (production).

Cast: Gerhard Riedmann (Sandor), Margit Saad (Saffi), Maria Sebaldt (Arsena), Oskar Sima (Zsupan).

Color. In German. 105 minutes.

Comment: Rabenalt made French and German versions simultaneously with different casts. Most of it was shot on location.

1954 Rabenalt French film

French feature film: Arthur Maria Rabenalt (director), Belgrade State Opera Ballet (dancers), Herzog Film (production).

Cast: Georges Guetary (Sandor), Margit Saad (Saffi).

Color. French. 105 minutes.

Comment: The French film of the operetta is called *Le baron tzigane*.

1962 Wilhelm film

German feature film: Kurt Wilhelm (director), Heinz Oskar Wuttig (screenplay), Willi Sohm (cinematographer).

Cast: Carlos Thompson (Sandor), Heidi Bruhl (Saffi), Willy Millowitsch (Zsupan).

Color. In German. 103 minutes.

***1975 Rabenalt TV film

German TV film: Arthur Maria Rabenalt (director), Kurt Eichhorn (conductor, Stuttgart Radio Orchestra and Chorus), Unitel (production).

Cast: Siegfried Jerusalem (Sandor), Ellen Shade (Saffi), Martha Mödl (Mirabella), Janet Perry (Arsena), Ivan Rebroff (Zsupan), Willi Brokmeier (Ottokar), Wolfgang Brendel (Homonay).

Video: Taurus (Germany) VHS. Color. In German. 97 minutes.

Comment: Wagnerian tenor Jerusalem began his singing career in this excellent film of the operetta.

1986 Seefestspiele Mörbisch

Austrian stage production: Sylvia Donch (director), Franz Bauer-Theussl (conductor, Seefestspiele Mörbisch Orchestra and Chorus).

Cast: Adolf Dallapozza (Sandor), Katalin Pitti (Saffi), Erika Schubert (Mirabella), Andrea Zsádon (Arsena), Peter Minich (Zsupan), Sibrand Basa (Ottokar), Harald Serafin (Homonay).

ORF (Austria) VHS. Sylvia Donch (director) Color. In German. 130 minutes.

Comment: Large-scale outdoor production.

Silent film

1927 Zelnick film

Rudolf Klein-Rogge plays Sandor with Lya Mara as Saffi in this German silent film usually screened with the music of the operetta. The supporting cast includes Michael Bohnen, Emil Fenyos, Wilhelm Dieterle, and Vivian Gibson. Friedrich Zelnick directed. Black and white. About 85 minutes.

ZIGEUNERLIEBE

1910 operetta by Lehár

Zigeunerliebe (Gypsy Love) is a tuneful operetta by FRANZ LEHÁR about Zorika, a young woman in a Romanian village who worries about whom she should marry. She is attracted to the gypsy violinist Jószi but she is engaged to dependable Jonel, so she steals away from her engagement party to think it over. When she falls asleep by the river, she dreams about what would happen if she went off with the gypsy. After the dream she is happy to pledge her love to husband-to-be Jonel without

reservation. The libretto is by A. M. Willner and Robert Bodanzky.

1930 The Rogue Song

American feature film: Lionel Barrymore (director), Frances Marion and John Colton (screenplay), Herbert Stothart (music director), MGM (studio).

Cast: Lawrence Tibbett (Yegor), Catherine Dale Owen (Princess Vera), Nance O'Neil (Princess Alexandra), Judith Vosselli (Countess Tatiana), Ullrich Haupt (Prince Serge), Elsa Alsen (Yegor's mother).

Technicolor. In English. 107 minutes.

Comment: Tibbett's first Hollywood film is lost but its soundtrack and a few minutes of footage survive. The plot is utterly changed, and much of Lehár's music is gone. Tibbett plays a bandit who steals from the Cossacks oppressing his people and falls in love with the sister of the Cossack leader.

1974 Kaslík film

German TV film: Václav Kaslík (director), Heinz Wallberg (conductor, Munich Radio-Television Orchestra and Bavarian Radio Choir), Theo Harisch (set designer), Unitel (production).

Cast: Janet Perry (Zorika), Ion Buzea (Jószi), Adolf Dallapozza (Jonel), Colette Lorand (Ilona), Heinz Friedrich (Dragotin), Kurt Grosskurth (Mihaly), Helmut Wallner (Kajetan), Marianne Becker (Jolan).

Video: Taurus (Germany) VHS. Color. In German. 87 minutes.

ZIMMERMANN, BERND

German composer (1918–1970)

Bernd Alois Zimmermann's opera DIE SOLDATEN (The Soldiers) has been called the most important German opera after *Lulu*. Zimmermann, who was brought up during the Nazi era, emerged as an important figure in avant-garde German music during the 1960s but then killed himself in 1970. His despair is reflected in his opera, which has established itself in the world repertory. It is complicated to produce as it requires a large cast, three screens for film scenes, and multiple stage levels. It is one of the few modern German operas available on video.

ZIRKUSPRINZESSIN, DIE

1926 operetta by Kálmán

Operettas had to compete with popular revues in Vienna, so librettists Julius Brammer and Alfred Grünwald added an exotic circus element to the usual princess in EMMERICH KÁLMÁN's operetta *Die Zirkusprinzessin* (The Circus Princess). The circus is Russian and so is wealthy Princess Fedora, who becomes involved with a circus performer called Mister X. He is actually a baron in disguise, so all can end romantically right. The New York production of the operetta in 1927 was held at the Winter Garden so the circus element could be emphasized.

1969 Köhler film

German TV film: Manfred R. Köhler (director), Werner Schmidt-Boelcke (conductor, Kurt Graunke Symphony Orchestra), Horst Hennicke (set designer), Unitel (production).

Cast: Rudolf Schock (Mister X), Ingeborg Hallstein (Princess Fedora), Isy Oren (Mabel), Peter Karner (Toni), Ernst-Fritz Fürbringer (Prince Sergius), Ernst Waldbrunn (Pelikan).

Color. In German. 111 minutes.

Silent film

1929 Janson film

Harry Liedtke plays the circus performer aristocrat in this German silent film, screened with the music of the operetta. The cast includes Vera Schmitterlöw, Adele Sandrock, Hans Junkermann, Fritz Kampers, Hilde Rosch, and Ernst Verebes. Guido Seeber was the cinematographer, and Victor Janson directed. Black and white. About 85 minutes.

ZURICH

The Zurich Operhaus, which began life in 1891 as the Stadttheater, is one of the major opera houses of Europe and has been innovative and influential during recent years. One of its major productions was the Monteverdi trio of operas by JEAN-PIERRE PONNELLE and NIKOLAUS HARNONCOURT, which were later filmed. Swiss feature film directors such as Daniel Schmid have also staged operas at the theater. Many of its recent productions are now on video. See IL BARBIERE DI SIVIGLIA (2001), LA BELLE HÉLÈNE (2000), COSÌ FAN TUTTE (2000), DON GIOVANNI (1999), GUILLAUME TELL (1987), HÄNSEL UND GRETEL (1998), IPHIGÉNIE EN TAURIDE (2001), L'INCORONAZIONE DI POPPEA (1979), LINDA DI CHAMOUNIX (1996), MACBETH (2001), LE NOZZE DI FIGARO (1996), ORFEO (1978), OTELLO (1961), IL RITORNO D'ULISSE IN PATRIA (1980), LES TROYENS (1992 film), and DIE ZAUBERFLÖTE (2000).

1984 OperaFest

This is a record of a gala concert at the Zurich Operhaus held to celebrate the reopening of the theater on December 1, 1984. The performers include Mirella Freni, José Carreras, Lucia Popp, Thomas Hampson, Gwyneth Jones, Alfredo Kraus, Nicolai Ghiaurov, Mara Zampieri, and Sona Ghazarian. The opera music is by Wagner, Mozart, Strauss, Donizetti, Offenbach, Verdi, Bizet, Rossini, and Dvořák. Gianni Paggi directed. Color. 92 minutes. VAI VHS.

1993 Der Opernhaus Direktor

The Opera House Director is a Swiss documentary film about Alexander Pereira, who became director of the Zurich Operhaus in 1991. It features excerpts from some of the productions. Color. In German. 29 minutes.

ZWEI HERZEN IN DREIVIERTELTAKT
1930 operetta by Stolz

Toni writes an operetta called *Zwei Herzen in Dreivierteltakt* but can't find a waltz for it. His librettist's beautiful sister Hedi helps out and the waltz is created and sung by opera singer Irene Eisinger. There are complications but all ends well in good operetta fashion. Robert Stolz's *Zwei Herzen in Dreivierteltakt* (Two Hearts in 3/4 Time) was an international success in its original version as a film. The movie struck a responsive chord around the world, and its title waltz was such a hit that sheet music for it can still found in U.S. flea markets. Even *The New York Times* loved it. Stolz later turned the film into a stage operetta, *Der Verlorene Walzer* (The Lost Waltz), which was produced in Zurich in 1933. He revised it again for a stage production in Vienna in 1948, this time going back to the original title.

1930 Super/Tobis film

German feature film: Geza von Bolvary (director), Walter Reisch and Franz Schulz (screenplay), Willy Goldberger and Max Brink (cinematographers), Super/Tobis Film (production).

Cast: Walter Janssen (Toni), Gretl Theimer (Hedi), Irene Eisinger (Anni), Willi Forst (Vicki), Oskar Karlweiss (Nicky), S. Z. Sakall (Theater Director), Paul Hörbiger (Ferdinand).

Black and white. In German. 91 minutes.

Selective Bibliography

There is no substantial bibliography of publications relating to opera on the screen, but Guy A. Marco's general bibliography *Opera A Research and Information Guide, Second Edition* is quite helpful and includes many relevant books. The selective and lightly annotated bibliography below is only a preliminary effort, but it may be helpful to those interested in obtaining further information about opera and opera music featured in films, television programs, and videos. It does not include most reviews or every general article, but hopefully it includes the most useful and relevant. The primary sources of information about opera on screen are the films and videos themselves when available, book and magazine reviews, national film indexes, film festival catalogs, and the databases at the Museum of Television and Radio (MTR) and Internationales Musikzentrum Wien (IMZ). Most film and opera reference books have information about opera and operetta on screen, the most helpful being *The New Grove Dictionary of Opera*. The best continuing sources are the DVD and video reviews in *BBC Music Magazine, Gramophone, Opera, Opera News, Opera Now,* and *The Opera Quarterly*.

1. OPERA ON FILM, TV, AND VIDEO

Adler, Peter Herman. "Opera on Television: The Beginning of an Era." *Musical America*, February 1952.

AFI National Film Theater. *Opera on Film* program booklet. Washington, D.C., 1974.

Ainsley, Rob, and Neil Evans (editors). *Music at the Movies: 100 Greatest Classical Cuts*. Classic CD special issue. September 1995.

Allen, Peter. "Broadcasting," in *The Metropolitan Opera Encyclopedia*. David Hamilton (editor). Simon and Schuster, New York, 1987. (Met telecasts)

Almquist, Sharon G. (editor). *Opera Mediagraphy: Video Recordings and Motion Pictures*. Greenwood, Westport, 1993. (Credits of operas on film and video)

———. *Opera Singers in Recital, Concert, and Feature Films: A Mediagraphy*. Greenwood, Westport, 1999. (Screen appearances of opera singers)

Anderson, Gillian B. *Music for Silent Films 1894–1929: A Guide*. Library of Congress, Washington, D.C., 1988.

Anderson, James. "Opera films." *Harper Dictionary of Opera and Operetta*. HarperCollins, New York, 1989.

Andreevsky, Alexander von. "Was soll der Opernfilm." *Weser Zeitung*, Bremen, May 15, 1930.

Annals of the Metropolitan Opera: Complete Chronicle of Performances and Artists. G. K. Hall, Boston, 1989. (Lists telecasts)

Annals of the Metropolitan Opera: Complete Chronicle of Performances and Artists. Performances and Artists 1883–2000. DiscEdition (CD-ROM). Metropolitan Opera Guild, 2001.

Ardoin, John "Opera and Television." *The Opera Quarterly*, Spring 1983.

———. "Operatic Shadows." *The Opera Quarterly*, Autumn 1988. (Opera singers in the movies)

———. *The Stages of Menotti*. Doubleday, Garden City, 1985. (Chapters on his TV operas)

Atkins, Irene Kahn. *Source Music in Motion Pictures*. Associated University Presses, East Brunswick, 1983. (Operas made for movies)

Ball, Robert Hamilton. *Shakespeare on Silent Film*. Allen & Unwin, London, 1968. (Shakespearean operas during the silent era)

Barcelona Filmoteca. *Òpera al Cinema*. 1981 program booklet with essays on opera films.

Barnes, John. *Manual of Television Opera Production*. CBC, Toronto, 1975.

Barnes, Jennifer. *Television Opera: The Fall of Opera Commissioned for Television*. London, 2002.

——— "Television Opera: A Non-History," in Tambling, *A Night in at the Opera*, 1994.

Barrios, Richard. *A Song in the Dark: The Birth of the Musical Film*. Oxford University Press, New York, 1995.

Batchelor, Joy. "From *Aida* to *Zauberflöte*." *Screen*, xxv/3, 1984.

Bate, Philip. "Ballet, Opera and Music," in *Television in the Making*, edited by Paul Rotha. Focal Press, London, 1956. (Opera at BBC-TV)

Bauer, L. "Twice Told Tales: Translating Opera into Film." *Theatre Arts*, xxxv/6, 1951.

Baxter, Joan. *Television Musicals, Plots, Critiques, Casts and Credits for 222 Shows 1944–1996*. McFarland, Jefferson, 1997.

Bebb, Richard. *Opera and the Cinema*. National Film Theatre program booklet. London, 1969.

Berchtold, William E. "Grand Opera Goes Hollywood." *North American Review*, February 1935.

Bernardini, Aldo. *Cinema italiano delle origini: Gli ambulati*. La Cineteca dei Friuli, 2001. (Early sound opera films in Italy)

Bernheimer, Martin. "TV Opera: The Great Debate." *Los Angeles Times*, October 8, 1978.

Bertz-Dostal, H. *Oper im Fernsehen*. Vienna, 1970.

Beyle, Claude, with Jean-Michel Brèque, Michèle Friche, Philipe Godefroid, and Fernand Leclercq. "Trente Classiques du Film-Opéra," in Duault, *Cinéma et Opéra*. (Essays on 30 opera films)

BFI National Film Theatre. *London International Opera Festival* annual programs.

Biamonte, S. G. (editor). *Musica e Film*. Edizioni dell'Ateneo, Rome, 1959. (Articles on opera and operetta in movies with filmography)

Bierstadt, E. H. "Opera in Moving Pictures." *Opera Magazine*, October 1915.

Blyth, Alan. *Opera on Video: The Essential Guide.* Kyle Cathie, London, 1995. (Reviews)

Boll, André. "L'Opéra Cinématographique." *Musica*, No. 38. Paris, May 1957. (UNESCO congress on "L'Opéra à la radio, à la télévision et dans le film")

Bourre, Jean-Paul. *Opéra et Cinéma.* Editions Artefact, Paris, 1987. (Opera film history)

Bradley, Edwin M. *The First Hollywood Musicals, A Critical Filmography of 171 Features, 1927 through 1932.* McFarland, Jefferson, 1996.

Bragaglia, Cristina, and Fernaldo di Giammatteo. *Italia 1900–1990. L'opera al cinema.* La Nuova Italia, Florence, 1990.

Breque, Jean-Michel. "Le Film-opera: vers une forme cinématographique autonome." See Duault, *Cinéma et Opéra.*

Brook, Peter. *The Shifting Point: Theatre, Film, Opera 1946–1987.* Harper & Row, New York, 1987.

Brooks, Tim, and Earle Marsh. *The Complete Directory to Prime Time Network TV Shows.* Ballantine Books, New York, 1963. (Operatic shows)

Brunel, Claude. "Opéra et Télévision." See Duault, *Cinéma et Opéra.*

Buchau, Stephanie von. "Jean-Pierre Ponnelle: The Sensual Stylist." *Opera News*, September 1977.

Burke, Richard C. *A History of Televised Opera in the United States.* Michigan University Ph.D. dissertation, 1963.

————. "The NBC Opera Theater." *Journal of Broadcasting*, Winter 1965–1966.

Burton, Jack. *The Blue Book of Hollywood Musicals.* Century House, New York, 1953. (Songs in Hollywood films from 1927 to 1952)

Buttava, Giovanni, and Aldo Grasso. "La camera lirica. Storia e tendenze della diffusione dell'opera lirico attraverso la television." Amici della Scala. March 2, 1986.

Cadars, Pierre. "Confession partielle d'un amoureux ambivalent." See Duault, *Cinéma et Opéra.*

Cannes Film Festival. *Cinéma et Opéra.* May 1987 program for opera film series.

Cartier, R. "Producing Television Opera." *Opera*, May 1957.

Casadio, Gianfranco. *Opera e cinema. La musica lirica nel cinema italiano dall'avvento del sonoro ad oggi.* Longo, Ravenna, 1995.

Castello, Giulio Cesare. "Canzoni, riviste, operette nella storia del cinema." In Biamonte, *Musica e Film.* (Survey of film operettas)

Chiarella, Anthony. "The DVD Generation." *Opera News*, May 1998.

Citron, Marcia J. "A Night at the Cinema: Zeffirelli's *Otello* and the Genre of Film Opera." *The Musical Quarterly*, Winter 1994.

————. *Opera on Screen.* Yale University Press, New Haven, 2000. (Academic study of the genre)

Colpi, Henri. *Defense et Illustration de la Musique dans le Film.* Société d'Édition, Lyon, 1963. (Chapters on screen operas, operettas, and composer biographies)

Comuzio, Ermanno. "Il Film-opera." *Colonna Sonora.* Formichiere, Rome, 1980. (Essay on opera and film)

————. "Opéra et Cinéma: des origines aux années soixante." In Duault, *Cinéma et Opéra.*

Crisp, Deborah, and Roger Hillman. "Verdi in Postwar Italian Cinema," in Joe, *Between Opera and Cinema.*

Croissant, Charles R. *Opera Performances in Video Format: A Check list of Commercially Released Recordings.* Music Library Association, Canton, Mass., 1991.

Crowther, Bosley. "Opera on the Screen." *New York Times*, November 14, 1954. (Film vs. TV opera)

Crutchfield, Will. "Karajan Faces Stiff Competition: Karajan." *New York Times*, July 18, 1993.

De Fries, Tjitte. "Sound-on-Disc Films 1900–1926." *FIAF Journal*, 1980. (Early sound opera films)

Deslandes, Jacques. "Le Phono-Cinéma-Théâtre." *Le Cinéma d'Aujord'hui*, August 1976.

Duault, Alain, and Claude Beylie (editors). *Cinéma et Opéra.* Double issue of *L'Avant-Scène Opéra* 98 and *L'Avant-Scène Cinéma* 360. Paris, 1987. (Opera film articles and opera filmography)

Durgat, Raymond. "Eternal Triangle: Opera, Film, Realism." *Monthly Film Bulletin*, October 1990.

Dwyer, Edward J. *American Video Opera: An Introduction and Guidebook to its Production.* Columbia University Ph.D. dissertation, 1963.

Eaton, Quaintance. "Great Opera Houses: NBC-TV." *Opera News*, February 8, 1964.

————. "Television Audience Sees First Video Opera." *Musical America*, December 15, 1948.

Englander, Roger. *Opera: What's All the Screaming About?* Walker, New York, 1994.

Evidon, Richard. "Film," in Sadie, *New Grove Dictionary of Opera.* (Opera on film)

Ewen, David. "Opera Performances: Motion Pictures." *The New Encyclopedia of the Opera.* Hill and Wang, New York, 1971.

————. "Opera Performance: Television." *The New Encyclopedia of the Opera.* Hill and Wang, New York, 1971.

Falkenburg, Claudia, and Andrew Wolt. *A Really Big Show: A Visual History of the Ed Sullivan Show.* Viking Studio Books, New York, 1992. (Opera singers on show)

Fawkes, Richard. "DVD, Your Flexible Friend?" *BBC Music Magazine*, February 2001.

————. "Opera for the Masses." *Opera Now*, April 1994. (Article on opera movies)

————. "Opera in View." *Opera Now.* (Opera on screen review column)

————. *Opera on Film.* Duckworth, London, 2000. (Excellent history of filmed opera and opera movies)

————. "Star Turns." *Opera Now*, March 1994. (Opera singers in the movies)

———. "To Boldly Go." *Opera Now*, September/October 2002. (Article on DVD advantages)

Franklin, Peter. "Movies as Opera (Behind the Great Divide)." in Tambling, *A Night in at the Opera*.

Gallone, Carmine. "Il Valore della music nel film e l'evoluzione dello spettacolo lirico sullo schermo." See Biamonte, *Musica e Film*. (Opera film director on opera in the cinema)

Garel, A., and M. Salmon. "Cinéma et Opéra." *La Revue du Cinéma*, No. 429, Paris, 1987.

Gelb, Arthur. "The Future of Video Opera." *New York Times*, December 28, 1952.

Gifford, Denis. *Entertainers in British Films: A Century of Showbiz in the Cinema*. Flick Books, Trowbridge, 1998.

Giudici, Elvio. *L'Opera in CD e video*. Il Saggiatore, Milano, 1999. (Useful Italian listings with plots and casts)

Giulianio, Elisabeth. "Opéra et Cinéma, un Union Légitime." See Duault, *Cinéma et Opéra*.

Graf, Herbert. *Opera for the People*. University of Minnesota Press, Minneapolis, 1951. (Chapter on TV opera in the 1940s)

Grief, Lyndal. *The Operas of Gian Carlo Menotti, 1937–1972: A Selective Bibliography*. Scarecrow Press, Metuchen, 1974. (Includes lists of articles about Menotti's screen operas)

Grimes, William. "Some Real Oldies Hit the Video Charts." *New York Times*, August 18, 1992. (Article about opera videos)

Grodman, Jeanette, and Maria De Monte. "Opera of the Future: Hollywood's Opera Films." *Opera News*, April 18, 1955.

Grover-Friedlander, Michal. "'There Ain't No Sanity Claus!' The Marx Brothers at the Opera," in Joe, *Between Opera and Cinema*.

Gruber, Paul (editor). *The Metropolitan Opera Guide to Opera on Video*. Norton, New York, 1997. (Useful guide but the quality of the opinions varies widely.)

Gutman, John. "The Case for Opera on Television." *Theatre Arts*, December 1953.

Hamilton, Mary. "Opera on Film," in *A–Z of Opera*. Facts on File, Oxford, 1990.

Halliwell, Leslie. *Halliwell's Teleguide*. Granada, London, 1979. (Includes opera programs)

Heinsheimer, Hans W. "Film Opera—Screen vs. Stage." *Modern Music*, March–April 1931.

Helm, Everett. "International Conference on Opera in Radio, TV and Film." *Musical Times*, February 1957.

Hornak, Richard. "Taster's Choice." *Opera News*. (Column of opera on video reviews)

Huckvale, David. "The Composing Machine: Wagner and Popular Culture," in Tambling, *A Night in at the Opera*.

Huntley, John. "Screen Opera." *British Film Music*. Skelton Robinson, London, 1947.

Internationales Musikzentrum. *Opera in Radio, TV and Film*. 1956 catalog, Salzburg.

Jahn, Melvin. "Sight and Sound: Laserdisc Wish List." *Opera News*, December 23, 1995. (Operas on laser)

———. *Tower Records Guide to the Classics on Video*. Tower Classics, Berkeley, November 1995. (Opera and classical music videos and laserdiscs on sale through Tower)

Joe, Jeongwon, and Rose Theresa (editors). *Between Opera and Cinema*. Routledge, New York, 2001. (Eleven essays about opera and cinema)

Johnson, Lawrence B. "When the Best Seat in the House Happens to Be at Home." *New York Times*, July 28, 1996. (On the joy of music and opera on laserdisc)

Johnson, Trevor. "Diva delights." *Sight and Sound*, November 1993. (Reviews of operas on video)

Kalbus, Oskar. "Der Operettenfilm." *Vom Werden Deutscher Filmkunst*. Altona, Berlin, 1935.

———. "Opern auf der Leinwand." Ibid.

Kauffmann, Stanley. "The Abduction from the Theater: Mozart Opera on Film," in *On Mozart*, edited by James M. Morris. Cambridge University Press, Cambridge, 1994. (On three Mozart opera films)

Kiepura, Jan. "L'Opera Lirica sullo Schermo." *Cinema* (Rome), No. 23, 1937.

Kirsten, Lincoln. "Television Opera in the USA." *Opera*, April 1952.

Kobal, John. *Gotta Sing, Gotta Dance*. Hamlyn, London, 1977. (Chapter on opera singers in Hollywood)

Kracauer, Siegfried. "Opera on the Screen." *Film Culture*, March–April 1955.

Kraft, Rebecca. *The Arts on Television 1976–1990*. NEA, Washington, D.C., 1991. (Operatic programs)

Kretschmer, Joan Thomson. "Face the Music." *Opera News*, June 1990. (On television opera)

Kuney, Jack. "Calling the Shots at the Metropolitan Opera." *Television Quarterly*, No. 4, 1984. (Interview with Kirk Browning)

Lacombe, Alain, and Claude Rocle. *La Musique du Film*. Editions van de Velde, Paris, 1979. (Biofilmographies of composers)

Large, Brian. "Filming, videotaping." See Sadie, *New Grove Dictionary of Opera*. (Video opera director on techniques of filming and videotaping opera)

Laser Video File. New Visions, Westwood, N.J. (Semiannual catalog with opera section)

Lee, M. Owen. "I Heard It at the Movies." *The Opera Quarterly*, Spring 1986, Winter 1991–1992. (Survey of opera scenes in non-operatic movies)

———. "Video: Live by Laser from the Met." *Opera Quarterly* 4, 1986.

Lehár, Franz. "L'Operetta Cinematografica." *Cinema* (Rome), No. 23, 1937.

Leonard, William Torbert. *Theatre: Stage to Screen to Television*. Scarecrow Press, Metuchen, 1981. (Operas and operettas that were staged, filmed, and televised)

Levin, David J. *Richard Wagner, Fritz Lang, and the Nibelungen: The Dramaturgy of Disavowal*. Princeton University Press, Princeton, 1998.

Levine, Robert. *Guide to Opera and Dance on Videocassette*. Consumers Union, Mount Vernon, 1989. (Reviews of operas on video)

Lipman, Samuel. "On the Air." *Commentary*, April 1980. (Survey of TV opera of the period)

Lunghi, Fernando Ludovico. "Il Film-opera." See Biamonte, *Musica e Film*. (History of opera on film)

Mackay, Harper. "Going Hollywood." *Opera News*, April 13, 1991. (Opera singers in Hollywood)

———. "Reel Sound." *Opera News*, February 15, 1992. (Opera composers in the movies)

Manvell, Roger, with John Huntley. *The Technique of Film Music*. Revised by Richard Arnell and Peter Day. Focal Press, London, 1975. (Sections on opera films)

Marchetti, Giuseppe, Luciano Pinelli, and Gabriele Rifilato. *VHS Film Guida*. Nuovi Eri, Rome, 1995. (Catalog of videos available in Italy with opera section)

Marco, Guy A. Opera: A Research and Information Guide, Second Edition. Garland, New York, 2001.

Marill, Alvin H. *Movies Made for Television: 1964–1986*. Baseline, New York, 1987.

McKee, David. "Video Trek: Lost In Space." *Opera News*, June 1995. (On the opera video industry)

McNeil, Alex. *Total Television*. Penguin Books, New York, 1984. (Entries on operatic programs)

Museum of Broadcasting. *Leonard Bernstein: The Television Work*. 1985 catalog, New York.

———. *Metropolitan Opera: The Radio and Television Legacy*. 1986 catalog, New York.

Musical America. "Problem of Film Opera Unresolved." March 1956.

Muziektheater, Amsterdam. *Bulletin Opera*, May 1994. (Issue devoted to opera on film programs)

Myers, Eric. "Hollywood Goes to the Opera." *Opera News*, January 8, 1994.

O'Connor, John J. "Putting Life into *Live from the Met*." *New York Times*, March 20, 1980. (About director Brian Large)

Parish, James Robert, and Michael R. Pitts. *Hollywood Songsters: A Biographical Dictionary*. Garland, New York, 1991. (Entries on opera singers in Hollywood)

Parker, David L. "Golden Voices, Silver Screen: Opera Singers as Movie Stars." *The Quarterly Journal of the Library of Congress*, Summer–Fall 1980. (Also includes European opera films)

Pasternak, Joe. *Easy the Hard Way*. W. H. Allen, London, 1956. (Life of opera/operetta film producer)

Perlmutter, Donna. "Camera Angles: Film Directors Are Bringing a Cinematic Eye to the Opera Stage." *Opera News*, February 18, 1995.

Philharmonic Hall, Lincoln Center. *Opera on Film*. Program booklet for July 15–27, 1970.

Phillips, Harvey E. "The Basics." *Opera News*, August 1991. (On collecting opera videos)

Ponnelle, Jean-Pierre. "Opera on the Small Screen." Essay in booklet with video of ZDF-TV's 1988 *Marriage of Figaro*.

Pratt, Douglas. *The Laser Video Disc Companion*. Baseline Books, New York, 1995. (Includes reviews of operas available on laserdisc)

Price, Walter. "Before MTV, There Was Opera." *Los Angeles Times*, November 1, 1992. (on *The Voice of Firestone*)

———. "Voice of Firestone." *Opera News*, December 8, 1990. (*The Voice of Firestone* telecasts and videos)

Rabenalt, Arthur Maria. *Der Operetten-Bildband Bühne Film Fernsehen*. Olms Press, Hildesheim, 1980. (History of German operettas on film and television)

Rattner, David S. "Opera and Films." *Film Music*, Spring 1956.

Reed, Robert M., and Maxine K. *The Encyclopedia of Television, Cable and Video*. Van Nostrand Reinhold. New York, 1992. (Opera items)

Rescigno, Eduardo. *Dizionario Rossiniano*. Biblioteca Universale Rizzoli, Milan, 2002. (Videos of Rossini operas)

Riley, Brooks. "Camera Angles." *Opera News*, June 1990. (Study of styles of TV opera directors Browning, Large, and Sellars)

Roberto, Antoine (project director). *Opera on Screen, The Catalogue of Opera, Operetta, Oratorio and Music Theatre on Television, Film and Video*. Ein Projekt im Aufgtrag des Österreichischen Bundesminsteriums für Wissenschaft und Forschung. Vienna, IMZ, 1995. (Collaborative project of the international TV companies with annual updates. Invaluable listings of programs.)

Robertson, Patrick. "Opera Films." *Guinness Film Facts and Feats*. Guinness Books, Enfield, 1985. (Descriptions of first opera films)

Rockwell, John. "The Impact of TV on Opera." *New York Times*, January 25, 1981.

———. "Why Does Opera Lure Filmmakers?" *New York Times*, May 8, 1983.

Rohan, Michael Scott (editor). *The Classical Video Guide*. Victor Gollancz, London, 1994. (Reviews of opera videos in England)

Rose, Brian G. *Television and the Performing Arts*. Greenwood Press, Westport, 1986. (History of opera on American TV and bibliography)

———. *Televising the Performing Arts: Interviews with Merrill Brockway, Kirk Browning, and Roger Englander*. Greenwood Press, Westport, 1992.

Rosson, Alex. "An Unequal Partner Raises Its Lovely Face." *New York Times*, March 12, 1995.

Rothstein, Edward. "The Sight of Music." *The New Republic*, September 2, 1991. (Opera on video)

SACIS International. *Straight to the Heart*. 1995 Italian TV catalog with opera programs.

Sadie, Stanley (editor). *The New Grove Dictionary of Opera*. Macmillan Press, London, 1992.

Salter, Lionel. "The Birth of TV Opera." *Opera,* March 1977. (BBC-TV opera history, 1936–1939)

———. "The Infancy of TV Opera." *Opera,* April 1977. (Continuation of above article)

———. "Opera on Television." *Opera,* April 1957.

———. "Television," in Sadie, *New Grove Dictionary of Opera.*

Schroeder, David. *Cinema's Illusions, Opera's Allure, The Operatic Impulse in Film.* Continuum Books, New York, 2002. (Fascinating study of how opera has influenced the movies)

Schwartz, Lloyd. "Opera on Television." *The Atlantic,* January 1983.

Serceau, M., and H. Puiseaux. "Cinéma et Opéra." *La Revue du Cinéma,* No. 430, Paris, 1987.

Stanbrook, Alan. "The Sight of Music. "*Sight and Sound,* lvi/2, 1987. (Essay on opera films)

Steane, John. "Real to reel..." *Opera Now,* May/June 1997. (Historical singers in early films)

Sturman, Janet L. *Zarzuela: Spanish Operetta, American Stage.* University of Illinois Press, Urbana, 2000.

Swed, Mark. "Lights...Aria...Action." *Los Angeles Times,* February 13, 1994.

Sykes, Margaret. *The Classical Catalog.* Gramophone, Harrow, 1995. (Opera videos in England)

Tambling, Jeremy. *Opera, Ideology and Film.* Manchester University Press, Manchester, 1957.

———. *A Night in at the Opera: Media Representations of Opera* (editor). John Libbey, London, 1994. (13 essays on screen opera)

———. "Introduction: Opera in the Distraction Culture." (Essay in *A Night in at the Opera*)

———. "Revisions and Re-vampings: Wagner, Marschner and Mozart on Television and Video." (Essay in *A Night in at the Opera*)

Taubman, Howard. "Televised Opera." *New York Times,* April 24, 1949.

Theresa, Rose. "From Méphistophélès to Méliès: Spectacle and Narrative in Opera and Early Film," in Joe, *Between Opera and Cinema.*

Toffetti, Sergio, and Stefano Della Casa (editors). *L'opera lirica nel cinema italiano.* Comune di Torino, Turin, 1977.

Topping, Graham. "Tune in to Opera on TV." *BBC Music Magazine,* January 2002.

Toscan du Plantier, Daniel. "Le Cinéma est l'(ardente) obligation de l'opéra," in Duault, *Cinéma et Opéra.*

Trask, C. Hooper. "Berlin Turns to the Film Operetta." *Variety,* November 13, 1932.

Turconi, David, and Antonio Sacchi. *Un bel dì vedemmo. Il melodramma dal palcoscenico allo schermo.* Amministrazione Provinciale, Pavia, 1984. (Operas on screen)

Turconi, David, with Catherine Schapira and Michel Pazdro. "Filmographie: Cinéma et Opéra: du film muet à la vidéo," in Duault, *Cinéma et Opéra.* (Opera filmography to 1987)

Uselton, Roi A. "Opera Singers on the Screen." *Films in Review,* April, May, June–July 1967. (Comprehensive three-part article on opera singers in Hollywood)

UCLA Film and Television Archive. *Hallmark Hall of Fame: The First Forty Years.* 1991 catalog. .

Unitel. *Unitel Television Catalog,* 1986. Sections on TV "Operas" and "Operettas."

Verna, Tony. *Live TV: An Inside Look at Directing and Producing.* Focal Press, Boston, 1987. (Articles on TV opera by director Kirk Browning and producer John Goberman)

Villien, Bruno. "Opéra et cinéma: le suspense continu." See Duault, *Cinéma et Opéra.*

Warrack, John, and Ewan West. "Film opera" and "Television Opera," in *The Concise Oxford Dictionary of Opera.* Oxford University Press, Oxford, 1992. (Brief histories of opera in film and TV)

Wells, William H. "Opera Video." *Opera Monthly.* (Column of opera video reviews)

Weiner, Marc A. "Why Does Hollywood Like Opera?" in Joe, *Between Opera and Cinema.*

Weir, Judith. "Memoirs of an Accidental Film Artist," in Tambling, *A Night in at the Opera.*

Wexler, J. "Opera Taken Out of Mothballs, Given Exciting Vitality by NBC." *Billboard,* October 13, 1951.

White, Jonathan. "Opera, Politics and Television: bel canto by Satellite," in Tambling, *A Night in at the Opera.*

Willey, George A. "Opera on Television." *The Music Review,* May 1959. (Survey of TV opera)

William Shaman. "The Operatic Vitaphone Shorts." *ARSC Journal,* Spring 1951.

Wlaschin, Ken. "The Glory of Opera Films That Hit the Right Notes." *Los Angeles Times,* November 15, 2000

———. *Opera on Screen: A Guide to 100 Years of Films and Videos Featuring Operas, Opera Singers and Operettas.* Beachwood Press, Los Angeles, 1997.

———. "Success Drives the Reluctant Actor Away." *Rome Daily American,* April 7, 1963.

Wynne, Peter. "Video Days: A historical survey of opera on television." *Opera News,* June 1998. (Excellent overview of opera on U.S. television)

Zeffirelli, Franco. "Une aventure exaltante mais risquée," in Duault, *Cinéma et Opéra.*

Zinger, Pablo. "An Operatic Armada Sweeps Ashore." *New York Times,* August 11, 1996. (On zarzuelas)

2. INDIVIDUAL OPERAS AND FILMS

Amadeus

—*Amadeus.* Peter Shaffer. Signet, New York, 1984. (Film edition with photos)

—*The Mozart Firmament.* Charles Kiselyak. 1996. (Booklet on film in laser edition)

Amahl and the Night Visitors—*The New York Times* critic Olin Downes on the television opera:

—"Menotti Opera, the First for TV, Has Its Premiere." December 25, 1951. (Front page)

—"Menotti's *Amahl* Is a Historic Step in the Development of a New Medium." December 30, 1951.

A Bayou Legend—"A Bayou Legend." *Opera News*, June 1981. (William Grant Still opera telecast)

The Beggar's Opera—"Beggar's Opera: A British Musical Film Version of Gay's Work." A. H. Weiler. *New York Times*, August 30, 1953.

Bed and Sofa—"New Life Off Broadway for Soviet Film of the 20s." Vincent Canby. *New York Times*, February 2, 1996.

La Belle et la Bête

—"The Cinematic Body in the Operatic Theater: Philip Glass's *La Belle et la Bête*." Jeongwon Joe, in Joe, *Between Opera and Cinema*.

—"Glass Meets Cocteau: Beauty or Beast." Chris Pasel and Kenneth Turan. *Los Angeles Times*, November 11, 1995.

Billy Budd—"Billy Budd Scores in TV Bow." Olin Downes. *New York Times*, October 20, 1952.

La Bohème—"*La bohème*: Fidelité et Originalité." See Luigi Comencini, in Duault, *Cinéma et Opéra*.

Boris Godunov—"A Propros de *Boris Godunov*." See Andrzej Wajda, in Duault, *Cinéma et Opéra*.

Carmen

—"The Carmen Connection." Glenn Loney. *Opera News*, September 1983. (Peter Brook's *Carmen*)

—"*Carmen Jones:* un film d'Otto Preminger." Olivier Eyquem. *Avant-Scene du Cinéma*, July–September 1978.

—"Fatal Charms." Peter Conrad. *Opera News*, 1986. (Carmen in the movies)

—"Gypsy." Leslie Rubinstein. *Opera News*, October 1984. (Francesco Rosi film)

Dalibor—"Prague." *Opera*, April 1957 (About film of the Smetana opera)

Diva—"Is There a Text in this Libido? *Diva* and the Rhetoric of Contemporary Opera Criticism." David J. Levin, in Joe, *Between Opera and Cinema*.

Don Giovanni

—"Don Juan." David S. Rattner. *Film Music*, January–February 1956. (Austrian film of the opera)

—"Liebermann, Losey and the Libertine: *Don Giovanni* on film." Roland Gelatt. *Opera News*, November 1979.

The Dream of Valentino—Washington Opera program 1994:

—"Creating the Dream." Charles Nolte.

—"The Memory, the Movie Star, the Myth." Ken Wlaschin.

Elektra—"*Elektra* on the Screen." *Moving Picture World*, April 23, 1910. (Vitagraph film of the opera)

Eugene Onegin—"*Eugene Onegin*." R. A. Tuggle. *Opera News*, December 12, 1959. (Soviet film of the opera)

Fitzcarraldo—*Fitzcarraldo: The Original Story*. Werner Herzog. Fjord Press, San Francisco, 1982.

Jeanne d'Arc au Bûcher—"Give It a Hearing: Public Should be Allowed to See Film Version of Claudel-Honegger work." Howard Taubman. *New York Times*, May 22, 1955.

Lucia di Lammermoor—"The Maddening Popularity Swings of Lucia di Lammermoor." Stephanie von Buchau. Los Angeles Opera Program 1994. (*Lucia* scene in *When Angels Fear to Tread*)

Macbeth—"Macbeth, la terrible parenthèse." Claude d'Anna on his film. See Duault, *Opéra et Cinéma*.

The Marriage—"Martinů Opera Scores in TV bow." Olin Downes. *New York Times*, February 8, 1953.

Marilyn—"New Milieu for Monroe: Some Like It Operatic." Edward Rothstein. *New York Times*, October 8, 1993.

McTeague—"Tarnishing the Gilded Age: Altman Directs *McTeague*." Carrie Rickey. *Opera News*, November 1992.

Meeting Venus—"Close Encounters." Glenn Close. *Opera News*, November 1991. (Film *Meeting Venus*)

The Medium—"Film Version of *The Medium* directed by Menotti in Rome." Robert Sabin. *Musical America*, April 15, 1951.

My Heart's in the Highlands—"Saroyan Story Charms as Opera." Raymond Ericson. *New York Times*, March 18, 1970.

A Night at the Opera

—"The Singing Salami: Unsystematic Reflections on the Marx Brothers' *A Night at the Opera*." Lawrence Kramer, in Tambling, *A Night in at the Opera*.

—"'There Ain't No Sanity Claus!' The Marx Brothers at the Opera." Michal Grover-Friedlander, in Joe, *Between Opera and Cinema*.

Nixon in China—"TV Adds New Dimension to *Nixon in China*." Alan Rich. *Los Angeles Herald Examiner*, April 10, 1988.

Noroît—"Sounding Out the Operatic, Jacques Rivette's *Noroît*." Mary M. Wiles, in Joe, *Between Opera and Cinema*.

Le Nozze di Figaro—"The Elusive Voice, Absence and Presence in Jean-Pierre Ponnelle's Film *Le nozze di Figaro*." Marcia J. Citron, in Joe, *Between Opera and Cinema*.

Orphée—"Mood Painting." Mark Swed. *Opera News*, May 1993. (Philip Glass opera)

Perfect Lives—*Perfect Lives, an Opera*. Robert Ashley. Burning Books, San Francisco, 1991.

The Phantom of the Opera—*The Complete Phantom of the Opera*. George Perry. Holt, New York, 1988.

Porgy and Bess

—*The Life and Times of Porgy and Bess*. Hollis Alpert. Knopf, New York, 1990. (Goldwyn film)

—"It Takes a Long Pull…" Richard Fawkes. *Opera Now*, December 1993. (Trevor Nunn film)

—"Porgy in Hollywood." Harper Mackay. *Opera News*, January 20, 1990. (Goldwyn film)

The Ring of the Nibelung

—"Live from Valhalla." Fred Plotkin. *Opera News*, June 1990. (Met videotaping of *Ring*)
—"A Ringing Response." Margaret Betley. *Opera News*, January 5, 1991. (Met *Ring* on TV)
—*Ring Resounding*. John Culshaw. Viking, New York, 1967. (Film *The Golden Ring*)
Rosa, A Horse Drama—"A Horse's Tale." Andrew Clements. *The Guardian*, November 5, 1994.
The Tales of Hoffmann
—*The Tales of Hoffmann: A Study of a Film*. Monk Gibbon. London, Saturn, 1951.
—"*The Tales of Hoffmann*, an Instance of Operatility." Lesley Stern, in Joe, *Between Opera and Cinema*.
The Threepenny Opera—"De la pièce et du film..." Lotte Eisner on Pabst, *Cahiers du Cinéma*, June 1954.
Three Tenors series—"The Three Tenors Juggernaut." Ralph Blumenthal. *New York Times*, March 24, 1996.
Il trovatore
—"*Trovatore* Begins Lyric Reform." *The Moving Picture World*, March 4, 1911.
—"Film Music." Lawrence Morton. *Hollywood Quarterly*, Summer 1950. (Problems of filming in Italy)
Turandot—"Opera and Post-modern Cultural Politics: *Turandot* in Beijing." Ping-Hui Liao, in Tambling, *A Night in at the Opera*.
War Requiem—*War Requiem, the Film*. Derek Jarman. Faber and Faber, London, 1989.
Willie Stark—"Hot Southern Politics Hits High-C on TV." Cynthia Lilley. *Los Angeles Reader*, October 16, 1981.

3. INDIVIDUAL SINGERS & DIRECTORS

Alberghetti—"She Keeps Her Music Life in Tune." Jack Hawn. *Los Angeles Times*, May 1, 1985.
Anderson—*Marian Anderson*. Anne Tedards. Chelsea House, New York, 1988.
Bertolucci—"The National Dimension? Verdi and Bernardo Bertolucci," in Tambling, *A Night in at the Opera*.
Caballé—*Monserrat Caballé, Casta Diva*. Robert Pullen and Stephen Taylor. Gollancz, London 1994. (Includes videography)
Callas—"TV Honors a Grand Diva in a Grand Way." Tim Page. *New York Times*, December 11, 1983.
Caruso—"Two Opera Stars in Silent Films." *New York Times*, December 2, 1918. (Caruso and Farrar)
Cebotari—*Maria Cebotari*. John Steane. *Opera News*, March 1994.
Chaliapin—*Chaliapin: An autobiography*. Nina Froud and James Hanley (editors). Macdonald, London, 1968.
Domingo—*My First Forty Years*. Plácido Domingo. Alfred A. Knopf, New York, 1983.
Durbin—*The Child Stars*. Norman J. Zierold. Chapter on Durbin. Coward-McCann, New York, 1965.
Eddy—"Nelson Eddy's Career in Opera." William Ashbrook. *Opera Quarterly*, Spring 1997.

Eggerth—"Queen of the Screen." Brendan Carroll on Marta Eggerth. *Opera Now*, October 1995.
Ellis—"I Sang with Caruso." Michael Scott on Mary Ellis. *Opera News*, June 1988.
Farrar—*Always First Class: The Career of Geraldine Farrar*. E. Nash. Washington, DC, 1982.
Flórez—"The Flowering of Juan Diego Flórez." *The Economist*, April 6, 2002.
Hendricks—"Mimì with a Method." Barbara Hendricks and *La bohème* film. *Opera News*, August 1988.
Jepson—"Another View." F. Paul Driscoll. Helen Jepson in *The Goldwyn Follies*. *Opera News*, February 18, 1995.
Jeritza—"Maria Jeritza." Gustl Breuer. *Opera News*, September 1982.
Kiepura—"Magnetic Pole." Brendan Carroll on Jan Kiepura. *Opera Now*, April 1984.
Lanza
—*Mario Lanza*. Derek Mannering. Robert Hale, London, 1993.
—*Mario Lanza: Tenor in Exile*. Roland L. Bassette. Amadeus Press, Portland, 1999.
Lewis—"An American Tragedy." Michael B. Dougan on Mary Lewis. *Opera News*, July 1984.
McCormack—"John McCormack: A Hit in Movietone." Mordaunt Hall. *New York Times*, March 12, 1930.
MacDonald and Eddy—*The Films of Jeanette MacDonald and Nelson Eddy*. Philip Castanza. Citadel Press, Secaucus, 1978.
Mariano—*Luis Mariano, Le Prince de Lumière*. Daniel Ringold, Philippe Guiboust, et al. TFI, Paris, 1995.
McCracken—Wlaschin, Ken. "The Yanks Are Coming to Top the Bill." *Rome Daily American*, January 6, 1963.
Melba—"Peach of a Diva, PBS miniseries salutes Nellie Melba." Jamie James. *Opera News*, January 7, 1989.
Melchior—"Lauritz Melchior," in Parish, *Hollywood Songsters*.
Mojica—"Watch this Hombre." *Photoplay*, January 1930. (About José Mojica in Hollywood)
Moore—*You're Only Human Once*. Grace Moore. Doubleday, Doran, Garden City, 1944.
Novello—*Ivor*. Sandy Wilson. London, Joseph, 1975. (Information on his films)
Novotná—"Jarmila Novotná 1907–1994." Walter Price. *Opera News*, April 2, 1994.
Pavarotti—"Pavarotti Goes Hollywood." Leslie Rubinstein on *Yes, Giorgio*. *Opera News*, September 1982.
Pons
—*Lily Pons: A Centennial Portrait*. James A. Drake and Kristin Beale Ludecke (editors). Amadeus Press, Portland, 1999.
—"Lily Pons," in Parish, *Hollywood Songsters*.
Ponselle
—"The Ponselle Legacy." George Jellinek. *Opera News*, March 12, 1977.

—*Rosa Ponselle: A Centenary Biography.* James A. Drake. Amadeus Press, Portland, 1997.

Printemps—"Yvonne Printemps: 100 Years of Springtime." Patrick O'Connor. *Opera,* July 1994.

Schroeter—"Excess and Yearning: The Operatic in Werner Schroeter's Cinema," in Tambling, *A Night in at the Opera.*

Schwarzkopf—*Elisabeth Schwarzkopf.* Alan Jefferson. Northeastern University Press, Boston, 1996.

Stevens—"Risë." Martin Mayer. *Opera News,* December 24, 1988.

Tagliavini—*Ferruccio Tagliavini, L'Uomo, la Voce.* Umberto Bonafini. Magis Books, Reggio Emilia, 1993.

Tauber—Tamino and Beyond." Michael Scott. *Opera News,* August 1991.

Tibbett
—*Lawrence Tibbett, Singing Actor.* A Farkas (editor). Amadeus Press, Portland, 1989.
—"Lawrence Tibbett," in Parrish, *Hollywood Songsters.*

Turner—"Call Me Madame." Brian Kelly. *Opera News,* December 24, 1994.

Vargas—"Ramón Vargas, Tenor: Music That Changed Me." *BBC Music Magazine,* May 2002.

Visconti—*Screen of Time, A: A Study of Luchino Visconti.* Monica Stirling. Secker & Warburg, London, 1979.

Van Dam—"Long Distance Master." Marylis Sevilla-Gonza. *Opera News,* January 22, 1994.

Vishnevskaya—*Galina: A Russian Story.* Galina Vishnevskaya. Harcourt Brace Jovanovich, New York, 1984.

Zeffirelli—*Zeffirelli, The Autobiography of Franco Zeffirelli.* Weidenfeld and Nicolson, London, 1986.

4. PERIODICALS (with screen opera reviews)
L'Avant-Scène Cinéma
L'Avant-Scène Opéra
Billboard
Classic Images
Classical Pulse
Film Facts
Film Music
Gramophone
The Hollywood Reporter
Journal of Broadcasting
Monthly Film Bulletin
Motion Picture Herald Production Digest
Musica
Musical America
The New York Times
   —*Directory of the Film.* Arno Press, New York, 1971.
   —*Film Reviews.* 1913–1980 (10 vols.). Arno Press, New York.
Opera
L'Opéra
Opera International
Opera Monthly
Opera News
Opera Now
The Opera Quarterly
Opérette
Theatre Arts
Variety
   —*Film Reviews.* 1907–2001 (25 vols.). Garland Press, New York and Bower, Providence.
   —*Television Reviews.* 1905–1986 (11 vols.). Garland, New York

5. FILM CATALOGS
American films

American Film-Index 1908-1915 and *1916–1920.* Einar Lauritzen and Gunnar Lundquist. Film-Index, Stockholm, 1976/1984.

The American Film Industry: A Historical Dictionary. Anthony Slide. Greenwood Press, Westport, 1986.

American Film Institute Catalog of Motion Pictures
—*Film Beginnings, 1893–1910* (2 vols.). Elias Savada (compiler), Scarecrow, Metuchen, 1995.
—*Feature Films, 1911–1920* (2 vols.). Patricia King Hanson (editor). UC Press, Berkeley, 1988.
—*Feature Films, 1921–1930* (2 vols.). Kenneth W. Munden (editor). R. W. Bowker, New York, 1971.
—*Feature Films, 1931–1940* (3 vols.). Patricia King Hanson (editor). UC Press, Berkeley, 1993.
—*Feature Films, 1961–1970* (2 vols.). Richard P. Krafsur (editor). R. W. Bowker, New York, 1976.

American Film Personnel and Company Credits, 1908–1920. Paul Spehr. McFarland, Jefferson, 1996.

Biograph Bulletins 1896–1908. Kemp R. Niven. Locare, Los Angeles, 1971.

Biograph Bulletins 1908–1912. Eileen Bowser. Museum of Modern Art, New York, 1972.

Feature Films, 1940–1949: United States Filmography. Alan G Fetrow. McFarland, Jefferson, 1994.

The First Twenty Years: A Segment of Film History. Kemp R. Niven. Locare, Los Angeles, 1968.

The Great Movie Shorts. Leonard Maltin. Bonanza Books, New York, 1972.

Animated films

The Animated Film. Ralph Stephenson. Tantivy Press, London, 1973.

British Animated Films 1895–1985: A Filmography. Denis Gifford. McFarland, Jefferson, 1987.

Fifty Greatest Cartoons. Jerry Beck (editor). Turner Publishing, Atlanta, 1994.

Full-Length Animated Features Films. Bruno Edera. Focas Press. London, 1977.

Looney Tunes and Merrie Melodies. Jerry Beck and Will Friedwald. Henry Holt, New York, 1989.

Argentina

Medio Signo de Cine: Argentina Sono Film. Claudio España. Editorial Abril, Buenos Aires, 1984.

Austria

Austrian Films. Annual catalog*s*. Austrian Film
  Commission
Österrecheschen Spielfilm der Stummfilmzeit (1907–
1930). Walter Fritz. Austrian Film Archive, Vienna,
1967.
Österrecheschen Spielfilm der Tonfilmzeit (1929–1944).
Walter Fritz. Austrian Film Archive, Vienna, 1968.

British films

The British Film Catalogue: 1895–1985. Dennis Gifford.
  Facts on File, Oxford, 1986.
British Film Catalogues. British Council, London
British Sound Films: The Studio Years 1928–1959. David
  Quinlan. B. T. Batsford, London, 1984.
The History of the British Film
—1896–1906. Rachel Low.Roger Manvell. Allen &
  Unwin, London, 1948.
—1906–1914. Rachel Low. Allen & Unwin, 1949.
—1914–1918. Rachel Low. Allen & Unwin, 1948.
—1918–1939. Rachel Low. Allen & Unwin, 1971.
Who's Who in British Cinema. Dennis Gifford.. Batsford,
  London, 1978.

Czechoslovakia

All the Bright Young Men and Women: Czech Cinema.
  Josef Skvorecky. Take One, Toronto, 1971.
Outline of Czechoslovakian Cinema. Langdon Dewey.
  Informatics, London, 1971.

Denmark

Danske Titler og Biografier: Filmens Hvem-Hvad-Hvor.
  Bjorn Rasmussen. Politikens, Copenhagen, 1968.
Danish Films. Annual catalogs. Danish Film Institute.

Finland

Finnish Cinema. Peter Cowie. VAPK Publishing,
  Helsinki, 1990.
Finnish Films. Annual catalogs. Finnish Film
  Foundation. Helsinki, 1984–2002.

France

Catalogue des Films Français de Long Métrage, Films de
Fiction. Raymond Chirat, (editor).
—*1919–1929.* Cinémathèque de Toulouse, 1984.
—*1929–1939.* Cinémathèque Royale de Belgique, 1975.
—*1940–1950.* Cinémathèque de Luxembourg, 1981.
Catalogue Pathé 1896 à 1914. Henri Bousquet. Edition
Henri Bousquet, Paris, 1993.
Cinéma Français, Les Années 50. Jean-Charles Sabria
(editor). Centre Pompidou, Paris, 1987.
Cinema Francese 1930–1993. Mario Guidorizzi. Casa
Editrice Mazziana, Verona, 1993.
Filmographie des Long Metrages Sonores du Cinéma
Français. Vincent Pinel. Cinémathèque, Paris, 1985.
French Films. Catalogs. Unifrance, Paris.

Germany

Deutscher Spielfilm Almanach 1929–1950. Alfred Bauer.
Christoph Winterberg, München, 1976.
Films of the Federal Republic of Germany. Annual
  catalogs. Export-Union des Deutschen Films.
Germany (Screen Series), Illustrated Guide and Index.
Felix Bucher. Zwemmer, London, 1970.
Reclams Deutsches Filmlexikon. Herbert Holba, Gunter
  Knorr/Peter Spegel. Reclam, Stuttgart, 1984.
West German Cinema Since 1945: Reference Handbook.
Richard and Marie Helt. Scarecrow, Metuchen, 1987.

Holland

Dutch Cinema: An Illustrated History. Peter Cowie.
  Tantivy Press, London, 1979.
Dutch Film. Annual catalogs. Holland Film Promotion,

Hungary

Pictorial Guide to Hungarian Cinema 1901–1984. Istvan
  Nemeskurty, Tibor Szanto. Revai, Budapest, 1985.
Word and Image: History of the Hungarian Cinema.
  Istvan Nemeskurty. Corvina Press, Budapest, 1968.

International—film encyclopedias

Dictionnaire du Cinéma. Two vols. Jean Tulard. Robert
  Laffont, Paris, 1984/1985.
Directors and Their Films, 1895–1990. Brooks Bushnell.
McFarland, Jefferson, 1993.
Encyclopedia of the Musical Film. Stanley Green. Oxford
University Press, New York, 1981.
The Faber Companion to Foreign Films. Ronald Bergan
  and Robyn Karney. Faber, London, 1992.
The Film Encyclopedia (3d ed.). Ephraim Katz.
HarperCollins, New York, 2002.
Film History. "A Chronology of Cinema 1889–1896."
  Deac Rossell. Vol. 7, No. 2, Summer 1995.
Halliwell's Filmgoer's and Video Viewer's Companion.
  John Walker (editor). HarperCollins, London, 2002.
Halliwell's Film Guide. John Walker (editor).
  HarperCollins, London, 2001.
The Hollywood Musical. John Russell Taylor and Arthur
Jackson. McGraw-Hill, New York, 1971.
International Film Guides. Peter Cowie (editor). Tantivy
  Press and Hamlyn Press, London, 1965–2003.
Leonard Maltin's Movie and Video Guide. Leonard
Maltin (editor). Signet, New York, 2003.
Musical, O (2 vols.). Joao Benard da Costa and Manuel
S. Fonseca (editors). Lisbon, 1985.
*National Film Archive Catalogue: Silent Fiction Films
1895–1930.* British Film Institute, London, 1960.
*National Film Archive Catalogue: Silent Non-Fiction
Films 1895–1934.* British Film Institute, 1966.
National Film Theatre Program Booklets. British Film
  Institute, 1952–2002.
The New York Times Encyclopedia of Film 1896–1979.
Gene Brown (editor). Times Books, New York, 1984.
*Treasures from the Film Archives: Short Silent Fiction
Films.* Ronald S. Magliozzi. Scarecrow, Metuchen, 1988.

Twenty Years of Silents, 1908–1928. John T. Weaver (compiler). Scarecrow, Metuchen, 1971.
The Time Out Film Guide. John Pym (editor). Penguin, London, 2002.
Variety Obituaries 1905–1990 (13 vols.). Garland, New York, 1988.
The World's Great Movie Stars and Their Films. Ken Wlaschin. Salamander Press, London, 1979.

International
Film festival catalogs: Annecy, Berlin, Cannes, Chicago, Denver, Edinburgh, Karlovy Vary, Los Angeles (AFI Fest and Filmex), Locarno, London, Montreal, Moscow, Pordenone, San Francisco, San Sebastian, Seattle, Sundance, Sydney, Toronto, Venice, Zagreb.

Italy
Il Cinema muto Italiano. 1910–1931 (19 vols.). Vittorio Martinelli, et al. Bianco e Nero, Rome.
Il Cinema muto italiano (3 vols.). Aldo Bernardini. Laterza, Rome/Bari, 1980–1983.
Davanti allo Schermo, Cinema Italiano 1931–43. Mario Gromo. La Stampa, Turin, 1993.
Dizionario del Cinema Italiano
—*I Film, Vol. 1, 1930 al 1944*. Roberto Chiti and Enrico Lancia. Gremese Editore, Rome, 1993.
—*I Film, Vol. 2, 1945 al 1959*. Roberto Chiti and Roberto Poppi. Gremese Editore, Rome, 1991.
—*I Film, Vol. 3, 1960 al 1969*. Roberto Poppi and Mario Pecorari. Gremese Editore, Rome, 1992.
—*I Film, Vol. 4, 1970 al 1979*. Roberto Poppi and Mario Pecorari. Gremese Editore, Rome, 1996.
—*I Film, Vol. 5, 1980 al 1989*. Roberto Poppi. Gremese Editore, Rome, 2000.
—*I Film, Vol. 6, 1990 al 2000*. Enrico Lancia. Gremese Editore, Rome, 2002.
—*I Registi, 1930 ai Giorni Nostri*. Roberto Poppi. Gremese Editore, Rome, 1993.
Italian Film: A Who's Who. John Stewart. McFarland, Jefferson, 1994.
Ma l'Amore No: Cinema Italiano di Regime (1930–1943). Francesco Savio. Sonzogno, Milan, 1975.
Storia del cinema muto. Vol. 1. Roberto Paolella. Giannini, Naples, 1956.
Storia del cinema muto italiana. Vol. 1. Maria Adriana Prolo. Poligono, Milano, 1951.

Mexico
Mexican Cinema: Reflections of a Society 1896–1980. Carl J. Mora. UC Press, Berkeley, 1982.

Norway
Norwegian Films. Annual catalogs. Norwegian Film Institute, 1975–present.

Poland
Contemporary Polish Film. Stansilaw Kuszewski. Interpress Publishers, Warsaw, 1978.

Poland (World Cinema 1). Frank Bren. Flicks Books, Trowbridge, 1990.

Romania
Contributii la Istoria Cinematografiei in Romania 1896–1948. Ion Cantacuzino. Academiei, Bucharest, 1971.

Spain
Cine Español 1896–1983. August M. Torres (editor). Ministerio de Cultura, Madrid, 1984.
Cine Español. Annual film catalogs. Ministerio de Cultura, Madrid, 1980–1996.
Diccionario del Cine Español 1896–1966. Fernando Vizcaino Casas. Editora Nacional, Madrid, 1968.
Literature Española: Una Historia de Cine. Cine Español para el Exterior, Madrid, 1999.

Sweden
Authors of Swedish Feature Films and Swedish TV Theatre. Sven G. Winquist. SFI, Stockholm, 1969.
Svensk Filmografi 1920–1969 (4 vols.). Swedish Film Institute, Stockholm, 1977.
Swedish Films. Annual catalogs. Swedish Film Institute.
Swedish Silent Pictures 1896–1931 and Their Directors. Sven G. Winquist (editor). SFI, Stockholm, 1967.
Swedish Sound Pictures 1929–69 and Their Directors. Sven G. Winquist (editor). SFI, Stockholm, 1969.

Switzerland
Cinéma Suisse Muet, Lumières et Ombres. Rémy Pithon (editor). Éditions Antipodes, Lausanne, 2002.
Swiss Films. Annual catalogs. Swiss Film Center, Zurich

USSR
Eastern Europe (Screen Series). Nina Hibbin. Zwemmer, London, 1969.
Kino, A History of the Russian and Soviet Film. Jay Leyda. Allen & Unwin, London, 1960.
Soviet Film Catalogs. Sovexport Film, Moscow, n.d.
Vingt Ans de Cinéma Sovietique. Luda and Jean Schnitzer. Editions C.I.B., Paris, 1963.
Who's Who in the Soviet Cinema. Galina Domatovskaya and Irina Shilova. Progress, Moscow, 1978.

6. OPERA/OPERETTA DICTIONARIES
Adam, Nicky. *Who's Who in British Opera*. Scolar Press, Aldershot, 1993.
Bloom, Ken. *American Song: Musical Theater Companion 1900–1984*. Facts on File, New York, 1985.
Bordman, Gerald. *American Operetta: From H.M.S. Pinafore to Sweeney Todd*. Oxford U Press, 1981.
Bradley, Edwin M. *The First Hollywood Musicals*. McFarland, Jefferson, 1996.
Bruyr, José. *L'Opérette*. Press Universitaires de France, Paris, 1962.
Ewen, David. *The Book of European Light Opera*. Holt, Rinehart & Winston, New York, 1962.

———.*Lighter Classics in Music.* Arco Publishing, New York, 1961.

———. *The New Encyclopedia of the Opera.* Hill and Wang, New York, 1971.

Gammond, Peter. *The Oxford Companion to Popular Music.* Oxford University Press, New York, 1991.

Gammon, Peter, with Peter Clayton. *A Guide to Popular Music.* Phonexis House, London, 1960.

Gänzl, Kurt. *The Blackwell Guide to the Musical Theater on Record.* Blackwell, Oxford, 1990.

———.*The Encyclopedia of The Musical Theatre.* Blackwell Publishers, London, 1994.

———. *Gänzl's Book of the Musical Theatre.* Schirmer Books, New York, 1989.

Gelli, Piero (editor). *Dizionario dell'opera 2002.* Baldini & Castoldi, Milan, 2001.

Glasser, Alfred (editor). *The Lyric Opera Companion.* Andrews and McMeel, Kansas City, 1991.

Green, Stanley. *Encyclopedia of the Musical.* Cassell, London, 1977.

Griffiths, Paul. *Encyclopedia of 20th Century Music.* Thames and Hudson, London, 1986.

Henken, John E. *Francisco Asenjo Barbieri and Spanish National Music.* UCLA Ph.D. dissertation, 1987.

Hischak, Thomas S. *The American Musical Theatre Song Encyclopedia.* Greenwood, Westport, 1995.

Ho, Allan, and Dmitry Feofanov. *Biographical Dictionary of Soviet Composers.* Greenwood, 1989.

Holden, Amanda (editor). The Viking Opera Guide. Viking, London, 1993.

—*The New Penguin Opera Guide.* Penguin Books, London, 2001.

Hughes, Gervase. *Composers of Operetta.* St. Martin's Press, New York, 1962.

Jacobs, Arthur. *The Penguin Dictionary of Musical Performers.* Penguin Books, London, 1991.

Johnson, H. Earle. *Operas on American Subjects.* Coleman-Ross, New York, 1964.

Kornick, Rebecca Hodell. *Recent American Opera: A Production Guide.* Columbia, New York, 1991.

LaRue, C. Steven (editor). *International Dictionary of Opera.* St. James Press, Detroit, 1993.

Lebrecht, Norman. *Companion to 20th Century Music.* Simon & Schuster, New York, 1992.

Machlisi, Joseph. *American Composers of Our Time.* Thomas Y. Crowell, New York, 1963.

McSpadden, J. Walker. *Operas and Musical Comedies.* Thomas Crowell, New York, 1946.

Martin, George. *The Opera Companion to Twentieth Century Opera.* Dodd Mead, New York, 1979.

Parker, Derek and Julia. *The Story and the Song: English Musical Plays, 1916–78.* Chappell, London, 1979.

Pokrovsky, Boris, and Yuri Grigorovich. *The Bolshoi.* William Morrow, New York, 1979.

Rich, Maria F. (editor). *Who's Who in Opera.* Arno Press, New York, 1976.

Rockwell, John. *All American Music.* Alfred Knopf, New York, 1983.

Sadie, Stanley (editor). *The New Grove Dictionary of Opera.* Macmillan Press, London, 1992.

Schmidgall, Gary. *Shakespeare and Opera.* Oxford University Press, New York, 1990.

Seeger, Horst. *Opernlexikon.* Florian Noetzel Verlag, Berlin, 1978.

Slonimsky, Nicolas. *The Concise Baker's Biographical Dictionary of Musicians.* Schirmer, New York, 1988.

———. *Lectionary of Music.* Doubleday, New York, 1989.

Stockdale, F. M., and M. R. Dreyer. *The International Opera Guide.* Trafalgar Square, North Pomfret, 1990.

Traubner, Richard. *Operetta, A Theatrical History.* Doubleday, Garden City, 1983.

Warrack, John, and West, Ewan. *Concise Oxford Dictionary of Opera.* Oxford University Press, 1992.

Wurz, Anton. *Reclams Operettenführer.* Philipp Reclam Jun, Stuttgart, 1988/

Zentner, Wilhelm. *Reclams Opernführer.* Philipp Reclam Jun, Stuttgart, 1988.

Zietz, Karyl Lynn. *Breve storia dei teatri d'opera italiani.* Gremese Editore, Rome, 2001

DVD/VHS Distributors

Allegro
www.allegro-music.com

Arte/La Sept
Fax: 011-44-14-80-67

ArtHaus Musik
www.arthaus.musik.com

Artisan Entertainment
Tel: 310-449-9200
www.live-entertainment.com

BBC/Opus Arte Media
www.opusarte.com

Bel Canto Society
Tel: 800-347-5056
www.belcantosociety.org

Bel Canto Paramount Video
Tel: 323-956-5000
www.paramount.com

Best Video
Fax: 203-248-4910
www.bestvideo.com

BMG Classics/RCA Victor
Tel: 212-930-4550

Buena Vista Home Video
Tel: 818-560-1000
www.disney.com

Castle Opera
Unit 12, Brunswick Ind Park
Brunswick Way, New Southgate
London N11 1HX, UK

CBS Fox Video
P.O. Box 900
Beverly Hills, CA 90013

Classics World
www.classicalmus.com

Columbia/TriStar Home Video
Tel: 310-244-8000
www.cthv.com

Consumer Video Marketing
Tel: 516-482-0022
Fax: 516-482-0097

Corinth Video
Tel: 800-221-4720
Fax: 212-929-0010

Criterion/Voyager
Tel: 800-446-2001
www.criterionco.com

Decca
www.deccaclassics.com

DG (Deutsche Grammophon)
www.deutschegrammophon.com

Digital Video Express
www.divx.com

Divisa Ediciones
Fax: 983.273083
www.divasared.es

Dreamlife
www.dreamlife.co.jp

Dream Time Entertainment
Fax: 93.459.28.03

EMI Classics
www.emiclassics.com

Euroarts
www.euroarts.com

EVS
(European Video Distributors)
Tel: 800-423-6752

Facets Multimedia
Tel: 800-331-6197
Fax: 312-929-5437
www.facets.org

Film America
Tel: 212-489-6347

Film Australia
www.filmaust.com.au

Films for the Humanities &
Sciences
Tel: 800-257-5126
Fax: 609-275-3767
www.films.com

German Language Video Center
Tel: 800-252-1957
Fax 317-547-1263

Hardy Classic Video
www.klassicon.com

HBO Home Video
Tel: 212-512-1000
www.hbo.com/hbohomevideo

Home Vision
Fax: 312-878-8748

House of Opera
Tel: 888-495-9742
www.houseofopera.com

Image Entertainment
Tel: 818-407-9100
www.image-entertainment.com
ww.dvdvideogroup.com

Jarvis Conservatory
Tel: 707-255-5445
www.jarvisconservatory.com

Kino
Tel: 212-629-6880
Fax: 212-714-0871

Kultur
Tel: 732-229-2343
Fax: 732-229-0066
www.kulturvideo.com

Legato Classics
No longer operational

Live Opera
P.O. Box 3141
Steinway Station
New York, NY 11103

Live Opera Heaven
Tel: 212-501-8196
liveoperaheaven@juno.com

Live Opera Videos
Tel: 516-484-5100
www.dinosaur.org

Lumivision
Tel: 303-446-0400

Lyric
No longer operational

Metropolitan Opera Guild
Tel: 800-453-2258

MGM-UA Home Video
Tel: 310-449-3000
www.mgm.com/dvd

Miramax
www.miramax.com

Multimedia San Paolo
www.stpaula.it

New Line Home Video
Tel: 310-854-5811
www.newline.com/homevideo

NVC Arts
Tel: 011-44-171-388-3833
Fax: 011-44-171-383-7174

Opera d'Oro
www.allegro-music.com

Opera Dubs
No longer operational

Operaworld
Tel: 800-996-7372
www.Operaworld.com

Orion Home Video
Tel: 310-282-0550
www.orionpictures.com/orion

Philips
www.universalclassic.com
www.deccaclassics.com/dvd

Pioneer Classics
2265 East 220th Street
P.O. Box 22782
Long Beach, CA 90801-5782

Polygram Home Video
Tel: 310-777-7700
www.polygram-us.com

Premiere Opera, Ltd.
Tel: 212-877-3331
Fax: 212877.0782
www.premiereopera.com

Promart
www.promart.it

Public Media Home Video
Tel: 800-826-3456

Pyramid Film & Video
Tel: 310-828-7577, ext. 314

RCA Victor/BMB Classics
Tel: 212-930-4550

Sight and Sound
Tel: 617-894-8633
Fax: 617-894-9329

Sony Music
www.sonymusic.com/Music

TDK
www.tdkmediactive.com

Teldec Classics International
www.teldec.com
Triton Multimedia
www.tritonmedia.com

Twentieth Century-Fox
Home Entertainment
Tel: 310-369-3900
www.tcfhe.com

Unitel
www.unitel.classicalmusic.com

Universal Home Video
Tel: 818-777-4400
www.universalstudios.com/dvd

VAI
(Video Artists International)
Tel: 800-477-7146
www.vaimusic.com

Video Yesteryear
Tel: 800-243-0987

VIEW Video
Tel: 212-674-5550
www.view.com

Voyager
Tel: 800-446-2001

Warner Home Video
Tel: 818-954-6000
www.dvdwb.com

Winstar Home Entertainment
Tel: 212-686-6777
Fax: 212-545-9931

This index contains only the names of persons and works that are not the subject of individual entries in the encyclopedia. Page numbers in italics refer to illustrations.

Allman, Robert, 241, 396, 441
Allonsafan, 682
All's Well That Ends Well (Castelnuovo-Tedesco), 127
All the King's Horses (Tuttle), 213, 362
All the King's Men (Warren), 254
Allyson, June, 1, 431
Almirante, Mario, 202
Almodovar, Cristian, 279
Almodóvar, Pedro, 226, 736, 737
Alone at Last, 626, 693
Alonso, Jesus Aguirre Ramon, 279
Alonso, José Luis, 186
Alonso, Luis R., 433
Alonso, Rámon, 45, 292, 398, 578
Alonzo, Virginia, 637
Alouf, David, 38
Alpar, Gita, 712
Alsen, Elsa, 786
Alsop, Marin, 721
Alstock, Bernice, 437
Alstrup, Oda, 711, 716
Altered States (Russell), 154
Altes Herz wird wieder Jung (Engel), 376
Alt Heidelberg, 665
Altmeyer, Jeannine, 295, 579, 590, 755
Alton, John, 304
Altringen, Heinz, 62
Alva, Luigi, 47, 156
Alvarado, Don, 116, 591
Alvarez, Carlos, 305
Álvarez, Enrique García, 15, 395
Álvarez, Marcelo, 379, 584, 739
Alvarez, Octavio, 87
Alver, Jonathan, 510
Amadé, Raymond, 46
Amadei, Maria Letizia, 393
Amadini, Maria, 23
Amado, Lizette, 7
Amadori, Luis Cesar, 118, 355
Amaducci, Bruno, 123, 141, 267, 581, 641
Amano, Shokichi, 295, 579, 639, 755
Amanti in fuga (Gentilomo), 60
Amaya (Guridi), 307
Amazing Mrs Holiday, The (Renoir), 203, 576
Ambition (Vincent), 352
Ambrose, Anna, 312, 589
Ambrosio, Arthur, 529
Ameche, Don, 610
Ameling, Elly, 613
American in Paris, An (Gershwin), 276, 378
American President, The (Reiner), 237, 369
Americana, Ibero, 297
America's Singing Sweethearts (Lorentz), 410
Ames, Lewis, 672
Ames, Louis, 527, 583
Ames, Preston, 360
Aminel, Georges, 745
Amiramashvili, Medea, 166
Amirante, Luigi, 81
Amman, Lukas, 434, 778
Amner, Richard, 686
Amore di Norma (Martino), 493
Amour médecin, L' (Lully and Molière), 400
Amster, Peter, 471
Anagnost, Dino, 751
Analyze This (Ramis), 431, 588
Anania, Michael, 84, 404, 488
Ananiashvili, Nina, 461

Andalousie (Lopez), 388
Andalousie (Vernay), 426
Andalusische Nachte (Maisch), 117
Anday, Rosette, 617
Andemicael, Awet, 783
Ander, Charlotte, 297, 481, 769
Andergast, Maria, 200, 749
Andermann, Andrea, 702, 710
Anders, Günther, 473
Anders, Peter, 630
Anders, Sylvie, 769
Andersen, Hans Christian, 490, 662
Andersen, Hilde, 288
Anderson, Challis, 394
Anderson, D., 382
Anderson, Daphne, 63
Anderson, David Maxwell, 510
Anderson, Delbert, 313
Anderson, Gillian, 115, 158
Anderson, Judith, 616
Anderson, Kevin, 663
Anderson, Linda, 383, 481
Anderson, Liz, 589
Anderson, Maxwell, 138, 140, 289, 426, 593, 763
Anderson, Paul Thomas, 120
Anderson, Roslyn, 215
Anderson, Stig, 295, 590, 640
Anderson, William, 618
Andersson, Hans, 717
Andersson-Palme, Laila, 39
Andes, Keith, 660
Andes, Oliver, 304
Andjaparidze, Zurab, 166
Andò, Roberto, 493
Andrae, Marc, 80
André, Francine, 781
André, Gaby, 738
André, Maurice, 312
André, Nick, 333
Andreani, Henri, 235
Andreani, Oscar, 563
Andrée, Hanna, 374
Andrée, Ingrid, 144
Andrei Rublev, 680
Andreiev, Andrei, 199
Andreolli, Florindo, 528
Andresen, Bjorn, 170
Andrew, Roger, 36
Andrews, Al, 340
Andrews, Julie, 172, 653

Andrews, Kenny, 198
Andrews, Roger, 196
Andrews, William C., 63
Andrey, Pauline, 152
Andriot, Lucien, 331
Andro, Brian, 768
Andrsova, Jana, 607
Andy Hardy's Private Secretary (Seitz), 301, 395
Andzhaparidze, Zurab, 27, 338, 567
Anelli, Angelo, 340
Anelli, Anne Maria, 651
Anema e core, 675
Angas, Richard, 456
Angel, Heather, 356
Angel, Marie, 273, 361, 564, 599
Angela's Ashes (Parker), 188
Angeli, Pier, 39, 419
Angelillo, 16
Angelo, Nick, 437
Angélo, tyran de Padou (Hugo), 283
Angelou, Maya, 555
Angerer, Kathrin, 763
Angerer, Paul, 626

Angyal, Ladislaus, 483
Anisimov, Alexander, 187
Anita Louise, 452
Annabella, 408
Anna Karenina (Brown), 223
Anneliese Rothenberger Honors Herself, 605
Anni, Anna, 131, 187, 522
Anni difficili (Zampa), 493
Annihilation of Fish, The (Burnett), 564
Annis, Francesca, 106
Annovazzi, Elisenda, 305
Anoush (Tigranian), 271
Anselmi, Susanna, 179, 230, 399
Ansen, Betty, 703
Ansoldi, Giorgio, 477
Anst, Margarete, 350
Antamoro, Giulio, 187
Antel, Franz, 503, 661
Anthony, Charles, 65, 269, 522, 523, 674
Anthony, Dean, 663
Anthony, Susan, 31
Anthony, Susan B., 655, 694
Anthony, Trevor, 36
Anthony, Walter, 292
Antigone (Honegger), 325
Antinori, Nazzareno, 412
Anton, Jorge, 556
Anton, Karl, 428, 602, 742
Antonacci, Anna Caterina, 210, 228, 594
Antonini, Alfredo, 22, 42, 173, 269, 438, 716
Antonini, Giovanni, 35, 748, 749
Antonio, José, 616
Antonucci, Stefano, 95, 238, 784
Any Given Sunday (Stone), 244
Anything for a Song, 675
Anywhere But Here (Wang), 423
Apel, Johann, 265
Apéstegui, Ilse, 186
Apfel, Ed, 555
Apfel, Oscar, 11
Aphrodite (Erlanger), 255
Apocalypse Now (Coppola), 154, 649
Appelgren, Curt, 241, 451
Applebaum, Louis, 323
Apples to You (Roach), 49
Aprea, Bruno, 95
Apreck, Rolf, 252
Ara, Gabriele, 181
Arand, Christine, 216
Aranda, J. F., 778
Aranda, Vincent, 120
Arangi-Lombardi, Giannina, 757
Arata, Ubaldo, 641, 757
Araya, Graciela, 584
Arbell, Lucy, 197, 435
Arbo, Manuel, 688
Arbuckle, Fatty, 575
Arc de Triomphe, 213
Archer, Neill, 164, 241, 542
Archetti, Alberto, 547
Ardant, Fanny, 105
Ardavin, Eusebio Fernandez, 145
Ardelli, Norberto, 133
Ardoin, John, 105, 591
Ardolino, Emile, 435
Arduini, Suzanne, 673
Arena, Maurizio, 5, 258, 399, 412, 440, 482, 727
Arestrup, Niels, 439, 680
Argenta, Nancy, 383
Argento, Asia, 548
Argyle, Pearl, 141
Aria (Jarman), 391

Arias, Alfredo, 573
Arias, Maria, 145
Ariostini, Armando, 211, 382
Arioosto, Ludovico, 15, 32, 518
Arkell, Reginald, 377, 378
Arko, Günther, 742
Arlésienne, L' (Daudet), 32
Arletty, 242
Armbruster, Robert, 672
Arme Jonathan, Der (Millöcker), 459
Armenian, Raffi, 632
Armetta, Henry, 377
Armiliato, Fabio, 440
Arms and the Man (Shaw), 138
Armstrong, Karan, 59, 66, 227, 385, 706, 751, 754
Armstrong, Louis, 232, 654
Armstrong, Rebecca, 34
Armstrong, Richard, 196, 209, 337, 495, 698
Armstrong, Robert, 285
Armstrong, Sheila, 17
Arnaldi, Giuseppina, 583
Arnaldo, Arnaldo, 382
Arnauld, Yvonne, 355
Arndt, Dietrich, 346
Arnell, Richard, 687
Arniches, Carlos, 16, 197
Arnold, Danny, 455
Arnold, Edward, 205, 386, 484, 610
Arnold, Imgart, 163
Arnold, John, 600
Arnold, Leonore, 460
Arnoldsen, Sigrid, 48, 234
Arnould, Bernard, 209
Arnoux, Robert, 242
Arnova, Alba, 284
Arnschtam, Lev, 288
Arnshteyn, Mark, 525
Arnstaedt, Hansl, 74
Arozamena, Eduardo, 188
Arozamena, Jesús María, 127, 355
Arrangement, The (Kazan), 22
Arrighi, Luciana, 722
Arrivederci, Papa! (Mastrocinque), 59–60
Arroyo, Alberto, 279
Arroyo, Eduardo, 268
Arroyo, Martina, 6
Arshak II (Tchukhatjian), 33, 272
Artanda, Vincente, 349
Artemieve, Dmitri, 782
Artero, Matilde, 16
Arteta, Aïnhoa, 238, 540, 599
Arthur, George, 206
Arthur, Johnny, 175
Arthur, Robert, 488
Arthur, Robert Alan, 575
Aruhn, Britt-Marie, 134, 245, 779
Arundell, Dennis, 150
Arunder, Dennis, 443
Arvey, Verna, 56, 657
Arvidson, Jerker, 145
Asagaroff, Grischa, 48
Asari, Keita, 412
Asaryova, Emilia, 392
Asawa, Brian, 573
Asche, Oscar, 141
Asensio, Enriques Garcia, 45, 183, 186
As Frozen Music, 672
Ashe, Oscar, 512
Ashe, Rosemary, 63
Asher, Nadine, 306, 382
Ashkenazy, Vladimir, 683
Ashley, Claudia, 663
Ashley, Paul, 322

Ashley, Sam, 204
Ashton, Frederick, 150
Aslan, Raoul, 40
Asmus, Rudolf, 45, 151, 163
Aspinall, Michael, 573
Assas, Madeleine, 475
Assassinat du Duc de Guise, L', 613
Asselin, Paul, 242
Assmann, Arno, 429
Astaire, Fred, 275, 558
Asther, Nils, 17
Astley, Edwin, 334
Astor, June, 5
Astor, Junie, 291
Astor, Mary, 90
Atchkinson, Richard, 304
Athena (Thorpe), 558
Atherton, David, 76, 451, 545, 564
Atherton, James, 472
Atienza, Edward, 227
Atkins, Irene Hahn, 137
Atkins, Norman, 614, 672, 775
Atkins, Zoë, 125
Atkinson, David, 721
Atkinson, Dorothy, 699
Atkinson, Lynton, 219, 782
Atkinson, Richard, 85
Atlantic City (Malle), 493
Atlas (Monk), 466
Atonissen, Heather, 186
Atsuma, Mr., 747
Attaway, Ruth, 555
Attree, Emily, 99
Attwell, Michael, 326
Atwill, Lionel, 41
Atys (Lully), 139, 140, 400
Aubrey, Cecile, 423
Auclair, Michel, 24, 244, 423
Audi, Pierre, 590
Audran, Stéphane, 194
Audret, Pascale, 178
Audus, Hilary, 509
Auer, Erich, 240
Auer, Mischa, 268, 671
Augér, Arleen, 15, 476, 626
Auger, Guillermo, 317
August, Edwin, 642
August, Joseph, 391
August der Starke (Wegener), 88
Augustyn, Frank, 223
Aulaulu, Carla, 207
Aulenti, Gae, 195, 580
Aulis Sallinen: Man, Music, Nature, 613
Aumont, Jean-Pierre, 365, 588
Aurenche, Jean, 419
Auric, Georges, 65
Auseni, Manuel, 48
Aussey, Germaine, 745, 778
Aussi Longue Absence, Une (Colpi), 51
Austerlitz (Gance), 462
Austin, Anson, 4, 126, 156, 163, 243, 250, 328, 403, 443, 566
Austin, Charles, 150
Austin, Leslie, 429
Autant-Lara, Claude, 142
Auvray, Jean-Claude, 209, 702
Avati, Pupi, 474
Avdeyeva, Larissa, 91, 222, 567, 726
Avedon, Doe, 171
Avemo, Kerrsti, 517
Aventure à Monte Carlo (Lopez), 388
Aventures du roi Pausole, Les (Honegger), 325
Aversano, Salvatore, 305
Avery, Margaret, 348
Avery, Tex, 25, 50, 760

Avestissian, Michael, 26
A Víg Özvegy (Curtiz), 405
Aviles, Abraham, 300
Avolant, Gianni, 344
Awakenings (Marshall), 86
Axel, Gabriel, 194
Axel an der Himmelstür (Benatzky), 67
Axt, William, 41, 84, 665
Axtner, Harald, 733
Axur, rè d'Ormus, 613, 680
Ayars, Ann, 150
Ayers, Vanessa, 732
Ayldon, John, 323
Ayres, Lew, 409
Ayres, Nat, 405
Ayrton, Norman, 368
Azaria, Hank, 160
Azcona, Rafael, 155
Azema, Sabine, 604
Azito, Tony, 550
Aznavour, Charles, 250, 745
Azzaretti, Jaël, 197
Azzarilli, Adele Bianchi, 7
Azzolini, Fernanda Cadoni, 134
Azzopardi, Anthony, 258

Baarova, Lida, 152, 249
Baas, Balduin, 759
Babatunde, Obba, 714
Babbitt, Milton, 650
Babel, Pierre, 498
Babel Opera (Delvaux), 194
Babes in Arms, 270, 271
Babette's Feast (Axel), 194
Babs, Alice, 78
Baby Peggy, 116
Bac, André, 390
Bacall, Lauren, 71, 673
Bacchini, Romolo, 493
Bacelli, Monica, 482, 503, 677
Bach, Annette, 59, 60, 173
Bach, Dalia, 471
Bach, Mechthild, 388
Bach, Simone, 569
Bachelor, The (Sinyor), 121
Bachlund, Gary, 31
Bachmann, Gabor, 80
Bachmann, Ingeborg, 350, 562
Bachmann, Karl, 163
Bachrich, Susanne, 163
Backes, Constanze, 782
Bäckman, Ilkka, 252
Backus, Jim, 25
Bacon, Lloyd, 530, 586, 587
Badalucco, Niccia, 604
Badalucco, Nicola, 170
Badea, Alexandru, 519
Badea, Christian, 425
Badel, Alan, 616, 753
Badel, Pierre, 112
Badet, Régine, 115
Bad News Bears (Ritchie), 119
Baechtel, Harry, 7
Baecker, Otto, 785
Baer, Harry, 397
Baglioni, Bruna, 187, 482
Bahn, Roma, 434
Bahner, Gert, 780
Bahr, Hermann, 596
Baier, Barbara, 706
Baigildin, Sergei, 393
Bailey, Anne Howard, 175, 715
Bailey, Dennis, 336
Bailey, Leslie, 282
Bailey, Norman, 68, 252, 400, 545, 614, 709, 757

Battersby, Martin, 337
Battiato, Giacomo, 179
Battistoni, Carlo, 523
Battle of Britain, 758
Battle of Kerzhenets, The (Ivanov-Vano and Norstein), 374
Battleship Potemkin (Eisenstein), 208
Battsitoni, Carlo, 191
Battu, Léon, 424
Batukov, Yuri, 706
Bauchau, Nicholas, 164
Bauchau, Patrick, 418
Baudo, Serge, 167, 234, 751
Baudour, Michel, 38
Bauer, Belinda, 619
Bauer, Harry, 188
Bauer, Joachim, 330
Bauer, Richard, 315
Bauer, Rita, 207
Bauer, Vladimir, 521
Bauer-Ecsy, Leni, 418
Bauer-Theussl, Franz, 150, 335, 786
Baugé, André, 46, 242, 496
Baugh, Christ, 99
Bauman, Philip J., 7, 16, 186, 279, 578, 737
Baumann, Ludwig, 626, 679, 753
Baumeister, Ernst, 62, 316
Baumgartner, Bernhard, 768
Baumgartner, Reinhard, 754
Baur, Harry, 61, 269
Baustian, Robert, 388
Bautista, Conchita, 145
Bava, Mario, 211, 254, 527
Bavaglio, Giovanni, 208
Baxter, Anne, 666, 719
Baxter, Jane, 200
Baxter, Keith, 453
Baxter, Warner, 332, 363, 769
Bay, Howard, 733
Bayadère, La, 40
Bayan, Daria, 82, 189
Bayard, Jean-François, 242
Baye, Natalie, 62
Bayley, Clive, 38, 76
Bayne, Beverly, 598
Bayo, Maria, 678
Bazemore, Raymond, 80
Bazzini, Ugo, 235, 574
Bazzoni, Camillo, 581
Beach, Olive Mae, 587
Beach of Falesa, The (Hoddinott), 324
Beahan, Charles, 507
Beamish, Stephen, 339, 550
Bean, Gweneth, 31, 295
Beardsley, Aubrey, 616
Beardsley, Karen, 768
Beaser, Robert, 136
Beattie, Herbert, 384, 490
Beatto, Javier, 279
Beatty, Warren, 178, 334, 697
Beaty, John Lee, 2
Beaudry, Jacques, 100
Beaumarchais (Cools), 59
Beaumont, Harry, 193, 302, 598, 642
Beauregard, Richard, 320
Beaussant, Philippe, 595
Beaux jours du roi Murat, Les (Pathé), 291
Because You're Mine (Hall), 132, 371, 395, 587
Beccaria, Bruno, 387, 482
Bech, Philip, 214
Becht, Hermann, 295, 579, 639, 717
Bechtler, Hildegard, 192, 545
Beck, Elisabeth, 517

Beck, Karen, 472
Beckenstein, Marion, 133
Becker, Alexandra, 298
Becker, Harold, 546
Becker, Marianne, 786
Becker, Rolf, 298
Beckett, Samuel, 238, 239
Beczala, Piotr, 645, 782
Bednar, Karel, 166
Bedros, Polita, 390
Beebe, Lucius, 772
Beenhakker, Hans, 216
Beery, Noah, 292, 650
Beery, Wallace, 381
Beeton, David, 751
Begalyi, Ferenc, 547
Begg, Heather, 4, 54, 177, 243, 250, 497, 519, 752
Beghi, Luisella, 472
Begley, Kim, 93, 290, 418, 488
Behharz, Norbert, 1
Behind the Legend (Peters), 443
Behn-Grund, Friedl, 256, 483
Behr, Randall, 314, 518
Behrendt, Hans, 186, 244, 665
Behrens, Detlef-Michael, 94
Behrens, Stefan, 182, 264
Behrman, David, 479
Beilharz, Norbert, 210, 219, 664, 783
Beineix, Jean-Jacques, 757
Being John Malkovich (Jonze), 258–59
Beirer, Hans, 209, 614
Bekaert, Herman, 422
Békeffy, István, 416
Bekiaris, Pavlos, 473
Belafonte, Harry, 121
Belasco, David, 229, 230, 284, 411
Belazs, Béla, 55
Belcher, Daniel, 383
Belcourt, Emile, 36, 423
Belén, Ana, 155
Beling, Maria, 264, 630
Bell, Donald, 451
Bell, Joe, 438
Bell, Marie, 49, 500
Bell, Marion, 198, 445
Bell, Monta, 642
Bella Donna (Milton), 213
Belle de Cadix, La (Bernard), 426
Belle de Cadix, La (Lopez), 388
Belle meunière, La, 628
Belle Noiseuse, La, 662
Bellincioni, Gemma, 131
Bellissima (Visconti), 213
Bellman, Gina, 326
Bello, Vincenzo, 584, 599
Bellochio, Marco, 713
Bellon, Leonida, 126
Bellot, Patrice, 691
Belloy, Dormont de, 785
Bellugi, Piero, 211
Belmont, Virginia, 624
Belohlavek, Jiri, 345, 372
Belov, Grigori, 589
Belshazzar's Feast, 690
Belsky, Vladimir, 373
Beltrán, José María, 16, 145, 197
Beltrán, Tito, 238, 597
Belushi, James, 39
Belyavsky, Alexander, 338
Beňačková, Gabriele, 24, 53, 241, 378, 440, 607, 608
Benamou, Roger, 104, 522, 700
Benassi, Memo, 641
Bence, Margarethe, 53
Bender, Howard, 691

Bender, Madeline, 517
Bender, William, 735
Bendl, Ingrid, 424
Bendow, Wilhelm, 251
Bene, Carmelo, 193, 616
Beneix, Jean-Jacques, 182
Benelli, Sem, 21
Benelli, Ugo, 48, 109, 246
Benét, Stephen Vincent, 138
Benetti, Adriana, 59
Benetti, Carlo, 161, 238
Benetti, Olga, 161, 238
Benfer, Friedrich, 117
Beni, Gimi, 134, 299
Benigni, Roberto, 532
Bening, Annette, 168, 237, 369
Benini, Maurizio, 539
Benítez, Daniel, 16
Benitz, Albert, 697
Benjamin, Christopher, 312
Benjamin, Richard, 395
Benke, Hermann, 585
Benkhoff, Fita, 515
Bennent, Anne, 401
Bennet, Bernard, 768
Bennett, Alan, 312
Bennett, Charles, 41
Bennett, Compton, 406, 500
Bennett, Michael, 164
Bennett, Richard Rodney, 329
Bennett, Robert Russell, 505
Bennett, Spencer C., 582
Bennett, Wilda, 415
Benny, Jack, 54, 546
Benson, Alan, 630, 698
Benson, Richard, 480, 481
Benson, Susan, 293, 339, 456, 550
Bentivoglio, Fabrizio, 616
Bentley, Bob, 14, 41
Benvenuti, Leo, 47
Benz, Hamilton, 319
Benzell, Mimi, 139
Beque, Lucy, 612
Bérangère, 422
Beransky, Frantisek, 54
Berberian, Ara, 22, 113, 450, 584, 716
Berbié, Jane, 460, 498
Berek, Robert, 313
Bérel (de Choudens), Paul, 21
Berenger, Tom, 368, 757
Berg, Elisabeth, 781
Berg, Fritz, 240
Bergby, Ingar, 288
Bergen, Elly Felisie, 600
Berger, Elisabeth, 165
Berger, Helmut, 307, 397, 545
Berger, Ludwig, 73, 721, 734, 759
Berger, Mariel, 142
Berger, Mark, 18
Berger, Norbert, 36
Berger, Senta, 661
Berger-Tuna, Helmut, 429, 777
Bergeson, Scott, 108, 163, 498
Berghaus, Ruth, 242
Bergis, Jean-Marie, 96
Bergman, Alan, 315, 334
Bergman, Andrew, 588
Bergman, Ingrid, 344, 395, 603, 646
Bergman, Luly, 186
Bergman, Marilyn, 315, 334
Bergner, Elisabeth, 224, 758
Bergon, René, 171
Bergsma, Deanne, 151, 170
Bergstrom, Oscar, 520
Beria di Salsa, Francesco, 520
Beringola, Manuel, 688

Cambridge, Godfrey, 348
Camerini, Mario, 49
Camero, Manuel, 273
Cameron, Allan, 160, 282, 293, 323, 339, 456, 519, 536, 550, 561, 606, 652, 715, 775
Cameron, James, 520
Cameron, John, 19, 677
Camille, 658
Cammarano, Salvatore, 64, 392, 399, 424, 722
Cammell, Donald, 502
Campa, A., 145
Campana, Joyce, 488
Campane, Le, 603
Campanella, Bruno, 110, 135, 341
Campanile, Pasquale Festa, 128
Campanini, Carlo, 254
Campbell, Alan, 671
Campbell, Elizabeth, 666
Campbell, Norman, 177, 223, 293, 322, 323, 405, 418, 455, 598
Campeotto, Dario, 250
Campigotto, G. Franco, 45
Campillo, Anita, 257
Campion, Cris, 91
Campion, Jane, 502
Campogalliani, Carlo, 281, 290, 386, 643
Campori, Angelo, 243, 399, 584
Campos y Zori, José, 145
Camprodan, Francisco, 426
Campus Carmen, 117
Camus, Germán, 116
Canales, Susanita, 335
Canali, Anna Maria, 412, 583
Can-Can (Lang), 520
Cancellieri, Edmondo, 46, 111, 196, 392, 497
Candia, Roberto de, 422, 540
Candyman, 287
Canettieri, Stefano, 223
Canfarelli, Gianni, 471
Cannan, Dennis, 63
Cannan, Phyllis, 607, 731
Canning, Hugh, 162
Cano, Meteo, 364
Canonici, Luca, 83, 195, 196, 740, 784
Canova, Judy, 712
Cantante con me (Brignone), 398
Cantante dell'opera, La (Malasomma), 174–75
Cantelo, April, 20, 223, 683
Canteloube, Joseph, 686
Cantini, Guido, 20, 419, 648, 742
Cantininelli, Paolo, 258
Canto per te (Girolami), 182
Cantor, Eddie, 95, 395
Canzoneri, Michele, 667
Canzoni a due voci (Vernuccio), 60
Cap, Franz, 757
Capasso, Camille, 328, 609
Capecchi, Renato, 211, 257, 421, 521
Cape Fear, 631
Čapek, Karel, 353, 418
Capellani, Albert, 5, 84, 192, 220, 261, 262, 422, 425, 585, 615, 618, 634, 711, 718, 724
Capellani, Paul, 84, 192, 220, 262, 585, 615, 634, 718
Capeyron, Jean-Pierre, 178
Capitan aventurero, El, 464
Capitan de cosacos, Un (Reinhardt), 464–65
Capitan Fracassa, Il (Costa), 158
Caplan, Joan, 92, 392

Capobianco, Tito, 349, 393, 403, 420, 584, 593, 644, 709, 730
Capolicchio, Lino, 474
Capozzi, Alberto, 394, 523, 535, 590, 640
Cappannelli, George, 63
Cappuccio, Ruggero, 228
Capra, Frank, 13, 436
Captain Corelli's Mandolin (Madden), 279
Captain January, 394
Captain Pirate (Murphy), 363
Captive, The (Akerman), 158
Capuana, Franco, 9, 23
Capuano, Luigi, 166
Caraccio, Giuseppe, 385
Carbonara, Gerard, 232, 332
Carcache, Marian Motley, 732
Carcia, Pilar, 183
Cardelli, Giovanni, 407
Carden, Joan, 705, 714
Cardiff, Jack, 414
Cardinal, The (Preminger), 383
Cardinale, Claudia, 12, 248, 462
Cardino, André, 361
Cards, Virginia, 82
Cardynin, Petr, 568
Carecchi, Renato, 48
Career in C Major (Cain), 118, 332, 363, 769
Carew, Arthur Edmund, 717
Carewe, Edwin, 229, 270
Carey, MacDonald, 650
Cargill, Patrick, 622
Cariaga, Marvalee, 150, 178, 334
Cariaggi, Pier Quinto, 538
Carignani, Paolo, 161
Carino, Gerard, 548
Cariou, Len, 671
Carl, Joseph, 188
Carl, Rudolf, 370, 503
Carle, Karen, 183
Carleton, Lloyd B., 253
Carlin, Mario, 527
Carlini, Carlo, 650
Carlini, Paolo, 284, 477
Carlisle, Kitty, 489, 530, 559, 644, 724
Carlisle, Peggy, 712
Carlito's Way (DePalma), 369
Carlos, Lenus, 328
Carlsen, Toril, 288
Carlson, Lenus, 441
Carlton, William P., 87
Car Man, The (MacGibbon), 120
Carmeli, Boris, 208, 727
Carmencita (Edison), 246
Carmi, Vera, 290
Carminati, Fabrizio Maria, 425
Carminati, Tullio, 213, 344, 507, 552, 633
Carné, Marcel, 350
Carnevale, Anna, 130
Carney, Art, 348
Carnivale di Venezia, Il (Gentilomo and Adami), 166
Carnovich, Daniel, 516
Caro, Alicia, 198
Carognani, Paolo, 482
Carol, Cecile, 322
Carol, Martine, 201, 462
Caroli, Paolo, 412
Caroll, Linda, 599
Caron, Leslie, 39, 462
Carosello Napoletano (Giannini), 281
Carosi, Mauro, 263, 482
Carosio, Margherita, 21, 28, 212, 434,

473, 575
Carossio, Natale, 28
Carpani, Giuseppe, 491
Carpenter, Francis, 457
Carr, Charmian, 653
Carr, Howard, 380
Carr, Martin, 269
Carrado, Gino, 84
Carral, Dora, 509
Carraro, Massimiliano, 230
Carraro, Tiziana, 230
Carré, Michel, 180, 233, 310, 424, 453, 460, 597, 745
Carreau, Brigitte, 552
Carreno, Ansel C., 145
Carreras, Enrique, 547
Carrey, Jim, 54, 396, 448, 600
Carrie Nation (Moore), 469
Carrière, Berthold, 112, 119, 168, 293, 339, 456, 550
Carriere, Mathieu, 62
Carrillo, Leo, 391, 432, 468, 470, 610, 725
Carrington, Blackford, 661
Carrington, John, 194
Carrión, Miguel Ramos, 7
Caroli, Silvano, 35, 229, 386, 740
Carroll, Carvel, 258
Carroll, Diahann, 121, 554, 555
Carroll, Joan, 31, 94
Carroll, John, 592
Carron, Elizabeth, 111
Carruthers, Bob, 475
Carson, Johnny, 643
Carste, Hans, 365
Carten, Sabrina Elayne, 555
Carter, Betty, 763
Carter, Janis, 319
Carter, Joyce, 666
Carter, Richard, 405, 406
Carteri, Rosanna, 521, 563, 708
Cartier, John, 293, 323, 339, 456, 550, 606, 775
Cartier, Rudolf, 58, 112, 150, 521, 612, 676, 677, 698
Carturan, Gabriella, 24
Caruso, Enrico, Jr., 6, 49, 108, 125, 126, 197, 257, 724
Caruso, Mariano, 521
Carvajal, Carlos, 183, 300, 399, 578, 737
Carver, Brent, 550
Cary, John, 580
Casadesus, Jean-Claude, 77, 317
Casal, Antonio, 186, 578
Casanova (Benatzky), 67
Casanova (Volkoff), 363 Casanova, Alberto, 84
Casanova, Montserrat, 781
Casanova '70 (Monicelli), 466
Casapietra, Celestina, 24, 70, 286
Casaravilla, Carlos, 292
Casarini, Pino, 9
Casarrubios, Carmen, 226
Casas, Anna, 516
Casciarri, Giorgio, 346
Case, Evelyn, 82
Casei, Nedda, 206
Caselin, Luca, 45
Caselli, Fabio, 416
Caserini, Mario, 396, 420, 535, 640
Cash, Jim, 178
Cash, Louise, 22
Cash, Tony, 119
Cashmore, John, 12

Casimira, Maria, 621
Casino Girls (Künneke), 365
Casino Paradise (Bolcom), 89
Caskey, Marilyn, 315
Casler, Dan, 340
Casolla, Giovanna, 484, 728
Cass, Henry, 288
Cass, Lee, 92, 240, 304, 407, 542
Cassan, Marguerite, 512, 576
Cassard, Franck, 519
Cassavetes, John, 614
Cassello, Kathleen, 475
Cassidy, Patrick, 312, 334
Cassilly, Richard, 36, 240, 441, 612, 679, 773
Cassimatis, Irene, 403
Cassinelli, Antonio, 9, 385
Cassinelli, Ricardo, 96, 544, 720
Cassis, Alessandro, 5
Cassuto, Alvaro, 22
Casta diva (Gallone), 67, 195, 206
Casta diva (Kuyper), 494

Castagna, Bruna, 449
Castagna-Fullin, Maria, 582
Castaing, Danièle, 299
Casta Susanna, La (Perojo), 355
Cast Away (Zemeckis), 223
Casteen, Lisa, 606, 715
Castel, Lou, 713
Castel, Nico, 20, 113, 196
Castellani, Renato, 483, 598, 738
Castelli, Carlo, 527
Castellitto, Sergio, 604
Castelnuovo, Nino, 713
Castiglione, Enrico, 271, 702
Castillo, Salvador, 16
Castle, Charles, 682
Castle, Joyce, 136, 199, 295
Castle, William, 363
Castor et Pollux (Rameau), 140
Casto Susano, El (Pardavé), 355
Castro, Estrillita, 50
Castro, Eva de, 595
Castro, Julio, 327
Catalá, Maruja, 16
Cataldi, Antonio, 115
Catani, Cesare, 523
Catani, Ilio, 156, 196, 520
Catania, Claudia, 726
Catelain, Jaque, 192, 235, 600
Caterina Cornaro (Donizetti), 195
Catlett, Walter, 323
Catley, Gwen, 506
Caton, Frédéric, 14, 781
Cattaneo, Amelia, 238
Cattaneo, Aurelia, 258
Cattano, Gabriele, 321
Caubère, Philippe, 465
Cauchetier, Patrice, 542
Caulfield, Anne, 326
Caurier, Patrice, 135, 216
Cava, Carlo, 9
Cavadini, Catherine, 39
Cavalcanti, Alberto, 758
Cavaliere, Emile de, 556
Cavalieri, Catarina, 621
Cavalli, Francesco, 137
Cavara, Paolo, 265
Cavassilas, Pierre, 109, 152, 228, 702, 703, 745, 781
Cavaz, Tullio, 722
Cavazza, Sebastian, 120
Caven, Ingrid, 397, 419, 624
Cazalet, Hal, 216
Cazpell, Barbara, 415

Cazzaniga, Renato, 202
Cebrián, Ramón, 145
Cecchele, Gianfranco, 130, 727
Cecchi, Nana, 727
Cechalova, Milada, 18, 22, 783
Cecil, Edward, 546
Cehanovsky, George, 449, 527
Cela, Alketa, 109
Celakovska, Magda, 18, 501
Celetti, Rodolfo, 373
Celi, Teresa, 302
Celibidache, Sergiu, 148, 491
Celli, Teresa, 302
Cellini, Benvenuto, 68
Celulari, Edson, 63
Cemy, Florian, 209
Cendrillon (Méliès), 246
Censio Savelli, Christian, 382
Centinela, Alerta! (Grémillon), 16
Cerchio, Fernando, 134, 565
Céresi, Ugo, 161
Cerha, Friedrich, 400
Cerny, Floria, 579
Cerny, Karel, 18
Ceroli, Mario, 10, 702, 722
Cerovsek, Corey, 748
Cerquetti, Anita, 557, 628, 652
Certain Age, The (Ludwig), 598
Cervantes, Miguel de, 197
Cervi, Gino, 307, 472
Cervinka, Milos, 730
Cesarini, Athos, 521
Cester, Elifah, 404
Chabert, Lacey, 39
Chabrol, Claude, 70, 396
Chadwick, Helene, 642
Chadwick, Hilary, 12
Chailly, Riccardo, 24, 135, 191, 284, 407, 452, 573, 580, 584, 742
Chakiris, George, 360, 766
Chalbaud, Roman, 119, 423
Chaliapin, Feodor, Jr., 136
Chalis, Christopher, 250
Chalker, Margaret, 306
Challender, Stuart, 752
Challis, Christopher, 150
Challis, Drummond, 605
Chamberlain, Douglas, 293, 339, 550
Chamberlain, Richard, 683
Champa, Jo, 616
Champagne Waltz, 670
Champion, Gower, 639
Champion, Marge, 639
Chandler, Michael, 18
Chaney, Lon, 533, 546
Chang, Michael, 412
Chang, Sarah, 185
Change, Michael, 633
Chanteur de Mexico, Le (Lopez), 388
Chantler, David, 754
Chapin, Alice, 691
Chapin, Anne Morrison, 596
Chaplin, Charlie, 115–16, 386
Chaplin, Saul, 338, 766
Chaplin, Sidney, 71
Chapman, Frank, 596
Chapman, Michael, 56
Chapman, William, 322, 663
Chappell, Herbert, 316, 741
Chard, Geoffrey, 177, 572, 752, 775
Charell, Erik, 73, 149, 335
Charisse, Cyd, 171, 595
Charkviani, Djansung, 166
Charles, Duke of Windsor, 6
Charles, John, 368, 396
Charles, Lester, 340
Charles, Ray, 460

Charnock, Helen, 303
Charpin, Fernand, 46, 496
Chase, Chevy, 457
Chase, Ronald, 215, 320, 401
Chase, The (Ripley), 363
Chaste Suzanne, La (Berthomieu), 355
Chateau, René, 778
Chatelais, Jean-Yves, 745
Chatterton, Vivienne, 313
Chausson, Carlos, 48, 66, 157, 162, 349, 499
Chautard, Emile, 129
Chauvelot, Sylvain, 703
Chavala, La (Chapí), 137
Chavrova, T., 332, 769
Chazalettes, Giulio, 412
Checchini, Dino Hobbes, 166
Checinski, Jan, 316
Cheek, John, 634
Cheetham, Keith, 9, 24, 28, 83, 219, 228, 284, 320, 421, 513, 522, 702, 723
Chekhov, Anton, 57, 324, 363
Chelieu, Arman, 108
Chenieux, Pierre-Laurent, 92
Cher, 469
Cherkassov, Nikolai, 341, 479, 589
Chernov, Vladimir, 258, 568, 645, 657, 760
Chérubin (Massenet), 59
Chester, Kenn, 528
Chetwyn, Lionel, 382
Chevalier, Maurice, 73, 140, 315, 402, 409, 759
Chevalier, Valérie, 96, 720
Chiamavan Capinera, La (Regnoli), 60
Chiara, Maria, 9, 10, 35, 306, 307, 738
Chiaranello, Gianfranco, 401
Chiari, Walter, 675
Chic, Antonio, 31, 102
Chieftains, 539
Chien andalou, Un (Buñuel), 100, 207
Chi è più felice di me!, 623
Chikamatsu, Monzaemon, 348, 458
Childs, Julia, 324
Chilpéric (Hervé), 319
Chin, Peter, 543
Chingari, Marco, 229
Chinn, Lori Tan, 654
Chirkov, Boris, 288
Chirot, Armanda, 712
Chishko, Oles Semenovich, 732
Chisholm, Robert, 390
Chissari, Santa, 211
Chitty, Alison, 54, 273
Chiummo, Umberto, 594
Chivot, Henri, 434
Chladek, Rosalia, 150
Chlostowa, Daniele, 741
Chomette, Henri, 785
Chookasian, Lili, 480, 490
Choux, Jean, 375
Christ, Rudolf, 217
Christen, Gudrun, 214
Christian-Jaque, 70, 118, 745
Christians, Mady, 267, 276, 759
Christie, Agatha, 96
Christie, Julie, 713
Christie, George, 290
Christie, Nan, 215, 293, 561, 622, 652
Christin, Judith, 14, 24, 277, 412, 440, 781
Christmas Carol, A (Hoiby), 324
Christmas Eve (Mussorgsky), 272
Christoa, Marianna, 113
Christofellis, Aris, 128
Christoff, Miroslav, 408

Darras, Jean-Pierre, 745
Darrenkamp, John, 42, 450
Darrieux, Danielle, 171, 328
D'Artegna, Francesco Ellera, 83
D'Artenga, Elero, 539
Darvas, János, 15, 533
Darvas, Lili, 571
Dassel, Karin, 369
Dassin, Jules, 23
Daszak, John, 396
Daub, Ewald, 526, 630
Daudet, Alphonse, 32
Daudier, Charlotte, 263
Daug, Edward, 749
Daugherty, Michael, 147
Dauphin, Claude, 171, 242
Davene, Sylvaine, 216
Davenport, Jack, 293
Davenport, Mary, 438, 521, 542
D'Aversa, Alberto, 60, 281, 290, 624
Davey, Allen, 77
Davey, Perry, 768
David, Andrew, 400
David, Antione, 221
David, Eleanor, 699
David Harem, 609
Davidson, Christopher, 474
Davidson, Lawford, 235
Davidson, Ruth, 179
Davies, Andrew, 167
Davies, Arthur, 303, 584, 746
Davies, Dennis Russell, 12, 36, 266, 411, 620
Davies, Eric, 179
Davies, Jack, 654, 681
Davies, Joan, 176, 252
Davies, John J., 47, 151, 528, 583, 708
Davies, Lynne, 358
Davies, Marion, 575, 721
Davies, Mary, 698
Davies, Menai, 731
Davies, Morgan, 527
Davies, Ryland, 109, 179, 196, 218, 354, 391, 451, 715
Davies, Terence, 158, 452
Davies, Wyn, 457, 729
Davin, Patrick, 519
da Vinci, Leonardo, 40
Davis, Andre, 222
Davis, Anthony, 6
Davis, Bette, 289, 593, 718
Davis, Carl, 198, 561, 686, 699
Davis, Charles K. L., 189
Davis, Curtis W., 57
Davis, Desmond, 714
Davis, Ellen, 374
Davis, Geena, 692
Davis, Joan, 395
Davis, Judy, 396
Davis, Luther, 360
Davis, Michael Rees, 467
Davis, Sammy, Jr., 199, 554
Davis, Thulani, 147
Davis, Will S., 352
Davison, Hugh, 250
Davison, Peter J., 498, 499
Davtyan, Yuri, 26
Davy (Relph), 442
Davydov, Rotislav, 366
Dawley, J. Searle, 11, 234, 697
Dawn, Isabel, 284
Dawson, Anna, 715
Dawson, Anne, 510, 525
Dawson, Lynn, 448
Day, Doris, 4
Day, Frances, 355

Day, James, 694
Day, Josette, 46, 65, 496
Day, Richard, 449
Dayde, Bernard, 519
Dayle, Lucien, 162
Day-Lewis, Daniel, 87, 157
Daymond, Karl, 179, 722
Dazely, William, 38
Déa, Maria, 517
Dead Man Walking (Heggie), 147
Dean, Amanda, 215
Dean, Basil, 768
Dean, Hector, 262
Dean, Roy, 31
Dean, Stafford, 189, 252, 337, 396, 456, 746
de Ana, Hugo, 142
Deane, Tessa, 636
De Angelis, Vincenzo, 163, 403
Deans, Marjorie, 654
Dearly, Max, 115, 159, 745
Death of Dido, The (Pepusch), 543
Death of Klinghoffer, The (Adams), 3, 483, 634
Death of Maria Malibran, The, 628
d'Eaubonne, Jean, 159
de Banos, Ramon, 15, 88
Debbaut, Denise, 38
De Benedetti, Aldo, 648, 682
De Bernardi, Piero, 47
de Blasis, James, 211
De Bosio, Gian Franco, 35, 114, 210, 482, 522, 701
De Brulier, Nigel, 616
De Cahusac, Louis, 91
de Carlo, Mario, 45
De Carlo, Yvonne, 87, 588, 616, 753
de Carolis, Natale, 191, 503
de Castellbajac, Jean-Charles, 66
de Castro Tank, Niza, 304
de Celis, Lilián, 145
DeChiazza, Mark, 216
de Choudens (Bérel), Paul, 21
De Cicco, Lucio, 544
Decker, Franz-Paul, 537, 717, 744
Decker, Geraldine, 233
Decker, Willy, 156
De Cordova, Frederick, 50, 203
DeCormier, Robert, 494
de Cristofor, Carlo, 346
de Croisset, Francis, 142
de Curtis, Ernesto, 108, 255
de Diego, Manuel, 390
Dee, Ruby, 555
Deegan, Dorothy, 150
Deegan, J. M., 31
Deep River (Harling), 79
Deesy, Alfred, 224, 347
de Fabritiis, Oliviero, 21, 43, 67, 83, 132, 134, 229, 237, 392, 583, 644, 700
De Felice, Lionello, 257
De Féraudy, Jacques, 429
De Filippo, Eduardo, 340, 484
De Filippo, Peppino, 340
de Flers, Robert, 142
Deflo, Gilbert, 134,˜197, 516, 566
de Francesca-Cavazza, Maria de, 110
Defranceschi, Carlo Prospero, 227
DeGaw, Boyce, 284
De Giorgi, Elsa, 283
de Giorgio, Americo, 202
Degl, Karel, 53
de Grésac, Fred, 671
de Groof, Carl, 401
de Haan, David, 388
de Havilland, Olivia, 28, 172, 226, 452

Dehelly, M., 420
Dehner, John, 659
Deho, Enzo, 9, 392
Deide, Manfred, 773
De Jong, Constance, 620
de Jouy, Étienne, 305
De Kanel, Vladimir, 579
Dekker, Jellie, 614
de Kowa, Victor, 764
de Laarboy, Suzanne, 615
de Lacey, Terry, 121
Delacorta (novelist), 182
Delacôte, Jacques, 44, 113, 124, 134, 581
Delacour, Alfred, 515
de la Cour, Jean, 159
Delahunt, Colette, 54
Delamare, Lise, 70, 741
Delamboye, Hubert, 354
Delaney, Robert, 245
Delany, Cathleen, 170, 566
de Larra, Luis Mariano, 45
Delavan, Mark, 388
Delavault, Hélène, 112, 745
Delavigne, Germain, 477
Delbo, Jean-Jacques, 401
Del Bosco, Carlo, 566, 573
del Campo, Enrique, 327
Del Carlo, John, 106, 227
Del Colle, Tonino, 7, 202, 373
Del Colle, Ubaldo Maria, 131
del Corno, Filippo, 147
De Leeuw, Reinbert, 599
DeLeone, Carmon, 382
Delescluse, Jean, 781
Delestre-Poirson, Charles-Gaspard, 148
Delevan, Mark, 702
Delgado, Asuncion, 433
De Lidda, Alfredo, 648
de l'Isle, Marie, 188
del la Marra, Luciano, 8
della Rosa, Evelyn, 42
Della Valle, Cesare, 424
Deller, Alfred, 159
Dell'Isola, Salvatore, 509, 527, 583
Dell'Oste, Annamaria, 341
Del Mar, Norman, 377, 698
Delmare, Fred, 62
Del Monaco, Giancarlo, 229, 257, 413, 645, 657
Delmoni, Arturo, 518
del Monte, Carlo, 87, 127, 279, 328, 398, 714
Del Nero, Cyro, 305
De Loguoro, Giuseppe, 238
De Lon, Jack, 123
De Lorde, A., 138, 255
Del Poggio, Carla, 445
del Portal, Enrique, 87, 127, 145, 183, 279, 300, 328
del Pozo, Antonio, 88, 186
Del Rio, Dolores, 116, 428
Del Ruth, Harrison, 542
Del Ruth, Roy, 97, 117, 139, 175, 680
del Signore, Gino, 134
Del Sol, Laura, 119
Del Sol, Maria, 186
del Sol, Marina, 279
Deltgen, René, 133, 473, 704
Del Torre, Giulio, 675
De Luca, Neil, 2
de Luguoro-Presicce, Giuseppe, 737
DeLuise, Dom, 44
Delunsch, Mireille, 251
de Lutry, Michael, 19
Delvair, Jeanne, 220, 262, 425

Feliú y Codina, José, 182
Felix, Maria, 713
Felix, Seymour, 409, 413
Fellbom, Claes, 10
Felle, Amelia, 106, 263, 306, 641
Feller, Carlos, 7, 48, 227, 274, 436, 498, 641
Fellous, Roger, 199
Fellows, Edith, 38, 193
Felty, Janice, 157, 663
Feltz, Kurt, 406, 489, 750
Fenby, Eric, 172
Fenchal, Heinz, 249
Fenivessy, Emil, 405
Fenn, Jean, 86, 635
Fenouillet, Christian, 135
Fenton, James, 584
Fenyos, Emil, 786
Feore, Donna, 597
Ferber, Edna, 638
Ferber, Mel, 71
Fercioni, Gian Maurizio, 96
Ferencsik, János, 315
Ferenz, Willi, 150
Ferguson, Michael, 252, 480
Ferida, Luisa, 238, 477
Fernandel, 419
Fernández, Adriana, 516
Fernández, Anselmo, 145
Fernandez, Christopher, 7
Fernandez, Luis, 145
Fernandino, Marisa, 330
Ferner-White, Nicola, 780
Ferracuti, Aldo, 392
Ferrant, Guy, 142
Ferrante, John, 2
Ferrara, Franco, 288, 291, 334, 636
Ferrara, Giuseppe, 604
Ferrara, Mario, 412
Ferrarese, Adriana, 169
Ferrari, Alain, 105
Ferrari, Angelo, 165, 197
Ferrari, Mario, 641
Ferrarini, Alida, 113, 584, 588
Ferrario, Luigi, 382
Ferreira, Marina, 58
Ferreira, Tony, 322
Ferrens, Maria, 474
Ferreol, Andrea, 548
Ferrer, Mel, 250
Ferrerari, Mario, 129
Ferrero, Anna Maria, 173
Ferrero, Lorenzo, 467
Ferretti, Dante, 710, 723
Ferretti, Jacopo, 134
Ferri, Liana, 445
Ferri, Ursula, 782
Ferrier, Kathleen, 524
Ferrier, Tim, 78
Ferrin, Agostino, 68, 393, 492
Ferris, Barbara, 661
Ferris, Paul, 177, 752
Ferro, Gabriele, 35, 48, 135, 196, 210, 566
Ferronetti, Ignazio, 398, 624
Ferroni, Giorgio, 281, 623
Ferry, Jean, 741
Ferzetti, Gabriele, 563, 564, 581
Fessl, Ulli, 240
Festival of Regrets, The (Drattell), 136
Fetchit, Stepin, 638
Feuer, Donya, 779
Feuillade, Louis, 328, 460, 472, 476, 691
Feuillère, Edwige, 152, 419
Feyder, Jacques, 116

Feytl, Robert, 322
Fiala, Karel, 18, 166, 193
Fialko, Oleg, 578
Fichman, Niv, 626
Fidesser, Hans, 81
Fiedler, Arthur, 462
Field, David, 312
Field, Helen, 303, 337, 488, 633, 731, 746
Field, Pamela, 323
Field, Rebecca, 303
Fielding, David, 145, 358, 663
Fields, Dorothy, 331, 552, 733
Fields, Lew, 505
Fiennes, Martha, 223
Fiennes, Ralph, 223
Fiermonte, Enzo, 262
Fifth Façade, The, 672
Figueras, Montserrat, 516
Filacurida, Nicola, 412, 708
Filatova, Ludmilla, 568
Filip, Frantisek, 53
Filippeschi, Mario, 392, 583
Fille mal gardée, La (Hérold), 319
Filmstern, Der, 511
Final Romance (Forque), 273–74
Finbow, Alexander, 266, 783
Finch, Jon, 408
Finch, Nigel, 734
Finch, Peter, 157, 282
Finch, Serner, 335
Finda, Henry, 331
Find the Woman (Terriss), 235
Fine, Sylvia, 333, 772
Fineschi, Onelia, 527, 708
Fingleton, David, 162
Fini, Gianfranco, 702
Fink, Harold, 149
Fink, Richard Paul, 618
Finkenzeller, Heli, 472, 515
Finlay, Frank, 661
Finley, Gerald, 170, 525, 782
Finnie, Linda, 580, 755
Finnila, Birgit, 579
Fino, Claudio, 722
Fiodorov, Vladimir, 608
Fioravanti, Giulio, 393
Fiorentini, Mirella, 392
Fiori d'arancio (Checchini), 166
Fiorini, Guido, 700
Fiorito, Fausto, 150
Fiorito, John, 245
Fioroni, Giovanna, 425, 432
Firebird, The (Ekman), 291
Fire Maidens from Outer Space (Roth), 561
Fireman's Ball, The (Forman), 255
Fireman's Street, 673
Firestone, Idabelle, 107, 172, 750
First Love (Koster), 203, 413
First Name Carmen (Godard), 119, 291
First of the Few, 758
Firth, Colin, 168
Firth, Tazeena, 545, 728
Fischer, Adam, 54, 80, 283, 382, 420, 491
Fischer, Angelika, 697
Fischer, Ehard, 286
Fischer, Gyorgy, 55
Fischer, Hans Conrad, 61, 473
Fischer, Jeanette, 341
Fischer, Michel, 626
Fischer, O. W., 397, 764
Fischer, Res, 150
Fischer, Robert, 58
Fischer, Sebastian, 591, 640

Fischer-Ledinice, Michael, 743
Fisher, Gerry, 190, 456
Fisher, Gillian, 18, 783
Fisher, Joely, 783
Fisher, Rob, 671
Fisher, Rodney, 443
Fisher, Sylvia, 525
Fisher, Terence, 547
Fisichella, Salvatore, 58, 306, 307, 566, 689
Fissore, Enrico, 257
Fitch, Bernard, 76
Fitch, Clyde, 61
Fitwater, William, 314
Fitz-Allen, Adelaide, 535
Fitzball, Edward, 427
Fitzgerald, Adair, 380
Fitzgerald, Edward, 198
Fitzgerald, Geraldine, 719
Fitzgerald, Patricia, 116
Fitzpatrick, James J., 77, 737
Fitzpatrick, Kate, 443
Fitzroy, Emily, 487
Fitzwater, William, 47, 565, 587, 714
Five Corners (Bill), 368
Five Girls to Deal with (Schorm), 266, 627
Five Graves to Cairo, 90
Fjeldsøe, Solborg, 214
Fjelmose, Grith, 97, 194
Fjord, Olaf, 396
Flagello, Ezio, 245, 504
Flaherty, Robert, 694
Flaiano, Ennio, 658
Flame of New Orleans, The (Clair), 17, 145, 395
Flame of the Desert (Barker), 231
Flamini, Giuseppe, 493
Flanagan, D. J., 84
Flanagan, Finnuala, 384
Flanders, Ed, 384
Flanigan, Lauren, 136, 482
Flateau, Serge, 355
Flatt, Kate, 10
Fleck, Jacob, 75, 152, 344, 374, 585, 778
Fleck, Luise, 75, 344, 374, 778
Fleckenstein, Günther, 519
Flederick, André, 341, 482, 644
Fleetwood, James, 567
Flegg, Edmund, 215
Fleischer, Stanley, 175
Fleischmann, Benjamin, 605, 638
Fleisher, Dave, 307
Fleisher, Max, 307
Fleming, Victor, 375
Fletcher, Bramwell, 717
Fletcher, Lucille, 319
Flimm, Jürgen, 157, 192, 241, 499, 523, 696
Flindt, Flemming, 237
Flintzner, Karl, 497
Flockhart, Calista, 452
Flood, James, 264
Florelle, 536
Florelle, Odette, 199
Florent, Hippolyte-Louis, 305
Florey, Robert, 175
Florimo, Enzo, 156
Floris, Gianluca, 739
Flowers, Kate, 339, 456, 715, 780
Flowers from Nice, 611
Flup . . .! (Szulc), 415
Flusser, Richard, 496
Flutter, Barry, 645
Flying Down to Rio, 275

Gaumont, Leon, 368
Gautier, Georges, 96, 221, 391, 548, 720
Gavaldon, Roberto, 713
Gavanelli, Paolo, 132, 584
Gavani, Ciro, 615
Gavani, Dino, 77
Gavazzi, Carla, 189, 652
Gavazzi, Ernesto, 35, 412
Gaveau, René, 434, 460
Gavilanes, Los (Guerrero), 305
Gavin, Barry, 226, 545
Gavin, Pat, 377, 721
Gavirolova, T., 366
Gavoni, Marcello, 583
Gavriliuk, Ivan, 578
Gavrilova, Maria, 417, 461
Gavzzeni, Gianandrea, 202
Gaxton, William, 715
Gay, Piergiorgio, 346
Gayarre (Viladomat), 537
Gay Desperado, The (Mamoulian), 432
Gayer, Josepha, 214, 662
Gaylen, Diana, 28
Gaynes, George, 688
Gaynor, Mitzi, 587, 653
Gebhard, George, 691
Gebhardt, Horst, 780
Gebuehr, Otto, 484
Gefangene des Königs, Der (Koch), 88
Gehetzte Menschen, 625
Geiger, Paul, 42
Geiger-Torel, Herman, 149
Geirot, Alexander, 476
Geister, Jutta, 475
Gelb, Peter, 56, 119, 194, 748
Gelein, Igor, 676
Geliot, Michael, 36, 323, 456
Geller, Harry, 455
Gelling, Philip, 151
Gelmetti, Gianluigi, 106, 340, 621, 641, 678
Gemignani, Paul, 671
Gemma, Irene, 47
Gemmill, John, 744
Gence, Denise, 500
Génia, Claude, 291
Geniat, Marcelle, 585
Genina, Augusto, 165, 255, 280, 611
Genni, Sergio, 80
Gentilomo, Giacomo, 60, 166, 217, 445, 591, 623, 640
Gentleman From Louisiana, The, 610
Genz, Stephan, 706
George, Andrew, 519
George, Günther, 552
George, Heinrich, 630
George, Helen, 156, 189
George, Jim, 48, 565
George, Michael, 627, 686
George, Muriel, 768
George, Russell, 149
George, Tricia, 499
George, Zelma, 149
George White Scandals of 1922, 79
Gerace, Liliana, 67, 419, 597
Geraldo, Pedro, 776
Gérard, Rolf, 82, 111, 156, 186, 249, 544
Gerault, Yvon, 144, 400, 741
Gerber, Joyce, 14
Gere, Richard, 714
Gerelo, Vassily, 760
Gergalov, Alexander, 568, 611, 760
Gerhardt, Paul, 472
Gering, Marion, 670
Geringer, Rose, 304

Gero, Costanzo, 583
Gerona, Maria Luisa, 688
Geronimi, Clyde, 159, 766
Gerrard, Henry, 734
Gerron, Kurt, 244
Gershwin, Ira, 276, 555, 762, 763, 767
Gerstad, Merritt B., 104, 489
Gerstenhaber, Cyrille, 781
Gert, Valeska, 199
Gertner, Heinrich, 355
Gerusalemme liberata, La (Guazzoni), 589
Gerusalemme liberata, La (Tasso), 33, 678
Gervasio, Raffaele, 497
Gessendorf, Mechtild, 31
Geszty, Sylvia, 52, 151, 483
Getting It Right (Kleiser), 12
Getting of Wisdom, The (Beresford), 68
Getty, Paul, 748
Geyer, Gwynne, 528
Ghazarian, Sona, 29, 163, 475, 740, 787
Gherardini, Giovanni, 274
Ghiglia, Lorenzo, 179
Ghini, Massimo, 564, 581
Ghione, Emilio, 33, 129, 575, 678
Ghislanzoni, Antonio, 8, 12
Ghiuselev, Nicola, 151, 152, 234, 561
Ghost Opera, 678
Giacchieri, Renzo, 346, 482
Giachetti, Fosco, 280, 530, 586, 648, 737
Giachetti, Gianfranco, 49
Giacomini, Giuseppe, 257
Giacosa, Giuseppe, 82, 411, 421
Giaiotti, Bonaldo, 9, 257, 742
Giammarrusco, Vittorio, 471
Giannella, Giuliano, 450
Gianni, Dusolina, 277–78
Giannini, Ettore, 281
Giannini, Giancarlo, 312, 334, 416
Giannini, Giulio, 274, 341
Gianpetro, Josef, 247, 435, 646
Giants in the Earth (Moore), 469
Giaotti, Bonaldo, 399
Giasone (Cavalli), 137
Gibault, Claire, 96, 109, 781
Gibbons, Cedric, 172, 246, 277, 360, 437, 485, 487, 489, 671
Gibbs, Raymond, 522
Gibert, Francisco, 15
Gibson, Alexander, 268, 709
Gibson, Barbara, 150
Gibson, James, 292
Gibson, Madeleine, 77
Gibson, Mel, 230
Gibson, Vivian, 261, 298, 394, 427, 786
Gielen, Michael, 471
Gielgud, John, 344, 661, 754
Gietzen, Herbert, 349
Gift of the Magi, The (Adler), 4
Gigi, Girolamo, 181
Gigli, Alexander, 489
Gigli, Renato, 493
Gigolette (Lehár), 168
G.I. Jane (Scott), 278
Gil, Ariadna, 135
Gil, Manuel, 328
Gilbert, Arthur, 115, 234, 247, 723
Gilbert, Billy, 49, 139, 246
Gilbert, Jean, 186
Gilbert, John, 84, 405
Gilbert, Lewis, 463
Gilbert, Olive, 168, 287
Gilbert, Robert, 335
Gilbert, Roy, 340

Gilbert, Terry, 561
Gilbert, Tony, 113
Gilchrist, Diana, 782
Giles, David, 661
Gilette, Priscilla, 381
Gilfry, Rodney, 157, 339, 498, 499, 662
Gille, Philippe, 368, 420
Gillelan, Liz, 527
Giller, Walter, 626
Gillespie, William, 555
Gillett, Christopher, 358, 599
Gillette, Priscilla, 381
Gillette, Ruth, 609, 610
Gilliat, Sidney, 141, 282, 480, 513, 573
Gillibrand, Nicky, 192
Gillie, Jean, 355
Gillingwater, Claude, 461
Gillis, Don, 227
Gilly, Renée, 46
Gilmore, Gail, 513, 557
Gilpin, Sally, 63
Gilroy, Frank, 318
Giménez, David, 647
Giménez, Edoardo, 743
Giménez, Raúl, 135, 678
Gimeno, José, 279
Gimpel, Jacob, 86, 635
Ginastera, Alberto, 123
Giner, Ana, 183
Ginn, Michael, 730
Ginsberg, Allen, 36
Ginsberg, Francis, 622
Ginzer, Frances, 493
Giordani, Aldo, 257, 445, 682, 722
Giordani, Marcello, 452
Giordano, Salvatore, 116, 762
Giorgi, Fiorenzo, 346, 701
Giovanetti, Reynald, 722
Girl and the Kaiser, The (Jarno), 256
Girl from Lorraine, The (Goretta), 294
Girl in the Taxi, The (Gilbert), 354, 355
Girl on the Film, The, 244, 361, 673
Girl Who Came to Supper, The (Coward), 239
Girl with a Suitcase, The (Zurlini), 12
Giro de lune tra terra e mare (Gaudino), 544
Giroflé-Girofla (Lecocq), 373
Girolami, Marino, 182
Girolami, Romolo, 463
Gish, Dorothy, 665
Gish, Lillian, 84, 259, 415, 643
Gismonda (Sardou), 129
Gitta endeckt ihr Herz (Fröhlich), 17
Giuffrida, Giuseppe, 422
Giulini, Carlo Maria, 194, 228
Giulio Cesare, 634
Giunchi, Lea, 161
Giuramento, Il (Mercadante), 446
Giuri, Alberto Maria, 201
Giuseppe, Enrico Di, 450, 457
Giuseppini, Giorgio, 5
Giusti, Girolamo, 468
Give Us Our Dream (Nickell), 558
Gizzi, Loris, 419, 738
Gjevang, Anne, 461, 590
Glagolitic Mass, The, 343
Glamour Boy (Murphy), 259
Glanzmann, Hans, 258
Glaser, Etienne, 97
Glassman, William, 318
Glatzeder, Winfried, 474
Glawatsch, Franz, 374
Glaze, Gary, 292
Glazer, Benjamin, 682
Glázrová, Marie, 345

Guggia, Mario, 229
Guglielmi, Margherita, 43, 135
Guglielminetti, Eugenio, 727
Guglielmo Ratcliff, 631
Gui, Vittorio, 9, 489, 544, 604
Guide, Jean, 747
Guignal, Alin, 234
Guillard, Nicolas François, 169, 339
Guillemaud, Marcel, 458
Guillot, Marius-Paul, 70
Guilty Melody (Potter), 17
Guilty Voice, The (Rehfisch), 17
Guimaraes, Leila, 83
Guimera, Angel, 697
Guingal, Alain, 152, 317, 593, 597, 765
Guiomar, Julie, 112
Guise, Janine, 434
Guissart, René, 171, 535
Guitar, Jane, 665
Guitry, Sacha, 59, 63, 170, 171, 419, 561
Guitty, Madeleine, 142
Guizar, Tito, 212
Gulak-Artemovsky, Semyon, 732
Guleghina, Maria, 24, 482, 540, 568, 703
Gulin, Angeles, 551
Gulke, Peter, 218
Gullan, Campbell, 530
Gult, Karel, 18, 501
Gulyás, Dénes, 44
Gulyas, Michael, 730
Gundlach, Robert, 38, 139, 462
Guniya, V., 166
Gunn, Nathan, 760
Gunn, Rosemary, 441, 566, 780
Gunsbourg, Raoul, 341
Gunter, John, 14, 555, 709, 731
Gunther, Egon, 766
Günther, Felix, 74
Gunther, John, 441
Gurgenidze, Tamara, 166
Gurney, A. R., 136
Gurwitch, Annabelle, 260
Gury, Jeremy, 453
Guryakova, Olga, 760
Guschlbauer, Theodor, 461, 475
Gussmann, Wolfgang, 67
Gustafson, Nancy, 191, 251, 354, 568, 579
Gustavson, Eva, 8
Güstorff, Max, 442
Guth, Klaus, 339
Guthrie, Tyrone, 111, 323
Guthro, James, 339
Gutiérrez, Horacio, 613
Gutknecht, Carol, 471
Gutman, John, 92, 104, 387, 412, 601, 699, 700
Guttenberg, Steve, 343
Gutteridge, Tom, 215
Guttierez, Carmen, 614
Guttman, Irving, 669
Guy, Maureen, 698
Guy-Blanché, Alice, 234, 246, 261, 405, 454, 460, 568
Guy-Bromley, Philip, 76, 176, 326
Guyer, Joyce, 135
Gvazava, Eteri, 710
Gwendoline (Chabrier), 136
Gwenn, Edmund, 665
Gwilym, Mike, 312
Gynt, Greta, 18, 333, 676
Gypsies, The (Pushkin), 16
Gypsy Baron, The, 646
Gypsy Princess, The (Kálmán), 162

Gys, Leda, 21, 84, 341, 568, 747
Gys, Robert, 46, 377, 378, 496

Haach, Gunther, 777
Haack, Käthe, 631
Haage, Peter, 519, 773, 777
Haas, Karl, 153
Haas, Waltraud, 74, 503, 625, 759
Habay, André, 116, 341, 434, 512, 574, 673
Habereder, Agnes, 70, 726
Haberlik, Christina, 300
Hacker, Alan, 15
Hackett, Albert, 246, 485, 600
Hackman, Gene, 757
Hadar, Mary, 374
Haddock, Marcus, 114, 599
Haddon, Judith, 412
Haden, Charlie, 763
Hadjimischer, Michael, 407
Hadley, Henry, 306
Haefliger, Ernst, 218
Haellstroem, Arto, 300
Haenchen, Harmut, 286, 517, 590
Haenning, Gitte, 782
Haffner, Carl, 249
Hagar, Paul, 528
Hagegard, Erland, 81
Hagel, Christoph, 782
Hagerty, Julie, 91
Hagerty, Mary, 722
Häggander, Mari Anne, 441, 562, 579
Haggard, Piers, 393, 544, 768
Haggard, Stephen, 472, 768
Hagley, Alison, 345, 498, 499, 542
Hagopian, Mary M., 179
Hahn, Brigitte, 31
Haid, Liane, 163, 182, 585, 768
Haijne, Erland von, 779
Hainisch, Leopold, 406, 472, 489, 582, 622
Hajna, Josef, 163
Hajos, Joe, 505
Hajóssyová, Magdaléna, 765
Hale, Creighton, 717
Hale, Georgina, 417, 661, 719
Hale, John, 426
Hale, Robert, 113, 253, 265, 349, 393, 420, 579, 590, 639, 755
Hale, Sonnie, 481
Halem, Victor von, 441
Halévy, Ludovic, 44, 66, 96, 110, 120, 249, 299, 302, 544, 745
Halfvarson, Eric, 28, 34, 187, 584
Halk, Heidrun, 780
Hall, Alexander, 132, 287, 371, 395, 587
Hall, Bruce, 732
Hall, Ella, 253
Hall, Evelyn, 323
Hall, Herbert, 129
Hall, Janice, 7, 106, 641
Hall, Josephine, 558
Hall, Juanita, 653
Hall, Ken G., 98
Hall, Kenneth J., 147
Hall, Meredith, 179
Hall, Peter J., 43, 189, 645, 657
Hall, Thurston, 391
Hall-Davis, Lilian, 530
Haller, Ernest, 754
Haller, Herman, 742
Halley, Ina, 405, 742
Halley, Sharon, 404
Halling, Pat, 738
Hallstein, Ingeborg, 21, 264, 415, 730, 769, 787

Halman, Ella, 322
Halmen, Pet, 121, 516, 592
Halper, Ross, 183
Halsey, Simon, 164
Halstan, Margaret, 74
Halton, Richard, 663
Halvorson, Gary, 114, 168, 192, 272, 404, 499
Hamada, RieAsari, Yo, 344
Hamari, Julia, 112, 222, 314
Hamburger Hill, 287
Hamel, Lambert, 75
Hamer, Robert, 193, 537, 592
Hamill, Mark, 783
Hamilton, Antony, 619
Hamilton, Charles, 722
Hamilton, Gene, 449
Hamilton, Guy, 758
Hamilton, John, 455, 778
Hamilton, Mark, 698
Hamilton, Neil, 745
Hamilton, Tom, 204
Hamman, Joe, 460
Hammar, Russell, 708
Hammerstein, Arthur, 390
Hammerstein, Elaine, 642
Hammerstein, Oscar, I, 292, 310, 352, 431, 442,485
Hammid, Alexander, 541, 705
Hammond, Tom, 425
Hammond-Stroud, Derek, 53, 339, 391, 536, 601
Hammons, Thomas, 492
Hamon, Deryck, 457
Hampden, Walter, 734
Hampton, Christopher, 168
Hanbury, Victor, 206
Hancke, Edith, 264
Hancock, John, 136
Hancock, Leonard, 250
Hancorn, John, 358
Hands across the Sky (Lefeaux), 325
Handt, Herbert, 432
Hangman, Hangman! (Balada), 41
Hanicinec, Petr, 366
Hankal, Bob, 694
Hankinson, Michael, 98
Hanks, Tom, 5, 25, 106, 223, 331, 395, 554, 757
Hannah, Daryl, 587
Hannah and Her Sisters (Allen), 423
Hannan, Eilene, 607, 666, 760
Hannan, Tom, 294
Hannemann, Gerda, 252
Hannes, Hans, 242
Hanray, Lawrence, 768
Hans, le joueur de flûte (Ganne), 269
Hansbury, Victor, 74
Hansel & Gretel & Ted & Alice, 623
Hansen, Gunnar Robert, 214
Hansen, Joachim, 285
Hansen, Kurt, 626
Hansen, Max, 207
Hansen, Teri, 663
Hanson, Curtis, 756
Hanson, Maricarol, 687
Hansson, Lena T., 97, 194
Hanus, Heinz, 374
Hao Jiang Tian, 305
Happy Wanderer, The, 625
Harakiri (Lang), 413
Harapes, Vlastimil, 78
Harari, Robert, 478
Harbaugh, Carl, 115
Harben, Hubert, 768
Harbison, John, 637

Harbord, Carl, 681
Harbou, Thea von, 590, 728
Harbour, Dennis, 8
Harder, Emil, 306
Harder, William, 721
Harders, Jane, 443
Harding, Ann, 96, 230, 484
Harding, Bertita, 753
Harding, Muriel, 322
Hardt-Warden, Bruno, 323
Hardwick, Cedric, 693
Hardy, Janis, 707
Hardy, Oliver, 38, 86, 261, 361
Hardy, Robert, 41
Hardy, Rosemary, 320
Harel, Philip, 541
Harell, Marte, 85, 249, 280, 326, 332, 333, 515, 749
Harewood, Lord, 105
Hargreaves, John, 674
Harisch, Theo, 786
Harismendy, François, 191
Harjanne, Jouko, 686
Harlan, Veit, 88, 267, 442, 526
Harling, William, 79
Harney, Fred, 338
Harney, Greg, 315
Harnick, Sheldon, 61
Harper, Daniel, 440
Harper, Heather, 97, 330, 420, 525, 545, 677, 730
Harper, James, 160
Harper, Kim, 688
Harper, Thomas, 188
Harrell, Lynn, 378
Harrhy, Eiddwen, 140
Harries, Kathryn, 400
Harriet, the Woman Called Moses (Musgrave), 478
Harrington, David, 613
Harrington, Gerard III, 480
Harrington, Nedda, 137
Harris, Augustus, 125, 443
Harris, Elmer, 622
Harris, Hilda, 569
Harris, John, 107
Harris, Lloyd, 257, 428
Harris, Neal Patrick, 671
Harris, Richard, 199
Harris, Stan, 538
Harrison, Jane, 124
Harrison, Michael, 22
Harrison, Rex, 573, 634, 680
Harrison, Tony, 53
Harrison, Wallace, 450
Harrison Loved His Umbrella (Hollingsworth), 324
Harrold, Kathryn, 538
Harroway, Richard, 124
Harsany, Zsolt, 315
Harsent, David, 273, 767
Harster, Ralf, 620
Hart, Charles, 734
Hart, Ferdinand, 81
Hart, Moss, 660, 762
Hartelius, Malin, 314, 782
Hartgelius, Malin, 251
Hartl, Karl, 61, 88, 473, 785
Hartley, Jan, 499
Hartman, Don, 549, 772
Hartman, Rudolf, 222
Hartman, Vernon, 113
Hartmann, Georges, 765
Hartmann, Paul, 224, 346, 600, 665
Hartmann, Rudolf A., 29, 340, 601, 753
Hartmann, Will, 782

Hartmenn, Rudolf, 337
Hartung, Robert, 291
Hartwell, William, 481
Hartwig, Hildegarde, 375
Hartzell, Raimo, 279
Harvánek, Zdenek, 191
Harvel, John, 74
Harvey, Anthony, 717
Harvey, Frank, 98
Harvey, Kit Hesketh, 54
Harvey, Laurence, 253, 598, 666
Harvey, Lillian, 149, 355, 628
Harvey, Olly Jean, 160
Harvey, Peter, 496
Harvey Milk (Wallace), 147
Harvuot, Clifford, 82
Harwood, Elizabeth, 493, 709
Haseleu, Werner, 218
Hasen, Eoinar, 264
Haskin, Howard, 80, 358, 639
Haskins, Virginia, 46, 217, 278, 313, 467, 497, 542, 601
Haslam, Micaela, 321
Hassall, Christopher, 112, 168, 287, 358, 403, 404, 698
Hasse, O. E., 378
Hasselbach, Ernst, 263
Hassell, George, 84, 505
Hassenstein, Peter, 773
Hassert, Günther, 285
Hasti, Robert, 747
Hatch, Frank, 235
Hatfield, Hurd, 193
Hatfield, Marcia, 48, 565
Hathaway, Henry, 484
Hatheyer, Heidemarie, 483, 757
Hatley, Marvin, 50
Hatot, Georges, 234, 246
Hatton, Fanny, 302
Hatton, Frederick, 302
Hatts, Clifford, 112, 521, 698
Hauer, Jochen, 256
Hauff, Angelika, 256, 497
Hauff, Eberhard, 335
Hauff, Wilhelm, 350
Haugland, Aage, 92, 295, 444, 590, 601, 755, 773
Hauman, Constance, 401
Haupt, Ullrich, 786
Hauptmann, Cornelius, 476, 781
Hauptmann, Elisabeth (pseud. Dorothy Lane), 315
Hauschild, Wolf-Dieter, 266, 429
Hauser, Armando, 332, 769
Hauxvell, John, 198
Havel, Václav, 64
Haver, June, 692, 768
Haverl, Leopold, 746
Hawaii Calls, 95
Hawkins, Eric, 33
Hawkins, Osia, 544
Hawks, Howard, 272, 307, 587, 673, 725
Hawley, Lowell, S., 39
Hawn, Goldie, 457
Hawthorne, James, 64, 403, 460
Hawthorne, Nathaniel, 314
Hay, Erzsebet, 298
Hay, Valerie, 63
Hayakawa, Sessue, 138, 255
Hayashi, Yasuko, 412
Haydn, Richard, 359
Hayer, Niklaus, 240
Hayes, Bill, 775
Hayes, Marvin, 121
Hayes, Michael, 20, 404

Hayes, Patricia, 761
Hayes, Quentin, 107, 164, 303
Hayes-McCoy, Felicity, 510
Haym, Nicola, 285, 677
Haym, Nicol Francesco, 524
Haymes, Dick, 258, 692, 761
Haymon, Cynthia, 290, 555
Hay que casar al principe (Seiler), 464
Hays, Bill, 721
Hays, Ron, 719
Hayton, Lennie, 508, 638
Hayward, Louis, 363
Hayward, Lydia, 77
Hayward, Robert, 510
Hayward, Thomas, 250, 521
Hayworth, Rita, 118, 128, 616
Hazlewood, Charles, 446
Hazy, Erzsebet, 349
Head, Murray, 157
Headley, Glenne, 178, 334
Headley, Lena, 223
Hearn, George, 671
Hearne, John, 340
Hearst, William Randolph, 144, 575
Heartbreakers (Mirkin), 518
Heart's Desire, 332, 681
Heartsease, 642
Heath, George, 98
Heatherington, Dianne, 543
Heatherton, Ray, 322
Heavenly Creatures (Jackson), 86, 372, 415
Hechelmann, Friedrich, 313
Hecht, Ben, 205, 346
Hecht, Joshua, 583
Hecht, Manfred, 601
Heckroth, Hein, 80, 150, 250, 733
Hee, T., 766
Heeley, Desmond, 196, 405, 421, 425
Heeno, Marvin, 199
Heesters, Johannes, 74, 162, 249, 272, 276, 335, 484, 515, 526, 749
Hegarty, Mary, 226
Hegerlikova, Antonie, 222
Heggie, Jake, 147
Heggie, O. P., 734
Hegierski, Kathleen, 457
Heginbotham, John, 216
Hehn, Albert, 630
Heiberg, Kirsten, 88
Heichele, Hildegarde, 28, 250
Heider, Fred, 513
Heidermann, Paul, 251
Heidt, Winifred, 428, 567, 667
Heier, Hilde, 563
Heifetz, Jascha, 122, 505
Heikinheima, Hannu, 279
Heilberg, Kirstein, 126
Heilinger, Heinrich, 261
Heinbücher, Elke, 330
Heindorf, Ray, 6, 33, 602, 635, 653, 654, 725, 729, 772
Heine, Heinrich, 252
Heinicke, Michael, 221
Heinrich, Reinhard, 374, 385, 441, 534, 580, 679
Heinrich, Richard, 755
Heinrich, Rudolf, 163, 209, 385, 631, 701, 780
Heisler, Stuart, 306
Heitmeyer Jayne, 382
Heitzinger, Robert, 471
Held, Alan, 579
Held, Ludwig, 749
Helfgot, Daniel, 7, 16, 183, 186, 279, 300, 399, 578, 737

Jandra, Gerhard, 313
Jane Eyre (Berkeley), 69
Janes, Fiona, 157
Janho-Abumrad, Eduardo, 304
Janice Beard 45 WPM (Kilner), 518
Janka, Gerd, 516, 592
Jankisch, Mara, 622
Jankova, Maartin, 314
Janková, Martina, 645, 782
Jankovic, Eleonora, 412, 566, 674
Jankovic, Jenő, 44
Jannings, Emil, 236, 302, 376, 401
János Vitéz (Kacsóh), 351
Janowitz, Hans, 103
Janowski, Marek, 176, 209, 439, 519, 607
Jansen, Cynthia, 136
Jansen, Jacques, 142
Janson, Victor, 74, 133, 185, 207, 276, 263, 497, 631, 646, 660, 778, 787
Janssen, Walter, 314, 473, 630, 631, 787
Jaoui, Agnès, 337, 524, 588
Jaráy, Hans, 42, 628
Jarboro, Caterina, 6
Jarman, Claude, Jr., 410
Jarnac, Dorothy, 38
Jaroszewic, Andrzej, 92
Jarowsiewicz, Jadwiga, 309
Jarre, Maurice, 619
Jarrett, Dan, 377
Jarrott, Charles, 426
Järvefelt, Göran, 80, 145, 157, 190, 220, 245, 498, 517, 780, 781
Järvenpää, Jussi, 164
Jarvis, William, 7, 16, 183, 186, 279, 300, 578, 737
Jary, Michael, 434
Jarzavek, Daniel, 99
Jasny, Vojtech, 296, 353
Jason, Leigh, 553
Jasset, Victorin, 131, 188, 192
Jászai, Mari, 44
Jaubert, Maurice, 745
Jaulin, Lucien, 242
Jaulin, Montéran, 242
Jaun, Elizabeth, 306
Jaune, Ray, 334–35
Javor, Paul, 302
Jaynes, Betty, 271
Jayston, Michael, 452
Jean, Gloria, 712
Jean, Loulie, 554
Jean, Vadim, 238
Jean de Florette   Manon of the Spring (Berri), 258
Jean de Nivelle (Delibes), 172
Jeanmaire, Zizi, 119
Jeavons, Colin, 12
Jedlicka, Dalibor, 191
Jefferson, Alan, 629
Jefferson in Paris (Ivory), 140, 169, 342
Jeffes, Peter, 451
Jefford, Barbara, 452
Jeffrey, Robert, 318, 495
Jeffreys, Anne, 403
Jelde, Erick, 335
Jelen, Zdenek, 18, 193
Jellinek, George, 69
Jenbach, Béla, 146, 380, 778
Jenis, Eva, 163
Jenkin, Nicola, 589
Jenkins, George, 111, 170
Jenkins, Neil, 320, 358
Jenkins, Terry, 536, 663, 775
Jennens, Charles, 447
Jennes, Charles, 67

Jennifer 8 (Robinson), 414–15
Jennings, Alex, 452
Jennings, Delvin, 292
Jennings, Ken, 671
Jenny Lind (Franklin), 244
Jensen, Julian, 238, 457
Jente, Martin, 657
Jepson, Kristine, 114
Jerger, Alfred, 660
Jerome, Timothy, 63
Jessner, Leopold, 401, 426
Je suis avec toi (Decoin), 562
Jewison, Norman, 469
Jian, Gao Guang, 728
Jillian, Ann, 39
Jiménez, Enrique, 183
Jimenez de Cisneros, Isabel, 248, 566
Jindrák, Indrich, 53
Jing Ma Fan, 413
Jo, Sumi, 210, 353
Joachim-Haas, Hans, 266
Joan the Woman, 231
Job, Enrico, 112, 641
Jobim, Antonio Carlos, 185
Jocelyn (Godard), 595
Joël, Nicolas, 24, 310, 597, 618
Joffe, Mark, 155
Joffe, Roland, 729
Joffrey, Robert, 304
Johannson, Eva, 441, 444, 580
Johannsson, Kristjan, 131
Johanson, Robert, 404, 488
John, Lindway, 780
John, Markus, 219
Johnny Corncob (Jankovic), 347
Johnny Stecchino (Benigni), 532
Johns, Stratford, 63, 616
Johnson, Alan, 60
Johnson, Amy, 391, 702
Johnson, Anthony Rolfe, 476, 627, 761
Johnson, Cora, 714
Johnson, Edward, 449, 527
Johnson, Elizabeth, 58
Johnson, James, 416
Johnson, Jim, 34
Johnson, Kevin, 592
Johnson, Lyndon, 21
Johnson, Mary Jane, 83
Johnson, Mimi, 479
Johnson, Nunnally, 225, 769
Johnson, Patricia, 14, 24, 404
Johnson, Pauline, 87
Johnson, Robert, 555
Johnson, Sidney, 490
Johnson, Van, 85, 118, 292, 301, 304, 443
Johnson, William, 42
Johnston, James, 82
Johnston, Roy, 198
Johnston, Susanne, 293, 328
Jókai, Mór, 785
Jokel, Hannes, 475
Joli, Henri, 296
Jolivet, André, 95
Jolivet, Pierre, 783
Jolivet, Rita, 548
Joll, Philip, 303
Jollife, Genevieve, 531
Jolson, Al, 530
Joly, Nathaline, 745
Jonas, Maria, 782
Jonásová, Hana, 372
Jonasson, Andrea, 345
Jones, Allan, 246, 259, 318, 409, 413, 489, 600, 638, 703, 724
Jones, Allyn C., 255

Jones, Bill T., 488
Jones, Carol, 614
Jones, Cherry, 160
Jones, Clark, 111
Jones, Della, 15, 191, 286, 323, 775
Jones, Flyn, 324
Jones, Gareth, 51
Jones, Geraint, 179
Jones, Grace Trester, 412
Jones, Griffith, 358
Jones, Gwendolyn, 42
Jones, Isola, 130, 257, 262, 583, 584, 669
Jones, Ivy Baker, 20
Jones, Jacqueline, 456
Jones, James Earl, 564
Jones, Jeffrey, 18, 34, 168
Jones, Junetta, 179
Jones, Lea-Marian, 135
Jones, Natalie, 666
Jones, Neil, 668
Jones, Nerys, 79
Jones, Peggy Ann, 606
Jones, Perry, 577
Jones, Robert, 20
Jones, Robert Owen, 716
Jones, Roderick, 699
Jones, Shirley, 505, 575
Jones, Warren, 56
Jonilowicz, Jakub, 309
Jonson, Ben, 631
Jonson, Tom, 719
Jonstorff, Fritz-Jüptner, 250
Jonze, Spike, 259
Jordan, Armin, 191, 534
Jordan, Dorothy, 104
Jordan, Egon von, 625
Jordan, Irene, 240
Jordan, June, 146
Jordan, Kirk, 19, 140
Jordan, Philippe, 114
Jory, Victor, 287, 452
José Alfonso, Maria, 328
José, Edward, 125, 129, 130, 232, 480, 703
Joseph, Francesca, 671, 684
Josephine vendue par ses soeurs (Roger), 595
Josephson, Julian, 146
Josephson, Kim, 76
Joslyn, Betsy, 671
Jossoud, Hélène, 595
Jost, Tibor, 785
Jotowa, Milena, 314
Joubé, Romuald, 422
Jourdan, Louis, 85, 783
Jourfier, Lucienne, 46
Journey of Mother Ann, The (Kastle), 353
Journey to Jerusalem, A, 71
Jouy, Etienne de, 463
Joyce, Alice, 235
Joyce, James, 170, 408, 566
Joyn, Scott, 19
Juarez, Benito, 304
Juárez, Pablo, 7, 183
Juárez, Pedro D., 279
Juárez, Pedro Pablo, 300
Judd, Sue, 114, 782
Judd, Wilf, 510
Judendchor, Wiener, 383
Jugo, Jenny, 481, 569
Juhl, Lars, 295, 580, 590, 640, 755
Juhnke, Harald, 264, 778
Juice (Monk), 466
Juiles, Karl, 375

Julia, Raul, 106, 199, 684
Julian, Julio, 433
Julian, Kimm, 142
Julian, Rupert, 477, 546, 673
Julien (Charpentier), 138
Julis, Gabriele de, 521
Jumping Frog of Calaveras County, The
(Foss), 259
June, Ava, 730
June, Ray, 664
Jung, André, 519
Jung, Jean-François, 382, 542, 735
Jung, Manfred, 295, 639
Junge, Friedrich-Wilhelm, 31
Jungwirth, Manfred, 241, 601
Junkermann, Hans, 75, 81, 185, 249,
264, 355, 419, 660, 787
Junkers, Herbert, 52, 503, 733
Jupiter, Marcus, 228, 288
Juray, Hans, 74
Jurgens, Helmut, 29, 222
Jurgens, Curt (aka Curd Jürgens), 199,
378, 459, 473, 514
Jürgensen, Edwin, 785
Jurosko, Keith, 300
Justin, Ursula, 81
Justitz, Emil, 62
Jutzi, Phil, 496
Juul-Hansen, Holger, 250
Juvenet, Pierre, 46, 496

Kabale und Lieb (Schiller), 399
Kabatu, Isabelle, 647
Kabelka, Franz, 566, 627
Kach, Hugo, 397, 494, 601, 620, 627,
728, 757
Käch, Ruth, 314
Kadamka, Jiri, 392, 512
Kadlecova, Zuzana, 18, 501
Kaduce, Kelly E., 136
Káel, Csaba, 44
Kagan, Jeremy Paul, 715
Kagan, Paul, 348
Kahn, Cédric, 640
Kahn, Gus, 275, 284, 507
Kahn, Gustav, 679
Kahn, Irene, 331
Kahn, Madeline, 485
Kahn, Otto, 653
Kaimbacher, Alexander, 424
Kain, Karen, 405
Kaiser, Dora, 472
Kaiser, George, 512
Kaiser-Titz, Erich, 152
Kaiserwalzer, 207
Kajdanovski, Alexander, 266
Kalbeck, Max, 54
Kaldenberg, Keith, 318
Kale, Stuart, 245, 330, 503
Kales, Elisabeth, 335, 369, 404
Kalinina, Galina, 92, 482
Kallisch, Cornelia, 382
Kallman, Chester, 36, 80, 189, 317, 572,
779
Kallstrom, Gunnar, 573
Kalous, Jan, 746
Kaludov, Kaludi, 35
Kammerloher, Katharina, 523
Kampers, Fritz, 74, 428, 785, 787
Kamsler, Deltra, 455
Kamu, Okko, 532
Kanakis, Anna, 581
Kanazawa, Tamiko, 411
Kandiba, Alex, 332
Kandinsky, Wassily, 626
Kane, Edward, 249

Kang, Philip, 295, 580, 640, 755
Kanin, Garson, 249
Kannen, Gunter von, 534, 580, 640, 773
Kanouse, Monroe, 183, 300
Kansas, Jimmy, 186
Kantorow, Jean-Jacques, 448
Kanturek, Otto, 200, 527
Kaos (Taviani), 501, 682
Kaper, Bronislaw, 681
Kaplunovsky, Vladimir, 288
Kapnist, Elisabeth, 137
Kapniste-Serko, Maria, 608
Kapplmüller, Herbert, 773
Kärch, Ruth, 781
Karczykowski, Ryszard, 416
Karen, Bedrich, 647
Karina, Anna, 336
Karlin, Miriam, 178
Karloff, Boris, 137, 146, 259, 332, 478
Karlowa, Elma, 74, 625
Karltaloff, Plamen, 305
Karlweis, Oskar, 256, 419, 787
Karner, Peter, 787
Karns, Virginia, 38
Karp, Barbara, 751
Karpatova, Mariana I., 314
Karr, Darwin, 261, 454
Karsavina, Jean, 567
Kartousch, Luise, 772
Karyo, Tchéky, 595
Kasarda, John, 14
Kasarova, Vesselina, 48, 66, 70, 167,
568, 593, 726
Kaschmann, Joseph, 306
Kaschmann, Truba, 313, 424, 505
Kasper, Gary, 587
Kasrashvili, Makvala, 27
Kassewitch, Helene, 306
Kassyra (Delibes), 172
Kastner, Bruno, 369
Kate and Leopold (Mangold), 551
Katia Ismailova (Todorovski), 367
Katona, József, 44
Katselli, Aleka, 210
Katt, Geraldine, 108, 280
Katz, Eberhard, 36
Katzer, M., 404
Kaufman, Andy, 54, 600
Kaufman, George S., 489
Kaufman, Julie, 31
Kaufman, Robert, 315
Kaufmann, Christine, 419, 625
Kaufmann, Jonas, 491
Kaufmann, Julie, 579, 639
Kaupova, Helena, 345
Kaurismäki, Aki, 86
Kautner, Helmut, 397
Kautsky, Hans, 600
Kavaliauskas, Maryte, 324
Kavrakos, Dimitri, 10, 566
Kawlata, Franz, 54
Kay, Alan, 770
Kay, Brian, 18, 686, 783
Kaye, Danny, 14, 39, 210, 307, 333,
450, 587, 725, 772
Kaye, Judy, 721
Kaye, Stubby, 314, 455
Kays, Alan, 663
Kayser, Manuel, 327
Kayukov, Sergei, 611
Kazan, Elia, 22
Kazansky, Gennadi, 589
Kazantzakis, Nikos, 303
Kazaras, Peter, 277, 569, 760
Kazarnovskaya, Ljuba, 27
Kazlaus, Nomeda, 317

Keane, John, 293
Kearnley, Robert, 321
Kearns, Janette, 151
Keates, Jonathan, 312
Keaton, Buster, 121
Keefe, Zena, 84
Keel, Howard, 171, 301, 360, 558, 596,
600, 639, 678
Keeley, James A., 446
Keen, Elizabeth, 614
Keen, Malcolm, 311
Keene, Christopher, 113, 150, 412, 735
Keesttulst, Fried, 253
Kehrhahn, Nico, 434
Keigel, Leonard, 569
Keighley, William, 11, 172, 430, 654
Keilberth, Joseph, 29, 47, 148, 222, 337
Keindorf, Eberhard, 484
Keith, Herbert, 98
Keith, Rosalind, 245
Kelb, Peter, 504
Kelber, Michel, 297
Kelch, Werner, 697
Kelemen, Zoltan, 579
Keleti, Márton, 416
Kelland, Clarence Budington, 436
Keller, Gottfried, 746
Keller, Marie-Thérèse, 109
Keller, Marthe, 178, 344, 754
Keller, Otto, 551
Keller, Sheldon, 39
Keller, Ulla, 631
Kellerman, Annette, 394
Kelley, Andrew, 652
Kelley, Frank, 157, 498, 639
Kelley, Fred, 171
Kellogg, Carl Stewart, 612
Kellogg, Ray, 408, 653
Kelly, David, 76
Kelly, Gene, 171, 301, 508, 595, 596,
713
Kelly, Janis, 226, 361, 550
Kelly, Kathleen, 681
Kelly, Paul Austin, 243
Kelsey, Richmond, 766
Kelso, Edmund, 582
Keltai, Jenö, 347
Keltner, Jim, 619
Kemalyan, Stephen, 118, 225, 333
Kemm, Jean, 46, 496
Kemp, Gary, 266, 453
Kemp, Martin, 453
Kemp, Paul, 53, 162, 611
Kempe, Rudolf, 57
Kendaka, Lila, 109
Kendall, Gary, 446
Kendall, Victor, 417
Kenkins, Timothy, 330
Kennedy, Burt, 659
Kennedy, Julie, 260
Kennedy, Margaret, 676, 768
Kennedy, Roderick, 135, 330, 536
Kennedy-Richardson, Louisa, 731
Ken Russell's ABC of British Music, 609
Kent, Carl, 46, 411, 567, 674
Kent, Crawford, 691
Kent, Don, 178, 706
Kent, Guy, 759
Kentish, John, 19, 521
Kenton, Earle C., 712
Kentucky Moonshine (Butler), 530
Kenyon, Charles, 452, 454, 638
Kenyon, Nancy, 513
Kenyon, Nicholas, 511
Kerima (actress), 132
Kerl, Torsten, 706

McCrew, Patricia, 81
McCulloch, Susan, 498
McCullough, Andrew, 687, 715
McDaniel, Barry, 157, 201, 350, 631, 730
McDaniel, Hattie, 638
MacDermott, Marc, 11
McDonald, Anne-Maree, 752
MacDonald, Ann-Marie, 177, 403, 456
McDonald, Antony, 76
McDonald, Audra, 71, 122, 160, 276
Macdonald, Brian, 134, 293, 339, 456, 550
McDonald, Donald, 443
McDonald, Iain, 751
MacDonald, Kenneth, 76
MacDonald, Peter, 312
MacDonald, Peter, 120
MacDonald, Raymond, 53
McDonald, Roger, 443
MacDonald, S., 542
McDonald, William, 243
McDonnell, Tom, 47, 293, 361, 715, 760, 775
MacDonough, Glen, 38, 358
McDormand, Frances, 502
McDougall, Jamie, 179
McDowell, Malcolm, 86, 416
Mace, Mary, 39
McEwen, Terry, 669
McFadden, Claron, 312, 594
Macfadyen, Angus, 160, 764
MacFarlane, John, 215, 760
McFerrin, Bobby, 6, 410
McGann, William, 197, 257
McGegan, Nicholas, 312
MacGibbon, Ross, 120
McGiffert, John, 2
McGill, Bernard, 175
McGowan, Jack, 97
McGrail, Walter, 642
McGrath, William, 11
McGraw, William, 198
McGreevy, Geraldine, 228
McGregor, Ewan, 408
McGrow, Sheila, 268
Mach, Manuela, 388
Machackova, Katerina, 353
Machado, Aquiles, 212, 584
Machlis, Joseph, 22, 82, 130, 240, 583, 708, 759
Machover, Tod, 327
McHugh, Frank, 462
McHugh, James, 553
Macias, Reinaldo, 48, 519
McIntyre, Joy, 179
McIver, Bill, 19, 542
Mack, Harold F., 382
Mack, Max, 251, 500, 782
MacKay, Ann, 400
McKay, Barry, 287
Mackay, Clarence H., 127
Mackay, Ellin, 127
McKay, Margery, 653
McKee, Joseph, 472, 498
McKee, Richard, 457, 599
McKeever, Jacquelyn, 71, 322
McKenna, T. P., 312
McKenna, Virginia, 564
Mackenzie, Tandy, 489, 619
McKern, Leo, 44, 669
Mackey, Hugh, 581
McKidd, Kevin, 699
McKinley, Andrew, 19, 76, 92, 304, 428, 601, 614, 779
McKinney, Florine, 654

McLaglen, Victor, 116
MacLaine, Shirley, 194, 219, 414, 520, 603
McLaughlin, Marie, 29, 113, 241, 476, 498, 508, 584, 597, 709, 781
McLean, Colin, 731
McLean, Douglas, 293, 456, 550
McLean, Susan, 340
McLeod, William, 288
McLocklin, William, 313
McLoughlin, Marianne, 258
Macmillan, Andrew, 149
MacMillan, Richard, 293
McMillan, Richard, 456
MacMurray, Fred, 333, 670, 767
McNair, Sylvia, 448, 577
McNally, Terrence, 104, 136, 147, 704
McNaughton, Linda, 759
MacNeil, Walter, 709
Macpherson, Jeanie, 115, 138, 231, 255, 261
MacRae, Gordon, 4, 123, 175, 301, 505
McRae, Hilton, 358
MacRory, Avril, 215
McShane, David, 486
McTiernan, John, 501
Macurdy, John, 10, 189, 190, 385, 573, 679, 726
McVicar, David, 114, 584, 782
MacWatters, Virginia, 31, 94, 506
MacWilliams, Glen, 480
Mad about Opera, 624
Madame Bovary (Chabrol), 396
Madame Bovary (Flaubert), 392
Madame Bovary (Renoir), 394, 576
Madame Chrysanthème (Messager), 447
Madame de . . . (Ophuls), 328, 515
Madame Sherry, 1
Mädchen in Weiss (Janson), 133
Maddalena, James, 157, 286, 383, 488, 492, 498
Madden, John, 279
Madeleine (Herbert), 318
Mademoiselle Docteur (Pabst), 325
Mademoiselle Modiste (Leonard), 462
Maderna, Bruno, 338, 773
Madgett, Brittany, 77
Madison, Cleo, 703
Madjarowa, Violetta, 286
Mad Love (Aranda), 349
Madness of King George, The (Hytner), 312, 329
Maestri, Ambrogio, 228
Maestro and the Diva, The, 649
Maeterlinck, Maurice, 58, 171, 542
Maffei, Andrea, 407
Maffeo, Gianni, 82
Magálová, Kamila, 222
Magee, Emily, 499, 523
Magg, Herbert, 74
Maggi, Angelo, 179
Maggi, Enrico, 383, 637
Maggi, Luigi, 49, 500, 529
Maggio, Florence, 695
Magic Fire, 362
Magic Hunter (Enyedi), 266
Magiera, Leone, 83, 538, 539
Magimel, Benoît, 58, 595
Magini-Coletti (baritone), 143
Magnani, Anna, 213, 533, 544, 603, 704, 751
Magni, Luigi, 704
Magnier, Pierre, 159, 165
Magnificent Rebel, The (Tressler), 61
Magnolia (Anderson), 120
Magnus, Elisabeth von, 499

Magnuson, Elizabeth, 645
Magnussen, Fritz, 703
Magnusson, Charles, 182, 520
Magnusson, Lars, 218
Magrath, Leueen, 768
Mahard, Francis, 268, 567
Mahé, Martine, 146
Mahin, John Lee, 485, 638
Mahler, Alma, 15, 252, 626
Mahler, Zdenek, 176, 474
Mahnke, Claudia, 15
Mahoney, John, 469
Maibaum, Richard, 650
Maiden, Cullen, 57
Maid Marian (De Koven), 172
Maid of Pskov, The (Rimsky-Korsakov), 341
Maigrot, Bernard, 221, 461
Main, Marjorie, 478, 600
Main, Stewart, 258
Maisch, Herbert, 117, 133, 484, 617, 704
Majano, Anton Giulio, 527
Majeroni, Achille, 67, 603, 757
Majestät Mimi (Granichstädten), 202
Major, Malvina, 246
Major Barbara, 758
Major Dundee (Ophuls), 21
Makavejev, Dusan, 322
Make a Wish, 95
Making Opera (Azzopardi), 258
Makis, Julie, 632
Makris, Cynthia, 407
Malachovsky, Ondrej, 474
Malagnini, Mario, 114, 689
Malagu, Stefania, 522, 587
Malakova, Petra, 349, 522
Malaniuk, Ira, 29
Malas, Spiro, 47, 92, 217, 243, 340, 480
Malas-Godlewska, Ewa, 556
Malasomma, Nunzio, 175, 261, 535, 596
Malberg, Pater, 214
Malberg, Urban, 779
Malbin, Elaine, 133, 177, 412, 527, 614, 667, 674, 698, 708, 715
Malenotti, Maleno, 217, 445
Malgharini, Pina, 46, 111, 196, 306, 497
Malgoire, Jean-Claude, 468, 680
Malherbe, Annet, 253
Malina, J. B., 592
Malina, Josef, 152
Malinson, Sarah, 509
Malinson, Sue, 509
Malinson, Tess, 509
Malipiero, Giovanni, 20
Malis, David, 48, 757
Malkames, Don, 524
Malkhassiants, Yulia, 461
Malkovich, John, 58, 168, 253, 636, 719
Mallas-Godlewska, Ewa, 230
Malle, Louis, 493, 719
Malleson, Miles, 356
Malo, Gina, 249, 380, 481
Malone, Carol, 779
Malouf, David, 69, 752
Malta, Alexander, 53, 190, 351, 777
Maltese, Michael, 347, 348, 571, 591, 760, 767
Malvezzi, Cristofano, 556
Mamelles de Terésias, Les (Poulenc), 557
Mamoulian, Rouben, 409, 432, 505, 692
Mampaso, Manuel, 492
Manacchini, Giuseppe, 126
Manager, Richetta, 488
Manahan, George, 84, 214, 702

844

Murray, Ann, 32, 134, 135, 167, 191, 461, 475, 606, 636, 780, 781
Murray, Bill, 160
Murray, J. Harold, 323, 650
Murray, James, 600
Murray, John Horton, 150
Murray, Mae, 405
Murray, Peter, 47, 282, 293, 323, 339, 456, 528, 550, 583, 606, 708, 715, 775
Murray, Thelma, 711
Murray, William, 706
Murrow, Edward R., 104, 541, 619
Musaccio, Martina, 15
Musial, Martha, 697
Music, Clarence, 255
Musica Proibita (Campgalliani), 290
Musical Story, A, 376
Music at the Court of Louis XIV, 400
Music for Marcel Duchamp (Cage), 103
Music Goes Round, The (Schertzinger), 55
Music Lovers, The (Russell), 223, 609, 683
Music Man, The (Willson), 735
Music of Terezin (Broughton), 351
Music of the Heart (Craven), 520
Musikalisches Rendezvous, 406
Musill, John, 698
Musilli, John, 372
Mussbach, Peter, 573
Mussolini, Benito, 290
Musy, Louis, 46
Muszely, Melita, 150, 151
Muth, Cornelia, 388
Muti, Lorenzo, 425, 432
Muti, Ornella, 173
Mutterliebe (Ucicy), 326
Muus, Niel, 212
Muzio, Claudia, 764
My Big Fat Greek Wedding, 386
Mycroft, Walter C., 111
Myerberg, Michael, 42, 313
Myers, Michael, 26
Myers, Pamela, 349
My Geisha (Cardiff), 414
My Left Foot (Sheridan), 157
My Life, My Songs: Robert Stolz, 657
Myrick, Rony, 783
Myrtil, Odette, 63
My Sister Eileen, 71
Mysteries of Venice, The, 624
Mystery Men (Usher), 278
Myung-Whung Chung, 534, 572
My War Years: Arnold Schoenberg, 626
My Wild Irish Rose, 610

Nabokov, Nicolas, 36
Nacht der grossen Liebe, Die (Bolvary), 496
Nacht ohne Abschied, 630
Nada, Juan, 198
Nadelmann, Noemi, 589
Nadhering, Ernst, 61
Nadler, Max, 53
Naef, Yvonne, 723, 726
Nagel, Conrad, 20, 633
Naghibin, Yuri, 683
Naglestad, Catherine, 15, 218
Naglio, Sandro, 468
Nagy, Elemer, 313, 424, 505
Nagy, Käthe von, 617, 728
Nagy, Robert, 209, 450, 679, 726
Naida, Sergei, 374
Naish, J. Carrol, 468
Nakajima, Akiko, 78
Nakamaru, Michie, 415

Naked Carmen (Corigliano), 154
Naldi, Ronald, 412
Nannuzzi, Armando, 83, 131, 397, 528
Naouri, Laurent, 66, 114
Napier, Alan, 85, 302
Napier, Diana, 370, 527, 681
Napier, John, 330, 482
Napierkowska, Stacia, 422, 615, 634, 718, 724
Napoleon (Gance), 269, 325
Napoleon (Guitry), 63
Nardi, Marcia, 58
Nardinocchi, Angelo, 484
Nares, Owen, 201, 206
Nash, Billie, 472
Nash, Damien, 451
Nash, Heddle, 677
Nash, N. Richard, 554
Nash, Ogden, 246, 763
Nash, Royston, 323
Nasrudel, Douglas, 627
Natalia Petrovna (Hoiby), 324
Natheaux, Louis, 663
Natoma (Herbert), 318
Natzler, Lizzie, 207, 625
Nau, Eugénie, 131
Nau, Hans-Martin, 286
Navarro, García, 9
Nave, La (Montemezzi), 468
Nave, Maria Luisa, 4, 257
Nawe, Isabelle, 70
Naylor, Gloria, 555
Nazimova, Alla, 199, 616, 711
Nazzari, Amadeo, 129, 195, 238, 262
Neagle, Anna, 77, 358, 556
Neame, Derek, 380
Neame, Ronald, 51, 414, 501, 559, 654, 676
Neate, Kenneth, 699
Neblett, Carol, 145, 229, 691, 706
Nebolsin, Vasily, 92
Nechipaylo, Vadim, 567
Necká, Václav, 366
Nedashkovskaya, Raissa, 726
Nedland, Paul, 377
Neely, James Bert, 481
Neeson, Liam, 285
Neff, Hildegarde, 18, 717
Negri, Pola, 116, 138, 711
Negri, Roberto, 2, 42, 81, 163, 168, 169, 202, 223, 251, 298, 299, 335, 370, 403, 415, 456, 526, 576, 600, 602, 632, 639, 746
Negri-Pouget, Fernanda, 33, 235, 589, 678
Negroni, Baldassare, 711
Negulesco, Jean, 673, 718
Neher, Caroline, 199
Neidinger, Gustav, 241
Neil, Hildegard, 29
Neil, Kelly, 665
Neilan, Marshall, 413
Neilendam, Nicolai, 214
Neill, Harriet, 322
Neilson-Terry, Phyllis, 716
Nekvasil, Jirí, 372
Nekvasil, Ondrej, 372
Nelepp, Gyorgy, 27, 91
Nelle, George, 322
Nelli, Herva, 8, 227, 705
Nelson, Alison, 438
Nelson, Bill, 65, 103
Nelson, Gene, 505
Nelson, John, 56
Nelson, Judith, 447
Nelson, Keith, 53

Nelson, Nelda, 383
Nelson, Ralph, 693
Nelson, Tim Blake, 524
Nelsson, Woldemar, 57, 252, 385
Nemecek, Jiri, 607
Németh, Marika, 74, 416
Németh, Sandor, 162, 163
Nemirovich-Danchenko, Vladimir, 16
Nemolyneva, Svetlana, 222
Nentwig, Franz Ferdinand, 31
Neopolitan Carousel (Giannini), 281
Nepoti, Alberto, 115
Nerbe, Kerstin, 10
Neri, Giulio, 47, 52, 67, 257, 385, 563, 581, 583, 604
Nero, Franco, 754
Nerone (Mascagni), 299
Neroni, Luciano, 196, 261, 392, 497
Neroni, Nicola Fausto, 596
Nesbitt, Cathleen, 425
Nesbitt, Miriam, 11
Neschling, John, 305, 602
Nessi, Giuseppe, 651
Netrebko, Anna, 74, 608
Neubach, Ernest, 481
Neubauer, Margit, 706
Neubert, Kurt, 242
Neuenfels, Hans, 218, 219, 251
Neufeld, Eugen, 152
Neufeld, Max, 109, 152, 283, 654, 659
Neufeld, Rudolf, 303
Neugebauer, Alfred, 556
Neukirch, Harald, 70
Neuman, Günter, 286
Neumann, Hans, 253
Neumann, Harry, 377
Neumann, Jörg, 227, 777
Neumann, Julius, 782
Neumann, Kurt, 377, 670
Neumann, Václav, 32, 163, 222
Neumann, Vyaceslaw, 61
Neumann, Wolfgang, 773
Neumeier, John, 679
Neve, Alexis, 657
Never Trust a Woman, 681
Neveux, Georges, 32, 349, 350
Neville, Grace, 245
Neville Brothers, 539
Nevin, Robyn, 125, 443
Newberry, William, 648
Newman, Alfred, 123, 357, 358, 653, 699, 767
Newman, Bill, 687
Newman, Chris, 18
Newman, Claire, 70, 365
Newman, Günter, 614
Newman, Henry, 38
Newman, Linda, 392
Newman, Mike, 687, 731, 751
Newman, Phyllis, 71
Newman, Sydney, 36, 149
Newmark, John, 100, 256
Newson, Jeremy, 377
Newton, Christopher, 561
New Voices for Man, 468
New Wine (Schunzel), 61, 628
New World Symphony (Dvorák), 204
Next of Kin, 758
Nibelungen, Die (Lang), 370, 590
Nibelungen, Die (Reinl), 591
Nibelungi, I (Bernacchi), 590
Niblo, Fred, 245, 711
Nichi, Annibale, 115, 529
Nicholas, Paul, 754
Nicholas, Roger, 432
Nicholls, Anthony, 168

Ralph, Louis, 617
Ramalho, Elba, 63
Ramati, Netta B., 503
Rambert, Marie, 662
Rambova, Natacha, 199, 616
Ramettre, Noël, 170
Ramicova, Dunya, 157, 387, 492, 498, 639
Ramirez, Alejandro, 593
Ramirez, Ariel, 123, 124
Ramirez, Carlo, 333
Ramirez, Carlos, 767
Ramirez, Elisa, 578
Ramirez, Estrella, 453
Ramírez, Maria Carmen, 45, 155, 578
Ramis, Harold, 588
Ramos, José Ortiz, 198
Ramos Carrión, Miguel, 647
Rampling, Charlotte, 783
Rampy, David, 303
Ramuz, Charles F., 321
Ranalow, Frederic, 63
Rancatore, Désirée, 219, 228, 602
Randa, Cesmir, 53
Randi, Ermanno, 125, 216
Randi, Lori, 134, 493
Randle, Thomas, 226, 677
Randle, Tom, 289, 722
Randova, Alice, 191
Randova, Eva, 534, 579
Rands, Leslie, 322
Ranson, Jeremy, 223
Ranzani, Stefano, 238, 393
Rapee, Erno, 461
Rape of Lucretia, The, 706
Raphael, 40
Raphael, Anna, 408
Raphaelson, Sam, 402
Raphaelson, Samson, 264, 759
Raphanel, Ghyslaine, 221, 594
Rapp, Jacques, 391, 720
Rappaport, Herbert, 376
Rappaport, Mark, 473
Rapper, Irving, 80, 276, 555, 718
Rapsodia Satanica (Oxilia), 434, 511–12
Rapuach, Ernest, 7
Rarahu (Loti), 368
Rasch, Ellen, 291
Rasinski, Connie, 25
Raskin, Judith, 51, 175, 177, 189, 240, 366
Rasky, Harry, 659
Rasp, Fritz, 199
Rastelbinder, Der (Lehár), 374
Rasumny, Alexander, 569
Rath, John, 112
Rathbone, Basil, 96, 140, 172, 693
Rathkolb, Dr. Oliver, 353
Ratiu, Dan, 64
Ratkai, Matton, 429
Ratner, Brett, 588, 621
Ratoff, Gregory, 692, 761, 768, 769
Ratti, Eugenia, 473
Rätz, Christian, 216
Raub, Wolfram, 266
Rauch, Franz, 630
Raucourt, Jules, 703
Raulet, Georges, 458, 536
Rausch, Wolfgang, 31, 266
Rautio, Nina, 417
Rautyavaara, Mariaheidi, 351
Ravel, Gaston, 49, 500
Ravina, Rachel, 188
Rawlence, Christopher, 358, 423
Rawlinson, Gerald, 429
Rawnsley, John, 47, 83, 190, 584

Ray, Nicholas, 363
Rayam, Curtis, 593, 714
Raye, Carol, 682
Raymond, Emily, 452
Raymond, Gene, 409, 410, 553
Raymond, William, 262
Rayner, Michael, 323
Rayner, Minnie, 235
Raz, Vladimir, 607
Ready to Rumble (Robbins), 386
Reagan, Ronald, 138
Reardon, Johan, 268
Reardon, John, 189, 253, 366, 567, 654, 666, 779
Rear Window (Hitchcock), 354
Rebmann, Liselotte, 579
Rebroff, Ivan, 66, 378, 786
Reconstructie (Andriessen et al.), 25
Redel, Jessica, 163
Redford, Robert, 200
Redgrave, Corin, 70
Redgrave, Lynn, 12, 564
Redgrave, Michael, 250, 587
Redgrave, Vanessa, 160, 177, 426, 754
Redkin, Vladimir, 417
Red Line, The, 613
Red Pony, The (Copland), 153
Red Shoes, The (Powell), 558
Reece, Arley, 37
Reed, Carol, 616, 764
Reed, John, 323, 456, 606
Reed, Lou, 763
Reed, Luther, 428, 591
Reed, Oliver, 171, 177
Reed, Tom, 638
Reeder, William, 383, 481
Rees, Deborah, 18, 320, 501
Rees Davis, Michael, 237
Reeves, George, 630
Reeves, Keanu, 39, 168
Reeves, Peter, 178
Reeves, Steve, 552
Regas, Jack, 360
Regazzo, Lorenzo, 45
Reggiani, Hilde, 449
Reggio, Godfrey, 287
Regnier, Mlle., 420
Regnoli, Piero, 60
Rehfisch, Hans, 17
Rehfuss, Heinz, 240
Reich, Günter, 471
Reichenbach, François, 112, 533
Reichert, Heinz, 200, 771, 778
Reichhardt, Poul, 250
Reichmann, Max, 369, 681
Reichmann, Wolfgang, 62, 773
Reich mir die Hand, mein Leben (Hartl), 473, 613
Reid, Alain, 636
Reid, Alastair, 303
Reid, Alex, 140
Reid, David, 661
Reid, Fiona, 62
Reid, Rex, 53
Reid, Robert, 455
Reid, Wallace, 115, 231, 404, 665
Reilly, Charles Nelson, 39
Reimer, Eva-Christine, 75
Reineck, Hans-Peter, 252
Reinecke, Hans-Jurgen, 151, 521
Reine de Chypre, La (Halévy), 309
Reiner, Fritz, 111, 148, 600
Reiner, Rob, 237
Reinert, Emile Edwin, 661
Reinhardt, Andreas, 110, 218
Reinhardt, Betty, 108

Reinhardt, John, 464–65
Reinhardt, Max, 221, 226, 329, 452
Reinhardt, Rolf, 388
Reinhardt-Kiss, Ursula, 498
Reinhart, Gregory, 15, 391
Reinhold, Gert, 750
Reinking, Wilhelm, 240
Reinl, Harald, 591
Reinshagen, Victor, 519
Reis, Cristina, 58
Reis, Irving, 505
Reisch, Walter, 67, 292, 365, 402, 787
Reisen, Mark, 355
Reisenfeld, Hugo, 231
Reiss, Janine, 41
Reiter, George, 240
Reizen, Mark, 16, 27, 89
Reka, V., 366
Relph, Michael, 442
Reluctant Angels, The (Bartlett), 363
Relyea, Gary, 2, 195
Relyea, John, 192
Remedios, Ramon, 47, 243, 523
Remick, Lee, 706
Remigio, Carmela, 425
Remo, Ken, 455
Remorques (Grémillon), 303
Remsberg, Calvin, 671
Renan, Emile, 46, 490, 497, 678
Renaud, Madeleine, 178
Renault, Monique, 509
Rendall, David, 167, 251, 425, 450, 781
Rendezvous in Wien, 646
Renee, Madelyn, 83
Renfield, Leslie, 64
Rennahan, Ray, 128, 734
Rennert, Guenther, 240, 548, 631, 773
Rennert, Wolfgang, 506
Rennie, James, 230
Renoir, Claude, 412
Renshaw, Bruce, 453
Renshaw, Christopher, 187, 339, 456, 519, 606
Renton, Edward, 420
Renzetti, Donato, 10, 135, 243, 346, 584, 641
Reoyo, Enrique, 327
Reppa, David, 10, 178, 187, 278, 667, 674, 720
Reppel, Carmen, 579
Rescigno, Joseph, 31, 348
Rescigno, Nicola, 34, 102, 104, 196, 211, 326
Resick, Georgine, 436, 498
Resing, Vladimir, 304
Resnais, Alain, 317
Ress, Ulrich, 253
Restless in Thought, Disturbed in Mind, 652
Resto, Guillermo, 179
Reti, Jozsef, 316
Retroscena, 684
Rettick, Justine, 150
Retty, Wolf-Albach, 749
Reuprecht, Albert, 750
Reuter, Rolf, 498
Reuterswärd, Mans, 40, 69
Revel, Harry, 213
Revelle, Hamilton, 691
Reveschini, Barbara, 474
Revill, Clive, 456, 652
Revolution (Hudson), 154
Révonne, Suzanne, 84
Rex, Eugen, 81, 630
Rex, Rut, 631
Rey, Fernando, 476, 756

Rey, Isabel, 192, 499, 593
Rey, Roberto, 50, 736
Rey de los gitanos, El (Strayer), 464
Reyes, Consuelo, 198
Reyes, Dulce, 131
Reynolds, Anna, 222, 548
Reynolds, Burt, 706
Reynolds, Debbie, 558
Rhapsody in Blue (Gershwin), 276, 378
Rhapsody in Blue (Rapper), 80, 98, 555
Rhodes, Elise, 453
Rhodes, Jane, 118
Rhodes, Marion, 130, 708
Rhodope (Ganne), 269
Rhotert, Bert, 36
Rhys-Williams, Stephen, 768
Ribemont-Dessaignes, Georges, 372, 720
Ribert, Peter, 657
Ribetti, Elda, 189
Ricceri, Luciano, 35
Ricci, Christine, 423
Ricci, Elena, 81
Ricci, Enrique, 372, 426
Ricci, Giorgio, 434, 511, 574
Ricci, Orlando, 84
Ricci, Renzo, 757
Ricciardi, Joseph, 480
Rice, Christine, 782
Rice, Elmer, 663
Rice, Peter, 775, 781
Rice, Simon, 226
Rich, Delphine, 91
Rich, Johannes, 214
Richard, Cyril, 322
Richard, Frieda, 625
Richard, Lawrence, 456, 550, 606, 715, 775
Richard and Cosima (Patzak), 94
Richards, Emily, 314
Richards, Richard L., 42
Richards, Tom, 139
Richardson, Donald, 693
Richardson, Ian, 452, 548
Richardson, John, 632
Richardson, Linda, 767
Richardson, Marilyn, 752
Richardson, Mark, 663
Richardson, Ralph, 754
Richardson, Stephen, 320, 720
Richardson, Tony, 336, 548, 719
Richard-Willm, Pierre, 152
Richebé, Roger, 778
Richfield, George, 27, 46, 111, 196, 261, 306, 392, 497, 597
Richman, Arthur, 318
Richman, Harry, 55
Richmond, Alice, 304
Richmond, Gwyn, 585
Richmond, Stella, 241
Richter, Hans, 602, 778
Richter, Karl, 312
Richter, Mike, 510
Richter, Paul, 256, 590
Richter, Renate, 62
Richter, Sviatoslav, 288, 654, 683
Rickhards, Steven, 491
Ricordi, Giovanni, 581
Ricordi, Giulio, 421
Ricordi, Tito, 262
Riddell, Richard, 12
Ridderbusch, Karl, 52, 54, 579, 777
Ridderstedt, Margareta, 10
Riddle, Cassandra, 84
Riddle, The: Woman, 232
Ridgely, Richard, 642

Ridgeway, Stan, 763
Ridgwell, George, 380
Ridout, Godfrey, 455
Riech, Arnold, 182
Riedel, Deborah, 163
Riedmann, Gerhard, 74, 298, 352, 742, 750, 785
Riefenstahl, Leni, 697
Riegel, Kenneth, 92, 400, 606, 614
Riemann, Johannes, 37, 223, 280
Riemannoper (Johnson), 347
Riesenfeld, Hugo, 115, 255, 377, 390
Riesman, Michael, 467
Rifkin, Joshua, 348
Rigacci, Susanna, 196
Rigal, Delia, 186
Rigaud, Georges, 745, 778
Rigby, Gordon, 650
Rigby, Jean, 14, 114, 312, 542, 584, 636
Rigg, Diana, 226, 452
Riggins, Norman, 496
Riggs, Lynn, 505
Riggs, Otis, 150, 428, 583, 759
Riggs, Ralph, 715
Righelli, Gennaro, 84, 717
Rigillo, Mariano, 581
Rigoghossian, Sonia, 678
Rigosa, Danilo, 202
Riley, Michael, 494, 543, 661, 707
Riley, Terry, 479
Rilla, Walter, 682
Rimini, Giacomo, 706, 724
Rimoldi, Adriano, 193
Rimsky, Nicolas, 536
Rinaldi, Alberto, 106, 274, 528, 621, 641
Rinaldi, Gerardo, 335
Rinaldi, Giuseppe, 212
Rinaldi, Joe, 39
Rinaldi, Margherita, 432
Rinaldi, Nadia, 548
Rinaldi, Rossana, 523
Rinaldi, Rossano, 739
Ringart, Anna, 597
Ringholz, Teresa, 14, 227
Ringo, Rolda, 245
Rintzler, Marius, 109, 497
Rio, Carmen, 108
Ripellino, Angelo Maria, 338
Ripley, Arthur, 363
Ripley, Gladys, 311
Rischert, Christian, 397
Riscica, Rosetta, 650
Rishoi, Neil, 122
Risi, Dino, 173
Risin, Vladimir, 118
Riskin, Robert, 281, 767
Risley, Patricia, 499
Ritchard, Cyril, 403, 544
Ritchie, June, 199
Ritchie, Michael, 119
Ritchie, Sam, 99
Ritholz, Gerald, 299
Ritman, William, 716
Ritorno de Cesare, Il (Castelnuovo-Tedesco), 127
Ritt, Martin, 553
Rittau, Günther, 304, 785
Ritter, Ilse, 144
Ritter, Rod, 272
Ritter, Rudo, 427
Ritter, Tex, 117, 582, 586, 772
Ritter Blaubart (Welsenstein), 45
Ritterbusch, Sabine, 266
Rittner, Rudolf, 442
Ritzmann, Martin, 70

Riva, Ambrogio, 566
Riva, Carlos, 358
Riva, Manuela, 419
Riva, Mario, 675
Riva, William, 721
Rivas, Isabel, 279, 292, 578
Rivelles, Rafael, 117, 297
Riven, Nicolas, 142
Rivenq, Nicolas, 179, 468, 710
River, The, 694
Rivera, Javier, 688
Rivers, Fernand, 562, 712
Rivers, Joan, 644
Rivers, Malcolm, 47, 151, 528, 583
Riviera Girl, The (Wodehouse, Bolton, and Kern), 162
Rivkin, Allen, 304
Rizzi, Carlo, 58, 710, 723
Rizzieri, Elena, 288, 291, 334
Rizzo, Francis, 612
Rizzone, Cinzia, 425, 739
Roa, Miguel, 272
Roach, Bert, 650
Roach, Hal, 38, 49, 86–87, 261, 361
Road to Reno, The (Sylvan Simon), 311
Roar, Leif, 385, 534, 579
Roaratorio (Cage), 103
Roark-Strummer, Linda, 31, 35, 202
Robarts, Harry, 752
Robbe-Grillet, Alain, 713
Röbbeling, Harald, 428
Robber Symphony, The (Feher), 512
Robbie, Seymour, 80, 403
Robbins, Brian, 386
Robbins, Carrie, 618
Robbins, Jerome, 12, 357, 508, 766
Robbins, John, 506
Robbins, Julien, 76, 148, 229, 450, 669
Robbins, Kate, 540
Robbins, Tim, 119, 160, 501, 764
Robert, Alfredo, 43, 493
Robert, Hélène, 46, 496
Robert, Richard, 164
Roberti, Roberto, 262
Robert le diable (Meyerbeer), 451
Roberts, Alice, 401
Roberts, Ben, 635
Roberts, Eric, 457
Roberts, George, 306
Roberts, Joan, 505
Roberts, Joy, 293
Roberts, Judith Anna, 315
Roberts, Julia, 714
Roberts, Rachel, 199
Roberts, Ralph Arthur, 197
Roberts, Stephen, 340
Roberts, Susan, 782
Roberts, Theodore, 229
Robertson, James, 503
Robertson, John, 268
Robertson, Margo, 33
Robertson, Patrick, 584
Robertson, Stewart, 136
Robert Stolz Gala, 657
Robey, George, 141, 197
Robidas, Evelyne, 560
Robin, Leo, 264
Robin Hood (De Koven), 172
Robinson, Armin, 720
Robinson, Bruce, 414–15
Robinson, Edward G., 50, 430, 587
Robinson, Eric, 149, 636
Robinson, Faye, 597
Robinson, Forbes, 19, 20, 140, 421
Robinson, Gail, 201
Robinson, James, 503

Robinson, Mabel, 714
Robinson, Madeleine, 142
Robinson, Marlene, 783
Robinson, Peter, 157, 271, 456, 690
Robinson, Phil Alden, 188, 729
Robinson, Richard, 253
Robinson, Stanford, 19
Robison, Arthur, 381, 421
Robison, Stanford, 506
Robson, Andrew, 454
Robson, Ann, 545
Robson, Elizabeth, 179
Robson, Mark, 673
Robson, Nigel, 361, 468, 564
Roc, Patricia, 432
Rocchio, Michael, 383
Rocha, Glauber, 305, 524
Rock-a-Bye Baby (Tashlin), 39
Rockwell, Sam, 452
Roda, Enrico, 281
Roddam, Franc, 30, 719
Rodde, Anne-Marie, 91
Roden, Anthony, 330, 418
Rodenbuch, Georges, 706
Rodewald, Elizabeth Bacon, 125
Rodgers, Doug, 8, 227
Rodgers, Joan, 32, 461, 510
Rodolfi, Eleuterio, 49, 500
Rodolfo, Eleutaria, 615
Rodrigo, Raquel, 50, 186, 578, 736
Rodriguez, Amalia, 578
Rodríguez, María, 145, 183, 279
Roelsgaard, Jenny, 214
Roger, David, 242
Roger, Germaine, 434
Rogers, Charles R., 38, 198
Rogers, David, 318
Rogers, Ginger, 275, 762
Rogers, Nigel, 557
Rogers, Paul, 452
Rogers, Roy, 212
Roggero, Margaret, 338
Rogier, Frank, 64, 313
Rogner, Eva Maria, 29
Rogue Song, The, 696
Rohr, Tony, 377
Roider, Michael, 163
Roi l'a dit, Le (Delibes), 172
Roi malgré lui, Le (Chabrier), 136
Roiné, Eric, 434
Roisum, Lee, 307
Rojas, Raquel, 198
Rojek, Hans Jürgen, 57
Rojo, Gustavo, 535
Rojo, Rubén, 198, 328
Rökk, Marika, 74, 162, 250, 272, 276, 378, 434
Roland, Gilbert, 85
Rolandi, Gianna, 29, 134, 163, 393
Rolfe, Anthony, 93, 289
Rolland, Monique, 46, 496
Roller, Alfred, 600
Roma, Enrico, 187
Romanca Final (Forque), 305
Romance, Viviane, 118
Romance on the High Seas, 378
Romanchine, Anatoli, 93
Romani, Augusto, 344
Romani, Felice, 25, 58, 110, 211, 396, 492, 650, 729
Romano, Carlo, 212, 582
Romanovsky, Vladislav, 355
Romanowsky, Richard, 434
Romea, Alberto, 117
Romei, Rolf, 15
Romensky, Mikhail, 732

Romere, Miguel, 140
Romero, Angelo, 132
Romero, Cesar, 264
Romero, Elisa Ruiz, 737
Romero, Federico, 107, 127, 186
Romito, Filippo, 684
Romm, Mikhail, 569
Rommer, Claire, 660
Roncato, Massimiliano, 461
Ronconi, Giorgio, 290
Ronconi, Luca, 10, 191, 219, 306, 407, 463, 580, 702, 742, 743
Ronde, La, 659
Ronet, Maurice, 67, 581
Roni, Luigi, 202, 229, 306
Ronis, David, 31
Ronny (Kálmán), 352
Ronse, Henri, 482
Ronson, Jon, 162
Ronstadt, Linda, 550
Roocroft, Amanda, 157
Rooley, Anthony, 15, 468
Room, Abram, 60, 512
Room with a View, A (Ivory), 278, 342, 599
Rooney, Mickey, 206, 301, 315, 395, 452, 595
Rootering, Jan-Hendrik, 534, 579, 679, 780
Roper, Sarah, 783
Rorem, Ned, 153
Rosa di granata, La (Ghione), 129
Rosado, Pepa, 465
Rosado, Pepe, 7, 183, 279
Rosales, Rachel, 781
Rosalie (Herbert and Gershwin), 317
Rosalie (Van Dyke), 205
Rosar, Annie, 268
Rosato, Mary Lou, 160
Rosay, Françoise, 381, 512
Rosch, Hilde, 787
Röschmann, Dorothea, 499, 782
Roscoe, Albert, 615
Rose, Bernard, 62, 719
Rose, George, 550
Rose, Helen, 338
Rose, Jurgen, 43, 210, 601, 679, 718, 780
Rose, Norman, 217
Rose, Peter, 146, 167, 219, 639
Rose, Reginald, 245
Rosell, Francisco Gómez, 16
Rosemond, Sarah, 300
Rosemont, Norman, 123, 360
Rosen, Albert, 176
Rosen, David, 626
Rosen, Norman, 322
Rosen, Peter, 122, 126, 541–42, 621, 705
Rosenbaum, Martin, 185, 305
Rosenberger, Robert, 609
Rosenkönig, 628
Rosenman, Leonard, 626
Rosenshein, Neil, 34, 504, 544
Rosenthal, Manuel, 178
Rosher, Charles, 638
Rosimino, Paolo, 737
Rosing, Vladimir, 527
Roskam, Clair, 622
Rösler, Jo Hanns, 434
Ross, Adrian, 244
Ross, Allan, 668
Ross, Eleanor, 620
Ross, Howard, 63
Ross, Jerry, 4
Ross, Lesley Echo, 457

Ross, Susanna, 572
Ross, Vera, 282, 285
Rossato, Arturo, 285
Rossdeutscher, Cedric, 780
Rosselli, John, 652
Rossen, Robert, 771
Rossi, Carlo, 422
Rossi, Gaetano, 95, 106, 382, 634, 678
Rossi, Giacomo, 589
Rossi, Kim, 581
Rossi, Liliana, 392
Rossi, Mario, 211
Rossi, Tino, 628
Rossi, Vittorio, 9, 522
Rossi-Drago, Eleanora, 764
Rossini, W., 529
Rossini! Rossini!, 604
Rossini's Ghost, 604
Rossmanith, Gabriele, 680
Rosso, Mino, 196
Rosson, Harold, 128, 508
Rost, Andrea, 44, 191, 375
Rost, Helmut, 102, 326
Rost, Leo, 178
Rostand, Edmund, 164, 165
Rosten, Norman, 147, 467
Rostropovich, Mstislav, 92, 97, 185, 414, 572, 613, 743
Roswaenge, Helge, 428, 689
Rosy-Rosy, 207
Rosza, Miklos, 143
Rota, Ernesto, 109
Roth, Annie, 34
Roth, Bobby, 494
Roth, Cy, 561
Roth, Lillian, 734
Roth, Philip, 541
Rotha, Paul, 97
Rothapfel, S. L., 115, 231
Rothauser, Eduard, 420–21
Rothemüller, Marko, 156
Rother, Arthur, 497
Rothier, Léon, 116, 762
Rothlisberger, Max, 303, 521
Rothschilds, Die (Waschneck), 88–89
Rotmil, Jacques, 309, 355
Rotmund, Ernst, 762
Rottrei, Lia, 32
Rotunno, Giuseppe, 208, 700
Rou, Alexander, 437
Roubaud, Charles, 584
Roudakoff, Nicolas, 536
Roudot, Jean-François, 534
Roue, La (Gance), 325
Rouillon, Philippe, 317, 691
Rouleau, Joseph, 187, 233, 391
Rouleau, Raymond, 516
Roulin, Pascal, 509
Round, Thomas, 3, 282, 293, 323, 339, 456, 550, 606, 715, 775
Rouse, Sarah, 379
Roussel, Anne, 418
Rousselières, Jean, 419
Roussell, Henry, 495
Rousset, Christophe, 230
Roussillon, François, 197, 760
Roussin, André, 85
Route fleurie, La (Lopez), 388
Routledge, Patricia, 63
Roux, Michel, 741
Rovi, Charles, 175
Roving Boys at the Opera, 609
Rovira, Juan, 673
Row, Charles, 688
Rowe, Cheryl Bensman, 132–33
Rowe, Frank, 723

Schonauer, Marianne, 61, 189, 240
Schönberg, Michel, 414
Schönbock, Karl, 256
Schöne, Wolfgang, 110, 135, 266, 400, 534, 590
Schöne Helena, Die (von Ambesser), 66
Schöne Müllerin, Die (Schubert), 628
Schöner, Sonja, 240
Schöne Saskia, Die (Nedbal), 485
Schön ist die Welt, 626
School for Wives (Liebermann), 465
Schorg, Gretl, 630
Schorlemmer, Heinz, 272
Schorm, Evald, 266
Schott, Benjamin, 781
Schottler, Harmut, 266
Schøyen, Hege, 12, 563
Schramm, David, 160
Schramm, Margit, 759
Schreck, Max, 369, 397
Schreiber, Marc, 418
Schreibmayer, Kurt, 75, 580
Schreyvogl, F., 503
Schröder, Arnulf, 660
Schroder, Harmut, 66
Schroeder, Barbet, 51, 719
Schroeder, Ingeborg, 473
Schroeder, Marieke, 6, 689
Schroeder-Feinen, Ursula, 503
Schröter, Gisela, 70
Schroth, Hannelore, 244
Schrott, Erwin, 212
Schubert, Bernard L., 139, 462
Schubert, Erika, 786
Schubert: Klassix 13, 629
Schuberts Unvollendete Symphonie, 628
Schüfftan, Eugen, 721
Schuh, Ernest von, 148
Schulbach, Jan, 29
Schulberg, B. P., 437
Schuller, Gunther, 714
Schulman, Arnold, 64
Schulte, Wilm, 441
Schultz, Andrew, 78
Schultz, Fritz, 249
Schultz, Julianne, 78
Schultze, Jeanette, 483
Schulz, Elisabetta Norberg, 408
Schulz, Franz, 787
Schulz, Fritz, 74
Schulz, Kurt, 369, 630
Schuman, Patricia, 336
Schündler, Rudolf, 297, 378, 746
Schunk, Robert, 110, 252, 679, 755
Schunzel, Reinhold, 41, 61, 117, 199, 352, 628
Schurath, Marion, 780
Schuricht, Carl, 148
Schuster, Friedel, 745
Schuster, Harold, 408
Schütte, Peter, 264
Schütz, Ernst, 405
Schützendorf, Leo, 253
Schwab, Laurence, 487
Schwaiger, Rosl, 605
Schwartz, Al, 93
Schwartz, Arthur, 553
Schwartz, Gerard, 322
Schwartz, John, 31, 94, 299
Schwartz, Lew, 455
Schwartz, Robert Joel, 688
Schwartz, Stephen, 435
Schwarz, Gerald, 613, 622
Schwarz, Hanna, 163, 579, 614, 639, 717, 718, 755, 781
Schwarz, Hans, 579

Schwarz, Vera, 526
Schwarzbach, Hans-Peter, 780
Schwarzenberger, Xaver, 461, 777
Schwarzenegger, Arnold, 501
Schweiger, Heinrich, 312
Schweiger, Peter, 37
Schwengel, Bruno, 760
Schwitzgebel, Georges, 167
Schygulla, Hanna, 381, 613
Scibelli, Carlo, 404
Scimone, Claudio, 424, 518
Sciutti, Graziella, 51, 84, 473
Scola, Ettore, 649
Scotese, Giuseppe Maria, 118
Scott, Carter, 399
Scott, Helen, 64, 759
Scott, Jan, 123
Scott, Jay, 175
Scott, Kevin, 455
Scott, Michael, 229, 258, 413, 599, 645, 657
Scott, Norman, 8, 82
Scott, Renata, 513
Scott, Ridley, 278, 312, 368, 757
Scott, Robin, 28
Scott, Steven, 599
Scott, Tom, 18
Scott, Tony, 368
Scott, Walter, 195, 392
Scotto, Aubrey, 255
Scotto, Luigi, 129
Scovotti, Jeanette, 92
Scribe, Eugène, 4, 5, 108, 201, 211, 260, 328, 349, 421, 451, 477, 503
Scuderi, Vincenzo, 689
Scully, Karl, 408
Seabourne, John, 282, 293, 323, 339, 456, 550, 606, 715, 775
Seabury, John, 22
Seagren, Danny, 768
Seagull, The (Pasatieri), 535
Sea Hawk, The, 362
Seaman, David, 580, 783
Search, The (Zinnemann), 496
Searle, Ronald, 178
Sears, Heather, 334, 547
Sebaldt, Maria, 264, 750, 778, 785
Sebastian, Bruno, 11, 32
Sebastian, Georges, 104, 700
Sebestyén, Ákos, 517
Secombe, Harry, 442
Secret of Macbeth, The (Raphael), 408
Secunde, Nadine, 679, 755
Sedláček, Stanislav, 345
Seebar, Guido, 74, 787
Seefriend, Imgard, 27
Seeman, Horst, 62
Seen, Marta, 184
Segal, Misha, 334, 547
Segal, Vivienne, 40, 128, 264, 292, 586, 694
Segar, Kathleen, 599
Segarra, Ramon, 253
Segatori, Anna Maria, 393
Segerstam, Leif, 252, 407
Segovia, Andrés, 389, 505
Segreto di Don Giovanni, Il (Costa), 60
Seguiré tus pasos (Crevenna), 465
Segura, Georgorio, 355
Sehnsucht des Herzens (Martin), 326
Sehrbrock, Thomas, 388
Seiber, Gudrun, 622, 780
Seibt, Tatja, 754
Seiffert, Peter, 253
Seigner, Louis, 95
Seiler, Lewis, 464

Seine beste Rolle (Pittermann), 326
Seiter, William A., 203, 258, 260, 461, 733
Seitz, Franz, 240
Seitz, George, 301, 395
Seitz, Herbert, 412
Selee, Marion, 313
Self Defense (Meyer), 126
Selfish Giant, The (Hollingsworth), 324
Selig, Franz-Josef, 782
Sell, David, 669
Seller, Lew, 117, 132, 509
Sellner, Gustav Rudolf, 240, 350
Selman, David, 245
Selt, Herbert, 481
Seltzer, Dov, 199
Sembach, Johannes, 234
Semenovich Chishko, Oles, 208
Sémiramis, 634
Semler, Dean, 443
Semmelrogge, Willy, 773
Semmelroth, Wilhelm, 82
Sempere, José, 689
Sempléni, Maria, 74
Semtschuk, Ludmila, 283, 356, 567
Senator, Boaz, 114
Sénéchal, Michel, 66, 110, 412, 498, 522
Senesina, 524
Senft, Derek, 661
Senkova, Eva, 18, 501
Senn, Herbert, 47
Senn, Marta, 12, 234
Senna, Orlando, 63
Sennett, Mack, 117
Senso (Visconti), 89
Senza une donna (Guarini), 398
September Affair, 90
Sequi, Sandro, 243, 492, 493
Serafin, Enzo, 438
Serafin, Harald, 66, 81, 106, 335, 515, 633, 786
Serban, André, 23, 215, 341, 561
Serda, Julia, 200, 660
Serebrier, José, 687, 751
Seregi, Laszlo, 74
Serena, Gustavo, 238, 262, 703, 711
Sérénade, 628
Sereni, Mario, 360
Sergi, Arturo, 36
Seriese, Astrid, 460
Serio, Renato, 102
Serkin, Rudolf, 525
Serova, Valentina, 288
Serra, Enrico, 4, 340, 422
Serra, Luciana, 151, 584, 621, 651, 781
Serrano de Osma, C., 535
Serravezza, Nella, 382
Servaes, Dagny, 152, 484
Servaës, Ernest, 460
Servais, Jean, 623
Servant of Two Masters, The (Gianini), 278
Serven, Arthur, 674
Serventi, Luigi, 84, 131
Servile, Robert, 83, 340, 593, 785
Sessions, Bob, 198
Seuffert, Peter, 521
Seven Chances (Keaton), 121
Seven Hills of Rome, The (Rowland), 371
07 . . . Tassi (Pagliero and D'Aversa), 290
Seventh Veil, The (Bennett), 406
Seven Waves Away (Bliss), 79
Severin, Ulla, 156
Severini, Tiziano, 83

Sevilla, Carmen, 388, 426, 578
Sexton, Anne, 667, 707
Seyfert, Wilfried, 434
Seyler, Athene, 63, 380
Seymour, Jane, 106, 547
Seymour, John, 345
Seymour, Madeleine, 244
Sfiris, Konstantin, 64
Shade, Ellen, 242, 786
Shade, Nancy, 416, 648
Shadow of a Doubt (Hitchcock), 322, 405
Shadow of Angels, 624
Shadow of the Vampire (Merhige), 253
Shadows (Barker), 231–32
Shaeffer, Emmerich, 218
Shaffer, Peter, 18, 474, 551, 622
Shakespeare, William, 229, 324
Shamroy, Leon, 232, 264, 357, 554, 653, 768
Shandrasekhar, Jay, 756
Shane, Rita, 781
Shanks, Donald, 441, 566, 722, 780
Shanley, John Patrick, 469
Shapiro, M., 376
Shapiro, Mikhail, 366
Shapiro, Yevgeny, 222
Sharaff, Irene, 555
Sharis, David, 221
Sharman, Jim, 752
Sharman, William, 748
Sharp, Albert, 733
Sharp, Frederick, 420, 577
Sharp, Henry, 660
Sharp, Norma, 295, 579, 639
Sharp, William, 721
Sharpe, Anne, 377
Sharpe, Ivan, 457
Sharpe, Terence, 457
Shatz, Willy, 378
Shaulis, Jane, 148, 393, 457, 488, 612
Shavelson, Mel, 39, 772
Shaw, Carlos Fernández, 578
Shaw, Dick, 25
Shaw, George Bernard, 138, 188, 764
Shaw, Guillermo Fernández, 107, 127, 186
Shaw, Harold, 716
Shaw, John, 4, 702, 760
Shaw, Muriel, 460
Shaw, Robert, 448
Shaw-Robinson, Charles, 160
Shawshank Redemption, The (Darabont), 501
Shayne, Irwin, 322
Shean, Al, 478
Shear, Barry, 322
Shearer, Moira, 150
Shearer, Norma, 277, 386, 598, 665
Shebalin, Vissarion, 288
Shebujeva, E., 568
Sheehan, Winfield, 346
Sheen, Charlie, 587
Sheerer, Robert, 450
Sheff, Robert, 479
Sheffield, Philip, 38, 645
Sheldon, Gene, 39, 767
Shelenkov, Alexander, 288
Shelley, Julia, 325
Shelton, Chad, 383
Shelton, Lucy, 451
She Married Her Boss (La Cava), 54
Shengelaya, Ariadna, 222
Shentall, Susan, 598
Shepherd of the Seven Hills, The, 408
Shepherdson, Sally-Ann, 734

Shepis, Anastasia Tomaszewska, 518
Sher, Jack, 213
Sherbedgia, Rade, 654
Sheridan, Jim, 157
Sheridan, Kirsten, 502
Sheridan, Richard, 73
Sherman, Martin, 106
Sherman, Robert, 99
Sherwood, Don, 619
Sherwood, Gale, 176, 205, 485
Sheybal, Vladek, 171, 661
Shicoff, Neil, 83, 119, 152, 349, 597, 710
Shikovsky, Konstantin, 221
Shilkret, Nathaniel, 86
Shilling, Eric, 325, 519, 687
Shin, Young Hoon, 493
Shin, Young Ok, 634
Shinall, Vern, 36, 130, 150
Shipman, Gertrude, 711
Shiraishi, Kayoko, 504
Shire, David, 315, 334
Shirley, Bill, 672
Shirley, Don, 189
Shirley, George, 6
Shirley-Quirk, John, 76, 112, 170, 525
Shore, Andrew, 418
Shore, Dinah, 354, 446
Shore, Howard, 438
Short, Kevin, 76
Short, Paul, 131
Show Business (Marin), 395
Shriner, William, 497
Shtokolov, Boris, 93
Shuard, Amy, 677
Shunkin-Sho (Miki), 458
Shust, Michael, 493
Shuttleworth, Anna, 318, 495
Shuttleworth, Barbara, 598
Shuvalov, Ivan, 93
Siberian Lady Macbeth, 367
Sicango, Eduardo V., 528
Sichel, John, 323
Siciliani, Alessandro, 599
Siciliani, Maria Francesca, 492
Sidelev, Serge, 16
Sidhom, Peter, 597
Sidimu, Joysann, 253
Sidney, George, 301, 638, 678
Sidney, Lorna, 614
Sidney, Sylvia, 413, 663
Sieber, Josef, 645
Sieber, Walter, 256
Sieczynski, Rudolph, 332, 681
Sieden, Cynthia, 782
Siege, Gustav, 772
Siège de Corinthe, Le, 604
Siegl, Gerda, 200
Siegler, Allen, 245
Siena, Jerold, 150, 392
Siesz, Wolfgang, 759
Sievewright, Alan, 564
Sieyes, Maurice, 556
Siff, Ira, 300
Sifrankova, Libuše, 63
Sighele, Mietta, 220, 248
Signoret, Simone, 659
Signorinella (Mattoli), 60
Signorini, Evaristo, 304
Silbersher, Marvin, 496
Siletti, Mario, 653
Silins, Egil, 589
Sills, Milton, 231–32
Silva, J. Lopez, 578
Silva, Maria, 292, 328
Silvani, Aldo, 583

Silvano, 631
Silvasti, Jorma, 54, 252, 532
Silver, Johnny, 411, 412
Silver, Joseph, 63
Silver, Marcel, 323, 464
Silver, Marisa, 323
Silver, Ron, 719
Silveri, Paolo, 237, 527
Silvers, Louis, 292
Silvers, Sid, 97
Silverstein, Elliott, 453
Silver Tassie, The, 730
Silvestre, Armand, 317
Silvestrelli, Andrea, 191, 679
Sima, Gabriele, 54, 498
Sima, Oskar, 249, 256, 272, 483, 484, 681, 785
Simenon, Georges, 783
Simeon, Ennio, 148
Simeonov, Konstantin, 366
Simerada, Tomás, 32, 185, 276, 303, 307, 345
Simmonds, Nicolas, 661
Simmons, Calvin, 349
Simmons, Joyce, 19
Simmons, Mary, 149, 744
Simon, Andrea, 475, 634
Simon, Charles, 699
Simon, Edward F., 63
Simon, Eric, 407
Simon, Gérard, 595
Simon, Jay, 294
Simon, Joanna, 535, 716
Simón, Julio M., 16
Simon, Michel, 586, 704
Simon, Neil, 38, 139, 485
Simon, Robert, 320
Simon, S. J., 508
Simon, S. Sylvan, 311, 591
Simon, Simone, 368, 419
Simón Bolívar (Musgrave), 478
Simoncic, Dodo, 222
Simone, Charles, 724
Simoneau, Léopold, 540
Simoneau, Yves, 543
Simonella, Liborio, 248, 566
Simonelli, Giorgio C., 262
Simonetto, Alfredo, 527
Simoni, Renato, 727
Simonian, Konstantin, 26
Simonov, Yuri, 355, 567
Simpson, Angela, 555
Simpson, Christian, 19, 506, 687
Simpson, Fanny, 261
Simpson, Helen, 294
Simpson, Marietta, 448, 555
Simpson, N. F., 448
Simpson, Olive, 321
Simpson, Russell, 229
Sinagra, Pilade, 529
Sinatra, Frank, 193, 301, 354, 368, 426, 508, 638, 696
Sinaz, Guglielmo, 161
Sinclair, Monica, 36, 150, 243
Sinfonia d'Amore, 629
Singer, Gideon, 404
Singer, Sergiu, 201, 415
Singher, Martial, 509, 691
Singing Fool, The (Bacon), 530
Singing Nun, The, 362
Singing Taxi Driver, The, 682
Singleton, Joe, 457
Sing Me a Love Song (Enright), 445
Sinimberghi, Aldo, 394
Sinopoli, Giuseppe, 614, 679, 702
Sinjen, Sabine, 256, 665

Visconti, Eriprando, 220
Visit of the Old Lady, The (Einem), 154
Visse, Dominique, 336, 468
Vitali Marini, Palmira, 237, 261, 388
Vitrotti, Giovanni, 340, 585, 636
Vitti, Achille, 258, 529, 615
Vitti, Monica, 704
Viva, Sim, 429
Vizzotto, C., 202
Vlad, Alessio, 401
Vlad, Roman, 738
Vladar, Stefan, 626
Vladimirov, Yuri, 342
Vlady, Marina, 629
Vlasenko, Lev, 683
Vlasov, Vitaly, 355
Voce bianche, Le (Franciosa), 128
Voce nel tuo cuore, Una (D'Aversa), 60
Vogel, Paul C., 338, 600, 665
Vogel, Rudolf, 515, 750
Vogel, Siegfried, 70, 221, 286, 385, 679
Vogel, Volker, 314, 499, 782
Vogl, Johann, 60, 629
Vogler, Rudiger, 454
Voglio vivere così, 675
Voice in Your Heart, A, 624
Voice of Love, The (Bragaglia), 59
Voice of Yearning, The, 625
Voigt, Deborah, 210, 388, 604
Voigtmann, Karl-Fritz, 44, 151
Voitenko, Andrei, 258
Voketaitis, Arnold, 618
Vokov, Solomon, 638
Volkoff, Alexandre, 363
Volkova, Svetlana, 16, 760
Volle, Michale, 645
Voller, Achille, 382
Vollmer, Josefin H., 629
Vollrath, Ernest, 116
Volshaninova, Nelli, 16
Volska, Anna, 443
Voltaire, 107
Volter, Philippe, 407, 418
von Alten, Charlotte, 297
von Ambesser, Axel, 66, 240
von Antalfy, Alexander, 401
von Backy, Josef, 89
von Bolvary, Geza, 244, 249, 268, 280
von Buchen, Alix, 207
von Czerserpy, Arzan, 401
von Cziffra, Geza, 81, 250, 370
von Ditmar, Marina, 326
von Dohnányi, Christoph, 241, 265
von Endert, Elizabeth, 385
von Gatti, Emmerich, 380
von Gierke, Henning, 252, 284, 344, 385
von Goth, Rolf, 207
von Kannen, Gunter, 7, 295, 340
von Koszian, Johanna, 256
von Meyendorff, Irene, 264
von Nagy, Käthe, 280, 352
Von Nagy, Käthe, 37
Vonnegut, Kurt, 94
von Praunheim, Rosa, 207
von Schillings, Max, 148
von Stroheim, Erich, 63
Von Sydow, Max, 322
von Tasnady, Maria, 216
Von Tschoudi, Ludwig, 205
Von Twardowski, Hans Heinrich, 397
von Winterstein, Eduard, 256
von Wymetal, Wilhelm Jr. (aka William), 331, 332, 333, 437, 468, 546, 547, 600, 619
von Zallinger, Menhard, 21
Voorhees, Donald, 65, 154, 161, 182,

389, 447, 455, 463, 559, 668, 685, 727, 744
Vorekamp, Pieter, 311
Vorhaus, Bernard, 98
Vorins, Henry, 433
Vorsody, Hans von, 189
Voss, Stephanie, 198, 687
Vosselli, Judith, 461, 786
Votti, Antonio, 699
Votto, Antonino, 105
Voulgaris, Virginia, 300
Voutsinos, Frangiskos, 516
Voyage, The (Glass), 287, 557
Voyage de Thésée, Le (Neveux), 32
Voyage en Amérique, Le (Lavorel), 562
Voyage of Edgar Allen Poe (Argento), 30
Voyage to America, 694
Voytek, 393, 768
Vozza, Corinna, 132, 349, 484
Vrenios, Anastasios, 598
Vroman, Lisa, 671
Vrublevskaya, Valerie, 578
Vyvyan, Jennifer, 226, 525, 730

Waage, Lars, 580, 590, 640, 755
Wabo, Manfred, 10, 482, 523, 782
Wachsfigurenkabinett, Das (Leni), 341
Wächter, Eberhard, 150, 250, 298, 506
Wada, Emi, 504
Waddell, Christopher, 33
Waddington, Patrick, 201
Wadsworth, Andrew, 499
Wadsworth, Michael, 28
Wadsworth, Stephen, 569
Waechter, Franz, 369
Wägele, Karl, 729
Wagemann, Rose, 607
Wagener, Paul, 717
Wagenknecht, Chritoph, 219
Wager, Michael, 504
Waggner, George, 146, 259, 333, 547
Wagner, Elsa, 442, 497
Wagner, Friedlind, 591
Wagner, Fritz Arno, 5, 199, 287, 582, 688
Wagner, Richard, 672
Wagner, Robin, 48
Wagner, Roger, 138
Wagner, Wieland, 57, 177, 643, 717
Wagner, William, 179
Wagner, Winifred, 754
Wagner, Winnifred, 295
Wagner, Wolfgang, 57, 441, 534, 591, 649, 679
Wagon, Virginie, 144
Wague, Georges, 235
Wahlgren, Per-Arne, 498
Wahlund, Sten, 39
Wahman, William, 707
Wajda, Andrzej, 367
Wakefield, Hugh, 255, 480
Wakeham, Michael, 47, 293, 323, 339, 528, 708, 715, 775
Wakhévitch, Georges, 63, 112, 189, 390, 438, 442, 528, 579
Walbrook, Anton, 250, 569, 659, 660, 785
Walczak, Diana, 467
Wald, Jerry, 654
Waldau, Gustav, 200, 472
Waldberg, Heinrich von, 515
Waldbrunn, Ernst, 787
Waldman, Michael, 326, 606
Waldmuller, Lizzi, 483
Waletzky, Joshua, 539

Walewska, Malgorzata, 114
Walker, Charles, 300
Walker, David, 589
Walker, Don, 575
Walker, Edyth, 692
Walker, George, 160, 282, 293, 316, 323, 339, 456, 519, 536, 550, 561, 606, 652, 715, 775
Walker, James, 606
Walker, John Edward, 598
Walker, Joseph, 391, 507, 767
Walker, Malcolm, 215
Walker, Mallory, 14
Walker, Martin, 85
Walker, Norman, 311
Walker, Penelope, 542
Walker, Phyllis, 455
Walker, Robert D., 354, 427
Walker, Sandra, 222, 457, 518, 612
Walker, Sarah, 286, 289, 358, 451, 581
Walker, William, 28, 51, 321, 597
Wallace, Hal, 93
Wallace, Ian, 82, 189
Wallace, Milt, 183, 186
Wallace, Stewart, 147, 327
Wallasch, Peter, 382
Wallberg, Heinz, 503, 777, 786
Wallburg, Otto, 242, 625
Wallenstein, Alfred, 22, 111, 140, 392
Waller, Fred, 470, 553
Wallin, Seppo, 351
Wallis, Delia, 134
Wallis, Hal B., 28
Wallman, Margarita, 21, 727
Wallner, Fritz, 335
Wallner, Helmut, 786
Wallner, Max, 377, 406, 489, 611, 749
Wall Street (Stone), 587
Wallström, Tord, 190
Walmesley, Clare, 179
Walmsley, Ryan, 326
Walmsley-Clark, Penelope, 273
Walsh, Frances, 372
Walsh, George, 299
Walsh, Jack, 2
Walsh, Kieron J., 120
Walsh, Mary Jane, 652, 720
Walsh, Raoul, 115, 116, 553
Walsh, Stephen, 511
Walston, Ray, 653
Walter, E., 382
Walters, J., 698
Walters, Jess, 612
Walters, Julie, 199
Walther, Ute, 441
Walton, William, 754
Waltzes from Vienna (Hitchcock), 322, 660
Waltz from Strauss, A, 659, 660
Waltz King, The, 660, 661
Waltz Time (Thiele), 249
Walzel, Camillo (F. Zell), 272, 275
Walzer aus Wien, 660
Walzerkönig, Der, 660
Wanamaker, Sam, 9, 760
Wang Yan Yan, 184
Wang, Wayne, 423, 619
Wanka, Rolf, 146
War and Peace (Bondarchuk), 93
War and Peace (Vidor), 563
Ward, Anthony, 289, 422
Ward, Bill, 104, 701
Ward, David, 14
Ward, Dorothy, 358
Ward, Eddie, 264
Ward, Edward, 146, 333, 547

869

Whitehouse, Elizabeth, 602, 781
Whitehouse, Paul, 510, 657
Whiteside, Karen, 164
Whiting, John, 176, 543
Whiting, Leonard, 598
Whiting, Margaret, 661
Whitmore, James, 371
Whitney, Fred C., 139
Whitney, Robert, 58
Whitred, Gladys, 19
Whittemore, Thomas, 435
Whittier, Robert, 535
Whittingham, Jack, 168
Who Is Happier Than Me?, 623
Whorf, Richard, 193, 271, 301, 310, 318, 354, 362, 378, 444, 638
Wich, Harry, 504
Wiche, Lela, 424
Wicherek, Antoni, 309
Wickes, Andrew, 456, 457
Wicki, Bernhard, 660
Wicks, Dennis, 330, 391, 775
Widdicombe, John, 634, 669
Widmer, Oliver, 66, 157, 192
Wiek, Dorothea, 297
Wieler, Jossi, 15
Wieman, Mathias, 240
Wiemann, Ernest, 240, 441
Wienberg, Peter, 591
Wiene, Conrad, 660
Wiene, Robert, 103, 483, 600, 625, 660
Wiener Liebschafter (Choux), 375
Wiens, Edith, 525
Wien Tanzt, 660
Wieth, Carlo, 214
Wightman, Robert, 392
Wilber, Robert, 233
Wilborn, Kip, 663
Wilcock, Gordon, 453, 544
Wilcox, Herbert, 77, 141, 358, 415
Wild, Ernst, 47, 112, 130, 187, 190, 228, 240, 352, 497, 579
Wildcat, The (Penella), 272
Wilde, Cornel, 363
Wilde, Oscar, 311
Wilden, Henri, 368
Wilder, Billy, 206, 207, 478, 713, 719
Wilder, Gene, 44
Wilder, Michael, 424
Wilder, Thornton, 320, 387
Wilderman, William, 241, 717
Wildfire, 609
Wildgruber, Ulrich, 218
Wildner, Johannes, 475
Wild Side (Cammell), 502
Wiles, Gordon, 692, 712
Wilheim, Hans, 641
Wilhelm, Horst, 176–77, 777
Wilhelm, Kurt, 759, 786
Wilk, Herbert, 741
Will, Jacob, 382
Willard, Amy, 261
Willemetz, Albert, 159, 171, 535, 548, 721
William, Warren, 246
William-King, Anne, 731
Williams, Billy Dee, 348, 714
Williams, C. Jay, 642
Williams, Charles, 350
Williams, Daniel Lewis, 602
Williams, David, 76
Williams, Eleanor, 460
Williams, Emlyn, 224, 481
Williams, Esther, 430, 443, 444
Williams, Howard, 361
Williams, Hugh, 676

Williams, J. Mervyn, 572
Williams, Jeremy Huw, 164
Williams, John, 71, 741
Williams, Juan, 23
Williams, La Verne, 80, 503
Williams, Malcolm, 323
Williams, Margaret, 336, 525
Williams, Morris, 150
Williams, Nancy, 721
Williams, Robin, 51, 86, 554, 608
Williams, Tennessee, 287, 324, 559, 662, 666
Williamson, Cecil H., 254
Williamson, Malcolm, 512–13
Williamson, Nicol, 336
Williamson, W. K., 77
Willink, Carel, 253
Willis, Constance, 455
Willis, Edmund B., 600
Willis, Lawrence, 632
Willis, Nuala, 573, 633, 652, 767
Willm, Pierre Richard, 241, 242, 765
Willner, A. M., 182, 200, 223, 298, 641, 771, 786
Willow Springs, 628
Wills, Ted, 455
Wilm, Eike, 385
Wilmot, Richard, 58
Wilsher, Toby, 164
Wilsing, Jörn W., 53, 429
Wilson, Al, 526
Wilson, Andrew, 545
Wilson, Angela Turner, 142, 599
Wilson, Charles, 610
Wilson, Frank, 235
Wilson, Georges, 344
Wilson, Gran, 26, 780
Wilson, Hugh, 194, 219
Wilson, I. James, 672
Wilson, Lanford, 666
Wilson, Lois, 235, 477, 633
Wilson, Marian, 63
Wilson, Marie, 38, 158
Wilson, Noble, 227
Wilson, Richard, 125
Wilson, Stuart, 661
Wilson-Johnson, David, 451
Wimmer, Horst, 631
Wimperis, Arthur, 255
Winbergh, Gösta, 190, 441, 461, 573
Wincer, Simon, 382
Windgassen, Peter, 780
Winding, Romain, 703
Windon, Stephen F., 654
Windt, Herbert, 306
Winge, Stein, 93
Wings of the Morning (Schuster), 408
Wings of the Serf (Tarich), 341
Winkelstern, Marianne, 681
Winkler, George C., 21
Winkler, Hermann, 252
Winkler, Margaret, 438
Winksa, Aga, 218
Winmann, Michael, 476
Winner, Michael, 455
Winninger, Charles, 638
Winograde, Joshua, 136
Winsauer, Waltraud, 393
Winslet, Kate, 86, 372, 520
Winslow, Herbert Hall, 422
Winter, Hélène, 182
Winter, Keith, 139
Winter, Louise, 215, 222, 354, 594
Winterreise (Schubert), 248
Winters, Jonathan, 39
Winters, Lawrence, 28

Winterstein, Eduard von, 526
Winterstein, Willy, 250, 515, 749, 750, 769
Winthrop, Christine, 616
Wirth, Franz Peter, 764
Wisbar, Frank, 473
Wischmann, Marianne, 240, 335
Wisconsin Death Trip, 667
Wise, Herbert, 453, 583, 768
Wise, Patricia, 517, 622
Wise, Robert, 653, 766
Wishy, Joseph, 704
With Words and Music (Stone), 285
Witkowska, Nadia, 64, 217
Witney, William, 212
Wittges, Max, 131
Wittstein, Ed, 22, 82, 92, 156, 708
Wixell, Ingvar, 9, 82, 584, 701, 702, 741
Wizard of Oz, The, 658
Wodehouse, P. G., 162, 430
Wohlafka, Louis, 211
Wöhlbruck, Adolf, 785
Wohlbrück, Wilhelm, 734
Wohlers, Rüdiger, 351, 429
Wohlfahrt, Erwin, 240
Wojcicki, Kazimierz, 309, 315
Wolansky, Raymond, 777
Woldd, Hans, 326
Wolf, Gusti, 406, 489
Wolf, Hans-Jürgen, 766
Wolf, Julia Ann, 199
Wolf, Roger, 392
Wolf, Sally, 622
Wolf, Steffen, 237
Wolff, Beverly, 366, 721
Wolff, Christian, 665, 764
Wolff, Hugh, 153
Wolff, Willi, 769
Wolf-Ferrari, Ermanno, 646
Wolfit, Donald, 717
Wolfkind, Peter, 416
Wolken, Jonathan, 768
Wollard, Rolf, 676
Woloshyn, Ilya, 62
Wolowsky, Kurt, 152
Wolski, Włodzimierz, 309
Wolter, Hella, 534
Wölzl, Katrin, 252
Woman and the Puppet, The (Barker), 232
Woman God Forget, The (De Mille), 231
Woman of Impulse, A (José), 130
Woman Parade, The, 646
Woman Who Dared, The, 235
Women and Bandits (Soldati), 262
Women and Divas, 651
Wonder, Erich, 192, 295, 356, 382, 499, 579, 614, 639, 755
Wonderful Town (Bernstein), 70, 71
Wonder Man, 333
Wong, Anna May, 141
Wong, Corey Gordon, 150
Wood, Charles, 564, 565, 754
Wood, John, 31, 94
Wood, Natalie, 766
Wood, Peggy, 653
Wood, Peter, 218, 293, 471
Wood, Sam, 489
Woodberry, Earle, 160
Woodland, Rae, 330
Woodrow, Alan, 545, 679
Woods, Janice, 710
Woods, Michele-Denise, 160
Woods, Sara, 671
Woods, Weston, 635

870